So That's Why! BIBLE

Making Sense of All the People, Places, and Events of the Bible

NKJV
NEW
KING
JAMES
VERSION

Contributors

Timothy B. Cargal, Ph.D.

Mark W. Chavalas, Ph.D.

James R. Edwards, Ph.D.

John O. Gooch, Ph.D.

Lowell K. Handy, Ph.D.

Craig S. Keener, Ph.D.

David T. Landry, Ph.D.

Robert Lintz, Th.D.

George Lyons, Ph.D.

John S. Mason, Th.M.

David Merling, Ph.D.

Gerald P. Morris, Ph.D.

John W. Wright, Ph.D.

THOMAS NELSON BIBLES
A Division of Thomas Nelson, Inc.
www.ThomasNelson.com

The So That's Why! Bible

formerly titled

The Life and Times Historical Reference Bible

Copyright © 1997 by Thomas Nelson, Inc.

Color timeline pages
Copyright © 2001 by Thomas Nelson, Inc.

The Holy Bible, New King James Version
Copyright © 1982 by Thomas Nelson, Inc.

4 5 6 7 8 9 — 07 06 05 04 03

TABLE OF CONTENTS

Contents: Features iv
Contributors. vi
Introduction. vii
Reading Theological History ix
Rearranging the Bible's Canonical Order xi
New King James Version xvii

Epoch 1 Before the Patriarchs (Creation–2000 B.C.) 1
   The Beginnings of Human Civilization. 3

Epoch 2 The Patriarchs, Israel's Ancestors (2000–1500 B.C.) 22
   The Changing of the Empires 24
   Egypt in the Middle Bronze Age 61

Epoch 3 The Rise of a Unified People (1500–1200 B.C.) 81
   Egypt and the Exodus 82
   The Conquest of Canaan 266

Epoch 4 From Tribes to a Nation (1200–930 B.C.) 298
   A Tribal Confederation in Israel 300
   The United Monarchy in Israel 350

Epoch 5 The Fall of Two Nations (930–586 B.C.) 601
   The Divided Monarchy in Israel 603
   The Neo-Assyrian Empire 674
   The Neo-Babylonian Empire 807

Epoch 6 Exile and Return (586–332 B.C.) 984
   Exile in Babylon 986
   Wisdom in the Ancient Near East 1049
   The Persian Empire 1101

Epoch 7 Between the Two Testaments (332–37 B.C.) 1237
   The Greek Empire. 1239
   The Roman Empire 1256

Epoch 8 The Coming of the Messiah (37 B.C.–A.D. 30) 1259
   Introductions to Jesus Christ. 1262
   Early Lives of John the Baptist and Jesus. 1264
   Beginning of Jesus' Ministry 1275
   The Galilean Ministry. 1282
   From Galilee to Jerusalem 1353
   Jesus' Final Journey. 1361
   Final Ministry in Judea. 1381
   Jesus' Final Week in Jerusalem 1394

Epoch 9 The Church Age (A.D. 30–100) 1456
   The Gospel to the Jews 1459
   The Gospel to the Gentiles 1473
   The Gospel to the Gentile World 1483
   The Gospel from Jerusalem to Rome 1568
   Apocalyptic Writings and the End Time 1643

Index of Scripture Passages. 1669
Cultural and Historical Topics 1675
Glossary 1691

CONTENTS: FEATURES

TIME CHARTS

Epoch 1
Egypt's First Dynasties 19
The Millenniums 21

Epoch 2
Dating Abraham from the Exodus 42
Egypt and the Middle Kingdom 49
The Old Babylonian Period 63

Epoch 3
Egypt and the New Kingdom 88
Two Dates for the Exodus 102
Israel's Annual Feasts 162
Israel's Sacred Times 210
Law Codes of Ancient Mesopotamia . . 236
The Literature of Ugarit 297

Epoch 4
The Cycles of the Judges (Part 1) . . . 307
The Cycles of the Judges (Part 2) . . . 322
Kingdoms of Syria and Palestine 417
Absalom's Crime and Rise to Power . . 447
Solomon the Builder 592

Epoch 5
Rehoboam and Jeroboam Divide the
  Kingdom 605
Kings of the Divided Monarchy 612
Asa and Baasha Fight over Ramah . . . 619
Omri Begins a New Dynasty 620
Jehoshaphat and Ahab Form an
  Alliance 624
Brothers, In-Laws, Uncles, and
  Nephews 635
Attacks on Judah's Royal Family 656
Hazael Attacks Judah and Israel 662
Israel Is Victorious over Judah 665
Coregencies, Long Reigns, and
  Prosperity 667

Assassinations in Israel 714
An Officer Assassinates the King 715
Assyria Comes to Judah and
  Israel 722
Judah After Israel's Fall 747
An Idolatrous King in Judah 790
Josiah Pursues Reform in Judah 826
The Sons of Josiah Rule in Judah . . . 866
Deportations from Jerusalem to
  Babylon 869
Jeremiah's Call and Ministry 916
The Last Kings of Judah 949

Epoch 6
Dates in the Book of Ezekiel 999
The Dates of Haggai and Zechariah . . 1117
The Ministries of Ezra and
  Nehemiah 1166
The Persian Kings 1185

Epoch 7
The 70 Years of Jeremiah 1248

Epoch 8
Luke and the Career of Quirinius . . . 1281
Herod and Judea Under Rome's
  Augustus 1334
The Temples of Yahweh 1387
Division of Herod's Kingdom 1403

Epoch 9
Evidence for Dating New Testament
  Events 1534
The Roman Empire Rules
  Palestine 1562
Writers of the Early Church 1594
The Persecution of the Church 1614
Quotations of Greek Literature 1621
The Fate of Jerusalem 1653

TIME PANELS

Epoch 2
Abraham's Life (Early Exodus) 31
Abraham's Life (Late Exodus) 32
Jacob in Egypt (Early Exodus) 50
Jacob in Egypt (Late Exodus) 51

Epoch 3
Moses and the Promised Land (Early
  Exodus) 104
Moses and the Promised Land (Late
  Exodus) 105

The Wilderness Years (Early Exodus) . 190
The Wilderness Years (Late Exodus) . . 191

Epoch 4
The Era of the Judges (Early
  Exodus) 308
The Era of the Judges (Late Exodus) . . 327
Saul of Israel Against the Philistines . . 357
The First Kings of Israel 401
Solomon and Hiram Build the
  Temple 474

Epoch 5

Israel's Kings Meet Shalmaneser III of
Assyria. 617
Assyria Revives Under Tiglath-
Pileser III 719
The Fall of Samaria 738
Assyrian Kings Campaign Against
Judah 801
Nahum Prophesies of Nineveh and
Nabopolassar 822
The Battle of Carchemish 840
The Fall of Jerusalem 885
Nebuchadnezzar and the Kings of
Judah 900
The Pharaohs and Judah 966

Epoch 6

Jehoiachin's Exile and Release 1011
Building and Dedicating the Second
Temple 1119
Cyrus the Great's Campaigns 1122
Artaxerxes I (Longimanus), King of
Persia. 1192

Epoch 7

Alexander the Great Conquers
Persia. 1242
The Maccabean Revolt 1255

Epoch 8

Augustus Brings Peace to the Roman
World 1265
The Young Jesus 1273
Jesus Ministers in Galilee 1338
Jesus' Passion Week in Jerusalem. . . 1431
Beginning of the Church 1451

Epoch 9

Paul Becomes a Missionary 1489
Paul in Athens and Ephesus. 1503
Paul Is Arrested and Sent to Rome . . 1568
The End of Paul's Life 1611
The Fall of Jerusalem 1629
The Book of Revelation in Troubled
Times 1645
The Romans Destroy Jerusalem. . . . 1667

IN-TEXT MAPS

Epoch 1

The Ancient Near East After 3000 B.C. . 10

Epoch 2

Journeys of Abraham 39
Changing Empires of the Near East . . . 45
Jacob Returns to Canaan 56
Joseph Goes to Egypt 62
The Hyksos Empire 69

Epoch 3

Moses' Flight and Return to Egypt. . . . 86
The Route of the Exodus 100
The Approach to Transjordan 216
The Conquest of Canaan (Central and
Southern Campaigns). 275
The Conquest of Canaan (Northern
Campaign). 281
Cities of Refuge 291

Epoch 4

Gideon's Campaign 311
The Ministry of Samuel 345
The Davidic Kingdom 519
Solomon's Administrative Districts . . . 546
Geography in the Song of Solomon . . . 582
The Spread of Solomon's Fame 593

Epoch 5

Assyrian Campaigns in Palestine. . . . 716
Assyrian Campaign Against Israel . . . 735
Assyrian Campaign Against Judah . . . 743
The Neo-Assyrian Empire. 824
The Neo-Babylonian Empire 879

Nebuchadnezzar's Campaigns Against
Judah 937
Jeremiah's Journey to Egypt 963

Epoch 6

The Persian Empire 1141
The Return from Exile 1158
Alexander's Greek Empire 1236

Epoch 7

Ptolemaic Control of Palestine. 1251
Seleucid Control of Palestine 1253
Expansion of Palestine Under the
Maccabees 1254

Epoch 8

Herod's Kingdom at Jesus' Birth . . . 1265
The Journeys of Jesus' Birth. 1273
Jesus' Baptism and Temptation 1283
Jesus' Galilean Ministry 1296
Last Journey to Jerusalem. 1365
Jewish Pilgrimage to Jerusalem. . . . 1379
Roman Control of Palestine 1389
Appearances of the Risen Christ . . . 1448

Epoch 9

The Nations of Pentecost. 1463
Paul Goes to Galatia 1484
Paul Goes to Greece 1489
Paul on the Road to Damascus 1491
Asia and Greece Revisited 1515
On to Rome 1585
Regions of the Dispersion 1612
Sites of the Transfiguration 1620
The Seven Churches of Revelation . . 1644

CONTRIBUTORS

Timothy B. Cargal, Ph.D., served as University Lecturer in Philosophy and Religion at Western Kentucky University (Bowling Green, KY), and is pastor of Northwood Presbyterian Church (Silver Spring, MD). Dr. Cargal is author of *Restoring the Diaspora: Discursive Structure and Purpose in the Epistle of James.*

Mark W. Chavalas, Ph.D., is Associate Professor of History at the University of Wisconsin—LaCrosse (La Crosse, WI). Dr. Chavalas is editor of *New Horizons in the Study of Ancient Syria* and *Emar: The History, Religion, and Culture of a Bronze Age Town in Syria.* He has had nine seasons of archaeological field work in Syria.

James R. Edwards, Ph.D., served as chair of the Department of Religion at Jamestown College (Jamestown, ND) and is Professor of Religion at Whitworth College (Spokane, WA). A specialist in New Testament studies, Dr. Edwards contributed to *Nelson's New Illustrated Bible Dictionary* and is author of *Romans* in *The New International Biblical Commentary.*

John O. Gooch, Ph.D., served as curriculum editor for the United Methodist Church (Nashville, TN) and as Assistant Professor of Religion, Metropolitan College, St. Louis University. He is the only known youth minister with a doctorate in Patristics. Dr. Gooch is coauthor of *A Pocket Guide to the Bible.*

Lowell K. Handy, Ph.D., serves as Senior Lecturer in Scripture at Loyola University Chicago (Chicago, IL), and is Indexer/Analyst for the American Theological Library Association (Evanston, IL). Dr. Handy is author of *Among the Host of Heaven: The Syro-Palestinian Pantheon as Bureaucracy* and *The Educated Person's Thumbnail Introduction to the Bible.*

Craig S. Keener, Ph.D., is Visiting Professor of Biblical Studies at Eastern Baptist Theological Seminary (Wynnewood, PA). Dr. Keener focuses on New Testament background and is author of *The IVP Bible Background Commentary: New Testament,* as well as seven other books. He remains active in campus ministry.

David T. Landry, Ph.D., is Assistant Professor of Theology at the University of St. Thomas (St. Paul, MN). Dr. Landry is co-author and coeditor of *The Christian Theological Tradition.*

Robert Lintz, Th.D., served as Bible editor for Thomas Nelson Publishers (Nashville, TN). Dr. Lintz is associate editor of *The Wesley Bible,* editor of *The Life and Times Historical Reference Bible,* and author of *Shepherd's Notes—Exodus, Ruth, Esther.*

George Lyons, Ph.D., served as Professor of Biblical Literature at Olivet Nazarene University (Kankakee, IL) and is Professor of Biblical Literature at Northwest Nazarene College (Nampa, ID). Dr. Lyons is author of *Pauline Autobiography* and *More Holiness in Everyday Life,* and is a specialist in the Gospels and Paul's letters.

John S. Mason, Th.M., served as Professor of Biblical Studies at Daystar University College, Nairobi, Kenya, and as a missionary in Eritrea. He is editor of the *Tigrinya Grammar,* and assistant editor of the *New Geneva Study Bible.*

David Merling, Ph.D., is Associate Professor of Archaeology and History of Antiquity and Associate Director of the Institute of Archaeology at Andrews University (Berrien Springs, MI). Dr. Merling has directed archaeological digs in Jordan, and is coeditor of *Hesban After 25 Years* and author of *The Book of Joshua: Its Theme and Role in Archaeological Discussions.*

Gerald P. Morris, Ph.D., served as adjunct Professor of Old Testament Interpretation at The Southern Baptist Theological Seminary (Louisville, KY) and as Assistant Professor of Biblical Studies at Ouachita Baptist University (Arkadelphia, AR). Dr. Morris is author of *Prophecy, Poetry and Hosea.*

John W. Wright, Ph.D., served as Visiting Assistant Professor at St. Mary's College (Notre Dame, IN) and the University of Notre Dame and as pastor of the Winamac (IN) Church of the Nazarene. Dr. Wright contributed to *The Anchor Bible Dictionary* as a specialist in Second Temple Judaism, and is Associate Professor of Religion at Point Loma Nazarene College (San Diego, CA).

INTRODUCTION

The Bible was not written at one time nor by one author. The books of the Old and New Testaments were written over a period of more than 1,000 years, and their contents cover a variety of ancient peoples and cultures. If we are to understand and appropriate the Bible's message today, we need some sense of the historical and cultural context in which its diverse parts appeared. We read the words of the Bible today under entirely different circumstances than those under which they were written. To neglect the historical and cultural background of the biblical books is to risk misunderstanding them.

Unfortunately for modern readers, the individual books of the Bible do not always provide the information necessary to understand the Bible's historical and cultural background. At the time that these books were written, readers would have already been familiar with the world the writings describe. But thousands of years later, the events and customs that the original readers would have recognized immediately are often confusing and only dimly understood by modern readers.

The So That's Why! Bible will take you on a journey through the history and culture of the Bible. It will allow you to step back into biblical times and discover the world out of which the Bible grew. It will help you follow the flow of events in the Scriptures and see where sacred and secular history converge into one story of salvation. You will learn how sacred history fits into the context of secular history—why an event happened, how events relate to each other, as well as the cultural, religious, political, and geographical background that influenced the events.

Features for Historical and Cultural Learning

Several features of The So That's Why! Bible will help you understand the history and culture of the Bible.

Chronological Bible Text The entire New King James Version text is rearranged according to the time of the events narrated in each book or passage. Every verse of the Bible is located in one of nine epochs of time.

Transition Commentary Transition Comments explain the placement and chronology of related passages of the Bible.

Each Transition Comment is identified by a Puzzle Icon because the transitions help you "to put the puzzle together." You will learn how different Bible passages relate to each other and how they relate to the history of the ancient Near East and the Greco-Roman world. For instance, chapters 7 and 26 of the Book of Jeremiah preserve two versions of a single sermon. In So That's Why!, these chapters appear together under "Jeremiah's Temple Sermon" (p. 831), along with one of Jeremiah's confessions that responds to the persecution he experienced as a result of his preaching.

Epoch Introductions An "epoch" is a period of time that is characterized by peculiar features or events. So That's Why! will lead you through nine epochs, beginning with Epoch 1 (from creation up to Israel's patriarchs) and finishing with Epoch 9 (the church age and the visions of the end time). Introductions to each epoch discuss the peoples of that time and reveal what archaeology and the biblical literature tell us concerning the period.

Historical Overviews The Bible story unfolds over thousands of years. Historical Overviews provide descriptions of the changing times, helping you to form a mental view of the steps along the way. You will learn the importance of happenings from "The Beginnings of Human Civilization" (p. 3) to "Apocalyptic Writings and the End Time" (p. 1643).

Background Notes At many points, the world we read about in the Bible is related to the world outside the Bible. Background Notes provide information on the events, the customs, the religions, the literature, the politics, the places, and the persons with which the people of Bible times were familiar. For example, in "The Flood Through Other Eyes" (p. 12) you will learn of great flood stories that were told and retold throughout the ancient Near East.

Daily Life Have you ever wondered what life was really like for Bible peoples? Many of their customs differ greatly from ours today. Daily Life insights will acquaint you with topics such as "Cults and Supernatural" and "Politics and Government." In "Marriage and Family" (pp. 46, 71) you will see why being the firstborn son was a privileged position in the ancient family.

Time Panels   It is easier to grasp the passage of time when events are plotted along a time line. Time Panels treat significant topics of the Bible, such as "Paul Becomes a Missionary" (p. 1489), which shows the important occurrences of Paul's life between his conversion and his earliest missionary journeys.

Time Capsules   While the Bible offers some information for determining the dates of particular events, many more events of ancient history find no mention whatsoever in Scripture. Time Capsules provide dates for important episodes and occasions, grouping events inside and outside of the Bible within specific time periods. The list of happenings in "Time Capsule 522 to 520 B.C." (p. 1104) and "Time Capsule 518 to 500 B.C." (p. 1108) shows why the reign of Darius I in Persia was an opportune time for the Jews to rebuild and rededicate the Jerusalem temple. The Time Capsules appear in chronological order throughout *So That's Why!*, but no attempt has been made to locate them at the exact chronological time of the Bible text. Because of uncertainties in establishing an exact date for the Bible narratives, the Time Capsules have been placed only within the approximate time period of a narrative.

Time Charts   How can you organize for your study the years and years of time that relate to what you read in Scripture? Time Charts provide visual overviews of important chronological topics in the Bible. The final pages of the New Testament warn of Jerusalem's demise, and "The Fate of Jerusalem" (p. 1653) charts Jerusalem's rocky course of events from the temple's desecration by Antiochus IV to the city being renamed Aelia Capitolina as a Roman colony.

Maps   Maps provide knowledge of the geography of biblical times. 48 in-text maps appear throughout *So That's Why!* showing the Bible lands as the ancient peoples knew them. In "The Hyksos Empire" (p. 69) you will see that during patriarchal times foreigners ruled a region encompassing Egypt as well as Palestine, which was then known as "Retenu."

Index of Scripture Passages   To find any particular passage of Scripture, turn to the page numbers listed for that Scripture in the *Index of Scripture Passages*. Every passage of the Bible is listed in canonical order.

Cultural and Historical Topics   Are you interested in the lives of ancient peoples? Do you want to learn about their daily customs? The gods and goddesses they worshiped? The places where they lived and worked? The writings they read? The peoples, rulers, and nations that affected their lives? *Cultural and Historical Topics* will help you locate such information in the Background Notes.

Glossary   The Background Notes mention certain names, places, and things that are unfamiliar to us today. The brief descriptions and explanations of these subjects in the *Glossary* provide clarification when you need it.

Scripture References   References at the top of each page help you locate the Bible passages appearing on a particular page. For example, references in capital letters (LUKE 2:28) indicate either the first or last verse on a page. References in lowercase letters (Luke 2:21) indicate the first verse that follows a Transition Commentary on that page.

Reading a Chronological Text

This study Bible's attempt to rearrange the Bible text in the order of the events it narrates will probably highlight some difficulties that many Bible readers have never noticed. The Bible as it really is, not as we have imaginatively harmonized it in our minds, may be a bit unsettling at first. But to recognize such problems will only help readers better appreciate the efforts of serious biblical scholars to interpret the Bible. One goal of *So That's Why!* is to help Bible readers join the scholars' quest for historical truth.

Rearranging the Bible is, of course, a fallible human effort. Even those who have earned advanced degrees in the various fields of biblical studies would disagree on any particular rearrangement. The editors of *So That's Why!* have been forced at times to make hard decisions, to choose one location at the neglect of another that is equally plausible. In such instances, an honest effort has been made to acknowledge another possible arrangement and to present its case fairly. This allows readers to decide the issues for themselves.

In the case of debated issues *So That's Why!* avoids presenting a single, biased perspective. Rather, it treats evenhandedly the entire spectrum of credible opinion on disputed matters. It takes with equal seriousness the views of traditional, conservative Bible students and those of modern, critical scholarship. No attempt is made to persuade readers that one particular view is correct; that determination is ultimately their prayerful and thoughtful responsibility.

Rearranging the order of the Bible's books may appear to some readers to be a violation of the integrity of the Bible. The goal of *So That's Why!* is not to replace the time-honored canonical arrangement, but instead to honor time as the setting in which the biblical record appeared. Readers who study this Bible will return to their traditional Bibles better equipped to read them. No longer will its words be disconnected holy pronouncements out of the blue. They will be seen for what they really are: words "fitly spoken . . . like apples of gold in settings of silver" (Prov. 25:11). To acquire a sense of the flow of the Bible's story will put flesh and blood on its message.

READING THEOLOGICAL HISTORY

One goal of *The So That's Why! Bible* is to help readers acquire a greater appreciation for the historical dimensions of the biblical message. The Bible is not a theology book arranged according to topics: God, man, sin, salvation, etc. Nor is it simply a chronicle of events from creation to the final consummation. Historical events are often the Bible's subject matter, but these events are always reported from a particular perspective. That perspective is theological history. It is in the arena of history that God has chosen to make Himself known.

History and the Old Testament

The Old Testament is centered in history. It describes historical events and is addressed, at one level at least, to a specific historical audience: the Hebrew people. This makes the faith taught in the Bible very different from the beliefs of other ancient Near Eastern peoples.

The peoples surrounding the Hebrews built their religious beliefs on the rhythms of nature. The world had visible patterns, but to its inhabitants these rhythms were unexplainable, uncontrollable, and therefore attributed to the gods. There were gods to represent all the phenomena of nature: gods of the sun, moon, rain, storms, rivers, seas, and the earth itself. The typical religious expression of such religion was the myth, a story that explained these unexplainable features of nature. For instance, almost every people had a myth of a deity who was dead for part of the year and alive for the rest of the year—a story that explained the recurring cycle of the seasons.

The God of the Old Testament is very different. Most importantly, He is one God. All the phenomena that other peoples regarded as gods are simply the creations of the one God. In the other religions of the ancient Near East, nature was divine; in the Bible, God both created nature and was more than nature. The God of the Bible deals with His creation not in recurring, regular patterns, but in one-time, extraordinary moments of self-revelation. Moreover, these moments when God acts on earth are not described in vague, mythic language ("long ago, in the land of the gods"), but occur in real time, in recognizable locations on earth.

For this reason, the Old Testament's primary mode of communication is not myth, but history. Israel was not interested in describing how God acts in continual repetition in nature; Israel wanted to tell how God had performed unique, one-time actions in human history. They wanted to tell how at specific moments in history, God chose Abraham, blessed Jacob, and saved Abraham's and Jacob's descendants from slavery in Egypt. They wanted to tell how God established His chosen king over Israel, how God allowed that kingdom to be destroyed, and how once again God rescued His people from captivity. To tell their very different sort of faith, the Israelites used the art of history writing, and the Old Testament itself contains some of the very earliest examples of this art.

Of course, not all of the Old Testament consists of history writing. But even the parts of the Old Testament that are not history writing themselves usually appear in some historical context. The oracles, speeches, and poetry of the prophets are not history, but they are addressed to real people in real historical situations. They recall God's mighty acts of the historical past; they promise that God can and will act in history again. Books of wisdom and philosophy that do not speak of history at all, like Proverbs and Ecclesiastes, are nevertheless identified with the historical context of King Solomon's court. Even the psalms, intended for regular repetition in public worship, often provide a historical background, such as Ps. 3, superscribed as "A Psalm of David when he fled from Absalom his son."

Israel understood God as a God who acts in history, and for this reason almost every religious utterance was read in light of the history of God's mighty acts. Therefore, to understand the Old Testament as it is meant to be understood, the reader must have some grasp of the historical events that lie behind each chapter and book. Unless the reader knows the history of Israel and the ancient Near East, the Bible will always be to some extent a closed book.

The New Testament and the Old

The Old Testament was the Bible of the New Testament writers. Old Testament images and concepts filled their minds. Allusions to the Old Testament appear on nearly every page of their writings. The teaching of the Old Testament was basic to their thought.

These New Testament writers also believed that Christ was God's final revelation, the One who brought the earlier revelation into proper focus (Heb. 1:1, 2). Indeed, the risen Christ Himself had explained to His disciples how He fulfilled the Scriptures (Luke 24:27). Thus New Testament writers understood Him to be the One who brought to completion God's plan of salvation recorded in the early chapters of Genesis.

History writing in the New Testament is certainly a theological history. The authors believed that the purpose and meaning of history could be found in Christ. Therefore, the history of which they wrote was salvation history. God's earlier saving works looked forward to the Cross. God's bringing His people out of Egypt became a pattern for Christ's atoning work. At the Passover meal commemorating this deliverance from bondage, Christ made the bread and wine symbols of His death and of the new covenant (Luke 22:19, 20). History had reached its highest point in Him. So Paul, the most influential teacher of Christianity, wrote about the Jesus who appeared to him on the Damascus Road, describing the risen Christ as the one "through whom are all things, and through whom we live" (1 Cor. 8:6).

The Message and the Historical Setting

While both the Old and New Testaments present their message on a historical frame, the message takes precedence to the historical setting. The writers of biblical history did not write in the same manner as a modern historian. Ancient history writers were not as interested in "when something happened" as they were in the meaning of the events they were recounting. Therefore the reader of biblical history must be aware that many of the concerns that dominate modern history writing (specific dates, discussions of natural causes) simply were not very important to most of the biblical writers.

The contributors to *The So That's Why! Bible* do not attempt to understand the theological history of the Bible in the same sense as modern history. Rather, *So That's Why!* follows the salvation story through a sequence of unfolding events across the epochs of time. Hopefully this unique presentation of Scripture will allow us to read theological history from a refreshing, new perspective.

REARRANGING THE BIBLE'S CANONICAL ORDER

The individual books included in the Old and New Testaments as authoritative are called "the canon." For some readers, the placement of these books in our English Bibles (called "canonical order") is slightly confusing, since it does not always follow chronological order. Rather, it follows the order of the Latin Vulgate translated by Jerome in the 4th century A.D.

A reader can follow the Old Testament chronology easily for the first dozen books (Genesis through 2 Kings), but after that the chronological order often disappears. The books of Chronicles through Esther backtrack and retell many of the events already described. Portions of the books of Psalms and Proverbs refer to times that are centuries apart, and the prophetic writings, speaking of widely different times, are not presented in straight chronological order.

The New Testament reader also faces some chronological uncertainty. The life of Jesus appears in four Gospels, and while all four Gospels report information about Jesus in general chronological order, none do so strictly. Certain sayings or events appear in differing sequences in the various Gospels. Each of the authors had a slightly different purpose and audience in mind, and structured his materials in order to achieve the greatest effectiveness. Determining the events of Paul's life is not simple since the information from his letters does not always connect directly with the narrative of the Book of Acts.

Thus the canonical order presents a dilemma. To understand the Bible the reader must understand something of the history to which the Bible refers. At the same time, though, that historical background is not readily apparent from the order of the books in the Bible itself. *The So That's Why! Bible* makes the Bible's historical background more accessible by rearranging the Bible text according to nine epochs of time.

Moving Whole Books. To begin with, whole books of the Bible are relocated according to the historical time period narrated in the books. This reordering disrupts the canonical order of the books, and though this might seem irreverent to some people, it actually continues an ancient practice. The order of books in the Septuagint (the Greek Old Testament) differs from that of the older Hebrew Bible, and some of the Septuagint reordering is reflected in our English Old Testaments.

The early Greek translators, thinking a chronological order would make more sense, moved such books as Ruth, Ezra, and Nehemiah from their positions in the Hebrew manuscripts. The Book of Ruth does not appear after the Book of Judges in the Hebrew Bible, but near the end of the Bible. The books of Ezra and Nehemiah come before the books of Chronicles, even though they narrate events occurring later in time than those narrated by Chronicles. When the Old Testament was translated into Greek during the Hellenistic era (336–37 B.C.), the confusing chronology of the Hebrew Bible was changed by relocating several of these books. The Book of Ruth, which tells of events during the final years of the judges, was inserted between the books of Judges and 1 Samuel, while Ezra and Nehemiah were placed after 2 Chronicles.

Moving Portions of Books. Chronological confusion is not restricted to the order of whole books, however. The contents of certain individual books are not in chronological order, making it difficult for a modern reader to comprehend the historical context. So in addition to reordering whole books, even the contents of individual books have been rearranged—quite extensively in books like Isaiah and Jeremiah—to follow a chronological outline.

Combining Portions of Books. Moreover, various books have been woven together. For instance, the historical books of Kings and Chronicles are often interrupted by prophetic books or passages that pertain to the time described in the history. The four Gospels are combined into one presentation following the sequence of the Gospel of Mark. Certain of Paul's letters are inserted into the Book of Acts.

Principles of Rearrangement

Rearranging the biblical books chronologically is by no means easily accomplished, since Bible scholars differ on almost every important point of chronology. The rearrangement in *So That's Why!* is based on two distinct chronological goals. First, it provides a *relative chronology,* placing related events together without fixed dates.

For instance, the prophet Amos spoke in the northern kingdom of Israel during the reign of Jeroboam II, and so the history of Jeroboam II is read alongside the words of Amos that refer to Jeroboam's time. Second, *So That's Why!* provides an *absolute chronology* tied to historical information and fixed dates (or at least tentative dates). An absolute chronology enables readers to place the biblical history in the larger context of world history.

There are imposing difficulties with any attempt to construct either relative or absolute chronologies. Many biblical passages offer no chronological specificity. Even among books and passages that provide some indication of a specific historical context, the intended context is not always clear. For instance, the oracle of Jer. 14 is dated to the time of "the droughts," and Jeremiah's original audience supposedly had no trouble identifying this time. Modern readers, however, are not so fortunate: Were these droughts during the reign of King Josiah or King Jehoiakim or King Zedekiah? Jeremiah's prophetic career spans the reigns of all three kings. In the Book of Joel another prophet responds to a locust plague that ravaged the land of Judah. But when was that plague? Different scholars place Joel in at least three different centuries. All one can do in selecting a time period for the Book of Joel is to look at clues within the prophecy itself and then, in all humility, guess.

Difficulties vary with the different books of the Bible because those books differ from each other in the type of chronological issues they raise. *The So That's Why! Bible* addresses the unique problems of each portion of the Bible.

Genesis Through Joshua

The books of the Bible that narrate the earliest events do not provide specific years or refer to specific events or names that can be dated by other means. Even such a central figure as the individual who was Egypt's pharaoh during the Exodus is never referred to by name. Moreover, the years that are given are often suspiciously round numbers—like 40 years, which may be simply a symbolic number representing one generation.

Due to this lack of specific chronological information, scholars disagree widely on exactly when to date many events of early Israelite history. The Hebrews' exodus from Egypt, for example, is dated by many scholars in the 15th century B.C., whereas other scholars place it 200 years later, during the

13th century. The choice of either of these dates does not affect the chronological sequence of the narrative: by either date the Exodus precedes the conquest. So in *So That's Why!* both dates are given without stating any preference. The dates of the Exodus, wilderness wandering, and the conquest under Joshua are interrelated; consequently, the date a person favors for the Exodus determines the dating of the other two events.

The Exodus and Wilderness Wandering

When presenting relative chronology, the passages of the Bible are ordered according to the history that is narrated in the passage, not according to the time of the book's writing. For instance, the books of Exodus through Deuteronomy narrate the events of Israel's departure from Egypt and the subsequent wilderness wanderings. In *So That's Why!*, these books appear in the historical context of the Exodus, although many scholars argue that parts of these books were written much later. Regardless of when these books were written, their narrative can be appreciated as marvelous literature telling a story set in the time of the Hebrew exodus from Egypt.

Samuel, Kings, and Chronicles

The books of 1 and 2 Kings represent historical accounts that were evidently put together in their current form during the Babylonian exile (597–539 B.C.). Yet, because they narrate events as far back in time as the death of King David (about 970 B.C.), the books of Kings are not located in *So That's Why!* during their time of writing (the Exile), but rather are divided up and associated with the various historical eras which they narrate.

The history of the Israelite kingdoms is recounted in two full-length histories. The first is recorded in the books of Samuel and Kings, and the second appears in the books of Chronicles. The two histories are very similar; indeed, 1 and 2 Chronicles often quote directly from the earlier history of Samuel/Kings. Yet there are some marked differences in perspective. Whereas Samuel and Kings emphasize the religious leadership of prophets, Chronicles emphasizes the role of the priests. In order to present both historical accounts in their entirety, while staying as close as possible to chronological order, the two histories alternate. The account of a particular historical time appears first as told in Samuel or Kings, being labeled "Prophetic Account." Then the same history as told in Chronicles follows, being labeled "Priestly Account." This dual history begins at the reign of King Saul and continues until the destruction of Jerusalem, at which time a single chronological account resumes.

The Kings of the Divided Monarchy

Israel and Judah kept careful records of the lengths of reign of their rulers. The Bible's dates for the kings are relative dates, cross-referencing them to each other: for instance, Ahab became king of Israel in the 38th year of Asa king of Judah (1 Kin. 16:29). Since no definite year is given for the beginning of Asa's reign, however, this information alone is not enough to establish Ahab's dates.

An additional problem occurs when the years of reign are totaled. When the years given for the kings of Israel and Judah are added up, Israel's totals do not always correspond to Judah's. These apparent inconsistencies may appear for various reasons. When one king dies and another is crowned, is that year counted twice—as the last year of the deceased king and also as the first year of the new king? When a crown prince rules as regent while his royal father is still alive, as happens more than once, are the years of the coregency counted in the reigns of both kings? These questions make it difficult to utilize the years of reign in calculating an overall chronology. To provide a consistent presentation, So That's Why! adapts the system of dates for the kings found in The Mysterious Numbers of the Hebrew Kings by Edwin R. Thiele.

In the later history of Israel, the dates are much more certain, though a few chronological problems remain. Occasionally a biblical historian will recount some event out of chronological order, usually to make a theological point. For instance, the very last event described in the life of Hezekiah king of Judah is his entertaining of ambassadors from Babylon (2 Kin. 20:12–19; Is. 39:1–8). Evidence from both inside and outside of the Bible reveals that that event actually occurred earlier, certainly not just before Hezekiah's death (2 Kin. 20:21). The biblical historian evidently moved the account to the end because of the prophet Isaiah's warning about Babylon. During Hezekiah's reign, God had delivered Judah from Assyria, but the historian foreshadows a coming time when God would allow Judah to fall to Babylon. Emphasizing chronological order, So That's Why! restores such temporal displacements to their probable chronological contexts.

The Prophets

Other biblical books also concern the time covered by the Samuel/Kings and Chronicles double history. In So That's Why! most of the prophetic books are inserted at the appropriate historical points in the "Prophetic Account." Several groups of psalms as well as the words of the priestly prophet Ezekiel appear within the "Priestly Account." Books are inserted within the Prophetic and the Priestly accounts according to the events which are narrated or prophesied, not according to the times when the books were written. The Book of Jonah, for instance, is often thought to have been composed some time in the Persian era (559–331 B.C.), but events in the book are set in the lifetime of the prophet Jonah, who lived centuries earlier, during the reign of Jeroboam II (793–753 B.C.). Thus, the Book of Jonah appears in the context of Jeroboam's reign.

Other prophetic passages speak of times later than the traditional date of composition for the passage itself. For example, parts of the Book of Isaiah refer to events that took place centuries after the prophet Isaiah lived. Though Isaiah prophesied in Jerusalem during the 8th century B.C., the passage of Is. 44:28; 45:1 refers by name to Cyrus, a Persian king who lived in the 6th century. For this reason, some chapters from the Book of Isaiah appear in the time of Cyrus (539–530 B.C.). While scholars disagree whether these chapters were written by Isaiah of Jerusalem or by a later prophet during the 6th century, they agree that the 6th century is the time to which these chapters refer.

The Book of Ezekiel provides many dates, most of which indicate when the prophet received a message from God. To calculate his dates Ezekiel began counting from the exile of Jehoiachin to Babylon in 597 B.C. Each date is expressed as a "year of King Jehoiachin's captivity" (Ezek. 1:2) or a "year of our captivity" (Ezek. 33:21). In providing modern equivalents for Ezekiel's dates, So That's Why! follows the system of dates compiled in Babylonian Chronology 626 B.C.–A.D. 75 by R. A. Parker and W. H. Dubberstein.

The Book of Jeremiah

The Book of Jeremiah, perhaps the most radically rearranged book in So That's Why!, is a prime example of a book that lacks chronological order in its canonical form. As one of the most history-conscious of the prophetic books, Jeremiah refers specifically to individual kings and officials and even includes several historical narratives. At the same time, though, these history-minded oracles and historical narratives are not presented in anything resembling chronological order. Even the historical narratives of Jer. 25—29; 32—40 skip back and forth in time (see Jer. 25:1; 26:1; 32:1; 36:1). Thus although the Book of Jeremiah is only understandable in light of the historical events surrounding the destruction of Jerusalem in 586 B.C., simply reading the book from start to finish does not give the reader that necessary understanding.

Messianic Prophecies

Messianic prophecies raise a question as to the time period to which a particular prophecy refers. The New Testament takes great care to demonstrate that many Old Testament passages ultimately refer to the person and work of Jesus Christ. It would make sense to locate such Old Testament passages at pertinent places in the life of Jesus. This has not been done, however. Without denying that messianic prophecies are ultimately fulfilled in Christ, most of them also have significance for their original Old Testament time period. For instance, the promise in Is. 7:14, "Behold, the virgin shall conceive and bear a Son," is quoted in Matt. 1:23 as a reference to Christ's virgin birth. In the context of Is. 7, though, the promise is a part of the prophet Isaiah's larger message to Judah's king Ahaz, providing a sign that he should not fear the nations of Syria and Israel, for they would soon be destroyed (Is. 7:16). This prophecy has significance for more than one time period, and in *So That's Why!* appears in its original context, during the reign of Ahaz, even though its prophetic significance extends to the later context at the birth of Christ.

Wisdom Literature and Psalms

Some of the most hotly contested debates among Old Testament scholars concern the date when this or that passage was composed. Fortunately, *So That's Why!* only seeks to place biblical passages according to the setting described, a question about which there is more agreement. Even so, complete scholarly consensus still is not possible, and sometimes it is not certain to which time period various passages refer.

The wisdom literature of Proverbs, Ecclesiastes, and Job is an example of such chronological uncertainty. While most of the Old Testament is centered in history, these writings are an exception. Wisdom speaks of universal, practical matters that apply to all people of all nations in all ages. A proverb like "Hatred stirs up strife, But love covers all sins" (Prov. 10:12), for example, applies just as well to every age. Most of the Book of Proverbs and all of the Book of Ecclesiastes are associated with the court of King Solomon, the revered head of the wisdom movement in Israel. So in *So That's Why!* these passages appear in Solomon's time. Some sections of Proverbs and the whole Book of Job, however, defy chronological placement. For this reason, these writings are separated from the chronology and located, somewhat arbitrarily, in the Babylonian exile.

The psalms also intentionally resist chronological placement. For the most part, they do not refer to any one time, but rather speak in general language, providing words for worship in the temple. Some psalms do have superscriptions that associate them with particular events—usually from the life of David—and these superscriptions have determined the placement of certain psalms. Most of the psalms, however, are timeless, and without a historical context to follow can be placed only in reaction to their content. David's hymns of praise appear, as a block, in a time when David praised God: when he brought the ark of the covenant into Jerusalem (1 Chr. 15:29). On the other hand, David's laments appear at a time when David lamented: during a plague (1 Chr. 21:30). Other psalms appear in other historical contexts, from the fall of Jerusalem (Ps. 89) to the Babylonian captivity (Ps. 137) to the rebuilding of Jerusalem under Nehemiah (Ps. 120—134).

The Gospels

A challenging task faces us when we attempt to arrange the Gospels into a chronological presentation of Jesus' life. If early Christian tradition is correct, Mark's Gospel was not written to provide a sequential account of the events in Jesus' life. If the other Synoptic Gospels—Matthew and Luke—are related to Mark, as most scholars believe, they are not organized primarily along chronological lines either. What has long been recognized about John's Gospel is probably also true of the Synoptic Gospels: the Gospel writers' theological interests and their communities' practical needs were more decisive than historical concerns.

None of the Gospels satisfy our modern expectations of a biography of Jesus. This is not the fault of the Gospel writers; they had different purposes for writing, which will disappoint those whose only interest is history. But when we do ask historical questions, what, for example, should we conclude about the Gospel authors reporting events in the life of Jesus in different sequences?

The Synoptic Problem

The first three Gospels are called the Synoptic Gospels. The word "Synoptic" comes from two Greek words meaning "seen together." Matthew, Mark, and Luke tell the story of Jesus in essentially the same sequence and in nearly identical terms. The similarities are especially obvious when these three Gospels are compared with John. But equally striking are their conspicuous differences when compared closely with each other. This creates what scholars call the "Synoptic Problem": How can both similarities and differences be satisfactorily explained?

Similarities might be explained by appeal to the Gospels' divine inspiration. But this fails to account for their differences. Virtually all scholars today agree that the similarities among the Synoptic Gospels are so close as to require a literary explanation. That is, either all three copied from a lost earlier gospel or two of the Gospels depended on the third.

Other gospels did exist, which are called "apocryphal" because the church never accepted them. The apocryphal gospels were never widely used. Some were rejected because they seemed to promote false doctrines. Others were dismissed as merely fanciful speculations designed to answer the curious questions of those familiar with the canonical Gospels. In any case, none of the apocryphal gospels that survive explain the similarities among the canonical Gospels.

Various theories have been proposed to explain how the Gospels might have depended on each other. St. Augustine proposed the theory that Matthew was the earliest Gospel and that Luke and Mark used it in writing theirs. Many modern scholars espouse a similar view. But since the 19th century most scholars have presumed that Mark was the earliest Gospel. Even assuming that Mark was written first still does not account for all the similarities among the Synoptic Gospels. To offer more explanation, most scholars assume that, in addition to Mark, Matthew and Luke depended on a now-lost source. This hypothetical source is generally called "Q," an abbreviation for the German word *Quelle,* meaning "source."

Both ancient tradition and scholarly opinion seem to agree that Mark was the earliest Gospel. Since we cannot be certain of the exact sequence of events, the life of Jesus in *So That's Why!* follows Mark's order. Additional information provided by the other Gospels is arranged in what seems to be the most plausible order around Mark's framework.

Acts of the Apostles

The second task in rearranging the New Testament books is to construct a chronology of important events that occurred during the lives of the apostles and during the early years of the Christian church. The Book of Acts and the New Testament letters serve as the basis for the chronology of the church age. References to the political leaders during this time help pinpoint certain dates.

The Book of Acts is the one book of the New Testament which traces the development of the early church after the ascension of Jesus. Standing between the Gospels and the New Testament letters, Acts is a bridge between the life of Jesus and the ministry of the apostle Paul. As such, the narrative of Acts is one source of historical information about the early church.

There is little doubt that the Book of Acts and the Gospel of Luke come from the same author. Since the author does not identify himself by name, scholars have ascribed the authorship of both books to Luke, the companion of Paul (2 Tim. 4:11). Luke was closely associated with many events of Paul's mission, and this results in greater vividness in the latter half of Acts. At places (see Acts 16:10–17), the narrative changes to the first person ("we"), indicating that Luke was personally present. Nevertheless, some scholars believe that the books of Luke and Acts were written by an anonymous writer who was later identified with Luke. Also questioned is whether Luke is a reliable historian, since his primary motive for writing was not to record history, but to inform his audience of the triumphant course of the gospel, beginning in Jesus and continuing in the church (Acts 1:1). Thus, other scholars look to Paul's letters for a chronology of his ministry.

Paul's Letters

Paul the apostle was the earliest and most influential interpreter of Christ's message and teaching. As an early Christian missionary, Paul founded and corresponded with several early Christian churches. Using Paul's letters, however, to determine a chronology of events in his life is difficult. The letters do not provide any specific dates or a sequence of events, but only offer pieces of information which scholars try to relate to the narrative of Acts. To make the task more difficult, scholars cannot agree on the sequence in which Paul wrote his letters, nor on whether all of the letters accredited to Paul were actually written by him.

The New Testament letters follow the general custom and form of letters which became an important form of communication in the Greek-speaking world about 300 years before the birth of Jesus. The Roman government provided postal service only for official documents, so private letters were sent by special messengers or friendly travelers. Letters normally were sent to designated parties, although some were "open" or circular letters. Paul's letters, with the possible exception of Ephesians, were addressed to specific congregations.

Ancient letters normally followed a pattern which included: (1) an introduction, listing the names of sender and recipient, followed by a formal greeting inquiring about the recipient's health and a thanksgiving formula; (2) a body, or purpose for writing; and (3) a conclusion, consisting of appropriate remarks and a farewell. Paul's letters follow this pattern, with some exceptions. Paul replaced the bland greeting of inquiry about health with a salutation combining Christian grace and Hebrew peace. His thanksgiving was likewise more than a formality; it was a sincere expression of gratitude for the well-being of his congregations. He also omitted the farewell in favor of personal greetings or a benediction.

Since Paul's letters do not provide a sequence of events, So That's Why! follows the narrative sequence of Acts. In the Old Testament, books were rearranged based on the description of the narrative. Since the New Testament letters describe themselves as communication written from a particular sender to intended recipients, individual letters have been placed according to this description, if possible. In canonical Bibles, the Pauline letters are arranged in the New Testament according to length, from the longest (Romans) to the shortest (Philemon). In So That's Why! they have been arranged, as much as possible, according to information given in the salutations, greetings, and bodies of the letters.

The Prison Epistles

The Book of Acts ends with Paul in prison in Rome. Four letters—Philippians, Philemon, Colossians, and Ephesians—are known as the Prison Epistles, since all make reference to Paul being in prison. Paul, however, was imprisoned in Caesarea and possibly in Ephesus, besides Rome, so the placement of any one of the Prison Epistles must be considered tentative.

The Pastoral Letters

The chronology from Paul's imprisonment on is drawn from inferences in the New Testament letters, which have been arranged in So That's Why! according to their salutations, where possible. The Pastoral Letters—1 and 2 Timothy and Titus—have been placed according to the belief of some that Paul was released from Roman imprisonment to continue missionary work in Macedonia. If Paul was martyred while in prison, however, possibly in A.D. 64., these letters would have been compiled much later, by an unknown editor.

The Last New Testament Writings

The final books of the New Testament offer little help in determining a chronology. According to tradition, Peter was martyred in A.D. 64, so the letters of 1 and 2 Peter have been placed in So That's Why! just before that time. Those who think one or both of the letters were written by an unknown author would place them later. Writings such as Hebrews and the letters of 1, 2, and 3 John indicate some time in the last half of the 1st century A.D., but a more precise dating is impossible. The Book of Revelation appears last in So That's Why! Its contents are not limited to a specific time; the author wrote about God's plan for his own day and for the far future.

NEW KING JAMES VERSION

The Bible Text

The format of the New King James Version is designed to enhance the vividness and devotional quality of the Holy Scriptures:

—Subject headings assist the reader to identify topics and transitions in the biblical content.

—Words or phrases in *italics* indicate expressions in the original language which require clarification by additional English words.

—*Oblique type* in the New Testament indicates a quotation from the Old Testament.

—Prose is divided into paragraphs to indicate the structure of thought.

—Poetry is structured as contemporary verse to reflect the poetic form and beauty of the passage in the original language.

—The covenant name of God was usually translated from the Hebrew as "LORD" or "GOD" (using capital letters as shown) in the King James Old Testament. This tradition is maintained. In the present edition the name is so capitalized whenever the covenant name is quoted in the New Testament from a passage in the Old Testament.

The Old Testament Text

For the New King James Version the Old Testament text used was the 1967/1977 Stuttgart edition of the *Biblia Hebraica,* with frequent comparisons being made with the Bomberg edition of 1524–25. The Septuagint (Greek) Version of the Old Testament and the Latin Vulgate also were consulted. In addition to referring to a variety of ancient versions of the Hebrew Scriptures, the New King James Version draws on the resources of relevant manuscripts from the Dead Sea caves. In the few places where the Hebrew was so obscure that the 1611 King James was compelled to follow one of the versions, but where information is now available to resolve the problems, the New King James Version follows the Hebrew text. Significant variations are recorded in the footnotes.

The New Testament Text

The King James New Testament was based on the traditional text of the Greek-speaking churches, first published in 1516, and later called the Textus Receptus or Received Text. Although based on the relatively few available manuscripts, these were representative of many more which existed at the time but only became known later. One viewpoint of New Testament scholarship holds that the Byzantine Text that largely supports the Textus Receptus has as much right as the Alexandrian or any other tradition to be weighed in determining the text of the New Testament.

Since the 1880s most contemporary translations of the New Testament have relied upon a relatively few manuscripts discovered chiefly in the late nineteenth and early twentieth centuries. Such translations depend primarily on two manuscripts, Codex Vaticanus and Codex Sinaiticus, because of their greater age. The Greek text obtained by using these sources and the related papyri (our most ancient manuscripts) is known as the Alexandrian Text. The Critical Text (so called because it is edited according to specific principles of textual criticism) depends heavily upon the Alexandrian type of text.

A third viewpoint of New Testament scholarship favors a text based on the consensus of the majority of existing Greek manuscripts. This text is called the Majority Text. Most of these manuscripts are in substantial agreement. Even though many are late, and none is earlier than the fifth century, usually their readings are verified by papyri, ancient versions, quotations from the early church fathers, or a combination of these. The Majority Text is similar to the Textus Receptus, but it corrects those readings which have little or no support in the Greek manuscript tradition.

Because the New King James Version is the fifth revision of a historic document translated from specific Greek texts, the editors decided to retain the traditional text in the body of the New Testament and to indicate major Critical and Majority Text variant readings in the footnotes. Although these variations are duly indicated in the footnotes of the present edition, it is most important to emphasize that fully eighty-five percent of the New Testament text is the same in the Textus Receptus, the Alexandrian Text, and the Majority Text.

New King James Footnotes

Significant explanatory notes, alternate translations, and cross-references, as well as New Testament citations of Old Testament passages, are supplied in the footnotes.

Important textual variants in the Old Testament are identified in a standard form.

The textual notes in the present edition of the New Testament make no evaluation of readings, but do clearly indicate the manuscript sources of readings. They objectively present the facts without such tendentious remarks as "the best manuscripts omit" or "the most reliable manuscripts read." Such notes are value judgments that differ according to varying viewpoints on the text. By giving a clearly defined set of variants the New King James Version benefits readers of all textual persuasions.

Where significant variations occur in the New Testament Greek manuscripts, textual notes are classified as follows:

1. **NU-Text**

   These variations from the traditional text generally represent the Alexandrian or Egyptian type of text described previously in "The New Testament Text." They are found in the Critical Text published in the twenty-seventh edition of the Nestle-Aland Greek New Testament (N) and in the United Bible Societies' fourth edition (U), hence the acronym, "NU-Text."

2. **M-Text**

   This symbol indicates points of variation in the Majority Text from the traditional text, as also previously discussed in "The New Testament Text." It should be noted that M stands for whatever reading is printed in the published *Greek New Testament According to the Majority Text,* whether supported by overwhelming, strong, or only a divided majority textual tradition.

The textual notes reflect the scholarship of the past 150 years and will assist the reader to observe the variations between the different manuscript traditions of the New Testament. Such information is generally not available in English translations of the New Testament.

BEFORE THE PATRIARCHS

(Creation—2000 B.C.)

Humankind's earliest ancestors appear in what is called "prehistory"—before events were recorded. Then humans pioneered writing, and "history" began.

The Bible begins its story with the accounts of creation and of humankind's early history. The epoch extending from undatable creation to about 2000 B.C. witnessed the beginning both of life itself and of humankind's first civilizations. This is the time before the patriarchs Abraham, Isaac, and Jacob, long before Israel became a specific people. It is the time of humankind's earliest ancestors.

The very earliest part of this epoch is called "prehistory" because it covers the story of humans before there were recorded events. The advent of writing around 3000 B.C. eventually ended "prehistory," as humans began preserving information concerning their economies, laws, and religions. The various written documents of this period, including lists of kings, inscriptions from buildings, and historical epics, mark the start of the historical era.

▶ Archaeology and the Past

Archaeologists arrange historical and cultural evidence according to the most vital metal of each period, such as stone, copper, bronze, or iron. The earliest period, called the Stone Age, is divided into the Old Stone, Middle Stone, and New Stone ages. A later period, the Bronze Age, is also divided into the Early Bronze, Middle Bronze, and Late Bronze ages. The dates for these periods are approximate, of course, because cultural changes always come gradually. Very early dates are based on theories of evolution and geology, and interpreters of the Bible differ on how such dates relate to the creation accounts in Genesis.

Old Stone Age	before 10,000 B.C.
Middle Stone Age	10,000 to 8000 B.C.
New Stone Age	8000 to 4000 B.C.
Copper-Stone Age	4000 to 3000 B.C.
Early Bronze Age	3000 to 2000 B.C.

The Old Stone Age is designated by the name "Paleolithic." It was an age of hunting and food-gathering. People lived in caves or temporary shelters. They made implements of flint or chipped stone, and subsisted from what they could gather from nature itself.

The Middle Stone Age is called the Mesolithic period. It was a transitional stage to a food-producing economy. During this period real settlements first appeared, and there was an evolution in the arts of civilization.

The New Stone Age, or Neolithic period, is distinguished by several advances. One of the most notable, the invention of pottery, divides the New Stone Age into a prepottery period (c. 8000–5500 B.C.) and a pottery period (c. 5500–4000 B.C.). Other developments included agriculture, textiles, and the domestication of animals.

The Copper-Stone Age, or Chalcolithic period, saw a transition to a significant use of copper. At some sites from this period, dwellings were underground, entered by shafts from the surface and connected by tunnels. Copper working was found in the many pits, ovens, and fireplaces common in such sites.

The Early Bronze Age is the period in which we leave "prehistory" and enter the "historical" period. This is the period in which written records appear. The Mesopotamians pioneered writing, but Egypt was quick to recognize the benefits of it. At the site of Arad in Palestine, archaeologists have uncovered a potsherd bearing the signature of Narmer, who is often identified with Menes, the pharaoh of Egypt's first dynasty.

▶ The Peoples and Groups

The story of the Bible is linked with the histories of two great lands: Mesopotamia and Egypt. In Mesopotamia two different cultures developed, one in the south and the other in the north.

The earliest known inhabitants of Mesopotamia lived in the southern part, the land of Sumer or southern Babylonia. Known as Sumerians, this culture greatly influenced all of the ancient Near East, including the Israelites. The Sumerians developed a township system of government, consisting of city-states, in which the temple of the local deity was the center of economic, cultural, and religious life.

The story of the Bible is linked with the histories of two great lands: Mesopotamia and Egypt.

In northern Babylonia lived the Accadians. This culture took its name from the town of Agade, also known as Accad. The Accadian culture did not develop the independent city-state system of the south, but seems to have existed as a single territory. While there were temples, the palace and household played the more important role in the Accadian economy. Around 2300 B.C. a northerner named Sargon of Agade was able to unify north and south Babylonia.

Egypt was a land divided into two kingdoms: Lower Egypt around the Nile Delta and Upper Egypt of the Nile Valley. Egypt's prehistory or predynastic period witnessed the development of rulership by pharaohs. This period ended around 3000 B.C. with the unification of Lower and Upper Egypt by the ruler Menes, resulting in the First Dynasty. During the following Archaic period, the country came to accept a divine monarchy in which the pharaoh was considered the incarnation of the sky god Horus. Later pharaohs of the Old Kingdom, beginning about 2700 B.C., became famous for their pyramids.

▶ The Biblical Literature

The Book of Genesis is usually divided at Gen. 12, where the story of the patriarch Abraham begins. The chapters of Gen. 1—11, which concern the time before the patriarchs, are called "primeval history" because they relate the first ages of the world. Primeval history tells of a time much different from what the patriarchs would later experience, and from what humans experience now.

The major narratives of this primeval history give an account of creation, a great Flood, and the tower at Babel. The creation account (Gen. 1—3) describes the creation of all things, including humankind. The newly created humans rebel against God, resulting in their expulsion from the Garden of Eden. The Flood account (Gen. 6—9) tells of the continued evil in human hearts, the Flood, and God's judgment upon humanity. The redemption of Noah's family offers a new beginning. Following the Flood, Gen. 11 narrates the spread of the human race and its arrogant attempt to build a tower to the heavens. God confuses their languages, forcing them to disperse.

The Beginnings of Human Civilization

Scholars have placed the first human settlements as early as 7,000 to 8,000 years before Christ.

Biblical and secular historians agree that human civilization began in the ancient Near East. The earliest large communities developed in Mesopotamia (modern Iraq and Iran) and in Egypt. Palestine, where biblical Israel is found, lies along the best road between Mesopotamia and Egypt, and so the Bible's own history appropriately begins with these two civilization centers.

The task of assigning specific dates to this ancient history is difficult and uncertain, but scholars have placed the first human settlements as early as 7,000 to 8,000 years before Christ. Although dating the early events of civilization is elusive, we can at least follow the general stages by which human communities developed.

Advances in technology made it possible for humans to live in large communities. First they developed stone tools, then discovered how to make clay vessels, how to extract and use copper ore, and, by about 3000 B.C., how to use bronze. In terms of food and support, humans moved from small family groups hunting and gathering their food to larger nomadic clans tending domesticated animals. Farming developed next, and by 3000 B.C. people in Mesopotamia and Egypt were using sophisticated irrigation techniques to harness the regular floods of the Tigris, Euphrates, and Nile rivers. Now for the first time, food could be produced in large supply, enough to support cities and even empires.

The period from 3000 to 2000 B.C. (called the Early Bronze Age) saw the development of several such empires: the civilizations of Sumer, Accad, and Ur in Mesopotamia and the Old Kingdom of Egypt. Towering monuments testify to the amazing technological sophistication of these cultures. This was the age of the great pyramids in Egypt and of similar structures in Mesopotamia, called ziggurats. These ancient peoples worshiped many gods: gods of light, darkness, skies, seas, the land, the sun, the moon and stars, plants, and animals. Ancient writings from this time describe not only these gods, but also the creation of the world and a great flood.

The Book of Genesis

The Old Testament as a whole chronicles the history of the nation of Israel. This nation does not emerge as an entity, though, until the Book of Exodus, when God appears to the twelve tribes at Sinai. Genesis, then, is the prologue to the history of Israel. Chapters 1—11 tell about the creation and earliest history of all humankind, and chs. 12—50 describe God's working within the chosen family of Abraham, from whom Israel descended.

Within the theological narratives of Gen. 1—11 are several brief comments that reflect the advancing civilizations of Mesopotamia and Egypt. There are conflicts between hunters and shepherds and between shepherds and farmers. Humans develop technology and craftsmanship and establish the first cities. Chapter 11 describes humanity's technical skill (and vaulting ambition) in its account of a tower, or ziggurat, in the plains of Shinar (Mesopotamia). As in the Mesopotamian and Egyptian writings, there are stories of creation and of a worldwide flood.

Genesis, along with the books of Exodus through Deuteronomy, has traditionally been attributed to Moses. Many scholars retain this view today, but others, noting abrupt changes in vocabulary and style and certain perspectives that appear to come from a later time, argue that the book contains several sources and traditions, some much older than others. In either case, whether written entirely by Moses or composed from 900 to 400 B.C. of

THE CREATOR GOD IS NOT SUN OR MOON (Gen. 1:16)

In Gen. 1:16 the two great lights created by God are called the "greater light" and "lesser light." The words "sun" and "moon" were not omitted by accident from this verse. The writer of Genesis was aware that two prominent gods worshiped in the ancient Near East were the sun and the moon.

In Egypt the sun was associated with several important gods, including Amon-Re, Re, and Aton. Egyptians believed that the sun, as the god Re, created the world by his own personified power. One of Re's "eyes" was the moon god Tefnut. Another Egyptian god was Ptah, who was also considered the creator of all things. Ptah's two eyes were the sun and moon.

In Mesopotamia the sun god Shamash was worshiped as the benefactor of the oppressed. Night was seen as the passing of the sun to the netherworld or underworld. Ancient peoples prayed to the hidden sun for mediation between the dead and the living.

Canaanite worshipers knew the sun as Shemesh. The appearance of this god's name in place names, such as Beth Shemesh (1 Sam. 6:12), hints at the importance of Shemesh to the polytheistic Canaanites. While they also worshiped the moon, a moon god was only of secondary importance in their pantheon of deities.

The author of Gen. 1:14–19 makes the case that the Creator of the world is on a different plane than the sun or the moon. They are only the "greater" and "lesser" lights. No one should acknowledge them as deities or confuse them with the true God. They are simply creations of the creator God.

---

various ancient strands, the Book of Genesis is a recounting of Israel's origins by one who knew that all this was leading to God's choice of Israel as "a special treasure . . . above all people" (Ex. 19:5).

■ Genesis 1:1—4:26

Genesis
The Story of Creation

1 :1 In the beginning God created the heavens and the earth. ²The earth was without form, and void; and darkness was[a] on the face of the deep. And the Spirit of God was hovering over the face of the waters.

³Then God said, "Let there be light"; and there was light. ⁴And God saw the light, that it was good; and God divided the light from the darkness. ⁵God called the light Day, and the darkness He called Night. So the evening and the morning were the first day.

⁶Then God said, "Let there be a firmament in the midst of the waters, and let it divide the waters from the waters." ⁷Thus God made the firmament, and divided the waters which were under the firmament from the waters which were above the firmament; and it was so. ⁸And God called the firmament Heaven. So the evening and the morning were the second day.

⁹Then God said, "Let the waters under the heavens be gathered together into one place, and let the dry land appear"; and it was so. ¹⁰And God called the dry land Earth, and the gathering together of the waters He called Seas. And God saw that it was good.

¹¹Then God said, "Let the earth bring forth grass, the herb that yields seed, and the fruit tree that yields fruit according to its kind, whose seed is in itself, on the earth"; and it was so. ¹²And the earth brought forth grass, the herb that yields seed according to its kind, and the tree that yields fruit, whose seed is in itself according to its kind. And God saw that it was good. ¹³So the evening and the morning were the third day.

¹⁴Then God said, "Let there be lights in the firmament of the heavens to divide the day from the night; and let them be for signs and seasons, and for days and years; ¹⁵and let them be for lights in the firmament of the heavens to give light on the earth"; and it was so. ¹⁶Then God made two great lights: the greater light to rule the day, and the lesser light to rule the night. He made the stars also. ¹⁷God set them in the firmament of the heavens to give light

1:2 ᵃWords in italic type have been added for clarity. They are not found in the original Hebrew or Aramaic.

CREATION BY CONQUEST IN BABYLON (Gen. 1:26–29)

In the Neo-Babylonian Empire (626–539 B.C.), the fourth day of the New Year's celebration was highlighted by reciting the Enuma Elish, a liturgical text relating the creation of the physical world. This Babylonian poem was originally composed sometime before or during the reign of Nebuchadnezzar I (1133–1116 B.C.) to glorify Marduk as the divine ruler and establisher of order in the universe.

According to the Babylonian epic, before the world existed there were only Apsu and Tiamat, the god and goddess of fresh and salt water. Apsu and Tiamat give birth to deities, and the noise of these younger gods upsets them so much that they plot to slay their children. However, Ea, god of wisdom, discovers the plan and kills Apsu before the slaughter of the gods can be carried out. From the corpse of the slain god, Ea creates a home for himself and his spouse, the goddess Damkina. Here Ea and Damkina bear a son—Marduk.

Meanwhile, Tiamat, finding her husband slain and her peace disturbed by the gods' continuing noise, creates for herself an army of venomous monsters. She musters this horrendous force, appointing Kingu as leader, to kill off the younger gods and wreak revenge for the death of Apsu. Overhearing this scheme, Ea is overwhelmed by the coming terror. All the younger deities assemble to discuss their fate; all appear hopeless. Then the youthful Marduk volunteers to defend the gods.

In the ensuing battle all the hordes of monsters are killed, ending with the deaths of Kingu and Tiamat herself. Marduk divides the corpse of Tiamat, providing for two heavens and the earth. From the blood of Kingu, Marduk creates humans.

Some aspects of creation in the Babylonian epic have counterparts in the Genesis creation story (Gen. 1:1—2:4a). The sun and moon are treated as physical, created entities and not as deities. Light is created before other objects. The heavens are populated with the sun, moon, and stars in order to mark off the months, days, and festivals. Humans are created only at the end of creation. Yet also important are the theological differences. In the Babylonian story, humans were created as slaves for the gods, so that the deities would not have to work anymore. Genesis offers a much higher estimation of the worth of humanity in the eyes of God (Gen. 1:26–29).

---

on the earth, 18and to rule over the day and over the night, and to divide the light from the darkness. And God saw that *it was* good. 19So the evening and the morning were the fourth day.

20Then God said, "Let the waters abound with an abundance of living creatures, and let birds fly above the earth across the face of the firmament of the heavens." 21So God created great sea creatures and every living thing that moves, with which the waters abounded, according to their kind, and every winged bird according to its kind. And God saw that *it was* good. 22And God blessed them, saying, "Be fruitful and multiply, and fill the waters in the seas, and let birds multiply on the earth." 23So the evening and the morning were the fifth day.

24Then God said, "Let the earth bring forth the living creature according to its kind: cattle and creeping thing and beast of the earth, *each* according to its kind"; and it was so. 25And God made the beast of the earth according to its kind, cattle according to its kind, and everything that creeps on the earth according to its kind. And God saw that *it was* good.

26Then God said, "Let Us make man in Our image, according to Our likeness; let them have dominion over the fish of the sea, over the birds of the air, and over the cattle, over all[a] the earth and over every creeping thing that creeps on the earth." 27So God created man in His *own* image; in the image of God He created him; male and female He created them. 28Then God blessed them, and God said to them, "Be fruitful and multiply; fill the earth and subdue it; have dominion over the fish of the sea, over the birds of the air, and over every living thing that moves on the earth."

1:26 aSyriac reads *all the wild animals of.*

WHERE WAS EDEN? (Gen. 2:10–14)

The Book of Genesis states that God planted a garden "eastward in Eden" (Gen. 2:8). The name "Eden" is used not only for the region where God placed the garden (2:10), but also for the garden itself (2:15). For centuries biblical commentators have speculated on the location of Eden, studying the description of the garden for possible hints.

The garden is associated with four rivers: Pishon, Gihon, Hiddekel, and Euphrates (2:10–14). The last two of these rivers are known, Hiddekel being the Hebrew name for the Tigris River. Thus the mention of the Tigris and Euphrates rivers would suggest a location for Eden somewhere in Mesopotamia.

Unfortunately, the other rivers, Pishon and Gihon, are obscure and defy absolute placement. Pishon was in the land of Havilah (2:11), which has been associated with Arabia (Gen. 25:18), as well as with India. Gihon was in Cush (2:13), which was an ancient name for the area south of Egypt. Some scholars have argued that Pishon and Gihon represent the Indus and Nile rivers, but others contend that they may have been canals.

To the ancient writer of Genesis, Eden was a place blessed with an abundant supply of water. Unfortunately, this writer's description of Eden's rivers will not help us pinpoint a location for Eden itself.

29And God said, "See, I have given you every herb *that* yields seed which *is* on the face of all the earth, and every tree whose fruit yields seed; to you it shall be for food. 30Also, to every beast of the earth, to every bird of the air, and to everything that creeps on the earth, in which *there is* life, *I have given* every green herb for food"; and it was so. 31Then God saw everything that He had made, and indeed *it was* very good. So the evening and the morning were the sixth day.

2 1Thus the heavens and the earth, and all the host of them, were finished. 2And on the seventh day God ended His work which He had done, and He rested on the seventh day from all His work which He had done. 3Then God blessed the seventh day and sanctified it, because in it He rested from all His work which God had created and made.

4This *is* the history[a] of the heavens and the earth when they were created, in the day that the LORD God made the earth and the heavens, 5before any plant of the field was in the earth and before any herb of the field had grown. For the LORD God had not caused it to rain on the earth, and *there was* no man to till the ground; 6but a mist went up from the earth and watered the whole face of the ground.

7And the LORD God formed man *of* the dust of the ground, and breathed into his nostrils the breath of life; and man became a living being.

Life in God's Garden

8The LORD God planted a garden eastward in Eden, and there He put the man whom He had formed. 9And out of the ground the LORD God made every tree grow that is pleasant to the sight and good for food. The tree of life *was* also in the midst of the garden, and the tree of the knowledge of good and evil.

10Now a river went out of Eden to water the garden, and from there it parted and became four riverheads. 11The name of the first *is* Pishon; it *is* the one which skirts the whole land of Havilah, where

2:4 aHebrew *toledoth*, literally *generations*

PLANTS AND ANIMALS

In relatively dry climates a flourishing tree is a conspicuous sign of adequate water (Gen. 2:9). Gardens have been cultivated in the Near East for thousands of years, and the success of the gardens of Babylon is proverbial. Egyptian rulers also gave attention to their gardens and to the fish and birds in them.

there is gold. ¹²And the gold of that land *is* good. Bdellium and the onyx stone *are* there. ¹³The name of the second river *is* Gihon; it *is* the one which goes around the whole land of Cush. ¹⁴The name of the third river *is* Hiddekel;ᵃ it *is* the one which goes toward the east of Assyria. The fourth river *is* the Euphrates.

¹⁵Then the LORD God took the man and put him in the garden of Eden to tend and keep it. ¹⁶And the LORD God commanded the man, saying, "Of every tree of the garden you may freely eat; ¹⁷but of the tree of the knowledge of good and evil you shall not eat, for in the day that you eat of it you shall surely die."

¹⁸And the LORD God said, "*It is* not good that man should be alone; I will make him a helper comparable to him." ¹⁹Out of the ground the LORD God formed every beast of the field and every bird of the air, and brought *them* to Adam to see what he would call them. And whatever Adam called each living creature, that *was* its name. ²⁰So Adam gave names to all cattle, to the birds of the air, and to every beast of the field. But for Adam there was not found a helper comparable to him.

²¹And the LORD God caused a deep sleep to fall on Adam, and he slept; and He took one of his ribs, and closed up the flesh in its place. ²²Then the rib which the LORD God had taken from man He made into a woman, and He brought her to the man.

²³And Adam said:

"This *is* now bone of my bones
And flesh of my flesh;
She shall be called Woman,
Because she was taken out of Man."

²⁴Therefore a man shall leave his father and mother and be joined to his wife, and they shall become one flesh.

²⁵And they were both naked, the man and his wife, and were not ashamed.

The Temptation and Fall of Man

3 ¹Now the serpent was more cunning than any beast of the field which the LORD God had made. And he said to the woman, "Has God indeed said, 'You shall not eat of every tree of the garden'?"

²And the woman said to the serpent, "We may eat the fruit of the trees of the garden; ³but of the fruit of the tree which *is* in the midst of the garden, God has said, 'You shall not eat it, nor shall you touch it, lest you die.' "

⁴Then the serpent said to the woman, "You will not surely die. ⁵For God knows that in the day you eat of it your eyes will be opened, and you will be like God, knowing good and evil."

⁶So when the woman saw that the tree *was* good for food, that it *was* pleasant to the eyes, and a tree desirable to make *one* wise, she took of its fruit and ate. She also gave to her husband with her, and he ate. ⁷Then the eyes of both of them were opened, and they knew that they *were* naked; and they sewed fig leaves together and made themselves coverings.

⁸And they heard the sound of the LORD God walking in the garden in the cool of the day, and Adam and his wife hid themselves from the presence of the LORD God among the trees of the garden.

⁹Then the LORD God called to Adam and said to him, "Where *are* you?"

¹⁰So he said, "I heard Your voice in the garden, and I was afraid because I was naked; and I hid myself."

¹¹And He said, "Who told you that you *were* naked? Have you eaten from the tree of which I commanded you that you should not eat?"

¹²Then the man said, "The woman whom You gave *to be* with me, she gave me of the tree, and I ate."

¹³And the LORD God said to the woman, "What *is* this you have done?"

The woman said, "The serpent deceived me, and I ate."

¹⁴So the LORD God said to the serpent:

2:14 ᵃOr *Tigris*

TIME CAPSULE *26,000 to 10,000 B.C.*	
26,000	Stone tools shaped by grinding, from Japan
23,000	Stone tools shaped by grinding, from Australia
20,000	First known ovens, in the Ukraine
13,000	Flutes known in France
12,000	Boomerang known in Australia
11,000	Wolves or dogs tamed in Palestine
10,000	Prehistoric cave paintings, Lascaux, France
10,000– 8000	Middle Stone Age

"Because you have done this,
  You *are* cursed more than all cattle,
  And more than every beast of the
    field;
  On your belly you shall go,
  And you shall eat dust
  All the days of your life.
15 And I will put enmity
  Between you and the woman,
  And between your seed and her Seed;
  He shall bruise your head,
  And you shall bruise His heel."

16To the woman He said:

"I will greatly multiply your sorrow
    and your conception;
  In pain you shall bring forth children;
  Your desire *shall be* for your husband,
  And he shall rule over you."

17Then to Adam He said, "Because you have heeded the voice of your wife, and have eaten from the tree of which I commanded you, saying, 'You shall not eat of it':

"Cursed *is* the ground for your sake;
  In toil you shall eat *of* it
  All the days of your life.
18 Both thorns and thistles it shall bring
    forth for you,
  And you shall eat the herb of the field.
19 In the sweat of your face you shall eat
    bread
  Till you return to the ground,
  For out of it you were taken;
  For dust you *are,*
  And to dust you shall return."

20And Adam called his wife's name Eve, because she was the mother of all living.

21Also for Adam and his wife the LORD God made tunics of skin, and clothed them. 22Then the LORD God said, "Behold, the man has become like one of Us, to know good and evil. And now, lest he put out his hand and take also of the tree of life, and eat, and live forever"— 23therefore the LORD God sent him out of the garden of Eden to till the ground from which he was taken. 24So He drove out the man; and He placed cherubim at the east of the garden of Eden, and a flaming sword which turned every way, to guard the way to the tree of life.

Cain Murders Abel

4 1Now Adam knew Eve his wife, and she conceived and bore Cain, and said, "I have acquired a man from the LORD." 2Then she bore again, this time his brother Abel. Now Abel was a keeper of sheep, but Cain was a tiller of the ground. 3And in the process of time it came to pass that Cain brought an offering of the fruit of the ground to the LORD. 4Abel also brought of the firstborn of his flock and of their fat. And the LORD respected Abel and his offering, 5but He did not respect Cain and his offering. And Cain was very angry, and his countenance fell.

6So the LORD said to Cain, "Why are you angry? And why has your countenance fallen? 7If you do well, will you not be accepted? And if you do not do well, sin lies at the door. And its desire *is* for you, but you should rule over it."

8Now Cain talked with Abel his brother;a and it came to pass, when they were in the field, that Cain rose up against Abel his brother and killed him.

9Then the LORD said to Cain, "Where *is* Abel your brother?"

He said, "I do not know. Am I my brother's keeper?"

10And He said, "What have you done? The voice of your brother's blood cries out to Me from the ground. 11So now you *are* cursed from the earth, which has opened its mouth to receive your brother's blood from your hand. 12When you till the ground, it shall no longer yield its strength to you. A fugitive and a vagabond you shall be on the earth."

4:8 aSamaritan Pentateuch, Septuagint, Syriac, and Vulgate add *"Let us go out to the field."*

TIME CAPSULE *8000 to 7000 B.C.*

8000	Archaeological evidence of settlement at Jericho
8000	Lentils and peas grown in the Middle East
8000–4000	New Stone Age
7500	Sheep domesticated in the Middle East
7500	Hatchet used in Europe to fell trees
7000	The oldest known fortifications, at Jericho

¹³And Cain said to the LORD, "My punishment *is* greater than I can bear! ¹⁴Surely You have driven me out this day from the face of the ground; I shall be hidden from Your face; I shall be a fugitive and a vagabond on the earth, and it will happen *that* anyone who finds me will kill me."

¹⁵And the LORD said to him, "Therefore,ᵃ whoever kills Cain, vengeance shall be taken on him sevenfold." And the LORD set a mark on Cain, lest anyone finding him should kill him.

The Family of Cain

¹⁶Then Cain went out from the presence of the LORD and dwelt in the land of Nod on the east of Eden. ¹⁷And Cain knew his wife, and she conceived and bore Enoch. And he built a city, and called the name of the city after the name of his son—Enoch. ¹⁸To Enoch was born Irad; and Irad begot Mehujael, and Mehujael begot Methushael, and Methushael begot Lamech.

¹⁹Then Lamech took for himself two wives: the name of one *was* Adah, and the name of the second *was* Zillah. ²⁰And Adah bore Jabal. He was the father of those who dwell in tents and have livestock. ²¹His brother's name *was* Jubal. He was the father of all those who play the harp and flute. ²²And as for Zillah, she also bore Tubal-Cain, an instructor of every craftsman in bronze and iron. And the sister of Tubal-Cain *was* Naamah.

²³Then Lamech said to his wives:

"Adah and Zillah, hear my voice;
    Wives of Lamech, listen to my speech!
For I have killed a man for wounding
    me,
Even a young man for hurting me.
24 If Cain shall be avenged sevenfold,
    Then Lamech seventy-sevenfold."

4:15 ᵃFollowing Masoretic Text and Targum; Septuagint, Syriac, and Vulgate read *Not so.*
4:26 ᵃGreek *Enos*

A New Son

²⁵And Adam knew his wife again, and she bore a son and named him Seth, "For God has appointed another seed for me instead of Abel, whom Cain killed." ²⁶And as for Seth, to him also a son was born; and he named him Enosh.ᵃ Then *men* began to call on the name of the LORD.

Records of the Descendants

Genesis 1—11 tells much of its story by means of genealogies. At the end of the Cain and Abel account is a list of eight descendants of Cain (Gen. 4:17–22), among whom are the ancestors of pastoral nomads (v. 20), musicians (v. 21), and metalworkers (v. 22). In Gen. 5 the line of Adam's descendants through Seth is given, breaking off just before the Flood. Finally, in Gen. 10 the peoples of the earth are listed under the three sons of Noah, categorized according to clans, languages, location, and nationality.

It is possible, using the numbers of these lists, to add up the years and thus date the creation of the world at about 4004 B.C. Such computations were published in A.D. 1650–1654 by the Archbishop James Ussher. Many scholars, though, argue that modern historical dating and chronological specificity were foreign to the ancient mind and suggest that the exact numbers should not be read so mechanically. Furthermore, the numbers themselves vary in different text traditions, showing many disagreements between the Hebrew Bible, Samaritan Pentateuch, and the Septuagint (Greek Old Testament).

Thus different interpreters treat the genealogies in different ways. Some add up the successive generations, as did Ussher, to arrive at a date for creation sometime around 4004 B.C. Others take the genealogies as the schemes of ancient mathematicians, with different purposes, and accept that a date for the creation of the world is impossible to determine.

▼ ■ Genesis 5:1—6:22

SCIENCE AND TECHNOLOGY

True bronze (Gen. 4:22) is an alloy of copper and tin. Iron is an element that in its pure state is soft. Its usefulness for making tools and weapons did not appear until it could be reliably combined with carbon to make steel. It was still rare in the time of Pharaoh Tutankhamun (1336–1327 B.C.). One dagger with an iron blade was discovered in his tomb.

THE SUMERIAN KING LIST (Gen. 5:1–32)

The Sumerian King List is a text from southern Mesopotamia, written sometime very early in the 2nd millennium B.C. The list presumably follows a tradition going back to the early 3rd millennium B.C. It has interesting parallels with the genealogical list in Gen. 5.

In its existing form, the Sumerian King List is a propaganda text designed by the kings of Isin to affirm their rule as legitimate. It delineates the history of Sumer (and Accad) by showing the succession of dynasties (or cities) from the beginning of time to the writer's present. Each monarch in the early period rules for a very lengthy period (thousands of years on the average). Similarly, six of Adam's descendants listed in Gen. 5 lived in excess of 900 years (e.g., Gen. 5:5, 8, 11).

The King List abruptly and tersely mentions the great flood, which cuts the dynastic lines in half. Interestingly, after the flood, the reigns of the monarchs begin to decrease from thousands to hundreds of years. Gilgamesh, the famous hero from Uruk, ruled a mere 126 years. The lengths of reigns finally fall within the normal span of a human lifetime. Likewise, the genealogy of Gen. 11:10–26 shows a continual diminishing of the human lifespan after the Genesis Flood.

The Sumerian literary tradition, like the biblical record, contains the account that humankind lived to an advanced age in pre-Flood antiquity. Both also agree in general that ages began to decline immediately after the Flood until, finally, modern lifespans were experienced. This shared characteristic of the Sumerian and biblical records lends credibility to the view that both cultures came from the same literary setting or environment.

Genesis
The Family of Adam

5 :1 This is the book of the genealogy of Adam. In the day that God created man, He made him in the likeness of God. ²He created them male and female, and blessed them and called them Mankind in the day they were created. ³And Adam lived one hundred and thirty years, and begot *a son* in his own likeness, after his image, and named him Seth. ⁴After he begot Seth, the days of Adam were eight hundred years; and he had sons and daughters. ⁵So all the days that Adam lived were nine hundred and thirty years; and he died.

⁶Seth lived one hundred and five years, and begot Enosh. ⁷After he begot Enosh, Seth lived eight hundred and seven years, and had sons and daughters. ⁸So all the days of Seth were nine hundred and twelve years; and he died.

⁹Enosh lived ninety years, and begot

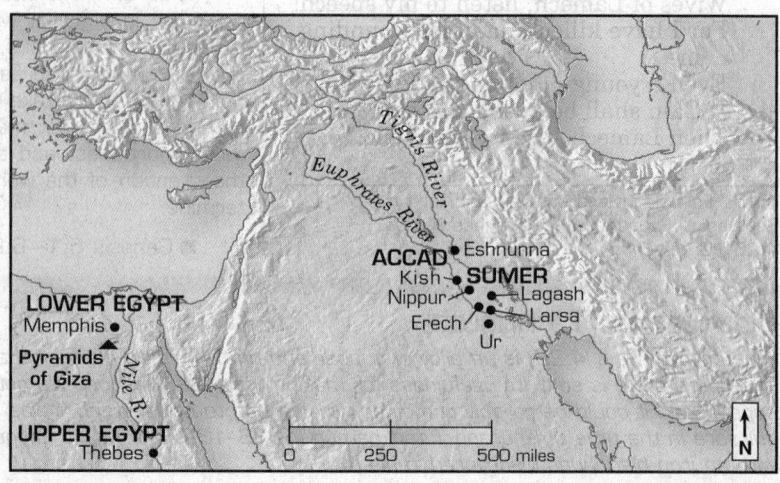

The Ancient Near East After 3000 B.C.

During the 3rd millennium Lower and Upper Egypt were united. Egypt's Old Kingdom (2700–2160 B.C.) produced the great pyramids, such as those at Giza. In Mesopotamia, the land of Sumer developed a system of independent city-states. Toward the end of the millennium this city-state rule was replaced by a more extensive territorial rule centered in Accad.

Cainan.[a] [10]After he begot Cainan, Enosh lived eight hundred and fifteen years, and had sons and daughters. [11]So all the days of Enosh were nine hundred and five years; and he died.

[12]Cainan lived seventy years, and begot Mahalalel. [13]After he begot Mahalalel, Cainan lived eight hundred and forty years, and had sons and daughters. [14]So all the days of Cainan were nine hundred and ten years; and he died.

[15]Mahalalel lived sixty-five years, and begot Jared. [16]After he begot Jared, Mahalalel lived eight hundred and thirty years, and had sons and daughters. [17]So all the days of Mahalalel were eight hundred and ninety-five years; and he died.

[18]Jared lived one hundred and sixty-two years, and begot Enoch. [19]After he begot Enoch, Jared lived eight hundred years, and had sons and daughters. [20]So all the days of Jared were nine hundred and sixty-two years; and he died.

[21]Enoch lived sixty-five years, and begot Methuselah. [22]After he begot Methuselah, Enoch walked with God three hundred years, and had sons and daughters. [23]So all the days of Enoch were three hundred and sixty-five years. [24]And Enoch walked with God; and he was not, for God took him.

[25]Methuselah lived one hundred and eighty-seven years, and begot Lamech. [26]After he begot Lamech, Methuselah lived seven hundred and eighty-two years, and had sons and daughters. [27]So all the days

of Methuselah were nine hundred and sixty-nine years; and he died.

[28]Lamech lived one hundred and eighty-two years, and had a son. [29]And he called his name Noah, saying, "This one will comfort us concerning our work and the toil of our hands, because of the ground which the LORD has cursed." [30]After he begot Noah, Lamech lived five hundred and ninety-five years, and had sons and daughters. [31]So all the days of Lamech were seven hundred and seventy-seven years; and he died.

[32]And Noah was five hundred years old, and Noah begot Shem, Ham, and Japheth.

The Wickedness and Judgment of Man

6 [1]Now it came to pass, when men began to multiply on the face of the earth, and daughters were born to them, [2]that the sons of God saw the daughters of men, that they were beautiful; and they took wives for themselves of all whom they chose.

[3]And the LORD said, "My Spirit shall not strive[a] with man forever, for he is indeed flesh; yet his days shall be one hundred and twenty years." [4]There were giants on the earth in those days, and also afterward, when the sons of God came in to the daughters of men and they bore children to them. Those were the mighty men who were of old, men of renown.

[5]Then the LORD[a] saw that the wickedness of man was great in the earth, and that every intent of the thoughts of his heart was only evil continually. [6]And the LORD was sorry that He had made man on the earth, and He was grieved in His heart. [7]So the LORD said, "I will destroy man

---

5:9 [a]Hebrew *Qenan*   6:3 [a]Septuagint, Syriac, Targum, and Vulgate read *abide*.   6:5 [a]Following Masoretic Text and Targum; Vulgate reads *God;* Septuagint reads LORD *God.*

TIME CAPSULE *7000 to 6000 B.C.*

7000	*Stone tools shaped by grinding, from Europe*
6770	*Carbon-14 dating of ashes at Jericho*
6500	*Cattle domesticated in Turkey*
6500	*Settlement at Ras Shamra (Ugarit) in Syria*
6500	*Paintings from Spain show people gathering wild honey*
6000	*Domestic cat is known, in Cyprus*
6000	*Skull with evidence of surgery (trepanning), from Europe*

TIME CAPSULE *6000 to 5000 B.C.*

6000	*Skull with evidence of surgery (trepanning), from Europe*
5859	*Carbon-14 dating of early fortification at Jericho*
5500	*Pottery is first known in Palestine*
5000	*Copper is melted (1083° C.) and cast in the Near East*
5000	*Evidence of temple at Eridu, Iraq*
5000	*Grapes are cultivated in Europe*
5000	*Mirrors found in graves in central Turkey*

THE FLOOD THROUGH OTHER EYES (Gen. 6:5–7)

Divine destruction of the world by means of a flood is a motif known in cultures from around the world. Most of these stories appear to have had their origin in the biblical account (Gen. 6:5–9:29). However, the ancient Near East has numerous myths of the great flood which are separate retellings of the same event.

Mesopotamian stories of the flood are first found written in the Sumerian language, in the earliest known literature (3rd millennium B.C.). A variety of retellings produced a number of versions. The two most famous flood stories outside the Bible are the Gilgamesh Epic and the story of Atrahasis.

Numerous other references and renditions of the flood are found scattered throughout the classical literature and other texts of the ancient Near East. The flood itself divides the history of the world into the period before it occurred and the current age. Things now are not as they were then.

whom I have created from the face of the earth, both man and beast, creeping thing and birds of the air, for I am sorry that I have made them." ⁸But Noah found grace in the eyes of the LORD.

Noah Pleases God

⁹This is the genealogy of Noah. Noah was a just man, perfect in his generations. Noah walked with God. ¹⁰And Noah begot three sons: Shem, Ham, and Japheth. ¹¹The earth also was corrupt before God, and the earth was filled with violence. ¹²So God looked upon the earth, and indeed it was corrupt; for all flesh had corrupted their way on the earth.

The Ark Prepared

¹³And God said to Noah, "The end of all flesh has come before Me, for the earth is filled with violence through them; and behold, I will destroy them with the earth. ¹⁴Make yourself an ark of gopherwood; make rooms in the ark, and cover it inside and outside with pitch. ¹⁵And this is how you shall make it: The length of the ark *shall be* three hundred cubits, its width fifty cubits, and its height thirty cubits. ¹⁶You shall make a window for the ark, and you shall finish it to a cubit from above; and set the door of the ark in its side. You shall make it *with* lower, second, and third *decks*. ¹⁷And behold, I Myself am bringing floodwaters on the earth, to destroy from under heaven all flesh in which *is* the breath of life; everything that *is* on the earth shall die. ¹⁸But I will establish My covenant with you; and you shall go into the ark—you, your sons, your wife, and ▼

your sons' wives with you. ¹⁹And of every living thing of all flesh you shall bring two of every *sort* into the ark, to keep *them* alive with you; they shall be male and female. ²⁰Of the birds after their kind, of animals after their kind, and of every creeping thing of the earth after its kind, two of every *kind* will come to you to keep *them* alive. ²¹And you shall take for yourself of all food that is eaten, and you shall gather *it* to yourself; and it shall be food for you and for them."

²²Thus Noah did; according to all that God commanded him, so he did.

How Long Was Noah in the Ark?

The narrator of the Flood tradition offers several dates, indicating when certain events took place. The time frame of these dates, cited by year, month, and day based on Noah's age, has Noah, his family, and the animals confined in the ark for more than a year—371 days.

In Gen. 7:11—8:19 are five dates. The first instance at 7:11 marks when the rain began. Five months later, the ark rested on Ararat (8:4). Two and a half months later the mountains were seen (8:5). After another three months Noah removed the covering of the ark (8:13). Finally, Noah, his family, and the animals went out of the ark 57 days later (8:14–19). The days between each date, assuming 30-day months as the narrator appears to do, are 150 + 74 + 90 + 57, totaling 371 days.

■ Genesis 7:1—11:32

WHEN THE GODS TIRE OF NOISY HUMANS (Gen. 7:1)

The story of Atrahasis, written during the reign of Ammisaduqa, king of Babylon (1646–1626 B.C.), is a variant of the Gilgamesh Epic. The title of the Atrahasis story means "When the gods like man." Yet the story, like that of the Genesis Flood story (Gen. 7:4), tells of the gods destroying much of humankind.

The reason given in this story for the flood was that the humans on the earth had become too numerous and their noise was disturbing the gods. The deities planned several devices to reduce the population including drought, plague, and famine, but each time the people survived. Finally, a flood was devised from which the people could not escape. It was Ea who warned the hero, Atrahasis, to save the animals and craftsmen in a boat, which he then did.

The humans had previously fed the gods by their sacrifices. As the seven days and nights of the flood raged and humans died, the deities became hungry and thirsty. Thus they were happy to have some people survive the flood.

The Mesopotamian legend contrasts with the ethical emphasis in Genesis. The Mesopotamian gods destroyed humans because they were noisy, yet wanted some humans left for service. The God of Genesis destroyed humans because they were wicked and corrupt (Gen. 6:5–7, 11–13). He allowed Noah and his family to live because they were righteous (Gen. 7:1).

Genesis
The Great Flood

7 :1 Then the LORD said to Noah, "Come into the ark, you and all your household, because I have seen *that* you *are* righteous before Me in this generation. ²You shall take with you seven each of every clean animal, a male and his female; two each of animals that *are* unclean, a male and his female; ³also seven each of birds of the air, male and female, to keep the species alive on the face of all the earth. ⁴For after seven more days I will cause it to rain on the earth forty days and forty nights, and I will destroy from the face of the earth all living things that I have made." ⁵And Noah did according to all that the LORD commanded him. ⁶Noah *was* six hundred years old when the floodwaters were on the earth.

⁷So Noah, with his sons, his wife, and his sons' wives, went into the ark because of the waters of the flood. ⁸Of clean animals, of animals that *are* unclean, of birds, and of everything that creeps on the earth, ⁹two by two they went into the ark to Noah, male and female, as God had commanded Noah. ¹⁰And it came to pass after seven days that the waters of the flood were on the earth. ¹¹In the six hundredth year of Noah's life, in the second month, the seventeenth day of the month, on that day all the fountains of the great deep were broken up, and the windows of heaven were opened. ¹²And the rain was on the earth forty days and forty nights.

¹³On the very same day Noah and Noah's sons, Shem, Ham, and Japheth, and Noah's wife and the three wives of his sons with them, entered the ark— ¹⁴they and every beast after its kind, all cattle after their kind, every creeping thing that creeps on the earth after its kind, and every bird after its kind, every bird of every sort. ¹⁵And they went into the ark to

TIME CAPSULE	*5000 to 4000 B.C.*
5000	*Copper is melted (1083° C.) and cast in the Near East*
4500	*Copper is known in Egypt*
4500	*Bronze and brass are derived from copper*
4500	*Sockets for hinging doors used in Sumer*
4300	*Village culture in the Fayum (Egypt), west of the Nile*
4004	*Ussher's date for the Creation*
4000	*Casting of molten silver and gold in the Near East*
4000	*Evidence of bits used for horses, from the Ukraine*

Noah, two by two, of all flesh in which *is* the breath of life. [16]So those that entered, male and female of all flesh, went in as God had commanded him; and the LORD shut him in.

[17]Now the flood was on the earth forty days. The waters increased and lifted up the ark, and it rose high above the earth. [18]The waters prevailed and greatly increased on the earth, and the ark moved about on the surface of the waters. [19]And the waters prevailed exceedingly on the earth, and all the high hills under the whole heaven were covered. [20]The waters prevailed fifteen cubits upward, and the mountains were covered. [21]And all flesh died that moved on the earth: birds and cattle and beasts and every creeping thing that creeps on the earth, and every man. [22]All in whose nostrils *was* the breath of the spirit[a] of life, all that *was* on the dry *land,* died. [23]So He destroyed all living things which were on the face of the ground: both man and cattle, creeping thing and bird of the air. They were destroyed from the earth. Only Noah and those who *were* with him in the ark remained *alive.* [24]And the waters prevailed on the earth one hundred and fifty days.

Noah's Deliverance

8 [1]Then God remembered Noah, and every living thing, and all the animals that *were* with him in the ark. And God made a wind to pass over the earth, and the waters subsided. [2]The fountains of the deep and the windows of heaven were also stopped, and the rain from heaven was restrained. [3]And the waters receded continually from the earth. At the end of the hundred and fifty days the waters decreased.

TIME CAPSULE   *4000 to 3500 B.C.*

4000	*Evidence of bits used for horses, from the Ukraine*
4000– 3000	*Copper-Stone Age*
3700	*Two villages combine to create Uruk, the earliest urban site*
3500	*Bronze is known in Ur*
3500	*Egyptian art shows greyhounds*
3500	*Village culture around Beersheba*
3500	*The olive is cultivated in Palestine*

---

[4]Then the ark rested in the seventh month, the seventeenth day of the month, on the mountains of Ararat. [5]And the waters decreased continually until the tenth month. In the tenth *month,* on the first *day* of the month, the tops of the mountains were seen.

[6]So it came to pass, at the end of forty days, that Noah opened the window of the ark which he had made. [7]Then he sent out a raven, which kept going to and fro until the waters had dried up from the earth. [8]He also sent out from himself a dove, to see if the waters had receded from the face of the ground. [9]But the dove found no resting place for the sole of her foot, and she returned into the ark to him, for the waters *were* on the face of the whole earth. So he put out his hand and took her, and drew her into the ark to himself. [10]And he waited yet another seven days, and again he sent the dove out from the ark. [11]Then the dove came to him in the evening, and behold, a freshly plucked olive leaf *was* in her mouth; and Noah knew that the waters had receded from the earth. [12]So he waited yet another seven days and sent out the dove, which did not return again to him anymore.

[13]And it came to pass in the six hundred and first year, in the first *month,* the first *day* of the month, that the waters were dried up from the earth; and Noah removed the covering of the ark and looked, and indeed the surface of the ground was dry. [14]And in the second month, on the twenty-seventh day of the month, the earth was dried.

[15]Then God spoke to Noah, saying, [16]"Go out of the ark, you and your wife, and your sons and your sons' wives with you. [17]Bring out with you every living thing of all flesh that *is* with you: birds and cattle and every creeping thing that creeps on the earth, so that they may abound on the earth, and be fruitful and multiply on the earth." [18]So Noah went out, and his sons and his wife and his sons' wives with him. [19]Every animal, every creeping thing, every bird, *and* whatever creeps on the earth, according to their families, went out of the ark.

God's Covenant with Creation

[20]Then Noah built an altar to the LORD, and took of every clean animal and

---

7:22 [a]Septuagint and Vulgate omit *of the spirit.*

WHEN THE BIRD DOES NOT RETURN (Gen. 8:6–12)

Both similarities and differences exist between the biblical Flood story in Gen. 6—9 and the Mesopotamian flood legend known as the Gilgamesh Epic. Among the similarities are the birds—doves, ravens, sparrows—that are sent out to determine if the floodwaters have receded (Gen. 8:6–12).

Though the Gilgamesh flood story appears already in the mid-3rd millennium Sumerian stories, the epic account most widely known comes from the library of the Assyrian king Ashurbanipal (668–627 B.C.). The story is related by the flood survivor, Utnapishtim, at the edge of the world, where Gilgamesh (king of Uruk around 2600 B.C.) had sought him to discover how to become immortal.

There is no reason given in this account for the decision by the council of the gods to destroy the earth. However, Ea, the god of wisdom, realizing that destruction was a mistake, warns Utnapishtim that a flood is coming. Utnapishtim tears down his house and builds a boat, into which he gathers animals in pairs, seeds of all plants, his relatives, and skilled craftsmen. The deities unleash the flood as a weapon for seven days, destroying everything which is not in the boat and terrifying themselves as well.

After the divine flood ceased, the boat rested on a mountaintop in the Zagros Mountains. Utnapishtim releases first a dove, then a sparrow, both of whom return without finding a place to land, and lastly a raven, who does not return. The flood is finally over and everything is allowed to leave the boat and repopulate the earth.

---

of every clean bird, and offered burnt offerings on the altar. ²¹And the LORD smelled a soothing aroma. Then the LORD said in His heart, "I will never again curse the ground for man's sake, although the imagination of man's heart *is* evil from his youth; nor will I again destroy every living thing as I have done.

22   "While the earth remains,
    Seedtime and harvest,
    Cold and heat,
    Winter and summer,
    And day and night
    Shall not cease."

9 ¹So God blessed Noah and his sons, and said to them: "Be fruitful and multiply, and fill the earth.ᵃ ²And the fear of you and the dread of you shall be on every beast of the earth, on every bird of the air, on all that move *on* the earth, and on all the fish of the sea. They are given into your hand. ³Every moving thing that lives shall be food for you. I have given you all things, even as the green herbs. ⁴But you shall not eat flesh with its life, *that is,* its blood. ⁵Surely for your lifeblood I will demand *a reckoning;* from the hand of every beast I will require it, and from the hand of man.

From the hand of every man's brother I will require the life of man.

6   "Whoever sheds man's blood,
    By man his blood shall be shed;
    For in the image of God
    He made man.
7   And as for you, be fruitful and
      multiply;
    Bring forth abundantly in the earth
    And multiply in it."

TIME CAPSULE   *3500 to 3000 B.C.*

3500	Evidence of village culture around Beersheba
3500	Sumerians develop advanced civilization in southern Mesopotamia
3300	Domestication of the horse
3250	Potter's wheel from Ur
3200	Earliest writing, from Uruk in the Sumerian language
3200	Earliest picture of a boat with a sail, from Egypt
3150	Pictographs from Uruk showing four-wheeled carts
3100	Earliest depiction of a chariot
3000	Egyptians write in hieroglyphic script

9:1 ᵃCompare Genesis 1:28

GOD'S BOW OR A GODDESS'S NECKLACE (Gen. 9:8–17)

The Genesis Flood narrative closes with a promise by God that the destruction of the human race would not occur again. In Gen. 9:8–17 the covenant between God and Noah represents a binding commitment between God and humans. God initiates a covenant never to destroy humanity with water again, and the sign of this covenant forever is God's rainbow placed in the sky.

At the end of the Mesopotamian flood narratives there are also speeches made by the deities that humans will not be destroyed again. There is also a sign established in the sky as a reminder. However, the purpose and context is quite different from that of the biblical Flood story. In both the Gilgamesh Epic and the story of Atrahasis the flood ends with the majority of gods glad to have the terror over.

The reaction of the deities varied. Ellil, the warrior god, is furious over the survival of the few remaining humans. On the other hand, the goddess Ninhursag (Nintu or Ishtar in some renditions), the goddess of both human and divine children, is devastated that her children have been destroyed. In an appeal made in highest heaven, Ninhursag declares that this deed by the gods is an evil against her and that her grief must be appeased. She takes the "big flies," created by Anu, makes them into a necklace, and sets it up as a daily reminder to the gods never to destroy the people, on whom the gods depend, again.

In the Mesopotamian flood narrative the covenant was made solely on the divine level, and the sign was for the gods alone. In Genesis God's rainbow is a visible sign of His covenant promises to Noah, to Noah's descendants, and to all living creatures of the earth (Gen. 9:12, 17).

[8]Then God spoke to Noah and to his sons with him, saying: [9]"And as for Me, behold, I establish My covenant with you and with your descendants[a] after you, [10]and with every living creature that *is* with you: the birds, the cattle, and every beast of the earth with you, of all that go out of the ark, every beast of the earth. [11]Thus I establish My covenant with you: Never again shall all flesh be cut off by the waters of the flood; never again shall there be a flood to destroy the earth."

[12]And God said: "This *is* the sign of the covenant which I make between Me and you, and every living creature that *is* with you, for perpetual generations: [13]I set My rainbow in the cloud, and it shall be for the sign of the covenant between Me and the earth. [14]It shall be, when I bring a cloud over the earth, that the rainbow shall be seen in the cloud; [15]and I will remember My covenant which *is* between Me and you and every living creature of all flesh; the waters shall never again become a flood to destroy all flesh. [16]The rainbow shall be in the cloud, and I will look on it to remember the everlasting covenant between God and every living creature of all flesh that *is* on the earth." [17]And God said to Noah, "This *is* the sign of the covenant which I have established between Me and all flesh that *is* on the earth."

Noah and His Sons

[18]Now the sons of Noah who went out of the ark were Shem, Ham, and Japheth. And Ham *was* the father of Canaan. [19]These three *were* the sons of Noah, and from these the whole earth was populated. [20]And Noah began *to be* a farmer, and

9:9 [a]Literally *seed*

AGRICULTURE AND HERDING

To be fruitful, vineyards require considerable care. When the grapes are crushed for their juice, organisms found on the outside of the peel reach the juice. The organisms multiply and cause the juice to ferment and become wine (Gen. 9:20, 21). If it ferments too long, it becomes vinegar. Ancient farmers had to balance these different factors.

THE FIRST WORLD EMPIRE (Gen. 10:8–10)

The city of Accad was one of the major urban centers in central Mesopotamia and, according to Gen. 10:10, one of the first cities in the kingdom of the legendary Nimrod. Although the precise location has not been found, Accad was most likely near Babylon.

The Sumerian name of the city was Agade. A certain Sargon of Agade (c. 2350 B.C.) founded the city and made it the capital of an early Semitic dynasty. Sargon and his successors (notably his grandson Naram-Sin) were able to control all of the Tigris-Euphrates basin and claimed to have even reached the Mediterranean Sea. The dynasty of Agade lasted for about two centuries and was in fact the first world empire. Evidently the city was then destroyed and not subsequently reoccupied. A Sumerian text from the late 3rd millennium B.C., *The Curse of Agade,* commemorates the city's demise.

The term "Accad" survived after the city was gone. The title "Sumer and Accad" continued to be used for the region of southern Mesopotamia until the late Achaemenid period (4th century B.C.). The language of the Semitic-speaking peoples of Accad is now known as "Accadian." Later peoples of Mesopotamia, including the Assyrians and Babylonians, employed Accadian as the written language of the region. Accadian texts have been discovered dating as late as the 1st century A.D.

---

he planted a vineyard. ²¹Then he drank of the wine and was drunk, and became uncovered in his tent. ²²And Ham, the father of Canaan, saw the nakedness of his father, and told his two brothers outside. ²³But Shem and Japheth took a garment, laid *it* on both their shoulders, and went backward and covered the nakedness of their father. Their faces *were* turned away, and they did not see their father's nakedness.

²⁴So Noah awoke from his wine, and knew what his younger son had done to him. ²⁵Then he said:

"Cursed *be* Canaan;
A servant of servants
He shall be to his brethren."

²⁶And he said:

"Blessed *be* the LORD,
The God of Shem,
And may Canaan be his servant.
²⁷   May God enlarge Japheth,
And may he dwell in the tents of
Shem;
And may Canaan be his servant."

²⁸And Noah lived after the flood three hundred and fifty years. ²⁹So all the days of Noah were nine hundred and fifty years; and he died.

10:3 ^aSpelled *Diphath* in 1 Chronicles 1:6

Nations Descended from Noah

10 ¹Now this *is* the genealogy of the sons of Noah: Shem, Ham, and Japheth. And sons were born to them after the flood.

²The sons of Japheth *were* Gomer, Magog, Madai, Javan, Tubal, Meshech, and Tiras. ³The sons of Gomer *were* Ashkenaz, Riphath,^a and Togarmah. ⁴The sons of Ja-

---

TIME CAPSULE *3000 to 2500 B.C.*

3000–2000	Early Bronze Age
3000	Menes unites Lower and Upper Egypt to found Egypt's First Dynasty
3000	Pottery is made on a wheel, Palestine
2900	Egyptians adopt a civil calendar of 365 days per year
2750	First stage of Stonehenge monument, Britain
2700–2160	The Old Kingdom in Egypt
2650	Step Pyramid of Djoser; the oldest building of cut stone
2600	Gilgamesh, a legendary king of Uruk
2550	The Great Pyramid at Giza, 481 feet high
2500	Alignments of huge stones (megaliths), Carnac, France

THE FIRST MAJOR CITY (Gen. 10:10)

Erech is the biblical form of Uruk, a Sumerian city on the Euphrates River in ancient Mesopotamia. Although the name "Erech" is cited only in Gen. 10:10 and Ezra 4:9, its historical importance far exceeds its scant mention in the Bible. Uruk (Erech) played a role in the origin of urbanization, as well as being one of the great religious centers of Mesopotamia.

Archaeological investigations have confirmed that the Ubaidian people, early inhabitants of Sumer, founded two villages in this area before 4000 B.C. By 3700 B.C. the two centers fused together to create Uruk, the first urban site in world history.

The first evidence of public architecture, cylinder seals, and the origins of writing come from this city. Building projects at Uruk included the earliest known ziggurat, a holy mound at the top of which was the White Temple. Cylinder seals, which were used to mark ownership, spread from Uruk throughout the ancient world. Picture writing (dated to about 3200 B.C.) expressed ideas through a series of pictures. This writing would later evolve into the script known as cuneiform, used first by the Sumerians, early inhabitants of the Tigris-Euphrates valley.

Religion was prominent in Uruk. An, the chief deity, was the head of the Sumerian pantheon of gods. Inanna, the goddess of love, was believed to bring fertility and prosperity to Sumer through her marriage to the god Dumuzi. The exploits of Gilgamesh, a legendary king of Uruk (c. 2600 B.C.), in search of immortality mention many of the Sumerian gods and goddesses.

Late in the 4th millennium the population of Uruk began to expand their culture, controlling major trade routes and the surrounding regions economically. It is not clear whether this also resulted in political domination. However, Uruk is the second city named in the Sumerian King List, a document that traces the succession of cities which ruled Sumer after the flood.

Uruk had a long history, existing until Hellenistic times (the end of the 1st millennium B.C.). Its longevity is apparent from the two occurrences of Erech in the Bible. It is mentioned very early as part of Nimrod's post-Flood kingdom (Gen. 10:8–10). Much later in time it is one of the cities and nations writing against Jerusalem during the reign of the Persian ruler Artaxerxes I (465–424 B.C.; Ezra 4:9).

van *were* Elishah, Tarshish, Kittim, and Dodanim.[a] 5From these the coastland *peoples* of the Gentiles were separated into their lands, everyone according to his language, according to their families, into their nations.

6The sons of Ham *were* Cush, Mizraim, Put,[a] and Canaan. 7The sons of Cush *were* Seba, Havilah, Sabtah, Raamah, and Sabtechah; and the sons of Raamah *were* Sheba and Dedan.

8Cush begot Nimrod; he began to be a mighty one on the earth. 9He was a mighty hunter before the LORD; therefore it is said, "Like Nimrod the mighty hunter before the LORD." 10And the beginning of his kingdom was Babel, Erech, Accad, and Calneh, in the land of Shinar. 11From that land he went to Assyria and built Nineveh, Rehoboth Ir, Calah, 12and Resen between Nineveh and Calah (that *is* the principal city).

13Mizraim begot Ludim, Anamim,

Lehabim, Naphtuhim, 14Pathrusim, and Casluhim (from whom came the Philistines and Caphtorim).

15Canaan begot Sidon his firstborn, and Heth; 16the Jebusite, the Amorite, and the Girgashite; 17the Hivite, the Arkite, and the Sinite; 18the Arvadite, the Zemarite, and the Hamathite. Afterward the families of the Canaanites were dispersed. 19And the border of the Canaanites was from Sidon as you go toward Gerar, as far as Gaza; then as you go toward Sodom, Gomorrah, Admah, and Zeboiim, as far as Lasha. 20These *were* the sons of Ham, according to their families, according to their languages, in their lands *and* in their nations.

21And *children* were born also to Shem, the father of all the children of Eber, the brother of Japheth the elder. 22The sons of

---

10:4 [a]Spelled *Rodanim* in Samaritan Pentateuch and 1 Chronicles 1:7   10:6 [a]Or *Phut*

EGYPT'S FIRST DYNASTIES

When the Egyptian priest Manetho (c. 305–285 B.C.) wrote a history of Egypt in Greek, he divided the history of the kings into 30 periods known as "dynasties." Manetho's dynasties are still used as an outline for Egypt's history, but have been divided into larger historical periods. The 1st and 2nd Dynasties are Egypt's formative age; the 3rd through 8th Dynasties are her pyramid age.

The Archaic Period
3000–2700 B.C.

The Dynasties
1st and 2nd Dynasties. Menes is the traditional founder of the 1st Dynasty. He unified the two predynastic kingdoms of Lower and Upper Egypt.

The Old Kingdom
2700–2600 B.C.

The Dynasties
3rd Dynasty. Pyramid age begins with the Step Pyramid of Pharaoh Djoser in 2650 B.C.

2600–2500 B.C.
4th Dynasty. The Great Pyramid becomes one of the seven wonders of the world.

2500–2350 B.C.
5th Dynasty. The sun god Re of Heliopolis is considered the father of the living ruler. The god Osiris is the god of the dead.

2350–2160 B.C.
6th–8th Dynasties. Weni, an Egyptian official, records 5 military expeditions against the "Sand-dwellers" of southern Palestine.

Shem *were* Elam, Asshur, Arphaxad, Lud, and Aram. ²³The sons of Aram *were* Uz, Hul, Gether, and Mash.ᵃ ²⁴Arphaxad begot Salah,ᵃ and Salah begot Eber. ²⁵To Eber were born two sons: the name of one *was* Peleg, for in his days the earth was divided; and his brother's name *was* Joktan. ²⁶Joktan begot Almodad, Sheleph, Hazarmaveth, Jerah, ²⁷Hadoram, Uzal, Diklah, ²⁸Obal,ᵃ Abimael, Sheba, ²⁹Ophir, Havilah, and Jobab. All these *were* the sons of Joktan. ³⁰And their dwelling place was from Mesha as you go toward Sephar, the mountain of the east. ³¹These *were* the sons of Shem, according to their families, according to their languages, in their lands, according to their nations.

³²These *were* the families of the sons of Noah, according to their generations, in their nations; and from these the nations were divided on the earth after the flood.

The Tower of Babel

11 ¹Now the whole earth had one language and one speech. ²And it came to pass, as they journeyed from the east,

that they found a plain in the land of Shinar, and they dwelt there. ³Then they said to one another, "Come, let us make bricks and bake *them* thoroughly." They had brick for stone, and they had asphalt for mortar. ⁴And they said, "Come, let us build ourselves a city, and a tower whose top *is* in the heavens; let us make a name for ourselves, lest we be scattered abroad over the face of the whole earth."

⁵But the LORD came down to see the

TIME CAPSULE   *2500 to 2400* B.C.

2500	Earliest surviving dam, in Egypt, 272 feet thick
2500	Stone temples built at Ggantija, Malta
2500	Egyptians use the sistrum, a metal percussion instrument
2500	Widespread use of axes with sockets for the handle
2450	Smelted iron from Mesopotamia
2450	Egyptians make copper pipes
2400	Egyptians use oars to propel large boats
2400–2250	Ebla, a Semitic city-state in northern Syria

BABEL AND ITS TOWER (Gen. 11:1–9)

Babel was one of the chief cities in Nimrod's kingdom (Gen. 10:8–10). The term "Babel" is the Hebrew form of the name "Babylon," the city on the Euphrates River in central Mesopotamia.

The city has a very ancient past. It is first mentioned by the Accadian king Sargon (c. 2350 B.C.), who, according to tradition, burned it. Shar-kali-sharri (c. 2200 B.C.) restored its temple tower. Hammurabi (1792–1750 B.C.), a king of the 1st Dynasty of Babylon, made it his capital city. Unfortunately, archaeologists have been able to find evidence only as far back as the period of the Neo-Babylonian king Nebuchadnezzar II (605 B.C. and later). The rising water table in the area has prevented much research into earlier periods.

Babel has received much attention over its tower (Gen. 11:4, 5). It likely was a staged temple tower, the distinctive Mesopotamian structure known by the Sumerian term "ziggurat." Ziggurats were developed in the 3rd millennium B.C. at Uruk (Erech) and Ur in Babylonia, as well as at Nineveh, and consisted of smaller and smaller stages or stories built on top of each other.

Those who believe the tower at Babel refers to temple ruins from Mesopotamia point especially to Etemenanki, the ziggurat of the Marduk temple in Babylon. A Babylonian text describes it as having a base of 295 feet square with seven platforms over 108 feet high. The top platform had a temple where the god met with humanity. Access was achieved by ramps or stairways.

In Genesis the tower was never completed (Gen. 11:8). The Etemenanki did not fair much better. It was repaired by the Assyrian king Esarhaddon (680–669 B.C.), severely damaged in the Assyrian civil war (652–648 B.C.), restored again by Nebuchadnezzar II (605–562 B.C.), but destroyed by the Persian king Xerxes I in 472 B.C. Alexander the Great (323 B.C.) cleared the area to rebuild it, but died prematurely.

city and the tower which the sons of men had built. ⁶And the LORD said, "Indeed the people *are* one and they all have one language, and this is what they begin to do; now nothing that they propose to do will be withheld from them. ⁷Come, let Us go down and there confuse their language, that they may not understand one another's speech." ⁸So the LORD scattered them abroad from there over the face of all the earth, and they ceased building the city. ⁹Therefore its name is called Babel, because there the LORD confused the language of all the earth; and from there the LORD scattered them abroad over the face of all the earth.

Shem's Descendants

¹⁰This *is* the genealogy of Shem: Shem *was* one hundred years old, and begot Arphaxad two years after the flood. ¹¹After he begot Arphaxad, Shem lived five hundred years, and begot sons and daughters.

¹²Arphaxad lived thirty-five years, and begot Salah. ¹³After he begot Salah, Arphaxad lived four hundred and three years, and begot sons and daughters.

¹⁴Salah lived thirty years, and begot Eber. ¹⁵After he begot Eber, Salah lived four hundred and three years, and begot sons and daughters.

¹⁶Eber lived thirty-four years, and begot Peleg. ¹⁷After he begot Peleg, Eber lived four hundred and thirty years, and begot sons and daughters.

¹⁸Peleg lived thirty years, and begot Reu. ¹⁹After he begot Reu, Peleg lived two hundred and nine years, and begot sons and daughters.

²⁰Reu lived thirty-two years, and begot Serug. ²¹After he begot Serug, Reu lived two hundred and seven years, and begot sons and daughters.

²²Serug lived thirty years, and begot Nahor. ²³After he begot Nahor, Serug lived two hundred years, and begot sons and daughters.

²⁴Nahor lived twenty-nine years, and begot Terah. ²⁵After he begot Terah, Nahor lived one hundred and nineteen years, and begot sons and daughters.

THE MILLENNIUMS

A millennium is a period of 1,000 years. Scholars of ancient history often refer to millenniums (or millennia) when speaking of time before the Common Era or Christian Era (before the year A.D. 1). The setting of the Old Testament books from the patriarchs through the prophet Malachi extends from the end of the 3rd millennium B.C. through most of the 1st millennium.

Millennium Designation	Range of Dates
3rd millennium B.C.	3000 to 2000 B.C.
2nd millennium B.C.	2000 to 1000 B.C.
1st millennium B.C.	1000 to 1 B.C.

26Now Terah lived seventy years, and begot Abram, Nahor, and Haran.

Terah's Descendants

27This *is* the genealogy of Terah: Terah begot Abram, Nahor, and Haran. Haran begot Lot. 28And Haran died before his father Terah in his native land, in Ur of the Chaldeans. 29Then Abram and Nahor took wives: the name of Abram's wife *was* Sarai, and the name of Nahor's wife, Milcah, the daughter of Haran the father of Milcah and the father of Iscah. 30But Sarai was barren; she had no child.

31And Terah took his son Abram and his grandson Lot, the son of Haran, and his daughter-in-law Sarai, his son Abram's wife, and they went out with them from Ur of the Chaldeans to go to the land of Canaan; and they came to Haran and dwelt there. 32So the days of Terah were two hundred and five years, and Terah died in Haran.

THE PATRIARCHS, ISRAEL'S ANCESTORS

(2000—1500 B.C.)

God chose from among the nations of the world a man, named Abraham, to whom He revealed Himself. In response, Abraham chose to be God's servant.

The term "patriarch" refers to the founder or ruler of a tribe, family, or clan. The Israelites traced their ancestry to one man—"the patriarch Abraham" (Is. 51:2; Heb. 7:4). They laid claim to Canaan based on the covenant God made with their first three patriarchs—Abraham, Isaac, Jacob—to "possess the land" (Deut. 1:8). The phrase "the patriarchs" eventually referred to Jacob's twelve sons as well (Acts 7:8, 9). Thus among figures of the Bible, the patriarchs were the ancestors of the Israelites from Abraham to Jacob's son Joseph.

Exact dates for the period in which the patriarchs lived cannot be established. The events of the patriarchal narratives in Genesis cannot be synchronized with any events outside of the Bible. As a result, scholars have suggested dates for the patriarchs ranging from 2000 B.C. to as late as 1200 B.C. The biblical context places Abraham long before Moses. In the genealogy of Ex. 6:16–20, Moses is the great-great-grandson of Jacob, who himself was the grandson of Abraham. The line of descent—Abraham, Isaac, Jacob, Levi, Kohath, Amram, Moses—would set Abraham somewhere around 2000 to 1900 B.C.

▶ Archaeology and the Past

The Middle Bronze Age (2000–1500 B.C.) produced one of the more archaeologically rewarding sites that have been discovered in Mesopotamia. The city of Mari owed its importance to being a focal point on caravan routes crossing the Syrian desert and linking Mari with Syria and the Mediterranean coasts, as well as with Assyria and Babylonia. In addition to the temple of Ishtar, the Mesopotamian goddess, and a ziggurat (or temple tower), archaeologists found a royal palace containing almost 300 rooms.

Some 20,000 clay tablets, known as the Mari letters, were dug up, which shed much light on the ancient biblical world. These documents were written in Accadian and date from the time of Hammurabi (c. 1750 B.C.). Some of the documents are diplomatic correspondence between Mari's king Zimri-Lim and Babylon's Hammurabi, who eventually destroyed Mari.

The Mari tablets refer to terms often associated with the patriarchs. The term "Habiru," found both at Mari and in the Nuzi texts, has been compared to Abraham being named a "Hebrew" (Gen. 14:13). The seminomadic group called "Bene-yamina" at Mari bears a similar name to the Israelite name "Benjamin." Mari also sheds light on the Amorites. Nahor, Haran, Mari, Qatna, and Ugarit all appear as Amorite cities with Amorite kings.

Another discovery related to the patriarchs dates from around the change from

Middle Bronze (2000–1500 B.C.) to Late Bronze (1500–1200 B.C.). Numerous clay tablets from the city of Nuzi are thought to illuminate customs and local practices found in the patriarchal narratives. Nuzi was a Hurrian city, and it was sometime after 1550 B.C. that the Hurrians established themselves in upper Mesopotamia and northern Syria, rapidly expanding to form the powerful kingdom of Mitanni.

Exact dates for Nuzi are difficult to determine, although the Nuzi tablets are usually dated between 1400 and 1330 B.C. The similarities of social and legal customs between the Nuzi texts and the patriarchal stories have led some scholars to place the patriarchs themselves after 1550 B.C. The Nuzi customs, however, may reflect social conditions of centuries before Nuzi, as well as those of much later times in the 1st millennium. Rather than demonstrating a date for the patriarchs, the Nuzi texts provide insights into cultural customs that help us understand daily life in the 2nd millennium B.C.

▶ The Peoples and Groups

The dynasty of Sargon of Agade lasted for only about a century before it declined. Mesopotamia experienced a period of anarchy, partly caused by invasions of the Gutians, foreigners from the Zagros Mountains. The strongest dynasty to emerge during this unstable time was the 3rd Dynasty of Ur, founded by Ur-Nammu about 2112 B.C. The connections that existed between Ur and various Syrian cities form one possible setting for Abraham's journeys.

Eventually, Ur too declined. The Ur empire collapsed with the invasion of the Elamites, bringing an end to Sumerian civilization. Tribes of Semitic peoples, called Amorites, migrated into Mesopotamia from the west in large numbers. Capturing major regions, they established Amorite dynasties in various city-states. Both Shamshi-Adad I (c. 1813–1781 B.C.), ruler of Asshur, and Hammurabi of Babylon (1792–1750 B.C.) were Amorite kings.

In Egypt, a period of decline and civil war ended gradually during the Middle Kingdom. King Amenemhet I of Thebes (1963–1934 B.C.) convinced the princes of the land to give their allegiance to him as the true heir to Egypt's throne. Another pharaoh, Sesostris III (1862–1843 B.C.) established a central government by restraining the powers of Egypt's provincial rulers and families.

Unity in Egypt continued for more than 200 years. Eventually, however, the country experienced a second period of weakness in which rival dynasties competed for control of limited areas. The most important of these dynasties was the Hyksos, who gained control of Lower Egypt, establishing a capital at Avaris. Toward the end of the Middle Bronze Age, King Kamose of Thebes broke the power of the Hyksos, and his younger brother Ahmose eventually drove them from Egypt.

Abraham is given the promise that he and his descendants will become a blessing to all humanity.

▶ The Biblical Literature

The second part of the Book of Genesis, chs. 12—50, tells the stories of Israel's patriarchs. The events from the lives of Abraham, Isaac, and Jacob (chs. 12—38) take place primarily in Canaan, although Abraham originated in Mesopotamia (Ur and Haran). The traditions concerning these ancestors are grouped into cycles of stories around Abraham (12:1—25:18) and around Jacob (25:19—36:43). Isaac appears in the Abraham and Jacob cycles, with much of his story in Gen. 26.

Abraham enters into covenant with God and is given the promise that he and his descendants will become a blessing to all humanity. In the stories of Abraham and Sarah, Isaac and Rebekah, Jacob and Leah and Rachel, and Joseph, the fulfillment of God's promises takes concrete form. The life of Joseph (chs. 37—50) is set primarily in Egypt, and in that foreign place we see God's unfailing providence and His determination to keep His promise to Abraham.

The Changing of the Empires

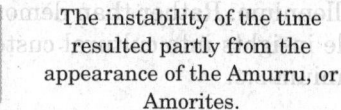

The instability of the time resulted partly from the appearance of the Amurru, or Amorites.

After about 2200 B.C. the great empires of the Early Bronze Age fell apart. Political instability and unrest spread throughout Egypt and Mesopotamia at the close of this age and the beginning of the Middle Bronze Age (2000–1500 B.C.).

In Egypt, the Old Kingdom was followed by over a century of political and social disarray. During this time, known in Egyptian history as the First Intermediate Period (2160–2010 B.C.), bedouins from Asia were able to infiltrate the Nile Delta. Civil strife between Egypt's city-states ended in 2040, when Mentuhotep II from Thebes reunified the land and began the prosperous and stable Middle Kingdom, which lasted until about 1786 B.C.

In Mesopotamia, no great empire arose to replace the 3rd Dynasty of Ur after that city-state fell in 2004 B.C. Smaller kingdoms such as Isin, Larsa, Assyria, Mari, and Babylon took turns dominating each other for brief periods. The greatest of these was the kingdom of Hammurabi I of Babylon (1792–1750 B.C.), whose famous law code parallels many of the Israelite laws. Hammurabi eventually brought all of Mesopotamia under Babylonian control. Even this kingdom was brief, though, declining during the rule of Hammurabi's son.

The instability of the time resulted partly from the appearance throughout the ancient Near East of a new ethnic group, the Amurru, or Amorites. This large group of Semitic people had personal names and customs that resemble those of the biblical Hebrews. Their influence was so pervasive that even some Mesopotamian kings had Amorite names.

After 2000 B.C. Amorites inhabited Palestine. Some settled in villages and established their own city-states, others lived as seminomadic shepherds, and still others lived on the fringes of society as warlike outcasts. Such outsiders, referred to as "Habiru," usually served as slaves or mercenaries to others, but on occasion fought their own battles.

Amorites worshiped many gods, but each city or clan identified its own particular deity. In Mesopotamia, in cities influenced by the Amorites, there even appeared prophets of these local gods, using language very similar to that of the much later Old Testament prophets. Away from the cities, among the seminomadic shepherds, great stress was given to the god of the clan's forefathers. Worship usually involved animal sacrifice, but child sacrifice was also common.

Abram the Amorite

The accounts of the patriarchs in Gen. 12—50 fit within the setting of Mesopotamia at this time. Abram was surely from an Amorite family, and that family's migration from Ur to Haran (in Syria) to southern Palestine follows the general pattern of the Amorite expansion. The patriarchs' way of life corresponds to that of the seminomadic shepherds, although occasionally they acted like the more warlike Habiru, as when Abram leads his men to battle in Gen. 14. The God who speaks to Abram is seen at least partly as the God of the clan, referred to often as "the God of the fathers" (Ex. 3:13).

Although Abram's relationship with his

THE GREAT PYRAMID AT GIZA (Gen. 12:14)

The famous pyramids at Giza functioned as individual tombs for some of the monarchs of Egypt's Old Kingdom (2700–2160 B.C.). Earliest among the monumental pyramid tombs appears to have been the Step Pyramid of Pharaoh Djoser (c. 2650 B.C.). The monarchs of the 4th Dynasty (2600–2500 B.C.), Khufu and his successor Khafre, built huge pyramids in imitation of the Step Pyramid. The Great Pyramid is slightly over 480 feet high, and each of the four sides at the base is about 756 feet wide. Such massive monuments demonstrate the great architectural precision and excellence of the Egyptian Old Kingdom.

The patriarch Abram traveled to Egypt during a time of famine in Canaan (Gen. 12:10). Exact dates for Abram's life are unknown, but scholars often place him around 2000 or 1900 B.C. Thus, the Great Pyramid at Giza was already centuries old when Abram and Sarai visited Egypt (Gen. 12:10—13:1).

God follows many of the Amorite patterns, it also differs from Amorite religion in significant ways. For instance, Abram's God repudiates child sacrifice (Gen. 22). Moreover, God is not just a local clan deity. Although He makes a covenant with a particular family, that covenant exists in order to bless "all the families of the earth" (Gen. 12:3).

■ Genesis 12:1—15:21

Genesis
Promises to Abram

12 :1 Now the LORD had said to Abram:

"Get out of your country,
From your family
And from your father's house,
To a land that I will show you.
2　I will make you a great nation;
I will bless you
And make your name great;
And you shall be a blessing.
3　I will bless those who bless you,
And I will curse him who curses you;
And in you all the families of the
earth shall be blessed."

⁴So Abram departed as the LORD had spoken to him, and Lot went with him. And Abram *was* seventy-five years old when he departed from Haran. ⁵Then Abram took Sarai his wife and Lot his brother's son, and all their possessions that they had gathered, and the people whom they had acquired in Haran, and they departed to go to the land of Canaan. So they came to the land of Canaan. ⁶Abram passed through the land to the place of Shechem, as far as the terebinth tree of Moreh.ᵃ And the Canaanites *were* then in the land.

⁷Then the LORD appeared to Abram and said, "To your descendants I will give this land." And there he built an altar to the LORD, who had appeared to him. ⁸And he moved from there to the mountain east of Bethel, and he pitched his tent *with* Bethel on the west and Ai on the east; there he built an altar to the LORD and called on the name of the LORD. ⁹So Abram journeyed, going on still toward the South.ᵃ

Abram in Egypt

¹⁰Now there was a famine in the land, and Abram went down to Egypt to dwell there, for the famine *was* severe in the land. ¹¹And it came to pass, when he was close to entering Egypt, that he said to Sarai his wife, "Indeed I know that you *are* a woman of beautiful countenance.

TIME CAPSULE　2350 to 2160 B.C.

2350	Instruction of Ptahhotep, wisdom literature from Egypt
2350	Sargon of Agade unifies Babylonia
2348	Ussher's date for the Flood of Noah
2300	Empire of the Old Accadian monarchs
2300	Map on clay tablet, with cardinal points marked, Iraq
2250	Evidence of nomads in Palestine
2160	Bronze is in general use in Egypt
2160	Collapse of Old Kingdom in Egypt

12:6 ᵃHebrew *Alon Moreh*　　12:9 ᵃHebrew *Negev*

¹²Therefore it will happen, when the Egyptians see you, that they will say, 'This *is* his wife'; and they will kill me, but they will let you live. ¹³Please say you *are* my sister, that it may be well with me for your sake, and that Iᵃ may live because of you."

¹⁴So it was, when Abram came into Egypt, that the Egyptians saw the woman, that she *was* very beautiful. ¹⁵The princes of Pharaoh also saw her and commended her to Pharaoh. And the woman was taken to Pharaoh's house. ¹⁶He treated Abram well for her sake. He had sheep, oxen, male donkeys, male and female servants, female donkeys, and camels.

¹⁷But the LORD plagued Pharaoh and his house with great plagues because of Sarai, Abram's wife. ¹⁸And Pharaoh called Abram and said, "What *is* this you have done to me? Why did you not tell me that she *was* your wife? ¹⁹Why did you say, 'She *is* my sister'? I might have taken her as my wife. Now therefore, here is your wife; take *her* and go your way." ²⁰So Pharaoh commanded *his* men concerning him; and they sent him away, with his wife and all that he had.

Abram Inherits Canaan

13 ¹Then Abram went up from Egypt, he and his wife and all that he had, and Lot with him, to the South.ᵃ ²Abram *was* very rich in livestock, in silver, and in gold. ³And he went on his journey from the South as far as Bethel, to the place where his tent had been at the beginning, between Bethel and Ai, ⁴to the place of the altar which he had made there at first. And there Abram called on the name of the LORD.

⁵Lot also, who went with Abram, had flocks and herds and tents. ⁶Now the land was not able to support them, that they might dwell together, for their possessions were so great that they could not dwell together. ⁷And there was strife between the herdsmen of Abram's livestock and the herdsmen of Lot's livestock. The Canaanites and the Perizzites then dwelt in the land.

⁸So Abram said to Lot, "Please let there be no strife between you and me, and between my herdsmen and your herdsmen; for we *are* brethren. ⁹*Is* not the whole land before you? Please separate from me. If *you take* the left, then I will go to the right; or, if *you go* to the right, then I will go to the left."

¹⁰And Lot lifted his eyes and saw all the plain of Jordan, that it *was* well watered everywhere (before the LORD destroyed Sodom and Gomorrah) like the garden of the LORD, like the land of Egypt as you go toward Zoar. ¹¹Then Lot chose for himself all the plain of Jordan, and Lot journeyed east. And they separated from each other. ¹²Abram dwelt in the land of Canaan, and Lot dwelt in the cities of the plain and pitched *his* tent even as far as Sodom. ¹³But the men of Sodom *were* exceedingly wicked and sinful against the LORD.

¹⁴And the LORD said to Abram, after Lot had separated from him: "Lift your eyes now and look from the place where you are—northward, southward, eastward, and westward; ¹⁵for all the land which you see I give to you and your descendantsᵃ forever. ¹⁶And I will make your descendants as the dust of the earth; so that if a man could number the dust of the earth, *then* your descendants also could be numbered. ¹⁷Arise, walk in the land through its length and its width, for I give it to you."

¹⁸Then Abram moved *his* tent, and went and dwelt by the terebinth trees of Mamre,ᵃ which *are* in Hebron, and built an altar there to the LORD.

Lot's Captivity and Rescue

14 ¹And it came to pass in the days of Amraphel king of Shinar, Arioch king of Ellasar, Chedorlaomer king of

---

12:13 ᵃLiterally *my soul*　　13:1 ᵃHebrew *Negev*　　13:15 ᵃLiterally *seed,* and so throughout the book　　13:18 ᵃHebrew *Alon Mamre*

TIME CAPSULE　*2166 to 2000 B.C.*

2166– 1991	Abraham's life (based on early Exodus)
2112– 2004	Ur-Nammu founds 3rd Dynasty of Ur
2095	Law code of Ur-Nammu
2040	Mentuhotep II from Thebes reunifies Egypt
2040– 1786	The Middle Kingdom in Egypt
2017– 1985	Ishbi-Erra founds Isin dynasty
2004	City-state of Ur falls to the Elamites
2000	Amorites inhabit Palestine

THE HABIRU—REFUGEES OR OUTLAWS? (Gen. 14:13)

The Habiru (also spelled Hapiru) were a class of fugitives found in the ancient Near East from about 2000 to 1000 B.C. Some of the Habiru were refugees who fled their homelands, while others included brigands, malcontents, and socially maladjusted individuals. Their geographic horizon extended from southern Mesopotamia, Anatolia, and Syro-Palestine to Egypt.

The obvious similarity between the words "Habiru" and "Hebrew" has led some to equate the Habiru with the early Israelites. Unfortunately, the original meaning of the Accadian term "Habiru" has never been satisfactorily determined. Most scholars, however, believe it concerns either refugees forced to leave their own land, or armed brigands who caused problems for local populations.

The Habiru are described at length in a great variety of texts, ranging from the Amarna letters in Egypt to the Hittite archives in central Anatolia. The Mari tablets describe the Habiru as brigands who were very mobile. The Nuzi documents identify them as foreigners who served the citizens of Nuzi. In all these texts, the Habiru are foreign to the Near Eastern society in which they are trying to survive. Some survived as servants or laborers; others as outlaws.

Abram was called "the Hebrew" (Gen. 14:13). In this context, he could be acting as an armed brigand with his own army to help his nephew Lot (14:14–16). On the other hand, David and his men are also called "Hebrews" (1 Sam. 29:3) when, in flight from King Saul, they sought refuge among the Philistines (1 Sam. 27:1–4). Although "Hebrew" is clearly an ethnic term in the Bible, it may have been originally a term describing the social condition of persons in flight or of those in armed gangs. Abram could have been called "the Hebrew" simply because of his status as a foreigner in Canaan.

Elam, and Tidal king of nations,[a] ²*that* they made war with Bera king of Sodom, Birsha king of Gomorrah, Shinab king of Admah, Shemeber king of Zeboiim, and the king of Bela (that is, Zoar). ³All these joined together in the Valley of Siddim (that is, the Salt Sea). ⁴Twelve years they served Chedorlaomer, and in the thirteenth year they rebelled.

⁵In the fourteenth year Chedorlaomer and the kings that *were* with him came and attacked the Rephaim in Ashteroth Karnaim, the Zuzim in Ham, the Emim in Shaveh Kiriathaim, ⁶and the Horites in their mountain of Seir, as far as El Paran, which *is* by the wilderness. ⁷Then they turned back and came to En Mishpat (that *is*, Kadesh), and attacked all the country of the Amalekites, and also the Amorites who dwelt in Hazezon Tamar.

⁸And the king of Sodom, the king of Gomorrah, the king of Admah, the king of Zeboiim, and the king of Bela (that *is*, Zoar) went out and joined together in battle in the Valley of Siddim ⁹against Chedorlaomer king of Elam, Tidal king of na-tions,[a] Amraphel king of Shinar, and Arioch king of Ellasar—four kings against five. ¹⁰Now the Valley of Siddim *was full of* asphalt pits; and the kings of Sodom and Gomorrah fled; *some* fell there, and the remainder fled to the mountains. ¹¹Then they took all the goods of Sodom and Gomorrah, and all their provisions, and went their way. ¹²They also took Lot, Abram's brother's son who dwelt in Sodom, and his goods, and departed.

¹³Then one who had escaped came and told Abram the Hebrew, for he dwelt by the terebinth trees of Mamre[a] the Amorite, brother of Eshcol and brother of Aner; and they *were* allies with Abram. ¹⁴Now when Abram heard that his brother was taken captive, he armed his three hundred and eighteen trained *servants* who were born in his own house, and went in pursuit as far as Dan. ¹⁵He divided his forces against them by night, and he and his servants attacked them and pursued them as far as Hobah, which *is* north of Damascus. ¹⁶So he brought back all the goods, and also brought back his brother Lot and his goods, as well as the women and the people.

¹⁷And the king of Sodom went out to

14:1 ᵃHebrew *goyim*   14:9 ᵃHebrew *goyim*
14:13 ᵃHebrew *Alon Mamre*

ABRAM'S CEREMONY AND A HITTITE RITUAL (Gen. 15:9, 10)

In a covenant ceremony Abram was instructed to cut animals in halves and arrange the pieces opposite each other (Gen. 15:9, 10). Abram's animal ritual has a literary parallel in a Hittite text from Anatolia, dated after the mid-2nd millennium B.C.

The Hittite text describes a ritual of purification to be used after a military defeat. The troops are required to perform the ritual "behind a river," where a man, a goat, a puppy, and a small pig are cut in half. The sections, thus divided, are arranged oppositely parallel on one side and on the other. In front of this array a gate of an unknown type of wood is built. Fires are lit on both sides of the arranged pieces. Then the troops are obliged to pass between the fires and are sprinkled with water upon reaching the bank of the river.

The procedure is not mentioned in any official Hittite state cult, but is recorded in the royal archives. Its similarities with the ceremony in Genesis, although superficial, show a common ritual tradition.

meet him at the Valley of Shaveh (that *is,* the King's Valley), after his return from the defeat of Chedorlaomer and the kings who *were* with him.

Abram and Melchizedek

18Then Melchizedek king of Salem brought out bread and wine; he *was* the priest of God Most High. 19And he blessed him and said:

"Blessed be Abram of God Most High,
Possessor of heaven and earth;
20 And blessed be God Most High,
Who has delivered your enemies into
your hand."

And he gave him a tithe of all.

21Now the king of Sodom said to Abram, "Give me the persons, and take the goods for yourself."

22But Abram said to the king of Sodom, "I have raised my hand to the LORD, God Most High, the Possessor of heaven and earth, 23that I *will take* nothing, from a thread to a sandal strap, and that I will not take anything that *is* yours, lest you should say, 'I have made Abram rich'— 24except only what the young men have eaten, and the portion of the men who went with me: Aner, Eshcol, and Mamre; let them take their portion."

God's Covenant with Abram

15 1After these things the word of the LORD came to Abram in a vision, saying, "Do not be afraid, Abram. I *am* your shield, your exceedingly great reward."

2But Abram said, "Lord GOD, what will You give me, seeing I go childless, and the heir of my house *is* Eliezer of Damascus?" 3Then Abram said, "Look, You have given me no offspring; indeed one born in my house is my heir!"

4And behold, the word of the LORD *came* to him, saying, "This one shall not be your heir, but one who will come from your own body shall be your heir." 5Then He brought him outside and said, "Look now toward heaven, and count the stars if you are able to number them." And He said to him, "So shall your descendants be." 6And he believed in the LORD, and He accounted it to him for righteousness.

7Then He said to him, "I *am* the LORD, who brought you out of Ur of the Chaldeans, to give you this land to inherit it."

8And he said, "Lord GOD, how shall I know that I will inherit it?"

9So He said to him, "Bring Me a three-

PASSING BETWEEN THE HALVES (Gen. 15:17–21)

There are no adequate modern parallels to the broad-ranging meanings of the term "covenant" as used in the Bible. The closest parallel probably resides in marriage, where a public gathering solemnizes an agreement between two people.

The type of covenant presented in the Bible is most often between two parties. The superior party was known as the suzerain; the inferior party as the vassal. Both the suzerain and vassal had specific responsibilities. Primarily, in ancient societies the suzerain provided protection for the vassal, while the vassal supported the suzerain with taxes and was loyal in time of war.

The Lord and Abram joined themselves in a suzerain and vassal covenant (Gen. 15:18). Like similar ancient Near Eastern covenants they held a public ceremony to ratify their relationship. The sacrifice of animals and a meal (15:9, 10) were typical components of covenant ceremonies, as were the promises of both parties. Abram's part of this agreement was to "believe" in the Lord (15:6), which meant to worship no other gods. The Lord promised Abram to make his descendants as numerous as the stars (15:5) and provide a homeland for them (15:18).

Two differences between ancient Near Eastern covenants and the Gen. 15 covenant are striking. Usually the list of the vassal's duties and responsibilities was much larger than that of the suzerain's. In fact, a covenant, including the duties of the vassal, was imposed on the vassal by the suzerain. In the Gen. 15 covenant almost nothing is said about Abram's responsibilities. The focus is on what the Lord promised to Abram, not what Abram promised the Lord.

In the second difference it was usually the vassal who cut the animals in two parts and walked between them (15:10, 17). The ritual symbolically demonstrated what would happen to the vassal if the covenant was broken. The "burning torch" passing between the pieces of flesh in the Gen. 15 covenant (15:17) was obviously a representation of the Lord. The symbolism of Him passing between the cut sacrifices implies that He would die before He would allow His covenant with Abram to fail.

year-old heifer, a three-year-old female goat, a three-year-old ram, a turtledove, and a young pigeon." ¹⁰Then he brought all these to Him and cut them in two, down the middle, and placed each piece opposite the other; but he did not cut the birds in two. ¹¹And when the vultures came down on the carcasses, Abram drove them away.

¹²Now when the sun was going down, a deep sleep fell upon Abram; and behold, horror *and* great darkness fell upon him. ¹³Then He said to Abram: "Know certainly that your descendants will be strangers in a land *that is* not theirs, and will serve them, and they will afflict them four hundred years. ¹⁴And also the nation whom they serve I will judge; afterward they shall come out with great possessions. ¹⁵Now as for you, you shall go to your fathers in peace; you shall be buried at a good old age. ¹⁶But in the fourth generation they shall return here, for the iniquity of the Amorites *is* not yet complete."

¹⁷And it came to pass, when the sun went down and it was dark, that behold, there appeared a smoking oven and a burning torch that passed between those pieces. ¹⁸On the same day the LORD made a covenant with Abram, saying:

"To your descendants I have given this land, from the river of Egypt to the great river, the River Euphrates— ¹⁹the Kenites, the Kenezzites, the Kadmonites, ²⁰the Hittites, the Perizzites, the Rephaim, ²¹the Amorites, the Canaanites, the Girgashites, and the Jebusites."

The Birth of Ishmael

None of the events of the patriarchs can be synchronized with any dates known from nonbiblical sources. Nevertheless, Genesis does provide a brief chronological outline of Abraham's life. Abram was 75 years old when he left Haran in Mesopotamia and journeyed to Canaan with his wife Sarai (Gen. 12:4, 5). After living 10 years in Canaan, Sarai made use of a typical ancient Near Eastern custom for a

barren wife. In this custom, the wife authorized her husband to obtain children by her
personal slave (Gen. 16:3). Thus, Abram at
age 86 fathered Ishmael through Sarai's maid
Hagar (16:16).

   Sarai's barrenness continued for 13 more
years, but God intervened before Abram, now
99 years old (Gen. 17:1), could announce Ishmael as his legal heir. Changing Abram's name
to Abraham, and Sarai's to Sarah, God
promised a child by Sarah (17:5, 15, 16).

▼   ■ Genesis 16:1—20:18

Genesis
Hagar and Ishmael

16 :1 Now Sarai, Abram's wife, had
borne him no *children*. And she had
an Egyptian maidservant whose name was
Hagar. ²So Sarai said to Abram, "See now,
the LORD has restrained me from bearing
children. Please, go in to my maid; perhaps
I shall obtain children by her." And Abram
heeded the voice of Sarai. ³Then Saraï,
Abram's wife, took Hagar her maid, the
Egyptian, and gave her to her husband
Abram to be his wife, after Abram had
dwelt ten years in the land of Canaan. ⁴So
he went in to Hagar, and she conceived.
And when she saw that she had conceived,
her mistress became despised in her eyes.
⁵Then Sarai said to Abram, "My wrong
be upon you! I gave my maid into your embrace; and when she saw that she had conceived, I became despised in her eyes. The
LORD judge between you and me."

⁶So Abram said to Sarai, "Indeed your
maid *is* in your hand; do to her as you
please." And when Sarai dealt harshly with
her, she fled from her presence.

⁷Now the Angel of the LORD found her
by a spring of water in the wilderness, by
the spring on the way to Shur. ⁸And He
said, "Hagar, Sarai's maid, where have you
come from, and where are you going?"

She said, "I am fleeing from the presence of my mistress Sarai."

⁹The Angel of the LORD said to her,
"Return to your mistress, and submit yourself under her hand." ¹⁰Then the Angel of
the LORD said to her, "I will multiply your
descendants exceedingly, so that they shall
not be counted for multitude." ¹¹And the
Angel of the LORD said to her:

"Behold, you *are* with child,
   And you shall bear a son.

You shall call his name Ishmael,
   Because the LORD has heard your
      affliction.
¹² He shall be a wild man;
   His hand *shall be* against every man,
   And every man's hand against him.
   And he shall dwell in the presence of
      all his brethren."

¹³Then she called the name of the LORD
who spoke to her, You-Are-the-God-Who-
Sees; for she said, "Have I also here seen
Him who sees me?" ¹⁴Therefore the well
was called Beer Lahai Roi;ᵃ observe, *it is*
between Kadesh and Bered.

¹⁵So Hagar bore Abram a son; and
Abram named his son, whom Hagar bore,
Ishmael. ¹⁶Abram *was* eighty-six years old
when Hagar bore Ishmael to Abram.

The Sign of the Covenant

17 ¹When Abram was ninety-nine years
old, the LORD appeared to Abram
and said to him, "I *am* Almighty God; walk
before Me and be blameless. ²And I will
make My covenant between Me and you,
and will multiply you exceedingly." ³Then
Abram fell on his face, and God talked with
him, saying: ⁴"As for Me, behold, My
covenant is with you, and you shall be a
father of many nations. ⁵No longer shall
your name be called Abram, but your name
shall be Abraham; for I have made you a
father of many nations. ⁶I will make you
exceedingly fruitful; and I will make nations of you, and kings shall come from
you. ⁷And I will establish My covenant between Me and you and your descendants
after you in their generations, for an everlasting covenant, to be God to you and your
descendants after you. ⁸Also I give to you
and your descendants after you the land in
which you are a stranger, all the land of
Canaan, as an everlasting possession; and
I will be their God."

⁹And God said to Abraham: "As for
you, you shall keep My covenant, you and
your descendants after you throughout
their generations. ¹⁰This *is* My covenant
which you shall keep, between Me and you
and your descendants after you: Every
male child among you shall be circumcised;
¹¹and you shall be circumcised in the flesh
of your foreskins, and it shall be a sign of
the covenant between Me and you. ¹²He

16:14 ᵃLiterally *Well of the One Who Lives and Sees
Me*

EPOCH 1
CREATION TO 2000 B.C.

BIBLICAL HISTORY

SECULAR HISTORY

26,000 B.C.

Creation, Adam and Eve (before 2500 B.C.):
God creates the universe and the earth. He creates Adam in His own image and creates woman (Eve) as Adam's life partner.

Stone tools shaped by grinding in Japan and Australia (c. 26,000–23,000 B.C.).

15,000 B.C.

First known ovens, in the Ukraine (c. 20,000 B.C.)

10,000 B.C.

Cain and Abel (before 2500 B.C.):
Cain, the oldest son of Adam and Eve, murders his brother Abel in a fit of jealous rage over God's favoring of Abel's offering and the rejection of his own.

Wolves or dogs tamed in Palestine (c. 11,000 B.C.).

7500 B.C.

Noah's Ark (before 2500 B.C.):
Displeased with sin in the world, God vows to destroy life on earth with a great flood, but saves Noah and his family, and pairs of "animals of every kind," wild and tame, in a great ship, called an ark. After the waters recede, the ark lands on Mount Ararat.

Hatchet used in Europe to fell trees; sheep domesticated in the Middle East (c. 7500 B.C.).

5000 B.C.

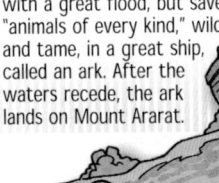

Pottery is first known in Palestine (c. 5500 B.C.).

3750 B.C.

Domestication of the horse; first chariots (c. 4000–3100 B.C.)

2500 B.C.

Tower of Babel (before 2500 B.C.):
Noah's descendants speak one language and begin building a great tower. God stops the construction project by confusing the people, making them speak many different languages, and scattering them across the earth.

First stage of Stonehenge monument in Britain (2750 B.C.).

❶ Adam and Eve

The first man and woman, God's crowning work of creation in the Garden of Eden. Adam and Eve sin and are expelled from Eden. Later, their son Cain kills his brother Abel. Another son, Seth, is born, plus many other sons and daughters.

❹ Isaac and Rebekah

Isaac journeys to Haran in Syria, marries his cousin Rebekah, and brings her back to Canaan. They have twin sons, Esau and Jacob.

❺ Jacob and Leah and Rachel

Jacob goes to Haran and marries both of his uncle Laban's daughters, Leah and Rachel, in Syria. With the two wives and with two concubines, Jacob produces sons who become the ancestors of the twelve tribes of Israel.

THE Patriarchs

❷ Noah and His Family

Noah, a descendant of Seth, builds an ark to save his family from the Flood at God's command. After the Flood, the ark rests on Mount Ararat (in Turkey) and Noah's sons Shem, Ham, and Japheth and their wives repopulate the earth. Subsequently, the people's attempt to build the Tower of Babel moves God to scatter the nations.

❸ Abraham and Sarah

Abraham, a descendant of Shem, leaves Ur (in southern Iraq) and travels to the land of Canaan with his wife Sarah. Two sons, Ishmael by Hagar and Isaac by Sarah, are born to him.

❻ Joseph

Jacob's son Joseph is sold into slavery in Egypt and becomes prime minister, enabling his family to be saved from famine. The Israelites come to Egypt. Joseph marries the Egyptian high priest's daughter Asenath, and she gives birth to sons, Ephraim and Manasseh, whose descendants become two tribes. Eventually, the Israelites are enslaved by the Egyptians.

EPOCH 2
2000 TO 1500 B.C.

BIBLICAL HISTORY

SECULAR HISTORY

Abram (Abraham) born (c. 2166 B.C.):
The patriarch Abram, later named Abraham, is born in Ur, located in southern Babylonia. His wife, Sarai (later named Sarah), is born about ten years later.

Abram moves to Canaan and later to Egypt (c. 2091 B.C.):
At God's command, Abram travels with his family from Ur to Haran and then to Canaan. Later they go to Egypt because of severe famine in the land. (Dates are based on early Exodus dating.)

Ishmael and Isaac born (c. 2080–2066 B.C.):
Back in Canaan, Abraham begets a son, Ishmael, by Sarah's slave Hagar with Sarah's approval. But later, Isaac is born to Abraham and Sarah when Abraham is in his 90s and Sarah is in her 80s.

Sodom and Gomorrah destroyed (c. 2066 B.C.):
God destroys these cities south of the Dead Sea because of their extreme depravity. The wife of Abraham's nephew Lot turns to a pillar of salt when she looks back at the burning cities.

Jacob born (c. 2006 B.C.):
Twins Jacob and Esau are born to Rebekah.

Jacob fathers twelve sons (c. 1950-1920 B.C.):
With two wives and two concubines, Jacob fathers the twelve sons who would beget the tribes of Israel: Reuben, Simeon, Levi, Judah, Dan, Naphtali, Gad, Asher, Issachar, Zebulun, Joseph (whose sons Ephraim and Manasseh would become tribes), and Benjamin. There is also a daughter, Dinah.

Joseph sold into slavery and taken to Egypt (c. 1890 B.C.):
Joseph's brothers, jealous of their father's favor for Joseph, sell him into slavery. He is taken to Egypt, where he later becomes a trusted official second only to Pharaoh.

2500 B.C.

2250 B.C.

2150 B.C.

2000 B.C.

1900 B.C.

1800 B.C.

1500 B.C.

The Great Pyramid at Giza demonstrates the architectural precision and advancement of the Egyptian Old Kingdom (c. 2550 B.C.).

Egyptians make copper pipes and use oars to propel large boats (c. 2450-2400 B.C.).

The Bronze Age is underway, with bronze in general use in Egypt (c. 2160 B.C.).

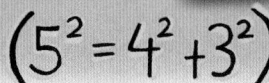

Mathematicians discover the Pythagorean Theorem (c. 1900 B.C.).

$$(5^2 = 4^2 + 3^2)$$

Astronomy and musical notation are developed in Babylon (c. 1800 B.C.).

Earliest evidence of spoked wheels (c. 1779 B.C.).

Phoenicians develop a consonantal alphabet (c. 1700 B.C.).

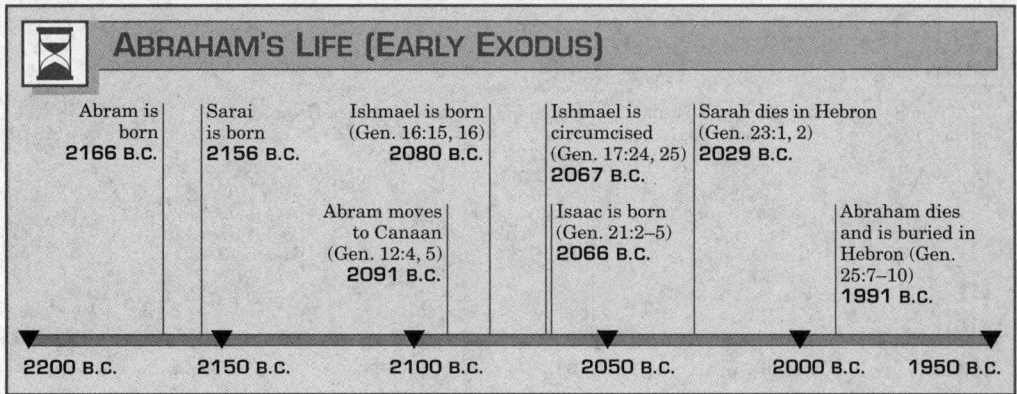

ABRAHAM'S LIFE (EARLY EXODUS)

| Abram is born 2166 B.C. | Sarai is born 2156 B.C. | Ishmael is born (Gen. 16:15, 16) 2080 B.C. | Ishmael is circumcised (Gen. 17:24, 25) 2067 B.C. | Sarah dies in Hebron (Gen. 23:1, 2) 2029 B.C. | |
| | | Abram moves to Canaan (Gen. 12:4, 5) 2091 B.C. | Isaac is born (Gen. 21:2–5) 2066 B.C. | | Abraham dies and is buried in Hebron (Gen. 25:7–10) 1991 B.C. |

| 2200 B.C. | 2150 B.C. | 2100 B.C. | 2050 B.C. | 2000 B.C. | 1950 B.C. |

who is eight days old among you shall be circumcised, every male child in your generations, he who is born in your house or bought with money from any foreigner who is not your descendant. [13]He who is born in your house and he who is bought with your money must be circumcised, and My covenant shall be in your flesh for an everlasting covenant. [14]And the uncircumcised male child, who is not circumcised in the flesh of his foreskin, that person shall be cut off from his people; he has broken My covenant."

[15]Then God said to Abraham, "As for Sarai your wife, you shall not call her name Sarai, but Sarah *shall be* her name. [16]And I will bless her and also give you a son by her; then I will bless her, and she shall be *a mother* of nations; kings of peoples shall be from her."

[17]Then Abraham fell on his face and laughed, and said in his heart, "Shall *a child* be born to a man who is one hundred years old? And shall Sarah, who is ninety years old, bear *a child?*" [18]And Abraham said to God, "Oh, that Ishmael might live before You!"

[19]Then God said: "No, Sarah your wife shall bear you a son, and you shall call his name Isaac; I will establish My covenant with him for an everlasting

covenant, *and* with his descendants after him. [20]And as for Ishmael, I have heard you. Behold, I have blessed him, and will make him fruitful, and will multiply him exceedingly. He shall beget twelve princes, and I will make him a great nation. [21]But My covenant I will establish with Isaac, whom Sarah shall bear to you at this set time next year." [22]Then He finished talking with him, and God went up from Abraham.

[23]So Abraham took Ishmael his son, all who were born in his house and all who were bought with his money, every male among the men of Abraham's house, and circumcised the flesh of their foreskins that very same day, as God had said to him. [24]Abraham *was* ninety-nine years old when he was circumcised in the flesh of his foreskin. [25]And Ishmael his son *was* thirteen years old when he was circumcised in the flesh of his foreskin. [26]That very same day Abraham was circumcised, and his son Ishmael; [27]and all the men of his house, born in the house or bought with money from a foreigner, were circumcised with him.

The Son of Promise

18 [1]Then the LORD appeared to him by the terebinth trees of Mamre,[a] as he was sitting in the tent door in the heat of the day. [2]So he lifted his eyes and looked, and behold, three men were standing by him; and when he saw *them,* he ran from

18:1 [a]Hebrew *Alon Mamre*

DAILY LIFE AND CUSTOMS

Circumcision is a minor operation that removes a piece of skin from the male organ. It was practiced in several nations of the ancient Near East, including Egypt. But for Israel it was a sign of membership in the community and was required of every male (Gen. 17:10, 11). Traditionally it was performed with a flint knife.

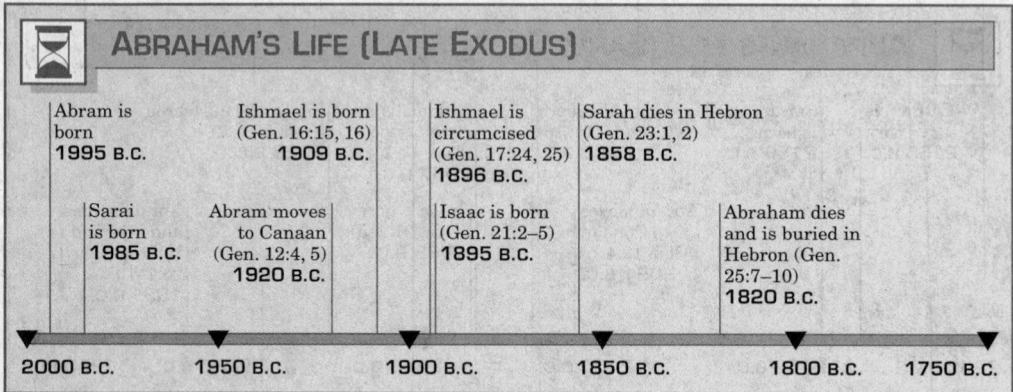

ABRAHAM'S LIFE (LATE EXODUS)

| Abram is born **1995 B.C.** | Ishmael is born (Gen. 16:15, 16) **1909 B.C.** | Ishmael is circumcised (Gen. 17:24, 25) **1896 B.C.** | Sarah dies in Hebron (Gen. 23:1, 2) **1858 B.C.** | |
| Sarai is born **1985 B.C.** | Abram moves to Canaan (Gen. 12:4, 5) **1920 B.C.** | Isaac is born (Gen. 21:2–5) **1895 B.C.** | | Abraham dies and is buried in Hebron (Gen. 25:7–10) **1820 B.C.** |

| 2000 B.C. | 1950 B.C. | 1900 B.C. | 1850 B.C. | 1800 B.C. | 1750 B.C. |

the tent door to meet them, and bowed himself to the ground, ³and said, "My Lord, if I have now found favor in Your sight, do not pass on by Your servant. ⁴Please let a little water be brought, and wash your feet, and rest yourselves under the tree. ⁵And I will bring a morsel of bread, that you may refresh your hearts. After that you may pass by, inasmuch as you have come to your servant."

They said, "Do as you have said."

⁶So Abraham hurried into the tent to Sarah and said, "Quickly, make ready three measures of fine meal; knead *it* and make cakes." ⁷And Abraham ran to the herd, took a tender and good calf, gave *it* to a young man, and he hastened to prepare it. ⁸So he took butter and milk and the calf which he had prepared, and set *it* before them; and he stood by them under the tree as they ate.

⁹Then they said to him, "Where *is* Sarah your wife?"

So he said, "Here, in the tent."

¹⁰And He said, "I will certainly return to you according to the time of life, and behold, Sarah your wife shall have a son."

(Sarah was listening in the tent door which *was* behind him.) ¹¹Now Abraham and Sarah were old, well advanced in age; *and* Sarah had passed the age of childbearing.ᵃ ¹²Therefore Sarah laughed within herself, saying, "After I have grown old, shall I have pleasure, my lord being old also?"

¹³And the LORD said to Abraham, "Why did Sarah laugh, saying, 'Shall I surely bear *a child,* since I am old?' ¹⁴Is anything too hard for the LORD? At the appointed time I will return to you, according to the time of life, and Sarah shall have a son."

¹⁵But Sarah denied *it,* saying, "I did not laugh," for she was afraid.

And He said, "No, but you did laugh!"

Abraham Intercedes for Sodom

¹⁶Then the men rose from there and looked toward Sodom, and Abraham went with them to send them on the way. ¹⁷And the LORD said, "Shall I hide from Abraham what I am doing, ¹⁸since Abraham shall surely become a great and mighty nation, and all the nations of the earth shall be blessed in him? ¹⁹For I have known him, in order that he may command his children and his household after him, that they keep the way of the LORD, to do righteousness and justice, that the LORD may bring to Abraham what He has spoken to him." ²⁰And the LORD said, "Because the outcry against Sodom and Gomorrah is great, and because their sin is very grave, ²¹I will go down now and see whether they have done altogether according to the outcry against it that has come to Me; and if not, I will know."

²²Then the men turned away from there and went toward Sodom, but Abraham still stood before the LORD. ²³And Abraham came near and said, "Would You also destroy the righteous with the wicked? ²⁴Suppose there were fifty righteous within the city; would You also destroy the place and not spare *it* for the fifty righteous that were in it? ²⁵Far be it from You to do such a thing as this, to slay the righteous with the wicked, so that the righteous should be as the wicked; far be it from You! Shall not the Judge of all the earth do right?"

²⁶So the LORD said, "If I find in Sodom

18:11 ᵃLiterally *the manner of women had ceased to be with Sarah* fifty righteous within the city, then I will spare all the place for their sakes."

²⁷Then Abraham answered and said, "Indeed now, I who *am but* dust and ashes have taken it upon myself to speak to the Lord: ²⁸Suppose there were five less than the fifty righteous; would You destroy all of the city for *lack of* five?"

So He said, "If I find there forty-five, I will not destroy *it.*"

²⁹And he spoke to Him yet again and said, "Suppose there should be forty found there?"

So He said, "I will not do *it* for the sake of forty."

³⁰Then he said, "Let not the Lord be angry, and I will speak: Suppose thirty should be found there?"

So He said, "I will not do *it* if I find thirty there."

³¹And he said, "Indeed now, I have taken it upon myself to speak to the Lord: Suppose twenty should be found there?"

So He said, "I will not destroy *it* for the sake of twenty."

³²Then he said, "Let not the Lord be angry, and I will speak but once more: Suppose ten should be found there?"

And He said, "I will not destroy *it* for the sake of ten." ³³So the LORD went His way as soon as He had finished speaking with Abraham; and Abraham returned to his place.

Sodom's Depravity

19 ¹Now the two angels came to Sodom in the evening, and Lot was sitting in the gate of Sodom. When Lot saw *them,* he rose to meet them, and he bowed himself with his face toward the ground. ²And he said, "Here now, my lords, please turn in to your servant's house and spend the night, and wash your feet; then you may rise early and go on your way."

And they said, "No, but we will spend the night in the open square."

³But he insisted strongly; so they turned in to him and entered his house. Then he made them a feast, and baked unleavened bread, and they ate. ⁴Now before they lay down, the men of the city, the men of Sodom, both old and young, all the people from every quarter, surrounded the house. ⁵And they called to Lot and said to him, "Where are the men

who came to you tonight? Bring them out to us that we may know them *carnally.*"

⁶So Lot went out to them through the doorway, shut the door behind him, ⁷and said, "Please, my brethren, do not do so wickedly! ⁸See now, I have two daughters who have not known a man; please, let me bring them out to you, and you may do to them as you wish; only do nothing to these men, since this is the reason they have come under the shadow of my roof."

⁹And they said, "Stand back!" Then they said, "This one came in to stay *here,* and he keeps acting as a judge; now we will deal worse with you than with them." So they pressed hard against the man Lot, and came near to break down the door. ¹⁰But the men reached out their hands and pulled Lot into the house with them, and shut the door. ¹¹And they struck the men who *were* at the doorway of the house with blindness, both small and great, so that they became weary *trying* to find the door.

Sodom and Gomorrah Destroyed

¹²Then the men said to Lot, "Have you anyone else here? Son-in-law, your sons, your daughters, and whomever you have in the city—take *them* out of this place! ¹³For we will destroy this place, because the outcry against them has grown great before the face of the LORD, and the LORD has sent us to destroy it."

¹⁴So Lot went out and spoke to his sons-in-law, who had married his daughters, and said, "Get up, get out of this place; for the LORD will destroy this city!" But to his sons-in-law he seemed to be joking.

¹⁵When the morning dawned, the angels urged Lot to hurry, saying, "Arise, take your wife and your two daughters who are here, lest you be consumed in the punishment of the city." ¹⁶And while he lingered, the men took hold of his hand, his wife's hand, and the hands of his two daughters, the LORD being merciful to him, and they brought him out and set him outside the city. ¹⁷So it came to pass, when they had brought them outside, that he[a] said, "Escape for your life! Do not look behind you nor stay anywhere in the plain. Escape to the mountains, lest you be destroyed."

¹⁸Then Lot said to them, "Please, no, my lords! ¹⁹Indeed now, your servant has found favor in your sight, and you have increased your mercy which you have shown

---

19:17 ᵃSeptuagint, Syriac, and Vulgate read *they.*

me by saving my life; but I cannot escape to the mountains, lest some evil overtake me and I die. ²⁰See now, this city *is* near *enough* to flee to, and it *is* a little one; please let me escape there (*is* it not a little one?) and my soul shall live."

²¹And he said to him, "See, I have favored you concerning this thing also, in that I will not overthrow this city for which you have spoken. ²²Hurry, escape there. For I cannot do anything until you arrive there."

Therefore the name of the city was called Zoar.

²³The sun had risen upon the earth when Lot entered Zoar. ²⁴Then the LORD rained brimstone and fire on Sodom and Gomorrah, from the LORD out of the heavens. ²⁵So He overthrew those cities, all the plain, all the inhabitants of the cities, and what grew on the ground.

²⁶But his wife looked back behind him, and she became a pillar of salt.

²⁷And Abraham went early in the morning to the place where he had stood before the LORD. ²⁸Then he looked toward Sodom and Gomorrah, and toward all the land of the plain; and he saw, and behold, the smoke of the land which went up like the smoke of a furnace. ²⁹And it came to pass, when God destroyed the cities of the plain, that God remembered Abraham, and sent Lot out of the midst of the overthrow, when He overthrew the cities in which Lot had dwelt.

The Descendants of Lot

³⁰Then Lot went up out of Zoar and dwelt in the mountains, and his two daughters were with him; for he was afraid to dwell in Zoar. And he and his two daughters dwelt in a cave. ³¹Now the firstborn said to the younger, "Our father *is* old, and *there is* no man on the earth to come in to us as is the custom of all the earth. ³²Come, let us make our father drink wine, and we will lie with him, that we may preserve the lineage of our father." ³³So they made their father drink wine that night. And the firstborn went in and lay with her father, and he did not know when she lay down or when she arose.

³⁴It happened on the next day that the firstborn said to the younger, "Indeed I lay with my father last night; let us make him drink wine tonight also, and you go in *and* lie with him, that we may preserve the lineage of our father." ³⁵Then they made their father drink wine that night also. And the younger arose and lay with him, and he did not know when she lay down or when she arose.

³⁶Thus both the daughters of Lot were with child by their father. ³⁷The firstborn bore a son and called his name Moab; he *is* the father of the Moabites to this day. ³⁸And the younger, she also bore a son and called his name Ben-Ammi; he *is* the father of the people of Ammon to this day.

Abraham and Abimelech

20 ¹And Abraham journeyed from there to the South, and dwelt between Kadesh and Shur, and stayed in Gerar. ²Now Abraham said of Sarah his wife, "She *is* my sister." And Abimelech king of Gerar sent and took Sarah.

³But God came to Abimelech in a dream by night, and said to him, "Indeed you *are* a dead man because of the woman whom you have taken, for she *is* a man's wife."

⁴But Abimelech had not come near her; and he said, "Lord, will You slay a righteous nation also? ⁵Did he not say to me, 'She *is* my sister'? And she, even she herself said, 'He *is* my brother.' In the integrity of my heart and innocence of my hands I have done this."

⁶And God said to him in a dream, "Yes, I know that you did this in the integrity of your heart. For I also withheld you from sinning against Me; therefore I did not let you touch her. ⁷Now therefore, restore the man's wife; for he *is* a prophet, and he will pray for you and you shall live. But if you do not restore *her,* know that you shall surely die, you and all who *are* yours."

⁸So Abimelech rose early in the morning, called all his servants, and told all these things in their hearing; and the men were very much afraid. ⁹And Abimelech called Abraham and said to him, "What have you done to us? How have I offended you, that you have brought on me and on my kingdom a great sin? You have done deeds to me that ought not to be done." ¹⁰Then Abimelech said to Abraham, "What did you have in view, that you have done this thing?"

¹¹And Abraham said, "Because I thought, surely the fear of God *is* not in this place; and they will kill me on account of my wife. ¹²But indeed *she is* truly my sister. She *is* the daughter of my father, but not the daughter of my mother; and she be-

came my wife. ¹³And it came to pass, when God caused me to wander from my father's house, that I said to her, 'This *is* your kindness that you should do for me: in every place, wherever we go, say of me, "He *is* my brother." ' "

¹⁴Then Abimelech took sheep, oxen, and male and female servants, and gave *them* to Abraham; and he restored Sarah his wife to him. ¹⁵And Abimelech said, "See, my land *is* before you; dwell where it pleases you." ¹⁶Then to Sarah he said, "Behold, I have given your brother a thousand *pieces* of silver; indeed this vindicates you[a] before all who *are* with you and before everybody." Thus she was rebuked.

¹⁷So Abraham prayed to God; and God healed Abimelech, his wife, and his female servants. Then they bore *children;* ¹⁸for the LORD had closed up all the wombs of the house of Abimelech because of Sarah, Abraham's wife.

20:16 ªLiterally *it is a covering of the eyes for you*

The Birth of Isaac

Both Abraham (Gen. 17:17) and Sarah (18:11, 12) laughed in disbelief that a couple well past childbearing age should bear a son. Yet in fulfillment of God's promise, Abraham, age 100, fathered Isaac through his wife Sarah, age 90 (Gen. 17:17; 21:1–5). Sarah's first concern was for her new son's status as Abraham's heir, a status threatened by Hagar's son Ishmael (21:9, 10). Ishmael was now about 14 years old, being 13 at his circumcision (17:24, 25).

An ancient Near Eastern law code describes the practice of giving one's maid as a second wife (see "The Birth of Ishmael" at Gen. 16:1). The law provided protection for children born to the second wife. It prohibited the disinheriting of a firstborn son of a slave wife (Ishmael) in the event that the barren upper-class wife should later bear a son (Isaac). However, the upper-class wife's son would supersede the slave wife's son as the legal "firstborn." Furthermore, the slave wife and her children could be offered their freedom, in which case they forfeited their inheritance. Isaac did become Abraham's heir, representing one case in which a younger son received the inheritance and blessing.

■ Genesis 21:1—24:67

Genesis
Isaac Is Born

21 :1 And the LORD visited Sarah as He had said, and the LORD did for Sarah as He had spoken. ²For Sarah conceived and bore Abraham a son in his old age, at the set time of which God had spoken to him. ³And Abraham called the name of his son who was born to him—whom Sarah bore to him—Isaac. ⁴Then Abraham circumcised his son Isaac when he was eight days old, as God had commanded him. ⁵Now Abraham was one hundred years old when his son Isaac was born to him. ⁶And Sarah said, "God has made me laugh, *and* all who hear will laugh with me." ⁷She also said, "Who would have said to Abraham that Sarah would nurse children? For I have borne *him* a son in his old age."

Hagar and Ishmael Depart

⁸So the child grew and was weaned. And Abraham made a great feast on the same day that Isaac was weaned.

⁹And Sarah saw the son of Hagar the Egyptian, whom she had borne to Abraham, scoffing. ¹⁰Therefore she said to Abraham, "Cast out this bondwoman and her son; for the son of this bondwoman shall not be heir with my son, *namely* with Isaac." ¹¹And the matter was very displeasing in Abraham's sight because of his son.

¹²But God said to Abraham, "Do not let it be displeasing in your sight because of the lad or because of your bondwoman. Whatever Sarah has said to you, listen to her voice; for in Isaac your seed shall be called. ¹³Yet I will also make a nation of the son of the bondwoman, because he *is* your seed."

¹⁴So Abraham rose early in the morning, and took bread and a skin of water; and putting *it* on her shoulder, he gave *it* and the boy to Hagar, and sent her away. Then she departed and wandered in the Wilderness of Beersheba. ¹⁵And the water in the skin was used up, and she placed the boy under one of the shrubs. ¹⁶Then she went and sat down across from *him* at a distance of about a bowshot; for she said to herself, "Let me not see the death of the boy." So she sat opposite *him,* and lifted her voice and wept.

¹⁷And God heard the voice of the lad. Then the angel of God called to Hagar out of heaven, and said to her, "What ails you,

A Slave of a Wife Becomes a Mother! (Gen. 21:9–11)

Sarai's condition of childlessness caused her to give her female servant to Abram for procreation (Gen. 16:1–3). It is obvious from Sarai's words, "perhaps I shall obtain children by her" (16:2), that she saw herself as the one who would be providing any eventual son from this union, even though the servant Hagar would be the mother of the child.

Ancient marriage contracts obligated wives to provide a son for the married couple. Contracts dating from the mid-2nd millennium B.C. have been discovered in the city of Nuzi which specify that if a wife bore no male child she had the obligation to provide a child via a female servant. If a child was thus born to a servant, the child would be considered the child of the wife in regards to the contract. Thus, even a barren wife could fulfill her marital contract.

Abram's reluctance to send Hagar away, when Sarai became jealous of her (Gen. 21:9–11), reflects another aspect of the Nuzi tablets. Servants who provided such children were not supposed to be sent away, but rather treated favorably. So it was that it took the voice of God to convince Abram to listen to Sarai's desire (21:12).

Hagar? Fear not, for God has heard the voice of the lad where he *is*. 18Arise, lift up the lad and hold him with your hand, for I will make him a great nation."

19Then God opened her eyes, and she saw a well of water. And she went and filled the skin with water, and gave the lad a drink. 20So God was with the lad; and he grew and dwelt in the wilderness, and became an archer. 21He dwelt in the Wilderness of Paran; and his mother took a wife for him from the land of Egypt.

A Covenant with Abimelech

22And it came to pass at that time that Abimelech and Phichol, the commander of his army, spoke to Abraham, saying, "God *is* with you in all that you do. 23Now therefore, swear to me by God that you will not deal falsely with me, with my offspring, or with my posterity; but that according to the kindness that I have done to you, you will do to me and to the land in which you have dwelt."

24And Abraham said, "I will swear."

25Then Abraham rebuked Abimelech because of a well of water which Abimelech's servants had seized. 26And Abimelech said, "I do not know who has done this thing; you did not tell me, nor had I heard *of it* until today." 27So Abraham took sheep and oxen and gave them to Abimelech, and the two of them made a covenant. 28And Abraham set seven ewe lambs of the flock by themselves.

29Then Abimelech asked Abraham, "What *is the meaning of* these seven ewe lambs which you have set by themselves?"

30And he said, "You will take *these* seven ewe lambs from my hand, that they may be my witness that I have dug this well." 31Therefore he called that place Beersheba,ᵃ because the two of them swore an oath there.

32Thus they made a covenant at Beersheba. So Abimelech rose with Phichol, the commander of his army, and they returned to the land of the Philistines. 33Then *Abraham* planted a tamarisk tree in Beersheba, and there called on the name of the LORD, the Everlasting God. 34And Abraham stayed in the land of the Philistines many days.

Abraham's Faith Confirmed

22 1Now it came to pass after these things that God tested Abraham, and said to him, "Abraham!"

And he said, "Here I am."

2Then He said, "Take now your son, your only *son* Isaac, whom you love, and go to the land of Moriah, and offer him there as a burnt offering on one of the mountains of which I shall tell you."

3So Abraham rose early in the morning and saddled his donkey, and took two of his young men with him, and Isaac his son; and he split the wood for the burnt offering, and arose and went to the place of which God had told him. 4Then on the third day Abraham lifted his eyes and saw the place afar off. 5And Abraham said to his young men, "Stay here with the don-

---

21:31 ᵃLiterally *Well of the Oath* or *Well of the Seven*

key; the lad[a] and I will go yonder and worship, and we will come back to you."

⁶So Abraham took the wood of the burnt offering and laid *it* on Isaac his son; and he took the fire in his hand, and a knife, and the two of them went together. ⁷But Isaac spoke to Abraham his father and said, "My father!"

And he said, "Here I am, my son."

Then he said, "Look, the fire and the wood, but where *is* the lamb for a burnt offering?"

⁸And Abraham said, "My son, God will provide for Himself the lamb for a burnt offering." So the two of them went together. ⁹Then they came to the place of which God had told him. And Abraham built an altar there and placed the wood in order; and he bound Isaac his son and laid him on the altar, upon the wood. ¹⁰And Abraham stretched out his hand and took the knife to slay his son.

¹¹But the Angel of the LORD called to him from heaven and said, "Abraham, Abraham!"

So he said, "Here I am."

¹²And He said, "Do not lay your hand on the lad, or do anything to him; for now I know that you fear God, since you have not withheld your son, your only *son,* from Me."

¹³Then Abraham lifted his eyes and looked, and there behind *him was* a ram caught in a thicket by its horns. So Abraham went and took the ram, and offered it up for a burnt offering instead of his son. ¹⁴And Abraham called the name of the place, The-LORD-Will-Provide;[a] as it is said *to* this day, "In the Mount of the LORD it shall be provided."

¹⁵Then the Angel of the LORD called to Abraham a second time out of heaven, ¹⁶and said: "By Myself I have sworn, says the LORD, because you have done this thing, and have not withheld your son,

your only *son*— ¹⁷blessing I will bless you, and multiplying I will multiply your descendants as the stars of the heaven and as the sand which *is* on the seashore; and your descendants shall possess the gate of their enemies. ¹⁸In your seed all the nations of the earth shall be blessed, because you have obeyed My voice." ¹⁹So Abraham returned to his young men, and they rose and went together to Beersheba; and Abraham dwelt at Beersheba.

The Family of Nahor

²⁰Now it came to pass after these things that it was told Abraham, saying, "Indeed Milcah also has borne children to your brother Nahor: ²¹Huz his firstborn, Buz his brother, Kemuel the father of Aram, ²²Chesed, Hazo, Pildash, Jidlaph, and Bethuel." ²³And Bethuel begot Rebekah.[a] These eight Milcah bore to Nahor, Abraham's brother. ²⁴His concubine, whose name was Reumah, also bore Tebah, Gaham, Thahash, and Maachah.

Sarah's Death and Burial

23 ¹Sarah lived one hundred and twenty-seven years; *these were* the years of the life of Sarah. ²So Sarah died in Kirjath Arba (that *is,* Hebron) in the land of Canaan, and Abraham came to mourn for Sarah and to weep for her.

³Then Abraham stood up from before his dead, and spoke to the sons of Heth, saying, ⁴"I *am* a foreigner and a visitor among you. Give me property for a burial place among you, that I may bury my dead out of my sight."

⁵And the sons of Heth answered Abraham, saying to him, ⁶"Hear us, my lord: You *are* a mighty prince among us; bury your dead in the choicest of our burial places. None of us will withhold from you his burial place, that you may bury your dead."

⁷Then Abraham stood up and bowed himself to the people of the land, the sons of Heth. ⁸And he spoke with them, saying, "If it is your wish that I bury my dead out

---

22:5 ªOr *young man*   22:14 ªHebrew *YHWH Yireh*   22:23 ªSpelled *Rebecca* in Romans 9:10

RELIGION AND WORSHIP

In the Bible, human sacrifice is regarded as one of the worst offenses against God and humankind (Gen. 22:12). It was one of the reasons the Canaanites were condemned. Archaeologists have dug up urns with ashes and the bones of children from the sacred precincts of Carthage. Apparently, the Carthaginians sacrificed children as part of their religion.

BUSINESS DOCUMENTS AT EBLA (Gen. 23:7–20)

The narrative in Gen. 23:7–20 is a picture of business being transacted during the late 3rd or early 2nd millennium B.C. Abraham purchases a property which is then deeded as his possession. Ancient texts dealing with business and commercial matters, as well as other types of texts, have been discovered at Ebla, a Semitic city-state in northern Syria that flourished from about 2400 to 2250 B.C.—prior to Abraham's time.

Although not mentioned in Scripture, Ebla casts its shadow over the history of northern Canaan. In the 3rd millennium B.C., Ebla controlled northern Canaan. By the time of Abraham (c. 2000 B.C.) this large urban center was long past its prime. Yet it was still an important center in the region.

Discoveries at Ebla, though not directly related to Scripture, have been invaluable in providing a larger context for understanding the cultural environment of the narratives in Genesis. Many of the personal names found at Ebla reveal a linguistic type very similar to that of the Old Testament patriarchs. Personal names discovered at Ebla include Ab-ra-mu (Abram), E-sa-um (Esau), Sa-u-lum (Saul), and Da-'u-dum (David).

The recording of business transactions was part of life in the ancient Near East, just as it is today. This is evident at Ebla where the largest portion of the texts found were administrative or business texts. More business recording is apparent in the narrative of Gen. 23: the deeding of the field of Ephron to Abraham would refer to a written deed of purchase that was signed by the purchaser and witnesses (23:17–20).

of my sight, hear me, and meet with Ephron the son of Zohar for me, ⁹that he may give me the cave of Machpelah which he has, which is at the end of his field. Let him give it to me at the full price, as property for a burial place among you."

¹⁰Now Ephron dwelt among the sons of Heth; and Ephron the Hittite answered Abraham in the presence of the sons of Heth, all who entered at the gate of his city, saying, ¹¹"No, my lord, hear me: I give you the field and the cave that is in it; I give it to you in the presence of the sons of my people. I give it to you. Bury your dead!"

¹²Then Abraham bowed himself down before the people of the land; ¹³and he spoke to Ephron in the hearing of the people of the land, saying, "If you will give it, please hear me. I will give you money for the field; take it from me and I will bury my dead there."

¹⁴And Ephron answered Abraham, saying to him, ¹⁵"My lord, listen to me; the land is worth four hundred shekels of silver. What is that between you and me? So bury your dead." ¹⁶And Abraham listened to Ephron; and Abraham weighed out the silver for Ephron which he had named in the hearing of the sons of Heth, four hundred shekels of silver, currency of the merchants.

¹⁷So the field of Ephron which was in Machpelah, which was before Mamre, the field and the cave which was in it, and all the trees that were in the field, which were within all the surrounding borders, were deeded ¹⁸to Abraham as a possession in the presence of the sons of Heth, before all who went in at the gate of his city.

¹⁹And after this, Abraham buried Sarah his wife in the cave of the field of Machpelah, before Mamre (that is, Hebron) in the land of Canaan. ²⁰So the field and the cave that is in it were deeded to Abraham by the sons of Heth as property for a burial place.

A Bride for Isaac

24 ¹Now Abraham was old, well advanced in age; and the LORD had blessed Abraham in all things. ²So Abraham said to the oldest servant of his house, who ruled over all that he had, "Please, put your hand under my thigh, ³and I will make you swear by the LORD, the God of heaven and the God of the earth, that you will not take a wife for my son from the daughters of the Canaanites, among whom I dwell; ⁴but you shall go to my country and to my family, and take a wife for my son Isaac."

⁵And the servant said to him, "Perhaps the woman will not be willing to follow me

MY SERVANT IS MY HEIR! (Gen. 24:2, 3)

When God promised Abram that his descendants were to grow into a great nation, He was addressing Abram's complaint in Gen. 15:2, 3. Abram was childless, so his property would have to go to a stranger. Eliezer, a man from Damascus, was going to be his heir (15:2), and it only maximized Abram's dilemma that Eliezer was his servant.

Tablets discovered in the ancient city of Nuzi reveal that childless couples regularly selected a servant as a replacement son. It was the duty of this servant to care for his adopted parents when they grew old and to perform the burial rites when they died. For his service the servant became the heir to the parents' property.

Ancient contracts have been found that specify the duties of an adopted son, and describe the relationship of the adoptee to any natural son born at a later time. Usually the natural son assumed the firstborn status. However, the adopted son was still treated well and not forsaken.

The relationship between Abram and Eliezer was a common relationship for that time. When Abram grew old, he made Eliezer his heir, probably with the usual stipulation that if a natural son was born, Eliezer would take second place. But even after the birth of Abram's sons, Ishmael and Isaac, Eliezer still maintained an important status in the household. He controlled all that Abram possessed (Gen. 24:2) and, as the oldest and most trusted of Abram's servants, even had the important task of selecting Isaac's wife (24:3).

---

to this land. Must I take your son back to the land from which you came?"

6But Abraham said to him, "Beware that you do not take my son back there. 7The LORD God of heaven, who took me from my father's house and from the land of my family, and who spoke to me and swore to me, saying, 'To your descendantsa

24:7 aLiterally *seed*

I give this land,' He will send His angel before you, and you shall take a wife for my son from there. 8And if the woman is not willing to follow you, then you will be released from this oath; only do not take my son back there." 9So the servant put his hand under the thigh of Abraham his master, and swore to him concerning this matter.

10Then the servant took ten of his

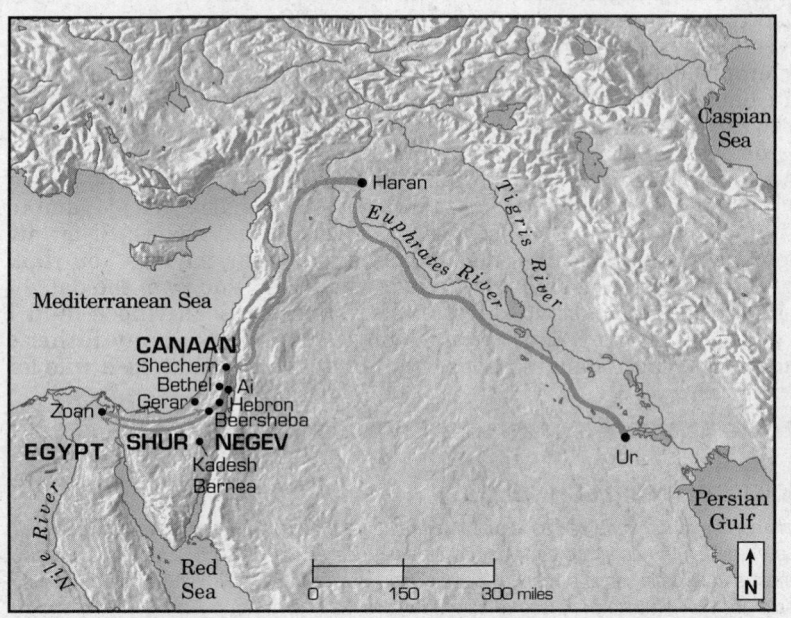

Journeys of Abraham
Abraham's birthplace has long been identified with Sumerian Ur in southern Mesopotamia. Ur may have sponsored colonies in northern Mesopotamia in the vicinity of Haran, from which Abraham's family possibly originated.

At Shechem in central Canaan, Abraham received the promise of God concerning the new land (Gen. 12:7). Famine, caused by unpredictable rains in Canaan, forced Abraham to Egypt, which was watered by the Nile River. Yet he would return to the land of promise.

master's camels and departed, for all his master's goods *were in* his hand. And he arose and went to Mesopotamia, to the city of Nahor. ¹¹And he made his camels kneel down outside the city by a well of water at evening time, the time when women go out to draw *water.* ¹²Then he said, "O LORD God of my master Abraham, please give me success this day, and show kindness to my master Abraham. ¹³Behold, *here* I stand by the well of water, and the daughters of the men of the city are coming out to draw water. ¹⁴Now let it be that the young woman to whom I say, 'Please let down your pitcher that I may drink,' and she says, 'Drink, and I will also give your camels a drink'—*let* her *be the one* You have appointed for Your servant Isaac. And by this I will know that You have shown kindness to my master."

¹⁵And it happened, before he had finished speaking, that behold, Rebekah, who was born to Bethuel, son of Milcah, the wife of Nahor, Abraham's brother, came out with her pitcher on her shoulder. ¹⁶Now the young woman *was* very beautiful to behold, a virgin; no man had known her. And she went down to the well, filled her pitcher, and came up. ¹⁷And the servant ran to meet her and said, "Please let me drink a little water from your pitcher."

¹⁸So she said, "Drink, my lord." Then she quickly let her pitcher down to her hand, and gave him a drink. ¹⁹And when she had finished giving him a drink, she said, "I will draw *water* for your camels also, until they have finished drinking." ²⁰Then she quickly emptied her pitcher into the trough, ran back to the well to draw *water,* and drew for all his camels. ²¹And the man, wondering at her, remained silent so as to know whether the LORD had made his journey prosperous or not.

²²So it was, when the camels had finished drinking, that the man took a golden nose ring weighing half a shekel, and two bracelets for her wrists weighing ten *shekels* of gold, ²³and said, "Whose daughter *are* you? Tell me, please, is there room *in* your father's house for us to lodge?"

²⁴So she said to him, "I *am* the daughter of Bethuel, Milcah's son, whom she bore to Nahor." ²⁵Moreover she said to him, "We have both straw and feed enough, and room to lodge."

²⁶Then the man bowed down his head and worshiped the LORD. ²⁷And he said, "Blessed *be* the LORD God of my master Abraham, who has not forsaken His mercy and His truth toward my master. As for me, being on the way, the LORD led me to the house of my master's brethren." ²⁸So the young woman ran and told her mother's household these things.

²⁹Now Rebekah had a brother whose name *was* Laban, and Laban ran out to the man by the well. ³⁰So it came to pass, when he saw the nose ring, and the bracelets on his sister's wrists, and when he heard the words of his sister Rebekah, saying, "Thus the man spoke to me," that he went to the man. And there he stood by the camels at the well. ³¹And he said, "Come in, O blessed of the LORD! Why do you stand outside? For I have prepared the house, and a place for the camels."

³²Then the man came to the house. And he unloaded the camels, and provided straw and feed for the camels, and water to wash his feet and the feet of the men who *were* with him. ³³*Food* was set before him to eat, but he said, "I will not eat until I have told about my errand."

And he said, "Speak on."

³⁴So he said, "I *am* Abraham's servant. ³⁵The LORD has blessed my master greatly, and he has become great; and He has given him flocks and herds, silver and gold, male and female servants, and camels and donkeys. ³⁶And Sarah my master's wife bore a son to my master when she was old; and to him he has given all that he has. ³⁷Now my master made me swear, saying, 'You shall not take a wife for my son from the daughters of the Canaanites, in whose land I dwell; ³⁸but you shall go to my father's house and to my family, and take a wife for

SCIENCE AND TECHNOLOGY

Gold can be found in nature as a metal, either pure or mixed with silver and copper. It is easily worked and does not corrode. It has been used as a measure of value from early times, and is a perennial symbol of wealth and rank (Gen. 24:22). Where there were no banks, gold could take the place of savings accounts.

my son.' ³⁹And I said to my master, 'Perhaps the woman will not follow me.' ⁴⁰But he said to me, 'The LORD, before whom I walk, will send His angel with you and prosper your way; and you shall take a wife for my son from my family and from my father's house. ⁴¹You will be clear from this oath when you arrive among my family; for if they will not give *her* to you, then you will be released from my oath.'

⁴²"And this day I came to the well and said, 'O LORD God of my master Abraham, if You will now prosper the way in which I go, ⁴³behold, I stand by the well of water; and it shall come to pass that when the virgin comes out to draw *water,* and I say to her, "Please give me a little water from your pitcher to drink," ⁴⁴and she says to me, "Drink, and I will draw for your camels also,"—*let* her *be* the woman whom the LORD has appointed for my master's son.'

⁴⁵"But before I had finished speaking in my heart, there was Rebekah, coming out with her pitcher on her shoulder; and she went down to the well and drew *water.* And I said to her, 'Please let me drink.' ⁴⁶And she made haste and let her pitcher down from her *shoulder,* and said, 'Drink, and I will give your camels a drink also.' So I drank, and she gave the camels a drink also. ⁴⁷Then I asked her, and said, 'Whose daughter *are* you?' And she said, 'The daughter of Bethuel, Nahor's son, whom Milcah bore to him.' So I put the nose ring on her nose and the bracelets on her wrists. ⁴⁸And I bowed my head and worshiped the LORD, and blessed the LORD God of my master Abraham, who had led me in the way of truth to take the daughter of my master's brother for his son. ⁴⁹Now if you will deal kindly and truly with my master, tell me. And if not, tell me, that I may turn to the right hand or to the left."

⁵⁰Then Laban and Bethuel answered and said, "The thing comes from the LORD; we cannot speak to you either bad or good. ⁵¹Here *is* Rebekah before you; take *her* and go, and let her be your master's son's wife, as the LORD has spoken."

⁵²And it came to pass, when Abraham's servant heard their words, that he worshiped the LORD, *bowing himself* to the earth. ⁵³Then the servant brought out jewelry of silver, jewelry of gold, and clothing, and gave *them* to Rebekah. He also gave precious things to her brother and to her mother.

⁵⁴And he and the men who *were* with him ate and drank and stayed all night. Then they arose in the morning, and he said, "Send me away to my master." ⁵⁵But her brother and her mother said, "Let the young woman stay with us *a few* days, at least ten; after that she may go." ⁵⁶And he said to them, "Do not hinder me, since the LORD has prospered my way; send me away so that I may go to my master." ⁵⁷So they said, "We will call the young woman and ask her personally." ⁵⁸Then they called Rebekah and said to her, "Will you go with this man?"

And she said, "I will go."

⁵⁹So they sent away Rebekah their sister and her nurse, and Abraham's servant and his men. ⁶⁰And they blessed Rebekah and said to her:

"Our sister, *may* you *become*
The *mother of* thousands of ten
    thousands;
And may your descendants possess
The gates of those who hate them."

⁶¹Then Rebekah and her maids arose, and they rode on the camels and followed the man. So the servant took Rebekah and departed.

⁶²Now Isaac came from the way of Beer Lahai Roi, for he dwelt in the South. ⁶³And Isaac went out to meditate in the field in the evening; and he lifted his eyes and looked, and there, the camels *were* coming. ⁶⁴Then Rebekah lifted her eyes, and when she saw Isaac she dismounted from her camel; ⁶⁵for she had said to the servant, "Who *is* this man walking in the field to meet us?"

TIME CAPSULE   *2000 to 1900 B.C.*

2000– 1000	*Habiru appear in the ancient Near East as a class of fugitives*
1995– 1820	*Abraham's life (based on late Exodus)*
1963– 1786	*12th Dynasty of Egypt*
1963– 1934	*Amenemhet I rules Egypt during time of prosperity*
1950	*Copper is mined by Egyptians in Nubia*
1900	*Mathematicians discover Pythagorean theorem*

DATING ABRAHAM FROM THE EXODUS

It is not known exactly when the patriarchs lived. The events narrated in Genesis cannot be synchronized with any events outside of the Bible. This has led scholars to propose dates for Abraham from about 2000 B.C. to as late as 1200 B.C. Others have used figures from the Bible to calculate Abraham's time backward from the Exodus.

Years	Chronological Information in Scripture
75	Abraham is 75 when leaving Haran (Gen. 12:4)
25	Abraham is 100 when Isaac is born (Gen. 21:5)
60	Isaac is 60 (and Abraham 160) when Jacob is born (Gen. 25:26)
130	Jacob is 130 when arriving in Egypt (Gen. 47:9)
	These figures represent a period of 290 years between Abraham's birth and Jacob's arrival in Egypt.
430	Israel's stay in Egypt is reported to be 430 years (Ex. 12:40), a number that is rounded to 400 in Gen. 15:13.

Following the early date for the Exodus in 1446 B.C., Abraham's birth is calculated at 2166 B.C. (1446 + 290 + 430 = 2166), and his death 175 years later at 1991 B.C.

Following the late date for the Exodus in 1275 B.C., Abraham's birth is calculated at 1995 B.C. (1275 + 290 + 430 = 1995), and his death at 1820 B.C.

The servant said, "It *is* my master." So she took a veil and covered herself.

⁶⁶And the servant told Isaac all the things that he had done. ⁶⁷Then Isaac brought her into his mother Sarah's tent; and he took Rebekah and she became his wife, and he loved her. So Isaac was comforted after his mother's *death.*

The Close of Abraham's Life

Genesis presents a concluding summary of Abraham's story before beginning that of his son Isaac and grandson Jacob. Abraham, who was 100 years old when Isaac was born, was 140 when Isaac married (Gen. 25:20) and 160 when Isaac fathered Jacob (25:26). Sometime during the 38 years between Sarah's death (Gen. 23:1) and his own, Abraham married Keturah (25:1), one of his concubines.

Ancient Near Eastern custom was for a man to divide his property among his sons before death. The major portion went to Isaac, Abraham's second son, born to his full wife Sarah, with smaller gifts to the other sons (25:5, 6). The Hebrew patriarch died at age 175 (25:7).

■ Genesis 25:1—36:43

Genesis
Abraham and Keturah

25 :1 Abraham again took a wife, and her name *was* Keturah. ²And she bore him Zimran, Jokshan, Medan, Midian, Ishbak, and Shuah. ³Jokshan begot Sheba and Dedan. And the sons of Dedan were Asshurim, Letushim, and Leummim. ⁴And the sons of Midian *were* Ephah, Epher, Hanoch, Abidah, and Eldaah. All these *were* the children of Keturah.

⁵And Abraham gave all that he had to Isaac. ⁶But Abraham gave gifts to the sons of the concubines which Abraham had; and while he was still living he sent them eastward, away from Isaac his son, to the country of the east.

Abraham's Death and Burial

⁷This *is* the sum of the years of Abraham's life which he lived: one hundred and seventy-five years. ⁸Then Abraham breathed his last and died in a good old age, an old man and full *of years,* and was gathered to his people. ⁹And his sons Isaac and Ishmael buried him in the cave of Machpelah, which *is* before Mamre, in the field of Ephron the son of Zohar the Hittite, ¹⁰the field which Abraham purchased from the sons of Heth. There Abraham was buried, and Sarah his wife. ¹¹And it came

BURIED IN THE CAVE OF MACHPELAH (Gen. 25:9, 10)

Abraham purchased a field from a Hittite man named Ephron to bury his wife Sarah (Gen. 23:4). His interest in the field was due to the presence of a cave on that property (23:9), making this the only account in the Old Testament of using a cave as a burial site.

Abraham's purchase of the cave of Machpelah began a burial tradition continued by his descendants. Not only was Sarah buried in the cave, but Abraham himself was buried there when he died (Gen. 25:9, 10). Abraham's son Isaac was living nearby in Hebron shortly before his death (Gen. 35:27; see 23:19), and was buried in the cave along with Rebekah his wife (Gen. 49:31). Isaac's son Jacob buried his wife Leah there, and was himself interred in the cave of Machpelah by his sons, who returned his body from Egypt for that purpose (Gen. 49:29–33; 50:13).

Caves were usually used not as burial sites, but as places of refuge. When Lot and his daughters fled Sodom and had nowhere else to live, they inhabited a cave (Gen. 19:30). Five Amorite kings who were fighting against the Israelites fled during the battle to hide in the cave at Makkedah (Josh. 10:16). Because hiding from King Saul occupied much of David's early military life, he seems to have spent more time living in a cave than anywhere else (1 Sam. 22:1; 24:1–3). Even Elijah, when he ran from the angry Queen Jezebel, found refuge in a desert cave (1 Kin. 19:13).

In ancient times caves were only infrequently used for burials. In some periods cadavers were buried in the floor of houses, but during most periods tombs were carved from the soft limestone rock in the Palestinian hills or dug into the dirt. Most often burials were grouped together, much like our modern tradition of cemeteries. Like the cave of Machpelah, burials were often family affairs, and burial sites were used for generations.

With little effort ancient peoples could utilize caves as ready-made houses or storage areas. It seems that only rarely would they give up this use of caves by making them burial sites. Perhaps, due to Abraham's "landlessness" as a foreigner (23:4), his only recourse was to purchase a plot of land for the burial of his family, and the cave was a ready-made tomb for that purpose.

---

to pass, after the death of Abraham, that God blessed his son Isaac. And Isaac dwelt at Beer Lahai Roi.

The Families of Ishmael and Isaac

¹²Now this *is* the genealogy of Ishmael, Abraham's son, whom Hagar the Egyptian, Sarah's maidservant, bore to Abraham. ¹³And these *were* the names of the sons of Ishmael, by their names, according to their generations: The firstborn of Ishmael, Nebajoth; then Kedar, Adbeel, Mibsam, ¹⁴Mishma, Dumah, Massa, ¹⁵Hadar,ᵃ Tema, Jetur, Naphish, and Kedemah. ¹⁶These *were* the sons of Ishmael and these *were* their names, by their towns and their settlements, twelve princes according to their nations. ¹⁷These *were* the years of the life of Ishmael: one hundred and thirty-seven years; and he breathed his last and died, and was gathered to his people. ¹⁸(They

dwelt from Havilah as far as Shur, which *is* east of Egypt as you go toward Assyria.) He died in the presence of all his brethren.

¹⁹This *is* the genealogy of Isaac, Abraham's son. Abraham begot Isaac. ²⁰Isaac was forty years old when he took Rebekah as wife, the daughter of Bethuel the Syrian of Padan Aram, the sister of Laban the Syrian. ²¹Now Isaac pleaded with the LORD for his wife, because she *was* barren; and the LORD granted his plea, and Rebekah his wife conceived. ²²But the children struggled together within her; and she said, "If *all is* well, why *am I* like this?" So she went to inquire of the LORD.

²³And the LORD said to her:

"Two nations *are* in your womb,
Two peoples shall be separated from
    your body;
One people shall be stronger than the
    other,
And the older shall serve the
    younger."

25:15 ᵃMasoretic Text reads *Hadad.*

24So when her days were fulfilled *for her* to give birth, indeed *there were* twins in her womb. 25And the first came out red. *He was* like a hairy garment all over; so they called his name Esau.ᵃ 26Afterward his brother came out, and his hand took hold of Esau's heel; so his name was called Jacob.ᵃ Isaac *was* sixty years old when she bore them.

27So the boys grew. And Esau was a skillful hunter, a man of the field; but Jacob was a mild man, dwelling in tents. 28And Isaac loved Esau because he ate *of* his game, but Rebekah loved Jacob.

Esau Sells His Birthright

29Now Jacob cooked a stew; and Esau came in from the field, and he *was* weary. 30And Esau said to Jacob, "Please feed me with that same red *stew,* for I *am* weary." Therefore his name was called Edom.ᵃ

31But Jacob said, "Sell me your birthright as of this day."

32And Esau said, "Look, I *am* about to die; so what *is* this birthright to me?"

33Then Jacob said, "Swear to me as of this day."

So he swore to him, and sold his birthright to Jacob. 34And Jacob gave Esau bread and stew of lentils; then he ate and drank, arose, and went his way. Thus Esau despised *his* birthright.

Isaac and Abimelech

26 1There was a famine in the land, besides the first famine that was in the days of Abraham. And Isaac went to Abimelech king of the Philistines, in Gerar. 2Then the LORD appeared to him and said: "Do not go down to Egypt; live in the land of which I shall tell you. 3Dwell in this land, and I will be with you and bless you; for to you and your descendants I give all these lands, and I will perform the oath which I swore to Abraham your father. 4And I will make your descendants multiply as the stars of heaven; I will give to your descendants all these lands; and in your seed all the nations of the earth shall be blessed; 5because Abraham obeyed My voice and kept My charge, My commandments, My statutes, and My laws."

6So Isaac dwelt in Gerar. 7And the men of the place asked about his wife. And he said, "She *is* my sister"; for he was afraid to say, "*She is* my wife," *because he thought,* "lest the men of the place kill me for Rebekah, because she *is* beautiful to behold."

8Now it came to pass, when he had been there a long time, that Abimelech king of the Philistines looked through a window, and saw, and there was Isaac, showing endearment to Rebekah his wife. 9Then Abimelech called Isaac and said, "Quite obviously she *is* your wife; so how could you say, 'She *is* my sister'?"

Isaac said to him, "Because I said, 'Lest I die on account of her.'"

10And Abimelech said, "What *is* this you have done to us? One of the people might soon have lain with your wife, and you would have brought guilt on us." 11So Abimelech charged all *his* people, saying, "He who touches this man or his wife shall surely be put to death."

12Then Isaac sowed in that land, and reaped in the same year a hundredfold; and the LORD blessed him. 13The man began to prosper, and continued prospering until he became very prosperous; 14for he had possessions of flocks and possessions of herds and a great number of servants. So the Philistines envied him. 15Now the Philistines had stopped up all the wells which his father's servants had dug in the days of Abraham his father, and they had filled them with earth. 16And Abimelech said to Isaac, "Go away from us, for you are much mightier than we."

17Then Isaac departed from there and pitched his tent in the Valley of Gerar, and dwelt there. 18And Isaac dug again the wells of water which they had dug in the days of Abraham his father, for the Philistines had stopped them up after the death of Abraham. He called them by the names which his father had called them.

19Also Isaac's servants dug in the valley, and found a well of running water there. 20But the herdsmen of Gerar quarreled with Isaac's herdsmen, saying, "The water *is* ours." So he called the name of the well Esek,ᵃ because they quarreled with him. 21Then they dug another well, and they quarreled over that *one* also. So he called its name Sitnah.ᵃ 22And he moved from there and dug another well, and they did not quarrel over it. So he called its name Rehoboth,ᵃ because he said, "For now the LORD has made room for us, and we shall be fruitful in the land."

25:25 ᵃLiterally *Hairy*   25:26 ᵃLiterally *Supplanter*   25:30 ᵃLiterally *Red*
26:20 ᵃLiterally *Quarrel*   26:21 ᵃLiterally *Enmity*   26:22 ᵃLiterally *Spaciousness*

²³Then he went up from there to Beer-sheba. ²⁴And the LORD appeared to him the same night and said, "I *am* the God of your father Abraham; do not fear, for I *am* with you. I will bless you and multiply your descendants for My servant Abraham's sake." ²⁵So he built an altar there and called on the name of the LORD, and he pitched his tent there; and there Isaac's servants dug a well.

²⁶Then Abimelech came to him from Gerar with Ahuzzath, one of his friends, and Phichol the commander of his army. ²⁷And Isaac said to them, "Why have you come to me, since you hate me and have sent me away from you?"

²⁸But they said, "We have certainly seen that the LORD is with you. So we said, 'Let there now be an oath between us, between you and us; and let us make a covenant with you, ²⁹that you will do us no harm, since we have not touched you, and since we have done nothing to you but good and have sent you away in peace. You *are* now the blessed of the LORD.' "

³⁰So he made them a feast, and they ate and drank. ³¹Then they arose early in the morning and swore an oath with one another; and Isaac sent them away, and they departed from him in peace.

³²It came to pass the same day that Isaac's servants came and told him about the well which they had dug, and said to him, "We have found water." ³³So he called it Shebah.ᵃ Therefore the name of the city *is* Beershebaᵇ to this day.

26:33 ᵃLiterally *Oath* or *Seven* ᵇLiterally *Well of the Oath* or *Well of the Seven*

³⁴When Esau was forty years old, he took as wives Judith the daughter of Beeri the Hittite, and Basemath the daughter of Elon the Hittite. ³⁵And they were a grief of mind to Isaac and Rebekah.

Isaac Blesses Jacob

27 ¹Now it came to pass, when Isaac was old and his eyes were so dim that he could not see, that he called Esau his older son and said to him, "My son."

And he answered him, "Here I am."

²Then he said, "Behold now, I am old. I do not know the day of my death. ³Now therefore, please take your weapons, your quiver and your bow, and go out to the field and hunt game for me. ⁴And make me savory food, such as I love, and bring *it* to me that I may eat, that my soul may bless you before I die."

⁵Now Rebekah was listening when Isaac spoke to Esau his son. And Esau went to the field to hunt game and to bring *it*. ⁶So Rebekah spoke to Jacob her son, saying, "Indeed I heard your father speak to Esau your brother, saying, ⁷'Bring me game and make savory food for me, that I may eat it and bless you in the presence of the LORD before my death.' ⁸Now therefore, my son, obey my voice according to what I command you. ⁹Go now to the flock and bring me from there two choice kids of the goats, and I will make savory food from them for your father, such as he loves. ¹⁰Then you shall take *it* to your father, that he may eat *it,* and that he may bless you before his death."

¹¹And Jacob said to Rebekah his mother, "Look, Esau my brother *is* a hairy

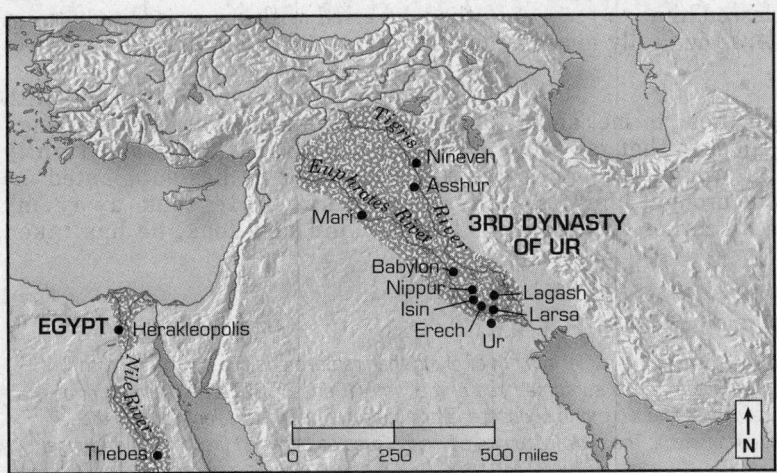

Changing Empires of the Near East

In Egypt the Old Kingdom was followed by civil strife between Herakleopolis and Thebes. Thebes eventually reunited Egypt in 2040 B.C.

In Mesopotamia, Ur-Nammu founded the 3rd Dynasty of Ur (2112–2004 B.C.). As this great city-state declined, smaller kingdoms, such as Isin, Larsa, Asshur, Mari, and Babylon, asserted their independence from Ur's control.

man, and I *am* a smooth-*skinned* man. ¹²Perhaps my father will feel me, and I shall seem to be a deceiver to him; and I shall bring a curse on myself and not a blessing."

¹³But his mother said to him, "*Let* your curse *be* on me, my son; only obey my voice, and go, get *them* for me." ¹⁴And he went and got *them* and brought *them* to his mother, and his mother made savory food, such as his father loved. ¹⁵Then Rebekah took the choice clothes of her elder son Esau, which *were* with her in the house, and put them on Jacob her younger son. ¹⁶And she put the skins of the kids of the goats on his hands and on the smooth part of his neck. ¹⁷Then she gave the savory food and the bread, which she had prepared, into the hand of her son Jacob.

¹⁸So he went to his father and said, "My father."

And he said, "Here I am. Who *are* you, my son?"

¹⁹Jacob said to his father, "I *am* Esau your firstborn; I have done just as you told me; please arise, sit and eat of my game, that your soul may bless me."

²⁰But Isaac said to his son, "How *is it* that you have found *it* so quickly, my son?"

And he said, "Because the LORD your God brought *it* to me."

²¹Isaac said to Jacob, "Please come near, that I may feel you, my son, whether you *are* really my son Esau or not." ²²So Jacob went near to Isaac his father, and he felt him and said, "The voice *is* Jacob's voice, but the hands *are* the hands of Esau." ²³And he did not recognize him, because his hands were hairy like his brother Esau's hands; so he blessed him.

²⁴Then he said, "*Are* you really my son Esau?"

He said, "I *am*."

²⁵He said, "Bring *it* near to me, and I will eat of my son's game, so that my soul may bless you." So he brought *it* near to him, and he ate; and he brought him wine, and he drank. ²⁶Then his father Isaac said

to him, "Come near now and kiss me, my son." ²⁷And he came near and kissed him; and he smelled the smell of his clothing, and blessed him and said:

> "Surely, the smell of my son
> *Is* like the smell of a field
> Which the LORD has blessed.
> 28 Therefore may God give you
> Of the dew of heaven,
> Of the fatness of the earth,
> And plenty of grain and wine.
> 29 Let peoples serve you,
> And nations bow down to you.
> Be master over your brethren,
> And let your mother's sons bow down
>   to you.
> Cursed *be* everyone who curses you,
> And blessed *be* those who bless you!"

Esau's Lost Hope

³⁰Now it happened, as soon as Isaac had finished blessing Jacob, and Jacob had scarcely gone out from the presence of Isaac his father, that Esau his brother came in from his hunting. ³¹He also had made savory food, and brought it to his father, and said to his father, "Let my father arise and eat of his son's game, that your soul may bless me."

³²And his father Isaac said to him, "Who *are* you?"

So he said, "I *am* your son, your firstborn, Esau."

³³Then Isaac trembled exceedingly, and said, "Who? Where *is* the one who hunted game and brought *it* to me? I ate all *of it* before you came, and I have blessed him— *and* indeed he shall be blessed."

³⁴When Esau heard the words of his father, he cried with an exceedingly great and bitter cry, and said to his father, "Bless me—me also, O my father!"

³⁵But he said, "Your brother came with deceit and has taken away your blessing."

³⁶And *Esau* said, "Is he not rightly named Jacob? For he has supplanted me these two times. He took away my birthright, and now look, he has taken

MARRIAGE AND FAMILY

Primogeniture is the social custom of giving the firstborn son the natural right to succeed his father as supreme head of the family (Gen. 27:32). Like the right of a prince to become king, primogeniture is not based on merit or talent, but on the accident of birth. The Bible recounts several struggles between firstborn and younger sons.

away my blessing!" And he said, "Have you not reserved a blessing for me?"

37Then Isaac answered and said to Esau, "Indeed I have made him your master, and all his brethren I have given to him as servants; with grain and wine I have sustained him. What shall I do now for you, my son?"

38And Esau said to his father, "Have you only one blessing, my father? Bless me—me also, O my father!" And Esau lifted up his voice and wept.

39Then Isaac his father answered and said to him:

"Behold, your dwelling shall be of the fatness of the earth,
And of the dew of heaven from above.
40 By your sword you shall live,
And you shall serve your brother;
And it shall come to pass, when you become restless,
That you shall break his yoke from your neck."

Jacob Escapes from Esau

41So Esau hated Jacob because of the blessing with which his father blessed him, and Esau said in his heart, "The days of mourning for my father are at hand; then I will kill my brother Jacob."

42And the words of Esau her older son were told to Rebekah. So she sent and called Jacob her younger son, and said to him, "Surely your brother Esau comforts himself concerning you by intending to kill you. 43Now therefore, my son, obey my voice: arise, flee to my brother Laban in Haran. 44And stay with him a few days, until your brother's fury turns away, 45until your brother's anger turns away from you, and he forgets what you have done to him; then I will send and bring you from there. Why should I be bereaved also of you both in one day?"

46And Rebekah said to Isaac, "I am weary of my life because of the daughters of Heth; if Jacob takes a wife of the daughters of Heth, like these who are the daughters of the land, what good will my life be to me?"

28 1Then Isaac called Jacob and blessed him, and charged him, and said to him: "You shall not take a wife from the daughters of Canaan. 2Arise, go to Padan Aram, to the house of Bethuel your mother's father; and take yourself a wife from there of the daughters of Laban your mother's brother.

3 "May God Almighty bless you,
And make you fruitful and multiply you,
That you may be an assembly of peoples;
4 And give you the blessing of Abraham,
To you and your descendants with you,
That you may inherit the land
In which you are a stranger,
Which God gave to Abraham."

5So Isaac sent Jacob away, and he went to Padan Aram, to Laban the son of Bethuel the Syrian, the brother of Rebekah, the mother of Jacob and Esau.

Esau Marries Mahalath

6Esau saw that Isaac had blessed Jacob and sent him away to Padan Aram to take himself a wife from there, and that as he blessed him he gave him a charge, saying, "You shall not take a wife from the daughters of Canaan," 7and that Jacob had obeyed his father and his mother and had gone to Padan Aram. 8Also Esau saw that the daughters of Canaan did not please his father Isaac. 9So Esau went to Ishmael and took Mahalath the daughter of Ishmael, Abraham's son, the sister of Nebajoth, to be his wife in addition to the wives he had.

Jacob's Vow at Bethel

10Now Jacob went out from Beersheba and went toward Haran. 11So he came to a certain place and stayed there all night, because the sun had set. And he took one of the stones of that place and put it at his

---

TIME CAPSULE   1900 to 1860 B.C.

1900–1750	Asshur establishes merchant colony at Kanesh in Anatolia
1900	Amorite dynasty rules the city of Ugarit
1900	Ionic-speaking people move into Greece
1876	Jacob enters Egypt (based on early Exodus; Gen. 46:3)
1862–1843	Sesostris III restrains the powers of Egypt's provincial families
1860–1750	Execration Texts of Egypt

THE MARI TABLET TOWNS (Gen. 28:10)

It is not known exactly when the patriarchs lived. Estimates for dating Abraham, Isaac, and Jacob range from about 2100 to 1800 B.C. Such dates would locate the patriarchal period sometime before, or simultaneous with, the Mari tablets, which themselves have been placed between 1813 and 1760 B.C.

Mari was once a powerful city located about halfway between Babylon and the Mediterranean Sea. Situated on the banks of the Euphrates River, Mari became rich through trading. Although the city is not named in the Bible, it is well known today because a large archive of official documents, now called the Mari tablets, was discovered there.

More than 20,000 clay tablets written in the Accadian language were dug up at the excavation site. The royal palace of Zimri-Lim, the last king of Mari, had more than 300 rooms, and it was in these rooms that archaeologists found the tablets.

Mari was very powerful for several hundred years, up to 1760 B.C., when it was destroyed by Hammurabi of Babylon. Hammurabi took away many documents, especially treaties and works on religion, before he abandoned the library. What remains is an extensive record dealing with many aspects of government.

The royal palace kept all kinds of administrative records, including lists of supplies, purchases, and expenses. Supplies and accounts for the women of the palace and the harem were kept separately. There are many letters to and from other cities.

The Mari tablets frequently mention the cities of Nahor and Haran. Both Abraham (Gen. 11:31) and Jacob (27:43; 28:10) lived in Haran at separate times during their lives. Abraham's servant is reported to have traveled to Nahor (24:10). Since cities mentioned in the Mari tablets are also named in the patriarchal stories, it is possible that the tablets reflect aspects of the culture known by the patriarchs.

---

head, and he lay down in that place to sleep. [12]Then he dreamed, and behold, a ladder *was* set up on the earth, and its top reached to heaven; and there the angels of God were ascending and descending on it.

[13]And behold, the LORD stood above it and said: "I *am* the LORD God of Abraham your father and the God of Isaac; the land on which you lie I will give to you and your descendants. [14]Also your descendants shall be as the dust of the earth; you shall spread abroad to the west and the east, to the north and the south; and in you and in your seed all the families of the earth shall be blessed. [15]Behold, I *am* with you and will keep you wherever you go, and will bring you back to this land; for I will not leave you until I have done what I have spoken to you."

[16]Then Jacob awoke from his sleep and said, "Surely the LORD is in this place, and I did not know *it*." [17]And he was afraid and said, "How awesome *is* this place! This *is* none other than the house of God, and this *is* the gate of heaven!"

[18]Then Jacob rose early in the morning, and took the stone that he had put at his head, set it up as a pillar, and poured oil on top of it. [19]And he called the name of that place Bethel;[a] but the name of that city had been Luz previously. [20]Then Jacob made a vow, saying, "If God will be with me, and keep me in this way that I am going, and give me bread to eat and clothing to put on, [21]so that I come back to my father's house in peace, then the LORD shall be my God. [22]And this stone which I have set as a pillar shall be God's house, and of all that You give me I will surely give a tenth to You."

Jacob Meets Rachel

29 [1]So Jacob went on his journey and came to the land of the people of the East. [2]And he looked, and saw a well in the field; and behold, there *were* three flocks of sheep lying by it; for out of that well they watered the flocks. A large stone *was* on the well's mouth. [3]Now all the flocks would be gathered there; and they would roll the stone from the well's mouth, water the sheep, and put the stone back in its place on the well's mouth.

28:19 [a]Literally *House of God*

EGYPT AND THE MIDDLE KINGDOM

Egypt's Old Kingdom was followed by the First Intermediate Period. This time of social upheaval saw the collapse of the central government.

First Intermediate Period	
First Intermediate Period **2160–2010 B.C.**	**The Dynasties** 9th–10th Dynasties. Local princes and barons vied for power. Territorial conflicts and disorder among the social classes replaced stability. Bedouins from Asia settled in the Delta region.
c. 2100 B.C.	Two city-states, Herakleopolis and Thebes, competed for power.
2040 B.C.	Thebes was victorious and brought an end to civil war in Egypt.
The Middle Kingdom **2106–1786 B.C.**	**The Dynasties** 11th and 12th Dynasties. Thebes' victory in 2040 allowed Egypt to pursue peacetime activities. But not until Amenemhet I began the 12th Dynasty in 1963 B.C. would Egypt experience peace and prosperity.

⁴And Jacob said to them, "My brethren, where *are* you from?"

And they said, "We *are* from Haran."

⁵Then he said to them, "Do you know Laban the son of Nahor?"

And they said, "We know him."

⁶So he said to them, "Is he well?"

And they said, "*He is* well. And look, his daughter Rachel is coming with the sheep."

⁷Then he said, "Look, *it is* still high day; *it is* not time for the cattle to be gathered together. Water the sheep, and go and feed *them*."

⁸But they said, "We cannot until all the flocks are gathered together, and they have rolled the stone from the well's mouth; then we water the sheep."

⁹Now while he was still speaking with them, Rachel came with her father's sheep, for she was a shepherdess. ¹⁰And it came to pass, when Jacob saw Rachel the daughter of Laban his mother's brother, and the sheep of Laban his mother's brother, that Jacob went near and rolled the stone from the well's mouth, and watered the flock of Laban his mother's brother. ¹¹Then Jacob kissed Rachel, and lifted up his voice and wept. ¹²And Jacob told Rachel that he *was* her father's relative and that he *was* Rebekah's son. So she ran and told her father.

¹³Then it came to pass, when Laban heard the report about Jacob his sister's son, that he ran to meet him, and embraced him and kissed him, and brought him to his house. So he told Laban all these things. ¹⁴And Laban said to him, "Surely you *are* my bone and my flesh." And he stayed with him for a month.

Jacob Marries Leah and Rachel

¹⁵Then Laban said to Jacob, "Because you *are* my relative, should you therefore serve me for nothing? Tell me, what *should* your wages *be?*" ¹⁶Now Laban had two daughters: the name of the elder *was* Leah, and the name of the younger *was* Rachel. ¹⁷Leah's eyes *were* delicate, but Rachel was beautiful of form and appearance.

¹⁸Now Jacob loved Rachel; so he said, "I will serve you seven years for Rachel your younger daughter."

¹⁹And Laban said, "*It is* better that I give her to you than that I should give her to another man. Stay with me." ²⁰So Jacob served seven years for Rachel, and they seemed *only* a few days to him because of the love he had for her.

²¹Then Jacob said to Laban, "Give *me* my wife, for my days are fulfilled, that I may go in to her." ²²And Laban gathered together all the men of the place and made a feast. ²³Now it came to pass in the evening, that he took Leah his daughter and brought her to Jacob; and he went in to her. ²⁴And Laban gave his maid Zilpah to his daughter Leah *as* a maid. ²⁵So it came to pass in the morning, that behold, it *was* Leah. And he said to Laban, "What is this you have done to me? Was it not for

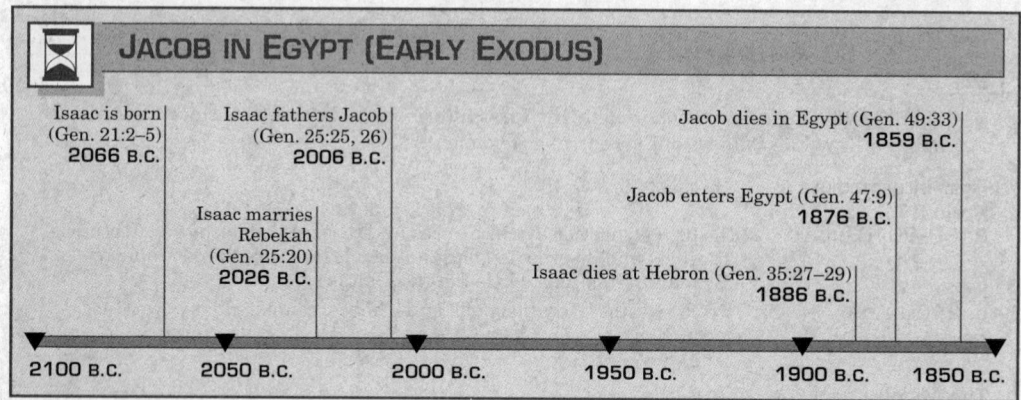

JACOB IN EGYPT (EARLY EXODUS)

Isaac is born
(Gen. 21:2–5)
2066 B.C.

Isaac fathers Jacob
(Gen. 25:25, 26)
2006 B.C.

Jacob dies in Egypt (Gen. 49:33)|
1859 B.C.

Isaac marries
Rebekah
(Gen. 25:20)
2026 B.C.

Jacob enters Egypt (Gen. 47:9)|
1876 B.C.

Isaac dies at Hebron (Gen. 35:27–29)|
1886 B.C.

2100 B.C.   2050 B.C.   2000 B.C.   1950 B.C.   1900 B.C.   1850 B.C.

Rachel that I served you? Why then have you deceived me?"

26And Laban said, "It must not be done so in our country, to give the younger before the firstborn. 27Fulfill her week, and we will give you this one also for the service which you will serve with me still another seven years."

28Then Jacob did so and fulfilled her week. So he gave him his daughter Rachel as wife also. 29And Laban gave his maid Bilhah to his daughter Rachel as a maid. 30Then *Jacob* also went in to Rachel, and he also loved Rachel more than Leah. And he served with Laban still another seven years.

The Children of Jacob

31When the LORD saw that Leah *was* unloved, He opened her womb; but Rachel *was* barren. 32So Leah conceived and bore a son, and she called his name Reuben;a for she said, "The LORD has surely looked on my affliction. Now therefore, my husband will love me." 33Then she conceived again and bore a son, and said, "Because the LORD has heard that I *am* unloved, He has therefore given me this *son* also." And she called his name Simeon.a 34She conceived again and bore a son, and said, "Now this time my husband will become attached to me, because I have borne him three sons." Therefore his name was called Levi.a 35And she conceived again and bore a son, and said, "Now I will praise the LORD." Therefore she called his name Judah.a Then she stopped bearing.

30 1Now when Rachel saw that she bore Jacob no children, Rachel envied her sister, and said to Jacob, "Give me children, or else I die!"

2And Jacob's anger was aroused against Rachel, and he said, "*Am* I in the place of God, who has withheld from you the fruit of the womb?"

3So she said, "Here is my maid Bilhah; go in to her, and she will bear *a child* on my knees, that I also may have children by her." 4Then she gave him Bilhah her maid as wife, and Jacob went in to her. 5And Bilhah conceived and bore Jacob a son. 6Then Rachel said, "God has judged my case; and He has also heard my voice and given me a son." Therefore she called his name Dan.a 7And Rachel's maid Bilhah conceived again and bore Jacob a second son. 8Then Rachel said, "With great wrestlings I have wrestled with my sister, *and* indeed I have prevailed." So she called his name Naphtali.a

9When Leah saw that she had stopped bearing, she took Zilpah her maid and gave her to Jacob as wife. 10And Leah's maid Zilpah bore Jacob a son. 11Then Leah said, "A troop comes!"a So she called his name Gad.b 12And Leah's maid Zilpah bore Jacob a second son. 13Then Leah said, "I am happy, for the daughters will call me blessed." So she called his name Asher.a

14Now Reuben went in the days of wheat harvest and found mandrakes in the field, and brought them to his mother Leah. Then Rachel said to Leah, "Please give me *some* of your son's mandrakes."

15But she said to her, "*Is it* a small matter that you have taken away my husband? Would you take away my son's mandrakes also?"

29:32 aLiterally *See, a Son*   29:33 aLiterally
Heard   29:34 aLiterally *Attached*
29:35 aLiterally *Praise*   30:6 aLiterally *Judge*
30:8 aLiterally *My Wrestling*   30:11 aFollowing
Qere, Syriac, and Targum; Kethib, Septuagint, and
Vulgate read *in fortune.* bLiterally *Troop* or
Fortune   30:13 aLiterally *Happy*

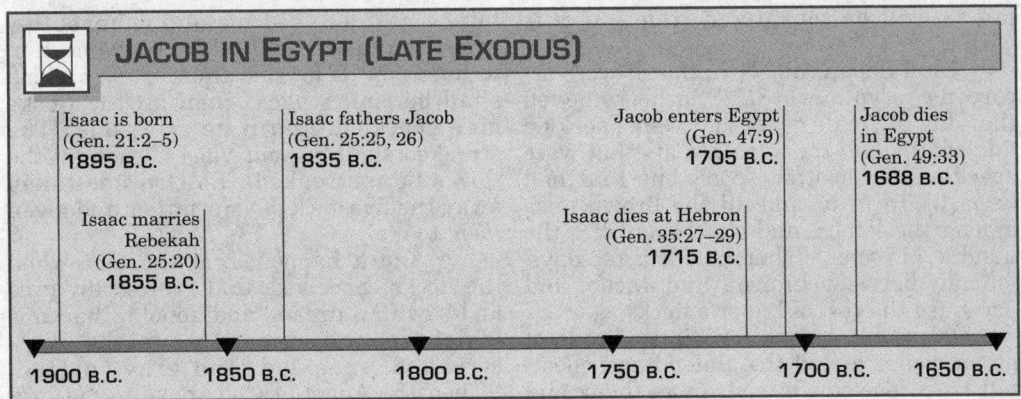

JACOB IN EGYPT (LATE EXODUS)

Isaac is born (Gen. 21:2–5) **1895 B.C.**	Isaac fathers Jacob (Gen. 25:25, 26) **1835 B.C.**	Jacob enters Egypt (Gen. 47:9) **1705 B.C.**	Jacob dies in Egypt (Gen. 49:33) **1688 B.C.**
Isaac marries Rebekah (Gen. 25:20) **1855 B.C.**		Isaac dies at Hebron (Gen. 35:27–29) **1715 B.C.**	

1900 B.C.   **1850 B.C.**   **1800 B.C.**   **1750 B.C.**   **1700 B.C.**   **1650 B.C.**

And Rachel said, "Therefore he will lie with you tonight for your son's mandrakes."

¹⁶When Jacob came out of the field in the evening, Leah went out to meet him and said, "You must come in to me, for I have surely hired you with my son's mandrakes." And he lay with her that night.

¹⁷And God listened to Leah, and she conceived and bore Jacob a fifth son. ¹⁸Leah said, "God has given me my wages, because I have given my maid to my husband." So she called his name Issachar.ᵃ ¹⁹Then Leah conceived again and bore Jacob a sixth son. ²⁰And Leah said, "God has endowed me *with* a good endowment; now my husband will dwell with me, because I have borne him six sons." So she called his name Zebulun.ᵃ ²¹Afterward she bore a daughter, and called her name Dinah.

²²Then God remembered Rachel, and God listened to her and opened her womb. ²³And she conceived and bore a son, and said, "God has taken away my reproach." ²⁴So she called his name Joseph,ᵃ and said, "The LORD shall add to me another son."

Jacob's Agreement with Laban

²⁵And it came to pass, when Rachel had borne Joseph, that Jacob said to La-

---

30:18 ᵃLiterally *Wages*   30:20 ᵃLiterally *Dwelling*   30:24 ᵃLiterally *He Will Add*

ban, "Send me away, that I may go to my own place and to my country. ²⁶Give *me* my wives and my children for whom I have served you, and let me go; for you know my service which I have done for you."

²⁷And Laban said to him, "Please *stay,* if I have found favor in your eyes, *for* I have learned by experience that the LORD has blessed me for your sake." ²⁸Then he said, "Name me your wages, and I will give *it.*"

²⁹So *Jacob* said to him, "You know how I have served you and how your livestock has been with me. ³⁰For what you had before I *came was* little, and it has increased to a great amount; the LORD has blessed you since my coming. And now, when shall I also provide for my own house?"

³¹So he said, "What shall I give you?"

And Jacob said, "You shall not give me anything. If you will do this thing for me, I will again feed and keep your flocks: ³²Let me pass through all your flock today, removing from there all the speckled and spotted sheep, and all the brown ones among the lambs, and the spotted and speckled among the goats; and *these* shall be my wages. ³³So my righteousness will answer for me in time to come, when the subject of my wages comes before you: every one that *is* not speckled and spotted among the goats, and brown among the

---

HEALTH AND MEDICINE

A mandrake (Gen. 30:14) is a small plant that blooms in the spring and has roots resembling a person's legs. It was by reputation an aphrodisiac, or aid to physical passion. Plants get their reputations as medicines or potions sometimes from science and sometimes from tradition or superstition, or from a mixture of these.

lambs, will be considered stolen, if *it is* with me."

34And Laban said, "Oh, that it were according to your word!" 35So he removed that day the male goats that were speckled and spotted, all the female goats that were speckled and spotted, every one that had *some* white in it, and all the brown ones among the lambs, and gave *them* into the hand of his sons. 36Then he put three days' journey between himself and Jacob, and Jacob fed the rest of Laban's flocks.

37Now Jacob took for himself rods of green poplar and of the almond and chestnut trees, peeled white strips in them, and exposed the white which *was* in the rods. 38And the rods which he had peeled, he set before the flocks in the gutters, in the watering troughs where the flocks came to drink, so that they should conceive when they came to drink. 39So the flocks conceived before the rods, and the flocks brought forth streaked, speckled, and spotted. 40Then Jacob separated the lambs, and made the flocks face toward the streaked and all the brown in the flock of Laban; but he put his own flocks by themselves and did not put them with Laban's flock.

41And it came to pass, whenever the stronger livestock conceived, that Jacob placed the rods before the eyes of the livestock in the gutters, that they might conceive among the rods. 42But when the flocks were feeble, he did not put *them* in; so the feebler were Laban's and the stronger Jacob's. 43Thus the man became exceedingly prosperous, and had large flocks, female and male servants, and camels and donkeys.

Jacob Flees from Laban

31 1Now *Jacob* heard the words of Laban's sons, saying, "Jacob has taken away all that was our father's, and from what was our father's he has acquired all this wealth." 2And Jacob saw the countenance of Laban, and indeed it *was* not *favorable* toward him as before. 3Then the LORD said to Jacob, "Return to the land of your fathers and to your family, and I will be with you."

4So Jacob sent and called Rachel and Leah to the field, to his flock, 5and said to them, "I see your father's countenance, that it *is* not *favorable* toward me as before; but the God of my father has been with me. 6And you know that with all my might I have served your father. 7Yet your father has deceived me and changed my wages ten times, but God did not allow him to hurt me. 8If he said thus: 'The speckled shall be your wages,' then all the flocks bore speckled. And if he said thus: 'The streaked shall be your wages,' then all the flocks bore streaked. 9So God has taken away the livestock of your father and given *them* to me.

10"And it happened, at the time when the flocks conceived, that I lifted my eyes and saw in a dream, and behold, the rams which leaped upon the flocks *were* streaked, speckled, and gray-spotted. 11Then the Angel of God spoke to me in a dream, saying, 'Jacob.' And I said, 'Here I am.' 12And He said, 'Lift your eyes now and see, all the rams which leap on the flocks *are* streaked, speckled, and gray-spotted; for I have seen all that Laban is doing to you. 13I *am* the God of Bethel, where you anointed the pillar *and* where you made a vow to Me. Now arise, get out of this land, and return to the land of your family.' "

14Then Rachel and Leah answered and said to him, "Is there still any portion or inheritance for us in our father's house? 15Are we not considered strangers by him? For he has sold us, and also completely consumed our money. 16For all these riches which God has taken from our father are *really* ours and our children's; now then, whatever God has said to you, do it."

17Then Jacob rose and set his sons and his wives on camels. 18And he carried away all his livestock and all his possessions which he had gained, his acquired livestock which he had gained in Padan Aram, to go to his father Isaac in the land of Canaan. 19Now Laban had gone to shear his sheep, and Rachel had stolen the household idols that were her father's. 20And Jacob stole away, unknown to Laban the Syrian, in that he did not tell him that he intended to flee. 21So he fled with all that he had. He arose and crossed the river, and headed toward the mountains of Gilead.

Laban Pursues Jacob

22And Laban was told on the third day that Jacob had fled. 23Then he took his brethren with him and pursued him for seven days' journey, and he overtook him in the mountains of Gilead. 24But God had come to Laban the Syrian in a dream by night, and said to him, "Be careful that you speak to Jacob neither good nor bad."

25So Laban overtook Jacob. Now Jacob

FAMILY LEADERSHIP AND HOUSEHOLD GODS (Gen. 31:30–34)

One of the most curious stories of the patriarchal accounts is the theft of Laban's gods by his daughter Rachel (Gen. 31:19). What makes this story seem so out of place is that these gods are never mentioned again after this episode, nor were they mentioned previously. Another oddity is Laban's insistence on finding the gods (31:33–35). After all, they were probably made of clay like the hundreds of household gods that have been found in archaeological excavations and had little intrinsic value.

Laban's accusation provoked reaction from Jacob centered on his mistreatment while with Laban (31:38–41). Jacob went so far as to claim that it was God alone who provided his wealth; he got nothing from Laban (31:42). Laban disputed that claim and suggested that all that Jacob possessed, including his wives, was actually Laban's (31:43). Certainly the two men could not agree on who owned what!

Conciliation was reached by making a covenant and establishing a boundary between Laban and Jacob (31:44–52). Since it was Laban who suggested the pillar of stones as a protective barrier, we can suppose that he had some fear of Jacob, even though it was Laban who had until this time been pursuing Jacob.

The story presents various puzzles: Laban's determination to recover the household gods; both men's claim of ownership of the wives, children and flocks; Laban's initiation of a boundary. Understanding these puzzles is helped by evidence that household gods served a purpose in addition to that of worship. Information gathered from one ancient tablet found at the 2nd millennium B.C. city of Nuzi suggests that, at times, household gods were used as evidence of family leadership.

The claim to leadership enlightens some aspects of this story. It explains why Rachel stole the gods: to give her husband the position of tribal leader. Why Laban was so insistent on getting them back: to make sure one of his own sons would become the family chief. Why Laban wanted to erect a boundary between Jacob and himself: to make sure that Jacob never returned with the household gods to claim the first rights to the family holdings.

---

had pitched his tent in the mountains, and Laban with his brethren pitched in the mountains of Gilead.

26And Laban said to Jacob: "What have you done, that you have stolen away unknown to me, and carried away my daughters like captives *taken* with the sword? 27Why did you flee away secretly, and steal away from me, and not tell me; for I might have sent you away with joy and songs, with timbrel and harp? 28And you did not allow me to kiss my sons and my daughters. Now you have done foolishly in *so* doing. 29It is in my power to do you harm, but the God of your father spoke to me last night, saying, 'Be careful that you speak to Jacob neither good nor bad.' 30And now you have surely gone because you greatly long for your father's house, *but* why did you steal my gods?"

31Then Jacob answered and said to Laban, "Because I was afraid, for I said, 'Perhaps you would take your daughters from me by force.' 32With whomever you find your gods, do not let him live. In the pres-

ence of our brethren, identify what I have of yours and take *it* with you." For Jacob did not know that Rachel had stolen them.

33And Laban went into Jacob's tent, into Leah's tent, and into the two maids' tents, but he did not find *them*. Then he went out of Leah's tent and entered Rachel's tent. 34Now Rachel had taken the household idols, put them in the camel's saddle, and sat on them. And Laban searched all about the tent but did not find *them*. 35And she said to her father, "Let it not displease my lord that I cannot rise before you, for the manner of women *is* with me." And he searched but did not find the household idols.

36Then Jacob was angry and rebuked Laban, and Jacob answered and said to Laban: "What *is* my trespass? What *is* my sin, that you have so hotly pursued me? 37Although you have searched all my things, what part of your household things have you found? Set *it* here before my brethren and your brethren, that they may judge between us both! 38These twenty years I *have*

LABAN OF ARAM-NAHARAIM (Gen. 31:47)

Padan Aram, also known as Aram-naharaim, was the home of Laban, a descendant of Abraham's brother Nahor (Gen. 28:2). Meaning literally "Aram between the Rivers," Aram-naharaim was the geographic name for upper Mesopotamia—the region between the Tigris and Euphrates rivers. Egyptian sources, including the Amarna archives from the 14th century, referred to the region as Naharina (without the 'Aram' prefix). English translations often translate it as "Mesopotamia" (Deut. 23:4).

Laban is described as an "Aramean" (Gen. 28:5, translated "Syrian" in the NKJV). The ethnic group known as the Arameans are not mentioned as inhabitants of this area until the 12th century B.C. But in the early 1st millennium B.C. numerous Aramean states were found in eastern Syria, and many individual Aramean tribes were causing great difficulty for both the Assyrian and Babylonian kingdoms in Mesopotamia.

When Laban speaks the words "Jegar Sahadutha," he is saying "Heap of Witness" in the Aramaic language (Gen. 31:47). Until the 1st millennium, Aramaic (a Semitic language closely related to biblical Hebrew) was spoken primarily by people from Aramean states. The Assyrians found Aramaic a convenient language for administering their conquered areas, thus it became an official language in portions of the Neo-Assyrian Empire from the 8th century on. The use of Aramaic spread until it later became the international language of commerce during the period of the Persian Empire's dominance (c. 559–331 B.C.).

The figure of Laban from upper Mesopotamia represents a people that had great influence on their world. The Arameans did not establish major kingdoms, as did the Assyrians and Babylonians. Nevertheless, the adjective "Aramean" was used long after the Aramean political states no longer existed. They left their mark through their language. Although Aramaic was later replaced by Greek in the Mediterranean world, the language continued to be used in the Near East by the Parthians (after 200 B.C.) and could be found as far east as India. It was the primary language of Palestine during the time of Jesus.

---

been with you; your ewes and your female goats have not miscarried their young, and I have not eaten the rams of your flock. ³⁹That which was torn *by beasts* I did not bring to you; I bore the loss of it. You required it from my hand, *whether* stolen by day or stolen by night. ⁴⁰*There* I was! In the day the drought consumed me, and the frost by night, and my sleep departed from my eyes. ⁴¹Thus I have been in your house twenty years; I served you fourteen years for your two daughters, and six years for your flock, and you have changed my wages ten times. ⁴²Unless the God of my father, the God of Abraham and the Fear of Isaac, had been with me, surely now you would have sent me away empty-handed. God has seen my affliction and the labor of my hands, and rebuked *you* last night."

Laban's Covenant with Jacob

⁴³And Laban answered and said to Jacob, "*These* daughters *are* my daughters, and *these* children *are* my children, and *this* flock *is* my flock; all that you see *is* mine. But what can I do this day to these my daughters or to their children whom they have borne? ⁴⁴Now therefore, come, let us make a covenant, you and I, and let it be a witness between you and me."

⁴⁵So Jacob took a stone and set it up *as* a pillar. ⁴⁶Then Jacob said to his brethren, "Gather stones." And they took stones and made a heap, and they ate there on the heap. ⁴⁷Laban called it Jegar Sahadutha,^a but Jacob called it Galeed.^b ⁴⁸And Laban said, "This heap *is* a witness between you and me this day." Therefore its name was called Galeed, ⁴⁹also Mizpah,^a because he said, "May the LORD watch between you and me when we are absent one from another. ⁵⁰If you afflict my daughters, or if you take *other* wives besides my daughters, *although* no man *is* with us—see, God *is* witness between you and me!"

⁵¹Then Laban said to Jacob, "Here is this heap and here is *this* pillar, which I have placed between you and me. ⁵²This

---

31:47 ^aLiterally, in Aramaic, *Heap of Witness*
^bLiterally, in Hebrew, *Heap of Witness*
31:49 ^aLiterally *Watch*

heap *is* a witness, and *this* pillar *is* a witness, that I will not pass beyond this heap to you, and you will not pass beyond this heap and this pillar to me, for harm. [53]The God of Abraham, the God of Nahor, and the God of their father judge between us." And Jacob swore by the Fear of his father Isaac. [54]Then Jacob offered a sacrifice on the mountain, and called his brethren to eat bread. And they ate bread and stayed all night on the mountain. [55]And early in the morning Laban arose, and kissed his sons and daughters and blessed them. Then Laban departed and returned to his place.

Esau Comes to Meet Jacob

32 [1]So Jacob went on his way, and the angels of God met him. [2]When Jacob saw them, he said, "This *is* God's camp." And he called the name of that place Mahanaim.[a]

[3]Then Jacob sent messengers before him to Esau his brother in the land of Seir, the country of Edom. [4]And he commanded them, saying, "Speak thus to my lord Esau, 'Thus your servant Jacob says: "I have dwelt with Laban and stayed there until now. [5]I have oxen, donkeys, flocks, and male and female servants; and I have sent to tell my lord, that I may find favor in your sight." ' "

[6]Then the messengers returned to Jacob, saying, "We came to your brother Esau, and he also is coming to meet you, and four hundred men *are* with him." [7]So Jacob was greatly afraid and distressed; and he divided the people that *were* with him, and the flocks and herds and camels, into two companies. [8]And he said, "If Esau comes to the one company and attacks it, then the other company which is left will escape."

[9]Then Jacob said, "O God of my father Abraham and God of my father Isaac, the LORD who said to me, 'Return to your country and to your family, and I will deal well with you': [10]I am not worthy of the least of all the mercies and of all the truth which You have shown Your servant; for I crossed over this Jordan with my staff, and now I have become two companies. [11]Deliver me, I pray, from the hand of my brother, from the hand of Esau; for I fear him, lest he come and attack me *and* the mother with the children. [12]For You said, 'I will surely treat you well, and make your descendants

as the sand of the sea, which cannot be numbered for multitude.' "

[13]So he lodged there that same night, and took what came to his hand as a present for Esau his brother: [14]two hundred female goats and twenty male goats, two hundred ewes and twenty rams, [15]thirty milk camels with their colts, forty cows and ten bulls, twenty female donkeys and ten foals. [16]Then he delivered *them* to the hand of his servants, every drove by itself, and said to his servants, "Pass over before me, and put some distance between successive droves." [17]And he commanded the first one, saying, "When Esau my brother meets you and asks you, saying, 'To whom do you belong, and where are you going? Whose *are* these in front of you?' [18]then you shall say, 'They *are* your servant Jacob's. It *is* a present sent to my lord Esau; and behold, he also *is* behind us.' " [19]So he commanded the second, the third, and all who followed the droves, saying, "In this manner you shall speak to Esau when you find him; [20]and also say, 'Behold, your servant Jacob *is* behind us.' " For he said, "I will appease him with the present that goes before me, and afterward I will see his face; perhaps he will accept me." [21]So the present went on over before him, but he himself lodged that night in the camp.

Wrestling with God

[22]And he arose that night and took his two wives, his two female servants, and his eleven sons, and crossed over the ford of

---

32:2 ªLiterally *Double Camp*

TIME CAPSULE	*1834 to 1800 B.C.*
1834	Amorite tribe captures city-state of Larsa
1834–1823	Warad-Sin is appointed by his father to be ruler of Larsa
1822–1763	Rim-Sin, king of Larsa
1813–1781	Shamshi-Adad I of Assyria rules city-state of Asshur and most of northern Mesopotamia
1813–1760	The Mari tablets
1804	King Rim-Sin of Larsa captures Isin
1800	Seminomadic tribe called Bene-yamina makes raids on Mari
1800	Musical notation used in Babylonia

Jabbok. 23He took them, sent them over the brook, and sent over what he had. 24Then Jacob was left alone; and a Man wrestled with him until the breaking of day. 25Now when He saw that He did not prevail against him, He touched the socket of his hip; and the socket of Jacob's hip was out of joint as He wrestled with him. 26And He said, "Let Me go, for the day breaks."

But he said, "I will not let You go unless You bless me!"

27So He said to him, "What *is* your name?"

He said, "Jacob."

28And He said, "Your name shall no longer be called Jacob, but Israel;ᵃ for you have struggled with God and with men, and have prevailed."

29Then Jacob asked, saying, "Tell *me* Your name, I pray."

And He said, "Why *is* it *that* you ask about My name?" And He blessed him there.

30So Jacob called the name of the place Peniel:ᵃ "For I have seen God face to face, and my life is preserved." 31Just as he crossed over Penuelᵃ the sun rose on him, and he limped on his hip. 32Therefore to this day the children of Israel do not eat the muscle that shrank, which *is* on the hip

socket, because He touched the socket of Jacob's hip in the muscle that shrank.

Jacob and Esau Meet

33 1Now Jacob lifted his eyes and looked, and there, Esau was coming, and with him were four hundred men. So he divided the children among Leah, Rachel, and the two maidservants. 2And he put the maidservants and their children in front, Leah and her children behind, and Rachel and Joseph last. 3Then he crossed over before them and bowed himself to the ground seven times, until he came near to his brother.

4But Esau ran to meet him, and embraced him, and fell on his neck and kissed him, and they wept. 5And he lifted his eyes and saw the women and children, and said, "Who *are* these with you?"

So he said, "The children whom God has graciously given your servant." 6Then the maidservants came near, they and their children, and bowed down. 7And Leah also came near with her children, and they bowed down. Afterward Joseph and Rachel came near, and they bowed down.

8Then Esau said, "What *do* you *mean by* all this company which I met?"

And he said, "*These are* to find favor in the sight of my lord."

9But Esau said, "I have enough, my brother; keep what you have for yourself."

10And Jacob said, "No, please, if I have now found favor in your sight, then receive my present from my hand, inasmuch as I have seen your face as though I had seen the face of God, and you were pleased with me. 11Please, take my blessing that is brought to you, because God has dealt graciously with me, and because I have enough." So he urged him, and he took *it*.

12Then Esau said, "Let us take our journey; let us go, and I will go before you."

13But Jacob said to him, "My lord knows that the children *are* weak, and the flocks and herds which are nursing *are* with me. And if the men should drive them hard one day, all the flock will die. 14Please let my lord go on ahead before his servant. I will lead on slowly at a pace which the livestock that go before me, and the children, are able to endure, until I come to my lord in Seir."

Jacob Returns to Canaan
After 20 years in northern Mesopotamia, Jacob returned to Canaan. He encountered the angels of God at Mahanaim and wrestled with a messenger of God at Penuel.

32:28 ᵃLiterally *Prince with God*   32:30 ᵃLiterally *Face of God*   32:31 ᵃSame as *Peniel*, verse 30

¹⁵And Esau said, "Now let me leave with you *some* of the people who *are* with me."

But he said, "What need is there? Let me find favor in the sight of my lord." ¹⁶So Esau returned that day on his way to Seir. ¹⁷And Jacob journeyed to Succoth, built himself a house, and made booths for his livestock. Therefore the name of the place is called Succoth.^a

Jacob Comes to Canaan

¹⁸Then Jacob came safely to the city of Shechem, which *is* in the land of Canaan, when he came from Padan Aram; and he pitched his tent before the city. ¹⁹And he bought the parcel of land, where he had pitched his tent, from the children of Hamor, Shechem's father, for one hundred pieces of money. ²⁰Then he erected an altar there and called it El Elohe Israel.^a

The Dinah Incident

34 ¹Now Dinah the daughter of Leah, whom she had borne to Jacob, went out to see the daughters of the land. ²And when Shechem the son of Hamor the Hivite, prince of the country, saw her, he took her and lay with her, and violated her. ³His soul was strongly attracted to Dinah the daughter of Jacob, and he loved the young woman and spoke kindly to the young woman. ⁴So Shechem spoke to his father Hamor, saying, "Get me this young woman as a wife."

⁵And Jacob heard that he had defiled Dinah his daughter. Now his sons were with his livestock in the field; so Jacob held his peace until they came. ⁶Then Hamor the father of Shechem went out to Jacob to speak with him. ⁷And the sons of Jacob came in from the field when they heard *it;* and the men were grieved and very angry, because he had done a disgraceful thing in Israel by lying with Jacob's daughter, a thing which ought not to be done. ⁸But Hamor spoke with them, saying, "The soul of my son Shechem longs for your daughter. Please give her to him as a wife. ⁹And make marriages with us; give your daughters to us, and take our daughters to yourselves. ¹⁰So you shall dwell with us, and the land shall be before you. Dwell and trade in it, and acquire possessions for yourselves in it."

¹¹Then Shechem said to her father and her brothers, "Let me find favor in your eyes, and whatever you say to me I will give. ¹²Ask me ever so much dowry and gift, and I will give according to what you say to me; but give me the young woman as a wife."

¹³But the sons of Jacob answered Shechem and Hamor his father, and spoke deceitfully, because he had defiled Dinah their sister. ¹⁴And they said to them, "We cannot do this thing, to give our sister to one who is uncircumcised, for that *would be* a reproach to us. ¹⁵But on this *condition* we will consent to you: If you will become as we *are,* if every male of you is circumcised, ¹⁶then we will give our daughters to you, and we will take your daughters to us; and we will dwell with you, and we will become one people. ¹⁷But if you will not heed us and be circumcised, then we will take our daughter and be gone."

¹⁸And their words pleased Hamor and Shechem, Hamor's son. ¹⁹So the young man did not delay to do the thing, because he delighted in Jacob's daughter. He *was* more honorable than all the household of his father.

²⁰And Hamor and Shechem his son came to the gate of their city, and spoke with the men of their city, saying: ²¹"These men *are* at peace with us. Therefore let them dwell in the land and trade in it. For indeed the land *is* large enough for them. Let us take their daughters to us as wives, and let us give them our daughters. ²²Only on this *condition* will the men consent to dwell with us, to be one people: if every male among us is circumcised as they *are* circumcised. ²³*Will* not their livestock, their property, and every animal of theirs *be* ours? Only let us consent to them, and they will dwell with us." ²⁴And all who went out of the gate of his city heeded Hamor and Shechem his son; every male was circumcised, all who went out of the gate of his city.

²⁵Now it came to pass on the third day, when they were in pain, that two of the sons of Jacob, Simeon and Levi, Dinah's brothers, each took his sword and came boldly upon the city and killed all the males. ²⁶And they killed Hamor and Shechem his son with the edge of the sword, and took Dinah from Shechem's house, and went out. ²⁷The sons of Jacob came upon the slain, and plundered the city, because their sister had been defiled.

33:17 ^aLiterally *Booths*   33:20 ^aLiterally *God, the God of Israel*

28They took their sheep, their oxen, and their donkeys, what *was* in the city and what *was* in the field, 29and all their wealth. All their little ones and their wives they took captive; and they plundered even all that *was* in the houses.

30Then Jacob said to Simeon and Levi, "You have troubled me by making me obnoxious among the inhabitants of the land, among the Canaanites and the Perizzites; and since I *am* few in number, they will gather themselves together against me and kill me. I shall be destroyed, my household and I."

31But they said, "Should he treat our sister like a harlot?"

Jacob's Return to Bethel

35 1Then God said to Jacob, "Arise, go up to Bethel and dwell there; and make an altar there to God, who appeared to you when you fled from the face of Esau your brother."

2And Jacob said to his household and to all who *were* with him, "Put away the foreign gods that *are* among you, purify yourselves, and change your garments. 3Then let us arise and go up to Bethel; and I will make an altar there to God, who answered me in the day of my distress and has been with me in the way which I have gone." 4So they gave Jacob all the foreign gods which *were* in their hands, and the earrings which *were* in their ears; and Jacob hid them under the terebinth tree which *was* by Shechem.

5And they journeyed, and the terror of God was upon the cities that *were* all around them, and they did not pursue the sons of Jacob. 6So Jacob came to Luz (that *is*, Bethel), which *is* in the land of Canaan, he and all the people who *were* with him. 7And he built an altar there and called the place El Bethel,[a] because there God appeared to him when he fled from the face of his brother.

8Now Deborah, Rebekah's nurse, died, and she was buried below Bethel under the terebinth tree. So the name of it was called Allon Bachuth.[a]

9Then God appeared to Jacob again, when he came from Padan Aram, and blessed him. 10And God said to him, "Your name *is* Jacob; your name shall not be called Jacob anymore, but Israel shall be your name." So He called his name Israel. 11Also God said to him: "I *am* God Almighty. Be fruitful and multiply; a nation and a company of nations shall proceed from you, and kings shall come from your body. 12The land which I gave Abraham and Isaac I give to you; and to your descendants after you I give this land." 13Then God went up from him in the place where He talked with him. 14So Jacob set up a pillar in the place where He talked with him, a pillar of stone; and he poured a drink offering on it, and he poured oil on it. 15And Jacob called the name of the place where God spoke with him, Bethel.

Death of Rachel

16Then they journeyed from Bethel. And when there was but a little distance to go to Ephrath, Rachel labored in *childbirth,* and she had hard labor. 17Now it came to pass, when she was in hard labor, that the midwife said to her, "Do not fear; you will have this son also." 18And so it was, as her soul was departing (for she died), that she called his name Ben-Oni;[a] but his father called him Benjamin.[b] 19So Rachel died and was buried on the way to Ephrath (that *is*, Bethlehem). 20And Jacob set a pillar on her grave, which *is* the pillar of Rachel's grave to this day.

21Then Israel journeyed and pitched his tent beyond the tower of Eder. 22And it happened, when Israel dwelt in that land, that Reuben went and lay with Bilhah his father's concubine; and Israel heard *about* it.

35:7 aLiterally *God of the House of God*
35:8 aLiterally *Terebinth of Weeping*
35:18 aLiterally *Son of My Sorrow* bLiterally *Son of the Right Hand*

ARCHITECTURE AND BUILDING

Pillars of stone are the oldest kind of monument (Gen. 35:14). There are more than 3,000 stone pillars at Carnac, France, from before 2000 B.C. When no writing accompanies a pillar, its meaning usually cannot be recovered. The pyramids and obelisks of Egypt are in effect elaborations of the pillar. Not all carved obelisks have writing on them.

BENJAMIN—SONS OF THE SOUTH (Gen. 35:18)

Benjamin was the youngest son of the biblical patriarch Jacob. Among the twelve tribes of Israel, the tribe of Benjamin bears his name as its tribal ancestor. Members of this tribe are thus called "Benjaminites" or "Benjamites," among whom the most famous were Saul, the first king of Israel (1 Sam. 9:1, 2), and Paul the apostle (Phil. 3:4, 5).

In the biblical narrative of Benjamin's birth, the baby is named by the mother as she was dying in childbirth. The name Rachel gave her son, "Ben-Oni," means "son of my sorrow." But the father, Jacob, named the baby "Benjamin" (Gen. 35:18). The English syllables "jamin" translate a Hebrew word meaning "right hand" or "south." (In Israel, the south is on the right-hand side as a person faces the east.) Thus the name "Benjamin" meant "son of the right hand" or "son of the south."

Another tribe with a similar name is known from ancient times. Clay tablets from the Amorite site of Mari in Syria give evidence that a tribe called "Bene-yamina" existed around 1800 B.C. The Bene-yamina were an unruly seminomadic group that were causing concern for Mari's king, Zimri-Lim.

The original meaning of the names "Benjamin" and "Bene-yamina" is undeniably the same; both mean literally "sons of the south." Nevertheless, there is no connection between the Israelite tribe and the tribe mentioned in the Mari sources. However, the similar names do suggest that both groups had a Semitic heritage and that "Benjamin" may very well have been a popular name for tribes in the Middle Bronze Age (2000–1500 B.C.).

Jacob's Twelve Sons

Now the sons of Jacob were twelve: ²³the sons of Leah *were* Reuben, Jacob's firstborn, and Simeon, Levi, Judah, Issachar, and Zebulun; ²⁴the sons of Rachel *were* Joseph and Benjamin; ²⁵the sons of Bilhah, Rachel's maidservant, *were* Dan and Naphtali; ²⁶and the sons of Zilpah, Leah's maidservant, *were* Gad and Asher. These *were* the sons of Jacob who were born to him in Padan Aram.

Death of Isaac

²⁷Then Jacob came to his father Isaac at Mamre, or Kirjath Arba[a] (that *is,* Hebron), where Abraham and Isaac had dwelt. ²⁸Now the days of Isaac were one hundred and eighty years. ²⁹So Isaac breathed his last and died, and was gathered to his people, *being* old and full of days. And his sons Esau and Jacob buried him.

The Family of Esau

36 ¹Now this *is* the genealogy of Esau, who is Edom. ²Esau took his wives from the daughters of Canaan: Adah the daughter of Elon the Hittite; Aholibamah the daughter of Anah, the daughter of Zibeon the Hivite; ³and Basemath, Ishmael's daughter, sister of Nebajoth. ⁴Now Adah bore Eliphaz to Esau, and Basemath bore Reuel. ⁵And Aholibamah bore Jeush, Jaalam, and Korah. These *were* the sons of Esau who were born to him in the land of Canaan.

⁶Then Esau took his wives, his sons, his daughters, and all the persons of his household, his cattle and all his animals, and all his goods which he had gained in the land of Canaan, and went to a country away from the presence of his brother Jacob. ⁷For their possessions were too great for them to dwell together, and the land where they were strangers could not support them because of their livestock. ⁸So Esau dwelt in Mount Seir. Esau *is* Edom.

⁹And this *is* the genealogy of Esau the father of the Edomites in Mount Seir. ¹⁰These *were* the names of Esau's sons: Eliphaz the son of Adah the wife of Esau, and Reuel the son of Basemath the wife of Esau. ¹¹And the sons of Eliphaz were Teman, Omar, Zepho,[a] Gatam, and Kenaz.

¹²Now Timna was the concubine of Eliphaz, Esau's son, and she bore Amalek to Eliphaz. These *were* the sons of Adah, Esau's wife.

¹³These *were* the sons of Reuel: Nahath, Zerah, Shammah, and Mizzah. These were the sons of Basemath, Esau's wife.

35:27 ᵃLiterally *Town of Arba*   36:11 ᵃSpelled *Zephi* in 1 Chronicles 1:36

THE HORITES OF MOUNT SEIR (Gen. 36:21)

At one time, Seir and Edom were possibly two separate geographical regions. Seir was a mountainous region; Edom was part of the Transjordanian plateau. Eventually Seir became a part of the Edomite state, and the names "Seir" and "Edom" came to be used interchangeably.

Two different peoples—the Horites and the Edomites—lived in this area known as Seir and Edom. The Horite genealogy in Gen. 36:20–30 is distinct from the Edomite genealogy in Gen. 36:9–19. The Horites appear to have been a more pastoral people, different from the agricultural Edomites. In the Bible the Horites are described as a group of tribes who inhabited the mountains of Seir until they were displaced by the Edomites (Gen. 14:6; Deut. 2:12, 22).

When in the 19th century scholars discovered a people called the Hurrians, they assumed a connection between Hurrians and the biblical Horites. But Hurrians were a cultural and political force in north Syria and the Tigris area, and their whereabouts in the northern regions does not correspond with the Horite association with Mount Seir.

The Horites should not be confused with either the Edomites or the Hurrians. All that can be determined about them now is that they were very early inhabitants of Seir.

14These were the sons of Aholibamah, Esau's wife, the daughter of Anah, the daughter of Zibeon. And she bore to Esau: Jeush, Jaalam, and Korah.

The Chiefs of Edom

15These *were* the chiefs of the sons of Esau. The sons of Eliphaz, the firstborn *son* of Esau, were Chief Teman, Chief Omar, Chief Zepho, Chief Kenaz, 16Chief Korah,a Chief Gatam, *and* Chief Amalek. These *were* the chiefs of Eliphaz in the land of Edom. They *were* the sons of Adah.

17These *were* the sons of Reuel, Esau's son: Chief Nahath, Chief Zerah, Chief Shammah, and Chief Mizzah. These *were* the chiefs of Reuel in the land of Edom. These *were* the sons of Basemath, Esau's wife.

18And these *were* the sons of Aholibamah, Esau's wife: Chief Jeush, Chief Jaalam, and Chief Korah. These *were* the chiefs *who descended* from Aholibamah, Esau's wife, the daughter of Anah. 19These *were* the sons of Esau, who is Edom, and these *were* their chiefs.

The Sons of Seir

20These *were* the sons of Seir the Horite who inhabited the land: Lotan, Shobal, Zibeon, Anah, 21Dishon, Ezer, and Dishan. These *were* the chiefs of the Horites, the sons of Seir, in the land of Edom.

22And the sons of Lotan were Hori and Hemam.a Lotan's sister *was* Timna. 23These *were* the sons of Shobal: Alvan,a Manahath, Ebal, Shepho,b and Onam.

24These *were* the sons of Zibeon: both Ajah and Anah. This *was the* Anah who found the watera in the wilderness as he pastured the donkeys of his father Zibeon. 25These *were* the children of Anah: Dishon and Aholibamah the daughter of Anah.

26These *were* the sons of Dishon:a Hemdan,b Eshban, Ithran, and Cheran. 27These *were* the sons of Ezer: Bilhan, Zaavan, and Akan.a 28These *were* the sons of Dishan: Uz and Aran.

29These *were* the chiefs of the Horites: Chief Lotan, Chief Shobal, Chief Zibeon, Chief Anah, 30Chief Dishon, Chief Ezer, and Chief Dishan. These *were* the chiefs of the Horites, according to their chiefs in the land of Seir.

The Kings of Edom

31Now these *were* the kings who reigned in the land of Edom before any

---

36:16 aSamaritan Pentateuch omits *Chief Korah.*
36:22 aSpelled *Homam* in 1 Chronicles 1:39
36:23 aSpelled *Alian* in 1 Chronicles 1:40   bSpelled *Shephi* in 1 Chronicles 1:40   36:24 aFollowing Masoretic Text and Vulgate (*hot springs*); Septuagint reads *Jamin;* Targum reads *mighty men;* Talmud interprets as *mules.*   36:26 aHebrew *Dishan* bSpelled *Hamran* in 1 Chronicles 1:41
36:27 aSpelled *Jaakan* in 1 Chronicles 1:42

king reigned over the children of Israel: [32]Bela the son of Beor reigned in Edom, and the name of his city *was* Dinhabah. [33]And when Bela died, Jobab the son of Zerah of Bozrah reigned in his place. [34]When Jobab died, Husham of the land of the Temanites reigned in his place. [35]And when Husham died, Hadad the son of Bedad, who attacked Midian in the field of Moab, reigned in his place. And the name of his city *was* Avith. [36]When Hadad died, Samlah of Masrekah reigned in his place. [37]And when Samlah died, Saul of Rehoboth-*by*-the-River reigned in his place. [38]When Saul died, Baal-Hanan the son of

Achbor reigned in his place. [39]And when Baal-Hanan the son of Achbor died, Hadar[a] reigned in his place; and the name of his city *was* Pau.[b] His wife's name *was* Mehetabel, the daughter of Matred, the daughter of Mezahab.

The Chiefs of Esau

[40]And these *were* the names of the chiefs of Esau, according to their families and their places, by their names: Chief Timnah, Chief Alvah,[a] Chief Jetheth, [41]Chief Aholibamah, Chief Elah, Chief Pinon, [42]Chief Kenaz, Chief Teman, Chief Mibzar, [43]Chief Magdiel, and Chief Iram. These *were* the chiefs of Edom, according to their dwelling places in the land of their possession. Esau *was* the father of the Edomites.

36:39 [a]Spelled *Hadad* in Samaritan Pentateuch, Syriac, and 1 Chronicles 1:50   [b]Spelled *Pai* in 1 Chronicles 1:50   36:40 [a]Spelled *Aliah* in 1 Chronicles 1:51

Egypt in the Middle Bronze Age

Egypt fell under the control of outsiders, a Semitic people known as the Hyksos.

The spread of the Amorite peoples evidently reached even to Egypt. After several prosperous centuries, the Middle Kingdom of Egypt ended, and the land again began to break up politically. In the Second Intermediate Period (1786–1550 B.C.) of Egyptian history, as in the First Intermediate Period, foreigners entered Egypt from Asia and settled in the Nile Delta (see "The Changing of the Empires" at Gen. 12:1). Eventually, Egypt fell under the control of these outsiders, a Semitic people, known as the Hyksos (meaning "foreign chiefs"). Although much despised by the native Egyptians, the Hyksos maintained their control from about 1648 to 1540 B.C., even expanding Egypt's control north into Palestine, which became an Egyptian province.

Joseph—a Hebrew in Egypt

The significance of the Hyksos dynasty for the Joseph narratives of Gen. 37—50 is debated. Some claim that Joseph's rise to power and the Hebrews' entry into Egypt took place during this time, while others say that the patriarchs must have entered Egypt earlier. In either case, an Egyptian dynasty with Semitic roots would have been a less hostile environment for the Hebrews, and might have contributed to their growth upon arriving there (Ex. 1:7).

▼   ■ Genesis 37:1—46:34

Genesis
Joseph Dreams of Greatness

37 :1 Now Jacob dwelt in the land where his father was a stranger, in the land of Canaan. [2]This *is* the history of Jacob.

Joseph, *being* seventeen years old, was feeding the flock with his brothers. And the lad *was* with the sons of Bilhah and the sons of Zilpah, his father's wives; and Joseph brought a bad report of them to his father.

[3]Now Israel loved Joseph more than all his children, because he *was* the son of his old age. Also he made him a tunic of *many* colors. [4]But when his brothers saw that their father loved him more than all his brothers, they hated him and could not speak peaceably to him.

[5]Now Joseph had a dream, and he told *it* to his brothers; and they hated him even more. [6]So he said to them, "Please hear this dream which I have dreamed: [7]There we were, binding sheaves in the field. Then behold, my sheaf arose and also stood

upright; and indeed your sheaves stood all around and bowed down to my sheaf."

⁸And his brothers said to him, "Shall you indeed reign over us? Or shall you indeed have dominion over us?" So they hated him even more for his dreams and for his words.

⁹Then he dreamed still another dream and told it to his brothers, and said, "Look, I have dreamed another dream. And this time, the sun, the moon, and the eleven stars bowed down to me."

¹⁰So he told *it* to his father and his brothers; and his father rebuked him and said to him, "What *is* this dream that you have dreamed? Shall your mother and I and your brothers indeed come to bow down to the earth before you?" ¹¹And his brothers envied him, but his father kept the matter *in mind.*

Joseph Sold by His Brothers

¹²Then his brothers went to feed their father's flock in Shechem. ¹³And Israel said to Joseph, "Are not your brothers feeding *the flock* in Shechem? Come, I will send you to them."

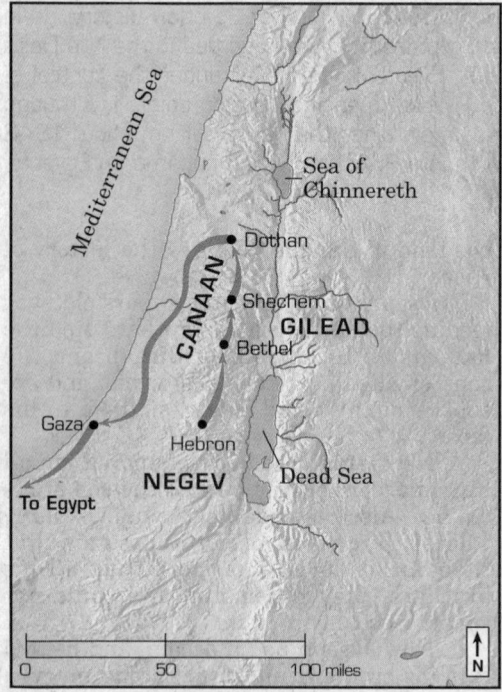

Joseph Goes to Egypt
Joseph searched for his brothers, eventually finding them at Dothan. His brothers sold him to a caravan of Midianites passing by en route from Gilead to Egypt.

So he said to him, "Here I am."

¹⁴Then he said to him, "Please go and see if it is well with your brothers and well with the flocks, and bring back word to me." So he sent him out of the Valley of Hebron, and he went to Shechem.

¹⁵Now a certain man found him, and there he was, wandering in the field. And the man asked him, saying, "What are you seeking?"

¹⁶So he said, "I am seeking my brothers. Please tell me where they are feeding *their flocks.*"

¹⁷And the man said, "They have departed from here, for I heard them say, 'Let us go to Dothan.' " So Joseph went after his brothers and found them in Dothan.

¹⁸Now when they saw him afar off, even before he came near them, they conspired against him to kill him. ¹⁹Then they said to one another, "Look, this dreamer is coming! ²⁰Come therefore, let us now kill him and cast him into some pit; and we shall say, 'Some wild beast has devoured him.' We shall see what will become of his dreams!"

²¹But Reuben heard *it,* and he delivered him out of their hands, and said, "Let us not kill him." ²²And Reuben said to them, "Shed no blood, *but* cast him into this pit which *is* in the wilderness, and do not lay a hand on him"—that he might deliver him out of their hands, and bring him back to his father.

²³So it came to pass, when Joseph had come to his brothers, that they stripped Joseph *of* his tunic, the tunic of *many* colors that *was* on him. ²⁴Then they took him and cast him into a pit. And the pit *was* empty; *there was* no water in it.

²⁵And they sat down to eat a meal. Then they lifted their eyes and looked, and there was a company of Ishmaelites, coming from Gilead with their camels, bearing spices, balm, and myrrh, on their way to carry *them* down to Egypt. ²⁶So Judah said to his brothers, "What profit *is there* if we kill our brother and conceal his blood? ²⁷Come and let us sell him to the Ishmaelites, and let not our hand be upon him, for he *is* our brother *and* our flesh." And his brothers listened. ²⁸Then Midianite traders passed by; so *the brothers* pulled Joseph up and lifted him out of the pit, and sold him to the Ishmaelites for twenty *shekels* of silver. And they took Joseph to Egypt.

²⁹Then Reuben returned to the pit, and

THE OLD BABYLONIAN PERIOD

Mesopotamia during the Old Babylonian period was characterized by various warring dynasties, each struggling for power over one another. Before this time, the strongest empire of southern Babylonia had been the 3rd Dynasty of Ur. The Ur dynasty was succeeded by others—primarily Isin and Larsa. Yet even these two dynasties did not last, eventually falling to Hammurabi, the greatest ruler of the time.

Key Dates	Key Events
2112–2004 B.C.	Ur-Nammu, founder of the 3rd Dynasty of Ur, constructs a ziggurat of Ur in honor of the god Nanna
2017 B.C.	Isin dynasty founded by an Amorite named Ishbi-Erra
2004 B.C.	City of Ur falls to the Elamites
c. 1804 B.C.	King Rim-Sin of Larsa defeats Isin
1792–1750 B.C.	Hammurabi is sixth king of the 1st Dynasty of Babylon
c. 1781 B.C.	Hammurabi defeats Isin
c. 1763 B.C.	Hammurabi defeats King Rim-Sin of Larsa
1760 B.C.	Hammurabi defeats King Zimri-Lim of Mari

indeed Joseph *was* not in the pit; and he tore his clothes. ³⁰And he returned to his brothers and said, "The lad *is* no *more;* and I, where shall I go?"

³¹So they took Joseph's tunic, killed a kid of the goats, and dipped the tunic in the blood. ³²Then they sent the tunic of *many* colors, and they brought *it* to their father and said, "We have found this. Do you know whether it *is* your son's tunic or not?"

³³And he recognized it and said, "*It is* my son's tunic. A wild beast has devoured him. Without doubt Joseph is torn to pieces." ³⁴Then Jacob tore his clothes, put sackcloth on his waist, and mourned for his son many days. ³⁵And all his sons and all his daughters arose to comfort him; but he refused to be comforted, and he said, "For I shall go down into the grave to my son in mourning." Thus his father wept for him.

³⁶Now the Midianites[a] had sold him in Egypt to Potiphar, an officer of Pharaoh *and* captain of the guard.

Judah and Tamar

38 ¹It came to pass at that time that Judah departed from his brothers, and visited a certain Adullamite whose name *was* Hirah. ²And Judah saw there a daughter of a certain Canaanite whose name *was* Shua, and he married her and went in to her. ³So she conceived and bore

a son, and he called his name Er. ⁴She conceived again and bore a son, and she called his name Onan. ⁵And she conceived yet again and bore a son, and called his name Shelah. He was at Chezib when she bore him.

⁶Then Judah took a wife for Er his firstborn, and her name *was* Tamar. ⁷But Er, Judah's firstborn, was wicked in the sight of the LORD, and the LORD killed him. ⁸And Judah said to Onan, "Go in to your brother's wife and marry her, and raise up an heir to your brother." ⁹But Onan knew that the heir would not be his; and it came to pass, when he went in to his brother's wife, that he emitted on the ground, lest he should give an heir to his brother. ¹⁰And the thing which he did displeased the LORD; therefore He killed him also.

¹¹Then Judah said to Tamar his daughter-in-law, "Remain a widow in your father's house till my son Shelah is grown." For he said, "Lest he also die like his brothers." And Tamar went and dwelt in her father's house.

¹²Now in the process of time the daughter of Shua, Judah's wife, died; and Judah was comforted, and went up to his sheepshearers at Timnah, he and his friend Hirah the Adullamite. ¹³And it was told Tamar, saying, "Look, your father-in-law is going up to Timnah to shear his sheep." ¹⁴So she took off her widow's garments, covered *herself* with a veil and wrapped herself, and sat in an open place

37:36 ªMasoretic Text reads *Medanites.*

which *was* on the way to Timnah; for she saw that Shelah was grown, and she was not given to him as a wife. [15]When Judah saw her, he thought she *was* a harlot, because she had covered her face. [16]Then he turned to her by the way, and said, "Please let me come in to you"; for he did not know that she *was* his daughter-in-law.

So she said, "What will you give me, that you may come in to me?"

[17]And he said, "I will send a young goat from the flock."

So she said, "Will you give *me* a pledge till you send *it?*"

[18]Then he said, "What pledge shall I give you?"

So she said, "Your signet and cord, and your staff that *is* in your hand." Then he gave *them* to her, and went in to her, and she conceived by him. [19]So she arose and went away, and laid aside her veil and put on the garments of her widowhood.

[20]And Judah sent the young goat by the hand of his friend the Adullamite, to receive *his* pledge from the woman's hand, but he did not find her. [21]Then he asked the men of that place, saying, "Where is the harlot who *was* openly by the roadside?"

And they said, "There was no harlot in this *place.*"

[22]So he returned to Judah and said, "I cannot find her. Also, the men of the place said there was no harlot in this *place.*"

[23]Then Judah said, "Let her take *them* for herself, lest we be shamed; for I sent this young goat and you have not found her."

[24]And it came to pass, about three months after, that Judah was told, saying, "Tamar your daughter-in-law has played the harlot; furthermore she *is* with child by harlotry."

So Judah said, "Bring her out and let her be burned!"

[25]When she *was* brought out, she sent to her father-in-law, saying, "By the man to whom these belong, I *am* with child." And she said, "Please determine whose these *are*—the signet and cord, and staff."

[26]So Judah acknowledged *them* and said, "She has been more righteous than I, because I did not give her to Shelah my son." And he never knew her again.

[27]Now it came to pass, at the time for giving birth, that behold, twins *were* in her womb. [28]And so it was, when she was giving birth, that *the one* put out *his* hand; and the midwife took a scarlet *thread* and bound it on his hand, saying, "This one came out first." [29]Then it happened, as he drew back his hand, that his brother came out unexpectedly; and she said, "How did you break through? *This* breach *be* upon you!" Therefore his name was called Perez.[a] [30]Afterward his brother came out who had the scarlet *thread* on his hand. And his name was called Zerah.

Joseph a Slave in Egypt

39 [1]Now Joseph had been taken down to Egypt. And Potiphar, an officer of Pharaoh, captain of the guard, an Egyptian, bought him from the Ishmaelites who had taken him down there. [2]The LORD was with Joseph, and he was a successful man; and he was in the house of his master the Egyptian. [3]And his master saw that the LORD *was* with him and that the LORD made all he did to prosper in his hand. [4]So Joseph found favor in his sight, and served him. Then he made him overseer of his house, and all *that* he had he put under his authority. [5]So it was, from the time *that* he had made him overseer of his house and all that he had, that the LORD blessed the Egyptian's house for Joseph's sake; and the blessing of the LORD was on all that he had in the house and in the field. [6]Thus he left all that he had in Joseph's hand, and he did not know what he had except for the bread which he ate.

Now Joseph was handsome in form and appearance.

38:29 [a]Literally *Breach* or *Breakthrough*

BELIEFS AND IDEAS

The name of Perez is explained by an incident at his birth (Gen. 38:29). In the Bible, names are often connected with memorable facts about the person named. In this case, the Hebrew word for "breach" is related to the name Perez. Ancient people thought that a person's name gave access to, or power over, that person.

JOSEPH GOES TO EGYPT (Gen. 39:1, 2)

After arriving in Egypt, Joseph became a slave of the Egyptian officer Potiphar (Gen. 39:1), but this slave's fortunes changed dramatically. Joseph's rise to power saw him become first the overseer of Potiphar's house (39:4), but eventually a ruler over all of Egypt, second in power to the Egyptian pharaoh himself (41:39–43). One possible setting for the Joseph story is the period when the Hyksos people ruled Egypt.

Before the Hyksos arrived, Egypt had been a united country. Under the 12th Dynasty (1963–1786 B.C.) Egypt enjoyed a flourishing mining industry and agricultural program, as well as a new capital established near Memphis by Pharaoh Amenemhet I. Another pharaoh, Sesostris III, was able to organize a strong central government for Egypt by controlling the families who ruled Egypt's territories.

Sometime after the 12th Dynasty the country began to fragment. Various rulers set up their own dynasties over portions of Egypt and ruled at the same time. The 13th Dynasty (1786–1633 B.C.) established a new capital at Thebes, while the 14th Dynasty (1786–1602 B.C.) consisted of several rulers in the Delta who proclaimed themselves "kings."

The political upheaval made Egypt ripe for the invasion of the Hyksos people, who subjugated the country and placed their own capital at Avaris in the Delta region. The Hyksos dynasty lasted more than a century (1648–1540 B.C.).

The ethnic background of the Hyksos is one reason for setting the Joseph story during this period. These invaders were a mixture of Semitic and Asiatic peoples. In an Egypt ruled by such foreigners, it is possible that someone like Joseph, himself being Semitic and foreign, could rise from a servant to a position of high office.

7And it came to pass after these things that his master's wife cast longing eyes on Joseph, and she said, "Lie with me."

8But he refused and said to his master's wife, "Look, my master does not know what *is* with me in the house, and he has committed all that he has to my hand. 9*There is* no one greater in this house than I, nor has he kept back anything from me but you, because you *are* his wife. How then can I do this great wickedness, and sin against God?"

10So it was, as she spoke to Joseph day by day, that he did not heed her, to lie with her *or* to be with her.

11But it happened about this time, when Joseph went into the house to do his work, and none of the men of the house *was* inside, 12that she caught him by his garment, saying, "Lie with me." But he left his garment in her hand, and fled and ran outside. 13And so it was, when she saw that he had left his garment in her hand and fled outside, 14that she called to the men of her house and spoke to them, saying, "See, he has brought in to us a Hebrew to mock us. He came in to me to lie with me, and I cried out with a loud voice. 15And it happened, when he heard that I lifted my voice and cried out, that he left his garment with me, and fled and went outside."

16So she kept his garment with her until his master came home. 17Then she spoke to him with words like these, saying, "The Hebrew servant whom you brought to us came in to me to mock me; 18so it happened, as I lifted my voice and cried out, that he left his garment with me and fled outside."

19So it was, when his master heard the words which his wife spoke to him, saying, "Your servant did to me after this manner," that his anger was aroused. 20Then Joseph's master took him and put him into the prison, a place where the king's prisoners *were* confined. And he was there in the prison. 21But the LORD was with Joseph and showed him mercy, and He gave him favor in the sight of the keeper of the prison. 22And the keeper of the prison committed to Joseph's hand all the prisoners who *were* in the prison; whatever they did there, it was his doing. 23The keeper of the prison did not look into anything *that was* under *Joseph's* authority,[a] because the LORD was with him; and whatever he did, the LORD made *it* prosper.

39:23 [a]Literally *his hand*

THE TALE OF TWO BROTHERS (Gen. 39:7–18)

Joseph's troubles with Potiphar's wife (Gen. 39:7–18) have a literary parallel in a folk tale from Egypt's New Kingdom (c. 1550–1069 B.C.). At best, the similarities between the *Tale of Two Brothers* and the Joseph story are superficial and confined to a few details. Nevertheless, both stories share a common plot.

The main characters in the *Tale of Two Brothers* are gods. Anubis asks his younger brother Bata to help him with the yearly sowing. While back home fetching grain, Bata is approached by Anubis's wife, who desires sexual relations with him. Like Joseph, Bata is appalled by the offer and leaves in haste. The wife makes it look as if she has been assaulted by Bata.

Readers of the 2nd millennium were familiar with this plot. An innocent servant or shepherd receives a sexual invitation from a seductive wife. His innocency triumphs by his refusal to participate, at which point he incurs the anger and false accusations of the wife. Though innocent, he must flee.

The Prisoners' Dreams

40 ¹It came to pass after these things *that* the butler and the baker of the king of Egypt offended their lord, the king of Egypt. ²And Pharaoh was angry with his two officers, the chief butler and the chief baker. ³So he put them in custody in the house of the captain of the guard, in the prison, the place where Joseph *was* confined. ⁴And the captain of the guard charged Joseph with them, and he served them; so they were in custody for a while.

⁵Then the butler and the baker of the king of Egypt, who *were* confined in the prison, had a dream, both of them, each man's dream in one night *and* each man's dream with its *own* interpretation. ⁶And Joseph came in to them in the morning and looked at them, and saw that they *were* sad. ⁷So he asked Pharaoh's officers who *were* with him in the custody of his lord's house, saying, "Why do you look *so* sad today?"

⁸And they said to him, "We each have had a dream, and *there is* no interpreter of it."

So Joseph said to them, "Do not interpretations belong to God? Tell *them* to me, please."

⁹Then the chief butler told his dream to Joseph, and said to him, "Behold, in my dream a vine *was* before me, ¹⁰and in the vine *were* three branches; it *was* as though it budded, its blossoms shot forth, and its clusters brought forth ripe grapes. ¹¹Then Pharaoh's cup *was* in my hand; and I took the grapes and pressed them into Pharaoh's cup, and placed the cup in Pharaoh's hand."

¹²And Joseph said to him, "This *is* the interpretation of it: The three branches *are* three days. ¹³Now within three days Pharaoh will lift up your head and restore you to your place, and you will put Pharaoh's cup in his hand according to the former manner, when you were his butler. ¹⁴But remember me when it is well with you, and please show kindness to me; make mention of me to Pharaoh, and get me out of this house. ¹⁵For indeed I was stolen away from the land of the Hebrews; and also I have done nothing here that they should put me into the dungeon."

¹⁶When the chief baker saw that the interpretation was good, he said to Joseph, "I also *was* in my dream, and there *were* three white baskets on my head. ¹⁷In the uppermost basket *were* all kinds of baked goods for Pharaoh, and the birds ate them out of the basket on my head."

¹⁸So Joseph answered and said, "This *is* the interpretation of it: The three baskets *are* three days. ¹⁹Within three days Pharaoh will lift off your head from you and hang you on a tree; and the birds will eat your flesh from you."

²⁰Now it came to pass on the third day, *which was* Pharaoh's birthday, that he made a feast for all his servants; and he lifted up the head of the chief butler and of the chief baker among his servants. ²¹Then he restored the chief butler to his butlership again, and he placed the cup in Pharaoh's hand. ²²But he hanged the chief baker, as Joseph had interpreted to them.

²³Yet the chief butler did not remember Joseph, but forgot him.

Pharaoh's Dreams

41 ¹Then it came to pass, at the end of two full years, that Pharaoh had a dream; and behold, he stood by the river. ²Suddenly there came up out of the river seven cows, fine looking and fat; and they fed in the meadow. ³Then behold, seven other cows came up after them out of the river, ugly and gaunt, and stood by the *other* cows on the bank of the river. ⁴And the ugly and gaunt cows ate up the seven fine looking and fat cows. So Pharaoh awoke. ⁵He slept and dreamed a second time; and suddenly seven heads of grain came up on one stalk, plump and good. ⁶Then behold, seven thin heads, blighted by the east wind, sprang up after them. ⁷And the seven thin heads devoured the seven plump and full heads. So Pharaoh awoke, and indeed, *it was* a dream. ⁸Now it came to pass in the morning that his spirit was troubled, and he sent and called for all the magicians of Egypt and all its wise men. And Pharaoh told them his dreams, but *there was* no one who could interpret them for Pharaoh.

⁹Then the chief butler spoke to Pharaoh, saying: "I remember my faults this day. ¹⁰When Pharaoh was angry with his servants, and put me in custody in the house of the captain of the guard, *both* me and the chief baker, ¹¹we each had a dream in one night, he and I. Each of us dreamed according to the interpretation of his *own* dream. ¹²Now there *was* a young Hebrew man with us there, a servant of the captain of the guard. And we told him, and he interpreted our dreams for us; to each man he interpreted according to his *own* dream. ¹³And it came to pass, just as he interpreted for us, so it happened. He restored me to my office, and he hanged him."

¹⁴Then Pharaoh sent and called Joseph, and they brought him quickly out of the dungeon; and he shaved, changed his clothing, and came to Pharaoh. ¹⁵And Pharaoh said to Joseph, "I have had a dream, and *there is* no one who can interpret it. But I have heard it said of you *that* you can understand a dream, to interpret it."

¹⁶So Joseph answered Pharaoh, saying, "*It is* not in me; God will give Pharaoh an answer of peace."

¹⁷Then Pharaoh said to Joseph: "Behold, in my dream I stood on the bank of the river. ¹⁸Suddenly seven cows came up out of the river, fine looking and fat; and they fed in the meadow. ¹⁹Then behold, seven other cows came up after them, poor and very ugly and gaunt, such ugliness as I have never seen in all the land of Egypt. ²⁰And the gaunt and ugly cows ate up the first seven, the fat cows. ²¹When they had eaten them up, no one would have known that they had eaten them, for they *were* just as ugly as at the beginning. So I awoke. ²²Also I saw in my dream, and suddenly seven heads came up on one stalk, full and good. ²³Then behold, seven heads, withered, thin, *and* blighted by the east wind, sprang up after them. ²⁴And the thin heads devoured the seven good heads. So I told *this* to the magicians, but *there was* no one who could explain *it* to me."

²⁵Then Joseph said to Pharaoh, "The dreams of Pharaoh *are* one; God has shown Pharaoh what He *is* about to do: ²⁶The seven good cows *are* seven years, and the seven good heads *are* seven years; the dreams *are* one. ²⁷And the seven thin and ugly cows which came up after them *are* seven years, and the seven empty heads blighted by the east wind are seven years of famine. ²⁸This *is* the thing which I have spoken to Pharaoh. God has shown Pharaoh what He *is* about to do. ²⁹Indeed seven years of great plenty will come throughout all the land of Egypt; ³⁰but after them seven years of famine will arise, and all the plenty will be forgotten in the

---

TIME CAPSULE   *1800 to 1779 B.C.*

1800	Wheel-thrown pottery in Greece
1792	Hammurabi ascends throne of Babylon
1790	First code of laws issued by Hammurabi
1790	Sumerian King List traces the history of Sumer and Accad from the flood to Hammurabi
1786–1633	13th Dynasty of Egypt establishes capital at Thebes
1786–1602	14th Dynasty of Egypt consists of local kings in the west Delta
1781	Hammurabi defeats Isin
1779	Earliest evidence for a wheel with spokes, from Syria

EGYPT'S SEVEN LEAN YEARS (Gen. 41:25–32)

Pharaoh's dreams involved seven fat cows and seven plump heads of grain which were devoured by seven ugly cows and seven thin heads, respectively (Gen. 41:1–7). In Joseph's interpretation, the ugly cows and thin heads symbolized seven years of famine (41:25–32). The record of the seven lean years in Egypt appears to have an antecedent in Egyptian literature.

A text called *The Tradition of the Seven Lean Years in Egypt* is attributed to Djoser, a pharaoh of the 3rd Dynasty of Egypt's Old Kingdom (c. 2650 B.C.). The text of this Egyptian story as it now exists came from scribes during the reign of Ptolemy V (204–180 B.C.), a ruler of the Macedonian dynasty established by the successors of Alexander the Great. While this text is much later than the account in Genesis, it is possible that it had been copied from an earlier text.

The Egyptian text recounts a letter that Djoser wrote to his overseer in Elephantine in southern Egypt, lamenting the fact that the "Nile has not come in my time for a space of seven years." Consequently grain was scarce, fruits were dried up, and "every man robbed his companion."

Imhotep, the renowned vizier or chief minister to Djoser, proceeds to tell him about the god Khnum, who resides at the birthplace of the Nile, namely Elephantine. Pharaoh Djoser then has a dream in which the god tells him that the Nile would soon "pour forth for you." Thus, plants would again grow and starvation would cease. The pharaoh awoke refreshed and presumably then drafted the text for his official at Elephantine.

land of Egypt; and the famine will deplete the land. ³¹So the plenty will not be known in the land because of the famine following, for it *will be* very severe. ³²And the dream was repeated to Pharaoh twice because the thing *is* established by God, and God will shortly bring it to pass.

³³"Now therefore, let Pharaoh select a discerning and wise man, and set him over the land of Egypt. ³⁴Let Pharaoh do *this,* and let him appoint officers over the land, to collect one-fifth *of the produce* of the land of Egypt in the seven plentiful years. ³⁵And let them gather all the food of those good years that are coming, and store up grain under the authority of Pharaoh, and let them keep food in the cities. ³⁶Then that food shall be as a reserve for the land for the seven years of famine which shall be in the land of Egypt, that the land may not perish during the famine."

Joseph's Rise to Power

³⁷So the advice was good in the eyes of Pharaoh and in the eyes of all his servants. ³⁸And Pharaoh said to his servants, "Can we find *such a one* as this, a man in whom *is* the Spirit of God?"

³⁹Then Pharaoh said to Joseph, "Inasmuch as God has shown you all this, *there is* no one as discerning and wise as you. ⁴⁰You shall be over my house, and all my people shall be ruled according to your word; only in regard to the throne will I be greater than you." ⁴¹And Pharaoh said to Joseph, "See, I have set you over all the land of Egypt."

⁴²Then Pharaoh took his signet ring off his hand and put it on Joseph's hand; and he clothed him in garments of fine linen and put a gold chain around his neck. ⁴³And he had him ride in the second char-

POLITICS AND GOVERNMENT

The Egyptians maintained large stone storehouses, primarily for grain (Gen. 41:48). This protected them from famine and also helped stabilize prices. The granaries were often associated with temples. The ruler was regarded as divine, and the department devoted to grain was one of the most important in the fundamentally religious government of Egypt.

iot which he had; and they cried out before him, "Bow the knee!" So he set him over all the land of Egypt. [44]Pharaoh also said to Joseph, "I *am* Pharaoh, and without your consent no man may lift his hand or foot in all the land of Egypt." [45]And Pharaoh called Joseph's name Zaphnath-Paaneah. And he gave him as a wife Asenath, the daughter of Poti-Pherah priest of On. So Joseph went out over *all* the land of Egypt.

[46]Joseph was thirty years old when he stood before Pharaoh king of Egypt. And Joseph went out from the presence of Pharaoh, and went throughout all the land of Egypt. [47]Now in the seven plentiful years the ground brought forth abundantly. [48]So he gathered up all the food of the seven years which were in the land of Egypt, and laid up the food in the cities; he laid up in every city the food of the fields which surrounded them. [49]Joseph gathered very much grain, as the sand of the sea, until he stopped counting, for *it was* immeasurable.

[50]And to Joseph were born two sons before the years of famine came, whom Asenath, the daughter of Poti-Pherah priest of

On, bore to him. [51]Joseph called the name of the firstborn Manasseh:[a] "For God has made me forget all my toil and all my father's house." [52]And the name of the second he called Ephraim:[a] "For God has caused me to be fruitful in the land of my affliction."

[53]Then the seven years of plenty which were in the land of Egypt ended, [54]and the seven years of famine began to come, as Joseph had said. The famine was in all lands, but in all the land of Egypt there was bread. [55]So when all the land of Egypt was famished, the people cried to Pharaoh for bread. Then Pharaoh said to all the Egyptians, "Go to Joseph; whatever he says to you, do." [56]The famine was over all the face of the earth, and Joseph opened all the storehouses[a] and sold to the Egyptians. And the famine became severe in the land of Egypt. [57]So all countries came to Joseph in Egypt to buy *grain,* because the famine was severe in all lands.

Joseph's Brothers Go to Egypt

42 [1]When Jacob saw that there was grain in Egypt, Jacob said to his sons, "Why do you look at one another?" [2]And he said, "Indeed I have heard that there is grain in Egypt; go down to that

41:51 [a]Literally *Making Forgetful*　　41:52 [a]Literally *Fruitfulness*　　41:56 [a]Literally *all that was in them*

The Hyksos Empire
After taking control of Lower Egypt, the Hyksos established a capital at Avaris. King Kamose of Thebes eventually broke the power of the Hyksos, and his younger brother Ahmose I drove them from Egypt. In 1540 B.C. Ahmose began a 3-year siege of Sharuhen, the Hyksos stronghold in south Palestine. At this time, Egyptian texts refer to the land of Palestine as "Retenu."

place and buy for us there, that we may live and not die."

³So Joseph's ten brothers went down to buy grain in Egypt. ⁴But Jacob did not send Joseph's brother Benjamin with his brothers, for he said, "Lest some calamity befall him." ⁵And the sons of Israel went to buy *grain* among those who journeyed, for the famine was in the land of Canaan.

⁶Now Joseph *was* governor over the land; and it was he who sold to all the people of the land. And Joseph's brothers came and bowed down before him with *their* faces to the earth. ⁷Joseph saw his brothers and recognized them, but he acted as a stranger to them and spoke roughly to them. Then he said to them, "Where do you come from?"

And they said, "From the land of Canaan to buy food."

⁸So Joseph recognized his brothers, but they did not recognize him. ⁹Then Joseph remembered the dreams which he had dreamed about them, and said to them, "You *are* spies! You have come to see the nakedness of the land!"

¹⁰And 'they said to him, "No, my lord, but your servants have come to buy food. ¹¹We *are* all one man's sons; we *are* honest *men;* your servants are not spies."

¹²But he said to them, "No, but you have come to see the nakedness of the land."

¹³And they said, "Your servants *are* twelve brothers, the sons of one man in the land of Canaan; and in fact, the youngest *is* with our father today, and one *is* no more."

¹⁴But Joseph said to them, "It *is* as I spoke to you, saying, 'You *are* spies!' ¹⁵In this *manner* you shall be tested: By the life of Pharaoh, you shall not leave this place unless your youngest brother comes here. ¹⁶Send one of you, and let him bring your brother; and you shall be kept in prison, that your words may be tested to see whether *there is* any truth in you; or else, by the life of Pharaoh, surely you *are* spies!" ¹⁷So he put them all together in prison three days.

¹⁸Then Joseph said to them the third day, "Do this and live, *for* I fear God: ¹⁹If you *are* honest *men,* let one of your brothers be confined to your prison house; but you, go and carry grain for the famine of your houses. ²⁰And bring your youngest brother to me; so your words will be verified, and you shall not die."

And they did so. ²¹Then they said to one another, "We *are* truly guilty concerning our brother, for we saw the anguish of his soul when he pleaded with us, and we would not hear; therefore this distress has come upon us."

²²And Reuben answered them, saying, "Did I not speak to you, saying, 'Do not sin against the boy'; and you would not listen? Therefore behold, his blood is now required of us." ²³But they did not know that Joseph understood *them,* for he spoke to them through an interpreter. ²⁴And he turned himself away from them and wept. Then he returned to them again, and talked with them. And he took Simeon from them and bound him before their eyes.

The Brothers Return to Canaan

²⁵Then Joseph gave a command to fill their sacks with grain, to restore every man's money to his sack, and to give them provisions for the journey. Thus he did for them. ²⁶So they loaded their donkeys with the grain and departed from there. ²⁷But as one *of them* opened his sack to give his donkey feed at the encampment, he saw his money; and there it was, in the mouth of his sack. ²⁸So he said to his brothers, "My money has been restored, and there it is, in my sack!" Then their hearts failed *them* and they were afraid, saying to one another, "What *is* this *that* God has done to us?"

²⁹Then they went to Jacob their father in the land of Canaan and told him all that had happened to them, saying: ³⁰"The man *who is* lord of the land spoke roughly to us, and took us for spies of the country. ³¹But we said to him, 'We *are* honest *men;* we are not spies. ³²We *are* twelve brothers, sons of our father; one *is* no *more,* and the youngest *is* with our father this day in the land of Canaan.' ³³Then the man, the lord of the country, said to us, 'By this I will know that you *are* honest *men:* Leave one of your brothers *here* with me, take *food for* the famine of your households, and be gone. ³⁴And bring your youngest brother to me; so I shall know that you *are* not spies, but *that* you *are* honest *men.* I will grant your brother to you, and you may trade in the land.' "

³⁵Then it happened as they emptied their sacks, that surprisingly each man's bundle of money *was* in his sack; and when they and their father saw the bundles of money, they were afraid. ³⁶And Jacob their father said to them, "You have bereaved

me: Joseph is no *more,* Simeon is no *more,* and you want to take Benjamin. All these things are against me."

³⁷Then Reuben spoke to his father, saying, "Kill my two sons if I do not bring him *back* to you; put him in my hands, and I will bring him back to you."

³⁸But he said, "My son shall not go down with you, for his brother is dead, and he is left alone. If any calamity should befall him along the way in which you go, then you would bring down my gray hair with sorrow to the grave."

Joseph's Brothers Return with Benjamin

43 ¹Now the famine *was* severe in the land. ²And it came to pass, when they had eaten up the grain which they had brought from Egypt, that their father said to them, "Go back, buy us a little food."

³But Judah spoke to him, saying, "The man solemnly warned us, saying, 'You shall not see my face unless your brother *is* with you.' ⁴If you send our brother with us, we will go down and buy you food. ⁵But if you will not send *him,* we will not go down; for the man said to us, 'You shall not see my face unless your brother *is* with you.' "

⁶And Israel said, "Why did you deal *so* wrongfully with me *as* to tell the man whether you had still *another* brother?"

⁷But they said, "The man asked us pointedly about ourselves and our family, saying, '*Is* your father still alive? Have you *another* brother?' And we told him according to these words. Could we possibly have known that he would say, 'Bring your brother down'?"

⁸Then Judah said to Israel his father, "Send the lad with me, and we will arise and go, that we may live and not die, both we and you *and* also our little ones. ⁹I myself will be surety for him; from my hand you shall require him. If I do not bring him *back* to you and set him before you, then let me bear the blame forever. ¹⁰For if we

had not lingered, surely by now we would have returned this second time."

¹¹And their father Israel said to them, "If *it must be* so, then do this: Take some of the best fruits of the land in your vessels and carry down a present for the man—a little balm and a little honey, spices and myrrh, pistachio nuts and almonds. ¹²Take double money in your hand, and take back in your hand the money that was returned in the mouth of your sacks; perhaps it was an oversight. ¹³Take your brother also, and arise, go back to the man. ¹⁴And may God Almighty give you mercy before the man, that he may release your other brother and Benjamin. If I am bereaved, I am bereaved!"

¹⁵So the men took that present and Benjamin, and they took double money in their hand, and arose and went down to Egypt; and they stood before Joseph. ¹⁶When Joseph saw Benjamin with them, he said to the steward of his house, "Take *these* men to my home, and slaughter an animal and make ready; for *these* men will dine with me at noon." ¹⁷Then the man did as Joseph ordered, and the man brought the men into Joseph's house.

¹⁸Now the men were afraid because they were brought into Joseph's house; and they said, "*It is* because of the money, which was returned in our sacks the first time, that we are brought in, so that he may make a case against us and seize us, to take us as slaves with our donkeys."

¹⁹When they drew near to the steward of Joseph's house, they talked with him at the door of the house, ²⁰and said, "O sir, we indeed came down the first time to buy food; ²¹but it happened, when we came to the encampment, that we opened our sacks, and there, *each* man's money *was* in the mouth of his sack, our money in full weight; so we have brought it back in our hand. ²²And we have brought down other money in our hands to buy food. We do not know who put our money in our sacks."

²³But he said, "Peace *be* with you, do not be afraid. Your God and the God of your

MARRIAGE AND FAMILY

Joseph seated his brothers in order of their age (Gen. 43:33). Rights of inheritance were almost inflexibly linked to the order of birth. In society as a whole, age was regarded as a title to respect. Contempt for one's parents or elders was a serious offense, in certain cases calling for extreme punishment (Ex. 21:17; Lev. 19:32).

father has given you treasure in your sacks; I had your money." Then he brought Simeon out to them.

24So the man brought the men into Joseph's house and gave *them* water, and they washed their feet; and he gave their donkeys feed. 25Then they made the present ready for Joseph's coming at noon, for they heard that they would eat bread there.

26And when Joseph came home, they brought him the present which *was* in their hand into the house, and bowed down before him to the earth. 27Then he asked them about *their* well-being, and said, "*Is* your father well, the old man of whom you spoke? *Is* he still alive?"

28And they answered, "Your servant our father *is* in good health; he *is* still alive." And they bowed their heads down and prostrated themselves.

29Then he lifted his eyes and saw his brother Benjamin, his mother's son, and said, "*Is* this your younger brother of whom you spoke to me?" And he said, "God be gracious to you, my son." 30Now his heart yearned for his brother; so Joseph made haste and sought *somewhere* to weep. And he went into *his* chamber and wept there. 31Then he washed his face and came out; and he restrained himself, and said, "Serve the bread."

32So they set him a place by himself, and them by themselves, and the Egyptians who ate with him by themselves; because the Egyptians could not eat food with the Hebrews, for that *is* an abomination to the Egyptians. 33And they sat before him, the firstborn according to his birthright and the youngest according to his youth; and the men looked in astonishment at one another. 34Then he took servings to them from before him, but Benjamin's serving was five times as much as any of theirs. So they drank and were merry with him.

Joseph's Cup

44 1And he commanded the steward of his house, saying, "Fill the men's sacks with food, as much as they can carry, and put each man's money in the mouth of his sack. 2Also put my cup, the silver cup, in the mouth of the sack of the youngest, and his grain money." So he did according to the word that Joseph had spoken. 3As soon as the morning dawned, the men were sent away, they and their donkeys. 4When they had gone out of the city, *and* were not

yet far off, Joseph said to his steward, "Get up, follow the men; and when you overtake them, say to them, 'Why have you repaid evil for good? 5*Is* not this *the one* from which my lord drinks, and with which he indeed practices divination? You have done evil in so doing.'"

6So he overtook them, and he spoke to them these same words. 7And they said to him, "Why does my lord say these words? Far be it from us that your servants should do such a thing. 8Look, we brought back to you from the land of Canaan the money which we found in the mouth of our sacks. How then could we steal silver or gold from your lord's house? 9With whomever of your servants it is found, let him die, and we also will be my lord's slaves."

10And he said, "Now also *let* it *be* according to your words; he with whom it is found shall be my slave, and you shall be blameless." 11Then each man speedily let down his sack to the ground, and each opened his sack. 12So he searched. He began with the oldest and left off with the youngest; and the cup was found in Benjamin's sack. 13Then they tore their clothes, and each man loaded his donkey and returned to the city.

14So Judah and his brothers came to Joseph's house, and he *was* still there; and they fell before him on the ground. 15And Joseph said to them, "What deed *is* this you have done? Did you not know that such a man as I can certainly practice divination?"

16Then Judah said, "What shall we say to my lord? What shall we speak? Or how shall we clear ourselves? God has found out the iniquity of your servants; here we are, my lord's slaves, both we and *he* also with whom the cup was found."

17But he said, "Far be it from me that I should do so; the man in whose hand the cup was found, he shall be my slave. And as for you, go up in peace to your father."

Judah Intercedes for Benjamin

18Then Judah came near to him and said: "O my lord, please let your servant speak a word in my lord's hearing, and do not let your anger burn against your servant; for you *are* even like Pharaoh. 19My lord asked his servants, saying, 'Have you a father or a brother?' 20And we said to my lord, 'We have a father, an old man, and a child of *his* old age, *who is* young; his brother is dead, and he alone is left of his mother's children, and his father loves him.' 21Then you said to your servants, 'Bring him down to me, that I may set my eyes on him.' 22And we said to my lord, 'The lad cannot leave his father, for *if* he should leave his father, *his father* would die.' 23But you said to your servants, 'Unless your youngest brother comes down with you, you shall see my face no more.'

24"So it was, when we went up to your servant my father, that we told him the words of my lord. 25And our father said, 'Go back *and* buy us a little food.' 26But we said, 'We cannot go down; if our youngest brother is with us, then we will go down; for we may not see the man's face unless our youngest brother *is* with us.' 27Then your servant my father said to us, 'You know that my wife bore me two sons; 28and the one went out from me, and I said, "Surely he is torn to pieces"; and I have not seen him since. 29But if you take this one also from me, and calamity befalls him, you shall bring down my gray hair with sorrow to the grave.'

30"Now therefore, when I come to your servant my father, and the lad *is* not with us, since his life is bound up in the lad's life, 31it will happen, when he sees that the lad *is* not *with us,* that he will die. So your servants will bring down the gray hair of your servant our father with sorrow to the grave. 32For your servant became surety for the lad to my father, saying, 'If I do not bring him *back* to you, then I shall bear the blame before my father forever.' 33Now therefore, please let your servant remain instead of the lad as a slave to my lord, and let the lad go up with his brothers. 34For how shall I go up to my father if the lad *is*

not with me, lest perhaps I see the evil that would come upon my father?"

Joseph Revealed to His Brothers

45 1Then Joseph could not restrain himself before all those who stood by him, and he cried out, "Make everyone go out from me!" So no one stood with him while Joseph made himself known to his brothers. 2And he wept aloud, and the Egyptians and the house of Pharaoh heard *it.*

3Then Joseph said to his brothers, "I *am* Joseph; does my father still live?" But his brothers could not answer him, for they were dismayed in his presence. 4And Joseph said to his brothers, "Please come near to me." So they came near. Then he said: "I *am* Joseph your brother, whom you sold into Egypt. 5But now, do not therefore be grieved or angry with yourselves because you sold me here; for God sent me before you to preserve life. 6For these two years the famine *has been* in the land, and *there are* still five years in which *there will be* neither plowing nor harvesting. 7And God sent me before you to preserve a posterity for you in the earth, and to save your lives by a great deliverance. 8So now *it was* not you *who* sent me here, but God; and He has made me a father to Pharaoh, and lord of all his house, and a ruler throughout all the land of Egypt.

9"Hurry and go up to my father, and say to him, 'Thus says your son Joseph: "God has made me lord of all Egypt; come down to me, do not tarry. 10You shall dwell in the land of Goshen, and you shall be near to me, you and your children, your children's children, your flocks and your herds, and all that you have. 11There I will provide for you, lest you and your household, and all that you have, come to poverty; for *there are* still five years of famine."'

12"And behold, your eyes and the eyes of my brother Benjamin see that *it is* my mouth that speaks to you. 13So you shall tell my father of all my glory in Egypt, and of all that you have seen; and you shall hurry and bring my father down here." 14Then he fell on his brother Benjamin's neck and wept, and Benjamin wept on his neck. 15Moreover he kissed all his brothers and wept over them, and after that his brothers talked with him.

16Now the report of it was heard in Pharaoh's house, saying, "Joseph's brothers

TIME CAPSULE	*1775 to 1700 B.C.*
1775	*Zimri-Lim regains control of Mari*
1760	*Hammurabi destroys palace at Mari*
1741– 1364	*Disunited, independent city-states in the region later called Assyria*
1728	*Ussher's date for the descent of Joseph into Egypt*
1705	*Jacob enters Egypt (based on late Exodus; Gen. 46:3)*
1700	*Phoenicians develop alphabet of consonants only*

have come." So it pleased Pharaoh and his servants well. [17]And Pharaoh said to Joseph, "Say to your brothers, 'Do this: Load your animals and depart; go to the land of Canaan. [18]Bring your father and your households and come to me; I will give you the best of the land of Egypt, and you will eat the fat of the land. [19]Now you are commanded—do this: Take carts out of the land of Egypt for your little ones and your wives; bring your father and come. [20]Also do not be concerned about your goods, for the best of all the land of Egypt is yours.'"

[21]Then the sons of Israel did so; and Joseph gave them carts, according to the command of Pharaoh, and he gave them provisions for the journey. [22]He gave to all of them, to each man, changes of garments; but to Benjamin he gave three hundred pieces of silver and five changes of garments. [23]And he sent to his father these things: ten donkeys loaded with the good things of Egypt, and ten female donkeys loaded with grain, bread, and food for his father for the journey. [24]So he sent his brothers away, and they departed; and he said to them, "See that you do not become troubled along the way."

[25]Then they went up out of Egypt, and came to the land of Canaan to Jacob their father. [26]And they told him, saying, "Joseph is still alive, and he is governor over all the land of Egypt." And Jacob's heart stood still, because he did not believe them. [27]But when they told him all the words which Joseph had said to them, and when he saw the carts which Joseph had sent to carry him, the spirit of Jacob their father revived. [28]Then Israel said, "It is enough. Joseph my son is still alive. I will go and see him before I die."

Jacob's Journey to Egypt

46 [1]So Israel took his journey with all that he had, and came to Beersheba, and offered sacrifices to the God of his father Isaac. [2]Then God spoke to Israel in the visions of the night, and said, "Jacob, Jacob!"

And he said, "Here I am."

[3]So He said, "I am God, the God of your father; do not fear to go down to Egypt, for I will make of you a great nation there. [4]I will go down with you to Egypt, and I will also surely bring you up again; and Joseph will put his hand on your eyes."

[5]Then Jacob arose from Beersheba;

and the sons of Israel carried their father Jacob, their little ones, and their wives, in the carts which Pharaoh had sent to carry him. [6]So they took their livestock and their goods, which they had acquired in the land of Canaan, and went to Egypt, Jacob and all his descendants with him. [7]His sons and his sons' sons, his daughters and his sons' daughters, and all his descendants he brought with him to Egypt.

[8]Now these were the names of the children of Israel, Jacob and his sons, who went to Egypt: Reuben was Jacob's firstborn. [9]The sons of Reuben were Hanoch, Pallu, Hezron, and Carmi. [10]The sons of Simeon were Jemuel,[a] Jamin, Ohad, Jachin,[b] Zohar,[c] and Shaul, the son of a Canaanite woman. [11]The sons of Levi were Gershon, Kohath, and Merari. [12]The sons of Judah were Er, Onan, Shelah, Perez, and Zerah (but Er and Onan died in the land of Canaan). The sons of Perez were Hezron and Hamul. [13]The sons of Issachar were Tola, Puvah,[a] Job,[b] and Shimron. [14]The sons of Zebulun were Sered, Elon, and Jahleel. [15]These were the sons of Leah, whom she bore to Jacob in Padan Aram, with his daughter Dinah. All the persons, his sons and his daughters, were thirty-three.

[16]The sons of Gad were Ziphion,[a] Haggi, Shuni, Ezbon,[b] Eri, Arodi,[c] and Areli. [17]The sons of Asher were Jimnah, Ishuah, Isui, Beriah, and Serah, their sister. And the sons of Beriah were Heber and Malchiel. [18]These were the sons of Zilpah, whom Laban gave to Leah his daughter; and these she bore to Jacob: sixteen persons.

[19]The sons of Rachel, Jacob's wife, were Joseph and Benjamin. [20]And to Joseph in the land of Egypt were born Manasseh and Ephraim, whom Asenath, the daughter of Poti-Pherah priest of On, bore to him. [21]The sons of Benjamin were Belah, Becher, Ashbel, Gera, Naaman, Ehi, Rosh, Muppim, Huppim,[a] and Ard. [22]These were the sons of Rachel, who were born to Jacob: fourteen persons in all.

46:10 [a]Spelled Nemuel in 1 Chronicles 4:24　[b]Called Jarib in 1 Chronicles 4:24　[c]Called Zerah in 1 Chronicles 4:24　46:13 [a]Spelled Puah in 1 Chronicles 7:1　[b]Same as Jashub in Numbers 26:24 and 1 Chronicles 7:1　46:16 [a]Spelled Zephon in Samaritan Pentateuch, Septuagint, and Numbers 26:15　[b]Called Ozni in Numbers 26:16　[c]Spelled Arod in Numbers 26:17　46:21 [a]Called Hupham in Numbers 26:39

²³The son of Dan *was* Hushim.ᵃ ²⁴The sons of Naphtali *were* Jahzeel,ᵃ Guni, Jezer, and Shillem.ᵇ ²⁵These *were* the sons of Bilhah, whom Laban gave to Rachel his daughter, and she bore these to Jacob: seven persons in all.

²⁶All the persons who went with Jacob to Egypt, who came from his body, besides Jacob's sons' wives, *were* sixty-six persons in all. ²⁷And the sons of Joseph who were born to him in Egypt *were* two persons. All the persons of the house of Jacob who went to Egypt were seventy.

Jacob Settles in Goshen

²⁸Then he sent Judah before him to Joseph, to point out before him *the way* to Goshen. And they came to the land of Goshen. ²⁹So Joseph made ready his chariot and went up to Goshen to meet his father Israel; and he presented himself to him, and fell on his neck and wept on his neck a good while.

³⁰And Israel said to Joseph, "Now let me die, since I have seen your face, because you *are* still alive."

³¹Then Joseph said to his brothers and to his father's household, "I will go up and tell Pharaoh, and say to him, 'My brothers and those of my father's house, who *were* in the land of Canaan, have come to me. ³²And the men *are* shepherds, for their occupation has been to feed livestock; and they have brought their flocks, their herds, and all that they have.' ³³So it shall be, when Pharaoh calls you and says, 'What is your occupation?' ³⁴that you shall say, 'Your servants' occupation has been with livestock from our youth even till now, both we *and* also our fathers,' that you may dwell in the land of Goshen; for every shepherd *is* an abomination to the Egyptians."

46:23 ᵃCalled *Shuham* in Numbers 26:42
46:24 ᵃSpelled *Jahziel* in 1 Chronicles 7:13   ᵇSpelled *Shallum* in 1 Chronicles 7:13

Jacob Enters Egypt

Jacob's journey from Canaan to Egypt is summarized in Gen. 47:27: "So Israel dwelt in the land of Egypt . . . and multiplied exceedingly." This event marks the move of the Israelite people from Canaan, the Promised Land, to Egypt, the land of slavery. As such, it became part of Israel's basic statement of faith. Israel's faith started with the retelling of her historical origins, often beginning with Jacob's descent to Egypt. For instance, the ritual retelling of Deut. 26:5–9 begins "My father was a Syrian, about to perish, and he went down to Egypt . . . ."

Jacob was 130 years old when he entered Egypt (Gen. 47:9). This figure is sometimes used to relate Abraham to the Israelite sojourn in Egypt. Abraham fathered Isaac when he was 100 years old (Gen. 21:5). Isaac fathered Jacob 60 years later (Gen. 25:26). Adding the numbers makes a passing of 290 years between Abraham's birth and this entry into Egypt (100 + 60 + 130 = 290).

▼ ■ Genesis 47:1—50:26

Genesis

47
:1 Then Joseph went and told Pharaoh, and said, "My father and my brothers, their flocks and their herds and all that they possess, have come from the land of Canaan; and indeed they *are* in the land of Goshen." ²And he took five men from among his brothers and presented them to Pharaoh. ³Then Pharaoh said to his brothers, "What *is* your occupation?"

And they said to Pharaoh, "Your servants *are* shepherds, both we *and* also our fathers." ⁴And they said to Pharaoh, "We have come to dwell in the land, because your servants have no pasture for their flocks, for the famine *is* severe in the land of Canaan. Now therefore, please let your servants dwell in the land of Goshen."

⁵Then Pharaoh spoke to Joseph, saying, "Your father and your brothers have come to you. ⁶The land of Egypt *is* before you. Have your father and brothers dwell in the best of the land; let them dwell in the land of Goshen. And if you know *any* competent men among them, then make them chief herdsmen over my livestock."

⁷Then Joseph brought in his father Jacob and set him before Pharaoh; and Jacob blessed Pharaoh. ⁸Pharaoh said to Jacob, "How old *are* you?"

⁹And Jacob said to Pharaoh, "The days of the years of my pilgrimage *are* one hundred and thirty years; few and evil have been the days of the years of my life, and they have not attained to the days of the years of the life of my fathers in the days of their pilgrimage." ¹⁰So Jacob blessed Pharaoh, and went out from before Pharaoh.

¹¹And Joseph situated his father and his brothers, and gave them a possession in the land of Egypt, in the best of the

BLESSED ARE THE BLESSED (Gen. 47:7, 10)

Bestowing a blessing on another was a common act in the ancient Near East. Inherent in the blessing process was the assumption, by both parties, that the one doing the blessing was superior to the one being blessed. Such superiority arose from a relationship to God, who was considered the source of the blessing. God occasionally gave a blessing directly (Gen. 2:3; 32:26).

To pronounce a blessing was not thought of as merely a ceremonial event. Rather the pronouncement was seen as actually conferring a specific change in status. Since the name and power of God was used, the blessing, once given, could not be retracted, even if bestowed by deceit. Once Isaac mistakenly pronounced the blessing for the firstborn son upon Jacob, his younger son (Gen. 27:27–29), he could not reverse the action in order to bless Esau, his firstborn (27:33–37).

A subordinate could also bless. Years later, Jacob, a foreigner in Egypt, blessed the pharaoh of Egypt. Since many died at a young age, old age was a sign that God's power resided with the one having a long life. Thus, Jacob, an old man, was superior to the younger pharaoh, who could benefit from Jacob's blessing him (Gen. 47:7, 10). Sometimes the Bible describes humans as "blessing" God (e.g., Ps. 34:1; 115:17, 18). In these cases "blessing God" probably conveys the idea of giving all that a human can rightfully give to God—praise.

land, in the land of Rameses, as Pharaoh had commanded. ¹²Then Joseph provided his father, his brothers, and all his father's household with bread, according to the number in *their* families.

Joseph Deals with the Famine

¹³Now *there was* no bread in all the land; for the famine *was* very severe, so that the land of Egypt and the land of Canaan languished because of the famine. ¹⁴And Joseph gathered up all the money that was found in the land of Egypt and in the land of Canaan, for the grain which they bought; and Joseph brought the money into Pharaoh's house. ¹⁵So when the money failed in the land of Egypt and in the land of Canaan, all the Egyptians came to Joseph and said, "Give us bread, for why should we die in your presence? For the money has failed." ¹⁶Then Joseph said, "Give your livestock, and I will give you *bread* for your livestock, if the money is gone." ¹⁷So they brought their livestock to Joseph, and Joseph gave them bread *in exchange* for the

horses, the flocks, the cattle of the herds, and for the donkeys. Thus he fed them with bread *in exchange* for all their livestock that year.

¹⁸When that year had ended, they came to him the next year and said to him, "We will not hide from my lord that our money is gone; my lord also has our herds of livestock. There is nothing left in the sight of my lord but our bodies and our lands. ¹⁹Why should we die before your eyes, both we and our land? Buy us and our land for bread, and we and our land will be servants of Pharaoh; give *us* seed, that we may live and not die, that the land may not be desolate."

²⁰Then Joseph bought all the land of Egypt for Pharaoh; for every man of the Egyptians sold his field, because the famine was severe upon them. So the land became Pharaoh's. ²¹And as for the people, he moved them into the cities,ᵃ from *one*

47:21 ᵃFollowing Masoretic Text and Targum; Samaritan Pentateuch, Septuagint, and Vulgate read *made the people virtual slaves.*

POLITICS AND GOVERNMENT

The Egyptian state supervised a bureaucracy capable of building pyramids and temples that required thousands of workers and years of effort. They kept meticulous records of commodities and of disbursements of food and drink to workers (Gen. 47:24). There were no coins, but they had standard-sized loaves of bread.

end of the borders of Egypt to the *other* end. ²²Only the land of the priests he did not buy; for the priests had rations *allotted to them* by Pharaoh, and they ate their rations which Pharaoh gave them; therefore they did not sell their lands.

²³Then Joseph said to the people, "Indeed I have bought you and your land this day for Pharaoh. Look, *here is* seed for you, and you shall sow the land. ²⁴And it shall come to pass in the harvest that you shall give one-fifth to Pharaoh. Four-fifths shall be your own, as seed for the field and for your food, for those of your households and as food for your little ones."

²⁵So they said, "You have saved our lives; let us find favor in the sight of my lord, and we will be Pharaoh's servants." ²⁶And Joseph made it a law over the land of Egypt to this day, *that* Pharaoh should have one-fifth, except for the land of the priests only, *which* did not become Pharaoh's.

Joseph's Vow to Jacob

²⁷So Israel dwelt in the land of Egypt, in the country of Goshen; and they had possessions there and grew and multiplied exceedingly. ²⁸And Jacob lived in the land of Egypt seventeen years. So the length of Jacob's life was one hundred and forty-seven years. ²⁹When the time drew near that Israel must die, he called his son Joseph and said to him, "Now if I have found favor in your sight, please put your hand under my thigh, and deal kindly and truly with me. Please do not bury me in Egypt, ³⁰but let me lie with my fathers; you shall carry me out of Egypt and bury me in their burial place."

And he said, "I will do as you have said."

³¹Then he said, "Swear to me." And he swore to him. So Israel bowed himself on the head of the bed.

Jacob Blesses Joseph's Sons

48 ¹Now it came to pass after these things that Joseph was told, "Indeed your father *is* sick"; and he took with him his two sons, Manasseh and Ephraim. ²And Jacob was told, "Look, your son Joseph is coming to you"; and Israel strengthened himself and sat up on the bed. ³Then Jacob said to Joseph: "God Almighty appeared to me at Luz in the land of Canaan and blessed me, ⁴and said to me, 'Behold, I will make you fruitful and multiply you,

and I will make of you a multitude of people, and give this land to your descendants after you *as* an everlasting possession.' ⁵And now your two sons, Ephraim and Manasseh, who were born to you in the land of Egypt before I came to you in Egypt, *are* mine; as Reuben and Simeon, they shall be mine. ⁶Your offspring whom you beget after them shall be yours; they will be called by the name of their brothers in their inheritance. ⁷But as for me, when I came from Padan, Rachel died beside me in the land of Canaan on the way, when *there was* but a little distance to go to Ephrath; and I buried her there on the way to Ephrath (that is, Bethlehem)."

⁸Then Israel saw Joseph's sons, and said, "Who *are* these?"

⁹Joseph said to his father, "They *are* my sons, whom God has given me in this *place.*"

And he said, "Please bring them to me, and I will bless them." ¹⁰Now the eyes of Israel were dim with age, *so that* he could not see. Then Joseph brought them near him, and he kissed them and embraced them. ¹¹And Israel said to Joseph, "I had not thought to see your face; but in fact, God has also shown me your offspring!"

¹²So Joseph brought them from beside his knees, and he bowed down with his face to the earth. ¹³And Joseph took them both, Ephraim with his right hand toward Israel's left hand, and Manasseh with his left hand toward Israel's right hand, and brought *them* near him. ¹⁴Then Israel stretched out his right hand and laid *it* on Ephraim's head, who *was* the younger, and his left hand on Manasseh's head, guiding his hands knowingly, for Manasseh *was* the firstborn. ¹⁵And he blessed Joseph, and said:

> "God, before whom my fathers
> Abraham and Isaac walked,
> The God who has fed me all my life
> long to this day,
> ¹⁶ The Angel who has redeemed me from
> all evil,
> Bless the lads;
> Let my name be named upon them,
> And the name of my fathers Abraham
> and Isaac;
> And let them grow into a multitude in
> the midst of the earth."

¹⁷Now when Joseph saw that his father laid his right hand on the head of

Ephraim, it displeased him; so he took hold of his father's hand to remove it from Ephraim's head to Manasseh's head. ¹⁸And Joseph said to his father, "Not so, my father, for this *one is* the firstborn; put your right hand on his head."

¹⁹But his father refused and said, "I know, my son, I know. He also shall become a people, and he also shall be great; but truly his younger brother shall be greater than he, and his descendants shall become a multitude of nations."

²⁰So he blessed them that day, saying, "By you Israel will bless, saying, 'May God make you as Ephraim and as Manasseh!'" And thus he set Ephraim before Manasseh.

²¹Then Israel said to Joseph, "Behold, I am dying, but God will be with you and bring you back to the land of your fathers. ²²Moreover I have given to you one portion above your brothers, which I took from the hand of the Amorite with my sword and my bow."

Jacob's Last Words to His Sons

49 ¹And Jacob called his sons and said, "Gather together, that I may tell you what shall befall you in the last days:

2   "Gather together and hear, you sons of Jacob,
    And listen to Israel your father.

3   "Reuben, you are my firstborn,
    My might and the beginning of my strength,
    The excellency of dignity and the excellency of power.
4   Unstable as water, you shall not excel,
    Because you went up to your father's bed;
    Then you defiled *it*—
    He went up to my couch.

5   "Simeon and Levi *are* brothers;
    Instruments of cruelty *are in* their dwelling place.
6   Let not my soul enter their council;
    Let not my honor be united to their assembly;
    For in their anger they slew a man,
    And in their self-will they hamstrung an ox.
7   Cursed *be* their anger, for *it is* fierce;
    And their wrath, for it is cruel!
    I will divide them in Jacob
    And scatter them in Israel.

8   "Judah, you *are he* whom your brothers shall praise;
    Your hand *shall be* on the neck of your enemies;
    Your father's children shall bow down before you.
9   Judah *is* a lion's whelp;
    From the prey, my son, you have gone up.
    He bows down, he lies down as a lion;
    And as a lion, who shall rouse him?
10   The scepter shall not depart from Judah,
    Nor a lawgiver from between his feet,
    Until Shiloh comes;
    And to Him *shall be* the obedience of the people.
11   Binding his donkey to the vine,
    And his donkey's colt to the choice vine,
    He washed his garments in wine,
    And his clothes in the blood of grapes.
12   His eyes *are* darker than wine,
    And his teeth whiter than milk.

13   "Zebulun shall dwell by the haven of the sea;
    He *shall become* a haven for ships,
    And his border shall adjoin Sidon.

14   "Issachar is a strong donkey,
    Lying down between two burdens;
15   He saw that rest *was* good,
    And that the land *was* pleasant;
    He bowed his shoulder to bear *a burden,*
    And became a band of slaves.

16   "Dan shall judge his people
    As one of the tribes of Israel.
17   Dan shall be a serpent by the way,
    A viper by the path,
    That bites the horse's heels
    So that its rider shall fall backward.
18   I have waited for your salvation,
    O Lord!

19   "Gad, a troop shall tramp upon him,
    But he shall triumph at last.

20   "Bread from Asher *shall be* rich,
    And he shall yield royal dainties.

21   "Naphtali *is* a deer let loose;
    He uses beautiful words.

22   "Joseph *is* a fruitful bough,
    A fruitful bough by a well;
    His branches run over the wall.

23 The archers have bitterly grieved him,
    Shot *at him* and hated him.
24 But his bow remained in strength,
    And the arms of his hands were made
      strong
    By the hands of the Mighty *God* of
      Jacob
    (From there *is* the Shepherd, the
      Stone of Israel),
25 By the God of your father who will
      help you,
    And by the Almighty who will bless
      you
    With blessings of heaven above,
    Blessings of the deep that lies
      beneath,
    Blessings of the breasts and of the
      womb.
26 The blessings of your father
    Have excelled the blessings of my
      ancestors,
    Up to the utmost bound of the
      everlasting hills.
    They shall be on the head of Joseph,
    And on the crown of the head of him
      who was separate from his brothers.

27 "Benjamin is a ravenous wolf;
    In the morning he shall devour the
      prey,
    And at night he shall divide the spoil."

28All these *are* the twelve tribes of Israel, and this *is* what their father spoke to them. And he blessed them; he blessed each one according to his own blessing.

Jacob's Death and Burial

29Then he charged them and said to them: "I am to be gathered to my people; bury me with my fathers in the cave that *is* in the field of Ephron the Hittite, 30in the cave that *is* in the field of Machpelah, which *is* before Mamre in the land of Canaan, which Abraham bought with the field of Ephron the Hittite as a possession for a burial place. 31There they buried Abraham and Sarah his wife, there they buried Isaac and Rebekah his wife, and there I buried Leah. 32The field and the cave that *is* there *were* purchased from the sons of Heth." 33And when Jacob had finished commanding his sons, he drew his feet up into the bed and breathed his last, and was gathered to his people.

50 1Then Joseph fell on his father's face and wept over him, and kissed him. 2And Joseph commanded his servants the physicians to embalm his father. So the physicians embalmed Israel. 3Forty days were required for him, for such are the days required for those who are embalmed; and the Egyptians mourned for him seventy days.

4Now when the days of his mourning were past, Joseph spoke to the household of Pharaoh, saying, "If now I have found favor in your eyes, please speak in the hearing of Pharaoh, saying, 5'My father made me swear, saying, "Behold, I am dying; in my grave which I dug for myself in the land of Canaan, there you shall bury me." Now therefore, please let me go up and bury my father, and I will come back.' "

6And Pharaoh said, "Go up and bury your father, as he made you swear."

7So Joseph went up to bury his father; and with him went up all the servants of Pharaoh, the elders of his house, and all the elders of the land of Egypt, 8as well as all the house of Joseph, his brothers, and his father's house. Only their little ones, their flocks, and their herds they left in the land of Goshen. 9And there went up with him both chariots and horsemen, and it was a very great gathering.

10Then they came to the threshing floor of Atad, which *is* beyond the Jordan, and they mourned there with a great and very solemn lamentation. He observed seven days of mourning for his father. 11And when the inhabitants of the land, the Canaanites, saw the mourning at the threshing floor of Atad, they said, "This *is* a deep mourning of the Egyptians." Therefore its name was called Abel Mizraim,[a] which *is* beyond the Jordan.

12So his sons did for him just as he had commanded them. 13For his sons carried him to the land of Canaan, and buried him in the cave of the field of Machpelah, before Mamre, which Abraham bought with the field from Ephron the Hittite as property for a burial place. 14And after he had buried his father, Joseph returned to Egypt, he and his brothers and all who went up with him to bury his father.

Joseph Reassures His Brothers

15When Joseph's brothers saw that their father was dead, they said, "Perhaps Joseph will hate us, and may actually repay us for all the evil which we did to him."

50:11 aLiterally *Mourning of Egypt*

16So they sent *messengers* to Joseph, saying, "Before your father died he commanded, saying, 17'Thus you shall say to Joseph: "I beg you, please forgive the trespass of your brothers and their sin; for they did evil to you." ' Now, please, forgive the trespass of the servants of the God of your father." And Joseph wept when they spoke to him.

18Then his brothers also went and fell down before his face, and they said, "Behold, we *are* your servants."

19Joseph said to them, "Do not be afraid, for *am* I in the place of God? 20But as for you, you meant evil against me; *but* God meant it for good, in order to bring it about as *it is* this day, to save many people alive. 21Now therefore, do not be afraid; I will provide for you and your little ones." And he comforted them and spoke kindly to them.

Death of Joseph

22So Joseph dwelt in Egypt, he and his father's household. And Joseph lived one hundred and ten years. 23Joseph saw Ephraim's children to the third *generation.* The children of Machir, the son of Manasseh, were also brought up on Joseph's knees.

24And Joseph said to his brethren, "I am dying; but God will surely visit you, and bring you out of this land to the land of which He swore to Abraham, to Isaac, and to Jacob." 25Then Joseph took an oath from the children of Israel, saying, "God will surely visit you, and you shall carry up my bones from here." 26So Joseph died, *being* one hundred and ten years old; and they embalmed him, and he was put in a coffin in Egypt.

BELIEFS AND IDEAS

Egyptian ideas about death and the afterlife emphasized preserving the dead body from decay (Gen. 50:26). The climate of Egypt is very dry, and the Egyptians were able to preserve bodies by drying them completely. This they did by burying them in natron, a naturally found combination of baking soda and sodium carbonate.

THE RISE OF A UNIFIED PEOPLE

(1500—1200 B.C.)

**God miraculously delivered His people from the hands
of the strongest nation of that day. These dramatic
events would forever be proof that the Israelites
were God's people.**

The Exodus marks the beginning of Israel as a people. The patriarchs were, at
most, an extended family, rather than a people. More such families undoubtedly
moved to Egypt either because of famine, or because of the migrations of peoples all
over the Middle East. When a dynasty of strong pharaohs returned to power, these
"foreigners" were oppressed and put to forced labor. The escape of a large band of
these slaves under the leadership of Moses was a new beginning for the Israelites.
Their experiences in the years of wandering in the wilderness—along with the great
covenant ceremony at Mount Sinai—began to mold them into both a distinct religious
entity and the nucleus of a nation. Their entry into Canaan and the struggle to maintain a separate identity in the face of cultural and religious temptations strengthened
their sense of being a people.

▶ Archaeology and the Past

The oldest written records of significance for Palestine come from the Late
Bronze Age (1500–1200 B.C.). The Amarna letters were part of the royal archive of
Amenhotep IV, also known as Akhenaten (1352–1336 B.C.). Akhenaten was more in-
terested in religious reform than in foreign policy. He abandoned Egyptian activity in
Palestine to pursue the introduction of monotheism, based on the worship of the sun
god, Aten.

Akhenaten's disinterest in administering the Egyptian empire resulted in turmoil and civil war in Palestine, and the Amarna letters reflect this disorder. Without
the stabilizing influence of the Egyptian military, the kings of the city-states were increasing their own power at the expense of their neighbors. There were also raids by
a people called the Habiru. Many of the Amarna letters appeal to the pharaoh for aid
against the incursions of these Habiru.

Other writings from the Late Bronze Age reflect a time of Egyptian power. An
inscription of Merenptah, who ruled Egypt from 1213 to 1203 B.C., includes the first
mention of Israel in Egyptian documents. Merenptah commemorates his victories
over the Libyans and other foreigners, boasting that all the peoples of Asia had submitted. One line reads, "Israel is laid waste, his seed is not."

▶ The Peoples and Groups

Early in this period, Egyptian armies marched through Palestine into Syria,
where they clashed with the Hurrians of Mitanni (in modern Iraq). The greatest political accomplishment of the Hurrians was the Mitanni Empire, which ruled Assyria
and lasted until the reign of Shalmaneser I of Assyria (1273–1244 B.C.). They were
even more important culturally, with their writings found from Assyria to Asia Minor
to Egypt.

Later in the Late Bronze Age, there were wars between Egyptians and the Hittites of Anatolia (modern Turkey). The Hittite Empire captured towns and regions, such as Ugarit and Amurru, from under Egypt's control. Hostilities with the Egyptians erupted again during the reign of Pharaoh Ramesses II (1279–1213 B.C.), who fought the Hittites to a stalemate in Syria and kept Palestine under Egyptian rule. Around 1200 B.C. the Hittite Empire collapsed, partly because of attacks by the "Sea Peoples" from the Aegean, and the rise of Assyria.

Two ethnic or political groups played roles in Israel's history during the Late Bronze Age—the Midianites and Canaanites. The Midianites lived in northwest Arabia, along the Gulf of Aqaba. They were shepherds but also copper miners and traders. Moses fled to the land of Midian, where he married into the family of Jethro, a priest of Midian (Ex. 18). Much later, a related tribe of Midianites were involved in the Israelite worship of Baal of Peor (Num. 25:16–18). The incident led to hostilities between Israel and Midian during the time of Moses (Num. 31:1–8).

The Canaanites were the inhabitants of Palestine west of the Jordan at the time of Joshua's invasion. They are first mentioned in an inscription of Amenhotep II (1427–1400 B.C.), and also in the Amarna letters. Originally, the term probably applied either to a Hurrian military aristocracy, or to a class of merchants. By the time of Joshua, the Canaanites were a mixed group of people. In the Old Testament the term "Canaanites" sometimes refers to all the people who lived west of Jordan. Other times the term is restricted to the Phoenicians who lived along the coast.

▶ The Biblical Literature

The biblical books of Exodus, Leviticus, Numbers, Deuteronomy, and Joshua relate the rise of the Israelites from slaves in Egypt to a unified people. The theme of these books is God's mighty acts on behalf of His people in the historical and political events of the Late Bronze Age. Though the focus of the biblical books is on God's activity, and the response of Israel to that activity, we still catch glimpses of the larger world of the Late Bronze Age.

> *The theme of these books is God's mighty acts on behalf of His people.*

Several pivotal events shaped Israel as a people. The Book of Exodus focuses on their escape from Egypt under the leadership of Moses and the making of the great covenant at Mount Sinai. The books of Leviticus and Numbers continue with the covenant, relating more divine instructions from Mount Sinai. Numbers also narrates the experiences the Israelites faced before coming to the Promised Land, most significantly the wilderness wanderings. Finally they were at the doorstep of Canaan. The Book of Deuteronomy is written as Moses' farewell speeches to the people of Israel. They would enter the land under a new generation of leaders, which is the story of the Book of Joshua.

Egypt and the Exodus

> The kings of this time were more expansionist than were previous Egyptian dynasties.

At last an Egyptian dynasty arose to expel the hated Hyksos rulers and begin the last great period of prosperity for ancient Egypt, the New Kingdom (c. 1550–1069 B.C.). Perhaps from a desire to keep all foreigners at bay, the kings of this time were more expansionist than were previous Egyptian dynasties. King Thutmose III (1479–1425 B.C.), for instance, expanded Egypt's boundaries through Palestine as far as the Euphrates River. These gains in Syria were soon challenged by an enemy from the north, the empire of the Hittites in Asia Minor.

One of Thutmose's descendants, Amenhotep IV (1352–1336 B.C.), is an especially remarkable New Kingdom ruler. Rejecting the many gods of Egyptian religion, this king worshiped one god, the sun god named Aten. He changed his own name to Akhenaten and built a new capital at Amarna. Letters found in the ruins of Amarna show that the city-states of Palestine were in varying degrees of rebellion during Akhenaten's reign. His religious reforms died when he did.

Another New Kingdom ruler, Ramesses II (1279–1213 B.C.), was especially notable for his many building projects. Egyptian sources suggest that Ramesses expanded the old Hyksos capital Avaris and renamed it "Raamses" after himself. The city became the royal residence for the 19th and 20th Dynasties. Ramesses reigned for more than 60 years, but his successors inherited a weaker Egypt and never equaled his glory.

The Book of Exodus

The Hebrews' exodus from bondage in Egypt is the defining event both in Israel's emergence as a nation and in the shape of that nation's faith. The Book of Exodus devotes about equal space to the events and to the ensuing covenant. The first half (chs. 1—19) tells the history, from Moses' birth through the Exodus itself up to Israel's climactic encounter with God on Mount Sinai. The second half of the book (chs. 20—40) consists mostly of God's instructions to His covenant people—both general, like the Ten Commandments, and specific, like the instructions for building the tabernacle, Israel's tent shrine.

It is no denial of the divine origin of this covenant to note how it is couched in the language and customs of its day. For instance, it is interesting to note that the covenant's emphasis on one God was preceded by the failed reforms of Akhenaten. Or again, the pattern for the giving of the covenant in Ex. 19—24 follows a very common Hittite treaty pattern, beginning with a prologue and continuing with a list of expectations (chs. 20—23), then concluding with a ratification ceremony (ch. 24).

■ Exodus 1:1—2:15

Exodus
Israel's Suffering in Egypt

1 :1 Now these *are* the names of the children of Israel who came to Egypt; each man and his household came with Jacob: ²Reuben, Simeon, Levi, and Judah; ³Issachar, Zebulun, and Benjamin; ⁴Dan, Naphtali, Gad, and Asher. ⁵All those who were descendants[a] of Jacob were seventy[b] persons (for Joseph was in Egypt *already*). ⁶And Joseph died, all his brothers, and all that generation. ⁷But the children of Israel were fruitful and increased abundantly, multiplied and grew exceedingly mighty; and the land was filled with them.

⁸Now there arose a new king over Egypt, who did not know Joseph. ⁹And he said to his people, "Look, the people of the children of Israel *are* more and mightier than we; ¹⁰come, let us deal shrewdly with them, lest they multiply, and it happen, in the event of war, that they also join our enemies and fight against us, and *so* go up out of the land." ¹¹Therefore they set taskmasters over them to afflict them with their burdens. And they built for Pharaoh supply cities, Pithom and Raamses. ¹²But the more they afflicted them, the more they multiplied and grew. And they were in dread of the children of Israel. ¹³So the Egyptians made the children of Israel serve with rigor. ¹⁴And they made their lives bitter with hard bondage—in mortar, in brick, and in all manner of service in the field. All their service in which they made them serve *was* with rigor.

¹⁵Then the king of Egypt spoke to the Hebrew midwives, of whom the name of one *was* Shiphrah and the name of the other Puah; ¹⁶and he said, "When you do the duties of a midwife for the Hebrew women, and see *them* on the birthstools, if it *is* a son, then you shall kill him; but if it *is* a daughter, then she shall live." ¹⁷But the midwives feared God, and did not do as the king of Egypt commanded them, but saved the male children alive. ¹⁸So the king of Egypt called for the midwives and said

1:5 ªLiterally *who came from the loins of* ᵇDead Sea Scrolls and Septuagint read *seventy-five* (compare Acts 7:14).

THE BIRTH OF SARGON (Ex. 2:1–10)

The birth story of Moses (Ex. 2:1–10) resembles a familiar theme in the ancient Near Eastern folklore: the exposure and rescue of an infant son, and his subsequent ascent to a position of royalty. One of the most famous versions of this theme is the birth legend of Sargon of Accad, a ruler in central Mesopotamia around 2350 B.C.

Although many legends of Sargon abound, the earliest record of these is from the late 8th century B.C. Some scholars maintain that the text was composed to commemorate the feats of a namesake of the Accadian Sargon—Sargon II of Assyria (721–705 B.C.).

According to the story, Sargon was born to a high priestess and an unknown father. Sargon's birth was kept secret, and his mother set him in a basket among bulrushes, where he was found by a drawer of water. From these humble beginnings, Sargon is said to have been granted the love of Ishtar, the goddess of love and war. The goddess's love is regarded as a token of Sargon's title to the throne. The apparent similarities between the Sargon and Moses birth accounts, though fascinating, are nevertheless superficial.

to them, "Why have you done this thing, and saved the male children alive?"

19And the midwives said to Pharaoh, "Because the Hebrew women *are* not like the Egyptian women; for they *are* lively and give birth before the midwives come to them."

20Therefore God dealt well with the midwives, and the people multiplied and grew very mighty. 21And so it was, because the midwives feared God, that He provided households for them.

22So Pharaoh commanded all his people, saying, "Every son who is born[a] you shall cast into the river, and every daughter you shall save alive."

Moses Is Born

2 1And a man of the house of Levi went and took *as wife* a daughter of Levi. 2So the woman conceived and bore a son. And when she saw that he *was* a beautiful *child,* she hid him three months. 3But when she could no longer hide him, she took an ark of bulrushes for him, daubed it with asphalt and pitch, put the child in it, and laid *it* in the reeds by the river's bank. 4And his sister stood afar off, to know what would be done to him.

5Then the daughter of Pharaoh came down to bathe at the river. And her maidens walked along the riverside; and when she saw the ark among the reeds, she sent her maid to get it. 6And when she opened *it,* she saw the child, and behold, the baby wept. So she had compassion on him, and said, "This is one of the Hebrews' children."

7Then his sister said to Pharaoh's daughter, "Shall I go and call a nurse for you from the Hebrew women, that she may nurse the child for you?"

8And Pharaoh's daughter said to her, "Go." So the maiden went and called the child's mother. 9Then Pharaoh's daughter said to her, "Take this child away and nurse him for me, and I will give *you* your wages." So the woman took the child and nursed him. 10And the child grew, and she brought him to Pharaoh's daughter, and he became her son. So she called his name Moses,[a] saying, "Because I drew him out of the water."

Moses Flees to Midian

11Now it came to pass in those days, when Moses was grown, that he went out

1:22 [a]Samaritan Pentateuch, Septuagint, and Targum add *to the Hebrews.*   2:10 [a]Literally *Drawn Out*

HEALTH AND MEDICINE

In traditional cultures births are usually attended only by women. A midwife is a woman with experience and training who can assist at births, recognize complications, and so forth. The most widespread practice, ancient and modern, is for mothers to deliver in a sitting position with a support like a birthstool (Ex. 1:16).

to his brethren and looked at their burdens. And he saw an Egyptian beating a Hebrew, one of his brethren. [12]So he looked this way and that way, and when he saw no one, he killed the Egyptian and hid him in the sand. [13]And when he went out the second day, behold, two Hebrew men were fighting, and he said to the one who did the wrong, "Why are you striking your companion?"

[14]Then he said, "Who made you a prince and a judge over us? Do you intend to kill me as you killed the Egyptian?"

So Moses feared and said, "Surely this thing is known!" [15]When Pharaoh heard of this matter, he sought to kill Moses. But Moses fled from the face of Pharaoh and dwelt in the land of Midian; and he sat down by a well.

Moses in Midian

Within the official boundaries of the Egyptian empire, in Palestine and the arid Sinai Peninsula, lived a diverse group called the Midianites. These people appeared sometime around the 13th century B.C. and were known as traders (cf. Gen. 37:36) and metalworkers. Less clearly known is their religion, but there is some evidence that they worshiped in tent shrines in the desert. The tabernacle that Moses was commanded to build (Ex. 26) may be related to Midianite practices. Moses' father-in-law Reuel (Ex. 2:18) was, after all, a priest of Midian. Elsewhere the names Jethro (Ex. 3:1) and Hobab (Judg. 4:11) are also given for the father-in-law of Moses.

▼　■ Exodus 2:16—6:30

Exodus

2 :16 Now the priest of Midian had seven daughters. And they came and drew water, and they filled the troughs to water their father's flock. [17]Then the shepherds came and drove them away; but Moses stood up and helped them, and watered their flock.

[18]When they came to Reuel their father, he said, "How *is it that* you have come so soon today?"

[19]And they said, "An Egyptian delivered us from the hand of the shepherds, and he also drew enough water for us and watered the flock."

[20]So he said to his daughters, "And where *is* he? Why *is* it *that* you have left the man? Call him, that he may eat bread."

[21]Then Moses was content to live with the man, and he gave Zipporah his daughter to Moses. [22]And she bore *him* a son. He called his name Gershom,[a] for he said, "I have been a stranger in a foreign land."

[23]Now it happened in the process of time that the king of Egypt died. Then the children of Israel groaned because of the bondage, and they cried out; and their cry came up to God because of the bondage. [24]So God heard their groaning, and God remembered His covenant with Abraham, with Isaac, and with Jacob. [25]And God looked upon the children of Israel, and God acknowledged *them.*

Moses at the Burning Bush

3 [1]Now Moses was tending the flock of Jethro his father-in-law, the priest of Midian. And he led the flock to the back of the desert, and came to Horeb, the mountain of God. [2]And the Angel of the LORD appeared to him in a flame of fire from the midst of a bush. So he looked, and behold, the bush was burning with fire, but the bush *was* not consumed. [3]Then Moses said, "I will now turn aside and see this great sight, why the bush does not burn."

[4]So when the LORD saw that he turned aside to look, God called to him from the midst of the bush and said, "Moses, Moses!"

And he said, "Here I am."

[5]Then He said, "Do not draw near this place. Take your sandals off your feet, for the place where you stand *is* holy ground." [6]Moreover He said, "I *am* the God of your father—the God of Abraham, the God of Isaac, and the God of Jacob." And Moses hid his face, for he was afraid to look upon God.

[7]And the LORD said: "I have surely seen the oppression of My people who *are* in Egypt, and have heard their cry because of their taskmasters, for I know their sorrows. [8]So I have come down to deliver them out of the hand of the Egyptians, and to bring them up from that land to a good and large land, to a land flowing with milk and honey, to the place of the Canaanites and the Hittites and the Amorites and the Perizzites and the Hivites and the Jebusites. [9]Now therefore, behold, the cry of the children of Israel has come to Me, and I have also seen the oppression with which the Egyptians oppress them. [10]Come now, therefore, and I will send you to Pharaoh

2:22 [a]Literally *Stranger There*

that you may bring My people, the children of Israel, out of Egypt."

11But Moses said to God, "Who *am* I that I should go to Pharaoh, and that I should bring the children of Israel out of Egypt?"

12So He said, "I will certainly be with you. And this *shall be* a sign to you that I have sent you: When you have brought the people out of Egypt, you shall serve God on this mountain."

13Then Moses said to God, "Indeed, *when* I come to the children of Israel and say to them, 'The God of your fathers has sent me to you,' and they say to me, 'What *is* His name?' what shall I say to them?"

14And God said to Moses, "I AM WHO I AM." And He said, "Thus you shall say to the children of Israel, 'I AM has sent me to you.' " 15Moreover God said to Moses, "Thus you shall say to the children of Israel: 'The LORD God of your fathers, the God of Abraham, the God of Isaac, and the God of Jacob, has sent me to you. This *is* My name forever, and this *is* My memorial to all generations.' 16Go and gather the elders of Israel together, and say to them, 'The LORD God of your fathers, the God of Abraham, of Isaac, and of Jacob, appeared to me, saying, "I have surely visited you and *seen* what is done to you in Egypt; 17and I have said I will bring you up out of the affliction of Egypt to the land of the Canaanites and the Hittites and the Amorites and the Perizzites and the Hivites and the Jebusites, to a land flowing with milk and honey." ' 18Then they will heed your voice; and you shall come, you and the elders of Israel, to the king of Egypt; and you shall say to him, 'The LORD God of the Hebrews has met with us; and now, please, let us go three days' journey into the wilderness, that we may sacrifice to the LORD our God.' 19But I am sure that the king of Egypt will not let you go, no, not even by a mighty hand. 20So I will stretch out My hand and strike Egypt with all My wonders which I will do in its midst; and after that he will let you go. 21And I will give this people favor in the sight of the Egyptians; and it shall be, when you go, that you shall not go empty-handed. 22But every woman shall ask of her neighbor, namely, of her who dwells near her house, articles of silver, articles of gold, and clothing; and you shall put *them* on your sons and on your daughters. So you shall plunder the Egyptians."

Miraculous Signs for Pharaoh

4 1Then Moses answered and said, "But suppose they will not believe me or listen to my voice; suppose they say, 'The LORD has not appeared to you.' "

2So the LORD said to him, "What *is* that in your hand?"

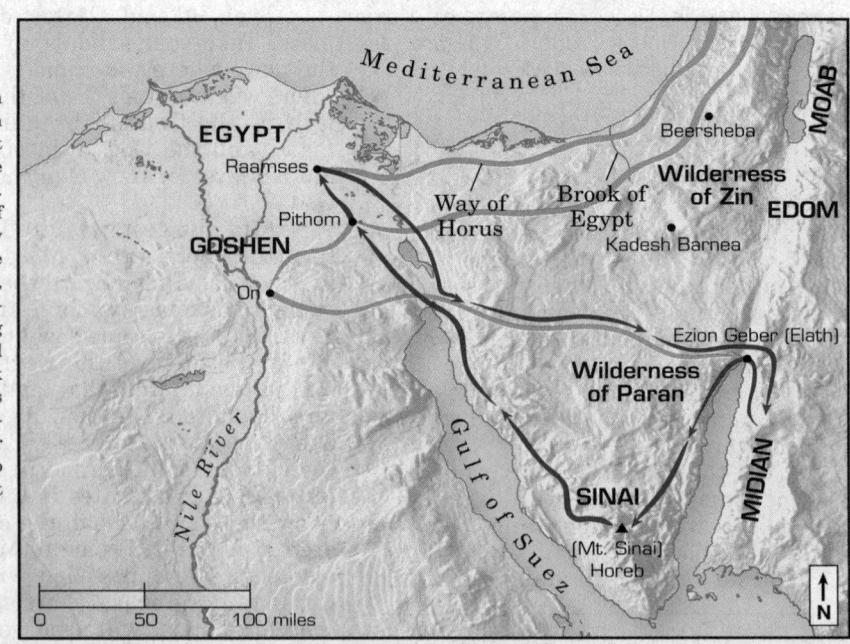

Moses' Flight and Return to Egypt

Moses fled from Pharaoh through the Sinai desert and settled in the land of Midian. In the vicinity of Horeb, located by tradition in the Sinai Peninsula, God revealed Himself in the burning bush and called Moses to go back to Egypt. Moses met Aaron at Horeb, and together they returned to Pharaoh's court in Raamses.

ENMERKAR AND THE HEAVY MOUTH (Ex. 4:10–16)

Among the objections Moses raised against his going to Pharaoh (Ex. 3:11) was that he considered himself "slow of speech and slow of tongue" (Ex. 4:10). In the Hebrew language this condition is expressed literally as "heavy of mouth" and "heavy of tongue." Moses' difficulties in speech are not unprecedented in ancient Near Eastern literature.

Enmerkar, the Sumerian king of Uruk and third successor to the famous Gilgamesh, is the main character of *Enmerkar and the Lord of Aratta,* an epic written in Sumerian near the end of the 3rd millennium B.C. In the brief passage, a messenger is unable to comprehend a message given to him by Enmerkar, and thus unable to verbally deliver it. Like Moses, Enmerkar was "slow in speech," expressed in the epic as "heavy of mouth." Therefore, the king of Uruk invented writing by putting the message on a piece of clay.

This epic seems to explain the origin of writing, implying that writing did not exist before Enmerkar (c. 2700–2500 B.C.). In actuality, writing preceded Enmerkar by at least 500 years.

He said, "A rod."

³And He said, "Cast it on the ground." So he cast it on the ground, and it became a serpent; and Moses fled from it. ⁴Then the LORD said to Moses, "Reach out your hand and take *it* by the tail" (and he reached out his hand and caught it, and it became a rod in his hand), ⁵"that they may believe that the LORD God of their fathers, the God of Abraham, the God of Isaac, and the God of Jacob, has appeared to you."

⁶Furthermore the LORD said to him, "Now put your hand in your bosom." And he put his hand in his bosom, and when he took it out, behold, his hand *was* leprous, like snow. ⁷And He said, "Put your hand in your bosom again." So he put his hand in his bosom again, and drew it out of his bosom, and behold, it was restored like his *other* flesh. ⁸"Then it will be, if they do not believe you, nor heed the message of the first sign, that they may believe the message of the latter sign. ⁹And it shall be, if they do not believe even these two signs, or listen to your voice, that you shall take water from the river[a] and pour *it* on the dry *land.* The water which you take from the river will become blood on the dry *land.*"

¹⁰Then Moses said to the LORD, "O my Lord, I *am* not eloquent, neither before nor since You have spoken to Your servant; but I *am* slow of speech and slow of tongue."

¹¹So the LORD said to him, "Who has made man's mouth? Or who makes the mute, the deaf, the seeing, or the blind? *Have* not I, the LORD? ¹²Now therefore, go, and I will be with your mouth and teach you what you shall say."

¹³But he said, "O my Lord, please send by the hand of whomever *else* You may send."

¹⁴So the anger of the LORD was kindled against Moses, and He said: "Is not Aaron the Levite your brother? I know that he can speak well. And look, he is also coming out to meet you. When he sees you, he will be glad in his heart. ¹⁵Now you shall speak to him and put the words in his mouth. And I will be with your mouth and with his mouth, and I will teach you what you shall do. ¹⁶So he shall be your spokesman to the people. And he himself shall be as a mouth for you, and you shall be to him as God. ¹⁷And you shall take this rod in your hand, with which you shall do the signs."

Moses Goes to Egypt

¹⁸So Moses went and returned to Jethro his father-in-law, and said to him, "Please let me go and return to my brethren who *are* in Egypt, and see whether they are still alive."

And Jethro said to Moses, "Go in peace."

¹⁹Now the LORD said to Moses in Midian, "Go, return to Egypt; for all the men who sought your life are dead." ²⁰Then Moses took his wife and his sons and set them on a donkey, and he returned to the land of Egypt. And Moses took the rod of God in his hand.

²¹And the LORD said to Moses, "When you go back to Egypt, see that you do all those wonders before Pharaoh which I

4:9 ᵃThat is, the Nile

EGYPT AND THE NEW KINGDOM

The Egyptian priest Manetho (c. 305–285 B.C.) describes the destructive invasion of Egypt by the Hyksos people, who seized control of Egypt and made Avaris, in the Delta region, their new capital.

Second Intermediate Period	The Dynasties
1786–1550 B.C.	13th–17th Dynasties. The weakening of the 13th Dynasty (1786–1633 B.C.) began a period in which rival dynasties vied for power.
1786–1602 B.C.	In the Delta several rulers proclaimed themselves "kings," representing the 14th Dynasty.
1648–1540 B.C.	The Hyksos dynasty controlled only Lower Egypt, while the kings of the Upper Nile Valley stood firm in their own local domains.
The New Kingdom	**The Dynasties**
1550–1069 B.C.	18th–20th Dynasties. The Egyptian kings Kamose and Ahmose I expelled the Hyksos from Egypt, beginning Egypt's "New Kingdom."
1550–1295 B.C.	18th Dynasty. Amenhotep I named himself after the god Amen or Amon. This universal god was linked with the sun god Re, and worshiped as Amon-Re.
1295–1186 B.C.	19th Dynasty. Seti I began new wars of conquest that pushed Egypt into Palestine, driving back the Hittites.
1186–1069 B.C.	20th Dynasty. Ramesses III fought off invasions by the Sea Peoples.

have put in your hand. But I will harden his heart, so that he will not let the people go. 22Then you shall say to Pharaoh, 'Thus says the LORD: "Israel *is* My son, My firstborn. 23So I say to you, let My son go that he may serve Me. But if you refuse to let him go, indeed I will kill your son, your firstborn." ' "

24And it came to pass on the way, at the encampment, that the LORD met him and sought to kill him. 25Then Zipporah took a sharp stone and cut off the foreskin of her son and cast *it* at *Moses'*[a] feet, and said, "Surely you *are* a husband of blood to me!" 26So He let him go. Then she said, "*You are* a husband of blood!"—because of the circumcision.

27And the LORD said to Aaron, "Go into the wilderness to meet Moses." So he went and met him on the mountain of God, and kissed him. 28So Moses told Aaron all the words of the LORD who had sent him, and all the signs which He had commanded him. 29Then Moses and Aaron went and gathered together all the elders of the children of Israel. 30And Aaron spoke all the words which the LORD had spoken to Moses. Then he did the signs in the sight of the people. 31So the people believed; and when they heard that the LORD had visited the children of Israel and that He had looked on their affliction, then they bowed their heads and worshiped.

First Encounter with Pharaoh

5 1Afterward Moses and Aaron went in and told Pharaoh, "Thus says the LORD God of Israel: 'Let My people go, that they may hold a feast to Me in the wilderness.' "

2And Pharaoh said, "Who *is* the LORD,

4:25 [a]Literally *his*

RELIGION AND WORSHIP

Animal sacrifice was practiced in all ancient cultures. It is a ritual killing of an animal as a part of religion (Ex. 5:3). Apparently the animal's moment of death and shedding of blood impressed on human beings that they were responsible to forces outside themselves. The Egyptians did not question the need to perform sacrifices.

that I should obey His voice to let Israel go? I do not know the LORD, nor will I let Israel go."

3So they said, "The God of the Hebrews has met with us. Please, let us go three days' journey into the desert and sacrifice to the LORD our God, lest He fall upon us with pestilence or with the sword."

4Then the king of Egypt said to them, "Moses and Aaron, why do you take the people from their work? Get *back* to your labor." 5And Pharaoh said, "Look, the people of the land *are* many now, and you make them rest from their labor!"

6So the same day Pharaoh commanded the taskmasters of the people and their officers, saying, 7"You shall no longer give the people straw to make brick as before. Let them go and gather straw for themselves. 8And you shall lay on them the quota of bricks which they made before. You shall not reduce it. For they are idle; therefore they cry out, saying, 'Let us go *and* sacrifice to our God.' 9Let more work be laid on the men, that they may labor in it, and let them not regard false words."

10And the taskmasters of the people and their officers went out and spoke to the people, saying, "Thus says Pharaoh: 'I will not give you straw. 11Go, get yourselves straw where you can find it; yet none of your work will be reduced.' " 12So the people were scattered abroad throughout all the land of Egypt to gather stubble instead of straw. 13And the taskmasters forced *them* to hurry, saying, "Fulfill your work, *your* daily quota, as when there was straw." 14Also the officers of the children of Israel, whom Pharaoh's taskmasters had set over them, were beaten *and* were asked, "Why have you not fulfilled your task in making brick both yesterday and today, as before?"

15Then the officers of the children of Israel came and cried out to Pharaoh, saying, "Why are you dealing thus with your servants? 16There is no straw given to your servants, and they say to us, 'Make brick!' And indeed your servants *are* beaten, but the fault *is* in your *own* people."

17But he said, "You *are* idle! Idle! Therefore you say, 'Let us go *and* sacrifice to the LORD.' 18Therefore go now *and* work; for no straw shall be given you, yet you shall deliver the quota of bricks." 19And the officers of the children of Israel saw *that*

they *were* in trouble after it was said, "You shall not reduce *any* bricks from your daily quota."

20Then, as they came out from Pharaoh, they met Moses and Aaron who stood there to meet them. 21And they said to them, "Let the LORD look on you and judge, because you have made us abhorrent in the sight of Pharaoh and in the sight of his servants, to put a sword in their hand to kill us."

Israel's Deliverance Assured

22So Moses returned to the LORD and said, "Lord, why have You brought trouble on this people? Why *is* it You have sent me? 23For since I came to Pharaoh to speak in Your name, he has done evil to this people; neither have You delivered Your people at all."

6 1Then the LORD said to Moses, "Now you shall see what I will do to Pharaoh. For with a strong hand he will let them go, and with a strong hand he will drive them out of his land."

2And God spoke to Moses and said to him: "I *am* the LORD. 3I appeared to Abraham, to Isaac, and to Jacob, as God Almighty, but *by* My name LORDa I was not known to them. 4I have also established My covenant with them, to give them the land of Canaan, the land of their pilgrimage, in which they were strangers. 5And I have also heard the groaning of the children of Israel whom the Egyptians keep in bondage, and I have remembered My covenant. 6Therefore say to the children of Israel: 'I *am* the LORD; I will bring you out from under the burdens of the Egyptians, I will rescue you from their bondage, and I

TIME CAPSULE	*1660 to 1633 B.C.*
1660	Horse in use in Nubia (southern Egypt)
1650	Hattusilis I makes Hattusa the Hittite capital
1648– 1540	The Hyksos dynasty controls Lower Egypt
1646– 1626	Ammisaduqa, king of Babylon
1634	Hittite king Hattusilis I destroys Alalakh
1633– 1550	Egypt's 17th Dynasty rules at Thebes

6:3 aHebrew YHWH, traditionally Jehovah

will redeem you with an outstretched arm and with great judgments. ⁷I will take you as My people, and I will be your God. Then you shall know that I *am* the LORD your God who brings you out from under the burdens of the Egyptians. ⁸And I will bring you into the land which I swore to give to Abraham, Isaac, and Jacob; and I will give it to you *as* a heritage: I *am* the LORD.' " ⁹So Moses spoke thus to the children of Israel; but they did not heed Moses, because of anguish of spirit and cruel bondage.

¹⁰And the LORD spoke to Moses, saying, ¹¹"Go in, tell Pharaoh king of Egypt to let the children of Israel go out of his land."

¹²And Moses spoke before the LORD, saying, "The children of Israel have not heeded me. How then shall Pharaoh heed me, for I *am* of uncircumcised lips?"

¹³Then the LORD spoke to Moses and Aaron, and gave them a command for the children of Israel and for Pharaoh king of Egypt, to bring the children of Israel out of the land of Egypt.

The Family of Moses and Aaron

¹⁴These *are* the heads of their fathers' houses: The sons of Reuben, the firstborn of Israel, *were* Hanoch, Pallu, Hezron, and Carmi. These are the families of Reuben. ¹⁵And the sons of Simeon *were* Jemuel,ᵃ Jamin, Ohad, Jachin, Zohar, and Shaul the son of a Canaanite woman. These *are* the families of Simeon. ¹⁶These *are* the names of the sons of Levi according to their generations: Gershon, Kohath, and Merari. And the years of the life of Levi *were* one hundred and thirty-seven. ¹⁷The sons of Gershon *were* Libni and Shimi according to their families. ¹⁸And the sons of Kohath *were* Amram, Izhar, Hebron, and Uzziel. And the years of the life of Kohath *were* one hundred and thirty-three. ¹⁹The sons of Merari *were* Mahli and Mushi. These *are* the families of Levi according to their generations.

²⁰Now Amram took for himself Jochebed, his father's sister, as wife; and she bore him Aaron and Moses. And the years of the life of Amram *were* one hundred and thirty-seven. ²¹The sons of Izhar *were* Korah, Nepheg, and Zichri. ²²And the sons of Uzziel *were* Mishael, Elzaphan, and Zithri. ²³Aaron took to himself Elisheba, daughter of Amminadab, sister of Nahshon, as wife; and she bore him Nadab, Abihu, Eleazar, and Ithamar. ²⁴And the sons of Korah *were* Assir, Elkanah, and

Abiasaph. These are the families of the Korahites. ²⁵Eleazar, Aaron's son, took for himself one of the daughters of Putiel as wife; and she bore him Phinehas. These *are* the heads of the fathers' houses of the Levites according to their families.

²⁶These *are the same* Aaron and Moses to whom the LORD said, "Bring out the children of Israel from the land of Egypt according to their armies." ²⁷These *are* the ones who spoke to Pharaoh king of Egypt, to bring out the children of Israel from Egypt. These *are the same* Moses and Aaron.

Aaron Is Moses' Spokesman

²⁸And it came to pass, on the day the LORD spoke to Moses in the land of Egypt, ²⁹that the LORD spoke to Moses, saying, "I *am* the LORD. Speak to Pharaoh king of Egypt all that I say to you."

³⁰But Moses said before the LORD, "Behold, I *am* of uncircumcised lips, and how shall Pharaoh heed me?"

6:15 ᵃSpelled *Nemuel* in Numbers 26:12

From Egypt to Midian to Egypt

The life of Moses is viewed by tradition in three periods: early life in Egypt; sojourn in Midian; appearance before Pharaoh in Egypt. The ages recorded for Moses in different biblical passages make each of the three periods to be 40 years long.

The first period, beginning with Moses' birth, ended abruptly when he was forced to flee Egypt. The Book of Exodus defines this time only as "when Moses was grown" (Ex. 2:11). However, Stephen's sermonic survey of Israel's history makes Moses "forty years old" at this time (Acts 7:23).

The second period, during which Moses found refuge in Midian, ended with Moses' return to Egypt, accompanied by Aaron. The Book of Exodus reports Moses to have been 80 years old when he and 83-year-old Aaron first approached Pharaoh (Ex. 7:7). Stephen's sermon agrees, placing the burning bush experience 40 years after Moses fled to Midian.

The last period of Moses' life ends, of course, with his death. That Moses was 80 when he stood before Pharaoh is consistent both with his age of 120 when he died (Deut. 34:7) and with the 40 years of wandering in the wilderness (Num. 14:33–35).

■ Exodus 7:1—12:36

DUELING DEITIES: MAGIC AND MAGICIANS IN EGYPT (Ex. 7:11)

Throughout the ancient Near East magicians were important members of royal courts. Magic was a means by which power could be transferred from the gods to humans. Magicians were well-educated, literate persons, who had studied the incantations and actions that were needed to cause gods or demons to honor human requests. Their official services were needed for understanding the will of the gods, bringing down curses on treaty-breakers, or creating catastrophes for enemies.

Egypt's magical traditions are the best known to us of all the traditions of the ancient world. This is partly because other civilizations were impressed by the Egyptian traditions, but mostly because a wealth of their magical texts have survived in the desert. The Egyptian magical texts extend in time from the Pyramid Texts (3rd millennium B.C.) to the end of the Roman Empire, and include incantations, amulets, secret signs, certain geometric shapes, acrostic word patterns, and the names of famous persons.

In Exodus, Moses is presented as directing the plagues in the same manner as the Egyptians understood their magic to work. Through the miracles Moses conveyed the power of his God. The Egyptian magicians, however, were engaged in the same enterprise. When they turned rods into snakes, water into blood, or called frogs out of the Nile, they believed it was the power of their gods working through them (Ex. 7:10, 11).

Pharaoh's magicians were unimpressed with Moses and his God as long as they were able to do the same tricks through their magical arts. But when they could not produce gnats, the Egyptians expressed their admiration for Moses with the words "This is the finger of God" (Ex. 8:18, 19), which quotes an actual Egyptian magical phrase. In this way they acknowledged that Moses' God was greater than their gods.

Exodus

7 :1 So the LORD said to Moses: "See, I have made you *as* God to Pharaoh, and Aaron your brother shall be your prophet. ²You shall speak all that I command you. And Aaron your brother shall tell Pharaoh to send the children of Israel out of his land. ³And I will harden Pharaoh's heart, and multiply My signs and My wonders in the land of Egypt. ⁴But Pharaoh will not heed you, so that I may lay My hand on Egypt and bring My armies *and* My people, the children of Israel, out of the land of Egypt by great judgments. ⁵And the Egyptians shall know that I *am* the LORD, when I stretch out My hand on Egypt and bring out the children of Israel from among them."

⁶Then Moses and Aaron did *so;* just as the LORD commanded them, so they did. ⁷And Moses *was* eighty years old and Aaron eighty-three years old when they spoke to Pharaoh.

Aaron's Miraculous Rod

⁸Then the LORD spoke to Moses and Aaron, saying, ⁹"When Pharaoh speaks to you, saying, 'Show a miracle for yourselves,' then you shall say to Aaron, 'Take your rod and cast *it* before Pharaoh, *and* let it become a serpent.'" ¹⁰So Moses and Aaron went in to Pharaoh, and they did so, just as the LORD commanded. And Aaron cast down his rod before Pharaoh and before his servants, and it became a serpent. ¹¹But Pharaoh also called the wise men and the sorcerers; so the magicians of Egypt, they also did in like manner with their enchantments. ¹²For every man threw down his rod, and they became serpents. But Aaron's rod swallowed up their rods. ¹³And Pharaoh's heart grew hard, and he did not heed them, as the LORD had said.

The First Plague: Waters Become Blood

¹⁴So the LORD said to Moses: "Pharaoh's heart *is* hard; he refuses to let the people go. ¹⁵Go to Pharaoh in the morning, when he goes out to the water, and you shall stand by the river's bank to meet him; and the rod which was turned to a serpent you shall take in your hand. ¹⁶And you shall say to him, 'The LORD God of the Hebrews has sent me to you, saying, "Let My people go, that they may serve Me in the wilderness"; but indeed, until now you

would not hear! ¹⁷Thus says the LORD: "By this you shall know that I *am* the LORD. Behold, I will strike the waters which *are* in the river with the rod that *is* in my hand, and they shall be turned to blood. ¹⁸And the fish that *are* in the river shall die, the river shall stink, and the Egyptians will loathe to drink the water of the river." ' "

¹⁹Then the LORD spoke to Moses, "Say to Aaron, 'Take your rod and stretch out your hand over the waters of Egypt, over their streams, over their rivers, over their ponds, and over all their pools of water, that they may become blood. And there shall be blood throughout all the land of Egypt, both in *buckets of* wood and *pitchers of* stone.' " ²⁰And Moses and Aaron did so, just as the LORD commanded. So he lifted up the rod and struck the waters that *were* in the river, in the sight of Pharaoh and in the sight of his servants. And all the waters that *were* in the river were turned to blood. ²¹The fish that *were* in the river died, the river stank, and the Egyptians could not drink the water of the river. So there was blood throughout all the land of Egypt.

²²Then the magicians of Egypt did so with their enchantments; and Pharaoh's heart grew hard, and he did not heed them, as the LORD had said. ²³And Pharaoh turned and went into his house. Neither was his heart moved by this. ²⁴So all the Egyptians dug all around the river for water to drink, because they could not drink the water of the river. ²⁵And seven days passed after the LORD had struck the river.

The Second Plague: Frogs

8 ¹And the LORD spoke to Moses, "Go to Pharaoh and say to him, 'Thus says the LORD: "Let My people go, that they may serve Me. ²But if you refuse to let *them* go, behold, I will smite all your territory with frogs. ³So the river shall bring forth frogs abundantly, which shall go up and come into your house, into your bedroom, on your bed, into the houses of your servants, on your people, into your ovens, and into your kneading bowls. ⁴And the frogs shall come up on you, on your people, and on all your servants." ' "

⁵Then the LORD spoke to Moses, "Say to Aaron, 'Stretch out your hand with your rod over the streams, over the rivers, and over the ponds, and cause frogs to come up on the land of Egypt.' " ⁶So Aaron stretched

out his hand over the waters of Egypt, and the frogs came up and covered the land of Egypt. ⁷And the magicians did so with their enchantments, and brought up frogs on the land of Egypt.

⁸Then Pharaoh called for Moses and Aaron, and said, "Entreat the LORD that He may take away the frogs from me and from my people; and I will let the people go, that they may sacrifice to the LORD."

⁹And Moses said to Pharaoh, "Accept the honor of saying when I shall intercede for you, for your servants, and for your people, to destroy the frogs from you and your houses, *that* they may remain in the river only."

¹⁰So he said, "Tomorrow." And he said, "*Let it be* according to your word, that you may know that *there is* no one like the LORD our God. ¹¹And the frogs shall depart from you, from your houses, from your servants, and from your people. They shall remain in the river only."

¹²Then Moses and Aaron went out from Pharaoh. And Moses cried out to the LORD concerning the frogs which He had brought against Pharaoh. ¹³So the LORD did according to the word of Moses. And the frogs died out of the houses, out of the courtyards, and out of the fields. ¹⁴They gathered them together in heaps, and the land stank. ¹⁵But when Pharaoh saw that there was relief, he hardened his heart and did not heed them, as the LORD had said.

The Third Plague: Lice

¹⁶So the LORD said to Moses, "Say to Aaron, 'Stretch out your rod, and strike the dust of the land, so that it may become lice throughout all the land of Egypt.' " ¹⁷And they did so. For Aaron stretched out his hand with his rod and struck the dust of the earth, and it became lice on man and beast. All the dust of the land became lice throughout all the land of Egypt.

¹⁸Now the magicians so worked with their enchantments to bring forth lice, but they could not. So there were lice on man and beast. ¹⁹Then the magicians said to Pharaoh, "This *is* the finger of God." But Pharaoh's heart grew hard, and he did not heed them, just as the LORD had said.

The Fourth Plague: Flies

²⁰And the LORD said to Moses, "Rise early in the morning and stand before Pharaoh as he comes out to the water. Then say to him, 'Thus says the LORD: "Let

My people go, that they may serve Me. [21]Or else, if you will not let My people go, behold, I will send swarms *of flies* on you and your servants, on your people and into your houses. The houses of the Egyptians shall be full of swarms *of flies,* and also the ground on which they *stand.* [22]And in that day I will set apart the land of Goshen, in which My people dwell, that no swarms *of flies* shall be there, in order that you may know that I *am* the LORD in the midst of the land. [23]I will make a difference[a] between My people and your people. Tomorrow this sign shall be." ' " [24]And the LORD did so. Thick swarms *of flies* came into the house of Pharaoh, *into* his servants' houses, and into all the land of Egypt. The land was corrupted because of the swarms *of flies.*

[25]Then Pharaoh called for Moses and Aaron, and said, "Go, sacrifice to your God in the land."

[26]And Moses said, "It is not right to do so, for we would be sacrificing the abomination of the Egyptians to the LORD our God. If we sacrifice the abomination of the Egyptians before their eyes, then will they not stone us? [27]We will go three days' journey into the wilderness and sacrifice to the LORD our God as He will command us."

[28]So Pharaoh said, "I will let you go, that you may sacrifice to the LORD your God in the wilderness; only you shall not go very far away. Intercede for me."

[29]Then Moses said, "Indeed I am going out from you, and I will entreat the LORD, that the swarms *of flies* may depart tomorrow from Pharaoh, from his servants, and from his people. But let Pharaoh not deal deceitfully anymore in not letting the people go to sacrifice to the LORD."

[30]So Moses went out from Pharaoh and entreated the LORD. [31]And the LORD did according to the word of Moses; He removed the swarms *of flies* from Pharaoh, from his servants, and from his people. Not one remained. [32]But Pharaoh hardened his heart at this time also; neither would he let the people go.

The Fifth Plague: Livestock Diseased

9 [1]Then the LORD said to Moses, "Go in to Pharaoh and tell him, 'Thus says the LORD God of the Hebrews: "Let My people go, that they may serve Me. [2]For if you re-

fuse to let *them* go, and still hold them, [3]behold, the hand of the LORD will be on your cattle in the field, on the horses, on the donkeys, on the camels, on the oxen, and on the sheep—a very severe pestilence. [4]And the LORD will make a difference between the livestock of Israel and the livestock of Egypt. So nothing shall die of all *that* belongs to the children of Israel." ' " [5]Then the LORD appointed a set time, saying, "Tomorrow the LORD will do this thing in the land."

[6]So the LORD did this thing on the next day, and all the livestock of Egypt died; but of the livestock of the children of Israel, not one died. [7]Then Pharaoh sent, and indeed, not even one of the livestock of the Israelites was dead. But the heart of Pharaoh became hard, and he did not let the people go.

The Sixth Plague: Boils

[8]So the LORD said to Moses and Aaron, "Take for yourselves handfuls of ashes from a furnace, and let Moses scatter it toward the heavens in the sight of Pharaoh. [9]And it will become fine dust in all the land of Egypt, and it will cause boils that break out in sores on man and beast throughout all the land of Egypt." [10]Then they took ashes from the furnace and stood before Pharaoh, and Moses scattered *them* toward heaven. And *they* caused boils that break out in sores on man and beast. [11]And the magicians could not stand before Moses because of the boils, for the boils were on the magicians and on all the Egyptians. [12]But the LORD hardened the heart of Pharaoh; and he did not heed them, just as the LORD had spoken to Moses.

The Seventh Plague: Hail

[13]Then the LORD said to Moses, "Rise early in the morning and stand before Pharaoh, and say to him, 'Thus says the LORD God of the Hebrews: "Let My people go, that they may serve Me, [14]for at this time I will send all My plagues to your very heart, and on your servants and on your people, that you may know that *there is* none like Me in all the earth. [15]Now if I had stretched out My hand and struck you and your people with pestilence, then you would have been cut off from the earth. [16]But indeed for this *purpose* I have raised you up, that I may show My power *in* you, and that My name may be declared in all the earth. [17]As yet you exalt yourself

8:23 [a]Literally *set a ransom* (compare Exodus 9:4 and 11:7)

against My people in that you will not let them go. ¹⁸Behold, tomorrow about this time I will cause very heavy hail to rain down, such as has not been in Egypt since its founding until now. ¹⁹Therefore send now *and* gather your livestock and all that you have in the field, for the hail shall come down on every man and every animal which is found in the field and is not brought home; and they shall die.” ’ ”

²⁰He who feared the word of the LORD among the servants of Pharaoh made his servants and his livestock flee to the houses. ²¹But he who did not regard the word of the LORD left his servants and his livestock in the field.

²²Then the LORD said to Moses, “Stretch out your hand toward heaven, that there may be hail in all the land of Egypt—on man, on beast, and on every herb of the field, throughout the land of Egypt.” ²³And Moses stretched out his rod toward heaven; and the LORD sent thunder and hail, and fire darted to the ground. And the LORD rained hail on the land of Egypt. ²⁴So there was hail, and fire mingled with the hail, so very heavy that there was none like it in all the land of Egypt since it became a nation. ²⁵And the hail struck throughout the whole land of Egypt, all that *was* in the field, both man and beast; and the hail struck every herb of the field and broke every tree of the field. ²⁶Only in the land of Goshen, where the children of Israel *were,* there was no hail.

²⁷And Pharaoh sent and called for Moses and Aaron, and said to them, “I have sinned this time. The LORD *is* righteous, and my people and I *are* wicked. ²⁸Entreat the LORD, that there may be no *more* mighty thundering and hail, for *it is* enough. I will let you go, and you shall stay no longer.”

²⁹So Moses said to him, “As soon as I have gone out of the city, I will spread out my hands to the LORD; the thunder will cease, and there will be no more hail, that you may know that the earth *is* the LORD’s.

³⁰But as for you and your servants, I know that you will not yet fear the LORD God.”

³¹Now the flax and the barley were struck, for the barley *was* in the head and the flax *was* in bud. ³²But the wheat and the spelt were not struck, for they *are* late crops.

³³So Moses went out of the city from Pharaoh and spread out his hands to the LORD; then the thunder and the hail ceased, and the rain was not poured on the earth. ³⁴And when Pharaoh saw that the rain, the hail, and the thunder had ceased, he sinned yet more; and he hardened his heart, he and his servants. ³⁵So the heart of Pharaoh was hard; neither would he let the children of Israel go, as the LORD had spoken by Moses.

The Eighth Plague: Locusts

10 ¹Now the LORD said to Moses, “Go in to Pharaoh; for I have hardened his heart and the hearts of his servants, that I may show these signs of Mine before him, ²and that you may tell in the hearing of your son and your son’s son the mighty things I have done in Egypt, and My signs which I have done among them, that you may know that I *am* the LORD.”

³So Moses and Aaron came in to Pharaoh and said to him, “Thus says the LORD God of the Hebrews: ‘How long will you refuse to humble yourself before Me? Let My people go, that they may serve Me. ⁴Or else, if you refuse to let My people go, behold, tomorrow I will bring locusts into your territory. ⁵And they shall cover the face of the earth, so that no one will be able to see the earth; and they shall eat the residue of what is left, which remains to you from the hail, and they shall eat every tree which grows up for you out of the field. ⁶They shall fill your houses, the houses of all your servants, and the houses of all the Egyptians—which neither your fathers nor your fathers’ fathers have seen, since the day that they were on the earth to this day.’ ” And he turned and went out from Pharaoh.

AGRICULTURE AND HERDING

Flax was grown mainly for its fibers, from which linen is made (Ex. 9:31). Spelt is a food grain similar to wheat, but it can grow in less fertile soil. Wheat and barley both have been grown in Egypt since 5000 B.C., and in Palestine since about 8000 B.C. All Egyptian agriculture depends on the Nile for water.

WHERE WAS THE RED SEA? (Ex. 10:19)

The Hebrew slaves escaped Egypt by way of the Red Sea. In antiquity this Red Sea also included the Gulf of Suez and the Gulf of Aqaba, the two gulfs into which it splits. The precise location of the Exodus crossing has been debated by scholars since antiquity without any agreement on a possible site.

The Red Sea is called *Yam Suph* in Hebrew, which is often translated as "sea of reeds." The Sea of Reeds would refer to the marshes where bulrushes or reeds grow plentifully. In a number of Old Testament passages, *Yam Suph* is associated with the Gulf of Aqaba, which marked the southern tip of King Solomon's empire (1 Kin. 9:26; Ex. 23:31). Yet in other passages *Yam Suph* probably refers to the Gulf of Suez, since the narrative indicates a body of water bordering on Egypt (Ex. 10:19; 13:18).

Although traditionally translated as "Red Sea," the Hebrew term *Yam Suph* probably means "Sea of Reeds." In various passages, *Yam Suph* is identified as the sea of the Exodus (Ex. 15:4, 22), where the Israelites crossed over on dry ground, escaping the Egyptians who were drowned. Nevertheless, the geographical location of this sea remains ambiguous, since descriptions of *Yam Suph* reflect the geography of Egypt as the biblical writer knew it. The majority of scholars favor a location somewhere in the eastern Delta region of Egypt, but the true location is still undetermined.

7Then Pharaoh's servants said to him, "How long shall this man be a snare to us? Let the men go, that they may serve the LORD their God. Do you not yet know that Egypt is destroyed?"

8So Moses and Aaron were brought again to Pharaoh, and he said to them, "Go, serve the LORD your God. Who *are* the ones that are going?"

9And Moses said, "We will go with our young and our old; with our sons and our daughters, with our flocks and our herds we will go, for we must hold a feast to the LORD."

10Then he said to them, "The LORD had better be with you when I let you and your little ones go! Beware, for evil is ahead of you. 11Not so! Go now, you *who are* men, and serve the LORD, for that is what you desired." And they were driven out from Pharaoh's presence.

12Then the LORD said to Moses, "Stretch out your hand over the land of Egypt for the locusts, that they may come upon the land of Egypt, and eat every herb of the land—all that the hail has left." 13So Moses stretched out his rod over the land of Egypt, and the LORD brought an east wind on the land all that day and all *that* night. When it was morning, the east wind brought the locusts. 14And the locusts went up over all the land of Egypt and rested on all the territory of Egypt. *They were* very severe; previously there had been no such locusts as they, nor shall there be such after them. 15For they covered the face of the whole earth, so that the land was darkened; and they ate every herb of the land and all the fruit of the trees which the hail had left. So there remained nothing green on the trees or on the plants of the field throughout all the land of Egypt.

16Then Pharaoh called for Moses and Aaron in haste, and said, "I have sinned against the LORD your God and against you. 17Now therefore, please forgive my sin only this once, and entreat the LORD your God, that He may take away from me this death only." 18So he went out from Pharaoh and entreated the LORD. 19And the LORD turned a very strong west wind, which took the locusts away and blew them into the Red Sea. There remained not one locust in all the territory of Egypt. 20But the LORD hardened Pharaoh's heart, and he did not let the children of Israel go.

The Ninth Plague: Darkness

21Then the LORD said to Moses, "Stretch out your hand toward heaven, that there may be darkness over the land of Egypt, darkness *which* may even be felt." 22So Moses stretched out his hand toward heaven, and there was thick darkness in all the land of Egypt three days. 23They did not see one another; nor did anyone rise from his place for three days.

But all the children of Israel had light in their dwellings.

24Then Pharaoh called to Moses and said, "Go, serve the LORD; only let your flocks and your herds be kept back. Let your little ones also go with you."

25But Moses said, "You must also give us sacrifices and burnt offerings, that we may sacrifice to the LORD our God. 26Our livestock also shall go with us; not a hoof shall be left behind. For we must take some of them to serve the LORD our God, and even we do not know with what we must serve the LORD until we arrive there."

27But the LORD hardened Pharaoh's heart, and he would not let them go. 28Then Pharaoh said to him, "Get away from me! Take heed to yourself and see my face no more! For in the day you see my face you shall die!"

29So Moses said, "You have spoken well. I will never see your face again."

Death of the Firstborn Announced

11 1And the LORD said to Moses, "I will bring one more plague on Pharaoh and on Egypt. Afterward he will let you go from here. When he lets *you* go, he will surely drive you out of here altogether. 2Speak now in the hearing of the people, and let every man ask from his neighbor and every woman from her neighbor, articles of silver and articles of gold." 3And the LORD gave the people favor in the sight of the Egyptians. Moreover the man Moses *was* very great in the land of Egypt, in the sight of Pharaoh's servants and in the sight of the people.

4Then Moses said, "Thus says the LORD: 'About midnight I will go out into the midst of Egypt; 5and all the firstborn in the land of Egypt shall die, from the firstborn of Pharaoh who sits on his throne, even to the firstborn of the female servant who *is* behind the handmill, and all the firstborn of the animals. 6Then there shall be a great cry throughout all the land of Egypt, such as was not like it *before,* nor shall be like it again. 7But against none of the children of Israel shall a dog move its tongue, against man or beast, that you may know that the LORD does make a difference between the Egyptians and Israel.' 8And all these your servants shall come down to me and bow down to me, saying, 'Get out, and all the people who follow you!' After that I will go out." Then he went out from Pharaoh in great anger.

9But the LORD said to Moses, "Pharaoh will not heed you, so that My wonders may be multiplied in the land of Egypt." 10So Moses and Aaron did all these wonders before Pharaoh; and the LORD hardened Pharaoh's heart, and he did not let the children of Israel go out of his land.

The Passover Instituted

12 1Now the LORD spoke to Moses and Aaron in the land of Egypt, saying, 2"This month *shall be* your beginning of months; it *shall be* the first month of the year to you. 3Speak to all the congregation of Israel, saying: 'On the tenth of this month every man shall take for himself a lamb, according to the house of *his* father, a lamb for a household. 4And if the household is too small for the lamb, let him and his neighbor next to his house take *it* according to the number of the persons; according to each man's need you shall make your count for the lamb. 5Your lamb shall be without blemish, a male of the first year. You may take *it* from the sheep or from the goats. 6Now you shall keep it until the fourteenth day of the same month. Then the whole assembly of the congregation of Israel shall kill it at twilight. 7And they shall take *some* of the blood and put *it* on the two doorposts and on the lintel of the houses where they eat it. 8Then they shall eat the flesh on that night; roasted in fire, with unleavened bread *and* with bitter *herbs* they shall eat it. 9Do not eat it raw, nor boiled at all with water, but roasted in fire—its head with its legs and its entrails. 10You shall let none of it remain until morning, and what remains of it until morning you shall burn with fire. 11And

TRADE AND ECONOMICS

Both silver and gold (Ex. 11:2) were used as a way of storing value long before coins were introduced in about 625 B.C. Ancient Egyptian bracelets and other items of gold jewelry were sometimes very thick and heavy. A necklace buried with Psusennes I in about 991 B.C. (and recovered in A.D. 1940) weighs more than 42 pounds.

ORIGINS OF THE PASSOVER MEAL   (Ex. 12:8)

Certain elements of the Passover ritual can be traced to ceremonies that celebrated the new agricultural year in farming cultures. These elements include a sacrifice to be eaten by the community, the eating of the new crop, bitter herbs, unleavened bread, thanksgiving for not dying during the period between harvests, and, of course, a new start. The Israelites would have known about these celebrations from farming in the Nile Delta.

God revealed through Moses a new meaning for the Israelite meal. Now the feast would symbolize salvation from Egyptian slavery and from death. The angel of death "passed over" the houses of the Israelites when He killed the firstborn of the Egyptians (Ex. 12:12, 13). The meal was to be prepared and eaten in haste, with the people ready to leave at a moment's notice. There was not time for bread to rise or for meat to be cooked slowly, so the lamb was to be roasted quickly over the fire (Ex. 12:8–10).

To this day the Passover Seder is celebrated by all Jewish families throughout the world. It is prepared and eaten according to the rules of Ex. 12. As the meal is eaten, the story of Passover is related—not as something which happened long ago to ancestors, but always as happening now. It is now that God brings every person who partakes of the meal to freedom and to salvation. The feast establishes identity: we are the people of God, because God did these things for us. Anticipating the coming of God's Messiah, Jewish tradition added to the service a place at the table for Elijah should the prophet come "this year" to proclaim the advent of the Messiah.

---

thus you shall eat it: *with* a belt on your waist, your sandals on your feet, and your staff in your hand. So you shall eat it in haste. It *is* the LORD's Passover.

12"For I will pass through the land of Egypt on that night, and will strike all the firstborn in the land of Egypt, both man and beast; and against all the gods of Egypt I will execute judgment: I *am* the LORD. 13Now the blood shall be a sign for you on the houses where you *are*. And when I see the blood, I will pass over you; and the plague shall not be on you to destroy *you* when I strike the land of Egypt.

14"So this day shall be to you a memorial; and you shall keep it as a feast to the LORD throughout your generations. You shall keep it as a feast by an everlasting ordinance. 15Seven days you shall eat unleavened bread. On the first day you shall remove leaven from your houses. For whoever eats leavened bread from the first day until the seventh day, that person shall be cut off from Israel. 16On the first day *there shall be* a holy convocation, and on the seventh day there shall be a holy convocation for you. No manner of work shall be done on them; but *that* which everyone must eat—that only may be prepared by you. 17So you shall observe *the Feast of* Unleavened Bread, for on this same day I will have brought your armies out of the land of Egypt. Therefore you shall observe this day throughout your generations as an everlasting ordinance. 18In the first *month,* on the fourteenth day of the month at evening, you shall eat unleavened bread, until the twenty-first day of the month at evening. 19For seven days no leaven shall be found in your houses, since whoever eats what is leavened, that same person shall be cut off from the congregation of Israel, whether *he is* a stranger or a native of the land. 20You shall eat nothing leavened; in all your dwellings you shall eat unleavened bread.'"

21Then Moses called for all the elders of Israel and said to them, "Pick out and take lambs for yourselves according to your families, and kill the Passover *lamb*. 22And you shall take a bunch of hyssop, dip *it* in the blood that *is* in the basin, and strike the lintel and the two doorposts with the blood that *is* in the basin. And none of you shall go out of the door of his house until morning. 23For the LORD will pass through to strike the Egyptians; and when He sees the blood on the lintel and on the two doorposts, the LORD will pass over the door and not allow the destroyer to come into your houses to strike *you*. 24And you shall observe this thing as an ordinance for you and your sons forever. 25It will come to pass when you come to the land which the

EGYPT AND ITS GOLD (Ex. 12:35, 36)

Gold and silver were considered precious metals from the beginning of history. In Egyptian society, the king or pharaoh (as he was called) had the power to concentrate wealth for himself. According to Egyptian custom, when kings or queens were buried their treasure went with them into the ground. This custom sometimes allows us to see from an Egyptian tomb what kind of wealth the deceased ruler possessed, of which gold was usually included.

Such was the case when archaeologists discovered the tomb of the Egyptian pharaoh Tutankhamun with its treasure intact. The tomb contained all kinds of furniture, clothing, and other articles. The coffin of the king himself was made of solid gold about ⅛ inch thick and was over 6 feet long, weighing 243 pounds (or about 4 talents).

The wealth of Tutankhamun's tomb is indicative of the wealth that the Hebrews must have observed while in Egypt. Tutankhamun became king in 1336 B.C., which places him about a 100 years before or after the Hebrew exodus from Egypt. The date of the Exodus is debated, but scholars locate it at either 1446 B.C. or later around 1275 B.C. When the Hebrews had an opportunity to take something of Egypt with them, Egyptian gold must have been hard to resist (Ex. 12:35, 36).

LORD will give you, just as He promised, that you shall keep this service. ²⁶And it shall be, when your children say to you, 'What do you mean by this service?' ²⁷that you shall say, 'It *is* the Passover sacrifice of the LORD, who passed over the houses of the children of Israel in Egypt when He struck the Egyptians and delivered our households.' " So the people bowed their heads and worshiped. ²⁸Then the children of Israel went away and did *so;* just as the LORD had commanded Moses and Aaron, so they did.

The Tenth Plague: Death of the Firstborn

²⁹And it came to pass at midnight that the LORD struck all the firstborn in the land of Egypt, from the firstborn of Pharaoh who sat on his throne to the firstborn of the captive who *was* in the dungeon, and all the firstborn of livestock. ³⁰So Pharaoh rose in the night, he, all his servants, and all the Egyptians; and there was a great cry in Egypt, for *there was* not a house where *there was* not one dead.

The Exodus

³¹Then he called for Moses and Aaron by night, and said, "Rise, go out from among my people, both you and the children of Israel. And go, serve the LORD as you have said. ³²Also take your flocks and your herds, as you have said, and be gone; and bless me also."

³³And the Egyptians urged the people, that they might send them out of the land in haste. For they said, "We *shall* all *be* dead." ³⁴So the people took their dough before it was leavened, having their kneading bowls bound up in their clothes on their shoulders. ³⁵Now the children of Israel had done according to the word of Moses, and they had asked from the Egyptians articles of silver, articles of gold, and clothing. ³⁶And the LORD had given the people favor in the sight of the Egyptians, so that they granted them *what they requested*. Thus they plundered the Egyptians.

The Exodus Begun

The actual date of the Exodus has been much debated. The two most frequently proposed possibilities are about 200 years apart: (1) in the 15th century B.C. during the reign of Thutmose III (1479–1425 B.C.) and (2) in the 13th century B.C. under Ramesses II (1279–1213 B.C.). The 15th-century date fits the numbers given in 1 Kin. 6:1 which places the Exodus 480 years before Solomon's temple, which would be about 1446 B.C. A 13th-century date, around 1275 B.C., seems to better fit other evidence (e.g., the building of the city of Raamses mentioned in Ex. 1:11) but requires understanding the 480 years of 1 Kings as a symbolic number.

Both dates place the Exodus in times of clear Egyptian supremacy, however, and this may be the essential point. The fact that the Book of Exodus does not name the Egyptian

king—the very fact that so frustrates historians—is peculiarly appropriate in a book that
tells how the ruler of the world's greatest empire is humbled before the mighty arm of Israel's God.

■ Exodus 12:37—18:27

Exodus

12 **:37** Then the children of Israel journeyed from Rameses to Succoth,
about six hundred thousand men on foot,
besides children. ³⁸A mixed multitude
went up with them also, and flocks and
herds—a great deal of livestock. ³⁹And they
baked unleavened cakes of the dough
which they had brought out of Egypt; for
it was not leavened, because they were
driven out of Egypt and could not wait, nor
had they prepared provisions for themselves.

⁴⁰Now the sojourn of the children of Is-
rael who lived in Egypt[a] *was* four hundred
and thirty years. ⁴¹And it came to pass at
the end of the four hundred and thirty
years—on that very same day—it came to
pass that all the armies of the LORD went
out from the land of Egypt. ⁴²It *is* a night of
solemn observance to the LORD for bringing
them out of the land of Egypt. This *is* that
night of the LORD, a solemn observance for
all the children of Israel throughout their
generations.

Passover Regulations

⁴³And the LORD said to Moses and
Aaron, "This *is* the ordinance of the
Passover: No foreigner shall eat it. ⁴⁴But
every man's servant who is bought for
money, when you have circumcised him,
then he may eat it. ⁴⁵A sojourner and a
hired servant shall not eat it. ⁴⁶In one
house it shall be eaten; you shall not carry
any of the flesh outside the house, nor shall
you break one of its bones. ⁴⁷All the congregation of Israel shall keep it. ⁴⁸And when a
stranger dwells with you *and wants* to
keep the Passover to the LORD, let all his
males be circumcised, and then let him
come near and keep it; and he shall be as a
native of the land. For no uncircumcised
person shall eat it. ⁴⁹One law shall be for
the native-born and for the stranger who
dwells among you."

⁵⁰Thus all the children of Israel did; as
the LORD commanded Moses and Aaron, so
they did. ⁵¹And it came to pass, on that
very same day, that the LORD brought the
children of Israel out of the land of Egypt
according to their armies.

The Firstborn Consecrated

13 ¹Then the LORD spoke to Moses, saying, ²"Consecrate to Me all the firstborn, whatever opens the womb among the
children of Israel, *both* of man and beast; it
is Mine."

The Feast of Unleavened Bread

³And Moses said to the people: "Re-
member this day in which you went out of
Egypt, out of the house of bondage; for by
strength of hand the LORD brought you out
of this *place*. No leavened bread shall be
eaten. ⁴On this day you are going out, in
the month Abib. ⁵And it shall be, when the
LORD brings you into the land of the
Canaanites and the Hittites and the Amorites and the Hivites and the Jebusites,
which He swore to your fathers to give you,
a land flowing with milk and honey, that
you shall keep this service in this month.
⁶Seven days you shall eat unleavened
bread, and on the seventh day *there shall
be* a feast to the LORD. ⁷Unleavened bread
shall be eaten seven days. And no leavened
bread shall be seen among you, nor shall
leaven be seen among you in all your quarters. ⁸And you shall tell your son in that
day, saying, '*This is done* because of what
the LORD did for me when I came up from
Egypt.' ⁹It shall be as a sign to you on
your hand and as a memorial between
your eyes, that the LORD's law may be
in your mouth; for with a strong hand
the LORD has brought you out of Egypt.
¹⁰You shall therefore keep this ordinance in
its season from year to year.

12:40 [a]Samaritan Pentateuch and Septuagint read
Egypt and Canaan.

TIME CAPSULE *1625 to 1600 B.C.*

1625   *Chariots used by the Hittites*

1600   *Chariot introduced to the Nile valley*

1600   *Labyrinthine palace of Knossos,
Crete*

1600   *Minoan palace of Phaistos, Crete*

1600– *The zenith of the Minoan civilization*
1400

The Law of the Firstborn

[11]"And it shall be, when the LORD brings you into the land of the Canaanites, as He swore to you and your fathers, and gives it to you, [12]that you shall set apart to the LORD all that open the womb, that is, every firstborn that comes from an animal which you have; the males *shall be* the LORD's. [13]But every firstborn of a donkey you shall redeem with a lamb; and if you will not redeem *it,* then you shall break its neck. And all the firstborn of man among your sons you shall redeem. [14]So it shall be, when your son asks you in time to come, saying, 'What *is* this?' that you shall say to him, 'By strength of hand the LORD brought us out of Egypt, out of the house of bondage. [15]And it came to pass, when Pharaoh was stubborn about letting us go, that the LORD killed all the firstborn in the land of Egypt, both the firstborn of man and the firstborn of beast. Therefore I sacrifice to the LORD all males that open the womb, but all the firstborn of my sons I redeem.' [16]It shall be as a sign on your hand and as frontlets between your eyes, for by strength of hand the LORD brought us out of Egypt."

The Wilderness Way

[17]Then it came to pass, when Pharaoh had let the people go, that God did not lead them *by* way of the land of the Philistines, although that *was* near; for God said, "Lest perhaps the people change their minds when they see war, and return to Egypt." [18]So God led the people around *by* way of the wilderness of the Red Sea. And the children of Israel went up in orderly ranks out of the land of Egypt.

[19]And Moses took the bones of Joseph with him, for he had placed the children of Israel under solemn oath, saying, "God will surely visit you, and you shall carry up my bones from here with you."[a]

[20]So they took their journey from Succoth and camped in Etham at the edge of the wilderness. [21]And the LORD went before them by day in a pillar of cloud to lead the way, and by night in a pillar of fire to give them light, so as to go by day and night. [22]He did not take away the pillar of cloud by day or the pillar of fire by night *from* before the people.

The Red Sea Crossing

14 [1]Now the LORD spoke to Moses, saying: [2]"Speak to the children of Israel, that they turn and camp before Pi Hahiroth, between Migdol and the sea, opposite Baal Zephon; you shall camp before it by the sea. [3]For Pharaoh will say of the children of Israel, 'They *are* bewildered by the land; the wilderness has closed them

---

13:19 [a]Genesis 50:25

The Route of the Exodus

Two routes have been proposed for the exodus of the Israelites from Egypt. A northern route moves east from Rameses along the northern Sinai coast. The southern route passes Succoth, continuing to the lower region of the Sinai Peninsula.

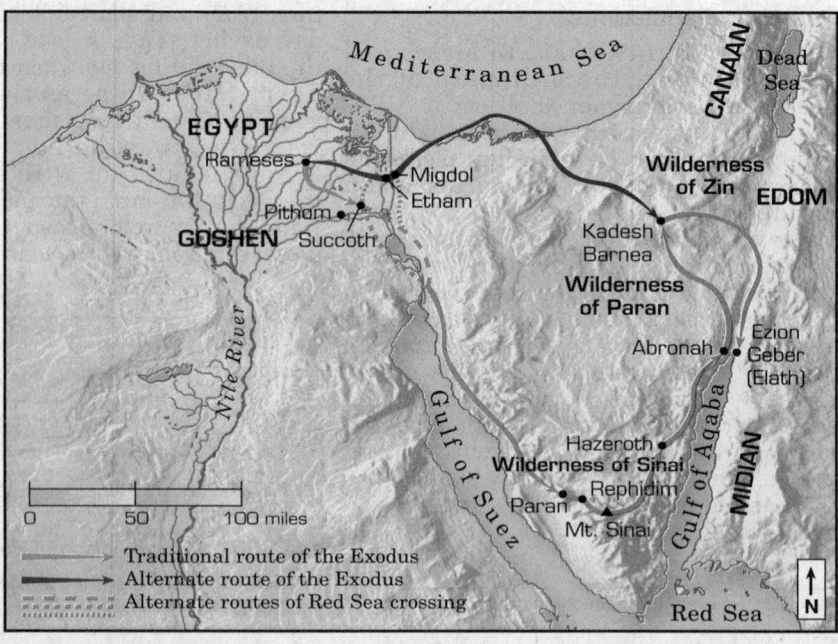

THE ROAD THROUGH PHILISTIA (Ex. 13:17)

There were three ancient routes between Asia and Egypt. One route went from Elath near Ezion Geber (1 Kin. 9:26) across the Sinai Peninsula to the area of the Suez around the city of On (Heliopolis). Another route stretched from near Beersheba in the Negev to the area of the Suez. The route most commonly used, however, especially by Egyptian armies, was the "way of the land of the Philistines" (Ex. 13:17).

In Egypt this roadway was called the "way of Horus," named for Egypt's earliest state god. The way of Horus was a coastal route that left Egypt from the northeast. It ran along the northern reaches of the Sinai Peninsula, and along the coast of Canaan. If a traveler was going toward Damascus, he would cut inland passing Megiddo and then down the Jezreel Valley to Hazor and from there cross into Transjordan. More northerly destinations would continue along the coast. The route did not actually lie within sight of the Mediterranean Sea, since the land closest to the water was marshy. Instead it lay inland a few miles where the soil was firmer.

The biblical name "way of the land of the Philistines" alludes to the coastal area where the Philistines lived and through which the way of Horus passed. From the point of view of the Israelites, the way of Horus came and went through Philistia and was, thus, the "way of the land of the Philistines." In later times, when the Philistines were not a distinguishable people, this route was known simply as the "way of the sea" (Is. 9:1).

---

in.' ⁴Then I will harden Pharaoh's heart, so that he will pursue them; and I will gain honor over Pharaoh and over all his army, that the Egyptians may know that I *am* the LORD." And they did so.

⁵Now it was told the king of Egypt that the people had fled, and the heart of Pharaoh and his servants was turned against the people; and they said, "Why have we done this, that we have let Israel go from serving us?" ⁶So he made ready his chariot and took his people with him. ⁷Also, he took six hundred choice chariots, and all the chariots of Egypt with captains over every one of them. ⁸And the LORD hardened the heart of Pharaoh king of Egypt, and he pursued the children of Israel; and the children of Israel went out with boldness. ⁹So the Egyptians pursued them, all the horses *and* chariots of Pharaoh, his horsemen and his army, and overtook them camping by the sea beside Pi Hahiroth, before Baal Zephon.

¹⁰And when Pharaoh drew near, the children of Israel lifted their eyes, and behold, the Egyptians marched after them. So they were very afraid, and the children of Israel cried out to the LORD. ¹¹Then they said to Moses, "Because *there were* no graves in Egypt, have you taken us away to die in the wilderness? Why have you so dealt with us, to bring us up out of Egypt? ¹²*Is* this not the word that we told you in Egypt, saying, 'Let us alone that we may serve the Egyptians'? For *it would have been* better for us to serve the Egyptians than that we should die in the wilderness."

¹³And Moses said to the people, "Do not be afraid. Stand still, and see the salvation of the LORD, which He will accomplish for you today. For the Egyptians whom you see today, you shall see again no more forever. ¹⁴The LORD will fight for you, and you shall hold your peace."

¹⁵And the LORD said to Moses, "Why do you cry to Me? Tell the children of Israel to go forward. ¹⁶But lift up your rod, and stretch out your hand over the sea and

---

SCIENCE AND TECHNOLOGY

Egyptian chariots were the finest in the ancient world. They were small and light, carrying a driver and one passenger (Ex. 14:6). The wheels were about 40 inches in diameter and 7 feet apart, for stability. The floor was a half-circle in front and straight in back along the axle. When the floor was made of woven leather, it provided some suspension for the riders.

TWO DATES FOR THE EXODUS

Two dating schemes have been proposed for the Exodus from Egypt—an "early" date and a "late" date. The early scheme considers the 480 years of 1 Kin. 6:1 to be a precise note of time; the late scheme considers it to be a symbolic figure, not an actual one.

A 15th–Century Exodus

When: Approximately 1446 B.C.

Ruling Pharaoh: Thutmose III (1479–1425 B.C.)

Reasons: 1 Kin. 6:1 states that the Exodus occurred 480 years before Solomon began building the temple.

Solomon, who reigned from 970 to 930 B.C., began the temple in the 4th year of his reign (about 966 B.C.).

The Exodus would then have occurred 480 years before 966 B.C., placing it in 1446 B.C.

A 13th–Century Exodus

When: Approximately 1275 B.C.

Ruling Pharaoh: Ramesses II (1279–1213 B.C.)

Reasons: Ex. 1:11 states that the Hebrew slaves built the supply cities, Pithom and Raamses.

Egyptian sources suggest that Pharaoh Ramesses renamed the city of Raamses after himself.

The 480 years of 1 Kin. 6:1 is a symbolic number, representing 12 generations of 40 years each.

---

divide it. And the children of Israel shall go on dry *ground* through the midst of the sea. [17]And I indeed will harden the hearts of the Egyptians, and they shall follow them. So I will gain honor over Pharaoh and over all his army, his chariots, and his horsemen. [18]Then the Egyptians shall know that I *am* the LORD, when I have gained honor for Myself over Pharaoh, his chariots, and his horsemen."

[19]And the Angel of God, who went before the camp of Israel, moved and went behind them; and the pillar of cloud went from before them and stood behind them. [20]So it came between the camp of the Egyptians and the camp of Israel. Thus it was a cloud and darkness *to the one,* and it gave light by night *to the other,* so that the one did not come near the other all that night.

[21]Then Moses stretched out his hand over the sea; and the LORD caused the sea to go *back* by a strong east wind all that night, and made the sea into dry *land,* and the waters were divided. [22]So the children of Israel went into the midst of the sea on the dry *ground,* and the waters *were* a wall to them on their right hand and on their left. [23]And the Egyptians pursued and went after them into the midst of the sea, all Pharaoh's horses, his chariots, and his horsemen.

[24]Now it came to pass, in the morning watch, that the LORD looked down upon the army of the Egyptians through the pillar of fire and cloud, and He troubled the army of the Egyptians. [25]And He took off[a] their chariot wheels, so that they drove them with difficulty; and the Egyptians said, "Let us flee from the face of Israel, for the LORD fights for them against the Egyptians."

[26]Then the LORD said to Moses, "Stretch out your hand over the sea, that the waters may come back upon the Egyptians, on their chariots, and on their horsemen." [27]And Moses stretched out his hand over the sea; and when the morning appeared, the sea returned to its full depth, while the Egyptians were fleeing into it. So the LORD overthrew the Egyptians in the midst of the sea. [28]Then the waters returned and covered the chariots, the horsemen, *and* all the army of Pharaoh that came into the sea after them. Not so much as one of them remained. [29]But the children of Israel had walked on dry *land* in the midst of the sea, and the waters *were* a wall to them on their right hand and on their left.

[30]So the LORD saved Israel that day out of the hand of the Egyptians, and Israel saw the Egyptians dead on the seashore. [31]Thus Israel saw the great work which the

---

14:25 [a]Samaritan Pentateuch, Septuagint, and Syriac read *bound.*

GOD AMONG THE WARRIOR DEITIES (Ex. 15:1–21)

The Song of Moses and Miriam in Ex. 15:1–21 is a victory song like those sung in many cultures in the ancient world. God is praised as a warrior going out to fight for Israel.

In the faith of the ancient world, armies did not go to battle alone. The deity or deities of the army fought in heaven and on earth against the opposing army and its gods. Nearly every culture had a deity of war. The Canaanite goddess Anath bedecked herself with parts of corpses from slain soldiers. The Mesopotamian goddess Ishtar led armies, along with the patron deities of the warring cities. All gods who were responsible for particular cities were expected to be able to defend their territory.

So Israel's God, bringing His people out of Egypt, is depicted in song as having defeated the army (and thus also the gods) of the Egyptians by Himself. The use of water to destroy enemies is ancient. Songs about the defeat of the Sumerian city of Ur early in the 2nd millennium B.C. tell about floods and roaring rivers sent by the gods to destroy the city. In Israel's song God picks up chariots and riders and throws them into the water like so many toys (Ex. 15:1, 4).

The language, symbols and imagery of Israel's song are those commonly used for war deities in the ancient Near East. Israel's enemies near and far are terrified (Ex. 15:14–16). Terror, or fear, was assumed to be a separate substance which went before the deity, defeating enemies even before the god arrived. The people of the victorious deity are established in their proper place, and the winning god is enthroned as ruler over the vanquished deities (15:16–18).

The peoples around Israel would understand such phrases familiar to ancient civilization. Thus, they would recognize the victory song of Moses and Miriam as praise for the work of a warrior deity who was mightier than any other deity ("Who is like You, O LORD, among the gods?" Ex. 15:11).

LORD had done in Egypt; so the people feared the LORD, and believed the LORD and His servant Moses.

The Song of Moses

15 ¹Then Moses and the children of Israel sang this song to the LORD, and spoke, saying:

"I will sing to the LORD,
For He has triumphed gloriously!
The horse and its rider
He has thrown into the sea!
2 The LORD *is* my strength and song,
And He has become my salvation;
He *is* my God, and I will praise Him;
My father's God, and I will exalt Him.
3 The LORD *is* a man of war;
The LORD *is* His name.
4 Pharaoh's chariots and his army He
has cast into the sea;
His chosen captains also are drowned
in the Red Sea.
5 The depths have covered them;
They sank to the bottom like a stone.

6 "Your right hand, O LORD, has become
glorious in power;
Your right hand, O LORD, has dashed
the enemy in pieces.
7 And in the greatness of Your
excellence
You have overthrown those who rose
against You;
You sent forth Your wrath;
It consumed them like stubble.
8 And with the blast of Your nostrils
The waters were gathered together;
The floods stood upright like a heap;
The depths congealed in the heart of
the sea.
9 The enemy said, 'I will pursue,
I will overtake,
I will divide the spoil;
My desire shall be satisfied on them.
I will draw my sword,
My hand shall destroy them.'
10 You blew with Your wind,
The sea covered them;
They sank like lead in the mighty
waters.

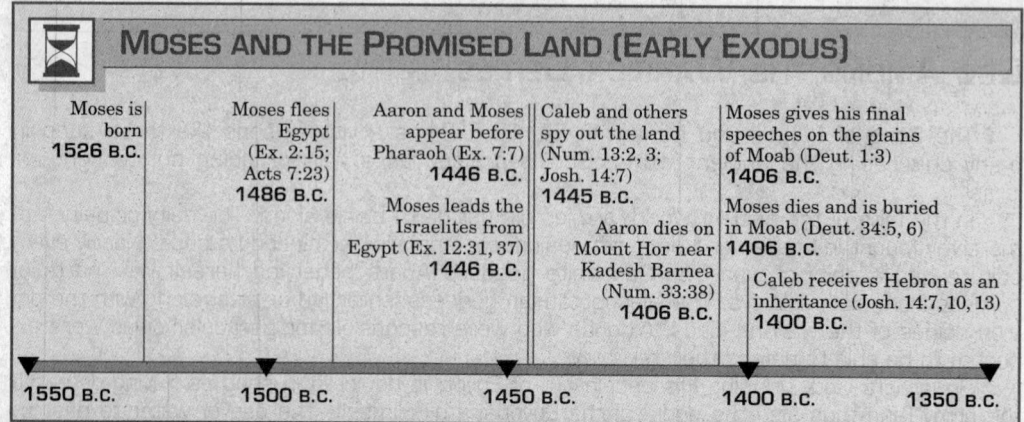

MOSES AND THE PROMISED LAND (EARLY EXODUS)

Moses is born 1526 B.C.	Moses flees Egypt (Ex. 2:15; Acts 7:23) 1486 B.C.	Aaron and Moses appear before Pharaoh (Ex. 7:7) 1446 B.C. Moses leads the Israelites from Egypt (Ex. 12:31, 37) 1446 B.C.	Caleb and others spy out the land (Num. 13:2, 3; Josh. 14:7) 1445 B.C. Aaron dies on Mount Hor near Kadesh Barnea (Num. 33:38) 1406 B.C.	Moses gives his final speeches on the plains of Moab (Deut. 1:3) 1406 B.C. Moses dies and is buried in Moab (Deut. 34:5, 6) 1406 B.C. Caleb receives Hebron as an inheritance (Josh. 14:7, 10, 13) 1400 B.C.

1550 B.C.	1500 B.C.	1450 B.C.	1400 B.C.	1350 B.C.

11 "Who *is* like You, O LORD, among the
    gods?
    Who *is* like You, glorious in holiness,
    Fearful in praises, doing wonders?
12 You stretched out Your right hand;
    The earth swallowed them.
13 You in Your mercy have led forth
    The people whom You have redeemed;
    You have guided *them* in Your
        strength
    To Your holy habitation.

14 "The people will hear *and* be afraid;
    Sorrow will take hold of the
        inhabitants of Philistia.
15 Then the chiefs of Edom will be
        dismayed;
    The mighty men of Moab,
    Trembling will take hold of them;
    All the inhabitants of Canaan will
        melt away.
16 Fear and dread will fall on them;
    By the greatness of Your arm
    They will be *as* still as a stone,
    Till Your people pass over, O LORD,
    Till the people pass over
    Whom You have purchased.
17 You will bring them in and plant them
    In the mountain of Your inheritance,
    In the place, O LORD, *which* You have
        made
    For Your own dwelling,
    The sanctuary, O LORD, *which* Your
        hands have established.

18 "The LORD shall reign forever and
        ever."

19 For the horses of Pharaoh went with
his chariots and his horsemen into the sea,

and the LORD brought back the waters of
the sea upon them. But the children of Israel went on dry *land* in the midst of the
sea.

The Song of Miriam

20 Then Miriam the prophetess, the sister of Aaron, took the timbrel in her hand;
and all the women went out after her with
timbrels and with dances. 21 And Miriam
answered them:

"Sing to the LORD,
    For He has triumphed gloriously!
    The horse and its rider
    He has thrown into the sea!"

Bitter Waters Made Sweet

22 So Moses brought Israel from the
Red Sea; then they went out into the
Wilderness of Shur. And they went three
days in the wilderness and found no water.
23 Now when they came to Marah, they
could not drink the waters of Marah, for
they *were* bitter. Therefore the name of it
was called Marah.[a] 24 And the people complained against Moses, saying, "What shall
we drink?" 25 So he cried out to the LORD,
and the LORD showed him a tree. When he
cast *it* into the waters, the waters were
made sweet.
    There He made a statute and an ordi-
nance for them, and there He tested them,
26 and said, "If you diligently heed the voice
of the LORD your God and do what is right
in His sight, give ear to His commandments and keep all His statutes, I will put
none of the diseases on you which I have

15:23 ª Literally *Bitter*

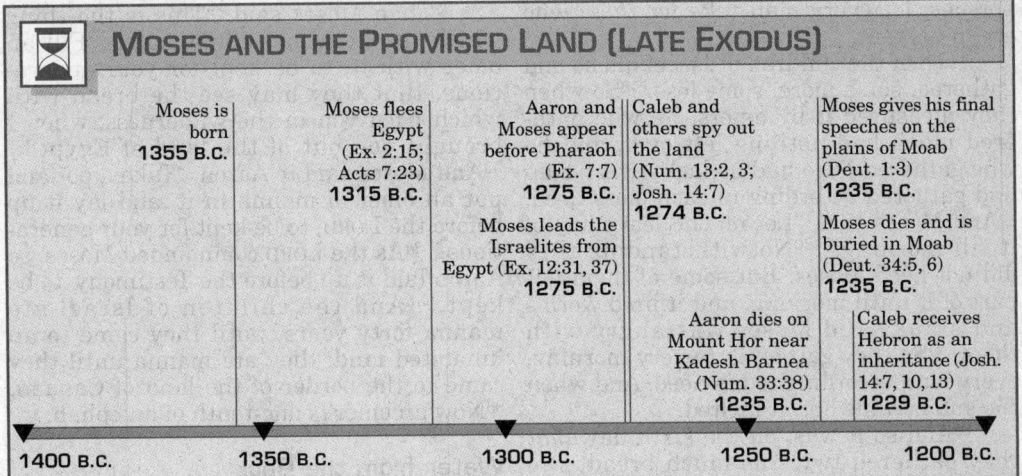

MOSES AND THE PROMISED LAND (LATE EXODUS)

Moses is born 1355 B.C.	Moses flees Egypt (Ex. 2:15; Acts 7:23) 1315 B.C.	Aaron and Moses appear before Pharaoh (Ex. 7:7) 1275 B.C.	Caleb and others spy out the land (Num. 13:2, 3; Josh. 14:7) 1274 B.C.	Moses gives his final speeches on the plains of Moab (Deut. 1:3) 1235 B.C.
		Moses leads the Israelites from Egypt (Ex. 12:31, 37) 1275 B.C.		Moses dies and is buried in Moab (Deut. 34:5, 6) 1235 B.C.
			Aaron dies on Mount Hor near Kadesh Barnea (Num. 33:38) 1235 B.C.	Caleb receives Hebron as an inheritance (Josh. 14:7, 10, 13) 1229 B.C.

| 1400 B.C. | 1350 B.C. | 1300 B.C. | 1250 B.C. | 1200 B.C. |

brought on the Egyptians. For I *am* the LORD who heals you."

27Then they came to Elim, where there *were* twelve wells of water and seventy palm trees; so they camped there by the waters.

Bread from Heaven

16 1And they journeyed from Elim, and all the congregation of the children of Israel came to the Wilderness of Sin, which is between Elim and Sinai, on the fifteenth day of the second month after they departed from the land of Egypt. 2Then the whole congregation of the children of Israel complained against Moses and Aaron in the wilderness. 3And the children of Israel said to them, "Oh, that we had died by the hand of the LORD in the land of Egypt, when we sat by the pots of meat *and* when we ate bread to the full! For you have brought us out into this wilderness to kill this whole assembly with hunger."

4Then the LORD said to Moses, "Behold, I will rain bread from heaven for you. And the people shall go out and gather a certain quota every day, that I may test them, whether they will walk in My law or not. 5And it shall be on the sixth day that they shall prepare what they bring in, and it shall be twice as much as they gather daily."

6Then Moses and Aaron said to all the children of Israel, "At evening you shall know that the LORD has brought you out of the land of Egypt. 7And in the morning you shall see the glory of the LORD; for He hears your complaints against the LORD.

But what *are* we, that you complain against us?" 8Also Moses said, "*This shall be seen* when the LORD gives you meat to eat in the evening, and in the morning bread to the full; for the LORD hears your complaints which you make against Him. And what *are* we? Your complaints *are* not against us but against the LORD."

9Then Moses spoke to Aaron, "Say to all the congregation of the children of Israel, 'Come near before the LORD, for He has heard your complaints.' " 10Now it came to pass, as Aaron spoke to the whole congregation of the children of Israel, that they looked toward the wilderness, and behold, the glory of the LORD appeared in the cloud.

11And the LORD spoke to Moses, saying, 12"I have heard the complaints of the children of Israel. Speak to them, saying, 'At twilight you shall eat meat, and in the morning you shall be filled with bread. And you shall know that I *am* the LORD your God.' "

13So it was that quails came up at evening and covered the camp, and in the morning the dew lay all around the camp. 14And when the layer of dew lifted, there, on the surface of the wilderness, was a small round substance, *as* fine as frost on the ground. 15So when the children of Israel saw *it,* they said to one another, "What is it?" For they did not know what it *was.*

And Moses said to them, "This *is* the bread which the LORD has given you to eat. 16This is the thing which the LORD has commanded: 'Let every man gather it according to each one's need, one omer for each person, *according to the* number of persons; let every man take for *those* who *are* in his tent.' "

17Then the children of Israel did so and gathered, some more, some less. 18So when they measured *it* by omers, he who gathered much had nothing left over, and he who gathered little had no lack. Every man had gathered according to each one's need. 19And Moses said, "Let no one leave any of it till morning." 20Notwithstanding they did not heed Moses. But some of them left part of it until morning, and it bred worms and stank. And Moses was angry with them. 21So they gathered it every morning, every man according to his need. And when the sun became hot, it melted.

22And so it was, on the sixth day, *that* they gathered twice as much bread, two omers for each one. And all the rulers of the congregation came and told Moses. 23Then he said to them, "This *is what* the LORD has said: 'Tomorrow *is* a Sabbath rest, a holy Sabbath to the LORD. Bake what you will bake *today,* and boil what you will boil; and lay up for yourselves all that remains, to be kept until morning.' " 24So they laid it up till morning, as Moses commanded; and it did not stink, nor were there any worms in it. 25Then Moses said, "Eat that today, for today *is* a Sabbath to the LORD; today you will not find it in the field. 26Six days you shall gather it, but on the seventh day, the Sabbath, there will be none."

27Now it happened *that some* of the people went out on the seventh day to gather, but they found none. 28And the LORD said to Moses, "How long do you refuse to keep My commandments and My laws? 29See! For the LORD has given you the Sabbath; therefore He gives you on the sixth day bread for two days. Let every man remain in his place; let no man go out of his place on the seventh day." 30So the people rested on the seventh day.

31And the house of Israel called its name Manna.ᵃ And it *was* like white coriander seed, and the taste of it *was* like wafers *made* with honey.

32Then Moses said, "This *is* the thing which the LORD has commanded: 'Fill an omer with it, to be kept for your generations, that they may see the bread with which I fed you in the wilderness, when I brought you out of the land of Egypt.' " 33And Moses said to Aaron, "Take a pot and put an omer of manna in it, and lay it up before the LORD, to be kept for your generations." 34As the LORD commanded Moses, so Aaron laid it up before the Testimony, to be kept. 35And the children of Israel ate manna forty years, until they came to an inhabited land; they ate manna until they came to the border of the land of Canaan. 36Now an omer *is* one-tenth of an ephah.

Water from the Rock

17 1Then all the congregation of the children of Israel set out on their journey from the Wilderness of Sin, according to the commandment of the LORD, and camped in Rephidim; but *there was* no water for the people to drink. 2Therefore the people contended with Moses, and said, "Give us water, that we may drink."

So Moses said to them, "Why do you contend with me? Why do you tempt the LORD?"

3And the people thirsted there for water, and the people complained against Moses, and said, "Why *is* it you have brought us up out of Egypt, to kill us and our children and our livestock with thirst?"

4So Moses cried out to the LORD, saying, "What shall I do with this people? They are almost ready to stone me!"

5And the LORD said to Moses, "Go on before the people, and take with you some of the elders of Israel. Also take in your hand your rod with which you struck the river, and go. 6Behold, I will stand before you there on the rock in Horeb; and you shall strike the rock, and water will come out of it, that the people may drink."

And Moses did so in the sight of the el-

16:31 ᵃLiterally *What?* (compare Exodus 16:15)

DAILY LIFE AND CUSTOMS

The 7-day week, with its rhythm of 6 days of work and 1 day of rest (Ex. 16:30), is revealed in Gen. 1 and in Ex. 20. The early Assyrians and the Egyptians divided time into periods of 10 days, while the Sumerians used 7. The recognized number of planets was 7, but this is not necessarily the reason for the length of the week.

ders of Israel. [7]So he called the name of the place Massah[a] and Meribah,[b] because of the contention of the children of Israel, and because they tempted the LORD, saying, "Is the LORD among us or not?"

Victory over the Amalekites

[8]Now Amalek came and fought with Israel in Rephidim. [9]And Moses said to Joshua, "Choose us some men and go out, fight with Amalek. Tomorrow I will stand on the top of the hill with the rod of God in my hand." [10]So Joshua did as Moses said to him, and fought with Amalek. And Moses, Aaron, and Hur went up to the top of the hill. [11]And so it was, when Moses held up his hand, that Israel prevailed; and when he let down his hand, Amalek prevailed. [12]But Moses' hands *became* heavy; so they took a stone and put *it* under him, and he sat on it. And Aaron and Hur supported his hands, one on one side, and the other on the other side; and his hands were steady until the going down of the sun. [13]So Joshua defeated Amalek and his people with the edge of the sword.

[14]Then the LORD said to Moses, "Write this *for* a memorial in the book and recount *it* in the hearing of Joshua, that I will utterly blot out the remembrance of Amalek from under heaven." [15]And Moses built an altar and called its name, The-LORD-Is-My-Banner;[a] [16]for he said, "Because the LORD has sworn: the LORD *will have* war with Amalek from generation to generation."

Jethro's Advice

18 [1]And Jethro, the priest of Midian, Moses' father-in-law, heard of all that God had done for Moses and for Israel His people—that the LORD had brought Israel out of Egypt. [2]Then Jethro, Moses' father-in-law, took Zipporah, Moses' wife, after he had sent her back, [3]with her two sons, of whom the name of one *was* Gershom (for he said, "I have been a stranger in a foreign land")[a] [4]and the name of the other *was* Eliezer[a] (for *he said,* "The God of my father *was* my help, and delivered me from the sword of Pharaoh"); [5]and Jethro, Moses' father-in-law, came with his sons and his wife to Moses in the wilderness,

where he was encamped at the mountain of God. [6]Now he had said to Moses, "I, your father-in-law Jethro, am coming to you with your wife and her two sons with her."

[7]So Moses went out to meet his father-in-law, bowed down, and kissed him. And they asked each other about *their* well-being, and they went into the tent. [8]And Moses told his father-in-law all that the LORD had done to Pharaoh and to the Egyptians for Israel's sake, all the hardship that had come upon them on the way, and *how* the LORD had delivered them. [9]Then Jethro rejoiced for all the good which the LORD had done for Israel, whom He had delivered out of the hand of the Egyptians. [10]And Jethro said, "Blessed *be* the LORD, who has delivered you out of the hand of the Egyptians and out of the hand of Pharaoh, *and* who has delivered the people from under the hand of the Egyptians. [11]Now I know that the LORD *is* greater than all the gods; for in the very thing in which they behaved proudly, *He was* above them." [12]Then Jethro, Moses' father-in-law, took[a] a burnt offering and *other* sacrifices *to offer* to God. And Aaron came with all the elders of Israel to eat bread with Moses' father-in-law before God.

[13]And so it was, on the next day, that Moses sat to judge the people; and the people stood before Moses from morning until evening. [14]So when Moses' father-in-law saw all that he did for the people, he said, "What *is* this thing that you are doing for the people? Why do you alone sit, and all the people stand before you from morning until evening?"

[15]And Moses said to his father-in-law, "Because the people come to me to inquire of God. [16]When they have a difficulty, they come to me, and I judge between one and another; and I make known the statutes of God and His laws."

17:7 [a]Literally *Tempted*   [b]Literally *Contention*
17:15 [a]Hebrew *YHWH Nissi*   18:3 [a]Compare
Exodus 2:22   18:4 [a]Literally *My God Is Help*
18:12 [a]Following Masoretic Text and Septuagint;
Syriac, Targum, and Vulgate read *offered.*

TIME CAPSULE   *1595 B.C.*

1595	Hittite king Mursilis I sacks Aleppo in northern Syria
1595	Mursilis I ends Old Babylonian dynasty of Hammurabi
1595–1000	Middle Babylonian period
1595	Agum II rules Babylon as first king of Kassite dynasty

¹⁷So Moses' father-in-law said to him, "The thing that you do *is* not good. ¹⁸Both you and these people who *are* with you will surely wear yourselves out. For this thing *is* too much for you; you are not able to perform it by yourself. ¹⁹Listen now to my voice; I will give you counsel, and God will be with you: Stand before God for the people, so that you may bring the difficulties to God. ²⁰And you shall teach them the statutes and the laws, and show them the way in which they must walk and the work they must do. ²¹Moreover you shall select from all the people able men, such as fear God, men of truth, hating covetousness; and place *such* over them *to be* rulers of thousands, rulers of hundreds, rulers of fifties, and rulers of tens. ²²And let them judge the people at all times. Then it will be *that* every great matter they shall bring to you, but every small matter they themselves shall judge. So it will be easier for you, for they will bear *the burden* with you. ²³If you do this thing, and God *so* commands you, then you will be able to endure, and all this people will also go to their place in peace."

²⁴So Moses heeded the voice of his father-in-law and did all that he had said. ²⁵And Moses chose able men out of all Israel, and made them heads over the people: rulers of thousands, rulers of hundreds, rulers of fifties, and rulers of tens. ²⁶So they judged the people at all times; the hard cases they brought to Moses, but they judged every small case themselves. ²⁷Then Moses let his father-in-law depart, and he went his way to his own land.

At Mount Sinai

The Israelites arrived at Mount Sinai in the 3rd month following their exodus from Egypt (Ex. 19:1). Here they would remain for several months while God's glory rested on the mountain. They completed work on the tabernacle in the 1st month of the 2nd year of the Exodus (Ex. 40:17), thus one year after leaving Egypt (Ex. 12:2, 3).

▼ ■ Exodus 19:1—40:38

Exodus
Israel at the Mountain

19:1 In the third month after the children of Israel had gone out of the land of Egypt, on the same day, they came *to* the Wilderness of Sinai. ²For they had departed from Rephidim, had come *to* the Wilderness of Sinai, and camped in the wilderness. So Israel camped there before the mountain.

³And Moses went up to God, and the LORD called to him from the mountain, saying, "Thus you shall say to the house of Jacob, and tell the children of Israel: ⁴'You have seen what I did to the Egyptians, and *how* I bore you on eagles' wings and brought you to Myself. ⁵Now therefore, if you will indeed obey My voice and keep My covenant, then you shall be a special treasure to Me above all people; for all the earth *is* Mine. ⁶And you shall be to Me a kingdom of priests and a holy nation.' These *are* the words which you shall speak to the children of Israel."

⁷So Moses came and called for the elders of the people, and laid before them all these words which the LORD commanded him. ⁸Then all the people answered together and said, "All that the LORD has spoken we will do." So Moses brought back the words of the people to the LORD. ⁹And the LORD said to Moses, "Behold, I come to you in the thick cloud, that the people may hear when I speak with you, and believe you forever."

So Moses told the words of the people to the LORD.

¹⁰Then the LORD said to Moses, "Go to the people and consecrate them today and tomorrow, and let them wash their clothes. ¹¹And let them be ready for the third day. For on the third day the LORD will come down upon Mount Sinai in the sight of all the people. ¹²You shall set bounds for the people all around, saying, 'Take heed to yourselves *that* you do *not* go up to the mountain or touch its base. Whoever touches the mountain shall surely be put to death. ¹³Not a hand shall touch him, but he shall surely be stoned or shot *with an arrow;* whether man or beast, he shall not live.' When the trumpet sounds long, they shall come near the mountain."

¹⁴So Moses went down from the mountain to the people and sanctified the people, and they washed their clothes. ¹⁵And he said to the people, "Be ready for the third day; do not come near *your* wives."

¹⁶Then it came to pass on the third day, in the morning, that there were thunderings and lightnings, and a thick cloud on the mountain; and the sound of the trumpet was very loud, so that all the peo-

WHERE THE GODS LIVE: SACRED MOUNTAINS (Ex. 19:2, 3)

Where heaven and earth met, humans and deities could come together. On the physical landscape of the ancient world, this meant mountains. Since ancient people thought deities actually lived on the peak of a sacred mountain, they built temples or altars on or near the mountain in honor of the gods.

So it was all over the Near East. The Canaanites and Phoenicians believed their gods lived on actual mountains near their cities. At Ugarit, El lived on Mount Zaphon. In Ex. 19:20, Israel's God Yahweh lives on Mount Sinai. Later, the Judeans believed Yahweh took up His residence on Mount Zion in Jerusalem, while the Samaritans said He lived on Mount Gerizim near Samaria. In the flat river valleys of Mesopotamia, worshipers of various deities built their own mountains, called ziggurats. The most famous ziggurat was that of Babylon, Etemenanki.

The appearance of the deity (called "theophany") at the sacred mountain often was accompanied by thunder, lightning, earthquakes, clouds, loud noises, lesser deities, and terror. Many of these characteristics are present in the description of God coming down on Sinai (Ex. 19:16–19).

Usually only priests were willing to risk experiencing such presence of the god. The actual appearance of the deity itself was thought to be dangerous to people who had not properly prepared themselves. The people of Israel were carefully prepared for the visit of God to the mountain (Ex. 19:10–13). Despite preparations, they were too terrified to actually meet God, and so Moses served as intermediary between God and the people (Ex. 19:23–25; 20:18–21).

---

ple who *were* in the camp trembled. ¹⁷And Moses brought the people out of the camp to meet with God, and they stood at the foot of the mountain. ¹⁸Now Mount Sinai *was* completely in smoke, because the LORD descended upon it in fire. Its smoke ascended like the smoke of a furnace, and the whole mountainᵃ quaked greatly. ¹⁹And when the blast of the trumpet sounded long and became louder and louder, Moses spoke, and God answered him by voice. ²⁰Then the LORD came down upon Mount Sinai, on the top of the mountain. And the LORD called Moses to the top of the mountain, and Moses went up.

²¹And the LORD said to Moses, "Go down and warn the people, lest they break through to gaze at the LORD, and many of them perish. ²²Also let the priests

who come near the LORD consecrate themselves, lest the LORD break out against them."

²³But Moses said to the LORD, "The people cannot come up to Mount Sinai; for You warned us, saying, 'Set bounds around the mountain and consecrate it.'"

²⁴Then the LORD said to him, "Away! Get down and then come up, you and Aaron with you. But do not let the priests and the people break through to come up to the LORD, lest He break out against them." ²⁵So Moses went down to the people and spoke to them.

The Ten Commandments

20 ¹And God spoke all these words, saying:

2 "I *am* the LORD your God, who brought you out of the land of Egypt, out of the house of bondage.

19:18 ᵃSeptuagint reads *all the people.*

GEOGRAPHY AND ENVIRONMENT

The Sinai Peninsula is a triangle of land between Egypt and Israel, about 125 miles east to west and 200 miles north to south. The traditional location of Mount Sinai (Ex. 19:18) is toward the south at Jebel Musa, a mountain 7,500 feet in altitude. This tradition is not early. The peninsula as a whole is inhospitable, desert land.

3 "You shall have no other gods before Me.

4 "You shall not make for yourself a carved image—any likeness *of anything* that *is* in heaven above, or that *is* in the earth beneath, or that *is* in the water under the earth; ⁵you shall not bow down to them nor serve them. For I, the LORD your God, *am* a jealous God, visiting the iniquity of the fathers upon the children to the third and fourth *generations* of those who hate Me, ⁶but showing mercy to thousands, to those who love Me and keep My commandments.

7 "You shall not take the name of the LORD your God in vain, for the LORD will not hold *him* guiltless who takes His name in vain.

8 "Remember the Sabbath day, to keep it holy. ⁹Six days you shall labor and do all your work, ¹⁰but the seventh day *is* the Sabbath of the LORD your God. *In it* you shall do no work: you, nor your son, nor your daughter, nor your male servant, nor your female servant, nor your cattle, nor your stranger who *is* within your gates. ¹¹For *in* six days the LORD made the heavens and the earth, the sea, and all that *is* in them, and rested the seventh day. Therefore the LORD blessed the Sabbath day and hallowed it.

12 "Honor your father and your mother, that your days may be long upon the land which the LORD your God is giving you.

13 "You shall not murder.

14 "You shall not commit adultery.

15 "You shall not steal.

16 "You shall not bear false witness against your neighbor.

17 "You shall not covet your neighbor's house; you shall not covet your neighbor's wife, nor his male servant, nor his female servant, nor his ox, nor his donkey, nor anything that *is* your neighbor's."

The People Afraid of God's Presence

¹⁸Now all the people witnessed the thunderings, the lightning flashes, the sound of the trumpet, and the mountain smoking; and when the people saw *it,* they trembled and stood afar off. ¹⁹Then they said to Moses, "You speak with us, and we will hear; but let not God speak with us, lest we die."

²⁰And Moses said to the people, "Do not fear; for God has come to test you, and that His fear may be before you, so that you may not sin." ²¹So the people stood afar off, but Moses drew near the thick darkness where God *was.*

The Law of the Altar

²²Then the LORD said to Moses, "Thus you shall say to the children of Israel: 'You have seen that I have talked with you from heaven. ²³You shall not make *anything to be* with Me—gods of silver or gods of gold you shall not make for yourselves. ²⁴An altar of earth you shall make for Me, and you shall sacrifice on it your burnt offerings and your peace offerings, your sheep and your oxen. In every place where I record My name I will come to you, and I will bless you. ²⁵And if you make Me an altar of stone, you shall not build it of hewn stone; for if you use your tool on it, you have profaned it. ²⁶Nor shall you go up by steps to My altar, that your nakedness may not be exposed on it.'

The Law Concerning Servants

21 ¹"Now these *are* the judgments which you shall set before them: ²If you buy a Hebrew servant, he shall serve six years; and in the seventh he shall go out free and pay nothing. ³If he comes in by himself, he shall go out by himself; if he *comes in* married, then his wife shall go out with him. ⁴If his master has given him a wife, and she has borne him sons or daughters, the wife and her children shall be her

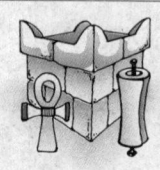

RELIGION AND WORSHIP

Almost all ancient worshipers had statues of one or more of their gods. The Israelites were the outstanding exception to this rule (Ex. 20:4). When Pompey the Great entered the temple in Jerusalem in 63 B.C., he and his men were deeply impressed that they found no image of God in the sanctuary.

THE OX THAT GORED (Ex. 21:28–32)

Certain laws found in the Law of Moses concern subject matter that is treated quite similarly in the laws of other ancient Near Eastern cultures. One example is the law dealing with an ox that gores a human causing personal injury or death (Ex. 21:28–32). A "goring-ox" law was not unique to Israel; at least four other ancient Near Eastern traditions had legislation on this issue.

The earliest appearance of ox-goring laws comes from Eshnunna, an early Old Babylonian period site (c. 2017–1793 B.C.) on the Diyala River in Mesopotamia. Such laws are also found in the Code of Hammurabi, a set of legal promulgations from Babylon (c. 1792–1750 B.C.). In these laws, there is no stipulation to stone an ox that gored habitually. The owner, rather, was heavily fined, especially if the ox had not been previously dehorned. In Israel, owners were also fined (21:30–32), but the ox was stoned (21:28).

Other examples of ox-goring legislation show that such laws existed over a long period of time. One letter comes from the Old Babylonian city of Mari on the Syrian side of the Euphrates River. The Mari tablets date from around 1813 to 1760 B.C., and demonstrate that goring-ox laws were actually put into practice in Syro-Mesopotamia during the time of the biblical patriarchs. Another letter from Nuzi in northern Mesopotamia places similar laws a few centuries later (c. 1450–1330 B.C.).

Apparently, Israel shared in a tradition of laws that were common in the ancient Near East. In the case of the goring-ox laws, Israel and the Old Babylonian cultures shared the principle of negligence and liability. Owners who failed to safeguard against potentially dangerous situations were held responsible (21:29).

---

master's, and he shall go out by himself. ⁵But if the servant plainly says, 'I love my master, my wife, and my children; I will not go out free,' ⁶then his master shall bring him to the judges. He shall also bring him to the door, or to the doorpost, and his master shall pierce his ear with an awl; and he shall serve him forever.

⁷"And if a man sells his daughter to be a female slave, she shall not go out as the male slaves do. ⁸If she does not please her master, who has betrothed her to himself, then he shall let her be redeemed. He shall have no right to sell her to a foreign people, since he has dealt deceitfully with her. ⁹And if he has betrothed her to his son, he shall deal with her according to the custom of daughters. ¹⁰If he takes another *wife,* he shall not diminish her food, her clothing, and her marriage rights. ¹¹And if he does not do these three for her, then she shall go out free, without *paying* money.

The Law Concerning Violence

¹²"He who strikes a man so that he dies shall surely be put to death. ¹³However, if he did not lie in wait, but God delivered *him* into his hand, then I will appoint for you a place where he may flee.

¹⁴"But if a man acts with premeditation against his neighbor, to kill him by treachery, you shall take him from My altar, that he may die.

¹⁵"And he who strikes his father or his mother shall surely be put to death.

¹⁶"He who kidnaps a man and sells him, or if he is found in his hand, shall surely be put to death.

¹⁷"And he who curses his father or his mother shall surely be put to death.

¹⁸"If men contend with each other, and one strikes the other with a stone or with *his* fist, and he does not die but is confined to *his* bed, ¹⁹if he rises again and walks about outside with his staff, then he who struck *him* shall be acquitted. He shall only pay *for* the loss of his time, and shall provide *for him* to be thoroughly healed.

²⁰"And if a man beats his male or female servant with a rod, so that he dies under his hand, he shall surely be punished. ²¹Notwithstanding, if he remains alive a day or two, he shall not be punished; for he *is* his property.

²²"If men fight, and hurt a woman with child, so that she gives birth prematurely, yet no harm follows, he shall surely be punished accordingly as the woman's husband imposes on him; and he shall pay as the judges *determine.* ²³But if *any* harm

follows, then you shall give life for life, [24]eye for eye, tooth for tooth, hand for hand, foot for foot, [25]burn for burn, wound for wound, stripe for stripe.

[26]"If a man strikes the eye of his male or female servant, and destroys it, he shall let him go free for the sake of his eye. [27]And if he knocks out the tooth of his male or female servant, he shall let him go free for the sake of his tooth.

Animal Control Laws

[28]"If an ox gores a man or a woman to death, then the ox shall surely be stoned, and its flesh shall not be eaten; but the owner of the ox *shall be* acquitted. [29]But if the ox tended to thrust with its horn in times past, and it has been made known to his owner, and he has not kept it confined, so that it has killed a man or a woman, the ox shall be stoned and its owner also shall be put to death. [30]If there is imposed on him a sum of money, then he shall pay to redeem his life, whatever is imposed on him. [31]Whether it has gored a son or gored a daughter, according to this judgment it shall be done to him. [32]If the ox gores a male or female servant, he shall give to their master thirty shekels of silver, and the ox shall be stoned.

[33]"And if a man opens a pit, or if a man digs a pit and does not cover it, and an ox or a donkey falls in it, [34]the owner of the pit shall make *it* good; he shall give money to their owner, but the dead *animal* shall be his.

[35]"If one man's ox hurts another's, so that it dies, then they shall sell the live ox and divide the money from it; and the dead *ox* they shall also divide. [36]Or if it was known that the ox tended to thrust in time past, and its owner has not kept it confined, he shall surely pay ox for ox, and the dead animal shall be his own.

Responsibility for Property

22 [1]"If a man steals an ox or a sheep, and slaughters it or sells it, he shall restore five oxen for an ox and four sheep for a sheep. [2]If the thief is found breaking in, and he is struck so that he dies, *there shall be* no guilt for his bloodshed. [3]If the sun has risen on him, *there shall be* guilt for his bloodshed. He should make full restitution; if he has nothing, then he shall be sold for his theft. [4]If the theft is certainly found alive in his hand, whether it is an ox or donkey or sheep, he shall restore double.

[5]"If a man causes a field or vineyard to be grazed, and lets loose his animal, and it feeds in another man's field, he shall make restitution from the best of his own field and the best of his own vineyard.

[6]"If fire breaks out and catches in thorns, so that stacked grain, standing grain, or the field is consumed, he who kindled the fire shall surely make restitution.

[7]"If a man delivers to his neighbor money or articles to keep, and it is stolen out of the man's house, if the thief is found, he shall pay double. [8]If the thief is not found, then the master of the house shall be brought to the judges *to see* whether he has put his hand into his neighbor's goods.

[9]"For any kind of trespass, *whether it concerns* an ox, a donkey, a sheep, or clothing, *or* for any kind of lost thing which *another* claims to be his, the cause of both parties shall come before the judges; *and* whomever the judges condemn shall pay double to his neighbor. [10]If a man delivers to his neighbor a donkey, an ox, a sheep, or any animal to keep, and it dies, is hurt, or driven away, no one seeing *it*, [11]*then* an oath of the Lord shall be between them both, that he has not put his hand into his neighbor's goods; and the owner of it shall accept *that,* and he shall not make *it* good. [12]But if, in fact, it is stolen from him, he shall make restitution to the owner of it. [13]If it is torn to pieces *by a beast, then* he shall bring it as evidence, *and* he shall not make good what was torn.

[14]"And if a man borrows *anything* from his neighbor, and it becomes injured or dies, the owner of it not *being* with it, he shall surely make *it* good. [15]If its owner

CULTURE AND SOCIETY

The law that requires a penalty equal to the damage caused by the crime is called Lex talionis. *This is a Latin term that means "law of retaliation." The idea is familiar to most people through its expression in the Hebrew Bible (Ex. 21:24). Some ancient codes called for penalties greater than the injury to be repaid.*

THE CODE OF HAMMURABI (Ex. 22:16, 17)

Babylon's king Hammurabi (1792–1750 B.C.) is best known for his law code. The Code of Hammurabi (as it is called) contains 282 laws and has numerous parallels with Scripture. Few of the laws, however, were ever cited in existing Old Babylonian court cases. At any rate, the collection of laws therein is incomplete and ignores many subjects. Hammurabi did not create these laws; rather, they appear to be a collection of diverse traditions.

The format of the Code of Hammurabi shows a similarity with laws in Exodus, Leviticus, and Deuteronomy. Both the Code of Hammurabi and the Covenant Code, found in Ex. 20:22—23:33, have a series of laws structured in an "if . . . then" format. These laws begin with the word "if," introducing a description of a potentially criminal situation. The format continues with the word "then," offering a description of the penalty. This format or style of law is often called case law since its format describes particular cases or situations.

The "if . . . then" format of the Code of Hammurabi appears frequently in the Covenant Code (with and without the word "then"; Ex. 22:8, 16, 17). The similarities of these two codes (and others) show there was a widespread legal tradition in the 2nd millennium B.C. In fact a number of situations mentioned in the Hammurabi code are virtually duplicated in the Mosaic code, often with different penalties.

---

was with it, he shall not make *it* good; if it *was* hired, it came for its hire.

Moral and Ceremonial Principles

16"If a man entices a virgin who is not betrothed, and lies with her, he shall surely pay the bride-price for her *to be* his wife. 17If her father utterly refuses to give her to him, he shall pay money according to the bride-price of virgins.

18"You shall not permit a sorceress to live.

19"Whoever lies with an animal shall surely be put to death.

20"He who sacrifices to *any* god, except to the LORD only, he shall be utterly destroyed.

21"You shall neither mistreat a stranger nor oppress him, for you were strangers in the land of Egypt.

22"You shall not afflict any widow or fatherless child. 23If you afflict them in any way, *and* they cry at all to Me, I will surely hear their cry; 24and My wrath will become hot, and I will kill you with the sword; your wives shall be widows, and your children fatherless.

25"If you lend money to *any of* My people *who are* poor among you, you shall not be like a moneylender to him; you shall not charge him interest. 26If you ever take your neighbor's garment as a pledge, you shall return it to him before the sun goes down. 27For that *is* his only covering, it *is* his garment for his skin. What will he sleep in? And it will be that when he cries to Me, I will hear, for I *am* gracious.

28"You shall not revile God, nor curse a ruler of your people.

29"You shall not delay *to offer* the first of your ripe produce and your juices. The firstborn of your sons you shall give to Me. 30Likewise you shall do with your oxen *and* your sheep. It shall be with its mother seven days; on the eighth day you shall give it to Me.

31"And you shall be holy men to Me: you shall not eat meat torn *by beasts* in the field; you shall throw it to the dogs.

Justice for All

23 1"You shall not circulate a false report. Do not put your hand with the wicked to be an unrighteous witness. 2You shall not follow a crowd to do evil; nor shall you testify in a dispute so as to turn aside after many to pervert *justice.* 3You shall not show partiality to a poor man in his dispute.

4"If you meet your enemy's ox or his donkey going astray, you shall surely bring it back to him again. 5If you see the donkey of one who hates you lying under its burden, and you would refrain from helping it, you shall surely help him with it.

6"You shall not pervert the judgment of your poor in his dispute. 7Keep yourself far from a false matter; do not kill the innocent and righteous. For I will not justify the wicked. 8And you shall take no bribe, for a bribe blinds the discerning and perverts the words of the righteous.

9"Also you shall not oppress a stranger, for you know the heart of a stranger, because you were strangers in the land of Egypt.

The Law of Sabbaths

10"Six years you shall sow your land and gather in its produce, 11but the seventh *year* you shall let it rest and lie fallow, that the poor of your people may eat; and what they leave, the beasts of the field may eat. In like manner you shall do with your vineyard *and* your olive grove. 12Six days you shall do your work, and on the seventh day you shall rest, that your ox and your donkey may rest, and the son of your female servant and the stranger may be refreshed.

13"And in all that I have said to you, be circumspect and make no mention of the name of other gods, nor let it be heard from your mouth.

Three Annual Feasts

14"Three times you shall keep a feast to Me in the year: 15You shall keep the Feast of Unleavened Bread (you shall eat unleavened bread seven days, as I commanded you, at the time appointed in the month of Abib, for in it you came out of Egypt; none shall appear before Me empty); 16and the Feast of Harvest, the firstfruits of your labors which you have sown in the field; and the Feast of Ingathering at the end of the year, when you have gathered in *the fruit of* your labors from the field.

17"Three times in the year all your males shall appear before the Lord GOD.ª

18"You shall not offer the blood of My sacrifice with leavened bread; nor shall the fat of My sacrifice remain until morning. 19The first of the firstfruits of your land you shall bring into the house of the LORD your God. You shall not boil a young goat in its mother's milk.

The Angel and the Promises

20"Behold, I send an Angel before you to keep you in the way and to bring you into the place which I have prepared. 21Beware of Him and obey His voice; do not provoke Him, for He will not pardon your transgressions; for My name *is* in Him. 22But if you indeed obey His voice and do all that I speak, then I will be an enemy to your enemies and an adversary to your ad-

versaries. 23For My Angel will go before you and bring you in to the Amorites and the Hittites and the Perizzites and the Canaanites and the Hivites and the Jebusites; and I will cut them off. 24You shall not bow down to their gods, nor serve them, nor do according to their works; but you shall utterly overthrow them and completely break down their *sacred* pillars.

25"So you shall serve the LORD your God, and He will bless your bread and your water. And I will take sickness away from the midst of you. 26No one shall suffer miscarriage or be barren in your land; I will fulfill the number of your days.

27"I will send My fear before you, I will cause confusion among all the people to whom you come, and will make all your enemies turn *their* backs to you. 28And I will send hornets before you, which shall drive out the Hivite, the Canaanite, and the Hittite from before you. 29I will not drive them out from before you in one year, lest the land become desolate and the beasts of the field become too numerous for you. 30Little by little I will drive them out from before you, until you have increased, and you inherit the land. 31And I will set your bounds from the Red Sea to the sea, Philistia, and from the desert to the River.ª For I will deliver the inhabitants of the land into your hand, and you shall drive them out before you. 32You shall make no covenant with them, nor with their gods. 33They shall not dwell in your land, lest they make you sin against Me. For *if* you serve their gods, it will surely be a snare to you."

Israel Affirms the Covenant

24 1Now He said to Moses, "Come up to the LORD, you and Aaron, Nadab and Abihu, and seventy of the elders of Israel, and worship from afar. 2And Moses alone shall come near the LORD, but they shall not come near; nor shall the people go up with him."

3So Moses came and told the people all the words of the LORD and all the judgments. And all the people answered with one voice and said, "All the words which the LORD has said we will do." 4And Moses wrote all the words of the LORD. And he rose early in the morning, and built an altar at the foot of the mountain, and twelve

---

23:17 ªHebrew YHWH, usually translated LORD
23:31 ªHebrew Nahar, the Euphrates

pillars according to the twelve tribes of Israel. [5]Then he sent young men of the children of Israel, who offered burnt offerings and sacrificed peace offerings of oxen to the LORD. [6]And Moses took half the blood and put *it* in basins, and half the blood he sprinkled on the altar. [7]Then he took the Book of the Covenant and read in the hearing of the people. And they said, "All that the LORD has said we will do, and be obedient." [8]And Moses took the blood, sprinkled *it* on the people, and said, "This is the blood of the covenant which the LORD has made with you according to all these words."

On the Mountain with God

[9]Then Moses went up, also Aaron, Nadab, and Abihu, and seventy of the elders of Israel, [10]and they saw the God of Israel. And *there was* under His feet as it were a paved work of sapphire stone, and it was like the very heavens in *its* clarity. [11]But on the nobles of the children of Israel He did not lay His hand. So they saw God, and they ate and drank.

[12]Then the LORD said to Moses, "Come up to Me on the mountain and be there; and I will give you tablets of stone, and the law and commandments which I have written, that you may teach them."

[13]So Moses arose with his assistant Joshua, and Moses went up to the mountain of God. [14]And he said to the elders, "Wait here for us until we come back to you. Indeed, Aaron and Hur *are* with you. If any man has a difficulty, let him go to them." [15]Then Moses went up into the mountain, and a cloud covered the mountain.

[16]Now the glory of the LORD rested on Mount Sinai, and the cloud covered it six days. And on the seventh day He called to Moses out of the midst of the cloud. [17]The sight of the glory of the LORD *was* like a consuming fire on the top of the mountain in the eyes of the children of Israel. [18]So Moses went into the midst of the cloud and went up into the mountain. And Moses was on the mountain forty days and forty nights.

Offerings for the Sanctuary

25 [1]Then the LORD spoke to Moses, saying: [2]"Speak to the children of Israel, that they bring Me an offering. From everyone who gives it willingly with his heart you shall take My offering. [3]And this *is* the offering which you shall take from them: gold, silver, and bronze; [4]blue, purple, and scarlet *thread,* fine linen, and goats' *hair;* [5]ram skins dyed red, badger skins, and acacia wood; [6]oil for the light, and spices for the anointing oil and for the sweet incense; [7]onyx stones, and stones to be set in the ephod and in the breastplate. [8]And let them make Me a sanctuary, that I may dwell among them. [9]According to all that I show you, *that is,* the pattern of the tabernacle and the pattern of all its furnishings, just so you shall make *it.*

The Ark of the Testimony

[10]"And they shall make an ark of acacia wood; two and a half cubits *shall be* its length, a cubit and a half its width, and a cubit and a half its height. [11]And you shall overlay it with pure gold, inside and out you shall overlay it, and shall make on it a molding of gold all around. [12]You shall cast four rings of gold for it, and put *them* in its four corners; two rings *shall be* on one side, and two rings on the other side. [13]And you shall make poles *of* acacia wood, and overlay them with gold. [14]You shall put the poles into the rings on the sides of the ark, that the ark may be carried by them. [15]The poles shall be in the rings of the ark; they shall not be taken from it. [16]And you shall put into the ark the Testimony which I will give you.

[17]"You shall make a mercy seat of pure gold; two and a half cubits *shall be* its length and a cubit and a half its width. [18]And you shall make two cherubim of gold; of hammered work you shall make them at the two ends of the mercy seat. [19]Make one cherub at one end, and the

---

CULTURE AND SOCIETY

The ark was a portable chest made of wood and covered with gold (Ex. 25:10). To this extent it resembles portable chests made by the Egyptians, displaying their skill in woodwork and decoration. The chests also provide examples of the way objects were carried with parallel bars arranged for the porters.

other cherub at the other end; you shall make the cherubim at the two ends of it *of one piece* with the mercy seat. ²⁰And the cherubim shall stretch out *their* wings above, covering the mercy seat with their wings, and they shall face one another; the faces of the cherubim *shall be* toward the mercy seat. ²¹You shall put the mercy seat on top of the ark, and in the ark you shall put the Testimony that I will give you. ²²And there I will meet with you, and I will speak with you from above the mercy seat, from between the two cherubim which *are* on the ark of the Testimony, about everything which I will give you in commandment to the children of Israel.

The Table for the Showbread

²³"You shall also make a table of acacia wood; two cubits *shall be* its length, a cubit its width, and a cubit and a half its height. ²⁴And you shall overlay it with pure gold, and make a molding of gold all around. ²⁵You shall make for it a frame of a handbreadth all around, and you shall make a gold molding for the frame all around. ²⁶And you shall make for it four rings of gold, and put the rings on the four corners that *are* at its four legs. ²⁷The rings shall be close to the frame, as holders for the poles to bear the table. ²⁸And you shall make the poles of acacia wood, and overlay them with gold, that the table may be carried with them. ²⁹You shall make its dishes, its pans, its pitchers, and its bowls for pouring. You shall make them of pure gold. ³⁰And you shall set the showbread on the table before Me always.

The Gold Lampstand

³¹"You shall also make a lampstand of pure gold; the lampstand shall be of hammered work. Its shaft, its branches, its bowls, its *ornamental* knobs, and flowers shall be *of one piece.* ³²And six branches shall come out of its sides: three branches of the lampstand out of one side, and three branches of the lampstand out of the other side. ³³Three bowls *shall be* made like almond *blossoms* on one branch, *with* an *ornamental* knob and a flower, and three bowls made like almond *blossoms* on the other branch, *with* an *ornamental* knob and a flower—and so for the six branches that come out of the lampstand. ³⁴On the lampstand itself four bowls *shall be* made like almond *blossoms, each with* its *ornamental* knob and flower. ³⁵And *there shall*

be a knob under the *first* two branches of the same, a knob under the *second* two branches of the same, and a knob under the *third* two branches of the same, according to the six branches that extend from the lampstand. ³⁶Their knobs and their branches *shall be of one piece;* all of it *shall be* one hammered piece of pure gold. ³⁷You shall make seven lamps for it, and they shall arrange its lamps so that they give light in front of it. ³⁸And its wick-trimmers and their trays *shall be* of pure gold. ³⁹It shall be made of a talent of pure gold, with all these utensils. ⁴⁰And see to it that you make *them* according to the pattern which was shown you on the mountain.

The Tabernacle

26 ¹"Moreover you shall make the tabernacle *with* ten curtains *of* fine woven linen and blue, purple, and scarlet *thread;* with artistic designs of cherubim you shall weave them. ²The length of each curtain *shall be* twenty-eight cubits, and the width of each curtain four cubits. And every one of the curtains shall have the same measurements. ³Five curtains shall be coupled to one another, and *the other* five curtains *shall be* coupled to one another. ⁴And you shall make loops of blue *yarn* on the edge of the curtain on the selvedge of *one* set, and likewise you shall do on the outer edge of *the other* curtain of the second set. ⁵Fifty loops you shall make in the one curtain, and fifty loops you shall make on the edge of the curtain that *is* on the end of the second set, that the loops may be clasped to one another. ⁶And you shall make fifty clasps of gold, and couple the curtains together with the clasps, so that it may be one tabernacle.

⁷"You shall also make curtains of goats' *hair,* to be a tent over the tabernacle. You shall make eleven curtains. ⁸The length of each curtain *shall be* thirty cubits, and the width of each curtain four cubits; and the eleven curtains shall all have the same measurements. ⁹And you shall couple five curtains by themselves and six curtains by themselves, and you shall double over the sixth curtain at the forefront of the tent. ¹⁰You shall make fifty loops on the edge of the curtain that is outermost in *one* set, and fifty loops on the edge of the curtain of the second set. ¹¹And you shall make fifty bronze clasps, put the clasps into the loops, and couple the tent together, that it may be one. ¹²The remnant that remains of the

curtains of the tent, the half curtain that remains, shall hang over the back of the tabernacle. ¹³And a cubit on one side and a cubit on the other side, of what remains of the length of the curtains of the tent, shall hang over the sides of the tabernacle, on this side and on that side, to cover it. ¹⁴"You shall also make a covering of ram skins dyed red for the tent, and a covering of badger skins above that.

¹⁵"And for the tabernacle you shall make the boards of acacia wood, standing upright. ¹⁶Ten cubits *shall be* the length of a board, and a cubit and a half *shall be* the width of each board. ¹⁷Two tenons *shall be* in each board for binding one to another. Thus you shall make for all the boards of the tabernacle. ¹⁸And you shall make the boards for the tabernacle, twenty boards for the south side. ¹⁹You shall make forty sockets of silver under the twenty boards: two sockets under each of the boards for its two tenons. ²⁰And for the second side of the tabernacle, the north side, *there shall be* twenty boards ²¹and their forty sockets of silver: two sockets under each of the boards. ²²For the far side of the tabernacle, westward, you shall make six boards. ²³And you shall also make two boards for the two back corners of the tabernacle. ²⁴They shall be coupled together at the bottom and they shall be coupled together at the top by one ring. Thus it shall be for both of them. They shall be for the two corners. ²⁵So there shall be eight boards with their sockets of silver—sixteen sockets— two sockets under each of the boards.

²⁶"And you shall make bars of acacia wood: five for the boards on one side of the tabernacle, ²⁷five bars for the boards on the other side of the tabernacle, and five bars for the boards of the side of the tabernacle, for the far side westward. ²⁸The middle bar shall pass through the midst of the boards from end to end. ²⁹You shall overlay the boards with gold, make their rings of gold *as* holders for the bars, and overlay the bars with gold. ³⁰And you shall raise up the tabernacle according to its pattern which you were shown on the mountain.

³¹"You shall make a veil woven of blue, purple, and scarlet *thread,* and fine woven linen. It shall be woven with an artistic design of cherubim. ³²You shall hang it upon the four pillars of acacia *wood* overlaid with gold. Their hooks *shall be* gold, upon four sockets of silver. ³³And you shall hang the veil from the clasps. Then you shall bring the ark of the Testimony in there, behind the veil. The veil shall be a divider for you between the holy *place* and the Most Holy. ³⁴You shall put the mercy seat upon the ark of the Testimony in the Most Holy. ³⁵You shall set the table outside the veil, and the lampstand across from the table on the side of the tabernacle toward the south; and you shall put the table on the north side.

³⁶"You shall make a screen for the door of the tabernacle, *woven of* blue, purple, and scarlet *thread,* and fine woven linen, made by a weaver. ³⁷And you shall make for the screen five pillars of acacia *wood,* and overlay them with gold; their hooks *shall be* gold, and you shall cast five sockets of bronze for them.

The Altar of Burnt Offering

27 ¹"You shall make an altar of acacia wood, five cubits long and five cubits wide—the altar shall be square—and its height *shall be* three cubits. ²You shall make its horns on its four corners; its horns shall be of one piece with it. And you shall overlay it with bronze. ³Also you shall make its pans to receive its ashes, and its shovels and its basins and its forks and its firepans; you shall make all its utensils of bronze. ⁴You shall make a grate for it, a network of bronze; and on the network you shall make four bronze rings at its four corners. ⁵You shall put it under the rim of the altar beneath, that the network may be midway up the altar. ⁶And you shall make poles for the altar, poles of acacia wood, and overlay them with bronze. ⁷The poles shall be put in the rings, and the poles shall be on the two sides of the altar to bear it. ⁸You shall make it hollow with

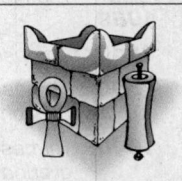

RELIGION AND WORSHIP

Ancient altars from the Middle East were often provided with projections on the four corners, called horns in the Bible (Ex. 27:2). Possibly these horns were used to hold the animal on the altar, as Ps. 118:27 would suggest. The bull was honored in different religions and the horn is a symbol of divine strength. But Exodus says nothing of this.

boards; as it was shown you on the mountain, so shall they make *it.*

The Court of the Tabernacle

9"You shall also make the court of the tabernacle. For the south side *there shall be* hangings for the court *made of* fine woven linen, one hundred cubits long for one side. 10And its twenty pillars and their twenty sockets *shall be* bronze. The hooks of the pillars and their bands *shall be* silver. 11Likewise along the length of the north side *there shall be* hangings one hundred *cubits* long, with its twenty pillars and their twenty sockets of bronze, and the hooks of the pillars and their bands of silver.

12"And along the width of the court on the west side *shall be* hangings of fifty cubits, with their ten pillars and their ten sockets. 13The width of the court on the east side *shall be* fifty cubits. 14The hangings on *one* side *of the gate shall be* fifteen cubits, *with* their three pillars and their three sockets. 15And on the other side *shall be* hangings of fifteen *cubits, with* their three pillars and their three sockets.

16"For the gate of the court *there shall be* a screen twenty cubits long, *woven of* blue, purple, and scarlet *thread,* and fine woven linen, made by a weaver. It *shall have* four pillars and four sockets. 17All the pillars around the court shall have bands of silver; their hooks *shall be* of silver and their sockets of bronze. 18The length of the court *shall be* one hundred cubits, the width fifty throughout, and the height five cubits, *made of* fine woven linen, and its sockets of bronze. 19All the utensils of the tabernacle for all its service, all its pegs, and all the pegs of the court, *shall be* of bronze.

TIME CAPSULE   *1553 to 1540 B.C.*

1553   *Kamose wars with Hyksos and reaches Avaris*

**1550–   *The New Kingdom in Egypt*
1069**

1540   *Ahmose I expels Hyksos from Egypt*

1540   *Ahmose I begins 3-year siege of Sharuhen in south Palestine*

1540   *Thebes becomes the family burying ground of the pharaohs*

The Care of the Lampstand

20"And you shall command the children of Israel that they bring you pure oil of pressed olives for the light, to cause the lamp to burn continually. 21In the tabernacle of meeting, outside the veil which *is* before the Testimony, Aaron and his sons shall tend it from evening until morning before the LORD. *It shall be* a statute forever to their generations on behalf of the children of Israel.

Garments for the Priesthood

28 1"Now take Aaron your brother, and his sons with him, from among the children of Israel, that he may minister to Me as priest, Aaron *and* Aaron's sons: Nadab, Abihu, Eleazar, and Ithamar. 2And you shall make holy garments for Aaron your brother, for glory and for beauty. 3So you shall speak to all *who are* gifted artisans, whom I have filled with the spirit of wisdom, that they may make Aaron's garments, to consecrate him, that he may minister to Me as priest. 4And these *are* the garments which they shall make: a breastplate, an ephod,[a] a robe, a skillfully woven tunic, a turban, and a sash. So they shall make holy garments for Aaron your brother and his sons, that he may minister to Me as priest.

The Ephod

5"They shall take the gold, blue, purple, and scarlet *thread,* and the fine linen, 6and they shall make the ephod of gold, blue, purple, *and* scarlet *thread,* and fine woven linen, artistically worked. 7It shall have two shoulder straps joined at its two edges, and *so* it shall be joined together. 8And the intricately woven band of the ephod, which *is* on it, shall be of the same workmanship, *made of* gold, blue, purple, and scarlet *thread,* and fine woven linen.

9"Then you shall take two onyx stones and engrave on them the names of the sons of Israel: 10six of their names on one stone and six names on the other stone, in order of their birth. 11With the work of an engraver in stone, *like* the engravings of a signet, you shall engrave the two stones with the names of the sons of Israel. You shall set them in settings of gold. 12And you shall put the two stones on the shoulders of the ephod *as* memorial stones for

---

28:4 aThat is, an ornamented vest

the sons of Israel. So Aaron shall bear their names before the LORD on his two shoulders as a memorial. ¹³You shall also make settings of gold, ¹⁴and you shall make two chains of pure gold like braided cords, and fasten the braided chains to the settings.

The Breastplate

¹⁵"You shall make the breastplate of judgment. Artistically woven according to the workmanship of the ephod you shall make it: of gold, blue, purple, and scarlet *thread,* and fine woven linen, you shall make it. ¹⁶It shall be doubled into a square: a span *shall be* its length, and a span *shall be* its width. ¹⁷And you shall put settings of stones in it, four rows of stones: *The first* row *shall be* a sardius, a topaz, and an emerald; *this shall be* the first row; ¹⁸the second row *shall be* a turquoise, a sapphire, and a diamond; ¹⁹the third row, a jacinth, an agate, and an amethyst; ²⁰and the fourth row, a beryl, an onyx, and a jasper. They shall be set in gold settings. ²¹And the stones shall have the names of the sons of Israel, twelve according to their names, *like* the engravings of a signet, each one with its own name; they shall be according to the twelve tribes.

²²"You shall make chains for the breastplate at the end, like braided cords of pure gold. ²³And you shall make two rings of gold for the breastplate, and put the two rings on the two ends of the breastplate. ²⁴Then you shall put the two braided *chains* of gold in the two rings which are on the ends of the breastplate; ²⁵and the *other* two ends of the two braided *chains* you shall fasten to the two settings, and put them on the shoulder straps of the ephod in the front.

²⁶"You shall make two rings of gold, and put them on the two ends of the breastplate, on the edge of it, which is on the inner side of the ephod. ²⁷And two *other* rings of gold you shall make, and put them on the two shoulder straps, underneath the ephod toward its front, right at the seam above the intricately woven band of the ephod. ²⁸They shall bind the breastplate by means of its rings to the rings of the ephod, using a blue cord, so that it is above the intricately woven band of the ephod, and so that the breastplate does not come loose from the ephod.

²⁹"So Aaron shall bear the names of the sons of Israel on the breastplate of judgment over his heart, when he goes into the holy *place,* as a memorial before the LORD continually. ³⁰And you shall put in the breastplate of judgment the Urim and the Thummim,ᵃ and they shall be over Aaron's heart when he goes in before the LORD. So Aaron shall bear the judgment of the children of Israel over his heart before the LORD continually.

Other Priestly Garments

³¹"You shall make the robe of the ephod all of blue. ³²There shall be an opening for his head in the middle of it; it shall have a woven binding all around its opening, like the opening in a coat of mail, so that it does not tear. ³³And upon its hem you shall make pomegranates of blue, purple, and scarlet, all around its hem, and bells of gold between them all around: ³⁴a golden bell and a pomegranate, a golden bell and a pomegranate, upon the hem of the robe all around. ³⁵And it shall be upon Aaron when he ministers, and its sound will be heard when he goes into the holy *place* before the LORD and when he comes out, that he may not die.

³⁶"You shall also make a plate of pure gold and engrave on it, *like* the engraving of a signet:

HOLINESS TO THE LORD.

³⁷And you shall put it on a blue cord, that it may be on the turban; it shall be on the front of the turban. ³⁸So it shall be on Aaron's forehead, that Aaron may bear the iniquity of the holy things which the children of Israel hallow in all their holy gifts; and

---

28:30 ᵃLiterally *the Lights and the Perfections* (compare Leviticus 8:8)

it shall always be on his forehead, that they may be accepted before the LORD.

39"You shall skillfully weave the tunic of fine linen *thread,* you shall make the turban of fine linen, and you shall make the sash of woven work.

40"For Aaron's sons you shall make tunics, and you shall make sashes for them. And you shall make hats for them, for glory and beauty. 41So you shall put them on Aaron your brother and on his sons with him. You shall anoint them, consecrate them, and sanctify them, that they may minister to Me as priests. 42And you shall make for them linen trousers to cover their nakedness; they shall reach from the waist to the thighs. 43They shall be on Aaron and on his sons when they come into the tabernacle of meeting, or when they come near the altar to minister in the holy *place,* that they do not incur iniquity and die. *It shall be* a statute forever to him and his descendants after him.

Aaron and His Sons Consecrated

29 1"And this is what you shall do to them to hallow them for ministering to Me as priests: Take one young bull and two rams without blemish, 2and unleavened bread, unleavened cakes mixed with oil, and unleavened wafers anointed with oil (you shall make them of wheat flour). 3You shall put them in one basket and bring them in the basket, with the bull and the two rams.

4"And Aaron and his sons you shall bring to the door of the tabernacle of meeting, and you shall wash them with water. 5Then you shall take the garments, put the tunic on Aaron, and the robe of the ephod, the ephod, and the breastplate, and gird him with the intricately woven band of the ephod. 6You shall put the turban on his head, and put the holy crown on the turban. 7And you shall take the anointing oil, pour *it* on his head, and anoint him. 8Then you shall bring his sons and put tunics on them. 9And you shall gird them with sashes, Aaron and his sons, and put the hats on them. The priesthood shall be theirs for a perpetual statute. So you shall consecrate Aaron and his sons.

10"You shall also have the bull brought before the tabernacle of meeting, and Aaron and his sons shall put their hands on the head of the bull. 11Then you shall kill the bull before the LORD, *by* the door of the tabernacle of meeting. 12You shall take

some of the blood of the bull and put *it* on the horns of the altar with your finger, and pour all the blood beside the base of the altar. 13And you shall take all the fat that covers the entrails, the fatty lobe *attached* to the liver, and the two kidneys and the fat that *is* on them, and burn *them* on the altar. 14But the flesh of the bull, with its skin and its offal, you shall burn with fire outside the camp. It *is* a sin offering.

15"You shall also take one ram, and Aaron and his sons shall put their hands on the head of the ram; 16and you shall kill the ram, and you shall take its blood and sprinkle *it* all around on the altar. 17Then you shall cut the ram in pieces, wash its entrails and its legs, and put *them* with its pieces and with its head. 18And you shall burn the whole ram on the altar. It *is* a burnt offering to the LORD; it *is* a sweet aroma, an offering made by fire to the LORD.

19"You shall also take the other ram, and Aaron and his sons shall put their hands on the head of the ram. 20Then you shall kill the ram, and take some of its blood and put *it* on the tip of the right ear of Aaron and on the tip of the right ear of his sons, on the thumb of their right hand and on the big toe of their right foot, and sprinkle the blood all around on the altar. 21And you shall take some of the blood that is on the altar, and some of the anointing oil, and sprinkle *it* on Aaron and on his garments, on his sons and on the garments of his sons with him; and he and his garments shall be hallowed, and his sons and his sons' garments with him.

22"Also you shall take the fat of the ram, the fat tail, the fat that covers the entrails, the fatty lobe *attached to* the liver, the two kidneys and the fat on them, the right thigh (for it *is* a ram of consecration), 23one loaf of bread, one cake *made with* oil, and one wafer from the basket of the unleavened bread that *is* before the LORD; 24and you shall put all these in the hands of Aaron and in the hands of his sons, and you shall wave them *as* a wave offering before the LORD. 25You shall receive them back from their hands and burn *them* on the altar as a burnt offering, as a sweet aroma before the LORD. It *is* an offering made by fire to the LORD.

26"Then you shall take the breast of the ram of Aaron's consecration and wave it *as* a wave offering before the LORD; and it shall be your portion. 27And from the ram of the consecration you shall consecrate the breast of the wave offering which is waved, and the thigh of the heave offering which is raised, of *that* which *is* for Aaron and of *that* which is for his sons. 28It shall be from the children of Israel *for* Aaron and his sons by a statute forever. For it is a heave offering; it shall be a heave offering from the children of Israel from the sacrifices of their peace offerings, *that is,* their heave offering to the LORD.

29"And the holy garments of Aaron shall be his sons' after him, to be anointed in them and to be consecrated in them. 30That son who becomes priest in his place shall put them on for seven days, when he enters the tabernacle of meeting to minister in the holy *place.*

31"And you shall take the ram of the consecration and boil its flesh in the holy place. 32Then Aaron and his sons shall eat the flesh of the ram, and the bread that *is* in the basket, *by* the door of the tabernacle of meeting. 33They shall eat those things with which the atonement was made, to consecrate *and* to sanctify them; but an outsider shall not eat *them,* because they *are* holy. 34And if any of the flesh of the consecration offerings, or of the bread, remains until the morning, then you shall burn the remainder with fire. It shall not be eaten, because it *is* holy.

35"Thus you shall do to Aaron and his sons, according to all that I have commanded you. Seven days you shall consecrate them. 36And you shall offer a bull every day *as* a sin offering for atonement. You shall cleanse the altar when you make atonement for it, and you shall anoint it to sanctify it. 37Seven days you shall make atonement for the altar and sanctify it. And the altar shall be most holy. Whatever touches the altar must be holy.[a]

The Daily Offerings

38"Now this *is* what you shall offer on the altar: two lambs of the first year, day by day continually. 39One lamb you shall offer in the morning, and the other lamb you shall offer at twilight. 40With the one lamb shall be one-tenth *of an ephah* of flour mixed with one-fourth of a hin of pressed oil, and one-fourth of a hin of wine *as* a drink offering. 41And the other lamb you shall offer at twilight; and you shall of-

fer with it the grain offering and the drink offering, as in the morning, for a sweet aroma, an offering made by fire to the LORD. 42*This shall be* a continual burnt offering throughout your generations *at* the door of the tabernacle of meeting before the LORD, where I will meet you to speak with you. 43And there I will meet with the children of Israel, and *the tabernacle* shall be sanctified by My glory. 44So I will consecrate the tabernacle of meeting and the altar. I will also consecrate both Aaron and his sons to minister to Me as priests. 45I will dwell among the children of Israel and will be their God. 46And they shall know that I *am* the LORD their God, who brought them up out of the land of Egypt, that I may dwell among them. I *am* the LORD their God.

The Altar of Incense

30 1"You shall make an altar to burn incense on; you shall make it of acacia wood. 2A cubit *shall be* its length and a cubit its width—it shall be square—and two cubits *shall be* its height. Its horns *shall be* of one piece with it. 3And you shall overlay its top, its sides all around, and its horns with pure gold; and you shall make for it a molding of gold all around. 4Two gold rings you shall make for it, under the molding on both its sides. You shall place *them* on its two sides, and they will be holders for the poles with which to bear it. 5You shall make the poles of acacia wood, and overlay them with gold. 6And you shall put it before the veil that *is* before the ark of the Testimony, before the mercy seat that *is* over the Testimony, where I will meet with you.

7"Aaron shall burn on it sweet incense every morning; when he tends the lamps, he shall burn incense on it. 8And when Aaron lights the lamps at twilight, he shall burn incense on it, a perpetual incense before the LORD throughout your generations. 9You shall not offer strange incense on it, or a burnt offering, or a grain offering; nor shall you pour a drink offering on it. 10And Aaron shall make atonement upon its horns once a year with the blood of the sin offering of atonement; once a year he shall make atonement upon it throughout your generations. It *is* most holy to the LORD."

The Ransom Money

11Then the LORD spoke to Moses, saying: 12"When you take the census of the

---

29:37 [a]Compare Numbers 4:15 and Haggai 2:11–13

children of Israel for their number, then every man shall give a ransom for himself to the LORD, when you number them, that there may be no plague among them when *you* number them. ¹³This is what everyone among those who are numbered shall give: half a shekel according to the shekel of the sanctuary (a shekel *is* twenty gerahs). The half-shekel *shall be* an offering to the LORD. ¹⁴Everyone included among those who are numbered, from twenty years old and above, shall give an offering to the LORD. ¹⁵The rich shall not give more and the poor shall not give less than half a shekel, when *you* give an offering to the LORD, to make atonement for yourselves. ¹⁶And you shall take the atonement money of the children of Israel, and shall appoint it for the service of the tabernacle of meeting, that it may be a memorial for the children of Israel before the LORD, to make atonement for yourselves."

The Bronze Laver

¹⁷Then the LORD spoke to Moses, saying: ¹⁸"You shall also make a laver of bronze, with its base also of bronze, for washing. You shall put it between the tabernacle of meeting and the altar. And you shall put water in it, ¹⁹for Aaron and his sons shall wash their hands and their feet in water from it. ²⁰When they go into the tabernacle of meeting, or when they come near the altar to minister, to burn an offering made by fire to the LORD, they shall wash with water, lest they die. ²¹So they shall wash their hands and their feet, lest they die. And it shall be a statute forever to them—to him and his descendants throughout their generations."

The Holy Anointing Oil

²²Moreover the LORD spoke to Moses, saying: ²³"Also take for yourself quality spices—five hundred *shekels* of liquid myrrh, half as much sweet-smelling cinnamon (two hundred and fifty *shekels*), two hundred and fifty *shekels* of sweet-smelling cane, ²⁴five hundred *shekels* of cassia, according to the shekel of the sanctuary, and a hin of olive oil. ²⁵And you shall make from these a holy anointing oil, an ointment compounded according to the art of the perfumer. It shall be a holy anointing oil. ²⁶With it you shall anoint the tabernacle of meeting and the ark of the Testimony; ²⁷the table and all its utensils, the lampstand and its utensils, and the altar of incense; ²⁸the altar of burnt offering with all its utensils, and the laver and its base. ²⁹You shall consecrate them, that they may be most holy; whatever touches them must be holy.ᵃ ³⁰And you shall anoint Aaron and his sons, and consecrate them, that *they* may minister to Me as priests.

³¹"And you shall speak to the children of Israel, saying: 'This shall be a holy anointing oil to Me throughout your generations. ³²It shall not be poured on man's flesh; nor shall you make *any other* like it, according to its composition. It *is* holy, *and* it shall be holy to you. ³³Whoever compounds *any* like it, or whoever puts *any* of it on an outsider, shall be cut off from his people.' "

The Incense

³⁴And the LORD said to Moses: "Take sweet spices, stacte and onycha and galbanum, and pure frankincense with *these* sweet spices; there shall be equal amounts of each. ³⁵You shall make of these an incense, a compound according to the art of the perfumer, salted, pure, *and* holy. ³⁶And you shall beat *some* of it very fine, and put some of it before the Testimony in the tabernacle of meeting where I will meet with you. It shall be most holy to you. ³⁷But *as for* the incense which you shall make, you shall not make any for yourselves, according to its composition. It shall be to you holy for the LORD. ³⁸Whoever makes *any* like it, to smell it, he shall be cut off from his people."

30:29 ᵃCompare Numbers 4:15 and Haggai 2:11–13

TRADE AND ECONOMICS

Spices (Ex. 30:34) were an important part of trade and commerce. They were imported from Arabia and from as far away as India, which could be reached from Egypt by sea. Most were plant products, such as gums and resins. Onycha was taken from a mollusk that lives in the Red Sea. Its exotic origin adds to its perceived value.

Artisans for Building the Tabernacle

31 [1]Then the LORD spoke to Moses, saying: [2]"See, I have called by name Bezalel the son of Uri, the son of Hur, of the tribe of Judah. [3]And I have filled him with the Spirit of God, in wisdom, in understanding, in knowledge, and in all *manner of* workmanship, [4]to design artistic works, to work in gold, in silver, in bronze, [5]in cutting jewels for setting, in carving wood, and to work in all *manner of* workmanship.

[6]"And I, indeed I, have appointed with him Aholiab the son of Ahisamach, of the tribe of Dan; and I have put wisdom in the hearts of all the gifted artisans, that they may make all that I have commanded you: [7]the tabernacle of meeting, the ark of the Testimony and the mercy seat that *is* on it, and all the furniture of the tabernacle— [8]the table and its utensils, the pure *gold* lampstand with all its utensils, the altar of incense, [9]the altar of burnt offering with all its utensils, and the laver and its base— [10]the garments of ministry,[a] the holy garments for Aaron the priest and the garments of his sons, to minister as priests, [11]and the anointing oil and sweet incense for the holy *place.* According to all that I have commanded you they shall do."

The Sabbath Law

[12]And the LORD spoke to Moses, saying, [13]"Speak also to the children of Israel, saying: 'Surely My Sabbaths you shall keep, for it *is* a sign between Me and you throughout your generations, that *you* may know that I *am* the LORD who sanctifies you. [14]You shall keep the Sabbath, therefore, for it *is* holy to you. Everyone who profanes it shall surely be put to death; for whoever does *any* work on it, that person shall be cut off from among his people. [15]Work shall be done for six days, but the seventh *is* the Sabbath of rest, holy to the LORD. Whoever does *any* work on the Sabbath day, he shall surely be put to death. [16]Therefore the children of Israel shall keep the Sabbath, to observe the Sabbath throughout their generations *as* a perpetual covenant. [17]It *is* a sign between Me and the children of Israel forever; for *in* six days the LORD made the heavens and the earth, and on the seventh day He rested and was refreshed.' "

[18]And when He had made an end of speaking with him on Mount Sinai, He gave Moses two tablets of the Testimony, tablets of stone, written with the finger of God.

The Gold Calf

32 [1]Now when the people saw that Moses delayed coming down from the mountain, the people gathered together to Aaron, and said to him, "Come, make us gods that shall go before us; for *as for* this Moses, the man who brought us up out of the land of Egypt, we do not know what has become of him."

[2]And Aaron said to them, "Break off the golden earrings which *are* in the ears of your wives, your sons, and your daughters, and bring *them* to me." [3]So all the people broke off the golden earrings which *were* in their ears, and brought *them* to Aaron. [4]And he received *the gold* from their hand, and he fashioned it with an engraving tool, and made a molded calf.

Then they said, "This *is* your god, O Israel, that brought you out of the land of Egypt!"

[5]So when Aaron saw *it,* he built an altar before it. And Aaron made a proclamation and said, "Tomorrow *is* a feast to the LORD." [6]Then they rose early on the next day, offered burnt offerings, and brought peace offerings; and the people sat down to eat and drink, and rose up to play.

[7]And the LORD said to Moses, "Go, get down! For your people whom you brought out of the land of Egypt have corrupted *themselves.* [8]They have turned aside quickly out of the way which I commanded them. They have made themselves a molded calf, and worshiped it and sacrificed to it, and said, 'This *is* your god, O Israel, that brought you out of the land of Egypt!' " [9]And the LORD said to Moses, "I have seen this people, and indeed it *is* a stiff-necked people! [10]Now therefore, let Me alone, that My wrath may burn hot against them and I may consume them. And I will make of you a great nation."

[11]Then Moses pleaded with the LORD his God, and said: "LORD, why does Your wrath burn hot against Your people whom You have brought out of the land of Egypt with great power and with a mighty hand? [12]Why should the Egyptians speak, and say, 'He brought them out to harm them, to kill them in the mountains, and to consume them from the face of the earth'?

CALVES, COWS, AND BULLS REPRESENTING THE DIVINE (Ex. 32:1–4)

The stories of Aaron molding the golden calf (Ex. 32:1–4) and Jeroboam building the golden calves for his new temples at Bethel and Dan (1 Kin. 12:28–31) are similar. Aaron's action, at the insistence of the people, came only 40 days after they received the commandments not to worship other gods nor to make images for worship. In almost no time the Israelites broke the rules given them by God. Similarly, God gave Jeroboam the northern kingdom with the provision that he be faithful to God. Jeroboam immediately broke the same commandments as the Israelites did in the wilderness.

But why make a calf? Cattle were common images for deities in the ancient Near East. In Egypt, Hathor, a very popular goddess, was represented as a cow, as a woman with cow horns or ears or both, and as a human with a cow's head. The usual manner of depicting a male deity in Syria-Palestine was to represent him either as a bull or with some features of a bull—usually horns. In Babylon the bull images of Hadad lined the main processional street.

The golden calf was possibly the representation of a Canaanite deity. Both El or Baal are connected with bulls in the Ugaritic texts. No large images of cattle deities have been recovered from Syria-Palestine, but a number of small bull images from the time of the Israelite occupation of the land demonstrate that larger statues could likely have been realistically fashioned in standing positions. If the golden calf represents a Canaanite god, such worship was a blatant rejection of Israel's God.

There is another possibility. In the ancient Near East, bulls, as well as other animals, were sometimes intended not as an image of the deity itself, but as mounts for the god who was understood to be present. Jeroboam's golden calves could have served the same purpose as the cherubim in the temple at Jerusalem. But even this would have been a rejection of the proper worship of Israel's God.

Turn from Your fierce wrath, and relent from this harm to Your people. 13Remember Abraham, Isaac, and Israel, Your servants, to whom You swore by Your own self, and said to them, 'I will multiply your descendants as the stars of heaven; and all this land that I have spoken of I give to your descendants, and they shall inherit *it* forever.' "a 14So the LORD relented from the harm which He said He would do to His people.

15And Moses turned and went down from the mountain, and the two tablets of the Testimony *were* in his hand. The tablets *were* written on both sides; on the one *side* and on the other they were written. 16Now the tablets *were* the work of God, and the writing *was* the writing of God engraved on the tablets.

17And when Joshua heard the noise of the people as they shouted, he said to Moses, "*There is* a noise of war in the camp."

18But he said:

"*It is* not the noise of the shout of victory,
Nor the noise of the cry of defeat,
But the sound of singing I hear."

19So it was, as soon as he came near the camp, that he saw the calf *and* the dancing. So Moses' anger became hot, and he cast the tablets out of his hands and broke them at the foot of the mountain. 20Then he took the calf which they had made, burned *it* in the fire, and ground *it* to powder; and he scattered *it* on the water and made the children of Israel drink *it*. 21And Moses said to Aaron, "What did this people do to you that you have brought *so* great a sin upon them?"

22So Aaron said, "Do not let the anger of my lord become hot. You know the people, that they *are set* on evil. 23For they said to me, 'Make us gods that shall go before us; *as for* this Moses, the man who brought us out of the land of Egypt, we do not know what has become of him.' 24And I said to them, 'Whoever has any gold, let them break *it* off.' So they gave *it* to me, and I cast it into the fire, and this calf came out."

25Now when Moses saw that the people *were* unrestrained (for Aaron had not restrained them, to *their* shame among their

32:13   aGenesis 13:15 and 22:17

enemies), [26]then Moses stood in the entrance of the camp, and said, "Whoever *is* on the LORD's side—*come* to me!" And all the sons of Levi gathered themselves together to him. [27]And he said to them, "Thus says the LORD God of Israel: 'Let every man put his sword on his side, and go in and out from entrance to entrance throughout the camp, and let every man kill his brother, every man his companion, and every man his neighbor.' " [28]So the sons of Levi did according to the word of Moses. And about three thousand men of the people fell that day. [29]Then Moses said, "Consecrate yourselves today to the LORD, that He may bestow on you a blessing this day, for every man has opposed his son and his brother."

[30]Now it came to pass on the next day that Moses said to the people, "You have committed a great sin. So now I will go up to the LORD; perhaps I can make atonement for your sin." [31]Then Moses returned to the LORD and said, "Oh, these people have committed a great sin, and have made for themselves a god of gold! [32]Yet now, if You will forgive their sin—but if not, I pray, blot me out of Your book which You have written."

[33]And the LORD said to Moses, "Whoever has sinned against Me, I will blot him out of My book. [34]Now therefore, go, lead the people to *the place* of which I have spoken to you. Behold, My Angel shall go before you. Nevertheless, in the day when I visit for punishment, I will visit punishment upon them for their sin."

[35]So the LORD plagued the people because of what they did with the calf which Aaron made.

The Command to Leave Sinai

33 [1]Then the LORD said to Moses, "Depart *and* go up from here, you and the people whom you have brought out of the land of Egypt, to the land of which I swore to Abraham, Isaac, and Jacob, saying, 'To your descendants I will give it.' [2]And I will send *My* Angel before you, and I will drive out the Canaanite and the Amorite and the Hittite and the Perizzite and the Hivite and the Jebusite. [3]*Go up* to a land flowing with milk and honey; for I will not go up in your midst, lest I consume you on the way, for you *are* a stiff-necked people."

[4]And when the people heard this bad news, they mourned, and no one put on his ornaments. [5]For the LORD had said to Moses, "Say to the children of Israel, 'You *are* a stiff-necked people. I could come up into your midst in one moment and consume you. Now therefore, take off your ornaments, that I may know what to do to you.' " [6]So the children of Israel stripped themselves of their ornaments by Mount Horeb.

Moses Meets with the LORD

[7]Moses took his tent and pitched it outside the camp, far from the camp, and called it the tabernacle of meeting. And it came to pass *that* everyone who sought the LORD went out to the tabernacle of meeting which *was* outside the camp. [8]So it was, whenever Moses went out to the tabernacle, *that* all the people rose, and each man stood *at* his tent door and watched Moses until he had gone into the tabernacle. [9]And it came to pass, when Moses entered the tabernacle, that the pillar of cloud descended and stood *at* the door of the tabernacle, and *the* LORD talked with Moses. [10]All the people saw the pillar of cloud standing *at* the tabernacle door, and all the people rose and worshiped, each man *in* his tent door. [11]So the LORD spoke to Moses face to face, as a man speaks to his friend. And he would return to the camp, but his servant Joshua the son of Nun, a young man, did not depart from the tabernacle.

The Promise of God's Presence

[12]Then Moses said to the LORD, "See, You say to me, 'Bring up this people.' But You have not let me know whom You will send with me. Yet You have said, 'I know you by name, and you have also found

---

DAILY LIFE AND CUSTOMS

Garments and ornaments for the body commonly signify a person's rank and status. It may be that the Israelites were removing such items, or it may be that they were removing whatever items were inappropriate for mourning, whether the items had special value or not (Ex. 33:5).

grace in My sight.' ¹³Now therefore, I pray, if I have found grace in Your sight, show me now Your way, that I may know You and that I may find grace in Your sight. And consider that this nation *is* Your people."

¹⁴And He said, "My Presence will go *with you,* and I will give you rest."

¹⁵Then he said to Him, "If Your Presence does not go *with us,* do not bring us up from here. ¹⁶For how then will it be known that Your people and I have found grace in Your sight, except You go with us? So we shall be separate, Your people and I, from all the people who *are* upon the face of the earth."

¹⁷So the LORD said to Moses, "I will also do this thing that you have spoken; for you have found grace in My sight, and I know you by name."

¹⁸And he said, "Please, show me Your glory."

¹⁹Then He said, "I will make all My goodness pass before you, and I will proclaim the name of the LORD before you. I will be gracious to whom I will be gracious, and I will have compassion on whom I will have compassion." ²⁰But He said, "You cannot see My face; for no man shall see Me, and live." ²¹And the LORD said, "Here is a place by Me, and you shall stand on the rock. ²²So it shall be, while My glory passes by, that I will put you in the cleft of the rock, and will cover you with My hand while I pass by. ²³Then I will take away My hand, and you shall see My back; but My face shall not be seen."

Moses Makes New Tablets

34 ¹And the LORD said to Moses, "Cut two tablets of stone like the first *ones,* and I will write on *these* tablets the words that were on the first tablets which you broke. ²So be ready in the morning, and come up in the morning to Mount Sinai, and present yourself to Me there on the top of the mountain. ³And no man shall come up with you, and let no man be seen throughout all the mountain; let neither flocks nor herds feed before that mountain."

⁴So he cut two tablets of stone like the first *ones.* Then Moses rose early in the morning and went up Mount Sinai, as the LORD had commanded him; and he took in his hand the two tablets of stone.

⁵Now the LORD descended in the cloud and stood with him there, and proclaimed the name of the LORD. ⁶And the LORD passed before him and proclaimed, "The LORD, the LORD God, merciful and gracious, longsuffering, and abounding in goodness and truth, ⁷keeping mercy for thousands, forgiving iniquity and transgression and sin, by no means clearing *the guilty,* visiting the iniquity of the fathers upon the children and the children's children to the third and the fourth generation."

⁸So Moses made haste and bowed his head toward the earth, and worshiped. ⁹Then he said, "If now I have found grace in Your sight, O Lord, let my Lord, I pray, go among us, even though we *are* a stiff-necked people; and pardon our iniquity and our sin, and take us as Your inheritance."

The Covenant Renewed

¹⁰And He said: "Behold, I make a covenant. Before all your people I will do marvels such as have not been done in all the earth, nor in any nation; and all the people among whom you *are* shall see the work of the LORD. For it *is* an awesome thing that I will do with you. ¹¹Observe what I command you this day. Behold, I am driving out from before you the Amorite and the Canaanite and the Hittite and the Perizzite and the Hivite and the Jebusite. ¹²Take heed to yourself, lest you make a covenant with the inhabitants of the land where you are going, lest it be a snare in your midst. ¹³But you shall destroy their altars, break their *sacred* pillars, and cut down their wooden images ¹⁴(for you shall worship no other god, for the LORD, whose name *is* Jealous, *is* a jealous God), ¹⁵lest you make a covenant with the inhabitants of the land, and they play the harlot with their gods and make sacrifice to their gods, and *one of them* invites you and you eat of his sacrifice, ¹⁶and you take of his daughters for your sons, and his daughters play the harlot with their gods and make your sons play the harlot with their gods.

¹⁷"You shall make no molded gods for yourselves.

¹⁸"The Feast of Unleavened Bread you shall keep. Seven days you shall eat unleavened bread, as I commanded you, in the appointed time of the month of Abib; for in the month of Abib you came out from Egypt.

¹⁹"All that open the womb *are* Mine, and every male firstborn among your livestock, *whether* ox or sheep. ²⁰But the firstborn of a donkey you shall redeem with a

FORBIDDEN RELIGIOUS OBJECTS (Ex. 34:13)

Altars, sacred pillars, and wooden images appear in the Bible as a recurring group of banned religious objects (Ex. 34:13). All three were common in the religious world of Syria-Palestine including Canaan.

Altars were used for making sacrifices to the god of the area. They were constructed where the deity was felt to be present, sometimes along with a temple, a shrine, or an open sanctuary. Many of the numerous ancient altars discovered in Palestine are carefully carved with stone horns on the four top corners. A depression was often carved around the outer top area to catch blood so that it could be ritually sprinkled on the altar itself, a standard sacrificial ritual. Only when devoted to God and restricted to certain locations were altars acceptable for Israel.

Sacred pillars were standing slabs of stone, sometimes carved, which stood in religious centers as representatives of deities. Such cultic items dating from the 3rd millennium B.C. have been recovered from Syria-Palestine. The tops often were shaped into a curve, and sometimes a divine symbol was carved into one of the flat surfaces. They functioned as divine images. Thus, to allow sacred pillars to remain standing would have breached the commandment not to worship other gods (Ex. 20:3).

The Hebrew *Asherim,* translated as "wooden images," were representations of the goddess Asherah. Because of the impermanence of wood and the lack of Old Testament descriptions, the form of the Asherim is uncertain. Some suggest these items were sacred trees or representations of sacred trees. Others suppose they were wooden objects made by humans, possibly poles or images. Since the Asherim stood for the goddess Asherah, it is understandable that the Judahites and Israelites were told to cut down, splinter, and burn them (Deut. 7:5; 12:3).

The many warnings against these forbidden objects suggest the appeal that Canaanite culture had for Judah and Israel. Incorporating indigenous religion into their worship of God posed a constant danger.

---

lamb. And if you will not redeem *him,* then you shall break his neck. All the firstborn of your sons you shall redeem.

"And none shall appear before Me empty-handed.

21"Six days you shall work, but on the seventh day you shall rest; in plowing time and in harvest you shall rest.

22"And you shall observe the Feast of Weeks, of the firstfruits of wheat harvest, and the Feast of Ingathering at the year's end.

23"Three times in the year all your men shall appear before the Lord, the LORD God of Israel. 24For I will cast out the nations before you and enlarge your borders; neither will any man covet your land when you go up to appear before the LORD your God three times in the year.

25"You shall not offer the blood of My sacrifice with leaven, nor shall the sacrifice of the Feast of the Passover be left until morning.

26"The first of the firstfruits of your land you shall bring to the house of the LORD your God. You shall not boil a young goat in its mother's milk."

27Then the LORD said to Moses, "Write these words, for according to the tenor of these words I have made a covenant with you and with Israel." 28So he was there with the LORD forty days and forty nights; he neither ate bread nor drank water. And He wrote on the tablets the words of the covenant, the Ten Commandments.[a]

The Shining Face of Moses

29Now it was so, when Moses came down from Mount Sinai (and the two tablets of the Testimony *were* in Moses' hand when he came down from the mountain), that Moses did not know that the skin of his face shone while he talked with Him. 30So when Aaron and all the children of Israel saw Moses, behold, the skin of his face shone, and they were afraid to come near him. 31Then Moses called to them, and Aaron and all the rulers of the

---

34:28 [a]Literally *Ten Words*

congregation returned to him; and Moses talked with them. ³²Afterward all the children of Israel came near, and he gave them as commandments all that the LORD had spoken with him on Mount Sinai. ³³And when Moses had finished speaking with them, he put a veil on his face. ³⁴But whenever Moses went in before the LORD to speak with Him, he would take the veil off until he came out; and he would come out and speak to the children of Israel whatever he had been commanded. ³⁵And whenever the children of Israel saw the face of Moses, that the skin of Moses' face shone, then Moses would put the veil on his face again, until he went in to speak with Him.

Sabbath Regulations

35 ¹Then Moses gathered all the congregation of the children of Israel together, and said to them, "These *are* the words which the LORD has commanded *you* to do: ²Work shall be done for six days, but the seventh day shall be a holy day for you, a Sabbath of rest to the LORD. Whoever does any work on it shall be put to death. ³You shall kindle no fire throughout your dwellings on the Sabbath day."

Offerings for the Tabernacle

⁴And Moses spoke to all the congregation of the children of Israel, saying, "This *is* the thing which the LORD commanded, saying: ⁵'Take from among you an offering to the LORD. Whoever *is* of a willing heart, let him bring it as an offering to the LORD: gold, silver, and bronze; ⁶blue, purple, and scarlet *thread,* fine linen, and goats' *hair;* ⁷ram skins dyed red, badger skins, and acacia wood; ⁸oil for the light, and spices for the anointing oil and for the sweet in-

cense; ⁹onyx stones, and stones to be set in the ephod and in the breastplate.

Articles of the Tabernacle

¹⁰'All *who are* gifted artisans among you shall come and make all that the LORD has commanded: ¹¹the tabernacle, its tent, its covering, its clasps, its boards, its bars, its pillars, and its sockets; ¹²the ark and its poles, *with* the mercy seat, and the veil of the covering; ¹³the table and its poles, all its utensils, and the showbread; ¹⁴also the lampstand for the light, its utensils, its lamps, and the oil for the light; ¹⁵the incense altar, its poles, the anointing oil, the sweet incense, and the screen for the door at the entrance of the tabernacle; ¹⁶the altar of burnt offering with its bronze grating, its poles, all its utensils, *and* the laver and its base; ¹⁷the hangings of the court, its pillars, their sockets, and the screen for the gate of the court; ¹⁸the pegs of the tabernacle, the pegs of the court, and their cords; ¹⁹the garments of ministry,ᵃ for ministering in the holy *place*—the holy garments for Aaron the priest and the garments of his sons, to minister as priests.' "

The Tabernacle Offerings Presented

²⁰And all the congregation of the children of Israel departed from the presence of Moses. ²¹Then everyone came whose heart was stirred, and everyone whose spirit was willing, *and* they brought the LORD's offering for the work of the tabernacle of meeting, for all its service, and for the holy garments. ²²They came, both men and women, as many as had a willing heart, *and* brought earrings and nose rings, rings and necklaces, all jewelry of gold, that is, every man who *made* an offering of gold to the LORD. ²³And every man, with whom was found blue, purple, and scarlet *thread*, fine linen, goats' *hair,* red skins of rams, and badger skins, brought *them.* ²⁴Everyone who offered an offering of silver or bronze brought the LORD's offering. And everyone with whom was found acacia wood for any work of the service, brought *it.* ²⁵All the women *who were* gifted artisans spun yarn with their hands, and brought what they had spun, of blue, purple, *and* scarlet, and fine linen. ²⁶And all the women whose hearts stirred with wisdom spun yarn of goats' *hair.* ²⁷The rulers

TIME CAPSULE	*1525 to 1511 B.C.*
1525	*Ilim-ilimma I establishes kingdom at Aleppo*
1525	*Ilim-ilimma's kingdom overthrown, and his son Idrimi flees to Phoenicia*
1525– 1504	*Amenhotep I, pharaoh of Egypt*
1518– 1480	*Idrimi returns victoriously and makes his capital at Alalakh*
1511	*Idrimi makes treaty with Mitanni in an alliance against the Hittites*

35:19 ᵃOr *woven garments*

brought onyx stones, and the stones to be set in the ephod and in the breastplate, [28]and spices and oil for the light, for the anointing oil, and for the sweet incense. [29]The children of Israel brought a freewill offering to the LORD, all the men and women whose hearts were willing to bring *material* for all kinds of work which the LORD, by the hand of Moses, had commanded to be done.

The Artisans Called by God

[30]And Moses said to the children of Israel, "See, the LORD has called by name Bezalel the son of Uri, the son of Hur, of the tribe of Judah; [31]and He has filled him with the Spirit of God, in wisdom and understanding, in knowledge and all manner of workmanship, [32]to design artistic works, to work in gold and silver and bronze, [33]in cutting jewels for setting, in carving wood, and to work in all manner of artistic workmanship.

[34]"And He has put in his heart the ability to teach, *in* him and Aholiab the son of Ahisamach, of the tribe of Dan. [35]He has filled them with skill to do all manner of work of the engraver and the designer and the tapestry maker, in blue, purple, and scarlet *thread,* and fine linen, and of the weaver—those who do every work and those who design artistic works.

36 [1]"And Bezalel and Aholiab, and every gifted artisan in whom the LORD has put wisdom and understanding, to know how to do all manner of work for the service of the sanctuary, shall do according to all that the LORD has commanded."

The People Give More than Enough

[2]Then Moses called Bezalel and Aholiab, and every gifted artisan in whose heart the LORD had put wisdom, everyone whose heart was stirred, to come and do the work. [3]And they received from Moses all the offering which the children of Israel had brought for the work of the service of making the sanctuary. So they continued bringing to him freewill offerings every morning. [4]Then all the craftsmen who were doing all the work of the sanctuary came, each from the work he was doing, [5]and they spoke to Moses, saying, "The people bring much more than enough for the service of the work which the LORD commanded *us* to do."

[6]So Moses gave a commandment, and they caused it to be proclaimed throughout the camp, saying, "Let neither man nor woman do any more work for the offering of the sanctuary." And the people were restrained from bringing, [7]for the material they had was sufficient for all the work to be done—indeed too much.

Building the Tabernacle

[8]Then all the gifted artisans among them who worked on the tabernacle made ten curtains woven of fine linen, and of blue, purple, and scarlet *thread; with* artistic designs of cherubim they made them. [9]The length of each curtain *was* twenty-eight cubits, and the width of each curtain four cubits; the curtains *were* all the same size. [10]And he coupled five curtains to one another, and *the other* five curtains he coupled to one another. [11]He made loops of blue *yarn* on the edge of the curtain on the selvedge of one set; likewise he did on the outer edge of *the other* curtain of the second set. [12]Fifty loops he made on one curtain, and fifty loops he made on the edge of the curtain on the end of the second set; the loops held one *curtain* to another. [13]And he made fifty clasps of gold, and coupled the curtains to one another with the clasps, that it might be one tabernacle.

[14]He made curtains of goats' *hair* for the tent over the tabernacle; he made eleven curtains. [15]The length of each curtain *was* thirty cubits, and the width of each curtain four cubits; the eleven curtains *were* the same size. [16]He coupled five curtains by themselves and six curtains by themselves. [17]And he made fifty loops on the edge of the curtain that is outermost in one set, and fifty loops he made on the edge of the curtain of the second set. [18]He also made fifty bronze clasps to couple the tent together, that it might be one. [19]Then he made a covering for the tent of ram skins dyed red, and a covering of badger skins above *that.*

[20]For the tabernacle he made boards of acacia wood, standing upright. [21]The length of each board *was* ten cubits, and the width of each board a cubit and a half. [22]Each board had two tenons for binding one to another. Thus he made for all the boards of the tabernacle. [23]And he made boards for the tabernacle, twenty boards for the south side. [24]Forty sockets of silver he made to go under the twenty boards: two sockets under each of the boards for its two tenons. [25]And for the other side of the

tabernacle, the north side, he made twenty boards ²⁶and their forty sockets of silver: two sockets under each of the boards. ²⁷For the west side of the tabernacle he made six boards. ²⁸He also made two boards for the two back corners of the tabernacle. ²⁹And they were coupled at the bottom and coupled together at the top by one ring. Thus he made both of them for the two corners. ³⁰So there were eight boards and their sockets—sixteen sockets of silver—two sockets under each of the boards.

³¹And he made bars of acacia wood: five for the boards on one side of the tabernacle, ³²five bars for the boards on the other side of the tabernacle, and five bars for the boards of the tabernacle on the far side westward. ³³And he made the middle bar to pass through the boards from one end to the other. ³⁴He overlaid the boards with gold, made their rings of gold *to be* holders for the bars, and overlaid the bars with gold.

³⁵And he made a veil of blue, purple, and scarlet *thread,* and fine woven linen; it was worked *with* an artistic design of cherubim. ³⁶He made for it four pillars of acacia *wood,* and overlaid them with gold, with their hooks of gold; and he cast four sockets of silver for them.

³⁷He also made a screen for the tabernacle door, of blue, purple, and scarlet *thread,* and fine woven linen, made by a weaver, ³⁸and its five pillars with their hooks. And he overlaid their capitals and their rings with gold, but their five sockets *were* bronze.

Making the Ark of the Testimony

37 ¹Then Bezalel made the ark of acacia wood; two and a half cubits *was* its length, a cubit and a half its width, and a cubit and a half its height. ²He overlaid it with pure gold inside and outside, and made a molding of gold all around it. ³And he cast for it four rings of gold *to be set* in its four corners: two rings on one side, and two rings on the other side of it. ⁴He made poles of acacia wood, and overlaid them

with gold. ⁵And he put the poles into the rings at the sides of the ark, to bear the ark. ⁶He also made the mercy seat of pure gold; two and a half cubits *was* its length and a cubit and a half its width. ⁷He made two cherubim of beaten gold; he made them of one piece at the two ends of the mercy seat: ⁸one cherub at one end on this side, and the other cherub at the *other* end on that side. He made the cherubim at the two ends *of one piece* with the mercy seat. ⁹The cherubim spread out *their* wings above, *and* covered the mercy seat with their wings. They faced one another; the faces of the cherubim were toward the mercy seat.

Making the Table for the Showbread

¹⁰He made the table of acacia wood; two cubits *was* its length, a cubit its width, and a cubit and a half its height. ¹¹And he overlaid it with pure gold, and made a molding of gold all around it. ¹²Also he made a frame of a handbreadth all around it, and made a molding of gold for the frame all around it. ¹³And he cast for it four rings of gold, and put the rings on the four corners that *were* at its four legs. ¹⁴The rings were close to the frame, as holders for the poles to bear the table. ¹⁵And he made the poles of acacia wood to bear the table, and overlaid them with gold. ¹⁶He made of pure gold the utensils which were on the table: its dishes, its cups, its bowls, and its pitchers for pouring.

Making the Gold Lampstand

¹⁷He also made the lampstand of pure gold; of hammered work he made the lampstand. Its shaft, its branches, its bowls, its *ornamental* knobs, and its flowers were of the same piece. ¹⁸And six branches came out of its sides: three branches of the lampstand out of one side, and three branches of the lampstand out of the other side. ¹⁹There were three bowls made like almond *blossoms* on one branch, with an *ornamental* knob and a flower, and three

---

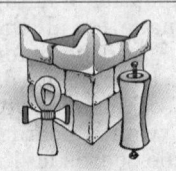

RELIGION AND WORSHIP

The lampstand (Ex. 37:17) was removed from Jerusalem by the Roman army in A.D. 70. It is depicted on the arch of Titus in Rome as part of a parade of spoils taken by the victorious soldiers. This was probably not the original lamp, but in any case it too is now lost. The seven-branched lampstand continues as a symbol of Judaism.

A Throne for God (Ex. 37:1–9)

The ark of the covenant was an object that reminded the Israelites of the presence of God in their midst. Although some nomadic peoples used small traveling casks for worship, no ancient people had a sacred object that compares to Israel's large box with its heavy adornment and sculptured cherubim on the lid (Ex. 37:1–9).

There are various ideas as to what the ark represents, often relating to each other in meaning. It has been described as a container or chest, as a portable throne for Israel's God, or as an extension of God's presence.

The construction of the ark is described in the shape of a chest, measuring 45 inches long by 27 inches wide by 27 inches tall (Ex. 37:1). As such, it served as a container to hold items. Similar to the temple thrones of gods in Egypt and the foundation deposits of temples in Mesopotamia, the ark also bore the words of the deity: the tablets of the Ten Commandments. Other items contained within the ark were Aaron's rod and a jar of manna (Heb. 9:4).

As a portable throne the ark provided the place where God would "sit" in the presence of the Israelites. The cherubim on the ark (Ex. 37:7) were not images of God, but rather divine attendants. They represented the type of throne which seated rulers and deities along the eastern Mediterranean coast as far back as the 2nd millennium B.C. A king sitting upon a cherubim throne is pictured in the sarcophagus of Ahiram, king of Byblos in the 10th century B.C.

Some scholars think that the ark represented the "footstool" of God's throne, rather than the throne itself. King David referred to the ark as a "footstool" (1 Chr. 28:2). The cherubim throne of Ahiram had a box-shaped footstool, and the Canaanite god El also had a footstool.

The ark was a symbol of the invisible presence of God. The possession of the ark in battle represented both the presence and the favor of God (1 Sam. 4:3–7). Its capture by the Philistines meant that the favor of God had been lost as well (1 Sam. 4:19–22).

---

bowls made like almond *blossoms* on the other branch, with an *ornamental* knob and a flower—and so for the six branches coming out of the lampstand. ²⁰And on the lampstand itself *were* four bowls made like almond *blossoms, each with* its *ornamental* knob and flower. ²¹*There was* a knob under the *first* two branches of the same, a knob under the *second* two branches of the same, and a knob under the *third* two branches of the same, according to the six branches extending from it. ²²Their knobs and their branches were of one piece; all of it *was* one hammered piece of pure gold. ²³And he made its seven lamps, its wick-trimmers, and its trays of pure gold. ²⁴Of a talent of pure gold he made it, with all its utensils.

Making the Altar of Incense

²⁵He made the incense altar of acacia wood. Its length *was* a cubit and its width a cubit—*it was* square—and two cubits *was* its height. Its horns were *of one piece* with it. ²⁶And he overlaid it with pure gold: its top, its sides all around, and its horns. He also made for it a molding of gold all around it. ²⁷He made two rings of gold for it under its molding, by its two corners on both sides, as holders for the poles with which to bear it. ²⁸And he made the poles of acacia wood, and overlaid them with gold.

Making the Anointing Oil and the Incense

²⁹He also made the holy anointing oil and the pure incense of sweet spices, according to the work of the perfumer.

Making the Altar of Burnt Offering

38 ¹He made the altar of burnt offering of acacia wood; five cubits *was* its length and five cubits its width—*it was* square—and its height *was* three cubits. ²He made its horns on its four corners; the horns were *of one piece* with it. And he overlaid it with bronze. ³He made all the utensils for the altar: the pans, the shovels, the basins, the forks, and the firepans; all its utensils he made of bronze. ⁴And he made a grate of bronze network for the altar, under its rim, midway from the bottom. ⁵He cast four rings for the four corners of the bronze grating, *as* holders for the poles. ⁶And he made the poles of acacia wood, and overlaid them with bronze. ⁷Then he put the poles into the rings on the sides of the altar, with which to bear it. He made the altar hollow with boards.

Making the Bronze Laver

⁸He made the laver of bronze and its base of bronze, from the bronze mirrors of the serving women who assembled at the door of the tabernacle of meeting.

Making the Court of the Tabernacle

⁹Then he made the court on the south side; the hangings of the court *were of* fine woven linen, one hundred cubits long. ¹⁰There *were* twenty pillars for them, with twenty bronze sockets. The hooks of the pillars and their bands *were* silver. ¹¹On the north side *the hangings were* one hundred cubits *long,* with twenty pillars and their twenty bronze sockets. The hooks of the pillars and their bands *were* silver. ¹²And on the west side *there were* hangings of fifty cubits, with ten pillars and their ten sockets. The hooks of the pillars and their bands *were* silver. ¹³For the east side *the hangings were* fifty cubits. ¹⁴The hangings of one side *of the gate were* fifteen cubits *long, with* their three pillars and their three sockets, ¹⁵and the same for the other side of the court gate; on this side and that *were* hangings of fifteen cubits, *with* their three pillars and their three sockets. ¹⁶All the hangings of the court all around *were of* fine woven linen. ¹⁷The sockets for the pillars *were* bronze, the hooks of the pillars and their bands *were* silver, and the overlay of their capitals *was* silver; and all the pillars of the court had bands of silver. ¹⁸The screen for the gate of the court *was* woven of blue, purple, and scarlet *thread,* and of fine woven linen. The length *was* twenty cubits, and the height along its width *was* five cubits, corresponding to the hangings of the court. ¹⁹And *there were* four pillars *with* their four sockets of bronze; their hooks *were* silver, and the overlay of their capitals and their bands *was* silver. ²⁰All the pegs of the tabernacle, and of the court all around, *were* bronze.

Materials of the Tabernacle

²¹This is the inventory of the tabernacle, the tabernacle of the Testimony, which was counted according to the commandment of Moses, for the service of the Levites, by the hand of Ithamar, son of Aaron the priest.

²²Bezalel the son of Uri, the son of Hur, of the tribe of Judah, made all that the LORD had commanded Moses. ²³And with him *was* Aholiab the son of Ahisamach, of the tribe of Dan, an engraver and designer, a weaver of blue, purple, and scarlet *thread,* and of fine linen.

²⁴All the gold that was used in all the work of the holy *place,* that is, the gold of the offering, was twenty-nine talents and seven hundred and thirty shekels, according to the shekel of the sanctuary. ²⁵And the silver from those who were numbered of the congregation *was* one hundred talents and one thousand seven hundred and seventy-five shekels, according to the shekel of the sanctuary: ²⁶a bekah for each man (*that is,* half a shekel, according to the shekel of the sanctuary), for everyone included in the numbering from twenty years old and above, for six hundred and three thousand, five hundred and fifty *men.* ²⁷And from the hundred talents of silver were cast the sockets of the sanctuary and the bases of the veil: one hundred sockets from the hundred talents, one talent for each socket. ²⁸Then from the one thousand seven hundred and seventy-five *shekels* he made hooks for the pillars, overlaid their capitals, and made bands for them.

²⁹The offering of bronze *was* seventy talents and two thousand four hundred shekels. ³⁰And with it he made the sockets for the door of the tabernacle of meeting, the bronze altar, the bronze grating for it, and all the utensils for the altar, ³¹the sockets for the court all around, the bases for the court gate, all the pegs for the tabernacle, and all the pegs for the court all around.

Making the Garments of the Priesthood

39 ¹Of the blue, purple, and scarlet thread they made garments of ministry,^a for ministering in the holy *place,* and made the holy garments for Aaron, as the LORD had commanded Moses.

Making the Ephod

²He made the ephod of gold, blue, purple, and scarlet *thread,* and of fine woven

39:1 ^aOr *woven garments*

linen. ³And they beat the gold into thin sheets and cut *it into* threads, to work *it* in *with* the blue, purple, and scarlet *thread,* and the fine linen, *into* artistic designs. ⁴They made shoulder straps for it to couple *it* together; it was coupled together at its two edges. ⁵And the intricately woven band of his ephod that *was* on it *was* of the same workmanship, *woven of* gold, blue, purple, and scarlet *thread,* and of fine woven linen, as the LORD had commanded Moses.

⁶And they set onyx stones, enclosed in settings of gold; they were engraved, as signets are engraved, with the names of the sons of Israel. ⁷He put them on the shoulders of the ephod *as* memorial stones for the sons of Israel, as the LORD had commanded Moses.

Making the Breastplate

⁸And he made the breastplate, artistically woven like the workmanship of the ephod, of gold, blue, purple, and scarlet *thread,* and of fine woven linen. ⁹They made the breastplate square by doubling it; a span *was* its length and a span its width when doubled. ¹⁰And they set in it four rows of stones: a row with a sardius, a topaz, and an emerald *was* the first row; ¹¹the second row, a turquoise, a sapphire, and a diamond; ¹²the third row, a jacinth, an agate, and an amethyst; ¹³the fourth row, a beryl, an onyx, and a jasper. *They were* enclosed in settings of gold in their mountings. ¹⁴*There were* twelve stones according to the names of the sons of Israel: according to their names, *engraved like* a signet, each one with its own name according to the twelve tribes. ¹⁵And they made chains for the breastplate at the ends, like braided cords of pure gold. ¹⁶They also made two settings of gold and two gold rings, and put the two rings on the two ends of the breastplate. ¹⁷And they put the two braided *chains* of gold in the two rings on the ends of the breastplate. ¹⁸The two ends of the two braided *chains* they fastened in the two settings, and put them on the shoulder straps of the ephod in the front. ¹⁹And they made two rings of gold and put *them* on the two ends of the breastplate, on the edge of it, which *was* on the inward side of the ephod. ²⁰They made two *other* gold rings and put them on the two shoulder straps, underneath the ephod toward its front, right at the seam above the intricately woven band of the ephod. ²¹And they bound the breastplate by means of its rings to the rings of the ephod with a blue cord, so that it would be above the intricately woven band of the ephod, and that the breastplate would not come loose from the ephod, as the LORD had commanded Moses.

Making the Other Priestly Garments

²²He made the robe of the ephod of woven work, all of blue. ²³And *there was* an opening in the middle of the robe, like the opening in a coat of mail, *with* a woven binding all around the opening, so that it would not tear. ²⁴They made on the hem of the robe pomegranates of blue, purple, and scarlet, and of fine woven *linen.* ²⁵And they made bells of pure gold, and put the bells between the pomegranates on the hem of the robe all around between the pomegranates: ²⁶a bell and a pomegranate, a bell and a pomegranate, all around the hem of the robe to minister in, as the LORD had commanded Moses.

²⁷They made tunics, artistically woven of fine linen, for Aaron and his sons, ²⁸a turban of fine linen, exquisite hats of fine linen, short trousers of fine woven linen, ²⁹and a sash of fine woven linen with blue, purple, and scarlet *thread,* made by a weaver, as the LORD had commanded Moses.

³⁰Then they made the plate of the holy crown of pure gold, and wrote on it an inscription *like* the engraving of a signet:

HOLINESS TO THE LORD.

³¹And they tied to it a blue cord, to fasten *it* above on the turban, as the LORD had commanded Moses.

SCIENCE AND TECHNOLOGY

Gold is the most malleable and ductile of metals. This means that it can be hammered into very thin sheets (Ex. 39:3), thinner than a piece of paper. Gold can be easily worked into different shapes and does not corrode. These characteristics help account for its value.

The Work Completed

³²Thus all the work of the tabernacle of the tent of meeting was finished. And the children of Israel did according to all that the LORD had commanded Moses; so they did. ³³And they brought the tabernacle to Moses, the tent and all its furnishings: its clasps, its boards, its bars, its pillars, and its sockets; ³⁴the covering of ram skins dyed red, the covering of badger skins, and the veil of the covering; ³⁵the ark of the Testimony with its poles, and the mercy seat; ³⁶the table, all its utensils, and the showbread; ³⁷the pure *gold* lampstand with its lamps (the lamps set in order), all its utensils, and the oil for light; ³⁸the gold altar, the anointing oil, and the sweet incense; the screen for the tabernacle door; ³⁹the bronze altar, its grate of bronze, its poles, and all its utensils; the laver with its base; ⁴⁰the hangings of the court, its pillars and its sockets, the screen for the court gate, its cords, and its pegs; all the utensils for the service of the tabernacle, for the tent of meeting; ⁴¹and the garments of ministry,ª to minister in the holy *place:* the holy garments for Aaron the priest, and his sons' garments, to minister as priests.

⁴²According to all that the LORD had commanded Moses, so the children of Israel did all the work. ⁴³Then Moses looked over all the work, and indeed they had done it; as the LORD had commanded, just so they had done it. And Moses blessed them.

The Tabernacle Erected and Arranged

40 ¹Then the LORD spoke to Moses, saying: ²"On the first day of the first month you shall set up the tabernacle of the tent of meeting. ³You shall put in it the ark of the Testimony, and partition off the ark with the veil. ⁴You shall bring in the table and arrange the things that are to be set in order on it; and you shall bring in the lampstand and light its lamps. ⁵You shall also set the altar of gold for the incense before the ark of the Testimony, and put up the screen for the door of the taber-

nacle. ⁶Then you shall set the altar of the burnt offering before the door of the tabernacle of the tent of meeting. ⁷And you shall set the laver between the tabernacle of meeting and the altar, and put water in it. ⁸You shall set up the court all around, and hang up the screen at the court gate.

⁹"And you shall take the anointing oil, and anoint the tabernacle and all that *is* in it; and you shall hallow it and all its utensils, and it shall be holy. ¹⁰You shall anoint the altar of the burnt offering and all its utensils, and consecrate the altar. The altar shall be most holy. ¹¹And you shall anoint the laver and its base, and consecrate it.

¹²"Then you shall bring Aaron and his sons to the door of the tabernacle of meeting and wash them with water. ¹³You shall put the holy garments on Aaron, and anoint him and consecrate him, that he may minister to Me as priest. ¹⁴And you shall bring his sons and clothe them with tunics. ¹⁵You shall anoint them, as you anointed their father, that they may minister to Me as priests; for their anointing shall surely be an everlasting priesthood throughout their generations."

¹⁶Thus Moses did; according to all that the LORD had commanded him, so he did.

¹⁷And it came to pass in the first month of the second year, on the first *day* of the month, *that* the tabernacle was raised up. ¹⁸So Moses raised up the tabernacle, fastened its sockets, set up its boards, put in its bars, and raised up its pillars. ¹⁹And he spread out the tent over the tabernacle and put the covering of the tent on top of it, as the LORD had commanded Moses. ²⁰He took the Testimony and put *it* into the ark, inserted the poles through the rings of the ark, and put the mercy seat on top of the ark. ²¹And he brought the ark into the tabernacle, hung up the veil of the covering, and partitioned off the ark of the Testimony, as the LORD had commanded Moses.

39:41 ªOr *woven garments*

CULTURE AND SOCIETY

Ancient treaties from the time of Moses have a recognizable form. Usually there is a provision for keeping the text of the treaty. In this case, the tablets of the law were deposited in the ark of the Testimony (Ex. 40:20), putting them at the center of the priestly rituals. Possibly the two tablets were identical, each a complete text of the law.

22He put the table in the tabernacle of meeting, on the north side of the tabernacle, outside the veil; 23and he set the bread in order upon it before the LORD, as the LORD had commanded Moses. 24He put the lampstand in the tabernacle of meeting, across from the table, on the south side of the tabernacle; 25and he lit the lamps before the LORD, as the LORD had commanded Moses. 26He put the gold altar in the tabernacle of meeting in front of the veil; 27and he burned sweet incense on it, as the LORD had commanded Moses. 28He hung up the screen *at* the door of the tabernacle. 29And he put the altar of burnt offering *before* the door of the tabernacle of the tent of meeting, and offered upon it the burnt offering and the grain offering, as the LORD had commanded Moses. 30He set the laver between the tabernacle of meeting and the altar, and put water there for washing; 31and Moses, Aaron, and his sons would wash their hands and their feet *with water* from it. 32Whenever they went into the tabernacle of meeting, and when they came near the altar, they washed, as the LORD had commanded Moses. 33And he raised up the court all around the tabernacle and the altar, and hung up the screen of the court gate. So Moses finished the work.

The Cloud and the Glory

34Then the cloud covered the tabernacle of meeting, and the glory of the LORD filled the tabernacle. 35And Moses was not able to enter the tabernacle of meeting, because the cloud rested above it, and the glory of the LORD filled the tabernacle. 36Whenever the cloud was taken up from above the tabernacle, the children of Israel would go onward in all their journeys. 37But if the cloud was not taken up, then they did not journey till the day that it was taken up. 38For the cloud of the LORD *was* above the tabernacle by day, and fire was over it by night, in the sight of all the house of Israel, throughout all their journeys.

The Book of Leviticus

Leviticus continues God's covenant instructions on Mount Sinai, begun in Ex. 20. The name "Leviticus" comes from the many laws and regulations of the book that concern the rights and duties of priests (who were of the tribe of Levi).

Certain clearly defined bodies of laws can be identified in the book. The first seven chapters prescribe the laws of sacrifices; chs. 11—15 distinguish between what is clean and unclean; ch. 16 describes the Day of Atonement; and the various laws of chs. 17—26 are unified by the distinct refrain "You shall be holy, for I the LORD your God am holy" (Lev. 19:2).

The entire Book of Leviticus is set in a relatively brief period of time. Only a month and a half passes between the erection of the tabernacle at Mount Sinai and the Hebrews' departure from Sinai. The tabernacle was finished on the *1st day* of the *1st month* in the 2nd year of the Exodus (Ex. 40:17); the departure was on the *20th day* of the *2nd month* of the same year (Num. 10:11, 12). Depending on whether the Hebrews left Egypt in the 15th or 13th century, the 2nd year of the Exodus would be about 1445 or 1274 B.C. (see "Egypt and the Exodus" at Ex. 1:1).

The content of Leviticus, however, extends beyond this short month and a half in the wilderness. Many of the laws clearly pertain to a time after the Israelites had entered their land, for instance, the laws for planting fields and cleansing houses. Partly for this reason, some suggest that at least the current form of the book was actually composed later than its context would suggest, perhaps from several different law codes. Of course, those who accept the traditional attribution of the first five books of the Bible to Moses disagree and understand these passages simply as laws given for a future time.

The animal sacrifices described so carefully in Leviticus fit properly in the historical context of the book. Animal sacrifice was universal in ancient Near Eastern religion, so Israel's sacrifice of animals is hardly surprising. More striking, though, is the absolute prohibition against the equally common practice of child sacrifice (see Lev. 18:21).

■ Leviticus 1:1—15:33

Leviticus
The Burnt Offering

1 :1 Now the LORD called to Moses, and spoke to him from the tabernacle of meeting, saying, 2"Speak to the children of Israel, and say to them: 'When any one of you brings an offering to the LORD, you shall bring your offering of the livestock— of the herd and of the flock.

3'If his offering *is* a burnt sacrifice of the herd, let him offer a male without blemish; he shall offer it of his own free will at the door of the tabernacle of meeting before the LORD. ⁴Then he shall put his hand on the head of the burnt offering, and it will be accepted on his behalf to make atonement for him. ⁵He shall kill the bull before the LORD; and the priests, Aaron's sons, shall bring the blood and sprinkle the blood all around on the altar that *is by* the door of the tabernacle of meeting. ⁶And he shall skin the burnt offering and cut it into its pieces. ⁷The sons of Aaron the priest shall put fire on the altar, and lay the wood in order on the fire. ⁸Then the priests, Aaron's sons, shall lay the parts, the head, and the fat in order on the wood that *is* on the fire upon the altar; ⁹but he shall wash its entrails and its legs with water. And the priest shall burn all on the altar as a burnt sacrifice, an offering made by fire, a sweet aroma to the LORD.

¹⁰If his offering *is* of the flocks—of the sheep or of the goats—as a burnt sacrifice, he shall bring a male without blemish. ¹¹He shall kill it on the north side of the altar before the LORD; and the priests, Aaron's sons, shall sprinkle its blood all around on the altar. ¹²And he shall cut it into its pieces, with its head and its fat; and the priest shall lay them in order on the wood that *is* on the fire upon the altar; ¹³but he shall wash the entrails and the legs with water. Then the priest shall bring *it* all and burn *it* on the altar; it *is* a burnt sacrifice, an offering made by fire, a sweet aroma to the LORD.

¹⁴"And if the burnt sacrifice of his offering to the LORD *is* of birds, then he shall bring his offering of turtledoves or young pigeons. ¹⁵The priest shall bring it to the altar, wring off its head, and burn *it* on the altar; its blood shall be drained out at the side of the altar. ¹⁶And he shall remove its crop with its feathers and cast it beside the altar on the east side, into the place for ashes. ¹⁷Then he shall split it at its wings, *but* shall not divide *it* completely; and the priest shall burn it on the altar, on the wood that *is* on the fire. It *is* a burnt sacri-

fice, an offering made by fire, a sweet aroma to the LORD.

The Grain Offering

2 ¹"When anyone offers a grain offering to the LORD, his offering shall be *of* fine flour. And he shall pour oil on it, and put frankincense on it. ²He shall bring it to Aaron's sons, the priests, one of whom shall take from it his handful of fine flour and oil with all the frankincense. And the priest shall burn *it as* a memorial on the altar, an offering made by fire, a sweet aroma to the LORD. ³The rest of the grain offering *shall be* Aaron's and his sons'. *It is* most holy of the offerings to the LORD made by fire.

⁴"And if you bring as an offering a grain offering baked in the oven, *it shall be* unleavened cakes of fine flour mixed with oil, or unleavened wafers anointed with oil. ⁵But if your offering *is* a grain offering *baked* in a pan, *it shall be of* fine flour, unleavened, mixed with oil. ⁶You shall break it in pieces and pour oil on it; it *is* a grain offering.

⁷"If your offering *is* a grain offering *baked* in a covered pan, it shall be made *of* fine flour with oil. ⁸You shall bring the grain offering that is made of these things to the LORD. And when it is presented to the priest, he shall bring it to the altar. ⁹Then the priest shall take from the grain offering a memorial portion, and burn *it* on the altar. *It is* an offering made by fire, a sweet aroma to the LORD. ¹⁰And what is left of the grain offering *shall be* Aaron's and his sons'. *It is* most holy of the offerings to the LORD made by fire.

¹¹"No grain offering which you bring to the LORD shall be made with leaven, for you shall burn no leaven nor any honey in any offering to the LORD made by fire. ¹²As for the offering of the firstfruits, you shall offer them to the LORD, but they shall not be burned on the altar for a sweet aroma. ¹³And every offering of your grain offering you shall season with salt; you shall not allow the salt of the covenant of your God to

RELIGION AND WORSHIP

Salt has a symbolic meaning in the sacrificial system (Lev. 2:13). It is a common substance and is an essential ingredient in bread. Leaven was not used in sacrifices but salt was required. The Bible does not explain the meaning of these symbols. Leaven is often said to be a symbol of decay, but its normal use is to improve bread, not destroy it.

be lacking from your grain offering. With all your offerings you shall offer salt.

¹⁴"If you offer a grain offering of your firstfruits to the LORD, you shall offer for the grain offering of your firstfruits green heads of grain roasted on the fire, grain beaten from full heads. ¹⁵And you shall put oil on it, and lay frankincense on it. It *is* a grain offering. ¹⁶Then the priest shall burn the memorial portion: *part* of its beaten grain and *part* of its oil, with all the frankincense, as an offering made by fire to the LORD.

The Peace Offering

3 ¹"When his offering *is* a sacrifice of a peace offering, if he offers *it* of the herd, whether male or female, he shall offer it without blemish before the LORD. ²And he shall lay his hand on the head of his offering, and kill it *at* the door of the tabernacle of meeting; and Aaron's sons, the priests, shall sprinkle the blood all around on the altar. ³Then he shall offer from the sacrifice of the peace offering an offering made by fire to the LORD. The fat that covers the entrails and all the fat that *is* on the entrails, ⁴the two kidneys and the fat that *is* on them by the flanks, and the fatty lobe *attached* to the liver above the kidneys, he shall remove; ⁵and Aaron's sons shall burn it on the altar upon the burnt sacrifice, which *is* on the wood that *is* on the fire, *as* an offering made by fire, a sweet aroma to the LORD.

⁶"If his offering as a sacrifice of a peace offering to the LORD *is* of the flock, *whether* male or female, he shall offer it without blemish. ⁷If he offers a lamb as his offering, then he shall offer it before the LORD. ⁸And

he shall lay his hand on the head of his offering, and kill it before the tabernacle of meeting; and Aaron's sons shall sprinkle its blood all around on the altar.

⁹"Then he shall offer from the sacrifice of the peace offering, as an offering made by fire to the LORD, its fat *and* the whole fat tail which he shall remove close to the backbone. And the fat that covers the entrails and all the fat that *is* on the entrails, ¹⁰the two kidneys and the fat that *is* on them by the flanks, and the fatty lobe *attached* to the liver above the kidneys, he shall remove; ¹¹and the priest shall burn *them* on the altar *as* food, an offering made by fire to the LORD.

¹²"And if his offering *is* a goat, then he shall offer it before the LORD. ¹³He shall lay his hand on its head and kill it before the tabernacle of meeting; and the sons of Aaron shall sprinkle its blood all around on the altar. ¹⁴Then he shall offer from it his offering, as an offering made by fire to the LORD. The fat that covers the entrails and all the fat that *is* on the entrails, ¹⁵the two kidneys and the fat that *is* on them by the flanks, and the fatty lobe *attached* to the liver above the kidneys, he shall remove; ¹⁶and the priest shall burn them on the altar *as* food, an offering made by fire for a sweet aroma; all the fat *is* the LORD's.

¹⁷"This shall be a perpetual statute throughout your generations in all your dwellings: you shall eat neither fat nor blood.' "

The Sin Offering

4 ¹Now the LORD spoke to Moses, saying, ²"Speak to the children of Israel, saying: 'If a person sins unintentionally against any of the commandments of the LORD *in anything* which ought not to be done, and does any of them, ³if the anointed priest sins, bringing guilt on the people, then let him offer to the LORD for his sin which he has sinned a young bull without blemish as a sin offering. ⁴He shall bring the bull to the door of the tabernacle of meeting before the LORD, lay his hand on the bull's head, and kill the bull before the LORD. ⁵Then the anointed priest shall take some of the bull's blood and bring it to the tabernacle of meeting. ⁶The priest shall dip his finger in the blood and sprinkle some of the blood seven times before the LORD, in front of the veil of the sanctuary. ⁷And the priest shall put some of the blood on the horns of the altar of sweet incense before

---

TIME CAPSULE　　*1504 to 1500 B.C.*

1504–1492	*Thutmose I, pharaoh of Egypt*
1500–1200	*Late Bronze Age*
1500	*Memphis again becomes the chosen royal residence for Egypt's pharaoh*
1500	*The priesthood of Thebes rises to power*
1500	*Map of Nippur, Iraq, on a clay tablet*
1500	*The best chariots are made in Egypt*

the LORD, which is in the tabernacle of meeting; and he shall pour the remaining blood of the bull at the base of the altar of the burnt offering, which is at the door of the tabernacle of meeting. ⁸He shall take from it all the fat of the bull as the sin offering. The fat that covers the entrails and all the fat which *is* on the entrails, ⁹the two kidneys and the fat that *is* on them by the flanks, and the fatty lobe *attached* to the liver above the kidneys, he shall remove, ¹⁰as it was taken from the bull of the sacrifice of the peace offering; and the priest shall burn them on the altar of the burnt offering. ¹¹But the bull's hide and all its flesh, with its head and legs, its entrails and offal— ¹²the whole bull he shall carry outside the camp to a clean place, where the ashes are poured out, and burn it on wood with fire; where the ashes are poured out it shall be burned.

¹³'Now if the whole congregation of Israel sins unintentionally, and the thing is hidden from the eyes of the assembly, and they have done *something against* any of the commandments of the LORD *in anything* which should not be done, and are guilty; ¹⁴when the sin which they have committed becomes known, then the assembly shall offer a young bull for the sin, and bring it before the tabernacle of meeting. ¹⁵And the elders of the congregation shall lay their hands on the head of the bull before the LORD. Then the bull shall be killed before the LORD. ¹⁶The anointed priest shall bring some of the bull's blood to the tabernacle of meeting. ¹⁷Then the priest shall dip his finger in the blood and sprinkle *it* seven times before the LORD, in front of the veil. ¹⁸And he shall put *some* of the blood on the horns of the altar which *is* before the LORD, which *is* in the tabernacle of meeting; and he shall pour the remaining blood at the base of the altar of burnt offering, which is at the door of the tabernacle of meeting. ¹⁹He shall take all the fat from it and burn *it* on the altar. ²⁰And he shall do with the bull as he did with the bull as a sin offering; thus he shall do with it. So the priest shall make atonement for them, and it shall be forgiven them. ²¹Then he shall carry the bull outside the camp, and burn it as he burned the first bull. It *is* a sin offering for the assembly.

²²'When a ruler has sinned, and done *something* unintentionally *against* any of the commandments of the LORD his God *in anything* which should not be done, and is guilty, ²³or if his sin which he has committed comes to his knowledge, he shall bring as his offering a kid of the goats, a male without blemish. ²⁴And he shall lay his hand on the head of the goat, and kill it at the place where they kill the burnt offering before the LORD. It *is* a sin offering. ²⁵The priest shall take some of the blood of the sin offering with his finger, put *it* on the horns of the altar of burnt offering, and pour its blood at the base of the altar of burnt offering. ²⁶And he shall burn all its fat on the altar, like the fat of the sacrifice of the peace offering. So the priest shall make atonement for him concerning his sin, and it shall be forgiven him.

²⁷'If anyone of the common people sins unintentionally by doing *something against* any of the commandments of the LORD *in anything* which ought not to be done, and is guilty, ²⁸or if his sin which he has committed comes to his knowledge, then he shall bring as his offering a kid of the goats, a female without blemish, for his sin which he has committed. ²⁹And he shall lay his hand on the head of the sin offering, and kill the sin offering at the place of the burnt offering. ³⁰Then the priest shall take *some* of its blood with his finger, put *it* on the horns of the altar of burnt offering, and pour all *the remaining* blood at the base of the altar. ³¹He shall remove all its fat, as fat is removed from the sacrifice of the peace offering; and the priest shall burn it on the altar for a sweet aroma to the LORD. So the priest shall make atonement for him, and it shall be forgiven him.

³²'If he brings a lamb as his sin offering, he shall bring a female without blemish. ³³Then he shall lay his hand on the head of the sin offering, and kill it as a sin offering at the place where they kill the burnt offering. ³⁴The priest shall take *some* of the blood of the sin offering with his finger, put *it* on the horns of the altar of burnt offering, and pour all *the remaining* blood at the base of the altar. ³⁵He shall remove all its fat, as the fat of the lamb is removed from the sacrifice of the peace offering. Then the priest shall burn it on the altar, according to the offerings made by fire to the LORD. So the priest shall make atonement for his sin that he has committed, and it shall be forgiven him.

The Trespass Offering

5 ¹'If a person sins in hearing the utterance of an oath, and *is* a witness, whether he has seen or known *of the matter*—if he does not tell *it,* he bears guilt.

²'Or if a person touches any unclean thing, whether *it is* the carcass of an unclean beast, or the carcass of unclean livestock, or the carcass of unclean creeping things, and he is unaware of it, he also shall be unclean and guilty. ³Or if he touches human uncleanness—whatever uncleanness with which a man may be defiled, and he is unaware of it—when he realizes *it,* then he shall be guilty.

⁴'Or if a person swears, speaking thoughtlessly with *his* lips to do evil or to do good, whatever *it is* that a man may pronounce by an oath, and he is unaware of it—when he realizes *it,* then he shall be guilty in any of these *matters.*

⁵'And it shall be, when he is guilty in any of these *matters,* that he shall confess that he has sinned in that *thing;* ⁶and he shall bring his trespass offering to the LORD for his sin which he has committed, a female from the flock, a lamb or a kid of the goats as a sin offering. So the priest shall make atonement for him concerning his sin.

⁷If he is not able to bring a lamb, then he shall bring to the LORD, for his trespass which he has committed, two turtledoves or two young pigeons: one as a sin offering and the other as a burnt offering. ⁸And he shall bring them to the priest, who shall offer *that* which *is* for the sin offering first, and wring off its head from its neck, but shall not divide *it* completely. ⁹Then he shall sprinkle *some* of the blood of the sin offering on the side of the altar, and the rest of the blood shall be drained out at the base of the altar. It *is* a sin offering. ¹⁰And he shall offer the second *as* a burnt offering according to the prescribed manner. So the priest shall make atonement on his behalf for his sin which he has committed, and it shall be forgiven him.

¹¹'But if he is not able to bring two turtledoves or two young pigeons, then he who sinned shall bring for his offering one-tenth of an ephah of fine flour as a sin of-fering. He shall put no oil on it, nor shall he put frankincense on it, for it *is* a sin offering. ¹²Then he shall bring it to the priest, and the priest shall take his handful of it as a memorial portion, and burn *it* on the altar according to the offerings made by fire to the LORD. It *is* a sin offering. ¹³The priest shall make atonement for him, for his sin that he has committed in any of these matters; and it shall be forgiven him. *The rest* shall be the priest's as a grain offering.' "

Offerings with Restitution

¹⁴Then the LORD spoke to Moses, saying: ¹⁵"If a person commits a trespass, and sins unintentionally in regard to the holy things of the LORD, then he shall bring to the LORD as his trespass offering a ram without blemish from the flocks, with your valuation in shekels of silver according to the shekel of the sanctuary, as a trespass offering. ¹⁶And he shall make restitution for the harm that he has done in regard to the holy thing, and shall add one-fifth to it and give it to the priest. So the priest shall make atonement for him with the ram of the trespass offering, and it shall be forgiven him.

¹⁷"If a person sins, and commits any of these things which are forbidden to be done by the commandments of the LORD, though he does not know *it,* yet he is guilty and shall bear his iniquity. ¹⁸And he shall bring to the priest a ram without blemish from the flock, with your valuation, as a trespass offering. So the priest shall make atonement for him regarding his ignorance in which he erred and did not know *it,* and it shall be forgiven him. ¹⁹It is a trespass offering; he has certainly trespassed against the LORD."

6 ¹And the LORD spoke to Moses, saying: ²"If a person sins and commits a trespass against the LORD by lying to his neighbor about what was delivered to him for safekeeping, or about a pledge, or about a robbery, or if he has extorted from his neighbor, ³or if he has found what was lost

---

RELIGION AND WORSHIP

The uncleanness treated in Leviticus is ritual uncleanness. Being unclean in this sense means to be excluded from normal participation in acts of religion. A person could become unclean by touching a corpse (Lev. 5:2), although this is not an immoral or sinful act. The offerings provided the means for removing uncleanness in this and other cases.

and lies concerning it, and swears falsely—in any one of these things that a man may do in which he sins: [4]then it shall be, because he has sinned and is guilty, that he shall restore what he has stolen, or the thing which he has extorted, or what was delivered to him for safekeeping, or the lost thing which he found, [5]or all that about which he has sworn falsely. He shall restore its full value, add one-fifth more to it, *and* give it to whomever it belongs, on the day of his trespass offering. [6]And he shall bring his trespass offering to the LORD, a ram without blemish from the flock, with your valuation, as a trespass offering, to the priest. [7]So the priest shall make atonement for him before the LORD, and he shall be forgiven for any one of these things that he may have done in which he trespasses."

The Law of the Burnt Offering

[8]Then the LORD spoke to Moses, saying, [9]"Command Aaron and his sons, saying, 'This *is* the law of the burnt offering: The burnt offering *shall be* on the hearth upon the altar all night until morning, and the fire of the altar shall be kept burning on it. [10]And the priest shall put on his linen garment, and his linen trousers he shall put on his body, and take up the ashes of the burnt offering which the fire has consumed on the altar, and he shall put them beside the altar. [11]Then he shall take off his garments, put on other garments, and carry the ashes outside the camp to a clean place. [12]And the fire on the altar shall be kept burning on it; it shall not be put out. And the priest shall burn wood on it every morning, and lay the burnt offering in order on it; and he shall burn on it the fat of the peace offerings. [13]A fire shall always be burning on the altar; it shall never go out.

The Law of the Grain Offering

[14]"This *is* the law of the grain offering: The sons of Aaron shall offer it on the altar before the LORD. [15]He shall take from it his handful of the fine flour of the grain offer-ing, with its oil, and all the frankincense which *is* on the grain offering, and shall burn *it* on the altar *for* a sweet aroma, as a memorial to the LORD. [16]And the remainder of it Aaron and his sons shall eat; with unleavened bread it shall be eaten in a holy place; in the court of the tabernacle of meeting they shall eat it. [17]It shall not be baked with leaven. I have given it *as* their portion of My offerings made by fire; it *is* most holy, like the sin offering and the trespass offering. [18]All the males among the children of Aaron may eat it. *It shall be* a statute forever in your generations concerning the offerings made by fire to the LORD. Everyone who touches them must be holy.' "[a]

[19]And the LORD spoke to Moses, saying, [20]"This *is* the offering of Aaron and his sons, which they shall offer to the LORD, *beginning* on the day when he is anointed: one-tenth of an ephah of fine flour as a daily grain offering, half of it in the morning and half of it at night. [21]It shall be made in a pan with oil. *When it is* mixed, you shall bring it in. The baked pieces of the grain offering you shall offer *for* a sweet aroma to the LORD. [22]The priest from among his sons, who is anointed in his place, shall offer it. *It is* a statute forever to the LORD. It shall be wholly burned. [23]For every grain offering for the priest shall be wholly burned. It shall not be eaten."

The Law of the Sin Offering

[24]Also the LORD spoke to Moses, saying, [25]"Speak to Aaron and to his sons, saying, 'This *is* the law of the sin offering: In the place where the burnt offering is killed, the sin offering shall be killed before the LORD. It *is* most holy. [26]The priest who offers it for sin shall eat it. In a holy place it shall be eaten, in the court of the tabernacle of meeting. [27]Everyone who touches its flesh must be holy.[a] And when its blood

---

6:18 [a]Compare Numbers 4:15 and Haggai 2:11–13   6:27 [a]Compare Numbers 4:15 and Haggai 2:11–13

SCIENCE AND TECHNOLOGY

Pottery was a common product of many cultures. The objects made of clay are baked to make them hard and permanent. Quality is determined by the type of clay and by the heat and evenness of firing. The firing process requires experience and skill. Still, the whole process is cheap enough that even in ancient times some pottery vessels were intended to be disposable (Lev. 6:28).

is sprinkled on any garment, you shall wash that on which it was sprinkled, in a holy place. 28But the earthen vessel in which it is boiled shall be broken. And if it is boiled in a bronze pot, it shall be both scoured and rinsed in water. 29All the males among the priests may eat it. It *is* most holy. 30But no sin offering from which *any* of the blood is brought into the tabernacle of meeting, to make atonement in the holy *place,*ᵃ shall be eaten. It shall be burned in the fire.

The Law of the Trespass Offering

7 1Likewise this *is* the law of the trespass offering (it *is* most holy): 2In the place where they kill the burnt offering they shall kill the trespass offering. And its blood he shall sprinkle all around on the altar. 3And he shall offer from it all its fat. The fat tail and the fat that covers the entrails, 4the two kidneys and the fat that *is* on them by the flanks, and the fatty lobe *attached* to the liver above the kidneys, he shall remove; 5and the priest shall burn them on the altar *as* an offering made by fire to the LORD. It *is* a trespass offering. 6Every male among the priests may eat it. It shall be eaten in a holy place. It *is* most holy. 7The trespass offering *is* like the sin offering; *there is* one law for them both: the priest who makes atonement with it shall have *it*. 8And the priest who offers anyone's burnt offering, that priest shall have for himself the skin of the burnt offering which he has offered. 9Also every grain offering that is baked in the oven and all that is prepared in the covered pan, or in a pan, shall be the priest's who offers it. 10Every grain offering, *whether* mixed with oil or dry, shall belong to all the sons of Aaron, to one *as much* as the other.

The Law of Peace Offerings

11This *is* the law of the sacrifice of peace offerings which he shall offer to the LORD: 12If he offers it for a thanksgiving, then he shall offer, with the sacrifice of thanksgiving, unleavened cakes mixed with oil, unleavened wafers anointed with oil, or cakes of blended flour mixed with oil. 13Besides the cakes, *as* his offering he shall offer leavened bread with the sacri-

fice of thanksgiving of his peace offering. 14And from it he shall offer one cake from each offering *as* a heave offering to the LORD. It shall belong to the priest who sprinkles the blood of the peace offering.

15The flesh of the sacrifice of his peace offering for thanksgiving shall be eaten the same day it is offered. He shall not leave any of it until morning. 16But if the sacrifice of his offering *is* a vow or a voluntary offering, it shall be eaten the same day that he offers his sacrifice; but on the next day the remainder of it also may be eaten; 17the remainder of the flesh of the sacrifice on the third day must be burned with fire. 18And if *any* of the flesh of the sacrifice of his peace offering is eaten at all on the third day, it shall not be accepted, nor shall it be imputed to him; it shall be an abomination *to* him who offers it, and the person who eats of it shall bear guilt.

19The flesh that touches any unclean thing shall not be eaten. It shall be burned with fire. And as for the *clean* flesh, all who are clean may eat of it. 20But the person who eats the flesh of the sacrifice of the peace offering that *belongs* to the LORD, while he is unclean, that person shall be cut off from his people. 21Moreover the person who touches any unclean thing, *such as* human uncleanness, *an* unclean animal, or any abominable unclean thing,ᵃ and who eats the flesh of the sacrifice of the peace offering that *belongs* to the LORD, that person shall be cut off from his people.' "

Fat and Blood May Not Be Eaten

22And the LORD spoke to Moses, saying, 23"Speak to the children of Israel, saying: 'You shall not eat any fat, of ox or sheep or goat. 24And the fat of an animal that dies *naturally,* and the fat of what is torn by wild beasts, may be used in any other way; but you shall by no means eat it. 25For whoever eats the fat of the animal of which men offer an offering made by fire to the LORD, the person who eats *it* shall be cut off from his people. 26Moreover you shall not eat any blood in any of your dwellings, *whether* of bird or beast. 27Whoever eats any blood, that person shall be cut off from his people.' "

The Portion for Aaron and His Sons

28Then the LORD spoke to Moses, saying, 29"Speak to the children of Israel, saying: 'He who offers the sacrifice of his peace offering to the LORD shall bring his

---

6:30 ᵃThe Most Holy Place when capitalized
7:21 ᵃFollowing Masoretic Text, Septuagint, and Vulgate; Samaritan Pentateuch, Syriac, and Targum read *swarming thing* (compare 5:2).

offering to the LORD from the sacrifice of his peace offering. ³⁰His own hands shall bring the offerings made by fire to the LORD. The fat with the breast he shall bring, that the breast may be waved *as* a wave offering before the LORD. ³¹And the priest shall burn the fat on the altar, but the breast shall be Aaron's and his sons'. ³²Also the right thigh you shall give to the priest *as* a heave offering from the sacrifices of your peace offerings. ³³He among the sons of Aaron, who offers the blood of the peace offering and the fat, shall have the right thigh for *his* part. ³⁴For the breast of the wave offering and the thigh of the heave offering I have taken from the children of Israel, from the sacrifices of their peace offerings, and I have given them to Aaron the priest and to his sons from the children of Israel by a statute forever.' "

³⁵This *is* the consecrated portion for Aaron and his sons, from the offerings made by fire to the LORD, on the day when *Moses* presented them to minister to the LORD as priests. ³⁶The LORD commanded this to be given to them by the children of Israel, on the day that He anointed them, *by* a statute forever throughout their generations.

³⁷This *is* the law of the burnt offering, the grain offering, the sin offering, the trespass offering, the consecrations, and the sacrifice of the peace offering, ³⁸which the LORD commanded Moses on Mount Sinai, on the day when He commanded the children of Israel to offer their offerings to the LORD in the Wilderness of Sinai.

Aaron and His Sons Consecrated

8 ¹And the LORD spoke to Moses, saying: ²"Take Aaron and his sons with him, and the garments, the anointing oil, a bull as the sin offering, two rams, and a basket of unleavened bread; ³and gather all the congregation together at the door of the tabernacle of meeting."

⁴So Moses did as the LORD commanded him. And the congregation was gathered together at the door of the tabernacle of meeting. ⁵And Moses said to the congregation, "This *is* what the LORD commanded to be done."

⁶Then Moses brought Aaron and his sons and washed them with water. ⁷And he put the tunic on him, girded him with the sash, clothed him with the robe, and put the ephod on him; and he girded him with the intricately woven band of the ephod, and with it tied *the ephod* on him. ⁸Then he put the breastplate on him, and he put the Urim and the Thummimᵃ in the breastplate. ⁹And he put the turban on his head. Also on the turban, on its front, he put the golden plate, the holy crown, as the LORD had commanded Moses.

¹⁰Also Moses took the anointing oil, and anointed the tabernacle and all that *was* in it, and consecrated them. ¹¹He sprinkled some of it on the altar seven times, anointed the altar and all its utensils, and the laver and its base, to consecrate them. ¹²And he poured some of the anointing oil on Aaron's head and anointed him, to consecrate him.

¹³Then Moses brought Aaron's sons and put tunics on them, girded them with sashes, and put hats on them, as the LORD had commanded Moses.

¹⁴And he brought the bull for the sin offering. Then Aaron and his sons laid their hands on the head of the bull for the sin offering, ¹⁵and Moses killed *it*. Then he took the blood, and put *some* on the horns of the altar all around with his finger, and purified the altar. And he poured the blood at the base of the altar, and consecrated it, to make atonement for it. ¹⁶Then he took all the fat that *was* on the entrails, the fatty lobe *attached to* the liver, and the two kidneys with their fat, and Moses burned *them* on the altar. ¹⁷But the bull, its hide, its flesh, and its offal, he burned with fire outside the camp, as the LORD had commanded Moses.

8:8 ᵃLiterally *the Lights and the Perfections* (compare Exodus 28:30)

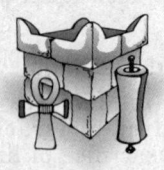

CULTS AND SUPERNATURAL

The Urim and Thummim (Lev. 8:8) were apparently some kind of lot that could be used to obtain an answer from God about certain questions (Num. 27:21). In the surrounding cultures, a common method of looking for such answers was to try to read them from the inside parts of a sacrificed animal, especially the liver. The Romans observed the flights of birds.

18Then he brought the ram as the burnt offering. And Aaron and his sons laid their hands on the head of the ram, 19and Moses killed *it*. Then he sprinkled the blood all around on the altar. 20And he cut the ram into pieces; and Moses burned the head, the pieces, and the fat. 21Then he washed the entrails and the legs in water. And Moses burned the whole ram on the altar. It *was* a burnt sacrifice for a sweet aroma, an offering made by fire to the LORD, as the LORD had commanded Moses.

22And he brought the second ram, the ram of consecration. Then Aaron and his sons laid their hands on the head of the ram, 23and Moses killed *it*. Also he took *some* of its blood and put it on the tip of Aaron's right ear, on the thumb of his right hand, and on the big toe of his right foot. 24Then he brought Aaron's sons. And Moses put *some* of the blood on the tips of their right ears, on the thumbs of their right hands, and on the big toes of their right feet. And Moses sprinkled the blood all around on the altar. 25Then he took the fat and the fat tail, all the fat that *was* on the entrails, the fatty lobe *attached to* the liver, the two kidneys and their fat, and the right thigh; 26and from the basket of unleavened bread that was before the LORD he took one unleavened cake, a cake of bread *anointed with* oil, and one wafer, and put *them* on the fat and on the right thigh; 27and he put all *these* in Aaron's hands and in his sons' hands, and waved them *as* a wave offering before the LORD. 28Then Moses took them from their hands and burned *them* on the altar, on the burnt offering. They *were* consecration offerings for a sweet aroma. That *was* an offering made by fire to the LORD. 29And Moses took the breast and waved it *as* a wave offering before the LORD. It was Moses' part of the ram of consecration, as the LORD had commanded Moses.

30Then Moses took some of the anointing oil and some of the blood which *was* on the altar, and sprinkled *it* on Aaron, on his garments, on his sons, and on the garments of his sons with him; and he consecrated Aaron, his garments, his sons, and the garments of his sons with him.

31And Moses said to Aaron and his sons, "Boil the flesh *at* the door of the tabernacle of meeting, and eat it there with the bread that *is* in the basket of consecration offerings, as I commanded, saying, 'Aaron and his sons shall eat it.' 32What remains of the flesh and of the bread you shall burn with fire. 33And you shall not go outside the door of the tabernacle of meeting *for* seven days, until the days of your consecration are ended. For seven days he shall consecrate you. 34As he has done this day, *so* the LORD has commanded to do, to make atonement for you. 35Therefore you shall stay *at* the door of the tabernacle of meeting day and night for seven days, and keep the charge of the LORD, so that you may not die; for so I have been commanded." 36So Aaron and his sons did all the things that the LORD had commanded by the hand of Moses.

The Priestly Ministry Begins

9 1It came to pass on the eighth day that Moses called Aaron and his sons and the elders of Israel. 2And he said to Aaron, "Take for yourself a young bull as a sin offering and a ram as a burnt offering, without blemish, and offer *them* before the LORD. 3And to the children of Israel you shall speak, saying, 'Take a kid of the goats as a sin offering, and a calf and a lamb, *both* of the first year, without blemish, as a burnt offering, 4also a bull and a ram as peace offerings, to sacrifice before the LORD, and a grain offering mixed with oil; for today the LORD will appear to you.' "

5So they brought what Moses commanded before the tabernacle of meeting. And all the congregation drew near and stood before the LORD. 6Then Moses said, "This *is* the thing which the LORD commanded you to do, and the glory of the LORD will appear to you." 7And Moses said to Aaron, "Go to the altar, offer your sin offering and your burnt offering, and make atonement for yourself and for the people. Offer the offering of the people, and make atonement for them, as the LORD commanded."

8Aaron therefore went to the altar and killed the calf of the sin offering, which *was* for himself. 9Then the sons of Aaron brought the blood to him. And he dipped his finger in the blood, put *it* on the horns of the altar, and poured the blood at the base of the altar. 10But the fat, the kidneys, and the fatty lobe from the liver of the sin offering he burned on the altar, as the LORD had commanded Moses. 11The flesh and the hide he burned with fire outside the camp.

12And he killed the burnt offering; and Aaron's sons presented to him the blood, which he sprinkled all around on the altar.

¹³Then they presented the burnt offering to him, with its pieces and head, and he burned *them* on the altar. ¹⁴And he washed the entrails and the legs, and burned *them* with the burnt offering on the altar.

¹⁵Then he brought the people's offering, and took the goat, which *was* the sin offering for the people, and killed it and offered it for sin, like the first one. ¹⁶And he brought the burnt offering and offered it according to the prescribed manner. ¹⁷Then he brought the grain offering, took a handful of it, and burned *it* on the altar, besides the burnt sacrifice of the morning.

¹⁸He also killed the bull and the ram *as* sacrifices of peace offerings, which *were* for the people. And Aaron's sons presented to him the blood, which he sprinkled all around on the altar, ¹⁹and the fat from the bull and the ram—the fatty tail, what covers *the entrails* and the kidneys, and the fatty lobe *attached to* the liver; ²⁰and they put the fat on the breasts. Then he burned the fat on the altar; ²¹but the breasts and the right thigh Aaron waved *as* a wave offering before the LORD, as Moses had commanded.

²²Then Aaron lifted his hand toward the people, blessed them, and came down from offering the sin offering, the burnt offering, and peace offerings. ²³And Moses and Aaron went into the tabernacle of meeting, and came out and blessed the people. Then the glory of the LORD appeared to all the people, ²⁴and fire came out from before the LORD and consumed the burnt offering and the fat on the altar. When all the people saw *it,* they shouted and fell on their faces.

The Profane Fire of Nadab and Abihu

10 ¹Then Nadab and Abihu, the sons of Aaron, each took his censer and put fire in it, put incense on it, and offered profane fire before the LORD, which He had not commanded them. ²So fire went out from the LORD and devoured them, and they died before the LORD. ³And Moses said to Aaron, "This is what the LORD spoke, saying:

'By those who come near Me
I must be regarded as holy;
And before all the people
I must be glorified.' "

So Aaron held his peace.

⁴Then Moses called Mishael and Elza-phan, the sons of Uzziel the uncle of Aaron, and said to them, "Come near, carry your brethren from before the sanctuary out of the camp." ⁵So they went near and carried them by their tunics out of the camp, as Moses had said.

⁶And Moses said to Aaron, and to Eleazar and Ithamar, his sons, "Do not uncover your heads nor tear your clothes, lest you die, and wrath come upon all the people. But let your brethren, the whole house of Israel, bewail the burning which the LORD has kindled. ⁷You shall not go out from the door of the tabernacle of meeting, lest you die, for the anointing oil of the LORD *is* upon you." And they did according to the word of Moses.

Conduct Prescribed for Priests

⁸Then the LORD spoke to Aaron, saying: ⁹"Do not drink wine or intoxicating drink, you, nor your sons with you, when you go into the tabernacle of meeting, lest you die. *It shall be* a statute forever throughout your generations, ¹⁰that you may distinguish between holy and unholy, and between unclean and clean, ¹¹and that you may teach the children of Israel all the statutes which the LORD has spoken to them by the hand of Moses."

¹²And Moses spoke to Aaron, and to Eleazar and Ithamar, his sons who were left: "Take the grain offering that remains of the offerings made by fire to the LORD, and eat it without leaven beside the altar; for it *is* most holy. ¹³You shall eat it in a holy place, because it *is* your due and your sons' due, of the sacrifices made by fire to the LORD; for so I have been commanded. ¹⁴The breast of the wave offering and the thigh of the heave offering you shall eat in a clean place, you, your sons, and your daughters with you; for *they are* your due and your sons' due, *which* are given from the sacrifices of peace offerings of the children of Israel. ¹⁵The thigh of the heave offering and the breast of the wave offering they shall bring with the offerings of fat made by fire, to offer *as* a wave offering before the LORD. And it shall be yours and your sons' with you, by a statute forever, as the LORD has commanded."

¹⁶Then Moses made careful inquiry about the goat of the sin offering, and there it was—burned up. And he was angry with Eleazar and Ithamar, the sons of Aaron *who were* left, saying, ¹⁷"Why have you not eaten the sin offering in a holy place, since

RIGHT OR WRONG RITUAL: LIFE OR DEATH (Lev. 10:1–7)

In the modern western world we tend to think of religious rituals as the procedures by which a group of people worship God. It is not a crisis of faith if some part of a ritual is not done exactly right. But in the ancient world the ritual was considered something to be performed correctly. The ritual, properly performed, was proper religion. To make an error in the prescribed forms of the rite was not just a mistake, but an act of impiety.

The priests, who were anointed and set apart to perform the rituals, were expected to live by a more stringent set of rules than were ordinary people. They had to memorize all the liturgy, hymns, and words for every religious service. The ancient world held services for the deities every day of the year, and so specialists were needed among the priesthood who could handle any service. These priests, it was believed, were chosen by the deity being worshiped.

Nadab and Abihu, Aaron's sons, were legitimate priests who chose on their own not to follow the ritual that was sanctioned by God (Lev. 10:1). Their deviation appears minor in the eyes of the modern western world; they simply lit their incense censers with a fire from an unapproved source. But for this breach of worship they were both destroyed by divine fire (10:2).

Israelites and Judahites would have understood these deaths as the proper consequence. A priest was supposed to follow the proper ritual, since the ritual was the way deity was honored and respected (10:3). Nadab's and Abihu's evil was their decision to determine for themselves right and wrong ways to worship. Even mourning for these dead priests was denied, lest it be seen as condoning their sin (10:6, 7).

---

it *is* most holy, and *God* has given it to you to bear the guilt of the congregation, to make atonement for them before the LORD? [18]See! Its blood was not brought inside the holy *place;*[a] indeed you should have eaten it in a holy *place,* as I commanded."

[19]And Aaron said to Moses, "Look, this day they have offered their sin offering and their burnt offering before the LORD, and such things have befallen me! *If* I had eaten the sin offering today, would it have been accepted in the sight of the LORD?" [20]So when Moses heard *that,* he was content.

Foods Permitted and Forbidden

11 [1]Now the LORD spoke to Moses and Aaron, saying to them, [2]"Speak to the children of Israel, saying, 'These *are* the animals which you may eat among

all the animals that *are* on the earth: [3]Among the animals, whatever divides the hoof, having cloven hooves *and* chewing the cud—that you may eat. [4]Nevertheless these you shall not eat among those that chew the cud or those that have cloven hooves: the camel, because it chews the cud but does not have cloven hooves, is unclean to you; [5]the rock hyrax, because it chews the cud but does not have cloven hooves, *is* unclean to you; [6]the hare, because it chews the cud but does not have cloven hooves, *is* unclean to you; [7]and the swine, though it divides the hoof, having cloven hooves, yet does not chew the cud, *is* unclean to you. [8]Their flesh you shall not eat, and their carcasses you shall not touch. They *are* unclean to you.

[9]These you may eat of all that *are* in the water: whatever in the water has fins and scales, whether in the seas or in the rivers—that you may eat. [10]But all in the

---

10:18 [a]The Most Holy Place when capitalized

PLANTS AND ANIMALS

The rationale for the distinctions between clean and unclean animals has been the subject of speculation. One suggestion is that unclean animals include those whose locomotion is improper or irregular, like the bat, which is a mammal that flies. Fish without fins are unclean (Lev. 11:10), as are animals that "creep" on the ground (11:41).

seas or in the rivers that do not have fins and scales, all that move in the water or any living thing which *is* in the water, they *are* an abomination to you. [11]They shall be an abomination to you; you shall not eat their flesh, but you shall regard their carcasses as an abomination. [12]Whatever in the water does not have fins or scales— that *shall be* an abomination to you.

[13]'And these you shall regard as an abomination among the birds; they shall not be eaten, they *are* an abomination: the eagle, the vulture, the buzzard, [14]the kite, and the falcon after its kind; [15]every raven after its kind, [16]the ostrich, the short-eared owl, the sea gull, and the hawk after its kind; [17]the little owl, the fisher owl, and the screech owl; [18]the white owl, the jackdaw, and the carrion vulture; [19]the stork, the heron after its kind, the hoopoe, and the bat.

[20]'All flying insects that creep on *all* fours *shall be* an abomination to you. [21]Yet these you may eat of every flying insect that creeps on *all* fours: those which have jointed legs above their feet with which to leap on the earth. [22]These you may eat: the locust after its kind, the destroying locust after its kind, the cricket after its kind, and the grasshopper after its kind. [23]But all *other* flying insects which have four feet *shall be* an abomination to you.

Unclean Animals

[24]'By these you shall become unclean; whoever touches the carcass of any of them shall be unclean until evening; [25]whoever carries part of the carcass of any of them shall wash his clothes and be unclean until evening: [26]*The carcass* of any animal which divides the foot, but is not cloven-hoofed or does not chew the cud, *is* unclean to you. Everyone who touches it shall be unclean. [27]And whatever goes on its paws, among all kinds of animals that go on *all* fours, those *are* unclean to you. Whoever touches any such carcass shall be unclean until evening. [28]Whoever carries *any such* carcass shall wash his clothes and be unclean until evening. It *is* unclean to you.

[29]'These also *shall be* unclean to you among the creeping things that creep on the earth: the mole, the mouse, and the large lizard after its kind; [30]the gecko, the monitor lizard, the sand reptile, the sand lizard, and the chameleon. [31]These *are* unclean to you among all that creep. Whoever touches them when they are dead shall be unclean until evening. [32]Anything on which *any* of them falls, when they are dead shall be unclean, whether *it is* any item of wood or clothing or skin or sack, whatever item *it is,* in which *any* work is done, it must be put in water. And it shall be unclean until evening; then it shall be clean. [33]Any earthen vessel into which *any* of them falls you shall break; and whatever *is* in it shall be unclean: [34]in such a vessel, any edible food upon which water falls becomes unclean, and any drink that may be drunk from it becomes unclean. [35]And everything on which *a part* of *any such* carcass falls shall be unclean; *whether it is* an oven or cooking stove, it shall be broken down; *for* they *are* unclean, and shall be unclean to you. [36]Nevertheless a spring or a cistern, *in which there is* plenty of water, shall be clean, but whatever touches any such carcass becomes unclean. [37]And if a part of *any such* carcass falls on any planting seed which is to be sown, it *remains* clean. [38]But if water is put on the seed, and if *a part* of *any such* carcass falls on it, it *becomes* unclean to you.

[39]'And if any animal which you may eat dies, he who touches its carcass shall be unclean until evening. [40]He who eats of its carcass shall wash his clothes and be unclean until evening. He also who carries its carcass shall wash his clothes and be unclean until evening.

[41]'And every creeping thing that creeps on the earth *shall be* an abomination. It shall not be eaten. [42]Whatever crawls on its belly, whatever goes on *all* fours, or whatever has many feet among all creeping things that creep on the earth—these you shall not eat, for they *are* an abomination. [43]You shall not make yourselves

TIME CAPSULE *1492 to 1479 B.C.*

1492– 1479 *Thutmose II, pharaoh of Egypt*

1486 *Moses flees Egypt (based on early Exodus; Ex. 2:15; Acts 7:23)*

1479– 1425 *Thutmose III, pharaoh of Egypt*

1479 *When Thutmose II dies, Queen Hatshepsut assumes a coregency with the very young Thutmose III*

1479– 1457 *Queen Hatshepsut reigns jointly with Thutmose III*

abominable with any creeping thing that creeps; nor shall you make yourselves unclean with them, lest you be defiled by them. ⁴⁴For I *am* the LORD your God. You shall therefore consecrate yourselves, and you shall be holy; for I *am* holy. Neither shall you defile yourselves with any creeping thing that creeps on the earth. ⁴⁵For I *am* the LORD who brings you up out of the land of Egypt, to be your God. You shall therefore be holy, for I *am* holy.

⁴⁶"This *is* the law of the animals and the birds and every living creature that moves in the waters, and of every creature that creeps on the earth, ⁴⁷to distinguish between the unclean and the clean, and between the animal that may be eaten and the animal that may not be eaten.'"

The Ritual After Childbirth

12 ¹Then the LORD spoke to Moses, saying, ²"Speak to the children of Israel, saying: 'If a woman has conceived, and borne a male child, then she shall be unclean seven days; as in the days of her customary impurity she shall be unclean. ³And on the eighth day the flesh of his foreskin shall be circumcised. ⁴She shall then continue in the blood of *her* purification thirty-three days. She shall not touch any hallowed thing, nor come into the sanctuary until the days of her purification are fulfilled.

⁵'But if she bears a female child, then she shall be unclean two weeks, as in her customary impurity, and she shall continue in the blood of *her* purification sixty-six days.

⁶'When the days of her purification are fulfilled, whether for a son or a daughter, she shall bring to the priest a lamb of the first year as a burnt offering, and a young pigeon or a turtledove as a sin offering, to the door of the tabernacle of meeting. ⁷Then he shall offer it before the LORD, and make atonement for her. And she shall be clean from the flow of her blood. This *is* the law for her who has borne a male or a female.

⁸'And if she is not able to bring a lamb, then she may bring two turtledoves or two young pigeons—one as a burnt offering and the other as a sin offering. So the priest

shall make atonement for her, and she will be clean.'"

The Law Concerning Leprosy

13 ¹And the LORD spoke to Moses and Aaron, saying: ²"When a man has on the skin of his body a swelling, a scab, or a bright spot, and it becomes on the skin of his body *like* a leprous^a sore, then he shall be brought to Aaron the priest or to one of his sons the priests. ³The priest shall examine the sore on the skin of the body; and if the hair on the sore has turned white, and the sore appears *to be* deeper than the skin of his body, it *is* a leprous sore. Then the priest shall examine him, and pronounce him unclean. ⁴But if the bright spot *is* white on the skin of his body, and does not appear *to be* deeper than the skin, and its hair has not turned white, then the priest shall isolate *the one who has* the sore seven days. ⁵And the priest shall examine him on the seventh day; and indeed *if* the sore appears to be as it was, *and* the sore has not spread on the skin, then the priest shall isolate him another seven days. ⁶Then the priest shall examine him again on the seventh day; and indeed *if* the sore has faded, *and* the sore has not spread on the skin, then the priest shall pronounce him clean; it *is only* a scab, and he shall wash his clothes and be clean. ⁷But if the scab should at all spread over the skin, after he has been seen by the priest for his cleansing, he shall be seen by the priest again. ⁸And *if* the priest sees that the scab has indeed spread on the skin, then the priest shall pronounce him unclean. It *is* leprosy.

⁹"When the leprous sore is on a person, then he shall be brought to the priest. ¹⁰And the priest shall examine *him;* and indeed *if* the swelling on the skin *is* white, and it has turned the hair white, and *there is* a spot of raw flesh in the swelling, ¹¹it *is* an old leprosy on the skin of his body. The priest shall pronounce him unclean, and shall not isolate him, for he *is* unclean.

¹²"And if leprosy breaks out all over the skin, and the leprosy covers all the skin of *the one who has* the sore, from his head to his foot, wherever the priest looks, ¹³then the priest shall consider; and indeed *if* the leprosy has covered all his body, he shall pronounce *him* clean *who has* the sore. It has all turned white. He *is* clean. ¹⁴But when raw flesh appears on him, he

13:2 ^aHebrew *saraath,* disfiguring skin diseases, including leprosy, and so in verses 2–46 and 14:2–32

shall be unclean. ¹⁵And the priest shall examine the raw flesh and pronounce him to be unclean; *for* the raw flesh *is* unclean. It *is* leprosy. ¹⁶Or if the raw flesh changes and turns white again, he shall come to the priest. ¹⁷And the priest shall examine him; and indeed *if* the sore has turned white, then the priest shall pronounce *him* clean *who has* the sore. He *is* clean.

¹⁸"If the body develops a boil in the skin, and it is healed, ¹⁹and in the place of the boil there comes a white swelling or a bright spot, reddish-white, then it shall be shown to the priest; ²⁰and *if*, when the priest sees it, it indeed *appears* deeper than the skin, and its hair has turned white, the priest shall pronounce him unclean. It *is* a leprous sore which has broken out of the boil. ²¹But if the priest examines it, and indeed *there are* no white hairs in it, and it *is* not deeper than the skin, but has faded, then the priest shall isolate him seven days; ²²and if it should at all spread over the skin, then the priest shall pronounce him unclean. It *is* a leprous sore. ²³But if the bright spot stays in one place, *and* has not spread, it *is* the scar of the boil; and the priest shall pronounce him clean.

²⁴"Or if the body receives a burn on its skin by fire, and the raw *flesh* of the burn becomes a bright spot, reddish-white or white, ²⁵then the priest shall examine it; and indeed *if* the hair of the bright spot has turned white, and it appears deeper than the skin, it *is* leprosy broken out in the burn. Therefore the priest shall pronounce him unclean. It *is* a leprous sore. ²⁶But if the priest examines it, and indeed *there are* no white hairs in the bright spot, and it *is* not deeper than the skin, but has faded, then the priest shall isolate him seven days. ²⁷And the priest shall examine him on the seventh day. If it has at all spread over the skin, then the priest shall pronounce him unclean. It *is* a leprous sore. ²⁸But if the bright spot stays in one place, *and* has not spread on the skin, but has faded, it *is* a swelling from the burn.

The priest shall pronounce him clean, for it *is* the scar from the burn.

²⁹"If a man or woman has a sore on the head or the beard, ³⁰then the priest shall examine the sore; and indeed if it appears deeper than the skin, *and there is* in it thin yellow hair, then the priest shall pronounce him unclean. It *is* a scaly leprosy of the head or beard. ³¹But if the priest examines the scaly sore, and indeed it does not appear deeper than the skin, and *there is* no black hair in it, then the priest shall isolate *the one who has* the scale seven days. ³²And on the seventh day the priest shall examine the sore; and indeed *if* the scale has not spread, and there is no yellow hair in it, and the scale does not appear deeper than the skin, ³³he shall shave himself, but the scale he shall not shave. And the priest shall isolate *the one who has* the scale another seven days. ³⁴On the seventh day the priest shall examine the scale; and indeed *if* the scale has not spread over the skin, and does not appear deeper than the skin, then the priest shall pronounce him clean. He shall wash his clothes and be clean. ³⁵But if the scale should at all spread over the skin after his cleansing, ³⁶then the priest shall examine him; and indeed *if* the scale has spread over the skin, the priest need not seek for yellow hair. He *is* unclean. ³⁷But if the scale appears to be at a standstill, and there is black hair grown up in it, the scale has healed. He *is* clean, and the priest shall pronounce him clean.

³⁸"If a man or a woman has bright spots on the skin of the body, *specifically* white bright spots, ³⁹then the priest shall look; and indeed *if* the bright spots on the skin of the body *are* dull white, it *is* a white spot *that* grows on the skin. He *is* clean.

⁴⁰"As for the man whose hair has fallen from his head, he *is* bald, *but* he *is* clean. ⁴¹He whose hair has fallen from his forehead, he *is* bald on the forehead, *but* he *is* clean. ⁴²And if there is on the bald head or bald forehead a reddish-white sore, it *is* leprosy breaking out on his bald head or his bald forehead. ⁴³Then the priest shall

HEALTH AND MEDICINE

Although there was no theory of communicable diseases, the isolation of the leper looks very much like quarantine (Lev. 13:45). The modern disease called leprosy is a particular infection called technically Hansen's disease. Its symptoms are different from the leprosy mentioned in the Bible.

examine it; and indeed *if* the swelling of the sore *is* reddish-white on his bald head or on his bald forehead, as the appearance of leprosy on the skin of the body, 44he is a leprous man. He *is* unclean. The priest shall surely pronounce him unclean; his sore *is* on his head.

45"Now the leper on whom the sore *is,* his clothes shall be torn and his head bare; and he shall cover his mustache, and cry, 'Unclean! Unclean!' 46He shall be unclean. All the days he has the sore he shall be unclean. He *is* unclean, and he shall dwell alone; his dwelling *shall be* outside the camp.

The Law Concerning Leprous Garments

47"Also, if a garment has a leprous plague[a] in it, *whether it is* a woolen garment or a linen garment, 48whether *it is* in the warp or woof of linen or wool, whether in leather or in anything made of leather, 49and if the plague is greenish or reddish in the garment or in the leather, whether in the warp or in the woof, or in anything made of leather, it *is* a leprous plague and shall be shown to the priest. 50The priest shall examine the plague and isolate *that which has* the plague seven days. 51And he shall examine the plague on the seventh day. If the plague has spread in the garment, either in the warp or in the woof, in the leather *or* in anything made of leather, the plague *is* an active leprosy. It *is* unclean. 52He shall therefore burn that garment in which is the plague, whether warp or woof, in wool or in linen, or anything of leather, for it *is* an active leprosy; *the garment* shall be burned in the fire.

53"But if the priest examines *it,* and indeed the plague has not spread in the garment, either in the warp or in the woof, or in anything made of leather, 54then the priest shall command that they wash *the thing* in which *is* the plague; and he shall isolate it another seven days. 55Then the priest shall examine the plague after it has been washed; and indeed *if* the plague has not changed its color, though the plague has not spread, it *is* unclean, and you shall burn it in the fire; it continues eating away, *whether* the damage *is* outside or inside. 56If the priest examines *it,* and indeed the plague has faded after washing it, then he

shall tear it out of the garment, whether out of the warp or out of the woof, or out of the leather. 57But if it appears again in the garment, either in the warp or in the woof, or in anything made of leather, it *is* a spreading *plague;* you shall burn with fire that in which is the plague. 58And if you wash the garment, either warp or woof, or whatever is made of leather, if the plague has disappeared from it, then it shall be washed a second time, and shall be clean.

59"This *is* the law of the leprous plague in a garment of wool or linen, either in the warp or woof, or in anything made of leather, to pronounce it clean or to pronounce it unclean."

The Ritual for Cleansing Healed Lepers

14 1Then the LORD spoke to Moses, saying, 2"This shall be the law of the leper for the day of his cleansing: He shall be brought to the priest. 3And the priest shall go out of the camp, and the priest shall examine *him;* and indeed, *if* the leprosy is healed in the leper, 4then the priest shall command to take for him who is to be cleansed two living *and* clean birds, cedar wood, scarlet, and hyssop. 5And the priest shall command that one of the birds be killed in an earthen vessel over running water. 6As for the living bird, he shall take it, the cedar wood and the scarlet and the hyssop, and dip them and the living bird in the blood of the bird *that was* killed over the running water. 7And he shall sprinkle it seven times on him who is to be cleansed from the leprosy, and shall pronounce him clean, and shall let the living bird loose in the open field. 8He who is to be cleansed shall wash his clothes, shave off all his hair, and wash himself in water, that he may be clean. After that he shall come into the camp, and shall stay outside his tent seven days. 9But on the seventh day he shall shave all the hair off his head and his beard and his eyebrows—all his hair he shall shave off. He shall wash his clothes and wash his body in water, and he shall be clean.

10"And on the eighth day he shall take two male lambs without blemish, one ewe lamb of the first year without blemish, three-tenths *of an ephah* of fine flour mixed with oil as a grain offering, and one log of oil. 11Then the priest who makes *him* clean shall present the man who is to be made clean, and those things, before the

---

13:47 [a] A mold, fungus, or similar infestation, and so in verses 47–59

RITUALS AGAINST FUNGUS (Lev. 14:33–53)

Israel's laws included regulations for dealing with a "leprous plague in a house" (Lev. 14:33–53). The Hebrew word translated "leprous plague" (14:33) is generic, pertaining to various infestations. When used to describe the deterioration of garments (Lev. 13:47) and houses, it probably refers to decay caused by fungus, mildew, mold, or dry rot.

In Israel, any house that was discolored with mildew caused by fungus-producing organisms was quarantined (14:36–38). The structure had to be cleansed both physically and ritually. Affected areas of stone were scraped, or replaced and remortared (14:40–42). If efforts were successful, the priest pronounced the house clean and performed a purification ritual (14:48–53).

This Mosaic dictum for quarantining and cleansing infected houses can be compared with two texts from Mesopotamia. One is a quotation from a Babylonian omen series, which prescribes a ritual to the Babylonian gods Ea and Ishum. Another ritual is mentioned in a letter to Esarhaddon, the king of Assyria from 680 to 669 B.C.

The omen reads, "If there is a fungus in a man's house, on the outer north wall, the owner of the house will die and his house will be scattered." In order to avert the evil, the individual is told to gather the fungus (in a particular manner) and burn it with a torch, placing mud and gypsum around it. The person then must recite an incantation to Ea (the god of wisdom) and slaughter a sheep to the god Ishum. Holy water is thrown on the person while another incantation is recited. Thus, the evil of the omen will be thwarted.

A letter to Esarhaddon confirms to the king the existence of a prayer and a ritual for two types of fungus that had appeared on the inner courtyard of the temple of Nabu. The author of the letter states that a technician, meaning a priest, will perform the appropriate ritual several times on the next morning.

LORD, *at* the door of the tabernacle of meeting. ¹²And the priest shall take one male lamb and offer it as a trespass offering, and the log of oil, and wave them *as* a wave offering before the LORD. ¹³Then he shall kill the lamb in the place where he kills the sin offering and the burnt offering, in a holy place; for as the sin offering *is* the priest's, so *is* the trespass offering. It *is* most holy. ¹⁴The priest shall take *some* of the blood of the trespass offering, and the priest shall put *it* on the tip of the right ear of him who is to be cleansed, on the thumb of his right hand, and on the big toe of his right foot. ¹⁵And the priest shall take *some* of the log of oil, and pour *it* into the palm of his own left hand. ¹⁶Then the priest shall dip his right finger in the oil that *is* in his left hand, and shall sprinkle some of the oil with his finger seven times before the LORD. ¹⁷And of the rest of the oil in his hand, the priest shall put *some* on the tip of the right ear of him who is to be cleansed, on the thumb of his right hand, and on the big toe of his right foot, on the blood of the trespass offering. ¹⁸The rest of the oil that *is* in the priest's hand he shall put on the head of him who is to be

cleansed. So the priest shall make atonement for him before the LORD.

¹⁹"Then the priest shall offer the sin offering, and make atonement for him who is to be cleansed from his uncleanness. Afterward he shall kill the burnt offering. ²⁰And the priest shall offer the burnt offering and the grain offering on the altar. So the priest shall make atonement for him, and he shall be clean.

²¹"But if he *is* poor and cannot afford it, then he shall take one male lamb *as* a trespass offering to be waved, to make atonement for him, one-tenth *of an ephah* of fine flour mixed with oil as a grain offering, a log of oil, ²²and two turtledoves or two young pigeons, such as he is able to afford: one shall be a sin offering and the other a burnt offering. ²³He shall bring them to the priest on the eighth day for his cleansing, to the door of the tabernacle of meeting, before the LORD. ²⁴And the priest shall take the lamb of the trespass offering and the log of oil, and the priest shall wave them *as* a wave offering before the LORD. ²⁵Then he shall kill the lamb of the trespass offering, and the priest shall take *some* of the blood of the trespass offering

and put *it* on the tip of the right ear of him who is to be cleansed, on the thumb of his right hand, and on the big toe of his right foot. 26And the priest shall pour some of the oil into the palm of his own left hand. 27Then the priest shall sprinkle with his right finger *some* of the oil that *is* in his left hand seven times before the LORD. 28And the priest shall put *some* of the oil that *is* in his hand on the tip of the right ear of him who is to be cleansed, on the thumb of the right hand, and on the big toe of his right foot, on the place of the blood of the trespass offering. 29The rest of the oil that *is* in the priest's hand he shall put on the head of him who is to be cleansed, to make atonement for him before the LORD. 30And he shall offer one of the turtledoves or young pigeons, such as he can afford— 31such as he is able to afford, the one *as* a sin offering and the other *as* a burnt offering, with the grain offering. So the priest shall make atonement for him who is to be cleansed before the LORD. 32This *is* the law *for one* who had a leprous sore, who cannot afford the usual cleansing."

The Law Concerning Leprous Houses

33And the LORD spoke to Moses and Aaron, saying: 34"When you have come into the land of Canaan, which I give you as a possession, and I put the leprous plague[a] in a house in the land of your possession, 35and he who owns the house comes and tells the priest, saying, 'It seems to me that *there is* some plague in the house,' 36then the priest shall command that they empty the house, before the priest goes *into it* to examine the plague, that all that *is* in the house may not be made unclean; and afterward the priest shall go in to examine the house. 37And he shall examine the plague; and indeed *if* the plague *is* on the walls of the house with ingrained streaks, greenish or reddish, which appear to be deep in the wall, 38then the priest shall go out of the house, to the door of the house, and shut up the house seven days. 39And the priest shall come again on the seventh day and look; and indeed *if* the plague has spread on the walls of the house, 40then the priest shall command that they take away the stones in which *is* the plague, and they shall cast them into an unclean place outside the city. 41And he shall cause the house to be scraped inside, all around, and the dust that they scrape off they shall pour out in an unclean place outside the city. 42Then they shall take other stones and put *them* in the place of *those* stones, and he shall take other mortar and plaster the house.

43"Now if the plague comes back and breaks out in the house, after he has taken away the stones, after he has scraped the house, and after it is plastered, 44then the priest shall come and look; and indeed *if* the plague has spread in the house, it *is* an active leprosy in the house. It *is* unclean. 45And he shall break down the house, its stones, its timber, and all the plaster of the house, and he shall carry *them* outside the city to an unclean place. 46Moreover he who goes into the house at all while it is shut up shall be unclean until evening. 47And he who lies down in the house shall wash his clothes, and he who eats in the house shall wash his clothes.

48"But if the priest comes in and examines *it,* and indeed the plague has not spread in the house after the house was plastered, then the priest shall pronounce the house clean, because the plague is healed. 49And he shall take, to cleanse the house, two birds, cedar wood, scarlet, and hyssop. 50Then he shall kill one of the birds in an earthen vessel over running water; 51and he shall take the cedar wood, the hyssop, the scarlet, and the living bird, and dip them in the blood of the slain bird and in the running water, and sprinkle the house seven times. 52And he shall cleanse the house with the blood of the bird and the running water and the living bird, with the cedar wood, the hyssop, and the scarlet. 53Then he shall let the living bird loose outside the city in the open field, and make atonement for the house, and it shall be clean.

54"This *is* the law for any leprous sore and scale, 55for the leprosy of a garment and of a house, 56for a swelling and a scab and a bright spot, 57to teach when *it is* unclean and when *it is* clean. This *is* the law of leprosy."

The Law Concerning Bodily Discharges

15 1And the LORD spoke to Moses and Aaron, saying, 2"Speak to the children of Israel, and say to them: 'When any man has a discharge from his body, his discharge *is* unclean. 3And this shall be his uncleanness in regard to his discharge—

14:34 [a]Decomposition by mildew, mold, dry rot, etc., and so in verses 34–53

whether his body runs with his discharge, or his body is stopped up by his discharge, it *is* his uncleanness. ⁴Every bed is unclean on which he who has the discharge lies, and everything on which he sits shall be unclean. ⁵And whoever touches his bed shall wash his clothes and bathe in water, and be unclean until evening. ⁶He who sits on anything on which he who has the discharge sat shall wash his clothes and bathe in water, and be unclean until evening. ⁷And he who touches the body of him who has the discharge shall wash his clothes and bathe in water, and be unclean until evening. ⁸If he who has the discharge spits on him who is clean, then he shall wash his clothes and bathe in water, and be unclean until evening. ⁹Any saddle on which he who has the discharge rides shall be unclean. ¹⁰Whoever touches anything that was under him shall be unclean until evening. He who carries *any of* those things shall wash his clothes and bathe in water, and be unclean until evening. ¹¹And whomever the one who has the discharge touches, and has not rinsed his hands in water, he shall wash his clothes and bathe in water, and be unclean until evening. ¹²The vessel of earth that he who has the discharge touches shall be broken, and every vessel of wood shall be rinsed in water.

¹³And when he who has a discharge is cleansed of his discharge, then he shall count for himself seven days for his cleansing, wash his clothes, and bathe his body in running water; then he shall be clean. ¹⁴On the eighth day he shall take for himself two turtledoves or two young pigeons, and come before the LORD, to the door of the tabernacle of meeting, and give them to the priest. ¹⁵Then the priest shall offer them, the one *as* a sin offering and the other *as* a burnt offering. So the priest shall make atonement for him before the LORD because of his discharge.

¹⁶'If any man has an emission of semen, then he shall wash all his body in water, and be unclean until evening. ¹⁷And any garment and any leather on which there is semen, it shall be washed with water, and be unclean until evening. ¹⁸Also, when a woman lies with a man, and *there is* an emission of semen, they shall bathe in water, and be unclean until evening.

¹⁹'If a woman has a discharge, *and* the discharge from her body is blood, she shall be set apart seven days; and whoever

touches her shall be unclean until evening. ²⁰Everything that she lies on during her impurity shall be unclean; also everything that she sits on shall be unclean. ²¹Whoever touches her bed shall wash his clothes and bathe in water, and be unclean until evening. ²²And whoever touches anything that she sat on shall wash his clothes and bathe in water, and be unclean until evening. ²³If *anything* is on *her* bed or on anything on which she sits, when he touches it, he shall be unclean until evening. ²⁴And if any man lies with her at all, so that her impurity is on him, he shall be unclean seven days; and every bed on which he lies shall be unclean.

²⁵'If a woman has a discharge of blood for many days, other than at the time of her *customary* impurity, or if it runs beyond her *usual time of* impurity, all the days of her unclean discharge shall be as the days of her *customary* impurity. She *shall be* unclean. ²⁶Every bed on which she lies all the days of her discharge shall be to her as the bed of her impurity; and whatever she sits on shall be unclean, as the uncleanness of her impurity. ²⁷Whoever touches those things shall be unclean; he shall wash his clothes and bathe in water, and be unclean until evening.

²⁸'But if she is cleansed of her discharge, then she shall count for herself seven days, and after that she shall be clean. ²⁹And on the eighth day she shall take for herself two turtledoves or two young pigeons, and bring them to the priest, to the door of the tabernacle of meeting. ³⁰Then the priest shall offer the one *as* a sin offering and the other *as* a burnt offering, and the priest shall make atonement for her before the LORD for the discharge of her uncleanness.

³¹'Thus you shall separate the children of Israel from their uncleanness, lest they die in their uncleanness when they defile My tabernacle that *is* among them. ³²This *is* the law for one who has a discharge, and *for him* who emits semen and is unclean thereby, ³³and for her who is indisposed because of her *customary* impurity, and for one who has a discharge, either man or woman, and for him who lies with her who is unclean.' "

The Day of Atonement

A description of the Day of Atonement, the most sacred event in the year, appears in Lev. 16 and also in Lev. 23:26–32. Postbiblical Judaism referred to this annual observance as "the day" or "the great day." In the New Testament Paul calls it "the Fast" (Acts 27:9). It was observed on the 10th day of the 7th month, Tishri, corresponding to October. See "Israel's Feasts" at Lev. 23:1.

■ Leviticus 16:1—22:33

Leviticus

16 :1 Now the LORD spoke to Moses after the death of the two sons of Aaron, when they offered *profane fire* before the LORD, and died; ²and the LORD said to Moses: "Tell Aaron your brother not to come at *just* any time into the Holy *Place* inside the veil, before the mercy seat which *is* on the ark, lest he die; for I will appear in the cloud above the mercy seat.

³"Thus Aaron shall come into the Holy *Place:* with *the blood of* a young bull as a sin offering, and *of* a ram as a burnt offering. ⁴He shall put the holy linen tunic and the linen trousers on his body; he shall be girded with a linen sash, and with the linen turban he shall be attired. These *are* holy garments. Therefore he shall wash his body in water, and put them on. ⁵And he shall take from the congregation of the children of Israel two kids of the goats as a sin offering, and one ram as a burnt offering.

⁶"Aaron shall offer the bull as a sin offering, which *is* for himself, and make atonement for himself and for his house. ⁷He shall take the two goats and present them before the LORD *at* the door of the tabernacle of meeting. ⁸Then Aaron shall cast lots for the two goats: one lot for the LORD and the other lot for the scapegoat. ⁹And Aaron shall bring the goat on which the LORD's lot fell, and offer it *as* a sin offering. ¹⁰But the goat on which the lot fell to be the scapegoat shall be presented alive before the LORD, to make atonement upon it, *and* to let it go as the scapegoat into the wilderness.

¹¹"And Aaron shall bring the bull of the sin offering, which is for himself, and make atonement for himself and for his house, and shall kill the bull as the sin offering which *is* for himself. ¹²Then he shall take a censer full of burning coals of fire from the altar before the LORD, with his hands full of sweet incense beaten fine, and bring *it* inside the veil. ¹³And he shall put the incense on the fire before the LORD, that the cloud of incense may cover the mercy seat that *is* on the Testimony, lest he die. ¹⁴He shall take some of the blood of the bull and sprinkle *it* with his finger on the mercy seat on the east *side;* and before the mercy seat he shall sprinkle some of the blood with his finger seven times.

¹⁵"Then he shall kill the goat of the sin offering, which *is* for the people, bring its blood inside the veil, do with that blood as he did with the blood of the bull, and sprinkle it on the mercy seat and before the mercy seat. ¹⁶So he shall make atonement for the Holy *Place,* because of the uncleanness of the children of Israel, and because of their transgressions, for all their sins; and so he shall do for the tabernacle of meeting which remains among them in the midst of their uncleanness. ¹⁷There shall be no man in the tabernacle of meeting when he goes in to make atonement in the Holy *Place,* until he comes out, that he may make atonement for himself, for his household, and for all the assembly of Israel. ¹⁸And he shall go out to the altar that *is* before the LORD, and make atonement for it, and shall take some of the blood of the bull and some of the blood of the goat, and put it on the horns of the altar all around. ¹⁹Then he shall sprinkle some of the blood on it with his finger seven times, cleanse it, and consecrate it from the uncleanness of the children of Israel.

²⁰"And when he has made an end of atoning for the Holy *Place,* the tabernacle of meeting, and the altar, he shall bring the live goat. ²¹Aaron shall lay both his hands on the head of the live goat, confess over it all the iniquities of the children of Israel, and all their transgressions,

---

BELIEFS AND IDEAS

The treatment of the scapegoat illustrates clearly how sins are transferred to the sacrificial animal by the laying on of hands by the priest (Lev. 16:21). The ritual described here is the origin of our idea of a "scapegoat." Sending a live animal away instead of killing it is a unique feature of the Day of Atonement.

ANIMALS THAT CARRY AWAY SIN (Lev. 16:7–10)

The Day of Atonement, observed on the 10th day of the 7th month, was the most sacred event in the year (Lev. 16:29, 34). One of the rituals for this annual day of fasting involved the cleansing of the sanctuary with blood. This was the only time in the year when the high priest entered the Most Holy Place to appear before the mercy seat (16:11–17). The other ritual involved the sending away of the scapegoat (16:7–10, 20–22).

In the scapegoat ritual, the scapegoat was sent into the wilderness. First, however, the priest placed his hands on the goat and confessed the sins of his people. The ritual symbolized the "removal" or "taking away" of the people's sin (16:21, 22).

The general form of the scapegoat ritual, as described in Leviticus, is not unique to Israel. Rituals from Anatolia and Mesopotamia attempt to appease an angry deity by using animals to carry away a plague or other evil suffering. A Hittite text from the mid-2nd millennium B.C. outlines what a monarch should do in case there is pestilence in his land caused by fighting in enemy territory.

In the Hittite ritual, the king is required to take an enemy bull (or ewe), "decorate the bull's ears with earrings and (fasten on it) red wool, green wool, black wool, and white wool." The bull is then driven into the enemy country, with the recitation, "Whatever god of the enemy country has caused this pestilence (if it be a male god), I have given thee a lusty, decorated bull with earrings. Be thou content with it. This bull shall take back the pestilence to the enemy country." An identical ceremony is performed with the ewe if the enemy's deity is a female.

In the Israelite ritual two goats were used. One was designated for the Lord and offered as a sin offering (16:9). The other goat, the scapegoat, bore the people's iniquities (16:22). In this ritual Israel released a live animal to carry away impurities, as other cultures did to eliminate sicknesses or sorceries.

---

concerning all their sins, putting them on the head of the goat, and shall send *it* away into the wilderness by the hand of a suitable man. ²²The goat shall bear on itself all their iniquities to an uninhabited land; and he shall release the goat in the wilderness.

²³"Then Aaron shall come into the tabernacle of meeting, shall take off the linen garments which he put on when he went into the Holy *Place,* and shall leave them there. ²⁴And he shall wash his body with water in a holy place, put on his garments, come out and offer his burnt offering and the burnt offering of the people, and make atonement for himself and for the people. ²⁵The fat of the sin offering he shall burn on the altar. ²⁶And he who released the goat as the scapegoat shall wash his clothes and bathe his body in water, and afterward he may come into the camp. ²⁷The bull *for* the sin offering and the goat *for* the sin offering, whose blood was brought in to make atonement in the Holy *Place,* shall be carried outside the camp. And they shall burn in the fire their skins, their flesh, and their offal. ²⁸Then he who

burns them shall wash his clothes and bathe his body in water, and afterward he may come into the camp.

²⁹"*This* shall be a statute forever for you: In the seventh month, on the tenth *day* of the month, you shall afflict your souls, and do no work at all, *whether* a native of your own country or a stranger who dwells among you. ³⁰For on that day *the priest* shall make atonement for you, to cleanse you, *that* you may be clean from all your sins before the LORD. ³¹It *is* a sabbath of solemn rest for you, and you shall afflict your souls. *It is* a statute forever. ³²And the priest, who is anointed and consecrated to minister as priest in his father's place, shall make atonement, and put on the linen clothes, the holy garments; ³³then he shall make atonement for the Holy Sanctuary,ᵃ and he shall make atonement for the tabernacle of meeting and for the altar, and he shall make atonement for the priests and for all the people of the assembly. ³⁴This shall be an everlasting statute for you, to make atonement for the children

16:33 ᵃThat is, the Most Holy Place

of Israel, for all their sins, once a year."
And he did as the LORD commanded Moses.

The Sanctity of Blood

17 ¹And the LORD spoke to Moses, saying, ²"Speak to Aaron, to his sons, and to all the children of Israel, and say to them, 'This is the thing which the LORD has commanded, saying: ³"Whatever man of the house of Israel who kills an ox or lamb or goat in the camp, or who kills it outside the camp, ⁴and does not bring it to the door of the tabernacle of meeting to offer an offering to the LORD before the tabernacle of the LORD, the guilt of bloodshed shall be imputed to that man. He has shed blood; and that man shall be cut off from among his people, ⁵to the end that the children of Israel may bring their sacrifices which they offer in the open field, that they may bring them to the LORD at the door of the tabernacle of meeting, to the priest, and offer them as peace offerings to the LORD. ⁶And the priest shall sprinkle the blood on the altar of the LORD at the door of the tabernacle of meeting, and burn the fat for a sweet aroma to the LORD. ⁷They shall no more offer their sacrifices to demons, after whom they have played the harlot. This shall be a statute forever for them throughout their generations." '

⁸"Also you shall say to them: 'Whatever man of the house of Israel, or of the strangers who dwell among you, who offers a burnt offering or sacrifice, ⁹and does not bring it to the door of the tabernacle of meeting, to offer it to the LORD, that man shall be cut off from among his people.

¹⁰"And whatever man of the house of Israel, or of the strangers who dwell among you, who eats any blood, I will set My face against that person who eats blood, and will cut him off from among his people. ¹¹For the life of the flesh is in the blood, and I have given it to you upon the altar to make atonement for your souls; for it is the blood that makes atonement for the soul.' ¹²Therefore I said to the children of Israel, 'No one among you shall eat blood, nor shall any stranger who dwells among you eat blood.'

¹³"Whatever man of the children of Israel, or of the strangers who dwell among you, who hunts and catches any animal or bird that may be eaten, he shall pour out its blood and cover it with dust; ¹⁴for it is the life of all flesh. Its blood sustains its life. Therefore I said to the children of Is-

rael, 'You shall not eat the blood of any flesh, for the life of all flesh is its blood. Whoever eats it shall be cut off.'

¹⁵"And every person who eats what died naturally or what was torn by beasts, whether he is a native of your own country or a stranger, he shall both wash his clothes and bathe in water, and be unclean until evening. Then he shall be clean. ¹⁶But if he does not wash them or bathe his body, then he shall bear his guilt."

Laws of Sexual Morality

18 ¹Then the LORD spoke to Moses, saying, ²"Speak to the children of Israel, and say to them: 'I am the LORD your God. ³According to the doings of the land of Egypt, where you dwelt, you shall not do; and according to the doings of the land of Canaan, where I am bringing you, you shall not do; nor shall you walk in their ordinances. ⁴You shall observe My judgments and keep My ordinances, to walk in them: I am the LORD your God. ⁵You shall therefore keep My statutes and My judgments, which if a man does, he shall live by them: I am the LORD.

⁶'None of you shall approach anyone who is near of kin to him, to uncover his nakedness: I am the LORD. ⁷The nakedness of your father or the nakedness of your mother you shall not uncover. She is your mother; you shall not uncover her nakedness. ⁸The nakedness of your father's wife you shall not uncover; it is your father's nakedness. ⁹The nakedness of your sister, the daughter of your father, or the daughter of your mother, whether born at home or elsewhere, their nakedness you shall not uncover. ¹⁰The nakedness of your son's

---

TIME CAPSULE   *1470 to 1448 B.C.*

1470   *Massive volcanic eruption on the Aegean island of Thera*

1458   *Thutmose III defeats coalition of Canaanite cities at Megiddo*

1450   *The city of Shechem is rebuilt after a century in ruins*

1450   *Earliest Egyptian shadow clock*

1450   *Thutmose III offers 27,000 pounds of gold to Amen, at Thebes*

1448   *Thutmose III campaigns on the Euphrates River against Mitanni*

daughter or your daughter's daughter, their nakedness you shall not uncover; for theirs *is* your own nakedness. ¹¹The nakedness of your father's wife's daughter, begotten by your father—she *is* your sister—you shall not uncover her nakedness. ¹²You shall not uncover the nakedness of your father's sister; she *is* near of kin to your father. ¹³You shall not uncover the nakedness of your mother's sister, for she *is* near of kin to your mother. ¹⁴You shall not uncover the nakedness of your father's brother. You shall not approach his wife; she *is* your aunt. ¹⁵You shall not uncover the nakedness of your daughter-in-law—she *is* your son's wife—you shall not uncover her nakedness. ¹⁶You shall not uncover the nakedness of your brother's wife; it *is* your brother's nakedness. ¹⁷You shall not uncover the nakedness of a woman and her daughter, nor shall you take her son's daughter or her daughter's daughter, to uncover her nakedness. They *are* near of kin to her. It *is* wickedness. ¹⁸Nor shall you take a woman as a rival to her sister, to uncover her nakedness while the other is alive.

¹⁹'Also you shall not approach a woman to uncover her nakedness as long as she is in her *customary* impurity. ²⁰Moreover you shall not lie carnally with your neighbor's wife, to defile yourself with her. ²¹And you shall not let any of your descendants pass through *the fire* to Molech, nor shall you profane the name of your God: I *am* the LORD. ²²You shall not lie with a male as with a woman. It *is* an abomination. ²³Nor shall you mate with any animal, to defile yourself with it. Nor shall any woman stand before an animal to mate with it. It *is* perversion.

²⁴'Do not defile yourselves with any of these things; for by all these the nations are defiled, which I am casting out before you. ²⁵For the land is defiled; therefore I visit the punishment of its iniquity upon it, and the land vomits out its inhabitants. ²⁶You shall therefore keep My statutes and My judgments, and shall not commit *any* of these abominations, *either* any of your own nation or any stranger who dwells among you ²⁷(for all these abominations the men of the land have done, who *were* before you, and thus the land is defiled), ²⁸lest the land vomit you out also when you defile it, as it vomited out the nations that *were* before you. ²⁹For whoever commits any of these abominations, the persons who commit *them* shall be cut off from among their people.

³⁰'Therefore you shall keep My ordinance, so that *you* do not commit *any* of these abominable customs which were committed before you, and that you do not defile yourselves by them: I *am* the LORD your God.' "

Moral and Ceremonial Laws

19 ¹And the LORD spoke to Moses, saying, ²"Speak to all the congregation of the children of Israel, and say to them: 'You shall be holy, for I the LORD your God *am* holy.

³'Every one of you shall revere his mother and his father, and keep My Sabbaths: I *am* the LORD your God.

⁴'Do not turn to idols, nor make for yourselves molded gods: I *am* the LORD your God.

⁵'And if you offer a sacrifice of a peace offering to the LORD, you shall offer it of your own free will. ⁶It shall be eaten the same day you offer *it,* and on the next day. And if any remains until the third day, it shall be burned in the fire. ⁷And if it is eaten at all on the third day, it *is* an abomination. It shall not be accepted. ⁸Therefore *everyone* who eats it shall bear his iniquity, because he has profaned the hallowed *offering* of the LORD; and that person shall be cut off from his people.

⁹'When you reap the harvest of your land, you shall not wholly reap the corners of your field, nor shall you gather the gleanings of your harvest. ¹⁰And you shall not glean your vineyard, nor shall you gather *every* grape of your vineyard; you

MARRIAGE AND FAMILY

The law provides a list of blood relatives with whom sexual intercourse is forbidden (Lev. 18:6). In some ancient societies the ruling class asserted for itself the right to marry sisters or brothers and flaunted this as a mark of nobility. This was the custom in Egypt. Over a period of time the practice is genetically harmful.

TECHNICAL PROPHECY SEEKS DIVINE KNOWLEDGE (Lev. 19:26)

Ancient people considered it important to know the will of the gods—on demand, if necessary. So there were specialists in the art of determining a deity's will through rituals or through the specialists' deep knowledge of the secret meaning of natural phenomena. Such specialized practices, which included divination and soothsaying, were aimed at foretelling the future and thus can be called "technical prophecy."

Most of what we know about divination and soothsaying comes from Mesopotamia—Babylonia and Assyria. Mesopotamian technical prophecy was carried out by highly educated, trained priests. A number of tablets survive which tell how to read natural events to determine the will of the gods. Wind, water, the blowing of grain, the appearance of animals, the position of the stars and planets, and indeed almost any natural occurrence had its divine meaning.

In a different method, Mesopotamian priests could obtain particular information by performing sacrifices. Archaeologists have found large numbers of clay models of livers taken from sheep sacrificed for the purpose of divination. By reading the bumps on the liver the priests could determine the answers to questions. The answers were then recorded on these clay models.

The peoples around Israel also sought knowledge from the gods. Sacred oracles from Syria-Palestine are found in Greek records such as *De Dea Syria* from the 2nd century A.D. These records indicate that answers to the questions of worshipers came through sounds from the openings of caves or from the flying of gods' statues (which skeptics claimed were rigged with ropes).

The Israelites themselves were forbidden to divine the will of God through these technical methods. They were allowed the oracular items called Urim and Thummim (Deut. 33:8; 1 Sam. 14:41), but Israel's law clearly instructed them not to "practice divination or soothsaying" (Lev. 19:26). For the Israelites the divine will would be disclosed by God through vision, dream, or prophet, and the Israelite worshiper was free to petition God for such revelation.

---

shall leave them for the poor and the stranger: I *am* the LORD your God.

11'You shall not steal, nor deal falsely, nor lie to one another. 12And you shall not swear by My name falsely, nor shall you profane the name of your God: I *am* the LORD.

13'You shall not cheat your neighbor, nor rob *him*. The wages of him who is hired shall not remain with you all night until morning. 14You shall not curse the deaf, nor put a stumbling block before the blind, but shall fear your God: I *am* the LORD.

15'You shall do no injustice in judgment. You shall not be partial to the poor, nor honor the person of the mighty. In righteousness you shall judge your neighbor. 16You shall not go about *as* a talebearer among your people; nor shall you take a stand against the life of your neighbor: I *am* the LORD.

17'You shall not hate your brother in your heart. You shall surely rebuke your neighbor, and not bear sin because of him. 18You shall not take vengeance, nor bear any grudge against the children of your people, but you shall love your neighbor as yourself: I *am* the LORD.

19'You shall keep My statutes. You shall not let your livestock breed with another kind. You shall not sow your field with mixed seed. Nor shall a garment of mixed linen and wool come upon you.

20'Whoever lies carnally with a woman who *is* betrothed to a man as a concubine, and who has not at all been redeemed nor given her freedom, for this there shall be scourging; *but* they shall not be put to death, because she was not free. 21And he shall bring his trespass offering to the LORD, to the door of the tabernacle of meeting, a ram as a trespass offering. 22The priest shall make atonement for him with the ram of the trespass offering before the LORD for his sin which he has committed. And the sin which he has committed shall be forgiven him.

23'When you come into the land, and have planted all kinds of trees for food, then you shall count their fruit as uncircumcised. Three years it shall be as uncircumcised to you. *It* shall not be eaten. ²⁴But in the fourth year all its fruit shall be holy, a praise to the LORD. ²⁵And in the fifth year you may eat its fruit, that it may yield to you its increase: I *am* the LORD your God.

²⁶'You shall not eat *anything* with the blood, nor shall you practice divination or soothsaying. ²⁷You shall not shave around the sides of your head, nor shall you disfigure the edges of your beard. ²⁸You shall not make any cuttings in your flesh for the dead, nor tattoo any marks on you: I *am* the LORD.

²⁹'Do not prostitute your daughter, to cause her to be a harlot, lest the land fall into harlotry, and the land become full of wickedness.

³⁰'You shall keep My Sabbaths and reverence My sanctuary: I *am* the LORD.

³¹'Give no regard to mediums and familiar spirits; do not seek after them, to be defiled by them: I *am* the LORD your God.

³²'You shall rise before the gray headed and honor the presence of an old man, and fear your God: I *am* the LORD.

³³'And if a stranger dwells with you in your land, you shall not mistreat him. ³⁴The stranger who dwells among you shall be to you as one born among you, and you shall love him as yourself; for you were strangers in the land of Egypt: I *am* the LORD your God.

³⁵'You shall do no injustice in judgment, in measurement of length, weight, or volume. ³⁶You shall have honest scales, honest weights, an honest ephah, and an honest hin: I *am* the LORD your God, who brought you out of the land of Egypt.

³⁷'Therefore you shall observe all My statutes and all My judgments, and perform them: I *am* the LORD.' "

Penalties for Breaking the Law

20 ¹Then the LORD spoke to Moses, saying, ²"Again, you shall say to the children of Israel: 'Whoever of the children of Israel, or of the strangers who dwell in Israel, who gives *any* of his descendants to Molech, he shall surely be put to death. The people of the land shall stone him with stones. ³I will set My face against that man, and will cut him off from his people, because he has given *some* of his descendants to Molech, to defile My sanctuary and profane My holy name. ⁴And if the people of the land should in any way hide their eyes from the man, when he gives *some* of his descendants to Molech, and they do not kill him, ⁵then I will set My face against that man and against his family; and I will cut him off from his people, and all who prostitute themselves with him to commit harlotry with Molech.

⁶'And the person who turns to mediums and familiar spirits, to prostitute himself with them, I will set My face against that person and cut him off from his people. ⁷Consecrate yourselves therefore, and be holy, for I *am* the LORD your God. ⁸And you shall keep My statutes, and perform them: I *am* the LORD who sanctifies you.

⁹'For everyone who curses his father or his mother shall surely be put to death. He has cursed his father or his mother. His blood *shall be* upon him.

¹⁰'The man who commits adultery with *another* man's wife, *he* who commits adultery with his neighbor's wife, the adulterer and the adulteress, shall surely be put to death. ¹¹The man who lies with his father's wife has uncovered his father's nakedness; both of them shall surely be put to death. Their blood *shall be* upon them. ¹²If a man lies with his daughter-in-law, both of them shall surely be put to death. They have committed perversion. Their blood *shall be* upon them. ¹³If a man lies with a male as he lies with a woman, both of them have committed an abomination. They shall surely be put to death. Their blood *shall be* upon them. ¹⁴If a man marries a woman and her mother, it *is* wickedness. They shall be burned with fire, both he and they, that there may be no wickedness among you. ¹⁵If a man mates with an animal, he shall surely be put to death, and you shall

CULTURE AND SOCIETY

There is undeniable evidence from Carthage in North Africa that the sacrifice of children was carried on there regularly. Sacrifice of adult human beings was the state religion of the Aztecs. It is sometimes said that human sacrifice never really occurred. The Law of Moses shows that it was a temptation at least (Lev. 20:2).

kill the animal. ¹⁶If a woman approaches any animal and mates with it, you shall kill the woman and the animal. They shall surely be put to death. Their blood *is* upon them.

¹⁷'If a man takes his sister, his father's daughter or his mother's daughter, and sees her nakedness and she sees his nakedness, it *is* a wicked thing. And they shall be cut off in the sight of their people. He has uncovered his sister's nakedness. He shall bear his guilt. ¹⁸If a man lies with a woman during her sickness and uncovers her nakedness, he has exposed her flow, and she has uncovered the flow of her blood. Both of them shall be cut off from their people.

¹⁹'You shall not uncover the nakedness of your mother's sister nor of your father's sister, for that would uncover his near of kin. They shall bear their guilt. ²⁰If a man lies with his uncle's wife, he has uncovered his uncle's nakedness. They shall bear their sin; they shall die childless. ²¹If a man takes his brother's wife, it *is* an unclean thing. He has uncovered his brother's nakedness. They shall be childless.

²²'You shall therefore keep all My statutes and all My judgments, and perform them, that the land where I am bringing you to dwell may not vomit you out. ²³And you shall not walk in the statutes of the nation which I am casting out before you; for they commit all these things, and therefore I abhor them. ²⁴But I have said to you, "You shall inherit their land, and I will give it to you to possess, a land flowing with milk and honey." I *am* the LORD your God, who has separated you from the peoples. ²⁵You shall therefore distinguish between clean animals and unclean, between unclean birds and clean, and you shall not make yourselves abominable by beast or by bird, or by any kind of living thing that creeps on the ground, which I have separated from you as unclean. ²⁶And you shall be holy to Me, for I the LORD *am* holy, and

have separated you from the peoples, that you should be Mine.

²⁷'A man or a woman who is a medium, or who has familiar spirits, shall surely be put to death; they shall stone them with stones. Their blood *shall be* upon them.' "

Regulations for Conduct of Priests

21 ¹And the LORD said to Moses, "Speak to the priests, the sons of Aaron, and say to them: 'None shall defile himself for the dead among his people, ²except for his relatives who are nearest to him: his mother, his father, his son, his daughter, and his brother; ³also his virgin sister who is near to him, who has had no husband, for her he may defile himself. ⁴*Otherwise* he shall not defile himself, *being* a chief man among his people, to profane himself.

⁵'They shall not make any bald *place* on their heads, nor shall they shave the edges of their beards nor make any cuttings in their flesh. ⁶They shall be holy to their God and not profane the name of their God, for they offer the offerings of the LORD made by fire, *and* the bread of their God; therefore they shall be holy. ⁷They shall not take a wife *who is* a harlot or a defiled woman, nor shall they take a woman divorced from her husband; for *the priest*ᵃ is holy to his God. ⁸Therefore you shall consecrate him, for he offers the bread of your God. He shall be holy to you, for I the LORD, who sanctify you, *am* holy. ⁹The daughter of any priest, if she profanes herself by playing the harlot, she profanes her father. She shall be burned with fire.

¹⁰'*He who is* the high priest among his brethren, on whose head the anointing oil was poured and who is consecrated to wear the garments, shall not uncover his head nor tear his clothes; ¹¹nor shall he go near any dead body, nor defile himself for his father or his mother; ¹²nor shall he go out of the sanctuary, nor profane the sanctuary of his God; for the consecration of the anointing oil of his God *is* upon him: I *am* the LORD. ¹³And he shall take a wife in her

21:7 ᵃLiterally *he*

CULTS AND SUPERNATURAL

The medium or spiritist is someone who pretends to find out things, especially about the future, through contact with dead persons or other kinds of spirits from the realm of the dead (Lev. 20:27). This is a common sort of magic that appears with many variations of method, in ancient and modern times. The Bible subjects it to ridicule and forbids it.

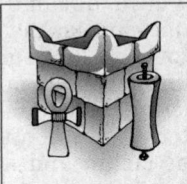

virginity. [14]A widow or a divorced woman or a defiled woman *or* a harlot—these he shall not marry; but he shall take a virgin of his own people as wife. [15]Nor shall he profane his posterity among his people, for I the LORD sanctify him.' "

[16]And the LORD spoke to Moses, saying, [17]"Speak to Aaron, saying: 'No man of your descendants in *succeeding* generations, who has *any* defect, may approach to offer the bread of his God. [18]For any man who has a defect shall not approach: a man blind or lame, who has a marred *face* or any *limb* too long, [19]a man who has a broken foot or broken hand, [20]or is a hunchback or a dwarf, or *a man* who has a defect in his eye, or eczema or scab, or is a eunuch. [21]No man of the descendants of Aaron the priest, who has a defect, shall come near to offer the offerings made by fire to the LORD. He has a defect; he shall not come near to offer the bread of his God. [22]He may eat the bread of his God, *both* the most holy and the holy; [23]only he shall not go near the veil or approach the altar, because he has a defect, lest he profane My sanctuaries; for I the LORD sanctify them.' "

[24]And Moses told *it* to Aaron and his sons, and to all the children of Israel.

22 [1]Then the LORD spoke to Moses, saying, [2]"Speak to Aaron and his sons, that they separate themselves from the holy things of the children of Israel, and that they do not profane My holy name *by* what they dedicate to Me: I *am* the LORD. [3]Say to them: 'Whoever of all your descendants throughout your generations, who goes near the holy things which the children of Israel dedicate to the LORD, while he has uncleanness upon him, that person shall be cut off from My presence: I *am* the LORD.

[4]'Whatever man of the descendants of Aaron, who *is* a leper or has a discharge, shall not eat the holy offerings until he is clean. And whoever touches anything made unclean *by* a corpse, or a man who has had an emission of semen, [5]or whoever touches any creeping thing by which he would be made unclean, or any person by whom he would become unclean, whatever his uncleanness may be— [6]the person who has touched any such thing shall be unclean until evening, and shall not eat the holy *offerings* unless he washes his body with water. [7]And when the sun goes down he shall be clean; and afterward he may eat the holy *offerings,* because it *is* his food. [8]What-

ever dies *naturally* or is torn *by beasts* he shall not eat, to defile himself with it: I *am* the LORD.

[9]'They shall therefore keep My ordinance, lest they bear sin for it and die thereby, if they profane it: I the LORD sanctify them.

[10]'No outsider shall eat the holy *offering;* one who dwells with the priest, or a hired servant, shall not eat the holy thing. [11]But if the priest buys a person with his money, he may eat it; and one who is born in his house may eat his food. [12]If the priest's daughter is married to an outsider, she may not eat of the holy offerings. [13]But if the priest's daughter is a widow or divorced, and has no child, and has returned to her father's house as in her youth, she may eat her father's food; but no outsider shall eat it.

[14]'And if a man eats the holy *offering* unintentionally, then he shall restore a holy *offering* to the priest, and add one-fifth to it. [15]They shall not profane the holy *offerings* of the children of Israel, which they offer to the LORD, [16]or allow them to bear the guilt of trespass when they eat their holy *offerings;* for I the LORD sanctify them.' "

Offerings Accepted and Not Accepted

[17]And the LORD spoke to Moses, saying, [18]"Speak to Aaron and his sons, and to all the children of Israel, and say to them: 'Whatever man of the house of Israel, or of the strangers in Israel, who offers his sacrifice for any of his vows or for any of his freewill offerings, which they offer to the LORD as a burnt offering— [19]*you shall offer* of your own free will a male without blemish from the cattle, from the sheep, or from the goats. [20]Whatever has a defect, you shall not offer, for it shall not be acceptable on your behalf. [21]And whoever offers a sacrifice of a peace offering to the LORD, to fulfill *his* vow, or a freewill offering from the cattle or the sheep, it must be perfect to be accepted; there shall be no defect in it. [22]Those *that are* blind or broken or maimed, or have an ulcer or eczema or scabs, you shall not offer to the LORD, nor make an offering by fire of them on the altar to the LORD. [23]Either a bull or a lamb that has any limb too long or too short you may offer *as* a freewill offering, but for a vow it shall not be accepted.

[24]'You shall not offer to the LORD what is bruised or crushed, or torn or cut; nor

shall you make *any offering of them* in your land. 25Nor from a foreigner's hand shall you offer any of these as the bread of your God, because their corruption *is* in them, *and* defects *are* in them. They shall not be accepted on your behalf.' "

26And the LORD spoke to Moses, saying: 27"When a bull or a sheep or a goat is born, it shall be seven days with its mother; and from the eighth day and thereafter it shall be accepted as an offering made by fire to the LORD. 28*Whether it is* a cow or ewe, do not kill both her and her young on the same day. 29And when you offer a sacrifice of thanksgiving to the LORD, offer *it* of your own free will. 30On the same day it shall be eaten; you shall leave none of it until morning: I *am* the LORD.

31"Therefore you shall keep My commandments, and perform them: I *am* the LORD. 32You shall not profane My holy name, but I will be hallowed among the children of Israel. I *am* the LORD who sanctifies you, 33who brought you out of the land of Egypt, to be your God: I *am* the LORD."

Israel's Feasts

In addition to the Sabbath (Lev. 23:3), Lev. 23 describes seven sacred festivals of the Hebrew calendar that were observed before the Babylonian exile. These feasts were occasions for nationwide gatherings which called the people to public worship.

Passover (23:5) and the Feast of Unleavened Bread (23:6–8) occurred in Abib (also called Nisan), the 1st month (March-April) of the sacred year. Combined they were one of Israel's three annual pilgrimage festivals for which every adult male was required to present himself at the tabernacle, and later, the temple. Passover may have been celebrated for one day at the beginning of the week-long Feast of Unleavened Bread, as it is in modern Judaism.

Firstfruits (23:9–21) was celebrated twice during the year as an expression of gratitude to God for His provision in the harvest. The first celebration occurred on the day following the Sabbath at the time of the Feast of Unleavened Bread. This fell during the barley harvest, sometime between the 16th and 22nd days of the 1st month (Abib). The second celebration occurred 50 days later during the Feast of Weeks.

The Feast of Weeks (23:15–22), also known as Harvest (Ex. 23:16), occurred 50 days after the offering of firstfruits at the barley harvest. Held in connection with the wheat harvest, this one-day celebration during the 3rd month (Sivan) involved the firstfruits observation as well as other sacrifices. It was the second festival with required attendance at the temple.

The Feast of Trumpets (23:23–25) was the first of three holy days of the 7th month (Tishri). It was a sacred celebration of the new civil year, calling attention to judgment for sin, and the need for penitence and forgiveness.

The Day of Atonement (23:26–32) was the second holy day of the 7th month. On this day sacrifice was made for the sin of the whole nation; thus, it was a time of true repentance and faith preparing for the Feast of Tabernacles.

The Feast of Tabernacles (23:33–36; or Booths, w. 39–43), the third holy day of the 7th month, was celebrated at the end of the grape harvest in September-October. Also known as Ingathering (Ex. 23:16), it was a time for great joy when all harvests were completed. It was also the third feast requiring a pilgrimage to Jerusalem.

■ Leviticus 23:1—24:23

Leviticus
Feasts of the LORD

23 :1 And the LORD spoke to Moses, saying, 2"Speak to the children of Israel, and say to them: 'The feasts of the LORD, which you shall proclaim *to be* holy convocations, these *are* My feasts.

The Sabbath

3'Six days shall work be done, but the seventh day *is* a Sabbath of solemn rest, a holy convocation. You shall do no work *on it;* it *is* the Sabbath of the LORD in all your dwellings.

The Passover and Unleavened Bread

4"These *are* the feasts of the LORD, holy convocations which you shall proclaim at their appointed times. 5On the fourteenth *day* of the first month at twilight *is* the LORD's Passover. 6And on the fifteenth day of the same month *is* the Feast of Unleavened Bread to the LORD; seven days you must eat unleavened bread. 7On the first day you shall have a holy convocation; you

ISRAEL'S ANNUAL FEASTS

Feast	Month of Sacred Year	Day	Corresponding Month
Passover	1 (Abib)	14	Mar.-Apr.
Ex. 12:1–14; Lev. 23:5; Num. 9:1–14; 28:16; Deut. 16:1–7			
*Unleavened Bread	1 (Abib)	15–21	Mar.-Apr.
Ex. 12:15–20; 13:3–10; Lev. 23:6–8; Num. 28:17–25; Deut. 16:3, 4, 8			
Firstfruits	1 (Abib) and	16	Mar.-Apr.
	3 (Sivan)	6	May-June
Lev. 23:9–14; Num. 28:26			
*Weeks	3 (Sivan)	6 (50 days after	May-June
(Harvest or Pentecost)		barley harvest)	
Ex. 23:16; 34:22; Lev. 23:15–21; Num. 28:26–31; Deut. 16:9–12			
Trumpets	7 (Tishri)	1	Sept.-Oct.
Rosh Hashanah			
Lev. 23:23–25; Num. 29:1–6			
Day of Atonement	7 (Tishri)	10	Sept.-Oct.
Yom Kippur			
Lev. 16; 23:26–32; Num. 29:7–11			
*Tabernacles	7 (Tishri)	15–22	Sept.-Oct.
(Booths or Ingathering)			
Ex. 23:16; 34:22; Lev. 23:33–36, 39–43; Num. 29:12–38; Deut. 16:13–15			

*The three major feasts for which all males of Israel were required to travel to the temple in Jerusalem (Ex. 23:14–19).

shall do no customary work on it. [8]But you shall offer an offering made by fire to the LORD for seven days. The seventh day *shall be* a holy convocation; you shall do no customary work *on it.*' "

The Feast of Firstfruits

[9]And the LORD spoke to Moses, saying, [10]"Speak to the children of Israel, and say to them: 'When you come into the land which I give to you, and reap its harvest, then you shall bring a sheaf of the firstfruits of your harvest to the priest. [11]He shall wave the sheaf before the LORD, to be accepted on your behalf; on the day after the Sabbath the priest shall wave it. [12]And you shall offer on that day, when you wave the sheaf, a male lamb of the first year, without blemish, as a burnt offering to the LORD. [13]Its grain offering *shall be* two-tenths *of an ephah* of fine flour mixed with oil, an offering made by fire to the LORD, for a sweet aroma; and its drink offering *shall be* of wine, one-fourth of a hin. [14]You shall eat neither bread nor parched grain nor fresh grain until the same day that you have brought an offering to your God; *it shall be* a statute forever throughout your generations in all your dwellings.

The Feast of Weeks

[15]'And you shall count for yourselves from the day after the Sabbath, from the day that you brought the sheaf of the wave offering: seven Sabbaths shall be completed. [16]Count fifty days to the day after the seventh Sabbath; then you shall offer a new grain offering to the LORD. [17]You shall bring from your dwellings two wave *loaves* of two-tenths *of an ephah.* They shall be of fine flour; they shall be baked with leaven. *They are* the firstfruits to the LORD. [18]And you shall offer with the bread seven lambs of the first year, without blemish, one young bull, and two rams. They shall be *as* a burnt offering to the LORD, with their grain offering and their drink offerings, an offering made by fire for a sweet aroma to the LORD. [19]Then you shall sacrifice one kid of the goats as a sin offering, and two male lambs of the first year as a sacrifice of a peace offering. [20]The priest shall wave them with the bread of the firstfruits *as* a wave offering before the LORD, with the two lambs. They shall be holy to the LORD for the priest. [21]And you shall proclaim on the same day *that* it is a holy convocation to you. You shall do no customary work *on it. It shall be* a statute forever in

all your dwellings throughout your generations.

²²"When you reap the harvest of your land, you shall not wholly reap the corners of your field when you reap, nor shall you gather any gleaning from your harvest. You shall leave them for the poor and for the stranger: I *am* the LORD your God.' "

The Feast of Trumpets

²³Then the LORD spoke to Moses, saying, ²⁴"Speak to the children of Israel, saying: 'In the seventh month, on the first *day* of the month, you shall have a sabbath-*rest,* a memorial of blowing of trumpets, a holy convocation. ²⁵You shall do no customary work *on it;* and you shall offer an offering made by fire to the LORD.' "

The Day of Atonement

²⁶And the LORD spoke to Moses, saying: ²⁷"Also the tenth *day* of this seventh month *shall be* the Day of Atonement. It shall be a holy convocation for you; you shall afflict your souls, and offer an offering made by fire to the LORD. ²⁸And you shall do no work on that same day, for it *is* the Day of Atonement, to make atonement for you before the LORD your God. ²⁹For any person who is not afflicted *in soul* on that same day shall be cut off from his people. ³⁰And any person who does any work on that same day, that person I will destroy from among his people. ³¹You shall do no manner of work; *it shall be* a statute forever throughout your generations in all your dwellings. ³²It *shall be* to you a sabbath of *solemn* rest, and you shall afflict your souls; on the ninth *day* of the month at evening, from evening to evening, you shall celebrate your sabbath."

The Feast of Tabernacles

³³Then the LORD spoke to Moses, saying, ³⁴"Speak to the children of Israel, saying: 'The fifteenth day of this seventh month *shall be* the Feast of Tabernacles *for* seven days to the LORD. ³⁵On the first day *there shall be* a holy convocation. You shall

do no customary work *on it.* ³⁶*For* seven days you shall offer an offering made by fire to the LORD. On the eighth day you shall have a holy convocation, and you shall offer an offering made by fire to the LORD. It *is* a sacred assembly, *and* you shall do no customary work *on it.*

³⁷"These *are* the feasts of the LORD which you shall proclaim *to be* holy convocations, to offer an offering made by fire to the LORD, a burnt offering and a grain offering, a sacrifice and drink offerings, everything on its day— ³⁸besides the Sabbaths of the LORD, besides your gifts, besides all your vows, and besides all your freewill offerings which you give to the LORD.

³⁹"Also on the fifteenth day of the seventh month, when you have gathered in the fruit of the land, you shall keep the feast of the LORD *for* seven days; on the first day *there shall be* a sabbath-*rest,* and on the eighth day a sabbath-*rest.* ⁴⁰And you shall take for yourselves on the first day the fruit of beautiful trees, branches of palm trees, the boughs of leafy trees, and willows of the brook; and you shall rejoice before the LORD your God for seven days. ⁴¹You shall keep it as a feast to the LORD for seven days in the year. *It shall be* a statute forever in your generations. You shall celebrate it in the seventh month. ⁴²You shall dwell in booths for seven days. All who are native Israelites shall dwell in booths, ⁴³that your generations may know that I made the children of Israel dwell in booths when I brought them out of the land of Egypt: I *am* the LORD your God.' "

⁴⁴So Moses declared to the children of Israel the feasts of the LORD.

Care of the Tabernacle Lamps

24 ¹Then the LORD spoke to Moses, saying: ²"Command the children of Israel that they bring to you pure oil of pressed olives for the light, to make the lamps burn continually. ³Outside the veil of the Testimony, in the tabernacle of meeting, Aaron shall be in charge of it from

DAILY LIFE AND CUSTOMS

Olives grow on small trees that live for many years. The oil is removed by crushing the fruit. Like honey, olive oil does not spoil in storage. It was commonly used as lamp oil (Lev. 24:2). A wick partly submerged in a small pool of oil burns like the wick of a wax candle. More oil can be added easily without blowing out the flame.

HAMMURABI'S "EYE FOR AN EYE" (Lev. 24:19, 20)

The punishments of Israel's legal system sometimes were based on a system of physical retaliation. The corporal punishments sentenced on the guilty offender were comparable to the injuries which the victim suffered. As the Law of Moses states, "so shall it be done to him" (Lev. 24:19), whether "eye for eye" or "tooth for tooth" (24:20).

Sometimes this law of "eye for eye, tooth for tooth" (Ex. 21:23–25) is considered to be primitive retaliations. It was designed, however, to protect the helpless from unfair reprisal by the powerful. Once a person had been judged guilty, justice was performed with complete impartiality. The rich man did not receive a lesser sentence for the same crime as did the poor man. This principle of physical reprisal may have come to Israel through the Amorites, as is suggested by laws from a prominent Amorite king.

Hammurabi (or Hammurapi) was the sixth king (1792–1750 B.C.) of the 1st Dynasty of Babylon. During his long reign Babylon rose to prominence in southern Mesopotamia. He was part of a group of Amorite rulers, some of whom had taken Babylon before his time. By the end of his reign, Hammurabi was successful in uniting the entire Tigris-Euphrates valley, although much of his empire was lost within a generation after his death.

A collection of laws that were sponsored by this Amorite king, now known as the Code of Hammurabi, reflect the same principle of retaliation found in the Law of Moses. If a citizen injured another citizen's eye or tooth, Hammurabi's code states: "his eye shall be destroyed" or "his tooth shall be knocked out." Such retribution is not found in law codes of the Sumerians and Hittites, nor in the Laws of Eshnunna. Possibly it comes from a time when Amorite tribes populated both Babylonia and Palestine.

---

evening until morning before the LORD continually; *it shall be* a statute forever in your generations. ⁴He shall be in charge of the lamps on the pure *gold* lampstand before the LORD continually.

The Bread of the Tabernacle

⁵"And you shall take fine flour and bake twelve cakes with it. Two-tenths *of an ephah* shall be in each cake. ⁶You shall set them in two rows, six in a row, on the pure *gold* table before the LORD. ⁷And you shall put pure frankincense on *each* row, that it may be on the bread for a memorial, an offering made by fire to the LORD. ⁸Every Sabbath he shall set it in order before the LORD continually, *being taken* from the children of Israel by an everlasting covenant. ⁹And it shall be for Aaron and his sons, and they shall eat it in a holy place; for it *is* most holy to him from the offerings of the LORD made by fire, by a perpetual statute."

The Penalty for Blasphemy

¹⁰Now the son of an Israelite woman, whose father *was* an Egyptian, went out among the children of Israel; and this Israelite *woman's* son and a man of Israel fought each other in the camp. ¹¹And the Israelite woman's son blasphemed the name *of the LORD* and cursed; and so they brought him to Moses. (His mother's name *was* Shelomith the daughter of Dibri, of the tribe of Dan.) ¹²Then they put him in custody, that the mind of the LORD might be shown to them.

¹³And the LORD spoke to Moses, saying, ¹⁴"Take outside the camp him who has cursed; then let all who heard *him* lay their hands on his head, and let all the congregation stone him. ¹⁵"Then you shall speak to the children of Israel, saying: 'Whoever curses his God shall bear his sin. ¹⁶And whoever blasphemes the name of the LORD shall surely be put to death. All the congregation shall certainly stone him, the stranger as well as him who is born in the land. When he blasphemes the name *of the LORD,* he shall be put to death.

¹⁷'Whoever kills any man shall surely be put to death. ¹⁸Whoever kills an animal shall make it good, animal for animal. ¹⁹'If a man causes disfigurement of his neighbor, as he has done, so shall it be done to him— ²⁰fracture for fracture, eye for eye, tooth for tooth; as he has caused disfigurement of a man, so shall it be done to him. ²¹And whoever kills an animal

shall restore it; but whoever kills a man shall be put to death. ²²You shall have the same law for the stranger and for one from your own country; for I *am* the LORD your God.' "

²³Then Moses spoke to the children of Israel; and they took outside the camp him who had cursed, and stoned him with stones. So the children of Israel did as the LORD commanded Moses.

The Sabbath Years and Year of Jubilee

Every 7th year was the Sabbath Year, in which the land was to lie fallow (Lev. 25:4). Among other things this practice would prevent soil depletion and the subsequent impoverishment of the farmer. The Year of Jubilee came every 50th year (Lev. 25:9, 11). Possibly no systematic harvesting of the produce of the fields was permitted during the 7th or Jubilee years. Although people might eat such produce in the fields (25:6, 7, 12), their regular meals were to come from the excess of the previous years (25:21).

■ Leviticus 25:1—27:34

Leviticus
The Sabbath of the Seventh Year

25 :1 And the LORD spoke to Moses on Mount Sinai, saying, ²"Speak to the children of Israel, and say to them: 'When you come into the land which I give you, then the land shall keep a sabbath to the LORD. ³Six years you shall sow your field, and six years you shall prune your vineyard, and gather its fruit; ⁴but in the seventh year there shall be a sabbath of solemn rest for the land, a sabbath to the LORD. You shall neither sow your field nor prune your vineyard. ⁵What grows of its own accord of your harvest you shall not reap, nor gather the grapes of your untended vine, *for* it is a year of rest for the land. ⁶And the sabbath *produce* of the land shall be food for you: for you, your male and female servants, your hired man, and the stranger who dwells with you, ⁷for your livestock and the beasts that *are* in your land—all its produce shall be for food.

The Year of Jubilee

⁸'And you shall count seven sabbaths of years for yourself, seven times seven years; and the time of the seven sabbaths

of years shall be to you forty-nine years. ⁹Then you shall cause the trumpet of the Jubilee to sound on the tenth *day* of the seventh month; on the Day of Atonement you shall make the trumpet to sound throughout all your land. ¹⁰And you shall consecrate the fiftieth year, and proclaim liberty throughout *all* the land to all its inhabitants. It shall be a Jubilee for you; and each of you shall return to his possession, and each of you shall return to his family. ¹¹That fiftieth year shall be a Jubilee to you; in it you shall neither sow nor reap what grows of its own accord, nor gather *the grapes* of your untended vine. ¹²For it *is* the Jubilee; it shall be holy to you; you shall eat its produce from the field.

¹³'In this Year of Jubilee, each of you shall return to his possession. ¹⁴And if you sell anything to your neighbor or buy from your neighbor's hand, you shall not oppress one another. ¹⁵According to the number of years after the Jubilee you shall buy from your neighbor, and according to the number of years of crops he shall sell to you. ¹⁶According to the multitude of years you shall increase its price, and according to the fewer number of years you shall diminish its price; for he sells to you *according* to the number *of the years* of the crops. ¹⁷Therefore you shall not oppress one another, but you shall fear your God; for I *am* the LORD your God.

Provisions for the Seventh Year

¹⁸'So you shall observe My statutes and keep My judgments, and perform them; and you will dwell in the land in safety. ¹⁹Then the land will yield its fruit, and you will eat your fill, and dwell there in safety.

TIME CAPSULE	*1446 to 1425 B.C.*
1446	*Moses leads exodus from Egypt (based on early Exodus)*
1446– 1406	*The 40 years of wilderness wandering (based on early Exodus)*
1445	*Israelites depart from Mount Sinai (based on early Exodus)*
1443	*Thutmose III receives tribute from Alalakh*
1439	*Mitanni recovers all of northern Syria from Egypt*
1425– 1180	*The New Kingdom of the Hittites*

PROTECTING THE WEAK IN THE JUBILEE YEAR (Lev. 25:8–17)

Every 50th year in Israel was the Year of Jubilee (Lev. 25:11–13). The provisions of this sacred time were intended to maintain economic equality and prevent the concentration of wealth in the hands of a few. In the Jubilee year, if property were not already redeemed, it was to be restored to the original owner (25:25–28). This prevented the creation of great hereditary estates that would have reduced the families of small landholders to the status of serfs.

The concept of the Jubilee year in Lev. 25 bears a general similarity to the suspension of debts, which was a widespread phenomenon in the Old Babylonian period (c. 2017–1595 B.C.). While the Old Babylonian peoples lived a few centuries before Israel inhabited Canaan, they too were concerned about the equitable distribution of land and the resultant wealth.

An Old Babylonian literary text (in the form of a letter) describes the conduct of judges during the suspension of debts on behalf of the sun god Shamash. The judges of two city-states, Babylon and nearby Sippar, met at Sippar to read the lawsuits of Sippar citizens. Also to be read were the sale documents for fields, houses, and orchards, which became invalid during the suspension of debts (the jubilee).

In both cultures there was an awareness that the accumulation of land could result in the oppression of those who were socially and economically weak. In the Old Babylonian letter, an individual who had been subsequently wronged wrote to the officials, asking that "the weak not be handed over to the strong in the presence of my lord, and for the strong not to oppress the weak." Israel's God Yahweh included a command amongst the stipulations of the Jubilee year: "you shall not oppress one another" (25:14, 17).

20'And if you say, "What shall we eat in the seventh year, since we shall not sow nor gather in our produce?" 21Then I will command My blessing on you in the sixth year, and it will bring forth produce enough for three years. 22And you shall sow in the eighth year, and eat old produce until the ninth year; until its produce comes in, you shall eat *of* the old *harvest.*

Redemption of Property

23'The land shall not be sold permanently, for the land *is* Mine; for you *are* strangers and sojourners with Me. 24And in all the land of your possession you shall grant redemption of the land.

25'If one of your brethren becomes poor, and has sold *some* of his possession, and if his redeeming relative comes to redeem it, then he may redeem what his brother sold. 26Or if the man has no one to redeem it, but he himself becomes able to redeem it, 27then let him count the years since its sale, and restore the remainder to the man to whom he sold it, that he may return to his possession. 28But if he is not able to have *it* restored to himself, then what was sold shall remain in the hand of him who bought it until the Year of Jubilee; and in the Jubilee it shall be re-leased, and he shall return to his possession.

29'If a man sells a house in a walled city, then he may redeem it within a whole year after it is sold; *within* a full year he may redeem it. 30But if it is not redeemed within the space of a full year, then the house in the walled city shall belong permanently to him who bought it, throughout his generations. It shall not be released in the Jubilee. 31However the houses of villages which have no wall around them shall be counted as the fields of the country. They may be redeemed, and they shall be released in the Jubilee. 32Nevertheless the cities of the Levites, *and* the houses in the cities of their possession, the Levites may redeem at any time. 33And if a man purchases a house from the Levites, then the house that was sold in the city of his possession shall be released in the Jubilee; for the houses in the cities of the Levites *are* their possession among the children of Israel. 34But the field of the common-land of their cities may not be sold, for it *is* their perpetual possession.

Lending to the Poor

35'If one of your brethren becomes poor, and falls into poverty among you, then you shall help him, like a stranger or a sojourner, that he may live with you. 36Take no usury or interest from him; but fear your God, that your brother may live with you. 37You shall not lend him your money for usury, nor lend him your food at a profit. 38I *am* the LORD your God, who brought you out of the land of Egypt, to give you the land of Canaan *and* to be your God.

The Law Concerning Slavery

39'And if *one of* your brethren *who dwells* by you becomes poor, and sells himself to you, you shall not compel him to serve as a slave. 40As a hired servant *and* a sojourner he shall be with you, *and* shall serve you until the Year of Jubilee. 41And *then* he shall depart from you—he and his children with him—and shall return to his own family. He shall return to the possession of his fathers. 42For they *are* My servants, whom I brought out of the land of Egypt; they shall not be sold as slaves. 43You shall not rule over him with rigor, but you shall fear your God. 44And as for your male and female slaves whom you may have—from the nations that are around you, from them you may buy male and female slaves. 45Moreover you may buy the children of the strangers who dwell among you, and their families who are with you, which they beget in your land; and they shall become your property. 46And you may take them as an inheritance for your children after you, to inherit *them as* a possession; they shall be your permanent slaves. But regarding your brethren, the children of Israel, you shall not rule over one another with rigor.

47'Now if a sojourner or stranger close to you becomes rich, and *one of* your brethren *who dwells* by him becomes poor, and sells himself to the stranger *or* sojourner close to you, or to a member of the stranger's family, 48after he is sold he may be redeemed again. One of his brothers may redeem him; 49or his uncle or his uncle's son may redeem him; or *anyone* who is near of kin to him in his family may re-

deem him; or if he is able he may redeem himself. 50Thus he shall reckon with him who bought him: The price of his release shall be according to the number of years, from the year that he was sold to him until the Year of Jubilee; *it shall be* according to the time of a hired servant for him. 51If *there are* still many years *remaining,* according to them he shall repay the price of his redemption from the money with which he was bought. 52And if there remain but a few years until the Year of Jubilee, then he shall reckon with him, *and* according to his years he shall repay him the price of his redemption. 53He shall be with him as a yearly hired servant, and he shall not rule with rigor over him in your sight. 54And if he is not redeemed in these *years,* then he shall be released in the Year of Jubilee—he and his children with him. 55For the children of Israel *are* servants to Me; they *are* My servants whom I brought out of the land of Egypt: I *am* the LORD your God.

Promise of Blessing and Retribution

26 1'You shall not make idols for yourselves;

neither a carved image nor a *sacred* pillar shall you rear up for yourselves;

nor shall you set up an engraved stone in your land, to bow down to it;

for I *am* the LORD your God.

2 You shall keep My Sabbaths and reverence My sanctuary:

I *am* the LORD.

3 'If you walk in My statutes and keep My commandments, and perform them,

4 then I will give you rain in its season, the land shall yield its produce, and the trees of the field shall yield their fruit.

5 Your threshing shall last till the time of vintage, and the vintage shall last till the time of sowing;

you shall eat your bread to the full, and dwell in your land safely.

6 I will give peace in the land, and you

PLANTS AND ANIMALS

The largest herds of domestic animals were sheep and goats. These could be attacked and killed by wolves and lions (Lev. 26:6), and also by birds of prey. Like the lion, the Syrian bear was dangerous to human beings. It reaches over 500 pounds in weight and would inspire terror in anyone it threatened.

shall lie down, and none will make *you* afraid;
I will rid the land of evil beasts,
and the sword will not go through your land.

7 You will chase your enemies, and they shall fall by the sword before you.

8 Five of you shall chase a hundred, and a hundred of you shall put ten thousand to flight;
your enemies shall fall by the sword before you.

9 'For I will look on you favorably and make you fruitful, multiply you and confirm My covenant with you.

10 You shall eat the old harvest, and clear out the old because of the new.

11 I will set My tabernacle among you, and My soul shall not abhor you.

12 I will walk among you and be your God, and you shall be My people.

13 I *am* the LORD your God, who brought you out of the land of Egypt, that *you* should not be their slaves;
I have broken the bands of your yoke and made you walk upright.

14 'But if you do not obey Me, and do not observe all these commandments,

15 and if you despise My statutes, or if your soul abhors My judgments, so that you do not perform all My commandments, *but* break My covenant,

16 I also will do this to you:
I will even appoint terror over you, wasting disease and fever which shall consume the eyes and cause sorrow of heart.
And you shall sow your seed in vain, for your enemies shall eat it.

17 I will set My face against you, and you shall be defeated by your enemies.
Those who hate you shall reign over you, and you shall flee when no one pursues you.

18 'And after all this, if you do not obey Me, then I will punish you seven times more for your sins.

19 I will break the pride of your power;
I will make your heavens like iron and your earth like bronze.

20 And your strength shall be spent in vain;
for your land shall not yield its produce, nor shall the trees of the land yield their fruit.

21 'Then, if you walk contrary to Me, and are not willing to obey Me, I will bring on you seven times more plagues, according to your sins.

22 I will also send wild beasts among you, which shall rob you of your children, destroy your livestock, and make you few in number;
and your highways shall be desolate.

23 'And if by these things you are not reformed by Me, but walk contrary to Me,

24 then I also will walk contrary to you, and I will punish you yet seven times for your sins.

25 And I will bring a sword against you that will execute the vengeance of the covenant;
when you are gathered together within your cities I will send pestilence among you;
and you shall be delivered into the hand of the enemy.

26 When I have cut off your supply of bread, ten women shall bake your bread in one oven, and they shall bring back your bread by weight, and you shall eat and not be satisfied.

27 'And after all this, if you do not obey Me, but walk contrary to Me,

28 then I also will walk contrary to you in fury;
and I, even I, will chastise you seven times for your sins.

29 You shall eat the flesh of your sons, and you shall eat the flesh of your daughters.

30 I will destroy your high places, cut down your incense altars, and cast your carcasses on the lifeless forms of your idols;
and My soul shall abhor you.

31 I will lay your cities waste and bring your sanctuaries to desolation, and I will not smell the fragrance of your sweet aromas.

32 I will bring the land to desolation, and your enemies who dwell in it shall be astonished at it.

33 I will scatter you among the nations and draw out a sword after you;
your land shall be desolate and your cities waste.

34 Then the land shall enjoy its sabbaths

as long as it lies desolate and you *are* in your enemies' land;

then the land shall rest and enjoy its sabbaths.

35 As long as *it* lies desolate it shall rest—

for the time it did not rest on your sabbaths when you dwelt in it.

36 'And as for those of you who are left, I will send faintness into their hearts in the lands of their enemies;

the sound of a shaken leaf shall cause them to flee;

they shall flee as though fleeing from a sword, and they shall fall when no one pursues.

37 They shall stumble over one another, as it were before a sword, when no one pursues;

and you shall have no *power* to stand before your enemies.

38 You shall perish among the nations, and the land of your enemies shall eat you up.

39 And those of you who are left shall waste away in their iniquity in your enemies' lands;

also in their fathers' iniquities, which are with them, they shall waste away.

40 'But if they confess their iniquity and the iniquity of their fathers, with their unfaithfulness in which they were unfaithful to Me, and that they also have walked contrary to Me,

41 and *that* I also have walked contrary to them and have brought them into the land of their enemies;

if their uncircumcised hearts are humbled, and they accept their guilt—

42 then I will remember My covenant with Jacob, and My covenant with Isaac and My covenant with Abraham I will remember;

I will remember the land.

43 The land also shall be left empty by them, and will enjoy its sabbaths while it lies desolate without them;

they will accept their guilt, because they despised My judgments and because their soul abhorred My statutes.

44 Yet for all that, when they are in the land of their enemies, I will not cast them away, nor shall I abhor them,

to utterly destroy them and break My covenant with them;

for I *am* the LORD their God.

45 But for their sake I will remember the covenant of their ancestors, whom I brought out of the land of Egypt in the sight of the nations, that I might be their God:

I *am* the LORD.'"

46These *are* the statutes and judgments and laws which the LORD made between Himself and the children of Israel on Mount Sinai by the hand of Moses.

Redeeming Persons and Property Dedicated to God

27 1Now the LORD spoke to Moses, saying, 2"Speak to the children of Israel, and say to them: 'When a man consecrates by a vow certain persons to the LORD, according to your valuation, 3if your valuation is of a male from twenty years old up to sixty years old, then your valuation shall be fifty shekels of silver, according to the shekel of the sanctuary. 4If it *is* a female, then your valuation shall be thirty shekels; 5and if from five years old up to twenty years old, then your valuation for a male shall be twenty shekels, and for a female ten shekels; 6and if from a month old up to five years old, then your valuation for a male shall be five shekels of silver, and for a female your valuation shall be three shekels of silver; 7and if from sixty years old and above, if *it is* a male, then your valuation shall be fifteen shekels, and for a female ten shekels.

8'But if he is too poor to pay your valuation, then he shall present himself before the priest, and the priest shall set a value for him; according to the ability of him who vowed, the priest shall value him.

9'If *it is* an animal that men may bring as an offering to the LORD, all that *anyone* gives to the LORD shall be holy. 10He shall not substitute it or exchange it, good for bad or bad for good; and if he at all exchanges animal for animal, then both it and the one exchanged for it shall be holy. 11If *it is* an unclean animal which they do not offer as a sacrifice to the LORD, then he shall present the animal before the priest; 12and the priest shall set a value for it, whether it is good or bad; as you, the priest, value it, so it shall be. 13But if he *wants* at all *to* redeem it, then he must add one-fifth to your valuation.

¹⁴'And when a man dedicates his house *to be* holy to the LORD, then the priest shall set a value for it, whether it is good or bad; as the priest values it, so it shall stand. ¹⁵If he who dedicated it *wants to* redeem his house, then he must add one-fifth of the money of your valuation to it, and it shall be his.

¹⁶'If a man dedicates to the LORD *part* of a field of his possession, then your valuation shall be according to the seed for it. A homer of barley seed *shall be valued* at fifty shekels of silver. ¹⁷If he dedicates his field from the Year of Jubilee, according to your valuation it shall stand. ¹⁸But if he dedicates his field after the Jubilee, then the priest shall reckon to him the money due according to the years that remain till the Year of Jubilee, and it shall be deducted from your valuation. ¹⁹And if he who dedicates the field ever wishes to redeem it, then he must add one-fifth of the money of your valuation to it, and it shall belong to him. ²⁰But if he does not want to redeem the field, or if he has sold the field to another man, it shall not be redeemed anymore; ²¹but the field, when it is released in the Jubilee, shall be holy to the LORD, as a devoted field; it shall be the possession of the priest.

²²'And if a man dedicates to the LORD a field which he has bought, which is not the field of his possession, ²³then the priest shall reckon to him the worth of your valuation, up to the Year of Jubilee, and he shall give your valuation on that day *as a* holy *offering* to the LORD. ²⁴In the Year of Jubilee the field shall return to him from whom it was bought, to the one who *owned* the land as a possession. ²⁵And all your valuations shall be according to the shekel of the sanctuary: twenty gerahs to the shekel.

²⁶'But the firstborn of the animals, which should be the LORD's firstborn, no man shall dedicate; whether *it is* an ox or sheep, it *is* the LORD's. ²⁷And if *it is* an unclean animal, then he shall redeem *it* according to your valuation, and shall add one-fifth to it; or if it is not redeemed, then it shall be sold according to your valuation.

²⁸'Nevertheless no devoted *offering* that a man may devote to the LORD of all that he has, *both* man and beast, or the field of his possession, shall be sold or redeemed; every devoted *offering is* most holy to the LORD. ²⁹No person under the ban, who may become doomed to destruction among men, shall be redeemed, *but* shall surely be put to death. ³⁰And all the tithe of the land, *whether* of the seed of the land *or* of the fruit of the tree, *is* the LORD's. It *is* holy to the LORD. ³¹If a man wants at all to redeem *any* of his tithes, he shall add one-fifth to it. ³²And concerning the tithe of the herd or the flock, of whatever passes under the rod, the tenth one shall be holy to the LORD. ³³He shall not inquire whether it is good or bad, nor shall he exchange it; and if he exchanges it at all, then both it and the one exchanged for it shall be holy; it shall not be redeemed.' "

³⁴These *are* the commandments which the LORD commanded Moses for the children of Israel on Mount Sinai.

The Book of Numbers

In the Hebrew Bible, this book is entitled "In the Wilderness." The name "Numbers" comes from the Greek translation of the Old Testament and refers specifically to the census figures given in two census reports: Num. 1:2–46 and 26:2–51.

The content of the Book of Numbers is diverse, moving back and forth between lists and laws and narratives, making it hard to identify any single outline or structure. The book begins in the same vein as Leviticus, with more divine instructions from Mount Sinai, still stressing priestly matters. These laws conclude in ch. 10, and the Israelites set out for the Promised Land.

Israel needed organization in order to reach that "land flowing with milk and honey," and God instructed Moses to take a census (Num. 1:2) so that the people would be organized both for travel and for warfare. This first census took place in the 2nd month of the 2nd year of the Exodus, either 1445 or 1274 B.C. (see "Egypt and the Exodus" at Ex. 1:1). In that same month and year, Moses and the people departed from Sinai (Num. 10:11–13).

The census numbers are surprisingly large, and interpreters have often been puzzled by them. For instance, how could 603,550 fighting men (Num. 1:45, 46) be intimidated by the tiny nation of Edom (Num. 20:14–21)? To answer such questions, many have noted that the Hebrew word for "thousand" is the same as the word for "clan." Understood that way, the numbers would be considerably lower.

The narratives of Num. 10—25 take up where those of Exodus leave off and in many ways parallel the accounts of Israel's grumbling against God in Ex. 16; 17. Indeed, the people appear even more dissatisfied in Numbers. In the end, God decrees that this complaining generation, including Moses himself, would not enter the Promised Land.

▼ ■ Numbers 1:1—8:26

Numbers
The First Census of Israel

1 :1 Now the LORD spoke to Moses in the Wilderness of Sinai, in the tabernacle of meeting, on the first *day* of the second month, in the second year after they had come out of the land of Egypt, saying: 2"Take a census of all the congregation of the children of Israel, by their families, by their fathers' houses, according to the number of names, every male individually, 3from twenty years old and above—all who *are able to* go to war in Israel. You and Aaron shall number them by their armies. 4And with you there shall be a man from every tribe, each one the head of his father's house.

5"These are the names of the men who shall stand with you: from Reuben, Elizur the son of Shedeur; 6from Simeon, Shelumiel the son of Zurishaddai; 7from Judah, Nahshon the son of Amminadab; 8from Issachar, Nethanel the son of Zuar; 9from Zebulun, Eliab the son of Helon; 10from the sons of Joseph: from Ephraim, Elishama the son of Ammihud; from Manasseh, Gamaliel the son of Pedahzur; 11from Benjamin, Abidan the son of Gideoni; 12from Dan, Ahiezer the son of Ammishaddai; 13from Asher, Pagiel the son of Ocran; 14from Gad, Eliasaph the son of Deuel;[a] 15from Naphtali, Ahira the son of Enan." 16These *were* chosen from the congregation, leaders of their fathers' tribes, heads of the divisions in Israel.

17Then Moses and Aaron took these men who had been mentioned by name, 18and they assembled all the congregation together on the first *day* of the second month; and they recited their ancestry by families, by their fathers' houses, according to the number of names, from twenty years old and above, each one individually. 19As the LORD commanded Moses, so he numbered them in the Wilderness of Sinai.

20Now the children of Reuben, Israel's oldest son, their genealogies by their families, by their fathers' house, according to the number of names, every male individually, from twenty years old and above, all who *were able to* go to war: 21those who were numbered of the tribe of Reuben *were* forty-six thousand five hundred.

22From the children of Simeon, their genealogies by their families, by their fathers' house, of those who were numbered, according to the number of names, every male individually, from twenty years old and above, all who *were able to* go to war: 23those who were numbered of the tribe of Simeon *were* fifty-nine thousand three hundred.

24From the children of Gad, their genealogies by their families, by their fathers' house, according to the number of names, from twenty years old and above, all who *were able to* go to war: 25those who were numbered of the tribe of Gad *were* forty-five thousand six hundred and fifty.

26From the children of Judah, their genealogies by their families, by their fathers' house, according to the number of names, from twenty years old and above, all who *were able to* go to war: 27those who were numbered of the tribe of Judah *were* seventy-four thousand six hundred.

28From the children of Issachar, their genealogies by their families, by their fathers' house, according to the number of names, from twenty years old and above, all who *were able to* go to war: 29those who were numbered of the tribe of Issachar *were* fifty-four thousand four hundred.

30From the children of Zebulun, their genealogies by their families, by their fathers' house, according to the number of names, from twenty years old and above,

---

1:14 aSpelled *Reuel* in 2:14

POLITICS AND GOVERNMENT

A census is an official count of a population and is usually understood as an assertion of government power. Frequently its purpose is taxation. In Num. 1:2 it is a means of raising an army. By 1800 B.C. the city of Mari on the Euphrates River had a military census in its archives.

all who *were able to* go to war: [31]those who were numbered of the tribe of Zebulun *were* fifty-seven thousand four hundred.

[32]From the sons of Joseph, the children of Ephraim, their genealogies by their families, by their fathers' house, according to the number of names, from twenty years old and above, all who *were able to* go to war: [33]those who were numbered of the tribe of Ephraim *were* forty thousand five hundred.

[34]From the children of Manasseh, their genealogies by their families, by their fathers' house, according to the number of names, from twenty years old and above, all who *were able to* go to war: [35]those who were numbered of the tribe of Manasseh *were* thirty-two thousand two hundred.

[36]From the children of Benjamin, their genealogies by their families, by their fathers' house, according to the number of names, from twenty years old and above, all who *were able to* go to war: [37]those who were numbered of the tribe of Benjamin *were* thirty-five thousand four hundred.

[38]From the children of Dan, their genealogies by their families, by their fathers' house, according to the number of names, from twenty years old and above, all who *were able to* go to war: [39]those who were numbered of the tribe of Dan *were* sixty-two thousand seven hundred.

[40]From the children of Asher, their genealogies by their families, by their fathers' house, according to the number of names, from twenty years old and above, all who *were able to* go to war: [41]those who were numbered of the tribe of Asher *were* forty-one thousand five hundred.

[42]From the children of Naphtali, their genealogies by their families, by their fathers' house, according to the number of names, from twenty years old and above, all who *were able to* go to war: [43]those who were numbered of the tribe of Naphtali *were* fifty-three thousand four hundred.

[44]These are the ones who were numbered, whom Moses and Aaron numbered, with the leaders of Israel, twelve men, each one representing his father's house. [45]So all who were numbered of the children of Israel, by their fathers' houses, from twenty years old and above, all who *were able to* go to war in Israel— [46]all who were numbered were six hundred and three thousand five hundred and fifty.

[47]But the Levites were not numbered among them by their fathers' tribe; [48]for the LORD had spoken to Moses, saying: [49]"Only the tribe of Levi you shall not number, nor take a census of them among the children of Israel; [50]but you shall appoint the Levites over the tabernacle of the Testimony, over all its furnishings, and over all things that belong to it; they shall carry the tabernacle and all its furnishings; they shall attend to it and camp around the tabernacle. [51]And when the tabernacle is to go forward, the Levites shall take it down; and when the tabernacle is to be set up, the Levites shall set it up. The outsider who comes near shall be put to death. [52]The children of Israel shall pitch their tents, everyone by his own camp, everyone by his own standard, according to their armies; [53]but the Levites shall camp around the tabernacle of the Testimony, that there may be no wrath on the congregation of the children of Israel; and the Levites shall keep charge of the tabernacle of the Testimony."

[54]Thus the children of Israel did; according to all that the LORD commanded Moses, so they did.

The Tribes and Leaders by Armies

2 [1]And the LORD spoke to Moses and Aaron, saying: [2]"Everyone of the children of Israel shall camp by his own standard, beside the emblems of his father's house; they shall camp some distance from the tabernacle of meeting. [3]On the east side, toward the rising of the sun, those of the standard of the forces with Judah shall camp according to their armies; and Nahshon the son of Amminadab *shall be* the leader of the children of Judah." [4]And his army was numbered at seventy-four thousand six hundred.

[5]"Those who camp next to him *shall be* the tribe of Issachar, and Nethanel the son of Zuar *shall be* the leader of the children of Issachar." [6]And his army was numbered at fifty-four thousand four hundred.

[7]"Then *comes* the tribe of Zebulun, and Eliab the son of Helon *shall be* the leader of the children of Zebulun." [8]And his army was numbered at fifty-seven thousand four hundred. [9]"All who were numbered according to their armies of the forces with Judah, one hundred and eighty-six thousand four hundred—these shall break camp first.

[10]"On the south side *shall be* the standard of the forces with Reuben according to their armies, and the leader of the children

of Reuben *shall be* Elizur the son of Shedeur." [11]And his army was numbered at forty-six thousand five hundred.

[12]"Those who camp next to him *shall be* the tribe of Simeon, and the leader of the children of Simeon *shall be* Shelumiel the son of Zurishaddai." [13]And his army was numbered at fifty-nine thousand three hundred.

[14]"Then *comes* the tribe of Gad, and the leader of the children of Gad *shall be* Eliasaph the son of Reuel."[a] [15]And his army was numbered at forty-five thousand six hundred and fifty. [16]"All who were numbered according to their armies of the forces with Reuben, one hundred and fifty-one thousand four hundred and fifty—they shall be the second to break camp.

[17]"And the tabernacle of meeting shall move out with the camp of the Levites in the middle of the camps; as they camp, so they shall move out, everyone in his place, by their standards.

[18]"On the west side *shall be* the standard of the forces with Ephraim according to their armies, and the leader of the children of Ephraim *shall be* Elishama the son of Ammihud." [19]And his army was numbered at forty thousand five hundred.

[20]"Next to him *comes* the tribe of Manasseh, and the leader of the children of Manasseh *shall be* Gamaliel the son of Pedahzur." [21]And his army was numbered at thirty-two thousand two hundred.

[22]"Then *comes* the tribe of Benjamin, and the leader of the children of Benjamin *shall be* Abidan the son of Gideoni." [23]And his army was numbered at thirty-five thousand four hundred. [24]"All who were numbered according to their armies of the forces with Ephraim, one hundred and eight thousand one hundred—they shall be the third to break camp.

[25]"The standard of the forces with Dan *shall be* on the north side according to their armies, and the leader of the children of Dan *shall be* Ahiezer the son of Ammishaddai." [26]And his army was numbered at sixty-two thousand seven hundred.

[27]"Those who camp next to him *shall be* the tribe of Asher, and the leader of the children of Asher *shall be* Pagiel the son of Ocran." [28]And his army was numbered at forty-one thousand five hundred.

[29]"Then *comes* the tribe of Naphtali, and the leader of the children of Naphtali *shall be* Ahira the son of Enan." [30]And his army was numbered at fifty-three thousand four hundred. [31]"All who were numbered of the forces with Dan, one hundred and fifty-seven thousand six hundred—they shall break camp last, with their standards."

[32]These *are* the ones who were numbered of the children of Israel by their fathers' houses. All who were numbered according to their armies of the forces *were* six hundred and three thousand five hundred and fifty. [33]But the Levites were not numbered among the children of Israel, just as the LORD commanded Moses.

[34]Thus the children of Israel did according to all that the LORD commanded Moses; so they camped by their standards and so they broke camp, each one by his family, according to their fathers' houses.

The Sons of Aaron

3 [1]Now these *are* the records of Aaron and Moses when the LORD spoke with Moses on Mount Sinai. [2]And these *are* the names of the sons of Aaron: Nadab, the firstborn, and Abihu, Eleazar, and Ithamar. [3]These *are* the names of the sons of Aaron, the anointed priests, whom he consecrated to minister as priests. [4]Nadab and Abihu had died before the LORD when they offered profane fire before the LORD in the Wilderness of Sinai; and they had no children. So Eleazar and Ithamar ministered as priests in the presence of Aaron their father.

The Levites Serve in the Tabernacle

[5]And the LORD spoke to Moses, saying: [6]"Bring the tribe of Levi near, and present them before Aaron the priest, that they may serve him. [7]And they shall attend to his needs and the needs of the whole congregation before the tabernacle of meeting, to do the work of the tabernacle. [8]Also they shall attend to all the furnishings of the tabernacle of meeting, and to the needs of the children of Israel, to do the work of the tabernacle. [9]And you shall give the Levites to Aaron and his sons; they *are* given entirely to him[a] from among the children of Israel. [10]So you shall appoint Aaron and his sons, and they shall attend to their priesthood; but the outsider who comes near shall be put to death."

[11]Then the LORD spoke to Moses, saying: [12]"Now behold, I Myself have taken

---

2:14 [a]Spelled *Deuel* in 1:14 and 7:42
3:9 [a]Samaritan Pentateuch and Septuagint read *Me.*

the Levites from among the children of Israel instead of every firstborn who opens the womb among the children of Israel. Therefore the Levites shall be Mine, ¹³because all the firstborn *are* Mine. On the day that I struck all the firstborn in the land of Egypt, I sanctified to Myself all the firstborn in Israel, both man and beast. They shall be Mine: I *am* the LORD."

Census of the Levites Commanded

¹⁴Then the LORD spoke to Moses in the Wilderness of Sinai, saying: ¹⁵"Number the children of Levi by their fathers' houses, by their families; you shall number every male from a month old and above."

¹⁶So Moses numbered them according to the word of the LORD, as he was commanded. ¹⁷These were the sons of Levi by their names: Gershon, Kohath, and Merari. ¹⁸And these *are* the names of the sons of Gershon by their families: Libni and Shimei. ¹⁹And the sons of Kohath by their families: Amram, Izehar, Hebron, and Uzziel. ²⁰And the sons of Merari by their families: Mahli and Mushi. These *are* the families of the Levites by their fathers' houses.

²¹From Gershon *came* the family of the Libnites and the family of the Shimites; these *were* the families of the Gershonites. ²²Those who were numbered, according to the number of all the males from a month old and above—of those who were numbered *there were* seven thousand five hundred. ²³The families of the Gershonites were to camp behind the tabernacle westward. ²⁴And the leader of the father's house of the Gershonites *was* Eliasaph the son of Lael. ²⁵The duties of the children of Gershon in the tabernacle of meeting *included* the tabernacle, the tent with its covering, the screen for the door of the tabernacle of meeting, ²⁶the screen for the door of the court, the hangings of the court which *are* around the tabernacle and the altar, and their cords, according to all the work relating to them.

²⁷From Kohath *came* the family of the Amramites, the family of the Izharites, the family of the Hebronites, and the family of the Uzzielites; these *were* the families of the Kohathites. ²⁸According to the number of all the males, from a month old and above, *there were* eight thousand six[a] hundred keeping charge of the sanctuary. ²⁹The families of the children of Kohath were to camp on the south side of the tabernacle. ³⁰And the leader of the fathers' house of the families of the Kohathites *was* Elizaphan the son of Uzziel. ³¹Their duty *included* the ark, the table, the lampstand, the altars, the utensils of the sanctuary with which they ministered, the screen, and all the work relating to them.

³²And Eleazar the son of Aaron the priest *was to be* chief over the leaders of the Levites, *with* oversight of those who kept charge of the sanctuary.

³³From Merari *came* the family of the Mahlites and the family of the Mushites; these *were* the families of Merari. ³⁴And those who were numbered, according to the number of all the males from a month old and above, *were* six thousand two hundred. ³⁵The leader of the fathers' house of the families of Merari *was* Zuriel the son of Abihail. These *were* to camp on the north side of the tabernacle. ³⁶And the appointed duty of the children of Merari *included* the boards of the tabernacle, its bars, its pillars, its sockets, its utensils, all the work relating to them, ³⁷and the pillars of the court all around, with their sockets, their pegs, and their cords.

³⁸Moreover those who were to camp before the tabernacle on the east, before the tabernacle of meeting, *were* Moses, Aaron, and his sons, keeping charge of the sanctuary, to meet the needs of the children of Israel; but the outsider who came near was to be put to death. ³⁹All who were numbered of the Levites, whom Moses and Aaron numbered at the commandment of the LORD, by their families, all the males

TIME CAPSULE   *1406 to 1405 B.C.*

1406   *Israelites reach the plains of Moab (based on early Exodus; Num. 22:1)*

1406   *Aaron dies on Mount Hor (early Exodus; Num. 33:38)*

1406   *Moses is buried in Moab (early Exodus; Deut. 34:5, 6)*

1405   *Joshua leads Israelite conquest of Canaan (based on early Exodus)*

1405– *Pharaoh Amenhotep II leads two*
1403   *campaigns into Canaan, quelling revolts*

3:28 ᵃSome manuscripts of the Septuagint read three.

from a month old and above, *were* twenty-two thousand.

Levites Dedicated Instead of the Firstborn

[40]Then the LORD said to Moses: "Number all the firstborn males of the children of Israel from a month old and above, and take the number of their names. [41]And you shall take the Levites for Me—I *am* the LORD—instead of all the firstborn among the children of Israel, and the livestock of the Levites instead of all the firstborn among the livestock of the children of Israel." [42]So Moses numbered all the firstborn among the children of Israel, as the LORD commanded him. [43]And all the firstborn males, according to the number of names from a month old and above, of those who were numbered of them, were twenty-two thousand two hundred and seventy-three.

[44]Then the LORD spoke to Moses, saying: [45]"Take the Levites instead of all the firstborn among the children of Israel, and the livestock of the Levites instead of their livestock. The Levites shall be Mine: I *am* the LORD. [46]And for the redemption of the two hundred and seventy-three of the firstborn of the children of Israel, who are more than the number of the Levites, [47]you shall take five shekels for each one individually; you shall take *them* in the currency of the shekel of the sanctuary, the shekel of twenty gerahs. [48]And you shall give the money, with which the excess number of them is redeemed, to Aaron and his sons."

[49]So Moses took the redemption money from those who were over and above those who were redeemed by the Levites. [50]From the firstborn of the children of Israel he took the money, one thousand three hundred and sixty-five *shekels,* according to the shekel of the sanctuary. [51]And Moses gave their redemption money to Aaron and his sons, according to the word of the LORD, as the LORD commanded Moses.

Duties of the Sons of Kohath

4 [1]Then the LORD spoke to Moses and Aaron, saying: [2]"Take a census of the sons of Kohath from among the children of Levi, by their families, by their fathers' house, [3]from thirty years old and above, even to fifty years old, all who enter the service to do the work in the tabernacle of meeting.

[4]"This *is* the service of the sons of Kohath in the tabernacle of meeting, *relating to* the most holy things: [5]When the camp prepares to journey, Aaron and his sons shall come, and they shall take down the covering veil and cover the ark of the Testimony with it. [6]Then they shall put on it a covering of badger skins, and spread over *that* a cloth entirely of blue; and they shall insert its poles.

[7]"On the table of showbread they shall spread a blue cloth, and put on it the dishes, the pans, the bowls, and the pitchers for pouring; and the showbread[a] shall be on it. [8]They shall spread over them a scarlet cloth, and cover the same with a covering of badger skins; and they shall insert its poles. [9]And they shall take a blue cloth and cover the lampstand of the light, with its lamps, its wick-trimmers, its trays, and all its oil vessels, with which they service it. [10]Then they shall put it with all its utensils in a covering of badger skins, and put *it* on a carrying beam.

[11]"Over the golden altar they shall spread a blue cloth, and cover it with a covering of badger skins; and they shall insert its poles. [12]Then they shall take all the utensils of service with which they minister in the sanctuary, put *them* in a blue cloth, cover them with a covering of badger skins, and put *them* on a carrying beam. [13]Also they shall take away the ashes from the altar, and spread a purple cloth over it. [14]They shall put on it all its implements with which they minister there—the firepans, the forks, the shovels, the basins, and all the utensils of the altar—and they shall spread on it a covering of badger skins, and insert its poles. [15]And when Aaron and his sons have finished covering the sanctuary and all the furnishings of the sanctuary, when the camp is set to go, then the sons of Kohath shall come to carry *them;* but they shall not touch any holy thing, lest they die.

"These *are* the things in the tabernacle of meeting which the sons of Kohath are to carry.

[16]"The appointed duty of Eleazar the son of Aaron the priest *is* the oil for the light, the sweet incense, the daily grain offering, the anointing oil, the oversight of all the tabernacle, of all that *is* in it, with the sanctuary and its furnishings."

[17]Then the LORD spoke to Moses and

4:7 [a]Literally *the continual bread*

Aaron, saying: ¹⁸"Do not cut off the tribe of the families of the Kohathites from among the Levites; ¹⁹but do this in regard to them, that they may live and not die when they approach the most holy things: Aaron and his sons shall go in and appoint each of them to his service and his task. ²⁰But they shall not go in to watch while the holy things are being covered, lest they die."

Duties of the Sons of Gershon

²¹Then the LORD spoke to Moses, saying: ²²"Also take a census of the sons of Gershon, by their fathers' house, by their families. ²³From thirty years old and above, even to fifty years old, you shall number them, all who enter to perform the service, to do the work in the tabernacle of meeting. ²⁴This *is* the service of the families of the Gershonites, in serving and carrying: ²⁵They shall carry the curtains of the tabernacle and the tabernacle of meeting *with* its covering, the covering of badger skins that *is* on it, the screen for the door of the tabernacle of meeting, ²⁶the screen for the door of the gate of the court, the hangings of the court which *are* around the tabernacle and altar, and their cords, all the furnishings for their service and all that is made for these things: so shall they serve.

²⁷"Aaron and his sons shall assign all the service of the sons of the Gershonites, all their tasks and all their service. And you shall appoint to them all their tasks as their duty. ²⁸This *is* the service of the families of the sons of Gershon in the tabernacle of meeting. And their duties *shall be* under the authority^a of Ithamar the son of Aaron the priest.

Duties of the Sons of Merari

²⁹"*As for* the sons of Merari, you shall number them by their families and by their fathers' house. ³⁰From thirty years old and above, even to fifty years old, you shall number them, everyone who enters the service to do the work of the tabernacle of meeting. ³¹And this *is* what they must carry as all their service for the tabernacle of meeting: the boards of the tabernacle, its bars, its pillars, its sockets, ³²and the pillars around the court with their sockets, pegs, and cords, with all their furnishings and all their service; and you shall assign *to each man* by name the items he must carry. ³³This *is* the service of the families of the sons of Merari, as all their service for

the tabernacle of meeting, under the authority^a of Ithamar the son of Aaron the priest."

Census of the Levites

³⁴And Moses, Aaron, and the leaders of the congregation numbered the sons of the Kohathites by their families and by their fathers' house, ³⁵from thirty years old and above, even to fifty years old, everyone who entered the service for work in the tabernacle of meeting; ³⁶and those who were numbered by their families were two thousand seven hundred and fifty. ³⁷These *were* the ones who were numbered of the families of the Kohathites, all who might serve in the tabernacle of meeting, whom Moses and Aaron numbered according to the commandment of the LORD by the hand of Moses.

³⁸And those who were numbered of the sons of Gershon, by their families and by their fathers' house, ³⁹from thirty years old and above, even to fifty years old, everyone who entered the service for work in the tabernacle of meeting— ⁴⁰those who were numbered by their families, by their fathers' house, were two thousand six hundred and thirty. ⁴¹These *are* the ones who were numbered of the families of the sons of Gershon, of all who might serve in the tabernacle of meeting, whom Moses and Aaron numbered according to the commandment of the LORD.

⁴²Those of the families of the sons of Merari who were numbered, by their families, by their fathers' house, ⁴³from thirty years old and above, even to fifty years old, everyone who entered the service for work in the tabernacle of meeting— ⁴⁴those who were numbered by their families were three thousand two hundred. ⁴⁵These *are* the ones who were numbered of the families of the sons of Merari, whom Moses and Aaron numbered according to the word of the LORD by the hand of Moses.

⁴⁶All who were numbered of the Levites, whom Moses, Aaron, and the leaders of Israel numbered, by their families and by their fathers' houses, ⁴⁷from thirty years old and above, even to fifty years old, everyone who came to do the work of service and the work of bearing burdens in the tabernacle of meeting— ⁴⁸those who were numbered were eight thousand five hundred and eighty.

4:28 ^aLiterally *hand*   4:33 ^aLiterally *hand*

49According to the commandment of the LORD they were numbered by the hand of Moses, each according to his service and according to his task; thus were they numbered by him, as the LORD commanded Moses.

Ceremonially Unclean Persons Isolated

5 1And the LORD spoke to Moses, saying: 2"Command the children of Israel that they put out of the camp every leper, everyone who has a discharge, and whoever becomes defiled by a corpse. 3You shall put out both male and female; you shall put them outside the camp, that they may not defile their camps in the midst of which I dwell." 4And the children of Israel did so, and put them outside the camp; as the LORD spoke to Moses, so the children of Israel did.

Confession and Restitution

5Then the LORD spoke to Moses, saying, 6"Speak to the children of Israel: 'When a man or woman commits any sin that men commit in unfaithfulness against the LORD, and that person is guilty, 7then he shall confess the sin which he has committed. He shall make restitution for his trespass in full, plus one-fifth of it, and give it to the one he has wronged. 8But if the man has no relative to whom restitution may be made for the wrong, the restitution for the wrong must go to the LORD for the priest, in addition to the ram of the atonement with which atonement is made for him. 9Every offering of all the holy things of the children of Israel, which they bring to the priest, shall be his. 10And every man's holy things shall be his; whatever any man gives the priest shall be his.'"

Concerning Unfaithful Wives

11And the LORD spoke to Moses, saying, 12"Speak to the children of Israel, and say to them: 'If any man's wife goes astray and behaves unfaithfully toward him, 13and a man lies with her carnally, and it is hidden from the eyes of her husband, and it is concealed that she has defiled herself, and there was no witness against her, nor was she caught— 14if the spirit of jealousy comes upon him and he becomes jealous of his wife, who has defiled herself; or if the spirit of jealousy comes upon him and he becomes jealous of his wife, although she has not defiled herself— 15then the man shall bring his wife to the priest. He shall bring the offering required for her, onetenth of an ephah of barley meal; he shall pour no oil on it and put no frankincense on it, because it is a grain offering of jealousy, an offering for remembering, for bringing iniquity to remembrance.

16'And the priest shall bring her near, and set her before the LORD. 17The priest shall take holy water in an earthen vessel, and take some of the dust that is on the floor of the tabernacle and put it into the water. 18Then the priest shall stand the woman before the LORD, uncover the woman's head, and put the offering for remembering in her hands, which is the grain offering of jealousy. And the priest shall have in his hand the bitter water that brings a curse. 19And the priest shall put her under oath, and say to the woman, "If no man has lain with you, and if you have not gone astray to uncleanness while under your husband's authority, be free from this bitter water that brings a curse. 20But if you have gone astray while under your husband's authority, and if you have defiled yourself and some man other than your husband has lain with you"— 21then the priest shall put the woman under the oath of the curse, and he shall say to the woman—"the LORD make you a curse and an oath among your people, when the LORD makes your thigh rot and your belly swell; 22and may this water that causes the curse go into your stomach, and make your belly swell and your thigh rot."

'Then the woman shall say, "Amen, so be it."

23'Then the priest shall write these curses in a book, and he shall scrape them off into the bitter water. 24And he shall make the woman drink the bitter water that brings a curse, and the water that brings the curse shall enter her to become bitter. 25Then the priest shall take the grain offering of jealousy from the woman's hand, shall wave the offering before the LORD, and bring it to the altar; 26and the priest shall take a handful of the offering, as its memorial portion, burn it on the altar, and afterward make the woman drink the water. 27When he has made her drink the water, then it shall be, if she has defiled herself and behaved unfaithfully toward her husband, that the water that brings a curse will enter her and become bitter, and her belly will swell, her thigh will rot, and the woman will become a curse among her people. ²⁸But if the woman has not defiled herself, and is clean, then she shall be free and may conceive children.

²⁹'This *is* the law of jealousy, when a wife, *while* under her husband's *authority,* goes astray and defiles herself, ³⁰or when the spirit of jealousy comes upon a man, and he becomes jealous of his wife; then he shall stand the woman before the LORD, and the priest shall execute all this law upon her. ³¹Then the man shall be free from iniquity, but that woman shall bear her guilt.'"

The Law of the Nazirite

6 ¹Then the LORD spoke to Moses, saying, ²"Speak to the children of Israel, and say to them: 'When either a man or woman consecrates an offering to take the vow of a Nazirite, to separate himself to the LORD, ³he shall separate himself from wine and *similar* drink; he shall drink neither vinegar made from wine nor vinegar made from *similar* drink; neither shall he drink any grape juice, nor eat fresh grapes or raisins. ⁴All the days of his separation he shall eat nothing that is produced by the grapevine, from seed to skin.

⁵'All the days of the vow of his separation no razor shall come upon his head; until the days are fulfilled for which he separated himself to the LORD, he shall be holy. *Then* he shall let the locks of the hair of his head grow. ⁶All the days that he separates himself to the LORD he shall not go near a dead body. ⁷He shall not make himself unclean even for his father or his mother, for his brother or his sister, when they die, because his separation to God *is* on his head. ⁸All the days of his separation he shall be holy to the LORD.

⁹'And if anyone dies very suddenly beside him, and he defiles his consecrated head, then he shall shave his head on the day of his cleansing; on the seventh day he shall shave it. ¹⁰Then on the eighth day he shall bring two turtledoves or two young pigeons to the priest, to the door of the tabernacle of meeting; ¹¹and the priest shall offer one as a sin offering and *the* other as a burnt offering, and make atonement for him, because he sinned in regard to the corpse; and he shall sanctify his head that same day. ¹²He shall consecrate to the LORD the days of his separation, and bring a male lamb in its first year as a trespass offering; but the former days shall be lost, because his separation was defiled.

¹³'Now this *is* the law of the Nazirite: When the days of his separation are fulfilled, he shall be brought to the door of the tabernacle of meeting. ¹⁴And he shall present his offering to the LORD: one male lamb in its first year without blemish as a burnt offering, one ewe lamb in its first year without blemish as a sin offering, one ram without blemish as a peace offering, ¹⁵a basket of unleavened bread, cakes of fine flour mixed with oil, unleavened wafers anointed with oil, and their grain offering with their drink offerings.

¹⁶'Then the priest shall bring *them* before the LORD and offer his sin offering and his burnt offering; ¹⁷and he shall offer the ram as a sacrifice of a peace offering to the LORD, with the basket of unleavened bread; the priest shall also offer its grain offering and its drink offering. ¹⁸Then the Nazirite shall shave his consecrated head *at* the door of the tabernacle of meeting, and shall take the hair from his consecrated head and put *it* on the fire which is under the sacrifice of the peace offering.

¹⁹'And the priest shall take the boiled shoulder of the ram, one unleavened cake from the basket, and one unleavened wafer, and put *them* upon the hands of the Nazirite after he has shaved his consecrated *hair,* ²⁰and the priest shall wave them as a wave offering before the LORD; they *are* holy for the priest, together with the breast of the wave offering and the thigh of the heave offering. After that the Nazirite may drink wine.'

²¹"This is the law of the Nazirite who vows to the LORD the offering for his separation, and besides that, whatever else his

CULTURE AND SOCIETY

An ordeal is a way of deciding whether a person is innocent or guilty. Whether the person is harmed or safe under a particular trial is supposed to reveal guilt or innocence. Ordeals were common in the ancient Middle East. The Bible describes only one ordeal (Num. 5:17–28). In it, the punishment as well as the determination of guilt is referred to God (5:21, 22, 27).

hand is able to provide; according to the vow which he takes, so he must do according to the law of his separation."

The Priestly Blessing

[22]And the LORD spoke to Moses, saying: [23]"Speak to Aaron and his sons, saying, 'This is the way you shall bless the children of Israel. Say to them:

24   "The LORD bless you and keep you;
25   The LORD make His face shine upon
         you,
      And be gracious to you;
26   The LORD lift up His countenance
         upon you,
      And give you peace." '

[27]"So they shall put My name on the children of Israel, and I will bless them."

Offerings of the Leaders

7 [1]Now it came to pass, when Moses had finished setting up the tabernacle, that he anointed it and consecrated it and all its furnishings, and the altar and all its utensils; so he anointed them and consecrated them. [2]Then the leaders of Israel, the heads of their fathers' houses, who *were* the leaders of the tribes and over those who were numbered, made an offering. [3]And they brought their offering before the LORD, six covered carts and twelve oxen, a cart for *every* two of the leaders, and for each one an ox; and they presented them before the tabernacle. [4]Then the LORD spoke to Moses, saying, [5]"Accept *these* from them, that they may be used in doing the work of the tabernacle of meeting; and you shall give them to the Levites, *to* every man according to his service." [6]So Moses took the carts and the oxen, and gave them to the Levites. [7]Two carts and four oxen he gave to the sons of Gershon, according to their service; [8]and four carts and eight oxen he gave to the sons of Merari, according to their ser-

vice, under the authority[a] of Ithamar the son of Aaron the priest. [9]But to the sons of Kohath he gave none, because theirs *was* the service of the holy things, *which* they carried on their shoulders.

[10]Now the leaders offered the dedication *offering* for the altar when it was anointed; so the leaders offered their offering before the altar. [11]For the LORD said to Moses, "They shall offer their offering, one leader each day, for the dedication of the altar."

[12]And the one who offered his offering on the first day *was* Nahshon the son of Amminadab, from the tribe of Judah. [13]His offering *was* one silver platter, the weight of which *was* one hundred and thirty *shekels,* and one silver bowl of seventy shekels, according to the shekel of the sanctuary, both of them full of fine flour mixed with oil as a grain offering; [14]one gold pan of ten *shekels,* full of incense; [15]one young bull, one ram, and one male lamb in its first year, as a burnt offering; [16]one kid of the goats as a sin offering; [17]and for the sacrifice of peace offerings: two oxen, five rams, five male goats, and five male lambs in their first year. This *was* the offering of Nahshon the son of Amminadab.

[18]On the second day Nethanel the son of Zuar, leader of Issachar, presented *an offering.* [19]*For* his offering he offered one silver platter, the weight of which *was* one hundred and thirty *shekels,* and one silver bowl of seventy shekels, according to the shekel of the sanctuary, both of them full of fine flour mixed with oil as a grain offering; [20]one gold pan of ten *shekels,* full of incense; [21]one young bull, one ram, and one male lamb in its first year, as a burnt offering; [22]one kid of the goats as a sin offering; [23]and as the sacrifice of peace offerings: two oxen, five rams, five male goats, and five male lambs in their first year. This *was* the offering of Nethanel the son of Zuar.

[24]On the third day Eliab the son of Helon, leader of the children of Zebulun,

7:8 [a]Literally *hand*

RELIGION AND WORSHIP

This list of the gifts presented to the Lord is highly formal and ceremonial (Num. 7:12). It resembles Egyptian pictures dating from 2650 B.C. that show servant after servant presenting trays of offerings to the temple. The ceremonial repetition produces an effect of order and abundance.

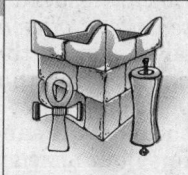

presented an offering. ²⁵His offering *was* one silver platter, the weight of which *was* one hundred and thirty *shekels,* and one silver bowl of seventy shekels, according to the shekel of the sanctuary, both of them full of fine flour mixed with oil as a grain offering; ²⁶one gold pan of ten *shekels,* full of incense; ²⁷one young bull, one ram, and one male lamb in its first year, as a burnt offering; ²⁸one kid of the goats as a sin offering; ²⁹and for the sacrifice of peace offerings: two oxen, five rams, five male goats, and five male lambs in their first year. This *was* the offering of Eliab the son of Helon.

³⁰On the fourth day Elizur the son of Shedeur, leader of the children of Reuben, *presented an offering.* ³¹His offering *was* one silver platter, the weight of which *was* one hundred and thirty *shekels,* and one silver bowl of seventy shekels, according to the shekel of the sanctuary, both of them full of fine flour mixed with oil as a grain offering; ³²one gold pan of ten *shekels,* full of incense; ³³one young bull, one ram, and one male lamb in its first year, as a burnt offering; ³⁴one kid of the goats as a sin offering; ³⁵and as the sacrifice of peace offerings: two oxen, five rams, five male goats, and five male lambs in their first year. This *was* the offering of Elizur the son of Shedeur.

³⁶On the fifth day Shelumiel the son of Zurishaddai, leader of the children of Simeon, *presented an offering.* ³⁷His offering *was* one silver platter, the weight of which *was* one hundred and thirty *shekels,* and one silver bowl of seventy shekels, according to the shekel of the sanctuary, both of them full of fine flour mixed with oil as a grain offering; ³⁸one gold pan of ten *shekels,* full of incense; ³⁹one young bull, one ram, and one male lamb in its first year, as a burnt offering; ⁴⁰one kid of the goats as a sin offering; ⁴¹and as the sacrifice of peace offerings: two oxen, five rams, five male goats, and five male lambs in their first year. This *was* the offering of Shelumiel the son of Zurishaddai.

⁴²On the sixth day Eliasaph the son of Deuel,ᵃ leader of the children of Gad, *presented an offering.* ⁴³His offering *was* one silver platter, the weight of which *was* one hundred and thirty *shekels,* and one silver bowl of seventy shekels, according to the shekel of the sanctuary, both of them full of fine flour mixed with oil as a grain offering; ⁴⁴one gold pan of ten *shekels,* full of in-

cense; ⁴⁵one young bull, one ram, and one male lamb in its first year, as a burnt offering; ⁴⁶one kid of the goats as a sin offering; ⁴⁷and as the sacrifice of peace offerings: two oxen, five rams, five male goats, and five male lambs in their first year. This *was* the offering of Eliasaph the son of Deuel.

⁴⁸On the seventh day Elishama the son of Ammihud, leader of the children of Ephraim, *presented an offering.* ⁴⁹His offering *was* one silver platter, the weight of which *was* one hundred and thirty *shekels,* and one silver bowl of seventy shekels, according to the shekel of the sanctuary, both of them full of fine flour mixed with oil as a grain offering; ⁵⁰one gold pan of ten *shekels,* full of incense; ⁵¹one young bull, one ram, and one male lamb in its first year, as a burnt offering; ⁵²one kid of the goats as a sin offering; ⁵³and as the sacrifice of peace offerings: two oxen, five rams, five male goats, and five male lambs in their first year. This *was* the offering of Elishama the son of Ammihud.

⁵⁴On the eighth day Gamaliel the son of Pedahzur, leader of the children of Manasseh, *presented an offering.* ⁵⁵His offering *was* one silver platter, the weight of which *was* one hundred and thirty *shekels,* and one silver bowl of seventy shekels, according to the shekel of the sanctuary, both of them full of fine flour mixed with oil as a grain offering; ⁵⁶one gold pan of ten *shekels,* full of incense; ⁵⁷one young bull, one ram, and one male lamb in its first year, as a burnt offering; ⁵⁸one kid of the goats as a sin offering; ⁵⁹and as the sacrifice of peace offerings: two oxen, five rams, five male goats, and five male lambs in their first year. This *was* the offering of Gamaliel the son of Pedahzur.

⁶⁰On the ninth day Abidan the son of Gideoni, leader of the children of Benjamin, *presented an offering.* ⁶¹His offering *was* one silver platter, the weight of which *was* one hundred and thirty *shekels,* and one silver bowl of seventy shekels, according to the shekel of the sanctuary, both of them full of fine flour mixed with oil as a grain offering; ⁶²one gold pan of ten *shekels,* full of incense; ⁶³one young bull, one ram, and one male lamb in its first year, as a burnt offering; ⁶⁴one kid of the goats as a sin offering; ⁶⁵and as the sacrifice of peace offerings: two oxen, five rams,

---

7:42 ᵃSpelled *Reuel* in 2:14

five male goats, and five male lambs in their first year. This *was* the offering of Abidan the son of Gideoni.

66On the tenth day Ahiezer the son of Ammishaddai, leader of the children of Dan, *presented an offering.* 67His offering *was* one silver platter, the weight of which *was* one hundred and thirty *shekels,* and one silver bowl of seventy shekels, according to the shekel of the sanctuary, both of them full of fine flour mixed with oil as a grain offering; 68one gold pan of ten *shekels,* full of incense; 69one young bull, one ram, and one male lamb in its first year, as a burnt offering; 70one kid of the goats as a sin offering; 71and as the sacrifice of peace offerings: two oxen, five rams, five male goats, and five male lambs in their first year. This *was* the offering of Ahiezer the son of Ammishaddai.

72On the eleventh day Pagiel the son of Ocran, leader of the children of Asher, *presented an offering.* 73His offering *was* one silver platter, the weight of which *was* one hundred and thirty *shekels,* and one silver bowl of seventy shekels, according to the shekel of the sanctuary, both of them full of fine flour mixed with oil as a grain offering; 74one gold pan of ten *shekels,* full of incense; 75one young bull, one ram, and one male lamb in its first year, as a burnt offering; 76one kid of the goats as a sin offering; 77and as the sacrifice of peace offerings: two oxen, five rams, five male goats, and five male lambs in their first year. This *was* the offering of Pagiel the son of Ocran.

78On the twelfth day Ahira the son of Enan, leader of the children of Naphtali, *presented an offering.* 79His offering *was* one silver platter, the weight of which *was* one hundred and thirty *shekels,* and one silver bowl of seventy shekels, according to the shekel of the sanctuary, both of them full of fine flour mixed with oil as a grain offering; 80one gold pan of ten *shekels,* full of incense; 81one young bull, one ram, and one male lamb in its first year, as a burnt offering; 82one kid of the goats as a sin offering; 83and as the sacrifice of peace offerings: two oxen, five rams, five male goats, and five male lambs in their first year. This *was* the offering of Ahira the son of Enan.

84This *was* the dedication *offering* for the altar from the leaders of Israel, when it was anointed: twelve silver platters, twelve silver bowls, and twelve gold pans. 85Each silver platter *weighed* one hundred and thirty *shekels* and each bowl seventy *shekels.* All the silver of the vessels *weighed* two thousand four hundred *shekels,* according to the shekel of the sanctuary. 86The twelve gold pans full of incense *weighed* ten *shekels* apiece, according to the shekel of the sanctuary; all the gold of the pans *weighed* one hundred and twenty *shekels.* 87All the oxen for the burnt offering *were* twelve young bulls, the rams twelve, the male lambs in their first year twelve, with their grain offering, and the kids of the goats as a sin offering twelve. 88And all the oxen for the sacrifice of peace offerings were twenty-four bulls, the rams sixty, the male goats sixty, and the lambs in their first year sixty. This *was* the dedication *offering* for the altar after it was anointed.

89Now when Moses went into the tabernacle of meeting to speak with Him, he heard the voice of One speaking to him from above the mercy seat that *was* on the ark of the Testimony, from between the two cherubim; thus He spoke to him.

Arrangement of the Lamps

8 1And the LORD spoke to Moses, saying: 2"Speak to Aaron, and say to him, 'When you arrange the lamps, the seven lamps shall give light in front of the lampstand.' " 3And Aaron did so; he arranged the lamps to face toward the front of the lampstand, as the LORD commanded Moses. 4Now this workmanship of the lampstand *was* hammered gold; from its shaft to its flowers it *was* hammered work. According to the pattern which the LORD had shown Moses, so he made the lampstand.

Cleansing and Dedication of the Levites

5Then the LORD spoke to Moses, saying: 6"Take the Levites from among the children of Israel and cleanse them *ceremonially.* 7Thus you shall do to them to cleanse them: Sprinkle water of purification on them, and let them shave all their body, and let them wash their clothes, and *so* make themselves clean. 8Then let them take a young bull with its grain offering of fine flour mixed with oil, and you shall take another young bull as a sin offering. 9And you shall bring the Levites before the tabernacle of meeting, and you shall gather together the whole congregation of the children of Israel. 10So you shall bring the Levites before the LORD, and the children of Israel shall lay their hands on the Levites; ¹¹and Aaron shall offer the Levites before the LORD *like* a wave offering from the children of Israel, that they may perform the work of the LORD. ¹²Then the Levites shall lay their hands on the heads of the young bulls, and you shall offer one as a sin offering and the other as a burnt offering to the LORD, to make atonement for the Levites.

¹³"And you shall stand the Levites before Aaron and his sons, and then offer them *like* a wave offering to the LORD. ¹⁴Thus you shall separate the Levites from among the children of Israel, and the Levites shall be Mine. ¹⁵After that the Levites shall go in to service the tabernacle of meeting. So you shall cleanse them and offer them *like* a wave offering. ¹⁶For they *are* wholly given to Me from among the children of Israel; I have taken them for Myself instead of all who open the womb, the firstborn of all the children of Israel. ¹⁷For all the firstborn among the children of Israel *are* Mine, *both* man and beast; on the day that I struck all the firstborn in the land of Egypt I sanctified them to Myself. ¹⁸I have taken the Levites instead of all the firstborn of the children of Israel. ¹⁹And I have given the Levites as a gift to Aaron and his sons from among the children of Israel, to do the work for the children of Israel in the tabernacle of meeting, and to make atonement for the children of Israel, that there be no plague among the children of Israel when the children of Israel come near the sanctuary."

²⁰Thus Moses and Aaron and all the congregation of the children of Israel did to the Levites; according to all that the LORD commanded Moses concerning the Levites, so the children of Israel did to them. ²¹And the Levites purified themselves and washed their clothes; then Aaron presented them *like* a wave offering before the LORD, and Aaron made atonement for them to cleanse them. ²²After that the Levites went in to do their work in the tabernacle of meeting before Aaron and his sons; as the LORD commanded Moses concerning the Levites, so they did to them.

²³Then the LORD spoke to Moses, saying, ²⁴"This *is* what *pertains* to the Levites: From twenty-five years old and above one may enter to perform service in the work of the tabernacle of meeting; ²⁵and at the age of fifty years they must cease performing this work, and shall work no more. ²⁶They

may minister with their brethren in the tabernacle of meeting, to attend to needs, but they *themselves* shall do no work. Thus you shall do to the Levites regarding their duties."

Observing the Rite of the Passover

In the 2nd month of the 2nd year of the Exodus, Moses took the first of two census reports, determining how many men were available for war (Num. 1:1–4). Just one month prior to this census, in the 1st month, the Israelites observed their first Passover since departing Egypt (Num. 9:1–5). Because the Passover was so important to the Israelite community, those who were not able to observe it in the 1st month were permitted to do so in the 2nd month (9:6, 7, 9, 11). Only 6 days after this second observance, Israel departed from Mount Sinai (10:12).

■ Numbers 9:1—12:16

Numbers
The Second Passover

9 :1 Now the LORD spoke to Moses in the Wilderness of Sinai, in the first month of the second year after they had come out of the land of Egypt, saying: ²"Let the children of Israel keep the Passover at its appointed time. ³On the fourteenth day of this month, at twilight, you shall keep it at its appointed time. According to all its rites and ceremonies you shall keep it." ⁴So Moses told the children of Israel that they should keep the Passover. ⁵And they kept the Passover on the fourteenth day of the first month, at twilight, in the Wilderness of Sinai; according to all that the LORD commanded Moses, so the children of Israel did.

⁶Now there were *certain* men who were defiled by a human corpse, so that they could not keep the Passover on that day; and they came before Moses and Aaron that day. ⁷And those men said to him, "We *became* defiled by a human corpse. Why are we kept from presenting the offering of the LORD at its appointed time among the children of Israel?"

⁸And Moses said to them, "Stand still, that I may hear what the LORD will command concerning you."

⁹Then the LORD spoke to Moses, say-

ing, ¹⁰"Speak to the children of Israel, saying: 'If anyone of you or your posterity is unclean because of a corpse, or *is* far away on a journey, he may still keep the LORD's Passover. ¹¹On the fourteenth day of the second month, at twilight, they may keep it. They shall eat it with unleavened bread and bitter herbs. ¹²They shall leave none of it until morning, nor break one of its bones. According to all the ordinances of the Passover they shall keep it. ¹³But the man who *is* clean and is not on a journey, and ceases to keep the Passover, that same person shall be cut off from among his people, because he did not bring the offering of the LORD at its appointed time; that man shall bear his sin.

¹⁴"And if a stranger dwells among you, and would keep the LORD's Passover, he must do so according to the rite of the Passover and according to its ceremony; you shall have one ordinance, both for the stranger and the native of the land.' "

The Cloud and the Fire

¹⁵Now on the day that the tabernacle was raised up, the cloud covered the tabernacle, the tent of the Testimony; from evening until morning it was above the tabernacle like the appearance of fire. ¹⁶So it was always: the cloud covered it *by day,* and the appearance of fire by night. ¹⁷Whenever the cloud was taken up from above the tabernacle, after that the children of Israel would journey; and in the place where the cloud settled, there the children of Israel would pitch their tents. ¹⁸At the command of the LORD the children of Israel would journey, and at the command of the LORD they would camp; as long as the cloud stayed above the tabernacle they remained encamped. ¹⁹Even when the cloud continued long, many days above the tabernacle, the children of Israel kept the charge of the LORD and did not journey. ²⁰So it was, when the cloud was above the tabernacle a few days: according to the command of the LORD they would remain encamped, and according to the command

of the LORD they would journey. ²¹So it was, when the cloud remained only from evening until morning: when the cloud was taken up in the morning, then they would journey; whether by day or by night, whenever the cloud was taken up, they would journey. ²²*Whether it was* two days, a month, or a year that the cloud remained above the tabernacle, the children of Israel would remain encamped and not journey; but when it was taken up, they would journey. ²³At the command of the LORD they remained encamped, and at the command of the LORD they journeyed; they kept the charge of the LORD, at the command of the LORD by the hand of Moses.

Two Silver Trumpets

10 ¹And the LORD spoke to Moses, saying: ²"Make two silver trumpets for yourself; you shall make them of hammered work; you shall use them for calling the congregation and for directing the movement of the camps. ³When they blow both of them, all the congregation shall gather before you at the door of the tabernacle of meeting. ⁴But if they blow *only* one, then the leaders, the heads of the divisions of Israel, shall gather to you. ⁵When you sound the advance, the camps that lie on the east side shall then begin their journey. ⁶When you sound the advance the second time, then the camps that lie on the south side shall begin their journey; they shall sound the call for them to begin their journeys. ⁷And when the assembly is to be gathered together, you shall blow, but not sound the advance. ⁸The sons of Aaron, the priests, shall blow the trumpets; and these shall be to you as an ordinance forever throughout your generations.

⁹"When you go to war in your land against the enemy who oppresses you, then you shall sound an alarm with the trumpets, and you will be remembered before the LORD your God, and you will be saved from your enemies. ¹⁰Also in the day of your gladness, in your appointed feasts, and at the beginning of your months, you

ARTS AND LITERATURE

Trumpets are wind instruments that can be made from shells or animal horns (Num. 10:2). They are known from very early times. Two metal trumpets, one made of silver, were buried with the pharaoh Tutankhamun in 1327 B.C. The trumpet seems to be a favorite signaling device for soldiers.

shall blow the trumpets over your burnt offerings and over the sacrifices of your peace offerings; and they shall be a memorial for you before your God: I *am* the LORD your God."

Departure from Sinai

¹¹Now it came to pass on the twentieth *day* of the second month, in the second year, that the cloud was taken up from above the tabernacle of the Testimony. ¹²And the children of Israel set out from the Wilderness of Sinai on their journeys; then the cloud settled down in the Wilderness of Paran. ¹³So they started out for the first time according to the command of the LORD by the hand of Moses.

¹⁴The standard of the camp of the children of Judah set out first according to their armies; over their army was Nahshon the son of Amminadab. ¹⁵Over the army of the tribe of the children of Issachar *was* Nethanel the son of Zuar. ¹⁶And over the army of the tribe of the children of Zebulun *was* Eliab the son of Helon.

¹⁷Then the tabernacle was taken down; and the sons of Gershon and the sons of Merari set out, carrying the tabernacle.

¹⁸And the standard of the camp of Reuben set out according to their armies; over their army *was* Elizur the son of Shedeur. ¹⁹Over the army of the tribe of the children of Simeon *was* Shelumiel the son of Zurishaddai. ²⁰And over the army of the tribe of the children of Gad *was* Eliasaph the son of Deuel.

²¹Then the Kohathites set out, carrying the holy things. (The tabernacle would be prepared for their arrival.)

²²And the standard of the camp of the children of Ephraim set out according to their armies; over their army *was* Elishama the son of Ammihud. ²³Over the army of the tribe of the children of Manasseh *was* Gamaliel the son of Pedahzur. ²⁴And over the army of the tribe of the children of Benjamin *was* Abidan the son of Gideoni.

²⁵Then the standard of the camp of the children of Dan (the rear guard of all the camps) set out according to their armies; over their army *was* Ahiezer the son of Ammishaddai. ²⁶Over the army of the tribe of the children of Asher *was* Pagiel the son of Ocran. ²⁷And over the army of the tribe of the children of Naphtali *was* Ahira the son of Enan.

²⁸Thus *was* the order of march of the children of Israel, according to their armies, when they began their journey.

²⁹Now Moses said to Hobab the son of Reuel[a] the Midianite, Moses' father-in-law, "We are setting out for the place of which the LORD said, 'I will give it to you.' Come with us, and we will treat you well; for the LORD has promised good things to Israel."

³⁰And he said to him, "I will not go, but I will depart to my *own* land and to my relatives."

³¹So *Moses* said, "Please do not leave, inasmuch as you know how we are to camp in the wilderness, and you can be our eyes. ³²And it shall be, if you go with us—indeed it shall be—that whatever good the LORD will do to us, the same we will do to you."

³³So they departed from the mountain of the LORD on a journey of three days; and the ark of the covenant of the LORD went before them for the three days' journey, to search out a resting place for them. ³⁴And the cloud of the LORD *was* above them by day when they went out from the camp. ³⁵So it was, whenever the ark set out, that Moses said:

"Rise up, O LORD!
Let Your enemies be scattered,
And let those who hate You flee before You."

TIME CAPSULE   *1400 B.C.*

1400–1330	Nuzi tablets illuminate patriarchal customs
1400	Population of Egypt is about 4 million
1400	Population of Palestine is about 200,000
1400	Egyptians begin to use chariot wheels with six spokes
1400	King Lab'ayu establishes small empire at Shechem
1400	Mycenaean Greeks invade Crete, destroying the palace at Knossos
1400–1200	Mythological texts from Ugarit

10:29 ᵃSeptuagint reads *Raguel* (compare Exodus 2:18).

EATING THE GOOD FOODS OF EGYPT (Num. 11:5)

The fresh fish eaten by the Israelites while in Egypt was a distant memory by the time they were wandering in the wilderness. They could recall other foods that Egypt had offered: "cucumbers, the melons, the leeks, the onions, and the garlic" (Num. 11:5). Now they were unhappy because they had no meat or the special foods they had enjoyed in Egypt. They complained about the lack of variety in their diet. The manna was rather bland, having the flower-like odor of coriander seed (Num. 11:6–9).

The delightful foods of Egypt are also mentioned in writings of that country. An Egyptian letter from the end of the New Kingdom period (1550–1069 B.C.) voices a similar bent towards the fruitful bounty at the city of Rameses. The scribe Pai-Bes writes to his master Amen-em-Opet that, upon arriving in Rameses, he found it a beautiful and pleasant district, full of fish in its ponds, grassy meadows, abundant dates, melons, leeks, onions, olives, figs, sweet wine, and many other good foods.

The Israelites had known the city of Rameses. It was one of the store cities they had built while slaves (Ex. 1:11; spelled Raamses). It was also the starting point of their exodus out of Egypt (Ex. 12:37). The ancient Egyptians called the city Per-Rameses-meri-Amon, the name used by the scribe in his letter. The scribe's naming of "melons, leeks, onions," along with several other foods, appears, at the very least, to authenticate the veracity of the Israelites' complaint. Like the scribe, they too had witnessed the abundance of Rameses and Egypt.

36And when it rested, he said:

"Return, O LORD,
To the many thousands of Israel."

The People Complain

11 1Now *when* the people complained, it displeased the LORD; for the LORD heard *it,* and His anger was aroused. So the fire of the LORD burned among them, and consumed *some* in the outskirts of the camp. 2Then the people cried out to Moses, and when Moses prayed to the LORD, the fire was quenched. 3So he called the name of the place Taberah,[a] because the fire of the LORD had burned among them.

4Now the mixed multitude who were among them yielded to intense craving; so the children of Israel also wept again and said: "Who will give us meat to eat? 5We remember the fish which we ate freely in Egypt, the cucumbers, the melons, the

11:3 aLiterally *Burning*

leeks, the onions, and the garlic; 6but now our whole being *is* dried up; *there is* nothing at all except this manna *before* our eyes!"

7Now the manna *was* like coriander seed, and its color like the color of bdellium. 8The people went about and gathered *it,* ground *it* on millstones or beat *it* in the mortar, cooked *it* in pans, and made cakes of it; and its taste was like the taste of pastry prepared with oil. 9And when the dew fell on the camp in the night, the manna fell on it.

10Then Moses heard the people weeping throughout their families, everyone at the door of his tent; and the anger of the LORD was greatly aroused; Moses also was displeased. 11So Moses said to the LORD, "Why have You afflicted Your servant? And why have I not found favor in Your sight, that You have laid the burden of all these people on me? 12Did I conceive all these people? Did I beget them, that You should say to me, 'Carry them in your bosom, as a

---

POLITICS AND GOVERNMENT

The Egyptians were proud of their ability to organize work. As is known from contemporary records, it was a point of pride with them that those who built monumental buildings like pyramids and tombs were well provided for (Num. 11:5). For one thing, it was proof of the general prosperity of the country.

guardian carries a nursing child,' to the land which You swore to their fathers? 13Where am I to get meat to give to all these people? For they weep all over me, saying, 'Give us meat, that we may eat.' 14I am not able to bear all these people alone, because the burden *is* too heavy for me. 15If You treat me like this, please kill me here and now—if I have found favor in Your sight—and do not let me see my wretchedness!"

The Seventy Elders

16So the LORD said to Moses: "Gather to Me seventy men of the elders of Israel, whom you know to be the elders of the people and officers over them; bring them to the tabernacle of meeting, that they may stand there with you. 17Then I will come down and talk with you there. I will take of the Spirit that *is* upon you and will put *the same* upon them; and they shall bear the burden of the people with you, that you may not bear *it* yourself alone. 18Then you shall say to the people, 'Consecrate yourselves for tomorrow, and you shall eat meat; for you have wept in the hearing of the LORD, saying, "Who will give us meat to eat? For *it was* well with us in Egypt." Therefore the LORD will give you meat, and you shall eat. 19You shall eat, not one day, nor two days, nor five days, nor ten days, nor twenty days, 20but *for* a whole month, until it comes out of your nostrils and becomes loathsome to you, because you have despised the LORD who is among you, and have wept before Him, saying, "Why did we ever come up out of Egypt?" ' "

21And Moses said, "The people whom I *am* among *are* six hundred thousand men on foot; yet You have said, 'I will give them meat, that they may eat *for* a whole month.' 22Shall flocks and herds be slaughtered for them, to provide enough for them? Or shall all the fish of the sea be gathered together for them, to provide enough for them?"

23And the LORD said to Moses, "Has the LORD's arm been shortened? Now you shall see whether what I say will happen to you or not."

24So Moses went out and told the people the words of the LORD, and he gathered the seventy men of the elders of the people and placed them around the tabernacle. 25Then the LORD came down in the cloud, and spoke to him, and took of the Spirit that *was* upon him, and placed *the same*

upon the seventy elders; and it happened, when the Spirit rested upon them, that they prophesied, although they never did *so* again.ª

26But two men had remained in the camp: the name of one *was* Eldad, and the name of the other Medad. And the Spirit rested upon them. Now they *were* among those listed, but who had not gone out to the tabernacle; yet they prophesied in the camp. 27And a young man ran and told Moses, and said, "Eldad and Medad are prophesying in the camp."

28So Joshua the son of Nun, Moses' assistant, *one* of his choice men, answered and said, "Moses my lord, forbid them!"

29Then Moses said to him, "Are you zealous for my sake? Oh, that all the LORD's people were prophets *and* that the LORD would put His Spirit upon them!" 30And Moses returned to the camp, he and the elders of Israel.

The LORD Sends Quail

31Now a wind went out from the LORD, and it brought quail from the sea and left *them* fluttering near the camp, about a day's journey on this side and about a day's journey on the other side, all around the camp, and about two cubits above the surface of the ground. 32And the people stayed up all that day, all night, and all the next day, and gathered the quail (he who gathered least gathered ten homers); and they spread *them* out for themselves all around the camp. 33But while the meat *was* still between their teeth, before it was chewed, the wrath of the LORD was aroused against the people, and the LORD struck the people with a very great plague. 34So he called the name of that place Kibroth Hattaavah,ª because there they buried the people who had yielded to craving.

35From Kibroth Hattaavah the people moved to Hazeroth, and camped at Hazeroth.

Dissension of Aaron and Miriam

12 1Then Miriam and Aaron spoke against Moses because of the Ethiopian woman whom he had married; for he had married an Ethiopian woman. 2So they said, "Has the LORD indeed spoken only through Moses? Has He not spoken through us also?" And the LORD heard *it*.

11:25 ªTargum and Vulgate read *did not cease.*
11:34 ªLiterally *Graves of Craving*

³(Now the man Moses *was* very humble, more than all men who *were* on the face of the earth.)

⁴Suddenly the LORD said to Moses, Aaron, and Miriam, "Come out, you three, to the tabernacle of meeting!" So the three came out. ⁵Then the LORD came down in the pillar of cloud and stood *in* the door of the tabernacle, and called Aaron and Miriam. And they both went forward. ⁶Then He said,

"Hear now My words:
If there is a prophet among you,
I, the LORD, make Myself known to
    him in a vision;
I speak to him in a dream.
⁷ Not so with My servant Moses;
He *is* faithful in all My house.
⁸ I speak with him face to face,
Even plainly, and not in dark sayings;
And he sees the form of the LORD.
Why then were you not afraid
To speak against My servant Moses?"

⁹So the anger of the LORD was aroused against them, and He departed. ¹⁰And when the cloud departed from above the tabernacle, suddenly Miriam *became* leprous, as *white as* snow. Then Aaron turned toward Miriam, and there she was, a leper. ¹¹So Aaron said to Moses, "Oh, my lord! Please do not lay *this* sin on us, in which we have done foolishly and in which we have sinned. ¹²Please do not let her be as one dead, whose flesh is half consumed when he comes out of his mother's womb!"

¹³So Moses cried out to the LORD, saying, "Please heal her, O God, I pray!"

¹⁴Then the LORD said to Moses, "If her father had but spit in her face, would she not be shamed seven days? Let her be shut out of the camp seven days, and afterward she may be received *again*." ¹⁵So Miriam was shut out of the camp seven days, and the people did not journey till Miriam was brought in *again*. ¹⁶And afterward the people moved from Hazeroth and camped in the Wilderness of Paran.

13:8 ᵃSeptuagint and Vulgate read *Oshea*.

Canaan Before the Conquest

From Kadesh Barnea the Israelites made their first attempt to penetrate the land of Canaan (Num. 13:17–20). Before the arrival of the Israelites, Canaan was divided between dozens of small, relatively independent city-states, each with its own king. After the conquests of the Egyptian pharaoh Thutmose I (1504–1492 B.C.), these Canaanite city-states were officially provinces of Egypt, but as letters from Palestine to Pharaoh Akhenaten show, Egyptian control was not always very firm.

Many of the Canaanite peoples were of Amorite descent, like the Israelites themselves, but later migrations had brought other ethnic groups into the land. Thus the Bible's frequent lists of the peoples to be conquered (Hittites, Hivites, Horites, Jebusites, Girgashites, Perizzites, etc., Num. 13:29) reflect a genuine ethnic mix. Nevertheless, the Bible often uses the term "Amorite" (or sometimes "Canaanite") in a general way, to refer to all or any of the peoples, nations, or tribes living in Palestine.

The city-states within Canaan were established and comparatively strong, while those to the east of the Jordan River were newer and weaker. Thus it makes sense that Israel established its control first in the east.

▪ Numbers 13:1–33

Numbers
Spies Sent into Canaan

13 :1 And the LORD spoke to Moses, saying, ²"Send men to spy out the land of Canaan, which I am giving to the children of Israel; from each tribe of their fathers you shall send a man, every one a leader among them."

³So Moses sent them from the Wilderness of Paran according to the command of the LORD, all of them men who *were* heads of the children of Israel. ⁴Now these *were* their names: from the tribe of Reuben, Shammua the son of Zaccur; ⁵from the tribe of Simeon, Shaphat the son of Hori; ⁶from the tribe of Judah, Caleb the son of Jephunneh; ⁷from the tribe of Issachar, Igal the son of Joseph; ⁸from the tribe of Ephraim, Hosheaᵃ the son of Nun; ⁹from the tribe of Benjamin, Palti the son of Raphu; ¹⁰from the tribe of Zebulun, Gaddiel the son of Sodi; ¹¹from the tribe of Joseph, *that is,* from the tribe of Manasseh, Gaddi the son of Susi; ¹²from the tribe of Dan, Ammiel the son of Gemalli; ¹³from the tribe of Asher, Sethur the son of Michael; ¹⁴from the tribe of Naphtali, Nahbi the son of Vophsi; ¹⁵from the tribe of Gad, Geuel the son of Machi.

¹⁶These *are* the names of the men

LONG GONE BUT NEVER FORGOTTEN—THE NEPHILIM (Num. 13:33)

When the Israelite scouts encountered the inhabitants of the land of Canaan, they reported that they had come across giants (Num. 13:32, 33). In their Hebrew language they referred to these giants as the Nephilim—the descendants of people who had lived before the Flood of Noah (Gen. 6:4). What frightened the spies was the immense size of their enemies: "Surely these people must descend from the intermarriage of the 'sons of God' and their human wives" (Gen. 6:2). The Israelites had thought the Nephilim existed only during the time before the Flood; they did not expect to find them in their own world.

The mythologies of the ancient Near East described a time, before the great flood, when things were different. In those days divinities and humans mated and produced semidivine, semihuman offspring who possessed superhuman qualities. They were the famous persons of ancient times, of which stories continued to be told (surviving in the mythologies of Egypt and Mesopotamia). These persons were considered to be stronger and larger than the current populace (see Num. 13:31).

Two of the spies, Joshua and Caleb, argued that the Nephilim were not too powerful to fight. Their size and lineage (even if they did come from the ancient deity-humans) were not matters to be taken into consideration since God had already promised the victory to the Israelites no matter what the odds (Num. 14:6–9). The people, unfortunately, voted with the other spies, being afraid to fight powerful and, perhaps, supernatural foes.

---

whom Moses sent to spy out the land. And Moses called Hoshea[a] the son of Nun, Joshua.

17Then Moses sent them to spy out the land of Canaan, and said to them, "Go up this *way* into the South, and go up to the mountains, 18and see what the land is like: whether the people who dwell in it *are* strong or weak, few or many; 19whether the land they dwell in *is* good or bad; whether the cities they inhabit *are* like camps or strongholds; 20whether the land *is* rich or poor; and whether there are forests there or not. Be of good courage. And bring some of the fruit of the land." Now the time *was* the season of the first ripe grapes.

21So they went up and spied out the land from the Wilderness of Zin as far as Rehob, near the entrance of Hamath. 22And they went up through the South and came to Hebron; Ahiman, Sheshai, and Talmai, the descendants of Anak, *were* there. (Now Hebron was built seven years before Zoan in Egypt.) 23Then they came to the Valley of Eshcol, and there cut down a branch with one cluster of grapes; they carried it between two of them on a pole. *They* also *brought* some of the pomegranates and figs. 24The place was called the Valley of Eshcol,[a] because of the cluster which the men of Israel cut down there. 25And they returned from spying out the land after forty days.

26Now they departed and came back to Moses and Aaron and all the congregation of the children of Israel in the Wilderness of Paran, at Kadesh; they brought back word to them and to all the congregation, and showed them the fruit of the land. 27Then they told him, and said: "We went to the land where you sent us. It truly flows with milk and honey, and this *is* its fruit. 28Nevertheless the people who dwell in the land *are* strong; the cities *are* fortified *and* very large; moreover we saw the descendants of Anak there. 29The Amalekites dwell in the land of the South; the Hittites, the Jebusites, and the Amorites dwell in the mountains; and the Canaanites dwell by the sea and along the banks of the Jordan."

30Then Caleb quieted the people before Moses, and said, "Let us go up at once and take possession, for we are well able to overcome it."

31But the men who had gone up with him said, "We are not able to go up against the people, for they *are* stronger than we." 32And they gave the children of Israel a bad report of the land which they had spied out, saying, "The land through which we have gone as spies *is* a land that devours its inhabitants, and all the people whom

---

13:16 aSeptuagint and Vulgate read *Oshea*.
13:24 aLiterally *Cluster*

we saw in it *are* men of *great* stature. [33]There we saw the giants[a] (the descendants of Anak came from the giants); and we were like grasshoppers in our own sight, and so we were in their sight."

Israel in the Wilderness

The story continues through the Israelites' tragic refusal at Kadesh Barnea to enter the Promised Land and through the consequent 40 years of wandering in the wilderness (Num. 14:33–35). While Numbers describes the Israelites' journey from Sinai to Kadesh Barnea, and then to the plains of Moab, it reports almost nothing about the 40 years of wandering which intervened between their first departure from Kadesh Barnea (Num. 14:25) and their second (Num. 20:22).

These gaps in the historical record arise because Numbers is not intended to be a history of the Hebrew people. It is a record of the faithfulness of God. Despite the failures of everyone, from the least of the people to Moses himself, God is faithful to His original promise to Abraham and his descendants. This does not mean that individuals escape the consequences of their sin, only that God's redemptive purposes in the world cannot be thwarted.

Thus the stagnant 40 years while the people were simply waiting are omitted as insignificant. Only the events occurring at the beginning and the end of the 40 years are mentioned: the Israelites' defeat when they tried to enter the land on their own strength (Num. 14:45), and their request for permission to pass through Edom (Num. 20:14). Between these events are only various laws and a few stories of the disobedience of key leaders.

▼ ■ Numbers 14:1—20:13

Numbers
Israel Refuses to Enter Canaan

14 :1 So all the congregation lifted up their voices and cried, and the people wept that night. [2]And all the children of Israel complained against Moses and Aaron, and the whole congregation said to them, "If only we had died in the land of Egypt! Or if only we had died in this wilderness! [3]Why has the LORD brought us to this land to fall by the sword, that our wives and children should become victims? Would it not be better for us to return to Egypt?" [4]So they said to one another, "Let us select a leader and return to Egypt."

[5]Then Moses and Aaron fell on their faces before all the assembly of the congregation of the children of Israel.

[6]But Joshua the son of Nun and Caleb the son of Jephunneh, *who were* among those who had spied out the land, tore their clothes; [7]and they spoke to all the congregation of the children of Israel, saying: "The land we passed through to spy out *is* an exceedingly good land. [8]If the LORD delights in us, then He will bring us into this land and give it to us, 'a land which flows with milk and honey.'[a] [9]Only do not rebel against the LORD, nor fear the people of the land, for they *are* our bread; their protection has departed from them, and the LORD *is* with us. Do not fear them."

[10]And all the congregation said to stone them with stones. Now the glory of the LORD appeared in the tabernacle of meeting before all the children of Israel.

Moses Intercedes for the People

[11]Then the LORD said to Moses: "How long will these people reject Me? And how long will they not believe Me, with all the signs which I have performed among them? [12]I will strike them with the pestilence and disinherit them, and I will make of you a nation greater and mightier than they."

[13]And Moses said to the LORD: "Then the Egyptians will hear *it*, for by Your might You brought these people up from among them, [14]and they will tell *it* to the inhabitants of this land. They have heard that You, LORD, *are* among these people; that You, LORD, are seen face to face and Your cloud stands above them, and You go before them in a pillar of cloud by day and in a pillar of fire by night. [15]Now *if* You kill these people as one man, then the nations which have heard of Your fame will speak, saying, [16]'Because the LORD was not able to bring this people to the land which He swore to give them, therefore He killed them in the wilderness.' [17]And now, I pray, let the power of my Lord be great, just as You have spoken, saying, [18]'The LORD is longsuffering and abundant in mercy, forgiving iniquity and transgression; but He by no means clears *the guilty*, visiting the iniquity of the fathers on the children to the third and fourth *generation.*'[a] [19]Pardon the iniquity of this people, I pray, according

13:33 [a]Hebrew *nephilim*   14:8 [a]Exodus 3:8
14:18 [a]Exodus 34:6, 7

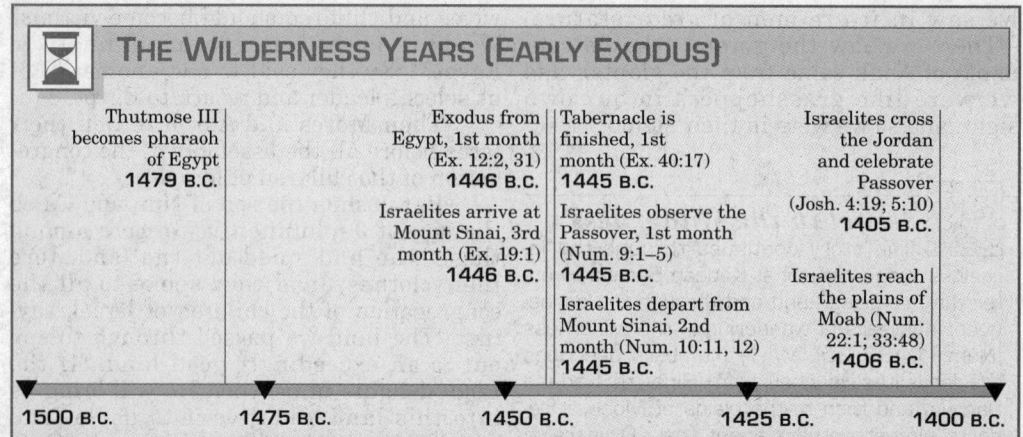

THE WILDERNESS YEARS (EARLY EXODUS)

Thutmose III becomes pharaoh of Egypt **1479 B.C.**	Exodus from Egypt, 1st month (Ex. 12:2, 31) **1446 B.C.** Israelites arrive at Mount Sinai, 3rd month (Ex. 19:1) **1446 B.C.**	Tabernacle is finished, 1st month (Ex. 40:17) **1445 B.C.** Israelites observe the Passover, 1st month (Num. 9:1–5) **1445 B.C.** Israelites depart from Mount Sinai, 2nd month (Num. 10:11, 12) **1445 B.C.**	Israelites cross the Jordan and celebrate Passover (Josh. 4:19; 5:10) **1405 B.C.** Israelites reach the plains of Moab (Num. 22:1; 33:48) **1406 B.C.**
1500 B.C.	**1475 B.C.**	**1450 B.C.**	**1425 B.C.**　　　　**1400 B.C.**

to the greatness of Your mercy, just as You have forgiven this people, from Egypt even until now."

20Then the LORD said: "I have pardoned, according to your word; 21but truly, as I live, all the earth shall be filled with the glory of the LORD— 22because all these men who have seen My glory and the signs which I did in Egypt and in the wilderness, and have put Me to the test now these ten times, and have not heeded My voice, 23they certainly shall not see the land of which I swore to their fathers, nor shall any of those who rejected Me see it. 24But My servant Caleb, because he has a different spirit in him and has followed Me fully, I will bring into the land where he went, and his descendants shall inherit it. 25Now the Amalekites and the Canaanites dwell in the valley; tomorrow turn and move out into the wilderness by the Way of the Red Sea."

Death Sentence on the Rebels

26And the LORD spoke to Moses and Aaron, saying, 27"How long *shall I bear with* this evil congregation who complain against Me? I have heard the complaints which the children of Israel make against Me. 28Say to them, 'As I live,' says the LORD, 'just as you have spoken in My hear-

ing, so I will do to you: 29The carcasses of you who have complained against Me shall fall in this wilderness, all of you who were numbered, according to your entire number, from twenty years old and above. 30Except for Caleb the son of Jephunneh and Joshua the son of Nun, you shall by no means enter the land which I swore I would make you dwell in. 31But your little ones, whom you said would be victims, I will bring in, and they shall know the land which you have despised. 32But *as for* you, your carcasses shall fall in this wilderness. 33And your sons shall be shepherds in the wilderness forty years, and bear the brunt of your infidelity, until your carcasses are consumed in the wilderness. 34According to the number of the days in which you spied out the land, forty days, for each day you shall bear your guilt one year, *namely* forty years, and you shall know My rejection. 35I the LORD have spoken this. I will surely do so to all this evil congregation who are gathered together against Me. In this wilderness they shall be consumed, and there they shall die.' "

36Now the men whom Moses sent to spy out the land, who returned and made all the congregation complain against him by bringing a bad report of the land, 37those very men who brought the evil re-

POLITICS AND GOVERNMENT

The nation-state is an invention of modern times. By contrast, the peoples mentioned in the Bible are usually tribes or single cities, often of very small size. The Amalekites (Num. 14:25) were nomads or seminomads who lived south and west of Canaan. They were traditionally enemies of the Israelites.

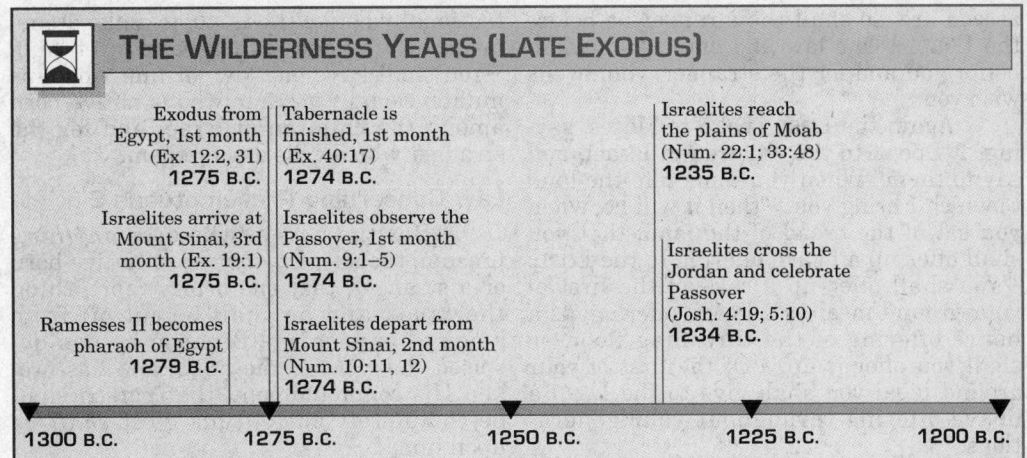

THE WILDERNESS YEARS (LATE EXODUS)

Exodus from Egypt, 1st month (Ex. 12:2, 31) **1275 B.C.**	Tabernacle is finished, 1st month (Ex. 40:17) **1274 B.C.**	Israelites reach the plains of Moab (Num. 22:1; 33:48) **1235 B.C.**
Israelites arrive at Mount Sinai, 3rd month (Ex. 19:1) **1275 B.C.**	Israelites observe the Passover, 1st month (Num. 9:1–5) **1274 B.C.**	Israelites cross the Jordan and celebrate Passover (Josh. 4:19; 5:10) **1234 B.C.**
Ramesses II becomes pharaoh of Egypt **1279 B.C.**	Israelites depart from Mount Sinai, 2nd month (Num. 10:11, 12) **1274 B.C.**	

1300 B.C.	1275 B.C.	1250 B.C.	1225 B.C.	1200 B.C.

port about the land, died by the plague before the LORD. ³⁸But Joshua the son of Nun and Caleb the son of Jephunneh remained alive, of the men who went to spy out the land.

A Futile Invasion Attempt

³⁹Then Moses told these words to all the children of Israel, and the people mourned greatly. ⁴⁰And they rose early in the morning and went up to the top of the mountain, saying, "Here we are, and we will go up to the place which the LORD has promised, for we have sinned!"

⁴¹And Moses said, "Now why do you transgress the command of the LORD? For this will not succeed. ⁴²Do not go up, lest you be defeated by your enemies, for the LORD *is* not among you. ⁴³For the Amalekites and the Canaanites *are* there before you, and you shall fall by the sword; because you have turned away from the LORD, the LORD will not be with you."

⁴⁴But they presumed to go up to the mountaintop. Nevertheless, neither the ark of the covenant of the LORD nor Moses departed from the camp. ⁴⁵Then the Amalekites and the Canaanites who dwelt in that mountain came down and attacked them, and drove them back as far as Hormah.

Laws of Grain and Drink Offerings

15 ¹And the LORD spoke to Moses, saying, ²"Speak to the children of Israel, and say to them: 'When you have come into the land you are to inhabit, which I am giving to you, ³and you make an offering by fire to the LORD, a burnt offering or a sacrifice, to fulfill a vow or as a

freewill offering or in your appointed feasts, to make a sweet aroma to the LORD, from the herd or the flock, ⁴then he who presents his offering to the LORD shall bring a grain offering of one-tenth *of an ephah* of fine flour mixed with one-fourth of a hin of oil; ⁵and one-fourth of a hin of wine as a drink offering you shall prepare with the burnt offering or the sacrifice, for each lamb. ⁶Or for a ram you shall prepare as a grain offering two-tenths *of an ephah* of fine flour mixed with one-third of a hin of oil; ⁷and as a drink offering you shall offer one-third of a hin of wine as a sweet aroma to the LORD. ⁸And when you prepare a young bull as a burnt offering, or as a sacrifice to fulfill a vow, or as a peace offering to the LORD, ⁹then shall be offered with the young bull a grain offering of three-tenths *of an ephah* of fine flour mixed with half a hin of oil; ¹⁰and you shall bring as the drink offering half a hin of wine as an offering made by fire, a sweet aroma to the LORD.

¹¹"Thus it shall be done for each young bull, for each ram, or for each lamb or young goat. ¹²According to the number that you prepare, so you shall do with everyone according to their number. ¹³All who are native-born shall do these things in this manner, in presenting an offering made by fire, a sweet aroma to the LORD. ¹⁴And if a stranger dwells with you, or whoever *is* among you throughout your generations, and would present an offering made by fire, a sweet aroma to the LORD, just as you do, so shall he do. ¹⁵One ordinance *shall be* for you of the assembly and for the stranger who dwells *with you,* an ordinance forever throughout your generations;

as you are, so shall the stranger be before the LORD. [16]One law and one custom shall be for you and for the stranger who dwells with you.' "[a]

[17]Again the LORD spoke to Moses, saying, [18]"Speak to the children of Israel, and say to them: 'When you come into the land to which I bring you, [19]then it will be, when you eat of the bread of the land, that you shall offer up a heave offering to the LORD. [20]You shall offer up a cake of the first of your ground meal *as* a heave offering; as a heave offering of the threshing floor, so shall you offer it up. [21]Of the first of your ground meal you shall give to the LORD a heave offering throughout your generations.

Laws Concerning Unintentional Sin

[22]'If you sin unintentionally, and do not observe all these commandments which the LORD has spoken to Moses— [23]all that the LORD has commanded you by the hand of Moses, from the day the LORD gave commandment and onward throughout your generations— [24]then it will be, if it is unintentionally committed, without the knowledge of the congregation, that the whole congregation shall offer one young bull as a burnt offering, as a sweet aroma to the LORD, with its grain offering and its drink offering, according to the ordinance, and one kid of the goats as a sin offering. [25]So the priest shall make atonement for the whole congregation of the children of Israel, and it shall be forgiven them, for it was unintentional; they shall bring their offering, an offering made by fire to the LORD, and their sin offering before the LORD, for their unintended sin. [26]It shall be forgiven the whole congregation of the children of Israel and the stranger who dwells among them, because all the people *did it* unintentionally.

[27]'And if a person sins unintentionally, then he shall bring a female goat in its first year as a sin offering. [28]So the priest shall make atonement for the person who sins unintentionally, when he sins unin-

tentionally before the LORD, to make atonement for him; and it shall be forgiven him. [29]You shall have one law for him who sins unintentionally, *for* him who is native-born among the children of Israel and for the stranger who dwells among them.

Law Concerning Presumptuous Sin

[30]'But the person who does *anything* presumptuously, *whether he is* native-born or a stranger, that one brings reproach on the LORD, and he shall be cut off from among his people. [31]Because he has despised the word of the LORD, and has broken His commandment, that person shall be completely cut off; his guilt *shall be* upon him.' "

Penalty for Violating the Sabbath

[32]Now while the children of Israel were in the wilderness, they found a man gathering sticks on the Sabbath day. [33]And those who found him gathering sticks brought him to Moses and Aaron, and to all the congregation. [34]They put him under guard, because it had not been explained what should be done to him.

[35]Then the LORD said to Moses, "The man must surely be put to death; all the congregation shall stone him with stones outside the camp." [36]So, as the LORD commanded Moses, all the congregation brought him outside the camp and stoned him with stones, and he died.

Tassels on Garments

[37]Again the LORD spoke to Moses, saying, [38]"Speak to the children of Israel: Tell them to make tassels on the corners of their garments throughout their generations, and to put a blue thread in the tassels of the corners. [39]And you shall have the tassel, that you may look upon it and remember all the commandments of the LORD and do them, and that you *may* not follow the harlotry to which your own heart and your own eyes are inclined, [40]and that

15:16 [a]Compare Exodus 12:49

DAILY LIFE AND CUSTOMS

The tassels were made by twisting and knotting the threads of the fabric in the outer garment. This element of the garment, still used today at prayer, was assigned a mnemonic (memory) function (Num. 15:39). The permanence of the Scripture text has assured the permanence of the mnemonic sign as well.

you may remember and do all My commandments, and be holy for your God. ⁴¹I *am* the LORD your God, who brought you out of the land of Egypt, to be your God: I *am* the LORD your God."

Rebellion Against Moses and Aaron

16 ¹Now Korah the son of Izhar, the son of Kohath, the son of Levi, with Dathan and Abiram the sons of Eliab, and On the son of Peleth, sons of Reuben, took *men;* ²and they rose up before Moses with some of the children of Israel, two hundred and fifty leaders of the congregation, representatives of the congregation, men of renown. ³They gathered together against Moses and Aaron, and said to them, "*You take* too much upon yourselves, for all the congregation *is* holy, every one of them, and the LORD *is* among them. Why then do you exalt yourselves above the assembly of the LORD?"

⁴So when Moses heard *it,* he fell on his face; ⁵and he spoke to Korah and all his company, saying, "Tomorrow morning the LORD will show who *is* His and *who is* holy, and will cause *him* to come near to Him. That one whom He chooses He will cause to come near to Him. ⁶Do this: Take censers, Korah and all your company; ⁷put fire in them and put incense in them before the LORD tomorrow, and it shall be *that* the man whom the LORD chooses *is* the holy one. *You take* too much upon yourselves, you sons of Levi!"

⁸Then Moses said to Korah, "Hear now, you sons of Levi: ⁹*Is it* a small thing to you that the God of Israel has separated you from the congregation of Israel, to bring you near to Himself, to do the work of the tabernacle of the LORD, and to stand before the congregation to serve them; ¹⁰and that He has brought you near *to Himself,* you and all your brethren, the sons of Levi, with you? And are you seeking the priesthood also? ¹¹Therefore you and all your company *are* gathered together against the LORD. And what *is* Aaron that you complain against him?"

¹²And Moses sent to call Dathan and Abiram the sons of Eliab, but they said, "We will not come up! ¹³*Is it* a small thing that you have brought us up out of a land flowing with milk and honey, to kill us in the wilderness, that you should keep acting like a prince over us? ¹⁴Moreover you have not brought us into a land flowing with milk and honey, nor given us inheritance of fields and vineyards. Will you put out the eyes of these men? We will not come up!"

¹⁵Then Moses was very angry, and said to the LORD, "Do not respect their offering. I have not taken one donkey from them, nor have I hurt one of them."

¹⁶And Moses said to Korah, "Tomorrow, you and all your company be present before the LORD—you and they, as well as Aaron. ¹⁷Let each take his censer and put incense in it, and each of you bring his censer before the LORD, two hundred and fifty censers; both you and Aaron, each *with* his censer." ¹⁸So every man took his censer, put fire in it, laid incense on it, and stood at the door of the tabernacle of meeting with Moses and Aaron. ¹⁹And Korah gathered all the congregation against them at the door of the tabernacle of meeting. Then the glory of the LORD appeared to all the congregation.

²⁰And the LORD spoke to Moses and Aaron, saying, ²¹"Separate yourselves from among this congregation, that I may consume them in a moment."

²²Then they fell on their faces, and said, "O God, the God of the spirits of all flesh, shall one man sin, and You be angry with all the congregation?"

²³So the LORD spoke to Moses, saying, ²⁴"Speak to the congregation, saying, 'Get away from the tents of Korah, Dathan, and Abiram.'"

²⁵Then Moses rose and went to Dathan and Abiram, and the elders of Israel followed him. ²⁶And he spoke to the congregation, saying, "Depart now from the tents of these wicked men! Touch nothing of theirs, lest you be consumed in all their sins." ²⁷So they got away from around the tents of Korah, Dathan, and Abiram; and Dathan and Abiram came out and stood at the door of their tents, with their wives, their sons, and their little children.

²⁸And Moses said: "By this you shall know that the LORD has sent me to do all these works, for *I have* not *done them* of my own will. ²⁹If these men die naturally like all men, or if they are visited by the common fate of all men, *then* the LORD has not sent me. ³⁰But if the LORD creates a new thing, and the earth opens its mouth and swallows them up with all that belongs to them, and they go down alive into the pit, then you will understand that these men have rejected the LORD."

³¹Now it came to pass, as he finished speaking all these words, that the ground

SINUHE VISITS A FERTILE PALESTINE (Num. 16:12, 13)

The report of the spies to Moses was that the land Palestine "flows with milk and honey" (Num. 13:23, 27). Although the sons of Eliab questioned the truth of this report (Num. 16:12, 13), the fertility of Palestine was known long before the Israelites arrived. A similar description is found in an Egyptian text of the Middle Kingdom which covers events from the reigns of two pharaohs—Amenemhet I (1963–1934 B.C.) and Sesostris I (1943–1898 B.C.). The *Tale of Sinuhe* describes the travels and ordeals in Palestine of an Egyptian official by the name Sinuhe.

Sinuhe, according to the text, was a high official in the court of Pharaoh Amenemhet I. During an unstable period of change in power in Egypt, Sinuhe fled to Palestine. The land of Palestine was then called "Retenu" in Egyptian texts, and was usually thought of as northern Canaan and southern and central Syria. Sinuhe records his many trials and tribulations in the region.

On one occasion, Sinuhe settles with a certain Ammienshi, called the ruler of Upper Retenu. The Egyptian official describes the area as having figs and grapes. "It had more wine than water. Plentiful was its honey, abundant its olives. Every kind of fruit was on its trees. Barley was there, and emmer." Milk was used in "every kind of cooking."

The Egyptian text is the earliest account of conditions in Palestine during the period of the biblical patriarchs. It appears to accord well with descriptions found in the five books of the Pentateuch. Both the *Tale of Sinuhe* and the Pentateuch describe Palestine during this time as fertile but politically unstable and sparsely populated.

---

split apart under them, ³²and the earth opened its mouth and swallowed them up, with their households and all the men with Korah, with all *their* goods. ³³So they and all those with them went down alive into the pit; the earth closed over them, and they perished from among the assembly. ³⁴Then all Israel who *were* around them fled at their cry, for they said, "Lest the earth swallow us up *also!*"

³⁵And a fire came out from the LORD and consumed the two hundred and fifty men who were offering incense.

³⁶Then the LORD spoke to Moses, saying: ³⁷"Tell Eleazar, the son of Aaron the priest, to pick up the censers out of the blaze, for they are holy, and scatter the fire some distance away. ³⁸The censers of these men who sinned against their own souls, let them be made into hammered plates as a covering for the altar. Because they presented them before the LORD, therefore they are holy; and they shall be a sign to the children of Israel." ³⁹So Eleazar the priest took the bronze censers, which those who were burned up had presented, and they were hammered out as a covering on the altar, ⁴⁰*to be* a memorial to the children of Israel that no outsider, who *is* not a descendant of Aaron, should come near to offer incense before the LORD, that he might not become like Korah and his companions, just as the LORD had said to him through Moses.

Complaints of the People

⁴¹On the next day all the congregation of the children of Israel complained against Moses and Aaron, saying, "You have killed the people of the LORD." ⁴²Now it happened, when the congregation had gathered against Moses and Aaron, that they turned toward the tabernacle of meeting; and suddenly the cloud covered it, and the glory of the LORD appeared. ⁴³Then Moses and Aaron came before the tabernacle of meeting.

⁴⁴And the LORD spoke to Moses, saying, ⁴⁵"Get away from among this congregation, that I may consume them in a moment."

And they fell on their faces.

⁴⁶So Moses said to Aaron, "Take a censer and put fire in it from the altar, put incense *on it,* and take it quickly to the congregation and make atonement for them; for wrath has gone out from the LORD. The plague has begun." ⁴⁷Then Aaron took *it* as Moses commanded, and ran into the midst of the assembly; and already the plague had begun among the people. So he put in the incense and made

atonement for the people. ⁴⁸And he stood between the dead and the living; so the plague was stopped. ⁴⁹Now those who died in the plague were fourteen thousand seven hundred, besides those who died in the Korah incident. ⁵⁰So Aaron returned to Moses at the door of the tabernacle of meeting, for the plague had stopped.

The Budding of Aaron's Rod

17 ¹And the LORD spoke to Moses, saying: ²"Speak to the children of Israel, and get from them a rod from each father's house, all their leaders according to their fathers' houses—twelve rods. Write each man's name on his rod. ³And you shall write Aaron's name on the rod of Levi. For there shall be one rod for the head of *each* father's house. ⁴Then you shall place them in the tabernacle of meeting before the Testimony, where I meet with you. ⁵And it shall be *that* the rod of the man whom I choose will blossom; thus I will rid Myself of the complaints of the children of Israel, which they make against you."

⁶So Moses spoke to the children of Israel, and each of their leaders gave him a rod apiece, for each leader according to their fathers' houses, twelve rods; and the rod of Aaron *was* among their rods. ⁷And Moses placed the rods before the LORD in the tabernacle of witness.

⁸Now it came to pass on the next day that Moses went into the tabernacle of witness, and behold, the rod of Aaron, of the house of Levi, had sprouted and put forth buds, had produced blossoms and yielded ripe almonds. ⁹Then Moses brought out all the rods from before the LORD to all the children of Israel; and they looked, and each man took his rod.

¹⁰And the LORD said to Moses, "Bring

Aaron's rod back before the Testimony, to be kept as a sign against the rebels, that you may put their complaints away from Me, lest they die." ¹¹Thus did Moses; just as the LORD had commanded him, so he did.

¹²So the children of Israel spoke to Moses, saying, "Surely we die, we perish, we all perish! ¹³Whoever even comes near the tabernacle of the LORD must die. Shall we all utterly die?"

Duties of Priests and Levites

18 ¹Then the LORD said to Aaron: "You and your sons and your father's house with you shall bear the iniquity *related to* the sanctuary, and you and your sons with you shall bear the iniquity *associated with* your priesthood. ²Also bring with you your brethren of the tribe of Levi, the tribe of your father, that they may be joined with you and serve you while you and your sons *are* with you before the tabernacle of witness. ³They shall attend to your needs and all the needs of the tabernacle; but they shall not come near the articles of the sanctuary and the altar, lest they die—they and you also. ⁴They shall be joined with you and attend to the needs of the tabernacle of meeting, for all the work of the tabernacle; but an outsider shall not come near you. ⁵And you shall attend to the duties of the sanctuary and the duties of the altar, that there *may* be no more wrath on the children of Israel. ⁶Behold, I Myself have taken your brethren the Levites from among the children of Israel; *they are* a gift to you, given by the LORD, to do the work of the tabernacle of meeting. ⁷Therefore you and your sons with you shall attend to your priesthood for everything at the altar and behind the veil; and you shall serve. I give your priesthood *to you* as a gift for service, but the outsider who comes near shall be put to death."

Offerings for Support of the Priests

⁸And the LORD spoke to Aaron: "Here, I Myself have also given you charge of My heave offerings, all the holy gifts of the children of Israel; I have given them as a portion to you and your sons, as an ordinance forever. ⁹This shall be yours of the most holy things *reserved* from the fire: every offering of theirs, every grain offering and every sin offering and every trespass offering which they render to Me, *shall be* most holy for you and your sons.

TIME CAPSULE　*1400 to 1366 B.C.*

1400　Oldest discovered water clock, from Egypt

1400　Spectators on a grandstand shown in a mural, Crete

1400–1390　Thutmose IV, pharaoh of Egypt

1390–1352　Amenhotep III, pharaoh of Egypt, rules during period of peace

1366　Hittite king Suppiluliumas invades Syria and captures Alalakh

[10]In a most holy *place* you shall eat it; every male shall eat it. It shall be holy to you.

[11]"This also *is* yours: the heave offering of their gift, with all the wave offerings of the children of Israel; I have given them to you, and your sons and daughters with you, as an ordinance forever. Everyone who is clean in your house may eat it.

[12]"All the best of the oil, all the best of the new wine and the grain, their first-fruits which they offer to the LORD, I have given them to you. [13]Whatever first ripe fruit is in their land, which they bring to the LORD, shall be yours. Everyone who is clean in your house may eat it.

[14]"Every devoted thing in Israel shall be yours.

[15]"Everything that first opens the womb of all flesh, which they bring to the LORD, whether man or beast, shall be yours; nevertheless the firstborn of man you shall surely redeem, and the firstborn of unclean animals you shall redeem. [16]And those redeemed of the devoted things you shall redeem when one month old, according to your valuation, for five shekels of silver, according to the shekel of the sanctuary, which *is* twenty gerahs. [17]But the firstborn of a cow, the firstborn of a sheep, or the firstborn of a goat you shall not redeem; they *are* holy. You shall sprinkle their blood on the altar, and burn their fat *as* an offering made by fire for a sweet aroma to the LORD. [18]And their flesh shall be yours, just as the wave breast and the right thigh are yours.

[19]"All the heave offerings of the holy things, which the children of Israel offer to the LORD, I have given to you and your sons and daughters with you as an ordinance forever; it *is* a covenant of salt forever before the LORD with you and your descendants with you."

[20]Then the LORD said to Aaron: "You shall have no inheritance in their land, nor shall you have any portion among them; I *am* your portion and your inheritance among the children of Israel.

Tithes for Support of the Levites

[21]"Behold, I have given the children of Levi all the tithes in Israel as an inheritance in return for the work which they perform, the work of the tabernacle of meeting. [22]Hereafter the children of Israel shall not come near the tabernacle of meeting, lest they bear sin and die. [23]But the Levites shall perform the work of the tabernacle of meeting, and they shall bear their iniquity; *it shall be* a statute forever, throughout your generations, that among the children of Israel they shall have no inheritance. [24]For the tithes of the children of Israel, which they offer up *as* a heave offering to the LORD, I have given to the Levites as an inheritance; therefore I have said to them, 'Among the children of Israel they shall have no inheritance.'"

The Tithe of the Levites

[25]Then the LORD spoke to Moses, saying, [26]"Speak thus to the Levites, and say to them: 'When you take from the children of Israel the tithes which I have given you from them as your inheritance, then you shall offer up a heave offering of it to the LORD, a tenth of the tithe. [27]And your heave offering shall be reckoned to you as though *it were* the grain of the threshing floor and as the fullness of the winepress. [28]Thus you shall also offer a heave offering to the LORD from all your tithes which you receive from the children of Israel, and you shall give the LORD's heave offering from it to Aaron the priest. [29]Of all your gifts you shall offer up every heave offering due to the LORD, from all the best of them, the consecrated part of them.' [30]Therefore you shall say to them: 'When you have lifted up the best of it, then *the rest* shall be accounted to the Levites as the produce of the threshing floor and as the produce of the winepress. [31]You may eat it in any place, you and your households, for it *is* your reward for your work in the tabernacle of meeting. [32]And you shall bear no sin because of it, when you have lifted up the best of it. But you shall not profane the holy gifts of the children of Israel, lest you die.'"

Laws of Purification

19 [1]Now the LORD spoke to Moses and Aaron, saying, [2]"This *is* the ordinance of the law which the LORD has commanded, saying: 'Speak to the children of Israel, that they bring you a red heifer without blemish, in which there *is* no defect *and* on which a yoke has never come. [3]You shall give it to Eleazar the priest, that he may take it outside the camp, and it shall be slaughtered before him; [4]and Eleazar the priest shall take some of its blood with his finger, and sprinkle some of its blood seven times directly in front of the tabernacle of meeting. ⁵Then the heifer shall be burned in his sight: its hide, its flesh, its blood, and its offal shall be burned. ⁶And the priest shall take cedar wood and hyssop and scarlet, and cast *them* into the midst of the fire burning the heifer. ⁷Then the priest shall wash his clothes, he shall bathe in water, and afterward he shall come into the camp; the priest shall be unclean until evening. ⁸And the one who burns it shall wash his clothes in water, bathe in water, and shall be unclean until evening. ⁹Then a man *who is* clean shall gather up the ashes of the heifer, and store *them* outside the camp in a clean place; and they shall be kept for the congregation of the children of Israel for the water of purification;ᵃ it *is* for purifying from sin. ¹⁰And the one who gathers the ashes of the heifer shall wash his clothes, and be unclean until evening. It shall be a statute forever to the children of Israel and to the stranger who dwells among them.

¹¹'He who touches the dead body of anyone shall be unclean seven days. ¹²He shall purify himself with the water on the third day and on the seventh day; *then* he will be clean. But if he does not purify himself on the third day and on the seventh day, he will not be clean. ¹³Whoever touches the body of anyone who has died, and does not purify himself, defiles the tabernacle of the LORD. That person shall be cut off from Israel. He shall be unclean, because the water of purification was not sprinkled on him; his uncleanness *is* still on him.

¹⁴'This *is* the law when a man dies in a tent: All who come into the tent and all who *are* in the tent shall be unclean seven days; ¹⁵and every open vessel, which has no cover fastened on it, *is* unclean. ¹⁶Whoever in the open field touches one who is slain by a sword or who has died, or a bone of a man, or a grave, shall be unclean seven days.

¹⁷'And for an unclean *person* they shall take some of the ashes of the heifer burnt for purification from sin, and running water shall be put on them in a vessel. ¹⁸A clean person shall take hyssop and dip *it* in the water, sprinkle *it* on the tent, on all the vessels, on the persons who were there, or on the one who touched a bone, the slain, the dead, or a grave. ¹⁹The clean *person* shall sprinkle the unclean on the third day and on the seventh day; and on the seventh day he shall purify himself, wash his clothes, and bathe in water; and at evening he shall be clean.

²⁰'But the man who is unclean and does not purify himself, that person shall be cut off from among the assembly, because he has defiled the sanctuary of the LORD. The water of purification has not been sprinkled on him; he *is* unclean. ²¹It shall be a perpetual statute for them. He who sprinkles the water of purification shall wash his clothes; and he who touches the water of purification shall be unclean until evening. ²²Whatever the unclean *person* touches shall be unclean; and the person who touches *it* shall be unclean until evening.' "

Moses' Error at Kadesh

20 ¹Then the children of Israel, the whole congregation, came into the Wilderness of Zin in the first month, and the people stayed in Kadesh; and Miriam died there and was buried there.

²Now there was no water for the congregation; so they gathered together against Moses and Aaron. ³And the people contended with Moses and spoke, saying: "If only we had died when our brethren died before the LORD! ⁴Why have you brought up the assembly of the LORD into this wilderness, that we and our animals should die here? ⁵And why have you made us come up out of Egypt, to bring us to this evil place? It *is* not a place of grain or figs or vines or pomegranates; nor *is* there any water to drink." ⁶So Moses and Aaron went from the presence of the assembly to the door of the tabernacle of meeting, and they

19:9 ᵃLiterally *impurity*

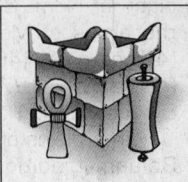

fell on their faces. And the glory of the LORD appeared to them.

7Then the LORD spoke to Moses, saying, 8"Take the rod; you and your brother Aaron gather the congregation together. Speak to the rock before their eyes, and it will yield its water; thus you shall bring water for them out of the rock, and give drink to the congregation and their animals." 9So Moses took the rod from before the LORD as He commanded him.

10And Moses and Aaron gathered the assembly together before the rock; and he said to them, "Hear now, you rebels! Must we bring water for you out of this rock?" 11Then Moses lifted his hand and struck the rock twice with his rod; and water came out abundantly, and the congregation and their animals drank.

12Then the LORD spoke to Moses and Aaron, "Because you did not believe Me, to hallow Me in the eyes of the children of Israel, therefore you shall not bring this assembly into the land which I have given them."

13This *was* the water of Meribah,a because the children of Israel contended with the LORD, and He was hallowed among them.

Moab: On the Doorstep of Canaan

The narrative of Numbers concludes with the Israelites once more at Kadesh Barnea (Num. 20:1, 14). The issue now is whether this new generation would believe after their fathers had not. As they prepare to journey from Kadesh toward the plains of Moab, they are ready to hear once more God's command to enter the land of Canaan.

The account of Aaron's death on Mount Hor (Num. 20:22–29) indicates the 40th year after the Exodus, and thus the last year of the wilderness wandering. In the list of Israel's wilderness journeys in ch. 33, Aaron's death is placed in the 5th month of the 40th year after the Israelites' departure from Egypt (Num. 33:3, 37, 38). Calculating by this tradition of Num. 33, Israel would have reached the plains of Moab either around 1406 B.C. (40 years = 1446–1406) or around 1235 B.C. (40 years = 1275–1235; see "Egypt and the Exodus" at Ex. 1:1).

The plains of Moab are the setting for the Balaam traditions. An Aramaic inscription found in the area east of the Jordan mentions a seer named Balaam. If this is the same Balaam described in Num. 22—24, then he was quite famous, which would explain King Balak's obvious respect for his powers (Num. 22:4-6).

■ Numbers 20:14—36:13

Numbers
Passage Through Edom Refused

20:14 Now Moses sent messengers from Kadesh to the king of Edom. "Thus says your brother Israel: 'You know all the hardship that has befallen us, 15how our fathers went down to Egypt, and we dwelt in Egypt a long time, and the Egyptians afflicted us and our fathers. 16When we cried out to the LORD, He heard our voice and sent the Angel and brought us up out of Egypt; now here we are in Kadesh, a city on the edge of your border. 17Please let us pass through your country. We will not pass through fields or vineyards, nor will we drink water from wells; we will go along the King's Highway; we will not turn aside to the right hand or to the left until we have passed through your territory.' "

18Then Edom said to him, "You shall not pass through my *land,* lest I come out against you with the sword."

19So the children of Israel said to him, "We will go by the Highway, and if I or my livestock drink any of your water, then I will pay for it; let me only pass through on foot, nothing *more.*"

20Then he said, "You shall not pass through." So Edom came out against them with many men and with a strong hand. 21Thus Edom refused to give Israel passage through his territory; so Israel turned away from him.

Death of Aaron

22Now the children of Israel, the whole congregation, journeyed from Kadesh and came to Mount Hor. 23And the LORD spoke to Moses and Aaron in Mount Hor by the border of the land of Edom, saying: 24"Aaron shall be gathered to his people, for he shall not enter the land which I have given to the children of Israel, because you rebelled against My word at the water of Meribah. 25Take Aaron and Eleazar his son, and bring them up to Mount Hor; 26and strip Aaron of his garments and put

20:13 aLiterally *Contention*

them on Eleazar his son; for Aaron shall be gathered *to his people* and die there." ²⁷So Moses did just as the LORD commanded, and they went up to Mount Hor in the sight of all the congregation. ²⁸Moses stripped Aaron of his garments and put them on Eleazar his son; and Aaron died there on the top of the mountain. Then Moses and Eleazar came down from the mountain. ²⁹Now when all the congregation saw that Aaron was dead, all the house of Israel mourned for Aaron thirty days.

Canaanites Defeated at Hormah

21 ¹The king of Arad, the Canaanite, who dwelt in the South, heard that Israel was coming on the road to Atharim. Then he fought against Israel and took *some* of them prisoners. ²So Israel made a vow to the LORD, and said, "If You will indeed deliver this people into my hand, then I will utterly destroy their cities." ³And the LORD listened to the voice of Israel and delivered up the Canaanites, and they utterly destroyed them and their cities. So the name of that place was called Hormah.ᵃ

The Bronze Serpent

⁴Then they journeyed from Mount Hor by the Way of the Red Sea, to go around the land of Edom; and the soul of the people became very discouraged on the way. ⁵And the people spoke against God and against Moses: "Why have you brought us up out of Egypt to die in the wilderness? For *there is* no food and no water, and our soul loathes this worthless bread." ⁶So the LORD sent fiery serpents among the people, and they bit the people; and many of the people of Israel died.

⁷Therefore the people came to Moses, and said, "We have sinned, for we have spoken against the LORD and against you; pray to the LORD that He take away the serpents from us." So Moses prayed for the people.

⁸Then the LORD said to Moses, "Make a fiery *serpent,* and set it on a pole; and it shall be that everyone who is bitten, when he looks at it, shall live." ⁹So Moses made a bronze serpent, and put it on a pole; and so it was, if a serpent had bitten anyone, when he looked at the bronze serpent, he lived.

From Mount Hor to Moab

¹⁰Now the children of Israel moved on and camped in Oboth. ¹¹And they journeyed from Oboth and camped at Ije Abarim, in the wilderness which *is* east of Moab, toward the sunrise. ¹²From there they moved and camped in the Valley of Zered. ¹³From there they moved and camped on the other side of the Arnon, which *is* in the wilderness that extends from the border of the Amorites; for the Arnon *is* the border of Moab, between Moab and the Amorites. ¹⁴Therefore it is said in the Book of the Wars of the LORD:

> "Waheb in Suphah,ᵃ
> The brooks of the Arnon,
> 15 And the slope of the brooks
> That reaches to the dwelling of Ar,
> And lies on the border of Moab."

¹⁶From there *they went* to Beer, which *is* the well where the LORD said to Moses, "Gather the people together, and I will give them water." ¹⁷Then Israel sang this song:

> "Spring up, O well!
> All of you sing to it—
> 18 The well the leaders sank,
> Dug by the nation's nobles,
> By the lawgiver, with their staves."

And from the wilderness *they went* to Mattanah, ¹⁹from Mattanah to Nahaliel, from Nahaliel to Bamoth, ²⁰and from Bamoth, *in* the valley that *is* in the country of Moab, to the top of Pisgah which looks down on the wasteland.ᵃ

21:3 ᵃLiterally *Utter Destruction*   21:14 ᵃAncient unknown places; Vulgate reads *What He did in the Red Sea.*   21:20 ᵃHebrew *Jeshimon*

Arts and Literature

The Book of the Wars of the LORD (Num. 21:14) has not been preserved, but part of its contents were evidently songs composed in the wilderness. Folk songs and even nursery rhymes can preserve names of places and historical events. Frequently the reference is brief or like a riddle, and the underlying history is then hard to discover.

A Quick Cure for Snakebite (Num. 21:4–9)

The bronze serpent on a pole that Moses made in the wilderness functioned as a cure for venomous snakebites (Num. 21:4–9). Scholars have suggested three explanations for what appears to be a type of magical medicine. Each of the three may express something about what the people of Israel understand concerning this serpent.

One suggestion is that the image of the fiery serpent was merely an object of sympathetic magic. The bronze serpent, representing the actual snake that bit the victim, was presented as a way of removing the poison from the snakebite. Magic amulets or charms for warding off and then curing illnesses and poisons were used everywhere in the ancient Near East. A number of copper and bronze serpent figures have been recovered, showing that the practice was widespread.

A second possibility is that the object symbolized God's power over the snakes. The bronze serpent would have been a sort of specialized worship item for those with snakebites. The "glance" toward the object would have been a plea or prayer to God for help. The bronze serpent was only an aid to the prayer, while the cure would have come from God.

Yet a third suggestion supposes the bronze serpent to have been an intermediary between God and the people. In the ancient Near East, the highest god of a pantheon could create new deities for specific purposes. The Israelites would have understood the bronze serpent as a lesser divine being created expressly to cure their particular kind of snakebites. Among the mythological texts of Ugarit (13th century B.C.) is the *Legend of Keret*. In this story the god El creates the goddess Shatiqatu solely to cure King Keret from an illness no other deity could handle.

This third understanding possibly explains what happened later as the bronze serpent was incorporated into the Israelite worship of God. It had been created by Moses and had been part of the religious world of Israel and Judah since before the settlement in Canaan. But by the time of Hezekiah (715–686 B.C.) Judahites worshiped it as Nehushtan (2 Kin. 18:4), possibly considering it a minor deity. The people's devotion to the bronze serpent was condemned by Hezekiah, who had it destroyed.

King Sihon Defeated

21Then Israel sent messengers to Sihon king of the Amorites, saying, 22"Let me pass through your land. We will not turn aside into fields or vineyards; we will not drink water from wells. We will go by the King's Highway until we have passed through your territory." 23But Sihon would not allow Israel to pass through his territory. So Sihon gathered all his people together and went out against Israel in the wilderness, and he came to Jahaz and fought against Israel. 24Then Israel defeated him with the edge of the sword, and took possession of his land from the Arnon to the Jabbok, as far as the people of Ammon; for the border of the people of Ammon *was* fortified. 25So Israel took all these cities, and Israel dwelt in all the cities of the Amorites, in Heshbon and in all its villages. 26For Heshbon *was* the city of Sihon king of the Amorites, who had fought against the former king of Moab, and had taken all his land from his hand as far as the Arnon. 27Therefore those who speak in proverbs say:

"Come to Heshbon, let it be built;
Let the city of Sihon be repaired.

28 "For fire went out from Heshbon,
A flame from the city of Sihon;
It consumed Ar of Moab,
The lords of the heights of the Arnon.
29 Woe to you, Moab!
You have perished, O people of
    Chemosh!
He has given his sons as fugitives,
And his daughters into captivity,
To Sihon king of the Amorites.

30 "But we have shot at them;
Heshbon has perished as far as Dibon.
Then we laid waste as far as Nophah,
Which *reaches* to Medeba."

³¹Thus Israel dwelt in the land of the Amorites. ³²Then Moses sent to spy out Jazer; and they took its villages and drove out the Amorites who *were* there.

King Og Defeated

³³And they turned and went up by the way to Bashan. So Og king of Bashan went out against them, he and all his people, to battle at Edrei. ³⁴Then the LORD said to Moses, "Do not fear him, for I have delivered him into your hand, with all his people and his land; and you shall do to him as you did to Sihon king of the Amorites, who dwelt at Heshbon." ³⁵So they defeated him, his sons, and all his people, until there was no survivor left him; and they took possession of his land.

Balak Sends for Balaam

22 ¹Then the children of Israel moved, and camped in the plains of Moab on the side of the Jordan *across from* Jericho.

²Now Balak the son of Zippor saw all that Israel had done to the Amorites. ³And Moab was exceedingly afraid of the people because they *were* many, and Moab was sick with dread because of the children of Israel. ⁴So Moab said to the elders of Midian, "Now this company will lick up everything around us, as an ox licks up the grass of the field." And Balak the son of Zippor *was* king of the Moabites at that time. ⁵Then he sent messengers to Balaam the son of Beor at Pethor, which *is* near the River[a] in the land of the sons of his people,[b] to call him, saying: "Look, a people has come from Egypt. See, they cover the face of the earth, and are settling next to me! ⁶Therefore please come at once, curse this people for me, for they *are* too mighty for me. Perhaps I shall be able to defeat them and drive them out of the land, for I know that he whom you bless *is* blessed, and he whom you curse is cursed."

⁷So the elders of Moab and the elders of Midian departed with the diviner's fee in their hand, and they came to Balaam and spoke to him the words of Balak. ⁸And he said to them, "Lodge here tonight, and I will bring back word to you, as the LORD speaks to me." So the princes of Moab stayed with Balaam.

⁹Then God came to Balaam and said, "Who *are* these men with you?"

¹⁰So Balaam said to God, "Balak the son of Zippor, king of Moab, has sent to me, *saying,* ¹¹'Look, a people has come out of Egypt, and they cover the face of the earth. Come now, curse them for me; perhaps I shall be able to overpower them and drive them out.' "

¹²And God said to Balaam, "You shall not go with them; you shall not curse the people, for they *are* blessed."

¹³So Balaam rose in the morning and said to the princes of Balak, "Go back to your land, for the LORD has refused to give me permission to go with you."

¹⁴And the princes of Moab rose and went to Balak, and said, "Balaam refuses to come with us."

¹⁵Then Balak again sent princes, more numerous and more honorable than they. ¹⁶And they came to Balaam and said to him, "Thus says Balak the son of Zippor: 'Please let nothing hinder you from coming to me; ¹⁷for I will certainly honor you greatly, and I will do whatever you say to me. Therefore please come, curse this people for me.' "

¹⁸Then Balaam answered and said to the servants of Balak, "Though Balak were to give me his house full of silver and gold, I could not go beyond the word of the LORD my God, to do less or more. ¹⁹Now therefore, please, you also stay here tonight, that I may know what more the LORD will say to me."

²⁰And God came to Balaam at night and said to him, "If the men come to call you, rise *and* go with them; but only the word which I speak to you—that you shall do." ²¹So Balaam rose in the morning, saddled his donkey, and went with the princes of Moab.

Balaam, the Donkey, and the Angel

²²Then God's anger was aroused because he went, and the Angel of the LORD took His stand in the way as an adversary against him. And he was riding on his donkey, and his two servants *were* with him. ²³Now the donkey saw the Angel of the LORD standing in the way with His drawn sword in His hand, and the donkey turned aside out of the way and went into the field. So Balaam struck the donkey to turn her back onto the road. ²⁴Then the Angel of the LORD stood in a narrow path between the vineyards, *with* a wall on this side and

22:5 [a]That is, the Euphrates [b]Or *the people of Amau*

BALAAM: PROPHET FOR HIRE (Num. 22:5, 6)

Balaam son of Beor is the famous prophet of Num. 22—24 whose services were requested by Balak, king of Moab. The Israelites were crossing through Moab at the time, and Balak was uncomfortable with such a large group of people in his land. So he called on the prophet to curse the Israelites in the name of God.

Normally a ruler would call on his own professional court prophets for such an undertaking. The blessing or cursing of neighboring kingdoms was standard duty for a court prophet. In contrast, prophets-for-hire were generally viewed unfavorably as unscrupulous persons who would say whatever their employer wished to hear. Nevertheless, Balak believed himself to be in sufficient danger to send for a famous and powerful prophet, whose work was known for its potency.

In the biblical traditions of Num. 22—24 Balaam is presented both favorably and unfavorably. Balaam, intending to keep his contract with Balak, attempted to curse the Israelites, but God kept him from doing so, insisting that Balaam bless them instead. In this way Balaam was a true prophet even in spite of himself and so, perhaps, was worthy of his fame. In a separate tradition (Num. 31:8, 16) Balaam is held responsible for the Israelite apostasy at Peor, and reported to have been killed by Israel.

An 8th-century B.C. inscription from Jordan confirms that Balaam was a renowned prophet at the time of Judah's and Israel's monarchies. The text, found at Tell Deir 'Alla, displays a heavenly pantheon, and tells how the prophet Balaam was called by the gods in the night through a vision or dream to witness to the divine will (see Num. 22:20). Thus Balaam's reliability as a prophet was remembered and recorded not only in the Bible, but also by the devotees who inscribed the Tell Deir 'Alla walls.

---

a wall on that side. 25And when the donkey saw the Angel of the LORD, she pushed herself against the wall and crushed Balaam's foot against the wall; so he struck her again. 26Then the Angel of the LORD went further, and stood in a narrow place where there *was* no way to turn either to the right hand or to the left. 27And when the donkey saw the Angel of the LORD, she lay down under Balaam; so Balaam's anger was aroused, and he struck the donkey with his staff.

28Then the LORD opened the mouth of the donkey, and she said to Balaam, "What have I done to you, that you have struck me these three times?"

29And Balaam said to the donkey, "Because you have abused me. I wish there were a sword in my hand, for now I would kill you!"

30So the donkey said to Balaam, "*Am I* not your donkey on which you have ridden, ever since *I became* yours, to this day? Was I ever disposed to do this to you?"

And he said, "No."

31Then the LORD opened Balaam's eyes, and he saw the Angel of the LORD standing in the way with His drawn sword in His hand; and he bowed his head and

fell flat on his face. 32And the Angel of the LORD said to him, "Why have you struck your donkey these three times? Behold, I have come out to stand against you, because *your* way is perverse before Me. 33The donkey saw Me and turned aside from Me these three times. If she had not turned aside from Me, surely I would also have killed you by now, and let her live."

34And Balaam said to the Angel of the LORD, "I have sinned, for I did not know You stood in the way against me. Now therefore, if it displeases You, I will turn back."

35Then the Angel of the LORD said to Balaam, "Go with the men, but only the word that I speak to you, that you shall speak." So Balaam went with the princes of Balak.

36Now when Balak heard that Balaam was coming, he went out to meet him at the city of Moab, which *is* on the border at the Arnon, the boundary of the territory. 37Then Balak said to Balaam, "Did I not earnestly send to you, calling for you? Why did you not come to me? Am I not able to honor you?"

38And Balaam said to Balak, "Look, I have come to you! Now, have I any power at all to say anything? The word that God puts in my mouth, that I must speak." ³⁹So Balaam went with Balak, and they came to Kirjath Huzoth. ⁴⁰Then Balak offered oxen and sheep, and he sent *some* to Balaam and to the princes who *were* with him.

Balaam's First Prophecy

⁴¹So it was, the next day, that Balak took Balaam and brought him up to the high places of Baal, that from there he might observe the extent of the people.

23 ¹Then Balaam said to Balak, "Build seven altars for me here, and prepare for me here seven bulls and seven rams."

²And Balak did just as Balaam had spoken, and Balak and Balaam offered a bull and a ram on *each* altar. ³Then Balaam said to Balak, "Stand by your burnt offering, and I will go; perhaps the LORD will come to meet me, and whatever He shows me I will tell you." So he went to a desolate height. ⁴And God met Balaam, and he said to Him, "I have prepared the seven altars, and I have offered on *each* altar a bull and a ram."

⁵Then the LORD put a word in Balaam's mouth, and said, "Return to Balak, and thus you shall speak." ⁶So he returned to him, and there he was, standing by his burnt offering, he and all the princes of Moab.

⁷And he took up his oracle and said:

"Balak the king of Moab has brought
　me from Aram,
From the mountains of the east.
'Come, curse Jacob for me,
And come, denounce Israel!'

8　"How shall I curse whom God has not
　　cursed?
And how shall I denounce *whom* the
　　LORD has not denounced?
9　For from the top of the rocks I see
　　him,
And from the hills I behold him;
There! A people dwelling alone,
Not reckoning itself among the
　　nations.

23:10 ^aOr *dust cloud*   23:15 ^aFollowing Masoretic Text, Targum, and Vulgate; Syriac reads *call;* Septuagint reads *go and ask God.*

10　"Who can count the dust^a of Jacob,
　　Or number one-fourth of Israel?
　　Let me die the death of the righteous,
　　And let my end be like his!"

¹¹Then Balak said to Balaam, "What have you done to me? I took you to curse my enemies, and look, you have blessed *them* bountifully!"

¹²So he answered and said, "Must I not take heed to speak what the LORD has put in my mouth?"

Balaam's Second Prophecy

¹³Then Balak said to him, "Please come with me to another place from which you may see them; you shall see only the outer part of them, and shall not see them all; curse them for me from there." ¹⁴So he brought him to the field of Zophim, to the top of Pisgah, and built seven altars, and offered a bull and a ram on *each* altar.

¹⁵And he said to Balak, "Stand here by your burnt offering while I meet^a *the* LORD over there."

¹⁶Then the LORD met Balaam, and put a word in his mouth, and said, "Go back to Balak, and thus you shall speak." ¹⁷So he came to him, and there he was, standing by his burnt offering, and the princes of Moab were with him. And Balak said to him, "What has the LORD spoken?"

¹⁸Then he took up his oracle and said:

"Rise up, Balak, and hear!
Listen to me, son of Zippor!

19　"God *is* not a man, that He should lie,
　　Nor a son of man, that He should
　　　repent.
　　Has He said, and will He not do?
　　Or has He spoken, and will He not
　　　make it good?
20　Behold, I have received *a command* to
　　　bless;
　　He has blessed, and I cannot reverse
　　　it.

21　"He has not observed iniquity in Jacob,
　　Nor has He seen wickedness in Israel.
　　The LORD his God *is* with him,
　　And the shout of a King *is* among
　　　them.
22　God brings them out of Egypt;
　　He has strength like a wild ox.

23 "For *there is* no sorcery against Jacob,
Nor any divination against Israel.
It now must be said of Jacob
And of Israel, 'Oh, what God has
done!'
24 Look, a people rises like a lioness,
And lifts itself up like a lion;
It shall not lie down until it devours
the prey,
And drinks the blood of the slain."

25Then Balak said to Balaam, "Neither curse them at all, nor bless them at all!"

26So Balaam answered and said to Balak, "Did I not tell you, saying, 'All that the LORD speaks, that I must do'?"

Balaam's Third Prophecy

27Then Balak said to Balaam, "Please come, I will take you to another place; perhaps it will please God that you may curse them for me from there." 28So Balak took Balaam to the top of Peor, that overlooks the wasteland.ᵃ 29Then Balaam said to Balak, "Build for me here seven altars, and prepare for me here seven bulls and seven rams." 30And Balak did as Balaam had said, and offered a bull and a ram on *every* altar.

24 1Now when Balaam saw that it pleased the LORD to bless Israel, he did not go as at other times, to seek to use sorcery, but he set his face toward the wilderness. 2And Balaam raised his eyes, and saw Israel encamped according to their tribes; and the Spirit of God came upon him.

3Then he took up his oracle and said:

"The utterance of Balaam the son of
Beor,
The utterance of the man whose eyes
are opened,
4 The utterance of him who hears the
words of God,
Who sees the vision of the Almighty,
Who falls down, with eyes wide open:

5 "How lovely are your tents, O Jacob!
Your dwellings, O Israel!

6 Like valleys that stretch out,
Like gardens by the riverside,
Like aloes planted by the LORD,
Like cedars beside the waters.
7 He shall pour water from his buckets,
And his seed *shall be* in many waters.

"His king shall be higher than Agag,
And his kingdom shall be exalted.

8 "God brings him out of Egypt;
He has strength like a wild ox;
He shall consume the nations, his
enemies;
He shall break their bones
And pierce *them* with his arrows.
9 'He bows down, he lies down as a lion;
And as a lion, who shall rouse him?'ᵃ

"Blessed *is* he who blesses you,
And cursed *is* he who curses you."

10Then Balak's anger was aroused against Balaam, and he struck his hands together; and Balak said to Balaam, "I called you to curse my enemies, and look, you have bountifully blessed *them* these three times! 11Now therefore, flee to your place. I said I would greatly honor you, but in fact, the LORD has kept you back from honor."

12So Balaam said to Balak, "Did I not also speak to your messengers whom you sent to me, saying, 13'If Balak were to give me his house full of silver and gold, I could not go beyond the word of the LORD, to do good or bad of my own will. What the LORD says, that I must speak'? 14And now, indeed, I am going to my people. Come, I will advise you what this people will do to your people in the latter days."

Balaam's Fourth Prophecy

15So he took up his oracle and said:

"The utterance of Balaam the son of
Beor,

23:28 ᵃHebrew *Jeshimon*   24:9 ᵃGenesis 49:9

PLANTS AND ANIMALS

The conventional assignment of different characteristics to different animals is partly dictated by nature, and partly traditional. For the ancient Near East the strength of the ox was a matter of observation (Num. 23:22). More important, the ox or bull was prominent in religion, as it was in Egypt and in Mycenae.

And the utterance of the man whose
eyes are opened;
16 The utterance of him who hears the
words of God,
And has the knowledge of the Most
High,
Who sees the vision of the Almighty,
Who falls down, with eyes wide open:

17 "I see Him, but not now;
I behold Him, but not near;
A Star shall come out of Jacob;
A Scepter shall rise out of Israel,
And batter the brow of Moab,
And destroy all the sons of tumult.[a]

18 "And Edom shall be a possession;
Seir also, his enemies, shall be a
possession,
While Israel does valiantly.
19 Out of Jacob One shall have dominion,
And destroy the remains of the city."

20Then he looked on Amalek, and he
took up his oracle and said:

"Amalek *was* first among the nations,
But *shall be* last until he perishes."

21Then he looked on the Kenites, and
he took up his oracle and said:

"Firm is your dwelling place,
And your nest is set in the rock;
22 Nevertheless Kain shall be burned.
How long until Asshur carries you
away captive?"

23Then he took up his oracle and said:

"Alas! Who shall live when God does
this?
24 But ships *shall come* from the coasts
of Cyprus,[a]
And they shall afflict Asshur and
afflict Eber,
And so shall *Amalek*,[b] until he
perishes."

25So Balaam rose and departed and returned to his place; Balak also went his
way.

24:17 [a]Hebrew *Sheth* (compare Jeremiah 48:45)
24:24 [a]Hebrew *Kittim*   [b]Literally *he* or *that one*
25:1 [a]Hebrew *Shittim*

Israel's Harlotry in Moab

25 1Now Israel remained in Acacia
Grove,[a] and the people began to
commit harlotry with the women of Moab.
2They invited the people to the sacrifices of
their gods, and the people ate and bowed
down to their gods. 3So Israel was joined to
Baal of Peor, and the anger of the LORD
was aroused against Israel.

4Then the LORD said to Moses, "Take
all the leaders of the people and hang the
offenders before the LORD, out in the sun,
that the fierce anger of the LORD may turn
away from Israel."

5So Moses said to the judges of Israel,
"Every one of you kill his men who were
joined to Baal of Peor."

6And indeed, one of the children of Israel came and presented to his brethren a
Midianite woman in the sight of Moses and
in the sight of all the congregation of the
children of Israel, who *were* weeping at the
door of the tabernacle of meeting. 7Now
when Phinehas the son of Eleazar, the son
of Aaron the priest, saw *it*, he rose from
among the congregation and took a javelin
in his hand; 8and he went after the man of
Israel into the tent and thrust both of them
through, the man of Israel, and the woman
through her body. So the plague was
stopped among the children of Israel. 9And
those who died in the plague were twenty-
four thousand.

10Then the LORD spoke to Moses, saying: 11"Phinehas the son of Eleazar, the son
of Aaron the priest, has turned back My
wrath from the children of Israel, because
he was zealous with My zeal among them,
so that I did not consume the children of
Israel in My zeal. 12Therefore say, 'Behold,
I give to him My covenant of peace; 13and
it shall be to him and his descendants
after him a covenant of an everlasting

TIME CAPSULE   *1363 to 1360 B.C.*

1363–	Ashur-uballit I is first ruler called
1328	"king of Assyria"
1360	Fire in the palace at Ugarit destroys
	the royal archives
1360	Ashur-uballit I writes two letters to
	Egyptian capital at Amarna
1360–	Amarna letters exchanged between
1333	Egypt and Canaanite vassal rulers

CHASING THE GODS OF MOAB (Num. 25:1–9)

The Israelites had no sooner been blessed by the prophet Balaam than they turned to the worship of the god Baal of Peor (Num. 25:1–9). Balaam had attempted to curse them, but God intervened. This was another in a series of events, beginning with the Exodus itself, in which God's salvation was repaid with complaints and apostasy.

What happened at the mountain called Peor in Moab? The Israelite men, being attracted to the Moabite women, accepted an invitation to their religious festivals where Baal of Peor, the god of the mountain, was worshiped. Baal of Peor was a prominent god of the Moabites, as well as of the Midianites and Ammonites.

The Israelites "ate" at the sacrifices (Num. 25:2). Whenever people in the ancient world killed animals for food, the slaughter was done in a ritual of sacrifice. The sacrifice gave honor to the deity to whom the meal was dedicated. Eating the meat served from the sacrifice was considered an act of worship of that deity, even if there were no other rituals or religious actions involved.

The Israelites who joined in the feast not only ate the sacrifice, but also "bowed down" to the Moabite gods (25:2). The men had not just gone along with the women for sexual favors and a free meal; rather they had joined the local cult devoted to the local god. For worshiping gods other than Israel's God, the punishment was death (25:4). Leaving the corpses of the offenders exposed was a practice used also by the Assyrian armies. It both disgraced the dead and served as a warning to others.

priesthood, because he was zealous for his God, and made atonement for the children of Israel.' "

14Now the name of the Israelite who was killed, who was killed with the Midianite woman, *was* Zimri the son of Salu, a leader of a father's house among the Simeonites. 15And the name of the Midianite woman who was killed *was* Cozbi the daughter of Zur; he *was* head of the people of a father's house in Midian.

16Then the LORD spoke to Moses, saying: 17"Harass the Midianites, and attack them; 18for they harassed you with their schemes by which they seduced you in the matter of Peor and in the matter of Cozbi, the daughter of a leader of Midian, their sister, who was killed in the day of the plague because of Peor."

The Second Census of Israel

26 1And it came to pass, after the plague, that the LORD spoke to Moses and Eleazar the son of Aaron the priest, saying: 2"Take a census of all the congregation of the children of Israel from twenty years old and above, by their fathers' houses, all who are able to go to war in Israel." 3So Moses and Eleazar the priest spoke with them in the plains of Moab by the Jordan, *across from* Jericho, saying: 4"Take a census of the people from twenty years old and above, just as the LORD commanded Moses and the children of Israel who came out of the land of Egypt."

5Reuben *was* the firstborn of Israel. The children of Reuben *were*: of Hanoch, the family of the Hanochites; *of* Pallu, the family of the Palluites; 6*of* Hezron, the family of the Hezronites; *of* Carmi, the family of the Carmites. 7These *are* the families of the Reubenites: those who were numbered of them were forty-three thousand seven hundred and thirty. 8And the son of Pallu *was* Eliab. 9The sons of Eliab *were* Nemuel, Dathan, and Abiram. These *are* the Dathan and Abiram, representatives of the congregation, who contended against Moses and Aaron in the company of Korah, when they contended against the LORD; 10and the earth opened its mouth and swallowed them up together with Korah when that company died, when the fire devoured two hundred and fifty men; and they became a sign. 11Nevertheless the children of Korah did not die.

12The sons of Simeon according to their families *were*: of Nemuel,[a] the family of the Nemuelites; *of* Jamin, the family of the Jaminites; *of* Jachin,[b] the family of the Ja-

26:12 [a]Spelled *Jemuel* in Genesis 46:10 and Exodus 6:15   [b]Called *Jarib* in 1 Chronicles 4:24

chinites; [13]*of* Zerah,[a] the family of the Zarhites; *of* Shaul, the family of the Shaulites. [14]These *are* the families of the Simeonites: twenty-two thousand two hundred.

[15]The sons of Gad according to their families *were:* of Zephon,[a] the family of the Zephonites; *of* Haggi, the family of the Haggites; *of* Shuni, the family of the Shunites; [16]*of* Ozni,[a] the family of the Oznites; *of* Eri, the family of the Erites; [17]*of* Arod,[a] the family of the Arodites; *of* Areli, the family of the Arelites. [18]These *are* the families of the sons of Gad according to those who were numbered of them: forty thousand five hundred.

[19]The sons of Judah *were* Er and Onan; and Er and Onan died in the land of Canaan. [20]And the sons of Judah according to their families were: *of* Shelah, the family of the Shelanites; *of* Perez, the family of the Parzites; *of* Zerah, the family of the Zarhites. [21]And the sons of Perez were: *of* Hezron, the family of the Hezronites; *of* Hamul, the family of the Hamulites. [22]These *are* the families of Judah according to those who were numbered of them: seventy-six thousand five hundred.

[23]The sons of Issachar according to their families *were:* of Tola, the family of the Tolaites; of Puah,[a] the family of the Punites;[b] [24]of Jashub, the family of the Jashubites; of Shimron, the family of the Shimronites. [25]These *are* the families of Issachar according to those who were numbered of them: sixty-four thousand three hundred.

[26]The sons of Zebulun according to their families *were:* of Sered, the family of the Sardites; of Elon, the family of the Elonites; of Jahleel, the family of the Jahleelites. [27]These *are* the families of the Zebulunites according to those who

were numbered of them: sixty thousand five hundred.

[28]The sons of Joseph according to their families, by Manasseh and Ephraim, *were:* [29]The sons of Manasseh: of Machir, the family of the Machirites; and Machir begot Gilead; of Gilead, the family of the Gileadites. [30]These *are* the sons of Gilead: *of* Jeezer,[a] the family of the Jeezerites; of Helek, the family of the Helekites; [31]*of* Asriel, the family of the Asrielites; *of* Shechem, the family of the Shechemites; [32]*of* Shemida, the family of the Shemidaites; *of* Hepher, the family of the Hepherites. [33]Now Zelophehad the son of Hepher had no sons, but daughters; and the names of the daughters of Zelophehad *were* Mahlah, Noah, Hoglah, Milcah, and Tirzah. [34]These *are* the families of Manasseh; and those who were numbered of them *were* fifty-two thousand seven hundred.

[35]These *are* the sons of Ephraim according to their families: of Shuthelah, the family of the Shuthalhites; of Becher,[a] the family of the Bachrites; of Tahan, the family of the Tahanites. [36]And these *are* the sons of Shuthelah: of Eran, the family of the Eranites. [37]These *are* the families of the sons of Ephraim according to those who were numbered of them: thirty-two thousand five hundred.

These *are* the sons of Joseph according to their families.

[38]The sons of Benjamin according to their families were: of Bela, the family of the Belaites; of Ashbel, the family of the Ashbelites; of Ahiram, the family of the Ahiramites; [39]of Shupham,[a] the family of the Shuphamites; of Hupham,[b] the family of the Huphamites. [40]And the sons of Bela were Ard[a] and Naaman: *of Ard,* the family of the Ardites; of Naaman, the family of the Naamites. [41]These *are* the sons of Benjamin according to their families; and those who were numbered of them *were* forty-five thousand six hundred.

[42]These *are* the sons of Dan according to their families: of Shuham,[a] the family of the Shuhamites. These *are* the families of Dan according to their families. [43]All the families of the Shuhamites, according to those who were numbered of them, *were* sixty-four thousand four hundred.

[44]The sons of Asher according to their families *were:* of Jimna, the family of the Jimnites; of Jesui, the family of the Jesuites; of Beriah, the family of the

---

26:13 [a]Called *Zohar* in Genesis 46:10
26:15 [a]Called *Ziphion* in Genesis 46:16
26:16 [a]Called *Ezbon* in Genesis 46:16
26:17 [a]Spelled *Arodi* in Samaritan Pentateuch, Syriac, and Genesis 46:16   26:23 [a]Hebrew *Puvah* (compare Genesis 46:13 and 1 Chronicles 7:1); Samaritan Pentateuch, Septuagint, Syriac, and Vulgate read *Puah.* [b]Samaritan Pentateuch, Septuagint, Syriac, and Vulgate read *Puaites.*   26:30 [a]Called *Abiezer* in Joshua 17:2   26:35 [a]Called *Bered* in 1 Chronicles 7:20   26:39 [a]Masoretic Text reads *Shephupham,* spelled *Shephuphan* in 1 Chronicles 8:5. [b]Called *Huppim* in Genesis 46:21   26:40 [a]Called *Addar* in 1 Chronicles 8:3   26:42 [a]Called *Hushim* in Genesis 46:23

Beriites. ⁴⁵Of the sons of Beriah: of Heber, the family of the Heberites; of Malchiel, the family of the Malchielites. ⁴⁶And the name of the daughter of Asher *was* Serah. ⁴⁷These *are* the families of the sons of Asher according to those who were numbered of them: fifty-three thousand four hundred.

⁴⁸The sons of Naphtali according to their families *were:* of Jahzeel,ᵃ the family of the Jahzeelites; of Guni, the family of the Gunites; ⁴⁹of Jezer, the family of the Jezerites; of Shillem, the family of the Shillemites. ⁵⁰These *are* the families of Naphtali according to their families; and those who were numbered of them *were* forty-five thousand four hundred.

⁵¹These *are* those who were numbered of the children of Israel: six hundred and one thousand seven hundred and thirty.

⁵²Then the LORD spoke to Moses, saying: ⁵³"To these the land shall be divided as an inheritance, according to the number of names. ⁵⁴To a large *tribe* you shall give a larger inheritance, and to a small *tribe* you shall give a smaller inheritance. Each shall be given its inheritance according to those who were numbered of them. ⁵⁵But the land shall be divided by lot; they shall inherit according to the names of the tribes of their fathers. ⁵⁶According to the lot their inheritance shall be divided between the larger and the smaller."

⁵⁷And these *are* those who were numbered of the Levites according to their families: of Gershon, the family of the Gershonites; of Kohath, the family of the Kohathites; of Merari, the family of the Merarites. ⁵⁸These *are* the families of the Levites: the family of the Libnites, the family of the Hebronites, the family of the Mahlites, the family of the Mushites, and the family of the Korathites. And Kohath begot Amram. ⁵⁹The name of Amram's wife *was* Jochebed the daughter of Levi, who was born to Levi in Egypt; and to Amram she bore Aaron and Moses and their sister Miriam. ⁶⁰To Aaron were born Nadab and Abihu, Eleazar and Ithamar. ⁶¹And Nadab

and Abihu died when they offered profane fire before the LORD.

⁶²Now those who were numbered of them were twenty-three thousand, every male from a month old and above; for they were not numbered among the other children of Israel, because there was no inheritance given to them among the children of Israel.

⁶³These *are* those who were numbered by Moses and Eleazar the priest, who numbered the children of Israel in the plains of Moab by the Jordan, *across from* Jericho. ⁶⁴But among these there was not a man of those who were numbered by Moses and Aaron the priest when they numbered the children of Israel in the Wilderness of Sinai. ⁶⁵For the LORD had said of them, "They shall surely die in the wilderness." So there was not left a man of them, except Caleb the son of Jephunneh and Joshua the son of Nun.

Inheritance Laws

27 ¹Then came the daughters of Zelophehad the son of Hepher, the son of Gilead, the son of Machir, the son of Manasseh, from the families of Manasseh the son of Joseph; and these *were* the names of his daughters: Mahlah, Noah, Hoglah, Milcah, and Tirzah. ²And they stood before Moses, before Eleazar the priest, and before the leaders and all the congregation, *by* the doorway of the tabernacle of meeting, saying: ³"Our father died in the wilderness; but he was not in the company of those who gathered together against the LORD, in company with Korah, but he died in his own sin; and he had no sons. ⁴Why should the name of our father be removed from among his family because he had no son? Give us a possession among our father's brothers."

⁵So Moses brought their case before the LORD.

⁶And the LORD spoke to Moses, saying: ⁷"The daughters of Zelophehad speak *what*

26:48 ᵃSpelled *Jahziel* in 1 Chronicles 7:13

CULTURE AND SOCIETY

The people of Israel are listed tribe by tribe, with the sons and families carefully named (Num. 26:51). In the tribal community, the facts of descent and physical relation have a much greater or a more obvious importance than in industrial societies. The Bible figures lines of descent over hundreds of years.

is right; you shall surely give them a possession of inheritance among their father's brothers, and cause the inheritance of their father to pass to them. ⁸And you shall speak to the children of Israel, saying: 'If a man dies and has no son, then you shall cause his inheritance to pass to his daughter. ⁹If he has no daughter, then you shall give his inheritance to his brothers. ¹⁰If he has no brothers, then you shall give his inheritance to his father's brothers. ¹¹And if his father has no brothers, then you shall give his inheritance to the relative closest to him in his family, and he shall possess it.' " And it shall be to the children of Israel a statute of judgment, just as the LORD commanded Moses.

Joshua the Next Leader of Israel

¹²Now the LORD said to Moses: "Go up into this Mount Abarim, and see the land which I have given to the children of Israel. ¹³And when you have seen it, you also shall be gathered to your people, as Aaron your brother was gathered. ¹⁴For in the Wilderness of Zin, during the strife of the congregation, you rebelled against My command to hallow Me at the waters before their eyes." (These *are* the waters of Meribah, at Kadesh in the Wilderness of Zin.)

¹⁵Then Moses spoke to the LORD, saying: ¹⁶"Let the LORD, the God of the spirits of all flesh, set a man over the congregation, ¹⁷who may go out before them and go in before them, who may lead them out and bring them in, that the congregation of the LORD may not be like sheep which have no shepherd."

¹⁸And the LORD said to Moses: "Take Joshua the son of Nun with you, a man in whom *is* the Spirit, and lay your hand on him; ¹⁹set him before Eleazar the priest and before all the congregation, and inaugurate him in their sight. ²⁰And you shall give *some* of your authority to him, that all the congregation of the children of Israel may be obedient. ²¹He shall stand before Eleazar the priest, who shall inquire before the LORD for him by the judgment of the Urim. At his word they shall go out, and at his word they shall come in, he and all the children of Israel with him—all the congregation."

²²So Moses did as the LORD commanded him. He took Joshua and set him before Eleazar the priest and before all the congregation. ²³And he laid his hands on him and inaugurated him, just as the LORD commanded by the hand of Moses.

Daily Offerings

28 ¹Now the LORD spoke to Moses, saying, ²"Command the children of Israel, and say to them, 'My offering, My food for My offerings made by fire as a sweet aroma to Me, you shall be careful to offer to Me at their appointed time.'

³"And you shall say to them, 'This *is* the offering made by fire which you shall offer to the LORD: two male lambs in their first year without blemish, day by day, as a regular burnt offering. ⁴The one lamb you shall offer in the morning, the other lamb you shall offer in the evening, ⁵and one-tenth of an ephah of fine flour as a grain offering mixed with one-fourth of a hin of pressed oil. ⁶*It is* a regular burnt offering which was ordained at Mount Sinai for a sweet aroma, an offering made by fire to the LORD. ⁷And its drink offering *shall be* one-fourth of a hin for each lamb; in a holy *place* you shall pour out the drink to the LORD as an offering. ⁸The other lamb you shall offer in the evening; as the morning grain offering and its drink offering, you shall offer *it* as an offering made by fire, a sweet aroma to the LORD.

Sabbath Offerings

⁹'And on the Sabbath day two lambs in their first year, without blemish, and two-tenths *of an ephah* of fine flour as a grain offering, mixed with oil, with its drink offering— ¹⁰*this is* the burnt offering for every Sabbath, besides the regular burnt offering with its drink offering.

Monthly Offerings

¹¹'At the beginnings of your months you shall present a burnt offering to the LORD: two young bulls, one ram, and seven lambs in their first year, without blemish; ¹²three-tenths *of an ephah* of fine flour as a grain offering, mixed with oil, for each bull; two-tenths *of an ephah* of fine flour as a grain offering, mixed with oil, for the one ram; ¹³and one-tenth *of an ephah* of fine flour, mixed with oil, as a grain offering for each lamb, as a burnt offering of sweet aroma, an offering made by fire to the LORD. ¹⁴Their drink offering shall be half a hin of wine for a bull, one-third of a hin for a ram, and one-fourth of a hin for a lamb; this *is* the burnt offering for each month

ISRAEL'S SACRED TIMES

Sabbath Ex. 20:8–11; 31:12–17; Lev. 23:3; Deut. 5:12–15	Every 7th day was a solemn rest from all work.
Sabbath Year Ex. 23:10, 11; Lev. 25:1–7	Every 7th year was designated a "year of release" to allow the land to lie fallow.
Year of Jubilee Lev. 25:8–55; 27:17–24; Ezek. 46:17	The 50th year, which followed seven Sabbath years, was to proclaim liberty to those who were servants because of debt, and to return lands to their former owners.
The New Moon Num. 28:11–15; Ps. 81:3	The 1st day of the Hebrew 29 or 30-day month was a day of rest, special sacrifices, and the blowing of trumpets
Dedication (Lights or *Hanukkah*) John 10:22	An 8-day feast in the 9th month (Chislev) commemorating the cleansing of the temple from defilement by Syria, and its rededication.
Purim (Lots) Esth. 9:18–32	A feast on the 14th and 15th of the 12th month (Adar). The name comes from Babylonian *Pur*, meaning "lot."

throughout the months of the year. ¹⁵Also one kid of the goats as a sin offering to the LORD shall be offered, besides the regular burnt offering and its drink offering.

Offerings at Passover

¹⁶'On the fourteenth day of the first month *is* the Passover of the LORD. ¹⁷And on the fifteenth day of this month *is* the feast; unleavened bread shall be eaten for seven days. ¹⁸On the first day *you shall have* a holy convocation. You shall do no customary work. ¹⁹And you shall present an offering made by fire as a burnt offering to the LORD: two young bulls, one ram, and seven lambs in their first year. Be sure they are without blemish. ²⁰Their grain offering shall be of fine flour mixed with oil: three-tenths *of an ephah* you shall offer for a bull, and two-tenths for a ram; ²¹you shall offer one-tenth *of an ephah* for each of the seven lambs; ²²also one goat *as* a sin offering, to make atonement for you. ²³You shall offer these besides the burnt offering of the morning, which *is* for a regular burnt offering. ²⁴In this manner you shall offer the food of the offering made by fire daily for seven days, as a sweet aroma to the LORD; it shall be offered besides the regular burnt offering and its drink offering. ²⁵And on the seventh day you shall

have a holy convocation. You shall do no customary work.

Offerings at the Feast of Weeks

²⁶'Also on the day of the firstfruits, when you bring a new grain offering to the LORD at your *Feast of* Weeks, you shall have a holy convocation. You shall do no customary work. ²⁷You shall present a burnt offering as a sweet aroma to the LORD: two young bulls, one ram, and seven lambs in their first year, ²⁸with their grain offering of fine flour mixed with oil: three-tenths *of an ephah* for each bull, two-tenths for the one ram, ²⁹and one-tenth for each of the seven lambs; ³⁰*also* one kid of the goats, to make atonement for you. ³¹Be sure they are without blemish. You shall present *them* with their drink offerings, besides the regular burnt offering with its grain offering.

Offerings at the Feast of Trumpets

29 ¹'And in the seventh month, on the first *day* of the month, you shall have a holy convocation. You shall do no customary work. For you it is a day of blowing the trumpets. ²You shall offer a burnt offering as a sweet aroma to the LORD: one young bull, one ram, *and* seven lambs in their first year, without blemish.

³Their grain offering *shall be* fine flour mixed with oil: three-tenths *of an ephah* for the bull, two-tenths for the ram, ⁴and one-tenth for each of the seven lambs; ⁵also one kid of the goats *as* a sin offering, to make atonement for you; ⁶besides the burnt offering with its grain offering for the New Moon, the regular burnt offering with its grain offering, and their drink offerings, according to their ordinance, as a sweet aroma, an offering made by fire to the LORD.

Offerings on the Day of Atonement

⁷'On the tenth *day* of this seventh month you shall have a holy convocation. You shall afflict your souls; you shall not do any work. ⁸You shall present a burnt offering to the LORD *as* a sweet aroma: one young bull, one ram, *and* seven lambs in their first year. Be sure they are without blemish. ⁹Their grain offering *shall be of* fine flour mixed with oil: three-tenths *of an ephah* for the bull, two-tenths for the one ram, ¹⁰and one-tenth for each of the seven lambs; ¹¹also one kid of the goats *as* a sin offering, besides the sin offering for atonement, the regular burnt offering with its grain offering, and their drink offerings.

Offerings at the Feast of Tabernacles

¹²'On the fifteenth day of the seventh month you shall have a holy convocation. You shall do no customary work, and you shall keep a feast to the LORD seven days. ¹³You shall present a burnt offering, an offering made by fire as a sweet aroma to the LORD: thirteen young bulls, two rams, *and* fourteen lambs in their first year. They shall be without blemish. ¹⁴Their grain offering *shall be of* fine flour mixed with oil: three-tenths *of an ephah* for each of the thirteen bulls, two-tenths for each of the two rams, ¹⁵and one-tenth for each of the fourteen lambs; ¹⁶also one kid of the goats *as* a sin offering, besides the regular burnt offering, its grain offering, and its drink offering.

¹⁷'On the second day *present* twelve young bulls, two rams, fourteen lambs in their first year without blemish, ¹⁸and their grain offering and their drink offerings for the bulls, for the rams, and for the lambs, by their number, according to the ordinance; ¹⁹also one kid of the goats *as* a sin offering, besides the regular burnt offering with its grain offering, and their drink offerings.

²⁰'On the third day *present* eleven bulls, two rams, fourteen lambs in their first year without blemish, ²¹and their grain offering and their drink offerings for the bulls, for the rams, and for the lambs, by their number, according to the ordinance; ²²also one goat *as* a sin offering, besides the regular burnt offering, its grain offering, and its drink offering.

²³'On the fourth day *present* ten bulls, two rams, *and* fourteen lambs in their first year, without blemish, ²⁴and their grain offering and their drink offerings for the bulls, for the rams, and for the lambs, by their number, according to the ordinance; ²⁵also one kid of the goats *as* a sin offering, besides the regular burnt offering, its grain offering, and its drink offering.

²⁶'On the fifth day *present* nine bulls, two rams, *and* fourteen lambs in their first year without blemish, ²⁷and their grain offering and their drink offerings for the bulls, for the rams, and for the lambs, by their number, according to the ordinance; ²⁸also one goat *as* a sin offering, besides the regular burnt offering, its grain offering, and its drink offering.

²⁹'On the sixth day *present* eight bulls, two rams, *and* fourteen lambs in their first year without blemish, ³⁰and their grain offering and their drink offerings for the bulls, for the rams, and for the lambs, by their number, according to the ordinance; ³¹also one goat *as* a sin offering, besides the regular burnt offering, its grain offering, and its drink offering.

³²'On the seventh day *present* seven bulls, two rams, *and* fourteen lambs in their first year without blemish, ³³and their grain offering and their drink offerings for the bulls, for the rams, and for the lambs, by their number, according to the ordinance; ³⁴also one goat *as* a sin offering, besides the regular burnt offering, its grain offering, and its drink offering.

³⁵'On the eighth day you shall have a sacred assembly. You shall do no customary work. ³⁶You shall present a burnt offering, an offering made by fire as a sweet aroma to the LORD: one bull, one ram, seven lambs in their first year without blemish, ³⁷and their grain offering and their drink offerings for the bull, for the ram, and for the lambs, by their number, according to the ordinance; ³⁸also one goat *as* a sin offering, besides the regular burnt offering, its grain offering, and its drink offering.

³⁹'These you shall present to the LORD

SWEARING TO THE GODS (Num. 30:2)

Emar has recently become a source for the understanding of Middle-Euphrates Syria in the Late Bronze Age (c. 1500–1200 B.C.). The city of Emar (or Imar, as it was apparently known) is indirectly referred to in texts from Ebla in the 3rd millennium B.C. and from Mari in the 18th century B.C. In later centuries (from about 1350 to 1187 B.C.) Emar was a Hittite protectorate, or dependent state.

Over 2,000 cuneiform texts, mostly written in Accadian, have been found at Emar. Many of these texts share distinct literary parallels with the Old Testament, and a number of features in the Emar textual collection appear to have a direct bearing on the understanding of the biblical text. These include the Emar installation festivals, calendar, rites for the dead, and rituals for the prophetic and priestly offices.

One such parallel between Emar and the Bible concerns vows made to the deity. According to Israel's law concerning vows to God, any Israelite who "swears an oath to bind himself by some agreement" (Num. 30:2) must carry out the oath and honor the agreement. At Emar, it seems that people swore by their ancestor's gods in order to protect their property rights. The inheritance clauses of certain texts from Emar show that heirs would swear by the gods of their deceased relative. Both cultures settled legal affairs by swearing to their deities.

at your appointed feasts (besides your vowed offerings and your freewill offerings) as your burnt offerings and your grain offerings, as your drink offerings and your peace offerings.' "

⁴⁰So Moses told the children of Israel everything, just as the LORD commanded Moses.

The Law Concerning Vows

30 ¹Then Moses spoke to the heads of the tribes concerning the children of Israel, saying, "This is the thing which the LORD has commanded: ²If a man makes a vow to the LORD, or swears an oath to bind himself by some agreement, he shall not break his word; he shall do according to all that proceeds out of his mouth.

³"Or if a woman makes a vow to the LORD, and binds herself by some agreement while in her father's house in her youth, ⁴and her father hears her vow and the agreement by which she has bound herself, and her father holds his peace, then all her vows shall stand, and every agreement with which she has bound herself shall stand. ⁵But if her father overrules her on the day that he hears, then none of her vows nor her agreements by which she has bound herself shall stand; and the LORD will release her, because her father overruled her.

⁶"If indeed she takes a husband, while bound by her vows or by a rash utterance from her lips by which she bound herself, ⁷and her husband hears it, and makes no response to her on the day that he hears, then her vows shall stand, and her agreements by which she bound herself shall stand. ⁸But if her husband overrules her on the day that he hears it, he shall make void her vow which she took and what she uttered with her lips, by which she bound herself, and the LORD will release her.

⁹"Also any vow of a widow or a divorced woman, by which she has bound herself, shall stand against her.

¹⁰"If she vowed in her husband's house, or bound herself by an agreement with an oath, ¹¹and her husband heard it, and made no response to her and did not overrule her, then all her vows shall stand, and

MARRIAGE AND FAMILY

In making and paying vows, the father or husband had a kind of veto power over what a wife or daughter could do (Num. 30:16). But when the veto power was not exercised within the time limit, or if it did not apply, a woman could make and pay vows that had the same absolute solemnity as vows made by a male.

every agreement by which she bound herself shall stand. ¹²But if her husband truly made them void on the day he heard *them,* then whatever proceeded from her lips concerning her vows or concerning the agreement binding her, it shall not stand; her husband has made them void, and the LORD will release her. ¹³Every vow and every binding oath to afflict her soul, her husband may confirm it, or her husband may make it void. ¹⁴Now if her husband makes no response whatever to her from day to day, then he confirms all her vows or all the agreements that bind her; he confirms them, because he made no response to her on the day that he heard *them.* ¹⁵But if he does make them void after he has heard *them,* then he shall bear her guilt."

¹⁶These *are* the statutes which the LORD commanded Moses, between a man and his wife, and between a father and his daughter in her youth in her father's house.

Vengeance on the Midianites

31 ¹And the LORD spoke to Moses, saying: ²"Take vengeance on the Midianites for the children of Israel. Afterward you shall be gathered to your people."

³So Moses spoke to the people, saying, "Arm some of yourselves for war, and let them go against the Midianites to take vengeance for the LORD on Midian. ⁴A thousand from each tribe of all the tribes of Israel you shall send to the war."

⁵So there were recruited from the divisions of Israel one thousand from *each* tribe, twelve thousand armed for war. ⁶Then Moses sent them to the war, one thousand from *each* tribe; he sent them to the war with Phinehas the son of Eleazar the priest, with the holy articles and the signal trumpets in his hand. ⁷And they warred against the Midianites, just as the LORD commanded Moses, and they killed all the males. ⁸They killed the kings of Midian with *the rest of* those who were killed—Evi, Rekem, Zur, Hur, and Reba, the five kings of Midian. Balaam the son of Beor they also killed with the sword.

⁹And the children of Israel took the women of Midian captive, with their little ones, and took as spoil all their cattle, all their flocks, and all their goods. ¹⁰They also burned with fire all the cities where they dwelt, and all their forts. ¹¹And they took all the spoil and all the booty—of man and beast.

Return from the War

¹²Then they brought the captives, the booty, and the spoil to Moses, to Eleazar the priest, and to the congregation of the children of Israel, to the camp in the plains of Moab by the Jordan, *across from* Jericho. ¹³And Moses, Eleazar the priest, and all the leaders of the congregation, went to meet them outside the camp. ¹⁴But Moses was angry with the officers of the army, *with* the captains over thousands and captains over hundreds, who had come from the battle.

¹⁵And Moses said to them: "Have you kept all the women alive? ¹⁶Look, these *women* caused the children of Israel, through the counsel of Balaam, to trespass against the LORD in the incident of Peor, and there was a plague among the congregation of the LORD. ¹⁷Now therefore, kill every male among the little ones, and kill every woman who has known a man intimately. ¹⁸But keep alive for yourselves all the young girls who have not known a man intimately. ¹⁹And as for you, remain outside the camp seven days; whoever has killed any person, and whoever has touched any slain, purify yourselves and your captives on the third day and on the seventh day. ²⁰Purify every garment, everything made of leather, everything woven of goats' *hair,* and everything made of wood."

²¹Then Eleazar the priest said to the men of war who had gone to the battle, "This *is* the ordinance of the law which the LORD commanded Moses: ²²Only the gold, the silver, the bronze, the iron, the tin, and the lead, ²³everything that can endure fire, you shall put through the fire, and it shall be clean; and it shall be purified with the water of purification. But all that cannot endure fire you shall put through water. ²⁴And you shall wash your clothes on the seventh day and be clean, and afterward you may come into the camp."

Division of the Plunder

²⁵Now the LORD spoke to Moses, saying: ²⁶"Count up the plunder that was taken—of man and beast—you and Eleazar the priest and the chief fathers of the congregation; ²⁷and divide the plunder into two parts, between those who took part in the war, who went out to battle, and all the congregation. ²⁸And levy a tribute for the LORD on the men of war who went out to battle: one of every five hundred of the

persons, the cattle, the donkeys, and the sheep; 29take *it* from their half, and give *it* to Eleazar the priest as a heave offering to the LORD. 30And from the children of Israel's half you shall take one of every fifty, drawn from the persons, the cattle, the donkeys, and the sheep, from all the livestock, and give them to the Levites who keep charge of the tabernacle of the LORD." 31So Moses and Eleazar the priest did as the LORD commanded Moses.

32The booty remaining from the plunder, which the men of war had taken, was six hundred and seventy-five thousand sheep, 33seventy-two thousand cattle, 34sixty-one thousand donkeys, 35and thirty-two thousand persons in all, of women who had not known a man intimately. 36And the half, the portion for those who had gone out to war, was in number three hundred and thirty-seven thousand five hundred sheep; 37and the LORD's tribute of the sheep was six hundred and seventy-five. 38The cattle *were* thirty-six thousand, of which the LORD's tribute *was* seventy-two. 39The donkeys *were* thirty thousand five hundred, of which the LORD's tribute *was* sixty-one. 40The persons *were* sixteen thousand, of which the LORD's tribute *was* thirty-two persons. 41So Moses gave the tribute *which was* the LORD's heave offering to Eleazar the priest, as the LORD commanded Moses.

42And from the children of Israel's half, which Moses separated from the men who fought— 43now the half belonging to the congregation was three hundred and thirty-seven thousand five hundred sheep, 44thirty-six thousand cattle, 45thirty thousand five hundred donkeys, 46and sixteen thousand persons— 47and from the children of Israel's half Moses took one of every fifty, drawn from man and beast, and gave them to the Levites, who kept charge of the tabernacle of the LORD, as the LORD commanded Moses.

48Then the officers who *were* over thousands of the army, the captains of thousands and captains of hundreds, came near to Moses; 49and they said to Moses, "Your servants have taken a count of the men of war who *are* under our command, and not a man of us is missing. 50Therefore we have brought an offering for the LORD, what every man found of ornaments of gold: armlets and bracelets and signet rings and earrings and necklaces, to make atonement for ourselves before the LORD." 51So Moses and Eleazar the priest received the gold from them, all the fashioned ornaments. 52And all the gold of the offering that they offered to the LORD, from the captains of thousands and captains of hundreds, was sixteen thousand seven hundred and fifty shekels. 53(The men of war had taken spoil, every man for himself.) 54And Moses and Eleazar the priest received the gold from the captains of thousands and of hundreds, and brought it into the tabernacle of meeting as a memorial for the children of Israel before the LORD.

The Tribes Settling East of the Jordan

32 1Now the children of Reuben and the children of Gad had a very great multitude of livestock; and when they saw the land of Jazer and the land of Gilead, that indeed the region *was* a place for livestock, 2the children of Gad and the children of Reuben came and spoke to Moses, to Eleazar the priest, and to the leaders of the congregation, saying, 3"Ataroth, Dibon, Jazer, Nimrah, Heshbon, Elealeh, Shebam, Nebo, and Beon, 4the country which the LORD defeated before the congregation of Israel, *is* a land for livestock, and your servants have livestock." 5Therefore they said, "If we have found favor in your sight, let this land be given to your servants as a possession. Do not take us over the Jordan."

6And Moses said to the children of Gad and to the children of Reuben: "Shall your brethren go to war while you sit here? 7Now why will you discourage the heart of the children of Israel from going over into the land which the LORD has given them? 8Thus your fathers did when I sent them away from Kadesh Barnea to see the land. 9For when they went up to the Valley of Eshcol and saw the land, they discouraged the heart of the children of Israel, so that they did not go into the land which the LORD had given them. 10So the LORD's anger was aroused on that day, and He swore an oath, saying, 11'Surely none of the men who came up from Egypt, from twenty years old and above, shall see the land of which I swore to Abraham, Isaac, and Jacob, because they have not wholly followed Me, 12except Caleb the son of Jephunneh, the Kenizzite, and Joshua the son of Nun, for they have wholly followed the LORD.' 13So the LORD's anger was aroused against Israel, and He made them wander in the wilderness forty years, until all the generation that had done evil in the sight of the

LORD was gone. [14]And look! You have risen in your fathers' place, a brood of sinful men, to increase still more the fierce anger of the LORD against Israel. [15]For if you turn away from following Him, He will once again leave them in the wilderness, and you will destroy all these people."

[16]Then they came near to him and said: "We will build sheepfolds here for our livestock, and cities for our little ones, [17]but we ourselves will be armed, ready *to go* before the children of Israel until we have brought them to their place; and our little ones will dwell in the fortified cities because of the inhabitants of the land. [18]We will not return to our homes until every one of the children of Israel has received his inheritance. [19]For we will not inherit with them on the other side of the Jordan and beyond, because our inheritance has fallen to us on this eastern side of the Jordan."

[20]Then Moses said to them: "If you do this thing, if you arm yourselves before the LORD for the war, [21]and all your armed men cross over the Jordan before the LORD until He has driven out His enemies from before Him, [22]and the land is subdued before the LORD, then afterward you may return and be blameless before the LORD and before Israel; and this land shall be your possession before the LORD. [23]But if you do not do so, then take note, you have sinned against the LORD; and be sure your sin will find you out. [24]Build cities for your little ones

---

32:41 [a]Literally *Towns of Jair*

---

and folds for your sheep, and do what has proceeded out of your mouth."

[25]And the children of Gad and the children of Reuben spoke to Moses, saying: "Your servants will do as my lord commands. [26]Our little ones, our wives, our flocks, and all our livestock will be there in the cities of Gilead; [27]but your servants will cross over, every man armed for war, before the LORD to battle, just as my lord says."

[28]So Moses gave command concerning them to Eleazar the priest, to Joshua the son of Nun, and to the chief fathers of the tribes of the children of Israel. [29]And Moses said to them: "If the children of Gad and the children of Reuben cross over the Jordan with you, every man armed for battle before the LORD, and the land is subdued before you, then you shall give them the land of Gilead as a possession. [30]But if they do not cross over armed with you, they shall have possessions among you in the land of Canaan."

[31]Then the children of Gad and the children of Reuben answered, saying: "As the LORD has said to your servants, so we will do. [32]We will cross over armed before the LORD into the land of Canaan, but the possession of our inheritance *shall remain* with us on this side of the Jordan."

[33]So Moses gave to the children of Gad, to the children of Reuben, and to half the tribe of Manasseh the son of Joseph, the kingdom of Sihon king of the Amorites and the kingdom of Og king of Bashan, the land with its cities within the borders, the cities of the surrounding country. [34]And the children of Gad built Dibon and Ataroth and Aroer, [35]Atroth and Shophan and Jazer and Jogbehah, [36]Beth Nimrah and Beth Haran, fortified cities, and folds for sheep. [37]And the children of Reuben built Heshbon and Elealeh and Kirjathaim, [38]Nebo and Baal Meon (*their* names being changed) and Shibmah; and they gave *other* names to the cities which they built.

[39]And the children of Machir the son of Manasseh went to Gilead and took it, and dispossessed the Amorites who *were* in it. [40]So Moses gave Gilead to Machir the son of Manasseh, and he dwelt in it. [41]Also Jair the son of Manasseh went and took its small towns, and called them Havoth Jair.[a] [42]Then Nobah went and took Kenath and its villages, and he called it Nobah, after his own name.

Israel's Journey from Egypt Reviewed

33 [1]These *are* the journeys of the children of Israel, who went out of the land of Egypt by their armies under the hand of Moses and Aaron. [2]Now Moses wrote down the starting points of their journeys at the command of the LORD. And these *are* their journeys according to their starting points:

[3]They departed from Rameses in the first month, on the fifteenth day of the first month; on the day after the Passover the children of Israel went out with boldness in the sight of all the Egyptians. [4]For the Egyptians were burying all *their* firstborn, whom the LORD had killed among them. Also on their gods the LORD had executed judgments.

[5]Then the children of Israel moved from Rameses and camped at Succoth. [6]They departed from Succoth and camped at Etham, which *is* on the edge of the wilderness. [7]They moved from Etham and turned back to Pi Hahiroth, which *is* east of Baal Zephon; and they camped near Migdol. [8]They departed from before Hahiroth[a] and passed through the midst of the sea into the wilderness, went three days' journey in the Wilderness of Etham, and camped at Marah. [9]They moved from Marah and came to Elim. At Elim *were* twelve springs of water and seventy palm trees; so they camped there.

[10]They moved from Elim and camped by the Red Sea. [11]They moved from the Red Sea and camped in the Wilderness of Sin. [12]They journeyed from the Wilderness of Sin and camped at Dophkah. [13]They departed from Dophkah and camped at Alush. [14]They moved from Alush and camped at Rephidim, where there was no water for the people to drink.

[15]They departed from Rephidim and camped in the Wilderness of Sinai. [16]They moved from the Wilderness of Sinai and camped at Kibroth Hattaavah. [17]They departed from Kibroth Hattaavah and camped at Hazeroth. [18]They departed from Hazeroth and camped at Rithmah. [19]They departed from Rithmah and camped at Rimmon Perez. [20]They departed from Rimmon Perez and camped at Libnah. [21]They moved from Libnah and camped at Rissah. [22]They journeyed from Rissah and camped at Kehelathah. [23]They went from Kehelathah and camped at Mount Shepher. [24]They moved from Mount Shepher and camped at Haradah. [25]They moved from Haradah and camped at Makheloth. [26]They moved from Makheloth and camped at Tahath. [27]They departed from Tahath and camped at Terah. [28]They moved from Terah and camped at Mithkah. [29]They went from Mithkah and camped at Hash-

---

33:8 [a]Many Hebrew manuscripts, Samaritan Pentateuch, Syriac, Targum, and Vulgate read *from Pi Hahiroth* (compare verse 7).

The Approach to Transjordan
From Kadesh Barnea Moses wanted to go east through Edom and north through Moab toward Canaan. Being refused passage through both territories, he instead went south to Elath, then north and east, bypassing Edom and Moab.

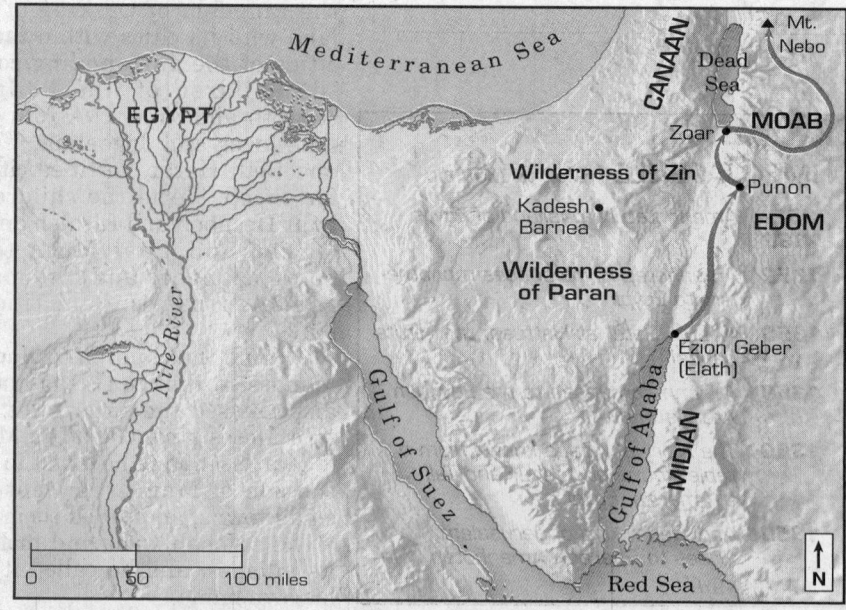

monah. [30]They departed from Hashmonah and camped at Moseroth. [31]They departed from Moseroth and camped at Bene Jaakan. [32]They moved from Bene Jaakan and camped at Hor Hagidgad. [33]They went from Hor Hagidgad and camped at Jotbathah. [34]They moved from Jotbathah and camped at Abronah. [35]They departed from Abronah and camped at Ezion Geber. [36]They moved from Ezion Geber and camped in the Wilderness of Zin, which *is* Kadesh. [37]They moved from Kadesh and camped at Mount Hor, on the boundary of the land of Edom.

[38]Then Aaron the priest went up to Mount Hor at the command of the LORD, and died there in the fortieth year after the children of Israel had come out of the land of Egypt, on the first *day* of the fifth month. [39]Aaron *was* one hundred and twenty-three years old when he died on Mount Hor.

[40]Now the king of Arad, the Canaanite, who dwelt in the South in the land of Canaan, heard of the coming of the children of Israel.

[41]So they departed from Mount Hor and camped at Zalmonah. [42]They departed from Zalmonah and camped at Punon. [43]They departed from Punon and camped at Oboth. [44]They departed from Oboth and camped at Ije Abarim, at the border of Moab. [45]They departed from Ijim[a] and camped at Dibon Gad. [46]They moved from Dibon Gad and camped at Almon Diblathaim. [47]They moved from Almon Diblathaim and camped in the mountains of Abarim, before Nebo. [48]They departed from the mountains of Abarim and camped in the plains of Moab by the Jordan, *across from* Jericho. [49]They camped by the Jordan, from Beth Jesimoth as far as the Abel Acacia Grove[a] in the plains of Moab.

Instructions for the Conquest of Canaan

[50]Now the LORD spoke to Moses in the plains of Moab by the Jordan, *across from* Jericho, saying, [51]"Speak to the children of Israel, and say to them: 'When you have crossed the Jordan into the land of Canaan, [52]then you shall drive out all the inhabitants of the land from before you, destroy all their engraved stones, destroy all their molded images, and demolish all

their high places; [53]you shall dispossess *the inhabitants of* the land and dwell in it, for I have given you the land to possess. [54]And you shall divide the land by lot as an inheritance among your families; to the larger you shall give a larger inheritance, and to the smaller you shall give a smaller inheritance; there everyone's *inheritance* shall be whatever falls to him by lot. You shall inherit according to the tribes of your fathers. [55]But if you do not drive out the inhabitants of the land from before you, then it shall be that those whom you let remain *shall be* irritants in your eyes and thorns in your sides, and they shall harass you in the land where you dwell. [56]Moreover it shall be *that* I will do to you as I thought to do to them.' "

The Appointed Boundaries of Canaan

34 [1]Then the LORD spoke to Moses, saying, [2]"Command the children of Israel, and say to them: 'When you come into the land of Canaan, this *is* the land that shall fall to you as an inheritance—the land of Canaan to its boundaries. [3]Your southern border shall be from the Wilderness of Zin along the border of Edom; then your southern border shall extend eastward to the end of the Salt Sea; [4]your border shall turn from the southern side of the Ascent of Akrabbim, continue to Zin, and be on the south of Kadesh Barnea; then it shall go on to Hazar Addar, and continue to Azmon; [5]the border shall turn from Azmon to the Brook of Egypt, and it shall end at the Sea.

[6]'As for the western border, you shall have the Great Sea for a border; this shall be your western border.

[7]'And this shall be your northern border: From the Great Sea you shall mark out your *border* line to Mount Hor; [8]from Mount Hor you shall mark out *your border* to the entrance of Hamath; then the direction of the border shall be toward Zedad; [9]the border shall proceed to Ziphron, and it shall end at Hazar Enan. This shall be your northern border.

[10]'You shall mark out your eastern border from Hazar Enan to Shepham; [11]the border shall go down from Shepham to Riblah on the east side of Ain; the border shall go down and reach to the eastern side of the Sea of Chinnereth; [12]the border shall go down along the Jordan, and it shall end at the Salt Sea. This shall be your land with its surrounding boundaries.' "

33:45 [a]Same as *Ije Abarim*, verse 44
33:49 [a]Hebrew *Abel Shittim*

THE RIVER OF EGYPT (Num. 34:1–5)

Numbers 34 describes the boundaries of the Promised Land—Canaan—which the Israelites would inherit. The southern border extended to the "Brook of Egypt" (Num. 34:3, 5), which is also known as "the river of Egypt" (Gen. 15:18). Without thought, one could confuse this "river of Egypt" with the Nile River, since the Nile is, and always has been, the life of Egyptian history and people.

The Nile River is, at times, intended by the biblical writer, but is called simply "the River" (Is. 19:7; Nah. 3:8). The name "Nile" comes from the Greco-Roman period (after 332 B.C.) and was unknown in earlier times. The Egyptians referred to the Nile by a word equivalent to "river," and a Hebrew modification of this Egyptian word appears most often in the Old Testament when the Nile is intended (Gen. 41:1; Ex. 1:22).

The phrases "river of Egypt" and "Brook of Egypt" are referring to the Wadi el-'Arish, a river that flows from the Sinai Peninsula's central high plateau to the low lying Mediterranean coast. Most people in ancient times came and left Egypt by traveling along the northern edge of the Sinai Peninsula. The Wadi el-'Arish intersects the peninsula on its eastern edge and, thus, marked for ancient people the eastern most boundary of Egypt. That is why the phrases "river of Egypt" and "Brook of Egypt" are found where geographic boundaries are described (Gen. 15:18; Num. 34:5).

---

¹³Then Moses commanded the children of Israel, saying: "This *is* the land which you shall inherit by lot, which the LORD has commanded to give to the nine tribes and to the half-tribe. ¹⁴For the tribe of the children of Reuben according to the house of their fathers, and the tribe of the children of Gad according to the house of their fathers, have received *their inheritance;* and the half-tribe of Manasseh has received its inheritance. ¹⁵The two tribes and the half-tribe have received their inheritance on this side of the Jordan, *across from* Jericho eastward, toward the sunrise."

The Leaders Appointed to Divide the Land

¹⁶And the LORD spoke to Moses, saying, ¹⁷"These *are* the names of the men who shall divide the land among you as an inheritance: Eleazar the priest and Joshua the son of Nun. ¹⁸And you shall take one leader of every tribe to divide the land for the inheritance. ¹⁹These *are* the names of the men: from the tribe of Judah, Caleb the son of Jephunneh; ²⁰from the tribe of the children of Simeon, Shemuel the son of Ammihud; ²¹from the tribe of Benjamin, Elidad the son of Chislon; ²²a leader from the tribe of the children of Dan, Bukki the son of Jogli; ²³from the sons of Joseph: a leader from the tribe of the children of Manasseh, Hanniel the son of Ephod, ²⁴and a leader from the tribe of the children of Ephraim, Kemuel the son of Shiphtan; ²⁵a leader from the tribe of the children of Zebulun, Elizaphan the son of Parnach; ²⁶a leader from the tribe of the children of Issachar, Paltiel the son of Azzan; ²⁷a leader from the tribe of the children of Asher, Ahihud the son of Shelomi; ²⁸and a leader from the tribe of the children of Naphtali, Pedahel the son of Ammihud."

²⁹These *are* the ones the LORD commanded to divide the inheritance among the children of Israel in the land of Canaan.

Cities for the Levites

35 ¹And the LORD spoke to Moses in the plains of Moab by the Jordan *across from* Jericho, saying: ²"Command the children of Israel that they give the Levites cities to dwell in from the inheritance of their possession, and you shall *also* give the Levites common-land around the cities. ³They shall have the cities to dwell in; and their common-land shall be for their cattle, for their herds, and for all their animals. ⁴The common-land of the cities which you will give the Levites *shall extend* from the wall of the city outward a thousand cubits all around. ⁵And you shall measure outside the city on the east side two thousand cubits, on the south side two thousand cubits, on the west side two thousand cubits, and on the north side two thousand cubits. The city *shall be* in the middle. This shall belong to them as common-land for the cities.

6"Now among the cities which you will give to the Levites *you shall appoint* six cities of refuge, to which a manslayer may flee. And to these you shall add forty-two cities. 7So all the cities you will give to the Levites *shall be* forty-eight; these *you shall give* with their common-land. 8And the cities which you will give *shall be* from the possession of the children of Israel; from the larger *tribe* you shall give many, from the smaller you shall give few. Each shall give some of its cities to the Levites, in proportion to the inheritance that each receives."

Cities of Refuge

9Then the LORD spoke to Moses, saying, 10"Speak to the children of Israel, and say to them: 'When you cross the Jordan into the land of Canaan, 11then you shall appoint cities to be cities of refuge for you, that the manslayer who kills any person accidentally may flee there. 12They shall be cities of refuge for you from the avenger, that the manslayer may not die until he stands before the congregation in judgment. 13And of the cities which you give, you shall have six cities of refuge. 14You shall appoint three cities on this side of the Jordan, and three cities you shall appoint in the land of Canaan, *which* will be cities of refuge. 15These six cities shall be for refuge for the children of Israel, for the stranger, and for the sojourner among them, that anyone who kills a person accidentally may flee there.

16"But if he strikes him with an iron implement, so that he dies, he *is* a murderer; the murderer shall surely be put to death. 17And if he strikes him with a stone in the hand, by which one could die, and he does die, he *is* a murderer; the murderer shall surely be put to death. 18Or *if* he strikes him with a wooden hand weapon, by which one could die, and he does die, he *is* a murderer; the murderer shall surely be

put to death. 19The avenger of blood himself shall put the murderer to death; when he meets him, he shall put him to death. 20If he pushes him out of hatred or, while lying in wait, hurls something at him so that he dies, 21or in enmity he strikes him with his hand so that he dies, the one who struck *him* shall surely be put to death. He *is* a murderer. The avenger of blood shall put the murderer to death when he meets him.

22"However, if he pushes him suddenly without enmity, or throws anything at him without lying in wait, 23or uses a stone, by which a man could die, throwing *it* at him without seeing *him,* so that he dies, while he was not his enemy or seeking his harm, 24then the congregation shall judge between the manslayer and the avenger of blood according to these judgments. 25So the congregation shall deliver the manslayer from the hand of the avenger of blood, and the congregation shall return him to the city of refuge where he had fled, and he shall remain there until the death of the high priest who was anointed with the holy oil. 26But if the manslayer at any time goes outside the limits of the city of refuge where he fled, 27and the avenger of blood finds him outside the limits of his city of refuge, and the avenger of blood kills the manslayer, he shall not be guilty of blood, 28because he should have remained in his city of refuge until the death of the high priest. But after the death of the high priest the manslayer may return to the land of his possession.

29"And these *things* shall be a statute of judgment to you throughout your generations in all your dwellings. 30Whoever kills a person, the murderer shall be put to death on the testimony of witnesses; but one witness is not *sufficient* testimony against a person for the death *penalty.* 31Moreover you shall take no ransom for the life of a murderer who *is* guilty of death, but he shall surely be put to death. 32And you shall take no ransom for him who has fled to his city of refuge, that he

---

POLITICS AND GOVERNMENT

The cities of refuge had the basic purpose of preventing private revenge, or vendetta (Num. 35:12). Criminal justice was the prerogative of the state, under the ultimate authority of God, who reserved vengeance for Himself (Deut. 32:35). The cities of refuge show how God delegated the right to punish to the state, and not to private parties.

may return to dwell in the land before the death of the priest. ³³So you shall not pollute the land where you *are;* for blood defiles the land, and no atonement can be made for the land, for the blood that is shed on it, except by the blood of him who shed it. ³⁴Therefore do not defile the land which you inhabit, in the midst of which I dwell; for I the LORD dwell among the children of Israel.' "

Marriage of Female Heirs

36 ¹Now the chief fathers of the families of the children of Gilead the son of Machir, the son of Manasseh, of the families of the sons of Joseph, came near and spoke before Moses and before the leaders, the chief fathers of the children of Israel. ²And they said: "The LORD commanded my lord *Moses* to give the land as an inheritance by lot to the children of Israel, and my lord was commanded by the LORD to give the inheritance of our brother Zelophehad to his daughters. ³Now if they are married to any of the sons of the *other* tribes of the children of Israel, then their inheritance will be taken from the inheritance of our fathers, and it will be added to the inheritance of the tribe into which they marry; so it will be taken from the lot of our inheritance. ⁴And when the Jubilee of the children of Israel comes, then their inheritance will be added to the inheritance of the tribe into which they marry; so their inheritance will be taken away from the inheritance of the tribe of our fathers."

⁵Then Moses commanded the children of Israel according to the word of the LORD, saying: "What the tribe of the sons of Joseph speaks is right. ⁶This *is* what the LORD commands concerning the daughters of Zelophehad, saying, 'Let them marry whom they think best, but they may marry only within the family of their father's tribe.' ⁷So the inheritance of the children of Israel shall not change hands from tribe to tribe, for every one of the children of Israel shall keep the inheritance of the tribe of his fathers. ⁸And every daughter who possesses an inheritance in any tribe of the children of Israel shall be the wife of one of the family of her father's tribe, so that the children of Israel each may possess the inheritance of his fathers. ⁹Thus no inheritance shall change hands from *one* tribe to another, but every tribe of the children of Israel shall keep its own inheritance."

¹⁰Just as the LORD commanded Moses,

so did the daughters of Zelophehad; ¹¹for Mahlah, Tirzah, Hoglah, Milcah, and Noah, the daughters of Zelophehad, were married to the sons of their father's brothers. ¹²They were married into the families of the children of Manasseh the son of Joseph, and their inheritance remained in the tribe of their father's family.

¹³These *are* the commandments and the judgments which the LORD commanded the children of Israel by the hand of Moses in the plains of Moab by the Jordan, *across from* Jericho.

The Book of Deuteronomy

Deuteronomy opens where the Book of Numbers closes: the Hebrew people are on the plains of Moab across the Jordan from Jericho (Num. 36:13; Deut. 1:1). The journey from Kadesh Barnea, which is reported to take 11 days (Deut. 1:2), was now over—after 40 years in the wilderness (1:3). Of the whole generation that refused to accept God's promise of the land of Canaan (Num. 14:26–32), only three persons were left: Joshua, Caleb and Moses.

Except for a few introductory and concluding statements referring to Moses in the third person, the Book of Deuteronomy consists of Moses' speeches to the people of Israel on the eve of their crossing the Jordan River to capture the Promised Land. In his first speech (chs. 1—4) he reviews the history of the people's travels from Egypt to their current place on the eastern banks of the Jordan. His second speech (chs. 5—28) summarizes the commandments that God had given on Mount Sinai, including a second presentation of the Ten Commandments in ch. 5. The name "Deuteronomy," which is derived from Latin and means "second law," refers to this speech. The third speech (chs. 29—33) is Moses' farewell and includes exhortations, songs, and blessings.

The structure of the book can be compared to a common ancient Near Eastern treaty format, found especially among the Hittites (see "The Book of Exodus" at Ex. 1:1). Such treaties began with a preamble and historical prologue (in Deuteronomy, the first speech), proceeded to the conditions and stipulations of the agreement (as in Moses' second speech), declared the blessings and curses that would result from obedience or disobedience (Deut. 27; 28), called on heavenly witnesses (31:28), and provided for the care of the treaty document (31:24–29).

Again we see God and His representative speaking in language and forms that would have been familiar to the original ancient Israelite audience.

The huge influence of Deuteronomy on the rest of the Old Testament is indisputable. Its highly distinct style appears throughout the historical books and in several of the Prophets, and it was very probably the book discovered in the temple that prompted the reforms of King Josiah (2 Kin. 22). Some scholars accept Moses as the author while others do not (particularly the account of Moses' death in ch. 34). Nevertheless, even those who consider the earlier books of Genesis through Numbers to be carefully edited composites from different sources agree on the fundamental unity of Deuteronomy.

 ■ Deuteronomy 1:1–4

Deuteronomy

1 :1 These *are* the words which Moses spoke to all Israel on this side of the Jordan in the wilderness, in the plain^a opposite Suph,^b between Paran, Tophel, Laban, Hazeroth, and Dizahab. ²*It is* eleven days' *journey* from Horeb by way of Mount Seir to Kadesh Barnea. ³Now it came to pass in the fortieth year, in the eleventh month, on the first *day* of the month, *that* Moses spoke to the children of Israel according to all that the Lord had given him as commandments to them, ⁴after he had killed Sihon king of the Amorites, who dwelt in Heshbon, and Og king of Bashan, who dwelt at Ashtaroth in^a Edrei.

1:1 ^aHebrew *arabah* ^bOne manuscript of the Septuagint, also Targum and Vulgate, read *Red Sea.* 1:4 ^aSeptuagint, Syriac, and Vulgate read *and* (compare Joshua 12:4). 1:7 ^aHebrew *arabah*

God's Mighty Acts

In his first speech (Deut. 1:6—4:43) Moses very carefully prepared his people to obey God and enter the land. He did so by showing what had brought them to this point—both disobedience (1:19–46) and obedience (2:1—3:22). Then he reminded them of the significance of those startling events at Sinai and of God's election of them to be His special people (4:1–43). This historical recital serves as the prologue to God's covenant with His chosen people (see "Covenantal Obedience" at Deut. 4:44).

 ■ Deuteronomy 1:5—4:43

Deuteronomy
The Previous Command to Enter Canaan

1 :5 On this side of the Jordan in the land of Moab, Moses began to explain this law, saying, ⁶"The Lord our God spoke to us in Horeb, saying: 'You have dwelt long enough at this mountain. ⁷Turn and take your journey, and go to the mountains of the Amorites, to all the neighboring *places* in the plain,^a in the mountains and in the lowland, in the South and on the seacoast, to the land of the Canaanites and to Lebanon, as far as the great river, the River Euphrates. ⁸See, I have set the land before you; go in and possess the land which the Lord swore to your fathers—to Abraham, Isaac, and Jacob—to give to them and their descendants after them.'

Tribal Leaders Appointed

⁹"And I spoke to you at that time, saying: 'I alone am not able to bear you. ¹⁰The Lord your God has multiplied you, and here you *are* today, as the stars of heaven in multitude. ¹¹May the Lord God of your fathers make you a thousand times more numerous than you are, and bless you as He has promised you! ¹²How can I alone bear your problems and your burdens and your complaints? ¹³Choose wise, understanding, and knowledgeable men from among your tribes, and I will make them heads over you.' ¹⁴And you answered me and said, 'The thing which you have told *us* to do *is* good.' ¹⁵So I took the heads of your tribes, wise and knowledgeable men, and made them heads over you, leaders of thousands, leaders of hundreds, leaders of fifties, leaders of tens, and officers for your tribes.

¹⁶"Then I commanded your judges at that time, saying, 'Hear *the cases* between your brethren, and judge righteously between a man and his brother or the stranger who is with him. ¹⁷You shall not show partiality in judgment; you shall hear the small as well as the great; you shall not be afraid in any man's presence, for the judgment *is* God's. The case that is too hard for you, bring to me, and I will hear it.' ¹⁸And I commanded you at that time all the things which you should do.

Israel's Refusal to Enter the Land

¹⁹"So we departed from Horeb, and went through all that great and terrible

wilderness which you saw on the way to the mountains of the Amorites, as the LORD our God had commanded us. Then we came to Kadesh Barnea. ²⁰And I said to you, 'You have come to the mountains of the Amorites, which the LORD our God is giving us. ²¹Look, the LORD your God has set the land before you; go up *and* possess *it,* as the LORD God of your fathers has spoken to you; do not fear or be discouraged.'

²²"And every one of you came near to me and said, 'Let us send men before us, and let them search out the land for us, and bring back word to us of the way by which we should go up, and of the cities into which we shall come.'

²³"The plan pleased me well; so I took twelve of your men, one man from *each* tribe. ²⁴And they departed and went up into the mountains, and came to the Valley of Eshcol, and spied it out. ²⁵They also took *some* of the fruit of the land in their hands and brought *it* down to us; and they brought back word to us, saying, '*It is* a good land which the LORD our God is giving us.'

²⁶"Nevertheless you would not go up, but rebelled against the command of the LORD your God; ²⁷and you complained in your tents, and said, 'Because the LORD hates us, He has brought us out of the land of Egypt to deliver us into the hand of the Amorites, to destroy us. ²⁸Where can we go up? Our brethren have discouraged our hearts, saying, "The people *are* greater and taller than we; the cities *are* great and fortified up to heaven; moreover we have seen the sons of the Anakim there." '

²⁹"Then I said to you, 'Do not be terrified, or afraid of them. ³⁰The LORD your God, who goes before you, He will fight for you, according to all He did for you in Egypt before your eyes, ³¹and in the wilderness where you saw how the LORD your God carried you, as a man carries his son, in all the way that you went until you came to this place.' ³²Yet, for all that, you did not believe the LORD your God, ³³who went in the way before you to search out a place for you to pitch your tents, to show you the way you should go, in the fire by night and in the cloud by day.

The Penalty for Israel's Rebellion

³⁴"And the LORD heard the sound of your words, and was angry, and took an oath, saying, ³⁵'Surely not one of these men of this evil generation shall see that good land of which I swore to give to your fathers, ³⁶except Caleb the son of Jephunneh; he shall see it, and to him and his children I am giving the land on which he walked, because he wholly followed the LORD.' ³⁷The LORD was also angry with me for your sakes, saying, 'Even you shall not go in there. ³⁸Joshua the son of Nun, who stands before you, he shall go in there. Encourage him, for he shall cause Israel to inherit it.

³⁹'Moreover your little ones and your children, who you say will be victims, who today have no knowledge of good and evil, they shall go in there; to them I will give it, and they shall possess it. ⁴⁰But *as for* you, turn and take your journey into the wilderness by the Way of the Red Sea.'

⁴¹"Then you answered and said to me, 'We have sinned against the LORD; we will go up and fight, just as the LORD our God commanded us.' And when everyone of you had girded on his weapons of war, you were ready to go up into the mountain.

⁴²"And the LORD said to me, 'Tell them, "Do not go up nor fight, for I *am* not among you; lest you be defeated before your enemies." ' ⁴³So I spoke to you; yet you would not listen, but rebelled against the command of the LORD, and presumptuously went up into the mountain. ⁴⁴And the Amorites who dwelt in that mountain came out against you and chased you as bees do, and drove you back from Seir to Hormah. ⁴⁵Then you returned and wept before the LORD, but the LORD would not listen to your voice nor give ear to you.

⁴⁶"So you remained in Kadesh many days, according to the days that you spent *there.*

The Desert Years

2 ¹"Then we turned and journeyed into the wilderness of the Way of the Red Sea, as the LORD spoke to me, and we skirted Mount Seir for many days.

²"And the LORD spoke to me, saying: ³'You have skirted this mountain long enough; turn northward. ⁴And command the people, saying, "You *are about to* pass through the territory of your brethren, the descendants of Esau, who live in Seir; and they will be afraid of you. Therefore watch yourselves carefully. ⁵Do not meddle with them, for I will not give you *any* of their land, no, not so much as one footstep, because I have given Mount Seir to Esau *as a* possession. ⁶You shall buy food from them

with money, that you may eat; and you shall also buy water from them with money, that you may drink.

7"For the LORD your God has blessed you in all the work of your hand. He knows your trudging through this great wilderness. These forty years the LORD your God *has been* with you; you have lacked nothing." '

8"And when we passed beyond our brethren, the descendants of Esau who dwell in Seir, away from the road of the plain, away from Elath and Ezion Geber, we turned and passed by way of the Wilderness of Moab. 9Then the LORD said to me, 'Do not harass Moab, nor contend with them in battle, for I will not give you *any* of their land *as* a possession, because I have given Ar to the descendants of Lot *as* a possession.' "

10(The Emim had dwelt there in times past, a people as great and numerous and tall as the Anakim. 11They were also regarded as giants,[a] like the Anakim, but the Moabites call them Emim. 12The Horites formerly dwelt in Seir, but the descendants of Esau dispossessed them and destroyed them from before them, and dwelt in their place, just as Israel did to the land of their possession which the LORD gave them.)

13" 'Now rise and cross over the Valley of the Zered.' So we crossed over the Valley of the Zered. 14And the time we took to come from Kadesh Barnea until we crossed over the Valley of the Zered *was* thirty-eight years, until all the generation of the men of war was consumed from the midst of the camp, just as the LORD had sworn to them. 15For indeed the hand of the LORD was against them, to destroy them from the midst of the camp until they were consumed.

16"So it was, when all the men of war had finally perished from among the people, 17that the LORD spoke to me, saying: 18This day you are to cross over at Ar, the boundary of Moab. 19And *when* you come near the people of Ammon, do not harass them or meddle with them, for I will not give you *any* of the land of the people of Ammon *as* a possession, because I have given it to the descendants of Lot *as* a possession.' "

20(That was also regarded as a land of giants;[a] giants formerly dwelt there. But the Ammonites call them Zamzummim, 21a people as great and numerous and tall as the Anakim. But the LORD destroyed them before them, and they dispossessed them and dwelt in their place, 22just as He had done for the descendants of Esau, who dwelt in Seir, when He destroyed the Horites from before them. They dispossessed them and dwelt in their place, even to this day. 23And the Avim, who dwelt in villages as far as Gaza—the Caphtorim, who came from Caphtor, destroyed them and dwelt in their place.)

24" 'Rise, take your journey, and cross over the River Arnon. Look, I have given into your hand Sihon the Amorite, king of Heshbon, and his land. Begin to possess *it,* and engage him in battle. 25This day I will begin to put the dread and fear of you upon the nations under the whole heaven, who shall hear the report of you, and shall tremble and be in anguish because of you.'

King Sihon Defeated

26"And I sent messengers from the Wilderness of Kedemoth to Sihon king of Heshbon, with words of peace, saying, 27'Let me pass through your land; I will keep strictly to the road, and I will turn neither to the right nor to the left. 28You shall sell me food for money, that I may eat, and give me water for money, that I may drink; only let me pass through on foot, 29just as the descendants of Esau who dwell in Seir and the Moabites who dwell in Ar did for me, until I cross the Jordan to the land which the LORD our God is giving us.'

30"But Sihon king of Heshbon would not let us pass through, for the LORD your

2:11 [a]Hebrew *rephaim*   2:20 [a]Hebrew *rephaim*

TRADE AND ECONOMICS

Coins were not struck until late in the 7th century B.C. However, it had long been possible to use pieces of gold, silver, or bronze in bartering and exchange (Deut. 2:6). Like the earliest coins, such pieces of metal were not tokens, but were used in consideration of their intrinsic value and exchanged by actual weight.

God hardened his spirit and made his heart obstinate, that He might deliver him into your hand, as *it is* this day.

³¹"And the LORD said to me, 'See, I have begun to give Sihon and his land over to you. Begin to possess *it,* that you may inherit his land.' ³²Then Sihon and all his people came out against us to fight at Jahaz. ³³And the LORD our God delivered him over to us; so we defeated him, his sons, and all his people. ³⁴We took all his cities at that time, and we utterly destroyed the men, women, and little ones of every city; we left none remaining. ³⁵We took only the livestock as plunder for ourselves, with the spoil of the cities which we took. ³⁶From Aroer, which *is* on the bank of the River Arnon, and *from* the city that *is* in the ravine, as far as Gilead, there was not one city too strong for us; the LORD our God delivered all to us. ³⁷Only you did not go near the land of the people of Ammon—anywhere along the River Jabbok, or to the cities of the mountains, or wherever the LORD our God had forbidden us.

King Og Defeated

3 ¹"Then we turned and went up the road to Bashan; and Og king of Bashan came out against us, he and all his people, to battle at Edrei. ²And the LORD said to me, 'Do not fear him, for I have delivered him and all his people and his land into your hand; you shall do to him as you did to Sihon king of the Amorites, who dwelt at Heshbon.'

³"So the LORD our God also delivered into our hands Og king of Bashan, with all his people, and we attacked him until he had no survivors remaining. ⁴And we took all his cities at that time; there was not a city which we did not take from them: sixty cities, all the region of Argob, the kingdom of Og in Bashan. ⁵All these cities *were* fortified with high walls, gates, and bars, besides a great many rural towns. ⁶And we utterly destroyed them, as we did to Sihon king of Heshbon, utterly destroying the men, women, and children of every city. ⁷But all the livestock and the spoil of the cities we took as booty for ourselves.

⁸"And at that time we took the land from the hand of the two kings of the Amorites who *were* on this side of the Jordan, from the River Arnon to Mount Hermon ⁹(the Sidonians call Hermon Sirion, and the Amorites call it Senir), ¹⁰all the cities of the plain, all Gilead, and all Bashan, as far as Salcah and Edrei, cities of the kingdom of Og in Bashan.

¹¹"For only Og king of Bashan remained of the remnant of the giants.[a] Indeed his bedstead *was* an iron bedstead. (*Is* it not in Rabbah of the people of Ammon?) Nine cubits *is* its length and four cubits its width, according to the standard cubit.

The Land East of the Jordan Divided

¹²"And this land, *which* we possessed at that time, from Aroer, which *is* by the River Arnon, and half the mountains of Gilead and its cities, I gave to the Reubenites and the Gadites. ¹³The rest of Gilead, and all Bashan, the kingdom of Og, I gave to half the tribe of Manasseh. (All the region of Argob, with all Bashan, was called the land of the giants.[a] ¹⁴Jair the son of Manasseh took all the region of Argob, as far as the border of the Geshurites and the Maachathites, and called Bashan after his own name, Havoth Jair,[a] to this day.)

¹⁵"Also I gave Gilead to Machir. ¹⁶And to the Reubenites and the Gadites I gave from Gilead as far as the River Arnon, the middle of the river as *the* border, as far as the River Jabbok, the border of the people of Ammon; ¹⁷the plain also, with the Jordan as *the* border, from Chinnereth as far as the east side of the Sea of the Arabah (the Salt Sea), below the slopes of Pisgah.

¹⁸"Then I commanded you at that time, saying: 'The LORD your God has given you this land to possess. All you men of valor shall cross over armed before your brethren, the children of Israel. ¹⁹But your wives, your little ones, and your livestock (I

TIME CAPSULE *1350 to 1345 B.C.*

1350   The Hurrian kingdom of Mitanni falls, and is ruled by Assyrians and Hittites

1350   King Niqmaddu II of Ugarit makes treaty with the king of Amurru

1348   Amenhotep IV changes his name to Akhenaten

1348   Pharaoh Akhenaten founds the city of Akhetaten (el-Amarna) in Egypt

1345   Pharaoh Akhenaten makes his residence in Akhetaten

3:11 ªHebrew *rephaim*   3:13 ªHebrew *rephaim*   3:14 ªLiterally *Towns of Jair*

know that you have much livestock) shall stay in your cities which I have given you, ²⁰until the LORD has given rest to your brethren as to you, and they also possess the land which the LORD your God is giving them beyond the Jordan. Then each of you may return to his possession which I have given you.'

²¹"And I commanded Joshua at that time, saying, 'Your eyes have seen all that the LORD your God has done to these two kings; so will the LORD do to all the kingdoms through which you pass. ²²You must not fear them, for the LORD your God Himself fights for you.'

Moses Forbidden to Enter the Land

²³"Then I pleaded with the LORD at that time, saying: ²⁴O Lord GOD, You have begun to show Your servant Your greatness and Your mighty hand, for what god *is there* in heaven or on earth who can do *anything* like Your works and Your mighty *deeds?* ²⁵I pray, let me cross over and see the good land beyond the Jordan, those pleasant mountains, and Lebanon.'

²⁶"But the LORD was angry with me on your account, and would not listen to me. So the LORD said to me: 'Enough of that! Speak no more to Me of this matter. ²⁷Go up to the top of Pisgah, and lift your eyes toward the west, the north, the south, and the east; behold *it* with your eyes, for you shall not cross over this Jordan. ²⁸But command Joshua, and encourage him and strengthen him; for he shall go over before this people, and he shall cause them to inherit the land which you will see.'

²⁹"So we stayed in the valley opposite Beth Peor.

Moses Commands Obedience

4 ¹"Now, O Israel, listen to the statutes and the judgments which I teach you to observe, that you may live, and go in and possess the land which the LORD God of your fathers is giving you. ²You shall not add to the word which I command you, nor take from it, that you may keep the commandments of the LORD your God which I command you. ³Your eyes have seen what the LORD did at Baal Peor; for the LORD your God has destroyed from among you all the men who followed Baal of Peor. ⁴But you who held fast to the LORD your God *are* alive today, every one of you.

⁵"Surely I have taught you statutes and judgments, just as the LORD my God commanded me, that you should act according *to them* in the land which you go to possess. ⁶Therefore be careful to observe *them;* for this *is* your wisdom and your understanding in the sight of the peoples who will hear all these statutes, and say, 'Surely this great nation *is* a wise and understanding people.'

⁷"For what great nation *is there* that has God *so* near to it, as the LORD our God *is* to us, for whatever *reason* we may call upon Him? ⁸And what great nation *is there* that has *such* statutes and righteous judgments as are in all this law which I set before you this day? ⁹Only take heed to yourself, and diligently keep yourself, lest you forget the things your eyes have seen, and lest they depart from your heart all the days of your life. And teach them to your children and your grandchildren, ¹⁰*especially concerning* the day you stood before the LORD your God in Horeb, when the LORD said to me, 'Gather the people to Me, and I will let them hear My words, that they may learn to fear Me all the days they live on the earth, and *that* they may teach their children.'

¹¹"Then you came near and stood at the foot of the mountain, and the mountain burned with fire to the midst of heaven, with darkness, cloud, and thick darkness. ¹²And the LORD spoke to you out of the midst of the fire. You heard the sound of the words, but saw no form; *you* only *heard* a voice. ¹³So He declared to you His covenant which He commanded you to perform, the Ten Commandments; and He wrote them on two tablets of stone. ¹⁴And the LORD commanded me at that time to teach you statutes and judgments, that you might observe them in the land which you cross over to possess.

Beware of Idolatry

¹⁵"Take careful heed to yourselves, for you saw no form when the LORD spoke to you at Horeb out of the midst of the fire, ¹⁶lest you act corruptly and make for yourselves a carved image in the form of any figure: the likeness of male or female, ¹⁷the likeness of any animal that *is* on the earth or the likeness of any winged bird that flies in the air, ¹⁸the likeness of anything that creeps on the ground or the likeness of any fish that *is* in the water beneath the earth. ¹⁹And *take heed,* lest you lift your eyes to heaven, and *when* you see the sun, the moon, and the stars, all the host of heaven,

you feel driven to worship them and serve them, which the LORD your God has given to all the peoples under the whole heaven as a heritage. 20But the LORD has taken you and brought you out of the iron furnace, out of Egypt, to be His people, an inheritance, as you are this day. 21Furthermore the LORD was angry with me for your sakes, and swore that I would not cross over the Jordan, and that I would not enter the good land which the LORD your God is giving you as an inheritance. 22But I must die in this land, I must not cross over the Jordan; but you shall cross over and possess that good land. 23Take heed to yourselves, lest you forget the covenant of the LORD your God which He made with you, and make for yourselves a carved image in the form of anything which the LORD your God has forbidden you. 24For the LORD your God is a consuming fire, a jealous God.

25"When you beget children and grandchildren and have grown old in the land, and act corruptly and make a carved image in the form of anything, and do evil in the sight of the LORD your God to provoke Him to anger, 26I call heaven and earth to witness against you this day, that you will soon utterly perish from the land which you cross over the Jordan to possess; you will not prolong your days in it, but will be utterly destroyed. 27And the LORD will scatter you among the peoples, and you will be left few in number among the nations where the LORD will drive you. 28And there you will serve gods, the work of men's hands, wood and stone, which neither see nor hear nor eat nor smell. 29But from there you will seek the LORD your God, and you will find Him if you seek Him with all your heart and with all your soul. 30When you are in distress, and all these things come upon you in the latter days, when you turn to the LORD your God and obey His voice 31(for the LORD your God is a merciful God), He will not forsake you nor destroy you, nor forget the covenant of your fathers which He swore to them.

32"For ask now concerning the days that are past, which were before you, since the day that God created man on the earth, and ask from one end of heaven to the other, whether any great thing like this has happened, or anything like it has been heard. 33Did any people ever hear the voice of God speaking out of the midst of the fire, as you have heard, and live? 34Or did God ever try to go and take for Himself a nation from the midst of another nation, by trials, by signs, by wonders, by war, by a mighty hand and an outstretched arm, and by great terrors, according to all that the LORD your God did for you in Egypt before your eyes? 35To you it was shown, that you might know that the LORD Himself is God; there is none other besides Him. 36Out of heaven He let you hear His voice, that He might instruct you; on earth He showed you His great fire, and you heard His words out of the midst of the fire. 37And because He loved your fathers, therefore He chose their descendants after them; and He brought you out of Egypt with His Presence, with His mighty power, 38driving out from before you nations greater and mightier than you, to bring you in, to give you their land as an inheritance, as it is this day. 39Therefore know this day, and consider it in your heart, that the LORD Himself is God in heaven above and on the earth beneath; there is no other. 40You shall therefore keep His statutes and His commandments which I command you today, that it may go well with you and with your children after you, and that you may prolong your days in the land which the LORD your God is giving you for all time."

Cities of Refuge East of the Jordan

41Then Moses set apart three cities on this side of the Jordan, toward the rising of the sun, 42that the manslayer might flee there, who kills his neighbor unintentionally, without having hated him in time past, and that by fleeing to one of these cities he might live: 43Bezer in the wilder-

ARTS AND LITERATURE

The art of the ancient Near East was fundamentally at the service of the nobility, who held the powers of religion and of government. For this reason most of the persons depicted are kings or gods (Deut. 4:16). In Egypt, the statues of kings were much bigger than the statues of the gods. The Jews did not make any statues of God.

ness on the plateau for the Reubenites, Ramoth in Gilead for the Gadites, and Golan in Bashan for the Manassites.

Covenantal Obedience

A brief introduction (Deut. 4:44–49) describes the setting for Moses' second speech, explaining how Israel arrived on the east side of the Jordan. The first section of the speech (chs. 5—11) summarizes the covenant obligations, and explains what the "statutes and judgments" are about and why obedience to them would be crucial for Israel to enjoy the covenant blessings. The second section (12:1—26:19) lists specific requirements, intermingling civil, ceremonial, and moral laws.

In this speech Moses reminds the people of their covenant obligations to be kept when they enter the land. It is plain, especially in chs. 6—11, that his purpose was not primarily informational, but motivational. His concern was to ensure that they would obey what they knew.

■ Deuteronomy 4:44—28:68

Deuteronomy
Introduction to God's Law

4 :44 Now this *is* the law which Moses set before the children of Israel. 45These *are* the testimonies, the statutes, and the judgments which Moses spoke to the children of Israel after they came out of Egypt, 46on this side of the Jordan, in the valley opposite Beth Peor, in the land of Sihon king of the Amorites, who dwelt at Heshbon, whom Moses and the children of Israel defeated after they came out of Egypt. 47And they took possession of his land and the land of Og king of Bashan, two kings of the Amorites, who *were* on this side of the Jordan, toward the rising of the sun, 48from Aroer, which *is* on the bank of the River Arnon, even to Mount Sion[a] (that is, Hermon), 49and all the plain on the east side of the Jordan as far as the Sea of the Arabah, below the slopes of Pisgah.

The Ten Commandments Reviewed

5 1And Moses called all Israel, and said to them: "Hear, O Israel, the statutes and judgments which I speak in your hearing today, that you may learn them and be

careful to observe them. 2The LORD our God made a covenant with us in Horeb. 3The LORD did not make this covenant with our fathers, but with us, those who *are* here today, all of us who *are* alive. 4The LORD talked with you face to face on the mountain from the midst of the fire. 5I stood between the LORD and you at that time, to declare to you the word of the LORD; for you were afraid because of the fire, and you did not go up the mountain. *He* said:

6 'I *am* the LORD your God who brought you out of the land of Egypt, out of the house of bondage.

7 'You shall have no other gods before Me.

8 'You shall not make for yourself a carved image—any likeness *of anything* that *is* in heaven above, or that *is* in the earth beneath, or that *is* in the water under the earth; 9you shall not bow down to them nor serve them. For I, the LORD your God, *am* a jealous God, visiting the iniquity of the fathers upon the children to the third and fourth *generations* of those who hate Me, 10but showing mercy to thousands, to those who love Me and keep My commandments.

11 'You shall not take the name of the LORD your God in vain, for the LORD will not hold *him* guiltless who takes His name in vain.

12 'Observe the Sabbath day, to keep it holy, as the LORD your God commanded you. 13Six days you shall labor and do all your work, 14but the seventh day *is* the Sabbath of the LORD your God. *In it* you shall do no work: you, nor your son, nor your daughter, nor your male servant, nor your female servant, nor your ox, nor your donkey, nor any of your cattle, nor your stranger who *is* within your gates, that your male servant and your female servant may rest as well as you. 15And remember that you were a slave in the land of Egypt, and the LORD your God brought you out from there by a mighty hand and by an outstretched arm; therefore the LORD your God commanded you to keep the Sabbath day.

16 'Honor your father and your mother, as the LORD your God has commanded

---

4:48 [a]Syriac reads *Sirion* (compare 3:9).

How Is an Idol a God? (Deut. 5:8, 9)

The prohibition of Deut. 5:8, 9 reflects a world where bowing down to idols meant worshiping not just images, but deities. Representations of gods in human, animal, or abstract forms were everywhere in the ancient Near East. Scattered from Egypt through Syria-Palestine and throughout Mesopotamia were local temples housing these images.

Beliefs differed as to whether or not gods were really there in the statues. In Egypt the gods were understood to be always in heaven above the human world, yet always in the images as well. The statues were considered to be the body of the god into which the presence of the deity entered. For this reason the body was clothed, bathed, and fed as one would care for a ruler. Since heavenly deities were invisible, the statues were normally kept in the dark, inner room of the temples away from the eyes of the people. Except for feast days when the image was brought out on procession, only the attending priests were allowed into the image's presence.

In Mesopotamia the understanding of images was slightly different. The image was considered only wood, stone, or metal as long as it was being fashioned. However, once it was set up in the temple, a lengthy ritual called "opening the mouth" changed the nature of the image. Through this religious ritual the deity supposedly entered the statue so that the idol became the god and, at that point, could receive praise, bestow blessings, and grant favors. The image was understood to be a gift of the god who dwelt within it. Therefore, any image that was looted in warfare was taken as absolute proof that the favor of the deity had passed to the victors.

In contrast to the Egyptians and Mesopotamians, Israel's worship was to be imageless. The commandment in Deut. 5:8, 9 condemns the fashioning of any image: "any likeness of anything." Moreover, the commandment even forbids making an image of the God of Israel.

---

you, that your days may be long, and that it may be well with you in the land which the LORD your God is giving you.

17 'You shall not murder.

18 'You shall not commit adultery.

19 'You shall not steal.

20 'You shall not bear false witness against your neighbor.

21 'You shall not covet your neighbor's wife; and you shall not desire your neighbor's house, his field, his male servant, his female servant, his ox, his donkey, or anything that *is* your neighbor's.'

22"These words the LORD spoke to all your assembly, in the mountain from the midst of the fire, the cloud, and the thick darkness, with a loud voice; and He added no more. And He wrote them on two tablets of stone and gave them to me.

The People Afraid of God's Presence

23"So it was, when you heard the voice from the midst of the darkness, while the mountain was burning with fire, that you came near to me, all the heads of your tribes and your elders. 24And you said: 'Surely the LORD our God has shown us His glory and His greatness, and we have heard His voice from the midst of the fire. We have seen this day that God speaks with man; yet he *still* lives. 25Now therefore, why should we die? For this great fire will consume us; if we hear the voice of the LORD our God anymore, then we shall die. 26For who *is there* of all flesh who has heard the voice of the living God speaking from the midst of the fire, as we *have,* and lived? 27You go near and hear all that the LORD our God may say, and tell us all that the LORD our God says to you, and we will hear and do *it.*'

28"Then the LORD heard the voice of your words when you spoke to me, and the LORD said to me: 'I have heard the voice of the words of this people which they have spoken to you. They are right *in* all that they have spoken. 29Oh, that they had such a heart in them that they would fear Me and always keep all My commandments, that it might be well with them and with their children forever! 30Go and say to them, "Return to your tents." 31But as for you, stand here by Me, and I will speak to you all the commandments, the statutes, and the judgments which you shall teach them, that they may observe *them* in the land which I am giving them to possess.'

32"Therefore you shall be careful to do as the LORD your God has commanded you; you shall not turn aside to the right hand or to the left. 33You shall walk in all the ways which the LORD your God has commanded you, that you may live and *that it may be* well with you, and *that* you may prolong *your* days in the land which you shall possess.

The Greatest Commandment

6 1"Now this *is* the commandment, *and these are* the statutes and judgments which the LORD your God has commanded to teach you, that you may observe *them* in the land which you are crossing over to possess, 2that you may fear the LORD your God, to keep all His statutes and His commandments which I command you, you and your son and your grandson, all the days of your life, and that your days may be prolonged. 3Therefore hear, O Israel, and be careful to observe *it*, that it may be well with you, and that you may multiply greatly as the LORD God of your fathers has promised you—'a land flowing with milk and honey.'a

4"Hear, O Israel: The LORD our God, the LORD *is* one!a 5You shall love the LORD your God with all your heart, with all your soul, and with all your strength.

6"And these words which I command you today shall be in your heart. 7You shall teach them diligently to your children, and shall talk of them when you sit in your house, when you walk by the way, when you lie down, and when you rise up. 8You shall bind them as a sign on your hand, and they shall be as frontlets between your eyes. 9You shall write them on the doorposts of your house and on your gates.

6:3 aExodus 3:8   6:4 aOr *The LORD is our God, the LORD alone* (that is, the only one)

Caution Against Disobedience

10"So it shall be, when the LORD your God brings you into the land of which He swore to your fathers, to Abraham, Isaac, and Jacob, to give you large and beautiful cities which you did not build, 11houses full of all good things, which you did not fill, hewn-out wells which you did not dig, vineyards and olive trees which you did not plant—when you have eaten and are full— 12*then* beware, lest you forget the LORD who brought you out of the land of Egypt, from the house of bondage. 13You shall fear the LORD your God and serve Him, and shall take oaths in His name. 14You shall not go after other gods, the gods of the peoples who *are* all around you 15(for the LORD your God *is* a jealous God among you), lest the anger of the LORD your God be aroused against you and destroy you from the face of the earth.

16"You shall not tempt the LORD your God as you tempted *Him* in Massah. 17You shall diligently keep the commandments of the LORD your God, His testimonies, and His statutes which He has commanded you. 18And you shall do *what is* right and good in the sight of the LORD, that it may be well with you, and that you may go in and possess the good land of which the LORD swore to your fathers, 19to cast out all your enemies from before you, as the LORD has spoken.

20"When your son asks you in time to come, saying, 'What *is the meaning of* the testimonies, the statutes, and the judgments which the LORD our God has commanded you?' 21then you shall say to your son: 'We were slaves of Pharaoh in Egypt, and the LORD brought us out of Egypt with a mighty hand; 22and the LORD showed signs and wonders before our eyes, great and severe, against Egypt, Pharaoh, and all his household. 23Then He brought us out from there, that He might bring us in, to give us the land of which He swore to our fathers. 24And the LORD commanded us to observe all these statutes, to fear the LORD our God, for our good always, that He

---

BELIEFS AND IDEAS

The words beginning "Hear, O Israel" are the basic confession of Jewish faith (Deut. 6:4). They are called the Shema (the Hebrew word meaning "hear"). They have been repeated privately and in public liturgy continuously, from the time that they were first revealed until today. Written on parchment scrolls, they are attached to doorposts in a special container.

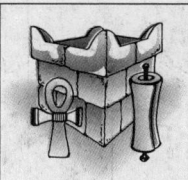

might preserve us alive, as *it is* this day. [25]Then it will be righteousness for us, if we are careful to observe all these commandments before the LORD our God, as He has commanded us.'

A Chosen People

7 [1]"When the LORD your God brings you into the land which you go to possess, and has cast out many nations before you, the Hittites and the Girgashites and the Amorites and the Canaanites and the Perizzites and the Hivites and the Jebusites, seven nations greater and mightier than you, [2]and when the LORD your God delivers them over to you, you shall conquer them *and* utterly destroy them. You shall make no covenant with them nor show mercy to them. [3]Nor shall you make marriages with them. You shall not give your daughter to their son, nor take their daughter for your son. [4]For they will turn your sons away from following Me, to serve other gods; so the anger of the LORD will be aroused against you and destroy you suddenly. [5]But thus you shall deal with them: you shall destroy their altars, and break down their *sacred* pillars, and cut down their wooden images,[a] and burn their carved images with fire.

[6]"For you *are* a holy people to the LORD your God; the LORD your God has chosen you to be a people for Himself, a special treasure above all the peoples on the face of the earth. [7]The LORD did not set His love on you nor choose you because you were more in number than any other people, for you were the least of all peoples; [8]but because the LORD loves you, and because He would keep the oath which He swore to your fathers, the LORD has brought you out with a mighty hand, and redeemed you from the house of bondage, from the hand of Pharaoh king of Egypt.

[9]"Therefore know that the LORD your God, He *is* God, the faithful God who keeps covenant and mercy for a thousand generations with those who love Him and keep His commandments; [10]and He repays those who hate Him to their face, to destroy them. He will not be slack with him who hates Him; He will repay him to his face. [11]Therefore you shall keep the commandment, the statutes, and the judgments which I command you today, to observe them.

Blessings of Obedience

[12]"Then it shall come to pass, because you listen to these judgments, and keep and do them, that the LORD your God will keep with you the covenant and the mercy which He swore to your fathers. [13]And He will love you and bless you and multiply you; He will also bless the fruit of your womb and the fruit of your land, your grain and your new wine and your oil, the increase of your cattle and the offspring of your flock, in the land of which He swore to your fathers to give you. [14]You shall be blessed above all peoples; there shall not be a male or female barren among you or among your livestock. [15]And the LORD will take away from you all sickness, and will afflict you with none of the terrible diseases of Egypt which you have known, but will lay *them* on all those who hate you. [16]Also you shall destroy all the peoples whom the LORD your God delivers over to you; your eye shall have no pity on them; nor shall you serve their gods, for that *will be* a snare to you.

[17]"If you should say in your heart, 'These nations are greater than I; how can I dispossess them?'— [18]you shall not be afraid of them, *but* you shall remember well what the LORD your God did to Pharaoh and to all Egypt: [19]the great trials which your eyes saw, the signs and the wonders, the mighty hand and the outstretched arm, by which the LORD your God brought you out. So shall the LORD your God do to all the peoples of whom you are afraid. [20]Moreover the LORD your God will send the hornet among them until those who are left, who hide themselves from

---

7:5 [a]Hebrew *Asherim*, Canaanite deities

GEOGRAPHY AND ENVIRONMENT

The list of seven nations (Deut. 7:1) is a traditional list of the enemies that Israel encountered in Palestine (Josh. 3:10). The Hittites were from what is today Turkey. The Jebusites dwelt in Jerusalem and were conquered by David. "Canaanite" and "Amorite" are often used loosely to include all or most of the seven peoples.

PHARAOH, KING OF EGYPT (Deut. 7:8)

Although the term "Pharaoh" is well known from Scripture, it was not the most common designation used by Egyptians for their monarch before the New Kingdom period (c. 1550 B.C.). In fact, it was not even used to refer to the Egyptian king until later in Egypt's history.

The Egyptian term for "Pharaoh" means literally the "Great House." Originally, it designated part of the large palatial complex at Memphis, one of the early capitals of Egypt in the 3rd millennium B.C. Soon thereafter, it denoted the Egyptian government itself—the king and his administration—not just the buildings from which they governed.

The process by which the king of Egypt became known as "Pharaoh" was gradual, involving various stages. In the first stage, sometime before Thutmose III became king (1479 B.C.), the title was occasionally applied to Egypt's monarch. A more advanced stage occurred before the end of the New Kingdom period (c. 1069 B.C.) when the use of "Pharaoh" referring to the king moved from everyday speech into the official language of the country. From the time of King Shoshenq I (or Sheshonk, 945–924 B.C.), "Pharaoh" was added to the king's official title.

The biblical writer uses the term as a common way of referring to the Egyptian king. God had delivered His people from bondage under "Pharaoh king of Egypt" (Deut. 7:8). This use reveals a knowledge of Egypt in the late 2nd and early 1st millenniums B.C.

The title "Pharaoh" highlights Israel's climactic experience with Egypt's king. The monarch of Egypt was considered the divine incarnation of Horus (the falcon god), as well as the son of Re (the sun god). Since Pharaoh was considered a god, the contest was between gods: the incarnate god of Egypt against the God of Israel, who spoke through His prophet Moses.

you, are destroyed. 21You shall not be terrified of them; for the LORD your God, the great and awesome God, *is* among you. 22And the LORD your God will drive out those nations before you little by little; you will be unable to destroy them at once, lest the beasts of the field become *too* numerous for you. 23But the LORD your God will deliver them over to you, and will inflict defeat upon them until they are destroyed. 24And He will deliver their kings into your hand, and you will destroy their name from under heaven; no one shall be able to stand against you until you have destroyed them. 25You shall burn the carved images of their gods with fire; you shall not covet the silver or gold *that is* on them, nor take *it* for yourselves, lest you be snared by it; for it *is* an abomination to the LORD your God. 26Nor shall you bring an abomination into your house, lest you be doomed to destruction like it. You shall utterly detest it and utterly abhor it, for it *is* an accursed thing.

Remember the LORD Your God

8 1"Every commandment which I command you today you must be careful to observe, that you may live and multiply, and go in and possess the land of which the LORD swore to your fathers. 2And you shall remember that the LORD your God led you all the way these forty years in the wilderness, to humble you *and* test you, to know what *was* in your heart, whether you would keep His commandments or not. 3So He humbled you, allowed you to hunger, and fed you with manna which you did not know nor did your fathers know, that He might make you know that man shall not live by bread alone; but man lives by every *word* that proceeds from the mouth of the LORD. 4Your garments did not wear out on you, nor did your foot swell these forty years. 5You should know in your heart that as a man chastens his son, *so* the LORD your God chastens you.

6"Therefore you shall keep the commandments of the LORD your God, to walk in His ways and to fear Him. 7For the LORD your God is bringing you into a good land, a land of brooks of water, of fountains and springs, that flow out of valleys and hills; 8a land of wheat and barley, of vines and fig trees and pomegranates, a land of olive oil and honey; 9a land in which you will eat bread without scarcity, in which you will lack nothing; a land whose stones *are* iron and out of whose hills you can dig copper. 10When you have eaten and are full, then you shall bless the LORD your God for the good land which He has given you.

11"Beware that you do not forget the LORD your God by not keeping His commandments, His judgments, and His statutes which I command you today, 12lest—*when* you have eaten and are full, and have built beautiful houses and dwell *in them;* 13and *when* your herds and your flocks multiply, and your silver and your gold are multiplied, and all that you have is multiplied; 14when your heart is lifted up, and you forget the LORD your God who brought you out of the land of Egypt, from the house of bondage; 15who led you through that great and terrible wilderness, *in which were* fiery serpents and scorpions and thirsty land where there was no water; who brought water for you out of the flinty rock; 16who fed you in the wilderness with manna, which your fathers did not know, that He might humble you and that He might test you, to do you good in the end— 17then you say in your heart, 'My power and the might of my hand have gained me this wealth.'

18"And you shall remember the LORD your God, for *it is* He who gives you power to get wealth, that He may establish His covenant which He swore to your fathers, as *it is* this day. 19Then it shall be, if you by any means forget the LORD your God, and follow other gods, and serve them and worship them, I testify against you this day that you shall surely perish. 20As the nations which the LORD destroys before you, so you shall perish, because you would not be obedient to the voice of the LORD your God.

Israel's Rebellions Reviewed

9 1"Hear, O Israel: You *are* to cross over the Jordan today, and go in to dispossess nations greater and mightier than yourself, cities great and fortified up to heaven, 2a people great and tall, the descendants of the Anakim, whom you know, and *of whom* you heard *it said,* 'Who can stand before the descendants of Anak?'

3Therefore understand today that the LORD your God *is* He who goes over before you *as* a consuming fire. He will destroy them and bring them down before you; so you shall drive them out and destroy them quickly, as the LORD has said to you.

4"Do not think in your heart, after the LORD your God has cast them out before you, saying, 'Because of my righteousness the LORD has brought me in to possess this land'; but *it is* because of the wickedness of these nations *that* the LORD is driving them out from before you. 5*It is* not because of your righteousness or the uprightness of your heart *that* you go in to possess their land, but because of the wickedness of these nations *that* the LORD your God drives them out from before you, and that He may fulfill the word which the LORD swore to your fathers, to Abraham, Isaac, and Jacob. 6Therefore understand that the LORD your God is not giving you this good land to possess because of your righteousness, for you *are* a stiff-necked people.

7"Remember! Do not forget how you provoked the LORD your God to wrath in the wilderness. From the day that you departed from the land of Egypt until you came to this place, you have been rebellious against the LORD. 8Also in Horeb you provoked the LORD to wrath, so that the LORD was angry *enough* with you to have destroyed you. 9When I went up into the mountain to receive the tablets of stone, the tablets of the covenant which the LORD made with you, then I stayed on the mountain forty days and forty nights. I neither ate bread nor drank water. 10Then the LORD delivered to me two tablets of stone written with the finger of God, and on them *were* all the words which the LORD had spoken to you on the mountain from the midst of the fire in the day of the assembly. 11And it came to pass, at the end of forty days and forty nights, *that* the LORD gave me the two tablets of stone, the tablets of the covenant.

12"Then the LORD said to me, 'Arise, go down quickly from here, for your people

DAILY LIFE AND CUSTOMS

Fasting appears in the Bible as a natural expression of feelings of distress, sorrow, and guilt (Deut. 9:18). It does not play a large part in the Law of Moses, where only one mandatory fast is found—on the Day of Atonement (Lev. 16:29-31). The apostle Paul called this day "the Fast" (Acts 27:9).

ANNIHILATION OF THE GOLDEN CALF (Deut. 9:21)

Moses did not want the people to forget their failure to remain devoted to Yahweh. He recalled for them the calf idol they had made, and that he had destroyed. Moses' actions in the matter possibly seem extreme: "I . . . burned it with fire and crushed it and ground it very small, until it was as fine as dust" (Deut. 9:21). Such actions, however, appear to have a parallel within Canaanite ritual.

Ritual annihilation of an enemy god was evidently common, at least in Canaan. A text from Ugarit (c. 1400–1200 B.C.), belonging to the Baal-Anath cycle of myths, describes a very similar destruction. The goddess Anath burns, grinds, and scatters the god Mot.

The Ugaritic ritual may not be the same ritual that is being described in Deut. 9:21. Nevertheless, the similarities suggest that Moses' annihilation of the idol calf was possibly a symbolic or ritualistic destruction known in Canaanite culture. It was not uncommon for Israelites and others to destroy enemy gods by breaking, burning, crushing, grinding, and scattering them, actions that possibly symbolized the utter defeat of the gods. In addition to Moses, two Judahite kings—Josiah (2 Kin. 23:4, 6, 15) and Asa (2 Chr. 15:16)—performed similar actions.

---

whom you brought out of Egypt have acted corruptly; they have quickly turned aside from the way which I commanded them; they have made themselves a molded image.'

13"Furthermore the LORD spoke to me, saying, 'I have seen this people, and indeed they are a stiff-necked people. 14Let Me alone, that I may destroy them and blot out their name from under heaven; and I will make of you a nation mightier and greater than they.'

15"So I turned and came down from the mountain, and the mountain burned with fire; and the two tablets of the covenant *were* in my two hands. 16And I looked, and behold, you had sinned against the LORD your God—had made for yourselves a molded calf! You had turned aside quickly from the way which the LORD had commanded you. 17Then I took the two tablets and threw them out of my two hands and broke them before your eyes. 18And I fell down before the LORD, as at the first, forty days and forty nights; I neither ate bread nor drank water, because of all your sin which you committed in doing wickedly in the sight of the LORD, to provoke Him to anger. 19For I was afraid of the anger and hot displeasure with which the LORD was angry with you, to destroy you. But the LORD listened to me at that time also. 20And the LORD was very angry with Aaron *and* would have destroyed him; so I prayed for Aaron also at the same time. 21Then I took your sin, the calf which you had made,

and burned it with fire and crushed it *and* ground *it* very small, until it was as fine as dust; and I threw its dust into the brook that descended from the mountain.

22"Also at Taberah and Massah and Kibroth Hattaavah you provoked the LORD to wrath. 23Likewise, when the LORD sent you from Kadesh Barnea, saying, 'Go up and possess the land which I have given you,' then you rebelled against the commandment of the LORD your God, and you did not believe Him nor obey His voice. 24You have been rebellious against the LORD from the day that I knew you.

25"Thus I prostrated myself before the LORD; forty days and forty nights I kept prostrating myself, because the LORD had said He would destroy you. 26Therefore I prayed to the LORD, and said: 'O Lord GOD, do not destroy Your people and Your inheritance whom You have redeemed through Your greatness, whom You have brought out of Egypt with a mighty hand. 27Remember Your servants, Abraham, Isaac, and Jacob; do not look on the stubbornness of this people, or on their wickedness or their sin, 28lest the land from which You brought us should say, "Because the LORD was not able to bring them to the land which He promised them, and because He hated them, He has brought them out to kill them in the wilderness." 29Yet they *are* Your people and Your inheritance, whom You brought out by Your mighty power and by Your outstretched arm.'

The Second Pair of Tablets

10 [1]"At that time the LORD said to me, 'Hew for yourself two tablets of stone like the first, and come up to Me on the mountain and make yourself an ark of wood. [2]And I will write on the tablets the words that were on the first tablets, which you broke; and you shall put them in the ark.'

[3]"So I made an ark of acacia wood, hewed two tablets of stone like the first, and went up the mountain, having the two tablets in my hand. [4]And He wrote on the tablets according to the first writing, the Ten Commandments, which the LORD had spoken to you in the mountain from the midst of the fire in the day of the assembly; and the LORD gave them to me. [5]Then I turned and came down from the mountain, and put the tablets in the ark which I had made; and there they are, just as the LORD commanded me."

[6](Now the children of Israel journeyed from the wells of Bene Jaakan to Moserah, where Aaron died, and where he was buried; and Eleazar his son ministered as priest in his stead. [7]From there they journeyed to Gudgodah, and from Gudgodah to Jotbathah, a land of rivers of water. [8]At that time the LORD separated the tribe of Levi to bear the ark of the covenant of the LORD, to stand before the LORD to minister to Him and to bless in His name, to this day. [9]Therefore Levi has no portion nor inheritance with his brethren; the LORD *is* his inheritance, just as the LORD your God promised him.)

[10]"As at the first time, I stayed in the mountain forty days and forty nights; the LORD also heard me at that time, *and*

the LORD chose not to destroy you. [11]Then the LORD said to me, 'Arise, begin *your* journey before the people, that they may go in and possess the land which I swore to their fathers to give them.'

The Essence of the Law

[12]"And now, Israel, what does the LORD your God require of you, but to fear the LORD your God, to walk in all His ways and to love Him, to serve the LORD your God with all your heart and with all your soul, [13]and to keep the commandments of the LORD and His statutes which I command you today for your good? [14]Indeed heaven and the highest heavens belong to the LORD your God, *also* the earth with all that *is* in it. [15]The LORD delighted only in your fathers, to love them; and He chose their descendants after them, you above all peoples, as *it is* this day. [16]Therefore circumcise the foreskin of your heart, and be stiffnecked no longer. [17]For the LORD your God *is* God of gods and Lord of lords, the great God, mighty and awesome, who shows no partiality nor takes a bribe. [18]He administers justice for the fatherless and the widow, and loves the stranger, giving him food and clothing. [19]Therefore love the stranger, for you were strangers in the land of Egypt. [20]You shall fear the LORD your God; you shall serve Him, and to Him you shall hold fast, and take oaths in His name. [21]He *is* your praise, and He *is* your God, who has done for you these great and awesome things which your eyes have seen. [22]Your fathers went down to Egypt with seventy persons, and now the LORD your God has made you as the stars of heaven in multitude.

TIME CAPSULE   *1336 to 1300 B.C.*

1336–1327	*Tutankhamun becomes pharaoh and reverses Akhenaten's reforms*
1323–1295	*Horemhab, pharaoh of Egypt*
1315	*Moses flees Egypt [based on late Exodus; Ex. 2:15; Acts 7:23]*
1321–1298	*Reign of Hittite king Mursilis II described in the "Text of Anittas"*
1308–1274	*Adad-nirari I of Assyria conducts campaigns against Mitanni*
1300	*Assyria loses control of Babylonia to the Kassites*

Love and Obedience Rewarded

11 [1]"Therefore you shall love the LORD your God, and keep His charge, His statutes, His judgments, and His commandments always. [2]Know today that *I do* not *speak* with your children, who have not known and who have not seen the chastening of the LORD your God, His greatness and His mighty hand and His outstretched arm— [3]His signs and His acts which He did in the midst of Egypt, to Pharaoh king of Egypt, and to all his land; [4]what He did to the army of Egypt, to their horses and their chariots: how He made the waters of the Red Sea overflow them as they pursued you, and *how* the LORD has destroyed them to this day; [5]what He did for you in the wilderness until you came to this place; [6]and what He did to Dathan and Abiram the sons of Eliab, the son of Reuben: how the earth opened its mouth and swallowed them up, their households, their tents, and all the substance that *was* in their possession, in the midst of all Israel— [7]but your eyes have seen every great act of the LORD which He did.

[8]"Therefore you shall keep every commandment which I command you today, that you may be strong, and go in and possess the land which you cross over to possess, [9]and that you may prolong *your* days in the land which the LORD swore to give your fathers, to them and their descendants, 'a land flowing with milk and honey.'[a] [10]For the land which you go to possess *is* not like the land of Egypt from which you have come, where you sowed your seed and watered *it* by foot, as a vegetable garden; [11]but the land which you cross over to possess *is* a land of hills and valleys, which drinks water from the rain of heaven, [12]a land for which the LORD your God cares; the eyes of the LORD your God *are* always on it, from the beginning of the year to the very end of the year.

[13]"And it shall be that if you earnestly obey My commandments which I command you today, to love the LORD your God and serve Him with all your heart and with all your soul, [14]then I[a] will give *you* the rain for your land in its season, the early rain and the latter rain, that you may gather in your grain, your new wine, and your oil. [15]And I will send grass in your fields for your livestock, that you may eat and be filled.' [16]Take heed to yourselves, lest your heart be deceived, and you turn aside and serve other gods and worship them, [17]lest the LORD's anger be aroused against you, and He shut up the heavens so that there be no rain, and the land yield no produce, and you perish quickly from the good land which the LORD is giving you.

[18]"Therefore you shall lay up these words of mine in your heart and in your soul, and bind them as a sign on your hand, and they shall be as frontlets between your eyes. [19]You shall teach them to your children, speaking of them when you

sit in your house, when you walk by the way, when you lie down, and when you rise up. [20]And you shall write them on the doorposts of your house and on your gates, [21]that your days and the days of your children may be multiplied in the land of which the LORD swore to your fathers to give them, like the days of the heavens above the earth.

[22]"For if you carefully keep all these commandments which I command you to do—to love the LORD your God, to walk in all His ways, and to hold fast to Him— [23]then the LORD will drive out all these nations from before you, and you will dispossess greater and mightier nations than yourselves. [24]Every place on which the sole of your foot treads shall be yours: from the wilderness and Lebanon, from the river, the River Euphrates, even to the Western Sea,[a] shall be your territory. [25]No man shall be able to stand against you; the LORD your God will put the dread of you and the fear of you upon all the land where you tread, just as He has said to you.

[26]"Behold, I set before you today a blessing and a curse: [27]the blessing, if you obey the commandments of the LORD your God which I command you today; [28]and the curse, if you do not obey the commandments of the LORD your God, but turn aside from the way which I command you today, to go after other gods which you have not known. [29]Now it shall be, when the LORD your God has brought you into the land which you go to possess, that you shall put the blessing on Mount Gerizim and the curse on Mount Ebal. [30]*Are* they not on the other side of the Jordan, toward the setting sun, in the land of the Canaanites who dwell in the plain opposite Gilgal, beside the terebinth trees of Moreh? [31]For you will cross over the Jordan and go in to possess the land which the LORD your God is giving you, and you will possess it and dwell in it. [32]And you shall be careful to observe all the statutes and judgments which I set before you today.

A Prescribed Place of Worship

12 [1]"These *are* the statutes and judgments which you shall be careful to observe in the land which the LORD God of your fathers is giving you to possess, all the days that you live on the earth. [2]You shall utterly destroy all the places where the nations which you shall dispossess served their gods, on the high mountains

---

11:9 [a]Exodus 3:8   11:14 [a]Following Masoretic Text and Targum; Samaritan Pentateuch, Septuagint, and Vulgate read *He*.   11:24 [a]That is, the Mediterranean

LAW CODES OF ANCIENT MESOPOTAMIA

The Hebrew laws of the Bible can be compared with several collections of laws (called "law codes") from other peoples of the ancient Near East. Many of the legal stipulations in the books of Exodus, Leviticus, Numbers, and Deuteronomy also appear in these other legal traditions.

Legal Collections in the Bible	Reference	
The Ten Commandments	Ex. 20:2–17; Deut. 5:6–21	
The Covenant Code	Ex. 20:22—23:33	
The Book of the Law	Deut. 12—26	
The Holiness Code	Lev. 17—26	

Law Codes of Ancient Cultures	Date	Language
Code of Ur-Nammu	c. 2112–2095 B.C.	Sumerian
Code of Lipit-Ishtar	c. 1934–1924 B.C.	Sumerian
Laws of Eshnunna	c. 1900 B.C.	Accadian
Code of Hammurabi	c. 1792–1750 B.C.	Accadian
Hittite laws	c. 1750–1200 B.C.	Hittite
Middle Assyrian laws	c. 1132–1076 B.C.	Accadian

and on the hills and under every green tree. ³And you shall destroy their altars, break their *sacred* pillars, and burn their wooden images with fire; you shall cut down the carved images of their gods and destroy their names from that place. ⁴You shall not worship the LORD your God *with* such *things.*

⁵"But you shall seek the place where the LORD your God chooses, out of all your tribes, to put His name for His dwelling place; and there you shall go. ⁶There you shall take your burnt offerings, your sacrifices, your tithes, the heave offerings of your hand, your vowed offerings, your freewill offerings, and the firstborn of your herds and flocks. ⁷And there you shall eat before the LORD your God, and you shall rejoice in all to which you have put your hand, you and your households, in which the LORD your God has blessed you.

⁸"You shall not at all do as we are doing here today—every man doing whatever *is* right in his own eyes— ⁹for as yet you have not come to the rest and the inheritance which the LORD your God is giving you. ¹⁰But *when* you cross over the Jordan and dwell in the land which the LORD your God is giving you to inherit, and He gives you rest from all your enemies round about, so that you dwell in safety, ¹¹then there will be the place where the LORD your God chooses to make His name abide. There you shall bring all that I command you: your burnt offerings, your sacrifices, your tithes, the heave offerings of your hand, and all your choice offerings which you vow to the LORD. ¹²And you shall rejoice before the LORD your God, you and your sons and your daughters, your male and female servants, and the Levite who *is* within your gates, since he has no portion nor inheritance with you. ¹³Take heed to yourself that you do not offer your burnt offerings in every place that you see; ¹⁴but in the place which the LORD chooses, in one of your tribes, there you shall offer your burnt offerings, and there you shall do all that I command you.

RELIGION AND WORSHIP

The religion of the Canaanites was centered on shrines located on hilltops scattered throughout the country (Deut. 12:3). The pillars or images were poles of some sort, wood or stone, sometimes decorated with carving, sometimes not (Deut. 16:21). They were not necessarily complete images like the statues of the Greeks and Romans.

15"However, you may slaughter and eat meat within all your gates, whatever your heart desires, according to the blessing of the LORD your God which He has given you; the unclean and the clean may eat of it, of the gazelle and the deer alike. 16Only you shall not eat the blood; you shall pour it on the earth like water. 17You may not eat within your gates the tithe of your grain or your new wine or your oil, of the firstborn of your herd or your flock, of any of your offerings which you vow, of your freewill offerings, or of the heave offering of your hand. 18But you must eat them before the LORD your God in the place which the LORD your God chooses, you and your son and your daughter, your male servant and your female servant, and the Levite who is within your gates; and you shall rejoice before the LORD your God in all to which you put your hands. 19Take heed to yourself that you do not forsake the Levite as long as you live in your land.

20"When the LORD your God enlarges your border as He has promised you, and you say, 'Let me eat meat,' because you long to eat meat, you may eat as much meat as your heart desires. 21If the place where the LORD your God chooses to put His name is too far from you, then you may slaughter from your herd and from your flock which the LORD has given you, just as I have commanded you, and you may eat within your gates as much as your heart desires. 22Just as the gazelle and the deer are eaten, so you may eat them; the unclean and the clean alike may eat them. 23Only be sure that you do not eat the blood, for the blood is the life; you may not eat the life with the meat. 24You shall not eat it; you shall pour it on the earth like water. 25You shall not eat it, that it may go well with you and your children after you, when you do what is right in the sight of the LORD. 26Only the holy things which you have, and your vowed offerings, you shall take and go to the place which the LORD chooses. 27And you shall offer your burnt offerings, the meat and the blood, on the altar of the LORD your God; and the blood of your sacrifices shall be poured out on the altar of the LORD your God, and you shall eat the meat. 28Observe and obey all these words which I command you, that it may go well with you and your children after you forever, when you do what is good and right in the sight of the LORD your God.

Beware of False Gods

29"When the LORD your God cuts off from before you the nations which you go to dispossess, and you displace them and dwell in their land, 30take heed to yourself that you are not ensnared to follow them, after they are destroyed from before you, and that you do not inquire after their gods, saying, 'How did these nations serve their gods? I also will do likewise.' 31You shall not worship the LORD your God in that way; for every abomination to the LORD which He hates they have done to their gods; for they burn even their sons and daughters in the fire to their gods.

32"Whatever I command you, be careful to observe it; you shall not add to it nor take away from it.

Punishment of Apostates

13 1"If there arises among you a prophet or a dreamer of dreams, and he gives you a sign or a wonder, 2and the sign or the wonder comes to pass, of which he spoke to you, saying, 'Let us go after other gods'—which you have not known—'and let us serve them,' 3you shall not listen to the words of that prophet or that dreamer of dreams, for the LORD your God is testing you to know whether you love the LORD your God with all your heart and with all your soul. 4You shall walk after the LORD your God and fear Him, and keep His commandments and obey His voice; you shall serve Him and hold fast to Him. 5But that prophet or that dreamer of dreams shall be put to death, because he has spoken in order to turn you away from the LORD your God, who brought you out of the land of Egypt and redeemed you from the house of bondage, to entice you from the way in which the LORD your God commanded you to walk. So you shall put away the evil from your midst.

6"If your brother, the son of your mother, your son or your daughter, the wife of your bosom, or your friend who is as your own soul, secretly entices you, saying, 'Let us go and serve other gods,' which you have not known, neither you nor your fathers, 7of the gods of the people which are all around you, near to you or far off from you, from one end of the earth to the other end of the earth, 8you shall not consent to him or listen to him, nor shall your eye pity him, nor shall you spare him or conceal him; ⁹but you shall surely kill him; your hand shall be first against him to put him to death, and afterward the hand of all the people. ¹⁰And you shall stone him with stones until he dies, because he sought to entice you away from the LORD your God, who brought you out of the land of Egypt, from the house of bondage. ¹¹So all Israel shall hear and fear, and not again do such wickedness as this among you.

¹²"If you hear someone in one of your cities, which the LORD your God gives you to dwell in, saying, ¹³'Corrupt men have gone out from among you and enticed the inhabitants of their city, saying, "Let us go and serve other gods"'—which you have not known— ¹⁴then you shall inquire, search out, and ask diligently. And *if it is* indeed true *and* certain *that* such an abomination was committed among you, ¹⁵you shall surely strike the inhabitants of that city with the edge of the sword, utterly destroying it, all that is in it and its livestock—with the edge of the sword. ¹⁶And you shall gather all its plunder into the middle of the street, and completely burn with fire the city and all its plunder, for the LORD your God. It shall be a heap forever; it shall not be built again. ¹⁷So none of the accursed things shall remain in your hand, that the LORD may turn from the fierceness of His anger and show you mercy, have compassion on you and multiply you, just as He swore to your fathers, ¹⁸because you have listened to the voice of the LORD your God, to keep all His commandments which I command you today, to do *what is* right in the eyes of the LORD your God.

Improper Mourning

14 ¹"You *are* the children of the LORD your God; you shall not cut yourselves nor shave the front of your head for the dead. ²For you *are* a holy people to the LORD your God, and the LORD has chosen you to be a people for Himself, a special treasure above all the peoples who *are* on the face of the earth.

Clean and Unclean Meat

³"You shall not eat any detestable thing. ⁴These *are* the animals which you may eat: the ox, the sheep, the goat, ⁵the deer, the gazelle, the roe deer, the wild goat, the mountain goat,^a the antelope, and the mountain sheep. ⁶And you may eat every animal with cloven hooves, having the hoof split into two parts, *and that* chews the cud, among the animals. ⁷Nevertheless, of those that chew the cud or have cloven hooves, you shall not eat, *such as* these: the camel, the hare, and the rock hyrax; for they chew the cud but do not have cloven hooves; they *are* unclean for you. ⁸Also the swine is unclean for you, because it has cloven hooves, yet *does* not *chew* the cud; you shall not eat their flesh or touch their dead carcasses.

⁹"These you may eat of all that *are* in the waters: you may eat all that have fins and scales. ¹⁰And whatever does not have fins and scales you shall not eat; it *is* unclean for you.

¹¹"All clean birds you may eat. ¹²But these you shall not eat: the eagle, the vulture, the buzzard, ¹³the red kite, the falcon, and the kite after their kinds; ¹⁴every raven after its kind; ¹⁵the ostrich, the short-eared owl, the sea gull, and the hawk after their kinds; ¹⁶the little owl, the screech owl, the white owl, ¹⁷the jackdaw, the carrion vulture, the fisher owl, ¹⁸the stork, the heron after its kind, and the hoopoe and the bat.

¹⁹"Also every creeping thing that flies is unclean for you; they shall not be eaten.

²⁰"You may eat all clean birds.

²¹"You shall not eat anything that dies *of itself;* you may give it to the alien who *is* within your gates, that he may eat it, or you may sell it to a foreigner; for you *are* a holy people to the LORD your God.

"You shall not boil a young goat in its mother's milk.

14:5 ^aOr *addax*

PLANTS AND ANIMALS

It is difficult to find a single principle that explains the rationale behind the specific assignment of animals to the clean and the unclean groups. The forbidden birds include all the birds of prey (Deut. 14:12). These birds eat food that they find already dead. This was considered objectionable for religion, though not necessarily unhealthy (Deut. 14:21).

TAXES IN UGARIT (Deut. 14:22–29)

At the site of Tell Ras Shamra, along the Syrian coast, archaeologists discovered the northern Canaanite city of Ugarit. This city was the capital of a 2nd millennium kingdom by the same name. A fertile agricultural countryside and a flourishing port used by seagoing trade ships helped the kingdom of Ugarit become a prosperous commercial center. But the sea was also the city's downfall; Ugarit was destroyed around 1180 B.C. by the raids of the Sea Peoples. The inhabitants abandoned their homes; no village or city ever occupied the area again.

Excavations at the site of Ugarit have uncovered over 1,000 texts in an alphabetic cuneiform script, all of which come from the 14th to 12th centuries B.C. Most of the documents were written in Ugaritic, a language until recently unknown. Like biblical Hebrew, it is a Northwest Semitic language, and thus shares many linguistic characteristics with the written language of the Old Testament.

The Ugaritic texts illuminate many mythical, religious, social, and cultural elements in the Old Testament. In Deut. 14:22–29 the Israelites are required to pay a tithe of their grain produce. Similarly, some Ugaritic texts mention a tax, or tithe, in the form of royal decrees imposed on royal dependents in outlying towns subject to Ugarit. Evidently, these royal dependents were required to perform various duties as well as pay certain taxes to royal authorities. Whether there was a religious significance to this tithe, as there was with the Israelite tithe (Deut. 14:23), is not known with certainty.

Tithing Principles

22"You shall truly tithe all the increase of your grain that the field produces year by year. 23And you shall eat before the LORD your God, in the place where He chooses to make His name abide, the tithe of your grain and your new wine and your oil, of the firstborn of your herds and your flocks, that you may learn to fear the LORD your God always. 24But if the journey is too long for you, so that you are not able to carry *the tithe, or* if the place where the LORD your God chooses to put His name is too far from you, when the LORD your God has blessed you, 25then you shall exchange *it* for money, take the money in your hand, and go to the place which the LORD your God chooses. 26And you shall spend that money for whatever your heart desires: for oxen or sheep, for wine or similar drink, for whatever your heart desires; you shall eat there before the LORD your God, and you shall rejoice, you and your household. 27You shall not forsake the Levite who *is* within your gates, for he has no part nor inheritance with you.

28"At the end of *every* third year you shall bring out the tithe of your produce of that year and store *it* up within your gates. 29And the Levite, because he has no portion nor inheritance with you, and the stranger and the fatherless and the widow who *are* within your gates, may come and eat and be satisfied, that the LORD your God may bless you in all the work of your hand which you do.

Debts Canceled Every Seven Years

15 1"At the end of *every* seven years you shall grant a release *of debts.* 2And this *is* the form of the release: Every creditor who has lent *anything* to his neighbor shall release *it;* he shall not require *it* of his neighbor or his brother, because it is called the LORD's release. 3Of a foreigner you may require *it;* but you shall give up your claim to what is owed by your brother, 4except when there may be no poor among you; for the LORD will greatly bless you in the land which the LORD your God is giving you to possess *as* an inheritance— 5only if you carefully obey the voice of the LORD your God, to observe with care all these commandments which I command you today. 6For the LORD your God will bless you just as He promised you; you shall lend to many nations, but you shall not borrow; you shall reign over many nations, but they shall not reign over you.

Generosity to the Poor

7"If there is among you a poor man of your brethren, within any of the gates in your land which the LORD your God is giving you, you shall not harden your heart nor shut your hand from your poor brother, [8]but you shall open your hand wide to him and willingly lend him sufficient for his need, whatever he needs. [9]Beware lest there be a wicked thought in your heart, saying, 'The seventh year, the year of release, is at hand,' and your eye be evil against your poor brother and you give him nothing, and he cry out to the LORD against you, and it become sin among you. [10]You shall surely give to him, and your heart should not be grieved when you give to him, because for this thing the LORD your God will bless you in all your works and in all to which you put your hand. [11]For the poor will never cease from the land; therefore I command you, saying, 'You shall open your hand wide to your brother, to your poor and your needy, in your land.'

The Law Concerning Bondservants

[12]"If your brother, a Hebrew man, or a Hebrew woman, is sold to you and serves you six years, then in the seventh year you shall let him go free from you. [13]And when you send him away free from you, you shall not let him go away empty-handed; [14]you shall supply him liberally from your flock, from your threshing floor, and from your winepress. *From what* the LORD has blessed you with, you shall give to him. [15]You shall remember that you were a slave in the land of Egypt, and the LORD your God redeemed you; therefore I command you this thing today. [16]And if it happens that he says to you, 'I will not go away from you,' because he loves you and your house, since he prospers with you, [17]then you shall take an awl and thrust *it* through his ear to the door, and he shall be your servant forever. Also to your female servant you shall do likewise. [18]It shall not seem hard to you when you send him away free from you; for he has been worth a double hired servant in serving you six years. Then the LORD your God will bless you in all that you do.

The Law Concerning Firstborn Animals

[19]"All the firstborn males that come from your herd and your flock you shall sanctify to the LORD your God; you shall do no work with the firstborn of your herd, nor shear the firstborn of your flock. [20]You and your household shall eat *it* before the LORD your God year by year in the place

which the LORD chooses. [21]But if there is a defect in it, *if it is* lame or blind *or has* any serious defect, you shall not sacrifice it to the LORD your God. [22]You may eat it within your gates; the unclean and the clean *person* alike *may eat it,* as *if it were* a gazelle or a deer. [23]Only you shall not eat its blood; you shall pour it on the ground like water.

The Passover Reviewed

16 [1]"Observe the month of Abib, and keep the Passover to the LORD your God, for in the month of Abib the LORD your God brought you out of Egypt by night. [2]Therefore you shall sacrifice the Passover to the LORD your God, from the flock and the herd, in the place where the LORD chooses to put His name. [3]You shall eat no leavened bread with it; seven days you shall eat unleavened bread with it, *that is,* the bread of affliction (for you came out of the land of Egypt in haste), that you may remember the day in which you came out of the land of Egypt all the days of your life. [4]And no leaven shall be seen among you in all your territory for seven days, nor shall *any* of the meat which you sacrifice the first day at twilight remain overnight until morning.

[5]"You may not sacrifice the Passover within any of your gates which the LORD your God gives you; [6]but at the place where the LORD your God chooses to make His name abide, there you shall sacrifice the Passover at twilight, at the going down of the sun, at the time you came out of Egypt. [7]And you shall roast and eat *it* in the place which the LORD your God chooses, and in the morning you shall turn and go to your tents. [8]Six days you shall eat unleavened bread, and on the seventh day there *shall be* a sacred assembly to the LORD your God. You shall do no work *on it.*

The Feast of Weeks Reviewed

[9]"You shall count seven weeks for yourself; begin to count the seven weeks from *the time* you begin *to put* the sickle to the grain. [10]Then you shall keep the Feast of Weeks to the LORD your God with the tribute of a freewill offering from your hand, which you shall give as the LORD your God blesses you. [11]You shall rejoice before the LORD your God, you and your son and your daughter, your male servant and your female servant, the Levite who *is* within your gates, the stranger and the fatherless

APPOINTING JUST JUDGES (Deut. 16:18–20)

The qualifications for choosing judges and officials were considered a serious matter in ancient cultures. Both Israel and Egypt had stipulations regarding the conduct of judges, emphasizing that a system of justice is only as good as the people who administer it.

Israel's law called for the selection of judges who would judge "with just judgment" (Deut. 16:18). The ideal of a just legal system was supported by prohibitions requiring that Israel's judges not "show partiality" or "take a bribe" (16:19).

The same ideal is evident in Egypt according to the Edict of Horemhab. Pharaoh Horemhab ruled for about 30 years (1323–1295 B.C.) in Egypt's 18th Dynasty, late in the 14th century B.C. For the administration of justice, the monarch looked for "people discreet and of good character, knowing how to judge the inmost thoughts, obedient to the instructions of the palace, and to the laws of the throne hall."

Horemhab claims to have taught these judges "the right course of life by guiding them to the truth." His advice to them was: "Do not associate with other people. Do not take bribes from others, for that will not turn out well." As the pharaoh advised his judges, he was clear in his warning concerning showing partiality: "Behold, (anyone) of you who makes common cause with another shall be for you as one who offends against truth."

These examples from Israel and Egypt demonstrate a common tradition in the ancient Near East about the appropriate administration of justice by legal officials. Bribes and partiality were not to be part of the system.

and the widow who *are* among you, at the place where the LORD your God chooses to make His name abide. 12And you shall remember that you were a slave in Egypt, and you shall be careful to observe these statutes.

The Feast of Tabernacles Reviewed

13"You shall observe the Feast of Tabernacles seven days, when you have gathered from your threshing floor and from your winepress. 14And you shall rejoice in your feast, you and your son and your daughter, your male servant and your female servant and the Levite, the stranger and the fatherless and the widow, who *are* within your gates. 15Seven days you shall keep a sacred feast to the LORD your God in the place which the LORD chooses, because the LORD your God will bless you in all your produce and in all the work of your hands, so that you surely rejoice.

16"Three times a year all your males shall appear before the LORD your God in the place which He chooses: at the Feast of Unleavened Bread, at the Feast of Weeks, and at the Feast of Tabernacles; and they shall not appear before the LORD empty-handed. 17Every man *shall give* as he is able, according to the blessing of the LORD your God which He has given you.

Justice Must Be Administered

18"You shall appoint judges and officers in all your gates, which the LORD your God gives you, according to your tribes, and they shall judge the people with just judgment. 19You shall not pervert justice; you shall not show partiality, nor take a bribe, for a bribe blinds the eyes of the wise and twists the words of the righteous. 20You shall follow what is altogether just, that you may live and inherit the land which the LORD your God is giving you.

21"You shall not plant for yourself any tree, as a wooden image, near the altar which you build for yourself to the LORD your God. 22You shall not set up a *sacred* pillar, which the LORD your God hates.

17 1"You shall not sacrifice to the LORD your God a bull or sheep which has any blemish *or* defect, for that *is* an abomination to the LORD your God.

2"If there is found among you, within any of your gates which the LORD your God gives you, a man or a woman who has been wicked in the sight of the LORD your God, in transgressing His covenant, 3who has gone and served other gods and worshiped them, either the sun or moon or any of the host of heaven, which I have not commanded, 4and it is told you, and you hear *of it*, then you shall inquire diligently. And if *it is* indeed true *and* certain that such an abomination has been committed in Israel, ⁵then you shall bring out to your gates that man or woman who has committed that wicked thing, and shall stone to death that man or woman with stones. ⁶Whoever is deserving of death shall be put to death on the testimony of two or three witnesses; he shall not be put to death on the testimony of one witness. ⁷The hands of the witnesses shall be the first against him to put him to death, and afterward the hands of all the people. So you shall put away the evil from among you.

⁸"If a matter arises which is too hard for you to judge, between degrees of guilt for bloodshed, between one judgment or another, or between one punishment or another, matters of controversy within your gates, then you shall arise and go up to the place which the LORD your God chooses. ⁹And you shall come to the priests, the Levites, and to the judge *there* in those days, and inquire *of them;* they shall pronounce upon you the sentence of judgment. ¹⁰You shall do according to the sentence which they pronounce upon you in that place which the LORD chooses. And you shall be careful to do according to all that they order you. ¹¹According to the sentence of the law in which they instruct you, according to the judgment which they tell you, you shall do; you shall not turn aside *to* the right hand or *to* the left from the sentence which they pronounce upon you. ¹²Now the man who acts presumptuously and will not heed the priest who stands to minister there before the LORD your God, or the judge, that man shall die. So you shall put away the evil from Israel. ¹³And all the people shall hear and fear, and no longer act presumptuously.

Principles Governing Kings

¹⁴"When you come to the land which the LORD your God is giving you, and possess it and dwell in it, and say, 'I will set a king over me like all the nations that *are* around me,' ¹⁵you shall surely set a king over you whom the LORD your God chooses;

one from among your brethren you shall set as king over you; you may not set a foreigner over you, who *is* not your brother. ¹⁶But he shall not multiply horses for himself, nor cause the people to return to Egypt to multiply horses, for the LORD has said to you, 'You shall not return that way again.' ¹⁷Neither shall he multiply wives for himself, lest his heart turn away; nor shall he greatly multiply silver and gold for himself.

¹⁸"Also it shall be, when he sits on the throne of his kingdom, that he shall write for himself a copy of this law in a book, from *the one* before the priests, the Levites. ¹⁹And it shall be with him, and he shall read it all the days of his life, that he may learn to fear the LORD his God and be careful to observe all the words of this law and these statutes, ²⁰that his heart may not be lifted above his brethren, that he may not turn aside from the commandment *to* the right hand or *to* the left, and that he may prolong *his* days in his kingdom, he and his children in the midst of Israel.

The Portion of the Priests and Levites

18 ¹"The priests, the Levites—all the tribe of Levi—shall have no part nor inheritance with Israel; they shall eat the offerings of the LORD made by fire, and His portion. ²Therefore they shall have no inheritance among their brethren; the LORD is their inheritance, as He said to them.

³"And this shall be the priest's due from the people, from those who offer a sacrifice, whether *it is* bull or sheep: they shall give to the priest the shoulder, the cheeks, and the stomach. ⁴The firstfruits of your grain and your new wine and your oil, and the first of the fleece of your sheep, you shall give him. ⁵For the LORD your God has chosen him out of all your tribes to stand to minister in the name of the LORD, him and his sons forever.

⁶"So if a Levite comes from any of your gates, from where he dwells among all Israel, and comes with all the desire of his mind to the place which the LORD chooses,

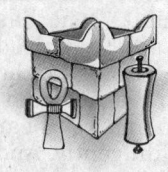

CULTS AND SUPERNATURAL

Ancient society was permeated with different kinds of magic (Deut. 18:10). It was practiced to foretell the future, to influence events, and to counter evil, including the magic of an enemy. The one God cannot be controlled or manipulated, and consequently His law forbids any magic, whatever its intent.

OMENS, SPELLS, AND OTHER ABOMINATIONS (Deut. 18:10, 11)

The Law of Moses banned all forms of foreign practices of divination. The various practices listed in Deut. 18:10, 11 were viewed as a subsidiary of magic. Often employed for divinatory oracles, these methods attempted to learn the will of the gods or to obtain knowledge of the future by other supernatural means. Sometimes the intent was to influence supernatural powers. All such practices were considered abominations of the Canaanite peoples (18:9, 13) and, as such, were forbidden in Israel.

All forms of divination were distinguished from inquiries of Israel's God. The use of the Urim and Thummim, the ephod, lots, and dreams were all legitimate methods of seeking Yahweh's will (1 Sam. 14:41; 23:9-12; 28:6). Divination practices, such as consulting a medium (1 Sam. 28:7-20), however, were illegitimate, even though some were believed to have power. They were not considered to be connected with the gods, but instead were seen as magic or wisdom arts, revealing secrets of God in a perverted way. Thus, the divinator trusted in signs and omens and in human wisdom rather than in God.

An example of pagan divination was teratoscopy, the omen interpretation of birth anomalies. One omen portends: "If an anomalous birth has eight feet and two tails, a prince will seize universal kingship." Moreover, the recorder of this omen mentions a hunter who claimed that when his sow gave birth, the offspring did in fact have eight feet and two tails. Thus, this omen was preserved for posterity. In Israel, the law was clear: "There shall not be found among you . . . one who interprets omens" (18:10).

7then he may serve in the name of the LORD his God as all his brethren the Levites *do,* who stand there before the LORD. 8They shall have equal portions to eat, besides what comes from the sale of his inheritance.

Avoid Wicked Customs

9"When you come into the land which the LORD your God is giving you, you shall not learn to follow the abominations of those nations. 10There shall not be found among you *anyone* who makes his son or his daughter pass through the fire, *or one* who practices witchcraft, *or* a soothsayer, or one who interprets omens, or a sorcerer, 11or one who conjures spells, or a medium, or a spiritist, or one who calls up the dead. 12For all who do these things *are* an abomination to the LORD, and because of these abominations the LORD your God drives them out from before you. 13You shall be blameless before the LORD your God. 14For these nations which you will dispossess listened to soothsayers and diviners; but as for you, the LORD your God has not appointed such for you.

A New Prophet Like Moses

15"The LORD your God will raise up for you a Prophet like me from your midst, from your brethren. Him you shall hear,

16according to all you desired of the LORD your God in Horeb in the day of the assembly, saying, 'Let me not hear again the voice of the LORD my God, nor let me see this great fire anymore, lest I die.' 17"And the LORD said to me: 'What they have spoken is good. 18I will raise up for them a Prophet like you from among their brethren, and will put My words in His mouth, and He shall speak to them all that I command Him. 19And it shall be *that* whoever will not hear My words, which He speaks in My name, I will require *it* of him. 20But the prophet who presumes to speak a word in My name, which I have not commanded him to speak, or who speaks in the name of other gods, that prophet shall die.' 21And if you say in your heart, 'How shall we know the word which the LORD has not spoken?'— 22when a prophet speaks in the name of the LORD, if the thing does not happen or come to pass, that *is* the thing which the LORD has not spoken; the prophet has spoken it presumptuously; you shall not be afraid of him.

Three Cities of Refuge

19 1"When the LORD your God has cut off the nations whose land the LORD your God is giving you, and you dispossess them and dwell in their cities and in their houses, 2you shall separate three cities for

yourself in the midst of your land which the LORD your God is giving you to possess. [3]You shall prepare roads for yourself, and divide into three parts the territory of your land which the LORD your God is giving you to inherit, that any manslayer may flee there.

[4]"And this *is* the case of the manslayer who flees there, that he may live: Whoever kills his neighbor unintentionally, not having hated him in time past— [5]as when *a man* goes to the woods with his neighbor to cut timber, and his hand swings a stroke with the ax to cut down the tree, and the head slips from the handle and strikes his neighbor so that he dies—he shall flee to one of these cities and live; [6]lest the avenger of blood, while his anger is hot, pursue the manslayer and overtake him, because the way is long, and kill him, though he *was* not deserving of death, since he had not hated the victim in time past. [7]Therefore I command you, saying, 'You shall separate three cities for yourself.'

[8]"Now if the LORD your God enlarges your territory, as He swore to your fathers, and gives you the land which He promised to give to your fathers, [9]and if you keep all these commandments and do them, which I command you today, to love the LORD your God and to walk always in His ways, then you shall add three more cities for yourself besides these three, [10]lest innocent blood be shed in the midst of your land which the LORD your God is giving you *as* an inheritance, and *thus* guilt of bloodshed be upon you.

[11]"But if anyone hates his neighbor, lies in wait for him, rises against him and strikes him mortally, so that he dies, and he flees to one of these cities, [12]then the elders of his city shall send and bring him from there, and deliver him over to the hand of the avenger of blood, that he may die. [13]Your eye shall not pity him, but you shall put away *the guilt of* innocent blood from Israel, that it may go well with you.

Property Boundaries

[14]"You shall not remove your neighbor's landmark, which the men of old have set, in your inheritance which you will inherit in the land that the LORD your God is giving you to possess.

The Law Concerning Witnesses

[15]"One witness shall not rise against a man concerning any iniquity or any sin that he commits; by the mouth of two or three witnesses the matter shall be established. [16]If a false witness rises against any man to testify against him of wrongdoing, [17]then both men in the controversy shall stand before the LORD, before the priests and the judges who serve in those days. [18]And the judges shall make careful inquiry, and indeed, *if* the witness *is* a false witness, who has testified falsely against his brother, [19]then you shall do to him as he thought to have done to his brother; so you shall put away the evil from among you. [20]And those who remain shall hear and fear, and hereafter they shall not again commit such evil among you. [21]Your eye shall not pity: life *shall be* for life, eye for eye, tooth for tooth, hand for hand, foot for foot.

Principles Governing Warfare

20 [1]"When you go out to battle against your enemies, and see horses and chariots *and* people more numerous than you, do not be afraid of them; for the LORD your God *is* with you, who brought you up from the land of Egypt. [2]So it shall be, when you are on the verge of battle, that the priest shall approach and speak to the people. [3]And he shall say to them, 'Hear, O Israel: Today you are on the verge of battle with your enemies. Do not let your heart faint, do not be afraid, and do not tremble or be terrified because of them; [4]for the LORD your God *is* He who goes with you, to fight for you against your enemies, to save you.'

[5]"Then the officers shall speak to the people, saying: 'What man *is there* who has

---

TIME CAPSULE   *1295 to 1275 B.C.*

1295– 1294	*Ramesses I founds Egypt's 19th Dynasty*
1294– 1279	*Seti I, pharaoh of Egypt*
1294	*Seti I drives Hittites from southern Syria*
1279– 1213	*Ramesses II, pharaoh of Egypt*
1279	*Ramesses II oversees a great building program in Egypt*
1275	*Moses leads exodus from Egypt (based on late Exodus)*

built a new house and has not dedicated it? Let him go and return to his house, lest he die in the battle and another man dedicate it. [6]Also what man *is there* who has planted a vineyard and has not eaten of it? Let him go and return to his house, lest he die in the battle and another man eat of it. [7]And what man *is there* who is betrothed to a woman and has not married her? Let him go and return to his house, lest he die in the battle and another man marry her.'

[8]"The officers shall speak further to the people, and say, 'What man *is there* who is fearful and fainthearted? Let him go and return to his house, lest the heart of his brethren faint[a] like his heart.' [9]And so it shall be, when the officers have finished speaking to the people, that they shall make captains of the armies to lead the people.

[10]"When you go near a city to fight against it, then proclaim an offer of peace to it. [11]And it shall be that if they accept your offer of peace, and open to you, then all the people *who are* found in it shall be placed under tribute to you, and serve you. [12]Now if *the city* will not make peace with you, but war against you, then you shall besiege it. [13]And when the LORD your God delivers it into your hands, you shall strike every male in it with the edge of the sword. [14]But the women, the little ones, the livestock, and all that is in the city, all its spoil, you shall plunder for yourself; and you shall eat the enemies' plunder which the LORD your God gives you. [15]Thus you shall do to all the cities *which are* very far from you, which *are* not of the cities of these nations.

[16]"But of the cities of these peoples which the LORD your God gives you *as* an inheritance, you shall let nothing that breathes remain alive, [17]but you shall utterly destroy them: the Hittite and the Amorite and the Canaanite and the Perizzite and the Hivite and the Jebusite, just as the LORD your God has commanded you, [18]lest they teach you to do according to all their abominations which they have done for their gods, and you sin against the LORD your God.

[19]"When you besiege a city for a long time, while making war against it to take it, you shall not destroy its trees by wield-ing an ax against them; if you can eat of them, do not cut them down to use in the siege, for the tree of the field *is* man's *food*. [20]Only the trees which you know *are* not trees for food you may destroy and cut down, to build siegeworks against the city that makes war with you, until it is subdued.

The Law Concerning Unsolved Murder

21 [1]"If *anyone* is found slain, lying in the field in the land which the LORD your God is giving you to possess, *and* it is not known who killed him, [2]then your elders and your judges shall go out and measure *the distance* from the slain man to the surrounding cities. [3]And it shall be *that* the elders of the city nearest to the slain man will take a heifer which has not been worked *and* which has not pulled with a yoke. [4]The elders of that city shall bring the heifer down to a valley with flowing water, which is neither plowed nor sown, and they shall break the heifer's neck there in the valley. [5]Then the priests, the sons of Levi, shall come near, for the LORD your God has chosen them to minister to Him and to bless in the name of the LORD; by their word every controversy and every assault shall be *settled*. [6]And all the elders of that city nearest to the slain *man* shall wash their hands over the heifer whose neck was broken in the valley. [7]Then they shall answer and say, 'Our hands have not shed this blood, nor have our eyes seen *it*. [8]Provide atonement, O LORD, for Your people Israel, whom You have redeemed, and do not lay innocent blood to the charge of Your people Israel.' And atonement shall be provided on their behalf for the blood. [9]So you shall put away the *guilt of* innocent blood from among you when you do *what is* right in the sight of the LORD.

Female Captives

[10]"When you go out to war against your enemies, and the LORD your God delivers them into your hand, and you take them captive, [11]and you see among the captives a beautiful woman, and desire her and would take her for your wife, [12]then you shall bring her home to your house, and she shall shave her head and trim her nails. [13]She shall put off the clothes of her captivity, remain in your house, and mourn her father and her mother a full month; after that you may go in to her and be her husband, and she shall be your wife. [14]And

---

20:8 [a]Following Masoretic Text and Targum; Samaritan Pentateuch, Septuagint, Syriac, and Vulgate read *lest he make his brother's heart faint*.

FINDING A DEAD BODY (Deut. 21:1–9)

If a dead person was found in an open field, the Israelite people performed a very specific ritual (Deut. 21:1–9). In the event that an innocent person was murdered and no one was apprehended, the whole nation was held responsible. Therefore a sacrifice had to be made for all the people.

Finding a slain stranger in the open country was not a phenomenon unique to Israel. Hittite laws, compiled in the mid-2nd millennium B.C. in central Anatolia, also dealt with this issue, but with a different response than that of Deut. 21.

One Hittite law reads: "If a man is killed on the field (or) fallow of another man, in case he is a free man, he shall give field (and) fallow, house (and) 1½ lbs. of silver. In case it is a woman, he shall give 3 pounds of silver." Thus, according to Hittite law, the family of a murder victim would be compensated by the property owner of the land where the murder occurred.

Both the Israelites and Hittites had provisions regarding the community nearest to where the body of a slain person was found. In Israel, the leaders were instructed to "measure the distance from the slain man to the surrounding cities" (Deut. 21:2), and the elders of the nearest city were required to perform a ritual, killing a heifer to remove guilt from the community. The Hittites also measured: "a distance of three leagues in one direction and a distance of three leagues in the other direction." The village that fell within the measured area was required to pay compensation.

The Israelite and Hittite laws differ in some aspects. The Hittite text is devoid of the ritual significance found in Deut. 21, and therefore no provisions were made to pacify a deity that may have been offended by the death (presumably a homicide). For her part, Israel made no attempt to compensate the victim's family. Both cultures, however, had a sense of corporate responsibility, requiring certain actions of the nearest community.

---

it shall be, if you have no delight in her, then you shall set her free, but you certainly shall not sell her for money; you shall not treat her brutally, because you have humbled her.

Firstborn Inheritance Rights

15"If a man has two wives, one loved and the other unloved, and they have borne him children, *both* the loved and the unloved, and *if* the firstborn son is of her who is unloved, 16then it shall be, on the day he bequeaths his possessions to his sons, *that* he must not bestow firstborn status on the son of the loved wife in preference to the son of the unloved, the *true* firstborn. 17But he shall acknowledge the son of the unloved wife *as* the firstborn by giving him a double portion of all that he has, for he *is* the beginning of his strength; the right of the firstborn *is* his.

The Rebellious Son

18"If a man has a stubborn and rebellious son who will not obey the voice of his father or the voice of his mother, and *who,* when they have chastened him, will not heed them, 19then his father and his mother shall take hold of him and bring him out to the elders of his city, to the gate of his city. 20And they shall say to the elders of his city, 'This son of ours is stubborn and rebellious; he will not obey our voice; he is a glutton and a drunkard.' 21Then all the men of his city shall stone him to death with stones; so you shall put away the evil from among you, and all Israel shall hear and fear.

Miscellaneous Laws

22"If a man has committed a sin deserving of death, and he is put to death, and you hang him on a tree, 23his body shall not remain overnight on the tree, but you shall surely bury him that day, so that you do not defile the land which the LORD your God is giving you *as* an inheritance; for he who is hanged *is* accursed of God.

22 1"You shall not see your brother's ox or his sheep going astray, and hide yourself from them; you shall certainly bring them back to your brother. 2And if your brother *is* not near you, or if you do not know him, then you shall bring it to

THE SLANDERED BRIDE FROM NIPPUR (Deut. 22:13–19)

Israelite society had laws governing how a husband could treat a new wife. The law of Deut. 22:13–19 prohibits a man from obtaining a divorce merely by questioning her virginity and slandering her name (22:14). A woman so accused was permitted to produce evidence of her fidelity. Should she be vindicated, the husband was fined 100 shekels of silver and forbidden to divorce her for the rest of his life (22:19).

Rejecting a new wife was not unique to Israel. A Sumerian marriage contract from Nippur describes a certain Enlil-issu, a priest of Enlil (the chief deity of the Sumerian pantheon). Enlil-issu took the woman Ama-sukkal as his wife, and the new wife brought 19 shekels of silver to her spouse. The contract stipulates that if Enlil-issu rejects his bride, the 19 shekels must be returned, as well as a half mina of silver (approximately 30 shekels). If the wife rejects her husband, the payment is exactly the same. No reasons are given for the potential separation.

All did not go well. Later on, the couple had their day in court, apparently before the consummation of the marriage. Ama-sukkal was not convicted of speaking against her husband, but Enlil-issu was convicted of slandering and abusing his wife, to which he responded, "You may convict me (even) more than now; (still) I will not marry her. Let them imprison me and (then) I will pay the money (instead)."

There are differences between the Israelite and Sumerian laws. The virginity of the Sumerian bride is not an issue in the Nippur contract, while virginity was the primary issue in the Israelite law. Nevertheless, we see that in both cultures a new bride was protected to some degree from being rejected unjustly, slandered, and consequently divorced.

---

your own house, and it shall remain with you until your brother seeks it; then you shall restore it to him. ³You shall do the same with his donkey, and so shall you do with his garment; with any lost thing of your brother's, which he has lost and you have found, you shall do likewise; you must not hide yourself.

⁴"You shall not see your brother's donkey or his ox fall down along the road, and hide yourself from them; you shall surely help him lift *them* up again.

⁵"A woman shall not wear anything that pertains to a man, nor shall a man put on a woman's garment, for all who do so *are* an abomination to the LORD your God.

⁶"If a bird's nest happens to be before you along the way, in any tree or on the ground, with young ones or eggs, with the mother sitting on the young or on the eggs, you shall not take the mother with the young; ⁷you shall surely let the mother go, and take the young for yourself, that it may be well with you and *that* you may prolong *your* days.

⁸"When you build a new house, then you shall make a parapet for your roof, that you may not bring guilt of bloodshed on your household if anyone falls from it.

⁹"You shall not sow your vineyard with different kinds of seed, lest the yield of the seed which you have sown and the fruit of your vineyard be defiled.

¹⁰"You shall not plow with an ox and a donkey together.

¹¹"You shall not wear a garment of different sorts, *such as* wool and linen mixed together.

¹²"You shall make tassels on the four corners of the clothing with which you cover *yourself.*

Laws of Sexual Morality

¹³"If any man takes a wife, and goes in to her, and detests her, ¹⁴and charges her with shameful conduct, and brings a bad name on her, and says, 'I took this woman, and when I came to her I found she *was* not a virgin,' ¹⁵then the father and mother of the young woman shall take and bring out *the evidence of* the young woman's virginity to the elders of the city at the gate. ¹⁶And the young woman's father shall say to the elders, 'I gave my daughter to this man as wife, and he detests her. ¹⁷Now he has charged her with shameful conduct, saying, "I found your daughter *was* not a virgin," and yet these *are* the evidences of my daughter's virginity.' And they shall spread the cloth before the elders of the

city. ¹⁸Then the elders of that city shall take that man and punish him; ¹⁹and they shall fine him one hundred *shekels* of silver and give *them* to the father of the young woman, because he has brought a bad name on a virgin of Israel. And she shall be his wife; he cannot divorce her all his days.

²⁰"But if the thing is true, *and evidences of* virginity are not found for the young woman, ²¹then they shall bring out the young woman to the door of her father's house, and the men of her city shall stone her to death with stones, because she has done a disgraceful thing in Israel, to play the harlot in her father's house. So you shall put away the evil from among you.

²²"If a man is found lying with a woman married to a husband, then both of them shall die—the man that lay with the woman, and the woman; so you shall put away the evil from Israel.

²³"If a young woman *who is* a virgin is betrothed to a husband, and a man finds her in the city and lies with her, ²⁴then you shall bring them both out to the gate of that city, and you shall stone them to death with stones, the young woman because she did not cry out in the city, and the man because he humbled his neighbor's wife; so you shall put away the evil from among you.

²⁵"But if a man finds a betrothed young woman in the countryside, and the man forces her and lies with her, then only the man who lay with her shall die. ²⁶But you shall do nothing to the young woman; *there is* in the young woman no sin *deserving* of death, for just as when a man rises against his neighbor and kills him, even so *is* this matter. ²⁷For he found her in the countryside, *and* the betrothed young woman cried out, but *there was* no one to save her.

²⁸"If a man finds a young woman *who is* a virgin, who is not betrothed, and he seizes her and lies with her, and they are found out, ²⁹then the man who lay with her shall give to the young woman's father fifty *shekels* of silver, and she shall be his

wife because he has humbled her; he shall not be permitted to divorce her all his days.

³⁰"A man shall not take his father's wife, nor uncover his father's bed.

Those Excluded from the Congregation

23 ¹"He who is emasculated by crushing or mutilation shall not enter the assembly of the LORD.

²"One of illegitimate birth shall not enter the assembly of the LORD; even to the tenth generation none of his *descendants* shall enter the assembly of the LORD.

³"An Ammonite or Moabite shall not enter the assembly of the LORD; even to the tenth generation none of his *descendants* shall enter the assembly of the LORD forever, ⁴because they did not meet you with bread and water on the road when you came out of Egypt, and because they hired against you Balaam the son of Beor from Pethor of Mesopotamia,^a to curse you. ⁵Nevertheless the LORD your God would not listen to Balaam, but the LORD your God turned the curse into a blessing for you, because the LORD your God loves you. ⁶You shall not seek their peace nor their prosperity all your days forever.

⁷"You shall not abhor an Edomite, for he *is* your brother. You shall not abhor an Egyptian, because you were an alien in his land. ⁸The children of the third generation born to them may enter the assembly of the LORD.

Cleanliness of the Campsite

⁹"When the army goes out against your enemies, then keep yourself from every wicked thing. ¹⁰If there is any man among you who becomes unclean by some occurrence in the night, then he shall go outside the camp; he shall not come inside the camp. ¹¹But it shall be, when evening comes, that he shall wash with water; and when the sun sets, he may come into the camp.

¹²"Also you shall have a place outside

23:4 ^aHebrew *Aram Naharaim*

CULTS AND SUPERNATURAL

Ritual harlots, known as cultic prostitutes, were forbidden in Israel (Deut. 23:17). Sacred prostitution and sexual rituals, practiced in shrines by the Phoenicians, and probably also by the Canaanites, were thought to bring fertility to the land. The connection of prostitutes with religion and ritual is hinted at in the Bible, but no details are explained, and little is really known about it.

the camp, where you may go out; [13]and you shall have an implement among your equipment, and when you sit down outside, you shall dig with it and turn and cover your refuse. [14]For the LORD your God walks in the midst of your camp, to deliver you and give your enemies over to you; therefore your camp shall be holy, that He may see no unclean thing among you, and turn away from you.

Miscellaneous Laws

[15]"You shall not give back to his master the slave who has escaped from his master to you. [16]He may dwell with you in your midst, in the place which he chooses within one of your gates, where it seems best to him; you shall not oppress him.

[17]"There shall be no *ritual* harlot[a] of the daughters of Israel, or a perverted[b] one of the sons of Israel. [18]You shall not bring the wages of a harlot or the price of a dog to the house of the LORD your God for any vowed offering, for both of these *are* an abomination to the LORD your God.

[19]"You shall not charge interest to your brother—interest on money *or* food or anything that is lent out at interest. [20]To a foreigner you may charge interest, but to your brother you shall not charge interest, that the LORD your God may bless you in all to which you set your hand in the land which you are entering to possess.

[21]"When you make a vow to the LORD your God, you shall not delay to pay it; for the LORD your God will surely require it of you, and it would be sin to you. [22]But if you abstain from vowing, it shall not be sin to you. [23]That which has gone from your lips you shall keep and perform, for you voluntarily vowed to the LORD your God what you have promised with your mouth.

[24]"When you come into your neighbor's vineyard, you may eat your fill of grapes at your pleasure, but you shall not put *any* in your container. [25]When you come into your neighbor's standing grain, you may pluck the heads with your hand, but you shall not use a sickle on your neighbor's standing grain.

Law Concerning Divorce

24 [1]"When a man takes a wife and marries her, and it happens that she finds no favor in his eyes because he has found some uncleanness in her, and he writes her a certificate of divorce, puts *it* in her hand, and sends her out of his house, [2]when she has departed from his house, and goes and becomes another man's *wife,* [3]*if* the latter husband detests her and writes her a certificate of divorce, puts *it* in her hand, and sends her out of his house, or if the latter husband dies who took her as his wife, [4]*then* her former husband who divorced her must not take her back to be his wife after she has been defiled; for that *is* an abomination before the LORD, and you shall not bring sin on the land which the LORD your God is giving you *as* an inheritance.

Miscellaneous Laws

[5]"When a man has taken a new wife, he shall not go out to war or be charged with any business; he shall be free at home one year, and bring happiness to his wife whom he has taken.

[6]"No man shall take the lower or the upper millstone in pledge, for he takes *one's* living in pledge.

[7]"If a man is found kidnapping any of his brethren of the children of Israel, and mistreats him or sells him, then that kidnapper shall die; and you shall put away the evil from among you.

[8]"Take heed in an outbreak of leprosy, that you carefully observe and do according to all that the priests, the Levites, shall teach you; just as I commanded them, *so* you shall be careful to do. [9]Remember what the LORD your God did to Miriam on the way when you came out of Egypt!

[10]"When you lend your brother anything, you shall not go into his house to get his pledge. [11]You shall stand outside, and the man to whom you lend shall bring the pledge out to you. [12]And if the man *is* poor, you shall not keep his pledge overnight. [13]You shall in any case return the pledge to him again when the sun goes down, that he may sleep in his own garment and bless you; and it shall be righteousness to you before the LORD your God.

[14]"You shall not oppress a hired servant *who is* poor and needy, *whether* one of your brethren or one of the aliens who *is* in your land within your gates. [15]Each day you shall give *him* his wages, and not let the sun go down on it, for he *is* poor and has set his heart on it; lest he cry out

---

23:17 [a]Hebrew *qedeshah,* feminine of *qadesh* (see note b)　[b]Hebrew *qadesh,* that is, one practicing sodomy and prostitution in religious rituals

TAKING OFF THE SANDALS (Deut. 25:5–10)

The countries of the Bible are warm and dry much of the year. Although shoes, covering the entire foot, are sometimes depicted in ancient pictures, sandals were the natural and more common foot covering for that climate. The simple act of removing a sandal carried symbolic meaning for ancient people.

Sandals were such personal items that they symbolically represented their owner in some legal transactions. In one type of business transaction, removal of the sandal confirmed an exchange of buying and selling. Such an exchange could even include the acquisition of a wife (Ruth 4:7–10). Yet a different legal transaction involved the breakdown of family and social obligations. A woman had a right to bear children to her deceased husband. If her brother-in-law refused her that right, she could publicly humiliate him, indicating such by removing his sandal (Deut. 25:7–10).

Sandals were also removed to symbolize the presence of holy ground. Because shoes tread through dust and dirt, they are symbolically dirty to Muslims; thus, they are taken off before entering holy places like mosques. This Muslim custom reflects the attitude that shoes, dirty as they are, should not desecrate holy places. This same attitude appears in the Old Testament. Both Moses before the burning bush (Ex. 3:5) and Joshua before the "Commander of the LORD's army" (Josh. 5:15) were instructed to remove their sandals, for they stood on "holy ground."

against you to the LORD, and it be sin to you.

16"Fathers shall not be put to death for *their* children, nor shall children be put to death for *their* fathers; a person shall be put to death for his own sin.

17"You shall not pervert justice due the stranger or the fatherless, nor take a widow's garment as a pledge. 18But you shall remember that you were a slave in Egypt, and the LORD your God redeemed you from there; therefore I command you to do this thing.

19"When you reap your harvest in your field, and forget a sheaf in the field, you shall not go back to get it; it shall be for the stranger, the fatherless, and the widow, that the LORD your God may bless you in all the work of your hands. 20When you beat your olive trees, you shall not go over the boughs again; it shall be for the stranger, the fatherless, and the widow. 21When you gather the grapes of your vineyard, you shall not glean *it* afterward; it shall be for the stranger, the fatherless, and the widow. 22And you shall remember that you were a slave in the land of Egypt; therefore I command you to do this thing.

25 1"If there is a dispute between men, and they come to court, that *the judges* may judge them, and they justify the righteous and condemn the wicked, 2then it shall be, if the wicked man de-

serves to be beaten, that the judge will cause him to lie down and be beaten in his presence, according to his guilt, with a certain number of blows. 3Forty blows he may give him *and* no more, lest he should exceed this and beat him with many blows above these, and your brother be humiliated in your sight.

4"You shall not muzzle an ox while it treads out *the grain.*

Marriage Duty of the Surviving Brother

5"If brothers dwell together, and one of them dies and has no son, the widow of the dead man shall not be *married* to a stranger outside *the family;* her husband's brother shall go in to her, take her as his wife, and perform the duty of a husband's brother to her. 6And it shall be *that* the firstborn son which she bears will succeed to the name of his dead brother, that his name may not be blotted out of Israel. 7But if the man does not want to take his brother's wife, then let his brother's wife go up to the gate to the elders, and say, 'My husband's brother refuses to raise up a name to his brother in Israel; he will not perform the duty of my husband's brother.' 8Then the elders of his city shall call him and speak to him. But *if* he stands firm and says, 'I do not want to take her,' 9then his brother's wife shall come to him in the

MIDDLE ASSYRIAN LAWS (Deut. 25:11, 12)

A number of the laws in the Pentateuch have literary parallels in the law codes of Mesopotamia. These codes include the Laws of Eshnunna and the Code of Hammurabi. The Middle Assyrian laws, however, are closer in time and subject matter to the biblical laws than are the compilations of Eshnunna and Hammurabi.

The law of Deut. 25:11, 12 addresses the case of a woman who intervenes in a fight between her husband and another man. The punishment—cutting off her hand—seems by modern standards to be both harsh and crude. This biblical law, however, was not out of place in the culture of that ancient time.

One Middle Assyrian law offers a fairly close parallel to the Deuteronomy law: "If a woman injures the testicles of a man in a fight, one of her fingers shall be cut off." The law establishes a more severe penalty if the man's "second testicle becomes affected from the first" or if the woman "injures the second testicle (too)." The Assyrian document is partly broken and unreadable, but possibly indicates that the woman who damages both of a man's testicles would have her eyes put out.

Such punishments are inappropriate in our legal systems today. Nevertheless, we can observe similarities between Israel's laws recorded in the Bible and the laws of other ancient cultures, such as the Sumerians, Babylonians, Assyrians, and Hittites. These parallels illustrate a shared legal tradition that existed throughout the ancient Near East. Apparently, certain social norms were accepted by both Israel and the neighboring peoples.

presence of the elders, remove his sandal from his foot, spit in his face, and answer and say, 'So shall it be done to the man who will not build up his brother's house.' ¹⁰And his name shall be called in Israel, 'The house of him who had his sandal removed.'

Miscellaneous Laws

¹¹"If *two* men fight together, and the wife of one draws near to rescue her husband from the hand of the one attacking him, and puts out her hand and seizes him by the genitals, ¹²then you shall cut off her hand; your eye shall not pity *her*.

¹³"You shall not have in your bag differing weights, a heavy and a light. ¹⁴You shall not have in your house differing measures, a large and a small. ¹⁵You shall have a perfect and just weight, a perfect and just measure, that your days may be lengthened in the land which the LORD your God is giving you. ¹⁶For all who do such things,

all who behave unrighteously, *are* an abomination to the LORD your God.

Destroy the Amalekites

¹⁷"Remember what Amalek did to you on the way as you were coming out of Egypt, ¹⁸how he met you on the way and attacked your rear ranks, all the stragglers at your rear, when you *were* tired and weary; and he did not fear God. ¹⁹Therefore it shall be, when the LORD your God has given you rest from your enemies all around, in the land which the LORD your God is giving you to possess *as* an inheritance, *that* you will blot out the remembrance of Amalek from under heaven. You shall not forget.

Offerings of Firstfruits and Tithes

26 ¹"And it shall be, when you come into the land which the LORD your God is giving you *as* an inheritance, and you possess it and dwell in it, ²that you

TRADE AND ECONOMICS

Without a bureau of standards, uniformity in weights and measures was difficult to achieve (Deut. 25:13). On the local level it was not impossible. Hellenistic cities put up standard measuring tables in public places. One from Thasos is made of stone with two basins cut into it, providing standards of about 8 and 16 quarts.

shall take some of the first of all the produce of the ground, which you shall bring from your land that the LORD your God is giving you, and put *it* in a basket and go to the place where the LORD your God chooses to make His name abide. ³And you shall go to the one who is priest in those days, and say to him, 'I declare today to the LORD your[a] God that I have come to the country which the LORD swore to our fathers to give us.'

⁴"Then the priest shall take the basket out of your hand and set it down before the altar of the LORD your God. ⁵And you shall answer and say before the LORD your God: 'My father *was* a Syrian,[a] about to perish, and he went down to Egypt and dwelt there, few in number; and there he became a nation, great, mighty, and populous. ⁶But the Egyptians mistreated us, afflicted us, and laid hard bondage on us. ⁷Then we cried out to the LORD God of our fathers, and the LORD heard our voice and looked on our affliction and our labor and our oppression. ⁸So the LORD brought us out of Egypt with a mighty hand and with an outstretched arm, with great terror and with signs and wonders. ⁹He has brought us to this place and has given us this land, "a land flowing with milk and honey";[a] ¹⁰and now, behold, I have brought the firstfruits of the land which you, O LORD, have given me.'

"Then you shall set it before the LORD your God, and worship before the LORD your God. ¹¹So you shall rejoice in every good *thing* which the LORD your God has given to you and your house, you and the Levite and the stranger who *is* among you.

¹²"When you have finished laying aside all the tithe of your increase in the third year—the year of tithing—and have given *it* to the Levite, the stranger, the fatherless, and the widow, so that they may eat within your gates and be filled, ¹³then you shall say before the LORD your God: 'I have removed the holy *tithe* from *my* house, and also have given them to the Levite, the stranger, the fatherless, and the widow, according to all Your commandments which You have commanded me; I have not transgressed Your commandments, nor have I forgotten *them*. ¹⁴I have not eaten any of it when in mourning, nor have I removed *any* of it for an unclean *use,* nor given *any* of it for the dead. I have obeyed the voice of the LORD my God, and have done according to all that You have commanded me. ¹⁵Look down from Your holy habitation, from heaven, and bless Your people Israel and the land which You have given us, just as You swore to our fathers, "a land flowing with milk and honey." '[a]

A Special People of God

¹⁶"This day the LORD your God commands you to observe these statutes and judgments; therefore you shall be careful to observe them with all your heart and with all your soul. ¹⁷Today you have proclaimed the LORD to be your God, and that you will walk in His ways and keep His statutes, His commandments, and His judgments, and that you will obey His voice. ¹⁸Also today the LORD has proclaimed you to be His special people, just as He promised you, that *you* should keep all His commandments, ¹⁹and that He will set you high above all nations which He has made, in praise, in name, and in honor, and that you may be a holy people to the LORD your God, just as He has spoken."

The Law Inscribed on Stones

27 ¹Now Moses, with the elders of Israel, commanded the people, saying: "Keep all the commandments which I command you today. ²And it shall be, on the day when you cross over the Jordan to the land which the LORD your God is giving you, that you shall set up for yourselves large stones, and whitewash them with

---

TIME CAPSULE   *1275 to 1273 B.C.*

1275–1235	*The 40 years of wilderness wandering (based on late Exodus)*
1274	*Israelites depart from Mount Sinai (based on late Exodus)*
1274	*Ramesses II fights the Hittites at Kadesh, both sides using chariots*
1274	*Ramesses II suffers defeat against the Hittites*
1273–1076	*Middle Assyrian Empire*
1273–1244	*Shalmaneser I of Assyria boasts of conquering the Hittites, the Arameans, and Mitanni*

26:3 [a]Septuagint reads *my.*   26:5 [a]Or
Aramean   26:9 [a]Exodus 3:8   26:15 [a]Exodus 3:8

lime. ³You shall write on them all the words of this law, when you have crossed over, that you may enter the land which the LORD your God is giving you, 'a land flowing with milk and honey,'ᵃ just as the LORD God of your fathers promised you. ⁴Therefore it shall be, when you have crossed over the Jordan, *that* on Mount Ebal you shall set up these stones, which I command you today, and you shall whitewash them with lime. ⁵And there you shall build an altar to the LORD your God, an altar of stones; you shall not use an iron *tool* on them. ⁶You shall build with whole stones the altar of the LORD your God, and offer burnt offerings on it to the LORD your God. ⁷You shall offer peace offerings, and shall eat there, and rejoice before the LORD your God. ⁸And you shall write very plainly on the stones all the words of this law."

⁹Then Moses and the priests, the Levites, spoke to all Israel, saying, "Take heed and listen, O Israel: This day you have become the people of the LORD your God. ¹⁰Therefore you shall obey the voice of the LORD your God, and observe His commandments and His statutes which I command you today."

Curses Pronounced from Mount Ebal

¹¹And Moses commanded the people on the same day, saying, ¹²"These shall stand on Mount Gerizim to bless the people, when you have crossed over the Jordan: Simeon, Levi, Judah, Issachar, Joseph, and Benjamin; ¹³and these shall stand on Mount Ebal to curse: Reuben, Gad, Asher, Zebulun, Dan, and Naphtali.

¹⁴"And the Levites shall speak with a loud voice and say to all the men of Israel: ¹⁵'Cursed *is* the one who makes a carved or molded image, an abomination to the LORD, the work of the hands of the craftsman, and sets *it* up in secret.'

"And all the people shall answer and say, 'Amen!'

¹⁶'Cursed *is* the one who treats his father or his mother with contempt.'

"And all the people shall say, 'Amen!'

¹⁷'Cursed *is* the one who moves his neighbor's landmark.'

"And all the people shall say, 'Amen!'

¹⁸'Cursed *is* the one who makes the blind to wander off the road.'

"And all the people shall say, 'Amen!'

¹⁹'Cursed *is* the one who perverts the justice due the stranger, the fatherless, and widow.'

"And all the people shall say, 'Amen!'

²⁰'Cursed *is* the one who lies with his father's wife, because he has uncovered his father's bed.'

"And all the people shall say, 'Amen!'

²¹'Cursed *is* the one who lies with any kind of animal.'

"And all the people shall say, 'Amen!'

²²'Cursed *is* the one who lies with his sister, the daughter of his father or the daughter of his mother.'

"And all the people shall say, 'Amen!'

²³'Cursed *is* the one who lies with his mother-in-law.'

"And all the people shall say, 'Amen!'

²⁴'Cursed *is* the one who attacks his neighbor secretly.'

"And all the people shall say, 'Amen!'

²⁵'Cursed *is* the one who takes a bribe to slay an innocent person.'

"And all the people shall say, 'Amen!'

²⁶'Cursed *is* the one who does not confirm *all* the words of this law by observing them.'

"And all the people shall say, 'Amen!' "

Blessings on Obedience

28 ¹"Now it shall come to pass, if you diligently obey the voice of the LORD your God, to observe carefully all His commandments which I command you today, that the LORD your God will set you high above all nations of the earth. ²And all these blessings shall come upon you and overtake you, because you obey the voice of the LORD your God:

³"Blessed *shall* you *be* in the city, and blessed *shall* you *be* in the country.

⁴"Blessed *shall be* the fruit of your body, the produce of your ground and the increase of your herds, the increase of your cattle and the offspring of your flocks.

⁵"Blessed *shall be* your basket and your kneading bowl.

⁶"Blessed *shall* you *be* when you come in, and blessed *shall* you *be* when you go out.

⁷"The LORD will cause your enemies who rise against you to be defeated before your face; they shall come out against you one way and flee before you seven ways.

⁸"The LORD will command the blessing on you in your storehouses and in all to which you set your hand, and He will bless you in the land which the LORD your God is giving you.

27:3 ᵃExodus 3:8

⁹"The LORD will establish you as a holy people to Himself, just as He has sworn to you, if you keep the commandments of the LORD your God and walk in His ways. ¹⁰Then all peoples of the earth shall see that you are called by the name of the LORD, and they shall be afraid of you. ¹¹And the LORD will grant you plenty of goods, in the fruit of your body, in the increase of your livestock, and in the produce of your ground, in the land of which the LORD swore to your fathers to give you. ¹²The LORD will open to you His good treasure, the heavens, to give the rain to your land in its season, and to bless all the work of your hand. You shall lend to many nations, but you shall not borrow. ¹³And the LORD will make you the head and not the tail; you shall be above only, and not be beneath, if you heed the commandments of the LORD your God, which I command you today, and are careful to observe *them*. ¹⁴So you shall not turn aside from any of the words which I command you this day, *to* the right or the left, to go after other gods to serve them.

Curses on Disobedience

¹⁵"But it shall come to pass, if you do not obey the voice of the LORD your God, to observe carefully all His commandments and His statutes which I command you today, that all these curses will come upon you and overtake you:

¹⁶"Cursed *shall* you *be* in the city, and cursed *shall* you *be* in the country.

¹⁷"Cursed *shall be* your basket and your kneading bowl.

¹⁸"Cursed *shall be* the fruit of your body and the produce of your land, the increase of your cattle and the offspring of your flocks.

¹⁹"Cursed *shall* you *be* when you come in, and cursed *shall* you *be* when you go out.

²⁰"The LORD will send on you cursing, confusion, and rebuke in all that you set your hand to do, until you are destroyed and until you perish quickly, because of the wickedness of your doings in which you have forsaken Me. ²¹The LORD will make the plague cling to you until He has consumed you from the land which you are going to possess. ²²The LORD will strike you with consumption, with fever, with inflammation, with severe burning fever, with the sword, with scorching, and with mildew; they shall pursue you until you perish. ²³And your heavens which *are* over your head shall be bronze, and the earth which is under you *shall be* iron. ²⁴The LORD will change the rain of your land to powder and dust; from the heaven it shall come down on you until you are destroyed.

²⁵"The LORD will cause you to be defeated before your enemies; you shall go out one way against them and flee seven ways before them; and you shall become troublesome to all the kingdoms of the earth. ²⁶Your carcasses shall be food for all the birds of the air and the beasts of the earth, and no one shall frighten *them* away. ²⁷The LORD will strike you with the boils of Egypt, with tumors, with the scab, and with the itch, from which you cannot be healed. ²⁸The LORD will strike you with madness and blindness and confusion of heart. ²⁹And you shall grope at noonday, as a blind man gropes in darkness; you shall not prosper in your ways; you shall be only oppressed and plundered continually, and no one shall save *you*.

³⁰"You shall betroth a wife, but another man shall lie with her; you shall build a house, but you shall not dwell in it; you shall plant a vineyard, but shall not gather its grapes. ³¹Your ox *shall be* slaughtered before your eyes, but you shall not eat of it; your donkey *shall be* violently taken away from before you, and shall not be restored to you; your sheep *shall be* given to your enemies, and you shall have no one to rescue *them*. ³²Your sons and your daughters *shall be* given to another people, and your eyes shall look and fail *with longing* for them all day long; and *there shall be* no strength in your hand. ³³A nation whom you have not known shall eat the fruit of

HEALTH AND MEDICINE

In modern times the human reaction to trauma and distress has been made the object of scientific study. It is not a topic for every time or every situation. In Deut. 28:34 the Bible shows a seemingly modern awareness of how the mind is assaulted and damaged by cruelty, thus "driven mad."

THE CURSES OF DISOBEDIENCE (Deut. 28:30–34)

The various commandments and statutes established in the Law of Moses were to be obeyed. The solemn message of Deut. 28:15–68 is that disobedience would not be tolerated in Israel. They could enjoy blessings from God, or they could experience curses: their carcasses eaten by birds (28:26); their bodies plagued by incurable diseases (28:27); their wives raped (28:30). The list of miseries goes on throughout Deut. 28.

Curses were a part of covenants in the ancient world, and were intended to enforce the stipulations of the covenant. What jars our modern concepts of God is Israel's belief that it was their deity who would cause these curses if they violated the covenant. Several times in Deuteronomy are the words, "The LORD will . . ." (28:20–22, 24, 25, etc.). Israel was not unique in these beliefs concerning covenant curses. The grave consequences for disobedience are formally similar to the consequences other peoples faced for breaking treaties with their monarchs.

Esarhaddon, king of Assyria (680–669 B.C.), required subject states to accept a treaty of fidelity to both Esarhaddon and his successor(s). *The Vassal Treaties of Esarhaddon* contain in explicit detail the consequences for breaking the oaths, and reflect traditional curses found in Mesopotamian texts for at least 1,000 years before Esarhaddon.

A selection of gods in the Assyrian pantheon were called upon to enact various curses (very similar to Deut. 28) upon a disobedient vassal and his heirs. For example: Nergal would extinguish the life of the vassal, along with bringing carnage and pestilence; Ishtar would break the bow of the vassal in battle; Ninurta would kill the vassal with his bow and feed his carcass to the birds; the god Sin would clothe the vassal with leprosy; and Shamash would cause the individual to walk about in darkness. Last, all of the gods listed on the tablet would work to turn the vassal's soil into iron, and turn the rain in the sky over his land into copper.

your land and the produce of your labor, and you shall be only oppressed and crushed continually. ³⁴So you shall be driven mad because of the sight which your eyes see. ³⁵The LORD will strike you in the knees and on the legs with severe boils which cannot be healed, and from the sole of your foot to the top of your head.

³⁶"The LORD will bring you and the king whom you set over you to a nation which neither you nor your fathers have known, and there you shall serve other gods—wood and stone. ³⁷And you shall become an astonishment, a proverb, and a byword among all nations where the LORD will drive you.

³⁸"You shall carry much seed out to the field but gather little in, for the locust shall consume it. ³⁹You shall plant vineyards and tend *them*, but you shall neither drink *of* the wine nor gather the *grapes;* for the worms shall eat them. ⁴⁰You shall have olive trees throughout all your territory, but you shall not anoint *yourself* with the oil; for your olives shall drop off. ⁴¹You shall beget sons and daughters, but they shall not be yours; for they shall go into captivity. ⁴²Locusts shall consume all your trees and the produce of your land.

⁴³"The alien who *is* among you shall rise higher and higher above you, and you shall come down lower and lower. ⁴⁴He shall lend to you, but you shall not lend to him; he shall be the head, and you shall be the tail.

⁴⁵"Moreover all these curses shall come upon you and pursue and overtake you, until you are destroyed, because you did not obey the voice of the LORD your God, to keep His commandments and His statutes which He commanded you. ⁴⁶And they shall be upon you for a sign and a wonder, and on your descendants forever.

⁴⁷"Because you did not serve the LORD your God with joy and gladness of heart, for the abundance of everything, ⁴⁸therefore you shall serve your enemies, whom the LORD will send against you, in hunger, in thirst, in nakedness, and in need of everything; and He will put a yoke of iron on your neck until He has destroyed you. ⁴⁹The LORD will bring a nation against you from afar, from the end of the earth, *as swift* as the eagle flies, a nation whose language you will not understand, ⁵⁰a nation of fierce countenance, which does not

respect the elderly nor show favor to the young. [51]And they shall eat the increase of your livestock and the produce of your land, until you are destroyed; they shall not leave you grain or new wine or oil, *or* the increase of your cattle or the offspring of your flocks, until they have destroyed you.

[52]"They shall besiege you at all your gates until your high and fortified walls, in which you trust, come down throughout all your land; and they shall besiege you at all your gates throughout all your land which the LORD your God has given you. [53]You shall eat the fruit of your own body, the flesh of your sons and your daughters whom the LORD your God has given you, in the siege and desperate straits in which your enemy shall distress you. [54]The sensitive and very refined man among you will be hostile toward his brother, toward the wife of his bosom, and toward the rest of his children whom he leaves behind, [55]so that he will not give any of them the flesh of his children whom he will eat, because he has nothing left in the siege and desperate straits in which your enemy shall distress you at all your gates. [56]The tender and delicate woman among you, who would not venture to set the sole of her foot on the ground because of her delicateness and sensitivity, will refuse[a] to the husband of her bosom, and to her son and her daughter, [57]her placenta which comes out from between her feet and her children whom she bears; for she will eat them secretly for lack of everything in the siege and desperate straits in which your enemy shall distress you at all your gates.

[58]"If you do not carefully observe all the words of this law that are written in this book, that you may fear this glorious and awesome name, THE LORD YOUR GOD, [59]then the LORD will bring upon you and your descendants extraordinary plagues—great and prolonged plagues—and serious and prolonged sicknesses. [60]Moreover He will bring back on you all the diseases of Egypt, of which you were afraid, and they shall cling to you. [61]Also every sickness and every plague, which *is* not written in this Book of the Law, will the LORD bring upon you until you are destroyed. [62]You shall be left few in number, whereas you were as the stars of heaven in multitude, because you would not obey the voice of the LORD your God. [63]And it shall be, *that* just as the LORD rejoiced over you

to do you good and multiply you, so the LORD will rejoice over you to destroy you and bring you to nothing; and you shall be plucked from off the land which you go to possess.

[64]"Then the LORD will scatter you among all peoples, from one end of the earth to the other, and there you shall serve other gods, which neither you nor your fathers have known—wood and stone. [65]And among those nations you shall find no rest, nor shall the sole of your foot have a resting place; but there the LORD will give you a trembling heart, failing eyes, and anguish of soul. [66]Your life shall hang in doubt before you; you shall fear day and night, and have no assurance of life. [67]In the morning you shall say, 'Oh, that it were evening!' And at evening you shall say, 'Oh, that it were morning!' because of the fear which terrifies your heart, and because of the sight which your eyes see.

[68]"And the LORD will take you back to Egypt in ships, by the way of which I said to you, 'You shall never see it again.' And there you shall be offered for sale to your enemies as male and female slaves, but no one will buy *you*."

Moses' Final Words

Moses' final speech (29:1—33:29) contains various materials. In a final charge Moses reviews Israel's recent God-given victories over idolatrous nations (29:1–19) and predicts their future apostasy (29:20–29), but also God's restoration and cleansing (30:1–10). In light of all of this, Moses calls on them to choose life (30:11—31:6). The Song of Moses (ch. 32) and the blessing of Moses (ch. 33) complete this leader's words to his people.

▪ Deuteronomy 29:1—33:29

Deuteronomy
The Covenant Renewed in Moab

29 :1 These *are* the words of the covenant which the LORD commanded Moses to make with the children of Israel in the land of Moab, besides the covenant which He made with them in Horeb.

[2]Now Moses called all Israel and said to them: "You have seen all that the LORD

28:56 [a]Literally *her eye shall be evil toward*

did before your eyes in the land of Egypt, to Pharaoh and to all his servants and to all his land— ³the great trials which your eyes have seen, the signs, and those great wonders. ⁴Yet the LORD has not given you a heart to perceive and eyes to see and ears to hear, to this *very* day. ⁵And I have led you forty years in the wilderness. Your clothes have not worn out on you, and your sandals have not worn out on your feet. ⁶You have not eaten bread, nor have you drunk wine or *similar* drink, that you may know that I *am* the LORD your God. ⁷And when you came to this place, Sihon king of Heshbon and Og king of Bashan came out against us to battle, and we conquered them. ⁸We took their land and gave it as an inheritance to the Reubenites, to the Gadites, and to half the tribe of Manasseh. ⁹Therefore keep the words of this covenant, and do them, that you may prosper in all that you do.

¹⁰"All of you stand today before the LORD your God: your leaders and your tribes and your elders and your officers, all the men of Israel, ¹¹your little ones and your wives—also the stranger who *is* in your camp, from the one who cuts your wood to the one who draws your water— ¹²that you may enter into covenant with the LORD your God, and into His oath, which the LORD your God makes with you today, ¹³that He may establish you today as a people for Himself, and *that* He may be God to you, just as He has spoken to you, and just as He has sworn to your fathers, to Abraham, Isaac, and Jacob.

¹⁴"I make this covenant and this oath, not with you alone, ¹⁵but with *him* who stands here with us today before the LORD our God, as well as with *him* who *is* not here with us today ¹⁶(for you know that we dwelt in the land of Egypt and that we came through the nations which you passed by, ¹⁷and you saw their abominations and their idols which *were* among them—wood and stone and silver and gold); ¹⁸so that there may not be among you man or woman or family or tribe, whose heart turns away today from the LORD our God, to go *and* serve the gods of these nations, and that there may not be among you a root bearing bitterness or wormwood; ¹⁹and so it may not happen, when he hears the words of this curse, that he blesses himself in his heart, saying, 'I

shall have peace, even though I follow the dictates[a] of my heart'—as though the drunkard could be included with the sober.

²⁰"The LORD would not spare him; for then the anger of the LORD and His jealousy would burn against that man, and every curse that is written in this book would settle on him, and the LORD would blot out his name from under heaven. ²¹And the LORD would separate him from all the tribes of Israel for adversity, according to all the curses of the covenant that are written in this Book of the Law, ²²so that the coming generation of your children who rise up after you, and the foreigner who comes from a far land, would say, when they see the plagues of that land and the sicknesses which the LORD has laid on it:

²³'The whole land *is* brimstone, salt, and burning; it is not sown, nor does it bear, nor does any grass grow there, like the overthrow of Sodom and Gomorrah, Admah, and Zeboiim, which the LORD overthrew in His anger and His wrath.' ²⁴All nations would say, 'Why has the LORD done so to this land? What does the heat of this great anger mean?' ²⁵Then *people* would say: 'Because they have forsaken the covenant of the LORD God of their fathers, which He made with them when He brought them out of the land of Egypt; ²⁶for they went and served other gods and worshiped them, gods that they did not know and that He had not given to them. ²⁷Then the anger of the LORD was aroused against this land, to bring on it every curse that is written in this book. ²⁸And the LORD uprooted them from their land in anger, in wrath, and in great indignation, and cast them into another land, as *it is* this day.'

²⁹"The secret *things belong* to the LORD our God, but those *things which are* revealed *belong* to us and to our children forever, that *we* may do all the words of this law.

The Blessing of Returning to God

30 ¹"Now it shall come to pass, when all these things come upon you, the blessing and the curse which I have set before you, and you call *them* to mind among all the nations where the LORD your God drives you, ²and you return to the LORD your God and obey His voice, according to all that I command you today, you and your children, with all your heart and with all your soul, ³that the LORD your God will

29:19 ᵃOr *stubbornness*

ADAPA MISSES OUT ON IMMORTALITY (Deut. 30:11, 12)

The Accadian myth of Adapa was found on a cuneiform text in the library at Tell el-Amarna, the Egyptian capital during the time of Pharaoh Akhenaten (1352–1336 B.C.). The story was uncovered also in various sites of Mesopotamia, including Asshur and Nineveh. The text relates the various adventures of the hero, Adapa, a priest of Ea at Eridu, a city in southern Mesopotamia.

According to the incomplete account, Adapa's boat sinks because of the divine South Wind as he is procuring food for the shrine at Eridu. He subsequently breaks the wings of the South Wind, causing a dramatic change in the climate, and resulting in a mandatory visit by Adapa to the divine high council, headed by Anu, the king of the gods.

Adapa's god, Ea, counsels him to refuse food or drink from the gods, as mortals often would be given food causing death. He is asked to try to win the favor of Tammuz and Gizzida, the divine gatekeepers. During his audience with Anu, Adapa is unexpectedly offered the bread and water of life. Heeding Ea's counsel, Adapa rejects the food, which amuses Anu. Adapa is then returned to his home. Whether Anu and Ea had conspired to trick Adapa, or whether Ea was ignorant of what Anu would offer the priest is not known, as the text is not complete.

The myth has the purpose of showing why humans had not achieved immortality. In ancient thought there was a distinction between the divine realm and the human realm. In general, humans did not belong in heaven. This belief is reflected in Deut. 30:11, 12 where Moses assures the Israelites that God's commands are not in heaven, lest they need someone to "ascend into heaven" for them to retrieve the commands.

bring you back from captivity, and have compassion on you, and gather you again from all the nations where the LORD your God has scattered you. ⁴If *any* of you are driven out to the farthest *parts* under heaven, from there the LORD your God will gather you, and from there He will bring you. ⁵Then the LORD your God will bring you to the land which your fathers possessed, and you shall possess it. He will prosper you and multiply you more than your fathers. ⁶And the LORD your God will circumcise your heart and the heart of your descendants, to love the LORD your God with all your heart and with all your soul, that you may live.

⁷"Also the LORD your God will put all these curses on your enemies and on those who hate you, who persecuted you. ⁸And you will again obey the voice of the LORD and do all His commandments which I command you today. ⁹The LORD your God will make you abound in all the work of your hand, in the fruit of your body, in the increase of your livestock, and in the produce of your land for good. For the LORD will again rejoice over you for good as He rejoiced over your fathers, ¹⁰if you obey the voice of the LORD your God, to keep His commandments and His statutes which are written in this Book of the Law, *and* if you turn to the LORD your God with all your heart and with all your soul.

The Choice of Life or Death

¹¹"For this commandment which I command you today *is* not *too* mysterious for you, nor *is* it far off. ¹²It *is* not in heaven, that you should say, 'Who will ascend into heaven for us and bring it to us, that we may hear it and do it?' ¹³Nor *is* it beyond the sea, that you should say, 'Who will go over the sea for us and bring it to us, that we may hear it and do it?' ¹⁴But the word *is* very near you, in your mouth and in your heart, that you may do it.

¹⁵"See, I have set before you today life and good, death and evil, ¹⁶in that I command you today to love the LORD your God, to walk in His ways, and to keep His commandments, His statutes, and His judgments, that you may live and multiply; and the LORD your God will bless you in the land which you go to possess. ¹⁷But if your heart turns away so that you do not hear, and are drawn away, and worship other gods and serve them, ¹⁸I announce to you today that you shall surely perish; you shall not prolong *your* days in the land which you cross over the Jordan to go in

and possess. [19]I call heaven and earth as witnesses today against you, *that* I have set before you life and death, blessing and cursing; therefore choose life, that both you and your descendants may live; [20]that you may love the LORD your God, that you may obey His voice, and that you may cling to Him, for He *is* your life and the length of your days; and that you may dwell in the land which the LORD swore to your fathers, to Abraham, Isaac, and Jacob, to give them."

Joshua the New Leader of Israel

31 [1]Then Moses went and spoke these words to all Israel. [2]And he said to them: "I *am* one hundred and twenty years old today. I can no longer go out and come in. Also the LORD has said to me, 'You shall not cross over this Jordan.' [3]The LORD your God Himself crosses over before you; He will destroy these nations from before you, and you shall dispossess them. Joshua himself crosses over before you, just as the LORD has said. [4]And the LORD will do to them as He did to Sihon and Og, the kings of the Amorites and their land, when He destroyed them. [5]The LORD will give them over to you, that you may do to them according to every commandment which I have commanded you. [6]Be strong and of good courage, do not fear nor be afraid of them; for the LORD your God, He *is* the One who goes with you. He will not leave you nor forsake you."

[7]Then Moses called Joshua and said to him in the sight of all Israel, "Be strong and of good courage, for you must go with this people to the land which the LORD has sworn to their fathers to give them, and you shall cause them to inherit it. [8]And the LORD, He *is* the One who goes before you. He will be with you, He will not leave you nor forsake you; do not fear nor be dismayed."

The Law to Be Read Every Seven Years

[9]So Moses wrote this law and delivered it to the priests, the sons of Levi, who bore the ark of the covenant of the LORD, and to all the elders of Israel. [10]And Moses commanded them, saying: "At the end of *every* seven years, at the appointed time in the year of release, at the Feast of Tabernacles, [11]when all Israel comes to appear before the LORD your God in the place which He chooses, you shall read this law before all Israel in their hearing. [12]Gather the people together, men and women and little ones, and the stranger who *is* within your gates, that they may hear and that they may learn to fear the LORD your God and carefully observe all the words of this law, [13]and *that* their children, who have not known it, may hear and learn to fear the LORD your God as long as you live in the land which you cross the Jordan to possess."

Prediction of Israel's Rebellion

[14]Then the LORD said to Moses, "Behold, the days approach when you must die; call Joshua, and present yourselves in the tabernacle of meeting, that I may inaugurate him."

So Moses and Joshua went and presented themselves in the tabernacle of meeting. [15]Now the LORD appeared at the tabernacle in a pillar of cloud, and the pillar of cloud stood above the door of the tabernacle.

[16]And the LORD said to Moses: "Behold, you will rest with your fathers; and this people will rise and play the harlot with the gods of the foreigners of the land, where they go *to be* among them, and they will forsake Me and break My covenant which I have made with them. [17]Then My anger shall be aroused against them in that day, and I will forsake them, and I will hide My face from them, and they shall be devoured. And many evils and troubles shall befall them, so that they will say in that day, 'Have not these evils come upon us because our God *is* not among us?' [18]And I will surely hide My face in that day because of all the evil which they have done, in that they have turned to other gods.

ARTS AND LITERATURE

In general, poetry is easier than prose to memorize and to transmit orally—to "put it in their mouths" (Deut. 31:19). This is so because a poem focuses on its own words as well as on what it talks about. Furthermore, the typical formal features of poetry, such as rhyming and balanced lines, make it easier to recite complete sections of a composition.

¹⁹"Now therefore, write down this song for yourselves, and teach it to the children of Israel; put it in their mouths, that this song may be a witness for Me against the children of Israel. ²⁰When I have brought them to the land flowing with milk and honey, of which I swore to their fathers, and they have eaten and filled themselves and grown fat, then they will turn to other gods and serve them; and they will provoke Me and break My covenant. ²¹Then it shall be, when many evils and troubles have come upon them, that this song will testify against them as a witness; for it will not be forgotten in the mouths of their descendants, for I know the inclination of their behavior today, even before I have brought them to the land of which I swore *to give them*."

²²Therefore Moses wrote this song the same day, and taught it to the children of Israel. ²³Then He inaugurated Joshua the son of Nun, and said, "Be strong and of good courage; for you shall bring the children of Israel into the land of which I swore to them, and I will be with you."

²⁴So it was, when Moses had completed writing the words of this law in a book, when they were finished, ²⁵that Moses commanded the Levites, who bore the ark of the covenant of the LORD, saying: ²⁶"Take this Book of the Law, and put it beside the ark of the covenant of the LORD your God, that it may be there as a witness against you; ²⁷for I know your rebellion and your stiff neck. *If* today, while I am yet alive with you, you have been rebellious against the LORD, then how much more after my death? ²⁸Gather to me all the elders of your tribes, and your officers, that I may speak these words in their hearing and call heaven and earth to witness against them. ²⁹For I know that after my death you will become utterly corrupt, and turn aside from the way which I have commanded you. And evil will befall you in the latter days, because you will do evil in the sight of the LORD, to provoke Him to anger through the work of your hands."

The Song of Moses

³⁰Then Moses spoke in the hearing of all the assembly of Israel the words of this song until they were ended:

32 ¹ "Give ear, O heavens, and I will speak;
And hear, O earth, the words of my mouth.
² Let my teaching drop as the rain,
My speech distill as the dew,
As raindrops on the tender herb,
And as showers on the grass.
³ For I proclaim the name of the LORD:
Ascribe greatness to our God.
⁴ *He is* the Rock, His work *is* perfect;
For all His ways *are* justice,
A God of truth and without injustice;
Righteous and upright *is* He.

⁵ "They have corrupted themselves;
They are not His children,
Because of their blemish:
A perverse and crooked generation.
⁶ Do you thus deal with the LORD,
O foolish and unwise people?
Is He not your Father, *who* bought you?
Has He not made you and established you?

⁷ "Remember the days of old,
Consider the years of many generations.
Ask your father, and he will show you;
Your elders, and they will tell you:
⁸ When the Most High divided their inheritance to the nations,
When He separated the sons of Adam,
He set the boundaries of the peoples
According to the number of the children of Israel.
⁹ For the LORD's portion *is* His people;
Jacob *is* the place of His inheritance.

¹⁰ "He found him in a desert land
And in the wasteland, a howling wilderness;
He encircled him, He instructed him,
He kept him as the apple of His eye.

PLANTS AND ANIMALS

The ideas of strength and protection, both inherent in the image of an eagle's wings, are combined in Deut. 32:11. The eagle displays strength and subtlety in the way it stays aloft in the wind. Secondly, wings were a traditional symbol of protection and refuge. Ancient Egyptian sculptures often have the wings of a falcon protecting a ruler or prince.

11 As an eagle stirs up its nest,
Hovers over its young,
Spreading out its wings, taking them up,
Carrying them on its wings,
12 *So* the LORD alone led him,
And *there was* no foreign god with him.

13 "He made him ride in the heights of the earth,
That he might eat the produce of the fields;
He made him draw honey from the rock,
And oil from the flinty rock;
14 Curds from the cattle, and milk of the flock,
With fat of lambs;
And rams of the breed of Bashan, and goats,
With the choicest wheat;
And you drank wine, the blood of the grapes.

15 "But Jeshurun grew fat and kicked;
You grew fat, you grew thick,
You are obese!
Then he forsook God *who* made him,
And scornfully esteemed the Rock of his salvation.
16 They provoked Him to jealousy with foreign *gods;*
With abominations they provoked Him to anger.
17 They sacrificed to demons, not to God,
To gods they did not know,
To new *gods,* new arrivals
That your fathers did not fear.
18 Of the Rock *who* begot you, you are unmindful,
And have forgotten the God who fathered you.

19 "And when the LORD saw *it,* He spurned *them,*
Because of the provocation of His sons and His daughters.
20 And He said: 'I will hide My face from them,
I will see what their end *will be,*
For they *are* a perverse generation,
Children in whom *is* no faith.
21 They have provoked Me to jealousy by *what* is not God;
They have moved Me to anger by their foolish idols.

But I will provoke them to jealousy by *those who are* not a nation;
I will move them to anger by a foolish nation.
22 For a fire is kindled in My anger,
And shall burn to the lowest hell;
It shall consume the earth with her increase,
And set on fire the foundations of the mountains.

23 'I will heap disasters on them;
I will spend My arrows on them.
24 *They shall be* wasted with hunger,
Devoured by pestilence and bitter destruction;
I will also send against them the teeth of beasts,
With the poison of serpents of the dust.
25 The sword shall destroy outside;
There shall be terror within
For the young man and virgin,
The nursing child with the man of gray hairs.
26 I would have said, "I will dash them in pieces,
I will make the memory of them to cease from among men,"
27 Had I not feared the wrath of the enemy,
Lest their adversaries should misunderstand,
Lest they should say, "Our hand *is* high;
And it is not the LORD who has done all this." '

28 "For they *are* a nation void of counsel,
Nor *is there any* understanding in them.
29 Oh, that they were wise, *that* they understood this,
That they would consider their latter end!
30 How could one chase a thousand,
And two put ten thousand to flight,
Unless their Rock had sold them,
And the LORD had surrendered them?
31 For their rock *is* not like our Rock,
Even our enemies themselves *being* judges.
32 For their vine *is* of the vine of Sodom
And of the fields of Gomorrah;
Their grapes *are* grapes of gall,
Their clusters *are* bitter.
33 Their wine *is* the poison of serpents,
And the cruel venom of cobras.

34 'Is this not laid up in store with Me,
Sealed up among My treasures?
35 Vengeance is Mine, and recompense;
Their foot shall slip in *due* time;
For the day of their calamity *is* at
hand,
And the things to come hasten upon
them.'

36 "For the LORD will judge His people
And have compassion on His servants,
When He sees that *their* power is
gone,
And *there is* no one *remaining,* bond
or free.
37 He will say: 'Where *are* their gods,
The rock in which they sought refuge?
38 Who ate the fat of their sacrifices,
And drank the wine of their drink
offering?
Let them rise and help you,
And be your refuge.

39 'Now see that I, *even* I, *am* He,
And *there is* no God besides Me;
I kill and I make alive;
I wound and I heal;
Nor *is there any* who can deliver from
My hand.
40 For I raise My hand to heaven,
And say, "*As* I live forever,
41 If I whet My glittering sword,
And My hand takes hold on judgment,
I will render vengeance to My
enemies,
And repay those who hate Me.
42 I will make My arrows drunk with
blood,
And My sword shall devour flesh,
With the blood of the slain and the
captives,
From the heads of the leaders of the
enemy." '

43 "Rejoice, O Gentiles, *with* His people;[a]
For He will avenge the blood of His
servants,
And render vengeance to His
adversaries;
He will provide atonement for His
land *and* His people."

[44]So Moses came with Joshua[a] the son
of Nun and spoke all the words of this song
in the hearing of the people. [45]Moses finished speaking all these words to all Israel,
[46]and he said to them: "Set your hearts on
all the words which I testify among you today, which you shall command your children to be careful to observe—all the words
of this law. [47]For it *is* not a futile thing for
you, because it *is* your life, and by this
word you shall prolong *your* days in the
land which you cross over the Jordan to
possess."

Moses to Die on Mount Nebo

[48]Then the LORD spoke to Moses that
very same day, saying: [49]"Go up this mountain of the Abarim, Mount Nebo, which *is*
in the land of Moab, across from Jericho;
view the land of Canaan, which I give to
the children of Israel as a possession; [50]and
die on the mountain which you ascend, and
be gathered to your people, just as Aaron
your brother died on Mount Hor and was
gathered to his people; [51]because you trespassed against Me among the children of
Israel at the waters of Meribah Kadesh, in
the Wilderness of Zin, because you did not
hallow Me in the midst of the children of
Israel. [52]Yet you shall see the land before
you, though you shall not go there, into the
land which I am giving to the children of
Israel."

Moses' Final Blessing on Israel

33 [1]Now this *is* the blessing with which
Moses the man of God blessed the
children of Israel before his death. [2]And he
said:

"The LORD came from Sinai,
And dawned on them from Seir;
He shone forth from Mount Paran,
And He came with ten thousands of
saints;

TIME CAPSULE   *1259 to 1250 B.C.*

1259   *Egyptians and Hittites conclude a
peace treaty*

1250   *Hittite letter mentions the iron
blade of a dagger*

1250   *"Lion Gate" of Mycenae*

1250   *Sea battle between Cyprus and the
Hittites*

1250   *Letter from King Hattusilis III shows
Hittite skills in producing smelted
iron*

32:43 [a]A Dead Sea Scroll fragment adds *And let all
the* gods *(angels) worship Him* (compare Septuagint
and Hebrews 1:6).   32:44 [a]Hebrew *Hoshea*
(compare Numbers 13:8, 16)

From His right hand
Came a fiery law for them.
3 Yes, He loves the people;
All His saints *are* in Your hand;
They sit down at Your feet;
Everyone receives Your words.
4 Moses commanded a law for us,
A heritage of the congregation of
Jacob.
5 And He was King in Jeshurun,
When the leaders of the people were
gathered,
All the tribes of Israel together.

6 "Let Reuben live, and not die,
Nor let his men be few."

7And this he said of Judah:

"Hear, LORD, the voice of Judah,
And bring him to his people;
Let his hands be sufficient for him,
And may You be a help against his
enemies."

8And of Levi he said:

"*Let* Your Thummim and Your Urim *be*
with Your holy one,
Whom You tested at Massah,
And with whom You contended at the
waters of Meribah,
9 Who says of his father and mother,
'I have not seen them';
Nor did he acknowledge his brothers,
Or know his own children;
For they have observed Your word
And kept Your covenant.
10 They shall teach Jacob Your
judgments,
And Israel Your law.
They shall put incense before You,
And a whole burnt sacrifice on Your
altar.
11 Bless his substance, LORD,
And accept the work of his hands;
Strike the loins of those who rise
against him,

And of those who hate him, that they
rise not again."

12Of Benjamin he said:

"The beloved of the LORD shall dwell in
safety by Him,
Who shelters him all the day long;
And he shall dwell between His
shoulders."

13And of Joseph he said:

"Blessed of the LORD *is* his land,
With the precious things of heaven,
with the dew,
And the deep lying beneath,
14 With the precious fruits of the sun,
With the precious produce of the
months,
15 With the best things of the ancient
mountains,
With the precious things of the
everlasting hills,
16 With the precious things of the earth
and its fullness,
And the favor of Him who dwelt in the
bush.
Let *the blessing* come 'on the head of
Joseph,
And on the crown of the head of him
who was separate from his
brothers.'a
17 His glory *is like* a firstborn bull,
And his horns *like* the horns of the
wild ox;
Together with them
He shall push the peoples
To the ends of the earth;
They *are* the ten thousands of
Ephraim,
And they *are* the thousands of
Manasseh."

18And of Zebulun he said:

"Rejoice, Zebulun, in your going out,
And Issachar in your tents!

33:16 aGenesis 49:26

BELIEFS AND IDEAS

*The gods of Canaan and Mesopotamia, unlike the gods of Egypt, were in constant
struggle and change. Over against them the Bible maintains the theme of the
incomparability of the Lord (Deut. 33:26), even when the Lord's power is expressed in a
conventional symbol, such as riding on the clouds.*

19 They shall call the peoples *to* the
    mountain;
    There they shall offer sacrifices of
    righteousness;
    For they shall partake *of* the
    abundance of the seas
    And *of* treasures hidden in the sand.”

20And of Gad he said:

“Blessed *is* he who enlarges Gad;
    He dwells as a lion,
    And tears the arm and the crown of
    his head.
21 He provided the first *part* for himself,
    Because a lawgiver’s portion was
    reserved there.
    He came *with* the heads of the people;
    He administered the justice of the
    LORD,
    And His judgments with Israel.”

22And of Dan he said:

“Dan *is* a lion’s whelp;
    He shall leap from Bashan.”

23And of Naphtali he said:

“O Naphtali, satisfied with favor,
    And full of the blessing of the LORD,
    Possess the west and the south.”

24And of Asher he said:

“Asher *is* most blessed of sons;
    Let him be favored by his brothers,
    And let him dip his foot in oil.
25 Your sandals *shall be* iron and bronze;
    As your days, *so shall* your strength
    be.

26 “*There is* no one like the God of
    Jeshurun,
    Who rides the heavens to help you,
    And in His excellency on the clouds.
27 The eternal God *is your* refuge,
    And underneath *are* the everlasting
    arms;
    He will thrust out the enemy from
    before you,
    And will say, ‘Destroy!’
28 Then Israel shall dwell in safety,
    The fountain of Jacob alone,
    In a land of grain and new wine;
    His heavens shall also drop dew.
29 Happy *are* you, O Israel!
    Who *is* like you, a people saved by the
    LORD,

The shield of your help
And the sword of your majesty!
Your enemies shall submit to you,
And you shall tread down their high
    places.”

The Death of Moses
Though he could not enter, Moses
was allowed to see the new land. He had been
the great spokesman for God. There would be
other prophets in Israel, but no one would ever
hold the place of the man who led them out of
Egypt to the Promised Land. As a crowning
honor, he is called for the first time the name
by which he is perhaps best remembered:
“Moses the servant of the LORD” (Deut. 34:5).

Israel had reached the plains of Moab
around either 1406 B.C. or 1235 B.C. (see
“Moab: On the Doorstep of Canaan” at Num.
20:14). Moses began his speeches in the
11th month of this 40th year after the Israelites’ departure from Egypt (Deut. 1:3; see
Num. 33:38). According to the chronological
scheme of the Book of Joshua, the Israelites
crossed the Jordan and celebrated Passover
in the 1st month of the next year (Josh. 4:19;
5:10). Sometime during the intervening two
months, Moses died at the age of 120 years
(Deut. 34:7).

■ Deuteronomy 34:1–12

Deuteronomy
Moses Dies on Mount Nebo

34 :1 Then Moses went up from the
    plains of Moab to Mount Nebo, to
the top of Pisgah, which is across from Jericho. And the LORD showed him all the land
of Gilead as far as Dan, 2all Naphtali and
the land of Ephraim and Manasseh, all the
land of Judah as far as the Western Sea,a
3the South, and the plain of the Valley of
Jericho, the city of palm trees, as far as
Zoar. 4Then the LORD said to him, “This *is*
the land of which I swore to give Abraham,
Isaac, and Jacob, saying, ‘I will give it to
your descendants.’ I have caused you to see
it with your eyes, but you shall not cross
over there.”

5So Moses the servant of the LORD died
there in the land of Moab, according to the
word of the LORD. 6And He buried him in a
valley in the land of Moab, opposite Beth
Peor; but no one knows his grave to this

34:2 aThat is, the Mediterranean

day. [7]Moses *was* one hundred and twenty years old when he died. His eyes were not dim nor his natural vigor diminished. [8]And the children of Israel wept for Moses in the plains of Moab thirty days. So the days of weeping *and* mourning for Moses ended.

[9]Now Joshua the son of Nun was full of the spirit of wisdom, for Moses had laid his hands on him; so the children of Israel heeded him, and did as the LORD had commanded Moses.

[10]But since then there has not arisen in Israel a prophet like Moses, whom the LORD knew face to face, [11]in all the signs and wonders which the LORD sent him to do in the land of Egypt, before Pharaoh, before all his servants, and in all his land, [12]and by all that mighty power and all the great terror which Moses performed in the sight of all Israel.

Teach Us to Number Our Days

Many of the psalms begin with a superscription associating that particular psalm with a specific historical person, usually David. Unfortunately the superscriptions do not settle questions of authorship because the terminology used in them is ambiguous. The Hebrew phrase of the superscriptions can be translated in various ways, possibly meaning "of David," "to David," "belonging to David," or "by David." Thus the Hebrew superscriptions do not necessarily refer to authorship, and scholars often differ on the precise dating of certain psalms.

The superscription of Ps. 90 describes this psalm as "A prayer of Moses the man of God." Many scholars consider Ps. 90 to be a late composition that was associated with Moses long after his death. The psalm is placed here after Deuteronomy not to decide the questions of authorship, but rather to allow it to be read in the context of Moses, as intended by the superscription. By reading Ps. 90 shortly after other poetic speeches accredited to Moses (Deut. 32; 33; see 31:30; 32:44; 33:1), we can understand it as a final comment on Moses' life and a prayer for God's help in the coming struggles. See "The Book of Psalms" at Ps. 8.

■ Psalm 90

PSALM 90

The Eternity of God, and Man's Frailty

A Prayer of Moses the man of God.

L ord, You have been our dwelling place[a]
  in all generations.
2 Before the mountains were brought
   forth,
  Or ever You had formed the earth and
   the world,
  Even from everlasting to everlasting,
   You *are* God.

3 You turn man to destruction,
  And say, "Return, O children of men."
4 For a thousand years in Your sight
  Are like yesterday when it is past,
  And *like* a watch in the night.
5 You carry them away *like* a flood;
  They are like a sleep.
  In the morning they are like grass
   which grows up:
6 In the morning it flourishes and grows
   up;
  In the evening it is cut down and
   withers.

7 For we have been consumed by Your
   anger,
  And by Your wrath we are terrified.
8 You have set our iniquities before You,
  Our secret *sins* in the light of Your
   countenance.
9 For all our days have passed away in
   Your wrath;
  We finish our years like a sigh.
10 The days of our lives *are* seventy
   years;
  And if by reason of strength *they are*
   eighty years,
  Yet their boast *is* only labor and
   sorrow;
  For it is soon cut off, and we fly away.
11 Who knows the power of Your anger?
  For as the fear of You, *so is* Your
   wrath.
12 So teach *us* to number our days,
  That we may gain a heart of wisdom.

13 Return, O LORD!
  How long?
  And have compassion on Your
   servants.
14 Oh, satisfy us early with Your mercy,
  That we may rejoice and be glad all
   our days!

90:1 [a]Septuagint, Targum, and Vulgate read *refuge.*

15 Make us glad according to the days *in
   which* You have afflicted us,
   The years *in which* we have seen evil.
16 Let Your work appear to Your
   servants,
   And Your glory to their children.

17 And let the beauty of the LORD our
   God be upon us,
   And establish the work of our hands
   for us;
   Yes, establish the work of our hands.

The Conquest of Canaan

The conquest of Palestine was not
the unstoppable, crushing tide of
invaders that is sometimes
pictured.

Historians disagree as to when the Israelites left Egypt (see "The Exodus Begun" at Ex.
12:37). The same historians disagree as to when Israel arrived in Canaan. Some place the
invasion at the end of the 15th century; others at the end of the 13th. Archaeological support
has been claimed for both dates, such as evidence that Jericho was destroyed at this or that
era. But assigning specific dates to physical remains is difficult, and, ultimately, archaeology
has not solved the question.

What can be agreed on, from evidence both within and outside of the Bible, is that the
conquest of Palestine was not the unstoppable, crushing tide of invaders that is sometimes
pictured. Despite sweeping statements that Joshua conquered "the whole land" (e.g., Josh.
11:16, 23), there are also descriptions of the land that "remains . . . to be possessed" (e.g.,
Josh. 13:1–6). Some of the Israelite conquests appear to have been by peaceful assimilation
of the native peoples into the Israelites' own group, such as happened with the Gibeonites
(Josh. 9).

The danger of such assimilation is that the Israelites' faith would be mixed with the
religious beliefs and practices of Canaan. The Canaanites recognized many deities, two of the
more prominent ones being El, the great sky god, and his female consort Asherah. By the time
of the conquest, the worship of El had been overshadowed by worship of a warrior storm god,
Baal.

Canaanite worship practices included child sacrifice and fertility rites, often involving
relations with cult prostitutes. Images of the gods were common in worship, as were the
wooden poles or objects called "Asherim" after the goddess Asherah. Much of Israel's religious
history dealt with the conflict between worshipers of the one God of the Exodus and worshipers
of these Canaanite deities.

The Book of Joshua

Although the Book of Joshua tells of
Israel's conquest of Canaan, it is not a typical
war story: little space is given to accounts of
actual fighting. Indeed, almost half of the book
(chs. 13—21) details how the land would be
divided between Israel's twelve tribes. Clearly
the focus is God's fulfillment of His promise of
land instead of on feats of arms.

God's command that Israel destroy every
creature living in the land (Josh. 6:17, 21)
poses a difficult ethical issue. This command is
moderated somewhat in Josh. 8:2 but is still
understandably troubling to many readers. We ▼

should not minimize the ethical question, but
should understand that the reason given for
the command involves the abominable and idolatrous Canaanite lifestyle. God ordains this total destruction so that Israel would not adopt
the religious practices of the Canaanites (see
Deut. 20:16–18).

The book concludes on the same theme.
In a covenant renewal ceremony (chs. 23;
24), Joshua demands that Israel choose
whether they will follow God or the gods of
Canaan.

■ Joshua 1:1—5:15

Joshua
God's Commission to Joshua

1 :1 After the death of Moses the servant of the LORD, it came to pass that the LORD spoke to Joshua the son of Nun, Moses' assistant, saying: 2"Moses My servant is dead. Now therefore, arise, go over this Jordan, you and all this people, to the land which I am giving to them—the children of Israel. 3Every place that the sole of your foot will tread upon I have given you, as I said to Moses. 4From the wilderness and this Lebanon as far as the great river, the River Euphrates, all the land of the Hittites, and to the Great Sea toward the going down of the sun, shall be your territory. 5No man shall *be able to* stand before you all the days of your life; as I was with Moses, *so* I will be with you. I will not leave you nor forsake you. 6Be strong and of good courage, for to this people you shall divide as an inheritance the land which I swore to their fathers to give them. 7Only be strong and very courageous, that you may observe to do according to all the law which Moses My servant commanded you; do not turn from it to the right hand or to the left, that you may prosper wherever you go. 8This Book of the Law shall not depart from your mouth, but you shall meditate in it day and night, that you may observe to do according to all that is written in it. For then you will make your way prosperous, and then you will have good success. 9Have I not commanded you? Be strong and of good courage; do not be afraid, nor be dismayed, for the LORD your God *is* with you wherever you go."

The Order to Cross the Jordan

10Then Joshua commanded the officers of the people, saying, 11"Pass through the camp and command the people, saying, 'Prepare provisions for yourselves, for within three days you will cross over this Jordan, to go in to possess the land which the LORD your God is giving you to possess.' "

12And to the Reubenites, the Gadites, and half the tribe of Manasseh Joshua spoke, saying, 13"Remember the word which Moses the servant of the LORD commanded you, saying, 'The LORD your God is giving you rest and is giving you this land.' 14Your wives, your little ones, and your livestock shall remain in the land which Moses gave you on this side of the Jordan. But you shall pass before your brethren armed, all your mighty men of valor, and help them, 15until the LORD has given your brethren rest, as He *gave* you, and they also have taken possession of the land which the LORD your God is giving them. Then you shall return to the land of your possession and enjoy it, which Moses the LORD's servant gave you on this side of the Jordan toward the sunrise."

16So they answered Joshua, saying, "All that you command us we will do, and wherever you send us we will go. 17Just as we heeded Moses in all things, so we will heed you. Only the LORD your God be with you, as He was with Moses. 18Whoever rebels against your command and does not heed your words, in all that you command him, shall be put to death. Only be strong and of good courage."

Rahab Hides the Spies

2 1Now Joshua the son of Nun sent out two men from Acacia Grove[a] to spy secretly, saying, "Go, view the land, especially Jericho."

So they went, and came to the house of a harlot named Rahab, and lodged there. 2And it was told the king of Jericho, saying, "Behold, men have come here tonight from the children of Israel to search out the country."

3So the king of Jericho sent to Rahab, saying, "Bring out the men who have come to you, who have entered your house, for they have come to search out all the country."

4Then the woman took the two men and hid them. So she said, "Yes, the men came to me, but I did not know where they *were* from. 5And it happened as the gate was being shut, when it was dark, that the men went out. Where the men went I do not know; pursue them quickly, for you may overtake them." 6(But she had brought them up to the roof and hidden them with the stalks of flax, which she had laid in order on the roof.) 7Then the men pursued them by the road to the Jordan, to the fords. And as soon as those who pursued them had gone out, they shut the gate.

8Now before they lay down, she came up to them on the roof, 9and said to the men: "I know that the LORD has given you the land, that the terror of you has fallen

2:1 ᵃHebrew *Shittim*

on us, and that all the inhabitants of the land are fainthearted because of you. [10]For we have heard how the LORD dried up the water of the Red Sea for you when you came out of Egypt, and what you did to the two kings of the Amorites who *were* on the other side of the Jordan, Sihon and Og, whom you utterly destroyed. [11]And as soon as we heard *these things,* our hearts melted; neither did there remain any more courage in anyone because of you, for the LORD your God, He *is* God in heaven above and on earth beneath. [12]Now therefore, I beg you, swear to me by the LORD, since I have shown you kindness, that you also will show kindness to my father's house, and give me a true token, [13]and spare my father, my mother, my brothers, my sisters, and all that they have, and deliver our lives from death."

[14]So the men answered her, "Our lives for yours, if none of you tell this business of ours. And it shall be, when the LORD has given us the land, that we will deal kindly and truly with you."

[15]Then she let them down by a rope through the window, for her house *was* on the city wall; she dwelt on the wall. [16]And she said to them, "Get to the mountain, lest the pursuers meet you. Hide there three days, until the pursuers have returned. Afterward you may go your way."

[17]So the men said to her: "We *will be* blameless of this oath of yours which you have made us swear, [18]unless, *when* we come into the land, you bind this line of scarlet cord in the window through which you let us down, and unless you bring your father, your mother, your brothers, and all your father's household to your own home. [19]So it shall be *that* whoever goes outside the doors of your house into the street, his blood *shall be* on his own head, and we *will be* guiltless. And whoever is with you in the house, his blood *shall be* on our head if a hand is laid on him. [20]And if you tell this business of ours, then we will be free from your oath which you made us swear."

[21]Then she said, "According to your words, so *be* it." And she sent them away, and they departed. And she bound the scarlet cord in the window.

[22]They departed and went to the mountain, and stayed there three days until the pursuers returned. The pursuers sought *them* all along the way, but did not find *them.* [23]So the two men returned, descended from the mountain, and crossed over; and they came to Joshua the son of Nun, and told him all that had befallen them. [24]And they said to Joshua, "Truly the LORD has delivered all the land into our hands, for indeed all the inhabitants of the country are fainthearted because of us."

Israel Crosses the Jordan

3 [1]Then Joshua rose early in the morning; and they set out from Acacia Grove[a] and came to the Jordan, he and all the children of Israel, and lodged there before they crossed over. [2]So it was, after three days, that the officers went through the camp; [3]and they commanded the people, saying, "When you see the ark of the covenant of the LORD your God, and the priests, the Levites, bearing it, then you shall set out from your place and go after it. [4]Yet there shall be a space between you and it, about two thousand cubits by measure. Do not come near it, that you may know the way by which you must go, for you have not passed *this* way before."

[5]And Joshua said to the people, "Sanctify yourselves, for tomorrow the LORD will do wonders among you." [6]Then Joshua spoke to the priests, saying, "Take up the ark of the covenant and cross over before the people."

So they took up the ark of the covenant and went before the people.

[7]And the LORD said to Joshua, "This day I will begin to exalt you in the sight of all Israel, that they may know that, as I was with Moses, *so* I will be with you. [8]You shall command the priests who bear the ark of the covenant, saying, 'When you

3:1 [a]Hebrew *Shittim*

ARCHITECTURE AND BUILDING

Like medieval castles, some cities of Palestine were surrounded with high, elaborate walls. Rahab's house was part of the wall of Jericho and she had a window facing out (Josh. 2:15). It would have been high enough above ground level to keep anyone from climbing in.

have come to the edge of the water of the Jordan, you shall stand in the Jordan.' "

⁹So Joshua said to the children of Israel, "Come here, and hear the words of the LORD your God." ¹⁰And Joshua said, "By this you shall know that the living God *is* among you, and *that* He will without fail drive out from before you the Canaanites and the Hittites and the Hivites and the Perizzites and the Girgashites and the Amorites and the Jebusites: ¹¹Behold, the ark of the covenant of the Lord of all the earth is crossing over before you into the Jordan. ¹²Now therefore, take for yourselves twelve men from the tribes of Israel, one man from every tribe. ¹³And it shall come to pass, as soon as the soles of the feet of the priests who bear the ark of the LORD, the Lord of all the earth, shall rest in the waters of the Jordan, *that* the waters of the Jordan shall be cut off, the waters that come down from upstream, and they shall stand as a heap."

¹⁴So it was, when the people set out from their camp to cross over the Jordan, with the priests bearing the ark of the covenant before the people, ¹⁵and as those who bore the ark came to the Jordan, and the feet of the priests who bore the ark dipped in the edge of the water (for the Jordan overflows all its banks during the whole time of harvest), ¹⁶that the waters which came down from upstream stood *still, and* rose in a heap very far away at Adam, the city that *is* beside Zaretan. So the waters that went down into the Sea of the Arabah, the Salt Sea, failed, *and* were cut off; and the people crossed over opposite Jericho. ¹⁷Then the priests who bore the ark of the covenant of the LORD stood firm on dry ground in the midst of the Jordan; and all Israel crossed over on dry ground, until all the people had crossed completely over the Jordan.

The Memorial Stones

4 ¹And it came to pass, when all the people had completely crossed over the Jordan, that the LORD spoke to Joshua,

saying: ²"Take for yourselves twelve men from the people, one man from every tribe, ³and command them, saying, 'Take for yourselves twelve stones from here, out of the midst of the Jordan, from the place where the priests' feet stood firm. You shall carry them over with you and leave them in the lodging place where you lodge tonight.' "

⁴Then Joshua called the twelve men whom he had appointed from the children of Israel, one man from every tribe; ⁵and Joshua said to them: "Cross over before the ark of the LORD your God into the midst of the Jordan, and each one of you take up a stone on his shoulder, according to the number of the tribes of the children of Israel, ⁶that this may be a sign among you when your children ask in time to come, saying, 'What do these stones *mean* to you?' ⁷Then you shall answer them that the waters of the Jordan were cut off before the ark of the covenant of the LORD; when it crossed over the Jordan, the waters of the Jordan were cut off. And these stones shall be for a memorial to the children of Israel forever."

⁸And the children of Israel did so, just as Joshua commanded, and took up twelve stones from the midst of the Jordan, as the LORD had spoken to Joshua, according to the number of the tribes of the children of Israel, and carried them over with them to the place where they lodged, and laid them down there. ⁹Then Joshua set up twelve stones in the midst of the Jordan, in the place where the feet of the priests who bore the ark of the covenant stood; and they are there to this day.

¹⁰So the priests who bore the ark stood in the midst of the Jordan until everything was finished that the LORD had commanded Joshua to speak to the people, according to all that Moses had commanded Joshua; and the people hurried and crossed over. ¹¹Then it came to pass, when all the people had completely crossed over, that the ark of the LORD and the priests crossed over in the presence of the people. ¹²And

BELIEFS AND IDEAS

The ark of the covenant resembles in some ways furniture found in both ancient Egypt and Palestine. Probably the ark represented the footstool of God's throne. Although by design it was portable (Josh. 3:6), it was not a charm or talisman that could guarantee the favor of God for those who possessed it or took it into battle.

CIRCUMCISED WITH FLINT KNIVES (Josh. 5:3)

Long before humans learned how to write or even make cooking vessels from clay, they discovered that flint, a kind of stone, could be split into smaller sharp and, thus, more useable pieces. Often large stones, called cores, were struck with other stones, or sometimes short sticks were placed on the worker's chest and pressed onto the core. Eventually, small pieces were split off of the larger cores.

A variety of tools were created with this method. The most common creation were long narrow blades used for knives. Other tools created were scrapers used to remove the flesh from hides, drills for poking holes, and knives. One of the most unusual designs was special crafted blades that were fitted on a curved wooden base, used as a sickle.

After the smaller pieces were forced from the core, they were sharpened by striking the edges with other flints. Flints can be sharper than scalpels. Modern surgeons have been known to use them in surgery.

In Gilgal, the Israelites' first camp after crossing the Jordan, this age old tool, the flint knife, was used to perform the sacred ceremony of circumcision (Josh. 4:19; 5:2, 3). Such a tool was commonly available and would have been sharper than any other cutting tool.

the men of Reuben, the men of Gad, and half the tribe of Manasseh crossed over armed before the children of Israel, as Moses had spoken to them. ¹³About forty thousand prepared for war crossed over before the LORD for battle, to the plains of Jericho. ¹⁴On that day the LORD exalted Joshua in the sight of all Israel; and they feared him, as they had feared Moses, all the days of his life.

¹⁵Then the LORD spoke to Joshua, saying, ¹⁶"Command the priests who bear the ark of the Testimony to come up from the Jordan." ¹⁷Joshua therefore commanded the priests, saying, "Come up from the Jordan." ¹⁸And it came to pass, when the priests who bore the ark of the covenant of the LORD had come from the midst of the Jordan, and the soles of the priests' feet touched the dry land, that the waters of the Jordan returned to their place and overflowed all its banks as before.

¹⁹Now the people came up from the Jordan on the tenth day of the first month, and they camped in Gilgal on the east border of Jericho. ²⁰And those twelve stones which they took out of the Jordan, Joshua set up in Gilgal. ²¹Then he spoke to the children of Israel, saying: "When your children ask their fathers in time to come, saying, 'What are these stones?' ²²then you shall let your children know, saying, 'Israel crossed over this Jordan on dry land'; ²³for the LORD your God dried up the waters of the Jordan before you until you had crossed over, as the LORD your God did to

the Red Sea, which He dried up before us until we had crossed over, ²⁴that all the peoples of the earth may know the hand of the LORD, that it is mighty, that you may fear the LORD your God forever."

The Second Generation Circumcised

5 ¹So it was, when all the kings of the Amorites who were on the west side of the Jordan, and all the kings of the Canaanites who were by the sea, heard that the LORD had dried up the waters of the Jordan from before the children of Israel until weᵃ had crossed over, that their heart melted; and there was no spirit in them any longer because of the children of Israel.

²At that time the LORD said to Joshua, "Make flint knives for yourself, and circumcise the sons of Israel again the second time." ³So Joshua made flint knives for himself, and circumcised the sons of Israel at the hill of the foreskins.ᵃ ⁴And this is the reason why Joshua circumcised them: All the people who came out of Egypt who were males, all the men of war, had died in the wilderness on the way, after they had come out of Egypt. ⁵For all the people who came out had been circumcised, but all the people born in the wilderness, on the way as they came out of Egypt, had not been cir-

5:1 ᵃFollowing Kethib; Qere, some Hebrew manuscripts and editions, Septuagint, Syriac, Targum, and Vulgate read they.   5:3 ᵃHebrew Gibeath Haaraloth

WHEN THE HEAVENS GO TO WAR (Josh. 5:13–15)

Joshua met the Commander of God's army, who spoke for God whom He served (Josh. 5:13–15). Being aware that he had, in effect, met God in this divine servant, Joshua's reaction was to bow down and worship the heavenly being. The Commander's instructions for Joshua to remove his sandals reminds us of the same command to Moses at the burning bush (Ex. 3:5).

That heaven should have its own army would not have seemed strange in the ancient world. While there were specific gods and goddesses of warfare, entire armies of gods could be found in the mythology of the ancient Near East, serving the desires of their superior gods. Mesopotamian myths of the 2nd and 1st millenniums B.C. describe heavenly armies waging war against both divine and human enemies. In the Babylonian epic, Enuma Elish, the god Marduk conquers the army of the goddess Tiamat.

Human wars were fought under the direction of the deities of the land over which a king reigned. The ancients believed that wars were not just between human armies, but also between heavenly armies. The patron deities of the rival states had their own armies to back their people.

Joshua believed that he would not be fighting alone. Egyptian letters from the Amarna period (c. 1360–1333 B.C.) reflect the belief that the king of Egypt went to war as part of a divine army. In a similar fashion, Joshua, having been asked by God to take the Promised Land, met his heavenly counterpart. The notification "I have now come" (Josh. 5:14) informed Joshua that the human conquest of the land was only a part of the real action. Crucial events of the battle would take place in heaven.

---

cumcised. ⁶For the children of Israel walked forty years in the wilderness, till all the people *who were* men of war, who came out of Egypt, were consumed, because they did not obey the voice of the LORD—to whom the LORD swore that He would not show them the land which the LORD had sworn to their fathers that He would give us, "a land flowing with milk and honey."ᵃ ⁷Then Joshua circumcised their sons *whom* He raised up in their place; for they were uncircumcised, because they had not been circumcised on the way.

⁸So it was, when they had finished circumcising all the people, that they stayed in their places in the camp till they were healed. ⁹Then the LORD said to Joshua, "This day I have rolled away the reproach of Egypt from you." Therefore the name of the place is called Gilgalᵃ to this day.

¹⁰Now the children of Israel camped in Gilgal, and kept the Passover on the fourteenth day of the month at twilight on the plains of Jericho. ¹¹And they ate of the produce of the land on the day after the Passover, unleavened bread and parched grain, on the very same day. ¹²Then the manna ceased on the day after they had eaten the produce of the land; and the children of Israel no longer had manna, but they ate the food of the land of Canaan that year.

The Commander of the Army of the LORD

¹³And it came to pass, when Joshua was by Jericho, that he lifted his eyes and looked, and behold, a Man stood opposite him with His sword drawn in His hand.

5:6 ᵃExodus 3:8   5:9 ᵃLiterally *Rolling*

BELIEFS AND IDEAS

The symbolism of removing the shoes in a holy place (Josh. 5:15) is followed today in Islamic mosques, where shoes may not be worn. In the 19th century A.D. it was required to be barefoot before the Emperor of Ethiopia. Perhaps shoes seem to represent the uncleanness of the workaday world.

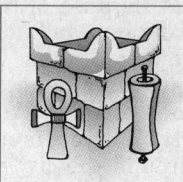

And Joshua went to Him and said to Him, "*Are* You for us or for our adversaries?"

[14]So He said, "No, but *as* Commander of the army of the LORD I have now come."

And Joshua fell on his face to the earth and worshiped, and said to Him, "What does my Lord say to His servant?"

[15]Then the Commander of the LORD's army said to Joshua, "Take your sandal off your foot, for the place where you stand *is* holy." And Joshua did so.

Conquering the Canaanite Cities

The detailed accounts in chs. 1—5 of the preparation, the Jordan crossing, and the camp at Gilgal show Israel mobilized to enter the land. The crossing of the Jordan and the Passover celebration are dated in the 1st month (Josh. 4:19; 5:10), suggesting that Joshua readied the people in less than two months after Moses' death. The conquest would have begun, then, around either 1405 B.C. or 1234 B.C. (see "The Death of Moses" at Deut. 34:1).

The conquest itself is described in three campaigns or stages: the thrust into central Canaan (Josh. 6:1—8:35), the southern campaign (9:1—10:43), and the northern campaign (11:1-15). The first stage relates the destruction of Jericho and Ai. Stages two and three present the long and complex military campaigns against coalitions of Canaanite cities.

The reader could easily assume that the whole operation took only a short time, whereas the process actually lasted several years. And even then the conquest was not complete (13:1). The campaigns are reported briefly in order to emphasize God's giving, rather than Israel's taking, the land. See "The Early Years of Conquest" at Josh. 14:6.

■ Joshua 6:1—14:5

Joshua
The Destruction of Jericho

6 :1 Now Jericho was securely shut up because of the children of Israel; none went out, and none came in. [2]And the LORD said to Joshua: "See! I have given Jericho into your hand, its king, *and* the mighty men of valor. [3]You shall march around the city, all *you* men of war; you shall go all around the city once. This you shall do six days. [4]And seven priests shall bear seven trumpets of rams' horns before the ark. But the seventh day you shall march around the city seven times, and the priests shall blow the trumpets. [5]It shall come to pass, when they make a long *blast* with the ram's horn, *and* when you hear the sound of the trumpet, that all the people shall shout with a great shout; then the wall of the city will fall down flat. And the people shall go up every man straight before him."

[6]Then Joshua the son of Nun called the priests and said to them, "Take up the ark of the covenant, and let seven priests bear seven trumpets of rams' horns before the ark of the LORD." [7]And he said to the people, "Proceed, and march around the city, and let him who is armed advance before the ark of the LORD."

[8]So it was, when Joshua had spoken to the people, that the seven priests bearing the seven trumpets of rams' horns before the LORD advanced and blew the trumpets, and the ark of the covenant of the LORD followed them. [9]The armed men went before the priests who blew the trumpets, and the rear guard came after the ark, while *the priests* continued blowing the trumpets. [10]Now Joshua had commanded the people, saying, "You shall not shout or make any noise with your voice, nor shall a word proceed out of your mouth, until the day I say to you, 'Shout!' Then you shall shout." [11]So he had the ark of the LORD circle the city, going around *it* once. Then they came into the camp and lodged in the camp.

[12]And Joshua rose early in the morning, and the priests took up the ark of the LORD. [13]Then seven priests bearing seven trumpets of rams' horns before the ark of the LORD went on continually and blew with the trumpets. And the armed men went before them. But the rear guard came after the ark of the LORD, while *the priests* continued blowing the trumpets. [14]And the second day they marched around the city once and returned to the camp. So they did six days.

[15]But it came to pass on the seventh day that they rose early, about the dawning of the day, and marched around the city seven times in the same manner. On that day only they marched around the city seven times. [16]And the seventh time it happened, when the priests blew the trumpets, that Joshua said to the people: "Shout, for the LORD has given you the city! [17]Now the city shall be doomed by the LORD to destruction, it and all who *are* in it. Only Ra-

hab the harlot shall live, she and all who *are* with her in the house, because she hid the messengers that we sent. ¹⁸And you, by all means abstain from the accursed things, lest you become accursed when you take of the accursed things, and make the camp of Israel a curse, and trouble it. ¹⁹But all the silver and gold, and vessels of bronze and iron, *are* consecrated to the Lord; they shall come into the treasury of the Lord."

²⁰So the people shouted when *the priests* blew the trumpets. And it happened when the people heard the sound of the trumpet, and the people shouted with a great shout, that the wall fell down flat. Then the people went up into the city, every man straight before him, and they took the city. ²¹And they utterly destroyed all that *was* in the city, both man and woman, young and old, ox and sheep and donkey, with the edge of the sword.

²²But Joshua had said to the two men who had spied out the country, "Go into the harlot's house, and from there bring out the woman and all that she has, as you swore to her." ²³And the young men who had been spies went in and brought out Rahab, her father, her mother, her brothers, and all that she had. So they brought out all her relatives and left them outside the camp of Israel. ²⁴But they burned the city and all that *was* in it with fire. Only the silver and gold, and the vessels of bronze and iron, they put into the treasury of the house of the Lord. ²⁵And Joshua spared Rahab the harlot, her father's household, and all that she had. So she dwells in Israel to this day, because she hid the messengers whom Joshua sent to spy out Jericho.

²⁶Then Joshua charged *them* at that time, saying, "Cursed *be* the man before the Lord who rises up and builds this city Jericho; he shall lay its foundation with his firstborn, and with his youngest he shall set up its gates."

7:1 ªCalled *Zimri* in 1 Chronicles 2:6

²⁷So the Lord was with Joshua, and his fame spread throughout all the country.

Defeat at Ai

7 ¹But the children of Israel committed a trespass regarding the accursed things, for Achan the son of Carmi, the son of Zabdi,ª the son of Zerah, of the tribe of Judah, took of the accursed things; so the anger of the Lord burned against the children of Israel.

²Now Joshua sent men from Jericho to Ai, which *is* beside Beth Aven, on the east side of Bethel, and spoke to them, saying, "Go up and spy out the country." So the men went up and spied out Ai. ³And they returned to Joshua and said to him, "Do not let all the people go up, but let about two or three thousand men go up and attack Ai. Do not weary all the people there, for *the people of Ai are* few." ⁴So about three thousand men went up there from the people, but they fled before the men of Ai. ⁵And the men of Ai struck down about thirty-six men, for they chased them *from* before the gate as far as Shebarim, and struck them down on the descent; therefore the hearts of the people melted and became like water.

⁶Then Joshua tore his clothes, and fell to the earth on his face before the ark of the Lord until evening, he and the elders of Israel; and they put dust on their heads. ⁷And Joshua said, "Alas, Lord God, why have You brought this people over the Jordan at all—to deliver us into the hand of the Amorites, to destroy us? Oh, that we had been content, and dwelt on the other side of the Jordan! ⁸O Lord, what shall I say when Israel turns its back before its enemies? ⁹For the Canaanites and all the inhabitants of the land will hear *it,* and surround us, and cut off our name from the earth. Then what will You do for Your great name?"

The Sin of Achan

¹⁰So the Lord said to Joshua: "Get up! Why do you lie thus on your face? ¹¹Israel

---

Beliefs and Ideas

Lev. 27:28, 29 explains that what is "accursed" (Josh. 6:18) has passed out of human hands and into the jurisdiction of God. This "cursing" or "devotion" to God, expressed by the Hebrew word herem, *is not a practice that can be applied outside the specific references of the Old Testament. It is little known outside these biblical passages.*

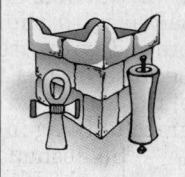

ACCURSED AND UNDER THE BAN (Josh. 7:1)

All of the inhabitants of Jericho, humans and animals, were killed as a sacrifice to God. They were "doomed by the LORD to destruction" (Josh. 6:17). In addition, all of Jericho's property was placed off limits to the Israelites and destroyed, except for items of iron, bronze, silver and gold, which went into the sacred treasury (6:18, 19). All of these things—people, property, valuables—were considered "accursed." The Hebrew word translated "accursed" referred to things that were completely destroyed or set apart for sacred use.

Accursed things were given to God. Of course, the items were not given to God physically, but rather by being totally destroyed or dedicated to sacred use. They were kept from the Israelites. They were for them "accursed" items. By not taking these items for themselves, the Israelites were acknowledging that such things belonged to God. God was the real conqueror of the city. Jericho was a kind of "tithe," the first city conquered in the Promised Land. Its possessions, therefore, belonged to God.

Achan's sin (Josh. 7:1) was that he took a garment from Jericho, even though he knew that everything in Jericho had been dedicated to God. He thus stole from God. By taking an "accursed" item, he himself became cursed.

This same Hebrew word for "accursed" is translated "the curse" in Is. 43:28. Israel (Jacob) would be given "to the curse." The Israelites had sinned against God, and would now themselves be dedicated to Him through their coming destruction.

---

has sinned, and they have also transgressed My covenant which I commanded them. For they have even taken some of the accursed things, and have both stolen and deceived; and they have also put *it* among their own stuff. ¹²Therefore the children of Israel could not stand before their enemies, *but* turned *their* backs before their enemies, because they have become doomed to destruction. Neither will I be with you anymore, unless you destroy the accursed from among you. ¹³Get up, sanctify the people, and say, 'Sanctify yourselves for tomorrow, because thus says the LORD God of Israel: "*There is* an accursed thing in your midst, O Israel; you cannot stand before your enemies until you take away the accursed thing from among you." ¹⁴In the morning therefore you shall be brought according to your tribes. And it shall be *that* the tribe which the LORD takes shall come according to families; and the family which the LORD takes shall come by households; and the household which the LORD takes shall come man by man. ¹⁵Then it shall be *that* he who is taken with the accursed thing shall be burned with fire, he and all that he has, because he has transgressed the covenant of the LORD, and because he has done a disgraceful thing in Israel.' "

¹⁶So Joshua rose early in the morning and brought Israel by their tribes, and the tribe of Judah was taken. ¹⁷He brought the clan of Judah, and he took the family of the Zarhites; and he brought the family of the Zarhites man by man, and Zabdi was taken. ¹⁸Then he brought his household man by man, and Achan the son of Carmi, the son of Zabdi, the son of Zerah, of the tribe of Judah, was taken.

¹⁹Now Joshua said to Achan, "My son, I beg you, give glory to the LORD God of Israel, and make confession to Him, and tell me now what you have done; do not hide *it* from me."

²⁰And Achan answered Joshua and said, "Indeed I have sinned against the LORD God of Israel, and this is what I have done: ²¹When I saw among the spoils a beautiful Babylonian garment, two hundred shekels of silver, and a wedge of gold weighing fifty shekels, I coveted them and took them. And there they are, hidden in the earth in the midst of my tent, with the silver under it."

²²So Joshua sent messengers, and they ran to the tent; and there it was, hidden in his tent, with the silver under it. ²³And they took them from the midst of the tent, brought them to Joshua and to all the children of Israel, and laid them out before the LORD. ²⁴Then Joshua, and all Israel with him, took Achan the son of Zerah, the silver, the garment, the wedge of gold, his sons, his daughters, his oxen, his donkeys,

his sheep, his tent, and all that he had, and they brought them to the Valley of Achor. 25And Joshua said, "Why have you troubled us? The LORD will trouble you this day." So all Israel stoned him with stones; and they burned them with fire after they had stoned them with stones.

26Then they raised over him a great heap of stones, still there to this day. So the LORD turned from the fierceness of His anger. Therefore the name of that place has been called the Valley of Achor^a to this day.

The Fall of Ai

8 1Now the LORD said to Joshua: "Do not be afraid, nor be dismayed; take all the people of war with you, and arise, go up to Ai. See, I have given into your hand the king of Ai, his people, his city, and his land. 2And you shall do to Ai and its king as you did to Jericho and its king. Only its spoil and its cattle you shall take as booty for yourselves. Lay an ambush for the city behind it."

3So Joshua arose, and all the people of war, to go up against Ai; and Joshua chose

7:26 ^aLiterally *Trouble*

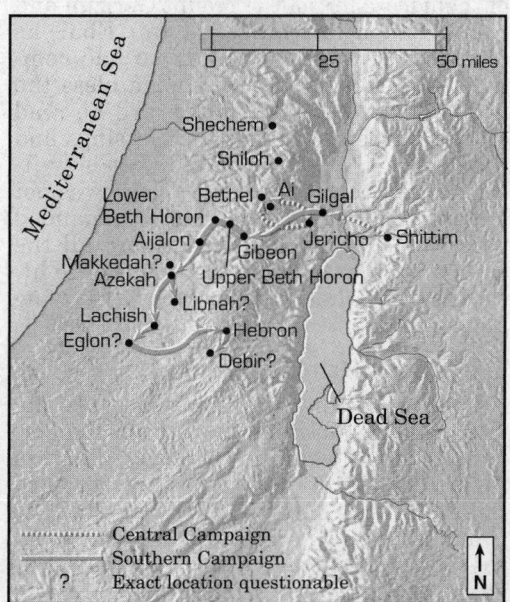

**The Conquest of Canaan
(Central and Southern Campaigns)**

From the camp at Gilgal, Joshua launched two campaigns. Jericho fell in the central campaign, which continued with an ambush of Bethel and Ai. Joshua launched the southern campaign against the Amorites assembled near Gibeon, and continued the assault all the way to Debir.

thirty thousand mighty men of valor and sent them away by night. 4And he commanded them, saying: "Behold, you shall lie in ambush against the city, behind the city. Do not go very far from the city, but all of you be ready. 5Then I and all the people who *are* with me will approach the city; and it will come about, when they come out against us as at the first, that we shall flee before them. 6For they will come out after us till we have drawn them from the city, for they will say, '*They are* fleeing before us as at the first.' Therefore we will flee before them. 7Then you shall rise from the ambush and seize the city, for the LORD your God will deliver it into your hand. 8And it will be, when you have taken the city, *that* you shall set the city on fire. According to the commandment of the LORD you shall do. See, I have commanded you."

9Joshua therefore sent them out; and they went to lie in ambush, and stayed between Bethel and Ai, on the west side of Ai; but Joshua lodged that night among the people. 10Then Joshua rose up early in the morning and mustered the people, and went up, he and the elders of Israel, before the people to Ai. 11And all the people of war who *were* with him went up and drew near; and they came before the city and camped on the north side of Ai. Now a valley *lay* between them and Ai. 12So he took about five thousand men and set them in ambush between Bethel and Ai, on the west side of the city. 13And when they had set the people, all the army that *was* on the north of the city, and its rear guard on the west of the city, Joshua went that night into the midst of the valley.

14Now it happened, when the king of Ai saw *it,* that the men of the city hurried and rose early and went out against Israel to battle, he and all his people, at an appointed place before the plain. But he did not know that *there was* an ambush against him behind the city. 15And Joshua and all Israel made as if they were beaten before them, and fled by the way of the wilderness. 16So all the people who *were* in Ai were called together to pursue them. And they pursued Joshua and were drawn away from the city. 17There was not a man left in Ai or Bethel who did not go out after Israel. So they left the city open and pursued Israel.

18Then the LORD said to Joshua, "Stretch out the spear that *is* in your hand toward Ai, for I will give it into your hand."

And Joshua stretched out the spear that *was* in his hand toward the city. ¹⁹So *those in* ambush arose quickly out of their place; they ran as soon as he had stretched out his hand, and they entered the city and took it, and hurried to set the city on fire. ²⁰And when the men of Ai looked behind them, they saw, and behold, the smoke of the city ascended to heaven. So they had no power to flee this way or that way, and the people who had fled to the wilderness turned back on the pursuers.

²¹Now when Joshua and all Israel saw that the ambush had taken the city and that the smoke of the city ascended, they turned back and struck down the men of Ai. ²²Then the others came out of the city against them; so they were *caught* in the midst of Israel, some on this side and some on that side. And they struck them down, so that they let none of them remain or escape. ²³But the king of Ai they took alive, and brought him to Joshua.

²⁴And it came to pass when Israel had made an end of slaying all the inhabitants of Ai in the field, in the wilderness where they pursued them, and when they all had fallen by the edge of the sword until they were consumed, that all the Israelites returned to Ai and struck it with the edge of the sword. ²⁵So it was *that* all who fell that day, both men and women, *were* twelve thousand—all the people of Ai. ²⁶For Joshua did not draw back his hand, with which he stretched out the spear, until he had utterly destroyed all the inhabitants of Ai. ²⁷Only the livestock and the spoil of that city Israel took as booty for themselves, according to the word of the LORD which He had commanded Joshua. ²⁸So

Joshua burned Ai and made it a heap forever, a desolation to this day. ²⁹And the king of Ai he hanged on a tree until evening. And as soon as the sun was down, Joshua commanded that they should take his corpse down from the tree, cast it at the entrance of the gate of the city, and raise over it a great heap of stones *that remains* to this day.

Joshua Renews the Covenant

³⁰Now Joshua built an altar to the LORD God of Israel in Mount Ebal, ³¹as Moses the servant of the LORD had commanded the children of Israel, as it is written in the Book of the Law of Moses: "an altar of whole stones over which no man has wielded an iron *tool.*"ª And they offered on it burnt offerings to the LORD, and sacrificed peace offerings. ³²And there, in the presence of the children of Israel, he wrote on the stones a copy of the law of Moses, which he had written. ³³Then all Israel, with their elders and officers and judges, stood on either side of the ark before the priests, the Levites, who bore the ark of the covenant of the LORD, the stranger as well as he who was born among them. Half of them *were* in front of Mount Gerizim and half of them in front of Mount Ebal, as Moses the servant of the LORD had commanded before, that they should bless the people of Israel. ³⁴And afterward he read all the words of the law, the blessings and the cursings, according to all that is written in the Book of the Law. ³⁵There was not a word of all that Moses had commanded which Joshua did not read before all the assembly of Israel, with the women, the little ones, and the strangers who were living among them.

The Treaty with the Gibeonites

9 ¹And it came to pass when all the kings who *were* on this side of the Jordan, in the hills and in the lowland and in all the coasts of the Great Sea toward Lebanon—the Hittite, the Amorite, the Canaanite, the Perizzite, the Hivite, and the Jebusite—heard *about it,* ²that they gathered together to fight with Joshua and Israel with one accord.

³But when the inhabitants of Gibeon heard what Joshua had done to Jericho and Ai, ⁴they worked craftily, and went and pretended to be ambassadors. And they

---

TIME CAPSULE   *1243 to 1234 B.C.*

1243–1207	*Tukulti-Ninurta I, king of Assyria*
1240	*Hittite Empire declines and vanishes by 1180 B.C.*
1235	*Israelites reach the plains of Moab (based on late Exodus; Num. 22:1)*
1235	*Aaron dies on Mount Hor (late Exodus; Num. 33:38)*
1235	*Moses is buried in Moab (late Exodus; Deut. 34:5, 6)*
1234	*Joshua leads Israelite conquest of Canaan (based on late Exodus)*

8:31 ªDeuteronomy 27:5, 6

GILGAL, PLACE OF COVENANT (Josh. 9:6)

Gilgal is a special holy place in the biblical stories. It was there that the newly arrived Israelites were circumcised. This act reestablished them as God's chosen people (Josh. 4:19; 5:7) and was supposed to prepare them spiritually for their conquest of Canaan. Gilgal was also where they celebrated their first Passover in the Promised Land (5:10). The "camp at Gilgal" (9:6) served as the Israelites' base of operations during their early military activities (Josh. 10:6, 7, 15, 43).

It is not surprising that Gilgal became a cultic center. At a later time both Samuel and Saul name Gilgal as a place where one went to offer sacrifices (1 Sam. 10:8; 15:21). Understandably, Saul used Gilgal as a place to intensify nationalistic feelings and loyalty (1 Sam. 11:14, 15). It was there that Saul was made king of Israel.

took old sacks on their donkeys, old wineskins torn and mended, ⁵old and patched sandals on their feet, and old garments on themselves; and all the bread of their provision was dry *and* moldy. ⁶And they went to Joshua, to the camp at Gilgal, and said to him and to the men of Israel, "We have come from a far country; now therefore, make a covenant with us."

⁷Then the men of Israel said to the Hivites, "Perhaps you dwell among us; so how can we make a covenant with you?"

⁸But they said to Joshua, "We *are* your servants."

And Joshua said to them, "Who *are* you, and where do you come from?"

⁹So they said to him: "From a very far country your servants have come, because of the name of the LORD your God; for we have heard of His fame, and all that He did in Egypt, ¹⁰and all that He did to the two kings of the Amorites who *were* beyond the Jordan—to Sihon king of Heshbon, and Og king of Bashan, who was at Ashtaroth. ¹¹Therefore our elders and all the inhabitants of our country spoke to us, saying, 'Take provisions with you for the journey, and go to meet them, and say to them, "We *are* your servants; now therefore, make a covenant with us." ' ¹²This bread of ours we took hot *for* our provision from our houses on the day we departed to come to you. But now look, it is dry and moldy. ¹³And these wineskins which we filled *were* new, and see, they are torn; and these our garments and our sandals have become old because of the very long journey."

¹⁴Then the men of Israel took some of their provisions; but they did not ask counsel of the LORD. ¹⁵So Joshua made peace with them, and made a covenant with

them to let them live; and the rulers of the congregation swore to them.

¹⁶And it happened at the end of three days, after they had made a covenant with them, that they heard that they *were* their neighbors who dwelt near them. ¹⁷Then the children of Israel journeyed and came to their cities on the third day. Now their cities *were* Gibeon, Chephirah, Beeroth, and Kirjath Jearim. ¹⁸But the children of Israel did not attack them, because the rulers of the congregation had sworn to them by the LORD God of Israel. And all the congregation complained against the rulers.

¹⁹Then all the rulers said to all the congregation, "We have sworn to them by the LORD God of Israel; now therefore, we may not touch them. ²⁰This we will do to them: We will let them live, lest wrath be upon us because of the oath which we swore to them." ²¹And the rulers said to them, "Let them live, but let them be woodcutters and water carriers for all the congregation, as the rulers had promised them."

²²Then Joshua called for them, and he spoke to them, saying, "Why have you deceived us, saying, 'We *are* very far from you,' when you dwell near us? ²³Now therefore, you *are* cursed, and none of you shall be freed from being slaves—woodcutters and water carriers for the house of my God."

²⁴So they answered Joshua and said, "Because your servants were clearly told that the LORD your God commanded His servant Moses to give you all the land, and to destroy all the inhabitants of the land from before you; therefore we were very much afraid for our lives because of you,

and have done this thing. ²⁵And now, here we are, in your hands; do with us as it seems good and right to do to us." ²⁶So he did to them, and delivered them out of the hand of the children of Israel, so that they did not kill them. ²⁷And that day Joshua made them woodcutters and water carriers for the congregation and for the altar of the LORD, in the place which He would choose, even to this day.

The Sun Stands Still

10 ¹Now it came to pass when Adoni-Zedek king of Jerusalem heard how Joshua had taken Ai and had utterly destroyed it—as he had done to Jericho and its king, so he had done to Ai and its king—and how the inhabitants of Gibeon had made peace with Israel and were among them, ²that they feared greatly, because Gibeon *was* a great city, like one of the royal cities, and because it *was* greater than Ai, and all its men *were* mighty. ³Therefore Adoni-Zedek king of Jerusalem sent to Hoham king of Hebron, Piram king of Jarmuth, Japhia king of Lachish, and Debir king of Eglon, saying, ⁴"Come up to me and help me, that we may attack Gibeon, for it has made peace with Joshua and with the children of Israel." ⁵Therefore the five kings of the Amorites, the king of Jerusalem, the king of Hebron, the king of Jarmuth, the king of Lachish, *and* the king of Eglon, gathered together and went up, they and all their armies, and camped before Gibeon and made war against it.

⁶And the men of Gibeon sent to Joshua at the camp at Gilgal, saying, "Do not forsake your servants; come up to us quickly, save us and help us, for all the kings of the Amorites who dwell in the mountains have gathered together against us."

⁷So Joshua ascended from Gilgal, he and all the people of war with him, and all the mighty men of valor. ⁸And the LORD said to Joshua, "Do not fear them, for I have delivered them into your hand; not a man of them shall stand before you." ⁹Joshua therefore came upon them sud-

denly, having marched all night from Gilgal. ¹⁰So the LORD routed them before Israel, killed them with a great slaughter at Gibeon, chased them along the road that goes to Beth Horon, and struck them down as far as Azekah and Makkedah. ¹¹And it happened, as they fled before Israel *and* were on the descent of Beth Horon, that the LORD cast down large hailstones from heaven on them as far as Azekah, and they died. *There were* more who died from the hailstones than the children of Israel killed with the sword.

¹²Then Joshua spoke to the LORD in the day when the LORD delivered up the Amorites before the children of Israel, and he said in the sight of Israel:

"Sun, stand still over Gibeon;
And Moon, in the Valley of Aijalon."
¹³   So the sun stood still,
And the moon stopped,
Till the people had revenge
Upon their enemies.

Is this not written in the Book of Jasher? So the sun stood still in the midst of heaven, and did not hasten to go *down* for about a whole day. ¹⁴And there has been no day like that, before it or after it, that the LORD heeded the voice of a man; for the LORD fought for Israel.

¹⁵Then Joshua returned, and all Israel with him, to the camp at Gilgal.

The Amorite Kings Executed

¹⁶But these five kings had fled and hidden themselves in a cave at Makkedah. ¹⁷And it was told Joshua, saying, "The five kings have been found hidden in the cave at Makkedah."

¹⁸So Joshua said, "Roll large stones against the mouth of the cave, and set men by it to guard them. ¹⁹And do not stay *there* yourselves, *but* pursue your enemies, and attack their rear *guard*. Do not allow them to enter their cities, for the LORD your God has delivered them into your hand." ²⁰Then it happened, while Joshua and the children

CULTURE AND SOCIETY

Hanging was not a way of putting someone to death, but a way of exposing the bodies of those executed (Josh. 10:26). The Law of Moses did not permit exposure past nightfall, but in many societies up to medieval times corpses were left exposed for days or weeks. The Romans exposed thousands of crucified Jews outside the walls of Jerusalem in A.D. 70.

WHEN GOD LISTENED TO A MAN (Josh. 10:12, 13)

Joshua's prayer, "Sun, stand still over Gibeon; And Moon, in the Valley of Aijalon" (Josh. 10:12), seems to request that somehow God stop the sun or perform some other miraculous heavenly event to lengthen the day. Joshua did not pray late in the evening: the sun "over Gibeon" would be in the east, while the moon "in the Valley of Aijalon" would be in the west. This positioning of the sun and moon indicates early morning, and for Joshua to utter a request for a longer day at that time of day seems unusual.

Joshua's asking the sun and moon to "stand still" (10:12) is a request typical of celestial omen texts from Mesopotamia. These texts are concerned with the 1st day of the full moon which came at the middle of the month and was observable by the location of the sun and moon in the early morning on opposite horizons. In Mesopotamian omen texts the sun and moon are asked to "wait" on each other, so that they would be on their respective horizons on the 14th day of the month.

When this positioning occurred, it was seen by the Mesopotamians as a sign of good fortune. For them it indicated that their calculations were accurate, that there would be exactly 30 days in the month, and that the days themselves would be full-length. On the other hand, when the sun and moon were on their respective horizons on any other day, it was considered a bad omen.

The position of the sun in the east (Gibeon) and moon in the west (Valley of Aijalon) suggests that this event occurred near the middle of the month. Joshua may be asking God to allow the sun and moon to "stand still" (10:12) or wait for each other so that they would be on their horizons on a day other than the 14th day of the month. That would cause the Canaanites to believe that that day was an evil day for fighting and give the Israelites the upper hand before the battle began. What made this occasion memorable is that "the LORD heeded the voice of a man" (10:14). God listened to Joshua, and the sun and moon were positioned for Israel's advantage—"the LORD fought for Israel."

---

of Israel made an end of slaying them with a very great slaughter, till they had finished, that those who escaped entered fortified cities. [21]And all the people returned to the camp, to Joshua at Makkedah, in peace.

No one moved his tongue against any of the children of Israel.

[22]Then Joshua said, "Open the mouth of the cave, and bring out those five kings to me from the cave." [23]And they did so, and brought out those five kings to him from the cave: the king of Jerusalem, the king of Hebron, the king of Jarmuth, the king of Lachish, *and* the king of Eglon. [24]So it was, when they brought out those kings to Joshua, that Joshua called for all the men of Israel, and said to the captains of the men of war who went with him, "Come near, put your feet on the necks of these kings." And they drew near and put their feet on their necks. [25]Then Joshua said to them, "Do not be afraid, nor be dismayed; be strong and of good courage, for thus the LORD will do to all your enemies against whom you fight." [26]And afterward Joshua struck them and killed them, and hanged them on five trees; and they were hanging on the trees until evening. [27]So it was at the time of the going down of the sun *that* Joshua commanded, and they took them down from the trees, cast them into the cave where they had been hidden, and laid large stones against the cave's mouth, *which remain* until this very day.

Conquest of the Southland

[28]On that day Joshua took Makkedah, and struck it and its king with the edge of the sword. He utterly destroyed them[a]—all the people who *were* in it. He let none remain. He also did to the king of Makkedah as he had done to the king of Jericho.

[29]Then Joshua passed from Makkedah, and all Israel with him, to Libnah; and they fought against Libnah. [30]And the

10:28 [a]Following Masoretic Text and most authorities; many Hebrew manuscripts, some manuscripts of the Septuagint, and some manuscripts of the Targum read *it.*

LORD also delivered it and its king into the hand of Israel; he struck it and all the people who *were* in it with the edge of the sword. He let none remain in it, but did to its king as he had done to the king of Jericho.

³¹Then Joshua passed from Libnah, and all Israel with him, to Lachish; and they encamped against it and fought against it. ³²And the LORD delivered Lachish into the hand of Israel, who took it on the second day, and struck it and all the people who *were* in it with the edge of the sword, according to all that he had done to Libnah. ³³Then Horam king of Gezer came up to help Lachish; and Joshua struck him and his people, until he left him none remaining.

³⁴From Lachish Joshua passed to Eglon, and all Israel with him; and they encamped against it and fought against it. ³⁵They took it on that day and struck it with the edge of the sword; all the people who *were* in it he utterly destroyed that day, according to all that he had done to Lachish.

³⁶So Joshua went up from Eglon, and all Israel with him, to Hebron; and they fought against it. ³⁷And they took it and struck it with the edge of the sword—its king, all its cities, and all the people who *were* in it; he left none remaining, according to all that he had done to Eglon, but utterly destroyed it and all the people who *were* in it.

³⁸Then Joshua returned, and all Israel with him, to Debir; and they fought against it. ³⁹And he took it and its king and all its cities; they struck them with the edge of the sword and utterly destroyed all the people who *were* in it. He left none remaining; as he had done to Hebron, so he did to Debir and its king, as he had done also to Libnah and its king.

⁴⁰So Joshua conquered all the land: the mountain country and the Southᵃ and the lowland and the wilderness slopes, and all their kings; he left none remaining, but utterly destroyed all that breathed, as the LORD God of Israel had commanded. ⁴¹And Joshua conquered them from Kadesh Barnea as far as Gaza, and all the country of Goshen, even as far as Gibeon. ⁴²All these kings and their land Joshua took at one time, because the LORD God of Israel fought for Israel. ⁴³Then Joshua returned, and all Israel with him, to the camp at Gilgal.

The Northern Conquest

11 ¹And it came to pass, when Jabin king of Hazor heard *these things,* that he sent to Jobab king of Madon, to the king of Shimron, to the king of Achshaph, ²and to the kings who *were* from the north, in the mountains, in the plain south of Chinneroth, in the lowland, and in the heights of Dor on the west, ³to the Canaanites in the east and in the west, the Amorite, the Hittite, the Perizzite, the Jebusite in the mountains, and the Hivite below Hermon in the land of Mizpah. ⁴So they went out, they and all their armies with them, *as* many people *as* the sand that *is* on the seashore in multitude, with very many horses and chariots. ⁵And when all these kings had met together, they came and camped together at the waters of Merom to fight against Israel.

⁶But the LORD said to Joshua, "Do not be afraid because of them, for tomorrow about this time I will deliver all of them slain before Israel. You shall hamstring their horses and burn their chariots with fire." ⁷So Joshua and all the people of war with him came against them suddenly by the waters of Merom, and they attacked them. ⁸And the LORD delivered them into the hand of Israel, who defeated them and chased them to Greater Sidon, to the Brook Misrephoth,ᵃ and to the Valley of Mizpah eastward; they attacked them until they left none of them remaining. ⁹So Joshua did to them as the LORD had told him: he

---

10:40 ᵃHebrew *Negev,* and so throughout this book   11:8 ᵃHebrew *Misrephoth Maim*

PLANTS AND ANIMALS

Before about 950 B.C. horses were not used for cavalry in battle, but for pulling chariots. To hamstring a horse is to cripple it by cutting the large tendon in the back of its leg (Josh. 11:6). The destroyed equipment of an enemy is an eloquent sign of their defeat, since they no longer control their means of fighting.

hamstrung their horses and burned their chariots with fire.

¹⁰Joshua turned back at that time and took Hazor, and struck its king with the sword; for Hazor was formerly the head of all those kingdoms. ¹¹And they struck all the people who *were* in it with the edge of the sword, utterly destroying *them*. There was none left breathing. Then he burned Hazor with fire.

¹²So all the cities of those kings, and all their kings, Joshua took and struck with the edge of the sword. He utterly destroyed them, as Moses the servant of the LORD had commanded. ¹³But *as for* the cities that stood on their mounds,ᵃ Israel burned none of them, except Hazor only, *which* Joshua burned. ¹⁴And all the spoil of these cities and the livestock, the children of Israel took as booty for themselves; but they struck every man with the edge of the sword until they had destroyed them, and they left none breathing. ¹⁵As the LORD had commanded Moses his servant, so Moses commanded Joshua, and so Joshua did. He left nothing undone of all that the LORD had commanded Moses.

Summary of Joshua's Conquests

¹⁶Thus Joshua took all this land: the mountain country, all the South, all the

---

11:13 ᵃHebrew *tel*, a heap of successive city ruins   11:16 ᵃHebrew *arabah*

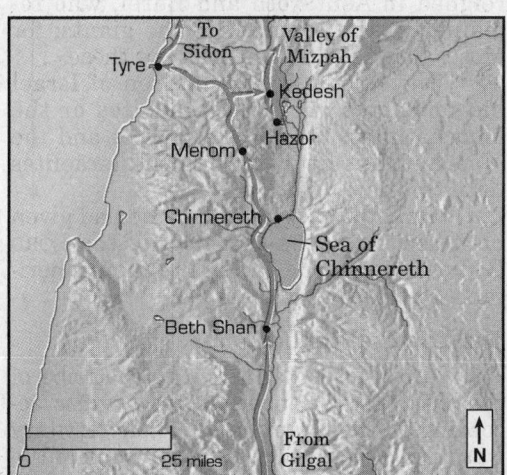

The Conquest of Canaan
(Northern Campaign)

A large coalition of kings gathered at the waters of Merom to fight against Joshua. In a surprise attack, Joshua's armies drove the forces back, some toward Tyre and Sidon, others toward Kedesh. Joshua divided his forces, destroying Hazor along the way.

---

land of Goshen, the lowland, and the Jordan plainᵃ—the mountains of Israel and its lowlands, ¹⁷from Mount Halak and the ascent to Seir, even as far as Baal Gad in the Valley of Lebanon below Mount Hermon. He captured all their kings, and struck them down and killed them. ¹⁸Joshua made war a long time with all those kings. ¹⁹There was not a city that made peace with the children of Israel, except the Hivites, the inhabitants of Gibeon. All *the others* they took in battle. ²⁰For it was of the LORD to harden their hearts, that they should come against Israel in battle, that He might utterly destroy them, *and* that they might receive no mercy, but that He might destroy them, as the LORD had commanded Moses.

²¹And at that time Joshua came and cut off the Anakim from the mountains: from Hebron, from Debir, from Anab, from all the mountains of Judah, and from all the mountains of Israel; Joshua utterly destroyed them with their cities. ²²None of the Anakim were left in the land of the children of Israel; they remained only in Gaza, in Gath, and in Ashdod. ²³So Joshua took the whole land, according to all that the LORD had said to Moses; and Joshua gave it as an inheritance to Israel according to their divisions by their tribes. Then the land rested from war.

The Kings Conquered by Moses

12 ¹These *are* the kings of the land whom the children of Israel defeated, and whose land they possessed on the other side of the Jordan toward the rising of the sun, from the River Arnon to Mount Hermon, and all the eastern Jordan plain: ²*One king was* Sihon king of the Amorites, who dwelt in Heshbon *and* ruled half of Gilead, from Aroer, which is on the bank of the River Arnon, from the middle of that river, even as far as the River Jabbok, *which is* the border of the Ammonites, ³and the eastern Jordan plain from the Sea of Chinneroth as far as the Sea of the Arabah (the Salt Sea), the road to Beth Jeshimoth, and southward below the slopes of Pisgah. ⁴*The other king was* Og king of Bashan and his territory, *who was* of the remnant of the giants, who dwelt at Ashtaroth and at Edrei, ⁵and reigned over Mount Hermon, over Salcah, over all Bashan, as far as the border of the Geshurites and the Maachathites, and over half of Gilead *to* the border of Sihon king of Heshbon.

⁶These Moses the servant of the LORD and the children of Israel had conquered; and Moses the servant of the LORD had given it *as* a possession to the Reubenites, the Gadites, and half the tribe of Manasseh.

The Kings Conquered by Joshua

⁷And these *are* the kings of the country which Joshua and the children of Israel conquered on this side of the Jordan, on the west, from Baal Gad in the Valley of Lebanon as far as Mount Halak and the ascent to Seir, which Joshua gave to the tribes of Israel *as* a possession according to their divisions, ⁸in the mountain country, in the lowlands, in the *Jordan* plain, in the slopes, in the wilderness, and in the South—the Hittites, the Amorites, the Canaanites, the Perizzites, the Hivites, and the Jebusites: ⁹the king of Jericho, one; the king of Ai, which *is* beside Bethel, one; ¹⁰the king of Jerusalem, one; the king of Hebron, one; ¹¹the king of Jarmuth, one; the king of Lachish, one; ¹²the king of Eglon, one; the king of Gezer, one; ¹³the king of Debir, one; the king of Geder, one; ¹⁴the king of Hormah, one; the king of Arad, one; ¹⁵the king of Libnah, one; the king of Adullam, one; ¹⁶the king of Makkedah, one; the king of Bethel, one; ¹⁷the king of Tappuah, one; the king of Hepher, one; ¹⁸the king of Aphek, one; the king of Lasharon, one; ¹⁹the king of Madon, one; the king of Hazor, one; ²⁰the king of Shimron Meron, one; the king of Achshaph, one; ²¹the king of Taanach, one; the king of Megiddo, one; ²²the king of Kedesh, one; the king of Jokneam in Carmel, one; ²³the king of Dor in the heights of Dor, one; the king of the people of Gilgal, one; ²⁴the king of Tirzah, one—all the kings, thirty-one.

Remaining Land to Be Conquered

13 ¹Now Joshua was old, advanced in years. And the LORD said to him: "You are old, advanced in years, and there remains very much land yet to be possessed. ²This is the land that yet remains: all the territory of the Philistines and all *that of* the Geshurites, ³from Sihor, which *is* east of Egypt, as far as the border of Ekron northward (*which* is counted as Canaanite); the five lords of the Philistines—the Gazites, the Ashdodites, the Ashkelonites, the Gittites, and the

Ekronites; also the Avites; ⁴from the south, all the land of the Canaanites, and Mearah that belongs to the Sidonians as far as Aphek, to the border of the Amorites; ⁵the land of the Gebalites,ª and all Lebanon, toward the sunrise, from Baal Gad below Mount Hermon as far as the entrance to Hamath; ⁶all the inhabitants of the mountains from Lebanon as far as the Brook Misrephoth,ª *and* all the Sidonians—them I will drive out from before the children of Israel; only divide it by lot to Israel as an inheritance, as I have commanded you. ⁷Now therefore, divide this land as an inheritance to the nine tribes and half the tribe of Manasseh."

The Land Divided East of the Jordan

⁸With the other half-tribe the Reubenites and the Gadites received their inheritance, which Moses had given them, beyond the Jordan eastward, as Moses the servant of the LORD had given them: ⁹from Aroer which *is* on the bank of the River Arnon, and the town that *is* in the midst of the ravine, and all the plain of Medeba as far as Dibon; ¹⁰all the cities of Sihon king of the Amorites, who reigned in Heshbon, as far as the border of the children of Ammon; ¹¹Gilead, and the border of the Geshurites and Maachathites, all Mount Hermon, and all Bashan as far as Salcah; ¹²all the kingdom of Og in Bashan, who reigned in Ashtaroth and Edrei, who remained of the remnant of the giants; for Moses had defeated and cast out these.

¹³Nevertheless the children of Israel did not drive out the Geshurites or the Maachathites, but the Geshurites and the Maachathites dwell among the Israelites until this day.

¹⁴Only to the tribe of Levi he had given no inheritance; the sacrifices of the LORD God of Israel made by fire *are* their inheritance, as He said to them.

The Land of Reuben

¹⁵And Moses had given to the tribe of the children of Reuben *an inheritance* according to their families. ¹⁶Their territory was from Aroer, which *is* on the bank of the River Arnon, and the city that *is* in the midst of the ravine, and all the plain by Medeba; ¹⁷Heshbon and all its cities that *are* in the plain: Dibon, Bamoth Baal,

THE SEA PEOPLES SETTLE IN PHILISTIA (Josh. 13:2, 3)

The Philistines were a people group whose origins are not clearly known. New Kingdom Egyptian sources from the 13th and 12th centuries B.C. mention them as one of the Sea Peoples who unsuccessfully invaded Egypt. The inscriptions of Pharaoh Merenptah (1213–1203 B.C.) report that when the Libyans attacked Egypt, there were "foreigners from the sea" fighting within the ranks of the Libyan armies. Egyptian descriptions of Pharaoh Ramesses' battles against the Sea Peoples list the Philistines among the opponents.

Some scholars believe that the Sea People groups came from the western regions of the Mediterranean and Aegean Seas—from Greece and Crete. Cities, regions and empires fell to these seaborne raiders: Cyprus, north Syria, the Hittite Empire, Ugarit. The Sea Peoples continued down the eastern Mediterranean coastal areas toward Canaan until Egypt's Ramesses III (1184–1153 B.C.) stopped their advance in 1175 B.C.

Ramesses did not win decisively. Later Egyptian sources record the settlement of some of the Sea Peoples in southern Palestine, which was in the Egyptian sphere of influence. The group called "Philistines" organized a confederation of five major cities: Gaza, Ashdod, Ashkelon, Gath, and Ekron. The Sea Peoples' invasion spawned a new culture in Palestine, one that the Israelites would experience as "Gazites, Ashdodites, Ashkelonites, Gittites, Ekronites" (Josh. 13:3).

Beth Baal Meon, ¹⁸Jahaza, Kedemoth, Mephaath, ¹⁹Kirjathaim, Sibmah, Zereth Shahar on the mountain of the valley, ²⁰Beth Peor, the slopes of Pisgah, and Beth Jeshimoth— ²¹all the cities of the plain and all the kingdom of Sihon king of the Amorites, who reigned in Heshbon, whom Moses had struck with the princes of Midian: Evi, Rekem, Zur, Hur, and Reba, who *were* princes of Sihon dwelling in the country. ²²The children of Israel also killed with the sword Balaam the son of Beor, the soothsayer, among those who were killed by them. ²³And the border of the children of Reuben was the bank of the Jordan. This *was* the inheritance of the children of Reuben according to their families, the cities and their villages.

The Land of Gad

²⁴Moses also had given *an inheritance* to the tribe of Gad, to the children of Gad according to their families. ²⁵Their territory was Jazer, and all the cities of Gilead, and half the land of the Ammonites as far as Aroer, which *is* before Rabbah, ²⁶and from Heshbon to Ramath Mizpah and Betonim, and from Mahanaim to the border of Debir, ²⁷and in the valley Beth Haram, Beth Nimrah, Succoth, and Zaphon, the rest of the kingdom of Sihon king of Heshbon, with the Jordan as *its* border, as far as the edge of the Sea of Chinnereth, on the other side of the Jordan eastward.

²⁸This *is* the inheritance of the children of Gad according to their families, the cities and their villages.

Half the Tribe of Manasseh (East)

²⁹Moses also had given *an inheritance* to half the tribe of Manasseh; it was for half the tribe of the children of Manasseh according to their families: ³⁰Their territory was from Mahanaim, all Bashan, all the kingdom of Og king of Bashan, and all the towns of Jair which are in Bashan, sixty cities; ³¹half of Gilead, and Ashtaroth and Edrei, cities of the kingdom of Og in Bashan, *were* for the children of Machir the son of Manasseh, for half of the children of Machir according to their families.

³²These *are the areas* which Moses had distributed as an inheritance in the plains of Moab on the other side of the Jordan, by Jericho eastward. ³³But to the tribe of Levi Moses had given no inheritance; the LORD God of Israel *was* their inheritance, as He had said to them.

The Land Divided West of the Jordan

14 ¹These *are the areas* which the children of Israel inherited in the land of Canaan, which Eleazar the priest, Joshua the son of Nun, and the heads of the fathers of the tribes of the children of Israel distributed as an inheritance to them. ²Their inheritance *was* by lot, as the LORD had commanded by the hand of

Moses, for the nine tribes and the half-tribe. ³For Moses had given the inheritance of the two tribes and the half-tribe on the other side of the Jordan; but to the Levites he had given no inheritance among them. ⁴For the children of Joseph were two tribes: Manasseh and Ephraim. And they gave no part to the Levites in the land, except cities to dwell *in,* with their common-lands for their livestock and their property. ⁵As the LORD had commanded Moses, so the children of Israel did; and they divided the land.

The Early Years of Conquest

The tradition in Josh. 14 emphasizes God's blessings to faithful Caleb. He was 40 years old when Moses sent him, along with the others, to spy out the land (Josh. 14:7). That event, recorded in Num. 13:1–6, is located in the 2nd year of the Exodus, either 1445 or 1274 B.C. (see "The Book of Numbers" at Num. 1:1).

Now Caleb had reached the age of 85 (Josh. 14:10). The passing time of 45 years suggests a date of around 1400 or 1229 B.C. This point in the conquest of Canaan was possibly 6 years after Israel's arrival on the plains of Moab in 1406 or 1235 B.C. (see "Moab: On the Doorstep of Canaan" at Num. 20:14).

The listing of Caleb's age is not meant to pinpoint calendar years. Rather, the example of Caleb is important for chs. 13—24 which narrate the distribution of the tribal territories and Joshua's final charge to the tribes. With Caleb we see both faithfulness to God and fulfillment of God's promises. The first inheritance of land would go to one who had been faithful. Furthermore, the granting of that inheritance would fulfill the promise made long before at the beginning of the Exodus (Num. 14:24).

■ Joshua 14:6—24:33

Joshua
Caleb Inherits Hebron

14 :6 Then the children of Judah came to Joshua in Gilgal. And Caleb the son of Jephunneh the Kenizzite said to him: "You know the word which the LORD said to Moses the man of God concerning you and me in Kadesh Barnea. ⁷I *was* forty years old when Moses the servant of the LORD sent me from Kadesh Barnea to spy out the land, and I brought back word to

him as *it was* in my heart. ⁸Nevertheless my brethren who went up with me made the heart of the people melt, but I wholly followed the LORD my God. ⁹So Moses swore on that day, saying, 'Surely the land where your foot has trodden shall be your inheritance and your children's forever, because you have wholly followed the LORD my God.' ¹⁰And now, behold, the LORD has kept me alive, as He said, these forty-five years, ever since the LORD spoke this word to Moses while Israel wandered in the wilderness; and now, here I am this day, eighty-five years old. ¹¹As yet I *am as* strong this day as on the day that Moses sent me; just as my strength *was* then, so now *is* my strength for war, both for going out and for coming in. ¹²Now therefore, give me this mountain of which the LORD spoke in that day; for you heard in that day how the Anakim *were* there, and *that* the cities *were* great *and* fortified. It may be that the LORD *will be* with me, and I shall be able to drive them out as the LORD said."

¹³And Joshua blessed him, and gave Hebron to Caleb the son of Jephunneh as an inheritance. ¹⁴Hebron therefore became the inheritance of Caleb the son of Jephunneh the Kenizzite to this day, because he wholly followed the LORD God of Israel. ¹⁵And the name of Hebron formerly was Kirjath Arba (*Arba was* the greatest man among the Anakim).

Then the land had rest from war.

The Land of Judah

15 ¹So *this* was the lot of the tribe of the children of Judah according to their families:

The border of Edom at the Wilderness of Zin southward *was* the extreme southern boundary. ²And their southern border began at the shore of the Salt Sea, from the bay that faces southward. ³Then it went out to the southern side of the Ascent of Akrabbim, passed along to Zin, ascended on the south side of Kadesh Barnea, passed along to Hezron, went up to Adar, and went around to Karkaa. ⁴*From there* it passed toward Azmon and went out to the Brook of Egypt; and the border ended at the sea. This shall be your southern border.

⁵The east border *was* the Salt Sea as far as the mouth of the Jordan.

And the border on the northern quarter *began* at the bay of the sea at the mouth of the Jordan. ⁶The border went up to Beth Hoglah and passed north of Beth

Arabah; and the border went up to the stone of Bohan the son of Reuben. ⁷Then the border went up toward Debir from the Valley of Achor, and it turned northward toward Gilgal, which *is* before the Ascent of Adummim, which *is* on the south side of the valley. The border continued toward the waters of En Shemesh and ended at En Rogel. ⁸And the border went up by the Valley of the Son of Hinnom to the southern slope of the Jebusite *city* (which *is* Jerusalem). The border went up to the top of the mountain that *lies* before the Valley of Hinnom westward, which *is* at the end of the Valley of Rephaimᵃ northward. ⁹Then the border went around from the top of the hill to the fountain of the water of Nephtoah, and extended to the cities of Mount Ephron. And the border went around to Baalah (which *is* Kirjath Jearim). ¹⁰Then the border turned westward from Baalah to Mount Seir, passed along to the side of Mount Jearim on the north (which *is* Chesalon), went down to Beth Shemesh, and passed on to Timnah. ¹¹And the border went out to the side of Ekron northward. Then the border went around to Shicron, passed along to Mount Baalah, and extended to Jabneel; and the border ended at the sea.

¹²The west border *was* the coastline of the Great Sea. This *is* the boundary of the children of Judah all around according to their families.

Caleb Occupies Hebron and Debir

¹³Now to Caleb the son of Jephunneh he gave a share among the children of Judah, according to the commandment of the LORD to Joshua, *namely,* Kirjath Arba, which *is* Hebron (*Arba was* the father of Anak). ¹⁴Caleb drove out the three sons of Anak from there: Sheshai, Ahiman, and Talmai, the children of Anak. ¹⁵Then he went up from there to the inhabitants of Debir (formerly the name of Debir *was* Kirjath Sepher).

15:8 ᵃLiterally *Giants*   15:40 ᵃOr *Lahmam*

¹⁶And Caleb said, "He who attacks Kirjath Sepher and takes it, to him I will give Achsah my daughter as wife." ¹⁷So Othniel the son of Kenaz, the brother of Caleb, took it; and he gave him Achsah his daughter as wife. ¹⁸Now it was so, when she came *to him,* that she persuaded him to ask her father for a field. So she dismounted from *her* donkey, and Caleb said to her, "What do you wish?" ¹⁹She answered, "Give me a blessing; since you have given me land in the South, give me also springs of water." So he gave her the upper springs and the lower springs.

The Cities of Judah

²⁰This *was* the inheritance of the tribe of the children of Judah according to their families:

²¹The cities at the limits of the tribe of the children of Judah, toward the border of Edom in the South, were Kabzeel, Eder, Jagur, ²²Kinah, Dimonah, Adadah, ²³Kedesh, Hazor, Ithnan, ²⁴Ziph, Telem, Bealoth, ²⁵Hazar, Hadattah, Kerioth, Hezron (which *is* Hazor), ²⁶Amam, Shema, Moladah, ²⁷Hazar Gaddah, Heshmon, Beth Pelet, ²⁸Hazar Shual, Beersheba, Bizjothjah, ²⁹Baalah, Ijim, Ezem, ³⁰Eltolad, Chesil, Hormah, ³¹Ziklag, Madmannah, Sansannah, ³²Lebaoth, Shilhim, Ain, and Rimmon: all the cities *are* twenty-nine, with their villages.

³³In the lowland: Eshtaol, Zorah, Ashnah, ³⁴Zanoah, En Gannim, Tappuah, Enam, ³⁵Jarmuth, Adullam, Socoh, Azekah, ³⁶Sharaim, Adithaim, Gederah, and Gederothaim: fourteen cities with their villages; ³⁷Zenan, Hadashah, Migdal Gad, ³⁸Dilean, Mizpah, Joktheel, ³⁹Lachish, Bozkath, Eglon, ⁴⁰Cabbon, Lahmas,ᵃ Kithlish, ⁴¹Gederoth, Beth Dagon, Naamah, and Makkedah: sixteen cities with their villages; ⁴²Libnah, Ether, Ashan, ⁴³Jiphtah, Ashnah, Nezib, ⁴⁴Keilah, Achzib, and Mareshah: nine cities with their villages; ⁴⁵Ekron, with its towns and villages; ⁴⁶from Ekron to the sea, all that *lay* near Ashdod, with their villages;

CULTURE AND SOCIETY

Arba is reported to be the ancestor of the people, or tribe, of the Anakim (Josh. 14:15; 15:13). Similarly the nomadic Arabs, or bedouin, are known by the name of a distant ancestor. For example, the name "Beni Amir" means the "sons of Amir." These names do not mean that a genealogy can be traced back to a certain person, but that a tribe associates itself with a certain famous name.

MERENPTAH, THE SUBDUER OF GEZER (Josh. 16:10)

Gezer was a major city in central Palestine, strategically located in the hills between the mountains and the coast. As the Israelites made incursions into Canaan, they were unable to occupy Gezer, and it remained a Canaanite-controlled city (Josh. 16:10; Judg. 1:29). The Canaanites of Gezer were not so fortunate in facing the pharaohs of Egypt, though.

In the days before Israel's monarchy, two different pharaohs waged victorious campaigns against Gezer. Thutmose III claims to have captured the city in his first campaign around 1458 B.C. Gezer is one of over 100 city names on Thutmoses' victory list inscribed on the walls of the temple of Amon at Karnak. Yet it was another pharaoh—Merenptah—who became known for his victory over Gezer.

Merenptah (also spelled Merneptah) succeeded the great builder Ramesses II to become the fourth king of Egypt's 19th Dynasty (c. 1213–1203 B.C.). This monarch appears to have kept the borders of the Egyptian empire intact. Early in his reign (1210 B.C.) he subdued the city of Gezer, and obtained the title, "Subduer of Gezer." Merenptah claims credit for Gezer's destruction in the Israel Stele, a victory inscription that also mentions the vanquishing of "Israel."

If there is any connection between the Gezer campaign and the boast against Israel in the stele, it is not known. "Israel" may simply have been loosely included in a list of Palestinian names. There is no evidence that Merenptah actually campaigned against Israel itself.

Although Israel could not conquer Gezer in Joshua's time, the city would later come to the Israelites through yet another Egyptian pharaoh. Some think that Siamun (978–959 B.C.) is the unnamed pharaoh of 1 Kin. 9:16 who captured Gezer and gave it to Israel's king Solomon as a wedding present.

47Ashdod with its towns and villages, Gaza with its towns and villages—as far as the Brook of Egypt and the Great Sea with *its* coastline.

48And in the mountain country: Shamir, Jattir, Sochoh, 49Dannah, Kirjath Sannah (which *is* Debir), 50Anab, Eshtemoh, Anim, 51Goshen, Holon, and Giloh: eleven cities with their villages; 52Arab, Dumah, Eshean, 53Janum, Beth Tappuah, Aphekah, 54Humtah, Kirjath Arba (which *is* Hebron), and Zior: nine cities with their villages; 55Maon, Carmel, Ziph, Juttah, 56Jezreel, Jokdeam, Zanoah, 57Kain, Gibeah, and Timnah: ten cities with their villages; 58Halhul, Beth Zur, Gedor, 59Maarath, Beth Anoth, and Eltekon: six cities with their villages; 60Kirjath Baal (which *is* Kirjath Jearim) and Rabbah: two cities with their villages.

61In the wilderness: Beth Arabah, Middin, Secacah, 62Nibshan, the City of Salt, and En Gedi: six cities with their villages.

63As for the Jebusites, the inhabitants of Jerusalem, the children of Judah could not drive them out; but the Jebusites dwell with the children of Judah at Jerusalem to this day.

Ephraim and West Manasseh

16 1The lot fell to the children of Joseph from the Jordan, by Jericho, to the waters of Jericho on the east, to the wilderness that goes up from Jericho through the mountains to Bethel, 2then went out from Bethel to Luz,[a] passed along to the border of the Archites at Ataroth, 3and went down westward to the boundary of the Japhletites, as far as the boundary of Lower Beth Horon to Gezer; and it ended at the sea.

4So the children of Joseph, Manasseh and Ephraim, took their inheritance.

The Land of Ephraim

5The border of the children of Ephraim, according to their families, was *thus:* The border of their inheritance on the east side was Ataroth Addar as far as Upper Beth Horon.

6And the border went out toward the sea on the north side of Michmethath; then the border went around eastward to Taanath Shiloh, and passed by it on the

16:2 [a]Septuagint reads *Bethel* (that is, Luz).

east of Janohah. [7]Then it went down from Janohah to Ataroth and Naarah,[a] reached to Jericho, and came out at the Jordan.

[8]The border went out from Tappuah westward to the Brook Kanah, and it ended at the sea. This *was* the inheritance of the tribe of the children of Ephraim according to their families. [9]The separate cities for the children of Ephraim *were* among the inheritance of the children of Manasseh, all the cities with their villages.

[10]And they did not drive out the Canaanites who dwelt in Gezer; but the Canaanites dwell among the Ephraimites to this day and have become forced laborers.

The Other Half-Tribe of Manasseh (West)

17 [1]There was also a lot for the tribe of Manasseh, for he *was* the firstborn of Joseph: *namely* for Machir the firstborn of Manasseh, the father of Gilead, because he was a man of war; therefore he was given Gilead and Bashan. [2]And there was *a lot* for the rest of the children of Manasseh according to their families: for the children of Abiezer,[a] the children of Helek, the children of Asriel, the children of Shechem, the children of Hepher, and the children of Shemida; these *were* the male children of Manasseh the son of Joseph according to their families.

[3]But Zelophehad the son of Hepher, the son of Gilead, the son of Machir, the son of Manasseh, had no sons, but only daughters. And these *are* the names of his daughters: Mahlah, Noah, Hoglah, Milcah, and Tirzah. [4]And they came near before Eleazar the priest, before Joshua the son of Nun, and before the rulers, saying, "The LORD commanded Moses to give us an inheritance among our brothers." Therefore, according to the commandment of the LORD, he gave them an inheritance among their father's brothers. [5]Ten shares fell to Manasseh, besides the land of Gilead and Bashan, which *were* on the other side of the Jordan, [6]because the daughters of Manasseh received an inheritance among his sons; and the rest of Manasseh's sons had the land of Gilead.

[7]And the territory of Manasseh was from Asher to Michmethath, that *lies* east of Shechem; and the border went along south to the inhabitants of En Tappuah. [8]Manasseh had the land of Tappuah, but Tappuah on the border of Manasseh *belonged* to the children of Ephraim. [9]And the border descended to the Brook Kanah, southward to the brook. These cities of Ephraim *are* among the cities of Manasseh. The border of Manasseh *was* on the north side of the brook; and it ended at the sea.

[10]Southward *it was* Ephraim's, northward *it was* Manasseh's, and the sea was its border. Manasseh's territory was adjoining Asher on the north and Issachar on the east. [11]And in Issachar and in Asher, Manasseh had Beth Shean and its towns, Ibleam and its towns, the inhabitants of Dor and its towns, the inhabitants of En Dor and its towns, the inhabitants of Taanach and its towns, and the inhabitants of Megiddo and its towns—three hilly regions. [12]Yet the children of Manasseh could not drive out *the inhabitants of* those cities, but the Canaanites were determined to dwell in that land. [13]And it happened, when the children of Israel grew strong, that they put the Canaanites to forced labor, but did not utterly drive them out.

More Land for Ephraim and Manasseh

[14]Then the children of Joseph spoke to Joshua, saying, "Why have you given us *only* one lot and one share to inherit, since we *are* a great people, inasmuch as the LORD has blessed us until now?"

[15]So Joshua answered them, "If you *are* a great people, *then* go up to the forest country and clear a place for yourself there in the land of the Perizzites and the giants,

---

16:7 [a]Or *Naaran* (compare 1 Chronicles 7:28)
17:2 [a]Called *Jeezer* in Numbers 26:30

SCIENCE AND TECHNOLOGY

The "iron chariots" of Josh. 17:18 is possibly a way of saying "cruel" or "invincible" chariots. A chariot during Joshua's time would not have had much iron in it. Perhaps the word refers to some kind of armor protecting the horse or chariot, or to armor or weapons brandished by the charioteer.

since the mountains of Ephraim are too confined for you."

16But the children of Joseph said, "The mountain country is not enough for us; and all the Canaanites who dwell in the land of the valley have chariots of iron, *both those* who *are* of Beth Shean and its towns and *those* who *are* of the Valley of Jezreel."

17And Joshua spoke to the house of Joseph—to Ephraim and Manasseh—saying, "You *are* a great people and have great power; you shall not have *only* one lot, 18but the mountain country shall be yours. Although it *is* wooded, you shall cut it down, and its farthest extent shall be yours; for you shall drive out the Canaanites, though they have iron chariots *and* are strong."

The Remainder of the Land Divided

18 1Now the whole congregation of the children of Israel assembled together at Shiloh, and set up the tabernacle of meeting there. And the land was subdued before them. 2But there remained among the children of Israel seven tribes which had not yet received their inheritance.

3Then Joshua said to the children of Israel: "How long will you neglect to go and possess the land which the LORD God of your fathers has given you? 4Pick out from among you three men for *each* tribe, and I will send them; they shall rise and go through the land, survey it according to their inheritance, and come *back* to me. 5And they shall divide it into seven parts. Judah shall remain in their territory on the south, and the house of Joseph shall remain in their territory on the north. 6You

shall therefore survey the land in seven parts and bring *the survey* here to me, that I may cast lots for you here before the LORD our God. 7But the Levites have no part among you, for the priesthood of the LORD *is* their inheritance. And Gad, Reuben, and half the tribe of Manasseh have received their inheritance beyond the Jordan on the east, which Moses the servant of the LORD gave them."

8Then the men arose to go away; and Joshua charged those who went to survey the land, saying, "Go, walk through the land, survey it, and come back to me, that I may cast lots for you here before the LORD in Shiloh." 9So the men went, passed through the land, and wrote the survey in a book in seven parts by cities; and they came to Joshua at the camp in Shiloh. 10Then Joshua cast lots for them in Shiloh before the LORD, and there Joshua divided the land to the children of Israel according to their divisions.

The Land of Benjamin

11Now the lot of the tribe of the children of Benjamin came up according to their families, and the territory of their lot came out between the children of Judah and the children of Joseph. 12Their border on the north side began at the Jordan, and the border went up to the side of Jericho on the north, and went up through the mountains westward; it ended at the Wilderness of Beth Aven. 13The border went over from there toward Luz, to the side of Luz (which *is* Bethel) southward; and the border descended to Ataroth Addar, near the hill that *lies* on the south side of Lower Beth Horon.

14Then the border extended around the west side to the south, from the hill that *lies* before Beth Horon southward; and it ended at Kirjath Baal (which *is* Kirjath Jearim), a city of the children of Judah. This *was* the west side.

15The south side *began* at the end of Kirjath Jearim, and the border extended on the west and went out to the spring of the waters of Nephtoah. 16Then the border came down to the end of the mountain that *lies* before the Valley of the Son of Hinnom, which *is* in the Valley of the Rephaim[a] on the north, descended to the Valley of Hinnom, to the side of the Jebusite *city* on the south, and descended to En Rogel. 17And it

TIME CAPSULE   *1213 to 1208 B.C.*

1213-1203	*Merenptah, pharaoh of Egypt*
1211	*Merenptah takes inventory of the wealth in Egypt's temples*
1210	*Merenptah captures the city of Gezer*
1208	*Libyan tribes and seaborne pirates attack Egypt*
1208	*Merenptah defeats the Libyans and Sea Peoples*
1208	*In the Israel Stele, Merenptah mentions Israel as one of his conquests*

18:16 aLiterally *Giants*

JEBUS, CITY OF THE JEBUSITES (Josh. 18:28)

In Josh. 18:21–28 the biblical writer lists the cities that made up the inheritance of the tribe of Benjamin. For one of those cities he adds an identification in parentheses: Jebus (which is Jerusalem). Jebus was the pre-Israelite name for Jerusalem, capital city of Israel. The inhabitants of Jebus, the Jebusites, are listed as one of the Canaanite tribes who dwelt in the region of central Palestine (Ex. 33:2). Some scholars believe that they were a non-Semitic people, possibly related to the Hurrians.

The name "Jebus" is not mentioned in any source outside of the Bible. The city's Hebrew name, Jerusalem, is found in the Egyptian Execration Texts (19th to 18th centuries B.C.) and in the documents from Tell el-Amarna in Egypt (14th to 13th centuries B.C.). Such evidence suggests that the city's name had been Jerusalem for several centuries.

Much remains unknown about Jebus. We do not know whether the Jebusites received their name from the city Jebus, or whether Jebus was named after the Jebusites who dwelt there. When the name was changed to Jebus is not known, nor whether, at some point, the city could have been called by both names. It is possible that David restored the earlier name, Jerusalem, when he became king of Israel and captured the city from the Jebusites (c. 1003 B.C.; 2 Sam. 5:6, 7).

---

went around from the north, went out to En Shemesh, and extended toward Geliloth, which is before the Ascent of Adummim, and descended to the stone of Bohan the son of Reuben. [18]Then it passed along toward the north side of Arabah,[a] and went down to Arabah. [19]And the border passed along to the north side of Beth Hoglah; then the border ended at the north bay at the Salt Sea, at the south end of the Jordan. This *was* the southern boundary.

[20]The Jordan was its border on the east side. This *was* the inheritance of the children of Benjamin, according to its boundaries all around, according to their families.

[21]Now the cities of the tribe of the children of Benjamin, according to their families, were Jericho, Beth Hoglah, Emek Keziz, [22]Beth Arabah, Zemaraim, Bethel, [23]Avim, Parah, Ophrah, [24]Chephar Haammoni, Ophni, and Gaba: twelve cities with their villages; [25]Gibeon, Ramah, Beeroth, [26]Mizpah, Chephirah, Mozah, [27]Rekem, Irpeel, Taralah, [28]Zelah, Eleph, Jebus (which *is* Jerusalem), Gibeath, *and* Kirjath: fourteen cities with their villages. This was the inheritance of the children of Benjamin according to their families.

Simeon's Inheritance with Judah

19 [1]The second lot came out for Simeon, for the tribe of the children of Simeon according to their families. And their inheritance was within the inheritance of the children of Judah. [2]They had in their inheritance Beersheba (Sheba), Moladah, [3]Hazar Shual, Balah, Ezem, [4]Eltolad, Bethul, Hormah, [5]Ziklag, Beth Marcaboth, Hazar Susah, [6]Beth Lebaoth, and Sharuhen: thirteen cities and their villages; [7]Ain, Rimmon, Ether, and Ashan: four cities and their villages; [8]and all the villages that *were* all around these cities as far as Baalath Beer, Ramah of the South. This *was* the inheritance of the tribe of the children of Simeon according to their families.

[9]The inheritance of the children of Simeon *was included* in the share of the children of Judah, for the share of the children of Judah was too much for them. Therefore the children of Simeon had *their* inheritance within the inheritance of that people.

The Land of Zebulun

[10]The third lot came out for the children of Zebulun according to their families, and the border of their inheritance was as far as Sarid. [11]Their border went toward the west and to Maralah, went to Dabbasheth, and extended along the brook that is east of Jokneam. [12]Then from Sarid it went eastward toward the sunrise along the border of Chisloth Tabor, and went out toward Daberath, bypassing Japhia. [13]And from there it passed along on the east of

---

18:18 [a]Or *Beth Arabah* (compare 15:6 and 18:22)

Gath Hepher, toward Eth Kazin, and extended to Rimmon, which borders on Neah. [14]Then the border went around it on the north side of Hannathon, and it ended in the Valley of Jiphthah El. [15]Included were Kattath, Nahallal, Shimron, Idalah, and Bethlehem: twelve cities with their villages. [16]This *was* the inheritance of the children of Zebulun according to their families, these cities with their villages.

The Land of Issachar

[17]The fourth lot came out to Issachar, for the children of Issachar according to their families. [18]And their territory went to Jezreel, and *included* Chesulloth, Shunem, [19]Haphraim, Shion, Anaharath, [20]Rabbith, Kishion, Abez, [21]Remeth, En Gannim, En Haddah, and Beth Pazzez. [22]And the border reached to Tabor, Shahazimah, and Beth Shemesh; their border ended at the Jordan: sixteen cities with their villages. [23]This *was* the inheritance of the tribe of the children of Issachar according to their families, the cities and their villages.

The Land of Asher

[24]The fifth lot came out for the tribe of the children of Asher according to their families. [25]And their territory included Helkath, Hali, Beten, Achshaph, [26]Alammelech, Amad, and Mishal; it reached to Mount Carmel westward, along *the Brook* Shihor Libnath. [27]It turned toward the sunrise to Beth Dagon; and it reached to Zebulun and to the Valley of Jiphthah El, then northward beyond Beth Emek and Neiel, bypassing Cabul *which was* on the left, [28]including Ebron,[a] Rehob, Hammon, and Kanah, as far as Greater Sidon. [29]And the border turned to Ramah and to the fortified city of Tyre; then the border turned to Hosah, and ended at the sea by the region of Achzib. [30]Also Ummah, Aphek, and Rehob *were included:* twenty-two cities with their villages. [31]This *was* the inheritance of the tribe of the children of Asher according to their families, these cities with their villages.

The Land of Naphtali

[32]The sixth lot came out to the children of Naphtali, for the children of Naphtali according to their families. [33]And their border began at Heleph, enclosing the territory from the terebinth tree in Zaanannim, Adami Nekeb, and Jabneel, as far as Lakkum; it ended at the Jordan. [34]From Heleph the border extended westward to Aznoth Tabor, and went out from there toward Hukkok; it adjoined Zebulun on the south side and Asher on the west side, and ended at Judah by the Jordan toward the sunrise. [35]And the fortified cities *are* Ziddim, Zer, Hammath, Rakkath, Chinnereth, [36]Adamah, Ramah, Hazor, [37]Kedesh, Edrei, En Hazor, [38]Iron, Migdal El, Horem, Beth Anath, and Beth Shemesh: nineteen cities with their villages. [39]This *was* the inheritance of the tribe of the children of Naphtali according to their families, the cities and their villages.

The Land of Dan

[40]The seventh lot came out for the tribe of the children of Dan according to their families. [41]And the territory of their inheritance was Zorah, Eshtaol, Ir Shemesh, [42]Shaalabbin, Aijalon, Jethlah, [43]Elon, Timnah, Ekron, [44]Eltekeh, Gibbethon, Baalath, [45]Jehud, Bene Berak, Gath Rimmon, [46]Me Jarkon, and Rakkon, with the region near Joppa. [47]And the border of the children of Dan went beyond these, because the children of Dan went up to fight against Leshem and took it; and they struck it with the edge of the sword, took possession of it, and dwelt in it. They called Leshem, Dan, after the name of Dan their father. [48]This *is* the inheritance of the tribe of the children of Dan according to their families, these cities with their villages.

Joshua's Inheritance

[49]When they had made an end of dividing the land as an inheritance according to their borders, the children of Israel gave an inheritance among them to Joshua the son of Nun. [50]According to the word of the LORD they gave him the city which he asked for, Timnath Serah in the mountains of Ephraim; and he built the city and dwelt in it.

[51]These *were* the inheritances which Eleazar the priest, Joshua the son of Nun, and the heads of the fathers of the tribes of the children of Israel divided as an inheritance by lot in Shiloh before the LORD, at the door of the tabernacle of meeting. So they made an end of dividing the country.

19:28 [a]Following Masoretic Text, Targum, and Vulgate; a few Hebrew manuscripts read *Abdon* (compare 21:30 and 1 Chronicles 6:74).

The Cities of Refuge

20 ¹The LORD also spoke to Joshua, saying, ²"Speak to the children of Israel, saying: 'Appoint for yourselves cities of refuge, of which I spoke to you through Moses, ³that the slayer who kills a person accidentally *or* unintentionally may flee there; and they shall be your refuge from the avenger of blood. ⁴And when he flees to one of those cities, and stands at the entrance of the gate of the city, and declares his case in the hearing of the elders of that city, they shall take him into the city as one of them, and give him a place, that he may dwell among them. ⁵Then if the avenger of blood pursues him, they shall not deliver the slayer into his hand, because he struck his neighbor unintentionally, but did not hate him beforehand. ⁶And he shall dwell in that city until he stands before the congregation for judgment, *and* until the death of the one who is high priest in those days. Then the slayer may return and come to his own city and his own house, to the city from which he fled.'"

⁷So they appointed Kedesh in Galilee,

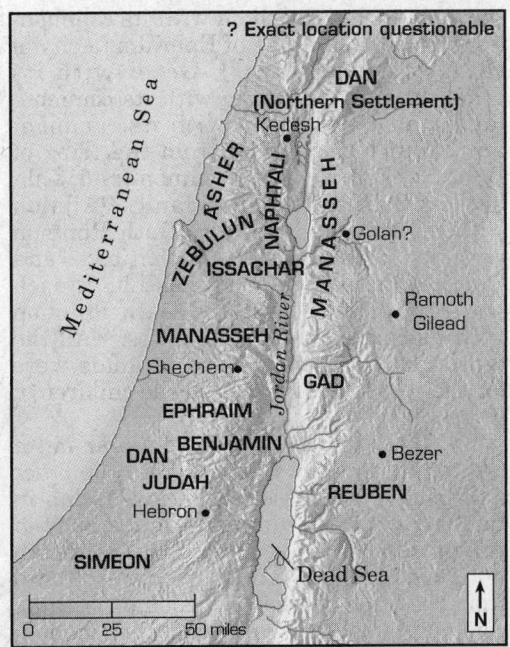

Cities of Refuge

The cities of refuge were established at strategic locations to provide a place of sanctuary for those who had killed someone unintentionally. There they remained until either being judged innocent by the congregation or until the death of the current high priest. Only then could they return to their original home without fear of reprisal.

in the mountains of Naphtali, Shechem in the mountains of Ephraim, and Kirjath Arba (which *is* Hebron) in the mountains of Judah. ⁸And on the other side of the Jordan, by Jericho eastward, they assigned Bezer in the wilderness on the plain, from the tribe of Reuben, Ramoth in Gilead, from the tribe of Gad, and Golan in Bashan, from the tribe of Manasseh. ⁹These were the cities appointed for all the children of Israel and for the stranger who dwelt among them, that whoever killed a person accidentally might flee there, and not die by the hand of the avenger of blood until he stood before the congregation.

Cities of the Levites

21 ¹Then the heads of the fathers' *houses* of the Levites came near to Eleazar the priest, to Joshua the son of Nun, and to the heads of the fathers' *houses* of the tribes of the children of Israel. ²And they spoke to them at Shiloh in the land of Canaan, saying, "The LORD commanded through Moses to give us cities to dwell in, with their common-lands for our livestock." ³So the children of Israel gave to the Levites from their inheritance, at the commandment of the LORD, these cities and their common-lands:

⁴Now the lot came out for the families of the Kohathites. And the children of Aaron the priest, *who were* of the Levites, had thirteen cities by lot from the tribe of Judah, from the tribe of Simeon, and from the tribe of Benjamin. ⁵The rest of the children of Kohath had ten cities by lot from the families of the tribe of Ephraim, from the tribe of Dan, and from the half-tribe of Manasseh.

⁶And the children of Gershon had thirteen cities by lot from the families of the tribe of Issachar, from the tribe of Asher, from the tribe of Naphtali, and from the half-tribe of Manasseh in Bashan.

⁷The children of Merari according to their families had twelve cities from the tribe of Reuben, from the tribe of Gad, and from the tribe of Zebulun.

⁸And the children of Israel gave these cities with their common-lands by lot to the Levites, as the LORD had commanded by the hand of Moses.

⁹So they gave from the tribe of the children of Judah and from the tribe of the children of Simeon these cities which are designated by name, ¹⁰which were for the

SUMERIAN CITIES OF REFUGE (Josh. 20:1–9)

When Israel entered Canaan, they appointed six locations to be "cities of refuge" (Josh. 20:2; Num. 35:13, 14). These cities were intended to stop the emergence of blood feuds, since the custom of blood revenge was long-standing (see Gen. 9:6). They were places where someone who had killed another by accident (Josh. 20:3) could go in order to escape the quick revenge of the dead person's family. These cities were not places where justice could be avoided, but places where further bloodshed could be prevented while an investigation took place (20:6).

Other Near Eastern peoples besides Israel provided places of refuge for its fugitives. A Sumerian incantation hymn dedicates a temple to the god Ninurta "on the battlefield by the cities of all the countries." The temple is described as the "house of refuge, wide house of the protective deity." As described in the Sumerian hymn, this house of refuge functioned as a "far-off ship moored in a foreign land" for the person who was confined to it. It was designated for "that person who in his own village, any man could cut him down."

The Sumerian text does not explicitly describe the reasons why the individual would need refuge in the temple of Ninurta. In contrast, the Israelite laws do specify what constituted an unintentional or accidental homicide (Num. 35:22, 23; Deut. 19:4, 5). Both the Sumerians and Israelites believed that their gods offered protection to certain persons. Ninurta is called "the protective deity," and Moses establishes the cities of refuge at the command of Yahweh (Num. 35:9–11). Both cultures knew that a place of refuge was needed to curb uncontrollable blood feuds.

children of Aaron, one of the families of the Kohathites, *who were* of the children of Levi; for the lot was theirs first. ¹¹And they gave them Kirjath Arba (*Arba was* the father of Anak), which *is* Hebron, in the mountains of Judah, with the common-land surrounding it. ¹²But the fields of the city and its villages they gave to Caleb the son of Jephunneh as his possession.

¹³Thus to the children of Aaron the priest they gave Hebron with its common-land (a city of refuge for the slayer), Libnah with its common-land, ¹⁴Jattir with its common-land, Eshtemoa with its common-land, ¹⁵Holon with its common-land, Debir with its common-land, ¹⁶Ain with its common-land, Juttah with its common-land, and Beth Shemesh with its common-land: nine cities from those two tribes; ¹⁷and from the tribe of Benjamin, Gibeon with its common-land, Geba with its common-land, ¹⁸Anathoth with its common-land, and Almon with its common-land: four cities. ¹⁹All the cities of the children of Aaron, the priests, *were* thirteen cities with their common-lands.

²⁰And the families of the children of Kohath, the Levites, the rest of the children of Kohath, even they had the cities of their lot from the tribe of Ephraim. ²¹For they gave them Shechem with its common-land in the mountains of Ephraim (a city of refuge for the slayer), Gezer with its common-land, ²²Kibzaim with its common-land, and Beth Horon with its common-land: four cities; ²³and from the tribe of Dan, Eltekeh with its common-land, Gibbethon with its common-land, ²⁴Aijalon with its common-land, *and* Gath Rimmon with its common-land: four cities; ²⁵and from the half-tribe of Manasseh, Tanach with its common-land and Gath Rimmon with its common-land: two cities. ²⁶All the ten cities with their common-lands were for the rest of the families of the children of Kohath.

²⁷Also to the children of Gershon, of the families of the Levites, from the *other* half-tribe of Manasseh, *they gave* Golan in Bashan with its common-land (a city of refuge for the slayer), and Be Eshterah with its common-land: two cities; ²⁸and from the tribe of Issachar, Kishion with its common-land, Daberath with its common-land, ²⁹Jarmuth with its common-land, *and* En Gannim with its common-land: four cities; ³⁰and from the tribe of Asher, Mishal with its common-land, Abdon with its common-land, ³¹Helkath with its common-land, and Rehob with its common-land: four cities; ³²and from the tribe of Naph-

tali, Kedesh in Galilee with its common-land (a city of refuge for the slayer), Hammoth Dor with its common-land, and Kartan with its common-land: three cities. [33]All the cities of the Gershonites according to their families *were* thirteen cities with their common-lands.

[34]And to the families of the children of Merari, the rest of the Levites, from the tribe of Zebulun, Jokneam with its common-land, Kartah with its common-land, [35]Dimnah with its common-land, *and* Nahalal with its common-land: four cities; [36]and from the tribe of Reuben, Bezer with its common-land, Jahaz with its common-land, [37]Kedemoth with its common-land, and Mephaath with its common-land: four cities;[a] [38]and from the tribe of Gad, Ramoth in Gilead with its common-land (a city of refuge for the slayer), Mahanaim with its common-land, [39]Heshbon with its common-land, *and* Jazer with its common-land: four cities in all. [40]So all the cities for the children of Merari according to their families, the rest of the families of the Levites, were *by* their lot twelve cities.

[41]All the cities of the Levites within the possession of the children of Israel *were* forty-eight cities with their common-lands. [42]Every one of these cities had its common-land surrounding it; thus *were* all these cities.

The Promise Fulfilled

[43]So the LORD gave to Israel all the land of which He had sworn to give to their fathers, and they took possession of it and dwelt in it. [44]The LORD gave them rest all around, according to all that He had sworn to their fathers. And not a man of all their enemies stood against them; the LORD delivered all their enemies into their hand. [45]Not a word failed of any good thing which the LORD had spoken to the house of Israel. All came to pass.

21:37 [a]Following Septuagint and Vulgate (compare 1 Chronicles 6:78, 79); Masoretic Text, Bomberg, and Targum omit verses 36 and 37.

Eastern Tribes Return to Their Lands

22 [1]Then Joshua called the Reubenites, the Gadites, and half the tribe of Manasseh, [2]and said to them: "You have kept all that Moses the servant of the LORD commanded you, and have obeyed my voice in all that I commanded you. [3]You have not left your brethren these many days, up to this day, but have kept the charge of the commandment of the LORD your God. [4]And now the LORD your God has given rest to your brethren, as He promised them; now therefore, return and go to your tents *and* to the land of your possession, which Moses the servant of the LORD gave you on the other side of the Jordan. [5]But take careful heed to do the commandment and the law which Moses the servant of the LORD commanded you, to love the LORD your God, to walk in all His ways, to keep His commandments, to hold fast to Him, and to serve Him with all your heart and with all your soul." [6]So Joshua blessed them and sent them away, and they went to their tents.

[7]Now to half the tribe of Manasseh Moses had given a possession in Bashan, but to the *other* half of it Joshua gave *a possession* among their brethren on this side of the Jordan, westward. And indeed, when Joshua sent them away to their tents, he blessed them, [8]and spoke to them, saying, "Return with much riches to your tents, with very much livestock, with silver, with gold, with bronze, with iron, and with very much clothing. Divide the spoil of your enemies with your brethren."

[9]So the children of Reuben, the children of Gad, and half the tribe of Manasseh returned, and departed from the children of Israel at Shiloh, which *is* in the land of Canaan, to go to the country of Gilead, to the land of their possession, which they had obtained according to the word of the LORD by the hand of Moses.

An Altar by the Jordan

[10]And when they came to the region of the Jordan which *is* in the land of Canaan,

---

GEOGRAPHY AND ENVIRONMENT

It is notoriously difficult to estimate the size of ancient populations for the cities inhabited by the Israelites (Josh. 21:43). Archaeological evidence suggests that the population of Palestine in the 14th century B.C. was not greater than 250,000 in all. The site of ancient Jericho is only eight and one-half acres in size, and most cities had fewer than 1,000 inhabitants.

the children of Reuben, the children of Gad, and half the tribe of Manasseh built an altar there by the Jordan—a great, impressive altar. ¹¹Now the children of Israel heard *someone* say, "Behold, the children of Reuben, the children of Gad, and half the tribe of Manasseh have built an altar on the frontier of the land of Canaan, in the region of the Jordan—on the children of Israel's side." ¹²And when the children of Israel heard *of it,* the whole congregation of the children of Israel gathered together at Shiloh to go to war against them.

¹³Then the children of Israel sent Phinehas the son of Eleazar the priest to the children of Reuben, to the children of Gad, and to half the tribe of Manasseh, into the land of Gilead, ¹⁴and with him ten rulers, one ruler each from the chief house of every tribe of Israel; and each one *was* the head of the house of his father among the divisionsᵃ of Israel. ¹⁵Then they came to the children of Reuben, to the children of Gad, and to half the tribe of Manasseh, to the land of Gilead, and they spoke with them, saying, ¹⁶"Thus says the whole congregation of the LORD: 'What treachery *is* this that you have committed against the God of Israel, to turn away this day from following the LORD, in that you have built for yourselves an altar, that you might rebel this day against the LORD? ¹⁷*Is* the iniquity of Peor not enough for us, from which we are not cleansed till this day, although there was a plague in the congregation of the LORD, ¹⁸but that you must turn away this day from following the LORD? And it shall be, if you rebel today against the LORD, that tomorrow He will be angry with the whole congregation of Israel. ¹⁹Nevertheless, if the land of your possession *is* unclean, *then* cross over to the land of the possession of the LORD, where the LORD's tabernacle stands, and take possession among us; but do not rebel against the LORD, nor rebel against us, by building yourselves an altar besides the altar of the LORD our God. ²⁰Did not Achan the son of Zerah commit a trespass in the accursed thing, and wrath fell on all the congregation of Israel? And that man did not perish alone in his iniquity.' "

²¹Then the children of Reuben, the children of Gad, and half the tribe of Manasseh answered and said to the heads of the divisionsᵃ of Israel: ²²"The LORD God of gods, the LORD God of gods, He knows, and let Israel itself know—if *it is* in rebellion, or if in treachery against the LORD, do not save us this day. ²³If we have built ourselves an altar to turn from following the LORD, or if to offer on it burnt offerings or grain offerings, or if to offer peace offerings on it, let the LORD Himself require *an account.* ²⁴But in fact we have done it for fear, for a reason, saying, 'In time to come your descendants may speak to our descendants, saying, "What have you to do with the LORD God of Israel? ²⁵For the LORD has made the Jordan a border between you and us, *you* children of Reuben and children of Gad. You have no part in the LORD." So your descendants would make our descendants cease fearing the LORD.' ²⁶Therefore we said, 'Let us now prepare to build ourselves an altar, not for burnt offering nor for sacrifice, ²⁷but *that* it *may be* a witness between you and us and our generations after us, that we may perform the service of the LORD before Him with our burnt offerings, with our sacrifices, and with our peace offerings; that your descendants may not say to our descendants in time to come, "You have no part in the LORD." ' ²⁸Therefore we said that it will be, when they say *this* to us or to our generations in time to come, that we may say, 'Here is the replica of the altar of the LORD which our fathers made, though not for burnt offerings nor for sacrifices; but it *is* a witness between you and us.' ²⁹Far be it from us that we should rebel against the LORD, and turn from following the LORD this day, to build an altar for burnt offerings, for grain offerings, or for sacrifices, besides the altar of the LORD our God which *is* before His tabernacle."

³⁰Now when Phinehas the priest and the rulers of the congregation, the heads of the divisionsᵃ of Israel who *were* with him, heard the words that the children of Reuben, the children of Gad, and the children of Manasseh spoke, it pleased them. ³¹Then Phinehas the son of Eleazar the priest said to the children of Reuben, the children of Gad, and the children of Manasseh, "This day we perceive that the LORD *is* among us, because you have not committed this treachery against the LORD. Now you have delivered the children of Israel out of the hand of the LORD."

³²And Phinehas the son of Eleazar the priest, and the rulers, returned from the

---

22:14 ᵃLiterally *thousands*   22:21 ᵃLiterally *thousands*   22:30 ᵃLiterally *thousands*

children of Reuben and the children of Gad, from the land of Gilead to the land of Canaan, to the children of Israel, and brought back word to them. ³³So the thing pleased the children of Israel, and the children of Israel blessed God; they spoke no more of going against them in battle, to destroy the land where the children of Reuben and Gad dwelt.

³⁴The children of Reuben and the children of Gadª called the altar, *Witness,* "For *it is* a witness between us that the LORD *is* God."

Joshua's Farewell Address

23 ¹Now it came to pass, a long time after the LORD had given rest to Israel from all their enemies round about, that Joshua was old, advanced in age. ²And Joshua called for all Israel, for their elders, for their heads, for their judges, and for their officers, and said to them:

"I am old, advanced in age. ³You have seen all that the LORD your God has done to all these nations because of you, for the LORD your God *is* He who has fought for you. ⁴See, I have divided to you by lot these nations that remain, to be an inheritance for your tribes, from the Jordan, with all the nations that I have cut off, as far as the Great Sea westward. ⁵And the LORD your God will expel them from before you and drive them out of your sight. So you shall possess their land, as the LORD your God promised you. ⁶Therefore be very courageous to keep and to do all that is written in the Book of the Law of Moses, lest you turn aside from it to the right hand or to the left, ⁷*and* lest you go among these nations, these who remain among you. You shall not make mention of the name of their gods, nor cause *anyone* to swear *by them;* you shall not serve them nor bow down to them, ⁸but you shall hold fast to the LORD your God, as you have done to this day. ⁹For the LORD has driven out from before you great and strong nations; but *as for* you, no one has been able to stand against you to this day. ¹⁰One man of you shall chase a thousand, for the LORD your God *is* He who fights for you, as He promised you. ¹¹Therefore take careful heed to yourselves, that you love the LORD your God. ¹²Or else, if indeed you do go

back, and cling to the remnant of these nations—these that remain among you—and make marriages with them, and go in to them and they to you, ¹³know for certain that the LORD your God will no longer drive out these nations from before you. But they shall be snares and traps to you, and scourges on your sides and thorns in your eyes, until you perish from this good land which the LORD your God has given you.

¹⁴"Behold, this day I *am* going the way of all the earth. And you know in all your hearts and in all your souls that not one thing has failed of all the good things which the LORD your God spoke concerning you. All have come to pass for you; not one word of them has failed. ¹⁵Therefore it shall come to pass, that as all the good things have come upon you which the LORD your God promised you, so the LORD will bring upon you all harmful things, until He has destroyed you from this good land which the LORD your God has given you. ¹⁶When you have transgressed the covenant of the LORD your God, which He commanded you, and have gone and served other gods, and bowed down to them, then the anger of the LORD will burn against you, and you shall perish quickly from the good land which He has given you."

The Covenant at Shechem

24 ¹Then Joshua gathered all the tribes of Israel to Shechem and called for the elders of Israel, for their heads, for their judges, and for their officers; and they presented themselves before God. ²And Joshua said to all the people, "Thus says the LORD God of Israel: 'Your fathers, *including* Terah, the father of Abraham and the father of Nahor, dwelt on the other side of the Riverª in old times; and they served other gods. ³Then I took your father Abraham from the other side of the River, led him throughout all the land of Canaan, and multiplied his descendants and gave him Isaac. ⁴To Isaac I gave Jacob and Esau. To Esau I gave the mountains of Seir to possess, but Jacob and his children went down to Egypt. ⁵Also I sent Moses and Aaron, and I plagued Egypt, according to what I did among them. Afterward I brought you out.

⁶"Then I brought your fathers out of Egypt, and you came to the sea; and the Egyptians pursued your fathers with chariots and horsemen to the Red Sea. ⁷So they cried out to the LORD; and He put darkness

---

22:34 ªSeptuagint adds *and half the tribe of Manasseh.*   24:2 ªHebrew *Nahar,* the Euphrates, and so in verses 3, 14, and 15

THE BROTHERS AND THE MOON GOD (Josh. 24:2)

Joshua reminded the people that their ancestors once lived in the region of the Euphrates River, where they "served other gods" (Josh. 24:2). The specific ancestors named are Terah and his two sons, Abraham and Nahor. In this ancestral family we witness a split, with one son continuing in his father's faith, while the other son pursued a new faith.

Terah lived at Ur in southern Mesopotamia. He moved about 600 miles north to Haran in northern Mesopotamia (Gen. 11:31), taking with him his son Abraham, Sarai (Abraham's wife), and Lot (Terah's grandson). Terah's other son, Nahor, is not reported to have made the journey to Haran at this time. Neither did Nahor take his brother Abraham's journey of faith to believe in the God Yahweh.

Who were the "other gods" (Josh. 24:2) that Terah and Nahor worshiped? Since these individuals were associated with the cities of Ur and Haran, it is likely that one of the "other gods" was Sin, the Mesopotamian moon god. Both Ur and Haran were centers for the worship of this lunar deity. The main temples at Haran and at Ur were dedicated to Sin. Living in the religious culture of these cities, Terah's family, being polytheists, were probably moon worshipers.

The brothers Abraham and Nahor took different directions of faith, and their respective decisions influenced their offspring. The participants in property agreements of ancient times often sealed their agreements by invoking the gods of their ancestors. In such an agreement, Laban, the descendant of Nahor, swore by his ancestor's gods, while Jacob swore by Yahweh, the God of his father Isaac and grandfather Abraham (Gen. 31:53).

---

between you and the Egyptians, brought the sea upon them, and covered them. And your eyes saw what I did in Egypt. Then you dwelt in the wilderness a long time. ⁸And I brought you into the land of the Amorites, who dwelt on the other side of the Jordan, and they fought with you. But I gave them into your hand, that you might possess their land, and I destroyed them from before you. ⁹Then Balak the son of Zippor, king of Moab, arose to make war against Israel, and sent and called Balaam the son of Beor to curse you. ¹⁰But I would not listen to Balaam; therefore he continued to bless you. So I delivered you out of his hand. ¹¹Then you went over the Jordan and came to Jericho. And the men of Jericho fought against you—*also* the Amorites, the Perizzites, the Canaanites, the Hittites, the Girgashites, the Hivites, and the Jebusites. But I delivered them into your hand. ¹²I sent the hornet before you which

drove them out from before you, *also* the two kings of the Amorites, *but* not with your sword or with your bow. ¹³I have given you a land for which you did not labor, and cities which you did not build, and you dwell in them; you eat of the vineyards and olive groves which you did not plant.'

¹⁴"Now therefore, fear the LORD, serve Him in sincerity and in truth, and put away the gods which your fathers served on the other side of the River and in Egypt. Serve the LORD! ¹⁵And if it seems evil to you to serve the LORD, choose for yourselves this day whom you will serve, whether the gods which your fathers served that *were* on the other side of the River, or the gods of the Amorites, in whose land you dwell. But as for me and my house, we will serve the LORD."

¹⁶So the people answered and said: "Far be it from us that we should forsake the LORD to serve other gods; ¹⁷for the

---

POLITICS AND GOVERNMENT

Ancient armies were compared to bees, wasps, and hornets (Josh. 24:12) because they traveled on foot and were dangerous when they were in great numbers, like a swarm of insects. The Greeks often decorated their shields with pictures of animals, and the hornet was used this way.

LORD our God *is* He who brought us and our fathers up out of the land of Egypt, from the house of bondage, who did those great signs in our sight, and preserved us in all the way that we went and among all the people through whom we passed. [18]And the LORD drove out from before us all the people, including the Amorites who dwelt in the land. We also will serve the LORD, for He *is* our God."

[19]But Joshua said to the people, "You cannot serve the LORD, for He *is* a holy God. He *is* a jealous God; He will not forgive your transgressions nor your sins. [20]If you forsake the LORD and serve foreign gods, then He will turn and do you harm and consume you, after He has done you good."

[21]And the people said to Joshua, "No, but we will serve the LORD!"

[22]So Joshua said to the people, "You *are* witnesses against yourselves that you have chosen the LORD for yourselves, to serve Him."

And they said, "*We are* witnesses!"

[23]"Now therefore," *he said,* "put away the foreign gods which *are* among you, and incline your heart to the LORD God of Israel."

[24]And the people said to Joshua, "The LORD our God we will serve, and His voice we will obey!"

[25]So Joshua made a covenant with the people that day, and made for them a statute and an ordinance in Shechem.

[26]Then Joshua wrote these words in the Book of the Law of God. And he took a large stone, and set it up there under the oak that *was* by the sanctuary of the LORD. [27]And Joshua said to all the people, "Behold, this stone shall be a witness to us, for it has heard all the words of the LORD which He spoke to us. It shall therefore be a witness to you, lest you deny your God." [28]So Joshua let the people depart, each to his own inheritance.

Death of Joshua and Eleazar

[29]Now it came to pass after these things that Joshua the son of Nun, the servant of the LORD, died, *being* one hundred and ten years old. [30]And they buried him within the border of his inheritance at Timnath Serah, which *is* in the mountains of Ephraim, on the north side of Mount Gaash.

[31]Israel served the LORD all the days of Joshua, and all the days of the elders who outlived Joshua, who had known all the works of the LORD which He had done for Israel.

[32]The bones of Joseph, which the children of Israel had brought up out of Egypt, they buried at Shechem, in the plot of ground which Jacob had bought from the sons of Hamor the father of Shechem for one hundred pieces of silver, and which had become an inheritance of the children of Joseph.

[33]And Eleazar the son of Aaron died. They buried him in a hill *belonging to* Phinehas his son, which was given to him in the mountains of Ephraim.

THE LITERATURE OF UGARIT

Writings of "the Canaanites" (Josh. 24:11) were discovered in Syria at Ras Shamra, known by its ancient name Ugarit. The Canaanite texts include myths, epics, and legends written in a unique alphabetic script, now called Ugaritic.

Ugaritic Legends and Myths

Legend of Keret　　Named for its major character, Keret, king of Hubur. Much of this story contains advice from El, the head of the gods, to Keret on where to find a new wife.

Legend of Aqhat　　The story of King Aqhat, who is the son of Daniel. The goddess Anath has Aqhat killed in order to obtain his beautiful bow for her arsenal. The father Daniel buries his son and mourns for a 7-year period.

Baal-Anath Cycle　　Various episodes describe cosmic battles between the divine forces of barrenness and productivity, sterility and fertility. The victor in these wars is sometimes Baal, sometimes Yam. Baal's consort, the goddess Anath, fights against Yam and Mot.

FROM TRIBES TO A NATION

(1200—930 B.C.)

A sweep of events marks Israel's rise from a loose confederation of tribes to a great kingdom. The fragmented tribes became the glory of Solomon.

The conquest of Canaan under Joshua is pictured as a united effort by the Israelite people. Yet because of natural boundaries and local concerns, Israel became an increasingly fragmented people. This was a time when international power in the ancient world was at a low ebb. Still Israel was barely surviving against such relatively insignificant peoples as the Moabites, Midianites, and Amalekites. The Israelite tribes were struggling to find a foothold in the new land.

Israel's story makes a transition, however, from the loose-knit group of tribes to a highly organized monarchy. The tribes that were governed by divinely selected judges eventually became a kingdom ruled by a dynasty also chosen under divine guidance. This story is told through a dramatic sweep of events that produced the most powerful empire in the ancient Middle East, in the golden age under the leadership of David and Solomon.

▶ Archaeology and the Past

Archaeological excavations reveal that such Canaanite cities as Bethel or Beth Shemesh were flourishing urban cultures. Houses were well built, with paved floors, and cities had public drainage systems and fortified walls. Sophisticated pottery, art, jewelry, and statues of gods are found in large numbers. The pottery and other goods discovered suggest that trade with Syria, Egypt, and the Aegean flourished. Stone bowls from ancient Egypt were found in the ruins, attesting to a trade in "antiques."

Archaeology offers a different picture of Israelite settlements during this period. Towns appeared in the hill country for the first time, including such places as Shiloh, Mizpah, and Gibeah, among others. The houses were built of stones stacked together, with no attempt to shape the stones to fit, and with no mortar to hold them together. Art and pottery were crude, and there are almost no signs of trade. This picture fits with that in the Book of Judges: the Israelites were poor, oppressed, and threatened by the superior cultures of their new neighbors; they were barely clinging to existence.

The transition from judges to kings can be seen in archaeology. Gibeah, Saul's fortress, has been excavated, revealing a two-story building, well built, with at least one watchtower. A higher quality pottery was found there, and—most important—an iron plowpoint. Israel was beginning to use iron. Yet it was David who "prepared iron in abundance" (1 Chr. 22:3) for the construction of a temple. All the iron fastenings that David stored up made the building of Solomon's temple possible. Iron nails held longer and tighter than those of bronze.

While David began various building projects in Jerusalem (2 Sam. 5:9, 11), very little has been uncovered by archaeologists. Excavations at Jerusalem do show an ingenious water system through which David's soldiers may have climbed to capture the city, when it was known as Jebus (2 Sam. 5:8). The situation changes, however, with David's son Solomon. Several archaeological finds lend support to the biblical picture of Solomon as Israel's first great builder.

Solomon was a trader in chariots and horses, buying chariots in Egypt and selling them farther north and east. Chariot cities built by Solomon include Megiddo, Hazor, and Gezer. All of these cities show evidence of fortifications dating to Solomon's time, particularly the six-chambered gates that were common in Solomon's building enterprises.

Excavations at Ezion Geber, on the Gulf of Aqaba, have uncovered the remains of a metal industry, apparently worked by slaves. Solomon controlled the mines of the Sinai and had a monopoly on the metal industry of his day. It was from these mines, most likely, that the great bronze doors and other metal trappings of the temple came. Ezion Geber was also a seaport, from which Solomon's ships went on trading expeditions to Africa every third year (1 Kin. 10:22). Some archaeological evidence of the spice trade with Arabia suggests that the famous queen of Sheba visited Solomon as much for economic reasons as to hear his wisdom.

Solomon's most significant building project was the temple and royal palace. The plan of Solomon's temple, as described in the Bible, is similar to plans of other temples in Canaan and Phoenicia. In fact, a temple dedicated to Yahweh has been excavated near the city of Arad in the Negev. It was part of a royal fortress from the time of Solomon, and differs from the Jerusalem temple mainly in having a broad room, rather than the long holy place. The 20-year temple-palace enterprise (2 Chr. 8:1) was impressive testimony that Israel had made the transition from tribes to a great nation.

> *The 20-year temple-palace enterprise was impressive testimony that Israel had become a great nation.*

▶ The Peoples and Groups

Much of Israel's history reflects the relative strength and weakness of Egypt and the empires of Mesopotamia. These major empires were weak during the reigns of David and Solomon, allowing both kings to expand their Israelite kingdoms. Yet other peoples interacted with Israel during the settlement and kingdom period.

The Sea Peoples were a great migration of seaborne groups coming out of Greece and the regions around the Aegean Sea. They overran ancient civilizations in Troy, Cyprus, and Asia Minor. They attacked Egypt by both land and sea, and Pharaoh Ramesses III (1184–1153 B.C.), while preventing their advance into Egypt, did allow them to settle in Egyptian strongholds on the Palestine coast. One of the Sea Peoples, the Philistines, controlled much of Palestine, and only under King David were the Israelites able to compete with and ultimately defeat the Philistines.

The Canaanites were a highly cultured people in the land when Israel arrived, with superiority in areas of building, art, trade, and economics. But their most important threat to Israel was in the area of religion. A nomadic people trying to settle in the land must have found it almost impossible not to think the gods of the Canaanites were powerful indeed, giving the Canaanite people such wealth and power. The documents found at Ugarit (Ras Shamra) include many of the myths, rituals, hymns, and prayers of the Canaanites.

The Arameans were the various tribes and kingdoms located in southern Syria, just northeast of Canaan. Cushan-Rishathaim, an unknown king from the early days of the judges (Judg. 3:8, 10), is sometimes identified as an Aramean. More definite references to Arameans (or Syrians), though, come from the time of David. Aram often refers to Aram-Damascus, the state whose capital was Damascus. David eventually conquered an alliance of Arameans from Damascus and from Zobah, an Aramean kingdom north of Damascus ruled by King Hadadezer (2 Sam. 8:3–8). Damascus regained its independence from Israel during Solomon's reign (1 Kin. 11:23–25).

Several nomadic or seminomadic groups raided the settled lands from time to time. The Amalekites are mentioned only in the Bible. The Midianites threatened Israel during the era of the judges and were opposed by Israel's judge Gideon (Judg. 6—8). What made such raids successful was the domestication of the camel, which freed travelers (and raiders) to range farther afield into the deserts. By David's reign these raiding groups were no longer serious threats.

▶ The Biblical Literature

Biblical books which relate Israel's transition to a kingdom include Judges, Ruth, 1 and 2 Samuel, 1 Chronicles, and parts of 1 Kings and 2 Chronicles. These books are a special kind of history: they not only give data about the past, but they try to explain what the data mean and how God was active in the history of the people. Judges is a collection of narratives about tribal heroes and heroines in the period between the death of Joshua and the time of Samuel. Ruth is about a foreign woman through whom God works to bring forth King David. 1 and 2 Samuel report the end of the judges and the rise of the monarchy in Israel. They include the lives of Samuel, Saul, and David.

The histories of Samuel, Kings, and Chronicles report the golden age of monarchy under David and Solomon. Many of Israel's writings were associated with these great kings. Traditionally, more of the Psalms were ascribed to David than to any other person. The glory years of Solomon are reflected in the love songs of the Song of Solomon, in the collections of sayings on the good life in Proverbs, and in the ultimate questions of life and death covered in Ecclesiastes.

A Tribal Confederation in Israel

Israel now organized itself into a loose confederation of independent tribes.

Having established at least a foothold in the land of Canaan, Israel now organized itself into a loose confederation of independent tribes. The link connecting these clans was their God. The tribes celebrated common religious festivals at the shrine where the ark of the covenant was kept. The shrine was movable, but it was most often located at Gilgal and Shiloh.

The tribal confederation had military purposes as well. When an outside people invaded, the clans were to join in a holy war. Some leader would take the initiative and summon the tribes to battle. These leaders, for the most part, we call the judges.

The judges led makeshift armies, but they did not have to face the forces of the major empires. Through most of the period of the judges, Egypt and the countries of Mesopotamia were weak and preoccupied with internal problems. The wars of the Book of Judges are waged against unconquered Canaanites and such small neighboring nations as Edom, Midian, and Ammon.

Toward the end of the Late Bronze Age (1500–1200 B.C.), though, a new group began to arrive in the land of Canaan, evidently from across the Mediterranean. They had war chariots and knew how to use iron, giving them a military advantage over the Israelites, who only had bronze. These seaborne bands, called the Sea Peoples, settled the fertile land along the southern coast. Among these peoples was the group called by the name "Philistines."

The presence of the Philistines helps to explain why the tribe of Dan, to whom Joshua allotted the Philistine coastland, never conquered any of its portion. Despite the uneven efforts of the Danite judge Samson, the tribe of Dan ultimately left the coast and found itself a new homeland far to the north (Judg. 18:1).

The Book of Judges

The brief introduction of the Book of Judges (Judg. 1:1—2:6) again makes clear that the Israelite invasion of Canaan was incomplete. The major portion of the book (3:7—16:31) focuses on the judges, the men and women by whom God delivered His people from oppressors. Though the judges were usually military leaders, they also exercised administrative duties, and some of them are not reported to have led armies at all (such as the "minor judges"; cf. Judg. 10:1–5; 12:8–15).

By the end of the book, the confederacy appears ready to collapse. The tribes had never been entirely unified either in worship or war. Four of them, Reuben, Gad (Gilead), Dan, and Asher, seem not to have responded to Deborah's summons to assist the other tribes in battle (Judg. 5:16, 17). By the latter stages of the judges' period, the tribes had fallen into idolatry and civil war. The refrain of the final chapters—"In those days there was no king in Israel; everyone did what was right in his own eyes" (17:6; 21:25)—points ahead to 1 Samuel and the beginning of the monarchy.

■ Judges 1:1—3:6

delivered the Canaanites and the Perizzites into their hand; and they killed ten thousand men at Bezek. ⁵And they found Adoni-Bezek in Bezek, and fought against him; and they defeated the Canaanites and the Perizzites. ⁶Then Adoni-Bezek fled, and they pursued him and caught him and cut off his thumbs and big toes. ⁷And Adoni-Bezek said, "Seventy kings with their thumbs and big toes cut off used to gather *scraps* under my table; as I have done, so God has repaid me." Then they brought him to Jerusalem, and there he died.

⁸Now the children of Judah fought against Jerusalem and took it; they struck it with the edge of the sword and set the city on fire. ⁹And afterward the children of Judah went down to fight against the Canaanites who dwelt in the mountains, in the South,ᵃ and in the lowland. ¹⁰Then Judah went against the Canaanites who dwelt in Hebron. (Now the name of Hebron *was* formerly Kirjath Arba.) And they killed Sheshai, Ahiman, and Talmai.

¹¹From there they went against the inhabitants of Debir. (The name of Debir *was* formerly Kirjath Sepher.)

¹²Then Caleb said, "Whoever attacks

Judges

The Continuing Conquest of Canaan

1 :1 Now after the death of Joshua it came to pass that the children of Israel asked the LORD, saying, "Who shall be first to go up for us against the Canaanites to fight against them?"

²And the LORD said, "Judah shall go up. Indeed I have delivered the land into his hand."

³So Judah said to Simeon his brother, "Come up with me to my allotted territory, that we may fight against the Canaanites; and I will likewise go with you to your allotted territory." And Simeon went with him. ⁴Then Judah went up, and the LORD

1:9 ᵃHebrew *Negev,* and so throughout this book

TIME CAPSULE	*1207 to 1200 B.C.*
1207	*Assyrian king Tukulti-Ninurta I assassinated in his own palace*
1203	*After Merenptah's death, Egypt declines into civil wars*
1200	*Mycenaean civilization of Greece is destroyed, possibly by invading Dorians*
1200– 800	*The Dark Age of Greece*
1200– 600	*Iron Age*
1200	*Rise of iron technology (carburization)*

ARAD IN THE INSCRIPTIONS (Judg. 1:16)

The southern region of Judah, a dry wilderness area, was known as "the Negev" (translated "the South" in Judg. 1:16). Arad was a Canaanite town in the Negev, thus the writer of Judges employs the description "in the South near Arad." The site of Arad was a large fortified town during the Early Bronze Age (c. 3000 B.C.) and showed extensive trade connections with Old Kingdom Egypt. This Arad was destroyed about 2700 B.C.

Another Arad emerged later during the Iron Age (c. 1200–600 B.C.), as is known from various inscriptions. Pieces of broken pottery (called by the Greek name *ostraca*) were used as inexpensive writing material, being inscribed with pen and ink. The name "Arad" appears on these pottery fragments or potsherds, as well as being mentioned in the records of Shishak, the Egyptian pharaoh (945–924 B.C.).

Over 200 ostraca have been found at the site of Arad. One inscription mentions a "House of Yahweh," using the personal name of Israel's God. This shrine or temple has in fact been found, containing a number of stone altars.

The inscriptions also list a number of Hebrew names of priestly families. The most prominent name is that of a particular "Eliashib," who held a leadership position. The common name "Eliashib" appears often in the Old Testament (1 Chr. 3:24; 24:12; Ezra 10:6, 24, 27; Neh. 3:1), although none are the same person as the Arad Eliashib.

Pharaoh Shishak claims to have captured Arad during a raid of Palestine in 925 B.C. An inscription on the walls of the temple of Karnak, listing over 150 towns which Shishak captured, includes the citadel of Arad. Archaeological excavations show that Arad was destroyed by fire during Shishak's time.

Kirjath Sepher and takes it, to him I will give my daughter Achsah as wife." [13]And Othniel the son of Kenaz, Caleb's younger brother, took it; so he gave him his daughter Achsah as wife. [14]Now it happened, when she came *to him,* that she urged him[a] to ask her father for a field. And she dismounted from *her* donkey, and Caleb said to her, "What do you wish?" [15]So she said to him, "Give me a blessing; since you have given me land in the South, give me also springs of water."

And Caleb gave her the upper springs and the lower springs.

[16]Now the children of the Kenite, Moses' father-in-law, went up from the City of Palms with the children of Judah into the Wilderness of Judah, which *lies* in the South *near* Arad; and they went and dwelt among the people. [17]And Judah went with his brother Simeon, and they attacked the Canaanites who inhabited Zephath, and utterly destroyed it. So the name of the city was called Hormah. [18]Also Judah took Gaza with its territory, Ashkelon with its territory, and Ekron with its territory. [19]So the LORD was with Judah. And they drove out the mountaineers, but they could not drive out the inhabitants of the lowland, because they had chariots of iron. [20]And they gave Hebron to Caleb, as Moses had said. Then he expelled from there the three sons of Anak. [21]But the children of Benjamin did not drive out the Jebusites who inhabited Jerusalem; so the Jebusites dwell with the children of Benjamin in Jerusalem to this day.

[22]And the house of Joseph also went up against Bethel, and the LORD *was* with them. [23]So the house of Joseph sent men to

---

1:14 [a]Septuagint and Vulgate read *he urged her.*

SCIENCE AND TECHNOLOGY

Chariots were lightweight vehicles used for carrying warriors into battle, or for supporting a bowman or spearman. The iron chariot (Judg. 1:19) possibly had iron reinforcement of some parts. Chariots were useful only on relatively flat terrain. They had wheels about 3 feet in diameter and 6 feet apart.

spy out Bethel. (The name of the city *was* formerly Luz.) 24And when the spies saw a man coming out of the city, they said to him, "Please show us the entrance to the city, and we will show you mercy." 25So he showed them the entrance to the city, and they struck the city with the edge of the sword; but they let the man and all his family go. 26And the man went to the land of the Hittites, built a city, and called its name Luz, which *is* its name to this day.

Incomplete Conquest of the Land

27However, Manasseh did not drive out *the inhabitants of* Beth Shean and its villages, or Taanach and its villages, or the inhabitants of Dor and its villages, or the inhabitants of Ibleam and its villages, or the inhabitants of Megiddo and its villages; for the Canaanites were determined to dwell in that land. 28And it came to pass, when Israel was strong, that they put the Canaanites under tribute, but did not completely drive them out.

29Nor did Ephraim drive out the Canaanites who dwelt in Gezer; so the Canaanites dwelt in Gezer among them.

30Nor did Zebulun drive out the inhabitants of Kitron or the inhabitants of Nahalol; so the Canaanites dwelt among them, and were put under tribute.

31Nor did Asher drive out the inhabitants of Acco or the inhabitants of Sidon, or of Ahlab, Achzib, Helbah, Aphik, or Rehob. 32So the Asherites dwelt among the Canaanites, the inhabitants of the land; for they did not drive them out.

33Nor did Naphtali drive out the inhabitants of Beth Shemesh or the inhabitants of Beth Anath; but they dwelt among the Canaanites, the inhabitants of the land. Nevertheless the inhabitants of Beth Shemesh and Beth Anath were put under tribute to them.

34And the Amorites forced the children of Dan into the mountains, for they would not allow them to come down to the valley; 35and the Amorites were determined to dwell in Mount Heres, in Aijalon, and in Shaalbim;[a] yet when the strength of the house of Joseph became greater, they were put under tribute.

36Now the boundary of the Amorites *was* from the Ascent of Akrabbim, from Sela, and upward.

Israel's Disobedience

2 1Then the Angel of the LORD came up from Gilgal to Bochim, and said: "I led you up from Egypt and brought you to the land of which I swore to your fathers; and I said, 'I will never break My covenant with you. 2And you shall make no covenant with the inhabitants of this land; you shall tear down their altars.' But you have not obeyed My voice. Why have you done this? 3Therefore I also said, 'I will not drive them out before you; but they shall be *thorns* in your side,[a] and their gods shall be a snare to you.'" 4So it was, when the Angel of the LORD spoke these words to all the children of Israel, that the people lifted up their voices and wept.

5Then they called the name of that place Bochim;[a] and they sacrificed there to the LORD. 6And when Joshua had dismissed the people, the children of Israel went each to his own inheritance to possess the land.

Death of Joshua

7So the people served the LORD all the days of Joshua, and all the days of the elders who outlived Joshua, who had seen all the great works of the LORD which He had done for Israel. 8Now Joshua the son of Nun, the servant of the LORD, died *when he was* one hundred and ten years old. 9And they buried him within the border of his inheritance at Timnath Heres, in the mountains of Ephraim, on the north side of Mount Gaash. 10When all that generation had been gathered to their fathers, another generation arose after them who did not know the LORD nor the work which He had done for Israel.

Israel's Unfaithfulness

11Then the children of Israel did evil in the sight of the LORD, and served the Baals; 12and they forsook the LORD God of their fathers, who had brought them out of the land of Egypt; and they followed other gods from *among* the gods of the people who *were* all around them, and they bowed down to them; and they provoked the LORD to anger. 13They forsook the LORD and served Baal and the Ashtoreths.[a] 14And the anger of the LORD was

---

1:35 [a]Spelled *Shaalabbin* in Joshua 19:42
2:3 [a]Septuagint, Targum, and Vulgate read *enemies to you*   2:5 [a]Literally *Weeping*
2:13 [a]Canaanite goddesses

ORGANIZING A PANTHEON OF MANY GODS (Judg. 2:11–13)

When the Israelites "served the Baals" (Judg. 2:11), they were buying into the mythological structure of the universe understood by the local culture. The gods of the religious world of Syria-Palestine were formed into a four-level hierarchy not unlike a small, localized bureaucracy.

The highest authorities of the Canaanite universe were the deities El and Asherah, the parents of all the other gods. They were the actual rulers of the cosmos and the final court of appeal for both gods and humans. As highest rulers, they assigned each of their offspring responsibility for specific tasks in governing the world.

The second level of deities was an especially rowdy group, as the myths recovered from Ugarit demonstrate. These gods were the powers behind the forces of nature, the political fates of cities and empires, and even behind abstractions, such as justice. Very powerful, they ordered the universe, promoted the welfare of their worshipers, and advanced themselves against other deities. Conflicting interests of their divine wills explained for devotees why the world did not always operate as it ought.

A third level of gods served as craftsmen and artisans for the higher deities. As specialists in the professions their expertise was unsurpassed. They might contradict and even argue with higher-level gods when ordered to do things they themselves knew to be folly. While they obeyed orders, they were not averse to mocking their superiors for the inferior knowledge those gods had of the work at hand.

At the bottom level of the divine hierarchy were the messenger deities—the angels. They were the slave labor of the Canaanite heaven. The position of any of the higher deities in the four-level bureaucracy was determined by El and Asherah and could be changed at any time, particularly for misuse of authority.

Israel's temptation to "try out" some of these deities sometimes was too great (Judg. 2:12). Besides Asherah (3:7), they knew of second-level gods and goddesses, such as Baal (3:7) and Anath (3:31). The idol that Hezekiah called Nehushtan (2 Kin. 18:4) represents a healing deity of the third level.

---

hot against Israel. So He delivered them into the hands of plunderers who despoiled them; and He sold them into the hands of their enemies all around, so that they could no longer stand before their enemies. 15Wherever they went out, the hand of the LORD was against them for calamity, as the LORD had said, and as the LORD had sworn to them. And they were greatly distressed.

16Nevertheless, the LORD raised up judges who delivered them out of the hand of those who plundered them. 17Yet they would not listen to their judges, but they played the harlot with other gods, and bowed down to them. They turned quickly from the way in which their fathers walked, in obeying the commandments of the LORD; they did not do so. 18And when the LORD raised up judges for them, the LORD was with the judge and delivered them out of the hand of their enemies all the days of the judge; for the LORD was

moved to pity by their groaning because of those who oppressed them and harassed them. 19And it came to pass, when the judge was dead, that they reverted and behaved more corruptly than their fathers, by following other gods, to serve them and bow down to them. They did not cease from their own doings nor from their stubborn way.

20Then the anger of the LORD was hot against Israel; and He said, "Because this nation has transgressed My covenant which I commanded their fathers, and has not heeded My voice, 21I also will no longer drive out before them any of the nations which Joshua left when he died, 22so that through them I may test Israel, whether they will keep the ways of the LORD, to walk in them as their fathers kept them, or not." 23Therefore the LORD left those nations, without driving them out immediately; nor did He deliver them into the hand of Joshua.

The Nations Remaining in the Land

3 ¹Now these *are* the nations which the LORD left, that He might test Israel by them, *that is,* all who had not known any of the wars in Canaan ²(*this was* only so that the generations of the children of Israel might be taught to know war, at least those who had not formerly known it), ³*namely,* five lords of the Philistines, all the Canaanites, the Sidonians, and the Hivites who dwelt in Mount Lebanon, from Mount Baal Hermon to the entrance of Hamath. ⁴And they were *left, that He might* test Israel by them, to know whether they would obey the commandments of the LORD, which He had commanded their fathers by the hand of Moses.

⁵Thus the children of Israel dwelt among the Canaanites, the Hittites, the Amorites, the Perizzites, the Hivites, and the Jebusites. ⁶And they took their daughters to be their wives, and gave their daughters to their sons; and they served their gods.

3:7 ªName or symbol for Canaanite goddesses

How Long Was the Era of the Judges?

After Joshua's death conditions changed quickly for the Israelite tribes. Their experiences are described in Judg. 2:11—3:6 as a recurring cycle of apostasy, oppression, supplication, and deliverance. The collection of stories in 3:7—16:31 reports the exploits of Israel's judges during 7 cycles of oppression and deliverance. Despite many attempts, scholars have not been able to determine the length of time represented in these stories.

The book provides various numbers for the years of the judges' period. Three types of chronological information indicate the number of years (1) that Israel was oppressed (e.g., Judg. 3:8), (2) that Israel had peace following a deliverance (e.g., Judg. 3:11), and (3) that particular individuals served as judge (e.g., Judg. 10:2). When tabulated, the total of these years is 410, but this figure does not necessarily represent the length of this period. Interpreting the numbers is complicated by the possibility of overlapping time periods and of symbolic numbers.

It was common to list periods chronologically which were either contemporaneous or overlapping. Since most of the judges were confined to particular tribes or regions, it is reasonable to assume considerable overlapping of the periods and events. The report that in one period Israel was oppressed by both Philistia and Ammon (Judg. 10:7) could suggest that Jephthah and Samson may have been living and working at the same time.

Many of the numbers in the Book of Judges may be symbolic, rather than chronological. Twelve judges are mentioned, although a detailed account is given for only six. While there were possibly many more judges than these, the number 12 speaks in symbolic fashion of the whole of an era. The same is true for the 7 cycles of oppression and deliverance, with 7 also depicting a sense of completeness. Also the duration of leadership ascribed to many of the judges is in units or multiples of 40, a number frequently denoting a generation of unspecified length.

An exact, precise dating of the judges' period will remain unknown. No references to contemporary events of this period are available. The figure of 300 years in Judg. 11:26 represents a period from Israel's victory over King Sihon of Heshbon (Num. 21:25, 26) to Jephthah's speech, but is difficult to coordinate with other evidence. All that can be said with certainty is that the period of Israel's judges stretches from the entry into Canaan (around 1406 or 1235 B.C.) until the establishment of the monarchy with Saul (around 1050 or 1020 B.C.).

■ Judges 3:7—21:25

Judges
Othniel

3 :7 So the children of Israel did evil in the sight of the LORD. They forgot the LORD their God, and served the Baals and Asherahs.ª ⁸Therefore the anger of the LORD was hot against Israel, and He sold them into the hand of Cushan-Rishathaim king of Mesopotamia; and the children of Israel served Cushan-Rishathaim eight years. ⁹When the children of Israel cried out to the LORD, the LORD raised up a deliverer for the children of Israel, who delivered them: Othniel the son of Kenaz, Caleb's younger brother. ¹⁰The Spirit of the LORD came upon him, and he judged Israel. He went out to war, and the LORD delivered Cushan-Rishathaim king of Mesopotamia into his hand; and his hand prevailed over Cushan-Rishathaim. ¹¹So the land had rest for forty years. Then Othniel the son of Kenaz died.

ANATH, GODDESS OF WAR (Judg. 3:31)

The judge Shamgar was known as "the son of Anath" (Judg. 3:31). Anath was the name of the Syro-Palestinian goddess of war, and it is not certain whether "Anath" in the judge's name refers to a location, a traditional family name, or the goddess herself. Regardless, it is noteworthy that the Bible, in recording the judge's military victory, has kept the goddess's name unchanged.

Anath is well known from the documents discovered at Ugarit. Daughter of the supreme god El, she was indulged by her father to the point of being spoiled. As a goddess Anath was greedy, self-consumed, ruthless, and violent. In a vivid symbol of the mayhem of war, she is described as crushing soldiers like grapes and draping herself with pieces of their corpses while she is in her own home. When she wanted something, she used violent brute force to attain it, without regard for the morality of the action.

Because of the close relationship of Anath with the storm god Baal, she is referred to either as Baal's sister or spouse. As his partner, Anath rescues him from the predicaments into which he rather stupidly entangled himself. In one case the goddess even killed Mot, the god of death, to reclaim Baal from the netherworld. Clearly dangerous to humans and deities, Anath's loyalty to Baal appears to remain constant.

The ruler of any city or nation considered it of great importance to have Anath's protection as the goddess of war. She is described in the Ugaritic texts as nursing the future king of the city in his youth. This was a way of saying that the heir to the throne was brought up properly to defend the area; that is, to be a warrior. The association of her name with Shamgar's may, in fact, have something to do with his status as such a leader and warrior.

Ehud

12And the children of Israel again did evil in the sight of the LORD. So the LORD strengthened Eglon king of Moab against Israel, because they had done evil in the sight of the LORD. 13Then he gathered to himself the people of Ammon and Amalek, went and defeated Israel, and took possession of the City of Palms. 14So the children of Israel served Eglon king of Moab eighteen years.

15But when the children of Israel cried out to the LORD, the LORD raised up a deliverer for them: Ehud the son of Gera, the Benjamite, a left-handed man. By him the children of Israel sent tribute to Eglon king of Moab. 16Now Ehud made himself a dagger (it was double-edged and a cubit in length) and fastened it under his clothes on his right thigh. 17So he brought the tribute to Eglon king of Moab. (Now Eglon was a very fat man.) 18And when he had finished presenting the tribute, he sent away the people who had carried the tribute. 19But he himself turned back from the stone images that were at Gilgal, and said, "I have a secret message for you, O king."

He said, "Keep silence!" And all who attended him went out from him. 20So Ehud came to him (now he was sitting upstairs in his cool private chamber). Then Ehud said, "I have a message from God for you." So he arose from his seat. 21Then Ehud reached with his left hand, took the dagger from his right thigh, and thrust it into his belly. 22Even the hilt went in after the blade, and the fat closed over the blade, for he did not draw the dagger out of his belly; and his entrails came out. 23Then Ehud went out through the porch and shut the doors of the upper room behind him and locked them.

24When he had gone out, Eglon'sa servants came to look, and to their surprise, the doors of the upper room were locked. So they said, "He is probably attending to his needs in the cool chamber." 25So they waited till they were embarrassed, and still he had not opened the doors of the upper room. Therefore they took the key and opened them. And there was their master, fallen dead on the floor.

26But Ehud had escaped while they delayed, and passed beyond the stone images and escaped to Seirah. 27And it happened, when he arrived, that he blew the trumpet in the mountains of Ephraim, and the chil-

3:24 aLiterally his

THE CYCLES OF THE JUDGES (PART 1)

The history of Israel's judges is told in two parts. An introduction (Judg. 2:11—3:6) describes a recurring cycle of apostasy, oppression, supplication, and deliverance. The numbers given for the years of oppression and deliverance may be symbolic or, if actual, may represent overlapping time periods. Part 1 (Judg. 3:7—10:5) covers seven judges and the king of Shechem.

Events and Judges	Years
Israel serves Cushan-Rishathaim (3:7, 8)	8
Peace follows Othniel's deliverance (3:9–11)	40
Israel serves Eglon (3:12–14)	18
Peace follows Ehud's deliverance (3:15–30)	80
Shamgar delivers Israel from Philistines (3:31)	?
Israel serves Jabin (4:1–3)	20
Peace follows deliverance by Deborah and Barak (4:4—5:31)	40
Israel serves Midian (6:1–6)	7
Peace follows Gideon's deliverance (6:7—8:35)	40
Abimelech, king of Shechem (9:1–57)	3
Tola's career (10:1, 2)	23
Jair's career (10:3–5)	22

dren of Israel went down with him from the mountains; and he led them. ²⁸Then he said to them, "Follow *me,* for the LORD has delivered your enemies the Moabites into your hand." So they went down after him, seized the fords of the Jordan leading to Moab, and did not allow anyone to cross over. ²⁹And at that time they killed about ten thousand men of Moab, all stout men of valor; not a man escaped. ³⁰So Moab was subdued that day under the hand of Israel. And the land had rest for eighty years.

Shamgar

³¹After him was Shamgar the son of Anath, who killed six hundred men of the Philistines with an ox goad; and he also delivered Israel.

Deborah

4 ¹When Ehud was dead, the children of Israel again did evil in the sight of the LORD. ²So the LORD sold them into the hand of Jabin king of Canaan, who reigned in Hazor. The commander of his army *was* Sisera, who dwelt in Harosheth Hagoyim. ³And the children of Israel cried out to the LORD; for Jabin had nine hundred chariots of iron, and for twenty years he had harshly oppressed the children of Israel.

⁴Now Deborah, a prophetess, the wife of Lapidoth, was judging Israel at that time. ⁵And she would sit under the palm tree of Deborah between Ramah and Bethel in the mountains of Ephraim. And the children of Israel came up to her for judgment. ⁶Then she sent and called for Barak the son of Abinoam from Kedesh in Naphtali, and said to him, "Has not the LORD God of Israel commanded, 'Go and deploy *troops* at Mount Tabor; take with you ten thousand men of the sons of Naphtali and of the sons of Zebulun; ⁷and against you I will deploy Sisera, the

SCIENCE AND TECHNOLOGY

The chariot was the main offensive weapon of the armies of that time (Judg. 4:3). It carried a soldier with a bow. As the famous paintings of Tutankhamun illustrate, archers could shoot from a chariot while it was moving at full speed. If they had compound bows, they could shoot beyond the range of ordinary bows.

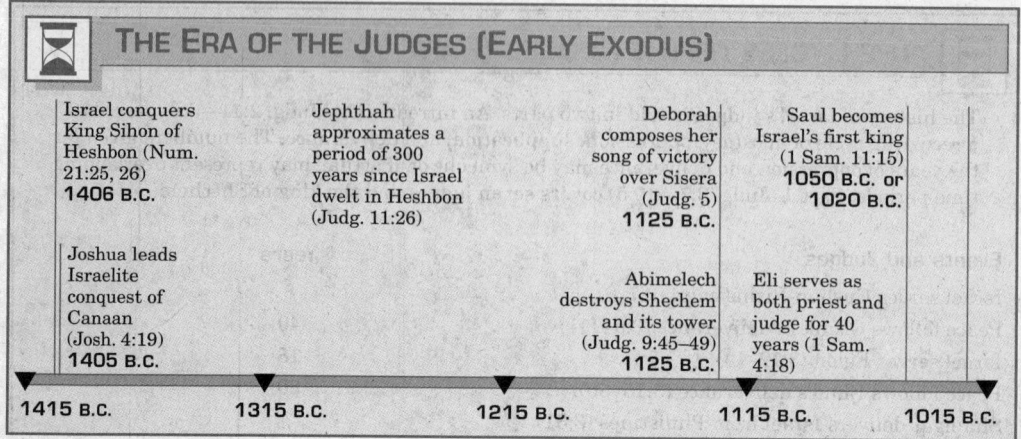

THE ERA OF THE JUDGES (EARLY EXODUS)

Israel conquers King Sihon of Heshbon (Num. 21:25, 26) **1406 B.C.**	Jephthah approximates a period of 300 years since Israel dwelt in Heshbon (Judg. 11:26)	Deborah composes her song of victory over Sisera (Judg. 5) **1125 B.C.**	Saul becomes Israel's first king (1 Sam. 11:15) **1050 B.C.** or **1020 B.C.**
Joshua leads Israelite conquest of Canaan (Josh. 4:19) **1405 B.C.**		Abimelech destroys Shechem and its tower (Judg. 9:45–49) **1125 B.C.**	Eli serves as both priest and judge for 40 years (1 Sam. 4:18)

1415 B.C.	1315 B.C.	1215 B.C.	1115 B.C.	1015 B.C.

commander of Jabin's army, with his chariots and his multitude at the River Kishon; and I will deliver him into your hand'?"

8And Barak said to her, "If you will go with me, then I will go; but if you will not go with me, I will not go!"

9So she said, "I will surely go with you; nevertheless there will be no glory for you in the journey you are taking, for the LORD will sell Sisera into the hand of a woman." Then Deborah arose and went with Barak to Kedesh. 10And Barak called Zebulun and Naphtali to Kedesh; he went up with ten thousand men under his command,ᵃ and Deborah went up with him.

11Now Heber the Kenite, of the children of Hobab the father-in-law of Moses, had separated himself from the Kenites and pitched his tent near the terebinth tree at Zaanaim, which is beside Kedesh.

12And they reported to Sisera that Barak the son of Abinoam had gone up to Mount Tabor. 13So Sisera gathered together all his chariots, nine hundred chariots of iron, and all the people who were with him, from Harosheth Hagoyim to the River Kishon.

14Then Deborah said to Barak, "Up! For this is the day in which the LORD has delivered Sisera into your hand. Has not the LORD gone out before you?" So Barak went down from Mount Tabor with ten thousand men following him. 15And the LORD routed Sisera and all his chariots and all his army with the edge of the sword before Barak; and Sisera alighted from his chariot and fled away on foot. 16But Barak pursued the chariots and the army as far as Harosheth Hagoyim, and all the army of Sisera fell by the edge of the sword; not a man was left.

17However, Sisera had fled away on foot to the tent of Jael, the wife of Heber the Kenite; for there was peace between Jabin king of Hazor and the house of Heber the Kenite. 18And Jael went out to meet Sisera, and said to him, "Turn aside, my lord, turn aside to me; do not fear." And when he had turned aside with her into the tent, she covered him with a blanket.

19Then he said to her, "Please give me a little water to drink, for I am thirsty." So she opened a jug of milk, gave him a drink, and covered him. 20And he said to her, "Stand at the door of the tent, and if any man comes and inquires of you, and says, 'Is there any man here?' you shall say, 'No.'"

21Then Jael, Heber's wife, took a tent

4:10 ᵃLiterally at his feet

DAILY LIFE AND CUSTOMS

Jael treated Sisera like a guest (Judg. 4:18). Her tent and her blanket were symbols of the protection he would enjoy through the laws of hospitality. The Kenites, to whom Jael's husband belonged, however, were a seminomadic tribe which was generally favorable to the Israelites (4:17). In a choice between conflicting loyalties, Jael rejected the relations established with Hazor by her husband, and killed Hazor's general Sisera.

peg and took a hammer in her hand, and went softly to him and drove the peg into his temple, and it went down into the ground; for he was fast asleep and weary. So he died. ²²And then, as Barak pursued Sisera, Jael came out to meet him, and said to him, "Come, I will show you the man whom you seek." And when he went into her *tent,* there lay Sisera, dead with the peg in his temple.

²³So on that day God subdued Jabin king of Canaan in the presence of the children of Israel. ²⁴And the hand of the children of Israel grew stronger and stronger against Jabin king of Canaan, until they had destroyed Jabin king of Canaan.

The Song of Deborah

5 ¹Then Deborah and Barak the son of Abinoam sang on that day, saying:

2 "When leaders lead in Israel,
    When the people willingly offer
      themselves,
    Bless the LORD!

3 "Hear, O kings! Give ear, O princes!
    I, *even* I, will sing to the LORD;
    I will sing praise to the LORD God of
      Israel.

4 "LORD, when You went out from Seir,
    When You marched from the field of
      Edom,
    The earth trembled and the heavens
      poured,
    The clouds also poured water;
5   The mountains gushed before the
      LORD,
    This Sinai, before the LORD God of
      Israel.

6 "In the days of Shamgar, son of Anath,
    In the days of Jael,
    The highways were deserted,
    And the travelers walked along the
      byways.
7   Village life ceased, it ceased in Israel,
    Until I, Deborah, arose,
    Arose a mother in Israel.
8   They chose new gods;
    Then *there was* war in the gates;

    Not a shield or spear was seen among
      forty thousand in Israel.
9   My heart *is* with the rulers of Israel
    Who offered themselves willingly with
      the people.
    Bless the LORD!

10 "Speak, you who ride on white
      donkeys,
    Who sit in judges' attire,
    And who walk along the road.
11 Far from the noise of the archers,
      among the watering places,
    There they shall recount the righteous
      acts of the LORD,
    The righteous acts *for* His villagers in
      Israel;
    Then the people of the LORD shall go
      down to the gates.

12 "Awake, awake, Deborah!
    Awake, awake, sing a song!
    Arise, Barak, and lead your captives
      away,
    O son of Abinoam!

13 "Then the survivors came down, the
      people against the nobles;
    The LORD came down for me against
      the mighty.
14 From Ephraim *were* those whose roots
      were in Amalek.
    After you, Benjamin, with your
      peoples,
    From Machir rulers came down,
    And from Zebulun those who bear the
      recruiter's staff.
15 And the princes of Issachar^a *were* with
      Deborah;
    As Issachar, so *was* Barak
    Sent into the valley under his
      command;^b
    Among the divisions of Reuben
    There were great resolves of heart.
16 Why did you sit among the sheepfolds,
    To hear the pipings for the flocks?
    The divisions of Reuben have great
      searchings of heart.
17 Gilead stayed beyond the Jordan,
    And why did Dan remain on ships?^a
    Asher continued at the seashore,
    And stayed by his inlets.
18 Zebulun *is* a people *who* jeopardized
      their lives to the point of death,
    Naphtali also, on the heights of the
      battlefield.

19 "The kings came *and* fought,
    Then the kings of Canaan fought

5:15 ^aFollowing Septuagint, Syriac, Targum, and Vulgate; Masoretic Text reads *And my princes in Issachar.* ^bLiterally *at his feet*   5:17 ^aOr *at ease*

In Taanach, by the waters of Megiddo;
They took no spoils of silver.
20 They fought from the heavens;
The stars from their courses fought
against Sisera.
21 The torrent of Kishon swept them
away,
That ancient torrent, the torrent of
Kishon.
O my soul, march on in strength!
22 Then the horses' hooves pounded,
The galloping, galloping of his steeds.
23 'Curse Meroz,' said the angel[a] of the
LORD,
'Curse its inhabitants bitterly,
Because they did not come to the help
of the LORD,
To the help of the LORD against the
mighty.'

24 "Most blessed among women is Jael,
The wife of Heber the Kenite;
Blessed is she among women in tents.
25 He asked for water, she gave milk;
She brought out cream in a lordly
bowl.
26 She stretched her hand to the tent
peg,
Her right hand to the workmen's
hammer;
She pounded Sisera, she pierced his
head,
She split and struck through his
temple.
27 At her feet he sank, he fell, he lay
still;
At her feet he sank, he fell;
Where he sank, there he fell dead.

28 "The mother of Sisera looked through
the window,
And cried out through the lattice,
'Why is his chariot so long in coming?
Why tarries the clatter of his
chariots?'
29 Her wisest ladies answered her,
Yes, she answered herself,
30 'Are they not finding and dividing the
spoil:

To every man a girl or two;
For Sisera, plunder of dyed garments,
Plunder of garments embroidered and
dyed,
Two pieces of dyed embroidery for the
neck of the looter?'

31 "Thus let all Your enemies perish,
O LORD!
But let those who love Him be like the
sun
When it comes out in full strength."

So the land had rest for forty years.

Midianites Oppress Israel

6 ¹Then the children of Israel did evil in
the sight of the LORD. So the LORD delivered them into the hand of Midian for
seven years, ²and the hand of Midian prevailed against Israel. Because of the Midianites, the children of Israel made for
themselves the dens, the caves, and the
strongholds which are in the mountains.
³So it was, whenever Israel had sown, Midianites would come up; also Amalekites
and the people of the East would come up
against them. ⁴Then they would encamp
against them and destroy the produce of
the earth as far as Gaza, and leave no sustenance for Israel, neither sheep nor ox nor
donkey. ⁵For they would come up with their
livestock and their tents, coming in as numerous as locusts; both they and their
camels were without number; and they
would enter the land to destroy it. ⁶So Israel was greatly impoverished because of
the Midianites, and the children of Israel
cried out to the LORD.

⁷And it came to pass, when the children of Israel cried out to the LORD because
of the Midianites, ⁸that the LORD sent a
prophet to the children of Israel, who said
to them, "Thus says the LORD God of Israel:
'I brought you up from Egypt and brought
you out of the house of bondage; ⁹and I delivered you out of the hand of the Egyp-

5:23 ᵃOr Angel

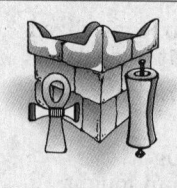

BELIEFS AND IDEAS

*Many people considered the stars to rule human affairs, either directly or as signs of
divine powers. When the stars had turned against Sisera (Judg. 5:20), it meant that
God ruled over all other powers, however they may be conceived. It seems also that God
stirred up the Kishon River against Sisera's chariots.*

tians and out of the hand of all who oppressed you, and drove them out before you and gave you their land. [10]Also I said to you, "I *am* the LORD your God; do not fear the gods of the Amorites, in whose land you dwell." But you have not obeyed My voice.' "

Gideon

[11]Now the Angel of the LORD came and sat under the terebinth tree which *was* in Ophrah, which *belonged* to Joash the Abiezrite, while his son Gideon threshed wheat in the winepress, in order to hide *it* from the Midianites. [12]And the Angel of the LORD appeared to him, and said to him, "The LORD *is* with you, you mighty man of valor!"

[13]Gideon said to Him, "O my lord,[a] if the LORD is with us, why then has all this happened to us? And where *are* all His miracles which our fathers told us about, saying, 'Did not the LORD bring us up from Egypt?' But now the LORD has forsaken us and delivered us into the hands of the Midianites."

[14]Then the LORD turned to him and said, "Go in this might of yours, and you shall save Israel from the hand of the Midianites. Have I not sent you?"

[15]So he said to Him, "O my Lord,[a] how can I save Israel? Indeed my clan *is* the weakest in Manasseh, and I *am* the least in my father's house."

[16]And the LORD said to him, "Surely I will be with you, and you shall defeat the Midianites as one man."

[17]Then he said to Him, "If now I have found favor in Your sight, then show me a sign that it is You who talk with me. [18]Do not depart from here, I pray, until I come to You and bring out my offering and set *it* before You."

And He said, "I will wait until you come back."

[19]So Gideon went in and prepared a young goat, and unleavened bread from an ephah of flour. The meat he put in a basket, and he put the broth in a pot; and he brought *them* out to Him under the terebinth tree and presented *them*. [20]The Angel of God said to him, "Take the meat and the unleavened bread and lay *them* on this

rock, and pour out the broth." And he did so.

[21]Then the Angel of the LORD put out the end of the staff that *was* in His hand, and touched the meat and the unleavened bread; and fire rose out of the rock and consumed the meat and the unleavened bread. And the Angel of the LORD departed out of his sight.

[22]Now Gideon perceived that He *was* the Angel of the LORD. So Gideon said, "Alas, O Lord GOD! For I have seen the Angel of the LORD face to face."

[23]Then the LORD said to him, "Peace *be* with you; do not fear, you shall not die." [24]So Gideon built an altar there to the LORD, and called it The-LORD-*Is*-Peace.[a] To this day it *is* still in Ophrah of the Abiezrites.

[25]Now it came to pass the same night that the LORD said to him, "Take your father's young bull, the second bull of seven years old, and tear down the altar of Baal that your father has, and cut down the wooden image[a] that *is* beside it; [26]and build an altar to the LORD your God on top of this rock in the proper arrangement, and take

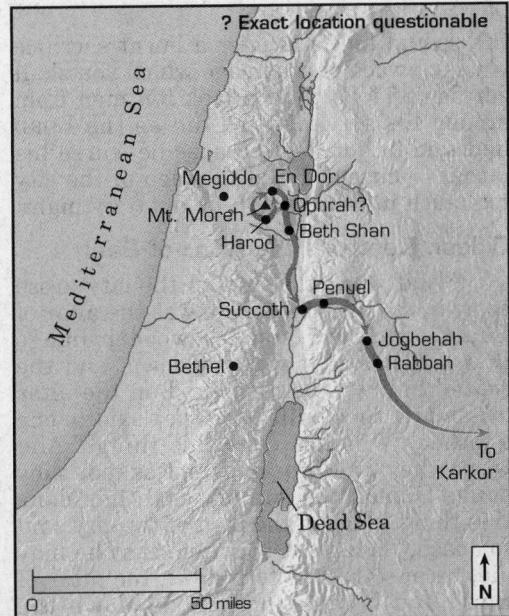

Gideon's Campaign

The Angel of the Lord appeared to Gideon in Ophrah, instructing him to rally the Israelites against the Midianites. With only 300 men Gideon left Harod and descended upon the sleeping armies just north of Mt. Moreh. He pursued the Midianites through Succoth and Penuel, finally capturing the Midianite kings in Karkor.

6:13 [a]Hebrew *adoni*, used of man   6:15 [a]Hebrew *Adonai*, used of God   6:24 [a]Hebrew *YHWH Shalom*   6:25 [a]Hebrew *Asherah*, a Canaanite goddess

BAAL, GOD OF STORMS (Judg. 6:25–32)

Of all the deities of Canaan, the Israelites were most drawn to Baal. Gideon's family had been devotees of the god (Judg. 6:25). So, when Gideon turned to worship God as the only God, he broke with the family tradition.

In Hebrew, "Baal" is the title "lord." This title was given to the storm god Hadad, who is widely known from Syria, Mesopotamia, and Egypt through inscriptions dating from the mid-3rd millennium to the last century B.C. Usually Hadad was simply called "Baal" and was understood to be the god of storms.

Since Baal brought rain, he was also credited with bringing the annual crops which were dependent on the rain. The gifts of rain and crops were so important that there were many sites devoted to the worship of Baal, each using the local version of the god's name.

In the Ugaritic myths Baal is portrayed as a mighty, lustful, and ambitious deity, but also as a god with decidedly more muscles than brains. His worshipers clearly enjoyed a good story about Baal charging into a situation through sheer bravado only to discover too late that it was a really dumb thing to do. Baal relied primarily on his sister Anath to rescue him from these difficulties of his own making, though others, such as Kothar-and-Hasis (a skilled artisan deity), Shapshu (the sun goddess), Asherah and El (rulers of the pantheon), helped him as well.

The seriousness with which some Israelites took their devotion to Baal is seen in their desire to kill Gideon for tearing down Baal's altar (Judg. 6:28–30). Joash, however, defends his son Gideon by making the deciding point: However entertaining the stories about Baal may be, if he is a god, he should be able to plead for himself. Thus Gideon is given the nickname "Jerubbaal," meaning "let Baal plead" (6:31, 32).

---

the second bull and offer a burnt sacrifice with the wood of the image which you shall cut down." 27So Gideon took ten men from among his servants and did as the LORD had said to him. But because he feared his father's household and the men of the city too much to do *it* by day, he did *it* by night.

Gideon Destroys the Altar of Baal

28And when the men of the city arose early in the morning, there was the altar of Baal, torn down; and the wooden image that *was* beside it was cut down, and the second bull was being offered on the altar *which had been* built. 29So they said to one another, "Who has done this thing?" And when they had inquired and asked, they said, "Gideon the son of Joash has done this thing." 30Then the men of the city said to Joash, "Bring out your son, that he may die, because he has torn down the altar of Baal, and because he has cut down the wooden image that *was* beside it."

31But Joash said to all who stood against him, "Would you plead for Baal? Would you save him? Let the one who would plead for him be put to death by morning! If he *is* a god, let him plead for himself, because his altar has been torn

down!" 32Therefore on that day he called him Jerubbaal,[a] saying, "Let Baal plead against him, because he has torn down his altar."

33Then all the Midianites and Amalekites, the people of the East, gathered together; and they crossed over and encamped in the Valley of Jezreel. 34But the Spirit of the LORD came upon Gideon; then he blew the trumpet, and the Abiezrites gathered behind him. 35And he sent messengers throughout all Manasseh, who also gathered behind him. He also sent messengers to Asher, Zebulun, and Naphtali; and they came up to meet them.

The Sign of the Fleece

36So Gideon said to God, "If You will save Israel by my hand as You have said— 37look, I shall put a fleece of wool on the threshing floor; if there is dew on the fleece only, and *it is* dry on all the ground, then I shall know that You will save Israel by my hand, as You have said." 38And it was so. When he rose early the next morning and squeezed the fleece together, he wrung the dew out of the fleece, a bowlful of water.

6:32 aLiterally *Let Baal Plead*

³⁹Then Gideon said to God, "Do not be angry with me, but let me speak just once more: Let me test, I pray, just once more with the fleece; let it now be dry only on the fleece, but on all the ground let there be dew." ⁴⁰And God did so that night. It was dry on the fleece only, but there was dew on all the ground.

Gideon's Valiant Three Hundred

7 ¹Then Jerubbaal (that *is,* Gideon) and all the people who *were* with him rose early and encamped beside the well of Harod, so that the camp of the Midianites was on the north side of them by the hill of Moreh in the valley.

²And the LORD said to Gideon, "The people who *are* with you *are* too many for Me to give the Midianites into their hands, lest Israel claim glory for itself against Me, saying, 'My own hand has saved me.' ³Now therefore, proclaim in the hearing of the people, saying, 'Whoever *is* fearful and afraid, let him turn and depart at once from Mount Gilead.' " And twenty-two thousand of the people returned, and ten thousand remained.

⁴But the LORD said to Gideon, "The people *are* still *too* many; bring them down to the water, and I will test them for you there. Then it will be, *that* of whom I say to you, 'This one shall go with you,' the same shall go with you; and of whomever I say to you, 'This one shall not go with you,' the same shall not go." ⁵So he brought the people down to the water. And the LORD said to Gideon, "Everyone who laps from the water with his tongue, as a dog laps, you shall set apart by himself; likewise everyone who gets down on his knees to drink." ⁶And the number of those who lapped, *putting* their hand to their mouth, was three hundred men; but all the rest of the people got down on their knees to drink water. ⁷Then the LORD said to Gideon, "By the three hundred men who lapped I will save you, and deliver the Midianites into your hand. Let all the *other* people go, every man to his place." ⁸So the people took provisions and their trumpets in their hands. And he sent away all *the rest of* Israel, every man to his tent, and retained those three hundred men. Now the camp of Midian was below him in the valley.

⁹It happened on the same night that the LORD said to him, "Arise, go down against the camp, for I have delivered it into your hand. ¹⁰But if you are afraid to go down, go down to the camp with Purah your servant, ¹¹and you shall hear what they say; and afterward your hands shall be strengthened to go down against the camp." Then he went down with Purah his servant to the outpost of the armed men who *were* in the camp. ¹²Now the Midianites and Amalekites, all the people of the East, were lying in the valley as numerous as locusts; and their camels *were* without number, as the sand by the seashore in multitude.

¹³And when Gideon had come, there was a man telling a dream to his companion. He said, "I have had a dream: *To my surprise,* a loaf of barley bread tumbled into the camp of Midian; it came to a tent and struck it so that it fell and overturned, and the tent collapsed."

¹⁴Then his companion answered and said, "This *is* nothing else but the sword of Gideon the son of Joash, a man of Israel! Into his hand God has delivered Midian and the whole camp."

¹⁵And so it was, when Gideon heard the telling of the dream and its interpretation, that he worshiped. He returned to the camp of Israel, and said, "Arise, for the LORD has delivered the camp of Midian into your hand." ¹⁶Then he divided the three hundred men *into* three companies, and he put a trumpet into every man's hand, with empty pitchers, and torches inside the pitchers. ¹⁷And he said to them, "Look at me and do likewise; watch, and when I come to the edge of the camp you shall do as I do: ¹⁸When I blow the trumpet, I and all who *are* with me, then you also blow the trumpets on every side of the whole camp, and say, '*The sword of* the LORD and of Gideon!' "

¹⁹So Gideon and the hundred men who *were* with him came to the outpost of the camp at the beginning of the middle watch, just as they had posted the watch; and they blew the trumpets and broke the pitchers that *were* in their hands. ²⁰Then the three companies blew the trumpets and broke the pitchers—they held the torches in their left hands and the trumpets in their right hands for blowing—and they cried, "The sword of the LORD and of Gideon!" ²¹And every man stood in his place all around the camp; and the whole army ran and cried out and fled. ²²When the three hundred blew the trumpets, the LORD set every man's sword against his companion throughout the whole camp; and the

army fled to Beth Acacia,[a] toward Zererah, as far as the border of Abel Meholah, by Tabbath.

23And the men of Israel gathered together from Naphtali, Asher, and all Manasseh, and pursued the Midianites. 24Then Gideon sent messengers throughout all the mountains of Ephraim, saying, "Come down against the Midianites, and seize from them the watering places as far as Beth Barah and the Jordan." Then all the men of Ephraim gathered together and seized the watering places as far as Beth Barah and the Jordan. 25And they captured two princes of the Midianites, Oreb and Zeeb. They killed Oreb at the rock of Oreb, and Zeeb they killed at the winepress of Zeeb. They pursued Midian and brought the heads of Oreb and Zeeb to Gideon on the other side of the Jordan.

Gideon Subdues the Midianites

8 1Now the men of Ephraim said to him, "Why have you done this to us by not calling us when you went to fight with the Midianites?" And they reprimanded him sharply.

2So he said to them, "What have I done now in comparison with you? Is not the gleaning of the grapes of Ephraim better than the vintage of Abiezer? 3God has delivered into your hands the princes of Midian, Oreb and Zeeb. And what was I able to do in comparison with you?" Then their anger toward him subsided when he said that.

4When Gideon came to the Jordan, he and the three hundred men who were with him crossed over, exhausted but still in pursuit. 5Then he said to the men of Succoth, "Please give loaves of bread to the people who follow me, for they are exhausted, and I am pursuing Zebah and Zalmunna, kings of Midian."

6And the leaders of Succoth said, "Are the hands of Zebah and Zalmunna now in your hand, that we should give bread to your army?"

7So Gideon said, "For this cause, when the LORD has delivered Zebah and Zalmunna into my hand, then I will tear your flesh with the thorns of the wilderness and with briers!" 8Then he went up from there to Penuel and spoke to them in the same way. And the men of Penuel answered him as the men of Succoth had answered. 9So he also spoke to the men of Penuel, saying, "When I come back in peace, I will tear down this tower!"

10Now Zebah and Zalmunna were at Karkor, and their armies with them, about fifteen thousand, all who were left of all the army of the people of the East; for one hundred and twenty thousand men who drew the sword had fallen. 11Then Gideon went up by the road of those who dwell in tents on the east of Nobah and Jogbehah; and he attacked the army while the camp felt secure. 12When Zebah and Zalmunna fled, he pursued them; and he took the two kings of Midian, Zebah and Zalmunna, and routed the whole army.

13Then Gideon the son of Joash returned from battle, from the Ascent of Heres. 14And he caught a young man of the men of Succoth and interrogated him; and he wrote down for him the leaders of Succoth and its elders, seventy-seven men. 15Then he came to the men of Succoth and said, "Here are Zebah and Zalmunna, about whom you ridiculed me, saying, 'Are the hands of Zebah and Zalmunna now in your hand, that we should give bread to your weary men?' " 16And he took the elders of the city, and thorns of the wilderness and briers, and with them he taught the men of Succoth. 17Then he tore down the tower of Penuel and killed the men of the city.

18And he said to Zebah and Zalmunna, "What kind of men were they whom you killed at Tabor?"

So they answered, "As you are, so were they; each one resembled the son of a king."

7:22 [a]Hebrew Beth Shittah

CULTURE AND SOCIETY

Fighting was largely hand to hand in ancient warfare, and a conventional part of battle was the warrior's boast (Judg. 8:9). Boasts and taunts of heroes are common in the Iliad, from about 850 B.C. In his Commentaries, Julius Caesar recorded several heroic sayings that affected the course of battle.

TOWERS OF SAFETY (Judg. 8:9, 17)

Towers were a standard feature of ancient cities. Often a city wall would be punctuated with regularly placed towers. Such towers were widened spaces in the wall where a larger number of defenders could withstand attackers attempting to gain entry. Towers allowed city residents to watch the other parts of the walls from a slightly forward position. They also provided a somewhat flanking position against attackers trying to scale or undermine the walls.

Towers were also built on hilltops. These served as watchtowers to detect approaching enemies or as signaling places for communication between larger communities.

Families also constructed towers for personal safety and storage of farming implements. Such towers have been found with the full range of household artifacts, symbolizing their domestic usefulness.

Citizens of smaller communities could not afford to build strong walls to protect their villages. They sometimes built one strong, tall building, a tower, to which they could flee in times of distress. Especially for smaller communities, the time investment for building towers was great, which made a tower a valuable prize of the citizenry.

Gideon was so distressed at the lack of support his effort received from the people of Penuel that he punished them by tearing down their tower (Judg. 8:8, 9, 17). They were left vulnerable and stripped of what must have been an object of community pride. Such a punishment would have been long remembered.

19Then he said, "They *were* my brothers, the sons of my mother. *As* the LORD lives, if you had let them live, I would not kill you." 20And he said to Jether his firstborn, "Rise, kill them!" But the youth would not draw his sword; for he *was* afraid, because he *was* still a youth.

21So Zebah and Zalmunna said, "Rise yourself, and kill us; for as a man *is, so is* his strength." So Gideon arose and killed Zebah and Zalmunna, and took the crescent ornaments that *were* on their camels' necks.

Gideon's Ephod

22Then the men of Israel said to Gideon, "Rule over us, both you and your son, and your grandson also; for you have delivered us from the hand of Midian."

23But Gideon said to them, "I will not rule over you, nor shall my son rule over you; the LORD shall rule over you." 24Then Gideon said to them, "I would like to make a request of you, that each of you would give me the earrings from his plunder." For they had golden earrings, because they *were* Ishmaelites.

25So they answered, "We will gladly give *them*." And they spread out a garment, and each man threw into it the earrings from his plunder. 26Now the weight of the gold earrings that he requested was one thousand seven hundred *shekels* of gold, besides the crescent ornaments, pendants,

and purple robes which *were* on the kings of Midian, and besides the chains that *were* around their camels' necks. 27Then Gideon made it into an ephod and set it up in his city, Ophrah. And all Israel played the harlot with it there. It became a snare to Gideon and to his house.

28Thus Midian was subdued before the children of Israel, so that they lifted their heads no more. And the country was quiet for forty years in the days of Gideon.

Death of Gideon

29Then Jerubbaal the son of Joash went and dwelt in his own house. 30Gideon had seventy sons who were his own offspring, for he had many wives. 31And his concubine who *was* in Shechem also bore him a son, whose name he called Abimelech. 32Now Gideon the son of Joash died at a good old age, and was buried in the tomb of Joash his father, in Ophrah of the Abiezrites.

33So it was, as soon as Gideon was dead, that the children of Israel again played the harlot with the Baals, and made Baal-Berith their god. 34Thus the children of Israel did not remember the LORD their God, who had delivered them from the hands of all their enemies on every side; 35nor did they show kindness to the house of Jerubbaal (Gideon) in accordance with the good he had done for Israel.

Abimelech's Conspiracy

9 ¹Then Abimelech the son of Jerubbaal went to Shechem, to his mother's brothers, and spoke with them and with all the family of the house of his mother's father, saying, ²"Please speak in the hearing of all the men of Shechem: 'Which is better for you, that all seventy of the sons of Jerubbaal reign over you, or that one reign over you?' Remember that I *am* your own flesh and bone."

³And his mother's brothers spoke all these words concerning him in the hearing of all the men of Shechem; and their heart was inclined to follow Abimelech, for they said, "He is our brother." ⁴So they gave him seventy *shekels* of silver from the temple of Baal-Berith, with which Abimelech hired worthless and reckless men; and they followed him. ⁵Then he went to his father's house at Ophrah and killed his brothers, the seventy sons of Jerubbaal, on one stone. But Jotham the youngest son of Jerubbaal was left, because he hid himself. ⁶And all the men of Shechem gathered together, all of Beth Millo, and they went and made Abimelech king beside the terebinth tree at the pillar that *was* in Shechem.

The Parable of the Trees

⁷Now when they told Jotham, he went and stood on top of Mount Gerizim, and lifted his voice and cried out. And he said to them:

"Listen to me, you men of Shechem,
That God may listen to you!

8 "The trees once went forth to anoint a
     king over them.
    And they said to the olive tree,
    'Reign over us!'
9 But the olive tree said to them,
    'Should I cease giving my oil,
     With which they honor God and men,
     And go to sway over trees?'

10 "Then the trees said to the fig tree,
    'You come *and* reign over us!'
11 But the fig tree said to them,
    'Should I cease my sweetness and my
      good fruit,
     And go to sway over trees?'

12 "Then the trees said to the vine,
    'You come *and* reign over us!'
13 But the vine said to them,

'Should I cease my new wine,
 Which cheers *both* God and men,
 And go to sway over trees?'

14 "Then all the trees said to the bramble,
    'You come *and* reign over us!'
15 And the bramble said to the trees,
    'If in truth you anoint me as king over
      you,
     Then come *and* take shelter in my
       shade;
     But if not, let fire come out of the
       bramble
     And devour the cedars of Lebanon!'

¹⁶"Now therefore, if you have acted in truth and sincerity in making Abimelech king, and if you have dealt well with Jerubbaal and his house, and have done to him as he deserves— ¹⁷for my father fought for you, risked his life, and delivered you out of the hand of Midian; ¹⁸but you have risen up against my father's house this day, and killed his seventy sons on one stone, and made Abimelech, the son of his female servant, king over the men of Shechem, because he is your brother— ¹⁹if then you have acted in truth and sincerity with Jerubbaal and with his house this day, *then* rejoice in Abimelech, and let him also rejoice in you. ²⁰But if not, let fire come from Abimelech and devour the men of Shechem and Beth Millo; and let fire come from the men of Shechem and from Beth Millo and devour Abimelech!" ²¹And Jotham ran away and fled; and he went to Beer and dwelt there, for fear of Abimelech his brother.

Downfall of Abimelech

²²After Abimelech had reigned over Israel three years, ²³God sent a spirit of ill will between Abimelech and the men of Shechem; and the men of Shechem dealt treacherously with Abimelech, ²⁴that the crime *done* to the seventy sons of Jerubbaal might be settled and their blood be laid on Abimelech their brother, who killed them, and on the men of Shechem, who aided him in the killing of his brothers. ²⁵And the men of Shechem set men in ambush against him on the tops of the mountains, and they robbed all who passed by them along that way; and it was told Abimelech.

²⁶Now Gaal the son of Ebed came with his brothers and went over to Shechem; and the men of Shechem put their confi-

SHECHEM IN THE AMARNA LETTERS (Judg. 9:6–31)

Nearly 400 cuneiform tablets (mostly letters) were found in Egypt at Tell el-Amarna (ancient Akhetaten) in the "office-house of the Pharaoh." These texts, called the Amarna letters, cover about a 30-year period (c. 1360–1333 B.C.) during the reigns of pharaohs Amenhotep III and Akhenaten. Most of the letters are written in Accadian, an East Semitic tongue that was the international language during this period.

Descriptions of Canaan in the Amarna letters fit well with the biblical portrayal. The land was politically decentralized, divided into separate, politically organized communities settled around larger cities and surrounding villages. The most prominent of these city-states were Gezer, Shechem, and Hazor. Some sites named in the Bible for this period, such as Hebron, Jericho, and Ai, are not mentioned in the Amarna letters. Jerusalem, however, is depicted as a modest city, and relatively unimportant.

The city of Shechem which is described for Abimelech's time (Judg. 9) bears similarity to the Canaanite town described in the Amarna letters. The Shechem of the Amarna letters has city lords and a mayor. Similarly, the city lords of Judg. 9, called the "men of Shechem," exercise the power to make Abimelech king (9:6), then later challenge his rule (9:23). The mayor who administered Shechem's affairs on behalf of King Abimelech was the city magistrate Zebul (9:30, 31).

The Amarna letters provide important information about the social and political world of Palestine during the era of Israel's judges. Often mentioned are the Habiru, roving bands of mercenaries, who are named in the Amarna letters as employed by Shechem. Similarly, a band of Habiru hired by the "men of Shechem" in Judg. 9 are represented as "Gaal and his brothers" (9:26, 41).

dence in him. ²⁷So they went out into the fields, and gathered *grapes* from their vineyards and trod *them,* and made merry. And they went into the house of their god, and ate and drank, and cursed Abimelech. ²⁸Then Gaal the son of Ebed said, "Who *is* Abimelech, and who *is* Shechem, that we should serve him? *Is he* not the son of Jerubbaal, and *is not* Zebul his officer? Serve the men of Hamor the father of Shechem; but why should we serve him? ²⁹If only this people were under my authority!ᵃ Then I would remove Abimelech." So heᵇ said to Abimelech, "Increase your army and come out!"

³⁰When Zebul, the ruler of the city, heard the words of Gaal the son of Ebed, his anger was aroused. ³¹And he sent messengers to Abimelech secretly, saying, "Take note! Gaal the son of Ebed and his brothers have come to Shechem; and here they are, fortifying the city against you. ³²Now therefore, get up by night, you and the people who *are* with you, and lie in wait in the field. ³³And it shall be, as soon

as the sun is up in the morning, *that* you shall rise early and rush upon the city; and *when* he and the people who are with him come out against you, you may then do to them as you find opportunity."

³⁴So Abimelech and all the people who *were* with him rose by night, and lay in wait against Shechem in four companies. ³⁵When Gaal the son of Ebed went out and stood in the entrance to the city gate, Abimelech and the people who *were* with him rose from lying in wait. ³⁶And when Gaal saw the people, he said to Zebul, "Look, people are coming down from the tops of the mountains!"

But Zebul said to him, "You see the shadows of the mountains as *if they were* men."

³⁷So Gaal spoke again and said, "See, people are coming down from the center of the land, and another company is coming from the Diviners'ᵃ Terebinth Tree."

³⁸Then Zebul said to him, "Where indeed *is* your mouth now, with which you said, 'Who is Abimelech, that we should serve him?' *Are* not these the people whom you despised? Go out, if you will, and fight with them now."

³⁹So Gaal went out, leading the men of

9:29 ᵃLiterally *hand* ᵇFollowing Masoretic Text and Targum; Dead Sea Scrolls read *they;* Septuagint reads *I.*
9:37 ᵃHebrew *Meonenim*

THE OLD-TIME BREAD MACHINE (Judg. 9:53)

Before flour was available in stores, individuals produced their own flour. After harvest, the grain was gathered in specially prepared areas for threshing. In this process the seed heads were broken from the stocks. Then the seeds were thrown into the air to allow the remaining bits of stock, which were lighter, to blow away.

The milling process, the final step, was accomplished by grinding the grain between two basalt stones. The bottom millstone most often had an outside edge to keep the flour from falling to the ground. The most common shapes for the "upper millstone" (Judg. 9:53) were either round or loaf-shaped.

Pairs of round millstones were custom fitted to each other. Both stones had a center hole and a protruding "collar" around the hole to keep the millstones aligned. The upper millstone also had one hole drilled on its outer edge. After the grain was placed between the two millstones, a small stick was inserted in the hole of the upper millstone and was used to slowly turn the upper millstone on the lower millstone, crushing the grain in the process.

Loaf-shaped upper millstones, with rounded tops and flat bottoms, were less complex in design but more effective in use. The grain was placed on the flat lower millstone, then, using two hands, the upper millstone was pushed back and forth crushing the grain.

Small basalt bowls and pestles, not unlike those used by pharmacists, were also used for grinding small amounts of grain. Though producing less flour than millstones, they were also less tiring to use, when only small amounts of flour were needed.

Millstones were part of everyday life for people of Old Testament times. Archaeologists find many samples of millstones wherever they dig. Judging from the many broken pieces found, millstones were easily broken and frequently discarded.

Any upper millstone weighed enough to produce a serious injury, if not death, when dropped from a high place. In the case of Abimelech (Judg. 9:53, 54) that is exactly what happened. He died because a household appliance was dropped on his head.

Shechem, and fought with Abimelech. 40And Abimelech chased him, and he fled from him; and many fell wounded, to the *very* entrance of the gate. 41Then Abimelech dwelt at Arumah, and Zebul drove out Gaal and his brothers, so that they would not dwell in Shechem.

42And it came about on the next day that the people went out into the field, and they told Abimelech. 43So he took his people, divided them into three companies, and lay in wait in the field. And he looked, and there were the people, coming out of the city; and he rose against them and attacked them. 44Then Abimelech and the company that *was* with him rushed forward and stood at the entrance of the gate of the city; and the *other* two companies rushed upon all who *were* in the fields and killed them. 45So Abimelech fought against the city all that day; he took the city and killed the people who *were* in it; and he demolished the city and sowed it with salt.

46Now when all the men of the tower of Shechem had heard *that*, they entered the stronghold of the temple of the god Berith.

47And it was told Abimelech that all the men of the tower of Shechem were gathered together. 48Then Abimelech went up to Mount Zalmon, he and all the people who *were* with him. And Abimelech took an ax in his hand and cut down a bough from the trees, and took it and laid *it* on his shoulder; then he said to the people who were with him, "What you have seen me do, make haste *and* do as I *have done*." 49So each of the people likewise cut down his own bough and followed Abimelech, put *them* against the stronghold, and set the stronghold on fire above them, so that all the people of the tower of Shechem died, about a thousand men and women.

50Then Abimelech went to Thebez, and he encamped against Thebez and took it. 51But there was a strong tower in the city, and all the men and women—all the people of the city—fled there and shut themselves in; then they went up to the top of the tower. 52So Abimelech came as far as the tower and fought against it; and he drew near the door of the tower to burn it with fire. 53But a certain woman dropped an up-

WORSHIPING YOUR NEIGHBORS' GODS (Judg. 10:6–16)

In the laws of Deuteronomy the Israelites were forbidden to worship the gods of the neighboring peoples (Deut. 6:14, 15). Yet as they settled in the new land, they took up the worship of the local deities, such as "the Baals and the Ashtoreths" (Judg. 10:6). The singular names "Baal" and "Ashtoreth" referred to widely revered deities. However, the plural "Baals" would seem to point generally to many various local male deities. Similarly, the plural "Ashtoreths" would signify all the local goddesses.

The popular belief of the ancient Near East was that particular deities owned particular sections of land. When people moved from one area to another, they were expected to worship the gods of their new area. They had to respect the local deity in order to be blessed by that deity.

By worshiping the Baals and Ashtoreths of Canaan, the Israelites were following the normal religious traditions of their day. They would have learned from the indigenous population that these gods were the owners of this land, and needed to be worshiped in order to prosper there. Thus the culture of the time made it difficult for many Israelites to ignore the gods of their new locality.

The Baals and Ashtoreths are only two examples of Israel turning away from God to the local deities. They are reported to have followed after gods from many areas, including Syria, Sidon, Moab, Ammon, and Philistia (Judg. 10:6). When eventually they cried, "we have . . . forsaken our God" (10:10), possibly they realized that they were His people no matter where they existed, and their obedience was to be toward Him alone. They must "put away the foreign gods" (10:16).

---

per millstone on Abimelech's head and crushed his skull. ⁵⁴Then he called quickly to the young man, his armorbearer, and said to him, "Draw your sword and kill me, lest men say of me, 'A woman killed him.'" So his young man thrust him through, and he died. ⁵⁵And when the men of Israel saw that Abimelech was dead, they departed, every man to his place.

⁵⁶Thus God repaid the wickedness of Abimelech, which he had done to his father by killing his seventy brothers. ⁵⁷And all the evil of the men of Shechem God returned on their own heads, and on them came the curse of Jotham the son of Jerubbaal.

Tola

10 ¹After Abimelech there arose to save Israel Tola the son of Puah, the son of Dodo, a man of Issachar; and he dwelt in Shamir in the mountains of Ephraim. ²He judged Israel twenty-three years; and he died and was buried in Shamir.

Jair

³After him arose Jair, a Gileadite; and he judged Israel twenty-two years. ⁴Now he had thirty sons who rode on thirty donkeys; they also had thirty towns, which are called "Havoth Jair"[a] to this day, which *are* in the land of Gilead. ⁵And Jair died and was buried in Camon.

Israel Oppressed Again

⁶Then the children of Israel again did evil in the sight of the LORD, and served the Baals and the Ashtoreths, the gods of Syria, the gods of Sidon, the gods of Moab, the gods of the people of Ammon, and the gods of the Philistines; and they forsook the LORD and did not serve Him. ⁷So the anger of the LORD was hot against Israel; and He sold them into the hands of the Philistines and into the hands of the people of Ammon. ⁸From that year they harassed and oppressed the children of Israel for eighteen years—all the children of Israel who *were* on the other side of the Jordan in the land of the Amorites, in Gilead. ⁹Moreover the people of Ammon crossed over the Jordan to fight against Judah also, against Benjamin, and against the house of Ephraim, so that Israel was severely distressed.

¹⁰And the children of Israel cried out to the LORD, saying, "We have sinned against You, because we have both forsaken our God and served the Baals!"

10:4 ^aLiterally *Towns of Jair* (compare Numbers 32:41 and Deuteronomy 3:14)

[11]So the LORD said to the children of Israel, "*Did I* not *deliver you* from the Egyptians and from the Amorites and from the people of Ammon and from the Philistines? [12]Also the Sidonians and Amalekites and Maonites[a] oppressed you; and you cried out to Me, and I delivered you from their hand. [13]Yet you have forsaken Me and served other gods. Therefore I will deliver you no more. [14]Go and cry out to the gods which you have chosen; let them deliver you in your time of distress."

[15]And the children of Israel said to the LORD, "We have sinned! Do to us whatever seems best to You; only deliver us this day, we pray." [16]So they put away the foreign gods from among them and served the LORD. And His soul could no longer endure the misery of Israel.

[17]Then the people of Ammon gathered together and encamped in Gilead. And the children of Israel assembled together and encamped in Mizpah. [18]And the people, the leaders of Gilead, said to one another, "Who *is* the man who will begin the fight against the people of Ammon? He shall be head over all the inhabitants of Gilead."

Jephthah

11 [1]Now Jephthah the Gileadite was a mighty man of valor, but he *was* the son of a harlot; and Gilead begot Jephthah. [2]Gilead's wife bore sons; and when his wife's sons grew up, they drove Jephthah out, and said to him, "You shall have no inheritance in our father's house, for you *are* the son of another woman." [3]Then Jephthah fled from his brothers and dwelt in the land of Tob; and worthless men banded together with Jephthah and went out *raiding* with him.

[4]It came to pass after a time that the people of Ammon made war against Israel.

[5]And so it was, when the people of Ammon made war against Israel, that the elders of Gilead went to get Jephthah from the land of Tob. [6]Then they said to Jephthah, "Come and be our commander, that we may fight against the people of Ammon."

[7]So Jephthah said to the elders of Gilead, "Did you not hate me, and expel me from my father's house? Why have you come to me now when you are in distress?"

[8]And the elders of Gilead said to Jephthah, "That is why we have turned again to you now, that you may go with us and fight against the people of Ammon, and be our head over all the inhabitants of Gilead."

[9]So Jephthah said to the elders of Gilead, "If you take me back home to fight against the people of Ammon, and the LORD delivers them to me, shall I be your head?"

[10]And the elders of Gilead said to Jephthah, "The LORD will be a witness between us, if we do not do according to your words." [11]Then Jephthah went with the elders of Gilead, and the people made him head and commander over them; and Jephthah spoke all his words before the LORD in Mizpah.

[12]Now Jephthah sent messengers to the king of the people of Ammon, saying, "What do you have against me, that you have come to fight against me in my land?"

[13]And the king of the people of Ammon answered the messengers of Jephthah, "Because Israel took away my land when they came up out of Egypt, from the Arnon as far as the Jabbok, and to the Jordan. Now therefore, restore those *lands* peaceably."

[14]So Jephthah again sent messengers to the king of the people of Ammon, [15]and said to him, "Thus says Jephthah: 'Israel did not take away the land of Moab, nor the land of the people of Ammon; [16]for when Israel came up from Egypt, they walked through the wilderness as far as the Red Sea and came to Kadesh. [17]Then Israel sent messengers to the king of Edom, saying, "Please let me pass through your land." But the king of Edom would not heed. And in like manner they sent to the king of Moab, but he would not *consent*. So Israel remained in Kadesh. [18]And they went along through the wilderness and bypassed the land of Edom and the land of Moab, came to the east side of the land of Moab, and encamped on the other side

---

TIME CAPSULE   *1200 to 1186 B.C.*

1200	*Copper mining and smelting in Austria*
1200	*Fall of Troy to the Greeks*
1200	*Civil struggles in Egypt end with accession of Seti II*
1188–1186	*Queen Tewosret rules Egypt*
1186	*A court official, Chancellor Baye, struggles for power in Egypt*

10:12   [a]Some Septuagint manuscripts read *Midianites*.

GODS' LANDS, GODS' PEOPLES (Judg. 11:24)

People of ancient cultures believed that the gods owned territory and could give it to whomever they wished. The gods also took care of particular peoples. When any ruler went out to battle, he proclaimed that he was fighting alongside his god or gods. The outcome of the battle was in the hands of the gods who were leading the kings. These two notions—gods giving lands and gods protecting their people—collide when two deities, Chemosh and Yahweh, are thought to possess the same land (Judg. 11:24).

Jephthah explained to the king of Ammon how Israel came to control the land which it was then inhabiting. The long explanation (Judg. 11:14–28) describes the entrance of Israel into the Promised Land. Jephthah's theological language was familiar throughout the ancient Near East. The God of Israel actually took the land from other gods and gave it to Israel.

Chemosh was the national god of Moab (Num. 21:22), but apparently was worshiped also by the Ammonites. The disagreement between Jephthah and the Ammonite king centered on what territory Chemosh had given the Ammonites (Judg. 11:24). The Ammonites claimed that they should have the land held by Israel, but Jephthah argues that both nations had received their lands from their gods and should accept what the gods had given them. The land really belonged to the gods, and not to the people who lived there.

The issue of land ownership, according to Jephthah, was already decided and the outcome of any battle was already decided. Israel had not broken faith with either Yahweh or the Ammonites. The land that Israel possessed was given to them by Yahweh, not to the Ammonites by Chemosh.

---

of the Arnon. But they did not enter the border of Moab, for the Arnon *was* the border of Moab. ¹⁹Then Israel sent messengers to Sihon king of the Amorites, king of Heshbon; and Israel said to him, "Please let us pass through your land into our place." ²⁰But Sihon did not trust Israel to pass through his territory. So Sihon gathered all his people together, encamped in Jahaz, and fought against Israel. ²¹And the LORD God of Israel delivered Sihon and all his people into the hand of Israel, and they defeated them. Thus Israel gained possession of all the land of the Amorites, who inhabited that country. ²²They took possession of all the territory of the Amorites, from the Arnon to the Jabbok and from the wilderness to the Jordan.

²³'And now the LORD God of Israel has dispossessed the Amorites from before His people Israel; should you then possess it? ²⁴Will you not possess whatever Chemosh your god gives you to possess? So whatever the LORD our God takes possession of before us, we will possess. ²⁵And now, *are* you any better than Balak the son of Zippor, king of Moab? Did he ever strive against Israel? Did he ever fight against them? ²⁶While Israel dwelt in Heshbon and its villages, in Aroer and its villages, and in all the cities along the banks of the Arnon, for three hundred years, why did you not recover *them* within that time? ²⁷Therefore I have not sinned against you, but you wronged me by fighting against me. May the LORD, the Judge, render judgment this day between the children of Israel and the people of Ammon.' " ²⁸However, the king of the people of Ammon did not heed the words which Jephthah sent him.

Jephthah's Vow and Victory

²⁹Then the Spirit of the LORD came upon Jephthah, and he passed through Gilead and Manasseh, and passed through Mizpah of Gilead; and from Mizpah of Gilead he advanced *toward* the people of Ammon. ³⁰And Jephthah made a vow to the LORD, and said, "If You will indeed deliver the people of Ammon into my hands, ³¹then it will be that whatever comes out of the doors of my house to meet me, when I return in peace from the people of Ammon, shall surely be the LORD's, and I will offer it up as a burnt offering."

³²So Jephthah advanced toward the people of Ammon to fight against them, and the LORD delivered them into his hands. ³³And he defeated them from Aroer as far as Minnith—twenty cities—and to

THE CYCLES OF THE JUDGES (PART 2)

Part 2 of the history of Israel's judges (Judg. 10:17—15:20) covers five more judges. The introduction (Judg. 10:6–16) depicts the Israelites as more and more undiscriminating in their worship of pagan gods.

Events and Judges	Years
Israel serves Ammon and Philistia (10:6–16)	18
Jephthah's career (10:17—12:7)	6
Ibzan's career (12:8–10)	7
Elon's career (12:11, 12)	10
Abdon's career (12:13–15)	8
Israel serves Philistia (13:1)	40
Samson's career (13:2—15:20)	20

Abel Keramim,[a] with a very great slaughter. Thus the people of Ammon were subdued before the children of Israel.

Jephthah's Daughter

[34]When Jephthah came to his house at Mizpah, there was his daughter, coming out to meet him with timbrels and dancing; and she *was his* only child. Besides her he had neither son nor daughter. [35]And it came to pass, when he saw her, that he tore his clothes, and said, "Alas, my daughter! You have brought me very low! You are among those who trouble me! For I have given my word to the LORD, and I cannot go back on it."

[36]So she said to him, "My father, *if* you have given your word to the LORD, do to me according to what has gone out of your mouth, because the LORD has avenged you of your enemies, the people of Ammon." [37]Then she said to her father, "Let this thing be done for me: let me alone for two months, that I may go and wander on the mountains and bewail my virginity, my friends and I." [38]So he said, "Go." And he sent her away *for* two months; and she went with her friends, and bewailed her virginity on the mountains. [39]And it was so at the end of two months that she returned to her fa-

ther, and he carried out his vow with her which he had vowed. She knew no man.

And it became a custom in Israel [40]*that* the daughters of Israel went four days each year to lament the daughter of Jephthah the Gileadite.

Jephthah's Conflict with Ephraim

12 [1]Then the men of Ephraim gathered together, crossed over toward Zaphon, and said to Jephthah, "Why did you cross over to fight against the people of Ammon, and did not call us to go with you? We will burn your house down on you with fire!"

[2]And Jephthah said to them, "My people and I were in a great struggle with the people of Ammon; and when I called you, you did not deliver me out of their hands. [3]So when I saw that you would not deliver *me,* I took my life in my hands and crossed over against the people of Ammon; and the LORD delivered them into my hand. Why then have you come up to me this day to fight against me?" [4]Now Jephthah gathered together all the men of Gilead and fought against Ephraim. And the men of Gilead defeated Ephraim, because they said, "You Gileadites *are* fugitives of

11:33 [a]Literally *Plain of Vineyards*

RELIGION AND WORSHIP

Human sacrifice is associated with the outcome of war in Greek literature, as it was with Jephthah (Judg. 11:30, 31). Agamemnon sacrificed his daughter in order to raise the wind for his ships. Greek literature also associates wandering in the mountains (Judg. 11:37) with the religious cult of the Bacchae, in the play of that name.

ISRAEL'S SOUTHERN DRAWL (Judg. 12:6)

Jephthah the Gileadite was the successful leader who enabled the Israelites east of the Jordan to defeat the antagonistic Ammonites (Judg. 11:4–33). As a result of Jephthah's activities, however, the tribe of Ephraim, which occupied the west side of the Jordan rift, and the Gileadites, who lived on the other side, came to war (12:1–4). In this war the pronunciation of one word could keep a man alive.

The word "Shibboleth" offers a rare opportunity to witness the sectional tensions that existed among the Israelites. The Old Testament accounts about a lineage that descended from one father can give the impression that the Israelites were afterwards a uniform nation. Jephthah, however, knew that there were distinct differences among the Israelite tribes. The most important, for this battle account, is that they were often so isolated from each other that at least one of the tribes developed its own Hebrew dialect.

It seems that the members of the central hill country tribe of Ephraim could not make a "sh" sound and, instead, pronounced an "s." Their attempts to say "Shibboleth" inevitably sounded as "Sibboleth" (12:6). Their effort, as they approached Jephthah's men, to hide themselves by claiming to be part of his troops failed. The impostors were exposed by their language.

This small glimpse into the everyday life of the Israelites shows us that some of them "talked funny." We can only wonder what other geographical differences may have existed among them.

Ephraim among the Ephraimites *and* among the Manassites." ⁵The Gileadites seized the fords of the Jordan before the Ephraimites *arrived*. And when *any* Ephraimite who escaped said, "Let me cross over," the men of Gilead would say to him, "*Are* you an Ephraimite?" If he said, "No," ⁶then they would say to him, "Then say, 'Shibboleth'!" And he would say, "Sibboleth," for he could not pronounce *it* right. Then they would take him and kill him at the fords of the Jordan. There fell at that time forty-two thousand Ephraimites.

⁷And Jephthah judged Israel six years. Then Jephthah the Gileadite died and was buried among the cities of Gilead.

Ibzan, Elon, and Abdon

⁸After him, Ibzan of Bethlehem judged Israel. ⁹He had thirty sons. And he gave away thirty daughters in marriage, and brought in thirty daughters from elsewhere for his sons. He judged Israel seven years. ¹⁰Then Ibzan died and was buried at Bethlehem.

¹¹After him, Elon the Zebulunite judged Israel. He judged Israel ten years. ¹²And Elon the Zebulunite died and was buried at Aijalon in the country of Zebulun.

¹³After him, Abdon the son of Hillel the Pirathonite judged Israel. ¹⁴He had forty sons and thirty grandsons, who rode on seventy young donkeys. He judged Israel eight years. ¹⁵Then Abdon the son of Hillel the Pirathonite died and was buried in Pirathon in the land of Ephraim, in the mountains of the Amalekites.

The Birth of Samson

13 ¹Again the children of Israel did evil in the sight of the LORD, and the LORD delivered them into the hand of the Philistines for forty years.

²Now there was a certain man from Zorah, of the family of the Danites, whose name *was* Manoah; and his wife *was* barren and had no children. ³And the Angel of the LORD appeared to the woman and said to her, "Indeed now, you are barren and have borne no children, but you shall conceive and bear a son. ⁴Now therefore, please be careful not to drink wine or *similar* drink, and not to eat anything unclean. ⁵For behold, you shall conceive and bear a son. And no razor shall come upon his head, for the child shall be a Nazirite to God from the womb; and he shall begin to deliver Israel out of the hand of the Philistines."

⁶So the woman came and told her husband, saying, "A Man of God came to me, and His countenance *was* like the countenance of the Angel of God, very awesome; but I did not ask Him where He *was* from,

and He did not tell me His name. ⁷And He said to me, 'Behold, you shall conceive and bear a son. Now drink no wine or *similar* drink, nor eat anything unclean, for the child shall be a Nazirite to God from the womb to the day of his death.' "

⁸Then Manoah prayed to the LORD, and said, "O my Lord, please let the Man of God whom You sent come to us again and teach us what we shall do for the child who will be born."

⁹And God listened to the voice of Manoah, and the Angel of God came to the woman again as she was sitting in the field; but Manoah her husband *was* not with her. ¹⁰Then the woman ran in haste and told her husband, and said to him, "Look, the Man who came to me the *other* day has just now appeared to me!"

¹¹So Manoah arose and followed his wife. When he came to the Man, he said to Him, "Are You the Man who spoke to this woman?"

And He said, "I *am*."

¹²Manoah said, "Now let Your words come *to pass!* What will be the boy's rule of life, and his work?"

¹³So the Angel of the LORD said to Manoah, "Of all that I said to the woman let her be careful. ¹⁴She may not eat anything that comes from the vine, nor may she drink wine or *similar* drink, nor eat anything unclean. All that I commanded her let her observe."

¹⁵Then Manoah said to the Angel of the LORD, "Please let us detain You, and we will prepare a young goat for You."

¹⁶And the Angel of the LORD said to Manoah, "Though you detain Me, I will not eat your food. But if you offer a burnt offering, you must offer it to the LORD." (For Manoah did not know He *was* the Angel of the LORD.)

¹⁷Then Manoah said to the Angel of the LORD, "What *is* Your name, that when Your words come *to pass* we may honor You?"

¹⁸And the Angel of the LORD said to him, "Why do you ask My name, seeing it *is* wonderful?"

¹⁹So Manoah took the young goat with the grain offering, and offered it upon the rock to the LORD. And He did a wondrous thing while Manoah and his wife looked on— ²⁰it happened as the flame went up toward heaven from the altar—the Angel of the LORD ascended in the flame of the altar! When Manoah and his wife saw *this,* they fell on their faces to the ground. ²¹When the Angel of the LORD appeared no more to Manoah and his wife, then Manoah knew that He *was* the Angel of the LORD.

²²And Manoah said to his wife, "We shall surely die, because we have seen God!"

²³But his wife said to him, "If the LORD had desired to kill us, He would not have accepted a burnt offering and a grain offering from our hands, nor would He have shown us all these *things,* nor would He have told us *such things* as these at this time."

²⁴So the woman bore a son and called his name Samson; and the child grew, and the LORD blessed him. ²⁵And the Spirit of the LORD began to move upon him at Mahaneh Danᵃ between Zorah and Eshtaol.

Samson's Philistine Wife

14 ¹Now Samson went down to Timnah, and saw a woman in Timnah of the daughters of the Philistines. ²So he went up and told his father and mother, saying, "I have seen a woman in Timnah of the daughters of the Philistines; now therefore, get her for me as a wife."

³Then his father and mother said to him, "*Is there* no woman among the daughters of your brethren, or among all my people, that you must go and get a wife from the uncircumcised Philistines?"

And Samson said to his father, "Get her for me, for she pleases me well."

⁴But his father and mother did not know that it was of the LORD—that He was seeking an occasion to move against the

---

13:25 ᵃLiterally *Camp of Dan* (compare 18:12)

BELIEFS AND IDEAS

The name of a person was considered as a key to their favor or influence. Often its meaning or possible associations expressed an essential truth about the person. Revealing a name meant offering a degree of intimacy. The name of a divine power gives a human being a way of calling on that power (Judg. 13:18).

Philistines. For at that time the Philistines had dominion over Israel.

⁵So Samson went down to Timnah with his father and mother, and came to the vineyards of Timnah.

Now *to his* surprise, a young lion *came* roaring against him. ⁶And the Spirit of the LORD came mightily upon him, and he tore the lion apart as one would have torn apart a young goat, though *he had* nothing in his hand. But he did not tell his father or his mother what he had done.

⁷Then he went down and talked with the woman; and she pleased Samson well. ⁸After some time, when he returned to get her, he turned aside to see the carcass of the lion. And behold, a swarm of bees and honey *were* in the carcass of the lion. ⁹He took some of it in his hands and went along, eating. When he came to his father and mother, he gave *some* to them, and they also ate. But he did not tell them that he had taken the honey out of the carcass of the lion.

¹⁰So his father went down to the woman. And Samson gave a feast there, for young men used to do so. ¹¹And it happened, when they saw him, that they brought thirty companions to be with him.

¹²Then Samson said to them, "Let me pose a riddle to you. If you can correctly solve and explain it to me within the seven days of the feast, then I will give you thirty linen garments and thirty changes of clothing. ¹³But if you cannot explain *it* to me, then you shall give me thirty linen garments and thirty changes of clothing."

And they said to him, "Pose your riddle, that we may hear it."

¹⁴So he said to them:

"Out of the eater came something to
     eat,
And out of the strong came something
     sweet."

Now for three days they could not explain the riddle.

¹⁵But it came to pass on the seventh[a] day that they said to Samson's wife, "Entice your husband, that he may explain the riddle to us, or else we will burn you and your father's house with fire. Have you invited us in order to take what is ours? *Is that* not *so?*"

¹⁶Then Samson's wife wept on him, and said, "You only hate me! You do not love me! You have posed a riddle to the sons of my people, but you have not explained *it* to me."

And he said to her, "Look, I have not explained *it* to my father or my mother; so should I explain *it* to you?" ¹⁷Now she had wept on him the seven days while their feast lasted. And it happened on the seventh day that he told her, because she pressed him so much. Then she explained the riddle to the sons of her people. ¹⁸So the men of the city said to him on the seventh day before the sun went down:

"What *is* sweeter than honey?
And what *is* stronger than a lion?"

And he said to them:

"If you had not plowed with my heifer,
You would not have solved my riddle!"

¹⁹Then the Spirit of the LORD came upon him mightily, and he went down to Ashkelon and killed thirty of their men, took their apparel, and gave the changes *of clothing* to those who had explained the riddle. So his anger was aroused, and he went back up to his father's house. ²⁰And Samson's wife was *given* to his companion, who had been his best man.

Samson Defeats the Philistines

15 ¹After a while, in the time of wheat harvest, it happened that Samson visited his wife with a young goat. And he said, "Let me go in to my wife, into *her* room." But her father would not permit him to go in.

14:15 ªFollowing Masoretic Text, Targum, and Vulgate; Septuagint and Syriac read *fourth*.

ARTS AND LITERATURE

Traditionally riddles were important tests of someone's wisdom, insight, and skill. In some cases a riddle was offered as a test whose outcome was of far-reaching importance, if not life and death. Though Samson was marrying a Philistine woman, relations between Israelites and Philistines were strained. The Philistines were serious about finding the answer to Samson's riddle (Judg. 14:14).

[2]Her father said, "I really thought that you thoroughly hated her; therefore I gave her to your companion. *Is* not her younger sister better than she? Please, take her instead."

[3]And Samson said to them, "This time I shall be blameless regarding the Philistines if I harm them!" [4]Then Samson went and caught three hundred foxes; and he took torches, turned *the foxes* tail to tail, and put a torch between each pair of tails. [5]When he had set the torches on fire, he let *the foxes* go into the standing grain of the Philistines, and burned up both the shocks and the standing grain, as well as the vineyards *and* olive groves.

[6]Then the Philistines said, "Who has done this?"

And they answered, "Samson, the son-in-law of the Timnite, because he has taken his wife and given her to his companion." So the Philistines came up and burned her and her father with fire.

[7]Samson said to them, "Since you would do a thing like this, I will surely take revenge on you, and after that I will cease." [8]So he attacked them hip and thigh with a great slaughter; then he went down and dwelt in the cleft of the rock of Etam.

[9]Now the Philistines went up, encamped in Judah, and deployed themselves against Lehi. [10]And the men of Judah said, "Why have you come up against us?"

So they answered, "We have come up to arrest Samson, to do to him as he has done to us."

[11]Then three thousand men of Judah went down to the cleft of the rock of Etam, and said to Samson, "Do you not know that the Philistines rule over us? What *is* this you have done to us?"

And he said to them, "As they did to me, so I have done to them."

[12]But they said to him, "We have come down to arrest you, that we may deliver you into the hand of the Philistines."

Then Samson said to them, "Swear to me that you will not kill me yourselves."

[13]So they spoke to him, saying, "No, but we will tie you securely and deliver you into their hand; but we will surely not kill you." And they bound him with two new ropes and brought him up from the rock.

[14]When he came to Lehi, the Philistines came shouting against him. Then the Spirit of the LORD came mightily upon him; and the ropes that *were* on his arms became like flax that is burned with fire, and his bonds broke loose from his hands. [15]He found a fresh jawbone of a donkey, reached out his hand and took it, and killed a thousand men with it. [16]Then Samson said:

> "With the jawbone of a donkey,
> Heaps upon heaps,
> With the jawbone of a donkey
> I have slain a thousand men!"

[17]And so it was, when he had finished speaking, that he threw the jawbone from his hand, and called that place Ramath Lehi.[a]

[18]Then he became very thirsty; so he cried out to the LORD and said, "You have given this great deliverance by the hand of Your servant; and now shall I die of thirst and fall into the hand of the uncircumcised?" [19]So God split the hollow place that *is* in Lehi,[a] and water came out, and he drank; and his spirit returned, and he revived. Therefore he called its name En Hakkore,[b] which is in Lehi to this day. [20]And he judged Israel twenty years in the days of the Philistines.

Samson and Delilah

16 [1]Now Samson went to Gaza and saw a harlot there, and went in to her. [2]*When* the Gazites *were told*, "Samson has come here!" they surrounded *the place* and lay in wait for him all night at the gate of the city. They were quiet all night, saying, "In the morning, when it is daylight, we

---

15:17 [a]Literally *Jawbone Height*   15:19 [a]Literally *Jawbone* (compare verse 14)   [b]Literally *Spring of the Caller*

GEOGRAPHY AND ENVIRONMENT

The names of places are interpreted so as to call to mind a significant incident that happened at that place. Sometimes the name is linked in a straightforward way to the event, as Samson chose the name "Ramath Lehi," meaning "jawbone height," to mark his victory with a jawbone (Judg. 15:17). Other times, the link is like a pun, making use of a fortuitous similarity of sound.

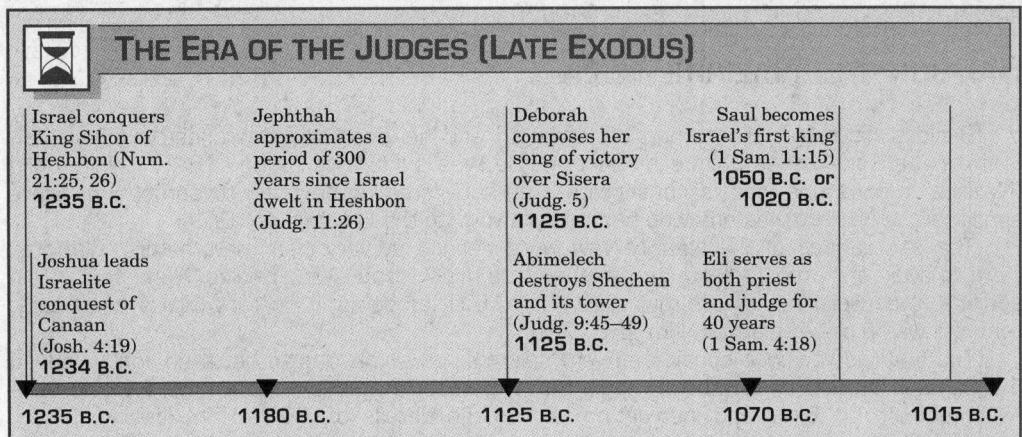

THE ERA OF THE JUDGES (LATE EXODUS)

Israel conquers King Sihon of Heshbon (Num. 21:25, 26) **1235 B.C.**	Jephthah approximates a period of 300 years since Israel dwelt in Heshbon (Judg. 11:26)	Deborah composes her song of victory over Sisera (Judg. 5) **1125 B.C.**	Saul becomes Israel's first king (1 Sam. 11:15) **1050 B.C. or 1020 B.C.**
Joshua leads Israelite conquest of Canaan (Josh. 4:19) **1234 B.C.**		Abimelech destroys Shechem and its tower (Judg. 9:45–49) **1125 B.C.**	Eli serves as both priest and judge for 40 years (1 Sam. 4:18)

| **1235 B.C.** | **1180 B.C.** | **1125 B.C.** | **1070 B.C.** | **1015 B.C.** |

will kill him." ³And Samson lay *low* till midnight; then he arose at midnight, took hold of the doors of the gate of the city and the two gateposts, pulled them up, bar and all, put *them* on his shoulders, and carried them to the top of the hill that faces Hebron.

⁴Afterward it happened that he loved a woman in the Valley of Sorek, whose name *was* Delilah. ⁵And the lords of the Philistines came up to her and said to her, "Entice him, and find out where his great strength *lies,* and by what *means* we may overpower him, that we may bind him to afflict him; and every one of us will give you eleven hundred *pieces* of silver."

⁶So Delilah said to Samson, "Please tell me where your great strength *lies,* and with what you may be bound to afflict you."

⁷And Samson said to her, "If they bind me with seven fresh bowstrings, not yet dried, then I shall become weak, and be like any *other* man."

⁸So the lords of the Philistines brought up to her seven fresh bowstrings, not yet dried, and she bound him with them. ⁹Now *men were* lying in wait, staying with her in the room. And she said to him, "The Philistines *are* upon you, Samson!" But he broke the bowstrings as a strand of yarn breaks when it touches fire. So the secret of his strength was not known.

¹⁰Then Delilah said to Samson, "Look, you have mocked me and told me lies. Now, please tell me what you may be bound with."

¹¹So he said to her, "If they bind me securely with new ropes that have never been used, then I shall become weak, and be like any *other* man."

¹²Therefore Delilah took new ropes and bound him with them, and said to him, "The Philistines *are* upon you, Samson!" And *men were* lying in wait, staying in the room. But he broke them off his arms like a thread.

¹³Delilah said to Samson, "Until now you have mocked me and told me lies. Tell me what you may be bound with."

And he said to her, "If you weave the seven locks of my head into the web of the loom"—

¹⁴So she wove *it* tightly with the batten of the loom, and said to him, "The Philistines *are* upon you, Samson!" But he awoke from his sleep, and pulled out the batten and the web from the loom.

¹⁵Then she said to him, "How can you say, 'I love you,' when your heart *is* not with me? You have mocked me these three times, and have not told me where your great strength *lies.*" ¹⁶And it came to pass, when she pestered him daily with her words and pressed him, *so* that his soul was vexed to death, ¹⁷that he told her all his heart, and said to her, "No razor has ever come upon my head, for I *have been* a Nazirite to God from my mother's womb. If I am shaven, then my strength will leave me, and I shall become weak, and be like any *other* man."

¹⁸When Delilah saw that he had told her all his heart, she sent and called for the lords of the Philistines, saying, "Come up once more, for he has told me all his heart." So the lords of the Philistines came up to her and brought the money in their hand. ¹⁹Then she lulled him to sleep on her knees, and called for a man and had him shave off the seven locks of his head. Then

SAMSON THE NAZIRITE (Judg. 16:17)

Besides his extraordinary physical strength and his spectacular wildness of character, Samson had one other unique distinction: he was a Nazirite (Judg. 16:17). The word "Nazirite" means one who is consecrated (or separated or devoted) to something. More specifically, a Nazirite was one who had taken a vow "to the LORD" (Num. 6:2).

The peculiarities of the Nazirite vow were defined by very clear parameters. Nazirites were to avoid any produce from grapevines: juice, fresh grapes and raisins (Num. 6:3, 4). In addition, they were not to cut their hair (Num. 6:5) or come in contact with a dead body, even if it was a close relative (Num. 6:6, 7).

The Nazirite vow was considered very solemn, not something to be taken lightly. Indeed the Samson stories open with an angel telling Samson's mother that her child would be a Nazirite from his birth and instructing her on the details of the Nazirite lifestyle (Judg. 13:3-5). Even Samson's mother was to keep herself from grapevine produce and food considered unclean (13:13, 14).

While Samson is the only Old Testament person specifically identified as a Nazirite, it is likely that many prophets were also Nazirites. The prophet Amos mentions prophets and Nazirites together (Amos 2:11, 12), and Samuel is an example of someone who was both. His mother Hannah made a vow that Samuel's hair would never be cut (1 Sam. 1:11). The Septuagint (the Greek translation of the Old Testament) adds to 1 Sam. 1:11 that Samuel would also abstain from grape juice. While not specifically said to be a Nazirite, it seems likely that, since Samuel followed the Nazirite rules, he was a Nazirite.

she began to torment him,[a] and his strength left him. ²⁰And she said, "The Philistines *are* upon you, Samson!" So he awoke from his sleep, and said, "I will go out as before, at other times, and shake myself free!" But he did not know that the LORD had departed from him.

²¹Then the Philistines took him and put out his eyes, and brought him down to Gaza. They bound him with bronze fetters, and he became a grinder in the prison. ²²However, the hair of his head began to grow again after it had been shaven.

Samson Dies with the Philistines

²³Now the lords of the Philistines gathered together to offer a great sacrifice to Dagon their god, and to rejoice. And they said:

"Our god has delivered into our hands
  Samson our enemy!"

²⁴When the people saw him, they praised their god; for they said:

"Our god has delivered into our hands
    our enemy,
The destroyer of our land,
And the one who multiplied our dead."

²⁵So it happened, when their hearts were merry, that they said, "Call for Samson, that he may perform for us." So they called for Samson from the prison, and he performed for them. And they stationed him between the pillars. ²⁶Then Samson said to the lad who held him by the hand, "Let me feel the pillars which support the temple, so that I can lean on them." ²⁷Now the temple was full of men and women. All the lords of the Philistines *were* there—about three thousand men and women on the roof watching while Samson performed.

²⁸Then Samson called to the LORD, saying, "O Lord GOD, remember me, I pray! Strengthen me, I pray, just this once, O God, that I may with one *blow* take vengeance on the Philistines for my two eyes!" ²⁹And Samson took hold of the two middle pillars which supported the temple, and he braced himself against them, one on his right and the other on his left. ³⁰Then Samson said, "Let me die with the Philistines!" And he pushed with *all his* might, and the temple fell on the lords and all the people who *were* in it. So the dead that he killed at his death were more than he had killed in his life.

16:19 ^aFollowing Masoretic Text, Targum, and Vulgate; Septuagint reads *he began to be weak.*

[31]And his brothers and all his father's household came down and took him, and brought *him* up and buried him between Zorah and Eshtaol in the tomb of his father Manoah. He had judged Israel twenty years.

Micah's Idolatry

17 [1]Now there was a man from the mountains of Ephraim, whose name *was* Micah. [2]And he said to his mother, "The eleven hundred *shekels* of silver that were taken from you, and on which you put a curse, even saying it in my ears—here *is* the silver with me; I took it."

And his mother said, *"May you be* blessed by the LORD, my son!" [3]So when he had returned the eleven hundred *shekels* of silver to his mother, his mother said, "I had wholly dedicated the silver from my hand to the LORD for my son, to make a carved image and a molded image; now therefore, I will return it to you." [4]Thus he returned the silver to his mother. Then his mother took two hundred *shekels* of silver and gave them to the silversmith, and he made it into a carved image and a molded image; and they were in the house of Micah.

[5]The man Micah had a shrine, and made an ephod and household idols;[a] and he consecrated one of his sons, who became his priest. [6]In those days *there was* no king in Israel; everyone did *what was* right in his own eyes.

[7]Now there was a young man from Bethlehem in Judah, of the family of Judah; he *was* a Levite, and was staying there. [8]The man departed from the city of Bethlehem in Judah to stay wherever he could find *a place*. Then he came to the mountains of Ephraim, to the house of Micah, as he journeyed. [9]And Micah said to him, "Where do you come from?"

So he said to him, "I *am* a Levite from Bethlehem in Judah, and I am on my way to find *a place* to stay."

[10]Micah said to him, "Dwell with me, and be a father and a priest to me, and I will give you ten *shekels* of silver per year, a suit of clothes, and your sustenance." So the Levite went in. [11]Then the Levite was content to dwell with the man; and the young man became like one of his sons to him. [12]So Micah consecrated the Levite, and the young man became his priest, and lived in the house of Micah. [13]Then Micah said, "Now I know that the LORD will be good to me, since I have a Levite as priest!"

The Danites Adopt Micah's Idolatry

18 [1]In those days *there was* no king in Israel. And in those days the tribe of the Danites was seeking an inheritance for itself to dwell in; for until that day *their* inheritance among the tribes of Israel had not fallen to them. [2]So the children of Dan sent five men of their family from their territory, men of valor from Zorah and Eshtaol, to spy out the land and search it. They said to them, "Go, search the land." So they went to the mountains of Ephraim, to the house of Micah, and lodged there. [3]While they *were* at the house of Micah, they recognized the voice of the young Levite. They turned aside and said to him, "Who brought you here? What are you doing in this *place?* What do you have here?"

[4]He said to them, "Thus and so Micah did for me. He has hired me, and I have become his priest."

[5]So they said to him, "Please inquire of God, that we may know whether the journey on which we go will be prosperous."

[6]And the priest said to them, "Go in peace. The presence of the LORD *be* with you on your way."

[7]So the five men departed and went to Laish. They saw the people who *were* there, how they dwelt safely, in the manner of the Sidonians, quiet and secure. *There were* no rulers in the land who might put *them* to shame for anything. They *were* far from the Sidonians, and they had no ties with anyone.[a]

17:5 [a]Hebrew *teraphim*   18:7 [a]Following Masoretic Text, Targum, and Vulgate; Septuagint reads *with Syria.*

RELIGION AND WORSHIP

Like Micah (Judg. 17:5), the Romans had the custom of displaying small images of their gods in their homes. They had them in private shrines, something like a window frame set into a wall, with a roof and columns. Such shrines and idols have been recovered undisturbed in Herculaneum and Pompeii, towns buried by a volcano in A.D. 79.

THE HOUSEHOLD GODS OF NUZI (Judg. 17:5; 18:14, 20)

Nuzi was an administrative center in the ancient land of Arraphe. It became prominent in the latter half of the 2nd millennium B.C. as part of the Hurrian kingdom of Mitanni. Over 3,500 cuneiform texts have been discovered at the site. These texts, written in a Hurrian style of Accadian, illuminate many social, legal, and religious customs of northern Mesopotamia around the 15th century B.C.

Many of these customs find parallels in the Old Testament. Servants were adopted by childless couples at Nuzi. As in the case of Abram's adopted servant Eliezer (Gen. 15:2, 3), the adopted servant at Nuzi became an heir to the foster parents' estate. Another Nuzi custom allows for a childless wife to furnish her husband with a handmaid as a concubine. As with Sarai and Hagar (Gen. 16:1, 2), the wife was entitled to treat the concubine's offspring as her own. A natural son born after a child by a handmaiden nevertheless became the primary heir, as it was with Ishmael and Isaac (Gen. 21:9–14).

The Nuzi texts reveal that household gods, called teraphim (Hos. 3:4), were a significant part of family life. Possession of these small household deities implied headship of the family. In the traditional line of inheritance, the eldest son normally received the family gods, as well as the largest share of the family property. Property inheritance possibly explains Rachel's stealing of her father Laban's household gods (Gen. 31:19).

The household gods of the Ephramite Micah also resemble those of Nuzi. Archaeological evidence from Nuzi suggests that houses had their own shrines, as did Micah (Judg. 17:5). A Nuzi court case concerns the loss of the family gods to someone outside of the family. Micah experienced the same misfortune (Judg. 18:14–17).

---

⁸Then *the spies* came back to their brethren at Zorah and Eshtaol, and their brethren said to them, "What *is* your report?"

⁹So they said, "Arise, let us go up against them. For we have seen the land, and indeed it *is* very good. *Would* you *do* nothing? Do not hesitate to go, *and* enter to possess the land. ¹⁰When you go, you will come to a secure people and a large land. For God has given it into your hands, a place where *there is* no lack of anything that *is* on the earth."

¹¹And six hundred men of the family of the Danites went from there, from Zorah and Eshtaol, armed with weapons of war. ¹²Then they went up and encamped in Kirjath Jearim in Judah. (Therefore they call that place Mahaneh Danᵃ to this day. There *it is,* west of Kirjath Jearim.) ¹³And they passed from there to the mountains of Ephraim, and came to the house of Micah.

¹⁴Then the five men who had gone to spy out the country of Laish answered and said to their brethren, "Do you know that there are in these houses an ephod, household idols, a carved image, and a molded image? Now therefore, consider what you should do." ¹⁵So they turned aside there, and came to the house of the young Levite man—to the house of Micah—and greeted him. ¹⁶The six hundred men armed with their weapons of war, who *were* of the children of Dan, stood by the entrance of the gate. ¹⁷Then the five men who had gone to spy out the land went up. Entering there, they took the carved image, the ephod, the household idols, and the molded image. The priest stood at the entrance of the gate with the six hundred men *who were* armed with weapons of war.

¹⁸When these went into Micah's house and took the carved image, the ephod, the household idols, and the molded image, the priest said to them, "What are you doing?"

¹⁹And they said to him, "Be quiet, put your hand over your mouth, and come with us; be a father and a priest to us. *Is it* better for you to be a priest to the household of one man, or that you be a priest to a tribe and a family in Israel?" ²⁰So the priest's heart was glad; and he took the ephod, the household idols, and the carved image, and took his place among the people.

²¹Then they turned and departed, and put the little ones, the livestock, and the

18:12 ᵃLiterally *Camp of Dan*

THEY WASHED THEIR FEET   (Judg. 19:21)

Footwashing was an expression of hospitality extended to guests of ancient Near Eastern homes. People traveling dusty roads needed to wash their feet for comfort and cleanliness. Guests were often offered water and vessels for washing their own feet. Such hospitality is described in Judg. 19:17–21 when a traveler and his two servants lodge with an old man in Gibeah. Footwashing could also be performed by a servant (Luke 7:44).

Customs varied. The earliest practice was to pour water over the guest's feet, while later practice used a basin. A portable footbath found at Samaria had a raised area in the middle to support the foot. In the town of Tell Beit Mirsim, identified with Debir (Josh. 10:38), archaeologists discovered built-in washing basins in rooms surrounding the court by one gate. The basins suggested that these rooms were part of the city's guesthouse.

goods in front of them. ²²When they were a good way from the house of Micah, the men who *were* in the houses near Micah's house gathered together and overtook the children of Dan. ²³And they called out to the children of Dan. So they turned around and said to Micah, "What ails you, that you have gathered such a company?"

²⁴So he said, "You have taken away my gods which I made, and the priest, and you have gone away. Now what more do I have? How can you say to me, 'What ails you?' "

²⁵And the children of Dan said to him, "Do not let your voice be heard among us, lest angry men fall upon you, and you lose your life, with the lives of your household!" ²⁶Then the children of Dan went their way. And when Micah saw that they *were* too strong for him, he turned and went back to his house.

Danites Settle in Laish

²⁷So they took *the things* Micah had made, and the priest who had belonged to him, and went to Laish, to a people quiet and secure; and they struck them with the edge of the sword and burned the city with fire. ²⁸*There was* no deliverer, because it *was* far from Sidon, and they had no ties with anyone. It was in the valley that belongs to Beth Rehob. So they rebuilt the city and dwelt there. ²⁹And they called the name of the city Dan, after the name of Dan their father, who was born to Israel. However, the name of the city formerly *was* Laish.

³⁰Then the children of Dan set up for themselves the carved image; and Jonathan the son of Gershom, the son of Ma-

nasseh,ᵃ and his sons were priests to the tribe of Dan until the day of the captivity of the land. ³¹So they set up for themselves Micah's carved image which he made, all the time that the house of God was in Shiloh.

The Levite's Concubine

19 ¹And it came to pass in those days, when *there was* no king in Israel, that there was a certain Levite staying in the remote mountains of Ephraim. He took for himself a concubine from Bethlehem in Judah. ²But his concubine played the harlot against him, and went away from him to her father's house at Bethlehem in Judah, and was there four whole months. ³Then her husband arose and went after her, to speak kindly to her *and* bring her back, having his servant and a couple of donkeys with him. So she brought him into her father's house; and when the father of the young woman saw him, he was glad to meet him. ⁴Now his father-in-law, the young woman's father, detained him; and he stayed with him three days. So they ate and drank and lodged there.

⁵Then it came to pass on the fourth day that they arose early in the morning, and he stood to depart; but the young woman's father said to his son-in-law, "Refresh your heart with a morsel of bread, and afterward go your way."

⁶So they sat down, and the two of them ate and drank together. Then the young woman's father said to the man, "Please be content to stay all night, and let your heart be merry." ⁷And when the man stood to depart, his father-in-law urged him; so he lodged there again. ⁸Then he arose early in the morning on the fifth day to depart, but the young woman's father said, "Please

---
18:30 ᵃSeptuagint and Vulgate read *Moses.*

refresh your heart." So they delayed until afternoon; and both of them ate.

⁹And when the man stood to depart—he and his concubine and his servant—his father-in-law, the young woman's father, said to him, "Look, the day is now drawing toward evening; please spend the night. See, the day is coming to an end; lodge here, that your heart may be merry. Tomorrow go your way early, so that you may get home."

¹⁰However, the man was not willing to spend that night; so he rose and departed, and came opposite Jebus (that is, Jerusalem). With him were the two saddled donkeys; his concubine was also with him. ¹¹They were near Jebus, and the day was far spent; and the servant said to his master, "Come, please, and let us turn aside into this city of the Jebusites and lodge in it."

¹²But his master said to him, "We will not turn aside here into a city of foreigners, who are not of the children of Israel; we will go on to Gibeah." ¹³So he said to his servant, "Come, let us draw near to one of these places, and spend the night in Gibeah or in Ramah." ¹⁴And they passed by and went their way; and the sun went down on them near Gibeah, which belongs to Benjamin. ¹⁵They turned aside there to go in to lodge in Gibeah. And when he went in, he sat down in the open square of the city, for no one would take them into his house to spend the night.

¹⁶Just then an old man came in from his work in the field at evening, who also was from the mountains of Ephraim; he was staying in Gibeah, whereas the men of the place were Benjamites. ¹⁷And when he raised his eyes, he saw the traveler in the open square of the city; and the old man said, "Where are you going, and where do you come from?"

¹⁸So he said to him, "We are passing from Bethlehem in Judah toward the remote mountains of Ephraim; I am from there. I went to Bethlehem in Judah; now I am going to the house of the LORD. But there is no one who will take me into his house, ¹⁹although we have both straw and fodder for our donkeys, and bread and wine for myself, for your female servant, and for the young man who is with your servant; there is no lack of anything."

²⁰And the old man said, "Peace be with you! However, let all your needs be my responsibility; only do not spend the night in the open square." ²¹So he brought him into his house, and gave fodder to the donkeys. And they washed their feet, and ate and drank.

Gibeah's Crime

²²As they were enjoying themselves, suddenly certain men of the city, perverted men,ᵃ surrounded the house and beat on the door. They spoke to the master of the house, the old man, saying, "Bring out the man who came to your house, that we may know him carnally!"

²³But the man, the master of the house, went out to them and said to them, "No, my brethren! I beg you, do not act so wickedly! Seeing this man has come into my house, do not commit this outrage. ²⁴Look, here is my virgin daughter and the man'sᵃ concubine; let me bring them out now. Humble them, and do with them as you please; but to this man do not do such a vile thing!" ²⁵But the men would not heed him. So the man took his concubine and brought her out to them. And they knew her and abused her all night until morning; and when the day began to break, they let her go.

²⁶Then the woman came as the day was dawning, and fell down at the door of the man's house where her master was, till it was light.

²⁷When her master arose in the morning, and opened the doors of the house and went out to go his way, there was his concubine, fallen at the door of the house with her hands on the threshold. ²⁸And he said to her, "Get up and let us be going." But

---

19:22 ᵃLiterally sons of Belial   19:24 ᵃLiterally his

CULTURE AND SOCIETY

In the traditional culture of the bedouin, or the nomadic Arabs, the "Law of the Tent" occupies a special place. Anyone who physically enters the tent of another person enjoys sanctuary there, and the owner will suffer extreme shame if any harm comes to his guest. The threatened sexual abuse of a guest by the citizens of Gibeah would have been an "outrage" (Judg. 19:22, 23).

there was no answer. So the man lifted her onto the donkey; and the man got up and went to his place.

29When he entered his house he took a knife, laid hold of his concubine, and divided her into twelve pieces, limb by limb,a and sent her throughout all the territory of Israel. 30And so it was that all who saw it said, "No such deed has been done or seen from the day that the children of Israel came up from the land of Egypt until this day. Consider it, confer, and speak up!"

Israel's War with the Benjamites

20 1So all the children of Israel came out, from Dan to Beersheba, as well as from the land of Gilead, and the congregation gathered together as one man before the LORD at Mizpah. 2And the leaders of all the people, all the tribes of Israel, presented themselves in the assembly of the people of God, four hundred thousand foot soldiers who drew the sword. 3(Now the children of Benjamin heard that the children of Israel had gone up to Mizpah.)

Then the children of Israel said, "Tell us, how did this wicked deed happen?"

4So the Levite, the husband of the woman who was murdered, answered and said, "My concubine and I went into Gibeah, which belongs to Benjamin, to spend the night. 5And the men of Gibeah rose against me, and surrounded the house at night because of me. They intended to kill me, but instead they ravished my concubine so that she died. 6So I took hold of my concubine, cut her in pieces, and sent her throughout all the territory of the inheritance of Israel, because they committed lewdness and outrage in Israel. 7Look! All of you are children of Israel; give your advice and counsel here and now!"

8So all the people arose as one man, saying, "None of us will go to his tent, nor will any turn back to his house; 9but now this is the thing which we will do to Gibeah: We will go up against it by lot. 10We will take ten men out of every hundred throughout all the tribes of Israel, a hundred out of every thousand, and a thousand out of every ten thousand, to make provisions for the people, that when they come to Gibeah in Benjamin, they may repay all the vileness that they have done in Israel." 11So all the men of Israel were gathered against the city, united together as one man.

12Then the tribes of Israel sent men through all the tribe of Benjamin, saying, "What is this wickedness that has occurred among you? 13Now therefore, deliver up the men, the perverted mena who are in Gibeah, that we may put them to death and remove the evil from Israel!" But the children of Benjamin would not listen to the voice of their brethren, the children of Israel. 14Instead, the children of Benjamin gathered together from their cities to Gibeah, to go to battle against the children of Israel. 15And from their cities at that time the children of Benjamin numbered twenty-six thousand men who drew the sword, besides the inhabitants of Gibeah, who numbered seven hundred select men. 16Among all this people were seven hundred select men who were left-handed; every one could sling a stone at a hair's breadth and not miss. 17Now besides Benjamin, the men of Israel numbered four hundred thousand men who drew the sword; all of these were men of war.

18Then the children of Israel arose and went up to the house of Goda to inquire of God. They said, "Which of us shall go up first to battle against the children of Benjamin?"

The LORD said, "Judah first!"

19So the children of Israel rose in the morning and encamped against Gibeah. 20And the men of Israel went out to battle against Benjamin, and the men of Israel put themselves in battle array to fight against them at Gibeah. 21Then the children of Benjamin came out of Gibeah, and on that day cut down to the ground twenty-two thousand men of the Israelites. 22And the people, that is, the men of Israel,

---

TIME CAPSULE	*1185 to 1180 B.C.*
1185	*Setnakht ends another civil war in Egypt and founds 20th Dynasty*
1184– 1153	*Ramesses III, pharaoh of Egypt*
1180	*Hattusa, the Hittite capital, is destroyed*
1180	*End of the New Kingdom of the Hittites*
1180	*Ugarit is destroyed*

19:29 aLiterally with her bones　　20:13 aLiterally sons of Belial　　20:18 aOr Bethel

encouraged themselves and again formed the battle line at the place where they had put themselves in array on the first day. 23Then the children of Israel went up and wept before the LORD until evening, and asked counsel of the LORD, saying, "Shall I again draw near for battle against the children of my brother Benjamin?"

And the LORD said, "Go up against him."

24So the children of Israel approached the children of Benjamin on the second day. 25And Benjamin went out against them from Gibeah on the second day, and cut down to the ground eighteen thousand more of the children of Israel; all these drew the sword.

26Then all the children of Israel, that is, all the people, went up and came to the house of Goda and wept. They sat there before the LORD and fasted that day until evening; and they offered burnt offerings and peace offerings before the LORD. 27So the children of Israel inquired of the LORD (the ark of the covenant of God was there in those days, 28and Phinehas the son of Eleazar, the son of Aaron, stood before it in those days), saying, "Shall I yet again go out to battle against the children of my brother Benjamin, or shall I cease?"

And the LORD said, "Go up, for tomorrow I will deliver them into your hand."

29Then Israel set men in ambush all around Gibeah. 30And the children of Israel went up against the children of Benjamin on the third day, and put themselves in battle array against Gibeah as at the other times. 31So the children of Benjamin went out against the people, and were drawn away from the city. They began to strike down and kill some of the people, as at the other times, in the highways (one of which goes up to Bethel and the other to Gibeah) and in the field, about thirty men of Israel. 32And the children of Benjamin said, "They are defeated before us, as at first."

But the children of Israel said, "Let us flee and draw them away from the city to the highways." 33So all the men of Israel rose from their place and put themselves in battle array at Baal Tamar. Then Israel's men in ambush burst forth from their position in the plain of Geba. 34And ten thousand select men from all Israel came against Gibeah, and the battle was fierce. But the Benjamitesa did not know that disaster was upon them. 35The LORD defeated Benjamin before Israel. And the children of Israel destroyed that day twenty-five thousand one hundred Benjamites; all these drew the sword.

36So the children of Benjamin saw that they were defeated. The men of Israel had given ground to the Benjamites, because they relied on the men in ambush whom they had set against Gibeah. 37And the men in ambush quickly rushed upon Gibeah; the men in ambush spread out and struck the whole city with the edge of the sword. 38Now the appointed signal between the men of Israel and the men in ambush was that they would make a great cloud of smoke rise up from the city, 39whereupon the men of Israel would turn in battle. Now Benjamin had begun to strike and kill about thirty of the men of Israel. For they said, "Surely they are defeated before us, as in the first battle." 40But when the cloud began to rise from the city in a column of smoke, the Benjamites looked behind them, and there was the whole city going up in smoke to heaven. 41And when the men of Israel turned back, the men of Benjamin panicked, for they saw that disaster had come upon them. 42Therefore they turned their backs before the men of Israel in the direction of the wilderness; but the battle overtook them, and whoever came out of the cities they destroyed in their midst. 43They surrounded the Benjamites, chased them, and easily trampled them down as far as the front of Gibeah toward the east. 44And eighteen thousand men of Benjamin fell; all these were men of valor. 45Then theya turned and fled toward the wilderness to the rock of Rimmon; and they cut down five thousand of them on the highways. Then they pursued them relentlessly up to Gidom, and killed two thousand of them. 46So all who fell of Benjamin that day were twenty-five thousand men who drew the sword; all these were men of valor.

47But six hundred men turned and fled toward the wilderness to the rock of Rimmon, and they stayed at the rock of Rimmon for four months. 48And the men of Israel turned back against the children of Benjamin, and struck them down with the edge of the sword—from every city, men and beasts, all who were found. They also set fire to all the cities they came to.

The Israel Stele of Merenptah (Judg. 21:25)

The Israel Stele was a monument set up by Pharaoh Merenptah of Egypt in the 5th year of his reign (c. 1208 B.C.), commemorating his victories in Palestine. The monument describes a clash between Egyptians and some Israelites, which is the first known mention of Israel from a source outside of the Bible.

Israel is depicted on the monument as "laid waste, his seed is not." The entirety of Palestine is described as conquered and controlled by the Egyptian monarch. Some scholars think that the name "Israel," as it appears in the stele, constitutes a people group, not a land. They suggest that Israel was not yet settled in Palestine, but rather, would have just left Egypt.

The text of the stele is not easily understood, so it is impossible to determine how long Israel had been in the land at the time Merenptah campaigned in Palestine. The Israel Stele does offer evidence that Israel was recognized as a people in Palestine around 1208 B.C. That the Egyptians did not know Israel as a nation or land fits with the description found in the Book of Judges: "In those days there was no king in Israel" (Judg. 21:25).

Wives Provided for the Benjamites

21 ¹Now the men of Israel had sworn an oath at Mizpah, saying, "None of us shall give his daughter to Benjamin as a wife." ²Then the people came to the house of God,ᵃ and remained there before God till evening. They lifted up their voices and wept bitterly, ³and said, "O LORD God of Israel, why has this come to pass in Israel, that today there should be one tribe *missing* in Israel?"

⁴So it was, on the next morning, that the people rose early and built an altar there, and offered burnt offerings and peace offerings. ⁵The children of Israel said, "Who *is there* among all the tribes of Israel who did not come up with the assembly to the LORD?" For they had made a great oath concerning anyone who had not come up to the LORD at Mizpah, saying, "He shall surely be put to death." ⁶And the children of Israel grieved for Benjamin their brother, and said, "One tribe is cut off from Israel today. ⁷What shall we do for wives for those who remain, seeing we have sworn by the LORD that we will not give them our daughters as wives?"

⁸And they said, "What one *is there* from the tribes of Israel who did not come up to Mizpah to the LORD?" And, in fact, no one had come to the camp from Jabesh Gilead to the assembly. ⁹For when the people were counted, indeed, not one of the inhabitants of Jabesh Gilead *was* there. ¹⁰So the congregation sent out there twelve thousand of their most valiant men, and commanded them, saying, "Go and strike the inhabitants of Jabesh Gilead with the edge of the sword, including the women and children. ¹¹And this *is* the thing that you shall do: You shall utterly destroy every male, and every woman who has known a man intimately." ¹²So they found among the inhabitants of Jabesh Gilead four hundred young virgins who had not known a man intimately; and they brought them to the camp at Shiloh, which is in the land of Canaan.

¹³Then the whole congregation sent *word* to the children of Benjamin who *were* at the rock of Rimmon, and announced peace to them. ¹⁴So Benjamin came back at that time, and they gave them the women whom they had saved alive of the women of Jabesh Gilead; and yet they had not found enough for them.

¹⁵And the people grieved for Benjamin, because the LORD had made a void in the tribes of Israel.

¹⁶Then the elders of the congregation said, "What shall we do for wives for those who remain, since the women of Benjamin have been destroyed?" ¹⁷And they said, "*There must be* an inheritance for the survivors of Benjamin, that a tribe may not be destroyed from Israel. ¹⁸However, we cannot give them wives from our daughters, for the children of Israel have sworn an oath, saying, 'Cursed *be* the one who gives a wife to Benjamin.' " ¹⁹Then they said, "In fact, *there is* a yearly feast of the LORD in Shiloh, which *is* north of Bethel, on the east side of the highway that goes

21:2 ᵃOr *Bethel*

up from Bethel to Shechem, and south of Lebonah."

²⁰Therefore they instructed the children of Benjamin, saying, "Go, lie in wait in the vineyards, ²¹and watch; and just when the daughters of Shiloh come out to perform their dances, then come out from the vineyards, and every man catch a wife for himself from the daughters of Shiloh; then go to the land of Benjamin. ²²Then it shall be, when their fathers or their brothers come to us to complain, that we will say to them, 'Be kind to them for our sakes, because we did not take a wife for any of them in the war; for *it is* not *as though* you have given the *women* to them at this time, making yourselves guilty of your oath.'"

²³And the children of Benjamin did so; they took enough wives for their number from those who danced, whom they caught. Then they went and returned to their inheritance, and they rebuilt the cities and dwelt in them. ²⁴So the children of Israel departed from there at that time, every man to his tribe and family; they went out from there, every man to his inheritance.

²⁵In those days *there was* no king in Israel; everyone did *what was* right in his own eyes.

The Book of Ruth

The Book of Judges, like many histories, presents only the wars and battles of its time. The Book of Ruth deals with what average people were doing between those wars. It describes a stable society, governed by wise elders, in which the laws of the covenant are respected and kept. For instance, the law demanded that if a man died before his wife had borne him children, his nearest male relative should marry the widow and raise up an heir to the one who had died (Deut. 25:5–10). Under this law Ruth eventually marries Boaz.

The book also pictures more peaceful relations with Israel's neighbors than does Judges. Naomi moves back and forth between Israel and Moab, and her sons take Moabite wives. This intermarriage alone is surprising, but even more startling is that the mixed marriage of Ruth and Boaz is blessed by God and produces Israel's greatest king, King David (Ruth 4:18–22).

■ Ruth 1:1—4:12

Ruth

Elimelech's Family Goes to Moab

1:1 Now it came to pass, in the days when the judges ruled, that there was a famine in the land. And a certain man of Bethlehem, Judah, went to dwell in the country of Moab, he and his wife and his two sons. ²The name of the man *was* Elimelech, the name of his wife *was* Naomi, and the names of his two sons *were* Mahlon and Chilion—Ephrathites of Bethlehem, Judah. And they went to the country of Moab and remained there. ³Then Elimelech, Naomi's husband, died; and she was left, and her two sons. ⁴Now they took wives of the women of Moab: the name of the one *was* Orpah, and the name of the other Ruth. And they dwelt there about ten years. ⁵Then both Mahlon and Chilion also died; so the woman survived her two sons and her husband.

Naomi Returns with Ruth

⁶Then she arose with her daughters-in-law that she might return from the country of Moab, for she had heard in the country of Moab that the LORD had visited His people by giving them bread. ⁷Therefore she went out from the place where she was, and her two daughters-in-law with her; and they went on the way to return to the land of Judah. ⁸And Naomi said to her two daughters-in-law, "Go, return each to her mother's house. The LORD deal kindly with you, as you have dealt with the dead and with me. ⁹The LORD grant that you may find rest, each in the house of her husband."

So she kissed them, and they lifted up their voices and wept. ¹⁰And they said to her, "Surely we will return with you to your people."

¹¹But Naomi said, "Turn back, my daughters; why will you go with me? *Are* there still sons in my womb, that they may be your husbands? ¹²Turn back, my daughters, go—for I am too old to have a husband. If I should say I have hope, *if* I should have a husband tonight and should also bear sons, ¹³would you wait for them till they were grown? Would you restrain yourselves from having husbands? No, my daughters; for it grieves me very much for your sakes that the hand of the LORD has gone out against me!"

¹⁴Then they lifted up their voices and wept again; and Orpah kissed her mother-in-law, but Ruth clung to her.

15And she said, "Look, your sister-in-law has gone back to her people and to her gods; return after your sister-in-law."

16But Ruth said:

"Entreat me not to leave you,
  Or to turn back from following after
    you;
  For wherever you go, I will go;
  And wherever you lodge, I will lodge;
  Your people *shall be* my people,
  And your God, my God.
17 Where you die, I will die,
  And there will I be buried.
  The LORD do so to me, and more also,
  If *anything but* death parts you and
    me."

18When she saw that she was determined to go with her, she stopped speaking to her.

19Now the two of them went until they came to Bethlehem. And it happened, when they had come to Bethlehem, that all the city was excited because of them; and the women said, "*Is* this Naomi?"

20But she said to them, "Do not call me Naomi;a call me Mara,b for the Almighty has dealt very bitterly with me. 21I went out full, and the LORD has brought me home again empty. Why do you call me Naomi, since the LORD has testified against me, and the Almighty has afflicted me?"

22So Naomi returned, and Ruth the Moabitess her daughter-in-law with her, who returned from the country of Moab. Now they came to Bethlehem at the beginning of barley harvest.

Ruth Meets Boaz

2 1There was a relative of Naomi's husband, a man of great wealth, of the family of Elimelech. His name *was* Boaz. 2So Ruth the Moabitess said to Naomi, "Please let me go to the field, and glean heads of grain after *him* in whose sight I may find favor."

And she said to her, "Go, my daughter."

3Then she left, and went and gleaned in the field after the reapers. And she happened to come to the part of the field *belonging* to Boaz, who *was* of the family of Elimelech.

4Now behold, Boaz came from Bethlehem, and said to the reapers, "The LORD *be* with you!"

And they answered him, "The LORD bless you!"

5Then Boaz said to his servant who was in charge of the reapers, "Whose young woman *is* this?"

6So the servant who was in charge of the reapers answered and said, "It *is* the young Moabite woman who came back with Naomi from the country of Moab. 7And she said, 'Please let me glean and gather after the reapers among the sheaves.' So she came and has continued from morning until now, though she rested a little in the house."

8Then Boaz said to Ruth, "You will listen, my daughter, will you not? Do not go to glean in another field, nor go from here, but stay close by my young women. 9*Let* your eyes *be* on the field which they reap, and go after them. Have I not commanded the young men not to touch you? And when you are thirsty, go to the vessels and drink from what the young men have drawn."

10So she fell on her face, bowed down to the ground, and said to him, "Why have I found favor in your eyes, that you should take notice of me, since I *am* a foreigner?"

11And Boaz answered and said to her, "It has been fully reported to me, all that you have done for your mother-in-law since the death of your husband, and *how* you have left your father and your mother and the land of your birth, and have come to a people whom you did not know before. 12The LORD repay your work, and a full reward be given you by the LORD God of Israel, under whose wings you have come for refuge."

13Then she said, "Let me find favor in your sight, my lord; for you have comforted me, and have spoken kindly to your maidservant, though I am not like one of your maidservants."

14Now Boaz said to her at mealtime, "Come here, and eat of the bread, and dip your piece of bread in the vinegar." So she sat beside the reapers, and he passed parched *grain* to her; and she ate and was satisfied, and kept some back. 15And when she rose up to glean, Boaz commanded his young men, saying, "Let her glean even among the sheaves, and do not reproach her. 16Also let *grain* from the bundles fall purposely for her; leave *it* that she may glean, and do not rebuke her."

17So she gleaned in the field until

1:20 aLiterally *Pleasant* bLiterally *Bitter*

NAOMI'S CLOSE RELATIVE (Ruth 2:20)

Naomi recognizes God's kindness in the person of Boaz, who is one of her "close relatives" (Ruth 2:20). The Hebrew word *goel,* translated "close relative," means "to redeem." Such relatives were redeemers because they had a legal obligation under the Law of Moses to redeem or buy back the property of destitute relatives from foreclosure (Lev. 25:25).

The close relative could redeem various types of obligations through a monetary payment. Individuals could reclaim their land or house. An indentured servant could be redeemed from servitude. A religious offering could be reclaimed. Yet some redemptions were not made with a sum of money. The closest male relative of a murdered Israelite was a "blood redeemer." This "avenger of blood" (2 Sam. 14:11) was required to avenge the blood of the dead kinsman with the life of the murderer.

The closest adult male relative of a deceased person was required to assure the economic welfare of the deceased's kin. In this case, the legal custom of the close relative was very similar to another legal custom—the levirate marriage. The close relative was to continue the name of his deceased male relative by legally acquiring the dead man's wife (Deut. 25:5, 6). The children of the new union then inherited the property of the deceased—the former husband.

Naomi hoped that Boaz would accept his dual responsibility as her close relative. One responsibility was to redeem Naomi's land, which she had sold in her destitute condition (Ruth 4:3, 4). Yet a second responsibility was to marry Naomi's daughter-in-law Ruth, continuing the name of Ruth's dead husband (4:5).

---

evening, and beat out what she had gleaned, and it was about an ephah of barley. ¹⁸Then she took *it* up and went into the city, and her mother-in-law saw what she had gleaned. So she brought out and gave to her what she had kept back after she had been satisfied.

¹⁹And her mother-in-law said to her, "Where have you gleaned today? And where did you work? Blessed be the one who took notice of you."

So she told her mother-in-law with whom she had worked, and said, "The man's name with whom I worked today *is* Boaz."

²⁰Then Naomi said to her daughter-in-law, "Blessed *be* he of the LORD, who has not forsaken His kindness to the living and the dead!" And Naomi said to her, "This man *is* a relation of ours, one of our close relatives."

²¹Ruth the Moabitess said, "He also said to me, 'You shall stay close by my young men until they have finished all my harvest.'"

²²And Naomi said to Ruth her daughter-in-law, "*It is* good, my daughter, that you go out with his young women, and that people do not meet you in any other field."

²³So she stayed close by the young women of Boaz, to glean until the end of barley harvest and wheat harvest; and she dwelt with her mother-in-law.

Ruth's Redemption Assured

3 ¹Then Naomi her mother-in-law said to her, "My daughter, shall I not seek security for you, that it may be well with you? ²Now Boaz, whose young women you were with, *is he* not our relative? In fact, he is winnowing barley tonight at the threshing floor. ³Therefore wash yourself and anoint yourself, put on your *best* garment and go down to the threshing floor; *but* do not make yourself known to the man until he has finished eating and drinking. ⁴Then it shall be, when he lies down, that you shall notice the place where he lies; and you shall go in, uncover his feet, and lie down; and he will tell you what you should do."

⁵And she said to her, "All that you say to me I will do."

⁶So she went down to the threshing floor and did according to all that her mother-in-law instructed her. ⁷And after Boaz had eaten and drunk, and his heart was cheerful, he went to lie down at the end of the heap of grain; and she came softly, uncovered his feet, and lay down.

⁸Now it happened at midnight that the man was startled, and turned himself; and

there, a woman was lying at his feet. [9]And he said, "Who *are* you?"

So she answered, "I *am* Ruth, your maidservant. Take your maidservant under your wing,[a] for you are a close relative."

[10]Then he said, "Blessed *are* you of the LORD, my daughter! For you have shown more kindness at the end than at the beginning, in that you did not go after young men, whether poor or rich. [11]And now, my daughter, do not fear. I will do for you all that you request, for all the people of my town know that you *are* a virtuous woman. [12]Now it is true that I *am* a close relative; however, there is a relative closer than I. [13]Stay this night, and in the morning it shall be *that* if he will perform the duty of a close relative for you—good; let him do it. But if he does not want to perform the duty for you, then I will perform the duty for you, *as* the LORD lives! Lie down until morning."

[14]So she lay at his feet until morning, and she arose before one could recognize another. Then he said, "Do not let it be known that the woman came to the threshing floor." [15]Also he said, "Bring the shawl that *is* on you and hold it." And when she held it, he measured six *ephahs* of barley, and laid *it* on her. Then she[a] went into the city.

[16]When she came to her mother-in-law, she said, "*Is* that you, my daughter?"

Then she told her all that the man had done for her. [17]And she said, "These six *ephahs* of barley he gave me; for he said to me, 'Do not go empty-handed to your mother-in-law.'"

[18]Then she said, "Sit still, my daughter, until you know how the matter will turn out; for the man will not rest until he has concluded the matter this day."

Boaz Redeems Ruth

4 [1]Now Boaz went up to the gate and sat down there; and behold, the close relative of whom Boaz had spoken came by. So Boaz said, "Come aside, friend,[a] sit down here." So he came aside and sat down. [2]And he took ten men of the elders of the city, and said, "Sit down here." So they sat down. [3]Then he said to the close relative, "Naomi, who has come back from the country of Moab, sold the piece of land which *belonged* to our brother Elimelech. [4]And I thought to inform you, saying, 'Buy *it* back in the presence of the inhabitants and the elders of my people. If you will redeem *it,* redeem *it;* but if you[a] will not redeem *it, then* tell me, that I may know; for *there is* no one but you to redeem *it,* and I *am* next after you.'"

And he said, "I will redeem *it.*"

[5]Then Boaz said, "On the day you buy the field from the hand of Naomi, you must also buy *it* from Ruth the Moabitess, the wife of the dead, to perpetuate[a] the name of the dead through his inheritance."

[6]And the close relative said, "I cannot redeem *it* for myself, lest I ruin my own inheritance. You redeem my right of redemption for yourself, for I cannot redeem *it.*"

[7]Now this *was the custom* in former times in Israel concerning redeeming and exchanging, to confirm anything: one man took off his sandal and gave *it* to the other, and this *was* a confirmation in Israel.

[8]Therefore the close relative said to Boaz, "Buy *it* for yourself." So he took off his sandal. [9]And Boaz said to the elders and all the people, "You *are* witnesses this day that I have bought all that was Elimelech's, and all that *was* Chilion's and Mahlon's, from the hand of Naomi. [10]Moreover, Ruth the Moabitess, the widow of Mahlon, I have acquired as my wife, to perpetuate the name of the dead through his inheritance, that the name of the dead may not be cut off from among his brethren and

---

3:9 [a]Or *Spread the corner of your garment over your maidservant*   3:15 [a]Many Hebrew manuscripts, Syriac, and Vulgate read *she;* Masoretic Text, Septuagint, and Targum read *he.*   4:1 [a]Hebrew *peloni almoni;* literally *so and so*   4:4 [a]Following many Hebrew manuscripts, Septuagint, Syriac, Targum, and Vulgate; Masoretic Text reads *he.*
4:5 [a]Literally *raise up*

MARRIAGE AND FAMILY

The "duty of a close relative" (Ruth 3:13) was a legal provision aimed at preserving the name and family line of the deceased relative. If a husband died without children, his brother had the duty of marrying the widow and raising a family for him. The custom illustrates how central genealogy was in that culture.

LEVIRATE MARRIAGE AND SANDAL CEREMONY (Ruth 4:1–10)

Levir is the Latin word for "brother-in-law." The levirate marriage is described in the legal text of Deut. 25:5–10. If a man died without leaving a male heir, his widow was to marry within the husband's family. Moreover, the husband's brother (i.e., the widow's brother-in-law) was required to perform the duty of the levir, that is, marry the woman and produce a son.

Preserving the family line was important in Israel. The levirate marriage was linked to laws of inheritance, so any offspring from the husband's brother were considered children of the deceased. The firstborn son would take the name of the dead former husband.

If the brother-in-law refused to perform the levir's duty, the woman was to perform the ceremony of the removal of his sandal (Deut. 25:8–10). A woman had a right to bear children to her deceased husband. If her brother-in-law refused her that right, she could publicly humiliate him. She was then allowed to marry outside of the family.

The primary purpose of the levirate marriage law was to protect the widow and help compensate the deceased husband's family for their personal loss. In Naomi's case, since she was beyond childbearing age, the levirate marriage would be to her widowed daughter-in-law Ruth. Naomi's closest relative was not willing to assume this obligation (Ruth 4:6). Perhaps he considered that if he had a son by Ruth who became his only surviving heir, all of his property would belong to the family of Elimelech, Naomi's deceased husband.

In the sandal ceremony of Ruth 4:6–8 there seems to be no disdain for the relative who declined to perform the duty of the levir. The significance of taking off the sandal seems to imply the passing of one's legal rights to another. Boaz thus gained the right to clear the property against any future claims, and to marry Ruth (4:9, 10).

from his position at the gate.[a] You *are* witnesses this day."

¹¹And all the people who *were* at the gate, and the elders, said, "*We are* witnesses. The Lord make the woman who is coming to your house like Rachel and Leah, the two who built the house of Israel; and may you prosper in Ephrathah and be famous in Bethlehem. ¹²May your house be like the house of Perez, whom Tamar bore to Judah, because of the offspring which the Lord will give you from this young woman."

From Turbulence to Rest

The story of Ruth takes place in the latter part of the judges' period ("in the days when the judges ruled," Ruth 1:1). Its rural setting and wholesome yet believable characters provide stark contrast to the violence and chaos of those days when "there was no king in Israel" (Judg. 21:25).

The genealogy at the end of the book (Ruth 4:18–22) reveals that the characters of this story are none other than the great-grandparents of King David. This story of faithfulness and family solidarity not only contrasts to the turbulence of the judges' period, but points forward to the reign of David (1010–970 B.C.)—

to a time when Israel would have "rest on every side" (1 Kin. 5:4).

■ Ruth 4:13–22

Ruth
Descendants of Boaz and Ruth

4 :13 So Boaz took Ruth and she became his wife; and when he went in to her, the Lord gave her conception, and she bore a son. ¹⁴Then the women said to Naomi, "Blessed *be* the Lord, who has not left you this day without a close relative; and may his name be famous in Israel! ¹⁵And may he be to you a restorer of life and a nourisher of your old age; for your daughter-in-law, who loves you, who is better to you than seven sons, has borne him." ¹⁶Then Naomi took the child and laid him on her bosom, and became a nurse to him. ¹⁷Also the neighbor women gave him a name, saying, "There is a son born to Naomi." And they called his name Obed. He *is* the father of Jesse, the father of David.

¹⁸Now this *is* the genealogy of Perez: Perez begot Hezron; ¹⁹Hezron begot Ram, and Ram begot Amminadab; ²⁰Amminadab begot Nahshon, and Nahshon begot

4:10 ᵃProbably his civic office

Salmon;[a] [21]Salmon begot Boaz, and Boaz begot Obed; [22]Obed begot Jesse, and Jesse begot David.

The Books of 1 and 2 Samuel

The books of Judges and Ruth point toward the beginning of an Israelite monarchy; in the books of Samuel the monarchy takes shape. In general terms, 1 Samuel tells of the beginning of the kingdom to the end of the reign of the first king, Saul. Then 2 Samuel is devoted to the career of David, Israel's second, and greatest, king.

But 1 Samuel begins not with a king, but with the imposing figure of Samuel. Samuel is priest and prophet and judge, indeed everything except king. It is from Samuel that the people seek a king. It is Samuel whom God sends to anoint first Saul, then David. It is Samuel who announces God's rejection of Saul (ch. 15), and when Saul's kingdom totters, it is from Samuel's ghost that Saul seeks advice (ch. 28).

The books of Samuel never identify an author, and may have been constructed from several different sources. For instance, the history from 2 Sam. 9 to 1 Kin. 2 gives such intimate detail of the inner workings of David's court that many have called it an independent eyewitness account. If so, it has been connected with other, more general, historical sources to form the present books.

■ 1 Samuel 1:1—6:21

1 Samuel
The Family of Elkanah

1 :1 Now there was a certain man of Ramathaim Zophim, of the mountains of Ephraim, and his name *was* Elkanah the son of Jeroham, the son of Elihu,[a] the son

of Tohu,[b] the son of Zuph, an Ephraimite. [2]And he had two wives: the name of one *was* Hannah, and the name of the other Peninnah. Peninnah had children, but Hannah had no children. [3]This man went up from his city yearly to worship and sacrifice to the LORD of hosts in Shiloh. Also the two sons of Eli, Hophni and Phinehas, the priests of the LORD, *were* there. [4]And whenever the time came for Elkanah to make an offering, he would give portions to Peninnah his wife and to all her sons and daughters. [5]But to Hannah he would give a double portion, for he loved Hannah, although the LORD had closed her womb. [6]And her rival also provoked her severely, to make her miserable, because the LORD had closed her womb. [7]So it was, year by year, when she went up to the house of the LORD, that she provoked her; therefore she wept and did not eat.

Hannah's Vow

[8]Then Elkanah her husband said to her, "Hannah, why do you weep? Why do you not eat? And why is your heart grieved? *Am* I not better to you than ten sons?"

[9]So Hannah arose after they had finished eating and drinking in Shiloh. Now Eli the priest was sitting on the seat by the doorpost of the tabernacle[a] of the LORD. [10]And she *was* in bitterness of soul, and prayed to the LORD and wept in anguish. [11]Then she made a vow and said, "O LORD of hosts, if You will indeed look on the affliction of Your maidservant and remember me, and not forget Your maidservant, but will give Your maidservant a male child, then I will give him to the LORD all the days of his life, and no razor shall come upon his head."

[12]And it happened, as she continued praying before the LORD, that Eli watched her mouth. [13]Now Hannah spoke in her heart; only her lips moved, but her voice was not heard. Therefore Eli thought she was drunk. [14]So Eli said to her, "How long will you be drunk? Put your wine away from you!"

4:20 [a]Hebrew *Salmah*   **1 Sam.** 1:1 [a]Spelled *Eliel* in 1 Chronicles 6:34   [b]Spelled *Toah* in 1 Chronicles 6:34   1:9 [a]Hebrew *heykal*, palace or temple

---

MARRIAGE AND FAMILY

Polygamy has flourished where women have occupied a low station in society. Israelites, such as Elkanah (1 Sam. 1:2), who had several wives were following the culture of that time. The rivalry of the wives was related to their desire for children, and was marked by jealousy, struggle, taunts, and scheming (1:6). Historically, the church has consistently opposed polygamy and seldom made even temporary concessions to it.

RITUAL FOR AN AUDIENCE WITH GOD (1 Sam. 1:8–18)

In the ancient Near East people believed that the gods would appear to you if you went to a sacred site. Worshipers followed a ritual that included a sacrifice, a meal dedicated to the god, and a prayer of petition, then spent the night in the holy place. Often the deity appeared to the worshiper in a dream (see 1 Kin. 3:5), but sometimes through the priests or a direct vision.

According to a text from about 2150 B.C., Gudea, king of Lagash, slept at the site of a proposed shrine. Gudea asked permission of the god Ningirsu to build a temple for the deity at that site. Ningirsu appeared to Gudea in a dream, giving him not only permission to build, but also the plans for the building itself. Other examples of this kind of prayer are found in Mesopotamia, Asia Minor, Egypt, Phoenicia, and the Greco-Roman world (including the epics of Homer).

Each year Elkanah and his wife Hannah visited the holy place at Shiloh (1 Sam. 1:3, 7). Hannah came to the sanctuary of Yahweh at Shiloh, where her husband Elkanah made a sacrifice for her (1:4, 5). After eating what was possibly a meal dedicated to Yahweh, Hannah made her prayer of petition (1:9–11). She was answered by Eli, God's priest, in God's name, and her request was granted in the birth of Samuel (1:20).

15But Hannah answered and said, "No, my lord, I *am* a woman of sorrowful spirit. I have drunk neither wine nor intoxicating drink, but have poured out my soul before the LORD. 16Do not consider your maidservant a wicked woman,a for out of the abundance of my complaint and grief I have spoken until now."

17Then Eli answered and said, "Go in peace, and the God of Israel grant your petition which you have asked of Him."

18And she said, "Let your maidservant find favor in your sight." So the woman went her way and ate, and her face was no longer *sad*.

Samuel Is Born and Dedicated

19Then they rose early in the morning and worshiped before the LORD, and returned and came to their house at Ramah. And Elkanah knew Hannah his wife, and the LORD remembered her. 20So it came to pass in the process of time that Hannah conceived and bore a son, and called his name Samuel,a *saying,* "Because I have asked for him from the LORD."

21Now the man Elkanah and all his house went up to offer to the LORD the yearly sacrifice and his vow. 22But Hannah did not go up, for she said to her husband, "*Not* until the child is weaned; then I will take him, that he may appear before the LORD and remain there forever."

23So Elkanah her husband said to her, "Do what seems best to you; wait until you have weaned him. Only let the LORD establish Hisa word." Then the woman stayed and nursed her son until she had weaned him.

24Now when she had weaned him, she took him up with her, with three bulls,a one ephah of flour, and a skin of wine, and brought him to the house of the LORD in Shiloh. And the child *was* young. 25Then they slaughtered a bull, and brought the child to Eli. 26And she said, "O my lord! As your soul lives, my lord, I *am* the woman who stood by you here, praying to the LORD. 27For this child I prayed, and the LORD has granted me my petition which I asked of Him. 28Therefore I also have lent him to the LORD; as long as he lives he shall be lent to the LORD." So they worshiped the LORD there.

Hannah's Prayer

2 1And Hannah prayed and said:

"My heart rejoices in the LORD;
My horna is exalted in the LORD.
I smile at my enemies,
Because I rejoice in Your salvation.

1:16 aLiterally *daughter of Belial*   1:20 aLiterally *Heard by God*   1:23 aFollowing Masoretic Text, Targum, and Vulgate; Dead Sea Scrolls, Septuagint, and Syriac read *your*.   1:24 aDead Sea Scrolls, Septuagint, and Syriac read *a three-year-old bull.*   2:1 aThat is, strength

2 "No one is holy like the LORD,
  For *there is* none besides You,
  Nor *is there* any rock like our God.

3 "Talk no more so very proudly;
  Let no arrogance come from your
   mouth,
  For the LORD *is* the God of knowledge;
  And by Him actions are weighed.

4 "The bows of the mighty men *are*
   broken,
  And those who stumbled are girded
   with strength.
5 *Those who were* full have hired
   themselves out for bread,
  And the hungry have ceased *to*
   hunger.
  Even the barren has borne seven,
  And she who has many children has
   become feeble.

6 "The LORD kills and makes alive;
  He brings down to the grave and
   brings up.
7 The LORD makes poor and makes rich;
  He brings low and lifts up.
8 He raises the poor from the dust
  And lifts the beggar from the ash
   heap,
  To set *them* among princes
  And make them inherit the throne of
   glory.

  "For the pillars of the earth *are* the
   LORD's,
  And He has set the world upon them.
9 He will guard the feet of His saints,
  But the wicked shall be silent in
   darkness.

  "For by strength no man shall prevail.
10 The adversaries of the LORD shall be
   broken in pieces;
  From heaven He will thunder against
   them.
  The LORD will judge the ends of the
   earth.

  "He will give strength to His king,
  And exalt the horn of His anointed."

11Then Elkanah went to his house at
Ramah. But the child ministered to the
LORD before Eli the priest.

The Wicked Sons of Eli

12Now the sons of Eli *were* corrupt;[a]
they did not know the LORD. 13And the
priests' custom with the people *was that*
when any man offered a sacrifice, the
priest's servant would come with a three-
pronged fleshhook in his hand while the
meat was boiling. 14Then he would thrust
it into the pan, or kettle, or caldron, or pot;
and the priest would take for himself all
that the fleshhook brought up. So they did
in Shiloh to all the Israelites who came
there. 15Also, before they burned the fat,
the priest's servant would come and say to
the man who sacrificed, "Give meat for
roasting to the priest, for he will not take
boiled meat from you, but raw."

16And *if* the man said to him, "They
should really burn the fat first; *then* you
may take *as much* as your heart desires,"
he would then answer him, "*No,* but you
must give *it* now; and if not, I will take *it*
by force."

17Therefore the sin of the young men
was very great before the LORD, for men
abhorred the offering of the LORD.

Samuel's Childhood Ministry

18But Samuel ministered before the
LORD, *even as* a child, wearing a linen
ephod. 19Moreover his mother used to
make him a little robe, and bring *it* to him
year by year when she came up with her
husband to offer the yearly sacrifice. 20And
Eli would bless Elkanah and his wife, and
say, "The LORD give you descendants from
this woman for the loan that was given to
the LORD." Then they would go to their own
home.

21And the LORD visited Hannah, so
that she conceived and bore three sons and

TIME CAPSULE *1178 to 1169 B.C.*

1178 Ramesses III defends Egypt against
   Libyan invasion

1175 Sea battle between Ramesses III
   and the Sea Peoples

1175 The Philistines settle on southern
   coast of Palestine

1172 Ramesses III repels another Libyan
   invasion of Egypt

1169 Wall carving from funerary temple
   near Thebes shows sea battle of
   Ramesses III

2:12 aLiterally *sons of Belial*

two daughters. Meanwhile the child Samuel grew before the LORD.

Prophecy Against Eli's Household

22Now Eli was very old; and he heard everything his sons did to all Israel,ª and how they lay with the women who assembled at the door of the tabernacle of meeting. 23So he said to them, "Why do you do such things? For I hear of your evil dealings from all the people. 24No, my sons! For it is not a good report that I hear. You make the LORD's people transgress. 25If one man sins against another, God will judge him. But if a man sins against the LORD, who will intercede for him?" Nevertheless they did not heed the voice of their father, because the LORD desired to kill them.

26And the child Samuel grew in stature, and in favor both with the LORD and men.

27Then a man of God came to Eli and said to him, "Thus says the LORD: 'Did I not clearly reveal Myself to the house of your father when they were in Egypt in Pharaoh's house? 28Did I not choose him out of all the tribes of Israel to be My priest, to offer upon My altar, to burn incense, and to wear an ephod before Me? And did I not give to the house of your father all the offerings of the children of Israel made by fire? 29Why do you kick at My sacrifice and My offering which I have commanded in My dwelling place, and honor your sons more than Me, to make yourselves fat with the best of all the offerings of Israel My people?' 30Therefore the LORD God of Israel says: 'I said indeed that your house and the house of your father would walk before Me forever.' But now the LORD says: 'Far be it from Me; for those who honor Me I will honor, and those who despise Me shall be lightly esteemed. 31Behold, the days are coming that I will cut off your arm and the arm of your father's house, so that there will not be an old man in your house. 32And you will see an enemy in My dwelling place, despite all the good

which God does for Israel. And there shall not be an old man in your house forever. 33But any of your men whom I do not cut off from My altar shall consume your eyes and grieve your heart. And all the descendants of your house shall die in the flower of their age. 34Now this shall be a sign to you that will come upon your two sons, on Hophni and Phinehas: in one day they shall die, both of them. 35Then I will raise up for Myself a faithful priest who shall do according to what is in My heart and in My mind. I will build him a sure house, and he shall walk before My anointed forever. 36And it shall come to pass that everyone who is left in your house will come and bow down to him for a piece of silver and a morsel of bread, and say, "Please, put me in one of the priestly positions, that I may eat a piece of bread." ' "

Samuel's First Prophecy

3 1Now the boy Samuel ministered to the LORD before Eli. And the word of the LORD was rare in those days; there was no widespread revelation. 2And it came to pass at that time, while Eli was lying down in his place, and when his eyes had begun to grow so dim that he could not see, 3and before the lamp of God went out in the tabernacleª of the LORD where the ark of God was, and while Samuel was lying down, 4that the LORD called Samuel. And he answered, "Here I am!" 5So he ran to Eli and said, "Here I am, for you called me."

And he said, "I did not call; lie down again." And he went and lay down.

6Then the LORD called yet again, "Samuel!"

So Samuel arose and went to Eli, and said, "Here I am, for you called me." He answered, "I did not call, my son; lie down again." 7(Now Samuel did not yet know the LORD, nor was the word of the LORD yet revealed to him.)

2:22 ªFollowing Masoretic Text, Targum, and Vulgate; Dead Sea Scrolls and Septuagint omit the rest of this verse.   3:3 ªHebrew heykal, palace or temple

CULTURE AND SOCIETY

The reply "Here I am!" (1 Sam. 3:4) is the reply a servant would give to an employer, like a soldier coming to attention and returning a salute. Samuel's attitude and immediate response to the voice of God is first his response to Eli. Moments later the young Samuel responded to God with the same willingness to serve (3:10).

⁸And the LORD called Samuel again the third time. So he arose and went to Eli, and said, "Here I am, for you did call me."

Then Eli perceived that the LORD had called the boy. ⁹Therefore Eli said to Samuel, "Go, lie down; and it shall be, if He calls you, that you must say, 'Speak, LORD, for Your servant hears.'" So Samuel went and lay down in his place.

¹⁰Now the LORD came and stood and called as at other times, "Samuel! Samuel!"

And Samuel answered, "Speak, for Your servant hears."

¹¹Then the LORD said to Samuel: "Behold, I will do something in Israel at which both ears of everyone who hears it will tingle. ¹²In that day I will perform against Eli all that I have spoken concerning his house, from beginning to end. ¹³For I have told him that I will judge his house forever for the iniquity which he knows, because his sons made themselves vile, and he did not restrain them. ¹⁴And therefore I have sworn to the house of Eli that the iniquity of Eli's house shall not be atoned for by sacrifice or offering forever."

¹⁵So Samuel lay down until morning,[a] and opened the doors of the house of the LORD. And Samuel was afraid to tell Eli the vision. ¹⁶Then Eli called Samuel and said, "Samuel, my son!"

He answered, "Here I am."

¹⁷And he said, "What *is* the word that *the* LORD spoke to you? Please do not hide *it* from me. God do so to you, and more also, if you hide anything from me of all the things that He said to you." ¹⁸Then Samuel told him everything, and hid nothing from him. And he said, "It *is* the LORD. Let Him do what seems good to Him."

¹⁹So Samuel grew, and the LORD was with him and let none of his words fall to the ground. ²⁰And all Israel from Dan to Beersheba knew that Samuel *had been* established as a prophet of the LORD. ²¹Then the LORD appeared again in Shiloh. For the LORD revealed Himself to Samuel in Shiloh by the word of the LORD.

4 ¹And the word of Samuel came to all Israel.[a]

The Ark of God Captured

Now Israel went out to battle against the Philistines, and encamped beside Ebenezer; and the Philistines encamped in Aphek. ²Then the Philistines put themselves in battle array against Israel. And when they joined battle, Israel was defeated by the Philistines, who killed about four thousand men of the army in the field. ³And when the people had come into the camp, the elders of Israel said, "Why has the LORD defeated us today before the Philistines? Let us bring the ark of the covenant of the LORD from Shiloh to us, that when it comes among us it may save us from the hand of our enemies." ⁴So the people sent to Shiloh, that they might bring from there the ark of the covenant of the LORD of hosts, who dwells *between* the cherubim. And the two sons of Eli, Hophni and Phinehas, *were* there with the ark of the covenant of God.

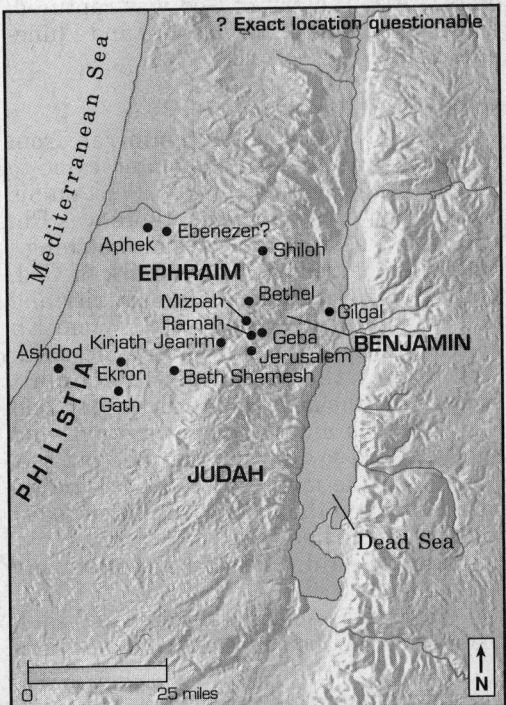

The Ministry of Samuel
At Shiloh God called Samuel to be His servant and prophet. Samuel called on Israel to put away their Baals and Ashtoreths, and to face judgment at Mizpah. Following Saul's defeat of the Ammonites, the people gathered at Gilgal where Samuel renewed the kingdom covenant with Israel and established Saul as king.

3:15 [a]Following Masoretic Text, Targum, and Vulgate; Septuagint adds *and he arose in the morning.*

4:1 [a]Following Masoretic Text and Targum; Septuagint and Vulgate add *And it came to pass in those days that the Philistines gathered themselves together to fight;* Septuagint adds further *against Israel.*

⁵And when the ark of the covenant of the LORD came into the camp, all Israel shouted so loudly that the earth shook. ⁶Now when the Philistines heard the noise of the shout, they said, "What *does* the sound of this great shout in the camp of the Hebrews *mean?*" Then they understood that the ark of the LORD had come into the camp. ⁷So the Philistines were afraid, for they said, "God has come into the camp!" And they said, "Woe to us! For such a thing has never happened before. ⁸Woe to us! Who will deliver us from the hand of these mighty gods? These *are* the gods who struck the Egyptians with all the plagues in the wilderness. ⁹Be strong and conduct yourselves like men, you Philistines, that you do not become servants of the Hebrews, as they have been to you. Conduct yourselves like men, and fight!"

¹⁰So the Philistines fought, and Israel was defeated, and every man fled to his tent. There was a very great slaughter, and there fell of Israel thirty thousand foot soldiers. ¹¹Also the ark of God was captured; and the two sons of Eli, Hophni and Phinehas, died.

Death of Eli

¹²Then a man of Benjamin ran from the battle line the same day, and came to Shiloh with his clothes torn and dirt on his head. ¹³Now when he came, there was Eli, sitting on a seat by the wayside watching,ᵃ for his heart trembled for the ark of God. And when the man came into the city and told *it,* all the city cried out. ¹⁴When Eli heard the noise of the outcry, he said, "What *does* the sound of this tumult *mean?*" And the man came quickly and told Eli. ¹⁵Eli was ninety-eight years old, and his eyes were so dim that he could not see.

¹⁶Then the man said to Eli, "I *am* he who came from the battle. And I fled today from the battle line."

And he said, "What happened, my son?"

¹⁷So the messenger answered and said, "Israel has fled before the Philistines, and there has been a great slaughter among the people. Also your two sons, Hophni and Phinehas, are dead; and the ark of God has been captured."

¹⁸Then it happened, when he made mention of the ark of God, that Eli fell off the seat backward by the side of the gate; and his neck was broken and he died, for the man was old and heavy. And he had judged Israel forty years.

Ichabod

¹⁹Now his daughter-in-law, Phinehas' wife, was with child, *due* to be delivered; and when she heard the news that the ark of God was captured, and that her father-in-law and her husband were dead, she bowed herself and gave birth, for her labor pains came upon her. ²⁰And about the time of her death the women who stood by her said to her, "Do not fear, for you have borne a son." But she did not answer, nor did she regard *it.* ²¹Then she named the child Ichabod,ᵃ saying, "The glory has departed from Israel!" because the ark of God had been captured and because of her father-in-law and her husband. ²²And she said, "The glory has departed from Israel, for the ark of God has been captured."

The Philistines and the Ark

5 ¹Then the Philistines took the ark of God and brought it from Ebenezer to Ashdod. ²When the Philistines took the ark of God, they brought it into the house of Dagonᵃ and set it by Dagon. ³And when the people of Ashdod arose early in the morning, there was Dagon, fallen on its face to the earth before the ark of the LORD. So they took Dagon and set it in its place again. ⁴And when they arose early the next morning, there was Dagon, fallen on its face to the ground before the ark of the LORD. The head of Dagon and both the

---

4:13 ᵃFollowing Masoretic Text and Vulgate; Septuagint reads *beside the gate watching the road.*   4:21 ᵃLiterally *Inglorious*   5:2 ᵃA Philistine idol

BELIEFS AND IDEAS

In Hebrew the name "Ichabod" means "inglorious," reflecting the departure of God's glory from Israel (1 Sam. 4:21). In the Old Testament, the glory of God is the radiance perceived when He is present, and is often associated with the ark of the covenant. In general, the glory of God is the appearance of what makes Him unique and admirable, especially His power and mercy.

DAGON BREAKS BEFORE GOD   (1 Sam. 5:1–5)

The Philistine community at Ashdod adopted one of the most widely worshiped gods arising from the middle Euphrates region. Dagon was known as a deity at two of the Philistine's five principal cities: Gaza (Judg. 16:21, 23) and Ashdod (1 Sam. 5:1–5). Dagon's temple at Ashdod still existed as late as the Hellenistic period (2nd century B.C.), when the city was known as Azotus (1 Macc. 10:83, 84).

The worship of Dagon is first recorded in the records of Sargon of Accad (c. 2350 B.C.), long before the time of the Philistines. The central temple of the cult was situated at Terqa, located just below the junction of the Habor and Euphrates rivers. Dagon was the patron deity of the territory governed from this city.

A lack of narrative materials makes it difficult to describe Dagon. The most reasonable theory—that he is the deity of grain—was suggested by Philo of Byblos, a 2nd-century A.D. Greek historian. The Hebrew noun *dagan* simply means "grain," and the central place of grain in the diet of all the cultures of the area might explain the popularity of the deity. A less likely, yet popular, theory connects Dagon to fish (Hebrew *dag* means "fish").

The Mari tablets (c. 1813–1760 B.C.) describe the activities of Dagon. As a ruling god, he led his people in warfare, provided for the fertility of the land and populace, protected the territory from human and divine encroachment, and took special care of the royal family. More interestingly, Dagon kept contact with his people by means of prophetic communication. Professional and nonprofessional prophets would report the will of the deity through those whom the god seized for such communication.

By Samuel's time the cult of Dagon had spread throughout Mesopotamia, Syria, and Palestine. Following ancient practice, a victorious Philistine city would bring booty taken from Israel's deity and place it before the image of their own deity. The breaking of Dagon's image in the presence of the ark of God (1 Sam. 5:3, 4) demonstrated the power Israel's God had over the Philistines' Dagon.

---

palms of its hands *were* broken off on the threshold; only Dagon's torso[a] was left of it. [5]Therefore neither the priests of Dagon nor any who come into Dagon's house tread on the threshold of Dagon in Ashdod to this day.

[6]But the hand of the LORD was heavy on the people of Ashdod, and He ravaged them and struck them with tumors,[a] *both* Ashdod and its territory. [7]And when the men of Ashdod saw how *it was,* they said, "The ark of the God of Israel must not remain with us, for His hand is harsh toward us and Dagon our god." [8]Therefore they sent and gathered to themselves all the lords of the Philistines, and said, "What shall we do with the ark of the God of Israel?"

And they answered, "Let the ark of the God of Israel be carried away to Gath." So they carried the ark of the God of Israel away. [9]So it was, after they had carried it away, that the hand of the LORD was against the city with a very great destruction; and He struck the men of the city, both small and great, and tumors broke out on them.

[10]Therefore they sent the ark of God to Ekron. So it was, as the ark of God came to Ekron, that the Ekronites cried out, saying, "They have brought the ark of the God of Israel to us, to kill us and our people!" [11]So they sent and gathered together all the lords of the Philistines, and said, "Send away the ark of the God of Israel, and let it go back to its own place, so that it does not kill us and our people." For there was a deadly destruction throughout all the city; the hand of God was very heavy there. [12]And the men who did not die were stricken with the tumors, and the cry of the city went up to heaven.

The Ark Returned to Israel

6 [1]Now the ark of the LORD was in the country of the Philistines seven

---

5:4 [a]Following Septuagint, Syriac, Targum, and Vulgate; Masoretic Text reads *Dagon.*
5:6 [a]Probably bubonic plague. Septuagint and Vulgate add here *And in the midst of their land rats sprang up, and there was a great death panic in the city.*

TESTING THE PRESENCE OF GOD (1 Sam. 6:1–9)

The Philistine reaction to the capture of the ark of God shows much about the theology of that ancient time. People believed that the deities behind the armies were the real military forces in a battle; the defeat of an enemy's army was also the defeat of the enemy's god. Because the Philistines had defeated the Israelite armies, they believed that their god Dagon was stronger than Yahweh, God of Israel. So they placed Yahweh's ark in Dagon's temple (1 Sam. 5:2).

The result was a plague (5:6) and a big embarrassment (5:4). The Philistines in Ashdod, Gath, and Ekron were defeated by Israel's God without the aid of human armies (5:6–10). Another ancient thought was that good or bad fortune could result from a sacred object. At first the Philistines believed that the plague was caused by the ark itself (5:10, 11). Though not certain that Israel's God was really behind these events, they decided to return the ark to the Israelites.

Before sending the ark out, the Philistines checked with their priests and diviners (6:2), a standard practice in the ancient Near East. Before any activity, official or mundane, worshipers inquired of the gods whether the action would be a good thing. The unexpected answer: send back the ark, along with gold images of tumors and rats, all in honor of Yahweh, God of Israel. Seeking cures, petitioners used models of disease as offerings to deities of healing. The objects served as a form of imitative magic, while the gold was a gift to the god.

Still not certain that Israel's God was really behind their problems, the Philistines set up a test. They yoked cows having calves (and untrained as draft animals) to the ark. If the cows turned back to their calves, as would be natural, so that the ark went nowhere, the Philistines would know the ark was no god, but just a gold-plated wooden box (6:9). The cows, of course, went where God directed them, and the Philistines witnessed a God who was more powerful than they (6:16).

---

months. ²And the Philistines called for the priests and the diviners, saying, "What shall we do with the ark of the LORD? Tell us how we should send it to its place."

³So they said, "If you send away the ark of the God of Israel, do not send it empty; but by all means return *it* to Him *with* a trespass offering. Then you will be healed, and it will be known to you why His hand is not removed from you."

⁴Then they said, "What *is* the trespass offering which we shall return to Him?"

They answered, "Five golden tumors and five golden rats, *according to* the number of the lords of the Philistines. For the same plague *was* on all of you and on your lords. ⁵Therefore you shall make images of your tumors and images of your rats that ravage the land, and you shall give glory to the God of Israel; perhaps He will lighten His hand from you, from your gods, and from your land. ⁶Why then do you harden your hearts as the Egyptians and Pharaoh hardened their hearts? When He did mighty things among them, did they not let the people go, that they might depart? ⁷Now therefore, make a new cart, take two milk cows which have never been yoked, and hitch the cows to the cart; and take their calves home, away from them. ⁸Then take the ark of the LORD and set it on the cart; and put the articles of gold which you are returning to Him *as* a trespass offering in a chest by its side. Then send it away, and let it go. ⁹And watch: if it goes up the road to its own territory, to Beth Shemesh, *then* He has done us this great evil. But if not, then we shall know that *it is* not His hand *that* struck us—it happened to us by chance."

¹⁰Then the men did so; they took two milk cows and hitched them to the cart, and shut up their calves at home. ¹¹And they set the ark of the LORD on the cart, and the chest with the gold rats and the images of their tumors. ¹²Then the cows headed straight for the road to Beth Shemesh, *and* went along the highway, lowing as they went, and did not turn aside to the right hand or the left. And the lords of the Philistines went after them to the border of Beth Shemesh.

¹³Now *the people of* Beth Shemesh *were* reaping their wheat harvest in the

valley; and they lifted their eyes and saw the ark, and rejoiced to see *it.* [14]Then the cart came into the field of Joshua of Beth Shemesh, and stood there; a large stone *was* there. So they split the wood of the cart and offered the cows as a burnt offering to the LORD. [15]The Levites took down the ark of the LORD and the chest that *was* with it, in which *were* the articles of gold, and put *them* on the large stone. Then the men of Beth Shemesh offered burnt offerings and made sacrifices the same day to the LORD. [16]So when the five lords of the Philistines had seen *it,* they returned to Ekron the same day.

[17]These *are* the golden tumors which the Philistines returned *as* a trespass offering to the LORD: one for Ashdod, one for Gaza, one for Ashkelon, one for Gath, one for Ekron; [18]and the golden rats, *according to* the number of all the cities of the Philistines *belonging* to the five lords, *both* fortified cities and country villages, even as far as the large *stone of* Abel on which they set the ark of the LORD, *which stone remains* to this day in the field of Joshua of Beth Shemesh.

[19]Then He struck the men of Beth Shemesh, because they had looked into the ark of the LORD. He struck fifty thousand and seventy men[a] of the people, and the people lamented because the LORD had struck the people with a great slaughter.

The Ark at Kirjath Jearim

[20]And the men of Beth Shemesh said, "Who is able to stand before this holy LORD God? And to whom shall it go up from us?" [21]So they sent messengers to the inhabitants of Kirjath Jearim, saying, "The Philistines have brought back the ark of the LORD; come down *and* take it up with you."

6:19 [a]Or *He struck seventy men of the people and fifty oxen of a man*   7:3 [a]Canaanite goddesses
7:4 [a]Canaanite goddesses

🧩 *Samuel's Public Ministry*

After the ark was returned from Philistine territory, it was taken to Kirjath Jearim (1 Sam. 7:1, 2). There it would remain for 20 years while Israel lamented under Philistine control (7:2). After these years, Samuel would begin what is recorded in 7:3–17 as his first public ministry.

The chronological comment of 7:2 is one

of a few such statements in 1 and 2 Samuel (see 1 Sam. 6:1; 2 Sam. 2:10, 11; 5:4, 5). Unfortunately, none of them allows us to establish dates for any of the primary events of this period. We do know that Samuel was an old man at the time he presented Saul as king in 1050 or 1020 B.C. (1 Sam. 8:1, 5; 10:24; see "When Did Saul Become King?" at 1 Sam. 13:1).

■ 1 Samuel 7:1–17

1 Samuel

7 :1 Then the men of Kirjath Jearim came and took the ark of the LORD, and brought it into the house of Abinadab on the hill, and consecrated Eleazar his son to keep the ark of the LORD.

Samuel Judges Israel

[2]So it was that the ark remained in Kirjath Jearim a long time; it was there twenty years. And all the house of Israel lamented after the LORD.

[3]Then Samuel spoke to all the house of Israel, saying, "If you return to the LORD with all your hearts, *then* put away the foreign gods and the Ashtoreths[a] from among you, and prepare your hearts for the LORD, and serve Him only; and He will deliver you from the hand of the Philistines." [4]So the children of Israel put away the Baals and the Ashtoreths,[a] and served the LORD only.

[5]And Samuel said, "Gather all Israel to Mizpah, and I will pray to the LORD for you." [6]So they gathered together at Mizpah, drew water, and poured *it* out before the LORD. And they fasted that day, and said there, "We have sinned against the LORD." And Samuel judged the children of Israel at Mizpah.

[7]Now when the Philistines heard that the children of Israel had gathered together at Mizpah, the lords of the Philistines went up against Israel. And when the children of Israel heard *of it,* they were afraid of the Philistines. [8]So the children of Israel said to Samuel, "Do not cease to cry out to the LORD our God for us, that He may save us from the hand of the Philistines."

[9]And Samuel took a suckling lamb and offered *it as* a whole burnt offering to the LORD. Then Samuel cried out to the LORD for Israel, and the LORD answered him. [10]Now as Samuel was offering up the burnt offering, the Philistines drew near to battle

against Israel. But the LORD thundered with a loud thunder upon the Philistines that day, and so confused them that they were overcome before Israel. ¹¹And the men of Israel went out of Mizpah and pursued the Philistines, and drove them back as far as below Beth Car. ¹²Then Samuel took a stone and set *it* up between Mizpah and Shen, and called its name Ebenezer,ᵃ saying, "Thus far the LORD has helped us."

¹³So the Philistines were subdued, and they did not come anymore into the territory of Israel. And the hand of the LORD was against the Philistines all the days of Samuel. ¹⁴Then the cities which the Philistines had taken from Israel were restored to Israel, from Ekron to Gath; and Israel recovered its territory from the hands of the Philistines. Also there was peace between Israel and the Amorites.

¹⁵And Samuel judged Israel all the days of his life. ¹⁶He went from year to year on a circuit to Bethel, Gilgal, and Mizpah, and judged Israel in all those places. ¹⁷But he always returned to Ramah, for his home *was* there. There he judged Israel, and there he built an altar to the LORD.

7:12 ᵃLiterally *Stone of Help*

The United Monarchy in Israel

Israel received what they had asked for: a king "like all the nations."

In the larger scope of ancient Near Eastern history, no time was more propitious for Israel to establish a monarchy. No great empire existed that might challenge a new kingdom. Assyria, the dominant power in Mesopotamia, was going through a temporary, but lengthy, period of weakness. Egypt's powerful New Kingdom (1550–1069 B.C.) was ending, and Egypt would never again be as strong.

Israel's major rivals during the united monarchy were the smaller kingdoms around Palestine. Of these, the Philistines on the coastal plain remained the greatest threat. Indeed, it was the Philistine threat that led the people to call for a king, and their first king, Saul, died fighting the Philistines. Not until Saul's successor, David, was this enemy finally subdued (2 Sam. 5:25).

David's rise to power as king attained high points in two events. First was his capture of the Jebusite city, Jerusalem (2 Sam. 5:6, 7). The city was well suited to be the capital of David's united nation. Second was his defeat of the Philistines, which enabled him to extend his rule across the Jordan River into Edom, Moab, and Ammon, and north into Syria (2 Sam. 8).

By the reign of Solomon, David's son and successor, Israel's borders had expanded to their greatest extent ever. Solomon consolidated his father's modest empire. By means of diplomatic ties, especially with the merchant city of Tyre to the north, Solomon became very successful in international trade. Within Israel, he constructed a new kind of state. The loose confederacy of independent tribes was replaced by a highly organized central bureaucracy, including military conscription and forced labor. Even Israel's worship center changed, from a movable tent shrine to a permanent temple, with the king himself performing some sacred functions. Israel received what they had asked for in 1 Sam. 8:5: a king "like all the nations."

Israel Asks for a King

Samuel's sons, as Eli's before him (1 Sam. 2:12–17), were not worthy of their father. In his old age Samuel had appointed his sons as judges, but nothing about their judging could be characterized as just (1 Sam. 8:1–3). The combination of Samuel's advancing age and his sons' corruption caused the people to seek a new type of leadership.

The people did not blame Samuel for his sons' ways. Nevertheless, they were ready to replace their corrupt judges with a king, following the pattern of other nations (8:4, 5). Samuel cautioned them about seeking a king. The picture he gave them was typical of Near Eastern kings: oppressive, greedy, and self-serving (8:10–18).

■ 1 Samuel 8:1–22

Is Beauty Judged by the Nose? (1 Sam. 8:13)

Samuel warned the people that a future king would take their daughters "to be perfumers, cooks, and bakers" (1 Sam. 8:13). Actually, perfumers were highly prized professionals, including priests among their ranks (1 Chr. 9:30). They are mentioned in the literatures of Ebla, Egypt, Mesopotamia, and Ugarit.

Due to the dry dusty atmosphere of the Near East, it is not surprising that a regular coating of moisturizing perfumed oils was applied to the body, including the hair. In such treatments, not only was the body covered with a fragrant potion, but more often the oily perfume served as a cosmetic. It was probably in this sphere that Esther received a six-month treatment of myrrh (perhaps, as a sunblock or skin softener) and "perfumes" (Esth. 2:12).

Among the perfumes available in Bible times were calamus, cassia, cinnamon, bdellium, frankincense, galbanum, myrrh, nard, and saffron. Many of these items were imported from distant lands, like Arabia, Nepal, Sri Lanka, India, and Somaliland. They were transported by caravans on overland routes, like the traders who bought Joseph while traveling from Gilead on their way to Egypt (Gen. 37:25). Perfumes probably also were transported by ship.

Among the specific uses of perfumes were preparations for the dead. When King Asa died (869 B.C.), he was laid in a bed in his tomb that was "filled with spices and various ingredients prepared in a mixture of ointments" (2 Chr. 16:14).

The medicinal use of perfumes and oils required specialists who knew not only how and when to apply these remedies, but also what to apply. This made professional perfumers an important part of ancient societies. Feeling good certainly does "delight" one's heart (Prov. 27:9).

1 Samuel

8 :1 Now it came to pass when Samuel was old that he made his sons judges over Israel. ²The name of his firstborn was Joel, and the name of his second, Abijah; *they were* judges in Beersheba. ³But his sons did not walk in his ways; they turned aside after dishonest gain, took bribes, and perverted justice.

⁴Then all the elders of Israel gathered together and came to Samuel at Ramah, ⁵and said to him, "Look, you are old, and your sons do not walk in your ways. Now make us a king to judge us like all the nations."

⁶But the thing displeased Samuel when they said, "Give us a king to judge us." So Samuel prayed to the LORD. ⁷And the LORD said to Samuel, "Heed the voice of the people in all that they say to you; for they have not rejected you, but they have rejected Me, that I should not reign over them. ⁸According to all the works which they have done since the day that I brought them up out of Egypt, even to this day—with which they have forsaken Me and served other gods—so they are doing to you also. ⁹Now therefore, heed their voice. However, you shall solemnly forewarn them, and show them the behavior of the king who will reign over them."

¹⁰So Samuel told all the words of the LORD to the people who asked him for a king. ¹¹And he said, "This will be the behavior of the king who will reign over you: He will take your sons and appoint *them* for his own chariots and *to be* his horsemen, and *some* will run before his chariots. ¹²He will appoint captains over his thousands and captains over his fifties, *will set some* to plow his ground and reap his harvest, and *some* to make his weapons of war and equipment for his chariots. ¹³He will take your daughters *to be* perfumers, cooks, and bakers. ¹⁴And he will take the best of your fields, your vineyards, and your olive groves, and give *them* to his servants. ¹⁵He will take a tenth of your grain and your vintage, and give it to his officers and servants. ¹⁶And he will take your male servants, your female servants, your finest young men,ᵃ and your donkeys, and put *them* to his work. ¹⁷He will take a tenth of your sheep. And you will be his servants. ¹⁸And you will cry out in that day because of your king whom you have chosen for yourselves, and the LORD will not hear you in that day."

8:16 ᵃSeptuagint reads *cattle.*

¹⁹Nevertheless the people refused to obey the voice of Samuel; and they said, "No, but we will have a king over us, ²⁰that we also may be like all the nations, and that our king may judge us and go out before us and fight our battles."

²¹And Samuel heard all the words of the people, and he repeated them in the hearing of the LORD. ²²So the LORD said to Samuel, "Heed their voice, and make them a king."

And Samuel said to the men of Israel, "Every man go to his city."

Prophetic Account: Saul and David

The Bible contains two separate histories of the Israelite monarchy. The first is found in the books of Samuel and Kings, and the second in the books of Chronicles. Although the account in Chronicles is based on the earlier history of Samuel and Kings, and often quotes directly from it, the two accounts tell the history from very different perspectives.

These two differing views of Israel's history could be described as the "prophetic view" in Samuel/Kings and the "priestly view" in Chronicles. Whereas Samuel and Kings are especially interested in prophets and prophecy, Chronicles is much more concerned with the temple and its priests. Because of such clear differences, the two accounts will be presented separately in alternating presentations, labeled "Prophetic" (Samuel/Kings) and "Priestly" (Chronicles).

The prophetic account begins with the prophet Samuel's meeting with Saul, the man from the tribe of Benjamin who would become the first king. At that time, the Philistines along the Mediterranean seacoast dominated the scene, but Saul was well suited to command Israel. He proved this by leading a military campaign against Ammon (1 Sam. 11). In this battle, Saul behaves like one of the judges of earlier years and is consequently accepted by both northern and southern Israel.

The account of Saul's career is woven together with the rise to power of Israel's next king, David. Saul's last years were clouded by periods of depression and gloom. By the time the young David entered Saul's court with his soothing music (1 Sam. 16:19–23), he had already been anointed Saul's successor (16:1, 13).

■ 1 Samuel 9:1—12:25

1 Samuel
Saul Chosen to Be King

9 :1 There was a man of Benjamin whose name *was* Kish the son of Abiel, the son of Zeror, the son of Bechorath, the son of Aphiah, a Benjamite, a mighty man of power. ²And he had a choice and handsome son whose name *was* Saul. *There was* not a more handsome person than he among the children of Israel. From his shoulders upward *he was* taller than any of the people.

³Now the donkeys of Kish, Saul's father, were lost. And Kish said to his son Saul, "Please take one of the servants with you, and arise, go and look for the donkeys." ⁴So he passed through the mountains of Ephraim and through the land of Shalisha, but they did not find *them*. Then they passed through the land of Shaalim, and *they were* not *there*. Then he passed through the land of the Benjamites, but they did not find *them*.

⁵When they had come to the land of Zuph, Saul said to his servant who *was* with him, "Come, let us return, lest my father cease *caring* about the donkeys and become worried about us."

⁶And he said to him, "Look now, *there is* in this city a man of God, and *he is* an honorable man; all that he says surely comes to pass. So let us go there; perhaps he can show us the way that we should go."

⁷Then Saul said to his servant, "But look, *if* we go, what shall we bring the man? For the bread in our vessels is all gone, and *there is* no present to bring to the man of God. What do we have?"

⁸And the servant answered Saul again and said, "Look, I have here at hand one-fourth of a shekel of silver. I will give *that* to the man of God, to tell us our way." ⁹(Formerly in Israel, when a man went to inquire of God, he spoke thus: "Come, let us go to the seer"; for *he who is* now *called* a prophet was formerly called a seer.)

¹⁰Then Saul said to his servant, "Well said; come, let us go." So they went to the city where the man of God *was*.

¹¹As they went up the hill to the city, they met some young women going out to draw water, and said to them, "Is the seer here?"

¹²And they answered them and said, "Yes, there he is, just ahead of you. Hurry now; for today he came to this city, because there is a sacrifice of the people today on the high place. ¹³As soon as you come into the city, you will surely find him before he

THE EVIL HIGH PLACES (1 Sam. 9:12)

High places were a regular part of religious life in Canaanite society. The Israelites were also attracted to these facilities, making them a common feature in their cities, both in Israel (2 Kin. 17:9) and in Judah (2 Kin. 23:5, 8).

The fullest description of a high place is of one near a city in the region of Zuph (1 Sam. 9:5). At this high place there was a hall large enough to hold at least 30 people (9:22), which was used, at least sometimes, as a place for eating (9:13). A cook was stationed there, which means the high place probably also had some type of kitchen and, presumably, storage rooms (9:23, 24). An altar was also present, allowing Samuel to attend a sacrifice at this high place (9:12).

Because of the word "high," many have assumed that high places were necessarily built on isolated hills or mountaintops. Such is suggested by comments that worshipers "go up to" or "come down from" the high place (1 Sam. 9:13, 25). Nevertheless, high places were probably just as often built within the walls of cities. The location of high places is said to be "in the cities" (2 Kin. 23:5) or "at the gates" of a city (2 Kin. 23:8). That cities most often were built on hilltops could mean that the highest point of a city may have been reserved for a high place.

On the other hand, archaeologists have discovered figurines and other cult objects in and around raised platforms, not so prominently located within cities. Small rooms and cooking areas have been found associated with these raised platforms, which possibly were the "high places" of Old Testament cities, even though not located on hilltops.

Worship in high places was later condemned. Hezekiah is reported to have been a good king partly because, among other things, he "removed the high places" (2 Kin. 18:4). The details of what transpired at these sites is now lost. What is clear is that high places became centers for the worship of foreign gods, where the Israelites engaged in evil practices (Jer. 19:4, 5).

---

goes up to the high place to eat. For the people will not eat until he comes, because he must bless the sacrifice; afterward those who are invited will eat. Now therefore, go up, for about this time you will find him." ¹⁴So they went up to the city. As they were coming into the city, there was Samuel, coming out toward them on his way up to the high place.

¹⁵Now the LORD had told Samuel in his ear the day before Saul came, saying, ¹⁶"Tomorrow about this time I will send you a man from the land of Benjamin, and you shall anoint him commander over My people Israel, that he may save My people from the hand of the Philistines; for I have looked upon My people, because their cry has come to Me."

¹⁷So when Samuel saw Saul, the LORD said to him, "There he is, the man of whom I spoke to you. This one shall reign over My people." ¹⁸Then Saul drew near to Samuel in the gate, and said, "Please tell me, where is the seer's house?"

¹⁹Samuel answered Saul and said, "I am the seer. Go up before me to the high place, for you shall eat with me today; and tomorrow I will let you go and will tell you all that is in your heart. ²⁰But as for your donkeys that were lost three days ago, do not be anxious about them, for they have been found. And on whom is all the desire of Israel? Is it not on you and on all your father's house?"

²¹And Saul answered and said, "Am I not a Benjamite, of the smallest of the tribes of Israel, and my family the least of all the families of the tribeᵃ of Benjamin? Why then do you speak like this to me?"

²²Now Samuel took Saul and his servant and brought them into the hall, and had them sit in the place of honor among those who were invited; there were about thirty persons. ²³And Samuel said to the cook, "Bring the portion which I gave you, of which I said to you, 'Set it apart.' " ²⁴So the cook took up the thigh with its upper part and set it before Saul. And Samuel said, "Here it is, what was kept back. It was set apart for you. Eat; for until this

9:21 ᵃLiterally tribes

WHERE WAS RACHEL'S TOMB? (1 Sam. 10:2)

Where was Rachel buried—near Bethlehem or farther north near Ramah? The answer to that question is not easily answered, but the confusion is easy to explain.

Jacob's wife Rachel was the mother of four sons, Joseph and Benjamin, her own children, and Dan and Naphtali, born to Rachel through her servant Bilhah (Gen. 35:24, 25). In giving birth to Benjamin she died.

According to Genesis, her death and burial occurred just north of Bethlehem, which is identified with the older settlement of Ephrath (Gen. 35:19, 20; 48:7). Yet in 1 Samuel the tomb of Rachel is located north of Jerusalem in the "territory of Benjamin" (1 Sam. 10:2), probably somewhere between Gibeah and Ramah. The confusion about where Rachel was buried very likely has something to do with intertribal rivalry.

In the days of the Israelite monarchy, the main rivals for the throne pitted the tribes of Judah and Benjamin against each other. David was from the tribe of Judah, which is the primary reason that his first capital was in Hebron, a Judahite city (2 Sam. 2:1, 11). Saul was from the tribe of Benjamin, so his headquarters were located in Benjamite territory, in the city known as "Gibeah of Benjamin" (1 Sam. 13:2) and as "Gibeah of Saul" (1 Sam. 15:34).

The anomaly concerning Rachel's tomb was that the mother of the Benjamites was buried in the heart of Judahite territory, Benjamin's major rival. Of course, Rachel's burial occurred long before the land was divided among the tribes. It seems logical that after the Benjamites possessed their own territory, they either reinterred their mother (if her burial site was still known), or created a new memorial place, within the territory of Benjamin. They were certainly not likely to admit that their mother was buried in Judah near Bethlehem. Whether physically or not, her burial spot was moved to Benjamin.

---

time it has been kept for you, since I said I invited the people." So Saul ate with Samuel that day.

25When they had come down from the high place into the city, *Samuel* spoke with Saul on the top of the house.ᵃ 26They arose early; and it was about the dawning of the day that Samuel called to Saul on the top of the house, saying, "Get up, that I may send you on your way." And Saul arose, and both of them went outside, he and Samuel.

Saul Anointed King

27As they were going down to the outskirts of the city, Samuel said to Saul, "Tell the servant to go on ahead of us." And he went on. "But you stand here awhile, that I may announce to you the word of God."

10 1Then Samuel took a flask of oil and poured *it* on his head, and kissed him and said: "*Is it* not because the LORD has anointed you commander over His inheritance?ᵃ 2When you have departed from me today, you will find two men by Rachel's tomb in the territory of Benjamin at Zelzah; and they will say to you, 'The donkeys which you went to look for have been found. And now your father has ceased caring about the donkeys and is worrying

about you, saying, "What shall I do about my son?" ' 3Then you shall go on forward from there and come to the terebinth tree of Tabor. There three men going up to God at Bethel will meet you, one carrying three young goats, another carrying three loaves of bread, and another carrying a skin of wine. 4And they will greet you and give you two *loaves* of bread, which you shall receive from their hands. 5After that you shall come to the hill of God where the Philistine garrison *is*. And it will happen, when you have come there to the city, that you will meet a group of prophets coming down from the high place with a stringed instrument, a tambourine, a flute, and a harp before them; and they will be prophesying. 6Then the Spirit of the LORD will come

9:25 ᵃFollowing Masoretic Text and Targum; Septuagint omits *He spoke with Saul on the top of the house;* Septuagint and Vulgate add *And he prepared a bed for Saul on the top of the house, and he slept.*
10:1 ᵃFollowing Masoretic Text, Targum, and Vulgate; Septuagint reads *His people Israel; and you shall rule the people of the Lord;* Septuagint and Vulgate add *And you shall deliver His people from the hands of their enemies all around them. And this shall be a sign to you, that God has anointed you to be a prince.*

upon you, and you will prophesy with them and be turned into another man. [7]And let it be, when these signs come to you, *that* you do as the occasion demands; for God *is* with you. [8]You shall go down before me to Gilgal; and surely I will come down to you to offer burnt offerings *and* make sacrifices of peace offerings. Seven days you shall wait, till I come to you and show you what you should do."

[9]So it was, when he had turned his back to go from Samuel, that God gave him another heart; and all those signs came to pass that day. [10]When they came there to the hill, there was a group of prophets to meet him; then the Spirit of God came upon him, and he prophesied among them. [11]And it happened, when all who knew him formerly saw that he indeed prophesied among the prophets, that the people said to one another, "What *is* this *that* has come upon the son of Kish? *Is* Saul also among the prophets?" [12]Then a man from there answered and said, "But who *is* their father?" Therefore it became a proverb: "*Is* Saul also among the prophets?" [13]And when he had finished prophesying, he went to the high place.

[14]Then Saul's uncle said to him and his servant, "Where did you go?"

So he said, "To look for the donkeys. When we saw that *they were* nowhere *to be found,* we went to Samuel."

[15]And Saul's uncle said, "Tell me, please, what Samuel said to you."

[16]So Saul said to his uncle, "He told us plainly that the donkeys had been found." But about the matter of the kingdom, he did not tell him what Samuel had said.

Saul Proclaimed King

[17]Then Samuel called the people together to the LORD at Mizpah, [18]and said to the children of Israel, "Thus says the LORD God of Israel: 'I brought up Israel out of Egypt, and delivered you from the hand of the Egyptians *and* from the hand of all

kingdoms and from those who oppressed you.' [19]But you have today rejected your God, who Himself saved you from all your adversities and your tribulations; and you have said to Him, 'No, set a king over us!' Now therefore, present yourselves before the LORD by your tribes and by your clans."[a]

[20]And when Samuel had caused all the tribes of Israel to come near, the tribe of Benjamin was chosen. [21]When he had caused the tribe of Benjamin to come near by their families, the family of Matri was chosen. And Saul the son of Kish was chosen. But when they sought him, he could not be found. [22]Therefore they inquired of the LORD further, "Has the man come here yet?"

And the LORD answered, "There he is, hidden among the equipment."

[23]So they ran and brought him from there; and when he stood among the people, he was taller than any of the people from his shoulders upward. [24]And Samuel said to all the people, "Do you see him whom the LORD has chosen, that *there is* no one like him among all the people?"

So all the people shouted and said, "Long live the king!"

[25]Then Samuel explained to the people the behavior of royalty, and wrote *it* in a book and laid *it* up before the LORD. And Samuel sent all the people away, every man to his house. [26]And Saul also went home to Gibeah; and valiant *men* went with him, whose hearts God had touched. [27]But some rebels said, "How can this man save us?" So they despised him, and brought him no presents. But he held his peace.

Saul Saves Jabesh Gilead

11 [1]Then Nahash the Ammonite came up and encamped against Jabesh Gilead; and all the men of Jabesh said to Nahash, "Make a covenant with us, and we will serve you."

[2]And Nahash the Ammonite answered them, "On this *condition* I will make a

---

10:19 [a]Literally *thousands*

SAUL THE KING? (1 Sam. 11:14, 15)

Gilgal held special significance for the relationship between Israel and her God Yahweh. It was there that the Israelites renewed their covenant with Yahweh before entering the Promised Land (Josh. 5:10). It was also at Gilgal that Saul was made king (1 Sam. 11:15). Yet despite the coronation ritual and celebration, a question hung over the new king: What kind of kingdom did he really have?

His standing army was relatively small and divided into two units, both of which were stationed within Benjamin, Saul's own tribal territory (1 Sam. 13:2). Even though Saul's soldiers are described as "men of Israel" (13:2), one wonders if most of them were not from his own tribe of Benjamin.

Before his coronation, Saul acted like a judge, calling together troops for a specific need (1 Sam. 11:7). Even though Samuel had already proclaimed Saul's kingship, the king-to-be met with opposition and rejection (10:24–27).

It appears that Saul's kingdom was an act of desperation on the part of the Israelites. The Ammonites were moving in on the tribes of Reuben and Gad (11:1–3), while the Philistines were controlling the heartland of Israel (13:3). The Israelites were ill prepared for war, lacking swords and spears, as well as a way to sharpen them, if they had them (13:19–22).

Saul's reign was one of defense and struggle. He is pictured as spending much of his time chasing David. The Bible says nothing about any building activities. Saul spent all of his time building a kingdom, with no time to build a palace. While there was great rejoicing in Gilgal at Saul's coronation (11:15), such things as palaces and royal cities would have to wait until the reign of his successor David.

---

covenant with you, that I may put out all your right eyes, and bring reproach on all Israel."

³Then the elders of Jabesh said to him, "Hold off for seven days, that we may send messengers to all the territory of Israel. And then, if *there is* no one to save us, we will come out to you."

⁴So the messengers came to Gibeah of Saul and told the news in the hearing of the people. And all the people lifted up their voices and wept. ⁵Now there was Saul, coming behind the herd from the field; and Saul said, "What *troubles* the people, that they weep?" And they told him the words of the men of Jabesh. ⁶Then the Spirit of God came upon Saul when he heard this news, and his anger was greatly aroused. ⁷So he took a yoke of oxen and cut them in pieces, and sent *them* throughout all the territory of Israel by the hands of messengers, saying, "Whoever does not go out with Saul and Samuel to battle, so it shall be done to his oxen."

And the fear of the LORD fell on the people, and they came out with one consent. ⁸When he numbered them in Bezek, the children of Israel were three hundred thousand, and the men of Judah thirty thousand. ⁹And they said to the messengers who came, "Thus you shall say to the men of Jabesh Gilead: 'Tomorrow, by *the time* the sun is hot, you shall have help.' " Then the messengers came and reported *it* to the men of Jabesh, and they were glad. ¹⁰Therefore the men of Jabesh said, "Tomorrow we will come out to you, and you may do with us whatever seems good to you."

¹¹So it was, on the next day, that Saul put the people in three companies; and they came into the midst of the camp in the morning watch, and killed Ammonites until the heat of the day. And it happened that those who survived were scattered, so that no two of them were left together.

¹²Then the people said to Samuel, "Who *is* he who said, 'Shall Saul reign over us?' Bring the men, that we may put them to death."

¹³But Saul said, "Not a man shall be put to death this day, for today the LORD has accomplished salvation in Israel."

¹⁴Then Samuel said to the people, "Come, let us go to Gilgal and renew the kingdom there." ¹⁵So all the people went to Gilgal, and there they made Saul king before the LORD in Gilgal. There they made

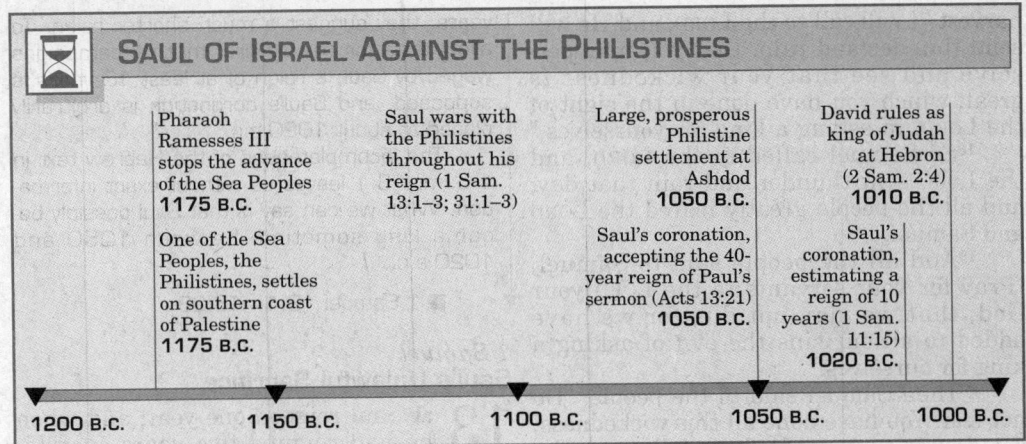

SAUL OF ISRAEL AGAINST THE PHILISTINES			
Pharaoh Ramesses III stops the advance of the Sea Peoples **1175 B.C.**	Saul wars with the Philistines throughout his reign (1 Sam. 13:1–3; 31:1–3)	Large, prosperous Philistine settlement at Ashdod **1050 B.C.**	David rules as king of Judah at Hebron (2 Sam. 2:4) **1010 B.C.**
One of the Sea Peoples, the Philistines, settles on southern coast of Palestine **1175 B.C.**		Saul's coronation, accepting the 40-year reign of Paul's sermon (Acts 13:21) **1050 B.C.**	Saul's coronation, estimating a reign of 10 years (1 Sam. 11:15) **1020 B.C.**

1200 B.C.	1150 B.C.	1100 B.C.	1050 B.C.	1000 B.C.

sacrifices of peace offerings before the LORD, and there Saul and all the men of Israel rejoiced greatly.

Samuel's Address at Saul's Coronation

12 ¹Now Samuel said to all Israel: "Indeed I have heeded your voice in all that you said to me, and have made a king over you. ²And now here is the king, walking before you; and I am old and gray-headed, and look, my sons *are* with you. I have walked before you from my childhood to this day. ³Here I am. Witness against me before the LORD and before His anointed: Whose ox have I taken, or whose donkey have I taken, or whom have I cheated? Whom have I oppressed, or from whose hand have I received *any* bribe with which to blind my eyes? I will restore *it* to you."

⁴And they said, "You have not cheated us or oppressed us, nor have you taken anything from any man's hand."

⁵Then he said to them, "The LORD *is* witness against you, and His anointed *is* witness this day, that you have not found anything in my hand."

And they answered, "*He is* witness."

⁶Then Samuel said to the people, "*It is* the LORD who raised up Moses and Aaron, and who brought your fathers up from the land of Egypt. ⁷Now therefore, stand still, that I may reason with you before the LORD concerning all the righteous acts of the

LORD which He did to you and your fathers: ⁸When Jacob had gone into Egypt,ᵃ and your fathers cried out to the LORD, then the LORD sent Moses and Aaron, who brought your fathers out of Egypt and made them dwell in this place. ⁹And when they forgot the LORD their God, He sold them into the hand of Sisera, commander of the army of Hazor, into the hand of the Philistines, and into the hand of the king of Moab; and they fought against them. ¹⁰Then they cried out to the LORD, and said, 'We have sinned, because we have forsaken the LORD and served the Baals and Ashtoreths;ᵃ but now deliver us from the hand of our enemies, and we will serve You.' ¹¹And the LORD sent Jerubbaal,ᵃ Bedan,ᵇ Jephthah, and Samuel,ᶜ and delivered you out of the hand of your enemies on every side; and you dwelt in safety. ¹²And when you saw that Nahash king of the Ammonites came against you, you said to me, 'No, but a king shall reign over us,' when the LORD your God *was* your king.

¹³"Now therefore, here is the king whom you have chosen *and* whom you have desired. And take note, the LORD has set a king over you. ¹⁴If you fear the LORD and serve Him and obey His voice, and do not rebel against the commandment of the LORD, then both you and the king who reigns over you will continue following the LORD your God. ¹⁵However, if you do not obey the voice of the LORD, but rebel against the commandment of the LORD, then the hand of the LORD will be against you, as *it was* against your fathers.

¹⁶"Now therefore, stand and see this great thing which the LORD will do before your eyes: ¹⁷*Is* today not the wheat

---

12:8 ᵃFollowing Masoretic Text, Targum, and Vulgate; Septuagint adds *and the Egyptians afflicted them.* 12:10 ᵃCanaanite goddesses 12:11 ᵃSyriac reads *Deborah;* Targum reads *Gideon.* ᵇSeptuagint and Syriac read *Barak;* Targum reads *Simson.* ᶜSyriac reads *Simson.*

harvest? I will call to the LORD, and He will send thunder and rain, that you may perceive and see that your wickedness *is* great, which you have done in the sight of the LORD, in asking a king for yourselves."

¹⁸So Samuel called to the LORD, and the LORD sent thunder and rain that day; and all the people greatly feared the LORD and Samuel.

¹⁹And all the people said to Samuel, "Pray for your servants to the LORD your God, that we may not die; for we have added to all our sins the evil of asking a king for ourselves."

²⁰Then Samuel said to the people, "Do not fear. You have done all this wickedness; yet do not turn aside from following the LORD, but serve the LORD with all your heart. ²¹And do not turn aside; for *then you would* go after empty things which cannot profit or deliver, for they *are* nothing. ²²For the LORD will not forsake His people, for His great name's sake, because it has pleased the LORD to make you His people. ²³Moreover, as for me, far be it from me that I should sin against the LORD in ceasing to pray for you; but I will teach you the good and the right way. ²⁴Only fear the LORD, and serve Him in truth with all your heart; for consider what great things He has done for you. ²⁵But if you still do wickedly, you shall be swept away, both you and your king."

When Did Saul Become King?

The Hebrew text of 1 Sam. 13:1 is in disarray. It says that Saul was a year old when he began to reign and reigned for two years. The translators of the NKJV have made a plausible surmise at what the original may have been in 13:1. Unfortunately, we do not know how old Saul was when he began to reign, nor in what year he became king.

In Antioch Paul preached a sermon in which he appealed to Israel's history. He comments that Saul was king "for forty years" (Acts 13:21), a number mentioned also by the Jewish historian Josephus. Some accept this number as the length of Saul's reign and, counting backward 40 years from the supposed date when David became king (1010 B.C.), place Saul's coronation in 1050 B.C.

Other scholars understand the 40 years of Acts 13:21 to be a symbolic round number representing one generation. Rather than 40

years, they suggest a much shorter reign. To allow time for the several military campaigns waged by Saul, a reign of at least 10 years is supposed, and Saul's coronation is arbitrarily placed at about 1020 B.C.

The incompleteness of the Hebrew text in 1 Sam. 13:1 leaves us without exact information. What we can say is that Saul possibly became king sometime between 1050 and 1020 B.C.

▼   ■ 1 Samuel 13:1—16:23

1 Samuel
Saul's Unlawful Sacrifice

13 :1 Saul reigned one year; and when he had reigned two years over Israel,ᵃ ²Saul chose for himself three thousand *men* of Israel. Two thousand were with Saul in Michmash and in the mountains of Bethel, and a thousand were with Jonathan in Gibeah of Benjamin. The rest of the people he sent away, every man to his tent.

³And Jonathan attacked the garrison of the Philistines that *was* in Geba, and the Philistines heard *of it*. Then Saul blew the trumpet throughout all the land, saying, "Let the Hebrews hear!" ⁴Now all Israel heard it said *that* Saul had attacked a garrison of the Philistines, and *that* Israel had also become an abomination to the Philistines. And the people were called together to Saul at Gilgal.

⁵Then the Philistines gathered together to fight with Israel, thirtyᵃ thousand chariots and six thousand horsemen, and people as the sand which *is* on the seashore in multitude. And they came up and encamped in Michmash, to the east of Beth Aven. ⁶When the men of Israel saw that they were in danger (for the people were distressed), then the people hid in caves, in thickets, in rocks, in holes, and in pits. ⁷And *some of* the Hebrews crossed over the Jordan to the land of Gad and Gilead.

As for Saul, he *was* still in Gilgal, and all the people followed him trembling. ⁸Then he waited seven days, according to the time set by Samuel. But Samuel did not come to Gilgal; and the people were scattered from him. ⁹So Saul said, "Bring a

---

13:1 ᵃThe Hebrew is difficult (compare 2 Samuel 5:4; 2 Kings 14:2; see also 2 Samuel 2:10; Acts 13:21).
13:5 ᵃFollowing Masoretic Text, Septuagint, Targum, and Vulgate; Syriac and some manuscripts of the Septuagint read *three*.

FROM COPPER TO BRONZE TO IRON (1 Sam. 13:19–22)

The first metals used by humans were gold, silver, and copper. Gold and silver were too soft to be used for tools or weapons. Copper in its native form is also soft, although it was hammered into a harder form. However, sometime around 3500 B.C. ancient metalworkers discovered that copper hardened when alloyed with tin to produce bronze, or with zinc to produce brass.

The harder bronze was not only a better metal for producing tools, but also resulted in more effective weapons. During the Early Bronze Age, from about 2300 B.C., bronze swords and ax heads were produced by bronzeworkers with increasing skill. Bronze instruments of warfare, such as the spear (2 Sam. 21:16), the bow (2 Sam. 22:35), and shield (2 Chr. 12:10), were still in use at the time of Israel's monarchy.

The next advance in metal technology came with the discovery of smelting to separate iron from its oxides. The ironworking process, which required fuel and heat, was slow to develop. Before 1200 B.C. iron was used mostly for jewelry and ceremonial weapons; however, there are a few examples of military use. An Accadian text from Nuzi in northern Mesopotamia, dating from about the 15th century B.C., gives evidence of a coat of scale armor, using iron scales, made for a horse. When the Israelites first arrived in Canaan, they were faced with the superiority of their opponents' iron-reinforced chariots (Judg. 1:19; 4:3).

Ironworking demanded the skill of a blacksmith. A letter of the Hittite king Hattusilis III, dating around 1250 B.C., shows that the Hittites had developed skills in the production of smelted iron. When Saul became Israel's king (1050 or 1020 B.C.), Philistine ironsmiths were able to control the actual working of iron in Canaan. They would sharpen the Hebrews' iron tools, but would not teach them to "make swords or spears" of iron (1 Sam. 13:19, 22).

---

burnt offering and peace offerings here to me." And he offered the burnt offering. [10]Now it happened, as soon as he had finished presenting the burnt offering, that Samuel came; and Saul went out to meet him, that he might greet him.

[11]And Samuel said, "What have you done?"

Saul said, "When I saw that the people were scattered from me, and *that* you did not come within the days appointed, and *that* the Philistines gathered together at Michmash, [12]then I said, 'The Philistines will now come down on me at Gilgal, and I have not made supplication to the LORD.' Therefore I felt compelled, and offered a burnt offering."

[13]And Samuel said to Saul, "You have done foolishly. You have not kept the commandment of the LORD your God, which He commanded you. For now the LORD would have established your kingdom over Israel

forever. [14]But now your kingdom shall not continue. The LORD has sought for Himself a man after His own heart, and the LORD has commanded him *to be* commander over His people, because you have not kept what the LORD commanded you."

[15]Then Samuel arose and went up from Gilgal to Gibeah of Benjamin.[a] And Saul numbered the people present with him, about six hundred men.

No Weapons for the Army

[16]Saul, Jonathan his son, and the people present with them remained in Gibeah of Benjamin. But the Philistines encamped in Michmash. [17]Then raiders came out of the camp of the Philistines in three companies. One company turned onto the road to Ophrah, to the land of Shual, [18]another company turned to the road *to* Beth Horon, and another company turned *to* the road of the border that overlooks the Valley of Zeboim toward the wilderness.

[19]Now there was no blacksmith to be found throughout all the land of Israel, for the Philistines said, "Lest the Hebrews make swords or spears." [20]But all the Israelites would go down to the Philistines to

---

13:15 [a]Following Masoretic Text and Targum; Septuagint and Vulgate add *And the rest of the people went up after Saul to meet the people who fought against them, going from Gilgal to Gibeah in the hill of Benjamin.*

sharpen each man's plowshare, his mattock, his ax, and his sickle; ²¹and the charge for a sharpening was a pim^a for the plowshares, the mattocks, the forks, and the axes, and to set the points of the goads. ²²So it came about, on the day of battle, that there was neither sword nor spear found in the hand of any of the people who *were* with Saul and Jonathan. But they were found with Saul and Jonathan his son. ²³And the garrison of the Philistines went out to the pass of Michmash.

Jonathan Defeats the Philistines

14 ¹Now it happened one day that Jonathan the son of Saul said to the young man who bore his armor, "Come, let us go over to the Philistines' garrison that *is* on the other side." But he did not tell his father. ²And Saul was sitting in the outskirts of Gibeah under a pomegranate tree which *is* in Migron. The people who *were* with him *were* about six hundred men. ³Ahijah the son of Ahitub, Ichabod's brother, the son of Phinehas, the son of Eli, the LORD's priest in Shiloh, was wearing an ephod. But the people did not know that Jonathan had gone.

⁴Between the passes, by which Jonathan sought to go over to the Philistines' garrison, *there was* a sharp rock on one side and a sharp rock on the other side. And the name of one *was* Bozez, and the name of the other Seneh. ⁵The front of one faced northward opposite Michmash, and the other southward opposite Gibeah.

⁶Then Jonathan said to the young man who bore his armor, "Come, let us go over to the garrison of these uncircumcised; it may be that the LORD will work for us. For nothing restrains the LORD from saving by many or by few."

⁷So his armorbearer said to him, "Do all that is in your heart. Go then; here I am with you, according to your heart."

⁸Then Jonathan said, "Very well, let us cross over to *these* men, and we will show ourselves to them. ⁹If they say thus to us, 'Wait until we come to you,' then we will

stand still in our place and not go up to them. ¹⁰But if they say thus, 'Come up to us,' then we will go up. For the LORD has delivered them into our hand, and this *will be* a sign to us."

¹¹So both of them showed themselves to the garrison of the Philistines. And the Philistines said, "Look, the Hebrews are coming out of the holes where they have hidden." ¹²Then the men of the garrison called to Jonathan and his armorbearer, and said, "Come up to us, and we will show you something."

Jonathan said to his armorbearer, "Come up after me, for the LORD has delivered them into the hand of Israel." ¹³And Jonathan climbed up on his hands and knees with his armorbearer after him; and they fell before Jonathan. And as he came after him, his armorbearer killed them. ¹⁴That first slaughter which Jonathan and his armorbearer made was about twenty men within about half an acre of land.^a

¹⁵And there was trembling in the camp, in the field, and among all the people. The garrison and the raiders also trembled; and the earth quaked, so that it was a very great trembling. ¹⁶Now the watchmen of Saul in Gibeah of Benjamin looked, and *there* was the multitude, melting away; and they went here and there. ¹⁷Then Saul said to the people who *were* with him, "Now call the roll and see who has gone from us." And when they had called the roll, surprisingly, Jonathan and his armorbearer *were* not *there*. ¹⁸And Saul said to Ahijah, "Bring the ark^a of God here" (for at that time the ark^b of God was with the children of Israel). ¹⁹Now it happened, while Saul talked to the priest, that the noise which *was* in the camp of the Philistines continued to increase; so Saul

---

13:21 ^aAbout two-thirds shekel weight
14:14 ^aLiterally *half the area plowed by a yoke* (of oxen in a day)   14:18 ^aFollowing Masoretic Text, Targum, and Vulgate; Septuagint reads *ephod.*
^bFollowing Masoretic Text, Targum, and Vulgate; Septuagint reads *ephod.*

SCIENCE AND TECHNOLOGY

Although the word "iron" does not occur in 1 Sam. 13:19–22, the Philistines are represented as having a certain skill that the Hebrews lacked. The technology of bronze was by this time centuries old. Approximately 50 percent of weapons recovered by archaeologists from the era of David and Solomon are iron and 50 percent bronze. A hundred years earlier, 80 percent were bronze.

said to the priest, "Withdraw your hand." [20]Then Saul and all the people who *were* with him assembled, and they went to the battle; and indeed every man's sword was against his neighbor, *and there was* very great confusion. [21]Moreover the Hebrews *who* were with the Philistines before that time, who went up with them into the camp *from the* surrounding *country,* they also joined the Israelites who *were* with Saul and Jonathan. [22]Likewise all the men of Israel who had hidden in the mountains of Ephraim, *when* they heard that the Philistines fled, they also followed hard after them in the battle. [23]So the LORD saved Israel that day, and the battle shifted to Beth Aven.

Saul's Rash Oath

[24]And the men of Israel were distressed that day, for Saul had placed the people under oath, saying, "Cursed *is* the man who eats *any* food until evening, before I have taken vengeance on my enemies." So none of the people tasted food. [25]Now all *the people* of the land came to a forest; and there was honey on the ground. [26]And when the people had come into the woods, there was the honey, dripping; but no one put his hand to his mouth, for the people feared the oath. [27]But Jonathan had not heard his father charge the people with the oath; therefore he stretched out the end of the rod that *was* in his hand and dipped it in a honeycomb, and put his hand to his mouth; and his countenance brightened. [28]Then one of the people said, "Your father strictly charged the people with an oath, saying, 'Cursed *is* the man who eats food this day.' " And the people were faint.

[29]But Jonathan said, "My father has troubled the land. Look now, how my countenance has brightened because I tasted a little of this honey. [30]How much better if the people had eaten freely today of the spoil of their enemies which they found! For now would there not have been a much greater slaughter among the Philistines?"

[31]Now they had driven back the Philistines that day from Michmash to Aijalon. So the people were very faint. [32]And

the people rushed on the spoil, and took sheep, oxen, and calves, and slaughtered *them* on the ground; and the people ate *them* with the blood. [33]Then they told Saul, saying, "Look, the people are sinning against the LORD by eating with the blood!"

So he said, "You have dealt treacherously; roll a large stone to me this day." [34]Then Saul said, "Disperse yourselves among the people, and say to them, 'Bring me here every man's ox and every man's sheep, slaughter *them* here, and eat; and do not sin against the LORD by eating with the blood.' " So every one of the people brought his ox with him that night, and slaughtered *it* there. [35]Then Saul built an altar to the LORD. This was the first altar that he built to the LORD.

[36]Now Saul said, "Let us go down after the Philistines by night, and plunder them until the morning light; and let us not leave a man of them."

And they said, "Do whatever seems good to you."

Then the priest said, "Let us draw near to God here."

[37]So Saul asked counsel of God, "Shall I go down after the Philistines? Will You deliver them into the hand of Israel?" But He did not answer him that day. [38]And Saul said, "Come over here, all you chiefs of the people, and know and see what this sin was today. [39]For *as* the LORD lives, who saves Israel, though it be in Jonathan my son, he shall surely die." But not a man among all the people answered him. [40]Then he said to all Israel, "You be on one side, and my son Jonathan and I will be on the other side."

And the people said to Saul, "Do what seems good to you."

[41]Therefore Saul said to the LORD God of Israel, "Give a perfect *lot.*"[a] So Saul and

---

14:41 [a]Following Masoretic Text and Targum; Septuagint and Vulgate read *Why do You not answer Your servant today? If the injustice is with me or Jonathan my son, O LORD God of Israel, give proof; and if You say it is with Your people Israel, give holiness.*

TIME CAPSULE *1169 to 1130 B.C.*

1169 Sea Peoples depicted in horse-drawn carts

1157 Elamites capture Babylonia and destroy the Kassite dynasty

1133–1116 Nebuchadnezzar I rules 2nd Isin dynasty of Babylon

1130 Egyptians lose control of southern Canaan

1130 Final destruction of Mycenae

Jonathan were taken, but the people escaped. ⁴²And Saul said, "Cast *lots* between my son Jonathan and me." So Jonathan was taken. ⁴³Then Saul said to Jonathan, "Tell me what you have done."

And Jonathan told him, and said, "I only tasted a little honey with the end of the rod that *was* in my hand. So now I must die!"

⁴⁴Saul answered, "God do so and more also; for you shall surely die, Jonathan."

⁴⁵But the people said to Saul, "Shall Jonathan die, who has accomplished this great deliverance in Israel? Certainly not! *As* the LORD lives, not one hair of his head shall fall to the ground, for he has worked with God this day." So the people rescued Jonathan, and he did not die.

⁴⁶Then Saul returned from pursuing the Philistines, and the Philistines went to their own place.

Saul's Continuing Wars

⁴⁷So Saul established his sovereignty over Israel, and fought against all his enemies on every side, against Moab, against the people of Ammon, against Edom, against the kings of Zobah, and against the Philistines. Wherever he turned, he harassed *them.*ᵃ ⁴⁸And he gathered an army and attacked the Amalekites, and delivered Israel from the hands of those who plundered them.

⁴⁹The sons of Saul were Jonathan, Jishui,ᵃ and Malchishua. And the names of his two daughters *were these:* the name of the firstborn Merab, and the name of the younger Michal. ⁵⁰The name of Saul's wife *was* Ahinoam the daughter of Ahimaaz. And the name of the commander of his army *was* Abner the son of Ner, Saul's uncle. ⁵¹Kish *was* the father of Saul, and Ner the father of Abner *was* the son of Abiel.

⁵²Now there was fierce war with the Philistines all the days of Saul. And when Saul saw any strong man or any valiant man, he took him for himself.

Saul Spares King Agag

15 ¹Samuel also said to Saul, "The LORD sent me to anoint you king over His people, over Israel. Now therefore, heed the voice of the words of the LORD. ²Thus says the LORD of hosts: 'I will punish Amalek *for* what he did to Israel, how he ambushed him on the way when he came up from Egypt. ³Now go and attack Amalek, and utterly destroy all that they have, and do not spare them. But kill both man and woman, infant and nursing child, ox and sheep, camel and donkey.' "

⁴So Saul gathered the people together and numbered them in Telaim, two hundred thousand foot soldiers and ten thousand men of Judah. ⁵And Saul came to a city of Amalek, and lay in wait in the valley.

⁶Then Saul said to the Kenites, "Go, depart, get down from among the Amalekites, lest I destroy you with them. For you showed kindness to all the children of Israel when they came up out of Egypt." So the Kenites departed from among the Amalekites. ⁷And Saul attacked the Amalekites, from Havilah all the way to Shur, which is east of Egypt. ⁸He also took Agag king of the Amalekites alive, and utterly destroyed all the people with the edge of the sword. ⁹But Saul and the people spared Agag and the best of the sheep, the oxen, the fatlings, the lambs, and all *that was* good, and were unwilling to utterly destroy them. But everything despised and worthless, that they utterly destroyed.

Saul Rejected as King

¹⁰Now the word of the LORD came to Samuel, saying, ¹¹"I greatly regret that I have set up Saul *as* king, for he has turned back from following Me, and has not performed My commandments." And it grieved

---

14:47 ᵃSeptuagint and Vulgate read *prospered.*
14:49 ᵃCalled *Abinadab* in 1 Chronicles 8:33 and 9:39

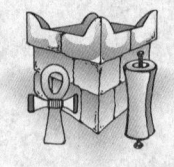

RELIGION AND WORSHIP

Samuel repeats God's demand that Amalek be destroyed (1 Sam. 15:3). The term for this decree in Hebrew is herem, *meaning "devoted" or "banned." As a religious demand, it is absolute, although in fact the inhabitants of Canaan were not at any time entirely exterminated (Deut. 7:22; Judg. 1:27–36). Throughout history, many wars have had an obvious religious component.*

Samuel, and he cried out to the LORD all night. 12So when Samuel rose early in the morning to meet Saul, it was told Samuel, saying, "Saul went to Carmel, and indeed, he set up a monument for himself; and he has gone on around, passed by, and gone down to Gilgal." 13Then Samuel went to Saul, and Saul said to him, "Blessed *are* you of the LORD! I have performed the commandment of the LORD."

14But Samuel said, "What then *is* this bleating of the sheep in my ears, and the lowing of the oxen which I hear?"

15And Saul said, "They have brought them from the Amalekites; for the people spared the best of the sheep and the oxen, to sacrifice to the LORD your God; and the rest we have utterly destroyed."

16Then Samuel said to Saul, "Be quiet! And I will tell you what the LORD said to me last night."

And he said to him, "Speak on."

17So Samuel said, "When you *were* little in your own eyes, *were* you not head of the tribes of Israel? And did not the LORD anoint you king over Israel? 18Now the LORD sent you on a mission, and said, 'Go, and utterly destroy the sinners, the Amalekites, and fight against them until they are consumed.' 19Why then did you not obey the voice of the LORD? Why did you swoop down on the spoil, and do evil in the sight of the LORD?"

20And Saul said to Samuel, "But I have obeyed the voice of the LORD, and gone on the mission on which the LORD sent me, and brought back Agag king of Amalek; I have utterly destroyed the Amalekites. 21But the people took of the plunder, sheep and oxen, the best of the things which should have been utterly destroyed, to sacrifice to the LORD your God in Gilgal."

22So Samuel said:

> "Has the LORD *as great* delight in burnt offerings and sacrifices,
> As in obeying the voice of the LORD?
> Behold, to obey is better than sacrifice,
> *And* to heed than the fat of rams.
> 23 For rebellion *is as* the sin of witchcraft,
> And stubbornness *is as* iniquity and idolatry.
> Because you have rejected the word of the LORD,
> He also has rejected you from *being* king."

24Then Saul said to Samuel, "I have sinned, for I have transgressed the commandment of the LORD and your words, because I feared the people and obeyed their voice. 25Now therefore, please pardon my sin, and return with me, that I may worship the LORD."

26But Samuel said to Saul, "I will not return with you, for you have rejected the word of the LORD, and the LORD has rejected you from being king over Israel."

27And as Samuel turned around to go away, *Saul* seized the edge of his robe, and it tore. 28So Samuel said to him, "The LORD has torn the kingdom of Israel from you today, and has given it to a neighbor of yours, *who is* better than you. 29And also the Strength of Israel will not lie nor relent. For He *is* not a man, that He should relent."

30Then he said, "I have sinned; *yet* honor me now, please, before the elders of my people and before Israel, and return with me, that I may worship the LORD your God." 31So Samuel turned back after Saul, and Saul worshiped the LORD.

32Then Samuel said, "Bring Agag king of the Amalekites here to me." So Agag came to him cautiously.

And Agag said, "Surely the bitterness of death is past."

33But Samuel said, "As your sword has made women childless, so shall your mother be childless among women." And Samuel hacked Agag in pieces before the LORD in Gilgal.

34Then Samuel went to Ramah, and Saul went up to his house at Gibeah of Saul. 35And Samuel went no more to see Saul until the day of his death. Nevertheless Samuel mourned for Saul, and the LORD regretted that He had made Saul king over Israel.

David Anointed King

16 1Now the LORD said to Samuel, "How long will you mourn for Saul, seeing I have rejected him from reigning over Israel? Fill your horn with oil, and go; I am sending you to Jesse the Bethlehemite. For I have provided Myself a king among his sons."

2And Samuel said, "How can I go? If Saul hears *it,* he will kill me."

But the LORD said, "Take a heifer with you, and say, 'I have come to sacrifice to the LORD.' 3Then invite Jesse to the sacrifice, and I will show you what you shall do; you shall anoint for Me the one I name to you."

⁴So Samuel did what the LORD said, and went to Bethlehem. And the elders of the town trembled at his coming, and said, "Do you come peaceably?"

⁵And he said, "Peaceably; I have come to sacrifice to the LORD. Sanctify yourselves, and come with me to the sacrifice." Then he consecrated Jesse and his sons, and invited them to the sacrifice.

⁶So it was, when they came, that he looked at Eliab and said, "Surely the LORD's anointed *is* before Him!"

⁷But the LORD said to Samuel, "Do not look at his appearance or at his physical stature, because I have refused him. For *the LORD does* not *see* as man sees;ᵃ for man looks at the outward appearance, but the LORD looks at the heart."

⁸So Jesse called Abinadab, and made him pass before Samuel. And he said, "Neither has the LORD chosen this one." ⁹Then Jesse made Shammah pass by. And he said, "Neither has the LORD chosen this one." ¹⁰Thus Jesse made seven of his sons pass before Samuel. And Samuel said to Jesse, "The LORD has not chosen these." ¹¹And Samuel said to Jesse, "Are all the young men here?" Then he said, "There remains yet the youngest, and there he is, keeping the sheep."

And Samuel said to Jesse, "Send and bring him. For we will not sit downᵃ till he comes here." ¹²So he sent and brought him in. Now he *was* ruddy, with bright eyes, and good-looking. And the LORD said, "Arise, anoint him; for this *is* the one!" ¹³Then Samuel took the horn of oil and anointed him in the midst of his brothers; and the Spirit of the LORD came upon David from that day forward. So Samuel arose and went to Ramah.

A Distressing Spirit Troubles Saul

¹⁴But the Spirit of the LORD departed from Saul, and a distressing spirit from the LORD troubled him. ¹⁵And Saul's servants said to him, "Surely, a distressing spirit from God is troubling you. ¹⁶Let our master now command your servants, *who are* before you, to seek out a man *who is* a skillful player on the harp. And it shall be that he will play it with his hand when the distressing spirit from God is upon you, and you shall be well."

¹⁷So Saul said to his servants, "Provide me now a man who can play well, and bring *him* to me."

¹⁸Then one of the servants answered and said, "Look, I have seen a son of Jesse the Bethlehemite, *who is* skillful in playing, a mighty man of valor, a man of war, prudent in speech, and a handsome person; and the LORD *is* with him."

¹⁹Therefore Saul sent messengers to Jesse, and said, "Send me your son David, who *is* with the sheep." ²⁰And Jesse took a donkey *loaded with* bread, a skin of wine, and a young goat, and sent *them* by his son David to Saul. ²¹So David came to Saul and stood before him. And he loved him greatly, and he became his armorbearer. ²²Then Saul sent to Jesse, saying, "Please let David stand before me, for he has found favor in my sight." ²³And so it was, whenever the spirit from God was upon Saul, that David would take a harp and play *it* with his hand. Then Saul would become refreshed and well, and the distressing spirit would depart from him.

The Shepherd's Psalm

Few of the psalms give any information about their historical context. Indeed, this is intentional: the psalms were designed for worship and were written to reflect the many different needs of many worshipers who would use them. The origination of the psalms in worship makes it difficult to place them in chronological order.

Although we cannot know exactly when Ps. 23 was composed, it is particularly appropriate to be read after 1 Sam. 16:14–23. With such a psalm the shepherd David might sing to his troubled, unstable king.

■ Psalm 23

PSALM 23

The LORD the Shepherd of His People

A Psalm of David.

The LORD *is* my shepherd;
  I shall not want.
2 He makes me to lie down in green
    pastures;

16:7 ᵃSeptuagint reads *For God does not see as man sees;* Targum reads *It is not by the appearance of a man;* Vulgate reads *Nor do I judge according to the looks of a man.*   16:11 ᵃFollowing Septuagint and Vulgate; Masoretic Text reads *turn around;* Targum and Syriac read *turn away.*

He leads me beside the still waters.
3 He restores my soul;
He leads me in the paths of
  righteousness
For His name's sake.

4 Yea, though I walk through the valley
  of the shadow of death,
I will fear no evil;
For You *are* with me;
Your rod and Your staff, they comfort
  me.

5 You prepare a table before me in the
  presence of my enemies;
You anoint my head with oil;
My cup runs over.
6 Surely goodness and mercy shall
  follow me
All the days of my life;
And I will dwell[a] in the house of the
  LORD
Forever.

David in Saul's Court

David's arrival in Saul's court as musician and armorbearer (1 Sam. 16:14–23) is followed immediately by a second arrival, this time as the boy slayer of the Philistine giant (1 Sam. 17). Though some details of these two accounts are puzzling, such as why Saul does not seem to recognize his own armorbearer (1 Sam. 17:55), the "two arrivals" are appropriate to David's character. He will always be remembered as both a great warrior, the lion of Judah, and as the sweet singer of Israel, the man after God's own heart.

Saul's and David's victories over the Philistines gave heart to Israel, but the Philistines continued pressing inland. Saul would spend the rest of his life at war with them. That strain, along with his jealousy of David's popularity, helped to overset an already troubled mind.

▼ ■ 1 Samuel 17:1—19:17

1 Samuel
David and Goliath

17 :1 Now the Philistines gathered their armies together to battle, and were gathered at Sochoh, which *belongs* to Judah; they encamped between Sochoh and Azekah, in Ephes Dammim. [2]And Saul and the men of Israel were gathered together, and they encamped in the Valley of Elah, and drew up in battle array against the Philistines. [3]The Philistines stood on a mountain on one side, and Israel stood on a mountain on the other side, with a valley between them.

[4]And a champion went out from the camp of the Philistines, named Goliath, from Gath, whose height *was* six cubits and a span. [5]*He had* a bronze helmet on his head, and he *was* armed with a coat of mail, and the weight of the coat *was* five thousand shekels of bronze. [6]And *he had* bronze armor on his legs and a bronze javelin between his shoulders. [7]Now the staff of his spear *was* like a weaver's beam, and his iron spearhead *weighed* six hundred shekels; and a shield-bearer went before him. [8]Then he stood and cried out to the armies of Israel, and said to them, "Why have you come out to line up for battle? *Am* I not a Philistine, and you the servants of Saul? Choose a man for yourselves, and let him come down to me. [9]If he is able to fight with me and kill me, then we will be your servants. But if I prevail against him and kill him, then you shall be our servants and serve us." [10]And the Philistine said, "I defy the armies of Israel this day; give me a man, that we may fight together." [11]When Saul and all Israel heard these words of the Philistine, they were dismayed and greatly afraid.

[12]Now David *was* the son of that Ephrathite of Bethlehem Judah, whose name *was* Jesse, and who had eight sons. And the man was old, advanced *in years,* in the days of Saul. [13]The three oldest sons of Jesse had gone to follow Saul to the battle. The names of his three sons who went to the battle *were* Eliab the firstborn, next to him Abinadab, and the third Shammah. [14]David *was* the youngest. And the three oldest followed Saul. [15]But David occasionally went and returned from Saul to feed his father's sheep at Bethlehem.

[16]And the Philistine drew near and presented himself forty days, morning and evening.

[17]Then Jesse said to his son David, "Take now for your brothers an ephah of this dried *grain* and these ten loaves, and run to your brothers at the camp. [18]And carry these ten cheeses to the captain of *their* thousand, and see how your brothers fare, and bring back news of them." [19]Now Saul and they and all the men of Israel

---

23:6 [a]Following Septuagint, Syriac, Targum, and Vulgate; Masoretic Text reads *return.*

How Big Is A Giant? (1 Sam. 17:4)

The height reported for the Philistine Goliath, "six cubits and a span" (1 Sam. 17:4), indicates a very big man: approximately 9 feet, 9 inches tall. If such a height seems tall now, it was much taller in ancient times. Biblical people averaged about 5 feet in height, judging from skeletons uncovered by archaeologists.

Other Old Testament sources offer a different measurement for Goliath's height. Some manuscripts of the Septuagint (the Greek Old Testament) and one of the Samuel manuscripts from the Dead Sea Scrolls read "*four* cubits and a span" in 1 Sam. 17:4. This height—about 6 feet, 9 inches—would still make Goliath a giant for David's time. It is difficult to know what caused the differing numbers of six cubits (9 feet) and four cubits (6 feet).

Some scholars have noticed a possible explanation in the Hebrew text. The Hebrew words for "six hundred" (17:7), a few lines below the "six cubits" line, look very similar to the Hebrew words for "six cubits." They suppose that the eye of an early copyist accidentally caught sight of "six hundred," and the similarity of those words in Hebrew caused him to write "six" instead of "four" with "cubits." In this way, "six cubits" may have replaced "four cubits," making Goliath appear to be 9 feet, 9 inches tall, when he was still a giant at 6 feet, 6 inches.

It cannot be known which of these manuscripts preserves the original number. Nevertheless, the youth David (1 Sam. 17:33) faced an opponent who, at either height, was truly a giant among warriors of his day.

---

were in the Valley of Elah, fighting with the Philistines.

20 So David rose early in the morning, left the sheep with a keeper, and took *the things* and went as Jesse had commanded him. And he came to the camp as the army was going out to the fight and shouting for the battle. 21 For Israel and the Philistines had drawn up in battle array, army against army. 22 And David left his supplies in the hand of the supply keeper, ran to the army, and came and greeted his brothers. 23 Then as he talked with them, there was the champion, the Philistine of Gath, Goliath by name, coming up from the armies of the Philistines; and he spoke according to the same words. So David heard *them.* 24 And all the men of Israel, when they saw the man, fled from him and were dreadfully afraid. 25 So the men of Israel said, "Have you seen this man who has come up? Surely he has come up to defy Israel; and it shall be *that* the man who kills

him the king will enrich with great riches, will give him his daughter, and give his father's house exemption *from taxes* in Israel."

26 Then David spoke to the men who stood by him, saying, "What shall be done for the man who kills this Philistine and takes away the reproach from Israel? For who *is* this uncircumcised Philistine, that he should defy the armies of the living God?"

27 And the people answered him in this manner, saying, "So shall it be done for the man who kills him."

28 Now Eliab his oldest brother heard when he spoke to the men; and Eliab's anger was aroused against David, and he said, "Why did you come down here? And with whom have you left those few sheep in the wilderness? I know your pride and the insolence of your heart, for you have come down to see the battle."

29 And David said, "What have I done

SCIENCE AND TECHNOLOGY

The description of Goliath's spear emphasizes his skill as a warrior (1 Sam. 17:7). In Homer, the "huge and heavy" spear of the heroic warrior is the proverbial indicator of strength on the battlefield. Hector's spear was 17 feet long. Soldiers of the Roman Empire used a throwing spear that came in light and heavy versions. The heavy version reportedly had a diameter of 3 inches.

IS THE ARMOR TOO BIG, OR THE CROWN? (1 Sam. 17:38–40)

There was more to Saul's offer of the royal armor and sword to David than meets the eye (1 Sam. 17:38, 39). Positions of authority in the ancient world were marked by formal insignia, or by special clothing. Even more important, the ruler's weapon, usually a sword, was seen as a gift of the deities and a mark of their favor toward the bearer as the legitimate ruler.

So when Saul offered David his armor, he would have been understood by Israelite culture as offering David his own position as king of Israel. The transfer of clothing signified a transfer of status. Elsewhere in the Bible, Elijah called Elisha to replace him as God's primary prophet simply by throwing his mantle upon his successor (1 Kin. 19:19).

Saul's sword was the mark of his position as defender of Israel; when the sword was given to David, Saul's kingship went with it. But David could not wear the armor or the sword; he was not ready to rule, even though he already had the favor of God and the courage to defend Israel. By returning the military gear, David showed that he did not intend to replace Saul as king. He held to this position firmly, even later avoiding confrontation with Saul (1 Sam. 24:6, 7).

Eventually, however, David would be king. When Saul's son Jonathan covenanted with David, the transfer of clothing and armor was repeated, but with a different result (1 Sam. 18:1–4).

---

now? *Is* there not a cause?" ³⁰Then he turned from him toward another and said the same thing; and these people answered him as the first ones *did.*

³¹Now when the words which David spoke were heard, they reported *them* to Saul; and he sent for him. ³²Then David said to Saul, "Let no man's heart fail because of him; your servant will go and fight with this Philistine."

³³And Saul said to David, "You are not able to go against this Philistine to fight with him; for you *are* a youth, and he a man of war from his youth."

³⁴But David said to Saul, "Your servant used to keep his father's sheep, and when a lion or a bear came and took a lamb out of the flock, ³⁵I went out after it and struck it, and delivered *the lamb* from its mouth; and when it arose against me, I caught *it* by its beard, and struck and killed it. ³⁶Your servant has killed both lion and bear; and this uncircumcised Philistine will be like one of them, seeing he has defied the armies of the living God." ³⁷Moreover David said, "The LORD, who delivered me from the paw of the lion and from the paw of the bear, He will deliver me from the hand of this Philistine."

And Saul said to David, "Go, and the LORD be with you!"

³⁸So Saul clothed David with his armor, and he put a bronze helmet on his head; he also clothed him with a coat of mail. ³⁹David fastened his sword to his armor and tried to walk, for he had not tested *them.* And David said to Saul, "I cannot walk with these, for I have not tested *them.*" So David took them off.

⁴⁰Then he took his staff in his hand; and he chose for himself five smooth stones from the brook, and put them in a shepherd's bag, in a pouch which he had, and his sling was in his hand. And he drew near to the Philistine. ⁴¹So the Philistine came, and began drawing near to David, and the man who bore the shield *went* before him. ⁴²And when the Philistine looked about and saw David, he disdained him; for he was *only* a youth, ruddy and good-looking. ⁴³So the Philistine said to David, "*Am* I a dog, that you come to me with sticks?" And the Philistine cursed David by his gods. ⁴⁴And the Philistine said to David, "Come to me, and I will give your flesh to the birds of the air and the beasts of the field!"

⁴⁵Then David said to the Philistine, "You come to me with a sword, with a spear, and with a javelin. But I come to you in the name of the LORD of hosts, the God of the armies of Israel, whom you have defied. ⁴⁶This day the LORD will deliver you into my hand, and I will strike you and take your head from you. And this day I will give the carcasses of the camp of the

JONATHAN TRANSFERS CLAIM TO THE THRONE (1 Sam. 18:1–4)

After he killed Goliath, David became a member of Saul's court. Jonathan, Saul's son and heir, took an immediate liking to David and saw this new friend as an equal. This, as it turns out, was central to the rise of David to the throne.

When Saul had offered David his armor and sword (1 Sam. 17:38, 39), David returned them. Now Jonathan handed over to David his robe and his military gear, including his sword and bow (1 Sam. 18:4). As with Saul's offer, Jonathan's offer entailed more than the clothes.

With David's acceptance of the sword of Jonathan, David became who Jonathan was. David was now the heir apparent to the throne of Israel. Jonathan was already an acknowledged military leader by this time; David is described as still a young man (17:58). But in this action the already established heir, Jonathan, acknowledged that God's decision had been made: David was to rule rather than himself, and he was willing to step aside.

Both Saul and Jonathan knew what had happened with this transfer of royal insignia (1 Sam. 20:30, 31). Saul began sending out David to battles he had previously fought himself or had sent Jonathan to fight (18:5). After this time, in another indication of David's new status, Saul began to refer to David as "my son" (1 Sam. 24:16; 26:21).

Philistines to the birds of the air and the wild beasts of the earth, that all the earth may know that there is a God in Israel. ⁴⁷Then all this assembly shall know that the LORD does not save with sword and spear; for the battle *is* the LORD's, and He will give you into our hands."

⁴⁸So it was, when the Philistine arose and came and drew near to meet David, that David hurried and ran toward the army to meet the Philistine. ⁴⁹Then David put his hand in his bag and took out a stone; and he slung *it* and struck the Philistine in his forehead, so that the stone sank into his forehead, and he fell on his face to the earth. ⁵⁰So David prevailed over the Philistine with a sling and a stone, and struck the Philistine and killed him. But *there was* no sword in the hand of David. ⁵¹Therefore David ran and stood over the Philistine, took his sword and drew it out of its sheath and killed him, and cut off his head with it.

And when the Philistines saw that their champion was dead, they fled. ⁵²Now the men of Israel and Judah arose and shouted, and pursued the Philistines as far as the entrance of the valley^a and to the gates of Ekron. And the wounded of the Philistines fell along the road to Shaaraim, even as far as Gath and Ekron. ⁵³Then the children of Israel returned from chasing the Philistines, and they plundered their tents. ⁵⁴And David took the head of the Philistine and brought it to Jerusalem, but he put his armor in his tent.

⁵⁵When Saul saw David going out against the Philistine, he said to Abner, the commander of the army, "Abner, whose son *is* this youth?"

And Abner said, "As your soul lives, O king, I do not know."

⁵⁶So the king said, "Inquire whose son this young man *is.*"

⁵⁷Then, as David returned from the slaughter of the Philistine, Abner took him and brought him before Saul with the head of the Philistine in his hand. ⁵⁸And Saul said to him, "Whose son *are* you, young man?"

So David answered, "*I am* the son of your servant Jesse the Bethlehemite."

Saul Resents David

18 ¹Now when he had finished speaking to Saul, the soul of Jonathan was knit to the soul of David, and Jonathan loved him as his own soul. ²Saul took him that day, and would not let him go home to his father's house anymore. ³Then Jonathan and David made a covenant, because he loved him as his own soul. ⁴And Jonathan took off the robe that *was* on him and gave it to David, with his armor, even to his sword and his bow and his belt.

⁵So David went out wherever Saul sent him, *and* behaved wisely. And Saul set him over the men of war, and he was accepted in the sight of all the people and also in the

---

17:52 ^aFollowing Masoretic Text, Syriac, Targum, and Vulgate; Septuagint reads *Gath.*

sight of Saul's servants. 6Now it had happened as they were coming *home,* when David was returning from the slaughter of the Philistine, that the women had come out of all the cities of Israel, singing and dancing, to meet King Saul, with tambourines, with joy, and with musical instruments. 7So the women sang as they danced, and said:

> "Saul has slain his thousands,
> And David his ten thousands."

8Then Saul was very angry, and the saying displeased him; and he said, "They have ascribed to David ten thousands, and to me they have ascribed *only* thousands. Now *what* more can he have but the kingdom?" 9So Saul eyed David from that day forward.

10And it happened on the next day that the distressing spirit from God came upon Saul, and he prophesied inside the house. So David played *music* with his hand, as at other times; but *there was* a spear in Saul's hand. 11And Saul cast the spear, for he said, "I will pin David to the wall!" But David escaped his presence twice.

12Now Saul was afraid of David, because the LORD was with him, but had departed from Saul. 13Therefore Saul removed him from his presence, and made him his captain over a thousand; and he went out and came in before the people. 14And David behaved wisely in all his ways, and the LORD *was* with him. 15Therefore, when Saul saw that he behaved very wisely, he was afraid of him. 16But all Israel and Judah loved David, because he went out and came in before them.

David Marries Michal

17Then Saul said to David, "Here is my older daughter Merab; I will give her to you as a wife. Only be valiant for me, and fight the LORD's battles." For Saul thought, "Let my hand not be against him, but let the hand of the Philistines be against him." 18So David said to Saul, "Who *am* I,

and what *is* my life *or* my father's family in Israel, that I should be son-in-law to the king?" 19But it happened at the time when Merab, Saul's daughter, should have been given to David, that she was given to Adriel the Meholathite as a wife.

20Now Michal, Saul's daughter, loved David. And they told Saul, and the thing pleased him. 21So Saul said, "I will give her to him, that she may be a snare to him, and that the hand of the Philistines may be against him." Therefore Saul said to David a second time, "You shall be my son-in-law today."

22And Saul commanded his servants, "Communicate with David secretly, and say, 'Look, the king has delight in you, and all his servants love you. Now therefore, become the king's son-in-law.'"

23So Saul's servants spoke those words in the hearing of David. And David said, "Does it seem to you *a* light *thing* to be a king's son-in-law, seeing I *am* a poor and lightly esteemed man?" 24And the servants of Saul told him, saying, "In this manner David spoke."

25Then Saul said, "Thus you shall say to David: 'The king does not desire any dowry but one hundred foreskins of the Philistines, to take vengeance on the king's enemies.'" But Saul thought to make David fall by the hand of the Philistines. 26So when his servants told David these words, it pleased David well to become the king's son-in-law. Now the days had not expired; 27therefore David arose and went, he and his men, and killed two hundred men of the Philistines. And David brought their foreskins, and they gave them in full count to the king, that he might become the king's son-in-law. Then Saul gave him Michal his daughter as a wife.

28Thus Saul saw and knew that the LORD *was* with David, and *that* Michal, Saul's daughter, loved him; 29and Saul was still more afraid of David. So Saul became David's enemy continually. 30Then the princes of the Philistines went out *to war.* And so it was, whenever they went out,

---

MARRIAGE AND FAMILY

The dowry or bride-price is a feature of traditional cultures. Sometimes the bride is accompanied by a gift from her father, and other times the prospective husband must give a gift to the father. Instead of a dowry, Saul requests that David present to him the tokens of a victory against their national enemy, the Philistines (1 Sam. 18:25).

that David behaved more wisely than all the servants of Saul, so that his name became highly esteemed.

Saul Persecutes David

19 ¹Now Saul spoke to Jonathan his son and to all his servants, that they should kill David; but Jonathan, Saul's son, delighted greatly in David. ²So Jonathan told David, saying, "My father Saul seeks to kill you. Therefore please be on your guard until morning, and stay in a secret *place* and hide. ³And I will go out and stand beside my father in the field where you *are,* and I will speak with my father about you. Then what I observe, I will tell you."

⁴Thus Jonathan spoke well of David to Saul his father, and said to him, "Let not the king sin against his servant, against David, because he has not sinned against you, and because his works *have been* very good toward you. ⁵For he took his life in his hands and killed the Philistine, and the LORD brought about a great deliverance for all Israel. You saw *it* and rejoiced. Why then will you sin against innocent blood, to kill David without a cause?"

⁶So Saul heeded the voice of Jonathan, and Saul swore, "*As* the LORD lives, he shall not be killed." ⁷Then Jonathan called David, and Jonathan told him all these things. So Jonathan brought David to Saul, and he was in his presence as in times past.

⁸And there was war again; and David went out and fought with the Philistines, and struck them with a mighty blow, and they fled from him.

⁹Now the distressing spirit from the LORD came upon Saul as he sat in his house with his spear in his hand. And David was playing *music* with *his* hand. ¹⁰Then Saul sought to pin David to the wall with the spear, but he slipped away from Saul's presence; and he drove the spear into the wall. So David fled and escaped that night.

¹¹Saul also sent messengers to David's house to watch him and to kill him in the morning. And Michal, David's wife, told him, saying, "If you do not save your life tonight, tomorrow you will be killed." ¹²So Michal let David down through a window. And he went and fled and escaped. ¹³And Michal took an image and laid *it* in the bed, put a cover of goats' *hair* for his head, and covered *it* with clothes. ¹⁴So when Saul sent messengers to take David, she said, "He *is* sick."

¹⁵Then Saul sent the messengers *back* to see David, saying, "Bring him up to me in the bed, that I may kill him." ¹⁶And when the messengers had come in, there was the image in the bed, with a cover of goats' *hair* for his head. ¹⁷Then Saul said to Michal, "Why have you deceived me like this, and sent my enemy away, so that he has escaped?"

And Michal answered Saul, "He said to me, 'Let me go! Why should I kill you?' "

Protection in the Night

While the language of the psalms themselves does not describe specific historical events, a few psalms have superscriptions that assign them to a particular historical context. These superscriptions are clearly separate from the actual psalm, and many scholars believe that they were added long after the original compositions.

Whether they were original to the psalms or were added later, the superscriptions do associate some psalms with specific events. They may indicate how certain psalms were understood or used by Israelites in worship and devotion. For that reason, psalms have been placed so as to preserve the associations of the superscriptions. Thus Ps. 59 was associated with Saul's attempt to capture David at his own house (1 Sam. 19:15).

■ Psalm 59

PSALM 59

The Assured Judgment of the Wicked

*To the Chief Musician. Set to "Do Not Destroy."*ᵃ
A Michtam of David when Saul sent men, and they watched the house in order to kill him.

Deliver me from my enemies, O my God;
    Defend me from those who rise up
        against me.
2   Deliver me from the workers of
        iniquity,
    And save me from bloodthirsty men.

3   For look, they lie in wait for my life;
    The mighty gather against me,
    Not *for* my transgression nor *for* my
        sin, O LORD.
4   They run and prepare themselves
        through no fault *of mine.*

59:title   ᵃHebrew *Al Tashcheth*

Awake to help me, and behold!
5 You therefore, O LORD God of hosts,
   the God of Israel,
Awake to punish all the nations;
Do not be merciful to any wicked
   transgressors.   Selah

6 At evening they return,
They growl like a dog,
And go all around the city.
7 Indeed, they belch with their mouth;
Swords *are* in their lips;
For *they say*, "Who hears?"

8 But You, O LORD, shall laugh at them;
You shall have all the nations in
   derision.
9 I will wait for You, O You his
   Strength;[a]
For God *is* my defense.
10 My God of mercy[a] shall come to meet
   me;
God shall let me see *my desire* on my
   enemies.

11 Do not slay them, lest my people
   forget;
Scatter them by Your power,
And bring them down,
O Lord our shield.
12 *For* the sin of their mouth *and* the
   words of their lips,
Let them even be taken in their pride,
And for the cursing and lying *which*
   they speak.
13 Consume *them* in wrath, consume
   them,
That they *may* not *be;*

And let them know that God rules in
   Jacob
To the ends of the earth.   Selah

14 And at evening they return,
They growl like a dog,
And go all around the city.
15 They wander up and down for food,
And howl[a] if they are not satisfied.

16 But I will sing of Your power;
Yes, I will sing aloud of Your mercy in
   the morning;
For You have been my defense
And refuge in the day of my trouble.
17 To You, O my Strength, I will sing
   praises;
For God *is* my defense,
My God of mercy.

David Flees from Saul

As David's popularity grows, even within Saul's inner circle, so does Saul's jealousy. The break is inevitable; David flees. Although he is a fugitive, he somehow keeps his influential supporters, among whom are Samuel (1 Sam. 19:18), Jonathan (Saul's son and heir, 20:1–42), and the priest Ahimelech (21:1–9).

Ahimelech's son, Abiathar, became one of David's primary supporters. Many years later the Gospel of Mark would refer to the event described in 1 Sam. 21, but instead of mentioning Ahimelech, it would use the better known name of the son, Abiathar (Mark 2:23–28).

■ 1 Samuel 19:18—21:15

59:9 [a]Following Masoretic Text and Syriac; some Hebrew manuscripts, Septuagint, Targum, and Vulgate read *my Strength.*   59:10 [a]Following Qere; some Hebrew manuscripts, Septuagint, and Vulgate read *My God, His mercy;* Kethib, some Hebrew manuscripts and Targum read *O God, my mercy;* Syriac reads *O God, Your mercy.*   59:15 [a]Following Septuagint and Vulgate; Masoretic Text, Syriac, and Targum read *spend the night.*

1 Samuel

19 **:18** So David fled and escaped, and went to Samuel at Ramah, and told him all that Saul had done to him. And he and Samuel went and stayed in Naioth. [19]Now it was told Saul, saying, "Take note, David *is* at Naioth in Ramah!" [20]Then Saul sent messengers to take David. And when they saw the group of prophets prophesying,

---

PLANTS AND ANIMALS

In the ancient Near East most dogs were not pets but wild dogs. They made their presence known at night, when there was no traffic or crowds to keep them away (Ps. 59:14). Since they ate whatever they could find, their diet was unclean and could even include dead bodies or blood. Having paws, they were considered unclean for food or sacrifice (Lev. 11:27).

MONTHS OF THE YEARLY CALENDAR (1 Sam. 20:5–24)

In Israel, the New Moon was an important festival. So important that Israelites expected this festival to continue in the new earth where all people will enjoy companionship with Yahweh (Is. 66:23).

The "New Moon" festival resulted from the practice of beginning a new month based on a new moon, the sighting of the first visible crescent of the moon. Virtually every society in the Near East marked their months by the new moon, Egypt being an exception. Since the actual amount of time occurring between new moons is more than 29 days, but less than 30 days, some months contained 29 days, and others 30. The time was determined by visual observation.

Most nations kept track of their years following an agricultural agenda with spring serving as the beginning of the year. The problem was that one year (12 months) of 29- or 30-day months quickly leads to a New Year's day out-of-sync with spring (12 months × 29½ days = 354 days in a year). Thus, in Babylon, on an irregular basis a king would add a 13th month to the year to adjust the New Year's day to the beginning of the spring season. By about 500 B.C. the Babylonians had worked out a regular 19-year cycle to regulate this correspondence.

How the problem was handled in Israel is not known. What is known is that very early in Israel's history, the New Moon day had become a monthly religious festival (1 Sam. 20:5, 18, 24). The importance of this day is suggested by its description as a "solemn feast day" (Ps. 81:3), and the claim that the New Moon festival was a "statute for Israel" (81:4). No wonder the prophet Amos complained about those who waited anxiously for the New Moon day to pass, so they could return to their regular business (Amos 8:5).

---

and Samuel standing *as* leader over them, the Spirit of God came upon the messengers of Saul, and they also prophesied. ²¹And when Saul was told, he sent other messengers, and they prophesied likewise. Then Saul sent messengers again the third time, and they prophesied also. ²²Then he also went to Ramah, and came to the great well that *is* at Sechu. So he asked, and said, "Where *are* Samuel and David?"

And *someone* said, "Indeed *they are* at Naioth in Ramah." ²³So he went there to Naioth in Ramah. Then the Spirit of God was upon him also, and he went on and prophesied until he came to Naioth in Ramah. ²⁴And he also stripped off his clothes and prophesied before Samuel in like manner, and lay down naked all that day and all that night. Therefore they say, "*Is* Saul also among the prophets?"[a]

Jonathan's Loyalty to David

20 ¹Then David fled from Naioth in Ramah, and went and said to Jonathan, "What have I done? What *is* my iniquity, and what *is* my sin before your father, that he seeks my life?"

²So Jonathan said to him, "By no means! You shall not die! Indeed, my father will do nothing either great or small without first telling me. And why should my father hide this thing from me? It *is* not *so!*"

³Then David took an oath again, and said, "Your father certainly knows that I have found favor in your eyes, and he has said, 'Do not let Jonathan know this, lest he be grieved.' But truly, *as* the LORD lives and *as* your soul lives, *there is* but a step between me and death."

⁴So Jonathan said to David, "Whatever you yourself desire, I will do *it* for you."

⁵And David said to Jonathan, "Indeed tomorrow *is* the New Moon, and I should not fail to sit with the king to eat. But let me go, that I may hide in the field until the third *day* at evening. ⁶If your father misses me at all, then say, 'David earnestly asked *permission* of me that he might run over to Bethlehem, his city, for *there is* a yearly sacrifice there for all the family.' ⁷If he says thus: '*It is* well,' your servant will be safe. But if he is very angry, be sure that evil is determined by him. ⁸Therefore you shall deal kindly with your servant, for you have brought your servant into a covenant of the LORD with you. Nevertheless, if there is in-

19:24 ^aCompare 1 Samuel 10:12

iquity in me, kill me yourself, for why should you bring me to your father?"

⁹But Jonathan said, "Far be it from you! For if I knew certainly that evil was determined by my father to come upon you, then would I not tell you?"

¹⁰Then David said to Jonathan, "Who will tell me, or what *if* your father answers you roughly?"

¹¹And Jonathan said to David, "Come, let us go out into the field." So both of them went out into the field. ¹²Then Jonathan said to David: "The LORD God of Israel *is* witness! When I have sounded out my father sometime tomorrow, *or* the third *day,* and indeed *there is* good toward David, and I do not send to you and tell you, ¹³may the LORD do so and much more to Jonathan. But if it pleases my father *to do* you evil, then I will report it to you and send you away, that you may go in safety. And the LORD be with you as He has been with my father. ¹⁴And you shall not only show me the kindness of the LORD while I still live, that I may not die; ¹⁵but you shall not cut off your kindness from my house forever, no, not when the LORD has cut off every one of the enemies of David from the face of the earth." ¹⁶So Jonathan made *a covenant* with the house of David, *saying,* "Let the LORD require *it* at the hand of David's enemies."

¹⁷Now Jonathan again caused David to vow, because he loved him; for he loved him as he loved his own soul. ¹⁸Then Jonathan said to David, "Tomorrow *is* the New Moon; and you will be missed, because your seat will be empty. ¹⁹And *when* you have stayed three days, go down quickly and come to the place where you hid on the day of the deed; and remain by the stone Ezel. ²⁰Then I will shoot three arrows to the side, as though I shot at a target; ²¹and there I will send a lad, *saying,* 'Go, find the arrows.' If I expressly say to the lad, 'Look, the arrows *are* on this side of you; get them and come'—then, as the LORD lives, *there is* safety for you and no harm. ²²But if I say thus to the young man, 'Look, the arrows *are* beyond you'—go your way, for the LORD has sent you away. ²³And as for the matter which you and I have spoken of, indeed the LORD *be* between you and me forever."

²⁴Then David hid in the field. And when the New Moon had come, the king sat down to eat the feast. ²⁵Now the king sat on his seat, as at other times, on a seat by the wall. And Jonathan arose,ᵃ and Abner sat by Saul's side, but David's place was empty. ²⁶Nevertheless Saul did not say anything that day, for he thought, "Something has happened to him; he *is* unclean, surely he *is* unclean." ²⁷And it happened the next day, the second *day* of the month, that David's place was empty. And Saul said to Jonathan his son, "Why has the son of Jesse not come to eat, either yesterday or today?"

²⁸So Jonathan answered Saul, "David earnestly asked *permission* of me *to go* to Bethlehem. ²⁹And he said, 'Please let me go, for our family has a sacrifice in the city, and my brother has commanded me *to be there.* And now, if I have found favor in your eyes, please let me get away and see my brothers.' Therefore he has not come to the king's table."

³⁰Then Saul's anger was aroused against Jonathan, and he said to him, "You son of a perverse, rebellious *woman!* Do I not know that you have chosen the son of Jesse to your own shame and to the shame of your mother's nakedness? ³¹For as long as the son of Jesse lives on the earth, you shall not be established, nor your kingdom. Now therefore, send and bring him to me, for he shall surely die."

³²And Jonathan answered Saul his father, and said to him, "Why should he be killed? What has he done?" ³³Then Saul cast a spear at him to kill him, by which Jonathan knew that it was determined by his father to kill David.

³⁴So Jonathan arose from the table in fierce anger, and ate no food the second day of the month, for he was grieved for David,

---

20:25 ᵃFollowing Masoretic Text, Syriac, Targum, and Vulgate; Septuagint reads *he sat across from Jonathan.*

TIME CAPSULE   *1125 to 1120 B.C.*

1125   *Deborah composes her song of victory over Sisera (Judg. 5)*

1125   *Archaeological remains at Shechem show Abimelech's destruction of the city and its tower (Judg. 9:45–49)*

1120   *Nebuchadnezzar I conquers Elam and returns statue of Marduk*

1120   *Babylonian temple of Esagil renovated and Marduk proclaimed king of the gods*

because his father had treated him shamefully.

³⁵And so it was, in the morning, that Jonathan went out into the field at the time appointed with David, and a little lad *was* with him. ³⁶Then he said to his lad, "Now run, find the arrows which I shoot." As the lad ran, he shot an arrow beyond him. ³⁷When the lad had come to the place where the arrow was which Jonathan had shot, Jonathan cried out after the lad and said, "*Is* not the arrow beyond you?" ³⁸And Jonathan cried out after the lad, "Make haste, hurry, do not delay!" So Jonathan's lad gathered up the arrows and came back to his master. ³⁹But the lad did not know anything. Only Jonathan and David knew of the matter. ⁴⁰Then Jonathan gave his weapons to his lad, and said to him, "Go, carry *them* to the city."

⁴¹As soon as the lad had gone, David arose from *a place* toward the south, fell on his face to the ground, and bowed down three times. And they kissed one another; and they wept together, but David more so. ⁴²Then Jonathan said to David, "Go in peace, since we have both sworn in the name of the LORD, saying, 'May the LORD be between you and me, and between your descendants and my descendants, forever.' " So he arose and departed, and Jonathan went into the city.

David and the Holy Bread

21 ¹Now David came to Nob, to Ahimelech the priest. And Ahimelech was afraid when he met David, and said to him, "Why *are* you alone, and no one is with you?"

²So David said to Ahimelech the priest, "The king has ordered me on some business, and said to me, 'Do not let anyone know anything about the business on which I send you, or what I have commanded you.' And I have directed *my* young men to such and such a place. ³Now therefore, what have you on hand? Give *me* five *loaves of* bread in my hand, or whatever can be found."

⁴And the priest answered David and said, "*There is* no common bread on hand; but there is holy bread, if the young men have at least kept themselves from women."

⁵Then David answered the priest, and said to him, "Truly, women *have been* kept from us about three days since I came out. And the vessels of the young men are holy, and *the bread is* in effect common, even though it was consecrated in the vessel this day."

⁶So the priest gave him holy *bread;* for there was no bread there but the showbread which had been taken from before the LORD, in order to put hot bread *in its place* on the day when it was taken away.

⁷Now a certain man of the servants of Saul *was* there that day, detained before the LORD. And his name *was* Doeg, an Edomite, the chief of the herdsmen who *belonged* to Saul.

⁸And David said to Ahimelech, "Is there not here on hand a spear or a sword? For I have brought neither my sword nor my weapons with me, because the king's business required haste."

⁹So the priest said, "The sword of Goliath the Philistine, whom you killed in the Valley of Elah, there it is, wrapped in a cloth behind the ephod. If you will take that, take *it.* For *there is* no other except that one here."

And David said, "*There is* none like it; give it to me."

David Flees to Gath

¹⁰Then David arose and fled that day from before Saul, and went to Achish the king of Gath. ¹¹And the servants of Achish said to him, "*Is* this not David the king of the land? Did they not sing of him to one another in dances, saying:

> 'Saul has slain his thousands,
> And David his ten thousands'?"ª

¹²Now David took these words to heart, and was very much afraid of Achish the king of Gath. ¹³So he changed his behavior before them, pretended madness in their hands, scratched on the doors of the gate, and let his saliva fall down on his beard. ¹⁴Then Achish said to his servants, "Look, you see the man is insane. Why have you brought him to me? ¹⁵Have I need of madmen, that you have brought this *fellow* to play the madman in my presence? Shall this *fellow* come into my house?"

21:11 ᵃCompare 1 Samuel 18:7

Among the Philistines at Gath

Two psalms have superscriptions that associate them with David's sojourn at Gath. The superscription to Ps. 56 remembers the time when the Philistines captured David. The superscription to Ps. 34 even mentions David's pretended madness before the Philistine king.

    The name of the Philistine king in Ps. 34 is Abimelech. In 1 Sam. 21:10–15 where this incident is reported, the king's name is given as Achish. Possibly "Abimelech" was a title or throne name used for all kings of the Philistine regions. The city of Gerar, which was a Philistine city after about 1200 B.C., shows a King Abimelech in the patriarchal stories of Abraham (Gen. 20:2) and of his son Isaac (Gen. 26:1, where Abimelech is even called "king of the Philistines"). The name "Abimelech" is translated "my father, the king" or "father of the king," an appropriate meaning for a throne name.

▼   ■ Psalms 56; 34

PSALM 56

Prayer for Relief from Tormentors

To the Chief Musician. Set to "The Silent Dove in Distant Lands."[a] *A Michtam of David when the Philistines captured him in Gath.*

Be merciful to me, O God, for man would swallow me up;
    Fighting all day he oppresses me.
2   My enemies would hound *me* all day,
    For *there are* many who fight against me, O Most High.

3   Whenever I am afraid,
    I will trust in You.
4   In God (I will praise His word),
    In God I have put my trust;
    I will not fear.
    What can flesh do to me?

5   All day they twist my words;
    All their thoughts *are* against me for evil.
6   They gather together,
    They hide, they mark my steps,
    When they lie in wait for my life.
7   Shall they escape by iniquity?
    In anger cast down the peoples,
      O God!

8   You number my wanderings;
    Put my tears into Your bottle;
    Are they not in Your book?
9   When I cry out *to You,*
    Then my enemies will turn back;
    This I know, because God *is* for me.

10   In God (I will praise *His* word),
    In the LORD (I will praise *His* word),
11   In God I have put my trust;
    I will not be afraid.
    What can man do to me?

12   Vows *made* to You *are binding* upon me, O God;
    I will render praises to You,
13   For You have delivered my soul from death.
    Have You not *kept* my feet from falling,
    That I may walk before God
    In the light of the living?

PSALM 34

The Happiness of Those Who Trust in God

A Psalm of David when he pretended madness before Abimelech, who drove him away, and he departed.

I will bless the LORD at all times;
    His praise *shall* continually *be* in my mouth.
2   My soul shall make its boast in the LORD;
    The humble shall hear *of it* and be glad.
3   Oh, magnify the LORD with me,
    And let us exalt His name together.

4   I sought the LORD, and He heard me,
    And delivered me from all my fears.
5   They looked to Him and were radiant,
    And their faces were not ashamed.
6   This poor man cried out, and the LORD heard *him,*
    And saved him out of all his troubles.
7   The angel[a] of the LORD encamps all around those who fear Him,
    And delivers them.

8   Oh, taste and see that the LORD *is* good;
    Blessed *is* the man *who* trusts in Him!
9   Oh, fear the LORD, you His saints!
    There is no want to those who fear Him.
10   The young lions lack and suffer hunger;
    But those who seek the LORD shall not lack any good *thing.*

11   Come, you children, listen to me;
    I will teach you the fear of the LORD.

56:title ªHebrew *Jonath Elem Rechokim*
34:7 ªOr *Angel*

ANGEL: MESSENGER AND PRESENCE OF GOD (Ps. 34:7)

Angels do the will of God. Both the Hebrew and Greek words for "angel" mean "messenger." In the ancient Near East the divine realm was viewed in terms of the structure of human society, and angels were the lowest level of society—the slave messengers. These lowest denizens of heaven did only what they were commanded to do by their superiors.

While other ancient Near Eastern cultures believed in pantheons of gods, the official religion of Israel accepted no other divine beings than God, save the angels. The gods of the pantheons could disagree with and disobey the authoritative deities of their own divine hierarchy. The psalmists, though, knew of no disagreement in heaven, since God is in control of all divine beings (Ps. 89:6, 7). The angels do the work of heaven in harmony with the will of God.

In narratives of the Bible and of the texts from Ugarit (1400–1200 B.C.), divine messengers carry messages in the form of living letters. The messengers repeat word for word what they are told to report to other gods or to humans. In this way the message given by an angel in the name of another deity was indeed the very words of the deity who sent the messenger.

An angel of any given deity was so closely associated with the god as to represent the actual presence of the god. Thus, as Moses experienced at the burning bush (Ex. 3:2–4), to speak with an angel was actually to speak with the deity. The Bible presents a similar situation with the activity of angels. Since the messenger could do only as ordered by God, whatever an angel did in the name of God was done by God. So in Israel's psalms, it is God who protects the faithful, even though the actual divine being standing guard is God's angel (Ps. 34:7).

---

12 Who *is* the man *who* desires life,
    And loves *many* days, that he may see
    good?
13 Keep your tongue from evil,
    And your lips from speaking deceit.
14 Depart from evil and do good;
    Seek peace and pursue it.

15 The eyes of the LORD *are* on the
    righteous,
    And His ears *are open* to their cry.
16 The face of the LORD *is* against those
    who do evil,
    To cut off the remembrance of them
    from the earth.

17 *The righteous* cry out, and the LORD
    hears,
    And delivers them out of all their
    troubles.
18 The LORD *is* near to those who have a
    broken heart,
    And saves such as have a contrite
    spirit.

19 Many *are* the afflictions of the
    righteous,
    But the LORD delivers him out of them
    all.
20 He guards all his bones;

Not one of them is broken.
21 Evil shall slay the wicked,
    And those who hate the righteous
    shall be condemned.
22 The LORD redeems the soul of His
    servants,
    And none of those who trust in Him
    shall be condemned.

Murder in the Holy Place

Saul's pursuit of David intensified, now involving actual murder. The time of Israel's tribal confederation, just before Saul was crowned king, was not very unified, but what unity there was came from Israel's common worship at the shrine where the ark of the covenant was kept. Reverence for the shrine continued, even after the confederation ended, and no sane Israelite would have dreamed of attacking that holy place or its priests. But Saul by this time could hardly be called sane.

■ 1 Samuel 22:1–23

1 Samuel
David's Four Hundred Men

22 :1 David therefore departed from there and escaped to the cave of Adullam. So when his brothers and all his father's house heard *it,* they went down there to him. ²And everyone *who was* in distress, everyone who *was* in debt, and everyone *who was* discontented gathered to him. So he became captain over them. And there were about four hundred men with him.

³Then David went from there to Mizpah of Moab; and he said to the king of Moab, "Please let my father and mother come here with you, till I know what God will do for me." ⁴So he brought them before the king of Moab, and they dwelt with him all the time that David was in the stronghold.

⁵Now the prophet Gad said to David, "Do not stay in the stronghold; depart, and go to the land of Judah." So David departed and went into the forest of Hereth.

Saul Murders the Priests

⁶When Saul heard that David and the men who *were* with him had been discovered—now Saul was staying in Gibeah under a tamarisk tree in Ramah, with his spear in his hand, and all his servants standing about him— ⁷then Saul said to his servants who stood about him, "Hear now, you Benjamites! Will the son of Jesse give every one of you fields and vineyards, *and* make you all captains of thousands and captains of hundreds? ⁸All of you have conspired against me, and *there is* no one who reveals to me that my son has made a covenant with the son of Jesse; and *there is* not one of you who is sorry for me or reveals to me that my son has stirred up my servant against me, to lie in wait, as *it is* this day."

⁹Then answered Doeg the Edomite, who was set over the servants of Saul, and said, "I saw the son of Jesse going to Nob, to Ahimelech the son of Ahitub. ¹⁰And he inquired of the LORD for him, gave him provisions, and gave him the sword of Goliath the Philistine."

¹¹So the king sent to call Ahimelech the priest, the son of Ahitub, and all his father's house, the priests who *were* in Nob. And they all came to the king. ¹²And Saul said, "Hear now, son of Ahitub!"

He answered, "Here I am, my lord."

¹³Then Saul said to him, "Why have you conspired against me, you and the son of Jesse, in that you have given him bread and a sword, and have inquired of God for him, that he should rise against me, to lie in wait, as it is this day?"

¹⁴So Ahimelech answered the king and said, "And who among all your servants *is as* faithful as David, who is the king's son-in-law, who goes at your bidding, and is honorable in your house? ¹⁵Did I then begin to inquire of God for him? Far be it from me! Let not the king impute anything to his servant, *or* to any in the house of my father. For your servant knew nothing of all this, little or much."

¹⁶And the king said, "You shall surely die, Ahimelech, you and all your father's house!" ¹⁷Then the king said to the guards who stood about him, "Turn and kill the priests of the LORD, because their hand also *is* with David, and because they knew when he fled and did not tell it to me." But the servants of the king would not lift their hands to strike the priests of the LORD. ¹⁸And the king said to Doeg, "You turn and kill the priests!" So Doeg the Edomite turned and struck the priests, and killed on that day eighty-five men who wore a linen ephod. ¹⁹Also Nob, the city of the priests, he struck with the edge of the sword, both men and women, children and nursing infants, oxen and donkeys and sheep—with the edge of the sword.

²⁰Now one of the sons of Ahimelech the son of Ahitub, named Abiathar, escaped and fled after David. ²¹And Abiathar told David that Saul had killed the LORD's priests. ²²So David said to Abiathar, "I knew that day, when Doeg the Edomite *was* there, that he would surely tell Saul. I have caused *the death* of all the persons of your father's house. ²³Stay with me; do not fear. For he who seeks my life seeks your life, but with me you *shall be* safe."

POLITICS AND GOVERNMENT

The administrative center was not a physical location, like a building, but the physical presence of the ruler, in this case, Saul (1 Sam. 22:6). With a spear as the symbol of his authority and his retainers surrounding him, Saul could establish a ruling center under a tamarisk tree. Deborah held court under a palm tree (Judg. 4:5).

Doeg, the Evildoer

An important player in the massacre of the priests was Saul's servant Doeg. He was the one who informed Saul about the priest Ahimelech's dealings with David (1 Sam. 22:9, 10). When Saul's own guards refused to strike the Lord's priests, the Edomite Doeg did not hesitate to carry out the evil deed, killing 85 priests, as well as people in the city of Nob (22:18, 19).

It is not surprising that Israel would reflect upon this tragedy in a psalm. The superscription of Ps. 52 associates this psalm's thoughts on evil and wickedness with the evildoer Doeg.

■ Psalm 52

PSALM 52

The End of the Wicked and the Peace of the Godly

To the Chief Musician. A Contemplation[a] of David when Doeg the Edomite went and told Saul, and said to him, "David has gone to the house of Ahimelech."

Why do you boast in evil, O mighty man?
The goodness of God *endures*
continually.
2 Your tongue devises destruction,
Like a sharp razor, working
deceitfully.
3 You love evil more than good,
Lying rather than speaking
righteousness.   Selah
4 You love all devouring words,
You deceitful tongue.

5 God shall likewise destroy you forever;
He shall take you away, and pluck you
out of *your* dwelling place,
And uproot you from the land of the
living.   Selah
6 The righteous also shall see and fear,
And shall laugh at him, *saying,*
7 "Here is the man *who* did not make
God his strength,
But trusted in the abundance of his
riches,
And strengthened himself in his
wickedness."

8 But I *am* like a green olive tree in the
house of God;
I trust in the mercy of God forever
and ever.
9 I will praise You forever,

Because You have done *it;*
And in the presence of Your saints
I will wait on Your name, for *it is*
good.

Seeking God's Guidance

In the ancient Near East, there were many ways of asking advice from the gods. Before battles, kings would consult with soothsayers and diviners to ensure divine favor. Mosaic law prohibited such divination (see Lev. 19:26), but even in Israel there were means of seeking a word from God. One of these evidently was the ephod that Abiathar the priest had brought to David's camp (1 Sam. 23:9–12).

In Exodus, the ephod refers to the linen apron worn by the high priest (Ex. 39:2–7). With Abiathar's ephod David would ask a yes-no question, and by some means that is not clear the ephod would reveal God's answer. The means is not important, in the end. The essential point is that David inquired of God, and God answered. Saul, by contrast, sought information from spies. When Saul did at last inquire of God, God would no longer answer (1 Sam. 28:6).

■ 1 Samuel 23:1–29

1 Samuel
David Saves the City of Keilah

23 :1 Then they told David, saying, "Look, the Philistines are fighting against Keilah, and they are robbing the threshing floors."

2Therefore David inquired of the LORD, saying, "Shall I go and attack these Philistines?"

And the LORD said to David, "Go and attack the Philistines, and save Keilah."

3But David's men said to him, "Look, we are afraid here in Judah. How much more then if we go to Keilah against the armies of the Philistines?" 4Then David inquired of the LORD once again.

And the LORD answered him and said, "Arise, go down to Keilah. For I will deliver the Philistines into your hand." 5And David and his men went to Keilah and fought with the Philistines, struck them with a mighty blow, and took away their livestock. So David saved the inhabitants of Keilah.

6Now it happened, when Abiathar the son of Ahimelech fled to David at Keilah,

---

52:title ªHebrew *Maschil*

that he went down *with* an ephod in his hand.

7And Saul was told that David had gone to Keilah. So Saul said, "God has delivered him into my hand, for he has shut himself in by entering a town that has gates and bars." 8Then Saul called all the people together for war, to go down to Keilah to besiege David and his men.

9When David knew that Saul plotted evil against him, he said to Abiathar the priest, "Bring the ephod here." 10Then David said, "O LORD God of Israel, Your servant has certainly heard that Saul seeks to come to Keilah to destroy the city for my sake. 11Will the men of Keilah deliver me into his hand? Will Saul come down, as Your servant has heard? O LORD God of Israel, I pray, tell Your servant."

And the LORD said, "He will come down."

12Then David said, "Will the men of Keilah deliver me and my men into the hand of Saul?"

And the LORD said, "They will deliver *you.*"

13So David and his men, about six hundred, arose and departed from Keilah and went wherever they could go. Then it was told Saul that David had escaped from Keilah; so he halted the expedition.

David in Wilderness Strongholds

14And David stayed in strongholds in the wilderness, and remained in the mountains in the Wilderness of Ziph. Saul sought him every day, but God did not deliver him into his hand. 15So David saw that Saul had come out to seek his life. And David *was* in the Wilderness of Ziph in a forest.a 16Then Jonathan, Saul's son, arose and went to David in the woods and strengthened his hand in God. 17And he said to him, "Do not fear, for the hand of Saul my father shall not find you. You shall be king over Israel, and I shall be next to you. Even my father Saul knows that." 18So the two of them made a covenant before the LORD. And David stayed in the woods, and Jonathan went to his own house.

19Then the Ziphites came up to Saul at Gibeah, saying, "Is David not hiding with us in strongholds in the woods, in the hill of Hachilah, which *is* on the south of Jeshimon? 20Now therefore, O king, come down according to all the desire of your soul to come down; and our part *shall be* to deliver him into the king's hand."

21And Saul said, "Blessed *are* you of the LORD, for you have compassion on me. 22Please go and find out for sure, and see the place where his hideout is, *and* who has seen him there. For I am told he is very crafty. 23See therefore, and take knowledge of all the lurking places where he hides; and come back to me with certainty, and I will go with you. And it shall be, if he is in the land, that I will search for him throughout all the clansa of Judah."

24So they arose and went to Ziph before Saul. But David and his men *were* in the Wilderness of Maon, in the plain on the south of Jeshimon. 25When Saul and his men went to seek *him,* they told David. Therefore he went down to the rock, and stayed in the Wilderness of Maon. And when Saul heard *that,* he pursued David in the Wilderness of Maon. 26Then Saul went on one side of the mountain, and David and his men on the other side of the mountain. So David made haste to get away from Saul, for Saul and his men were encircling David and his men to take them.

27But a messenger came to Saul, saying, "Hurry and come, for the Philistines have invaded the land!" 28Therefore Saul returned from pursuing David, and went against the Philistines; so they called that place the Rock of Escape.a 29Then David went up from there and dwelt in strongholds at En Gedi.

David in the Wilderness

The "wilderness of Judah," mentioned in the superscription of Ps. 63, is the arid, rocky region along the western shore of the Dead Sea, southeast of Jerusalem. On the western edge of this wilderness area are the towns Ziph, Maon, and Carmel (not to be confused with Mount Carmel on the Mediterranean Sea). The town of En Gedi, sitting on the shore of the Dead Sea, is an oasis of the area.

Most of these places are mentioned in the account of David's flight from Saul (1 Sam. 23:13–29). The rugged terrain of the wilderness made it difficult for Saul to track David. Such terrain is reflected in the language of the psalmist who seeks God "in a dry and thirsty land" (Ps. 63:1).

■ Psalm 63

23:15 aOr *in Horesh*   23:23 aLiterally *thousands*
23:28 aHebrew *Sela Hammahlekoth*

PSALM 63

Joy in the Fellowship of God

A Psalm of David when he was in the wilderness of Judah.

O God, You *are* my God;
Early will I seek You;
My soul thirsts for You;
My flesh longs for You
In a dry and thirsty land
Where there is no water.

2 So I have looked for You in the
sanctuary,
To see Your power and Your glory.

3 Because Your lovingkindness *is* better
than life,
My lips shall praise You.

4 Thus I will bless You while I live;
I will lift up my hands in Your name.

5 My soul shall be satisfied as with
marrow and fatness,
And my mouth shall praise *You* with
joyful lips.

6 When I remember You on my bed,
I meditate on You in the *night*
watches.

7 Because You have been my help,
Therefore in the shadow of Your wings
I will rejoice.

8 My soul follows close behind You;
Your right hand upholds me.

9 But those *who* seek my life, to destroy
it,
Shall go into the lower parts of the
earth.

10 They shall fall by the sword;
They shall be a portion for jackals.

11 But the king shall rejoice in God;
Everyone who swears by Him shall
glory;
But the mouth of those who speak lies
shall be stopped.

Hiding in the Caves

David is not the only illustrious refugee who has found haven among the caves and crags of the Judean wilderness. In later years such people as Herod the Great and the Jewish zealots who rebelled against the Roman Empire would hide there also. The many caves were particularly useful hiding places—the Dead Sea Scrolls lay undiscovered in some of these caves for hundreds of years.

David clearly made the most of the cave environment while avoiding Saul's pursuit. The superscriptions of two psalms—Ps. 57 and Ps. 142—associate these psalms' laments with the stressful circumstances surrounding David's days of hiding.

- 1 Samuel 24:1–22
- Psalms 57; 142

1 Samuel 24:1–22
David Spares Saul

24 **:1** Now it happened, when Saul had returned from following the Philistines, that it was told him, saying, "Take note! David *is* in the Wilderness of En Gedi." ²Then Saul took three thousand chosen men from all Israel, and went to seek David and his men on the Rocks of the Wild Goats. ³So he came to the sheepfolds by the road, where there *was* a cave; and Saul went in to attend to his needs. (David and his men were staying in the recesses of the cave.) ⁴Then the men of David said to him, "This is the day of which the LORD said to you, 'Behold, I will deliver your enemy into your hand, that you may do to him as it seems good to you.'" And David arose and secretly cut off a corner of Saul's robe. ⁵Now it happened afterward that David's heart troubled him because he had cut Saul's *robe.* ⁶And he said to his men, "The LORD forbid that I should do this thing to my master, the LORD's anointed, to stretch out my hand against him, seeing he *is* the anointed of the LORD." ⁷So David restrained his servants with *these* words, and did not allow them to rise against Saul. And Saul got up from the cave and went on *his* way.

⁸David also arose afterward, went out of the cave, and called out to Saul, saying, "My lord the king!" And when Saul looked behind him, David stooped with his face to the earth, and bowed down. ⁹And David said to Saul: "Why do you listen to the words of men who say, 'Indeed David seeks your harm'? ¹⁰Look, this day your eyes have seen that the LORD delivered you today into my hand in the cave, and *someone* urged *me* to kill you. But *my eye* spared you, and I said, 'I will not stretch out my hand against my lord, for he *is* the LORD's anointed.' ¹¹Moreover, my father, see! Yes, see the corner of your robe in my hand! For in that I cut off the corner of your robe, and did not kill you, know and see that *there is* neither evil nor rebellion in my hand, and I

have not sinned against you. Yet you hunt my life to take it. ¹²Let the LORD judge between you and me, and let the LORD avenge me on you. But my hand shall not be against you. ¹³As the proverb of the ancients says, 'Wickedness proceeds from the wicked.' But my hand shall not be against you. ¹⁴After whom has the king of Israel come out? Whom do you pursue? A dead dog? A flea? ¹⁵Therefore let the LORD be judge, and judge between you and me, and see and plead my case, and deliver me out of your hand."

¹⁶So it was, when David had finished speaking these words to Saul, that Saul said, "*Is* this your voice, my son David?" And Saul lifted up his voice and wept. ¹⁷Then he said to David: "You *are* more righteous than I; for you have rewarded me with good, whereas I have rewarded you with evil. ¹⁸And you have shown this day how you have dealt well with me; for when the LORD delivered me into your hand, you did not kill me. ¹⁹For if a man finds his enemy, will he let him get away safely? Therefore may the LORD reward you with good for what you have done to me this day. ²⁰And now I know indeed that you shall surely be king, and that the kingdom of Israel shall be established in your hand. ²¹Therefore swear now to me by the LORD that you will not cut off my descendants after me, and that you will not destroy my name from my father's house."

²²So David swore to Saul. And Saul went home, but David and his men went up to the stronghold.

PSALM 57

Prayer for Safety from Enemies

To the Chief Musician. Set to "Do Not Destroy."^a *A Michtam of David when he fled from Saul into the cave.*

Be merciful to me, O God, be merciful to me!
  For my soul trusts in You;
  And in the shadow of Your wings I will make my refuge,
  Until *these* calamities have passed by.

2 I will cry out to God Most High,
  To God who performs *all things* for me.

3 He shall send from heaven and save me;
  He reproaches the one who would swallow me up.   Selah
  God shall send forth His mercy and His truth.

4 My soul *is* among lions;
  I lie *among* the sons of men
  Who are set on fire,
  Whose teeth *are* spears and arrows,
  And their tongue a sharp sword.

5 Be exalted, O God, above the heavens;
  Let Your glory *be* above all the earth.

6 They have prepared a net for my steps;
  My soul is bowed down;
  They have dug a pit before me;
  Into the midst of it they *themselves* have fallen.   Selah

7 My heart is steadfast, O God, my heart is steadfast;
  I will sing and give praise.

8 Awake, my glory!
  Awake, lute and harp!
  I will awaken the dawn.

9 I will praise You, O Lord, among the peoples;
  I will sing to You among the nations.

10 For Your mercy reaches unto the heavens,
  And Your truth unto the clouds.

11 Be exalted, O God, above the heavens;
  Let Your glory *be* above all the earth.

PSALM 142

A Plea for Relief from Persecutors

A Contemplation^a *of David. A Prayer when he was in the cave.*

I cry out to the LORD with my voice;
  With my voice to the LORD I make my supplication.

2 I pour out my complaint before Him;
  I declare before Him my trouble.

3 When my spirit was overwhelmed within me,
  Then You knew my path.
  In the way in which I walk
  They have secretly set a snare for me.

4 Look on *my* right hand and see,
  For *there is* no one who acknowledges me;

57:title ªHebrew *Al Tashcheth*   142:title ªHebrew *Maschil*

Refuge has failed me;
No one cares for my soul.

5   I cried out to You, O LORD:
     I said, "You *are* my refuge,
     My portion in the land of the living.
6   Attend to my cry,
     For I am brought very low;
     Deliver me from my persecutors,
     For they are stronger than I.
7   Bring my soul out of prison,
     That I may praise Your name;
     The righteous shall surround me,
     For You shall deal bountifully with
     me."

What's in a Name?

Names in the Old Testament are often significant clues to interpretation. Hebrew names had meaning. For instance, according to a popular interpretation given in 1 Sam. 1:20, the name "Samuel" came from the Hebrew word meaning "to ask." Hannah named her son Samuel because she had "asked for him from the LORD."

In 1 Sam. 25 the wordplay is more obvious. The name "Nabal," in popular interpretation, meant literally "fool" or "folly" (1 Sam. 25:25). Nabal lives up to his name. Having refused to give David's men provisions, he ends up providing David with his own wife.

■ 1 Samuel 25:1-44

1 Samuel
Death of Samuel

25 :1 Then Samuel died; and the Israelites gathered together and lamented for him, and buried him at his home in Ramah. And David arose and went down to the Wilderness of Paran.[a]

David and the Wife of Nabal

2Now *there was* a man in Maon whose business *was* in Carmel, and the man *was* very rich. He had three thousand sheep and a thousand goats. And he was shearing his sheep in Carmel. 3The name of the man *was* Nabal, and the name of his wife Abigail. And *she was* a woman of good understanding and beautiful appearance; but the man *was* harsh and evil in *his* doings. He *was of the house of* Caleb.

4When David heard in the wilderness that Nabal was shearing his sheep, 5David sent ten young men; and David said to the young men, "Go up to Carmel, go to Nabal,

and greet him in my name. 6And thus you shall say to him who lives *in prosperity:* 'Peace *be* to you, peace to your house, and peace to all that you have! 7Now I have heard that you have shearers. Your shepherds were with us, and we did not hurt them, nor was there anything missing from them all the while they were in Carmel. 8Ask your young men, and they will tell you. Therefore let *my* young men find favor in your eyes, for we come on a feast day. Please give whatever comes to your hand to your servants and to your son David.' "

9So when David's young men came, they spoke to Nabal according to all these words in the name of David, and waited.

10Then Nabal answered David's servants, and said, "Who *is* David, and who *is* the son of Jesse? There are many servants nowadays who break away each one from his master. 11Shall I then take my bread and my water and my meat that I have killed for my shearers, and give *it* to men when I do not know where they *are* from?"

12So David's young men turned on their heels and went back; and they came and told him all these words. 13Then David said to his men, "Every man gird on his sword." So every man girded on his sword, and David also girded on his sword. And about four hundred men went with David, and two hundred stayed with the supplies.

14Now one of the young men told Abigail, Nabal's wife, saying, "Look, David sent messengers from the wilderness to greet our master; and he reviled them. 15But the men *were* very good to us, and we were not hurt, nor did we miss anything as long as we accompanied them, when we were in the fields. 16They were a wall to us both by night and day, all the time we were with them keeping the sheep. 17Now therefore, know and consider what you will do, for harm is determined against our master and against all his household. For he *is* such a scoundrel[a] that *one* cannot speak to him."

18Then Abigail made haste and took two hundred *loaves* of bread, two skins of wine, five sheep already dressed, five seahs of roasted *grain,* one hundred clusters of raisins, and two hundred cakes of figs, and loaded *them* on donkeys. 19And she said to her servants, "Go on before me; see, I am

25:1 aFollowing Masoretic Text, Syriac, Targum, and Vulgate; Septuagint reads *Maon.*   25:17 aLiterally *son of Belial*

FROM THE POCKET OF A SLING (1 Sam. 25:29)

The most common image of a sling is that of the slingshot, a weapon built from a Y-shaped piece of wood. That is not what David used in his confrontation with Goliath (1 Sam. 17:40), nor what Abigail means by "the pocket of a sling" (1 Sam. 25:29).

The type of sling that David used was made from either leather or goat's hair. This sling had two long, thin straps with a pouch or pocket in the middle. The stone would be placed in the pocket after which the two straps were held in the same hand and swung around in the air to gain velocity while the slinger took aim.

At the ready, the slinger released one strap from his hand, sending the stone flying with great speed toward the target. Some slings had a small loop on one of the straps that could be placed around a finger to reduce the chance of accidental release of the entire sling. Abigail's well-chosen words, declaring that God would "sling out" David's enemies as from a sling's pocket (25:29), would communicate clearly to a king who had been a slinger himself.

coming after you." But she did not tell her husband Nabal.

20So it was, *as* she rode on the donkey, that she went down under cover of the hill; and there were David and his men, coming down toward her, and she met them. 21Now David had said, "Surely in vain I have protected all that this *fellow* has in the wilderness, so that nothing was missed of all that *belongs* to him. And he has repaid me evil for good. 22May God do so, and more also, to the enemies of David, if I leave one male of all who *belong* to him by morning light."

23Now when Abigail saw David, she dismounted quickly from the donkey, fell on her face before David, and bowed down to the ground. 24So she fell at his feet and said: "On me, my lord, *on* me *let* this iniquity *be!* And please let your maidservant speak in your ears, and hear the words of your maidservant. 25Please, let not my lord regard this scoundrel Nabal. For as his name *is,* so *is* he: Nabal[a] *is* his name, and folly *is* with him! But I, your maidservant, did not see the young men of my lord whom you sent. 26Now therefore, my lord, *as* the LORD lives and *as* your soul lives, since the LORD has held you back from coming to bloodshed and from avenging yourself with

your own hand, now then, let your enemies and those who seek harm for my lord be as Nabal. 27And now this present which your maidservant has brought to my lord, let it be given to the young men who follow my lord. 28Please forgive the trespass of your maidservant. For the LORD will certainly make for my lord an enduring house, because my lord fights the battles of the LORD, and evil is not found in you throughout your days. 29Yet a man has risen to pursue you and seek your life, but the life of my lord shall be bound in the bundle of the living with the LORD your God; and the lives of your enemies He shall sling out, *as from* the pocket of a sling. 30And it shall come to pass, when the LORD has done for my lord according to all the good that He has spoken concerning you, and has appointed you ruler over Israel, 31that this will be no grief to you, nor offense of heart to my lord, either that you have shed blood without cause, or that my lord has avenged himself. But when the LORD has dealt well with my lord, then remember your maidservant."

32Then David said to Abigail: "Blessed *is* the LORD God of Israel, who sent you this day to meet me! 33And blessed *is* your advice and blessed *are* you, because you have kept me this day from coming to bloodshed

25:25 ªLiterally *Fool*

FOOD AND DRINK

Raisins and fig cakes are made by drying fruit, with the result being a concentration of sugar. This is naturally attractive to the taste, and it acts as a preservative. The absence of processed sugars made dried fruits more desirable (1 Sam. 25:18). Honey is another source of sugar and it too is prominent in the Bible as a symbol of prosperity.

and from avenging myself with my own hand. [34]For indeed, *as* the LORD God of Israel lives, who has kept me back from hurting you, unless you had hurried and come to meet me, surely by morning light no males would have been left to Nabal!" [35]So David received from her hand what she had brought him, and said to her, "Go up in peace to your house. See, I have heeded your voice and respected your person."

[36]Now Abigail went to Nabal, and there he was, holding a feast in his house, like the feast of a king. And Nabal's heart *was* merry within him, for he *was* very drunk; therefore she told him nothing, little or much, until morning light. [37]So it was, in the morning, when the wine had gone from Nabal, and his wife had told him these things, that his heart died within him, and he became *like* a stone. [38]Then it happened, *after* about ten days, that the LORD struck Nabal, and he died.

[39]So when David heard that Nabal was dead, he said, "Blessed *be* the LORD, who has pleaded the cause of my reproach from the hand of Nabal, and has kept His servant from evil! For the LORD has returned the wickedness of Nabal on his own head."

And David sent and proposed to Abigail, to take her as his wife. [40]When the servants of David had come to Abigail at Carmel, they spoke to her saying, "David sent us to you, to ask you to become his wife."

[41]Then she arose, bowed her face to the earth, and said, "Here is your maidservant, a servant to wash the feet of the servants of my lord." [42]So Abigail rose in haste and rode on a donkey, attended by five of her maidens; and she followed the messengers of David, and became his wife. [43]David also took Ahinoam of Jezreel, and so both of them were his wives.

[44]But Saul had given Michal his daughter, David's wife, to Palti[a] the son of Laish, who *was* from Gallim.

Saul's Last Days

Saul was clearly aware that David would succeed him as king. This fear he had revealed early on to his son Jonathan (1 Sam. 20:30, 31). Later, in a unique encounter with the man who would become his successor, Saul extracted a promise that his family be spared the usual fate of the families of displaced dynasties (24:20, 21). David's in-

evitable kingship did mean that no reconciliation would be possible between Saul and David.

The last chapters of 1 Samuel (26:1—30:31) record David's activities during Saul's last years. When it became clear that Saul's hatred would not allow David to participate in the life of his people, David contemplated going over to the Philistines, a step he finally accepted (27:1–4). David would spend much of his exile among the Philistines at the town of Ziklag.

Saul received information on David's movements from informers, more than once from the residents of Ziph in the Judean wilderness (1 Sam. 23:19; 26:1). Saul did not receive any message from God, however. Faced with this silence, he resorted to necromancy, the summoning of the spirits of the dead (28:7–20). Though common in the ancient Near East, the practice was prohibited in Israel (see Lev. 19:31; 20:27).

In his efforts to escape Saul's grasp, David often hid in the deserted region east of Ziph, known as the Wilderness of Ziph (1 Sam. 23:14; 26:2). The people of Ziph remained loyal to Saul, and their messages to Gibeah telling him of David's whereabouts are remembered in the superscription of Ps. 54.

■ Psalm 54
■ 1 Samuel 26:1—30:31

PSALM 54

Answered Prayer for Deliverance from Adversaries

To the Chief Musician. With stringed instruments.[a] A Contemplation[b] of David when the Ziphites went and said to Saul, "Is David not hiding with us?"

Save me, O God, by Your name,
  And vindicate me by Your strength.
[2] Hear my prayer, O God;
  Give ear to the words of my mouth.
[3] For strangers have risen up against me,
  And oppressors have sought after my life;
  They have not set God before them.
                                    Selah

[4] Behold, God *is* my helper;
  The Lord *is* with those who uphold my life.

25:44 [a]Spelled *Paltiel* in 2 Samuel 3:15
Ps. 54:title [a]Hebrew *neginoth* [b]Hebrew *Maschil*

5 He will repay my enemies for their
    evil.
    Cut them off in Your truth.

6 I will freely sacrifice to You;
    I will praise Your name, O LORD, for *it
    is* good.
7 For He has delivered me out of all
    trouble;
    And my eye has seen *its desire* upon
    my enemies.

1 Samuel 26:1—30:31
David Spares Saul a Second Time

26 :1 Now the Ziphites came to Saul at Gibeah, saying, "Is David not hiding in the hill of Hachilah, opposite Jeshimon?" ²Then Saul arose and went down to the Wilderness of Ziph, having three thousand chosen men of Israel with him, to seek David in the Wilderness of Ziph. ³And Saul encamped in the hill of Hachilah, which *is* opposite Jeshimon, by the road. But David stayed in the wilderness, and he saw that Saul came after him into the wilderness. ⁴David therefore sent out spies, and understood that Saul had indeed come.

⁵So David arose and came to the place where Saul had encamped. And David saw the place where Saul lay, and Abner the son of Ner, the commander of his army. Now Saul lay within the camp, with the people encamped all around him. ⁶Then David answered, and said to Ahimelech the Hittite and to Abishai the son of Zeruiah, brother of Joab, saying, "Who will go down with me to Saul in the camp?"

And Abishai said, "I will go down with you."

⁷So David and Abishai came to the people by night; and there Saul lay sleeping within the camp, with his spear stuck in the ground by his head. And Abner and the people lay all around him. ⁸Then Abishai said to David, "God has delivered your enemy into your hand this day. Now therefore, please, let me strike him at once with the spear, right to the earth; and I will not *have to strike* him a second time!"

⁹But David said to Abishai, "Do not destroy him; for who can stretch out his hand against the LORD's anointed, and be guiltless?" ¹⁰David said furthermore, "*As* the LORD lives, the LORD shall strike him, or his day shall come to die, or he shall go out to battle and perish. ¹¹The LORD forbid that I should stretch out my hand against the LORD's anointed. But please, take now the spear and the jug of water that *are* by his head, and let us go." ¹²So David took the spear and the jug of water *by* Saul's head, and they got away; and no man saw or knew *it* or awoke. For they *were* all asleep, because a deep sleep from the LORD had fallen on them.

¹³Now David went over to the other side, and stood on the top of a hill afar off, a great distance *being* between them. ¹⁴And David called out to the people and to Abner the son of Ner, saying, "Do you not answer, Abner?"

Then Abner answered and said, "Who *are* you, calling out to the king?"

¹⁵So David said to Abner, "*Are* you not a man? And who *is* like you in Israel? Why then have you not guarded your lord the king? For one of the people came in to destroy your lord the king. ¹⁶This thing that you have done *is* not good. *As* the LORD lives, you deserve to die, because you have not guarded your master, the LORD's anointed. And now see where the king's spear *is,* and the jug of water that *was* by his head."

¹⁷Then Saul knew David's voice, and said, "*Is* that your voice, my son David?"

David said, "*It is* my voice, my lord, O king." ¹⁸And he said, "Why does my lord thus pursue his servant? For what have I done, or what evil *is* in my hand? ¹⁹Now therefore, please, let my lord the king hear the words of his servant: If the LORD has stirred you up against me, let Him accept an offering. But if *it is* the children of men, *may* they *be* cursed before the LORD, for they have driven me out this day from sharing in the inheritance of the LORD, saying, 'Go, serve other gods.' ²⁰So now, do not let my blood fall to the earth before the face of the LORD. For the king of Israel has come out to seek a flea, as when one hunts a partridge in the mountains."

²¹Then Saul said, "I have sinned. Return, my son David. For I will harm you no more, because my life was precious in your eyes this day. Indeed I have played the fool and erred exceedingly."

²²And David answered and said, "Here is the king's spear. Let one of the young men come over and get it. ²³May the LORD repay every man *for* his righteousness and his faithfulness; for the LORD delivered you into *my* hand today, but I would not stretch out my hand against the LORD's anointed. ²⁴And indeed, as your life was valued much this day in my eyes, so let my life be valued

ROYAL CITIES OF THE PHILISTINE LORDS (1 Sam. 27:5)

The activities of the Philistines, as they settled in Canaan by the middle of the 12th century B.C., were centered on five cities: Ashdod, Ashkelon, Ekron, Gath, and Gaza (Josh. 13:3; 1 Sam. 6:17). These cities are all located in the southern coastal plain. It is natural that this region was selected by the Philistines, since they were part of a larger group of peoples called the Sea Peoples, all of whom came from coastal areas.

The fighting between the Philistines and the Israelites was in many ways a geographical struggle. The Philistines resided in the coastal plain, while the Israelites were the people of the central hill country. The Philistine encroachment into the hill country was so forceful that Israel was provoked into a change of leadership from the religious leader Samuel to the political and military leader Saul (1 Sam. 9:16).

While only five cities are specifically designated as Philistine, each of these royal cities oversaw the activities of nearby smaller towns or villages. Ziklag, which was given to David by the Philistine king Achish, was probably a vassal town to the Philistine royal city of Gath (1 Sam. 27:5, 6). In this way the sphere of the Philistine cities was much wider than might be supposed. Five Philistine lords ruled over the many country villages affiliated with the five royal cities (1 Sam. 8:18).

Philistine pottery appears in Canaan about the middle of the 12th century B.C. While centered in the coastal area, some pottery has also been found in the Shephelah (the foothills of the hill country) and even in the hill country. This should not be surprising, since Philistine military outposts spread to the very hometowns of both Saul and David (1 Sam. 14:1; 2 Sam. 23:14). The five Philistine cities sought to add subservient cities to their realm, but Saul, David, and their kinsmen, ardent opponents, stood in the way.

---

much in the eyes of the LORD, and let Him deliver me out of all tribulation."

²⁵Then Saul said to David, *"May* you *be* blessed, my son David! You shall both do great things and also still prevail."

So David went on his way, and Saul returned to his place.

David Allied with the Philistines

27 ¹And David said in his heart, "Now I shall perish someday by the hand of Saul. *There is* nothing better for me than that I should speedily escape to the land of the Philistines; and Saul will despair of me, to seek me anymore in any part of Israel. So I shall escape out of his hand." ²Then David arose and went over with the six hundred men who *were* with him to Achish the son of Maoch, king of Gath. ³So David dwelt with Achish at Gath, he and his men, each man with his household, *and* David with his two wives, Ahinoam the Jezreelitess, and Abigail the Carmelitess, Nabal's widow. ⁴And it was told Saul that David had fled to Gath; so he sought him no more.

⁵Then David said to Achish, "If I have now found favor in your eyes, let them give me a place in some town in the country,

that I may dwell there. For why should your servant dwell in the royal city with you?" ⁶So Achish gave him Ziklag that day. Therefore Ziklag has belonged to the kings of Judah to this day. ⁷Now the time that David dwelt in the country of the Philistines was one full year and four months.

⁸And David and his men went up and raided the Geshurites, the Girzites,ᵃ and the Amalekites. For those nations were the inhabitants of the land from of old, as you go to Shur, even as far as the land of Egypt. ⁹Whenever David attacked the land, he left neither man nor woman alive, but took away the sheep, the oxen, the donkeys, the camels, and the apparel, and returned and came to Achish. ¹⁰Then Achish would say, "Where have you made a raid today?" And David would say, "Against the southern *area* of Judah, or against the southern *area* of the Jerahmeelites, or against the southern *area* of the Kenites." ¹¹David would save neither man nor woman alive, to bring *news* to Gath, saying, "Lest they should inform on us, saying, 'Thus David did.'" And thus *was* his behavior all the time he dwelt in the country of

27:8 ᵃOr *Gezrites*

A GUIDE FOR DIVINE WISDOM (1 Sam. 28:6)

In a revelation to Moses at Mount Sinai, God not only established Israel's priesthood, but also provided a means for direct communication between the priesthood and Himself. The vehicle for this communication was located on the "breastplate of judgment" (Ex. 28:29, 30), a decorative, square, linen piece that hung across the high priest's chest. It was attached to the priest's gown by two gold chains that were connected at the shoulders. On this breastplate were twelve stones inscribed with the names of the twelve Israelite tribes (Ex. 28:17–21). The most remarkable feature of the breastplate, however, was the two additional stones called the Urim and Thummim.

The Urim and Thummim were used to ask God specific questions. A leader with a question would go to the high priest, who would "inquire before the LORD" (Num. 27:21) for the questioner. Questions were formed so that a yes or no answer could be given (1 Sam. 23:9–12). Presumably, the appropriate stone glowed. In the stories of David, the Urim and Thummim stones are often indicated by the calling for "the ephod," the high priest's garment to which they were attached (1 Sam. 30:7, 8).

Saul's diminished relationship with his God is starkly underlined by his failure to receive a divine answer "either by dreams or by Urim or by the prophets" (1 Sam. 28:6, 15). The picture is of a desperate Saul being ignored by his deity. Eventually, Saul turned to witchcraft for guidance (1 Sam. 28:7).

Obtaining answers from God via the Urim and Thummim seems to have ceased or at least become out of vogue after the time of David. From Solomon's reign until the Jews' return from Babylon, the Urim and Thummim are mentioned only by the governor of Judah (Ezra 2:63; Neh. 7:65). Whether they actually were used even at that time is questionable. The governor may have referred to the Urim and Thummim as a way of stalling would-be priests who lacked evidence of the proper priestly genealogy (Ezra 2:62).

---

the Philistines. ¹²So Achish believed David, saying, "He has made his people Israel utterly abhor him; therefore he will be my servant forever."

28 ¹Now it happened in those days that the Philistines gathered their armies together for war, to fight with Israel. And Achish said to David, "You assuredly know that you will go out with me to battle, you and your men."

²So David said to Achish, "Surely you know what your servant can do."

And Achish said to David, "Therefore I will make you one of my chief guardians forever."

Saul Consults a Medium

³Now Samuel had died, and all Israel had lamented for him and buried him in Ramah, in his own city. And Saul had put the mediums and the spiritists out of the land.

⁴Then the Philistines gathered together, and came and encamped at Shunem. So Saul gathered all Israel together, and they encamped at Gilboa. ⁵When Saul saw the army of the Philistines, he was afraid, and his heart trembled greatly. ⁶And when Saul inquired of the LORD, the LORD did not answer him, either by dreams or by Urim or by the prophets.

⁷Then Saul said to his servants, "Find me a woman who is a medium, that I may go to her and inquire of her."

And his servants said to him, "In fact, *there is* a woman who is a medium at En Dor."

⁸So Saul disguised himself and put on other clothes, and he went, and two men with him; and they came to the woman by night. And he said, "Please conduct a séance for me, and bring up for me the one I shall name to you."

⁹Then the woman said to him, "Look, you know what Saul has done, how he has cut off the mediums and the spiritists from the land. Why then do you lay a snare for my life, to cause me to die?"

¹⁰And Saul swore to her by the LORD, saying, "*As* the LORD lives, no punishment shall come upon you for this thing."

¹¹Then the woman said, "Whom shall I bring up for you?"

And he said, "Bring up Samuel for me."

¹²When the woman saw Samuel, she cried out with a loud voice. And the woman spoke to Saul, saying, "Why have you deceived me? For you *are* Saul!"

¹³And the king said to her, "Do not be afraid. What did you see?"

And the woman said to Saul, "I saw a spirit[a] ascending out of the earth."

¹⁴So he said to her, "What *is* his form?"

And she said, "An old man is coming up, and he *is* covered with a mantle." And Saul perceived that it *was* Samuel, and he stooped with *his* face to the ground and bowed down.

¹⁵Now Samuel said to Saul, "Why have you disturbed me by bringing me up?"

And Saul answered, "I am deeply distressed; for the Philistines make war against me, and God has departed from me and does not answer me anymore, neither by prophets nor by dreams. Therefore I have called you, that you may reveal to me what I should do."

¹⁶Then Samuel said: "So why do you ask me, seeing the LORD has departed from you and has become your enemy? ¹⁷And the LORD has done for Himself[a] as He spoke by me. For the LORD has torn the kingdom out of your hand and given it to your neighbor, David. ¹⁸Because you did not obey the voice of the LORD nor execute His fierce wrath upon Amalek, therefore the LORD has done this thing to you this day. ¹⁹Moreover the LORD will also deliver Israel with you into the hand of the Philistines. And tomorrow you and your sons *will be* with me. The LORD will also deliver the army of Israel into the hand of the Philistines."

²⁰Immediately Saul fell full length on the ground, and was dreadfully afraid because of the words of Samuel. And there was no strength in him, for he had eaten no food all day or all night.

²¹And the woman came to Saul and saw that he was severely troubled, and said to him, "Look, your maidservant has obeyed your voice, and I have put my life in my hands and heeded the words which you spoke to me. ²²Now therefore, please, heed also the voice of your maidservant, and let me set a piece of bread before you; and eat, that you may have strength when you go on *your* way."

²³But he refused and said, "I will not eat."

So his servants, together with the woman, urged him; and he heeded their voice. Then he arose from the ground and sat on the bed. ²⁴Now the woman had a fatted calf in the house, and she hastened to kill it. And she took flour and kneaded *it,* and baked unleavened bread from it. ²⁵So she brought *it* before Saul and his servants, and they ate. Then they rose and went away that night.

The Philistines Reject David

29 ¹Then the Philistines gathered together all their armies at Aphek, and the Israelites encamped by a fountain which *is* in Jezreel. ²And the lords of the Philistines passed in review by hundreds and by thousands, but David and his men passed in review at the rear with Achish. ³Then the princes of the Philistines said, "What *are* these Hebrews *doing here?*"

And Achish said to the princes of the Philistines, "*Is* this not David, the servant of Saul king of Israel, who has been with me these days, or these years? And to this day I have found no fault in him since he defected *to me.*"

⁴But the princes of the Philistines were angry with him; so the princes of the Philistines said to him, "Make this fellow return, that he may go back to the place which you have appointed for him, and do not let him go down with us to battle, lest in the battle he become our adversary. For with what could he reconcile himself to his master, if not with the heads of these men? ⁵*Is* this not David, of whom they sang to one another in dances, saying:

28:13 ªHebrew *elohim*   28:17 ªOr *him,* that is, David

BEDOUINS AND THEIR CAMELS (1 Sam. 30:1–18)

The bedouins were pastoral nomads in western Asia in the 1st millennium B.C., who specialized in camel breeding. The camel was first domesticated in east and south Arabia in the 3rd millennium B.C. By the end of the Late Bronze Age (c. 1200 B.C.), the animal was used for transport and food in Syro-Palestine.

The first literary evidence of bedouin tribes comes from Assyrian royal inscriptions and reliefs (9th to 7th centuries B.C.). These tribes are described as large and combative, but subject to the Assyrian state. A thousand Arab bedouins were conscripted to fight along with Assyria at the battle of Qarqar against the Syro-Palestinian coalition (853 B.C.). The Assyrian king Tiglath-Pileser III (744–727 B.C.) was given 10,000 camels as tribute from the bedouins.

The first bedouin political state emerged in the 7th century B.C. According to Assyrian annals, it was a tribal confederacy centered in northern Arabia, led by the tribe of Qedar. These camel-breeding tribes are associated with the Ishmaelites, who were descended from Ishmael, the first son of Abraham (Gen. 16:15).

The camel allowed the pastoral nomads to travel greater distances, giving them the ability to penetrate the desert, away from politically organized communities. The Amalekites, whose attributes are similar in nature to the bedouin, seem to have traversed a large geographical region from the western Sinai to Arabia (1 Sam. 15:7). Their seasonal migrations as camel herders brought them into contact with other peoples, contact that sometimes became raiding opportunities. Some of the Amalekites who raided David's Ziklag were able to escape by fleeing on their camels (1 Sam. 30:1, 16, 17).

'Saul has slain his thousands,
And David his ten thousands'?"[a]

6Then Achish called David and said to him, "Surely, *as* the LORD lives, you have been upright, and your going out and your coming in with me in the army *is* good in my sight. For to this day I have not found evil in you since the day of your coming to me. Nevertheless the lords do not favor you. 7Therefore return now, and go in peace, that you may not displease the lords of the Philistines."

8So David said to Achish, "But what have I done? And to this day what have you found in your servant as long as I have been with you, that I may not go and fight against the enemies of my lord the king?"

9Then Achish answered and said to David, "I know that you *are* as good in my sight as an angel of God; nevertheless the princes of the Philistines have said, 'He shall not go up with us to the battle.' 10Now therefore, rise early in the morning with your master's servants who have come

with you.[a] And as soon as you are up early in the morning and have light, depart."

11So David and his men rose early to depart in the morning, to return to the land of the Philistines. And the Philistines went up to Jezreel.

David's Conflict with the Amalekites

30 1Now it happened, when David and his men came to Ziklag, on the third day, that the Amalekites had invaded the South and Ziklag, attacked Ziklag and burned it with fire, 2and had taken captive the women and those who *were* there, from small to great; they did not kill anyone, but carried *them* away and went their way. 3So David and his men came to the city, and there it was, burned with fire; and their wives, their sons, and their daughters had been taken captive. 4Then David and the people who *were* with him lifted up their voices and wept, until they had no more power to weep. 5And David's two wives, Ahinoam the Jezreelitess, and Abigail the widow of Nabal the Carmelite, had been taken captive. 6Now David was greatly distressed, for the people spoke of stoning him, because the soul of all the people was grieved, every man for his sons and his daughters. But David strengthened himself in the LORD his God.

29:5 [a]Compare 1 Samuel 18:7   29:10 [a]Following Masoretic Text, Targum, and Vulgate; Septuagint adds *and go to the place which I have selected for you there; and set no bothersome word in your heart, for you are good before me. And rise on your way.*

⁷Then David said to Abiathar the priest, Ahimelech's son, "Please bring the ephod here to me." And Abiathar brought the ephod to David. ⁸So David inquired of the LORD, saying, "Shall I pursue this troop? Shall I overtake them?"

And He answered him, "Pursue, for you shall surely overtake *them* and without fail recover *all*."

⁹So David went, he and the six hundred men who *were* with him, and came to the Brook Besor, where those stayed who were left behind. ¹⁰But David pursued, he and four hundred men; for two hundred stayed *behind,* who were so weary that they could not cross the Brook Besor.

¹¹Then they found an Egyptian in the field, and brought him to David; and they gave him bread and he ate, and they let him drink water. ¹²And they gave him a piece of a cake of figs and two clusters of raisins. So when he had eaten, his strength came back to him; for he had eaten no bread nor drunk water for three days and three nights. ¹³Then David said to him, "To whom do you *belong,* and where *are* you from?"

And he said, "I *am* a young man from Egypt, servant of an Amalekite; and my master left me behind, because three days ago I fell sick. ¹⁴We made an invasion of the southern *area* of the Cherethites, in the *territory* which *belongs* to Judah, and of the southern *area* of Caleb; and we burned Ziklag with fire."

¹⁵And David said to him, "Can you take me down to this troop?"

So he said, "Swear to me by God that you will neither kill me nor deliver me into the hands of my master, and I will take you down to this troop."

¹⁶And when he had brought him down, there they were, spread out over all the land, eating and drinking and dancing, because of all the great spoil which they had taken from the land of the Philistines and from the land of Judah. ¹⁷Then David attacked them from twilight until the evening of the next day. Not a man of them escaped, except four hundred young men who rode on camels and fled. ¹⁸So David recovered all that the Amalekites had carried away, and David rescued his two wives. ¹⁹And nothing of theirs was lacking, either small or great, sons or daughters, spoil or anything which they had taken from them; David recovered all. ²⁰Then David took all the flocks and herds they had driven before those *other* livestock, and said, "This *is* David's spoil."

²¹Now David came to the two hundred men who had been so weary that they could not follow David, whom they also had made to stay at the Brook Besor. So they went out to meet David and to meet the people who *were* with him. And when David came near the people, he greeted them. ²²Then all the wicked and worthless menᵃ of those who went with David answered and said, "Because they did not go with us, we will not give them *any* of the spoil that we have recovered, except for every man's wife and children, that they may lead *them* away and depart."

²³But David said, "My brethren, you shall not do so with what the LORD has given us, who has preserved us and delivered into our hand the troop that came against us. ²⁴For who will heed you in this matter? But as his part *is* who goes down to the battle, so *shall* his part *be* who stays by the supplies; they shall share alike." ²⁵So it was, from that day forward; he made it a statute and an ordinance for Israel to this day.

²⁶Now when David came to Ziklag, he sent *some* of the spoil to the elders of Judah, to his friends, saying, "Here is a present for you from the spoil of the enemies of the LORD"— ²⁷to *those* who *were* in Bethel, *those* who *were* in Ramoth of the South, *those* who *were* in Jattir, ²⁸*those* who *were* in Aroer, *those* who *were* in Siphmoth, *those* who *were* in Eshtemoa, ²⁹*those* who *were* in Rachal, *those* who *were* in the cities of the Jerahmeelites, *those* who *were* in the cities

---

30:22 ᵃLiterally *men of Belial*

RELIGION AND WORSHIP

The ephod was a kind of garment worn by the high priest (1 Sam. 30:7). Its function was to permit a questioner to inquire of God concerning what actions to take in particular situations. Attached to the ephod was a breastplate containing the Urim and Thummim. These were special objects, accessible to the high priest and the king, used to convey God's answer.

of the Kenites, ³⁰*those* who *were* in Hormah, *those* who *were* in Chorashan,ᵃ *those* who *were* in Athach, ³¹*those* who *were* in Hebron, and to all the places where David himself and his men were accustomed to rove.

Israel's First King Is Dead

The final chapter of 1 Samuel depicts the sad end to a life of progressive alienation from God. Saul's rebellion was his own, but his defeat included other people as well. A last grim service (31:11–13) for the fallen king and his sons was performed in memory of Saul's deliverance of Jabesh Gilead many years before (see 1 Sam. 11). Israel's first king was dead, clearing the way for David's accession in about 1010 B.C.

The story of Saul's death continues from 1 Samuel to 2 Samuel without interruption. Modern sensitivities are repulsed at David's actions in 2 Sam. 1:1–16. Nonetheless, there is every reason to believe he was acting in integrity. Believing the Amalekite's report that he had killed Saul, David, far from rewarding the man, executed him for his wanton act (1:14–16). David himself had twice refused to kill Saul. He refused to allow his men to kill the king. Even if it would give him the throne, David would not approve the murder of his predecessor.

- 1 Samuel 31:1–13
- 2 Samuel 1:1–27

---

1 Samuel 31:1–13
The Tragic End of Saul and His Sons

31 :1 Now the Philistines fought against Israel; and the men of Israel fled from before the Philistines, and fell slain on Mount Gilboa. ²Then the Philistines followed hard after Saul and his sons. And the Philistines killed Jonathan,

Abinadab, and Malchishua, Saul's sons. ³The battle became fierce against Saul. The archers hit him, and he was severely wounded by the archers.

⁴Then Saul said to his armorbearer, "Draw your sword, and thrust me through with it, lest these uncircumcised men come and thrust me through and abuse me."

But his armorbearer would not, for he was greatly afraid. Therefore Saul took a sword and fell on it. ⁵And when his armorbearer saw that Saul was dead, he also fell on his sword, and died with him. ⁶So Saul, his three sons, his armorbearer, and all his men died together that same day.

⁷And when the men of Israel who *were* on the other side of the valley, and *those* who *were* on the other side of the Jordan, saw that the men of Israel had fled and that Saul and his sons were dead, they forsook the cities and fled; and the Philistines came and dwelt in them. ⁸So it happened the next day, when the Philistines came to strip the slain, that they found Saul and his three sons fallen on Mount Gilboa. ⁹And they cut off his head and stripped off his armor, and sent *word* throughout the land of the Philistines, to proclaim *it in* the temple of their idols and among the people. ¹⁰Then they put his armor in the temple of the Ashtoreths, and they fastened his body to the wall of Beth Shan.ᵃ

¹¹Now when the inhabitants of Jabesh Gilead heard what the Philistines had done to Saul, ¹²all the valiant men arose and traveled all night, and took the body of Saul and the bodies of his sons from the wall of Beth Shan; and they came to Jabesh and burned them there. ¹³Then they took their bones and buried *them* under the tamarisk tree at Jabesh, and fasted seven days.

2 Samuel 1:1–27
The Report of Saul's Death

1 :1 Now it came to pass after the death of Saul, when David had returned from the slaughter of the Amalekites, and David had stayed two days in Ziklag, ²on the

---

30:30 ᵃOr *Borashan*   31:10 ᵃSpelled *Beth Shean* in Joshua 17:11 and elsewhere

---

CULTURE AND SOCIETY

A standard feature of ancient warfare was to make a display of the fallen enemy. A suit of armor taken on the field of battle would be set up as a kind of sculptural monument. Still more terrible was to leave the enemy unburied. The people of Jabesh Gilead were brave because they performed a sacred duty in the face of great danger (1 Sam. 31:8–13).

third day, behold, it happened that a man came from Saul's camp with his clothes torn and dust on his head. So it was, when he came to David, that he fell to the ground and prostrated himself.

³And David said to him, "Where have you come from?"

So he said to him, "I have escaped from the camp of Israel."

⁴Then David said to him, "How did the matter go? Please tell me."

And he answered, "The people have fled from the battle, many of the people are fallen and dead, and Saul and Jonathan his son are dead also."

⁵So David said to the young man who told him, "How do you know that Saul and Jonathan his son are dead?"

⁶Then the young man who told him said, "As I happened by chance to be on Mount Gilboa, there was Saul, leaning on his spear; and indeed the chariots and horsemen followed hard after him. ⁷Now when he looked behind him, he saw me and called to me. And I answered, 'Here I am.' ⁸And he said to me, 'Who are you?' So I answered him, 'I am an Amalekite.' ⁹He said to me again, 'Please stand over me and kill me, for anguish has come upon me, but my life still remains in me.' ¹⁰So I stood over him and killed him, because I was sure that he could not live after he had fallen. And I took the crown that was on his head and the bracelet that was on his arm, and have brought them here to my lord."

¹¹Therefore David took hold of his own clothes and tore them, and so did all the men who were with him. ¹²And they mourned and wept and fasted until evening for Saul and for Jonathan his son, for the people of the LORD and for the house of Israel, because they had fallen by the sword.

¹³Then David said to the young man who told him, "Where are you from?"

And he answered, "I am the son of an alien, an Amalekite."

¹⁴So David said to him, "How was it you were not afraid to put forth your hand to destroy the LORD's anointed?" ¹⁵Then David called one of the young men and said, "Go near, and execute him!" And he struck him so that he died. ¹⁶So David said to him, "Your blood is on your own head, for your own mouth has testified against you, saying, 'I have killed the LORD's anointed.' "

The Song of the Bow

¹⁷Then David lamented with this lamentation over Saul and over Jonathan his son, ¹⁸and he told them to teach the children of Judah the Song of the Bow; indeed it is written in the Book of Jasher:

19 "The beauty of Israel is slain on your
        high places!
     How the mighty have fallen!
20   Tell it not in Gath,
     Proclaim it not in the streets of
        Ashkelon—
     Lest the daughters of the Philistines
        rejoice,
     Lest the daughters of the
        uncircumcised triumph.

21 "O mountains of Gilboa,
     Let there be no dew nor rain upon you,
     Nor fields of offerings.
     For the shield of the mighty is cast
        away there!
     The shield of Saul, not anointed with
        oil.
22   From the blood of the slain,
     From the fat of the mighty,
     The bow of Jonathan did not turn
        back,
     And the sword of Saul did not return
        empty.

23 "Saul and Jonathan were beloved and
        pleasant in their lives,
     And in their death they were not
        divided;
     They were swifter than eagles,
     They were stronger than lions.

24 "O daughters of Israel, weep over Saul,
     Who clothed you in scarlet, with
        luxury;
     Who put ornaments of gold on your
        apparel.

25 "How the mighty have fallen in the
        midst of the battle!
     Jonathan was slain in your high
        places.
26   I am distressed for you, my brother
        Jonathan;
     You have been very pleasant to me;
     Your love to me was wonderful,
     Surpassing the love of women.

27 "How the mighty have fallen,
     And the weapons of war perished!"

Deliverance from Saul

The superscription to Ps. 18 is not very specific. It associates the psalm with a time when David celebrated deliverance, especially deliverance from Saul. Since no reconciliation with Saul took place before he died, it makes some sense to read this psalm in the context of Saul's death.

This psalm also appears, with only minor changes, in 2 Sam. 22. There, although 2 Sam. 22:1 still notes David's deliverance from Saul, the song refers to a wider range of enemies.

■ Psalm 18

PSALM 18

God the Sovereign Savior

To the Chief Musician. A Psalm of David the servant of the LORD, who spoke to the LORD the words of this song on the day that the LORD delivered him from the hand of all his enemies and from the hand of Saul. And he said:

I will love You, O LORD, my strength.
2 The LORD is my rock and my fortress and my deliverer;
My God, my strength, in whom I will trust;
My shield and the horn of my salvation, my stronghold.
3 I will call upon the LORD, *who is worthy* to be praised;
So shall I be saved from my enemies.

4 The pangs of death surrounded me,
And the floods of ungodliness made me afraid.
5 The sorrows of Sheol surrounded me;
The snares of death confronted me.
6 In my distress I called upon the LORD,
And cried out to my God;
He heard my voice from His temple,
And my cry came before Him, *even* to His ears.

18:13 ᵃFollowing Masoretic Text, Targum, and Vulgate; a few Hebrew manuscripts and Septuagint omit *Hailstones and coals of fire.*

7 Then the earth shook and trembled;
The foundations of the hills also quaked and were shaken,
Because He was angry.
8 Smoke went up from His nostrils,
And devouring fire from His mouth;
Coals were kindled by it.
9 He bowed the heavens also, and came down
With darkness under His feet.
10 And He rode upon a cherub, and flew;
He flew upon the wings of the wind.
11 He made darkness His secret place;
His canopy around Him *was* dark waters
And thick clouds of the skies.
12 From the brightness before Him,
His thick clouds passed with hailstones and coals of fire.

13 The LORD thundered from heaven,
And the Most High uttered His voice,
Hailstones and coals of fire.ᵃ
14 He sent out His arrows and scattered the foe,
Lightnings in abundance, and He vanquished them.
15 Then the channels of the sea were seen,
The foundations of the world were uncovered
At Your rebuke, O LORD,
At the blast of the breath of Your nostrils.

16 He sent from above, He took me;
He drew me out of many waters.
17 He delivered me from my strong enemy,
From those who hated me,
For they were too strong for me.
18 They confronted me in the day of my calamity,
But the LORD was my support.
19 He also brought me out into a broad place;
He delivered me because He delighted in me.

BELIEFS AND IDEAS

God's appearance at Mount Sinai when Moses received the law was marked by thunder, lightning, earthquake, and smoke. The phenomena of earthquake, volcano, and thunderstorm came together (Ex. 19:16–19). The Canaanites regarded their god Baal as the ruler of storms, and in Greek literature Zeus is called the "cloud gatherer." The display of natural power was considered a sign of divine power (Ps. 18:7).

20 The LORD rewarded me according to
my righteousness;
According to the cleanness of my
hands
He has recompensed me.
21 For I have kept the ways of the LORD,
And have not wickedly departed from
my God.
22 For all His judgments *were* before me,
And I did not put away His statutes
from me.
23 I was also blameless before Him,
And I kept myself from my iniquity.
24 Therefore the LORD has recompensed
me according to my righteousness,
According to the cleanness of my
hands in His sight.

25 With the merciful You will show
Yourself merciful;
With a blameless man You will show
Yourself blameless;
26 With the pure You will show Yourself
pure;
And with the devious You will show
Yourself shrewd.
27 For You will save the humble people,
But will bring down haughty looks.

28 For You will light my lamp;
The LORD my God will enlighten my
darkness.
29 For by You I can run against a troop,
By my God I can leap over a wall.
30 *As for* God, His way *is* perfect;
The word of the LORD is proven;
He *is* a shield to all who trust in Him.

31 For who *is* God, except the LORD?
And who *is* a rock, except our God?
32 *It is* God who arms me with strength,
And makes my way perfect.

33 He makes my feet like the *feet of* deer,
And sets me on my high places.
34 He teaches my hands to make war,
So that my arms can bend a bow of
bronze.

35 You have also given me the shield of
Your salvation;
Your right hand has held me up,
Your gentleness has made me great.
36 You enlarged my path under me,
So my feet did not slip.

37 I have pursued my enemies and
overtaken them;
Neither did I turn back again till they
were destroyed.
38 I have wounded them,
So that they could not rise;
They have fallen under my feet.
39 For You have armed me with strength
for the battle;
You have subdued under me those
who rose up against me.
40 You have also given me the necks of
my enemies,
So that I destroyed those who hated
me.
41 They cried out, but *there was* none to
save;
Even to the LORD, but He did not
answer them.
42 Then I beat them as fine as the dust
before the wind;
I cast them out like dirt in the streets.

43 You have delivered me from the
strivings of the people;
You have made me the head of the
nations;
A people I have not known shall serve
me.
44 As soon as they hear of me they obey
me;
The foreigners submit to me.
45 The foreigners fade away,
And come frightened from their
hideouts.

46 The LORD lives!
Blessed *be* my Rock!
Let the God of my salvation be
exalted.
47 *It is* God who avenges me,
And subdues the peoples under me;
48 He delivers me from my enemies.
You also lift me up above those who
rise against me;

TIME CAPSULE   *1114 to 1100 B.C.*

1114–1076	Tiglath-Pileser I rules Assyria and expands Assyrian influence
1114	Tiglath-Pileser I stops attack by Assyria's enemy, the Mushku
1100	Tiglath-Pileser I defeats a coalition of Aramean tribes in Syria
1100	Iron becomes common in Palestine
1100	Egyptians use carrier pigeons

You have delivered me from the
    violent man.
49 Therefore I will give thanks to You,
    O LORD, among the Gentiles,
    And sing praises to Your name.

50 Great deliverance He gives to His
    king,
    And shows mercy to His anointed,
    To David and his descendants
    forevermore.

2:8 ªCalled *Esh-Baal* in 1 Chronicles 8:33 and 9:39

Who Will Succeed Saul as King?

Most ancient Near Eastern kingdoms had established dynasties in which successive rulers came from the same family. The practice of dynastic succession meant that when a king died, his eldest son normally reigned in his place. The exceptions were those rather frequent cases when a powerful general seized control for himself.

But dynastic succession was foreign to Israel. During the earlier tribal confederacy, the judges had been inspired specifically for times of crisis, and their inspiration was not transferred to their sons. When Gideon was asked to reign, he refused, saying, "I will not rule over you, nor shall my son rule over you; the LORD shall rule over you" (Judg. 8:23).

When Israel's first king died, the question of succession became crucial. Some favored a dynastic succession, placing Saul's son Ishbosheth on the throne (2 Sam. 2:8–10). Others, perhaps remembering the pattern of the judges, preferred to crown the man who had shown himself most able, David (2 Sam. 2:10, 11).

In addition, both Ishbosheth and David had ambitious generals. Abner, who was commander of Saul's army, as well as a cousin of Saul, naturally supported Ishbosheth to succeed his father as king. In the same way, Joab, commander of David's army and the son of David's sister Zeruiah, was a powerful element in David's campaign for the throne. In the ensuing years of civil war, the plots and maneuverings of these generals became extremely significant.

Equally significant are the brief lists in 2 Sam. 3:2–5 and 5:13–16 of the sons born to David. The question of royal succession would apply to the next generation as well.

David's first and third sons, Amnon and Absalom (3:2, 3), would prove themselves unworthy of the throne and be eliminated (2 Sam. 13—18). Two other sons, Adonijah (3:4) and Solomon (5:14), would later challenge each other for their father's throne (1 Kin. 1; 2).

▼   ■ 2 Samuel 2:1—4:12

2 Samuel
David Anointed King of Judah

2 :1 It happened after this that David inquired of the LORD, saying, "Shall I go up to any of the cities of Judah?"

And the LORD said to him, "Go up."

David said, "Where shall I go up?"

And He said, "To Hebron." ²So David went up there, and his two wives also, Ahinoam the Jezreelitess, and Abigail the widow of Nabal the Carmelite. ³And David brought up the men who *were* with him, every man with his household. So they dwelt in the cities of Hebron. ⁴Then the men of Judah came, and there they anointed David king over the house of Judah. And they told David, saying, "The men of Jabesh Gilead *were* the ones who buried Saul." ⁵So David sent messengers to the men of Jabesh Gilead, and said to them, "You *are* blessed of the LORD, for you have shown this kindness to your lord, to Saul, and have buried him. ⁶And now may the LORD show kindness and truth to you. I also will repay you this kindness, because you have done this thing. ⁷Now therefore, let your hands be strengthened, and be valiant; for your master Saul is dead, and also the house of Judah has anointed me king over them."

Ishbosheth Made King of Israel

⁸But Abner the son of Ner, commander of Saul's army, took Ishboshethª the son of Saul and brought him over to Mahanaim; ⁹and he made him king over Gilead, over the Ashurites, over Jezreel, over Ephraim, over Benjamin, and over all Israel. ¹⁰Ishbosheth, Saul's son, *was* forty years old when he began to reign over Israel, and he reigned two years. Only the house of Judah followed David. ¹¹And the time that David was king in Hebron over the house of Judah was seven years and six months.

Israel and Judah at War

¹²Now Abner the son of Ner, and the servants of Ishbosheth the son of Saul, went out from Mahanaim to Gibeon. ¹³And

Joab the son of Zeruiah, and the servants of David, went out and met them by the pool of Gibeon. So they sat down, one on one side of the pool and the other on the other side of the pool. 14Then Abner said to Joab, "Let the young men now arise and compete before us."

And Joab said, "Let them arise."

15So they arose and went over by number, twelve from Benjamin, *followers* of Ish-bosheth the son of Saul, and twelve from the servants of David. 16And each one grasped his opponent by the head and *thrust* his sword in his opponent's side; so they fell down together. Therefore that place was called the Field of Sharp Swords,a which *is* in Gibeon. 17So there was a very fierce battle that day, and Abner and the men of Israel were beaten before the servants of David.

18Now the three sons of Zeruiah were there: Joab and Abishai and Asahel. And Asahel *was* as fleet of foot as a wild gazelle. 19So Asahel pursued Abner, and in going he did not turn to the right hand or to the left from following Abner.

20Then Abner looked behind him and said, "*Are* you Asahel?"

He answered, "I *am*."

21And Abner said to him, "Turn aside to your right hand or to your left, and lay hold on one of the young men and take his armor for yourself." But Asahel would not turn aside from following him. 22So Abner said again to Asahel, "Turn aside from following me. Why should I strike you to the ground? How then could I face your brother Joab?" 23However, he refused to turn aside. Therefore Abner struck him in the stomach with the blunt end of the spear, so that the spear came out of his back; and he fell down there and died on the spot. So it was *that* as many as came to the place where Asahel fell down and died, stood still.

24Joab and Abishai also pursued Abner. And the sun was going down when they came to the hill of Ammah, which *is* before Giah by the road to the Wilderness of Gibeon. 25Now the children of Benjamin gathered together behind Abner and became a unit, and took their stand on top of a hill. 26Then Abner called to Joab and said, "Shall the sword devour forever? Do you not know that it will be bitter in the latter end? How long will it be then until you tell the people to return from pursuing their brethren?"

27And Joab said, "*As* God lives, unless you had spoken, surely then by morning all the people would have given up pursuing their brethren." 28So Joab blew a trumpet; and all the people stood still and did not pursue Israel anymore, nor did they fight anymore. 29Then Abner and his men went on all that night through the plain, crossed over the Jordan, and went through all Bithron; and they came to Mahanaim.

30So Joab returned from pursuing Abner. And when he had gathered all the people together, there were missing of David's servants nineteen men and Asahel. 31But the servants of David had struck down, of Benjamin and Abner's men, three hundred and sixty men who died. 32Then they took up Asahel and buried him in his father's tomb, which *was in* Bethlehem. And Joab and his men went all night, and they came to Hebron at daybreak.

3 1Now there was a long war between the house of Saul and the house of David. But David grew stronger and stronger, and the house of Saul grew weaker and weaker.

Sons of David

2Sons were born to David in Hebron: His firstborn was Amnon by Ahinoam the Jezreelitess; 3his second, Chileab, by Abigail the widow of Nabal the Carmelite; the third, Absalom the son of Maacah, the daughter of Talmai, king of Geshur; 4the fourth, Adonijah the son of Haggith; the fifth, Shephatiah the son of Abital; 5and the sixth, Ithream, by David's wife Eglah. These were born to David in Hebron.

2:16 aHebrew *Helkath Hazzurim*

CULTURE AND SOCIETY

In the hand-to-hand combat of the nomad, the final stage was to seize the opponent and deliver the fatal blow (2 Sam. 2:16). The fighting match between Saul's and David's warriors illustrates a particular technique of fighting. The contest displays a social idea of combat in which the number of contestants is fixed and the fighting is by arrangement (2:14, 15).

THE SORT OF WIFE (2 Sam. 3:7)

The word "concubine" is difficult to define for people of western culture since there is no analogous relationship in Western European society. In the ancient Near East a concubine was a woman who had legal status within a family and who shared the sexual attentions of the husband, while having somewhat lesser authority than a wife. The presence of concubines in a household was openly acknowledged without any pejorative implication (2 Sam. 19:5). In other words, they were accepted like other family members. The sons of a concubine were treated as heirs, though with, perhaps, somewhat lesser status (Gen. 25:6).

For one to take another man's concubine was seen as usurping the husband's authority. This was especially true of a king's concubines. To gain possession of a king's harem was to gain title to the king's throne. After David became king, he took possession of Saul's concubines (2 Sam. 12:8). When Absalom usurped his father David's rule of Jerusalem, one of his first acts to publicly claim royal authority was to establish sexual relations with David's concubines (2 Sam. 16:21, 22).

After Saul died, his son Ishbosheth struggled to secure his position as Saul's successor. There were battles between Ishbosheth's Israel and David's Judah (2 Sam. 3:6). In light of Ishbosheth's shaky kingship, it is quite natural that he would be alarmed at the possibility of anyone, especially the army commander Abner, having relations with Saul's concubine, Rizpah (3:7).

Abner Joins Forces with David

⁶Now it was so, while there was war between the house of Saul and the house of David, that Abner was strengthening *his hold* on the house of Saul.

⁷And Saul had a concubine, whose name *was* Rizpah, the daughter of Aiah. So *Ishbosheth* said to Abner, "Why have you gone in to my father's concubine?"

⁸Then Abner became very angry at the words of Ishbosheth, and said, "*Am* I a dog's head that belongs to Judah? Today I show loyalty to the house of Saul your father, to his brothers, and to his friends, and have not delivered you into the hand of David; and you charge me today with a fault concerning this woman? ⁹May God do so to Abner, and more also, if I do not do for David as the LORD has sworn to him— ¹⁰to transfer the kingdom from the house of Saul, and set up the throne of David over Israel and over Judah, from Dan to Beersheba." ¹¹And he could not answer Abner another word, because he feared him.

¹²Then Abner sent messengers on his behalf to David, saying, "Whose *is* the land?" saying *also,* "Make your covenant with me, and indeed my hand *shall be* with you to bring all Israel to you."

¹³And *David* said, "Good, I will make a covenant with you. But one thing I require of you: you shall not see my face unless you first bring Michal, Saul's daughter, when you come to see my face." ¹⁴So David sent messengers to Ishbosheth, Saul's son, saying, "Give *me* my wife Michal, whom I betrothed to myself for a hundred foreskins of the Philistines." ¹⁵And Ishbosheth sent and took her from *her* husband, from Paltiel[a] the son of Laish. ¹⁶Then her husband went along with her to Bahurim, weeping behind her. So Abner said to him, "Go, return!" And he returned.

¹⁷Now Abner had communicated with the elders of Israel, saying, "In time past you were seeking for David *to be* king over you. ¹⁸Now then, do *it!* For the LORD has spoken of David, saying, 'By the hand of My servant David, I[a] will save My people Israel from the hand of the Philistines and the hand of all their enemies.'" ¹⁹And Abner also spoke in the hearing of Benjamin. Then Abner also went to speak in the hearing of David in Hebron all that seemed good to Israel and the whole house of Benjamin.

²⁰So Abner and twenty men with him came to David at Hebron. And David made a feast for Abner and the men who *were* with him. ²¹Then Abner said to David, "I

3:15 ᵃSpelled *Palti* in 1 Samuel 25:44
3:18 ᵃFollowing many Hebrew manuscripts, Septuagint, Syriac, and Targum; Masoretic Text reads *he.*

will arise and go, and gather all Israel to my lord the king, that they may make a covenant with you, and that you may reign over all that your heart desires." So David sent Abner away, and he went in peace.

Joab Murders Abner

22At that moment the servants of David and Joab came from a raid and brought much spoil with them. But Abner *was* not with David in Hebron, for he had sent him away, and he had gone in peace. 23When Joab and all the troops that *were* with him had come, they told Joab, saying, "Abner the son of Ner came to the king, and he sent him away, and he has gone in peace." 24Then Joab came to the king and said, "What have you done? Look, Abner came to you; why *is* it *that* you sent him away, and he has already gone? 25Surely you realize that Abner the son of Ner came to deceive you, to know your going out and your coming in, and to know all that you are doing."

26And when Joab had gone from David's presence, he sent messengers after Abner, who brought him back from the well of Sirah. But David did not know *it.* 27Now when Abner had returned to Hebron, Joab took him aside in the gate to speak with him privately, and there stabbed him in the stomach, so that he died for the blood of Asahel his brother.

28Afterward, when David heard *it,* he said, "My kingdom and I *are* guiltless before the LORD forever of the blood of Abner the son of Ner. 29Let it rest on the head of Joab and on all his father's house; and let there never fail to be in the house of Joab one who has a discharge or is a leper, who leans on a staff or falls by the sword, or who lacks bread." 30So Joab and Abishai his brother killed Abner, because he had killed their brother Asahel at Gibeon in the battle.

David's Mourning for Abner

31Then David said to Joab and to all the people who were with him, "Tear your clothes, gird yourselves with sackcloth, and mourn for Abner." And King David followed the coffin. 32So they buried Abner in Hebron; and the king lifted up his voice and wept at the grave of Abner, and all the people wept. 33And the king sang *a lament* over Abner and said:

"Should Abner die as a fool dies?
34   Your hands were not bound
        Nor your feet put into fetters;
        As a man falls before wicked men, *so*
            you fell."

Then all the people wept over him again.

35And when all the people came to persuade David to eat food while it was still day, David took an oath, saying, "God do so to me, and more also, if I taste bread or anything else till the sun goes down!" 36Now all the people took note *of it,* and it pleased them, since whatever the king did pleased all the people. 37For all the people and all Israel understood that day that it had not been the king's *intent* to kill Abner the son of Ner. 38Then the king said to his servants, "Do you not know that a prince and a great man has fallen this day in Israel? 39And I *am* weak today, though anointed king; and these men, the sons of Zeruiah, *are* too harsh for me. The LORD shall repay the evildoer according to his wickedness."

Ishbosheth Is Murdered

4 1When Saul's son[a] heard that Abner had died in Hebron, he lost heart, and all Israel was troubled. 2Now Saul's son *had* two men *who were* captains of troops. The name of one *was* Baanah and the name of the other Rechab, the sons of Rimmon the Beerothite, of the children of Benjamin. (For Beeroth also was *part* of Benjamin, 3because the Beerothites fled to Gittaim and have been sojourners there until this day.)

4Jonathan, Saul's son, had a son *who was* lame in *his* feet. He was five years old

4:1 aThat is, Ishbosheth

CULTURE AND SOCIETY

Before the monarchy there was a long-standing custom of blood revenge. The "blood avenger" would avenge the death of a relative by killing the relative's slayer (Josh. 20:3). Blood vengeance was not allowed, however, for persons killed in battle (2 Sam. 2:21–23). Joab ignores this exception and avenges his younger brother Asahel's death by killing Abner (2 Sam. 3:27).

when the news about Saul and Jonathan came from Jezreel; and his nurse took him up and fled. And it happened, as she made haste to flee, that he fell and became lame. His name *was* Mephibosheth.[a]

5Then the sons of Rimmon the Beerothite, Rechab and Baanah, set out and came at about the heat of the day to the house of Ishbosheth, who was lying on his bed at noon. 6And they came there, all the way into the house, *as though* to get wheat, and they stabbed him in the stomach. Then Rechab and Baanah his brother escaped. 7For when they came into the house, he was lying on his bed in his bedroom; then they struck him and killed him, beheaded him and took his head, and were all night escaping through the plain. 8And they brought the head of Ishbosheth to David at Hebron, and said to the king, "Here is the head of Ishbosheth, the son of Saul your enemy, who sought your life; and the LORD has avenged my lord the king this day of Saul and his descendants."

9But David answered Rechab and Baanah his brother, the sons of Rimmon the Beerothite, and said to them, "*As* the LORD lives, who has redeemed my life from all adversity, 10when someone told me, saying, 'Look, Saul is dead,' thinking to have brought good news, I arrested him and had him executed in Ziklag—the one who *thought* I would give him a reward for *his* news. 11How much more, when wicked men have killed a righteous person in his own house on his bed? Therefore, shall I not now require his blood at your hand and remove you from the earth?" 12So David commanded his young men, and they executed them, cut off their hands and feet, and hanged *them* by the pool in Hebron. But they took the head of Ishbosheth and buried *it* in the tomb of Abner in Hebron.

4:4 aCalled *Merib-Baal* in 1 Chronicles 8:34 and 9:40

When Did David Become King?

The exact dates of David's kingship are unknown. In fact, exact dates for Israel's first three kings—Saul, David, Solomon—are not known (see "When Did Saul Become King?" at 1 Sam. 13:1). The text of 2 Samuel records that David reigned first over Judah for 7½ years at Hebron, then over Israel and Judah

for 33 years at Jerusalem. These figures are rounded to a total reign of 40 years (2 Sam. 5:4, 5). However, an absolute date for when David began to rule is lacking.

David's reign could be estimated backward from his son Solomon, but Solomon's dates too are uncertain. Like Saul and David, Solomon also is reported to have reigned 40 years (1 Kin. 11:42). However, the 40-year figure given for Saul, David, and Solomon could be a symbolic round number representing the length of a generation. In addition, we are not sure how long Solomon ruled as a coregent with his father (1 Kin. 1:32-35; 2:1, 10).

If we accept that any dates for David are only approximate, his reign can be figured by starting from Solomon's son Rehoboam. The beginning of Rehoboam's rule over Judah can be placed at 930 B.C. Counting backward 40 years would date Solomon's reign from 970 to 930 B.C. Backing up another 40 years would place the beginning of David's rule in Judah at about 1010 B.C. and in Jerusalem at about 1003 B.C.

▼

■ 2 Samuel 5:1—7:29

---

2 Samuel
David Reigns over All Israel

5 :1 Then all the tribes of Israel came to David at Hebron and spoke, saying, "Indeed we *are* your bone and your flesh. 2Also, in time past, when Saul was king over us, you were the one who led Israel out and brought them in; and the LORD said to you, 'You shall shepherd My people Israel, and be ruler over Israel.' " 3Therefore all the elders of Israel came to the king at Hebron, and King David made a covenant with them at Hebron before the LORD. And they anointed David king over Israel. 4David *was* thirty years old when he began to reign, *and* he reigned forty years. 5In Hebron he reigned over Judah seven years and six months, and in Jerusalem he reigned thirty-three years over all Israel and Judah.

The Conquest of Jerusalem

6And the king and his men went to Jerusalem against the Jebusites, the inhabitants of the land, who spoke to David, saying, "You shall not come in here; but the blind and the lame will repel you," thinking, "David cannot come in here." 7Nevertheless David took the stronghold of Zion (that *is*, the City of David).

8Now David said on that day, "Whoever

UP THE JEBUSITE WATER SHAFT (2 Sam. 5:8)

The City of David was built on a hill over the Gihon spring, the main water source for the Jerusalem area (2 Chr. 32:30). Before David conquered the city, a people called the Jebusites lived there and dug a shaft down to the spring, which flowed from the mountain's base.

This water shaft was the key to the long-lived freedom of the Jebusites (Josh. 15:63). It gave the city's inhabitants access to water, even when enemies surrounded them. That plus the steep mountain on which the city was built made the city nearly impossible to conquer.

The digging of the Jebusite shaft was no easy task. In fact, the Jebusites actually first dug a tunnel that after some time had to be abandoned. Their second attempt produced two descending steps and one horizontal step before finally reaching water level. Once there, the Jebusites tunneled an additional 65 feet to the mouth of the spring.

David discovered the Jebusite shaft and realized that it was the easiest and least-expected way for his soldiers to enter Jerusalem. By climbing up the shaft (the same shaft still visible to visitors today), David and his men conquered the Jebusites and gained a new capital city (2 Sam. 5:8, 9).

---

climbs up by way of the water shaft and defeats the Jebusites (the lame and the blind, *who are* hated by David's soul), *he shall be chief and captain.*"a Therefore they say, "The blind and the lame shall not come into the house."

9Then David dwelt in the stronghold, and called it the City of David. And David built all around from the Milloa and inward. 10So David went on and became great, and the LORD God of hosts *was* with him.

11Then Hiram king of Tyre sent messengers to David, and cedar trees, and carpenters and masons. And they built David a house. 12So David knew that the LORD had established him as king over Israel, and that He had exalted His kingdom for the sake of His people Israel.

13And David took more concubines and wives from Jerusalem, after he had come from Hebron. Also more sons and daughters were born to David. 14Now these *are* the names of those who were born to him in Jerusalem: Shammua,a Shobab, Nathan, Solomon, 15Ibhar, Elishua,a Nepheg, Japhia, 16Elishama, Eliada, and Eliphelet.

The Philistines Defeated

17Now when the Philistines heard that they had anointed David king over Israel, all the Philistines went up to search for David. And David heard *of it* and went down to the stronghold. 18The Philistines also went and deployed themselves in the Valley of Rephaim. 19So David inquired of the LORD, saying, "Shall I go up against the Philistines? Will You deliver them into my hand?"

And the LORD said to David, "Go up, for I will doubtless deliver the Philistines into your hand."

20So David went to Baal Perazim, and David defeated them there; and he said, "The LORD has broken through my enemies before me, like a breakthrough of water." Therefore he called the name of that place Baal Perazim.a 21And they left their images there, and David and his men carried them away.

22Then the Philistines went up once again and deployed themselves in the Valley of Rephaim. 23Therefore David inquired of the LORD, and He said, "You shall not go up; circle around behind them, and come upon them in front of the mulberry trees. 24And it shall be, when you hear the sound of marching in the tops of the mulberry trees, then you shall advance quickly. For then the LORD will go out before you to strike the camp of the Philistines." 25And David did so, as the LORD commanded him; and he drove back the Philistines from Gebaa as far as Gezer.

5:8 aCompare 1 Chronicles 11:6   5:9 aLiterally *The Landfill*   5:14 aSpelled *Shimea* in 1 Chronicles 3:5   5:15 aSpelled *Elishama* in 1 Chronicles 3:6   5:20 aLiterally *Master of Breakthroughs*   5:25 aFollowing Masoretic Text, Targum, and Vulgate; Septuagint reads *Gibeon.*

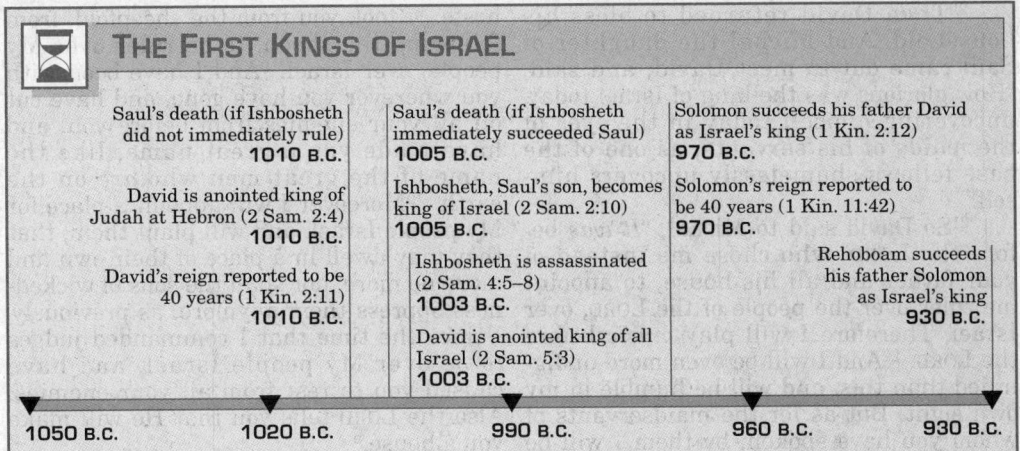

THE FIRST KINGS OF ISRAEL

Saul's death (if Ishbosheth did not immediately rule) **1010 B.C.**	Saul's death (if Ishbosheth immediately succeeded Saul) **1005 B.C.**	Solomon succeeds his father David as Israel's king (1 Kin. 2:12) **970 B.C.**
David is anointed king of Judah at Hebron (2 Sam. 2:4) **1010 B.C.**	Ishbosheth, Saul's son, becomes king of Israel (2 Sam. 2:10) **1005 B.C.**	Solomon's reign reported to be 40 years (1 Kin. 11:42) **970 B.C.**
David's reign reported to be 40 years (1 Kin. 2:11) **1010 B.C.**	Ishbosheth is assassinated (2 Sam. 4:5–8) **1003 B.C.**	Rehoboam succeeds his father Solomon as Israel's king **930 B.C.**
	David is anointed king of all Israel (2 Sam. 5:3) **1003 B.C.**	

1050 B.C.	1020 B.C.	990 B.C.	960 B.C.	930 B.C.

The Ark Brought to Jerusalem

6 ¹Again David gathered all *the* choice men of Israel, thirty thousand. ²And David arose and went with all the people who *were* with him from Baale Judah to bring up from there the ark of God, whose name is called by the Name,ᵃ the LORD of Hosts, who dwells *between* the cherubim. ³So they set the ark of God on a new cart, and brought it out of the house of Abinadab, which *was* on the hill; and Uzzah and Ahio, the sons of Abinadab, drove the new cart.ᵃ ⁴And they brought it out of the house of Abinadab, which *was* on the hill, accompanying the ark of God; and Ahio went before the ark. ⁵Then David and all the house of Israel played *music* before the LORD on all kinds of *instruments of* fir wood, on harps, on stringed instruments, on tambourines, on sistrums, and on cymbals.

⁶And when they came to Nachon's threshing floor, Uzzah put out *his* hand to the ark of God and took hold of it, for the oxen stumbled. ⁷Then the anger of the LORD was aroused against Uzzah, and God struck him there for *his* error; and he died there by the ark of God. ⁸And David became angry because of the LORD's outbreak against Uzzah; and he called the name of the place Perez Uzzahᵃ to this day.

⁹David was afraid of the LORD that day; and he said, "How can the ark of the LORD come to me?" ¹⁰So David would not move the ark of the LORD with him into the City of David; but David took it aside into the house of Obed-Edom the Gittite. ¹¹The ark of the LORD remained in the house of Obed-Edom the Gittite three months. And the LORD blessed Obed-Edom and all his household.

¹²Now it was told King David, saying, "The LORD has blessed the house of Obed-Edom and all that *belongs* to him, because of the ark of God." So David went and brought up the ark of God from the house of Obed-Edom to the City of David with gladness. ¹³And so it was, when those bearing the ark of the LORD had gone six paces, that he sacrificed oxen and fatted sheep. ¹⁴Then David danced before the LORD with all *his* might; and David *was* wearing a linen ephod. ¹⁵So David and all the house of Israel brought up the ark of the LORD with shouting and with the sound of the trumpet.

¹⁶Now as the ark of the LORD came into the City of David, Michal, Saul's daughter, looked through a window and saw King David leaping and whirling before the LORD; and she despised him in her heart. ¹⁷So they brought the ark of the LORD, and set it in its place in the midst of the tabernacle that David had erected for it. Then David offered burnt offerings and peace offerings before the LORD. ¹⁸And when David had finished offering burnt offerings and peace offerings, he blessed the people in the name of the LORD of hosts. ¹⁹Then he distributed among all the people, among the whole multitude of Israel, both the women and the men, to everyone a loaf of bread, a piece *of meat,* and a cake of raisins. So all the people departed, everyone to his house.

6:2 ᵃSeptuagint, Targum, and Vulgate omit *by the Name;* many Hebrew manuscripts and Syriac read *there.*   6:3 ᵃSeptuagint adds *with the ark.*
6:8 ᵃLiterally *Outburst Against Uzzah*

²⁰Then David returned to bless his household. And Michal the daughter of Saul came out to meet David, and said, "How glorious was the king of Israel today, uncovering himself today in the eyes of the maids of his servants, as one of the base fellows shamelessly uncovers himself!"

²¹So David said to Michal, "*It was* before the LORD, who chose me instead of your father and all his house, to appoint me ruler over the people of the LORD, over Israel. Therefore I will play *music* before the LORD. ²²And I will be even more undignified than this, and will be humble in my own sight. But as for the maidservants of whom you have spoken, by them I will be held in honor."

²³Therefore Michal the daughter of Saul had no children to the day of her death.

God's Covenant with David

7 ¹Now it came to pass when the king was dwelling in his house, and the LORD had given him rest from all his enemies all around, ²that the king said to Nathan the prophet, "See now, I dwell in a house of cedar, but the ark of God dwells inside tent curtains."

³Then Nathan said to the king, "Go, do all that *is* in your heart, for the LORD *is* with you."

⁴But it happened that night that the word of the LORD came to Nathan, saying, ⁵"Go and tell My servant David, 'Thus says the LORD: "Would you build a house for Me to dwell in? ⁶For I have not dwelt in a house since the time that I brought the children of Israel up from Egypt, even to this day, but have moved about in a tent and in a tabernacle. ⁷Wherever I have moved about with all the children of Israel, have I ever spoken a word to anyone from the tribes of Israel, whom I commanded to shepherd My people Israel, saying, 'Why have you not built Me a house of cedar?' " '

⁸Now therefore, thus shall you say to My servant David, 'Thus says the LORD of hosts: "I took you from the sheepfold, from following the sheep, to be ruler over My people, over Israel. ⁹And I have been with you wherever you have gone, and have cut off all your enemies from before you, and have made you a great name, like the name of the great men who *are* on the earth. ¹⁰Moreover I will appoint a place for My people Israel, and will plant them, that they may dwell in a place of their own and move no more; nor shall the sons of wickedness oppress them anymore, as previously, ¹¹since the time that I commanded judges *to be* over My people Israel, and have caused you to rest from all your enemies. Also the LORD tells you that He will make you a house.ᵃ

¹²"When your days are fulfilled and you rest with your fathers, I will set up your seed after you, who will come from your body, and I will establish his kingdom. ¹³He shall build a house for My name, and I will establish the throne of his kingdom forever. ¹⁴I will be his Father, and he shall be My son. If he commits iniquity, I will chasten him with the rod of men and with the blows of the sons of men. ¹⁵But My mercy shall not depart from him, as I took *it* from Saul, whom I removed from before you. ¹⁶And your house and your kingdom shall be established forever before you.ᵃ Your throne shall be established forever." ' "

¹⁷According to all these words and according to all this vision, so Nathan spoke to David.

David's Thanksgiving to God

¹⁸Then King David went in and sat before the LORD; and he said: "Who *am* I, O Lord GOD? And what is my house, that You have brought me this far? ¹⁹And yet this was a small thing in Your sight, O Lord GOD; and You have also spoken of Your servant's house for a great while to come. *Is* this the manner of man, O Lord GOD?

7:11 ᵃThat is, a royal dynasty   7:16 ᵃSeptuagint reads *Me.*

AGRICULTURE AND HERDING

David is one of several shepherds who eventually became great leaders (2 Sam. 7:8). Amos was called to be a prophet while he was tending sheep (Amos 7:14). Moses noticed the burning bush when he was "tending the flock of Jethro his father-in-law" (Ex. 3:1). One of Greece's earliest poets, Hesiod (c. 700 B.C.) received his call to write poetry while he was a shepherd on Mount Helicon.

20Now what more can David say to You? For You, Lord GOD, know Your servant. 21For Your word's sake, and according to Your own heart, You have done all these great things, to make Your servant know *them.* 22Therefore You are great, O Lord GOD.[a] For *there is* none like You, nor *is there any* God besides You, according to all that we have heard with our ears. 23And who *is* like Your people, like Israel, the one nation on the earth whom God went to redeem for Himself as a people, to make for Himself a name—and to do for Yourself great and awesome deeds for Your land—before Your people whom You redeemed for Yourself from Egypt, the nations, and their gods? 24For You have made Your people Israel Your very own people forever; and You, LORD, have become their God.

25"Now, O LORD God, the word which You have spoken concerning Your servant and concerning his house, establish *it* forever and do as You have said. 26So let Your name be magnified forever, saying, 'The LORD of hosts *is* the God over Israel.' And let the house of Your servant David be established before You. 27For You, O LORD of hosts, God of Israel, have revealed *this* to Your servant, saying, 'I will build you a house.' Therefore Your servant has found it in his heart to pray this prayer to You.

28"And now, O Lord GOD, You are God, and Your words are true, and You have promised this goodness to Your servant. 29Now therefore, let it please You to bless the house of Your servant, that it may continue before You forever; for You, O Lord GOD, have spoken *it,* and with Your blessing let the house of Your servant be blessed forever."

7:22 [a]Targum and Syriac read *O LORD God.*
1 Chr. 9:37 [a]Called *Zecher* in 8:31
9:38 [a]Spelled *Shimeah* in 8:32 　 9:41 [a]Spelled *Tarea* in 8:35 　 [b]Following Arabic, Syriac, Targum, and Vulgate (compare 8:35); Masoretic Text and Septuagint omit *and Ahaz.* 　 9:42 [a]Spelled *Jehoaddah* in 8:36 　 9:43 [a]Spelled *Raphah* in 8:37

The Books of Chronicles

While Chronicles has a different emphasis than Samuel and Kings, the Chronicler is able to use a good deal of those earlier books. In fact, Chronicles often quotes the other histories, especially Kings. But Chronicles also extends farther in time. Whereas Kings ends during the Babylonian exile, Chronicles concludes with the Persian king Cyrus's proclamation that allowed the exiled Jews to return to Jerusalem. See "Prophetic Account: Saul and David" at 1 Sam. 9:1.

Although the books of Chronicles are especially concerned with the monarchy, they begin much earlier, with Adam. In the historical shorthand of genealogies of 1 Chr. 1—9, the Chronicler covers the time span between Adam and King Saul (and a good deal beyond Saul). These genealogical lists actually go as far as the postexilic period and provide an important backdrop for that era (see "Priestly Genealogies" at 1 Chr. 1:1).

The final genealogy (1 Chr. 9:35–44), however, covers Saul's family and introduces the narrative of his tragic death in 1 Chr. 10. Within the list are what was probably the original names of Saul's son (Esh-Baal, 9:39) and grandson (Merib-Baal, 9:40). The prophetic story of Saul's family in 2 Samuel consistently spells these names as Ishbosheth (2 Sam. 2:8) and Mephibosheth (2 Sam. 4:4). The author of Samuel replaced the name of the Canaanite god Baal with *bosheth,* the Hebrew word for "shame."

■ 1 Chronicles 9:35–44

---

1 Chronicles
The Family of King Saul

9 :35 Jeiel the father of Gibeon, whose wife's name *was* Maacah, dwelt at Gibeon. 36His firstborn son *was* Abdon, then Zur, Kish, Baal, Ner, Nadab, 37Gedor, Ahio, Zechariah,[a] and Mikloth. 38And Mikloth begot Shimeam.[a] They also dwelt alongside their relatives in Jerusalem, with their brethren. 39Ner begot Kish, Kish begot Saul, and Saul begot Jonathan, Malchishua, Abinadab, and Esh-Baal. 40The son of Jonathan *was* Merib-Baal, and Merib-Baal begot Micah. 41The sons of Micah *were* Pithon, Melech, Tahrea,[a] and Ahaz.[b] 42And Ahaz begot Jarah;[a] Jarah begot Alemeth, Azmaveth, and Zimri; and Zimri begot Moza; 43Moza begot Binea, Rephaiah[a] his son, Eleasah his son, and Azel his son.

44And Azel had six sons whose names *were* these: Azrikam, Bocheru, Ishmael, Sheariah, Obadiah, and Hanan; these *were* the sons of Azel.

Priestly Account: Saul and David

The books of Chronicles cover the same historical time period as the books of Samuel and Kings, but they do so very differently. The author of Chronicles, often called "the Chronicler," wrote at a later time and with a different purpose, and thus omitted episodes that would detract from that purpose. Saul is allotted very little space, and the Chronicler consistently ignores the civil war between the houses of Saul and David. Only Saul's ignominious end is recorded (1 Chr. 10) as background to David's rise to the throne.

The Chronicler is mainly interested in Davidic kingship, Jerusalem, and the temple. In Chronicles, David is above all the devout founder of the Jerusalem temple. Perhaps for this reason, he is consistently presented in a positive light. In telling David's story, the Chronicler emphasizes the king's concern for the ark of the covenant and for his capital at Jerusalem (1 Chr. 13; 15). Both the ark and the capital are prerequisites for the temple.

■ 1 Chronicles 10:1—11:47

1 Chronicles
Tragic End of Saul and His Sons

10 :1 Now the Philistines fought against Israel; and the men of Israel fled from before the Philistines, and fell slain on Mount Gilboa. ²Then the Philistines followed hard after Saul and his sons. And the Philistines killed Jonathan, Abinadab, and Malchishua, Saul's sons. ³The battle became fierce against Saul. The archers hit him, and he was wounded by the archers. ⁴Then Saul said to his armorbearer, "Draw your sword, and thrust me through with it, lest these uncircumcised men come and abuse me." But his armorbearer would not, for he was greatly afraid. Therefore Saul took a sword and fell on it. ⁵And when his armorbearer saw that Saul was dead, he also fell on his sword and

died. ⁶So Saul and his three sons died, and all his house died together. ⁷And when all the men of Israel who *were* in the valley saw that they had fled and that Saul and his sons were dead, they forsook their cities and fled; then the Philistines came and dwelt in them.

⁸So it happened the next day, when the Philistines came to strip the slain, that they found Saul and his sons fallen on Mount Gilboa. ⁹And they stripped him and took his head and his armor, and sent word *throughout* the land of the Philistines to proclaim the news *in the temple* of their idols and among the people. ¹⁰Then they put his armor in the temple of their gods, and fastened his head in the temple of Dagon.

¹¹And when all Jabesh Gilead heard all that the Philistines had done to Saul, ¹²all the valiant men arose and took the body of Saul and the bodies of his sons; and they brought them to Jabesh, and buried their bones under the tamarisk tree at Jabesh, and fasted seven days.

¹³So Saul died for his unfaithfulness which he had committed against the LORD, because he did not keep the word of the LORD, and also because he consulted a medium for guidance. ¹⁴But *he* did not inquire of the LORD; therefore He killed him, and turned the kingdom over to David the son of Jesse.

David Made King over All Israel

11 ¹Then all Israel came together to David at Hebron, saying, "Indeed we *are* your bone and your flesh. ²Also, in time past, even when Saul was king, you *were* the one who led Israel out and brought them in; and the LORD your God said to you, 'You shall shepherd My people Israel, and be ruler over My people Israel.' " ³Therefore all the elders of Israel came to the king at Hebron, and David made a covenant with them at Hebron before the LORD. And they anointed David king over Israel, according to the word of the LORD by Samuel.

ARTS AND LITERATURE

In the ancient world, the proper disposition of the bodies of the dead was of extreme importance (1 Chr. 10:11, 12). In the Greek tragedy Antigone, *the lead character, Antigone, decides against the law of the state that she must provide a decent burial for her brother. She makes this choice of divine law over human law, even though she knows that the penalty for doing what is right is death.*

WHAT WAS THE MILLO? (1 Chr. 11:8)

David's building of the Millo was considered by the biblical writers to be one of this king's major accomplishments. Likewise his son Solomon was known for significant building activities, including the temple, Solomon's palace, the wall of Jerusalem, the rebuilding of the cities of Hazor, Megiddo, and Gezer, as well as the Millo (1 Kin. 9:15). The building of the Millo was certainly seen as a major building feat. Unfortunately, the biblical writers never describe what the Millo was.

The Millo is first associated with David; therefore, we can assume that the Millo was located in the City of David (1 Chr. 11:8). The later account of the Millo's rebuilding by King Hezekiah (715–686 B.C.) specifies this location (2 Chr. 32:5). Whatever the Millo was, it appears to have been a major construction project.

Archaeological excavations in the City of David discovered terraces built on its steep eastern slope. These terraces served as retaining walls for the buildings constructed above. This innovative support structure was probably what Jerusalemites knew as "the Millo."

The City of David

4And David and all Israel went to Jerusalem, which is Jebus, where the Jebusites *were,* the inhabitants of the land. 5But the inhabitants of Jebus said to David, "You shall not come in here!" Nevertheless David took the stronghold of Zion (that is, the City of David). 6Now David said, "Whoever attacks the Jebusites first shall be chief and captain." And Joab the son of Zeruiah went up first, and became chief. 7Then David dwelt in the stronghold; therefore they called it the City of David. 8And he built the city around it, from the Millo[a] to the surrounding area. Joab repaired the rest of the city. 9So David went on and became great, and the LORD of hosts *was* with him.

The Mighty Men of David

10Now these *were* the heads of the mighty men whom David had, who strengthened themselves with him in his kingdom, with all Israel, to make him king, according to the word of the LORD concerning Israel. 11And this *is* the number of the mighty men whom David had: Jashobeam the son of a Hachmonite, chief of the captains;[a] he had lifted up his spear against three hundred, killed *by him* at one time.

12After him *was* Eleazar the son of Dodo, the Ahohite, who *was* one of the three mighty men. 13He was with David at Pasdammim. Now there the Philistines were gathered for battle, and there was a piece of ground full of barley. So the people fled from the Philistines. 14But they stationed themselves in the middle of *that* field, defended it, and killed the Philistines. So the LORD brought about a great victory.

15Now three of the thirty chief men went down to the rock to David, into the cave of Adullam; and the army of the Philistines encamped in the Valley of Rephaim. 16David *was* then in the stronghold, and the garrison of the Philistines *was* then in Bethlehem. 17And David said with longing, "Oh, that someone would give me a drink of water from the well of Bethlehem, which is by the gate!" 18So the three broke through the camp of the Philistines, drew water from the well of Bethlehem that *was* by the gate, and took *it* and brought *it* to David. Nevertheless David would not drink it, but poured it out to the LORD. 19And he said, "Far be it from me, O my God, that I should do this! Shall I drink the blood of these men *who have put* their lives *in jeopardy?* For at the risk of their lives they brought it." Therefore he would not drink it. These things were done by the three mighty men.

20Abishai the brother of Joab was chief of *another* three.[a] He had lifted up his spear against three hundred *men,* killed *them,* and won a name among *these* three.

11:8 aLiterally *The Landfill*   11:11 aFollowing Qere; Kethib, Septuagint, and Vulgate read *the thirty* (compare 2 Samuel 23:8).   11:20 aFollowing Masoretic Text, Septuagint, and Vulgate; Syriac reads *thirty.*

21Of the three he was more honored than the other two men. Therefore he became their captain. However he did not attain to the *first* three.

22Benaiah was the son of Jehoiada, the son of a valiant man from Kabzeel, who had done many deeds. He had killed two lion-like heroes of Moab. He also had gone down and killed a lion in the midst of a pit on a snowy day. 23And he killed an Egyptian, a man of *great* height, five cubits tall. In the Egyptian's hand *there was* a spear like a weaver's beam; and he went down to him with a staff, wrested the spear out of the Egyptian's hand, and killed him with his own spear. 24These *things* Benaiah the son of Jehoiada did, and won a name among three mighty men. 25Indeed he was more honored than the thirty, but he did not attain to the *first* three. And David appointed him over his guard.

26Also the mighty warriors *were* Asahel the brother of Joab, Elhanan the son of Dodo of Bethlehem, 27Shammoth the Harorite,ª Helez the Pelonite,ᵇ 28Ira the son of Ikkesh the Tekoite, Abiezer the Anathothite, 29Sibbechai the Hushathite, Ilai the Ahohite, 30Maharai the Netophathite, Heledª the son of Baanah the Netophathite, 31Ithaiª the son of Ribai of Gibeah, of the sons of Benjamin, Benaiah the Pirathonite, 32Huraiª of the brooks of Gaash, Abielᵇ the Arbathite, 33Azmaveth the Baharumite,ª Eliahba the Shaalbonite, 34the sons of Hashem the Gizonite, Jonathan the son of Shageh the Hararite, 35Ahiam the son of Sacar the Hararite, Eliphal the son of Ur, 36Hepher the Mecherathite, Ahijah the Pelonite, 37Hezro the Carmelite, Naarai the son of Ezbai, 38Joel the brother of Nathan, Mibhar the son of Hagri, 39Zelek the Ammonite, Naharai the Berothiteª (the armorbearer of Joab the son of Zeruiah), 40Ira the Ithrite, Gareb the Ithrite, 41Uriah the Hittite, Zabad the son of Ahlai, 42Adina the son of Shiza the Reubenite (a chief of the Reubenites) and thirty with him, 43Hanan the son of Maachah, Joshaphat the Mithnite, 44Uzzia the Ashterathite, Shama and Jeiel the sons of Hotham the Aroerite, 45Jediael the son of Shimri, and Joha his brother, the Tizite, 46Eliel the Mahavite, Jeribai and Joshaviah the sons of Elnaam, Ithmah the Moabite, 47Eliel, Obed, and Jaasiel the Mezobaite.

David the Fugitive

Chronicles makes no mention of Saul's opposition to David's rise to kingship (see "Priestly Account: Saul and David" at 1 Chr. 10:1). But in 1 Chr. 12, in material not found in the prophetic account, the Chronicler does describe the days before David was king when he was pursued by Saul in the wilderness. During this time David had established his stronghold and military headquarters at Ziklag in the extreme south of Judah (12:1, 8, 16).

The Chronicler's account emphasizes the support that gathered around David. Even some of Saul's own kinsmen from the tribe of Benjamin came to David's aid (12:2). Even men from two of the northern tribes, Gad (12:8–15) and Manasseh (12:19–22), came. This description of David's fugitive days shows that the support he had then had culminated in the joy and celebration now surrounding his coronation as king of all Israel. All the mighty warriors and all Israelites now came to Hebron "to turn over the kingdom of Saul" to David (12:23–40).

■ 1 Chronicles 12:1—15:29

1 Chronicles
The Growth of David's Army

12 :1 Now these *were* the men who came to David at Ziklag while he was still a fugitive from Saul the son of Kish; and they *were* among the mighty men, helpers in the war, 2armed with bows, using both the right hand and the left in *hurling* stones and *shooting* arrows with the bow. *They were* of Benjamin, Saul's brethren.

3The chief *was* Ahiezer, then Joash, the sons of Shemaah the Gibeathite; Jeziel and Pelet the sons of Azmaveth; Berachah, and Jehu the Anathothite; 4Ishmaiah the Gibeonite, a mighty man among the thirty, and over the thirty; Jeremiah, Jahaziel, Johanan, and Jozabad the Gederathite; 5Eluzai, Jerimoth, Bealiah, Shemariah, and Shephatiah the Haruphite; 6Elkanah, Jisshiah, Azarel, Joezer, and Jashobeam,

---

11:27 ªSpelled *Harodite* in 2 Samuel 23:25   ᵇCalled *Paltite* in 2 Samuel 23:26   11:30 ªSpelled *Heleb* in 2 Samuel 23:29 and *Heldai* in 1 Chronicles 27:15   11:31 ªSpelled *Ittai* in 2 Samuel 23:29   11:32 ªSpelled *Hiddai* in 2 Samuel 23:30 ᵇSpelled *Abi-Albon* in 2 Samuel 23:31 11:33 ªSpelled *Barhumite* in 2 Samuel 23:31 11:39 ªSpelled *Beerothite* in 2 Samuel 23:37

the Korahites; [7]and Joelah and Zebadiah the sons of Jeroham of Gedor.

[8]*Some* Gadites joined David at the stronghold in the wilderness, mighty men of valor, men trained for battle, who could handle shield and spear, whose faces *were like* the faces of lions, and *were* as swift as gazelles on the mountains: [9]Ezer the first, Obadiah the second, Eliab the third, [10]Mishmannah the fourth, Jeremiah the fifth, [11]Attai the sixth, Eliel the seventh, [12]Johanan the eighth, Elzabad the ninth, [13]Jeremiah the tenth, and Machbanai the eleventh. [14]These *were* from the sons of Gad, captains of the army; the least was over a hundred, and the greatest was over a thousand. [15]These *are* the ones who crossed the Jordan in the first month, when it had overflowed all its banks; and they put to flight all *those* in the valleys, to the east and to the west.

[16]Then some of the sons of Benjamin and Judah came to David at the stronghold. [17]And David went out to meet them, and answered and said to them, "If you have come peaceably to me to help me, my heart will be united with you; but if to betray me to my enemies, since *there is* no wrong in my hands, may the God of our fathers look and bring judgment." [18]Then the Spirit came upon Amasai, chief of the captains, *and he said:*

"*We are* yours, O David;
 We *are* on your side, O son of Jesse!
Peace, peace to you,
And peace to your helpers!
For your God helps you."

So David received them, and made them captains of the troop.

[19]And *some* from Manasseh defected to David when he was going with the Philistines to battle against Saul; but they did not help them, for the lords of the Philistines sent him away by agreement, saying, "He may defect to his master Saul *and endanger* our heads." [20]When he went to Ziklag, those of Manasseh who defected to him were Adnah, Jozabad, Jediael, Michael, Jozabad, Elihu, and Zillethai, captains of the thousands who *were* from Manasseh. [21]And they helped David against the bands *of raiders,* for they *were* all mighty men of valor, and they were captains in the army. [22]For at *that* time they came to David day by day to help him, until *it was* a great army, like the army of God.

David's Army at Hebron

[23]Now these *were* the numbers of the divisions *that were* equipped for war, *and* came to David at Hebron to turn *over* the kingdom of Saul to him, according to the word of the LORD: [24]of the sons of Judah bearing shield and spear, six thousand eight hundred armed for war; [25]of the sons of Simeon, mighty men of valor fit for war, seven thousand one hundred; [26]of the sons of Levi four thousand six hundred; [27]Jehoiada, the leader of the Aaronites, and with him three thousand seven hundred; [28]Zadok, a young man, a valiant warrior, and from his father's house twenty-two captains; [29]of the sons of Benjamin, relatives of Saul, three thousand (until then the greatest part of them had remained loyal to the house of Saul); [30]of the sons of Ephraim twenty thousand eight hundred, mighty men of valor, famous men throughout their father's house; [31]of the half-tribe of Manasseh eighteen thousand, who were designated by name to come and make David king; [32]of the sons of Issachar who had understanding of the times, to know what Israel ought to do, their chiefs were two hundred; and all their brethren were at their command; [33]of Zebulun there were fifty thousand who went out to battle, expert in war with all weapons of war, stouthearted men who could keep ranks; [34]of Naphtali one thousand captains, and with them thirty-seven thousand with shield and spear; [35]of the Danites who could keep battle formation, twenty-eight thousand six hundred; [36]of Asher, those who could go out to war, able to keep battle formation, forty thousand; [37]of the Reubenites and the Gadites and the half-tribe of Manasseh, from the other side of the Jordan, one hundred and twenty thousand armed for battle with every *kind* of weapon of war.

TIME CAPSULE   *1100 to 1076 B.C.*

1100   *Wen-amon sails on official mission to Byblos to purchase lumber*

1098   *Rebellion in Upper Egypt against the high priest of Amon*

1086   *Ussher's date for the birth of David*

1076   *Assyria's power declines after death of Tiglath-Pileser I*

1076   *Wen-amon reports that high priest of Amon controls southern Egypt*

38All these men of war, who could keep ranks, came to Hebron with a loyal heart, to make David king over all Israel; and all the rest of Israel *were* of one mind to make David king. 39And they were there with David three days, eating and drinking, for their brethren had prepared for them. 40Moreover those who were near to them, from as far away as Issachar and Zebulun and Naphtali, were bringing food on donkeys and camels, on mules and oxen— provisions of flour and cakes of figs and cakes of raisins, wine and oil and oxen and sheep abundantly, for *there was* joy in Israel.

The Ark Brought from Kirjath Jearim

13 1Then David consulted with the captains of thousands and hundreds, *and* with every leader. 2And David said to all the assembly of Israel, "If *it seems* good to you, and if it is of the LORD our God, let us send out to our brethren everywhere *who are* left in all the land of Israel, and with them to the priests and Levites *who are* in their cities *and* their common-lands, that they may gather together to us; 3and let us bring the ark of our God back to us, for we have not inquired at it since the days of Saul." 4Then all the assembly said that they would do so, for the thing was right in the eyes of all the people.

5So David gathered all Israel together, from Shihor in Egypt to as far as the entrance of Hamath, to bring the ark of God from Kirjath Jearim. 6And David and all Israel went up to Baalah,a to Kirjath Jearim, which belonged to Judah, to bring up from there the ark of God the LORD, who dwells *between* the cherubim, where *His* name is proclaimed. 7So they carried the ark of God on a new cart from the house of Abinadab, and Uzza and Ahio drove the cart. 8Then David and all Israel played *music* before God with all *their* might, with singing, on harps, on stringed instruments, on tambourines, on cymbals, and with trumpets.

9And when they came to Chidon'sa threshing floor, Uzza put out his hand to hold the ark, for the oxen stumbled. 10Then the anger of the LORD was aroused against Uzza, and He struck him because he put his hand to the ark; and he died there before God. 11And David became angry because of the LORD's outbreak against Uzza; therefore that place is called Perez Uzzaa to this day. 12David was afraid of God that day, saying, "How can I bring the ark of God to me?"

13So David would not move the ark with him into the City of David, but took it aside into the house of Obed-Edom the Gittite. 14The ark of God remained with the family of Obed-Edom in his house three months. And the LORD blessed the house of Obed-Edom and all that he had.

David Established at Jerusalem

14 1Now Hiram king of Tyre sent messengers to David, and cedar trees, with masons and carpenters, to build him a house. 2So David knew that the LORD had established him as king over Israel, for his kingdom was highly exalted for the sake of His people Israel.

3Then David took more wives in Jerusalem, and David begot more sons and daughters. 4And these are the names of his children whom he had in Jerusalem: Shammua,a Shobab, Nathan, Solomon, 5Ibhar, Elishua,a Elpelet,b 6Nogah, Nepheg, Japhia, 7Elishama, Beeliada,a and Eliphelet.

The Philistines Defeated

8Now when the Philistines heard that David had been anointed king over all Israel, all the Philistines went up to search for David. And David heard *of it* and went out against them. 9Then the Philistines

---

13:6 aCalled *Baale Judah* in 2 Samuel 6:2
13:9 aCalled *Nachon* in 2 Samuel 6:6
13:11 aLiterally *Outburst Against Uzza*
14:4 aSpelled *Shimea* in 3:5   14:5 aSpelled *Elishama* in 3:6   bSpelled *Eliphelet* in 3:6
14:7 aSpelled *Eliada* in 3:8

ARTS AND LITERATURE

The ancient world had wind, percussion, and stringed instruments. The main instruments of the Israelites seem to have been small harps and percussion instruments, not including drums (1 Chr. 13:8). The percussion instruments include the metal rattle called a sistrum that was a favorite in Egypt. The titles of the psalms probably include some names of musical tunes.

PELESETS, PHILISTINES, AND PALESTINE (1 Chr. 14:8)

The name "Sea Peoples" was coined by the Egyptians to denote groups of people that migrated to Canaan beginning at the end of the 13th century B.C. They came to the Near East in two major waves, traveling along the coast via Asia Minor and Canaan before reaching Egypt.

At the mortuary temple of Ramesses III, Medinet Habu, graphic pictures of the Sea Peoples were incised in the temple walls. These pictures provide an Egyptian view of what the Sea Peoples looked like, the kind of ships they used, their weapons, and how they dressed. The text that goes with the pictures even records the names of the individual subgroups. Although most of the names are unfamiliar, like the Denyen, Thekel, Shekelesh, Sherden, and Weshesh, one group—the Pelesets—are known in the Bible as "the Philistines" (1 Chr. 14:8).

Ramesses III also described how the Sea Peoples devastated the nations that were in their path. Nations like the Hittites and major cities like Ugarit collapsed after the Sea Peoples passed their way. The Sea Peoples' manner of travel was by ship and on foot. Those who sailed along the coast were supported by those who followed along coastal roads. Some of the Sea Peoples seem to have settled newly conquered territory as others pressed on toward Egypt.

According to Ramesses III, in Egypt they met their match. He stopped their advance, then settled them on the coast of Canaan. Why the Sea Peoples began their epic migration is not known. It has been suggested that famine in their homelands or the force of other peoples made them begin their trek. Whatever the cause, one of their groups, the Pelesets (Philistines), so dominated the history of the coastal regions of Canaan that their name became the name of the region—Palestine.

went and made a raid on the Valley of Rephaim. ¹⁰And David inquired of God, saying, "Shall I go up against the Philistines? Will You deliver them into my hand?"

The LORD said to him, "Go up, for I will deliver them into your hand."

¹¹So they went up to Baal Perazim, and David defeated them there. Then David said, "God has broken through my enemies by my hand like a breakthrough of water." Therefore they called the name of that place Baal Perazim.ᵃ ¹²And when they left their gods there, David gave a commandment, and they were burned with fire.

¹³Then the Philistines once again made a raid on the valley. ¹⁴Therefore David inquired again of God, and God said to him, "You shall not go up after them; circle around them, and come upon them in front of the mulberry trees. ¹⁵And it shall be, when you hear a sound of marching in the tops of the mulberry trees, then you shall go out to battle, for God has gone out before you to strike the camp of the Philistines." ¹⁶So David did as God commanded him, and they drove back the army of the Philistines from Gibeon as far as Gezer. ¹⁷Then the fame of David went out into all lands, and the LORD brought the fear of him upon all nations.

The Ark Brought to Jerusalem

15 ¹David built houses for himself in the City of David; and he prepared a place for the ark of God, and pitched a tent for it. ²Then David said, "No one may carry the ark of God but the Levites, for the LORD has chosen them to carry the ark of God and to minister before Him forever." ³And David gathered all Israel together at Jerusalem, to bring up the ark of the LORD to its place, which he had prepared for it. ⁴Then David assembled the children of Aaron and the Levites: ⁵of the sons of Kohath, Uriel the chief, and one hundred and twenty of his brethren; ⁶of the sons of Merari, Asaiah the chief, and two hundred and twenty of his brethren; ⁷of the sons of Gershom, Joel the chief, and one hundred and thirty of his brethren; ⁸of the sons of Elizaphan, Shemaiah the chief, and two hundred of his brethren; ⁹of the sons of Hebron, Eliel the chief, and eighty of his brethren; ¹⁰of the sons of Uzziel,

14:11 ᵃLiterally *Master of Breakthroughs*

Amminadab the chief, and one hundred and twelve of his brethren.

¹¹And David called for Zadok and Abiathar the priests, and for the Levites: for Uriel, Asaiah, Joel, Shemaiah, Eliel, and Amminadab. ¹²He said to them, "You *are* the heads of the fathers' *houses* of the Levites; sanctify yourselves, you and your brethren, that you may bring up the ark of the LORD God of Israel to *the place* I have prepared for it. ¹³For because you *did* not *do it* the first *time,* the LORD our God broke out against us, because we did not consult Him about the proper order."

¹⁴So the priests and the Levites sanctified themselves to bring up the ark of the LORD God of Israel. ¹⁵And the children of the Levites bore the ark of God on their shoulders, by its poles, as Moses had commanded according to the word of the LORD.

¹⁶Then David spoke to the leaders of the Levites to appoint their brethren *to be* the singers accompanied by instruments of music, stringed instruments, harps, and cymbals, by raising the voice with resounding joy. ¹⁷So the Levites appointed Heman the son of Joel; and of his brethren, Asaph the son of Berechiah; and of their brethren, the sons of Merari, Ethan the son of Kushaiah; ¹⁸and with them their brethren of the second *rank:* Zechariah, Ben,ᵃ Jaaziel, Shemiramoth, Jehiel, Unni, Eliab, Benaiah, Maaseiah, Mattithiah, Elipheleh, Mikneiah, Obed-Edom, and Jeiel, the gatekeepers; ¹⁹the singers, Heman, Asaph, and Ethan, *were* to sound the cymbals of bronze; ²⁰Zechariah, Aziel, Shemiramoth, Jehiel, Unni, Eliab, Maaseiah, and Benaiah, with strings according to Alamoth; ²¹Mattithiah, Elipheleh, Mikneiah, Obed-Edom, Jeiel, and Azaziah, to direct with harps on the Sheminith; ²²Chenaniah, leader of the Levites, was instructor *in charge of* the music, because he *was* skillful; ²³Berechiah and Elkanah *were* doorkeepers for the ark; ²⁴Shebaniah, Joshaphat, Nethanel, Amasai, Zechariah, Benaiah, and Eliezer, the priests, were to blow the trumpets before the ark of God;

and Obed-Edom and Jehiah, doorkeepers for the ark.

²⁵So David, the elders of Israel, and the captains over thousands went to bring up the ark of the covenant of the LORD from the house of Obed-Edom with joy. ²⁶And so it was, when God helped the Levites who bore the ark of the covenant of the LORD, that they offered seven bulls and seven rams. ²⁷David was clothed with a robe of fine linen, as were all the Levites who bore the ark, the singers, and Chenaniah the music master *with* the singers. David also wore a linen ephod. ²⁸Thus all Israel brought up the ark of the covenant of the LORD with shouting and with the sound of the horn, with trumpets and with cymbals, making music with stringed instruments and harps.

²⁹And it happened, *as* the ark of the covenant of the LORD came to the City of David, that Michal, Saul's daughter, looked through a window and saw King David whirling and playing music; and she despised him in her heart.

15:18 ᵃFollowing Masoretic Text and Vulgate; Septuagint omits *Ben.*

The Book of Psalms

The psalms, almost without exception, are difficult to tie to a specific historical context. They are the worship songs of Israel and are intended to apply to the needs of all worshipers across time. Some psalms do have historical superscriptions that make it possible to associate them with specific events, but these make up only about ten percent of all the psalms.

The rest of the psalms must follow some other criteria by which to read them within the history of Israel. One criterion is to place the psalms ascribed to David (or Solomon or Moses) during the life of that person (see "Teach Us to Number Our Days" at Ps. 90). A second criterion is to place psalms according to their type.

POLITICS AND GOVERNMENT

David was clothed in a robe of fine linen as he danced to music during the procession of the ark into Jerusalem (1 Chr. 15:27–29). The reaction of Michal (2 Sam. 6:20) may suggest that he discarded the robe during the dancing. By participating in the dance and procession, David possibly demonstrated to the people his authority to rule before Yahweh his God.

While there are various classifications of psalm types, two prominent types are hymns and laments. Hymns are songs of praise to God, and laments are appeals for God's help in times of trouble. In the Bible, the psalms are arranged in five distinct books (perhaps to parallel the five books of the Pentateuch). In general, the movement through the five books progresses from lament (in the early books) to praise (in the fifth book).

There was joy and shouting and music as David and Israel moved the ark to Jerusalem (1 Chr. 15:25–28). Such a setting favors the reading of psalms that are hymns of praise, and which are ascribed to David. Several psalms (Ps. 8; 19; 29; 32; 65; 68; 103; 108; 138) are appropriate for the context of David's joyous entry into Jerusalem before the ark. A psalm of thanksgiving, such as Ps. 32, expresses gratitude to God for deliverance. The joy that accompanies God's deliverance could also reflect the joy of the ark event.

■ Psalms 8; 19; 29; 32; 65; 68; 103; 108; 138

PSALM 8

The Glory of the LORD in Creation

To the Chief Musician. On the instrument of Gath.[a] *A Psalm of David.*

O LORD, our Lord,
How excellent *is* Your name in all the earth,
Who have set Your glory above the heavens!

2 Out of the mouth of babes and nursing infants
You have ordained strength,
Because of Your enemies,
That You may silence the enemy and the avenger.

3 When I consider Your heavens, the work of Your fingers,
The moon and the stars, which You have ordained,

4 What is man that You are mindful of him,
And the son of man that You visit him?

5 For You have made him a little lower than the angels,[a]
And You have crowned him with glory and honor.

6 You have made him to have dominion over the works of Your hands;
You have put all *things* under his feet,

7 All sheep and oxen—
Even the beasts of the field,

8 The birds of the air,
And the fish of the sea
That pass through the paths of the seas.

9 O LORD, our Lord,
How excellent *is* Your name in all the earth!

PSALM 19

The Perfect Revelation of the LORD

To the Chief Musician. A Psalm of David.

The heavens declare the glory of God;
And the firmament shows His handiwork.

2 Day unto day utters speech,
And night unto night reveals knowledge.

3 *There is* no speech nor language
Where their voice is not heard.

4 Their line[a] has gone out through all the earth,
And their words to the end of the world.

In them He has set a tabernacle for the sun,

5 Which *is* like a bridegroom coming out of his chamber,

8:title [a]Hebrew *Al Gittith*   8:5 [a]Hebrew *Elohim, God*; Septuagint, Syriac, Targum, and Jewish tradition translate as *angels*.   19:4 [a]Septuagint, Syriac, and Vulgate read *sound*; Targum reads *business*.

RELIGION AND WORSHIP

The sun illustrates God's energy and power, and it is linked with a bridegroom as representing natural life in its bloom (Ps. 19:4, 5). Some ancient peoples worshiped the sun. The Egyptian pharaoh Akhenaten (1352–1336 B.C.) tried to make the sun god the only deity in Egypt's state religion, but his successors reversed his innovation as soon as he died.

STORM GOD IMAGERY   (Ps. 29:3–9)

Hymns offering praise for deities in the ancient Near East often used common language, even though the hymns praised different gods. For example, Ps. 29 glorifies Yahweh as a storm god, using language very similar to the descriptions in the Ugaritic texts of the Canaanite and Phoenician god Baal.

Phrases like "voice of the LORD" (or "voice of Yahweh"; 29:5) and "voice of Baal" are common Semitic language. They refer to thunder as the sound of a god's speech, whether that deity was a storm god or not. The thunder or voice announced both the power and the presence of the deity. All of nature and of humanity was affected by the sound and reverberation of the approaching god.

Place names in Ps. 29 describe a geography north of Israel. "Lebanon and Sirion" (29:6) are mountain ranges of Phoenicia. The "many waters" (29:3) appear to picture the Mediterranean Sea. The Wilderness of Kadesh (29:8) possibly refers to the Kadesh on the Orontes River in Syria. A hymn composed for a Phoenician deity, such as Baal, would most likely refer to these same places. Possibly Ps. 29 adapts Phoenician language, describing a storm passing eastward from the waters of the Mediterranean, across Lebanon, and over the land through the wilderness.

And rejoices like a strong man to run its race.

6 Its rising *is* from one end of heaven,
And its circuit to the other end;
And there is nothing hidden from its heat.

7 The law of the LORD *is* perfect,
converting the soul;
The testimony of the LORD *is* sure,
making wise the simple;

8 The statutes of the LORD *are* right,
rejoicing the heart;
The commandment of the LORD *is*
pure, enlightening the eyes;

9 The fear of the LORD *is* clean,
enduring forever;
The judgments of the LORD *are* true
and righteous altogether.

10 More to be desired *are they* than gold,
Yea, than much fine gold;
Sweeter also than honey and the honeycomb.

11 Moreover by them Your servant is warned,
And in keeping them *there is* great reward.

12 Who can understand *his* errors?
Cleanse me from secret *faults.*

13 Keep back Your servant also from presumptuous *sins;*
Let them not have dominion over me.
Then I shall be blameless,
And I shall be innocent of great transgression.

14 Let the words of my mouth and the meditation of my heart
Be acceptable in Your sight,
O LORD, my strength and my Redeemer.

PSALM 29

Praise to God in His Holiness and Majesty

A Psalm of David.

Give unto the LORD, O you mighty ones,
Give unto the LORD glory and strength.

2 Give unto the LORD the glory due to His name;
Worship the LORD in the beauty of holiness.

3 The voice of the LORD *is* over the waters;
The God of glory thunders;
The LORD *is* over many waters.

4 The voice of the LORD *is* powerful;
The voice of the LORD *is* full of majesty.

5 The voice of the LORD breaks the cedars,
Yes, the LORD splinters the cedars of Lebanon.

6 He makes them also skip like a calf,
Lebanon and Sirion like a young wild ox.

KING OF THE UNIVERSE (Ps. 29:10, 11)

The last two verses of Ps. 29 are a classic ending for hymns in the ancient world. They define Yahweh as the God who rules above all other gods. Cultures that believed in pantheons of many gods commonly honored one deity as the ruler of all the others. While the official religion of Israel considered Yahweh to be the only God, hymns could reflect Yahweh's power over the gods of popular religion.

The heavenly throne room is pictured much like the throne room of a human ruler. The king sat upon a throne raised above all others in the reception hall. Similarly, the psalmist describes Yahweh as King, sitting above "the Flood" forever (29:10). For ancient people the Flood meant the waters of chaos which still surround the created order. The waters of chaos were terrifying; they were the waters unleashed in the Flood. But as long as God reigns, He keeps them in check.

The power which is described in Ps. 29 as belonging to Yahweh is also given to God's people (29:11). Just as rulers empower people who live under their rule, so the Israelites, God's chosen people, are promised the strength of Yahweh. The psalm ends with a sense of order, kept for the benefit of Israel.

---

7 The voice of the LORD divides the
   flames of fire.

8 The voice of the LORD shakes the
   wilderness;
   The LORD shakes the Wilderness of
   Kadesh.

9 The voice of the LORD makes the deer
   give birth,
   And strips the forests bare;
   And in His temple everyone says,
   "Glory!"

10 The LORD sat *enthroned* at the Flood,
   And the LORD sits as King forever.

11 The LORD will give strength to His
   people;
   The LORD will bless His people with
   peace.

PSALM 32

The Joy of Forgiveness

A Psalm of David. A Contemplation.[a]

Blessed *is he whose* transgression *is*
   forgiven,
   Whose sin *is* covered.

2 Blessed *is* the man to whom the LORD
   does not impute iniquity,
   And in whose spirit *there is* no deceit.

3 When I kept silent, my bones grew old
   Through my groaning all the day long.

4 For day and night Your hand was
   heavy upon me;
   My vitality was turned into the
   drought of summer.   Selah

5 I acknowledged my sin to You,
   And my iniquity I have not hidden.
   I said, "I will confess my
   transgressions to the LORD,"
   And You forgave the iniquity of my
   sin.   Selah

6 For this cause everyone who is godly
   shall pray to You
   In a time when You may be found;
   Surely in a flood of great waters
   They shall not come near him.

7 You *are* my hiding place;
   You shall preserve me from trouble;
   You shall surround me with songs of
   deliverance.   Selah

8 I will instruct you and teach you in
   the way you should go;
   I will guide you with My eye.

9 Do not be like the horse *or* like the
   mule,
   Which have no understanding,
   Which must be harnessed with bit and
   bridle,
   Else they will not come near you.

10 Many sorrows *shall be* to the wicked;
   But he who trusts in the LORD, mercy
   shall surround him.

11 Be glad in the LORD and rejoice, you
   righteous;

32:title ªHebrew *Maschil*

And shout for joy, all *you* upright in
heart!

PSALM 65

Praise to God for His Salvation and Providence

To the Chief Musician. A Psalm of David.
A Song.

Praise is awaiting You, O God, in Zion;
And to You the vow shall be
performed.
2 O You who hear prayer,
To You all flesh will come.
3 Iniquities prevail against me;
As for our transgressions,
You will provide atonement for them.

4 Blessed *is the man* You choose,
And cause to approach *You,*
That he may dwell in Your courts.
We shall be satisfied with the
goodness of Your house,
Of Your holy temple.

5 *By* awesome deeds in righteousness
You will answer us,
O God of our salvation,
You who are the confidence of all the
ends of the earth,
And of the far-off seas;
6 Who established the mountains by His
strength,
Being clothed with power;
7 You who still the noise of the seas,
The noise of their waves,
And the tumult of the peoples.
8 They also who dwell in the farthest
parts are afraid of Your signs;
You make the outgoings of the
morning and evening rejoice.

9 You visit the earth and water it,
You greatly enrich it;
The river of God is full of water;
You provide their grain,
For so You have prepared it.
10 You water its ridges abundantly,
You settle its furrows;
You make it soft with showers,
You bless its growth.

11 You crown the year with Your
goodness,
And Your paths drip *with* abundance.
12 They drop *on* the pastures of the
wilderness,
And the little hills rejoice on every
side.
13 The pastures are clothed with flocks;
The valleys also are covered with
grain;
They shout for joy, they also sing.

PSALM 68

The Glory of God in His Goodness to Israel

To the Chief Musician. A Psalm of David.
A Song.

Let God arise,
Let His enemies be scattered;
Let those also who hate Him flee
before Him.
2 As smoke is driven away,
So drive *them* away;
As wax melts before the fire,
So let the wicked perish at the
presence of God.
3 But let the righteous be glad;
Let them rejoice before God;
Yes, let them rejoice exceedingly.

4 Sing to God, sing praises to His name;
Extol Him who rides on the clouds,[a]
By His name YAH,
And rejoice before Him.

5 A father of the fatherless, a defender
of widows,
Is God in His holy habitation.
6 God sets the solitary in families;

68:4 [a]Masoretic Text reads *deserts;* Targum reads
heavens (compare verse 34 and Isaiah 19:1).

GEOGRAPHY AND ENVIRONMENT

The seasons of Palestine are more accurately called wet and dry than winter and
summer. There are two rainy seasons each year. However, the variation of rain from
year to year is great, and the population was continually reminded of their dependence
on the heavens (Ps. 65:9). With no refrigeration and little distant transportation of food,
the products of the earth and the cycles of gardening were known to everyone.

EPOCH 3
1500 TO 1200 B.C.

BIBLICAL HISTORY

Moses born and taken into Pharaoh's household (c. 1526 B.C.):
Moses' mother hides her baby to save him from Pharaoh's command that all Hebrew baby boys should be killed. Pharaoh's daughter finds Moses and raises him as her own.

Moses leads the Israelites out of Egypt (c. 1446 B.C.):
Having fled from Egypt 40 years earlier, Moses returns at God's command to free his people from slavery. Pharaoh refuses, God sends plagues on the Egyptians, and the Israelites leave Egypt. God parts the Red Sea for them and they enter the Sinai Peninsula. (Dated according to the early date for the Exodus.)

The Israelites enter the Promised Land (c. 1406 B.C.):
After God gives the Law to Moses at Mount Sinai, the people refuse to enter the Promised Land and God makes them travel in the wilderness for 40 years. Finally, a new generation led by Joshua crosses the Jordan River and enters the land.

The wall of Jericho falls (c. 1406 B.C.):
The Israelites are able to conquer the walled city of Jericho when God makes its wall fall so the Israelites can end their siege of the city. Rahab the harlot, who helped the Israelites, is spared with her family.

The sun stands still for Joshua (c. 1405 B.C.):
In a battle with the Amorites, Joshua pursues them to Gibeon, but he needs more time to defeat them. So God causes the sun to stand still, extending the hours of daylight for Joshua to complete his victory.

SECULAR HISTORY

1500 B.C.

1450 B.C.

1400 B.C.

1350 B.C.

1300 B.C.

1250 B.C.

1200 B.C.

Horses are in use in Nubia in southern Egypt (c. 1660 B.C.).

The Hittites and the Egyptians are using chariots (c. 1600 B.C.).

The New Kingdom is in power in Egypt; Pharaoh moves to Memphis (c. 1500 B.C.).

Massive volcanic eruption on the Aegean island of Thera (c. 1470 B.C.).

Earliest Egyptian shadow clock (c. 1450 B.C.).

Mycenaean Greeks invade Crete, destroying the palace at Knossos (c. 1400 B.C.).

Fire in the palace at Ugarit destroys royal archives (c. 1360 B.C.).

THE EXODUS TO THE

❶ Moses, Aaron, and Miriam

These siblings provide leadership for the Israelites as they head toward the Promised Land. Moses is sent by God to tell the Pharaoh to "let my people go." Aaron is his spokesman. After the Israelites miraculously cross the Red Sea, God gives his law to Moses atop Mount Sinai.

❷ Caleb and Joshua

Israelites are sent into Canaan to "spy out the land," and most of them are intimidated by the Canaanites they find there. But Caleb and Joshua have faith in God, and they alone of the adults in Israel are allowed to live long enough to enter the Promised Land. Joshua becomes the military leader of the new generation.

❸ Deborah

The wife of Lapidoth, Deborah the prophetess and Israel's only female judge sits under a palm tree and advises her people. Deborah and her general Barak defeat the Canaanite general Sisera. The Song of Deborah in Judges 5 is a remarkable early example of Hebrew poetry.

❹ Samson

Physically strong and morally weak, this judge with a weakness for pagan women is tricked by Delilah. His strength gone, he is captured and blinded by the Philistines. Samson and many Philistines are killed when he pulls down the temple of Dagon.

United Monarchy

1500 TO 930 B.C.)

❺ Ruth

Born in Moab, Ruth returns to Bethlehem with her mother-in-law Naomi even though her husband has died. While there, she meets and marries Boaz, a wealthy farmer, and they become ancestors of David and Jesus.

❻ Samuel

Hannah prays earnestly for God to grant her a child, promising to dedicate him to God, and Samuel is born. The boy serves God under the priest Eli, then grows up to become a traveling judge and anointer of kings.

❼ Saul

The people insist on having a king, so Samuel anoints Saul of the tribe of Benjamin. He is an impressive leader, but his rashness and disobedience toward God are his undoing.

❽ David

The youngest of eight sons of Jesse of Bethlehem, David is anointed by Samuel to replace Saul. After a struggle in which David becomes a fugitive, he becomes Israel's most famous king. Many psalms are attributed to him. He has sins and weaknesses, yet he repents and God honors him and his descendants.

❾ Solomon

This son of David and Bathsheba succeeds to the throne of Israel, and is renowned for his wisdom and the wealth and splendor of his kingdom.

BIBLICAL HISTORY

For an extended time following Joshua's death, the Israelites are ruled by judges.

Deborah defeats Sisera (c. 1125 B.C.):
The judge Deborah and her general Barak battle the Canaanite king Sisera and are victorious. Deborah composes her famous victory song.

Samson defeats the Philistines (c. 1120 B.C.):
The judge Samson is tricked by Delilah and captured by the Philistines and blinded, but he brings down their temple on them as his strength returns, sacrificing his own life in the process.

Eli serves as priest and judge (c. 1100 B.C.):
Eli is priest at Shiloh. His sons are unworthy, but young Samuel is brought up under Eli's care and becomes Israel's leading prophet.

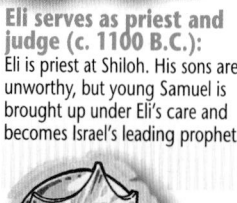

Saul becomes Israel's first king (c. 1050 B.C.):
The people demand a king like the other nations have, so against his judgment the prophet Samuel anoints Saul, a Benjamite, to be king.

David is king of Israel (c. 1010-970 B.C.):
Saul proves unworthy, so God has Samuel anoint David to be king. David slays Goliath. Later, Saul turns on David and they become enemies. Saul dies in battle, and David becomes the great king of a united kingdom.

Solomon is king of Israel (c. 970-930 B.C.):
The son of David and Bathsheba, Solomon comes to the throne as his father's successor. He gets to build the Temple in Jerusalem that had been planned by David. Solomon is known for his wealth and his wisdom.

1200 B.C.

1150 B.C.

1100 B.C.

1050 B.C.

1000 B.C.

950 B.C.

900 B.C.

SECULAR HISTORY

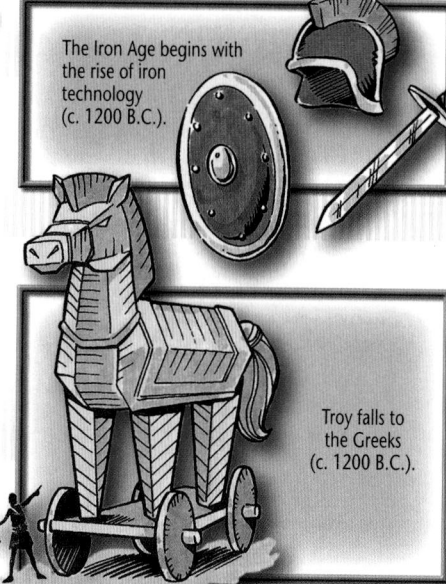

The Iron Age begins with the rise of iron technology (c. 1200 B.C.).

Troy falls to the Greeks (c. 1200 B.C.).

Lumber trade by sea between Lebanon and Egypt thrives (c. 1100 B.C.).

The temple of Hera is constructed at Olympia in Greece (c. 975 B.C.).

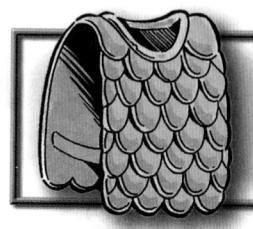

Assyrians make armor with iron scales (c. 950 B.C.).

He brings out those who are bound
   into prosperity;
But the rebellious dwell in a dry *land.*

7 O God, when You went out before Your
      people,
   When You marched through the
      wilderness,   Selah
8 The earth shook;
   The heavens also dropped *rain* at the
      presence of God;
   Sinai itself *was moved* at the presence
      of God, the God of Israel.
9 You, O God, sent a plentiful rain,
   Whereby You confirmed Your
      inheritance,
   When it was weary.
10 Your congregation dwelt in it;
   You, O God, provided from Your
      goodness for the poor.

11 The Lord gave the word;
   Great *was* the company of those who
      proclaimed *it:*
12 "Kings of armies flee, they flee,
   And she who remains at home divides
      the spoil.
13 Though you lie down among the
      sheepfolds,
   You will be like the wings of a dove
      covered with silver,
   And her feathers with yellow gold."
14 When the Almighty scattered kings in
      it,
   It was *white* as snow in Zalmon.

15 A mountain of God *is* the mountain of
      Bashan;
   A mountain *of many* peaks *is* the
      mountain of Bashan.
16 Why do you fume with envy, you
      mountains of *many* peaks?
   This is the mountain *which* God
      desires to dwell in;
   Yes, the LORD will dwell *in it* forever.

17 The chariots of God *are* twenty
      thousand,
   Even thousands of thousands;
   The Lord is among them *as in* Sinai,
      in the Holy *Place.*
18 You have ascended on high,
   You have led captivity captive;
   You have received gifts among men,
   Even *from* the rebellious,
   That the LORD God might dwell *there.*

19 Blessed *be* the Lord,
   Who daily loads us *with benefits,*
   The God of our salvation!   Selah
20 Our God *is* the God of salvation;
   And to GOD the Lord *belong* escapes
      from death.

21 But God will wound the head of His
      enemies,
   The hairy scalp of the one who still
      goes on in his trespasses.
22 The Lord said, "I will bring back from
      Bashan,
   I will bring *them* back from the depths
      of the sea,
23 That your foot may crush *them*[a] in
      blood,
   And the tongues of your dogs *may
      have* their portion from *your*
      enemies."

24 They have seen Your procession,
      O God,
   The procession of my God, my King,
      into the sanctuary.
25 The singers went before, the players
      on instruments *followed* after;
   Among *them were* the maidens playing
      timbrels.
26 Bless God in the congregations,
   The Lord, from the fountain of Israel.
27 There *is* little Benjamin, their leader,
   The princes of Judah *and* their
      company,
   The princes of Zebulun *and* the
      princes of Naphtali.

28 Your God has commanded[a] your
      strength;

68:23 [a]Septuagint, Syriac, Targum, and Vulgate read
you may dip your foot.   68:28 [a]Septuagint, Syriac,
Targum, and Vulgate read *Command, O God.*

GEOGRAPHY AND ENVIRONMENT

*Zalmon is evidently a mountain in Bashan, but is not positively identified (Ps. 68:14).
Bashan was east of the Sea of Galilee and reached as far as Mount Hermon, the
highest mountain in Palestine. Usually there is snow on Mount Hermon, and its beauty is
proverbial. The very striking poetic imagery of Ps. 68 sometimes presents difficulties for
interpretation.*

WHEN GOD IS ANGRY (Ps. 103:8, 9)

Stilling the gods' anger is a common theme in ancient Near Eastern literature. An Accadian epic text from at least the 8th century B.C. in Mesopotamia is *The Epic of Erra*, a narrative poem about the chief deity Marduk; his protagonist, the god Erra; and Erra's advisor, the god Ishum. The anger displayed by Erra can be contrasted with the anger that characterizes Yahweh in the Old Testament.

At one point in the Accadian poem, Erra becomes enraged and decides to ravage countries and their populations. Ishum pacifies him and a remnant escapes. Erra recognizes his blunder in attacking the divine leadership of Marduk and his subjects—humankind. Thus, Erra praises Ishum for his rational calm in the face of Erra's great rage.

Although this text shares a common literary theme with the Bible, the incipient polytheism of the text betrays a marked difference from the monotheism of Israel. The anger of various ancient Near Eastern deities had to be restrained, usually by other deities who intervened on behalf of humans. In contrast, Israel understood that there were no other gods who could intervene when Yahweh was angry. Yet Yahweh restrains His own anger. The psalmist declares that Yahweh is "slow to anger" and will not "keep His anger forever" (Ps. 103:8, 9).

Ancient Near Eastern gods often became angry for petty reasons. The god Erra makes mistakes and allows his anger to get the best of him. The God of Israel neither makes a mistake nor becomes so infuriated that He loses control. Anger is not a basic part of Yahweh's personality; rather, He is "merciful and gracious" (Ps. 103:8).

Strengthen, O God, what You have
done for us.
29 Because of Your temple at Jerusalem,
Kings will bring presents to You.
30 Rebuke the beasts of the reeds,
The herd of bulls with the calves of the
peoples,
Till everyone submits himself with
pieces of silver.
Scatter the peoples *who* delight in
war.
31 Envoys will come out of Egypt;
Ethiopia will quickly stretch out her
hands to God.

32 Sing to God, you kingdoms of the
earth;
Oh, sing praises to the Lord,   Selah
33 To Him who rides on the heaven of
heavens, *which were* of old!
Indeed, He sends out His voice, a
mighty voice.
34 Ascribe strength to God;
His excellence *is* over Israel,
And His strength *is* in the clouds.
35 O God, *You are* more awesome than
Your holy places.
The God of Israel *is* He who gives
strength and power to *His* people.

Blessed *be* God!

PSALM 103

Praise for the LORD's Mercies

A Psalm *of David*.

Bless the LORD, O my soul;
And all that is within me, *bless* His
holy name!
2 Bless the LORD, O my soul,
And forget not all His benefits:
3 Who forgives all your iniquities,
Who heals all your diseases,
4 Who redeems your life from
destruction,
Who crowns you with lovingkindness
and tender mercies,
5 Who satisfies your mouth with good
things,
So that your youth is renewed like the
eagle's.

6 The LORD executes righteousness
And justice for all who are oppressed.
7 He made known His ways to Moses,
His acts to the children of Israel.
8 The LORD *is* merciful and gracious,
Slow to anger, and abounding in
mercy.
9 He will not always strive *with us,*
Nor will He keep *His anger* forever.
10 He has not dealt with us according to
our sins,

KINGDOMS OF SYRIA AND PALESTINE

Syria refers to the region north of Palestine, which was associated with the city-state of Damascus. In ancient times Syria was known as Aram. Since Syria and Palestine rarely knew political unity, various kingdoms inhabited these regions.

Kingdom	Approximate Period	Important Rulers
Ebla	2400–2250 B.C.	Igris-Halam, Irkab-Damu
Alalakh	1800–1400 B.C.	Yamhad, Yarim-Lim, Idrimi
Ugarit	1400–1180 B.C.	Niqmaddu II
Sea Peoples	1200–1050 B.C.	Seafaring peoples including the Philistines
Aram-Damascus	1050–732 B.C.	Rezon, Hadad-ezer (Ben-Hadad), Hazael
Phoenicia	1050–340 B.C.	Hiram I, Ethbaal I
United Israel	1050 (or 1020)–930 B.C.	Saul, David, Solomon
Israel	930–722 B.C.	Jeroboam I, Ahab, Jehu
Judah	930–586 B.C.	Rehoboam, Hezekiah, Josiah

Nor punished us according to our
iniquities.
11 For as the heavens are high above the
earth,
So great is His mercy toward those
who fear Him;
12 As far as the east is from the west,
So far has He removed our
transgressions from us.
13 As a father pities *his* children,
So the LORD pities those who fear
Him.
14 For He knows our frame;
He remembers that we *are* dust.

15 *As for* man, his days *are* like grass;
As a flower of the field, so he
flourishes.
16 For the wind passes over it, and it is
gone,
And its place remembers it no more.[a]
17 But the mercy of the LORD *is* from
everlasting to everlasting
On those who fear Him,
And His righteousness to children's
children,
18 To such as keep His covenant,
And to those who remember His
commandments to do them.

19 The LORD has established His throne
in heaven,
And His kingdom rules over all.

20 Bless the LORD, you His angels,
Who excel in strength, who do His
word,
Heeding the voice of His word.
21 Bless the LORD, all *you* His hosts,
You ministers of His, who do His
pleasure.
22 Bless the LORD, all His works,
In all places of His dominion.

Bless the LORD, O my soul!

PSALM 108

Assurance of God's Victory over Enemies

A Song. A Psalm of David.

O God, my heart is steadfast;
I will sing and give praise, even with
my glory.
2 Awake, lute and harp!
I will awaken the dawn.
3 I will praise You, O LORD, among the
peoples,
And I will sing praises to You among
the nations.
4 For Your mercy *is* great above the
heavens,
And Your truth *reaches* to the clouds.

5 Be exalted, O God, above the heavens,
And Your glory above all the earth;
6 That Your beloved may be delivered,
Save *with* Your right hand, and hear
me.

103:16 ªCompare Job 7:10

7   God has spoken in His holiness:
    "I will rejoice;
    I will divide Shechem
    And measure out the Valley of
        Succoth.
8   Gilead *is* Mine; Manasseh *is* Mine;
    Ephraim also *is* the helmet for My
        head;
    Judah *is* My lawgiver.
9   Moab *is* My washpot;
    Over Edom I will cast My shoe;
    Over Philistia I will triumph."

10 Who will bring me *into* the strong
        city?
    Who will lead me to Edom?
11 *Is it* not *You,* O God, *who* cast us off?
    And *You,* O God, *who* did not go out
        with our armies?
12 Give us help from trouble,
    For the help of man is useless.
13 Through God we will do valiantly,
    For *it is* He *who* shall tread down our
        enemies.[a]

PSALM 138

The LORD's Goodness to the Faithful

A Psalm *of David.*

I will praise You with my whole heart;
    Before the gods I will sing praises to
        You.
2   I will worship toward Your holy
        temple,
    And praise Your name
    For Your lovingkindness and Your
        truth;
    For You have magnified Your word
        above all Your name.
3   In the day when I cried out, You
        answered me,
    And made me bold *with* strength in
        my soul.

4   All the kings of the earth shall praise
        You, O LORD,
    When they hear the words of Your
        mouth.
5   Yes, they shall sing of the ways of the
        LORD,
    For great *is* the glory of the LORD.
6   Though the LORD *is* on high,
    Yet He regards the lowly;
    But the proud He knows from afar.

7   Though I walk in the midst of trouble,
        You will revive me;

You will stretch out Your hand
    Against the wrath of my enemies,
    And Your right hand will save me.
8   The LORD will perfect *that which*
        concerns me;
    Your mercy, O LORD, *endures* forever;
    Do not forsake the works of Your
        hands.

Music in the Temple

One aspect of the Chronicler's emphasis on the temple is his interest in the different priestly duties, particularly in the musical service. In the genealogical introduction to 1 Chronicles (1 Chr. 1:1—9:34), more space is given to the Levitical musicians than to some entire tribes (see 6:31–48 and "Priestly Genealogies" at 1 Chr. 1:1).

The prophetic account in 2 Sam. 6:12–19 mentions the sound of music when the ark was brought to Jerusalem. The Chronicler, however, provides much more detail about that music and stresses the role of the Levites in this event. There were Levites carrying the ark, as well as singing and playing instruments (1 Chr. 15:2, 15, 16, 28). Once the ark was in Jerusalem, David began to organize the service of the Jerusalem sanctuary. One of his first actions was to appoint the Levitical musicians and their three leaders: Asaph, Heman, and Jeduthun (1 Chr. 16:37, 41, 42; see 2 Chr. 5:12).

■ 1 Chronicles 16:1–43

1 Chronicles
The Ark Placed in the Tabernacle

16 :1 So they brought the ark of God, and set it in the midst of the tabernacle that David had erected for it. Then they offered burnt offerings and peace offerings before God. ²And when David had finished offering the burnt offerings and the peace offerings, he blessed the people in the name of the LORD. ³Then he distributed to everyone of Israel, both man and woman, to everyone a loaf of bread, a piece *of meat,* and a cake of raisins.

⁴And he appointed some of the Levites to minister before the ark of the LORD, to commemorate, to thank, and to praise the LORD God of Israel: ⁵Asaph the chief, and next to him Zechariah, *then* Jeiel, Shemiramoth, Jehiel, Mattithiah, Eliab,

---

108:13 ᵃCompare verses 6–13 with 60:5–12

Benaiah, and Obed-Edom: Jeiel with stringed instruments and harps, but Asaph made music with cymbals; [6]Benaiah and Jahaziel the priests regularly *blew* the trumpets before the ark of the covenant of God.

David's Song of Thanksgiving

[7]On that day David first delivered *this psalm* into the hand of Asaph and his brethren, to thank the LORD:

8 Oh, give thanks to the LORD!
Call upon His name;
Make known His deeds among the peoples!

9 Sing to Him, sing psalms to Him;
Talk of all His wondrous works!

10 Glory in His holy name;
Let the hearts of those rejoice who seek the LORD!

11 Seek the LORD and His strength;
Seek His face evermore!

12 Remember His marvelous works which He has done,
His wonders, and the judgments of His mouth,

13 O seed of Israel His servant,
You children of Jacob, His chosen ones!

14 He *is* the LORD our God;
His judgments *are* in all the earth.

15 Remember His covenant forever,
The word which He commanded, for a thousand generations,

16 *The* covenant which He made with Abraham,
And His oath to Isaac,

17 And confirmed it to Jacob for a statute,
To Israel *for* an everlasting covenant,

18 Saying, "To you I will give the land of Canaan
As the allotment of your inheritance,"

19 When you were few in number,
Indeed very few, and strangers in it.

20 When they went from one nation to another,
And from *one* kingdom to another people,

21 He permitted no man to do them wrong;
Yes, He rebuked kings for their sakes,

22 *Saying,* "Do not touch My anointed ones,
And do My prophets no harm."[a]

23 Sing to the LORD, all the earth;
Proclaim the good news of His salvation from day to day.

24 Declare His glory among the nations,
His wonders among all peoples.

25 For the LORD *is* great and greatly to be praised;
He *is* also to be feared above all gods.

26 For all the gods of the peoples *are* idols,
But the LORD made the heavens.

27 Honor and majesty *are* before Him;
Strength and gladness are in His place.

28 Give to the LORD, O families of the peoples,
Give to the LORD glory and strength.

29 Give to the LORD the glory *due* His name;
Bring an offering, and come before Him.
Oh, worship the LORD in the beauty of holiness!

30 Tremble before Him, all the earth.
The world also is firmly established,
It shall not be moved.

31 Let the heavens rejoice, and let the earth be glad;
And let them say among the nations,
"The LORD reigns."

32 Let the sea roar, and all its fullness;
Let the field rejoice, and all that *is* in it.

33 Then the trees of the woods shall rejoice before the LORD,
For He is coming to judge the earth.[a]

34 Oh, give thanks to the LORD, for *He is* good!
For His mercy *endures* forever.[a]

35 And say, "Save us, O God of our salvation;
Gather us together, and deliver us from the Gentiles,
To give thanks to Your holy name,
To triumph in Your praise."

16:22 [a]Compare verses 8–22 with Psalm 105:1–15   16:33 [a]Compare verses 23–33 with Psalm 96:1–13   16:34 [a]Compare verse 34 with Psalm 106:1

THERE ARE GODS AND THEN THERE IS GOD (Ps. 96:5)

Hymns of praise in the ancient Near East often declared the god being praised to be superior to all other gods. The Bible occasionally uses that kind of language, but more often goes beyond it and says that Yahweh is the only God.

One way of dismissing other gods was to say they were only statues. The supposed "gods of the peoples" are nothing more than the inanimate idols themselves (Ps. 96:5). Yahweh is declared the true deity because only He created the world—"the LORD made the heavens" (96:5). All other gods are impotent and unworthy of adoration; they should be ignored. People who could mistake stone, metal, or wood for a real god are foolish.

A second way of dismissing other gods was to leave open the possibility they existed, yet maintain that they had no serious power and therefore were not to be taken seriously. The prophet Jeremiah, for example, says that other gods did not create the world and will therefore cease to exist (Jer. 10:11). Their insignificance is stressed by their being placed lower than Yahweh in divine authority.

In this way, the Hebrew poets were able to adapt the usual language of Near Eastern hymns into the worship of Yahweh. To Israel and Judah only Yahweh mattered. The other deities either did not exist or were so meaningless that whether they existed was irrelevant. Yahweh was "to be feared above all gods" (Ps. 96:4).

---

36 Blessed *be* the LORD God of Israel
From everlasting to everlasting![a]

And all the people said, "Amen!" and praised the LORD.

Regular Worship Maintained

37So he left Asaph and his brothers there before the ark of the covenant of the LORD to minister before the ark regularly, as every day's work required; 38and Obed-Edom with his sixty-eight brethren, including Obed-Edom the son of Jeduthun, and Hosah, *to be* gatekeepers; 39and Zadok the priest and his brethren the priests, before the tabernacle of the LORD at the high place that *was* at Gibeon, 40to offer burnt offerings to the LORD on the altar of burnt offering regularly morning and evening, and *to do* according to all that is written in the Law of the LORD which He commanded Israel; 41and with them Heman and Jeduthun and the rest who were chosen, who were designated by name, to give thanks to the LORD, because His mercy *endures* forever; 42and with them Heman and Jeduthun, to sound aloud with trumpets and cymbals and the musical instruments of God. Now the sons of Jeduthun *were* gatekeepers.

43Then all the people departed, every man to his house; and David returned to bless his house.

Psalms of the Musicians

When the ark was placed in the tabernacle, David gave a psalm to the Levitical singers under Asaph, Heman, and Jeduthun to perform (1 Chr. 16:1, 7–36). The various sections of this psalm also appear in three independent psalms: Ps. 96; 105; 106. (1 Chr. 16:8–22 = Ps. 105:1–15; 1 Chr. 16:23–33 = Ps. 96:1–13; 1 Chr. 16:34–36 = Ps. 106:1, 47, 48.)

The names of Asaph, Heman, and Jeduthun appear in the superscriptions of several psalms. Two psalms (Ps. 39; 62) are identified as being by David and given by name to Jeduthun. Another psalm (Ps. 77) is ascribed to Asaph, but given to Jeduthun. Many other psalms are ascribed to Asaph (Ps. 50; 73—83) and one (Ps. 88) to Heman.

■ Psalms 96; 105; 106; 39; 62; 50; 73—83; 88

PSALM 96

A Song of Praise to God Coming in Judgment

Oh, sing to the LORD a new song!
Sing to the LORD, all the earth.
2 Sing to the LORD, bless His name;
Proclaim the good news of His
salvation from day to day.

16:36 [a]Compare verses 35, 36 with Psalm 106:47, 48

3 Declare His glory among the nations,
   His wonders among all peoples.

4 For the LORD *is* great and greatly to
      be praised;
   He *is* to be feared above all gods.
5 For all the gods of the peoples *are*
      idols,
   But the LORD made the heavens.
6 Honor and majesty *are* before Him;
   Strength and beauty *are* in His
      sanctuary.

7 Give to the LORD, O families of the
      peoples,
   Give to the LORD glory and strength.
8 Give to the LORD the glory *due* His
      name;
   Bring an offering, and come into His
      courts.
9 Oh, worship the LORD in the beauty of
      holiness!
   Tremble before Him, all the earth.

10 Say among the nations, "The LORD
      reigns;
   The world also is firmly established,
   It shall not be moved;
   He shall judge the peoples
      righteously."

11 Let the heavens rejoice, and let the
      earth be glad;
   Let the sea roar, and all its fullness;
12 Let the field be joyful, and all that *is*
      in it.
   Then all the trees of the woods will
      rejoice before the LORD.
13 For He is coming, for He is coming to
      judge the earth.
   He shall judge the world with
      righteousness,
   And the peoples with His truth.

PSALM 105

The Eternal Faithfulness of the LORD

Oh, give thanks to the LORD!
   Call upon His name;
   Make known His deeds among the
      peoples!
2 Sing to Him, sing psalms to Him;
   Talk of all His wondrous works!
3 Glory in His holy name;
   Let the hearts of those rejoice who
      seek the LORD!
4 Seek the LORD and His strength;
   Seek His face evermore!

5 Remember His marvelous works
      which He has done,
   His wonders, and the judgments of
      His mouth,
6 O seed of Abraham His servant,
   You children of Jacob, His chosen
      ones!

7 He *is* the LORD our God;
   His judgments *are* in all the earth.
8 He remembers His covenant forever,
   The word *which* He commanded, for a
      thousand generations,
9 *The covenant* which He made with
      Abraham,
   And His oath to Isaac,
10 And confirmed it to Jacob for a
      statute,
   To Israel *as* an everlasting covenant,
11 Saying, "To you I will give the land of
      Canaan
   As the allotment of your inheritance,"
12 When they were few in number,
   Indeed very few, and strangers in it.

13 When they went from one nation to
      another,
   From *one* kingdom to another people,
14 He permitted no one to do them
      wrong;
   Yes, He rebuked kings for their sakes,
15 *Saying,* "Do not touch My anointed
      ones,
   And do My prophets no harm."

16 Moreover He called for a famine in the
      land;
   He destroyed all the provision of
      bread.
17 He sent a man before them—
   Joseph—*who* was sold as a slave.
18 They hurt his feet with fetters,
   He was laid in irons.
19 Until the time that his word came to
      pass,
   The word of the LORD tested him.
20 The king sent and released him,
   The ruler of the people let him go free.
21 He made him lord of his house,
   And ruler of all his possessions,
22 To bind his princes at his pleasure,
   And teach his elders wisdom.

23 Israel also came into Egypt,
   And Jacob dwelt in the land of Ham.
24 He increased His people greatly,
   And made them stronger than their
      enemies.

25 He turned their heart to hate His
    people,
    To deal craftily with His servants.

26 He sent Moses His servant,
    And Aaron whom He had chosen.
27 They performed His signs among them,
    And wonders in the land of Ham.
28 He sent darkness, and made *it* dark;
    And they did not rebel against His
    word.
29 He turned their waters into blood,
    And killed their fish.
30 Their land abounded with frogs,
    Even in the chambers of their kings.
31 He spoke, and there came swarms of
    flies,
    And lice in all their territory.
32 He gave them hail for rain,
    And flaming fire in their land.
33 He struck their vines also, and their
    fig trees,
    And splintered the trees of their
    territory.
34 He spoke, and locusts came,
    Young locusts without number,
35 And ate up all the vegetation in their
    land,
    And devoured the fruit of their ground.
36 He also destroyed all the firstborn in
    their land,
    The first of all their strength.

37 He also brought them out with silver
    and gold,
    And *there was* none feeble among His
    tribes.
38 Egypt was glad when they departed,
    For the fear of them had fallen upon
    them.
39 He spread a cloud for a covering,
    And fire to give light in the night.
40 *The people* asked, and He brought
    quail,
    And satisfied them with the bread of
    heaven.
41 He opened the rock, and water gushed
    out;
    It ran in the dry places *like* a river.

42 For He remembered His holy promise,
    And Abraham His servant.
43 He brought out His people with joy,
    His chosen ones with gladness.
44 He gave them the lands of the
    Gentiles,
    And they inherited the labor of the
    nations,
45 That they might observe His statutes
    And keep His laws.

Praise the LORD!

PSALM 106

Joy in Forgiveness of Israel's Sins

Praise the LORD!

Oh, give thanks to the LORD, for *He is*
    good!
For His mercy *endures* forever.

2 Who can utter the mighty acts of the
    LORD?
    Who can declare all His praise?
3 Blessed *are* those who keep justice,
    And he who does[a] righteousness at all
    times!

4 Remember me, O LORD, with the favor
    You have toward Your people.
    Oh, visit me with Your salvation,
5 That I may see the benefit of Your
    chosen ones,
    That I may rejoice in the gladness of
    Your nation,
    That I may glory with Your
    inheritance.

6 We have sinned with our fathers,
    We have committed iniquity,
    We have done wickedly.
7 Our fathers in Egypt did not
    understand Your wonders;

106:3 [a]Septuagint, Syriac, Targum, and Vulgate read
those who do.

ARTS AND LITERATURE

*The Hebrew Bible contains several references to Israel's past, especially to God's past
works on the people's behalf. Certain of the psalms rehearse in some detail the history
that is related to the exodus from Egypt, asserting its relevance to the succeeding
generations. In Ps. 106, not only the Exodus, but also the rebellion in the wilderness is
recounted (106:7–33).*

Worshiping Ancestors as Gods (Ps. 106:28)

The deification of ancestors was common throughout the ancient world. The mythological texts from Ugarit (1400–1200 B.C.) make reference to "rulers" in the netherworld who formerly had been monarchs in the human realm. These deceased humans were treated as minor deities, having religious feasts held in their honor. Even in ancient Palestine, the excavations of graves have sometimes uncovered tubes built into the ground so that communication and food could be delivered to the deceased.

Ancestor worship is not common in the Bible. There is one Canaanite practice mentioned, however, by which famous or important dead persons had become deities of the underworld. The psalmist reports that the Israelites "ate sacrifices made to the dead" (Ps. 106:28). The practice is associated with the "Baal of Peor" incident, indicating that the Israelites encountered the custom as they moved toward the Promised Land.

The Law of Moses made it unacceptable to treat any human as a god, whether living or dead (Ex. 20:2; Deut. 26:14). The Israelites who engaged in the regional religious belief of eating sacrifices for the dead were considered to have turned away from the one true God and "provoked Him to anger" (Ps. 106:29). To honor the memory of one's ancestors was desirable, but such honor must not pass over into worship.

They did not remember the multitude of Your mercies,
But rebelled by the sea—the Red Sea.

8 Nevertheless He saved them for His name's sake,
That He might make His mighty power known.

9 He rebuked the Red Sea also, and it dried up;
So He led them through the depths,
As through the wilderness.

10 He saved them from the hand of him who hated *them,*
And redeemed them from the hand of the enemy.

11 The waters covered their enemies;
There was not one of them left.

12 Then they believed His words;
They sang His praise.

13 They soon forgot His works;
They did not wait for His counsel,

14 But lusted exceedingly in the wilderness,
And tested God in the desert.

15 And He gave them their request,
But sent leanness into their soul.

16 When they envied Moses in the camp,
And Aaron the saint of the LORD,

17 The earth opened up and swallowed Dathan,
And covered the faction of Abiram.

18 A fire was kindled in their company;
The flame burned up the wicked.

19 They made a calf in Horeb,
And worshiped the molded image.

20 Thus they changed their glory
Into the image of an ox that eats grass.

21 They forgot God their Savior,
Who had done great things in Egypt,

22 Wondrous works in the land of Ham,
Awesome things by the Red Sea.

23 Therefore He said that He would destroy them,
Had not Moses His chosen one stood before Him in the breach,
To turn away His wrath, lest He destroy *them.*

24 Then they despised the pleasant land;
They did not believe His word,

25 But complained in their tents,
And did not heed the voice of the LORD.

26 Therefore He raised His hand *in an oath* against them,
To overthrow them in the wilderness,

27 To overthrow their descendants among the nations,
And to scatter them in the lands.

28 They joined themselves also to Baal of Peor,
And ate sacrifices made to the dead.

29 Thus they provoked *Him* to anger with their deeds,
And the plague broke out among them.

30 Then Phinehas stood up and
  intervened,
  And the plague was stopped.
31 And that was accounted to him for
  righteousness
  To all generations forevermore.

32 They angered *Him* also at the waters
  of strife,[a]
  So that it went ill with Moses on
  account of them;
33 Because they rebelled against His
  Spirit,
  So that he spoke rashly with his lips.

34 They did not destroy the peoples,
  Concerning whom the LORD had
  commanded them,
35 But they mingled with the Gentiles
  And learned their works;
36 They served their idols,
  Which became a snare to them.
37 They even sacrificed their sons
  And their daughters to demons,
38 And shed innocent blood,
  The blood of their sons and daughters,
  Whom they sacrificed to the idols of
  Canaan;
  And the land was polluted with blood.
39 Thus they were defiled by their own
  works,
  And played the harlot by their own
  deeds.

40 Therefore the wrath of the LORD was
  kindled against His people,
  So that He abhorred His own
  inheritance.
41 And He gave them into the hand of
  the Gentiles,
  And those who hated them ruled over
  them.
42 Their enemies also oppressed them,
  And they were brought into subjection
  under their hand.
43 Many times He delivered them;
  But they rebelled in their counsel,
  And were brought low for their
  iniquity.

44 Nevertheless He regarded their
  affliction,
  When He heard their cry;
45 And for their sake He remembered
  His covenant,
  And relented according to the
  multitude of His mercies.
46 He also made them to be pitied
  By all those who carried them away
  captive.

47 Save us, O LORD our God,
  And gather us from among the
  Gentiles,
  To give thanks to Your holy name,
  To triumph in Your praise.

48 Blessed *be* the LORD God of Israel
  From everlasting to everlasting!
  And let all the people say, "Amen!"

  Praise the LORD!

PSALM 39

Prayer for Wisdom and Forgiveness

*To the Chief Musician. To Jeduthun. A Psalm of
David.*

I said, "I will guard my ways,
  Lest I sin with my tongue;
  I will restrain my mouth with a
  muzzle,
  While the wicked are before me."
2 I was mute with silence,
  I held my peace *even* from good;
  And my sorrow was stirred up.
3 My heart was hot within me;
  While I was musing, the fire burned.
  Then I spoke with my tongue:

4 "LORD, make me to know my end,
  And what *is* the measure of my days,
  That I may know how frail I *am*.
5 Indeed, You have made my days *as*
  handbreadths,
  And my age *is* as nothing before You;
  Certainly every man at his best state
    is but vapor.   Selah
6 Surely every man walks about like a
  shadow;
  Surely they busy themselves in vain;
  He heaps up *riches,*
  And does not know who will gather
  them.

7 "And now, Lord, what do I wait for?
  My hope *is* in You.
8 Deliver me from all my transgressions;
  Do not make me the reproach of the
  foolish.
9 I was mute, I did not open my mouth,
  Because it was You who did *it.*
10 Remove Your plague from me;
  I am consumed by the blow of Your
  hand.

106:32 [a]Or *Meribah*

11 When with rebukes You correct man
    for iniquity,
  You make his beauty melt away like a
    moth;
  Surely every man *is* vapor.   Selah

12 "Hear my prayer, O LORD,
  And give ear to my cry;
  Do not be silent at my tears;
  For I *am* a stranger with You,
  A sojourner, as all my fathers *were.*
13 Remove Your gaze from me, that I
    may regain strength,
  Before I go away and am no more."

PSALM 62

A Calm Resolve to Wait for the Salvation of God

To the Chief Musician. To Jeduthun. A Psalm of David.

Truly my soul silently *waits* for God;
  From Him *comes* my salvation.
2 He only *is* my rock and my salvation;
  He is my defense;
  I shall not be greatly moved.

3 How long will you attack a man?
  You shall be slain, all of you,
  Like a leaning wall and a tottering
    fence.
4 They only consult to cast *him* down
    from his high position;
  They delight in lies;
  They bless with their mouth,
  But they curse inwardly.   Selah

5 My soul, wait silently for God alone,
  For my expectation *is* from Him.
6 He only *is* my rock and my salvation;
  He is my defense;
  I shall not be moved.
7 In God *is* my salvation and my glory;
  The rock of my strength,
  And my refuge, *is* in God.

8 Trust in Him at all times, you people;
  Pour out your heart before Him;
  God *is* a refuge for us.   Selah

9 Surely men of low degree *are* a vapor,
  Men of high degree *are* a lie;
  If they are weighed on the scales,
  They *are* altogether *lighter* than vapor.
10 Do not trust in oppression,
  Nor vainly hope in robbery;

If riches increase,
Do not set *your* heart *on them.*

11 God has spoken once,
  Twice I have heard this:
  That power *belongs* to God.
12 Also to You, O Lord, *belongs* mercy;
  For You render to each one according
    to his work.

PSALM 50

God the Righteous Judge

A Psalm of Asaph.

The Mighty One, God the LORD,
  Has spoken and called the earth
  From the rising of the sun to its going
    down.
2 Out of Zion, the perfection of beauty,
  God will shine forth.
3 Our God shall come, and shall not
    keep silent;
  A fire shall devour before Him,
  And it shall be very tempestuous all
    around Him.

4 He shall call to the heavens from
    above,
  And to the earth, that He may judge
    His people:
5 "Gather My saints together to Me,
  Those who have made a covenant with
    Me by sacrifice."
6 Let the heavens declare His
    righteousness,
  For God Himself *is* Judge.   Selah

7 "Hear, O My people, and I will speak,
  O Israel, and I will testify against you;
  I *am* God, your God!
8 I will not rebuke you for your sacrifices
  Or your burnt offerings,
  Which are continually before Me.
9 I will not take a bull from your house,
  Nor goats out of your folds.
10 For every beast of the forest *is* Mine,
  And the cattle on a thousand hills.
11 I know all the birds of the mountains,
  And the wild beasts of the field *are*
    Mine.

12 "If I were hungry, I would not tell you;
  For the world *is* Mine, and all its
    fullness.
13 Will I eat the flesh of bulls,
  Or drink the blood of goats?
14 Offer to God thanksgiving,

And pay your vows to the Most High.

15 Call upon Me in the day of trouble;
I will deliver you, and you shall
glorify Me."

16 But to the wicked God says:
"What *right* have you to declare My
statutes,
Or take My covenant in your mouth,
17 Seeing you hate instruction
And cast My words behind you?
18 When you saw a thief, you consented[a]
with him,
And have been a partaker with
adulterers.
19 You give your mouth to evil,
And your tongue frames deceit.
20 You sit *and* speak against your
brother;
You slander your own mother's son.
21 These *things* you have done, and I
kept silent;
You thought that I was altogether like
you;
But I will rebuke you,
And set *them* in order before your
eyes.

22 "Now consider this, you who forget
God,
Lest I tear *you* in pieces,
And *there be* none to deliver:
23 Whoever offers praise glorifies Me;
And to him who orders *his* conduct
aright
I will show the salvation of God."

PSALM 73

The Tragedy of the Wicked, and the Blessedness of Trust in God

A Psalm of Asaph.

Truly God *is* good to Israel,
To such as are pure in heart.
2 But as for me, my feet had almost
stumbled;
My steps had nearly slipped.
3 For I *was* envious of the boastful,

When I saw the prosperity of the
wicked.

4 For *there are* no pangs in their death,
But their strength *is* firm.
5 They *are* not in trouble *as other* men,
Nor are they plagued like *other* men.
6 Therefore pride serves as their
necklace;
Violence covers them *like* a garment.
7 Their eyes bulge[a] with abundance;
They have more than heart could
wish.
8 They scoff and speak wickedly
concerning oppression;
They speak loftily.
9 They set their mouth against the
heavens,
And their tongue walks through the
earth.

10 Therefore his people return here,
And waters of a full *cup* are drained by
them.
11 And they say, "How does God know?
And is there knowledge in the Most
High?"
12 Behold, these *are* the ungodly,
Who are always at ease;
They increase *in* riches.
13 Surely I have cleansed my heart *in*
vain,
And washed my hands in innocence.
14 For all day long I have been plagued,
And chastened every morning.

15 If I had said, "I will speak thus,"
Behold, I would have been untrue to
the generation of Your children.
16 When I thought *how* to understand
this,
It *was* too painful for me—
17 Until I went into the sanctuary of
God;
Then I understood their end.

50:18 [a]Septuagint, Syriac, Targum, and Vulgate read
ran. 73:7 [a]Targum reads *face bulges;* Septuagint,
Syriac, and Vulgate read *iniquity bulges*.

RELIGION AND WORSHIP

*When food, whether meat or vegetable, was offered in sacrifice, there was a natural
suggestion that the worshiper was providing sustenance for the god or gods being
worshiped. In the Old Testament sacrifices were required by Israel's God. Yet the Psalms
reveal a sharp polemic against any such misinterpretation of the sacrifices. Yahweh
declares, "If I were hungry, I would not tell you" (Ps. 50:12).*

18 Surely You set them in slippery
    places;
    You cast them down to destruction.
19 Oh, how they are *brought* to
    desolation, as in a moment!
    They are utterly consumed with
    terrors.
20 As a dream when *one* awakes,
    So, Lord, when You awake,
    You shall despise their image.

21 Thus my heart was grieved,
    And I was vexed in my mind.
22 I *was* so foolish and ignorant;
    I was *like* a beast before You.
23 Nevertheless I *am* continually with
    You;
    You hold *me* by my right hand.
24 You will guide me with Your counsel,
    And afterward receive me *to* glory.

25 Whom have I in heaven *but You?*
    And *there is* none upon earth *that* I
    desire besides You.
26 My flesh and my heart fail;
    But God *is* the strength of my heart
    and my portion forever.

27 For indeed, those who are far from
    You shall perish;
    You have destroyed all those who
    desert You for harlotry.
28 But *it is* good for me to draw near to
    God;
    I have put my trust in the Lord GOD,
    That I may declare all Your works.

PSALM 74

A Plea for Relief from Oppressors

A Contemplation[a] *of Asaph.*

O God, why have You cast *us* off forever?
    Why does Your anger smoke against
    the sheep of Your pasture?
2 Remember Your congregation, *which*
    You have purchased of old,

74:title [a]Hebrew *Maschil*

    The tribe of Your inheritance, *which*
    You have redeemed—
    This Mount Zion where You have
    dwelt.
3 Lift up Your feet to the perpetual
    desolations.
    The enemy has damaged everything
    in the sanctuary.
4 Your enemies roar in the midst of Your
    meeting place;
    They set up their banners *for* signs.
5 They seem like men who lift up
    Axes among the thick trees.
6 And now they break down its carved
    work, all at once,
    With axes and hammers.
7 They have set fire to Your sanctuary;
    They have defiled the dwelling place
    of Your name to the ground.
8 They said in their hearts,
    "Let us destroy them altogether."
    They have burned up all the meeting
    places of God in the land.

9 We do not see our signs;
    There is no longer any prophet;
    Nor *is there* any among us who knows
    how long.
10 O God, how long will the adversary
    reproach?
    Will the enemy blaspheme Your name
    forever?
11 Why do You withdraw Your hand, even
    Your right hand?
    Take it out of Your bosom and destroy
    them.
12 For God *is* my King from of old,
    Working salvation in the midst of the
    earth.
13 You divided the sea by Your strength;
    You broke the heads of the sea
    serpents in the waters.
14 You broke the heads of Leviathan in
    pieces,
    And gave him *as* food to the people
    inhabiting the wilderness.
15 You broke open the fountain and the
    flood;
    You dried up mighty rivers.

CULTURE AND SOCIETY

Standards of physical beauty have a natural and a social component. In many cultures fat is praised, presumably because it is a sign of wealth to have enough to eat. The psalm writer's judgment concerning prosperity is influenced by moral considerations of the pride, arrogance, and cruelty that wealth seems to encourage. The prosperity of wicked persons is transitory, no more permanent than a dream (Ps. 73:3, 19, 20).

16 The day *is* Yours, the night also *is*
    Yours;
    You have prepared the light and the
    sun.
17 You have set all the borders of the
    earth;
    You have made summer and winter.

18 Remember this, *that* the enemy has
    reproached, O LORD,
    And *that* a foolish people has
    blasphemed Your name.
19 Oh, do not deliver the life of Your
    turtledove to the wild beast!
    Do not forget the life of Your poor
    forever.
20 Have respect to the covenant;
    For the dark places of the earth are
    full of the haunts of cruelty.
21 Oh, do not let the oppressed return
    ashamed!
    Let the poor and needy praise Your
    name.

22 Arise, O God, plead Your own cause;
    Remember how the foolish man
    reproaches You daily.
23 Do not forget the voice of Your
    enemies;
    The tumult of those who rise up
    against You increases continually.

PSALM 75

Thanksgiving for God's Righteous Judgment

To the Chief Musician. Set to "Do Not Destroy."[a]
A Psalm of Asaph. A Song.

We give thanks to You, O God, we give
thanks!
    For Your wondrous works declare *that*
    Your name is near.

2   "When I choose the proper time,
    I will judge uprightly.
3   The earth and all its inhabitants are
    dissolved;
    I set up its pillars firmly.   Selah

4   "I said to the boastful, 'Do not deal
    boastfully,'
    And to the wicked, 'Do not lift up the
    horn.
5   Do not lift up your horn on high;
    Do *not* speak with a stiff neck.' "

6   For exaltation *comes* neither from the
    east
    Nor from the west nor from the south.
7   But God *is* the Judge:
    He puts down one,
    And exalts another.
8   For in the hand of the LORD *there is* a
    cup,
    And the wine is red;
    It is fully mixed, and He pours it out;
    Surely its dregs shall all the wicked of
    the earth
    Drain *and* drink down.

9   But I will declare forever,
    I will sing praises to the God of Jacob.

10 "All the horns of the wicked I will also
    cut off,
    But the horns of the righteous shall be
    exalted."

PSALM 76

The Majesty of God in Judgment

*To the Chief Musician. On stringed
instruments.*[a] *A Psalm of Asaph. A Song.*

In Judah God *is* known;
    His name *is* great in Israel.
2   In Salem[a] also is His tabernacle,
    And His dwelling place in Zion.
3   There He broke the arrows of the bow,
    The shield and sword of battle.   Selah

4   You *are* more glorious and excellent
    Than the mountains of prey.
5   The stouthearted were plundered;
    They have sunk into their sleep;
    And none of the mighty men have
    found the use of their hands.
6   At Your rebuke, O God of Jacob,
    Both the chariot and horse were cast
    into a dead sleep.

7   You, Yourself, *are* to be feared;
    And who may stand in Your presence
    When once You are angry?
8   You caused judgment to be heard from
    heaven;
    The earth feared and was still,
9   When God arose to judgment,
    To deliver all the oppressed of the
    earth.   Selah

75:title [a]Hebrew *Al Tashcheth*   76:title [a]Hebrew
neginoth   76:2 [a]That is, Jerusalem

10 Surely the wrath of man shall praise
     You;
     With the remainder of wrath You shall
     gird Yourself.

11 Make vows to the LORD your God, and
     pay *them;*
     Let all who are around Him bring
     presents to Him who ought to be
     feared.
12 He shall cut off the spirit of princes;
     He is awesome to the kings of the
     earth.

PSALM 77

The Consoling Memory of God's Redemptive Works

To the Chief Musician. To Jeduthun. A Psalm of Asaph.

I cried out to God with my voice—
     To God with my voice;
     And He gave ear to me.
2 In the day of my trouble I sought the
     Lord;
     My hand was stretched out in the
     night without ceasing;
     My soul refused to be comforted.
3 I remembered God, and was troubled;
     I complained, and my spirit was
     overwhelmed.   Selah

4 You hold my eyelids *open;*
     I am so troubled that I cannot speak.
5 I have considered the days of old,
     The years of ancient times.
6 I call to remembrance my song in the
     night;
     I meditate within my heart,
     And my spirit makes diligent search.

7 Will the Lord cast off forever?
     And will He be favorable no more?
8 Has His mercy ceased forever?
     Has *His* promise failed forevermore?
9 Has God forgotten to be gracious?
     Has He in anger shut up His tender
     mercies?   Selah

10 And I said, "This *is* my anguish;
     But I will remember the years of the
     right hand of the Most High."
11 I will remember the works of the
     LORD;
     Surely I will remember Your wonders
     of old.

12 I will also meditate on all Your work,
     And talk of Your deeds.
13 Your way, O God, *is* in the sanctuary;
     Who *is* so great a God as *our* God?
14 You *are* the God who does wonders;
     You have declared Your strength
     among the peoples.
15 You have with *Your* arm redeemed
     Your people,
     The sons of Jacob and Joseph.   Selah

16 The waters saw You, O God;
     The waters saw You, they were afraid;
     The depths also trembled.
17 The clouds poured out water;
     The skies sent out a sound;
     Your arrows also flashed about.
18 The voice of Your thunder *was* in the
     whirlwind;
     The lightnings lit up the world;
     The earth trembled and shook.
19 Your way *was* in the sea,
     Your path in the great waters,
     And Your footsteps were not known.
20 You led Your people like a flock
     By the hand of Moses and Aaron.

PSALM 78

God's Kindness to Rebellious Israel

A Contemplation[a] *of Asaph.*

G ive ear, O my people, *to* my law;
     Incline your ears to the words of my
     mouth.
2 I will open my mouth in a parable;
     I will utter dark sayings of old,
3 Which we have heard and known,
     And our fathers have told us.
4 We will not hide *them* from their
     children,
     Telling to the generation to come the
     praises of the LORD,
     And His strength and His wonderful
     works that He has done.

5 For He established a testimony in
     Jacob,
     And appointed a law in Israel,
     Which He commanded our fathers,
     That they should make them known
     to their children;
6 That the generation to come might
     know *them,*
     The children *who* would be born,
     That they may arise and declare *them*
     to their children,

78:title ªHebrew *Maschil*

7 That they may set their hope in God,
And not forget the works of God,
But keep His commandments;
8 And may not be like their fathers,
A stubborn and rebellious generation,
A generation *that* did not set its heart
aright,
And whose spirit was not faithful to
God.

9 The children of Ephraim, *being* armed
and carrying bows,
Turned back in the day of battle.
10 They did not keep the covenant of God;
They refused to walk in His law,
11 And forgot His works
And His wonders that He had shown
them.

12 Marvelous things He did in the sight
of their fathers,
In the land of Egypt, *in* the field of
Zoan.
13 He divided the sea and caused them
to pass through;
And He made the waters stand up like
a heap.
14 In the daytime also He led them with
the cloud,
And all the night with a light of fire.
15 He split the rocks in the wilderness,
And gave *them* drink in abundance
like the depths.
16 He also brought streams out of the
rock,
And caused waters to run down like
rivers.

17 But they sinned even more against
Him
By rebelling against the Most High in
the wilderness.
18 And they tested God in their heart
By asking for the food of their fancy.
19 Yes, they spoke against God:
They said, "Can God prepare a table
in the wilderness?
20 Behold, He struck the rock,
So that the waters gushed out,
And the streams overflowed.
Can He give bread also?
Can He provide meat for His people?"

21 Therefore the LORD heard *this* and
was furious;
So a fire was kindled against Jacob,
And anger also came up against
Israel,

22 Because they did not believe in God,
And did not trust in His salvation.
23 Yet He had commanded the clouds
above,
And opened the doors of heaven,
24 Had rained down manna on them to
eat,
And given them of the bread of heaven.
25 Men ate angels' food;
He sent them food to the full.

26 He caused an east wind to blow in the
heavens;
And by His power He brought in the
south wind.
27 He also rained meat on them like the
dust,
Feathered fowl like the sand of the
seas;
28 And He let *them* fall in the midst of
their camp,
All around their dwellings.
29 So they ate and were well filled,
For He gave them their own desire.
30 They were not deprived of their
craving;
But while their food *was* still in their
mouths,
31 The wrath of God came against them,
And slew the stoutest of them,
And struck down the choice *men* of
Israel.

32 In spite of this they still sinned,
And did not believe in His wondrous
works.
33 Therefore their days He consumed in
futility,
And their years in fear.

34 When He slew them, then they sought
Him;
And they returned and sought
earnestly for God.
35 Then they remembered that God *was*
their rock,
And the Most High God their
Redeemer.
36 Nevertheless they flattered Him with
their mouth,
And they lied to Him with their
tongue;
37 For their heart was not steadfast with
Him,
Nor were they faithful in His
covenant.
38 But He, *being* full of compassion,
forgave *their* iniquity,

And did not destroy *them.*
Yes, many a time He turned His anger
away,
And did not stir up all His wrath;
39 For He remembered that they *were
but* flesh,
A breath that passes away and does
not come again.

40 How often they provoked Him in the
wilderness,
And grieved Him in the desert!
41 Yes, again and again they tempted
God,
And limited the Holy One of Israel.
42 They did not remember His power:
The day when He redeemed them
from the enemy,
43 When He worked His signs in Egypt,
And His wonders in the field of Zoan;
44 Turned their rivers into blood,
And their streams, that they could not
drink.
45 He sent swarms of flies among them,
which devoured them,
And frogs, which destroyed them.
46 He also gave their crops to the
caterpillar,
And their labor to the locust.
47 He destroyed their vines with hail,
And their sycamore trees with frost.
48 He also gave up their cattle to the hail,
And their flocks to fiery lightning.
49 He cast on them the fierceness of His
anger,
Wrath, indignation, and trouble,
By sending angels of destruction
among them.
50 He made a path for His anger;
He did not spare their soul from
death,
But gave their life over to the plague,
51 And destroyed all the firstborn in
Egypt,
The first of *their* strength in the tents
of Ham.
52 But He made His own people go forth
like sheep,
And guided them in the wilderness
like a flock;
53 And He led them on safely, so that
they did not fear;
But the sea overwhelmed their
enemies.
54 And He brought them to His holy
border,
This mountain *which* His right hand
had acquired.

55 He also drove out the nations before
them,
Allotted them an inheritance by
survey,
And made the tribes of Israel dwell in
their tents.

56 Yet they tested and provoked the Most
High God,
And did not keep His testimonies,
57 But turned back and acted
unfaithfully like their fathers;
They were turned aside like a
deceitful bow.
58 For they provoked Him to anger with
their high places,
And moved Him to jealousy with their
carved images.
59 When God heard *this,* He was furious,
And greatly abhorred Israel,
60 So that He forsook the tabernacle of
Shiloh,
The tent He had placed among men,
61 And delivered His strength into
captivity,
And His glory into the enemy's hand.
62 He also gave His people over to the
sword,
And was furious with His inheritance.
63 The fire consumed their young men,
And their maidens were not given in
marriage.
64 Their priests fell by the sword,
And their widows made no
lamentation.

65 Then the Lord awoke as *from* sleep,
Like a mighty man who shouts
because of wine.
66 And He beat back His enemies;
He put them to a perpetual reproach.

67 Moreover He rejected the tent of
Joseph,
And did not choose the tribe of
Ephraim,
68 But chose the tribe of Judah,
Mount Zion which He loved.
69 And He built His sanctuary like the
heights,
Like the earth which He has
established forever.
70 He also chose David His servant,
And took him from the sheepfolds;
71 From following the ewes that had
young He brought him,
To shepherd Jacob His people,
And Israel His inheritance.

72 So he shepherded them according to
    the integrity of his heart,
And guided them by the skillfulness of
    his hands.

PSALM 79

A Dirge and a Prayer for Israel, Destroyed by Enemies

A Psalm of Asaph.

O God, the nations have come into Your
    inheritance;
Your holy temple they have defiled;
They have laid Jerusalem in heaps.
2 The dead bodies of Your servants
They have given *as* food for the birds
    of the heavens,
The flesh of Your saints to the beasts
    of the earth.
3 Their blood they have shed like water
    all around Jerusalem,
And *there was* no one to bury *them.*
4 We have become a reproach to our
    neighbors,
A scorn and derision to those who are
    around us.

5 How long, LORD?
Will You be angry forever?
Will Your jealousy burn like fire?
6 Pour out Your wrath on the nations
    that do not know You,
And on the kingdoms that do not call
    on Your name.
7 For they have devoured Jacob,
And laid waste his dwelling place.

8 Oh, do not remember former iniquities
    against us!
Let Your tender mercies come speedily
    to meet us,
For we have been brought very low.
9 Help us, O God of our salvation,
For the glory of Your name;
And deliver us, and provide
    atonement for our sins,
For Your name's sake!
10 Why should the nations say,

"Where *is* their God?"
Let there be known among the nations
    in our sight
The avenging of the blood of Your
    servants *which has been* shed.

11 Let the groaning of the prisoner come
    before You;
According to the greatness of Your
    power
Preserve those who are appointed to
    die;
12 And return to our neighbors sevenfold
    into their bosom
Their reproach with which they have
    reproached You, O Lord.

13 So we, Your people and sheep of Your
    pasture,
Will give You thanks forever;
We will show forth Your praise to all
    generations.

PSALM 80

Prayer for Israel's Restoration

To the Chief Musician. Set to "The Lilies."[a]
A Testimony[b] *of Asaph. A Psalm.*

G ive ear, O Shepherd of Israel,
You who lead Joseph like a flock;
You who dwell *between* the cherubim,
    shine forth!
2 Before Ephraim, Benjamin, and
    Manasseh,
Stir up Your strength,
And come *and* save us!

3 Restore us, O God;
Cause Your face to shine,
And we shall be saved!

4 O LORD God of hosts,
How long will You be angry
Against the prayer of Your people?
5 You have fed them with the bread of
    tears,

80:title [a]Hebrew *Shoshannim*   [b]Hebrew *Eduth*

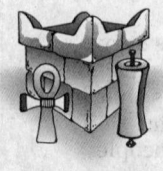

BELIEFS AND IDEAS

*Like David (Ps. 78:70), the prophet Amos received the call of God while he was tending
sheep (Amos 7:14, 15). The Greek poet Hesiod, a contemporary of Homer, relates how
he heard the divine call to be a poet while he was shepherding. The gift of writing poetry
was not given to all and was not to be refused when offered.*

CHERUBIM, THE DIVINE GUARDIANS (Ps. 80:1)

The religious and royal art of ancient Near Eastern civilizations shows a number of winged, mythological creatures being depicted as composites of several different animals. These supernatural beings appear as guardians for thrones, gateways, palaces, and temples, as well as serving as stands for the images of deities.

The cherubim of the Bible are representatives of these creatures. They acted as guardians of the garden of Eden (Gen. 3:24); they formed the moving throne of God (Ezek. 1—3); their likenesses were molded at the top of the ark of the covenant (Ex. 25:18). In the Most Holy Place of Solomon's temple were two large cherubim, and images of cherubim were carved into the temple walls by order of Solomon (1 Kin. 6:23–29). Clearly, the artistic representation of the cherubim was associated with the worship of God in Jerusalem.

Cherubim are always described in the Bible as having wings, but we lack a full description of their appearance. From similar creatures found in the art of Phoenicia, Mesopotamia, and even in the Samaritan ivory fragments (not to mention Egyptian sphinxes), cherubim appear to have animal bodies with human heads and a pair of wings extending from the shoulders. While human heads appear on all examples, as well as wings, the bodies may be those of lions or bulls or a combination of both. Phoenician artistic examples exist from the 2nd millennium B.C. through the biblical period, so it is possible that the figures carved in the Jerusalem temple were designed by Phoenician craftsmen based on their understanding of such figures.

In religious art cherubim formed mounts, guardians, or companions of the deities, but did not represent the gods themselves. Likewise, the cherubim in Solomon's temple were not intended to be images of God, but were displayed to demonstrate the holiness of the sanctuary and the majesty of the deity worshiped there. Ps. 80:1 reflects the place where God's presence was most revered: in the temple, dwelling between the cherubim of the mercy seat (see Num. 7:89).

And given them tears to drink in great measure.

6 You have made us a strife to our neighbors,
And our enemies laugh among themselves.

7 Restore us, O God of hosts;
Cause Your face to shine,
And we shall be saved!

8 You have brought a vine out of Egypt;
You have cast out the nations, and planted it.

9 You prepared *room* for it,
And caused it to take deep root,
And it filled the land.

10 The hills were covered with its shadow,
And the mighty cedars with its boughs.

11 She sent out her boughs to the Sea,[a]
And her branches to the River.[b]

12 Why have You broken down her hedges,
So that all who pass by the way pluck her *fruit?*

13 The boar out of the woods uproots it,
And the wild beast of the field devours it.

14 Return, we beseech You, O God of hosts;
Look down from heaven and see,
And visit this vine

15 And the vineyard which Your right hand has planted,
And the branch *that* You made strong for Yourself.

16 *It is* burned with fire, *it is* cut down;
They perish at the rebuke of Your countenance.

17 Let Your hand be upon the man of Your right hand,
Upon the son of man *whom* You made strong for Yourself.

18 Then we will not turn back from You;
Revive us, and we will call upon Your name.

80:11 [a]That is, the Mediterranean   [b]That is, the Euphrates

19 Restore us, O LORD God of hosts;
    Cause Your face to shine,
    And we shall be saved!

PSALM 81

An Appeal for Israel's Repentance

To the Chief Musician. On an instrument of Gath.[a] *A Psalm of Asaph.*

Sing aloud to God our strength;
    Make a joyful shout to the God of
        Jacob.
2 Raise a song and strike the timbrel,
    The pleasant harp with the lute.

3 Blow the trumpet at the time of the
        New Moon,
    At the full moon, on our solemn feast
        day.
4 For this *is* a statute for Israel,
    A law of the God of Jacob.
5 This He established in Joseph *as* a
        testimony,
    When He went throughout the land of
        Egypt,
    Where I heard a language I did not
        understand.

6 "I removed his shoulder from the
        burden;
    His hands were freed from the
        baskets.
7 You called in trouble, and I delivered
        you;
    I answered you in the secret place of
        thunder;
    I tested you at the waters of Meribah.
                                    Selah

8 "Hear, O My people, and I will
        admonish you!
    O Israel, if you will listen to Me!
9 There shall be no foreign god among
        you;
    Nor shall you worship any foreign god.
10 I *am* the LORD your God,
    Who brought you out of the land of
        Egypt;
    Open your mouth wide, and I will fill it.

11 "But My people would not heed My
        voice,
    And Israel would *have* none of Me.
12 So I gave them over to their own
        stubborn heart,
    To walk in their own counsels.

13 "Oh, that My people would listen to
        Me,
    That Israel would walk in My ways!
14 I would soon subdue their enemies,
    And turn My hand against their
        adversaries.
15 The haters of the LORD would pretend
        submission to Him,
    But their fate would endure forever.
16 He would have fed them also with the
        finest of wheat;
    And with honey from the rock I would
        have satisfied you."

PSALM 82

A Plea for Justice

A Psalm of Asaph.

God stands in the congregation of the
        mighty;
    He judges among the gods.[a]
2 How long will you judge unjustly,
    And show partiality to the wicked?
                                    Selah
3 Defend the poor and fatherless;
    Do justice to the afflicted and needy.
4 Deliver the poor and needy;
    Free *them* from the hand of the
        wicked.

5 They do not know, nor do they
        understand;
    They walk about in darkness;
    All the foundations of the earth are
        unstable.

6 I said, "You *are* gods,[a]
    And all of you *are* children of the Most
        High.
7 But you shall die like men,
    And fall like one of the princes."

8 Arise, O God, judge the earth;
    For You shall inherit all nations.

PSALM 83

Prayer to Frustrate Conspiracy Against Israel

A Song. A Psalm of Asaph.

Do not keep silent, O God!
    Do not hold Your peace,

81:title [a]Hebrew *Al Gittith*   82:1 [a]Hebrew *elohim,*
mighty *ones;* that is, the judges   82:6 [a]Hebrew
elohim, mighty *ones;* that is, the judges

WHEN GODS GO BAD (Ps. 82:1)

Among the psalms, Ps. 82 uniquely offers the only reference to Yahweh taking direct control of the world from the heavenly beings. These "gods," who previously controlled the world under Yahweh's authority, had perpetuated injustice to the poor (82:2–4).

The scene of Yahweh among the gods resembles the assembly of Canaanite gods in the Ugaritic myths (c. 1400–1200 B.C.). At Ugarit the gods were answerable to El, head of the pantheon, for their behavior. The lesser gods were responsible for keeping order in the universe, supposedly working together to run the cosmos according to El's plan. If they did not, El could remove them from power or even condemn them to death.

The psalmist's "congregation of the mighty" (82:1) appears to have originally referred to the heavenly council. The "mighty" were "gods, . . . children of the Most High" (82:6). They have been interpreted to be either angels or judges.

In this psalm Yahweh condemns the "mighty" gods or judges. They were supposed to defend the powerless, but instead condoned the wicked behavior of the powerful. Because the heavenly powers have acted improperly, knowledge and order have collapsed, and the cosmos hovers on the edge of a return to chaos (82:5).

Instead of justice and order, the gods or judges have created injustice and chaos. Yahweh, who gave them their power in the beginning, now condemns them to death (82:6, 7). The congregation sings praises to God for taking over sole rule of the universe (82:8). Like the god El of the Ugaritic texts, Yahweh is the principal figure, whose justice and order can no longer be thwarted by lesser gods.

And do not be still, O God!

2 For behold, Your enemies make a tumult;
And those who hate You have lifted up their head.

3 They have taken crafty counsel against Your people,
And consulted together against Your sheltered ones.

4 They have said, "Come, and let us cut them off from *being* a nation,
That the name of Israel may be remembered no more."

5 For they have consulted together with one consent;
They form a confederacy against You:

6 The tents of Edom and the Ishmaelites;
Moab and the Hagrites;

7 Gebal, Ammon, and Amalek;
Philistia with the inhabitants of Tyre;

8 Assyria also has joined with them;
They have helped the children of Lot.
Selah

9 Deal with them as *with* Midian,
As *with* Sisera,
As *with* Jabin at the Brook Kishon,

10 Who perished at En Dor,
Who became *as* refuse on the earth.

11 Make their nobles like Oreb and like Zeeb,
Yes, all their princes like Zebah and Zalmunna,

12 Who said, "Let us take for ourselves
The pastures of God for a possession."

13 O my God, make them like the whirling dust,
Like the chaff before the wind!

14 As the fire burns the woods,
And as the flame sets the mountains on fire,

15 So pursue them with Your tempest,
And frighten them with Your storm.

16 Fill their faces with shame,
That they may seek Your name, O LORD.

17 Let them be confounded and dismayed forever;
Yes, let them be put to shame and perish,

18 That they may know that You, whose name alone *is* the LORD,
Are the Most High over all the earth.

AN ARABIAN TRIBAL CONFEDERACY (Ps. 83:6)

The name "Ishmael" became the representative name for the entire tribe of Ishmaelites. Ishmael was the son of Abraham by Sarah's maid, Hagar (Gen. 16:15). The twelve sons of Ishmael are well known, both in the Bible (Gen. 25:12–16) and in sources outside of the Bible. It is not certain whether these sources are speaking about the same group or groups, or if the sources refer to different groups. The psalmist was aware of one group of "Ishmaelites" (Ps. 83:6) that were enemies of Israel.

The Ishmaelites were the first known power from the central Arabian desert. An Ishmaelite tribal confederacy reached its greatest power during the Late Assyrian period. The first reference to them comes from the 8th-century B.C. records of Tiglath-Pileser III, describing his campaigns in Syria. The Ishmaelites sent tribute of camels to this Assyrian king after his campaign against them in 738 B.C. Again in 733 B.C. they paid tribute of camels, incense, and spices to Tiglath-Pileser. Another Assyrian king, Sargon II received tribute from a variety of Ishmaelite tribes in 716 B.C.

The Ishmaelite tribes evidently lived along the trade routes used to transport incense and controlled the trade of incense and aromatic goods. Assyrian attempts to create vassal states in northern Arabia were unsuccessful. The annals of the Assyrian king Ashurbanipal (668–627 B.C.) offer much description of Ishmaelite tribes that were encroaching upon Assyrian territory.

The term "Ishmaelite" disappeared at the end of the 7th century B.C. Many of the splinter tribes, however, continued to exist, including the Arab tribes in central Arabia.

PSALM 88

A Prayer for Help in Despondency

A Song. A Psalm of the sons of Korah. To the Chief Musician. Set to "Mahalath Leannoth."
A Contemplation[a] of Heman the Ezrahite.

O Lord, God of my salvation,
I have cried out day and night before You.

2 Let my prayer come before You;
Incline Your ear to my cry.

3 For my soul is full of troubles,
And my life draws near to the grave.

4 I am counted with those who go down to the pit;
I am like a man *who has* no strength,

5 Adrift among the dead,
Like the slain who lie in the grave,
Whom You remember no more,
And who are cut off from Your hand.

6 You have laid me in the lowest pit,
In darkness, in the depths.

7 Your wrath lies heavy upon me,
And You have afflicted *me* with all Your waves.   Selah

8 You have put away my acquaintances far from me;
You have made me an abomination to them;

9 *I am* shut up, and I cannot get out;
My eye wastes away because of affliction.

Lord, I have called daily upon You;
I have stretched out my hands to You.

10 Will You work wonders for the dead?
Shall the dead arise *and* praise You?   Selah

11 Shall Your lovingkindness be declared in the grave?
Or Your faithfulness in the place of destruction?

12 Shall Your wonders be known in the dark?
And Your righteousness in the land of forgetfulness?

13 But to You I have cried out, O Lord,
And in the morning my prayer comes before You.

14 Lord, why do You cast off my soul?
Why do You hide Your face from me?

15 I *have been* afflicted and ready to die from *my* youth;
I suffer Your terrors;
I am distraught.

16 Your fierce wrath has gone over me;
Your terrors have cut me off.

88:title ªHebrew *Maschil*

17 They came around me all day long
　　like water;
　They engulfed me altogether.
18 Loved one and friend You have put far
　　from me,
　And my acquaintances into darkness.

A Desire to Build the Temple

The Chronicler shows David establishing everything about the temple except the temple itself. One reason David could not build the temple was because he was a man of war, who had shed blood (1 Chr. 22:8; 28:1–3). However, in 2 Sam. 7 and 1 Chr. 17 a more basic reason is given: during all the years of the tribal confederation, God's ark had been in a movable shrine. He had never been restricted to a single site. David, while establishing the new patterns of kingship, would nevertheless respect the old covenant traditions, one of which was the tabernacle.

■ 1 Chronicles 17:1–27

1 Chronicles
God's Covenant with David

17 :1 Now it came to pass, when David was dwelling in his house, that David said to Nathan the prophet, "See now, I dwell in a house of cedar, but the ark of the covenant of the LORD *is* under tent curtains."

2Then Nathan said to David, "Do all that *is* in your heart, for God *is* with you."

3But it happened that night that the word of God came to Nathan, saying, 4"Go and tell My servant David, 'Thus says the LORD: "You shall not build Me a house to dwell in. 5For I have not dwelt in a house since the time that I brought up Israel, even to this day, but have gone from tent to tent, and from *one* tabernacle *to another.* 6Wherever I have moved about with all Israel, have I ever spoken a word to any of the judges of Israel, whom I commanded to shepherd My people, saying, 'Why have you not built Me a house of cedar?' " ' 7Now therefore, thus shall you say to My servant David, 'Thus says the LORD of hosts: "I took you from the sheepfold, from following the sheep, to be ruler over My people Israel. 8And I have been with you wherever you have gone, and have cut off all your ene-

mies from before you, and have made you a name like the name of the great men who *are* on the earth. 9Moreover I will appoint a place for My people Israel, and will plant them, that they may dwell in a place of their own and move no more; nor shall the sons of wickedness oppress them anymore, as previously, 10since the time that I commanded judges *to be* over My people Israel. Also I will subdue all your enemies. Furthermore I tell you that the LORD will build you a house.[a] 11And it shall be, when your days are fulfilled, when you must go *to be* with your fathers, that I will set up your seed after you, who will be of your sons; and I will establish his kingdom. 12He shall build Me a house, and I will establish his throne forever. 13I will be his Father, and he shall be My son; and I will not take My mercy away from him, as I took *it* from *him* who was before you. 14And I will establish him in My house and in My kingdom forever; and his throne shall be established forever." ' "

15According to all these words and according to all this vision, so Nathan spoke to David.

16Then King David went in and sat before the LORD; and he said: "Who *am* I, O LORD God? And what is my house, that You have brought me this far? 17And *yet* this was a small thing in Your sight, O God; and You have *also* spoken of Your servant's house for a great while to come, and have regarded me according to the rank of a man of high degree, O LORD God. 18What more can David *say* to You for the honor of Your servant? For You know Your servant. 19O LORD, for Your servant's sake, and according to Your own heart, You have done all this greatness, in making known all these great things. 20O LORD, *there is* none like You, nor *is there any* God besides You, according to all that we have heard with our ears. 21And who *is* like Your people Israel, the one nation on the earth whom God went to redeem for Himself *as* a people—to make for Yourself a name by great and awesome deeds, by driving out nations from before Your people whom You redeemed from Egypt? 22For You have made Your people Israel Your very own people forever; and You, LORD, have become their God.

23"And now, O LORD, the word which You have spoken concerning Your servant and concerning his house, *let it* be established forever, and do as You have said. 24So let it be established, that Your name

17:10　ªThat is, a royal dynasty

may be magnified forever, saying, 'The LORD of hosts, the God of Israel, *is* Israel's God.' And let the house of Your servant David be established before You. 25For You, O my God, have revealed to Your servant that You will build him a house. Therefore Your servant has found it *in his heart* to pray before You. 26And now, LORD, You are God, and have promised this goodness to Your servant. 27Now You have been pleased to bless the house of Your servant, that it may continue before You forever; for You have blessed it, O LORD, and *it shall be* blessed forever."

Prophetic Account: David's Reign

When Saul died, the Philistines must have assumed that their victory over Israel was complete. The government of Ishbosheth, Saul's son, had virtually no power, and David's rule over Judah was probably condoned by the Philistines. After all, David had been living in their land, and they considered him their man.

If those were the Philistines' assumptions, they were wrong. Within an astonishingly brief time, David had constructed an impressive empire. First, he drove the Philistines from Israelite territory (2 Sam. 5). Then, responding to an insult from Ammon, he sent his armies across the Jordan. By the time he was done, he had defeated the Ammonites, several Aramean (Syrian) kingdoms, Moab, and Edom (2 Sam. 8; 10). He was aided, no doubt, by the decline of the empires of Egypt and Mesopotamia, but his achievements are still impressive, by any standards.

In typical fashion, though, the biblical history pays scant attention to such feats of arms. Instead, the text focuses on David's behavior while his armies were off at war—especially on his affair with Bathsheba. This incident and its aftermath forms the heart of what is often called the "Succession Document" (2 Sam. 9—1 Kin. 2). The history of the "Succession Document" gives a unified and very detailed record of events in David's court up until Solomon, the son of Bathsheba, was crowned David's successor.

■ 2 Samuel 8:1—12:15a

2 Samuel
David's Further Conquests

8 :1 After this it came to pass that David attacked the Philistines and subdued

them. And David took Metheg Ammah from the hand of the Philistines.

2Then he defeated Moab. Forcing them down to the ground, he measured them off with a line. With two lines he measured off those to be put to death, and with one full line those to be kept alive. So the Moabites became David's servants, *and* brought tribute.

3David also defeated Hadadezer the son of Rehob, king of Zobah, as he went to recover his territory at the River Euphrates. 4David took from him one thousand *chariots,* seven hundredª horsemen, and twenty thousand foot soldiers. Also David hamstrung all the chariot horses, except that he spared *enough* of them for one hundred chariots.

5When the Syrians of Damascus came to help Hadadezer king of Zobah, David killed twenty-two thousand of the Syrians. 6Then David put garrisons in Syria of Damascus; and the Syrians became David's servants, *and* brought tribute. So the LORD preserved David wherever he went. 7And David took the shields of gold that had belonged to the servants of Hadadezer, and brought them to Jerusalem. 8Also from Betahª and from Berothai, cities of Hadadezer, King David took a large amount of bronze.

9When Toiª king of Hamath heard that David had defeated all the army of Hadadezer, 10then Toi sent Joramª his son to King David, to greet him and bless him, because he had fought against Hadadezer and defeated him (for Hadadezer had been at war with Toi); and *Joram* brought with him articles of silver, articles of gold, and articles of bronze. 11King David also dedicated these to the LORD, along with the silver and gold that he had dedicated from all the nations which he had subdued— 12from Syria,ª from Moab, from the people of Ammon, from the Philistines, from Amalek, and from the spoil of Hadadezer the son of Rehob, king of Zobah.

13And David made *himself* a name when he returned from killing eighteen thousand Syriansª in the Valley of Salt.

HADADEZER FALLS TO KING DAVID (2 Sam. 8:3)

Hadadezer was the Aramean king defeated by David. As the "king of Zobah" (2 Sam. 8:3, 5), Hadadezer ruled a territory assumed to be north of Damascus in Syria. It is possible, however, that Hadadezer also controlled territory "beyond the River," meaning beyond the Euphrates (2 Sam. 10:16). Aramean tribes were being used as mercenaries by the Ammonites against Israel, and Hadadezer appears to have commanded several mercenary troops.

Scholars are not certain whether David fought against Hadadezer one, two, or even three times. The various battle reports in Scripture could refer to different battles or to the same battle. At some point, the Arameans became subject to David (10:19).

Hadadezer has not been identified in presently known sources outside of the Bible. He should not be confused with his namesake Hadad-ezer, the later king of Damascus who was part of the coalition opposing Shalmaneser III at the battle of Qarqar in 853 B.C.

---

¹⁴He also put garrisons in Edom; throughout all Edom he put garrisons, and all the Edomites became David's servants. And the LORD preserved David wherever he went.

David's Administration

¹⁵So David reigned over all Israel; and David administered judgment and justice to all his people. ¹⁶Joab the son of Zeruiah *was* over the army; Jehoshaphat the son of Ahilud *was* recorder; ¹⁷Zadok the son of Ahitub and Ahimelech the son of Abiathar *were* the priests; Seraiah[a] *was* the scribe; ¹⁸Benaiah the son of Jehoiada *was over* both the Cherethites and the Pelethites; and David's sons were chief ministers.

David's Kindness to Mephibosheth

9 ¹Now David said, "Is there still anyone who is left of the house of Saul, that I may show him kindness for Jonathan's sake?"

²And *there was* a servant of the house of Saul whose name *was* Ziba. So when they had called him to David, the king said to him, "*Are* you Ziba?"

He said, "At your service!"

³Then the king said, "*Is* there not still someone of the house of Saul, to whom I may show the kindness of God?"

And Ziba said to the king, "There is still a son of Jonathan *who is* lame in *his* feet."

⁴So the king said to him, "Where *is* he?"

And Ziba said to the king, "Indeed he *is* in the house of Machir the son of Ammiel, in Lo Debar."

⁵Then King David sent and brought him out of the house of Machir the son of Ammiel, from Lo Debar.

⁶Now when Mephibosheth the son of Jonathan, the son of Saul, had come to David, he fell on his face and prostrated himself. Then David said, "Mephibosheth?"

And he answered, "Here is your servant!"

⁷So David said to him, "Do not fear, for I will surely show you kindness for Jonathan your father's sake, and will restore to you all the land of Saul your grandfather; and you shall eat bread at my table continually."

⁸Then he bowed himself, and said, "What *is* your servant, that you should look upon such a dead dog as I?"

⁹And the king called to Ziba, Saul's servant, and said to him, "I have given to your master's son all that belonged to Saul and to all his house. ¹⁰You therefore, and your sons and your servants, shall work the land for him, and you shall bring in *the harvest,* that your master's son may have food to eat. But Mephibosheth your master's son shall eat bread at my table always." Now Ziba had fifteen sons and twenty servants.

¹¹Then Ziba said to the king, "According to all that my lord the king has commanded his servant, so will your servant do."

"As for Mephibosheth," *said the king,* "he shall eat at my table[a] like one of the king's sons." ¹²Mephibosheth had a young

---

8:17 ᵃSpelled *Shavsha* in 1 Chronicles 18:16
9:11 ᵃSeptuagint reads *David's table.*

You Dirty Dead Dog! (2 Sam. 9:8)

The dog was the earliest domesticated animal, providing companionship for humans. Yet, in the Bible, the term "dog" is often applied figuratively to worthless or wicked persons. The profit from the sale of a dog was compared to the price of a prostitute and neither was supposed to be donated to the sanctuary because both dogs and prostitutes were "an abomination" to Israel's God (Deut. 23:18).

In important ways, dogs and pigs were thought by ancient people to be alike. Both were scavengers and both ran wild, if not controlled. In some ancient Near Eastern societies dogs and pigs were associated with or substituted for each other in religious rituals. Interestingly enough, the part dogs or pigs played in these rituals was as agents for cleansing, with impurities and disease being transferred from the human to the animal.

The Law of Moses contained various dietary laws. Food restrictions permitted the eating of "clean" animals, while forbidding the eating of "unclean" animals. The distinction of which animals were clean and which were not clean is detailed in Lev. 11. Both the pig and the dog, by the criteria of Leviticus (11:7, 27), would be unclean.

When Mephibosheth called himself a "dead dog" (2 Sam. 9:8), he was lowering himself to the lowest possible realm. Not only did he liken himself to an unclean scavenger (Ex. 22:31; 1 Kin. 14:11), but he portrayed himself as a dog in its worse possible state—death. The Levitical rule was that a dead dog (or any dead unclean animal) should not be touched. If it was touched, even accidentally, it made the one who touched it "unclean until evening" (Lev. 11:24, 25).

As a verbal sign of humility, Mephibosheth could have said nothing more to King David to show the differences in their positions. David was the king, while Mephibosheth, Saul's grandson, was a dead dog.

---

son whose name *was* Micha. And all who dwelt in the house of Ziba *were* servants of Mephibosheth. ¹³So Mephibosheth dwelt in Jerusalem, for he ate continually at the king's table. And he was lame in both his feet.

The Ammonites and Syrians Defeated

10 ¹It happened after this that the king of the people of Ammon died, and Hanun his son reigned in his place. ²Then David said, "I will show kindness to Hanun the son of Nahash, as his father showed kindness to me."

So David sent by the hand of his servants to comfort him concerning his father. And David's servants came into the land of the people of Ammon. ³And the princes of the people of Ammon said to Hanun their lord, "Do you think that David really honors your father because he has sent comforters to you? Has David not *rather* sent his servants to you to search the city, to spy it out, and to overthrow it?"

⁴Therefore Hanun took David's servants, shaved off half of their beards, cut off their garments in the middle, at their buttocks, and sent them away. ⁵When they told David, he sent to meet them, because the men were greatly ashamed. And the king said, "Wait at Jericho until your beards have grown, and *then* return."

⁶When the people of Ammon saw that they had made themselves repulsive to David, the people of Ammon sent and hired the Syrians of Beth Rehob and the Syrians

CULTURE AND SOCIETY

Israelites regarded a man's beard as a mark of his worth and status. To have it forcibly removed or disfigured was not just a question of appearances, but a mark of defeat. Since a leader was personally responsible for his followers, the humiliation of David's servants was a humiliation for him as well (2 Sam. 10:4–6).

of Zoba, twenty thousand foot soldiers; and from the king of Maacah one thousand men, and from Ish-Tob twelve thousand men. [7]Now when David heard *of it,* he sent Joab and all the army of the mighty men. [8]Then the people of Ammon came out and put themselves in battle array at the entrance of the gate. And the Syrians of Zoba, Beth Rehob, Ish-Tob, and Maacah *were* by themselves in the field.

[9]When Joab saw that the battle line was against him before and behind, he chose some of Israel's best and put *them* in battle array against the Syrians. [10]And the rest of the people he put under the command of Abishai his brother, that he might set *them* in battle array against the people of Ammon. [11]Then he said, "If the Syrians are too strong for me, then you shall help me; but if the people of Ammon are too strong for you, then I will come and help you. [12]Be of good courage, and let us be strong for our people and for the cities of our God. And may the LORD do *what is* good in His sight."

[13]So Joab and the people who *were* with him drew near for the battle against the Syrians, and they fled before him. [14]When the people of Ammon saw that the Syrians were fleeing, they also fled before Abishai, and entered the city. So Joab returned from the people of Ammon and went to Jerusalem.

[15]When the Syrians saw that they had been defeated by Israel, they gathered together. [16]Then Hadadezer[a] sent and brought out the Syrians who *were* beyond the River,[b] and they came to Helam. And Shobach the commander of Hadadezer's army *went* before them. [17]When it was told David, he gathered all Israel, crossed over the Jordan, and came to Helam. And the Syrians set themselves in battle array against David and fought with him. [18]Then the Syrians fled before Israel; and David killed seven hundred charioteers and forty thousand horsemen of the Syrians, and struck Shobach the commander of their army, who died there. [19]And when all the kings *who were* servants to Hadadezer[a] saw that they were defeated by Israel, they made peace with Israel and served them. So the Syrians were afraid to help the people of Ammon anymore.

David, Bathsheba, and Uriah

11 [1]It happened in the spring of the year, at the time when kings go out *to battle,* that David sent Joab and his servants with him, and all Israel; and they destroyed the people of Ammon and besieged Rabbah. But David remained at Jerusalem.

[2]Then it happened one evening that David arose from his bed and walked on the roof of the king's house. And from the roof he saw a woman bathing, and the woman *was* very beautiful to behold. [3]So David sent and inquired about the woman. And *someone* said, "*Is* this not Bathsheba, the daughter of Eliam, the wife of Uriah the Hittite?" [4]Then David sent messengers, and took her; and she came to him, and he lay with her, for she was cleansed from her impurity; and she returned to her house. [5]And the woman conceived; so she sent and told David, and said, "I *am* with child."

[6]Then David sent to Joab, *saying,* "Send me Uriah the Hittite." And Joab sent Uriah to David. [7]When Uriah had come to him, David asked how Joab was doing, and how the people were doing, and how the war prospered. [8]And David said to Uriah, "Go down to your house and wash your feet." So Uriah departed from the king's house, and a gift *of food* from the king followed him. [9]But Uriah slept at the door of the king's house with all the servants of his lord, and did not go down to his house. [10]So when they told David, saying, "Uriah did not go down to his house," David said to Uriah, "Did you not come from a journey? Why did you not go down to your house?"

TIME CAPSULE   *1073 to 1050 B.C.*

1073–1056   *Assyrian king Assur-bel-kala encounters Arameans at the River Habur*

1069   *End of New Kingdom in Egypt*

1069   *Smendes I becomes pharaoh and makes Zoan (Tanis) Egypt's new capital*

1054   *Pinudjem I becomes first pharaoh of southern Egypt*

1050–930   *Arameans bring "Dark Age" to Assyrian royal reports*

1050   *Philistines have prosperous settlement at Ashdod*

10:16 [a]Hebrew *Hadarezer*   [b]That is, the Euphrates   10:19 [a]Hebrew *Hadarezer*

¹¹And Uriah said to David, "The ark and Israel and Judah are dwelling in tents, and my lord Joab and the servants of my lord are encamped in the open fields. Shall I then go to my house to eat and drink, and to lie with my wife? *As* you live, and *as* your soul lives, I will not do this thing."

¹²Then David said to Uriah, "Wait here today also, and tomorrow I will let you depart." So Uriah remained in Jerusalem that day and the next. ¹³Now when David called him, he ate and drank before him; and he made him drunk. And at evening he went out to lie on his bed with the servants of his lord, but he did not go down to his house.

¹⁴In the morning it happened that David wrote a letter to Joab and sent *it* by the hand of Uriah. ¹⁵And he wrote in the letter, saying, "Set Uriah in the forefront of the hottest battle, and retreat from him, that he may be struck down and die." ¹⁶So it was, while Joab besieged the city, that he assigned Uriah to a place where he knew there *were* valiant men. ¹⁷Then the men of the city came out and fought with Joab. And *some* of the people of the servants of David fell; and Uriah the Hittite died also.

¹⁸Then Joab sent and told David all the things concerning the war, ¹⁹and charged the messenger, saying, "When you have finished telling the matters of the war to the king, ²⁰if it happens that the king's wrath rises, and he says to you: 'Why did you approach so near to the city when you fought? Did you not know that they would shoot from the wall? ²¹Who struck Abimelech the son of Jerubbesheth?ᵃ Was it not a woman who cast a piece of a millstone on him from the wall, so that he died in Thebez? Why did you go near the wall?'—then you shall say, 'Your servant Uriah the Hittite is dead also.' "

²²So the messenger went, and came and told David all that Joab had sent by him. ²³And the messenger said to David, "Surely the men prevailed against us and came out to us in the field; then we drove them back as far as the entrance of the gate. ²⁴The archers shot from the wall at your servants; and *some* of the king's servants are dead, and your servant Uriah the Hittite is dead also."

²⁵Then David said to the messenger, "Thus you shall say to Joab: 'Do not let this thing displease you, for the sword devours one as well as another. Strengthen your at-tack against the city, and overthrow it.' So encourage him."

²⁶When the wife of Uriah heard that Uriah her husband was dead, she mourned for her husband. ²⁷And when her mourning was over, David sent and brought her to his house, and she became his wife and bore him a son. But the thing that David had done displeased the LORD.

Nathan's Parable and David's Confession

12 ¹Then the LORD sent Nathan to David. And he came to him, and said to him: "There were two men in one city, one rich and the other poor. ²The rich *man* had exceedingly many flocks and herds. ³But the poor *man* had nothing, except one little ewe lamb which he had bought and nourished; and it grew up together with him and with his children. It ate of his own food and drank from his own cup and lay in his bosom; and it was like a daughter to him. ⁴And a traveler came to the rich man, who refused to take from his own flock and from his own herd to prepare one for the wayfaring man who had come to him; but he took the poor man's lamb and prepared it for the man who had come to him."

⁵So David's anger was greatly aroused against the man, and he said to Nathan, "*As* the LORD lives, the man who has done this shall surely die! ⁶And he shall restore fourfold for the lamb, because he did this thing and because he had no pity."

⁷Then Nathan said to David, "You *are* the man! Thus says the LORD God of Israel: 'I anointed you king over Israel, and I delivered you from the hand of Saul. ⁸I gave you your master's house and your master's wives into your keeping, and gave you the house of Israel and Judah. And if *that had been* too little, I also would have given you much more! ⁹Why have you despised the commandment of the LORD, to do evil in His sight? You have killed Uriah the Hittite with the sword; you have taken his wife *to be* your wife, and have killed him with the sword of the people of Ammon. ¹⁰Now therefore, the sword shall never depart from your house, because you have despised Me, and have taken the wife of Uriah the Hittite to be your wife.' ¹¹Thus says the LORD: 'Behold, I will raise up adversity against you from your own house;

11:21 ᵃSame as *Jerubbaal* (Gideon), Judges 6:32ff

and I will take your wives before your eyes and give *them* to your neighbor, and he shall lie with your wives in the sight of this sun. [12]For you did *it* secretly, but I will do this thing before all Israel, before the sun.' "

[13]So David said to Nathan, "I have sinned against the LORD."

And Nathan said to David, "The LORD also has put away your sin; you shall not die. [14]However, because by this deed you have given great occasion to the enemies of the LORD to blaspheme, the child also *who is* born to you shall surely die." [15]Then Nathan departed to his house.

Create in Me a Clean Heart

No psalm is more clearly tied to a historical context than Ps. 51. Not only is its superscription unusually explicit, but there are even internal echoes within the psalm (cf. Ps. 51:4 and 2 Sam. 12:13). Many scholars argue that this psalm was actually composed long after David. Regardless of the question of authorship, however, there can be little doubt that Ps. 51 is meant to be read in light of David's adultery with Bathsheba and murder of her husband (2 Sam. 11; 12).

■ Psalm 51

PSALM 51

A Prayer of Repentance

To the Chief Musician. A Psalm of David when Nathan the prophet went to him, after he had gone in to Bathsheba.

Have mercy upon me, O God,
According to Your lovingkindness;
According to the multitude of Your
     tender mercies,
Blot out my transgressions.
2   Wash me thoroughly from my iniquity,
And cleanse me from my sin.

3   For I acknowledge my transgressions,
And my sin *is* always before me.
4   Against You, You only, have I sinned,
And done *this* evil in Your sight—
That You may be found just when You
     speak,[a]
And blameless when You judge.

5   Behold, I was brought forth in
     iniquity,
And in sin my mother conceived me.
6   Behold, You desire truth in the inward
     parts,
And in the hidden *part* You will make
     me to know wisdom.

7   Purge me with hyssop, and I shall be
     clean;
Wash me, and I shall be whiter than
     snow.
8   Make me hear joy and gladness,
That the bones You have broken may
     rejoice.
9   Hide Your face from my sins,
And blot out all my iniquities.

10   Create in me a clean heart, O God,
And renew a steadfast spirit within
     me.
11   Do not cast me away from Your
     presence,
And do not take Your Holy Spirit from
     me.

12   Restore to me the joy of Your
     salvation,
And uphold me *by Your* generous
     Spirit.
13   *Then* I will teach transgressors Your
     ways,
And sinners shall be converted to You.

14   Deliver me from the guilt of
     bloodshed, O God,
The God of my salvation,
And my tongue shall sing aloud of
     Your righteousness.
15   O Lord, open my lips,
And my mouth shall show forth Your
     praise.
16   For You do not desire sacrifice, or else
     I would give *it;*
You do not delight in burnt offering.
17   The sacrifices of God *are* a broken
     spirit,
A broken and a contrite heart—
These, O God, You will not despise.

18   Do good in Your good pleasure to Zion;
Build the walls of Jerusalem.
19   Then You shall be pleased with the
     sacrifices of righteousness,
With burnt offering and whole burnt
     offering;
Then they shall offer bulls on Your
     altar.

51:4 [a]Septuagint, Targum, and Vulgate, read *in Your words.*

The Sons of David

Counting the children named in Scripture, David fathered 19 sons and 1 daughter. His six oldest sons (listed in 2 Sam. 3:2–5) were all born in Hebron, all with different mothers. The eldest, and therefore the logical choice to reign after David, was Amnon. The second, Chileab, is never mentioned again and may have died young. Third was Absalom, and fourth was Adonijah.

None of the four eldest sons would succeed David on Israel's throne. That honor would fall to a much younger son, just born and by that token the least likely to reign: Solomon, the son of Bathsheba. When reading of the complicated interactions between these sons, we should always remember where they stood in line to the throne. It is certain that the sons themselves never forgot.

▼   ■ 2 Samuel 12:15b—14:33

2 Samuel
The Death of David's Son

12 :15b And the LORD struck the child that Uriah's wife bore to David, and it became ill. 16David therefore pleaded with God for the child, and David fasted and went in and lay all night on the ground. 17So the elders of his house arose *and went* to him, to raise him up from the ground. But he would not, nor did he eat food with them. 18Then on the seventh day it came to pass that the child died. And the servants of David were afraid to tell him that the child was dead. For they said, "Indeed, while the child was alive, we spoke to him, and he would not heed our voice. How can we tell him that the child is dead? He may do some harm!"

19When David saw that his servants were whispering, David perceived that the child was dead. Therefore David said to his servants, "Is the child dead?"

And they said, "He is dead."

20So David arose from the ground, washed and anointed himself, and changed his clothes; and he went into the house of the LORD and worshiped. Then he went to his own house; and when he requested, they set food before him, and he ate. 21Then his servants said to him, "What *is* this that you have done? You fasted and wept for the child *while he was* alive, but when the child died, you arose and ate food."

22And he said, "While the child was alive, I fasted and wept; for I said, 'Who can tell *whether* the LORD[a] will be gracious to me, that the child may live?' 23But now he is dead; why should I fast? Can I bring him back again? I shall go to him, but he shall not return to me."

Solomon Is Born

24Then David comforted Bathsheba his wife, and went in to her and lay with her. So she bore a son, and he[a] called his name Solomon. Now the LORD loved him, 25and He sent *word* by the hand of Nathan the prophet: So he[a] called his name Jedidiah,[b] because of the LORD.

Rabbah Is Captured

26Now Joab fought against Rabbah of the people of Ammon, and took the royal city. 27And Joab sent messengers to David, and said, "I have fought against Rabbah, and I have taken the city's water *supply*. 28Now therefore, gather the rest of the people together and encamp against the city and take it, lest I take the city and it be called after my name." 29So David gathered all the people together and went to Rabbah, fought against it, and took it. 30Then he took their king's crown from his head. Its weight *was* a talent of gold, with precious stones. And it was *set* on David's head. Also he brought out the spoil of the city in great abundance. 31And he brought

---

12:22 [a]A few Hebrew manuscripts and Syriac read *God.*   12:24 [a]Following Kethib, Septuagint, and Vulgate; Qere, a few Hebrew manuscripts, Syriac, and Targum read *she.*   12:25 [a]Qere, some Hebrew manuscripts, Syriac, and Targum read *she.*   [b]Literally *Beloved of the LORD*

POLITICS AND GOVERNMENT

Slavery was the usual fate of people defeated in war. Labor in mines and quarries was hard and dangerous. The Greek silver mines at Laurium were operated by slaves, and the Romans punished slaves by sending them to the mines. It may be that the first job David required of the people of Rabbah was to destroy the defenses of their own city (2 Sam. 12:31).

RABBAH, CAPITAL OF THE AMMONITES (2 Sam. 12:26)

The Ammonites inhabited the mountainous area in Transjordan directly east of Jerusalem. Their capital was at Rabbah, which was also known as "Rabbah of the people of Ammon" (Deut. 3:11). The city is designated a "royal city," meaning that a king resided there (2 Sam. 12:26). Since this Ammonite royal city was only about 40 miles from Jerusalem, Israel's capital city, King David had to capture Rabbah in order to control the region for Israel. This he eventually did, assuming the Ammonite king's crown for himself (12:29, 30).

Rabbah has one of the most impressive natural settings. Its L-shaped citadel sits high above the center of modern Amman, Jordan. Because of extensive building in later times, principally in Roman and Byzantine periods, much of the city from David's time has not been uncovered. Nevertheless, Rabbah's natural defensive position is obvious.

When Joab, David's general, captured the city, he was careful to send word to David that he had not only captured the city but also its water source (12:27). In the area of the citadel archaeologists have discovered a large underground cistern. Dated by nearby structures, it appears to be the main water source from the time when Joab besieged the city. Some think that a fortified citadel protected the Ammonite king's royal residence as well as the water supply. If so, then Joab was indicating to David that Israel's army had broken down Ammon's strongest defenses.

---

out the people who *were* in it, and put *them to work* with saws and iron picks and iron axes, and made them cross over to the brick works. So he did to all the cities of the people of Ammon. Then David and all the people returned to Jerusalem.

Amnon and Tamar

13 ¹After this Absalom the son of David had a lovely sister, whose name *was* Tamar; and Amnon the son of David loved her. ²Amnon was so distressed over his sister Tamar that he became sick; for she *was* a virgin. And it was improper for Amnon to do anything to her. ³But Amnon had a friend whose name *was* Jonadab the son of Shimeah, David's brother. Now Jonadab *was* a very crafty man. ⁴And he said to him, "Why *are* you, the king's son, becoming thinner day after day? Will you not tell me?"

Amnon said to him, "I love Tamar, my brother Absalom's sister."

⁵So Jonadab said to him, "Lie down on your bed and pretend to be ill. And when your father comes to see you, say to him, 'Please let my sister Tamar come and give me food, and prepare the food in my sight, that I may see *it* and eat it from her hand.' " ⁶Then Amnon lay down and pretended to be ill; and when the king came to see him, Amnon said to the king, "Please let Tamar my sister come and make a couple of cakes for me in my sight, that I may eat from her hand."

⁷And David sent home to Tamar, saying, "Now go to your brother Amnon's house, and prepare food for him." ⁸So Tamar went to her brother Amnon's house; and he was lying down. Then she took flour and kneaded *it,* made cakes in his sight, and baked the cakes. ⁹And she took the pan and placed *them* out before him, but he refused to eat. Then Amnon said, "Have everyone go out from me." And they all went out from him. ¹⁰Then Amnon said to Tamar, "Bring the food into the bedroom, that I may eat from your hand." And Tamar took the cakes which she had made, and brought *them* to Amnon her brother in the bedroom. ¹¹Now when she had brought *them* to him to eat, he took hold of her and said to her, "Come, lie with me, my sister."

¹²But she answered him, "No, my brother, do not force me, for no such thing should be done in Israel. Do not do this disgraceful thing! ¹³And I, where could I take my shame? And as for you, you would be like one of the fools in Israel. Now therefore, please speak to the king; for he will not withhold me from you." ¹⁴However, he would not heed her voice; and being stronger than she, he forced her and lay with her.

¹⁵Then Amnon hated her exceedingly, so that the hatred with which he hated her *was* greater than the love with which he had loved her. And Amnon said to her, "Arise, be gone!"

ASHES OF SORROW (2 Sam. 13:19)

People of biblical times often figuratively expressed their feelings. One way this was done was by joining their feelings to an unusual striking act. For example, accidentally tearing a favorite article of clothing would make some people angry, sad, or frustrated. But in Bible times distraught people sometimes tore their clothes in a dramatic expression of their feelings. We should remember that long before the industrial revolution every piece of clothing was handmade. This only reinforces how much sorrow a person must have felt to tear a garment, especially if it was a precious one.

Tamar's tragic story is one of a sister being sexually violated by her brother Amnon, even though she pled with him that "no such thing should be done in Israel" (2 Sam. 13:12). In disgrace she tore her robe, a special possession as indicated by its description as "of many colors." In addition, she put "ashes on her head" (2 Sam. 13:19).

In the cooking process the usual endeavor was to remain clean, meaning to keep the ashes in the firepit and not on one's person. Ashes were refuse and dirty. Tamar, like other ancient persons (Esth. 4:1; Job 2:8; Dan. 9:3), covered herself with ashes by putting them on her head. By tearing her beautiful robe and covering her head in ashes, Tamar expressed, even better than with words, how distraught she was.

16So she said to him, "No, indeed! This evil of sending me away *is* worse than the other that you did to me."

But he would not listen to her. 17Then he called his servant who attended him, and said, "Here! Put this *woman* out, away from me, and bolt the door behind her." 18Now she had on a robe of many colors, for the king's virgin daughters wore such apparel. And his servant put her out and bolted the door behind her.

19Then Tamar put ashes on her head, and tore her robe of many colors that *was* on her, and laid her hand on her head and went away crying bitterly. 20And Absalom her brother said to her, "Has Amnon your brother been with you? But now hold your peace, my sister. He *is* your brother; do not take this thing to heart." So Tamar remained desolate in her brother Absalom's house.

21But when King David heard of all these things, he was very angry. 22And Absalom spoke to his brother Amnon neither good nor bad. For Absalom hated Amnon, because he had forced his sister Tamar.

Absalom Murders Amnon

23And it came to pass, after two full years, that Absalom had sheepshearers in Baal Hazor, which *is* near Ephraim; so Absalom invited all the king's sons. 24Then Absalom came to the king and said, "Kindly note, your servant has sheepshearers; please, let the king and his servants go with your servant."

25But the king said to Absalom, "No, my son, let us not all go now, lest we be a burden to you." Then he urged him, but he would not go; and he blessed him.

26Then Absalom said, "If not, please let my brother Amnon go with us."

And the king said to him, "Why should he go with you?" 27But Absalom urged him; so he let Amnon and all the king's sons go with him.

28Now Absalom had commanded his servants, saying, "Watch now, when Amnon's heart is merry with wine, and when I say to you, 'Strike Amnon!' then kill him. Do not be afraid. Have I not commanded you? Be courageous and valiant." 29So the servants of Absalom did to Amnon as Absa-

DAILY LIFE AND CUSTOMS

Concerning Tamar's "robe of many colors" is the comment that "the king's virgin daughters wore such apparel" (2 Sam. 13:18). Clothing has always been used as a means of distinguishing royalty and the nobility from the population at large. Frequently societies have passed laws, called sumptuary laws, that enforce such distinctions.

ABSALOM'S CRIME AND RISE TO POWER

Chronological notes in the Book of 2 Samuel trace the quick rise of Absalom as he attempts to take the kingship from his father by force.

Passing Years	Event
	Amnon defiles his half sister Tamar (2 Sam. 13:1–22)
2 years later	Absalom has his brother Amnon killed (2 Sam. 13:23–29)
	Absalom banished to Geshur for 3 years (2 Sam. 13:37–39)
3 years later	Absalom returns to Jerusalem (2 Sam. 14:21–24)
	Absalom dwells in Jerusalem for 2 years (2 Sam. 14:28)
2 years later	Absalom burns Joab's field (2 Sam. 14:29–32)
	Absalom courts the men of Israel for 4 years (2 Sam. 15:1–6)
4 years later	Absalom goes to Hebron to declare himself king (2 Sam. 15:7–12)

The Hebrew Old Testament reads "40 years" in 2 Sam. 15:7. Yet David's entire reign was only 40 years long (1 Kin. 2:11). The chronological difficulty is solved if we read "4 years" in 2 Sam. 15:7, as do the Septuagint (Greek Old Testament), Syriac manuscripts, and the historian Josephus.

lom had commanded. Then all the king's sons arose, and each one got on his mule and fled.

30And it came to pass, while they were on the way, that news came to David, saying, "Absalom has killed all the king's sons, and not one of them is left!" 31So the king arose and tore his garments and lay on the ground, and all his servants stood by with their clothes torn. 32Then Jonadab the son of Shimeah, David's brother, answered and said, "Let not my lord suppose they have killed all the young men, the king's sons, for only Amnon is dead. For by the command of Absalom this has been determined from the day that he forced his sister Tamar. 33Now therefore, let not my lord the king take the thing to his heart, to think that all the king's sons are dead. For only Amnon is dead."

Absalom Flees to Geshur

34Then Absalom fled. And the young man who was keeping watch lifted his eyes and looked, and there, many people were coming from the road on the hillside behind him.a 35And Jonadab said to the king, "Look, the king's sons are coming; as your servant said, so it is." 36So it was, as soon as he had finished speaking, that the king's sons indeed came, and they lifted up their voice and wept. Also the king and all his servants wept very bitterly.

37But Absalom fled and went to Talmai the son of Ammihud, king of Geshur. And David mourned for his son every day. 38So Absalom fled and went to Geshur, and was there three years. 39And King Davida longed to go tob Absalom. For he had been comforted concerning Amnon, because he was dead.

Absalom Returns to Jerusalem

14 1So Joab the son of Zeruiah perceived that the king's heart was concerned about Absalom. 2And Joab sent to Tekoa and brought from there a wise woman, and said to her, "Please pretend to be a mourner, and put on mourning apparel; do not anoint yourself with oil, but act like a woman who has been mourning a long time for the dead. 3Go to the king and speak to him in this manner." So Joab put the words in her mouth.

4And when the woman of Tekoa spokea to the king, she fell on her face to the ground and prostrated herself, and said, "Help, O king!"

5Then the king said to her, "What troubles you?"

13:34 aSeptuagint adds And the watchman went and told the king, and said, "I see men from the way of Horonaim, from the regions of the mountains."
13:39 aFollowing Masoretic Text, Syriac, and Vulgate; Septuagint reads the spirit of the king; Targum reads the soul of King David. bFollowing Masoretic Text and Targum; Septuagint and Vulgate read ceased to pursue after. 14:4 aMany Hebrew manuscripts, Septuagint, Syriac, and Vulgate read came.

And she answered, "Indeed I *am* a widow, my husband is dead. [6]Now your maidservant had two sons; and the two fought with each other in the field, and *there was* no one to part them, but the one struck the other and killed him. [7]And now the whole family has risen up against your maidservant, and they said, 'Deliver him who struck his brother, that we may execute him for the life of his brother whom he killed; and we will destroy the heir also.' So they would extinguish my ember that is left, and leave to my husband *neither* name nor remnant on the earth."

[8]Then the king said to the woman, "Go to your house, and I will give orders concerning you."

[9]And the woman of Tekoa said to the king, "My lord, O king, *let* the iniquity *be* on me and on my father's house, and the king and his throne *be* guiltless."

[10]So the king said, "Whoever says *anything* to you, bring him to me, and he shall not touch you anymore."

[11]Then she said, "Please let the king remember the LORD your God, and do not permit the avenger of blood to destroy anymore, lest they destroy my son."

And he said, "*As* the LORD lives, not one hair of your son shall fall to the ground."

[12]Therefore the woman said, "Please, let your maidservant speak *another* word to my lord the king."

And he said, "Say on."

[13]So the woman said: "Why then have you schemed such a thing against the people of God? For the king speaks this thing as one who is guilty, *in that* the king does not bring his banished one home again. [14]For we will surely die and *become* like water spilled on the ground, which cannot be gathered up again. Yet God does not take away a life; but He devises means, so that His banished ones are not expelled from Him. [15]Now therefore, I have come to speak of this thing to my lord the king because the people have made me afraid. And your maidservant said, 'I will now speak to the king; it may be that the king will perform the request of his maidservant. [16]For the king will hear and deliver his maidservant from the hand of the man *who would* destroy me and my son together from the inheritance of God.' [17]Your maidservant said, 'The word of my lord the king will now be comforting; for as the angel of God, so *is* my lord the king in dis-

cerning good and evil. And may the LORD your God be with you.' "

[18]Then the king answered and said to the woman, "Please do not hide from me anything that I ask you."

And the woman said, "Please, let my lord the king speak."

[19]So the king said, "*Is* the hand of Joab with you in all this?" And the woman answered and said, "*As* you live, my lord the king, no one can turn to the right hand or to the left from anything that my lord the king has spoken. For your servant Joab commanded me, and he put all these words in the mouth of your maidservant. [20]To bring about this change of affairs your servant Joab has done this thing; but my lord *is* wise, according to the wisdom of the angel of God, to know everything that *is* in the earth."

[21]And the king said to Joab, "All right, I have granted this thing. Go therefore, bring back the young man Absalom."

[22]Then Joab fell to the ground on his face and bowed himself, and thanked the king. And Joab said, "Today your servant knows that I have found favor in your sight, my lord, O king, in that the king has fulfilled the request of his servant." [23]So Joab arose and went to Geshur, and brought Absalom to Jerusalem. [24]And the king said, "Let him return to his own house, but do not let him see my face." So Absalom returned to his own house, but did not see the king's face.

David Forgives Absalom

[25]Now in all Israel there was no one who was praised as much as Absalom for his good looks. From the sole of his foot to the crown of his head there was no blemish in him. [26]And when he cut the hair of his head—at the end of every year he cut *it* because it was heavy on him—when he cut it, he weighed the hair of his head at two hundred shekels according to the king's standard. [27]To Absalom were born three sons, and one daughter whose name *was* Tamar. She was a woman of beautiful appearance.

[28]And Absalom dwelt two full years in Jerusalem, but did not see the king's face. [29]Therefore Absalom sent for Joab, to send him to the king, but he would not come to him. And when he sent again the second time, he would not come. [30]So he said to his servants, "See, Joab's field is near mine, and he has barley there; go and set it on fire." And Absalom's servants set the field on fire.

[31]Then Joab arose and came to Absa-

lom's house, and said to him, "Why have your servants set my field on fire?"

³²And Absalom answered Joab, "Look, I sent to you, saying, 'Come here, so that I may send you to the king, to say, "Why have I come from Geshur? *It would be* better for me *to be* there still." ' Now therefore, let me see the king's face; but if there is iniquity in me, let him execute me."

³³So Joab went to the king and told him. And when he had called for Absalom, he came to the king and bowed himself on his face to the ground before the king. Then the king kissed Absalom.

Absalom Subverts the Nation

David's advancing years and his preoccupation with war and his family problems may have delayed the administration of justice. In this Absalom saw the opportunity to work his way into the good graces of the people of Israel, eventually building a conspiracy to become king himself (2 Sam. 15:1–6, 10–12). When David received word of this conspiracy, however, he did not delay. His hasty departure from the city to escape Absalom may have been in part to save Jerusalem from siege and possible damage.

A chronological note in 2 Sam. 15:7 suggests that 40 years passed before Absalom made his move in Hebron. However, since David's entire reign is reported to have been 40 years (1 Kin. 2:11), we should probably read "4 years" in 2 Sam. 15:7, as does the Septuagint (the Greek Old Testament), Syriac manuscripts, and the Jewish historian Josephus (see footnote at 2 Sam. 15:7).

▼　■ 2 Samuel 15:1–37

2 Samuel
Absalom's Treason

15 :1 After this it happened that Absalom provided himself with chariots and horses, and fifty men to run before him. ²Now Absalom would rise early and stand beside the way to the gate. *So* it was, whenever anyone who had a lawsuit came to the king for a decision, that Absalom would call to him and say, "What city *are* you from?" And he would say, "Your servant *is* from such and such a tribe of Israel."

³Then Absalom would say to him, "Look, your case *is* good and right; but *there is* no deputy of the king to hear you." ⁴Moreover Absalom would say, "Oh, that I were made judge in the land, and everyone who has any suit or cause would come to me; then I would give him justice." ⁵And *so* it was, whenever anyone came near to bow down to him, that he would put out his hand and take him and kiss him. ⁶In this manner Absalom acted toward all Israel who came to the king for judgment. So Absalom stole the hearts of the men of Israel.

⁷Now it came to pass after forty[a] years that Absalom said to the king, "Please, let me go to Hebron and pay the vow which I made to the LORD. ⁸For your servant took a vow while I dwelt at Geshur in Syria, saying, 'If the LORD indeed brings me back to Jerusalem, then I will serve the LORD.' "

⁹And the king said to him, "Go in peace." So he arose and went to Hebron.

¹⁰Then Absalom sent spies throughout all the tribes of Israel, saying, "As soon as you hear the sound of the trumpet, then you shall say, 'Absalom reigns in Hebron!' " ¹¹And with Absalom went two hundred men invited from Jerusalem, and they went along innocently and did not know anything. ¹²Then Absalom sent for Ahithophel the Gilonite, David's counselor, from his city—from Giloh—while he offered sacrifices. And the conspiracy grew strong, for the people with Absalom continually increased in number.

David Escapes from Jerusalem

¹³Now a messenger came to David, saying, "The hearts of the men of Israel are with Absalom."

¹⁴So David said to all his servants who *were* with him at Jerusalem, "Arise, and let us flee, or we shall not escape from Absalom. Make haste to depart, lest he overtake us suddenly and bring disaster upon us, and strike the city with the edge of the sword."

¹⁵And the king's servants said to the king, "We *are* your servants, *ready to do* whatever my lord the king commands." ¹⁶Then the king went out with all his household after him. But the king left ten women, concubines, to keep the house. ¹⁷And the king went out with all the people after him, and stopped at the outskirts. ¹⁸Then all his servants passed before him; and all the Cherethites, all the Pelethites,

---

15:7 ᵃSeptuagint manuscripts, Syriac, and Josephus read *four.*

GITTITES FIGHT WITH DAVID (2 Sam. 15:18)

Gath was one of the five principal Philistine cities and was the closest to Judahite territory (1 Sam. 17:52). According to the report of the Book of Joshua, Gath was formerly inhabited by a race of giants called the Anakim (Josh. 11:22), and it was the home of the giant Goliath whom David killed (1 Sam. 17:4).

David of Israel had personal connections with Gath. While Saul was king of Israel, David had sought asylum by fleeing to Gath, where he was received by the city's king, Achish (1 Sam. 27:2). Later, when David became king of Israel himself, he regularly employed soldiers from Gath (known as "the Gittites") in his army (2 Sam. 15:18). In addition to 600 Gittite mercenaries under the command of Ittai the Gittite (2 Sam. 18:2), David also employed Obed-Edom the Gittite (2 Sam. 6:10).

Employing foreign mercenaries, or whole contingents of foreign troops, in one's army was fairly common in the ancient Near East. The Assyrian king Tiglath-Pileser III (744–727 B.C.) used archers and shield-bearing troops from both Syria and Elam. Thus it is not surprising that David would use foreign auxiliaries, such as the Gittites, in his own armies.

---

and all the Gittites, six hundred men who had followed him from Gath, passed before the king.

19Then the king said to Ittai the Gittite, "Why are you also going with us? Return and remain with the king. For you *are* a foreigner and also an exile from your own place. 20In fact, you came *only* yesterday. Should I make you wander up and down with us today, since I go I know not where? Return, and take your brethren back. Mercy and truth *be* with you."

21But Ittai answered the king and said, "As the LORD lives, and *as* my lord the king lives, surely in whatever place my lord the king shall be, whether in death or life, even there also your servant will be."

22So David said to Ittai, "Go, and cross over." Then Ittai the Gittite and all his men and all the little ones who *were* with him crossed over. 23And all the country wept with a loud voice, and all the people crossed over. The king himself also crossed over the Brook Kidron, and all the people crossed over toward the way of the wilderness.

24There was Zadok also, and all the Levites with him, bearing the ark of the covenant of God. And they set down the ark of God, and Abiathar went up until all the people had finished crossing over from the city. 25Then the king said to Zadok, "Carry the ark of God back into the city. If I find favor in the eyes of the LORD, He will bring me back and show me *both* it and His dwelling place. 26But if He says thus: 'I have no delight in you,' here I am, let Him do to me as seems good to Him." 27The king also said to Zadok the priest, "*Are* you *not* a seer? Return to the city in peace, and your two sons with you, Ahimaaz your son, and Jonathan the son of Abiathar. 28See, I will wait in the plains of the wilderness until word comes from you to inform me." 29Therefore Zadok and Abiathar carried the ark of God back to Jerusalem. And they remained there.

30So David went up by the Ascent of the *Mount of* Olives, and wept as he went up; and he had his head covered and went barefoot. And all the people who *were* with him covered their heads and went up, weeping as they went up. 31Then *someone* told David, saying, "Ahithophel *is* among the conspirators with Absalom." And David said, "O LORD, I pray, turn the counsel of Ahithophel into foolishness!"

POLITICS AND GOVERNMENT

The Cherethites and Pelethites were professional soldiers working for King David (2 Sam. 15:18). Their names are often taken to mean that they came from Crete and from Palestine. The advantage of mercenary soldiers is that they are not torn by local loyalties, but the related disadvantage is that their loyalty may become nothing more than money.

³²Now it happened when David had come to the top *of the mountain,* where he worshiped God—there was Hushai the Archite coming to meet him with his robe torn and dust on his head. ³³David said to him, "If you go on with me, then you will become a burden to me. ³⁴But if you return to the city, and say to Absalom, 'I will be your servant, O king; *as I was* your father's servant previously, so I *will* now also *be* your servant,' then you may defeat the counsel of Ahithophel for me. ³⁵And *do* you not *have* Zadok and Abiathar the priests with you there? Therefore it will be *that* whatever you hear from the king's house, you shall tell to Zadok and Abiathar the priests. ³⁶Indeed *they have* there with them their two sons, Ahimaaz, Zadok's *son,* and Jonathan, Abiathar's *son;* and by them you shall send me everything you hear."

³⁷So Hushai, David's friend, went into the city. And Absalom came into Jerusalem.

A Prayer in Time of Darkness

As he fled Jerusalem, David sent the ark of the covenant back into the city. He was convinced that if God favored his cause, he would return and see it again (2 Sam. 15:24–26). Such trust in God's care is a proper setting in which to read Ps. 3. The superscription of the psalm associates this lament with David's flight from his own son.

■ Psalm 3

PSALM 3

The LORD Helps His Troubled People

A Psalm of David when he fled from Absalom his son.

L ORD, how they have increased who
    trouble me!
  Many *are* they who rise up against
    me.
2 Many *are* they who say of me,
  "*There is* no help for him in God."
                 Selah

3 But You, O LORD, *are* a shield for me,
  My glory and the One who lifts up my
    head.
4 I cried to the LORD with my voice,
  And He heard me from His holy hill.
                 Selah

5 I lay down and slept;
  I awoke, for the LORD sustained me.
6 I will not be afraid of ten thousands of
    people
  Who have set *themselves* against me
    all around.

7 Arise, O LORD;
  Save me, O my God!
  For You have struck all my enemies on
    the cheekbone;
  You have broken the teeth of the
    ungodly.
8 Salvation *belongs* to the LORD.
  Your blessing *is* upon Your people.
                 Selah

David Flees Jerusalem

Although David had gone to considerable trouble to unite the land of Israel, the tribal distinctions remained. Of all the tribes, the one that resented David most was the tribe of Benjamin, Saul's tribe. As David fled his stronghold in Jerusalem, seemingly deposed, he personally encountered Benjamite hostility. Shimei, a kinsman of Saul, wrongly blamed David for the misfortunes of Saul's last days (2 Sam. 16:5–8).

■ 2 Samuel 16:1–14

2 Samuel
Mephibosheth's Servant

16 :1 When David was a little past the top *of the mountain,* there was Ziba the servant of Mephibosheth, who met him with a couple of saddled donkeys, and on them two hundred *loaves* of bread, one hundred clusters of raisins, one hundred summer fruits, and a skin of wine. ²And the king said to Ziba, "What do you mean to do with these?"

So Ziba said, "The donkeys *are* for the king's household to ride on, the bread and summer fruit for the young men to eat, and the wine for those who are faint in the wilderness to drink."

³Then the king said, "And where *is* your master's son?"

And Ziba said to the king, "Indeed he is staying in Jerusalem, for he said, 'Today the house of Israel will restore the kingdom of my father to me.'"

⁴So the king said to Ziba, "Here, all that *belongs* to Mephibosheth *is* yours."

And Ziba said, "I humbly bow before you, *that* I may find favor in your sight, my lord, O king!"

Shimei Curses David

[5]Now when King David came to Bahurim, there was a man from the family of the house of Saul, whose name *was* Shimei the son of Gera, coming from there. He came out, cursing continuously as he came. [6]And he threw stones at David and at all the servants of King David. And all the people and all the mighty men *were* on his right hand and on his left. [7]Also Shimei said thus when he cursed: "Come out! Come out! You bloodthirsty man, you rogue! [8]The LORD has brought upon you all the blood of the house of Saul, in whose place you have reigned; and the LORD has delivered the kingdom into the hand of Absalom your son. So now you *are caught* in your own evil, because you are a bloodthirsty man!"

[9]Then Abishai the son of Zeruiah said to the king, "Why should this dead dog curse my lord the king? Please, let me go over and take off his head!"

[10]But the king said, "What have I to do with you, you sons of Zeruiah? So let him curse, because the LORD has said to him, 'Curse David.' Who then shall say, 'Why have you done so?' "

[11]And David said to Abishai and all his servants, "See how my son who came from my own body seeks my life. How much more now *may this* Benjamite? Let him alone, and let him curse; for so the LORD has ordered him. [12]It may be that the LORD will look on my affliction,[a] and that the LORD will repay me with good for his cursing this day." [13]And as David and his men went along the road, Shimei went along the hillside opposite him and cursed as he went, threw stones at him and kicked up dust. [14]Now the king and all the people who *were* with him became weary; so they refreshed themselves there.

Persecution from a Benjamite

The superscription to Ps. 7 does not identify a specific time. Nor does it identify "Cush, a Benjamite," who is mentioned only here in the Bible. Nevertheless, the reference to the insults of this Benjamite Cush corresponds rather neatly with the insults of the Benjamite Shimei in 2 Sam. 16. The content of Ps. 7 suggests that Cush was an enemy of David; his affiliation with the tribe of Benjamin makes it likely he followed Saul. Whenever and whatever this unknown Cush spoke, the lament of Ps. 7 makes increasingly clear the rivalry between Saul's tribe and David's tribe of Judah.

■ Psalm 7

PSALM 7

Prayer and Praise for Deliverance from Enemies

A Meditation[a] of David, which he sang to the LORD concerning the words of Cush, a Benjamite.

O LORD my God, in You I put my trust;
  Save me from all those who persecute me;
  And deliver me,
2 Lest they tear me like a lion,
  Rending *me* in pieces, while *there is* none to deliver.

3 O LORD my God, if I have done this:
  If there is iniquity in my hands,
4 If I have repaid evil to him who was at peace with me,
  Or have plundered my enemy without cause,
5 Let the enemy pursue me and overtake *me;*
  Yes, let him trample my life to the earth,
  And lay my honor in the dust.   Selah

6 Arise, O LORD, in Your anger;
  Lift Yourself up because of the rage of my enemies;
  Rise up for me[a] *to* the judgment You have commanded!
7 So the congregation of the peoples shall surround You;
  For their sakes, therefore, return on high.
8 The LORD shall judge the peoples;
  Judge me, O LORD, according to my righteousness,
  And according to my integrity within me.

16:12 [a]Following Kethib, Septuagint, Syriac, and Vulgate; Qere reads *my eyes;* Targum reads *tears of my eyes.*   **Ps. 7:title** [a]Hebrew *Shiggaion*
7:6 [a]Following Masoretic Text, Targum, and Vulgate; Septuagint reads *O LORD my God.*

9 Oh, let the wickedness of the wicked
come to an end,
But establish the just;
For the righteous God tests the hearts
and minds.
10 My defense *is* of God,
Who saves the upright in heart.

11 God *is* a just judge,
And God is angry *with the wicked*
every day.
12 If he does not turn back,
He will sharpen His sword;
He bends His bow and makes it ready.
13 He also prepares for Himself
instruments of death;
He makes His arrows into fiery shafts.

14 Behold, *the wicked* brings forth
iniquity;
Yes, he conceives trouble and brings
forth falsehood.
15 He made a pit and dug it out,
And has fallen into the ditch *which* he
made.
16 His trouble shall return upon his own
head,
And his violent dealing shall come
down on his own crown.

17 I will praise the Lord according to His
righteousness,
And will sing praise to the name of
the Lord Most High.

Who Will Be Captain?

In the ancient Near East, the captain
of the army was extremely powerful, almost on
a level with the king himself. Indeed, when a
king was overthrown, the captain of the army
was generally involved. In this period when first
Absalom took over Jerusalem as king (2 Sam.
16:15, 16), and then David returned to the
city as king (2 Sam. 19:15), two captains—
Joab and Amasa—vied for control of the army.
Amasa was a cousin of Joab, and both
men were nephews of David (1 Chr. 2:13–17).

Although earlier defending Absalom (2 Sam.
14:1–24), Joab went into exile with the king,
to whom was his first loyalty. When Absalom
entered Jerusalem, he installed Amasa as captain in place of Joab (2 Sam. 17:25; 18:1, 2).

David's captain, Joab, is one of the most
complex figures in the Bible. On the one hand
he seems to be fiercely loyal to David, but on
the other hand he repeatedly acts on his own
initiative, even against David's express wishes.
His conduct in the battle against Absalom is
the best example of Joab's independent nature
(2 Sam. 18:5, 14).

Returning to the throne, David sought to
heal the wounds of war. He forgave Absalom's
captain, Amasa, and made him captain in
place of Joab (2 Sam. 19:11–13). David may
have blamed Joab for the death of Absalom
as well as for the earlier murder of Abner
(2 Sam. 3:27). But Joab, though loyal to
David, was also brutally single-minded in his determination to lead David's armies, and he destroyed yet another rival (2 Sam. 20:8–10).

■ 2 Samuel 16:15—20:26

2 Samuel
The Advice of Ahithophel

16 :15 Meanwhile Absalom and all the
people, the men of Israel, came to
Jerusalem; and Ahithophel *was* with him.
16And so it was, when Hushai the Archite,
David's friend, came to Absalom, that
Hushai said to Absalom, "*Long* live the
king! *Long* live the king!"
17So Absalom said to Hushai, "*Is* this
your loyalty to your friend? Why did you
not go with your friend?"
18And Hushai said to Absalom, "No,
but whom the Lord and this people and all
the men of Israel choose, his I will be, and
with him I will remain. 19"Furthermore,
whom should I serve? *Should I* not *serve* in
the presence of his son? As I have served in
your father's presence, so will I be in your
presence."
20Then Absalom said to Ahithophel,
"Give advice as to what we should do."
21And Ahithophel said to Absalom, "Go

BELIEFS AND IDEAS

*The bow and arrow was the most effective long-range weapon until the introduction of
firearms. In Homer's Iliad, divine arrows fall on the Greeks when Apollo wishes to punish
them for disrespect. The arrows bring sickness and death. Similarly, arrows also appear
in the Bible as appropriate symbols of wounding, suffering, and death. If they come from
God, they are His judgment (Ps. 7:13).*

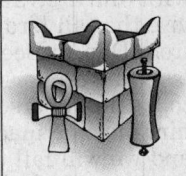

in to your father's concubines, whom he has left to keep the house; and all Israel will hear that you are abhorred by your father. Then the hands of all who are with you will be strong." ²²So they pitched a tent for Absalom on the top of the house, and Absalom went in to his father's concubines in the sight of all Israel.

²³Now the advice of Ahithophel, which he gave in those days, *was* as if one had inquired at the oracle of God. So *was* all the advice of Ahithophel both with David and with Absalom.

17 ¹Moreover Ahithophel said to Absalom, "Now let me choose twelve thousand men, and I will arise and pursue David tonight. ²I will come upon him while he *is* weary and weak, and make him afraid. And all the people who *are* with him will flee, and I will strike only the king. ³Then I will bring back all the people to you. When all return except the man whom you seek, all the people will be at peace." ⁴And the saying pleased Absalom and all the elders of Israel.

The Advice of Hushai

⁵Then Absalom said, "Now call Hushai the Archite also, and let us hear what he says too." ⁶And when Hushai came to Absalom, Absalom spoke to him, saying, "Ahithophel has spoken in this manner. Shall we do as he says? If not, speak up."

⁷So Hushai said to Absalom: "The advice that Ahithophel has given *is* not good at this time. ⁸For," said Hushai, "you know your father and his men, that they *are* mighty men, and they *are* enraged in their minds, like a bear robbed of her cubs in the field; and your father *is* a man of war, and will not camp with the people. ⁹Surely by now he is hidden in some pit, or in some *other* place. And it will be, when some of them are overthrown at the first, that whoever hears *it* will say, 'There is a slaughter among the people who follow Absalom.' ¹⁰And even he *who is* valiant, whose heart *is* like the heart of a lion, will melt completely. For all Israel knows that your father *is* a mighty man, and *those* who *are* with him *are* valiant men. ¹¹Therefore I advise that all Israel be fully gathered to you, from Dan to Beersheba, like the sand that *is* by the sea for multitude, and that you go to battle in person. ¹²So we will come upon him in some place where he may be found, and we will fall on him as the dew falls on the ground. And of him and all the men

who *are* with him there shall not be left so much as one. ¹³Moreover, if he has withdrawn into a city, then all Israel shall bring ropes to that city; and we will pull it into the river, until there is not one small stone found there."

¹⁴So Absalom and all the men of Israel said, "The advice of Hushai the Archite *is* better than the advice of Ahithophel." For the LORD had purposed to defeat the good advice of Ahithophel, to the intent that the LORD might bring disaster on Absalom.

Hushai Warns David to Escape

¹⁵Then Hushai said to Zadok and Abiathar the priests, "Thus and so Ahithophel advised Absalom and the elders of Israel, and thus and so I have advised. ¹⁶Now therefore, send quickly and tell David, saying, 'Do not spend this night in the plains of the wilderness, but speedily cross over, lest the king and all the people who *are* with him be swallowed up.' " ¹⁷Now Jonathan and Ahimaaz stayed at En Rogel, for they dared not be seen coming into the city; so a female servant would come and tell them, and they would go and tell King David. ¹⁸Nevertheless a lad saw them, and told Absalom. But both of them went away quickly and came to a man's house in Bahurim, who had a well in his court; and they went down into it. ¹⁹Then the woman took and spread a covering over the well's mouth, and spread ground grain on it; and the thing was not known. ²⁰And when Absalom's servants came to the woman at the house, they said, "Where *are* Ahimaaz and Jonathan?"

So the woman said to them, "They have gone over the water brook."

And when they had searched and could not find *them,* they returned to Jerusalem. ²¹Now it came to pass, after they had departed, that they came up out of the well and went and told King David, and said to David, "Arise and cross over the water quickly. For thus has Ahithophel advised against you." ²²So David and all the people who *were* with him arose and crossed over the Jordan. By morning light not one of them was left who had not gone over the Jordan.

²³Now when Ahithophel saw that his advice was not followed, he saddled a donkey, and arose and went home to his house, to his city. Then he put his household in order, and hanged himself, and died; and he was buried in his father's tomb.

24Then David went to Mahanaim. And Absalom crossed over the Jordan, he and all the men of Israel with him. 25And Absalom made Amasa captain of the army instead of Joab. This Amasa *was* the son of a man whose name *was* Jithra,[a] an Israelite,[b] who had gone in to Abigail the daughter of Nahash, sister of Zeruiah, Joab's mother. 26So Israel and Absalom encamped in the land of Gilead.

27Now it happened, when David had come to Mahanaim, that Shobi the son of Nahash from Rabbah of the people of Ammon, Machir the son of Ammiel from Lo Debar, and Barzillai the Gileadite from Rogelim, 28brought beds and basins, earthen vessels and wheat, barley and flour, parched *grain* and beans, lentils and parched *seeds,* 29honey and curds, sheep and cheese of the herd, for David and the people who *were* with him to eat. For they said, "The people are hungry and weary and thirsty in the wilderness."

Absalom's Defeat and Death

18 1And David numbered the people who *were* with him, and set captains of thousands and captains of hundreds over them. 2Then David sent out one third of the people under the hand of Joab, one third under the hand of Abishai the son of Zeruiah, Joab's brother, and one third under the hand of Ittai the Gittite. And the king said to the people, "I also will surely go out with you myself."

3But the people answered, "You shall not go out! For if we flee away, they will not care about us; nor if half of us die, will they care about us. But *you are* worth ten thousand of us now. For you are now more help to us in the city."

17:25 ªSpelled *Jether* in 1 Chronicles 2:17 and elsewhere ᵇFollowing Masoretic Text, some manuscripts of the Septuagint, and Targum; some manuscripts of the Septuagint read *Ishmaelite* (compare 1 Chronicles 2:17); Vulgate reads *of Jezrael.* 18:12 ªThe ancient versions read *'Protect the young man Absalom for me!'*

4Then the king said to them, "Whatever seems best to you I will do." So the king stood beside the gate, and all the people went out by hundreds and by thousands. 5Now the king had commanded Joab, Abishai, and Ittai, saying, "*Deal* gently for my sake with the young man Absalom." And all the people heard when the king gave all the captains orders concerning Absalom.

6So the people went out into the field of battle against Israel. And the battle was in the woods of Ephraim. 7The people of Israel were overthrown there before the servants of David, and a great slaughter of twenty thousand took place there that day. 8For the battle there was scattered over the face of the whole countryside, and the woods devoured more people that day than the sword devoured.

9Then Absalom met the servants of David. Absalom rode on a mule. The mule went under the thick boughs of a great terebinth tree, and his head caught in the terebinth; so he was left hanging between heaven and earth. And the mule which *was* under him went on. 10Now a certain man saw *it* and told Joab, and said, "I just saw Absalom hanging in a terebinth tree!"

11So Joab said to the man who told him, "You just saw *him!* And why did you not strike him there to the ground? I would have given you ten *shekels* of silver and a belt."

12But the man said to Joab, "Though I were to receive a thousand *shekels* of silver in my hand, I would not raise my hand against the king's son. For in our hearing the king commanded you and Abishai and Ittai, saying, 'Beware lest anyone *touch* the young man Absalom!'[a] 13Otherwise I would have dealt falsely against my own life. For there is nothing hidden from the king, and you yourself would have set yourself against *me.*"

14Then Joab said, "I cannot linger with you." And he took three spears in his hand and thrust them through Absalom's heart, while he was *still* alive in the midst of the

PLANTS AND ANIMALS

Animals are normally ranked in order of prestige. In the Bible the mule appears next to the horse as a favored mount of kings (1 Kin. 1:33; 2 Sam. 18:9). Mules are the offspring of a female horse and a donkey; they resemble horses, but are hardier. The Law of Moses forbade breeding one species with another (Lev. 19:19). To obey this law mules had to be brought into Israel from the outside.

ABSALOM'S MONUMENT (2 Sam. 18:18)

Absalom wanted to be king in his father's place but ended his life under an obscure terebinth tree (2 Sam. 18:14, 15). He did not even have a son to carry on his name. In the end, he had no kingdom and no heir.

During his lifetime Absalom reflected on his lack of a son to remember him. Apparently, all three sons born to Absalom must have died early in life (2 Sam. 14:27). Without a male heir, Absalom decided to erect a monument in one of the most traveled valleys. Thus, as people walked through the "King's Valley" (also called the Kidron Valley), they would see his monument and remember Absalom (2 Sam. 18:18).

Today, visitors to modern Jerusalem can see "the Tomb of Absalom" in the Kidron Valley. While that is the tomb's popular name, it has no real connection to Absalom. The monument called the Tomb of Absalom was actually built during the Roman period (37 B.C.–A.D. 325), almost 1,000 years after the time of Absalom. Even the monument that Absalom himself built as a memorial to his life has been forgotten.

---

terebinth tree. ¹⁵And ten young men who bore Joab's armor surrounded Absalom, and struck and killed him.

¹⁶So Joab blew the trumpet, and the people returned from pursuing Israel. For Joab held back the people. ¹⁷And they took Absalom and cast him into a large pit in the woods, and laid a very large heap of stones over him. Then all Israel fled, everyone to his tent.

¹⁸Now Absalom in his lifetime had taken and set up a pillar for himself, which *is* in the King's Valley. For he said, "I have no son to keep my name in remembrance." He called the pillar after his own name. And to this day it is called Absalom's Monument.

David Hears of Absalom's Death

¹⁹Then Ahimaaz the son of Zadok said, "Let me run now and take the news to the king, how the LORD has avenged him of his enemies."

²⁰And Joab said to him, "You shall not take the news this day, for you shall take the news another day. But today you shall take no news, because the king's son is dead." ²¹Then Joab said to the Cushite, "Go, tell the king what you have seen." So the Cushite bowed himself to Joab and ran.

²²And Ahimaaz the son of Zadok said again to Joab, "But whatever happens, please let me also run after the Cushite."

So Joab said, "Why will you run, my son, since you have no news ready?"

²³"But whatever happens," *he said,* "let me run."

So he said to him, "Run." Then Ahimaaz ran by way of the plain, and outran the Cushite.

²⁴Now David was sitting between the two gates. And the watchman went up to the roof over the gate, to the wall, lifted his eyes and looked, and there was a man, running alone. ²⁵Then the watchman cried out and told the king. And the king said, "If he *is* alone, *there is* news in his mouth." And he came rapidly and drew near.

²⁶Then the watchman saw *another* man running, and the watchman called to the gatekeeper and said, "There is *another* man, running alone!"

And the king said, "He also brings news."

²⁷So the watchman said, "I think the running of the first is like the running of Ahimaaz the son of Zadok."

And the king said, "He *is* a good man, and comes with good news."

²⁸So Ahimaaz called out and said to the king, "All is well!" Then he bowed down with his face to the earth before the king, and said, "Blessed *be* the LORD your God, who has delivered up the men who raised their hand against my lord the king!"

²⁹The king said, "Is the young man Absalom safe?"

Ahimaaz answered, "When Joab sent the king's servant and *me* your servant, I saw a great tumult, but I did not know what *it was about.*"

³⁰And the king said, "Turn aside *and* stand here." So he turned aside and stood still.

31Just then the Cushite came, and the Cushite said, "There is good news, my lord the king! For the LORD has avenged you this day of all those who rose against you." 32And the king said to the Cushite, "Is the young man Absalom safe?"

So the Cushite answered, "May the enemies of my lord the king, and all who rise against you to do harm, be like *that* young man!"

David's Mourning for Absalom

33Then the king was deeply moved, and went up to the chamber over the gate, and wept. And as he went, he said thus: "O my son Absalom—my son, my son Absalom—if only I had died in your place! O Absalom my son, my son!"

19 1And Joab was told, "Behold, the king is weeping and mourning for Absalom." 2So the victory that day was *turned* into mourning for all the people. For the people heard it said that day, "The king is grieved for his son." 3And the people stole back into the city that day, as people who are ashamed steal away when they flee in battle. 4But the king covered his face, and the king cried out with a loud voice, "O my son Absalom! O Absalom, my son, my son!"

5Then Joab came into the house to the king, and said, "Today you have disgraced all your servants who today have saved your life, the lives of your sons and daughters, the lives of your wives and the lives of your concubines, 6in that you love your enemies and hate your friends. For you have declared today that you regard neither princes nor servants; for today I perceive that if Absalom had lived and all of us had died today, then it would have pleased you well. 7Now therefore, arise, go out and speak comfort to your servants. For I swear by the LORD, if you do not go out, not one will stay with you this night. And that will be worse for you than all the evil that has befallen you from your youth until now." 8Then the king arose and sat in the gate. And they told all the people, saying, "There is the king, sitting in the gate." So all the people came before the king.

For everyone of Israel had fled to his tent.

David Returns to Jerusalem

9Now all the people were in a dispute throughout all the tribes of Israel, saying, "The king saved us from the hand of our enemies, he delivered us from the hand of the Philistines, and now he has fled from the land because of Absalom. 10But Absalom, whom we anointed over us, has died in battle. Now therefore, why do you say nothing about bringing back the king?"

11So King David sent to Zadok and Abiathar the priests, saying, "Speak to the elders of Judah, saying, 'Why are you the last to bring the king back to his house, since the words of all Israel have come to the king, to his *very* house? 12You *are* my brethren, you *are* my bone and my flesh. Why then are you the last to bring back the king?' 13And say to Amasa, 'Are you not my bone and my flesh? God do so to me, and more also, if you are not commander of the army before me continually in place of Joab.' " 14So he swayed the hearts of all the men of Judah, just as *the heart of* one man, so that they sent *this word* to the king: "Return, you and all your servants!"

15Then the king returned and came to the Jordan. And Judah came to Gilgal, to go to meet the king, to escort the king across the Jordan. 16And Shimei the son of Gera, a Benjamite, who *was* from Bahurim, hurried and came down with the men of Judah to meet King David. 17*There were* a thousand men of Benjamin with him, and Ziba the servant of the house of Saul, and his fifteen sons and his twenty servants with him; and they went over the Jordan before the king. 18Then a ferryboat went across to carry over the king's household, and to do what he thought good.

David's Mercy to Shimei

Now Shimei the son of Gera fell down before the king when he had crossed the Jordan. 19Then he said to the king, "Do not let my lord impute iniquity to me, or remember what wrong your servant did on the day that my lord the king left Jerusalem, that the king should take *it* to heart. 20For I, your servant, know that I have sinned. Therefore here I am, the first to come today of all the house of Joseph to go down to meet my lord the king."

21But Abishai the son of Zeruiah answered and said, "Shall not Shimei be put to death for this, because he cursed the LORD's anointed?"

22And David said, "What have I to do with you, you sons of Zeruiah, that you

IDRIMI RETURNS TO HIS KINGDOM   (2 Sam. 19:30)

Alalakh was a city that carried on commercial relations with various cities of Mesopotamia and Syria during the 17th and 16th centuries B.C. Cities on the Euphrates River, such as Emar and Carchemish, as well as Ebla and Ugarit to the west, were trading partners of Alalakh. Various cuneiform texts and an autobiographical inscription found at Alalakh relate the story of Idrimi, king of Alalakh from about 1518 to 1480 B.C.

Idrimi's father established a kingdom at the city of Aleppo. The "autobiography," dated two centuries after Idrimi's death, recounts how he fled with his family from Aleppo when his father was overthrown around 1525 B.C. For 7 years he lived among the Habiru, who helped him eventually regain the throne. He located the capital of his kingdom at Alalakh.

There are elements of folklore in the story of Idrimi's rise to power and the justification of his reign that are similar to the story of King David. Both Idrimi and David were forced to flee their homes. Both lived among foreigners: Idrimi with the Habiru; David as a "Hebrew" among the Philistines (1 Sam. 29:2, 3). Both spent time in exile, but both were able to regain their thrones: Idrimi at Alalakh; David at Jerusalem (2 Sam. 19:30; 20:22).

---

should be adversaries to me today? Shall any man be put to death today in Israel? For do I not know that today I *am* king over Israel?" ²³Therefore the king said to Shimei, "You shall not die." And the king swore to him.

David and Mephibosheth Meet

²⁴Now Mephibosheth the son of Saul came down to meet the king. And he had not cared for his feet, nor trimmed his mustache, nor washed his clothes, from the day the king departed until the day he returned in peace. ²⁵So it was, when he had come to Jerusalem to meet the king, that the king said to him, "Why did you not go with me, Mephibosheth?"

²⁶And he answered, "My lord, O king, my servant deceived me. For your servant said, 'I will saddle a donkey for myself, that I may ride on it and go to the king,' because your servant *is* lame. ²⁷And he has slandered your servant to my lord the king, but my lord the king *is* like the angel of God. Therefore do *what is* good in your eyes. ²⁸For all my father's house were but dead men before my lord the king. Yet you set your servant among those who eat at your own table. Therefore what right have I still to cry out anymore to the king?"

²⁹So the king said to him, "Why do you speak anymore of your matters? I have said, 'You and Ziba divide the land.'"

³⁰Then Mephibosheth said to the king, "Rather, let him take it all, inasmuch as my lord the king has come back in peace to his own house."

David's Kindness to Barzillai

³¹And Barzillai the Gileadite came down from Rogelim and went across the Jordan with the king, to escort him across the Jordan. ³²Now Barzillai was a very aged man, eighty years old. And he had provided the king with supplies while he stayed at Mahanaim, for he *was* a very rich man. ³³And the king said to Barzillai, "Come across with me, and I will provide for you while you are with me in Jerusalem."

³⁴But Barzillai said to the king, "How long have I to live, that I should go up with the king to Jerusalem? ³⁵I *am* today eighty years old. Can I discern between the good and bad? Can your servant taste what I eat or what I drink? Can I hear any longer the voice of singing men and singing women? Why then should your servant be a further burden to my lord the king? ³⁶Your servant will go a little way across the Jordan with the king. And why should the king repay me *with* such a reward? ³⁷Please let your servant turn back again, that I may die in my own city, near the grave of my father and mother. But here is your servant Chimham; let him cross over with my lord the king, and do for him what seems good to you."

³⁸And the king answered, "Chimham shall cross over with me, and I will do for him what seems good to you. Now whatever you request of me, I will do for you." ³⁹Then all the people went over the Jordan. And when the king had crossed over, the king kissed Barzillai and

blessed him, and he returned to his own place.

The Quarrel About the King

40Now the king went on to Gilgal, and Chimham[a] went on with him. And all the people of Judah escorted the king, and also half the people of Israel. 41Just then all the men of Israel came to the king, and said to the king, "Why have our brethren, the men of Judah, stolen you away and brought the king, his household, and all David's men with him across the Jordan?"

42So all the men of Judah answered the men of Israel, "Because the king is a close relative of ours. Why then are you angry over this matter? Have we ever eaten at the king's expense? Or has he given us any gift?"

43And the men of Israel answered the men of Judah, and said, "We have ten shares in the king; therefore we also have more right to David than you. Why then do you despise us—were we not the first to advise bringing back our king?"

Yet the words of the men of Judah were fiercer than the words of the men of Israel.

The Rebellion of Sheba

20 1And there happened to be there a rebel,[a] whose name was Sheba the son of Bichri, a Benjamite. And he blew a trumpet, and said:

"We have no share in David,
   Nor do we have inheritance in the son
      of Jesse;
Every man to his tents, O Israel!"

2So every man of Israel deserted David, and followed Sheba the son of Bichri. But the men of Judah, from the Jordan as far as Jerusalem, remained loyal to their king.

3Now David came to his house at Jerusalem. And the king took the ten women, his concubines whom he had left to keep the house, and put them in seclusion and supported them, but did not go in to them. So they were shut up to the day of their death, living in widowhood.

4And the king said to Amasa, "Assemble the men of Judah for me within three days, and be present here yourself." 5So Amasa went to assemble the men of Judah. But he delayed longer than the set time which David had appointed him. 6And David said to Abishai, "Now Sheba the son of Bichri will do us more harm than Absalom. Take your lord's servants and pursue him, lest he find for himself fortified cities, and escape us." 7So Joab's men, with the Cherethites, the Pelethites, and all the mighty men, went out after him. And they went out of Jerusalem to pursue Sheba the son of Bichri. 8When they were at the large stone which is in Gibeon, Amasa came before them. Now Joab was dressed in battle armor; on it was a belt with a sword fastened in its sheath at his hips; and as he was going forward, it fell out. 9Then Joab said to Amasa, "Are you in health, my brother?" And Joab took Amasa by the beard with his right hand to kiss him. 10But Amasa did not notice the sword that was in Joab's hand. And he struck him with it in the stomach, and his entrails poured out on the ground; and he did not strike him again. Thus he died.

Then Joab and Abishai his brother pursued Sheba the son of Bichri. 11Meanwhile one of Joab's men stood near Amasa, and said, "Whoever favors Joab and whoever is for David—follow Joab!" 12But Amasa wallowed in his blood in the middle of the highway. And when the man saw that all the people stood still, he moved Amasa from the highway to the field and threw a garment over him, when he saw that everyone who came upon him halted. 13When he was removed from the highway, all the people went on after Joab to pursue Sheba the son of Bichri.

14And he went through all the tribes of Israel to Abel and Beth Maachah and all the Berites. So they were gathered together and also went after Sheba.[a] 15Then they came and besieged him in Abel of Beth Maachah; and they cast up a siege mound against the city, and it stood by the rampart. And all the people who were with Joab battered the wall to throw it down.

16Then a wise woman cried out from the city, "Hear, hear! Please say to Joab, 'Come nearby, that I may speak with you.'" 17When he had come near to her, the woman said, "Are you Joab?"

He answered, "I am."

19:40 aMasoretic Text reads Chimhan.
20:1 aLiterally man of Belial   20:14 aLiterally him

CHERETHITES AND PELETHITES   (2 Sam. 20:23)

The Cherethites and the Pelethites were core troops of David's personal guard. Their Canaanite home territory in southern Judah was close to the Philistines near the Mediterranean coast (1 Sam. 30:14).

The Cherethites and the Pelethites had become attached to David while he lived in Gath (2 Sam. 15:18). Somehow they felt closer to David than to the Philistines. Their origin near Gath suggests that their ancestors may have been part of the Sea Peoples and, thus, had migrated from the Aegean area. On the other hand, they may have been the remnant of peoples that were replaced by the Philistines who moved into the coastal area. We have no documented evidence to settle this question.

The Cherethites and the Pelethites were extremely loyal to David, accompanying him when he fled from Absalom (2 Sam. 15:18) and pursuing the rebel Sheba who threatened David's kingdom (2 Sam. 20:7). They were also instrumental in the events that established Solomon as king (1 Kin. 1:38, 44).

The Cherethites, Pelethites, and David were in a near perfect relationship. The protection and loyalty which the Cherethites and Pelethites offered David assured them of his goodwill. Yet because they were foreigners, there was no possibility of this personal guard—those closest to David—replacing him as king with one of their own.

Then she said to him, "Hear the words of your maidservant."

And he answered, "I am listening."

[18]So she spoke, saying, "They used to talk in former times, saying, 'They shall surely seek *guidance* at Abel,' and so they would end *disputes*. [19]I *am among the* peaceable *and* faithful in Israel. You seek to destroy a city and a mother in Israel. Why would you swallow up the inheritance of the LORD?"

[20]And Joab answered and said, "Far be it, far be it from me, that I should swallow up or destroy! [21]That *is* not so. But a man from the mountains of Ephraim, Sheba the son of Bichri by name, has raised his hand against the king, against David. Deliver him only, and I will depart from the city."

So the woman said to Joab, "Watch, his head will be thrown to you over the wall." [22]Then the woman in her wisdom went to all the people. And they cut off the head of Sheba the son of Bichri, and threw *it* out to Joab. Then he blew a trumpet, and they withdrew from the city, every man to his tent. So Joab returned to the king at Jerusalem.

David's Government Officers

[23]And Joab *was* over all the army of Israel; Benaiah the son of Jehoiada *was* over the Cherethites and the Pelethites; [24]Ado- ▼

ram *was* in charge of revenue; Jehoshaphat the son of Ahilud *was* recorder; [25]Sheva *was* scribe; Zadok and Abiathar *were* the priests; [26]and Ira the Jairite was a chief minister under David.

The Gibeonites Are Avenged

The precise time when this 3-year famine occurred is unknown, but it must have been sometime after David brought Mephibosheth to Jerusalem (2 Sam. 21:7; 9:13). Some scholars suggest that the Gibeonite incident answers the charge of Shimei against David as a bloodthirsty man (2 Sam. 16:7, 8). The famine is interpreted to David as caused by an otherwise unreported slaughter of the Gibeonites by Saul. Such a slaughter would have been a breach of a divinely sanctioned covenant (21:2). Shimei's kinsman Saul was more bloodthirsty than David.

At a loss to find a way to cleanse the land of its bloodguilt, David accepted the vengeful demand of the remaining Gibeonites and ordered the execution of seven of Saul's descendants. Shimei had assumed that God was punishing David (16:8), but after the Gibeonites' anger had been assuaged, God does not punish David but rather hears his prayer (21:14).

■ 2 Samuel 21:1–22

2 Samuel

21

:1 Now there was a famine in the days of David for three years, year after year; and David inquired of the LORD. And the LORD answered, "It is because of Saul and *his* bloodthirsty house, because he killed the Gibeonites." 2So the king called the Gibeonites and spoke to them. Now the Gibeonites *were* not of the children of Israel, but of the remnant of the Amorites; the children of Israel had sworn protection to them, but Saul had sought to kill them in his zeal for the children of Israel and Judah.

3Therefore David said to the Gibeonites, "What shall I do for you? And with what shall I make atonement, that you may bless the inheritance of the LORD?"

4And the Gibeonites said to him, "We will have no silver or gold from Saul or from his house, nor shall you kill any man in Israel for us."

So he said, "Whatever you say, I will do for you."

5Then they answered the king, "As for the man who consumed us and plotted against us, *that* we should be destroyed from remaining in any of the territories of Israel, 6let seven men of his descendants be delivered to us, and we will hang them before the LORD in Gibeah of Saul, *whom* the LORD chose."

And the king said, "I will give *them.*"

7But the king spared Mephibosheth the son of Jonathan, the son of Saul, because of the LORD's oath that *was* between them, between David and Jonathan the son of Saul. 8So the king took Armoni and Mephibosheth, the two sons of Rizpah the daughter of Aiah, whom she bore to Saul, and the five sons of Michal[a] the daughter of Saul, whom she brought up for Adriel the son of Barzillai the Meholathite; 9and he delivered them into the hands of the Gibeonites, and they hanged them on the hill before the LORD. So they fell, *all* seven together, and were put to death in the days of harvest, in the first *days,* in the beginning of barley harvest.

10Now Rizpah the daughter of Aiah took sackcloth and spread it for herself on the rock, from the beginning of harvest until the late rains poured on them from heaven. And she did not allow the birds of the air to rest on them by day nor the beasts of the field by night.

11And David was told what Rizpah the daughter of Aiah, the concubine of Saul, had done. 12Then David went and took the bones of Saul, and the bones of Jonathan his son, from the men of Jabesh Gilead who had stolen them from the street of Beth Shan,[a] where the Philistines had hung them up, after the Philistines had struck down Saul in Gilboa. 13So he brought up the bones of Saul and the bones of Jonathan his son from there; and they gathered the bones of those who had been hanged. 14They buried the bones of Saul and Jonathan his son in the country of Benjamin in Zelah, in the tomb of Kish his father. So they performed all that the king commanded. And after that God heeded the prayer for the land.

Philistine Giants Destroyed

15When the Philistines were at war again with Israel, David and his servants with him went down and fought against the Philistines; and David grew faint. 16Then Ishbi-Benob, who *was* one of the sons of the giant, the weight of whose bronze spear *was* three hundred *shekels,* who was bearing a new *sword,* thought he could kill David. 17But Abishai the son of Zeruiah came to his aid, and struck the Philistine and killed him. Then the men of David swore to him, saying, "You shall go out no more with us to battle, lest you quench the lamp of Israel."

18Now it happened afterward that there was again a battle with the Philistines at Gob. Then Sibbechai the

---

21:8 [a]Or *Merab* (compare 1 Samuel 18:19 and 25:44; 2 Samuel 3:14 and 6:23)   21:12 [a]Spelled *Beth Shean* in Joshua 17:11 and elsewhere

---

CULTURE AND SOCIETY

The Gibeonites requested seven sons to be given to them to be killed and hanged up "before the LORD" (2 Sam. 21:6). The offering of these sons as some sort of sacrifice by the Gibeonites shows how complex the issues of guilt and justice were in ancient cultures. In the Iliad, Achilles is said to offer twelve sons of the enemy on the funeral pyre of his friend Patroclus.

Hushathite killed Saph,[a] who *was* one of the sons of the giant. [19]Again there was war at Gob with the Philistines, where El-hanan the son of Jaare-Oregim[a] the Beth-lehemite killed *the brother of* Goliath the Gittite, the shaft of whose spear *was* like a weaver's beam.

[20]Yet again there was war at Gath, where there was a man of *great* stature, who had six fingers on each hand and six toes on each foot, twenty-four in number; and he also was born to the giant. [21]So when he defied Israel, Jonathan the son of Shimea,[a] David's brother, killed him.

[22]These four were born to the giant in Gath, and fell by the hand of David and by the hand of his servants.

David's Song of Praise

Because the superscription of Ps. 18 refers to David's deliverance "from the hand of Saul," that psalm appears with the narrative of Saul's death, to be read in that context. Nevertheless, an almost exact duplicate of Ps. 18 occurs here in 2 Sam. 22, reflecting the end of David's life. In this context, the psalm must be read as David's thanks for a lifetime of deliverance, from many more enemies than just Saul.

David's song of praise is followed by his "last words" (2 Sam. 23:1–7). Since the Hebrew term translated "says" in "Thus says David" (23:1) is used elsewhere in the Old Testament to describe divinely inspired utterance, especially prophetic speeches, these "last words" have some of the tone and authority of a divine oracle.

■ 2 Samuel 22:1—23:39

2 Samuel
Praise for God's Deliverance

22 :1 Then David spoke to the LORD the words of this song, on the day when the LORD had delivered him from the hand of all his enemies, and from the hand of Saul. [2]And he said:[a]

"The LORD *is* my rock and my fortress and my deliverer;
[3] The God of my strength, in whom I will trust;
My shield and the horn of my salvation,
My stronghold and my refuge;
My Savior, You save me from violence.

[4] I will call upon the LORD, *who is worthy* to be praised;
So shall I be saved from my enemies.

[5] "When the waves of death surrounded me,
The floods of ungodliness made me afraid.
[6] The sorrows of Sheol surrounded me;
The snares of death confronted me.
[7] In my distress I called upon the LORD,
And cried out to my God;
He heard my voice from His temple,
And my cry *entered* His ears.

[8] "Then the earth shook and trembled;
The foundations of heaven[a] quaked and were shaken,
Because He was angry.
[9] Smoke went up from His nostrils,
And devouring fire from His mouth;
Coals were kindled by it.
[10] He bowed the heavens also, and came down
With darkness under His feet.
[11] He rode upon a cherub, and flew;
And He was seen[a] upon the wings of the wind.
[12] He made darkness canopies around Him,
Dark waters *and* thick clouds of the skies.
[13] From the brightness before Him
Coals of fire were kindled.

[14] "The LORD thundered from heaven,
And the Most High uttered His voice.
[15] He sent out arrows and scattered them;
Lightning bolts, and He vanquished them.
[16] Then the channels of the sea were seen,
The foundations of the world were uncovered,
At the rebuke of the LORD,
At the blast of the breath of His nostrils.

21:18 [a]Spelled *Sippai* in 1 Chronicles 20:4
21:19 [a]Spelled *Jair* in 1 Chronicles 20:5
21:21 [a]Spelled *Shammah* in 1 Samuel 16:9 and elsewhere   22:2 [a]Compare Psalm 18
22:8 [a]Following Masoretic Text, Septuagint, and Targum; Syriac and Vulgate read *hills* (compare Psalm 18:7).   22:11 [a]Following Masoretic Text and Septuagint; many Hebrew manuscripts, Syriac, and Vulgate read *He flew* (compare Psalm 18:10); Targum reads *He spoke with power*.

17 "He sent from above, He took me,
He drew me out of many waters.
18 He delivered me from my strong
enemy,
From those who hated me;
For they were too strong for me.
19 They confronted me in the day of my
calamity,
But the LORD was my support.
20 He also brought me out into a broad
place;
He delivered me because He delighted
in me.

21 "The LORD rewarded me according to
my righteousness;
According to the cleanness of my
hands
He has recompensed me.
22 For I have kept the ways of the LORD,
And have not wickedly departed from
my God.
23 For all His judgments *were* before me;
And *as for* His statutes, I did not
depart from them.
24 I was also blameless before Him,
And I kept myself from my iniquity.
25 Therefore the LORD has recompensed
me according to my righteousness,
According to my cleanness in His
eyes.[a]

26 "With the merciful You will show
Yourself merciful;
With a blameless man You will show
Yourself blameless;
27 With the pure You will show Yourself
pure;
And with the devious You will show
Yourself shrewd.
28 You will save the humble people;
But Your eyes *are* on the haughty, *that*
You may bring *them* down.

29 "For You *are* my lamp, O LORD;
The LORD shall enlighten my darkness.

30 For by You I can run against a troop;
By my God I can leap over a wall.
31 *As for* God, His way *is* perfect;
The word of the LORD *is* proven;
He *is* a shield to all who trust in Him.

32 "For who *is* God, except the LORD?
And who *is* a rock, except our God?
33 God *is* my strength *and* power,[a]
And He makes my[b] way perfect.
34 He makes my[a] feet like the *feet* of
deer,
And sets me on my high places.
35 He teaches my hands to make war,
So that my arms can bend a bow of
bronze.

36 "You have also given me the shield of
Your salvation;
Your gentleness has made me great.
37 You enlarged my path under me;
So my feet did not slip.

38 "I have pursued my enemies and
destroyed them;
Neither did I turn back again till they
were destroyed.
39 And I have destroyed them and
wounded them,
So that they could not rise;
They have fallen under my feet.
40 For You have armed me with strength
for the battle;
You have subdued under me those
who rose against me.
41 You have also given me the necks of
my enemies,
So that I destroyed those who hated
me.
42 They looked, but *there was* none to
save;
Even to the LORD, but He did not
answer them.
43 Then I beat them as fine as the dust
of the earth;
I trod them like dirt in the streets,
And I spread them out.

44 "You have also delivered me from the
strivings of my people;
You have kept me as the head of the
nations.
A people I have not known shall serve
me.
45 The foreigners submit to me;
As soon as they hear, they obey me.
46 The foreigners fade away,

22:25 [a]Septuagint, Syriac, and Vulgate read *the
cleanness of my hands in His sight* (compare Psalm
18:24); Targum reads *my cleanness before His
word.*   22:33 [a]Dead Sea Scrolls, Septuagint,
Syriac, and Vulgate read *It is God who arms me with
strength* (compare Psalm 18:32); Targum reads *It is
God who sustains me with strength.*   [b]Following Qere,
Septuagint, Syriac, Targum, and Vulgate (compare
Psalm 18:32); Kethib reads *His.*
22:34 [a]Following Qere, Septuagint, Syriac, Targum,
and Vulgate (compare Psalm 18:33); Kethib reads
His.

DAVID THE SWEET PSALMIST (2 Sam. 23:1)

The last words of David are introduced by the epitaph, "the son of Jesse . . . the man raised up on high, The anointed of the God of Jacob, And the sweet psalmist of Israel" (2 Sam. 23:1). David and psalms are ever considered together in the tradition of Israel.

Psalms are often thought of as poems or songs. In the Hebrew tradition the psalms are known as "songs of praise." While other themes are exhibited in the psalms, praise is the most pronounced feature. Music was a regular part of ancient life, accompanying mourners at funerals, priests at temples, brides at weddings, and the solitary individual in contemplation. Within this musical culture, the psalms were Israel's worship songs, offering reflection on the experiences of life.

In the stories that surround David, psalms are shown to be an integral part of his life (2 Sam. 1:17). His skill at playing the harp was widely known and highly appreciated (1 Sam. 16:16–23). When David became king, he appointed professional singers to perform religious duties (1 Chr. 6:31, 32; 15:16–24). David himself rendered "songs of praise" at special religious occasions (1 Chr. 16:7–36). In these services, music was used as a vehicle for prophesying (1 Chr. 25:1).

The Book of Psalms is often associated with David because the superscriptions (or psalm titles) ascribe a large number of the psalms to David or to an event in his life. After his death, David's fame as a psalmist grew ever larger. While the Hebrew Bible associates David with 73 psalms, later translations increase the number of psalms ascribed to him. The Dead Sea Psalms Scroll claims that David wrote 4,050 psalms and songs, all given him by divine inspiration from the Lord.

And come frightened[a] from their
hideouts.

47 "The LORD lives!
Blessed *be* my Rock!
Let God be exalted,
The Rock of my salvation!
48 *It is* God who avenges me,
And subdues the peoples under me;
49 He delivers me from my enemies.
You also lift me up above those who
rise against me;
You have delivered me from the
violent man.
50 Therefore I will give thanks to You,
O LORD, among the Gentiles,
And sing praises to Your name.

51 "*He is* the tower of salvation to His
king,
And shows mercy to His anointed,
To David and his descendants
forevermore."

David's Last Words

23 ¹Now these *are* the last words of David.

Thus says David the son of Jesse;
Thus says the man raised up on high,

The anointed of the God of Jacob,
And the sweet psalmist of Israel:

2 "The Spirit of the LORD spoke by me,
And His word *was* on my tongue.
3 The God of Israel said,
The Rock of Israel spoke to me:
'He who rules over men *must be* just,
Ruling in the fear of God.
4 And *he shall be* like the light of the
morning *when* the sun rises,
A morning without clouds,
Like the tender grass *springing* out of
the earth,
By clear shining after rain.'

5 "Although my house *is* not so with God,
Yet He has made with me an
everlasting covenant,
Ordered in all *things* and secure.
For *this is* all my salvation and all *my*
desire;
Will He not make *it* increase?
6 But *the sons* of rebellion *shall* all *be* as
thorns thrust away,

22:46 ᵃFollowing Septuagint, Targum, and Vulgate (compare Psalm 18:45); Masoretic Text reads *gird themselves*.

Because they cannot be taken with
hands.
7 But the man *who* touches them
Must be armed with iron and the
shaft of a spear,
And they shall be utterly burned with
fire in *their* place."

David's Mighty Men

8These *are* the names of the mighty
men whom David had: Josheb-Basshebeth[a]
the Tachmonite, chief among the captains.[b]
He was called Adino the Eznite, because
he had killed eight hundred men at one
time. 9And after him *was* Eleazar the
son of Dodo,[a] the Ahohite, *one* of the
three mighty men with David when they
defied the Philistines *who* were gathered
there for battle, and the men of Israel
had retreated. 10He arose and attacked
the Philistines until his hand was weary,
and his hand stuck to the sword. The
LORD brought about a great victory that
day; and the people returned after him
only to plunder. 11And after him *was*
Shammah the son of Agee the Hararite.
The Philistines had gathered together into
a troop where there was a piece of ground
full of lentils. So the people fled from the
Philistines. 12But he stationed himself in
the middle of the field, defended it, and
killed the Philistines. So the LORD brought
about a great victory.

13Then three of the thirty chief men
went down at harvest time and came to
David at the cave of Adullam. And
the troop of Philistines encamped in the
Valley of Rephaim. 14David *was* then in
the stronghold, and the garrison of
the Philistines *was* then *in* Bethlehem.
15And David said with longing, "Oh, that
someone would give me a drink of the
water from the well of Bethlehem, which
is by the gate!" 16So the three mighty
men broke through the camp of the
Philistines, drew water from the well of
Bethlehem that *was* by the gate, and took
it and brought *it* to David. Nevertheless he
would not drink it, but poured it out to the
LORD. 17And he said, "Far be it from me,
O LORD, that I should do this! Is *this not*
the blood of the men who went in *jeopardy
of* their lives?" Therefore he would not
drink it.

These things were done by the three
mighty men.

18Now Abishai the brother of Joab, the
son of Zeruiah, was chief of *another* three.[a]
He lifted his spear against three hundred
men, killed *them,* and won a name among
these three. 19Was he not the most honored
of three? Therefore he became their captain. However, he did not attain to the *first*
three.

20Benaiah *was* the son of Jehoiada, the
son of a valiant man from Kabzeel, who
had done many deeds. He had killed
two lion-like heroes of Moab. He also
had gone down and killed a lion in the
midst of a pit on a snowy day. 21And he
killed an Egyptian, a spectacular man. The
Egyptian *had* a spear in his hand; so
he went down to him with a staff, wrested
the spear out of the Egyptian's hand, and
killed him with his own spear. 22These
things Benaiah the son of Jehoiada
did, and won a name among three mighty
men. 23He was more honored than the
thirty, but he did not attain to the *first*
three. And David appointed him over his
guard.

24Asahel the brother of Joab *was* one of
the thirty; Elhanan the son of Dodo of
Bethlehem, 25Shammah the Harodite,
Elika the Harodite, 26Helez the Paltite, Ira
the son of Ikkesh the Tekoite, 27Abiezer the
Anathothite, Mebunnai the Hushathite,
28Zalmon the Ahohite, Maharai the Netophathite, 29Heleb the son of Baanah (the
Netophathite), Ittai the son of Ribai from
Gibeah of the children of Benjamin, 30Be-
naiah a Pirathonite, Hiddai from the
brooks of Gaash, 31Abi-Albon the Arbathite, Azmaveth the Barhumite, 32Eli-
ahba the Shaalbonite (of the sons of
Jashen), Jonathan, 33Shammah the
Hararite, Ahiam the son of Sharar the
Hararite, 34Eliphelet the son of Ahasbai,
the son of the Maachathite, Eliam the son
of Ahithophel the Gilonite, 35Hezrai[a] the
Carmelite, Paarai the Arbite, 36Igal the son
of Nathan of Zobah, Bani the Gadite,
37Zelek the Ammonite, Naharai the
Beerothite (armorbearer of Joab the son of
Zeruiah), 38Ira the Ithrite, Gareb the
Ithrite, 39*and* Uriah the Hittite: thirty-
seven in all.

23:8 [a]Literally *One Who Sits in the Seat* (compare
1 Chronicles 11:11)   [b]Following Masoretic Text and
Targum; Septuagint and Vulgate read *the three.*
23:9 [a]Spelled *Dodai* in 1 Chronicles 27:4
23:18 [a]Following Masoretic Text, Septuagint, and
Vulgate; some Hebrew manuscripts and Syriac read
thirty; Targum reads *the mighty men.*
23:35 [a]Spelled *Hezro* in 1 Chronicles 11:37

Priestly Account: David's Reign

The historian of Chronicles presents a very different picture of David than does the historian of Samuel. A small example of the Chronicler's work is David's victory over Moab. In 1 Sam. 8:2, David summarily executes two-thirds of his Moabite prisoners of war. The Chronicler, however, concerned to show David in his very best light, tells of the victory while omitting these brutal executions (1 Chr. 18:2).

The Chronicler goes to greater lengths to avoid David's failures. For instance, Chronicles completely omits any reference either to David's sin with Bathsheba or to the civil war with Absalom. Avoiding all unpleasantness in this way, the Chronicler is able to tell of David's reign rather quickly.

▼   ■ 1 Chronicles 18:1–13

1 Chronicles
David's Further Conquests

18 :1 After this it came to pass that David attacked the Philistines, subdued them, and took Gath and its towns from the hand of the Philistines. ²Then he defeated Moab, and the Moabites became David's servants, *and* brought tribute.

³And David defeated Hadadezer[a] king of Zobah *as far as* Hamath, as he went to establish his power by the River Euphrates. ⁴David took from him one thousand chariots, seven thousand[a] horsemen, and twenty thousand foot soldiers. Also David hamstrung all the chariot *horses,* except that he spared enough of them for one hundred chariots.

⁵When the Syrians of Damascus came to help Hadadezer king of Zobah, David killed twenty-two thousand of the Syrians. ⁶Then David put *garrisons* in Syria of Damascus; and the Syrians became David's servants, *and* brought tribute. So the LORD preserved David wherever he went. ⁷And David took the shields of gold that were on the servants of Hadadezer, and brought them to Jerusalem. ⁸Also from Tibhath[a] and from Chun, cities of Hadadezer, David brought a large amount of bronze, with which Solomon made the bronze Sea, the pillars, and the articles of bronze.

⁹Now when Tou[a] king of Hamath heard that David had defeated all the army of Hadadezer king of Zobah, ¹⁰he sent Hadoram[a] his son to King David, to greet him and bless him, because he had fought against Hadadezer and defeated him (for Hadadezer had been at war with Tou); and *Hadoram brought with him* all kinds of articles of gold, silver, and bronze. ¹¹King David also dedicated these to the LORD, along with the silver and gold that he had brought from all *these* nations—from Edom, from Moab, from the people of Ammon, from the Philistines, and from Amalek.

¹²Moreover Abishai the son of Zeruiah killed eighteen thousand Edomites[a] in the Valley of Salt. ¹³He also put garrisons in Edom, and all the Edomites became David's servants. And the LORD preserved David wherever he went.

18:3 [a]Hebrew *Hadarezer,* and so throughout chapters 18 and 19   18:4 [a]Or *seven hundred* (compare 2 Samuel 8:4)   18:8 [a]Spelled *Betah* in 2 Samuel 8:8   18:9 [a]Spelled *Toi* in 2 Samuel 8:9, 10   18:10 [a]Spelled *Joram* in 2 Samuel 8:10   18:12 [a]Or *Syrians* (compare 2 Samuel 8:13)

The Promise of Military Victory

Not only does the superscription of Ps. 60 place this psalm precisely, but so also does the text of the psalm itself. Most psalms intentionally use very general language, referring to unspecified "enemies." In contrast, Ps. 60 names particular surrounding kingdoms, the nations that David conquered, in its superscription and text.

The psalm expresses the hope that God will bring future victory over enemies (Ps. 60:12). In ch. 18 the Chronicler summarized David's victories over Philistia, Moab, Aram (Syria), and Edom with the report that "the LORD preserved David wherever he went" (1 Chr. 18:13). In the final account of David's wars with the Ammonites, Philistines, and descendants of the giant (1 Chr. 19; 20), Chronicles continues to show that God's blessing was upon David (1 Chr. 19:13).

▼   ■ Psalm 60
       ■ 1 Chronicles 18:14—20:8

PSALM 60

Urgent Prayer for the Restored Favor of God

To the Chief Musician. Set to "Lily of the Testimony."ᵃ A Michtam of David. For teaching. When he fought against Mesopotamia and Syria of Zobah, and Joab returned and killed twelve thousand Edomites in the Valley of Salt.

O God, You have cast us off;
  You have broken us down;
  You have been displeased;
  Oh, restore us again!
2 You have made the earth tremble;
  You have broken it;
  Heal its breaches, for it is shaking.
3 You have shown Your people hard
    things;
  You have made us drink the wine of
    confusion.

4 You have given a banner to those who
    fear You,
  That it may be displayed because of
    the truth.   Selah
5 That Your beloved may be delivered,
  Save *with* Your right hand, and hear
    me.

6 God has spoken in His holiness:
  "I will rejoice;
  I will divide Shechem
  And measure out the Valley of
    Succoth.
7 Gilead *is* Mine, and Manasseh *is*
    Mine;
  Ephraim also *is* the helmet for My
    head;
  Judah *is* My lawgiver.
8 Moab *is* My washpot;
  Over Edom I will cast My shoe;
  Philistia, shout in triumph because
    of Me."

9 Who will bring me *to* the strong city?
  Who will lead me to Edom?
10 *Is it* not You, O God, *who* cast us off?
  And You, O God, *who* did not go out
    with our armies?
11 Give us help from trouble,
  For the help of man *is* useless.
12 Through God we will do valiantly,

For *it is* He *who* shall tread down our
  enemies.ᵃ

1 Chronicles 18:14—20:8
David's Administration

18 :14 So David reigned over all Israel, and administered judgment and justice to all his people. 15Joab the son of Zeruiah *was* over the army; Jehoshaphat the son of Ahilud *was* recorder; 16Zadok the son of Ahitub and Abimelech the son of Abiathar *were* the priests; Shavshaᵃ *was* the scribe; 17Benaiah the son of Jehoiada *was* over the Cherethites and the Pelethites; and David's sons *were* chief ministers at the king's side.

The Ammonites and Syrians Defeated

19 1It happened after this that Nahash the king of the people of Ammon died, and his son reigned in his place. 2Then David said, "I will show kindness to Hanun the son of Nahash, because his father showed kindness to me." So David sent messengers to comfort him concerning his father. And David's servants came to Hanun in the land of the people of Ammon to comfort him.
  3And the princes of the people of Ammon said to Hanun, "Do you think that David really honors your father because he has sent comforters to you? Did his servants not come to you to search and to overthrow and to spy out the land?"
  4Therefore Hanun took David's servants, shaved them, and cut off their garments in the middle, at their buttocks, and sent them away. 5Then *some* went and told David about the men; and he sent to meet them, because the men were greatly

---

60:title ᵃHebrew *Shushan Eduth*
60:12 ᵃCompare verses 5–12 with 108:6–13
1 Chr. 18:16 ᵃSpelled *Seraiah* in 2 Samuel 8:17

TIME CAPSULE	*1050 to 1003 B.C.*
1050	*Saul becomes first king of Israel (or 1020)*
1020	*Saul becomes first king of Israel (or 1050)*
1010– 1003	*David rules as king of Judah at Hebron (2 Sam. 2:4)*
1005	*Ishbosheth succeeds Saul as king of Israel (2 Sam. 2:10)*
1003	*Ishbosheth is assassinated (2 Sam. 4:5–8)*
1003– 970	*David rules as king of Israel at Jerusalem*

GATES AND FORTIFIED CITIES (1 Chr. 19:9)

Battles were often fought near the gate of a city (1 Chr. 19:9), which was its most vulnerable defensive feature. City gates were made of wood, so it was easier for enemies to gain access to the city by beating them down or setting them on fire, than by storming or undermining the stone walls. For this reason a number of developments were added to city gates to make them a stronger part of a fortified city's overall defense (2 Chr. 8:5).

One building strategy was to make the approach to the city a long narrow ramp. Such ramps ran parallel to one of the city's walls, and were often built along the wall from right to left. Enemy soldiers carrying shields were forced to turn nearly backwards to defend themselves (even in ancient times people were mostly right-handed). Furthermore, enemies had to run the length of the wall before they came to the first gate. This process exposed them to observation and attack from the city's defenders.

Cities also had more than one gate in the gatehouse or main-gate complex. The outer gate was built well outside the city and at a right angle to the city. It was placed directly in front of the approach ramp and was the first major obstacle for attackers.

These gatehouses were part of a castlelike building similar to towers. Defenders were stationed on the roofs of these complexes and behind the doors. If enemy soldiers succeeded in gaining entrance, they found themselves confined to a narrow passage that made a sharp right turn toward the main gate. Of course, defenders were not only blocking the passage but were also stationed above on the walls of the passage. If enemies survived this gauntlet, they still faced the city's primary gate.

The main gate was a multichambered structure resembling an extralarge tower. It consisted of up to four separate sets of gates, behind which were chambers for defending soldiers. The roofs of these gate structures were designed so that the defenders had clear aim at the attackers.

---

ashamed. And the king said, "Wait at Jericho until your beards have grown, and *then* return."

⁶When the people of Ammon saw that they had made themselves repulsive to David, Hanun and the people of Ammon sent a thousand talents of silver to hire for themselves chariots and horsemen from Mesopotamia,ᵃ from Syrian Maacah, and from Zobah.ᵇ ⁷So they hired for themselves thirty-two thousand chariots, with the king of Maacah and his people, who came and encamped before Medeba. Also the people of Ammon gathered together from their cities, and came to battle.

⁸Now when David heard *of it,* he sent Joab and all the army of the mighty men. ⁹Then the people of Ammon came out and put themselves in battle array before the gate of the city, and the kings who had come *were* by themselves in the field. ¹⁰When Joab saw that the battle line was against him before and behind, he chose some of Israel's best, and put *them* in battle array against the Syrians. ¹¹And the rest of the people he put under the command of Abishai his brother, and they set

themselves in battle array against the people of Ammon. ¹²Then he said, "If the Syrians are too strong for me, then you shall help me; but if the people of Ammon are too strong for you, then I will help you. ¹³Be of good courage, and let us be strong for our people and for the cities of our God. And may the LORD do *what is* good in His sight."

¹⁴So Joab and the people who *were* with him drew near for the battle against the Syrians, and they fled before him. ¹⁵When the people of Ammon saw that the Syrians were fleeing, they also fled before Abishai his brother, and entered the city. So Joab went to Jerusalem.

¹⁶Now when the Syrians saw that they had been defeated by Israel, they sent messengers and brought the Syrians who were beyond the River,ᵃ and Shophachᵇ the commander of Hadadezer's army *went* before them. ¹⁷When it was told David, he gathered all Israel, crossed over the Jordan and

---

19:6 ᵃHebrew *Aram Naharaim* ᵇSpelled *Zoba* in 2 Samuel 10:6   19:16 ᵃThat is, the Euphrates ᵇSpelled *Shobach* in 2 Samuel 10:16

came upon them, and set up in battle array against them. So when David had set up in *battle* array against the Syrians, they fought with him. ¹⁸Then the Syrians fled before Israel; and David killed seven thousandᵃ charioteers and forty thousand foot soldiersᵇ of the Syrians, and killed Shophach the commander of the army. ¹⁹And when the servants of Hadadezer saw that they were defeated by Israel, they made peace with David and became his servants. So the Syrians were not willing to help the people of Ammon anymore.

Rabbah Is Conquered

20 ¹It happened in the spring of the year, at the time kings go out *to battle,* that Joab led out the armed forces and ravaged the country of the people of Ammon, and came and besieged Rabbah. But David stayed at Jerusalem. And Joab defeated Rabbah and overthrew it. ²Then David took their king's crown from his head, and found it to weigh a talent of gold, and *there were* precious stones in it. And it was set on David's head. Also he brought out the spoil of the city in great abundance. ³And he brought out the people who *were* in it, and put *them* to workᵃ with saws, with iron picks, and with axes. So David did to all the cities of the people of Ammon. Then David and all the people returned *to* Jerusalem.

Philistine Giants Destroyed

⁴Now it happened afterward that war broke out at Gezer with the Philistines, at which time Sibbechai the Hushathite killed Sippai,ᵃ *who was one* of the sons of the giant. And they were subdued. ⁵Again there was war with the Philistines, and Elhanan the son of Jairᵃ

19:18 ᵃOr *seven hundred* (compare 2 Samuel 10:18)
ᵇOr *horsemen* (compare 2 Samuel 10:18)
20:3 ᵃSeptuagint reads *cut them.*   20:4 ᵃSpelled
Saph in 2 Samuel 21:18   20:5 ᵃSpelled *Jaare-Oregim* in 2 Samuel 21:19   20:7 ᵃSpelled
Shimeah in 2 Samuel 21:21 and *Shammah* in
1 Samuel 16:9

killed Lahmi the brother of Goliath the Gittite, the shaft of whose spear *was* like a weaver's beam.

⁶Yet again there was war at Gath, where there was a man of *great* stature, with twenty-four fingers and toes, six *on each hand* and six *on each foot;* and he also was born to the giant. ⁷So when he defied Israel, Jonathan the son of Shimea,ᵃ David's brother, killed him.

⁸These were born to the giant in Gath, and they fell by the hand of David and by the hand of his servants.

Prophetic Account: David's Final Years

The ancient world knew of only two reasons for taking a census: to draft citizens into the military or to draft them into forced labor. Both types of conscription were common among Near Eastern kingdoms, but neither had ever been a part of Israel's life. During the tribal confederation, war had been a voluntary action and only foreigners had been enslaved. When David took a census, it was a clear step away from those covenant traditions and a clear step toward the usual patterns of kingship. Even Joab, David's pragmatic commander in chief, was surprised at David's decision (2 Sam. 24:3).

The census takers followed a route from Jerusalem to Aroer (east of the Dead Sea), north to Dan, west to Tyre, south to Beersheba, then back to Jerusalem. While it took nearly 10 months to complete this circuit (24:8), it is not certain when the census occurred.

■ 2 Samuel 24:1–25

---

2 Samuel
David's Census of Israel and Judah

24 :1 Again the anger of the LORD was aroused against Israel, and He moved David against them to say, "Go, number Israel and Judah."

²So the king said to Joab the commander of the army who *was* with him,

---

"Now go throughout all the tribes of Israel, from Dan to Beersheba, and count the people, that I may know the number of the people."

³And Joab said to the king, "Now may the LORD your God add to the people a hundred times more than there are, and may the eyes of my lord the king see it. But why does my lord the king desire this thing?" ⁴Nevertheless the king's word prevailed against Joab and against the captains of the army. Therefore Joab and the captains of the army went out from the presence of the king to count the people of Israel.

⁵And they crossed over the Jordan and camped in Aroer, on the right side of the town which is in the midst of the ravine of Gad, and toward Jazer. ⁶Then they came to Gilead and to the land of Tahtim Hodshi; they came to Dan Jaan and around to Sidon; ⁷and they came to the stronghold of Tyre and to all the cities of the Hivites and the Canaanites. Then they went out to South Judah as far as Beersheba. ⁸So when they had gone through all the land, they came to Jerusalem at the end of nine months and twenty days. ⁹Then Joab gave the sum of the number of the people to the king. And there were in Israel eight hundred thousand valiant men who drew the sword, and the men of Judah were five hundred thousand men.

The Judgment on David's Sin

¹⁰And David's heart condemned him after he had numbered the people. So David said to the LORD, "I have sinned greatly in what I have done; but now, I pray, O LORD, take away the iniquity of Your servant, for I have done very foolishly."

¹¹Now when David arose in the morning, the word of the LORD came to the prophet Gad, David's seer, saying, ¹²"Go and tell David, 'Thus says the LORD: "I offer you three things; choose one of them for yourself, that I may do it to you." ' " ¹³So Gad came to David and told him; and he said to him, "Shall seven[a] years of famine come to you in your land? Or shall you flee

three months before your enemies, while they pursue you? Or shall there be three days' plague in your land? Now consider and see what answer I should take back to Him who sent me."

¹⁴And David said to Gad, "I am in great distress. Please let us fall into the hand of the LORD, for His mercies are great; but do not let me fall into the hand of man."

¹⁵So the LORD sent a plague upon Israel from the morning till the appointed time. From Dan to Beersheba seventy thousand men of the people died. ¹⁶And when the angel[a] stretched out His hand over Jerusalem to destroy it, the LORD relented from the destruction, and said to the angel who was destroying the people, "It is enough; now restrain your hand." And the angel of the LORD was by the threshing floor of Araunah[b] the Jebusite.

¹⁷Then David spoke to the LORD when he saw the angel who was striking the people, and said, "Surely I have sinned, and I have done wickedly; but these sheep, what have they done? Let Your hand, I pray, be against me and against my father's house."

The Altar on the Threshing Floor

¹⁸And Gad came that day to David and said to him, "Go up, erect an altar to the LORD on the threshing floor of Araunah the Jebusite." ¹⁹So David, according to the word of Gad, went up as the LORD commanded. ²⁰Now Araunah looked, and saw the king and his servants coming toward him. So Araunah went out and bowed before the king with his face to the ground.

²¹Then Araunah said, "Why has my lord the king come to his servant?"

And David said, "To buy the threshing floor from you, to build an altar to the

---

24:13 ªFollowing Masoretic Text, Syriac, Targum, and Vulgate; Septuagint reads three (compare 1 Chronicles 21:12).   24:16 ªOr Angel ᵇSpelled Ornan in 1 Chronicles 21:15

POLITICS AND GOVERNMENT

The Bible contains numerous lists of persons and tribes, as well as censuses of fighting men. In many cases the purpose of a census was taxation or a military draft. For this and other reasons censuses were often offensive to the population being counted (2 Sam. 24:2). A census taken by the Romans caused riots in Palestine around A.D. 6 or 7.

COUNTING HEADS (2 Sam. 24:10–14)

One case of census taking is presented in the Old Testament as at best a mistake and at worst a sin. King David wanted to count his population, but his census is presented as an evil act that would bring punishment on the Israelites (2 Sam. 24:10–13). The Chronicler even suggests that the idea for David's census came from Satan himself (1 Chr. 21:1).

A number of census records have been found among ancient Near Eastern tablets. Empires, stretching over large areas, needed to be able to calculate taxes and assign supplies for their soldiers. They met these obligations by counting and recording the numbers of their people. For propaganda purposes, the Assyrians calculated that they had resettled in different parts of their kingdom 4.5 million conquered people.

An interesting example of an ancient census is the Assyrian Doomsday Book. In these 21 tablets families are registered by the father's name. After the families are listed, the children's height is provided as a means of calculating relative age. A separate section provided a description of land that belonged to each family and how the land was used. Not all families were included in this register, since the Assyrian Doomsday Book was used as a regional guide to noble families who were exempt from Assyrian taxes. From these records it has become clear that early censuses were not used for long-range planning but had specific, immediate purposes.

The Bible nowhere specifies why census taking was considered evil. Nevertheless, David felt guilty over the census he ordered, confessing that he had "sinned greatly" (2 Sam. 24:10). Since it seems obvious that the counting in itself was not bad, the sin had to do with the motivation for counting the people. We can only guess that if David knew the size of his population he might either trust in the size of his army or fear the size of his enemy's army. The census would thus interfere with dependence on God to give victory over Israel's enemies.

LORD, that the plague may be withdrawn from the people."

²²Now Araunah said to David, "Let my lord the king take and offer up whatever *seems* good to him. Look, *here are* oxen for burnt sacrifice, and threshing implements and the yokes of the oxen for wood. ²³All these, O king, Araunah has given to the king."

And Araunah said to the king, "May the LORD your God accept you."

²⁴Then the king said to Araunah, "No, but I will surely buy *it* from you for a price; nor will I offer burnt offerings to the LORD my God with that which costs me nothing." So David bought the threshing floor and the oxen for fifty shekels of silver. ²⁵And David built there an altar to the LORD, and offered burnt offerings and peace offerings. So the LORD heeded the prayers for the land, and the plague was withdrawn from Israel.

The Books of Kings

Although the books of Kings present a unified history, they clearly consist of many smaller strands, woven together by an editor. These strands include a detailed account of Solomon's court, a history of the kings of the northern kingdom, a history of the kings of the southern kingdom, and narratives about the prophets Elijah and Elisha.

All these strands are woven together and unified by theological comments that interpret the history. The interpretations evaluate the different kings and kingdoms in terms of the requirements found in the Book of Deuteronomy. For instance, 2 Kin. 17, which explains in some detail why God allowed the northern kingdom to be destroyed, uses thoughts and even specific expressions from Deuteronomy. For this reason, Kings is often described as part of a "Deuteronomistic History."

The history concludes during the Babylonian exile, with the last recorded event occurring in 561 B.C. (2 Kin. 25:27–30). However, there is no mention of the Persian king Cyrus and his edict of 539 B.C. that freed the exiled Jews (see 2 Chr. 36:22, 23). Therefore, it is reasonable to assume that the editing process was done sometime between 561 and 539 B.C.

The Book of 1 Kings begins with the story

of how Solomon became David's successor instead of Adonijah, the crown prince. An exact date for when Solomon began his reign is impossible to determine. The 40 years given as the length of his reign (1 Kin. 11:42) could be a symbolic number, and, furthermore, it is not known how long Solomon ruled as a coregent while his father, David, was still alive (1 Kin. 1:32–35; 2:10). Accepting these uncertainties, we can set the date for Solomon's enthronement at approximately 970 B.C. See "When Did David Become King?" at 2 Sam. 5:1.

▼   ■ 1 Kings 1:1—2:35

1 Kings
Adonijah Presumes to Be King

1 :1 Now King David was old, advanced in years; and they put covers on him, but he could not get warm. ²Therefore his servants said to him, "Let a young woman, a virgin, be sought for our lord the king, and let her stand before the king, and let her care for him; and let her lie in your bosom, that our lord the king may be warm." ³So they sought for a lovely young woman throughout all the territory of Israel, and found Abishag the Shunammite, and brought her to the king. ⁴The young woman *was* very lovely; and she cared for the king, and served him; but the king did not know her.

⁵Then Adonijah the son of Haggith exalted himself, saying, "I will be king"; and he prepared for himself chariots and horsemen, and fifty men to run before him. ⁶(And his father had not rebuked him at any time by saying, "Why have you done so?" He *was* also very good-looking. *His mother* had borne him after Absalom.) ⁷Then he conferred with Joab the son of Zeruiah and with Abiathar the priest, and they followed and helped Adonijah. ⁸But Zadok the priest, Benaiah the son of Jehoiada, Nathan the prophet, Shimei, Rei, and the mighty men who *belonged* to David were not with Adonijah.

⁹And Adonijah sacrificed sheep and oxen and fattened cattle by the stone of Zoheleth, which *is* by En Rogel; he also invited all his brothers, the king's sons, and all the men of Judah, the king's servants. ¹⁰But he did not invite Nathan the prophet, Benaiah, the mighty men, or Solomon his brother.

¹¹So Nathan spoke to Bathsheba the mother of Solomon, saying, "Have you not heard that Adonijah the son of Haggith has become king, and David our lord does not know *it?* ¹²Come, please, let me now give you advice, that you may save your own life and the life of your son Solomon. ¹³Go immediately to King David and say to him, 'Did you not, my lord, O king, swear to your maidservant, saying, "Assuredly your son Solomon shall reign after me, and he shall sit on my throne"? Why then has Adonijah become king?' ¹⁴Then, while you are still talking there with the king, I also will come in after you and confirm your words."

¹⁵So Bathsheba went into the chamber to the king. (Now the king was very old, and Abishag the Shunammite was serving the king.) ¹⁶And Bathsheba bowed and did homage to the king. Then the king said, "What is your wish?"

¹⁷Then she said to him, "My lord, you swore by the LORD your God to your maidservant, *saying,* 'Assuredly Solomon your son shall reign after me, and he shall sit on my throne.' ¹⁸So now, look! Adonijah has become king; and now, my lord the king, you do not know about *it.* ¹⁹He has sacrificed oxen and fattened cattle and sheep in abundance, and has invited all the sons of the king, Abiathar the priest, and Joab the commander of the army; but Solomon your servant he has not invited. ²⁰And as for you, my lord, O king, the eyes of all Israel *are* on you, that you should tell them who will sit on the throne of my lord the king after him. ²¹Otherwise it will happen, when my lord the king rests with his fathers, that I and my son Solomon will be counted as offenders."

²²And just then, while she was still talking with the king, Nathan the prophet also came in. ²³So they told the king, saying, "Here is Nathan the prophet." And when he came in before the king, he bowed down before the king with his face to the ground. ²⁴And Nathan said, "My lord, O king, have you said, 'Adonijah shall reign after me, and he shall sit on my throne'? ²⁵For he has gone down today, and has sacrificed oxen and fattened cattle and sheep in abundance, and has invited all the king's sons, and the commanders of the army, and Abiathar the priest; and look! They are eating and drinking before him; and they say, '*Long* live King Adonijah!' ²⁶But he has not invited me—me your servant—nor Zadok the priest, nor Benaiah the son of Jehoiada, nor your servant Sol-

omon. ²⁷Has this thing been done by my lord the king, and you have not told your servant who should sit on the throne of my lord the king after him?"

David Proclaims Solomon King

²⁸Then King David answered and said, "Call Bathsheba to me." So she came into the king's presence and stood before the king. ²⁹And the king took an oath and said, "*As* the LORD lives, who has redeemed my life from every distress, ³⁰just as I swore to you by the LORD God of Israel, saying, 'Assuredly Solomon your son shall be king after me, and he shall sit on my throne in my place,' so I certainly will do this day."

³¹Then Bathsheba bowed with *her* face to the earth, and paid homage to the king, and said, "Let my lord King David live forever!"

³²And King David said, "Call to me Zadok the priest, Nathan the prophet, and Benaiah the son of Jehoiada." So they came before the king. ³³The king also said to them, "Take with you the servants of your lord, and have Solomon my son ride on my own mule, and take him down to Gihon. ³⁴There let Zadok the priest and Nathan the prophet anoint him king over Israel; and blow the horn, and say, '*Long* live King Solomon!' ³⁵Then you shall come up after him, and he shall come and sit on my throne, and he shall be king in my place. For I have appointed him to be ruler over Israel and Judah."

³⁶Benaiah the son of Jehoiada answered the king and said, "Amen! May the LORD God of my lord the king say so *too*. ³⁷As the LORD has been with my lord the king, even so may He be with Solomon, and make his throne greater than the throne of my lord King David."

³⁸So Zadok the priest, Nathan the prophet, Benaiah the son of Jehoiada, the Cherethites, and the Pelethites went down and had Solomon ride on King David's mule, and took him to Gihon. ³⁹Then Zadok the priest took a horn of oil from the tabernacle and anointed Solomon. And they

blew the horn, and all the people said, "*Long* live King Solomon!" ⁴⁰And all the people went up after him; and the people played the flutes and rejoiced with great joy, so that the earth *seemed to* split with their sound.

⁴¹Now Adonijah and all the guests who *were* with him heard *it* as they finished eating. And when Joab heard the sound of the horn, he said, "Why *is* the city in such a noisy uproar?" ⁴²While he was still speaking, there came Jonathan, the son of Abiathar the priest. And Adonijah said to him, "Come in, for you *are* a prominent man, and bring good news."

⁴³Then Jonathan answered and said to Adonijah, "No! Our lord King David has made Solomon king. ⁴⁴The king has sent with him Zadok the priest, Nathan the prophet, Benaiah the son of Jehoiada, the Cherethites, and the Pelethites; and they have made him ride on the king's mule. ⁴⁵So Zadok the priest and Nathan the prophet have anointed him king at Gihon; and they have gone up from there rejoicing, so that the city is in an uproar. This *is* the noise that you have heard. ⁴⁶Also Solomon sits on the throne of the kingdom. ⁴⁷And moreover the king's servants have gone to bless our lord King David, saying, 'May God make the name of Solomon better than your name, and may He make his throne greater than your throne.' Then the king bowed himself on the bed. ⁴⁸Also the king said thus, 'Blessed *be* the LORD God of Israel, who has given *one* to sit on my throne this day, while my eyes see *it!'* "

⁴⁹So all the guests who were with Adonijah were afraid, and arose, and each one went his way.

⁵⁰Now Adonijah was afraid of Solomon; so he arose, and went and took hold of the horns of the altar. ⁵¹And it was told Solomon, saying, "Indeed Adonijah is afraid of King Solomon; for look, he has taken hold of the horns of the altar, saying, 'Let King Solomon swear to me today that he will not put his servant to death with the sword.' "

⁵²Then Solomon said, "If he proves

POLITICS AND GOVERNMENT

The ritual act of anointing was accompanied with shouts of praise, called acclamation. Like anointing, acclamation was a particular symbolic action. It was an essential part of raising a person to the throne to become king. When the priest Zadok and prophet Nathan anointed Solomon, they shouted "Long live King Solomon!" to which the people answered the same (1 Kin. 1:34, 39).

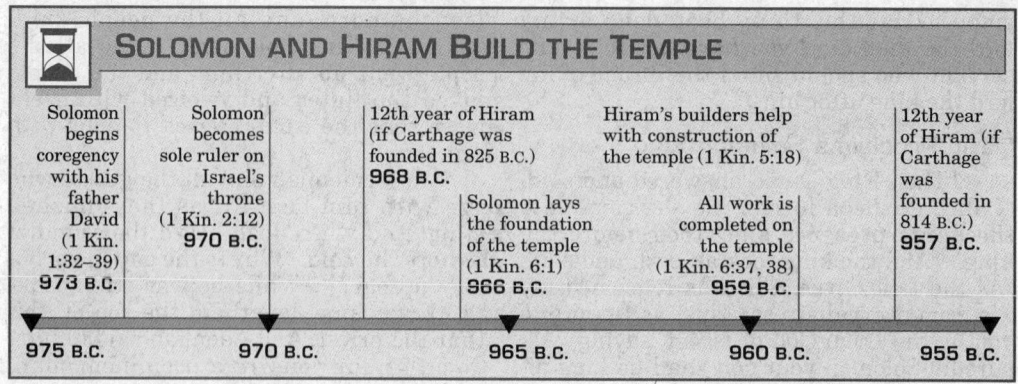

⧗ SOLOMON AND HIRAM BUILD THE TEMPLE				
Solomon begins coregency with his father David (1 Kin. 1:32–39) **973 B.C.**	Solomon becomes sole ruler on Israel's throne (1 Kin. 2:12) **970 B.C.**	12th year of Hiram (if Carthage was founded in 825 B.C.) **968 B.C.** Solomon lays the foundation of the temple (1 Kin. 6:1) **966 B.C.**	Hiram's builders help with construction of the temple (1 Kin. 5:18) All work is completed on the temple (1 Kin. 6:37, 38) **959 B.C.**	12th year of Hiram (if Carthage was founded in 814 B.C.) **957 B.C.**
▼ 975 B.C.	▼ 970 B.C.	▼ 965 B.C.	▼ 960 B.C.	▼ 955 B.C.

himself a worthy man, not one hair of him shall fall to the earth; but if wickedness is found in him, he shall die." ⁵³So King Solomon sent them to bring him down from the altar. And he came and fell down before King Solomon; and Solomon said to him, "Go to your house."

David's Instructions to Solomon

2 ¹Now the days of David drew near that he should die, and he charged Solomon his son, saying: ²"I go the way of all the earth; be strong, therefore, and prove yourself a man. ³And keep the charge of the LORD your God: to walk in His ways, to keep His statutes, His commandments, His judgments, and His testimonies, as it is written in the Law of Moses, that you may prosper in all that you do and wherever you turn; ⁴that the LORD may fulfill His word which He spoke concerning me, saying, 'If your sons take heed to their way, to walk before Me in truth with all their heart and with all their soul,' He said, 'you shall not lack a man on the throne of Israel.'

⁵"Moreover you know also what Joab the son of Zeruiah did to me, *and* what he did to the two commanders of the armies of Israel, to Abner the son of Ner and Amasa the son of Jether, whom he killed. And he shed the blood of war in peacetime, and put the blood of war on his belt that *was* around his waist, and on his sandals that *were* on his feet. ⁶Therefore do according to your wisdom, and do not let his gray hair go down to the grave in peace.

⁷"But show kindness to the sons of Barzillai the Gileadite, and let them be among those who eat at your table, for so they came to me when I fled from Absalom your brother.

⁸"And see, *you have* with you Shimei the son of Gera, a Benjamite from Bahurim, who cursed me with a malicious curse in the day when I went to Mahanaim. But he came down to meet me at the Jordan, and I swore to him by the LORD, saying, 'I will not put you to death with the sword.' ⁹Now therefore, do not hold him guiltless, for you *are* a wise man and know what you ought to do to him; but bring his gray hair down to the grave with blood."

Death of David

¹⁰So David rested with his fathers, and was buried in the City of David. ¹¹The period that David reigned over Israel *was* forty years; seven years he reigned in Hebron, and in Jerusalem he reigned thirty-three years. ¹²Then Solomon sat on the throne of his father David; and his kingdom was firmly established.

Solomon Executes Adonijah

¹³Now Adonijah the son of Haggith came to Bathsheba the mother of Solomon. So she said, "Do you come peaceably?"

And he said, "Peaceably." ¹⁴Moreover he said, "I have something *to say* to you."

And she said, "Say it."

¹⁵Then he said, "You know that the kingdom was mine, and all Israel had set their expectations on me, that I should reign. However, the kingdom has been turned over, and has become my brother's; for it was his from the LORD. ¹⁶Now I ask one petition of you; do not deny me."

And she said to him, "Say it."

¹⁷Then he said, "Please speak to King Solomon, for he will not refuse you, that he may give me Abishag the Shunammite as wife."

[18]So Bathsheba said, "Very well, I will speak for you to the king."

[19]Bathsheba therefore went to King Solomon, to speak to him for Adonijah. And the king rose up to meet her and bowed down to her, and sat down on his throne and had a throne set for the king's mother; so she sat at his right hand. [20]Then she said, "I desire one small petition of you; do not refuse me."

And the king said to her, "Ask it, my mother, for I will not refuse you."

[21]So she said, "Let Abishag the Shunammite be given to Adonijah your brother as wife."

[22]And King Solomon answered and said to his mother, "Now why do you ask Abishag the Shunammite for Adonijah? Ask for him the kingdom also—for he *is* my older brother—for him, and for Abiathar the priest, and for Joab the son of Zeruiah." [23]Then King Solomon swore by the LORD, saying, "May God do so to me, and more also, if Adonijah has not spoken this word against his own life! [24]Now therefore, *as* the LORD lives, who has confirmed me and set me on the throne of David my father, and who has established a house[a] for me, as He promised, Adonijah shall be put to death today!"

[25]So King Solomon sent by the hand of Benaiah the son of Jehoiada; and he struck him down, and he died.

Abiathar Exiled, Joab Executed

[26]And to Abiathar the priest the king said, "Go to Anathoth, to your own fields, for you *are* deserving of death; but I will not put you to death at this time, because you carried the ark of the Lord GOD before my father David, and because you were afflicted every time my father was afflicted." [27]So Solomon removed Abiathar from being priest to the LORD, that he might fulfill the word of the LORD which He spoke concerning the house of Eli at Shiloh.

[28]Then news came to Joab, for Joab had defected to Adonijah, though he had not defected to Absalom. So Joab fled to the tabernacle of the LORD, and took hold of the horns of the altar. [29]And King Solomon was told, "Joab has fled to the tabernacle of the LORD; there *he is,* by the altar." Then Solomon sent Benaiah the son of Jehoiada, saying, "Go, strike him down." [30]So Benaiah went to the tabernacle of the LORD, and

said to him, "Thus says the king, 'Come out!' "

And he said, "No, but I will die here." And Benaiah brought back word to the king, saying, "Thus said Joab, and thus he answered me."

[31]Then the king said to him, "Do as he has said, and strike him down and bury him, that you may take away from me and from the house of my father the innocent blood which Joab shed. [32]So the LORD will return his blood on his head, because he struck down two men more righteous and better than he, and killed them with the sword—Abner the son of Ner, the commander of the army of Israel, and Amasa the son of Jether, the commander of the army of Judah—though my father David did not know *it.* [33]Their blood shall therefore return upon the head of Joab and upon the head of his descendants forever. But upon David and his descendants, upon his house and his throne, there shall be peace forever from the LORD."

[34]So Benaiah the son of Jehoiada went up and struck and killed him; and he was buried in his own house in the wilderness. [35]The king put Benaiah the son of Jehoiada in his place over the army, and the king put Zadok the priest in the place of Abiathar.

Shimei Before King Solomon

Twice David prevented Shimei from being killed (2 Sam. 16:9–12; 19:21–23). On his deathbed, however, David asked Solomon to see to it that Shimei did not remain unpunished (1 Kin. 2:8, 9). Now, at least 3 years after David's death, Solomon executed Shimei the Benjamite for violating the oath he took before the new king (1 Kin. 2:36–46).

■ 1 Kings 2:36–46

1 Kings
Shimei Executed

2 :36 Then the king sent and called for Shimei, and said to him, "Build yourself a house in Jerusalem and dwell there, and do not go out from there anywhere. [37]For it shall be, on the day you go out and cross the Brook Kidron, know for certain you shall surely die; your blood shall be on your own head."

[38]And Shimei said to the king, "The

2:24 [a]That is, a royal dynasty

saying *is* good. As my lord the king has said, so your servant will do." So Shimei dwelt in Jerusalem many days.

39Now it happened at the end of three years, that two slaves of Shimei ran away to Achish the son of Maachah, king of Gath. And they told Shimei, saying, "Look, your slaves *are* in Gath!" 40So Shimei arose, saddled his donkey, and went to Achish at Gath to seek his slaves. And Shimei went and brought his slaves from Gath. 41And Solomon was told that Shimei had gone from Jerusalem to Gath and had come back. 42Then the king sent and called for Shimei, and said to him, "Did I not make you swear by the LORD, and warn you, saying, 'Know for certain that on the day you go out and travel anywhere, you shall surely die'? And you said to me, 'The word I have heard *is* good.' 43Why then have you not kept the oath of the LORD and the commandment that I gave you?" 44The king said moreover to Shimei, "You know, as your heart acknowledges, all the wickedness that you did to my father David; therefore the LORD will return your wickedness on your own head. 45But King Solomon *shall be* blessed, and the throne of David shall be established before the LORD forever."

46So the king commanded Benaiah the son of Jehoiada; and he went out and struck him down, and he died. Thus the kingdom was established in the hand of Solomon.

Priestly Account: David's Final Years

One place where Chronicles is sharply distinct from Samuel is in the account of David's census. In 2 Sam. 24, God was angry and stirred David to this sin. In 1 Chr. 21, Satan prompts the census. Whatever theological reason there may be for this change, it is consistent with Chronicles's concern for David's good reputation. Satan, not an angry God, incited David to sin.

▼   ■ 1 Chronicles 21:1–30

1 Chronicles
The Census of Israel and Judah

21 :1 Now Satan stood up against Israel, and moved David to number Israel. 2So David said to Joab and to the leaders of the people, "Go, number Israel

from Beersheba to Dan, and bring the number of them to me that I may know *it*." 3And Joab answered, "May the LORD make His people a hundred times more than they are. But, my lord the king, *are* they not all my lord's servants? Why then does my lord require this thing? Why should he be a cause of guilt in Israel?"

4Nevertheless the king's word prevailed against Joab. Therefore Joab departed and went throughout all Israel and came to Jerusalem. 5Then Joab gave the sum of the number of the people to David. All Israel *had* one million one hundred thousand men who drew the sword, and Judah *had* four hundred and seventy thousand men who drew the sword. 6But he did not count Levi and Benjamin among them, for the king's word was abominable to Joab.

7And God was displeased with this thing; therefore He struck Israel. 8So David said to God, "I have sinned greatly, because I have done this thing; but now, I pray, take away the iniquity of Your servant, for I have done very foolishly."

9Then the LORD spoke to Gad, David's seer, saying, 10"Go and tell David, saying, 'Thus says the LORD: "I offer you three *things;* choose one of them for yourself, that I may do *it* to you." ' "

11So Gad came to David and said to him, "Thus says the LORD: 'Choose for yourself, 12either threea years of famine, or three months to be defeated by your foes with the sword of your enemies overtaking *you*, or else for three days the sword of the LORD—the plague in the land, with the angelb of the LORD destroying throughout all the territory of Israel.' Now consider what answer I should take back to Him who sent me."

13And David said to Gad, "I am in great distress. Please let me fall into the hand of the LORD, for His mercies *are* very great; but do not let me fall into the hand of man."

14So the LORD sent a plague upon Israel, and seventy thousand men of Israel fell. 15And God sent an angel to Jerusalem to destroy it. As hea was destroying, the LORD looked and relented of the disaster, and said to the angel who was destroying,

21:12 aOr *seven* (compare 2 Samuel 24:13) bOr *Angel*, and so elsewhere in this chapter
21:15 aOr *He*

Satan, Initiating Evil for Israel (1 Chr. 21:1)

The Chronicler uses "Satan" as the proper name of a celestial being, who is operating independently of Yahweh. This Satan who "stood up against Israel" (1 Chr. 21:1) is related to the divine functionary who appears as an adversary or accuser of humans (Job 1:6; 2:1; Zech. 3:1). The Chronicler's Satan, however, differs by being a divine being in opposition to the will of God.

Ancient Near Eastern civilizations had many demons, as well as deities who often did horrendous things to humans. The only deity, though, who can reasonably be compared to the figure of Satan (as Satan developed in early Judaism and appears in Christianity) is found in Persia's dualistic religion, Zoroastrianism.

The Iranian prophet Zoroaster lived possibly between the 10th and 6th centuries B.C. (although exact dates are unknown). He taught that the cosmos was divided into two warring factions, one good and one evil. Those who struggle on behalf of good worship Ahura Mazda, the god of light; those seeking evil worship Angra Mainyu (also called Ahriman). These two deities, with their followers, were destined to vie for control of the universe until a final cosmic battle in which good will triumph over evil. Those humans who served Ahura Mazda would find rewards in heaven; those who served Angra Mainyu would be cast into a burning hell.

Zoroastrianism became the official religion of the Persian Empire during the Achaemenid dynasty (c. 559–331 B.C.). It was publicly declared the royal faith in a huge inscription by Darius I (522–486 B.C.). The Chronicler wrote during the approximately 200 years that Judah was a territory within the Persian province called "beyond the River" (1 Chr. 19:16), and his notion of Satan as the evil counterpart of God compares to the evil Angra Mainyu of Zoroastrianism.

"It is enough; now restrain your[b] hand." And the angel of the LORD stood by the threshing floor of Ornan[c] the Jebusite.

16Then David lifted his eyes and saw the angel of the LORD standing between earth and heaven, having in his hand a drawn sword stretched out over Jerusalem. So David and the elders, clothed in sackcloth, fell on their faces. 17And David said to God, "Was it not I who commanded the people to be numbered? I am the one who has sinned and done evil indeed; but these sheep, what have they done? Let Your hand, I pray, O LORD my God, be against me and my father's house, but not against Your people that they should be plagued."

18Therefore, the angel of the LORD commanded Gad to say to David that David should go and erect an altar to the LORD on the threshing floor of Ornan the Jebusite. 19So David went up at the word of Gad, which he had spoken in the name of the LORD. 20Now Ornan turned and saw the angel; and his four sons who were with him hid themselves, but Ornan continued threshing wheat. 21So David came to Ornan, and Ornan looked and saw David. And he went out from the threshing floor, and bowed before David with his face to the ground. 22Then David said to Ornan, "Grant me the place of this threshing floor, that I may build an altar on it to the LORD. You shall grant it to me at the full price, that the plague may be withdrawn from the people."

23But Ornan said to David, "Take it to yourself, and let my lord the king do what is good in his eyes. Look, I also give you the oxen for burnt offerings, the threshing implements for wood, and the wheat for the grain offering; I give it all."

24Then King David said to Ornan, "No, but I will surely buy it for the full price, for I will not take what is yours for the LORD, nor offer burnt offerings with that which costs me nothing." 25So David gave Ornan six hundred shekels of gold by weight for the place. 26And David built there an altar to the LORD, and offered burnt offerings and peace offerings, and called on the LORD; and He answered him from heaven by fire on the altar of burnt offering.

27So the LORD commanded the angel, and he returned his sword to its sheath.

28At that time, when David saw that

21:15 bOr Your cSpelled Araunah in 2 Samuel 24:16

the LORD had answered him on the threshing floor of Ornan the Jebusite, he sacrificed there. ²⁹For the tabernacle of the LORD and the altar of the burnt offering, which Moses had made in the wilderness, *were* at that time at the high place in Gibeon. ³⁰But David could not go before it to inquire of God, for he was afraid of the sword of the angel of the LORD.

David's Laments

David's hymns of praise were associated with the time when David rejoiced before the ark of the covenant (see "The Book of Psalms" at Ps. 8). The other major category of psalms is laments, in which the singer complains to God and asks for help. Related to the lament is the song of trust, in which the singer expresses faith in God's ability to deliver.

Several of the psalms associated with specific points in David's life are laments or songs of trust. For example, Ps. 57 and 142 reflect David's days of hiding in caves from Saul, while Ps. 3 and 7 reflect his flight from Jerusalem. All of these psalms are laments. Many other laments and songs of trust, however, are attributed to David, but provide no historical context. Nevertheless, these psalms can be read in light of this time in David's life.

The arrangement of psalms in the Bible shows a movement from lament to praise (see "The Book of Psalms" at Ps. 8). If we read David's laments according to the five "Books" of the psalms, we see the concentration of laments in Books I and II. In Book I (Ps. 1—41) itself are 22 more laments associated with David.

■ Psalms 4—6; 9—14; 16; 17; 22; 25—28; 31; 35; 36; 38; 40; 41

PSALM 4

The Safety of the Faithful

To the Chief Musician. With stringed instruments. A Psalm of David.

Hear me when I call, O God of my
    righteousness!
    You have relieved me in *my* distress;
    Have mercy on me, and hear my
    prayer.

2   How long, O you sons of men,
    Will you turn my glory to shame?
    How long will you love worthlessness
    And seek falsehood?   Selah

3   But know that the LORD has set
        apart[a] for Himself him who is godly;
    The LORD will hear when I call to
        Him.

4   Be angry, and do not sin.
    Meditate within your heart on your
        bed, and be still.   Selah
5   Offer the sacrifices of righteousness,
    And put your trust in the LORD.

6   *There are* many who say,
    "Who will show us *any* good?"
    LORD, lift up the light of Your
        countenance upon us.
7   You have put gladness in my heart,
    More than in the season that their
        grain and wine increased.
8   I will both lie down in peace, and
        sleep;
    For You alone, O LORD, make me dwell
        in safety.

PSALM 5

A Prayer for Guidance

To the Chief Musician. With flutes.[a] A Psalm of David.

Give ear to my words, O LORD,
    Consider my meditation.
2   Give heed to the voice of my cry,
    My King and my God,
    For to You I will pray.
3   My voice You shall hear in the
        morning, O LORD;
    In the morning I will direct *it* to You,
    And I will look up.

4   For You *are* not a God who takes
        pleasure in wickedness,
    Nor shall evil dwell with You.
5   The boastful shall not stand in Your
        sight;
    You hate all workers of iniquity.
6   You shall destroy those who speak
        falsehood;
    The LORD abhors the bloodthirsty and
        deceitful man.

7   But as for me, I will come into Your
        house in the multitude of Your
        mercy;
    In fear of You I will worship toward
        Your holy temple.

4:3 ªMany Hebrew manuscripts, Septuagint, Targum, and Vulgate read *made wonderful.*   5:title ªHebrew *nehiloth*

8   Lead me, O LORD, in Your
         righteousness because of my
         enemies;
     Make Your way straight before my
         face.

9   For *there is* no faithfulness in their
         mouth;
     Their inward part *is* destruction;
     Their throat *is* an open tomb;
     They flatter with their tongue.
10   Pronounce them guilty, O God!
     Let them fall by their own counsels;
     Cast them out in the multitude of
         their transgressions,
     For they have rebelled against You.

11   But let all those rejoice who put their
         trust in You;
     Let them ever shout for joy, because
         You defend them;
     Let those also who love Your name
     Be joyful in You.
12   For You, O LORD, will bless the
         righteous;
     With favor You will surround him as
         with a shield.

PSALM 6

A Prayer of Faith in Time of Distress

*To the Chief Musician. With stringed
instruments. On an eight-stringed harp.*[a]
A Psalm of David.

O LORD, do not rebuke me in Your anger,
     Nor chasten me in Your hot
         displeasure.
2   Have mercy on me, O LORD, for I *am*
         weak;
     O LORD, heal me, for my bones are
         troubled.
3   My soul also is greatly troubled;
     But You, O LORD—how long?

4   Return, O LORD, deliver me!
     Oh, save me for Your mercies' sake!
5   For in death *there is* no remembrance
         of You;
     In the grave who will give You
         thanks?

6   I am weary with my groaning;
     All night I make my bed swim;
     I drench my couch with my tears.

7   My eye wastes away because of grief;
     It grows old because of all my
         enemies.

8   Depart from me, all you workers of
         iniquity;
     For the LORD has heard the voice of
         my weeping.
9   The LORD has heard my supplication;
     The LORD will receive my prayer.
10   Let all my enemies be ashamed and
         greatly troubled;
     Let them turn back *and* be ashamed
         suddenly.

PSALM 9

Prayer and Thanksgiving for the LORD's Righteous Judgments

*To the Chief Musician. To the tune of "Death of
the Son."*[a] *A Psalm of David.*

I will praise *You,* O LORD, with my whole
         heart;
     I will tell of all Your marvelous works.
2   I will be glad and rejoice in You;
     I will sing praise to Your name,
         O Most High.

3   When my enemies turn back,
     They shall fall and perish at Your
         presence.
4   For You have maintained my right
         and my cause;
     You sat on the throne judging in
         righteousness.
5   You have rebuked the nations,
     You have destroyed the wicked;
     You have blotted out their name
         forever and ever.

6   O enemy, destructions are finished
         forever!
     And you have destroyed cities;
     Even their memory has perished.
7   But the LORD shall endure forever;
     He has prepared His throne for
         judgment.
8   He shall judge the world in
         righteousness,
     And He shall administer judgment for
         the peoples in uprightness.

9   The LORD also will be a refuge for the
         oppressed,
     A refuge in times of trouble.
10   And those who know Your name will
         put their trust in You;

6:title [a]Hebrew *sheminith*   9:title [a]Hebrew *Muth
Labben*

For You, LORD, have not forsaken
those who seek You.

11 Sing praises to the LORD, who dwells
in Zion!
Declare His deeds among the people.
12 When He avenges blood, He
remembers them;
He does not forget the cry of the
humble.

13 Have mercy on me, O LORD!
Consider my trouble from those who
hate me,
You who lift me up from the gates of
death,
14 That I may tell of all Your praise
In the gates of the daughter of Zion.
I will rejoice in Your salvation.

15 The nations have sunk down in the pit
which they made;
In the net which they hid, their own
foot is caught.
16 The LORD is known by the judgment
He executes;
The wicked is snared in the work of
his own hands.
              Meditation.ᵃ   Selah

17 The wicked shall be turned into hell,
And all the nations that forget God.
18 For the needy shall not always be
forgotten;
The expectation of the poor shall not
perish forever.

19 Arise, O LORD,
Do not let man prevail;
Let the nations be judged in Your sight.
20 Put them in fear, O LORD,
That the nations may know
themselves to be but men.   Selah

PSALM 10

A Song of Confidence in God's Triumph over Evil

Why do You stand afar off, O LORD?
Why do You hide in times of trouble?
2 The wicked in his pride persecutes the
poor;
Let them be caught in the plots which
they have devised.

3 For the wicked boasts of his heart's
desire;
He blesses the greedy and renounces
the LORD.

4 The wicked in his proud countenance
does not seek God;
God is in none of his thoughts.
5 His ways are always prospering;
Your judgments are far above, out of
his sight;
As for all his enemies, he sneers at
them.
6 He has said in his heart, "I shall not
be moved;
I shall never be in adversity."
7 His mouth is full of cursing and deceit
and oppression;
Under his tongue is trouble and
iniquity.
8 He sits in the lurking places of the
villages;
In the secret places he murders the
innocent;
His eyes are secretly fixed on the
helpless.
9 He lies in wait secretly, as a lion in his
den;
He lies in wait to catch the poor;
He catches the poor when he draws
him into his net.
10 So he crouches, he lies low,
That the helpless may fall by his
strength.
11 He has said in his heart,
"God has forgotten;
He hides His face;
He will never see."

12 Arise, O LORD!
O God, lift up Your hand!
Do not forget the humble.
13 Why do the wicked renounce God?
He has said in his heart,
"You will not require an account."

14 But You have seen, for You observe
trouble and grief,
To repay it by Your hand.
The helpless commits himself to You;
You are the helper of the fatherless.
15 Break the arm of the wicked and the
evil man;
Seek out his wickedness until You find
none.

16 The LORD is King forever and ever;
The nations have perished out of His
land.
17 LORD, You have heard the desire of the
humble;

9:16 ᵃHebrew *Higgaion*

You will prepare their heart;
You will cause Your ear to hear,
18 To do justice to the fatherless and the
oppressed,
That the man of the earth may
oppress no more.

PSALM 11

Faith in the LORD's Righteousness

To the Chief Musician. A Psalm of David.

In the LORD I put my trust;
How can you say to my soul,
"Flee *as* a bird to your mountain"?
2 For look! The wicked bend *their* bow,
They make ready their arrow on the
string,
That they may shoot secretly at the
upright in heart.
3 If the foundations are destroyed,
What can the righteous do?

4 The LORD *is* in His holy temple,
The LORD's throne *is* in heaven;
His eyes behold,
His eyelids test the sons of men.
5 The LORD tests the righteous,
But the wicked and the one who loves
violence His soul hates.
6 Upon the wicked He will rain coals;
Fire and brimstone and a burning wind
Shall be the portion of their cup.

7 For the LORD *is* righteous,
He loves righteousness;
His countenance beholds the upright.[a]

PSALM 12

Man's Treachery and God's Constancy

*To the Chief Musician. On an eight-stringed
harp.[a] A Psalm of David.*

Help, LORD, for the godly man ceases!
For the faithful disappear from among
the sons of men.

11:7 [a]Or *The upright beholds His countenance*
12:title [a]Hebrew *sheminith*

2 They speak idly everyone with his
neighbor;
With flattering lips *and* a double heart
they speak.

3 May the LORD cut off all flattering
lips,
And the tongue that speaks proud
things,
4 Who have said,
"With our tongue we will prevail;
Our lips *are* our own;
Who *is* lord over us?"

5 "For the oppression of the poor, for the
sighing of the needy,
Now I will arise," says the LORD;
"I will set *him* in the safety for which
he yearns."

6 The words of the LORD *are* pure words,
Like silver tried in a furnace of earth,
Purified seven times.
7 You shall keep them, O LORD,
You shall preserve them from this
generation forever.

8 The wicked prowl on every side,
When vileness is exalted among the
sons of men.

PSALM 13

Trust in the Salvation of the LORD

To the Chief Musician. A Psalm of David.

How long, O LORD? Will You forget me
forever?
How long will You hide Your face from
me?
2 How long shall I take counsel in my
soul,
Having sorrow in my heart daily?
How long will my enemy be exalted
over me?

3 Consider *and* hear me, O LORD my
God;
Enlighten my eyes,

MARRIAGE AND FAMILY

*The basic economic unit of ancient society was the family, with the father at its head.
Under him were his immediate relatives as well as more distant relatives, servants, and
still others, depending on the family's wealth. A fatherless person was someone who fell
outside this circle of defense and provision (Ps. 10:14).*

THE SLEEP OF DEATH (Ps. 13:3)

Death is a universal dilemma. In one ancient Near Eastern story, the Gilgamesh Epic, the hero Gilgamesh is suddenly struck by the pain of death, when his friend Enkidu dies. Gilgamesh then begins a long journey in search of the secret of eternal life. Even when he finds it in a thorny plant, it is stolen from him, and Gilgamesh concludes that seeking immortality is useless because all must die.

The Israelites had a unique focus on the here and now. While the Egyptians prepared elaborate tombs, including paintings and figures that would supposedly benefit the dead one, the Hebrew scriptures stressed the importance of living life to its fullness because death was the end of human activity. Hebrew wisdom offered this advice: Find joy in the daily rounds of life, "for there is no work or device or knowledge or wisdom in the grave where you are going" (Eccl. 9:10).

Death was often equated with a kind of sleep, thus the psalmist uses the image of "the sleep of death" (Ps. 13:3). When the kings of Israel died, we are told they went to sleep or "rested" with their fathers (1 Kin. 2:10; 11:43; 14:31).

The Hebrews described death with visual imagery as the abode of the dead. A person who dies, goes to Sheol (sometimes translated as "hell," "grave," or the "pit"), which clearly represents the grave (Job 21:13; Prov. 7:27). In Sheol there is no human activity, not even the praising of the Lord (Ps. 146:3, 4; 115:17). Or as the author of Ecclesiastes wrote, "For the living know that they will die; But the dead know nothing" (Eccl. 9:5).

Death was not to be dreaded; it was the expected, normal end of life. Indeed, death was considered good for the person who was "full of years" and had reached "a good old age" (Gen. 25:8; Job 42:17).

Lest I sleep the *sleep of* death;
4   Lest my enemy say,
"I have prevailed against him";
Lest those who trouble me rejoice
    when I am moved.

5   But I have trusted in Your mercy;
My heart shall rejoice in Your
    salvation.
6   I will sing to the LORD,
Because He has dealt bountifully with
    me.

PSALM 14

Folly of the Godless, and God's Final Triumph

To the Chief Musician. A Psalm of David.

The fool has said in his heart,
"*There is* no God."
They are corrupt,
They have done abominable works,
There is none who does good.

2   The LORD looks down from heaven
    upon the children of men,
To see if there are any who
    understand, who seek God.

3   They have all turned aside,
They have together become corrupt;
There is none who does good,
No, not one.

4   Have all the workers of iniquity no
    knowledge,
Who eat up my people *as* they eat
    bread,
And do not call on the LORD?
5   There they are in great fear,
For God *is* with the generation of the
    righteous.
6   You shame the counsel of the poor,
But the LORD *is* his refuge.

7   Oh, that the salvation of Israel *would*
    come out of Zion!
When the LORD brings back the
    captivity of His people,
Let Jacob rejoice *and* Israel be glad.

PSALM 16

The Hope of the Faithful, and the Messiah's Victory

A Michtam of David.

Preserve me, O God, for in You I put my
    trust.

2 *O my soul,* you have said to the LORD,
"You *are* my Lord,
My goodness is nothing apart from
You."
3 As for the saints who *are* on the earth,
"They are the excellent ones, in whom
is all my delight."

4 Their sorrows shall be multiplied who
hasten *after* another *god;*
Their drink offerings of blood I will
not offer,
Nor take up their names on my lips.

5 O LORD, *You are* the portion of my
inheritance and my cup;
You maintain my lot.
6 The lines have fallen to me in
pleasant *places;*
Yes, I have a good inheritance.

7 I will bless the LORD who has given
me counsel;
My heart also instructs me in the
night seasons.
8 I have set the LORD always before me;
Because *He is* at my right hand I shall
not be moved.

9 Therefore my heart is glad, and my
glory rejoices;
My flesh also will rest in hope.
10 For You will not leave my soul in
Sheol,
Nor will You allow Your Holy One to
see corruption.
11 You will show me the path of life;
In Your presence *is* fullness of joy;
At Your right hand *are* pleasures
forevermore.

PSALM 17

Prayer with Confidence in Final Salvation

A Prayer of David.

Hear a just cause, O LORD,
Attend to my cry;

Give ear to my prayer *which is* not
from deceitful lips.
2 Let my vindication come from Your
presence;
Let Your eyes look on the things that
are upright.

3 You have tested my heart;
You have visited *me* in the night;
You have tried me and have found
nothing;
I have purposed that my mouth shall
not transgress.
4 Concerning the works of men,
By the word of Your lips,
I have kept away from the paths of
the destroyer.
5 Uphold my steps in Your paths,
That my footsteps may not slip.

6 I have called upon You, for You will
hear me, O God;
Incline Your ear to me, *and* hear my
speech.
7 Show Your marvelous lovingkindness
by Your right hand,
O You who save those who trust *in You*
From those who rise up *against them.*
8 Keep me as the apple of Your eye;
Hide me under the shadow of Your
wings,
9 From the wicked who oppress me,
From my deadly enemies who
surround me.

10 They have closed up their fat *hearts;*
With their mouths they speak proudly.
11 They have now surrounded us in our
steps;
They have set their eyes, crouching
down to the earth,
12 As a lion is eager to tear his prey,
And like a young lion lurking in secret
places.

13 Arise, O LORD,
Confront him, cast him down;
Deliver my life from the wicked with
Your sword,

BELIEFS AND IDEAS

*The "apple" of the eye is the pupil, the dark opening through which light enters the eye.
Its beauty, its function, and its delicacy make the eye the object of protection, and a
source of anxiety if threatened. The use of this metaphor in the Bible expresses faith
that God treats His own as especially precious (Ps. 17:8; Deut. 32:10).*

14 With Your hand from men, O LORD,
From men of the world *who have* their
   portion in *this* life,
And whose belly You fill with Your
   hidden treasure.
They are satisfied with children,
And leave the rest of their *possession*
   for their babes.

15 As for me, I will see Your face in
   righteousness;
I shall be satisfied when I awake in
   Your likeness.

PSALM 22

The Suffering, Praise, and Posterity of the Messiah

To the Chief Musician. Set to "The Deer of the Dawn."[a] *A Psalm of David.*

M**y God, My God, why have You
   forsaken Me?**
Why are You so far from helping Me,
And from the words of My groaning?
2 O My God, I cry in the daytime, but
   You do not hear;
And in the night season, and am not
   silent.

3 But You *are* holy,
Enthroned in the praises of Israel.
4 Our fathers trusted in You;
They trusted, and You delivered them.
5 They cried to You, and were delivered;
They trusted in You, and were not
   ashamed.

6 But I *am* a worm, and no man;
A reproach of men, and despised by
   the people.
7 All those who see Me ridicule Me;
They shoot out the lip, they shake the
   head, *saying,*
8 "He trusted[a] in the LORD, let Him
   rescue Him;
Let Him deliver Him, since He
   delights in Him!"

9 But You *are* He who took Me out of
   the womb;
You made Me trust *while* on My
   mother's breasts.
10 I was cast upon You from birth.
From My mother's womb
You *have been* My God.
11 Be not far from Me,
For trouble *is* near;
For *there is* none to help.

12 Many bulls have surrounded Me;
Strong *bulls* of Bashan have encircled
   Me.
13 They gape at Me *with* their mouths,
Like a raging and roaring lion.

14 I am poured out like water,
And all My bones are out of joint;
My heart is like wax;
It has melted within Me.
15 My strength is dried up like a
   potsherd,
And My tongue clings to My jaws;
You have brought Me to the dust of
   death.

16 For dogs have surrounded Me;
The congregation of the wicked has
   enclosed Me.
They pierced[a] My hands and My feet;
17 I can count all My bones.
They look *and* stare at Me.
18 They divide My garments among
   them,
And for My clothing they cast lots.

19 But You, O LORD, do not be far from
   Me;
O My Strength, hasten to help Me!
20 Deliver Me from the sword,
My precious *life* from the power of the
   dog.
21 Save Me from the lion's mouth
And from the horns of the wild oxen!

You have answered Me.

22 I will declare Your name to My
   brethren;
In the midst of the assembly I will
   praise You.
23 You who fear the LORD, praise Him!
All you descendants of Jacob, glorify
   Him,
And fear Him, all you offspring of
   Israel!
24 For He has not despised nor abhorred
   the affliction of the afflicted;
Nor has He hidden His face from Him;
But when He cried to Him, He heard.

25 My praise *shall be* of You in the great
   assembly;

22:title [a]Hebrew *Aijeleth Hashahar*
22:8 [a]Septuagint, Syriac, and Vulgate read *hoped;*
Targum reads *praised.*   22:16 [a]Following some
Hebrew manuscripts, Septuagint, Syriac, Vulgate;
Masoretic Text reads *Like a lion.*

I will pay My vows before those who
  fear Him.
26 The poor shall eat and be satisfied;
  Those who seek Him will praise the
  LORD.
  Let your heart live forever!

27 All the ends of the world
  Shall remember and turn to the LORD,
  And all the families of the nations
  Shall worship before You.[a]
28 For the kingdom *is* the LORD's,
  And He rules over the nations.

29 All the prosperous of the earth
  Shall eat and worship;
  All those who go down to the dust
  Shall bow before Him,
  Even he who cannot keep himself
  alive.

30 A posterity shall serve Him.
  It will be recounted of the Lord to the
  next generation,
31 They will come and declare His
  righteousness to a people who will
  be born,
  That He has done *this*.

PSALM 25

A Plea for Deliverance and Forgiveness

A Psalm of David.

To You, O LORD, I lift up my soul.
  2 O my God, I trust in You;
  Let me not be ashamed;
  Let not my enemies triumph over me.
3 Indeed, let no one who waits on You be
  ashamed;
  Let those be ashamed who deal
  treacherously without cause.

4 Show me Your ways, O LORD;
  Teach me Your paths.
5 Lead me in Your truth and teach me,
  For You *are* the God of my salvation;
  On You I wait all the day.

6 Remember, O LORD, Your tender
  mercies and Your lovingkindnesses,
  For they *are* from of old.
7 Do not remember the sins of my
  youth, nor my transgressions;

According to Your mercy remember
  me,
  For Your goodness' sake, O LORD.

8 Good and upright *is* the LORD;
  Therefore He teaches sinners in the
  way.
9 The humble He guides in justice,
  And the humble He teaches His way.
10 All the paths of the LORD *are* mercy
  and truth,
  To such as keep His covenant and His
  testimonies.
11 For Your name's sake, O LORD,
  Pardon my iniquity, for it *is* great.

12 Who *is* the man that fears the LORD?
  Him shall He[a] teach in the way He[b]
  chooses.
13 He himself shall dwell in prosperity,
  And his descendants shall inherit the
  earth.
14 The secret of the LORD *is* with those
  who fear Him,
  And He will show them His covenant.
15 My eyes *are* ever toward the LORD,
  For He shall pluck my feet out of the
  net.

16 Turn Yourself to me, and have mercy
  on me,
  For I *am* desolate and afflicted.
17 The troubles of my heart have
  enlarged;
  Bring me out of my distresses!
18 Look on my affliction and my pain,
  And forgive all my sins.
19 Consider my enemies, for they are
  many;
  And they hate me with cruel hatred.
20 Keep my soul, and deliver me;
  Let me not be ashamed, for I put my
  trust in You.
21 Let integrity and uprightness preserve
  me,
  For I wait for You.

22 Redeem Israel, O God,
  Out of all their troubles!

PSALM 26

A Prayer for Divine Scrutiny and Redemption

A Psalm of David.

Vindicate me, O LORD,
  For I have walked in my integrity.

22:27 [a]Following Masoretic Text, Septuagint, and
Targum; Arabic, Syriac, and Vulgate read *Him.*
25:12 [a]Or *he*   [b]Or *he*

I have also trusted in the LORD;
I shall not slip.
2 Examine me, O LORD, and prove me;
Try my mind and my heart.
3 For Your lovingkindness *is* before my
   eyes,
And I have walked in Your truth.
4 I have not sat with idolatrous mortals,
Nor will I go in with hypocrites.
5 I have hated the assembly of evildoers,
And will not sit with the wicked.

6 I will wash my hands in innocence;
So I will go about Your altar, O LORD,
7 That I may proclaim with the voice of
   thanksgiving,
And tell of all Your wondrous works.
8 LORD, I have loved the habitation of
   Your house,
And the place where Your glory
   dwells.

9 Do not gather my soul with sinners,
Nor my life with bloodthirsty men,
10 In whose hands *is* a sinister scheme,
And whose right hand is full of bribes.

11 But as for me, I will walk in my
   integrity;
Redeem me and be merciful to me.
12 My foot stands in an even place;
In the congregations I will bless the
   LORD.

PSALM 27

An Exuberant Declaration of Faith

A Psalm of David.

The LORD *is* my light and my salvation;
   Whom shall I fear?
The LORD *is* the strength of my life;
Of whom shall I be afraid?
2 When the wicked came against me
To eat up my flesh,
My enemies and foes,
They stumbled and fell.
3 Though an army may encamp against
   me,

My heart shall not fear;
Though war may rise against me,
In this I *will be* confident.

4 One *thing* I have desired of the LORD,
That will I seek:
That I may dwell in the house of the
   LORD
All the days of my life,
To behold the beauty of the LORD,
And to inquire in His temple.
5 For in the time of trouble
He shall hide me in His pavilion;
In the secret place of His tabernacle
He shall hide me;
He shall set me high upon a rock.

6 And now my head shall be lifted up
   above my enemies all around me;
Therefore I will offer sacrifices of joy
   in His tabernacle;
I will sing, yes, I will sing praises to
   the LORD.

7 Hear, O LORD, *when* I cry with my
   voice!
Have mercy also upon me, and answer
   me.
8 *When You said,* "Seek My face,"
My heart said to You, "Your face,
   LORD, I will seek."
9 Do not hide Your face from me;
Do not turn Your servant away in
   anger;
You have been my help;
Do not leave me nor forsake me,
O God of my salvation.
10 When my father and my mother
   forsake me,
Then the LORD will take care of me.

11 Teach me Your way, O LORD,
And lead me in a smooth path,
   because of my enemies.
12 Do not deliver me to the will of my
   adversaries;
For false witnesses have risen against
   me,
And such as breathe out violence.

CULTURE AND SOCIETY

In the nomadic culture of the bedouin, one of the most sacred laws, related to the laws of hospitality, is the "law of the tent." According to this custom, a host is bound to protect any guest who enters his dwelling. The host's personal honor is turned to shame if he is unable to secure his guests from harm, even under extreme circumstances. The psalmist finds similar protection in God's "pavilion" (Ps. 27:5).

13 *I would have lost heart,* unless I had
　　believed
　That I would see the goodness of the
　　LORD
　In the land of the living.

14 Wait on the LORD;
　Be of good courage,
　And He shall strengthen your heart;
　Wait, I say, on the LORD!

PSALM 28

Rejoicing in Answered Prayer

A Psalm of David.

To You I will cry, O LORD my Rock:
　Do not be silent to me,
　Lest, if You *are* silent to me,
　I become like those who go down to
　　the pit.
2 Hear the voice of my supplications
　When I cry to You,
　When I lift up my hands toward Your
　　holy sanctuary.

3 Do not take me away with the wicked
　And with the workers of iniquity,
　Who speak peace to their neighbors,
　But evil *is* in their hearts.
4 Give them according to their deeds,
　And according to the wickedness of
　　their endeavors;
　Give them according to the work of
　　their hands;
　Render to them what they deserve.
5 Because they do not regard the works
　　of the LORD,
　Nor the operation of His hands,
　He shall destroy them
　And not build them up.

6 Blessed *be* the LORD,
　Because He has heard the voice of my
　　supplications!
7 The LORD *is* my strength and my
　　shield;
　My heart trusted in Him, and I am
　　helped;
　Therefore my heart greatly rejoices,
　And with my song I will praise Him.

8 The LORD *is* their strength,[a]
　And He *is* the saving refuge of His
　　anointed.

28:8 [a]Following Masoretic Text and Targum;
Septuagint, Syriac, and Vulgate read *the strength of*
His people.

9 Save Your people,
　And bless Your inheritance;
　Shepherd them also,
　And bear them up forever.

PSALM 31

The LORD a Fortress in Adversity

To the Chief Musician. A Psalm of David.

In You, O LORD, I put my trust;
　Let me never be ashamed;
　Deliver me in Your righteousness.
2 Bow down Your ear to me,
　Deliver me speedily;
　Be my rock of refuge,
　A fortress of defense to save me.

3 For You *are* my rock and my fortress;
　Therefore, for Your name's sake,
　Lead me and guide me.
4 Pull me out of the net which they
　　have secretly laid for me,
　For You *are* my strength.
5 Into Your hand I commit my spirit;
　You have redeemed me, O LORD God of
　　truth.

6 I have hated those who regard useless
　　idols;
　But I trust in the LORD.
7 I will be glad and rejoice in Your
　　mercy,
　For You have considered my trouble;
　You have known my soul in
　　adversities,
8 And have not shut me up into the
　　hand of the enemy;
　You have set my feet in a wide place.

9 Have mercy on me, O LORD, for I am
　　in trouble;
　My eye wastes away with grief,
　Yes, my soul and my body!
10 For my life is spent with grief,
　And my years with sighing;
　My strength fails because of my
　　iniquity,
　And my bones waste away.
11 I am a reproach among all my
　　enemies,
　But especially among my neighbors,
　And *am* repulsive to my
　　acquaintances;
　Those who see me outside flee from
　　me.
12 I am forgotten like a dead man, out of
　　mind;

I am like a broken vessel.
13 For I hear the slander of many;
Fear *is* on every side;
While they take counsel together
against me,
They scheme to take away my life.

14 But as for me, I trust in You, O LORD;
I say, "You *are* my God."
15 My times *are* in Your hand;
Deliver me from the hand of my
enemies,
And from those who persecute me.
16 Make Your face shine upon Your
servant;
Save me for Your mercies' sake.
17 Do not let me be ashamed, O LORD, for
I have called upon You;
Let the wicked be ashamed;
Let them be silent in the grave.
18 Let the lying lips be put to silence,
Which speak insolent things proudly
and contemptuously against the
righteous.

19 Oh, how great *is* Your goodness,
Which You have laid up for those who
fear You,
Which You have prepared for those
who trust in You
In the presence of the sons of men!
20 You shall hide them in the secret
place of Your presence
From the plots of man;
You shall keep them secretly in a
pavilion
From the strife of tongues.

21 Blessed *be* the LORD,
For He has shown me His marvelous
kindness in a strong city!
22 For I said in my haste,
"I am cut off from before Your eyes";
Nevertheless You heard the voice of
my supplications
When I cried out to You.

23 Oh, love the LORD, all you His saints!
For the LORD preserves the faithful,

And fully repays the proud person.
24 Be of good courage,
And He shall strengthen your heart,
All you who hope in the LORD.

PSALM 35

The LORD the Avenger of His People

A Psalm of David.

Plead *my cause,* O LORD, with those who
strive with me;
Fight against those who fight against
me.
2 Take hold of shield and buckler,
And stand up for my help.
3 Also draw out the spear,
And stop those who pursue me.
Say to my soul,
"I *am* your salvation."

4 Let those be put to shame and
brought to dishonor
Who seek after my life;
Let those be turned back and brought
to confusion
Who plot my hurt.
5 Let them be like chaff before the wind,
And let the angel[a] of the LORD chase
them.
6 Let their way be dark and slippery,
And let the angel of the LORD pursue
them.
7 For without cause they have hidden
their net for me *in* a pit,
Which they have dug without cause
for my life.
8 Let destruction come upon him
unexpectedly,
And let his net that he has hidden
catch himself;
Into that very destruction let him fall.

9 And my soul shall be joyful in the
LORD;
It shall rejoice in His salvation.
10 All my bones shall say,

35:5 [a]Or *Angel*

POLITICS AND GOVERNMENT

*Lying "witnesses" (Ps. 35:11) appeared in the law courts to destroy private enemies.
Jezebel hired false witnesses to testify against one of her enemies in order to put him to
death (1 Kin. 21:13). In the New Testament, Jesus' enemies found witnesses to testify
against Him (Matt. 26:60). The Ten Commandments refer directly to the courts when
they say, "You shall not bear false witness against your neighbor" (Ex. 20:16).*

"LORD, who *is* like You,
Delivering the poor from him who is
too strong for him,
Yes, the poor and the needy from him
who plunders him?"

11 Fierce witnesses rise up;
They ask me *things* that I do not know.
12 They reward me evil for good,
To the sorrow of my soul.
13 But as for me, when they were sick,
My clothing *was* sackcloth;
I humbled myself with fasting;
And my prayer would return to my
own heart.
14 I paced about as though *he were* my
friend *or* brother;
I bowed down heavily, as one who
mourns *for his* mother.

15 But in my adversity they rejoiced
And gathered together;
Attackers gathered against me,
And I did not know *it;*
They tore *at me* and did not cease;
16 With ungodly mockers at feasts
They gnashed at me with their teeth.

17 Lord, how long will You look on?
Rescue me from their destructions,
My precious *life* from the lions.
18 I will give You thanks in the great
assembly;
I will praise You among many people.

19 Let them not rejoice over me who are
wrongfully my enemies;
Nor let them wink with the eye who
hate me without a cause.
20 For they do not speak peace,
But they devise deceitful matters
Against *the* quiet ones in the land.
21 They also opened their mouth wide
against me,
And said, "Aha, aha!
Our eyes have seen *it.*"

22 *This* You have seen, O LORD;
Do not keep silence.
O Lord, do not be far from me.
23 Stir up Yourself, and awake to my
vindication,
To my cause, my God and my Lord.
24 Vindicate me, O LORD my God,
according to Your righteousness;
And let them not rejoice over me.
25 Let them not say in their hearts, "Ah,
so we would have it!"

Let them not say, "We have swallowed
him up."
26 Let them be ashamed and brought to
mutual confusion
Who rejoice at my hurt;
Let them be clothed with shame and
dishonor
Who exalt themselves against me.

27 Let them shout for joy and be glad,
Who favor my righteous cause;
And let them say continually,
"Let the LORD be magnified,
Who has pleasure in the prosperity of
His servant."
28 And my tongue shall speak of Your
righteousness
And of Your praise all the day long.

PSALM 36

Man's Wickedness and God's Perfections

To the Chief Musician. A Psalm of David the servant of the LORD.

An oracle within my heart concerning
the transgression of the wicked:
There is no fear of God before his eyes.
2 For he flatters himself in his own
eyes,
When he finds out his iniquity *and*
when he hates.
3 The words of his mouth *are*
wickedness and deceit;
He has ceased to be wise *and* to do
good.
4 He devises wickedness on his bed;
He sets himself in a way *that is* not
good;
He does not abhor evil.

5 Your mercy, O LORD, *is* in the heavens;
Your faithfulness *reaches* to the
clouds.
6 Your righteousness *is* like the great
mountains;
Your judgments *are* a great deep;
O LORD, You preserve man and beast.

7 How precious *is* Your lovingkindness,
O God!
Therefore the children of men put
their trust under the shadow of
Your wings.
8 They are abundantly satisfied with
the fullness of Your house,

And You give them drink from the
river of Your pleasures.
9 For with You *is* the fountain of life;
In Your light we see light.

10 Oh, continue Your lovingkindness to
those who know You,
And Your righteousness to the upright
in heart.
11 Let not the foot of pride come against
me,
And let not the hand of the wicked
drive me away.
12 There the workers of iniquity have
fallen;
They have been cast down and are not
able to rise.

PSALM 38

Prayer in Time of Chastening

A Psalm of David. To bring to remembrance.

O LORD, do not rebuke me in Your wrath,
Nor chasten me in Your hot
displeasure!
2 For Your arrows pierce me deeply,
And Your hand presses me down.

3 *There is* no soundness in my flesh
Because of Your anger,
Nor *any* health in my bones
Because of my sin.
4 For my iniquities have gone over my
head;
Like a heavy burden they are too
heavy for me.
5 My wounds are foul *and* festering
Because of my foolishness.

6 I am troubled, I am bowed down
greatly;
I go mourning all the day long.
7 For my loins are full of inflammation,
And *there is* no soundness in my flesh.
8 I am feeble and severely broken;
I groan because of the turmoil of my
heart.

9 Lord, all my desire *is* before You;
And my sighing is not hidden from
You.
10 My heart pants, my strength fails me;
As for the light of my eyes, it also has
gone from me.

11 My loved ones and my friends stand
aloof from my plague,
And my relatives stand afar off.
12 Those also who seek my life lay snares
for me;
Those who seek my hurt speak of
destruction,
And plan deception all the day long.

13 But I, like a deaf *man,* do not hear;
And *I am* like a mute *who* does not
open his mouth.
14 Thus I am like a man who does not
hear,
And in whose mouth *is* no response.

15 For in You, O LORD, I hope;
You will hear, O Lord my God.
16 For I said, "*Hear me,* lest they rejoice
over me,
Lest, when my foot slips, they exalt
themselves against me."

17 For I *am* ready to fall,
And my sorrow *is* continually before
me.
18 For I will declare my iniquity;
I will be in anguish over my sin.
19 But my enemies *are* vigorous, *and*
they are strong;
And those who hate me wrongfully
have multiplied.
20 Those also who render evil for good,
They are my adversaries, because I
follow *what is* good.

21 Do not forsake me, O LORD;
O my God, be not far from me!
22 Make haste to help me,
O Lord, my salvation!

PSALM 40

Faith Persevering in Trial

To the Chief Musician. A Psalm of David.

I waited patiently for the LORD;
And He inclined to me,
And heard my cry.
2 He also brought me up out of a
horrible pit,
Out of the miry clay,
And set my feet upon a rock,
And established my steps.
3 He has put a new song in my mouth—
Praise to our God;
Many will see *it* and fear,
And will trust in the LORD.

4 Blessed *is* that man who makes the
LORD his trust,

And does not respect the proud, nor
such as turn aside to lies.
5 Many, O LORD my God, *are* Your
wonderful works
Which You have done;
And Your thoughts toward us
Cannot be recounted to You in order;
If I would declare and speak *of them,*
They are more than can be numbered.

6 Sacrifice and offering You did not
desire;
My ears You have opened.
Burnt offering and sin offering You did
not require.
7 Then I said, "Behold, I come;
In the scroll of the book *it is* written of
me.
8 I delight to do Your will, O my God,
And Your law *is* within my heart."

9 I have proclaimed the good news of
righteousness
In the great assembly;
Indeed, I do not restrain my lips,
O LORD, You Yourself know.
10 I have not hidden Your righteousness
within my heart;
I have declared Your faithfulness and
Your salvation;
I have not concealed Your
lovingkindness and Your truth
From the great assembly.

11 Do not withhold Your tender mercies
from me, O LORD;
Let Your lovingkindness and Your
truth continually preserve me.
12 For innumerable evils have
surrounded me;
My iniquities have overtaken me, so
that I am not able to look up;
They are more than the hairs of my
head;
Therefore my heart fails me.

13 Be pleased, O LORD, to deliver me;
O LORD, make haste to help me!
14 Let them be ashamed and brought to
mutual confusion
Who seek to destroy my life;
Let them be driven backward and
brought to dishonor
Who wish me evil.
15 Let them be confounded because of
their shame,
Who say to me, "Aha, aha!"

16 Let all those who seek You rejoice and
be glad in You;
Let such as love Your salvation say
continually,
"The LORD be magnified!"
17 But I *am* poor and needy;
Yet the LORD thinks upon me.
You *are* my help and my deliverer;
Do not delay, O my God.

PSALM 41

The Blessing and Suffering of the Godly

To the Chief Musician. A Psalm of David

B lessed *is* he who considers the poor;
The LORD will deliver him in time of
trouble.
2 The LORD will preserve him and keep
him alive,
And he will be blessed on the earth;
You will not deliver him to the will of
his enemies.
3 The LORD will strengthen him on his
bed of illness;
You will sustain him on his sickbed.

4 I said, "LORD, be merciful to me:
Heal my soul, for I have sinned
against You."
5 My enemies speak evil of me:
"When will he die, and his name
perish?"
6 And if he comes to see *me,* he speaks
lies;
His heart gathers iniquity to itself;
When he goes out, he tells *it.*

7 All who hate me whisper together
against me;
Against me they devise my hurt.
8 "An evil disease," *they say,* clings to
him.
And *now* that he lies down, he will
rise up no more."
9 Even my own familiar friend in whom
I trusted,
Who ate my bread,
Has lifted up *his* heel against me.

10 But You, O LORD, be merciful to me,
and raise me up,
That I may repay them.
11 By this I know that You are well
pleased with me,
Because my enemy does not triumph
over me.

12   As for me, You uphold me in my
         integrity,
       And set me before Your face forever.

13   Blessed *be* the LORD God of Israel
       From everlasting to everlasting!
       Amen and Amen.

David's Laments (Book II)

Psalm 41 ends Book I (Ps. 1—41) of the psalms, with Ps. 41:13 offering a doxology to this first segment of the Psalter. Again in Book II (Ps. 42—72) we see the emphasis on lament in the early part of the Psalter, with 7 additional laments associated with David and one unidentified lament (Ps. 71).

■ Psalms 53; 55; 58; 61; 64; 69; 70; 71

PSALM 53

Folly of the Godless, and the Restoration of Israel

To the Chief Musician. Set to "Mahalath."
A Contemplation[a] *of David.*

The fool has said in his heart,
       "There is no God."
       They are corrupt, and have done
         abominable iniquity;
       There is none who does good.

2   God looks down from heaven upon the
         children of men,
       To see if there are *any* who
         understand, who seek God.

3   Every one of them has turned aside;
       They have together become corrupt;
       There is none who does good,
       No, not one.

4   Have the workers of iniquity no
         knowledge,
       Who eat up my people *as* they eat
         bread,
       And do not call upon God?

5   There they are in great fear
       Where no fear was,
       For God has scattered the bones of
         him who encamps against you;
       You have put *them* to shame,
       Because God has despised them.

6   Oh, that the salvation of Israel would
         come out of Zion!
       When God brings back the captivity of
         His people,
       Let Jacob rejoice *and* Israel be glad.

PSALM 55

Trust in God Concerning the Treachery of Friends

To the Chief Musician. With stringed
instruments.[a] *A Contemplation*[b] *of David.*

Give ear to my prayer, O God,
       And do not hide Yourself from my
         supplication.
2   Attend to me, and hear me;
       I am restless in my complaint, and
         moan noisily,
3   Because of the voice of the enemy,
       Because of the oppression of the
         wicked;
       For they bring down trouble upon me,
       And in wrath they hate me.

4   My heart is severely pained within me,
       And the terrors of death have fallen
         upon me.
5   Fearfulness and trembling have come
         upon me,
       And horror has overwhelmed me.
6   So I said, "Oh, that I had wings like a
         dove!
       I would fly away and be at rest.
7   Indeed, I would wander far off,
       And remain in the wilderness.   Selah
8   I would hasten my escape
       From the windy storm *and* tempest."

9   Destroy, O Lord, *and* divide their
         tongues,
       For I have seen violence and strife in
         the city.
10   Day and night they go around it on its
         walls;
       Iniquity and trouble *are* also in the
         midst of it.
11   Destruction *is* in its midst;
       Oppression and deceit do not depart
         from its streets.

12   For *it is* not an enemy *who* reproaches
         me;
       Then I could bear *it.*
       Nor *is it* one *who* hates me who has
         exalted *himself* against me;
       Then I could hide from him.
13   But *it was* you, a man my equal,
       My companion and my acquaintance.
14   We took sweet counsel together,
       And walked to the house of God in the
         throng.

53:title [a]Hebrew *Maschil*   55:title [a]Hebrew
neginoth   [b]Hebrew *Maschil*

15 Let death seize them;
Let them go down alive into hell,
For wickedness *is* in their dwellings
and among them.

16 As for me, I will call upon God,
And the LORD shall save me.
17 Evening and morning and at noon
I will pray, and cry aloud,
And He shall hear my voice.
18 He has redeemed my soul in peace
from the battle *that was* against
me,
For there were many against me.
19 God will hear, and afflict them,
Even He who abides from of old.
                          Selah

Because they do not change,
Therefore they do not fear God.

20 He has put forth his hands against
those who were at peace with him;
He has broken his covenant.
21 *The words* of his mouth were
smoother than butter,
But war *was* in his heart;
His words were softer than oil,
Yet they *were* drawn swords.

22 Cast your burden on the LORD,
And He shall sustain you;
He shall never permit the righteous to
be moved.

23 But You, O God, shall bring them
down to the pit of destruction;
Bloodthirsty and deceitful men shall
not live out half their days;
But I will trust in You.

PSALM 58

The Just Judgment of the Wicked

To the Chief Musician. Set to "Do Not Destroy."[a]
A Michtam of David.

Do you indeed speak righteousness, you
silent ones?
Do you judge uprightly, you sons of
men?
2 No, in heart you work wickedness;
You weigh out the violence of your
hands in the earth.

3 The wicked are estranged from the
womb;

They go astray as soon as they are
born, speaking lies.
4 Their poison *is* like the poison of a
serpent;
They are like the deaf cobra *that* stops
its ear,
5 Which will not heed the voice of
charmers,
Charming ever so skillfully.

6 Break their teeth in their mouth,
O God!
Break out the fangs of the young
lions, O LORD!
7 Let them flow away as waters *which*
run continually;
When he bends *his* bow,
Let his arrows be as if cut in pieces.
8 *Let them be* like a snail which melts
away as it goes,
Like a stillborn child of a woman, that
they may not see the sun.

9 Before your pots can feel *the burning*
thorns,
He shall take them away as with a
whirlwind,
As in His living and burning wrath.
10 The righteous shall rejoice when he
sees the vengeance;
He shall wash his feet in the blood of
the wicked,
11 So that men will say,
"Surely *there is* a reward for the
righteous;
Surely He is God who judges in the
earth."

PSALM 61

Assurance of God's Eternal Protection

*To the Chief Musician. On a stringed
instrument.*[a] *A Psalm of David.*

Hear my cry, O God;
Attend to my prayer.
2 From the end of the earth I will cry to
You,
When my heart is overwhelmed;
Lead me to the rock that is higher
than I.

3 For You have been a shelter for me,
A strong tower from the enemy.
4 I will abide in Your tabernacle forever;
I will trust in the shelter of Your
wings.   **Selah**

58:title [a]Hebrew *Al Tashcheth*   61:title [a]Hebrew
neginah

5 For You, O God, have heard my vows;
   You have given *me* the heritage of
      those who fear Your name.
6 You will prolong the king's life,
   His years as many generations.
7 He shall abide before God forever.
   Oh, prepare mercy and truth, *which*
      may preserve him!

8 So I will sing praise to Your name
      forever,
   That I may daily perform my vows.

PSALM 64

Oppressed by the Wicked but Rejoicing in the LORD

To the Chief Musician. A Psalm of David.

Hear my voice, O God, in my
      meditation;
   Preserve my life from fear of the
      enemy.
2 Hide me from the secret plots of the
      wicked,
   From the rebellion of the workers of
      iniquity,
3 Who sharpen their tongue like a
      sword,
   And bend *their bows to shoot* their
      arrows—bitter words,
4 That they may shoot in secret at the
      blameless;
   Suddenly they shoot at him and do
      not fear.

5 They encourage themselves *in* an evil
      matter;
   They talk of laying snares secretly;
   They say, "Who will see them?"
6 They devise iniquities:
   "We have perfected a shrewd scheme."
   Both the inward thought and the
      heart of man are deep.

7 But God shall shoot at them *with* an
      arrow;
   Suddenly they shall be wounded.
8 So He will make them stumble over
      their own tongue;
   All who see them shall flee away.
9 All men shall fear,
   And shall declare the work of God;
   For they shall wisely consider His
      doing.

10 The righteous shall be glad in the
      LORD, and trust in Him.

And all the upright in heart shall
      glory.

PSALM 69

An Urgent Plea for Help in Trouble

To the Chief Musician. Set to "The Lilies."[a]
A Psalm of David.

Save me, O God!
   For the waters have come up to *my*
      neck.
2 I sink in deep mire,
   Where *there is* no standing;
   I have come into deep waters,
   Where the floods overflow me.
3 I am weary with my crying;
   My throat is dry;
   My eyes fail while I wait for my God.

4 Those who hate me without a cause
   Are more than the hairs of my head;
   They are mighty who would destroy
      me,
   Being my enemies wrongfully;
   Though I have stolen nothing,
   I *still* must restore *it.*

5 O God, You know my foolishness;
   And my sins are not hidden from You.
6 Let not those who wait for You,
      O Lord GOD of hosts, be ashamed
      because of me;
   Let not those who seek You be
      confounded because of me, O God of
      Israel.
7 Because for Your sake I have borne
      reproach;
   Shame has covered my face.
8 I have become a stranger to my
      brothers,
   And an alien to my mother's children;
9 Because zeal for Your house has eaten
      me up,
   And the reproaches of those who
      reproach You have fallen on me.
10 When I wept *and chastened* my soul
      with fasting,
   That became my reproach.
11 I also made sackcloth my garment;
   I became a byword to them.
12 Those who sit in the gate speak
      against me,
   And I *am* the song of the drunkards.

13 But as for me, my prayer *is* to You,
   O LORD, *in* the acceptable time;

69:title ªHebrew *Shoshannim*

O God, in the multitude of Your mercy,
Hear me in the truth of Your
    salvation.
14 Deliver me out of the mire,
And let me not sink;
Let me be delivered from those who
    hate me,
And out of the deep waters.
15 Let not the floodwater overflow me,
Nor let the deep swallow me up;
And let not the pit shut its mouth on
    me.

16 Hear me, O LORD, for Your
    lovingkindness *is* good;
Turn to me according to the multitude
    of Your tender mercies.
17 And do not hide Your face from Your
    servant,
For I am in trouble;
Hear me speedily.
18 Draw near to my soul, *and* redeem it;
Deliver me because of my enemies.

19 You know my reproach, my shame,
    and my dishonor;
My adversaries *are* all before You.
20 Reproach has broken my heart,
And I am full of heaviness;
I looked *for someone* to take pity, but
    there was none;
And for comforters, but I found none.
21 They also gave me gall for my food,
And for my thirst they gave me
    vinegar to drink.

22 Let their table become a snare before
    them,
And their well-being a trap.
23 Let their eyes be darkened, so that
    they do not see;
And make their loins shake
    continually.
24 Pour out Your indignation upon them,
And let Your wrathful anger take hold
    of them.
25 Let their dwelling place be desolate;
Let no one live in their tents.
26 For they persecute the *ones* You have
    struck,
And talk of the grief of those You have
    wounded.
27 Add iniquity to their iniquity,
And let them not come into Your
    righteousness.

28 Let them be blotted out of the book of
    the living,
And not be written with the righteous.

29 But I *am* poor and sorrowful;
Let Your salvation, O God, set me up
    on high.
30 I will praise the name of God with a
    song,
And will magnify Him with
    thanksgiving.
31 *This* also shall please the LORD better
    than an ox *or* bull,
Which has horns and hooves.
32 The humble shall see *this and* be glad;
And you who seek God, your hearts
    shall live.
33 For the LORD hears the poor,
And does not despise His prisoners.

34 Let heaven and earth praise Him,
The seas and everything that moves
    in them.
35 For God will save Zion
And build the cities of Judah,
That they may dwell there and
    possess it.
36 Also, the descendants of His servants
    shall inherit it,
And those who love His name shall
    dwell in it.

PSALM 70

Prayer for Relief from Adversaries

*To the Chief Musician. A Psalm of David. To
bring to remembrance.*

Make haste, O God, to deliver me!
Make haste to help me, O LORD!

2 Let them be ashamed and confounded
Who seek my life;
Let them be turned back[a] and
    confused
Who desire my hurt.
3 Let them be turned back because of
    their shame,
Who say, "Aha, aha!"

4 Let all those who seek You rejoice and
    be glad in You;
And let those who love Your salvation
    say continually,
"Let God be magnified!"

5 But I *am* poor and needy;
Make haste to me, O God!

70:2 ᵃFollowing Masoretic Text, Septuagint, Targum,
and Vulgate; some Hebrew manuscripts and Syriac
read *be appalled* (compare 40:15).

You *are* my help and my deliverer;
O LORD, do not delay.

PSALM 71

God the Rock of Salvation

In You, O LORD, I put my trust;
Let me never be put to shame.
2 Deliver me in Your righteousness, and
cause me to escape;
Incline Your ear to me, and save me.
3 Be my strong refuge,
To which I may resort continually;
You have given the commandment to
save me,
For You *are* my rock and my fortress.

4 Deliver me, O my God, out of the hand
of the wicked,
Out of the hand of the unrighteous
and cruel man.
5 For You are my hope, O Lord GOD;
You are my trust from my youth.
6 By You I have been upheld from birth;
You are He who took me out of my
mother's womb.
My praise *shall be* continually of You.

7 I have become as a wonder to many,
But You *are* my strong refuge.
8 Let my mouth be filled *with* Your
praise
And with Your glory all the day.

9 Do not cast me off in the time of old
age;
Do not forsake me when my strength
fails.
10 For my enemies speak against me;
And those who lie in wait for my life
take counsel together,
11 Saying, "God has forsaken him;
Pursue and take him, for *there is* none
to deliver *him*."

12 O God, do not be far from me;
O my God, make haste to help me!
13 Let them be confounded *and*
consumed
Who are adversaries of my life;
Let them be covered *with* reproach
and dishonor
Who seek my hurt.

14 But I will hope continually,
And will praise You yet more and
more.

15 My mouth shall tell of Your
righteousness
And Your salvation all the day,
For I do not know *their* limits.
16 I will go in the strength of the Lord
GOD;
I will make mention of Your
righteousness, of Yours only.

17 O God, You have taught me from my
youth;
And to this *day* I declare Your
wondrous works.
18 Now also when *I am* old and
grayheaded,
O God, do not forsake me,
Until I declare Your strength to *this*
generation,
Your power to everyone *who* is to
come.

19 Also Your righteousness, O God, *is*
very high,
You who have done great things;
O God, who *is* like You?
20 *You,* who have shown me great and
severe troubles,
Shall revive me again,
And bring me up again from the
depths of the earth.
21 You shall increase my greatness,
And comfort me on every side.

22 Also with the lute I will praise You—
And Your faithfulness, O my God!
To You I will sing with the harp,
O Holy One of Israel.
23 My lips shall greatly rejoice when I
sing to You,
And my soul, which You have
redeemed.
24 My tongue also shall talk of Your
righteousness all the day long;
For they are confounded,
For they are brought to shame
Who seek my hurt.

David's Laments (Books III–V)

The end of Book II (Ps. 42—72) of the psalms is clearly indicated by Ps. 72:20, "The prayers of David the son of Jesse are ended." At one time this verse possibly marked the end of a collection of David's psalms, and most psalms associated with David do appear in Books I and II. In the last three books of the psalms (Books III–V), only a few Davidic laments are found. One additional lament, Ps. 102, presents the prayer of an unknown suffering saint.

■ Psalms 86; 102; 109; 139—141; 143

PSALM 86

Prayer for Mercy, with Meditation on the Excellencies of the LORD

A Prayer of David.

Bow down Your ear, O LORD, hear me;
   For I *am* poor and needy.
2 Preserve my life, for I *am* holy;
   You are my God;
   Save Your servant who trusts in You!
3 Be merciful to me, O Lord,
   For I cry to You all day long.
4 Rejoice the soul of Your servant,
   For to You, O Lord, I lift up my soul.
5 For You, Lord, *are* good, and ready to forgive,
   And abundant in mercy to all those who call upon You.

6 Give ear, O LORD, to my prayer;
   And attend to the voice of my supplications.
7 In the day of my trouble I will call upon You,
   For You will answer me.

8 Among the gods *there is* none like You, O Lord;
   Nor *are there any works* like Your works.
9 All nations whom You have made
   Shall come and worship before You, O Lord,
   And shall glorify Your name.
10 For You *are* great, and do wondrous things;
   You alone *are* God.

11 Teach me Your way, O LORD;
   I will walk in Your truth;
   Unite my heart to fear Your name.
12 I will praise You, O Lord my God, with all my heart,

And I will glorify Your name forevermore.
13 For great *is* Your mercy toward me,
   And You have delivered my soul from the depths of Sheol.

14 O God, the proud have risen against me,
   And a mob of violent *men* have sought my life,
   And have not set You before them.
15 But You, O Lord, *are* a God full of compassion, and gracious,
   Longsuffering and abundant in mercy and truth.

16 Oh, turn to me, and have mercy on me!
   Give Your strength to Your servant,
   And save the son of Your maidservant.
17 Show me a sign for good,
   That those who hate me may see *it* and be ashamed,
   Because You, LORD, have helped me and comforted me.

PSALM 102

The LORD's Eternal Love

A Prayer of the afflicted, when he is overwhelmed and pours out his complaint before the LORD.

Hear my prayer, O LORD,
   And let my cry come to You.
2 Do not hide Your face from me in the day of my trouble;
   Incline Your ear to me;
   In the day that I call, answer me speedily.

3 For my days are consumed like smoke,
   And my bones are burned like a hearth.
4 My heart is stricken and withered like grass,
   So that I forget to eat my bread.
5 Because of the sound of my groaning
   My bones cling to my skin.
6 I am like a pelican of the wilderness;
   I am like an owl of the desert.

PLANTS AND ANIMALS

In the ancient Near East solitude was considered dangerous and unpleasant, not as a welcome retreat from a busy life. The desert was a place of hunger (Ps. 107:4, 5), and the cries of the birds there (Ps. 102:6) made the atmosphere eerie. Security was found in being surrounded with the life of the town and city.

7   I lie awake,
And am like a sparrow alone on the
    housetop.
8   My enemies reproach me all day long;
Those who deride me swear an oath
    against me.
9   For I have eaten ashes like bread,
And mingled my drink with weeping,
10   Because of Your indignation and Your
    wrath;
For You have lifted me up and cast me
    away.
11   My days *are* like a shadow that
    lengthens,
And I wither away like grass.

12   But You, O LORD, shall endure forever,
And the remembrance of Your name to
    all generations.
13   You will arise *and* have mercy on
    Zion;
For the time to favor her,
Yes, the set time, has come.
14   For Your servants take pleasure in her
    stones,
And show favor to her dust.
15   So the nations shall fear the name of
    the LORD,
And all the kings of the earth Your
    glory.
16   For the LORD shall build up Zion;
He shall appear in His glory.
17   He shall regard the prayer of the
    destitute,
And shall not despise their prayer.

18   This will be written for the generation
    to come,
That a people yet to be created may
    praise the LORD.
19   For He looked down from the height of
    His sanctuary;
From heaven the LORD viewed the
    earth,
20   To hear the groaning of the prisoner,
To release those appointed to death,
21   To declare the name of the LORD in
    Zion,
And His praise in Jerusalem,
22   When the peoples are gathered
    together,
And the kingdoms, to serve the LORD.

23   He weakened my strength in the way;
He shortened my days.
24   I said, "O my God,
Do not take me away in the midst of
    my days;

Your years *are* throughout all
    generations.
25   Of old You laid the foundation of the
    earth,
And the heavens *are* the work of Your
    hands.
26   They will perish, but You will endure;
Yes, they will all grow old like a
    garment;
Like a cloak You will change them,
And they will be changed.
27   But You *are* the same,
And Your years will have no end.
28   The children of Your servants will
    continue,
And their descendants will be
    established before You."

PSALM 109

Plea for Judgment of False Accusers

To the Chief Musician. A Psalm of David.

Do not keep silent,
O God of my praise!
2   For the mouth of the wicked and the
    mouth of the deceitful
Have opened against me;
They have spoken against me with a
    lying tongue.
3   They have also surrounded me with
    words of hatred,
And fought against me without a cause.
4   In return for my love they are my
    accusers,
But I *give myself to* prayer.
5   Thus they have rewarded me evil for
    good,
And hatred for my love.

6   Set a wicked man over him,
And let an accuser[a] stand at his right
    hand.
7   When he is judged, let him be found
    guilty,
And let his prayer become sin.
8   Let his days be few,
And let another take his office.
9   Let his children be fatherless,
And his wife a widow.
10   Let his children continually be
    vagabonds, and beg;
Let them seek *their bread*[a] also from
    their desolate places.

109:6 [a]Hebrew *satan*   109:10 [a]Following
Masoretic Text and Targum; Septuagint and Vulgate
read *be cast out.*

11 Let the creditor seize all that he has,
And let strangers plunder his labor.
12 Let there be none to extend mercy to
him,
Nor let there be any to favor his
fatherless children.
13 Let his posterity be cut off,
And in the generation following let
their name be blotted out.

14 Let the iniquity of his fathers be
remembered before the LORD,
And let not the sin of his mother be
blotted out.
15 Let them be continually before the
LORD,
That He may cut off the memory of
them from the earth;
16 Because he did not remember to show
mercy,
But persecuted the poor and needy
man,
That he might even slay the broken in
heart.
17 As he loved cursing, so let it come to
him;
As he did not delight in blessing, so
let it be far from him.
18 As he clothed himself with cursing as
with his garment,
So let it enter his body like water,
And like oil into his bones.
19 Let it be to him like the garment
which covers him,
And for a belt with which he girds
himself continually.
20 *Let* this *be* the LORD's reward to my
accusers,
And to those who speak evil against
my person.

21 But You, O GOD the Lord,
Deal with me for Your name's sake;
Because Your mercy *is* good, deliver
me.
22 For I *am* poor and needy,
And my heart is wounded within me.
23 I am gone like a shadow when it
lengthens;

I am shaken off like a locust.
24 My knees are weak through fasting,
And my flesh is feeble from lack of
fatness.
25 I also have become a reproach to
them;
When they look at me, they shake
their heads.

26 Help me, O LORD my God!
Oh, save me according to Your mercy,
27 That they may know that this *is* Your
hand—
That You, LORD, have done it!
28 Let them curse, but You bless;
When they arise, let them be
ashamed,
But let Your servant rejoice.
29 Let my accusers be clothed with
shame,
And let them cover themselves with
their own disgrace as with a
mantle.

30 I will greatly praise the LORD with my
mouth;
Yes, I will praise Him among the
multitude.
31 For He shall stand at the right hand
of the poor,
To save *him* from those who condemn
him.

PSALM 139

God's Perfect Knowledge of Man

For the Chief Musician. A Psalm of David.

O LORD, You have searched me and
known *me*.
2 You know my sitting down and my
rising up;
You understand my thought afar off.
3 You comprehend my path and my
lying down,
And are acquainted with all my ways.
4 For *there is* not a word on my tongue,
But behold, O LORD, You know it
altogether.

BELIEFS AND IDEAS

*Curses were common in the ancient world. A curse is a formula of words that when
recited or written is supposed to influence the course of another person's life. A person
who suspected that an enemy was using curses could reply with countercurses designed
to resist the influence of the curse (Ps. 109:17).*

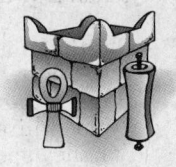

5 You have hedged me behind and
     before,
  And laid Your hand upon me.
6 *Such* knowledge *is* too wonderful for
     me;
  It is high, I cannot *attain* it.

7 Where can I go from Your Spirit?
  Or where can I flee from Your
     presence?
8 If I ascend into heaven, You *are* there;
  If I make my bed in hell, behold, You
     are there.
9 *If* I take the wings of the morning,
  And dwell in the uttermost parts of
     the sea,
10 Even there Your hand shall lead me,
   And Your right hand shall hold me.
11 If I say, "Surely the darkness shall
      fall[a] on me,"
   Even the night shall be light about
      me;
12 Indeed, the darkness shall not hide
      from You,
   But the night shines as the day;
   The darkness and the light *are* both
      alike *to You.*

13 For You formed my inward parts;
   You covered me in my mother's womb.
14 I will praise You, for I am fearfully
      and wonderfully made;[a]
   Marvelous are Your works,
   And *that* my soul knows very well.
15 My frame was not hidden from You,
   When I was made in secret,
   And skillfully wrought in the lowest
      parts of the earth.
16 Your eyes saw my substance, being yet
      unformed.
   And in Your book they all were
      written,
   The days fashioned for me,
   When *as yet there were* none of them.

17 How precious also are Your thoughts
      to me, O God!
   How great is the sum of them!
18 *If* I should count them, they would be
      more in number than the sand;
   When I awake, I am still with You.

19 Oh, that You would slay the wicked,
      O God!
   Depart from me, therefore, you
      bloodthirsty men.
20 For they speak against You wickedly;
   Your enemies take *Your name* in vain.[a]

21 Do I not hate them, O LORD, who hate
      You?
   And do I not loathe those who rise up
      against You?
22 I hate them with perfect hatred;
   I count them my enemies.

23 Search me, O God, and know my
      heart;
   Try me, and know my anxieties;
24 And see if *there is any* wicked way in
      me,
   And lead me in the way everlasting.

PSALM 140

Prayer for Deliverance from Evil Men

To the Chief Musician. A Psalm of David.

Deliver me, O LORD, from evil men;
   Preserve me from violent men,
2 Who plan evil things in *their* hearts;
   They continually gather together *for*
      war.
3 They sharpen their tongues like a
      serpent;
   The poison of asps *is* under their lips.
                                          Selah

4 Keep me, O LORD, from the hands of
      the wicked;
   Preserve me from violent men,
   Who have purposed to make my steps
      stumble.
5 The proud have hidden a snare for
      me, and cords;
   They have spread a net by the
      wayside;
   They have set traps for me.   Selah

6 I said to the LORD: "You *are* my God;
   Hear the voice of my supplications,
      O LORD.
7 O GOD the Lord, the strength of my
      salvation,
   You have covered my head in the day
      of battle.
8 Do not grant, O LORD, the desires of
      the wicked;
   Do not further his *wicked* scheme,
   Lest they be exalted.   Selah

139:11 [a]Vulgate and Symmachus read *cover.*
139:14 [a]Following Masoretic Text and Targum;
Septuagint, Syriac, and Vulgate read *You are fearfully
wonderful.*   139:20 [a]Septuagint and Vulgate read
They take Your cities in vain.

9   "*As for* the head of those who surround
me,
Let the evil of their lips cover them;
10   Let burning coals fall upon them;
Let them be cast into the fire,
Into deep pits, that they rise not up
again.
11   Let not a slanderer be established in
the earth;
Let evil hunt the violent man to
overthrow *him*."

12   I know that the LORD will maintain
The cause of the afflicted,
And justice for the poor.
13   Surely the righteous shall give thanks
to Your name;
The upright shall dwell in Your
presence.

PSALM 141

Prayer for Safekeeping from Wickedness

A Psalm of David.

L ORD, I cry out to You;
Make haste to me!
Give ear to my voice when I cry out to
You.
2   Let my prayer be set before You *as*
incense,
The lifting up of my hands *as* the
evening sacrifice.

3   Set a guard, O LORD, over my mouth;
Keep watch over the door of my lips.
4   Do not incline my heart to any evil
thing,
To practice wicked works
With men who work iniquity;
And do not let me eat of their
delicacies.

5   Let the righteous strike me;
It shall be a kindness.
And let him rebuke me;
It shall be as excellent oil;
Let my head not refuse it.

For still my prayer *is* against the
deeds of the wicked.
6   Their judges are overthrown by the
sides of the cliff,
And they hear my words, for they are
sweet.
7   Our bones are scattered at the mouth
of the grave,
As when one plows and breaks up the
earth.

8   But my eyes *are* upon You, O GOD the
Lord;
In You I take refuge;
Do not leave my soul destitute.
9   Keep me from the snares they have
laid for me,
And from the traps of the workers of
iniquity.
10   Let the wicked fall into their own
nets,
While I escape safely.

PSALM 143

An Earnest Appeal for Guidance and Deliverance

A Psalm of David.

H ear my prayer, O LORD,
Give ear to my supplications!
In Your faithfulness answer me,
And in Your righteousness.
2   Do not enter into judgment with Your
servant,
For in Your sight no one living is
righteous.

3   For the enemy has persecuted my
soul;
He has crushed my life to the ground;
He has made me dwell in darkness,
Like those who have long been dead.
4   Therefore my spirit is overwhelmed
within me;
My heart within me is distressed.

5   I remember the days of old;
I meditate on all Your works;

RELIGION AND WORSHIP

The Bible describes more than one posture suitable for praying. The most basic is to fall down or bow before the Creator. The hands reach out to God when begging, in giving praise, and possibly in greeting (Ps. 141:2). The raised hands may also be a sign of amazement and reverence for the awesomeness of God.

I muse on the work of Your hands.

6 I spread out my hands to You;
My soul *longs* for You like a thirsty
land.   Selah

7 Answer me speedily, O LORD;
My spirit fails!
Do not hide Your face from me,
Lest I be like those who go down into
the pit.

8 Cause me to hear Your lovingkindness
in the morning,
For in You do I trust;
Cause me to know the way in which I
should walk,
For I lift up my soul to You.

9 Deliver me, O LORD, from my enemies;
In You I take shelter.[a]

10 Teach me to do Your will,
For You *are* my God;
Your Spirit *is* good.
Lead me in the land of uprightness.

11 Revive me, O LORD, for Your name's
sake!
For Your righteousness' sake bring my
soul out of trouble.

12 In Your mercy cut off my enemies,
And destroy all those who afflict my
soul;
For I *am* Your servant.

The Prosperity of the Wicked

One psalm associated with David is neither a hymn nor a lament, but rather a wisdom psalm (see "Wisdom Psalms" at Ps. 1). The collection of wise sayings in Ps. 37 is often compared to the Book of Proverbs. Its basic theme is to commend trust in God for everyday living in the face of wickedness and temptation. Despite temporary prosperity, the wicked must ultimately fail.

■ Psalm 37

PSALM 37

The Heritage of the Righteous and the Calamity of the Wicked

A Psalm of David.

D o not fret because of evildoers,
Nor be envious of the workers of
iniquity.

2 For they shall soon be cut down like
the grass,
And wither as the green herb.

3 Trust in the LORD, and do good;
Dwell in the land, and feed on His
faithfulness.

4 Delight yourself also in the LORD,
And He shall give you the desires of
your heart.

5 Commit your way to the LORD,
Trust also in Him,
And He shall bring *it* to pass.

6 He shall bring forth your
righteousness as the light,
And your justice as the noonday.

7 Rest in the LORD, and wait patiently
for Him;
Do not fret because of him who
prospers in his way,
Because of the man who brings wicked
schemes to pass.

8 Cease from anger, and forsake wrath;
Do not fret—*it* only *causes* harm.

9 For evildoers shall be cut off;
But those who wait on the LORD,
They shall inherit the earth.

10 For yet a little while and the wicked
shall be no *more;*
Indeed, you will look carefully for his
place,
But it *shall be* no *more.*

11 But the meek shall inherit the earth,
And shall delight themselves in the
abundance of peace.

12 The wicked plots against the just,
And gnashes at him with his teeth.

13 The Lord laughs at him,
For He sees that his day is coming.

14 The wicked have drawn the sword
And have bent their bow,
To cast down the poor and needy,
To slay those who are of upright
conduct.

15 Their sword shall enter their own
heart,
And their bows shall be broken.

16 A little that a righteous man has
Is better than the riches of many
wicked.

143:9 [a]Septuagint and Vulgate read *To You I flee.*

17 For the arms of the wicked shall be
     broken,
   But the LORD upholds the righteous.
18 The LORD knows the days of the
     upright,
   And their inheritance shall be forever.
19 They shall not be ashamed in the evil
     time,
   And in the days of famine they shall
     be satisfied.
20 But the wicked shall perish;
   And the enemies of the LORD,
   Like the splendor of the meadows,
     shall vanish.
   Into smoke they shall vanish away.

21 The wicked borrows and does not
     repay,
   But the righteous shows mercy and
     gives.
22 For *those* blessed by Him shall inherit
     the earth,
   But *those* cursed by Him shall be cut
     off.

23 The steps of a *good* man are ordered
     by the LORD,
   And He delights in his way.
24 Though he fall, he shall not be utterly
     cast down;
   For the LORD upholds *him with* His
     hand.

25 I have been young, and *now* am old;
   Yet I have not seen the righteous
     forsaken,
   Nor his descendants begging bread.
26 *He is* ever merciful, and lends;
   And his descendants *are* blessed.

27 Depart from evil, and do good;
   And dwell forevermore.
28 For the LORD loves justice,
   And does not forsake His saints;
   They are preserved forever,

   But the descendants of the wicked
     shall be cut off.
29 The righteous shall inherit the land,
   And dwell in it forever.

30 The mouth of the righteous speaks
     wisdom,
   And his tongue talks of justice.
31 The law of his God *is* in his heart;
   None of his steps shall slide.

32 The wicked watches the righteous,
   And seeks to slay him.
33 The LORD will not leave him in his
     hand,
   Nor condemn him when he is judged.

34 Wait on the LORD,
   And keep His way,
   And He shall exalt you to inherit the
     land;
   When the wicked are cut off, you shall
     see *it.*
35 I have seen the wicked in great power,
   And spreading himself like a native
     green tree.
36 Yet he passed away,[a] and behold, he
     was no *more;*
   Indeed I sought him, but he could not
     be found.

37 Mark the blameless *man,* and observe
     the upright;
   For the future of *that* man *is* peace.
38 But the transgressors shall be
     destroyed together;
   The future of the wicked shall be cut
     off.

39 But the salvation of the righteous *is*
     from the LORD;
   He is their strength in the time of
     trouble.
40 And the LORD shall help them and
     deliver them;
   He shall deliver them from the
     wicked,
   And save them,
   Because they trust in Him.

37:36 [a]Following Masoretic Text, Septuagint, and Targum; Syriac and Vulgate read *I passed by.*

DAILY LIFE AND CUSTOMS

In village life a person's affairs are more visible than in modern cities. In the Bible, righteous persons are considered responsible to support their society according to their means. Their acts of generosity are not occasional, special displays, but part of the household budget. Although outsiders might not see it, the reputation of a generous person would be common knowledge, as visible as the light of day at noon (Ps. 37:6).

Preparations for the Temple

In both 2 Sam. 24 and 1 Chr. 21, David took the census and was punished. The two accounts differ after that point, though. The Samuel account is immediately followed by the description of David's feeble last years (1 Kin. 1; 2), a pathetic end to a great life. The Chronicles account focuses on David's victories, and to the Chronicler, none of David's achievements is as great as his founding of the temple and his appointment of the priests who would serve there.

The superscription of Ps. 30 associates the psalm with "the dedication of the house of David." The Hebrew could also be translated as "the dedication of the house. Of David." Although it is not certain that the word "house" refers to the temple, the superscription may suggest that at some point Ps. 30 was associated with the temple.

- ■ 1 Chronicles 22:1–19
- ■ Psalm 30

1 Chronicles 22:1–19
David Prepares to Build the Temple

22 :1 Then David said, "This *is* the house of the LORD God, and this *is* the altar of burnt offering for Israel." ²So David commanded to gather the aliens who *were* in the land of Israel; and he appointed masons to cut hewn stones to build the house of God. ³And David prepared iron in abundance for the nails of the doors of the gates and for the joints, and bronze in abundance beyond measure, ⁴and cedar trees in abundance; for the Sidonians and those from Tyre brought much cedar wood to David.

⁵Now David said, "Solomon my son *is* young and inexperienced, and the house to be built for the LORD *must be* exceedingly magnificent, famous and glorious throughout all countries. I will now make preparation for it." So David made abundant preparations before his death.

⁶Then he called for his son Solomon, and charged him to build a house for the LORD God of Israel. ⁷And David said to Solomon: "My son, as for me, it was in my mind to build a house to the name of the LORD my God; ⁸but the word of the LORD came to me, saying, 'You have shed much blood and have made great wars; you shall not build a house for My name, because you have shed much blood on the earth in My sight. ⁹Behold, a son shall be born to you, who shall be a man of rest; and I will give him rest from all his enemies all around. His name shall be Solomon,ᵃ for I will give peace and quietness to Israel in his days. ¹⁰He shall build a house for My name, and he shall be My son, and I *will be* his Father; and I will establish the throne of his kingdom over Israel forever.' ¹¹Now, my son, may the LORD be with you; and may you prosper, and build the house of the LORD your God, as He has said to you. ¹²Only may the LORD give you wisdom and understanding, and give you charge concerning Israel, that you may keep the law of the LORD your God. ¹³Then you will prosper, if you take care to fulfill the statutes and judgments with which the LORD charged Moses concerning Israel. Be strong and of good courage; do not fear nor be dismayed. ¹⁴Indeed I have taken much trouble to prepare for the house of the LORD one hundred thousand talents of gold and one million talents of silver, and bronze and iron beyond measure, for it is so abundant. I have prepared timber and stone also, and you may add to them. ¹⁵Moreover *there are* workmen with you in abundance: woodsmen and stonecutters, and all types of skillful men for every kind of work. ¹⁶Of gold and silver and bronze and iron *there is* no limit. Arise and begin working, and the LORD be with you."

¹⁷David also commanded all the leaders of Israel to help Solomon his son, *saying,* ¹⁸"Is not the LORD your God with you? And has He *not* given you rest on every

22:9 ᵃLiterally *Peaceful*

ARCHITECTURE AND BUILDING

Gates were often made of wood fortified with many nails (1 Chr. 22:3). The doorway of the Parthenon in Athens was nearly 14 feet wide and 32 feet high, and the doors were made of wood plated with bronze. The doorway of Solomon's temple was somewhat smaller. Architects used bronze and iron for structural reinforcement as well as for ornamentation in building.

side? For He has given the inhabitants of the land into my hand, and the land is subdued before the LORD and before His people. [19]Now set your heart and your soul to seek the LORD your God. Therefore arise and build the sanctuary of the LORD God, to bring the ark of the covenant of the LORD and the holy articles of God into the house that is to be built for the name of the LORD."

PSALM 30

The Blessedness of Answered Prayer

A Psalm. A Song at the dedication of the house of David.

I will extol You, O LORD, for You have
  lifted me up,
  And have not let my foes rejoice over
  me.
[2] O LORD my God, I cried out to You,
  And You healed me.
[3] O LORD, You brought my soul up from
  the grave;
  You have kept me alive, that I should
  not go down to the pit.[a]

[4] Sing praise to the LORD, you saints of
  His,
  And give thanks at the remembrance
  of His holy name.[a]
[5] For His anger *is but for* a moment,
  His favor *is for* life;
  Weeping may endure for a night,
  But joy *comes* in the morning.

[6] Now in my prosperity I said,
  "I shall never be moved."
[7] LORD, by Your favor You have made
  my mountain stand strong;
  You hid Your face, *and* I was troubled.

[8] I cried out to You, O LORD;
  And to the LORD I made supplication:
[9] "What profit *is there* in my blood,
  When I go down to the pit?
  Will the dust praise You?
  Will it declare Your truth?
[10] Hear, O LORD, and have mercy on me;
  LORD, be my helper!"

Ps. 30:3 [a]Following Qere and Targum; Kethib, Septuagint, Syriac, and Vulgate read *from those who descend to the pit.*   30:4 [a]Or *His holiness*
1 Chr. 23:7 [a]Spelled *Libni* in Exodus 6:17
23:10 [a]Septuagint and Vulgate read *Zizah* (compare verse 11).

[11] You have turned for me my mourning
  into dancing;
  You have put off my sackcloth and
  clothed me with gladness,
[12] To the end that *my* glory may sing
  praise to You and not be silent.
  O LORD my God, I will give thanks to
  You forever.

Divisions of the Temple Personnel

In the Chronicler's emphasis upon temple affairs, other matters get pushed aside. For instance, all the complicated court intrigues that led up to Solomon's coronation in 1 Kings are replaced in the priestly account with a single sentence (1 Chr. 23:1). Then the Chronicler returns to his temple theme.

The organization of the temple arranged the personnel into family groups. The Levites (ch. 23), priests (ch. 24), musicians (ch. 25), and gatekeepers (ch. 26) are listed by divisions. Although these lists are frustrating to modern readers, such details of organization were not trivial to the Chronicler.

■ 1 Chronicles 23:1—26:19

1 Chronicles
The Divisions of the Levites

23 :1 So when David was old and full of days, he made his son Solomon king over Israel.

[2]And he gathered together all the leaders of Israel, with the priests and the Levites. [3]Now the Levites were numbered from the age of thirty years and above; and the number of individual males was thirty-eight thousand. [4]Of these, twenty-four thousand *were* to look after the work of the house of the LORD, six thousand *were* officers and judges, [5]four thousand *were* gatekeepers, and four thousand praised the LORD with *musical* instruments, "which I made," *said David,* "for giving praise."

[6]Also David separated them into divisions among the sons of Levi: Gershon, Kohath, and Merari.

[7]Of the Gershonites: Laadan[a] and Shimei. [8]The sons of Laadan: the first Jehiel, then Zetham and Joel—three *in all.* [9]The sons of Shimei: Shelomith, Haziel, and Haran—three *in all.* These were the heads of the fathers' *houses* of Laadan. [10]And the sons of Shimei: Jahath, Zina,[a] Jeush, and Beriah. These *were* the four sons of Shimei. [11]Jahath was the first and

Zizah the second. But Jeush and Beriah did not have many sons; therefore they were assigned as one father's house.

[12]The sons of Kohath: Amram, Izhar, Hebron, and Uzziel—four *in all.* [13]The sons of Amram: Aaron and Moses; and Aaron was set apart, he and his sons forever, that he should sanctify the most holy things, to burn incense before the LORD, to minister to Him, and to give the blessing in His name forever. [14]Now the sons of Moses the man of God were reckoned to the tribe of Levi. [15]The sons of Moses *were* Gershon[a] and Eliezer. [16]Of the sons of Gershon, She-buel[a] *was* the first. [17]Of the descendants of Eliezer, Rehabiah was the first. And Eliezer had no other sons, but the sons of Rehabiah were very many. [18]Of the sons of Izhar, Shelomith *was* the first. [19]Of the sons of Hebron, Jeriah *was* the first, Amariah the second, Jahaziel the third, and Jekameam the fourth. [20]Of the sons of Uzziel, Michah *was* the first and Jesshiah the second.

[21]The sons of Merari *were* Mahli and Mushi. The sons of Mahli *were* Eleazar and Kish. [22]And Eleazar died, and had no sons, but only daughters; and their brethren, the sons of Kish, took them *as* wives. [23]The sons of Mushi *were* Mahli, Eder, and Jere-moth—three *in all.*

[24]These *were* the sons of Levi by their fathers' houses—the heads of the fathers' *houses* as they were counted individually by the number of their names, who did the work for the service of the house of the LORD, from the age of twenty years and above.

[25]For David said, "The LORD God of Is-rael has given rest to His people, that they may dwell in Jerusalem forever"; [26]and also to the Levites, "They shall no longer carry the tabernacle, or any of the articles for its service." [27]For by the last words of David the Levites *were* numbered from twenty years old and above; [28]because their duty *was* to help the sons of Aaron in the service of the house of the LORD, in the courts and in the chambers, in the purify-ing of all holy things and the work of the service of the house of God, [29]both with the showbread and the fine flour for the grain offering, with the unleavened cakes and *what is baked in* the pan, with what is mixed and with all kinds of measures and sizes; [30]to stand every morning to thank and praise the LORD, and likewise at evening; [31]and at every presentation of a burnt offering to the LORD on the Sabbaths and on the New Moons and on the set feasts, by number according to the ordi-nance governing them, regularly before the LORD; [32]and that they should attend to the needs of the tabernacle of meeting, the needs of the holy *place,* and the needs of the sons of Aaron their brethren in the work of the house of the LORD.

The Divisions of the Priests

24 [1]Now *these are* the divisions of the sons of Aaron. The sons of Aaron *were* Nadab, Abihu, Eleazar, and Ithamar. [2]And Nadab and Abihu died before their father, and had no children; therefore Eleazar and Ithamar ministered as priests. [3]Then David with Zadok of the sons of Eleazar, and Ahimelech of the sons of Ithamar, divided them according to the schedule of their service.

[4]There were more leaders found of the sons of Eleazar than of the sons of Ithamar, and *thus* they were divided. Among the sons of Eleazar *were* sixteen heads of *their* fathers' houses, and eight heads of their fathers' houses among the sons of Ithamar. [5]Thus they were divided by lot, one group as another, for there were officials of the sanctuary and officials *of the house* of God, from the sons of Eleazar and from the sons of Ithamar. [6]And the scribe, Shemaiah the son of Nethanel, *one of* the Levites, wrote them down before the king, the leaders, Zadok the priest, Ahimelech the son of Abi-athar, and the heads of the fathers' *houses* of the priests and Levites, one father's house taken for Eleazar and *one* for Ithamar.

23:15 [a]Hebrew *Gershom* (compare 6:16)
23:16 [a]Spelled *Shubael* in 24:20

TIME CAPSULE   *1000* B.C.

1000   *Example of steel hardened by quenching, from Cyprus*

1000   *Growth of coastal trade under Phoenicians*

1000   *Hebrew and Greek alphabets de-velop from Phoenician*

1000   *Nubia becomes an independent state*

1000   *Semitic peoples migrate from Ara-bia to Ethiopia*

⁷Now the first lot fell to Jehoiarib, the second to Jedaiah, ⁸the third to Harim, the fourth to Seorim, ⁹the fifth to Malchijah, the sixth to Mijamin, ¹⁰the seventh to Hakkoz, the eighth to Abijah, ¹¹the ninth to Jeshua, the tenth to Shecaniah, ¹²the eleventh to Eliashib, the twelfth to Jakim, ¹³the thirteenth to Huppah, the fourteenth to Jeshebeab, ¹⁴the fifteenth to Bilgah, the sixteenth to Immer, ¹⁵the seventeenth to Hezir, the eighteenth to Happizzez,[a] ¹⁶the nineteenth to Pethahiah, the twentieth to Jehezekel,[a] ¹⁷the twenty-first to Jachin, the twenty-second to Gamul, ¹⁸the twenty-third to Delaiah, the twenty-fourth to Maaziah.

¹⁹This *was* the schedule of their service for coming into the house of the LORD according to their ordinance by the hand of Aaron their father, as the LORD God of Israel had commanded him.

Other Levites

²⁰And the rest of the sons of Levi: of the sons of Amram, Shubael;[a] of the sons of Shubael, Jehdeiah. ²¹Concerning Rehabiah, of the sons of Rehabiah, the first *was* Isshiah. ²²Of the Izharites, Shelomoth;[a] of the sons of Shelomoth, Jahath. ²³Of the sons *of* Hebron,[a] Jeriah *was the first,*[b] Amariah the second, Jahaziel the third, *and* Jekameam the fourth. ²⁴*Of* the sons of Uzziel, Michah; of the sons of Michah, Shamir. ²⁵The brother of Michah, Isshiah; of the sons of Isshiah, Zechariah. ²⁶The sons of Merari *were* Mahli and Mushi; the son of Jaaziah, Beno. ²⁷The sons of Merari by Jaaziah *were* Beno, Shoham, Zaccur, and Ibri. ²⁸Of Mahli: Eleazar, who had no sons. ²⁹Of Kish: the son of Kish, Jerahmeel.

³⁰Also the sons of Mushi *were* Mahli,

Eder, and Jerimoth. These *were* the sons of the Levites according to their fathers' houses.

³¹These also cast lots just as their brothers the sons of Aaron did, in the presence of King David, Zadok, Ahimelech, and the heads of the fathers' *houses* of the priests and Levites. The chief fathers *did* just as their younger brethren.

The Musicians

25 ¹Moreover David and the captains of the army separated for the service *some* of the sons of Asaph, of Heman, and of Jeduthun, who *should* prophesy with harps, stringed instruments, and cymbals. And the number of the skilled men performing their service was: ²Of the sons of Asaph: Zaccur, Joseph, Nethaniah, and Asharelah;[a] the sons of Asaph *were* under the direction of Asaph, who prophesied according to the order of the king. ³Of Jeduthun, the sons of Jeduthun: Gedaliah, Zeri,[a] Jeshaiah, Shimei, Hashabiah, and Mattithiah, six,[b] under the direction of their father Jeduthun, ,who prophesied with a harp to give thanks and to praise the LORD. ⁴Of Heman, the sons of Heman: Bukkiah, Mattaniah, Uzziel,[a] Shebuel,[b] Jerimoth,[c] Hananiah, Hanani, Eliathah, Giddalti, Romamti-Ezer, Joshbekashah, Mallothi, Hothir, *and* Mahazioth. ⁵All these *were* the sons of Heman the king's seer in the words of God, to exalt his horn.[a] For God gave Heman fourteen sons and three daughters.

⁶All these *were* under the direction of their father for the music *in* the house of the LORD, with cymbals, stringed instruments, and harps, for the service of the house of God. Asaph, Jeduthun, and Heman *were* under the authority of the king. ⁷So the number of them, with their brethren who were instructed in the songs of the LORD, all who were skillful, *was* two hundred and eighty-eight.

⁸And they cast lots for their duty, the small as well as the great, the teacher with the student.

⁹Now the first lot for Asaph came out for Joseph; the second for Gedaliah, him with his brethren and sons, twelve; ¹⁰the third for Zaccur, his sons and his brethren, twelve; ¹¹the fourth for Jizri,[a] his sons and his brethren, twelve; ¹²the fifth for Nethaniah, his sons and his brethren, twelve; ¹³the sixth for Bukkiah, his sons and his brethren, twelve; ¹⁴the seventh for

---

24:15 ªSeptuagint and Vulgate read *Aphses.*
24:16 ªMasoretic Text reads *Jehezkel.*
24:20 ªSpelled *Shebuel* in 23:16   24:22 ªSpelled *Shelomith* in 23:18   24:23 ªSupplied from 23:19 (following some Hebrew manuscripts and Septuagint manuscripts) ᵇSupplied from 23:19 (following some Hebrew manuscripts and Septuagint manuscripts)
25:2 ªSpelled *Jesharelah* in verse 14
25:3 ªSpelled *Jizri* in verse 11 ᵇ*Shimei,* appearing in one Hebrew and several Septuagint manuscripts, completes the total of six sons (compare verse 17).   25:4 ªSpelled *Azarel* in verse 18 ᵇSpelled *Shubael* in verse 20 ᶜSpelled *Jeremoth* in verse 22   25:5 ªThat is, to increase his power or influence   25:11 ªSpelled *Zeri* in verse 3

PROPHETS BETWEEN GOD AND HUMANITY (1 Chr. 25:5)

Prophets were common in the ancient Near East. In most royal courts, they were specialists whose occupation was to act as a mediator between God (or the gods) and the human world. These prophets were understood to have been seized by the divinities who used them to convey their very words to the human listeners. Kings employed court prophets in order to be informed of the divine will any time it was deemed necessary. Some of these professional prophets were not trustworthy, since they might claim as divine word whatever would advance their own positions in court.

A historical note in the Book of 1 Samuel indicates that the prophet had earlier been known as a "seer" (1 Sam. 9:9). The term "seer" refers to the experience of the prophet being allowed to see the deliberations of the divine council and to relate the decisions made there in accurate detail. Thus one who was called a "seer," a term related to the prophet's vision, came to be called a prophet, a term related to the public proclamation of the message.

In David's court Heman is described as "the king's seer" (1 Chr. 25:5). This Heman was also one of David's temple musicians (1 Chr. 16:42). Possibly a group of cultic prophets became part of the temple musical guild, and so David appointed this group to "prophesy with harps, stringed instruments, and cymbals" (25:1).

Jesharelah,[a] his sons and his brethren, twelve; [15]the eighth for Jeshaiah, his sons and his brethren, twelve; [16]the ninth for Mattaniah, his sons and his brethren, twelve; [17]the tenth for Shimei, his sons and his brethren, twelve; [18]the eleventh for Azarel,[a] his sons and his brethren, twelve; [19]the twelfth for Hashabiah, his sons and his brethren, twelve; [20]the thirteenth for Shubael,[a] his sons and his brethren, twelve; [21]the fourteenth for Mattithiah, his sons and his brethren, twelve; [22]the fifteenth for Jeremoth,[a] his sons and his brethren, twelve; [23]the sixteenth for Hananiah, his sons and his brethren, twelve; [24]the seventeenth for Joshbekashah, his sons and his brethren, twelve; [25]the eighteenth for Hanani, his sons and his brethren, twelve; [26]the nineteenth for Mallothi, his sons and his brethren, twelve; [27]the twentieth for Eliathah, his sons and his brethren, twelve; [28]the twenty-first for Hothir, his sons and his brethren, twelve; [29]the twenty-second for Giddalti, his sons and his brethren, twelve; [30]the twenty-third for Mahazioth, his sons and his brethren, twelve; [31]the twenty-fourth for Romamti-Ezer, his sons and his brethren, twelve.

The Gatekeepers

26 [1]Concerning the divisions of the gatekeepers: of the Korahites, Meshelemiah the son of Kore, of the sons of Asaph. [2]And the sons of Meshelemiah were Zechariah the firstborn, Jediael the second, Zebadiah the third, Jathniel the fourth, [3]Elam the fifth, Jehohanan the sixth, Eliehoenai the seventh.

[4]Moreover the sons of Obed-Edom were Shemaiah the firstborn, Jehozabad the second, Joah the third, Sacar the fourth, Nethanel the fifth, [5]Ammiel the sixth, Issachar the seventh, Peulthai the eighth; for God blessed him.

[6]Also to Shemaiah his son were sons born who governed their fathers' houses, because they were men of great ability. [7]The sons of Shemaiah were Othni, Rephael, Obed, and Elzabad, whose brothers Elihu and Semachiah were able men.

[8]All these were of the sons of Obed-Edom, they and their sons and their brethren, able men with strength for the work: sixty-two of Obed-Edom.

[9]And Meshelemiah had sons and brethren, eighteen able men.

[10]Also Hosah, of the children of Merari, had sons: Shimri the first (for though he was not the firstborn, his father made him the first), [11]Hilkiah the second, Tebaliah the third, Zechariah the fourth; all the sons and brethren of Hosah were thirteen.

[12]Among these were the divisions of the gatekeepers, among the chief men, hav-

25:14 [a]Spelled *Asharelah* in verse 2
25:18 [a]Spelled *Uzziel* in verse 4   25:20 [a]Spelled *Shebuel* in verse 4   25:22 [a]Spelled *Jerimoth* in verse 4

ing duties just like their brethren, to serve in the house of the LORD. [13]And they cast lots for each gate, the small as well as the great, according to their father's house. [14]The lot for the East *Gate* fell to Shelemiah. Then they cast lots *for* his son Zechariah, a wise counselor, and his lot came out for the North Gate; [15]to Obed-Edom the South Gate, and to his sons the storehouse.[a] [16]To Shuppim and Hosah *the lot came out* for the West Gate, with the Shallecheth Gate on the ascending highway—watchman opposite watchman. [17]On the east were *six* Levites, on the north four each day, on the south four each day, and for the storehouse[a] two by two. [18]As for the Parbar[a] on the west, *there were* four on the highway *and* two at the Parbar. [19]These were the divisions of the gatekeepers among the sons of Korah and among the sons of Merari.

The Sons of Korah

Among the lists of Levites in Chronicles, two groups receive particular attention. The first is the Levitical singers, led by Asaph, Heman, and Jeduthun (1 Chr. 25:1). The second is the gatekeepers. It is hard to be sure what duties were assigned these gatekeepers, but 1 Chr. 26:1 identifies them with the group called the "Korahites." The superscriptions of many psalms refer to this group, associating those psalms with "the sons of Korah."

The psalms "of the sons of Korah" (Ps. 42—49; 84; 85; 87), as well as two others (Ps. 15; 24), speak of the requirements for entry into the temple and thus seem appropriate for gatekeepers. Psalm 43, while it does not have a superscription, is clearly a continuation of Ps. 42, which is ascribed to the sons of Korah. Psalm 88 is associated with Heman the Ezrahite, as well as the sons of Korah (see "Psalms of the Musicians" at Ps. 96).

■ Psalms 15; 24; 42—49; 84; 85; 87

PSALM 15

The Character of Those Who May Dwell with the LORD

A Psalm of David.

LORD, who may abide in Your
   tabernacle?
   Who may dwell in Your holy hill?

[2] He who walks uprightly,
   And works righteousness,
   And speaks the truth in his heart;
[3] He *who* does not backbite with his
   tongue,
   Nor does evil to his neighbor,
   Nor does he take up a reproach
   against his friend;
[4] In whose eyes a vile person is
   despised,
   But he honors those who fear the
   LORD;
   He *who* swears to his own hurt and
   does not change;
[5] He *who* does not put out his money at
   usury,
   Nor does he take a bribe against the
   innocent.

He who does these *things* shall never
   be moved.

PSALM 24

The King of Glory and His Kingdom

A Psalm of David.

The earth *is* the LORD's, and all its
   fullness,
   The world and those who dwell
   therein.
[2] For He has founded it upon the seas,
   And established it upon the waters.

[3] Who may ascend into the hill of the
   LORD?
   Or who may stand in His holy place?
[4] He who has clean hands and a pure
   heart,
   Who has not lifted up his soul to an
   idol,
   Nor sworn deceitfully.
[5] He shall receive blessing from the
   LORD,
   And righteousness from the God of his
   salvation.
[6] This *is* Jacob, the generation of those
   who seek Him,
   Who seek Your face.   Selah

[7] Lift up your heads, O you gates!
   And be lifted up, you everlasting
   doors!
   And the King of glory shall come in.
[8] Who *is* this King of glory?
   The LORD strong and mighty,
   The LORD mighty in battle.
[9] Lift up your heads, O you gates!

26:15 [a]Hebrew *asuppim*   26:17 [a]Hebrew
asuppim   26:18 [a]Probably a court or colonnade
extending west of the temple

Lift up, you everlasting doors!
And the King of glory shall come in.
10 Who is this King of glory?
The LORD of hosts,
He *is* the King of glory.   Selah

PSALM 42

Yearning for God in the Midst of Distresses

To the Chief Musician. A Contemplation[a] *of the sons of Korah.*

A s the deer pants for the water brooks,
So pants my soul for You, O God.
2 My soul thirsts for God, for the living
God.
When shall I come and appear before
God?[a]
3 My tears have been my food day and
night,
While they continually say to me,
"Where *is* your God?"

4 When I remember these *things,*
I pour out my soul within me.
For I used to go with the multitude;
I went with them to the house of God,
With the voice of joy and praise,
With a multitude that kept a pilgrim
feast.

5 Why are you cast down, O my soul?
And *why* are you disquieted within
me?
Hope in God, for I shall yet praise Him
For the help of His countenance.[a]

6 O my God,[a] my soul is cast down
within me;
Therefore I will remember You from
the land of the Jordan,
And from the heights of Hermon,
From the Hill Mizar.
7 Deep calls unto deep at the noise of
Your waterfalls;
All Your waves and billows have gone
over me.
8 The LORD will command His
lovingkindness in the daytime,

And in the night His song *shall be*
with me—
A prayer to the God of my life.
9 I will say to God my Rock,
"Why have You forgotten me?
Why do I go mourning because of the
oppression of the enemy?"
10 *As* with a breaking of my bones,
My enemies reproach me,
While they say to me all day long,
"Where *is* your God?"

11 Why are you cast down, O my soul?
And why are you disquieted within
me?
Hope in God;
For I shall yet praise Him,
The help of my countenance and my
God.

PSALM 43

Prayer to God in Time of Trouble

V indicate me, O God,
And plead my cause against an
ungodly nation;
Oh, deliver me from the deceitful and
unjust man!
2 For You *are* the God of my strength;
Why do You cast me off?
Why do I go mourning because of the
oppression of the enemy?

3 Oh, send out Your light and Your
truth!
Let them lead me;
Let them bring me to Your holy hill

42:title [a]Hebrew *Maschil*   42:2 [a]Following
Masoretic Text and Vulgate; some Hebrew
manuscripts, Septuagint, Syriac, and Targum read *I
see the face of God.*   42:5 [a]Following Masoretic
Text and Targum; a few Hebrew manuscripts,
Septuagint, Syriac, and Vulgate read *The help of my
countenance, my God.*   42:6 [a]Following Masoretic
Text and Targum; a few Hebrew manuscripts,
Septuagint, Syriac, and Vulgate put *my God* at the end
of verse 5.

ARCHITECTURE AND BUILDING

*To the psalmist, the "everlasting doors" (Ps. 24:7) were the gates of heaven. On earth
they were represented by the gates of the temple. God enters the temple in order to
take up His residence there in the inmost sanctuary. The moment of passage through a
door was an occasion for ceremonies or rituals at every level, from the doorway of a
cottage to the cordon of guards that protected access to a king.*

And to Your tabernacle.
4 Then I will go to the altar of God,
   To God my exceeding joy;
   And on the harp I will praise You,
   O God, my God.

5 Why are you cast down, O my soul?
   And why are you disquieted within
      me?
   Hope in God;
   For I shall yet praise Him,
   The help of my countenance and my
      God.

PSALM 44

Redemption Remembered in Present Dishonor

To the Chief Musician. A Contemplation[a] *of the sons of Korah.*

We have heard with our ears, O God,
   Our fathers have told us,
   The deeds You did in their days,
   In days of old:
2 You drove out the nations with Your
      hand,
   But them You planted;
   You afflicted the peoples, and cast
      them out.
3 For they did not gain possession of the
      land by their own sword,
   Nor did their own arm save them;
   But it was Your right hand, Your arm,
      and the light of Your countenance,
   Because You favored them.

4 You are my King, O God;[a]
   Command[b] victories for Jacob.
5 Through You we will push down our
      enemies;
   Through Your name we will trample
      those who rise up against us.

44:title [a]Hebrew *Maschil*   44:4 [a]Following Masoretic Text and Targum; Septuagint and Vulgate read *and my God.*   [b]Following Masoretic Text and Targum; Septuagint, Syriac, and Vulgate read *Who commands.*

6 For I will not trust in my bow,
   Nor shall my sword save me.
7 But You have saved us from our
      enemies,
   And have put to shame those who
      hated us.
8 In God we boast all day long,
   And praise Your name forever.   Selah

9 But You have cast *us* off and put us to
      shame,
   And You do not go out with our
      armies.
10 You make us turn back from the
      enemy,
   And those who hate us have taken
      spoil for themselves.
11 You have given us up like sheep
      intended for food,
   And have scattered us among the
      nations.
12 You sell Your people for *next to*
      nothing,
   And are not enriched by selling them.

13 You make us a reproach to our
      neighbors,
   A scorn and a derision to those all
      around us.
14 You make us a byword among the
      nations,
   A shaking of the head among the
      peoples.
15 My dishonor *is* continually before me,
   And the shame of my face has covered
      me,
16 Because of the voice of him who
      reproaches and reviles,
   Because of the enemy and the avenger.

17 All this has come upon us;
   But we have not forgotten You,
   Nor have we dealt falsely with Your
      covenant.
18 Our heart has not turned back,
   Nor have our steps departed from Your
      way;
19 But You have severely broken us in
      the place of jackals,

BELIEFS AND IDEAS

The English word "shame" means an inner attitude or feeling. But the Hebrew word refers more to public disgrace. Shame accompanies the experience of defeat and applies even to those who are not personally responsible for what happened (Ps. 44:9). Trouble resulting from a natural cause or providential act that no one could foresee or prevent could still be said to "shame" or "confuse" the one who suffered.

And covered us with the shadow of
death.

20 If we had forgotten the name of our
God,
Or stretched out our hands to a
foreign god,
21 Would not God search this out?
For He knows the secrets of the heart.
22 Yet for Your sake we are killed all day
long;
We are accounted as sheep for the
slaughter.

23 Awake! Why do You sleep, O Lord?
Arise! Do not cast *us* off forever.
24 Why do You hide Your face,
And forget our affliction and our
oppression?
25 For our soul is bowed down to the
dust;
Our body clings to the ground.
26 Arise for our help,
And redeem us for Your mercies' sake.

PSALM 45

The Glories of the Messiah and His Bride

To the Chief Musician. Set to "The Lilies."[a]
A Contemplation[b] *of the sons of Korah. A Song
of Love.*

My heart is overflowing with a good
theme;
I recite my composition concerning the
King;
My tongue *is* the pen of a ready
writer.

2 You are fairer than the sons of men;
Grace is poured upon Your lips;
Therefore God has blessed You forever.
3 Gird Your sword upon *Your* thigh,
O Mighty One,
With Your glory and Your majesty.
4 And in Your majesty ride prosperously
because of truth, humility, *and*
righteousness;

And Your right hand shall teach You
awesome things.
5 Your arrows *are* sharp in the heart of
the King's enemies;
The peoples fall under You.

6 Your throne, O God, *is* forever and
ever;
A scepter of righteousness *is* the
scepter of Your kingdom.
7 You love righteousness and hate
wickedness;
Therefore God, Your God, has
anointed You
With the oil of gladness more than
Your companions.
8 All Your garments are scented with
myrrh and aloes *and* cassia,
Out of the ivory palaces, by which
they have made You glad.
9 Kings' daughters *are* among Your
honorable women;
At Your right hand stands the queen
in gold from Ophir.

10 Listen, O daughter,
Consider and incline your ear;
Forget your own people also, and your
father's house;
11 So the King will greatly desire your
beauty;
Because He *is* your Lord, worship
Him.
12 And the daughter of Tyre *will come*
with a gift;
The rich among the people will seek
your favor.

13 The royal daughter *is* all glorious
within *the palace;*
Her clothing *is* woven with gold.
14 She shall be brought to the King in
robes of many colors;
The virgins, her companions who
follow her, shall be brought to You.
15 With gladness and rejoicing they shall
be brought;
They shall enter the King's palace.

45:title [a]Hebrew *Shoshannim* [b]Hebrew *Maschil*

TRADE AND ECONOMICS

*Wealth and luxury is expressed in the Bible by means of the products available to the
rich and powerful in ancient times. Such products included perfumes and ivory (Ps.
45:8). Ivory was difficult to obtain, usually being imported from foreign places. Perfumes
were compounded using substances that came from as far away as the Himalaya
mountains in India.*

GOD IS IN THE MIDST OF HIS CITY (Ps. 46:4, 5)

Ancient people understood a relationship between their land and their deities. Gods owned territory and allotted it to human rulers. The residence of the god was the main temple in the capital of the land under the deity's control. This city of the god could only be transferred from one human ruler to another with the blessing of the god, or if the deity was defeated in heaven by another deity.

The people of Mesopotamia never doubted that their god Marduk controlled Babylon. Even when the city was overrun by the Elamites (c. 1157 B.C.) and later destroyed by the Assyrians (689 B.C.), the people believed that Marduk had declared this fate for his city because the population had breached its loyalty to its patron deity.

Just so, Jerusalem was God's capital in Judah. The people of Jerusalem commonly believed that as long as they obeyed God, God would save their city from any human invasion. This is what Isaiah proclaimed to the Assyrians (Is. 37:33–35) and what certain false prophets twisted into a belief that Jerusalem could not be conquered at all (Jer. 23:16, 17). The theology of the psalmist, however, is clear: if the people were righteous, God would not allow the city to be taken from them, no matter the size or power of the enemy attacking. The "city of God . . . shall not be moved" (Ps. 46:4, 5).

God was understood to dwell in a special way in the temple at Jerusalem. Since God is the only deity, there would never be a way to defeat Jerusalem unless God abandoned the temple and city. This central article of Judean theology was modified by a vision of the prophet Ezekiel: when God could no longer tolerate the evil of Jerusalem's population, He moved out of the city. It ceased to be God's city and was destroyed by mere humans with ease (Ezek. 10).

---

16 Instead of Your fathers shall be Your
    sons,
    Whom You shall make princes in all
    the earth.
17 I will make Your name to be
    remembered in all generations;
    Therefore the people shall praise You
    forever and ever.

PSALM 46

God the Refuge of His People and Conqueror of the Nations

To the Chief Musician. A Psalm of the sons of Korah. A Song for Alamoth.

God *is* our refuge and strength,
    A very present help in trouble.
2 Therefore we will not fear,
    Even though the earth be removed,
    And though the mountains be carried
    into the midst of the sea;
3 *Though* its waters roar *and* be
    troubled,
    Though the mountains shake with its
    swelling.   Selah

4 *There is* a river whose streams shall
    make glad the city of God,
    The holy *place* of the tabernacle of the
    Most High.
5 God *is* in the midst of her, she shall
    not be moved;
    God shall help her, just at the break of
    dawn.
6 The nations raged, the kingdoms were
    moved;
    He uttered His voice, the earth
    melted.

7 The LORD of hosts *is* with us;
    The God of Jacob *is* our refuge.   Selah

8 Come, behold the works of the LORD,
    Who has made desolations in the
    earth.
9 He makes wars cease to the end of the
    earth;
    He breaks the bow and cuts the spear
    in two;
    He burns the chariot in the fire.

10 Be still, and know that I *am* God;
    I will be exalted among the nations,
    I will be exalted in the earth!

11 The LORD of hosts *is* with us;
    The God of Jacob *is* our refuge.   Selah

PSALM 47

Praise to God, the Ruler of the Earth

To the Chief Musician. A Psalm of the sons of Korah.

Oh, clap your hands, all you peoples!
Shout to God with the voice of
triumph!
2 For the LORD Most High *is* awesome;
He is a great King over all the earth.
3 He will subdue the peoples under us,
And the nations under our feet.
4 He will choose our inheritance for us,
The excellence of Jacob whom He
loves.   Selah

5 God has gone up with a shout,
The LORD with the sound of a
trumpet.
6 Sing praises to God, sing praises!
Sing praises to our King, sing praises!
7 For God *is* the King of all the earth;
Sing praises with understanding.

8 God reigns over the nations;
God sits on His holy throne.
9 The princes of the people have
gathered together,
The people of the God of Abraham.
For the shields of the earth *belong* to
God;
He is greatly exalted.

PSALM 48

The Glory of God in Zion

A Song. A Psalm of the sons of Korah.

Great *is* the LORD, and greatly to be
praised
In the city of our God,
In His holy mountain.
2 Beautiful in elevation,
The joy of the whole earth,
Is Mount Zion *on* the sides of the
north,
The city of the great King.

3 God *is* in her palaces;
He is known as her refuge.

4 For behold, the kings assembled,
They passed by together.
5 They saw *it, and* so they marveled;
They were troubled, they hastened
away.
6 Fear took hold of them there,
And pain, as of a woman in birth
pangs,
7 *As when* You break the ships of
Tarshish
With an east wind.

8 As we have heard,
So we have seen
In the city of the LORD of hosts,
In the city of our God:
God will establish it forever.   Selah

9 We have thought, O God, on Your
lovingkindness,
In the midst of Your temple.
10 According to Your name, O God,
So *is* Your praise to the ends of the
earth;
Your right hand is full of
righteousness.
11 Let Mount Zion rejoice,
Let the daughters of Judah be glad,
Because of Your judgments.

12 Walk about Zion,
And go all around her.
Count her towers;
13 Mark well her bulwarks;
Consider her palaces;
That you may tell *it* to the generation
following.
14 For this *is* God,
Our God forever and ever;
He will be our guide
Even to death.[a]

48:14 [a]Following Masoretic Text and Syriac;
Septuagint and Vulgate read *Forever.*

GEOGRAPHY AND ENVIRONMENT

The "east wind" is a hot, dry wind that blows across Palestine from the east. It can continue for days or weeks, and therefore can become very unpleasant. In the Bible the east wind often symbolizes an exercise of divine judgment. It withers crops (Gen. 41:27), destroys gardens (Ezek. 17:10), and brings locusts (Ex. 10:13). It is said to shatter ships on the sea (Ps. 48:7; Ezek. 27:26).

PSALM 49

The Confidence of the Foolish

To the Chief Musician. A Psalm of the sons of Korah.

Hear this, all peoples;
Give ear, all inhabitants of the world,
2 Both low and high,
Rich and poor together.
3 My mouth shall speak wisdom,
And the meditation of my heart *shall give* understanding.
4 I will incline my ear to a proverb;
I will disclose my dark saying on the harp.

5 Why should I fear in the days of evil,
When the iniquity at my heels surrounds me?
6 Those who trust in their wealth
And boast in the multitude of their riches,
7 None *of them* can by any means redeem *his* brother,
Nor give to God a ransom for him—
8 For the redemption of their souls *is* costly,
And it shall cease forever—
9 That he should continue to live eternally,
And not see the Pit.

10 For he sees wise men die;
Likewise the fool and the senseless person perish,
And leave their wealth to others.
11 Their inner thought *is that* their houses *will last* forever,[a]
Their dwelling places to all generations;
They call *their* lands after their own names.
12 Nevertheless man, *though* in honor, does not remain;[a]
He is like the beasts *that* perish.

13 This is the way of those who *are* foolish,
And of their posterity who approve their sayings.   Selah

14 Like sheep they are laid in the grave;
Death shall feed on them;
The upright shall have dominion over them in the morning;
And their beauty shall be consumed in the grave, far from their dwelling.
15 But God will redeem my soul from the power of the grave,
For He shall receive me.   Selah

16 Do not be afraid when one becomes rich,
When the glory of his house is increased;
17 For when he dies he shall carry nothing away;
His glory shall not descend after him.
18 Though while he lives he blesses himself
(For *men* will praise you when you do well for yourself),
19 He shall go to the generation of his fathers;
They shall never see light.
20 A man *who is* in honor, yet does not understand,
Is like the beasts *that* perish.

PSALM 84

The Blessedness of Dwelling in the House of God

To the Chief Musician. On an instrument of Gath.[a] A Psalm of the sons of Korah.

How lovely *is* Your tabernacle,
O LORD of hosts!
2 My soul longs, yes, even faints
For the courts of the LORD;
My heart and my flesh cry out for the living God.

3 Even the sparrow has found a home,
And the swallow a nest for herself,
Where she may lay her young—
Even Your altars, O LORD of hosts,
My King and my God.
4 Blessed *are* those who dwell in Your house;
They will still be praising You.   Selah

5 Blessed *is* the man whose strength *is* in You,
Whose heart *is* set on pilgrimage.
6 *As they* pass through the Valley of Baca,
They make it a spring;
The rain also covers it with pools.

49:11 [a]Septuagint, Syriac, Targum, and Vulgate read *Their graves shall be their houses forever.*
49:12 [a]Following Masoretic Text and Targum; Septuagint, Syriac, and Vulgate read *understand* (compare verse 20).   84:title [a]Hebrew *Al Gittith*

7   They go from strength to strength;
    Each one appears before God in Zion.[a]

8   O LORD God of hosts, hear my prayer;
    Give ear, O God of Jacob!   Selah
9   O God, behold our shield,
    And look upon the face of Your
      anointed.

10   For a day in Your courts *is* better than
     a thousand.
    I would rather be a doorkeeper in the
     house of my God
    Than dwell in the tents of wickedness.
11   For the LORD God *is* a sun and shield;
    The LORD will give grace and glory;
    No good *thing* will He withhold
    From those who walk uprightly.

12   O LORD of hosts,
    Blessed *is* the man who trusts in You!

PSALM 85

Prayer that the LORD Will Restore Favor to the Land

To the Chief Musician. A Psalm of the sons of Korah.

LORD, You have been favorable to Your
    land;
    You have brought back the captivity of
     Jacob.
2   You have forgiven the iniquity of Your
     people;
    You have covered all their sin.   Selah
3   You have taken away all Your wrath;
    You have turned from the fierceness of
     Your anger.

4   Restore us, O God of our salvation,
    And cause Your anger toward us to
     cease.
5   Will You be angry with us forever?
    Will You prolong Your anger to all
     generations?
6   Will You not revive us again,
    That Your people may rejoice in You?

7   Show us Your mercy, LORD,
    And grant us Your salvation.

8   I will hear what God the LORD will
     speak,
    For He will speak peace
    To His people and to His saints;
    But let them not turn back to folly.
9   Surely His salvation *is* near to those
     who fear Him,
    That glory may dwell in our land.

10   Mercy and truth have met together;
    Righteousness and peace have kissed.
11   Truth shall spring out of the earth,
    And righteousness shall look down
     from heaven.
12   Yes, the LORD will give *what is* good;
    And our land will yield its increase.
13   Righteousness will go before Him,
    And shall make His footsteps *our*
     pathway.

PSALM 87

The Glories of the City of God

A Psalm of the sons of Korah. A Song.

His foundation *is* in the holy
    mountains.
2   The LORD loves the gates of Zion
    More than all the dwellings of Jacob.
3   Glorious things are spoken of you,
    O city of God!   Selah

4   "I will make mention of Rahab and
     Babylon to those who know Me;
    Behold, O Philistia and Tyre, with
     Ethiopia:
    'This *one* was born there.' "

5   And of Zion it will be said,
    "This *one* and that *one* were born in
     her;
    And the Most High Himself shall
     establish her."

84:7 [a]Septuagint, Syriac, and Vulgate read *The God of gods shall be seen.*

PLANTS AND ANIMALS

In the Bible, "sparrow" (Ps. 84:3) is not the name of a single species of bird, but refers to several kinds of small birds that frequent human habitations. These birds, like the English sparrow found everywhere in the United States, are able to adapt to changing conditions and the presence of human beings.

6 The LORD will record,
    When He registers the peoples:
    "This *one* was born there."   Selah

7 Both the singers and the players on
    instruments *say,*
    "All my springs *are* in you."

David's Counsel to Solomon

The organization of David's kingdom concludes in 1 Chr. 26:20—27:34 with lists of the temple treasurers, judicial officers, military captains and officers, tribal officers, administrators, and counselors. David is credited with organizing Israel's religious life, military power, and civil government. One thing remained—building the temple.

Both Samuel/Kings and Chronicles agree that David did not build the temple. Solomon, his son and successor, did that. The two accounts differ, however, in the extent to which David is involved. The Chronicler spares no effort to show that David did everything except build the temple. When David hands over the building plans to Solomon (1 Chr. 28:11), it is clear that the Chronicler sees David, not his son, as the true founder of the temple.

■ 1 Chronicles 26:20—29:30

1 Chronicles
The Treasuries and Other Duties

26 :20 Of the Levites, Ahijah *was* over the treasuries of the house of God and over the treasuries of the dedicated things. 21The sons of Laadan, the descendants of the Gershonites of Laadan, heads of their fathers' *houses,* of Laadan the Gershonite: Jehieli. 22The sons of Jehieli, Zetham and Joel his brother, *were* over the treasuries of the house of the LORD. 23Of the Amramites, the Izharites, the Hebronites, and the Uzzielites: 24Shebuel the son of Gershom, the son of Moses, *was* overseer of the treasuries. 25And his brethren by Eliezer *were* Rehabiah his son,

Jeshaiah his son, Joram his son, Zichri his son, and Shelomith his son.

26This Shelomith and his brethren *were* over all the treasuries of the dedicated things which King David and the heads of fathers' *houses,* the captains over thousands and hundreds, and the captains of the army, had dedicated. 27Some of the spoils won in battles they dedicated to maintain the house of the LORD. 28And all that Samuel the seer, Saul the son of Kish, Abner the son of Ner, and Joab the son of Zeruiah had dedicated, every dedicated *thing,* was under the hand of Shelomith and his brethren.

29Of the Izharites, Chenaniah and his sons *performed* duties as officials and judges over Israel outside Jerusalem.

30Of the Hebronites, Hashabiah and his brethren, one thousand seven hundred able men, had the oversight of Israel on the west side of the Jordan for all the business of the LORD, and in the service of the king. 31Among the Hebronites, Jerijah *was* head of the Hebronites according to his genealogy of the fathers. In the fortieth year of the reign of David they were sought, and there were found among them capable men at Jazer of Gilead. 32And his brethren *were* two thousand seven hundred able men, heads of fathers' *houses,* whom King David made officials over the Reubenites, the Gadites, and the half-tribe of Manasseh, for every matter pertaining to God and the affairs of the king.

The Military Divisions

27 1And the children of Israel, according to their number, the heads of fathers' *houses,* the captains of thousands and hundreds and their officers, served the king in every matter of the *military* divisions. *These divisions* came in and went out month by month throughout all the months of the year, each division *having* twenty-four thousand.

2Over the first division for the first month *was* Jashobeam the son of Zabdiel, and in his division *were* twenty-four

thousand; ³*he was* of the children of Perez, and the chief of all the captains of the army for the first month. ⁴Over the division of the second month *was* Dodai[a] an Ahohite, and of his division Mikloth also *was* the leader; in his division *were* twenty-four thousand. ⁵The third captain of the army for the third month *was* Benaiah, the son of Jehoiada the priest, who was chief; in his division *were* twenty-four thousand. ⁶This was the Benaiah *who was* mighty *among* the thirty, and was over the thirty; in his division *was* Ammizabad his son. ⁷The fourth *captain* for the fourth month *was* Asahel the brother of Joab, and Zebadiah his son after him; in his division *were* twenty-four thousand. ⁸The fifth *captain* for the fifth month *was* Shamhuth[a] the Izrahite; in his division were twenty-four thousand. ⁹The sixth *captain* for the sixth month *was* Ira the son of Ikkesh the Tekoite; in his division *were* twenty-four thousand. ¹⁰The seventh *captain* for the seventh month *was* Helez the Pelonite, of the children of Ephraim; in his division *were* twenty-four thousand. ¹¹The eighth *captain* for the eighth month *was* Sibbechai the Hushathite, of the Zarhites; in his division *were* twenty-four thousand. ¹²The ninth *captain* for the ninth month *was* Abiezer the Anathothite, of the Benjamites; in his division *were* twenty-four thousand. ¹³The tenth *captain* for the tenth month *was* Maharai the Netophathite, of the Zarhites; in his division *were* twenty-four thousand. ¹⁴The eleventh *captain* for the eleventh month *was* Benaiah the Pirathonite, of the children of Ephraim; in his division *were* twenty-four thousand. ¹⁵The twelfth *captain* for the twelfth month *was* Heldai[a] the Netophathite, of Othniel; in his division *were* twenty-four thousand.

Leaders of Tribes

¹⁶Furthermore, over the tribes of Israel: the officer over the Reubenites *was* Eliezer the son of Zichri; over the Simeonites, Shephatiah the son of Maachah; ¹⁷*over* the Levites, Hashabiah the son of Kemuel; over the Aaronites, Zadok; ¹⁸*over* Judah, Elihu, *one* of David's brothers; *over* Issachar, Omri the son of Michael; ¹⁹*over* Zebulun, Ishmaiah the son of Obadiah; *over* Naphtali, Jerimoth the son of Azriel; ²⁰*over* the children of Ephraim, Hoshea the son of Azaziah; *over* the half-tribe of Manasseh, Joel the son of Pedaiah; ²¹*over* the half-*tribe* of Manasseh in Gilead, Iddo the son of Zechariah; *over* Benjamin, Jaasiel the son of Abner; ²²*over* Dan, Azarel the son of Jeroham. These *were* the leaders of the tribes of Israel.

²³But David did not take the number of those twenty years old and under, because the LORD had said He would multiply Israel like the stars of the heavens. ²⁴Joab the son of Zeruiah began a census, but he did not finish, for wrath came upon Israel because of this census; nor was the number recorded in the account of the chronicles of King David.

Other State Officials

²⁵And Azmaveth the son of Adiel *was* over the king's treasuries; and Jehonathan the son of Uzziah was over the storehouses in the field, in the cities, in the villages, and in the fortresses. ²⁶Ezri the son of Chelub was over those who did the work of the field for tilling the ground. ²⁷And Shimei the Ramathite *was* over the vineyards, and Zabdi the Shiphmite was over the produce of the vineyards for the supply of wine. ²⁸Baal-Hanan the Gederite was over the olive trees and the sycamore trees that *were* in the lowlands, and Joash *was* over the store of oil. ²⁹And Shitrai the Sharonite *was* over the herds that fed in Sharon, and Shaphat the son of Adlai was over the herds *that were* in the valleys. ³⁰Obil the Ishmaelite *was* over the camels, Jehdeiah the Meronothite *was* over the

---

27:4 [a]Hebrew *Dodai,* usually spelled *Dodo* (compare 2 Samuel 23:9)   27:8 [a]Spelled *Shammoth* in 11:27 and *Shammah* in 2 Samuel 23:11   27:15 [a]Spelled *Heled* in 11:30 and *Heleb* in 2 Samuel 23:29

ARCHITECTURE AND BUILDING

It was customary for part of the spoils won in wars to be dedicated to the temples, whether in Israel (1 Chr. 26:27) or in Greece and Rome. The accumulated wealth in the temple would form a strategic reserve for the city, making the temple a public treasury. As a result, temples became attractive targets in wartime, being raided by friends or plundered by enemies.

donkeys, [31]and Jaziz the Hagrite *was* over the flocks. All these *were* the officials over King David's property.

[32]Also Jehonathan, David's uncle, *was* a counselor, a wise man, and a scribe; and Jehiel the son of Hachmoni *was* with the king's sons. [33]Ahithophel *was* the king's counselor, and Hushai the Archite *was* the king's companion. [34]After Ahithophel *was* Jehoiada the son of Benaiah, then Abiathar. And the general of the king's army *was* Joab.

Solomon Instructed to Build the Temple

28 [1]Now David assembled at Jerusalem all the leaders of Israel: the officers of the tribes and the captains of the divisions who served the king, the captains over thousands and captains over hundreds, and the stewards over all the substance and possessions of the king and of his sons, with the officials, the valiant men, and all the mighty men of valor.

[2]Then King David rose to his feet and said, "Hear me, my brethren and my people: I *had* it in my heart to build a house of rest for the ark of the covenant of the LORD, and for the footstool of our God, and had made preparations to build it. [3]But God said to me, 'You shall not build a house for My name, because you *have been* a man of war and have shed blood.' [4]However the LORD God of Israel chose me above all the house of my father to be king over Israel forever, for He has chosen Judah *to be* the ruler. And of the house of Judah, the house of my father, and among the sons of my father, He was pleased with me to make *me* king over all Israel. [5]And of all my sons (for the LORD has given me many sons) He has chosen my son Solomon to sit on the throne of the kingdom of the LORD over Israel. [6]Now He said to me, 'It is your son Solomon *who* shall build My house and My courts; for I have chosen him *to be* My son, and I will be his Father. [7]Moreover I will establish his kingdom forever, if he is steadfast to observe My commandments and My judgments, as it is this day.' [8]Now therefore, in the sight of all Israel, the assembly of the LORD, and in the hearing of our God, be careful to seek out all the commandments of the LORD your God, that you may possess this good land, and leave *it* as an inheritance for your children after you forever.

[9]"As for you, my son Solomon, know the God of your father, and serve Him with a loyal heart and with a willing mind; for the LORD searches all hearts and understands all the intent of the thoughts. If you seek Him, He will be found by you; but if you forsake Him, He will cast you off forever. [10]Consider now, for the LORD has chosen you to build a house for the sanctuary; be strong, and do it."

[11]Then David gave his son Solomon the

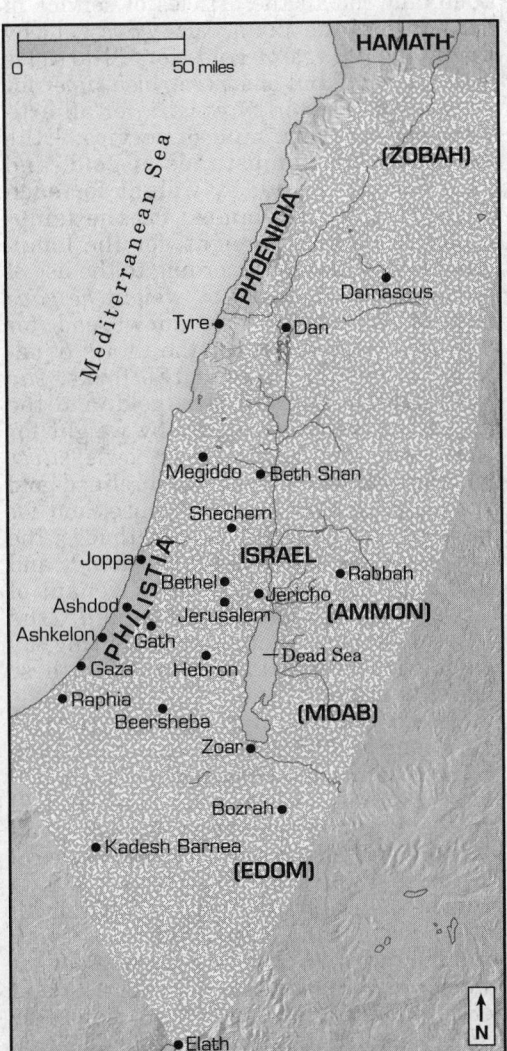

The Davidic Kingdom

The military successes of David against the Moabites and Edomites expanded and solidified his control to the east and south of Jerusalem. He also succeeded in isolating the Philistines to a few coastal cities. Victories against Zobah and the Arameans in the northeast and against the Ammonites in the central region greatly extended his borders.

plans for the vestibule, its houses, its treasuries, its upper chambers, its inner chambers, and the place of the mercy seat; 12and the plans for all that he had by the Spirit, of the courts of the house of the LORD, of all the chambers all around, of the treasuries of the house of God, and of the treasuries for the dedicated things; 13also for the division of the priests and the Levites, for all the work of the service of the house of the LORD, and for all the articles of service in the house of the LORD. 14*He gave* gold by weight for *things* of gold, for all articles used in every kind of service; also *silver* for all articles of silver by weight, for all articles used in every kind of service; 15the weight for the lampstands of gold, and their lamps of gold, by weight for each lampstand and its lamps; for the lampstands of silver by weight, for the lampstand and its lamps, according to the use of each lampstand. 16And by weight *he gave* gold for the tables of the showbread, for each table, and silver for the tables of silver; 17also pure gold for the forks, the basins, the pitchers of pure gold, and the golden bowls—*he gave gold* by weight for every bowl; and for the silver bowls, *silver* by weight for every bowl; 18and refined gold by weight for the altar of incense, and for the construction of the chariot, that is, the gold cherubim that spread *their wings* and overshadowed the ark of the covenant of the LORD. 19"All *this*," said David, "the LORD made me understand in writing, by *His* hand upon me, all the works of these plans."

20And David said to his son Solomon, "Be strong and of good courage, and do *it;* do not fear nor be dismayed, for the LORD God—my God—*will be* with you. He will not leave you nor forsake you, until you have finished all the work for the service of the house of the LORD. 21*Here are* the divisions of the priests and the Levites for all the service of the house of God; and every willing craftsman *will be* with you for all manner of workmanship, for every kind of service; also the leaders and all the people *will be* completely at your command."

Offerings for Building the Temple

29 1Furthermore King David said to all the assembly: "My son Solomon, whom alone God has chosen, *is* young and inexperienced; and the work *is* great, because the temple[a] *is* not for man but for the LORD God. 2Now for the house of my God I have prepared with all my might: gold for *things to be made of* gold, silver for *things of* silver, bronze for *things of* bronze, iron for *things of* iron, wood for *things of* wood, onyx stones, *stones* to be set, glistening stones of various colors, all kinds of precious stones, and marble slabs in abundance. 3Moreover, because I have set my affection on the house of my God, I have given to the house of my God, over and above all that I have prepared for the holy house, my own special treasure of gold and silver: 4three thousand talents of gold, of the gold of Ophir, and seven thousand talents of refined silver, to overlay the walls of the houses; 5the gold for *things of* gold and the silver for *things of* silver, and for all kinds of work *to be done* by the hands of craftsmen. Who *then* is willing to consecrate himself this day to the LORD?"

6Then the leaders of the fathers' *houses,* leaders of the tribes of Israel, the captains of thousands and of hundreds, with the officers over the king's work, offered willingly. 7They gave for the work of the house of God five thousand talents and ten thousand darics of gold, ten thousand talents of silver, eighteen thousand talents of bronze, and one hundred thousand talents of iron. 8And whoever had *precious* stones gave *them* to the treasury of the house of the LORD, into the hand of Jehiel[a] the Gershonite. 9Then the people rejoiced, for they had offered willingly, because with a loyal heart they had offered willingly to the LORD; and King David also rejoiced greatly.

David's Praise to God

10Therefore David blessed the LORD before all the assembly; and David said:

"Blessed are You, LORD God of Israel,
  our Father, forever and ever.
11 Yours, O LORD, *is* the greatness,
  The power and the glory,
  The victory and the majesty;
  For all *that is* in heaven and in earth
    is Yours;
  Yours *is* the kingdom, O LORD,
  And You are exalted as head over all.
12 Both riches and honor *come* from You,
  And You reign over all.
  In Your hand *is* power and might;

29:1 aLiterally *palace*   29:8 aPossibly the same as *Jehieli* (compare 26:21, 22)

In Your hand *it is* to make great
And to give strength to all.

13 "Now therefore, our God,
We thank You
And praise Your glorious name.
14 But who *am* I, and who *are* my people,
That we should be able to offer so
willingly as this?
For all things *come* from You,
And of Your own we have given You.
15 For we *are* aliens and pilgrims before
You,
As *were* all our fathers;
Our days on earth *are* as a shadow,
And without hope.

16"O LORD our God, all this abundance that we have prepared to build You a house for Your holy name is from Your hand, and *is* all Your own. 17I know also, my God, that You test the heart and have pleasure in uprightness. As for me, in the uprightness of my heart I have willingly offered all these *things;* and now with joy I have seen Your people, who are present here to offer willingly to You. 18O LORD God of Abraham, Isaac, and Israel, our fathers, keep this forever in the intent of the thoughts of the heart of Your people, and fix their heart toward You. 19And give my son Solomon a loyal heart to keep Your commandments and Your testimonies and Your statutes, to do all *these things,* and to build the temple[a] for which I have made provision."

20Then David said to all the assembly, "Now bless the LORD your God." So all the assembly blessed the LORD God of their fathers, and bowed their heads and prostrated themselves before the LORD and the king.

Solomon Anointed King

21And they made sacrifices to the LORD and offered burnt offerings to the LORD on the next day: a thousand bulls, a thousand rams, a thousand lambs, with their drink offerings, and sacrifices in abundance for all Israel. 22So they ate and drank before the LORD with great gladness on that day. And they made Solomon the son of David king the second time, and anointed *him* before the LORD *to be* the leader, and Zadok *to be* priest. 23Then Solomon sat on the throne of the LORD as king instead of David his father, and prospered; and all Israel obeyed him. 24All the leaders and the mighty men,

and also all the sons of King David, submitted themselves to King Solomon. 25So the LORD exalted Solomon exceedingly in the sight of all Israel, and bestowed on him *such* royal majesty as had not been on any king before him in Israel.

The Close of David's Reign

26Thus David the son of Jesse reigned over all Israel. 27And the period that he reigned over Israel *was* forty years; seven years he reigned in Hebron, and thirty-three *years* he reigned in Jerusalem. 28So he died in a good old age, full of days and riches and honor; and Solomon his son reigned in his place. 29Now the acts of King David, first and last, indeed they *are* written in the book of Samuel the seer, in the book of Nathan the prophet, and in the book of Gad the seer, 30with all his reign and his might, and the events that happened to him, to Israel, and to all the kingdoms of the lands.

Royal and Enthronement Psalms

In addition to the two general types of psalms, the hymns and laments, there are several smaller categories or subtypes. One category consists of those psalms which focus particularly on the position of the king, and thus are known as "royal" or "enthronement" psalms. A few of them (Ps. 2; 20) speak of the earthly king as God's chosen son, His anointed one. Others (Ps. 93—99) describe God Himself as King. Yet others are fitting either for the king's coronation (Ps. 110), as prayers for him (Ps. 21; 72), or as promises or prayers by him (Ps. 101; 144). The theme of these psalms is best expressed in the recurring declaration, "The LORD reigns!" (Ps. 93:1; 97:1).

The royal or enthronement psalms may have been used in royal festivals in the temple, or during coronations. It is impossible to be sure of this, but it nevertheless seems appropriate to read these psalms in light of Solomon's coronation. The Chronicler relates Solomon's assumption of the throne above all in the context of the temple. One royal psalm, Ps. 96, appears with some differences as part of the psalm David presented to the Levitical musicians (see "Psalms of the Musicians" at Ps. 96).

■ Psalms 2; 20; 21; 72; 93—95; 97—99; 101; 110; 144

KINGS AS VICE-REGENTS (Ps. 2:7)

The position of king in the ancient Near East was the point at which heaven and earth came together. The Egyptians believed their pharaoh was divine and returned to the gods when he died. From about 1500 B.C. the pharaoh was thought to be the son of the god Amon-Re, as well as the "image of god," both physically and in his actions. Egyptian kings had their own priests, and their palace was treated as a temple. The pharaoh counted on the help of the other gods in ruling his kingdom. As long as he did not alienate the other deities, they would fight with him to protect or expand the kingdom of Egypt.

In Mesopotamia, rulers were not considered divine, but they were understood to have been appointed king by the patron deity of their city or empire. Since the god had chosen him, the king ruled as vice-regent of the god and was accountable to the god for all his actions. As long as the king did what was expected of a good ruler, the gods would protect him and guarantee victory over his enemies.

Such ancient Near Eastern theology was used by Judah to celebrate the crowning of Davidic kings in Jerusalem. The psalmist describes Yahweh speaking to Judah's new king in words parallel to the Mesopotamian royal texts: "You are My Son, Today I have begotten You" (Ps. 2:7). The early Christians understood Ps. 2 to refer to Jesus as the Messiah (Acts 4:25, 26; 13:33). But originally Ps. 2:7 meant that Judah's king was the legitimate heir to the throne (other rulers were "adopted"). The king was the vice-regent of Yahweh, seated at His right hand, and Yahweh would guarantee victories for the king over Judah's enemies.

PSALM 2

The Messiah's Triumph and Kingdom

Why do the nations rage,
And the people plot a vain thing?
2   The kings of the earth set themselves,
And the rulers take counsel together,
Against the LORD and against His
    Anointed, *saying,*
3   "Let us break Their bonds in pieces
And cast away Their cords from us."

4   He who sits in the heavens shall
    laugh;
The LORD shall hold them in derision.
5   Then He shall speak to them in His
    wrath,
And distress them in His deep
    displeasure:
6   "Yet I have set My King
On My holy hill of Zion."

7   "I will declare the decree:
The LORD has said to Me,
'You *are* My Son,
Today I have begotten You.
8   Ask of Me, and I will give *You*
The nations *for* Your inheritance,
And the ends of the earth *for* Your
    possession.
9   You shall break[a] them with a rod of
    iron;

You shall dash them to pieces like a
    potter's vessel.'"

10   Now therefore, be wise, O kings;
Be instructed, you judges of the earth.
11   Serve the LORD with fear,
And rejoice with trembling.
12   Kiss the Son,[a] lest He[b] be angry,
And you perish *in* the way,
When His wrath is kindled but a
    little.
Blessed *are* all those who put their
    trust in Him.

PSALM 20

The Assurance of God's Saving Work

To the Chief Musician. A Psalm of David.

May the LORD answer you in the day of
    trouble;
May the name of the God of Jacob
    defend you;
2   May He send you help from the
    sanctuary,
And strengthen you out of Zion;

2:9 [a]Following Masoretic Text and Targum;
Septuagint, Syriac, and Vulgate read *rule* (compare
Revelation 2:27).   2:12 [a]Septuagint and Vulgate
read *Embrace discipline;* Targum reads *Receive
instruction.*   [b]Septuagint reads *the LORD.*

3   May He remember all your offerings,
    And accept your burnt sacrifice. Selah

4   May He grant you according to your
        heart's *desire,*
    And fulfill all your purpose.
5   We will rejoice in your salvation,
    And in the name of our God we will
        set up *our* banners!
    May the LORD fulfill all your petitions.

6   Now I know that the LORD saves His
        anointed;
    He will answer him from His holy
        heaven
    With the saving strength of His right
        hand.

7   Some *trust* in chariots, and some in
        horses;
    But we will remember the name of the
        LORD our God.
8   They have bowed down and fallen;
    But we have risen and stand upright.

9   Save, LORD!
    May the King answer us when we call.

PSALM 21

Joy in the Salvation of the LORD

To the Chief Musician. A Psalm of David.

The king shall have joy in Your strength,
        O LORD;
    And in Your salvation how greatly
        shall he rejoice!
2   You have given him his heart's desire,
    And have not withheld the request of
        his lips.   Selah

3   For You meet him with the blessings
        of goodness;
    You set a crown of pure gold upon his
        head.
4   He asked life from You, *and* You gave
        it to him—
    Length of days forever and ever.
5   His glory *is* great in Your salvation;
    Honor and majesty You have placed
        upon him.
6   For You have made him most blessed
        forever;
    You have made him exceedingly glad
        with Your presence.

7   For the king trusts in the LORD,
    And through the mercy of the Most
        High he shall not be moved.

8   Your hand will find all Your enemies;
    Your right hand will find those who
        hate You.
9   You shall make them as a fiery oven
        in the time of Your anger;
    The LORD shall swallow them up in
        His wrath,
    And the fire shall devour them.
10 Their offspring You shall destroy from
        the earth,
    And their descendants from among
        the sons of men.
11 For they intended evil against You;
    They devised a plot *which* they are
        not able *to perform.*
12 Therefore You will make them turn
        their back;
    You will make ready *Your arrows* on
        Your string toward their faces.

13 Be exalted, O LORD, in Your own
        strength!
    We will sing and praise Your power.

PSALM 72

Glory and Universality of the Messiah's Reign

A Psalm of Solomon.

Give the king Your judgments, O God,
    And Your righteousness to the king's
        Son.
2   He will judge Your people with
        righteousness,
    And Your poor with justice.
3   The mountains will bring peace to the
        people,
    And the little hills, by righteousness.
4   He will bring justice to the poor of the
        people;
    He will save the children of the needy,
    And will break in pieces the oppressor.

5   They shall fear You[a]
    As long as the sun and moon endure,
    Throughout all generations.
6   He shall come down like rain upon the
        grass before mowing,
    Like showers *that* water the earth.
7   In His days the righteous shall
        flourish,
    And abundance of peace,
    Until the moon is no more.

72:5 [a]Following Masoretic Text and Targum;
Septuagint and Vulgate read *They shall continue.*

8 He shall have dominion also from sea
to sea,
And from the River to the ends of the
earth.
9 Those who dwell in the wilderness
will bow before Him,
And His enemies will lick the dust.
10 The kings of Tarshish and of the isles
Will bring presents;
The kings of Sheba and Seba
Will offer gifts.
11 Yes, all kings shall fall down before
Him;
All nations shall serve Him.

12 For He will deliver the needy when he
cries,
The poor also, and *him* who has no
helper.
13 He will spare the poor and needy,
And will save the souls of the needy.
14 He will redeem their life from
oppression and violence;
And precious shall be their blood in
His sight.

15 And He shall live;
And the gold of Sheba will be given to
Him;
Prayer also will be made for Him
continually,
And daily He shall be praised.

16 There will be an abundance of grain
in the earth,
On the top of the mountains;
Its fruit shall wave like Lebanon;
And *those* of the city shall flourish like
grass of the earth.

17 His name shall endure forever;
His name shall continue as long as
the sun.
And *men* shall be blessed in Him;
All nations shall call Him blessed.

18 Blessed *be* the LORD God, the God of
Israel,
Who only does wondrous things!

19 And blessed *be* His glorious name
forever!
And let the whole earth be filled *with*
His glory.
Amen and Amen.

20 The prayers of David the son of Jesse
are ended.

PSALM 93

The Eternal Reign of the LORD

The LORD reigns, He is clothed with
majesty;
The LORD is clothed,
He has girded Himself with strength.
Surely the world is established, so
that it cannot be moved.
2 Your throne *is* established from of old;
You *are* from everlasting.

3 The floods have lifted up, O LORD,
The floods have lifted up their voice;
The floods lift up their waves.
4 The LORD on high *is* mightier
Than the noise of many waters,
Than the mighty waves of the sea.

5 Your testimonies are very sure;
Holiness adorns Your house,
O LORD, forever.

PSALM 94

God the Refuge of the Righteous

O LORD God, to whom vengeance
belongs—
O God, to whom vengeance belongs,
shine forth!
2 Rise up, O Judge of the earth;
Render punishment to the proud.
3 LORD, how long will the wicked,
How long will the wicked triumph?

4 They utter speech, *and* speak insolent
things;
All the workers of iniquity boast in
themselves.

GEOGRAPHY AND ENVIRONMENT

The psalmist uses geographical names as conventional references to the most distant
corners of the earth (Ps. 72:10). Tarshish and "the isles" are probably Spain and islands
in the Mediterranean, west of Israel. Sheba and Seba were in south Arabia and possibly
east Africa. These places could be reached by sea. The Jews were not sailors, but their
neighbors the Phoenicians were.

5   They break in pieces Your people,
        O Lord,
    And afflict Your heritage.
6   They slay the widow and the stranger,
    And murder the fatherless.
7   Yet they say, "The Lord does not see,
    Nor does the God of Jacob
        understand."

8   Understand, you senseless among the
        people;
    And *you* fools, when will you be wise?
9   He who planted the ear, shall He not
        hear?
    He who formed the eye, shall He not
        see?
10 He who instructs the nations, shall He
        not correct,
    He who teaches man knowledge?
11 The Lord knows the thoughts of man,
    That they *are* futile.

12 Blessed *is* the man whom You
        instruct, O Lord,
    And teach out of Your law,
13 That You may give him rest from the
        days of adversity,
    Until the pit is dug for the wicked.
14 For the Lord will not cast off His
        people,
    Nor will He forsake His inheritance.
15 But judgment will return to
        righteousness,
    And all the upright in heart will
        follow it.

16 Who will rise up for me against the
        evildoers?
    Who will stand up for me against the
        workers of iniquity?
17 Unless the Lord *had been* my help,
    My soul would soon have settled in
        silence.
18 If I say, "My foot slips,"
    Your mercy, O Lord, will hold me up.
19 In the multitude of my anxieties
        within me,
    Your comforts delight my soul.

20 Shall the throne of iniquity, which
        devises evil by law,
    Have fellowship with You?
21 They gather together against the life
        of the righteous,
    And condemn innocent blood.

22 But the Lord has been my defense,
    And my God the rock of my refuge.
23 He has brought on them their own
        iniquity,
    And shall cut them off in their own
        wickedness;
    The Lord our God shall cut them off.

PSALM 95

A Call to Worship and Obedience

Oh come, let us sing to the Lord!
    Let us shout joyfully to the Rock of
        our salvation.
2   Let us come before His presence with
        thanksgiving;
    Let us shout joyfully to Him with
        psalms.
3   For the Lord *is* the great God,
    And the great King above all gods.
4   In His hand *are* the deep places of the
        earth;
    The heights of the hills *are* His also.
5   The sea *is* His, for He made it;
    And His hands formed the dry *land*.

6   Oh come, let us worship and bow
        down;
    Let us kneel before the Lord our
        Maker.
7   For He *is* our God,
    And we *are* the people of His pasture,
    And the sheep of His hand.

    Today, if you will hear His voice:
8   "Do not harden your hearts, as in the
        rebellion,[a]
    As *in* the day of trial[b] in the
        wilderness,
9   When your fathers tested Me;
    They tried Me, though they saw My
        work.
10 For forty years I was grieved with *that*
        generation,
    And said, 'It *is* a people who go astray
        in their hearts,
    And they do not know My ways.'
11 So I swore in My wrath,
    'They shall not enter My rest.' "

PSALM 97

A Song of Praise to the Sovereign
Lord

The Lord reigns;
    Let the earth rejoice;
    Let the multitude of isles be glad!

95:8 [a]Or *Meribah* [b]Or *Massah*

2 Clouds and darkness surround Him;
Righteousness and justice *are* the
foundation of His throne.
3 A fire goes before Him,
And burns up His enemies round
about.
4 His lightnings light the world;
The earth sees and trembles.
5 The mountains melt like wax at the
presence of the LORD,
At the presence of the Lord of the
whole earth.
6 The heavens declare His
righteousness,
And all the peoples see His glory.

7 Let all be put to shame who serve
carved images,
Who boast of idols.
Worship Him, all *you* gods.
8 Zion hears and is glad,
And the daughters of Judah rejoice
Because of Your judgments, O LORD.
9 For You, LORD, *are* most high above all
the earth;
You are exalted far above all gods.

10 You who love the LORD, hate evil!
He preserves the souls of His saints;
He delivers them out of the hand of
the wicked.
11 Light is sown for the righteous,
And gladness for the upright in heart.
12 Rejoice in the LORD, you righteous,
And give thanks at the remembrance
of His holy name.[a]

PSALM 98

A Song of Praise to the LORD for His Salvation and Judgment

A Psalm.

Oh, sing to the LORD a new song!
For He has done marvelous things;
His right hand and His holy arm have
gained Him the victory.
2 The LORD has made known His
salvation;
His righteousness He has revealed in
the sight of the nations.
3 He has remembered His mercy and
His faithfulness to the house of
Israel;
All the ends of the earth have seen the
salvation of our God.

4 Shout joyfully to the LORD, all the
earth;

Break forth in song, rejoice, and sing
praises.
5 Sing to the LORD with the harp,
With the harp and the sound of a
psalm,
6 With trumpets and the sound of a
horn;
Shout joyfully before the LORD, the
King.

7 Let the sea roar, and all its fullness,
The world and those who dwell in it;
8 Let the rivers clap *their* hands;
Let the hills be joyful together before
the LORD,
9 For He is coming to judge the earth.
With righteousness He shall judge the
world,
And the peoples with equity.

PSALM 99

Praise to the LORD for His Holiness

The LORD reigns;
Let the peoples tremble!
He dwells *between* the cherubim;
Let the earth be moved!
2 The LORD *is* great in Zion,
And He *is* high above all the peoples.
3 Let them praise Your great and
awesome name—
He *is* holy.

4 The King's strength also loves justice;
You have established equity;
You have executed justice and
righteousness in Jacob.
5 Exalt the LORD our God,
And worship at His footstool—
He *is* holy.

6 Moses and Aaron were among His
priests,
And Samuel was among those who
called upon His name;
They called upon the LORD, and He
answered them.
7 He spoke to them in the cloudy pillar;
They kept His testimonies and the
ordinance He gave them.

8 You answered them, O LORD our God;
You were to them God-Who-Forgives,
Though You took vengeance on their
deeds.

97:12 [a]Or *His holiness*

DAVIDIC KINGS IN THE COSMIC ORDER (Ps. 110:1–4)

In the pantheons of the ancient Near East, superior gods appointed lesser gods to their positions in the cosmic hierarchy. Similarly, human rulers were given their thrones by the patron gods of their lands. In Syria-Palestine and Mesopotamia, kings were understood to be ruling on behalf of the gods. Kings were not divine, but they held a special position of power and trust in relationship to their god.

The psalmist of Ps. 110 expresses such a relationship between Yahweh and a Davidic king: "The LORD said to my Lord" (Yahweh said to my king; 110:1). The king is placed in the honored position at the right hand of Yahweh.

Ancient people believed that the god of the land chose the human ruler, and also defended that ruler and land against other kings and their gods. Wars fought on earth by kings and their armies were actually fought in heaven by the gods. Any ruler who obeyed his patron deity would never go out to battle alone, but would always have the aid of his god.

Yahweh's words to the king, "You are a priest forever" (110:4), reflects an ancient Near Eastern concept of kingship not found in the rest of the Bible. Kings in Mesopotamia and Syria-Palestine were also considered the official high priest of their patron deities, even though kings did not perform routine priestly functions. Yet in Judah, kings were not priests and were not allowed to function as priests (2 Chr. 26:18).

In contrast, however, the psalmist announces that the Davidic king is a priest "according to the order of Melchizedek" (110:4). Melchizedek was a Canaanite priest-king, the king of Salem, but also a "priest of God Most High" (Gen. 14:18). Perhaps at some point in history Israel's king did serve as honorary priest of Yahweh.

---

9   Exalt the LORD our God,
    And worship at His holy hill;
    For the LORD our God *is* holy.

PSALM 101

Promised Faithfulness to the LORD

A Psalm of David.

I will sing of mercy and justice;
  To You, O LORD, I will sing praises.

2   I will behave wisely in a perfect way.
    Oh, when will You come to me?
    I will walk within my house with a
      perfect heart.

3   I will set nothing wicked before my
      eyes;
    I hate the work of those who fall away;
    It shall not cling to me.

4   A perverse heart shall depart from
      me;
    I will not know wickedness.

5   Whoever secretly slanders his
      neighbor,
    Him I will destroy;
    The one who has a haughty look and a
      proud heart,
    Him I will not endure.

6   My eyes *shall be* on the faithful of the
      land,
    That they may dwell with me;
    He who walks in a perfect way,
    He shall serve me.

7   He who works deceit shall not dwell
      within my house;
    He who tells lies shall not continue in
      my presence.

8   Early I will destroy all the wicked of
      the land,
    That I may cut off all the evildoers
      from the city of the LORD.

PSALM 110

Announcement of the Messiah's Reign

A Psalm of David.

The LORD said to my Lord,
  "Sit at My right hand,
    Till I make Your enemies Your
      footstool."

2   The LORD shall send the rod of Your
      strength out of Zion.
    Rule in the midst of Your enemies!

3   Your people *shall be* volunteers
    In the day of Your power;

In the beauties of holiness, from the
    womb of the morning,
You have the dew of Your youth.

4 The LORD has sworn
And will not relent,
"You *are* a priest forever
According to the order of Melchizedek."

5 The Lord *is* at Your right hand;
He shall execute kings in the day of
    His wrath.
6 He shall judge among the nations,
He shall fill *the places* with dead
    bodies,
He shall execute the heads of many
    countries.
7 He shall drink of the brook by the
    wayside;
Therefore He shall lift up the head.

PSALM 144

A Song to the LORD Who Preserves and Prospers His People

A Psalm of David.

Blessed *be* the LORD my Rock,
  Who trains my hands for war,
And my fingers for battle—
2 My lovingkindness and my fortress,
My high tower and my deliverer,
My shield and *the One* in whom I take
    refuge,
Who subdues my people[a] under me.

3 LORD, what *is* man, that You take
    knowledge of him?
Or the son of man, that You are
    mindful of him?
4 Man is like a breath;
His days *are* like a passing shadow.

5 Bow down Your heavens, O LORD, and
    come down;
Touch the mountains, and they shall
    smoke.
6 Flash forth lightning and scatter them;
Shoot out Your arrows and destroy
    them.
7 Stretch out Your hand from above;
Rescue me and deliver me out of great
    waters,
From the hand of foreigners,
8 Whose mouth speaks lying words,
And whose right hand *is* a right hand
    of falsehood.

9 I will sing a new song to You, O God;
On a harp of ten strings I will sing
    praises to You,

10 *The One* who gives salvation to kings,
Who delivers David His servant
From the deadly sword.

11 Rescue me and deliver me from the
    hand of foreigners,
Whose mouth speaks lying words,
And whose right hand *is* a right hand
    of falsehood—
12 That our sons *may be* as plants grown
    up in their youth;
That our daughters *may be* as pillars,
Sculptured in palace style;
13 *That* our barns *may be* full,
Supplying all kinds of produce;
That our sheep may bring forth
    thousands
And ten thousands in our fields;
14 *That* our oxen *may be* well laden;
That there be no breaking in or going
    out;
That there be no outcry in our streets.
15 Happy *are* the people who are in such
    a state;
Happy *are* the people whose God *is*
    the LORD!

144:2 [a]Following Masoretic Text, Septuagint, and Vulgate; Syriac and Targum read *the peoples* (compare 18:47).

Prophetic Account: Solomon's Reign

David will always be remembered in two contexts. On the one hand he is the "sweet singer of Israel," the psalmist, but on the other hand he is the man of war who defeated Israel's enemies. His son Solomon also has a dual claim to fame in the Bible. First, he is the one who constructed the temple. Second, Solomon is particularly tied to the wisdom tradition of Israel.

The term "wisdom tradition" refers to a phenomenon that was widespread in the ancient Near East, especially in royal courts. This kind of "wisdom" stressed observation of the world and the search for the underlying principles of reality. Wisdom, in this restricted definition, is not very concerned with eternity; its focus is always on this world and on human relationships. In both the narratives of Solomon's judgment (1 Kin. 3:16–28) and the literature attributed to him (1 Kin. 4:29–34), Solomon is Israel's original model for the wise man.

■ 1 Kings 3:1—4:34

1 Kings

Solomon Requests Wisdom

3 **:1** Now Solomon made a treaty with Pharaoh king of Egypt, and married Pharaoh's daughter; then he brought her to the City of David until he had finished building his own house, and the house of the LORD, and the wall all around Jerusalem. ²Meanwhile the people sacrificed at the high places, because there was no house built for the name of the LORD until those days. ³And Solomon loved the LORD, walking in the statutes of his father David, except that he sacrificed and burned incense at the high places.

⁴Now the king went to Gibeon to sacrifice there, for that *was* the great high place: Solomon offered a thousand burnt offerings on that altar. ⁵At Gibeon the LORD appeared to Solomon in a dream by night; and God said, "Ask! What shall I give you?"

⁶And Solomon said: "You have shown great mercy to Your servant David my father, because he walked before You in truth, in righteousness, and in uprightness of heart with You; You have continued this great kindness for him, and You have given him a son to sit on his throne, as *it is* this day. ⁷Now, O LORD my God, You have made Your servant king instead of my father David, but I *am* a little child; I do not know *how* to go out or come in. ⁸And Your servant *is* in the midst of Your people whom You have chosen, a great people, too numerous to be numbered or counted. ⁹Therefore give to Your servant an understanding heart to judge Your people, that I may discern between good and evil. For who is able to judge this great people of Yours?"

¹⁰The speech pleased the LORD, that Solomon had asked this thing. ¹¹Then God said to him: "Because you have asked this thing, and have not asked long life for yourself, nor have asked riches for yourself, nor have asked the life of your enemies, but have asked for yourself understanding to discern justice, ¹²behold, I have done according to your words; see, I have given you a wise and understanding heart, so that there has not been anyone like you before you, nor shall any like you arise after you. ¹³And I have also given you what you have not asked: both riches and honor, so that there shall not be anyone like you among the kings all your days. ¹⁴So if you walk in My ways, to keep My statutes and My commandments, as your father David walked, then I will lengthen your days."

¹⁵Then Solomon awoke; and indeed it had been a dream. And he came to Jerusalem and stood before the ark of the covenant of the LORD, offered up burnt offerings, offered peace offerings, and made a feast for all his servants.

Solomon's Wise Judgment

¹⁶Now two women *who were* harlots came to the king, and stood before him. ¹⁷And one woman said, "O my lord, this woman and I dwell in the same house; and I gave birth while she *was* in the house. ¹⁸Then it happened, the third day after I had given birth, that this woman also gave birth. And we *were* together; no one *was* with us in the house, except the two of us in the house. ¹⁹And this woman's son died in the night, because she lay on him. ²⁰So she arose in the middle of the night and took my son from my side, while your maidservant slept, and laid him in her bosom, and laid her dead child in my bosom. ²¹And when I rose in the morning to nurse my son, there he was, dead. But when I had examined him in the morning, indeed, he was not my son whom I had borne."

²²Then the other woman said, "No! But the living one *is* my son, and the dead one *is* your son."

And the first woman said, "No! But the dead one *is* your son, and the living one *is* my son."

Thus they spoke before the king.

²³And the king said, "The one says, 'This *is* my son, who lives, and your son *is* the dead one'; and the other says, 'No! But your son *is* the dead one, and my son *is* the living one.' " ²⁴Then the king said, "Bring me a sword." So they brought a sword before the king. ²⁵And the king said, "Divide

---

TIME CAPSULE　*980 to 970 B.C.*

980	*Hiram becomes king of Tyre (or 969)*
978–959	*Siamun, pharaoh of Egypt*
975	*The temple of Hera is constructed at Olympia in Greece*
973	*Solomon is coregent with David (1 Kin. 1:32–39)*
970–930	*Solomon, king of Israel (1 Kin. 1:39)*

SOLOMON MARRIES PHARAOH'S DAUGHTER (1 Kin. 3:1)

Marriage was an effective means for creating alliances among ancient nations. The idea behind such marriages was that two nations, by marriage, became one larger extended family. The hope was that one would deal more kindly with kin than with strangers.

No greater evidence of Solomon's importance among the nearby countries could be given than to record his marriage to an Egyptian pharaoh's daughter. As policy, Egypt's pharaohs did not give their daughters in marriage to foreign kings. In one tablet from Tell el-Amarna, Egypt (1360–1333 B.C.), the Egyptians respond to a request by a Babylonian king for one of pharaoh's daughters, "From of old a daughter of the king of Egypt has not been given to anyone." At the same time, the pharaohs themselves did marry royal, foreign wives. Solomon's marriage to one of pharaoh's daughters (1 Kin. 3:1; 9:16) is a major testimony to Solomon's unusual esteem.

On the other hand, in the time of Solomon Egypt had seen its better days. Solomon's Egyptian father-in-law is not named, but Siamun (978–959 B.C.), who reigned during Egypt's Third Intermediate Period, is the likely pharaoh. This period was characterized by weakness and instability. The pharaohs were so politically weak that they did all they could to assure support from important Egyptians, including allowing the marriage of their daughters to Egyptian commoners. In the case of Solomon, Siamun sought the support of Israel by doing the extraordinary—marrying one of his daughters to a foreign king.

the living child in two, and give half to one, and half to the other."

²⁶Then the woman whose son *was* living spoke to the king, for she yearned with compassion for her son; and she said, "O my lord, give her the living child, and by no means kill him!"

But the other said, "Let him be neither mine nor yours, *but* divide *him*."

²⁷So the king answered and said, "Give the first woman the living child, and by no means kill him; she *is* his mother."

²⁸And all Israel heard of the judgment which the king had rendered; and they feared the king, for they saw that the wisdom of God *was* in him to administer justice.

Solomon's Administration

4 ¹So King Solomon was king over all Israel. ²And these *were* his officials: Azariah the son of Zadok, the priest; ³Elihoreph and Ahijah, the sons of Shisha, scribes; Jehoshaphat the son of Ahilud, the recorder; ⁴Benaiah the son of Jehoiada, over the army; Zadok and Abiathar, the priests; ⁵Azariah the son of Nathan, over the officers; Zabud the son of Nathan, a priest *and* the king's friend; ⁶Ahishar, over the household; and Adoniram the son of Abda, over the labor force.

⁷And Solomon had twelve governors over all Israel, who provided food for the king and his household; each one made provision for one month of the year. ⁸These *are* their names: Ben-Hur,ᵃ in the mountains of Ephraim; ⁹Ben-Deker,ᵃ in Makaz, Shaalbim, Beth Shemesh, and Elon Beth Hanan; ¹⁰Ben-Hesed,ᵃ in Arubboth; to him *belonged* Sochoh and all the land of Hepher; ¹¹Ben-Abinadab,ᵃ *in* all the regions of Dor; he had Taphath the daughter of Solomon as wife; ¹²Baana the son of Ahilud, *in* Taanach, Megiddo, and all Beth Shean, which *is* beside Zaretan below Jezreel, from Beth Shean to Abel Meholah, as far as the other side of Jokneam; ¹³Ben-Geber,ᵃ in Ramoth Gilead; to him *belonged* the towns of Jair the son of Manasseh, in Gilead; to him *also belonged* the region of Argob in Bashan—sixty large cities with walls and bronze gate-bars; ¹⁴Ahinadab the son of Iddo, *in* Mahanaim; ¹⁵Ahimaaz, in Naphtali; he also took Basemath the daughter of Solomon as wife; ¹⁶Baanah the son of Hushai, in Asher and Aloth; ¹⁷Jehoshaphat the son of Paruah, in Issachar; ¹⁸Shimei the son of Elah, in Benjamin; ¹⁹Geber the son of Uri, in the land of Gilead, *in* the country of Sihon king of the Amorites, and of Og king of Bashan.

4:8 ᵃLiterally *Son of Hur*   4:9 ᵃLiterally *Son of Deker*   4:10 ᵃLiterally *Son of Hesed*
4:11 ᵃLiterally *Son of Abinadab*   4:13 ᵃLiterally *Son of Geber*

MEGIDDO IN SOLOMON'S DISTRICTS (1 Kin. 4:7, 12)

Outside of Judah, Solomon's kingdom was divided into 12 administrative districts, each ruled by a governor (1 Kin. 4:7–19). Many districts were primarily geographic and not tribal entities, thus breaking with Israel's earlier tradition. The districts were set up to provide administrative tax collections for the crown, and the appointed governor was in charge of raising revenue to support Solomon's administration in Jerusalem (1 Kin. 4:20, 21). The district of Judah appears to have been exempt from this taxation, a situation which did not create good feeling for Judah among the other tribes.

Megiddo was a Canaanite town in the valley of Jezreel in northern Palestine. It apparently came under Israel's control by Solomon's time and was likely the seat of his 5th administrative district (1 Kin. 4:12). It was also one of the major cities rebuilt by Solomon, along with Jerusalem, Hazor, and Gezer.

Megiddo is listed among the cities which Pharaoh Shishak (945–924 B.C.) claims to have conquered in his Palestinian campaign of 925 B.C. A number of buildings at Megiddo, including a palace, appear to have been destroyed by fire during this invasion. A portion of a stele (standing stone slab or pillar) recording Shishak's invasion was found at the site. That Shishak (also spelled Sheshonk or Shoshenq) set up a triumphal stele possibly indicates that he desired to reassert Egyptian control in Canaan.

He was the only governor who *was* in the land.

Prosperity and Wisdom of Solomon's Reign

20Judah and Israel *were* as numerous as the sand by the sea in multitude, eating and drinking and rejoicing. 21So Solomon reigned over all kingdoms from the Rivera *to* the land of the Philistines, as far as the border of Egypt. *They* brought tribute and served Solomon all the days of his life.

22Now Solomon's provision for one day was thirty kors of fine flour, sixty kors of meal, 23ten fatted oxen, twenty oxen from the pastures, and one hundred sheep, besides deer, gazelles, roebucks, and fatted fowl.

24For he had dominion over all *the region* on this side of the Rivera from Tiph-sah even to Gaza, namely over all the kings on this side of the River; and he had peace on every side all around him. 25And Judah and Israel dwelt safely, each man under his vine and his fig tree, from Dan as far as Beersheba, all the days of Solomon.

26Solomon had fortya thousand stalls of horses for his chariots, and twelve thousand horsemen. 27And these governors, each man in his month, provided food for King Solomon and for all who came to King Solomon's table. There was no lack in their supply. 28They also brought barley and straw to the proper place, for the horses and steeds, each man according to his charge.

29And God gave Solomon wisdom and exceedingly great understanding, and largeness of heart like the sand on the seashore. 30Thus Solomon's wisdom excelled the wisdom of all the men of the East and all the wisdom of Egypt. 31For he was wiser than all men—than Ethan the Ezrahite, and Heman, Chalcol, and Darda,

---

4:21 ªThat is, the Euphrates   4:24 ªThat is, the Euphrates   4:26 ªFollowing Masoretic Text and most other authorities; some manuscripts of the Septuagint read *four* (compare 2 Chronicles 9:25).

FOOD AND DRINK

Grapevines and fig trees yielded the more pleasant, if less essential, parts of the diet. The peaceful cultivation of these plants by individual householders is a miniature but vigorous sketch of the life of peace (1 Kin. 4:25). The multitude of animals provided for the king's table (1 Kin. 4:22) expresses the higher level of life in the royal court.

the sons of Mahol; and his fame was in all the surrounding nations. ³²He spoke three thousand proverbs, and his songs were one thousand and five. ³³Also he spoke of trees, from the cedar tree of Lebanon even to the hyssop that springs out of the wall; he spoke also of animals, of birds, of creeping things, and of fish. ³⁴And men of all nations, from all the kings of the earth who had heard of his wisdom, came to hear the wisdom of Solomon.

The Book of Proverbs

The wisdom tradition of Israel influences several different biblical books, but its heart is in the Book of Proverbs. The proverbs are short, poetically matched comments on the world. They do not claim to be universal truth, but rather situational advice to be applied to different contexts. (For instance, two adjacent proverbs in Prov. 26:4, 5 give directly contradictory advice.)

The Book of Proverbs is actually several different collections of proverbs. Chapters 1—9 contain relatively long strings of interconnected proverbs and a few extended "wisdom poems." The sayings of Prov. 10:1—22:16 are a less unified collection of individual proverbs, though there is some organization around themes, such as human behavior and the inner person. Other collections in the Book of Proverbs are to be dated later than Solomon's reign (see "Wisdom in the Ancient Near East" at Prov. 22:17).

Both of the first two collections (1:1—9:18 and 10:1—22:16) are ascribed to Solomon. Many interpreters suggest that the attributions in Prov. 1:1 and 10:1 do not necessarily refer to authorship but are rather tributes to Solomon, the greatest of all the wise. Especially the longer poems of chs. 1—9 have been considered to be later than Solomon's time. Other interpreters, though, accept the attributions of 1:1 and 10:1 as simple statements of fact. In either case, it is appropriate to read these wise sayings following the comment of 1 Kings that Solomon was "wiser than all men" (1 Kin. 4:31).

The collection of chs. 1—9 is a picture of the value of wisdom. Wisdom is personified as a woman pleading with men and women to pursue her. A strong contrast is developed between the fruits of pursuing wisdom and the corruption of following folly.

▼   ■ Proverbs 1:1—9:18

Proverbs
The Beginning of Knowledge

1 **:1** The proverbs of Solomon the son of David, king of Israel:

2   To know wisdom and instruction,
To perceive the words of understanding,
3   To receive the instruction of wisdom,
Justice, judgment, and equity;
4   To give prudence to the simple,
To the young man knowledge and discretion—
5   A wise *man* will hear and increase learning,
And a man of understanding will attain wise counsel,
6   To understand a proverb and an enigma,
The words of the wise and their riddles.

7   The fear of the LORD *is* the beginning of knowledge,
But fools despise wisdom and instruction.

Shun Evil Counsel

8   My son, hear the instruction of your father,
And do not forsake the law of your mother;
9   For they *will be* a graceful ornament on your head,
And chains about your neck.

10   My son, if sinners entice you,
Do not consent.
11   If they say, "Come with us,
Let us lie in wait to *shed* blood;
Let us lurk secretly for the innocent without cause;
12   Let us swallow them alive like Sheol,ᵃ
And whole, like those who go down to the Pit;
13   We shall find all *kinds* of precious possessions,
We shall fill our houses with spoil;
14   Cast in your lot among us,
Let us all have one purse"—
15   My son, do not walk in the way with them,
Keep your foot from their path;
16   For their feet run to evil,
And they make haste to shed blood.

1:12 ᵃOr *the grave*

17 Surely, in vain the net is spread
In the sight of any bird;
18 But they lie in wait for their *own*
blood,
They lurk secretly for their *own* lives.
19 So *are* the ways of everyone who is
greedy for gain;
It takes away the life of its owners.

The Call of Wisdom

20 Wisdom calls aloud outside;
She raises her voice in the open
squares.
21 She cries out in the chief concourses,[a]
At the openings of the gates in the
city
She speaks her words:
22 "How long, you simple ones, will you
love simplicity?
For scorners delight in their scorning,
And fools hate knowledge.
23 Turn at my rebuke;
Surely I will pour out my spirit on
you;
I will make my words known to you.
24 Because I have called and you refused,
I have stretched out my hand and no
one regarded,
25 Because you disdained all my counsel,
And would have none of my rebuke,
26 I also will laugh at your calamity;
I will mock when your terror comes,
27 When your terror comes like a storm,
And your destruction comes like a
whirlwind,
When distress and anguish come upon
you.

28 "Then they will call on me, but I will
not answer;
They will seek me diligently, but they
will not find me.
29 Because they hated knowledge
And did not choose the fear of the
LORD,
30 They would have none of my counsel
And despised my every rebuke.
31 Therefore they shall eat the fruit of
their own way,
And be filled to the full with their own
fancies.
32 For the turning away of the simple
will slay them,
And the complacency of fools will
destroy them;

33 But whoever listens to me will dwell
safely,
And will be secure, without fear of
evil."

The Value of Wisdom

2 ¹ My son, if you receive my words,
And treasure my commands within
you,
2 So that you incline your ear to
wisdom,
And apply your heart to
understanding;
3 Yes, if you cry out for discernment,
And lift up your voice for
understanding,
4 If you seek her as silver,
And search for her as *for* hidden
treasures;
5 Then you will understand the fear of
the LORD,
And find the knowledge of God.
6 For the LORD gives wisdom;
From His mouth *come* knowledge and
understanding;
7 He stores up sound wisdom for the
upright;
He is a shield to those who walk
uprightly;
8 He guards the paths of justice,
And preserves the way of His saints.
9 Then you will understand
righteousness and justice,
Equity *and* every good path.

10 When wisdom enters your heart,
And knowledge is pleasant to your
soul,
11 Discretion will preserve you;
Understanding will keep you,
12 To deliver you from the way of evil,
From the man who speaks perverse
things,
13 From those who leave the paths of
uprightness
To walk in the ways of darkness;
14 Who rejoice in doing evil,
And delight in the perversity of the
wicked;
15 Whose ways *are* crooked,
And *who are* devious in their paths;
16 To deliver you from the immoral
woman,
From the seductress *who* flatters with
her words,
17 Who forsakes the companion of her
youth,
And forgets the covenant of her God.

1:21 ªSeptuagint, Syriac, and Targum read *top of the
walls;* Vulgate reads *the head of multitudes.*

18 For her house leads down to death,
And her paths to the dead;
19 None who go to her return,
Nor do they regain the paths of life—
20 So you may walk in the way of
goodness,
And keep *to* the paths of
righteousness.
21 For the upright will dwell in the land,
And the blameless will remain in it;
22 But the wicked will be cut off from the
earth,
And the unfaithful will be uprooted
from it.

Guidance for the Young

3 1 My son, do not forget my law,
But let your heart keep my
commands;
2 For length of days and long life
And peace they will add to you.

3 Let not mercy and truth forsake you;
Bind them around your neck,
Write them on the tablet of your
heart,
4 *And* so find favor and high esteem
In the sight of God and man.

5 Trust in the LORD with all your heart,
And lean not on your own
understanding;
6 In all your ways acknowledge Him,
And He shall direct[a] your paths.

7 Do not be wise in your own eyes;
Fear the LORD and depart from evil.
8 It will be health to your flesh,[a]
And strength[b] to your bones.

9 Honor the LORD with your
possessions,
And with the firstfruits of all your
increase;
10 So your barns will be filled with
plenty,
And your vats will overflow with new
wine.

11 My son, do not despise the chastening
of the LORD,
Nor detest His correction;
12 For whom the LORD loves He corrects,
Just as a father the son *in whom* he
delights.

13 Happy *is* the man *who* finds wisdom,
And the man *who* gains
understanding;

14 For her proceeds *are* better than the
profits of silver,
And her gain than fine gold.
15 She *is* more precious than rubies,
And all the things you may desire
cannot compare with her.
16 Length of days *is* in her right hand,
In her left hand riches and honor.
17 Her ways *are* ways of pleasantness,
And all her paths *are* peace.
18 She *is* a tree of life to those who take
hold of her,
And happy *are all* who retain her.

19 The LORD by wisdom founded the
earth;
By understanding He established the
heavens;
20 By His knowledge the depths were
broken up,
And clouds drop down the dew.

21 My son, let them not depart from your
eyes—
Keep sound wisdom and discretion;
22 So they will be life to your soul
And grace to your neck.
23 Then you will walk safely in your way,
And your foot will not stumble.
24 When you lie down, you will not be
afraid;
Yes, you will lie down and your sleep
will be sweet.
25 Do not be afraid of sudden terror,
Nor of trouble from the wicked when
it comes;
26 For the LORD will be your confidence,
And will keep your foot from being
caught.

27 Do not withhold good from those to
whom it is due,
When it is in the power of your hand
to do *so.*
28 Do not say to your neighbor,
"Go, and come back,
And tomorrow I will give *it,*"
When *you have* it with you.
29 Do not devise evil against your
neighbor,
For he dwells by you for safety's sake.
30 Do not strive with a man without
cause,
If he has done you no harm.

3:6 [a]Or *make smooth* or *straight*   3:8 [a]Literally
navel, figurative of the body   [b]Literally *drink* or
refreshment

31 Do not envy the oppressor,
And choose none of his ways;
32 For the perverse *person is* an
abomination to the LORD,
But His secret counsel *is* with the
upright.
33 The curse of the LORD *is* on the house
of the wicked,
But He blesses the home of the just.
34 Surely He scorns the scornful,
But gives grace to the humble.
35 The wise shall inherit glory,
But shame shall be the legacy of fools.

Security in Wisdom

4 1 Hear, *my* children, the instruction of
a father,
And give attention to know
understanding;
2 For I give you good doctrine:
Do not forsake my law.
3 When I was my father's son,
Tender and the only one in the sight of
my mother,
4 He also taught me, and said to me:
"Let your heart retain my words;
Keep my commands, and live.
5 Get wisdom! Get understanding!
Do not forget, nor turn away from the
words of my mouth.
6 Do not forsake her, and she will
preserve you;
Love her, and she will keep you.
7 Wisdom *is* the principal thing;
Therefore get wisdom.
And in all your getting, get
understanding.
8 Exalt her, and she will promote you;
She will bring you honor, when you
embrace her.
9 She will place on your head an
ornament of grace;
A crown of glory she will deliver to
you."

10 Hear, my son, and receive my sayings,
And the years of your life will be
many.

4:18 ªLiterally *light*

11 I have taught you in the way of
wisdom;
I have led you in right paths.
12 When you walk, your steps will not be
hindered,
And when you run, you will not
stumble.
13 Take firm hold of instruction, do not
let go;
Keep her, for she *is* your life.

14 Do not enter the path of the wicked,
And do not walk in the way of evil.
15 Avoid it, do not travel on it;
Turn away from it and pass on.
16 For they do not sleep unless they have
done evil;
And their sleep is taken away unless
they make *someone* fall.
17 For they eat the bread of wickedness,
And drink the wine of violence.

18 But the path of the just *is* like the
shining sun,ª
That shines ever brighter unto the
perfect day.
19 The way of the wicked *is* like
darkness;
They do not know what makes them
stumble.

20 My son, give attention to my words;
Incline your ear to my sayings.
21 Do not let them depart from your
eyes;
Keep them in the midst of your heart;
22 For they *are* life to those who find
them,
And health to all their flesh.
23 Keep your heart with all diligence,
For out of it *spring* the issues of life.
24 Put away from you a deceitful mouth,
And put perverse lips far from you.
25 Let your eyes look straight ahead,
And your eyelids look right before you.
26 Ponder the path of your feet,
And let all your ways be established.
27 Do not turn to the right or the left;
Remove your foot from evil.

MARRIAGE AND FAMILY

*In the instruction of the wisdom literature is the traditional advice from father to son
(Prov. 4:3, 4). A predominant purpose is to advise young men on how to follow a career
in business or the court, as opposed for example to agriculture or the army. Several
proverbs tell explicitly how to deal with kings (Prov. 24:21).*

The Peril of Adultery

5 [1] My son, pay attention to my
wisdom;
Lend your ear to my understanding,

[2] That you may preserve discretion,
And your lips may keep knowledge.

[3] For the lips of an immoral woman
drip honey,
And her mouth *is* smoother than oil;

[4] But in the end she is bitter as
wormwood,
Sharp as a two-edged sword.

[5] Her feet go down to death,
Her steps lay hold of hell.[a]

[6] Lest you ponder *her* path of life—
Her ways are unstable;
You do not know *them.*

[7] Therefore hear me now, *my* children,
And do not depart from the words of
my mouth.

[8] Remove your way far from her,
And do not go near the door of her
house,

[9] Lest you give your honor to others,
And your years to the cruel *one;*

[10] Lest aliens be filled with your wealth,
And your labors *go* to the house of a
foreigner;

[11] And you mourn at last,
When your flesh and your body are
consumed,

[12] And say:
"How I have hated instruction,
And my heart despised correction!

[13] I have not obeyed the voice of my
teachers,
Nor inclined my ear to those who
instructed me!

[14] I was on the verge of total ruin,
In the midst of the assembly and
congregation."

[15] Drink water from your own cistern,
And running water from your own
well.

[16] Should your fountains be dispersed
abroad,
Streams of water in the streets?

[17] Let them be only your own,
And not for strangers with you.

[18] Let your fountain be blessed,
And rejoice with the wife of your
youth.

[19] *As a* loving deer and a graceful doe,
Let her breasts satisfy you at all
times;

And always be enraptured with her
love.

[20] For why should you, my son, be
enraptured by an immoral woman,
And be embraced in the arms of a
seductress?

[21] For the ways of man *are* before the
eyes of the LORD,
And He ponders all his paths.

[22] His own iniquities entrap the wicked
man,
And he is caught in the cords of his
sin.

[23] He shall die for lack of instruction,
And in the greatness of his folly he
shall go astray.

Dangerous Promises

6 [1] My son, if you become surety for
your friend,
If you have shaken hands in pledge
for a stranger,

[2] You are snared by the words of your
mouth;
You are taken by the words of your
mouth.

[3] So do this, my son, and deliver
yourself;
For you have come into the hand of
your friend:
Go and humble yourself;
Plead with your friend.

[4] Give no sleep to your eyes,
Nor slumber to your eyelids.

[5] Deliver yourself like a gazelle from
the hand *of the hunter,*
And like a bird from the hand of the
fowler.[a]

The Folly of Indolence

[6] Go to the ant, you sluggard!
Consider her ways and be wise,

[7] Which, having no captain,
Overseer or ruler,

[8] Provides her supplies in the summer,
And gathers her food in the harvest.

[9] How long will you slumber,
O sluggard?
When will you rise from your sleep?

[10] A little sleep, a little slumber,
A little folding of the hands to sleep—

[11] So shall your poverty come on you like
a prowler,
And your need like an armed man.

5:5 [a]Or *Sheol*   6:5 [a]That is, one who catches
birds in a trap or snare

The Wicked Man

12 A worthless person, a wicked man,
Walks with a perverse mouth;
13 He winks with his eyes,
He shuffles his feet,
He points with his fingers;
14 Perversity *is* in his heart,
He devises evil continually,
He sows discord.
15 Therefore his calamity shall come
suddenly;
Suddenly he shall be broken without
remedy.

16 These six *things* the LORD hates,
Yes, seven *are* an abomination to Him:
17 A proud look,
A lying tongue,
Hands that shed innocent blood,
18 A heart that devises wicked plans,
Feet that are swift in running to evil,
19 A false witness *who* speaks lies,
And one who sows discord among
brethren.

Beware of Adultery

20 My son, keep your father's command,
And do not forsake the law of your
mother.
21 Bind them continually upon your
heart;
Tie them around your neck.
22 When you roam, they[a] will lead you;
When you sleep, they will keep you;
And *when* you awake, they will speak
with you.
23 For the commandment *is* a lamp,
And the law a light;
Reproofs of instruction *are* the way of
life,
24 To keep you from the evil woman,
From the flattering tongue of a
seductress.
25 Do not lust after her beauty in your
heart,
Nor let her allure you with her
eyelids.
26 For by means of a harlot
A man is reduced to a crust of bread;
And an adulteress[a] will prey upon his
precious life.
27 Can a man take fire to his bosom,
And his clothes not be burned?
28 Can one walk on hot coals,
And his feet not be seared?

29 So *is* he who goes in to his neighbor's
wife;
Whoever touches her shall not be
innocent.

30 *People* do not despise a thief
If he steals to satisfy himself when he
is starving.
31 Yet *when* he is found, he must restore
sevenfold;
He may have to give up all the
substance of his house.
32 Whoever commits adultery with a
woman lacks understanding;
He *who* does so destroys his own soul.
33 Wounds and dishonor he will get,
And his reproach will not be wiped
away.
34 For jealousy *is* a husband's fury;
Therefore he will not spare in the day
of vengeance.
35 He will accept no recompense,
Nor will he be appeased though you
give many gifts.

7 1 My son, keep my words,
And treasure my commands within
you.
2 Keep my commands and live,
And my law as the apple of your eye.
3 Bind them on your fingers;
Write them on the tablet of your
heart.
4 Say to wisdom, "You *are* my sister,"
And call understanding *your* nearest
kin,
5 That they may keep you from the
immoral woman,
From the seductress *who* flatters with
her words.

The Crafty Harlot

6 For at the window of my house
I looked through my lattice,
7 And saw among the simple,
I perceived among the youths,
A young man devoid of understanding,
8 Passing along the street near her
corner;
And he took the path to her house
9 In the twilight, in the evening,
In the black and dark night.

10 And there a woman met him,
With the attire of a harlot, and a
crafty heart.
11 She *was* loud and rebellious,
Her feet would not stay at home.

6:22 ªLiterally *it* 6:26 ªLiterally *a man's wife,*
that is, of another

12 At times *she was* outside, at times in
    the open square,
    Lurking at every corner.
13 So she caught him and kissed him;
    With an impudent face she said to
    him:
14 "*I have* peace offerings with me;
    Today I have paid my vows.
15 So I came out to meet you,
    Diligently to seek your face,
    And I have found you.
16 I have spread my bed with tapestry,
    Colored coverings of Egyptian linen.
17 I have perfumed my bed
    With myrrh, aloes, and cinnamon.
18 Come, let us take our fill of love until
    morning;
    Let us delight ourselves with love.
19 For my husband *is* not at home;
    He has gone on a long journey;
20 He has taken a bag of money with
    him,
    And will come home on the appointed
    day."

21 With her enticing speech she caused
    him to yield,
    With her flattering lips she seduced
    him.
22 Immediately he went after her, as an
    ox goes to the slaughter,
    Or as a fool to the correction of the
    stocks,[a]
23 Till an arrow struck his liver.
    As a bird hastens to the snare,
    He did not know it *would cost* his life.

24 Now therefore, listen to me, *my*
    children;
    Pay attention to the words of my
    mouth:
25 Do not let your heart turn aside to her
    ways,
    Do not stray into her paths;
26 For she has cast down many wounded,
    And all who were slain by her were
    strong *men.*
27 Her house *is* the way to hell,[a]
    Descending to the chambers of death.

The Excellence of Wisdom

8 1 Does not wisdom cry out,
    And understanding lift up her voice?
2 She takes her stand on the top of the
    high hill,
    Beside the way, where the paths meet.
3 She cries out by the gates, at the
    entry of the city,
    At the entrance of the doors:
4 "To you, O men, I call,
    And my voice *is* to the sons of men.
5 O you simple ones, understand
    prudence,
    And you fools, be of an understanding
    heart.
6 Listen, for I will speak of excellent
    things,
    And from the opening of my lips *will
    come* right things;
7 For my mouth will speak truth;
    Wickedness *is* an abomination to my
    lips.
8 All the words of my mouth *are* with
    righteousness;
    Nothing crooked or perverse *is* in
    them.
9 They *are* all plain to him who
    understands,
    And right to those who find
    knowledge.
10 Receive my instruction, and not silver,
    And knowledge rather than choice
    gold;
11 For wisdom *is* better than rubies,
    And all the things one may desire
    cannot be compared with her.

12 "I, wisdom, dwell with prudence,
    And find out knowledge *and*
    discretion.
13 The fear of the LORD *is* to hate evil;
    Pride and arrogance and the evil way
    And the perverse mouth I hate.
14 Counsel *is* mine, and sound wisdom;
    I *am* understanding, I have strength.

7:22 [a]Septuagint, Syriac, and Targum read *as a dog
to bonds;* Vulgate reads *as a lamb . . . to bonds.*
7:27 [a]Or *Sheol*

POLITICS AND GOVERNMENT

*The gates of ancient cities were large structures that often included several rooms
where business could be conducted. It is appropriate to find the figure of Wisdom calling
for her students in this location (Prov. 8:3), since the city gate was a place where legal
as well as commercial transactions took place (Ruth 4:1, 11; Amos 5:12, 15).*

THE PERSON OF LADY WISDOM (Prov. 8:22–31)

God's first possession, which He possessed before the universe was created, is the figure of Wisdom (Prov. 8:22). In Prov. 8:1–9:12 Wisdom is portrayed as a woman who seeks to teach all humans how to live properly in this world in accordance with the will of God and in harmony with the design of creation. She knows from direct involvement both God's will and creation's design, for it was by Wisdom that God created the world (8:27–31) so that humans can understand it and live well in it.

The poem in Proverbs insists that acquiring wisdom is easy, since Wisdom herself seeks out persons, both wise and foolish, to teach them (8:1–4). The ways of God are not hidden, neither are the ways which lead to a good human life. Anyone who wishes to succeed is welcomed to learn this way of life. For wisdom, it is asserted, leads to a good life, while foolishness leads to death.

The Hebrew Bible represents God's wisdom as a person, the feminine figure of Wisdom, but not as a separate deity. It remains unknown whether some Israelites and Judeans may have related her to the goddess Asherah. The Ugaritic myths (1400–1200 B.C.) present Asherah as the spouse of El, the head of the pantheon, and as having great wisdom of her own.

Wisdom became increasingly identified with God and with the Torah, the first five books of Israel's Scripture. Her traits accumulated through a tradition of poems written later than Proverbs, such as Ecclesiasticus (Wisdom of Jesus ben Sirach), Baruch, and the Wisdom of Solomon. By the time the Wisdom of Solomon was written, Wisdom could be portrayed as creator of the world, the giver of life, and even the source of eternal life. Later, these same notions appear in the prologue of the Gospel of John (John 1:1–18), describing the preexistence of Christ, the divine Word.

---

15 By me kings reign,
And rulers decree justice.
16 By me princes rule, and nobles,
All the judges of the earth.[a]
17 I love those who love me,
And those who seek me diligently will
find me.
18 Riches and honor *are* with me,
Enduring riches and righteousness.
19 My fruit *is* better than gold, yes, than
fine gold,
And my revenue than choice silver.
20 I traverse the way of righteousness,
In the midst of the paths of justice,
21 That I may cause those who love me
to inherit wealth,
That I may fill their treasuries.

22 "The LORD possessed me at the
beginning of His way,
Before His works of old.
23 I have been established from
everlasting,

From the beginning, before there was
ever an earth.
24 When *there were* no depths I was
brought forth,
When *there were* no fountains
abounding with water.
25 Before the mountains were settled,
Before the hills, I was brought forth;
26 While as yet He had not made the
earth or the fields,
Or the primal dust of the world.
27 When He prepared the heavens, I *was*
there,
When He drew a circle on the face of
the deep,
28 When He established the clouds
above,
When He strengthened the fountains
of the deep,
29 When He assigned to the sea its limit,
So that the waters would not
transgress His command,
When He marked out the foundations
of the earth,
30 Then I was beside Him *as* a master
craftsman;[a]
And I was daily *His* delight,
Rejoicing always before Him,

8:16 [a]Masoretic Text, Syriac, Targum, and Vulgate
read *righteousness;* Septuagint, Bomberg, and some
manuscripts and editions read *earth.*   8:30 [a]A
Jewish tradition reads *one brought up.*

31   Rejoicing in His inhabited world,
      And my delight *was* with the sons of
         men.

32   "Now therefore, listen to me, *my*
         children,
      For blessed *are those who* keep my
         ways.
33   Hear instruction and be wise,
      And do not disdain *it.*
34   Blessed is the man who listens to me,
      Watching daily at my gates,
      Waiting at the posts of my doors.
35   For whoever finds me finds life,
      And obtains favor from the LORD;
36   But he who sins against me wrongs
         his own soul;
      All those who hate me love death."

The Way of Wisdom

9 ¹ Wisdom has built her house,
      She has hewn out her seven pillars;
2   She has slaughtered her meat,
      She has mixed her wine,
      She has also furnished her table.
3   She has sent out her maidens,
      She cries out from the highest places
         of the city,
4   "Whoever *is* simple, let him turn in
         here!"
      As for him who lacks understanding,
         she says to him,
5   "Come, eat of my bread
      And drink of the wine I have mixed.
6   Forsake foolishness and live,
      And go in the way of understanding.

7   "He who corrects a scoffer gets shame
         for himself,
      And he who rebukes a wicked *man*
         only harms himself.
8   Do not correct a scoffer, lest he hate
         you;
      Rebuke a wise *man,* and he will love
         you.
9   Give *instruction* to a wise *man,* and he
         will be still wiser;
      Teach a just *man,* and he will increase
         in learning.
10   "The fear of the LORD *is* the beginning
         of wisdom,
      And the knowledge of the Holy One *is*
         understanding.
11   For by me your days will be
         multiplied,
      And years of life will be added to you.
12   If you are wise, you are wise for
         yourself,

And *if* you scoff, you will bear *it*
   alone."

The Way of Folly

13   A foolish woman is clamorous;
      She is simple, and knows nothing.
14   For she sits at the door of her house,
      On a seat *by* the highest places of the
         city,
15   To call to those who pass by,
      Who go straight on their way:
16   "Whoever *is* simple, let him turn in
         here";
      And *as for* him who lacks
         understanding, she says to him,
17   "Stolen water is sweet,
      And bread *eaten* in secret is pleasant."
18   But he does not know that the dead
         are there,
      That her guests *are* in the depths of
         hell.[a]

More Proverbs Ascribed to Solomon

The value and the practice of wisdom are encouraged throughout Prov. 10:1—22:16, the second collection of proverbs ascribed to Solomon. Chapters 10—15 are characterized by proverbs which contrast wise and foolish behavior. In Proverbs this contrast is more than just a comment on intelligence. Wisdom meant living in harmony with the good and orderly creation of God. Thus for the wisdom teachers, wisdom was almost a synonym for virtue, and folly and wickedness were interchangeable.

■ Proverbs 10:1—15:33

Proverbs
Wise Sayings of Solomon

10 **:1** The proverbs of Solomon:

A wise son makes a glad father,
But a foolish son *is* the grief of his
   mother.

2   Treasures of wickedness profit
         nothing,
      But righteousness delivers from
         death.
3   The LORD will not allow the righteous
         soul to famish,

9:18 [a]Or *Sheol*

But He casts away the desire of the
wicked.

4 He who has a slack hand becomes
poor,
But the hand of the diligent makes
rich.

5 He who gathers in summer *is* a wise
son;
He who sleeps in harvest *is* a son who
causes shame.

6 Blessings *are* on the head of the
righteous,
But violence covers the mouth of the
wicked.

7 The memory of the righteous *is*
blessed,
But the name of the wicked will rot.

8 The wise in heart will receive
commands,
But a prating fool will fall.

9 He who walks with integrity walks
securely,
But he who perverts his ways will
become known.

10 He who winks with the eye causes
trouble,
But a prating fool will fall.

11 The mouth of the righteous *is* a well of
life,
But violence covers the mouth of the
wicked.

12 Hatred stirs up strife,
But love covers all sins.

13 Wisdom is found on the lips of him
who has understanding,
But a rod *is* for the back of him who is
devoid of understanding.

14 Wise *people* store up knowledge,
But the mouth of the foolish *is* near
destruction.

15 The rich man's wealth *is* his strong
city;
The destruction of the poor *is* their
poverty.

16 The labor of the righteous *leads* to life,
The wages of the wicked to sin.

17 He who keeps instruction *is in* the
way of life,
But he who refuses correction goes
astray.

18 Whoever hides hatred *has* lying lips,
And whoever spreads slander *is* a fool.

19 In the multitude of words sin is not
lacking,
But he who restrains his lips *is* wise.

20 The tongue of the righteous *is* choice
silver;
The heart of the wicked *is worth* little.

21 The lips of the righteous feed many,
But fools die for lack of wisdom.[a]

22 The blessing of the LORD makes *one*
rich,
And He adds no sorrow with it.

23 To do evil *is* like sport to a fool,
But a man of understanding has
wisdom.

24 The fear of the wicked will come upon
him,
And the desire of the righteous will be
granted.

25 When the whirlwind passes by, the
wicked *is* no *more,*
But the righteous *has* an everlasting
foundation.

26 As vinegar to the teeth and smoke to
the eyes,
So *is* the lazy *man* to those who send
him.

27 The fear of the LORD prolongs days,
But the years of the wicked will be
shortened.

28 The hope of the righteous *will be*
gladness,
But the expectation of the wicked will
perish.

29 The way of the LORD *is* strength for
the upright,
But destruction *will come* to the
workers of iniquity.

30 The righteous will never be removed,
But the wicked will not inhabit the
earth.

31 The mouth of the righteous brings
forth wisdom,

10:21 [a]Literally *heart*

But the perverse tongue will be cut
out.

32 The lips of the righteous know what is
acceptable,
But the mouth of the wicked *what is*
perverse.

11

¹ Dishonest scales *are* an
abomination to the LORD,
But a just weight *is* His delight.

2 When pride comes, then comes shame;
But with the humble *is* wisdom.

3 The integrity of the upright will guide
them,
But the perversity of the unfaithful
will destroy them.

4 Riches do not profit in the day of
wrath,
But righteousness delivers from
death.

5 The righteousness of the blameless
will direct[a] his way aright,
But the wicked will fall by his own
wickedness.

6 The righteousness of the upright will
deliver them,
But the unfaithful will be caught by
their lust.

7 When a wicked man dies, *his*
expectation will perish,
And the hope of the unjust perishes.

8 The righteous is delivered from
trouble,
And it comes to the wicked instead.

9 The hypocrite with *his* mouth destroys
his neighbor,
But through knowledge the righteous
will be delivered.

10 When it goes well with the righteous,
the city rejoices;
And when the wicked perish, *there is*
jubilation.

11 By the blessing of the upright the city
is exalted,
But it is overthrown by the mouth of
the wicked.

12 He who is devoid of wisdom despises
his neighbor,
But a man of understanding holds his
peace.

13 A talebearer reveals secrets,
But he who is of a faithful spirit
conceals a matter.

14 Where *there is* no counsel, the people
fall;
But in the multitude of counselors
there is safety.

15 He who is surety for a stranger will
suffer,
But one who hates being surety is
secure.

16 A gracious woman retains honor,
But ruthless *men* retain riches.

17 The merciful man does good for his
own soul,
But *he who is* cruel troubles his own
flesh.

18 The wicked *man* does deceptive work,
But he who sows righteousness *will
have* a sure reward.

19 As righteousness *leads* to life,
So he who pursues evil *pursues it* to
his own death.

20 Those who are of a perverse heart *are*
an abomination to the LORD,
But *the* blameless in their ways *are*
His delight.

21 *Though they join* forces,[a] the wicked
will not go unpunished;
But the posterity of the righteous will
be delivered.

22 As a ring of gold in a swine's snout,
So is a lovely woman who lacks
discretion.

23 The desire of the righteous *is* only
good,
But the expectation of the wicked *is*
wrath.

24 There is *one* who scatters, yet
increases more;
And there is *one* who withholds more
than is right,
But it *leads* to poverty.

25 The generous soul will be made rich,
And he who waters will also be
watered himself.

26 The people will curse him who
withholds grain,
But blessing *will be* on the head of
him who sells *it*.

27 He who earnestly seeks good finds
favor,

11:5 ᵃOr *make smooth* or *straight*
11:21 ᵃLiterally *hand to hand*

But trouble will come to him who
seeks *evil.*

28 He who trusts in his riches will fall,
But the righteous will flourish like
foliage.

29 He who troubles his own house will
inherit the wind,
And the fool *will be* servant to the
wise of heart.

30 The fruit of the righteous *is a* tree of
life,
And he who wins souls *is* wise.

31 If the righteous will be recompensed
on the earth,
How much more the ungodly and the
sinner.

12 ¹ Whoever loves instruction loves
knowledge,
But he who hates correction *is* stupid.

2 A good *man* obtains favor from the
LORD,
But a man of wicked intentions He
will condemn.

3 A man is not established by
wickedness,
But the root of the righteous cannot
be moved.

4 An excellent[a] wife *is* the crown of her
husband,
But she who causes shame *is* like
rottenness in his bones.

5 The thoughts of the righteous *are*
right,
But the counsels of the wicked *are*
deceitful.

6 The words of the wicked *are,* "Lie in
wait for blood,"

But the mouth of the upright will
deliver them.

7 The wicked are overthrown and *are* no
more,
But the house of the righteous will
stand.

8 A man will be commended according
to his wisdom,
But he who is of a perverse heart will
be despised.

9 Better *is the one* who is slighted but
has a servant,
Than he who honors himself but lacks
bread.

10 A righteous *man* regards the life of his
animal,
But the tender mercies of the wicked
are cruel.

11 He who tills his land will be satisfied
with bread,
But he who follows frivolity *is* devoid
of understanding.[a]

12 The wicked covet the catch of evil
men,
But the root of the righteous yields
fruit.

13 The wicked is ensnared by the
transgression of *his* lips,
But the righteous will come through
trouble.

14 A man will be satisfied with good by
the fruit of *his* mouth,
And the recompense of a man's hands
will be rendered to him.

15 The way of a fool *is* right in his own
eyes,
But he who heeds counsel *is* wise.

16 A fool's wrath is known at once,
But a prudent *man* covers shame.

17 He *who* speaks truth declares
righteousness,
But a false witness, deceit.

12:4 [a]Literally *A wife of valor*   12:11 [a]Literally
heart

POLITICS AND GOVERNMENT

*The emphasis of the wisdom literature on the power of speech and the need to watch
carefully what one says suggests that the instruction originated in court circles (Prov.
12:17). In the royal court, policy would be discussed and decided. Also in the court,
spies would be a danger, as the warning about "little birds" indicates (Eccl. 10:20).*

18 There is one who speaks like the
    piercings of a sword,
But the tongue of the wise *promotes*
    health.
19 The truthful lip shall be established
    forever,
But a lying tongue *is* but for a
    moment.
20 Deceit is in the heart of those who
    devise evil,
But counselors of peace have joy.
21 No grave trouble will overtake the
    righteous,
But the wicked shall be filled with
    evil.
22 Lying lips *are* an abomination to the
    LORD,
But those who deal truthfully *are* His
    delight.

23 A prudent man conceals knowledge,
But the heart of fools proclaims
    foolishness.

24 The hand of the diligent will rule,
But the lazy *man* will be put to forced
    labor.

25 Anxiety in the heart of man causes
    depression,
But a good word makes it glad.

26 The righteous should choose his
    friends carefully,
For the way of the wicked leads them
    astray.

27 The lazy *man* does not roast what he
    took in hunting,
But diligence *is* man's precious
    possession.

28 In the way of righteousness *is* life,
And in *its* pathway *there is* no death.

13

1 A wise son *heeds* his father's
    instruction,
But a scoffer does not listen to rebuke.

2 A man shall eat well by the fruit of *his*
    mouth,
But the soul of the unfaithful feeds on
    violence.
3 He who guards his mouth preserves
    his life,
But he who opens wide his lips shall
    have destruction.

4 The soul of a lazy *man* desires, and
    has nothing;
But the soul of the diligent shall be
    made rich.

5 A righteous *man* hates lying,
But a wicked *man* is loathsome and
    comes to shame.
6 Righteousness guards *him whose* way
    is blameless,
But wickedness overthrows the sinner.

7 There is one who makes himself rich,
    yet *has* nothing;
And one who makes himself poor, yet
    has great riches.

8 The ransom of a man's life *is* his
    riches,
But the poor does not hear rebuke.

9 The light of the righteous rejoices,
But the lamp of the wicked will be put
    out.

10 By pride comes nothing but strife,
But with the well-advised *is* wisdom.

11 Wealth *gained by* dishonesty will be
    diminished,
But he who gathers by labor will
    increase.

12 Hope deferred makes the heart sick,
But *when* the desire comes, *it is* a tree
    of life.

13 He who despises the word will be
    destroyed,
But he who fears the commandment
    will be rewarded.
14 The law of the wise *is* a fountain of
    life,
To turn *one* away from the snares of
    death.

15 Good understanding gains favor,
But the way of the unfaithful *is* hard.
16 Every prudent *man* acts with
    knowledge,
But a fool lays open *his* folly.

17 A wicked messenger falls into trouble,
But a faithful ambassador *brings*
    health.

18 Poverty and shame *will come* to him
    who disdains correction,

But he who regards a rebuke will be honored.

19 A desire accomplished is sweet to the soul,
But *it is* an abomination to fools to depart from evil.

20 He who walks with wise *men* will be wise,
But the companion of fools will be destroyed.

21 Evil pursues sinners,
But to the righteous, good shall be repaid.

22 A good *man* leaves an inheritance to his children's children,
But the wealth of the sinner is stored up for the righteous.

23 Much food *is in* the fallow *ground* of the poor,
And for lack of justice there is waste.[a]

24 He who spares his rod hates his son,
But he who loves him disciplines him promptly.

25 The righteous eats to the satisfying of his soul,
But the stomach of the wicked shall be in want.

14

1 The wise woman builds her house,
But the foolish pulls it down with her hands.

2 He who walks in his uprightness fears the LORD,
But *he who is* perverse in his ways despises Him.

3 In the mouth of a fool *is* a rod of pride,
But the lips of the wise will preserve them.

4 Where no oxen *are,* the trough *is* clean;
But much increase *comes* by the strength of an ox.

5 A faithful witness does not lie,
But a false witness will utter lies.

6 A scoffer seeks wisdom and does not *find it,*
But knowledge *is* easy to him who understands.

7 Go from the presence of a foolish man,
When you do not perceive *in him* the lips of knowledge.

8 The wisdom of the prudent *is* to understand his way,
But the folly of fools *is* deceit.

9 Fools mock at sin,
But among the upright *there is* favor.

10 The heart knows its own bitterness,
And a stranger does not share its joy.

11 The house of the wicked will be overthrown,
But the tent of the upright will flourish.

12 There is a way *that seems* right to a man,
But its end *is* the way of death.

13 Even in laughter the heart may sorrow,
And the end of mirth *may be* grief.

14 The backslider in heart will be filled with his own ways,
But a good man *will be satisfied* from above.[a]

15 The simple believes every word,
But the prudent considers well his steps.

16 A wise *man* fears and departs from evil,
But a fool rages and is self-confident.

17 A quick-tempered *man* acts foolishly,
And a man of wicked intentions is hated.

18 The simple inherit folly,
But the prudent are crowned with knowledge.

19 The evil will bow before the good,
And the wicked at the gates of the righteous.

20 The poor *man* is hated even by his own neighbor,
But the rich *has* many friends.

13:23 [a]Literally *what is swept away*
14:14 [a]Literally *from above himself*

21 He who despises his neighbor sins;
   But he who has mercy on the poor,
       happy *is* he.

22 Do they not go astray who devise evil?
   But mercy and truth *belong* to those
       who devise good.

23 In all labor there is profit,
   But idle chatter[a] *leads* only to poverty.

24 The crown of the wise is their riches,
   But the foolishness of fools *is* folly.

25 A true witness delivers souls,
   But a deceitful *witness* speaks lies.

26 In the fear of the LORD *there is* strong
       confidence,
   And His children will have a place of
       refuge.

27 The fear of the LORD *is* a fountain of
       life,
   To turn *one* away from the snares of
       death.

28 In a multitude of people *is* a king's
       honor,
   But in the lack of people *is* the
       downfall of a prince.

14:23 ªLiterally *talk of the lips*

Solomon's Administrative Districts

"A multitude of people is a king's honor" (Prov. 14:28). The growth and extension of Israel's borders under Solomon's leadership resulted in a very large kingdom (1 Kin. 4:20, 21). Solomon faced an urgent need for ever-increasing revenues to meet expenditures on building and commercial projects throughout his expanding kingdom. To address this need, the king divided Israel into 12 districts and appointed over each district a governor responsible for levying and collecting taxes.

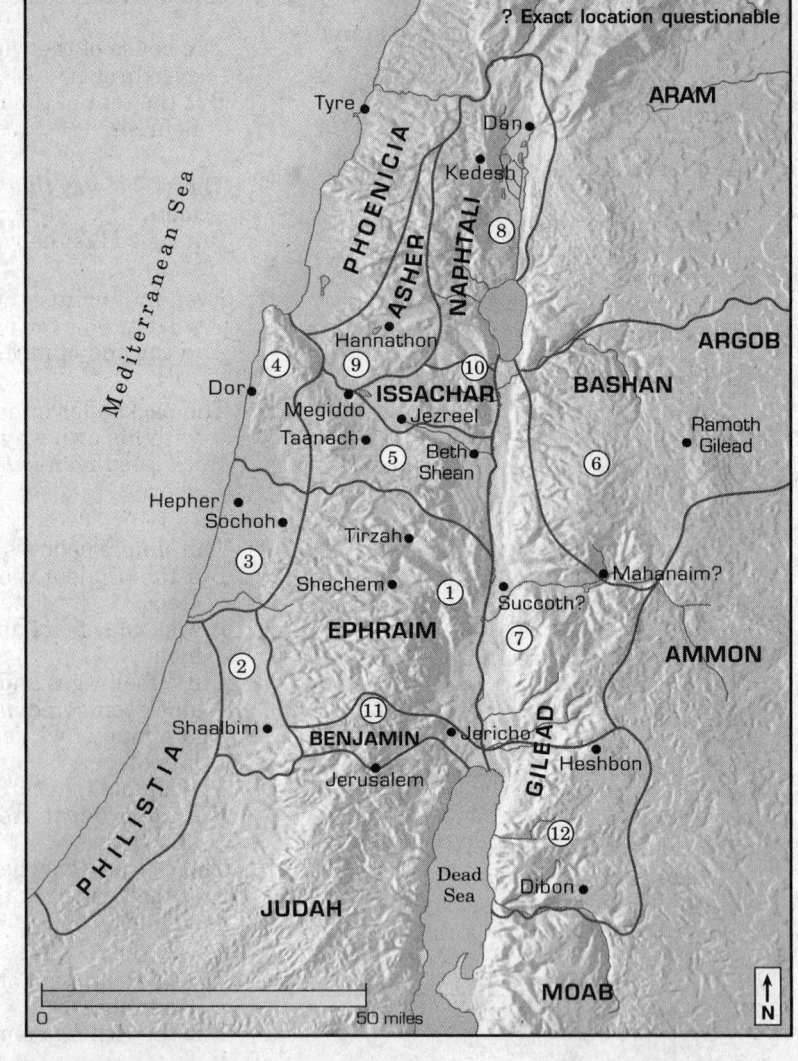

29 *He who is* slow to wrath has great
   understanding,
   But *he who is* impulsive[a] exalts folly.

30 A sound heart *is* life to the body,
   But envy *is* rottenness to the bones.

31 He who oppresses the poor reproaches
   his Maker,
   But he who honors Him has mercy on
   the needy.

32 The wicked is banished in his
   wickedness,
   But the righteous has a refuge in his
   death.

33 Wisdom rests in the heart of him who
   has understanding,
   But *what is* in the heart of fools is
   made known.

34 Righteousness exalts a nation,
   But sin *is* a reproach to *any* people.

35 The king's favor *is* toward a wise
   servant,
   But his wrath *is against* him who
   causes shame.

15

1 A soft answer turns away
   wrath,
   But a harsh word stirs up anger.
2 The tongue of the wise uses
   knowledge rightly,
   But the mouth of fools pours forth
   foolishness.

3 The eyes of the LORD *are* in every
   place,
   Keeping watch on the evil and the
   good.

4 A wholesome tongue *is* a tree of life,
   But perverseness in it breaks the
   spirit.

5 A fool despises his father's instruction,
   But he who receives correction is
   prudent.

6 *In* the house of the righteous *there is*
   much treasure,
   But in the revenue of the wicked is
   trouble.

7 The lips of the wise disperse
   knowledge,
   But the heart of the fool *does* not *do*
   so.

8 The sacrifice of the wicked *is* an
   abomination to the LORD,
   But the prayer of the upright *is* His
   delight.

9 The way of the wicked *is* an
   abomination to the LORD,
   But He loves him who follows
   righteousness.

10 Harsh discipline *is* for him who
   forsakes the way,
   And he who hates correction will die.

11 Hell[a] and Destruction[b] *are* before the
   LORD;
   So how much more the hearts of the
   sons of men.

12 A scoffer does not love one who
   corrects him,
   Nor will he go to the wise.

13 A merry heart makes a cheerful
   countenance,
   But by sorrow of the heart the spirit is
   broken.

14 The heart of him who has
   understanding seeks knowledge,
   But the mouth of fools feeds on
   foolishness.

15 All the days of the afflicted *are* evil,
   But he who is of a merry heart *has* a
   continual feast.

14:29 [a]Literally *short of spirit*   15:11 [a]Or *Sheol*
[b]Hebrew *Abaddon*

BELIEFS AND IDEAS

*The Old Testament commonly refers to the dead as inhabitants of Sheol, sometimes
translated as "Hell" (Prov. 15:11). As a place, Sheol is a shadowy region where the
dead, although not unconscious, are unable to participate in the affairs of the living.
Ancient people thought of Sheol or Hell as a person, as well as a place. The personified
Hell was never satisfied (Prov. 27:20).*

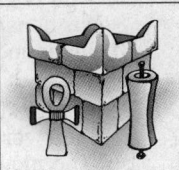

16 Better *is* a little with the fear of the
Lord,
Than great treasure with trouble.

17 Better *is* a dinner of herbs[a] where love
is,
Than a fatted calf with hatred.

18 A wrathful man stirs up strife,
But *he who is* slow to anger allays
contention.

19 The way of the lazy *man is* like a
hedge of thorns,
But the way of the upright *is* a
highway.

20 A wise son makes a father glad,
But a foolish man despises his mother.

21 Folly *is* joy *to him who is* destitute of
discernment,
But a man of understanding walks
uprightly.

22 Without counsel, plans go awry,
But in the multitude of counselors
they are established.

23 A man has joy by the answer of his
mouth,
And a word *spoken* in due season, how
good *it is!*

24 The way of life *winds* upward for the
wise,
That he may turn away from hell[a]
below.

25 The Lord will destroy the house of the
proud,
But He will establish the boundary of
the widow.

26 The thoughts of the wicked *are* an
abomination to the Lord,
But *the words* of the pure *are*
pleasant.

27 He who is greedy for gain troubles his
own house,
But he who hates bribes will live.

28 The heart of the righteous studies how
to answer,
But the mouth of the wicked pours
forth evil.

29 The Lord *is* far from the wicked,
But He hears the prayer of the
righteous.

30 The light of the eyes rejoices the
heart,
And a good report makes the bones
healthy.[a]

31 The ear that hears the rebukes of life
Will abide among the wise.

32 He who disdains instruction despises
his own soul,
But he who heeds rebuke gets
understanding.

33 The fear of the Lord *is* the instruction
of wisdom,
And before honor *is* humility.

Miscellaneous Proverbs

A cluster of sayings (Prov. 16:10–15)
deals with the responsibilities and desired
characteristics of the king and his reign. For
the most part, however, Prov. 16:1—22:16
are a collection of miscellaneous, self-
contained proverbs.

■ Proverbs 16:1—22:16

Proverbs

16

:1 The preparations of the heart
belong to man,
But the answer of the tongue *is* from
the Lord.

2 All the ways of a man *are* pure in his
own eyes,
But the Lord weighs the spirits.

3 Commit your works to the Lord,
And your thoughts will be established.

4 The Lord has made all for Himself,
Yes, even the wicked for the day of
doom.

5 Everyone proud in heart *is* an
abomination to the Lord;
Though they join forces,[a] none will go
unpunished.

6 In mercy and truth
Atonement is provided for iniquity;

15:17 [a]Or *vegetables*   15:24 [a]Or *Sheol*
15:30 [a]Literally *fat*   16:5 [a]Literally *hand to
hand*

And by the fear of the LORD *one*
　departs from evil.

7　When a man's ways please the LORD,
　He makes even his enemies to be at
　　peace with him.

8　Better *is* a little with righteousness,
　Than vast revenues without justice.

9　A man's heart plans his way,
　But the LORD directs his steps.

10　Divination *is* on the lips of the king;
　His mouth must not transgress in
　　judgment.
11　Honest weights and scales *are* the
　　LORD's;
　All the weights in the bag *are* His
　　work.
12　*It is* an abomination for kings to
　　commit wickedness,
　For a throne is established by
　　righteousness.
13　Righteous lips *are* the delight of kings,
　And they love him who speaks *what is*
　　right.
14　As messengers of death *is* the king's
　　wrath,
　But a wise man will appease it.
15　In the light of the king's face *is* life,
　And his favor *is* like a cloud of the
　　latter rain.

16　How much better to get wisdom than
　　gold!
　And to get understanding is to be
　　chosen rather than silver.

17　The highway of the upright *is* to
　　depart from evil;
　He who keeps his way preserves his
　　soul.

18　Pride *goes* before destruction,
　And a haughty spirit before a fall.
19　Better *to be* of a humble spirit with
　　the lowly,
　Than to divide the spoil with the
　　proud.

20　He who heeds the word wisely will
　　find good,
　And whoever trusts in the LORD,
　　happy *is* he.

21　The wise in heart will be called
　　prudent,
　And sweetness of the lips increases
　　learning.

22　Understanding *is* a wellspring of life
　　to him who has it.
　But the correction of fools *is* folly.

23　The heart of the wise teaches his
　　mouth,
　And adds learning to his lips.

24　Pleasant words *are like* a honeycomb,
　Sweetness to the soul and health to
　　the bones.

25　There is a way *that seems* right to a
　　man,
　But its end *is* the way of death.

26　The person who labors, labors for
　　himself,
　For his *hungry* mouth drives him *on.*

27　An ungodly man digs up evil,
　And *it is* on his lips like a burning
　　fire.
28　A perverse man sows strife,
　And a whisperer separates the best of
　　friends.
29　A violent man entices his neighbor,
　And leads him in a way *that is* not
　　good.
30　He winks his eye to devise perverse
　　things;
　He purses his lips *and* brings about
　　evil.

31　The silver-haired head *is* a crown of
　　glory,
　If it is found in the way of
　　righteousness.

32　*He who is* slow to anger *is* better than
　　the mighty,
　And he who rules his spirit than he
　　who takes a city.

33　The lot is cast into the lap,
　But its every decision *is* from the
　　LORD.

17

1　Better *is* a dry morsel with
　　quietness,
　Than a house full of feasting[a] *with*
　　strife.

17:1　[a]Or *sacrificial meals*

2 A wise servant will rule over a son
who causes shame,
And will share an inheritance among
the brothers.

3 The refining pot *is* for silver and the
furnace for gold,
But the LORD tests the hearts.

4 An evildoer gives heed to false lips;
A liar listens eagerly to a spiteful
tongue.

5 He who mocks the poor reproaches his
Maker;
He who is glad at calamity will not go
unpunished.

6 Children's children *are* the crown of
old men,
And the glory of children *is* their
father.

7 Excellent speech is not becoming to a
fool,
Much less lying lips to a prince.

8 A present *is* a precious stone in the
eyes of its possessor;
Wherever he turns, he prospers.

9 He who covers a transgression seeks
love,
But he who repeats a matter
separates friends.

10 Rebuke is more effective for a wise
man
Than a hundred blows on a fool.

11 An evil *man* seeks only rebellion;
Therefore a cruel messenger will be
sent against him.

12 Let a man meet a bear robbed of her
cubs,
Rather than a fool in his folly.

13 Whoever rewards evil for good,
Evil will not depart from his house.

14 The beginning of strife *is like*
releasing water;
Therefore stop contention before a
quarrel starts.

15 He who justifies the wicked, and he
who condemns the just,

Both of them alike *are* an abomination
to the LORD.

16 Why *is there* in the hand of a fool the
purchase price of wisdom,
Since *he has* no heart *for it?*

17 A friend loves at all times,
And a brother is born for adversity.

18 A man devoid of understanding
shakes hands in a pledge,
And becomes surety for his friend.

19 He who loves transgression loves
strife,
And he who exalts his gate seeks
destruction.

20 He who has a deceitful heart finds no
good,
And he who has a perverse tongue
falls into evil.

21 He who begets a scoffer *does so* to his
sorrow,
And the father of a fool has no joy.

22 A merry heart does good, *like*
medicine,[a]
But a broken spirit dries the bones.

23 A wicked *man* accepts a bribe behind
the back[a]
To pervert the ways of justice.

24 Wisdom *is* in the sight of him who has
understanding,
But the eyes of a fool *are* on the ends
of the earth.

25 A foolish son *is* a grief to his father,
And bitterness to her who bore him.

26 Also, to punish the righteous *is* not
good,
Nor to strike princes for *their*
uprightness.

27 He who has knowledge spares his
words,
And a man of understanding is of a
calm spirit.

28 Even a fool is counted wise when he
holds his peace;

17:22 [a]Or *makes medicine even better*
17:23 [a]Literally *from the bosom*

When he shuts his lips, *he is considered* perceptive.

18

1 A man who isolates himself
   seeks his own desire;
 He rages against all wise judgment.

2 A fool has no delight in
   understanding,
 But in expressing his own heart.

3 When the wicked comes, contempt
   comes also;
 And with dishonor *comes* reproach.

4 The words of a man's mouth *are* deep
   waters;
 The wellspring of wisdom *is* a flowing
   brook.

5 *It is* not good to show partiality to the
   wicked,
 Or to overthrow the righteous in
   judgment.

6 A fool's lips enter into contention,
 And his mouth calls for blows.

7 A fool's mouth *is* his destruction,
 And his lips *are* the snare of his soul.

8 The words of a talebearer *are* like
   tasty trifles,[a]
 And they go down into the inmost
   body.

9 He who is slothful in his work
 Is a brother to him who is a great
   destroyer.

10 The name of the LORD *is* a strong
   tower;
 The righteous run to it and are safe.

11 The rich man's wealth *is* his strong
   city,
 And like a high wall in his own
   esteem.

12 Before destruction the heart of a man
   is haughty,
 And before honor *is* humility.

13 He who answers a matter before he
   hears *it,*
 It *is* folly and shame to him.

14 The spirit of a man will sustain him in
   sickness,
 But who can bear a broken spirit?

15 The heart of the prudent acquires
   knowledge,
 And the ear of the wise seeks
   knowledge.

16 A man's gift makes room for him,
 And brings him before great men.

17 The first *one* to plead his cause *seems*
   right,
 Until his neighbor comes and
   examines him.

18 Casting lots causes contentions to
   cease,
 And keeps the mighty apart.

19 A brother offended *is harder to win*
   than a strong city,
 And contentions *are* like the bars of a
   castle.

20 A man's stomach shall be satisfied
   from the fruit of his mouth;
 From the produce of his lips he shall
   be filled.

21 Death and life *are* in the power of the
   tongue,
 And those who love it will eat its fruit.

22 *He who* finds a wife finds a good
   thing,
 And obtains favor from the LORD.

23 The poor *man* uses entreaties,
 But the rich answers roughly.

18:8 [a]A Jewish tradition reads *wounds.*

ARCHITECTURE AND BUILDING

The main defense of cities was a high, thick wall (Prov. 18:11). At the time of Solomon these walls were built thick enough to be in effect a double wall with internal walls making rooms inside. Dirt or rubble was used to make the surrounding ground slope so enemies had to attack uphill.

24 A man *who has* friends must himself
be friendly,[a]
But there is a friend *who* sticks closer
than a brother.

19 [1] Better *is* the poor who walks in
his integrity
Than *one who is* perverse in his lips,
and is a fool.

2 Also it is not good *for* a soul *to be*
without knowledge,
And he sins who hastens with *his* feet.

3 The foolishness of a man twists his
way,
And his heart frets against the LORD.

4 Wealth makes many friends,
But the poor is separated from his
friend.

5 A false witness will not go
unpunished,
And *he who* speaks lies will not
escape.

6 Many entreat the favor of the nobility,
And every man *is* a friend to one who
gives gifts.

7 All the brothers of the poor hate him;
How much more do his friends go far
from him!
He may pursue *them with* words, *yet*
they abandon *him.*

8 He who gets wisdom loves his own
soul;
He who keeps understanding will find
good.

9 A false witness will not go
unpunished,
And *he who* speaks lies shall perish.

10 Luxury is not fitting for a fool,
Much less for a servant to rule over
princes.

11 The discretion of a man makes him
slow to anger,
And his glory *is* to overlook a
transgression.

12 The king's wrath *is* like the roaring of
a lion,
But his favor *is* like dew on the grass.

13 A foolish son *is* the ruin of his father,
And the contentions of a wife *are* a
continual dripping.

14 Houses and riches *are* an inheritance
from fathers,
But a prudent wife *is* from the LORD.

15 Laziness casts *one* into a deep sleep,
And an idle person will suffer hunger.

16 He who keeps the commandment
keeps his soul,
But he who is careless[a] of his ways
will die.

17 He who has pity on the poor lends to
the LORD,
And He will pay back what he has
given.

18 Chasten your son while there is hope,
And do not set your heart on his
destruction.[a]

19 *A man of* great wrath will suffer
punishment;
For if you rescue *him,* you will have to
do it again.

20 Listen to counsel and receive
instruction,
That you may be wise in your latter
days.

21 There are many plans in a man's
heart,
Nevertheless the LORD's counsel—that
will stand.

22 What is desired in a man is kindness,
And a poor man is better than a liar.

23 The fear of the LORD *leads* to life,
And *he who has it* will abide in
satisfaction;
He will not be visited with evil.

24 A lazy *man* buries his hand in the
bowl,[a]

18:24 [a]Following Greek manuscripts, Syriac, Targum,
and Vulgate; Masoretic Text reads *may come to
ruin.*   19:16 [a]Literally *despises,* figurative of
recklessness or carelessness   19:18 [a]Literally *to
put him to death;* a Jewish tradition reads *on his
crying.*   19:24 [a]Septuagint and Syriac read
bosom; Targum and Vulgate read *armpit.*

And will not so much as bring it to his mouth again.

25 Strike a scoffer, and the simple will become wary;
Rebuke one who has understanding, *and* he will discern knowledge.

26 He who mistreats *his* father *and* chases away *his* mother
Is a son who causes shame and brings reproach.

27 Cease listening to instruction, my son,
And you will stray from the words of knowledge.

28 A disreputable witness scorns justice,
And the mouth of the wicked devours iniquity.

29 Judgments are prepared for scoffers,
And beatings for the backs of fools.

20 1 Wine *is* a mocker,
Strong drink *is* a brawler,
And whoever is led astray by it is not wise.

2 The wrath[a] of a king *is* like the roaring of a lion;
Whoever provokes him to anger sins *against* his own life.

3 *It is* honorable for a man to stop striving,
Since any fool can start a quarrel.

4 The lazy *man* will not plow because of winter;
He will beg during harvest and *have* nothing.

5 Counsel in the heart of man *is like* deep water,
But a man of understanding will draw it out.

6 Most men will proclaim each his own goodness,
But who can find a faithful man?

7 The righteous *man* walks in his integrity;
His children *are* blessed after him.

8 A king who sits on the throne of judgment
Scatters all evil with his eyes.

9 Who can say, "I have made my heart clean,
I am pure from my sin"?

10 Diverse weights *and* diverse measures,
They *are* both alike, an abomination to the LORD.

11 Even a child is known by his deeds,
Whether what he does *is* pure and right.

12 The hearing ear and the seeing eye,
The LORD has made them both.

13 Do not love sleep, lest you come to poverty;
Open your eyes, *and* you will be satisfied with bread.

14 "*It is* good for nothing,"[a] cries the buyer;
But when he has gone his way, then he boasts.

15 There is gold and a multitude of rubies,
But the lips of knowledge *are* a precious jewel.

16 Take the garment of one who is surety *for* a stranger,
And hold it as a pledge *when it* is for a seductress.

17 Bread gained by deceit *is* sweet to a man,
But afterward his mouth will be filled with gravel.

18 Plans are established by counsel;
By wise counsel wage war.

19 He who goes about *as* a talebearer reveals secrets;
Therefore do not associate with one who flatters with his lips.

20 Whoever curses his father or his mother,
His lamp will be put out in deep darkness.

20:2 [a]Literally *fear* or *terror* which is produced by the king's wrath   20:14 [a]Literally *evil, evil*

21 An inheritance gained hastily at the
beginning
Will not be blessed at the end.

22 Do not say, "I will recompense evil";
Wait for the LORD, and He will save
you.

23 Diverse weights *are* an abomination to
the LORD,
And dishonest scales *are* not good.

24 A man's steps *are* of the LORD;
How then can a man understand his
own way?

25 *It is* a snare for a man to devote
rashly *something as* holy,
And afterward to reconsider *his* vows.

26 A wise king sifts out the wicked,
And brings the threshing wheel over
them.

27 The spirit of a man *is* the lamp of the
LORD,
Searching all the inner depths of his
heart.[a]

28 Mercy and truth preserve the king,
And by lovingkindness he upholds his
throne.

29 The glory of young men *is* their
strength,
And the splendor of old men *is* their
gray head.

30 Blows that hurt cleanse away evil,
As *do* stripes the inner depths of the
heart.[a]

21 ¹ The king's heart *is* in the hand
of the LORD,
Like the rivers of water;
He turns it wherever He wishes.

2 Every way of a man *is* right in his
own eyes,
But the LORD weighs the hearts.

3 To do righteousness and justice
Is more acceptable to the LORD than
sacrifice.

4 A haughty look, a proud heart,
And the plowing[a] of the wicked *are*
sin.

5 The plans of the diligent *lead* surely to
plenty,
But *those of* everyone *who is* hasty,
surely to poverty.

6 Getting treasures by a lying tongue
Is the fleeting fantasy of those who
seek death.[a]

7 The violence of the wicked will destroy
them,[a]
Because they refuse to do justice.

8 The way of a guilty man *is* perverse;[a]
But *as for* the pure, his work *is* right.

9 Better to dwell in a corner of a
housetop,
Than in a house shared with a
contentious woman.

10 The soul of the wicked desires evil;
His neighbor finds no favor in his
eyes.

11 When the scoffer is punished, the
simple is made wise;
But when the wise is instructed, he
receives knowledge.

12 The righteous *God* wisely considers
the house of the wicked,
Overthrowing the wicked for *their*
wickedness.

13 Whoever shuts his ears to the cry of
the poor
Will also cry himself and not be heard.

14 A gift in secret pacifies anger,
And a bribe behind the back,[a] strong
wrath.

15 *It is* a joy for the just to do justice,
But destruction *will come* to the
workers of iniquity.

20:27 [a]Literally *the rooms of the belly*
20:30 [a]Literally *the rooms of the belly*   21:4 [a]Or
lamp   21:6 [a]Septuagint reads *Pursue vanity on
the snares of death;* Vulgate reads *Is vain and foolish,
and shall stumble on the snares of death;* Targum
reads *They shall be destroyed, and they shall fall who
seek death.*   21:7 [a]Literally *drag them away*
21:8 [a]Or *The way of a man is perverse and
strange*   21:14 [a]Literally *in the bosom*

16 A man who wanders from the way of
    understanding
    Will rest in the assembly of the dead.

17 He who loves pleasure *will be* a poor
    man;
    He who loves wine and oil will not be
    rich.

18 The wicked *shall be* a ransom for the
    righteous,
    And the unfaithful for the upright.

19 Better to dwell in the wilderness,
    Than with a contentious and angry
    woman.

20 *There is* desirable treasure,
    And oil in the dwelling of the wise,
    But a foolish man squanders it.

21 He who follows righteousness and
    mercy
    Finds life, righteousness and honor.

22 A wise *man* scales the city of the
    mighty,
    And brings down the trusted
    stronghold.

23 Whoever guards his mouth and
    tongue
    Keeps his soul from troubles.

24 A proud *and* haughty *man*—"Scoffer"
    is his name;
    He acts with arrogant pride.

25 The desire of the lazy *man* kills him,
    For his hands refuse to labor.
26 He covets greedily all day long,
    But the righteous gives and does not
    spare.

27 The sacrifice of the wicked *is* an
    abomination;
    How much more *when* he brings it
    with wicked intent!

28 A false witness shall perish,
    But the man who hears *him* will
    speak endlessly.

29 A wicked man hardens his face,
    But *as for* the upright, he establishes[a]
    his way.

30 *There is* no wisdom or understanding
    Or counsel against the LORD.

31 The horse *is* prepared for the day of
    battle,
    But deliverance *is* of the LORD.

22 ¹ A *good* name is to be chosen
    rather than great riches,
    Loving favor rather than silver and
    gold.

2   The rich and the poor have this in
    common,
    The LORD *is* the maker of them all.

3   A prudent *man* foresees evil and hides
    himself,
    But the simple pass on and are
    punished.

4   By humility *and* the fear of the LORD
    Are riches and honor and life.

5   Thorns *and* snares *are* in the way of
    the perverse;
    He who guards his soul will be far
    from them.

6   Train up a child in the way he should
    go,
    And when he is old he will not depart
    from it.

7   The rich rules over the poor,
    And the borrower *is* servant to the
    lender.

8   He who sows iniquity will reap sorrow,
    And the rod of his anger will fail.

9   He who has a generous eye will be
    blessed,
    For he gives of his bread to the poor.

10 Cast out the scoffer, and contention
    will leave;
    Yes, strife and reproach will cease.

11 He who loves purity of heart
    And has grace on his lips,
    The king *will be* his friend.

12 The eyes of the LORD preserve
    knowledge,
    But He overthrows the words of the
    faithless.

21:29 ªQere and Septuagint read *understands.*

13 The lazy *man* says, "*There is* a lion
    outside!
    I shall be slain in the streets!"

14 The mouth of an immoral woman *is* a
    deep pit;
    He who is abhorred by the LORD will
    fall there.

15 Foolishness *is* bound up in the heart
    of a child;
    The rod of correction will drive it far
    from him.

16 He who oppresses the poor to increase
    his *riches,*
    And he who gives to the rich, *will*
    surely *come* to poverty.

Solomon the Builder

In addition to being the quintessential
wise man, Solomon is famed for his building
projects. He made the most of his father
David's alliance with the merchant city of Tyre
(2 Sam. 5:11; 1 Kin. 5:1) and also used Israel's strategic position on several trade
routes to his advantage. Solomon quickly became wealthier than any Israelite king before
or since, and much of this wealth he poured
into construction.

▼   ■ 1 Kings 5:1–18

1 Kings
Solomon Prepares to Build the Temple

5 :1 Now Hiram king of Tyre sent his
servants to Solomon, because he heard
that they had anointed him king in place of
his father, for Hiram had always loved David. 2Then Solomon sent to Hiram, saying:

3   You know how my father David could
    not build a house for the name of the
    LORD his God because of the wars
    which were fought against him on
    every side, until the LORD put *his foes*[a]
    under the soles of his feet.
4   But now the LORD my God has given
    me rest on every side; *there is* neither
    adversary nor evil occurrence.
5   And behold, I propose to build a house
    for the name of the LORD my God, as
    the LORD spoke to my father David,
    saying, "Your son, whom I will set on
    your throne in your place, he shall
    build the house for My name."

6   Now therefore, command that they cut
    down cedars for me from Lebanon; and
    my servants will be with your
    servants, and I will pay you wages for
    your servants according to whatever
    you say. For you know *there is* none
    among us who has skill to cut timber
    like the Sidonians.

7So it was, when Hiram heard the
words of Solomon, that he rejoiced greatly
and said,

Blessed *be* the LORD this day, for He
has given David a wise son over this
great people!

8Then Hiram sent to Solomon, saying:

I have considered *the message* which
you sent me, *and* I will do all you
desire concerning the cedar and
cypress logs.
9   My servants shall bring *them* down
    from Lebanon to the sea; I will float
    them in rafts by sea to the place you
    indicate to me, and will have them
    broken apart there; then you can take
    them away. And you shall fulfill my
    desire by giving food for my household.

10Then Hiram gave Solomon cedar and
cypress logs *according to* all his desire.
11And Solomon gave Hiram twenty thousand kors of wheat *as* food for his household, and twenty[a] kors of pressed oil. Thus
Solomon gave to Hiram year by year.
12So the LORD gave Solomon wisdom,
as He had promised him; and there was
peace between Hiram and Solomon, and
the two of them made a treaty together.
13Then King Solomon raised up a labor
force out of all Israel; and the labor force
was thirty thousand men. 14And he sent
them to Lebanon, ten thousand a month in
shifts: they were one month in Lebanon
and two months at home; Adoniram *was* in
charge of the labor force. 15Solomon had
seventy thousand who carried burdens,
and eighty thousand who quarried *stone* in
the mountains, 16besides three thousand
three hundred[a] from the chiefs of Sol-

5:3 [a]Literally *them*   5:11 [a]Following Masoretic
Text, Targum, and Vulgate; Septuagint and Syriac read
twenty thousand.   5:16 [a]Following Masoretic Text,
Targum, and Vulgate; Septuagint reads *three thousand
six hundred.*

omon's deputies, who supervised the people who labored in the work. ¹⁷And the king commanded them to quarry large stones, costly stones, *and* hewn stones, to lay the foundation of the temple.ᵃ ¹⁸So Solomon's builders, Hiram's builders, and the Gebalites quarried *them;* and they prepared timber and stones to build the temple.

Laying the Temple's Foundation

Solomon laid the foundation of the temple in the 4th year of his reign, which was about 966 B.C. (see "The Books of Kings" at 1 Kin. 1:1). This 4th year is said to have been 480 years after the Exodus from Egypt (1 Kin. 6:1).

Scholars approach this chronological information in different ways. Some interpret the 480 years as figurative—perhaps the result of multiplying the 12 tribes by the standard length of a generation, which was 40 years (12 × 40 = 480). These interpreters then do not use the figure of 1 Kin. 6:1 to calculate the time of the Exodus. Others take the 480 years literally, and a simple calculation from the 4th year of Solomon (966 B.C.) would then date the Israelite exodus from Egypt at 1446 B.C. (966 + 480 = 1446). On the different dates proposed for the Exodus, see "The Exodus Begun" at Ex. 12:37.

The temple was built according to David's plans. The description in 1 Kin. 6 of the actual construction includes many details which are now known to have been common in temple designs of that time.

■ 1 Kings 6:1–38

1 Kings
Solomon Builds the Temple

6 :1 And it came to pass in the four hundred and eightiethᵃ year after the children of Israel had come out of the land of Egypt, in the fourth year of Solomon's reign over Israel, in the month of Ziv, which *is* the second month, that he began to build the house of the LORD. ²Now the house which King Solomon built for the LORD, its length *was* sixty cubits, its width twenty, and its height thirty cubits. ³The vestibule in front of the sanctuaryᵃ of the house *was* twenty cubits long across the width of the house, *and* the width of *the vestibule*ᵇ *extended* ten cubits from the front of the house. ⁴And he made for the house windows with beveled frames.

⁵Against the wall of the temple he built chambers all around, *against* the walls of the temple, all around the sanctuary and the inner sanctuary.ᵃ Thus he made side chambers all around. ⁶The lowest chamber *was* five cubits wide, the middle *was* six cubits wide, and the third *was* seven cubits wide; for he made narrow ledges around the outside of the temple, so that *the support beams* would not be fastened into the walls of the temple. ⁷And the temple, when it was being built, was built with stone finished at the quarry, so that no hammer or chisel *or* any iron tool was heard in the temple while it was being built. ⁸The doorway for the middle storyᵃ *was* on the right side of the temple. They went up by stairs to the middle *story,* and from the middle to the third.

⁹So he built the temple and finished it, and he paneled the temple with beams and boards of cedar. ¹⁰And he built side chambers against the entire temple, each five cubits high; they were attached to the temple with cedar beams.

¹¹Then the word of the LORD came to Solomon, saying: ¹²"*Concerning* this temple which you are building, if you walk in My statutes, execute My judgments, keep all My commandments, and walk in them, then I will perform My word with you, which I spoke to your father David. ¹³And I will dwell among the children of Israel, and will not forsake My people Israel."

¹⁴So Solomon built the temple and finished it. ¹⁵And he built the inside walls of the temple with cedar boards; from the floor of the temple to the ceiling he paneled the inside with wood; and he covered the floor of the temple with planks of cypress. ¹⁶Then he built the twenty-cubit room at the rear of the temple, from floor to ceiling, with cedar boards; he built *it* inside as the inner sanctuary, as the Most Holy *Place.* ¹⁷And in front of it the temple sanctuary

5:17 ᵃLiterally *house,* and so frequently throughout this book　　6:1 ᵃFollowing Masoretic Text, Targum, and Vulgate; Septuagint reads *fortieth.*
6:3 ᵃHebrew *heykal;* here the main room of the temple, elsewhere called the holy place (compare Exodus 26:33 and Ezekiel 41:1)　　ᵇLiterally *it*
6:5 ᵃHebrew *debir;* here the inner room of the temple, elsewhere called the Most Holy Place (compare verse 16)　　6:8 ᵃFollowing Masoretic Text and Vulgate; Septuagint reads *upper story;* Targum reads *ground story.*

FOUNDING SOLOMON'S TEMPLE (1 Kin. 6:1)

According to 1 Kings, the construction of the Jerusalem temple began in the 4th year of Solomon's reign. The Jewish historian Josephus (A.D. 37–100) lived long after Solomon, but wrote in his work titled *Against Apion* concerning the date of the temple's foundation.

Josephus's accounts of Hiram, king of Tyre, provide information that could be instrumental in approximating a date for the building of the temple, as well as for Solomon's own rule. Josephus quotes from a lost work of the historian Menander of Ephesus, who provided a list of Tyrian kings.

Scholars do debate whether Josephus's chronological information is reliable. In addition to the list of kings, Menander wrote that the time from Hiram's coronation as king to the founding of the north African city of Carthage was 155 years and 8 months. Josephus also tells us, via Menander, that the temple of Jerusalem was built in Hiram's 12th year. Unfortunately, Josephus's own calculations do not add to his totals.

We cannot obtain a precise date for Solomon's 4th year from Josephus's information. Scholars do not agree on when Carthage was founded: some say 825 B.C.; others say 814 B.C. Combining Josephus's calculations would date Solomon's temple building in either 968 or 957 B.C. In the absence of absolute chronological data, Solomon's 4th year is usually estimated to have been about 966 B.C.

---

was forty cubits *long.* ¹⁸The inside of the temple was cedar, carved with ornamental buds and open flowers. All *was* cedar; there was no stone *to be* seen.

¹⁹And he prepared the inner sanctuary inside the temple, to set the ark of the covenant of the LORD there. ²⁰The inner sanctuary *was* twenty cubits long, twenty cubits wide, and twenty cubits high. He overlaid it with pure gold, and overlaid the altar of cedar. ²¹So Solomon overlaid the inside of the temple with pure gold. He stretched gold chains across the front of the inner sanctuary, and overlaid it with gold. ²²The whole temple he overlaid with gold, until he had finished all the temple; also he overlaid with gold the entire altar that *was* by the inner sanctuary.

²³Inside the inner sanctuary he made two cherubim *of* olive wood, *each* ten cubits high. ²⁴One wing of the cherub *was* five cubits, and the other wing of the cherub five cubits: ten cubits from the tip of one wing to the tip of the other. ²⁵And the other cherub *was* ten cubits; both cherubim *were*

of the same size and shape. ²⁶The height of one cherub *was* ten cubits, and so *was* the other cherub. ²⁷Then he set the cherubim inside the inner room;ᵃ and they stretched out the wings of the cherubim so that the wing of the one touched *one* wall, and the wing of the other cherub touched the other wall. And their wings touched each other in the middle of the room. ²⁸Also he overlaid the cherubim with gold.

²⁹Then he carved all the walls of the temple all around, both the inner and outer *sanctuaries,* with carved figures of cherubim, palm trees, and open flowers. ³⁰And the floor of the temple he overlaid with gold, both the inner and outer *sanctuaries.*

³¹For the entrance of the inner sanctuary he made doors *of* olive wood; the lintel *and* doorposts *were* one-fifth *of the wall.* ³²The two doors *were of* olive wood; and he carved on them figures of cherubim, palm trees, and open flowers, and overlaid *them*

6:27 ᵃLiterally *house*

ARCHITECTURE AND BUILDING

A cherub is a supernatural creature that was represented in the decor of Solomon's temple (1 Kin. 6:23). Its wings are mentioned often. The visions of Ezekiel (Ezek. 1:5–14; 10:20) suggest that the cherub was part human, part animal, with prominent wings. Figures of this description are familiar from the art of the ancient Middle East.

with gold; and he spread gold on the cherubim and on the palm trees. 33So for the door of the sanctuary he also made doorposts *of* olive wood, one-fourth *of the wall.* 34And the two doors *were of* cypress wood; two panels *comprised* one folding door, and two panels *comprised* the other folding door. 35Then he carved cherubim, palm trees, and open flowers *on them,* and overlaid *them* with gold applied evenly on the carved work.

36And he built the inner court with three rows of hewn stone and a row of cedar beams.

37In the fourth year the foundation of the house of the LORD was laid, in the month of Ziv. 38And in the eleventh year, in the month of Bul, which is the eighth month, the house was finished in all its details and according to all its plans. So he was seven years in building it.

Building the King's Palace

The construction of the temple was a 7-year process, lasting from 966 to 959 B.C. (1 Kin. 6:37, 38). The palace complex, however, took longer to complete because it included several buildings south of the temple. The House of the Forest of Lebanon (1 Kin. 7:2–5) served as a treasury and armory (1 Kin. 10:17, 21; Is. 22:8). Other buildings were the Hall of Pillars (7:6), the Hall of Judgment (7:7), and residences for Solomon and Pharaoh's daughter (7:8).

The account in 1 Kings records the length of time it took Solomon to complete the temple and palace. In addition to the 7 years of temple construction were another 13 years for the palace (1 Kin. 7:1). Thus, these two major projects covered a period of 20 years (966–946 B.C.; see 1 Kin. 9:10).

▪ 1 Kings 7:1—9:14

---

1 Kings
Solomon's Other Buildings

7 :1 But Solomon took thirteen years to build his own house; so he finished all his house.

2He also built the House of the Forest of Lebanon; its length *was* one hundred cubits, its width fifty cubits, and its height thirty cubits, with four rows of cedar pillars, and cedar beams on the pillars. 3And *it was* paneled with cedar above the beams that *were* on forty-five pillars, fifteen *to* a row. 4*There were* windows *with beveled frames in* three rows, and window *was* opposite window *in* three tiers. 5And all the doorways and doorposts *had* rectangular frames; and window *was* opposite window *in* three tiers.

6He also made the Hall of Pillars: its length *was* fifty cubits, and its width thirty cubits; and in front of them *was* a portico with pillars, and a canopy *was* in front of them.

7Then he made a hall for the throne, the Hall of Judgment, where he might judge; and *it was* paneled with cedar from floor to ceiling.[a]

8And the house where he dwelt *had* another court inside the hall, of like workmanship. Solomon also made a house like this hall for Pharaoh's daughter, whom he had taken *as wife.*

9All these *were of* costly stones cut to size, trimmed with saws, inside and out, from the foundation to the eaves, and also on the outside to the great court. 10The foundation *was of* costly stones, large stones, some ten cubits and some eight cubits. 11And above *were* costly stones, hewn to size, and cedar wood. 12The great court *was* enclosed with three rows of hewn stones and a row of cedar beams. So were the inner court of the house of the LORD and the vestibule of the temple.

Huram the Craftsman

13Now King Solomon sent and brought Huram[a] from Tyre. 14He *was* the son of a widow from the tribe of Naphtali, and his father *was* a man of Tyre, a bronze worker; he was filled with wisdom and understanding and skill in working with all kinds of bronze work. So he came to King Solomon and did all his work.

The Bronze Pillars for the Temple

15And he cast two pillars of bronze, each one eighteen cubits high, and a line of twelve cubits measured the circumference of each. 16Then he made two capitals *of* cast bronze, to set on the tops of the pillars. The height of one capital *was* five cubits, and the height of the other capital *was* five cubits. 17*He made* a lattice network, with wreaths of chainwork, for the capitals

---

7:7 aLiterally *floor,* that is, of the upper level
7:13 aHebrew *Hiram* (compare 2 Chronicles 2:13, 14)

THEOLOGY OF PALACE AND TEMPLE DISTRICTS (1 Kin. 7:1–12)

The extensive details about the construction of Solomon's royal residence are similar to the royal districts of capital cities in Syria-Palestine during the first half of the 1st millennium B.C. The site required an impressive palace for the king's family, a reception hall for greeting foreign dignitaries, and a private royal temple (which served also as the central temple of the kingdom).

The capital cities of ancient empires were built both for protection and to impress those who approached them. To this end there were walls around the city and walls around the royal complex within the city itself. Ancient people understood that the deity who had created the kingdom dwelt within the town along with the ruler, who was chosen by the deity. Within the inner wall would be the dual dwellings of the king and the god.

In the theology behind the town structure, the deity and king ruled together and so dwelt together. Should the kingdom be invaded, the nation was not yet defeated as long as the royal complex could be defended. Should the temple be overrun, however, the people understood that the patron deity had turned the land over to the invading peoples and their invading deity.

Since the temple was part of the palace complex, the king could consult the patron deity at any time. The temple itself was usually restricted to the use of the royal family and the royal priesthood, except for holy days when the courts would be opened for public worship. Even then the inner sanctuary of the temple was usually restricted to the higher levels of priests.

A palace complex similar to that which Solomon built in Jerusalem was uncovered intact at Tell Ta'yinat in northern Syria. A large palace building with a reception throne room stood beside a smaller temple with an entryway, a main room, and a most holy place, just like the ground plan of Solomon's temple.

---

which *were* on top of the pillars: seven chains for one capital and seven for the other capital. [18]So he made the pillars, and two rows of pomegranates above the network all around to cover the capitals that *were* on top; and thus he did for the other capital.

[19]The capitals which *were* on top of the pillars in the hall *were* in the shape of lilies, four cubits. [20]The capitals on the two pillars also *had pomegranates* above, by the convex surface which *was* next to the network; and there *were* two hundred such pomegranates in rows on each of the capitals all around.

[21]Then he set up the pillars by the vestibule of the temple; he set up the pillar on the right and called its name Jachin, and he set up the pillar on the left and called its name Boaz. [22]The tops of the pillars were in the shape of lilies. So the work of the pillars was finished.

The Sea and the Oxen

[23]And he made the Sea of cast bronze, ten cubits from one brim to the other; *it was* completely round. Its height *was* five cubits, and a line of thirty cubits measured its circumference.

[24]Below its brim *were* ornamental buds encircling it all around, ten to a cubit, all the way around the Sea. The ornamental buds *were* cast in two rows when it was cast. [25]It stood on twelve oxen: three looking toward the north, three looking toward the west, three looking toward the south, and three looking toward the east; the Sea *was set* upon them, and all their back parts *pointed* inward. [26]It *was* a handbreadth thick; and its brim was shaped like the brim of a cup, *like* a lily blossom. It contained two thousand[a] baths.

The Carts and the Lavers

[27]He also made ten carts of bronze; four cubits *was* the length of each cart, four cubits its width, and three cubits its height. [28]And this *was* the design of the carts: They had panels, and the panels *were* between frames; [29]on the panels that *were* between the frames *were* lions, oxen,

---

7:26 [a]Or *three thousand* (compare 2 Chronicles 4:5)

and cherubim. And on the frames *was* a pedestal on top. Below the lions and oxen *were* wreaths of plaited work. ³⁰Every cart had four bronze wheels and axles of bronze, and its four feet had supports. Under the laver *were* supports of cast *bronze* beside each wreath. ³¹Its opening inside the crown at the top *was* one cubit in diameter; and the opening *was* round, shaped *like* a pedestal, one and a half cubits in outside diameter; and also on the opening *were* engravings, but the panels were square, not round. ³²Under the panels *were* the four wheels, and the axles of the wheels *were joined* to the cart. The height of a wheel *was* one and a half cubits. ³³The workmanship of the wheels *was* like the workmanship of a chariot wheel; their axle pins, their rims, their spokes, and their hubs *were* all of cast *bronze*. ³⁴And *there were* four supports at the four corners of each cart; its supports *were* part of the cart itself. ³⁵On the top of the cart, at the height of half a cubit, *it was* perfectly round. And on the top of the cart, its flanges and its panels *were* of the same casting. ³⁶On the plates of its flanges and on its panels he engraved cherubim, lions, and palm trees, wherever there was a clear space on each, with wreaths all around. ³⁷Thus he made the ten carts. All of them were of the same mold, one measure, *and* one shape.

³⁸Then he made ten lavers of bronze; each laver contained forty baths, *and* each laver *was* four cubits. On each of the ten carts *was* a laver. ³⁹And he put five carts on the right side of the house, and five on the left side of the house. He set the Sea on the right side of the house, toward the southeast.

Furnishings of the Temple

⁴⁰Huramª made the lavers and the shovels and the bowls. So Huram finished doing all the work that he was to do for King Solomon *for* the house of the LORD: ⁴¹the two pillars, the *two* bowl-shaped capitals that *were* on top of the two pillars; the two networks covering the two bowl-shaped capitals which *were* on top of the pillars; ⁴²four hundred pomegranates for the two networks (two rows of pomegranates for each network, to cover the two

bowl-shaped capitals that *were* on top of the pillars); ⁴³the ten carts, and ten lavers on the carts; ⁴⁴one Sea, and twelve oxen under the Sea; ⁴⁵the pots, the shovels, and the bowls.

All these articles which Huramª made for King Solomon *for* the house of the LORD *were of* burnished bronze. ⁴⁶In the plain of Jordan the king had them cast in clay molds, between Succoth and Zaretan. ⁴⁷And Solomon did not weigh all the articles, because *there were* so many; the weight of the bronze was not determined.

⁴⁸Thus Solomon had all the furnishings made for the house of the LORD: the altar of gold, and the table of gold on which *was* the showbread; ⁴⁹the lampstands of pure gold, five on the right *side* and five on the left in front of the inner sanctuary, with the flowers and the lamps and the wick-trimmers of gold; ⁵⁰the basins, the trimmers, the bowls, the ladles, and the censers of pure gold; and the hinges of gold, *both* for the doors of the inner room (the Most Holy *Place*) *and* for the doors of the main hall of the temple.

⁵¹So all the work that King Solomon had done for the house of the LORD was finished; and Solomon brought in the things which his father David had dedicated: the silver and the gold and the furnishings. He put them in the treasuries of the house of the LORD.

The Ark Brought into the Temple

8 ¹Now Solomon assembled the elders of Israel and all the heads of the tribes, the chief fathers of the children of Israel, to King Solomon in Jerusalem, that they might bring up the ark of the covenant of the LORD from the City of David, which *is* Zion. ²Therefore all the men of Israel assembled with King Solomon at the feast in the month of Ethanim, which *is* the seventh month. ³So all the elders of Israel came, and the priests took up the ark. ⁴Then they brought up the ark of the LORD, the tabernacle of meeting, and all the holy furnishings that *were* in the tabernacle. The priests and the Levites brought them up. ⁵Also King Solomon, and all the congregation of Israel who were assembled with him, *were* with him before the ark, sacrificing sheep and oxen that could not be counted or numbered for multitude. ⁶Then the priests brought in the ark of the covenant of the LORD to its place, into the inner sanctuary of the temple, to the Most

---

7:40 ªHebrew *Hiram* (compare 2 Chronicles 2:13, 14) 7:45 ªHebrew *Hiram* (compare 2 Chronicles 2:13, 14)

Holy *Place,* under the wings of the cherubim. ⁷For the cherubim spread *their* two wings over the place of the ark, and the cherubim overshadowed the ark and its poles. ⁸The poles extended so that the ends of the poles could be seen from the holy *place,* in front of the inner sanctuary; but they could not be seen from outside. And they are there to this day. ⁹Nothing *was* in the ark except the two tablets of stone which Moses put there at Horeb, when the LORD made *a covenant* with the children of Israel, when they came out of the land of Egypt.

¹⁰And it came to pass, when the priests came out of the holy *place,* that the cloud filled the house of the LORD, ¹¹so that the priests could not continue ministering because of the cloud; for the glory of the LORD filled the house of the LORD.

¹²Then Solomon spoke:

"The LORD said He would dwell in the dark cloud.
¹³ I have surely built You an exalted house,
And a place for You to dwell in forever."

Solomon's Speech at Completion of the Work

¹⁴Then the king turned around and blessed the whole assembly of Israel, while all the assembly of Israel was standing. ¹⁵And he said: "Blessed *be* the LORD God of Israel, who spoke with His mouth to my father David, and with His hand has fulfilled *it,* saying, ¹⁶'Since the day that I brought My people Israel out of Egypt, I have chosen no city from any tribe of Israel *in which* to build a house, that My name might be there; but I chose David to be over My people Israel.' ¹⁷Now it was in the heart of my father David to build a temple[a] for the name of the LORD God of Israel. ¹⁸But the LORD said to my father David, 'Whereas it was in your heart to build a temple for My name, you did well that it was in your heart. ¹⁹Nevertheless you shall not build the temple, but your son who will

come from your body, he shall build the temple for My name.' ²⁰So the LORD has fulfilled His word which He spoke; and I have filled the position of my father David, and sit on the throne of Israel, as the LORD promised; and I have built a temple for the name of the LORD God of Israel. ²¹And there I have made a place for the ark, in which *is* the covenant of the LORD which He made with our fathers, when He brought them out of the land of Egypt."

Solomon's Prayer of Dedication

²²Then Solomon stood before the altar of the LORD in the presence of all the assembly of Israel, and spread out his hands toward heaven; ²³and he said: "LORD God of Israel, *there is* no God in heaven above or on earth below like You, who keep *Your* covenant and mercy with Your servants who walk before You with all their hearts. ²⁴You have kept what You promised Your servant David my father; You have both spoken with Your mouth and fulfilled *it* with Your hand, as *it is* this day. ²⁵Therefore, LORD God of Israel, now keep what You promised Your servant David my father, saying, 'You shall not fail to have a man sit before Me on the throne of Israel, only if your sons take heed to their way, that they walk before Me as you have walked before Me.' ²⁶And now I pray, O God of Israel, let Your word come true, which You have spoken to Your servant David my father.

²⁷"But will God indeed dwell on the earth? Behold, heaven and the heaven of heavens cannot contain You. How much less this temple which I have built! ²⁸Yet regard the prayer of Your servant and his supplication, O LORD my God, and listen to the cry and the prayer which Your servant is praying before You today: ²⁹that Your eyes may be open toward this temple night and day, toward the place of which You said, 'My name shall be there,' that You

---

8:17 ᵃLiterally *house,* and so in verses 18–20

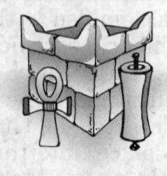

RELIGION AND WORSHIP

The normal position for public prayer was to stand and to stretch out the hands (Ps. 134:2; 1 Tim. 2:8). In this position Solomon prayed (1 Kin. 8:22), though he also kneeled facing the altar before standing to bless the people (1 Kin. 8:54, 55). The position taken for prayer at home or in private could well have been different.

may hear the prayer which Your servant makes toward this place. [30]And may You hear the supplication of Your servant and of Your people Israel, when they pray toward this place. Hear in heaven Your dwelling place; and when You hear, forgive.

[31]"When anyone sins against his neighbor, and is forced to take an oath, and comes *and* takes an oath before Your altar in this temple, [32]then hear in heaven, and act, and judge Your servants, condemning the wicked, bringing his way on his head, and justifying the righteous by giving him according to his righteousness.

[33]"When Your people Israel are defeated before an enemy because they have sinned against You, and when they turn back to You and confess Your name, and pray and make supplication to You in this temple, [34]then hear in heaven, and forgive the sin of Your people Israel, and bring them back to the land which You gave to their fathers.

[35]"When the heavens are shut up and there is no rain because they have sinned against You, when they pray toward this place and confess Your name, and turn from their sin because You afflict them, [36]then hear in heaven, and forgive the sin of Your servants, Your people Israel, that You may teach them the good way in which they should walk; and send rain on Your land which You have given to Your people as an inheritance.

[37]"When there is famine in the land, pestilence *or* blight *or* mildew, locusts *or* grasshoppers; when their enemy besieges them in the land of their cities; whatever plague or whatever sickness *there is;* [38]whatever prayer, whatever supplication is made by anyone, *or* by all Your people Israel, when each one knows the plague of his own heart, and spreads out his hands toward this temple: [39]then hear in heaven Your dwelling place, and forgive, and act, and give to everyone according to all his ways, whose heart You know (for You alone know the hearts of all the sons of men), [40]that they may fear You all the days that they live in the land which You gave to our fathers.

[41]"Moreover, concerning a foreigner, who *is* not of Your people Israel, but has come from a far country for Your name's sake [42](for they will hear of Your great name and Your strong hand and Your outstretched arm), when he comes and prays toward this temple, [43]hear in heaven Your dwelling place, and do according to all for which the foreigner calls to You, that all peoples of the earth may know Your name and fear You, as *do* Your people Israel, and that they may know that this temple which I have built is called by Your name.

[44]"When Your people go out to battle against their enemy, wherever You send them, and when they pray to the LORD toward the city which You have chosen and the temple which I have built for Your name, [45]then hear in heaven their prayer and their supplication, and maintain their cause.

[46]"When they sin against You (for *there is* no one who does not sin), and You become angry with them and deliver them to the enemy, and they take them captive to the land of the enemy, far or near; [47]*yet* when they come to themselves in the land where they were carried captive, and repent, and make supplication to You in the land of those who took them captive, saying, 'We have sinned and done wrong, we have committed wickedness'; [48]and *when* they return to You with all their heart and with all their soul in the land of their enemies who led them away captive, and pray to You toward their land which You gave to their fathers, the city which You have chosen and the temple which I have built for Your name: [49]then hear in heaven Your dwelling place their prayer and their supplication, and maintain their cause, [50]and forgive Your people who have sinned against You, and all their transgressions which they have transgressed against You; and grant them compassion before those who took them captive, that they may have compassion on them [51](for they *are* Your people and Your inheritance, whom You brought out of Egypt, out of the iron furnace), [52]that Your eyes may be open to the supplication of Your servant and the supplication of Your people Israel, to listen to them whenever they call to You. [53]For You separated them from among all the peoples of the earth *to be* Your inheritance, as You spoke by Your servant Moses, when You brought our fathers out of Egypt, O Lord GOD."

Solomon Blesses the Assembly

[54]And so it was, when Solomon had finished praying all this prayer and supplication to the LORD, that he arose from before the altar of the LORD, from kneeling on his knees with his hands spread up to heaven.

55Then he stood and blessed all the assembly of Israel with a loud voice, saying: 56"Blessed *be* the LORD, who has given rest to His people Israel, according to all that He promised. There has not failed one word of all His good promise, which He promised through His servant Moses. 57May the LORD our God be with us, as He was with our fathers. May He not leave us nor forsake us, 58that He may incline our hearts to Himself, to walk in all His ways, and to keep His commandments and His statutes and His judgments, which He commanded our fathers. 59And may these words of mine, with which I have made supplication before the LORD, be near the LORD our God day and night, that He may maintain the cause of His servant and the cause of His people Israel, as each day may require, 60that all the peoples of the earth may know that the LORD *is* God; *there is* no other. 61Let your heart therefore be loyal to the LORD our God, to walk in His statutes and keep His commandments, as at this day."

Solomon Dedicates the Temple

62Then the king and all Israel with him offered sacrifices before the LORD. 63And Solomon offered a sacrifice of peace offerings, which he offered to the LORD, twenty-two thousand bulls and one hundred and twenty thousand sheep. So the king and all the children of Israel dedicated the house of the LORD. 64On the same day the king consecrated the middle of the court that *was* in front of the house of the LORD; for there he offered burnt offerings, grain offerings, and the fat of the peace offerings, because the bronze altar that *was* before the LORD *was* too small to receive the burnt offerings, the grain offerings, and the fat of the peace offerings.

65At that time Solomon held a feast, and all Israel with him, a great assembly from the entrance of Hamath to the Brook of Egypt, before the LORD our God, seven days and seven *more* days—fourteen days. 66On the eighth day he sent the people away; and they blessed the king, and went to their tents joyful and glad of heart for all the good that the LORD had done for His servant David, and for Israel His people.

God's Second Appearance to Solomon

9 1And it came to pass, when Solomon had finished building the house of the LORD and the king's house, and all Solomon's desire which he wanted to do, 2that the LORD appeared to Solomon the second time, as He had appeared to him at Gibeon. 3And the LORD said to him: "I have heard your prayer and your supplication that you have made before Me; I have consecrated this house which you have built to put My name there forever, and My eyes and My heart will be there perpetually. 4Now if you walk before Me as your father David walked, in integrity of heart and in uprightness, to do according to all that I have commanded you, *and* if you keep My statutes and My judgments, 5then I will establish the throne of your kingdom over Israel forever, as I promised David your father, saying, 'You shall not fail to have a man on the throne of Israel.' 6But if you or your sons at all turn from following Me, and do not keep My commandments *and* My statutes which I have set before you, but go and serve other gods and worship them, 7then I will cut off Israel from the land which I have given them; and this house which I have consecrated for My name I will cast out of My sight. Israel will be a proverb and a byword among all peoples. 8And *as for* this house, *which* is exalted, everyone who passes by it will be astonished and will hiss, and say, 'Why has the LORD done thus to this land and to this house?' 9Then they will answer, 'Because they forsook the LORD their God, who brought their fathers out of the land of Egypt, and have embraced other gods, and worshiped them and served them; therefore the LORD has brought all this calamity on them.' "

Solomon and Hiram Exchange Gifts

10Now it happened at the end of twenty years, when Solomon had built the two houses, the house of the LORD and the king's house 11(Hiram the king of Tyre had supplied Solomon with cedar and cypress and gold, as much as he desired), *that* King Solomon then gave Hiram twenty cities in the land of Galilee. 12Then Hiram went from Tyre to see the cities which Solomon had given him, but they did not please him. 13So he said, "What *kind of* cities *are* these which you have given me, my brother?" And he called them the land of Cabul,a as they are to this day. 14Then Hiram sent the king one hundred and twenty talents of gold.

9:13 aLiterally *Good for Nothing*

SOLOMON AND HIS ARCHITECTURE (1 Kin. 9:15)

Three cities that were rebuilt by Solomon—Hazor, Megiddo, Gezer—provide one of the most striking correlations between archaeology and the Bible (1 Kin. 9:15). At each of these cities, archaeologists have dug down to layers that are assigned to Solomon's time period. They have uncovered a striking similarity in the fortifications that these cities had at that time.

Hazor, Megiddo, and Gezer all had nearly identical six-chambered gates. The chambers were part of a gate complex and part of a larger tower structure. They were constructed by building four parallel piers on each side of the entranceway. These piers were connected and made into rooms by an outside wall on each set of piers. There were, then, three rooms on each side, with an aisle down the middle.

Wooden gates were placed between the piers, which meant that the entire gate complex had four separate gates. The multiple gates, and chambers behind each gate, assured a difficult access for those trying to take the city by force.

At both Hazor and Gezer, a casemate wall was connected to the unique gateways. Casemate walls were two closely parallel walls which were subdivided into rooms. While these walls were rather narrow and not very thick, dirt from within the city could be quickly placed between the walls, transforming the two walls into one thick, strong wall. The architectural similarities found at Hazor, Megiddo, and Gezer suggest that six-chambered gates and casemate walls were characteristic of Solomon's building strategy.

Solomon's Other Accomplishments

Solomon's most important building project was the Jerusalem temple, but he had other projects that were similarly impressive. Excavations in Palestine have uncovered several fortified cities that Solomon built along Israel's borders.

▼ ■ 1 Kings 9:15—10:29

1 Kings

9 **:15** And this *is* the reason for the labor force which King Solomon raised: to build the house of the LORD, his own house, the Millo,[a] the wall of Jerusalem, Hazor, Megiddo, and Gezer. 16(Pharaoh king of Egypt had gone up and taken Gezer and burned it with fire, had killed the Canaanites who dwelt in the city, and had given it *as* a dowry to his daughter, Solomon's wife.) 17And Solomon built Gezer, Lower Beth Horon, 18Baalath, and Tadmor in the wilderness, in the land *of Judah,* 19all the storage cities that Solomon had, cities for his chariots and cities for his cavalry, and whatever Solomon desired to build in Jerusalem, in Lebanon, and in all the land of his dominion.

20All the people *who were* left of the Amorites, Hittites, Perizzites, Hivites, and Jebusites, who *were* not of the children of Israel— 21that is, their descendants who were left in the land after them, whom the children of Israel had not been able to destroy completely—from these Solomon raised forced labor, as it is to this day. 22But of the children of Israel Solomon made no forced laborers, because they *were* men of war and his servants: his officers, his captains, commanders of his chariots, and his cavalry.

23Others *were* chiefs of the officials who *were* over Solomon's work: five hundred and fifty, who ruled over the people who did the work.

24But Pharaoh's daughter came up from the City of David to her house which *Solomon*[a] had built for her. Then he built the Millo.

25Now three times a year Solomon offered burnt offerings and peace offerings on the altar which he had built for the LORD, and he burned incense with them *on the altar* that *was* before the LORD. So he finished the temple.

26King Solomon also built a fleet of ships at Ezion Geber, which *is* near Elath[a]

9:15 [a]Literally *The Landfill*   9:24 [a]Literally *he*
(compare 2 Chronicles 8:11)   9:26 [a]Hebrew *Eloth*
(compare 2 Kings 14:22)

on the shore of the Red Sea, in the land of Edom. ²⁷Then Hiram sent his servants with the fleet, seamen who knew the sea, to work with the servants of Solomon. ²⁸And they went to Ophir, and acquired four hundred and twenty talents of gold from there, and brought *it* to King Solomon.

The Queen of Sheba's Praise of Solomon

10 ¹Now when the queen of Sheba heard of the fame of Solomon concerning the name of the LORD, she came to test him with hard questions. ²She came to Jerusalem with a very great retinue, with camels that bore spices, very much gold, and precious stones; and when she came to Solomon, she spoke with him about all that was in her heart. ³So Solomon answered all her questions; there was nothing so difficult for the king that he could not explain *it* to her. ⁴And when the queen of Sheba had seen all the wisdom of Solomon, the house that he had built, ⁵the food on his table, the seating of his servants, the service of his waiters and their apparel, his cupbearers, and his entryway by which he went up to the house of the LORD, there was no more spirit in her. ⁶Then she said to the king: "It was a true report which I heard in my own land about your words and your wisdom. ⁷However I did not believe the words until I came and saw with my own eyes; and indeed the half was not told me. Your wisdom and prosperity exceed the fame of which I heard. ⁸Happy *are* your men and happy *are* these your servants, who stand continually before you *and* hear your wisdom! ⁹Blessed be the LORD your God, who delighted in you, setting you on the throne of Israel! Because the LORD has loved Israel forever, therefore He made you king, to do justice and righteousness."

¹⁰Then she gave the king one hundred and twenty talents of gold, spices in great quantity, and precious stones. There never again came such abundance of spices as the queen of Sheba gave to King Solomon. ¹¹Also, the ships of Hiram, which brought gold from Ophir, brought great *quantities* of almugᵃ wood and precious stones from Ophir. ¹²And the king made steps of the almug wood for the house of the LORD and for the king's house, also harps and stringed instruments for singers. There never again came such almug wood, nor has the like been seen to this day.

¹³Now King Solomon gave the queen of Sheba all she desired, whatever she asked, besides what Solomon had given her according to the royal generosity. So she turned and went to her own country, she and her servants.

Solomon's Great Wealth

¹⁴The weight of gold that came to Solomon yearly was six hundred and sixty-six talents of gold, ¹⁵besides *that* from the traveling merchants, from the income of traders, from all the kings of Arabia, and from the governors of the country.

¹⁶And King Solomon made two hundred large shields *of* hammered gold; six hundred *shekels* of gold went into each shield. ¹⁷He also *made* three hundred shields *of* hammered gold; three minas of gold went into each shield. The king put them in the House of the Forest of Lebanon.

¹⁸Moreover the king made a great throne of ivory, and overlaid it with pure gold. ¹⁹The throne had six steps, and the top of the throne *was* round at the back; *there were* armrests on either side of the place of the seat, and two lions stood beside the armrests. ²⁰Twelve lions stood there, one on each side of the six steps; nothing like *this* had been made for any *other* kingdom.

²¹All King Solomon's drinking vessels *were* gold, and all the vessels of the House of the Forest of Lebanon *were* pure gold.

10:11 ᵃOr *algum* (compare 2 Chronicles 9:10, 11)

TRADE AND ECONOMICS

A throne is the symbolic point from which a kingdom is ruled, and its magnificent construction indicates the greatness of that kingdom. Ivory was imported, and Solomon's use of it shows his power to buy material from distant places (see 1 Kin. 10:22; Prov. 31:14). The lion figures around the throne also demonstrate the wealth of Solomon's kingdom (1 Kin. 10:19, 20).

Not *one was* silver, for this was accounted as nothing in the days of Solomon. 22For the king had merchant ships[a] at sea with the fleet of Hiram. Once every three years the merchant ships came bringing gold, silver, ivory, apes, and monkeys.[b] 23So King Solomon surpassed all the kings of the earth in riches and wisdom.

24Now all the earth sought the presence of Solomon to hear his wisdom, which God had put in his heart. 25Each man brought his present: articles of silver and gold, garments, armor, spices, horses, and mules, at a set rate year by year.

26And Solomon gathered chariots and horsemen; he had one thousand four hundred chariots and twelve thousand horsemen, whom he stationed[a] in the chariot cities and with the king at Jerusalem. 27The king made silver *as common* in Jerusalem as stones, and he made cedar trees as abundant as the sycamores which *are* in the lowland.

28Also Solomon had horses imported from Egypt and Keveh; the king's merchants bought them in Keveh at the *current* price. 29Now a chariot that was imported from Egypt cost six hundred *shekels* of silver, and a horse one hundred and fifty; and thus, through their agents,[a] they exported *them* to all the kings of the Hittites and the kings of Syria.

10:22 [a]Literally *ships of Tarshish*, deep-sea vessels
[b]Or *peacocks*　　　10:26 [a]Following Septuagint,
Syriac, Targum, and Vulgate (compare
2 Chronicles 9:25); Masoretic Text reads *led.*
10:29 [a]Literally *by their hands*　　　**Eccl.** 1:2 [a]Or
Absurdity, Frustration, Futility, Nonsense; and so
throughout this book

The Book of Ecclesiastes

No book in the Bible is more surprising than this one. In its secular worldview, its purely philosophical approach to reality, and especially its thoroughgoing pessimism, it is unlike any other biblical text. To be sure, it concludes with an orthodox statement of faith (Eccl. 12:13, 14), but this glimmer of faith follows chapter upon chapter of anguished doubt.

Perhaps equally surprising is the book's attribution to Solomon. Though Solomon's name is not mentioned, the author calls himself "the Preacher, the son of David, king in Jerusalem" (1:1; see 1:12). Because of this identification, and even more because of Solomon's traditional position as the master

sage and model wise man, some scholars suggest that the Preacher's words are indeed Solomon's. Other scholars, however, note that except for the references to the Preacher's wisdom and wealth (2:4–9), the book hardly fits the Bible's portrait of Solomon. This fact, along with the late style and grammar used in the book, suggests to them that someone else wrote the book, assuming the role of Solomon.

Whether Solomon or another writer, the author who appears in the pages of the book itself is above all a teacher. The Hebrew word for "Preacher," *Qoheleth,* means "one who leads an assembly." The Book of Ecclesiastes consists of the words of this preacher (12:9, 10). He diligently produced many proverbs (12:9) and other words of truth (12:10), so that the people might be admonished. He was a wise man, a teacher, a skilled writer, a seeker of truth, and an exhorter of his flock (12:11, 12).

Regardless of whether Solomon wrote the original, the book can be read in light of Solomon's greatness. Read in this way, Ecclesiastes offers a striking contrast between Solomon at the peak of his power and worldly success and this bleak and weary book. The writer's thesis is "Vanity of vanities, all is vanity" (1:2). There are inexplicable mysteries about life which defy easy solutions. Human wisdom is only partial; it cannot fathom the mysteries of God's creation. Only at the end, almost as an afterthought, does the Preacher appear to make his peace with his world and his God (12:13).

▼

■ Ecclesiastes 1:1—12:14

Ecclesiastes
The Vanity of Life

1 :1 The words of the Preacher, the son of David, king in Jerusalem.

2　"Vanity[a] of vanities," says the
　　　Preacher;
　　"Vanity of vanities, all *is* vanity."

3　What profit has a man from all his
　　　labor
　　In which he toils under the sun?
4　*One* generation passes away, and
　　　another generation comes;
　　But the earth abides forever.
5　The sun also rises, and the sun goes
　　　down,
　　And hastens to the place where it
　　　arose.

6   The wind goes toward the south,
    And turns around to the north;
    The wind whirls about continually,
    And comes again on its circuit.
7   All the rivers run into the sea,
    Yet the sea *is* not full;
    To the place from which the rivers
        come,
    There they return again.
8   All things *are* full of labor;
    Man cannot express *it.*
    The eye is not satisfied with seeing,
    Nor the ear filled with hearing.

9   That which has been *is* what will be,
    That which *is* done is what will be
        done,
    And *there is* nothing new under the
        sun.
10 Is there anything of which it may be
        said,
    "See, this *is* new"?
    It has already been in ancient times
        before us.
11 *There is* no remembrance of former
        things,
    Nor will there be any remembrance of
        things that are to come
    By *those* who will come after.

The Grief of Wisdom

12I, the Preacher, was king over Israel
in Jerusalem. 13And I set my heart to seek
and search out by wisdom concerning all
that is done under heaven; this burdensome task God has given to the sons of
man, by which they may be exercised. 14I
have seen all the works that are done under the sun; and indeed, all *is* vanity and
grasping for the wind.

15 *What is* crooked cannot be made
        straight,
    And what is lacking cannot be
        numbered.

16I communed with my heart, saying,
"Look, I have attained greatness, and have
gained more wisdom than all who were before me in Jerusalem. My heart has understood great wisdom and knowledge." 17And
I set my heart to know wisdom and to
know madness and folly. I perceived that
this also is grasping for the wind.

18 For in much wisdom *is* much grief,
    And he who increases knowledge
        increases sorrow.

The Vanity of Pleasure

2 1I said in my heart, "Come now, I will
    test you with mirth; therefore enjoy
pleasure"; but surely, this also *was* vanity.
2I said of laughter—"Madness!"; and of
mirth, "What does it accomplish?" 3I
searched in my heart *how* to gratify my
flesh with wine, while guiding my heart
with wisdom, and how to lay hold on folly,
till I might see what *was* good for the sons
of men to do under heaven all the days of
their lives.

4I made my works great, I built myself
houses, and planted myself vineyards. 5I
made myself gardens and orchards, and I
planted all *kinds* of fruit trees in them.
6I made myself water pools from which to
water the growing trees of the grove. 7I acquired male and female servants, and had
servants born in my house. Yes, I had
greater possessions of herds and flocks
than all who were in Jerusalem before me.
8I also gathered for myself silver and gold
and the special treasures of kings and of
the provinces. I acquired male and female
singers, the delights of the sons of men,
and musical instruments[a] of all kinds.

9So I became great and excelled more
than all who were before me in Jerusalem.
Also my wisdom remained with me.

10 Whatever my eyes desired I did not
        keep from them.
    I did not withhold my heart from any
        pleasure,
    For my heart rejoiced in all my labor;

2:8 [a]Exact meaning unknown

PLANTS AND ANIMALS

*The kings of the ancient Near East, like the pharaohs of Egypt, placed great importance
on their gardens (Eccl. 2:5). The "king's garden" (2 Kin. 25:4) was probably part of the
royal residence. The tradition of royal gardens has been continued especially by the
Arabs. A famous example is the Alhambra in Spain, with its courtyards and fountains,
built in the 13th century* A.D.

And this was my reward from all my labor.

11 Then I looked on all the works that my hands had done
And on the labor in which I had toiled;
And indeed all *was* vanity and grasping for the wind.
There was no profit under the sun.

The End of the Wise and the Fool

12 Then I turned myself to consider wisdom and madness and folly;
For what *can* the man *do* who succeeds the king?—
Only what he has already done.

13 Then I saw that wisdom excels folly
As light excels darkness.

14 The wise man's eyes *are* in his head,
But the fool walks in darkness.
Yet I myself perceived
That the same event happens to them all.

15 So I said in my heart,
"As it happens to the fool,
It also happens to me,
And why was I then more wise?"
Then I said in my heart,
"This also *is* vanity."

16 For *there is* no more remembrance of the wise than of the fool forever,
Since all that now *is* will be forgotten in the days to come.
And how does a wise *man* die?
As the fool!

17Therefore I hated life because the work that was done under the sun *was* distressing to me, for all *is* vanity and grasping for the wind. 18Then I hated all my labor in which I had toiled under the sun, because I must leave it to the man who will come after me. 19And who knows whether he will be wise or a fool? Yet he will rule over all my labor in which I toiled and in which I have shown myself wise under the sun. This also *is* vanity. 20Therefore I turned my heart and despaired of all the labor in which I had toiled under the sun. 21For there is a man whose labor *is* with wisdom, knowledge, and skill; yet he must leave his heritage to a man who has not labored for it. This also *is* vanity and a great evil. 22For

what has man for all his labor, and for the striving of his heart with which he has toiled under the sun? 23For all his days *are* sorrowful, and his work burdensome; even in the night his heart takes no rest. This also is vanity.

24Nothing *is* better for a man *than* that he should eat and drink, and *that* his soul should enjoy good in his labor. This also, I saw, was from the hand of God. 25For who can eat, or who can have enjoyment, more than I?[a] 26For *God* gives wisdom and knowledge and joy to a man who *is* good in His sight; but to the sinner He gives the work of gathering and collecting, that he may give to *him who is* good before God. This also *is* vanity and grasping for the wind.

Everything Has Its Time

3 1 To everything *there is* a season,
A time for every purpose under heaven:

2 A time to be born,
And a time to die;
A time to plant,
And a time to pluck *what is* planted;

3 A time to kill,
And a time to heal;
A time to break down,
And a time to build up;

4 A time to weep,
And a time to laugh;
A time to mourn,
And a time to dance;

5 A time to cast away stones,
And a time to gather stones;
A time to embrace,
And a time to refrain from embracing;

6 A time to gain,
And a time to lose;
A time to keep,
And a time to throw away;

7 A time to tear,
And a time to sew;
A time to keep silence,
And a time to speak;

8 A time to love,
And a time to hate;
A time of war,
And a time of peace.

The God-Given Task

9What profit has the worker from that in which he labors? 10I have seen the God-given task with which the sons of men are

---

2:25 aFollowing Masoretic Text, Targum, and Vulgate; some Hebrew manuscripts, Septuagint, and Syriac read *without Him.*

to be occupied. [11]He has made everything beautiful in its time. Also He has put eternity in their hearts, except that no one can find out the work that God does from beginning to end.

[12]I know that nothing *is* better for them than to rejoice, and to do good in their lives, [13]and also that every man should eat and drink and enjoy the good of all his labor—it *is* the gift of God.

14   I know that whatever God does,
     It shall be forever.
     Nothing can be added to it,
     And nothing taken from it.
     God does *it,* that men should fear
       before Him.
15   That which is has already been,
     And what is to be has already been;
     And God requires an account of what
       is past.

Injustice Seems to Prevail

[16]Moreover I saw under the sun:

   In the place of judgment,
   Wickedness *was* there;
   And *in* the place of righteousness,
   Iniquity *was* there.

[17]I said in my heart,

   "God shall judge the righteous and the
     wicked,
   For *there is* a time there for every
     purpose and for every work."

[18]I said in my heart, "Concerning the condition of the sons of men, God tests them, that they may see that they themselves are *like* animals." [19]For what happens to the sons of men also happens to animals; one thing befalls them: as one dies, so dies the other. Surely, they all have one breath; man has no advantage over animals, for all *is* vanity. [20]All go to one place: all are from the dust, and all return to dust. [21]Who knows the spirit of the sons of men, which goes upward, and the spirit of the animal, which goes down to the earth?[a] [22]So I perceived that nothing *is* better than that a man should rejoice in his own works, for that *is* his heritage. For who can bring him to see what will happen after him?

4 [1]Then I returned and considered all the oppression that is done under the sun:

   And look! The tears of the oppressed,
   But they have no comforter—
   On the side of their oppressors *there is*
     power,
   But they have no comforter.
2   Therefore I praised the dead who were
     already dead,
   More than the living who are still
     alive.
3   Yet, better than both *is he* who has
     never existed,
   Who has not seen the evil work that is
     done under the sun.

The Vanity of Selfish Toil

[4]Again, I saw that for all toil and every skillful work a man is envied by his neighbor. This also *is* vanity and grasping for the wind.

5   The fool folds his hands
     And consumes his own flesh.
6   Better a handful *with* quietness
     Than both hands full, *together with*
     toil and grasping for the wind.

[7]Then I returned, and I saw vanity under the sun:

8   There is one alone, without
     companion:
   He has neither son nor brother.
   Yet *there is* no end to all his labors,
   Nor is his eye satisfied with riches.
   But he never asks,
   "For whom do I toil and deprive myself
     of good?"
   This also *is* vanity and a grave
     misfortune.

The Value of a Friend

9   Two *are* better than one,
     Because they have a good reward for
     their labor.
10   For if they fall, one will lift up his
     companion.
   But woe to him *who is* alone when he
     falls,
   For *he has* no one to help him up.
11   Again, if two lie down together, they
     will keep warm;
   But how can one be warm *alone?*
12   Though one may be overpowered by
     another, two can withstand him.

3:21 [a]Septuagint, Syriac, Targum, and Vulgate read *Who knows whether the spirit . . . goes upward, and whether . . . goes downward to the earth?*

And a threefold cord is not quickly
broken.

Popularity Passes Away

13 Better a poor and wise youth
Than an old and foolish king who will
be admonished no more.
14 For he comes out of prison to be king,
Although he was born poor in his
kingdom.
15 I saw all the living who walk under
the sun;
They were with the second youth who
stands in his place.
16 *There was* no end of all the people
over whom he was made king;
Yet those who come afterward will not
rejoice in him.
Surely this also *is* vanity and grasping
for the wind.

Fear God, Keep Your Vows

5 ¹Walk prudently when you go to the
house of God; and draw near to hear
rather than to give the sacrifice of fools, for
they do not know that they do evil.

2 Do not be rash with your mouth,
And let not your heart utter anything
hastily before God.
For God *is* in heaven, and you on
earth;
Therefore let your words be few.
3 For a dream comes through much
activity,
And a fool's voice *is known* by *his*
many words.

4 When you make a vow to God, do not
delay to pay it;
For *He has* no pleasure in fools.
Pay what you have vowed—
5 Better not to vow than to vow and not
pay.

⁶Do not let your mouth cause your flesh to
sin, nor say before the messenger *of God*
that it *was* an error. Why should God be
angry at your excuseᵃ and destroy the work
of your hands? ⁷For in the multitude of
dreams and many words *there is* also vanity. But fear God.

The Vanity of Gain and Honor

⁸If you see the oppression of the poor,
and the violent perversion of justice and

righteousness in a province, do not marvel
at the matter; for high official watches over
high official, and higher officials are over
them.
⁹Moreover the profit of the land is for
all; *even* the king is served from the field.

10 He who loves silver will not be
satisfied with silver;
Nor he who loves abundance, with
increase.
This also *is* vanity.

11 When goods increase,
They increase who eat them;
So what profit have the owners
Except to see *them* with their eyes?

12 The sleep of a laboring man *is* sweet,
Whether he eats little or much;
But the abundance of the rich will not
permit him to sleep.

13 There is a severe evil *which* I have
seen under the sun:
Riches kept for their owner to his
hurt.
14 But those riches perish through
misfortune;
When he begets a son, *there is* nothing
in his hand.
15 As he came from his mother's womb,
naked shall he return,
To go as he came;
And he shall take nothing from his
labor
Which he may carry away in his hand.

16 And this also *is* a severe evil—
Just exactly as he came, so shall he
go.
And what profit has he who has
labored for the wind?
17 All his days he also eats in darkness,
And *he has* much sorrow and sickness
and anger.

¹⁸Here is what I have seen: *It is* good
and fitting *for one* to eat and drink, and to
enjoy the good of all his labor in which he
toils under the sun all the days of his life
which God gives him; for it *is* his heritage.
¹⁹As for every man to whom God has given
riches and wealth, and given him power to
eat of it, to receive his heritage and rejoice
in his labor—this *is* the gift of God. ²⁰For
he will not dwell unduly on the days of his

5:6 ᵃLiterally *voice*

life, because God keeps *him* busy with the joy of his heart.

6 ¹There is an evil which I have seen under the sun, and it *is* common among men: ²A man to whom God has given riches and wealth and honor, so that he lacks nothing for himself of all he desires; yet God does not give him power to eat of it, but a foreigner consumes it. This *is* vanity, and it *is* an evil affliction.

³If a man begets a hundred *children* and lives many years, so that the days of his years are many, but his soul is not satisfied with goodness, or indeed he has no burial, I say *that* a stillborn child *is* better than he— ⁴for it comes in vanity and departs in darkness, and its name is covered with darkness. ⁵Though it has not seen the sun or known *anything,* this has more rest than that man, ⁶even if he lives a thousand years twice—but has not seen goodness. Do not all go to one place?

7 All the labor of man *is* for his mouth,
   And yet the soul is not satisfied.
8 For what more has the wise *man* than
      the fool?
   What does the poor man have,
   Who knows *how* to walk before the
      living?
9 Better *is* the sight of the eyes than the
      wandering of desire.
   This also *is* vanity and grasping for
      the wind.

10 Whatever one is, he has been named
      already,
   For it is known that he *is* man;
   And he cannot contend with Him who
      is mightier than he.
11 Since there are many things that
      increase vanity,
   How *is* man the better?

¹²For who knows what *is* good for man in life, all the days of his vain life which he passes like a shadow? Who can tell a man what will happen after him under the sun?

The Value of Practical Wisdom

7 ¹ A good name *is* better than precious
      ointment,
   And the day of death than the day of
      one's birth;
2 Better to go to the house of mourning
   Than to go to the house of feasting,
   For that *is* the end of all men;
   And the living will take *it* to heart.
3 Sorrow *is* better than laughter,
   For by a sad countenance the heart is
      made better.
4 The heart of the wise *is* in the house
      of mourning,
   But the heart of fools *is* in the house
      of mirth.

5 *It is* better to hear the rebuke of the
      wise
   Than for a man to hear the song of
      fools.
6 For like the crackling of thorns under
      a pot,
   So *is* the laughter of the fool.
   This also is vanity.
7 Surely oppression destroys a wise
      man's reason,
   And a bribe debases the heart.

8 The end of a thing *is* better than its
      beginning;
   The patient in spirit *is* better than the
      proud in spirit.
9 Do not hasten in your spirit to be
      angry,
   For anger rests in the bosom of fools.
10 Do not say,
   "Why were the former days better than
      these?"
   For you do not inquire wisely
      concerning this.

11 Wisdom *is* good with an inheritance,
   And profitable to those who see the
      sun.
12 For wisdom *is* a defense *as* money *is* a
      defense,

CULTURE AND SOCIETY

In several cultures typical of the Mediterranean area, a person's chief goal is to maintain personal honor, their perceived reputation as a person of substance and consequence (Eccl. 7:1). This is achieved mainly through family and social relations and interactions, rather than through learning skills or accumulating wealth.

But the excellence of knowledge *is*
that wisdom gives life to those who
have it.

13 Consider the work of God;
For who can make straight what He
has made crooked?
14 In the day of prosperity be joyful,
But in the day of adversity consider:
Surely God has appointed the one as
well as the other,
So that man can find out nothing *that*
will come after him.

15I have seen everything in my days of
vanity:

There is a just *man* who perishes in
his righteousness,
And there is a wicked *man* who
prolongs *life* in his wickedness.

16 Do not be overly righteous,
Nor be overly wise:
Why should you destroy yourself?
17 Do not be overly wicked,
Nor be foolish:
Why should you die before your time?
18 *It is* good that you grasp this,
And also not remove your hand from
the other;
For he who fears God will escape
them all.

19 Wisdom strengthens the wise
More than ten rulers of the city.

20 For *there is* not a just man on earth
who does good
And does not sin.

21 Also do not take to heart everything
people say,
Lest you hear your servant cursing
you.
22 For many times, also, your own heart
has known
That even you have cursed others.

23 All this I have proved by wisdom.
I said, "I will be wise";
But it *was* far from me.
24 As for that which is far off and
exceedingly deep,
Who can find it out?
25 I applied my heart to know,
To search and seek out wisdom and
the reason *of things,*

To know the wickedness of folly,
Even of foolishness *and* madness.
26 And I find more bitter than death
The woman whose heart *is* snares and
nets,
Whose hands *are* fetters.
He who pleases God shall escape from
her,
But the sinner shall be trapped by
her.

27 "Here is what I have found," says the
Preacher,
"*Adding* one thing to the other to find
out the reason,
28 Which my soul still seeks but I cannot
find:
One man among a thousand I have
found,
But a woman among all these I have
not found.
29 Truly, this only I have found:
That God made man upright,
But they have sought out many
schemes."

8 1 Who *is* like a wise *man?*
And who knows the interpretation
of a thing?
A man's wisdom makes his face shine,
And the sternness of his face is
changed.

Obey Authorities for God's Sake

2I *say,* "Keep the king's commandment
for the sake of your oath to God. 3Do not be
hasty to go from his presence. Do not take
your stand for an evil thing, for he does
whatever pleases him."

4 Where the word of a king *is, there is*
power;
And who may say to him, "What are
you doing?"
5 He who keeps his command will
experience nothing harmful;
And a wise man's heart discerns both
time and judgment,
6 Because for every matter there is a
time and judgment,
Though the misery of man increases
greatly.
7 For he does not know what will
happen;
So who can tell him when it will
occur?
8 No one has power over the spirit to
retain the spirit,

DEATH IS OUR LOT; ENJOY LIFE (Eccl. 8:8)

Ancient people reflected on the inevitability of death. As the Book of Ecclesiastes expresses: "no one has power in the day of death" (Eccl. 8:8). Similar reflections are found in the Gilgamesh Epic, the adventures of Gilgamesh, king of Uruk around 2600 B.C.

The Gilgamesh Epic, composed in Accadian, has been preserved in two major versions, one from late in the Old Babylonian period (1750–1600 B.C.) and a second by Neo-Assyrian scribes (750–612 B.C.). The Neo-Assyrian version contains a scene in which Gilgamesh, in his search for immortality, passes by Siduri, the divine alewife (who is tending her beer stand on the seacoast). Her advice (in the Old Babylonian version) on the futility of his quest is quite similar to the advice of Ecclesiastes: "Live joyfully" (Eccl. 9:9).

Siduri begins by reminding Gilgamesh that it is impossible for humans to find eternal life, which the gods have reserved for themselves. Her advice to Gilgamesh is to eat, make merry, and rejoice in the feasting while he can. She tells him to enjoy the daily rounds of life: wear fresh, clean clothing, bathe himself, play with his children, and enjoy his wife. That is all, she tells him, that is allowed by the gods. Old age and death will overtake everyone. Gilgamesh continued on his search, but found that Siduri's words reflected reality.

The writer of Ecclesiastes offers readers much the same advice: eat and drink with joy, wear clean ("white") garments, attend to your body ("oil on your head"), and enjoy your wife (Eccl. 9:7–9). The passage in the Gilgamesh Epic shows that these ideas of Ecclesiastes were known in the ancient Near East as early as the Israelite and Judean kingdoms. Siduri's speech proves that the idea of resignation to mortality was pondered in the ancient Near East in almost the same terms as it was by the preacher of Ecclesiastes.

And no one has power in the day of
death.
There is no release from that war,
And wickedness will not deliver those
who are given to it.

⁹All this I have seen, and applied my heart to every work that is done under the sun: *There is* a time in which one man rules over another to his own hurt.

Death Comes to All

¹⁰Then I saw the wicked buried, who had come and gone from the place of holiness, and they were forgottenᵃ in the city where they had so done. This also *is* vanity. ¹¹Because the sentence against an evil work is not executed speedily, therefore the heart of the sons of men is fully set in them to do evil. ¹²Though a sinner does evil a hundred *times,* and his *days* are prolonged, yet I surely know that it will be well with those who fear God, who fear before Him. ¹³But it will not be well with the wicked; nor will he prolong *his* days, *which are* as a shadow, because he does not fear before God.

¹⁴There is a vanity which occurs on earth, that there are just *men* to whom it happens according to the work of the wicked; again, there are wicked *men* to whom it happens according to the work of the righteous. I said that this also *is* vanity.

¹⁵So I commended enjoyment, because a man has nothing better under the sun than to eat, drink, and be merry; for this will remain with him in his labor *all* the days of his life which God gives him under the sun.

¹⁶When I applied my heart to know wisdom and to see the business that is done on earth, even though one sees no sleep day or night, ¹⁷then I saw all the work of God, that a man cannot find out the work that is done under the sun. For though a man labors to discover *it,* yet he will not find *it;* moreover, though a wise *man* attempts to know *it,* he will not be able to find *it.*

9 ¹For I considered all this in my heart, so that I could declare it all: that the righteous and the wise and their works *are* in the hand of God. People know neither love nor hatred *by* anything *they see* before them. ²All things *come* alike to all:

8:10 ᵃSome Hebrew manuscripts, Septuagint, and Vulgate read *praised.*

WHAT THE DEAD KNOW (Eccl. 9:5, 10)

Necromancy was the contacting of the dead on behalf of the living. It is found in ancient literature from the Sumerian period (late 3rd millennium B.C.), such as the Mesopotamian story of Gilgamesh and Enkidu in the netherworld. Heroes would make their way to the edge of the land of the dead to speak with those who had passed into the land of Death. Or they consulted a medium who connected them to the spirit to whom they wished to speak. Hebrew wisdom literature, however, presented a different view: "the dead know nothing" (Eccl. 9:5).

The Law of Moses forbade such practices (Deut. 18:11). Nevertheless, a famous case of an Israelite seeking information from the spirits of the dead is that of Saul asking the medium of En Dor to call up the ghost of Samuel. Saul, desperate for information from God, thought he could learn the will of God from the dead Samuel (1 Sam. 28:8–19). Not only did this act violate God's law, but also Saul's own proclamation against necromancy (28:3, 9).

What did the dead know? Sometimes it appears from ancient literature that the dead were expected to know the future or events which were happening at a great distance. Gilgamesh asked Enkidu about the meaning of life and the possibility of avoiding death, but the query was of no avail, only confirming Gilgamesh's mortality. The usual conversation between the living and the dead seems to involve the desire of a living person to learn the fates that relatives and loved ones faced in the afterworld.

The Hebrew scriptures not only prohibited consulting the dead, but said it was futile. The dead have no "knowledge or wisdom" whatsoever (Eccl. 9:10). Samuel's response to Saul revealed both God's will and the future of Saul's family (1 Sam. 28:16–19), but this is unusual. God had departed from Saul (28:15), and whatever the king's experience with necromancy involved was a violation of Israel's religious traditions.

One event *happens* to the righteous
　　and the wicked;
To the good,[a] the clean, and the
　　unclean;
To him who sacrifices and him who
　　does not sacrifice.
As is the good, so *is* the sinner;
He who takes an oath as *he* who fears
　　an oath.

³This *is* an evil in all that is done under the sun: that one thing *happens* to all. Truly the hearts of the sons of men are full of evil; madness *is* in their hearts while they live, and after that *they* go to the dead. ⁴But for him who is joined to all the living there is hope, for a living dog is better than a dead lion.

5　For the living know that they will die;
　　But the dead know nothing,
　　And they have no more reward,
　　For the memory of them is forgotten.
6　Also their love, their hatred, and their
　　envy have now perished;

Nevermore will they have a share
In anything done under the sun.

7　Go, eat your bread with joy,
　　And drink your wine with a merry
　　　heart;
　　For God has already accepted your
　　　works.
8　Let your garments always be white,
　　And let your head lack no oil.

⁹Live joyfully with the wife whom you love all the days of your vain life which He has given you under the sun, all your days of vanity; for that *is* your portion in life, and in the labor which you perform under the sun. ¹⁰Whatever your hand finds to do, do *it* with your might; for *there is* no work or device or knowledge or wisdom in the grave where you are going.

¹¹I returned and saw under the sun that—

The race *is* not to the swift,
Nor the battle to the strong,
Nor bread to the wise,
Nor riches to men of understanding,
Nor favor to men of skill;

9:2 ^aSeptuagint, Syriac, and Vulgate read *good and bad.*

But time and chance happen to them all.

12 For man also does not know his time:
Like fish taken in a cruel net,
Like birds caught in a snare,
So the sons of men *are* snared in an evil time,
When it falls suddenly upon them.

Wisdom Superior to Folly

13 This wisdom I have also seen under the sun, and it *seemed* great to me: 14 *There was* a little city with few men in it; and a great king came against it, besieged it, and built great snares[a] around it. 15 Now there was found in it a poor wise man, and he by his wisdom delivered the city. Yet no one remembered that same poor man. 16 Then I said:

"Wisdom *is* better than strength.
Nevertheless the poor man's wisdom *is* despised,
And his words are not heard.
17 Words of the wise, *spoken* quietly, *should be* heard
Rather than the shout of a ruler of fools.
18 Wisdom *is* better than weapons of war;
But one sinner destroys much good."

10

1 Dead flies putrefy[a] the perfumer's ointment,
And cause it to give off a foul odor;
So does a little folly to one respected for wisdom *and* honor.
2 A wise man's heart *is* at his right hand,
But a fool's heart at his left.
3 Even when a fool walks along the way,
He lacks wisdom,
And he shows everyone *that* he *is* a fool.
4 If the spirit of the ruler rises against you,
Do not leave your post;
For conciliation pacifies great offenses.

5 There is an evil I have seen under the sun,
As an error proceeding from the ruler:
6 Folly is set in great dignity,
While the rich sit in a lowly place.
7 I have seen servants on horses,
While princes walk on the ground like servants.

8 He who digs a pit will fall into it,
And whoever breaks through a wall will be bitten by a serpent.
9 He who quarries stones may be hurt by them,
And he who splits wood may be endangered by it.
10 If the ax is dull,
And one does not sharpen the edge,
Then he must use more strength;
But wisdom brings success.

11 A serpent may bite when *it is* not charmed;
The babbler is no different.
12 The words of a wise man's mouth *are* gracious,
But the lips of a fool shall swallow him up;
13 The words of his mouth begin with foolishness,
And the end of his talk *is* raving madness.
14 A fool also multiplies words.
No man knows what is to be;
Who can tell him what will be after him?
15 The labor of fools wearies them,
For they do not even know how to go to the city!

16 Woe to you, O land, when your king *is* a child,
And your princes feast in the morning!

9:14 [a]Septuagint, Syriac, and Vulgate read *bulwarks.*   10:1 [a]Targum and Vulgate omit *putrefy.*

POLITICS AND GOVERNMENT

Ecclesiastes stresses the wisdom of not talking against the government or the powerful (Eccl. 10:20). In the ancient Near East the king's privilege and power were often without theoretical limit. In Israel the word of Yahweh was supreme, but the prophets sometimes had to risk their lives to proclaim this liberating truth.

17 Blessed *are* you, O land, when your
  king *is* the son of nobles,
  And your princes feast at the proper
    time—
  For strength and not for drunkenness!
18 Because of laziness the building
    decays,
  And through idleness of hands the
    house leaks.
19 A feast is made for laughter,
  And wine makes merry;
  But money answers everything.

20 Do not curse the king, even in your
    thought;
  Do not curse the rich, even in your
    bedroom;
  For a bird of the air may carry your
    voice,
  And a bird in flight may tell the
    matter.

The Value of Diligence

11 ¹ Cast your bread upon the
    waters,
  For you will find it after many days.
2 Give a serving to seven, and also to
    eight,
  For you do not know what evil will be
    on the earth.

3 If the clouds are full of rain,
  They empty *themselves* upon the
    earth;
  And if a tree falls to the south or the
    north,
  In the place where the tree falls, there
    it shall lie.
4 He who observes the wind will not
    sow,
  And he who regards the clouds will
    not reap.

5 As you do not know what *is* the way of
    the wind,[a]
  Or how the bones *grow* in the womb of
    her who is with child,
  So you do not know the works of God
    who makes everything.
6 In the morning sow your seed,
  And in the evening do not withhold
    your hand;
  For you do not know which will
    prosper,

Either this or that,
  Or whether both alike *will be* good.

7 Truly the light is sweet,
  And *it is* pleasant for the eyes to
    behold the sun;
8 But if a man lives many years
  And rejoices in them all,
  Yet let him remember the days of
    darkness,
  For they will be many.
  All that is coming *is* vanity.

Seek God in Early Life

9 Rejoice, O young man, in your youth,
  And let your heart cheer you in the
    days of your youth;
  Walk in the ways of your heart,
  And in the sight of your eyes;
  But know that for all these
  God will bring you into judgment.
10 Therefore remove sorrow from your
    heart,
  And put away evil from your flesh,
  For childhood and youth *are* vanity.

12 ¹ Remember now your Creator in
    the days of your youth,
  Before the difficult days come,
  And the years draw near when you
    say,
  "I have no pleasure in them":
2 While the sun and the light,
  The moon and the stars,
  Are not darkened,
  And the clouds do not return after the
    rain;
3 In the day when the keepers of the
    house tremble,
  And the strong men bow down;
  When the grinders cease because they
    are few,
  And those that look through the
    windows grow dim;
4 When the doors are shut in the
    streets,
  And the sound of grinding is low;
  When one rises up at the sound of a
    bird,
  And all the daughters of music are
    brought low.
5 Also they are afraid of height,
  And of terrors in the way;
  When the almond tree blossoms,
  The grasshopper is a burden,
  And desire fails.

11:5 ªOr *spirit*

SOLOMON WORSHIPS THE GODS OF HIS WIVES (1 Kin. 11:1–8)

Most royal marriages in the ancient world were political. A treaty would be finalized with a wedding, one ruler's child marrying a child of the other ruler. Family ties between kingdoms meant that warfare between them would be a family matter, and thus less likely to happen. Solomon's wives (who numbered 700 according to 1 Kin. 11:3) were all princesses. Apparently Solomon was considered an important international partner by numerous kingdoms within and around his empire.

Each of these women had come from a country that worshiped gods different from the national God of Israel. Each woman would wish to remain true to her own heritage and her own protective deity. They would have worshiped the God of Israel as the ruling god of the land in which they now lived, yet they remained devoted to the gods of their homelands.

Solomon allowed his wives to worship their own deities, but it is not for this that the author of Kings condemns him. Rather, Solomon's desire for his wives was strong, and he himself eventually began to worship the deities his wives worshiped. Even in the theology of the time this would have been unnecessary; Solomon had no tradition or relationship with these foreign gods, as did his wives. Yet, in his old age he shifted from an exclusive monotheism to the worship of many gods. For this he is condemned; it was apostasy from Yahweh, his own God (1 Kin. 11:4).

For man goes to his eternal home,
And the mourners go about the
  streets.

6 *Remember your Creator* before the
  silver cord is loosed,[a]
Or the golden bowl is broken,
Or the pitcher shattered at the
  fountain,
Or the wheel broken at the well.
7 Then the dust will return to the earth
  as it was,
And the spirit will return to God who
  gave it.

8 "Vanity of vanities," says the Preacher,
  "All *is* vanity."

The Whole Duty of Man

9And moreover, because the Preacher was wise, he still taught the people knowledge; yes, he pondered and sought out *and* set in order many proverbs. 10The Preacher sought to find acceptable words; and *what was* written *was* upright—words of truth. 11The words of the wise are like goads, and the words of scholars[a] are like well-driven nails, given by one Shepherd. 12And further, my son, be admonished by these. Of making many books *there is* no end, and much study *is* wearisome to the flesh.

13Let us hear the conclusion of the whole matter:

Fear God and keep His
  commandments,
For this is man's all.
14 For God will bring every work into
  judgment,
Including every secret thing,
Whether good or evil.

12:6 aFollowing Qere and Targum; Kethib reads *removed;* Septuagint and Vulgate read *broken.*   12:11 aLiterally *masters of the assemblies*

Solomon's Political Wives

Much of Solomon's economic success was built on diplomatic alliances. In the ancient world, such alliances were generally sealed with marriage relations, and Solomon's thousand wives and concubines included many women from foreign courts. One of the most important of Solomon's diplomatic wives was an Egyptian princess (1 Kin. 3:1; 7:8; 9:16). She is thought to have been the daughter of Pharaoh Siamun (978–959 B.C.), a ruler of the Egyptian 21st Dynasty.

■ 1 Kings 11:1–8

---

1 Kings

Solomon's Heart Turns from the LORD

11 :1 But King Solomon loved many foreign women, as well as the daughter of Pharaoh: women of the Moabites, Ammonites, Edomites, Sidonians, *and* Hittites— [2]from the nations of whom the LORD had said to the children of Israel, "You shall not intermarry with them, nor they with you. Surely they will turn away your hearts after their gods." Solomon clung to these in love. [3]And he had seven hundred wives, princesses, and three hundred concubines; and his wives turned away his heart. [4]For it was so, when Solomon was old, that his wives turned his heart after other gods; and his heart was not loyal to the LORD his God, as *was* the heart of his father David. [5]For Solomon went after Ashtoreth the goddess of the Sidonians, and after Milcom the abomination of the Ammonites. [6]Solomon did evil in the sight of the LORD, and did not fully follow the LORD, as *did* his father David. [7]Then Solomon built a high place for Chemosh the abomination of Moab, on the hill that *is* east of Jerusalem, and for Molech the abomination of the people of Ammon. [8]And he did likewise for all his foreign wives, who burned incense and sacrificed to their gods.

1:2 [a]A Palestinian young woman (compare 6:13). The speaker and audience are identified according to the number, gender, and person of the Hebrew words. Occasionally the identity is not certain. [b]Masculine singular, that is, the Beloved

The Song of Solomon

This book is an extended dialogue between two lovers (the Shulamite and her beloved), written in sumptuous and often erotic poetry. The speakers are not identified by name in the text, but in the Hebrew it is clear when a speech is addressed to a man and when to a woman. A few other voices chime in: the daughters of Jerusalem (Song 1:5), the beloved's friends (6:13), and the Shulamite's brothers (8:8, 9). Still, most of the speeches come from the two lovers.

Solomon is mentioned by name, not only in the superscription (1:1) but also in the speeches (3:7–11; 8:11, 12). Some suggest that the book is actually a three-person conversation, with Solomon being one of the speakers. This is uncertain, as indeed are most things about this book, where luxurious description overpowers plot and logic. Jews and Christians alike have often interpreted the poem as an allegory of God's love affair with

His people. Many, though, read it literally and accept it as the Bible's blessing on the delights of human love.

The superscription does not necessarily mean that Solomon wrote the book. The Hebrew construction of Song 1:1 is ambiguous and could mean "to Solomon," "for Solomon," or simply "in the manner of Solomon." The other references to Solomon are in the third person, which make it possible that the book is in honor of an "ideal Solomon," and refers to the style in which Solomon may have composed love songs (1 Kin. 4:32).

Regardless of whether the book was authored by Solomon or compiled late, it nevertheless reflects the setting of Solomon's era. The pomp and circumstance described in the book calls to mind Solomon's royal court. His association with the song warrants reading it in light of his relations with women described in 1 Kin. 11:1–8.

■ Song of Solomon 1:1—8:14

Song of Solomon

1 :1 The song of songs, which *is* Solomon's.

The Banquet

THE SHULAMITE[a]

2 Let him kiss me with the kisses of his
    mouth—
For your[b] love *is* better than wine.
3 Because of the fragrance of your good
    ointments,
Your name *is* ointment poured forth;
Therefore the virgins love you.
4 Draw me away!

TIME CAPSULE *969 to 950 B.C.*

969 Hiram becomes king of Tyre (or 980)

966 Solomon begins to build the temple (1 Kin. 6:1)

966– 959 Solomon completes the temple in 7 years (1 Kin. 6:38)

959– 946 Solomon completes the palace in 13 years (1 Kin. 7:1)

954 Shishak serves as commander in chief of Egypt's army

950 Assyrians make armor with iron scales

En Gedi, an Oasis in a Mountain (Song 1:14)

En Gedi is the strongest of the perennial springs that flow from the Judean wilderness down to the Dead Sea. This spring cascades down the face of the mountain in stages with small pools between falls. Its path down the mountain is surrounded by lush vegetation, which has a uniquely compelling beauty well known to the writer of the Song of Solomon (Song 1:14).

The rough terrain from which the spring comes is extremely rugged, making it an ideal hideout for David when he was running from King Saul (1 Sam. 23:29; 24:1). In the mountains surrounding the spring are many caves and hiding places.

The site of En Gedi was enjoyed as an oasis on the shore of the Dead Sea long before David's time. On the top of one of the nearby hills lies the ruins of an ancient temple which dates back to the 4th millennium B.C. Cultic copper implements from the temple were found buried just a few miles south, hidden in a cave.

THE DAUGHTERS OF JERUSALEM

    We will run after you.[a]

THE SHULAMITE

    The king has brought me into his chambers.

THE DAUGHTERS OF JERUSALEM

    We will be glad and rejoice in you.[b]

    We will remember your[c] love more than wine.

THE SHULAMITE

    Rightly do they love you.[d]

5   I *am* dark, but lovely,
    O daughters of Jerusalem,
    Like the tents of Kedar,
    Like the curtains of Solomon.

6   Do not look upon me, because I *am* dark,
    Because the sun has tanned me.
    My mother's sons were angry with me;
    They made me the keeper of the vineyards,
    But my own vineyard I have not kept.

(TO HER BELOVED)

7   Tell me, O you whom I love,
    Where you feed *your flock,*
    Where you make *it* rest at noon.
    For why should I be as one who veils herself[a]
    By the flocks of your companions?

THE BELOVED

8   If you do not know, O fairest among women,
    Follow in the footsteps of the flock,
    And feed your little goats
    Beside the shepherds' tents.

9   I have compared you, my love,
    To my filly among Pharaoh's chariots.

10   Your cheeks are lovely with ornaments,
    Your neck with chains *of gold.*

THE DAUGHTERS OF JERUSALEM

11   We will make you[a] ornaments of gold
    With studs of silver.

THE SHULAMITE

12   While the king *is* at his table,
    My spikenard sends forth its fragrance.

13   A bundle of myrrh *is* my beloved to me,
    That lies all night between my breasts.

14   My beloved *is* to me a cluster of henna *blooms*
    In the vineyards of En Gedi.

THE BELOVED

15   Behold, you *are* fair, my love!
    Behold, you *are* fair!
    You *have* dove's eyes.

THE SHULAMITE

16   Behold, you *are* handsome, my beloved!

1:4 [a]Masculine singular, that is, the Beloved [b]Feminine singular, that is, the Shulamite [c]Masculine singular, that is, the Beloved [d]Masculine singular, that is, the Beloved 1:7 [a]Septuagint, Syriac, and Vulgate read *wanders.* 1:11 [a]Feminine singular, that is, the Shulamite

Yes, pleasant!
Also our bed *is* green.
17 The beams of our houses *are* cedar,
And our rafters of fir.

2 1 I *am* the rose of Sharon,
And the lily of the valleys.

THE BELOVED
2 Like a lily among thorns,
So is my love among the daughters.

THE SHULAMITE
3 Like an apple tree among the trees of
the woods,
So *is* my beloved among the sons.
I sat down in his shade with great
delight,
And his fruit *was* sweet to my taste.

THE SHULAMITE TO THE DAUGHTERS OF
JERUSALEM
4 He brought me to the banqueting
house,
And his banner over me *was* love.
5 Sustain me with cakes of raisins,
Refresh me with apples,
For I *am* lovesick.

6 His left hand *is* under my head,
And his right hand embraces me.
7 I charge you, O daughters of
Jerusalem,
By the gazelles or by the does of the
field,
Do not stir up nor awaken love
Until it pleases.

The Beloved's Request

THE SHULAMITE
8 The voice of my beloved!
Behold, he comes
Leaping upon the mountains,
Skipping upon the hills.
9 My beloved is like a gazelle or a young
stag.
Behold, he stands behind our wall;
He is looking through the windows,
Gazing through the lattice.

10 My beloved spoke, and said to me:
"Rise up, my love, my fair one,
And come away.
11 For lo, the winter is past,
The rain is over *and* gone.

12 The flowers appear on the earth;
The time of singing has come,
And the voice of the turtledove
Is heard in our land.
13 The fig tree puts forth her green figs,
And the vines *with* the tender grapes
Give a good smell.
Rise up, my love, my fair one,
And come away!

14 "O my dove, in the clefts of the rock,
In the secret *places* of the cliff,
Let me see your face,
Let me hear your voice;
For your voice *is* sweet,
And your face *is* lovely."

HER BROTHERS
15 Catch us the foxes,
The little foxes that spoil the vines,
For our vines *have* tender grapes.

THE SHULAMITE
16 My beloved *is* mine, and I *am* his.
He feeds *his flock* among the lilies.

(TO HER BELOVED)
17 Until the day breaks
And the shadows flee away,
Turn, my beloved,
And be like a gazelle
Or a young stag
Upon the mountains of Bether.[a]

A Troubled Night

THE SHULAMITE

3 1 By night on my bed I sought the one
I love;
I sought him, but I did not find him.
2 "I will rise now," *I said,*
"And go about the city;
In the streets and in the squares
I will seek the one I love."
I sought him, but I did not find him.
3 The watchmen who go about the city
found me;
I said,
"Have you seen the one I love?"

4 Scarcely had I passed by them,
When I found the one I love.
I held him and would not let him go,
Until I had brought him to the house
of my mother,
And into the chamber of her who
conceived me.

2:17 ªLiterally *Separation*

5 I charge you, O daughters of
    Jerusalem,
  By the gazelles or by the does of the
    field,
  Do not stir up nor awaken love
  Until it pleases.

The Coming of Solomon

THE SHULAMITE

6 Who *is* this coming out of the
    wilderness
  Like pillars of smoke,
  Perfumed with myrrh and
    frankincense,
  With all the merchant's fragrant
    powders?
7 Behold, it *is* Solomon's couch,
  With sixty valiant men around it,
  Of the valiant of Israel.

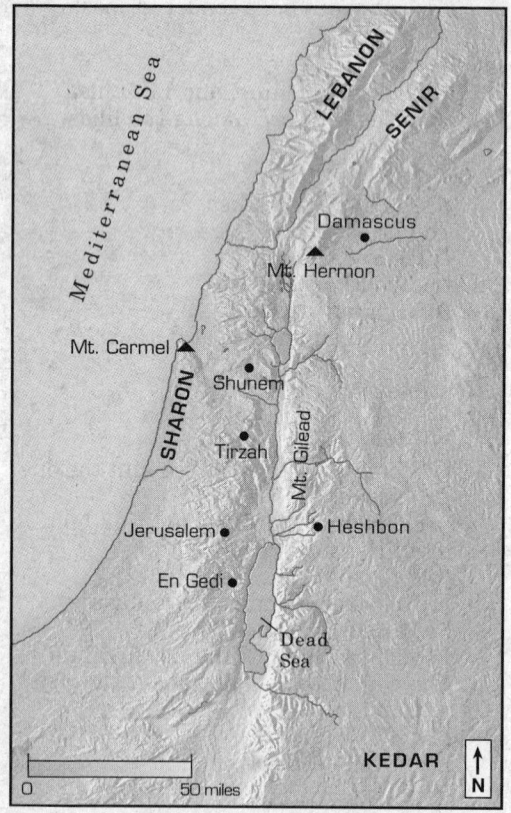

Geography in the Song of Solomon
The beautiful love story that unfolds in the Song of Solomon
takes place in a variety of settings. With several word
pictures the lovers speak of, and to, each other: "rose of
Sharon"; "lily of the valleys"; "vineyards of En Gedi." Love
grows and flourishes in the pastoral setting of the pastures
and valleys, on the mountains and hillsides.

8 They all hold swords,
  Being expert in war.
  Every man *has* his sword on his thigh
  Because of fear in the night.

9 Of the wood of Lebanon
  Solomon the King
  Made himself a palanquin:[a]
10 He made its pillars *of* silver,
  Its support *of* gold,
  Its seat *of* purple,
  Its interior paved *with* love
  By the daughters of Jerusalem.
11 Go forth, O daughters of Zion,
  And see King Solomon with the crown
  With which his mother crowned him
  On the day of his wedding,
  The day of the gladness of his heart.

THE BELOVED

4 ¹ Behold, you *are* fair, my love!
    Behold, you *are* fair!
  You *have* dove's eyes behind your veil.
  Your hair *is* like a flock of goats,
  Going down from Mount Gilead.
2 Your teeth *are* like a flock of shorn
    sheep
  Which have come up from the
    washing,
  Every one of which bears twins,
  And none *is* barren among them.
3 Your lips *are* like a strand of scarlet,
  And your mouth is lovely.
  Your temples behind your veil
  Are like a piece of pomegranate.
4 Your neck *is* like the tower of David,
  Built for an armory,
  On which hang a thousand bucklers,
  All shields of mighty men.
5 Your two breasts *are* like two fawns,
  Twins of a gazelle,
  Which feed among the lilies.

6 Until the day breaks
  And the shadows flee away,
  I will go my way to the mountain of
    myrrh
  And to the hill of frankincense.

7 You *are* all fair, my love,
  And *there is* no spot in you.
8 Come with me from Lebanon, *my*
    spouse,

3:9 ᵃA portable enclosed chair

With me from Lebanon.
Look from the top of Amana,
From the top of Senir and Hermon,
From the lions' dens,
From the mountains of the leopards.

9 You have ravished my heart,
My sister, *my* spouse;
You have ravished my heart
With one *look* of your eyes,
With one link of your necklace.
10 How fair is your love,
My sister, *my* spouse!
How much better than wine is your
love,
And the scent of your perfumes
Than all spices!
11 Your lips, O *my* spouse,
Drip as the honeycomb;
Honey and milk *are* under your
tongue;
And the fragrance of your garments
Is like the fragrance of Lebanon.

12 A garden enclosed
Is my sister, *my* spouse,
A spring shut up,
A fountain sealed.
13 Your plants *are* an orchard of
pomegranates
With pleasant fruits,
Fragrant henna with spikenard,
14 Spikenard and saffron,
Calamus and cinnamon,
With all trees of frankincense,
Myrrh and aloes,
With all the chief spices—
15 A fountain of gardens,
A well of living waters,
And streams from Lebanon.

THE SHULAMITE
16 Awake, O north *wind,*
And come, O south!
Blow upon my garden,
That its spices may flow out.
Let my beloved come to his garden
And eat its pleasant fruits.

THE BELOVED

5 1 I have come to my garden, my sister,
my spouse;
I have gathered my myrrh with my
spice;
I have eaten my honeycomb with my
honey;
I have drunk my wine with my milk.

(TO HIS FRIENDS)
Eat, O friends!
Drink, yes, drink deeply,
O beloved ones!

The Shulamite's Troubled Evening

THE SHULAMITE
2 I sleep, but my heart is awake;
It is the voice of my beloved!
He knocks, *saying,*
"Open for me, my sister, my love,
My dove, my perfect one;
For my head is covered with dew,
My locks with the drops of the night."

3 I have taken off my robe;
How can I put it on *again?*
I have washed my feet;
How can I defile them?
4 My beloved put his hand
By the latch *of the door,*
And my heart yearned for him.
5 I arose to open for my beloved,
And my hands dripped *with* myrrh,
My fingers with liquid myrrh,
On the handles of the lock.

6 I opened for my beloved,
But my beloved had turned away *and*
was gone.
My heart leaped up when he spoke.
I sought him, but I could not find him;
I called him, but he gave me no
answer.
7 The watchmen who went about the
city found me.
They struck me, they wounded me;
The keepers of the walls
Took my veil away from me.

ARTS AND LITERATURE

In Near Eastern poetry, the appeal of a metaphor or simile is often intellectual, offering a puzzle rather than a picture. The teeth are like sheep because none are missing (Song 4:2), not because there is much visual similarity. Such images can become conventional clichés, and difficult to interpret.

8   I charge you, O daughters of
        Jerusalem,
    If you find my beloved,
    That you tell him I *am* lovesick!

THE DAUGHTERS OF JERUSALEM
9   What *is* your beloved
    More than *another* beloved,
    O fairest among women?
    What *is* your beloved
    More than *another* beloved,
    That you so charge us?

THE SHULAMITE
10 My beloved *is* white and ruddy,
    Chief among ten thousand.
11 His head *is like* the finest gold;
    His locks *are* wavy,
    And black as a raven.
12 His eyes *are* like doves
    By the rivers of waters,
    Washed with milk,
    And fitly set.
13 His cheeks *are* like a bed of spices,
    Banks of scented herbs.
    His lips *are* lilies,
    Dripping liquid myrrh.

14 His hands *are* rods of gold
    Set with beryl.
    His body *is* carved ivory
    Inlaid *with* sapphires.
15 His legs *are* pillars of marble
    Set on bases of fine gold.
    His countenance *is* like Lebanon,
    Excellent as the cedars.
16 His mouth *is* most sweet,
    Yes, he *is* altogether lovely.
    This *is* my beloved,
    And this *is* my friend,
    O daughters of Jerusalem!

THE DAUGHTERS OF JERUSALEM

6 ¹ Where has your beloved gone,
        O fairest among women?
    Where has your beloved turned aside,
    That we may seek him with you?

THE SHULAMITE
2   My beloved has gone to his garden,
    To the beds of spices,
    To feed *his flock* in the gardens,
    And to gather lilies.
3   I *am* my beloved's,
    And my beloved *is* mine.
    He feeds *his flock* among the lilies.

Praise of the Shulamite's Beauty

THE BELOVED
4   O my love, you *are as* beautiful as
        Tirzah,
    Lovely as Jerusalem,
    Awesome as *an army* with banners!
5   Turn your eyes away from me,
    For they have overcome me.
    Your hair *is* like a flock of goats
    Going down from Gilead.
6   Your teeth *are* like a flock of sheep
    Which have come up from the
        washing;
    Every one bears twins,
    And none *is* barren among them.
7   Like a piece of pomegranate
    Are your temples behind your veil.

8   There are sixty queens
    And eighty concubines,
    And virgins without number.
9   My dove, my perfect one,
    Is the only one,
    The only one of her mother,
    The favorite of the one who bore her.
    The daughters saw her
    And called her blessed,
    The queens and the concubines,
    And they praised her.

10 Who is she who looks forth as the
        morning,
    Fair as the moon,
    Clear as the sun,
    Awesome as *an army* with banners?

THE SHULAMITE
11 I went down to the garden of nuts
    To see the verdure of the valley,

ARTS AND LITERATURE

The comparisons of Song 6:4 are good illustrations of the puzzling imagery of Israelite poetry. The woman's beauty is compared to cities, and to the flags of a marching army. The point of comparison is not explained, but perhaps it reflects the woman's importance to the writer and her power over his emotions.

THE POOLS OF HESHBON (Song 7:4)

The biblical city of Heshbon was situated at a major north-south, east-west crossroad on the King's Highway (Num. 20:17) in Transjordan. It was there that a battle was fought between the Israelites, led by Moses, and the Amorites, led by Sihon (Num. 21:21–31). The Israelites successfully defeated the Amorites, after which Israel's tribes of Reuben and Gad settled in Transjordan (Num. 32).

The Iron Age (1200–600 B.C.) location of Heshbon was established in an area that had no perennial spring. Those who built the city had to construct water cisterns beneath the houses and public buildings. By this means the inhabitants were able to collect the water from the roofs and streets during the winter rainy season.

Archaeologists have found many cisterns at Tell Hesban, the modern name of Heshbon. The largest water facility from the time of the Song of Solomon was a reservoir that would hold about 600,000 gallons of water, if filled. Certainly the pools of Heshbon were a good choice for the biblical writer when he sought figurative language to describe a Shulamite girl's beauty. Possibly he had in mind deep and dark eyes in referring to the Shulamite's eyes as "like the pools in Heshbon" (Song 7:4).

To see whether the vine had budded
And the pomegranates had bloomed.
12 Before I was even aware,
My soul had made me
As the chariots of my noble people.[a]

THE BELOVED AND HIS FRIENDS

13 Return, return, O Shulamite;
Return, return, that we may look
upon you!

THE SHULAMITE

What would you see in the
Shulamite—
As it were, the dance of the two
camps?[a]

Expressions of Praise

THE BELOVED

7 1 How beautiful are your feet in
sandals,
O prince's daughter!
The curves of your thighs *are* like
jewels,
The work of the hands of a skillful
workman.
2 Your navel *is* a rounded goblet;
It lacks no blended beverage.
Your waist *is* a heap of wheat
Set about with lilies.
3 Your two breasts *are* like two fawns,
Twins of a gazelle.

4 Your neck *is* like an ivory tower,
Your eyes *like* the pools in Heshbon
By the gate of Bath Rabbim.
Your nose *is* like the tower of Lebanon
Which looks toward Damascus.
5 Your head *crowns* you like *Mount
Carmel*,
And the hair of your head *is* like
purple;
A king *is* held captive by *your* tresses.

6 How fair and how pleasant you are,
O love, with your delights!
7 This stature of yours is like a palm
tree,
And your breasts *like* its clusters.
8 I said, "I will go up to the palm tree,
I will take hold of its branches."
Let now your breasts be like clusters
of the vine,
The fragrance of your breath like
apples,
9 And the roof of your mouth like the
best wine.

THE SHULAMITE

The wine goes *down* smoothly for my
beloved,
Moving gently the lips of sleepers.[a]
10 I *am* my beloved's,
And his desire *is* toward me.

11 Come, my beloved,
Let us go forth to the field;
Let us lodge in the villages.
12 Let us get up early to the vineyards;
Let us see if the vine has budded,

6:12 [a]Hebrew *Ammi Nadib*   6:13 [a]Hebrew
Mahanaim   7:9 [a]Septuagint, Syriac, and Vulgate
read *lips and teeth*.

Whether the grape blossoms are open,
And the pomegranates are in bloom.
There I will give you my love.
13 The mandrakes give off a fragrance,
And at our gates *are* pleasant *fruits,*
All manner, new and old,
Which I have laid up for you, my
    beloved.

8 1 Oh, that you were like my brother,
    Who nursed at my mother's breasts!
If I should find you outside,
I would kiss you;
I would not be despised.
2 I would lead you *and* bring you
Into the house of my mother,
She *who* used to instruct me.
I would cause you to drink of spiced
    wine,
Of the juice of my pomegranate.

(TO THE DAUGHTERS OF JERUSALEM)

3 His left hand *is* under my head,
And his right hand embraces me.
4 I charge you, O daughters of
    Jerusalem,
Do not stir up nor awaken love
Until it pleases.

Love Renewed in Lebanon

A RELATIVE

5 Who *is* this coming up from the
    wilderness,
Leaning upon her beloved?

I awakened you under the apple tree.
There your mother brought you forth;
There she *who* bore you brought *you*
    forth.

THE SHULAMITE TO HER BELOVED

6 Set me as a seal upon your heart,
As a seal upon your arm;
For love *is as* strong as death,
Jealousy *as* cruel as the grave;[a]
Its flames *are* flames of fire,
A most vehement[b] flame.

7 Many waters cannot quench love,
Nor can the floods drown it.
If a man would give for love
All the wealth of his house,
It would be utterly despised.

THE SHULAMITE'S BROTHERS

8 We have a little sister,
And she has no breasts.

What shall we do for our sister
In the day when she is spoken for?
9 If she *is* a wall,
We will build upon her
A battlement of silver;
And if she *is* a door,
We will enclose her
With boards of cedar.

THE SHULAMITE

10 I *am* a wall,
And my breasts like towers;
Then I became in his eyes
As one who found peace.
11 Solomon had a vineyard at Baal
    Hamon;
He leased the vineyard to keepers;
Everyone was to bring for its fruit
A thousand silver coins.

(TO SOLOMON)

12 My own vineyard *is* before me.
You, O Solomon, *may have a*
    thousand,
And those who tend its fruit two
    hundred.

THE BELOVED

13 You who dwell in the gardens,
The companions listen for your voice—
Let me hear it!

THE SHULAMITE

14 Make haste, my beloved,
And be like a gazelle
Or a young stag
On the mountains of spices.

8:6 [a]Or *Sheol* [b]Literally *A flame of YAH* (a poetic form
of *YHWH, the* LORD)

Solomon's Decline

Solomon's many foreign wives led to
his downfall. The more he resembled the other
kings of the ancient world, the further he got
from Israel's covenant relationship with God.
Besides worshiping his wives' foreign gods,
Solomon also established forced labor for his
citizens. This was unheard of among free Israelites, and Israel would not bear it long. As
Pharaoh Shishak (known as Sheshonk I), who
ruled from 945 to 924 B.C., led a new dynasty
in Egypt, King Solomon of Israel was in the declining years of his reign (1 Kin. 11:40).

■ 1 Kings 11:9–43

1 Kings

11
:9 So the LORD became angry with Solomon, because his heart had turned from the LORD God of Israel, who had appeared to him twice, ¹⁰and had commanded him concerning this thing, that he should not go after other gods; but he did not keep what the LORD had commanded. ¹¹Therefore the LORD said to Solomon, "Because you have done this, and have not kept My covenant and My statutes, which I have commanded you, I will surely tear the kingdom away from you and give it to your servant. ¹²Nevertheless I will not do it in your days, for the sake of your father David; I will tear it out of the hand of your son. ¹³However I will not tear away the whole kingdom; I will give one tribe to your son for the sake of My servant David, and for the sake of Jerusalem which I have chosen."

Adversaries of Solomon

¹⁴Now the LORD raised up an adversary against Solomon, Hadad the Edomite; he *was* a descendant of the king in Edom. ¹⁵For it happened, when David was in Edom, and Joab the commander of the army had gone up to bury the slain, after he had killed every male in Edom ¹⁶(because for six months Joab remained there with all Israel, until he had cut down every male in Edom), ¹⁷that Hadad fled to go to Egypt, he and certain Edomites of his father's servants with him. Hadad *was* still a little child. ¹⁸Then they arose from Midian and came to Paran; and they took men with them from Paran and came to Egypt, to Pharaoh king of Egypt, who gave him a house, apportioned food for him, and gave him land. ¹⁹And Hadad found great favor in the sight of Pharaoh, so that he gave him as wife the sister of his own wife, that is, the sister of Queen Tahpenes. ²⁰Then the sister of Tahpenes bore him Genubath his son, whom Tahpenes weaned in Pharaoh's house. And Genubath was in Pharaoh's household among the sons of Pharaoh.

²¹So when Hadad heard in Egypt that David rested with his fathers, and that Joab the commander of the army was dead, Hadad said to Pharaoh, "Let me depart, that I may go to my own country."

²²Then Pharaoh said to him, "But what have you lacked with me, that suddenly you seek to go to your own country?"

So he answered, "Nothing, but do let me go anyway."

²³And God raised up *another* adversary against him, Rezon the son of Eliadah, who had fled from his lord, Hadadezer king of Zobah. ²⁴So he gathered men to him and became captain over a band *of raiders,* when David killed those *of Zobah.* And they went to Damascus and dwelt there, and reigned in Damascus. ²⁵He was an adversary of Israel all the days of Solomon (besides the trouble that Hadad *caused*); and he abhorred Israel, and reigned over Syria.

Jeroboam's Rebellion

²⁶Then Solomon's servant, Jeroboam the son of Nebat, an Ephraimite from Zereda, whose mother's name *was* Zeruah, a widow, also rebelled against the king.

²⁷And this *is* what caused him to rebel against the king: Solomon had built the Millo *and* repaired the damages to the City of David his father. ²⁸The man Jeroboam *was* a mighty man of valor; and Solomon, seeing that the young man was industrious, made him the officer over all the labor force of the house of Joseph.

²⁹Now it happened at that time, when Jeroboam went out of Jerusalem, that the prophet Ahijah the Shilonite met him on the way; and he had clothed himself with a new garment, and the two *were* alone in the field. ³⁰Then Ahijah took hold of the new garment that *was* on him, and tore it *into* twelve pieces. ³¹And he said to Jeroboam, "Take for yourself ten pieces, for thus says the LORD, the God of Israel: 'Behold, I will tear the kingdom out of the hand of Solomon and will give ten tribes to you ³²(but he shall have one tribe for the sake of My servant David, and for the sake of Jerusalem, the city which I have chosen out of all the tribes of Israel), ³³because they have[a] forsaken Me, and worshiped Ashtoreth the goddess of the Sidonians, Chemosh the god of the Moabites, and Milcom the god of the people of Ammon, and have not walked in My ways to do *what is* right in My eyes and *keep* My statutes and My judgments, as *did* his father David. ³⁴However I will not take the whole kingdom out of his hand, because I have made him ruler all the days of his life for the sake of My servant David, whom I chose

---

11:33 [a]Following Masoretic Text and Targum; Septuagint, Syriac, and Vulgate read *he has.*

because he kept My commandments and My statutes. ³⁵But I will take the kingdom out of his son's hand and give it to you— ten tribes. ³⁶And to his son I will give one tribe, that My servant David may always have a lamp before Me in Jerusalem, the city which I have chosen for Myself, to put My name there. ³⁷So I will take you, and you shall reign over all your heart desires, and you shall be king over Israel. ³⁸Then it shall be, if you heed all that I command you, walk in My ways, and do *what is* right in My sight, to keep My statutes and My commandments, as My servant David did, then I will be with you and build for you an enduring house, as I built for David, and will give Israel to you. ³⁹And I will afflict the descendants of David because of this, but not forever.' "

⁴⁰Solomon therefore sought to kill Jeroboam. But Jeroboam arose and fled to Egypt, to Shishak king of Egypt, and was in Egypt until the death of Solomon.

Death of Solomon

⁴¹Now the rest of the acts of Solomon, all that he did, and his wisdom, *are* they not written in the book of the acts of Solomon? ⁴²And the period that Solomon reigned in Jerusalem over all Israel *was* forty years. ⁴³Then Solomon rested with his fathers, and was buried in the City of David his father. And Rehoboam his son reigned in his place.

Priestly Account: Solomon's Reign

The second book of Chronicles continues the story of the monarchy from the beginning of Solomon's reign (c. 970 B.C.). The Chronicler takes a much more positive view of Solomon than does the historian of Kings. In the priestly history, Solomon is above all the builder of the temple. Anything that might distract from that central role (such as Solomon's wisdom) is downplayed, and anything that might tarnish it (such as Solomon's worship of foreign gods) is simply omitted.

■ 2 Chronicles 1:1—2:18

2 Chronicles
Solomon Requests Wisdom

1 :1 Now Solomon the son of David was strengthened in his kingdom, and the LORD his God *was* with him and exalted him exceedingly.

²And Solomon spoke to all Israel, to the captains of thousands and of hundreds, to the judges, and to every leader in all Israel, the heads of the fathers' *houses.* ³Then Solomon, and all the assembly with him, went to the high place that *was* at Gibeon; for the tabernacle of meeting with God was there, which Moses the servant of the LORD had made in the wilderness. ⁴But David had brought up the ark of God from Kirjath Jearim to *the place* David had prepared for it, for he had pitched a tent for it at Jerusalem. ⁵Now the bronze altar that Bezalel the son of Uri, the son of Hur, had made, he put[a] before the tabernacle of the LORD; Solomon and the assembly sought Him *there.* ⁶And Solomon went up there to the bronze altar before the LORD, which *was* at the tabernacle of meeting, and offered a thousand burnt offerings on it.

⁷On that night God appeared to Solomon, and said to him, "Ask! What shall I give you?"

⁸And Solomon said to God: "You have shown great mercy to David my father, and have made me king in his place. ⁹Now, O LORD God, let Your promise to David my father be established, for You have made me king over a people like the dust of the earth in multitude. ¹⁰Now give me wisdom and knowledge, that I may go out and come in before this people; for who can judge this great people of Yours?"

¹¹Then God said to Solomon: "Because this was in your heart, and you have not asked riches or wealth or honor or the life of your enemies, nor have you asked long life—but have asked wisdom and knowl-

---

1:5 ªSome authorities read *it was there.*

TIME CAPSULE   *945 to 930 B.C.*

945–924	Shishak, pharaoh of Egypt (Shoshenq I or Sheshonk)
945	The term "Pharaoh" is added to the Egyptian king's official title
934–612	Neo-Assyrian period
934	Ashur-dan, king of Assyria, fortifies city of Asshur
930	Solomon dies and is succeeded by his son Rehoboam (1 Kin. 11:43)

KINGS OF THE NEO-HITTITES (2 Chr. 1:17)

The Hittites were a major Indo-European people centered in Anatolia. Their political power extended from about 1700 to 1180 B.C., and the Hittite Empire at its height comprised most of present-day Turkey, Armenia, Syria, and northern Palestine. They fought numerous battles with Egypt for supremacy in Palestine. The Hittites adopted the cuneiform writing system from Mesopotamia to write their own language, also known as Hittite.

References to Hittites in the Bible do not refer to the great Hittite Empire of the Late Bronze Age (1500–1200 B.C.), but to the political successors of the Hittites in north Syria. These so-called Neo-Hittite kingdoms, which were centered at Carchemish, Malatya, and other cities, survived in north Syria until the Assyrian conquest in the 8th century B.C. The Neo-Hittite states were a mixture of a variety of ethnic components, including Hittite, Luwian (native Anatolian), Hurrian, and Northwest Semitic elements.

The "kings of the Hittites" with whom Solomon conducted business (2 Chr. 1:17) apparently refers to these petty Neo-Hittite states in north Syria. Since they were composed of small kingdoms lacking a united political structure, it would be appropriate to speak of several Hittite "kings." By the time of Solomon (970–930 B.C.), the Neo-Hittite kingdoms had been substantially weakened, but were still able to import horses and chariots from Israel's wealthy king.

---

edge for yourself, that you may judge My people over whom I have made you king— [12]wisdom and knowledge *are* granted to you; and I will give you riches and wealth and honor, such as none of the kings have had who *were* before you, nor shall any after you have the like."

Solomon's Military and Economic Power

[13]So Solomon came to Jerusalem from the high place that *was* at Gibeon, from before the tabernacle of meeting, and reigned over Israel. [14]And Solomon gathered chariots and horsemen; he had one thousand four hundred chariots and twelve thousand horsemen, whom he stationed in the chariot cities and with the king in Jerusalem. [15]Also the king made silver and gold as common in Jerusalem as stones, and he made cedars as abundant as the sycamores which *are* in the lowland. [16]And Solomon

had horses imported from Egypt and Keveh; the king's merchants bought them in Keveh at the *current* price. [17]They also acquired and imported from Egypt a chariot for six hundred *shekels* of silver, and a horse for one hundred and fifty; thus, through their agents,[a] they exported them to all the kings of the Hittites and the kings of Syria.

Solomon Prepares to Build the Temple

2 [1]Then Solomon determined to build a temple for the name of the LORD, and a royal house for himself. [2]Solomon selected seventy thousand men to bear burdens, eighty thousand to quarry *stone* in the mountains, and three thousand six hundred to oversee them.

[3]Then Solomon sent to Hiram[a] king of Tyre, saying:

As you have dealt with David my father, and sent him cedars to build himself a house to dwell in, *so deal with me.* [4]Behold, I am building a

---

1:17 [a]Literally *by their hands*   2:3 [a]Hebrew *Huram* (compare 1 Kings 5:1)

SCIENCE AND TECHNOLOGY

The Egyptians met the horse and chariot when fighting against the Hyksos in around 1648 B.C., and within a hundred years were using the same weapon themselves. They became masters in using it, and distinguished themselves as chariot makers (2 Chr. 1:17). In a land where wood was scarce, they became expert in joinery, and their chariots were light, flexible, and strong.

HIRAM, KING OF TYRE (2 Chr. 2:11)

Hiram, who became king of Tyre in either 980 or 969 B.C., had a special relationship with Solomon, king of Israel (2 Chr. 2:11). They were business partners in several efforts. This association continued a friendship that had existed previously between Solomon's father and Hiram (2 Sam. 5:11).

A treaty between Hiram and Solomon involved several acts of cooperation (1 Kin. 5:12). One was the rebuilding of Jerusalem, the capital of Israel. Craftsmen of Israel and Tyre worked together in building the temple, Solomon's palace, as well as other projects (1 Kin. 5:18; 2 Chr. 2:12-14). The two kings were also joint participants in a commercial shipping business (1 Kin. 10:11, 22).

Additional information about Hiram comes from Josephus, the Jewish historian of the 1st century A.D. Josephus in turn draws information from a historian named Dius, whose work has not survived to modern times. Supposedly, Hiram and Solomon competed with each other in solving riddles. Wagers were made between them as to who could solve whose riddles. At first Solomon won large sums of money from Hiram. As time went on, however, Hiram gained the help of a certain Abdemon, who not only won for Hiram his losses but also an additional great amount from Solomon.

One might suppose that Hiram was helping Solomon only because of his friendship with David (1 Kin. 5:1). In fact, Hiram was helping, at least in part, because of the wealth it brought him. Not only did he receive a yearly payment in kind (1 Kin. 5:11), but, at the end of the major building projects, Solomon gave Hiram 20 cities, which were probably located on the Mediterranean coast (1 Kin. 9:11). Indeed, the Phoenicians became one of the most wealthy people in the 1st millennium B.C.

---

temple for the name of the LORD my God, to dedicate *it* to Him, to burn before Him sweet incense, for the continual showbread, for the burnt offerings morning and evening, on the Sabbaths, on the New Moons, and on the set feasts of the LORD our God. This *is an ordinance* forever to Israel.

5 And the temple which I build *will be* great, for our God is greater than all gods. 6But who is able to build Him a temple, since heaven and the heaven of heavens cannot contain Him? Who *am* I then, that I should build Him a temple, except to burn sacrifice before Him?

7 Therefore send me at once a man skillful to work in gold and silver, in bronze and iron, in purple and crimson and blue, who has skill to engrave with the skillful men who are with me in Judah and Jerusalem, whom David my father provided. 8Also send me cedar and cypress and algum logs from Lebanon, for I know that your servants have skill to cut timber in Lebanon; and indeed my servants

will be with your servants, 9to prepare timber for me in abundance, for the temple which I am about to build *shall be* great and wonderful.

10 And indeed I will give to your servants, the woodsmen who cut timber, twenty thousand kors of ground wheat, twenty thousand kors of barley, twenty thousand baths of wine, and twenty thousand baths of oil.

11Then Hiram king of Tyre answered in writing, which he sent to Solomon:

Because the LORD loves His people, He has made you king over them.

12Hiram[a] also said:

Blessed *be* the LORD God of Israel, who made heaven and earth, for He has given King David a wise son, endowed with prudence and understanding, who will build a temple for the LORD and a royal house for himself!

2:12 [a]Hebrew *Huram* (compare 1 Kings 5:1)

13 And now I have sent a skillful man, endowed with understanding, Huram[a] my master[b] *craftsman* [14](the son of a woman of the daughters of Dan, and his father was a man of Tyre), skilled to work in gold and silver, bronze and iron, stone and wood, purple and blue, fine linen and crimson, and to make any engraving and to accomplish any plan which may be given to him, with your skillful men and with the skillful men of my lord David your father.

15 Now therefore, the wheat, the barley, the oil, and the wine which my lord has spoken of, let him send to his servants. [16]And we will cut wood from Lebanon, as much as you need; we will bring it to you in rafts by sea to Joppa, and you will carry it up to Jerusalem.

[17]Then Solomon numbered all the aliens who *were* in the land of Israel, after the census in which David his father had numbered them; and there were found to be one hundred and fifty-three thousand six hundred. [18]And he made seventy thousand of them bearers of burdens, eighty thousand stonecutters in the mountain, and three thousand six hundred overseers to make the people work.

2:13 [a]Spelled *Hiram* in 1 Kings 7:13   [b]Literally *father* (compare 1 Kings 7:13, 14)   3:1 [a]Literally *He,* following Masoretic Text and Vulgate; Septuagint reads *the LORD;* Targum reads *the Angel of the LORD.* [b]Spelled *Araunah* in 2 Samuel 24:16ff   3:4 [a]The main room of the temple; elsewhere called the holy place (compare 1 Kings 6:3)   [b]Following Masoretic Text, Septuagint, and Vulgate; Arabic, some manuscripts of the Septuagint, and Syriac omit *one hundred and.*   3:5 [a]Literally *house* 3:15 [a]Literally *house*   [b]Or *eighteen* (compare 1 Kings 7:15; 2 Kings 25:17; and Jeremiah 52:21)

Solomon Begins Building the Temple

Work on the foundation of the temple began in the 4th year of Solomon's reign, which was about 966 B.C. (2 Chr. 3:2). The Chronicler shortens the Kings account of the construction of the temple. His main interest is in the institutions and worship connected with the building.

■ 2 Chronicles 3:1—4:22

2 Chronicles
Foundation of the Temple

3 :1 Now Solomon began to build the house of the LORD at Jerusalem on Mount Moriah, where *the LORD*[a] had appeared to his father David, at the place that David had prepared on the threshing floor of Ornan[b] the Jebusite. [2]And he began to build on the second *day* of the second month in the fourth year of his reign.

[3]This is the foundation which Solomon laid for building the house of God: The length *was* sixty cubits (by cubits according to the former measure) and the width twenty cubits. [4]And the vestibule that *was* in front *of* the sanctuary[a] was twenty cubits long across the width of the house, and the height *was* one hundred and[b] twenty. He overlaid the inside with pure gold. [5]The larger room[a] he paneled with cypress which he overlaid with fine gold, and he carved palm trees and chainwork on it. [6]And he decorated the house with precious stones for beauty, and the gold *was* gold from Parvaim. [7]He also overlaid the house—the beams and doorposts, its walls and doors—with gold; and he carved cherubim on the walls.

[8]And he made the Most Holy Place. Its length was according to the width of the house, twenty cubits, and its width twenty cubits. He overlaid it with six hundred talents of fine gold. [9]The weight of the nails *was* fifty shekels of gold; and he overlaid the upper area with gold. [10]In the Most Holy Place he made two cherubim, fashioned by carving, and overlaid them with gold. [11]The wings of the cherubim *were* twenty cubits in *overall* length: one wing *of* the one cherub *was* five cubits, touching the wall of the room, and the other wing *was* five cubits, touching the wing of the other cherub; [12]one wing of the other cherub *was* five cubits, touching the wall of the room, and the other wing *also was* five cubits, touching the wing of the other cherub. [13]The wings of these cherubim spanned twenty cubits overall. They stood on their feet, and they faced inward. [14]And he made the veil of blue, purple, crimson, and fine linen, and wove cherubim into it.

[15]Also he made in front of the temple[a] two pillars thirty-five[b] cubits high, and the capital that *was* on the top of each of *them* was five cubits. [16]He made wreaths of chainwork, as in the inner sanctuary, and put *them* on top of the pillars; and he made

SOLOMON THE BUILDER

Solomon is reported to have laid the foundation of the temple in the 4th year of his reign (1 Kin. 6:1). It took 7 years to build the temple (1 Kin. 6:37, 38) and an additional 13 years to build the king's palace (1 Kin. 7:1). In all, Solomon spent 20 years in two great building projects (1 Kin. 9:10; 2 Chr. 8:1). These chronological figures are possibly symbolic, rather than actual, but they do stress the architectural accomplishments of one of Israel's great leaders.

Year	Event
970	Solomon becomes king (1 Kin. 1:32–40; 1 Chr. 29:22)
966	Solomon begins to build the temple (1 Kin. 6:1; 2 Chr. 3:1)
959	Solomon completes construction of the temple (1 Kin. 6:37, 38; 2 Chr. 5:1)
946	Solomon completes construction of the royal palace (1 Kin. 7:1; 2 Chr. 8:1)
930	Solomon dies and is succeeded by his son Rehoboam (1 Kin. 11:43; 2 Chr. 9:31)

one hundred pomegranates, and put *them* on the wreaths of chainwork. [17]Then he set up the pillars before the temple, one on the right hand and the other on the left; he called the name of the one on the right hand Jachin, and the name of the one on the left Boaz.

Furnishings of the Temple

4 [1]Moreover he made a bronze altar: twenty cubits was its length, twenty cubits its width, and ten cubits its height. [2]Then he made the Sea of cast *bronze,* ten cubits from one brim to the other; *it was* completely round. Its height *was* five cubits, and a line of thirty cubits measured its circumference. [3]And under it *was* the likeness of oxen encircling it all around, ten to a cubit, all the way around the Sea. The oxen *were* cast in two rows, when it was cast. [4]It stood on twelve oxen: three looking toward the north, three looking toward the west, three looking toward the south, and three looking toward the east; the Sea *was set* upon them, and all their back parts *pointed* inward. [5]It *was* a handbreadth thick; and its brim was shaped like the brim of a cup, *like* a lily blossom. It contained three thousand[a] baths.

[6]He also made ten lavers, and put five on the right side and five on the left, to wash in them; such things as they offered for the burnt offering they would wash in them, but the Sea *was* for the priests to wash in. [7]And he made ten lampstands of gold according to their design, and set *them* in the temple, five on the right side and five on the left. [8]He also made ten tables, and placed *them* in the temple, five on the right side and five on the left. And he made one hundred bowls of gold.

[9]Furthermore he made the court of the priests, and the great court and doors for the court; and he overlaid these doors with bronze. [10]He set the Sea on the right side, toward the southeast.

[11]Then Huram made the pots and the shovels and the bowls. So Huram finished doing the work that he was to do for King Solomon for the house of God: [12]the two pillars and the bowl-shaped capitals *that were* on top of the two pillars; the two networks

---

4:5 [a]Or *two thousand* (compare 1 Kings 7:26)

 **ARCHITECTURE AND BUILDING**

The pillars erected by Solomon were freestanding and made of bronze, probably about 27 feet high (2 Chr. 3:17). Pillars were commonly used in this way to mark the entrance to ancient temples. Since pillars are sometimes decorated like plants, the pillars could have represented trees. Their names seem to make them symbolic of God's presence in His strength.

covering the two bowl-shaped capitals which *were* on top of the pillars; [13]four hundred pomegranates for the two networks (two rows of pomegranates for each network, to cover the two bowl-shaped capitals that *were* on the pillars); [14]he also made carts and the lavers on the carts; [15]one Sea and twelve oxen under it; [16]also the pots, the shovels, the forks—and all their articles Huram his master[a] *craftsman* made of burnished bronze for King Solomon for the house of the LORD.

[17]In the plain of Jordan the king had them cast in clay molds, between Succoth and Zeredah.[a] [18]And Solomon had all these articles made in such great abundance that the weight of the bronze was not determined.

[19]Thus Solomon had all the furnishings made for the house of God: the altar of gold and the tables on which *was* the showbread; [20]the lampstands with their lamps of pure gold, to burn in the prescribed manner in front of the inner sanctuary, [21]with the flowers and the lamps and the wick-trimmers of gold, of purest gold; [22]the trimmers, the bowls, the ladles, and the censers of pure gold. As for the entry of the sanctuary, its inner doors to the Most Holy *Place,* and the doors of the main hall of the temple, *were* gold.

4:16 [a]Literally *father*   4:17 [a]Spelled *Zaretan* in 1 Kings 7:46

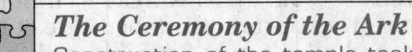

The Ceremony of the Ark

Construction of the temple took 7 years to complete, lasting from 966 to 959 B.C. (1 Kin. 6:37, 38). The Chronicler associates the temple site with Mount Moriah on which Abraham was asked to sacrifice Isaac (2 Chr. 3:1; Gen. 22:2). Since this mound was north of the ancient City of David, upon completion of the temple the city limits were extended to include the temple area. It was then necessary to bring the ark up from its former resting place (2 Chr. 1:4; 5:2).

■ 2 Chronicles 5:1—7:22

2 Chronicles

5 :1 So all the work that Solomon had done for the house of the LORD was finished; and Solomon brought in the things which his father David had dedicated: the silver and the gold and all the furnishings. And he put *them* in the treasuries of the house of God.

The Ark Brought into the Temple

[2]Now Solomon assembled the elders of Israel and all the heads of the tribes, the chief fathers of the children of Israel, in Jerusalem, that they might bring the ark of the covenant of the LORD up from the City of David, which *is* Zion. [3]Therefore all the men of Israel assembled with the king at the feast, which *was* in the seventh month. [4]So all the elders of Israel came, and the

---

The Spread of Solomon's Fame

Solomon's influence in economic and political affairs was enhanced by the transportation and trade routes that intersected his kingdom. That Solomon acquired much through trade is suggested by the response of the queen of Sheba on her visit to Solomon, and by the mention of traders and merchants (2 Chr. 9:14) in the account of his wealth.

Major route
Other route

Tiphsah

PHOENICIA HAMATH

Mediterranean Sea

Tyre
Hazor   Tadmor
Joppa   Damascus
Gaza
Raphia

To Tarshish

Jerusalem

EGYPT

PHILISTIA

Memphis

Ezion Geber

Babylon

Ur

Nile R.

Red Sea

Arabian Desert

N

0   200 miles

To Ophir   To SHEBA

Levites took up the ark. 5Then they brought up the ark, the tabernacle of meeting, and all the holy furnishings that *were* in the tabernacle. The priests and the Levites brought them up. 6Also King Solomon, and all the congregation of Israel who were assembled with him before the ark, were sacrificing sheep and oxen that could not be counted or numbered for multitude. 7Then the priests brought in the ark of the covenant of the LORD to its place, into the inner sanctuary of the temple,a to the Most Holy *Place,* under the wings of the cherubim. 8For the cherubim spread *their* wings over the place of the ark, and the cherubim overshadowed the ark and its poles. 9The poles extended so that the ends of the poles of the ark could be seen from *the holy place,* in front of the inner sanctuary; but they could not be seen from outside. And they are there to this day. 10Nothing was in the ark except the two tablets which Moses put *there* at Horeb, when the LORD made *a covenant* with the children of Israel, when they had come out of Egypt.

11And it came to pass when the priests came out of the *Most* Holy *Place* (for all the priests who *were* present had sanctified themselves, without keeping to their divisions), 12and the Levites *who were* the singers, all those of Asaph and Heman and Jeduthun, with their sons and their brethren, stood at the east end of the altar, clothed in white linen, having cymbals, stringed instruments and harps, and with them one hundred and twenty priests sounding with trumpets— 13indeed it came to pass, when the trumpeters and singers *were* as one, to make one sound to be heard in praising and thanking the LORD, and when they lifted up their voice with the trumpets and cymbals and instruments of music, and praised the LORD, *saying:*

"*For He is* good,
  For His mercy *endures* forever,"a

that the house, the house of the LORD, was filled with a cloud, 14so that the priests could not continue ministering because of the cloud; for the glory of the LORD filled the house of God.

6 1Then Solomon spoke:

"The LORD said He would dwell in the dark cloud.
2 I have surely built You an exalted house,

And a place for You to dwell in forever."

Solomon's Speech upon Completion of the Work

3Then the king turned around and blessed the whole assembly of Israel, while all the assembly of Israel was standing. 4And he said: "Blessed *be* the LORD God of Israel, who has fulfilled with His hands *what* He spoke with His mouth to my father David, saying, 5'Since the day that I brought My people out of the land of Egypt, I have chosen no city from any tribe of Israel *in which* to build a house, that My name might be there, nor did I choose any man to be a ruler over My people Israel. 6Yet I have chosen Jerusalem, that My name may be there, and I have chosen David to be over My people Israel.' 7Now it was in the heart of my father David to build a templea for the name of the LORD God of Israel. 8But the LORD said to my father David, 'Whereas it was in your heart to build a temple for My name, you did well in that it was in your heart. 9Nevertheless you shall not build the temple, but your son who will come from your body, he shall build the temple for My name.' 10So the LORD has fulfilled His word which He spoke, and I have filled the position of my father David, and sit on the throne of Israel, as the LORD promised; and I have built the temple for the name of the LORD God of Israel. 11And there I have put the ark, in which *is* the covenant of the LORD which He made with the children of Israel."

Solomon's Prayer of Dedication

12Then *Solomon*a stood before the altar of the LORD in the presence of all the assembly of Israel, and spread out his hands 13(for Solomon had made a bronze platform five cubits long, five cubits wide, and three cubits high, and had set it in the midst of the court; and he stood on it, knelt down on his knees before all the assembly of Israel, and spread out his hands toward heaven); 14and he said: "LORD God of Israel, *there is* no God in heaven or on earth like You, who keep *Your* covenant and mercy with Your servants who walk before You with all their

---

5:7 aLiterally *house*   5:13 aCompare Psalm 106:1   6:7 aLiterally *house,* and so in verses 8–10   6:12 aLiterally *he* (compare 1 Kings 8:22)

hearts. [15]You have kept what You promised Your servant David my father; You have both spoken with Your mouth and fulfilled *it* with Your hand, as *it is* this day. [16]Therefore, LORD God of Israel, now keep what You promised Your servant David my father, saying, 'You shall not fail to have a man sit before Me on the throne of Israel, only if your sons take heed to their way, that they walk in My law as you have walked before Me.' [17]And now, O LORD God of Israel, let Your word come true, which You have spoken to Your servant David.

[18]"But will God indeed dwell with men on the earth? Behold, heaven and the heaven of heavens cannot contain You. How much less this temple[a] which I have built! [19]Yet regard the prayer of Your servant and his supplication, O LORD my God, and listen to the cry and the prayer which Your servant is praying before You: [20]that Your eyes may be open toward this temple day and night, toward the place where *You* said *You would* put Your name, that You may hear the prayer which Your servant makes toward this place. [21]And may You hear the supplications of Your servant and of Your people Israel, when they pray toward this place. Hear from heaven Your dwelling place, and when You hear, forgive.

[22]"If anyone sins against his neighbor, and is forced to take an oath, and comes *and* takes an oath before Your altar in this temple, [23]then hear from heaven, and act, and judge Your servants, bringing retribution on the wicked by bringing his way on his own head, and justifying the righteous by giving him according to his righteousness.

[24]"Or if Your people Israel are defeated before an enemy because they have sinned against You, and return and confess Your name, and pray and make supplication before You in this temple, [25]then hear from heaven and forgive the sin of Your people Israel, and bring them back to the land which You gave to them and their fathers.

[26]"When the heavens are shut up and there is no rain because they have sinned against You, when they pray toward this place and confess Your name, and turn from their sin because You afflict them, [27]then hear *in* heaven, and forgive the sin of Your servants, Your people Israel, that You may teach them the good way in which

they should walk; and send rain on Your land which You have given to Your people as an inheritance.

[28]"When there is famine in the land, pestilence or blight or mildew, locusts or grasshoppers; when their enemies besiege them in the land of their cities; whatever plague or whatever sickness *there is;* [29]whatever prayer, whatever supplication is *made* by anyone, or by all Your people Israel, when each one knows his own burden and his own grief, and spreads out his hands to this temple: [30]then hear from heaven Your dwelling place, and forgive, and give to everyone according to all his ways, whose heart You know (for You alone know the hearts of the sons of men), [31]that they may fear You, to walk in Your ways as long as they live in the land which You gave to our fathers.

[32]"Moreover, concerning a foreigner, who is not of Your people Israel, but has come from a far country for the sake of Your great name and Your mighty hand and Your outstretched arm, when they come and pray in this temple; [33]then hear from heaven Your dwelling place, and do according to all for which the foreigner calls to You, that all peoples of the earth may know Your name and fear You, as *do* Your people Israel, and that they may know that this temple which I have built is called by Your name.

[34]"When Your people go out to battle against their enemies, wherever You send them, and when they pray to You toward this city which You have chosen and the temple which I have built for Your name, [35]then hear from heaven their prayer and their supplication, and maintain their cause.

[36]"When they sin against You (for *there is* no one who does not sin), and You become angry with them and deliver them to the enemy, and they take them captive to a land far or near; [37]*yet* when they come to themselves in the land where they were carried captive, and repent, and make supplication to You in the land of their captivity, saying, 'We have sinned, we have done wrong, and have committed wickedness'; [38]and *when* they return to You with all their heart and with all their soul in the land of their captivity, where they have been carried captive, and pray toward their land which You gave to their fathers, the city which You have chosen, and toward the temple which I have built for Your

---

6:18 [a]Literally *house*

name: [39]then hear from heaven Your dwelling place their prayer and their supplications, and maintain their cause, and forgive Your people who have sinned against You. [40]Now, my God, I pray, let Your eyes be open and *let* Your ears *be* attentive to the prayer *made* in this place.

[41] "Now therefore,
    Arise, O LORD God, to Your resting place,
    You and the ark of Your strength.
    Let Your priests, O LORD God, be clothed with salvation,
    And let Your saints rejoice in goodness.

[42] "O LORD God, do not turn away the face of Your Anointed;
    Remember the mercies of Your servant David."[a]

Solomon Dedicates the Temple

7 [1]When Solomon had finished praying, fire came down from heaven and consumed the burnt offering and the sacrifices; and the glory of the LORD filled the temple.[a] [2]And the priests could not enter the house of the LORD, because the glory of the LORD had filled the LORD's house. [3]When all the children of Israel saw how the fire came down, and the glory of the LORD on the temple, they bowed their faces to the ground on the pavement, and worshiped and praised the LORD, *saying:*

    "For *He is* good,
    For His mercy *endures* forever."[a]

[4]Then the king and all the people offered sacrifices before the LORD. [5]King Solomon offered a sacrifice of twenty-two thousand bulls and one hundred and twenty thousand sheep. So the king and all the people dedicated the house of God. [6]And the priests attended to their services; the Levites also with instruments of the music of the LORD, which King David had made to praise the LORD, saying, "For His mercy *endures* forever,"[a] whenever David offered praise by their ministry. The priests sounded trumpets opposite them, while all Israel stood.

[7]Furthermore Solomon consecrated the middle of the court that *was* in front of the house of the LORD; for there he offered burnt offerings and the fat of the peace offerings, because the bronze altar which Solomon had made was not able to receive the burnt offerings, the grain offerings, and the fat.

[8]At that time Solomon kept the feast seven days, and all Israel with him, a very great assembly from the entrance of Hamath to the Brook of Egypt.[a] [9]And on the eighth day they held a sacred assembly, for they observed the dedication of the altar seven days, and the feast seven days. [10]On the twenty-third day of the seventh month he sent the people away to their tents, joyful and glad of heart for the good that the LORD had done for David, for Solomon, and for His people Israel. [11]Thus Solomon finished the house of the LORD and the king's house; and Solomon successfully accomplished all that came into his heart to make in the house of the LORD and in his own house.

God's Second Appearance to Solomon

[12]Then the LORD appeared to Solomon by night, and said to him: "I have heard your prayer, and have chosen this place for Myself as a house of sacrifice. [13]When I shut up heaven and there is no rain, or command the locusts to devour the land, or send pestilence among My people, [14]if My people who are called by My name will humble themselves, and pray and seek My face, and turn from their wicked ways, then I will hear from heaven, and will forgive their sin and heal their land. [15]Now My eyes will be open and My ears attentive to prayer *made* in this place. [16]For now I have chosen and sanctified this house, that My name may be there forever; and My eyes and My heart will be there perpetually. [17]As for you, if you walk before Me as your father David walked, and do according to all that I have commanded you, and if you keep My statutes and My judgments, [18]then I will establish the throne of your kingdom, as I covenanted with David your father, saying, 'You shall not fail *to have* a man as ruler in Israel.'

[19]"But if you turn away and forsake My statutes and My commandments which I have set before you, and go and serve other gods, and worship them, [20]then I will uproot them from My land which I have given them; and this house which I have

---

6:42 [a]Compare Psalm 132:8–10   7:1 [a]Literally *house*   7:3 [a]Compare Psalm 106:1
7:6 [a]Compare Psalm 106:1   7:8 [a]That is, the Shihor (compare 1 Chronicles 13:5)

sanctified for My name I will cast out of My sight, and will make it a proverb and a byword among all peoples.

21"And *as for* this house, which is exalted, everyone who passes by it will be astonished and say, 'Why has the LORD done thus to this land and this house?' 22Then they will answer, 'Because they forsook the LORD God of their fathers, who brought them out of the land of Egypt, and embraced other gods, and worshiped them and served them; therefore He has brought all this calamity on them.' "

Building the Royal Palaces

The period of 20 years from 966 to 946 B.C. included 7 years of temple construction and an additional 13 years for the king's palace (1 Kin. 6:37—7:1). Besides these two major projects, other buildings were erected (see "Building the King's Palace" at 1 Kin. 7:1).

One particular house was built for Solomon's wife from Egypt, the daughter of Pharaoh. While both the historian of Kings (1 Kin. 9:24) and the Chronicler (2 Chr. 8:11) record this event, Chronicles emphasizes that the pagan princess must not dwell in the sacred places near the ark. As usual, the priestly history shows great concern for the ritual holiness of the temple of Israel's God.

▼   ■ 2 Chronicles 8:1—9:31

2 Chronicles
Solomon's Additional Achievements

8 :1 It came to pass at the end of twenty years, when Solomon had built the house of the LORD and his own house, 2that the cities which Hiram[a] had given to Solomon, Solomon built them; and he settled the children of Israel there. 3And Solomon went to Hamath Zobah and seized it. 4He also built Tadmor in the wilderness, and all the storage cities which he built in Hamath. 5He built Upper Beth Horon and Lower Beth Horon, fortified cities *with* walls, gates, and bars, 6also Baalath and all the storage cities that Solomon had, and all the chariot cities and the cities of the cavalry, and all that Solomon desired to build in Jerusalem, in Lebanon, and in all the land of his dominion.

7All the people *who were* left of the Hittites, Amorites, Perizzites, Hivites, and Jebusites, who *were* not of Israel— 8that is, their descendants who were left in the land after them, whom the children of Israel did not destroy—from these Solomon raised forced labor, as it is to this day. 9But Solomon did not make the children of Israel servants for his work. Some *were* men of war, captains of his officers, captains of his chariots, and his cavalry. 10And others *were* chiefs of the officials of King Solomon: two hundred and fifty, who ruled over the people.

11Now Solomon brought the daughter of Pharaoh up from the City of David to the house he had built for her, for he said, "My wife shall not dwell in the house of David king of Israel, because *the places* to which the ark of the LORD has come are holy."

12Then Solomon offered burnt offerings to the LORD on the altar of the LORD which he had built before the vestibule, 13according to the daily rate, offering according to the commandment of Moses, for the Sabbaths, the New Moons, and the three appointed yearly feasts—the Feast of Unleavened Bread, the Feast of Weeks, and the Feast of Tabernacles. 14And, according to the order of David his father, he appointed the divisions of the priests for their service, the Levites for their duties (to praise and serve before the priests) as the duty of each day required, and the gatekeepers by their divisions at each gate; for so David the man of God had commanded. 15They did not depart from the command of the king to the priests and Levites concerning any matter or concerning the treasuries.

8:2 ªHebrew *Huram* (compare 2 Chronicles 2:3)

GEOGRAPHY AND ENVIRONMENT

Ophir is the name of a remote source of gold (2 Chr. 8:18), probably in the direction of Yemen and across the Indian Ocean to the east. Apart from this, it is not possible to identify its location. There was some ancient gold production in the biblical Cush, roughly corresponding to Upper Egypt and the Sudan. As is still true, remoteness of origin adds glamor to luxury products.

CHARIOTS AND CHARIOT CITIES (2 Chr. 8:5, 6)

The first chariots were apparently four-wheeled wagons or carts used to transport soldiers into battle. Pictures of such vehicles have been found from as early as 3100 B.C. The Egyptians, the Assyrians, and the Romans all used chariots in war. They were symbols of mobility and power.

In its classic form, the chariot is a two-wheeled, horse-drawn vehicle from which a soldier rides and fights. Through the centuries, most chariots carried two passengers, a driver and a fighter, and were drawn by two horses. The best chariots were made in Egypt starting about 1500 B.C., before the Hebrews' Egyptian service. Several complete Egyptian chariots from this time were recovered in A.D. 1922 from the tomb of Tutankhamun, one of the pharaohs whose goods were buried with him.

Tutankhamun's chariots are made of carefully shaped wood, glued and tied together with rawhide. The platform carried two riders side by side; it was a wooden frame with woven straps of leather for the floor. All this made the chariot light in weight, very strong, and as springy as engineering would allow. The "chariots of iron" driven by Israel's enemies (Josh. 17:16, 18; Judg. 1:19; 4:3, 13) were probably wood with iron tires or metal reinforcement at certain points.

Chariot forces became a crucial part of an adequate defense in the ancient Near East. King David confiscated chariots from his conquered enemies (2 Sam. 8:3, 4). But it was his son Solomon who realized the military potential of the chariot. He not only imported Egyptian chariots, but also established "chariot cities" (2 Chr. 8:6). Archaeological excavations at Hazor, one of the cities fortified by Solomon (1 Kin. 9:15, 17–19), shows the remains of chariot enclosures dating to Solomon's time.

16Now all the work of Solomon was well-ordered from[a] the day of the foundation of the house of the LORD until it was finished. So the house of the LORD was completed.

17Then Solomon went to Ezion Geber and Elath[a] on the seacoast, in the land of Edom. 18And Hiram sent him ships by the hand of his servants, and servants who knew the sea. They went with the servants of Solomon to Ophir, and acquired four hundred and fifty talents of gold from there, and brought it to King Solomon.

The Queen of Sheba's Praise of Solomon

9 1Now when the queen of Sheba heard of the fame of Solomon, she came to Jerusalem to test Solomon with hard questions, having a very great retinue, camels that bore spices, gold in abundance, and precious stones; and when she came to Solomon, she spoke with him about all that was in her heart. 2So Solomon answered all her questions; there was nothing so difficult for Solomon that he could not explain it to her. 3And when the queen of Sheba had seen the wisdom of Solomon, the house that he had built, 4the food on his table,

the seating of his servants, the service of his waiters and their apparel, his cupbearers and their apparel, and his entryway by which he went up to the house of the LORD, there was no more spirit in her. 5Then she said to the king: "It was a true report which I heard in my own land about your words and your wisdom. 6However I did not believe their words until I came and saw with my own eyes; and indeed the half of the greatness of your wisdom was not told me. You exceed the fame of which I heard. 7Happy are your men and happy are these your servants, who stand continually before you and hear your wisdom! 8Blessed be the LORD your God, who delighted in you, setting you on His throne to be king for the LORD your God! Because your God has loved Israel, to establish them forever, therefore He made you king over them, to do justice and righteousness."

9And she gave the king one hundred and twenty talents of gold, spices in great abundance, and precious stones; there

8:16 ªFollowing Septuagint, Syriac, and Vulgate; Masoretic Text reads as far as.   8:17 ªHebrew Eloth (compare 2 Kings 14:22)

SOLOMON AND THE QUEEN OF SHEBA (2 Chr. 9:1–9)

The queen of Sheba who visited Solomon at Jerusalem (2 Chr. 9:1) is otherwise unnamed in Scripture. Presumably, Sheba was a land in the southwestern Arabian peninsula, and was known in native sources as Saba. The kingdom of Saba was a complex society by the end of the 1st millennium B.C.

The term "Saba," referring to the people called Sabeans, is mentioned in the inscriptions of two Assyrian kings: Tiglath-Pileser III (744–727 B.C.) and Sargon II (721–705 B.C.). Although these Sabeans were in northern Arabia, it is possible that they had originated in south Arabia (in Sheba) and later expanded along important northern trade routes.

Sabean civilization appears to have been sophisticated, having large urban centers, irrigation systems, and a myriad of trade connections throughout the Near East and southern Asia. Sabean merchants (or "merchants from Sheba") were well known for their trade items (Is. 60:6; Ezek. 27:22, 23).

It is possible that the queen of Sheba came to Jerusalem, not only to visit socially with Solomon, but also to strengthen trade relations with him. Solomon had just built a cargo fleet that traversed the Gulf of Aqaba (1 Kin. 9:26–28), and the queen's abundant gifts to him (1 Chr. 9:9) may have been in exchange for trade concessions.

never were any spices such as those the queen of Sheba gave to King Solomon.

10Also, the servants of Hiram and the servants of Solomon, who brought gold from Ophir, brought algum[a] wood and precious stones. 11And the king made walkways *of* the algum[a] wood for the house of the LORD and for the king's house, also harps and stringed instruments for singers; and there were none such *as these* seen before in the land of Judah.

12Now King Solomon gave to the queen of Sheba all she desired, whatever she asked, *much more* than she had brought to the king. So she turned and went to her own country, she and her servants.

Solomon's Great Wealth

13The weight of gold that came to Solomon yearly was six hundred and sixty-six talents of gold, 14besides *what* the traveling merchants and traders brought. And all the kings of Arabia and governors of the country brought gold and silver to Solomon. 15And King Solomon made two hundred large shields of hammered gold; six hundred *shekels* of hammered gold went into each shield. 16He also *made* three hundred shields of hammered gold; three hundred *shekels*[a] of gold went into each shield. The king put them in the House of the Forest of Lebanon.

17Moreover the king made a great throne of ivory, and overlaid it with pure gold. 18The throne *had* six steps, with a footstool of gold, *which were* fastened to the throne; there were armrests on either side of the place of the seat, and two lions stood beside the armrests. 19Twelve lions stood there, one on each side of the six steps; nothing like *this* had been made for any *other* kingdom.

20All King Solomon's drinking vessels *were* gold, and all the vessels of the House of the Forest of Lebanon *were* pure gold. Not *one was* silver, for this was accounted as nothing in the days of Solomon. 21For

9:10 [a]Or *almug* (compare 1 Kings 10:11, 12)
9:11 [a]Or *almug* (compare 1 Kings 10:11, 12)
9:16 [a]Or *three minas* (compare 1 Kings 10:17)

ARCHITECTURE AND BUILDING

Public display of wealth is a driving force in the human psychology, and gold has often been the choice of kings to draw attention to their power. There is evidence of gold shields being used as ceremonial display in temples elsewhere in the Middle East, from about 200 years after Solomon's time. The total weight of Solomon's shields was about 5,000 pounds (2 Chr. 9:16).

the king's ships went to Tarshish with the servants of Hiram.[a] Once every three years the merchant ships[b] came, bringing gold, silver, ivory, apes, and monkeys.[c]

[22]So King Solomon surpassed all the kings of the earth in riches and wisdom. [23]And all the kings of the earth sought the presence of Solomon to hear his wisdom, which God had put in his heart. [24]Each man brought his present: articles of silver and gold, garments, armor, spices, horses, and mules, at a set rate year by year.

[25]Solomon had four thousand stalls for horses and chariots, and twelve thousand horsemen whom he stationed in the chariot cities and with the king at Jerusalem.

[26]So he reigned over all the kings from the River[a] to the land of the Philistines, as far as the border of Egypt. [27]The king made silver as common in Jerusalem as stones, and he made cedar trees as abundant as the sycamores which are in the lowland. [28]And they brought horses to Solomon from Egypt and from all lands.

Death of Solomon

[29]Now the rest of the acts of Solomon, first and last, are they not written in the book of Nathan the prophet, in the prophecy of Ahijah the Shilonite, and in the visions of Iddo the seer concerning Jeroboam the son of Nebat? [30]Solomon reigned in Jerusalem over all Israel forty years. [31]Then Solomon rested with his fathers, and was buried in the City of David his father. And Rehoboam his son reigned in his place.

9:21 [a]Hebrew *Huram* (compare 1 Kings 10:22) [b]Literally *ships of Tarshish*, deep-sea vessels   [c]Or *peacocks*   9:26 [a]That is, the Euphrates

THE FALL OF TWO NATIONS

(930—586 B.C.)

**The positive accomplishments of the united monarchy
slowly began to unravel, and Solomon's kingdom
eventually divided into Israel and Judah.**

The brokenness of God's people led to brokenness in the world. Solomon's empire
broke apart partly because Solomon and Rehoboam failed to be instruments of justice
for their people. The many positive accomplishments of the united monarchy now
slowly began to unravel, eventually resulting in the division of Solomon's kingdom
into Israel (north) and Judah (south).

The story of the divided monarchy is one of gradual decay, with only brief interludes of hope. The two little nations of Israel and Judah spent most of their existence
as vassal states, serving first the Neo-Assyrian Empire (934–612 B.C.) and then the
Neo-Babylonian Empire (626–539 B.C.). Israel was destroyed by the Neo-Assyrians;
Judah by the Neo-Babylonians.

▶ Archaeology and the Past

The Iron Age (1200–600 B.C.) spans the united and divided monarchies, and
remains and records of this age often relate to the Bible. For example, Pharaoh Shishak I left inscriptions listing the cities and towns that he conquered in Palestine
after the division of the kingdoms. While Egypt was not a strong force in the region,
the records of other empires, especially those of Assyria, provide more details to sup-
plement the biblical accounts.

Israelite kings built a new capital for the northern kingdom at Samaria. Excavations there have revealed great city walls on bedrock, dating from this period.
Large numbers of ivory inlays from furniture were also found, reminding us that the
ruling classes in Israel were incredibly wealthy. The prophets criticized the upper
classes because their "houses of ivory" (Amos 3:15) were built by exploiting the poor.

King Ahab rebuilt the stables at Megiddo, and made it once again a great city.
He also built a palace at Hazor as part of the renovation of that city. His economic
power made him an international force. According to an inscription of Shalmaneser III of Assyria, "Ahab the Israelite" brought 2,000 chariots and 10,000 infantry to
the battle of Qarqar (853 B.C.). Ahab apparently had picked up on Solomon's trade in
horses and chariots. Certainly he was a force in halting Assyria's advance toward
Palestine.

Israel appears in other important inscriptions of the period. The famous
Moabite Stone tells how King Mesha of Moab rebelled successfully against Israel in
the 9th century B.C. The Black Obelisk of Shalmaneser III (841 B.C.) shows, in a series
of carvings, conquered kings paying tribute to the Neo-Assyrian emperor. In the first
"picture" of an Israelite king, Jehu of Israel is shown kissing the feet of Shalmaneser.

Records and annals of Assyrian kings reveal contact between the Neo-Assyrian
Empire and the divided kingdoms of Israel and Judah. King Azariah (Uzziah) of Judah is listed in the records of Tiglath-Pileser III as leading a revolt against Assyria.

Both Assyrian inscriptions and excavated cities in Israel record that Tiglath-Pileser overran Israel (about 732 B.C.), laying waste cities, making Galilee an Assyrian province, and deporting the population to other parts of his empire.

Ironically, one of the more important archaeological finds related to the fall of Israel is found to the south, in Jerusalem. The "Broad Wall" of Judah's king Hezekiah was a city wall built on the western hills of Jerusalem. It tells us that, at this time, Jerusalem was greatly enlarged, partly to handle the flood of refugees from Israel.

Judah herself experienced Assyrian power through Assyria's king Sennacherib. Hezekiah undertook a massive water project to carry water from the Gihon spring, outside the city walls, through a tunnel into the city. The tunnel was dug to ensure the water supply at the time of Sennacherib's invasion in 701 B.C. Sennacherib also left a long document describing his siege of Jerusalem. The carvings on Sennacherib's palace walls included large pictures of the siege and destruction of Lachish, an important Judahite fortress. The carvings show both the siege process, the storming of the city, and the surrender of the citizens.

The Neo-Assyrian Empire fell around 612 B.C., but in its place arose the Neo-Babylonian Empire, which would ultimately destroy Jerusalem and carry the kings of Judah into exile. From the period of the Babylonian invasions are the Lachish Letters. These messages are written on pieces of broken pottery to the military commander at Lachish (which had been rebuilt). In them, an officer describes how he can no longer see the signals from other outposts, a sign of the advance of the Babylonian army.

In Jerusalem itself, recent excavations in the City of David have uncovered what is called the House of Ahiel, a 6th-century house that was destroyed by the Babylonians in their attacks on the city. The house had been burned, and there were Babylonian arrowheads in the ruins.

On a more peaceful note are the many seals and seal impressions from this period found in Jerusalem. One seal belongs to Gedaliah, the governor, who may have been the governor put in place by the Babylonians after they destroyed Jerusalem. Another fascinating seal impression bears the name of Baruch, son of Neriah, the name of the prophet Jeremiah's friend and scribe.

▶ The Peoples and Groups

The Assyrians were one of the great superpowers of the ancient world, with an empire centered on the Tigris River. One of the keys to Assyrian power was a large, permanent army, with soldiers trained in every specialty needed for war. Artists were important in Assyria, and literature and architecture flourished. The most spectacular work was stone carving, and Assyrian palaces and monuments are filled with carvings, showing the nation at war, at work, and in the daily round of life. On the other side of their character, the Assyrians were unspeakably cruel and tortured prisoners as a regular practice. The Assyrian Empire was overthrown by the Medes and Babylonians in the years between 612 and 609 B.C.

The other superpower in the East was Babylon. One of their greatest kings was Nebuchadnezzar, whose armies destroyed Jerusalem in 586 B.C. In addition to his military and political ambitions, Nebuchadnezzar rebuilt Babylon to make it one of the most beautiful cities in the world. The Ishtar Gate was a double gate, faced with enameled bricks, in patterns of flowers, animals, and dragons. The palace was also built of enameled bricks, and contained one room decorated with bricks of gold and blue. The "hanging gardens," a set of gardens built on terraces that thrust up into the air, is one of the wonders of the ancient world. Babylon was taken by the Persians in 539 B.C.

▶ The Biblical Literature

Biblical books that relate this period come from three groups, the first consisting of portions from Kings and Chronicles. The history of the kingdoms of Judah and Israel shows their alternation between faithfulness and faithlessness in their relationships with Yahweh.

A second group relates to the Neo-Assyrian period and includes the prophetic writings of Amos, Hosea, Isaiah, Micah, Jonah, and Zephaniah. Amos and Hosea preached in Israel, with an emphasis on social and economic justice. They warned of the coming punishment of Yahweh because of Israel's failure to keep the covenant. Isaiah was a counselor to the kings of Judah. He worked through two major international crises, which he saw as signs of God's rule over the nations, and of God's displeasure over Judah's failure to bring about social justice. Micah was a rural contemporary of Isaiah who also preached against injustice, but lifted up a vision of a day of peace and salvation. Zephaniah began preaching sometime after 640 B.C., condemning idolatry and injustice. All these prophets were conscious of God's concern for justice and the failure of their nation to bring justice to the people.

The history of Judah and Israel shows their alternation between faithfulness and faithlessness towards Yahweh.

The third group relates to the Neo-Babylonian period. Parts of the Book of Daniel tell the story of a Jewish youth exiled to Babylon, while the Book of Lamentations mourns the destruction of Jerusalem. Also included are prophecies from Jeremiah, Habakkuk, Nahum, Ezekiel, and Obadiah. Jeremiah lived through the destruction of Jerusalem in 586 B.C. He continued to call for social justice and loyalty to Yahweh, but also introduced the vision of a new covenant and of hope. Habakkuk records the pain of seeing the Babylonians on the march and wonders where God is in these events. Nahum rejoices over the defeat of Assyria. Ezekiel was the first prophet to write from exile in Babylon. He first preached a message of doom and judgment but, after the destruction of Jerusalem, began to preach hope. Obadiah is a song of anger against the people of Edom for their part in the destruction of Jerusalem.

The Divided Monarchy in Israel

The glory years of Solomon were ended, replaced by a monarchy divided into North and South.

Israel was more united under the monarchy than ever before, but the old tribal loyalties remained, at least under the surface. Saul, from the tribe of Benjamin, had surrounded himself with other Benjamites (1 Sam. 22:7), as had David with members of his own tribe of Judah. These two tribes remained rivals throughout the united monarchy. While resentment over the forced labor imposed by Solomon precipitated the division of Israel into different parts (1 Kin. 12:1–17), the divisions were there already.

The division of Israel into two kingdoms led to some resentment and even the threat of war, but war was averted and before long the two new nations were diplomatic allies. However, the glory years of Solomon's united monarchy were ended, replaced by a divided monarchy—

a northern kingdom, which from this time on assumed the old name "Israel," and a southern kingdom of Judah.

The division of the kingdom left David's empire in shambles. Not only was Israel split, but the other nations that David had conquered soon achieved independence. The continuing weakness of the Egyptian and Assyrian empires allowed the weakened land of Israel to survive, but Aram-Damascus (Syria), just to the northeast was a growing threat.

Prophetic Account: The Kingdom Divides

The books of Kings are an anonymous writer's reflections on the history of the Israelite monarchy from the accession of Solomon to the end. The story of the uneasy coexistence of Israel and Judah continues from 1 Kin. 12:1 until the fall of the northern kingdom (2 Kin. 17:41). The unity between North (Israel) and South (Judah) under Saul, David, and Solomon had been held together by the charisma and strength of its leaders. Now the tribes went separate ways, following separate leaders: Jeroboam I for the northern tribes and Rehoboam, Solomon's son, for the southern tribes of Judah and Simeon.

▼   ■ 1 Kings 12:1–24

1 Kings
The Revolt Against Rehoboam

12 :1 And Rehoboam went to Shechem, for all Israel had gone to Shechem to make him king. ²So it happened, when Jeroboam the son of Nebat heard *it* (he was still in Egypt, for he had fled from the presence of King Solomon and had been dwelling in Egypt), ³that they sent and called him. Then Jeroboam and the whole assembly of Israel came and spoke to Rehoboam, saying, ⁴"Your father made our yoke heavy; now therefore, lighten the burdensome service of your father, and his heavy yoke which he put on us, and we will serve you."

⁵So he said to them, "Depart *for* three days, then come back to me." And the people departed.

⁶Then King Rehoboam consulted the elders who stood before his father Solomon while he still lived, and he said, "How do you advise *me* to answer these people?"

⁷And they spoke to him, saying, "If you will be a servant to these people today, and serve them, and answer them, and speak good words to them, then they will be your servants forever."

⁸But he rejected the advice which the elders had given him, and consulted the young men who had grown up with him, who stood before him. ⁹And he said to them, "What advice do you give? How should we answer this people who have spoken to me, saying, 'Lighten the yoke which your father put on us'?"

¹⁰Then the young men who had grown up with him spoke to him, saying, "Thus you should speak to this people who have spoken to you, saying, 'Your father made our yoke heavy, but you make *it* lighter on us'—thus you shall say to them: 'My little *finger* shall be thicker than my father's waist! ¹¹And now, whereas my father put a heavy yoke on you, I will add to your yoke; my father chastised you with whips, but I will chastise you with scourges!' "[a]

¹²So Jeroboam and all the people came to Rehoboam the third day, as the king had directed, saying, "Come back to me the third day." ¹³Then the king answered the people roughly, and rejected the advice which the elders had given him; ¹⁴and he spoke to them according to the advice of the young men, saying, "My father made your yoke heavy, but I will add to your yoke; my father chastised you with whips, but I will chastise you with scourges!"[a] ¹⁵So the king did not listen to the people; for the turn *of events* was from the LORD, that He might fulfill His word, which the LORD had spoken by Ahijah the Shilonite to Jeroboam the son of Nebat.

¹⁶Now when all Israel saw that the king did not listen to them, the people answered the king, saying:

"What share have we in David?
We have no inheritance in the son of Jesse.
To your tents, O Israel!
Now, see to your own house, O David!"

So Israel departed to their tents. ¹⁷But Rehoboam reigned over the children of Israel who dwelt in the cities of Judah.

¹⁸Then King Rehoboam sent Adoram,

12:11 [a]Literally *scorpions*   12:14 [a]Literally *scorpions*

REHOBOAM AND JEROBOAM DIVIDE THE KINGDOM

The discontent and unrest that existed in Solomon's kingdom was like a powder keg awaiting a spark. When Solomon died, the occasion for the explosion came because of the foolish insensitivity of his son Rehoboam. The 10 northern tribes revolted against Rehoboam and appointed Jeroboam as their king.

Judah (southern kingdom)	Israel (northern kingdom)
Rehoboam fought border wars against Jeroboam, probably over the territory of Benjamin which was a buffer zone between the two kingdoms (1 Kin. 14:30).	**Jeroboam** established his capital at Tirzah. He was succeeded by his son Nadab, but the dynasty was soon cut off by Nadab's assassination.
Abijah (or Abijam), son of Rehoboam, continued the border wars against Jeroboam (1 Kin. 15:7).	**Nadab** besieged the Philistine city of Gibbethon, but during the siege was assassinated by his successor Baasha (1 Kin. 15:27).

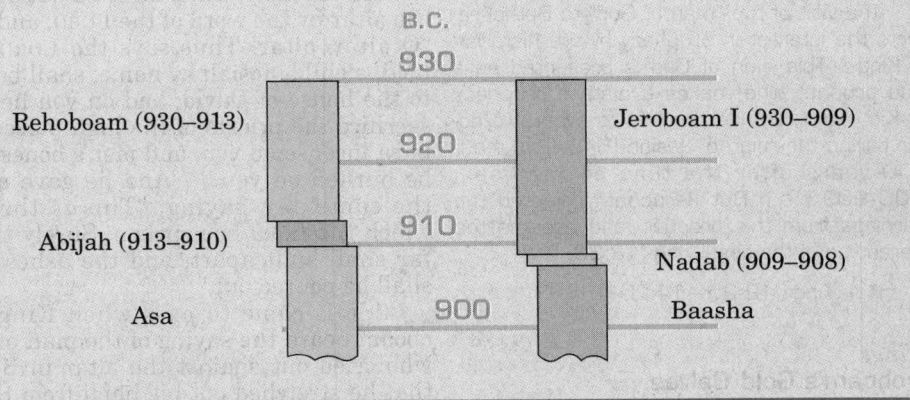

who *was* in charge of the revenue; but all Israel stoned him with stones, and he died. Therefore King Rehoboam mounted his chariot in haste to flee to Jerusalem. [19]So Israel has been in rebellion against the house of David to this day.

[20]Now it came to pass when all Israel heard that Jeroboam had come back, they sent for him and called him to the congregation, and made him king over all Israel. There was none who followed the house of David, but the tribe of Judah only.

[21]And when Rehoboam came to Jerusalem, he assembled all the house of Judah with the tribe of Benjamin, one hundred and eighty thousand chosen *men* who were warriors, to fight against the house of Israel, that he might restore the kingdom to Rehoboam the son of Solomon. [22]But the word of God came to Shemaiah the man of God, saying, [23]"Speak to Rehoboam the son of Solomon, king of Judah, to all the house of Judah and Benjamin, and to the rest of the people, saying, [24]'Thus says the LORD:

"You shall not go up nor fight against your brethren the children of Israel. Let every man return to his house, for this thing is from Me." ' " Therefore they obeyed the

TIME CAPSULE   930 to 925 B.C.

930	Rehoboam succeeds Solomon as king of Israel
930	The kingdom of Israel splits into northern Israel and southern Judah
930	Jeroboam I becomes king in northern Israel
930–722	The northern kingdom of Israel
930–586	The southern kingdom of Judah
925	Pharaoh Shishak captures Arad during a raid of Palestine
925	Shishak sacks the temple in Jerusalem

word of the LORD, and turned back, according to the word of the LORD.

First Dynasty of the Northern Kingdom

Israel in the north was much larger and stronger than the southern Judah. But Israel was also less unified than Judah. Not only did it include more tribes, but it had neither a central shrine, like the temple in Jerusalem, nor the ark of the covenant. To remedy this lack, Israel's first king, Jeroboam I, built replacement shrines at Dan and Bethel. These were probably dedicated to Israel's one God, but the golden calves Jeroboam set there were soon regarded as idols (1 Kin. 12:25–33).

The visit of the "man of God" to Bethel reflects the interest in prophecy by the historian of Kings. This man of God is presented as a true prophet who makes a distant prophecy (1 Kin. 13:1, 2). He prophesies events to occur during the reign of Josiah (640–609 B.C.), 300 years after the time of Jeroboam (930–909 B.C.). But Jeroboam rejected the warnings from this prophet, and became the stereotype of the sinful king (13:33, 34).

■ 1 Kings 12:25—14:20

1 Kings
Jeroboam's Gold Calves

12 **:25** Then Jeroboam built Shechem in the mountains of Ephraim, and dwelt there. Also he went out from there and built Penuel. 26And Jeroboam said in his heart, "Now the kingdom may return to the house of David: 27If these people go up to offer sacrifices in the house of the LORD at Jerusalem, then the heart of this people will turn back to their lord, Rehoboam king of Judah, and they will kill me and go back to Rehoboam king of Judah."

28Therefore the king asked advice, made two calves of gold, and said to the people, "It is too much for you to go up to Jerusalem. Here are your gods, O Israel, which brought you up from the land of Egypt!" 29And he set up one in Bethel, and the other he put in Dan. 30Now this thing became a sin, for the people went *to worship* before the one as far as Dan. 31He made shrines^a on the high places, and made priests from every class of people, who were not of the sons of Levi.

32Jeroboam ordained a feast on the fifteenth day of the eighth month, like the feast that *was* in Judah, and offered sacrifices on the altar. So he did at Bethel, sacrificing to the calves that he had made. And at Bethel he installed the priests of the high places which he had made. 33So he made offerings on the altar which he had made at Bethel on the fifteenth day of the eighth month, in the month which he had devised in his own heart. And he ordained a feast for the children of Israel, and offered sacrifices on the altar and burned incense.

The Message of the Man of God

13 1And behold, a man of God went from Judah to Bethel by the word of the LORD, and Jeroboam stood by the altar to burn incense. 2Then he cried out against the altar by the word of the LORD, and said, "O altar, altar! Thus says the LORD: 'Behold, a child, Josiah by name, shall be born to the house of David; and on you he shall sacrifice the priests of the high places who burn incense on you, and men's bones shall be burned on you.'" 3And he gave a sign the same day, saying, "This *is* the sign which the LORD has spoken: Surely the altar shall split apart, and the ashes on it shall be poured out."

4So it came to pass when King Jeroboam heard the saying of the man of God, who cried out against the altar in Bethel, that he stretched out his hand from the altar, saying, "Arrest him!" Then his hand, which he stretched out toward him, withered, so that he could not pull it back to himself. 5The altar also was split apart, and the ashes poured out from the altar, according to the sign which the man of God had given by the word of the LORD. 6Then the king answered and said to the man of God, "Please entreat the favor of the LORD your God, and pray for me, that my hand may be restored to me."

So the man of God entreated the LORD, and the king's hand was restored to him, and became as before. 7Then the king said to the man of God, "Come home with me and refresh yourself, and I will give you a reward."

8But the man of God said to the king, "If you were to give me half your house, I would not go in with you; nor would I eat bread nor drink water in this place. 9For so it was commanded me by the word of the LORD, saying, 'You shall not eat bread, nor

12:31 ^aLiterally *a house*

HOLY COWS (1 Kin. 12:28)

The act of Jeroboam in crafting images of cows for worship was not unique. Not only did he repeat the actions of Aaron by creating a golden calf, but he quoted the words of Aaron, "Here are your gods, O Israel, which brought you up from the land of Egypt" (Ex. 32:4; 1 Kin. 12:28).

Exactly which god was represented by the calves is not known. The Hebrew word for "calves" in 1 Kin. 12:28 suggests that the animal was a young bull, as was used for sacrifices (Mic. 6:6). A number of small bull images have been found by archaeologists, testifying to the common worship of such images. Calf worship was still prominent among the Israelites of the northern kingdom when Hosea prophesied (Hos. 8:5; 10:5, 6), during the reign of Jeroboam II (793–753 B.C.).

Jeroboam I placed his two idol calves in the two geographical extremes of his empire (1 Kin. 12:29). Bethel, just a few miles north of Jerusalem, means "house of god" and had been a traditional place of worship since the days of the patriarchs (Gen. 31:13). Dan lies in the most northerly extreme of Israel. In so doing Jeroboam made sure that one of his worship centers was closer to the Israelites than was Jerusalem.

To completely separate the Israelites from the worship of God in Jerusalem, Jeroboam even began a new priesthood. In Israel's covenant the Levites were assigned as priests for the nation's worship (Num. 3:5–10), but Jeroboam appointed non-Levitical priests, causing the Levites to flee to Judah (1 Kin. 12:31; 2 Chr. 11:14, 15). He even inaugurated separate feasts (1 Kin. 12:32). By encouraging the worship of the golden bull Jeroboam hoped to keep the hearts of his people from returning to King Rehoboam, the grandson of David (12:26, 27).

---

drink water, nor return by the same way you came.'" [10]So he went another way and did not return by the way he came to Bethel.

Death of the Man of God

[11]Now an old prophet dwelt in Bethel, and his sons came and told him all the works that the man of God had done that day in Bethel; they also told their father the words which he had spoken to the king. [12]And their father said to them, "Which way did he go?" For his sons had seen[a] which way the man of God went who came from Judah. [13]Then he said to his sons, "Saddle the donkey for me." So they saddled the donkey for him; and he rode on it, [14]and went after the man of God, and found him sitting under an oak. Then he said to him, "*Are* you the man of God who came from Judah?"

And he said, "I *am*."

[15]Then he said to him, "Come home with me and eat bread."

[16]And he said, "I cannot return with you nor go in with you; neither can I eat bread nor drink water with you in this place. [17]For I have been told by the word of the LORD, 'You shall not eat bread nor drink water there, nor return by going the way you came.'"

[18]He said to him, "I too *am* a prophet as you *are,* and an angel spoke to me by the word of the LORD, saying, 'Bring him back with you to your house, that he may eat bread and drink water.'" (He was lying to him.)

[19]So he went back with him, and ate bread in his house, and drank water.

[20]Now it happened, as they sat at the table, that the word of the LORD came to the prophet who had brought him back; [21]and he cried out to the man of God who came from Judah, saying, "Thus says the LORD: 'Because you have disobeyed the word of the LORD, and have not kept the commandment which the LORD your God commanded you, [22]but you came back, ate bread, and drank water in the place of which *the* LORD said to you, "Eat no bread and drink no water," your corpse shall not come to the tomb of your fathers.'"

[23]So it was, after he had eaten bread

13:12 [a]Septuagint, Syriac, Targum, and Vulgate read *showed him.*

and after he had drunk, that he saddled the donkey for him, the prophet whom he had brought back. ²⁴When he was gone, a lion met him on the road and killed him. And his corpse was thrown on the road, and the donkey stood by it. The lion also stood by the corpse. ²⁵And there, men passed by and saw the corpse thrown on the road, and the lion standing by the corpse. Then they went and told *it* in the city where the old prophet dwelt.

²⁶Now when the prophet who had brought him back from the way heard *it,* he said, "It *is* the man of God who was disobedient to the word of the LORD. Therefore the LORD has delivered him to the lion, which has torn him and killed him, according to the word of the LORD which He spoke to him." ²⁷And he spoke to his sons, saying, "Saddle the donkey for me." So they saddled *it.* ²⁸Then he went and found his corpse thrown on the road, and the donkey and the lion standing by the corpse. The lion had not eaten the corpse nor torn the donkey. ²⁹And the prophet took up the corpse of the man of God, laid it on the donkey, and brought it back. So the old prophet came to the city to mourn, and to bury him. ³⁰Then he laid the corpse in his own tomb; and they mourned over him, *saying,* "Alas, my brother!" ³¹So it was, after he had buried him, that he spoke to his sons, saying, "When I am dead, then bury me in the tomb where the man of God *is* buried; lay my bones beside his bones. ³²For the saying which he cried out by the word of the LORD against the altar in Bethel, and against all the shrinesᵃ on the high places which *are* in the cities of Samaria, will surely come to pass."

³³After this event Jeroboam did not turn from his evil way, but again he made priests from every class of people for the high places; whoever wished, he consecrated him, and he became *one* of the priests of the high places. ³⁴And this thing was the sin of the house of Jeroboam, so as to exterminate and destroy *it* from the face of the earth.

Judgment on the House of Jeroboam

14 ¹At that time Abijah the son of Jeroboam became sick. ²And Jeroboam said to his wife, "Please arise, and disguise yourself, that they may not recognize you as the wife of Jeroboam, and go to Shiloh. Indeed, Ahijah the prophet *is* there, who told me that *I would be* king over this peo-

ple. ³Also take with you ten loaves, *some* cakes, and a jar of honey, and go to him; he will tell you what will become of the child." ⁴And Jeroboam's wife did so; she arose and went to Shiloh, and came to the house of Ahijah. But Ahijah could not see, for his eyes were glazed by reason of his age.

⁵Now the LORD had said to Ahijah, "Here is the wife of Jeroboam, coming to ask you something about her son, for he *is* sick. Thus and thus you shall say to her; for it will be, when she comes in, that she will pretend *to be* another *woman.*"

⁶And so it was, when Ahijah heard the sound of her footsteps as she came through the door, he said, "Come in, wife of Jeroboam. Why do you pretend *to be* another *person?* For I *have been* sent to you *with* bad *news.* ⁷Go, tell Jeroboam, 'Thus says the LORD God of Israel: "Because I exalted you from among the people, and made you ruler over My people Israel, ⁸and tore the kingdom away from the house of David, and gave it to you; and *yet* you have not been as My servant David, who kept My commandments and who followed Me with all his heart, to do only *what was* right in My eyes; ⁹but you have done more evil than all who were before you, for you have gone and made for yourself other gods and molded images to provoke Me to anger, and have cast Me behind your back— ¹⁰therefore behold! I will bring disaster on the house of Jeroboam, and will cut off from Jeroboam every male in Israel, bond and free; I will take away the remnant of the house of Jeroboam, as one takes away refuse until it is all gone. ¹¹The dogs shall eat whoever belongs to Jeroboam and dies in the city, and the birds of the air shall eat whoever dies in the field; for the LORD has spoken!" ' ¹²Arise therefore, go to your own house. When your feet enter the city, the child shall die. ¹³And all Israel shall mourn for him and bury him, for he is the only one of Jeroboam who shall come to the grave, because in him there is found something good toward the LORD God of Israel in the house of Jeroboam.

¹⁴"Moreover the LORD will raise up for Himself a king over Israel who shall cut off the house of Jeroboam; this is the day. What? Even now! ¹⁵For the LORD will strike Israel, as a reed is shaken in the water. He will uproot Israel from this good land which He gave to their fathers, and

---

13:32 ᵃLiterally *houses*

will scatter them beyond the River,[a] because they have made their wooden images,[b] provoking the LORD to anger. 16And He will give Israel up because of the sins of Jeroboam, who sinned and who made Israel sin."

17Then Jeroboam's wife arose and departed, and came to Tirzah. When she came to the threshold of the house, the child died. 18And they buried him; and all Israel mourned for him, according to the word of the LORD which He spoke through His servant Ahijah the prophet.

Death of Jeroboam

19Now the rest of the acts of Jeroboam, how he made war and how he reigned, indeed they *are* written in the book of the chronicles of the kings of Israel. 20The period that Jeroboam reigned *was* twenty-two years. So he rested with his fathers. Then Nadab his son reigned in his place.

14:15 [a]That is, the Euphrates [b]Hebrew *Asherim*, Canaanite deities   14:24 [a]Hebrew *qadesh*, that is, one practicing sodomy and prostitution in religious rituals

---

The Davidic Dynasty in Judah

The descendants of David continued to rule in Judah during the divided monarchy, represented first by Solomon's son Rehoboam. During Rehoboam's reign (930–913 B.C.), the Egyptian pharaoh Shishak (or Sheshonk) marched against Judah and Jerusalem, taking tribute from the temple and palace (1 Kin. 14:25, 26). Shishak's own records report a devastating attack on Israel as well. Ruling Egypt's 22nd Dynasty from 945 to 924 B.C., Shishak led his campaign into Palestine during Rehoboam's 5th year (c. 925 B.C.).

In the first account of Judah during the divided kingdom, the historian of Kings presents three kings: Rehoboam, Abijam (or Abijah, 913–910 B.C.), and Asa (910–869 B.C.). He dates each king by synchronizing his accession year with the reign of the monarch in the other kingdom (see 1 Kin. 15:1, 9).

Because Kings alternates between accounts of Israel and Judah, some unusual historical sequences result. For example, the border wars between Asa and Israel's Baasha (15:16–21) are discussed before Baasha is formally introduced (15:27–30). During the 9th century B.C. Damascus (Syria) allied itself with various Aramean kingdoms and became a serious threat to Israel's northeast. Asa enticed Ben-Hadad I of Aram-Damascus to invade Israel, hoping to relieve Israel's military pressure on Jerusalem.

■ 1 Kings 14:21—15:24

1 Kings
Rehoboam Reigns in Judah

14:21 And Rehoboam the son of Solomon reigned in Judah. Rehoboam *was* forty-one years old when he became king. He reigned seventeen years in Jerusalem, the city which the LORD had chosen out of all the tribes of Israel, to put His name there. His mother's name *was* Naamah, an Ammonitess. 22Now Judah did evil in the sight of the LORD, and they provoked Him to jealousy with their sins which they committed, more than all that their fathers had done. 23For they also built for themselves high places, *sacred* pillars, and wooden images on every high hill and under every green tree. 24And there were also perverted persons[a] in the land. They did according to all the abominations of the nations which the LORD had cast out before the children of Israel.

25It happened in the fifth year of King Rehoboam *that* Shishak king of Egypt came up against Jerusalem. 26And he took away the treasures of the house of the LORD and the treasures of the king's house; he took away everything. He also took away all the gold shields which Solomon had made. 27Then King Rehoboam made bronze shields in their place, and committed *them* to the hands of the captains of the guard, who guarded the doorway of the

---

CULTS AND SUPERNATURAL

The Hebrew word qadesh *is spelled the same as the Hebrew word meaning "separated" or "set apart." In 1 Kin. 14:24 the word describes persons connected with the hilltop sites of Canaanite worship. It is usually assumed that these persons were prostitutes, male and female, whose acts were associated with the religious worship carried out at the sanctuary.*

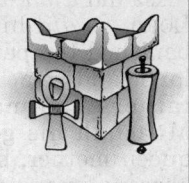

king's house. ²⁸And whenever the king entered the house of the LORD, the guards carried them, then brought them back into the guardroom.

²⁹Now the rest of the acts of Rehoboam, and all that he did, *are* they not written in the book of the chronicles of the kings of Judah? ³⁰And there was war between Rehoboam and Jeroboam all *their* days. ³¹So Rehoboam rested with his fathers, and was buried with his fathers in the City of David. His mother's name *was* Naamah, an Ammonitess. Then Abijam[a] his son reigned in his place.

Abijam Reigns in Judah

15 ¹In the eighteenth year of King Jeroboam the son of Nebat, Abijam became king over Judah. ²He reigned three years in Jerusalem. His mother's name *was* Maachah the granddaughter of Abishalom. ³And he walked in all the sins of his father, which he had done before him; his heart was not loyal to the LORD his God, as was the heart of his father David. ⁴Nevertheless for David's sake the LORD his God gave him a lamp in Jerusalem, by setting up his son after him and by establishing Jerusalem; ⁵because David did *what was* right in the eyes of the LORD, and had not turned aside from anything that He commanded him all the days of his life, except in the matter of Uriah the Hittite. ⁶And there was war between Rehoboam[a] and Jeroboam all the days of his life. ⁷Now the rest of the acts of Abijam, and all that he did, *are* they not written in the book of the chronicles of the kings of Judah? And there was war between Abijam and Jeroboam.

⁸So Abijam rested with his fathers, and they buried him in the City of David. Then Asa his son reigned in his place.

Asa Reigns in Judah

⁹In the twentieth year of Jeroboam king of Israel, Asa became king over Judah. ¹⁰And he reigned forty-one years in Jerusalem. His grandmother's name *was* Maachah the granddaughter of Abishalom. ¹¹Asa did *what was* right in the eyes of the LORD, as *did* his father David. ¹²And he banished the perverted persons[a] from the land, and removed all the idols that his fathers had made. ¹³Also he removed Maachah his grandmother from *being* queen mother, because she had made an obscene image of Asherah.[a] And Asa cut

down her obscene image and burned *it* by the Brook Kidron. ¹⁴But the high places were not removed. Nevertheless Asa's heart was loyal to the LORD all his days. ¹⁵He also brought into the house of the LORD the things which his father had dedicated, and the things which he himself had dedicated: silver and gold and utensils.

¹⁶Now there was war between Asa and Baasha king of Israel all their days. ¹⁷And Baasha king of Israel came up against Judah, and built Ramah, that he might let none go out or come in to Asa king of Judah. ¹⁸Then Asa took all the silver and gold *that was* left in the treasuries of the house of the LORD and the treasuries of the king's house, and delivered them into the hand of his servants. And King Asa sent them to Ben-Hadad the son of Tabrimmon, the son of Hezion, king of Syria, who dwelt in Damascus, saying, ¹⁹"*Let there be* a treaty between you and me, as there was between my father and your father. See, I have sent you a present of silver and gold. Come and break your treaty with Baasha king of Israel, so that he will withdraw from me."

²⁰So Ben-Hadad heeded King Asa, and sent the captains of his armies against the cities of Israel. He attacked Ijon, Dan, Abel Beth Maachah, and all Chinneroth, with all the land of Naphtali. ²¹Now it happened, when Baasha heard *it,* that he stopped building Ramah, and remained in Tirzah.

²²Then King Asa made a proclamation

14:31 [a]Spelled *Abijah* in 2 Chronicles 12:16ff
15:6 [a]Following Masoretic Text, Septuagint, Targum, and Vulgate; some Hebrew manuscripts and Syriac read *Abijam*.   15:12 [a]Hebrew *qedeshim*, that is, those practicing sodomy and prostitution in religious rituals   15:13 [a]A Canaanite goddess

---

TIME CAPSULE *924 to 900* B.C.

924– 889	Osorkon I, pharaoh of Egypt, provides wealth for the temple of Thebes
913	Abijah becomes king in Judah
910	Asa becomes king in Judah
909	Nadab becomes king in Israel
908	Baasha assassinates Nadab and becomes king in Israel
900	Phoenicians establish trading colonies as far away as Spain

throughout all Judah; none *was* exempted. And they took away the stones and timber of Ramah, which Baasha had used for building; and with them King Asa built Geba of Benjamin, and Mizpah.

23The rest of all the acts of Asa, all his might, all that he did, and the cities which he built, *are* they not written in the book of the chronicles of the kings of Judah? But in the time of his old age he was diseased in his feet. 24So Asa rested with his fathers, and was buried with his fathers in the City of David his father. Then Jehoshaphat his son reigned in his place.

Unrest in Israel

Instability characterized the northern kingdom. Despite Jeroboam's long reign (930–909 B.C.), his dynasty would continue to rule Israel for only two more years under his son Nadab (909–908 B.C.) before being cut off by Baasha. The new dynasty would also last for only two rulers: Baasha himself (908–886 B.C.) and his son Elah (886–885 B.C.). One of Elah's military commanders, Zimri, assassinated the king and assumed the throne himself. But Zimri's conspiracy lasted only 7 days (1 Kin. 16:15–30), and Israel sank into civil war.

■ 1 Kings 15:25—16:20

---

1 Kings
Nadab Reigns in Israel

15 :25 Now Nadab the son of Jeroboam became king over Israel in the second year of Asa king of Judah, and he reigned over Israel two years. 26And he did evil in the sight of the LORD, and walked in the way of his father, and in his sin by which he had made Israel sin.

27Then Baasha the son of Ahijah, of the house of Issachar, conspired against him. And Baasha killed him at Gibbethon, which *belonged* to the Philistines, while Nadab and all Israel laid siege to Gibbethon. 28Baasha killed him in the third year of Asa king of Judah, and reigned in his place. 29And it was so, when he became king, *that* he killed all the house of Jeroboam. He did not leave to Jeroboam anyone that breathed, until he had destroyed him, according to the word of the LORD which He had spoken by His servant Ahijah the Shilonite, 30because of the sins of Jeroboam, which he had sinned and by

which he had made Israel sin, because of his provocation with which he had provoked the LORD God of Israel to anger.

31Now the rest of the acts of Nadab, and all that he did, *are* they not written in the book of the chronicles of the kings of Israel? 32And there was war between Asa and Baasha king of Israel all their days.

Baasha Reigns in Israel

33In the third year of Asa king of Judah, Baasha the son of Ahijah became king over all Israel in Tirzah, and *reigned* twenty-four years. 34He did evil in the sight of the LORD, and walked in the way of Jeroboam, and in his sin by which he had made Israel sin.

16 1Then the word of the LORD came to Jehu the son of Hanani, against Baasha, saying: 2"Inasmuch as I lifted you out of the dust and made you ruler over My people Israel, and you have walked in the way of Jeroboam, and have made My people Israel sin, to provoke Me to anger with their sins, 3surely I will take away the posterity of Baasha and the posterity of his house, and I will make your house like the house of Jeroboam the son of Nebat. 4The dogs shall eat whoever belongs to Baasha and dies in the city, and the birds of the air shall eat whoever dies in the fields."

5Now the rest of the acts of Baasha, what he did, and his might, *are* they not written in the book of the chronicles of the kings of Israel? 6So Baasha rested with his fathers and was buried in Tirzah. Then Elah his son reigned in his place.

7And also the word of the LORD came by the prophet Jehu the son of Hanani against Baasha and his house, because of all the evil that he did in the sight of the LORD in provoking Him to anger with the work of his hands, in being like the house of Jeroboam, and because he killed them.

Elah Reigns in Israel

8In the twenty-sixth year of Asa king of Judah, Elah the son of Baasha became king over Israel, *and reigned* two years in Tirzah. 9Now his servant Zimri, commander of half *his* chariots, conspired against him as he was in Tirzah drinking himself drunk in the house of Arza, steward of *his* house in Tirzah. 10And Zimri went in and struck him and killed him in the twenty-seventh year of Asa king of Judah, and reigned in his place.

11Then it came to pass, when he began

KINGS OF THE DIVIDED MONARCHY

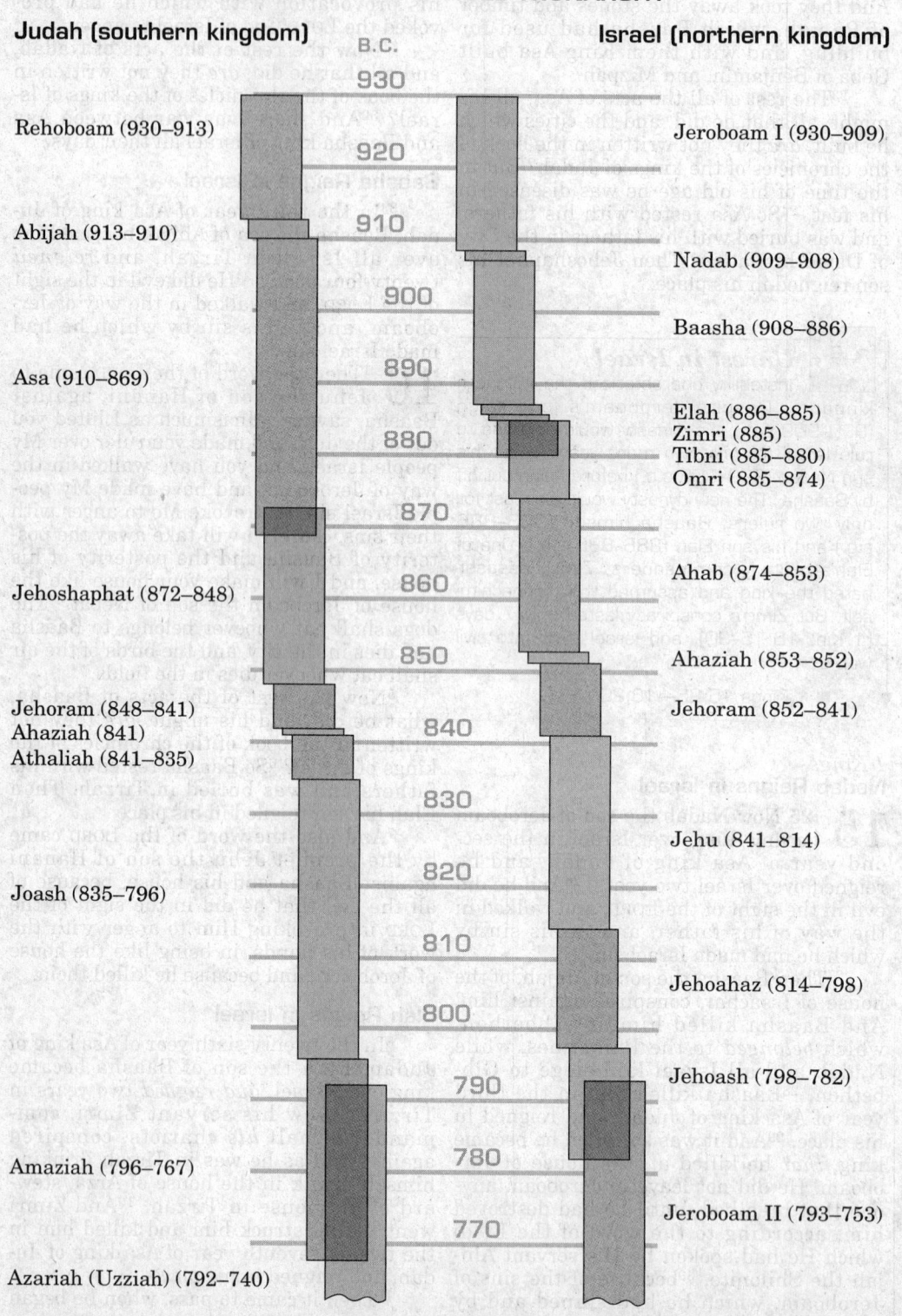

Judah (southern kingdom)   **Israel (northern kingdom)**

B.C.

930

Rehoboam (930–913)   Jeroboam I (930–909)

920

910

Abijah (913–910)   Nadab (909–908)

900

Baasha (908–886)

890

Asa (910–869)

Elah (886–885)
880   Zimri (885)
                                                Tibni (885–880)
                                                Omri (885–874)

870

Ahab (874–853)
860

Jehoshaphat (872–848)

850   Ahaziah (853–852)

Jehoram (848–841)   Jehoram (852–841)
Ahaziah (841)   840
Athaliah (841–835)

830

Jehu (841–814)
820

Joash (835–796)

810

Jehoahaz (814–798)
800

790   Jehoash (798–782)

780

Amaziah (796–767)

770   Jeroboam II (793–753)

Azariah (Uzziah) (792–740)

Judah (southern kingdom)

Israel (northern kingdom)

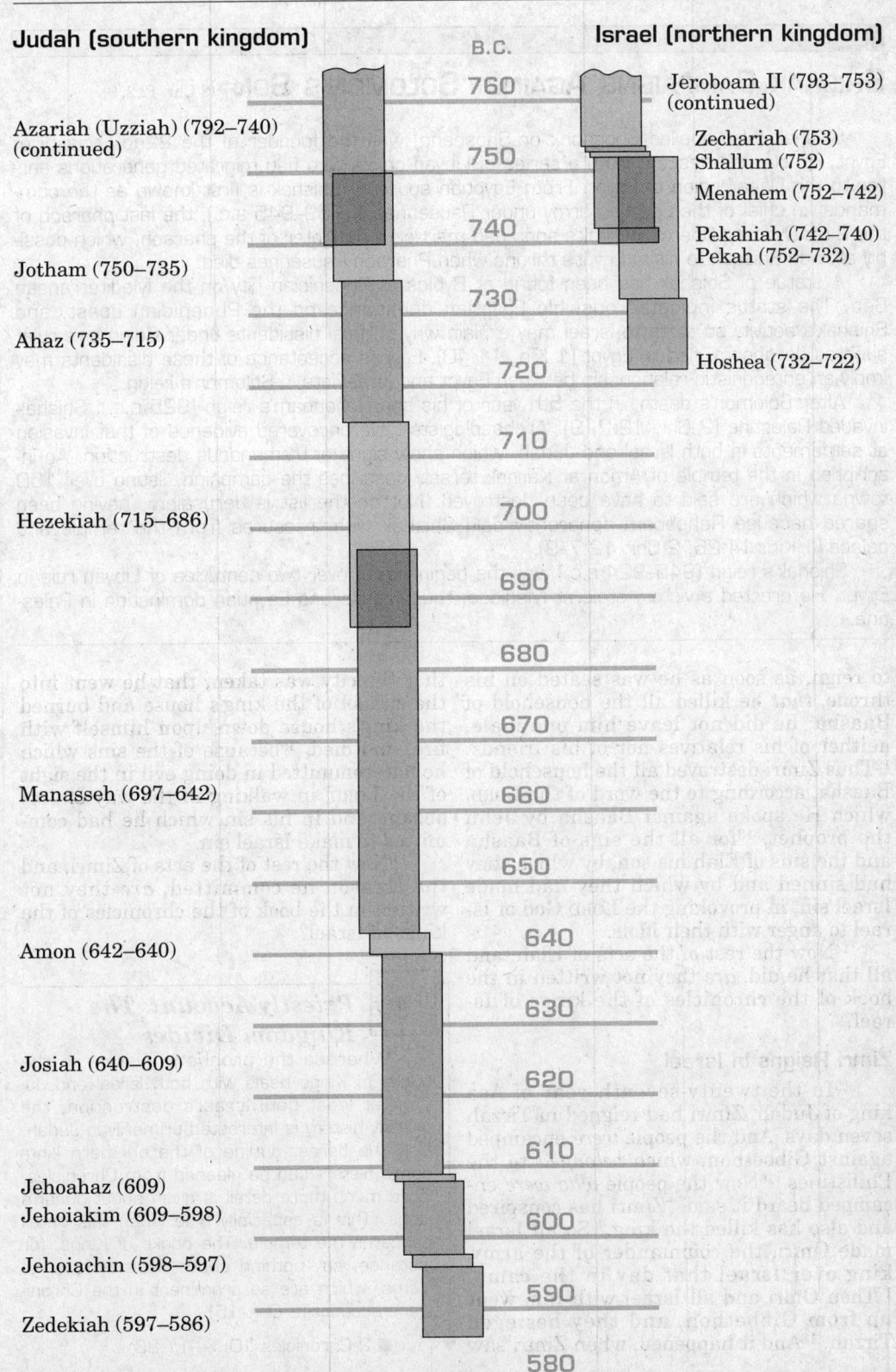

B.C.

760

Jeroboam II (793–753)
(continued)

Azariah (Uzziah) (792–740)
(continued)

750

Zechariah (753)
Shallum (752)

Menahem (752–742)

740

Pekahiah (742–740)
Pekah (752–732)

Jotham (750–735)

730

Ahaz (735–715)

720

Hoshea (732–722)

710

700

Hezekiah (715–686)

690

680

670

660

Manasseh (697–642)

650

640

Amon (642–640)

630

Josiah (640–609)

620

610

Jehoahaz (609)
Jehoiakim (609–598)

600

Jehoiachin (598–597)

590

Zedekiah (597–586)

580

SHISHAK CAMPAIGNS AGAINST SOLOMON'S SON (2 Chr. 12:2, 9)

Shishak (also spelled Sheshonk or Shoshenq) was the founder of the 22nd Dynasty of Egypt. He claimed descent from a series of Libyan chiefs who had migrated generations earlier to the Delta region of Egypt. From Egyptian sources, Shishak is first known as the commander in chief of the Egyptian army under Psusennes II (959–945 B.C.), the last pharaoh of the 21st Dynasty. One of Shishak's sons had married a daughter of the pharaoh, which possibly allowed Shishak to claim Egypt's throne when Pharaoh Psusennes died.

A statue of Shishak has been found at Byblos, a Phoenician city on the Mediterranean Sea. The statue indicates possible Egyptian dominance on the Phoenician coast, and Shishak's activity so close to Israel may explain why political dissidents under Solomon's rule, such as Jeroboam, fled to Egypt (1 Kin. 11:40). Egypt's acceptance of these dissidents may imply an antagonistic relationship between Egypt and Israel late in Solomon's reign.

After Solomon's death, in the 5th year of his son Rehoboam's reign (925 B.C.), Shishak invaded Palestine (2 Chr. 12:2, 9). Archaeologists have uncovered evidence of that invasion at settlements in both Israel and Judah, which show signs of tremendous destruction. An inscription in the temple of Amon at Karnak tersely describes the campaign, listing over 150 towns which are said to have been destroyed. Not on the list is Jerusalem, having been spared because Rehoboam apparently paid Shishak with treasures from the temple and palace (1 Kin. 14:26; 2 Chr. 12:7–9).

Shishak's reign (945–924 B.C.) was the beginning of over two centuries of Libyan rule in Egypt. He erected a victory stele at Megiddo, thus reasserting Egyptian domination in Palestine.

to reign, as soon as he was seated on his throne, *that* he killed all the household of Baasha; he did not leave him one male, neither of his relatives nor of his friends. 12Thus Zimri destroyed all the household of Baasha, according to the word of the LORD, which He spoke against Baasha by Jehu the prophet, 13for all the sins of Baasha and the sins of Elah his son, by which they had sinned and by which they had made Israel sin, in provoking the LORD God of Israel to anger with their idols.

14Now the rest of the acts of Elah, and all that he did, *are* they not written in the book of the chronicles of the kings of Israel?

Zimri Reigns in Israel

15In the twenty-seventh year of Asa king of Judah, Zimri had reigned in Tirzah seven days. And the people *were* encamped against Gibbethon, which *belonged* to the Philistines. 16Now the people who *were* encamped heard it said, "Zimri has conspired and also has killed the king." So all Israel made Omri, the commander of the army, king over Israel that day in the camp. 17Then Omri and all Israel with him went up from Gibbethon, and they besieged Tirzah. 18And it happened, when Zimri saw ▼

that the city was taken, that he went into the citadel of the king's house and burned the king's house down upon himself with fire, and died, 19because of the sins which he had committed in doing evil in the sight of the LORD, in walking in the way of Jeroboam, and in his sin which he had committed to make Israel sin.

20Now the rest of the acts of Zimri, and the treason he committed, *are* they not written in the book of the chronicles of the kings of Israel?

 Priestly Account: The Kingdom Divides

Whereas the prophetic history in the books of Kings deals with both Israel and Judah, at least until Israel's destruction, the priestly history is interested primarily in Judah. Only the barest outline of the northern kingdom's history can be gleaned from Chronicles, while much more detail is given about Judah's kings. This is especially true when this detail concerns the temple. The books of Kings, for instance, say nothing about Asa's temple reforms, which are so prominent in the Chronicler's account (2 Chr. 15).

■ 2 Chronicles 10:1—11:23

2 Chronicles
The Revolt Against Rehoboam

10 :1 And Rehoboam went to Shechem, for all Israel had gone to Shechem to make him king. ²So it happened, when Jeroboam the son of Nebat heard *it* (he was in Egypt, where he had fled from the presence of King Solomon), that Jeroboam returned from Egypt. ³Then they sent for him and called him. And Jeroboam and all Israel came and spoke to Rehoboam, saying, ⁴"Your father made our yoke heavy; now therefore, lighten the burdensome service of your father and his heavy yoke which he put on us, and we will serve you."

⁵So he said to them, "Come back to me after three days." And the people departed.

⁶Then King Rehoboam consulted the elders who stood before his father Solomon while he still lived, saying, "How do you advise *me* to answer these people?"

⁷And they spoke to him, saying, "If you are kind to these people, and please them, and speak good words to them, they will be your servants forever."

⁸But he rejected the advice which the elders had given him, and consulted the young men who had grown up with him, who stood before him. ⁹And he said to them, "What advice do you give? How should we answer this people who have spoken to me, saying, 'Lighten the yoke which your father put on us'?"

¹⁰Then the young men who had grown up with him spoke to him, saying, "Thus you should speak to the people who have spoken to you, saying, 'Your father made our yoke heavy, but you make *it* lighter on us'—thus you shall say to them: 'My little *finger* shall be thicker than my father's waist! ¹¹And now, whereas my father put a heavy yoke on you, I will add to your yoke; my father chastised you with whips, but I *will chastise you* with scourges!' "ᵃ

¹²So Jeroboam and all the people came to Rehoboam on the third day, as the king had directed, saying, "Come back to me the third day." ¹³Then the king answered them roughly. King Rehoboam rejected the advice of the elders, ¹⁴and he spoke to them according to the advice of the young men, saying, "My fatherᵃ made your yoke heavy,

but I will add to it; my father chastised you with whips, but I *will chastise you* with scourges!"ᵇ ¹⁵So the king did not listen to the people; for the turn *of events* was from God, that the LORD might fulfill His word, which He had spoken by the hand of Ahijah the Shilonite to Jeroboam the son of Nebat.

¹⁶Now when all Israel *saw* that the king did not listen to them, the people answered the king, saying:

"What share have we in David?
We have no inheritance in the son of
  Jesse.
Every man to your tents, O Israel!
Now see to your own house, O David!"

So all Israel departed to their tents. ¹⁷But Rehoboam reigned over the children of Israel who dwelt in the cities of Judah. ¹⁸Then King Rehoboam sent Hadoram, who *was* in charge of revenue; but the children of Israel stoned him with stones, and he died. Therefore King Rehoboam mounted *his* chariot in haste to flee to Jerusalem. ¹⁹So Israel has been in rebellion against the house of David to this day.

11 ¹Now when Rehoboam came to Jerusalem, he assembled from the house of Judah and Benjamin one hundred and eighty thousand chosen *men* who were warriors, to fight against Israel, that he might restore the kingdom to Rehoboam.

²But the word of the LORD came to Shemaiah the man of God, saying, ³"Speak to Rehoboam the son of Solomon, king of Judah, and to all Israel in Judah and Benjamin, saying, ⁴'Thus says the LORD: "You shall not go up or fight against your brethren! Let every man return to his house, for this thing is from Me." ' " Therefore they obeyed the words of the LORD, and turned back from attacking Jeroboam.

Rehoboam Fortifies the Cities

⁵So Rehoboam dwelt in Jerusalem, and built cities for defense in Judah. ⁶And he built Bethlehem, Etam, Tekoa, ⁷Beth Zur, Sochoh, Adullam, ⁸Gath, Mareshah, Ziph, ⁹Adoraim, Lachish, Azekah, ¹⁰Zorah, Aijalon, and Hebron, which are in Judah and Benjamin, fortified cities. ¹¹And he fortified the strongholds, and put captains in them, and stores of food, oil, and wine. ¹²Also in every city *he put* shields and spears, and made them very strong, having Judah and Benjamin on his side.

10:11 ªLiterally *scorpions*   10:14 ªFollowing many Hebrew manuscripts, Septuagint, Syriac, and Vulgate (compare verse 10 and 1 Kings 12:14); Masoretic Text reads *I*.   ᵇLiterally *scorpions*

Priests and Levites Move to Judah

¹³And from all their territories the priests and the Levites who *were* in all Israel took their stand with him. ¹⁴For the Levites left their common-lands and their possessions and came to Judah and Jerusalem, for Jeroboam and his sons had rejected them from serving as priests to the LORD. ¹⁵Then he appointed for himself priests for the high places, for the demons, and the calf idols which he had made. ¹⁶And after *the Levites left,*ᵃ those from all the tribes of Israel, such as set their heart to seek the LORD God of Israel, came to Jerusalem to sacrifice to the LORD God of their fathers. ¹⁷So they strengthened the kingdom of Judah, and made Rehoboam the son of Solomon strong for three years, because they walked in the way of David and Solomon for three years.

The Family of Rehoboam

¹⁸Then Rehoboam took for himself as wife Mahalath the daughter of Jerimoth the son of David, *and of* Abihail the daughter of Eliah the son of Jesse. ¹⁹And she bore him children: Jeush, Shamariah, and Zaham. ²⁰After her he took Maachah the granddaughterᵃ of Absalom; and she bore him Abijah, Attai, Ziza, and Shelomith. ²¹Now Rehoboam loved Maachah the granddaughter of Absalom more than all his wives and his concubines; for he took eighteen wives and sixty concubines, and begot twenty-eight sons and sixty daughters. ²²And Rehoboam appointed Abijah the son of Maachah as chief, *to be* leader among his brothers; for he *intended* to make him king. ²³He dealt wisely, and dispersed some of his sons throughout all the territories of Judah and Benjamin, to every fortified city; and he gave them provisions in abundance. He also sought many wives *for them.*

Rehoboam's Apostasy

As the Chronicler traces the kings of Judah starting with Rehoboam (930–913 B.C.) and Abijah (913–910 B.C.), he emphasizes the consequences of disobedience. While both Kings and Chronicles mention Shishak's invasion of Judah in 925 B.C., the Chronicler offers an explanation for the attack that is not found in the parallel account of 1 Kin. 14:25, 26. In Chronicles the underlying cause of this invasion was Rehoboam's and Judah's sin (12:5–8).

Chronicles also notes Jeroboam's disobedience. In a sermon, Judah's king Abijah challenged the legitimacy of Jeroboam's reign (2 Chr. 13:5, 6) and the validity of his religious innovations (13:8, 9). Jeroboam had led Israel to abandon Yahweh, the God of their fathers (13:12).

▼ ■ 2 Chronicles 12:1—13:22

2 Chronicles
Egypt Attacks Judah

12 :1 Now it came to pass, when Rehoboam had established the kingdom and had strengthened himself, that he forsook the law of the LORD, and all Israel along with him. ²And it happened in the fifth year of King Rehoboam *that* Shishak king of Egypt came up against Jerusalem, because they had transgressed against the LORD, ³with twelve hundred chariots, sixty thousand horsemen, and people without number who came with him out of Egypt— the Lubim and the Sukkiim and the Ethiopians. ⁴And he took the fortified cities of Judah and came to Jerusalem.

⁵Then Shemaiah the prophet came to Rehoboam and the leaders of Judah, who were gathered together in Jerusalem because of Shishak, and said to them, "Thus says the LORD: 'You have forsaken Me, and therefore I also have left you in the hand of Shishak.'"

⁶So the leaders of Israel and the king humbled themselves; and they said, "The LORD *is* righteous."

⁷Now when the LORD saw that they humbled themselves, the word of the LORD came to Shemaiah, saying, "They have humbled themselves; *therefore* I will not destroy them, but I will grant them some deliverance. My wrath shall not be poured out on Jerusalem by the hand of Shishak. ⁸Nevertheless they will be his servants, that they may distinguish My service from the service of the kingdoms of the nations."

⁹So Shishak king of Egypt came up against Jerusalem, and took away the treasures of the house of the LORD and the treasures of the king's house; he took everything. He also carried away the gold shields which Solomon had made. ¹⁰Then King Rehoboam made bronze shields in

---

11:16 ᵃLiterally *after them*   11:20 ᵃLiterally *daughter,* but in the broader sense of granddaughter (compare 2 Chronicles 13:2)

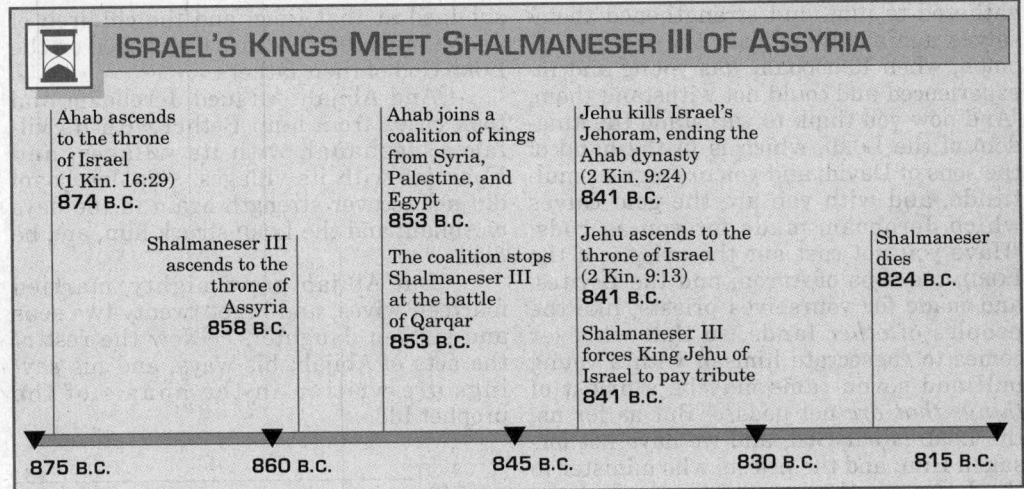

ISRAEL'S KINGS MEET SHALMANESER III OF ASSYRIA

Ahab ascends to the throne of Israel (1 Kin. 16:29) **874 B.C.**	Ahab joins a coalition of kings from Syria, Palestine, and Egypt **853 B.C.**	Jehu kills Israel's Jehoram, ending the Ahab dynasty (2 Kin. 9:24) **841 B.C.**
Shalmaneser III ascends to the throne of Assyria **858 B.C.**	The coalition stops Shalmaneser III at the battle of Qarqar **853 B.C.**	Jehu ascends to the throne of Israel (2 Kin. 9:13) **841 B.C.** · Shalmaneser III forces King Jehu of Israel to pay tribute **841 B.C.** · Shalmaneser dies **824 B.C.**

875 B.C.   **860 B.C.**   **845 B.C.**   **830 B.C.**   **815 B.C.**

their place, and committed *them* to the hands of the captains of the guard, who guarded the doorway of the king's house. ¹¹And whenever the king entered the house of the LORD, the guard would go and bring them out; then they would take them back into the guardroom. ¹²When he humbled himself, the wrath of the LORD turned from him, so as not to destroy *him* completely; and things also went well in Judah.

The End of Rehoboam's Reign

¹³Thus King Rehoboam strengthened himself in Jerusalem and reigned. Now Rehoboam *was* forty-one years old when he became king; and he reigned seventeen years in Jerusalem, the city which the LORD had chosen out of all the tribes of Israel, to put His name there. His mother's name *was* Naamah, an Ammonitess. ¹⁴And he did evil, because he did not prepare his heart to seek the LORD.

¹⁵The acts of Rehoboam, first and last, *are* they not written in the book of Shemaiah the prophet, and of Iddo the seer concerning genealogies? And *there were* wars between Rehoboam and Jeroboam all their days. ¹⁶So Rehoboam rested with his fathers, and was buried in the City of David. Then Abijah[a] his son reigned in his place.

Abijah Reigns in Judah

13 ¹In the eighteenth year of King Jeroboam, Abijah became king over Ju-

dah. ²He reigned three years in Jerusalem. His mother's name *was* Michaiah[a] the daughter of Uriel of Gibeah.

And there was war between Abijah and Jeroboam. ³Abijah set the battle in order with an army of valiant warriors, four hundred thousand choice men. Jeroboam also drew up in battle formation against him with eight hundred thousand choice men, mighty men of valor.

⁴Then Abijah stood on Mount Zemaraim, which *is* in the mountains of Ephraim, and said, "Hear me, Jeroboam and all Israel: ⁵Should you not know that the LORD God of Israel gave the dominion over Israel to David forever, to him and his sons, by a covenant of salt? ⁶Yet Jeroboam the son of Nebat, the servant of Solomon the son of David, rose up and rebelled against his lord. ⁷Then worthless rogues

---

TIME CAPSULE   *900 to 885 B.C.*

900 Earliest example of laminated steel

895 Asa leads covenant renewal celebration in Judah (2 Chr. 15:10–15)

895 Osorkon I of Egypt invades Palestine

887 Ethbaal I, priest of Astarte, seizes throne of Tyre

886 Elah becomes king in Israel

885 Zimri murders Elah and becomes king in Israel

885 Zimri commits suicide after 7 days as king

12:16 ᵃSpelled *Abijam* in 1 Kings 14:31
13:2 ᵃSpelled *Maachah* in 11:20, 21 and 1 Kings 15:2

gathered to him, and strengthened themselves against Rehoboam the son of Solomon, when Rehoboam was young and inexperienced and could not withstand them. [8]And now you think to withstand the kingdom of the LORD, which is in the hand of the sons of David; and you *are* a great multitude, and with you are the gold calves which Jeroboam made for you as gods. [9]Have you not cast out the priests of the LORD, the sons of Aaron, and the Levites, and made for yourselves priests, like the peoples of *other* lands, so that whoever comes to consecrate himself with a young bull and seven rams may be a priest of *things that are* not gods? [10]But as for us, the LORD *is* our God, and we have not forsaken Him; and the priests who minister to the LORD *are* the sons of Aaron, and the Levites *attend* to *their* duties. [11]And they burn to the LORD every morning and every evening burnt sacrifices and sweet incense; *they* also *set* the showbread *in order on* the pure *gold* table, and the lampstand of gold with its lamps to burn every evening; for we keep the command of the LORD our God, but you have forsaken Him. [12]Now look, God Himself is with us as *our* head, and His priests with sounding trumpets to sound the alarm against you. O children of Israel, do not fight against the LORD God of your fathers, for you shall not prosper!"

[13]But Jeroboam caused an ambush to go around behind them; so they were in front of Judah, and the ambush *was* behind them. [14]And when Judah looked around, to their surprise the battle line *was* at both front and rear; and they cried out to the LORD, and the priests sounded the trumpets. [15]Then the men of Judah gave a shout; and as the men of Judah shouted, it happened that God struck Jeroboam and all Israel before Abijah and Judah. [16]And the children of Israel fled before Judah, and God delivered them into their hand. [17]Then Abijah and his people struck them with a great slaughter; so five hundred thousand choice men of Israel fell slain. [18]Thus the children of Israel were subdued at that time; and the children of Judah prevailed, because they relied on the LORD God of their fathers.

[19]And Abijah pursued Jeroboam and took cities from him: Bethel with its villages, Jeshanah with its villages, and Ephrain[a] with its villages. [20]So Jeroboam did not recover strength again in the days of Abijah; and the LORD struck him, and he died.

[21]But Abijah grew mighty, married fourteen wives, and begot twenty-two sons and sixteen daughters. [22]Now the rest of the acts of Abijah, his ways, and his sayings *are* written in the annals of the prophet Iddo.

Asa's Revival

According to the Chronicler, the beginning of Asa's reign (910–869 B.C.) was peaceful (2 Chr. 14:1). It was a time of religious reform in which Asa removed the shrines of the Canaanite nature religions (2 Chr. 14:3, 5). The Chronicler provides a more detailed account of the reform in 2 Chr. 15. The covenant renewal celebration (15:10–15) was held in Asa's 15th year (895 B.C.). Despite these successful reforms, Asa was unable to rid the land completely of the pagan high places (15:17).

■ 2 Chronicles 14:1—16:14

2 Chronicles

14

:1 So Abijah rested with his fathers, and they buried him in the City of David. Then Asa his son reigned in his place. In his days the land was quiet for ten years.

Asa Reigns in Judah

[2]Asa did *what was* good and right in the eyes of the LORD his God, [3]for he removed the altars of the foreign *gods* and the high places, and broke down the *sacred* pillars and cut down the wooden images.

13:19 [a]Or *Ephron*

MARRIAGE AND FAMILY

Cases of polygamy, a man having more than one wife, were usually a sign that a person was rich and powerful, such as King Abijah (2 Chr. 13:21). Polygamy may have been practiced only by the upper class. The Greeks were monogamous, and the Romans regarded polygamy as degenerate or barbarian. The Jews by the New Testament period were generally monogamous.

ASA AND BAASHA FIGHT OVER RAMAH

Judah (southern kingdom)

Asa, the son of Abijah, had two encounters with foreign nations. First, he stopped an invasion by the Ethiopian king Zerah (2 Chr. 14:12, 13). Later, when Baasha tried to blockade Asa by fortifying the city of Ramah, Asa hired Ben-Hadad, king of Syria (Aram), to thwart Baasha's plans (2 Chr. 16:1–6).

Israel (northern kingdom)

Baasha secured himself on Israel's throne by assassinating Nadab and then murdering every member of Jeroboam's and Nadab's royal house (1 Kin. 15:27–29). In order to defend his kingdom against Ben-Hadad of Syria (Aram), Baasha was forced to withdraw from Ramah.

Elah succeeded his father Baasha, but a brief 2-year reign was ended when Zimri, one of his captains, murdered him while Elah was in a drunken stupor (1 Kin. 16:8–10).

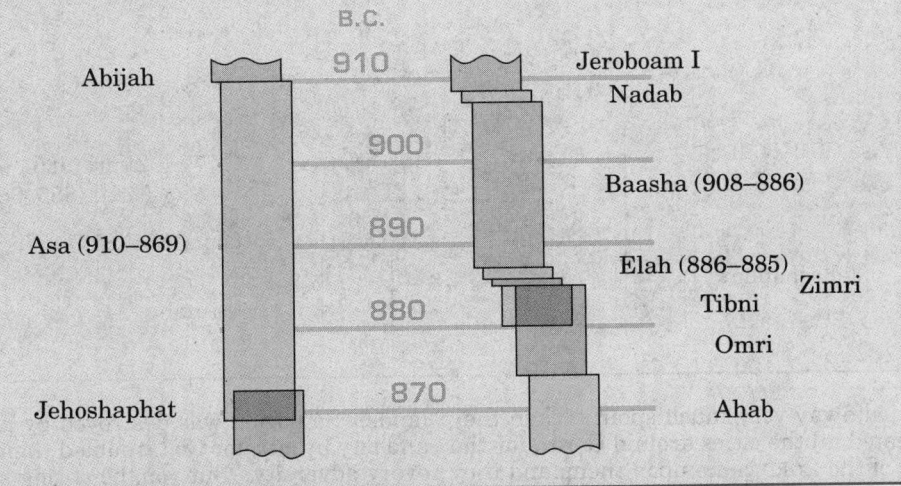

4He commanded Judah to seek the LORD God of their fathers, and to observe the law and the commandment. 5He also removed the high places and the incense altars from all the cities of Judah, and the kingdom was quiet under him. 6And he built fortified cities in Judah, for the land had rest; he had no war in those years, because the LORD had given him rest. 7Therefore he said to Judah, "Let us build these cities and make walls around *them,* and towers, gates, and bars, *while* the land *is* yet before us, because we have sought the LORD our God; we have sought *Him,* and He has given us rest on every side." So they built and prospered. 8And Asa had an army of three hundred thousand from Judah who carried shields and spears, and from Benjamin two hundred and eighty thousand men who carried shields and drew bows; all these *were* mighty men of valor.

9Then Zerah the Ethiopian came out against them with an army of a million men and three hundred chariots, and he came to Mareshah. 10So Asa went out against him, and they set the troops in battle array in the Valley of Zephathah at Mareshah. 11And Asa cried out to the LORD his God, and said, "LORD, *it is* nothing for You to help, whether with many or with those who have no power; help us, O LORD our God, for we rest on You, and in Your name we go against this multitude. O LORD, You *are* our God; do not let man prevail against You!"

12So the LORD struck the Ethiopians before Asa and Judah, and the Ethiopians fled. 13And Asa and the people who *were* with him pursued them to Gerar. So the Ethiopians were overthrown, and they could not recover, for they were broken before the LORD and His army. And they

⧗ OMRI BEGINS A NEW DYNASTY

Judah (southern kingdom)	**Israel (northern kingdom)**
Asa contracted a disease in his feet in the 39th year of his reign (871 B.C.). He would live about 2 years longer (2 Chr. 16:12, 13). During his last years, Asa's son Jehoshaphat ruled with his father as a coregent.	**Zimri,** the king's chariot commander, ended the Baasha-Elah dynasty without support of the army. Immediately Omri, the army commander, besieged the capital Tirzah. After only 7 days as king, Zimri was forced to commit suicide (1 Kin. 16:15).
	Tibni challenged Omri for the throne for at least 4 or 5 years, but Omri emerged victorious.
	Omri reigned for 6 years in Tirzah, but built a new city, Samaria, and made it Israel's new capital.

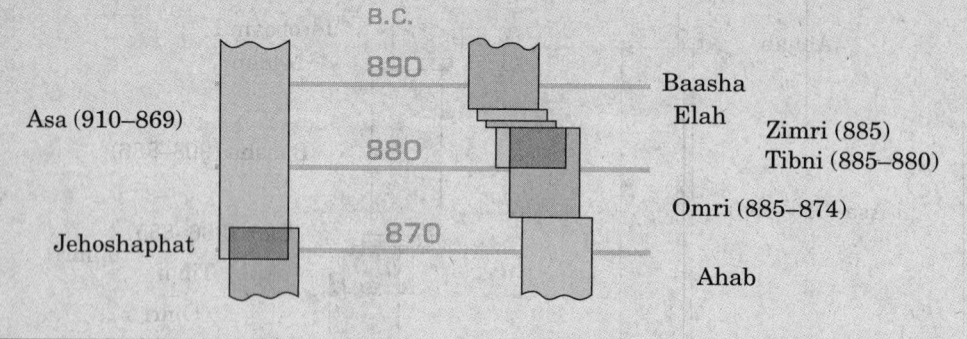

carried away very much spoil. ¹⁴Then they defeated all the cities around Gerar, for the fear of the LORD came upon them; and they plundered all the cities, for there was exceedingly much spoil in them. ¹⁵They also attacked the livestock enclosures, and carried off sheep and camels in abundance, and returned to Jerusalem.

The Reforms of Asa

15 ¹Now the Spirit of God came upon Azariah the son of Oded. ²And he went out to meet Asa, and said to him: "Hear me, Asa, and all Judah and Benjamin. The LORD *is* with you while you are with Him. If you seek Him, He will be found by you; but if you forsake Him, He will forsake you. ³For a long time Israel *has been* without the true God, without a teaching priest, and without law; ⁴but when in their trouble they turned to the LORD God of Israel, and sought Him, He was found by them. ⁵And in those times *there was* no peace to the one who went out, nor to the one who came in, but great turmoil *was* on all the inhabitants of the

lands. ⁶So nation was destroyed by nation, and city by city, for God troubled them with every adversity. ⁷But you, be strong and do not let your hands be weak, for your work shall be rewarded!"

⁸And when Asa heard these words and the prophecy of Oded[a] the prophet, he took courage, and removed the abominable idols from all the land of Judah and Benjamin and from the cities which he had taken in the mountains of Ephraim; and he restored the altar of the LORD that *was* before the vestibule of the LORD. ⁹Then he gathered all Judah and Benjamin, and those who dwelt with them from Ephraim, Manasseh, and Simeon, for they came over to him in great numbers from Israel when they saw that the LORD his God was with him.

¹⁰So they gathered together at Jerusalem in the third month, in the fifteenth year of the reign of Asa. ¹¹And they offered to the LORD at that time seven hundred

15:8 ªFollowing Masoretic Text and Septuagint; Syriac and Vulgate read *Azariah the son of Oded* (compare verse 1).

ASHERAH, QUEEN MOTHER OF THE GODS (2 Chr. 15:16)

King Asa of Judah removed his mother Maachah from her position as queen mother of Judah because she made sacred objects for the goddess Asherah (2 Chr. 15:16). The worship of any deity beside Yahweh was forbidden, so Asa was fulfilling the cultic laws by removing even the work of his mother from the royal precinct. It was urgent then to replace Maachah as queen mother since any such high position should be held by one true to Yahweh.

Asherah was a widely worshiped goddess throughout Syria-Palestine and even into Egypt. In the myths recovered from Ugarit, she is the spouse of El, head of the pantheon, and thus the queen mother of the gods. She chose which deities were to be established in what positions of authority in the cosmos. In the chain of authority she was the final resort for petitions to El. She is portrayed as fairly well in control of herself and the world which she owns with her spouse. Unquestionably, Asherah was the most politically powerful goddess in the Canaanite pantheon.

It appears that at times Judahites worshiped Asherah as the spouse of Yahweh, who was also called El (Gen. 33:20; 35:7). Inscriptions dating from the time of the divided monarchy (after 930 B.C.) name Yahweh and refer to "His Asherah." These inscriptions were found in northeast Sinai at Kuntillet 'Ajrud and within Judah's borders at Khirbet el-Qom. The goddess clearly was popular in the land among populace and royalty alike, who continued worshiping her even down to the reign of Josiah (640–609 B.C.; 2 Kin. 23:4).

A human queen mother was the queen who, among other duties, advised the king, helped appoint princes and princesses to official positions, and helped choose the heir apparent to the throne. It was a position of considerable power and prestige. That King Asa's mother, Maachah, worshiped Asherah, and dedicated some cultic object to her, possibly shows that this queen mother of Judah acknowledged her role as a representative of the goddess, the queen mother of heaven.

bulls and seven thousand sheep from the spoil they had brought. ¹²Then they entered into a covenant to seek the LORD God of their fathers with all their heart and with all their soul; ¹³and whoever would not seek the LORD God of Israel was to be put to death, whether small or great, whether man or woman. ¹⁴Then they took an oath before the LORD with a loud voice, with shouting and trumpets and rams' horns. ¹⁵And all Judah rejoiced at the oath, for they had sworn with all their heart and sought Him with all their soul; and He was found by them, and the LORD gave them rest all around.

¹⁶Also he removed Maachah, the mother of Asa the king, from *being* queen mother, because she had made an obscene image of Asherah;[a] and Asa cut down her obscene image, then crushed and burned *it* by the Brook Kidron. ¹⁷But the high places were not removed from Israel. Nevertheless the heart of Asa was loyal all his days.

¹⁸He also brought into the house of God the things that his father had dedicated and that he himself had dedicated: silver and gold and utensils. ¹⁹And there was no war until the thirty-fifth year of the reign of Asa.

Asa's Treaty with Syria

16 ¹In the thirty-sixth year of the reign of Asa, Baasha king of Israel came up against Judah and built Ramah, that he might let none go out or come in to Asa king of Judah. ²Then Asa brought silver and gold from the treasuries of the house of the LORD and of the king's house, and sent to Ben-Hadad king of Syria, who dwelt in Damascus, saying, ³"*Let there be* a treaty between you and me, as there was between my father and your father. See, I have sent you silver and gold; come, break your treaty with Baasha king of Israel, so that he will withdraw from me."

⁴So Ben-Hadad heeded King Asa, and sent the captains of his armies against the cities of Israel. They attacked Ijon, Dan, Abel Maim, and all the storage cities of

15:16 ᵃA Canaanite deity

Naphtali. ⁵Now it happened, when Baasha heard *it,* that he stopped building Ramah and ceased his work. ⁶Then King Asa took all Judah, and they carried away the stones and timber of Ramah, which Baasha had used for building; and with them he built Geba and Mizpah.

Hanani's Message to Asa

⁷And at that time Hanani the seer came to Asa king of Judah, and said to him: "Because you have relied on the king of Syria, and have not relied on the LORD your God, therefore the army of the king of Syria has escaped from your hand. ⁸Were the Ethiopians and the Lubim not a huge army with very many chariots and horsemen? Yet, because you relied on the LORD, He delivered them into your hand. ⁹For the eyes of the LORD run to and fro throughout the whole earth, to show Himself strong on behalf of *those* whose heart *is* loyal to Him. In this you have done foolishly; therefore from now on you shall have wars." ¹⁰Then Asa was angry with the seer, and put him in prison, for *he was* enraged at him because of this. And Asa oppressed *some* of the people at that time.

Illness and Death of Asa

¹¹Note that the acts of Asa, first and last, are indeed written in the book of the kings of Judah and Israel. ¹²And in the thirty-ninth year of his reign, Asa became diseased in his feet, and his malady was severe; yet in his disease he did not seek the LORD, but the physicians. ¹³So Asa rested with his fathers; he died in the forty-first year of his reign. ¹⁴They buried him in his own tomb, which he had made for himself in the City of David; and they laid him in the bed which was filled with spices and various ingredients prepared in a mixture of ointments. They made a very great burning for him.

Prophetic Account: Ahab and Jehoshaphat

Zimri's assassination of King Elah (see "Unrest in Israel" at 1 Kin. 15:25) resulted in a few chaotic years for Israel. The chariot commander Zimri had little support, but merely took advantage of the king's drunken stupor (1 Kin. 16:9). Another military commander, Omri, assuming kingship himself, ended Zimri's conspiracy after only 7 days

(16:15, 16). However, civil war broke out for about five years (885–880 B.C.), with Omri and a rival named Tibni competing for the throne (16:21). Omri eventually won.

The turbulent history of the northern kingdom stabilized somewhat under the rule of Omri (885–874 B.C.). Although the Bible says little about this king beyond his founding of the capital city of Samaria, he was very successful in material terms. He expanded Israel's borders and established a reputation for himself. Even after Omri's dynasty had disappeared, Assyria would refer to the nation of Israel as "the house of Omri." Certainly, he was successful enough to establish a dynasty: his son Ahab reigned in his place.

The historian of Kings is much more concerned with Ahab, primarily because of his wife, Jezebel. Jezebel was from the merchant city of Tyre and brought with her an evangelistic zeal for her god, Baal (1 Kin. 16:31). She established her own shrines, priests, and prophets, and ruthlessly persecuted those who remained faithful to Yahweh, the God of Israel. Foremost among these faithful was a rough and austere prophet named Elijah.

Israel and Judah had often warred against each other during the first years following the monarchy's division in 930 B.C. Their political relations calmed somewhat when Ahab of Israel and Jehoshaphat of Judah formed an alliance. Eventually, the two kingdoms even joined themselves militarily in battle against Aram (Syria; 1 Kin. 22).

▼ ■ 1 Kings 16:21–34

1 Kings
Omri Reigns in Israel

16 **:21** Then the people of Israel were divided into two parts: half of the people followed Tibni the son of Ginath, to make him king, and half followed Omri. ²²But the people who followed Omri prevailed over the people who followed Tibni the son of Ginath. So Tibni died and Omri reigned. ²³In the thirty-first year of Asa king of Judah, Omri became king over Israel, *and reigned* twelve years. Six years he reigned in Tirzah. ²⁴And he bought the hill of Samaria from Shemer for two talents of silver; then he built on the hill, and called the name of the city which he built, Samaria, after the name of Shemer, owner of the hill. ²⁵Omri did evil in the eyes of the LORD, and did worse than all who *were* before him. ²⁶For he walked in all the ways of Jeroboam the son of Nebat, and in his sin

---

Aʜᴀʙ ᴛʜᴇ Rᴇʟɪɢɪᴏᴜs Cᴏᴍᴘʀᴏᴍɪsᴇʀ (1 Kin. 16:28–33)

Ahab was the second king of a dynasty founded by his father Omri in the northern kingdom of Israel. He ruled from 874 to 853 B.C. and is possibly alluded to in an inscription from c. 850 B.C. The royal inscription, called the Moabite Stone, does not mention Ahab by name. However, the Moabite king Mesha does claim to have freed the Moabites from Israelite domination during the reign of the "son of Omri."

The writer of the books of Kings gives a very negative evaluation of Ahab. His sin was that of religious compromise: he allowed Baal worship to continue in Israel.

Religious compromise was the consequence of a political move. Much of Ahab's reign saw tension between Israel and the Aramean kingdom of Damascus to the northeast. Continuing his father's policies of thwarting the Aramean presence in Israel, Ahab sought a series of alliances with neighboring Judah to the south and with Phoenicia on the coast.

Ahab's alliances were strengthened by political marriages. His daughter Athaliah was married in 867 B.C. to Jehoram, the son of Judah's King Jehoshaphat (2 Kin. 8:16–18; 2 Chr. 21:5, 6). The marriage helped to end hostile relations between Israel and Judah. The historian Josephus records that Ahab himself married Jezebel, whose father Ethbaal ruled the Phoenician kingdom including Tyre and Sidon (1 Kin. 16:31, 32).

Ahab thus solidified peace with Phoenicia through his marriage to the infamous Phoenician princess Jezebel. This foreign queen remained true to her foreign background: Josephus reports that her father was a priest in the Phoenician cult of Baal; his name "Ethbaal" means "with Baal." The writer of Israel's history strongly condemned Ahab for supporting Jezebel's worship of the Phoenician and Canaanite god and compromising the Israelite worship of Yahweh (1 Kin. 16:30–33).

---

by which he had made Israel sin, provoking the Lᴏʀᴅ God of Israel to anger with their idols.

27Now the rest of the acts of Omri which he did, and the might that he showed, *are* they not written in the book of the chronicles of the kings of Israel?

28So Omri rested with his fathers and was buried in Samaria. Then Ahab his son reigned in his place.

Ahab Reigns in Israel

29In the thirty-eighth year of Asa king of Judah, Ahab the son of Omri became king over Israel; and Ahab the son of Omri reigned over Israel in Samaria twenty-two years. 30Now Ahab the son of Omri did evil in the sight of the Lᴏʀᴅ, more than all who *were* before him. 31And it came to pass, as though it had been a trivial thing for him to walk in the sins of Jeroboam the son of Nebat, that he took as wife Jezebel the daughter of Ethbaal, king of the Sidonians;

and he went and served Baal and worshiped him. 32Then he set up an altar for Baal in the temple of Baal, which he had built in Samaria. 33And Ahab made a wooden image.ᵃ Ahab did more to provoke the Lᴏʀᴅ God of Israel to anger than all the kings of Israel who were before him. 34In his days Hiel of Bethel built Jericho. He laid its foundation with Abiram his firstborn, and with his youngest *son* Segub he set up its gates, according to the word of the Lᴏʀᴅ, which He had spoken through Joshua the son of Nun.ᵃ

🧩 ***Elijah in Israel***

Kings expands the brief summary of Ahab's reign (1 Kin. 16:29–34) with stories about the prophet Elijah. During Ahab's rule (874–853 B.C.), the struggle of Hebrew faith with Baalism inaugurates a new era of prophetic revelation. Elijah's struggle against, and eventual victory over, Baalism (1 Kin. 17; 18) leads to Jezebel's threat on Elijah's life and his depressive reaction (1 Kin. 19).

■ 1 Kings 17:1—19:21

16:33 ᵃHebrew *Asherah*, a Canaanite goddess
16:34 ᵃCompare Joshua 6:26

⧖ JEHOSHAPHAT AND AHAB FORM AN ALLIANCE

Judah (southern kingdom)
Jehoshaphat, son of Asa, allied himself with Israel's king Ahab. The alliance was sealed with the marriage of Jehoshaphat's son Jehoram and Ahab's daughter Athaliah (2 Kin. 8:18).

Israel (northern kingdom)
Ahab, son of Omri, was the first king of Israel to establish peaceful relations with Judah. He had frequent conflicts with Ben-Hadad, king of Aram (Syria). Jehoshaphat and Ahab joined forces against the Syrians in a battle at Ramoth Gilead, where Ahab lost his life (1 Kin. 22).

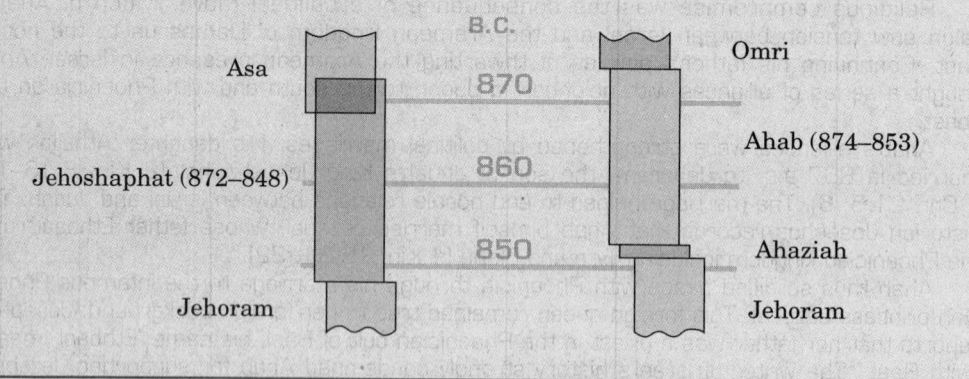

Asa

Jehoshaphat (872–848)

Jehoram

B.C.
870
860
850

Omri

Ahab (874–853)

Ahaziah

Jehoram

1 Kings
Elijah Proclaims a Drought

17 :1 And Elijah the Tishbite, of the inhabitants of Gilead, said to Ahab, "As the LORD God of Israel lives, before whom I stand, there shall not be dew nor rain these years, except at my word."

²Then the word of the LORD came to him, saying, ³"Get away from here and turn eastward, and hide by the Brook Cherith, which flows into the Jordan. ⁴And it will be *that* you shall drink from the brook, and I have commanded the ravens to feed you there."

⁵So he went and did according to the word of the LORD, for he went and stayed by the Brook Cherith, which flows into the Jordan. ⁶The ravens brought him bread and meat in the morning, and bread and meat in the evening; and he drank from the brook. ⁷And it happened after a while that the brook dried up, because there had been no rain in the land.

Elijah and the Widow

⁸Then the word of the LORD came to him, saying, ⁹"Arise, go to Zarephath, which *belongs* to Sidon, and dwell there. See, I have commanded a widow there to provide for you." ¹⁰So he arose and went to Zarephath. And when he came to the gate of the city, indeed a widow *was* there gathering sticks. And he called to her and said, "Please bring me a little water in a cup, that I may drink." ¹¹And as she was going to get *it,* he called to her and said, "Please bring me a morsel of bread in your hand."

¹²So she said, "As the LORD your God lives, I do not have bread, only a handful of flour in a bin, and a little oil in a jar; and see, I *am* gathering a couple of sticks that I

🌄 GEOGRAPHY AND ENVIRONMENT

Gathering sticks for a fire was common when the only fuel available for heating was wood (1 Kin. 17:10). The climate of Palestine is mild enough that heating is not absolutely necessary in winter. However, fuel is required year-round for cooking. In modern times there is often danger of deforestation, but when the population was smaller, wood was a renewable supply.

may go in and prepare it for myself and my son, that we may eat it, and die."

13And Elijah said to her, "Do not fear; go *and* do as you have said, but make me a small cake from it first, and bring *it* to me; and afterward make *some* for yourself and your son. 14For thus says the LORD God of Israel: 'The bin of flour shall not be used up, nor shall the jar of oil run dry, until the day the LORD sends rain on the earth.' "

15So she went away and did according to the word of Elijah; and she and he and her household ate for *many* days. 16The bin of flour was not used up, nor did the jar of oil run dry, according to the word of the LORD which He spoke by Elijah.

Elijah Revives the Widow's Son

17Now it happened after these things *that* the son of the woman who owned the house became sick. And his sickness was so serious that there was no breath left in him. 18So she said to Elijah, "What have I to do with you, O man of God? Have you come to me to bring my sin to remembrance, and to kill my son?"

19And he said to her, "Give me your son." So he took him out of her arms and carried him to the upper room where he was staying, and laid him on his own bed. 20Then he cried out to the LORD and said, "O LORD my God, have You also brought tragedy on the widow with whom I lodge, by killing her son?" 21And he stretched himself out on the child three times, and cried out to the LORD and said, "O LORD my God, I pray, let this child's soul come back to him." 22Then the LORD heard the voice of Elijah; and the soul of the child came back to him, and he revived.

23And Elijah took the child and brought him down from the upper room into the house, and gave him to his mother. And Elijah said, "See, your son lives!" 24Then the woman said to Elijah, "Now by this I know that you *are* a man of God, *and* that the word of the LORD in your mouth *is* the truth."

Elijah's Message to Ahab

18 1And it came to pass *after* many days that the word of the LORD came to Elijah, in the third year, saying, "Go, present yourself to Ahab, and I will send rain on the earth."

2So Elijah went to present himself to Ahab; and *there was* a severe famine in Samaria. 3And Ahab had called Obadiah, who

was in charge of *his* house. (Now Obadiah feared the LORD greatly. 4For so it was, while Jezebel massacred the prophets of the LORD, that Obadiah had taken one hundred prophets and hidden them, fifty to a cave, and had fed them with bread and water.) 5And Ahab had said to Obadiah, "Go into the land to all the springs of water and to all the brooks; perhaps we may find grass to keep the horses and mules alive, so that we will not have to kill any livestock." 6So they divided the land between them to explore it; Ahab went one way by himself, and Obadiah went another way by himself.

7Now as Obadiah was on his way, suddenly Elijah met him; and he recognized him, and fell on his face, and said, "*Is* that you, my lord Elijah?"

8And he answered him, "*It is* I. Go, tell your master, 'Elijah *is here.*' "

9So he said, "How have I sinned, that you are delivering your servant into the hand of Ahab, to kill me? 10As the LORD your God lives, there is no nation or kingdom where my master has not sent someone to hunt for you; and when they said, '*He is* not *here,*' he took an oath from the kingdom or nation that they could not find you. 11And now you say, 'Go, tell your master, "Elijah *is here*" '! 12And it shall come to pass, *as soon as* I am gone from you, that the Spirit of the LORD will carry you to a place I do not know; so when I go and tell Ahab, and he cannot find you, he will kill me. But I your servant have feared the LORD from my youth. 13Was it not reported to my lord what I did when Jezebel killed the prophets of the LORD, how I hid one hundred men of the LORD's prophets, fifty

---

TIME CAPSULE   *885 to 879 B.C.*

885–880	*Civil war between Omri and Tibni, competing for Israel's throne*
883–859	*Ashurnasirpal II of Assyria campaigns every year of his reign*
883	*Ashurnasirpal rebuilds Calah as his capital in Assyria*
880	*Omri becomes sole king in Israel*
880	*Assyrian troops fight on horseback in pairs*
879	*Omri builds city of Samaria and makes it Israel's new capital city*

MOCKING CANAANITE RELIGIOUS RITUAL (1 Kin. 18:17–29)

The confrontation between Elijah and the 450 prophets of Baal on Mount Carmel (1 Kin. 18) demonstrates the power of Israel's God Yahweh over against the weakness, even unreality, of the god Baal. After King Ahab of Israel married Jezebel, the princess of Sidon, the foreign queen promoted the worship of her Sidonian god, Baal (1 Kin. 16:31, 32). The goddess Asherah, symbolized by trees or wooden images (16:33), was also part of this cult, being represented by 400 prophets of her own (18:19).

The prophets of Baal and Asherah are said to "eat at Jezebel's table" (18:19), meaning they were on the government payroll. Professional prophets were standard personnel in many courts, though the number, 850, in Jezebel's court suggests either a rich kingdom or extravagance on her part.

Elijah chose a ritual for the contest that was common to the opposing prophets. An animal sacrifice (18:23) was a central cultic ritual used to honor deities, and bull sacrifices are well known from the clay tablets found at Ugarit. Both Yahweh and Baal were worshiped by the proper sacrifice of bulls.

Elijah's request that each deity light the fire for its own sacrifice (18:24) may reflect the staging of "miracles" in Phoenician temples. The 2nd-century A.D. writer Lucian from Samosata records in *De Dea Syria* how Phoenician priests would rig idols with hidden ropes. Pulling on the ropes would make the idols appear to move and thus amaze worshipers. On the mountain, at a new altar, there would be no chance to fool people with a staged "miraculous" divine intervention.

The prophets of Baal cried aloud and cut themselves in a frenzy (18:28). Self-laceration and mutilation, considered a sign of submission to the deity, appears in a number of religious cult activities. Lucian of Samosata reports worshipers of the goddess at Hierapolis falling into a frenzy and cutting off parts of their own flesh in honor of the deity. On Mount Carmel such actions failed to elicit any divine response (18:29).

---

to a cave, and fed them with bread and water? ¹⁴And now you say, 'Go, tell your master, "Elijah *is here.*" ' He will kill me!"

¹⁵Then Elijah said, "*As* the LORD of hosts lives, before whom I stand, I will surely present myself to him today."

¹⁶So Obadiah went to meet Ahab, and told him; and Ahab went to meet Elijah.

¹⁷Then it happened, when Ahab saw Elijah, that Ahab said to him, "*Is that* you, O troubler of Israel?"

¹⁸And he answered, "I have not troubled Israel, but you and your father's house *have,* in that you have forsaken the commandments of the LORD and have followed the Baals. ¹⁹Now therefore, send *and* gather all Israel to me on Mount Carmel, the four hundred and fifty prophets of Baal, and the four hundred prophets of Asherah,ᵃ who eat at Jezebel's table."

Elijah's Mount Carmel Victory

²⁰So Ahab sent for all the children of Israel, and gathered the prophets together on Mount Carmel. ²¹And Elijah came to all the people, and said, "How long will you falter between two opinions? If the LORD *is* God, follow Him; but if Baal, follow him." But the people answered him not a word. ²²Then Elijah said to the people, "I alone am left a prophet of the LORD; but Baal's prophets *are* four hundred and fifty men. ²³Therefore let them give us two bulls; and let them choose one bull for themselves, cut it in pieces, and lay *it* on the wood, but put no fire *under it;* and I will prepare the other bull, and lay *it* on the wood, but put no fire *under it.* ²⁴Then you call on the name of your gods, and I will call on the name of the LORD; and the God who answers by fire, He is God."

So all the people answered and said, "It is well spoken."

²⁵Now Elijah said to the prophets of Baal, "Choose one bull for yourselves and prepare *it* first, for you *are* many; and call on the name of your god, but put no fire *under it.*"

18:19 ᵃA Canaanite goddess

26So they took the bull which was given them, and they prepared *it,* and called on the name of Baal from morning even till noon, saying, "O Baal, hear us!" But *there was* no voice; no one answered. Then they leaped about the altar which they had made.

27And so it was, at noon, that Elijah mocked them and said, "Cry aloud, for he *is* a god; either he is meditating, or he is busy, or he is on a journey, *or* perhaps he is sleeping and must be awakened." 28So they cried aloud, and cut themselves, as was their custom, with knives and lances, until the blood gushed out on them. 29And when midday was past, they prophesied until the *time* of the offering of the *evening* sacrifice. But *there was* no voice; no one answered, no one paid attention.

30Then Elijah said to all the people, "Come near to me." So all the people came near to him. And he repaired the altar of the LORD *that was* broken down. 31And Elijah took twelve stones, according to the number of the tribes of the sons of Jacob, to whom the word of the LORD had come, saying, "Israel shall be your name."a 32Then with the stones he built an altar in the name of the LORD; and he made a trench around the altar large enough to hold two seahs of seed. 33And he put the wood in order, cut the bull in pieces, and laid *it* on the wood, and said, "Fill four waterpots with water, and pour *it* on the burnt sacrifice and on the wood." 34Then he said, "Do *it* a second time," and they did *it* a second time; and he said, "Do *it* a third time," and they did *it* a third time. 35So the water ran all around the altar; and he also filled the trench with water.

36And it came to pass, at *the time of* the offering of the *evening* sacrifice, that Elijah the prophet came near and said, "LORD God of Abraham, Isaac, and Israel, let it be known this day that You *are* God in Israel and I *am* Your servant, and *that* I have done all these things at Your word. 37Hear me, O LORD, hear me, that this people may know that You *are* the LORD God, and *that* You have turned their hearts back *to You* again."

38Then the fire of the LORD fell and consumed the burnt sacrifice, and the wood and the stones and the dust, and it licked up the water that *was* in the trench. 39Now when all the people saw *it,* they fell on their faces; and they said, "The LORD, He *is* God! The LORD, He *is* God!"

40And Elijah said to them, "Seize the prophets of Baal! Do not let one of them escape!" So they seized them; and Elijah brought them down to the Brook Kishon and executed them there.

The Drought Ends

41Then Elijah said to Ahab, "Go up, eat and drink; for *there is* the sound of abundance of rain." 42So Ahab went up to eat and drink. And Elijah went up to the top of Carmel; then he bowed down on the ground, and put his face between his knees, 43and said to his servant, "Go up now, look toward the sea."

So he went up and looked, and said, "*There is* nothing." And seven times he said, "Go again."

44Then it came to pass the seventh *time,* that he said, "There is a cloud, as small as a man's hand, rising out of the sea!" So he said, "Go up, say to Ahab, 'Prepare *your chariot,* and go down before the rain stops you.' "

45Now it happened in the meantime that the sky became black with clouds and wind, and there was a heavy rain. So Ahab rode away and went to Jezreel. 46Then the hand of the LORD came upon Elijah; and he girded up his loins and ran ahead of Ahab to the entrance of Jezreel.

Elijah Escapes from Jezebel

19 1And Ahab told Jezebel all that Elijah had done, also how he had executed all the prophets with the sword. 2Then Jezebel sent a messenger to Elijah, saying, "So let the gods do *to me,* and more also, if I do not make your life as the life of one of them by tomorrow about this time." 3And when he saw *that,* he arose and ran for his life, and went to Beersheba, which *belongs* to Judah, and left his servant there.

4But he himself went a day's journey into the wilderness, and came and sat down under a broom tree. And he prayed that he might die, and said, "It is enough! Now, LORD, take my life, for I *am* no better than my fathers!"

5Then as he lay and slept under a broom tree, suddenly an angela touched him, and said to him, "Arise *and* eat." 6Then he looked, and there by his head *was* a cake baked on coals, and a jar of water. So he ate and drank, and lay down again.

18:31 aGenesis 32:28   19:5 aOr *Angel*

THE UPTOWN GIRL (1 Kin. 19:2, 3)

The marriage between Israel's king Ahab and Sidon's princess Jezebel was politically motivated. Unfortunately, the union had an ill effect on Israel's worship of Yahweh. Even today, the name "Jezebel" is associated with all that is evil.

Jezebel, it should be remembered, killed the prophets of Yahweh (1 Kin. 18:13). She was also the one who frightened Yahweh's prophet Elijah so much that he fled for safety (1 Kin. 19:2, 3). She also caused the man Naboth to be killed so her husband could possess Naboth's field (1 Kin. 21:8–13). Her evil deeds led Elijah to predict that Jezebel would be eaten by dogs after her death (1 Kin. 21:23; 2 Kin. 9:35–37). Since Jezebel was so evil, how could she have had so much power?

That her influence came from being the wife of Ahab, making her the queen, is true but not the whole story. She was also the daughter of Ethbaal, the king of Sidon (1 Kin. 16:31). During Ahab's time Sidon was one of the most powerful and certainly richest areas in and around Israel. The material culture of the Sidonians is one of the highest of those found in ancient Canaan. Their ceramic dishes are artistically beautiful, making the typical pots of the Israelites look clumsy and backwoodish.

As a princess from Sidon, Jezebel might have been the original "uptown" girl. She came from the richest and most advanced culture, as the daughter of a king, to Israel, a simple hill-country kingdom. Her aristocratic presence overwhelmed those around her; all eyes and hearts turned in her direction. They swooned in following her god Baal and deserted Yahweh, God of Israel. Not surprisingly, this original "uptown" girl also influenced her husband Ahab's worship of Baal (1 Kin. 16:31).

---

[7]And the angel[a] of the LORD came back the second time, and touched him, and said, "Arise *and* eat, because the journey *is* too great for you." [8]So he arose, and ate and drank; and he went in the strength of that food forty days and forty nights as far as Horeb, the mountain of God.

[9]And there he went into a cave, and spent the night in that place; and behold, the word of the LORD *came* to him, and He said to him, "What are you doing here, Elijah?"

[10]So he said, "I have been very zealous for the LORD God of hosts; for the children of Israel have forsaken Your covenant, torn down Your altars, and killed Your prophets with the sword. I alone am left; and they seek to take my life."

God's Revelation to Elijah

[11]Then He said, "Go out, and stand on the mountain before the LORD." And behold, the LORD passed by, and a great and strong wind tore into the mountains and broke the rocks in pieces before the LORD, *but* the LORD *was* not in the wind; and after the wind an earthquake, *but* the LORD *was* not in the earthquake; [12]and after the earthquake a fire, *but* the LORD *was* not in

the fire; and after the fire a still small voice.

[13]So it was, when Elijah heard *it,* that he wrapped his face in his mantle and went out and stood in the entrance of the cave. Suddenly a voice *came* to him, and said, "What are you doing here, Elijah?"

[14]And he said, "I have been very zealous for the LORD God of hosts; because the children of Israel have forsaken Your covenant, torn down Your altars, and killed Your prophets with the sword. I alone am left; and they seek to take my life."

[15]Then the LORD said to him: "Go, return on your way to the Wilderness of Damascus; and when you arrive, anoint Hazael *as* king over Syria. [16]Also you shall anoint Jehu the son of Nimshi *as* king over Israel. And Elisha the son of Shaphat of Abel Meholah you shall anoint *as* prophet in your place. [17]It shall be *that* whoever escapes the sword of Hazael, Jehu will kill; and whoever escapes the sword of Jehu, Elisha will kill. [18]Yet I have reserved seven thousand in Israel, all whose knees have not bowed to Baal, and every mouth that has not kissed him."

19:7 [a]Or *Angel*

Elisha Follows Elijah

¹⁹So he departed from there, and found Elisha the son of Shaphat, who *was* plowing *with* twelve yoke *of oxen* before him, and he was with the twelfth. Then Elijah passed by him and threw his mantle on him. ²⁰And he left the oxen and ran after Elijah, and said, "Please let me kiss my father and my mother, and *then* I will follow you."

And he said to him, "Go back again, for what have I done to you?"

²¹So *Elisha* turned back from him, and took a yoke of oxen and slaughtered them and boiled their flesh, using the oxen's equipment, and gave it to the people, and they ate. Then he arose and followed Elijah, and became his servant.

Ahab Wars with Damascus

Towards the end of Ahab's reign, one of Israel's primary threats was the state of Aram (or Syria), with its center in Damascus. In 853 B.C. Damascus led a coalition of Syro-Palestinian states (including Ahab and Israel) which was able to resist an advancing Assyrian army at the town of Qarqar. Ahab and Damascus were allies in that encounter with Assyria, but they became enemies soon afterward. The wars that Ahab fought against Aram-Damascus are recounted in 1 Kin. 20; 22.

The identity of King Ben-Hadad who led the Aramean (Syrian) forces against Israel (1 Kin. 20:1) is uncertain. Since the Arameans' main deity was Hadad, god of rain, several of Aram's kings were named "Ben-Hadad," meaning "son of Hadad." Some think that Ahab's opponent was the same Ben-Hadad who aided Judah's King Asa (1 Kin. 15:18), or possibly the King Hadad-ezer of Damascus who led the coalition at Qarqar. Others even suggest that the name "Ben-Hadad" reflects the Aramean king of 2 Kin. 13:24, 25. Thus the actual events surrounding Ahab's death in 853 B.C. remain unidentified.

■ 1 Kings 20:1—22:40

1 Kings
Ahab Defeats the Syrians

20 :1 Now Ben-Hadad the king of Syria gathered all his forces together; thirty-two kings *were* with him, with horses and chariots. And he went up and besieged Samaria, and made war against it. ²Then he sent messengers into the city to Ahab king of Israel, and said to him, "Thus says Ben-Hadad: ³'Your silver and your gold *are* mine; your loveliest wives and children are mine.'"

⁴And the king of Israel answered and said, "My lord, O king, just as you say, I and all that I have *are* yours."

⁵Then the messengers came back and said, "Thus speaks Ben-Hadad, saying, 'Indeed I have sent to you, saying, "You shall deliver to me your silver and your gold, your wives and your children"; ⁶but I will send my servants to you tomorrow about this time, and they shall search your house and the houses of your servants. And it shall be, *that* whatever is pleasant in your eyes, they will put *it* in their hands and take *it*.'"

⁷So the king of Israel called all the elders of the land, and said, "Notice, please, and see how this *man* seeks trouble, for he sent to me for my wives, my children, my silver, and my gold; and I did not deny him."

⁸And all the elders and all the people said to him, "Do not listen or consent."

⁹Therefore he said to the messengers of Ben-Hadad, "Tell my lord the king, 'All that you sent for to your servant the first time I will do, but this thing I cannot do.'"

And the messengers departed and brought back word to him.

¹⁰Then Ben-Hadad sent to him and said, "The gods do so to me, and more also, if enough dust is left of Samaria for a handful for each of the people who follow me."

¹¹So the king of Israel answered and said, "Tell *him,* 'Let not the one who puts on *his* armor boast like the one who takes *it off.*'"

¹²And it happened when *Ben-Hadad* heard this message, as he and the kings *were* drinking at the command post, that he said to his servants, "Get ready." And they got ready to attack the city.

¹³Suddenly a prophet approached Ahab king of Israel, saying, "Thus says the LORD: 'Have you seen all this great multitude? Behold, I will deliver it into your hand today, and you shall know that I *am* the LORD.'"

¹⁴So Ahab said, "By whom?"

And he said, "Thus says the LORD: 'By the young leaders of the provinces.'"

Then he said, "Who will set the battle in order?"

And he answered, "You."

¹⁵Then he mustered the young leaders of the provinces, and there were two hundred and thirty-two; and after them he mustered all the people, all the children of Israel—seven thousand.

¹⁶So they went out at noon. Meanwhile Ben-Hadad and the thirty-two kings helping him were getting drunk at the command post. ¹⁷The young leaders of the provinces went out first. And Ben-Hadad sent out *a patrol,* and they told him, saying, "Men are coming out of Samaria!" ¹⁸So he said, "If they have come out for peace, take them alive; and if they have come out for war, take them alive."

¹⁹Then these young leaders of the provinces went out of the city with the army which followed them. ²⁰And each one killed his man; so the Syrians fled, and Israel pursued them; and Ben-Hadad the king of Syria escaped on a horse with the cavalry. ²¹Then the king of Israel went out and attacked the horses and chariots, and killed the Syrians with a great slaughter.

²²And the prophet came to the king of Israel and said to him, "Go, strengthen yourself; take note, and see what you should do, for in the spring of the year the king of Syria will come up against you."

The Syrians Again Defeated

²³Then the servants of the king of Syria said to him, "Their gods *are* gods of the hills. Therefore they were stronger than we; but if we fight against them in the plain, surely we will be stronger than they. ²⁴So do this thing: Dismiss the kings, each from his position, and put captains in their places; ²⁵and you shall muster an army like the army that you have lost, horse for horse and chariot for chariot. Then we will fight against them in the plain; surely we will be stronger than they."

And he listened to their voice and did so.

²⁶So it was, in the spring of the year, that Ben-Hadad mustered the Syrians and went up to Aphek to fight against Is-

rael. ²⁷And the children of Israel were mustered and given provisions, and they went against them. Now the children of Israel encamped before them like two little flocks of goats, while the Syrians filled the countryside.

²⁸Then a man of God came and spoke to the king of Israel, and said, "Thus says the LORD: 'Because the Syrians have said, "The LORD *is* God of the hills, but He *is* not God of the valleys," therefore I will deliver all this great multitude into your hand, and you shall know that I *am* the LORD.' "

²⁹And they encamped opposite each other for seven days. So it was that on the seventh day the battle was joined; and the children of Israel killed one hundred thousand foot soldiers *of* the Syrians in one day. ³⁰But the rest fled to Aphek, into the city; then a wall fell on twenty-seven thousand of the men *who were* left.

And Ben-Hadad fled and went into the city, into an inner chamber.

Ahab's Treaty with Ben-Hadad

³¹Then his servants said to him, "Look now, we have heard that the kings of the house of Israel *are* merciful kings. Please, let us put sackcloth around our waists and ropes around our heads, and go out to the king of Israel; perhaps he will spare your life." ³²So they wore sackcloth around their waists and *put* ropes around their heads, and came to the king of Israel and said, "Your servant Ben-Hadad says, 'Please let me live.' "

And he said, "*Is* he still alive? He *is* my brother."

³³Now the men were watching closely to see whether *any sign of mercy would come* from him; and they quickly grasped *at this word* and said, "Your brother Ben-Hadad."

So he said, "Go, bring him." Then Ben-Hadad came out to him; and he had him come up into the chariot.

³⁴So *Ben-Hadad* said to him, "The cities which my father took from your father I will restore; and you may set up

RELIGION AND WORSHIP

The prophets occasionally performed "prophetic actions" of some sort, dramatizing an aspect of their message. Such actions might include "striking" (1 Kin. 20:35), symbolic items, such as Zedekiah's "horns of iron" (1 Kin. 22:11), as well as more elaborate activity like Ezekiel's actions (Ezek. 4; 5). There is at least one example of prophetic action in the New Testament (Acts 21:11).

marketplaces for yourself in Damascus, as my father did in Samaria."

Then *Ahab said,* "I will send you away with this treaty." So he made a treaty with him and sent him away.

Ahab Condemned

³⁵Now a certain man of the sons of the prophets said to his neighbor by the word of the LORD, "Strike me, please." And the man refused to strike him. ³⁶Then he said to him, "Because you have not obeyed the voice of the LORD, surely, as soon as you depart from me, a lion shall kill you." And as soon as he left him, a lion found him and killed him.

³⁷And he found another man, and said, "Strike me, please." So the man struck him, inflicting a wound. ³⁸Then the prophet departed and waited for the king by the road, and disguised himself with a bandage over his eyes. ³⁹Now as the king passed by, he cried out to the king and said, "Your servant went out into the midst of the battle; and there, a man came over and brought a man to me, and said, 'Guard this man; if by any means he is missing, your life shall be for his life, or else you shall pay a talent of silver.' ⁴⁰While your servant was busy here and there, he was gone."

Then the king of Israel said to him, "So *shall* your judgment *be;* you yourself have decided *it.*"

⁴¹And he hastened to take the bandage away from his eyes; and the king of Israel recognized him as one of the prophets. ⁴²Then he said to him, "Thus says the LORD: 'Because you have let slip out of *your* hand a man whom I appointed to utter destruction, therefore your life shall go for his life, and your people for his people.' "

⁴³So the king of Israel went to his house sullen and displeased, and came to Samaria.

Naboth Is Murdered for His Vineyard

21 ¹And it came to pass after these things *that* Naboth the Jezreelite had a vineyard which *was* in Jezreel, next to the palace of Ahab king of Samaria. ²So Ahab spoke to Naboth, saying, "Give me your vineyard, that I may have it for a vegetable garden, because it *is* near, next to my house; and for it I will give you a vineyard better than it. *Or,* if it seems good to you, I will give you its worth in money."

³But Naboth said to Ahab, "The LORD forbid that I should give the inheritance of my fathers to you!"

⁴So Ahab went into his house sullen and displeased because of the word which Naboth the Jezreelite had spoken to him; for he had said, "I will not give you the inheritance of my fathers." And he lay down on his bed, and turned away his face, and would eat no food. ⁵But Jezebel his wife came to him, and said to him, "Why is your spirit so sullen that you eat no food?"

⁶He said to her, "Because I spoke to Naboth the Jezreelite, and said to him, 'Give me your vineyard for money; or else, if it pleases you, I will give you *another* vineyard for it.' And he answered, 'I will not give you my vineyard.' "

⁷Then Jezebel his wife said to him, "You now exercise authority over Israel! Arise, eat food, and let your heart be cheerful; I will give you the vineyard of Naboth the Jezreelite."

⁸And she wrote letters in Ahab's name, sealed *them* with his seal, and sent the letters to the elders and the nobles who *were* dwelling in the city with Naboth. ⁹She wrote in the letters, saying,

Proclaim a fast, and seat Naboth with high honor among the people; ¹⁰and seat two men, scoundrels, before him to bear witness against him, saying, "You have blasphemed God and the king." *Then* take him out, and stone him, that he may die.

¹¹So the men of his city, the elders and nobles who were inhabitants of his city, did as Jezebel had sent to them, as it *was* written in the letters which she had sent to them. ¹²They proclaimed a fast, and seated Naboth with high honor among the people.

TIME CAPSULE   *874 to 867 B.C.*

874– 850	*Osorkon II of Egypt completes extensive temple construction at Tanis*
874	*Ahab becomes king in Israel*
872	*Jehoshaphat serves as coregent with Asa in Judah*
869	*Jehoshaphat becomes sole king in Judah*
867	*Israel's King Ahab marries daughter Athaliah to Jehoram, the son of Judah's King Jehoshaphat*

13And two men, scoundrels, came in and sat before him; and the scoundrels witnessed against him, against Naboth, in the presence of the people, saying, "Naboth has blasphemed God and the king!" Then they took him outside the city and stoned him with stones, so that he died. 14Then they sent to Jezebel, saying, "Naboth has been stoned and is dead."

15And it came to pass, when Jezebel heard that Naboth had been stoned and was dead, that Jezebel said to Ahab, "Arise, take possession of the vineyard of Naboth the Jezreelite, which he refused to give you for money; for Naboth is not alive, but dead." 16So it was, when Ahab heard that Naboth was dead, that Ahab got up and went down to take possession of the vineyard of Naboth the Jezreelite.

The LORD Condemns Ahab

17Then the word of the LORD came to Elijah the Tishbite, saying, 18"Arise, go down to meet Ahab king of Israel, who *lives* in Samaria. There *he is,* in the vineyard of Naboth, where he has gone down to take possession of it. 19You shall speak to him, saying, 'Thus says the LORD: "Have you murdered and also taken possession?" ' And you shall speak to him, saying, 'Thus says the LORD: "In the place where dogs licked the blood of Naboth, dogs shall lick your blood, even yours." ' "

20So Ahab said to Elijah, "Have you found me, O my enemy?"

And he answered, "I have found *you,* because you have sold yourself to do evil in the sight of the LORD: 21Behold, I will bring calamity on you. I will take away your posterity, and will cut off from Ahab every male in Israel, both bond and free. 22I will make your house like the house of Jeroboam the son of Nebat, and like the house of Baasha the son of Ahijah, because of the provocation with which you have provoked *Me* to anger, and made Israel sin.' 23And concerning Jezebel the LORD also spoke, saying, 'The dogs shall eat Jezebel by the walla of Jezreel.' 24The dogs shall eat who-

ever belongs to Ahab and dies in the city, and the birds of the air shall eat whoever dies in the field."

25But there was no one like Ahab who sold himself to do wickedness in the sight of the LORD, because Jezebel his wife stirred him up. 26And he behaved very abominably in following idols, according to all *that* the Amorites had done, whom the LORD had cast out before the children of Israel.

27So it was, when Ahab heard those words, that he tore his clothes and put sackcloth on his body, and fasted and lay in sackcloth, and went about mourning.

28And the word of the LORD came to Elijah the Tishbite, saying, 29"See how Ahab has humbled himself before Me? Because he has humbled himself before Me, I will not bring the calamity in his days. In the days of his son I will bring the calamity on his house."

Micaiah Warns Ahab

22 1Now three years passed without war between Syria and Israel. 2Then it came to pass, in the third year, that Jehoshaphat the king of Judah went down to *visit* the king of Israel.

3And the king of Israel said to his servants, "Do you know that Ramoth in Gilead *is* ours, but we hesitate to take it out of the hand of the king of Syria?" 4So he said to Jehoshaphat, "Will you go with me to fight at Ramoth Gilead?"

Jehoshaphat said to the king of Israel, "I *am* as you *are,* my people as your people, my horses as your horses." 5Also Jehoshaphat said to the king of Israel, "Please inquire for the word of the LORD today."

6Then the king of Israel gathered the prophets together, about four hundred

---

21:23 aFollowing Masoretic Text and Septuagint; some Hebrew manuscripts, Syriac, Targum, and Vulgate read *plot of ground* (compare 2 Kings 9:36).

BELIEFS AND IDEAS

In several visions of God described by the prophets, God is enthroned and surrounded by a court consisting of His servants. Among those attending the court are spirits prepared to perform works, such as deceiving King Ahab (1 Kin. 22:19–23). In one case, even Satan, the Adversary, attends God's court, obtaining permission to afflict Job with misfortune and sickness (Job 1:6–12).

men, and said to them, "Shall I go against Ramoth Gilead to fight, or shall I refrain?"

So they said, "Go up, for the Lord will deliver *it* into the hand of the king."

7And Jehoshaphat said, "*Is there* not still a prophet of the LORD here, that we may inquire of Him?"a

8So the king of Israel said to Jehoshaphat, "*There is* still one man, Micaiah the son of Imlah, by whom we may inquire of the LORD; but I hate him, because he does not prophesy good concerning me, but evil."

And Jehoshaphat said, "Let not the king say such things!"

9Then the king of Israel called an officer and said, "Bring Micaiah the son of Imlah quickly!"

10The king of Israel and Jehoshaphat the king of Judah, having put on *their* robes, sat each on his throne, at a threshing floor at the entrance of the gate of Samaria; and all the prophets prophesied before them. 11Now Zedekiah the son of Chenaanah had made horns of iron for himself; and he said, "Thus says the LORD: 'With these you shall gore the Syrians until they are destroyed.'" 12And all the prophets prophesied so, saying, "Go up to Ramoth Gilead and prosper, for the LORD will deliver *it* into the king's hand."

13Then the messenger who had gone to call Micaiah spoke to him, saying, "Now listen, the words of the prophets with one accord encourage the king. Please, let your word be like the word of one of them, and speak encouragement."

14And Micaiah said, "*As* the LORD lives, whatever the LORD says to me, that I will speak."

15Then he came to the king; and the king said to him, "Micaiah, shall we go to war against Ramoth Gilead, or shall we refrain?"

And he answered him, "Go and prosper, for the LORD will deliver *it* into the hand of the king!"

16So the king said to him, "How many times shall I make you swear that you tell me nothing but the truth in the name of the LORD?"

17Then he said, "I saw all Israel scattered on the mountains, as sheep that have no shepherd. And the LORD said, 'These have no master. Let each return to his house in peace.'"

18And the king of Israel said to Jehoshaphat, "Did I not tell you he would not prophesy good concerning me, but evil?"

19Then *Micaiah* said, "Therefore hear the word of the LORD: I saw the LORD sitting on His throne, and all the host of heaven standing by, on His right hand and on His left. 20And the LORD said, 'Who will persuade Ahab to go up, that he may fall at Ramoth Gilead?' So one spoke in this manner, and another spoke in that manner. 21Then a spirit came forward and stood before the LORD, and said, 'I will persuade him.' 22The LORD said to him, 'In what way?' So he said, 'I will go out and be a lying spirit in the mouth of all his prophets.' And the LORD said, 'You shall persuade *him,* and also prevail. Go out and do so.' 23Therefore look! The LORD has put a lying spirit in the mouth of all these prophets of yours, and the LORD has declared disaster against you."

24Now Zedekiah the son of Chenaanah went near and struck Micaiah on the cheek, and said, "Which way did the spirit from the LORD go from me to speak to you?"

25And Micaiah said, "Indeed, you shall see on that day when you go into an inner chamber to hide!"

26So the king of Israel said, "Take Micaiah, and return him to Amon the governor of the city and to Joash the king's son; 27and say, 'Thus says the king: "Put this *fellow* in prison, and feed him with bread of affliction and water of affliction, until I come in peace."'"

28But Micaiah said, "If you ever return in peace, the LORD has not spoken by me." And he said, "Take heed, all you people!"

Ahab Dies in Battle

29So the king of Israel and Jehoshaphat the king of Judah went up to Ramoth Gilead. 30And the king of Israel said to Jehoshaphat, "I will disguise myself and go into battle; but you put on your robes." So the king of Israel disguised himself and went into battle.

31Now the king of Syria had commanded the thirty-two captains of his chariots, saying, "Fight with no one small or great, but only with the king of Israel." 32So it was, when the captains of the chariots saw Jehoshaphat, that they said, "Surely it *is* the king of Israel!" Therefore they turned aside to fight against him, and Jehoshaphat cried out. 33And it happened, when the captains of the chariots saw that

22:7 aOr *him*

THE IVORY HOUSE (1 Kin. 22:39)

The city of Samaria holds two distinctions. First, it was the only city that the Israelites are specifically credited with building from the ground up (1 Kin. 16:24); all others they took from some other people. Samaria's second claim to fame is the amazingly large number of ivories that were found in the rubble of King Ahab's palace (1 Kin. 22:39).

The ivories have been found in destruction layers that had been Ahab's house, but exactly how they were used is not certain. Among the pieces found were a large number of plaques, suggesting that they were hung on walls. Some of these plaques were themselves decorated with gold, colored glass, and jewels. Other pieces of ivory were used as inlays for furniture, which recalls the "beds of ivory" mentioned by the prophet Amos (Amos 6:4).

The motifs of these ivory pieces included animals like lions and goats; foreign gods like the Egyptian gods Horus and Re; Hebrew letters; and winged creatures. No doubt such unusual and expensive decoration spread the fame of Ahab, who ruled from 874 to 853 B.C. Ivory houses also characterized the prosperity that the prophet Amos decried during the later reign of Jeroboam II (793–753 B.C.). The kings of Israel had a summer palace in Jezreel and a winter palace at Samaria, both being examples of luxury and extravagance (Amos 3:15).

---

it *was* not the king of Israel, that they turned back from pursuing him. ³⁴Now a *certain* man drew a bow at random, and struck the king of Israel between the joints of his armor. So he said to the driver of his chariot, "Turn around and take me out of the battle, for I am wounded."

³⁵The battle increased that day; and the king was propped up in his chariot, facing the Syrians, and died at evening. The blood ran out from the wound onto the floor of the chariot. ³⁶Then, as the sun was going down, a shout went throughout the army, saying, "Every man to his city, and every man to his own country!"

³⁷So the king died, and was brought to Samaria. And they buried the king in Samaria. ³⁸Then *someone* washed the chariot at a pool in Samaria, and the dogs licked up his blood while the harlots bathed,ᵃ according to the word of the LORD which He had spoken.

³⁹Now the rest of the acts of Ahab, and all that he did, the ivory house which he built and all the cities that he built, *are* they not written in the book of the chronicles of the kings of Israel? ⁴⁰So Ahab rested with his fathers. Then Ahaziah his son reigned in his place.

The Alliance of Judah and Israel

In a summary of Jehoshaphat's reign (872–848 B.C.), the author of Kings comments that Jehoshaphat "made peace with the king of Israel" (1 Kin. 22:44). This alliance resulted in both a joint military campaign with Israel's Ahab and later a commercial enterprise with Ahab's son Ahaziah—neither of which was successful. The campaign against the Arameans at Ramoth Gilead was aborted after Ahab was killed (1 Kin. 22:35, 36), and the trading venture with Ahaziah ended in shipwreck (1 Kin. 22:48; 2 Chr. 20:35–37). After two such failures, Jehoshaphat was understandably reluctant to continue working with Israel (1 Kin. 22:49).

■ 1 Kings 22:41–50

1 Kings
Jehoshaphat Reigns in Judah

22 :41 Jehoshaphat the son of Asa had become king over Judah in the fourth year of Ahab king of Israel. ⁴²Jehoshaphat *was* thirty-five years old when he became king, and he reigned twenty-five years in Jerusalem. His mother's name *was* Azubah the daughter of Shilhi. ⁴³And he walked in all the ways of his father Asa. He did not turn aside from them, doing *what was* right in the eyes of the LORD. Nevertheless the high places were not taken away, *for* the people offered sacrifices and burned incense on the high places. ⁴⁴Also Jehoshaphat made peace with the king of Israel.

⁴⁵Now the rest of the acts of Je-

22:38 ᵃSyriac and Targum read *they washed his armor.*

BROTHERS, IN-LAWS, UNCLES, AND NEPHEWS

Judah (southern kingdom)

Jehoram (or Joram) was the son of Jehoshaphat and brother-in-law to Israel's Ahaziah and Jehoram. He married their sister Athaliah (2 Chr. 21:6).

Ahaziah was the son of Jehoram and the nephew of Israel's Ahaziah and Jehoram. He joined his uncle, Israel's Jehoram, in a campaign against Syria (2 Kin. 8:28).

Israel (northern kingdom)

Ahaziah was the son of Ahab, brother of Israel's Jehoram, and uncle to Judah's Ahaziah. He continued the alliance with Jehoshaphat, building ships and conducting an unsuccessful joint trading venture (2 Chr. 20:35–37).

Jehoram (or Joram) was the son of Ahab, brother of Israel's Ahaziah, and uncle to Judah's Ahaziah. He allied himself with Jehoshaphat to fight Moab (2 Kin. 3:6). Later he allied with Judah's Ahaziah, his nephew, to fight Syria (2 Kin. 8:28, 29).

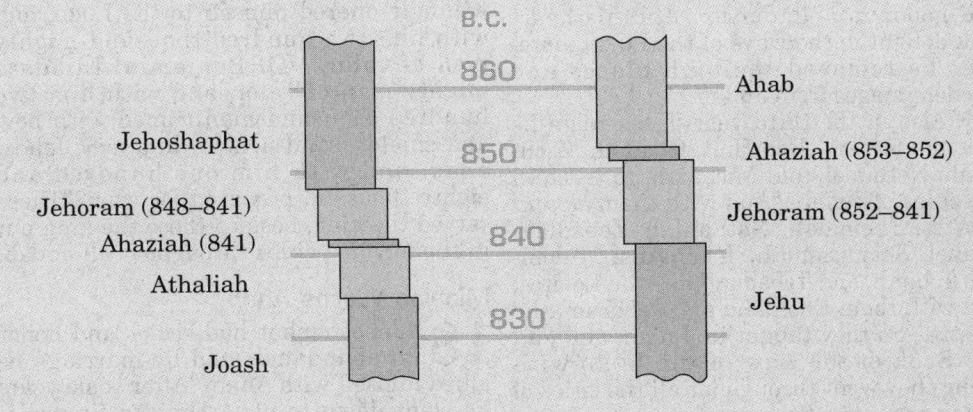

B.C.
860 — Ahab
Jehoshaphat
850 — Ahaziah (853–852)
Jehoram (848–841)　　Jehoram (852–841)
Ahaziah (841)
840
Athaliah
　　　　Jehu
830
Joash

hoshaphat, the might that he showed, and how he made war, *are* they not written in the book of the chronicles of the kings of Judah? ⁴⁶And the rest of the perverted persons,ᵃ who remained in the days of his father Asa, he banished from the land. ⁴⁷*There was* then no king in Edom, only a deputy of the king.

⁴⁸Jehoshaphat made merchant shipsᵃ to go to Ophir for gold; but they never sailed, for the ships were wrecked at Ezion Geber. ⁴⁹Then Ahaziah the son of Ahab said to Jehoshaphat, "Let my servants go with your servants in the ships." But Jehoshaphat would not.

⁵⁰And Jehoshaphat rested with his fathers, and was buried with his fathers in the City of David his father. Then Jehoram his son reigned in his place.

Priestly Account: Ahab and Jehoshaphat

The historian of Kings offered a short summary of Jehoshaphat's reign (1 Kin. 22:41–50), while covering Ahab's reign in the northern kingdom much more thoroughly. The Chronicler reverses that emphasis, concentrating on Judah's king Jehoshaphat (872–848 B.C.), and mentioning Ahab only at the campaign against Ramoth Gilead (2 Chr. 18).

Chronicles relates the battle of Ramoth Gilead almost word for word from Kings, but adds comments that present Jehoshaphat in a good light. The feast hosted by Ahab (2 Chr. 18:2) is not mentioned in 1 Kin. 22:2; perhaps the Chronicler wanted to show that Ahab was primarily responsible for the military defeat. While Jehoshaphat is rebuked for his alliance with "the wicked," meaning Ahab, he is praised for his religious reforms (2 Chr. 19:1–3).

■ 2 Chronicles 17:1—19:11

22:46 ᵃHebrew *qadesh*, that is, one practicing sodomy and prostitution in religious rituals
22:48 ᵃOr *ships of Tarshish*

2 Chronicles
Jehoshaphat Reigns in Judah

17 :1 Then Jehoshaphat his son reigned in his place, and strengthened himself against Israel. ²And he placed troops in all the fortified cities of Judah, and set garrisons in the land of Judah and in the cities of Ephraim which Asa his father had taken. ³Now the LORD was with Jehoshaphat, because he walked in the former ways of his father David; he did not seek the Baals, ⁴but sought the God^a of his father, and walked in His commandments and not according to the acts of Israel. ⁵Therefore the LORD established the kingdom in his hand; and all Judah gave presents to Jehoshaphat, and he had riches and honor in abundance. ⁶And his heart took delight in the ways of the LORD; moreover he removed the high places and wooden images from Judah.

⁷Also in the third year of his reign he sent his leaders, Ben-Hail, Obadiah, Zechariah, Nethanel, and Michaiah, to teach in the cities of Judah. ⁸And with them *he sent* Levites: Shemaiah, Nethaniah, Zebadiah, Asahel, Shemiramoth, Jehonathan, Adonijah, Tobijah, and Tobadonijah—the Levites; and with them Elishama and Jehoram, the priests. ⁹So they taught in Judah, and *had* the Book of the Law of the LORD with them; they went throughout all the cities of Judah and taught the people.

¹⁰And the fear of the LORD fell on all the kingdoms of the lands that *were* around Judah, so that they did not make war against Jehoshaphat. ¹¹Also *some* of the Philistines brought Jehoshaphat presents and silver as tribute; and the Ara-bians brought him flocks, seven thousand seven hundred rams and seven thousand seven hundred male goats.

¹²So Jehoshaphat became increasingly powerful, and he built fortresses and storage cities in Judah. ¹³He had much property in the cities of Judah; and the men of war, mighty men of valor, *were* in Jerusalem.

¹⁴These *are* their numbers, according to their fathers' houses. Of Judah, the captains of thousands: Adnah the captain, and with him three hundred thousand mighty men of valor; ¹⁵and next to him *was* Jehohanan the captain, and with him two hundred and eighty thousand; ¹⁶and next to him *was* Amasiah the son of Zichri, who willingly offered himself to the LORD, and with him two hundred thousand mighty men of valor. ¹⁷Of Benjamin: Eliada a mighty man of valor, and with him two hundred thousand men armed with bow and shield; ¹⁸and next to him *was* Jehozabad, and with him one hundred and eighty thousand prepared for war. ¹⁹These served the king, besides those the king put in the fortified cities throughout all Judah.

Micaiah Warns Ahab

18 ¹Jehoshaphat had riches and honor in abundance; and by marriage he allied himself with Ahab. ²After some years he went down to *visit* Ahab in Samaria; and Ahab killed sheep and oxen in abundance for him and the people who were with him, and persuaded him to go up *with him* to Ramoth Gilead. ³So Ahab king of Israel said to Jehoshaphat king of Judah, "Will you go with me *against* Ramoth Gilead?"

And he answered him, "I *am* as you *are,* and my people as your people; *we will be* with you in the war."

⁴Also Jehoshaphat said to the king of Israel, "Please inquire for the word of the LORD today."

⁵Then the king of Israel gathered the prophets together, four hundred men, and said to them, "Shall we go to war against Ramoth Gilead, or shall I refrain?"

So they said, "Go up, for God will deliver it into the king's hand."

⁶But Jehoshaphat said, "*Is there* not still a prophet of the LORD here, that we may inquire of Him?"^a

TIME CAPSULE   858 to 853 B.C.

858–824	Shalmaneser III of Assyria campaigns against Urartu and Damascus
858	Assyrian Empire reaches to the Mediterranean
856	Shalmaneser captures many cities of Urartu
853–845	Urhilina, king of Hamath, is part of coalition that stops Assyrian advances to the west
853	Anti-Assyrian coalition fights against Assyria's Shalmaneser at the battle of Qarqar

17:4 ^aSeptuagint reads LORD God.   18:6 ^aOr him

7So the king of Israel said to Jehoshaphat, "*There is* still one man by whom we may inquire of the LORD; but I hate him, because he never prophesies good concerning me, but always evil. He *is* Micaiah the son of Imla."

And Jehoshaphat said, "Let not the king say such things!"

8Then the king of Israel called one *of his* officers and said, "Bring Micaiah the son of Imla quickly!"

9The king of Israel and Jehoshaphat king of Judah, clothed in *their* robes, sat each on his throne; and they sat at a threshing floor at the entrance of the gate of Samaria; and all the prophets prophesied before them. 10Now Zedekiah the son of Chenaanah had made horns of iron for himself; and he said, "Thus says the LORD: 'With these you shall gore the Syrians until they are destroyed.' "

11And all the prophets prophesied so, saying, "Go up to Ramoth Gilead and prosper, for the LORD will deliver *it* into the king's hand."

12Then the messenger who had gone to call Micaiah spoke to him, saying, "Now listen, the words of the prophets with one accord encourage the king. Therefore please let your word be like *the word of* one of them, and speak encouragement."

13And Micaiah said, "*As* the LORD lives, whatever my God says, that I will speak."

14Then he came to the king; and the king said to him, "Micaiah, shall we go to war against Ramoth Gilead, or shall I refrain?"

And he said, "Go and prosper, and they shall be delivered into your hand!"

15So the king said to him, "How many times shall I make you swear that you tell me nothing but the truth in the name of the LORD?"

16Then he said, "I saw all Israel scattered on the mountains, as sheep that have no shepherd. And the LORD said, 'These have no master. Let each return to his house in peace.' "

17And the king of Israel said to Jehoshaphat, "Did I not tell you he would not prophesy good concerning me, but evil?"

18Then *Micaiah* said, "Therefore hear the word of the LORD: I saw the LORD sitting on His throne, and all the host of heaven standing on His right hand and His left. 19And the LORD said, 'Who will persuade Ahab king of Israel to go up, that he may fall at Ramoth Gilead?' So one spoke in this manner, and another spoke in that manner. 20Then a spirit came forward and stood before the LORD, and said, 'I will persuade him.' The LORD said to him, 'In what way?' 21So he said, 'I will go out and be a lying spirit in the mouth of all his prophets.' And *the* LORD said, 'You shall persuade *him* and also prevail; go out and do so.' 22Therefore look! The LORD has put a lying spirit in the mouth of these prophets of yours, and the LORD has declared disaster against you."

23Then Zedekiah the son of Chenaanah went near and struck Micaiah on the cheek, and said, "Which way did the spirit from the LORD go from me to speak to you?"

24And Micaiah said, "Indeed you shall see on that day when you go into an inner chamber to hide!"

25Then the king of Israel said, "Take Micaiah, and return him to Amon the governor of the city and to Joash the king's son; 26and say, 'Thus says the king: "Put this *fellow* in prison, and feed him with bread of affliction and water of affliction, until I return in peace." ' "

27But Micaiah said, "If you ever return in peace, the LORD has not spoken by me." And he said, "Take heed, all you people!"

Ahab Dies in Battle

28So the king of Israel and Jehoshaphat the king of Judah went up to Ramoth Gilead. 29And the king of Israel said to Jehoshaphat, "I will disguise myself and go into battle; but you put on your robes." So the king of Israel disguised himself, and they went into battle.

30Now the king of Syria had commanded the captains of the chariots who

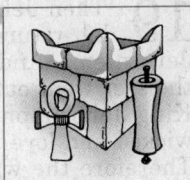

BELIEFS AND IDEAS

Zedekiah's horns of iron (2 Chr. 18:10) were part of a public display of prophets before the royal court of Israel. The symbolic action makes the prophetic word visible and unforgettable. The royal court itself resembles the heavenly court described by Micaiah (2 Chr. 18:18) in one respect: the agents before the throne are not unanimous, but include differing opinions.

HEAVEN PLANS AN ASSASSINATION (2 Chr. 18:18–22)

Ahab, king of Israel (874–853 B.C.), asked Jehoshaphat, king of Judah, to join him in an attack on Syria (2 Chr. 18:3). The two kings then consulted the professional court prophets, inquiring about the will of the deity in the matter. This was normal practice throughout the ancient Near East, especially during military campaigns, and kings kept staffs of professional prophets in their courts just for this purpose.

The 400 professional prophets who answered Ahab spoke with one voice (18:5). Prophets usually determined the will of the deity by means of set observations which were written down in manuals. This kept individual interpretation to a minimum. However, one prophet, Micaiah, spoke independently for Yahweh, claiming to have seen and heard the heavenly court procedure.

Usually the divine council was made up of gods. In Canaanite religion, El, the head of the pantheon, would be in charge of such a council, but the deities in attendance were the ones who debated the course of action. Once a plan was determined, these lesser deities were also the ones to carry out the action in the world. In Micaiah's vision Yahweh is the head of the council (18:18), and the members are called spirits. The spirit who devised the plan to lead the king of Israel into a battle where he would die was also the one assigned to carry out the plan (18:21).

Neo-Assyrian texts show that court prophets continued to be consulted by the Assyrian kings Esarhaddon (680–669 B.C.) and Ashurbanipal (668–627 B.C.). The prophets, who are called "proclaimers," reported oracles to the king from such Assyrian deities as Asshur, Ishtar, and Ninlil. The oracles themselves were preserved in the official royal annals.

---

were with him, saying, "Fight with no one small or great, but only with the king of Israel."

31So it was, when the captains of the chariots saw Jehoshaphat, that they said, "It *is* the king of Israel!" Therefore they surrounded him to attack; but Jehoshaphat cried out, and the LORD helped him, and God diverted them from him. 32For so it was, when the captains of the chariots saw that it was not the king of Israel, that they turned back from pursuing him. 33Now a certain man drew a bow at random, and struck the king of Israel between the joints of his armor. So he said to the driver of his chariot, "Turn around and take me out of the battle, for I am wounded." 34The battle increased that day, and the king of Israel propped *himself* up in *his* chariot facing the Syrians until evening; and about the time of sunset he died.

19 1Then Jehoshaphat the king of Judah returned safely to his house in Jerusalem. 2And Jehu the son of Hanani the seer went out to meet him, and said to King Jehoshaphat, "Should you help the wicked and love those who hate the LORD? Therefore the wrath of the LORD *is* upon you. 3Nevertheless good things are found in

you, in that you have removed the wooden images from the land, and have prepared your heart to seek God."

The Reforms of Jehoshaphat

4So Jehoshaphat dwelt at Jerusalem; and he went out again among the people from Beersheba to the mountains of Ephraim, and brought them back to the LORD God of their fathers. 5Then he set judges in the land throughout all the fortified cities of Judah, city by city, 6and said to the judges, "Take heed to what you are doing, for you do not judge for man but for the LORD, who *is* with you in the judgment. 7Now therefore, let the fear of the LORD be upon you; take care and do *it,* for *there is* no iniquity with the LORD our God, no partiality, nor taking of bribes."

8Moreover in Jerusalem, for the judgment of the LORD and for controversies, Jehoshaphat appointed some of the Levites and priests, and some of the chief fathers of Israel, when they returned to Jerusalem.a 9And he commanded them, saying, "Thus you shall act in the fear of the LORD, faithfully and with a loyal heart: 10What-

---

19:8 aSeptuagint and Vulgate read *for the inhabitants of Jerusalem.*

ever case comes to you from your brethren who dwell in their cities, whether of bloodshed or offenses against law or commandment, against statutes or ordinances, you shall warn them, lest they trespass against the LORD and wrath come upon you and your brethren. Do this, and you will not be guilty. ¹¹And take notice: Amariah the chief priest *is* over you in all matters of the LORD; and Zebadiah the son of Ishmael, the ruler of the house of Judah, for all the king's matters; also the Levites *will be* officials before you. Behave courageously, and the LORD will be with the good."

Holy War Against the Transjordan Coalition

Elijah, in many ways the hero of the Book of 1 Kings, appears only once in Chronicles (2 Chr. 21:12). This is partly because Elijah prophesied in the northern kingdom, whereas the Chronicler writes mostly about Judah. Another reason, though, is that the Chronicler simply is not as interested in prophets—even Elijah—as he is in priests and the temple. For instance, Jehoshaphat's battle against a coalition of Transjordanian forces, including Moab, Ammon, and Edom, is not recorded in Kings. The account in Chronicles relates a royal speech in the temple court (2 Chr. 20:5, 14–17), and describes the battle as fought not by warriors but by, of all people, the temple musicians (20:21–23, 27–29).

■ 2 Chronicles 20:1–37

2 Chronicles
Ammon, Moab, and Mount Seir Defeated

20 :1 It happened after this *that* the people of Moab with the people of Ammon, and *others* with them besides the Ammonites,ᵃ came to battle against Jehoshaphat. ²Then some came and told Jehoshaphat, saying, "A great multitude is coming against you from beyond the sea, from Syria;ᵃ and they are in Hazazon Tamar" (which *is* En Gedi). ³And Jehoshaphat feared, and set himself to seek the LORD, and proclaimed a fast through-

out all Judah. ⁴So Judah gathered together to ask *help* from the LORD; and from all the cities of Judah they came to seek the LORD.

⁵Then Jehoshaphat stood in the assembly of Judah and Jerusalem, in the house of the LORD, before the new court, ⁶and said: "O LORD God of our fathers, *are* You not God in heaven, and do You *not* rule over all the kingdoms of the nations, and in Your hand *is there not* power and might, so that no one is able to withstand You? ⁷*Are* You not our God, *who* drove out the inhabitants of this land before Your people Israel, and gave it to the descendants of Abraham Your friend forever? ⁸And they dwell in it, and have built You a sanctuary in it for Your name, saying, ⁹'If disaster comes upon us—sword, judgment, pestilence, or famine—we will stand before this temple and in Your presence (for Your name *is* in this temple), and cry out to You in our affliction, and You will hear and save.' ¹⁰And now, here are the people of Ammon, Moab, and Mount Seir—whom You would not let Israel invade when they came out of the land of Egypt, but they turned from them and did not destroy them— ¹¹here they are, rewarding us by coming to throw us out of Your possession which You have given us to inherit. ¹²O our God, will You not judge them? For we have no power against this great multitude that is coming against us; nor do we know what to do, but our eyes *are* upon You."

¹³Now all Judah, with their little ones, their wives, and their children, stood before the LORD.

¹⁴Then the Spirit of the LORD came upon Jahaziel the son of Zechariah, the son of Benaiah, the son of Jeiel, the son of Mattaniah, a Levite of the sons of Asaph, in the midst of the assembly. ¹⁵And he said, "Listen, all you of Judah and you inhabitants of Jerusalem, and you, King Jehoshaphat! Thus says the LORD to you: 'Do not be afraid nor dismayed because of this great multitude, for the battle *is* not yours, but God's. ¹⁶Tomorrow go down against them. They will surely come up by the Ascent of Ziz, and you will find them at the end of the brook before the Wilderness of Jeruel. ¹⁷You will not *need* to fight in this *battle.* Position yourselves, stand still and see the salvation of the LORD, who is with you, O Judah and Jerusalem!' Do not fear or be dismayed; tomorrow go out against them, for the LORD *is* with you."

¹⁸And Jehoshaphat bowed his head

20:1 ᵃFollowing Masoretic Text and Vulgate; Septuagint reads *Meunites* (compare 26:7).
20:2 ᵃFollowing Masoretic Text, Septuagint, and Vulgate; some Hebrew manuscripts and Old Latin read *Edom.*

SEIR IS EDOM   (2 Chr. 20:23)

Seir was a geographic region within the territory of the Edomites (Gen. 36:21). The central and southern highlands of Transjordan were, in biblical times, divided among three peoples, the Ammonites, Moabites, and Edomites, with the Edomites living in the southern-most region.

The association between Edom and Seir was so close that, at times, the name of Seir was used as an alternative name for Edom (Num. 24:18). Sometimes Seir is referred to as Mount Seir, suggesting that its territory was mountainous.

Exactly where this region is located is unknown. The name "Seir" means "hairy," which provides no geographical clues. On the other hand, "Edom" means "red," which has caused some scholars to speculate that Edom itself was in the area of the reddish sandstone mountains around Petra, with Seir being one of those mountains. This location is unlikely, however, since Seir seems to be connected with a major passageway up to the Transjordanian plateau (Josh. 12:7).

The Chronicler apparently uses "Mount Seir" to represent Edom (2 Chr. 20:23). The Ammonites and Moabites joined forces to destroy the Edomites, before turning on each other.

with *his* face to the ground, and all Judah and the inhabitants of Jerusalem bowed before the LORD, worshiping the LORD. ¹⁹Then the Levites of the children of the Kohathites and of the children of the Korahites stood up to praise the LORD God of Israel with voices loud and high.

²⁰So they rose early in the morning and went out into the Wilderness of Tekoa; and as they went out, Jehoshaphat stood and said, "Hear me, O Judah and you inhabitants of Jerusalem: Believe in the LORD your God, and you shall be established; believe His prophets, and you shall prosper." ²¹And when he had consulted with the people, he appointed those who should sing to the LORD, and who should praise the beauty of holiness, as they went out before the army and were saying:

"Praise the LORD,
For His mercy *endures* forever."ᵃ

²²Now when they began to sing and to praise, the LORD set ambushes against the people of Ammon, Moab, and Mount Seir, who had come against Judah; and they were defeated. ²³For the people of Ammon and Moab stood up against the inhabitants of Mount Seir to utterly kill and destroy *them*. And when they had made an end of the inhabitants of Seir, they helped to destroy one another.

²⁴So when Judah came to a place overlooking the wilderness, they looked toward the multitude; and there *were* their dead bodies, fallen on the earth. No one had escaped.

²⁵When Jehoshaphat and his people came to take away their spoil, they found among them an abundance of valuables on the dead bodies,ᵃ and precious jewelry, which they stripped off for themselves, more than they could carry away; and they were three days gathering the spoil because there was so much. ²⁶And on the fourth day they assembled in the Valley of Berachah, for there they blessed the LORD; therefore the name of that place was called The Valley of Berachahᵃ until this day. ²⁷Then they returned, every man of Judah and Jerusalem, with Jehoshaphat in front of them, to go back to Jerusalem with joy, for the LORD had made them rejoice over their enemies. ²⁸So they came to Jerusalem, with stringed instruments and harps and trumpets, to the house of the LORD. ²⁹And the fear of God was on all the kingdoms of *those* countries when they heard that the LORD had fought against the enemies of Israel. ³⁰Then the realm of Jehoshaphat was quiet, for his God gave him rest all around.

20:21 ᵃCompare Psalm 106:1   20:25 ᵃA few Hebrew manuscripts, Old Latin, and Vulgate read *garments;* Septuagint reads *armor.*
20:26 ᵃLiterally *Blessing*

The End of Jehoshaphat's Reign

³¹So Jehoshaphat was king over Judah. *He was* thirty-five years old when he became king, and he reigned twenty-five years in Jerusalem. His mother's name *was* Azubah the daughter of Shilhi. ³²And he walked in the way of his father Asa, and did not turn aside from it, doing *what was* right in the sight of the LORD. ³³Nevertheless the high places were not taken away, for as yet the people had not directed their hearts to the God of their fathers.

³⁴Now the rest of the acts of Jehoshaphat, first and last, indeed they *are* written in the book of Jehu the son of Hanani, which *is* mentioned in the book of the kings of Israel.

³⁵After this Jehoshaphat king of Judah allied himself with Ahaziah king of Israel, who acted very wickedly. ³⁶And he allied himself with him to make ships to go to Tarshish, and they made the ships in Ezion Geber. ³⁷But Eliezer the son of Dodavah of Mareshah prophesied against Jehoshaphat, saying, "Because you have allied yourself with Ahaziah, the LORD has destroyed your works." Then the ships were wrecked, so that they were not able to go to Tarshish.

1:3 ᵃOr *Angel*

🧩 *Prophetic Account: Fall of Omri's Dynasty*

The Omride dynasty lasted almost 50 years through the reigns of four Israelite kings. Omri and his son Ahab were followed on the throne by Ahaziah (853–852 B.C.) and Jehoram (or Joram; 852–841 B.C.). Both Ahaziah and Jehoram were sons of Ahab; since Ahaziah was childless, he was succeeded as king by his brother (2 Kin. 1:17).

The historian of Kings introduces Ahaziah's reign in 1 Kin. 22:51–53 with criticism of the king's religious policies. Ahaziah was guilty of perpetuating both the Canaanite fertility religion of his parents, Ahab and Jezebel, and the idolatrous calf worship of Jeroboam. The story of Ahaziah's involvement with Canaanite religion continues in the Book of 2 Kings, recounting the king's encounter with the prophet Elijah (2 Kin. 1).

■ 1 Kings 22:51–53
■ 2 Kings 1:1–18

1 Kings 22:51–53
Ahaziah Reigns in Israel

22 :51 Ahaziah the son of Ahab became king over Israel in Samaria in the seventeenth year of Jehoshaphat king of Judah, and reigned two years over Israel. ⁵²He did evil in the sight of the LORD, and walked in the way of his father and in the way of his mother and in the way of Jeroboam the son of Nebat, who had made Israel sin; ⁵³for he served Baal and worshiped him, and provoked the LORD God of Israel to anger, according to all that his father had done.

2 Kings 1:1–18
God Judges Ahaziah

1 :1 Moab rebelled against Israel after the death of Ahab.

²Now Ahaziah fell through the lattice of his upper room in Samaria, and was injured; so he sent messengers and said to them, "Go, inquire of Baal-Zebub, the god of Ekron, whether I shall recover from this injury." ³But the angelᵃ of the LORD said to Elijah the Tishbite, "Arise, go up to meet the messengers of the king of Samaria, and say to them, 'Is it because *there is* no God in Israel *that* you are going to inquire of Baal-Zebub, the god of Ekron?' ⁴Now therefore, thus says the LORD: 'You shall not come down from the bed to which you have gone up, but you shall surely die.' " So Elijah departed.

⁵And when the messengers returned to him, he said to them, "Why have you come back?"

⁶So they said to him, "A man came up to meet us, and said to us, 'Go, return to the king who sent you, and say to him, "Thus says the LORD: 'Is it because *there is* no God in Israel *that* you are sending to inquire of Baal-Zebub, the god of Ekron? Therefore you shall not come down from the bed to which you have gone up, but you shall surely die.' " ' "

⁷Then he said to them, "What kind of man *was it* who came up to meet you and told you these words?"

⁸So they answered him, "A hairy man wearing a leather belt around his waist."

And he said, "It *is* Elijah the Tishbite."

⁹Then the king sent to him a captain of fifty with his fifty men. So he went up to him; and there he was, sitting on the top of a hill. And he spoke to him: "Man of God, the king has said, 'Come down!' "

THE LORD OF THE FLIES (2 Kin. 1:2–16)

Baal-Zebub, a Philistine deity at Ekron, is unknown outside of 2 Kin. 1:2–16. The deity is often confused with Beelzebub (or Beelzebul) mentioned in the New Testament (Matt. 12:24). The name "Baal-Zebub" means "lord of the flies," and a deity by this name likely was worshiped in the Philistine city of Ekron.

Ahaziah, due to an accidental injury (2 Kin. 1:2), did not rule long as king of Israel (853–852 B.C.). Having been wounded, he sent messengers to the deity Baal-Zebub, seeking information about his chances of recovery. One method by which professional prophets determined the will of the gods was to watch the ways in which flies swarmed. So probably Baal-Zebub was a god from whom knowledge of future events was sought by means of the flight of insects. Ahaziah sought divine knowledge from Ekron, just as people from all over the ancient world visited the Greek shrine at Delphi to inquire of the oracle there.

Elijah, the prophet of Yahweh, stopped the messengers (and a few armies) from consulting Baal-Zebub and then confronted Ahaziah with his lack of faithfulness. This was a demonstration that Yahweh is all Israel needs; there is no need for foreign gods (1:6). That the king did not trust the God of Israel enough to inquire of Him was enough to cause the king to die. The ancients believed that rulers were given their kingdoms by their patron gods. When a king abandoned his patron god, he risked being abandoned by the god.

---

¹⁰So Elijah answered and said to the captain of fifty, "If I *am* a man of God, then let fire come down from heaven and consume you and your fifty men." And fire came down from heaven and consumed him and his fifty. ¹¹Then he sent to him another captain of fifty with his fifty men.

And he answered and said to him: "Man of God, thus has the king said, 'Come down quickly!' "

¹²So Elijah answered and said to them, "If I *am* a man of God, let fire come down from heaven and consume you and your fifty men." And the fire of God came down from heaven and consumed him and his fifty.

¹³Again, he sent a third captain of fifty with his fifty men. And the third captain of fifty went up, and came and fell on his knees before Elijah, and pleaded with him, and said to him: "Man of God, please let my life and the life of these fifty servants of yours be precious in your sight. ¹⁴Look, fire has come down from heaven and burned up the first two captains of fifties with their fifties. But let my life now be precious in your sight."

¹⁵And the angelª of the LORD said to Elijah, "Go down with him; do not be afraid of him." So he arose and went down with him to the king. ¹⁶Then he said to him, "Thus says the LORD: 'Because you have sent messengers to inquire of Baal-Zebub, the god of Ekron, *is it* because *there is* no God in Israel to inquire of His word? Therefore you shall not come down from the bed to which you have gone up, but you shall surely die.' "

¹⁷So *Ahaziah* died according to the word of the LORD which Elijah had spoken. Because he had no son, Jehoramª became king in his place, in the second year of Jehoram the son of Jehoshaphat, king of Judah.

¹⁸Now the rest of the acts of Ahaziah which he did, *are* they not written in the

1:15 ªOr *Angel*   1:17 ªThe son of Ahab king of Israel (compare 3:1)

CULTURE AND SOCIETY

Clothing is used universally to indicate the status and function of persons in society. The prophet's calling is shown by unsophisticated garments, including a leather belt (2 Kin. 1:8; Mark 1:6). Among other things, this clothing proves that the prophet is not on the king's payroll, but owes allegiance only to God (Luke 7:25).

book of the chronicles of the kings of Israel?

Elisha in Israel

Elijah's role in 1 Kings is assumed in 2 Kings by his disciple and successor Elisha. The two prophets are presented quite differently, however. Elijah is always a messenger, pronouncing God's words, whereas Elisha speaks briefly or not at all. Instead, Elisha performs miracles, and his ministry is marked more with actions than words.

The Elisha narratives are often indifferent to political powers. For instance, the story in 2 Kin. 6:8–23 speaks of the kings of Israel and Syria but never bothers to identify which ones. Elisha himself was very involved in politics, however. Indeed, he personally inaugurated two new royal dynasties: that of Hazael, king of Syria (2 Kin. 8:7–15), and that of Jehu, king of Israel (2 Kin. 9:1–13).

The last king of the Omride dynasty, Jehoram, also called Joram (852–841 B.C.), came to the throne during the period of Elisha's ministry (2 Kin. 1:17; 3:1). Jehoram removed a cultic pillar of Baal that was set up by his father, Ahab (3:2). However, he did not rid Israel of Baal worship; the temple of Baal continued to stand through Jehoram's reign until destroyed by Jehu (2 Kin. 10:25–28).

■ 2 Kings 2:1—8:15

2 Kings
Elijah Ascends to Heaven

2 :1 And it came to pass, when the LORD was about to take up Elijah into heaven by a whirlwind, that Elijah went with Elisha from Gilgal. ²Then Elijah said to Elisha, "Stay here, please, for the LORD has sent me on to Bethel."

But Elisha said, "*As* the LORD lives, and *as* your soul lives, I will not leave you!" So they went down to Bethel.

³Now the sons of the prophets who *were* at Bethel came out to Elisha, and said to him, "Do you know that the LORD will take away your master from over you today?"

And he said, "Yes, I know; keep silent!"

⁴Then Elijah said to him, "Elisha, stay here, please, for the LORD has sent me on to Jericho."

But he said, "*As* the LORD lives, and *as* your soul lives, I will not leave you!" So they came to Jericho.

⁵Now the sons of the prophets who *were* at Jericho came to Elisha and said to him, "Do you know that the LORD will take away your master from over you today?"

So he answered, "Yes, I know; keep silent!"

⁶Then Elijah said to him, "Stay here, please, for the LORD has sent me on to the Jordan."

But he said, "*As* the LORD lives, and *as* your soul lives, I will not leave you!" So the two of them went on. ⁷And fifty men of the sons of the prophets went and stood facing *them* at a distance, while the two of them stood by the Jordan. ⁸Now Elijah took his mantle, rolled *it* up, and struck the water; and it was divided this way and that, so that the two of them crossed over on dry ground.

⁹And so it was, when they had crossed over, that Elijah said to Elisha, "Ask! What may I do for you, before I am taken away from you?"

Elisha said, "Please let a double portion of your spirit be upon me."

¹⁰So he said, "You have asked a hard thing. *Nevertheless,* if you see me *when I am* taken from you, it shall be so for you; but if not, it shall not be *so.*" ¹¹Then it happened, as they continued on and talked, that suddenly a chariot of fire *appeared* with horses of fire, and separated the two of them; and Elijah went up by a whirlwind into heaven.

¹²And Elisha saw *it,* and he cried out, "My father, my father, the chariot of Israel and its horsemen!" So he saw him no more. And he took hold of his own clothes and tore them into two pieces. ¹³He also took up

TIME CAPSULE   *853 to 848 B.C.*

853	Ahaziah becomes king in Israel
853	Jehoram (or Joram) serves as coregent with Jehoshaphat in Judah
852	Joram (or Jehoram) becomes king in Israel
850–750	Gradual breakup of the Libyan Dynasty in Egypt
850	The royal inscription called the Moabite Stone
848	Jehoram (or Joram) becomes sole king in Judah

LIFE FROM A SPRING (2 Kin. 2:19–22)

The men of Jericho approached the prophet Elisha concerning their city's spring, remarking "the water is bad" (2 Kin. 2:19). The spring referred to in this story is today commonly known as "Elisha's spring." It lies across the modern road from the ancient ruin of Jericho, called by archaeologists Tell es-Sultan. The more formal name of the spring is thus En es-Sultan (*En* being the Arabic word for spring).

This spring is vitally important to the region, partly because Jericho has the lowest elevation of any city on earth (about 840 feet below sea level). Such a low elevation, combined with the naturally arid climate of Israel, makes the area very hot in summer and pleasantly warm in winter. Its geographical location on the east side of the Judean hills and wilderness means that what moisture is blown in from the Mediterranean Sea is emptied well before it reaches the Jordan valley.

Settlers in the Jericho area were attracted by this spring, which still gushes forth at about 1,000 gallons of water per minute. It waters the Jericho region by an ingenious and complex system of gravity-flow irrigation channels. En es-Sultan thus provides a year-round source of water that has been used for agriculture for thousands of years. Archaeological evidence suggests that Jericho is the oldest city in the world, thanks to En es-Sultan.

If the waters of En es-Sultan were to go bad or stop, all ancient settlement in this area would have ceased, since the spring was the major source of water. One can then understand the desperation of the city elders who pled with Elisha for help. With the waters of En es-Sultan turning bad, the very existence of Jericho was at stake. Elisha "healed" the waters (2 Kin. 2:21), and the city was saved.

the mantle of Elijah that had fallen from him, and went back and stood by the bank of the Jordan. ¹⁴Then he took the mantle of Elijah that had fallen from him, and struck the water, and said, "Where *is* the LORD God of Elijah?" And when he also had struck the water, it was divided this way and that; and Elisha crossed over.

¹⁵Now when the sons of the prophets who *were* from Jericho saw him, they said, "The spirit of Elijah rests on Elisha." And they came to meet him, and bowed to the ground before him. ¹⁶Then they said to him, "Look now, there are fifty strong men with your servants. Please let them go and search for your master, lest perhaps the Spirit of the LORD has taken him up and cast him upon some mountain or into some valley."

And he said, "You shall not send anyone."

¹⁷But when they urged him till he was ashamed, he said, "Send *them!*" Therefore they sent fifty men, and they searched for three days but did not find him. ¹⁸And when they came back to him, for he had stayed in Jericho, he said to them, "Did I not say to you, 'Do not go'?"

Elisha Performs Miracles

¹⁹Then the men of the city said to Elisha, "Please notice, the situation of this city *is* pleasant, as my lord sees; but the water *is* bad, and the ground barren."

²⁰And he said, "Bring me a new bowl, and put salt in it." So they brought *it* to him. ²¹Then he went out to the source of the water, and cast in the salt there, and said, "Thus says the LORD: 'I have healed this water; from it there shall be no more death or barrenness.' " ²²So the water re-

CULTURE AND SOCIETY

Society's convictions about what sort of behavior is appropriate for persons of different ages varies for good and bad reasons. Frequently, the age at which young men became warriors in ancient societies was younger than in modern Western armies. The "youths" of 2 Kin. 2:23, like the "young man" of Gen. 4:23, could have been armed and dangerous.

mains healed to this day, according to the word of Elisha which he spoke.

23Then he went up from there to Bethel; and as he was going up the road, some youths came from the city and mocked him, and said to him, "Go up, you baldhead! Go up, you baldhead!"

24So he turned around and looked at them, and pronounced a curse on them in the name of the LORD. And two female bears came out of the woods and mauled forty-two of the youths.

25Then he went from there to Mount Carmel, and from there he returned to Samaria.

Moab Rebels Against Israel

3 1Now Jehoram the son of Ahab became king over Israel at Samaria in the eighteenth year of Jehoshaphat king of Judah, and reigned twelve years. 2And he did evil in the sight of the LORD, but not like his father and mother; for he put away the *sacred* pillar of Baal that his father had made. 3Nevertheless he persisted in the sins of Jeroboam the son of Nebat, who had made Israel sin; he did not depart from them.

4Now Mesha king of Moab was a sheepbreeder, and he regularly paid the king of Israel one hundred thousand lambs and the wool of one hundred thousand rams. 5But it happened, when Ahab died, that the king of Moab rebelled against the king of Israel.

6So King Jehoram went out of Samaria at that time and mustered all Israel. 7Then he went and sent to Jehoshaphat king of Judah, saying, "The king of Moab has rebelled against me. Will you go with me to fight against Moab?"

And he said, "I will go up; I *am* as you *are,* my people as your people, my horses as your horses." 8Then he said, "Which way shall we go up?"

And he answered, "By way of the Wilderness of Edom."

9So the king of Israel went with the king of Judah and the king of Edom, and they marched on that roundabout route seven days; and there was no water for the army, nor for the animals that followed them. 10And the king of Israel said, "Alas! For the LORD has called these three kings together to deliver them into the hand of Moab."

11But Jehoshaphat said, "*Is there* no prophet of the LORD here, that we may inquire of the LORD by him?"

So one of the servants of the king of Israel answered and said, "Elisha the son of Shaphat *is* here, who poured water on the hands of Elijah."

12And Jehoshaphat said, "The word of the LORD is with him." So the king of Israel and Jehoshaphat and the king of Edom went down to him.

13Then Elisha said to the king of Israel, "What have I to do with you? Go to the prophets of your father and the prophets of your mother."

But the king of Israel said to him, "No, for the LORD has called these three kings *together* to deliver them into the hand of Moab."

14And Elisha said, "*As* the LORD of hosts lives, before whom I stand, surely were it not that I regard the presence of Jehoshaphat king of Judah, I would not look at you, nor see you. 15But now bring me a musician."

Then it happened, when the musician played, that the hand of the LORD came upon him. 16And he said, "Thus says the LORD: 'Make this valley full of ditches.' 17For thus says the LORD: 'You shall not see wind, nor shall you see rain; yet that valley shall be filled with water, so that you, your cattle, and your animals may drink.' 18And this is a simple matter in the sight of the LORD; He will also deliver the Moabites into your hand. 19Also you shall attack every fortified city and every choice city, and shall cut down every good tree, and stop up every spring of water, and ruin every good piece of land with stones."

20Now it happened in the morning, when the grain offering was offered, that suddenly water came by way of Edom, and the land was filled with water.

21And when all the Moabites heard that the kings had come up to fight against them, all who were able to bear arms and older were gathered; and they stood at the border. 22Then they rose up early in the morning, and the sun was shining on the water; and the Moabites saw the water on the other side *as* red as blood. 23And they said, "This is blood; the kings have surely struck swords and have killed one another; now therefore, Moab, to the spoil!"

24So when they came to the camp of Israel, Israel rose up and attacked the Moabites, so that they fled before them;

A HUMAN SACRIFICE FOR A HOPELESS WAR (2 Kin. 3:21-27)

When Mesha, king of Moab, waged a war of liberation against Israelite overlordship, he found himself fighting three armies: the Israelites and their allies Judah and Edom. The author of Kings uses a series of statements in 2 Kin. 3:21–27 to convey the increasingly hopeless situation of the Moabite forces.

The military undertaking was over before it began. The Moabites mistook the red reflection of the sunrise in the river to be blood from the three armies. Moab moved upon the Israelite encampment as scavengers rather than as military personnel and were themselves taken by surprise and routed (vv. 21–24).

Israel's army devastated the entire land of Moab, forcing the Moabite survivors to retreat into Kir Haraseth, their only city left standing. In a last military tactic, a Moabite force of 700 hand-to-hand combat soldiers were led out of the walled city to confront the Edomite army. It was a futile effort (vv. 25, 26).

All military strategy having failed, the King of Moab sacrificed his heir-apparent on the city wall in view of the attacking coalition (v. 27). The amazing result of this maneuver was "great indignation against Israel," and the attacking armies departed to their homes, leaving the Moabite army victorious on the field of battle. In the face of overwhelming odds, the King of Moab had won the war.

This passage may not seem so weird when compared to an incantation text from Ugarit, a Mediterranean Sea coastal city destroyed in the 12th century B.C. The text explains what needed to be done if the city was besieged and the battle was hopeless. Baal, the patron deity of Ugarit, is addressed, and a horse and a human son are sacrificed to the deity along with a libation poured out in the deity's honor. Upon hearing the shout of the city's people, Baal would respond by "throwing" the besiegers away from the city gates and saving the day.

Certainly this was a ritual to be used only when it was clear to the defenders that the war was lost. It effectively removed Moab's next generation of political rule, the king's firstborn son. Sacrificing the child to Chemosh, Moab's deity, demonstrated how serious the sacrificers were.

The result was exactly what Mesha's religious tradition told him would happen: the supposedly victorious armies fled. Their flight may have been influenced by the absolute condemnation of human sacrifice in the divine law of Judah and Israel (Ex. 34:20; Deut. 18:10). Child sacrifice was so appalling and detestable that they fled what was to them a place of absolute apostasy.

and they entered *their* land, killing the Moabites. 25Then they destroyed the cities, and each man threw a stone on every good piece of land and filled it; and they stopped up all the springs of water and cut down all the good trees. But they left the stones of Kir Haraseth *intact.* However the slingers surrounded and attacked it.

26And when the king of Moab saw that the battle was too fierce for him, he took with him seven hundred men who drew swords, to break through to the king of Edom, but they could not. 27Then he took his eldest son who would have reigned in his place, and offered him *as* a burnt offering upon the wall; and there was great indignation against Israel. So they departed from him and returned to *their own* land.

Elisha and the Widow's Oil

4 1A certain woman of the wives of the sons of the prophets cried out to Elisha, saying, "Your servant my husband is dead, and you know that your servant feared the LORD. And the creditor is coming to take my two sons to be his slaves."

2So Elisha said to her, "What shall I do for you? Tell me, what do you have in the house?" And she said, "Your maidservant has nothing in the house but a jar of oil."

3Then he said, "Go, borrow vessels from everywhere, from all your neighbors—empty vessels; do not gather just a few. 4And when you have come in, you shall shut the door behind you and your sons; then pour it into all those vessels, and set aside the full ones."

⁵So she went from him and shut the door behind her and her sons, who brought *the vessels* to her; and she poured *it* out. ⁶Now it came to pass, when the vessels were full, that she said to her son, "Bring me another vessel."

And he said to her, "*There is* not another vessel." So the oil ceased. ⁷Then she came and told the man of God. And he said, "Go, sell the oil and pay your debt; and you *and* your sons live on the rest."

Elisha Raises the Shunammite's Son

⁸Now it happened one day that Elisha went to Shunem, where there *was* a notable woman, and she persuaded him to eat some food. So it was, as often as he passed by, he would turn in there to eat some food. ⁹And she said to her husband, "Look now, I know that this *is* a holy man of God, who passes by us regularly. ¹⁰Please, let us make a small upper room on the wall; and let us put a bed for him there, and a table and a chair and a lampstand; so it will be, whenever he comes to us, he can turn in there."

¹¹And it happened one day that he came there, and he turned in to the upper room and lay down there. ¹²Then he said to Gehazi his servant, "Call this Shunammite woman." When he had called her, she stood before him. ¹³And he said to him, "Say now to her, 'Look, you have been concerned for us with all this care. What *can I* do for you? Do you want me to speak on your behalf to the king or to the commander of the army?' "

She answered, "I dwell among my own people."

¹⁴So he said, "What then *is* to be done for her?"

And Gehazi answered, "Actually, she has no son, and her husband is old."

¹⁵So he said, "Call her." When he had called her, she stood in the doorway. ¹⁶Then he said, "About this time next year you shall embrace a son."

And she said, "No, my lord. Man of God, do not lie to your maidservant!"

¹⁷But the woman conceived, and bore a son when the appointed time had come, of which Elisha had told her.

¹⁸And the child grew. Now it happened one day that he went out to his father, to the reapers. ¹⁹And he said to his father, "My head, my head!"

So he said to a servant, "Carry him to his mother." ²⁰When he had taken him and brought him to his mother, he sat on her knees till noon, and *then* died. ²¹And she went up and laid him on the bed of the man of God, shut *the door* upon him, and went out. ²²Then she called to her husband, and said, "Please send me one of the young men and one of the donkeys, that I may run to the man of God and come back."

²³So he said, "Why are you going to him today? *It is* neither the New Moon nor the Sabbath."

And she said, "*It is* well." ²⁴Then she saddled a donkey, and said to her servant, "Drive, and go forward; do not slacken the pace for me unless I tell you." ²⁵And so she departed, and went to the man of God at Mount Carmel.

So it was, when the man of God saw her afar off, that he said to his servant Gehazi, "Look, the Shunammite woman! ²⁶Please run now to meet her, and say to her, '*Is it* well with you? *Is it* well with your husband? *Is it* well with the child?' "

And she answered, "*It is* well." ²⁷Now when she came to the man of God at the hill, she caught him by the feet, but Gehazi came near to push her away. But the man of God said, "Let her alone; for her soul *is* in deep distress, and the LORD has hidden *it* from me, and has not told me."

²⁸So she said, "Did I ask a son of my lord? Did I not say, 'Do not deceive me'?"

²⁹Then he said to Gehazi, "Get yourself ready, and take my staff in your hand, and be on your way. If you meet anyone, do not greet him; and if anyone greets you, do not answer him; but lay my staff on the face of the child."

³⁰And the mother of the child said, "As the LORD lives, and *as* your soul lives, I will not leave you." So he arose and followed

---

TIME CAPSULE *842 to 841 B.C.*

842–800	*Hazael, king of Aram-Damascus*
841	*Ahaziah becomes king in Judah*
841	*Jehu exterminates the Ahab dynasty and becomes king in Israel*
841	*Athaliah murders her grandsons and gains Judah's throne*
841	*The Black Obelisk of Shalmaneser III*
841	*Shalmaneser forces King Jehu of Israel to pay tribute*

her. ³¹Now Gehazi went on ahead of them, and laid the staff on the face of the child; but *there was* neither voice nor hearing. Therefore he went back to meet him, and told him, saying, "The child has not awakened."

³²When Elisha came into the house, there was the child, lying dead on his bed. ³³He went in therefore, shut the door behind the two of them, and prayed to the LORD. ³⁴And he went up and lay on the child, and put his mouth on his mouth, his eyes on his eyes, and his hands on his hands; and he stretched himself out on the child, and the flesh of the child became warm. ³⁵He returned and walked back and forth in the house, and again went up and stretched himself out on him; then the child sneezed seven times, and the child opened his eyes. ³⁶And he called Gehazi and said, "Call this Shunammite woman." So he called her. And when she came in to him, he said, "Pick up your son." ³⁷So she went in, fell at his feet, and bowed to the ground; then she picked up her son and went out.

Elisha Purifies the Pot of Stew

³⁸And Elisha returned to Gilgal, and *there was* a famine in the land. Now the sons of the prophets *were* sitting before him; and he said to his servant, "Put on the large pot, and boil stew for the sons of the prophets." ³⁹So one went out into the field to gather herbs, and found a wild vine, and gathered from it a lapful of wild gourds, and came and sliced *them* into the pot of stew, though they did not know *what they were.* ⁴⁰Then they served it to the men to eat. Now it happened, as they were eating the stew, that they cried out and said, "Man of God, *there is* death in the pot!" And they could not eat *it.*

⁴¹So he said, "Then bring some flour." And he put *it* into the pot, and said, "Serve *it* to the people, that they may eat." And there was nothing harmful in the pot.

Elisha Feeds One Hundred Men

⁴²Then a man came from Baal Shalisha, and brought the man of God bread of the firstfruits, twenty loaves of barley bread, and newly ripened grain in his knapsack. And he said, "Give *it* to the people, that they may eat."

⁴³But his servant said, "What? Shall I set this before one hundred men?"

He said again, "Give it to the people, that they may eat; for thus says the LORD: 'They shall eat and have *some* left over.' " ⁴⁴So he set *it* before them; and they ate and had *some* left over, according to the word of the LORD.

Naaman's Leprosy Healed

5 ¹Now Naaman, commander of the army of the king of Syria, was a great and honorable man in the eyes of his master, because by him the LORD had given victory to Syria. He was also a mighty man of valor, *but* a leper. ²And the Syrians had gone out on raids, and had brought back captive a young girl from the land of Israel. She waited on Naaman's wife. ³Then she said to her mistress, "If only my master *were* with the prophet who *is* in Samaria! For he would heal him of his leprosy." ⁴And *Naaman* went in and told his master, saying, "Thus and thus said the girl who *is* from the land of Israel."

⁵Then the king of Syria said, "Go now, and I will send a letter to the king of Israel."

So he departed and took with him ten talents of silver, six thousand *shekels* of gold, and ten changes of clothing. ⁶Then he brought the letter to the king of Israel, which said,

Now be advised, when this letter
comes to you, that I have sent
Naaman my servant to you, that you
may heal him of his leprosy.

⁷And it happened, when the king of Israel read the letter, that he tore his clothes and said, "*Am* I God, to kill and make alive, that this man sends a man to me to heal him of his leprosy? Therefore please consider, and see how he seeks a quarrel with me."

⁸So it was, when Elisha the man of God heard that the king of Israel had torn his clothes, that he sent to the king, saying, "Why have you torn your clothes? Please let him come to me, and he shall know that there is a prophet in Israel."

⁹Then Naaman went with his horses and chariot, and he stood at the door of Elisha's house. ¹⁰And Elisha sent a messenger to him, saying, "Go and wash in the Jordan seven times, and your flesh shall be restored to you, and *you shall* be clean." ¹¹But Naaman became furious, and went away and said, "Indeed, I said to myself, 'He will surely come out *to me,* and stand

and call on the name of the LORD his God, and wave his hand over the place, and heal the leprosy.' ¹²*Are* not the Abanah[a] and the Pharpar, the rivers of Damascus, better than all the waters of Israel? Could I not wash in them and be clean?" So he turned and went away in a rage. ¹³And his servants came near and spoke to him, and said, "My father, *if* the prophet had told you *to do* something great, would you not have done *it?* How much more then, when he says to you, 'Wash, and be clean'?" ¹⁴So he went down and dipped seven times in the Jordan, according to the saying of the man of God; and his flesh was restored like the flesh of a little child, and he was clean.

¹⁵And he returned to the man of God, he and all his aides, and came and stood before him; and he said, "Indeed, now I know that *there is* no God in all the earth, except in Israel; now therefore, please take a gift from your servant."

¹⁶But he said, "*As* the LORD lives, before whom I stand, I will receive nothing." And he urged him to take *it,* but he refused.

¹⁷So Naaman said, "Then, if not, please let your servant be given two mule-loads of earth; for your servant will no longer offer either burnt offering or sacrifice to other gods, but to the LORD. ¹⁸Yet in this thing may the LORD pardon your servant: when my master goes into the temple of Rimmon to worship there, and he leans on my hand, and I bow down in the temple of Rimmon— when I bow down in the temple of Rimmon, may the LORD please pardon your servant in this thing."

¹⁹Then he said to him, "Go in peace." So he departed from him a short distance.

Gehazi's Greed

²⁰But Gehazi, the servant of Elisha the man of God, said, "Look, my master has spared Naaman this Syrian, while not receiving from his hands what he brought; but *as* the LORD lives, I will run after him and take something from him." ²¹So Gehazi pursued Naaman. When Naaman saw *him* running after him, he got down from the chariot to meet him, and said, "*Is* all well?"

²²And he said, "All *is* well. My master has sent me, saying, 'Indeed, just now two young men of the sons of the prophets have come to me from the mountains of Ephraim. Please give them a talent of silver and two changes of garments.' "

²³So Naaman said, "Please, take two talents." And he urged him, and bound two talents of silver in two bags, with two changes of garments, and handed *them* to two of his servants; and they carried *them* on ahead of him. ²⁴When he came to the citadel, he took *them* from their hand, and stored *them* away in the house; then he let the men go, and they departed. ²⁵Now he went in and stood before his master. Elisha said to him, "Where *did you go,* Gehazi?"

And he said, "Your servant did not go anywhere."

²⁶Then he said to him, "Did not my heart go *with you* when the man turned back from his chariot to meet you? *Is it* time to receive money and to receive clothing, olive groves and vineyards, sheep and oxen, male and female servants? ²⁷Therefore the leprosy of Naaman shall cling to you and your descendants forever." And he went out from his presence leprous, *as white* as snow.

The Floating Ax Head

6 ¹And the sons of the prophets said to Elisha, "See now, the place where we dwell with you is too small for us. ²Please, let us go to the Jordan, and let every man take a beam from there, and let us make there a place where we may dwell."

So he answered, "Go."

³Then one said, "Please consent to go with your servants."

And he answered, "I will go." ⁴So he went with them. And when they came to the Jordan, they cut down trees. ⁵But as one was cutting down a tree, the iron *ax*

5:12 [a]Following Kethib, Septuagint, and Vulgate; Qere, Syriac, and Targum read *Amanah.*

BELIEFS AND IDEAS

Taking money in exchange for religious services, as did Gehazi (2 Kin. 5:20–27), is not forbidden in the Bible, but is regarded as dangerous. The basic principle that money and possessions are potentially corrupting is already expressed in Gen. 14:23 and reaches a climax in the cleansing of the temple (Mark 11:15–17) and the death of Ananias and Sapphira (Acts 5:1–11).

head fell into the water; and he cried out and said, "Alas, master! For it was borrowed."

6So the man of God said, "Where did it fall?" And he showed him the place. So he cut off a stick, and threw *it* in there; and he made the iron float. 7Therefore he said, "Pick *it* up for yourself." So he reached out his hand and took it.

The Blinded Syrians Captured

8Now the king of Syria was making war against Israel; and he consulted with his servants, saying, "My camp *will be* in such and such a place." 9And the man of God sent to the king of Israel, saying, "Beware that you do not pass this place, for the Syrians are coming down there." 10Then the king of Israel sent *someone* to the place of which the man of God had told him. Thus he warned him, and he was watchful there, not just once or twice.

11Therefore the heart of the king of Syria was greatly troubled by this thing; and he called his servants and said to them, "Will you not show me which of us *is* for the king of Israel?"

12And one of his servants said, "None, my lord, O king; but Elisha, the prophet who *is* in Israel, tells the king of Israel the words that you speak in your bedroom."

13So he said, "Go and see where he *is,* that I may send and get him."

And it was told him, saying, "Surely *he is* in Dothan."

14Therefore he sent horses and chariots and a great army there, and they came by night and surrounded the city. 15And when the servant of the man of God arose early and went out, there was an army, surrounding the city with horses and chariots. And his servant said to him, "Alas, my master! What shall we do?"

16So he answered, "Do not fear, for those who *are* with us *are* more than those who *are* with them." 17And Elisha prayed, and said, "LORD, I pray, open his eyes that he may see." Then the LORD opened the eyes of the young man, and he saw. And behold, the mountain *was* full of horses and chariots of fire all around Elisha. 18So when *the Syrians* came down to him, Elisha prayed to the LORD, and said, "Strike this people, I pray, with blindness." And He struck them with blindness according to the word of Elisha.

19Now Elisha said to them, "This *is* not the way, nor *is* this the city. Follow me, and I will bring you to the man whom you seek." But he led them to Samaria.

20So it was, when they had come to Samaria, that Elisha said, "LORD, open the eyes of these *men,* that they may see." And the LORD opened their eyes, and they saw; and there *they were,* inside Samaria!

21Now when the king of Israel saw them, he said to Elisha, "My father, shall I kill *them?* Shall I kill *them?*"

22But he answered, "You shall not kill *them.* Would you kill those whom you have taken captive with your sword and your bow? Set food and water before them, that they may eat and drink and go to their master." 23Then he prepared a great feast for them; and after they ate and drank, he sent them away and they went to their master. So the bands of Syrian *raiders* came no more into the land of Israel.

Syria Besieges Samaria in Famine

24And it happened after this that Ben-Hadad king of Syria gathered all his army, and went up and besieged Samaria. 25And there was a great famine in Samaria; and indeed they besieged it until a donkey's head was *sold* for eighty *shekels* of silver, and one-fourth of a kab of dove droppings for five *shekels* of silver.

26Then, as the king of Israel was passing by on the wall, a woman cried out to him, saying, "Help, my lord, O king!"

27And he said, "If the LORD does not help you, where can I find help for you? From the threshing floor or from the winepress?" 28Then the king said to her, "What is troubling you?"

And she answered, "This woman said to me, 'Give your son, that we may eat him today, and we will eat my son tomorrow.' 29So we boiled my son, and ate him. And I said to her on the next day, 'Give your son, that we may eat him'; but she has hidden her son."

30Now it happened, when the king heard the words of the woman, that he tore his clothes; and as he passed by on the wall, the people looked, and there underneath *he had* sackcloth on his body. 31Then he said, "God do so to me and more also, if the head of Elisha the son of Shaphat remains on him today!"

32But Elisha was sitting in his house, and the elders were sitting with him. And *the king* sent a man ahead of him, but before the messenger came to him, he said to the elders, "Do you see how this son of a murderer has sent someone to take away my head? Look, when the messenger comes, shut the door, and hold him fast at the door. *Is* not the sound of his master's feet behind him?" 33And while he was still talking with them, there was the messenger, coming down to him; and then *the king* said, "Surely this calamity *is* from the LORD; why should I wait for the LORD any longer?"

7 1Then Elisha said, "Hear the word of the LORD. Thus says the LORD: 'Tomorrow about this time a seah of fine flour *shall be sold* for a shekel, and two seahs of barley for a shekel, at the gate of Samaria.'"

2So an officer on whose hand the king leaned answered the man of God and said, "Look, *if* the LORD would make windows in heaven, could this thing be?"

And he said, "In fact, you shall see *it* with your eyes, but you shall not eat of it."

The Syrians Flee

3Now there were four leprous men at the entrance of the gate; and they said to one another, "Why are we sitting here until we die? 4If we say, 'We will enter the city,' the famine *is* in the city, and we shall die there. And if we sit here, we die also. Now therefore, come, let us surrender to the army of the Syrians. If they keep us alive, we shall live; and if they kill us, we shall only die." 5And they rose at twilight to go to the camp of the Syrians; and when they had come to the outskirts of the Syrian camp, to their surprise no one *was* there. 6For the LORD had caused the army of the Syrians to hear the noise of chariots and the noise of horses—the noise of a great army; so they said to one another, "Look, the king of Israel has hired against us the kings of the Hittites and the kings of the Egyptians to attack us!" 7Therefore they arose and fled at twilight, and left the camp intact—their tents, their horses, and their donkeys—and they fled for their lives. 8And when these lepers came to the outskirts of the camp, they went into one tent and ate and drank, and carried from it silver and gold and clothing, and went and hid *them;* then they came back and entered another tent, and carried *some* from there *also,* and went and hid *it.*

9Then they said to one another, "We are not doing right. This day *is* a day of good news, and we remain silent. If we wait until morning light, some punishment will come upon us. Now therefore, come, let us go and tell the king's household." 10So they went and called to the gatekeepers of the city, and told them, saying, "We went to the Syrian camp, and surprisingly no one *was* there, not a human sound—only horses and donkeys tied, and the tents intact." 11And the gatekeepers called out, and they told *it* to the king's household inside.

12So the king arose in the night and said to his servants, "Let me now tell you what the Syrians have done to us. They know that we *are* hungry; therefore they have gone out of the camp to hide themselves in the field, saying, 'When they come out of the city, we shall catch them alive, and get into the city.'"

13And one of his servants answered and said, "Please, let several *men* take five of the remaining horses which are left in the city. Look, they *may either become* like all the multitude of Israel that are left in it; or indeed, *I say,* they *may become* like all the multitude of Israel left from those who are consumed; so let us send them and see." 14Therefore they took two chariots with horses; and the king sent them in the direction of the Syrian army, saying, "Go and see." 15And they went after them to the Jordan; and indeed all the road *was* full of garments and weapons which the Syrians had thrown away in their haste. So the messengers returned and told the king. 16Then the people went out and plundered the tents of the Syrians. So a seah of fine flour was *sold* for a shekel, and two seahs of barley for a shekel, according to the word of the LORD.

17Now the king had appointed the officer on whose hand he leaned to have

---

TIME CAPSULE   *841 to 814 B.C.*

841	Shalmaneser III besieges Damascus and destroys the surrounding countryside
838	Shalmaneser invades Damascus but fails to overthrow Hazael
835	Athaliah is killed, and Joash becomes king in Judah
825	Founding of city of Carthage (or 814)
814	Founding of city of Carthage (or 825)
814	Jehoahaz becomes king in Israel

KING, DOG, AND SON OF A NOBODY (2 Kin. 8:7–15)

Hazael was a king of Aram-Damascus (Syria) and an archenemy of Israel. The devastation that he would inflict upon Israel and Judah was graphically depicted by the prophet Elisha even before Hazael became Aram's king (2 Kin. 8:11–13). Though a king, Hazael really was a "dog" who would commit a "gross thing" (8:13).

Events of Hazael's reign (c. 842–800 B.C.) are known from biblical and Assyrian sources. The Bible records that he usurped the throne of Damascus, killing Ben-Hadad, the previous king (2 Kin. 8:7–15). The annals of the Assyrian king Shalmaneser III support this picture by describing Hazael as "the son of a nobody," an expression referring to a usurper.

The Syro-Palestinian coalition of Hamath, Aram-Damascus, Israel, and others had earlier blocked the advances of Shalmaneser III of Assyria in 853 B.C. This coalition evidently broke down during the reign of Hazael. He alone met an invading Assyrian army in 841 B.C. and was defeated. Damascus was besieged but not taken, although the countryside surrounding it was devastated. The Assyrians returned twice again in 837 and 836 B.C., but Hazael survived these attacks also.

Sometime after 836 B.C. Hazael became free of Assyrian advances, and was able to concentrate his efforts on the south, terrorizing both Israel and Judah. He took the Transjordan—the territory east of the Jordan River—from Israel (2 Kin. 10:32, 33). Apparently Israel under King Jehoahaz (814–798 B.C.) became a vassal of Aram after Hazael had reduced the Israelite army (2 Kin. 13:7). Likewise, Judah under King Joash (835–796 B.C.) also paid tribute to Hazael (2 Kin. 12:17, 18). Both Jehoahaz and Joash were probably relieved when Hazael died near the ends of their reigns (2 Kin. 13:24).

---

charge of the gate. But the people trampled him in the gate, and he died, just as the man of God had said, who spoke when the king came down to him. ¹⁸So it happened just as the man of God had spoken to the king, saying, "Two seahs of barley for a shekel, and a seah of fine flour for a shekel, shall be *sold* tomorrow about this time in the gate of Samaria."

¹⁹Then that officer had answered the man of God, and said, "Now look, *if* the LORD would make windows in heaven, could such a thing be?"

And he had said, "In fact, you shall see *it* with your eyes, but you shall not eat of it." ²⁰And so it happened to him, for the people trampled him in the gate, and he died.

The King Restores the Shunammite's Land

8 ¹Then Elisha spoke to the woman whose son he had restored to life, saying, "Arise and go, you and your household, and stay wherever you can; for the LORD has called for a famine, and furthermore, it will come upon the land for seven years." ²So the woman arose and did according to the saying of the man of God, and she went with her household and dwelt in the land of the Philistines seven years.

³It came to pass, at the end of seven years, that the woman returned from the land of the Philistines; and she went to make an appeal to the king for her house and for her land. ⁴Then the king talked with Gehazi, the servant of the man of God, saying, "Tell me, please, all the great things Elisha has done." ⁵Now it happened, as he was telling the king how he had restored the dead to life, that there was the woman whose son he had restored to life, appealing to the king for her house and for her land. And Gehazi said, "My lord, O king, this *is* the woman, and this *is* her son whom Elisha restored to life." ⁶And when the king asked the woman, she told him.

So the king appointed a certain officer for her, saying, "Restore all that *was* hers, and all the proceeds of the field from the day that she left the land until now."

Death of Ben-Hadad

⁷Then Elisha went to Damascus, and Ben-Hadad king of Syria was sick; and it was told him, saying, "The man of God has come here." ⁸And the king said to Hazael, "Take a present in your hand, and go to

meet the man of God, and inquire of the LORD by him, saying, 'Shall I recover from this disease?' " 9So Hazael went to meet him and took a present with him, of every good thing of Damascus, forty camel-loads; and he came and stood before him, and said, "Your son Ben-Hadad king of Syria has sent me to you, saying, 'Shall I recover from this disease?' "

10And Elisha said to him, "Go, say to him, 'You shall certainly recover.' However the LORD has shown me that he will really die." 11Then he set his countenance in a stare until he was ashamed; and the man of God wept. 12And Hazael said, "Why is my lord weeping?"

He answered, "Because I know the evil that you will do to the children of Israel: Their strongholds you will set on fire, and their young men you will kill with the sword; and you will dash their children, and rip open their women with child."

13So Hazael said, "But what is your servant—a dog, that he should do this gross thing?"

And Elisha answered, "The LORD has shown me that you will become king over Syria."

14Then he departed from Elisha, and came to his master, who said to him, "What did Elisha say to you?" And he answered, "He told me you would surely recover." 15But it happened on the next day that he took a thick cloth and dipped it in water, and spread it over his face so that he died; and Hazael reigned in his place.

8:21 ªSpelled *Jehoram* in verse 16

🧩 The Royal Marriage

The alliance between King Jehoshaphat of Judah and King Ahab of Israel was secured by a diplomatic marriage: Jehoshaphat's son, Prince Jehoram, married Ahab's daughter, Princess Athaliah (2 Kin. 8:18). The marriage was a seal of the political alliance between their families that fostered peace and cooperation between the nations Judah and Israel.

The two families even gave their sons some of the same names. While Ahab's sons Ahaziah and Jehoram were ruling in Israel (853–841 B.C.), Jehoshaphat's son Jehoram (848–841 B.C.) and grandson Ahaziah (841 B.C.) were ruling in Judah.

▪ 2 Kings 8:16–29

2 Kings
Jehoram Reigns in Judah

8 :16 Now in the fifth year of Joram the son of Ahab, king of Israel, Jehoshaphat *having been* king of Judah, Jehoram the son of Jehoshaphat began to reign as king of Judah. 17He was thirty-two years old when he became king, and he reigned eight years in Jerusalem. 18And he walked in the way of the kings of Israel, just as the house of Ahab had done, for the daughter of Ahab was his wife; and he did evil in the sight of the LORD. 19Yet the LORD would not destroy Judah, for the sake of His servant David, as He promised him to give a lamp to him *and* his sons forever.

20In his days Edom revolted against Judah's authority, and made a king over themselves. 21So Joramª went to Zair, and all his chariots with him. Then he rose by night and attacked the Edomites who had surrounded him and the captains of the chariots; and the troops fled to their tents. 22Thus Edom has been in revolt against Judah's authority to this day. And Libnah revolted at that time.

23Now the rest of the acts of Joram, and all that he did, *are* they not written in the book of the chronicles of the kings of Judah? 24So Joram rested with his fathers, and was buried with his fathers in the City of David. Then Ahaziah his son reigned in his place.

Ahaziah Reigns in Judah

25In the twelfth year of Joram the son of Ahab, king of Israel, Ahaziah the son of Jehoram, king of Judah, began to reign. 26Ahaziah *was* twenty-two years old when he became king, and he reigned one year in Jerusalem. His mother's name *was* Athaliah the granddaughter of Omri, king of Israel. 27And he walked in the way of the house of Ahab, and did evil in the sight of the LORD, like the house of Ahab, for he *was* the son-in-law of the house of Ahab.

28Now he went with Joram the son of Ahab to war against Hazael king of Syria at Ramoth Gilead; and the Syrians wounded Joram. 29Then King Joram went back to Jezreel to recover from the wounds which the Syrians had inflicted on him at Ramah, when he fought against Hazael king of Syria. And Ahaziah the son of Jehoram, king of Judah, went down to see Joram the son of Ahab in Jezreel, because he was sick.

Jehu Destroys Ahab's Family

Jehu (841–814 B.C.) came to power with Elisha's charge to end the dynasty of Omri and its Baal worship (2 Kin. 9:1–10). He completed the destruction of official Baalism (10:28), but his methods were so bloody that a century later the prophet Hosea would still be denouncing them (Hos. 1:4).

Jehu's persecution of Ahab's family broke up Israel's military alliances. Phoenicia to the north was the homeland of Ahab's wife Jezebel. Judah to the south was greatly influenced by Ahab's daughter Athaliah, who was queen mother in Jerusalem. Jehu's Israel was now estranged from both Phoenicia and Judah.

Without these alliances, Israel was vulnerable to more powerful nations, such as Aram-Damascus (Syria) and Assyria. Aram under King Hazael succeeded in capturing much Israelite territory (10:32, 33). Farther to the north, the long dormant Assyrian Empire was beginning to awake. The resurgent Assyria compelled Jehu to pay tribute, an event recorded on the Black Obelisk of the Assyrian king Shalmaneser III.

■ 2 Kings 9:1—10:36

2 Kings
Jehu Anointed King of Israel

9 :1 And Elisha the prophet called one of the sons of the prophets, and said to him, "Get yourself ready, take this flask of oil in your hand, and go to Ramoth Gilead. ²Now when you arrive at that place, look there for Jehu the son of Jehoshaphat, the son of Nimshi, and go in and make him rise up from among his associates, and take him to an inner room. ³Then take the flask of oil, and pour *it* on his head, and say, 'Thus says the LORD: "I have anointed you king over Israel." ' Then open the door and flee, and do not delay."

⁴So the young man, the servant of the prophet, went to Ramoth Gilead. ⁵And when he arrived, there *were* the captains of the army sitting; and he said, "I have a message for you, Commander."

Jehu said, "For which *one* of us?"

And he said, "For you, Commander." ⁶Then he arose and went into the house. And he poured the oil on his head, and said to him, "Thus says the LORD God of Israel: 'I have anointed you king over the people of the LORD, over Israel. ⁷You shall strike down the house of Ahab your master, that I may avenge the blood of My servants the prophets, and the blood of all the servants of the LORD, at the hand of Jezebel. ⁸For the whole house of Ahab shall perish; and I will cut off from Ahab all the males in Israel, both bond and free. ⁹So I will make the house of Ahab like the house of Jeroboam the son of Nebat, and like the house of Baasha the son of Ahijah. ¹⁰The dogs shall eat Jezebel on the plot *of ground* at Jezreel, and *there shall be* none to bury her.' " And he opened the door and fled.

¹¹Then Jehu came out to the servants of his master, and *one* said to him, "*Is* all well? Why did this madman come to you?"

And he said to them, "You know the man and his babble."

¹²And they said, "A lie! Tell us now."

So he said, "Thus and thus he spoke to me, saying, 'Thus says the LORD: "I have anointed you king over Israel." ' "

¹³Then each man hastened to take his garment and put *it* under him on the top of the steps; and they blew trumpets, saying, "Jehu is king!"

Joram of Israel Killed

¹⁴So Jehu the son of Jehoshaphat, the son of Nimshi, conspired against Joram. (Now Joram had been defending Ramoth Gilead, he and all Israel, against Hazael king of Syria. ¹⁵But King Joram had returned to Jezreel to recover from the wounds which the Syrians had inflicted on him when he fought with Hazael king of Syria.) And Jehu said, "If you are so minded, let no one leave *or* escape from the city to go and tell *it* in Jezreel." ¹⁶So Jehu

POLITICS AND GOVERNMENT

Becoming a king in Israel required formal public acknowledgment and proclamation. This was done by anointing and public acclamation. In the anointing of Jehu (2 Kin. 9:12, 13), a trumpet was used in a typical way to emphasize a pronouncement that was new, important, and authoritative. In effect, the trumpet magnified the human voice.

JEHU ENCOUNTERS SHALMANESER AND HAZEL (2 Kin. 9:13)

Jehu was the individual who became king after overthrowing the dynasty of Omri in Israel. To complete his bloody revolution he attempted to eradicate the Baal cult from Samaria. Followers of Baal would have naturally supported the Omri-Ahab family, and thus would have been a constant threat to Jehu (2 Kin. 10:18–27).

The Assyrian king Shalmaneser III conducted his fourth campaign against Syro-Palestine in 841 B.C., the first year of Jehu's reign (841–814 B.C.). Jehu was apparently part of a coalition of kings that included King Hazael of Aram-Damascus. The Assyrians wreaked great havoc in the area, but did not take either Damascus or Samaria.

Details of Shalmaneser's campaign are found in Assyrian inscriptions. Among the annals and on the Black Obelisk of Shalmaneser are records that Jehu was reduced to vassaldom and was required to pay a heavy tribute to the Assyrian monarch. The Assyrian writings describe Jehu as the "son of Omri." Either the Omri dynasty enjoyed an international reputation or the Assyrians were ignorant of the hostile relationship between Jehu and the Omri royal family.

The encounter between Shalmaneser and Jehu must have been significant for both kings. Shalmaneser carved a scene on his Black Obelisk depicting Jehu bowing in submission to the Assyrian ruler, bringing with him many articles of tribute. Jehu, by submitting to the Assyrians, gained protection against Aram-Damascus. In fact, Shalmaneser invaded Damascus again in 838 B.C. but failed to overthrow Hazael.

No Assyrian sources mention Jehu again, implying that he had been successfully subjugated, requiring no further Assyrian incursions. Years later, however, as the Assyrian Empire declined, Hazael of Aram-Damascus attacked Israel, conquering parts of Jehu's kingdom (2 Kin. 10:32, 33).

---

rode in a chariot and went to Jezreel, for Joram was laid up there; and Ahaziah king of Judah had come down to see Joram.

17Now a watchman stood on the tower in Jezreel, and he saw the company of Jehu as he came, and said, "I see a company of men."

And Joram said, "Get a horseman and send him to meet them, and let him say, '*Is it* peace?' "

18So the horseman went to meet him, and said, "Thus says the king: '*Is it* peace?' "

And Jehu said, "What have you to do with peace? Turn around and follow me."

So the watchman reported, saying, "The messenger went to them, but is not coming back."

19Then he sent out a second horseman who came to them, and said, "Thus says the king: '*Is it* peace?' "

And Jehu answered, "What have you to do with peace? Turn around and follow me."

20So the watchman reported, saying, "He went up to them and is not coming back; and the driving *is* like the driving of Jehu the son of Nimshi, for he drives furiously!"

21Then Joram said, "Make ready." And his chariot was made ready. Then Joram king of Israel and Ahaziah king of Judah went out, each in his chariot; and they went out to meet Jehu, and met him on the property of Naboth the Jezreelite. 22Now it happened, when Joram saw Jehu, that he said, "*Is it* peace, Jehu?"

So he answered, "What peace, as long as the harlotries of your mother Jezebel and her witchcraft *are so* many?"

23Then Joram turned around and fled, and said to Ahaziah, "Treachery, Ahaziah!" 24Now Jehu drew his bow with full strength and shot Jehoram between his arms; and the arrow came out at his heart, and he sank down in his chariot. 25Then *Jehu* said to Bidkar his captain, "Pick *him* up, *and* throw him into the tract of the field of Naboth the Jezreelite; for remember, when you and I were riding together behind Ahab his father, that the LORD laid this burden upon him: 26'Surely I saw yesterday the blood of Naboth and the blood of his sons,' says the LORD, 'and I will repay you in this plot,' says the LORD. Now therefore, take *and* throw him on the plot *of* ground, according to the word of the LORD."

ATTACKS ON JUDAH'S ROYAL FAMILY

Judah (southern kingdom)

Athaliah was the daughter of Israel's king Ahab and sister of Israel's king Jehoram. She was married to Judah's king Jehoram. When her husband died, Athaliah's son Ahaziah became king, but was killed after one year.

Desiring Judah's throne for herself, Athaliah ruthlessly tried to kill all her grandsons (2 Kin. 11:1). Had she succeeded, there would not have been a descendant of David to sit on Judah's throne. One grandson survived, the infant Joash (2 Kin. 11:2).

Israel (northern kingdom)

Jehu led a violent extermination of the Ahab dynasty. After killing Israel's king Jehoram (2 Kin. 9:24), the son of Ahab, Jehu also influenced the deaths of Ahab's wife Jezebel (9:33) and 70 sons (2 Kin. 10:1, 7).

The slaughter of Ahab's family continued with the killing of Judah's king Ahaziah (9:27), who was Ahab's grandson. Jehu continued an attack against Judah's royal family by executing Ahaziah's brothers (10:12–14). These attacks on Judah's royalty allowed Athaliah to seize Judah's throne.

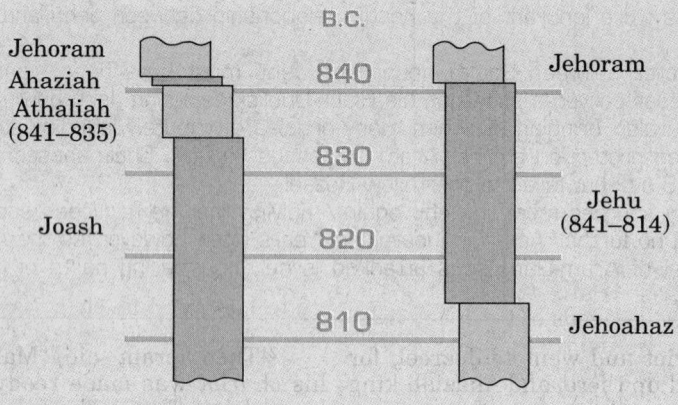

Jehoram
Ahaziah
Athaliah
(841–835)

Joash

B.C.
840
830
820
810

Jehoram

Jehu
(841–814)

Jehoahaz

Ahaziah of Judah Killed

27But when Ahaziah king of Judah saw *this,* he fled by the road to Beth Haggan.a So Jehu pursued him, and said, "Shoot him also in the chariot." *And they shot him* at the Ascent of Gur, which is by Ibleam. Then he fled to Megiddo, and died there. 28And his servants carried him in the chariot to Jerusalem, and buried him in his tomb with his fathers in the City of David. 29In the eleventh year of Joram the son of Ahab, Ahaziah had become king over Judah.

Jezebel's Violent Death

30Now when Jehu had come to Jezreel, Jezebel heard *of it;* and she put paint on her eyes and adorned her head, and looked through a window. 31Then, as Jehu entered at the gate, she said, "*Is it* peace, Zimri, murderer of your master?"

32And he looked up at the window, and said, "Who *is* on my side? Who?" So two *or* three eunuchs looked out at him. 33Then he said, "Throw her down." So they threw her down, and *some* of her blood spattered on the wall and on the horses; and he trampled her underfoot. 34And when he had gone in, he ate and drank. Then he said, "Go now, see to this accursed *woman,* and bury her, for she was a king's daughter." 35So they went to bury her, but they found no more of her than the skull and the feet and the palms of *her* hands. 36Therefore they came back and told him. And he said, "This *is* the word of the LORD, which He spoke by His servant Elijah the Tishbite, saying, 'On the plot *of ground* at Jezreel dogs shall eat the flesh of Jezebel;a 37and the corpse of Jezebel shall be as refuse on the surface of the field, in the plot at Jezreel, so that they shall not say, "Here *lies* Jezebel." ' "

9:27 aLiterally *The Garden House*   9:36 a1 Kings 21:23

Ahab's Seventy Sons Killed

10 ¹Now Ahab had seventy sons in Samaria. And Jehu wrote and sent letters to Samaria, to the rulers of Jezreel,[a] to the elders, and to those who reared Ahab's *sons,* saying:

2　　Now as soon as this letter comes to you, since your master's sons *are* with you, and you have chariots and horses, a fortified city also, and weapons, ³choose the best qualified of your master's sons, set *him* on his father's throne, and fight for your master's house.

⁴But they were exceedingly afraid, and said, "Look, two kings could not stand up to him; how then can we stand?" ⁵And he who *was* in charge of the house, and he who *was* in charge of the city, the elders also, and those who reared *the sons,* sent to Jehu, saying, "We *are* your servants, we will do all you tell us; but we will not make anyone king. Do *what is* good in your sight." ⁶Then he wrote a second letter to them, saying:

If you *are* for me and will obey my voice, take the heads of the men, your master's sons, and come to me at Jezreel by this time tomorrow.

Now the king's sons, seventy persons, *were* with the great men of the city, *who* were rearing them. ⁷So it was, when the letter came to them, that they took the king's sons and slaughtered seventy persons, put their heads in baskets and sent *them* to him at Jezreel.

⁸Then a messenger came and told him, saying, "They have brought the heads of the king's sons."

And he said, "Lay them in two heaps at the entrance of the gate until morning." ⁹So it was, in the morning, that he went out and stood, and said to all the people, "You *are* righteous. Indeed I conspired against my master and killed him; but who killed all these? ¹⁰Know now that nothing shall fall to the earth of the word of the LORD which the LORD spoke concerning the house of Ahab; for the LORD has done what He spoke by His servant Elijah." ¹¹So Jehu killed all who remained of the house of Ahab in Jezreel, and all his great men and his close acquaintances and his priests, until he left him none remaining.

Ahaziah's Forty-two Brothers Killed

¹²And he arose and departed and went to Samaria. On the way, at Beth Eked[a] of the Shepherds, ¹³Jehu met with the brothers of Ahaziah king of Judah, and said, "Who *are* you?"

So they answered, "We *are* the brothers of Ahaziah; we have come down to greet the sons of the king and the sons of the queen mother."

¹⁴And he said, "Take them alive!" So they took them alive, and killed them at the well of Beth Eked, forty-two men; and he left none of them.

The Rest of Ahab's Family Killed

¹⁵Now when he departed from there, he met Jehonadab the son of Rechab, *coming* to meet him; and he greeted him and said to him, "Is your heart right, as my heart *is* toward your heart?"

And Jehonadab answered, "It is."

Jehu said, "If it is, give *me* your hand." So he gave *him* his hand, and he took him up to him into the chariot. ¹⁶Then he said, "Come with me, and see my zeal for the LORD." So they had him ride in his chariot. ¹⁷And when he came to Samaria, he killed all who remained to Ahab in Samaria, till he had destroyed them, according to the word of the LORD which He spoke to Elijah.

Worshipers of Baal Killed

¹⁸Then Jehu gathered all the people together, and said to them, "Ahab served

---

> **TIME CAPSULE**　*810 to 796 B.C.*
>
> | | |
> |---|---|
> | **810–783** | *Adad-nirari III of Assyria influenced by his mother Semiramis* |
> | **800** | *Earliest reference to hardening steel by quenching, Odyssey Book 9* |
> | **798** | *Jehoash (or Joash) becomes king in Israel* |
> | **796** | *Adad-nirari III of Assyria successfully assaults the Aramean capital, Damascus* |
> | **796** | *Ben-Hadad (called Mar'i) of Damascus pays tribute to Adad-nirari* |
> | **796** | *King Jehoash of Israel pays tribute to Adad-nirari* |

10:1 ᵃFollowing Masoretic Text, Syriac, and Targum; Septuagint reads *Samaria;* Vulgate reads *city.*
10:12 ᵃOr *The Shearing House*

BAAL WORSHIP IN SAMARIA (2 Kin. 10:18–28)

During Ahab's reign (874–853 B.C.), Yahweh continued to be the official God of Israel, but Baal was clearly the main deity worshiped by the royal family. The temple of Baal was located in Samaria, the capital city (2 Kin. 10:21), while the national temples of Yahweh were in Bethel and Dan, away from the center of the kingdom.

The god Baal that was worshiped in Samaria had been introduced from Sidon by Ahab's queen Jezebel (1 Kin. 16:31, 32). Since the worship of Yahweh continued in the country, the two deities—Baal and Yahweh—were seen as part of a pantheon of gods for the northern kingdom. But the god whom the royal court consulted regularly was Baal; it was Baal's temple that was part of the palace complex in Samaria. The authority given to Baal in Ahab's northern kingdom is evident by the large number of prophets and priests of Baal, and by the throngs of worshipers.

The worshipers would not have considered worshiping both Baal and Yahweh to be a problem. They would have seen Baal as Yahweh's representative in charge of ruling their kingdom. The Law of Moses, however, forbade the worship of other gods even if one believed these gods existed. Israelites were not to bow down to anything in heaven or on earth (Ex. 20:4, 5).

The worship of Baal was a problem. Baal had become the heart of the national religion. This was an apostasy that called for the overthrow of the rulers and even the kingdom itself. In a very real sense, Sidon had conquered Israel religiously. The apostasy was ended by Jehu, whose bloody purge of Baalism destroyed the royal family of Ahab, as well as massacring the worshipers of Baal (2 Kin. 10:18–28).

Baal a little, Jehu will serve him much. [19]Now therefore, call to me all the prophets of Baal, all his servants, and all his priests. Let no one be missing, for I have a great sacrifice for Baal. Whoever is missing shall not live." But Jehu acted deceptively, with the intent of destroying the worshipers of Baal. [20]And Jehu said, "Proclaim a solemn assembly for Baal." So they proclaimed *it.* [21]Then Jehu sent throughout all Israel; and all the worshipers of Baal came, so that there was not a man left who did not come. So they came into the temple[a] of Baal, and the temple of Baal was full from one end to the other. [22]And he said to the one in charge of the wardrobe, "Bring out vestments for all the worshipers of Baal." So he brought out vestments for them. [23]Then Jehu and Jehonadab the son of Rechab went into the temple of Baal, and said to the worshipers of Baal, "Search and see that no servants of the LORD are here with you, but only the worshipers of Baal." [24]So they went in to offer sacrifices and burnt offerings. Now Jehu had appointed for himself eighty men on the outside, and had said, "If any of the men whom I have brought into your hands escapes, *whoever lets him escape, it shall be* his life for the life of the other."

[25]Now it happened, as soon as he had made an end of offering the burnt offering, that Jehu said to the guard and to the captains, "Go in *and* kill them; let no one come out!" And they killed them with the edge of the sword; then the guards and the officers threw *them* out, and went into the inner room of the temple of Baal. [26]And they brought the *sacred* pillars out of the temple of Baal and burned them. [27]Then they broke down the *sacred* pillar of Baal, and tore down the temple of Baal and made it a refuse dump to this day. [28]Thus Jehu destroyed Baal from Israel.

[29]However Jehu did not turn away from the sins of Jeroboam the son of Nebat, who had made Israel sin, *that is,* from the golden calves that *were* at Bethel and Dan. [30]And the LORD said to Jehu, "Because you have done well in doing *what is* right in My sight, *and* have done to the house of Ahab all that *was* in My heart, your sons shall sit on the throne of Israel to the fourth *generation.*" [31]But Jehu took no heed to walk in the law of the LORD God of Israel with all his heart; for he did not depart from the sins of Jeroboam, who had made Israel sin.

10:21 ªLiterally *house,* and so elsewhere in this chapter

Death of Jehu

³²In those days the LORD began to cut off *parts* of Israel; and Hazael conquered them in all the territory of Israel ³³from the Jordan eastward: all the land of Gilead—Gad, Reuben, and Manasseh—from Aroer, which *is* by the River Arnon, including Gilead and Bashan.

³⁴Now the rest of the acts of Jehu, all that he did, and all his might, *are* they not written in the book of the chronicles of the kings of Israel? ³⁵So Jehu rested with his fathers, and they buried him in Samaria. Then Jehoahaz his son reigned in his place. ³⁶And the period that Jehu reigned over Israel in Samaria *was* twenty-eight years.

Priestly Account: Fall of Omri's Dynasty

Because the northern kingdom lay outside the purview of the Chronicler, he only briefly mentions that Jehu destroyed the dynasty of Omri and Ahab (2 Chr. 22:7, 8). He is much more concerned about the impact that Ahab's family had on two of Judah's kings: Jehoram (848–841 B.C.) and Ahaziah (841 B.C.). Athaliah, the daughter of Ahab, apparently had much influence on her husband, Jehoram (2 Chr. 21:6), and then seized power after his death. In her role as queen mother, Athaliah could exert power in the government of her son, Ahaziah (2 Chr. 22:2, 3).

▼　■ 2 Chronicles 21:1—22:9

2 Chronicles
Jehoram Reigns in Judah

21 :1 And Jehoshaphat rested with his fathers, and was buried with his fathers in the City of David. Then Jehoram his son reigned in his place. ²He had brothers, the sons of Jehoshaphat: Azariah, Jehiel, Zechariah, Azaryahu, Michael, and Shephatiah; all these *were* the sons of Jehoshaphat king of Israel. ³Their father gave them great gifts of silver and gold and precious things, with fortified cities in Judah; but he gave the kingdom to Jehoram, because he *was* the firstborn.

⁴Now when Jehoram was established over the kingdom of his father, he strengthened himself and killed all his brothers with the sword, and also *others* of the princes of Israel.

⁵Jehoram *was* thirty-two years old when he became king, and he reigned eight years in Jerusalem. ⁶And he walked in the way of the kings of Israel, just as the house of Ahab had done, for he had the daughter of Ahab as a wife; and he did evil in the sight of the LORD. ⁷Yet the LORD would not destroy the house of David, because of the covenant that He had made with David, and since He had promised to give a lamp to him and to his sons forever.

⁸In his days Edom revolted against Judah's authority, and made a king over themselves. ⁹So Jehoram went out with his officers, and all his chariots with him. And he rose by night and attacked the Edomites who had surrounded him and the captains of the chariots. ¹⁰Thus Edom has been in revolt against Judah's authority to this day. At that time Libnah revolted against his rule, because he had forsaken the LORD God of his fathers. ¹¹Moreover he made high places in the mountains of Judah, and caused the inhabitants of Jerusalem to commit harlotry, and led Judah astray.

¹²And a letter came to him from Elijah the prophet, saying,

> Thus says the LORD God of your
> father David:
> Because you have not walked in the
> ways of Jehoshaphat your father, or in
> the ways of Asa king of Judah, ¹³but
> have walked in the way of the kings of
> Israel, and have made Judah and the
> inhabitants of Jerusalem to play the
> harlot like the harlotry of the house of
> Ahab, and also have killed your
> brothers, those of your father's
> household, *who were* better than
> yourself, ¹⁴behold, the LORD will strike
> your people with a serious affliction—
> your children, your wives, and all
> your possessions; ¹⁵and you *will
> become* very sick with a disease of
> your intestines, until your intestines
> come out by reason of the sickness,
> day by day.

¹⁶Moreover the LORD stirred up against Jehoram the spirit of the Philistines and the Arabians who *were* near the Ethiopians. ¹⁷And they came up into Judah and invaded it, and carried away all the possessions that were found in the king's house, and also his sons and his wives, so that there was not a son left to

him except Jehoahaz,[a] the youngest of his sons.

[18]After all this the LORD struck him in his intestines with an incurable disease. [19]Then it happened in the course of time, after the end of two years, that his intestines came out because of his sickness; so he died in severe pain. And his people made no burning for him, like the burning for his fathers.

[20]He was thirty-two years old when he became king. He reigned in Jerusalem eight years and, to no one's sorrow, departed. However they buried him in the City of David, but not in the tombs of the kings.

Ahaziah Reigns in Judah

22 [1]Then the inhabitants of Jerusalem made Ahaziah his youngest son king in his place, for the raiders who came with the Arabians into the camp had killed all the older *sons*. So Ahaziah the son of Jehoram, king of Judah, reigned. [2]Ahaziah *was* forty-two[a] years old when he became king, and he reigned one year in Jerusalem. His mother's name *was* Athaliah the granddaughter of Omri. [3]He also walked in the ways of the house of Ahab, for his mother advised him to do wickedly. [4]Therefore he did evil in the sight of the LORD, like the house of Ahab; for they were his counselors after the death of his father, to his destruction. [5]He also followed their advice, and went with Jehoram[a] the son of Ahab king of Israel to war against Hazael king of Syria at Ramoth Gilead; and the Syrians wounded Joram. [6]Then he returned to Jezreel to recover from the wounds which he had received at Ramah, when he fought against Hazael king of Syria. And Azariah[a] the son of Jehoram, king of Judah, went down to see Jehoram the son of Ahab in Jezreel, because he was sick.

[7]His going to Joram was God's occasion for Ahaziah's downfall; for when he arrived, he went out with Jehoram against Jehu the son of Nimshi, whom the LORD had anointed to cut off the house of Ahab. [8]And it happened, when Jehu was executing judgment on the house of Ahab, and found the princes of Judah and the sons of Ahaziah's brothers who served Ahaziah, that he killed them. [9]Then he searched for Ahaziah; and they caught him (he was hiding in Samaria), and brought him to Jehu. When they had killed him, they buried

him, "because," they said, "he is the son of Jehoshaphat, who sought the LORD with all his heart."

So the house of Ahaziah had no one to assume power over the kingdom.

Prophetic Account: Athaliah Seizes Judah's Throne

Jehu exceeded his role of destroying the Israelite house of Ahab and killed even Judah's king, Ahaziah (2 Kin. 9:27, 28). It is not hard to explain Jehu's actions. Ahaziah was related to Ahab's family through his mother, Athaliah. Israel's king Joram was the uncle of Judah's king Ahaziah, so Jehu killed them both.

With her son dead, Athaliah seized the throne of Judah herself and nearly exterminated the Davidic line. She wanted to make sure that no surviving male of David's royal family could challenge her rule. For the first and only time, a queen ruled Judah on her own.

Athaliah's reign (841–835 B.C.) would be brief, for one young prince, Joash, was saved from the massacre (2 Kin. 11:2, 3). Jehoiada, the chief priest for many years in Jerusalem, organized the conspiracy that brought the young Joash (or Jehoash) to the throne. The accession of Joash (835–796 B.C.) restored the Davidic monarchy to the southern kingdom.

▼ ■ 2 Kings 11:1—12:21

2 Kings
Athaliah Reigns in Judah

11 :1 When Athaliah the mother of Ahaziah saw that her son was dead, she arose and destroyed all the royal heirs. [2]But Jehosheba, the daughter of King Joram, sister of Ahaziah, took Joash the son of Ahaziah, and stole him away from among the king's sons *who were* being murdered; and they hid him and his nurse in the bedroom, from Athaliah, so that he was not killed. [3]So he was hidden with her in the house of the LORD for six years, while Athaliah reigned over the land.

21:17 [a]Elsewhere called *Ahaziah* (compare 2 Chronicles 22:1)   22:2 [a]Or *twenty-two* (compare 2 Kings 8:26)   22:5 [a]Also spelled *Joram* (compare verses 5 and 7; 2 Kings 8:28; and elsewhere)   22:6 [a]Some Hebrew manuscripts, Septuagint, Syriac, Vulgate, and 2 Kings 8:29 read *Ahaziah*

Joash Crowned King of Judah

[4]In the seventh year Jehoiada sent and brought the captains of hundreds—of the bodyguards and the escorts—and brought them into the house of the LORD to him. And he made a covenant with them and took an oath from them in the house of the LORD, and showed them the king's son. [5]Then he commanded them, saying, "This is what you shall do: One-third of you who come on duty on the Sabbath shall be keeping watch over the king's house, [6]one-third shall be at the gate of Sur, and one-third at the gate behind the escorts. You shall keep the watch of the house, lest it be broken down. [7]The two contingents of you who go off duty on the Sabbath shall keep the watch of the house of the LORD for the king. [8]But you shall surround the king on all sides, every man with his weapons in his hand; and whoever comes within range, let him be put to death. You are to be with the king as he goes out and as he comes in."

[9]So the captains of the hundreds did according to all that Jehoiada the priest commanded. Each of them took his men who were to be on duty on the Sabbath, with those who were going off duty on the Sabbath, and came to Jehoiada the priest. [10]And the priest gave the captains of hundreds the spears and shields which had belonged to King David, that were in the temple of the LORD. [11]Then the escorts stood, every man with his weapons in his hand, all around the king, from the right side of the temple to the left side of the temple, by the altar and the house. [12]And he brought out the king's son, put the crown on him, and gave him the Testimony;[a] they made him king and anointed him, and they clapped their hands and said, "Long live the king!"

Death of Athaliah

[13]Now when Athaliah heard the noise of the escorts and the people, she came to the people in the temple of the LORD. [14]When she looked, there was the king standing by a pillar according to custom; and the leaders and the trumpeters were by the king. All the people of the land were rejoicing and blowing trumpets. So

Athaliah tore her clothes and cried out, "Treason! Treason!"

[15]And Jehoiada the priest commanded the captains of the hundreds, the officers of the army, and said to them, "Take her outside under guard, and slay with the sword whoever follows her." For the priest had said, "Do not let her be killed in the house of the LORD." [16]So they seized her; and she went by way of the horses' entrance into the king's house, and there she was killed.

[17]Then Jehoiada made a covenant between the LORD, the king, and the people, that they should be the LORD's people, and also between the king and the people. [18]And all the people of the land went to the temple of Baal, and tore it down. They thoroughly broke in pieces its altars and images, and killed Mattan the priest of Baal before the altars. And the priest appointed officers over the house of the LORD. [19]Then he took the captains of hundreds, the bodyguards, the escorts, and all the people of the land; and they brought the king down from the house of the LORD, and went by way of the gate of the escorts to the king's house. Then he sat on the throne of the kings. [20]So all the people of the land rejoiced; and the city was quiet, for they had slain Athaliah with the sword in the king's house. [21]Jehoash was seven years old when he became king.

Jehoash Repairs the Temple

12 [1]In the seventh year of Jehu, Jehoash[a] became king, and he reigned forty years in Jerusalem. His mother's name was Zibiah of Beersheba. [2]Jehoash did what was right in the sight of the LORD

TIME CAPSULE *796 to 767 B.C.*	
796	Amaziah becomes king in Judah
793	Jeroboam II serves as coregent with Jehoash in Israel
792	Azariah (or Uzziah) serves as co-regent with Amaziah in Judah
782	Jeroboam II becomes sole king in Israel
782– 745	Assyria is fragmented into various governor-ruled states
776	Athletic contests begin at Olympia
767	Azariah (or Uzziah) becomes sole king in Judah

11:12 [a]That is, the Law (compare Exodus 25:16, 21 and Deuteronomy 31:9)   12:1 [a]Spelled *Joash* in 11:2ff

HAZEL ATTACKS JUDAH AND ISRAEL

Judah (southern kingdom)

Joash was the son of Ahaziah and grandson of Judah's royal couple, Jehoram and Athaliah. When King Ahaziah died, Athaliah killed all the royal heirs to the throne except for one. Hidden by his aunt Jehosheba, Joash (or Jehoash) survived to become king at 7 years old (2 Chr. 22:12; 24:1).

About 812 B.C. Joash made repairs to the temple (2 Kin. 12:6–16). Unfortunately, he was forced to pay tribute to Hazael of Aram (Syria), which included sacred items and wealth from the temple treasuries (12:17, 18).

Israel (northern kingdom)

Jehoahaz, son of Jehu, continued the dynasty begun by his father. The kingdom that Jehoahaz inherited from Jehu was beset by wars against Aram-Damascus (2 Kin. 10:32, 33). King Hazael of Aram (Syria) and his son Ben-Hadad severely punished Israel during Jehoahaz's reign (2 Kin. 13:3, 25).

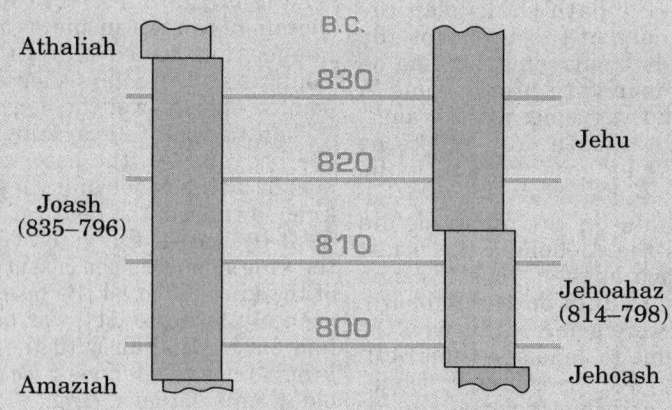

all the days in which Jehoiada the priest instructed him. ³But the high places were not taken away; the people still sacrificed and burned incense on the high places.

⁴And Jehoash said to the priests, "All the money of the dedicated gifts that are brought into the house of the LORD—each man's census money, each man's assessment moneyª—*and* all the money that a man purposes in his heart to bring into the house of the LORD, ⁵let the priests take *it* themselves, each from his constituency; and let them repair the damages of the temple, wherever any dilapidation is found."

⁶Now it was so, by the twenty-third year of King Jehoash, *that* the priests had not repaired the damages of the temple. ⁷So King Jehoash called Jehoiada the priest and the *other* priests, and said to them, "Why have you not repaired the damages of the temple? Now therefore, do not take *more* money from your constituency, but deliver it for repairing the damages of the temple." ⁸And the priests agreed that they would neither receive *more* money from the people, nor repair the damages of the temple.

⁹Then Jehoiada the priest took a chest,

12:4 ªCompare Leviticus 27:2ff

TRADE AND ECONOMICS

In the absence of banks, religious temples were used as treasuries or storehouses (2 Kin. 12:9). This was true in Egypt and Greece as well as in Israel, resulting in a close association of civil and religious government. The practice of keeping written records of the ownership of goods goes back as far as the history of writing itself.

bored a hole in its lid, and set it beside the altar, on the right side as one comes into the house of the LORD; and the priests who kept the door put there all the money brought into the house of the LORD. ¹⁰So it was, whenever they saw that *there was* much money in the chest, that the king's scribe and the high priest came up and put it in bags, and counted the money that was found in the house of the LORD. ¹¹Then they gave the money, which had been apportioned, into the hands of those who did the work, who had the oversight of the house of the LORD; and they paid it out to the carpenters and builders who worked on the house of the LORD, ¹²and to masons and stonecutters, and for buying timber and hewn stone, to repair the damage of the house of the LORD, and for all that was paid out to repair the temple. ¹³However there were not made for the house of the LORD basins of silver, trimmers, sprinkling-bowls, trumpets, any articles of gold or articles of silver, from the money brought into the house of the LORD. ¹⁴But they gave that to the workmen, and they repaired the house of the LORD with it. ¹⁵Moreover they did not require an account from the men into whose hand they delivered the money to be paid to workmen, for they dealt faithfully. ¹⁶The money from the trespass offerings and the money from the sin offerings was not brought into the house of the LORD. It belonged to the priests.

Hazael Threatens Jerusalem

¹⁷Hazael king of Syria went up and fought against Gath, and took it; then Hazael set his face to go up to Jerusalem. ¹⁸And Jehoash king of Judah took all the sacred things that his fathers, Jehoshaphat and Jehoram and Ahaziah, kings of Judah, had dedicated, and his own sacred things, and all the gold found in the treasuries of the house of the LORD and in the king's house, and sent *them* to Hazael king of Syria. Then he went away from Jerusalem.

Death of Joash

¹⁹Now the rest of the acts of Joash,ᵃ and all that he did, *are* they not written in

12:19 ᵃSpelled *Jehoash* in 12:1ff
12:20 ᵃLiterally *The Landfill* 12:21 ᵃCalled *Zabad* in 2 Chronicles 24:26 ᵇCalled *Shimrith* in 2 Chronicles 24:26 13:1 ᵃSpelled *Jehoash* in 12:1ff

the book of the chronicles of the kings of Judah?

²⁰And his servants arose and formed a conspiracy, and killed Joash in the house of the Millo,ᵃ which goes down to Silla. ²¹For Jozacharᵃ the son of Shimeath and Jehozabad the son of Shomer,ᵇ his servants, struck him. So he died, and they buried him with his fathers in the City of David. Then Amaziah his son reigned in his place.

The Dynasty of Jehu in Israel

Jehu overthrew the Omride dynasty and established a new dynasty that would last for almost a century (841–753 B.C.). Four successors followed Jehu on Israel's throne: Jehoahaz, Jehoash, Jeroboam II, and Zechariah. The reigns of Jehoahaz (814–798 B.C.) and Jehoash (798–782 B.C.) were marked by constant wars with Aram-Damascus (Syria; 2 Kin. 13:3).

While Jehu was king, Aram's King Hazael had been able to take from Israel territories on the east side of the Jordan (2 Kin. 10:31–33). Apparently, Hazael continued to reduce Israel's territory during Jehoahaz's rule. However, the situation changed by the time Jehoash became king. Aram's powerful king Hazael (c. 842–800 B.C.) had died, and about 796 B.C. Aram was besieged by the Assyrian king Adad-nirari III. These events allowed Jehoash to find some success against a weaker Aram (2 Kin. 13:24, 25).

■ 2 Kings 13:1–25

2 Kings
Jehoahaz Reigns in Israel

13 :1 In the twenty-third year of Joashᵃ the son of Ahaziah, king of Judah, Jehoahaz the son of Jehu became king over Israel in Samaria, *and reigned* seventeen years. ²And he did evil in the sight of the LORD, and followed the sins of Jeroboam the son of Nebat, who had made Israel sin. He did not depart from them.

³Then the anger of the LORD was aroused against Israel, and He delivered them into the hand of Hazael king of Syria, and into the hand of Ben-Hadad the son of Hazael, all *their* days. ⁴So Jehoahaz pleaded with the LORD, and the LORD listened to him; for He saw the oppression of Israel, because the king of Syria oppressed them. ⁵Then the LORD gave Israel

THE DECLINING KINGDOM OF BEN-HADAD (2 Kin. 13:3)

The name "Ben-Hadad" was used for at least two kings of Aram-Damascus, and possibly three. The Ben-Hadad named in 2 Kin. 13:3 as the son of Hazael should not be confused with the Ben-Hadad mentioned in 1 Kin. 15:18–20. Ben-Hadad, son of Hazael, ruled Aram-Damascus (translated "Syria" in 2 Kin. 13:3) in the late 9th or early 8th century B.C. While his father had been probably the most powerful monarch of the Aram-Damascus kingdom, sources outside of the Bible describe the decline of the kingdom under Ben-Hadad's own reign.

In the early 8th century B.C. Ben-Hadad led an assault against Zakkur, the king of the lands of Hamath and Luash. According to Zakkur's own inscription, he was saved from Ben-Hadad's siege by divine intervention. Although Ben-Hadad led a coalition of ten allies, he was in fact unable to defeat Zakkur.

The Neo-Assyrian annals describe another failure of Ben-Hadad. These texts tell how the Assyrian king Adad-nirari III (810–783 B.C.) waged a successful assault upon the Aramean capital, Damascus, in 796 B.C. The Assyrians entered the city and forced the king to pay tribute. While the Aramean king mentioned in the texts is called Mar'i, some scholars now identify him with Ben-Hadad, who ruled Damascus at that time.

While Ben-Hadad's Aramean state was suffering these defeats against Hamath and Assyria, it was also losing territory on its southern border to Israel. Israel had been a vassal state of Aram-Damascus under Ben-Hadad's father, Hazael (see 2 Kin. 10:32, 33; 13:3–7). However, during Ben-Hadad's reign this Aramean domination was overthrown by King Joash (or Jehoash) of Israel. In three campaigns during his reign (798–782 B.C.), Joash was successful in recapturing cities from Ben-Hadad that Israel had lost previously (2 Kin. 13:24, 25).

---

a deliverer, so that they escaped from under the hand of the Syrians; and the children of Israel dwelt in their tents as before. [6]Nevertheless they did not depart from the sins of the house of Jeroboam, who had made Israel sin, *but* walked in them; and the wooden image[a] also remained in Samaria. [7]For He left of the army of Jehoahaz only fifty horsemen, ten chariots, and ten thousand foot soldiers; for the king of Syria had destroyed them and made them like the dust at threshing.

[8]Now the rest of the acts of Jehoahaz, all that he did, and his might, *are* they not written in the book of the chronicles of the kings of Israel? [9]So Jehoahaz rested with his fathers, and they buried him in Samaria. Then Joash his son reigned in his place.

Jehoash Reigns in Israel

[10]In the thirty-seventh year of Joash king of Judah, Jehoash[a] the son of Jehoahaz became king over Israel in Samaria, *and reigned* sixteen years. [11]And he did evil in the sight of the LORD. He did not depart from all the sins of Jeroboam the son

of Nebat, who made Israel sin, *but* walked in them.

[12]Now the rest of the acts of Joash, all that he did, and his might with which he fought against Amaziah king of Judah, *are* they not written in the book of the chronicles of the kings of Israel? [13]So Joash rested with his fathers. Then Jeroboam sat on his throne. And Joash was buried in Samaria with the kings of Israel.

Death of Elisha

[14]Elisha had become sick with the illness of which he would die. Then Joash the king of Israel came down to him, and wept over his face, and said, "O my father, my father, the chariots of Israel and their horsemen!"

[15]And Elisha said to him, "Take a bow and some arrows." So he took himself a bow and some arrows. [16]Then he said to the king of Israel, "Put your hand on the bow." So he put his hand *on it,* and Elisha

---

13:6 [a]Hebrew *Asherah,* a Canaanite goddess
13:10 [a]Spelled *Joash* in verse 9

ISRAEL IS VICTORIOUS OVER JUDAH

Judah (southern kingdom)

Amaziah, son of Joash, became king when his father was assassinated (2 Chr. 24:25). He built up the army of Judah, enabling him to gain a stunning victory over the Edomites (24:5, 11). Possibly this success led Amaziah to challenge Jehoash (or Joash) of Israel to war, an effort with disastrous results. Israel defeated Judah at Beth Shemesh; destroyed part of Jerusalem's wall; and looted both Jerusalem's temple and royal treasury (2 Chr. 25:22–24). Like his father, Amaziah was assassinated (25:27).

Israel (northern kingdom)

Jehoash (or Joash), son of Jehoahaz, continued the Jehu dynasty. Israel was revived during his reign, following a long period of suffering at the hands of the Arameans (Syrians). The Assyrian king Adad-nirari III captured the Aramean capital, Damascus, in 796 B.C., and that event possibly enabled Jehoash to recover cities from Aram that Israel had lost while Jehoash's father ruled (2 Kin. 13:24, 25). Jehoash also defeated King Amaziah of Judah.

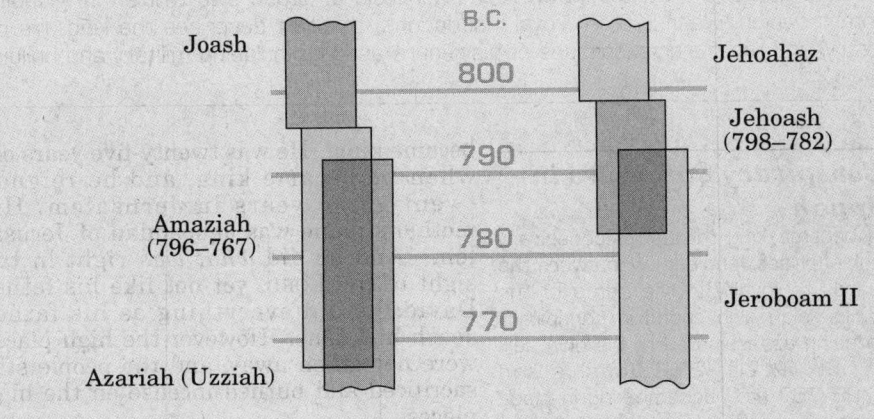

put his hands on the king's hands. [17]And he said, "Open the east window"; and he opened it. Then Elisha said, "Shoot"; and he shot. And he said, "The arrow of the LORD's deliverance and the arrow of deliverance from Syria; for you must strike the Syrians at Aphek till you have destroyed *them.*" [18]Then he said, "Take the arrows"; so he took *them.* And he said to the king of Israel, "Strike the ground"; so he struck three times, and stopped. [19]And the man of God was angry with him, and said, "You should have struck five or six times; then you would have struck Syria till you had destroyed *it!* But now you will strike Syria *only* three times."

[20]Then Elisha died, and they buried him. And the *raiding* bands from Moab invaded the land in the spring of the year. [21]So it was, as they were burying a man, that suddenly they spied a band *of raiders;* and they put the man in the tomb of Elisha; and when the man was let down and touched the bones of Elisha, he revived and stood on his feet.

Israel Recaptures Cities from Syria

[22]And Hazael king of Syria oppressed Israel all the days of Jehoahaz. [23]But the LORD was gracious to them, had compassion on them, and regarded them, because of His covenant with Abraham, Isaac, and Jacob, and would not yet destroy them or cast them from His presence.

[24]Now Hazael king of Syria died. Then Ben-Hadad his son reigned in his place. [25]And Jehoash[a] the son of Jehoahaz recaptured from the hand of Ben-Hadad, the son of Hazael, the cities which he had taken out of the hand of Jehoahaz his father by war. Three times Joash defeated him and recaptured the cities of Israel.

13:25 [a]Spelled *Joash* in verses 12–14, 25

THE MOABITE STONE AND KING MESHA (2 Kin. 13:20)

Moab was a nation located in the area southeast of the Dead Sea. Its inhabitants were descended from one of the daughters of Lot, a nephew of Abraham (Gen. 11:27; 19:36, 37), and thus were related to the Israelites. Relations, however, did not produce peace between the two peoples.

It is understandable that there were "raiding bands from Moab" (2 Kin. 13:20) in Israel sometime after Elisha died in the early 8th century B.C. The Moabite Stone, a royal inscription on a basalt slab dating from about 850 B.C., tells of the Moabite king Mesha, who ruled Moab while Ahab was king in Israel. After Ahab died in 853 B.C. (2 Kin. 3:4, 5), Mesha was able to recover Moabite territory in Medeba from the control of Israel. In fact, Mesha claims that three of Israel's cities were taken: Ataroth, Nebo, and Jahaz. He likely resettled the three cities with Moabites.

The Moabite Stone is the only known memorial stele or stone slab written in Moabite. Similar to other ancient Near Eastern royal inscriptions, this text describes the king, his paternal ancestry, and the major successes of his tenure as king, including military and building exploits.

Conspiracy Continues in Judah

Joash became king through a conspiracy led by the chief priest Jehoiada, who swore the temple guards to loyalty in the name of the child king. His reign also ended in conspiracy with Joash being assassinated by his own servants (2 Kin. 12:20, 21). Joash's son Amaziah (796–767 B.C.) became king in place of his assassinated father. But like his father, Amaziah's reign and life also would be ended by conspiracy and assassination (2 Kin. 14:17–20). The Davidic dynasty was still on shaky ground.

When Jehu became Israel's king, the alliance between Israel and Judah ended immediately. Under Judah's king Amaziah, war broke out once again between the two nations. The outcome for Judah was disastrous: Amaziah was captured, and Israel's army invaded Jerusalem, looting treasures from the temple and palace (2 Kin. 14:12–14). A people's conspiracy against Amaziah is understandable since his war against Israel and the loss of temple treasures would have made him an unpopular king.

▼   ■ 2 Kings 14:1–22

2 Kings
Amaziah Reigns in Judah

14 :1 In the second year of Joash the son of Jehoahaz, king of Israel, Amaziah the son of Joash, king of Judah,

became king. 2He was twenty-five years old when he became king, and he reigned twenty-nine years in Jerusalem. His mother's name was Jehoaddan of Jerusalem. 3And he did *what was* right in the sight of the LORD, yet not like his father David; he did everything as his father Joash had done. 4However the high places were not taken away, and the people still sacrificed and burned incense on the high places.

5Now it happened, as soon as the kingdom was established in his hand, that he executed his servants who had murdered his father the king. 6But the children of the murderers he did not execute, according to what is written in the Book of the Law of Moses, in which the LORD commanded, saying, "Fathers shall not be put to death for their children, nor shall children be put to death for their fathers; but a person shall be put to death for his own sin."[a]

7He killed ten thousand Edomites in the Valley of Salt, and took Sela by war, and called its name Joktheel to this day.

8Then Amaziah sent messengers to Jehoash[a] the son of Jehoahaz, the son of Jehu, king of Israel, saying, "Come, let us face one another *in battle*." 9And Jehoash king of Israel sent to Amaziah king of Judah, saying, "The thistle that *was* in Lebanon sent to the cedar that *was* in Lebanon, saying, 'Give your daughter to my son as

---

14:6 ªDeuteronomy 24:16   14:8 ªSpelled *Joash*
in 13:12ff and 2 Chronicles 25:17ff

COREGENCIES, LONG REIGNS, AND PROSPERITY

Judah (southern kingdom)

Azariah (or Uzziah) became king at 16 years old, and his long reign of 52 years suggests that he served as a coregent with his father Amaziah. Possibly the people placed the young Azariah on the throne when his father Amaziah was taken prisoner by Israel (2 Kin. 14:13, 21).

Ruling a prosperous Judah, Azariah secured the defenses of both his capital and country. About 750 B.C. the disease of leprosy forced him to live the rest of his life in a separate place, while his son Jotham ruled as coregent (2 Chr. 26:21).

Israel (northern kingdom)

Jeroboam II, son of Jehoash, was the 4th king of the Jehu dynasty. His long reign of 41 years began as a coregent with his father. Possibly Jehoash placed Jeroboam on the throne when war broke out against King Amaziah of Judah (2 Kin. 13:12).

Successful military adventures helped Jeroboam expand the boundaries of Israel to their greatest extent since the days of David and Solomon (2 Kin. 14:25, 28). The prophet Amos prophesied against social abuses in Jeroboam's Israel (Amos 7:9–11).

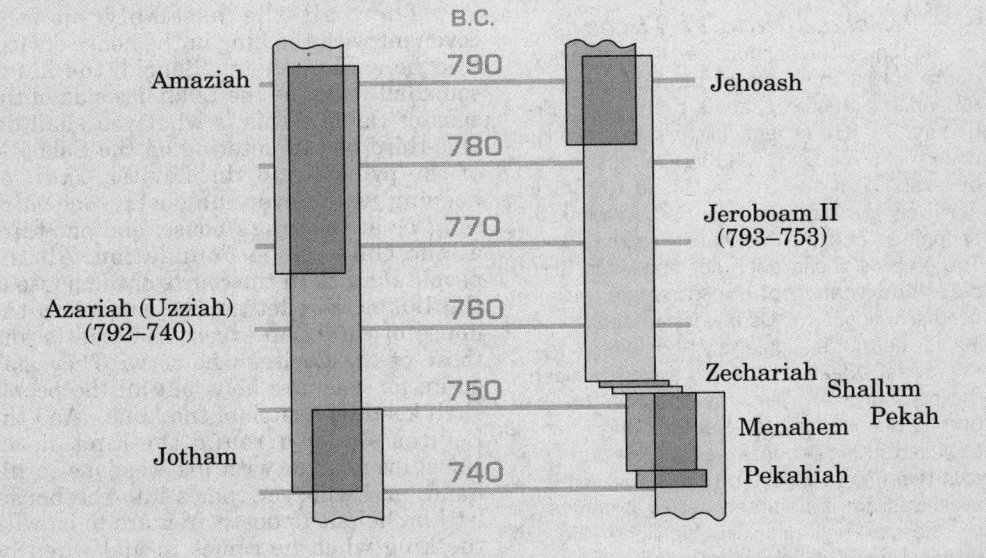

wife'; and a wild beast that *was* in Lebanon passed by and trampled the thistle. ¹⁰You have indeed defeated Edom, and your heart has lifted you up. Glory *in that,* and stay at home; for why should you meddle with trouble so that you fall—you and Judah with you?"

¹¹But Amaziah would not heed. Therefore Jehoash king of Israel went out; so he and Amaziah king of Judah faced one another at Beth Shemesh, which *belongs* to Judah. ¹²And Judah was defeated by Israel, and every man fled to his tent. ¹³Then Jehoash king of Israel captured Amaziah king of Judah, the son of Jehoash, the son of Ahaziah, at Beth Shemesh; and he went to Jerusalem, and broke down the wall of Jerusalem from the Gate of Ephraim to the

Corner Gate—four hundred cubits. ¹⁴And he took all the gold and silver, all the articles that were found in the house of the LORD and in the treasuries of the king's house, and hostages, and returned to Samaria.

¹⁵Now the rest of the acts of Jehoash which he did—his might, and how he fought with Amaziah king of Judah—*are* they not written in the book of the chronicles of the kings of Israel? ¹⁶So Jehoash rested with his fathers, and was buried in Samaria with the kings of Israel. Then Jeroboam his son reigned in his place.

¹⁷Amaziah the son of Joash, king of Judah, lived fifteen years after the death of Jehoash the son of Jehoahaz, king of Israel. ¹⁸Now the rest of the acts of Amaziah,

are they not written in the book of the chronicles of the kings of Judah? ¹⁹And they formed a conspiracy against him in Jerusalem, and he fled to Lachish; but they sent after him to Lachish and killed him there. ²⁰Then they brought him on horses, and he was buried at Jerusalem with his fathers in the City of David.

²¹And all the people of Judah took Azariah,ᵃ who *was* sixteen years old, and made him king instead of his father Amaziah. ²²He built Elath and restored it to Judah, after the king rested with his fathers.

Priestly Account: Athaliah Seizes Judah's Throne

In Kings, the account of the northern kingdom's rulers from Joram through Jehoash is expanded with stories about the prophet Elisha (2 Kin. 2—13). In fact, Elisha's final prophecy occurs in a meeting with King Jehoash (Joash) of Israel (2 Kin. 13:14–21). In Chronicles, however, the focus is on priests rather than prophets, and on Judah rather than Israel. The prophet Elisha does not appear in Chronicles, and the prophetic struggle with the northern kingdom's Baal worship appears only insofar as that struggle touched Judah.

Israel's Baal worship did arrive in Judah in the person of Athaliah, the daughter of Ahab. She no doubt promoted Baalism while married to Judah's King Jehoram, as well as during her own reign (841–835 B.C.). In Chronicles, however, Baalism is defeated not by prophets but by priests. The Chronicler highlights the part played by the religious personnel in making Joash king (2 Chr. 23:4–7) and in leading a purge of Baal worship (23:16–19).

▼   ■ 2 Chronicles 22:10—23:21

---

2 Chronicles
Athaliah Reigns in Judah

22 :10 Now when Athaliah the mother of Ahaziah saw that her son was dead, she arose and destroyed all the royal heirs of the house of Judah. ¹¹But Jehoshabeath,ᵃ the daughter of the king, took Joash the son of Ahaziah, and stole him away from among the king's sons who were being murdered, and put him and his nurse in a bedroom. So Jehoshabeath, the daughter of King Jehoram, the wife of Jehoiada the priest (for she was the sister of Ahaziah), hid him from Athaliah so that she did not kill him. ¹²And he was hidden with them in the house of God for six years, while Athaliah reigned over the land.

Joash Crowned King of Judah

23 ¹In the seventh year Jehoiada strengthened himself, *and made a* covenant with the captains of hundreds: Azariah the son of Jeroham, Ishmael the son of Jehohanan, Azariah the son of Obed, Maaseiah the son of Adaiah, and Elishaphat the son of Zichri. ²And they went throughout Judah and gathered the Levites from all the cities of Judah, and the chief fathers of Israel, and they came to Jerusalem.

³Then all the assembly made a covenant with the king in the house of God. And he said to them, "Behold, the king's son shall reign, as the LORD has said of the sons of David. ⁴This *is* what you shall do: One-third of you entering on the Sabbath, of the priests and the Levites, *shall be* keeping watch over the doors; ⁵one-third *shall be* at the king's house; and one-third at the Gate of the Foundation. All the people *shall be* in the courts of the house of the LORD. ⁶But let no one come into the house of the LORD except the priests and those of the Levites who serve. They may go in, for they *are* holy; but all the people shall keep the watch of the LORD. ⁷And the Levites shall surround the king on all sides, every man with his weapons in his hand; and whoever comes into the house, let him be put to death. You are to be with the king when he comes in and when he goes out."

⁸So the Levites and all Judah did according to all that Jehoiada the priest commanded. And each man took his men who were to be on duty on the Sabbath, with those who were going *off duty* on the Sabbath; for Jehoiada the priest had not dismissed the divisions. ⁹And Jehoiada the priest gave to the captains of hundreds the spears and the large and small shields which *had belonged* to King David, that *were* in the temple of God. ¹⁰Then he set all the people, every man with his weapon in his hand, from the right side of the temple to the left side of the temple, along by the altar and by the temple, all around the

---

14:21 ᵃCalled *Uzziah* in 2 Chronicles 26:1ff, Isaiah 6:1, and elsewhere   **2 Chr.** 22:11 ᵃSpelled *Jehosheba* in 2 Kings 11:2

BAAL WORSHIP IN JERUSALEM (2 Chr. 23:17)

Just as Israel's capital Samaria featured a temple of Baal, so also was there a temple built for Baal in Jerusalem, the capital of Judah (2 Chr. 23:17). It is possible that this building was built by Judah's king Jehoram for his bride Athaliah, the daughter of Jezebel. The new queen brought to Judah the Baal religion of Sidon, her mother's home city, and influenced her husband Jehoram toward the religious behaviors of her father Ahab's kingdom (2 Chr. 21:5, 6).

Unlike in Samaria, however, Yahweh remained the major deity in the capital Jerusalem. The Baal temple was built for a foreign deity worshiped by the royal family, like the temples built by Solomon for his foreign wives (1 Kin. 11:7, 8). Most likely, those who worshiped Baal understood him to be under the control of Yahweh, whose temple remained the central shrine of the kingdom and who would still have been considered the direct ruler of Judah.

When Athaliah seized the throne, however, the god she worshiped became the major deity of the country. Her murder of the descendants of David (2 Chr. 22:10) shows that she exercised her power primarily for her own protection. She did not rule as a regent for Yahweh, and was perhaps responsible for the deterioration of Yahweh's temple, mentioned by the Chronicler (2 Chr. 24:7).

Opposition to Athaliah's rule was instigated by the priests of Yahweh's temple. The "people of the land," who were probably the landowning countrymen (2 Chr. 23:13) remained loyal to Yahweh and joined the revolt to overthrow the queen. Returning to the worship of Yahweh was vital, so that Yahweh would continue to protect the land, and not allow it to be devastated as the northern kingdom was.

---

king. ¹¹And they brought out the king's son, put the crown on him, *gave him* the Testimony,^a and made him king. Then Jehoiada and his sons anointed him, and said, "*Long* live the king!"

Death of Athaliah

¹²Now when Athaliah heard the noise of the people running and praising the king, she came to the people *in* the temple of the LORD. ¹³*When* she looked, there was the king standing by his pillar at the entrance; and the leaders and the trumpeters *were* by the king. All the people of the land were rejoicing and blowing trumpets, also the singers with musical instruments, and those who led in praise. So Athaliah tore her clothes and said, "Treason! Treason!"

23:11 ^aThat is, the Law (compare Exodus 25:16, 21; 31:18)   23:17 ^aLiterally *house*

¹⁴And Jehoiada the priest brought out the captains of hundreds who were set over the army, and said to them, "Take her outside under guard, and slay with the sword whoever follows her." For the priest had said, "Do not kill her in the house of the LORD."

¹⁵So they seized her; and she went by way of the entrance of the Horse Gate *into* the king's house, and they killed her there.

¹⁶Then Jehoiada made a covenant between himself, the people, and the king, that they should be the LORD's people. ¹⁷And all the people went to the temple^a of Baal, and tore it down. They broke in pieces its altars and images, and killed Mattan the priest of Baal before the altars. ¹⁸Also Jehoiada appointed the oversight of the house of the LORD to the hand of the priests, the Levites, whom David had assigned in the house of the LORD, to offer the

---

RELIGION AND WORSHIP

In the Bible, any area belonging to God is marked by His purity and righteousness. God does not permit wrongdoing in His presence, and the earthly king who reigns in His name must also exclude wrongdoing. The priest in 2 Chr. 23:14 considers it obvious that killing is not permitted in the temple, even though in some circumstances killing is permitted before God (1 Sam. 15:33).

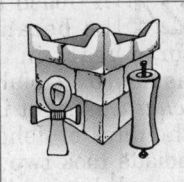

burnt offerings of the LORD, as *it is* written in the Law of Moses, with rejoicing and with singing, *as it was established* by David. ¹⁹And he set the gatekeepers at the gates of the house of the LORD, so that no one *who was* in any way unclean should enter.

²⁰Then he took the captains of hundreds, the nobles, the governors of the people, and all the people of the land, and brought the king down from the house of the LORD; and they went through the Upper Gate to the king's house, and set the king on the throne of the kingdom. ²¹So all the people of the land rejoiced; and the city was quiet, for they had slain Athaliah with the sword.

The Apostasy of Joash and Amaziah

The Chronicler's emphasis on priests and the temple is reflected in the details that he alone presents. His account of Joash's reign (835–796 B.C.), for instance, stresses the role of the king's different advisors. Joash did right while following the lead of the priest Jehoiada, but when the priest was gone, he fell under the wrongful influence of Judah's leaders (2 Chr. 24:15–18). Worse, the king murdered Jehoiada's son Zechariah (24:20–22), a murder still remembered in Jesus' time (Matt. 23:35).

Similarly, only the Chronicler tells us about idolatry during the reign of Amaziah (796–767 B.C.). While both Kings and Chronicles report Judah's victory over Edom (2 Kin. 14:7; 2 Chr. 25:11, 12), the Chronicler notes Amaziah's involvement with Edomite gods (25:14, 15, 20). Amaziah's actions were typical of kings of the ancient world in that he sought to incorporate the captured gods into his own religion. But such behavior was neither normal nor acceptable for a Judahite king.

■ 2 Chronicles 24:1—25:28

2 Chronicles
Joash Repairs the Temple

24 :1 Joash *was* seven years old when he became king, and he reigned forty years in Jerusalem. His mother's name *was* Zibiah of Beersheba. ²Joash did *what was* right in the sight of the LORD all the days of Jehoiada the priest. ³And Jehoiada took two wives for him, and he had sons and daughters.

⁴Now it happened after this *that* Joash set his heart on repairing the house of the LORD. ⁵Then he gathered the priests and the Levites, and said to them, "Go out to the cities of Judah, and gather from all Israel money to repair the house of your God from year to year, and see that you do it quickly."

However the Levites did not do it quickly. ⁶So the king called Jehoiada the chief *priest,* and said to him, "Why have you not required the Levites to bring in from Judah and from Jerusalem the collection, *according to the commandment* of Moses the servant of the LORD and of the assembly of Israel, for the tabernacle of witness?" ⁷For the sons of Athaliah, that wicked woman, had broken into the house of God, and had also presented all the dedicated things of the house of the LORD to the Baals.

⁸Then at the king's command they made a chest, and set it outside at the gate of the house of the LORD. ⁹And they made a proclamation throughout Judah and Jerusalem to bring to the LORD the collection *that* Moses the servant of God *had imposed* on Israel in the wilderness. ¹⁰Then all the leaders and all the people rejoiced, brought their contributions, and put *them* into the chest until all had given. ¹¹So it was, at that time, when the chest was brought to the king's official by the hand of the Levites, and when they saw that *there was* much money, that the king's scribe and the high priest's officer came and emptied the chest, and took it and returned it to its place. Thus they did day by day, and gathered money in abundance.

¹²The king and Jehoiada gave it to those who did the work of the service of the house of the LORD; and they hired masons

TIME CAPSULE   *763 to 752 B.C.*

763	*City of Haran rebels against Assyrians and is destroyed by Asshurdan III*
753	*Zechariah becomes king in Israel*
752	*Shallum assassinates Zechariah and becomes king in Israel*
752	*Menahem assassinates Shallum and becomes king in Israel*
752	*Pekah is an officer in Israel's royal court*

PRIESTS WIELDING POLITICAL POWER (2 Chr. 24:1–3)

In the power structures of the ancient Near East, priests carried both political and religious authority. They were consulted by rulers and free citizens to determine the will of the gods. They were responsible for teaching the moral rules decreed by the gods. In both Mesopotamia and Egypt priests controlled large tracts of land and their temples played the role of modern banks for storing money and making loans. At times in Egypt the priests were said to wield more power than the pharaoh. So priesthoods were able to bring both political and sacred authority to bear on the rulers of their societies.

In Israel and Judah priests also exercised power in relation to kings and rulers. The most important office of the priest was as the intermediary between God and the people; this meant also between God and the king. Priests were expected to bring up future rulers in the proper service and worship of God.

The potential political power of the priesthood is witnessed in the Jerusalem priest Jehoiada. He organized the palace guard to bring about the downfall and execution of Queen Athaliah, resulting in the enthronement of Joash (Jehoash) as king (2 Kin. 11:4–21). Since the new king was so young, the priest Jehoiada served in the influential position of regent and advisor to the king, even securing wives for him (2 Chr. 24:1–3).

---

and carpenters to repair the house of the LORD, and also those who worked in iron and bronze to restore the house of the LORD. ¹³So the workmen labored, and the work was completed by them; they restored the house of God to its original condition and reinforced it. ¹⁴When they had finished, they brought the rest of the money before the king and Jehoiada; they made from it articles for the house of the LORD, articles for serving and offering, spoons and vessels of gold and silver. And they offered burnt offerings in the house of the LORD continually all the days of Jehoiada.

Apostasy of Joash

¹⁵But Jehoiada grew old and was full of days, and he died; *he was* one hundred and thirty years old when he died. ¹⁶And they buried him in the City of David among the kings, because he had done good in Israel, both toward God and His house.

¹⁷Now after the death of Jehoiada the leaders of Judah came and bowed down to the king. And the king listened to them. ¹⁸Therefore they left the house of the LORD God of their fathers, and served wooden images and idols; and wrath came upon Judah and Jerusalem because of their trespass. ¹⁹Yet He sent prophets to them, to bring them back to the LORD; and they

testified against them, but they would not listen.

²⁰Then the Spirit of God came upon Zechariah the son of Jehoiada the priest, who stood above the people, and said to them, "Thus says God: 'Why do you transgress the commandments of the LORD, so that you cannot prosper? Because you have forsaken the LORD, He also has forsaken you.' " ²¹So they conspired against him, and at the command of the king they stoned him with stones in the court of the house of the LORD. ²²Thus Joash the king did not remember the kindness which Jehoiada his father had done to him, but killed his son; and as he died, he said, "The LORD look on *it,* and repay!"

Death of Joash

²³So it happened in the spring of the year *that* the army of Syria came up against him; and they came to Judah and Jerusalem, and destroyed all the leaders of the people from among the people, and sent all their spoil to the king of Damascus. ²⁴For the army of the Syrians came with a small company of men; but the LORD delivered a very great army into their hand, because they had forsaken the LORD God of their fathers. So they executed judgment against Joash. ²⁵And when they had withdrawn from him (for they left him severely wounded), his own servants conspired against him because of the blood of the sonsᵃ of Jehoiada the priest, and killed

24:25 ᵃSeptuagint and Vulgate read *son* (compare verses 20–22).

him on his bed. So he died. And they buried him in the City of David, but they did not bury him in the tombs of the kings.

²⁶These are the ones who conspired against him: Zabad[a] the son of Shimeath the Ammonitess, and Jehozabad the son of Shimrith[b] the Moabitess. ²⁷Now *concerning* his sons, and the many oracles about him, and the repairing of the house of God, indeed they *are* written in the annals of the book of the kings. Then Amaziah his son reigned in his place.

Amaziah Reigns in Judah

25 ¹Amaziah *was* twenty-five years old *when* he became king, and he reigned twenty-nine years in Jerusalem. His mother's name *was* Jehoaddan of Jerusalem. ²And he did *what was* right in the sight of the LORD, but not with a loyal heart.

³Now it happened, as soon as the kingdom was established for him, that he executed his servants who had murdered his father the king. ⁴However he did not execute their children, but *did* as *it is* written in the Law in the Book of Moses, where the LORD commanded, saying, "The fathers shall not be put to death for their children, nor shall the children be put to death for their fathers; but a person shall die for his own sin."[a]

The War Against Edom

⁵Moreover Amaziah gathered Judah together and set over them captains of thousands and captains of hundreds, according to *their* fathers' houses, throughout all Judah and Benjamin; and he numbered them from twenty years old and above, and found them to be three hundred thousand choice *men, able* to go to war, who could handle spear and shield. ⁶He also hired one hundred thousand mighty men of valor from Israel for one hundred talents of silver. ⁷But a man of God came to him, saying, "O king, do not let the army of Israel go with you, for the LORD *is* not with Israel—*not with* any of the children of Ephraim. ⁸But if you go, be gone! Be strong in battle! *Even so,* God shall make you fall before the enemy; for God has power to help and to overthrow."

⁹Then Amaziah said to the man of God, "But what *shall we* do about the hundred talents which I have given to the troops of Israel?"

And the man of God answered, "The

LORD is able to give you much more than this." ¹⁰So Amaziah discharged the troops that had come to him from Ephraim, to go back home. Therefore their anger was greatly aroused against Judah, and they returned home in great anger.

¹¹Then Amaziah strengthened himself, and leading his people, he went to the Valley of Salt and killed ten thousand of the people of Seir. ¹²Also the children of Judah took captive ten thousand alive, brought them to the top of the rock, and cast them down from the top of the rock, so that they all were dashed in pieces.

¹³But as for the soldiers of the army which Amaziah had discharged, so that they would not go with him to battle, they raided the cities of Judah from Samaria to Beth Horon, killed three thousand in them, and took much spoil.

¹⁴Now it was so, after Amaziah came from the slaughter of the Edomites, that he brought the gods of the people of Seir, set them up *to be* his gods, and bowed down before them and burned incense to them. ¹⁵Therefore the anger of the LORD was aroused against Amaziah, and He sent him a prophet who said to him, "Why have you sought the gods of the people, which could not rescue their own people from your hand?"

¹⁶So it was, as he talked with him, that *the king* said to him, "Have we made you the king's counselor? Cease! Why should you be killed?"

Then the prophet ceased, and said, "I know that God has determined to destroy you, because you have done this and have not heeded my advice."

Israel Defeats Judah

¹⁷Now Amaziah king of Judah asked advice and sent to Joash[a] the son of Jehoahaz, the son of Jehu, king of Israel, saying, "Come, let us face one another *in battle.*" ¹⁸And Joash king of Israel sent to Amaziah king of Judah, saying, "The thistle that *was* in Lebanon sent to the cedar that *was* in Lebanon, saying, 'Give your daughter to my son as wife'; and a wild beast that *was* in Lebanon passed by and trampled the thistle. ¹⁹Indeed you say that you have defeated the Edomites, and your

---

24:26 [a]Or *Jozachar* (compare 2 Kings 12:21)
[b]Or *Shomer* (compare 2 Kings 12:21)
25:4 [a]Deuteronomy 24:16   25:17 [a]Spelled *Jehoash* in 2 Kings 14:8ff

ADOPTING THEIR IDOLS (2 Chr. 25:14)

The booty taken in war from defeated peoples often included the statues and images of their gods. Two kings of Judah took idols as booty, David from the Philistines (2 Sam. 5:19–21) and Amaziah from the Edomites (2 Chr. 25:14–16).

Captured idols often were treated as symbols of the gods themselves, as they had been by their own peoples. Such idols were taken to the temples of the victors and placed in positions of honor. It was believed that these gods had chosen the conquerors to rule the invaded territories for the gods. In such cases the gods became a part of the divine bureaucracy of the empire.

Theologically, taking these objects could be good propaganda. When Nebuchadnezzar I (1133–1116 B.C.) returned the image of Marduk to Babylon from Elam, where it had been taken previously as booty, the event was treated as the glorious return of the god and as showing the greatness of Babylon. This return sparked an explosion of theological writing of hymns and poems.

Cyrus II, king of Persia (559–530 B.C.), also realized political advantage by respecting the local gods of conquered peoples. At the beginning of his reign over Babylon he declared that all the images of the peoples conquered by the Neo-Babylonian kings would be returned to their respective lands and their respective peoples. Cyrus believed that all the gods had accepted him as the true ruler for their lands.

When Amaziah adopted the Edomite gods (2 Chr. 25:14), he was following the common practice of victorious kings. But the resulting wrath of Yahweh would show that Amaziah had made the wrong choice (25:16).

heart is lifted up to boast. Stay at home now; why should you meddle with trouble, that you should fall—you and Judah with you?"

20But Amaziah would not heed, for it *came* from God, that He might give them into the hand *of their enemies,* because they sought the gods of Edom. 21So Joash king of Israel went out; and he and Amaziah king of Judah faced one another at Beth Shemesh, which *belongs* to Judah. 22And Judah was defeated by Israel, and every man fled to his tent. 23Then Joash the king of Israel captured Amaziah king of Judah, the son of Joash, the son of Jehoahaz, at Beth Shemesh; and he brought him to Jerusalem, and broke down the wall of Jerusalem from the Gate of Ephraim to the Corner Gate—four hundred cubits. 24And *he took* all the gold and silver, all the arti-cles that were found in the house of God with Obed-Edom, the treasures of the king's house, and hostages, and returned to Samaria.

Death of Amaziah

25Amaziah the son of Joash, king of Judah, lived fifteen years after the death of Joash the son of Jehoahaz, king of Israel. 26Now the rest of the acts of Amaziah, from first to last, indeed *are* they not written in the book of the kings of Judah and Israel? 27After the time that Amaziah turned away from following the LORD, they made a conspiracy against him in Jerusalem, and he fled to Lachish; but they sent after him to Lachish and killed him there. 28Then they brought him on horses and buried him with his fathers in the City of Judah.

POLITICS AND GOVERNMENT

Lachish was the second largest city in Palestine during the 9th and 8th centuries B.C. Solomon's son Rehoboam made it one of his fortified cities (2 Chr. 11:5–10). Two other Judahite kings probably strengthened Lachish's fortifications: Asa (2 Chr. 14:6) and Jehoshaphat (17:2). This fortified city was thus a logical place for Amaziah to seek protection (2 Chr. 25:27).

The Neo-Assyrian Empire

> Assyria quickly established supremacy over Mesopotamia, even over her old rival Babylon.

Most of Israel's national history took place in a power vacuum. The great New Kingdom of Egypt, from which the Israelites had escaped in the Exodus, faded away shortly after Ramesses II (1279–1213 B.C.). The Egyptian dynasties that followed were much weaker. In Mesopotamia, the major power was Assyria, but Assyria remained too busy with internal problems to worry about outlying nations like Israel.

A few times Assyria seemed to revive and look beyond its borders. A monument to the Assyrian king Shalmaneser III (858–824 B.C.) describes how he swept through Israel and forced the Israelite king Jehu to pay tribute to Assyria. Such triumphs were rare, though, until the Assyrian Tiglath-Pileser III (744–727 B.C.) came to power during the reigns of Uzziah in Judah and Jeroboam II in Israel. Tiglath-Pileser quickly established his supremacy over Mesopotamia, even over Assyria's old rival Babylon, and began to expand Assyria's borders.

Few armies were as hated as the Assyrian army. Even in a time and culture that was not known for respecting human life, Assyrian tactics and policies toward their enemies were notoriously brutal. The surrounding nations began to watch Tiglath-Pileser nervously.

Prophetic Account: Jeroboam and Azariah (Uzziah)

The prophetic history, found in 2 Kings, places particular emphasis on the history of the northern kingdom and kings, such as Jeroboam II. Jeroboam was the fourth generation of the Jehu dynasty in Israel, following his grandfather Jehoahaz and father Jehoash to the throne. His long reign of about 41 years (793–753 B.C.) began with an 11-year coregency, during which time Jeroboam ruled together with his father. Upon the death of Jehoash (Joash) in 782 B.C., Jeroboam "sat on his (father's) throne" (2 Kin. 13:13), now a king in his own right.

It was a good time to take leadership in Israel. The Assyrian Empire led by Shalmaneser III had forced Jeroboam's great-grandfather Jehu to pay tribute in 841 B.C. But that empire was now greatly weakened. During the years from 782 to 745 B.C., Assyria was fragmented into various governor-ruled states, and threatened by an expanding kingdom of Urartu to its north. Assyria's weakness allowed Jeroboam to pursue an expansionist policy himself, restoring territory on Israel's northern border (2 Kin. 14:25).

■ 2 Kings 14:23–29

2 Kings
Jeroboam II Reigns in Israel

14 :23 In the fifteenth year of Amaziah the son of Joash, king of Judah, Jeroboam the son of Joash, king of Israel, became king in Samaria, *and reigned* forty-one years. 24And he did evil in the sight of the LORD; he did not depart from all the sins of Jeroboam the son of Nebat, who had made Israel sin. 25He restored the territory of Israel from the entrance of Hamath to the Sea of the Arabah, according to the word of the LORD God of Israel, which He had spoken through His servant Jonah the son of Amittai, the prophet who *was* from Gath Hepher. 26For the LORD saw *that* the affliction of Israel *was* very bitter; and whether bond or free, there was no helper for Israel. 27And the LORD did not say that He would blot out the name of Israel from under heaven; but He saved them by the hand of Jeroboam the son of Joash.

28Now the rest of the acts of Jeroboam, and all that he did—his might, how he made war, and how he recaptured for Israel, from Damascus and Hamath, *what had belonged* to Judah—*are* they not written in the book of the chronicles of the kings of Israel? 29So Jeroboam rested with his fathers, the kings of Israel. Then Zechariah his son reigned in his place.

The Book of Jonah

Jonah the son of Amittai is mentioned in 2 Kin. 14:25, prophesying a victory for the Israelite king Jeroboam II. The book devoted to this prophet does not mention Jonah's activities in Israel. Instead, it tells of a message God gives Jonah to deliver to Nineveh, the capital of Assyria.

Certain details of the Book of Jonah have troubled historians. Leaving aside Jonah's extraordinary encounter with the great fish, scholars have noted that Assyrian records do not mention a mass repentance in Nineveh at this time. Also the title "king of Nineveh" (Jon. 3:6) seems rather small for the ruler of an empire. For these reasons, many have treated the book as an extended parable, not intended to be read as history. Others though, not troubled by accounts of God doing miracles, find no reason to doubt the book's facticity.

Jonah is distinct among prophetic books in that it is a narrative, not a collection of poetic oracles. The message of the book, that God is concerned with all His creation, not just with Israel, is not unique, though. It also appears with other prophets, including Jonah's contemporary Amos.

Two features stand out in the book's theology. One is the universal love and compassion of God for all nations. Another is the sovereignty of God. The relatively unimpressive title "king of Nineveh" serves above all to humble Nineveh's great monarch before the power of Israel's God.

■ Jonah 1:1—4:11

Jonah
Jonah's Disobedience

1 :1 Now the word of the LORD came to Jonah the son of Amittai, saying, ²"Arise, go to Nineveh, that great city, and cry out against it; for their wickedness has come up before Me." ³But Jonah arose to flee to Tarshish from the presence of the LORD. He went down to Joppa, and found a ship going to Tarshish; so he paid the fare, and went down into it, to go with them to Tarshish from the presence of the LORD.

The Storm at Sea

⁴But the LORD sent out a great wind on the sea, and there was a mighty tempest on the sea, so that the ship was about to be broken up.

⁵Then the mariners were afraid; and every man cried out to his god, and threw the cargo that *was* in the ship into the sea, to lighten the load.ᵃ But Jonah had gone down into the lowest parts of the ship, had lain down, and was fast asleep.

⁶So the captain came to him, and said to him, "What do you mean, sleeper? Arise, call on your God; perhaps your God will consider us, so that we may not perish."

⁷And they said to one another, "Come, let us cast lots, that we may know for whose cause this trouble *has come* upon us." So they cast lots, and the lot fell on Jonah. ⁸Then they said to him, "Please tell us! For whose cause *is* this trouble upon us? What is your occupation? And where do you come from? What is your country? And of what people are you?"

⁹So he said to them, "I *am* a Hebrew; and I fear the LORD, the God of heaven, who made the sea and the dry *land.*"

Jonah Thrown into the Sea

¹⁰Then the men were exceedingly afraid, and said to him, "Why have you done this?" For the men knew that he fled from the presence of the LORD, because he had told them. ¹¹Then they said to him, "What shall we do to you that the sea may be calm for us?"—for the sea was growing more tempestuous.

¹²And he said to them, "Pick me up and throw me into the sea; then the sea will become calm for you. For I know that this great tempest *is* because of me."

¹³Nevertheless the men rowed hard to return to land, but they could not, for the sea continued to grow more tempestuous against them. ¹⁴Therefore they cried out to the LORD and said, "We pray, O LORD, please do not let us perish for this man's life, and do not charge us with innocent blood; for You, O LORD, have done as it pleased You." ¹⁵So they picked up Jonah and threw him into the sea, and the sea ceased from its raging. ¹⁶Then the men feared the LORD exceedingly, and offered a sacrifice to the LORD and took vows.

Jonah's Prayer and Deliverance

¹⁷Now the LORD had prepared a great fish to swallow Jonah. And Jonah was in the belly of the fish three days and three nights.

1:5 ᵃLiterally *from upon them*

JONAH SAILS FOR TARSHISH (Jon. 1:3)

When Jonah decided to flee from God, he boarded a "ship going to Tarshish" (Jon. 1:3). The narrative about Jonah indicates that Tarshish was in an opposite direction from Nineveh, but the specific direction is not given.

Tarshish is mentioned over thirty times in Scripture, yet its exact location is uncertain. The kings Jehoshaphat and Ahaziah built ships at Ezion Geber, near the Red Sea, which were intended to "go to Tarshish" (2 Chr. 20:36, 37). Nevertheless, the location of Tarshish was not necessarily in the vicinity of the Red Sea.

The most likely candidate for a location is the Phoenician colony Tartessus in southwestern Spain. This colony was known to the Greek historian Herodotus and the Latin writers Strabo and Pliny. Their writings refer to its rich metal resources. Assyrian records from the 7th century B.C. also mention a place called Tarsisi, but its location is unknown.

Some scholars suppose that the term "Tarshish" may well describe an activity associated with a place rather than a specific geographic location. Besides Strabo and Pliny, the prophets Jeremiah (Jer. 10:9) and Ezekiel (Ezek. 27:12) also knew that Tarshish was a source for metals. In the Hebrew language the word "Tarshish" often refers to a precious stone, usually translated as "beryl" (Ex. 28:20; Ezek. 28:13). Possibly then, "Tarshish" did not identify one specific location, but rather several places where the activity of metalworking took place.

In the Bible, ships are frequently called "ships of Tarshish" (Is. 23:1, 14; 60:9). Tarshish ships were often found in the Mediterranean area, carrying goods from Tyre (Ezek. 27:25). We may never know whether the destination of the Tarshish ship in the Jonah story was one site known as "Tarshish" or one of several sites referred to by that name.

---

2 ¹Then Jonah prayed to the LORD his God from the fish's belly. ²And he said:

"I cried out to the LORD because of my affliction,
And He answered me.

"Out of the belly of Sheol I cried,
And You heard my voice.
³ For You cast me into the deep,
Into the heart of the seas,
And the floods surrounded me;
All Your billows and Your waves passed over me.
⁴ Then I said, 'I have been cast out of Your sight;
Yet I will look again toward Your holy temple.'
⁵ The waters surrounded me, *even* to my soul;
The deep closed around me;
Weeds were wrapped around my head.
⁶ I went down to the moorings of the mountains;
The earth with its bars *closed* behind me forever;
Yet You have brought up my life from the pit,
O LORD, my God.

⁷ "When my soul fainted within me,
I remembered the LORD;
And my prayer went *up* to You,
Into Your holy temple.

⁸ "Those who regard worthless idols
Forsake their own Mercy.
⁹ But I will sacrifice to You
With the voice of thanksgiving;
I will pay what I have vowed.
Salvation *is* of the LORD."

¹⁰So the LORD spoke to the fish, and it vomited Jonah onto dry *land.*

Jonah Preaches at Nineveh

3 ¹Now the word of the LORD came to Jonah the second time, saying, ²"Arise, go to Nineveh, that great city, and preach to it the message that I tell you." ³So Jonah arose and went to Nineveh, according to the word of the LORD. Now Nineveh was an exceedingly great city, a three-day journey[a] *in extent.* ⁴And Jonah began to enter the city on the first day's walk. Then he cried out and said, "Yet forty days, and Nineveh shall be overthrown!"

3:3 ᵃExact meaning unknown

The People of Nineveh Believe

[5]So the people of Nineveh believed God, proclaimed a fast, and put on sackcloth, from the greatest to the least of them. [6]Then word came to the king of Nineveh; and he arose from his throne and laid aside his robe, covered *himself* with sackcloth and sat in ashes. [7]And he caused *it* to be proclaimed and published throughout Nineveh by the decree of the king and his nobles, saying,

Let neither man nor beast, herd nor flock, taste anything; do not let them eat, or drink water. [8]But let man and beast be covered with sackcloth, and cry mightily to God; yes, let every one turn from his evil way and from the violence that is in his hands. [9]Who can tell *if* God will turn and relent, and turn away from His fierce anger, so that we may not perish?

[10]Then God saw their works, that they turned from their evil way; and God relented from the disaster that He had said He would bring upon them, and He did not do it.

Jonah's Anger and God's Kindness

4 [1]But it displeased Jonah exceedingly, and he became angry. [2]So he prayed to the LORD, and said, "Ah, LORD, was not this what I said when I was still in my country? Therefore I fled previously to Tarshish; for I know that You *are* a gracious and merciful God, slow to anger and abundant in lovingkindness, One who relents from doing harm. [3]Therefore now, O LORD, please take my life from me, for *it is* better for me to die than to live!"

[4]Then the LORD said, "*Is it* right for you to be angry?"

[5]So Jonah went out of the city and sat on the east side of the city. There he made himself a shelter and sat under it in the shade, till he might see what would become of the city. [6]And the LORD God prepared a plant[a] and made it come up over Jonah, that it might be shade for his head to deliver him from his misery. So Jonah was very grateful for the plant. [7]But as morning dawned the next day God prepared a worm, and it *so* damaged the plant that it withered. [8]And it happened, when the sun arose, that God prepared a vehement east wind; and the sun beat on Jonah's head, so that he grew faint. Then he wished death for himself, and said, "*It is* better for me to die than to live."

[9]Then God said to Jonah, "*Is it* right for you to be angry about the plant?"

And he said, "*It is* right for me to be angry, even to death!"

[10]But the LORD said, "You have had pity on the plant for which you have not labored, nor made it grow, which came up in a night and perished in a night. [11]And should I not pity Nineveh, that great city, in which are more than one hundred and twenty thousand persons who cannot discern between their right hand and their left—and much livestock?"

4:6 [a]Hebrew *kikayon*, exact identity unknown

The Book of Amos

Two of the minor prophets, Amos and Hosea, spoke to the northern kingdom of Israel during the rise of the Neo-Assyrian Empire. Both took the Assyrian threat very seriously, but their messages were unheard. Comparative prosperity in Israel during the reign of Jeroboam II (793–753 B.C.) had fed complacency.

Amos spoke harshly about this complacency. Although he himself was from Tekoa in the land of Judah (Amos 1:1), Amos was sent by God to prophesy to Israel (see 7:10–17), and he brought with him a deep intolerance for oppression. He raged against the lavish lives of the rich (4:1–3), the oppression of the poor (5:11–15), and the ostentatious religious ceremony of the oppressors (5:21–24).

Even more startling, Amos belittles Israel's precious Exodus heritage. Yes, Israel was chosen from among all the nations, he says, but that just means God will judge Israel more harshly (3:1, 2). Besides, Amos adds,

GEOGRAPHY AND ENVIRONMENT

Nineveh was the capital of the Assyrian Empire and certainly a "great city" by ancient standards (Jon. 3:3). Archaeologists have uncovered a very large temple of Ishtar as well as other public buildings in Nineveh. More than 25,000 tablets were discovered in the palace of Ashurbanipal. Among these tablets were several that related the Mesopotamian flood legend.

God works among other nations, too, such as Ethiopia, Philistia, and Syria (9:7). Given Amos's message, it is not surprising that he was eventually sent home to Judah (7:12, 13).

▼   ■ Amos 1:1—6:7

Amos

1 :1 The words of Amos, who was among the sheepbreeders[a] of Tekoa, which he saw concerning Israel in the days of Uzziah king of Judah, and in the days of Jeroboam the son of Joash, king of Israel, two years before the earthquake. 2And he said:

"The LORD roars from Zion,
And utters His voice from Jerusalem;
The pastures of the shepherds mourn,
And the top of Carmel withers."

Judgment on the Nations

3Thus says the LORD:

"For three transgressions of Damascus,
    and for four,
I will not turn away its *punishment,*
Because they have threshed Gilead
    with implements of iron.
4   But I will send a fire into the house of
        Hazael,
Which shall devour the palaces of
    Ben-Hadad.
5   I will also break the *gate* bar of
        Damascus,
And cut off the inhabitant from the
    Valley of Aven,
And the one who holds the scepter
    from Beth Eden.
The people of Syria shall go captive to
    Kir,"
Says the LORD.

6Thus says the LORD:

"For three transgressions of Gaza, and
    for four,
I will not turn away its *punishment,*
Because they took captive the whole
    captivity
To deliver *them* up to Edom.
7   But I will send a fire upon the wall of
        Gaza,
Which shall devour its palaces.
8   I will cut off the inhabitant from
        Ashdod,
And the one who holds the scepter
    from Ashkelon;

I will turn My hand against Ekron,
And the remnant of the Philistines
    shall perish,"
Says the Lord GOD.

9Thus says the LORD:

"For three transgressions of Tyre, and
    for four,
I will not turn away its *punishment,*
Because they delivered up the whole
    captivity to Edom,
And did not remember the covenant of
    brotherhood.
10   But I will send a fire upon the wall of
        Tyre,
Which shall devour its palaces."

11Thus says the LORD:

"For three transgressions of Edom, and
    for four,
I will not turn away its *punishment,*
Because he pursued his brother with
    the sword,
And cast off all pity;
His anger tore perpetually,
And he kept his wrath forever.
12   But I will send a fire upon Teman,
Which shall devour the palaces of
    Bozrah."

13Thus says the LORD:

"For three transgressions of the people
    of Ammon, and for four,
I will not turn away its *punishment,*

1:1 ᵃCompare 2 Kings 3:4

TIME CAPSULE   *750 B.C.*

750   *Jotham serves as coregent with
          Azariah (Uzziah) in Judah*

750   *Archaeological work at the city of
          Hazor shows occurrence of earth-
          quake*

750   *Clay tablet presents Gilgamesh
          story as a drama*

750   *Earliest description of a chariot
          race, in the Iliad*

750   *Greek city-state culture in Aegean*

750   *Iliad and Odyssey come from oral
          tradition*

FROM A CAPITAL TO A VASSAL CITY (Amos 1:6–8)

During a period from about 1550 to 1150 B.C., Egypt ruled over Canaan, with Gaza serving as the capital city of the Egyptian province. The earliest inscriptional evidence of Gaza shows that it was a well-fortified town as far back as the reign of Seti I of Egypt (1294–1279 B.C.).

During the time of Pharaoh Ramesses III (1184–1153 B.C.), the Sea Peoples invaded Canaan. Although Ramesses stopped their further advance in 1175 B.C., he allowed them to settle in southern Palestine. One group of the Sea Peoples, the Philistines, formed a confederation of five city-states, and Gaza, which had been Canaan's capital under Egypt, continued as the foremost Philistine city.

During the 8th century B.C., when the Neo-Assyrian Empire was threatening nations to the west, the prophet Amos pronounced various judgments on Gaza and on other Philistine cities (Amos 1:6–8). Amos had foreboding news for Gaza: both its walls and palaces would be destroyed by fire (1:7).

The troubles started for Gaza when Tiglath-Pileser was king of Assyria (744–727 B.C.) and a certain Hanno was king of Gaza. Hanno is mentioned in an Assyrian tribute list from 738 B.C. as one king who paid tribute to Assyria. The Assyrian annals note Tiglath-Pileser's campaign in 734 B.C. in which he marched through Syria and Palestine, conquering the city of Gaza. Gaza's royal family was captured and a large tribute imposed. Hanno apparently fled at this time, although he was reinstated later during Tiglath-Pileser's reign.

During the reign of Sargon II of Assyria (721–705 B.C.), Hanno again rebelled and was subsequently led in chains to Assyria. Amos's prophecy (1:7) probably points toward either Gaza's fall in 734 B.C. or to the later campaign by Sargon II. The city that had been a capital of Canaan and a leading Philistine city was now merely a vassal of Assyria.

Because they ripped open the women
  with child in Gilead,
That they might enlarge their
  territory.
14 But I will kindle a fire in the wall of
  Rabbah,
And it shall devour its palaces,
Amid shouting in the day of battle,
And a tempest in the day of the
  whirlwind.
15 Their king shall go into captivity,
He and his princes together,"
Says the LORD.

2 ¹Thus says the LORD:

"For three transgressions of Moab, and
  for four,

I will not turn away its *punishment,*
Because he burned the bones of the
  king of Edom to lime.
2 But I will send a fire upon Moab,
And it shall devour the palaces of
  Kerioth;
Moab shall die with tumult,
With shouting *and* trumpet sound.
3 And I will cut off the judge from its
  midst,
And slay all its princes with him,"
Says the LORD.

Judgment on Judah

⁴Thus says the LORD:

"For three transgressions of Judah,
  and for four,
I will not turn away its *punishment,*

TRADE AND ECONOMICS

In the ancient world, fibers were prepared and woven into fabrics by hand. The complexities of keeping sheep for wool or growing flax for linen only added to the value of cloth. For the poor, the outer garment doubled as a blanket. It could be offered as security for a loan (Amos 2:8), but the law required lenders not to keep this essential item overnight (Ex. 22:26, 27).

Because they have despised the law of
the LORD,
And have not kept His
commandments.
Their lies lead them astray,
Lies which their fathers followed.
5 But I will send a fire upon Judah,
And it shall devour the palaces of
Jerusalem."

Judgment on Israel

⁶Thus says the LORD:

"For three transgressions of Israel, and
for four,
I will not turn away its *punishment,*
Because they sell the righteous for
silver,
And the poor for a pair of sandals.
7 They pant afterᵃ the dust of the earth
which is on the head of the poor,
And pervert the way of the humble.
A man and his father go in to the
same girl,
To defile My holy name.
8 They lie down by every altar on
clothes taken in pledge,
And drink the wine of the condemned
in the house of their god.

9 "Yet *it was* I *who* destroyed the
Amorite before them,
Whose height *was* like the height of
the cedars,
And he *was as* strong as the oaks;
Yet I destroyed his fruit above
And his roots beneath.
10 Also *it was* I *who* brought you up from
the land of Egypt,
And led you forty years through the
wilderness,
To possess the land of the Amorite.
11 I raised up some of your sons as
prophets,
And some of your young men as
Nazirites.
Is it not so, O you children of Israel?"
Says the LORD.
12 "But you gave the Nazirites wine to
drink,
And commanded the prophets saying,
'Do not prophesy!'

13 "Behold, I am weighed down by you,
As a cart full of sheaves is weighed
down.
14 Therefore flight shall perish from the
swift,

The strong shall not strengthen his
power,
Nor shall the mighty deliver himself;
15 He shall not stand who handles the
bow,
The swift of foot shall not escape,
Nor shall he who rides a horse deliver
himself.
16 The most courageous men of might
Shall flee naked in that day,"
Says the LORD.

Authority of the Prophet's Message

3 ¹Hear this word that the LORD has spoken against you, O children of Israel,
against the whole family which I brought
up from the land of Egypt, saying:

2 "You only have I known of all the
families of the earth;
Therefore I will punish you for all
your iniquities."

3 Can two walk together, unless they
are agreed?
4 Will a lion roar in the forest, when he
has no prey?
Will a young lion cry out of his den, if
he has caught nothing?
5 Will a bird fall into a snare on the
earth, where there is no trap for it?
Will a snare spring up from the earth,
if it has caught nothing at all?
6 If a trumpet is blown in a city, will not
the people be afraid?
If there is calamity in a city, will not
the LORD have done *it?*

7 Surely the Lord GOD does nothing,
Unless He reveals His secret to His
servants the prophets.
8 A lion has roared!
Who will not fear?
The Lord GOD has spoken!
Who can but prophesy?

Punishment of Israel's Sins

9 "Proclaim in the palaces at Ashdod,ᵃ
And in the palaces in the land of
Egypt, and say:
'Assemble on the mountains of
Samaria;
See great tumults in her midst,
And the oppressed within her.

2:7 ᵃOr *trample on*   3:9 ᵃFollowing Masoretic
Text; Septuagint reads *Assyria.*

10   For they do not know to do right,'
     Says the LORD,
     'Who store up violence and robbery in
       their palaces.' "

11Therefore thus says the Lord GOD:

"An adversary *shall be* all around the
     land;
He shall sap your strength from you,
And your palaces shall be plundered."

12Thus says the LORD:

"As a shepherd takes from the mouth
     of a lion
Two legs or a piece of an ear,
So shall the children of Israel be
     taken out
Who dwell in Samaria—
In the corner of a bed and on the
     edge[a] of a couch!
13   Hear and testify against the house of
     Jacob,"
     Says the Lord GOD, the God of hosts,
14   "That in the day I punish Israel for
     their transgressions,
I will also visit *destruction* on the
     altars of Bethel;
And the horns of the altar shall be cut
     off
And fall to the ground.
15   I will destroy the winter house along
     with the summer house;
The houses of ivory shall perish,
And the great houses shall have an
     end,"
Says the LORD.

4   1   Hear this word, you cows of Bashan,
     who *are* on the mountain of
     Samaria,
Who oppress the poor,
Who crush the needy,
Who say to your husbands,[a] "Bring
     wine, let us drink!"
2   The Lord GOD has sworn by His
     holiness:
"Behold, the days shall come upon you
When He will take you away with
     fishhooks,
And your posterity with fishhooks.
3   You will go out *through* broken *walls,*
Each one straight ahead of her,

And you will be cast into Harmon,"
     Says the LORD.

4   "Come to Bethel and transgress,
At Gilgal multiply transgression;
Bring your sacrifices every morning,
Your tithes every three days.[a]
5   Offer a sacrifice of thanksgiving with
     leaven,
Proclaim *and* announce the freewill
     offerings;
For this you love,
You children of Israel!"
     Says the Lord GOD.

Israel Did Not Accept Correction

6   "Also I gave you cleanness of teeth in
     all your cities.
And lack of bread in all your places;
Yet you have not returned to Me,"
     Says the LORD.

7   "I also withheld rain from you,
When *there were* still three months to
     the harvest.
I made it rain on one city,
I withheld rain from another city.
One part was rained upon,
And where it did not rain the part
     withered.
8   So two *or* three cities wandered to
     another city to drink water,
But they were not satisfied;
Yet you have not returned to Me,"
     Says the LORD.

9   "I blasted you with blight and mildew.
When your gardens increased,
Your vineyards,
Your fig trees,
And your olive trees,
The locust devoured *them;*
Yet you have not returned to Me,"
     Says the LORD.

10   "I sent among you a plague after the
     manner of Egypt;
Your young men I killed with a sword,
Along with your captive horses;
I made the stench of your camps come
     up into your nostrils;
Yet you have not returned to Me,"
     Says the LORD.

11   "I overthrew *some* of you,
As God overthrew Sodom and
     Gomorrah,

3:12 [a]The Hebrew is uncertain.   4:1 [a]Literally
their lords or *their masters*   4:4 [a]*Or years*
(compare Deuteronomy 14:28)

And you were like a firebrand plucked
    from the burning;
Yet you have not returned to Me,"
Says the LORD.

12 "Therefore thus will I do to you,
        O Israel;
Because I will do this to you,
Prepare to meet your God, O Israel!"

13   For behold,
    He who forms mountains,
    And creates the wind,
    Who declares to man what his[a]
        thought is,
    And makes the morning darkness,
    Who treads the high places of the
        earth—
    The LORD God of hosts is His name.

A Lament for Israel

5 ¹Hear this word which I take up
    against you, a lamentation, O house of
Israel:

2   The virgin of Israel has fallen;
    She will rise no more.
    She lies forsaken on her land;
    There is no one to raise her up.

³For thus says the Lord GOD:

"The city that goes out by a thousand
    Shall have a hundred left,
    And that which goes out by a hundred
    Shall have ten left to the house of
        Israel."

A Call to Repentance

⁴For thus says the LORD to the house of
Israel:

"Seek Me and live;
5   But do not seek Bethel,
    Nor enter Gilgal,
    Nor pass over to Beersheba;
    For Gilgal shall surely go into
        captivity,
    And Bethel shall come to nothing.

6   Seek the LORD and live,
    Lest He break out like fire in the
        house of Joseph,
    And devour it,
    With no one to quench it in Bethel—
7   You who turn justice to wormwood,
    And lay righteousness to rest in the
        earth!"

8   He made the Pleiades and Orion;
    He turns the shadow of death into
        morning
    And makes the day dark as night;
    He calls for the waters of the sea
    And pours them out on the face of the
        earth;
    The LORD is His name.
9   He rains ruin upon the strong,
    So that fury comes upon the fortress.

10   They hate the one who rebukes in the
        gate,
    And they abhor the one who speaks
        uprightly.
11   Therefore, because you tread down the
        poor
    And take grain taxes from him,
    Though you have built houses of hewn
        stone,
    Yet you shall not dwell in them;
    You have planted pleasant vineyards,
    But you shall not drink wine from
        them.
12   For I know your manifold
        transgressions
    And your mighty sins:
    Afflicting the just and taking bribes;
    Diverting the poor from justice at the
        gate.
13   Therefore the prudent keep silent at
        that time,
    For it is an evil time.

14   Seek good and not evil,
    That you may live;
    So the LORD God of hosts will be with
        you,
    As you have spoken.

4:13 ᵃOr His

BELIEFS AND IDEAS

*The "day of the LORD" is a phrase used especially by such prophets as Isaiah, Joel, and
Zephaniah (Is. 13:6; Joel 2:1; Zeph. 1:14). These prophets expected this day to witness
the decisive intervention of God. The day would be a day of darkness and judgment
(Amos 5:18). God would bring history to a full and proper conclusion.*

CELESTIAL IDOLS (Amos 5:26)

"Sikkuth" and "Chiun" (Amos 5:26) are the Hebrew words which correspond to two Accadian terms (*sakkud* and *kayamanu*), both referring to the planet Saturn. Saturn is usually depicted in Mesopotamian texts as the physical planet used for sightings in astrological and astronomical observations. This would not be a reason for Israelites to carry around symbols of Saturn, however.

Some evidence suggests that the god represented by Saturn in Mesopotamia was Ninurta (also called Nimrod). Ninurta was a warrior deity, which may explain why the Israelites were carrying Saturn's image with them. It would have made sense to carry the sign of a divine protector into battle on a standard. This was common practice with ancient armies.

The prophet Amos appears to condemn a god who would have been only vaguely familiar to Israelites. Possibly, then, Amos uses the general terms for Saturn—Sikkuth and Chiun—rather than a specific name of the god, such as Ninurta. His choice does emphasize the foreignness of the Israelites' behavior: they were involving themselves with Assyrian religious elements. By naming a deity of Assyrian and Babylonian religion, Amos was able to refer obliquely to the coming exile of Israel to Assyria (5:27).

15   Hate evil, love good;
      Establish justice in the gate.
      It may be that the LORD God of hosts
      Will be gracious to the remnant of
            Joseph.

The Day of the LORD

16Therefore the LORD God of hosts, the Lord, says this:

      "*There shall be* wailing in all streets,
      And they shall say in all the
            highways,
      'Alas! Alas!'
      They shall call the farmer to
            mourning,
      And skillful lamenters to wailing.
17   In all vineyards *there shall be*
            wailing,
      For I will pass through you,"
      Says the LORD.

18   Woe to you who desire the day of the
            LORD!
      For what good *is* the day of the LORD
            to you?
      It *will be* darkness, and not light.
19   It *will be* as though a man fled from a
            lion,
      And a bear met him!
      Or *as though* he went into the house,
      Leaned his hand on the wall,
      And a serpent bit him!
20   *Is* not the day of the LORD darkness,
            and not light?
      Is it not very dark, with no brightness
            in it?

21   "I hate, I despise your feast days,
      And I do not savor your sacred
            assemblies.
22   Though you offer Me burnt offerings
            and your grain offerings,
      I will not accept *them,*
      Nor will I regard your fattened peace
            offerings.
23   Take away from Me the noise of your
            songs,
      For I will not hear the melody of your
            stringed instruments.
24   But let justice run down like water,
      And righteousness like a mighty
            stream.

25   "Did you offer Me sacrifices and
            offerings
      In the wilderness forty years, O house
            of Israel?
26   You also carried Sikkuth[a] your king[b]
      And Chiun,[c] your idols,
      The star of your gods,
      Which you made for yourselves.
27   Therefore I will send you into
            captivity beyond Damascus,"
      Says the LORD, whose name *is* the God
            of hosts.

5:26 [a]A pagan deity   [b]Septuagint and Vulgate read *tabernacle of Moloch.*   [c]A pagan deity

THE DECLINE OF HAMATH THE GREAT (Amos 6:2, 14)

Hamath was a Syro-Hittite city in central Syria, which had a past going back as far as the 6th millennium B.C. The city is mentioned in the Syrian Ebla texts from the 3rd millennium B.C. and in Hittite texts of the 2nd millennium B.C. The prophet Amos warned that the Assyrians would attack Israel "from the entrance of Hamath" (Amos 6:14), which represented Israel's northern border during the reign of King Jeroboam II (793–753 B.C.).

The city of Hamath had numerous dealings with Israel to its south. During the period of David and Solomon (after 1000 B.C.), Hamath was apparently subordinate to Israel. Later, however, Hamath became independent. The Assyrian sources of Shalmaneser III (858–824 B.C.) say that King Urhilina of Hamath was a ringleader in the coalition against Assyria at the battle of Qarqar in 853 B.C. Under King Zakkur, Hamath enjoyed a period of strength during the early 8th century B.C.

Yet the Bible indicates weakness for Hamath sometime later in the same century. Amos, who prophesied during the reign of Jeroboam II, points out that since "Hamath the great" had fallen, Israel should not think that she herself would survive (Amos 6:2). Furthermore, the writer of Kings records a victory by Jeroboam II over Hamath (2 Kin. 14:28).

If Jeroboam II did in fact defeat Hamath, it is possible that this Syro-Hittite kingdom began to decline during the 8th century B.C. According to Assyrian annals, Hamath was forced to surrender 19 provinces to Assyria in 738 B.C., 15 years after the death of Jeroboam II. By 720 B.C. Hamath had lost its independence and had become a province of Assyria.

Warnings to Zion and Samaria

6 ¹ Woe to you *who are* at ease in Zion,
And trust in Mount Samaria,
Notable persons in the chief nation,
To whom the house of Israel comes!

² Go over to Calneh and see;
And from there go to Hamath the
great;
Then go down to Gath of the
Philistines.
Are you better than these kingdoms?
Or is their territory greater than your
territory?

³ *Woe to* you who put far off the day of
doom,
Who cause the seat of violence to come
near;

⁴ Who lie on beds of ivory,
Stretch out on your couches,
Eat lambs from the flock
And calves from the midst of the stall;

⁵ Who sing idly to the sound of stringed
instruments,
And invent for yourselves musical
instruments like David;

⁶ Who drink wine from bowls,
And anoint yourselves with the best
ointments,
But are not grieved for the affliction of
Joseph.

⁷ Therefore they shall now go captive as
the first of the captives,
And those who recline at banquets
shall be removed.

Destruction to Come

Part of Israel's pride during Amos's time came from the military victories of Jeroboam II (2 Kin. 14:25). Lo Debar and Karnaim, mentioned in Amos 6:13, may have been cities of the Transjordan captured in these campaigns. Amos is scornful of such

FOOD AND DRINK

The custom of eating while reclining seems to have come to Palestine from the East. People ate from common dishes on a low table as they reclined on large couches. The banquets of the rich included musicians, fine foods, and perfumes for the guests. Ivory inlays decorated the wooden parts of luxurious furniture (Amos 6:4). Examples of such inlay survive, showing how it was carved by artisans.

petty boasting. Victory over these insignificant cities pales before the destruction and slaughter that approaches Israel (Amos 6:8–11).

■ Amos 6:8—7:9

Amos

6

:8 The Lord GOD has sworn by Himself,
The LORD God of hosts says:
"I abhor the pride of Jacob,
And hate his palaces;
Therefore I will deliver up *the* city
And all that is in it."

9Then it shall come to pass, that if ten men remain in one house, they shall die. 10And when a relative *of the dead,* with one who will burn *the bodies,* picks up the bodiesa to take them out of the house, he will say to one inside the house, "*Are there* any more with you?"
Then someone will say, "None."
And he will say, "Hold your tongue! For we dare not mention the name of the LORD."

11   For behold, the LORD gives a command:
He will break the great house into bits,
And the little house into pieces.

12   Do horses run on rocks?
Does *one* plow *there* with oxen?
Yet you have turned justice into gall,
And the fruit of righteousness into wormwood,

13   You who rejoice over Lo Debar,a
Who say, "Have we not taken Karnaimb for ourselves
By our own strength?"

14   "But, behold, I will raise up a nation against you,
O house of Israel,"
Says the LORD God of hosts;
"And they will afflict you from the entrance of Hamath
To the Valley of the Arabah."

Vision of the Locusts

7

1Thus the Lord GOD showed me: Behold, He formed locust swarms at the beginning of the late crop; indeed *it was* the late crop after the king's mowings. 2And so it was, when they had finished eating the grass of the land, that I said:

"O Lord GOD, forgive, I pray!
Oh, that Jacob may stand,
For he *is* small!"

3   *So* the LORD relented concerning this.
"It shall not be," said the LORD.

Vision of the Fire

4Thus the Lord GOD showed me: Behold, the Lord GOD called for conflict by fire, and it consumed the great deep and devoured the territory. 5Then I said:

"O Lord GOD, cease, I pray!
Oh, that Jacob may stand,
For he *is* small!"

6   *So* the LORD relented concerning this.
"This also shall not be," said the Lord GOD.

Vision of the Plumb Line

7Thus He showed me: Behold, the Lord stood on a wall *made* with a plumb line, with a plumb line in His hand. 8And the LORD said to me, "Amos, what do you see?"
And I said, "A plumb line."
Then the Lord said:

"Behold, I am setting a plumb line
In the midst of My people Israel;
I will not pass by them anymore.

9   The high places of Isaac shall be desolate,
And the sanctuaries of Israel shall be laid waste.
I will rise with the sword against the house of Jeroboam."

TIME CAPSULE   *750 to 744 B.C.*

750	*Picture of a pulley, from Assyria*
747– 664	*The Cushite Era in Egypt*
747– 716	*Ethiopian ruler named Piankhy is pharaoh in Egypt*
747– 539	*The Babylonian Chronicle*
745	*Political structure of the Neo-Assyrian Empire is fragmented*
744– 727	*Tiglath-Pileser III of Assyria, also called "Pul" (2 Kin. 15:19)*

6:10 aLiterally *bones*   6:13 aLiterally *Nothing*
bLiterally *Horns,* symbol of strength

Confrontation with Amaziah

The account in Amos 7:10–17 of Amos's encounter with Amaziah, the priest of Bethel, includes the message that Amaziah sent to Jeroboam II (7:10, 11). The message reports a prophecy in which Amos predicts that Jeroboam will die violently and that Israel will go into exile. This prophecy thus dates Amos's ministry sometime before the end of Jeroboam's reign in 753 B.C.

Attempts have been made to date Amos's ministry by an earthquake which occurred during the reign of Judah's King Azariah (or Uzziah), but which was still remembered hundreds of years later (see Zech. 14:5). Amos received his vision "two years before the earthquake" (Amos 1:1).

Unfortunately, an exact date for this earthquake is uncertain. Archaeological work at the city of Hazor shows evidence that it happened sometime in the mid-8th century B.C. The Jewish historian Josephus connects the earthquake with the violation of the priest's office by Azariah (2 Chr. 26:16–20). When Azariah's violation resulted in leprosy, his son Jotham governed with him as coregent (2 Kin. 15:5). Jotham's 10-year coregency with Azariah began in 750 B.C., so following Josephus would place Amos's ministry a few years before 750.

▼   ■ Amos 7:10—9:15

Amos
Amaziah's Complaint

7 **:10** Then Amaziah the priest of Bethel sent to Jeroboam king of Israel, saying, "Amos has conspired against you in the midst of the house of Israel. The land is not able to bear all his words. ¹¹For thus Amos has said:

'Jeroboam shall die by the sword,
And Israel shall surely be led away captive
From their own land.' "

¹²Then Amaziah said to Amos:

"Go, you seer!
Flee to the land of Judah.
There eat bread,
And there prophesy.
13   But never again prophesy at Bethel,
For it *is* the king's sanctuary,
And it *is* the royal residence."

¹⁴Then Amos answered, and said to Amaziah:

"I *was* no prophet,
Nor *was* I a son of a prophet,
But I *was* a sheepbreeder[a]
And a tender of sycamore fruit.
15   Then the LORD took me as I followed the flock,
And the LORD said to me,
'Go, prophesy to My people Israel.'
16   Now therefore, hear the word of the LORD:
You say, 'Do not prophesy against Israel,
And do not spout against the house of Isaac.'

¹⁷"Therefore thus says the LORD:

'Your wife shall be a harlot in the city;
Your sons and daughters shall fall by the sword;
Your land shall be divided by *survey* line;
You shall die in a defiled land;
And Israel shall surely be led away captive
From his own land.' "

Vision of the Summer Fruit

8 ¹Thus the Lord GOD showed me: Behold, a basket of summer fruit. ²And He said, "Amos, what do you see?"
So I said, "A basket of summer fruit."
Then the LORD said to me:

7:14   ᵃCompare 2 Kings 3:4

AGRICULTURE AND HERDING

The sycamore fruit of Amos was a kind of fig (ficus sycomorus). When the fruit is young, small cuts are made in it. Experience has shown that doing this improves the quality of the mature fruit. It is a tedious process, and the "tender of sycamore fruit" (Amos 7:14) was not considered to be employed in a high status job.

"The end has come upon My people
Israel;
I will not pass by them anymore.
3   And the songs of the temple
Shall be wailing in that day,"
Says the Lord GOD—
"Many dead bodies everywhere,
They shall be thrown out in silence."

4   Hear this, you who swallow up[a] the
needy,
And make the poor of the land fail,

5Saying:

"When will the New Moon be past,
That we may sell grain?
And the Sabbath,
That we may trade wheat?
Making the ephah small and the
shekel large,
Falsifying the scales by deceit,
6   That we may buy the poor for silver,
And the needy for a pair of sandals—
Even sell the bad wheat?"

7   The LORD has sworn by the pride of
Jacob:
"Surely I will never forget any of their
works.
8   Shall the land not tremble for this,
And everyone mourn who dwells in it?
All of it shall swell like the River,[a]
Heave and subside
Like the River of Egypt.

9   "And it shall come to pass in that day,"
says the Lord GOD,
"That I will make the sun go down at
noon,
And I will darken the earth in broad
daylight;
10   I will turn your feasts into mourning,
And all your songs into lamentation;
I will bring sackcloth on every waist,
And baldness on every head;
I will make it like mourning for an
only *son*,
And its end like a bitter day.

11   "Behold, the days are coming," says the
Lord GOD,

"That I will send a famine on the land,
Not a famine of bread,
Nor a thirst for water,
But of hearing the words of the LORD.
12   They shall wander from sea to sea,
And from north to east;
They shall run to and fro, seeking the
word of the LORD,
But shall not find *it*.

13   "In that day the fair virgins
And strong young men
Shall faint from thirst.
14   Those who swear by the sin[a] of
Samaria,
Who say,
'As your god lives, O Dan!'
And, 'As the way of Beersheba lives!'
They shall fall and never rise again."

The Destruction of Israel

9 1I saw the Lord standing by the altar,
and He said:

"Strike the doorposts, that the
thresholds may shake,
And break them on the heads of them
all.
I will slay the last of them with the
sword.
He who flees from them shall not get
away,
And he who escapes from them shall
not be delivered.

2   "Though they dig into hell,[a]
From there My hand shall take them;
Though they climb up to heaven,
From there I will bring them down;
3   And though they hide themselves on
top of Carmel,
From there I will search and take
them;
Though they hide from My sight at
the bottom of the sea,
From there I will command the
serpent, and it shall bite them;
4   Though they go into captivity before
their enemies,
From there I will command the sword,
And it shall slay them.
I will set My eyes on them for harm
and not for good."

5   The Lord GOD of hosts,
He who touches the earth and it
melts,

8:4 [a]Or *trample on* (compare 2:7)   8:8 [a]That is,
the Nile; some Hebrew manuscripts, Septuagint,
Syriac, Targum, and Vulgate read *River;* Masoretic
Text reads *the light.*   8:14 [a]Or *Ashima,* a Syrian
goddess   9:2 [a]Or *Sheol*

GOD IS THE GOD OF ALL PEOPLES (Amos 9:7)

The prophet Amos recognized that Israel was not the only people who had received Yahweh's mercy. In a series of short poetic statements, Amos describes the universal power of Yahweh and reminds the Israelites that God is not concerned with them alone (Amos 9:7).

The prophet cites examples of three other peoples for whom Yahweh cares and for whom He has acted in the past. This places the sin of Israel in a much broader context. There are others for whom God needs to work, and Israel must not put herself above the other nations or assume that she will be treated differently from the other nations.

The three peoples named by Amos are the Ethiopians, Philistines, and Syrians. Yahweh's mercy thus reaches to a distant people (the Ethiopians), as well as to Israel's neighboring enemies (the Philistines and Syrians). He has brought to Canaan people from the centers of differing cultures: from Egypt (Egyptian cultural sphere), from Caphtor (East Mediterranean cultural sphere), and from Kir (Mesopotamian cultural sphere). Yahweh's concern is for all people.

It is not important to Amos that none of the other three peoples worshiped Yahweh. Israel had been called to be God's special people and to worship Yahweh alone, but had not done so. Now, as easily as God had brought these peoples into the land, He would scatter the Israelites from out of the land and into the world.

And all who dwell there mourn;
All of it shall swell like the River,[a]
And subside like the River of Egypt.
6 He who builds His layers in the sky,
And has founded His strata in the
      earth;
Who calls for the waters of the sea,
And pours them out on the face of the
      earth—
The LORD *is* His name.

7 "*Are* you not like the people of Ethiopia
      to Me,
O children of Israel?" says the LORD.
"Did I not bring up Israel from the
      land of Egypt,
The Philistines from Caphtor,
And the Syrians from Kir?

8 "Behold, the eyes of the Lord GOD *are*
      on the sinful kingdom,
And I will destroy it from the face of
      the earth;
Yet I will not utterly destroy the house
      of Jacob,"
Says the LORD.

9 "For surely I will command,
And will sift the house of Israel
      among all nations,
As *grain* is sifted in a sieve;
Yet not the smallest grain shall fall to
      the ground.

10 All the sinners of My people shall die
      by the sword,
Who say, 'The calamity shall not
      overtake nor confront us.'

Israel Will Be Restored

11 "On that day I will raise up
The tabernacle[a] of David, which has
      fallen down,
And repair its damages;
I will raise up its ruins,
And rebuild it as in the days of old;
12 That they may possess the remnant of
      Edom,[a]
And all the Gentiles who are called by
      My name,"
Says the LORD who does this thing.

13 "Behold, the days are coming," says the
      LORD,
"When the plowman shall overtake the
      reaper,
And the treader of grapes him who
      sows seed;
The mountains shall drip with sweet
      wine,
And all the hills shall flow *with it.*
14 I will bring back the captives of My
      people Israel;

9:5 [a]That is, the Nile   9:11 [a]Literally *booth*, figure
of a deposed dynasty   9:12 [a]Septuagint reads
mankind.

They shall build the waste cities and
   inhabit *them;*
They shall plant vineyards and drink
   wine from them;
They shall also make gardens and eat
   fruit from them.
15 I will plant them in their land,
And no longer shall they be pulled up
From the land I have given them,"
Says the LORD your God.

The Book of Hosea

Hosea is the only native northern Israelite among the writing prophets. Although
active at the same time as Amos, Hosea's
message is quite different in its focus. Where
Amos spoke about oppression, poverty, and injustice, Hosea speaks against the worship of
the Canaanite deities, such as Baal and
Asherah. These religions stressed rituals that
were designed to promote the fertility of the
land; among these rituals was sexual intercourse with official cult prostitutes.

Prostitution, or harlotry, becomes a major
theme in Hosea, partly through the prophet's
own family experience (Hos. 1—3). Israel is
the bride of God, and once the marriage was
happy (Hos. 2:14, 15; 11:1). By worshiping
other gods, though, Israel has become a harlot. God alternately rages against His unfaithful
wife and tenderly longs for reconciliation (6:4;
11:8, 9). The book ends with an impassioned
appeal for Israel to "return" and a promise
that, if she will, then God will become the true
fertility God to His wayward people.

■ Hosea 1:1—3:5

Hosea

1 :1 The word of the LORD that came to
Hosea the son of Beeri, in the days of
Uzziah, Jotham, Ahaz, *and* Hezekiah,

1:6 ªLiterally *No-Mercy* ᵇOr *That I may forgive them
at all*   1:9 ªLiterally *Not-My-People*

---

kings of Judah, and in the days of Jeroboam the son of Joash, king of Israel.

The Family of Hosea

2When the LORD began to speak by Hosea,
the LORD said to Hosea:

> "Go, take yourself a wife of harlotry
> And children of harlotry,
> For the land has committed great
>   harlotry
> *By departing* from the LORD."

3So he went and took Gomer the daughter
of Diblaim, and she conceived and bore him
a son. 4Then the LORD said to him:

> "Call his name Jezreel,
> For in a little *while*
> I will avenge the bloodshed of Jezreel
>   on the house of Jehu,
> And bring an end to the kingdom of
>   the house of Israel.
> 5 It shall come to pass in that day
> That I will break the bow of Israel in
>   the Valley of Jezreel."

6And she conceived again and bore a
daughter. Then *God* said to him:

> "Call her name Lo-Ruhamah,ª
> For I will no longer have mercy on the
>   house of Israel,
> But I will utterly take them away.ᵇ
> 7 Yet I will have mercy on the house of
>   Judah,
> Will save them by the LORD their God,
> And will not save them by bow,
> Nor by sword or battle,
> By horses or horsemen."

8Now when she had weaned Lo-
Ruhamah, she conceived and bore a son.
9Then *God* said:

> "Call his name Lo-Ammi,ª
> For you *are* not My people,
> And I will not be your *God.*

ARTS AND LITERATURE

*The prophet revealed what God had said through the names given to the children (Hos.
1:4–7). By themselves, these names convey little, but when their meaning was known,
the children became a perpetual reminder of what God was saying to the people. The
prophets used actions with particular symbolic meanings, making their words public,
memorable, and definite.*

The Restoration of Israel

10 "Yet the number of the children of
     Israel
  Shall be as the sand of the sea,
  Which cannot be measured or
     numbered.
  And it shall come to pass
  In the place where it was said to
     them,
  'You *are* not My people,'a
  There it shall be said to them,
  '*You are* sons of the living God.'
11 Then the children of Judah and the
     children of Israel
  Shall be gathered together,
  And appoint for themselves one head;
  And they shall come up out of the
     land,
  For great *will be* the day of Jezreel!

2 ¹ Say to your brethren, 'My people,'a
   And to your sisters, 'Mercyb *is
   shown.*'

God's Unfaithful People

2 "Bring charges against your mother,
     bring charges;
  For she *is* not My wife, nor *am* I her
     Husband!
  Let her put away her harlotries from
     her sight,
  And her adulteries from between her
     breasts;
3 Lest I strip her naked
  And expose her, as in the day she was
     born,
  And make her like a wilderness,
  And set her like a dry land,
  And slay her with thirst.

4 "I will not have mercy on her children,
  For they *are* the children of harlotry.

---

5 For their mother has played the
     harlot;
  She who conceived them has behaved
     shamefully.
  For she said, 'I will go after my lovers,
  Who give *me* my bread and my water,
  My wool and my linen,
  My oil and my drink.'

6 "Therefore, behold,
  I will hedge up your way with thorns,
  And wall her in,
  So that she cannot find her paths.
7 She will chase her lovers,
  But not overtake them;
  Yes, she will seek them, but not find
     them.
  Then she will say,
  'I will go and return to my first
     husband,
  For then *it was* better for me than
     now.'
8 For she did not know
  That I gave her grain, new wine, and
     oil,
  And multiplied her silver and gold—
  Which they prepared for Baal.

9 "Therefore I will return and take away
  My grain in its time
  And My new wine in its season,
  And will take back My wool and My
     linen,
  Given to cover her nakedness.
10 Now I will uncover her lewdness in
     the sight of her lovers,
  And no one shall deliver her from My
     hand.
11 I will also cause all her mirth to cease,
  Her feast days,
  Her New Moons,
  Her Sabbaths—
  All her appointed feasts.

12 "And I will destroy her vines and her
     fig trees,
  Of which she has said,
  'These *are* my wages that my lovers
     have given me.'
  So I will make them a forest,
  And the beasts of the field shall eat
     them.
13 I will punish her
  For the days of the Baals to which she
     burned incense.

TIME CAPSULE 743 to 740 B.C.

743   Tiglath-Pileser III wins battle against
      Ararat's Sarduri II

742– Period of Assyria's greatest impe-
630   rial power

742   Pekahiah becomes king in Israel

740   Jotham becomes sole king in Judah

740   Pekah assassinates Pekahiah and
      becomes sole king in Israel

740   Isaiah's call consists of a vision of
      God

1:10 aHebrew *lo-ammi* (compare verse 9)
2:1 aHebrew *Ammi* (compare 1:9, 10) bHebrew
Ruhamah (compare 1:6)

She decked herself with her earrings
   and jewelry,
And went after her lovers;
But Me she forgot," says the LORD.

God's Mercy on His People

14   "Therefore, behold, I will allure her,
   Will bring her into the wilderness,
   And speak comfort to her.
15   I will give her her vineyards from
      there,
   And the Valley of Achor as a door of
      hope;
   She shall sing there,
   As in the days of her youth,
   As in the day when she came up from
      the land of Egypt.

16   "And it shall be, in that day,"
   Says the LORD,
   "*That* you will call Me 'My Husband,'[a]
   And no longer call Me 'My Master,'[b]
17   For I will take from her mouth the
      names of the Baals,
   And they shall be remembered by
      their name no more.
18   In that day I will make a covenant for
      them
   With the beasts of the field,
   With the birds of the air,
   And *with* the creeping things of the
      ground.
   Bow and sword of battle I will shatter
      from the earth,
   To make them lie down safely.

19   "I will betroth you to Me forever;
   Yes, I will betroth you to Me
   In righteousness and justice,
   In lovingkindness and mercy;
20   I will betroth you to Me in
      faithfulness,
   And you shall know the LORD.

21   "It shall come to pass in that day
   That I will answer," says the LORD;
   "I will answer the heavens,
   And they shall answer the earth.
22   The earth shall answer
   With grain,
   With new wine,
   And with oil;
   They shall answer Jezreel.[a]

23   Then I will sow her for Myself in the
      earth,
   And I will have mercy on *her who had*
      not obtained mercy;[a]
   Then I will say to *those who were* not
      My people,[b]
   'You *are* My people!'
   And they shall say, '*You are* my God!'"

Israel Will Return to God

3 [1]Then the LORD said to me, "Go again,
love a woman *who is* loved by a lover[a]
and is committing adultery, just like the
love of the LORD for the children of Israel,
who look to other gods and love *the* raisin
cakes *of the pagans.*"

[2]So I bought her for myself for fifteen
shekels of silver, and one and one-half
homers of barley. [3]And I said to her, "You
shall stay with me many days; you shall
not play the harlot, nor shall you have a
man—so, too, *will* I *be* toward you."

[4]For the children of Israel shall abide
many days without king or prince, without
sacrifice or *sacred* pillar, without ephod or
teraphim. [5]Afterward the children of Israel
shall return and seek the LORD their God
and David their king. They shall fear the
LORD and His goodness in the latter days.

The Dates of Hosea's Ministry

The names of five kings indicate the historical period during which Hosea prophesied. According to Hos. 1:1, his ministry is dated by the reign of Israel's Jeroboam II (793–753 B.C.), and by Judah's kings Uzziah, Jotham, Ahaz, and Hezekiah. The total period of the Judahite kings was from about 792 to 686 B.C., although there is no reason to believe Hosea's ministry extended past the fall of Israel in 722 B.C.

The words of Hosea are not arranged in the book chronologically, but rather by thematic and poetic connections. Moreover, it is almost impossible to suggest a chronology for Hosea's oracles, since they are vague concerning their historical context. Most could apply to any of a number of historical situations. Knowing some details about the last years of the northern kingdom, however, does help to illuminate a few of Hosea's many obscure passages.

The account of Hosea's unhappy marriage (Hos. 1—3) traces Israel's apostasy from Yahweh, and serves as an introduction to the themes and language of the book. This section

---

2:16 [a]Hebrew *Ishi*   [b]Hebrew *Baali*   2:22 [a]Literally
God Will Sow   2:23 [a]Hebrew *lo-ruhamah*
[b]Hebrew *lo-ammi*   3:1 [a]Literally *friend* or *husband*

is followed by a statement of God's charges against Israel (4:1—5:7), which possibly reflects the political stability and prosperity of the last years of Jeroboam's rule up to 753 B.C. As already indicated by Hosea's contemporary Amos (see "The Book of Amos" at Amos 1:1), the people had become complacent and comfortable with the social inequality and religious apostasy of their time (Hos. 2:8; 4:11–13).

■ Hosea 4:1—5:7

Hosea

God's Charge Against Israel

4 :1 Hear the word of the LORD,
      You children of Israel,
   For the LORD *brings* a charge against
      the inhabitants of the land:

   "There is no truth or mercy
      Or knowledge of God in the land.
2 *By* swearing and lying,
      Killing and stealing and committing
         adultery,
      They break all restraint,
      With bloodshed upon bloodshed.
3 Therefore the land will mourn;
      And everyone who dwells there will
         waste away
      With the beasts of the field
      And the birds of the air;
      Even the fish of the sea will be taken
         away.

4 "Now let no man contend, or rebuke
      another;
      For your people *are* like those who
         contend with the priest.
5 Therefore you shall stumble in the
         day;
      The prophet also shall stumble with
         you in the night;
      And I will destroy your mother.
6 My people are destroyed for lack of
         knowledge.
      Because you have rejected knowledge,
      I also will reject you from being priest
         for Me;

   Because you have forgotten the law of
      your God,
   I also will forget your children.

7 "The more they increased,
      The more they sinned against Me;
   I will change[a] their glory[b] into shame.
8 They eat up the sin of My people;
   They set their heart on their iniquity.
9 And it shall be: like people, like priest.
   So I will punish them for their ways,
   And reward them for their deeds.
10 For they shall eat, but not have
      enough;
   They shall commit harlotry, but not
      increase;
   Because they have ceased obeying the
      LORD.

The Idolatry of Israel

11 "Harlotry, wine, and new wine enslave
      the heart.
12 My people ask counsel from their
      wooden *idols,*
   And their staff informs them.
   For the spirit of harlotry has caused
      them to stray,
   And they have played the harlot
      against their God.
13 They offer sacrifices on the
      mountaintops,
   And burn incense on the hills,
   Under oaks, poplars, and terebinths,
   Because their shade *is* good.
   Therefore your daughters commit
      harlotry,
   And your brides commit adultery.

14 "I will not punish your daughters when
      they commit harlotry,
   Nor your brides when they commit
      adultery;

4:7 [a]Following Masoretic Text, Septuagint, and Vulgate; scribal tradition, Syriac, and Targum read *They will change.* [b]Following Masoretic Text, Septuagint, Syriac, Targum, and Vulgate; scribal tradition reads *My glory.*

CULTS AND SUPERNATURAL

The religion of Canaan was practiced in innumerable small shrines located on hilltops and in groves of trees. The idols consisted of stone pillars and wooden poles. There were prostitutes of both sexes present at the shrines, and their activities were encouraged and protected, if not required, by the local gods (Hos. 4:14).

For *the men* themselves go apart with
harlots,
And offer sacrifices with a ritual
harlot.[a]
Therefore people *who* do not
understand will be trampled.

15 "Though you, Israel, play the harlot,
Let not Judah offend.
Do not come up to Gilgal,
Nor go up to Beth Aven,
Nor swear an oath, *saying,* 'As the
LORD lives'—

16 "For Israel is stubborn
Like a stubborn calf;
Now the LORD will let them forage
Like a lamb in open country.

17 "Ephraim *is* joined to idols,
Let him alone.
18 Their drink is rebellion,
They commit harlotry continually.
Her rulers dearly[a] love dishonor.
19 The wind has wrapped her up in its
wings,
And they shall be ashamed because of
their sacrifices.

Impending Judgment on Israel and Judah

5 1 "Hear this, O priests!
Take heed, O house of Israel!
Give ear, O house of the king!
For yours *is* the judgment,
Because you have been a snare to
Mizpah
And a net spread on Tabor.
2 The revolters are deeply involved in
slaughter,
Though I rebuke them all.
3 I know Ephraim,
And Israel is not hidden from Me;
For now, O Ephraim, you commit
harlotry;
Israel is defiled.

4 "They do not direct their deeds
Toward turning to their God,
For the spirit of harlotry is in their
midst,
And they do not know the LORD.
5 The pride of Israel testifies to his face;

Therefore Israel and Ephraim stumble
in their iniquity;
Judah also stumbles with them.

6 "With their flocks and herds
They shall go to seek the LORD,
But they will not find *Him;*
He has withdrawn Himself from them.
7 They have dealt treacherously with
the LORD,
For they have begotten pagan
children.
Now a New Moon shall devour them
and their heritage."

Hosea and Assyria

During the 30 years from the end of
Jeroboam's reign in 753 B.C. to Samaria's fall
in 722, the situation in northern Israel
changed drastically. Political life suffered a
rapid change of rulers occasioned by intrigue
and assassinations. A resurgent Assyria, in
successive attacks, succeeded in stripping
away more and more of Israel's territory.

Some of Hosea's oracles may reflect the
confusion of this time. In 743 B.C. Tiglath-
Pileser III of Assyria campaigned against the
Syro-Palestinian states. Israel under King
Pekah (752–732 B.C.) joined Aram (Syria),
hoping to stop the Assyrian advance. Pekah
and Aram also pressured Judah to join them,
prompting the Syro-Ephraimite War from 735
to 732 B.C. (see "Israel and Syria Besiege Judah" at Is. 7:1). Both Judah and Israel (called
"Ephraim") suffer, fighting each other (Hos.
5:10–14).

■ Hosea 5:8—6:11

Hosea

5 :8 "Blow the ram's horn in Gibeah,
The trumpet in Ramah!
Cry aloud *at* Beth Aven,
'*Look* behind you, O Benjamin!'
9 Ephraim shall be desolate in the day
of rebuke;
Among the tribes of Israel I make
known what is sure.

10 "The princes of Judah are like those
who remove a landmark;
I will pour out My wrath on them like
water.
11 Ephraim is oppressed *and* broken in
judgment,

4:14 ᵃCompare Deuteronomy 23:18
4:18 ᵃHebrew is difficult; a Jewish tradition reads
Her rulers shamefully love, 'Give!'

Because he willingly walked by
human precept.

12 Therefore I *will be* to Ephraim like a
moth,
And to the house of Judah like
rottenness.

13 "When Ephraim saw his sickness,
And Judah *saw* his wound,
Then Ephraim went to Assyria
And sent to King Jareb;
Yet he cannot cure you,
Nor heal you of your wound.

14 For I *will be* like a lion to Ephraim,
And like a young lion to the house of
Judah.
I, *even* I, will tear *them* and go away;
I will take *them* away, and no one
shall rescue.

15 I will return again to My place
Till they acknowledge their offense.
Then they will seek My face;
In their affliction they will earnestly
seek Me."

A Call to Repentance

6 1 Come, and let us return to the LORD;
For He has torn, but He will heal us;
He has stricken, but He will bind us
up.

2 After two days He will revive us;
On the third day He will raise us up,
That we may live in His sight.

3 Let us know,
Let us pursue the knowledge of the
LORD.
His going forth is established as the
morning;
He will come to us like the rain,
Like the latter *and* former rain to the
earth.

Impenitence of Israel and Judah

4 "O Ephraim, what shall I do to you?
O Judah, what shall I do to you?
For your faithfulness is like a morning
cloud,
And like the early dew it goes away.

5 Therefore I have hewn *them* by the
prophets,
I have slain them by the words of My
mouth;
And your judgments *are like* light *that*
goes forth.

6 For I desire mercy and not sacrifice,
And the knowledge of God more than
burnt offerings.

7 "But like men[a] they transgressed the
covenant;
There they dealt treacherously with
Me.

8 Gilead *is* a city of evildoers
And defiled with blood.

9 As bands of robbers lie in wait for a
man,
So the company of priests murder on
the way to Shechem;
Surely they commit lewdness.

10 I have seen a horrible thing in the
house of Israel:
There *is* the harlotry of Ephraim;
Israel is defiled.

11 Also, O Judah, a harvest is appointed
for you,
When I return the captives of My
people."

6:7 [a]Or *like Adam*

Hosea and Israel's Kings

"All their kings have fallen" (Hos. 7:7).
This was an appropriate description of instability in the declining northern kingdom. Within 20 years, four of Israel's kings had been assassinated: Zechariah in 753 B.C., Shallum in 752 (within 7 months of Zechariah), Pekahiah in 740, and Pekah in 732. After the Syro-Ephraimite War ended in 732, Israel was in its final years as a kingdom.

Hoshea (732–722 B.C.) was the last king of northern Israel. He led a pro-Assyrian conspiracy against Israel's king Pekah, assassinating him and seizing the throne himself (2 Kin. 15:30). At first Israel, under Hoshea, became a vassal of Assyria (Hos. 5:13; 14:3). Sometime after the death of the Assyrian king Tiglath-Pileser III in 727 B.C., Hoshea stopped paying tribute and turned to Egypt for help (2 Kin. 17:4). The prophet Hosea warns that an alliance with Egypt will be of no avail (Hos. 7:11, 16).

Hoshea's refusal to pay tribute to Assyria had dire consequences. The Assyrian king Shalmaneser V (726–722 B.C.) laid siege to Samaria from 725 to 722 B.C. and, at some point, imprisoned Hoshea. Samaria lost her king (Hos. 10:3, 7; 13:10, 11). The policy pursued by King Hoshea to lean upon Egypt for help against Assyria would not succeed in preserving the nation from destruction (11:5, 6; 13:16).

■ Hosea 7:1—14:9

Hosea

7 :1 "When I would have healed Israel,
Then the iniquity of Ephraim was
uncovered,
And the wickedness of Samaria.
For they have committed fraud;
A thief comes in;
A band of robbers takes spoil outside.

2 They do not consider in their hearts
That I remember all their wickedness;
Now their own deeds have surrounded
them;
They are before My face.

3 They make a king glad with their
wickedness,
And princes with their lies.

4 "They *are* all adulterers.
Like an oven heated by a baker—
He ceases stirring *the fire* after
kneading the dough,
Until it is leavened.

5 In the day of our king
Princes have made *him* sick, inflamed
with wine;
He stretched out his hand with
scoffers.

6 They prepare their heart like an oven,
While they lie in wait;
Their baker[a] sleeps all night;
In the morning it burns like a flaming
fire.

7 They are all hot, like an oven,
And have devoured their judges;
All their kings have fallen.
None among them calls upon Me.

8 "Ephraim has mixed himself among
the peoples;
Ephraim is a cake unturned.

9 Aliens have devoured his strength,
But he does not know *it;*
Yes, gray hairs are here and there on
him,
Yet he does not know *it.*

10 And the pride of Israel testifies to his
face,

But they do not return to the LORD
their God,
Nor seek Him for all this.

Futile Reliance on the Nations

11 "Ephraim also is like a silly dove,
without sense—
They call to Egypt,
They go to Assyria.

12 Wherever they go, I will spread My
net on them;
I will bring them down like birds of
the air;
I will chastise them
According to what their congregation
has heard.

13 "Woe to them, for they have fled from
Me!
Destruction to them,
Because they have transgressed
against Me!
Though I redeemed them,
Yet they have spoken lies against Me.

14 They did not cry out to Me with their
heart
When they wailed upon their beds.

"They assemble together for[a] grain and
new wine,
They rebel against Me;[b]

15 Though I disciplined *and*
strengthened their arms,
Yet they devise evil against Me;

16 They return, *but* not to the Most
High;[a]
They are like a treacherous bow.
Their princes shall fall by the sword
For the cursings of their tongue.
This *shall be* their derision in the land
of Egypt.

7:6 [a]Following Masoretic Text and Vulgate; Syriac and
Targum read *Their anger;* Septuagint reads
Ephraim.   7:14 [a]Following Masoretic Text and
Targum; Vulgate reads *thought upon;* Septuagint reads
slashed themselves for (compare 1 Kings 18:28).
[b]Following Masoretic Text, Syriac, and Targum;
Septuagint omits *They rebel against Me;* Vulgate reads
They departed from Me.   7:16 [a]Or *upward*

TIME CAPSULE   *738 to 735 B.C.*

738   *King Enel of Hamath loses 19
provinces to the Assyrians*

738   *Samaria, Damascus, and Tyre pay
tribute to Assyria*

**737–
735**   *Rezin of Damascus leads coalition
against Assyria*

**735–
732**   *The Syro-Ephraimite War*

735   *Ahaz serves as coregent with
Jotham in Judah*

DESTROYING THEIR IDOLS (Hos. 8:5, 6)

The spoils of war in the ancient world often included statues and images of the gods of defeated peoples. The prophet Hosea dismisses the golden calves of Samaria (Israel) by prophesying that they are worthless and fated to become Assyrian spoils of war (Hos. 10:5, 6).

The Neo-Assyrian kings regularly listed the images of gods, as well as gold and silver, as part of the spoils of war taken from conquered temples. In an inscription, Sargon II includes the images of Samaria's gods among the tally of spoils taken from Samaria in 721 B.C. These were not the golden calves referred to by Hosea, but other idols used by the royal house of Israel.

Captured idols were most valuable as sources of precious metal and gems. If the conquerors wished to show disdain for the conquered people, they would dismantle the idols and use the gold, silver, and gems as raw material for other projects. The wooden or stone parts of the idol would be burned or broken. Extreme contempt for the images meant that the entire object was totally destroyed. No wonder there would be mourning (Hos. 10:5) when the once-worshiped idol was "broken to pieces" (Hos. 8:6).

The Apostasy of Israel

8 1 "*Set* the trumpet[a] to your mouth!
He shall come like an eagle against
the house of the LORD,
Because they have transgressed My
covenant
And rebelled against My law.
2 Israel will cry to Me,
'My God, we know You!'
3 Israel has rejected the good;
The enemy will pursue him.

4 "They set up kings, but not by Me;
They made princes, but I did not
acknowledge *them.*
From their silver and gold
They made idols for themselves—
That they might be cut off.
5 Your calf is rejected, O Samaria!
My anger is aroused against them—
How long until they attain to
innocence?
6 For from Israel *is* even this:
A workman made it, and it *is* not God;
But the calf of Samaria shall be
broken to pieces.

7 "They sow the wind,
And reap the whirlwind.
The stalk has no bud;
It shall never produce meal.
If it should produce,
Aliens would swallow it up.
8 Israel is swallowed up;
Now they are among the Gentiles
Like a vessel in which *is* no pleasure.

9 For they have gone up to Assyria,
Like a wild donkey alone by itself;
Ephraim has hired lovers.
10 Yes, though they have hired among
the nations,
Now I will gather them;
And they shall sorrow a little,[a]
Because of the burden[b] of the king of
princes.

11 "Because Ephraim has made many
altars for sin,
They have become for him altars for
sinning.
12 I have written for him the great
things of My law,
But they were considered a strange
thing.
13 *For* the sacrifices of My offerings they
sacrifice flesh and eat *it,*
But the LORD does not accept them.
Now He will remember their iniquity
and punish their sins.
They shall return to Egypt.

14 "For Israel has forgotten his Maker,
And has built temples;[a]
Judah also has multiplied fortified
cities;
But I will send fire upon his cities,
And it shall devour his palaces."

8:1 [a]Hebrew *shophar,* ram's horn   8:10 [a]Or *begin
to diminish*   [b]Or *oracle*   8:14 [a]Or *palaces*

Judgment of Israel's Sin

9 1 Do not rejoice, O Israel, with joy like
other peoples,
For you have played the harlot
against your God.
You have made love *for* hire on every
threshing floor.
2 The threshing floor and the winepress
Shall not feed them,
And the new wine shall fail in her.

3 They shall not dwell in the LORD's
land,
But Ephraim shall return to Egypt,
And shall eat unclean *things* in
Assyria.
4 They shall not offer wine *offerings* to
the LORD,
Nor shall their sacrifices be pleasing
to Him.
It shall be like bread of mourners to
them;
All who eat it shall be defiled.
For their bread *shall be* for their *own*
life;
It shall not come into the house of the
LORD.

5 What will you do in the appointed day,
And in the day of the feast of the
LORD?
6 For indeed they are gone because of
destruction.
Egypt shall gather them up;
Memphis shall bury them.
Nettles shall possess their valuables
of silver;
Thorns *shall be* in their tents.

7 The days of punishment have come;
The days of recompense have come.
Israel knows!
The prophet *is* a fool,
The spiritual man *is* insane,

8 Because of the greatness of your
iniquity and great enmity.
The watchman of Ephraim *is* with my
God;
But the prophet *is* a fowler'sᵃ snare in
all his ways—
Enmity in the house of his God.
9 They are deeply corrupted,
As in the days of Gibeah.
He will remember their iniquity;
He will punish their sins.

10 "I found Israel
Like grapes in the wilderness;
I saw your fathers
As the firstfruits on the fig tree in its
first season.
But they went to Baal Peor,
And separated themselves *to that*
shame;
They became an abomination like the
thing they loved.
11 *As for* Ephraim, their glory shall fly
away like a bird—
No birth, no pregnancy, and no
conception!
12 Though they bring up their children,
Yet I will bereave them to the last
man.
Yes, woe to them when I depart from
them!
13 Just as I saw Ephraim like Tyre,
planted in a pleasant place,
So Ephraim will bring out his children
to the murderer."

14 Give them, O LORD—
What will You give?
Give them a miscarrying womb
And dry breasts!

15 "All their wickedness *is* in Gilgal,
For there I hated them.
Because of the evil of their deeds
I will drive them from My house;
I will love them no more.
All their princes *are* rebellious.
16 Ephraim is stricken,
Their root is dried up;

9:8 ᵃThat is, one who catches birds in a trap or
snare

MARRIAGE AND FAMILY

*Societies in ancient Israel considered it extremely important for people to have families.
Barrenness was a universally understood cause of personal misery. When Hosea invoked
an evil fate on Ephraim, he chose "a miscarrying womb" (Hos. 9:14) and the death of
any newborn that escaped miscarriage. The last of the plagues on Egypt involved the
death of the firstborn (Ex. 4:23).*

REMEMBER THE BRUTAL SHALMAN (Hos. 10:14)

The person whom the prophet Hosea identifies as "Shalman" (Hos. 10:14) must have been well known to Hosea and his contemporaries. Evidently Shalman's army destroyed a fortress named Beth Arbel, treating the victims mercilessly. The dark memories which Hosea recalls include mothers being "dashed in pieces" upon their children (10:14).

Unfortunately, both Shalman and Beth Arbel are mentioned in the Bible only by Hosea, and defy absolute identification. Beth Arbel has been identified with Arbela, a town in the Transjordan, near Pella. The site is mentioned by the early Christian historian Eusebius, who locates the town on a very strategic trade route. Josephus, the 1st-century A.D. Jewish historian, also lists an Arbela west of the Sea of Galilee, but this site is not considered important enough to be remembered for such massive destruction as described by Hosea. There is no literary evidence that either of these sites was destroyed during Hosea's time.

"Shalman" has most often been interpreted as a short form of the name "Shalmaneser." Five kings of Assyria were known as Shalmaneser, two of whom could have been the king mentioned by Hosea. Shalmaneser III (858–824 B.C.) fought at the battle of Qarqar (853 B.C.), and in fact may have invaded Israel in 841 B.C. Shalmaneser V (726–722 B.C.) laid siege to Samaria and was the primary force that brought down the northern kingdom of Israel. Neither of these Shalmanesers, however, lists a Beth Arbel in his records.

Another possibility is a certain Moabite king, Salmanu, a contemporary of Hosea. Salmanu is listed as a tribute bearer in the annals of Assyria's King Tiglath-Pileser III (744–727 B.C.). Whether the prophet speaks of Shalmaneser or Salmanu, he warns Israel that she will face the same brutality that Beth Arbel once suffered from the now unidentified Shalman (Hos. 10:15).

They shall bear no fruit.
Yes, were they to bear children,
I would kill the darlings of their
    womb."

17 My God will cast them away,
Because they did not obey Him;
And they shall be wanderers among
    the nations.

Israel's Sin and Captivity

10 ¹ Israel empties *his* vine;
He brings forth fruit for himself.
According to the multitude of his fruit
He has increased the altars;
According to the bounty of his land
They have embellished *his sacred*
    pillars.

² Their heart is divided;
Now they are held guilty.
He will break down their altars;
He will ruin their *sacred* pillars.

³ For now they say,
"We have no king,
Because we did not fear the LORD.
And as for a king, what would he do
    for us?"

4 They have spoken words,
Swearing falsely in making a
    covenant.
Thus judgment springs up like
    hemlock in the furrows of the field.

5 The inhabitants of Samaria fear
Because of the calf[a] of Beth Aven.
For its people mourn for it,
And its priests shriek for it—
Because its glory has departed from it.

6 *The idol* also shall be carried to
    Assyria
As a present for King Jareb.
Ephraim shall receive shame,
And Israel shall be ashamed of his
    own counsel.

7 *As for* Samaria, her king is cut off
Like a twig on the water.

8 Also the high places of Aven, the sin of
    Israel,
Shall be destroyed.
The thorn and thistle shall grow on
    their altars;

10:5 ªLiterally *calves*

They shall say to the mountains,
 "Cover us!"
And to the hills, "Fall on us!"

9 "O Israel, you have sinned from the
  days of Gibeah;
 There they stood.
 The battle in Gibeah against the
  children of iniquity[a]
 Did not overtake them.
10 When *it is* My desire, I will chasten
  them.
 Peoples shall be gathered against
  them
 When I bind them for their two
  transgressions.[a]
11 Ephraim *is* a trained heifer
 That loves to thresh *grain;*
 But I harnessed her fair neck,
 I will make Ephraim pull *a plow.*
 Judah shall plow;
 Jacob shall break his clods."

12 Sow for yourselves righteousness;
 Reap in mercy;
 Break up your fallow ground,
 For *it is* time to seek the LORD,
 Till He comes and rains righteousness
  on you.

13 You have plowed wickedness;
 You have reaped iniquity.
 You have eaten the fruit of lies,
 Because you trusted in your own way,
 In the multitude of your mighty men.
14 Therefore tumult shall arise among
  your people,
 And all your fortresses shall be
  plundered
 As Shalman plundered Beth Arbel in
  the day of battle—
 A mother dashed in pieces upon *her*
  children.
15 Thus it shall be done to you, O Bethel,
 Because of your great wickedness.

At dawn the king of Israel
Shall be cut off utterly.

God's Continuing Love for Israel

11 1 "When Israel *was* a child, I loved
  him,
 And out of Egypt I called My son.
2 *As* they called them,[a]
 So they went from them;[b]
 They sacrificed to the Baals,
 And burned incense to carved images.

3 "I taught Ephraim to walk,
 Taking them by their arms;[a]
 But they did not know that I healed
  them.
4 I drew them with gentle cords,[a]
 With bands of love,
 And I was to them as those who take
  the yoke from their neck.[b]
 I stooped *and* fed them.

5 "He shall not return to the land of
  Egypt;
 But the Assyrian shall be his king,
 Because they refused to repent.
6 And the sword shall slash in his cities,
 Devour his districts,
 And consume *them,*
 Because of their own counsels.
7 My people are bent on backsliding
  from Me.
 Though they call to the Most High,[a]
 None at all exalt *Him.*

8 "How can I give you up, Ephraim?
 How can I hand you over, Israel?
 How can I make you like Admah?
 How can I set you like Zeboiim?
 My heart churns within Me;
 My sympathy is stirred.
9 I will not execute the fierceness of My
  anger;
 I will not again destroy Ephraim.
 For I *am* God, and not man,
 The Holy One in your midst;
 And I will not come with terror.[a]

10 "They shall walk after the LORD.
 He will roar like a lion.
 When He roars,
 Then *His* sons shall come trembling
  from the west;
11 They shall come trembling like a bird
  from Egypt,
 Like a dove from the land of Assyria.
 And I will let them dwell in their
  houses,"
 Says the LORD.

10:9 [a]So read many Hebrew manuscripts,
Septuagint, and Vulgate; Masoretic Text reads
unruliness. 10:10 [a]Or *in their two habitations*
11:2 [a]Following Masoretic Text and Vulgate;
Septuagint reads *Just as I called them;* Targum
interprets as *I sent prophets to a thousand of them.*
[b]Following Masoretic Text, Targum, and Vulgate;
Septuagint reads *from My face.* 11:3 [a]Some
Hebrew manuscripts, Septuagint, Syriac, and Vulgate
read *My arms.* 11:4 [a]Literally *cords of a man*
[b]Literally *jaws* 11:7 [a]Or *upward* 11:9 [a]Or *I
will not enter a city*

THE ASSYRIANS MAKE A COMEBACK (Hos. 11:5)

Assyria was not always a political state. It originated around the city of Asshur along the Tigris River and is first mentioned in Accadian sources in the late 3rd millennium B.C. The Assyrians evidently forged an independent state in the early 2nd millennium B.C. (c. 1800 B.C.), but did not become a lasting political force until the 14th century B.C. The reign of Ashur-uballit I (c. 1363–1328 B.C.) marked the beginning of a stable empire.

Even though Assyria was now an influential kingdom, it was not yet a major power. Assyrian expansionist tendencies did not begin until the late 13th century B.C. under Tukulti-Ninurta I (c. 1243–1207 B.C.). It was not until the 9th century B.C. that Assyria threatened Syria-Palestine, primarily under Shalmaneser III (858–824 B.C.) and his successors.

After Shalmaneser, the Neo-Assyrian Empire declined to a low point. By 745 B.C. its political structure was fragmented, and the kingdom of Urartu threatened its northern territory. At this crucial time for the empire a new king took power, beginning a revival of Assyrian strength. From 744 to 681 B.C. four Assyrian kings, all of whom appear in the Bible, led Assyria to its greatest period of imperial power: Tiglath-Pileser III, Shalmaneser V, Sargon II, Sennacherib.

The revived Assyria threatened the very existence of the small states to the west. In 734 B.C. Tiglath-Pileser III mounted a ferocious offensive against the western states. This campaign culminated in the conquest of Damascus in 732 B.C. and forced most other states to pay tribute to Assyria.

A decade later the Assyrians laid siege to Samaria, the capital of Israel, and ended its existence. Shalmaneser V conducted a 3-year siege, climaxing in Samaria's fall in 722 B.C. Sargon II succeeded Shalmaneser in that same year and probably was the king who carried the Israelite people into exile. Israel experienced the reality of Hosea's prophecy: "The Assyrian shall be his king" (Hos. 11:5).

Assyria had come back as a major power, and she would flex her new strength quickly. Sennacherib (704–681 B.C.) seized most of the major towns in Judah in his campaign of 701 B.C., then destroyed Babylon in 689 B.C.

God's Charge Against Ephraim

12 "Ephraim has encircled Me with lies,
  And the house of Israel with deceit;
  But Judah still walks with God,
  Even with the Holy One^a *who is*
    faithful.

12 1 "Ephraim feeds on the wind,
  And pursues the east wind;
He daily increases lies and desolation.
Also they make a covenant with the
  Assyrians,
And oil is carried to Egypt.

2 "The LORD also *brings* a charge against
    Judah,
  And will punish Jacob according to his
    ways;
  According to his deeds He will
    recompense him.
3 He took his brother by the heel in the
    womb,
  And in his strength he struggled with
    God.^a

4 Yes, he struggled with the Angel and
    prevailed;
  He wept, and sought favor from Him.
  He found Him *in* Bethel,
  And there He spoke to us—
5 That is, the LORD God of hosts.
  The LORD *is* His memorable name.
6 So you, by *the help of* your God,
    return;
  Observe mercy and justice,
  And wait on your God continually.

7 "A cunning Canaanite!
  Deceitful scales *are* in his hand;
  He loves to oppress.
8 And Ephraim said,
  'Surely I have become rich,
  I have found wealth for myself;
  In all my labors
  They shall find in me no iniquity that
    is sin.'

11:12 ^aOr *holy ones*   12:3 ^aCompare Genesis
32:28

9 "But I *am* the LORD your God,
Ever since the land of Egypt;
I will again make you dwell in tents,
As in the days of the appointed feast.
10 I have also spoken by the prophets,
And have multiplied visions;
I have given symbols through the
witness of the prophets."

11 Though Gilead *has* idols—
Surely they are vanity—
Though they sacrifice bulls in Gilgal,
Indeed their altars *shall be* heaps in
the furrows of the field.

12 Jacob fled to the country of Syria;
Israel served for a spouse,
And for a wife he tended *sheep.*
13 By a prophet the LORD brought Israel
out of Egypt,
And by a prophet he was preserved.
14 Ephraim provoked *Him* to anger most
bitterly;
Therefore his Lord will leave the guilt
of his bloodshed upon him,
And return his reproach upon him.

Relentless Judgment on Israel

13 1 When Ephraim spoke,
trembling,
He exalted *himself* in Israel;
But when he offended through Baal
worship, he died.
2 Now they sin more and more,
And have made for themselves molded
images,
Idols of their silver, according to their
skill;
All of it *is* the work of craftsmen.
They say of them,
"Let the men who sacrifice[a] kiss the
calves!"
3 Therefore they shall be like the
morning cloud
And like the early dew that passes
away,
Like chaff blown off from a threshing
floor
And like smoke from a chimney.

4 "Yet I *am* the LORD your God
Ever since the land of Egypt,

And you shall know no God but Me;
For *there is* no savior besides Me.
5 I knew you in the wilderness,
In the land of great drought.
6 When they had pasture, they were
filled;
They were filled and their heart was
exalted;
Therefore they forgot Me.

7 "So I will be to them like a lion;
Like a leopard by the road I will lurk;
8 I will meet them like a bear deprived
of her cubs;
I will tear open their rib cage,
And there I will devour them like a
lion.
The wild beast shall tear them.

9 "O Israel, you are destroyed,[a]
But your help[b] *is* from Me.
10 I will be your King;[a]
Where *is any other,*
That he may save you in all your
cities?
And your judges to whom you said,
'Give me a king and princes'?
11 I gave you a king in My anger,
And took *him* away in My wrath.

12 "The iniquity of Ephraim *is* bound up;
His sin *is* stored up.
13 The sorrows of a woman in childbirth
shall come upon him.
He *is* an unwise son,
For he should not stay long where
children are born.

14 "I will ransom them from the power of
the grave;[a]
I will redeem them from death.
O Death, I will be your plagues![b]

13:2 [a]Or *those who offer human sacrifice*
13:9 [a]Literally *it* or *he destroyed you* [b]Literally *in
your help* 13:10 [a]Septuagint, Syriac, Targum, and
Vulgate read *Where is your king?* 13:14 [a]Or
Sheol [b]Septuagint reads *where is your punishment?*

<table>
<tr><td colspan="2">**TIME CAPSULE** 735 to 733 B.C.</td></tr>
<tr><td>**735**</td><td>Tiglath-Pileser III lays siege to capital of Ararat</td></tr>
<tr><td>**734**</td><td>Tiglath-Pileser mounts offensive campaign against western states</td></tr>
<tr><td>**734**</td><td>Tiglath-Pileser marches through Palestine and conquers city of Gaza</td></tr>
<tr><td>**733**</td><td>Shanip of Bit-Ammon pays tribute to the Assyrian king Tiglath-Pileser</td></tr>
<tr><td>**733**</td><td>Ishmaelites pay tribute to Tiglath-Pileser of Assyria</td></tr>
</table>

O Grave,[c] I will be your destruction![d]
Pity is hidden from My eyes."

15 Though he is fruitful among *his*
      brethren,
   An east wind shall come;
   The wind of the LORD shall come up
      from the wilderness.
   Then his spring shall become dry,
   And his fountain shall be dried up.
   He shall plunder the treasury of every
      desirable prize.
16 Samaria is held guilty,[a]
   For she has rebelled against her God.
   They shall fall by the sword,
   Their infants shall be dashed in
      pieces,
   And their women with child ripped
      open.

Israel Restored at Last

14 1 O Israel, return to the LORD
         your God,
   For you have stumbled because of
      your iniquity;
2 Take words with you,
   And return to the LORD.
   Say to Him,
   "Take away all iniquity;
   Receive *us* graciously,
   For we will offer the sacrifices[a] of our
      lips.
3 Assyria shall not save us,
   We will not ride on horses,
   Nor will we say anymore to the work
      of our hands, '*You are* our gods.'
   For in You the fatherless finds mercy."

4 "I will heal their backsliding,
   I will love them freely,
   For My anger has turned away from
      him.
5 I will be like the dew to Israel;
   He shall grow like the lily,
   And lengthen his roots like Lebanon.
6 His branches shall spread;
   His beauty shall be like an olive tree,
   And his fragrance like Lebanon.
7 Those who dwell under his shadow
      shall return;
   They shall be revived *like* grain,
   And grow like a vine.
   Their scent[a] *shall be* like the wine of
      Lebanon.

8 "Ephraim *shall say,* 'What have I to do
      anymore with idols?'
   I have heard and observed him.

I *am* like a green cypress tree;
Your fruit is found in Me."

9 Who *is* wise?
   Let him understand these things.
   Who is prudent?
   Let him know them.
   For the ways of the LORD *are* right;
   The righteous walk in them,
   But transgressors stumble in them.

Azariah (Uzziah) King of Judah

The long reign of Jeroboam II in the northern kingdom coincided with the even longer reign of Azariah in Judah (792–740 B.C.). Indeed, Azariah (called Uzziah in Chronicles and Isaiah) almost outlived Judah's time of peace. The skin disease of leprosy forced him to relinquish administration of his kingdom to his son Jotham around 750 B.C. The disruptions associated with the resurgent Assyrian Empire began in earnest sometime during the 10-year coregency (750–740 B.C.) while Jotham ruled with his father.

■ 2 Kings 15:1–7

2 Kings
Azariah Reigns in Judah

15 :1 In the twenty-seventh year of Jeroboam king of Israel, Azariah the son of Amaziah, king of Judah, became king. 2He was sixteen years old when he became king, and he reigned fifty-two years in Jerusalem. His mother's name *was* Jecholiah of Jerusalem. 3And he did *what was* right in the sight of the LORD, according to all that his father Amaziah had done, 4except that the high places were not removed; the people still sacrificed and burned incense on the high places. 5Then the LORD struck the king, so that he was a leper until the day of his death; so he dwelt in an isolated house. And Jotham the king's son *was* over the *royal* house, judging the people of the land.

6Now the rest of the acts of Azariah, and all that he did, *are* they not written in the book of the chronicles of the kings of

---

13:14 [c]Or *Sheol* [d]Septuagint reads *where is your sting?*   13:16 [a]Septuagint reads *shall be disfigured.*   14:2 [a]Literally *bull calves;* Septuagint reads *fruit.*   14:7 [a]Literally *remembrance*

Judah? ⁷So Azariah rested with his fathers, and they buried him with his fathers in the City of David. Then Jotham his son reigned in his place.

🧩 The Book of Isaiah

Few books have inspired more debate in terms of their historical context. Isaiah the prophet lived in Judah in the 8th century B.C., the time of Assyria's resurgence. He prophesied in Jerusalem, especially to kings Ahaz (735–715 B.C.) and Hezekiah (715–686 B.C.), and many of his prophecies speak clearly of the political situation of their time. His message to both kings, in brief, was that no human power could stand in the way of Assyria. Thus Judah was not to rely on alliances with Egypt or any other nation. Judah's only hope was faith in God's power to protect Zion, His chosen city.

The judgments recorded in Is. 1—35 can almost all be placed in this 8th-century Assyrian context. Chapters 36—39 is a historical narrative about that time period, almost identical to 2 Kin. 18:13—20:19. The setting changes, however, in Is. 40—55. These chapters are oracles of salvation that specifically speak of Cyrus the Persian and the restoration of Jerusalem in 538 B.C., some 200 years after Isaiah's time. Another change of setting occurs in Is. 56—66, chapters that appear to speak of the restored temple during Persian rule (c. 538–515 B.C.).

For almost a thousand years, some scholars have noted these shifts and suggested that the Book of Isaiah is the work of at least two different prophets. One would have been the prophet Isaiah himself, but the other an anonymous prophet of the late Babylonian exile (Cyrus's time) who consciously traced his spiritual roots to the original Isaiah. Other scholars, while acknowledging that chs. 40—66 speak of a later time, maintain that they are still the work of the prophet Isaiah, a divine vision of the salvation to come in the distant future.

But historical context concerns more than just the question of authorship. The sense of the various chapters of Isaiah should be considered in the context of which they speak. During Isaiah's own lifetime the threat was Assyria, and the prophet had to speak forcefully to his people and their kings, because they tended to trust in their own political and military maneuverings rather than in the power of God. This is the setting for most of Is. 1—39.

The prophecies of Is. 40—66 demonstrate that Judah's God is superior to other nations that would come. God promises to deliver His people, His chosen servants, from their captivity in Babylon. He will do something unheard of: through the mighty Persian emperor Cyrus, God will set an exiled people free to go home. Beyond all this, God will prepare His people to make His glory known to the Gentiles, who will come to the Lord's house to learn His ways (49:6; 56:3–8). These later chapters of Isaiah should be read in this context.

The first five chapters of Isaiah contain many representative oracles and may be intended as a thematic introduction to the book. Chronologically, though, Isaiah's ministry begins with his call, recounted in Is. 6. The prophet's call consists of a vision of God which he received "in the year that King Uzziah died" (6:1), about 740 B.C.

Chapters 1—5 present God's case against Judah. She has been seduced by the folly of human independence. Because Judah placed her faith in human leadership instead of in God, she was doomed to experience weaker and weaker leadership. This was exactly what happened in Judah's final years.

■ Isaiah 6:1–13
■ Isaiah 1:1—5:30

Isaiah 6:1–13
Isaiah Called to Be a Prophet

6 :1 In the year that King Uzziah died, I saw the Lord sitting on a throne, high and lifted up, and the train of His *robe* filled the temple. ²Above it stood seraphim; each one had six wings: with two he covered his face, with two he covered his feet, and with two he flew. ³And one cried to another and said:

"Holy, holy, holy *is* the LORD of hosts;
The whole earth *is* full of His glory!"

⁴And the posts of the door were shaken by the voice of him who cried out, and the house was filled with smoke.
⁵So I said:

"Woe *is* me, for I am undone!
Because I *am* a man of unclean lips,
And I dwell in the midst of a people of
    unclean lips;
For my eyes have seen the King,
The LORD of hosts."

ISAIAH ENCOUNTERS THE SERAPHIM (Is. 6:2–7)

In Judaism and Christianity the seraphim have been considered to be angels high in the heavenly court. The only account in the Bible where seraphim appear (Is. 6:2–7) suggests they were guardians of the throne room of Yahweh.

The translation "seraphim" comes from the Hebrew word *saraph,* which often refers to a "fiery flying serpent" (Is. 14:29; 30:6). Therefore some scholars assume that the flying beings which Isaiah saw guarding the throne of Yahweh had some type of serpents' bodies.

Ancient Near Eastern mythologies commonly present snakelike creatures guarding deities and their possessions. In Egypt the uraeus ("fiery snake") was not only a guardian of the god-king, but also a symbol of divine-kingship itself. The artifacts of Elam are rich in cobra symbolism. Mesopotamian artists used a serpent with legs liberally in public artwork. Further to the east, Indian mythology had nagas guarding the food and treasures of the gods. These cobra people could appear either as snakes or humans, or even with aspects of both. They also shot fire from their eyes and mouths.

The six wings of the seraphim (Is. 6:2) correspond to the six wings of the god El. The Greek writer Philo of Byblos (A.D. 64–141) explains in his *History of Phoenicia* that these wings represent eternal vigilance, mind, and understanding—all appropriate attributes for those closest to Yahweh.

The seraphim in Isaiah act for God and stand in God's presence, giving God glory and praise. They also act for God in relationship to the prophet. Inspiring both reverence and awe, the seraphim were able to make Isaiah acceptable in the presence of Yahweh (2:7), an activity which reflects their position as throne room guards.

---

⁶Then one of the seraphim flew to me, having in his hand a live coal *which* he had taken with the tongs from the altar. ⁷And he touched my mouth *with it,* and said:

"Behold, this has touched your lips;
    Your iniquity is taken away,
    And your sin purged."

⁸Also I heard the voice of the Lord, saying:

"Whom shall I send,
    And who will go for Us?"

Then I said, "Here *am* I! Send me."
⁹And He said, "Go, and tell this people:

'Keep on hearing, but do not
        understand;
    Keep on seeing, but do not perceive.'

¹⁰ "Make the heart of this people dull,
    And their ears heavy,
    And shut their eyes;
    Lest they see with their eyes,
    And hear with their ears,
    And understand with their heart,
    And return and be healed."

¹¹Then I said, "Lord, how long?"
    And He answered:

"Until the cities are laid waste and
        without inhabitant,
    The houses are without a man,
    The land is utterly desolate,
¹² The LORD has removed men far away,
    And the forsaken places *are* many in
        the midst of the land.
¹³ But yet a tenth *will be* in it,
    And will return and be for consuming,
    As a terebinth tree or as an oak,

ARTS AND LITERATURE

A stone relief made between 894 and 808 B.C. shows a figure with six wings, something like the seraphim seen by Isaiah (Is. 6:2). The relief was found at Tell Halaf, about halfway between Nineveh and Carchemish in northern Mesopotamia. Unfortunately, there is no writing on the relief to say what it represents.

Whose stump *remains* when it is cut
down.
So the holy seed *shall be* its stump."

Isaiah 1:1—5:30

1 :1 The vision of Isaiah the son of Amoz,
which he saw concerning Judah and
Jerusalem in the days of Uzziah, Jotham,
Ahaz, *and* Hezekiah, kings of Judah.

The Wickedness of Judah

2   Hear, O heavens, and give ear,
O earth!
For the LORD has spoken:
"I have nourished and brought up
children,
And they have rebelled against Me;
3   The ox knows its owner
And the donkey its master's crib;
But Israel does not know,
My people do not consider."

4   Alas, sinful nation,
A people laden with iniquity,
A brood of evildoers,
Children who are corrupters!
They have forsaken the LORD,
They have provoked to anger
The Holy One of Israel,
They have turned away backward.

5   Why should you be stricken again?
You will revolt more and more.
The whole head is sick,
And the whole heart faints.
6   From the sole of the foot even to the
head,
There is no soundness in it,
But wounds and bruises and
putrefying sores;
They have not been closed or bound
up,
Or soothed with ointment.

7   Your country *is* desolate,
Your cities *are* burned with fire;
Strangers devour your land in your
presence;

And *it is* desolate, as overthrown by
strangers.
8   So the daughter of Zion is left as a
booth in a vineyard,
As a hut in a garden of cucumbers,
As a besieged city.
9   Unless the LORD of hosts
Had left to us a very small remnant,
We would have become like Sodom,
We would have been made like
Gomorrah.

10 Hear the word of the LORD,
You rulers of Sodom;
Give ear to the law of our God,
You people of Gomorrah:
11 "To what purpose *is* the multitude of
your sacrifices to Me?"
Says the LORD.
"I have had enough of burnt offerings
of rams
And the fat of fed cattle.
I do not delight in the blood of bulls,
Or of lambs or goats.

12 "When you come to appear before Me,
Who has required this from your
hand,
To trample My courts?
13 Bring no more futile sacrifices;
Incense is an abomination to Me.
The New Moons, the Sabbaths, and
the calling of assemblies—
I cannot endure iniquity and the
sacred meeting.
14 Your New Moons and your appointed
feasts
My soul hates;
They are a trouble to Me,
I am weary of bearing *them.*
15 When you spread out your hands,
I will hide My eyes from you;
Even though you make many prayers,
I will not hear.
Your hands are full of blood.

16 "Wash yourselves, make yourselves
clean;

RELIGION AND WORSHIP

*Worship in Old Testament times involved daily sacrifices of animals, as well as various
feasts and assemblies held during the year (Is. 1:13). In many cultures today, as also in
ancient Rome, the number of religious holidays accounts for practically half of the days in
a year. Although God had instituted Israel's religious meetings, He took no delight in
them unless they represented genuine worship.*

Put away the evil of your doings from
  before My eyes.
Cease to do evil,
17 Learn to do good;
Seek justice,
Rebuke the oppressor;[a]
Defend the fatherless,
Plead for the widow.

18 "Come now, and let us reason
    together,"
Says the LORD,
"Though your sins are like scarlet,
They shall be as white as snow;
Though they are red like crimson,
They shall be as wool.
19 If you are willing and obedient,
You shall eat the good of the land;
20 But if you refuse and rebel,
You shall be devoured by the sword";
For the mouth of the LORD has
  spoken.

The Degenerate City
21 How the faithful city has become a
    harlot!
It was full of justice;
Righteousness lodged in it,
But now murderers.
22 Your silver has become dross,
Your wine mixed with water.
23 Your princes *are* rebellious,
And companions of thieves;
Everyone loves bribes,
And follows after rewards.
They do not defend the fatherless,
Nor does the cause of the widow come
  before them.

24 Therefore the Lord says,
The LORD of hosts, the Mighty One of
  Israel,
"Ah, I will rid Myself of My
  adversaries,
And take vengeance on My enemies.
25 I will turn My hand against you,
And thoroughly purge away your
  dross,
And take away all your alloy.
26 I will restore your judges as at the
    first,
And your counselors as at the
  beginning.
Afterward you shall be called the city
  of righteousness, the faithful city."

27 Zion shall be redeemed with justice,
And her penitents with righteousness.

28 The destruction of transgressors and
  of sinners *shall be* together,
And those who forsake the LORD shall
  be consumed.
29 For they[a] shall be ashamed of the
  terebinth trees
Which you have desired;
And you shall be embarrassed because
  of the gardens
Which you have chosen.
30 For you shall be as a terebinth whose
  leaf fades,
And as a garden that has no water.
31 The strong shall be as tinder,
And the work of it as a spark;
Both will burn together,
And no one shall quench *them*.

The Future House of God

2 ¹The word that Isaiah the son of Amoz
saw concerning Judah and Jerusalem.

2 Now it shall come to pass in the latter
    days
That the mountain of the LORD's
  house
Shall be established on the top of the
  mountains,
And shall be exalted above the hills;
And all nations shall flow to it.
3 Many people shall come and say,
"Come, and let us go up to the
  mountain of the LORD,
To the house of the God of Jacob;
He will teach us His ways,
And we shall walk in His paths."
For out of Zion shall go forth the law,
And the word of the LORD from
  Jerusalem.
4 He shall judge between the nations,
And rebuke many people;
They shall beat their swords into
  plowshares,
And their spears into pruning hooks;
Nation shall not lift up sword against
  nation,
Neither shall they learn war anymore.

The Day of the LORD
5 O house of Jacob, come and let us
  walk
In the light of the LORD.

1:17 [a]Some ancient versions read *the oppressed*.
1:29 [a]Following Masoretic Text, Septuagint, and
Vulgate; some Hebrew manuscripts and Targum read
you.

WORSHIPING MOLES AND BATS (Is. 2:20)

Isaiah focuses on two extremely repugnant examples of idol worship. Moles and bats were not usually the animals used as images to represent deities. In order to show how ridiculous Judah's apostasy was, Isaiah contrasted the precious metals, gold and silver, with the images of "moles and bats" made from them (Is. 2:20).

The Hebrew word translated "moles" (2:20) refers to a digging animal and is sometimes translated as "mice." Rodents, particularly mice, were mummified in Egypt as a part of the worship of various deities, but mice themselves were not worshiped there.

Bats, on the other hand, were regularly worshiped in Egypt as a part of the cult of the dead. The peak of devotion to bats came in the late Egyptian period (1069–525 B.C.), which was contemporary with the kingdoms of Israel and Judah. Egyptian statues of bats for use in the religious cult are very lifelike, displaying much attention to the detail of the natural animal.

Some deity statues in Egypt were part animal and part human, but the idols which Isaiah mentions were simply molded in the shape of rodents and bats. Isaiah reminds his hearers, with these particularly repugnant examples, that they had broken the Law of Moses which prohibited the making of an image in the likeness of anything on the earth (Ex. 20:4).

---

6 For You have forsaken Your people,
   the house of Jacob,
Because they are filled with eastern
   ways;
They *are* soothsayers like the
   Philistines,
And they are pleased with the
   children of foreigners.

7 Their land is also full of silver and
   gold,
And there is no end to their treasures;
Their land is also full of horses,
And there is no end to their chariots.

8 Their land is also full of idols;
They worship the work of their own
   hands,
That which their own fingers have
   made.

9 People bow down,
And each man humbles himself;
Therefore do not forgive them.

10 Enter into the rock, and hide in the
   dust,
From the terror of the LORD
And the glory of His majesty.

11 The lofty looks of man shall be
   humbled,
The haughtiness of men shall be
   bowed down,
And the LORD alone shall be exalted in
   that day.

12 For the day of the LORD of hosts
Shall come upon everything proud and
   lofty,

Upon everything lifted up—
And it shall be brought low—

13 Upon all the cedars of Lebanon *that
   are* high and lifted up,
And upon all the oaks of Bashan;

14 Upon all the high mountains,
And upon all the hills *that are* lifted
   up;

15 Upon every high tower,
And upon every fortified wall;

16 Upon all the ships of Tarshish,
And upon all the beautiful sloops.

17 The loftiness of man shall be bowed
   down,
And the haughtiness of men shall be
   brought low;
The LORD alone will be exalted in that
   day,

18 But the idols He shall utterly abolish.

19 They shall go into the holes of the
   rocks,
And into the caves of the earth,
From the terror of the LORD
And the glory of His majesty,
When He arises to shake the earth
   mightily.

20 In that day a man will cast away his
   idols of silver
And his idols of gold,
Which they made, *each* for himself to
   worship,
To the moles and bats,

21 To go into the clefts of the rocks,
And into the crags of the rugged rocks,

From the terror of the LORD
And the glory of His majesty,
When He arises to shake the earth
    mightily.

22 Sever yourselves from such a man,
    Whose breath *is* in his nostrils;
    For of what account is he?

Judgment on Judah and Jerusalem

3 ¹ For behold, the Lord, the LORD of
       hosts,
    Takes away from Jerusalem and from
       Judah
    The stock and the store,
    The whole supply of bread and the
       whole supply of water;
2   The mighty man and the man of war,
    The judge and the prophet,
    And the diviner and the elder;
3   The captain of fifty and the honorable
       man,
    The counselor and the skillful artisan,
    And the expert enchanter.

4   "I will give children *to be* their princes,
    And babes shall rule over them.
5   The people will be oppressed,
    Every one by another and every one
       by his neighbor;
    The child will be insolent toward the
       elder,
    And the base toward the honorable."

6   When a man takes hold of his brother
    In the house of his father, *saying,*
    "You have clothing;
    You be our ruler,
    And *let* these ruins *be* under your
       power,"ᵃ
7   In that day he will protest, saying,
    "I cannot cure *your* ills,
    For in my house *is* neither food nor
       clothing;
    Do not make me a ruler of the people."

8   For Jerusalem stumbled,
    And Judah is fallen,
    Because their tongue and their doings

Are against the LORD,
To provoke the eyes of His glory.
9   The look on their countenance
       witnesses against them,
    And they declare their sin as Sodom;
    They do not hide *it.*
    Woe to their soul!
    For they have brought evil upon
       themselves.

10 "Say to the righteous that *it shall be*
       well *with them,*
    For they shall eat the fruit of their
       doings.
11 Woe to the wicked! *It shall be* ill *with
       him,*
    For the reward of his hands shall be
       given him.
12 *As for* My people, children *are* their
       oppressors,
    And women rule over them.
    O My people! Those who lead you
       cause *you* to err,
    And destroy the way of your paths."

Oppression and Luxury Condemned

13 The LORD stands up to plead,
    And stands to judge the people.
14 The LORD will enter into judgment
    With the elders of His people
    And His princes:
    "For you have eaten up the vineyard;
    The plunder of the poor *is* in your
       houses.
15 What do you mean by crushing My
       people
    And grinding the faces of the poor?"
    Says the Lord GOD of hosts.

¹⁶Moreover the LORD says:

"Because the daughters of Zion are
       haughty,
    And walk with outstretched necks
    And wanton eyes,
    Walking and mincing *as* they go,
    Making a jingling with their feet,

3:6 ᵃLiterally *hand*

DAILY LIFE AND CUSTOMS

*Since there is no description of most of the items in Isaiah's list of finery (Is. 3:18), it is
often impossible to tell exactly what these items were. Despite the difficulty faced by
modern scholars to learn the precise meaning of the Hebrew words, those words were
not rare or difficult when written. To the Hebrew writer, they were too familiar to think of
anyone not knowing them.*

17 Therefore the Lord will strike with a
scab
The crown of the head of the
daughters of Zion,
And the LORD will uncover their secret
parts."

18 In that day the Lord will take away
the finery:
The jingling anklets, the scarves, and
the crescents;
19 The pendants, the bracelets, and the
veils;
20 The headdresses, the leg ornaments,
and the headbands;
The perfume boxes, the charms,
21 and the rings;
The nose jewels,
22 the festal apparel, and the mantles;
The outer garments, the purses,
23 and the mirrors;
The fine linen, the turbans, and the
robes.

24And so it shall be:

Instead of a sweet smell there will be
a stench;
Instead of a sash, a rope;
Instead of well-set hair, baldness;
Instead of a rich robe, a girding of
sackcloth;
And branding instead of beauty.
25 Your men shall fall by the sword,
And your mighty in the war.

26 Her gates shall lament and mourn,
And she *being* desolate shall sit on the
ground.

4 ¹ And in that day seven women shall
take hold of one man, saying,
"We will eat our own food and wear our
own apparel;
Only let us be called by your name,
To take away our reproach."

The Renewal of Zion

2 In that day the Branch of the LORD
shall be beautiful and glorious;
And the fruit of the earth *shall be*
excellent and appealing
For those of Israel who have escaped.

³And it shall come to pass that *he who
is* left in Zion and remains in Jerusalem
will be called holy—everyone who is recorded among the living in Jerusalem.

⁴When the Lord has washed away the filth
of the daughters of Zion, and purged the
blood of Jerusalem from her midst, by the
spirit of judgment and by the spirit of
burning, ⁵then the LORD will create above
every dwelling place of Mount Zion, and
above her assemblies, a cloud and smoke
by day and the shining of a flaming fire by
night. For over all the glory there *will be* a
covering. ⁶And there will be a tabernacle
for shade in the daytime from the heat, for
a place of refuge, and for a shelter from
storm and rain.

God's Disappointing Vineyard

5 ¹ Now let me sing to my Well-beloved
A song of my Beloved regarding His
vineyard:

My Well-beloved has a vineyard
On a very fruitful hill.
2 He dug it up and cleared out its
stones,
And planted it with the choicest vine.
He built a tower in its midst,
And also made a winepress in it;
So He expected *it* to bring forth *good*
grapes,
But it brought forth wild grapes.

3 "And now, O inhabitants of Jerusalem
and men of Judah,
Judge, please, between Me and My
vineyard.
4 What more could have been done to
My vineyard
That I have not done in it?
Why then, when I expected *it* to bring
forth *good* grapes,
Did it bring forth wild grapes?

TIME CAPSULE *733 to 732 B.C.*

733–732	Rezin of Damascus leads rebellion against Assyria
733	Tiglath-Pileser III is victorious against Rezin's army and lays siege to Damascus
732	Tiglath-Pileser conquers the Aramean state of Damascus
732	The Syro-Ephraimite War
732	Hoshea assassinates Pekah and becomes king in Israel
732	Ahaz becomes sole king in Judah

5 And now, please let Me tell you what I
    will do to My vineyard:
  I will take away its hedge, and it shall
    be burned;
  And break down its wall, and it shall
    be trampled down.
6 I will lay it waste;
  It shall not be pruned or dug,
  But there shall come up briers and
    thorns.
  I will also command the clouds
  That they rain no rain on it."

7 For the vineyard of the LORD of hosts
    is the house of Israel,
  And the men of Judah are His
    pleasant plant.
  He looked for justice, but behold,
    oppression;
  For righteousness, but behold, a cry
    for help.

Impending Judgment on Excesses

8 Woe to those who join house to house;
  They add field to field,
  Till *there is* no place
  Where they may dwell alone in the
    midst of the land!
9 In my hearing the LORD of hosts *said,*
  "Truly, many houses shall be desolate,
  Great and beautiful ones, without
    inhabitant.
10 For ten acres of vineyard shall yield
    one bath,
  And a homer of seed shall yield one
    ephah."

11 Woe to those who rise early in the
    morning,
  That they may follow intoxicating
    drink;
  Who continue until night, *till* wine
    inflames them!
12 The harp and the strings,
  The tambourine and flute,
  And wine are in their feasts;
  But they do not regard the work of the
    LORD,
  Nor consider the operation of His
    hands.

13 Therefore my people have gone into
    captivity,
  Because *they have* no knowledge;
  Their honorable men *are* famished,
  And their multitude dried up with
    thirst.
14 Therefore Sheol has enlarged itself

  And opened its mouth beyond
    measure;
  Their glory and their multitude and
    their pomp,
  And he who is jubilant, shall descend
    into it.
15 People shall be brought down,
  Each man shall be humbled,
  And the eyes of the lofty shall be
    humbled.
16 But the LORD of hosts shall be exalted
    in judgment,
  And God who is holy shall be hallowed
    in righteousness.
17 Then the lambs shall feed in their
    pasture,
  And in the waste places of the fat ones
    strangers shall eat.

18 Woe to those who draw iniquity with
    cords of vanity,
  And sin as if with a cart rope;
19 That say, "Let Him make speed *and*
    hasten His work,
  That we may see *it;*
  And let the counsel of the Holy One of
    Israel draw near and come,
  That we may know *it.*"

20 Woe to those who call evil good, and
    good evil;
  Who put darkness for light, and light
    for darkness;
  Who put bitter for sweet, and sweet
    for bitter!

21 Woe to *those who are* wise in their
    own eyes,
  And prudent in their own sight!

22 Woe to men mighty at drinking wine,
  Woe to men valiant for mixing
    intoxicating drink,
23 Who justify the wicked for a bribe,
  And take away justice from the
    righteous man!

24 Therefore, as the fire devours the
    stubble,
  And the flame consumes the chaff,
  So their root will be as rottenness,
  And their blossom will ascend like
    dust;
  Because they have rejected the law of
    the LORD of hosts,
  And despised the word of the Holy
    One of Israel.

25 Therefore the anger of the LORD is
  aroused against His people;
He has stretched out His hand against
  them
And stricken them,
And the hills trembled.
Their carcasses *were* as refuse in the
  midst of the streets.

For all this His anger is not turned
  away,
But His hand *is* stretched out still.

26 He will lift up a banner to the nations
  from afar,
And will whistle to them from the end
  of the earth;
Surely they shall come with speed,
  swiftly.
27 No one will be weary or stumble
  among them,
No one will slumber or sleep;
Nor will the belt on their loins be
  loosed,
Nor the strap of their sandals be
  broken;
28 Whose arrows *are* sharp,
And all their bows bent;
Their horses' hooves will seem like
  flint,
And their wheels like a whirlwind.
29 Their roaring *will be* like a lion,
They will roar like young lions;
Yes, they will roar
And lay hold of the prey;
They will carry *it* away safely,
And no one will deliver.
30 In that day they will roar against
  them
Like the roaring of the sea.
And if *one* looks to the land,
Behold, darkness *and* sorrow;
And the light is darkened by the
  clouds.

26:1 ªCalled *Azariah* in 2 Kings 14:21ff
26:2 ªHebrew *Eloth* 26:5 ªSeveral Hebrew
manuscripts, Septuagint, Syriac, Targum, and Arabic
read *fear.*

Priestly Account: Jeroboam and Uzziah (Azariah)

Under the long reign of Jeroboam II
(793–753 B.C.), Israel experienced prosperity
and political success to a degree it had not
known since the monarchy divided. Yet the
Chronicler, who never shows much interest in
the northern kingdom, does not mention this
king. Jeroboam's contemporary—King Uzziah
of Judah (792–740 B.C.)—was also a great
ruler. Like Jeroboam, Uzziah led his southern
kingdom to a time of prosperity and expansion.

Chronicles, telling the story from a priestly
perspective, devotes much more space to Judah's Uzziah (Azariah in Kings) than does the
prophetic account. The most significant difference between the two histories concerns
Uzziah's leprosy. The Book of 2 Kings does not
explicitly say why Uzziah contracted the disease, but it does say that Uzziah's sin was that
of allowing the "high places" to remain. The
Chronicler, by contrast, focuses on Uzziah's sin
against the temple and against the prerogatives of the priests.

■ 2 Chronicles 26:1–23

2 Chronicles
Uzziah Reigns in Judah

26 :1 Now all the people of Judah took
Uzziah,ª who *was* sixteen years old,
and made him king instead of his father
Amaziah. ²He built Elathª and restored it
to Judah, after the king rested with his
fathers.

³Uzziah *was* sixteen years old when he
became king, and he reigned fifty-two
years in Jerusalem. His mother's name
was Jecholiah of Jerusalem. ⁴And he did
what was right in the sight of the LORD, according to all that his father Amaziah had
done. ⁵He sought God in the days of
Zechariah, who had understanding in the
visionsª of God; and as long as he sought
the LORD, God made him prosper.

⁶Now he went out and made war
against the Philistines, and broke down
the wall of Gath, the wall of Jabneh, and
the wall of Ashdod; and he built cities
around Ashdod and among the Philistines.
⁷God helped him against the Philistines,
against the Arabians who lived in Gur
Baal, and against the Meunites. ⁸Also the
Ammonites brought tribute to Uzziah. His
fame spread as far as the entrance of
Egypt, for he became exceedingly strong.

⁹And Uzziah built towers in Jerusalem
at the Corner Gate, at the Valley Gate, and
at the corner buttress of the wall; then he
fortified them. ¹⁰Also he built towers in the
desert. He dug many wells, for he had
much livestock, both in the lowlands and
in the plains; *he also had* farmers and

NO KING-PRIESTS IN JUDAH   (2 Chr. 26:16–21)

The Law of Moses stipulated that only the priests could perform the ritual sacrifices (Num. 3:5–10). The interior of the temple in Jerusalem was forbidden to all except for certain orders of Levitical priests. Unlike the kings of neighboring nations, the king of Judah was not allowed into his own private temple, for he was not a priest as were most kings in the ancient Near East.

The common Near Eastern belief was that the most significant person in the community should also be the one to represent the people before the god. Egyptian kings were considered embodied gods, and had responsibilities for religious rituals within the cult. Mesopotamian and Syro-Palestinian rulers were seen as both vice-regents of their patron deities as well as high priests of the deities' cults. Certain public holy days could be carried out only by the king, serving as high priest. One of the reasons Nabonidus, king of Babylonia (556–539 B.C.), was so unpopular was that he did not perform the New Year's rituals for several years, but left them to his son. This made the ritual improper and without value.

During Abraham's time, the person of Melchizedek is described as both "*king* of Salem" and "*priest* of God Most High" (Gen. 14:18). Possibly the earlier rulers of Jerusalem (identified with Salem) had been king-priests, but this was a practice not allowed in Yahweh's Jerusalem cult. There, political rule and religious practice were strictly separate.

Judah's king Uzziah was trying to act like the other kings of the ancient world by burning incense on the altar of the temple (2 Chr. 26:16–20). His actions, however, were usurping the role of the priest. The antagonistic encounter between Uzziah and 81 priests of Yahweh (26:17, 18) reveals the power struggles between king and priests that probably occurred often in Judah's politics.

---

vinedressers in the mountains and in Carmel, for he loved the soil.

¹¹Moreover Uzziah had an army of fighting men who went out to war by companies, according to the number on their roll as prepared by Jeiel the scribe and Maaseiah the officer, under the hand of Hananiah, *one* of the king's captains. ¹²The total number of chief officers[a] of the mighty men of valor *was* two thousand six hundred. ¹³And under their authority *was* an army of three hundred and seven thousand five hundred, that made war with mighty power, to help the king against the enemy. ¹⁴Then Uzziah prepared for them, for the entire army, shields, spears, helmets, body armor, bows, and slings *to cast* stones. ¹⁵And he made devices in Jerusalem, invented by skillful men, to be on the towers and the corners, to shoot arrows and large stones. So his fame spread far and wide, for he was marvelously helped till he became strong.

The Penalty for Uzziah's Pride

¹⁶But when he was strong his heart was lifted up, to *his* destruction, for he transgressed against the LORD his God by entering the temple of the LORD to burn incense on the altar of incense. ¹⁷So Azariah the priest went in after him, and with him were eighty priests of the LORD—valiant men. ¹⁸And they withstood King Uzziah, and said to him, "*It* is not for you, Uzziah, to burn incense to the LORD, but for the priests, the sons of Aaron, who are consecrated to burn incense. Get out of the sanctuary, for you have trespassed! You *shall have* no honor from the LORD God."

¹⁹Then Uzziah became furious; and he *had* a censer in his hand to burn incense. And while he was angry with the priests, leprosy broke out on his forehead, before the priests in the house of the LORD, beside the incense altar. ²⁰And Azariah the chief priest and all the priests looked at him, and there, on his forehead, he *was* leprous; so they thrust him out of that place. Indeed he also hurried to get out, because the LORD had struck him.

²¹King Uzziah was a leper until the day of his death. He dwelt in an isolated house, because he was a leper; for he was cut off from the house of the LORD. Then Jotham his son *was* over the king's house, judging the people of the land.

26:12 ªLiterally *chief fathers*

22Now the rest of the acts of Uzziah, from first to last, the prophet Isaiah the son of Amoz wrote. 23So Uzziah rested with his fathers, and they buried him with his fathers in the field of burial which *belonged* to the kings, for they said, "He is a leper." Then Jotham his son reigned in his place.

Prophetic Account: Pekah Attacks Ahaz

After Jeroboam II, the northern kingdom that had been so prosperous and comfortable fell apart. Four different kings ruled in rapid succession; only two were related, and only one was able to hold the throne for longer than a couple of years.

Assassination was commonplace in Israel for 20 years. Zechariah (753 B.C.) ruled only 6 months before his assassination ended the dynasty of Jehu. Shallum (752 B.C.), the assassin, ruled only 1 month before he himself was assassinated by the next king, Menahem. After a 10-year rule (752–742 B.C.), Menahem was succeeded by his son Pekahiah (742–740 B.C.). A military officer, Pekah, assassinated Pekahiah, only to be assassinated himself in 732 B.C. by Israel's last king, Hoshea.

The fifth king, Pekah, evidently came to power with the support of those who wanted to resist the growing power of Assyria. The previous two kings, Menahem and his son Pekahiah, had been sympathetic to Assyria, at least to the extent of paying tribute (2 Kin. 15:19, 20). Pekah's anti-Assyrian party probably resented Menahem's and Pekahiah's conciliatory attitude toward Assyria. Pekah would later form an alliance with Rezin, king of Syria, which pitted Israel and Syria against Judah and Assyria (see 2 Kin. 15:37; 16:5, 7–9).

■ 2 Kings 15:8–31

2 Kings
Zechariah Reigns in Israel

15 :8 In the thirty-eighth year of Azariah king of Judah, Zechariah the son of Jeroboam reigned over Israel in Samaria six months. 9And he did evil in the sight of the LORD, as his fathers had done; he did not depart from the sins of Jeroboam the son of Nebat, who had made Israel sin. 10Then Shallum the son of

Jabesh conspired against him, and struck and killed him in front of the people; and he reigned in his place.

11Now the rest of the acts of Zechariah, indeed they *are* written in the book of the chronicles of the kings of Israel. 12This *was* the word of the LORD which He spoke to Jehu, saying, "Your sons shall sit on the throne of Israel to the fourth *generation.*"a And so it was.

Shallum Reigns in Israel

13Shallum the son of Jabesh became king in the thirty-ninth year of Uzziah a king of Judah; and he reigned a full month in Samaria. 14For Menahem the son of Gadi went up from Tirzah, came to Samaria, and struck Shallum the son of Jabesh in Samaria and killed him; and he reigned in his place.

15Now the rest of the acts of Shallum, and the conspiracy which he led, indeed they *are* written in the book of the chronicles of the kings of Israel. 16Then from Tirzah, Menahem attacked Tiphsah, all who *were* there, and its territory. Because they did not surrender, therefore he attacked *it.* All the women there who were with child he ripped open.

Menahem Reigns in Israel

17In the thirty-ninth year of Azariah king of Judah, Menahem the son of Gadi became king over Israel, *and reigned* ten years in Samaria. 18And he did evil in the sight of the LORD; he did not depart all his days from the sins of Jeroboam the son of Nebat, who had made Israel sin. 19Pul a king of Assyria came against the land; and Menahem gave Pul a thousand talents of silver, that his hand might be with him to strengthen the kingdom under his control. 20And Menahem exacted the money from Israel, from all the very wealthy, from each man fifty shekels of silver, to give to the king of Assyria. So the king of Assyria turned back, and did not stay there in the land.

21Now the rest of the acts of Menahem, and all that he did, *are* they not written in the book of the chronicles of the kings of Israel? 22So Menahem rested with his fathers. Then Pekahiah his son reigned in his place.

Pekahiah Reigns in Israel

23In the fiftieth year of Azariah king of Judah, Pekahiah the son of Menahem

15:12 a2 Kings 10:30　　15:13 aCalled *Azariah* in 14:21ff and 15:1ff　　15:19 aThat is, Tiglath-Pileser III (compare verse 29)

ASSASSINATIONS IN ISRAEL

Judah (southern kingdom)
Azariah (or Uzziah) extended Judah's territory and brought the nation to a time of great prosperity. In the south he maintained control over Edom; to the west he warred against the Philistines, seizing several cities (2 Chr. 26:2, 6). While Judah enjoyed a stable period under Azariah's leadership, the northern kingdom, Israel, faced much instability as one king after another was assassinated.

Israel (northern kingdom)
Zechariah, son of Jeroboam II, was the last king of the Jehu dynasty. He reigned only 6 months before being assassinated by Shallum (2 Kin. 15:8, 10).

Shallum claimed the throne by assassinating Zechariah, but after only 1 month as king was himself assassinated by Menahem.

Menahem quickly killed the assassin Shallum and assumed the throne himself. But his kingship was probably challenged by a rival named Pekah. Another threat was the advancing Assyrian army of Tiglath-Pileser III which forced Menahem to pay tribute to the Assyrian king (2 Kin. 15:19).

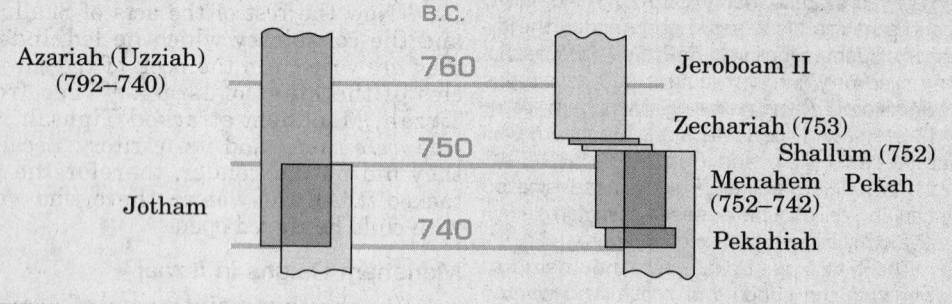

became king over Israel in Samaria, *and reigned* two years. [24]And he did evil in the sight of the LORD; he did not depart from the sins of Jeroboam the son of Nebat, who had made Israel sin. [25]Then Pekah the son of Remaliah, an officer of his, conspired against him and killed him in Samaria, in the citadel of the king's house, along with Argob and Arieh; and with him were fifty men of Gilead. He killed him and reigned in his place.

[26]Now the rest of the acts of Pekahiah, and all that he did, indeed they *are* written in the book of the chronicles of the kings of Israel.

Pekah Reigns in Israel

[27]In the fifty-second year of Azariah king of Judah, Pekah the son of Remaliah became king over Israel in Samaria, *and reigned* twenty years. [28]And he did evil in the sight of the LORD; he did not depart from the sins of Jeroboam the son of Nebat, who had made Israel sin. [29]In the days of Pekah king of Israel, Tiglath-Pileser king

of Assyria came and took Ijon, Abel Beth Maachah, Janoah, Kedesh, Hazor, Gilead, and Galilee, all the land of Naphtali; and he carried them captive to Assyria. [30]Then Hoshea the son of Elah led a conspiracy against Pekah the son of Remaliah, and struck and killed him; so he reigned in his place in the twentieth year of Jotham the son of Uzziah.

[31]Now the rest of the acts of Pekah, and all that he did, indeed they *are* written in the book of the chronicles of the kings of Israel.

 ### *Jotham and Ahaz in Judah*

While political instability plagued Israel, the calm succession of David's descendants on the throne of Judah continued. After a co-regency with his father Uzziah (750–740 B.C.), Jotham ruled Judah alone until being succeeded by his own son Ahaz (735–715 B.C.). A coalition between Israel's king Pekah and

AN OFFICER ASSASSINATES THE KING

Judah (southern kingdom)

Jotham began ruling as a coregent when it was discovered that his father Azariah had leprosy (2 Chr. 26:21). He inherited a prosperous kingdom from his father and continued to strengthen Judah, building cities and fortifications throughout the countryside. A threat to Judah began to develop during Jotham's reign when Pekah of Israel and Rezin of Aram (Syria) formed a coalition (2 Kin. 15:37).

Israel (northern kingdom)

Pekah is reported to have ruled 20 years (2 Kin. 15:27). If so, his reign began at the same time Menahem took the throne. Possibly Pekah was an officer of the royal court while Menahem and Pekahiah were kings.

Pekahiah, son of Menahem, reigned only 2 years before being assassinated by Pekah (2 Kin. 15:25).

Pekah became sole king by assassinating Pekahiah. His reign ended when he himself was assassinated by Hoshea (2 Kin. 15:30).

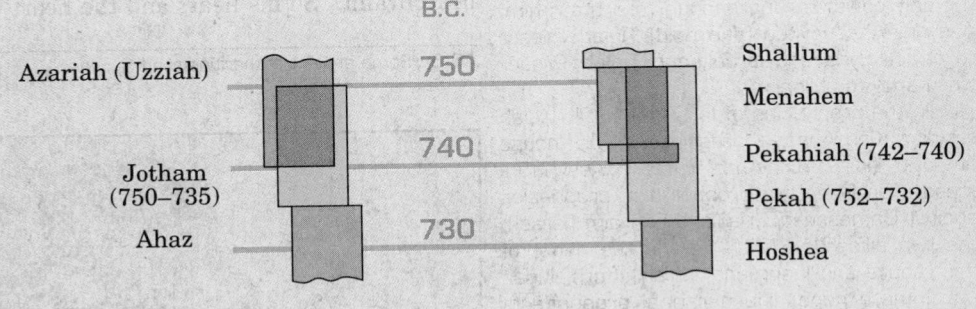

	B.C.	
Azariah (Uzziah)	750	Shallum
		Menahem
Jotham (750–735)	740	Pekahiah (742–740)
		Pekah (752–732)
Ahaz	730	Hoshea

Aram's king Rezin had some impact upon Jotham's kingdom, but would present a serious crisis for Ahaz's kingdom (2 Kin. 15:37; 16:5).

■ 2 Kings 15:32—16:4

2 Kings
Jotham Reigns in Judah

15 **:32** In the second year of Pekah the son of Remaliah, king of Israel, Jotham the son of Uzziah, king of Judah, began to reign. [33]He was twenty-five years old when he became king, and he reigned sixteen years in Jerusalem. His mother's name *was* Jerusha[a] the daughter of Zadok. [34]And he did *what was* right in the sight of the LORD; he did according to all that his father Uzziah had done. [35]However the high places were not removed; the people still sacrificed and burned incense on the high places. He built the Upper Gate of the house of the LORD.

[36]Now the rest of the acts of Jotham, and all that he did, *are* they not written in the book of the chronicles of the kings of Judah? [37]In those days the LORD began to send Rezin king of Syria and Pekah the son of Remaliah against Judah. [38]So Jotham rested with his fathers, and was buried with his fathers in the City of David his father. Then Ahaz his son reigned in his place.

Ahaz Reigns in Judah

16 [1]In the seventeenth year of Pekah the son of Remaliah, Ahaz the son of Jotham, king of Judah, began to reign. [2]Ahaz *was* twenty years old when he became king, and he reigned sixteen years in Jerusalem; and he did not do *what was* right in the sight of the LORD his God, as his father David *had* done. [3]But he walked in the way of the kings of Israel; indeed he made his son pass through the fire, according to the abominations of the nations whom the LORD had cast out from before the children of Israel. [4]And he sacrificed and burned incense on the high places, on the hills, and under every green tree.

15:33 [a]Spelled *Jerushah* in 2 Chronicles 27:1

Israel and Syria Besiege Judah

Assyria's growing power under Tiglath-Pileser III could no longer be ignored. Israel and Syria formed a defensive alliance, and their kings, Pekah and Rezin, demanded that Judah join the alliance as well. Ahaz declined, perhaps influenced by the prophet Isaiah's assurances that the Syro-Israelite coalition was doomed (Is. 7:3–9; 8:5–8).

Syria and Israel, then, decided to secure their flank by attacking Judah. Thus Ahaz, trying to avoid war with Assyria, had incited Israel and Syria to besiege his land. Isaiah told him to depend on God (Is. 7:4), but Ahaz preferred more pragmatic steps. He made a treaty with the only power strong enough to protect him: Assyria. Ahaz invited (and paid) Tiglath-Pileser to attack Syria and Israel, and Tiglath-Pileser was happy to oblige.

In the prophecies of Is. 7:1—10:4, Isaiah rebukes King Ahaz, addressing him as "house of David" (Is. 7:13). Ahaz trusts in Assyria instead of in God. The prophet also prophesies against Damascus (Syria) and Ephraim (Israel), the two allies (Is. 17:1–14). In the midst of this rebuke and judgment, Isaiah offers Judah its ultimate hope: the personal presence of God (Hebrew *Immanuel*, "God with us," 7:14; 8:8, 10). This promise of God's personal presence forms the core of the New Testament's understanding of Christ (see Matt. 1:23, quoting Is. 7:14).

- 2 Kings 16:5–9
- Isaiah 7:1–10:4
- Isaiah 17:1–14

2 Kings 16:5–9

16 :5 Then Rezin king of Syria and Pekah the son of Remaliah, king of Israel, came up to Jerusalem to *make* war; and they besieged Ahaz but could not overcome *him*. 6At that time Rezin king of Syria captured Elath for Syria, and drove the men of Judah from Elath. Then the Edomites[a] went to Elath, and dwell there to this day.

7So Ahaz sent messengers to Tiglath-Pileser king of Assyria, saying, "I *am* your servant and your son. Come up and save me from the hand of the king of Syria and from the hand of the king of Israel, who rise up against me." 8And Ahaz took the silver and gold that was found in the house of the LORD, and in the treasuries of the

king's house, and sent *it as* a present to the king of Assyria. 9So the king of Assyria heeded him; for the king of Assyria went up against Damascus and took it, carried *its people* captive to Kir, and killed Rezin.

Isaiah 7:1—10:4
Isaiah Sent to King Ahaz

7 :1 Now it came to pass in the days of Ahaz the son of Jotham, the son of Uzziah, king of Judah, *that* Rezin king of Syria and Pekah the son of Remaliah, king of Israel, went up to Jerusalem to *make* war against it, but could not prevail against it. 2And it was told to the house of David, saying, "Syria's forces are deployed in Ephraim." So his heart and the heart of

---

16:6 ªSome ancient authorities read *Syrians*.

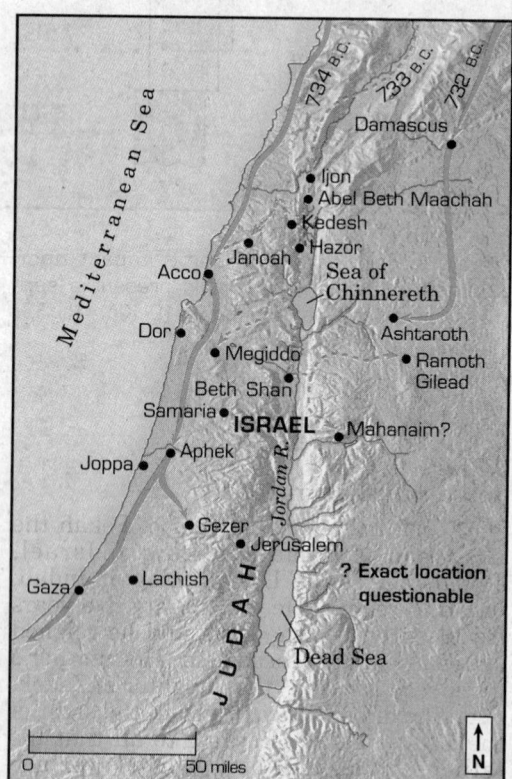

Assyrian Campaigns in Palestine

In 734 B.C. Tiglath-Pileser III of Assyria moved along the coast through Philistia, conquering Gaza, and placing his forces on the Egyptian border. In 733 B.C. much of Galilee was conquered, deporting many Israelites in the process. The Aramean capital of Damascus fell to Assyria in 732 B.C.

Vassal to Sovereign to Vassal (2 Kin. 16:9)

Aram was an important state in southern Syria from the 11th to 8th centuries B.C. The state was connected with the larger ethnic group of Arameans, who inhabited this area in the late 2nd and 1st millenniums B.C. Reflecting this region, the NKJV and some other translations render the Hebrew name *Aram* as "Syria" or "Syrians."

Many Aramean tribal states attached the designation "Aram" to their names, as in the compound name "Padan Aram" (Gen. 25:20). Biblical writers usually used the Hebrew word *Aram* to refer specifically to Aram-Damascus, the Aramean state whose capital was Damascus. But occasionally *Aram* refers to the Aramean states in general (Judg. 10:6; 1 Kin. 10:29; Amos 9:7).

Early in the 10th century B.C., the Aram-Damascus kingdom was incorporated as a vassal into King David's state (2 Sam. 8:5, 6). During the reign of Solomon (970–930 B.C.), Rezon usurped the throne of Damascus and was able to free himself of Israelite control (1 Kin. 11:23–25).

Aram-Damascus took advantage of the split of the Israelite kingdom in 930 B.C. and became the most powerful state in the region. Soon thereafter, Ahab of Israel became vassal to Ben-Hadad of Aram (1 Kin. 20:1–9) who ruled a kingdom that controlled much of southern Syria and Palestine.

Aram-Damascus was instrumental in originating the anti-Assyrian coalition against Assyria's Shalmaneser III in 853 B.C., culminating in the battle of Qarqar. Assyrian annals tell us that Ahab of Israel furnished 2,000 chariots and 10,000 infantry, while King Hadad-ezer of Aram-Damascus contributed 1,200 chariots and 20,000 infantry. The coalition lasted about a decade. For the next century, intermittent war was fought between Aram-Damascus and Israel, with Aram usually the dominant power in this struggle.

Aram-Damascus continued to be a threat to the existence of both Israel and Judah until the mid-8th century B.C. During the state's last years of independence, Rezin, the last Aramean king, formed a second anti-Assyrian coalition. In what is known as the Syro-Ephraimite War, Rezin, in alliance with Israel, attacked Judah with the apparent goal of coercing Judah into the coalition.

The result was not as Rezin hoped. Assyrian annals tell of Aram falling to Assyria in 732 B.C. and becoming a vassal to the Assyrian king, Tiglath-Pileser III. Aram-Damascus was annexed to Assyria, ending the former state's sovereignty (2 Kin. 16:9).

---

his people were moved as the trees of the woods are moved with the wind.

³Then the LORD said to Isaiah, "Go out now to meet Ahaz, you and Shear-Jashub[a] your son, at the end of the aqueduct from the upper pool, on the highway to the Fuller's Field, ⁴and say to him: 'Take heed, and be quiet; do not fear or be fainthearted for these two stubs of smoking firebrands, for the fierce anger of Rezin and Syria, and the son of Remaliah. ⁵Because Syria, Ephraim, and the son of Remaliah have plotted evil against you, saying, ⁶"Let us go up against Judah and trouble it, and let us make a gap in its wall for ourselves, and set a king over them, the son of Tabel"— ⁷thus says the Lord GOD:

"It shall not stand,
Nor shall it come to pass.
8 For the head of Syria *is* Damascus,
And the head of Damascus *is* Rezin.
Within sixty-five years Ephraim will
    be broken,
So that it will not *be* a people.
9 The head of Ephraim *is* Samaria,
And the head of Samaria *is*
    Remaliah's son.
If you will not believe,
Surely you shall not be
    established." ' "

The Immanuel Prophecy

¹⁰Moreover the LORD spoke again to Ahaz, saying, ¹¹"Ask a sign for yourself from the LORD your God; ask it either in the depth or in the height above."

7:3 aLiterally *A Remnant Shall Return*

SMOLDERING ENDS OF BURNT-OUT LOGS (Is. 7:1–9)

The term "Syro-Ephraimite War" is a modern expression referring to the major conflict in which the kingdom of Judah was opposed by the Syro-Ephraimite coalition of Syria and Israel. King Rezin of Syria (centered in Damascus) and King Pekah of northern Israel (known as Ephraim) tried to force Judah to join them in an alliance against Assyria. The resulting war is reported in the biblical historical narratives (2 Kin. 16:5–9; 2 Chr. 28:5–21).

The importance of this struggle in Israel's history is evident from numerous references to the conflict in the prophets. Some of Hosea's prophecies probably picture the period during the war, reflecting military engagements between Israel and Judah (Hos. 5:8–15). The prophet Isaiah told Judah's king Ahaz not to fear the kings of Syria and Israel, calling them "two stubs of smoking firebrands" (Is. 7:1–9); they were burnt-out logs.

Before the war, a coalition of Syro-Palestinian states, including Syria, Tyre, Ashkelon, and Israel, had formed to defend against the rising power of Assyria. When Ahaz of Judah refused to enter the group, they plotted to replace this Davidic king with a puppet ruler, who was the son of a certain Tabel (Is. 7:5, 6). Scholars suppose Tabel refers to Tubail, who later himself became king of Tyre.

As the prophet Isaiah had announced (Is. 7:1–9), the Syro-Ephraimite coalition failed. Judah and Jerusalem were attacked, however, the Assyrians under Tiglath-Pileser III (744–727 B.C.), responding to Ahaz's call for help, invaded Syria, destroying Damascus in 732 B.C. Tyre lost significant territory, and the rulers of the Philistine states Ashkelon and Gaza were replaced. Pekah of Israel was subsequently assassinated, and Israel was required to continue paying tribute to Assyria.

---

¹²But Ahaz said, "I will not ask, nor will I test the LORD!"

¹³Then he said, "Hear now, O house of David! *Is it* a small thing for you to weary men, but will you weary my God also? ¹⁴Therefore the Lord Himself will give you a sign: Behold, the virgin shall conceive and bear a Son, and shall call His name Immanuel.ᵃ ¹⁵Curds and honey He shall eat, that He may know to refuse the evil and choose the good. ¹⁶For before the Child shall know to refuse the evil and choose the good, the land that you dread will be forsaken by both her kings. ¹⁷The LORD will bring the king of Assyria upon you and your people and your father's house—days that have not come since the day that Ephraim departed from Judah."

¹⁸ And it shall come to pass in that day
  That the LORD will whistle for the fly
  That *is* in the farthest part of the
    rivers of Egypt,
  And for the bee that *is* in the land of
    Assyria.
¹⁹ They will come, and all of them will
    rest
  In the desolate valleys and in the
    clefts of the rocks,
  And on all thorns and in all pastures.

²⁰ In the same day the Lord will shave
    with a hired razor,
  With those from beyond the River,ᵃ
    with the king of Assyria,
  The head and the hair of the legs,
  And will also remove the beard.

²¹ It shall be in that day
  That a man will keep alive a young
    cow and two sheep;
²² So it shall be, from the abundance of
    milk they give,
  That he will eat curds;
  For curds and honey everyone will eat
    who is left in the land.

²³ It shall happen in that day,
  That wherever there could be a
    thousand vines
  Worth a thousand *shekels* of silver,
  It will be for briers and thorns.
²⁴ With arrows and bows men will come
    there,
  Because all the land will become
    briers and thorns.

²⁵ And to any hill which could be dug
    with the hoe,

7:14 ᵃLiterally *God-With-Us*   7:20 ᵃThat is, the Euphrates

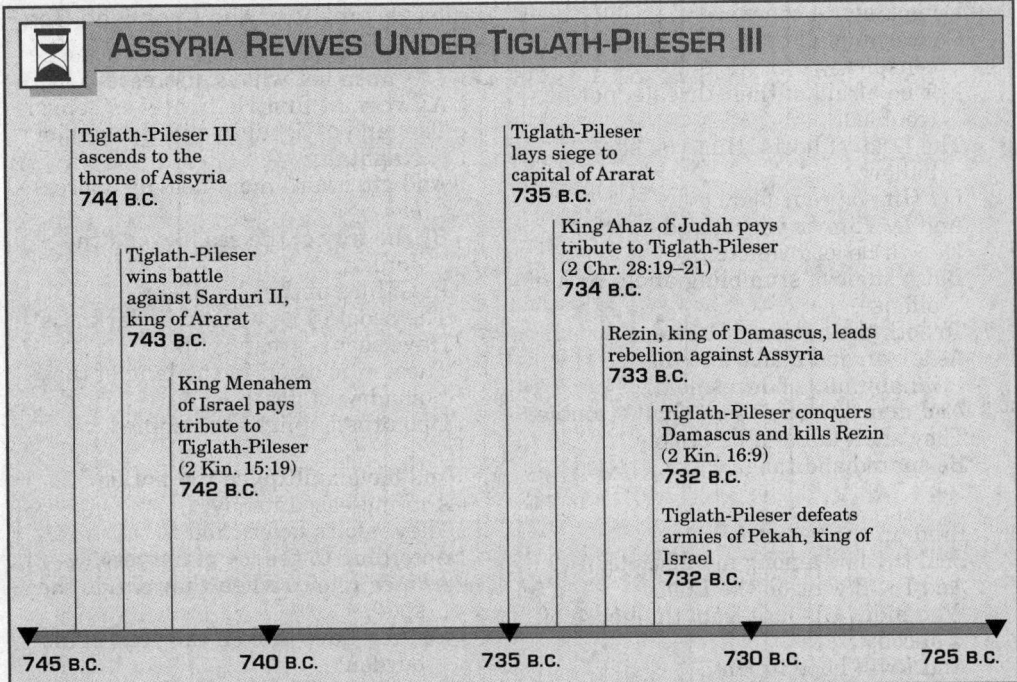

ASSYRIA REVIVES UNDER TIGLATH-PILESER III

Tiglath-Pileser III
ascends to the
throne of Assyria
744 B.C.

Tiglath-Pileser
wins battle
against Sarduri II,
king of Ararat
743 B.C.

King Menahem
of Israel pays
tribute to
Tiglath-Pileser
(2 Kin. 15:19)
742 B.C.

Tiglath-Pileser
lays siege to
capital of Ararat
735 B.C.

King Ahaz of Judah pays
tribute to Tiglath-Pileser
(2 Chr. 28:19–21)
734 B.C.

Rezin, king of Damascus, leads
rebellion against Assyria
733 B.C.

Tiglath-Pileser conquers
Damascus and kills Rezin
(2 Kin. 16:9)
732 B.C.

Tiglath-Pileser defeats
armies of Pekah, king of
Israel
732 B.C.

745 B.C.   **740 B.C.**   **735 B.C.**   **730 B.C.**   **725 B.C.**

You will not go there for fear of briers
    and thorns;
But it will become a range for oxen
And a place for sheep to roam.

Assyria Will Invade the Land

8 ¹Moreover the LORD said to me, "Take a large scroll, and write on it with a man's pen concerning Maher-Shalal-Hash-Baz.ᵃ ²And I will take for Myself faithful witnesses to record, Uriah the priest and Zechariah the son of Jeberechiah."

³Then I went to the prophetess, and she conceived and bore a son. Then the LORD said to me, "Call his name Maher-Shalal-Hash-Baz; ⁴for before the child shall have knowledge to cry 'My father' and 'My mother,' the riches of Damascus and the spoil of Samaria will be taken away before the king of Assyria."

⁵The LORD also spoke to me again, saying:

6 "Inasmuch as these people refused
    The waters of Shiloah that flow softly,
    And rejoice in Rezin and in
        Remaliah's son;

7 Now therefore, behold, the Lord
        brings up over them
    The waters of the River,ᵃ strong and
        mighty—
    The king of Assyria and all his glory;
    He will go up over all his channels
    And go over all his banks.
8 He will pass through Judah,
    He will overflow and pass over,
    He will reach up to the neck;
    And the stretching out of his wings
    Will fill the breadth of Your land,
        O Immanuel.ᵃ

9 "Be shattered, O you peoples, and be
        broken in pieces!
    Give ear, all you from far countries.
    Gird yourselves, but be broken in
        pieces;
    Gird yourselves, but be broken in
        pieces.
10 Take counsel together, but it will come
        to nothing;
    Speak the word, but it will not stand,
    For God is with us."ᵃ

Fear God, Heed His Word

¹¹For the LORD spoke thus to me with a strong hand, and instructed me that I should not walk in the way of this people, saying:

8:1 ᵃLiterally *Speed the Spoil, Hasten the Booty*
8:7 ᵃThat is, the Euphrates   8:8 ᵃLiterally *God-With-Us*   8:10 ᵃHebrew *Immanuel*

12 "Do not say, 'A conspiracy,'
   Concerning all that this people call a
      conspiracy,
   Nor be afraid of their threats, nor be
      troubled.
13 The LORD of hosts, Him you shall
      hallow;
   Let Him *be* your fear,
   And *let* Him *be* your dread.
14 He will be as a sanctuary,
   But a stone of stumbling and a rock of
      offense
   To both the houses of Israel,
   As a trap and a snare to the
      inhabitants of Jerusalem.
15 And many among them shall stumble;
   They shall fall and be broken,
   Be snared and taken."

16 Bind up the testimony,
   Seal the law among my disciples.
17 And I will wait on the LORD,
   Who hides His face from the house of
      Jacob;
   And I will hope in Him.
18 Here am I and the children whom the
      LORD has given me!
   We are for signs and wonders in
      Israel
   From the LORD of hosts,
   Who dwells in Mount Zion.

19And when they say to you, "Seek those who are mediums and wizards, who whisper and mutter," should not a people seek their God? *Should they* seek the dead on behalf of the living? 20To the law and to the testimony! If they do not speak according to this word, *it is* because *there* is no light in them. 21They will pass through it hardpressed and hungry; and it shall happen, when they are hungry, that they will be enraged and curse their king and their God, and look upward. 22Then they will look to the earth, and see trouble and darkness, gloom of anguish; and *they will be* driven into darkness.

The Government of the Promised Son

9 1 Nevertheless the gloom *will* not *be*
      upon her who *is* distressed,
   As when at first He lightly esteemed
   The land of Zebulun and the land of
      Naphtali,
   And afterward more heavily oppressed
      her,
   By the way of the sea, beyond the
      Jordan,
   In Galilee of the Gentiles.
2 The people who walked in darkness
   Have seen a great light;
   Those who dwelt in the land of the
      shadow of death,
   Upon them a light has shined.

3 You have multiplied the nation
   And increased its joy;[a]
   They rejoice before You
   According to the joy of harvest,
   As *men* rejoice when they divide the
      spoil.
4 For You have broken the yoke of his
      burden
   And the staff of his shoulder,
   The rod of his oppressor,
   As in the day of Midian.
5 For every warrior's sandal from the
      noisy battle,
   And garments rolled in blood,
   Will be used for burning *and* fuel of
      fire.

6 For unto us a Child is born,
   Unto us a Son is given;
   And the government will be upon His
      shoulder.
   And His name will be called
   Wonderful, Counselor, Mighty God,
   Everlasting Father, Prince of Peace.
7 Of the increase of *His* government and
      peace
   There will be no end,

9:3 aFollowing Qere and Targum; Kethib and Vulgate read *not increased joy;* Septuagint reads *Most of the people You brought down in Your joy.*

CULTS AND SUPERNATURAL

The spirits of the dead, and the mediums who pretend to speak for them, can only talk in whispers and squeaks (Is. 8:19). This is appropriate for those who have left their body behind. When Odysseus visited Hades, the spirits there lamented their increasing separation from the life of physical vitality. The prophets struggled to keep the people from resorting to spiritism.

Upon the throne of David and over
   His kingdom,
To order it and establish it with
   judgment and justice
From that time forward, even forever.
The zeal of the Lord of hosts will
   perform this.

The Punishment of Samaria

8 The Lord sent a word against Jacob,
   And it has fallen on Israel.
9 All the people will know—
   Ephraim and the inhabitant of
     Samaria—
   Who say in pride and arrogance of
     heart:
10 "The bricks have fallen down,
   But we will rebuild with hewn stones;
   The sycamores are cut down,
   But we will replace *them* with cedars."
11 Therefore the LORD shall set up
   The adversaries of Rezin against him,
   And spur his enemies on,
12 The Syrians before and the Philistines
     behind;
   And they shall devour Israel with an
     open mouth.

For all this His anger is not turned
   away,
But His hand *is* stretched out still.

13 For the people do not turn to Him who
     strikes them,
   Nor do they seek the LORD of hosts.
14 Therefore the LORD will cut off head
     and tail from Israel,
   Palm branch and bulrush in one day.
15 The elder and honorable, he *is* the
     head;
   The prophet who teaches lies, he *is*
     the tail.

16 For the leaders of this people cause
     them to err,
   And *those who are* led by them are
     destroyed.
17 Therefore the Lord will have no joy in
     their young men,
   Nor have mercy on their fatherless
     and widows;
   For everyone *is* a hypocrite and an
     evildoer,
   And every mouth speaks folly.

For all this His anger is not turned
   away,
But His hand *is* stretched out still.

18 For wickedness burns as the fire;
   It shall devour the briers and thorns,
   And kindle in the thickets of the
     forest;
   They shall mount up *like* rising
     smoke.
19 Through the wrath of the LORD of
     hosts
   The land is burned up,
   And the people shall be as fuel for the
     fire;
   No man shall spare his brother.
20 And he shall snatch on the right hand
     And be hungry;
   He shall devour on the left hand
     And not be satisfied;
   Every man shall eat the flesh of his
     own arm.
21 Manasseh *shall devour* Ephraim, and
     Ephraim Manasseh;
   Together they *shall be* against Judah.

For all this His anger is not turned
   away,
But His hand *is* stretched out still.

10

1 "Woe to those who decree
     unrighteous decrees,
   Who write misfortune,
   Which they have prescribed
2 To rob the needy of justice,
   And to take what is right from the
     poor of My people,
   That widows may be their prey,
   And *that* they may rob the fatherless.
3 What will you do in the day of
     punishment,
   And in the desolation *which* will come
     from afar?
   To whom will you flee for help?
   And where will you leave your glory?

TIME CAPSULE   *727 to 722 B.C.*

727   *Tiglath-Pileser III dies, and Hoshea withholds tribute from Assyria*

726–
722   *The reign of Shalmaneser V of Assyria ends during a revolution*

725–
722   *Shalmaneser lays siege to Samaria*

724   *Hoshea of Israel shifts his loyalty from Assyria to Egypt*

722   *Fall of Samaria to the Assyrians*

ASSYRIA COMES TO JUDAH AND ISRAEL

Judah (southern kingdom)

Ahaz, son of Jotham, adopted policies as king that favored Assyria. He refused to join the anti-Assyrian alliance that kings Pekah of Israel and Rezin of Aram (Syria) were supporting. Pekah and Rezin besieged Jerusalem, threatening to dethrone Ahaz.

In defense, Ahaz requested help from the king of Assyria. The plan worked when Assyria invaded Israel and Aram, but Ahaz had to pay tribute to Assyria's king (2 Kin. 16:9, 10; 2 Chr. 28:21).

Israel (northern kingdom)

Hoshea became king after assassinating the former king, Pekah. At first Hoshea served as a puppet king under Assyria. But eventually he rebelled against Assyria, negotiating an alliance with Egypt (2 Kin. 17:4).

The Assyrian king, Shalmaneser V, besieged the capital, Samaria, and Hoshea was captured and imprisoned. After 3 years of siege, Assyria finally captured Samaria, and its inhabitants were exiled to locations in the Assyrian Empire.

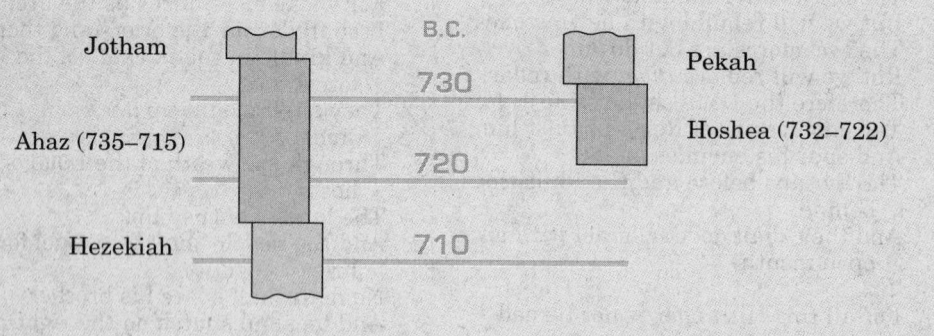

4 Without Me they shall bow down
     among the prisoners,
And they shall fall among the slain."

For all this His anger is not turned
     away,
But His hand *is* stretched out still.

Isaiah 17:1–14
Proclamation Against Syria and Israel

17 :1 The burden against Damascus.

"Behold, Damascus will cease from
     being a city,
And it will be a ruinous heap.
2 The cities of Aroer *are* forsaken;[a]
They will be for flocks
Which lie down, and no one will make
     them afraid.
3 The fortress also will cease from
     Ephraim,
The kingdom from Damascus,
And the remnant of Syria;
They will be as the glory of the
     children of Israel,"
Says the LORD of hosts.

4 "In that day it shall come to pass
That the glory of Jacob will wane,
And the fatness of his flesh grow
     lean.
5 It shall be as when the harvester
     gathers the grain,
And reaps the heads with his arm;
It shall be as he who gathers heads of
     grain
In the Valley of Rephaim.
6 Yet gleaning grapes will be left in it,
Like the shaking of an olive tree,
Two *or* three olives at the top of the
     uppermost bough,
Four *or* five in its most fruitful
     branches,"
Says the LORD God of Israel.

7 In that day a man will look to his
     Maker,
And his eyes will have respect for the
     Holy One of Israel.

17:2 aFollowing Masoretic Text and Vulgate; Septuagint reads *It shall be forsaken forever;* Targum reads *Its cities shall be forsaken and desolate.*

IS THIS A RITUAL FOR A DYING GOD? (Is. 17:10, 11)

Isaiah prophesied that a harvest of "pleasant plants" would reap "a heap of ruins" (Is. 17:10, 11). Scholars have often suggested that the prophet refers to a ritual for the worship of the god Adonis. All we know about the worship of Adonis comes from Greek sources, but it is claimed that the Greek cult of Adonis was based on a Phoenician cult practiced primarily by women in Phoenicia.

As a part of the ritual in honor of Adonis, seedlings were planted on potsherds (broken pieces of pottery). The plants would sprout, but because they had no soil, would grow only for a day or two and then die. The short life of the plant symbolized the short and tragic life of the god Adonis, who is said to have died young in a hunting accident. The women then mourned for the dead god with public wailing.

Isaiah intensifies the meaning of the ritual. The worshipers think they are mourning for the god, but Isaiah asserts that they are really mourning their own demise. They will surely die because they have abandoned Yahweh (17:10).

8 He will not look to the altars,
The work of his hands;
He will not respect what his fingers
have made,
Nor the wooden images[a] nor the
incense altars.

9 In that day his strong cities will be as
a forsaken bough[a]
And an uppermost branch,[b]
Which they left because of the
children of Israel;
And there will be desolation.

10 Because you have forgotten the God of
your salvation,
And have not been mindful of the
Rock of your stronghold,
Therefore you will plant pleasant
plants
And set out foreign seedlings;

11 In the day you will make your plant to
grow,
And in the morning you will make
your seed to flourish;
But the harvest *will be* a heap of
ruins
In the day of grief and desperate
sorrow.

12 Woe to the multitude of many
people
Who make a noise like the roar of the
seas,
And to the rushing of nations
That make a rushing like the rushing
of mighty waters!

13 The nations will rush like the rushing
of many waters;
But *God* will rebuke them and they
will flee far away,
And be chased like the chaff of the
mountains before the wind,
Like a rolling thing before the
whirlwind.

14 Then behold, at eventide, trouble!
And before the morning, he *is* no
more.
This *is* the portion of those who
plunder us,
And the lot of those who rob us.

17:8 [a]Hebrew *Asherim,* Canaanite deities
17:9 [a]Septuagint reads *Hivites;* Targum reads *laid waste;* Vulgate reads *as the plows.* [b]Septuagint reads *Amorites;* Targum reads *in ruins;* Vulgate reads *corn.*

TIME CAPSULE *722 to 720 B.C.*

722 Sargon II usurps the throne of Assyria

721 First official year of Sargon's reign

721– 705 Israelites transported to Assyria during early years of Sargon's reign

721– 710 Merodach-Baladan's first reign in Babylon

720 Elamites assist Merodach-Baladan against Assyria

After the Syro-Ephraimite War

The Syro-Ephraimite War ended in 732 B.C. when Tiglath-Pileser and Assyria destroyed Damascus, the capital of Aram (Syria). The Assyrian armies made their presence felt throughout Palestine, from Syria in the northeast to the Philistine coastlands in the southwest. Isaiah warns Assyria that her hold on Palestine will not last forever (Is. 14:24–27), but before Assyria's power would be broken, that power would stretch even to the land of the Philistines (14:28–32).

Judah too, which had avoided war by making diplomatic concessions, was under Assyrian sovereignty. Ahaz's Assyrian-inspired temple modifications (2 Kin. 16:10–18) should perhaps be seen as a sign of the Judean king's loyalty to his Assyrian overlords (16:18).

- Isaiah 14:24–32
- 2 Kings 16:10–20

Isaiah 14:24–32
Assyria Destroyed

14 :24 The LORD of hosts has sworn,
saying,
"Surely, as I have thought, so it shall
come to pass,
And as I have purposed, *so* it shall
stand:
25 That I will break the Assyrian in My
land,
And on My mountains tread him
underfoot.
Then his yoke shall be removed from
them,
And his burden removed from their
shoulders.
26 This *is* the purpose that is purposed
against the whole earth,
And this *is* the hand that is stretched
out over all the nations.
27 For the LORD of hosts has purposed,
And who will annul *it*?
His hand *is* stretched out,
And who will turn it back?"

Philistia Destroyed

28This is the burden which came in the year that King Ahaz died.

29 "Do not rejoice, all you of Philistia,
Because the rod that struck you is
broken;
For out of the serpent's roots will come
forth a viper,

And its offspring *will be* a fiery flying
serpent.
30 The firstborn of the poor will feed,
And the needy will lie down in safety;
I will kill your roots with famine,
And it will slay your remnant.
31 Wail, O gate! Cry, O city!
All you of Philistia *are* dissolved;
For smoke will come from the north,
And no one *will be* alone in his
appointed times."

32 What will they answer the
messengers of the nation?
That the LORD has founded Zion,
And the poor of His people shall take
refuge in it.

2 Kings 16:10–20

16 :10 Now King Ahaz went to Damascus to meet Tiglath-Pileser king of Assyria, and saw an altar that *was* at Damascus; and King Ahaz sent to Urijah the priest the design of the altar and its pattern, according to all its workmanship. 11Then Urijah the priest built an altar according to all that King Ahaz had sent from Damascus. So Urijah the priest made *it* before King Ahaz came back from Damascus. 12And when the king came back from Damascus, the king saw the altar; and the king approached the altar and made offerings on it. 13So he burned his burnt offering and his grain offering; and he poured his drink offering and sprinkled the blood of his peace offerings on the altar. 14He also brought the bronze altar which *was* before the LORD, from the front of the temple— from between the *new* altar and the house of the LORD—and put it on the north side of the *new* altar. 15Then King Ahaz commanded Urijah the priest, saying, "On the great *new* altar burn the morning burnt offering, the evening grain offering, the king's burnt sacrifice, and his grain offering, with the burnt offering of all the people of the land, their grain offering, and their drink offerings; and sprinkle on it all the blood of the burnt offering and all the blood of the sacrifice. And the bronze altar shall be for me to inquire *by*." 16Thus did Urijah the priest, according to all that King Ahaz commanded.

17And King Ahaz cut off the panels of the carts, and removed the lavers from them; and he took down the Sea from the bronze oxen that *were* under it, and put it on a pavement of stones. 18Also he removed the Sabbath pavilion which they had built in the temple, and he removed the king's outer entrance from the house of the LORD, on account of the king of Assyria.

19Now the rest of the acts of Ahaz which he did, *are* they not written in the book of the chronicles of the kings of Judah? 20So Ahaz rested with his fathers, and was buried with his fathers in the City of David. Then Hezekiah his son reigned in his place.

The Book of Micah

Micah, like Isaiah, prophesied in Judah during the reigns of Jotham, Ahaz, and Hezekiah (Mic. 1:1). Indeed, there are even some parallels between the two prophets. Both spoke of God's plan for Zion (Jerusalem) and said that salvation would come through the line of David (cf. Is. 11:1–5; Mic. 5:2–5). There is even one shared prophecy: Is. 2:2–4 is almost identical to Mic. 4:1–3.

Micah has a few distinctives, however. Perhaps because he is not from Jerusalem itself, he is less convinced of Jerusalem's invulnerability than Isaiah seems. Micah prophesies Jerusalem's destruction (Mic. 3:12; see Jer. 26:17–19 for the results of this prophecy). In addition, Micah rejects religious hypocrisy and calls for the protection of the helpless in language that is more like that of Amos than that of Isaiah (Mic. 6:1–8).

■ Micah 1:1—2:13

Micah

1 :1 The word of the LORD that came to Micah of Moresheth in the days of Jotham, Ahaz, *and* Hezekiah, kings of Judah, which he saw concerning Samaria and Jerusalem.

The Coming Judgment on Israel

2　　Hear, all you peoples!
　　Listen, O earth, and all that is in it!
　　Let the Lord GOD be a witness against
　　　you,
　　The Lord from His holy temple.

3　　For behold, the LORD is coming out of
　　　His place;
　　He will come down
　　And tread on the high places of the
　　　earth.

4　The mountains will melt under Him,
　　And the valleys will split
　　Like wax before the fire,
　　Like waters poured down a steep
　　　place.

5　All this is for the transgression of
　　　Jacob
　　And for the sins of the house of Israel.
　　What *is* the transgression of Jacob?
　　Is it not Samaria?
　　And what *are* the high places of
　　　Judah?
　　Are they not Jerusalem?

6　"Therefore I will make Samaria a heap
　　　of ruins in the field,
　　Places for planting a vineyard;
　　I will pour down her stones into the
　　　valley,
　　And I will uncover her foundations.

7　All her carved images shall be beaten
　　　to pieces,
　　And all her pay as a harlot shall be
　　　burned with the fire;
　　All her idols I will lay desolate,
　　For she gathered *it* from the pay of a
　　　harlot,
　　And they shall return to the pay of a
　　　harlot."

Mourning for Israel and Judah

8　Therefore I will wail and howl,
　　I will go stripped and naked;
　　I will make a wailing like the jackals
　　And a mourning like the ostriches,

9　For her wounds *are* incurable.
　　For it has come to Judah;
　　It has come to the gate of My people—
　　To Jerusalem.

10　Tell *it* not in Gath,
　　Weep not at all;
　　In Beth Aphrah[a]
　　Roll yourself in the dust.

11　Pass by in naked shame, you
　　　inhabitant of Shaphir;
　　The inhabitant of Zaanan[a] does not go
　　　out.
　　Beth Ezel mourns;
　　Its place to stand is taken away from
　　　you.

12　For the inhabitant of Maroth pined[a]
　　　for good,
　　But disaster came down from the
　　　LORD
　　To the gate of Jerusalem.

1:10 ᵃLiterally *House of Dust*　　1:11 ᵃLiterally *Going Out*　　1:12 ᵃLiterally *was sick*

13 O inhabitant of Lachish,
Harness the chariot to the swift steeds
(She *was* the beginning of sin to the
daughter of Zion),
For the transgressions of Israel were
found in you.

14 Therefore you shall give presents to
Moresheth Gath;[a]
The houses of Achzib[b] *shall be* a lie to
the kings of Israel.

15 I will yet bring an heir to you,
O inhabitant of Mareshah;[a]
The glory of Israel shall come to
Adullam.

16 Make yourself bald and cut off your
hair,
Because of your precious children;
Enlarge your baldness like an eagle,
For they shall go from you into
captivity.

Woe to Evildoers

2 1 Woe to those who devise iniquity,
And work out evil on their beds!
At morning light they practice it,
Because it is in the power of their
hand.

2 They covet fields and take *them* by
violence,
Also houses, and seize *them.*
So they oppress a man and his house,
A man and his inheritance.

3Therefore thus says the LORD:

"Behold, against this family I am
devising disaster,
From which you cannot remove your
necks;

Nor shall you walk haughtily,
For this *is* an evil time.

4 In that day *one* shall take up a
proverb against you,
And lament with a bitter lamentation,
saying:
'We are utterly destroyed!
He has changed the heritage of my
people;
How He has removed *it* from me!
To a turncoat He has divided our
fields.' "

5 Therefore you will have no one to
determine boundaries[a] by lot
In the assembly of the LORD.

Lying Prophets

6 "Do not prattle," *you say to those* who
prophesy.
So they shall not prophesy to you;[a]
They shall not return insult for
insult.[b]

7 *You who are* named the house of
Jacob:
"Is the Spirit of the LORD restricted?
Are these His doings?
Do not My words do good
To him who walks uprightly?

8 "Lately My people have risen up as an
enemy—
You pull off the robe with the garment
From those who trust *you,* as they
pass by,
Like men returned from war.

9 The women of My people you cast out
From their pleasant houses;
From their children
You have taken away My glory
forever.

10 "Arise and depart,
For this *is* not *your* rest;
Because it is defiled, it shall destroy,
Yes, with utter destruction.

11 If a man should walk in a false spirit
And speak a lie, *saying,*
'I will prophesy to you of wine and
drink,'
Even he would be the prattler of this
people.

TIME CAPSULE   *720 to 716 B.C.*

720   *After a victory at Qarqar Sargon II
marches through Gaza and Israel to
Egypt's border*

720   *Hamath is incorporated into the Assyrian Empire*

717   *Assyrians conquer and destroy Carchemish*

717   *Memphis is besieged by the Nubian
ruler Piankhy*

716   *Ishmaelite tribes pay tribute to Sargon II of Assyria*

1:14 [a]Literally *Possession of Gath*   [b]Literally *Lie*
1:15 [a]Literally *Inheritance*   2:5 [a]Literally *one
casting a surveyor's line*   2:6 [a]Literally *to these*
[b]Vulgate reads *He shall not take shame.*

Israel Restored

12 "I will surely assemble all of you,
O Jacob,
I will surely gather the remnant of
Israel;
I will put them together like sheep of
the fold,[a]
Like a flock in the midst of their
pasture;
They shall make a loud noise because
of *so many* people.

13 The one who breaks open will come up
before them;
They will break out,
Pass through the gate,
And go out by it;
Their king will pass before them,
With the LORD at their head."

Micah's Ministry

Like Hosea's oracles, Micah's words provide only vague references to the historical events which may form their background. The kings mentioned in Mic. 1:1 (Jotham, Ahaz, Hezekiah) place Micah's ministry in the second half of the 8th century B.C. (750–686 B.C.). Specific dates within that period are not possible to determine.

A few passages in the book suggest approximate times. References to Samaria (Mic. 1:1, 6) imply that at least part of Micah's preaching occurred before the fall of the northern kingdom in 722 B.C. Two other passages point to a later time during Hezekiah's reign (715–686 B.C.). The cities named in Mic. 1:10–16 seem to picture a military invasion from the south such as that conducted by the Assyrian king Sennacherib in 701 B.C. (see "Sennacherib's Invasion" at Is. 36:1). Quoting the words of Mic. 3:12, Jeremiah places Micah in "the days of Hezekiah" (Jer. 26:18), prophesying the fall of Jerusalem.

■ Micah 3:1—7:20

Micah
Wicked Rulers and Prophets

3 :1 And I said:

"Hear now, O heads of Jacob,
And you rulers of the house of Israel:
Is it not for you to know justice?
2 You who hate good and love evil;

Who strip the skin from My people,[a]
And the flesh from their bones;
3 Who also eat the flesh of My people,
Flay their skin from them,
Break their bones,
And chop *them* in pieces
Like *meat* for the pot,
Like flesh in the caldron."

4 Then they will cry to the LORD,
But He will not hear them;
He will even hide His face from them
at that time,
Because they have been evil in their
deeds.

5 Thus says the LORD concerning the
prophets
Who make my people stray;
Who chant "Peace"
While they chew with their teeth,
But who prepare war against him
Who puts nothing into their mouths:
6 "Therefore you shall have night
without vision,
And you shall have darkness without
divination;
The sun shall go down on the
prophets,
And the day shall be dark for them.
7 So the seers shall be ashamed,
And the diviners abashed;
Indeed they shall all cover their lips;
For *there is* no answer from God."

8 But truly I am full of power by the
Spirit of the LORD,
And of justice and might,
To declare to Jacob his transgression
And to Israel his sin.
9 Now hear this,
You heads of the house of Jacob
And rulers of the house of Israel,
Who abhor justice
And pervert all equity,
10 Who build up Zion with bloodshed
And Jerusalem with iniquity:
11 Her heads judge for a bribe,
Her priests teach for pay,
And her prophets divine for money.
Yet they lean on the LORD, and say,
"Is not the LORD among us?
No harm can come upon us."
12 Therefore because of you
Zion shall be plowed *like* a field,
Jerusalem shall become heaps of
ruins,
And the mountain of the temple[a]
Like the bare hills of the forest.

2:12 [a]Hebrew *Bozrah*   3:2 [a]Literally *them*
3:12 [a]Literally *house*

A PROPHET PROPHESIES AGAINST THE PROPHETS (Mic. 3:5–8)

Kings usually employed the services of professional prophets, who kept the king informed of the will of the gods. Yet despite the prevalence of such court prophets, it was widely believed that gods could use any human, from slave to ruler, as a prophet. The Mari tablets (c. 1813–1760 B.C.) record a prophecy from the deity Dagon as it was spoken by a slave woman who served one of the princesses. The prophetic frenzy of King Saul is an example of prophetic actions on the part of royalty (1 Sam. 19:23, 24).

Those persons who were seized by God and forced to speak the divine word are known as ecstatic prophets. For example, Amos insists that God had made him speak, though he was definitely not a prophet, only a sheepbreeder (Amos 7:14, 15). Similarly, Micah received power to prophesy "by the Spirit of the LORD" (Mic. 3:8). Yet Micah's prophecies denounced the professional prophets and seers who themselves could obtain "no answer from God" (Mic. 3:5–7).

Generally, the ecstatic prophets were different individuals from the professional court prophets, and the Bible distinguishes between true and false prophets. The true prophet was forced to speak the very word supplied by God whether or not the human wished to do so, as was Jeremiah's prophetic experience (Jer. 20:7–9). To hear the words of a true prophet was to hear the very word of God. False prophets, however, made up their own prophecies and then spoke them as if they were from the divine world. One seldom actually encountered a court prophet who was also ecstatic, though such was the prophet Micaiah in King Ahab's court (1 Kin. 22:8, 14).

The LORD's Reign in Zion

4 1 Now it shall come to pass in the latter days
That the mountain of the LORD's house
Shall be established on the top of the mountains,
And shall be exalted above the hills;
And peoples shall flow to it.
2 Many nations shall come and say,
"Come, and let us go up to the mountain of the LORD,
To the house of the God of Jacob;
He will teach us His ways,
And we shall walk in His paths."
For out of Zion the law shall go forth,
And the word of the LORD from Jerusalem.
3 He shall judge between many peoples,
And rebuke strong nations afar off;
They shall beat their swords into plowshares,
And their spears into pruning hooks;
Nation shall not lift up sword against nation,
Neither shall they learn war anymore.[a]
4 But everyone shall sit under his vine and under his fig tree,

And no one shall make *them* afraid;
For the mouth of the LORD of hosts has spoken.
5 For all people walk each in the name of his god,
But we will walk in the name of the LORD our God
Forever and ever.

Zion's Future Triumph

6 "In that day," says the LORD,
"I will assemble the lame,
I will gather the outcast
And those whom I have afflicted;
7 I will make the lame a remnant,
And the outcast a strong nation;
So the LORD will reign over them in Mount Zion
From now on, even forever.
8 And you, O tower of the flock,
The stronghold of the daughter of Zion,
To you shall it come,
Even the former dominion shall come,
The kingdom of the daughter of Jerusalem."

9 Now why do you cry aloud?
Is there no king in your midst?

4:3 [a]Compare Isaiah 2:2–4

EACH WITH THEIR OWN GOD (Mic. 4:5)

Micah recognized that each people had its own gods. Each state or group had its own patron deity or deities to whom it was devoted, and whom the civil authorities honored in public ritual. The theology of the ancient Near East held that patron deities provided for their people protection, abundance, and guidance for moral and ritual conduct.

Around Judah were cities with patron deities, like Tyre and her god Baal-Melqart. There were also states, such as Moab with her ethnic deity Chemosh, and empires, which, though they had vast pantheons, still had a national deity, such as Re in Egypt, Asshur in Assyria, and Marduk in Babylonia.

Micah says that Judah will "walk" in Yahweh's name forever, though other nations walk in the name of their own gods (Mic. 4:5). The import of his statement is that Yahweh was one God among many deities. That there were other gods for other peoples, however, does not alter Judah's situation: Yahweh was to be their only God, and it was by the laws of Yahweh that Judah must live.

Has your counselor perished?
For pangs have seized you like a
woman in labor.
10 Be in pain, and labor to bring forth,
O daughter of Zion,
Like a woman in birth pangs.
For now you shall go forth from the
city,
You shall dwell in the field,
And to Babylon you shall go.
There you shall be delivered;
There the LORD will redeem you
From the hand of your enemies.

11 Now also many nations have gathered
against you,
Who say, "Let her be defiled,
And let our eye look upon Zion."
12 But they do not know the thoughts of
the LORD,
Nor do they understand His counsel;
For He will gather them like sheaves
to the threshing floor.

13 "Arise and thresh, O daughter of Zion;
For I will make your horn iron,
And I will make your hooves bronze;
You shall beat in pieces many peoples;
I will consecrate their gain to the
LORD,

And their substance to the Lord of the
whole earth."

5 1 Now gather yourself in troops,
O daughter of troops;
He has laid siege against us;
They will strike the judge of Israel
with a rod on the cheek.

The Coming Messiah

2 "But you, Bethlehem Ephrathah,
Though you are little among the
thousands of Judah,
Yet out of you shall come forth to Me
The One to be Ruler in Israel,
Whose goings forth *are* from of old,
From everlasting."

3 Therefore He shall give them up,
Until the time *that* she who is in labor
has given birth;
Then the remnant of His brethren
Shall return to the children of Israel.
4 And He shall stand and feed *His flock*
In the strength of the LORD,
In the majesty of the name of the
LORD His God;
And they shall abide,

HEALTH AND MEDICINE

In the ancient world, children were born at home, not in a hospital. The pains of labor and delivery, extreme as they are, were familiar to many people. The writers of the Bible use birth pains to suggest the sufferings that must take place before the salvation of God appears (Mic. 4:10). The distress that accompanies the unfolding of the divine plan has been called "the birth pangs of the Messiah" (compare John 16:21, 22).

For now He shall be great
To the ends of the earth;
5   And this *One* shall be peace.

Judgment on Israel's Enemies

When the Assyrian comes into our
  land,
And when he treads in our palaces,
Then we will raise against him
Seven shepherds and eight princely
  men.
6   They shall waste with the sword the
  land of Assyria,
And the land of Nimrod at its
  entrances;
Thus He shall deliver *us* from the
  Assyrian,
When he comes into our land
And when he treads within our
  borders.

7   Then the remnant of Jacob
Shall be in the midst of many peoples,
Like dew from the LORD,
Like showers on the grass,
That tarry for no man
Nor wait for the sons of men.
8   And the remnant of Jacob
Shall be among the Gentiles,
In the midst of many peoples,
Like a lion among the beasts of the
  forest,
Like a young lion among flocks of
  sheep,
Who, if he passes through,
Both treads down and tears in pieces,
And none can deliver.
9   Your hand shall be lifted against your
  adversaries,
And all your enemies shall be cut off.

10   "And it shall be in that day," says the
  LORD,
"That I will cut off your horses from
  your midst
And destroy your chariots.
11   I will cut off the cities of your land
And throw down all your strongholds.
12   I will cut off sorceries from your hand,
And you shall have no soothsayers.
13   Your carved images I will also cut off,
And your *sacred* pillars from your
  midst;
You shall no more worship the work of
  your hands;
14   I will pluck your wooden images[a] from
  your midst;
Thus I will destroy your cities.

15   And I will execute vengeance in anger
  and fury
On the nations that have not heard."[a]

God Pleads with Israel

6   ¹Hear now what the LORD says:

"Arise, plead your case before the
  mountains,
And let the hills hear your voice.
2   Hear, O you mountains, the LORD's
  complaint,
And you strong foundations of the
  earth;
For the LORD has a complaint against
  His people,
And He will contend with Israel.

3   "O My people, what have I done to
  you?
And how have I wearied you?
Testify against Me.
4   For I brought you up from the land of
  Egypt,
I redeemed you from the house of
  bondage;
And I sent before you Moses, Aaron,
  and Miriam.
5   O My people, remember now
What Balak king of Moab counseled,
And what Balaam the son of Beor
  answered him,
From Acacia Grove[a] to Gilgal,
That you may know the righteousness
  of the LORD."

6   With what shall I come before the
  LORD,
And bow myself before the High God?
Shall I come before Him with burnt
  offerings,
With calves a year old?
7   Will the LORD be pleased with
  thousands of rams,
Ten thousand rivers of oil?
Shall I give my firstborn *for* my
  transgression,
The fruit of my body *for* the sin of my
  soul?

8   He has shown you, O man, what *is*
  good;
And what does the LORD require of
  you

5:14 [a]Hebrew *Asherim,* Canaanite deities
5:15 [a]Or *obeyed*   6:5 [a]Hebrew *Shittim* (compare
Numbers 25:1; Joshua 2:1; 3:1)

OMRI'S NAME LIVES ON (Mic. 6:16)

Omri was the king of Israel (885–874 B.C.) who established Samaria as the capital of the Israelite kingdom. He also founded a dynasty in Israel that lasted four generations, with Omri being followed on Israel's throne by his son Ahab, and Ahab's sons Ahaziah and Joram.

Omri and his dynasty achieved international importance. Illustrating Omri's influence are references to him in two sources outside of the Bible. The Moabite Stone is a basalt slab dating from about 850 B.C. which records some of Omri's military accomplishments. In the inscription on the stone, King Mesha of Moab mentions Omri as occupying parts of the land of Moab. Moreover, Omri is indirectly mentioned in the Assyrian annals of Shalmaneser III (858–824 B.C.). Although Jehu was not of Omri's family and had even overthrown the Omri dynasty, he is described in the annals as a "son of Omri," and the land of Israel is called the "house of Omri."

This Israelite king also impacted neighboring Judah, and his name was known to Micah, who prophesied more than 125 years after Omri's death. Micah's mention of "the statutes of Omri" (Mic. 6:16) possibly alludes to Omri's importance in at least legal declarations, although there is no other reference to Omri's legal code, even in sources outside of the Bible. Despite impressive political accomplishments, Omri is condemned for his religious policies (1 Kin. 16:25, 26), and Micah announces judgment on the people because they have kept Omri's statutes.

But to do justly,
To love mercy,
And to walk humbly with your God?

Punishment of Israel's Injustice

9 The LORD's voice cries to the city—
Wisdom shall see Your name:

"Hear the rod!
Who has appointed it?
10 Are there yet the treasures of wickedness
In the house of the wicked,
And the short measure *that is* an abomination?
11 Shall I count pure *those* with the wicked scales,
And with the bag of deceitful weights?
12 For her rich men are full of violence,
Her inhabitants have spoken lies,
And their tongue is deceitful in their mouth.

13 "Therefore I will also make *you* sick by striking you,
By making *you* desolate because of your sins.

14 You shall eat, but not be satisfied;
Hunger[a] *shall be* in your midst.
You may carry *some* away,[b] but shall not save *them;*
And what you do rescue I will give over to the sword.

15 "You shall sow, but not reap;
You shall tread the olives, but not anoint yourselves with oil;
And *make* sweet wine, but not drink wine.
16 For the statutes of Omri are kept;
All the works of Ahab's house *are done;*
And you walk in their counsels,
That I may make you a desolation,
And your inhabitants a hissing.
Therefore you shall bear the reproach of My people."[a]

Sorrow for Israel's Sins

7 1 Woe is me!
For I am like those who gather summer fruits,
Like those who glean vintage grapes;
There is no cluster to eat
Of the first-ripe fruit *which* my soul desires.
2 The faithful *man* has perished from the earth,
And *there is* no one upright among men.

6:14 [a]Or *Emptiness* or *Humiliation*   [b]Targum and Vulgate read *You shall take hold.*   6:16 [a]Following Masoretic Text, Targum, and Vulgate; Septuagint reads *of nations.*

They all lie in wait for blood;
Every man hunts his brother with a
    net.

3 That they may successfully do evil
    with both hands—
The prince asks *for gifts,*
The judge *seeks* a bribe,
And the great *man* utters his evil
    desire;
So they scheme together.
4 The best of them *is* like a brier;
The most upright *is sharper* than a
    thorn hedge;
The day of your watchman and your
    punishment comes;
Now shall be their perplexity.

5 Do not trust in a friend;
Do not put your confidence in a
    companion;
Guard the doors of your mouth
From her who lies in your bosom.
6 For son dishonors father,
Daughter rises against her mother,
Daughter-in-law against her mother-
    in-law;
A man's enemies *are* the men of his
    own household.
7 Therefore I will look to the LORD;
I will wait for the God of my salvation;
My God will hear me.

Israel's Confession and Comfort

8 Do not rejoice over me, my enemy;
When I fall, I will arise;
When I sit in darkness,
The LORD *will be* a light to me.
9 I will bear the indignation of the
    LORD,
Because I have sinned against Him,
Until He pleads my case
And executes justice for me.
He will bring me forth to the light;
I will see His righteousness.
10 Then *she who is* my enemy will see,
And shame will cover her who said to
    me,
  "Where is the LORD your God?"
My eyes will see her;
Now she will be trampled down
Like mud in the streets.

11 *In* the day when your walls are to be
    built,
In that day the decree shall go far and
    wide.[a]

12 *In* that day they[a] shall come to you
From Assyria and the fortified cities,[b]
From the fortress[c] to the River,[d]
From sea to sea,
And mountain *to* mountain.
13 Yet the land shall be desolate
Because of those who dwell in it,
And for the fruit of their deeds.

God Will Forgive Israel

14 Shepherd Your people with Your staff,
The flock of Your heritage,
Who dwell solitarily *in* a woodland,
In the midst of Carmel;
Let them feed *in* Bashan and Gilead,
As in days of old.

15 "As in the days when you came out of
    the land of Egypt,
I will show them[a] wonders."

16 The nations shall see and be ashamed
    of all their might;
They shall put *their* hand over *their*
    mouth;
Their ears shall be deaf.
17 They shall lick the dust like a serpent;
They shall crawl from their holes like
    snakes of the earth.
They shall be afraid of the LORD our
    God,
And shall fear because of You.
18 Who *is* a God like You,
Pardoning iniquity
And passing over the transgression of
    the remnant of His heritage?

He does not retain His anger forever,
Because He delights *in* mercy.
19 He will again have compassion on us,
And will subdue our iniquities.

You will cast all our[a] sins
Into the depths of the sea.
20 You will give truth to Jacob
And mercy to Abraham,
Which You have sworn to our fathers
From days of old.

7:11 [a]Or *the boundary shall be extended*
7:12 [a]Literally *he,* collective of the captives   [b]Hebrew
arey mazor, possibly *cities of Egypt*   [c]Hebrew *mazor,*
possibly *Egypt*   [d]That is, the Euphrates
7:15 [a]Literally *him,* collective for the captives
7:19 [a]Literally *their*

Priestly Account: Pekah Attacks Ahaz

As usual, the Chronicler gives more detail about the kings of Judah and much less detail about the kings of Israel, than does the Book of Kings. The succession of kings in Israel is not mentioned; only Pekah appears in relation to the attack on Judah (2 Chr. 28:5, 6). On the other hand, Chronicles expands the account of King Jotham in Judah, relating more of his building activities (27:3, 4) and his victory over Ammon (27:5).

The differences between Kings and Chronicles, though, are more than just detail. In 2 Kings, Syria and Israel could not overcome Ahaz (2 Kin. 16:5), but 2 Chronicles describes their victory over Judah, emphasizing Judah's losses (2 Chr. 28:5–15). Perhaps 2 Kin. 16:5 only means that the Syro-Israelite coalition could not take Jerusalem itself.

In Chronicles the two kingdoms, Israel and Judah, are still "brethren," even though they are at war (28:11). For Israel to have enslaved their brethren from Judah would have been in violation of the Mosaic law (see Lev. 25:39–43). The Israelites of Ephraim were sensitive to the guilt involved (2 Chr. 28:13), which influenced the kind treatment of the Judahite captives (28:15).

The two histories agree, however, in their condemnation of Ahaz and his worship of foreign deities. "This is that King Ahaz" (2 Chr. 28:22–25) who did not turn to God, but, in fact, turned farther from Him.

■ 2 Chronicles 27:1—28:27

2 Chronicles
Jotham Reigns in Judah

27 :1 Jotham *was* twenty-five years old when he became king, and he reigned sixteen years in Jerusalem. His mother's name *was* Jerushah[a] the daughter of Zadok. ²And he did *what was* right in the sight of the LORD, according to all that his father Uzziah had done (although he did not enter the temple of the LORD). But still the people acted corruptly.

³He built the Upper Gate of the house of the LORD, and he built extensively on the wall of Ophel. ⁴Moreover he built cities in the mountains of Judah, and in the forests

he built fortresses and towers. ⁵He also fought with the king of the Ammonites and defeated them. And the people of Ammon gave him in that year one hundred talents of silver, ten thousand kors of wheat, and ten thousand of barley. The people of Ammon paid this to him in the second and third years also. ⁶So Jotham became mighty, because he prepared his ways before the LORD his God.

⁷Now the rest of the acts of Jotham, and all his wars and his ways, indeed they *are* written in the book of the kings of Israel and Judah. ⁸He was twenty-five years old when he became king, and he reigned sixteen years in Jerusalem. ⁹So Jotham rested with his fathers, and they buried him in the City of David. Then Ahaz his son reigned in his place.

Ahaz Reigns in Judah

28 ¹Ahaz *was* twenty years old when he became king, and he reigned sixteen years in Jerusalem; and he did not do *what was* right in the sight of the LORD, as his father David *had done*. ²For he walked in the ways of the kings of Israel, and made molded images for the Baals. ³He burned incense in the Valley of the Son of Hinnom, and burned his children in the fire, according to the abominations of the nations whom the LORD had cast out before the children of Israel. ⁴And he sacrificed and burned incense on the high places, on the hills, and under every green tree.

Syria and Israel Defeat Judah

⁵Therefore the LORD his God delivered him into the hand of the king of Syria.

TIME CAPSULE	715 to 710 B.C.
715	*Hezekiah becomes king in Judah*
714–712	*Ashkelon joins with other Philistine cities in coalition against Assyria*
713	*Sargon II places his brother on throne in Ashdod*
712	*Sargon forces Yamani of Ashdod to flee to Egypt*
710	*Merodach-Baladan driven from Babylon by Sargon*

They defeated him, and carried away a great multitude of them as captives, and brought *them* to Damascus. Then he was also delivered into the hand of the king of Israel, who defeated him with a great slaughter. 6For Pekah the son of Remaliah killed one hundred and twenty thousand in Judah in one day, all valiant men, because they had forsaken the LORD God of their fathers. 7Zichri, a mighty man of Ephraim, killed Maaseiah the king's son, Azrikam the officer over the house, and Elkanah *who was* second to the king. 8And the children of Israel carried away captive of their brethren two hundred thousand women, sons, and daughters; and they also took away much spoil from them, and brought the spoil to Samaria.

Israel Returns the Captives

9But a prophet of the LORD was there, whose name *was* Oded; and he went out before the army that came to Samaria, and said to them: "Look, because the LORD God of your fathers was angry with Judah, He has delivered them into your hand; but you have killed them in a rage *that* reaches up to heaven. 10And now you propose to force the children of Judah and Jerusalem to be your male and female slaves; *but are* you not also guilty before the LORD your God? 11Now hear me, therefore, and return the captives, whom you have taken captive from your brethren, for the fierce wrath of the LORD *is* upon you."

12Then some of the heads of the children of Ephraim, Azariah the son of Johanan, Berechiah the son of Meshillemoth, Jehizkiah the son of Shallum, and Amasa the son of Hadlai, stood up against those who came from the war, 13and said to them, "You shall not bring the captives here, for we *already* have offended the LORD. You intend to add to our sins and to our guilt; for our guilt is great, and *there is* fierce wrath against Israel." 14So the armed men left the captives and the spoil before the leaders and all the assembly. 15Then the men who were designated by name rose up and took the captives, and from the spoil they clothed all who were naked among them, dressed them and gave them sandals, gave them food and drink, and anointed them; and they let all the feeble ones ride on donkeys. So they brought them to their brethren at Jericho, the city of palm trees. Then they returned to Samaria.

Assyria Refuses to Help Judah

16At the same time King Ahaz sent to the kings[a] of Assyria to help him. 17For again the Edomites had come, attacked Judah, and carried away captives. 18The Philistines also had invaded the cities of the lowland and of the South of Judah, and had taken Beth Shemesh, Aijalon, Gederoth, Sochoh with its villages, Timnah with its villages, and Gimzo with its villages; and they dwelt there. 19For the LORD brought Judah low because of Ahaz king of Israel, for he had encouraged moral decline in Judah and had been continually unfaithful to the LORD. 20Also Tiglath-Pileser[a] king of Assyria came to him and distressed him, and did not assist him. 21For Ahaz took part *of the treasures* from the house of the LORD, from the house of the king, and from the leaders, and he gave *it* to the king of Assyria; but he did not help him.

Apostasy and Death of Ahaz

22Now in the time of his distress King Ahaz became increasingly unfaithful to the LORD. This *is that* King Ahaz. 23For he sacrificed to the gods of Damascus which had defeated him, saying, "Because the gods of the kings of Syria help them, I will sacrifice to them that they may help me." But they were the ruin of him and of all Israel. 24So Ahaz gathered the articles of the house of God, cut in pieces the articles of the house of God, shut up the doors of the house of the LORD, and made for himself altars in every corner of Jerusalem. 25And in every single city of Judah he made high places to burn incense to other gods, and provoked to anger the LORD God of his fathers.

26Now the rest of his acts and all his ways, from first to last, indeed they *are* written in the book of the kings of Judah and Israel. 27So Ahaz rested with his fathers, and they buried him in the city, in Jerusalem; but they did not bring him into the tombs of the kings of Israel. Then Hezekiah his son reigned in his place.

28:16 aSeptuagint, Syriac, and Vulgate read *king* (compare verse 20).   28:20 aHebrew *Tilgath-Pilneser*

Prophetic Account: Assyria's Invasions

The alliance made by Pekah of Israel and Rezin of Syria failed. As Isaiah had foretold (Is. 17:1–11), Tiglath-Pileser of Assyria overcame Syria and crushed it, destroying 591 towns in the campaign that ended in 732 B.C. Israel, however, survived briefly after the Syro-Ephraimite War, now under King Hoshea (732–722 B.C.). When Tiglath-Pileser died, Hoshea rebelled against Assyria, depending on help from Egypt. Tiglath-Pileser's successor, Shalmaneser V (726–722 B.C.), moved quickly.

■ 2 Kings 17:1–4

2 Kings
Hoshea Reigns in Israel

17 **:1** In the twelfth year of Ahaz king of Judah, Hoshea the son of Elah became king of Israel in Samaria, *and he*

Damascus●
● Ijon
● Abel Beth Maachah
● Kedesh
Janoah ● Hazor
Acco● Sea of
Chinnereth
Dor ● ● Ashtaroth
● Megiddo ● Ramoth
Beth Shan● Gilead
ISRAEL
Samaria ●
● Mahanaim?
Joppa● ●Aphek
● Gezer
● Jerusalem
Gaza● **? Exact location questionable**
Lachish ●
Dead Sea

Mediterranean Sea

Jordan R.

JUDAH

0   50 miles   ↑N

Assyrian Campaign Against Israel
In 725 B.C. Shalmaneser V of Assyria invaded Israel and besieged the capital city of Samaria for 3 years. Shalmaneser died shortly before Samaria fell in 722 B.C. Sargon II, his successor, claimed the credit for the Assyrian victory.

reigned nine years. ²And he did evil in the sight of the Lᴏʀᴅ, but not as the kings of Israel who were before him. ³Shalmaneser king of Assyria came up against him; and Hoshea became his vassal, and paid him tribute money. ⁴And the king of Assyria uncovered a conspiracy by Hoshea; for he had sent messengers to So, king of Egypt, and brought no tribute to the king of Assyria, as *he had done* year by year. Therefore the king of Assyria shut him up, and bound him in prison.

A Warning to Jerusalem's Leaders

To Isaiah, in southern Judah, northern Israel's approaching end was the result of the people's refusal to listen to the word of the Lord. There was no reason for Judah to rejoice. Instead, Isaiah used the "fading flower" of Ephraim (another name for Israel) as an object lesson for the rulers in Jerusalem (Is. 28:1–29). Jerusalem too can be punished, he declares, though it will not be destroyed (29:6–9). And someday, perhaps, those who had refused to hear will hear; even Israel, the house of Jacob, might be restored (29:17–24).

■ Isaiah 28:1—29:24

Isaiah
Woe to Ephraim and Jerusalem

28 **:1** Woe to the crown of pride, to the drunkards of Ephraim,
Whose glorious beauty *is* a fading flower
Which *is* at the head of the verdant valleys,
To those who are overcome with wine!
2 Behold, the Lord has a mighty and strong one,
Like a tempest of hail and a destroying storm,
Like a flood of mighty waters overflowing,
Who will bring *them* down to the earth with *His* hand.
3 The crown of pride, the drunkards of Ephraim,
Will be trampled underfoot;
4 And the glorious beauty is a fading flower
Which *is* at the head of the verdant valley,
Like the first fruit before the summer,

KING SO OR DYNASTY SO (2 Kin. 17:4)

King Hoshea of Israel attempted to procure military aid from "So, king of Egypt" (2 Kin. 17:4) for a rebellion against Assyria, but was unsuccessful. The positive identification of this king with monarchs listed in Egyptian records also has been unsuccessful.

Though no Egyptian king is known by the name "So," two kings are possible candidates. Both ruled in Egypt during Hoshea's reign in Israel (732–722 B.C.), and both ruled at a time when Egypt was politically divided. In fact, they were contemporaries: Osorkon IV (730–715 B.C.) and Tefnakht I (727–720 B.C.).

Osorkon IV was the last ruler of the 22nd Dynasty (c. 945–715 B.C.). The Egypt of his time was no longer a united kingdom, but rather consisted of small, rival Libyan dynasties. Some scholars suggest that "So" was a short form of the name "Osorkon."

Tefnakht I was able to consolidate a kingdom in Egypt's West Delta, establishing a capital at Sais. Scholars have supposed that "So" could be a place name corresponding to Sais, or to "the Saite," a name referring to the dynasty of pharaohs who ruled from the city of Sais. If this were the case, then the writer of 2 Kings possibly meant that Hoshea sent "to Sais (So), to the king of Egypt," emphasizing the Egyptian monarch's dynasty rather than his personal name.

These two contemporary monarchs are the most likely candidates to be King So of Egypt. Although Osorkon IV would have been physically closer to Palestine, Tefnakht campaigned in Arabia, according to tradition.

Which an observer sees;
He eats it up while it is still in his
  hand.

5 In that day the LORD of hosts will be
For a crown of glory and a diadem of
  beauty
To the remnant of His people,
6 For a spirit of justice to him who sits
  in judgment,
And for strength to those who turn
  back the battle at the gate.

7 But they also have erred through
  wine,
And through intoxicating drink are
  out of the way;
The priest and the prophet have erred
  through intoxicating drink,
They are swallowed up by wine,
They are out of the way through
  intoxicating drink;

They err in vision, they stumble *in*
  judgment.
8 For all tables are full of vomit *and*
  filth;
No place *is clean.*

9 "Whom will he teach knowledge?
And whom will he make to
  understand the message?
Those *just* weaned from milk?
Those *just* drawn from the breasts?
10 For precept *must be* upon precept,
  precept upon precept,
Line upon line, line upon line,
Here a little, there a little."

11 For with stammering lips and another
  tongue
He will speak to this people,
12 To whom He said, "This *is* the rest
  with which
You may cause the weary to rest,"

FOOD AND DRINK

There is a natural limit to the strength of alcohol that can be obtained without distilling, a process unknown in biblical times. Great quantities of grain were used to make beer, which was more of a food or thin gruel than today's beer. Numerous warnings in Scripture show that drunkenness was a problem (Is. 28:7).

A COVENANT WITH DEATH (Is. 28:15, 18)

In the ancient world worshipers prayed to both demons and deities of death to spare them, or they wore amulets to protect them from death by warding off the divine beings. Such amulets are commonly found in Middle Eastern archaeological digs, including Judah and Israel.

The god of death in Syria-Palestine was Mot. The Ugaritic myths from Ras Shamra, Syria, depict Mot as having an insatiable appetite for living beings and, in the end, devouring all life. In Canaanite thought, Mot, the bringer of death, struggles with Baal, the bringer of life. Mot's victories result in death and destruction on earth, while Baal's victories bring life-giving rains and good crops.

Isaiah confronted some leaders of Jerusalem who anticipated a coming destruction (Is. 28:14–22). The "overflowing scourge" (28:15) pictures a "flood," a metaphor used throughout the ancient Near East for military destruction. These leaders believed that by making a covenant with Mot they would be safe. Mot, they supposed, would protect them when the devastation passed through.

Isaiah answers that their "covenant with death," their bargain with Mot, offers no real security (28:18, 19). All Mot can deliver is death itself.

And, "This *is* the refreshing";
Yet they would not hear.

13 But the word of the LORD was to them,
"Precept upon precept, precept upon precept,
Line upon line, line upon line,
Here a little, there a little,"
That they might go and fall backward, and be broken
And snared and caught.

14 Therefore hear the word of the LORD, you scornful men,
Who rule this people who *are* in Jerusalem,

15 Because you have said, "We have made a covenant with death,
And with Sheol we are in agreement.
When the overflowing scourge passes through,
It will not come to us,
For we have made lies our refuge,
And under falsehood we have hidden ourselves."

A Cornerstone in Zion

16 Therefore thus says the Lord GOD:

"Behold, I lay in Zion a stone for a foundation,
A tried stone, a precious cornerstone, a sure foundation;
Whoever believes will not act hastily.

17 Also I will make justice the measuring line,

And righteousness the plummet;
The hail will sweep away the refuge of lies,
And the waters will overflow the hiding place.

18 Your covenant with death will be annulled,
And your agreement with Sheol will not stand;
When the overflowing scourge passes through,
Then you will be trampled down by it.

19 As often as it goes out it will take you;
For morning by morning it will pass over,
And by day and by night;
It will be a terror just to understand the report."

20 For the bed is too short to stretch out *on,*
And the covering so narrow that one cannot wrap himself *in it.*

21 For the LORD will rise up as *at* Mount Perazim,
He will be angry as in the Valley of Gibeon—
That He may do His work, His awesome work,
And bring to pass His act, His unusual act.

22 Now therefore, do not be mockers,
Lest your bonds be made strong;
For I have heard from the Lord GOD of hosts,

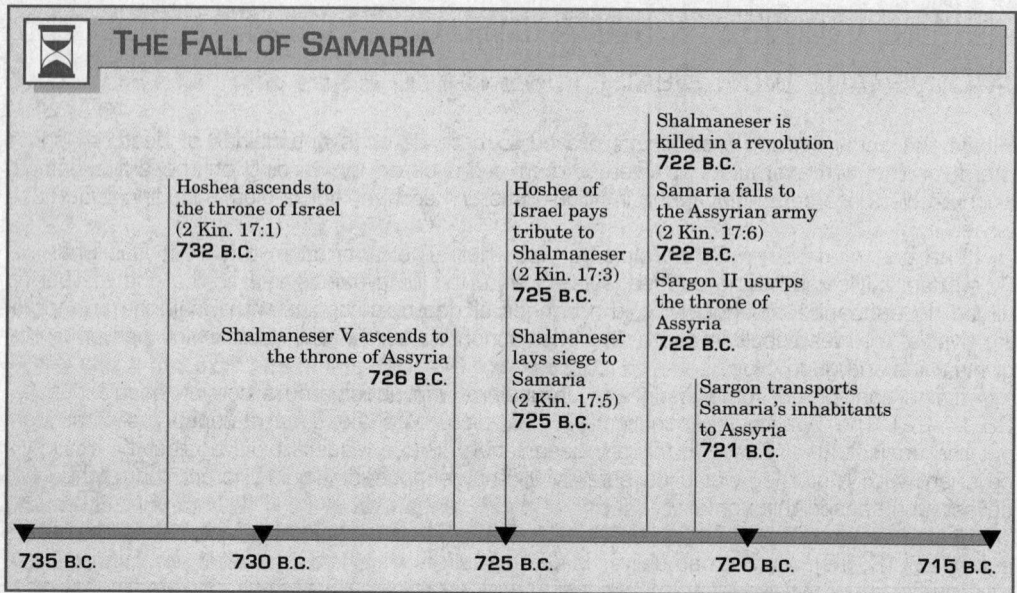

THE FALL OF SAMARIA

Hoshea ascends to the throne of Israel (2 Kin. 17:1) **732 B.C.**

Shalmaneser V ascends to the throne of Assyria **726 B.C.**

Hoshea of Israel pays tribute to Shalmaneser (2 Kin. 17:3) **725 B.C.**

Shalmaneser lays siege to Samaria (2 Kin. 17:5) **725 B.C.**

Shalmaneser is killed in a revolution **722 B.C.**

Samaria falls to the Assyrian army (2 Kin. 17:6) **722 B.C.**

Sargon II usurps the throne of Assyria **722 B.C.**

Sargon transports Samaria's inhabitants to Assyria **721 B.C.**

735 B.C.   **730 B.C.**   **725 B.C.**   **720 B.C.**   **715 B.C.**

A destruction determined even upon the whole earth.

Listen to the Teaching of God

23 Give ear and hear my voice,
Listen and hear my speech.
24 Does the plowman keep plowing all day to sow?
Does he keep turning his soil and breaking the clods?
25 When he has leveled its surface,
Does he not sow the black cummin
And scatter the cummin,
Plant the wheat in rows,
The barley in the appointed place,
And the spelt in its place?
26 For He instructs him in right judgment,
His God teaches him.

27 For the black cummin is not threshed with a threshing sledge,
Nor is a cartwheel rolled over the cummin;
But the black cummin is beaten out with a stick,
And the cummin with a rod.
28 Bread *flour* must be ground;
Therefore he does not thresh it forever,
Break *it with* his cartwheel,
Or crush it *with* his horsemen.
29 This also comes from the LORD of hosts,

Who is wonderful in counsel *and* excellent in guidance.

Woe to Jerusalem

29 1 "Woe to Ariel,[a] to Ariel, the city *where* David dwelt!
Add year to year;
Let feasts come around.
2 Yet I will distress Ariel;
There shall be heaviness and sorrow,
And it shall be to Me as Ariel.
3 I will encamp against you all around,
I will lay siege against you with a mound,
And I will raise siegeworks against you.
4 You shall be brought down,
You shall speak out of the ground;
Your speech shall be low, out of the dust;
Your voice shall be like a medium's, out of the ground;
And your speech shall whisper out of the dust.

5 "Moreover the multitude of your foes
Shall be like fine dust,
And the multitude of the terrible ones
Like chaff that passes away;
Yes, it shall be in an instant, suddenly.

29:1   aThat is, Jerusalem

6 You will be punished by the LORD of
hosts
With thunder and earthquake and
great noise,
With storm and tempest
And the flame of devouring fire.
7 The multitude of all the nations who
fight against Ariel,
Even all who fight against her and
her fortress,
And distress her,
Shall be as a dream of a night vision.
8 It shall even be as when a hungry
man dreams,
And look—he eats;
But he awakes, and his soul is still
empty;
Or as when a thirsty man dreams,
And look—he drinks;
But he awakes, and indeed *he is* faint,
And his soul still craves:
So the multitude of all the nations
shall be,
Who fight against Mount Zion."

The Blindness of Disobedience

9 Pause and wonder!
Blind yourselves and be blind!
They are drunk, but not with wine;
They stagger, but not with
intoxicating drink.
10 For the LORD has poured out on you
The spirit of deep sleep,
And has closed your eyes, namely, the
prophets;
And He has covered your heads,
namely, the seers.

11The whole vision has become to you
like the words of a book that is sealed,
which *men* deliver to one who is literate,
saying, "Read this, please."
And he says, "I cannot, for it *is* sealed."
12Then the book is delivered to one who
is illiterate, saying, "Read this, please."
And he says, "I am not literate."
13Therefore the Lord said:

"Inasmuch as these people draw near
with their mouths
And honor Me with their lips,
But have removed their hearts far
from Me,
And their fear toward Me is taught by
the commandment of men,
14 Therefore, behold, I will again do a
marvelous work
Among this people,

A marvelous work and a wonder;
For the wisdom of their wise *men*
shall perish,
And the understanding of their
prudent *men* shall be hidden."
15 Woe to those who seek deep to hide
their counsel far from the LORD,
And their works are in the dark;
They say, "Who sees us?" and, "Who
knows us?"
16 Surely you have things turned
around!
Shall the potter be esteemed as the
clay;
For shall the thing made say of him
who made it,
"He did not make me"?
Or shall the thing formed say of him
who formed it,
"He has no understanding"?

Future Recovery of Wisdom

17 *Is* it not yet a very little while
Till Lebanon shall be turned into a
fruitful field,
And the fruitful field be esteemed as a
forest?
18 In that day the deaf shall hear the
words of the book,
And the eyes of the blind shall see out
of obscurity and out of darkness.
19 The humble also shall increase *their*
joy in the LORD,
And the poor among men shall rejoice
In the Holy One of Israel.
20 For the terrible one is brought to
nothing,
The scornful one is consumed,
And all who watch for iniquity are cut
off—
21 Who make a man an offender by a
word,
And lay a snare for him who reproves
in the gate,
And turn aside the just by empty
words.

22Therefore thus says the LORD, who
redeemed Abraham, concerning the house
of Jacob:

"Jacob shall not now be ashamed,
Nor shall his face now grow pale;
23 But when he sees his children,
The work of My hands, in his midst,
They will hallow My name,

And hallow the Holy One of Jacob,
And fear the God of Israel.
24 These also who erred in spirit will
come to understanding,
And those who complained will learn
doctrine."

The Fall of Samaria

Modern history-writing aims at objectivity and tries to present only what can be independently verified. This is a new notion. Ancient historians invariably had their own polemic purposes and—more to the point—were quite open about it. The historian of the Book of Kings cannot tell of such an event as the fall of the northern kingdom without giving the theological reason that such a thing could have happened.

Practical reasons for the fall, such as Assyria's superior armies, are unimportant to the biblical historian. Israel had broken the statutes and commandments of the Lord (2 Kin. 17:15, 16). Ultimately it was Israel's rejection by her God that brought about her fall (17:18, 20, 23).

The identity of the Assyrian king who captured Samaria in 722 B.C. is not clear. Shalmaneser V died sometime during or after the 3-year siege. His brother and successor, Sargon II (721–705 B.C.), was probably the king who actually entered the city and led the conquered Israelites into exile.

In an inscription Sargon claims credit for deporting 27,290 captives. The custom of many Assyrian kings was to replace the deported captives with inhabitants from other conquered areas. The mixture of races broke rebellious tendencies and blended religious practices (17:24–41). This ethnic and religious blending in Samaria is the reason for the Jewish prejudice against Samaritans that is so evident in the New Testament.

■ 2 Kings 17:5–41

2 Kings
Israel Carried Captive to Assyria

17 :5 Now the king of Assyria went throughout all the land, and went up to Samaria and besieged it for three years. [6]In the ninth year of Hoshea, the king of Assyria took Samaria and carried Israel away to Assyria, and placed them in Halah and by the Habor, the River of Gozan, and in the cities of the Medes. [7]For so it was that the children of Is-

rael had sinned against the LORD their God, who had brought them up out of the land of Egypt, from under the hand of Pharaoh king of Egypt; and they had feared other gods, [8]and had walked in the statutes of the nations whom the LORD had cast out from before the children of Israel, and of the kings of Israel, which they had made. [9]Also the children of Israel secretly did against the LORD their God things that *were* not right, and they built for themselves high places in all their cities, from watchtower to fortified city. [10]They set up for themselves *sacred* pillars and wooden images[a] on every high hill and under every green tree. [11]There they burned incense on all the high places, like the nations whom the LORD had carried away before them; and they did wicked things to provoke the LORD to anger, [12]for they served idols, of which the LORD had said to them, "You shall not do this thing."

[13]Yet the LORD testified against Israel and against Judah, by all of His prophets, every seer, saying, "Turn from your evil ways, and keep My commandments *and* My statutes, according to all the law which I commanded your fathers, and which I sent to you by My servants the prophets." [14]Nevertheless they would not hear, but stiffened their necks, like the necks of their fathers, who did not believe in the LORD their God. [15]And they rejected His statutes and His covenant that He had made with their fathers, and His testimonies which He had testified against them; they followed idols, became idolaters, and *went* after the nations who *were* all around them, *concerning* whom the LORD had charged

17:10 [a]Hebrew *Asherim*, Canaanite deities

TIME CAPSULE   *710 to 703 B.C.*

710	*Assyrian troops fight on horseback individually*
705	*Hezekiah revolts against Assyria*
705	*Earliest pin-tumbler lock mechanism, Assyria*
704– 681	*Sennacherib of Assyria faces alliance of Chaldeans, Arameans, and Elamites early in his reign*
703– 702?	*Merodach-Baladan's second reign in Babylon*

ASSYRIANS WORSHIP YAHWEH (2 Kin. 17:25, 28)

In the theology of the ancient world, gods owned territory. When Assyria overran Samaria, it was understood that Asshur, god of Assyria, was then in control of an empire which included Israel. Since the land of Israel still technically belonged to Yahweh, in the eyes of the Assyrians Yahweh was now a lesser deity in their pantheon, who would serve their god Asshur.

The Assyrians desired to be on good terms with the deities who owned the territories which Asshur and the Assyrian armies had conquered. It was important, therefore, to acknowledge Yahweh as God of Israel. Immediately after the conquest, however, busy with the resettling of peoples from other parts of their empire into Israel, the Assyrian army failed to retain the official rites in honor of Yahweh. As would any slighted god in the ancient world, Yahweh responded with a "gentle" reminder not to ignore the real power of the land; lions were sent which attacked people (2 Kin. 17:25).

Assyria attempted to correct this slight by finding among the exiled Israelites an official priest of Yahweh and returning him to Samaria. The king of Assyria hoped that the people who had been resettled in Israel would learn the proper religion for the territory they now inhabited. This would ensure that the local God, Yahweh, would remain happy with Assyria.

The people whom the Assyrians had forcibly relocated to Israel did what the Judeans would do approximately 136 years later when they were exiled to Babylonia. The new transplanted inhabitants brought their own gods with them to Israel and continued the worship they had practiced in their previous home territories (2 Kin. 17:29–33).

them that they should not do like them. 16So they left all the commandments of the LORD their God, made for themselves a molded image *and* two calves, made a wooden image and worshiped all the host of heaven, and served Baal. 17And they caused their sons and daughters to pass through the fire, practiced witchcraft and soothsaying, and sold themselves to do evil in the sight of the LORD, to provoke Him to anger. 18Therefore the LORD was very angry with Israel, and removed them from His sight; there was none left but the tribe of Judah alone.

19Also Judah did not keep the commandments of the LORD their God, but walked in the statutes of Israel which they made. 20And the LORD rejected all the descendants of Israel, afflicted them, and delivered them into the hand of plunderers, until He had cast them from His sight. 21For He tore Israel from the house of Da-

vid, and they made Jeroboam the son of Nebat king. Then Jeroboam drove Israel from following the LORD, and made them commit a great sin. 22For the children of Israel walked in all the sins of Jeroboam which he did; they did not depart from them, 23until the LORD removed Israel out of His sight, as He had said by all His servants the prophets. So Israel was carried away from their own land to Assyria, *as it is* to this day.

Assyria Resettles Samaria

24Then the king of Assyria brought *people* from Babylon, Cuthah, Ava, Hamath, and from Sepharvaim, and placed *them* in the cities of Samaria instead of the children of Israel; and they took possession of Samaria and dwelt in its cities. 25And it was so, at the beginning of their dwelling there, *that* they did not fear the LORD; therefore the LORD sent lions among them,

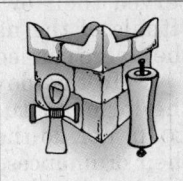

CULTS AND SUPERNATURAL

The native religion of Canaan had an obvious focus on trees, whether living trees or the wooden poles made from them (2 Kin. 17:10). These poles were carved in some way, probably not as freestanding statues like those of classical Greece and Rome. The Israelites were familiar with trees being a popular and widespread symbol of divinity, but were not to represent their God by any image.

GODS OF THE ASSYRIAN EXILES IN ISRAEL (2 Kin. 17:29–33)

The people whom Assyria forcibly resettled in Israel did not worship Yahweh exclusively when they arrived. Nor did they accept the gods of Canaan. Instead the immigrants took over the sacred places of the Israelites and established the cults of their own gods where the Israelites had worshiped Canaanite gods (2 Kin. 17:29).

Most of the deities listed in 2 Kin. 17:30, 31 (Ashima, Nibhaz, Tartak, Adrammelech, Anammelech) cannot be clearly identified with any known gods of the ancient Near East. Only Nergal (and perhaps Succoth Benoth) can be associated with Babylonian or Assyrian religion.

The new immigrants to Samaria were not impressed with the local rural deities. While they did begin to worship Yahweh (17:33), they also kept the worship of other gods from cultured areas of Mesopotamia and Elam. Because they made statues of their deities, their first religious actions were forbidden by the local patron deity of the land, Yahweh.

which killed *some* of them. ²⁶So they spoke to the king of Assyria, saying, "The nations whom you have removed and placed in the cities of Samaria do not know the rituals of the God of the land; therefore He has sent lions among them, and indeed, they are killing them because they do not know the rituals of the God of the land." ²⁷Then the king of Assyria commanded, saying, "Send there one of the priests whom you brought from there; let him go and dwell there, and let him teach them the rituals of the God of the land." ²⁸Then one of the priests whom they had carried away from Samaria came and dwelt in Bethel, and taught them how they should fear the LORD.

²⁹However every nation continued to make gods of its own, and put *them* in the shrines on the high places which the Samaritans had made, *every* nation in the cities where they dwelt. ³⁰The men of Babylon made Succoth Benoth, the men of Cuth made Nergal, the men of Hamath made Ashima, ³¹and the Avites made Nibhaz and Tartak; and the Sepharvites burned their children in fire to Adrammelech and Anammelech, the gods of Sepharvaim. ³²So they feared the LORD, and from every class they appointed for themselves priests of the high places, who sacrificed for them in the shrines of the high places. ³³They feared the LORD, yet served their own gods—according to the rituals of the nations from among whom they were carried away.

³⁴To this day they continue practicing the former rituals; they do not fear the LORD, nor do they follow their statutes or their ordinances, or the law and commandment which the LORD had commanded the children of Jacob, whom He named Israel, ³⁵with whom the LORD had made a covenant and charged them, saying: "You shall not fear other gods, nor bow down to them nor serve them nor sacrifice to them; ³⁶but the LORD, who brought you up from the land of Egypt with great power and an outstretched arm, Him you shall fear, Him you shall worship, and to Him you shall offer sacrifice. ³⁷And the statutes, the ordinances, the law, and the commandment which He wrote for you, you shall be careful to observe forever; you shall not fear other gods. ³⁸And the covenant that I have made with you, you shall not forget, nor shall you fear other gods. ³⁹But the LORD your God you shall fear; and He will deliver you from the hand of all your enemies." ⁴⁰However they did not obey, but they followed their former rituals. ⁴¹So these nations feared the LORD, yet served their carved images; also their children and their children's children have continued doing as their fathers did, even to this day.

A New King in Judah

The reign of Ahaz had not been good for Judah. His pro-Assyrian policy resulted in Judah becoming a vassal to Assyria. He compromised Judah's worship of Yahweh through his worship of foreign deities. During Ahaz's rule, Judah lost the port of Elath to Aram, and it became inhabited by Edomites. Furthermore, Chronicles records invasions by the Philistines into southern Judah at this time (2 Chr. 28:18).

Judah needed a change of direction, and

it came in Hezekiah, the son and successor of Ahaz. During his reign (715–686 B.C.), Hezekiah led an unparalleled reformation of worship (2 Kin. 18:4–6); revolted against Assyria, reversing the policy of Ahaz (18:7); and reconquered Philistia (18:8). This first rebellion against Assyria may have occurred in 705 B.C. when the Assyrian king Sargon died.

▼   ■ 2 Kings 18:1–12

2 Kings
Hezekiah Reigns in Judah

18 :1 Now it came to pass in the third year of Hoshea the son of Elah, king of Israel, *that* Hezekiah the son of Ahaz, king of Judah, began to reign. ²He was twenty-five years old when he became king, and he reigned twenty-nine years in Jerusalem. His mother's name *was* Abi[a] the daughter of Zechariah. ³And he did *what was* right in the sight of the LORD, according to all that his father David had done.

⁴He removed the high places and broke the *sacred* pillars, cut down the wooden image[a] and broke in pieces the bronze serpent that Moses had made; for until those days the children of Israel burned incense to it, and called it Nehushtan.[b] ⁵He trusted in the LORD God of Israel, so that after him was none like him among all the kings of Judah, nor who were before him. ⁶For he held fast to the LORD; he did not depart from following Him, but kept His commandments, which the LORD had commanded Moses. ⁷The LORD was with him; he prospered wherever he went. And he rebelled against the king of Assyria and did not serve him. ⁸He subdued the Philistines, as far as Gaza and its territory, from watchtower to fortified city.

⁹Now it came to pass in the fourth year of King Hezekiah, which *was* the seventh year of Hoshea the son of Elah, king of Israel, *that* Shalmaneser king of Assyria came up against Samaria and besieged it. ¹⁰And at the end of three years they took it. In the sixth year of Hezekiah, that *is,* the ninth year of Hoshea king of Israel, Samaria was taken. ¹¹Then the king of Assyria carried Israel away captive to Assyria, and put them in Halah and by the Habor, the River of Gozan, and in the cities of the Medes, ¹²because they did not obey the voice of the LORD their God, but transgressed His covenant *and* all that Moses the servant of the LORD had commanded; and they would neither hear nor do *them.*

18:2 [a]Called *Abijah* in 2 Chronicles 29:1ff
18:4 [a]Hebrew *Asherah,* a Canaanite goddess
[b]Literally *Bronze Thing*

Assyrian Campaign Against Judah
In 701 B.C. Sennacherib of Assyria moved southward along the coastal plains, defeated an Egyptian army, and then turned his attention toward Judah. From his camp at Lachish he moved against Jerusalem, but did not capture the city.

Assyria, Tool in God's Hand

The prophet Isaiah had declared that Assyria was (unwittingly) serving God's purposes in punishing Israel. When that punishment was complete, however, Isaiah had a new message: a message of judgment for Assyria and of possible hope for the remnant of Israel and to Judah.

The Assyrians had made people submit to their yoke (Is. 10:27) and boasted of their strength (10:13, 14). God would now punish His arrogant tool, Assyria (10:5–34). He would reveal a ruler "from the stem of Jesse," that is, from the line of David, to rule in peace (11:1–9), and would gather His people from every place to which they may have been scattered by His judgment (11:10–16). Such deliverance prompts a hymn of praise to God (12:1–6).

■ Isaiah 10:5—12:6

Isaiah
Arrogant Assyria Also Judged

10 :5 "Woe to Assyria, the rod of My anger
And the staff in whose hand is My indignation.
6 I will send him against an ungodly nation,
And against the people of My wrath
I will give him charge,
To seize the spoil, to take the prey,
And to tread them down like the mire of the streets.
7 Yet he does not mean so,
Nor does his heart think so;
But *it is* in his heart to destroy,
And cut off not a few nations.
8 For he says,
'*Are* not my princes altogether kings?
9 *Is* not Calno like Carchemish?
Is not Hamath like Arpad?
Is not Samaria like Damascus?
10 As my hand has found the kingdoms of the idols,
Whose carved images excelled those of Jerusalem and Samaria,
11 As I have done to Samaria and her idols,
Shall I not do also to Jerusalem and her idols?' "

12Therefore it shall come to pass, when the Lord has performed all His work on Mount Zion and on Jerusalem, *that He will say,* "I will punish the fruit of the arrogant heart of the king of Assyria, and the glory of his haughty looks." 13For he says:

"By the strength of my hand I have done *it,*
And by my wisdom, for I am prudent;
Also I have removed the boundaries of the people,
And have robbed their treasuries;
So I have put down the inhabitants like a valiant *man.*

14 My hand has found like a nest the riches of the people,
And as one gathers eggs *that are* left,
I have gathered all the earth;
And there was no one who moved *his* wing,
Nor opened *his* mouth with even a peep."

15 Shall the ax boast itself against him who chops with it?
Or shall the saw exalt itself against him who saws with it?
As if a rod could wield *itself* against those who lift it up,
Or as if a staff could lift up, *as if it were* not wood!
16 Therefore the Lord, the Lord[a] of hosts,
Will send leanness among his fat ones;
And under his glory
He will kindle a burning
Like the burning of a fire.
17 So the Light of Israel will be for a fire,
And his Holy One for a flame;
It will burn and devour
His thorns and his briers in one day.
18 And it will consume the glory of his forest and of his fruitful field,
Both soul and body;
And they will be as when a sick man wastes away.
19 Then the rest of the trees of his forest
Will be so few in number
That a child may write them.

The Returning Remnant of Israel

20 And it shall come to pass in that day
That the remnant of Israel,
And such as have escaped of the house of Jacob,
Will never again depend on him who defeated them,
But will depend on the LORD, the Holy One of Israel, in truth.
21 The remnant will return, the remnant of Jacob,
To the Mighty God.
22 For though your people, O Israel, be as the sand of the sea,
A remnant of them will return;
The destruction decreed shall overflow with righteousness.
23 For the Lord GOD of hosts
Will make a determined end
In the midst of all the land.

10:16 aFollowing Bomberg; Masoretic Text and Dead Sea Scrolls read *YHWH* (*the LORD*).

OMRI BUILDS A CAPITAL AT SAMARIA (Is. 10:10, 11)

The name "Samaria" originally referred to the city chosen by King Omri to be the capital city of Israel in the early 9th century B.C. The site was excellent for establishing a capital because it was militarily defensible and close to a major international highway. Later in time, the name "Samaria" was associated with the region otherwise known as the northern kingdom of Israel.

It has been presumed that Omri built the city Samaria to create an atmosphere of stability and security during a period when it was uncertain who had rights to the throne. Several of the previous kings—Nadab, Elah, Zimri, and Tibni—ruled for very short periods before being overthrown by the succeeding monarch. Omri, a military commander who in fact himself usurped the throne, survived a civil war lasting about 5 years (885–880 B.C.), during which Tibni also claimed to be king (1 Kin. 16:21). Following Tibni's death, Omri moved Israel's capital from Tirzah, where the earlier kings Baasha, Elah, and Zimri had ruled (1 Kin. 16:22–24).

Samaria became a center for worship of the Phoenician god Baal. The cult of Baal was officially established in Samaria by Omri's son Ahab, who built a temple of Baal in the city.

The capital of the northern kingdom remained in Samaria until the nation fell in 722 B.C. More than a century after Omri had founded Samaria, the prophet Isaiah recalled the city in his message to Jerusalem. The idols and images of Jerusalem, the capital of Judah, Isaiah warned, would meet the same fate as had the idols and images of Samaria, the capital of Israel (Is. 10:10, 11).

24Therefore thus says the Lord GOD of hosts: "O My people, who dwell in Zion, do not be afraid of the Assyrian. He shall strike you with a rod and lift up his staff against you, in the manner of Egypt. 25For yet a very little while and the indignation will cease, as will My anger in their destruction." 26And the LORD of hosts will stir up a scourge for him like the slaughter of Midian at the rock of Oreb; *as* His rod was on the sea, so will He lift it up in the manner of Egypt.

27   It shall come to pass in that day
      That his burden will be taken away
         from your shoulder,
      And his yoke from your neck,
      And the yoke will be destroyed
         because of the anointing oil.

28   He has come to Aiath,
      He has passed Migron;
      At Michmash he has attended to his
         equipment.
29   They have gone along the ridge,
      They have taken up lodging at Geba.
      Ramah is afraid,
      Gibeah of Saul has fled.

30   Lift up your voice,
      O daughter of Gallim!
      Cause it to be heard as far as Laish—
      O poor Anathoth![a]
31   Madmenah has fled,
      The inhabitants of Gebim seek refuge.
32   As yet he will remain at Nob that day;
      He will shake his fist at the mount of
         the daughter of Zion,
      The hill of Jerusalem.

33   Behold, the Lord,
      The LORD of hosts,
      Will lop off the bough with terror;
      Those of high stature *will be* hewn
         down,
      And the haughty will be humbled.
34   He will cut down the thickets of the
         forest with iron,
      And Lebanon will fall by the Mighty
         One.

The Reign of Jesse's Offspring

11 1 There shall come forth a Rod
            from the stem of Jesse,
         And a Branch shall grow out of his
            roots.
2   The Spirit of the LORD shall rest upon
            Him,
         The Spirit of wisdom and
            understanding,
         The Spirit of counsel and might,

10:30 [a]Following Masoretic Text, Targum, and Vulgate; Septuagint and Syriac read *Listen to her, O Anathoth.*

EDOM—JUDAH'S UNWANTED NEIGHBOR (Is. 11:14)

"They shall lay their hand on Edom" (Is. 11:14). The prophet describes a time when Judah and Israel (Ephraim), once again united, would conquer the Edomites. In the last years of the 8th century B.C., this message would have been welcomed by Judahites. Their sister nation Israel had fallen in 722 B.C., and Edom offered Judah no cooperation in confronting the Assyrians in 713 and 701 B.C.

Edom was south and east of the Dead Sea. According to Israelite tradition, the Edomites were descended from Jacob's brother Esau, and a list of early Edomite monarchs appears in Gen. 36:31–39. Judah's relationship to their Edomite neighbors, however, was normally hostile.

King Ahaz took the throne of Judah in 735 B.C., and the first few years of his reign were marked by war. To his north he had to withstand a coalition of two nations—Syria and Israel. To his south he faced a smaller yet real threat from Edom. In fact, the nation of Edom played a role in the events following the invasion of Judah by Syria and northern Israel.

In what is called the Syro-Ephraimite War, Syria and Israel (Ephraim) attempted to depose King Ahaz of Judah (2 Kin. 16:5). Ahaz subsequently asked Assyria for help, and evidently entered into a treaty which reduced Judah to the status of an Assyrian vassal (16:7, 8). Edom was able to take advantage of this unstable international situation to invade southern Judah and occupy Elath, formerly an Edomite possession (2 Chr. 28:16, 17; 2 Kin. 16:6).

Edom is listed in Assyrian annals as among the nations who sent tribute to Assyria after the Syro-Ephraimite War of 732 B.C. Having become a vassal of Assyria, Edom was occasionally required to commit troops and unpaid labor for the Assyrians. No wonder she refused to ally with Judah against mighty Assyria.

The Spirit of knowledge and of the
   fear of the LORD.

3 His delight *is* in the fear of the LORD,
  And He shall not judge by the sight of
   His eyes,
  Nor decide by the hearing of His ears;
4 But with righteousness He shall judge
   the poor,
  And decide with equity for the meek of
   the earth;
  He shall strike the earth with the rod
   of His mouth,
  And with the breath of His lips He
   shall slay the wicked.
5 Righteousness shall be the belt of His
   loins,
  And faithfulness the belt of His waist.

6 "The wolf also shall dwell with the
   lamb,
  The leopard shall lie down with the
   young goat,
  The calf and the young lion and the
   fatling together;
  And a little child shall lead them.
7 The cow and the bear shall graze;

Their young ones shall lie down
   together;
And the lion shall eat straw like the
   ox.
8 The nursing child shall play by the
   cobra's hole,
And the weaned child shall put his
   hand in the viper's den.
9 They shall not hurt nor destroy in all
   My holy mountain,
For the earth shall be full of the
   knowledge of the LORD
As the waters cover the sea.

10 "And in that day there shall be a Root
   of Jesse,
Who shall stand as a banner to the
   people;
For the Gentiles shall seek Him,
And His resting place shall be
   glorious."

11 It shall come to pass in that day
That the Lord shall set His hand
   again the second time
To recover the remnant of His people
   who are left,

JUDAH AFTER ISRAEL'S FALL

Judah (southern kingdom)

Hezekiah, son of Ahaz, faced a golden opportunity to bring some unity between Judah and Israel. In the north, Israel had fallen to Assyria, so Hezekiah invited the northern tribes to a Passover celebration in Jerusalem.

There is no indication that Hezekiah joined the rebellion against Assyria that Ashdod led in 712 B.C. Eventually he did rebel, and the Assyrian king Sennacherib besieged Jerusalem in 701 B.C.

Hezekiah suffered a serious illness 15 years before he died. It is possible that his son Manasseh served as a coregent with him during the last 11 or 12 years of Hezekiah's life.

Israel (northern kingdom)

Fell to the Assyrian Empire in 722 B.C.

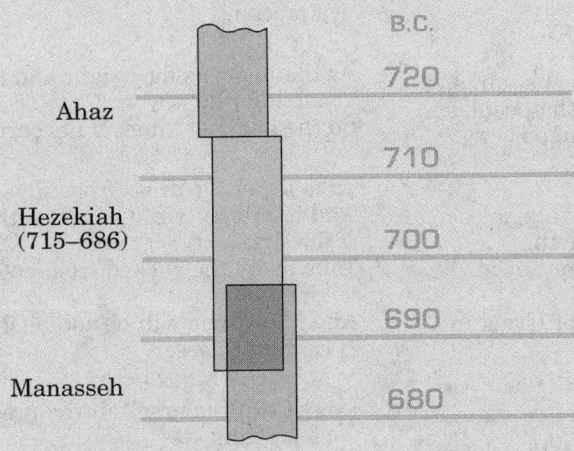

	B.C.
	720
Ahaz	
	710
Hezekiah (715–686)	700
	690
Manasseh	680

From Assyria and Egypt,
From Pathros and Cush,
From Elam and Shinar,
From Hamath and the islands of the
    sea.

12 He will set up a banner for the
        nations,
    And will assemble the outcasts of
        Israel,
    And gather together the dispersed of
        Judah
    From the four corners of the earth.
13 Also the envy of Ephraim shall depart,
    And the adversaries of Judah shall be
        cut off;
    Ephraim shall not envy Judah,
    And Judah shall not harass Ephraim.

14 But they shall fly down upon the
        shoulder of the Philistines toward
        the west;
    Together they shall plunder the people
        of the East;
    They shall lay their hand on Edom
        and Moab;
    And the people of Ammon shall obey
        them.
15 The LORD will utterly destroy[a] the
        tongue of the Sea of Egypt;
    With His mighty wind He will shake
        His fist over the River,[b]
    And strike it in the seven
        streams,
    And make *men* cross over dryshod.
16 There will be a highway for the
        remnant of His people
    Who will be left from Assyria,
    As it was for Israel
    In the day that he came up from the
        land of Egypt.

11:15 [a]Following Masoretic Text and Vulgate; Septuagint, Syriac, and Targum read *dry up.*   [b]That is, the Euphrates

A Hymn of Praise

12 [1]And in that day you will say:

"O LORD, I will praise You;
Though You were angry with me,
Your anger is turned away, and You
    comfort me.
2   Behold, God *is* my salvation,
I will trust and not be afraid;
'For YAH, the LORD, *is* my strength and
    song;
He also has become my salvation.' "[a]

3   Therefore with joy you will draw
    water
From the wells of salvation.

[4]And in that day you will say:

"Praise the LORD, call upon His name;
Declare His deeds among the peoples,
Make mention that His name is
    exalted.
5   Sing to the LORD,
For He has done excellent things;
This *is* known in all the earth.
6   Cry out and shout, O inhabitant of
    Zion,
For great *is* the Holy One of Israel in
    your midst!"

Hezekiah's Proverbs

Shalmaneser V of Assyria conquered Israel, but died himself about the same time. He was replaced by Sargon II (721–705 B.C.). Shortly after Sargon took the throne, a certain Merodach-Baladan led a successful rebellion in the city of Babylon. The first several years of Sargon's rule would pass (721–710 B.C.) before he was able to drive Merodach-Baladan into hiding.

Sargon was involved in various campaigns. In 720 a victory at Qarqar was followed by a march through Gaza and Israel to Egypt's border. In 713 and 712 he defeated separate rebellions in Ashdod. During Sargon's military activities, Judah somehow escaped his attention. This allowed King Hezekiah to establish a fairly prosperous court and apparently to sponsor some literary work, the collections of wisdom traditions.

The attribution of Prov. 25:1 identifies a collection of proverbs (Prov. 25—29) which was copied by "the men of Hezekiah king of Judah." Perhaps some of the sayings connected with Solomon's name were copied and pre-

served for future generations. The reference to the "men of Hezekiah" may reflect Hezekiah's support of the sages who collected and copied the earlier proverbs.

■ Proverbs 25:1—29:27

Proverbs
Further Wise Sayings of Solomon

25 :1 These also *are* proverbs of Solomon which the men of Hezekiah king of Judah copied:

2   *It is* the glory of God to conceal a
    matter,
But the glory of kings *is* to search out
    a matter.

3   *As* the heavens for height and the
    earth for depth,
So the heart of kings *is* unsearchable.

4   Take away the dross from silver,
And it will go to the silversmith *for*
    jewelry.
5   Take away the wicked from before the
    king,
And his throne will be established in
    righteousness.

6   Do not exalt yourself in the presence
    of the king,
And do not stand in the place of the
    great;
7   For *it is* better that he say to you,
"Come up here,"
Than that you should be put lower in
    the presence of the prince,
Whom your eyes have seen.

8   Do not go hastily to court;
For what will you do in the end,
When your neighbor has put you to
    shame?
9   Debate your case with your neighbor,
And do not disclose the secret to
    another;
10 Lest he who hears *it* expose your
    shame,
And your reputation be ruined.

11 A word fitly spoken *is like* apples of
    gold
In settings of silver.

12:2 [a]Exodus 15:2

12 *Like* an earring of gold and an
   ornament of fine gold
   Is a wise rebuker to an obedient ear.

13 Like the cold of snow in time of
   harvest
   Is a faithful messenger to those who
   send him,
   For he refreshes the soul of his
   masters.

14 Whoever falsely boasts of giving
   Is like clouds and wind without rain.

15 By long forbearance a ruler is
   persuaded,
   And a gentle tongue breaks a bone.

16 Have you found honey?
   Eat only as much as you need,
   Lest you be filled with it and vomit.

17 Seldom set foot in your neighbor's
   house,
   Lest he become weary of you and hate
   you.

18 A man who bears false witness
   against his neighbor
   Is like a club, a sword, and a sharp
   arrow.

19 Confidence in an unfaithful *man* in
   time of trouble
   Is like a bad tooth and a foot out of
   joint.

20 *Like* one who takes away a garment in
   cold weather,
   And like vinegar on soda,
   Is one who sings songs to a heavy
   heart.

21 If your enemy is hungry, give him
   bread to eat;
   And if he is thirsty, give him water to
   drink;
22 For *so* you will heap coals of fire on
   his head,
   And the LORD will reward you.

23 The north wind brings forth rain,
   And a backbiting tongue an angry
   countenance.

24 *It is* better to dwell in a corner of a
   housetop,

Than in a house shared with a
contentious woman.

25 *As* cold water to a weary soul,
   So *is* good news from a far country.

26 A righteous *man* who falters before
   the wicked
   Is like a murky spring and a polluted
   well.

27 *It is* not good to eat much honey;
   So to seek one's own glory *is not* glory.

28 Whoever *has* no rule over his own
   spirit
   Is like a city broken down, without
   walls.

26 ¹ As snow in summer and rain in
   harvest,
   So honor is not fitting for a fool.

2 Like a flitting sparrow, like a flying
   swallow,
   So a curse without cause shall not
   alight.

3 A whip for the horse,
   A bridle for the donkey,
   And a rod for the fool's back.
4 Do not answer a fool according to his
   folly,
   Lest you also be like him.
5 Answer a fool according to his folly,
   Lest he be wise in his own eyes.
6 He who sends a message by the hand
   of a fool
   Cuts off *his own* feet *and* drinks
   violence.
7 *Like* the legs of the lame that hang
   limp
   Is a proverb in the mouth of fools.
8 Like one who binds a stone in a sling
   Is he who gives honor to a fool.

TIME CAPSULE   *701 to 700 B.C.*

701   *Assyrian king Sennacherib stops rebellion in Ashkelon*

701   *Sennacherib seizes major towns in Judah and besieges Jerusalem*

700   *Malta is a Phoenician trading colony*

700–200   *Rituals of sacrifice of children at the Phoenician colony of Carthage*

Sumerian Abominations (Prov. 26:25)

The Book of Proverbs describes the person who pretends kindness but is motivated by hatred and deceit: "There are seven abominations in his heart" (Prov. 26:25). Other proverbs list murder (Prov. 6:16, 17), dishonest scales (11:1), and pride (16:5) as abominations. "Lying lips" are specifically called an "abomination to the Lord" (12:22). Whatever offended the moral sense of a person was considered an abomination, not only by Israel's God, but also by the gods of Sumer, located in the southern Tigris-Euphrates valley.

A Sumerian text lists a series of abominations to the gods. A judge who perverts justice, or a firstborn son who drives a younger son out of his rightful inheritance, are abominations to the god Utu. Also offensive to Utu are eating at a banquet without washing the hands, spitting without stamping on the spittle, and blowing the nose without returning the mucus to dust. Reaching for alms was an abomination to the god Ninurta. Bringing unwashed hands to the mouth was offensive presumably to any god.

The abominations in the Sumerian list are cultic and ethical in nature, but do not address idolatry as an abomination. The Law of Moses, however, was forthright: the toleration or bringing of carved images into one's house was an abomination to the God of Israel (Deut. 7:25, 26).

---

9 Like a thorn *that* goes into the hand of
    a drunkard
    Is a proverb in the mouth of fools.

10 The great *God* who formed everything
    Gives the fool *his* hire and the
      transgressor *his* wages.[a]

11 As a dog returns to his own vomit,
    So a fool repeats his folly.

12 Do you see a man wise in his own
      eyes?
    There is more hope for a fool than for
      him.

13 The lazy *man* says, "*There is* a lion in
      the road!
    A fierce lion *is* in the streets!"

14 As a door turns on its hinges,
    So *does* the lazy *man* on his bed.

15 The lazy *man* buries his hand in the
      bowl;[a]
    It wearies him to bring it back to his
      mouth.

16 The lazy *man is* wiser in his own eyes
    Than seven men who can answer
      sensibly.

17 He who passes by *and* meddles in a
      quarrel not his own
    Is like one who takes a dog by the
      ears.

18 Like a madman who throws
      firebrands, arrows, and death,

19 *Is* the man *who* deceives his neighbor,
    And says, "I was only joking!"

20 Where *there is* no wood, the fire goes
      out;
    And where *there is* no talebearer,
      strife ceases.

21 As charcoal *is* to burning coals, and
      wood to fire,
    So *is* a contentious man to kindle
      strife.

22 The words of a talebearer *are* like
      tasty trifles,
    And they go down into the inmost
      body.

23 Fervent lips with a wicked heart
    Are like earthenware covered with
      silver dross.

24 He who hates, disguises *it* with his
      lips,
    And lays up deceit within himself;

25 When he speaks kindly, do not believe
      him,
    For *there are* seven abominations in
      his heart;

26 *Though his* hatred is covered by
      deceit,
    His wickedness will be revealed before
      the assembly.

27 Whoever digs a pit will fall into it,
    And he who rolls a stone will have it
      roll back on him.

26:10 [a]The Hebrew is difficult; ancient and modern translators differ greatly.   26:15 [a]Compare 19:24

28 A lying tongue hates *those who are*
　　crushed by it,
　And a flattering mouth works ruin.

27

1 Do not boast about tomorrow,
　　For you do not know what a day
　　may bring forth.

2 Let another man praise you, and not
　　your own mouth;
　A stranger, and not your own lips.

3 A stone *is* heavy and sand *is* weighty,
　But a fool's wrath *is* heavier than both
　　of them.

4 Wrath *is* cruel and anger a torrent,
　But who *is* able to stand before
　　jealousy?

5 Open rebuke *is* better
　Than love carefully concealed.

6 Faithful *are* the wounds of a friend,
　But the kisses of an enemy *are*
　　deceitful.

7 A satisfied soul loathes the
　　honeycomb,
　But to a hungry soul every bitter
　　thing *is* sweet.

8 Like a bird that wanders from its nest
　Is a man who wanders from his place.

9 Ointment and perfume delight the
　　heart,
　And the sweetness of a man's friend
　　gives delight by hearty counsel.

10 Do not forsake your own friend or
　　your father's friend,
　Nor go to your brother's house in the
　　day of your calamity;
　Better *is* a neighbor nearby than a
　　brother far away.

27:20 [a]Or *Sheol*　[b]Hebrew *Abaddon*

11 My son, be wise, and make my heart
　　glad,
　That I may answer him who
　　reproaches me.

12 A prudent *man* foresees evil *and*
　　hides himself;
　The simple pass on *and* are punished.

13 Take the garment of him who is
　　surety for a stranger,
　And hold it in pledge *when* he is
　　surety for a seductress.

14 He who blesses his friend with a loud
　　voice, rising early in the morning,
　It will be counted a curse to him.

15 A continual dripping on a very rainy
　　day
　And a contentious woman are alike;
16 Whoever restrains her restrains the
　　wind,
　And grasps oil with his right hand.

17 *As* iron sharpens iron,
　So a man sharpens the countenance of
　　his friend.

18 Whoever keeps the fig tree will eat its
　　fruit;
　So he who waits on his master will be
　　honored.

19 As in water face *reflects* face,
　So a man's heart *reveals* the man.

20 Hell[a] and Destruction[b] are never full;
　So the eyes of man are never satisfied.

21 The refining pot *is* for silver and the
　　furnace for gold,
　And a man *is valued* by what others
　　say of him.

22 Though you grind a fool in a mortar
　　with a pestle along with crushed
　　grain,

AGRICULTURE AND HERDING

*In addition to careers in court or business, Proverbs also presents the farmer (Prov.
27:18) and the shepherd (Prov. 27:23) as typical or acceptable ways of life. Those
employed in these occupations are exhorted to pay attention to the day-to-day affairs of
their labor. For such diligence they would enjoy the fruits of their work.*

Yet his foolishness will not depart
from him.

23 Be diligent to know the state of your
flocks,
And attend to your herds;
24 For riches *are* not forever,
Nor does a crown *endure* to all
generations.
25 *When* the hay is removed, and the
tender grass shows itself,
And the herbs of the mountains are
gathered in,
26 The lambs *will provide* your clothing,
And the goats the price of a field;
27 *You shall have* enough goats' milk for
your food,
For the food of your household,
And the nourishment of your
maidservants.

28

1 The wicked flee when no one
pursues,
But the righteous are bold as a lion.

2 Because of the transgression of a land,
many *are* its princes;
But by a man of understanding *and*
knowledge
Right will be prolonged.

3 A poor man who oppresses the poor
Is like a driving rain which leaves no
food.

4 Those who forsake the law praise the
wicked,
But such as keep the law contend
with them.

5 Evil men do not understand justice,
But those who seek the LORD
understand all.

6 Better *is* the poor who walks in his
integrity
Than one perverse *in his* ways,
though he *be* rich.

7 Whoever keeps the law *is* a discerning
son,
But a companion of gluttons shames
his father.

8 One who increases his possessions by
usury and extortion
Gathers it for him who will pity the
poor.

9 One who turns away his ear from
hearing the law,
Even his prayer *is* an abomination.

10 Whoever causes the upright to go
astray in an evil way,
He himself will fall into his own pit;
But the blameless will inherit good.

11 The rich man *is* wise in his own eyes,
But the poor who has understanding
searches him out.

12 When the righteous rejoice, *there is*
great glory;
But when the wicked arise, men hide
themselves.

13 He who covers his sins will not
prosper,
But whoever confesses and forsakes
them will have mercy.

14 Happy *is* the man who is always
reverent,
But he who hardens his heart will fall
into calamity.

15 *Like* a roaring lion and a charging
bear
Is a wicked ruler over poor people.

16 A ruler who lacks understanding *is* a
great oppressor,
But he who hates covetousness will
prolong *his* days.

17 A man burdened with bloodshed will
flee into a pit;
Let no one help him.

18 Whoever walks blamelessly will be
saved,
But *he who is* perverse *in his* ways
will suddenly fall.

19 He who tills his land will have plenty
of bread,
But he who follows frivolity will have
poverty enough!

20 A faithful man will abound with
blessings,
But he who hastens to be rich will not
go unpunished.

21 To show partiality *is* not good,
Because for a piece of bread a man
will transgress.

22 A man with an evil eye hastens after
   riches,
   And does not consider that poverty
   will come upon him.

23 He who rebukes a man will find more
   favor afterward
   Than he who flatters with the tongue.

24 Whoever robs his father or his mother,
   And says, "*It is* no transgression,"
   The same *is* companion to a destroyer.

25 He who is of a proud heart stirs up
   strife,
   But he who trusts in the LORD will be
   prospered.

26 He who trusts in his own heart is a
   fool,
   But whoever walks wisely will be
   delivered.

27 He who gives to the poor will not lack,
   But he who hides his eyes will have
   many curses.

28 When the wicked arise, men hide
   themselves;
   But when they perish, the righteous
   increase.

29 ¹ He who is often rebuked, *and*
       hardens *his* neck,
   Will suddenly be destroyed, and that
   without remedy.

2 When the righteous are in authority,
   the people rejoice;
   But when a wicked *man* rules, the
   people groan.

3 Whoever loves wisdom makes his
   father rejoice,
   But a companion of harlots wastes *his*
   wealth.

4 The king establishes the land by
   justice,
   But he who receives bribes overthrows
   it.

5 A man who flatters his neighbor
   Spreads a net for his feet.

6 By transgression an evil man is
   snared,
   But the righteous sings and rejoices.

7 The righteous considers the cause of
   the poor,
   But the wicked does not understand
   such knowledge.

8 Scoffers set a city aflame,
   But wise *men* turn away wrath.

9 *If* a wise man contends with a foolish
   man,
   Whether *the fool* rages or laughs,
   there is no peace.

10 The bloodthirsty hate the blameless,
   But the upright seek his well-being.ᵃ

11 A fool vents all his feelings,ᵃ
   But a wise *man* holds them back.

12 If a ruler pays attention to lies,
   All his servants *become* wicked.

13 The poor *man* and the oppressor have
   this in common:
   The LORD gives light to the eyes of
   both.

14 The king who judges the poor with
   truth,
   His throne will be established forever.

15 The rod and rebuke give wisdom,
   But a child left *to himself* brings
   shame to his mother.

16 When the wicked are multiplied,
   transgression increases;
   But the righteous will see their fall.

17 Correct your son, and he will give you
   rest;
   Yes, he will give delight to your soul.

18 Where *there is* no revelation,ᵃ the
   people cast off restraint;
   But happy *is* he who keeps the law.

19 A servant will not be corrected by
   mere words;
   For though he understands, he will
   not respond.

20 Do you see a man hasty in his words?
   There is more hope for a fool than for
   him.

29:10 ᵃLiterally *soul*   29:11 ᵃLiterally *spirit*
29:18 ᵃOr *prophetic vision*

21   He who pampers his servant from
       childhood
       Will have him as a son in the end.

22   An angry man stirs up strife,
       And a furious man abounds in
       transgression.

23   A man's pride will bring him low,
       But the humble in spirit will retain
       honor.

24   Whoever is a partner with a thief
       hates his own life;
       He swears to tell the truth,[a] but
       reveals nothing.

25   The fear of man brings a snare,
       But whoever trusts in the LORD shall
       be safe.

26   Many seek the ruler's favor,
       But justice for man *comes* from the
       LORD.

27   An unjust man *is* an abomination to
       the righteous,
       And *he who is* upright in the way *is*
       an abomination to the wicked.

The Ashdod Rebellion

While Sargon, king of Assyria, was occupied with Babylon, a new dynasty came to power in Egypt. An Ethiopian ruler named Piankhy (747–716 B.C.) swept through the land, uniting Egypt under one ruler for the first time in generations. The new power in Egypt gave hope to the nations of Palestine, who formed a coalition to rebel against Sargon. From 714 to 712 B.C. this rebellion was centered in Ashdod, on the Philistine coast, but it involved Moab, Edom, and certain promises from Egypt.

Judah was invited to join the anti-Assyrian coalition, but opinion on the matter was divided. Many thought this was Judah's chance, but Isaiah disagreed. Perhaps one of Isaiah's opponents was Shebna the scribe, mentioned in Is. 22:15–25. The exact nature of Shebna's conduct which caused him to be demoted from his office (22:19) is unknown. He represents the blindness of Judah's leaders.

Some of Isaiah's harshest messages were directed against Egypt (18:1—20:6) and against all those who trusted in Egypt's help (30:1—32:20). Neither would a relationship with Moab help Judah (15:1—16:14). God would save Zion, he agreed, but the way to salvation was through faith in God, not through alliances.

- Isaiah 18:1—20:6
- Isaiah 15:1—16:14
- Isaiah 22:15–25
- Isaiah 30:1—32:20

Isaiah 18:1—20:6
Proclamation Against Ethiopia

18 :1   Woe to the land shadowed with
       buzzing wings,
       Which *is* beyond the rivers of
       Ethiopia,
2   Which sends ambassadors by sea,
       Even in vessels of reed on the waters,
       saying,
   "Go, swift messengers, to a nation tall
       and smooth *of skin,*
       To a people terrible from their
       beginning onward,
       A nation powerful and treading down,
       Whose land the rivers divide."

3   All inhabitants of the world and
       dwellers on the earth:
       When he lifts up a banner on the
       mountains, you see *it;*
       And when he blows a trumpet, you
       hear *it.*
4   For so the LORD said to me,
   "I will take My rest,
       And I will look from My dwelling
       place
       Like clear heat in sunshine,
       Like a cloud of dew in the heat of
       harvest."
5   For before the harvest, when the bud
       is perfect
       And the sour grape is ripening in the
       flower,
       He will both cut off the sprigs with
       pruning hooks
       And take away *and* cut down the
       branches.
6   They will be left together for the
       mountain birds of prey
       And for the beasts of the earth;
       The birds of prey will summer on
       them,
       And all the beasts of the earth will
       winter on them.

29:24 [a]Literally *hears the adjuration*

7 In that time a present will be brought
to the LORD of hosts
From[a] a people tall and smooth *of
skin,*
And from a people terrible from their
beginning onward,
A nation powerful and treading down,
Whose land the rivers divide—
To the place of the name of the LORD
of hosts,
To Mount Zion.

Proclamation Against Egypt

19

¹The burden against Egypt.

Behold, the LORD rides on a swift
cloud,
And will come into Egypt;
The idols of Egypt will totter at His
presence,
And the heart of Egypt will melt in its
midst.

2 "I will set Egyptians against
Egyptians;
Everyone will fight against his
brother,
And everyone against his neighbor,
City against city, kingdom against
kingdom.
3 The spirit of Egypt will fail in its
midst;
I will destroy their counsel,
And they will consult the idols and
the charmers,
The mediums and the sorcerers.
4 And the Egyptians I will give
Into the hand of a cruel master,
And a fierce king will rule over them,"
Says the Lord, the LORD of hosts.

5 The waters will fail from the sea,
And the river will be wasted and dried
up.

6 The rivers will turn foul;
The brooks of defense will be emptied
and dried up;
The reeds and rushes will wither.
7 The papyrus reeds by the River,[a] by
the mouth of the River,
And everything sown by the River,
Will wither, be driven away, and be no
more.
8 The fishermen also will mourn;
All those will lament who cast hooks
into the River,
And they will languish who spread
nets on the waters.
9 Moreover those who work in fine
flax
And those who weave fine fabric will
be ashamed;
10 And its foundations will be broken.
All who make wages *will be* troubled
of soul.

11 Surely the princes of Zoan *are* fools;
Pharaoh's wise counselors give foolish
counsel.
How do you say to Pharaoh, "I *am* the
son of the wise,
The son of ancient kings?"
12 Where *are* they?
Where are your wise men?
Let them tell you now,
And let them know what the LORD of
hosts has purposed against Egypt.
13 The princes of Zoan have become
fools;
The princes of Noph[a] are deceived;
They have also deluded Egypt,
Those who are the mainstay of its
tribes.
14 The LORD has mingled a perverse
spirit in her midst;
And they have caused Egypt to err in
all her work,
As a drunken man staggers in his
vomit.
15 Neither will there be *any* work for
Egypt,
Which the head or tail,
Palm branch or bulrush, may do.[a]

18:7 [a]Following Dead Sea Scrolls, Septuagint, and
Vulgate; Masoretic Text omits *From;* Targum reads
To.　19:7 [a]That is, the Nile　19:13 [a]That is,
ancient Memphis　19:15 [a]Compare Isaiah
9:14–16

GEOGRAPHY AND ENVIRONMENT

*The White Nile flows from Lake Tanzania, and near Khartoum it joins the Blue Nile that
originates in Ethiopia. The Nile is 4,132 miles long, the longest river in the world. All the
inhabited land of Egypt depends directly on the Nile (Is. 19:7), since there is practically
no rainfall in that country.*

THE TARTAN COMES TO ASHDOD (Is. 20:1)

Back in the period of Israel's judges, Ashdod had been a major Philistine city. Ashdod was prominent in the Philistine capture of the ark of the covenant (1 Sam. 5:1-7), and it is also mentioned in Ugaritic sources of that time (15th to 13th centuries B.C.).

In the 8th century B.C. the threat of Assyria loomed large on the Palestinian horizon. The Assyrian king Tiglath-Pileser III had conquered the Aramean state of Damascus in 732 B.C., and there is evidence that the Assyrians also campaigned against the Philistines at that time. Ashdod and other cities in Palestine certainly felt the presence of Assyrian imperial power.

The Assyrian annals of Sargon II report how Ashdod revolted against Assyria a generation later. Ashdod's king Aziru formed an alliance with Egypt, Gaza, Ekron, Judah (under Hezekiah), Moab, Ammon, and Edom. But the alliance failed, and Sargon came to Palestine in 713 B.C., placing his own brother on Ashdod's throne in place of Aziru.

The people of Ashdod did not give up. Overthrowing Sargon's brother, they appointed a certain commoner, named Yamani. Yamani was successful in organizing another coalition against Assyria, this time consisting of the Philistine city-states Judah, Moab, Edom, Ammon, and possibly Cyprus. But Sargon returned again in 712 B.C., and Yamani was forced to flee to Egypt.

Ashdod did not recover this time. Sargon's annals mention an unnamed king of Egypt who sent Yamani in chains back to Assyria. The Assyrians returned, this time under the leadership of the Tartan, a commander called *turtanu* in the Assyrian language. The Tartan seized the city of Ashdod and deported the royal family, the gods of Ashdod, and its people, gold, and silver to Assyria (Is. 20:1). Ashdod was made into an Assyrian province. Fragments of a victory stele of Sargon have been found at the site of ancient Ashdod.

---

[16]In that day Egypt will be like women, and will be afraid and fear because of the waving of the hand of the LORD of hosts, which He waves over it. [17]And the land of Judah will be a terror to Egypt; everyone who makes mention of it will be afraid in himself, because of the counsel of the LORD of hosts which He has determined against it.

Egypt, Assyria, and Israel Blessed

[18]In that day five cities in the land of Egypt will speak the language of Canaan and swear by the LORD of hosts; one will be called the City of Destruction.[a]

[19]In that day there will be an altar to the LORD in the midst of the land of Egypt, and a pillar to the LORD at its border. [20]And it will be for a sign and for a witness to the LORD of hosts in the land of Egypt; for they will cry to the LORD because of the oppressors, and He will send them a Savior and a Mighty One, and He will deliver them. [21]Then the LORD will be known to Egypt, and the Egyptians will know the LORD in that day, and will make sacrifice and offering; yes, they will make a vow to the LORD and perform *it*. [22]And the LORD will strike Egypt, He will strike and heal *it;* they will return to the LORD, and He will be entreated by them and heal them.

[23]In that day there will be a highway from Egypt to Assyria, and the Assyrian will come into Egypt and the Egyptian into Assyria, and the Egyptians will serve with the Assyrians.

[24]In that day Israel will be one of three with Egypt and Assyria—a blessing in the

---

TIME CAPSULE   *697 to 686 B.C.*

697	Manasseh serves as coregent with Hezekiah in Judah
690–664	Tirhakah leads rebuilding program in Egypt
689	Assyrian king Sennacherib demolishes Babylon
689	Statue of Marduk disturbed at Babylon
686	Manasseh becomes sole king in Judah

19:18 [a]Some Hebrew manuscripts, Arabic, Dead Sea Scrolls, Targum, and Vulgate read *Sun;* Septuagint reads *Asedek* (literally *Righteousness*).

ETHIOPIANS RULING IN EGYPT (Is. 20:2–6)

The prophet Isaiah acted out Egypt's and Ethiopia's fate of being taken naked into Assyrian captivity (Is. 20:2–6). The Assyrian invasion, which Isaiah describes as an attack on both Ethiopians and Egyptians, would result in the "shame of Egypt" (20:4). The attack is against one "territory" whose inhabitants consider "Ethiopia their expectation and Egypt their glory" (20:5, 6).

The name "Ethiopia" is a translation of the Hebrew *Cush,* a land south of Egypt and east of the Nile. Later the Romans knew the land as Nubia. The Egyptians had extensive trading relations with the Cushites, and often dominated them politically. The Bible also mentions important trading connections with this area (Job 28:19). A close blood tie is observed in the Bible, as Cush was a brother of Mizraim, the ancestor of Egypt (Gen. 10:6).

By the 8th century B.C. the Cushites were successful in conquering Egypt and creating the Egyptian 25th Dynasty (c. 780–656 B.C.). They brought a certain degree of unity to Egypt, but faced a threat from the expanding Assyrian Empire. When Sennacherib and the Assyrians sought to conquer Judah, the Cushites, under Tirhakah, attempted to halt the advance of the Assyrian army (Is. 37:9). This event occurred either in 701 B.C., when Tirhakah was the Cushite crown prince, or a decade later in 688 B.C., when Tirhakah was himself king of Cushite Egypt.

Clashes between Egypt and two Assyrian kings continued during Tirhakah's reign (690–664 B.C.). Esarhaddon drove Tirhakah from Memphis in 671 B.C., and Ashurbanipal recaptured Memphis in 667 B.C. While the Ethiopians (Cushites) ruled Egypt, they surely wondered how they might be "delivered from the king of Assyria" (Is. 20:6).

---

midst of the land, ²⁵whom the LORD of hosts shall bless, saying, "Blessed *is* Egypt My people, and Assyria the work of My hands, and Israel My inheritance."

The Sign Against Egypt and Ethiopia

20 ¹In the year that Tartanᵃ came to Ashdod, when Sargon the king of Assyria sent him, and he fought against Ashdod and took it, ²at the same time the LORD spoke by Isaiah the son of Amoz, saying, "Go, and remove the sackcloth from your body, and take your sandals off your feet." And he did so, walking naked and barefoot.

³Then the LORD said, "Just as My servant Isaiah has walked naked and barefoot three years *for* a sign and a wonder against Egypt and Ethiopia, ⁴so shall the king of Assyria lead away the Egyptians as prisoners and the Ethiopians as captives, young and old, naked and barefoot, with their buttocks uncovered, to the shame of Egypt. ⁵Then they shall be afraid and ashamed of Ethiopia their expectation and Egypt their glory. ⁶And the inhabitant of this territory will say in that day, 'Surely such *is* our ex-

pectation, wherever we flee for help to be delivered from the king of Assyria; and how shall we escape?'"

Isaiah 15:1—16:14
Proclamation Against Moab

15 :1 The burden against Moab.

Because in the night Ar of Moab is
     laid waste
And destroyed,
Because in the night Kir of Moab is
     laid waste
And destroyed,

2 He has gone up to the templeᵃ and
     Dibon,
To the high places to weep.
Moab will wail over Nebo and over
     Medeba;
On all their heads *will be* baldness,
And every beard cut off.

3 In their streets they will clothe
     themselves with sackcloth;
On the tops of their houses
And in their streets
Everyone will wail, weeping bitterly.

4 Heshbon and Elealeh will cry out,
Their voice shall be heard as far as
     Jahaz;

20:1 ᵃOr *the Commander in Chief*   15:2 ᵃHebrew *bayith,* literally *house*

Therefore the armed soldiers[a] of Moab
will cry out;
His life will be burdensome to him.

5 "My heart will cry out for Moab;
His fugitives *shall flee* to Zoar,
Like a three-year-old heifer.[a]
For by the Ascent of Luhith
They will go up with weeping;
For in the way of Horonaim
They will raise up a cry of destruction,
6 For the waters of Nimrim will be
desolate,
For the green grass has withered
away;
The grass fails, there is nothing green.
7 Therefore the abundance they have
gained,
And what they have laid up,
They will carry away to the Brook of
the Willows.
8 For the cry has gone all around the
borders of Moab,
Its wailing to Eglaim
And its wailing to Beer Elim.
9 For the waters of Dimon[a] will be full
of blood;
Because I will bring more upon
Dimon,[b]
Lions upon him who escapes from
Moab,
And on the remnant of the land."

Moab Destroyed

16 1 Send the lamb to the ruler of the
land,
From Sela to the wilderness,
To the mount of the daughter of Zion.
2 For it shall be as a wandering bird
thrown out of the nest;
So shall be the daughters of Moab at
the fords of the Arnon.

3 "Take counsel, execute judgment;
Make your shadow like the night in
the middle of the day;
Hide the outcasts,
Do not betray him who escapes.
4 Let My outcasts dwell with you,
O Moab;
Be a shelter to them from the face of
the spoiler.
For the extortioner is at an end,
Devastation ceases,
The oppressors are consumed out of
the land.
5 In mercy the throne will be
established;

And One will sit on it in truth, in the
tabernacle of David,
Judging and seeking justice and
hastening righteousness."

6 We have heard of the pride of Moab—
He is very proud—
Of his haughtiness and his pride and
his wrath;
But his lies *shall* not *be* so.
7 Therefore Moab shall wail for Moab;
Everyone shall wail.
For the foundations of Kir Hareseth
you shall mourn;
Surely *they are* stricken.

8 For the fields of Heshbon languish,
And the vine of Sibmah;
The lords of the nations have broken
down its choice plants,
Which have reached to Jazer
And wandered through the
wilderness.
Her branches are stretched out,
They are gone over the sea.
9 Therefore I will bewail the vine of
Sibmah,
With the weeping of Jazer;
I will drench you with my tears,
O Heshbon and Elealeh;
For battle cries have fallen
Over your summer fruits and your
harvest.
10 Gladness is taken away,
And joy from the plentiful field;
In the vineyards there will be no
singing,
Nor will there be shouting;
No treaders will tread out wine in the
presses;
I have made their shouting cease.
11 Therefore my heart shall resound like
a harp for Moab,
And my inner being for Kir Heres.

12 And it shall come to pass,
When it is seen that Moab is weary on
the high place,

15:4 [a]Following Masoretic Text, Targum, and Vulgate;
Septuagint and Syriac read *loins.* 15:5 [a]Or *The
Third Eglath,* an unknown city (compare Jeremiah
48:34) 15:9 [a]Following Masoretic Text and
Targum; Dead Sea Scrolls and Vulgate read *Dibon;*
Septuagint reads *Rimon.* [b]Following Masoretic Text
and Targum; Dead Sea Scrolls and Vulgate read *Dibon;*
Septuagint reads *Rimon.*

That he will come to his sanctuary to
pray;
But he will not prevail.

¹³This *is* the word which the LORD has
spoken concerning Moab since that time.
¹⁴But now the LORD has spoken, saying,
"Within three years, as the years of a hired
man, the glory of Moab will be despised
with all that great multitude, and the remnant *will be* very small *and* feeble."

Isaiah 22:15–25
The Judgment on Shebna

22 :15 Thus says the Lord GOD of
hosts:

"Go, proceed to this steward,
To Shebna, who *is* over the house, *and*
say:
16 'What have you here, and whom have
you here,
That you have hewn a sepulcher here,
As he who hews himself a sepulcher
on high,
Who carves a tomb for himself in a
rock?
17 Indeed, the LORD will throw you away
violently,
O mighty man,
And will surely seize you.
18 He will surely turn violently and toss
you like a ball
Into a large country;
There you shall die, and there your
glorious chariots
Shall be the shame of your master's
house.
19 So I will drive you out of your office,
And from your position he will pull
you down.ᵃ

20 'Then it shall be in that day,
That I will call My servant Eliakim
the son of Hilkiah;
21 I will clothe him with your robe
And strengthen him with your belt;

22:19 ᵃSeptuagint omits *he will pull you down;* Syriac,
Targum, and Vulgate read *I will pull you down.*

I will commit your responsibility into
his hand.
He shall be a father to the inhabitants
of Jerusalem
And to the house of Judah.
22 The key of the house of David
I will lay on his shoulder;
So he shall open, and no one shall
shut;
And he shall shut, and no one shall
open.
23 I will fasten him *as* a peg in a secure
place,
And he will become a glorious throne
to his father's house.

24"They will hang on him all the glory
of his father's house, the offspring and the
posterity, all vessels of small quantity, from
the cups to all the pitchers. 25In that day,'
says the LORD of hosts, 'the peg that is fastened in the secure place will be removed
and be cut down and fall, and the burden
that *was* on it will be cut off; for the LORD
has spoken.' "

Isaiah 30:1—32:20
Futile Confidence in Egypt

30 :1 "Woe to the rebellious children,"
says the LORD,
"Who take counsel, but not of Me,
And who devise plans, but not of My
Spirit,
That they may add sin to sin;
2 Who walk to go down to Egypt,
And have not asked My advice,
To strengthen themselves in the
strength of Pharaoh,
And to trust in the shadow of Egypt!
3 Therefore the strength of Pharaoh
Shall be your shame,
And trust in the shadow of Egypt
Shall be *your* humiliation.
4 For his princes were at Zoan,
And his ambassadors came to Hanes.
5 They were all ashamed of a people
who could not benefit them,
Or be help or benefit,
But a shame and also a reproach."

ARCHITECTURE AND BUILDING

*Many of the tombs dating from the time of Isaiah are cut into the rocks in the hills
surrounding Jerusalem. Some tombs were made with an entrance area leading to the
rooms where family members could be buried. Only a rich person could afford to prepare
such an impressive tomb. Shebna built a memorial to himself instead of paying attention
to the desperate condition of his nation (Is. 22:15, 16).*

⁶The burden against the beasts of the South.

Through a land of trouble and
    anguish,
From which *came* the lioness and lion,
The viper and fiery flying serpent,
They will carry their riches on the
    backs of young donkeys,
And their treasures on the humps of
    camels,
To a people *who* shall not profit;
7 For the Egyptians shall help in vain
    and to no purpose.
Therefore I have called her
Rahab-Hem-Shebeth.ᵃ

A Rebellious People

8 Now go, write it before them on a
    tablet,
And note it on a scroll,
That it may be for time to come,
Forever and ever:
9 That this *is* a rebellious people,
Lying children,
Children *who* will not hear the law of
    the LORD;
10 Who say to the seers, "Do not see,"
And to the prophets, "Do not prophesy
    to us right things;
Speak to us smooth things, prophesy
    deceits.
11 Get out of the way,
Turn aside from the path,
Cause the Holy One of Israel
To cease from before us."

¹²Therefore thus says the Holy One of
Israel:

"Because you despise this word,
And trust in oppression and
    perversity,
And rely on them,
13 Therefore this iniquity shall be to you
Like a breach ready to fall,
A bulge in a high wall,
Whose breaking comes suddenly, in an
    instant.

14 And He shall break it like the
        breaking of the potter's vessel,
Which is broken in pieces;
He shall not spare.
So there shall not be found among its
    fragments
A shard to take fire from the hearth,
Or to take water from the cistern."

¹⁵For thus says the Lord GOD, the Holy
One of Israel:

"In returning and rest you shall be
    saved;
In quietness and confidence shall be
    your strength."
But you would not,
16 And you said, "No, for we will flee on
    horses"—
Therefore you shall flee!
And, "We will ride on swift *horses*"—
Therefore those who pursue you shall
    be swift!
17 One thousand *shall flee* at the threat
    of one,
At the threat of five you shall flee,
Till you are left as a pole on top of a
    mountain
And as a banner on a hill.

God Will Be Gracious

18 Therefore the LORD will wait, that He
        may be gracious to you;
And therefore He will be exalted, that
    He may have mercy on you.
For the LORD *is* a God of justice;
Blessed *are* all those who wait for
    Him.

19 For the people shall dwell in Zion at
        Jerusalem;
You shall weep no more.
He will be very gracious to you at the
    sound of your cry;
When He hears it, He will answer
    you.

30:7 ᵃLiterally *Rahab Sits Idle*

ARTS AND LITERATURE

*The oldest writing tablets (Is. 30:8) discovered so far can be dated to about 1350 B.C.
They were found in A.D. 1986 in a shipwreck off the coast of southern Turkey. Until this
discovery, the oldest tablets were those found in a well at Nimrud, near Nineveh, dating
from about 700 B.C. The original writing surface was a coating of wax.*

TOPHET BURNS WITH MUCH WOOD (Is. 30:33)

Tophet (or Topheth) was a cultic site installed in the Valley of the Son of Hinnom (2 Kin. 23:10). It was connected to the worship of the god Molech and involved rituals that allowed children to be burned with fire (Jer. 7:31). The Valley of Hinnom runs roughly in a curving form, east-west, on the south side of the city of Jerusalem. To this day, no archaeological evidence of Tophet has been found.

The prophets often mentioned the fire of Tophet that was used to destroy children, but for the prophets Tophet was symbolical of the judgment God would bring on those not faithful to Him. Jeremiah proclaims that God would make Jerusalem and the towns around it like Tophet—like a place of burning—because their inhabitants had "stiffened their necks" against God's will (Jer. 19:12–15).

Another prophet, Isaiah, announces that a similar punishment would befall Assyria (Is. 30:31–33). Tophet is pictured by Isaiah as a funeral pyre that God had prepared "of old," ages before Assyria existed. It was "deep and large," a place of burning "with much wood," certainly adequate to punish Assyria (30:31) and its king (30:33).

The rites of child sacrifice at Tophet left their mark long after worship at that spot had been forgotten. By New Testament times, the Aramaic term *gehinnam,* meaning "Valley of Hinnom," was known in Greek as Gehenna, the "hell fire" (Matt. 5:22). In Jesus' warnings about hell fire (Matt. 18:9), Gehenna would be a fiery judgment, recalling the judgment and burning at Tophet proclaimed by Isaiah.

---

20 And *though* the Lord gives you
   The bread of adversity and the water
     of affliction,
   Yet your teachers will not be moved
     into a corner anymore,
   But your eyes shall see your teachers.
21 Your ears shall hear a word behind
     you, saying,
   "This *is* the way, walk in it,"
   Whenever you turn to the right hand
   Or whenever you turn to the left.
22 You will also defile the covering of
     your images of silver,
   And the ornament of your molded
     images of gold.
   You will throw them away as an
     unclean thing;
   You will say to them, "Get away!"

23 Then He will give the rain for your
     seed
   With which you sow the ground,
   And bread of the increase of the earth;
   It will be fat and plentiful.
   In that day your cattle will feed
   In large pastures.
24 Likewise the oxen and the young
     donkeys that work the ground
   Will eat cured fodder,
   Which has been winnowed with the
     shovel and fan.
25 There will be on every high mountain

And on every high hill
Rivers *and* streams of waters,
In the day of the great slaughter,
When the towers fall.
26 Moreover the light of the moon will be
     as the light of the sun,
   And the light of the sun will be
     sevenfold,
   As the light of seven days,
   In the day that the LORD binds up the
     bruise of His people
   And heals the stroke of their wound.

Judgment on Assyria

27 Behold, the name of the LORD comes
     from afar,
   Burning *with* His anger,
   And *His* burden *is* heavy;
   His lips are full of indignation,
   And His tongue like a devouring fire.
28 His breath is like an overflowing
     stream,
   Which reaches up to the neck,
   To sift the nations with the sieve of
     futility;
   And *there shall be* a bridle in the jaws
     of the people,
   Causing *them* to err.

29 You shall have a song
   As in the night *when* a holy festival is
     kept,

And gladness of heart as when one
    goes with a flute,
To come into the mountain of the
    LORD,
To the Mighty One of Israel.
30 The LORD will cause His glorious voice
    to be heard,
And show the descent of His arm,
With the indignation of *His* anger
And the flame of a devouring fire,
With scattering, tempest, and
    hailstones.
31 For through the voice of the LORD
Assyria will be beaten down,
    As He strikes with the rod.
32 And *in* every place where the staff of
    punishment passes,
Which the LORD lays on him,
It will be with tambourines and harps;
And in battles of brandishing He will
    fight with it.
33 For Tophet *was* established of old,
Yes, for the king it is prepared.
He has made *it* deep and large;
Its pyre *is* fire with much wood;
The breath of the LORD, like a stream
    of brimstone,
Kindles it.

The Folly of Not Trusting God

31 ¹ Woe to those who go down to
    Egypt for help,
And rely on horses,
Who trust in chariots because *they are*
    many,
And in horsemen because they are
    very strong,
But who do not look to the Holy One
    of Israel,
Nor seek the LORD!
2 Yet He also *is* wise and will bring
    disaster,
And will not call back His words,

But will arise against the house of
    evildoers,
And against the help of those who
    work iniquity.
3 Now the Egyptians *are* men, and not
    God;
And their horses are flesh, and not
    spirit.
When the LORD stretches out His
    hand,
Both he who helps will fall,
And he who is helped will fall down;
They all will perish together.

God Will Deliver Jerusalem

⁴For thus the LORD has spoken to me:

"As a lion roars,
And a young lion over his prey
(When a multitude of shepherds is
    summoned against him,
He will not be afraid of their voice
Nor be disturbed by their noise),
So the LORD of hosts will come down
To fight for Mount Zion and for its
    hill.
5 Like birds flying about,
So will the LORD of hosts defend
    Jerusalem.
Defending, He will also deliver *it;*
Passing over, He will preserve *it.*"

⁶Return *to Him* against whom the children of Israel have deeply revolted. ⁷For in that day every man shall throw away his idols of silver and his idols of gold—sin, which your own hands have made for yourselves.

8 "Then Assyria shall fall by a sword not
    of man,
And a sword not of mankind shall
    devour him.
But he shall flee from the sword,
And his young men shall become
    forced labor.
9 He shall cross over to his stronghold
    for fear,
And his princes shall be afraid of the
    banner,"
Says the LORD,
Whose fire *is* in Zion
And whose furnace *is* in Jerusalem.

A Reign of Righteousness

32 ¹ Behold, a king will reign in
    righteousness,
And princes will rule with justice.

TIME CAPSULE   *684 to 677 B.C.*

684	*Inundation of the Nile results in bumper crop in Egypt*
683– 680	*Tirhakah of Egypt conducts military campaigns in Libya and Palestine*
681	*Sennacherib's death*
680– 669	*Esarhaddon's mother Naqi'a exercises authority during her son's reign*
677	*Esarhaddon marches against Sidon*

2   A man will be as a hiding place from
     the wind,
    And a cover from the tempest,
    As rivers of water in a dry place,
    As the shadow of a great rock in a
     weary land.

3   The eyes of those who see will not be
     dim,
    And the ears of those who hear will
     listen.

4   Also the heart of the rash will
     understand knowledge,
    And the tongue of the stammerers will
     be ready to speak plainly.

5   The foolish person will no longer be
     called generous,
    Nor the miser said *to be* bountiful;

6   For the foolish person will speak
     foolishness,
    And his heart will work iniquity:
    To practice ungodliness,
    To utter error against the LORD,
    To keep the hungry unsatisfied,
    And he will cause the drink of the
     thirsty to fail.

7   Also the schemes of the schemer *are*
     evil;
    He devises wicked plans
    To destroy the poor with lying words,
    Even when the needy speaks justice.

8   But a generous man devises generous
     things,
    And by generosity he shall stand.

Consequences of Complacency

9   Rise up, you women who are at ease,
    Hear my voice;
    You complacent daughters,
    Give ear to my speech.

10   In a year and *some* days
    You will be troubled, you complacent
     women;
    For the vintage will fail,
    The gathering will not come.

11   Tremble, you *women* who are at ease;
    Be troubled, you complacent ones;
    Strip yourselves, make yourselves
     bare,
    And gird *sackcloth* on *your* waists.

12   People shall mourn upon their breasts
    For the pleasant fields, for the fruitful
     vine.

13   On the land of my people will come up
     thorns *and* briers,
    Yes, on all the happy homes *in* the
     joyous city;

14   Because the palaces will be forsaken,
    The bustling city will be deserted.
    The forts and towers will become lairs
     forever,
    A joy of wild donkeys, a pasture of
     flocks—

15   Until the Spirit is poured upon us
     from on high,
    And the wilderness becomes a fruitful
     field,
    And the fruitful field is counted as a
     forest.

The Peace of God's Reign

16   Then justice will dwell in the
     wilderness,
    And righteousness remain in the
     fruitful field.

17   The work of righteousness will be
     peace,
    And the effect of righteousness,
     quietness and assurance forever.

18   My people will dwell in a peaceful
     habitation,
    In secure dwellings, and in quiet
     resting places,

19   Though hail comes down on the forest,
    And the city is brought low in
     humiliation.

20   Blessed *are* you who sow beside all
     waters,
    Who send out freely the feet of the ox
     and the donkey.

Hezekiah's Illness and Recovery

Sargon of Assyria decisively put down the Ashdod rebellion in 712 B.C., and as Isaiah had expected, Egypt did not keep its promises of aid. King Hezekiah must not have been too involved in the rebellion, however, because Judah was not punished as Ashdod was. Nevertheless, a few years later he began to consider rebellion again. He even received overtures of friendship from Merodach-Baladan, who had been driven from Babylon by Sargon around 710 B.C. but had managed to regain control and was planning another rebellion against Assyria.

The biblical history of the next few years appears not only in 2 Kin. 18:13—20:21 but also in Is. 36—39. The order of events in the biblical text is not strictly chronological. Hezekiah's illness (Is. 38) and the visit by ambassadors from the Babylonian ruler Merodach-

Baladan (Is. 39) are described at the end of this section but must have come before Sennacherib withdrew from Jerusalem (Is. 37:37; see 2 Kin. 20:6).

The name "Berodach-Baladan" in 2 Kin. 20:12 appears to be a corrupted spelling of Merodach-Baladan. He was the Babylonian ruler at two separate times (721–710 and 703–702 B.C.), and specialized in forming alliances to support his fight against Assyrian control. He may still have been known by the title "king of Babylon" at the time of Hezekiah's sickness, although he might then have been in exile. Hezekiah died in 686 B.C.; his illness 15 years earlier would have been approximately 701 B.C. (2 Kin. 20:6).

- 2 Kings 20:1–11
- Isaiah 38:1–22
- 2 Kings 20:12–19
- Isaiah 39:1–8

2 Kings 20:1–11
Hezekiah's Life Extended

20 :1 In those days Hezekiah was sick and near death. And Isaiah the prophet, the son of Amoz, went to him and said to him, "Thus says the LORD: 'Set your house in order, for you shall die, and not live.'"

2Then he turned his face toward the wall, and prayed to the LORD, saying, 3"Remember now, O LORD, I pray, how I have walked before You in truth and with a loyal heart, and have done *what was* good in Your sight." And Hezekiah wept bitterly.

4And it happened, before Isaiah had gone out into the middle court, that the word of the LORD came to him, saying, 5"Return and tell Hezekiah the leader of My people, 'Thus says the LORD, the God of David your father: "I have heard your prayer, I have seen your tears; surely I will heal you. On the third day you shall go up to the house of the LORD. 6And I will add to your days fifteen years. I will deliver you and this city from the hand of the king of Assyria; and I will defend this city for My own sake, and for the sake of My servant David."'"

7Then Isaiah said, "Take a lump of figs." So they took and laid *it* on the boil, and he recovered.

8And Hezekiah said to Isaiah, "What *is* the sign that the LORD will heal me, and that I shall go up to the house of the LORD the third day?"

9Then Isaiah said, "This is the sign to you from the LORD, that the LORD will do the thing which He has spoken: *shall* the shadow go forward ten degrees or go backward ten degrees?"

10And Hezekiah answered, "It is an easy thing for the shadow to go down ten degrees; no, but let the shadow go backward ten degrees."

11So Isaiah the prophet cried out to the LORD, and He brought the shadow ten degrees backward, by which it had gone down on the sundial of Ahaz.

Isaiah 38:1–22
Hezekiah's Life Extended

38 :1 In those days Hezekiah was sick and near death. And Isaiah the prophet, the son of Amoz, went to him and said to him, "Thus says the LORD: 'Set your house in order, for you shall die and not live.'"

2Then Hezekiah turned his face toward the wall, and prayed to the LORD, 3and said, "Remember now, O LORD, I pray, how I have walked before You in truth and with a loyal heart, and have done *what is* good in Your sight." And Hezekiah wept bitterly.

4And the word of the LORD came to Isaiah, saying, 5"Go and tell Hezekiah, 'Thus says the LORD, the God of David your father: "I have heard your prayer, I have seen your tears; surely I will add to your days fifteen years. 6I will deliver you and this city from the hand of the king of Assyria, and I will defend this city."' 7And this *is* the sign to you from the LORD, that the LORD will do this thing which He has spoken: 8Behold, I will bring the shadow on the sundial, which has gone down with the sun on the sundial of Ahaz, ten degrees backward." So the sun returned ten degrees on the dial by which it had gone down.

9This is the writing of Hezekiah king of Judah, when he had been sick and had recovered from his sickness:

10   I said,
"In the prime of my life
I shall go to the gates of Sheol;
I am deprived of the remainder of my
    years."
11   I said,
"I shall not see YAH,
The LORD[a] in the land of the living;

38:11 [a]Hebrew YAH, YAH

SENNACHERIB FAILS TO OPEN THE CAGE (Is. 38:6)

Sennacherib was the king of Assyria who mounted a ferocious military campaign against Syro-Palestine at the end of the 8th century B.C. The invasion is described in Sennacherib's annals as his third military campaign. There are a number of copies referring to this attack, as well as carved stone reliefs at Nineveh which relate the Assyrian siege of Lachish (an important fortified town in Judah).

The annals describe the destruction of a wide area of Judah, but do not mention the taking of Jerusalem. Military operations against the capital of Judah were never completed, although Sennacherib claims to have encircled Jerusalem with watchtowers. Outside of Jerusalem, the land of Judah was plundered: 46 cities were conquered, many of which were given over to Philistia, a rival of Judah. The annals claim that over 200,000 captives were taken from Judah (though not necessarily into permanent or extended captivity).

Sennacherib placed responsibility for Judah's fate in the hands of Hezekiah (the Assyrians typically blamed the enemy monarch for the invasion). We are told that the Assyrians demanded from Hezekiah his daughters, weapons, women, gold, and numerous other artifacts. The lists of tribute are the longest and most detailed of any of Sennacherib's inscriptions, possibly to downplay the failure to take Jerusalem.

The reassuring message to Hezekiah from the prophet Isaiah was that God would deliver his "city from the hand of the king of Assyria" (Is. 38:6). The Assyrian annals boast of victories but make no mention of defeats. Thus Sennacherib boasts of imprisoning Hezekiah like a "bird in a cage," but fails to say that the Assyrians had to withdraw from the cage without capturing the bird.

I shall observe man no more among
   the inhabitants of the world.[b]
12 My life span is gone,
   Taken from me like a shepherd's tent;
   I have cut off my life like a weaver.
   He cuts me off from the loom;
   From day until night You make an
      end of me.
13 I have considered until morning—
   Like a lion,
   So He breaks all my bones;
   From day until night You make an
      end of me.

14 Like a crane or a swallow, so I
   chattered;
   I mourned like a dove;
   My eyes fail from looking upward.
   O LORD,[a] I am oppressed;
   Undertake for me!

15 "What shall I say?
   He has both spoken to me,[a]
   And He Himself has done it.
   I shall walk carefully all my years
   In the bitterness of my soul.
16 O Lord, by these things men live;
   And in all these things is the life of
      my spirit;
   So You will restore me and make me
      live.
17 Indeed it was for my own peace
   That I had great bitterness;
   But You have lovingly delivered my
      soul from the pit of corruption,

38:11 [b]Following some Hebrew manuscripts; Masoretic Text and Vulgate read rest; Septuagint omits among the inhabitants of the world; Targum reads land. 38:14 [a]Following Bomberg; Masoretic Text and Dead Sea Scrolls read Lord. 38:15 [a]Following Masoretic Text and Vulgate; Dead Sea Scrolls and Targum read And shall I say to Him; Septuagint omits first half of this verse.

SCIENCE AND TECHNOLOGY

Sundials were in use in Egypt from at least 1300 B.C. The scale on which the shadow traveled was straight, like a ruler. There are also sundials made in which the shadow travels up or down a series of steps, like a flight of stairs. Ahaz's sundial may have been of this type (Is. 38:8), with a pillar on the top.

A CHALDEAN THORN PRICKS MIGHTY ASSYRIA (Is. 39:1)

Merodach-Baladan (also known by his Accadian name, Mardukapal-iddina) was a Chaldean tribal leader from southern Babylonia during the late 8th century B.C. Except for the biblical references (2 Kin. 20:12; Is. 39:1), this Chaldean ruler is mentioned primarily in hostile Assyrian sources, although a few Chaldean sources do exist.

While Assyria was expanding its control of southern Babylonia, Merodach-Baladan sent tribute to the Assyrian king Tiglath-Pileser III (744–727 B.C.). Later, during the confusing period in which the Assyrian throne was usurped by Sargon II (722–721 B.C.), the Chaldean leader formed a coalition of Chaldean and Aramean tribes and claimed independence from Assyria. He was evidently appreciated by the local inhabitants of Babylonia, who flourished under his kingship for the next 10 years until 710 B.C.

After 710 B.C. Merodach-Baladan was forced to engage in an ancient equivalent of guerrilla warfare against Assyrian advances. Although he was deposed from the throne of Babylon in this period, the Chaldean chieftain was never captured by the Assyrians. He, along with Hezekiah of Judah and others, was instrumental in leading a rebellion against Assyria during the early reign of Sennacherib (704–701 B.C.).

The alliance against Assyria was eventually defeated. Sennacherib drove Merodach-Baladan out of Babylon, and the Chaldean is last mentioned as fleeing east to Elam about 700 B.C. For a half-century, this ruler had been a constant thorn in the side of the Assyrian Empire.

For You have cast all my sins behind
  Your back.
18 For Sheol cannot thank You,
  Death cannot praise You;
  Those who go down to the pit cannot
    hope for Your truth.
19 The living, the living man, he shall
    praise You,
  As I *do* this day;
  The father shall make known Your
    truth to the children.

20 "The LORD *was ready* to save me;
  Therefore we will sing my songs with
    stringed instruments
  All the days of our life, in the house of
    the LORD."

21Now Isaiah had said, "Let them take a lump of figs, and apply *it* as a poultice on the boil, and he shall recover."

22And Hezekiah had said, "What *is* the sign that I shall go up to the house of the LORD?"

2 Kings 20:12–19
The Babylonian Envoys

20 :12 At that time Berodach-Baladan[a] the son of Baladan, king of Babylon, sent letters and a present to Hezekiah, for he heard that Hezekiah had been sick. 13And Hezekiah was attentive to them, and

showed them all the house of his treasures—the silver and gold, the spices and precious ointment, and all[a] his armory—all that was found among his treasures. There was nothing in his house or in all his dominion that Hezekiah did not show them.

14Then Isaiah the prophet went to King Hezekiah, and said to him, "What did these men say, and from where did they come to you?"

So Hezekiah said, "They came from a far country, from Babylon."

15And he said, "What have they seen in your house?"

So Hezekiah answered, "They have seen all that *is* in my house; there is nothing among my treasures that I have not shown them."

16Then Isaiah said to Hezekiah, "Hear the word of the LORD: 17'Behold, the days are coming when all that *is* in your house, and what your fathers have accumulated until this day, shall be carried to Babylon; nothing shall be left,' says the LORD. 18'And they shall take away some of your sons who will descend from you, whom you will

---

20:12 [a]Spelled *Merodach-Baladan* in Isaiah 39:1
20:13 [a]Following many Hebrew manuscripts, Syriac, and Targum; Masoretic Text omits *all.*

beget; and they shall be eunuchs in the palace of the king of Babylon.'"

¹⁹So Hezekiah said to Isaiah, "The word of the LORD which you have spoken *is* good!" For he said, "Will there not be peace and truth at least in my days?"

Isaiah 39:1–8
The Babylonian Envoys

39 :1 At that time Merodach-Baladan[a] the son of Baladan, king of Babylon, sent letters and a present to Hezekiah, for he heard that he had been sick and had recovered. ²And Hezekiah was pleased with them, and showed them the house of his treasures—the silver and gold, the spices and precious ointment, and all his armory—all that was found among his treasures. There was nothing in his house or in all his dominion that Hezekiah did not show them.

³Then Isaiah the prophet went to King Hezekiah, and said to him, "What did these men say, and from where did they come to you?"

So Hezekiah said, "They came to me from a far country, from Babylon."

⁴And he said, "What have they seen in your house?"

So Hezekiah answered, "They have seen all that *is* in my house; there is nothing among my treasures that I have not shown them."

⁵Then Isaiah said to Hezekiah, "Hear the word of the LORD of hosts: ⁶'Behold, the days are coming when all that *is* in your house, and what your fathers have accumulated until this day, shall be carried to Babylon; nothing shall be left,' says the LORD. ⁷'And they shall take away *some* of your sons who will descend from you, whom you will beget; and they shall be eunuchs in the palace of the king of Babylon.'"

⁸So Hezekiah said to Isaiah, "The word of the LORD which you have spoken *is* good!" For he said, "At least there will be peace and truth in my days."

39:1 ᵃSpelled *Berodach-Baladan* in 2 Kings 20:12

Sennacherib's Invasion

After flirting with the idea for years, Hezekiah finally rebelled against Assyria. The Assyrian king, Sennacherib (704–681 B.C.), promptly attacked Judah.

The chronology of Sennacherib's invasion is difficult. The 14th year of Hezekiah (2 Kin. 18:13; Is. 36:1) would be 701 B.C., but the siege was interrupted by an attack from Tirhakah of Egypt (2 Kin. 19:9; Is. 37:9), whose reign (690–664 B.C.) did not begin until about 10 years after this date. Some suggest that the Bible uses the name "Tirhakah," the most famous of the Ethiopian pharaohs, for a different and less well known king. Others argue that Hezekiah actually rebelled against Sennacherib twice, and the two accounts have been compressed into one narrative.

The suggestion that there were two invasions would also explain why there are two different reasons given for Jerusalem's deliverance. Hezekiah rebelled and was invaded in 701 B.C. He survived this first invasion only by paying exorbitant tribute to Sennacherib (2 Kin. 18:14–16). This payment is corroborated by Assyrian records, but interestingly enough, the parallel passage in Isaiah (Is. 36:1, 2) does not mention Hezekiah's tribute.

- Isaiah 36:1
- 2 Kings 18:13–16

Isaiah 36:1

36 :1 Now it came to pass in the fourteenth year of King Hezekiah *that* Sennacherib king of Assyria came up against all the fortified cities of Judah and took them.

2 Kings 18:13–16

18 :13 And in the fourteenth year of King Hezekiah, Sennacherib king of Assyria came up against all the fortified cities of Judah and took them. ¹⁴Then Hezekiah king of Judah sent to the king of Assyria at Lachish, saying, "I have done wrong; turn away from me; whatever you

---

TIME CAPSULE   *676 to 672 B.C.*

676	*Edom, Moab, and Ammon become vassals of Assyria*
675	*Temple of the moon god at Haran is repaired by Assyrian king Esarhaddon*
674	*Esarhaddon makes his first attack on Egypt*
672	*Esarhaddon appoints one son as heir to Assyria's throne and another son to Babylonia's throne*

impose on me I will pay." And the king of Assyria assessed Hezekiah king of Judah three hundred talents of silver and thirty talents of gold. ¹⁵So Hezekiah gave *him* all the silver that was found in the house of the LORD and in the treasuries of the king's house. ¹⁶At that time Hezekiah stripped *the gold from* the doors of the temple of the LORD, and *from* the pillars which Hezekiah king of Judah had overlaid, and gave it to the king of Assyria.

A Second Invasion

Hezekiah survived his rebellion of 701 B.C., but some 12 or 13 years later he tried again. Maybe around 688 B.C. Sennacherib again invaded and laid siege to Jerusalem (Is. 36:2—37:7). This time Tirhakah, the Ethiopian king of Egypt, interrupted the siege briefly but was driven back. This time there was no tribute paid; Jerusalem was spared by a miraculous plague that swept the Assyrian camp (Is. 37:8—38). A second invasion by Sennacherib is not recorded in Assyrian annals, but it has been suggested by scholars to account for the appearance of Pharaoh Tirhakah, who was not yet in power when Sennacherib invaded Judah in 701 B.C.

■ 2 Kings 18:17—19:7
■ Isaiah 36:2—37:7
■ 2 Kings 19:8-37
■ Isaiah 37:8-38
■ 2 Kings 20:20, 21

2 Kings 18:17—19:7
Sennacherib Boasts Against the LORD

18 :17 Then the king of Assyria sent *the* Tartan,^a *the* Rabsaris,^b *and the* Rabshakeh^c from Lachish, with a great army against Jerusalem, to King Hezekiah. And they went up and came to Jerusalem. When they had come up, they went and stood by the aqueduct from the upper pool, which *was* on the highway to the Fuller's Field. ¹⁸And when they had called to the king, Eliakim the son of Hilkiah, who *was* over the household, Shebna the scribe, and Joah the son of Asaph, the recorder, came out to them. ¹⁹Then *the* Rabshakeh said to them, "Say now to Hezekiah, 'Thus says the great king, the king of Assyria: "What confidence *is* this in which you trust? ²⁰You speak of *having* plans and power for war; but *they are* mere words. And in whom do you trust, that you rebel

against me? ²¹Now look! You are trusting in the staff of this broken reed, Egypt, on which if a man leans, it will go into his hand and pierce it. So *is* Pharaoh king of Egypt to all who trust in him. ²²But if you say to me, 'We trust in the LORD our God,' *is* it not He whose high places and whose altars Hezekiah has taken away, and said to Judah and Jerusalem, 'You shall worship before this altar in Jerusalem'?" ' ²³Now therefore, I urge you, give a pledge to my master the king of Assyria, and I will give you two thousand horses—if you are able on your part to put riders on them! ²⁴How then will you repel one captain of the least of my master's servants, and put your trust in Egypt for chariots and horsemen? ²⁵Have I now come up without the LORD against this place to destroy it? The LORD said to me, 'Go up against this land, and destroy it.' "

²⁶Then Eliakim the son of Hilkiah, Shebna, and Joah said to *the* Rabshakeh, "Please speak to your servants in Aramaic, for we understand *it;* and do not speak to us in Hebrew^a in the hearing of the people who *are* on the wall."

²⁷But *the* Rabshakeh said to them, "Has my master sent me to your master and to you to speak these words, and not to the men who sit on the wall, who will eat and drink their own waste with you?"

²⁸Then *the* Rabshakeh stood and called out with a loud voice in Hebrew, and spoke, saying, "Hear the word of the great king, the king of Assyria! ²⁹Thus says the king: 'Do not let Hezekiah deceive you, for he shall not be able to deliver you from his hand; ³⁰nor let Hezekiah make you trust in the LORD, saying, "The LORD will surely deliver us; this city shall not be given into the hand of the king of Assyria." ' ³¹Do not listen to Hezekiah; for thus says the king of Assyria: 'Make *peace* with me by a present and come out to me; and every one of you eat from his own vine and every one from his own fig tree, and every one of you drink the waters of his own cistern; ³²until I come and take you away to a land like your own land, a land of grain and new wine, a land of bread and vineyards, a land of olive groves and honey, that you may live and not die. But do not listen to Hezekiah, lest he persuade you, saying, "The LORD will

---

18:17 ^aA title, probably *Commander in Chief* ^bA title, probably *Chief Officer* ^cA title, probably *Chief of Staff* or *Governor*   18:26 ^aLiterally *Judean*

THE ASSYRIANS SERVE GOD, SO THEY SAY (2 Kin. 18:25; Is. 36:10)

One of the high-ranking officers in the Assyrian army was titled the Rabshakeh (2 Kin. 18:17; Is. 36:2), a position possibly similar to a Chief of Staff. As the Assyrian army laid siege to Jerusalem, the Rabshakeh urged King Hezekiah and his people to surrender. He further intimidated the Jerusalemites by claiming that Jerusalem's own God, Yahweh, had given him authority to take the city (2 Kin. 18:25; Is. 36:10).

The Rabshakeh supported his claim by asserting that Yahweh was displeased with Hezekiah as king of Judah. The altars and high places that had been purged in Hezekiah's earlier reform (2 Kin. 18:4) belonged to Yahweh, so the Rabshakeh thought (2 Kin. 18:22; Is. 36:7). Therefore, Yahweh had given Judah to Sennacherib, king of Assyria (704–681 B.C.), who would become Yahweh's new vice-regent for the land. According to the Rabshakeh's logic, the Judahites should recognize their own God's right to transfer the land from Hezekiah's control to Sennacherib's, as well as understand that Yahweh had brought the Assyrian army to take possession.

The Rabshakeh's speech plays on the common Near Eastern belief that gods owned the land and could give it to whomever they chose. A frequently used propaganda device in the Neo-Assyrian period was to claim that a god had chosen to destroy his own nation or turn it over to another people. Sennacherib himself used this argument when he destroyed Babylon in 689 B.C., claiming that Marduk (Babylon's god) had ordered the destruction of his own city.

deliver us." [33]Has any of the gods of the nations at all delivered its land from the hand of the king of Assyria? [34]Where *are* the gods of Hamath and Arpad? Where *are* the gods of Sepharvaim and Hena and Ivah? Indeed, have they delivered Samaria from my hand? [35]Who among all the gods of the lands have delivered their countries from my hand, that the LORD should deliver Jerusalem from my hand?' "

[36]But the people held their peace and answered him not a word; for the king's commandment was, "Do not answer him." [37]Then Eliakim the son of Hilkiah, who *was* over the household, Shebna the scribe, and Joah the son of Asaph, the recorder, came to Hezekiah with *their* clothes torn, and told him the words of *the* Rabshakeh.

Isaiah Assures Deliverance

19 [1]And so it was, when King Hezekiah heard *it,* that he tore his clothes, covered himself with sackcloth, and went into the house of the LORD. [2]Then he sent Eliakim, who *was* over the household, Shebna the scribe, and the elders of the priests, covered with sackcloth, to Isaiah the prophet, the son of Amoz. [3]And they said to him, "Thus says Hezekiah: 'This day *is* a day of trouble, and rebuke, and

blasphemy; for the children have come to birth, but *there is* no strength to bring them forth. [4]It may be that the LORD your God will hear all the words of *the* Rabshakeh, whom his master the king of Assyria has sent to reproach the living God, and will rebuke the words which the LORD your God has heard. Therefore lift up *your* prayer for the remnant that is left.' "

[5]So the servants of King Hezekiah came to Isaiah. [6]And Isaiah said to them, "Thus you shall say to your master, 'Thus says the LORD: "Do not be afraid of the words which you have heard, with which the servants of the king of Assyria have blasphemed Me. [7]Surely I will send a spirit upon him, and he shall hear a rumor and return to his own land; and I will cause him to fall by the sword in his own land." ' "

Isaiah 36:2—37:7
Sennacherib Boasts Against the LORD

36 :2 Then the king of Assyria sent *the* Rabshakeh[a] with a great army from Lachish to King Hezekiah at Jerusalem. And he stood by the aqueduct from the upper pool, on the highway to the Fuller's Field. [3]And Eliakim the son of Hilkiah, who was over the household, Shebna the scribe, and Joah the son of Asaph, the recorder, came out to him.

[4]Then *the* Rabshakeh said to them,

36:2 [a]A title, probably *Chief of Staff* or *Governor*

OKAY, THE ASSYRIANS REALLY SERVE ASSHUR (2 Kin. 18:35; Is. 36:20)

The Rabshakeh continued his propaganda speech with a shift in emphasis. The king of Assyria, Sennacherib, was considered the vice-regent of the god Asshur, patron deity of Assyria. The common belief was that conquering armies were preceded by their gods, who defeated the local gods of the lands being invaded. The divine presence (of Asshur, in this case) went before the king, defeating his enemies.

Clearly, the Rabshakeh argues, none of the gods of other lands had been able to help their people against the Assyrian army (2 Kin. 18:33–35; Is. 36:18–20). Hamath, Arpad, Sepharvaim, Hena, and Ivah had all fallen to Assyria's power. So Asshur must be the highest ruling deity of all gods, otherwise why would Sennacherib's armies be so successful?

The unbroken list of conquests (2 Kin. 18:34; Is. 36:19) was given to Jerusalem as proof that Asshur and his Assyrians controlled the world. If all other gods had given up their land and handed their territories over to Asshur, it would follow logically that Yahweh should do the same. The Judahites were defying both Asshur and Yahweh by their refusal to surrender.

The prophet Isaiah, however, assured Hezekiah that the Rabshakeh had "blasphemed" Yahweh both by misunderstanding the order of the universe and by misrepresenting the current situation. Whether Assyria knew it or not, she existed only at the command of the sovereign God Yahweh (Is. 37:26, 27).

"Say now to Hezekiah, 'Thus says the great king, the king of Assyria: "What confidence is this in which you trust? ⁵I say you speak of having plans and power for war; but *they are* mere words. Now in whom do you trust, that you rebel against me? ⁶Look! You are trusting in the staff of this broken reed, Egypt, on which if a man leans, it will go into his hand and pierce it. So *is* Pharaoh king of Egypt to all who trust in him.

⁷"But if you say to me, 'We trust in the LORD our God,' *is it* not He whose high places and whose altars Hezekiah has taken away, and said to Judah and Jerusalem, 'You shall worship before this altar'?" ' ⁸Now therefore, I urge you, give a pledge to my master the king of Assyria, and I will give you two thousand horses—if you are able on your part to put riders on them! ⁹How then will you repel one captain of the least of my master's servants, and put your trust in Egypt for chariots and horsemen? ¹⁰Have I now come up without the LORD against this land to destroy it? The LORD said to me, 'Go up against this land, and destroy it.' "

¹¹Then Eliakim, Shebna, and Joah said to *the* Rabshakeh, "Please speak to your servants in Aramaic, for we understand *it;* and do not speak to us in Hebrewᵃ in the hearing of the people who *are* on the wall."

¹²But *the* Rabshakeh said, "Has my master sent me to your master and to you to speak these words, and not to the men who sit on the wall, who will eat and drink their own waste with you?"

¹³Then *the* Rabshakeh stood and called out with a loud voice in Hebrew, and said, "Hear the words of the great king, the king of Assyria! ¹⁴Thus says the king: 'Do not let Hezekiah deceive you, for he will not be able to deliver you; ¹⁵nor let Hezekiah make you trust in the LORD, saying, "The LORD will surely deliver us; this city will not be given into the hand of the king of Assyria." ' ¹⁶Do not listen to Hezekiah; for thus says the king of Assyria: 'Make *peace* with me *by a* present and come out to me; and every one of you eat from his own vine and every one from his own fig tree, and every one of you drink the waters of his own cistern; ¹⁷until I come and take you away to a land like your own land, a land of grain and new wine, a land of bread and vineyards. ¹⁸*Beware* lest Hezekiah persuade you, saying, "The LORD will deliver us." Has any one of the gods of the nations delivered its land from the hand of the king of Assyria? ¹⁹Where *are* the gods of Hamath and Arpad? Where *are* the gods of Sepharvaim? Indeed, have they delivered Samaria from my hand? ²⁰Who among all the gods of these lands have delivered their

---

36:11 ᵃLiterally *Judean*

TIRHAKAH, KING OF ETHIOPIA AND EGYPT (2 Kin. 19:9; Is. 37:9)

Tirhakah was from a Nubian line of kings of Egypt in the 25th Dynasty. Isaiah calls him the "king of Ethiopia" (or Cush; Is. 37:9), a correct title since Tirhakah originated in Nubia, a region of northeast Africa along the Nile.

Upon attaining the Egyptian throne, Tirhakah began numerous building projects, especially at the Egyptian city of Thebes. Egyptian inscriptions provide evidence of his military campaigns both in Libya and in Palestine early in his reign (c. 683–680 B.C.). He allied with Tyre and Sidon against the continued advance of Assyria.

After 680 B.C. Tirhakah finally faced attacks from Assyria. Assyrian sources describe the invasion and conquest of the Phoenician city-states by Esarhaddon (680–669 B.C.), who then invaded the Delta region of Egypt. Though Esarhaddon's forces were repulsed in 674 B.C., his army succeeded 3 years later (671 B.C.) in taking Memphis, Tirhakah's capital city.

Tirhakah was able to regain control of Memphis. However, another Assyrian king, Ashurbanipal (668–627 B.C.), also sent armies to Egypt early in his reign in 667 and 664 B.C. The Assyrians forced Tirhakah to flee southward to Nubia, where he died in 664 B.C. Nevertheless, he continued to be considered the king of Egypt even while in his southern exile.

Tirhakah's role in the Assyrian invasion of Judah is unknown in sources outside of the Bible. Assyria's king Sennacherib first invaded Judah in 701 B.C. (Is. 36:2), and Tirhakah was not officially king of Egypt for another decade (690–664 B.C.). Some scholars suppose that Sennacherib besieged Jerusalem during a second invasion around 688 B.C. During that year Tirhakah was ruling Egypt and could have interrupted the siege (Is. 37:9), though Assyrian sources do not report a campaign in 688.

countries from my hand, that the LORD should deliver Jerusalem from my hand?' "

21But they held their peace and answered him not a word; for the king's commandment was, "Do not answer him." 22Then Eliakim the son of Hilkiah, who *was* over the household, Shebna the scribe, and Joah the son of Asaph, the recorder, came to Hezekiah with *their* clothes torn, and told him the words of *the* Rabshakeh.

Isaiah Assures Deliverance

37 1And so it was, when King Hezekiah heard *it,* that he tore his clothes, covered himself with sackcloth, and went into the house of the LORD. 2Then he sent Eliakim, who *was* over the household, Shebna the scribe, and the elders of the priests, covered with sackcloth, to Isaiah the prophet, the son of Amoz. 3And they said to him, "Thus says Hezekiah: 'This day *is* a day of trouble and rebuke and blasphemy; for the children have come to birth, but *there is* no strength to bring them forth. 4It may be that the LORD your God will hear the words of *the* Rabshakeh, whom his master the king of Assyria has sent to reproach the living God, and will rebuke the words which the LORD your God

has heard. Therefore lift up *your* prayer for the remnant that is left.' "

5So the servants of King Hezekiah came to Isaiah. 6And Isaiah said to them, "Thus you shall say to your master, 'Thus says the LORD: "Do not be afraid of the words which you have heard, with which the servants of the king of Assyria have blasphemed Me. 7Surely I will send a spirit upon him, and he shall hear a rumor and return to his own land; and I will cause him to fall by the sword in his own land." ' "

2 Kings 19:8–37
Sennacherib's Threat and Hezekiah's Prayer

19 :8 Then *the* Rabshakeh returned and found the king of Assyria warring against Libnah, for he heard that he had departed from Lachish. 9And the king heard concerning Tirhakah king of Ethiopia, "Look, he has come out to make war with you." So he again sent messengers to Hezekiah, saying, 10"Thus you shall speak to Hezekiah king of Judah, saying: 'Do not let your God in whom you trust deceive you, saying, "Jerusalem shall not be given into the hand of the king of Assyria." 11Look! You have heard what the kings of

Assyria have done to all lands by utterly destroying them; and shall you be delivered? ¹²Have the gods of the nations delivered those whom my fathers have destroyed, Gozan and Haran and Rezeph, and the people of Eden who *were* in Telassar? ¹³Where *is* the king of Hamath, the king of Arpad, and the king of the city of Sepharvaim, Hena, and Ivah?' "

¹⁴And Hezekiah received the letter from the hand of the messengers, and read it; and Hezekiah went up to the house of the LORD, and spread it before the LORD. ¹⁵Then Hezekiah prayed before the LORD, and said: "O LORD God of Israel, *the One* who dwells *between* the cherubim, You are God, You alone, of all the kingdoms of the earth. You have made heaven and earth. ¹⁶Incline Your ear, O LORD, and hear; open Your eyes, O LORD, and see; and hear the words of Sennacherib, which he has sent to reproach the living God. ¹⁷Truly, LORD, the kings of Assyria have laid waste the nations and their lands, ¹⁸and have cast their gods into the fire; for they *were* not gods, but the work of men's hands—wood and stone. Therefore they destroyed them. ¹⁹Now therefore, O LORD our God, I pray, save us from his hand, that all the kingdoms of the earth may know that You *are* the LORD God, You alone."

The Word of the LORD Concerning Sennacherib

²⁰Then Isaiah the son of Amoz sent to Hezekiah, saying, "Thus says the LORD God of Israel: 'Because you have prayed to Me against Sennacherib king of Assyria, I have heard.' ²¹This *is* the word which the LORD has spoken concerning him:

'The virgin, the daughter of Zion,
Has despised you, laughed you to scorn;
The daughter of Jerusalem
Has shaken *her* head behind your back!

²² 'Whom have you reproached and blasphemed?
Against whom have you raised *your* voice,
And lifted up your eyes on high?
Against the Holy *One* of Israel.
²³ By your messengers you have reproached the Lord,
And said: "By the multitude of my chariots
I have come up to the height of the mountains,
To the limits of Lebanon;
I will cut down its tall cedars
And its choice cypress trees;
I will enter the extremity of its borders,
To its fruitful forest.
²⁴ I have dug and drunk strange water,
And with the soles of my feet I have dried up
All the brooks of defense."

²⁵ 'Did you not hear long ago
How I made it,
From ancient times that I formed it?
Now I have brought it to pass,
That you should be
For crushing fortified cities *into* heaps of ruins.
²⁶ Therefore their inhabitants had little power;
They were dismayed and confounded;
They were *as* the grass of the field
And the green herb,
As the grass on the housetops
And *grain* blighted before it is grown.

²⁷ 'But I know your dwelling place,
Your going out and your coming in,
And your rage against Me.
²⁸ Because your rage against Me and your tumult
Have come up to My ears,
Therefore I will put My hook in your nose
And My bridle in your lips,

SCIENCE AND TECHNOLOGY

An army attacking a city would typically lay siege to it, or surround it and try to starve it into submission. Within its walls a city had to have food and water to resist a siege. The attacking army could try to build a "siege mound" (2 Kin. 19:32), a ramp of dirt leading up to the top of the city walls. Using such a ramp, the soldiers could march over the fortifications.

And I will turn you back
By the way which you came.

29"This *shall be* a sign to you:

You shall eat this year such as grows
    of itself,
And in the second year what springs
    from the same;
Also in the third year sow and reap,
Plant vineyards and eat the fruit of
    them.
30 And the remnant who have escaped of
    the house of Judah
Shall again take root downward,
And bear fruit upward.
31 For out of Jerusalem shall go a
    remnant,
And those who escape from Mount
    Zion.
The zeal of the LORD of hosts[a] will do
    this.'

32"Therefore thus says the LORD concerning the king of Assyria:

'He shall not come into this city,
Nor shoot an arrow there,
Nor come before it with shield,
Nor build a siege mound against it.
33 By the way that he came,
By the same shall he return;
And he shall not come into this city,'
Says the LORD.
34 'For I will defend this city, to save it
For My own sake and for My servant
    David's sake.' "

Sennacherib's Defeat and Death

35And it came to pass on a certain
night that the angel[a] of the LORD went out,
and killed in the camp of the Assyrians one
hundred and eighty-five thousand; and
when *people* arose early in the morning,
there were the corpses—all dead. 36So Sennacherib king of Assyria departed and
went away, returned *home,* and remained
at Nineveh. 37Now it came to pass, as he
was worshiping in the temple of Nisroch
his god, that his sons Adrammelech and
Sharezer struck him down with the sword;
and they escaped into the land of Ararat.

Then Esarhaddon his son reigned in his
place.

Isaiah 37:8–38
Sennacherib's Threat and Hezekiah's Prayer

37 :8 Then *the* Rabshakeh returned,
and found the king of Assyria warring against Libnah, for he heard that he
had departed from Lachish. 9And the king
heard concerning Tirhakah king of Ethiopia, "He has come out to make war with
you." So when he heard *it,* he sent messengers to Hezekiah, saying, 10"Thus you shall
speak to Hezekiah king of Judah, saying:
'Do not let your God in whom you trust deceive you, saying, "Jerusalem shall not be
given into the hand of the king of Assyria."
11Look! You have heard what the kings of
Assyria have done to all lands by utterly
destroying them; and shall you be delivered? 12Have the gods of the nations delivered those whom my fathers have destroyed, Gozan and Haran and Rezeph,
and the people of Eden who *were* in Telassar? 13Where *is* the king of Hamath, the
king of Arpad, and the king of the city of
Sepharvaim, Hena, and Ivah?' "

14And Hezekiah received the letter
from the hand of the messengers, and read
it; and Hezekiah went up to the house of
the LORD, and spread it before the LORD.
15Then Hezekiah prayed to the LORD, saying: 16"O LORD of hosts, God of Israel, *the*
One who dwells *between* the cherubim, You
are God, You alone, of all the kingdoms of
the earth. You have made heaven and
earth. 17Incline Your ear, O LORD, and hear;
open Your eyes, O LORD, and see; and hear
all the words of Sennacherib, which he has
sent to reproach the living God. 18Truly,
LORD, the kings of Assyria have laid waste
all the nations and their lands, 19and have
cast their gods into the fire; for they *were*
not gods, but the work of men's hands—
wood and stone. Therefore they destroyed
them. 20Now therefore, O LORD our God,
save us from his hand, that all the kingdoms of the earth may know that You *are*
the LORD, You alone."

The Word of the LORD Concerning Sennacherib

21Then Isaiah the son of Amoz sent to
Hezekiah, saying, "Thus says the LORD
God of Israel, 'Because you have prayed to
Me against Sennacherib king of Assyria,

19:31 [a]Following many Hebrew manuscripts and
ancient versions (compare Isaiah 37:32); Masoretic
Text omits *of hosts.*   19:35 [a]Or *Angel*

ARARAT—ASSYRIA'S ENEMY TO THE NORTH   (2 Kin. 19:37; Is. 37:38)

Ararat is best known as the region where Noah's ark landed, described by Gen. 8:4 as "on the mountains of Ararat." The country of Ararat was located in eastern Anatolia, and, at its greatest extent, included parts of what today is Iran, Iraq, and southern Russia. Assyrian records called this country Urartu. During the 9th to 6th centuries B.C. the kingdom of Urartu or Ararat flourished as an independent political entity, posing a constant threat to the Assyrian Empire.

The Assyrian annals first mention Ararat as a geographic region during the reign of Shalmaneser I (13th century B.C.). By the 9th century B.C. Ararat was ruled as a unified state by a certain Sarduri I. The expansion of the kingdom to the south posed a direct threat to Assyrian economic security, resulting in two centuries of conflict between the two powers. The Assyrian king Shalmaneser III (858–824 B.C.) conducted several campaigns against Ararat, commemorating his victories on the large bronze gates of the Assyrian city Imgur-Enlil, southeast of Nineveh.

The 8th century witnessed more Assyrian victories. Tiglath-Pileser III (744–727 B.C.) won a primary battle against Ararat's Sarduri II in 743. His Assyrian army destroyed the Ararat countryside while laying siege to Sarduri's capital in 735 B.C. Another Assyrian king, Sargon II (721–705 B.C.), claims to have invaded Ararat, raided its sacred city, Musasir, and carried off the national god of Ararat.

Relations between Ararat and Assyria were no better during the reign of Assyria's Sennacherib (704–681 B.C.). It makes sense that those who murdered Sennacherib in 681 would flee to Ararat, the political enemies of Assyria, in order to find refuge. Both Assyrian and later Babylonian sources appear to confirm the biblical account of Sennacherib's death in 2 Kin. 19:37; Is. 37:38. The Babylonian Chronicle reports Sennacherib's death by his son.

The Assyrians never completely conquered Ararat. However, the Medes, who with the Babylonians ended the Assyrian Empire in 612 B.C., also brought an end to Ararat. With the help of the Scythians, the Medes incorporated the kingdom of Ararat into the Median Empire in 585 B.C.

---

²²this *is* the word which the LORD has spoken concerning him:

"The virgin, the daughter of Zion,
Has despised you, laughed you to scorn;
The daughter of Jerusalem
Has shaken *her* head behind your back!

23 "Whom have you reproached and blasphemed?
Against whom have you raised *your* voice,
And lifted up your eyes on high?
Against the Holy One of Israel.
24 By your servants you have reproached the Lord,
And said, 'By the multitude of my chariots
I have come up to the height of the mountains,
To the limits of Lebanon;

I will cut down its tall cedars
And its choice cypress trees;
I will enter its farthest height,
To its fruitful forest.
25 I have dug and drunk water,
And with the soles of my feet I have dried up
All the brooks of defense.'

26 "Did you not hear long ago
How I made it,
From ancient times that I formed it?
Now I have brought it to pass,
That you should be
For crushing fortified cities *into* heaps of ruins.
27 Therefore their inhabitants *had* little power;
They were dismayed and confounded;
They were *as* the grass of the field
And the green herb,
As the grass on the housetops
And grain blighted before it is grown.

28 "But I know your dwelling place,
   Your going out and your coming in,
   And your rage against Me.
29 Because your rage against Me and
   your tumult
   Have come up to My ears,
   Therefore I will put My hook in your
   nose
   And My bridle in your lips,
   And I will turn you back
   By the way which you came." '

30"This *shall be* a sign to you:

   You shall eat this year such as grows
   of itself,
   And the second year what springs
   from the same;
   Also in the third year sow and reap,
   Plant vineyards and eat the fruit of
   them.
31 And the remnant who have escaped of
   the house of Judah
   Shall again take root downward,
   And bear fruit upward.
32 For out of Jerusalem shall go a
   remnant,
   And those who escape from Mount
   Zion.
   The zeal of the LORD of hosts will do
   this.

33"Therefore thus says the LORD concerning the king of Assyria:

   'He shall not come into this city,
   Nor shoot an arrow there,
   Nor come before it with shield,
   Nor build a siege mound against it.
34 By the way that he came,
   By the same shall he return;
   And he shall not come into this city,'
   Says the LORD.
35 'For I will defend this city, to save it
   For My own sake and for My servant
   David's sake.' "

Sennacherib's Defeat and Death

36Then the angel[a] of the LORD went
out, and killed in the camp of the Assyrians
one hundred and eighty-five thousand; and
when *people* arose early in the morning,
there were the corpses—all dead. 37So Sennacherib king of Assyria departed and
went away, returned *home*, and remained
at Nineveh. 38Now it came to pass, as he
was worshiping in the house of Nisroch his

37:36 [a]Or Angel

god, that his sons Adrammelech and
Sharezer struck him down with the sword;
and they escaped into the land of Ararat.
Then Esarhaddon his son reigned in his
place.

2 Kings 20:20, 21
Death of Hezekiah

20 :20 Now the rest of the acts of
Hezekiah—all his might, and how
he made a pool and a tunnel and brought
water into the city—*are* they not written in
the book of the chronicles of the kings of
Judah? 21So Hezekiah rested with his
fathers. Then Manasseh his son reigned in
his place.

After Sennacherib's Campaign

Jerusalem had been spared, just as Isaiah
had repeatedly promised (see Is. 31:4, 5), but
the land had not escaped unscathed by Sennacherib's invasion (Is. 22:1–14). The prophet
condemns Judah's leadership, perhaps even
including Hezekiah, for paying more attention
to the defenses of the city than to seeking
their "Maker" (22:8–11). The lands around
Jerusalem had been desolated, as had the
northern lands of Phoenicia, particularly the
city of Sidon (23:1–18).

The historical setting of Is. 24—27 is difficult to determine. The judgments and salva-
tions described in these chapters are not
specifically tied to the political events of the
8th century. For this reason, many suggest
that chs. 24—27 actually refer to a much
later time, perhaps to the destruction of
Jerusalem in 586 B.C. It is true that the style
of these chapters is more like the apocalyptic
prophecies in Ezekiel and Daniel than like the
other prophecies of Isaiah. Nevertheless, the
woe described here well suits the time after
Assyria's armies had destroyed Israel and ravaged Judah, as does the reference in Is.
27:13 to the ones "who are about to perish in
the land of Assyria."

■ Isaiah 22:1–14
■ Isaiah 23:1–18
■ Isaiah 24:1—27:13

Isaiah 22:1–14
Proclamation Against Jerusalem

22 :1 The burden against the Valley of
Vision.

   What ails you now, that you have all
   gone up to the housetops,

HEZEKIAH'S TUNNEL (Is. 22:11)

Beginning in the 8th century B.C. the kingdoms of Judah and Israel were continuously threatened by the Neo-Assyrian Empire. Assyrian kings came to Canaan to collect taxes and to intimidate the local rulers. In 722 B.C. Samaria, the capital of Israel, was destroyed (2 Kin. 17:6), and those Israelites that could, fled toward Jerusalem. Upon becoming king of Judah in 715 B.C., Hezekiah did his best to prepare Jerusalem for the eventual attack by the Assyrians. His most lasting project involved water.

Rain in Judah usually comes only in the winter. Thus, Judahites built their cities near perennial springs, and in Jerusalem the main water source was the Gihon spring (1 Kin. 1:33, 38). Like most springs, the Gihon flowed in the valley, while the city sat on the hill above. Thus the spring that served Jerusalem water was, then, at the foot of the hill, outside the walls of the city. That location would be a problem if an enemy army surrounded the city.

Hezekiah camouflaged the spring and ordered that a tunnel be carved into the hillside to bring the water under the city. Shafts were then dug down to the flowing water in the tunnel, which when finished was 1,750 feet long and emptied into the Pool of Siloam (2 Chr. 32:2–4, 30).

A dedication inscription was discovered in A.D. 1880 near the southern exit of the tunnel. Called the Siloam inscription, it describes the 8-month effort of two teams of diggers working toward each other from opposite ends of the tunnel. As the workmen came close together they could hear the other team, and they dug, according to the inscription, "pickaxe against pickaxe" until the water flowed from the spring to the reservoir.

Hezekiah's tunnel was a remarkable building project. The height of the tunnel varies greatly but averages 6 feet, and the water is most often less than knee deep. Even today, visitors to Jerusalem can wade through the s-shaped tunnel in the cool waters of the Gihon spring. Hezekiah was successful in securing the city's water supply. But the prophet (Is. 22:9–11) warns Judah's leaders that dependence on defense projects would not be sufficient to secure the city itself.

---

2 You who are full of noise,
A tumultuous city, a joyous city?
Your slain *men are* not slain with the sword,
Nor dead in battle.

3 All your rulers have fled together;
They are captured by the archers.
All who are found in you are bound together;
They have fled from afar.

4 Therefore I said, "Look away from me,
I will weep bitterly;
Do not labor to comfort me
Because of the plundering of the daughter of my people."

5 For *it is* a day of trouble and treading down and perplexity
By the Lord GOD of hosts
In the Valley of Vision—
Breaking down the walls
And of crying to the mountain.

6 Elam bore the quiver
With chariots of men *and* horsemen,
And Kir uncovered the shield.

7 It shall come to pass *that* your choicest valleys
Shall be full of chariots,
And the horsemen shall set themselves in array at the gate.

8 He removed the protection of Judah.
You looked in that day to the armor of the House of the Forest;

9 You also saw the damage to the city of David,
That it was great;
And you gathered together the waters of the lower pool.

10 You numbered the houses of Jerusalem,
And the houses you broke down
To fortify the wall.

11 You also made a reservoir between the two walls
For the water of the old pool.
But you did not look to its Maker,
Nor did you have respect for Him who fashioned it long ago.

12   And in that day the Lord GOD of
hosts
Called for weeping and for mourning,
For baldness and for girding with
sackcloth.

13   But instead, joy and gladness,
Slaying oxen and killing sheep,
Eating meat and drinking wine:
"Let us eat and drink, for tomorrow we
die!"

14   Then it was revealed in my hearing by
the LORD of hosts,
"Surely for this iniquity there will be
no atonement for you,
Even to your death," says the Lord
GOD of hosts.

Isaiah 23:1–18
Proclamation Against Tyre

23 :1 The burden against Tyre.

Wail, you ships of Tarshish!
For it is laid waste,
So that there is no house, no harbor;
From the land of Cyprus[a] it is
revealed to them.

2   Be still, you inhabitants of the
coastland,
You merchants of Sidon,
Whom those who cross the sea have
filled.[a]

3   And on great waters the grain of
Shihor,
The harvest of the River,[a] *is* her
revenue;
And she is a marketplace for the
nations.

4   Be ashamed, O Sidon;
For the sea has spoken,
The strength of the sea, saying,
"I do not labor, nor bring forth
children;
Neither do I rear young men,
Nor bring up virgins."

5   When the report *reaches* Egypt,
They also will be in agony at the
report of Tyre.

6   Cross over to Tarshish;
Wail, you inhabitants of the coastland!

7   *Is* this your joyous *city,*
Whose antiquity *is* from ancient
days,
Whose feet carried her far off to
dwell?

8   Who has taken this counsel against
Tyre, the crowning *city,*
Whose merchants *are* princes,
Whose traders *are* the honorable of
the earth?

9   The LORD of hosts has purposed it,
To bring to dishonor the pride of all
glory,
To bring into contempt all the
honorable of the earth.

10   Overflow through your land like the
River,[a]
O daughter of Tarshish;
There is no more strength.

11   He stretched out His hand over the
sea,
He shook the kingdoms;
The LORD has given a commandment
against Canaan
To destroy its strongholds.

12   And He said, "You will rejoice no
more,
O you oppressed virgin daughter of
Sidon.
Arise, cross over to Cyprus;
There also you will have no rest."

13   Behold, the land of the Chaldeans,
This people *which* was not;
Assyria founded it for wild beasts of
the desert.
They set up its towers,
They raised up its palaces,
And brought it to ruin.

23:1 [a]Hebrew *Kittim,* western lands, especially
Cyprus   23:2 [a]Following Masoretic Text and
Vulgate; Septuagint and Targum read *Passing over the
water;* Dead Sea Scrolls read *Your messengers
passing over the sea.*   23:3 [a]That is, the Nile
23:10 [a]That is, the Nile

TIME CAPSULE   *671 to 667 B.C.*

671	*Esarhaddon invades Egypt and captures Memphis*
671	*Esarhaddon drives the Egyptian ruler Tirhakah from Memphis*
669	*Esarhaddon dies en route to Egypt*
668–627	*Ashurbanipal rules in Assyria*
667–648	*Shamash-shuma-ukin rules Babylonia*

14   Wail, you ships of Tarshish!
     For your strength is laid waste.

15Now it shall come to pass in that day
that Tyre will be forgotten seventy years,
according to the days of one king. At the
end of seventy years it will happen to Tyre
as *in* the song of the harlot:

16   "Take a harp, go about the city,
     You forgotten harlot;
     Make sweet melody, sing many songs,
     That you may be remembered."

17And it shall be, at the end of seventy
years, that the LORD will deal with Tyre.
She will return to her hire, and commit fornication with all the kingdoms of the world
on the face of the earth. 18Her gain and her
pay will be set apart for the LORD; it will
not be treasured nor laid up, for her gain
will be for those who dwell before the LORD,
to eat sufficiently, and for fine clothing.

Isaiah 24:1—27:13

Impending Judgment on the Earth

24 :1   Behold, the LORD makes the
            earth empty and makes it
            waste,
     Distorts its surface
     And scatters abroad its inhabitants.
2   And it shall be:
     As with the people, so with the priest;
     As with the servant, so with his
            master;
     As with the maid, so with her
            mistress;
     As with the buyer, so with the seller;
     As with the lender, so with the
            borrower;
     As with the creditor, so with the
            debtor.
3   The land shall be entirely emptied
            and utterly plundered,
     For the LORD has spoken this word.

4   The earth mourns *and* fades away,
     The world languishes *and* fades
            away;

     The haughty people of the earth
            languish.
5   The earth is also defiled under its
            inhabitants,
     Because they have transgressed the
            laws,
     Changed the ordinance,
     Broken the everlasting covenant.
6   Therefore the curse has devoured the
            earth,
     And those who dwell in it are
            desolate.
     Therefore the inhabitants of the earth
            are burned,
     And few men *are* left.

7   The new wine fails, the vine
            languishes,
     All the merry-hearted sigh.
8   The mirth of the tambourine ceases,
     The noise of the jubilant ends,
     The joy of the harp ceases.
9   They shall not drink wine with a song;
     Strong drink is bitter to those who
            drink it.
10   The city of confusion is broken down;
     Every house is shut up, so that none
            may go in.
11   *There is* a cry for wine in the streets,
     All joy is darkened,
     The mirth of the land is gone.
12   In the city desolation is left,
     And the gate is stricken with
            destruction.
13   When it shall be thus in the midst of
            the land among the people,
     It shall be like the shaking of an olive
            tree,
     Like the gleaning of grapes when the
            vintage is done.

14   They shall lift up their voice, they
            shall sing;
     For the majesty of the LORD
     They shall cry aloud from the sea.
15   Therefore glorify the LORD in the
            dawning light,
     The name of the LORD God of Israel in
            the coastlands of the sea.

POLITICS AND GOVERNMENT

*Pits have often been used for punishment (Is. 24:22). In 413 B.C. Athens suffered a
terrible defeat at Syracuse, and 7,000 prisoners were held in the quarries at Syracuse
before being sold into slavery. The Romans executed prisoners condemned to death in
an underground cell called the Tullianum.*

GOD PUNISHES GODS AND KINGS (Is. 24:21–23)

Worshipers held special feast days dedicated to their gods, at which time the duty of the gods was to bring justice to all. Such justice included punishing evildoers. Patron deities of cities and empires, as well as the sun gods and goddesses, were expected to punish the wicked at any time. Nevertheless, humans would also pray to gods of all kinds and at all levels of the divine hierarchy, requesting that justice be done.

Isaiah expects that Yahweh will sweep the wicked completely from ruling over His righteous worshipers (Is. 24:21–23). All who have misbehaved will be punished. Divine rulers "on high" ("the host of exalted ones") as well as human rulers ("the kings of the earth") will lose the offices they have abused. They will be placed in the Pit, usually meaning the land of the dead (Sheol), a place where they will be physically restrained from ever gaining power again.

The myths of Ugarit contain similar threats against the gods by El, the chief god of the pantheon. El reminds the other gods that he can and will remove them from their positions for improper behavior. Such behavior occurs in the Ugaritic *Legend of Aqhat* when the goddess Anath kills Aqhat. Aqhat's father, Daniel, requests the god Baal to intercede with El so that Anath might be punished.

Similarly, Isaiah expects Yahweh to punish the idols. The moon god Yareah and the sun god Shemesh were widely worshiped deities throughout Syria-Palestine, and Isaiah prophesies that they will be debased (24:23). Instead, God alone will reign in Jerusalem (the holy city) on Mount Zion (the holy mountain; see Ps. 82).

---

16 From the ends of the earth we have
    heard songs:
"Glory to the righteous!"
But I said, "I am ruined, ruined!
Woe to me!
The treacherous dealers have dealt
    treacherously,
Indeed, the treacherous dealers have
    dealt very treacherously."

17 Fear and the pit and the snare
Are upon you, O inhabitant of the
    earth.
18 And it shall be
That he who flees from the noise of
    the fear
Shall fall into the pit,
And he who comes up from the midst
    of the pit
Shall be caught in the snare;
For the windows from on high are
    open,
And the foundations of the earth are
    shaken.

19 The earth is violently broken,
The earth is split open,
The earth is shaken exceedingly.
20 The earth shall reel to and fro like a
    drunkard,
And shall totter like a hut;

Its transgression shall be heavy upon
    it,
And it will fall, and not rise again.

21 It shall come to pass in that day
That the LORD will punish on high the
    host of exalted ones,
And on the earth the kings of the
    earth.
22 They will be gathered together,
As prisoners are gathered in the pit,
And will be shut up in the prison;
After many days they will be
    punished.
23 Then the moon will be disgraced
And the sun ashamed;
For the LORD of hosts will reign
On Mount Zion and in Jerusalem
And before His elders, gloriously.

Praise to God

25 1 O LORD, You *are* my God.
    I will exalt You,
I will praise Your name,
For You have done wonderful *things;*
Your counsels of old *are* faithfulness
    and truth.
2 For You have made a city a ruin,
A fortified city a ruin,
A palace of foreigners to be a city no
    more;
It will never be rebuilt.

3 Therefore the strong people will
glorify You;
The city of the terrible nations will
fear You.
4 For You have been a strength to the
poor,
A strength to the needy in his distress,
A refuge from the storm,
A shade from the heat;
For the blast of the terrible ones *is* as
a storm *against* the wall.
5 You will reduce the noise of aliens,
As heat in a dry place;
As heat in the shadow of a cloud,
The song of the terrible ones will be
diminished.

6 And in this mountain
The LORD of hosts will make for all
people
A feast of choice pieces,
A feast of wines on the lees,
Of fat things full of marrow,
Of well-refined wines on the lees.
7 And He will destroy on this mountain
The surface of the covering cast over
all people,
And the veil that is spread over all
nations.
8 He will swallow up death forever,
And the Lord GOD will wipe away
tears from all faces;
The rebuke of His people
He will take away from all the earth;
For the LORD has spoken.

9 And it will be said in that day:
"Behold, this *is* our God;
We have waited for Him, and He will
save us.
This *is* the LORD;
We have waited for Him;
We will be glad and rejoice in His
salvation."

10 For on this mountain the hand of the
LORD will rest,
And Moab shall be trampled down
under Him,
As straw is trampled down for the
refuse heap.
11 And He will spread out His hands in
their midst
As a swimmer reaches out to swim,
And He will bring down their pride
Together with the trickery of their
hands.

12 The fortress of the high fort of your
walls
He will bring down, lay low,
And bring to the ground, down to the
dust.

A Song of Salvation

26 [1]In that day this song will be sung
in the land of Judah:

"We have a strong city;
God will appoint salvation *for* walls
and bulwarks.
2 Open the gates,
That the righteous nation which keeps
the truth may enter in.
3 You will keep *him* in perfect peace,
Whose mind *is* stayed *on You,*
Because he trusts in You.
4 Trust in the LORD forever,
For in YAH, the LORD, *is* everlasting
strength.[a]
5 For He brings down those who dwell
on high,
The lofty city;
He lays it low,
He lays it low to the ground,
He brings it down to the dust.
6 The foot shall tread it down—
The feet of the poor
And the steps of the needy."

7 The way of the just *is* uprightness;
O Most Upright,
You weigh the path of the just.
8 Yes, in the way of Your judgments,
O LORD, we have waited for You;
The desire of *our* soul *is* for Your name
And for the remembrance of You.
9 With my soul I have desired You in
the night,
Yes, by my spirit within me I will seek
You early;
For when Your judgments *are* in the
earth,
The inhabitants of the world will
learn righteousness.

10 Let grace be shown to the wicked,
Yet he will not learn righteousness;
In the land of uprightness he will deal
unjustly,
And will not behold the majesty of the
LORD.
11 LORD, *when* Your hand is lifted up,
they will not see.

26:4 [a]Or *Rock of Ages*

But they will see and be ashamed
For *their* envy of people;
Yes, the fire of Your enemies shall
    devour them.

12 LORD, You will establish peace for us,
For You have also done all our works
    in us.
13 O LORD our God, masters besides You
Have had dominion over us;
But by You only we make mention of
    Your name.
14 *They are* dead, they will not live;
They are deceased, they will not rise.
Therefore You have punished and
    destroyed them,
And made all their memory to perish.
15 You have increased the nation,
    O LORD,
You have increased the nation;
You are glorified;
You have expanded all the borders of
    the land.

16 LORD, in trouble they have visited You,
They poured out a prayer *when* Your
    chastening *was* upon them.
17 As a woman with child
Is in pain and cries out in her pangs,
When she draws near the time of her
    delivery,
So have we been in Your sight,
    O LORD.
18 We have been with child, we have
    been in pain;
We have, as it were, brought forth
    wind;
We have not accomplished any
    deliverance in the earth,
Nor have the inhabitants of the world
    fallen.

19 Your dead shall live;
Together with my dead body[a] they
    shall arise.
Awake and sing, you who dwell in
    dust;
For your dew *is like* the dew of herbs,
And the earth shall cast out the dead.

Take Refuge from the Coming Judgment

20 Come, my people, enter your
    chambers,
And shut your doors behind you;
Hide yourself, as it were, for a little
    moment,
Until the indignation is past.
21 For behold, the LORD comes out of His
    place
To punish the inhabitants of the earth
    for their iniquity;
The earth will also disclose her
    blood,
And will no more cover her slain.

27 1 In that day the LORD with His
    severe sword, great and strong,
Will punish Leviathan the fleeing
    serpent,
Leviathan that twisted serpent;
And He will slay the reptile that *is* in
    the sea.

The Restoration of Israel

2 In that day sing to her,
"A vineyard of red wine![a]
3 I, the LORD, keep it,
I water it every moment;
Lest any hurt it,
I keep it night and day.
4 Fury *is* not in Me.
Who would set briers *and* thorns
Against Me in battle?
I would go through them,
I would burn them together.
5 Or let him take hold of My strength,
That he may make peace with Me;
And he shall make peace with Me."

26:19 [a]Following Masoretic Text and Vulgate; Syriac and Targum read *their dead bodies;* Septuagint reads *those in the tombs.*   27:2 [a]Following Masoretic Text (Kittel's *Biblia Hebraica*), Bomberg, and Vulgate; Masoretic Text (*Biblia Hebraica Stuttgartensia*), some Hebrew manuscripts, and Septuagint read *delight;* Targum reads *choice vineyard.*

TIME CAPSULE   *667 to 656 B.C.*

667   *Ashurbanipal captures Memphis*

665   *Elamite ruler Urtak attacks Babylonia and is pushed back*

664   *Ethiopia controls Egypt until 664*

664   *Ashurbanipal drives Cushites from Thebes and Memphis*

664–525   *Egypt is united under pharaohs from Sais*

656   *Psammetichus I begins united dynasty in Egypt by annexing Upper Egypt*

6   Those who come He shall cause to
      take root in Jacob;
   Israel shall blossom and bud,
   And fill the face of the world with
      fruit.

7   Has He struck Israel as He struck
      those who struck him?
   Or has He been slain according to the
      slaughter of those who were slain
      by Him?
8   In measure, by sending it away,
   You contended with it.
   He removes *it* by His rough wind
   In the day of the east wind.
9   Therefore by this the iniquity of Jacob
      will be covered;
   And this *is* all the fruit of taking away
      his sin:
   When he makes all the stones of the
      altar
   Like chalkstones that are beaten to
      dust,
   Wooden images[a] and incense altars
      shall not stand.

10   Yet the fortified city *will be* desolate,
   The habitation forsaken and left like a
      wilderness;
   There the calf will feed, and there it
      will lie down
   And consume its branches.
11   When its boughs are withered, they
      will be broken off;
   The women come *and* set them on fire.
   For it *is* a people of no understanding;
   Therefore He who made them will not
      have mercy on them,
   And He who formed them will show
      them no favor.

12   And it shall come to pass in that day
   That the LORD will thresh,
   From the channel of the River[a] to the
      Brook of Egypt;
   And you will be gathered one by
      one,
   O you children of Israel.

13   So it shall be in that day:
   The great trumpet will be blown;
   They will come, who are about to
      perish in the land of Assyria,
   And they who are outcasts in the land
      of Egypt,
   And shall worship the LORD in the
      holy mount at Jerusalem.

Priestly Account: Assyria's Invasions

The Chronicler has comparatively little interest in Hezekiah's rebellion against Assyria. Political matters are never as important in Chronicles as are temple concerns. The historian of Kings only briefly covered Hezekiah's reform before devoting most of his account to the king's illness and the Assyrian invasions. The Chronicler reverses the emphasis, expanding the account of the reforms (2 Chr. 29—31), then offering a shortened version of the illness and invasions (2 Chr. 32).

Indeed, the Chronicler describes Hezekiah's greatness entirely in terms of his temple reforms. Hezekiah's reforms are even more highly praised than the more famous reforms of his great-grandson Josiah (2 Kin. 22; 23; 2 Chr. 34; 35). Hezekiah is even given credit for resuming the Passover celebration (2 Chr. 30:26), something that 2 Kin. 23:22 attributes to Josiah. As usual, Chronicles shows a keen interest in the priests and Levites and in their duties (2 Chr. 31).

■ 2 Chronicles 29:1—31:21

2 Chronicles
Hezekiah Reigns in Judah

29 :1 Hezekiah became king *when he was* twenty-five years old, and he reigned twenty-nine years in Jerusalem. His mother's name *was* Abijah[a] the daughter of Zechariah. 2And he did *what was* right in the sight of the LORD, according to all that his father David had done.

Hezekiah Cleanses the Temple

3In the first year of his reign, in the first month, he opened the doors of the house of the LORD and repaired them. 4Then he brought in the priests and the Levites, and gathered them in the East Square, 5and said to them: "Hear me, Levites! Now sanctify yourselves, sanctify the house of the LORD God of your fathers, and carry out the rubbish from the holy *place.* 6For our fathers have trespassed and done evil in the eyes of the LORD our God; they have forsaken Him, have turned their faces away from the dwelling place of the LORD, and turned *their* backs *on Him.*

27:9 [a]Hebrew *Asherim,* Canaanite deities
27:12 [a]That is, the Euphrates
2 Chr. 29:1 [a]Spelled *Abi* in 2 Kings 18:2

⁷They have also shut up the doors of the vestibule, put out the lamps, and have not burned incense or offered burnt offerings in the holy *place* to the God of Israel. ⁸Therefore the wrath of the LORD fell upon Judah and Jerusalem, and He has given them up to trouble, to desolation, and to jeering, as you see with your eyes. ⁹For indeed, because of this our fathers have fallen by the sword; and our sons, our daughters, and our wives *are* in captivity.

¹⁰"Now *it is* in my heart to make a covenant with the LORD God of Israel, that His fierce wrath may turn away from us. ¹¹My sons, do not be negligent now, for the LORD has chosen you to stand before Him, to serve Him, and that you should minister to Him and burn incense."

¹²Then these Levites arose: Mahath the son of Amasai and Joel the son of Azariah, of the sons of the Kohathites; of the sons of Merari, Kish the son of Abdi and Azariah the son of Jehallelel; of the Gershonites, Joah the son of Zimmah and Eden the son of Joah; ¹³of the sons of Elizaphan, Shimri and Jeiel; of the sons of Asaph, Zechariah and Mattaniah; ¹⁴of the sons of Heman, Jehiel and Shimei; and of the sons of Jeduthun, Shemaiah and Uzziel.

¹⁵And they gathered their brethren, sanctified themselves, and went according to the commandment of the king, at the words of the LORD, to cleanse the house of the LORD. ¹⁶Then the priests went into the inner part of the house of the LORD to cleanse *it,* and brought out all the debris that they found in the temple of the LORD to the court of the house of the LORD. And the Levites took *it* out and carried *it* to the Brook Kidron.

¹⁷Now they began to sanctify on the first *day* of the first month, and on the eighth day of the month they came to the vestibule of the LORD. So they sanctified the house of the LORD in eight days, and on the sixteenth day of the first month they finished.

¹⁸Then they went in to King Hezekiah and said, "We have cleansed all the house of the LORD, the altar of burnt offerings with all its articles, and the table of the showbread with all its articles. ¹⁹Moreover all the articles which King Ahaz in his reign had cast aside in his transgression we have prepared and sanctified; and there they *are,* before the altar of the LORD."

Hezekiah Restores Temple Worship

²⁰Then King Hezekiah rose early, gathered the rulers of the city, and went up to the house of the LORD. ²¹And they brought seven bulls, seven rams, seven lambs, and seven male goats for a sin offering for the kingdom, for the sanctuary, and for Judah. Then he commanded the priests, the sons of Aaron, to offer *them* on the altar of the LORD. ²²So they killed the bulls, and the priests received the blood and sprinkled *it* on the altar. Likewise they killed the rams and sprinkled the blood on the altar. They also killed the lambs and sprinkled the blood on the altar. ²³Then they brought out the male goats *for* the sin offering before the king and the assembly, and they laid their hands on them. ²⁴And the priests killed them; and they presented their blood on the altar as a sin offering to make an atonement for all Israel, for the king commanded *that* the burnt offering and the sin offering *be made* for all Israel.

²⁵And he stationed the Levites in the house of the LORD with cymbals, with stringed instruments, and with harps, according to the commandment of David, of Gad the king's seer, and of Nathan the prophet; for thus *was* the commandment of the LORD by His prophets. ²⁶The Levites stood with the instruments of David, and the priests with the trumpets. ²⁷Then Hezekiah commanded *them* to offer the burnt offering on the altar. And when the burnt offering began, the song of the LORD *also* began, with the trumpets and with the instruments of David king of Israel. ²⁸So all the assembly worshiped, the singers sang, and the trumpeters sounded; all *this continued* until the burnt offering was finished. ²⁹And when they had finished offering, the king and all who were present with him bowed and worshiped. ³⁰Moreover King Hezekiah and the leaders commanded the Levites to sing praise to the LORD with the words of David and of Asaph the seer. So they sang praises with gladness, and they bowed their heads and worshiped.

³¹Then Hezekiah answered and said, "Now *that* you have consecrated yourselves to the LORD, come near, and bring sacrifices and thank offerings into the house of the LORD." So the assembly brought in sacrifices and thank offerings, and as many as were of a willing heart *brought* burnt offerings. ³²And the number of the burnt

offerings which the assembly brought was seventy bulls, one hundred rams, *and* two hundred lambs; all these *were* for a burnt offering to the LORD. 33The consecrated things *were* six hundred bulls and three thousand sheep. 34But the priests were too few, so that they could not skin all the burnt offerings; therefore their brethren the Levites helped them until the work was ended and until the *other* priests had sanctified themselves, for the Levites were more diligent in sanctifying themselves than the priests. 35Also the burnt offerings *were* in abundance, with the fat of the peace offerings and *with* the drink offerings for *every* burnt offering.

So the service of the house of the LORD was set in order. 36Then Hezekiah and all the people rejoiced that God had prepared the people, since the events took place so suddenly.

Hezekiah Keeps the Passover

30 1And Hezekiah sent to all Israel and Judah, and also wrote letters to Ephraim and Manasseh, that they should come to the house of the LORD at Jerusalem, to keep the Passover to the LORD God of Israel. 2For the king and his leaders and all the assembly in Jerusalem had agreed to keep the Passover in the second month. 3For they could not keep it at the regular time,a because a sufficient number of priests had not consecrated themselves, nor had the people gathered together at Jerusalem. 4And the matter pleased the king and all the assembly. 5So they resolved to make a proclamation throughout all Israel, from Beersheba to Dan, that they should come to keep the Passover to the LORD God of Israel at Jerusalem, since they had not done *it* for a long *time* in the *prescribed* manner.

6Then the runners went throughout all Israel and Judah with the letters from the king and his leaders, and spoke according to the command of the king: "Children of Israel, return to the LORD God of Abraham, Isaac, and Israel; then He will return to the remnant of you who have escaped from the hand of the kings of Assyria. 7And do not be like your fathers and your brethren, who trespassed against the LORD God of their fathers, so that He gave them up to desolation, as you see. 8Now do not be stiff-necked, as your fathers *were, but* yield yourselves to the LORD; and enter His sanctuary, which He has sanctified forever, and

serve the LORD your God, that the fierceness of His wrath may turn away from you. 9For if you return to the LORD, your brethren and your children *will be treated* with compassion by those who lead them captive, so that they may come back to this land; for the LORD your God *is* gracious and merciful, and will not turn *His* face from you if you return to Him."

10So the runners passed from city to city through the country of Ephraim and Manasseh, as far as Zebulun; but they laughed at them and mocked them. 11Nevertheless some from Asher, Manasseh, and Zebulun humbled themselves and came to Jerusalem. 12Also the hand of God was on Judah to give them singleness of heart to obey the command of the king and the leaders, at the word of the LORD.

13Now many people, a very great assembly, gathered at Jerusalem to keep the Feast of Unleavened Bread in the second month. 14They arose and took away the altars that *were* in Jerusalem, and they took away all the incense altars and cast *them* into the Brook Kidron. 15Then they slaughtered the Passover *lambs* on the fourteenth *day* of the second month. The priests and the Levites were ashamed, and sanctified themselves, and brought the burnt offerings to the house of the LORD. 16They stood in their place according to their custom, according to the Law of Moses the man of God; the priests sprinkled the blood *received* from the hand of the Levites. 17For *there were* many in the assembly who had not sanctified themselves; therefore the Levites had charge of the slaughter of the Passover *lambs* for everyone *who was* not clean, to sanctify *them* to the LORD. 18For a multitude of the people, many from Ephraim, Manasseh, Issachar, and Zebulun, had not cleansed themselves, yet they ate the Passover contrary to what was written. But Hezekiah prayed for them, saying, "May the good LORD provide atonement for everyone 19*who* prepares his heart to seek God, the LORD God of his fathers, though *he is* not *cleansed* according to the purification of the sanctuary." 20And the LORD listened to Hezekiah and healed the people.

21So the children of Israel who were present at Jerusalem kept the Feast of Unleavened Bread seven days with great

30:3 aThat is, the first month (compare Leviticus 23:5); literally *at that time*

HEZEKIAH BRINGS REVIVAL TO JUDAH (2 Chr. 30:26)

King Hezekiah of Judah (715–686 B.C.) is given very high marks as a monarch by the writer of 2 Kings. The works of this king (2 Kin. 18:3) and those of Josiah (2 Kin. 22:1, 2) are favorably compared with those of their ancestor King David. Hezekiah is credited with sweeping reforms of Judah's temple worship (2 Chr. 29—31). The Passover observance which he restored was such a time of joy that the Chronicler reports, "Since the time of Solomon the son of David, king of Israel, there had been nothing like this in Jerusalem" (2 Chr. 30:26).

Hezekiah is a focus of attention in the Assyrian annals. It is probable that he joined the alliance of Chaldeans, Arameans, and Elamites that rebelled against Assyrian rule after the death of Sargon II in 705 B.C. Sargon's successor, Sennacherib, invaded Palestine in 701 B.C., ravaging Judah and taking all of its fortified towns—except Jerusalem. The Assyrian records claim that over 200,000 Judahites were deported, and that Hezekiah was "like a caged bird" in his capital city. Though Jerusalem had to pay large amounts of tribute, the city was not captured (2 Kin. 18:13–16).

gladness; and the Levites and the priests praised the LORD day by day, *singing* to the LORD, accompanied by loud instruments. 22And Hezekiah gave encouragement to all the Levites who taught the good knowledge of the LORD; and they ate throughout the feast seven days, offering peace offerings and making confession to the LORD God of their fathers.

23Then the whole assembly agreed to keep *the feast* another seven days, and they kept it *another* seven days with gladness. 24For Hezekiah king of Judah gave to the assembly a thousand bulls and seven thousand sheep, and the leaders gave to the assembly a thousand bulls and ten thousand sheep; and a great number of priests sanctified themselves. 25The whole assembly of Judah rejoiced, also the priests and Levites, all the assembly that came from Israel, the sojourners who came from the land of Israel, and those who dwelt in Judah. 26So there was great joy in Jerusalem, for since the time of Solomon the son of David, king of Israel, *there had* been nothing

like this in Jerusalem. 27Then the priests, the Levites, arose and blessed the people, and their voice was heard; and their prayer came *up* to His holy dwelling place, to heaven.

The Reforms of Hezekiah

31 1Now when all this was finished, all Israel who were present went out to the cities of Judah and broke the *sacred* pillars in pieces, cut down the wooden images, and threw down the high places and the altars—from all Judah, Benjamin, Ephraim, and Manasseh—until they had utterly destroyed them all. Then all the children of Israel returned to their own cities, every man to his possession.

2And Hezekiah appointed the divisions of the priests and the Levites according to their divisions, each man according to his service, the priests and Levites for burnt offerings and peace offerings, to serve, to give thanks, and to praise in the gates of the campa of the LORD. 3The king also *appointed* a portion of his possessions for the burnt offerings: for the morning and evening burnt offerings, the burnt offerings for the Sabbaths and the New Moons and

31:2 aThat is, the temple

FOOD AND DRINK

In biblical times practically all meat was slaughtered in a religious ritual, if not as a special sacrifice (2 Chr. 30:24). A large feast using such meat was part of the religious event. Among the nomadic Arabs (the bedouin) of modern times, meat was seldom eaten except for a festival or to welcome a guest. As nomads they kept large herds of sheep and goats, while hunting and eating gazelle.

the set feasts, as *it is* written in the Law of the LORD.

⁴Moreover he commanded the people who dwelt in Jerusalem to contribute support for the priests and the Levites, that they might devote themselves to the Law of the LORD.

⁵As soon as the commandment was circulated, the children of Israel brought in abundance the firstfruits of grain and wine, oil and honey, and of all the produce of the field; and they brought in abundantly the tithe of everything. ⁶And the children of Israel and Judah, who dwelt in the cities of Judah, brought the tithe of oxen and sheep; also the tithe of holy things which were consecrated to the LORD their God they laid in heaps.

⁷In the third month they began laying them in heaps, and they finished in the seventh month. ⁸And when Hezekiah and the leaders came and saw the heaps, they blessed the LORD and His people Israel. ⁹Then Hezekiah questioned the priests and the Levites concerning the heaps. ¹⁰And Azariah the chief priest, from the house of Zadok, answered him and said, "Since *the people* began to bring the offerings into the house of the LORD, we have had enough to eat and have plenty left, for the LORD has blessed His people; and what is left *is* this great abundance."

¹¹Now Hezekiah commanded *them* to prepare rooms in the house of the LORD, and they prepared them. ¹²Then they faithfully brought in the offerings, the tithes, and the dedicated things; Cononiah the Levite had charge of them, and Shimei his brother *was* the next. ¹³Jehiel, Azaziah, Nahath, Asahel, Jerimoth, Jozabad, Eliel, Ismachiah, Mahath, and Benaiah *were* overseers under the hand of Cononiah and Shimei his brother, at the commandment of Hezekiah the king and Azariah the ruler of the house of God. ¹⁴Kore the son of Imnah the Levite, the keeper of the East Gate, *was* over the freewill offerings to God, to distribute the offerings of the LORD and the most holy things. ¹⁵And under him *were* Eden, Miniamin, Jeshua, Shemaiah, Amariah, and Shecaniah, *his* faithful assistants in the cities of the priests, to distribute allotments to their brethren by divisions, to the great as well as the small.

¹⁶Besides those males from three years old and up who were written in the genealogy, they distributed to everyone who entered the house of the LORD his daily portion for the work of his service, by his division, ¹⁷and to the priests who were written in the genealogy according to their father's house, and to the Levites from twenty years old and up according to their work, by their divisions, ¹⁸and to all who were written in the genealogy—their little ones and their wives, their sons and daughters, the whole company of them— for in their faithfulness they sanctified themselves in holiness.

¹⁹Also for the sons of Aaron the priests, *who were* in the fields of the common-lands of their cities, in every single city, *there were* men who were designated by name to distribute portions to all the males among the priests and to all who were listed by genealogies among the Levites.

²⁰Thus Hezekiah did throughout all Judah, and he did what *was* good and right and true before the LORD his God. ²¹And in every work that he began in the service of the house of God, in the law and in the commandment, to seek his God, he did *it* with all his heart. So he prospered.

Hezekiah's Sickness and Rebellion

When the Chronicler finally deals with Hezekiah's rebellion against Assyria, it is a much condensed account. Among other omissions, Chronicles does not mention that Hezekiah paid tribute to Sennacherib (2 Kin. 18:13–16). As in Kings and Isaiah, the accounts of Hezekiah's illness and of the ambassadors from Babylon appear to be out of chronological order. Given the known dates for the Babylonian ruler Merodach-Baladan (721–710 and 703–702 B.C.), the "ambassadors of the princes of Babylon" (2 Chr. 32:31) probably visited before Sennacherib's withdrawal from Jerusalem in 701 B.C., and certainly before his death in 681 B.C.

- 2 Chronicles 32:24–31
- 2 Chronicles 32:1–23
- 2 Chronicles 32:32, 33

2 Chronicles 32:24–31
Hezekiah Humbles Himself

32 :24 In those days Hezekiah was sick and near death, and he prayed to the LORD; and He spoke to him and gave him a sign. ²⁵But Hezekiah did not repay according to the favor *shown* him, for his heart was lifted up; therefore wrath was looming over him and over Judah and Jerusalem. [26]Then Hezekiah humbled himself for the pride of his heart, he and the inhabitants of Jerusalem, so that the wrath of the LORD did not come upon them in the days of Hezekiah.

Hezekiah's Wealth and Honor

[27]Hezekiah had very great riches and honor. And he made himself treasuries for silver, for gold, for precious stones, for spices, for shields, and for all kinds of desirable items; [28]storehouses for the harvest of grain, wine, and oil; and stalls for all kinds of livestock, and folds for flocks.[a] [29]Moreover he provided cities for himself, and possessions of flocks and herds in abundance; for God had given him very much property. [30]This same Hezekiah also stopped the water outlet of Upper Gihon, and brought the water by tunnel[a] to the west side of the City of David. Hezekiah prospered in all his works.

[31]However, *regarding* the ambassadors of the princes of Babylon, whom they sent to him to inquire about the wonder that was *done* in the land, God withdrew from him, in order to test him, that He might know all *that was* in his heart.

2 Chronicles 32:1–23

Sennacherib Boasts Against the LORD

32 :1 After these deeds of faithfulness, Sennacherib king of Assyria came and entered Judah; he encamped against the fortified cities, thinking to win them over to himself. [2]And when Hezekiah saw that Sennacherib had come, and that his purpose was to make war against Jerusalem, [3]he consulted with his leaders and commanders[a] to stop the water from the springs which were outside the city; and they helped him. [4]Thus many people gathered together who stopped all the springs and the brook that ran through the land, saying, "Why should the kings[a] of Assyria come and find much water?" [5]And he strengthened himself, built up all the wall that was broken, raised it up to the towers, and built another wall outside; also he re-

paired the Millo[a] in the City of David, and made weapons and shields in abundance. [6]Then he set military captains over the people, gathered them together to him in the open square of the city gate, and gave them encouragement, saying, [7]"Be strong and courageous; do not be afraid nor dismayed before the king of Assyria, nor before all the multitude that is with him; for there are more with us than with him. [8]With him is an arm of flesh; but with us is the Lord our God, to help us and to fight our battles." And the people were strengthened by the words of Hezekiah king of Judah.

[9]After this Sennacherib king of Assyria sent his servants to Jerusalem (but he and all the forces with him *laid siege* against Lachish), to Hezekiah king of Judah, and to all Judah who *were* in Jerusalem, saying, [10]"Thus says Sennacherib king of Assyria: 'In what do you trust, that you remain under siege in Jerusalem? [11]Does not Hezekiah persuade you to give yourselves over to die by famine and by thirst, saying, "The LORD our God will deliver us from the hand of the king of Assyria"? [12]Has not the same Hezekiah taken away His high places and His altars, and commanded Judah and Jerusalem, saying, "You shall worship before one altar and burn incense on it"? [13]Do you not know what I and my fathers have done to all the peoples of *other* lands? Were the gods of the nations of those lands in any way able to deliver their lands out of my hand? [14]Who *was there* among all the gods of those nations that my fathers utterly destroyed that could deliver his people from my hand, that your God should be able to deliver you from my hand? [15]Now therefore, do not let Hezekiah deceive you or persuade you like this, and do not

---

32:28 [a]Following Septuagint and Vulgate; Arabic and Syriac omit *folds for flocks;* Masoretic Text reads *flocks for sheepfolds.*   32:30 [a]Literally *brought it straight* (compare 2 Kings 20:20)   32:3 [a]Literally *mighty men*   32:4 [a]Following Masoretic Text and Vulgate; Arabic, Septuagint, and Syriac read *king.* 32:5 [a]Literally *The Landfill*

TIME CAPSULE   *653 to 648 B.C.*

653   *Ashurbanipal campaigns against Elam at the river Ulai*

652–648   *The Assyrian civil war between Ashurbanipal and his brother Shamash-shuma-ukin*

650   *Greeks use molds for making things out of clay*

648   *Ashurbanipal captures Babylon, and his brother Shamash-shuma-ukin dies in the palace fire*

THE SIEGE OF LACHISH (2 Chr. 32:9)

One of the more dramatic military efforts in Assyrian history is only barely mentioned in the Bible. This event was the conquest of Lachish by the Assyrian king Sennacherib. Some scholars think Sennacherib may have invaded Palestine twice: An invasion in 701 B.C. that is reported in Assyrian annals, and a supposed second invasion in 688 B.C. After attacking and defeating Lachish, the Assyrian king set up his headquarters there, from which he sent Assyrian forces to Jerusalem (2 Kin. 18:17).

The Bible only reports the destruction of Lachish in small details. It tells us that Sennacherib was "at Lachish" (2 Kin. 18:14), that he "laid siege against Lachish" (2 Chr. 32:9), and implies that he eventually captured that city (Is. 37:8). Fortunately, the Assyrian record of that conquest is much more detailed.

On the walls of his Nineveh palace Sennacherib had carved stone reliefs of the siege of Lachish. In these artistic works one can see how the Assyrians built a siege mound for their use in breaching the walls. The captive Judahites are also shown being led into captivity, giving us the earliest pictures of the common dress of the day. We also gain an interesting insight into the military efforts of the time, including the defensive features of Lachish, the Assyrian siege engines equipped with battering rams, contingents of archers, and soldiers using slings in combat.

believe him; for no god of any nation or kingdom was able to deliver his people from my hand or the hand of my fathers. How much less will your God deliver you from my hand?' "

16Furthermore, his servants spoke against the LORD God and against His servant Hezekiah.

17He also wrote letters to revile the LORD God of Israel, and to speak against Him, saying, "As the gods of the nations of *other* lands have not delivered their people from my hand, so the God of Hezekiah will not deliver His people from my hand." 18Then they called out with a loud voice in Hebrew[a] to the people of Jerusalem who *were* on the wall, to frighten them and trouble them, that they might take the city. 19And they spoke against the God of Jerusalem, as against the gods of the people of the earth—the work of men's hands.

Sennacherib's Defeat and Death

20Now because of this King Hezekiah and the prophet Isaiah, the son of Amoz, prayed and cried out to heaven. 21Then the LORD sent an angel who cut down every mighty man of valor, leader, and captain in the camp of the king of Assyria. So he returned shamefaced to his own land. And when he had gone into the temple of his god, some of his own offspring struck him down with the sword there.

22Thus the LORD saved Hezekiah and the inhabitants of Jerusalem from the hand of Sennacherib the king of Assyria, and from the hand of all *others,* and guided them[a] on every side. 23And many brought gifts to the LORD at Jerusalem, and presents to Hezekiah king of Judah, so that he was exalted in the sight of all nations thereafter.

2 Chronicles 32:32, 33
Death of Hezekiah

32 :32 Now the rest of the acts of Hezekiah, and his goodness, indeed

32:18 [a]Literally *Judean*   32:22 [a]Septuagint reads *gave them rest;* Vulgate reads *gave them treasures.*

ARCHITECTURE AND BUILDING

Hezekiah's tunnel (2 Chr. 32:30) still exists and is a tourist attraction today. It is 1,750 feet long. Workmen dug simultaneously from the two ends, and a surviving inscription tells how they met in the middle. They could hear shouts from the other team, enabling them to find each other. The tunnel was dug sometime between 715 and 701 B.C.

A BIRD IN A CAGE (2 Chr. 32:9, 21, 22)

In the 8th century B.C. the Assyrians were the dominant power in the Near East, so it is no wonder that several books report about the Assyrian period (Isaiah, Jonah, Nahum, 2 Kings, 2 Chronicles). One of the most amazing accounts is that of the confrontation between Hezekiah and Sennacherib. What makes this incident so unusual is that it is mentioned not only in the Bible but also by the Assyrians in the annals of Sennacherib.

Sennacherib, the Assyrian king, invaded Judah in 701 B.C. He conquered Lachish, one of Judah's strongest cities, and was plaguing the entire area (2 Kin. 18:13, 14). The seriousness of this threat to Judah can be seen from Sennacherib's records where he claims to have destroyed 46 walled cities and to have conquered smaller towns "without number." In addition, Sennacherib boasted of taking 200,150 people captive. Undoubtedly, the Assyrian conquest was a catastrophic blow to Judah.

Whether in 701 B.C. or later, as some scholars suppose, in 688 B.C., Sennacherib finally focused his attention on Jerusalem. After surrounding the city, the Assyrian Chief of Staff Rabshakeh tried to convince the city's leaders to petition King Hezekiah for peace (2 Kin. 18:17–19). Sennacherib's records report about Hezekiah, "Himself, like a caged bird, I shut up in Jerusalem, his royal city."

Though the city was terrified, Isaiah prophesied the ultimate demise of Sennacherib and retreat of his army (2 Kin. 19:6, 7). The Chronicler records the destruction of Sennacherib's army as the work of the angel of the Lord (2 Chr. 32:21). Sennacherib himself, in his own records, does not say why he did not complete his conquest of Jerusalem. He only states that he had made preparation to do so, but then went away.

they *are* written in the vision of Isaiah the prophet, the son of Amoz, *and* in the book of the kings of Judah and Israel. [33]So Hezekiah rested with his fathers, and they buried him in the upper tombs of the sons of David; and all Judah and the inhabitants of Jerusalem honored him at his death. Then Manasseh his son reigned in his place.

probably Assyrian) deities as completely as Manasseh. According to tradition, Manasseh had the prophet Isaiah executed by placing him in a log and sawing it in half. The legend is uncertain, but it may be referred to in Heb. 11:37. The historian of Kings is very clear concerning this ruler's influence: Judah's eventual destruction can be attributed to the sins of Manasseh (2 Kin. 21:10–15; 23:26, 27).

■ 2 Kings 21:1–18

21:3 [a]Hebrew *Asherah*, a Canaanite goddess   [b]The gods of the Assyrians

Prophetic Account: Bad and Good Kings

After his illness, Hezekiah probably began preparing his son Manasseh to succeed him as king. It is likely that Manasseh ruled as a coregent during the last 11 or 12 years of Hezekiah's life (697–686 B.C.). After Hezekiah died, Manasseh quickly surrendered to Assyria. His long reign (697–642 B.C.) is presented as the blackest period in Judah's history. Hezekiah received praise as a king (2 Kin. 18:5); his son did not (21:11).

Manasseh seems to have set about dismantling the faith of the Judahites. No king of Judah would ever embrace the Canaanite (and

2 Kings
Manasseh Reigns in Judah

21 :1 Manasseh *was* twelve years old when he became king, and he reigned fifty-five years in Jerusalem. His mother's name *was* Hephzibah. [2]And he did evil in the sight of the LORD, according to the abominations of the nations whom the LORD had cast out before the children of Israel. [3]For he rebuilt the high places which Hezekiah his father had destroyed; he raised up altars for Baal, and made a wooden image,[a] as Ahab king of Israel had done; and he worshiped all the host of heaven[b] and served them. [4]He also built altars in the house of the LORD, of which the LORD had said, "In Jerusalem I will put My name." [5]And he built altars for all the host

⌛ AN IDOLATROUS KING IN JUDAH

Judah (southern kingdom)

Manasseh probably served as coregent with his father Hezekiah for about 11 or 12 years. During his own reign, Manasseh restored the idolatry that Hezekiah had abolished.

   Those who protested Manasseh's actions were killed (2 Kin. 21:16). It is possible that he executed the prophet Isaiah. Rabbinical tradition states that Manasseh gave the command that Isaiah be sawn in two.

Amon, son of Manasseh, reigned for only 2 years. His own servants conspired to kill him; however, after Amon's assassination the people of Judah executed the conspirators and placed Amon's son Josiah on the throne (2 Chr. 33:25).

Israel (northern kingdom)

Fell to the Assyrian Empire in 722 B.C.

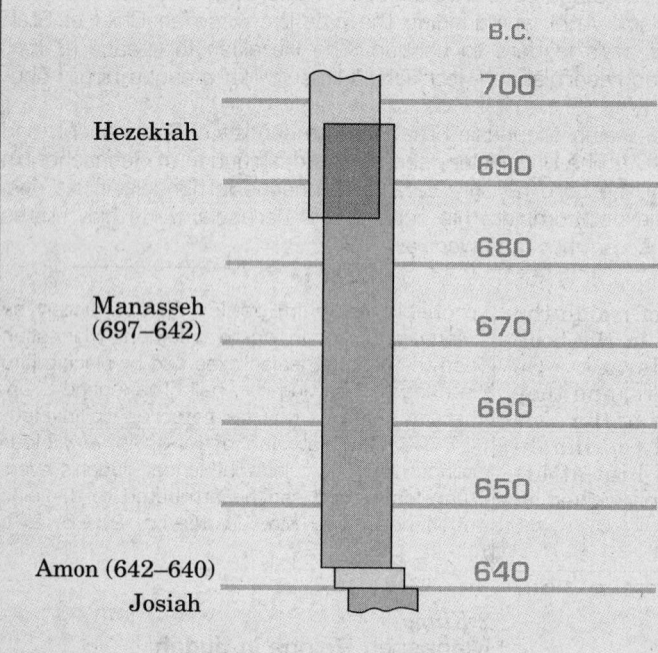

B.C.

Hezekiah	700
	690
	680
Manasseh (697–642)	670
	660
	650
Amon (642–640)	640
Josiah	

of heaven in the two courts of the house of the LORD. ⁶Also he made his son pass through the fire, practiced soothsaying, used witchcraft, and consulted spiritists and mediums. He did much evil in the sight of the LORD, to provoke *Him* to anger. ⁷He even set a carved image of Asherah[a] that he had made, in the house of which the LORD had said to David and to Solomon his son, "In this house and in Jerusalem, which I have chosen out of all the tribes of Israel, I will put My name forever; ⁸and I will not make the feet of Israel wander anymore from the land which I gave their fathers—only if they are careful to do ac-

cording to all that I have commanded them, and according to all the law that My servant Moses commanded them." ⁹But they paid no attention, and Manasseh seduced them to do more evil than the nations whom the LORD had destroyed before the children of Israel.

   ¹⁰And the LORD spoke by His servants the prophets, saying, ¹¹"Because Manasseh king of Judah has done these abominations (he has acted more wickedly than all the Amorites who *were* before him, and has

---

21:7 ᵃA Canaanite goddess

The Long, Dark Years of Manasseh (2 Kin. 21:16)

Manasseh's reign (697–642 B.C.) was the longest in the history of the Judean kingdom. In his first 11 or 12 years he ruled as a minor, serving as a coregent with his father Hezekiah. His 55-year rule must have seemed even longer to some. The writer of Kings gives Manasseh very low marks as a monarch, cataloging the king's many sins (2 Kin. 21:1–18).

Assyrian sources from the 7th century B.C. mention Manasseh. Judah had become a vassal state of Assyria after Sennacherib's invasion of Judah in 701 B.C. The annals of Sennacherib's son, Esarhaddon (680–669 B.C.) name Manasseh among 22 vassal kings who were obligated to transport materials to Nineveh. The records of Ashurbanipal (668–627 B.C.) also list Manasseh in an account of vassal kings who presented gifts to Assyria and helped to defeat Egypt.

Among the criticisms leveled at Manasseh was that he worshiped the stars—the "host of heaven" (2 Kin. 21:3). Some scholars assume that Manasseh's religious practices were due to the direction of Assyria. Vassal states were obligated to pay tribute and take loyalty oaths, demonstrating Assyrian rulership. But there is no evidence that the Assyrians imposed their religion upon these states. Possibly Manasseh willingly incorporated Assyrian cultic practices in the temple to show his loyalty to Assyria.

The writer of Chronicles reports that Manasseh was taken prisoner by the Assyrians to Babylon (2 Chr. 33:11). The city of Babylon did not gain power until after about 625 B.C., several years after Manasseh's reign. After the death of Esarhaddon, however, the Assyrians had corulers at Nineveh and Babylon for 16 years (668–652 B.C.), so it is plausible that Manasseh could have been sent to Babylon.

also made Judah sin with his idols), ¹²therefore thus says the LORD God of Israel: 'Behold, I am bringing *such* calamity upon Jerusalem and Judah, that whoever hears of it, both his ears will tingle. ¹³And I will stretch over Jerusalem the measuring line of Samaria and the plummet of the house of Ahab; I will wipe Jerusalem as *one* wipes a dish, wiping *it* and turning *it* upside down. ¹⁴So I will forsake the remnant of My inheritance and deliver them into the hand of their enemies; and they shall become victims of plunder to all their enemies, ¹⁵because they have done evil in My sight, and have provoked Me to anger since the day their fathers came out of Egypt, even to this day.' "

¹⁶Moreover Manasseh shed very much innocent blood, till he had filled Jerusalem from one end to another, besides his sin by which he made Judah sin, in doing evil in the sight of the LORD.

¹⁷Now the rest of the acts of Manasseh—all that he did, and the sin that he committed—*are* they not written in the book of the chronicles of the kings of Judah? ¹⁸So Manasseh rested with his fathers, and was buried in the garden of his own house, in the garden of Uzza. Then his son Amon reigned in his place.

Assassination in the Palace

Manasseh was followed to the throne by his son Amon, who was assassinated after only 2 years as king (642–640 B.C.). The conspiracy against Amon was probably a palace intrigue rather than a popular revolt (2 Kin. 21:23, 24). He was assassinated in the royal palace, and "the people of the land" quickly enacted vengeance upon the conspirators.

■ 2 Kings 21:19–26

2 Kings
Amon's Reign and Death

21:19 Amon *was* twenty-two years old when he became king, and he reigned two years in Jerusalem. His mother's name *was* Meshullemeth the daughter of Haruz of Jotbah. ²⁰And he did evil in the sight of the LORD, as his father Manasseh had done. ²¹So he walked in all the ways that his father had walked; and he served the idols that his father had served, and worshiped them. ²²He forsook the LORD God of his fathers, and did not walk in the way of the LORD.

SHOULD WE CORRECT A CULT GONE ASTRAY? (2 Kin. 22:8–20)

Josiah was confronted with the "Book of the Law," revealing that the temple cult in Jerusalem had been corrupted (2 Kin. 22:8). His response was to check with the prophetess Huldah to find out if this was truly the word of God (22:13). The caution of the king appears to be part of standard cult reform procedure in the ancient Near East.

The Assyrian king Sennacherib demolished the city of Babylon in 689 B.C. Later, his son Esarhaddon ruled Assyria and undertook the rebuilding of Babylon and the temple cult of the god Marduk. According to inscriptions relating the events of Esarhaddon's reign (680–669 B.C.), Marduk caused omens to appear to the king, revealing that the cult should be reinstated. The king, however, worried about such an undertaking since it was Marduk himself who had ordered his own city destroyed. Following Mesopotamian customs, the king went to the temples of the deities in charge of omens, Shamash and Adad, as well as to Marduk, and kneeled before them. Each deity supplied yet more omens to confirm that the temple reform should be instigated.

In the same way, the Babylonian king Nabonidus (556–539 B.C.) observed an eclipse of the moon, which was interpreted (by means of an omen book) to mean that the moon god, Sin, wished a new high priestess and a refurbished cult. As with Esarhaddon and Josiah, Nabonidus wanted to confirm the message. The king checked three times with the gods Shamash and Adad, the omen deities, to confirm the need for a new high priestess, the restoration of the Sin temples throughout Babylonia, and the choice of his daughter for priestess of Sin.

---

²³Then the servants of Amon conspired against him, and killed the king in his own house. ²⁴But the people of the land executed all those who had conspired against King Amon. Then the people of the land made his son Josiah king in his place.

²⁵Now the rest of the acts of Amon which he did, *are* they not written in the book of the chronicles of the kings of Judah? ²⁶And he was buried in his tomb in the garden of Uzza. Then Josiah his son reigned in his place.

Josiah, the Religious Reformer

Sennacherib, king of Assyria, died in 681 B.C., a few years after Hezekiah. His reign ended violently when some of his own sons assassinated him, and he was replaced by another son Esarhaddon (680–669 B.C.). Under Esarhaddon and his successor, Ashurbanipal (668–627 B.C.), Assyria was at its peak of power. These kings even conquered Egypt, something that no Mesopotamian power had ever done before. Esarhaddon captured Memphis in 671 B.C., and Ashurbanipal captured Memphis again in 667 B.C. and Thebes in 664 B.C.

By the end of Ashurbanipal's long reign ▼

(627 B.C.), however, the great Neo-Assyrian Empire was near collapse. Many factors explain this rapid decline, but ultimately one may say that the Assyrians were better at building an empire than at maintaining it. In particular, the nation of Babylon, which had never completely accepted Assyrian supremacy, began to assert itself.

Assyria's preoccupation with internal matters allowed the new king of Judah, Josiah (640–609 B.C.), to assert his independence. In 628 B.C. (his 12th year, 2 Chr. 34:3), he began to purge Judah and Jerusalem of the pagan high places. While this was surely a religious action, it would also have made a political statement. Manasseh had shown his allegiance to Assyria by worshiping Assyrian gods; Josiah's return to the worship of Israel's God was a declaration of independence.

A discovery in 622 B.C. (Josiah's 18th year, 2 Kin. 22:3), as the young king began to repair and renovate the temple, greatly affected him. His reforms gained their greatest impetus from the Book of the Law that Hilkiah the priest found in the temple. From the kinds of reforms that Josiah put into effect, it seems likely that this book was part or all of the Book of Deuteronomy. No religious reforms in Israel's history were so comprehensive.

■ 2 Kings 22:1–20

2 Kings
Josiah Reigns in Judah

22 :1 Josiah *was* eight years old when he became king, and he reigned thirty-one years in Jerusalem. His mother's name *was* Jedidah the daughter of Adaiah of Bozkath. ²And he did *what was* right in the sight of the LORD, and walked in all the ways of his father David; he did not turn aside to the right hand or to the left.

Hilkiah Finds the Book of the Law

³Now it came to pass, in the eighteenth year of King Josiah, *that* the king sent Shaphan the scribe, the son of Azaliah, the son of Meshullam, to the house of the LORD, saying: ⁴"Go up to Hilkiah the high priest, that he may count the money which has been brought into the house of the LORD, which the doorkeepers have gathered from the people. ⁵And let them deliver it into the hand of those doing the work, who are the overseers in the house of the LORD; let them give it to those who *are* in the house of the LORD doing the work, to repair the damages of the house— ⁶to carpenters and builders and masons—and to buy timber and hewn stone to repair the house. ⁷However there need be no accounting made with them of the money delivered into their hand, because they deal faithfully."

⁸Then Hilkiah the high priest said to Shaphan the scribe, "I have found the Book of the Law in the house of the LORD." And Hilkiah gave the book to Shaphan, and he read it. ⁹So Shaphan the scribe went to the king, bringing the king word, saying, "Your servants have gathered the money that was found in the house, and have delivered it into the hand of those who do the work, who oversee the house of the LORD." ¹⁰Then Shaphan the scribe showed the king, saying, "Hilkiah the priest has given me a book." And Shaphan read it before the king.

¹¹Now it happened, when the king heard the words of the Book of the Law, that he tore his clothes. ¹²Then the king commanded Hilkiah the priest, Ahikam the son of Shaphan, Achbor[a] the son of Michaiah, Shaphan the scribe, and Asaiah a servant of the king, saying, ¹³"Go, inquire of the LORD for me, for the people and for all Judah, concerning the words of this book that has been found; for great *is* the wrath of the LORD that is aroused against us, because our fathers have not obeyed the words of this book, to do according to all that is written concerning us."

¹⁴So Hilkiah the priest, Ahikam, Achbor, Shaphan, and Asaiah went to Huldah the prophetess, the wife of Shallum the son of Tikvah, the son of Harhas, keeper of the wardrobe. (She dwelt in Jerusalem in the Second Quarter.) And they spoke with her. ¹⁵Then she said to them, "Thus says the LORD God of Israel, 'Tell the man who sent you to Me, ¹⁶"Thus says the LORD: 'Behold, I will bring calamity on this place and on its inhabitants—all the words of the book which the king of Judah has read— ¹⁷because they have forsaken Me and burned incense to other gods, that they might provoke Me to anger with all the works of their hands. Therefore My wrath shall be aroused against this place and shall not be quenched.' " ' ¹⁸But as for the king of Judah, who sent you to inquire of the LORD, in this manner you shall speak to him, 'Thus says the LORD God of Israel: "*Concerning* the words which you have heard— ¹⁹because your heart was tender, and you humbled yourself before the LORD when you heard what I spoke against this place and against its inhabitants, that they would become a desolation and a curse, and you tore your clothes and wept before Me, I also have heard *you*," says the LORD. ²⁰"Surely, therefore, I will gather you to your fathers, and you shall be gathered to your grave in peace; and your eyes shall not see all the calamity which I will bring on this place." ' " So they brought back word to the king.

22:12 ᵃ*Abdon the son of Micah* in 2 Chronicles 34:20

The Book of Zephaniah
The superscription to the Book of Zephaniah (Zeph. 1:1) places this prophet during the reign of Josiah (640–609 B.C.). Although Josiah's reforms are not mentioned specifically within the book, Zephaniah clearly sympathizes with Josiah's aims. In one oracle, the prophet pronounces doom on the idolatrous priests and pagan worshipers that Josiah sought to destroy (Zeph. 1:4–6). Zephaniah may have been one of the prophetic voices that encouraged the reform efforts (2 Kin. 23:2, 3), and his prophecies were

probably delivered before the reforms of 622 B.C.

Zephaniah's message extended beyond Judah, however. He also pronounces judgment on foreign nations, most significantly on Ethiopia (which had controlled Egypt until about 664 B.C.) and on Assyria itself. The "day of the LORD," Zephaniah declares, will come to all the nations. Jerusalem itself is not exempt (Zeph. 3:6, 7), but in the end God will establish justice and comfort for His city.

■ Zephaniah 1:1—3:20

Zephaniah

1 :1 The word of the LORD which came to Zephaniah the son of Cushi, the son of Gedaliah, the son of Amariah, the son of Hezekiah, in the days of Josiah the son of Amon, king of Judah.

The Great Day of the LORD

2 "I will utterly consume everything
    From the face of the land,"
    Says the LORD;
3 "I will consume man and beast;
    I will consume the birds of the
        heavens,
    The fish of the sea,
    And the stumbling blocks[a] along with
        the wicked.
    I will cut off man from the face of the
        land,"
    Says the LORD.

4 "I will stretch out My hand against
        Judah,
    And against all the inhabitants of
        Jerusalem.
    I will cut off every trace of Baal from
        this place,
    The names of the idolatrous priests[a]
        with the *pagan* priests—

---

5 Those who worship the host of heaven
        on the housetops;
    Those who worship and swear *oaths*
        by the LORD,
    But who *also* swear by Milcom;[a]
6 Those who have turned back from
        following the LORD,
    And have not sought the LORD, nor
        inquired of Him."

7 Be silent in the presence of the Lord
        GOD;
    For the day of the LORD *is* at hand,
    For the LORD has prepared a sacrifice;
    He has invited[a] His guests.

8 "And it shall be,
    In the day of the LORD's sacrifice,
    That I will punish the princes and the
        king's children,
    And all such as are clothed with
        foreign apparel.
9 In the same day I will punish
    All those who leap over the threshold,[a]
    Who fill their masters' houses with
        violence and deceit.

10 "And there shall be on that day," says
        the LORD,
    "The sound of a mournful cry from the
        Fish Gate,
    A wailing from the Second Quarter,
    And a loud crashing from the hills.
11 Wail, you inhabitants of Maktesh![a]
    For all the merchant people are cut
        down;
    All those who handle money are cut
        off.

12 "And it shall come to pass at that time
    That I will search Jerusalem with
        lamps,
    And punish the men
    Who are settled in complacency,[a]
    Who say in their heart,
    'The LORD will not do good,
    Nor will He do evil.'
13 Therefore their goods shall become
        booty,

TIME CAPSULE *647 to 630 B.C.*

647 *Ashurbanipal invades Elam*

642 *Amon becomes king in Judah*

640 *Josiah becomes king in Judah*

640 *Assyrians under Ashurbanipal conquer Elamites*

630 *All of Philistia comes under Egyptian control*

1:3 [a]Figurative of idols   1:4 [a]Hebrew *chemarim*   1:5 [a]Or *Malcam*, an Ammonite god, also called *Molech* (compare Leviticus 18:21)
1:7 [a]Literally *set apart, consecrated*
1:9 [a]Compare 1 Samuel 5:5   1:11 [a]Literally *Mortar*, a market district of Jerusalem
1:12 [a]Literally *on their lees*, that is, settled like the dregs of wine

JERUSALEM'S APOSTASIES AND OTHER GODS (Zeph. 1:4–6)

The prophet Zephaniah announces judgment upon the people of Judah. Apostasies are the cause for Yahweh's wrath; the people had been in pursuit of other deities.

The deity Baal, also known as the storm god Hadad, had long been a part of Jerusalem worship. This popular Canaanite deity was reintroduced during the reign of Manasseh (2 Kin. 21:3). The threat to "cut off every trace of Baal" (Zeph. 1:4) parallels actions in Egypt after the Amarna period (c. 1336 B.C.). The name of the god Aten was removed from Egyptian monuments, manuscripts, and even from hieroglyphics where "Aten" formed part of someone's name. Workmen took chisels and actually chipped the divine name out of the stone. Zephaniah threatens even more drastic measures—not just the name, but the worshipers of Baal will be destroyed.

Besides Baal worshipers, there were those who worshiped the host of heaven in their homes. This means they accepted a pantheon of gods, while worshiping "on the housetops" (Zeph. 1:5), perhaps as they watched the stars. Since these people used their personal homes instead of cultic centers, they were possibly holding family worship services for various deities.

Many in Judah attempted to worship other gods in addition to Yahweh. Zephaniah particularly raises the example of Milcom (or Molech), no doubt chosen because he was understood by most Judahites to be unsavory (1:5). For Judah, Yahweh was to have been the only God and thus the only deity one could swear by. In most other nations, though, oaths were taken more seriously when the swearer swore by more and more deities. For Zephaniah, however, any oath that appealed beyond Yahweh to another god was already false.

And their houses a desolation;
They shall build houses, but not
    inhabit *them;*
They shall plant vineyards, but not
    drink their wine."

14 The great day of the LORD *is* near;
    It is near and hastens quickly.
    The noise of the day of the LORD is
        bitter;
    There the mighty men shall cry out.
15 That day *is* a day of wrath,
    A day of trouble and distress,
    A day of devastation and desolation,
    A day of darkness and gloominess,
    A day of clouds and thick darkness,
16 A day of trumpet and alarm
    Against the fortified cities
    And against the high towers.

17 "I will bring distress upon men,
    And they shall walk like blind men,
    Because they have sinned against the
        LORD;
    Their blood shall be poured out like
        dust,
    And their flesh like refuse."

18 Neither their silver nor their gold
    Shall be able to deliver them
    In the day of the LORD's wrath;
    But the whole land shall be devoured
    By the fire of His jealousy,
    For He will make speedy riddance
    Of all those who dwell in the land.

A Call to Repentance

2 1 Gather yourselves together, yes,
        gather together,
    O undesirable[a] nation,
2 Before the decree is issued,
    Or the day passes like chaff,
    Before the LORD's fierce anger comes
        upon you,
    Before the day of the LORD's anger
        comes upon you!

3 Seek the LORD, all you meek of the
        earth,
    Who have upheld His justice.
    Seek righteousness, seek humility.
    It may be that you will be hidden
    In the day of the LORD's anger.

Judgment on Nations

4 For Gaza shall be forsaken,
    And Ashkelon desolate;
    They shall drive out Ashdod at
        noonday,

2:1 [a]Or *shameless*

A New King Rises and a Capital Dies (Zeph. 2:13)

At the time the Assyrians destroyed Israel (722 B.C.) and then plagued Judah (701 B.C.), Nineveh was the proud capital of the Assyrian Empire (2 Kin. 18:9–13; 19:36). The Assyrian kingdom eventually spread from Egypt to the Persian Gulf. The size of Nineveh itself can be imagined from the description of the city in the Book of Jonah: "an exceedingly great city, a three-day journey in extent" (Jon. 3:3). A city with a population of 120,000 inhabitants (Jon. 4:11) would certainly have been one of the largest cities of ancient times.

As far as the prophet Nahum was concerned, Nineveh, the great city, had one chief characteristic—sinfulness. The Assyrians, with Nineveh as their capital, had waged terrible military campaigns against Israel and Judah. Nahum prophesies the invasion, siege, and sack of this "bloody city" that had looted so many others (Nah. 1—3).

Nineveh was most influential at the time when her last major king, Ashurbanipal, took the throne. During Ashurbanipal's reign (668–627 B.C.), Assyria continued to control Babylonia, as she had since the Assyrian king Sennacherib captured the city of Babylon in 689 B.C. The death of a ruler, however, is a common time for revolt, and after Ashurbanipal's death a Babylonian named Nabopolassar seized the throne of Babylon. Nabopolassar was not from the Babylonian royal family but did receive the support of the populace.

Nabopolassar's kingdom grew quickly. He claimed Uruk in 623 B.C. and Nippur in 622 B.C., but failed to conquer Nineveh and Asshur in 615 B.C. Yet the prophet Zephaniah announced that Assyria and Nineveh would be destroyed (Zeph. 2:13). In 612 B.C. Nabopolassar's son Nebuchadnezzar led the armies of Babylon, in alliance with the Medes, and destroyed Nineveh. The destruction was so complete that the once-great capital never rose from the ashes.

And Ekron shall be uprooted.
5 Woe to the inhabitants of the seacoast,
The nation of the Cherethites!
The word of the LORD *is* against you,
O Canaan, land of the Philistines:
"I will destroy you;
So there shall be no inhabitant."

6 The seacoast shall be pastures,
With shelters[a] for shepherds and folds for flocks.
7 The coast shall be for the remnant of the house of Judah;
They shall feed *their* flocks there;
In the houses of Ashkelon they shall lie down at evening.
For the LORD their God will intervene for them,
And return their captives.

8 "I have heard the reproach of Moab,
And the insults of the people of Ammon,
With which they have reproached My people,
And made arrogant threats against their borders.
9 Therefore, as I live,"
Says the LORD of hosts, the God of Israel,
"Surely Moab shall be like Sodom,
And the people of Ammon like Gomorrah—
Overrun with weeds and saltpits,
And a perpetual desolation.
The residue of My people shall plunder them,

2:6 [a]Literally *excavations*, either underground huts or cisterns

Beliefs and Ideas

In Old Testament times the goal of human civilization was typically the city. The uninhabited desert or wilderness was considered to be undesirable and hostile, a suitable picture of God's curse (Zeph. 2:13). Ruined buildings did not seem romantic or full of interesting memories. They were evidence that something had gone wrong and that God had rejected the people that once lived in them.

And the remnant of My people shall
    possess them."

10 This they shall have for their pride,
    Because they have reproached and
      made arrogant threats
    Against the people of the LORD of
      hosts.
11 The LORD *will be* awesome to them,
    For He will reduce to nothing all the
      gods of the earth;
    People shall worship Him,
    Each one from his place,
    Indeed all the shores of the nations.

12 "You Ethiopians also,
    You shall be slain by My sword."

13 And He will stretch out His hand
      against the north,
    Destroy Assyria,
    And make Nineveh a desolation,
    As dry as the wilderness.
14 The herds shall lie down in her midst,
    Every beast of the nation.
    Both the pelican and the bittern
    Shall lodge on the capitals *of* her
      pillars;
    Their voice shall sing in the windows;
    Desolation *shall be* at the threshold;
    For He will lay bare the cedar work.
15 This is the rejoicing city
    That dwelt securely,
    That said in her heart,
    "I *am it,* and *there is* none besides me."
    How has she become a desolation,
    A place for beasts to lie down!
    Everyone who passes by her
    Shall hiss and shake his fist.

The Wickedness of Jerusalem

3 1 Woe to her who is rebellious and
      polluted,
    To the oppressing city!
2 She has not obeyed *His* voice,
    She has not received correction;
    She has not trusted in the LORD,
    She has not drawn near to her God.

3 Her princes in her midst *are* roaring
      lions;

Her judges *are* evening wolves
    That leave not a bone till morning.
4 Her prophets are insolent, treacherous
      people;
    Her priests have polluted the
      sanctuary,
    They have done violence to the law.
5 The LORD *is* righteous in her midst,
    He will do no unrighteousness.
    Every morning He brings His justice
      to light;
    He never fails,
    But the unjust knows no shame.

6 "I have cut off nations,
    Their fortresses are devastated;
    I have made their streets desolate,
    With none passing by.
    Their cities are destroyed;
    There is no one, no inhabitant.
7 I said, 'Surely you will fear Me,
    You will receive instruction'—
    So that her dwelling would not be cut
      off,
    Despite everything for which I
      punished her.
    But they rose early and corrupted all
      their deeds.

A Faithful Remnant

8 "Therefore wait for Me," says the LORD,
    "Until the day I rise up for plunder;[a]
    My determination *is* to gather the
      nations
    To My assembly of kingdoms,
    To pour on them My indignation,
    All My fierce anger;
    All the earth shall be devoured
    With the fire of My jealousy.

9 "For then I will restore to the peoples a
      pure language,
    That they all may call on the name of
      the LORD,
    To serve Him with one accord.
10 From beyond the rivers of Ethiopia
    My worshipers,
    The daughter of My dispersed ones,
    Shall bring My offering.
11 In that day you shall not be shamed
      for any of your deeds
    In which you transgress against Me;
    For then I will take away from your
      midst
    Those who rejoice in your pride,
    And you shall no longer be haughty
    In My holy mountain.

3:8 [a]Septuagint and Syriac read *for witness;* Targum
reads *for the day of My revelation for judgment;*
Vulgate reads *for the day of My resurrection that is to
come.*

12 I will leave in your midst
A meek and humble people,
And they shall trust in the name of
the LORD.
13 The remnant of Israel shall do no
unrighteousness
And speak no lies,
Nor shall a deceitful tongue be found
in their mouth;
For they shall feed *their* flocks and lie
down,
And no one shall make *them* afraid."

Joy in God's Faithfulness

14 Sing, O daughter of Zion!
Shout, O Israel!
Be glad and rejoice with all *your*
heart,
O daughter of Jerusalem!
15 The LORD has taken away your
judgments,
He has cast out your enemy.
The King of Israel, the LORD, *is* in
your midst;
You shall see[a] disaster no more.

16 In that day it shall be said to
Jerusalem:
"Do not fear;
Zion, let not your hands be weak.
17 The LORD your God in your midst,
The Mighty One, will save;
He will rejoice over you with
gladness,
He will quiet *you* with His love,
He will rejoice over you with singing."

18 "I will gather those who sorrow over
the appointed assembly,
Who are among you,
To whom its reproach *is* a burden.
19 Behold, at that time
I will deal with all who afflict you;
I will save the lame,
And gather those who were driven
out;
I will appoint them for praise and
fame
In every land where they were put to
shame.
20 At that time I will bring you back,
Even at the time I gather you;
For I will give you fame and praise
Among all the peoples of the earth,
When I return your captives before
your eyes,"
Says the LORD.

Josiah Keeps the Passover

The historian of Kings describes Josiah's religious reforms in some detail, and in 2 Kin. 23:25 gives Josiah by far the most complimentary evaluation of any of Judah's kings. Josiah's reign brought great hope to Judah, first to the priests and prophets who hoped to see a genuine renewal of worship. The celebration of the Passover in 622 B.C. formed a climax to Josiah's religious reforms (2 Kin. 23:21–23).

Josiah's reign also gave hope to Judahites with more secular goals. There were evidently many who dreamed of reunifying Israel. Josiah began to expand Judah's borders into what had been the northern kingdom of Israel before Assyria captured it. In these efforts, Josiah was helped by the sharp decline of the Assyrian Empire, which created a power vacuum in the area of the former northern kingdom. Among other actions, Josiah destroyed the idolatrous Israelite shrine of Bethel from which the prophet Amos had been expelled over a century before (Amos 7:10–17).

■ 2 Kings 23:1–25

2 Kings
Josiah Restores True Worship

23 :1 Now the king sent them to gather all the elders of Judah and Jerusalem to him. [2]The king went up to the house of the LORD with all the men of Judah, and with him all the inhabitants of Jerusalem—the priests and the prophets and all the people, both small and great. And he read in their hearing all the words of the Book of the Covenant which had been found in the house of the LORD.

[3]Then the king stood by a pillar and made a covenant before the LORD, to follow the LORD and to keep His commandments and His testimonies and His statutes, with all *his* heart and all *his* soul, to perform the words of this covenant that were written in this book. And all the people took a stand for the covenant. [4]And the king commanded Hilkiah the high priest, the priests of the second order, and the doorkeepers, to bring out of the temple of the LORD all the articles that were made for Baal, for Asherah,[a] and for all the host of heaven;[b]

3:15 [a]Some Hebrew manuscripts, Septuagint, and Bomberg read *see;* Masoretic Text and Vulgate read *fear.*   **2 Kin. 23:4** [a]A Canaanite goddess   [b]The gods of the Assyrians

and he burned them outside Jerusalem in the fields of Kidron, and carried their ashes to Bethel. ⁵Then he removed the idolatrous priests whom the kings of Judah had ordained to burn incense on the high places in the cities of Judah and in the places all around Jerusalem, and those who burned incense to Baal, to the sun, to the moon, to the constellations, and to all the host of heaven. ⁶And he brought out the wooden imageᵃ from the house of the LORD, to the Brook Kidron outside Jerusalem, burned it at the Brook Kidron and ground *it* to ashes, and threw its ashes on the graves of the common people. ⁷Then he tore down the *ritual* booths of the perverted personsᵃ that *were* in the house of the LORD, where the women wove hangings for the wooden image. ⁸And he brought all the priests from the cities of Judah, and defiled the high places where the priests had burned incense, from Geba to Beersheba; also he broke down the high places at the gates which *were* at the entrance of the Gate of Joshua the governor of the city, which *were* to the left of the city gate. ⁹Nevertheless the priests of the high places did not come up to the altar of the LORD in Jerusalem, but they ate unleavened bread among their brethren.

¹⁰And he defiled Topheth, which *is* in the Valley of the Sonᵃ of Hinnom, that no man might make his son or his daughter pass through the fire to Molech. ¹¹Then he removed the horses that the kings of Judah had dedicated to the sun, at the entrance to the house of the LORD, by the chamber of Nathan-Melech, the officer who *was* in the court; and he burned the chariots of the sun with fire. ¹²The altars that *were* on the roof, the upper chamber of Ahaz, which the kings of Judah had made, and the al-

tars which Manasseh had made in the two courts of the house of the LORD, the king broke down and pulverized there, and threw their dust into the Brook Kidron. ¹³Then the king defiled the high places that *were* east of Jerusalem, which *were* on the south of the Mount of Corruption, which Solomon king of Israel had built for Ashtoreth the abomination of the Sidonians, for Chemosh the abomination of the Moabites, and for Milcom the abomination of the people of Ammon. ¹⁴And he broke in pieces the *sacred* pillars and cut down the wooden images, and filled their places with the bones of men.

¹⁵Moreover the altar that *was* at Bethel, *and* the high place which Jeroboam the son of Nebat, who made Israel sin, had made, both that altar and the high place he broke down; and he burned the high place *and* crushed *it* to powder, and burned the wooden image. ¹⁶As Josiah turned, he saw the tombs that *were* there on the mountain. And he sent and took the bones out of the tombs and burned *them* on the altar, and defiled it according to the word of the LORD which the man of God proclaimed, who proclaimed these words. ¹⁷Then he said, "What gravestone *is* this that I see?"

So the men of the city told him, "*It is* the tomb of the man of God who came from Judah and proclaimed these things which you have done against the altar of Bethel."

¹⁸And he said, "Let him alone; let no one move his bones." So they let his bones alone, with the bones of the prophet who came from Samaria.

¹⁹Now Josiah also took away all the shrines of the high places that *were* in the cities of Samaria, which the kings of Israel had made to provoke the LORDᵃ to anger; and he did to them according to all the deeds he had done in Bethel. ²⁰He executed all the priests of the high places who *were* there, on the altars, and burned men's bones on them; and he returned to Jerusalem.

²¹Then the king commanded all the people, saying, "Keep the Passover to the

23:6 ᵃHebrew *Asherah*, a Canaanite goddess
23:7 ᵃHebrew *qedeshim*, that is, those practicing sodomy and prostitution in religious rituals
23:10 ᵃKethib reads *Sons*.   23:19 ᵃFollowing Septuagint, Syriac, and Vulgate; Masoretic Text and Targum omit *the LORD*.

Arts and Literature

The sun can be compared to a flaming chariot traveling across the sky, and the horses of this chariot are convenient symbols of its daily journey. Small statues of horses decorated with solar disks have been excavated near Jerusalem. Live horses pulling chariots in processions honoring the sun may have been thought to be "dedicated to the sun" (2 Kin. 23:11).

CLEANING OUT SOLOMON'S HIGH PLACES (2 Kin. 23:13)

Josiah achieved fame as the king responsible for reforming Judah's cultic worship (2 Kin. 23:25). Part of his reform involved purging the temple and temple precincts of pagan images (see "The Temple Pantheon of Jerusalem" at 2 Chr. 34:33). Yet another part of the reform linked the famous Josiah with another king who, more than 300 years earlier, had also attained great fame—Solomon. Josiah destroyed the high places east of Jerusalem that Solomon himself had built (2 Kin. 23:13).

The Hebrew word translated "high place" refers to a sanctuary; what Solomon did was to build temples to foreign gods in the vicinity of Jerusalem. In the ancient Near East any temple, sanctuary, or shrine constructed by the rightful ruler was a state religious site. So Solomon had officially included foreign gods in the religion of Israel. Furthermore, his sanctuary construction was extensive; he actually built such shrines for "all his foreign wives" (1 Kin. 11:5-8).

Three gods—Ashtoreth, Chemosh, Milcom—are recorded by name as having a high place constructed for them by Solomon (2 Kin. 23:13). Ashtoreth (or Astarte) was the patron goddess in Sidon, a very powerful Phoenician city-state. Chemosh was the patron deity of Moab. An inscription set up by the Moabites around 850 B.C. tells about the defeat of Israel by Chemosh and his chosen Moabite king, Mesha. Milcom (or Molech), the god of Ammon, required human sacrifice. The famous Solomon allowed these deities into Israel; now the famous Josiah cleaned them out.

LORD your God, as *it is* written in this Book of the Covenant." ²²Such a Passover surely had never been held since the days of the judges who judged Israel, nor in all the days of the kings of Israel and the kings of Judah. ²³But in the eighteenth year of King Josiah this Passover was held before the LORD in Jerusalem. ²⁴Moreover Josiah put away those who consulted mediums and spiritists, the household gods and idols, all the abominations that were seen in the land of Judah and in Jerusalem, that he might perform the words of the law which were written in the book that Hilkiah the priest found in the house of the LORD. ²⁵Now before him there was no king like him, who turned to the LORD with all his heart, with all his soul, and with all his might, according to all the Law of Moses; nor after him did *any* arise like him.

Priestly Account: Bad and Good Kings

Both Kings and Chronicles evaluate the kings of Israel and Judah in simple terms: the kings either do evil or do right. There is little or no middle ground. The kings of Judah during the Neo-Assyrian Empire were, in order, Ahaz (bad, 2 Chr. 28:1); Hezekiah (good, 2 Chr. 29:2); Manasseh, Amon (bad, 2 Chr. 33:2, 22); Josiah (good, 2 Chr. 34:2).

One of the most fascinating differences between the histories of Kings and Chronicles concerns King Manasseh (697–642 B.C.). In Kings his sinfulness is cited as the ultimate reason that God would allow Jerusalem to be destroyed (2 Kin. 21:11–13; 23:26, 27). No redeeming quality is allowed to disturb this black portrait. In Chronicles, however, Manasseh is captured by Assyria and eventually humbles himself before God and is forgiven (2 Chr. 33:11–13). Such repentance is, to say the least, striking.

The Chronicler carries the theme of Manasseh's repentance into the account of Amon

---

TIME CAPSULE   628 to 626 B.C.

628   Josiah begins to repair and renovate the temple

627   Jeremiah is born; or becomes aware of his divine calling; or begins to prophesy

626–ͅ539   The Neo-Babylonian Empire

626–605   Nabopolassar is founder of the Neo-Babylonian Dynasty

626   Nabopolassar lays siege to Assyrian garrison at Nippur

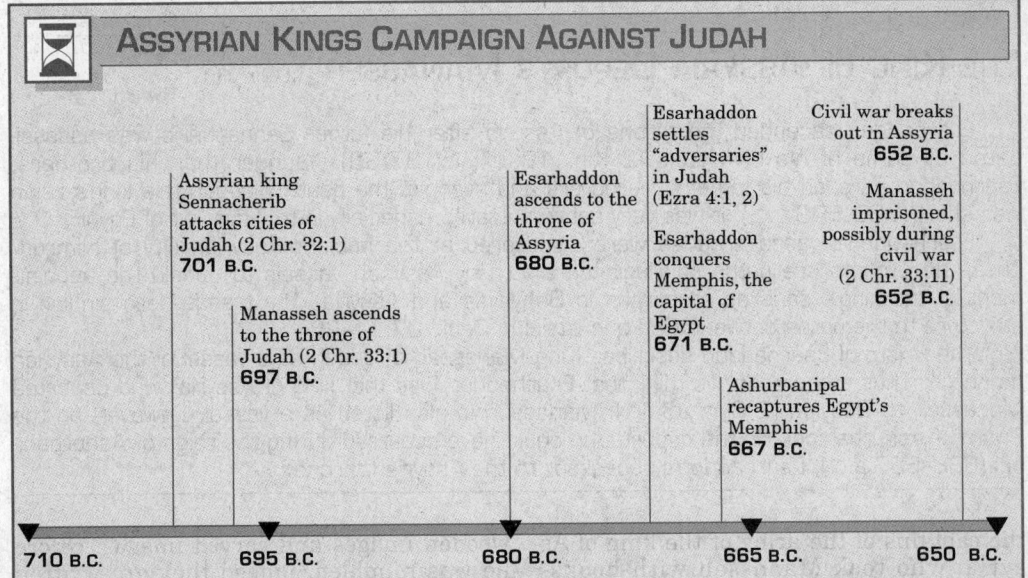

ASSYRIAN KINGS CAMPAIGN AGAINST JUDAH

Assyrian king
Sennacherib
attacks cities of
Judah (2 Chr. 32:1)
701 B.C.

Manasseh ascends
to the throne of
Judah (2 Chr. 33:1)
697 B.C.

Esarhaddon
ascends to the
throne of
Assyria
680 B.C.

Esarhaddon
settles
"adversaries"
in Judah
(Ezra 4:1, 2)

Esarhaddon
conquers
Memphis, the
capital of
Egypt
671 B.C.

Ashurbanipal
recaptures Egypt's
Memphis
667 B.C.

Civil war breaks
out in Assyria
652 B.C.

Manasseh
imprisoned,
possibly during
civil war
(2 Chr. 33:11)
652 B.C.

710 B.C.   **695 B.C.**   **680 B.C.**   **665 B.C.**   **650 B.C.**

(642–640 B.C.). Kings criticized Amon for doing evil "as his father Manasseh had done" (2 Kin. 21:20). Chronicles changes this report to say that Amon did not humble himself "as his father Manasseh had humbled himself" (2 Chr. 33:23). The "Prayer of Manasseh" of the Apocrypha is based on the Chronicler's repentance account, though it was almost certainly written centuries later.

The Chronicler's account of Josiah (640–609 B.C.) follows the Kings account very closely, except that it lays more stress on the Passover celebration. Since the Passover is a temple festival, this is completely consistent with Chronicles's priestly focus. Much more information is provided concerning the duties of the Levites and the details of the Passover ritual itself (2 Chr. 35:1–19).

■ 2 Chronicles 33:1—35:19

2 Chronicles
Manasseh Reigns in Judah

33 :1 Manasseh *was* twelve years old when he became king, and he reigned fifty-five years in Jerusalem. ²But he did evil in the sight of the LORD, according to the abominations of the nations whom the LORD had cast out before the children of Israel. ³For he rebuilt the high places which Hezekiah his father had broken down; he raised up altars for the

Baals, and made wooden images; and he worshiped all the host of heaven[a] and served them. ⁴He also built altars in the house of the LORD, of which the LORD had said, "In Jerusalem shall My name be forever." ⁵And he built altars for all the host of heaven in the two courts of the house of the LORD. ⁶Also he caused his sons to pass through the fire in the Valley of the Son of Hinnom; he practiced soothsaying, used witchcraft and sorcery, and consulted mediums and spiritists. He did much evil in the sight of the LORD, to provoke Him to anger. ⁷He even set a carved image, the idol which he had made, in the house of God, of which God had said to David and to Solomon his son, "In this house and in Jerusalem, which I have chosen out of all the tribes of Israel, I will put My name forever; ⁸and I will not again remove the foot of Israel from the land which I have appointed for your fathers—only if they are careful to do all that I have commanded them, according to the whole law and the statutes and the ordinances by the hand of Moses." ⁹So Manasseh seduced Judah and the inhabitants of Jerusalem to do more evil than the nations whom the LORD had destroyed before the children of Israel.

Manasseh Restored After Repentance

¹⁰And the LORD spoke to Manasseh and his people, but they would not listen. ¹¹Therefore the LORD brought upon them

33:3 ᵃThe gods of the Assyrians

THE KING OF ASSYRIA DEPORTS MANASSEH (2 Chr. 33:11)

Esarhaddon ascended the throne of Assyria after his father Sennacherib was assassinated by some of his own sons (2 Kin. 19:37; Is. 37:38). Younger than his brothers, Esarhaddon pursued his father's murderers and avenged the death. Though this king's reign was short (680–669 B.C.), it was very active militarily, especially in the invasion of Egypt.

Esarhaddon's vassal treaties were discovered at the ancient Assyrian city of Nimrud. These documents are oaths of allegiance sworn by Assyrian vassals to uphold the appointment of the king's sons as monarchs in Babylonia and Assyria. The treaties are similar in structure to the oaths between God and Israel in Deut. 27:11–26.

The Prism of Esarhaddon describes King Manasseh of Judah as a vassal of the Assyrian monarch. Thus some scholars think that Esarhaddon was the "king of Assyria" who deported Manasseh to Babylon (2 Chr. 33:11). Manasseh is also listed as a vassal, however, on the Prism of Ashurbanipal. So the deportation could have occurred during the reign of Ashurbanipal (668–627 B.C.), Esarhaddon's successor to the Assyrian throne.

the captains of the army of the king of Assyria, who took Manasseh with hooks,[a] bound him with bronze *fetters,* and carried him off to Babylon. [12]Now when he was in affliction, he implored the LORD his God, and humbled himself greatly before the God of his fathers, [13]and prayed to Him; and He received his entreaty, heard his supplication, and brought him back to Jerusalem into his kingdom. Then Manasseh knew that the LORD *was* God.

[14]After this he built a wall outside the City of David on the west side of Gihon, in the valley, as far as the entrance of the Fish Gate; and *it* enclosed Ophel, and he raised it to a very great height. Then he put military captains in all the fortified cities of Judah. [15]He took away the foreign gods and the idol from the house of the LORD, and all the altars that he had built in the mount of the house of the LORD and in Jerusalem; and he cast *them* out of the city. [16]He also repaired the altar of the LORD, sacrificed peace offerings and thank offerings on it, and commanded Judah to serve the LORD God of Israel. [17]Nevertheless the people still sacrificed on the high places, *but* only to the LORD their God.

Death of Manasseh

[18]Now the rest of the acts of Manasseh, his prayer to his God, and the words of the seers who spoke to him in the name of the LORD God of Israel, indeed they *are written* in the book[a] of the kings of Israel. [19]Also his prayer and *how God* received his entreaty, and all his sin and trespass, and the sites where he built high places and set up wooden images and carved images, before he was humbled, indeed they *are* written among the sayings of Hozai.[a] [20]So Manasseh rested with his fathers, and they buried him in his own house. Then his son Amon reigned in his place.

Amon's Reign and Death

[21]Amon *was* twenty-two years old when he became king, and he reigned two years in Jerusalem. [22]But he did evil in the sight of the LORD, as his father Manasseh had done; for Amon sacrificed to all the carved images which his father Manasseh had made, and served them. [23]And he did not humble himself before the LORD, as his father Manasseh had humbled himself; but Amon trespassed more and more.

[24]Then his servants conspired against him, and killed him in his own house. [25]But the people of the land executed all those who had conspired against King Amon. Then the people of the land made his son Josiah king in his place.

Josiah Reigns in Judah

34 [1]Josiah *was* eight years old when he became king, and he reigned thirty-one years in Jerusalem. [2]And he did *what was* right in the sight of the LORD, and walked in the ways of his father David; *he* did *not* turn aside to the right hand or to the left.

[3]For in the eighth year of his reign,

33:11 [a]That is, nose hooks (compare 2 Kings 19:28)   33:18 [a]Literally *words*
33:19 [a]Septuagint reads *the seers.*

THE TEMPLE PANTHEON OF JERUSALEM (2 Chr. 34:31, 33)

Josiah's covenant with Yahweh meant that there would be only one deity worshiped in Judah, for Josiah "removed all the abominations" from the country (2 Chr. 34:31, 33). The reform began in 622 B.C. by removing the idols that had been placed in the Jerusalem temple. These images, representing gods such as Baal and Asherah (2 Kin. 23:4), were of Syro-Palestinian (Canaanite) origin. The expression "host of heaven" (2 Kin. 23:4) referred to an entire pantheon of gods; Josiah's reform was thorough.

It is significant that there were images of these various deities in the royal temple. Through the reigns of Manasseh and Amon, Josiah's predecessors, the local gods had been incorporated into Judah's royal cult. Probably both Canaanite and Assyrian deities were worshiped, for Assyria was then the ruling power over the vassal state of Judah. Many of the traditional Canaanite gods had been worshiped in the northern kingdom, and an association of these gods with Israel may explain why Josiah took the cult images to Bethel for disposal (23:4). Bethel had been a national temple of Israel.

The sanctity of the temple space was retained during the reform efforts. Only priests were allowed to clean out the images. Hilkiah had been the high priest of the cult involving all these deities, but, under orders from the king (23:4), he removed the gods that he had served.

---

while he was still young, he began to seek the God of his father David; and in the twelfth year he began to purge Judah and Jerusalem of the high places, the wooden images, the carved images, and the molded images. ⁴They broke down the altars of the Baals in his presence, and the incense altars which *were* above them he cut down; and the wooden images, the carved images, and the molded images he broke in pieces, and made dust of them and scattered *it* on the graves of those who had sacrificed to them. ⁵He also burned the bones of the priests on their altars, and cleansed Judah and Jerusalem. ⁶And *so he did* in the cities of Manasseh, Ephraim, and Simeon, as far as Naphtali and all around, with axes.ᵃ ⁷When he had broken down the altars and the wooden images, had beaten the carved images into powder, and cut down all the incense altars throughout all the land of Israel, he returned to Jerusalem.

Hilkiah Finds the Book of the Law

⁸In the eighteenth year of his reign, when he had purged the land and the temple,ᵃ he sent Shaphan the son of Azaliah, Maaseiah the governor of the city, and Joah the son of Joahaz the recorder, to repair the house of the LORD his God. ⁹When they came to Hilkiah the high priest, they delivered the money that was brought into the house of God, which the Levites who kept the doors had gathered from the hand of Manasseh and Ephraim, from all the remnant of Israel, from all Judah and Benjamin, and *which* they had brought back to Jerusalem. ¹⁰Then they put *it* in the hand of the foremen who had the oversight of the house of the LORD; and they gave it to the workmen who worked in the house of the LORD, to repair and restore the house. ¹¹They gave *it* to the craftsmen and builders to buy hewn stone and timber for beams, and to floor the houses which the kings of Judah had destroyed. ¹²And the men did the work faithfully. Their overseers *were* Jahath and Obadiah the Levites, of the sons of Merari, and Zechariah and Meshullam, of the sons of the Kohathites, to supervise. *Others of* the Levites, all of whom were skillful with instruments of music, ¹³*were* over the burden bearers and *were* overseers of all who did work in any kind of service. And *some* of the Levites *were* scribes, officers, and gatekeepers.

¹⁴Now when they brought out the money that was brought into the house of the LORD, Hilkiah the priest found the Book of the Law of the LORD *given* by Moses. ¹⁵Then Hilkiah answered and said to Shaphan the scribe, "I have found the Book of the Law in the house of the LORD." And Hilkiah gave the book to Shaphan. ¹⁶So Shaphan carried the book to the king,

---

34:6 ᵃLiterally *swords*   34:8 ᵃLiterally *house*

bringing the king word, saying, "All that was committed to your servants they are doing. [17]And they have gathered the money that was found in the house of the LORD, and have delivered it into the hand of the overseers and the workmen." [18]Then Shaphan the scribe told the king, saying, "Hilkiah the priest has given me a book." And Shaphan read it before the king.

[19]Thus it happened, when the king heard the words of the Law, that he tore his clothes. [20]Then the king commanded Hilkiah, Ahikam the son of Shaphan, Abdon[a] the son of Micah, Shaphan the scribe, and Asaiah a servant of the king, saying, [21]"Go, inquire of the LORD for me, and for those who are left in Israel and Judah, concerning the words of the book that is found; for great *is* the wrath of the LORD that is poured out on us, because our fathers have not kept the word of the LORD, to do according to all that is written in this book."

[22]So Hilkiah and those the king *had appointed* went to Huldah the prophetess, the wife of Shallum the son of Tokhath,[a] the son of Hasrah,[b] keeper of the wardrobe. (She dwelt in Jerusalem in the Second Quarter.) And they spoke to her to that *effect.*

[23]Then she answered them, "Thus says the LORD God of Israel, 'Tell the man who sent you to Me, [24]"Thus says the LORD: 'Behold, I will bring calamity on this place and on its inhabitants, all the curses that are written in the book which they have read before the king of Judah, [25]because they have forsaken Me and burned incense to other gods, that they might provoke Me to anger with all the works of their hands. Therefore My wrath will be poured out on this place, and not be quenched.' " ' [26]But as for the king of Judah, who sent you to inquire of the LORD, in this manner you shall speak to him, 'Thus says the LORD God of Israel: "Concerning the words which you have heard— [27]because your heart was tender, and you humbled yourself before God when you heard His words against this place and against its inhabitants, and you humbled yourself before Me, and you tore your clothes and wept before Me, I also have heard *you,*" says the LORD. [28]"Surely I will gather you to your fathers, and you shall be gathered to your grave in peace; and your eyes shall not see all the calamity which I will bring on this place and its inhabitants." ' " So they brought back word to the king.

Josiah Restores True Worship

[29]Then the king sent and gathered all the elders of Judah and Jerusalem. [30]The king went up to the house of the LORD, with all the men of Judah and the inhabitants of Jerusalem—the priests and the Levites, and all the people, great and small. And he read in their hearing all the words of the Book of the Covenant which had been found in the house of the LORD. [31]Then the king stood in his place and made a covenant before the LORD, to follow the LORD, and to keep His commandments and His testimonies and His statutes with all his heart and all his soul, to perform the words of the covenant that were written in this book. [32]And he made all who were present in Jerusalem and Benjamin take a stand. So the inhabitants of Jerusalem did according to the covenant of God, the God of their fathers. [33]Thus Josiah removed all the abominations from all the country that *belonged* to the children of Israel, and made all who were present in Israel diligently serve the LORD their God. All his days they did not depart from following the LORD God of their fathers.

Josiah Keeps the Passover

35 [1]Now Josiah kept a Passover to the LORD in Jerusalem, and they slaughtered the Passover *lambs* on the fourteenth *day* of the first month. [2]And he set the priests in their duties and encouraged them for the service of the house of the LORD. [3]Then he said to the Levites who taught all Israel, who were holy to the LORD: "Put the holy ark in the house which Solomon the son of David, king of Israel, built. *It shall* no longer *be* a burden on *your* shoulders. Now serve the LORD your God and His people Israel. [4]Prepare *yourselves* according to your fathers' houses, according to your divisions, following the written instruction of David king of Israel and the written instruction of Solomon his son. [5]And stand in the holy *place* according to the divisions of the fathers' houses of your brethren the *lay* people, and *according to* the division of the father's house of the Levites. [6]So slaughter the Passover *offerings,* consecrate yourselves, and prepare *them* for your brethren, that *they* may do according to the word of the LORD by the hand of Moses."

7Then Josiah gave the *lay* people lambs and young goats from the flock, all for Passover *offerings* for all who were present, to the number of thirty thousand, as well as three thousand cattle; these *were* from the king's possessions. 8And his leaders gave willingly to the people, to the priests, and to the Levites. Hilkiah, Zechariah, and Jehiel, rulers of the house of God, gave to the priests for the Passover *offerings* two thousand six hundred *from the flock,* and three hundred cattle. 9Also Conaniah, his brothers Shemaiah and Nethanel, and Hashabiah and Jeiel and Jozabad, chief of the Levites, gave to the Levites for Passover *offerings* five thousand *from the flock* and five hundred cattle.

10So the service was prepared, and the priests stood in their places, and the Levites in their divisions, according to the king's command. 11And they slaughtered the Passover *offerings;* and the priests sprinkled *the blood* with their hands, while the Levites skinned *the animals.* 12Then they removed the burnt offerings that *they* might give them to the divisions of the fathers' houses of the *lay* people, to offer to the LORD, as *it is* written in the Book of Moses. And so *they did* with the cattle. 13Also they roasted the Passover *offerings* with fire according to the ordinance; but the *other* holy *offerings* they boiled in pots, in caldrons, and in pans, and divided *them* quickly among all the *lay* people. 14Then afterward they prepared portions for themselves and for the priests, because the priests, the sons of Aaron, *were busy* in offering burnt offerings and fat until night; therefore the Levites prepared portions for themselves and for the priests, the sons of Aaron. 15And the singers, the sons of Asaph, *were* in their places, according to the command of David, Asaph, Heman, and Jeduthun the king's seer. Also the gatekeepers were at each gate; they did not have to leave their position, because their brethren the Levites prepared portions for them.

16So all the service of the LORD was prepared the same day, to keep the Passover and to offer burnt offerings on the altar of the LORD, according to the command of King Josiah. 17And the children of Israel who were present kept the Passover at that time, and the Feast of Unleavened Bread for seven days. 18There had been no

Passover kept in Israel like that since the days of Samuel the prophet; and none of the kings of Israel had kept such a Passover as Josiah kept, with the priests and the Levites, all Judah and Israel who were present, and the inhabitants of Jerusalem. 19In the eighteenth year of the reign of Josiah this Passover was kept.

Psalms of Joy and Praise

Josiah reinstated the celebration of Passover in Jerusalem, which had been neglected for years. The Chronicler emphasizes the role of the priests and Levites in Josiah's observance (2 Chr. 35:10), and also comments that the singers were "in their places" at the celebration (2 Chr. 35:15). Passover became a time of joy and feasting as God's people remembered His deliverance from Egypt. It was a time of singing and of giving praise to God. In such a context it is appropriate to recall some of the psalms that reflect joy and praise. The beautiful hymn of Ps. 33 begins with a call to praise. Two psalms of thanksgiving (Ps. 66; 67) celebrate the greatness of God in exuberant tones. The hymn of procession in Ps. 100 was probably sung by pilgrims coming to worship in the temple.

▼

■ Psalms 33; 66; 67; 100

PSALM 33

The Sovereignty of the LORD in Creation and History

Rejoice in the LORD, O you righteous!
   For praise from the upright is
     beautiful.
2 Praise the LORD with the harp;
   Make melody to Him with an
     instrument of ten strings.
3 Sing to Him a new song;
   Play skillfully with a shout of joy.

4 For the word of the LORD *is* right,
   And all His work *is done* in truth.
5 He loves righteousness and justice;
   The earth is full of the goodness of
     the LORD.

6 By the word of the LORD the heavens
     were made,
   And all the host of them by the breath
     of His mouth.

7 He gathers the waters of the sea
     together as a heap;[a]
   He lays up the deep in storehouses.

8 Let all the earth fear the LORD;
   Let all the inhabitants of the world
     stand in awe of Him.

9 For He spoke, and it was *done;*
   He commanded, and it stood fast.

10 The LORD brings the counsel of the
     nations to nothing;
   He makes the plans of the peoples of
     no effect.

11 The counsel of the LORD stands forever,
   The plans of His heart to all
     generations.

12 Blessed *is* the nation whose God *is*
     the LORD,
   The people He has chosen as His own
     inheritance.

13 The LORD looks from heaven;
   He sees all the sons of men.

14 From the place of His dwelling He
     looks
   On all the inhabitants of the earth;

15 He fashions their hearts individually;
   He considers all their works.

16 No king *is* saved by the multitude of
     an army;
   A mighty man is not delivered by
     great strength.

17 A horse *is* a vain hope for safety;
   Neither shall it deliver *any* by its
     great strength.

18 Behold, the eye of the LORD *is* on those
     who fear Him,
   On those who hope in His mercy,

19 To deliver their soul from death,
   And to keep them alive in famine.

20 Our soul waits for the LORD;
   He *is* our help and our shield.

21 For our heart shall rejoice in Him,
   Because we have trusted in His holy
     name.

22 Let Your mercy, O LORD, be upon us,
   Just as we hope in You.

PSALM 66

Praise to God for His Awesome Works

To the Chief Musician. A Song. A Psalm.

Make a joyful shout to God, all the
   earth!

2 Sing out the honor of His name;
   Make His praise glorious.

3 Say to God,
   "How awesome are Your works!
   Through the greatness of Your power
   Your enemies shall submit themselves
     to You.

4 All the earth shall worship You
   And sing praises to You;
   They shall sing praises *to* Your name."
                                    Selah

5 Come and see the works of God;
   He is awesome *in His* doing toward
     the sons of men.

6 He turned the sea into dry *land;*
   They went through the river on foot.
   There we will rejoice in Him.

7 He rules by His power forever;
   His eyes observe the nations;
   Do not let the rebellious exalt
     themselves.   Selah

8 Oh, bless our God, you peoples!
   And make the voice of His praise to be
     heard,

9 Who keeps our soul among the living,
   And does not allow our feet to be
     moved.

10 For You, O God, have tested us;
   You have refined us as silver is
     refined.

11 You brought us into the net;
   You laid affliction on our backs.

12 You have caused men to ride over our
     heads;
   We went through fire and through
     water;
   But You brought us out to rich
     fulfillment.

13 I will go into Your house with burnt
     offerings;
   I will pay You my vows,

14 Which my lips have uttered
   And my mouth has spoken when I
     was in trouble.

15 I will offer You burnt sacrifices of fat
     animals,
   With the sweet aroma of rams;
   I will offer bulls with goats.   Selah

16 Come *and* hear, all you who fear God,
   And I will declare what He has done
     for my soul.

17 I cried to Him with my mouth,
   And He was extolled with my tongue.

33:7 [a]Septuagint, Targum, and Vulgate read *in a vessel.*

18 If I regard iniquity in my heart,
    The Lord will not hear.
19 *But* certainly God has heard *me;*
    He has attended to the voice of my
        prayer.

20 Blessed *be* God,
    Who has not turned away my prayer,
    Nor His mercy from me!

PSALM 67

An Invocation and a Doxology

*To the Chief Musician. On stringed
instruments.*[a] *A Psalm. A Song.*

God be merciful to us and bless us,
And cause His face to shine upon us,
                                    Selah
2   That Your way may be known on
        earth,
    Your salvation among all nations.

3   Let the peoples praise You, O God;
    Let all the peoples praise You.
4   Oh, let the nations be glad and sing
        for joy!
    For You shall judge the people
        righteously,
    And govern the nations on earth.
                                    Selah

67:title [a]Hebrew *neginoth*   100:3 [a]Following
Kethib, Septuagint, and Vulgate; Qere, many Hebrew
manuscripts, and Targum read *we are His.*

5   Let the peoples praise You, O God;
    Let all the peoples praise You.
6   *Then* the earth shall yield her
        increase;
    God, our own God, shall bless us.
7   God shall bless us,
    And all the ends of the earth shall
        fear Him.

PSALM 100

A Song of Praise for the LORD's Faithfulness to His People

A Psalm of Thanksgiving.

Make a joyful shout to the LORD, all you
        lands!
2   Serve the LORD with gladness;
    Come before His presence with singing.
3   Know that the LORD, He *is* God;
    It is He *who* has made us, and not we
        ourselves;[a]
    We are His people and the sheep of His
        pasture.

4   Enter into His gates with
        thanksgiving,
    And into His courts with praise.
    Be thankful to Him, *and* bless His
        name.
5   For the LORD *is* good;
    His mercy *is* everlasting,
    And His truth *endures* to all
        generations.

The Neo-Babylonian Empire

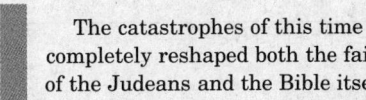

The catastrophes of this time
completely reshaped both the faith
of the Judeans and the Bible itself.

The events of the approximately 30 years following Josiah's reform of 622 B.C. lie behind a wide range of biblical books. The most important are probably the books of Jeremiah and Ezekiel, but other prophetic books, historical accounts, psalms, and poems also refer to this critical era. The catastrophes of this time would completely reshape both the faith of the Judeans and the Bible itself. These disasters were even more staggering in that they came so suddenly after the optimistic years of Josiah's reign in Judah (640–609 B.C.).

Under Ashurbanipal (668–627 B.C.) the Assyrian Empire that had once made the world its own had grown old and surprisingly weak. Constant rebellions from outlying provinces had sapped its resources. Egypt, for instance, had effectively declared its independence and appeared to be regaining some of its former strength. Even more disturbing for Assyria, though, were rebellions closer to home. After Ashurbanipal died, Babylon rebelled once more, joined by the northeastern nation of Media. This time Assyria would not be able to quell the revolt.

The effect of these stirring events on Judah was virtually to give King Josiah complete independence from his official overlords in Assyria. He could pursue his religious reforms and expand his political boundaries at will.

Prophetic Account: Josiah's Last Years

Josiah's reforms would not allow Judah to avoid the consequences of Manasseh's sins. Judgment upon Judah was inevitable, though for a brief time delayed. Israel, the northern kingdom, had fallen in 722 B.C.; Judah's fall would come.

The word of Yahweh announcing the approaching judgment (2 Kin. 23:27) was likely preached by one of the prophets. While the identity of that prophet (or prophets) is not given, the theme of Yahweh rejecting His chosen people appears again in the prophecies of Jeremiah (Jer. 6:27-30).

■ 2 Kings 23:26, 27

2 Kings
Impending Judgment on Judah

23 :26 Nevertheless the LORD did not turn from the fierceness of His great wrath, with which His anger was aroused against Judah, because of all the provocations with which Manasseh had provoked Him. 27And the LORD said, "I will also remove Judah from My sight, as I have removed Israel, and will cast off this city Jerusalem which I have chosen, and the house of which I said, 'My name shall be there.' "a

23:27 a1 Kings 8:29

The Book of Jeremiah

No prophet is more important in this crucial time period than Jeremiah. He was from a priestly family, from the small town of Anathoth near Jerusalem. He may have been a descendant of David's priest Abiathar, who had been banished to Anathoth by King Solomon (1 Kin. 2:26). In any case, Jeremiah's relationship with the Jerusalem establishment—temple, priests, prophets, and kings—was strained, to say the least. Unlike Isaiah, who was evidently acknowledged and respected throughout Jerusalem in his day, Jeremiah's long ministry was marked by persecution, banishment from the temple, and threats of death.

Jeremiah's very unpopular message was

that Jerusalem had sinned so long and so grievously that God was about to destroy the temple, the city, and the land. In language very close to that of the northern prophet Hosea, Jeremiah called for the people to turn from their wickedness. Even after almost all of Jeremiah's prophecies had been fulfilled, though, few listened.

No book in the Old Testament presents more difficulties to chronological arrangement. In its usual order, the book is divided into three general sections: oracles against Judah and Jerusalem (chs. 1—25), narratives about Jeremiah (chs. 26—45), and oracles against other nations (chs. 46—51). The final chapter (ch. 52) is an almost exact reproduction of 2 Kin. 25. Not one of these three general sections follows a chronological arrangement, however. Even the historical narratives of the central portion skip back and forth in time. As for the oracles of the first section, it is almost impossible to decide the time period to which some of these refer.

Any attempt to arrange chronologically the various portions of Jeremiah must be both very different from the usual order and very tentative. On the other hand, no other Old Testament book benefits more from such a rearrangement. To read Jeremiah's words in light of his life and the history of his land is a completely new experience.

The first chronological difficulty concerns the beginning of Jeremiah's ministry. In Jer. 1:2 the prophet is reported to have received the word of the Lord in the 13th year of Josiah's reign (627 B.C.). If this is when he began his prophetic task, then the time of his ministry spans all of Josiah's reforms. It is odd then that Jeremiah never mentions these reforms or any other sign of religious faithfulness in Jerusalem.

The year 627 B.C. marks a beginning for this prophet, but was it the beginning of his ministry? Some think this is when Jeremiah became aware of his divine calling, and not necessarily when he began to prophesy. Others suggest that Jer. 1:2 actually refers to the date of Jeremiah's birth, noting that Jeremiah was called as a prophet even before he was born (Jer. 1:5). If he was born in 627, Jeremiah could have begun his prophetic ministry near the end of Josiah's reforms, when he was between the ages of 12 and 18. Many of the oracles found in chs. 1—6 rebuke the people and the priests for backsliding, perhaps indicating that Josiah's reforms were falling apart even during Josiah's reign.

The end of Jeremiah's ministry is dated by

Jer. 1:3 in King Zedekiah's 11th year [586 B.C.]. This prophet continued his work until Jerusalem fell and the city's people were exiled.

■ Jeremiah 1:1—6:30

Jeremiah

1 **:1** The words of Jeremiah the son of Hilkiah, of the priests who *were* in Anathoth in the land of Benjamin, [2]to whom the word of the LORD came in the days of Josiah the son of Amon, king of Judah, in the thirteenth year of his reign. [3]It came also in the days of Jehoiakim the son of Josiah, king of Judah, until the end of the eleventh year of Zedekiah the son of Josiah, king of Judah, until the carrying away of Jerusalem captive in the fifth month.

The Prophet Is Called

[4]Then the word of the LORD came to me, saying:

5   "Before I formed you in the womb I
      knew you;
     Before you were born I sanctified you;
     I ordained you a prophet to the
      nations."

[6]Then said I:

"Ah, Lord GOD!
   Behold, I cannot speak, for I *am* a
    youth."

[7]But the LORD said to me:

"Do not say, 'I *am* a youth,'
   For you shall go to all to whom I send
    you,
   And whatever I command you, you
    shall speak.
8   Do not be afraid of their faces,
   For I *am* with you to deliver you,"
    says the LORD.

[9]Then the LORD put forth His hand and touched my mouth, and the LORD said to me:

"Behold, I have put My words in your
    mouth.
10   See, I have this day set you over the
     nations and over the kingdoms,
   To root out and to pull down,
   To destroy and to throw down,
   To build and to plant."

[11]Moreover the word of the LORD came to me, saying, "Jeremiah, what do you see?"

And I said, "I see a branch of an almond tree."

[12]Then the LORD said to me, "You have seen well, for I am ready to perform My word."

[13]And the word of the LORD came to me the second time, saying, "What do you see?"

And I said, "I see a boiling pot, and it is facing away from the north."

[14]Then the LORD said to me:

"Out of the north calamity shall break
    forth
   On all the inhabitants of the land.
15   For behold, I am calling
   All the families of the kingdoms of the
    north," says the LORD;
"They shall come and each one set his
    throne
   At the entrance of the gates of
    Jerusalem,
   Against all its walls all around,
   And against all the cities of Judah.
16   I will utter My judgments
   Against them concerning all their
    wickedness,
   Because they have forsaken Me,
   Burned incense to other gods,
   And worshiped the works of their own
    hands.

17   "Therefore prepare yourself and arise,
   And speak to them all that I command
    you.

CULTURE AND SOCIETY

Like Moses (Ex. 3:11), Jeremiah protested that he was unable to perform the task that God was asking him to do (Jer. 1:6). A "youth" was not someone underage, but someone without experience, an apprentice. The time of childhood ended sooner than in some Western societies, and males could become fighters while still considered "youths" (see 2 Kin. 2:23).

Do not be dismayed before their faces,
Lest I dismay you before them.
18 For behold, I have made you this day
A fortified city and an iron pillar,
And bronze walls against the whole
    land—
Against the kings of Judah,
Against its princes,
Against its priests,
And against the people of the land.
19 They will fight against you,
But they shall not prevail against you.
For I *am* with you," says the LORD, "to
    deliver you."

God's Case Against Israel

2 ¹Moreover the word of the LORD came
to me, saying, ²"Go and cry in the hearing of Jerusalem, saying, 'Thus says the
LORD:

"I remember you,
The kindness of your youth,
The love of your betrothal,
When you went after Me in the
    wilderness,
In a land not sown.
3 Israel *was* holiness to the LORD,
The firstfruits of His increase.
All that devour him will offend;
Disaster will come upon them," says
    the LORD.' "

⁴Hear the word of the LORD, O house of
Jacob and all the families of the house of
Israel. ⁵Thus says the LORD:

"What injustice have your fathers
    found in Me,
That they have gone far from Me,
Have followed idols,
And have become idolaters?

---

6 Neither did they say, 'Where *is* the
    LORD,
Who brought us up out of the land of
    Egypt,
Who led us through the wilderness,
Through a land of deserts and pits,
Through a land of drought and the
    shadow of death,
Through a land that no one crossed
And where no one dwelt?'
7 I brought you into a bountiful country,
To eat its fruit and its goodness.
But when you entered, you defiled My
    land
And made My heritage an
    abomination.
8 The priests did not say, 'Where *is* the
    LORD?'
And those who handle the law did not
    know Me;
The rulers also transgressed against
    Me;
The prophets prophesied by Baal,
And walked after *things that* do not
    profit.
9 "Therefore I will yet bring charges
    against you," says the LORD,
"And against your children's children I
    will bring charges.
10 For pass beyond the coasts of Cyprusᵃ
    and see,
Send to Kedarᵇ and consider
    diligently,
And see if there has been such *a
    thing*.
11 Has a nation changed *its* gods,
Which *are* not gods?
But My people have changed their
    Glory
For *what* does not profit.
12 Be astonished, O heavens, at this,
And be horribly afraid;
Be very desolate," says the LORD.
13 "For My people have committed two
    evils:
They have forsaken Me, the fountain
    of living waters,
And hewn themselves cisterns—
    broken cisterns that can hold no
    water.

14 "*Is* Israel a servant?
Is he a homeborn *slave?*
Why is he plundered?

TIME CAPSULE   *625 to 622 B.C.*

625 *Earliest coinage, found in Ephesus*

623 *Nabopolassar claims Uruk for the
Babylonians*

622 *Nabopolassar claims Nippur for the
Babylonians*

622 *Hilkiah the priest finds Book of the
Law in the temple*

622 *The reforms of Josiah*

622 *Celebration of the Passover as a
climax to Josiah's reform effort*

2:10 ᵃHebrew *Kittim*, western lands, especially
Cyprus ᵇIn the northern Arabian desert,
representative of the eastern cultures

BROKEN CISTERNS (Jer. 2:13)

In Old Testament times cisterns were an everyday part of life. The seasonal rainfall of the Bible lands necessitated extraordinary strategies for securing water. In some cities virtually every household had its own cistern, arranged so as to collect runoff water from the streets as well as from the roofs of the houses.

Cisterns were dug into the bedrock foundation of the houses, and could be plastered or unplastered depending on the type of rock into which they had been dug. Sometimes two or more cisterns were connected by water channels. In the middle of many of these cisterns were stone-carved sumps where the larger impurities could be collected and periodically removed. Even in the best of times, however, the stored waters, while usable, were not very pleasant.

In Jer. 2:13 the prophet makes a contrast between the true God and the false gods of Canaan. He describes Israel's God as fresh, sweet water from a living or moving spring that could give life to all. The Israelites are charged with ignoring this refreshing source and turning instead to water from a cistern.

The irony of Jeremiah's prophecy is even greater. The cisterns from which the Israelites were seeking satisfaction were broken cisterns that really could not collect water. Jeremiah's contrast would be understood by those who daily sought drinking water from cisterns. God is a living sustaining water source that satisfies, while the false gods of Canaan are like broken, unusable cisterns that promise refreshment but leave those who try to drink there thirsty and without hope.

---

15 The young lions roared at him, *and* growled;
They made his land waste;
His cities are burned, without inhabitant.

16 Also the people of Noph[a] and Tahpanhes
Have broken the crown of your head.

17 Have you not brought this on yourself,
In that you have forsaken the LORD your God
When He led you in the way?

18 And now why take the road to Egypt,
To drink the waters of Sihor?
Or why take the road to Assyria,
To drink the waters of the River?[a]

19 Your own wickedness will correct you,
And your backslidings will rebuke you.

Know therefore and see that *it is* an evil and bitter *thing*
That you have forsaken the LORD your God,
And the fear of Me *is* not in you,"
Says the Lord GOD of hosts.

20 "For of old I have broken your yoke *and* burst your bonds;
And you said, 'I will not transgress,'
When on every high hill and under every green tree
You lay down, playing the harlot.

21 Yet I had planted you a noble vine, a seed of highest quality.
How then have you turned before Me
Into the degenerate plant of an alien vine?

22 For though you wash yourself with lye, and use much soap,
Yet your iniquity is marked before Me," says the Lord GOD.

2:16 ᵃThat is, Memphis in ancient Egypt
2:18 ᵃThat is, the Euphrates

SCIENCE AND TECHNOLOGY

Lye and soap are both alkaline. In practice this means that they can remove grease and oil from clothing, something that water alone will not do (Jer. 2:22). Naturally occurring soda is also alkaline and was used in the ancient world as well. The difficulty of washing clothes in ancient times is apparent from the way the whiteness of clean clothes is used as a metaphor in the Bible.

AVOIDING UNGODLY ALLIANCES (Jer. 2:18)

In the years between 627 and 605 B.C. many important events occurred in Judah. For instance, King Josiah undertook his reforms to centralize all worship of Yahweh at the Jerusalem temple and outlawed all idolatrous worship (2 Kin. 23:1–25). On the international scene, major changes were under way as well.

For over a century, the great Assyrian Empire had reigned supreme throughout the ancient Near East. At the beginning of the 7th century B.C., the Assyrian king Sennacherib had conquered all of Judah, except for Jerusalem, which miraculously withstood his siege (2 Kin. 18:13—19:37). By the late 7th century, however, Assyria's influence had begun to wane. King Josiah took advantage of Assyria's loss of power to exert Judah's independence.

The Babylonians quickly arose to contest the Assyrians for control of Mesopotamia. In an attempt to hold on to power and stop the Babylonians, Assyria entered an alliance with a more distant power—Egypt. They hoped this alliance with the pharaohs of the 26th Dynasty (664–525 B.C.) would change the balance of power back into their favor.

While all these events happened far from Judah, no doubt Assyrian, and possibly also Egyptian, diplomats lobbied in Jerusalem for the Judahites to join with them. The Egyptian pharaoh Psammetichus II even visited Judah in 591 B.C. The offer to join forces with the two oldest and most powerful, prestigious states in that century would have looked very tempting. Surely this was the path to security and prosperity for the kingdom of Judah!

Jeremiah did not think so. The "road to Egypt" and the "road to Assyria" were dead ends. Help would not come from the part of the Nile River known as Sihor (or Shihor, Is. 23:3), nor from Assyria's Euphrates River (Jer. 2:18). Political alliances were not the way to security, but rather faithfulness to Yahweh and Yahweh alone. Rather than entering an alliance with the Assyrians and the Egyptians, Jeremiah counseled Judah to maintain the independence achieved during the reign of King Josiah (640–609 B.C.).

---

23 "How can you say, 'I am not polluted,
I have not gone after the Baals'?
See your way in the valley;
Know what you have done:
You are a swift dromedary breaking
   loose in her ways,
24 A wild donkey used to the wilderness,
That sniffs at the wind in her desire;
In her time of mating, who can turn
   her away?
All those who seek her will not weary
   themselves;
In her month they will find her.
25 Withhold your foot from being unshod,
   and your throat from thirst.
But you said, 'There is no hope.
No! For I have loved aliens, and after
   them I will go.'

26 "As the thief is ashamed when he is
   found out,
So is the house of Israel ashamed;
They and their kings and their
   princes, and their priests and their
   prophets,
27 Saying to a tree, 'You *are* my father,'
And to a stone, 'You gave birth to me.'

For they have turned *their* back to
   Me, and not *their* face.
But in the time of their trouble
They will say, 'Arise and save us.'
28 But where *are* your gods that you
   have made for yourselves?
Let them arise,
If they can save you in the time of
   your trouble;
For *according to* the number of your
   cities
Are your gods, O Judah.

29 "Why will you plead with Me?
You all have transgressed against
   Me," says the LORD.
30 "In vain I have chastened your
   children;
They received no correction.
Your sword has devoured your
   prophets
Like a destroying lion.

31 "O generation, see the word of the
   LORD!
Have I been a wilderness to Israel,
Or a land of darkness?

Why do My people say, 'We are lords;
We will come no more to You'?
32 Can a virgin forget her ornaments,
Or a bride her attire?
Yet My people have forgotten Me days
without number.

33 "Why do you beautify your way to seek
love?
Therefore you have also taught
The wicked women your ways.
34 Also on your skirts is found
The blood of the lives of the poor
innocents.
I have not found it by secret search,
But plainly on all these things.
35 Yet you say, 'Because I am innocent,
Surely His anger shall turn from me.'
Behold, I will plead My case against
you,
Because you say, 'I have not sinned.'
36 Why do you gad about so much to
change your way?
Also you shall be ashamed of Egypt as
you were ashamed of Assyria.
37 Indeed you will go forth from him
With your hands on your head;
For the LORD has rejected your
trusted allies,
And you will not prosper by them.

Israel Is Shameless

3 1 "They say, 'If a man divorces his wife,
And she goes from him
And becomes another man's,
May he return to her again?'
Would not that land be greatly
polluted?
But you have played the harlot with
many lovers;
Yet return to Me," says the LORD.

2 "Lift up your eyes to the desolate
heights and see:
Where have you not lain *with men?*
By the road you have sat for them
Like an Arabian in the wilderness;
And you have polluted the land
With your harlotries and your
wickedness.
3 Therefore the showers have been
withheld,
And there has been no latter rain.
You have had a harlot's forehead;
You refuse to be ashamed.
4 Will you not from this time cry to Me,
'My Father, You *are* the guide of my
youth?

5 Will He remain angry forever?
Will He keep it to the end?'
Behold, you have spoken and done evil
things,
As you were able."

A Call to Repentance

6 The LORD said also to me in the days of Josiah the king: "Have you seen what backsliding Israel has done? She has gone up on every high mountain and under every green tree, and there played the harlot. 7 And I said, after she had done all these *things,* 'Return to Me.' But she did not return. And her treacherous sister Judah saw it. 8 Then I saw that for all the causes for which backsliding Israel had committed adultery, I had put her away and given her a certificate of divorce; yet her treacherous sister Judah did not fear, but went and played the harlot also. 9 So it came to pass, through her casual harlotry, that she defiled the land and committed adultery with stones and trees. 10 And yet for all this her treacherous sister Judah has not turned to Me with her whole heart, but in pretense," says the LORD.

11 Then the LORD said to me, "Backsliding Israel has shown herself more righteous than treacherous Judah. 12 Go and proclaim these words toward the north, and say:

'Return, backsliding Israel,' says the
LORD;
'I will not cause My anger to fall on
you.
For I *am* merciful,' says the LORD;
'I will not remain angry forever.
13 Only acknowledge your iniquity,
That you have transgressed against
the LORD your God,
And have scattered your charms
To alien deities under every green
tree,
And you have not obeyed My voice,'
says the LORD.

14 "Return, O backsliding children," says the LORD; "for I am married to you. I will take you, one from a city and two from a family, and I will bring you to Zion. 15 And I will give you shepherds according to My heart, who will feed you with knowledge and understanding.

16 "Then it shall come to pass, when you are multiplied and increased in the land in those days," says the LORD, "that they will

JEREMIAH IN THE DAYS OF KING JOSIAH (Jer. 3:6)

Jeremiah received messages from Yahweh "in the days of Josiah the king" (Jer. 3:6). His prophetic call is dated specifically in Josiah's 13th year, which was 627 B.C. (Jer. 1:1, 2). The peace and prosperity of Josiah's kingship is thus the setting for the early years of Jeremiah's ministry.

Josiah, who reigned from 640 to 609 B.C., was the last major king of the Davidic dynasty in Judah. He is given high marks by the historian of Kings (2 Kin. 23:25), equaled only by Josiah's great-grandfather Hezekiah (2 Kin. 18:5) and by David himself. It was in 622 B.C., Josiah's 18th year, that the Book of the Law, apparently including at least a portion of the Book of Deuteronomy, was discovered.

Some of the most significant achievements of King Josiah were in the area of religious reform. In 632 B.C. he began to seek the God of his ancestors, and in 628 B.C. he initiated his earliest reforms (2 Chr. 34:3). The crucial year, however, was 622. A project to repair the temple resulted in the discovery of the law book, which in turn provided a new momentum for the reformation already in progress.

These reform efforts seem to have coincided with a civil war in Assyria. The Neo-Assyrian Empire was in decline, and the reforms may have been an expression of Judah's independence from Assyrian rule. Josiah removed all pagan elements from the temple, again an act that could have been interpreted as a claim of autonomy from Assyria. Though the king may have had some political motives, the main impetus for reform was religious—a desire to seek Yahweh and adhere to His law (2 Kin. 23:3). In the days of such a king, Yahweh called and spoke to Jeremiah.

---

say no more, 'The ark of the covenant of the LORD.' It shall not come to mind, nor shall they remember it, nor shall they visit *it,* nor shall it be made anymore.

17"At that time Jerusalem shall be called The Throne of the LORD, and all the nations shall be gathered to it, to the name of the LORD, to Jerusalem. No more shall they follow the dictates of their evil hearts.

18"In those days the house of Judah shall walk with the house of Israel, and they shall come together out of the land of the north to the land that I have given as an inheritance to your fathers.

19"But I said:

'How can I put you among the children
And give you a pleasant land,
A beautiful heritage of the hosts of
    nations?'

"And I said:

'You shall call Me, "My Father,"
And not turn away from Me.'
20 Surely, *as* a wife treacherously departs
    from her husband,
So have you dealt treacherously with
    Me,
O house of Israel," says the LORD.

21 A voice was heard on the desolate
    heights,
Weeping *and* supplications of the
    children of Israel.
For they have perverted their way;
They have forgotten the LORD their
    God.

22 "Return, you backsliding children,
And I will heal your backslidings."

"Indeed we do come to You,
For You are the LORD our God.
23 Truly, in vain *is salvation hoped for*
    from the hills,
And from the multitude of
    mountains;
Truly, in the LORD our God
Is the salvation of Israel.
24 For shame has devoured
The labor of our fathers from our
    youth—
Their flocks and their herds,
Their sons and their daughters.
25 We lie down in our shame,
And our reproach covers us.
For we have sinned against the LORD
    our God,
We and our fathers,
From our youth even to this day,

And have not obeyed the voice of the
LORD our God."

4 ¹"If you will return, O Israel," says
the LORD,
"Return to Me;
And if you will put away your
abominations out of My sight,
Then you shall not be moved.
² And you shall swear, 'The LORD lives,'
In truth, in judgment, and in
righteousness;
The nations shall bless themselves in
Him,
And in Him they shall glory."

³For thus says the LORD to the men of
Judah and Jerusalem:

"Break up your fallow ground,
And do not sow among thorns.
⁴ Circumcise yourselves to the LORD,
And take away the foreskins of your
hearts,
You men of Judah and inhabitants of
Jerusalem,
Lest My fury come forth like fire,
And burn so that no one can quench
it,
Because of the evil of your doings."

An Imminent Invasion

⁵Declare in Judah and proclaim in Jerusalem, and say:

"Blow the trumpet in the land;
Cry, 'Gather together,'
And say, 'Assemble yourselves,
And let us go into the fortified cities.'
⁶ Set up the standard toward Zion.
Take refuge! Do not delay!
For I will bring disaster from the
north,
And great destruction."

⁷ The lion has come up from his thicket,
And the destroyer of nations is on his
way.
He has gone forth from his place
To make your land desolate.
Your cities will be laid waste,
Without inhabitant.
⁸ For this, clothe yourself with
sackcloth,
Lament and wail.
For the fierce anger of the LORD
Has not turned back from us.

⁹ "And it shall come to pass in that day,"
says the LORD,
"*That* the heart of the king shall
perish,
And the heart of the princes;
The priests shall be astonished,
And the prophets shall wonder."

¹⁰ Then I said, "Ah, Lord GOD!
Surely You have greatly deceived this
people and Jerusalem,
Saying, 'You shall have peace,'
Whereas the sword reaches to the
heart."

¹¹ At that time it will be said
To this people and to Jerusalem,
"A dry wind of the desolate heights
blows in the wilderness
Toward the daughter of My people—
Not to fan or to cleanse—
¹² A wind too strong for these will come
for Me;
Now I will also speak judgment
against them."

¹³ "Behold, he shall come up like clouds,
And his chariots like a whirlwind.
His horses are swifter than eagles.
Woe to us, for we are plundered!"

¹⁴ O Jerusalem, wash your heart from
wickedness,
That you may be saved.
How long shall your evil thoughts
lodge within you?
¹⁵ For a voice declares from Dan
And proclaims affliction from Mount
Ephraim:
¹⁶ "Make mention to the nations,
Yes, proclaim against Jerusalem,
That watchers come from a far
country
And raise their voice against the cities
of Judah.
¹⁷ Like keepers of a field they are
against her all around,
Because she has been rebellious
against Me," says the LORD.
¹⁸ "Your ways and your doings
Have procured these *things* for you.
This *is* your wickedness,
Because it is bitter,
Because it reaches to your heart."

Sorrow for the Doomed Nation

¹⁹ O my soul, my soul!
I am pained in my very heart!

My heart makes a noise in me;
I cannot hold my peace,
Because you have heard, O my soul,
The sound of the trumpet,
The alarm of war.
20 Destruction upon destruction is cried,
For the whole land is plundered.
Suddenly my tents are plundered,
And my curtains in a moment.
21 How long will I see the standard,
And hear the sound of the trumpet?

22 "For My people *are* foolish,
They have not known Me.
They *are* silly children,
And they have no understanding.
They *are* wise to do evil,
But to do good they have no
knowledge."

23 I beheld the earth, and indeed *it was*
without form, and void;
And the heavens, they *had* no light.
24 I beheld the mountains, and indeed
they trembled,
And all the hills moved back and
forth.
25 I beheld, and indeed *there was* no
man,
And all the birds of the heavens had
fled.
26 I beheld, and indeed the fruitful land
was a wilderness,
And all its cities were broken down
At the presence of the LORD,
By His fierce anger.

27For thus says the LORD:

"The whole land shall be desolate;
Yet I will not make a full end.
28 For this shall the earth mourn,
And the heavens above be black,
Because I have spoken.
I have purposed and will not relent,
Nor will I turn back from it.
29 The whole city shall flee from the
noise of the horsemen and bowmen.
They shall go into thickets and climb
up on the rocks.
Every city *shall be* forsaken,
And not a man shall dwell in it.

30 "And *when* you *are* plundered,
What will you do?
Though you clothe yourself with
crimson,

Though you adorn *yourself* with
ornaments of gold,
Though you enlarge your eyes with
paint,
In vain you will make yourself fair;
Your lovers will despise you;
They will seek your life.

31 "For I have heard a voice as of a
woman in labor,
The anguish as of her who brings
forth her first child,
The voice of the daughter of Zion
bewailing herself;
She spreads her hands, *saying,*
'Woe *is* me now, for my soul is weary
Because of murderers!'

The Justice of God's Judgment

5 1 "Run to and fro through the streets
of Jerusalem;
See now and know;
And seek in her open places
If you can find a man,
If there is *anyone* who executes
judgment,
Who seeks the truth,
And I will pardon her.
2 Though they say, 'As the LORD lives,'
Surely they swear falsely."

3 O LORD, *are* not Your eyes on the
truth?
You have stricken them,
But they have not grieved;
You have consumed them,
But they have refused to receive
correction.
They have made their faces harder
than rock;
They have refused to return.

4 Therefore I said, "Surely these *are*
poor.
They are foolish;
For they do not know the way of the
LORD,
The judgment of their God.
5 I will go to the great men and speak
to them,
For they have known the way of the
LORD,
The judgment of their God."

But these have altogether broken the
yoke
And burst the bonds.

6 Therefore a lion from the forest shall
slay them,
A wolf of the deserts shall destroy
them;
A leopard will watch over their cities.
Everyone who goes out from there
shall be torn in pieces,
Because their transgressions are
many;
Their backslidings have increased.

7 "How shall I pardon you for this?
Your children have forsaken Me
And sworn by *those that are* not gods.
When I had fed them to the full,
Then they committed adultery
And assembled themselves by troops
in the harlots' houses.
8 They were *like* well-fed lusty stallions;
Every one neighed after his neighbor's
wife.
9 Shall I not punish *them* for these
things?" says the LORD.
"And shall I not avenge Myself on such
a nation as this?

10 "Go up on her walls and destroy,
But do not make a complete end.
Take away her branches,
For they *are* not the LORD's.
11 For the house of Israel and the house
of Judah
Have dealt very treacherously with
Me," says the LORD.

12 They have lied about the LORD,
And said, "*It is* not He.
Neither will evil come upon us,
Nor shall we see sword or famine.
13 And the prophets become wind,
For the word *is* not in them.
Thus shall it be done to them."

14Therefore thus says the LORD God of
hosts:

"Because you speak this word,
Behold, I will make My words in your
mouth fire,

And this people wood,
And it shall devour them.
15 Behold, I will bring a nation against
you from afar,
O house of Israel," says the LORD.
"It *is* a mighty nation,
It *is* an ancient nation,
A nation whose language you do not
know,
Nor can you understand what they
say.
16 Their quiver *is* like an open tomb;
They *are* all mighty men.
17 And they shall eat up your harvest
and your bread,
Which your sons and daughters
should eat.
They shall eat up your flocks and your
herds;
They shall eat up your vines and your
fig trees;
They shall destroy your fortified cities,
In which you trust, with the sword.

18"Nevertheless in those days," says
the LORD, "I will not make a complete end
of you. 19And it will be when you say, 'Why
does the LORD our God do all these *things*
to us?' then you shall answer them, 'Just as
you have forsaken Me and served foreign
gods in your land, so you shall serve aliens
in a land *that is* not yours.'

20 "Declare this in the house of Jacob
And proclaim it in Judah, saying,
21 'Hear this now, O foolish people,
Without understanding,
Who have eyes and see not,
And who have ears and hear not:
22 Do you not fear Me?' says the LORD.
'Will you not tremble at My presence,
Who have placed the sand as the
bound of the sea,
By a perpetual decree, that it cannot
pass beyond it?
And though its waves toss to and fro,
Yet they cannot prevail;
Though they roar, yet they cannot
pass over it.

BELIEFS AND IDEAS

*One of the notable themes of the Bible is the doctrine of the "remnant," the part of the
people that God reserves (Jer. 5:18). Only what remained of the people after the
devastation of Jerusalem by the Babylonians in 586 B.C. was able to return 70 years
later. But it was foretold that there would be a remnant to return (Jer. 46:28).*

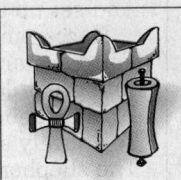

23 But this people has a defiant and
        rebellious heart;
    They have revolted and departed.
24 They do not say in their heart,
    "Let us now fear the LORD our God,
    Who gives rain, both the former and
        the latter, in its season.
    He reserves for us the appointed
        weeks of the harvest."
25 Your iniquities have turned these
        things away,
    And your sins have withheld good
        from you.

26 'For among My people are found
        wicked *men;*
    They lie in wait as one who sets
        snares;
    They set a trap;
    They catch men.
27 As a cage is full of birds,
    So their houses *are* full of deceit.
    Therefore they have become great and
        grown rich.
28 They have grown fat, they are sleek;
    Yes, they surpass the deeds of the
        wicked;
    They do not plead the cause,
    The cause of the fatherless;
    Yet they prosper,
    And the right of the needy they do not
        defend.
29 Shall I not punish *them* for these
        things?' says the LORD.
    'Shall I not avenge Myself on such a
        nation as this?'

30 "An astonishing and horrible thing
    Has been committed in the land:
31 The prophets prophesy falsely,
    And the priests rule by their *own*
        power;
    And My people love *to have it* so.
    But what will you do in the end?

Impending Destruction from the North

6 1 "O you children of Benjamin,
        Gather yourselves to flee from the
        midst of Jerusalem!
    Blow the trumpet in Tekoa,
    And set up a signal-fire in Beth
        Haccerem;
    For disaster appears out of the north,
    And great destruction.
2 I have likened the daughter of Zion
    To a lovely and delicate woman.
3 The shepherds with their flocks shall
        come to her.

    They shall pitch *their* tents against
        her all around.
    Each one shall pasture in his own
        place."

4 "Prepare war against her;
    Arise, and let us go up at noon.
    Woe to us, for the day goes away,
    For the shadows of the evening are
        lengthening.
5 Arise, and let us go by night,
    And let us destroy her palaces."

6 For thus has the LORD of hosts said:

    "Cut down trees,
    And build a mound against
        Jerusalem.
    This *is* the city to be punished.
    She *is* full of oppression in her midst.
7 As a fountain wells up with water,
    So she wells up with her wickedness.
    Violence and plundering are heard in
        her.
    Before Me continually *are* grief and
        wounds.
8 Be instructed, O Jerusalem,
    Lest My soul depart from you;
    Lest I make you desolate,
    A land not inhabited."

9 Thus says the LORD of hosts:

    "They shall thoroughly glean as a vine
        the remnant of Israel;
    As a grape-gatherer, put your hand
        back into the branches."

10 To whom shall I speak and give
        warning,
    That they may hear?
    Indeed their ear *is* uncircumcised,
    And they cannot give heed.
    Behold, the word of the LORD is a
        reproach to them;
    They have no delight in it.
11 Therefore I am full of the fury of the
        LORD.
    I am weary of holding *it* in.
    "I will pour it out on the children
        outside,
    And on the assembly of young men
        together;
    For even the husband shall be taken
        with the wife,
    The aged with *him who is* full of days.
12 And their houses shall be turned over
        to others,

SIGNAL-FIRES IN BETH HACCEREM (Jer. 6:1)

In the 1930s archaeologists discovered a group of ostraca in the ruins of the outer gate at the site of Lachish, the ancient Judahite city. All the evidence suggests that these ostraca (broken pieces of pottery used to write on) were written in the last days of the kingdom of Judah before the Babylonian king Nebuchadnezzar utterly destroyed Jerusalem in 586 B.C. The ostraca are now known as the Lachish Letters.

The letters address a man named "Yaosh." Yaosh, always called "my lord" in the letters, probably commanded Lachish's defenses and participated in the frantic diplomatic and military attempts to stave off the Babylonian invasion. Letter IV has a particularly harrowing tone as it ends: "and let (my lord) know that we are watching for the signals of Lachish, according to all the indications which my lord has given, for we cannot see Azekah." The "signals of Lachish" were a fire lit on top of a high point or tower, as part of the national defense system—early technology to warn of an impending attack.

The only thing worse than the lighting of a signal was seeing it no more. That could mean only one thing: the enemy was approaching. Having lost sight of the signal-fire in Azekah, those in Jerusalem strained in hope to see the signal-fire of Lachish. Maybe the Babylonians would be stopped there! Judging by the destruction at Lachish, however, such a hope was in vain.

The Lachish Letters therefore provide a chilling background for Jeremiah's warning: "set up a signal-fire in Beth Haccerem" (Jer. 6:1). Scholars have recently suggested that Beth Haccerem was a site about 3 miles southwest of Jerusalem, almost exactly halfway between Jerusalem and Bethlehem. It thus represented the last stop before the invading Babylonian army reached Jerusalem. Jeremiah's point is clear: destruction of Jerusalem had drawn very near. God's judgment was about to ring forth.

Fields and wives together;
For I will stretch out My hand
Against the inhabitants of the land,"
  says the LORD.
13 "Because from the least of them even
    to the greatest of them,
  Everyone *is* given to covetousness;
  And from the prophet even to the
    priest,
  Everyone deals falsely.
14 They have also healed the hurt of My
    people slightly,
  Saying, 'Peace, peace!'
  When *there is* no peace.
15 Were they ashamed when they had
    committed abomination?
  No! They were not at all ashamed;
  Nor did they know how to blush.

Therefore they shall fall among those
  who fall;
At the time I punish them,
They shall be cast down," says the
  LORD.

16 Thus says the LORD:

"Stand in the ways and see,
And ask for the old paths, where the
  good way *is*,
And walk in it;
Then you will find rest for your souls.
But they said, 'We will not walk *in it.*'
17 Also, I set watchmen over you, *saying*,
'Listen to the sound of the trumpet!'
But they said, 'We will not listen.'

SCIENCE AND TECHNOLOGY

Silver commonly occurs in nature mixed with lead (Jer. 6:29). The two metals are separated by a process called cupellation, in which the ore is heated in a ceramic vessel over a flame blown by a bellows. The process is repeated to increase the purity of the silver. With practice the technique can achieve a high degree of purity with silver, as well as recover the lead for its uses.

18 Therefore hear, you nations,
And know, O congregation, what *is*
among them.
19 Hear, O earth!
Behold, I will certainly bring calamity
on this people—
The fruit of their thoughts,
Because they have not heeded My
words
Nor My law, but rejected it.
20 For what purpose to Me
Comes frankincense from Sheba,
And sweet cane from a far country?
Your burnt offerings *are* not
acceptable,
Nor your sacrifices sweet to Me."

21Therefore thus says the LORD:

"Behold, I will lay stumbling blocks
before this people,
And the fathers and the sons together
shall fall on them.
The neighbor and his friend shall
perish."

22Thus says the LORD:

"Behold, a people comes from the north
country,
And a great nation will be raised from
the farthest parts of the earth.
23 They will lay hold on bow and spear;
They *are* cruel and have no mercy;
Their voice roars like the sea;
And they ride on horses,
As men of war set in array against
you, O daughter of Zion."

24 We have heard the report of it;
Our hands grow feeble.
Anguish has taken hold of us,
Pain as of a woman in labor.
25 Do not go out into the field,
Nor walk by the way.
Because of the sword of the enemy,
Fear *is* on every side.
26 O daughter of my people,
Dress in sackcloth
And roll about in ashes!
Make mourning *as for* an only son,
most bitter lamentation;
For the plunderer will suddenly come
upon us.

27 "I have set you *as* an assayer *and* a
fortress among My people,
That you may know and test their
way.

28 They *are* all stubborn rebels, walking
as slanderers.
They are bronze and iron,
They *are* all corrupters;
29 The bellows blow fiercely,
The lead is consumed by the fire;
The smelter refines in vain,
For the wicked are not drawn off.
30 *People* will call them rejected silver,
Because the LORD has rejected them."

The Book of Nahum

In 612 B.C. the rebel alliance of the Babylonians and the Medes, under the leadership of the Babylonian king Nabopolassar (626–605 B.C.), drove the Assyrians out of their own capital, Nineveh. The Assyrians were not entirely defeated, and they were able to regroup in the northwest, at the ancient city of Haran. Nevertheless, Nineveh, once a symbol of Assyrian splendor, was gone. The nations that had once been so terrorized by Assyria could only be delighted.

Nothing is known of the prophet named Nahum, nor of the exact time of his prophecy. It is clear, however, that the book speaks of the events of 612 B.C., when the Medes and Babylonians drove the Assyrians out of Nineveh. Nahum's glee at Nineveh's downfall can sound vindictive to modern ears, but it is understandable. Assyria's reputation for brutality and torture was well established; Nineveh was referred to as "the bloody city" [Nah. 3:1]. More than one person had wondered how such cruelty could go unpunished, including the prophet Habakkuk (see "The Book of Habakkuk" at Hab. 1:1]. Nahum's delight comes primarily from seeing that the Lord does punish the wicked after all [see Nah. 1:2, 3].

Nahum's mention of "No Amon" [3:8] refers to Thebes, the Egyptian capital which Assyria herself had sacked in 664 B.C. Nahum recalls that Assyrian victory as a warning that Assyria also must face judgment, and would fall as had her victims.

■ Nahum 1:1—3:19

Nahum

1 :1 The burden[a] against Nineveh. The book of the vision of Nahum the Elkoshite.

1:1 [a]Or *oracle*

ASSYRIA'S CAPITAL IS DESTROYED (Nah. 1:1)

Nineveh was the chief city of the Assyrian Empire in the last century of the empire's power (c. 705–612 B.C.). It is this 7th-century Nineveh that is known from accounts in the books of Nahum and Jonah. Yet the city had a very long history, and there are substantial archaeological material remains of Nineveh from the New Stone Age (c. 5000–4000 B.C.).

The city is not mentioned in written records until the mid-3rd millennium B.C. when it was under control of the Accadian kings. It is named again briefly during the reign of Shamshi-Adad I (1813–1781 B.C.), who ruled the city-state of Asshur and most of northern Mesopotamia. Though it is listed in Gen. 10:11 along with Calah, there is no evidence of Nineveh being politically linked with other Assyrian cities until later in time.

Nineveh was incorporated into Assyria during the reign of Ashur-uballit I (1363–1328 B.C.). The city thus played a prominent role in the Middle Assyrian Empire after 1273 B.C., and Assyrian kings spent much time in building activity there.

The Nineveh against which Nahum prophesies was more than just a major city. The Assyrian king Sennacherib (705–681 B.C.) decided to make Nineveh the capital of Assyria, and it was then transformed into the capital of a world state. Like the Babylonian king Nebuchadnezzar II a century later, Sennacherib spent a great deal of time in monumental building projects at the site.

Despite being protected by an enormous city wall, Nineveh was captured and destroyed by an alliance of Medes and Chaldeans in 612 B.C. The fall of this great city, which is recorded in the Babylonian Chronicle and described in Nahum's prophecy (Nah. 2:3–13), effectively ended the Assyrian Empire.

God's Wrath on His Enemies

2   God *is* jealous, and the LORD avenges;
The LORD avenges and *is* furious.
The LORD will take vengeance on His adversaries,
And He reserves *wrath* for His enemies;

3   The LORD *is* slow to anger and great in power,
And will not at all acquit *the wicked.*

The LORD has His way
In the whirlwind and in the storm,
And the clouds *are* the dust of His feet.

4   He rebukes the sea and makes it dry,
And dries up all the rivers.
Bashan and Carmel wither,
And the flower of Lebanon wilts.

5   The mountains quake before Him,
The hills melt,
And the earth heaves[a] at His presence,
Yes, the world and all who dwell in it.

6   Who can stand before His indignation?
And who can endure the fierceness of His anger?

His fury is poured out like fire,
And the rocks are thrown down by Him.

7   The LORD *is* good,
A stronghold in the day of trouble;
And He knows those who trust in Him.

8   But with an overflowing flood
He will make an utter end of its place,
And darkness will pursue His enemies.

9   What do you conspire against the LORD?
He will make an utter end *of it.*
Affliction will not rise up a second time.

10   For while tangled *like* thorns,
And while drunken *like* drunkards,
They shall be devoured like stubble fully dried.

11   From you comes forth *one*
Who plots evil against the LORD,
A wicked counselor.

12Thus says the LORD:

"Though *they are* safe, and likewise many,

1:5 ^aTargum reads *burns.*

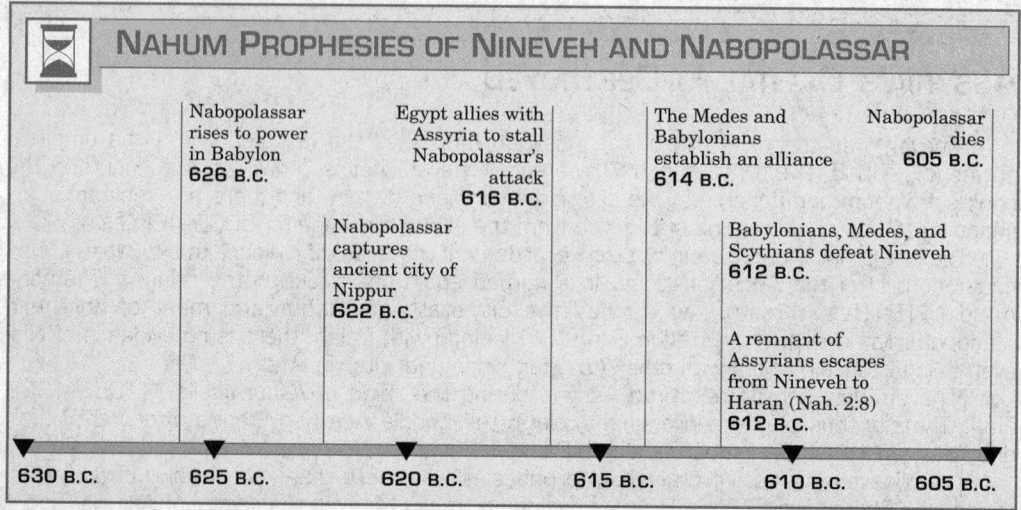

NAHUM PROPHESIES OF NINEVEH AND NABOPOLASSAR

Nabopolassar rises to power in Babylon **626 B.C.**	Egypt allies with Assyria to stall Nabopolassar's attack **616 B.C.**	The Medes and Babylonians establish an alliance **614 B.C.**	Nabopolassar dies **605 B.C.**
	Nabopolassar captures ancient city of Nippur **622 B.C.**	Babylonians, Medes, and Scythians defeat Nineveh **612 B.C.**	
		A remnant of Assyrians escapes from Nineveh to Haran (Nah. 2:8) **612 B.C.**	

630 B.C.   625 B.C.   620 B.C.   615 B.C.   610 B.C.   605 B.C.

Yet in this manner they will be cut down
When he passes through.
Though I have afflicted you,
I will afflict you no more;
13 For now I will break off his yoke from you,
And burst your bonds apart."

14 The LORD has given a command concerning you:
"Your name shall be perpetuated no longer.
Out of the house of your gods
I will cut off the carved image and the molded image.
I will dig your grave,
For you are vile."

15 Behold, on the mountains
The feet of him who brings good tidings,
Who proclaims peace!
O Judah, keep your appointed feasts,
Perform your vows.
For the wicked one shall no more pass through you;
He is utterly cut off.

The Destruction of Nineveh

2 1 He who scatters[a] has come up before your face.
Man the fort!
Watch the road!
Strengthen your flanks!
Fortify your power mightily.

2 For the LORD will restore the excellence of Jacob
Like the excellence of Israel,
For the emptiers have emptied them out
And ruined their vine branches.

3 The shields of his mighty men are made red,
The valiant men are in scarlet.
The chariots come with flaming torches
In the day of his preparation,
And the spears are brandished.[a]
4 The chariots rage in the streets,
They jostle one another in the broad roads;
They seem like torches,
They run like lightning.

5 He remembers his nobles;
They stumble in their walk;
They make haste to her walls,
And the defense is prepared.
6 The gates of the rivers are opened,
And the palace is dissolved.
7 It is decreed:[a]
She shall be led away captive,
She shall be brought up;
And her maidservants shall lead her as with the voice of doves,
Beating their breasts.

2:1 [a]Vulgate reads *he who destroys.*
2:3 [a]Literally *the cypresses are shaken;* Septuagint and Syriac read *the horses rush about;* Vulgate reads *the drivers are stupefied.*   2:7 [a]Hebrew *Huzzab*

8 Though Nineveh of old *was* like a pool
    of water,
  Now they flee away.
  "Halt! Halt!" *they cry;*
  But no one turns back.
9 Take spoil of silver!
  Take spoil of gold!
  There is no end of treasure,
  Or wealth of every desirable prize.
10 She is empty, desolate, and waste!
  The heart melts, and the knees shake;
  Much pain *is* in every side,
  And all their faces are drained of
    color.[a]

11 Where *is* the dwelling of the lions,
  And the feeding place of the young
    lions,
  Where the lion walked, the lioness
    and lion's cub,
  And no one made *them* afraid?
12 The lion tore in pieces enough for his
    cubs,
  Killed for his lionesses,
  Filled his caves with prey,
  And his dens with flesh.

13 "Behold, I *am* against you," says the
LORD of hosts, "I will burn your[a] chariots in
smoke, and the sword shall devour your
young lions; I will cut off your prey from
the earth, and the voice of your messengers
shall be heard no more."

The Woe of Nineveh

3 1 Woe to the bloody city!
    It *is* all full of lies *and* robbery.
    Its victim never departs.
2 The noise of a whip
  And the noise of rattling wheels,
  Of galloping horses,
  Of clattering chariots!
3 Horsemen charge with bright sword
    and glittering spear.
  There is a multitude of slain,

  A great number of bodies,
  Countless corpses—
  They stumble over the corpses—
4 Because of the multitude of harlotries
    of the seductive harlot,
  The mistress of sorceries,
  Who sells nations through her
    harlotries,
  And families through her sorceries.

5 "Behold, I *am* against you," says the
    LORD of hosts;
  "I will lift your skirts over your face,
  I will show the nations your
    nakedness,
  And the kingdoms your shame.
6 I will cast abominable filth upon you,
  Make you vile,
  And make you a spectacle.
7 It shall come to pass *that* all who look
    upon you
  Will flee from you, and say,
  'Nineveh is laid waste!
  Who will bemoan her?'
  Where shall I seek comforters for
    you?"

8 Are you better than No Amon[a]
  That was situated by the River,[b]
  That had the waters around her,
  Whose rampart *was* the sea,
  Whose wall *was* the sea?
9 Ethiopia and Egypt *were* her strength,
  And *it was* boundless;
  Put and Lubim were your[a] helpers.
10 Yet she *was* carried away,
  She went into captivity;
  Her young children also were dashed
    to pieces
  At the head of every street;
  They cast lots for her honorable men,
  And all her great men were bound in
    chains.
11 You also will be drunk;
  You will be hidden;
  You also will seek refuge from the
    enemy.

12 All your strongholds *are* fig trees with
    ripened figs:

2:10 [a]Compare Joel 2:6   2:13 [a]Literally *her*
3:8 [a]That is, ancient Thebes; Targum and Vulgate
read *populous Alexandria.*   [b]Literally *rivers,* that is, the
Nile and the surrounding canals   3:9 [a]Septuagint
reads *her.*

ARTS AND LITERATURE

*The public art of the Assyrians depicted the humiliation, mutilation, and death of
prisoners of war. In the 9th century B.C. an Assyrian king boasted of his unrestrained
cruelty to his enemies, recording his exploits by writing them in stone at the door of a
temple. Ironically, Nahum's prophecy describes the fall of Assyria's capital, Nineveh (Nah.
3:3). It was conquered in 612 B.C. by the Babylonians and the Medes.*

If they are shaken,
They fall into the mouth of the eater.
13 Surely, your people in your midst *are*
women!
The gates of your land are wide open
for your enemies;
Fire shall devour the bars of your
gates.

14 Draw your water for the siege!
Fortify your strongholds!
Go into the clay and tread the
mortar!
Make strong the brick kiln!
15 There the fire will devour you,
The sword will cut you off;
It will eat you up like a locust.

Make yourself many—like the locust!
Make yourself many—like the
swarming locusts!
16 You have multiplied your merchants
more than the stars of heaven.
The locust plunders and flies away.
17 Your commanders *are* like *swarming*
locusts,
And your generals like great
grasshoppers,
Which camp in the hedges on a cold
day;
When the sun rises they flee away,
And the place where they *are* is not
known.

18 Your shepherds slumber, O king of
Assyria;

Your nobles rest *in the dust.*
Your people are scattered on the
mountains,
And no one gathers them.
19 Your injury *has* no healing,
Your wound is severe.
All who hear news of you
Will clap *their* hands over you,
For upon whom has not your
wickedness passed continually?

The Death of Josiah

Assyria, driven out of its capital, Nineveh, in 612 B.C., had established a capital-in-exile at Haran. In 610, the Assyrians were expelled even from there. In an attempt to recapture Haran, Assyria made an alliance with its former enemy Egypt. The Egyptian king, Necho II (610–595 B.C.) evidently feared the new strength of Babylon more than the aging power of Assyria, and he marched north through the land of Judah to join forces with Assyria in the assault of Haran.

On the way to Haran, Pharaoh Necho was met by Judah's King Josiah, who attacked the Egyptian army at Megiddo in 609 B.C. Exactly why Josiah did so is unclear. Perhaps he feared a resurgence of Egyptian power. Whatever the reason, Josiah and Judah paid for his attack. Josiah himself was killed, and Judah became an Egyptian vassal. Josiah's son Jehoahaz became the new king of Judah, but ruled only 3 months.

■ 2 Kings 23:28–34

**The Neo-Assyrian
Empire**

By 650 B.C. the Assyrian Empire, with its capital in Nineveh, stretched from the Persian Gulf in the east throughout the fertile crescent into Palestine and beyond, embracing for a short time all of Egypt in the southwest. Judah, while a free zone, still paid tribute to Assyria. The prophet Nahum mentions Assyria's victory over Thebes (or No Amon, Nah. 3:8). But Nahum also prophesies the destruction of Nineveh, Assyria's great capital (Nah. 3:18).

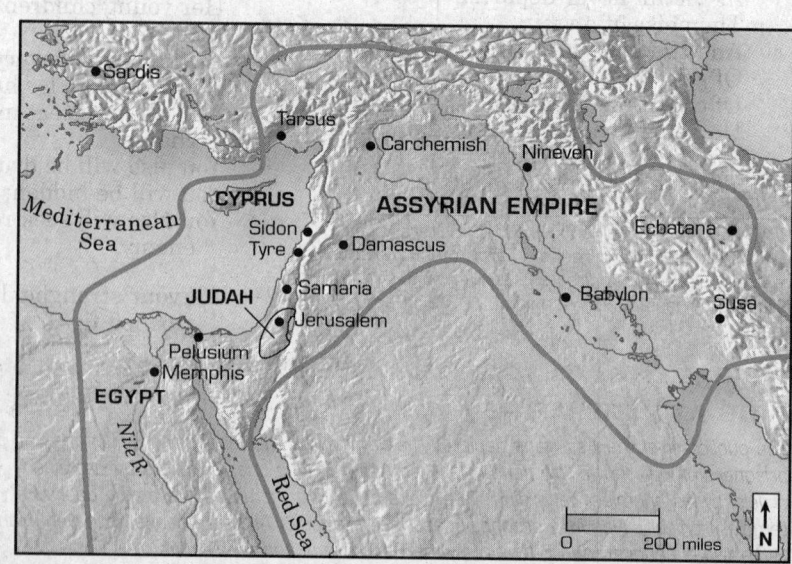

2 Kings
Josiah Dies in Battle

23 :28 Now the rest of the acts of Josiah, and all that he did, *are* they not written in the book of the chronicles of the kings of Judah? [29]In his days Pharaoh Necho king of Egypt went to the aid of the king of Assyria, to the River Euphrates; and King Josiah went against him. And *Pharaoh Necho* killed him at Megiddo when he confronted him. [30]Then his servants moved his body in a chariot from Megiddo, brought him to Jerusalem, and buried him in his own tomb. And the people of the land took Jehoahaz the son of Josiah, anointed him, and made him king in his father's place.

The Reign and Captivity of Jehoahaz

[31]Jehoahaz *was* twenty-three years old when he became king, and he reigned three months in Jerusalem. His mother's name *was* Hamutal the daughter of Jeremiah of Libnah. [32]And he did evil in the sight of the LORD, according to all that his fathers had done. [33]Now Pharaoh Necho put him in prison at Riblah in the land of Hamath, that he might not reign in Jerusalem; and he imposed on the land a tribute of one hundred talents of silver and a talent of gold. [34]Then Pharaoh Necho made Eliakim the son of Josiah king in place of his father Josiah, and changed his name to Jehoiakim. And *Pharaoh* took Jehoahaz and went to Egypt, and he[a] died there.

23:34 [a]That is, Jehoahaz   **Jer.** 22:11 [a]Also called *Jehoahaz*

---

weeping for the dead King Josiah, but rather to weep for Jehoahaz who was exiled to Egypt by Pharaoh Necho and would not return. Another reason to weep for Jehoahaz was the greed and rapacity of Jehoiakim who took his place (22:13–17).

■ Jeremiah 22:10–17

Jeremiah

22 :10   Weep not for the dead, nor
       bemoan him;
     Weep bitterly for him who goes away,
     For he shall return no more,
     Nor see his native country.

Message to the Son of Josiah

[11]For thus says the LORD concerning Shallum[a] the son of Josiah, king of Judah, who reigned instead of Josiah his father, who went from this place: "He shall not return here anymore, [12]but he shall die in the place where they have led him captive, and shall see this land no more.

13   "Woe to him who builds his house by
      unrighteousness
     And his chambers by injustice,
     Who uses his neighbor's service
      without wages
     And gives him nothing for his work,
14   Who says, 'I will build myself a wide
      house with spacious chambers,
     And cut out windows for it,
     Paneling *it* with cedar
     And painting *it* with vermilion.'

15   "Shall you reign because you enclose
      yourself in cedar?
     Did not your father eat and drink,
     And do justice and righteousness?
     Then *it was* well with him.

🧩 A Dirge for an Exiled King

Josiah's attack may have at least slowed the Egyptian armies under Necho. At any rate, the Assyrian-Egyptian alliance failed to recapture Haran. Assyria was driven further north, and Necho returned south. It was on this return trip that Necho asserted his new authority over Judah by removing the new king, Jehoahaz, from the throne and replacing him with his brother Eliakim.

In another demonstration of power, Necho changed Eliakim's name to the throne name "Jehoiakim." Similarly, Jehoahaz was an official throne name; Jehoahaz's personal name was Shallum (Jer. 22:11). The prophet's dirge (Jer. 22:10–12) instructs Judah not to continue

---

TIME CAPSULE   616 to 614 B.C.

616–594	*Babylonian Chronicle records campaigns of Nebuchadnezzar*
616	*Egypt sends help to Assyria to stop the Babylonian attack*
615	*Nabopolassar fails to conquer Nineveh and Asshur*
614	*Nabopolassar establishes peace treaty with Cyaxeres, king of the Medes*
614	*The Medes and Scythians capture city of Asshur*

JOSIAH PURSUES REFORM IN JUDAH

Judah (southern kingdom)
Josiah, son of Amon, ruled during 3 decades of peace and prosperity for Judah. The death of the great Assyrian king, Ashurbanipal, brought about a serious decline in Assyria's power and allowed Josiah freedom to pursue various reforms.

In 609 B.C. Josiah attempted to block Pharaoh Necho II of Egypt as he marched north to assist Assyria in a fight against Babylon. Possibly Necho's northern campaign appeared a threat to Judah. Nevertheless, in a battle against Necho at Megiddo, Josiah suffered serious injuries and eventually died.

Israel (northern kingdom)
Fell to the Assyrian Empire in 722 B.C.

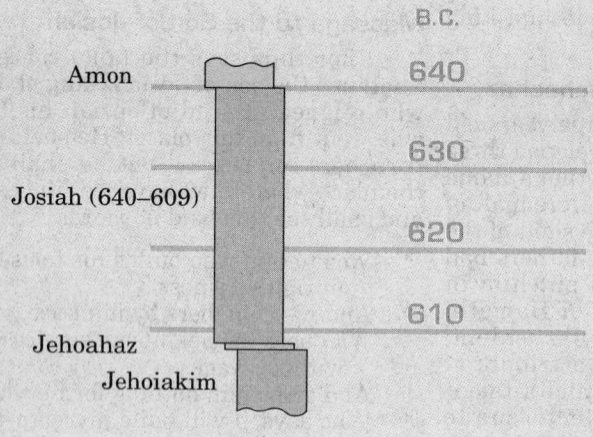

16 He judged the cause of the poor and
      needy;
   Then *it was* well.
   Was not this knowing Me?" says the
      LORD.
17 "Yet your eyes and your heart *are* for
      nothing but your covetousness,
   For shedding innocent blood,
   And practicing oppression and
      violence."

 Priestly Account: Josiah's
Last Years

The Chronicler's account of Josiah's death in 609 B.C. is very close to the account in Kings. One difference is the curious note that Necho fought "against Carchemish" (2 Chr. 35:20). An important battle was fought by Assyria and Babylon at Carchemish in 605 B.C., 4 years after Josiah's death, but in 609 B.C. Necho was advancing to fight at Haran. The Chronicler may be referring to Necho's plans in 609 to join the Assyrian army near Carche-

mish on the Euphrates River, and use that city as a base of operations for the siege of Haran.

Chronicles also provides more detail about Josiah's death. The Chronicler reports that God accomplishes His purposes even through a foreigner, the Egyptian pharaoh Necho (35:21). The tragedy of Josiah's death is accentuated by the lamentations of Judah and of the prophet Jeremiah, mourning for the king whose reign would be remembered forever as the kingdom's last moment of glory.

▼ ■ 2 Chronicles 35:20—36:4

2 Chronicles
Josiah Dies in Battle

35 :20 After all this, when Josiah had prepared the temple, Necho king of Egypt came up to fight against Carchemish by the Euphrates; and Josiah went out against him. 21But he sent messengers to him, saying, "What have I to do with you, king of Judah? *I have* not *come* against you this day, but against the house with which I have war; for God commanded me to make haste. Refrain *from meddling with* God, who *is* with me, lest He destroy you." ²²Nevertheless Josiah would not turn his face from him, but disguised himself so that he might fight with him, and did not heed the words of Necho from the mouth of God. So he came to fight in the Valley of Megiddo.

²³And the archers shot King Josiah; and the king said to his servants, "Take me away, for I am severely wounded." ²⁴His servants therefore took him out of that chariot and put him in the second chariot that he had, and they brought him to Jerusalem. So he died, and was buried in *one of* the tombs of his fathers. And all Judah and Jerusalem mourned for Josiah.

²⁵Jeremiah also lamented for Josiah. And to this day all the singing men and the singing women speak of Josiah in their lamentations. They made it a custom in Israel; and indeed they *are* written in the Laments.

²⁶Now the rest of the acts of Josiah and his goodness, according to *what was* written in the Law of the LORD, ²⁷and his deeds from first to last, indeed they *are* written in the book of the kings of Israel and Judah.

The Reign and Captivity of Jehoahaz

36 ¹Then the people of the land took Jehoahaz the son of Josiah, and made him king in his father's place in Jerusalem. ²Jehoahazᵃ *was* twenty-three years old when he became king, and he reigned three months in Jerusalem. ³Now the king of Egypt deposed him at Jerusalem; and he imposed on the land a tribute of one hundred talents of silver and a talent of gold. ⁴Then the king of Egypt made *Jehoahaz's*ᵃ brother Eliakim king over Judah and Jerusalem, and changed his name to Jehoiakim. And Necho took Jehoahazᵇ his brother and carried him off to Egypt.

36:2 ᵃMasoretic Text reads *Joahaz.*
36:4 ᵃLiterally *his* ᵇMasoretic Text reads
Joahaz. **Hab.** 1:1 ᵃOr *oracle*

The Book of Habakkuk

In the final years of Josiah's reign, while Assyria fought the Babylonian alliance in Mesopotamia, the prophet Habakkuk pondered the forces behind these events. Like Nahum, Habakkuk felt the injustice of Assyria's power. In a dialogue with God, he asks how such violence could go unpunished. Unlike Nahum, though, Habakkuk is not satisfied with Assyria's punishment at the hands of Babylon. Is Babylon any better than Assyria, after all? How can a pure God use such impure tools? In reply, God tells Habakkuk to wait, for in such faithful waiting is true righteousness (Hab. 2:4).

Habakkuk's forthright questioning has earned him the title "the philosopher prophet." He might just as well be described as a priestly prophet. He uses priestly language (ch. 3 is a psalm, complete with musical directions). Even the questions he asks of God sound priestly, very similar in tone and content to the questions asked by the psalmist of Ps. 73, a psalm associated with the priestly singer Asaph.

■ Habakkuk 1:1—3:19

Habakkuk

1 :1 The burdenᵃ which the prophet Habakkuk saw.

The Prophet's Question

2 O LORD, how long shall I cry,
And You will not hear?
Even cry out to You, "Violence!"
And You will not save.

3 Why do You show me iniquity,
And cause *me* to see trouble?
For plundering and violence *are* before me;
There is strife, and contention arises.

4 Therefore the law is powerless,
And justice never goes forth.
For the wicked surround the righteous;
Therefore perverse judgment proceeds.

The LORD's Reply

5 "Look among the nations and watch—
Be utterly astounded!
For *I will* work a work in your days
Which you would not believe, though it were told *you.*

6 For indeed I am raising up the Chaldeans,
A bitter and hasty nation
Which marches through the breadth of the earth,
To possess dwelling places *that are* not theirs.

7 They are terrible and dreadful;
Their judgment and their dignity proceed from themselves.

8 Their horses also are swifter than leopards,

CHALDEANS BECOME BABYLONIANS (Hab. 1:6)

As early as the 9th century B.C. the Chaldeans as a people are known from cuneiform records, the wedge-shaped characters etched in blocks of clay with styluses. The Chaldeans originally inhabited the southern portion of Babylonia on the west border of Elam. There was possibly a relationship between them and the Arameans, but that relationship is not clear. Both were tribal groups in southern Babylonia, and there is no difference between Aramean and Chaldean personal names. Yet the Arameans and Chaldeans were often described as distinct peoples.

For over 2 centuries of the Neo-Assyrian period (934–612 B.C.) the Chaldeans were at odds with the powerful Assyrians in the north. They often successfully waged guerrilla warfare against this foe. Merodach-Baladan II was a Chaldean king who twice occupied the throne of Babylon (721–710 and 703–702 B.C.). Evidently he also enlisted the support of Hezekiah, king of Judah, during a revolt against the Assyrians (Is. 39:1, 2).

By the 7th century B.C., the Chaldean tribes were able to control Babylonia and its capital city, Babylon. At that point, the terms "Babylonian" and "Chaldean" appear to be synonymous. Thus, Scripture uses these terms interchangeably: Nebuchadnezzar II, king of Babylon (c. 605–562 B.C.) and the destroyer of Jerusalem, was himself a Chaldean (see Ezra 5:12).

And more fierce than evening wolves.
Their chargers charge ahead;
Their cavalry comes from afar;
They fly as the eagle *that* hastens to eat.

9 "They all come for violence;
Their faces are set *like* the east wind.
They gather captives like sand.
10 They scoff at kings,
And princes are scorned by them.
They deride every stronghold,
For they heap up earthen *mounds* and seize it.
11 Then *his* mind[a] changes, and he transgresses;
He commits offense,
Ascribing this power to his god."

The Prophet's Second Question

12 Are You not from everlasting,
O LORD my God, my Holy One?
We shall not die.
O LORD, You have appointed them for judgment;
O Rock, You have marked them for correction.
13 *You are* of purer eyes than to behold evil,
And cannot look on wickedness.
Why do You look on those who deal treacherously,
And hold Your tongue when the wicked devours
A *person* more righteous than he?
14 *Why* do You make men like fish of the sea,
Like creeping things *that have* no ruler over them?

15 They take up all of them with a hook,
They catch them in their net,
And gather them in their dragnet.
Therefore they rejoice and are glad.
16 Therefore they sacrifice to their net,
And burn incense to their dragnet;
Because by them their share *is* sumptuous
And their food plentiful.
17 Shall they therefore empty their net,
And continue to slay nations without pity?

TIME CAPSULE *612 to 609 B.C.*

612 The Medes and Babylonians drive the Assyrians out of Nineveh

612 Fall of Assyria to the Medes and Babylonians

610 Nabopolassar of Babylon attacks Haran and scatters the Assyrian and Egyptian armies

610–595 Pharaoh Necho II of Egypt is foe of Babylon

609 The last Assyrian king, Ashur-uballit II, fails to recover the city of Haran from the Babylonians

1:11 [a]Literally *spirit* or *wind*

2 ¹ I will stand my watch
   And set myself on the rampart,
   And watch to see what He will say to
      me,
   And what I will answer when I am
      corrected.

The Just Live by Faith

²Then the LORD answered me and said:

"Write the vision
And make *it* plain on tablets,
That he may run who reads it.
³ For the vision *is* yet for an appointed
      time;
   But at the end it will speak, and it
      will not lie.
   Though it tarries, wait for it;
   Because it will surely come,
   It will not tarry.

⁴ "Behold the proud,
   His soul is not upright in him;
   But the just shall live by his faith.

Woe to the Wicked

⁵ "Indeed, because he transgresses by
      wine,
   He is a proud man,
   And he does not stay at home.
   Because he enlarges his desire as
      hell,ᵃ
   And he *is* like death, and cannot be
      satisfied,
   He gathers to himself all nations
   And heaps up for himself all peoples.

⁶ "Will not all these take up a proverb
      against him,
   And a taunting riddle against him,
      and say,
   'Woe to him who increases
   What is not his—how long?

And to him who loads himself with
      many pledges"?ᵃ
⁷ Will not your creditorsᵃ rise up
      suddenly?
   Will they not awaken who oppress
      you?
   And you will become their booty.
⁸ Because you have plundered many
      nations,
   All the remnant of the people shall
      plunder you,
   Because of men's blood
   And the violence of the land *and* the
      city,
   And of all who dwell in it.

⁹ "Woe to him who covets evil gain for
      his house,
   That he may set his nest on high,
   That he may be delivered from the
      power of disaster!
¹⁰ You give shameful counsel to your
      house,
   Cutting off many peoples,
   And sin *against* your soul.
¹¹ For the stone will cry out from the
      wall,
   And the beam from the timbers will
      answer it.

¹² "Woe to him who builds a town with
      bloodshed,
   Who establishes a city by iniquity!
¹³ Behold, *is it* not of the LORD of hosts
   That the peoples labor to feed the
      fire,ᵃ
   And nations weary themselves in
      vain?
¹⁴ For the earth will be filled
   With the knowledge of the glory of the
      LORD,
   As the waters cover the sea.

¹⁵ "Woe to him who gives drink to his
      neighbor,
   Pressingᵃ *him to* your bottle,
   Even to make *him* drunk,
   That you may look on his nakedness!

2:5 ᵃOr *Sheol*   2:6 ᵃSyriac and Vulgate read *thick
clay.*   2:7 ᵃLiterally *those who bite you*
2:13 ᵃLiterally *for what satisfies fire,* that is, for what
is of no lasting value   2:15 ᵃLiterally *Attaching* or
Joining

BELIEFS AND IDEAS

*The land of the dead in general is presented in the Old Testament as it seemed from the
point of view of the living. The dead were excluded from the energy of life and were
reduced to weak, unhappy shadows. In its terrible aspect death was compared to the
mouth of a gigantic monster. The appetite of death could never be satisfied (Hab. 2:5),
requiring that all must die.*

16 You are filled with shame instead of
   glory.
   You also—drink!
   And be exposed as uncircumcised!ᵃ
   The cup of the Lord's right hand *will
   be* turned against you,
   And utter shame will be on your glory.
17 For the violence *done to* Lebanon will
   cover you,
   And the plunder of beasts *which* made
   them afraid,
   Because of men's blood
   And the violence of the land *and* the
   city,
   And of all who dwell in it.

18 "What profit is the image, that its
   maker should carve it,
   The molded image, a teacher of lies,
   That the maker of its mold should
   trust in it,
   To make mute idols?
19 Woe to him who says to wood, 'Awake!'
   To silent stone, 'Arise! It shall teach!'
   Behold, it is overlaid with gold and
   silver,
   Yet in it there is no breath at all.

20 "But the Lord is in His holy temple.
   Let all the earth keep silence before
   Him."

The Prophet's Prayer

3 ¹A prayer of Habakkuk the prophet, on
   Shigionoth.ᵃ

2 O Lord, I have heard Your speech *and*
   was afraid;
   O Lord, revive Your work in the midst
   of the years!
   In the midst of the years make *it*
   known;
   In wrath remember mercy.

3 God came from Teman,
   The Holy One from Mount Paran.
                                   Selah

   His glory covered the heavens,
   And the earth was full of His praise.
4 *His* brightness was like the light;
   He had rays *flashing* from His hand,
   And there His power *was* hidden.
5 Before Him went pestilence,
   And fever followed at His feet.

6 He stood and measured the earth;
   He looked and startled the nations.

And the everlasting mountains were
   scattered,
The perpetual hills bowed.
His ways *are* everlasting.
7 I saw the tents of Cushan in affliction;
   The curtains of the land of Midian
   trembled.

8 O Lord, were *You* displeased with the
   rivers,
   Was Your anger against the rivers,
   Was Your wrath against the sea,
   That You rode on Your horses,
   Your chariots of salvation?
9 Your bow was made quite ready;
   Oaths were sworn over *Your* arrows.ᵃ
                                   Selah

   You divided the earth with rivers.
10 The mountains saw You *and* trembled;
   The overflowing of the water passed
   by.
   The deep uttered its voice,
   And lifted its hands on high.
11 The sun and moon stood still in their
   habitation;
   At the light of Your arrows they went,
   At the shining of Your glittering spear.

12 You marched through the land in
   indignation;
   You trampled the nations in anger.
13 You went forth for the salvation of
   Your people,
   For salvation with Your Anointed.
   You struck the head from the house of
   the wicked,
   By laying bare from foundation to
   neck.   Selah

14 You thrust through with his own
   arrows
   The head of his villages.
   They came out like a whirlwind to
   scatter me;
   Their rejoicing was like feasting on
   the poor in secret.
15 You walked through the sea with Your
   horses,
   Through the heap of great waters.

16 When I heard, my body trembled;
   My lips quivered at *the* voice;

2:16 ᵃDead Sea Scrolls and Septuagint read *And
reel!*; Syriac and Vulgate read *And fall fast asleep!*
3:1 ᵃExact meaning unknown   3:9 ᵃLiterally *rods*
or *tribes* (compare verse 14)

Rottenness entered my bones;
And I trembled in myself,
That I might rest in the day of
  trouble.
When he comes up to the people,
He will invade them with his troops.

A Hymn of Faith

17 Though the fig tree may not blossom,
  Nor fruit be on the vines;
  Though the labor of the olive may fail,
  And the fields yield no food;
  Though the flock may be cut off from
    the fold,
  And there be no herd in the stalls—
18 Yet I will rejoice in the LORD,
  I will joy in the God of my salvation.

19 The LORD God^a is my strength;
  He will make my feet like deer's *feet,*
  And He will make me walk on my
    high hills.

To the Chief Musician. With my
stringed instruments.

Prophetic Account: Jehoiakim and Jehoiachin

The exile of King Jehoahaz to Egypt by Pharaoh Necho (2 Kin. 23:34) was the end for Judah as an independent nation. Her next king, Jehoiakim, would rule as a vassal first to Egypt and then to Babylon. His son, Jehoiachin, would rule only long enough to surrender to Babylon.

When Pharaoh Necho of Egypt placed Jehoiakim on Judah's throne in 609 B.C., it was with the understanding that he would be loyal to Egypt. This gave Egypt a buffer between its own land and the armies of Babylon, but it placed Judah in a precarious position, caught between two warring empires. Of these, Babylon was the strongest, but Egypt was the nearest. Jehoiakim wavered between alliances, but generally remained loyal to Egypt.

▼ ■ 2 Kings 23:35–37

2 Kings
Jehoiakim Reigns in Judah

23 :35 So Jehoiakim gave the silver and gold to Pharaoh; but he taxed the land to give money according to the

command of Pharaoh; he exacted the silver and gold from the people of the land, from every one according to his assessment, to give *it* to Pharaoh Necho. ³⁶Jehoiakim *was* twenty-five years old when he became king, and he reigned eleven years in Jerusalem. His mother's name *was* Zebudah the daughter of Pedaiah of Rumah. ³⁷And he did evil in the sight of the LORD, according to all that his fathers had done.

Jeremiah's Temple Sermon

Jeremiah's ministry entered its most active stage when Jehoiakim became king in 609 B.C., when Jeremiah was (by one proposed chronology) about 18 years old. In Jehoiakim's first year, Jeremiah preached what is known as his Temple Sermon. The events surrounding this sermon and a short version of the sermon itself are recounted in Jer. 26. A much longer version of the sermon appears in Jer. 7:1—8:3. That Jeremiah was from Anathoth, not from Jerusalem, may explain why he was so scornful of those who put their trust in "the temple of the LORD, the temple of the LORD" (7:4). It may also explain why the Jerusalem hierarchy reacted so strongly to his condemnations.

At various points in the first half of the Book of Jeremiah appear the prophet's complaints to God concerning the difficulty of his calling. These are usually called Jeremiah's Confessions. They are couched in the language of the psalms, and like the psalms give few clues as to their precise historical context. These laments can be read where complaints would be appropriate. The first of these, Jer. 12:1–17, is appropriate in the context of Jeremiah's near execution after preaching his Temple Sermon (Jer. 26:8–19).

■ Jeremiah 26:1–6
■ Jeremiah 7:1—8:3
■ Jeremiah 26:7–24
■ Jeremiah 11:1—12:17

Jeremiah 26:1–6

26 :1 In the beginning of the reign of Jehoiakim the son of Josiah, king of Judah, this word came from the LORD, saying, ²"Thus says the LORD: 'Stand in the court of the LORD's house, and speak to all the cities of Judah, which come to worship *in* the LORD's house, all the words that I command you to speak to them. Do not diminish a word. ³Perhaps everyone will listen and turn from his evil way, that I may

3:19 ᵃHebrew *YHWH Adonai*

relent concerning the calamity which I purpose to bring on them because of the evil of their doings.' 4And you shall say to them, 'Thus says the LORD: "If you will not listen to Me, to walk in My law which I have set before you, 5to heed the words of My servants the prophets whom I sent to you, both rising up early and sending *them* (but you have not heeded), 6then I will make this house like Shiloh, and will make this city a curse to all the nations of the earth." ' "

Jeremiah 7:1—8:3
Trusting in Lying Words

7 :1 The word that came to Jeremiah from the LORD, saying, 2"Stand in the gate of the LORD's house, and proclaim there this word, and say, 'Hear the word of the LORD, all *you of* Judah who enter in at these gates to worship the LORD!' " 3Thus says the LORD of hosts, the God of Israel: "Amend your ways and your doings, and I will cause you to dwell in this place. 4Do not trust in these lying words, saying, 'The temple of the LORD, the temple of the LORD, the temple of the LORD *are* these.'

5"For if you thoroughly amend your ways and your doings, if you thoroughly execute judgment between a man and his neighbor, 6if you do not oppress the stranger, the fatherless, and the widow, and do not shed innocent blood in this place, or walk after other gods to your hurt, 7then I will cause you to dwell in this place, in the land that I gave to your fathers forever and ever.

8"Behold, you trust in lying words that cannot profit. 9Will you steal, murder, commit adultery, swear falsely, burn incense to Baal, and walk after other gods whom you do not know, 10and *then* come and stand before Me in this house which is called by My name, and say, 'We are delivered to do all these abominations'? 11Has this house, which is called by My name, become a den of thieves in your eyes? Behold, I, even I, have seen *it*," says the LORD.

12"But go now to My place which *was* in Shiloh, where I set My name at the first, and see what I did to it because of the wickedness of My people Israel. 13And now, because you have done all these works," says the LORD, "and I spoke to you, rising up early and speaking, but you did not hear, and I called you, but you did not answer, 14therefore I will do to the house which is called by My name, in which you trust, and to this place which I gave to you and your fathers, as I have done to Shiloh. 15And I will cast you out of My sight, as I have cast out all your brethren—the whole posterity of Ephraim.

16"Therefore do not pray for this people, nor lift up a cry or prayer for them, nor make intercession to Me; for I will not hear you. 17Do you not see what they do in the cities of Judah and in the streets of Jerusalem? 18The children gather wood, the fathers kindle the fire, and the women knead dough, to make cakes for the queen of heaven; and *they* pour out drink offerings to other gods, that they may provoke Me to anger. 19Do they provoke Me to anger?" says the LORD. "*Do they* not *provoke* themselves, to the shame of their own faces?"

20Therefore thus says the Lord GOD: "Behold, My anger and My fury will be poured out on this place—on man and on beast, on the trees of the field and on the fruit of the ground. And it will burn and not be quenched."

21Thus says the LORD of hosts, the God of Israel: "Add your burnt offerings to your sacrifices and eat meat. 22For I did not speak to your fathers, or command them in the day that I brought them out of the land of Egypt, concerning burnt offerings or sacrifices. 23But this is what I commanded them, saying, 'Obey My voice, and I will be your God, and you shall be My people. And walk in all the ways that I have commanded you, that it may be well with you.' 24Yet they did not obey or incline their ear, but followed the counsels *and* the dictates of their evil hearts, and went backward and not forward. 25Since the day that your fathers came out of the land of Egypt until

---

TIME CAPSULE   609 B.C.

609   Pharaoh Necho of Egypt moves army northward to help the Assyrians against Nebuchadnezzar of Babylon

609   Pharaoh Necho kills King Josiah of Judah at Megiddo

609   Jehoahaz becomes king in Judah

609   Necho replaces Jehoahaz with his half brother Eliakim

609   Necho gives Eliakim the throne name "Jehoiakim" (2 Chr. 36:4)

FAMILY WORSHIP OF THE QUEEN OF HEAVEN (Jer. 7:17-20)

Still unknown is the identity of the "queen of heaven" who was worshiped in Judah (Jer. 7:18; 44:18). She could have been Asherah, Anath, or Astarte, all popular Canaanite goddesses. The only reference to "queen of heaven" outside the Bible is in a 6th-century B.C. letter found at Hermopolis in Egypt; there Anath is given the title. Since Anath was a popular deity in Hermopolis, it is possible she acquired the title "queen of heaven" there.

Whichever goddess was the queen of heaven, she seems to have been worshiped in homes, rather than in a temple. The activities of her worshipers mentioned in the Book of Jeremiah picture a family cultic meal and not a congregational service. The entire family was involved: women, men, and children all took part in the worship, though each had specific roles related to age and gender (Jer. 7:18). The women were particularly associated with, and possibly blamed for, such worship, but they defended themselves to Jeremiah by reminding him that wives did nothing without their "husbands' permission" (Jer. 44:19).

The worship ritual does not identify the goddess. The Hebrew word for the cakes that the women made (Jer. 7:18) seems to come from an Accadian word referring to a sweet pastry which was offered to the Mesopotamian goddess Ishtar. Yet this would not necessarily connect the queen of heaven cult to Mesopotamia. It simply shows that important goddesses were honored with festival bakery goods.

The other ritual activities also fail to identify the queen of heaven. Both burning incense and pouring out drink offerings (Jer. 44:18) were standard parts of religious rituals in Syria-Palestine. Judah's own God Yahweh was honored with incense and drink offerings.

Worship of the queen of heaven was carried to Egypt by refugees fleeing from Jerusalem's destruction. They apparently credited her with bringing the peace and well-being they enjoyed when Judah was independent under King Josiah (44:17). For Jeremiah, however, her worship was part of the cause of the past disaster, as well as that to come (44:20-27).

---

this day, I have even sent to you all My servants the prophets, daily rising up early and sending *them*. ²⁶Yet they did not obey Me or incline their ear, but stiffened their neck. They did worse than their fathers.

²⁷"Therefore you shall speak all these words to them, but they will not obey you. You shall also call to them, but they will not answer you.

Judgment on Obscene Religion

²⁸"So you shall say to them, 'This *is* a nation that does not obey the voice of the LORD their God nor receive correction. Truth has perished and has been cut off from their mouth. ²⁹Cut off your hair and cast *it* away, and take up a lamentation on the desolate heights; for the LORD has rejected and forsaken the generation of His wrath.' ³⁰For the children of Judah have done evil in My sight," says the LORD. "They have set their abominations in the house which is called by My name, to pollute it. ³¹And they have built the high places of Tophet, which *is* in the Valley of

the Son of Hinnom, to burn their sons and their daughters in the fire, which I did not command, nor did it come into My heart.

³²"Therefore behold, the days are coming," says the LORD, "when it will no more be called Tophet, or the Valley of the Son of Hinnom, but the Valley of Slaughter; for they will bury in Tophet until there is no room. ³³The corpses of this people will be food for the birds of the heaven and for the beasts of the earth. And no one will frighten *them away*. ³⁴Then I will cause to cease from the cities of Judah and from the streets of Jerusalem the voice of mirth and the voice of gladness, the voice of the bridegroom and the voice of the bride. For the land shall be desolate.

8 ¹"At that time," says the LORD, "they shall bring out the bones of the kings of Judah, and the bones of its princes, and the bones of the priests, and the bones of the prophets, and the bones of the inhabitants of Jerusalem, out of their graves. ²They shall spread them before the sun and the moon and all the host of heaven,

A Place for Burning Babies to the Gods (Jer. 7:31)

A firepit in the Valley of the Son of Hinnom called Tophet was built for the sole purpose of sacrificing young children to one or more deities. Probably the god worshiped there was Molech, but his cult may have been adapted to the worship of Yahweh. Jeremiah's prophecy of judgment (Jer. 7:31) condemns the practice, but also reveals that the sacrifice of children was popular in Jerusalem.

The worship complex for these rituals must have been large. Jeremiah's reference to the "high places of Tophet" (7:31) describes dedicated sanctuaries serving as cultic centers. There would have been an altar, a place for cremating the sacrificial victims, and probably a burial area for the bones and ashes. Such a center has been excavated at the Phoenician colony of Carthage, where the bones of children and animals have been found in urns.

which they have loved and which they have served and after which they have walked, which they have sought and which they have worshiped. They shall not be gathered nor buried; they shall be like refuse on the face of the earth. ³Then death shall be chosen rather than life by all the residue of those who remain of this evil family, who remain in all the places where I have driven them," says the LORD of hosts.

Jeremiah 26:7-24
Jeremiah Saved from Death

26 :7 So the priests and the prophets and all the people heard Jeremiah speaking these words in the house of the LORD. ⁸Now it happened, when Jeremiah had made an end of speaking all that the LORD had commanded *him* to speak to all the people, that the priests and the prophets and all the people seized him, saying, "You will surely die! ⁹Why have you prophesied in the name of the LORD, saying, 'This house shall be like Shiloh, and this city shall be desolate, without an inhabitant'?" And all the people were gathered against Jeremiah in the house of the LORD.

¹⁰When the princes of Judah heard these things, they came up from the king's house to the house of the LORD and sat down in the entry of the New Gate of the LORD's *house.* ¹¹And the priests and the prophets spoke to the princes and all the people, saying, "This man deserves to die! For he has prophesied against this city, as you have heard with your ears."

¹²Then Jeremiah spoke to all the princes and all the people, saying: "The LORD sent me to prophesy against this house and against this city with all the

words that you have heard. ¹³Now therefore, amend your ways and your doings, and obey the voice of the LORD your God; then the LORD will relent concerning the doom that He has pronounced against you. ¹⁴As for me, here I am, in your hand; do with me as seems good and proper to you. ¹⁵But know for certain that if you put me to death, you will surely bring innocent blood on yourselves, on this city, and on its inhabitants; for truly the LORD has sent me to you to speak all these words in your hearing."

¹⁶So the princes and all the people said to the priests and the prophets, "This man does not deserve to die. For he has spoken to us in the name of the LORD our God."

¹⁷Then certain of the elders of the land rose up and spoke to all the assembly of the people, saying: ¹⁸"Micah of Moresheth prophesied in the days of Hezekiah king of Judah, and spoke to all the people of Judah, saying, 'Thus says the LORD of hosts:

"Zion shall be plowed *like* a field,
    Jerusalem shall become heaps of
        ruins,
    And the mountain of the temple[a]
    Like the bare hills of the forest." '[b]

¹⁹Did Hezekiah king of Judah and all Judah ever put him to death? Did he not fear the LORD and seek the LORD's favor? And the LORD relented concerning the doom which He had pronounced against them. But we are doing great evil against ourselves."

²⁰Now there was also a man who

26:18 [a]Literally *house* [b]Compare Micah 3:12

prophesied in the name of the LORD, Urijah the son of Shemaiah of Kirjath Jearim, who prophesied against this city and against this land according to all the words of Jeremiah. 21And when Jehoiakim the king, with all his mighty men and all the princes, heard his words, the king sought to put him to death; but when Urijah heard *it,* he was afraid and fled, and went to Egypt. 22Then Jehoiakim the king sent men to Egypt: Elnathan the son of Achbor, and *other* men *who went* with him to Egypt. 23And they brought Urijah from Egypt and brought him to Jehoiakim the king, who killed him with the sword and cast his dead body into the graves of the common people.

24Nevertheless the hand of Ahikam the son of Shaphan was with Jeremiah, so that they should not give him into the hand of the people to put him to death.

Jeremiah 11:1—12:17
The Broken Covenant

11 :1 The word that came to Jeremiah from the LORD, saying, 2"Hear the words of this covenant, and speak to the men of Judah and to the inhabitants of Jerusalem; 3and say to them, 'Thus says the LORD God of Israel: "Cursed *is* the man who does not obey the words of this covenant 4which I commanded your fathers in the day I brought them out of the land of Egypt, from the iron furnace, saying, 'Obey My voice, and do according to all that I command you; so shall you be My people, and I will be your God,' 5that I may establish the oath which I have sworn to your fathers, to give them 'a land flowing with milk and honey,'a as *it is* this day." ' "

And I answered and said, "So be it, LORD."

6Then the LORD said to me, "Proclaim all these words in the cities of Judah and in the streets of Jerusalem, saying: 'Hear the words of this covenant and do them. 7For I earnestly exhorted your fathers in the day I brought them up out of the land of Egypt, until this day, rising early and exhorting, saying, "Obey My voice." 8Yet they did not obey or incline their ear, but everyone followed the dictates of his evil heart; therefore I will bring upon them all the words of this covenant, which I commanded *them* to do, but *which* they have not done.' "

9And the LORD said to me, "A conspiracy has been found among the men of Judah and among the inhabitants of Jerusalem. 10They have turned back to the iniquities of their forefathers who refused to hear My words, and they have gone after other gods to serve them; the house of Israel and the house of Judah have broken My covenant which I made with their fathers."

11Therefore thus says the LORD: "Behold, I will surely bring calamity on them which they will not be able to escape; and though they cry out to Me, I will not listen to them. 12Then the cities of Judah and the inhabitants of Jerusalem will go and cry out to the gods to whom they offer incense, but they will not save them at all in the time of their trouble. 13For *according to* the number of your cities were your gods, O Judah; and *according to* the number of the streets of Jerusalem you have set up altars to *that* shameful thing, altars to burn incense to Baal.

14"So do not pray for this people, or lift up a cry or prayer for them; for I will not hear *them* in the time that they cry out to Me because of their trouble.

15 "What has My beloved to do in My
            house,
       Having done lewd deeds with many?
       And the holy flesh has passed from
            you.
       When you do evil, then you rejoice.
16   The LORD called your name,
       Green Olive Tree, Lovely *and* of Good
            Fruit.
       With the noise of a great tumult
       He has kindled fire on it,
       And its branches are broken.

17"For the LORD of hosts, who planted you, has pronounced doom against you for the evil of the house of Israel and of the house of Judah, which they have done against themselves to provoke Me to anger in offering incense to Baal."

Jeremiah's Life Threatened

18Now the LORD gave me knowledge *of it,* and I know *it;* for You showed me their doings. 19But I *was* like a docile lamb brought to the slaughter; and I did not know that they had devised schemes against me, *saying,* "Let us destroy the tree with its fruit, and let us cut him off from

the land of the living, that his name may
be remembered no more."

20 But, O LORD of hosts,
    You who judge righteously,
    Testing the mind and the heart,
    Let me see Your vengeance on them,
    For to You I have revealed my cause.

21"Therefore thus says the LORD concerning the men of Anathoth who seek your
life, saying, 'Do not prophesy in the name
of the LORD, lest you die by our hand'—
22therefore thus says the LORD of hosts:
'Behold, I will punish them. The young
men shall die by the sword, their sons and
their daughters shall die by famine; 23and
there shall be no remnant of them, for I
will bring catastrophe on the men of
Anathoth, even the year of their punishment.'"

Jeremiah's Question

12 1 Righteous are You, O LORD, when
       I plead with You;
    Yet let me talk with You about Your
       judgments.
    Why does the way of the wicked
       prosper?
    Why are those happy who deal so
       treacherously?
2   You have planted them, yes, they have
       taken root;
    They grow, yes, they bear fruit.
    You are near in their mouth
    But far from their mind.

3   But You, O LORD, know me;
    You have seen me,
    And You have tested my heart toward
       You.
    Pull them out like sheep for the
       slaughter,
    And prepare them for the day of
       slaughter.
4   How long will the land mourn,
    And the herbs of every field wither?
    The beasts and birds are consumed,
    For the wickedness of those who dwell
       there,
    Because they said, "He will not see
       our final end."

The LORD Answers Jeremiah

5   "If you have run with the footmen, and
       they have wearied you,
    Then how can you contend with
       horses?

And if in the land of peace,
In which you trusted, they wearied
   you,
Then how will you do in the
   floodplain[a] of the Jordan?
6 For even your brothers, the house of
      your father,
   Even they have dealt treacherously
      with you;
   Yes, they have called a multitude after
      you.
   Do not believe them,
   Even though they speak smooth words
      to you.

7 "I have forsaken My house, I have left
      My heritage;
   I have given the dearly beloved of My
      soul into the hand of her enemies.
8 My heritage is to Me like a lion in the
      forest;
   It cries out against Me;
   Therefore I have hated it.
9 My heritage is to Me like a speckled
      vulture;
   The vultures all around are against
      her.
   Come, assemble all the beasts of the
      field,
   Bring them to devour!

10 "Many rulers[a] have destroyed My
      vineyard,
   They have trodden My portion
      underfoot;
   They have made My pleasant portion
      a desolate wilderness.
11 They have made it desolate;
   Desolate, it mourns to Me;
   The whole land is made desolate,
   Because no one takes it to heart.
12 The plunderers have come
   On all the desolate heights in the
      wilderness,
   For the sword of the LORD shall
      devour
   From one end of the land to the other
      end of the land;
   No flesh shall have peace.
13 They have sown wheat but reaped
      thorns;
   They have put themselves to pain but
      do not profit.
   But be ashamed of your harvest

12:5 aOr thicket   12:10 aLiterally shepherds or
pastors

Because of the fierce anger of the
   LORD."

14Thus says the LORD: "Against all My
evil neighbors who touch the inheritance
which I have caused My people Israel to inherit—behold, I will pluck them out of
their land and pluck out the house of Judah from among them. 15Then it shall be,
after I have plucked them out, that I will
return and have compassion on them and
bring them back, everyone to his heritage
and everyone to his land. 16And it shall be,
if they will learn carefully the ways of My
people, to swear by My name, 'As the LORD
lives,' as they taught My people to swear by
Baal, then they shall be established in the
midst of My people. 17But if they do not
obey, I will utterly pluck up and destroy
that nation," says the LORD.

The Battle of Carchemish

In Jehoiakim's 4th year (605 B.C.),
the exiled nation of Assyria again made an alliance with Egypt and attacked the Babylonian
army, which was led by the crown prince of
Babylon, Nebuchadnezzar (also spelled Nebuchadrezzar). On the way through Canaan,
Pharaoh Necho evidently attacked Gaza and
Ashkelon in the Philistine coastlands.

The battle, fought at Carchemish on the
northern Euphrates River, was a rout. Nebuchadnezzar's armies destroyed the Assyrians
once and for all and sent Necho fleeing back
through Palestine toward Egypt. Nebuchadnezzar was unable to follow up his advantage,
however. Receiving word that his father
Nabopolassar had died, Nebuchadnezzar returned to Babylon to assume the throne, now
the undisputed ruler over all Mesopotamia.

Jeremiah was a keen observer of world
events and frequently spoke to and about the
nations around Judah. His announcements
of judgment against Philistia (Jer. 47:17)
and Egypt (46:1–12) may have referred to
the events surrounding the battle at Carchemish. His political advice to Jehoiakim, which
the king invariably ignored, was to accept
Babylonian supremacy and reject alliances with
Egypt.

Jeremiah's essential theme, though, was
that all these events were part of God's plan,
and that God was working through all the nations to perform His will. The object lessons of
the ruined linen sash (13:1–11), the bottle
filled with wine (13:12–14), and the potter's

clay (18:1–17) illustrated clearly that no nation, not even Judah, could escape His judgment.

- Jeremiah 47:1–7
- Jeremiah 46:1–12
- Jeremiah 13:1–14
- Jeremiah 18:1–17

Jeremiah 47:1–7
Judgment on Philistia

47 :1 The word of the LORD that came
to Jeremiah the prophet against the
Philistines, before Pharaoh attacked Gaza.
2Thus says the LORD:

"Behold, waters rise out of the north,
   And shall be an overflowing flood;
They shall overflow the land and all
      that is in it,
   The city and those who dwell within;
Then the men shall cry,
   And all the inhabitants of the land
      shall wail.
3 At the noise of the stamping hooves of
      his strong horses,
   At the rushing of his chariots,
   At the rumbling of his wheels,
   The fathers will not look back for *their*
      children,
   Lacking courage,
4 Because of the day that comes to
      plunder all the Philistines,
   To cut off from Tyre and Sidon every
      helper who remains;
   For the LORD shall plunder the
      Philistines,
   The remnant of the country of
      Caphtor.
5 Baldness has come upon Gaza,
   Ashkelon is cut off
   With the remnant of their valley.
   How long will you cut yourself?

TIME CAPSULE   *609 to 605 B.C.*

609   *Jehoiakim becomes king in Judah*

605   *Jehoiakim's 3rd year according to
          the Babylonian method of counting
          in Book of Daniel*

605   *Jehoiakim's 4th year according to
          the Judean method of counting in
          Book of Jeremiah*

**605–
562**   *Nebuchadnezzar II is 2nd king of
          Chaldean dynasty in Babylon*

THE CITY OF FAILED REVOLTS (Jer. 47:5–7)

The large seaport town of Ashkelon, 13 miles north of Gaza along the coast of Philistia, was often controlled by other powers: Egypt, Assyria, Babylon. The history of this Philistine city is one of numerous rebellions against stronger forces, but also of numerous failures.

The name of the city appears in the Egyptian Execration Texts (19th to 18th centuries B.C.), as well as in the Amarna letters and various royal inscriptions from Egypt (14th to 13th centuries B.C.). A rebellion against Egyptian control was not successful, and a picture of Ashkelon's fall to Egyptian troops is inscribed in the wall of the temple of Karnak at Thebes. The inscription was once credited to the pharaoh Ramesses II (1279–1213 B.C.), but now is thought to be that of his son Merenptah (1213–1203 B.C.).

According to the Assyrian annals of Sargon II (721–705 B.C.), Ashkelon played a role (along with other Philistine cities) in a coalition against Assyria from 714 to 712 B.C. The rebellion did not work. Another overthrow of Assyrian control was attempted in 701 B.C. against the Assyrian ruler Sennacherib, but was stopped in the same year. The Philistine city would continue to pay tribute to Assyria until the collapse of the reign of the last great Assyrian monarch, Ashurbanipal (668–627 B.C.).

After the Assyrian Empire declined, other powers became interested in Ashkelon. All of Philistia, including this city, briefly came under Egyptian control about 630 B.C. However, in 605 B.C. Nebuchadnezzar II of Babylon celebrated a decisive victory over Egypt at the battle of Carchemish. When Nebuchadnezzar claimed Egyptian-held territory in the region of Ashkelon, the city resisted.

Jeremiah correctly prophesied that Ashkelon would be taken by Babylon (Jer. 47:5–7). In 604 B.C. Ashkelon's king, Aga, was killed and many prisoners were captured and deported to Babylon. The Babylonian Chronicle describes these prisoners as receiving rations at the Babylonian court. Jeremiah's call, "Ashkelon is cut off" (47:5), marked one more fall for a city that had fallen several times before.

---

6 "O you sword of the LORD,
How long until you are quiet?
Put yourself up into your scabbard,
Rest and be still!
7 How can it be quiet,
Seeing the LORD has given it a charge
Against Ashkelon and against the
seashore?
There He has appointed it."

Jeremiah 46:1–12
Judgment on Egypt

46 :1 The word of the LORD which came to Jeremiah the prophet against the nations. ²Against Egypt.

Concerning the army of Pharaoh Necho, king of Egypt, which was by the River Euphrates in Carchemish, and which Nebuchadnezzar king of Babylon defeated in the fourth year of Jehoiakim the son of Josiah, king of Judah:

3 "Order the buckler and shield,
And draw near to battle!
4 Harness the horses,
And mount up, you horsemen!

Stand forth with *your* helmets,
Polish the spears,
Put on the armor!
5 Why have I seen them dismayed *and*
turned back?
Their mighty ones are beaten down;
They have speedily fled,
And did not look back,
For fear *was* all around," says the
LORD.
6 "Do not let the swift flee away,
Nor the mighty man escape;
They will stumble and fall
Toward the north, by the River
Euphrates.

7 "Who *is* this coming up like a flood,
Whose waters move like the rivers?
8 Egypt rises up like a flood,
And *its* waters move like the rivers;
And he says, 'I will go up *and* cover
the earth,
I will destroy the city and its
inhabitants.'
9 Come up, O horses, and rage,
O chariots!

WHO'S CONTROLLING CARCHEMISH? (Jer. 46:2)

Carchemish was a major city with a strategic location on the Upper Euphrates River. Its position 120 miles inland from the northeastern corner of the Mediterranean put it near the main route from Egypt through Palestine to Assyria and Babylonia.

The city was sometimes independent and sometimes under foreign control. The Egyptians controlled it in the 15th century B.C., and the Hittites in the 13th century. Later on the Assyrians forced Carchemish to pay them taxes, and in 717 B.C. they conquered and destroyed the city (see Is. 10:9).

Carchemish was a key site in the struggle of Assyria and Egypt against Babylon. In 609 B.C. Pharaoh Necho of Egypt moved his army northward to help the Assyrians against Nebuchadnezzar of Babylon. King Josiah of Judah for some reason tried to stop Necho, engaging the Egyptians at Megiddo, but was killed in the attempt (2 Kin. 23:29, 30; 2 Chr. 35:20–25).

Eventually, Necho was able to occupy and fortify Carchemish for Egypt. But in 605 B.C. Nebuchadnezzar and the Babylonians defeated Necho at the battle of Carchemish. This defeat, which Jeremiah mentions (Jer. 46:2), put the Egyptians out of the way and allowed the Babylonians to bring their forces down to Judah.

Judah was a small nation pressed between the Egyptians to the south and the Assyrians and Babylonians to the north. Josiah's Judean army was no match for the more powerful Egyptians in 609. However, Jeremiah prophesies that Judah's God, who is sovereign over political powers, would end Egypt's control of Carchemish in 605. God had planned a sacrifice "in the north country by the River Euphrates" (Jer. 46:10).

And let the mighty men come forth:
The Ethiopians and the Libyans who
    handle the shield,
And the Lydians who handle *and* bend
    the bow.
10 For this *is* the day of the Lord GOD of
    hosts,
A day of vengeance,
That He may avenge Himself on His
    adversaries.
The sword shall devour;
It shall be satiated and made drunk
    with their blood;
For the Lord GOD of hosts has a
    sacrifice
In the north country by the River
    Euphrates.

11 "Go up to Gilead and take balm,
O virgin, the daughter of Egypt;
In vain you will use many medicines;
You shall not be cured.
12 The nations have heard of your
    shame,
And your cry has filled the land;
For the mighty man has stumbled
    against the mighty;
They both have fallen together."

13:4 ᵃHebrew *Perath*

Jeremiah 13:1–14
Symbol of the Linen Sash

13 :1 Thus the LORD said to me: "Go and get yourself a linen sash, and put it around your waist, but do not put it in water." ²So I got a sash according to the word of the LORD, and put *it* around my waist.

³And the word of the LORD came to me the second time, saying, ⁴"Take the sash that you acquired, which *is* around your waist, and arise, go to the Euphrates,ᵃ and hide it there in a hole in the rock." ⁵So I went and hid it by the Euphrates, as the LORD commanded me.

⁶Now it came to pass after many days that the LORD said to me, "Arise, go to the Euphrates, and take from there the sash which I commanded you to hide there." ⁷Then I went to the Euphrates and dug, and I took the sash from the place where I had hidden it; and there was the sash, ruined. It was profitable for nothing.

⁸Then the word of the LORD came to me, saying, ⁹"Thus says the LORD: 'In this manner I will ruin the pride of Judah and the great pride of Jerusalem. ¹⁰This evil people, who refuse to hear My words, who follow the dictates of their hearts, and

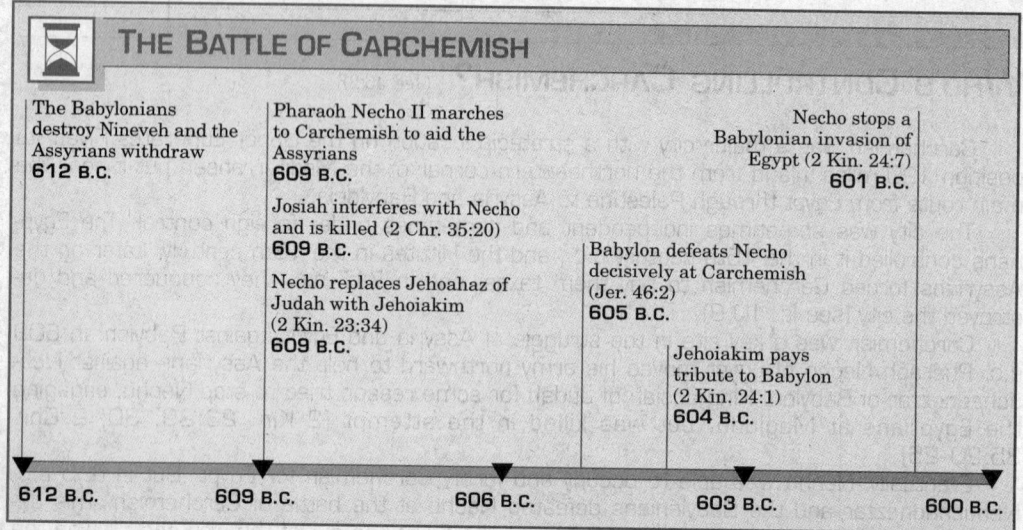

THE BATTLE OF CARCHEMISH

The Babylonians destroy Nineveh and the Assyrians withdraw **612 B.C.**

Pharaoh Necho II marches to Carchemish to aid the Assyrians **609 B.C.**

Josiah interferes with Necho and is killed (2 Chr. 35:20) **609 B.C.**

Necho replaces Jehoahaz of Judah with Jehoiakim (2 Kin. 23:34) **609 B.C.**

Necho stops a Babylonian invasion of Egypt (2 Kin. 24:7) **601 B.C.**

Babylon defeats Necho decisively at Carchemish (Jer. 46:2) **605 B.C.**

Jehoiakim pays tribute to Babylon (2 Kin. 24:1) **604 B.C.**

612 B.C.   **609 B.C.**   **606 B.C.**   **603 B.C.**   **600 B.C.**

walk after other gods to serve them and worship them, shall be just like this sash which is profitable for nothing. 11For as the sash clings to the waist of a man, so I have caused the whole house of Israel and the whole house of Judah to cling to Me,' says the LORD, 'that they may become My people, for renown, for praise, and for glory; but they would not hear.'

Symbol of the Wine Bottles

12"Therefore you shall speak to them this word: 'Thus says the LORD God of Israel: "Every bottle shall be filled with wine." '

"And they will say to you, 'Do we not certainly know that every bottle will be filled with wine?'

13"Then you shall say to them, 'Thus says the LORD: "Behold, I will fill all the inhabitants of this land—even the kings who sit on David's throne, the priests, the prophets, and all the inhabitants of Jerusalem—with drunkenness! 14And I will dash them one against another, even the fathers and the sons together," says the LORD. "I will not pity nor spare nor have mercy, but will destroy them." ' "

Jeremiah 18:1–17
The Potter and the Clay

18 :1 The word which came to Jeremiah from the LORD, saying: 2"Arise and go down to the potter's house, and there I will cause you to hear My words." 3Then I went down to the potter's house, and there he was, making something at the wheel. 4And the vessel that he made of clay was marred in the hand of the potter; so he made it again into another vessel, as it seemed good to the potter to make.

5Then the word of the LORD came to me, saying: 6"O house of Israel, can I not do with you as this potter?" says the LORD. "Look, as the clay *is* in the potter's hand, so *are* you in My hand, O house of Israel! 7The instant I speak concerning a nation and concerning a kingdom, to pluck up, to pull down, and to destroy *it,* 8if that nation against whom I have spoken turns from its evil, I will relent of the disaster that I thought to bring upon it. 9And the instant I speak concerning a nation and concerning a kingdom, to build and to plant *it,* 10if it does evil in My sight so that it does not obey My voice, then I will relent concerning

SCIENCE AND TECHNOLOGY

A potter's wheel (Jer. 18:3) is a horizontal platform that rotates and allows the workman to form circular vessels accurately. If the rotation is fast enough and has adequate momentum, the potter makes the vessel by pressing and pulling the clay as it turns. A half-shaped vessel can be folded down and remolded into a new one with no particular effort (18:4).

the good with which I said I would benefit it.

11"Now therefore, speak to the men of Judah and to the inhabitants of Jerusalem, saying, 'Thus says the LORD: "Behold, I am fashioning a disaster and devising a plan against you. Return now every one from his evil way, and make your ways and your doings good." ' "

God's Warning Rejected

12And they said, "That is hopeless! So we will walk according to our own plans, and we will every one obey the dictates of his evil heart."

13Therefore thus says the LORD:

> "Ask now among the Gentiles,
> Who has heard such things?
> The virgin of Israel has done a very
>   horrible thing.

14 Will *a man* leave the snow water of
        Lebanon,
    Which comes from the rock of the
        field?
    Will the cold flowing waters be
        forsaken for strange waters?

15 "Because My people have forgotten Me,
    They have burned incense to
        worthless idols.
    And they have caused themselves to
        stumble in their ways,
    From the ancient paths,
    To walk in pathways and not on a
        highway,

16 To make their land desolate *and* a
        perpetual hissing;
    Everyone who passes by it will be
        astonished
    And shake his head.

17 I will scatter them as with an east
        wind before the enemy;
    I will show them[a] the back and not
        the face
    In the day of their calamity."

18:17 [a]Following Septuagint, Syriac, Targum, and Vulgate; Masoretic Text reads *look them in.*

Jeremiah's Scroll

By the 4th year of Jehoiakim's reign (605 B.C.), when Babylon affirmed its supremacy at the battle of Carchemish, Jeremiah was well known to the Jerusalem leadership. Indeed, his constant condemnations of Judah's leaders had led them to banish him from the temple. There would be no more sermons at the temple gates (see "Jeremiah's Temple Sermon" at Jer. 26:1). Jeremiah was not so easily silenced, though. The prophet dictated a message to his friend and scribe, Baruch, and sent him to read the scroll on the day of fasting (Jer. 36:1–10). Baruch had to wait over a year before a day of fasting was proclaimed. The 9th month of Jehoiakim's 5th year (36:9, 22), following the Babylonian calendar, would place the fast in December, 604 B.C.

The exact contents of this scroll are uncertain, although it may have contained large portions of what is now Jer. 1—25. The message of Jer. 25:1–14 must have been a part of the scroll, since the superscription (25:1) dates these verses in Jehoiakim's 4th year, and the phrase "this book" (25:13) may refer to the scroll. Jeremiah reminds the people (25:3) that 23 years have passed since his calling in the 13th year of Josiah's reign (627 B.C.), and he has spoken to them repeatedly.

The second of Jeremiah's Confessions (15:10–21) can be read as an appropriate response to the king's rejection and burning of Jeremiah's written oracle (36:11–32). Jeremiah's friend Baruch also suffered and made his complaint, to which Jeremiah responds strongly (45:1–5). Baruch's brother, Seraiah, served as a high official under King Zedekiah. Baruch had good reason to believe that he, too, could have gained a responsible position in Judah's court (both were sons of Neriah, 32:12; 51:59). He forfeited that dream by siding with Jeremiah and alienating Judah's rulers.

- Jeremiah 36:1–10
- Jeremiah 25:1–14
- Jeremiah 36:11–32
- Jeremiah 45:1–5
- Jeremiah 15:10–21

Jeremiah 36:1–10
The Scroll Read in the Temple

36 :1 Now it came to pass in the fourth year of Jehoiakim the son of Josiah, king of Judah, *that* this word came to Jeremiah from the LORD, saying: 2"Take a scroll of a book and write on it all the words that I have spoken to you against Israel, against Judah, and against all the nations, from the day I spoke to you, from the days of Josiah even to this day. 3It may be that the house of Judah will hear all the adversities which I purpose to bring upon them, that everyone may turn from his evil way, that I may forgive their iniquity and their sin."

JEHOIAKIM RESISTS BABYLON'S CONTROL (Jer. 36:1)

Jehoiakim, whose personal name was Eliakim, was one of the last three kings of the Judean monarchy (609–598 B.C.). He began his reign as a vassal to Egypt. After the death of his father Josiah at the battle of Megiddo (609 B.C.), Jehoiakim's brother Jehoahaz became Judah's new king. The Egyptian pharaoh Necho II removed Jehoahaz from the throne, deporting him to Egypt and replacing him with his brother Jehoiakim. Paying tribute to Egypt was Jehoiakim's task as a puppet ruler under Egypt's control.

After the battle of Carchemish, which took place in Jehoiakim's 4th year (605 B.C.; Jer. 25:1; 36:1), the Judean king was obliged to shift allegiance to the new power in the area, Chaldean Babylon. The Babylonian Chronicle records that Nebuchadnezzar II marched to the west in 605 B.C. and conducted campaigns in Syria-Palestine from 605 to 601 B.C. It was probably the campaign of 604–603 B.C. for which the Babylonian Chronicle notes that Nebuchadnezzar exacted tribute from many of the Palestinian rulers, which would have included Jehoiakim.

The Judean monarch subsequently continued to pay tribute for the next 3 or 4 years, until the Babylonians suffered setbacks from Egypt. Jehoiakim then rebelled. Nebuchadnezzar did not immediately move against Jerusalem, possibly because, according to the Babylonian Chronicle, he remained in Babylon resupplying his army during his 5th year (599 B.C.).

Jehoiakim's luck would not last forever. The Babylonian Chronicle relates the capture of Jerusalem 2 years later (597 B.C.) by the Babylonian forces. Jehoiakim died either during or as a result of the siege. His son Jehoiachin was deposed, and enormous amounts of tribute were sent to Babylon.

⁴Then Jeremiah called Baruch the son of Neriah; and Baruch wrote on a scroll of a book, at the instruction of Jeremiah,ᵃ all the words of the LORD which He had spoken to him. ⁵And Jeremiah commanded Baruch, saying, "I *am* confined, I cannot go into the house of the LORD. ⁶You go, therefore, and read from the scroll which you have written at my instruction,ᵃ the words of the LORD, in the hearing of the people in the LORD's house on the day of fasting. And you shall also read them in the hearing of all Judah who come from their cities. ⁷It may be that they will present their supplication before the LORD, and everyone will turn from his evil way. For great *is* the anger and the fury that the LORD has pronounced against this people." ⁸And Baruch the son of Neriah did according to all that Jeremiah the prophet commanded him, reading from the book the words of the LORD in the LORD's house.

⁹Now it came to pass in the fifth year of Jehoiakim the son of Josiah, king of Judah, in the ninth month, *that* they proclaimed a fast before the LORD to all the people in Jerusalem, and to all the people who came from the cities of Judah to Jerusalem. ¹⁰Then Baruch read from the book the words of Jeremiah in the house of the LORD, in the chamber of Gemariah the son of Shaphan the scribe, in the upper court at the entry of the New Gate of the LORD's house, in the hearing of all the people.

Jeremiah 25:1–14
Seventy Years of Desolation

25 :1 The word that came to Jeremiah concerning all the people of Judah, in the fourth year of Jehoiakim the son of Josiah, king of Judah (which *was* the first year of Nebuchadnezzar king of Babylon), ²which Jeremiah the prophet spoke to all the people of Judah and to all the inhabitants of Jerusalem, saying: ³"From the thirteenth year of Josiah the son of Amon, king of Judah, even to this day, this *is* the twenty-third year in which the word of the LORD has come to me; and I have spoken to you, rising early and speaking, but you have not listened. ⁴And the LORD has sent to you all His servants the prophets, rising early and sending *them,* but you have not listened nor inclined your ear to hear. ⁵They said, 'Repent now everyone of his evil way and his evil doings, and dwell in the land that the LORD has given to you

36:4 ᵃLiterally *from Jeremiah's mouth*
36:6 ᵃLiterally *from my mouth*

and your fathers forever and ever. ⁶Do not go after other gods to serve them and worship them, and do not provoke Me to anger with the works of your hands; and I will not harm you.' ⁷Yet you have not listened to Me," says the LORD, "that you might provoke Me to anger with the works of your hands to your own hurt.

⁸"Therefore thus says the LORD of hosts: 'Because you have not heard My words, ⁹behold, I will send and take all the families of the north,' says the LORD, 'and Nebuchadnezzar the king of Babylon, My servant, and will bring them against this land, against its inhabitants, and against these nations all around, and will utterly destroy them, and make them an astonishment, a hissing, and perpetual desolations. ¹⁰Moreover I will take from them the voice of mirth and the voice of gladness, the voice of the bridegroom and the voice of the bride, the sound of the millstones and the light of the lamp. ¹¹And this whole land shall be a desolation *and* an astonishment, and these nations shall serve the king of Babylon seventy years.

¹²'Then it will come to pass, when seventy years are completed, *that* I will punish the king of Babylon and that nation, the land of the Chaldeans, for their iniquity,' says the LORD; 'and I will make it a perpetual desolation. ¹³So I will bring on that land all My words which I have pronounced against it, all that is written in this book, which Jeremiah has prophesied concerning all the nations. ¹⁴(For many nations and great kings shall be served by them also; and I will repay them according to their deeds and according to the works of their own hands.)' "

Jeremiah 36:11–32
The Scroll Read in the Palace

36 :11 When Michaiah the son of Gemariah, the son of Shaphan, heard all the words of the LORD from the book, ¹²he then went down to the king's house, into the scribe's chamber; and there all the princes were sitting—Elishama the scribe, Delaiah the son of Shemaiah, Elnathan the son of Achbor, Gemariah the son of Shaphan, Zedekiah the son of Hananiah, and all the princes. ¹³Then Michaiah declared to them all the words that he had heard when Baruch read the book in the

hearing of the people. ¹⁴Therefore all the princes sent Jehudi the son of Nethaniah, the son of Shelemiah, the son of Cushi, to Baruch, saying, "Take in your hand the scroll from which you have read in the hearing of the people, and come." So Baruch the son of Neriah took the scroll in his hand and came to them. ¹⁵And they said to him, "Sit down now, and read it in our hearing." So Baruch read *it* in their hearing.

¹⁶Now it happened, when they had heard all the words, that they looked in fear from one to another, and said to Baruch, "We will surely tell the king of all these words." ¹⁷And they asked Baruch, saying, "Tell us now, how did you write all these words—at his instruction?"ᵃ

¹⁸So Baruch answered them, "He proclaimed with his mouth all these words to me, and I wrote *them* with ink in the book."

¹⁹Then the princes said to Baruch, "Go and hide, you and Jeremiah; and let no one know where you are."

The King Destroys Jeremiah's Scroll

²⁰And they went to the king, into the court; but they stored the scroll in the chamber of Elishama the scribe, and told all the words in the hearing of the king. ²¹So the king sent Jehudi to bring the scroll, and he took it from Elishama the scribe's chamber. And Jehudi read it in the hearing of the king and in the hearing of all the princes who stood beside the king. ²²Now the king was sitting in the winter house in the ninth month, with *a fire* burning on the hearth before him. ²³And it happened, when Jehudi had read three or four columns, *that the king* cut it with the scribe's knife and cast *it* into the fire that *was* on the hearth, until all the scroll was consumed in the fire that *was* on the hearth. ²⁴Yet they were not afraid, nor did they tear their garments, the king nor any of his servants who heard all these words. ²⁵Nevertheless Elnathan, Delaiah, and Gemariah implored the king not to burn the scroll; but he would not listen to them. ²⁶And the king commanded Jerahmeel the king'sᵃ son, Seraiah the son of Azriel, and Shelemiah the son of Abdeel, to seize Baruch the scribe and Jeremiah the prophet, but the LORD hid them.

Jeremiah Rewrites the Scroll

²⁷Now after the king had burned the scroll with the words which Baruch had

---

36:17 ᵃLiterally *with his mouth*   36:26 ᵃHebrew *Hammelech*

A FAITHFUL FRIEND AND SCRIBE (Jer. 36:4, 32)

Jeremiah dictated his prophetic message to a certain Baruch, the son of Neriah (Jer. 36:4). When temple officials forbade Jeremiah to enter the temple with his message of judgment, Baruch took the scroll into the temple courtyard and faithfully read it there (36:9, 10). Ultimately, the king destroyed the scroll, only to have Jeremiah dictate another to Baruch (36:20–24, 32). For his efforts, Baruch received a warrant for his arrest, and had to go into hiding (36:26).

Throughout the Book of Jeremiah, Baruch is pictured as Jeremiah's loyal friend, scribe, and lawyer. Baruch witnessed and sealed the legal transaction for Jeremiah's purchase of land and personally held the deed for Jeremiah (36:12–16). When the military forced Jeremiah to move to Egypt as a refugee following the destruction of Jerusalem, Baruch went with him (43:5, 6). Baruch was evidently Jeremiah's "right-hand man."

Yet Baruch was also a very important person in Jerusalem's society. A seal impression reading "Belonging to Berechiah, son of Neriah, the scribe" has been found in a royal archive. This seal of "Berechiah" (the long form of the name "Baruch") identifies Baruch's profession as a scribe, yet also suggests that he was probably a royal scribe from a prominent scribal family.

Not just anyone had a seal, only those with wealth and influence. Such a seal was a ring used to grant legal status to documents and transactions. Pressed into soft clay, it made the document legally binding based upon the status and character of the person. Baruch's seal impression matches two imprints, or bullae, which were made by the seal. Apparently, Jeremiah's friend and scribe had important connections within Jerusalem's society.

---

written at the instruction of Jeremiah,[a] the word of the LORD came to Jeremiah, saying: ²⁸"Take yet another scroll, and write on it all the former words that were in the first scroll which Jehoiakim the king of Judah has burned. ²⁹And you shall say to Jehoiakim king of Judah, 'Thus says the LORD: "You have burned this scroll, saying, 'Why have you written in it that the king of Babylon will certainly come and destroy this land, and cause man and beast to cease from here?'" ³⁰Therefore thus says the LORD concerning Jehoiakim king of Judah: "He shall have no one to sit on the throne of David, and his dead body shall be cast out to the heat of the day and the frost of the night. ³¹I will punish him, his family, and his servants for their iniquity; and I will bring on them, on the inhabitants of Jerusalem, and on the men of Judah all

the doom that I have pronounced against them; but they did not heed." ' "

³²Then Jeremiah took another scroll and gave it to Baruch the scribe, the son of Neriah, who wrote on it at the instruction of Jeremiah[a] all the words of the book which Jehoiakim king of Judah had burned in the fire. And besides, there were added to them many similar words.

Jeremiah 45:1–5
Assurance to Baruch

45 :1 The word that Jeremiah the prophet spoke to Baruch the son of Neriah, when he had written these words in a book at the instruction of Jeremiah,[a]

36:27 ªLiterally *from Jeremiah's mouth*
36:32 ªLiterally *from Jeremiah's mouth*
45:1 ªLiterally *from Jeremiah's mouth*

ARTS AND LITERATURE

Before the time of Christ, books were written on scrolls made of leather or papyrus, a kind of paper. A typical papyrus scroll was 10 inches high and 15 feet long, with the text written in columns. The scroll that Baruch wrote and then rewrote probably included a significant part of the present Book of Jeremiah, though it is impossible to know which sections exactly (Jer. 36:27).

in the fourth year of Jehoiakim the son of Josiah, king of Judah, saying, [2]"Thus says the LORD, the God of Israel, to you, O Baruch: [3]'You said, "Woe is me now! For the LORD has added grief to my sorrow. I fainted in my sighing, and I find no rest." '

[4]"Thus you shall say to him, 'Thus says the LORD: "Behold, what I have built I will break down, and what I have planted I will pluck up, that is, this whole land. [5]And do you seek great things for yourself? Do not seek *them;* for behold, I will bring adversity on all flesh," says the LORD. "But I will give your life to you as a prize in all places, wherever you go." ' "

Jeremiah 15:10–21
Jeremiah's Dejection

15 :10 Woe is me, my mother,
              That you have borne me,
A man of strife and a man of
        contention to the whole earth!
I have neither lent for interest,
Nor have men lent to me for interest.
Every one of them curses me.

[11]The LORD said:

"Surely it will be well with your
        remnant;
Surely I will cause the enemy to
        intercede with you
In the time of adversity and in the
        time of affliction.
12 Can anyone break iron,
        The northern iron and the bronze?
13 Your wealth and your treasures
        I will give as plunder without price,
Because of all your sins,
        Throughout your territories.
14 And I will make *you* cross over with[a]
        your enemies
Into a land *which* you do not know;
For a fire is kindled in My anger,
Which shall burn upon you."

15 O LORD, You know;
        Remember me and visit me,
And take vengeance for me on my
        persecutors.
In Your enduring patience, do not take
        me away.
Know that for Your sake I have
        suffered rebuke.

16 Your words were found, and I ate
        them,
And Your word was to me the joy and
        rejoicing of my heart;
For I am called by Your name,
O LORD God of hosts.
17 I did not sit in the assembly of the
        mockers,
Nor did I rejoice;
I sat alone because of Your hand,
For You have filled me with
        indignation.
18 Why is my pain perpetual
And my wound incurable,
Which refuses to be healed?
Will You surely be to me like an
        unreliable stream,
As waters *that* fail?

The LORD Reassures Jeremiah

[19]Therefore thus says the LORD:

"If you return,
        Then I will bring you back;
You shall stand before Me;
If you take out the precious from the
        vile,
You shall be as My mouth.
Let them return to you,
But you must not return to them.
20 And I will make you to this people a
        fortified bronze wall;
And they will fight against you,
But they shall not prevail against you;
For I *am* with you to save you
And deliver you," says the LORD.
21 "I will deliver you from the hand of the
        wicked,
And I will redeem you from the grip of
        the terrible."

15:14 [a]Following Masoretic Text and Vulgate; Septuagint, Syriac, and Targum read *cause you to serve* (compare 17:4).

The Droughts

In his early prophecies, Jeremiah calls repeatedly for the people to return to the Lord (e.g., 4:1–4), but in his later oracles he seems less hopeful that the people can repent. Perhaps the continual rejection of his message by the people and the king led to this bleak new perspective.

The mention of "the droughts" (Jer. 14:1) does not specify when these droughts occurred; however, the oracles that follow fit the later years of Jehoiakim's reign. These passages are difficult to place historically, but because of their similarity in theme and their recurring images of deserts and desolation, they can be read in the context of those droughts.

This was a time for weeping, not just by the doomed nation but by the prophet who proclaimed that doom. Jeremiah's laments in Jer. 14:1—15:9 emphasize that Judah's reality would be droughts, war, and famine. The prophet's lifestyle—forbidding marriage, childbearing, attendance at funerals and weddings—was to be a constant reminder of Judah's imminent tragedy (16:1—17:27). Themes of Judah's evil and the consequences of judgment continue in Jer. 8:4—10:16. At times Jeremiah could weep without ceasing (9:1); at other times he wanted to flee from his people (9:2). His discouragement is especially evident in 17:14–18, the third of his "Confessions."

- Jeremiah 14:1—15:9
- Jeremiah 16:1—17:27
- Jeremiah 8:4—10:16

Jeremiah 14:1—15:9
Sword, Famine, and Pestilence

14 :1 The word of the LORD that came to Jeremiah concerning the droughts.

2 "Judah mourns,
   And her gates languish;
   They mourn for the land,
   And the cry of Jerusalem has gone up.
3 Their nobles have sent their lads for water;
   They went to the cisterns *and* found no water.
   They returned with their vessels empty;
   They were ashamed and confounded
   And covered their heads.
4 Because the ground is parched,
   For there was no rain in the land,
   The plowmen were ashamed;
   They covered their heads.
5 Yes, the deer also gave birth in the field,
   But left because there was no grass.
6 And the wild donkeys stood in the desolate heights;

They sniffed at the wind like jackals;
   Their eyes failed because *there was* no grass."

7 O LORD, though our iniquities testify against us,
   Do it for Your name's sake;
   For our backslidings are many,
   We have sinned against You.
8 O the Hope of Israel, his Savior in time of trouble,
   Why should You be like a stranger in the land,
   And like a traveler *who* turns aside to tarry for a night?
9 Why should You be like a man astonished,
   Like a mighty one *who* cannot save?
   Yet You, O LORD, *are* in our midst,
   And we are called by Your name;
   Do not leave us!

¹⁰Thus says the LORD to this people:

"Thus they have loved to wander;
   They have not restrained their feet.
   Therefore the LORD does not accept them;
   He will remember their iniquity now,
   And punish their sins."

¹¹Then the LORD said to me, "Do not pray for this people, for *their* good. ¹²When they fast, I will not hear their cry; and when they offer burnt offering and grain offering, I will not accept them. But I will consume them by the sword, by the famine, and by the pestilence."

¹³Then I said, "Ah, Lord GOD! Behold, the prophets say to them, 'You shall not see the sword, nor shall you have famine, but I will give you assured peace in this place.'"

¹⁴And the LORD said to me, "The prophets prophesy lies in My name. I have not sent them, commanded them, nor spoken to them; they prophesy to you a false vision, divination, a worthless thing, and the deceit of their heart. ¹⁵Therefore thus says the LORD concerning the prophets who

BELIEFS AND IDEAS

The famine resulting from lack of water was a natural calamity, yet the people responded with shame (Jer. 14:4). They felt responsibility for the famine because they considered it to be a punishment for their sins (14:7, 10). The control of the weather and especially rain was exclusively reserved to Judah's God Yahweh (14:22), while surrounding religions attributed this power to Baal.

prophesy in My name, whom I did not send, and who say, 'Sword and famine shall not be in this land'—'By sword and famine those prophets shall be consumed! ¹⁶And the people to whom they prophesy shall be cast out in the streets of Jerusalem because of the famine and the sword; they will have no one to bury them—them nor their wives, their sons nor their daughters—for I will pour their wickedness on them.'

¹⁷"Therefore you shall say this word to them:

'Let my eyes flow with tears night and
    day,
And let them not cease;
For the virgin daughter of my people
Has been broken with a mighty
    stroke, with a very severe blow.
18 If I go out to the field,
Then behold, those slain with the
    sword!
And if I enter the city,
Then behold, those sick from famine!
Yes, both prophet and priest go about
    in a land they do not know.' "

The People Plead for Mercy

19 Have You utterly rejected Judah?
Has Your soul loathed Zion?
Why have You stricken us so that
    there is no healing for us?
We looked for peace, but *there was* no
    good;
And for the time of healing, and there
    was trouble.
20 We acknowledge, O LORD, our
    wickedness
And the iniquity of our fathers,
For we have sinned against You.
21 Do not abhor *us,* for Your name's sake;
Do not disgrace the throne of Your
    glory.
Remember, do not break Your
    covenant with us.
22 Are there any among the idols of the
    nations that can cause rain?
Or can the heavens give showers?
Are You not He, O LORD our God?
Therefore we will wait for You,
Since You have made all these.

The LORD Will Not Relent

15 ¹Then the LORD said to me, "*Even* if Moses and Samuel stood before Me, My mind *would* not *be* favorable toward this people. Cast *them* out of My sight, and let them go forth. ²And it shall be, if they say to you, 'Where should we go?' then you shall tell them, 'Thus says the LORD:

"Such as *are* for death, to death;
And such as *are* for the sword, to the
    sword;
And such as *are* for the famine, to the
    famine;
And such as *are* for the captivity, to
    the captivity." '

³"And I will appoint over them four forms *of destruction,*" says the LORD: "the sword to slay, the dogs to drag, the birds of the heavens and the beasts of the earth to devour and destroy. ⁴I will hand them over to trouble, to all kingdoms of the earth, because of Manasseh the son of Hezekiah, king of Judah, for what he did in Jerusalem.

5 "For who will have pity on you,
    O Jerusalem?
Or who will bemoan you?
Or who will turn aside to ask how you
    are doing?
6 You have forsaken Me," says the LORD,
"You have gone backward.
Therefore I will stretch out My hand
    against you and destroy you;
I am weary of relenting!
7 And I will winnow them with a
    winnowing fan in the gates of the
    land;
I will bereave *them* of children;
I will destroy My people,
Since they do not return from their
    ways.
8 Their widows will be increased to Me
    more than the sand of the seas;
I will bring against them,
Against the mother of the young men,
A plunderer at noonday;
I will cause anguish and terror to fall
    on them suddenly.
9 "She languishes who has borne seven;
She has breathed her last;
Her sun has gone down
While *it was* yet day;
She has been ashamed and
    confounded.
And the remnant of them I will
    deliver to the sword
Before their enemies," says the LORD.

MANASSEH'S REPENTANCE AND FORGIVENESS (Jer. 15:4)

Many of the prayers and hymns of the ancient Near East concern forgiveness for sins committed against a certain deity. The gods could be petitioned for forgiveness because they were viewed as merciful to those who freely confessed their sins. Restoration of health, property, or position were considered signs that forgiveness had been granted. Proper devotion to the god seems to have been enough in ancient times to cancel almost any kind of sin, whether committed with or without knowledge.

One example of a forgiveness prayer is *Ludlul bel Nemeqi,* a Mesopotamian text from the Kassite period (c. 1595–1157 B.C.). The text describes the sufferings of the author and his prayer to the Babylonian god Marduk for relief. The writer admits that he has sinned against the god, even though he is not exactly certain what the transgression was, and asks for mercy. Marduk accepts the petitioner's prayer, forgives his sin, and restores him to health and fortune.

During a long reign (697–642 B.C.) King Manasseh had infuriated Yahweh with his heretical cult innovations. The devastating influence of this king's actions on Judah's national course was still remembered a half-century later by the prophet Jeremiah (Jer. 15:4). The Chronicler records Manasseh's punishment by exile, his prayer of repentance, and acceptance by Yahweh (2 Chr. 33:11–13). As with other Near Eastern forgiveness prayers, Manasseh is restored to his kingdom (33:13).

Jeremiah 16:1—17:27
Jeremiah's Lifestyle and Message

16 :1 The word of the LORD also came to me, saying, 2"You shall not take a wife, nor shall you have sons or daughters in this place." 3For thus says the LORD concerning the sons and daughters who are born in this place, and concerning their mothers who bore them and their fathers who begot them in this land: 4"They shall die gruesome deaths; they shall not be lamented nor shall they be buried, *but* they shall be like refuse on the face of the earth. They shall be consumed by the sword and by famine, and their corpses shall be meat for the birds of heaven and for the beasts of the earth."

5For thus says the LORD: "Do not enter the house of mourning, nor go to lament or bemoan them; for I have taken away My peace from this people," says the LORD, "lovingkindness and mercies. 6Both the great and the small shall die in this land. They shall not be buried; neither shall men lament for them, cut themselves, nor make themselves bald for them. 7Nor shall *men* break *bread* in mourning for them, to comfort them for the dead; nor shall *men* give them the cup of consolation to drink for their father or their mother. 8Also you shall not go into the house of feasting to sit with them, to eat and drink."

9For thus says the LORD of hosts, the God of Israel: "Behold, I will cause to cease from this place, before your eyes and in your days, the voice of mirth and the voice of gladness, the voice of the bridegroom and the voice of the bride.

10"And it shall be, when you show this people all these words, and they say to you, 'Why has the LORD pronounced all this great disaster against us? Or what *is* our iniquity? Or what *is* our sin that we have committed against the LORD our God?' 11then you shall say to them, 'Because your fathers have forsaken Me,' says the LORD; 'they have walked after other gods and have served them and worshiped them, and have forsaken Me and not kept My law. 12And you have done worse than your fathers, for behold, each one follows the dictates of his own evil heart, so that no one listens to Me. 13Therefore I will cast you out of this land into a land that you do not know, neither you nor your fathers; and there you shall serve other gods day and night, where I will not show you favor.'

God Will Restore Israel

14"Therefore behold, the days are coming," says the LORD, "that it shall no more be said, 'The LORD lives who brought up the children of Israel from the land of Egypt,' 15but, 'The LORD lives who brought

A Prophet Without a Family (Jer. 16:2)

A prophet's life often characterized the message that God had given that prophet to proclaim. The symbolism of the single life takes on dark overtones for Jeremiah (Jer. 16:2–13).

God prohibited Jeremiah from marrying, and thus from having children: "You shall not take a wife, nor shall you have sons or daughters in this place" (Jer. 16:2). By prohibiting marriage, God emptied the prophet's life of any future significance from the perspective of his society.

Israelite society was grounded upon the social institution of the family. Not only did the family provide stability for the present, it also carried the status of the family into the future. The man governed the family, and heirs provided the means for his "name," his status and honor, to continue into new generations.

Marriage, then, represented the first step toward achieving an honorable future. Marriage was not so much about "falling in love" as it was a social compact between two families in the hope of gaining more status (honor) for both. Children were the expected fruit of a marriage, cementing the relationship between the families and providing an inheritor to carry on the family's name into the future. With no children, one's household had no future; without a wife, a man had no legitimate children.

By depriving Jeremiah of a family, God symbolically pronounced the depth and extent of His judgment upon Israel. Even without a family, Jeremiah would be better off than his peers. The children of his peers would die "gruesome deaths" (16:3, 4) so frequently that even the parents would not observe the proper mourning rituals (16:5–7). Given the depth of destruction, even celebrations, such as those at weddings, would not occur (16:9). Such would be the price for Judah forsaking Yahweh and walking after other gods (16:10, 11).

---

up the children of Israel from the land of the north and from all the lands where He had driven them.' For I will bring them back into their land which I gave to their fathers.

16"Behold, I will send for many fishermen," says the LORD, "and they shall fish them; and afterward I will send for many hunters, and they shall hunt them from every mountain and every hill, and out of the holes of the rocks. 17For My eyes *are* on all their ways; they are not hidden from My face, nor is their iniquity hidden from My eyes. 18And first I will repay double for their iniquity and their sin, because they have defiled My land; they have filled My inheritance with the carcasses of their detestable and abominable idols."

19   O LORD, my strength and my fortress,
  My refuge in the day of affliction,
  The Gentiles shall come to You
  From the ends of the earth and say,
  "Surely our fathers have inherited lies,
  Worthlessness and unprofitable
    things."

20   Will a man make gods for himself,
  Which *are* not gods?

21   "Therefore behold, I will this once
    cause them to know,
  I will cause them to know
  My hand and My might;
  And they shall know that My name *is*
    the LORD.

Judah's Sin and Punishment

17 1 "The sin of Judah *is* written with a
    pen of iron;
  With the point of a diamond *it is*
    engraved
  On the tablet of their heart,
  And on the horns of your altars,
2   While their children remember
  Their altars and their wooden images[a]
  By the green trees on the high hills.
3   O My mountain in the field,
  I will give as plunder your wealth, all
    your treasures,
  And your high places of sin within all
    your borders.
4   And you, even yourself,
  Shall let go of your heritage which I
    gave you;

17:2 ᵃHebrew *Asherim,* Canaanite deities

MOURNING AT THE BANQUET HALL (Jer. 16:5, 8)

Banqueting houses were common in ancient times, as evidenced by the texts and material remains of the ancient Near East. They were places where individuals (as well as "gods") came for the express purpose of drinking. The writer of Ecclesiastes planted "vineyards" and built "houses" (Eccl. 2:4), by which he could be referring to wine cellars, places where wine was drunk, ritual banquet houses, or even taverns. The prophet Jeremiah was commanded by God not to enter a "house of feasting . . . to eat and drink" (Jer. 16:8) because of the impending doom upon the nation.

The Hebrew term *marzeah* refers to some type of "house," but is ambiguous in meaning. It is translated both as "banquets" (Amos 6:7) and as a "house of mourning" (Jer. 16:5). Whatever its meaning, it is apparently synonymous with the "house of feasting" in Jer. 16:8. The common denominator between the "house of mourning" in Jeremiah and the "banquets" in Amos may be drinking, and not mourning, as scholars have traditionally understood *marzeah*.

The house represented by *marzeah* is found in many written records outside of the Bible. At Ugarit, a Canaanite town with writings dating from 1400 to 1200 B.C., the *marzeah* appears to have been a meeting place for some kind of organization. The primary activity there was drinking. The *marzeah* organization owned much property, including vineyards, and often made large real estate transactions, as recorded in the Ugaritic texts.

The *marzeah* is also found in Phoenician writings from Carthage, as well as in Aramaic texts from Elephantine in Egypt, Palmyra, and Nabatea. It is also mentioned in a text from the Transjordan and in later Hebrew rabbinic writings. From this information, it appears that the *marzeah* was an organization known for its drinking festivals. Sometimes it was associated with funeral feasts, as many there would drink in order to console themselves. Jeremiah's "house of mourning" (Jer. 16:5) and "house of feasting" (16:8) were possibly the same house.

And I will cause you to serve your
enemies
In the land which you do not know;
For you have kindled a fire in My
anger *which* shall burn forever."

⁵Thus says the LORD:

"Cursed *is* the man who trusts in man
And makes flesh his strength,
Whose heart departs from the LORD.
6 For he shall be like a shrub in the
desert,
And shall not see when good comes,
But shall inhabit the parched places
in the wilderness,
In a salt land *which is* not inhabited.

7 "Blessed *is* the man who trusts in the
LORD,
And whose hope is the LORD.
8 For he shall be like a tree planted by
the waters,
Which spreads out its roots by the
river,

And will not fear[a] when heat comes;
But its leaf will be green,
And will not be anxious in the year of
drought,
Nor will cease from yielding fruit.

9 "The heart *is* deceitful above all *things,*
And desperately wicked;
Who can know it?
10 I, the LORD, search the heart,
I test the mind,
Even to give every man according to
his ways,
According to the fruit of his doings.

11 "*As* a partridge that broods but does
not hatch,
So is he who gets riches, but not by
right;
It will leave him in the midst of his
days,
And at his end he will be a fool."

17:8 ᵃQere and Targum read *see.*

12 A glorious high throne from the
  beginning
  Is the place of our sanctuary.
13 O LORD, the hope of Israel,
  All who forsake You shall be ashamed.

"Those who depart from Me
Shall be written in the earth,
Because they have forsaken the LORD,
The fountain of living waters."

Jeremiah Prays for Deliverance

14 Heal me, O LORD, and I shall be
  healed;
  Save me, and I shall be saved,
  For You *are* my praise.
15 Indeed they say to me,
  "Where *is* the word of the LORD?
  Let it come now!"
16 As for me, I have not hurried away
  from *being* a shepherd *who* follows
  You,
  Nor have I desired the woeful day;
  You know what came out of my lips;
  It was right there before You.
17 Do not be a terror to me;
  You *are* my hope in the day of doom.
18 Let them be ashamed who persecute
  me,
  But do not let me be put to shame;
  Let them be dismayed,
  But do not let me be dismayed.
  Bring on them the day of doom,
  And destroy them with double
  destruction!

Hallow the Sabbath Day

¹⁹Thus the LORD said to me: "Go and stand in the gate of the children of the people, by which the kings of Judah come in and by which they go out, and in all the gates of Jerusalem; ²⁰and say to them, 'Hear the word of the LORD, you kings of Judah, and all Judah, and all the inhabitants of Jerusalem, who enter by these gates. ²¹Thus says the LORD: "Take heed to yourselves, and bear no burden on the Sabbath day, nor bring *it* in by the gates of Jerusalem; ²²nor carry a burden out of your houses on the Sabbath day, nor do any work, but hallow the Sabbath day, as I commanded your fathers. ²³But they did not obey nor incline their ear, but made their neck stiff, that they might not hear nor receive instruction.

²⁴"And it shall be, if you heed Me carefully," says the LORD, "to bring no burden through the gates of this city on the Sab-

bath day, but hallow the Sabbath day, to do no work in it, ²⁵then shall enter the gates of this city kings and princes sitting on the throne of David, riding in chariots and on horses, they and their princes, accompanied by the men of Judah and the inhabitants of Jerusalem; and this city shall remain forever. ²⁶And they shall come from the cities of Judah and from the places around Jerusalem, from the land of Benjamin and from the lowland, from the mountains and from the South, bringing burnt offerings and sacrifices, grain offerings and incense, bringing sacrifices of praise to the house of the LORD.

²⁷"But if you will not heed Me to hallow the Sabbath day, such as not carrying a burden when entering the gates of Jerusalem on the Sabbath day, then I will kindle a fire in its gates, and it shall devour the palaces of Jerusalem, and it shall not be quenched." ' "

Jeremiah 8:4—10:16
The Peril of False Teaching

8 :4 "Moreover you shall say to them, 'Thus says the LORD:

"Will they fall and not rise?
Will one turn away and not return?
5 Why has this people slidden back,
  Jerusalem, in a perpetual backsliding?
  They hold fast to deceit,
  They refuse to return.
6 I listened and heard,
  But they do not speak aright.
  No man repented of his wickedness,
  Saying, 'What have I done?'
  Everyone turned to his own course,
  As the horse rushes into the battle.

7 "Even the stork in the heavens
  Knows her appointed times;
  And the turtledove, the swift, and the
  swallow
  Observe the time of their coming.
  But My people do not know the
  judgment of the LORD.

8 "How can you say, 'We *are* wise,
  And the law of the LORD *is* with us'?
  Look, the false pen of the scribe
  certainly works falsehood.
9 The wise men are ashamed,
  They are dismayed and taken.
  Behold, they have rejected the word of
  the LORD;
  So what wisdom do they have?

10 Therefore I will give their wives to
     others,
   And their fields to those who will
     inherit *them;*
   Because from the least even to the
     greatest
   Everyone is given to covetousness;
   From the prophet even to the priest
   Everyone deals falsely.
11 For they have healed the hurt of the
     daughter of My people slightly,
   Saying, 'Peace, peace!'
   When *there is* no peace.
12 Were they ashamed when they had
     committed abomination?
   No! They were not at all ashamed,
   Nor did they know how to blush.
   Therefore they shall fall among those
     who fall;
   In the time of their punishment
   They shall be cast down," says the
     LORD.

13 "I will surely consume them," says the
     LORD.
   "No grapes *shall be* on the vine,
   Nor figs on the fig tree,
   And the leaf shall fade;
   And *the things* I have given them
     shall pass away from them." ' "

14 "Why do we sit still?
   Assemble yourselves,
   And let us enter the fortified cities,
   And let us be silent there.
   For the LORD our God has put us to
     silence
   And given us water of gall to drink,
   Because we have sinned against the
     LORD.

15 "*We* looked for peace, but no good *came;*
   And for a time of health, and there
     was trouble!
16 The snorting of His horses was heard
     from Dan.
   The whole land trembled at the sound
     of the neighing of His strong ones;
   For they have come and devoured the
     land and all that is in it,
   The city and those who dwell in it."

17 "For behold, I will send serpents
     among you,
   Vipers which cannot be charmed,
   And they shall bite you," says the
     LORD.

The Prophet Mourns for the People

18 I would comfort myself in sorrow;
   My heart *is* faint in me.
19 Listen! The voice,
   The cry of the daughter of my people
   From a far country:
   "*Is* not the LORD in Zion?
   Is not her King in her?"

   "Why have they provoked Me to anger
   With their carved images—
   With foreign idols?"

20 "The harvest is past,
   The summer is ended,
   And we are not saved!"

21 For the hurt of the daughter of my
     people I am hurt.
   I am mourning;
   Astonishment has taken hold of me.
22 *Is there* no balm in Gilead,
   Is there no physician there?
   Why then is there no recovery
   For the health of the daughter of my
     people?

9 ¹ Oh, that my head were waters,
      And my eyes a fountain of tears,
   That I might weep day and night
   For the slain of the daughter of my
     people!
2 Oh, that I had in the wilderness
   A lodging place for travelers;
   That I might leave my people,
   And go from them!
   For they *are* all adulterers,
   An assembly of treacherous men.

3 "And *like* their bow they have bent
     their tongues *for* lies.
   They are not valiant for the truth on
     the earth.
   For they proceed from evil to evil,
   And they do not know Me," says the
     LORD.
4 "Everyone take heed to his neighbor,
   And do not trust any brother;
   For every brother will utterly
     supplant,
   And every neighbor will walk with
     slanderers.
5 Everyone will deceive his neighbor,
   And will not speak the truth;
   They have taught their tongue to
     speak lies;
   They weary themselves to commit
     iniquity.

DEATH COMES THROUGH YOUR WINDOWS (Jer. 9:21)

The prophet warns Jerusalem to prepare for deep mourning. The city will be so shattered by the death toll of war that its women will wail with grief. As Jeremiah explains, death will no longer be outside, but rather inside the city. Indeed, death will come through the "windows" into the very homes of the people (Jer. 9:20, 21).

The Hebrew word for "death" is *mot.* In the Hebrew Bible, *mot* not only refers to the place of death, but is also personified, referring to the person "Death." The prophets knew that Yahweh could redeem His people from the plagues of Death (Hos. 13:14). In Ugaritic mythology, Mot was the god of death, who was understood to have final power over all humans, since all people die.

Throughout the ancient Near East there were numerous deities of death. The notion that Death creeps into personal dwellings to steal away the living can be found expressed in almost the same terms in an elegy from Assyria. Written as if by a woman who has died, the poem describes how Death crept into her bedroom and drove her away from her husband.

In both the Bible and the Assyrian text, Death is unwelcome and, like a thief, breaks into one's seemingly safe home to kill without mercy or warning. Jerusalem's women would certainly mourn, "Death has come through our windows" (Jer. 9:21).

---

6 Your dwelling place *is* in the midst of
        deceit;
    Through deceit they refuse to know
        Me," says the LORD.

7Therefore thus says the LORD of hosts:

    "Behold, I will refine them and try
        them;
    For how shall I deal with the
        daughter of My people?
8   Their tongue *is* an arrow shot out;
    It speaks deceit;
    One speaks peaceably to his neighbor
        with his mouth,
    But in his heart he lies in wait.
9   Shall I not punish them for these
        things?" says the LORD.
    "Shall I not avenge Myself on such a
        nation as this?"

10 I will take up a weeping and wailing
        for the mountains,
    And for the dwelling places of the
        wilderness a lamentation,
    Because they are burned up,
    So that no one can pass through;
    Nor can *men* hear the voice of the
        cattle.
    Both the birds of the heavens and the
        beasts have fled;
    They are gone.

11 "I will make Jerusalem a heap of ruins,
        a den of jackals.

    I will make the cities of Judah
        desolate, without an inhabitant."

12Who *is* the wise man who may understand this? And *who is he* to whom the mouth of the LORD has spoken, that he may declare it? Why does the land perish *and* burn up like a wilderness, so that no one can pass through?

13And the LORD said, "Because they have forsaken My law which I set before them, and have not obeyed My voice, nor walked according to it, 14but they have walked according to the dictates of their own hearts and after the Baals, which their fathers taught them," 15therefore thus says the LORD of hosts, the God of Israel: "Behold, I will feed them, this people, with wormwood, and give them water of gall to drink. 16I will scatter them also among the Gentiles, whom neither they nor their fathers have known. And I will send a sword after them until I have consumed them."

The People Mourn in Judgment

17Thus says the LORD of hosts:

    "Consider and call for the mourning
        women,
    That they may come;
    And send for skillful wailing women,
    That they may come.
18 Let them make haste
    And take up a wailing for us,

ORACLES IN HEAVEN (Jer. 10:2)

Jeremiah dismisses the idea of reading the future by looking at the skies. Even though Gentile nations studied the "signs of heaven" and were "dismayed at them" (Jer. 10:2), Judah was not to follow their example. Ancient people had two ways of trying to read the future in the skies: one way studied atmospheric conditions; the other, the movement of planets and stars.

The atmospheric method looked to various weather-related conditions as indicators of what events would occur on earth. The way the wind blew, how the rain fell, the formation of clouds, or the color of the morning or evening sky were recorded and checked against the omen books to see what they meant. People did not think that these weather conditions caused the earthly events. Rather, the event was simply associated with a particular weather condition.

More famous, because it has been retained to the present age, is the reading of the stars and planets. Early forms of astronomy and astrology merged to tell both time and the future. By the 1st Dynasty in Egypt (c. 3000 B.C.) scribes associated the flooding of the Nile with the rising of the star Sirius. From the 9th Dynasty (c. 2160 B.C.) onward a series of stars (known as "rams" in Egypt) were thought to control individual destinies.

The zodiac and other familiar forms of astrology were developed in Mesopotamia. The earliest Mesopotamian astrological references date from the Dynasty of Accad (c. 2300 B.C.). The Old Babylonian period (c. 2017–1595 B.C.) provides the first extensive series of celestial "charts," collected in a work entitled *Enuma Anu Enlil*.

At first the system was used to predict events for the nation itself and for the royal family. By the Neo-Assyrian period (934–612 B.C.) all the elements which now make up the zodiac appeared in an Assyrian text. The formal 12-sign, 4-season structure appeared later in the Neo-Babylonian (626–539 B.C.) or early Persian (539–530 B.C.) periods. The prophets dismissed the endeavors of astrologers and stargazers as meaningless (Jer. 10:2; Is. 47:13).

That our eyes may run with tears,
And our eyelids gush with water.

19 For a voice of wailing is heard from
    Zion:
'How we are plundered!
We are greatly ashamed,
Because we have forsaken the land,
Because we have been cast out of our
    dwellings.' "

20 Yet hear the word of the LORD,
    O women,
And let your ear receive the word of
    His mouth;
Teach your daughters wailing,
And everyone her neighbor a
    lamentation.

21 For death has come through our
    windows,
Has entered our palaces,
To kill off the children—*no longer to
be* outside!
And the young men—*no longer* on the
    streets!

22 Speak, "Thus says the LORD:

'Even the carcasses of men shall fall as
    refuse on the open field,
Like cuttings after the harvester,
And no one shall gather *them.*' "

23 Thus says the LORD:

"Let not the wise *man* glory in his
    wisdom,
Let not the mighty *man* glory in his
    might,
Nor let the rich *man* glory in his
    riches;

24 But let him who glories glory in this,
That he understands and knows Me,
That I *am* the LORD, exercising
    lovingkindness, judgment, and
    righteousness in the earth.
For in these I delight," says the LORD.

25 "Behold, the days are coming," says
the LORD, "that I will punish all *who are*

circumcised with the uncircumcised—
26Egypt, Judah, Edom, the people of Ammon, Moab, and all *who are* in the farthest corners, who dwell in the wilderness. For all *these* nations *are* uncircumcised, and all the house of Israel *are* uncircumcised in the heart."

Idols and the True God

10 1Hear the word which the Lord speaks to you, O house of Israel.
2Thus says the Lord:

"Do not learn the way of the Gentiles;
Do not be dismayed at the signs of heaven,
For the Gentiles are dismayed at them.
3 For the customs of the peoples *are* futile;
For *one* cuts a tree from the forest,
The work of the hands of the workman, with the ax.
4 They decorate it with silver and gold;
They fasten it with nails and hammers
So that it will not topple.
5 They *are* upright, like a palm tree,
And they cannot speak;
They must be carried,
Because they cannot go *by themselves*.
Do not be afraid of them,
For they cannot do evil,
Nor can they do any good."

6 Inasmuch as *there is* none like You,
O Lord
(You *are* great, and Your name *is* great in might),
7 Who would not fear You, O King of the nations?
For this is Your rightful due.
For among all the wise *men* of the nations,
And in all their kingdoms,
There is none like You.

8 But they are altogether dull-hearted and foolish;
A wooden idol *is* a worthless doctrine.
9 Silver is beaten into plates;
It is brought from Tarshish,
And gold from Uphaz,
The work of the craftsman
And of the hands of the metalsmith;
Blue and purple *are* their clothing;
They *are* all the work of skillful *men*.
10 But the Lord *is* the true God;
He *is* the living God and the everlasting King.
At His wrath the earth will tremble,
And the nations will not be able to endure His indignation.

11Thus you shall say to them: "The gods that have not made the heavens and the earth shall perish from the earth and from under these heavens."

12 He has made the earth by His power,
He has established the world by His wisdom,
And has stretched out the heavens at His discretion.
13 When He utters His voice,
There is a multitude of waters in the heavens:
"And He causes the vapors to ascend from the ends of the earth.
He makes lightning for the rain,
He brings the wind out of His treasuries."a

14 Everyone is dull-hearted, without knowledge;
Every metalsmith is put to shame by an image;
For his molded image *is* falsehood,
And *there is* no breath in them.
15 They *are* futile, a work of errors;
In the time of their punishment they shall perish.
16 The Portion of Jacob *is* not like them,
For He *is* the Maker of all *things*,
And Israel *is* the tribe of His inheritance;
The Lord of hosts *is* His name.

10:13 aPsalm 135:7

ARCHITECTURE AND BUILDING

The people of Canaan worshiped in many centers. The most prominent element in their worship was the wooden poles set up in honor of their female goddess (Jer. 10:3–5). It is doubtful that these poles were freestanding sculpture, but they could have been carved in low relief. Except under unusual circumstances, such as the dry climate of Egypt, wood does not survive for archaeologists to discover.

Jehoiakim's Rebellion Against Babylon

Despite his promises to remain faithful to Egypt, Jehoiakim had to bow to Babylonian authority. The Babylonian Chronicle reports that Babylon's King Nebuchadnezzar campaigned in Syria-Palestine each year from 605 to 601 B.C. It was probably during the long campaign of 604–603 that Nebuchadnezzar showed his power in Jerusalem, and Jehoiakim became his subject. Jehoiakim always preferred alliances with Egypt though, and he rebelled against Babylon as soon as he thought he could get away with it. Sometime around 601 B.C. the Babylonian army suffered a military setback while fighting Pharaoh Necho in Egypt. Jehoiakim thought that this was his opportunity. He was mistaken.

■ 2 Kings 24:1–4

2 Kings
Judah Overrun by Enemies

24 :1 In his days Nebuchadnezzar king of Babylon came up, and Jehoiakim became his vassal *for* three years. Then he turned and rebelled against him. ²And the LORD sent against him *raiding* bands of Chaldeans, bands of Syrians, bands of Moabites, and bands of the people of Ammon; He sent them against Judah to destroy it, according to the word of the LORD which He had spoken by His servants the prophets. ³Surely at the commandment of the LORD *this* came upon Judah, to remove *them* from His sight because of the sins of Manasseh, according to all that he had done, ⁴and also because of the innocent blood that he had shed; for he had filled Jerusalem with innocent blood, which the LORD would not pardon.

The Rechabites

When Nebuchadnezzar swept through the land of Judah on the way to Jerusalem, he drove all the inhabitants before him. One family that was driven to take refuge in Jerusalem was the family of Rechab (Jer. 35:11). This family, the Rechabites, had rigorously obeyed the arbitrary injunctions of their ancestor Jonadab, and Jer. 35 highlights their obedience as an example of loyalty not found in Judah in its last days.

The notable member of this family, who appears to be the founder, was Jonadab (Jer.

35:6; also spelled Jehonadab). He is mentioned in 2 Kin. 10:15, 16 as one who opposed the worship of Baal in Israel, joining Jehu in his "zeal for the LORD." Jonadab and his Rechabite descendants displayed a faithfulness and devotion towards Yahweh that was lacking in disobedient Judah.

■ Jeremiah 35:1–19

Jeremiah
The Obedient Rechabites

35 :1 The word which came to Jeremiah from the LORD in the days of Jehoiakim the son of Josiah, king of Judah, saying, ²"Go to the house of the Rechabites, speak to them, and bring them into the house of the LORD, into one of the chambers, and give them wine to drink."

³Then I took Jaazaniah the son of Jeremiah, the son of Habazziniah, his brothers and all his sons, and the whole house of the Rechabites, ⁴and I brought them into the house of the LORD, into the chamber of the sons of Hanan the son of Igdaliah, a man of God, which *was* by the chamber of the princes, above the chamber of Maaseiah the son of Shallum, the keeper of the door. ⁵Then I set before the sons of the house of the Rechabites bowls full of wine, and cups; and I said to them, "Drink wine."

⁶But they said, "We will drink no wine, for Jonadab the son of Rechab, our father, commanded us, saying, 'You shall drink no wine, you nor your sons, forever. ⁷You shall not build a house, sow seed, plant a vineyard, nor have *any of these;* but all your days you shall dwell in tents, that you may live many days in the land where you are sojourners.' ⁸Thus we have obeyed the voice of Jonadab the son of Rechab, our father, in all that he charged us, to drink no wine all

THE OBEDIENT RECHABITES (Jer. 35:2)

The Rechabites are an enigmatic people mentioned by name only in Jeremiah 35. We can assume that the Rechabite family members encountered by Jeremiah were quite few in number, since all of them were able to fit in just one area of the temple (Jer. 35:2).

The Rechabites were not usually city dwellers, since they did not build, or live, in houses, nor plant gardens or vineyards (Jer. 35:7). They lived in tents as seasonal nomads, following the available water sources for their animals. In addition to the usual nomadic lifestyle, the Rechabites did not drink wine because Rechab (the ancestor from whom they derived their name) had commanded them saying "You shall drink no wine, you nor your sons, forever" (Jer. 35:6). It is possible that, in some way, the Rechabites were related to the Kenites (1 Chr. 2:55). This link with the Kenites would make the Rechabites distant relatives of Moses (Judg. 1:16).

Jeremiah pays special attention to the Rechabites partly because of their loyalty to their father. The prophet cites the example of the Rechabites as the basis for an earnest plea to a disobedient Judah (Jer. 35:12–16). This family had rigorously obeyed the arbitrary injunctions of an earthly father. Why could not Judah obey the injunctions of their God Yahweh?

The reward for the Rechabites was the promise that their family would always continue (Jer. 35:19; Neh. 3:14). Implicit in this promise was hope that, if the Judahites would return to Yahweh, they too would continue to exist.

---

our days, we, our wives, our sons, or our daughters, 9nor to build ourselves houses to dwell in; nor do we have vineyard, field, or seed. 10But we have dwelt in tents, and have obeyed and done according to all that Jonadab our father commanded us. 11But it came to pass, when Nebuchadnezzar king of Babylon came up into the land, that we said, 'Come, let us go to Jerusalem for fear of the army of the Chaldeans and for fear of the army of the Syrians.' So we dwell at Jerusalem."

12Then came the word of the LORD to Jeremiah, saying, 13"Thus says the LORD of hosts, the God of Israel: 'Go and tell the men of Judah and the inhabitants of Jerusalem, "Will you not receive instruction to obey My words?" says the LORD. 14"The words of Jonadab the son of Rechab, which he commanded his sons, not to drink wine, are performed; for to this day they drink none, and obey their father's commandment. But although I have spoken to you, rising early and speaking, you did not obey Me. 15I have also sent to you all My servants the prophets, rising up early and sending them, saying, 'Turn now everyone from his evil way, amend your doings, and do not go after other gods to serve them; then you will dwell in the land which I have given you and your fathers.' But you have not inclined your ear, nor obeyed Me. 16Surely the sons of Jonadab the son of

Rechab have performed the commandment of their father, which he commanded them, but this people has not obeyed Me."'

17"Therefore thus says the LORD God of hosts, the God of Israel: 'Behold, I will bring on Judah and on all the inhabitants of Jerusalem all the doom that I have pronounced against them; because I have spoken to them but they have not heard, and I have called to them but they have not answered.'"

18And Jeremiah said to the house of the Rechabites, "Thus says the LORD of hosts, the God of Israel: 'Because you have obeyed the commandment of Jonadab your father, and kept all his precepts and done according to all that he commanded you, 19therefore thus says the LORD of hosts, the God of Israel: "Jonadab the son of Rechab shall not lack a man to stand before Me forever."'"

False Prophets

No prophet since Elijah had more trouble with false prophets than Jeremiah. As Nebuchadnezzar approached Jerusalem, Jeremiah declared that God would give the city to the armies of Babylon, but other prophets proclaimed that Jerusalem could never be captured, never be destroyed. These false prophets of Judah would bear responsibility for

Jerusalem's coming fall, for they had confirmed the people in their sinful ways (Jer. 23:9–40).

Jeremiah's message of imminent doom led inevitably to more persecution. The narratives of chs. 18—20 show both the message and the response it was given. The last two of Jeremiah's Confessions also appear here (18:19–23 and 20:7–18). The final Confession, especially, is a wrenching cry from a man who never wanted to be a prophet but who could not stop, from a messenger whose greatness as a prophet is only magnified by his human frailty.

■ Jeremiah 23:9–40
■ Jeremiah 18:18—20:18

Jeremiah 23:9–40
False Prophets and Empty Oracles

23 :9 My heart within me is broken
Because of the prophets;
All my bones shake.
I am like a drunken man,
And like a man whom wine has
overcome,
Because of the LORD,
And because of His holy words.
10 For the land is full of adulterers;
For because of a curse the land
mourns.
The pleasant places of the wilderness
are dried up.
Their course of life is evil,
And their might *is* not right.

11 "For both prophet and priest are
profane;
Yes, in My house I have found their
wickedness," says the LORD.
12 "Therefore their way shall be to them
Like slippery *ways;*
In the darkness they shall be
driven on
And fall in them;
For I will bring disaster on them,
The year of their punishment," says
the LORD.
13 "And I have seen folly in the prophets
of Samaria:
They prophesied by Baal
And caused My people Israel to err.
14 Also I have seen a horrible thing in
the prophets of Jerusalem:
They commit adultery and walk in
lies;
They also strengthen the hands of
evildoers,

So that no one turns back from his
wickedness.
All of them are like Sodom to Me,
And her inhabitants like Gomorrah.

15 "Therefore thus says the LORD of
hosts concerning the prophets:

'Behold, I will feed them with
wormwood,
And make them drink the water of
gall;
For from the prophets of Jerusalem
Profaneness has gone out into all the
land.' "

16 Thus says the LORD of hosts:

"Do not listen to the words of the
prophets who prophesy to you.
They make you worthless;
They speak a vision of their own
heart,
Not from the mouth of the LORD.
17 They continually say to those who
despise Me,
'The LORD has said, "You shall have
peace" ';
And *to* everyone who walks according
to the dictates of his own heart,
they say,
'No evil shall come upon you.' "

18 For who has stood in the counsel of
the LORD,
And has perceived and heard His
word?
Who has marked His word and heard
it?
19 Behold, a whirlwind of the LORD has
gone forth in fury—
A violent whirlwind!
It will fall violently on the head of the
wicked.
20 The anger of the LORD will not turn
back
Until He has executed and performed
the thoughts of His heart.
In the latter days you will understand
it perfectly.

21 "I have not sent these prophets, yet
they ran.
I have not spoken to them, yet they
prophesied.
22 But if they had stood in My counsel,
And had caused My people to hear My
words,

TRUE OR FALSE PROPHET? (Jer. 23:16–27)

Jeremiah relentlessly proclaimed a message of God's judgment, warning that the Babylonians would come and completely devastate Judah and Jerusalem. The sufferings he described of the Babylonian siege and subsequent victory were terrifying (Jer. 18:21).

To say the least, this did not exactly make him a popular speaker in Jerusalem. People then, as now, wanted an optimistic, upbeat message. Jeremiah, therefore, often had conflict with others, especially the aristocracy of Jerusalem, over the content of his prophecy. Among other things, Jeremiah once ended up in stocks outside the temple as the leaders of Jerusalem tried to get him to change his vision of the future (Jer. 20:1–6).

Jeremiah, however, was not the only prophet at work in Jerusalem at that time. Other prophets worked the streets as well, and they were a little more sensitive to public sentiments than Jeremiah. As one might expect, these prophets were much more popular.

These other prophets recalled that the prophet Isaiah had correctly prophesied that God would save Jerusalem from the Assyrians merely a century earlier (Is. 37:21–35). From this they concluded, and publicly prophesied, that God again would save Jerusalem, and His temple, from defeat. Even though the Babylonians pressed near, there would be "peace" (Jer. 23:17).

In Jeremiah's time it was not easy to distinguish between a false prophet and a true prophet: Which prophet had really received counsel from God? The key difference, claimed Jeremiah, was moral: the false prophets' oracles had brought about no change in the Judahites' evil lifestyle (23:22). This indicated that these prophets spoke "a vision of their own heart, not from the mouth of the LORD" (23:16).

Then they would have turned them
  from their evil way
And from the evil of their doings.

23 "Am I a God near at hand," says the
    LORD,
  "And not a God afar off?
24 Can anyone hide himself in secret
    places,
  So I shall not see him?" says the LORD;
  "Do I not fill heaven and earth?" says
    the LORD.

25"I have heard what the prophets have said who prophesy lies in My name, saying, 'I have dreamed, I have dreamed!' 26How long will *this* be in the heart of the prophets who prophesy lies? Indeed *they are* prophets of the deceit of their own heart, 27who try to make My people forget My name by their dreams which everyone tells his neighbor, as their fathers forgot My name for Baal.

28 "The prophet who has a dream, let him
    tell a dream;
  And he who has My word, let him
    speak My word faithfully.
  What *is* the chaff to the wheat?" says
    the LORD.
29 "*Is* not My word like a fire?" says the
    LORD,
  "And like a hammer *that* breaks the
    rock in pieces?

30"Therefore behold, I *am* against the prophets," says the LORD, "who steal My words every one from his neighbor. 31Behold, I *am* against the prophets," says the LORD, "who use their tongues and say, 'He

---

RELIGION AND WORSHIP

People knew the prophets by their appearance and way of life (2 Kin. 1:8), their visible experiences (1 Sam. 19:24), and their prophetic word (2 Chr. 18:7). Evidently some or most of these signs could be counterfeited by false prophets, claiming to speak for Yahweh (Jer. 23:25). Priests and diviners who publicly claimed to represent other gods were more easily identified and excluded (Deut. 13:2).

says.' ³²Behold, I *am* against those who prophesy false dreams," says the LORD, "and tell them, and cause My people to err by their lies and by their recklessness. Yet I did not send them or command them; therefore they shall not profit this people at all," says the LORD.

³³"So when these people or the prophet or the priest ask you, saying, 'What is the oracle of the LORD?' you shall then say to them, 'What oracle?'ᵃ I will even forsake you," says the LORD. ³⁴"And *as for* the prophet and the priest and the people who say, 'The oracle of the LORD!' I will even punish that man and his house. ³⁵Thus every one of you shall say to his neighbor, and every one to his brother, 'What has the LORD answered?' and, 'What has the LORD spoken?' ³⁶And the oracle of the LORD you shall mention no more. For every man's word will be his oracle, for you have perverted the words of the living God, the LORD of hosts, our God. ³⁷Thus you shall say to the prophet, 'What has the LORD answered you?' and, 'What has the LORD spoken?' ³⁸But since you say, 'The oracle of the LORD!' therefore thus says the LORD: 'Because you say this word, "The oracle of the LORD!" and I have sent to you, saying, "Do not say, 'The oracle of the LORD!' " ³⁹therefore behold, I, even I, will utterly forget you and forsake you, and the city that I gave you and your fathers, and *will cast you* out of My presence. ⁴⁰And I will bring an everlasting reproach upon you, and a perpetual shame, which shall not be forgotten.' "

Jeremiah 18:18—20:18
Jeremiah Persecuted

18 :18 Then they said, "Come and let us devise plans against Jeremiah; for the law shall not perish from the priest, nor counsel from the wise, nor the word from the prophet. Come and let us attack him with the tongue, and let us not give heed to any of his words."

19   Give heed to me, O LORD,
      And listen to the voice of those who
          contend with me!
20   Shall evil be repaid for good?
      For they have dug a pit for my life.
      Remember that I stood before You
      To speak good for them,
      To turn away Your wrath from them.
21   Therefore deliver up their children to
          the famine,
      And pour out their *blood*

      By the force of the sword;
      Let their wives *become* widows
      And bereaved of their children.
      Let their men be put to death,
      Their young men *be* slain
      By the sword in battle.
22   Let a cry be heard from their houses,
      When You bring a troop suddenly
          upon them;
      For they have dug a pit to take me,
      And hidden snares for my feet.
23   Yet, LORD, You know all their counsel
      Which is against me, to slay *me*.
      Provide no atonement for their
          iniquity,
      Nor blot out their sin from Your sight;
      But let them be overthrown before
          You.
      Deal *thus* with them
      In the time of Your anger.

The Sign of the Broken Flask

19 ¹Thus says the LORD: "Go and get a potter's earthen flask, and *take* some of the elders of the people and some of the elders of the priests. ²And go out to the Valley of the Son of Hinnom, which *is* by the entry of the Potsherd Gate; and proclaim there the words that I will tell you, ³and say, 'Hear the word of the LORD, O kings of Judah and inhabitants of Jerusalem. Thus says the LORD of hosts, the God of Israel: "Behold, I will bring such a catastrophe on this place, that whoever hears of it, his ears will tingle.

⁴"Because they have forsaken Me and made this an alien place, because they have burned incense in it to other gods whom neither they, their fathers, nor the kings of Judah have known, and have filled this place with the blood of the innocents ⁵(they have also built the high places of Baal, to burn their sons with fire *for* burnt offerings to Baal, which I did not command or speak, nor did it come into My mind), ⁶therefore behold, the days are coming," says the LORD, "that this place shall no more be called Tophet or the Valley of the Son of Hinnom, but the Valley of Slaughter. ⁷And I will make void the counsel of Judah and Jerusalem in this place, and I will cause them to fall by the sword before their enemies and by the hands of those who seek their lives; their corpses I will give as meat for the birds of the heaven and for

23:33 ᵃSeptuagint, Targum, and Vulgate read *You are the burden.*

BROKEN PIECES IN THE GARBAGE DUMP (Jer. 19:1–13)

Refuse disposal is a necessity not only for contemporary society, but was also for urban life in ancient Israel. Much like pioneer America where the refuse pile was just off the back step of the house, Jerusalemite society used a valley just outside its walls, the Valley of Hinnom, to dispose of its garbage.

Large pots served as the "garbage cans" to deliver the refuse to its proper place. Therefore, the gate that provided access to this valley was called the Potsherd Gate. In postexilic Judah, in the time of Nehemiah, the same gate was called the Refuse Gate (Neh. 2:13; 3:14). It probably was not a pleasant place to spend an afternoon!

The Valley of Hinnom was also not a place that the "elders of the people" and "the elders of the priests" (Jer. 19:1), the leaders of Jerusalemite society, frequented very often. They, no doubt, had others to carry out their garbage. Yet it was in the midst of the city dump that Jeremiah called these important leaders of Jerusalem and Judah (19:2).

If the elders were not pleased at the location, they probably were not pleased with Jeremiah's message, either. Jeremiah used the setting to proclaim the tragedy that would soon befall Jerusalem, a tragedy so great as to make the ears "tingle" (19:3). The gist of Jeremiah's oracle is that all Judah and Jerusalem will become like broken pots in the garbage dump (19:6–9, 11–13). Jeremiah punctuated this oracle of judgment by shattering a pot in front of the elders (19:10, 11).

Through the combination of location and action, therefore, Jeremiah made God's coming judgment of Judah clear. Destruction awaited.

---

the beasts of the earth. ⁸I will make this city desolate and a hissing; everyone who passes by it will be astonished and hiss because of all its plagues. ⁹And I will cause them to eat the flesh of their sons and the flesh of their daughters, and everyone shall eat the flesh of his friend in the siege and in the desperation with which their enemies and those who seek their lives shall drive them to despair." '

¹⁰"Then you shall break the flask in the sight of the men who go with you, ¹¹and say to them, 'Thus says the LORD of hosts: "Even so I will break this people and this city, as *one* breaks a potter's vessel, which cannot be made whole again; and they shall bury *them* in Tophet till *there is* no place to bury. ¹²Thus I will do to this place," says the LORD, "and to its inhabitants, and make this city like Tophet. ¹³And the houses of Jerusalem and the houses of the kings of Judah shall be de-

filed like the place of Tophet, because of all the houses on whose roofs they have burned incense to all the host of heaven, and poured out drink offerings to other gods." ' "

¹⁴Then Jeremiah came from Tophet, where the LORD had sent him to prophesy; and he stood in the court of the Lord's house and said to all the people, ¹⁵"Thus says the LORD of hosts, the God of Israel: 'Behold, I will bring on this city and on all her towns all the doom that I have pronounced against it, because they have stiffened their necks that they might not hear My words.' "

The Word of God to Pashhur

20 ¹Now Pashhur the son of Immer, the priest who *was* also chief governor in the house of the LORD, heard that Jeremiah prophesied these things. ²Then Pashhur struck Jeremiah the prophet, and put

---

ARCHITECTURE AND BUILDING

In the Middle East the roofs of houses can be used like the deck or porch of a North American house. Archaeologists have discovered evidence that the people of Ashkelon, a Philistine town, burned incense on the roofs of their houses (Jer. 19:13). In ancient societies, religious rituals were carried out not just by the state, but also by individuals and households.

him in the stocks that *were* in the high gate of Benjamin, which *was* by the house of the LORD.

³And it happened on the next day that Pashhur brought Jeremiah out of the stocks. Then Jeremiah said to him, "The LORD has not called your name Pashhur, but Magor-Missabib.ᵃ ⁴For thus says the LORD: 'Behold, I will make you a terror to yourself and to all your friends; and they shall fall by the sword of their enemies, and your eyes shall see *it*. I will give all Judah into the hand of the king of Babylon, and he shall carry them captive to Babylon and slay them with the sword. ⁵Moreover I will deliver all the wealth of this city, all its produce, and all its precious things; all the treasures of the kings of Judah I will give into the hand of their enemies, who will plunder them, seize them, and carry them to Babylon. ⁶And you, Pashhur, and all who dwell in your house, shall go into captivity. You shall go to Babylon, and there you shall die, and be buried there, you and all your friends, to whom you have prophesied lies.' "

Jeremiah's Unpopular Ministry

7   O LORD, You induced me, and I was
       persuaded;
     You are stronger than I, and have
       prevailed.
     I am in derision daily;
     Everyone mocks me.
8   For when I spoke, I cried out;
     I shouted, "Violence and plunder!"
     Because the word of the LORD was
       made to me
     A reproach and a derision daily.
9   Then I said, "I will not make mention
       of Him,
     Nor speak anymore in His name."
     But *His word* was in my heart like a
       burning fire
     Shut up in my bones;
     I was weary of holding *it* back,
     And I could not.
10   For I heard many mocking:
     "Fear on every side!"

"Report," *they say,* "and we will report
     it!"
All my acquaintances watched for my
     stumbling, *saying,*
"Perhaps he can be induced;
     Then we will prevail against him,
     And we will take our revenge on him."

11   But the LORD *is* with me as a mighty,
     awesome One.
     Therefore my persecutors will
     stumble, and will not prevail.
     They will be greatly ashamed, for they
     will not prosper.
     Their everlasting confusion will never
     be forgotten.
12   But, O LORD of hosts,
     You who test the righteous,
     And see the mind and heart,
     Let me see Your vengeance on them;
     For I have pleaded my cause before
     You.

13   Sing to the LORD! Praise the LORD!
     For He has delivered the life of the
     poor
     From the hand of evildoers.

14   Cursed *be* the day in which I was
     born!
     Let the day not be blessed in which
     my mother bore me!
15   Let the man *be* cursed
     Who brought news to my father,
     saying,
"A male child has been born to you!"
     Making him very glad.
16   And let that man be like the cities
     Which the LORD overthrew, and did
     not relent;
     Let him hear the cry in the morning
     And the shouting at noon,
17   Because he did not kill me from the
     womb,
     That my mother might have been my
     grave,

20:3 ᵃLiterally *Fear on Every Side*

BELIEFS AND IDEAS

Although the Romans dignified suicide, regarding it as an acceptable way of leaving this world, the Judeans were much less approving of it. They did not criticize Saul for taking his own life in the wake of defeat in war, thus escaping abuse from his enemies (1 Sam. 31:4). Yet to curse the gift of life was understood to be an extreme act, practically an insult to God (Jer. 20:14; Job 2:9, 10).

PHARAOH NECHO BATTLES THE BABYLONIANS (2 Kin. 24:7)

Pharaoh Necho II, who reigned from 610 to 595 B.C., was the second king of the 26th Dynasty of Egypt. He is known for his defeat of Judah and killing of King Josiah at Megiddo in 609 B.C., and for his own defeat at the hands of Babylon at Carchemish in 605 B.C.

During the last years of the Assyrian Empire, Necho assisted the weakened Assyrians in their struggles against the rising power of the Babylonians. Accadian sources relate that in 609 Necho was moving his army north to help the Assyrians recapture Haran from the Babylonians. On the way, he encountered Josiah. In 605, Babylon completely annihilated Necho's Egyptian army at Carchemish.

The pharaoh was successful in repelling a Babylonian invasion deep into Palestine in 601 B.C. This evidently caused Judah's king Jehoiakim to rebel against Babylonian control (2 Kin. 24:1). Apparently Necho's forces could not recover from the 601 battle in order to conduct future campaigns: Necho "did not come out of his land anymore" (2 Kin. 24:7). After 601, it appears that Egypt and Babylon were not hostile, but nothing more is mentioned about Necho, who died in 595 B.C.

And her womb always enlarged *with me.*

18 Why did I come forth from the womb
to see labor and sorrow,
That my days should be consumed
with shame?

Do Not Hope in King Jehoiachin

The attack on Egypt's border in 601 B.C. by Nebuchadnezzar's Babylonian army was repelled by Pharaoh Necho. Babylon recovered from this battle, but Egypt did not. In the last few years before his death in 595 B.C., Pharaoh Necho could do no more than keep Babylon from invading Egypt (2 Kin. 24:7).

Before Nebuchadnezzar could capture Jerusalem, Jehoiakim died. Given the situation, one could speculate that he was assassinated, but such an event is unknown. In any case, he does not appear to have been much missed, if Jeremiah's comments on his death are representative (Jer. 22:18–23).

Jehoiakim was succeeded by his son Coniah (also spelled Jeconiah), who is very often mentioned alongside his mother Nehushta. When Coniah became king, he assumed the throne name Jehoiachin. Though pleased to be rid of Jehoiakim, Jeremiah did not greet the new king with optimism. His warnings now carried with them the conviction that it was too late (Jer. 13:15–27). The king and his mother would be taken into exile (Jer. 22:24–30; 13:18, 19). Jehoiachin ruled for only 3

months in 598–597 B.C. before surrendering to Nebuchadnezzar.

- 2 Kings 24:5–9
- Jeremiah 22:18–30
- Jeremiah 13:15–27

2 Kings 24:5–9

24 **:5** Now the rest of the acts of Jehoiakim, and all that he did, *are* they not written in the book of the chronicles of the kings of Judah? **6**So Jehoiakim rested with his fathers. Then Jehoiachin his son reigned in his place.

7And the king of Egypt did not come out of his land anymore, for the king of Babylon had taken all that belonged to the king of Egypt from the Brook of Egypt to the River Euphrates.

The Reign of Jehoiachin

8Jehoiachin *was* eighteen years old when he became king, and he reigned in Jerusalem three months. His mother's name *was* Nehushta the daughter of Elnathan of Jerusalem. **9**And he did evil in the sight of the LORD, according to all that his father had done.

Jeremiah 22:18–30
Message to Jehoiakim

22 **:18** Therefore thus says the LORD concerning Jehoiakim the son of Josiah, king of Judah:

"They shall not lament for him,
Saying, 'Alas, my brother!' or 'Alas, my sister!'

They shall not lament for him,
Saying, 'Alas, master!' or 'Alas, his
glory!'
19   He shall be buried with the burial of a
donkey,
Dragged and cast out beyond the
gates of Jerusalem.

20   "Go up to Lebanon, and cry out,
And lift up your voice in Bashan;
Cry from Abarim,
For all your lovers are destroyed.
21   I spoke to you in your prosperity,
But you said, 'I will not hear.'
This *has been* your manner from your
youth,
That you did not obey My voice.
22   The wind shall eat up all your rulers,
And your lovers shall go into captivity;
Surely then you will be ashamed and
humiliated
For all your wickedness.
23   O inhabitant of Lebanon,
Making your nest in the cedars,
How gracious will you be when pangs
come upon you,
Like the pain of a woman in labor?

Message to Coniah

24 *"As* I live," says the LORD, "though
Coniah[a] the son of Jehoiakim, king of Judah, were the signet on My right hand, yet
I would pluck you off; 25and I will give you
into the hand of those who seek your life,
and into the hand *of those* whose face you
fear—the hand of Nebuchadnezzar king of
Babylon and the hand of the Chaldeans.
26So I will cast you out, and your mother
who bore you, into another country where
you were not born; and there you shall die.
27But to the land to which they desire to return, there they shall not return.

28   "Is this man Coniah a despised, broken
idol—
A vessel in which *is* no pleasure?
Why are they cast out, he and his
descendants,
And cast into a land which they do not
know?
29   O earth, earth, earth,
Hear the word of the LORD!
30   Thus says the LORD:
'Write this man down as childless,
A man *who* shall not prosper in his
days;
For none of his descendants shall
prosper,

Sitting on the throne of David,
And ruling anymore in Judah.' "

Jeremiah 13:15–27
Pride Precedes Captivity

13 :15   Hear and give ear:
Do not be proud,
For the LORD has spoken.
16   Give glory to the LORD your God
Before He causes darkness,
And before your feet stumble
On the dark mountains,
And while you are looking for light,
He turns it into the shadow of death
And makes *it* dense darkness.
17   But if you will not hear it,
My soul will weep in secret for *your*
pride;
My eyes will weep bitterly
And run down with tears,
Because the LORD's flock has been
taken captive.

18   Say to the king and to the queen
mother,
"Humble yourselves;
Sit down,
For your rule shall collapse, the crown
of your glory."
19   The cities of the South shall be shut
up,
And no one shall open *them;*
Judah shall be carried away captive,
all of it;
It shall be wholly carried away
captive.

20   Lift up your eyes and see
Those who come from the north.
Where *is* the flock *that* was given to
you,
Your beautiful sheep?
21   What will you say when He punishes
you?
For you have taught them
To be chieftains, to be head over you.
Will not pangs seize you,
Like a woman in labor?
22   And if you say in your heart,
"Why have these things come upon
me?"
For the greatness of your iniquity
Your skirts have been uncovered,
Your heels made bare.
23   Can the Ethiopian change his skin or
the leopard its spots?

22:24 [a]Also called *Jeconiah* and *Jehoiachin*

JEHOIACHIN'S EXILE IN BABYLON (2 Kin. 24:10–17)

Jehoiachin ruled briefly as king of Judah for 3 months, from about December, 598 to March, 597 B.C. He was the son of Jehoiakim, the previous king who had rebelled against Babylonian rule around 601 B.C. Jehoiachin was the unfortunate successor who was but 18 years old when the Babylonians returned to take the city of Jerusalem and dethrone Judah's monarch.

The Babylonian Chronicle records that the Babylonian king Nebuchadnezzar left Babylon in the month of Kislev in his 7th year (December, 598 B.C.) on a campaign against Judah, and ultimately captured Jerusalem and its king. The text states that the king was deported, although his name is not explicitly mentioned, and that another king was appointed in his place. Obviously, the Babylonian Chronicle refers to Jehoiachin being deposed and deported to Babylon, while Mattaniah was put on the throne and given the throne name "Zedekiah" (2 Kin. 24:10–17).

Babylonian cuneiform texts, which date between 595 and 570 B.C., thus contemporary with the reign of Nebuchadnezzar II (605–562 B.C.), list rations distributed to several captives and skilled workers. Named among them is Jehoiachin. It is probable that the Judean king and his family were under house arrest, but enjoyed relative freedom.

Jehoiachin continued to be imprisoned until the reign of Evil-Merodach, successor to Nebuchadnezzar. This release from prison is dated in the 37th year of Jehoiachin's captivity (2 Kin. 25:27; Jer. 52:31), which corresponds to about 561 B.C., at the beginning of Evil-Merodach's reign. Neither the Babylonian nor biblical sources describe Jehoiachin's fate, though he apparently dined in Babylon with other exiled kings until he died (Jer. 52:34).

Then may you also do good who are
accustomed to do evil.

24 "Therefore I will scatter them like
   stubble
   That passes away by the wind of the
   wilderness.
25 This is your lot,
   The portion of your measures from
   Me," says the LORD,
   "Because you have forgotten Me
   And trusted in falsehood.
26 Therefore I will uncover your skirts
   over your face,
   That your shame may appear.
27 I have seen your adulteries
   And your *lustful* neighings,
   The lewdness of your harlotry,
   Your abominations on the hills in the
   fields.
   Woe to you, O Jerusalem!
   Will you still not be made clean?"

Jehoiachin Is Taken Captive

The new king Jehoiachin had little time to enjoy his throne. The Babylonian Chronicle reports that Nebuchadnezzar left Babylon in December, 598 B.C. on a campaign against Judah and besieged the city. Jeremiah's call to submit to Babylon was finally obeyed, though unwillingly, when it was clear that defeat was inevitable. In March, 597 B.C., Jehoiachin and his mother went into exile, and Mattaniah, another son of Josiah's and therefore uncle to Jehoiachin, was placed on the throne, changing his name to Zedekiah.

■ 2 Kings 24:10–17

2 Kings

24 :10 At that time the servants of Nebuchadnezzar king of Babylon came up against Jerusalem, and the city was besieged. ¹¹And Nebuchadnezzar king of Babylon came against the city, as his servants were besieging it. ¹²Then Jehoiachin king of Judah, his mother, his servants, his princes, and his officers went out to the king of Babylon; and the king of Babylon, in the eighth year of his reign, took him prisoner.

The Captivity of Jerusalem

¹³And he carried out from there all the treasures of the house of the LORD and the treasures of the king's house, and he cut in pieces all the articles of gold which

THE SONS OF JOSIAH RULE IN JUDAH

Judah (southern kingdom)

Jehoahaz, son of Josiah, ruled for only 3 months (2 Chr. 36:2). Pharaoh Necho of Egypt, who defeated and killed Josiah, also deposed Jehoahaz from Judah's throne. Jehoahaz is also known as Shallum (1 Chr. 3:15).

Jehoiakim, also a son of Josiah, was a half brother to Jehoahaz. When Pharaoh Necho deported Jehoahaz to Egypt, he placed Eliakim on the throne, giving him the throne name "Jehoiakim" (2 Chr. 36:4). Jehoiakim was forced to pay tribute to Necho. Later in his reign, Jehoiakim became a vassal of Nebuchadnezzar of Babylon (2 Kin. 24:1).

Israel (northern kingdom)

Fell to the Assyrian Empire in 722 B.C.

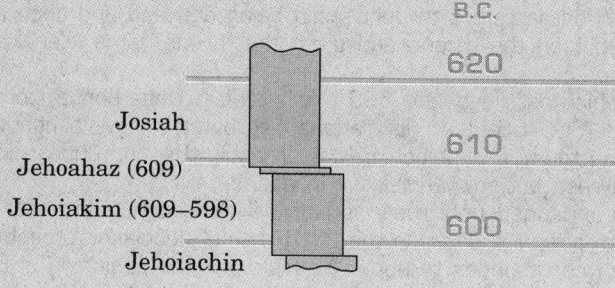

B.C.

620

Josiah

610

Jehoahaz (609)

Jehoiakim (609–598)

600

Jehoiachin

Solomon king of Israel had made in the temple of the LORD, as the LORD had said. ¹⁴Also he carried into captivity all Jerusalem: all the captains and all the mighty men of valor, ten thousand captives, and all the craftsmen and smiths. None remained except the poorest people of the land. ¹⁵And he carried Jehoiachin captive to Babylon. The king's mother, the king's wives, his officers, and the mighty of the land he carried into captivity from Jerusalem to Babylon. ¹⁶All the valiant men, seven thousand, and craftsmen and smiths, one thousand, all *who were* strong *and* fit for war, these the king of Babylon brought captive to Babylon.

Zedekiah Reigns in Judah

¹⁷Then the king of Babylon made Mattaniah, *Jehoiachin's*ᵃ uncle, king in his place, and changed his name to Zedekiah.

Priestly Account: Jehoiakim and Jehoiachin

Chronicles, which normally gives more detail about the kings of Judah, is surprisingly brief in its account of Jehoiakim. The Chronicler adds one detail, that Jehoiakim was bound

in chains to be taken to Babylon. It is not clear whether the king died before the Babylonians could carry him into captivity.

Chronicles also omits many details of Jehoiachin's reign, providing no reference to Nebuchadnezzar's siege of Jerusalem. True to his priestly focus, the Chronicler does include comment about the treasures which were taken from the temple for tribute (2 Chr. 36:10).

■ 2 Chronicles 36:5–10

2 Chronicles
The Reign and Captivity of Jehoiakim

36 :5 Jehoiakim *was* twenty-five years old when he became king, and he reigned eleven years in Jerusalem. And he did evil in the sight of the LORD his God. ⁶Nebuchadnezzar king of Babylon came up against him, and bound him in bronze *fetters* to carry him off to Babylon. ⁷Nebuchadnezzar also carried off *some* of the articles from the house of the LORD to Babylon, and put them in his temple at Babylon. ⁸Now the rest of the acts of Jehoiakim, the abominations which he did, and what was found against him, indeed they *are* written in the book of the kings of

24:17 ᵃLiterally *his*

Israel and Judah. Then Jehoiachin his son reigned in his place.

The Reign and Captivity of Jehoiachin

⁹Jehoiachin *was* eight[a] years old when he became king, and he reigned in Jerusalem three months and ten days. And he did evil in the sight of the LORD. ¹⁰At the turn of the year King Nebuchadnezzar summoned *him* and took him to Babylon, with the costly articles from the house of the LORD, and made Zedekiah, *Jehoiakim's*[a] brother, king over Judah and Jerusalem.

Prophetic Account: Zedekiah and Jeremiah

Judah was divided. Its leadership had been removed from the land with Jehoiachin in 597 B.C., leaving in Jerusalem those of lesser importance. One who stayed was Jeremiah. Although the prophet had had only strained relations with the leaders of Judah, now that they were gone, Jeremiah considered them Jerusalem's best hope. It was the exiles, not the people remaining in Judah, whom God would use to redeem His land and His people. In a vision (Jer. 24:1–10) Jeremiah sees that the exiled people are actually "good figs." It is the survivors in Jerusalem, the "bad figs," who will face a terrible fate.

■ Jeremiah 24:1–10

Jeremiah
The Sign of Two Baskets of Figs

24 :1 The LORD showed me, and there were two baskets of figs set before the temple of the LORD, after Nebuchadnezzar king of Babylon had carried away captive Jeconiah the son of Jehoiakim, king of Judah, and the princes of Judah with the craftsmen and smiths, from Jerusalem, and had brought them to Babylon.

36:9 ªSome Hebrew manuscripts, Septuagint, Syriac, and 2 Kings 24:8 read *eighteen*.   36:10 ªLiterally *his* (compare 2 Kings 24:17)

²One basket *had* very good figs, like the figs *that are* first ripe; and the other basket *had* very bad figs which could not be eaten, they were so bad. ³Then the LORD said to me, "What do you see, Jeremiah?"

And I said, "Figs, the good figs, very good; and the bad, very bad, which cannot be eaten, they are so bad."

⁴Again the word of the LORD came to me, saying, ⁵"Thus says the LORD, the God of Israel: 'Like these good figs, so will I acknowledge those who are carried away captive from Judah, whom I have sent out of this place for *their own* good, into the land of the Chaldeans. ⁶For I will set My eyes on them for good, and I will bring them back to this land; I will build them and not pull *them* down, and I will plant them and not pluck *them* up. ⁷Then I will give them a heart to know Me, that I *am* the LORD; and they shall be My people, and I will be their God, for they shall return to Me with their whole heart.

⁸'And as the bad figs which cannot be eaten, they are so bad'—surely thus says the LORD—'so will I give up Zedekiah the king of Judah, his princes, the residue of Jerusalem who remain in this land, and those who dwell in the land of Egypt. ⁹I will deliver them to trouble into all the kingdoms of the earth, for *their* harm, *to be* a reproach and a byword, a taunt and a curse, in all places where I shall drive them. ¹⁰And I will send the sword, the famine, and the pestilence among them, till they are consumed from the land that I gave to them and their fathers.' "

The Book of Daniel

Among the exiles taken to Babylon was the young man Daniel, who began immediately his training to become a courtier in Nebuchadnezzar's court (Dan. 1). His long life as a faithful Jew in a pagan land is told in chs. 1—6 of the Book of Daniel, while chs. 7—12 consist of Daniel's symbolic visions of the future.

POLITICS AND GOVERNMENT

The Babylonian Chronicle is an official writing covering events of southern Mesopotamia, dating from Sargon of Accad (c. 2350 B.C.) to the Persian period (c. 539 B.C.). The entries include a selection of events and are brief. Only parts of the Chronicle survive. The date that Jerusalem fell to Nebuchadnezzar (2 Chr. 36:10) is given as 2 Adar, or March 16, 597 B.C.

The Book of Daniel presents many difficulties to chronological arrangement. To begin with, Dan. 1:1 places Nebuchadnezzar's siege and the beginning of Daniel's exile in the "third year of the reign of Jehoiakim" (605 B.C.). No other text describes a siege and captivity in that year, which was Nebuchadnezzar's 1st year. To resolve the difficulty, some scholars favor an otherwise unknown siege in 605 B.C. when, it is suggested, Nebuchadnezzar sent Chaldean (Babylonian) armies against Judah (2 Kin. 24:2), bound Jehoiakim in chains, and carried off vessels from the Jerusalem temple (2 Chr. 36:6, 7), along with Daniel and other exiles. Then another, final, siege in 597 B.C. led to the much larger deportation described in other biblical accounts.

Other interpreters are more skeptical about an unknown event in 605 B.C. The historian of Kings recounts only the sieges of 597 B.C. (2 Kin. 24:10, 11) and of 588 B.C. (2 Kin. 25:1, 2). The prophet Jeremiah summarized the deportations of Judeans from Jerusalem (Jer. 52:28–30), recording three deportations that possibly correspond to 597, 586, and 581 B.C. (see "Various Deportations to Babylon" at Jer. 52:28). Jeremiah does not list a deportation for 605 B.C.

It is difficult to imagine why both Kings and Jeremiah neglect to mention such an important event as an invasion and deportation. Perhaps the dates given in Dan. 1:1; 2:1, locating these narratives at the beginning of King Nebuchadnezzar's reign, serve a thematic purpose—to shift the focus away from Judah's history to Babylon's. Indeed, in many ways, the main character in Dan. 1—4 is not Daniel but Nebuchadnezzar.

The first large deportation, and thus the beginning of the Babylonian exile, occurred in Nebuchadnezzar's 8th year (597 B.C.; 2 Kin. 24:12), when Jehoiachin was taken captive to Babylon. Regardless of when Daniel was deported, the experiences of this most famous Judean exile can be read in that context.

A second chronological difficulty has to do with identifying the times referred to in the visions of Daniel (chs. 7—12). On the one hand, the visions themselves say that they refer to the "latter time" (8:19), and they are even today very often interpreted as referring to events that have not yet occurred. On the other hand, the more explicit visions (chs. 10—12) quite clearly refer to the end of the Persian Empire and the rise of the Greek Empire of the 4th through 2nd centuries B.C. (e.g., 11:2, 3; see "Daniel and the Greeks" at Dan. 10:1).

To say that Daniel's visions speak specifically of events in the Persian-Greek period does not, however, mean that they cannot also refer to the "latter time." Daniel's visions are densely packed with obscure and surprising images; they resist being restricted to any single meaning. For this reason, many scholars understand them to have multiple fulfillments. Thus, Dan. 7—12 can be read in light of historical events at the end of the 1st millennium B.C., while keeping in mind the possible references to an ultimate fulfillment. See "The Apocalyptic Visions of Daniel" at Dan. 7:1.

Because the visions describe the events of the Greek era so clearly and in such detail, scholars often suggest that they were actually written during Greek times and attributed to the historical figure of Daniel. Other scholars, though, less puzzled by such explicit foretelling of future events among the prophets, accept the traditional attribution of the book to Daniel himself.

▼   ■ Daniel 1:1–21

Daniel
Daniel and His Friends Obey God

1 :1 In the third year of the reign of Jehoiakim king of Judah, Nebuchadnezzar king of Babylon came to Jerusalem and besieged it. ²And the Lord gave Jehoiakim king of Judah into his hand, with some of the articles of the house of God, which he carried into the land of Shinar to the house of his god; and he brought the articles into the treasure house of his god.

³Then the king instructed Ashpenaz, the master of his eunuchs, to bring some of the children of Israel and some of the king's descendants and some of the nobles, ⁴young men in whom *there was* no blemish, but good-looking, gifted in all wisdom, possessing knowledge and quick to understand, who *had* ability to serve in the king's palace, and whom they might teach the language and literature of the Chaldeans. ⁵And the king appointed for them a daily provision of the king's delicacies and of the wine which he drank, and three years of training for them, so that at the end of *that time* they might serve before the king. ⁶Now from among those of the sons of Judah were Daniel, Hananiah, Mishael, and Azariah. ⁷To them the chief of the eunuchs gave names: he gave Daniel *the name* Belteshazzar; to Hananiah,

DEPORTATIONS FROM JERUSALEM TO BABYLON

The armies of Babylon under King Nebuchadnezzar besieged Jerusalem on different occasions, taking parts of the population away into exile. The Babylonian Chronicle records the campaigns of Nebuchadnezzar between the years 616 and 594 B.C., including the siege of Jerusalem in 597 B.C.

A Proposed Early Deportation

605 B.C. Nebuchadnezzar besieges Jerusalem, captures King Jehoiakim, and deports captives, including Daniel, into exile.

Source: The Book of Daniel is the only record of a deportation in this year. Dan. 1:1, 2 dates the siege in Jehoiakim's 3rd year, which according to the Babylonian method of counting would be 605 B.C. Some think that 2 Chr. 36:6, 7 refers to this event.

(Jeremiah, writing in Judah and using the Judean method of counting, reckons 605 B.C. as Jehoiakim's 4th year, Jer. 46:2.)

The Deportation of Jehoiachin

597 B.C. Nebuchadnezzar captures King Jehoiachin, loots the temple treasures, and deports captives, including Ezekiel, into exile.

Source: The Babylonian Chronicle, as well as 2 Kin. 24:10–16; 2 Chr. 36:10; and probably Jer. 52:28. The reason for the large difference in the numbers of deported captives is not known.

The Fall of Jerusalem

588 to 586 B.C. Nebuchadnezzar besieges Judah's cities, including Jerusalem, during these years. In 586, his army captures King Zedekiah, burns down the temple, and deports Jerusalem's people into exile.

Source: The Lachish Letters, as well as 2 Kin. 25:1–21; 2 Chr. 36:17–20; and probably Jer. 52:29.

A Final Deportation

581 B.C. Nebuzaradan, captain of the guard for the Babylonians, deports 745 persons from Jerusalem.

Source: The Book of Jeremiah (Jer. 50:30) is the only record of a deportation in this year. It could have been a reprisal for the murder of the governor Gedaliah, who was appointed by the Babylonians.

Shadrach; to Mishael, Meshach; and to Azariah, Abed-Nego.

⁸But Daniel purposed in his heart that he would not defile himself with the portion of the king's delicacies, nor with the wine which he drank; therefore he requested of the chief of the eunuchs that he might not defile himself. ⁹Now God had brought Daniel into the favor and goodwill of the chief of the eunuchs. ¹⁰And the chief of the eunuchs said to Daniel, "I fear my lord the king, who has appointed your food

---

CULTURE AND SOCIETY

Some people were born into slavery, but many others lost their freedom as a result of war. In this way the rich and the nobility could be enslaved as well as the poor. Nebuchadnezzar chose slaves for his palace from the defeated Judeans, requiring them to be physically healthy, wellborn, and well-educated (Dan. 1:3, 4). They received new names as a token of his authority over them.

and drink. For why should he see your faces looking worse than the young men who *are* your age? Then you would endanger my head before the king."

[11]So Daniel said to the steward[a] whom the chief of the eunuchs had set over Daniel, Hananiah, Mishael, and Azariah, [12]"Please test your servants for ten days, and let them give us vegetables to eat and water to drink. [13]Then let our appearance be examined before you, and the appearance of the young men who eat the portion of the king's delicacies; and as you see fit, *so* deal with your servants." [14]So he consented with them in this matter, and tested them ten days.

[15]And at the end of ten days their features appeared better and fatter in flesh than all the young men who ate the portion of the king's delicacies. [16]Thus the steward took away their portion of delicacies and the wine that they were to drink, and gave them vegetables.

[17]As for these four young men, God gave them knowledge and skill in all literature and wisdom; and Daniel had understanding in all visions and dreams.

[18]Now at the end of the days, when the king had said that they should be brought in, the chief of the eunuchs brought them in before Nebuchadnezzar. [19]Then the king interviewed them,[a] and among them all none was found like Daniel, Hananiah, Mishael, and Azariah; therefore they served before the king. [20]And in all matters of wisdom *and* understanding about which the king examined them, he found them ten times better than all the magicians *and* astrologers who *were* in all his realm. [21]Thus Daniel continued until the first year of King Cyrus.

TIME CAPSULE   *604 to 601 B.C.*

604 *Baruch reads Jeremiah's scroll at the temple (Jer. 36:10)*

604 *Jehoiakim burns Jeremiah's scroll (Jer. 36:22, 23)*

603 *Nebuchadnezzar destroys Philistine city during campaign in Palestine*

601 *Necho repels a Babylonian invasion of Egypt's border*

601 *King Jehoiakim rebels against Babylonian rule*

Daniel's Time in Babylon

Two different contexts appear in Dan. 2. The narrative of ch. 2 includes a symbolic dream that is, in many ways, parallel to Daniel's visions of the future in chs. 7 and 8. Thus the dream could be read alongside those two visions, in light of their future reference (see "The Apocalyptic Visions of Daniel" at Dan. 7:1). Because Nebuchadnezzar's dream is essential to the story set in his time, though, it should be read with chs. 1—6, rather than in the Greek period with the visions of chs. 7; 8.

The chronological note in Dan. 2:1 places the narrative in Nebuchadnezzar's 2nd year (604 B.C.) and assumes that Daniel and his three friends were taken captive a year earlier in 605 B.C. Besides the historical questions that surround these dates and make them puzzling to many scholars (see "The Book of Daniel" at Dan. 1:1), there are a few other chronological features of Daniel's career evident in Dan. 1; 2.

The Book of Daniel provides information that pictures a long life for the Judean Daniel in Babylon. Whether one begins with Nebuchadnezzar's 1st year (605 B.C.; Dan. 1:1) or with the first year of the exile as reported in Kings and Jeremiah (597 B.C.; Jer. 28:1-4), Daniel's longevity in the court was remarkable. He is reported to have continued his public ministry in the royal court until the "first year of King Cyrus" (Dan. 1:21). Cyrus took the throne of Persia in 559 B.C.; however, this 1st year very likely refers to 539 B.C. when Cyrus defeated Babylon and became its ruler. The Book of Daniel thus describes an impressive record of from 60 to 70 years for Daniel in Babylon.

The story of Dan. 1 places the Hebrew exiles in "training" for 3 years after coming to Babylon (Dan. 1:5). Thus, Daniel's interpretation of the king's dream in 604 (his 2nd year; Dan. 2:1) is set before the end of the 3 years of training, and one must picture a very youthful Daniel in the king's court.

▼   ■ Daniel 2:1—4:37

Daniel
Nebuchadnezzar's Dream

2 :1 Now in the second year of Nebuchadnezzar's reign, Nebuchadnezzar had dreams; and his spirit was *so* troubled that his sleep left him. [2]Then the king gave

---

1:11 [a]Hebrew *Melzar,* also in verse 16
1:19 [a]Literally *talked with them*

the command to call the magicians, the astrologers, the sorcerers, and the Chaldeans to tell the king his dreams. So they came and stood before the king. ³And the king said to them, "I have had a dream, and my spirit is anxious to know the dream."

⁴Then the Chaldeans spoke to the king in Aramaic,ᵃ "O king, live forever! Tell your servants the dream, and we will give the interpretation."

⁵The king answered and said to the Chaldeans, "My decision is firm: if you do not make known the dream to me, and its interpretation, you shall be cut in pieces, and your houses shall be made an ash heap. ⁶However, if you tell the dream and its interpretation, you shall receive from me gifts, rewards, and great honor. Therefore tell me the dream and its interpretation."

⁷They answered again and said, "Let the king tell his servants the dream, and we will give its interpretation."

⁸The king answered and said, "I know for certain that you would gain time, because you see that my decision is firm: ⁹if you do not make known the dream to me, *there is only* one decree for you! For you have agreed to speak lying and corrupt words before me till the time has changed. Therefore tell me the dream, and I shall know that you can give me its interpretation."

¹⁰The Chaldeans answered the king, and said, "There is not a man on earth who can tell the king's matter; therefore no king, lord, or ruler has *ever* asked such things of any magician, astrologer, or Chaldean. ¹¹*It is* a difficult thing that the king requests, and there is no other who can tell it to the king except the gods, whose dwelling is not with flesh."

¹²For this reason the king was angry and very furious, and gave the command to destroy all the wise *men* of Babylon. ¹³So the decree went out, and they began killing the wise *men;* and they sought Daniel and his companions, to kill *them.*

God Reveals Nebuchadnezzar's Dream

¹⁴Then with counsel and wisdom Daniel answered Arioch, the captain of the king's guard, who had gone out to kill the wise *men* of Babylon; ¹⁵he answered and

said to Arioch the king's captain, "Why is the decree from the king so urgent?" Then Arioch made the decision known to Daniel.

¹⁶So Daniel went in and asked the king to give him time, that he might tell the king the interpretation. ¹⁷Then Daniel went to his house, and made the decision known to Hananiah, Mishael, and Azariah, his companions, ¹⁸that they might seek mercies from the God of heaven concerning this secret, so that Daniel and his companions might not perish with the rest of the wise *men* of Babylon. ¹⁹Then the secret was revealed to Daniel in a night vision. So Daniel blessed the God of heaven.

²⁰Daniel answered and said:

"Blessed be the name of God forever
　　and ever,
For wisdom and might are His.
21　And He changes the times and the
　　　seasons;
He removes kings and raises up kings;
He gives wisdom to the wise
And knowledge to those who have
　　understanding.
22　He reveals deep and secret things;
He knows what *is* in the darkness,
And light dwells with Him.

23　"I thank You and praise You,
O God of my fathers;
You have given me wisdom and might,
And have now made known to me
　　what we asked of You,
For You have made known to us the
　　king's demand."

Daniel Explains the Dream

²⁴Therefore Daniel went to Arioch, whom the king had appointed to destroy the wise *men* of Babylon. He went and said thus to him: "Do not destroy the wise *men* of Babylon; take me before the king, and I will tell the king the interpretation."

²⁵Then Arioch quickly brought Daniel before the king, and said thus to him, "I have found a man of the captivesᵃ of Judah, who will make known to the king interpretation."

²⁶The king answered and said to Daniel, whose name *was* Belteshazzar, "Are you able to make known to me the dream which I have seen, and its interpretation?"

²⁷Daniel answered in the presence of the king, and said, "The secret which the king has demanded, the wise *men,* the astrologers, the magicians, and the

2:4 ᵃThe original language of Daniel 2:4b through 7:28 is Aramaic.　　2:25 ᵃLiterally *of the sons of the captivity*

soothsayers cannot declare to the king. 28But there is a God in heaven who reveals secrets, and He has made known to King Nebuchadnezzar what will be in the latter days. Your dream, and the visions of your head upon your bed, were these: 29As for you, O king, thoughts came *to* your *mind while* on your bed, *about* what would come to pass after this; and He who reveals secrets has made known to you what will be. 30But as for me, this secret has not been revealed to me because I have more wisdom than anyone living, but for *our* sakes who make known the interpretation to the king, and that you may know the thoughts of your heart.

31"You, O king, were watching; and behold, a great image! This great image, whose splendor *was* excellent, stood before you; and its form *was* awesome. 32This image's head *was* of fine gold, its chest and arms of silver, its belly and thighs[a] of bronze, 33its legs of iron, its feet partly of iron and partly of clay.[a] 34You watched while a stone was cut out without hands, which struck the image on its feet of iron and clay, and broke them in pieces. 35Then the iron, the clay, the bronze, the silver, and the gold were crushed together, and became like chaff from the summer threshing floors; the wind carried them away so that no trace of them was found. And the stone that struck the image became a great mountain and filled the whole earth.

36"This *is* the dream. Now we will tell the interpretation of it before the king. 37You, O king, *are* a king of kings. For the God of heaven has given you a kingdom, power, strength, and glory; 38and wherever the children of men dwell, or the beasts of the field and the birds of the heaven, He has given *them* into your hand, and has made you ruler over them all—you *are* this head of gold. 39But after you shall arise another kingdom inferior to yours; then another, a third kingdom of bronze, which shall rule over all the earth. 40And the fourth kingdom shall be as strong as iron, inasmuch as iron breaks in pieces and shatters everything; and like iron that crushes, *that kingdom* will break in pieces and crush all the others. 41Whereas you saw the feet and toes, partly of potter's clay and partly of iron, the kingdom shall be divided; yet the strength of the iron shall be in it, just as you saw the iron mixed with ceramic clay. 42And *as* the toes of the feet *were* partly of iron and partly of clay, *so* the kingdom shall be partly strong and partly fragile. 43As you saw iron mixed with ceramic clay, they will mingle with the seed of men; but they will not adhere to one another, just as iron does not mix with clay. 44And in the days of these kings the God of heaven will set up a kingdom which shall never be destroyed; and the kingdom shall not be left to other people; it shall break in pieces and consume all these kingdoms, and it shall stand forever. 45Inasmuch as you saw that the stone was cut out of the mountain without hands, and that it broke in pieces the iron, the bronze, the clay, the silver, and the gold—the great God has made known to the king what will come to pass after this. The dream is certain, and its interpretation is sure."

Daniel and His Friends Promoted

46Then King Nebuchadnezzar fell on his face, prostrate before Daniel, and commanded that they should present an offering and incense to him. 47The king answered Daniel, and said, "Truly your God *is* the God of gods, the Lord of kings, and a revealer of secrets, since you could reveal this secret." 48Then the king promoted Daniel and gave him many great gifts; and he made him ruler over the whole province of Babylon, and chief administrator over all the wise *men* of Babylon. 49Also Daniel petitioned the king, and he set Shadrach, Meshach, and Abed-Nego over the affairs of the province of Babylon; but Daniel *sat* in the gate[a] of the king.

2:32 [a]Or *sides*   2:33 [a]Or *baked clay*, and so in verses 34, 35, and 42   2:49 [a]That is, the king's court

SCIENCE AND TECHNOLOGY

Iron replaced bronze as the most common metal for tool and weapons, starting about 1200 B.C. The process of replacement lasted some time. For one thing, iron has to have some carbon in it, then it can be hardened by heating and quenching. Weapons were known to bend during use and the soldiers had to straighten them in the midst of battle. Yet in the end iron was recognized as the common symbol of war (Dan. 2:40).

NEBUCHADNEZZAR, KING OF BABYLON (Dan. 3:1)

Nebuchadnezzar II reigned from 605 to 562 B.C., becoming the second and most famous king of the Neo-Babylonian or Chaldean dynasty (Dan. 3:1). As crown prince, he orchestrated the victory over the Egyptians at the crucial battle of Carchemish in 605 B.C.

The Chaldean king spent a great deal of effort in campaigning to the west—in Syria and Palestine—primarily to check Egyptian influence in the region. The Babylonian Chronicle, the primary historical source for the early periods of the Chaldean kingdom, records how Nebuchadnezzar laid siege to Jerusalem in 597 B.C. and deposed King Jehoiachin of Judah.

The destruction of Jerusalem in 586 B.C., related by the historian of Kings (2 Kin. 25:1–21), is not mentioned in cuneiform records, since the Babylonian Chronicle breaks off after 594 B.C. The Jewish historian Josephus (A.D. 37–100) does record Jerusalem's end in an account that apparently depends upon the Book of 2 Kings as a source.

Nebuchadnezzar was also known for his great building projects, especially in Babylon. These included a summer palace, a fortification of the city, the ziggurat (sometimes associated with the tower of Babel described in Gen. 11), and the famous royal hanging gardens.

This Chaldean king is also well known from later Greek, Latin, and Jewish sources. The classical writers were impressed with his monumental building activity, while the Jewish writers, understandably, condemned him for his destruction of Jerusalem and the temple.

The Image of Gold

3 ¹Nebuchadnezzar the king made an image of gold, whose height *was* sixty cubits *and* its width six cubits. He set it up in the plain of Dura, in the province of Babylon. ²And King Nebuchadnezzar sent *word* to gather together the satraps, the administrators, the governors, the counselors, the treasurers, the judges, the magistrates, and all the officials of the provinces, to come to the dedication of the image which King Nebuchadnezzar had set up. ³So the satraps, the administrators, the governors, the counselors, the treasurers, the judges, the magistrates, and all the officials of the provinces gathered together for the dedication of the image that King Nebuchadnezzar had set up; and they stood before the image that Nebuchadnezzar had set up. ⁴Then a herald cried aloud: "To you it is commanded, O peoples, nations, and languages, ⁵*that* at the time you hear the sound of the horn, flute, harp, lyre, *and* psaltery, in symphony with all kinds of music, you shall fall down and worship the gold image that King Nebuchadnezzar has set up; ⁶and whoever does not fall down and worship shall be cast immediately into the midst of a burning fiery furnace."

⁷So at that time, when all the people heard the sound of the horn, flute, harp, *and* lyre, in symphony with all kinds of music, all the people, nations, and languages fell down *and* worshiped the gold image which King Nebuchadnezzar had set up.

Daniel's Friends Disobey the King

⁸Therefore at that time certain Chaldeans came forward and accused the Jews. ⁹They spoke and said to King Nebuchadnezzar, "O king, live forever! ¹⁰You, O king, have made a decree that everyone who hears the sound of the horn, flute, harp, lyre, *and* psaltery, in symphony with all kinds of music, shall fall down and worship the gold image; ¹¹and whoever does not fall down and worship shall be cast into the midst of a burning fiery furnace. ¹²There are certain Jews whom you have set over the affairs of the province of Babylon: Shadrach, Meshach, and Abed-Nego; these men, O king, have not paid due regard to you. They do not serve your gods or worship the gold image which you have set up."

¹³Then Nebuchadnezzar, in rage and fury, gave the command to bring Shadrach, Meshach, and Abed-Nego. So they brought these men before the king. ¹⁴Nebuchadnezzar spoke, saying to them, "*Is it* true, Shadrach, Meshach, and Abed-Nego, *that* you do not serve my gods or worship the gold image which I have set up? ¹⁵Now if you are ready at the time you hear the

sound of the horn, flute, harp, lyre, *and* psaltery, in symphony with all kinds of music, and you fall down and worship the image which I have made, *good!* But if you do not worship, you shall be cast immediately into the midst of a burning fiery furnace. And who *is* the god who will deliver you from my hands?"

[16]Shadrach, Meshach, and Abed-Nego answered and said to the king, "O Nebuchadnezzar, we have no need to answer you in this matter. [17]If that *is the case,* our God whom we serve is able to deliver us from the burning fiery furnace, and He will deliver *us* from your hand, O king. [18]But if not, let it be known to you, O king, that we do not serve your gods, nor will we worship the gold image which you have set up."

Saved in Fiery Trial

[19]Then Nebuchadnezzar was full of fury, and the expression on his face changed toward Shadrach, Meshach, and Abed-Nego. He spoke and commanded that they heat the furnace seven times more than it was usually heated. [20]And he commanded certain mighty men of valor who *were* in his army to bind Shadrach, Meshach, and Abed-Nego, *and* cast *them* into the burning fiery furnace. [21]Then these men were bound in their coats, their trousers, their turbans, and their *other* garments, and were cast into the midst of the burning fiery furnace. [22]Therefore, because the king's command was urgent, and the furnace exceedingly hot, the flame of the fire killed those men who took up Shadrach, Meshach, and Abed-Nego. [23]And these three men, Shadrach, Meshach, and Abed-Nego, fell down bound into the midst of the burning fiery furnace.

[24]Then King Nebuchadnezzar was astonished; and he rose in haste *and* spoke, saying to his counselors, "Did we not cast three men bound into the midst of the fire?"

They answered and said to the king, "True, O king."

[25]"Look!" he answered, "I see four men loose, walking in the midst of the fire; and they are not hurt, and the form of the fourth is like the Son of God."[a]

Nebuchadnezzar Praises God

[26]Then Nebuchadnezzar went near the mouth of the burning fiery furnace *and* spoke, saying, "Shadrach, Meshach, and Abed-Nego, servants of the Most High God,

come out, and come *here.*" Then Shadrach, Meshach, and Abed-Nego came from the midst of the fire. [27]And the satraps, administrators, governors, and the king's counselors gathered together, and they saw these men on whose bodies the fire had no power; the hair of their head was not singed nor were their garments affected, and the smell of fire was not on them.

[28]Nebuchadnezzar spoke, saying, "Blessed be the God of Shadrach, Meshach, and Abed-Nego, who sent His Angel[a] and delivered His servants who trusted in Him, and they have frustrated the king's word, and yielded their bodies, that they should not serve nor worship any god except their own God! [29]Therefore I make a decree that any people, nation, or language which speaks anything amiss against the God of Shadrach, Meshach, and Abed-Nego shall be cut in pieces, and their houses shall be made an ash heap; because there is no other God who can deliver like this."

[30]Then the king promoted Shadrach, Meshach, and Abed-Nego in the province of Babylon.

Nebuchadnezzar's Second Dream

4 [1]   Nebuchadnezzar the king,

To all peoples, nations, and languages that dwell in all the earth:

Peace be multiplied to you.

[2]   I thought it good to declare the signs and wonders that the Most High God has worked for me.

[3]   How great *are* His signs,
And how mighty His wonders!
His kingdom *is* an everlasting kingdom,
And His dominion *is* from generation to generation.

[4]   I, Nebuchadnezzar, was at rest in my house, and flourishing in my palace. [5]I saw a dream which made me afraid, and the thoughts on my bed and the visions of my head troubled me. [6]Therefore I issued a decree to bring in all the wise *men* of Babylon before me, that they might make known to me the interpretation of the dream. [7]Then the magicians, the astrologers, the

---

3:25 [a]Or *a son of the gods*   3:28 [a]Or *angel*

Chaldeans, and the soothsayers came in, and I told them the dream; but they did not make known to me its interpretation. 8But at last Daniel came before me (his name *is* Belteshazzar, according to the name of my god; in him *is* the Spirit of the Holy God), and I told the dream before him, *saying:* 9"Belteshazzar, chief of the magicians, because I know that the Spirit of the Holy God *is* in you, and no secret troubles you, explain to me the visions of my dream that I have seen, and its interpretation.

10 "These *were* the visions of my head *while* on my bed:

I was looking, and behold,
A tree in the midst of the earth,
And its height was great.
11 The tree grew and became strong;
Its height reached to the heavens,
And it could be seen to the ends of all the earth.
12 Its leaves *were* lovely,
Its fruit abundant,
And in it *was* food for all.
The beasts of the field found shade under it,
The birds of the heavens dwelt in its branches,
And all flesh was fed from it.

13 "I saw in the visions of my head *while* on my bed, and there was a watcher, a holy one, coming down from heaven. 14He cried aloud and said thus:

'Chop down the tree and cut off its branches,
Strip off its leaves and scatter its fruit.
Let the beasts get out from under it,
And the birds from its branches.

15 Nevertheless leave the stump and roots in the earth,
Bound with a band of iron and bronze,
In the tender grass of the field.
Let it be wet with the dew of heaven,
And *let* him graze with the beasts
On the grass of the earth.
16 Let his heart be changed from *that of* a man,
Let him be given the heart of a beast,
And let seven times[a] pass over him.

17 'This decision *is* by the decree of the watchers,
And the sentence by the word of the holy ones,
In order that the living may know
That the Most High rules in the kingdom of men,
Gives it to whomever He will,
And sets over it the lowest of men.'

18 "This dream I, King Nebuchadnezzar, have seen. Now you, Belteshazzar, declare its interpretation, since all the wise *men* of my kingdom are not able to make known to me the interpretation; but you *are* able, for the Spirit of the Holy God *is* in you."

Daniel Explains the Second Dream

19 Then Daniel, whose name was Belteshazzar, was astonished for a time, and his thoughts troubled him. *So* the king spoke, and said, "Belteshazzar, do not let the dream or its interpretation trouble you."

Belteshazzar answered and said, "My lord, *may* the dream concern those who hate you, and its interpretation concern your enemies!

20 "The tree that you saw, which grew and became strong, whose height reached to the heavens and which *could be seen* by all the earth, 21whose leaves *were* lovely and its fruit abundant, in which *was* food for all, under which the beasts of the field

4:16 [a]Possibly *seven years*, and so in verses 23, 25, and 32

BELIEFS AND IDEAS

A "watcher" is a kind of angel not mentioned anywhere in the Bible except Dan. 4:13, 23. Nevertheless, watchers are a prominent part of Jewish speculation of the last few centuries B.C. The medieval Jewish scholar Rashi explained the name by its similarity to the Hebrew word for "awake." Like God, the angels do not sleep (Ps. 121:3, 4).

dwelt, and in whose branches the birds of the heaven had their home— 22it *is* you, O king, who have grown and become strong; for your greatness has grown and reaches to the heavens, and your dominion to the end of the earth.

23 "And inasmuch as the king saw a watcher, a holy one, coming down from heaven and saying, 'Chop down the tree and destroy it, but leave its stump and roots in the earth, *bound* with a band of iron and bronze in the tender grass of the field; let it be wet with the dew of heaven, and let him graze with the beasts of the field, till seven times pass over him'; 24this is the interpretation, O king, and this is the decree of the Most High, which has come upon my lord the king: 25They shall drive you from men, your dwelling shall be with the beasts of the field, and they shall make you eat grass like oxen. They shall wet you with the dew of heaven, and seven times shall pass over you, till you know that the Most High rules in the kingdom of men, and gives it to whomever He chooses.

26 "And inasmuch as they gave the command to leave the stump *and* roots of the tree, your kingdom shall be assured to you, after you come to know that Heaven rules. 27Therefore, O king, let my advice be acceptable to you; break off your sins by *being* righteous, and your iniquities by showing mercy to *the* poor. Perhaps there may be a lengthening of your prosperity."

Nebuchadnezzar's Humiliation

28 All *this* came upon King Nebuchadnezzar. 29At the end of the twelve months he was walking about the royal palace of Babylon. 30The king spoke, saying, "Is not this great Babylon, that I have built for a royal dwelling by my mighty power and for the honor of my majesty?"

31 While the word *was still* in the king's mouth, a voice fell from heaven: "King Nebuchadnezzar, to you it is spoken: the kingdom has departed from you! 32And they shall drive you from men,

and your dwelling *shall be* with the beasts of the field. They shall make you eat grass like oxen; and seven times shall pass over you, until you know that the Most High rules in the kingdom of men, and gives it to whomever He chooses."

33 That very hour the word was fulfilled concerning Nebuchadnezzar; he was driven from men and ate grass like oxen; his body was wet with the dew of heaven till his hair had grown like eagles' *feathers* and his nails like birds' *claws*.

Nebuchadnezzar Praises God

34 And at the end of the timea I, Nebuchadnezzar, lifted my eyes to heaven, and my understanding returned to me; and I blessed the Most High and praised and honored Him who lives forever:

For His dominion *is* an everlasting dominion,
And His kingdom *is* from generation to generation.
35 All the inhabitants of the earth *are* reputed as nothing;
He does according to His will in the army of heaven
And *among* the inhabitants of the earth.
No one can restrain His hand
Or say to Him, "What have You done?"

36 At the same time my reason returned to me, and for the glory of my kingdom, my honor and splendor returned to me. My counselors and nobles resorted to me, I was restored to my kingdom, and excellent majesty was added to me. 37Now I, Nebuchadnezzar, praise and extol and honor the King of heaven, all of whose works *are* truth, and His ways justice. And those who walk in pride He is able to put down.

4:34 aLiterally *days*

Zedekiah's Alliances

While the exiles, including King Jehoiachin, were taken to Babylon, Nebuchadnezzar placed Jehoiachin's uncle Mattaniah on the throne, no doubt with clear instructions to remain faithful to Babylon. Mattaniah was given the throne name "Zedekiah."

Although Zedekiah was placed on the throne in Jerusalem by the Babylonians, and certainly swore fidelity to Babylon, his was a weak allegiance. Like his brother Jehoiakim before him, Zedekiah was often tempted by promises from Egypt. As far as Israel's political alliances were concerned, Zedekiah could just as well have been Jehoiakim again.

The final chapter of the Book of Jeremiah (ch. 52) appears to have been taken almost word for word from 2 Kin. 24:18—25:30. Some scholars suggest that a later editor, noting how the Book of Jeremiah jumps back and forth in time, felt the need to provide a chronological overview of Jeremiah's times.

- 2 Kings 24:18, 19
- Jeremiah 52:1, 2

2 Kings 24:18, 19

24 :18 Zedekiah *was* twenty-one years old when he became king, and he reigned eleven years in Jerusalem. His mother's name *was* Hamutal the daughter of Jeremiah of Libnah. ¹⁹He also did evil in the sight of the LORD, according to all that Jehoiakim had done.

Jeremiah 52:1, 2

52 :1 Zedekiah *was* twenty-one years old when he became king, and he reigned eleven years in Jerusalem. His mother's name *was* Hamutal the daughter of Jeremiah of Libnah. ²He also did evil in the sight of the LORD, according to all that Jehoiakim had done.

27:1 ªFollowing Masoretic Text, Targum, and Vulgate; some Hebrew manuscripts, Arabic, and Syriac read *Zedekiah* (compare 27:3, 12; 28:1).   ᵇSeptuagint omits verse 1.

Zedekiah's Jerusalem Conference

Almost immediately after becoming king, Zedekiah sponsored a conference of local nations. At this conference in Jerusalem, messengers from these neighboring lands discussed the possibility of a united rebellion against their Babylonian master. Excited by the possibilities, many prophets in Jerusalem began to foretell a great victory and the restoration of all that Nebuchadnezzar had taken from the city. As usual, Jeremiah was the lone dis-

senting voice. He declared that Nebuchadnezzar of Babylon was only doing God's will (Jer. 27:6), and prophesied disaster on all who opposed Babylon.

Many of the oracles against the foreign nations (chs. 46—51) fit in this context. Jeremiah's message to Judah's neighbors was that the Lord would allow them to survive if they surrendered to the control of Babylon (Jer. 27:1–11). Those who did not would fall to the invading Babylonian armies (48:1—49:39; 25:15–38). He had the same message for Zedekiah and Judah, despite the predictions of peace by such false prophets as Hananiah (27:12—28:17).

This conference is placed by Jer. 27:1 at "the beginning" of Jehoiakim's reign. Some Hebrew manuscripts and some major versions read "Zedekiah" in place of "Jehoiakim," and Jer. 27:3 refers to King Zedekiah. Since the oracle takes place after Nebuchadnezzar had plundered the temple in 597 B.C. (27:20), it should be dated with Jer. 28:1 in Zedekiah's 4th year (593 B.C.).

- Jeremiah 27:1–11
- Jeremiah 48:1—49:39
- Jeremiah 25:15–38
- Jeremiah 27:12—28:17

Jeremiah 27:1–11
Symbol of the Bonds and Yokes

27 :1 In the beginning of the reign of Jehoiakimª the son of Josiah, king of Judah, this word came to Jeremiah from the LORD, saying,ᵇ ²"Thus says the LORD to me: 'Make for yourselves bonds and yokes, and put them on your neck, ³and send them to the king of Edom, the king of Moab, the king of the Ammonites, the king of Tyre, and the king of Sidon, by the hand of the messengers who come to Jerusalem to Zedekiah king of Judah. ⁴And command them to say to their masters, "Thus says the LORD of hosts, the God of Israel—thus you shall say to your masters: ⁵'I have made the earth, the man and the beast that *are* on the ground, by My great power and by My outstretched arm, and have given it to whom it seemed proper to Me. ⁶And now I have given all these lands into the hand of Nebuchadnezzar the king of Babylon, My servant; and the beasts of the field I have also given him to serve him. ⁷So all nations shall serve him and his son and his son's son, until the time of his land comes; and then many nations and great kings shall make him serve them. ⁸And it shall be, *that* the nation and kingdom which will not serve Nebuchadnezzar the king of Babylon, and which will not put its neck under the yoke of the king of Babylon, that nation I will punish,' says the LORD, with the sword, the famine, and the pestilence, until I have consumed them by his hand. 9Therefore do not listen to your prophets, your diviners, your dreamers, your soothsayers, or your sorcerers, who speak to you, saying, "You shall not serve the king of Babylon." 10For they prophesy a lie to you, to remove you far from your land; and I will drive you out, and you will perish. 11But the nations that bring their necks under the yoke of the king of Babylon and serve him, I will let them remain in their own land,' says the LORD, 'and they shall till it and dwell in it.' " ' "

Jeremiah 48:1—49:39

Judgment on Moab

48

:1 Against Moab.
Thus says the LORD of hosts, the God of Israel:

"Woe to Nebo!
For it is plundered,
Kirjathaim is shamed *and* taken;
The high stronghold[a] is shamed and
    dismayed—
2   No more praise of Moab.
In Heshbon they have devised evil
    against her:
'Come, and let us cut her off as a
    nation.'
You also shall be cut down,
    O Madmen![a]
The sword shall pursue you;
3   A voice of crying *shall be* from
    Horonaim:
'Plundering and great destruction!'

4   "Moab is destroyed;
Her little ones have caused a cry to be
    heard;[a]
5   For in the Ascent of Luhith they
    ascend with continual weeping;

For in the descent of Horonaim the
    enemies have heard a cry of
    destruction.

6   "Flee, save your lives!
And be like the juniper[a] in the
    wilderness.
7   For because you have trusted in your
    works and your treasures,
You also shall be taken.
And Chemosh shall go forth into
    captivity,
His priests and his princes together.
8   And the plunderer shall come against
    every city;
No one shall escape.
The valley also shall perish,
And the plain shall be destroyed,
As the LORD has spoken.

9   "Give wings to Moab,
That she may flee and get away;
For her cities shall be desolate,
Without any to dwell in them.
10 Cursed *is* he who does the work of the
    LORD deceitfully,
And cursed *is* he who keeps back his
    sword from blood.

11 "Moab has been at ease from his[a]
    youth;
He has settled on his dregs,
And has not been emptied from vessel
    to vessel,
Nor has he gone into captivity.
Therefore his taste remained in him,
And his scent has not changed.

12 "Therefore behold, the days are
    coming," says the LORD,
"That I shall send him wine-workers
Who will tip him over

48:1 [a]Hebrew *Misgab*   48:2 [a]A city of Moab
48:4 [a]Following Masoretic Text, Targum, and Vulgate;
Septuagint reads *Proclaim it in Zoar*.   48:6 [a]Or
Aroer, a city of Moab   48:11 [a]The Hebrew uses
masculine and feminine pronouns interchangeably in
this chapter.

SCIENCE AND TECHNOLOGY

The basic motor power available for agriculture was the muscles of humans and animals. Animals pulled loads by means of a wooden yoke, a basic item known to everyone (Jer. 27:2). The yoke was thus a symbol for doing work at the command of another. At its worst this was slavery or humiliation in war (Lev. 26:13). At the other extreme it was a symbol for following the commandments of God (Lam. 3:27; Matt. 11:29).

And empty his vessels
And break the bottles.
13 Moab shall be ashamed of Chemosh,
As the house of Israel was ashamed of
Bethel, their confidence.

14 "How can you say, 'We *are* mighty
And strong men for the war'?
15 Moab is plundered and gone up *from*
her cities;
Her chosen young men have gone
down to the slaughter," says the
King,
Whose name *is* the LORD of hosts.

16 "The calamity of Moab *is* near at hand,
And his affliction comes quickly.
17 Bemoan him, all you who are around
him;
And all you who know his name,
Say, 'How the strong staff is broken,
The beautiful rod!'

18 "O daughter inhabiting Dibon,
Come down from *your* glory,
And sit in thirst;
For the plunderer of Moab has come
against you,
He has destroyed your strongholds.
19 O inhabitant of Aroer,
Stand by the way and watch;
Ask him who flees
And her who escapes;
Say, 'What has happened?'
20 Moab is shamed, for he is broken
down.

Wail and cry!
Tell it in Arnon, that Moab is
plundered.

21 "And judgment has come on the plain
country:
On Holon and Jahzah and Mephaath,
22 On Dibon and Nebo and Beth
Diblathaim,
23 On Kirjathaim and Beth Gamul and
Beth Meon,
24 On Kerioth and Bozrah,
On all the cities of the land of Moab,
Far or near.
25 The horn of Moab is cut off,
And his arm is broken," says the
LORD.

26 "Make him drunk,
Because he exalted *himself* against
the LORD.
Moab shall wallow in his vomit,
And he shall also be in derision.
27 For was not Israel a derision to you?
Was he found among thieves?
For whenever you speak of him,
You shake *your head in* scorn.
28 You who dwell in Moab,
Leave the cities and dwell in the rock,
And be like the dove *which* makes her
nest
In the sides of the cave's mouth.

29 "We have heard the pride of Moab
(He *is* exceedingly proud),

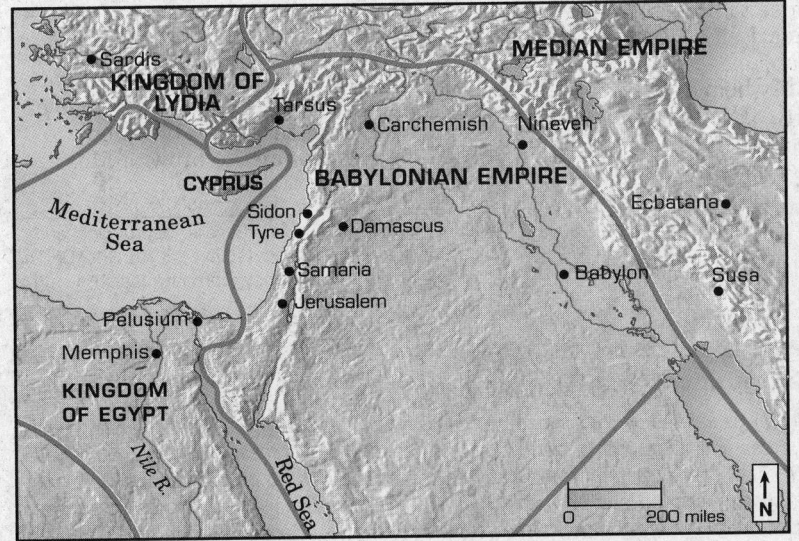

**The Neo-Babylonian
Empire**
In 605 B.C. Nebuchad-
nezzar's 2-year siege of
Carchemish proved suc-
cessful, and most of the
Assyrian Empire rapidly
became the Babylonian
Empire. In 586 B.C.
Nebuchadnezzar con-
quered all of Judah,
besieging and destroying
Jerusalem and the Jewish
temple in the process. At
its zenith in 560 B.C.
Babylon ruled the entire
fertile crescent and
Arabia, although Egypt
regained autonomy.

Of his loftiness and arrogance and
    pride,
And of the haughtiness of his heart."

30 "I know his wrath," says the LORD,
"But it *is* not right;
His lies have made nothing right.
31 Therefore I will wail for Moab,
And I will cry out for all Moab;
I[a] will mourn for the men of Kir
    Heres.
32 O vine of Sibmah! I will weep for you
    with the weeping of Jazer.
Your plants have gone over the sea,
They reach to the sea of Jazer.
The plunderer has fallen on your
    summer fruit and your vintage.
33 Joy and gladness are taken
From the plentiful field
And from the land of Moab;
I have caused wine to fail from the
    winepresses;
No one will tread with joyous
    shouting—
Not joyous shouting!

34 "From the cry of Heshbon to Elealeh
    and to Jahaz
They have uttered their voice,
From Zoar to Horonaim,
Like a three-year-old heifer;[a]
For the waters of Nimrim also shall be
    desolate.

35 "Moreover," says the LORD,
"I will cause to cease in Moab
The one who offers *sacrifices* in the
    high places
And burns incense to his gods.
36 Therefore My heart shall wail like
    flutes for Moab,
And like flutes My heart shall wail
For the men of Kir Heres.
Therefore the riches they have
    acquired have perished.

37 "For every head *shall be* bald, and
    every beard clipped;
On all the hands *shall be* cuts, and on
    the loins sackcloth—

38 A general lamentation
On all the housetops of Moab,
And in its streets;
For I have broken Moab like a vessel
    in which *is* no pleasure," says the
    LORD.
39 "They shall wail:
'How she is broken down!
How Moab has turned her back with
    shame!'
So Moab shall be a derision
And a dismay to all those about her."

40For thus says the LORD:

"Behold, one shall fly like an eagle,
And spread his wings over Moab.
41 Kerioth is taken,
And the strongholds are surprised;
The mighty men's hearts in Moab on
    that day shall be
Like the heart of a woman in birth
    pangs.
42 And Moab shall be destroyed as a
    people,
Because he exalted *himself* against
    the LORD.
43 Fear and the pit and the snare *shall
    be* upon you,
O inhabitant of Moab," says the LORD.
44 "He who flees from the fear shall fall
    into the pit,
And he who gets out of the pit shall be
    caught in the snare.
For upon Moab, upon it I will bring
The year of their punishment," says
    the LORD.

45 "Those who fled stood under the
    shadow of Heshbon
Because of exhaustion.
But a fire shall come out of Heshbon,
A flame from the midst of Sihon,
And shall devour the brow of Moab,

48:31 [a]Following Dead Sea Scrolls, Septuagint, and
Vulgate; Masoretic Text reads *He.*   48:34 [a]Or *The
Third Eglath,* an unknown city (compare Isaiah
15:5)

GEOGRAPHY AND ENVIRONMENT

*Moab was located on the plateau southeast of the Dead Sea. The Moabites kept herds
of sheep and goats and farmed wheat and barley. They worshiped the god Chemosh (Jer.
48:13). A stone celebrating the victories of the king of Moab over Israel was discovered
at Dibon, near the Dead Sea (48:18). The stone records how the Moabites consecrated
Ataroth, an Israelite town, to Chemosh, thus killing the inhabitants.*

The crown of the head of the sons of
tumult.
46 Woe to you, O Moab!
The people of Chemosh perish;
For your sons have been taken
captive,
And your daughters captive.

47 "Yet I will bring back the captives of
Moab
In the latter days," says the LORD.

Thus far *is* the judgment of Moab.

Judgment on Ammon

49 ¹Against the Ammonites.
Thus says the LORD:

"Has Israel no sons?
Has he no heir?
Why *then* does Milcomᵃ inherit Gad,
And his people dwell in its cities?
2 Therefore behold, the days are
coming," says the LORD,
"That I will cause to be heard an alarm
of war
In Rabbah of the Ammonites;
It shall be a desolate mound,
And her villages shall be burned with
fire.
Then Israel shall take possession of
his inheritance," says the LORD.

3 "Wail, O Heshbon, for Ai is plundered!
Cry, you daughters of Rabbah,
Gird yourselves with sackcloth!
Lament and run to and fro by the
walls;
For Milcom shall go into captivity
With his priests and his princes
together.
4 Why do you boast in the valleys,
Your flowing valley, O backsliding
daughter?
Who trusted in her treasures, *saying,*
'Who will come against me?'
5 Behold, I will bring fear upon you,"
Says the Lord GOD of hosts,
"From all those who are around you;
You shall be driven out, everyone
headlong,
And no one will gather those who
wander off.

6 But afterward I will bring back
The captives of the people of Ammon,"
says the LORD.

Judgment on Edom

⁷Against Edom.
Thus says the LORD of hosts:

"*Is* wisdom no more in Teman?
Has counsel perished from the
prudent?
Has their wisdom vanished?
8 Flee, turn back, dwell in the depths,
O inhabitants of Dedan!
For I will bring the calamity of Esau
upon him,
The time *that* I will punish him.
9 If grape-gatherers came to you,
Would they not leave *some* gleaning
grapes?
If thieves by night,
Would they not destroy until they
have enough?
10 But I have made Esau bare;
I have uncovered his secret places,ᵃ
And he shall not be able to hide
himself.
His descendants are plundered,
His brethren and his neighbors,
And he *is* no more.
11 Leave your fatherless children,
I will preserve *them* alive;
And let your widows trust in Me."

¹²For thus says the LORD: "Behold,
those whose judgment *was* not to drink of
the cup have assuredly drunk. And *are* you
the one who will altogether go unpunished?
You shall not go unpunished, but you shall
surely drink *of it.* ¹³For I have sworn by
Myself," says the LORD, "that Bozrah shall
become a desolation, a reproach, a waste,
and a curse. And all its cities shall be perpetual wastes."

14 I have heard a message from the
LORD,
And an ambassador has been sent to
the nations:
"Gather together, come against her,
And rise up to battle!

15 "For indeed, I will make you small
among nations,
Despised among men.
16 Your fierceness has deceived you,
The pride of your heart,

49:1 ᵃHebrew *Malcam,* literally *their king,* a god of
the Ammonites; also called *Molech* (compare verse
3)   49:10 ᵃCompare Obadiah 1:5, 6

O you who dwell in the clefts of the
   rock,
Who hold the height of the hill!
Though you make your nest as high as
   the eagle,
I will bring you down from there,"
   says the LORD.^a

17 "Edom also shall be an astonishment;
   Everyone who goes by it will be
     astonished
   And will hiss at all its plagues.
18 As in the overthrow of Sodom and
     Gomorrah
   And their neighbors," says the LORD,
"No one shall remain there,
   Nor shall a son of man dwell in it.

19 "Behold, he shall come up like a lion
     from the floodplain^a of the Jordan
   Against the dwelling place of the
     strong;
   But I will suddenly make him run
     away from her.
   And who *is* a chosen *man that* I may
     appoint over her?
   For who *is* like Me?
   Who will arraign Me?
   And who *is* that shepherd
   Who will withstand Me?"

20 Therefore hear the counsel of the
     LORD that He has taken against
     Edom,
   And His purposes that He has
     proposed against the inhabitants of
     Teman:
   Surely the least of the flock shall draw
     them out;
   Surely He shall make their dwelling
     places desolate with them.
21 The earth shakes at the noise of their
     fall;
   At the cry its noise is heard at the
     Red Sea.
22 Behold, He shall come up and fly like
     the eagle,
   And spread His wings over Bozrah;

The heart of the mighty men of Edom
   in that day shall be
Like the heart of a woman in birth
   pangs.

Judgment on Damascus

23Against Damascus.

"Hamath and Arpad are shamed,
   For they have heard bad news.
They are fainthearted;
There is trouble on the sea;
   It cannot be quiet.
24 Damascus has grown feeble;
   She turns to flee,
   And fear has seized *her.*
   Anguish and sorrows have taken her
     like a woman in labor.
25 Why is the city of praise not deserted,
     the city of My joy?
26 Therefore her young men shall fall in
     her streets,
   And all the men of war shall be cut off
     in that day," says the LORD of hosts.
27 "I will kindle a fire in the wall of
     Damascus,
   And it shall consume the palaces of
     Ben-Hadad."^a

Judgment on Kedar and Hazor

28Against Kedar and against the kingdoms of Hazor, which Nebuchadnezzar
king of Babylon shall strike.
  Thus says the LORD:

"Arise, go up to Kedar,
   And devastate the men of the East!
29 Their tents and their flocks they shall
     take away.
   They shall take for themselves their
     curtains,
   All their vessels and their camels;
   And they shall cry out to them,
   'Fear *is* on every side!'

30 "Flee, get far away! Dwell in the
     depths,

49:16 ^aCompare Obadiah 1:3, 4   49:19 ^aOr
thicket   49:27 ^aCompare Amos 1:4

GEOGRAPHY AND ENVIRONMENT

The people of Kedar were basically the same people later called Arabs (Jer. 49:28).
They were nomads, living in tents made of black goat hair (Ps. 120:5; Song 1:5). They
kept sheep and goats (Ezek. 27:21), but lived in the wilderness rather than in towns or
pasturelands. Isaiah recalls their archers (Is. 21:17). Their traditional ancestor was one
of the sons of Ishmael (Gen. 25:13).

O inhabitants of Hazor!" says the
LORD.
"For Nebuchadnezzar king of Babylon
    has taken counsel against you,
And has conceived a plan against you.

31 "Arise, go up to the wealthy nation
    that dwells securely," says the
    LORD,
"Which has neither gates nor bars,
    Dwelling alone.
32 Their camels shall be for booty,
And the multitude of their cattle for
    plunder.
I will scatter to all winds those in the
    farthest corners,
And I will bring their calamity from
    all its sides," says the LORD.
33 "Hazor shall be a dwelling for jackals,
    a desolation forever;
No one shall reside there,
Nor son of man dwell in it."

Judgment on Elam

34The word of the LORD that came to
Jeremiah the prophet against Elam, in the
beginning of the reign of Zedekiah king of
Judah, saying, 35"Thus says the LORD of
hosts:

'Behold, I will break the bow of Elam,
    The foremost of their might.
36 Against Elam I will bring the four
    winds
From the four quarters of heaven,
And scatter them toward all those
    winds;
There shall be no nations where the
    outcasts of Elam will not go.
37 For I will cause Elam to be dismayed
    before their enemies
And before those who seek their life.
I will bring disaster upon them,
    My fierce anger,' says the LORD;
'And I will send the sword after
    them
Until I have consumed them.
38 I will set My throne in Elam,
And will destroy from there the king
    and the princes,' says the LORD.

39 'But it shall come to pass in the latter
    days:
I will bring back the captives of Elam,'
    says the LORD."

25:26 ªA code word for Babylon (compare
51:41)

Jeremiah 25:15–38
Judgment on the Nations

25 :15 For thus says the LORD God of
Israel to me: "Take this wine cup of
fury from My hand, and cause all the nations, to whom I send you, to drink it.
16And they will drink and stagger and go
mad because of the sword that I will send
among them."
17Then I took the cup from the LORD's
hand, and made all the nations drink, to
whom the LORD had sent me: 18Jerusalem
and the cities of Judah, its kings and its
princes, to make them a desolation, an astonishment, a hissing, and a curse, as *it is*
this day; 19Pharaoh king of Egypt, his servants, his princes, and all his people; 20all
the mixed multitude, all the kings of the
land of Uz, all the kings of the land of the
Philistines (namely, Ashkelon, Gaza, Ekron, and the remnant of Ashdod); 21Edom,
Moab, and the people of Ammon; 22all the
kings of Tyre, all the kings of Sidon, and
the kings of the coastlands which *are*
across the sea; 23Dedan, Tema, Buz, and
all *who are* in the farthest corners; 24all
the kings of Arabia and all the kings of the
mixed multitude who dwell in the desert;
25all the kings of Zimri, all the kings of
Elam, and all the kings of the Medes; 26all
the kings of the north, far and near, one
with another; and all the kingdoms of the
world which *are* on the face of the earth.
Also the king of Sheshachª shall drink after them.
27"Therefore you shall say to them,
'Thus says the LORD of hosts, the God of Israel: "Drink, be drunk, and vomit! Fall and
rise no more, because of the sword which I
will send among you." ' 28And it shall be, if
they refuse to take the cup from your hand
to drink, then you shall say to them, 'Thus
says the LORD of hosts: "You shall certainly
drink! 29For behold, I begin to bring
calamity on the city which is called by My
name, and should you be utterly unpunished? You shall not be unpunished, for I
will call for a sword on all the inhabitants
of the earth," says the LORD of hosts.'
30"Therefore prophesy against them all
these words, and say to them:

'The LORD will roar from on high,
    And utter His voice from His holy
    habitation;
He will roar mightily against His fold.
He will give a shout, as those who
    tread *the grapes,*

EKRON DRINKS GOD'S WINE CUP OF FURY (Jer. 25:20)

Ekron was one of the cities of the Philistine Pentapolis—an alliance of five cities which also included Ashkelon, Gath, Ashdod, and Gaza. It was located in the Shephelah, bordering on Judah's territory.

By the time of Jeremiah the Pentapolis was reduced by one, as Gath is no longer mentioned by the prophets Jeremiah (Jer. 25:20), Zephaniah (Zeph. 2:4), or Zechariah (Zech. 9:5). The remainder of the Philistine cities were also in danger of being destroyed, as Jeremiah's prophecy suggests. The kings of Ashkelon, Gaza, Ekron, and Ashdod are included among those Jeremiah made to drink God's "wine cup of fury" (Jer. 25:15-17, 20).

Moreover, an Aramaic letter, known as the Saqqara Papyrus in Egypt, supports Jeremiah's warnings of coming destruction. The letter, written by a certain King Adon of one of the Philistine city-states, urgently requests aid from Egypt because of an approaching Babylonian invasion of Palestine. Such a letter could have been sent during or shortly after the time of Egypt's King Psammetichus I (664–610 B.C.), who had reunited Egypt and then aided Assyria against the rising power of Babylon. Some scholars suppose that Adon may indeed have been the king at Ekron.

The Babylonian Chronicle describes the destruction of a Philistine city during the campaign in 603 B.C. by Nebuchadnezzar II. The name of the Philistine city, however, is not mentioned, and so possibly could have been Ekron. That Ekron did drink the "wine cup of fury" is possible, since the city is not named in any records again until the late Hellenistic period (after 150 B.C.).

Against all the inhabitants of the earth.

31 A noise will come to the ends of the earth—
For the LORD has a controversy with the nations;
He will plead His case with all flesh.
He will give those *who are* wicked to the sword,' says the LORD."

32Thus says the LORD of hosts:

"Behold, disaster shall go forth
From nation to nation,
And a great whirlwind shall be raised up
From the farthest parts of the earth.

33"And at that day the slain of the LORD shall be from *one* end of the earth even to the *other* end of the earth. They shall not be lamented, or gathered, or buried; they shall become refuse on the ground.

34 "Wail, shepherds, and cry!
Roll about *in the ashes,*
You leaders of the flock!
For the days of your slaughter and your dispersions are fulfilled;
You shall fall like a precious vessel.
35 And the shepherds will have no way to flee,

Nor the leaders of the flock to escape.
36 A voice of the cry of the shepherds,
And a wailing of the leaders to the flock *will be heard.*
For the LORD has plundered their pasture,
37 And the peaceful dwellings are cut down
Because of the fierce anger of the LORD.
38 He has left His lair like the lion;
For their land is desolate
Because of the fierceness of the Oppressor,
And because of His fierce anger."

Jeremiah 27:12—28:17

27 :12 I also spoke to Zedekiah king of Judah according to all these words, saying, "Bring your necks under the yoke of the king of Babylon, and serve him and his people, and live! 13Why will you die, you and your people, by the sword, by the famine, and by the pestilence, as the LORD has spoken against the nation that will not serve the king of Babylon? 14Therefore do not listen to the words of the prophets who speak to you, saying, 'You shall not serve the king of Babylon,' for they prophesy a lie to you; 15for I have not sent them," says the LORD, "yet they prophesy a lie in My name,

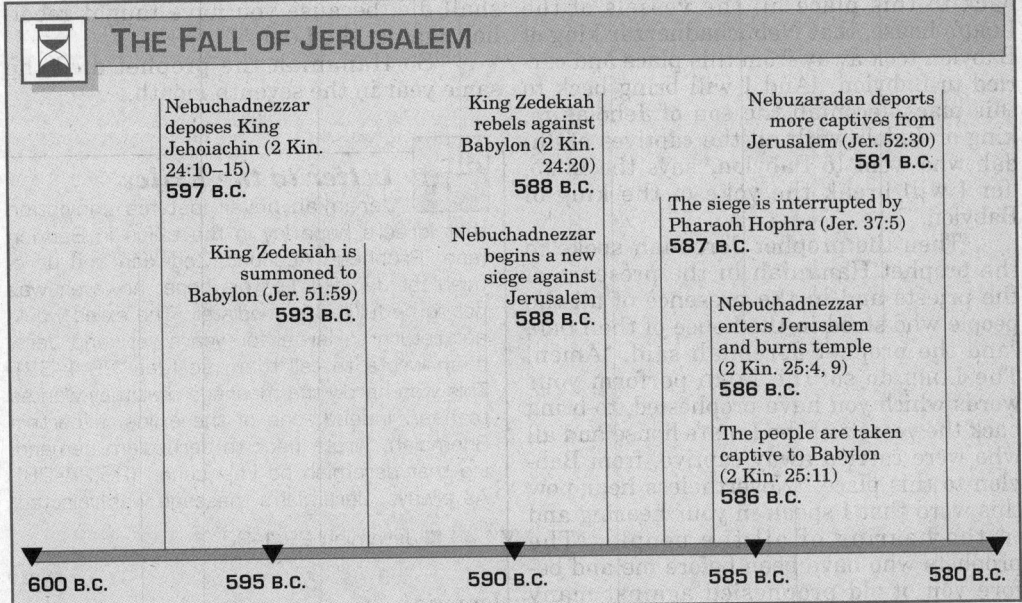

that I may drive you out, and that you may perish, you and the prophets who prophesy to you."

16Also I spoke to the priests and to all this people, saying, "Thus says the LORD: 'Do not listen to the words of your prophets who prophesy to you, saying, "Behold, the vessels of the LORD's house will now shortly be brought back from Babylon"; for they prophesy a lie to you. 17Do not listen to them; serve the king of Babylon, and live! Why should this city be laid waste? 18But if they *are* prophets, and if the word of the LORD is with them, let them now make intercession to the LORD of hosts, that the vessels which are left in the house of the LORD, *in* the house of the king of Judah, and at Jerusalem, do not go to Babylon.'

19"For thus says the LORD of hosts concerning the pillars, concerning the Sea, concerning the carts, and concerning the remainder of the vessels that remain in this city, 20which Nebuchadnezzar king of Babylon did not take, when he carried away captive Jeconiah the son of Jehoiakim, king of Judah, from Jerusalem to Babylon, and all the nobles of Judah and Jerusalem— 21yes, thus says the LORD of hosts, the God of Israel, concerning the vessels that remain in the house of the LORD, and in the house of the king of Judah and of Jerusalem: 22"They shall be carried to Babylon, and there they shall be until the day that I visit them,' says the

LORD. 'Then I will bring them up and restore them to this place.' "

Hananiah's Falsehood and Doom

28 1And it happened in the same year, at the beginning of the reign of Zedekiah king of Judah, in the fourth year *and* in the fifth month, *that* Hananiah the son of Azur the prophet, who *was* from Gibeon, spoke to me in the house of the LORD in the presence of the priests and of all the people, saying, 2"Thus speaks the LORD of hosts, the God of Israel, saying: 'I have broken the yoke of the king of Babylon. 3Within two full years I will bring back to this place all the vessels of the LORD's house, that Nebuchadnezzar king of Babylon took away from this place and carried to Babylon. 4And I will bring back to this place Jeconiah the son of Jehoiakim, king of Judah, with all the captives of Judah who went to Babylon,' says the LORD, 'for I will break the yoke of the king of Babylon.' "

5Then the prophet Jeremiah spoke to the prophet Hananiah in the presence of the priests and in the presence of all the people who stood in the house of the LORD, 6and the prophet Jeremiah said, "Amen! The LORD do so; the LORD perform your words which you have prophesied, to bring back the vessels of the LORD's house and all who were carried away captive, from Babylon to this place. 7Nevertheless hear now this word that I speak in your hearing and in the hearing of all the people: 8The prophets who have been before me and before you of old prophesied against many countries and great kingdoms—of war and disaster and pestilence. 9As for the prophet who prophesies of peace, when the word of the prophet comes to pass, the prophet will be known as one whom the LORD has truly sent."

10Then Hananiah the prophet took the yoke off the prophet Jeremiah's neck and broke it. 11And Hananiah spoke in the presence of all the people, saying, "Thus says the LORD: 'Even so I will break the yoke of Nebuchadnezzar king of Babylon from the neck of all nations within the space of two full years.' " And the prophet Jeremiah went his way.

12Now the word of the LORD came to Jeremiah, after Hananiah the prophet had broken the yoke from the neck of the prophet Jeremiah, saying, 13"Go and tell Hananiah, saying, 'Thus says the LORD: "You have broken the yokes of wood, but you have made in their place yokes of iron." 14For thus says the LORD of hosts, the God of Israel: "I have put a yoke of iron on the neck of all these nations, that they may serve Nebuchadnezzar king of Babylon; and they shall serve him. I have given him the beasts of the field also." ' "

15Then the prophet Jeremiah said to Hananiah the prophet, "Hear now, Hananiah, the LORD has not sent you, but you make this people trust in a lie. 16Therefore thus says the LORD: 'Behold, I will cast you from the face of the earth. This year you

shall die, because you have taught rebellion against the LORD.' "

17So Hananiah the prophet died the same year in the seventh month.

Letter to the Exiles

Jeremiah never lost his conviction that Israel's hope lay in the exiles in Babylon (see "Prophetic Account: Zedekiah and Jeremiah" at Jer. 24:1). This hope, however, was not to be fulfilled immediately. The exiles would not return to Israel for years yet, and Jeremiah wrote to tell them so (Jer. 29:1–32). This was hardly the message that they wanted to hear. Indeed, one of the exiles, a certain Shemaiah, wrote back to Jerusalem demanding that Jeremiah be imprisoned (29:24–28). As always, Jeremiah's message was rejected.

■ Jeremiah 29:1–32

Jeremiah
Jeremiah's Letter

29 :1 Now these *are* the words of the letter that Jeremiah the prophet sent from Jerusalem to the remainder of the elders who were carried away captive— to the priests, the prophets, and all the people whom Nebuchadnezzar had carried away captive from Jerusalem to Babylon. 2(This happened after Jeconiah the king, the queen mother, the eunuchs, the princes of Judah and Jerusalem, the craftsmen, and the smiths had departed from Jerusalem.) 3*The letter was sent* by the hand of Elasah the son of Shaphan, and Gemariah the son of Hilkiah, whom Zedekiah king of Judah sent to Babylon, to Nebuchadnezzar king of Babylon, saying,

4   Thus says the LORD of hosts, the God of Israel, to all who were carried away captive, whom I have caused to be carried away from Jerusalem to Babylon:

5   Build houses and dwell *in them;* plant gardens and eat their fruit. 6Take wives and beget sons and daughters; and take wives for your sons and give your daughters to husbands, so that they may bear sons and daughters— that you may be increased there, and not diminished. 7And seek the peace of the city where I have caused you to be carried away captive, and pray to the LORD for it; for in its peace you will

have peace. [8]For thus says the LORD of hosts, the God of Israel: Do not let your prophets and your diviners who are in your midst deceive you, nor listen to your dreams which you cause to be dreamed. [9]For they prophesy falsely to you in My name; I have not sent them, says the LORD.

[10] For thus says the LORD: After seventy years are completed at Babylon, I will visit you and perform My good word toward you, and cause you to return to this place. [11]For I know the thoughts that I think toward you, says the LORD, thoughts of peace and not of evil, to give you a future and a hope. [12]Then you will call upon Me and go and pray to Me, and I will listen to you. [13]And you will seek Me and find *Me,* when you search for Me with all your heart. [14]I will be found by you, says the LORD, and I will bring you back from your captivity; I will gather you from all the nations and from all the places where I have driven you, says the LORD, and I will bring you to the place from which I cause you to be carried away captive.

[15] Because you have said, "The LORD has raised up prophets for us in Babylon"— [16]therefore thus says the LORD concerning the king who sits on the throne of David, concerning all the people who dwell in this city, and concerning your brethren who have not gone out with you into captivity— [17]thus says the LORD of hosts: Behold, I will send on them the sword, the famine, and the pestilence, and will make them like rotten figs that cannot be eaten, they are so bad. [18]And I will pursue them with the sword, with famine, and with pestilence; and I will deliver them to trouble among all the kingdoms of the earth—to be a curse, an astonishment, a hissing, and a reproach among all the nations where I have driven them, [19]because they have not heeded My words, says the LORD, which I sent to them by My servants the prophets, rising up early and sending *them;* neither would you heed, says the LORD. [20]Therefore hear the word of the LORD, all you of the captivity, whom I have sent from Jerusalem to Babylon.

[21] Thus says the LORD of hosts, the God of Israel, concerning Ahab the son of Kolaiah, and Zedekiah the son of Maaseiah, who prophesy a lie to you in My name: Behold, I will deliver them into the hand of Nebuchadnezzar king of Babylon, and he shall slay them before your eyes. [22]And because of them a curse shall be taken up by all the captivity of Judah who *are* in Babylon, saying, "The LORD make you like Zedekiah and Ahab, whom the king of Babylon roasted in the fire"; [23]because they have done disgraceful things in Israel, have committed adultery with their neighbors' wives, and have spoken lying words in My name, which I have not commanded them. Indeed I know, and *am* a witness, says the LORD.

[24] You shall also speak to Shemaiah the Nehelamite, saying, [25]Thus speaks the LORD of hosts, the God of Israel, saying: You have sent letters in your name to all the people who *are* at Jerusalem, to Zephaniah the son of Maaseiah the priest, and to all the priests, saying, [26]"The LORD has made you priest instead of Jehoiada the priest, so that there should be officers *in* the house of the LORD over every man *who* is demented and considers himself a prophet, that you should put him in prison and in the stocks. [27]Now therefore, why have you not rebuked Jeremiah of Anathoth who makes himself a prophet to you? [28]For he has sent to us *in* Babylon, saying, 'This *captivity is* long; build houses and dwell *in them,* and plant gardens and eat their fruit.' "

[29] Now Zephaniah the priest read this letter in the hearing of Jeremiah the prophet. [30]Then the word of the LORD came to Jeremiah, saying: [31]Send to all those in captivity, saying, Thus says the LORD concerning Shemaiah the Nehelamite: Because Shemaiah has prophesied to you, and I have not sent him, and he has caused you to trust in a lie— [32]therefore thus says the LORD: Behold, I will punish Shemaiah the Nehelamite and his family: he shall not have anyone to dwell among this people, nor shall he see the good that I will do for My

people, says the LORD, because he has taught rebellion against the LORD.

Oracles Against Babylon

Jeremiah had declared that Babylon was only doing what God wanted, but this did not mean that Babylon would never be punished for its own sins. In Zedekiah's 4th year (593 B.C.), the king was summoned to Babylon (Jer. 51:59–64). Perhaps Nebuchadnezzar had heard about Zedekiah's Jerusalem conference (Jer. 27) and wanted an explanation. In any case, Jeremiah used the king's journey to send another letter, this one filled with his oracles about Babylon's coming judgment (50:1—51:58).

■ Jeremiah 50:1—51:64

Jeremiah
Judgment on Babylon and Babylonia

50 :1 The word that the LORD spoke against Babylon *and* against the land of the Chaldeans by Jeremiah the prophet.

2 "Declare among the nations,
Proclaim, and set up a standard;
Proclaim—do not conceal *it*—
Say, 'Babylon is taken, Bel is shamed.
Merodach[a] is broken in pieces;
Her idols are humiliated,
Her images are broken in pieces.'
3 For out of the north a nation comes up against her,
Which shall make her land desolate,
And no one shall dwell therein.

TIME CAPSULE   *598 to 597 B.C.*

598   *Jehoiachin becomes king in Judah*

597   *Nebuchadnezzar captures Jerusalem and deposes King Jehoiachin*

597   *The prophet Ezekiel is among Judeans deported to Babylon*

597   *Nebuchadnezzar replaces Jehoiachin with his uncle Mattaniah*

597   *Nebuchadnezzar gives Mattaniah the throne name "Zedekiah" (2 Kin. 24:17)*

597   *Zedekiah becomes king in Judah*

They shall move, they shall depart,
Both man and beast.

4 "In those days and in that time," says the LORD,
"The children of Israel shall come,
They and the children of Judah together;
With continual weeping they shall come,
And seek the LORD their God.
5 They shall ask the way to Zion,
With their faces toward it, *saying,*
'Come and let us join ourselves to the LORD
In a perpetual covenant
That will not be forgotten.'

6 "My people have been lost sheep.
Their shepherds have led them astray;
They have turned them away *on* the mountains.
They have gone from mountain to hill;
They have forgotten their resting place.
7 All who found them have devoured them;
And their adversaries said, 'We have not offended,
Because they have sinned against the LORD, the habitation of justice,
The LORD, the hope of their fathers.'

8 "Move from the midst of Babylon,
Go out of the land of the Chaldeans;
And be like the rams before the flocks.
9 For behold, I will raise and cause to come up against Babylon
An assembly of great nations from the north country,
And they shall array themselves against her;
From there she shall be captured.
Their arrows *shall be* like *those* of an expert warrior;[a]
None shall return in vain.
10 And Chaldea shall become plunder;
All who plunder her shall be satisfied," says the LORD.

11 "Because you were glad, because you rejoiced,

50:2 [a]A Babylonian god; sometimes spelled *Marduk*   50:9 [a]Following some Hebrew manuscripts, Septuagint, and Syriac; Masoretic Text, Targum, and Vulgate read *a warrior who makes childless.*

MARDUK ASCENDS THE DIVINE RANKS (Jer. 50:2)

Jeremiah announced the utter defeat of Babylon in the theological language of the people he had spent so much of his prophetic career confronting. The patron deity they believed in would prove to be the nothing Jeremiah had always proclaimed him to be: "Bel is shamed. Merodach is broken in pieces" (Jer. 50:2). The downfall of Babylon, the city whose armies destroyed Judah and Jerusalem, would mean also the downfall of her deities and their images.

"Merodach" is the Hebrew variant of "Marduk." Before 2000 B.C. Marduk, one of the sons of the god Enki, was a minor deity in the pantheon of the Sumerians. He became the patron deity of Babylon, and then rose in status during the reign of Hammurabi, sixth king of the 1st Dynasty of Babylon (1792–1750 B.C.). When Hammurabi gained control over all of Mesopotamia, Marduk, the god of the ruling city, became the ruling god of the conquered territory as well. The 1st Dynasty built the temple area called Esagila to honor Marduk for the victorious expansion of power.

Marduk's prestige waned after the 1st Dynasty. The victory of Nebuchadnezzar I over Elam (c. 1120 B.C.), however, brought new theological activity in Babylon, producing a cult with Marduk worshiped as the great cosmic ruler. The Babylonian creation epic, the Enuma Elish, relates Marduk's creation of the universe and celebrates the order which the god maintained. The title "Bel" (meaning "lord") became synonymous with Marduk, and from this period Bel Marduk was considered the divine lord of the universe.

In the early 1st millennium B.C. Assyria became the prominent power in Mesopotamia. Marduk was incorporated into the Assyrian pantheon, and, when the Assyrian king Sennacherib demolished Babylon in 689 B.C., the image of Marduk was reverently taken to the Assyrian capital. In accordance with ancient theology, Marduk was made subordinate to the victorious Asshur, patron deity of Assyria.

By Jeremiah's time the Neo-Babylonian Empire (626–539 B.C.) had reestablished Babylon's supremacy in Mesopotamia and beyond. Marduk was again seen by all the conquered people as the supreme deity whose city was victorious because of his might. Jeremiah used this theology, believed even by his contemporaries in Judah, to declare the coming end of Babylon and its god. For Jeremiah there was no doubt that Marduk was nothing; he was "broken in pieces" (Jer. 50:2). Furthermore, Israel's God was in charge, declaring, "I will punish Bel in Babylon" (Jer. 51:44).

You destroyers of My heritage,
Because you have grown fat like a
   heifer threshing grain,
And you bellow like bulls,
12 Your mother shall be deeply
   ashamed.
She who bore you shall be ashamed.
Behold, the least of the nations *shall
be* a wilderness,
A dry land and a desert.
13 Because of the wrath of the LORD
She shall not be inhabited,
But she shall be wholly desolate.
Everyone who goes by Babylon shall
   be horrified
And hiss at all her plagues.

14 "Put yourselves in array against
   Babylon all around,
All you who bend the bow;

Shoot at her, spare no arrows,
For she has sinned against the LORD.
15 Shout against her all around;
She has given her hand,
Her foundations have fallen,
Her walls are thrown down;
For it *is* the vengeance of the LORD.
Take vengeance on her.
As she has done, so do to her.
16 Cut off the sower from Babylon,
And him who handles the sickle at
   harvest time.
For fear of the oppressing sword
Everyone shall turn to his own
   people,
And everyone shall flee to his own
   land.

17 "Israel *is* like scattered sheep;
The lions have driven *him* away.

SARGON II DEVOURS ISRAEL (Jer. 50:17)

Sargon was the throne name of an Assyrian king who probably usurped the throne in the late 8th century (c. 722 B.C.). His name is mentioned only once in the Bible: the prophet Isaiah records that he received an oracle in about 712 B.C., the year that "Sargon the king of Assyria" campaigned against Ashdod (Is. 20:1).

Like his two immediate predecessors, Tiglath-Pileser III and Shalmaneser V, Sargon II mounted extensive military campaigns in Syro-Palestine. Though the Bible appears to give credit to Shalmaneser for besieging and taking Samaria (2 Kin. 17:3–6; 18:9, 10), Sargon in his annals claims to have conquered the city in 722 B.C. It is likely that both kings played a role in the conquest, with Shalmaneser conducting the siege and Sargon actually leading the Israelites into exile.

In his annals and inscriptions Sargon boasts about Samaria's fall. One claim tallies over 27,000 inhabitants of Samaria who were deported. Another claim states that Sargon subsequently rebuilt the city "better than it was before," and placed an Assyrian official there, as well as inhabitants brought from other lands. Archaeological excavations at Samaria from this period have revealed a fragment of a stele (stone slab) dedicated to Sargon, and a cuneiform text that mentions a local Assyrian governor.

As the prophet Jeremiah pictures Israel as "scattered sheep," he reflects on Sargon's capture of the northern kingdom's capital at Samaria. Just as lions attack sheep, so did Sargon "the king of Assyria devour" Israel (Jer. 50:17).

First the king of Assyria devoured
  him;
Now at last this Nebuchadnezzar king
  of Babylon has broken his bones."

18Therefore thus says the LORD of
hosts, the God of Israel:

"Behold, I will punish the king of
  Babylon and his land,
As I have punished the king of
  Assyria.
19 But I will bring back Israel to his
  home,
And he shall feed on Carmel and
  Bashan;
His soul shall be satisfied on Mount
  Ephraim and Gilead.
20 In those days and in that time," says
  the LORD,
"The iniquity of Israel shall be sought,
  but there shall be none;
And the sins of Judah, but they shall
  not be found;
For I will pardon those whom I
  preserve.

21 "Go up against the land of Merathaim,
  against it,
And against the inhabitants of Pekod.
Waste and utterly destroy them," says
  the LORD,

"And do according to all that I have
  commanded you.
22 A sound of battle is in the land,
And of great destruction.
23 How the hammer of the whole earth
  has been cut apart and broken!
How Babylon has become a desolation
  among the nations!
I have laid a snare for you;
24 You have indeed been trapped,
  O Babylon,
And you were not aware;
You have been found and also caught,
Because you have contended against
  the LORD.
25 The LORD has opened His armory,
And has brought out the weapons of
  His indignation;
For this is the work of the Lord GOD of
  hosts
In the land of the Chaldeans.
26 Come against her from the farthest
  border;
Open her storehouses;
Cast her up as heaps of ruins,
And destroy her utterly;
Let nothing of her be left.
27 Slay all her bulls,
Let them go down to the slaughter.
Woe to them!
For their day has come, the time of
  their punishment.

28 The voice of those who flee and escape
from the land of Babylon
Declares in Zion the vengeance of the
LORD our God,
The vengeance of His temple.

29 "Call together the archers against
Babylon.
All you who bend the bow, encamp
against it all around;
Let none of them escape.ᵃ
Repay her according to her work;
According to all she has done, do to
her;
For she has been proud against the
LORD,
Against the Holy One of Israel.
30 Therefore her young men shall fall in
the streets,
And all her men of war shall be cut off
in that day," says the LORD.
31 "Behold, I *am* against you,
O most haughty one!" says the Lord
GOD of hosts;
"For your day has come,
The time *that* I will punish you.ᵃ
32 The most proud shall stumble and
fall,
And no one will raise him up;
I will kindle a fire in his cities,
And it will devour all around him."

33Thus says the LORD of hosts:

"The children of Israel *were* oppressed,
Along with the children of Judah;
All who took them captive have held
them fast;
They have refused to let them go.
34 Their Redeemer *is* strong;
The LORD of hosts *is* His name.
He will thoroughly plead their case,
That He may give rest to the land,
And disquiet the inhabitants of
Babylon.

35 "A sword *is* against the Chaldeans,"
says the LORD,
"Against the inhabitants of Babylon,
And against her princes and her wise
men.

36 A sword *is* against the soothsayers,
and they will be fools.
A sword *is* against her mighty men,
and they will be dismayed.
37 A sword *is* against their horses,
Against their chariots,
And against all the mixed peoples who
are in her midst;
And they will become like women.
A sword *is* against her treasures, and
they will be robbed.
38 A droughtᵃ *is* against her waters, and
they will be dried up.
For it *is* the land of carved images,
And they are insane with *their* idols.

39 "Therefore the wild desert beasts shall
dwell *there* with the jackals,
And the ostriches shall dwell in it.
It shall be inhabited no more forever,
Nor shall it be dwelt in from
generation to generation.
40 As God overthrew Sodom and
Gomorrah
And their neighbors," says the LORD,
"*So* no one shall reside there,
Nor son of man dwell in it.

41 "Behold, a people shall come from the
north,
And a great nation and many kings
Shall be raised up from the ends of
the earth.
42 They shall hold the bow and the lance;
They *are* cruel and shall not show
mercy.
Their voice shall roar like the sea;
They shall ride on horses,
Set in array, like a man for the battle,
Against you, O daughter of Babylon.

43 "The king of Babylon has heard the
report about them,
And his hands grow feeble;
Anguish has taken hold of him,
Pangs as of a woman in childbirth.

44 "Behold, he shall come up like a lion
from the floodplainᵃ of the Jordan
Against the dwelling place of the
strong;
But I will make them suddenly run
away from her.
And who *is* a chosen *man that* I may
appoint over her?
For who *is* like Me?
Who will arraign Me?
And who *is* that shepherd
Who will withstand Me?"

50:29 ᵃQere, some Hebrew manuscripts, Septuagint,
and Targum add *to her.*   50:31 ᵃFollowing
Masoretic Text and Targum; Septuagint and Vulgate
read *The time of your punishment.*
50:38 ᵃFollowing Masoretic Text, Targum, and
Vulgate; Syriac reads *sword;* Septuagint omits *A
drought is.*   50:44 ᵃOr *thicket*

45 Therefore hear the counsel of the
    LORD that He has taken against
    Babylon,
    And His purposes that He has
    proposed against the land of the
    Chaldeans:
    Surely the least of the flock shall draw
    them out;
    Surely He will make their dwelling
    place desolate with them.
46 At the noise of the taking of Babylon
    The earth trembles,
    And the cry is heard among the
    nations.

The Utter Destruction of Babylon

51 ¹Thus says the LORD:

    "Behold, I will raise up against
    Babylon,
    Against those who dwell in Leb
    Kamai,ᵃ
    A destroying wind.
2   And I will send winnowers to Babylon,
    Who shall winnow her and empty her
    land.
    For in the day of doom
    They shall be against her all around.
3   Against *her* let the archer bend his
    bow,
    And lift himself up against *her* in his
    armor.
    Do not spare her young men;
    Utterly destroy all her army.
4   Thus the slain shall fall in the land of
    the Chaldeans,
    And *those* thrust through in her
    streets.
5   For Israel *is* not forsaken, nor Judah,
    By his God, the LORD of hosts,
    Though their land was filled with sin
    against the Holy One of Israel."

6   Flee from the midst of Babylon,
    And every one save his life!
    Do not be cut off in her iniquity,
    For this *is* the time of the LORD's
    vengeance;
    He shall recompense her.

7   Babylon *was* a golden cup in the
    LORD's hand,
    That made all the earth drunk.
    The nations drank her wine;
    Therefore the nations are deranged.
8   Babylon has suddenly fallen and been
    destroyed.
    Wail for her!
    Take balm for her pain;
    Perhaps she may be healed.

9   We would have healed Babylon,
    But she is not healed.
    Forsake her, and let us go everyone to
    his own country;
    For her judgment reaches to heaven
    and is lifted up to the skies.
10 The LORD has revealed our
    righteousness.
    Come and let us declare in Zion the
    work of the LORD our God.

11 Make the arrows bright!
    Gather the shields!
    The LORD has raised up the spirit of
    the kings of the Medes.
    For His plan *is* against Babylon to
    destroy it,
    Because it *is* the vengeance of the
    LORD,
    The vengeance for His temple.
12 Set up the standard on the walls of
    Babylon;
    Make the guard strong,
    Set up the watchmen,
    Prepare the ambushes.
    For the LORD has both devised and
    done
    What He spoke against the
    inhabitants of Babylon.
13 O you who dwell by many waters,
    Abundant in treasures,
    Your end has come,
    The measure of your covetousness.

51:1 ᵃA code word for Chaldea (Babylonia); may be
translated *The Midst of Those Who Rise Up Against
Me*

SCIENCE AND TECHNOLOGY

*Archers riding in chariots could shoot their arrows without stopping (Jer. 51:3). One
kind of armor for chariot archers was a long-sleeved leather shirt coming to the knees.
Scales were sewn to the shirt, like fish scales, and a suit of armor might contain 500 to
1,000 scales and weigh about 50 pounds. This kind of armor appears in ancient
Assyrian art, and many copper scales have also been discovered.*

14 The LORD of hosts has sworn by
        Himself:
    "Surely I will fill you with men, as with
        locusts,
    And they shall lift up a shout against
        you."

15 He has made the earth by His power;
    He has established the world by His
        wisdom,
    And stretched out the heaven by His
        understanding.
16 When He utters *His* voice—
    There is a multitude of waters in the
        heavens:
    "He causes the vapors to ascend from
        the ends of the earth;
    He makes lightnings for the rain;
    He brings the wind out of His
        treasuries."a

17 Everyone is dull-hearted, without
        knowledge;
    Every metalsmith is put to shame by
        the carved image;
    For his molded image *is* falsehood,
    And *there is* no breath in them.
18 They *are* futile, a work of errors;
    In the time of their punishment they
        shall perish.
19 The Portion of Jacob *is* not like them,
    For He *is* the Maker of all things;
    And *Israel is* the tribe of His
        inheritance.
    The LORD of hosts *is* His name.

20 "You *are* My battle-ax *and* weapons of
        war:
    For with you I will break the nation in
        pieces;
    With you I will destroy kingdoms;
21 With you I will break in pieces the
        horse and its rider;
    With you I will break in pieces the
        chariot and its rider;
22 With you also I will break in pieces
        man and woman;

With you I will break in pieces old and
    young;
With you I will break in pieces the
    young man and the maiden;
23 With you also I will break in pieces
        the shepherd and his flock;
    With you I will break in pieces the
        farmer and his yoke of oxen;
    And with you I will break in pieces
        governors and rulers.

24 "And I will repay Babylon
    And all the inhabitants of Chaldea
    For all the evil they have done
    In Zion in your sight," says the LORD.

25 "Behold, I *am* against you,
        O destroying mountain,
    Who destroys all the earth," says the
        LORD.
    "And I will stretch out My hand
        against you,
    Roll you down from the rocks,
    And make you a burnt mountain.
26 They shall not take from you a stone
        for a corner
    Nor a stone for a foundation,
    But you shall be desolate forever,"
        says the LORD.

27 Set up a banner in the land,
    Blow the trumpet among the nations!
    Prepare the nations against her,
    Call the kingdoms together against
        her:
    Ararat, Minni, and Ashkenaz.
    Appoint a general against her;
    Cause the horses to come up like the
        bristling locusts.
28 Prepare against her the nations,
    With the kings of the Medes,
    Its governors and all its rulers,
    All the land of his dominion.
29 And the land will tremble and sorrow;
    For every purpose of the LORD shall be
        performed against Babylon,
    To make the land of Babylon a
        desolation without inhabitant.

51:16 aPsalm 135:7

HEALTH AND MEDICINE

*Balm is a kind of resin taken from trees by cutting the bark. It was used as a perfume
and was considered effective as a medicine (Jer. 51:8). Although Gilead is mentioned
together with balm (Jer. 8:22; 46:11), the substance was not produced in Gilead. It
may have been transported through Gilead or sold there. Ancient pharmaceuticals
consisted mainly of plant products recommended by tradition.*

A FESTIVAL FOR BEL MARDUK (Jer. 51:44)

Bel Marduk was seen by the Babylonians as the creator god and the head of the pantheon of gods. Not only was the earth created long ago, but to the Babylonians that creation was temporary, needing to be reconfirmed each year less the cosmos return to chaos.

The New Year's Festival was an 11- to 12-day process of securing a continued creation. It is not known what happened on each day of the festival, but we do know that Marduk's temple was prepared on the 1st day, with the incantation priest washing himself with water from the Euphrates River, praying, and singing on the 2nd day. On the 3rd day, three craftsmen were given materials to make two images of wood, which represented evil, and adorn them with precious stones and red garments. On the 4th day, in the late afternoon, the story of creation (called the Enuma Elish) was recited.

On the 5th day, Marduk's temple was purified by sprinkling its walls with water from the Tigris River and smearing them with a tree sap. After the temple was cleansed, a sheep was slaughtered and, after taking the body into the temple, both head and body were thrown into the Euphrates River, supposedly taking away the sins of the previous year. That evening the king presented himself before Marduk and surrendered his kingship. The officiating priest struck the face of the king, pulled his ears, and forced him to bow before Marduk's image. The king confessed his innocence from evil and recognized the supremacy of Marduk.

On the 6th day, the two wooden images made by the craftsmen were decapitated and burned. On following days, gods from surrounding areas were brought to Marduk's temple with more songs and prayers. A grand banquet finished the New Year celebration, and the gods were returned to their own temples. This entire festival revolved around the idea that Marduk controlled the world.

The prophet Jeremiah proclaimed, however, that one day, as retribution for what Babylon did to Jerusalem, Yahweh would punish Marduk and Babylon (Jer. 51:44). When that happened, the world would know which god was really in control.

---

30 The mighty men of Babylon have
    ceased fighting,
They have remained in their
    strongholds;
Their might has failed,
They became *like* women;
They have burned her dwelling places,
The bars of her *gate* are broken.

31 One runner will run to meet another,
And one messenger to meet another,
To show the king of Babylon that his
    city is taken on *all* sides;

32 The passages are blocked,
The reeds they have burned with fire,
And the men of war are terrified.

33For thus says the LORD of hosts, the
God of Israel:

"The daughter of Babylon *is* like a
    threshing floor
When it is time to thresh her;
Yet a little while
And the time of her harvest will
    come."

34 "Nebuchadnezzar the king of Babylon
Has devoured me, he has crushed me;
He has made me an empty vessel,
He has swallowed me up like a
    monster;
He has filled his stomach with my
    delicacies,
He has spit me out.

35 Let the violence *done* to me and my
    flesh *be* upon Babylon,"
The inhabitant of Zion will say;
"And my blood be upon the inhabitants
    of Chaldea!"
Jerusalem will say.

36Therefore thus says the LORD:

"Behold, I will plead your case and
    take vengeance for you.
I will dry up her sea and make her
    springs dry.

37 Babylon shall become a heap,
A dwelling place for jackals,
An astonishment and a hissing,
Without an inhabitant.

BIBLICAL HISTORY

Rehoboam and Jeroboam divide the kingdom (c. 930 B.C.):
After Solomon's death, his son Rehoboam alienates his supporters and gets to be king only of the southern kingdom of Judah. Jeroboam sets up a rival kingdom in the north, known as Israel.

Ahab and Jezebel (874-853 B.C.):
King Ahab of Israel is influenced badly by his Phoenician princess wife Jezebel, a Baal-worshiper. Ahab builds shrines to the Phoenician god and brings many of his false priests to Israel. Corruption reigns.

Elijah and Elisha (c. 870–835 B.C.):
The prophet Elijah stands against the Baal worship in Ahab's Israel. He works miracles and finally is taken to heaven without dying, in a chariot of fire. Elijah's protégé Elisha takes over for him after he leaves. Elisha travels throughout Israel and also works many miracles.

Isaiah (c. 740–680 B.C.):
The greatest of the writing prophets, Isaiah has been called "the fifth evangelist," because his book refers in so many ways to the coming Messiah. Isaiah pronounces judgments on surrounding nations for opposing God, and warns his own.

Israel falls to the Assyrians (722 B.C.):
The mighty armies of Assyria conquer the northern kingdom of Israel. Most of the Israelites are deported to Assyria and other groups are brought in to repopulate the land. The southern kingdom of Judah is miraculously spared, but they have to pay tribute.

Josiah's reforms (c. 622 B.C.):
The Book of the Law is found and king Josiah leads a revival of godly worship in Judah. The Passover is kept again.

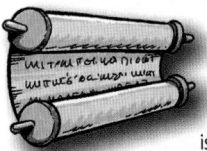

Judah falls to the Babylonians (586 B.C.):
The southern kingdom of Judah is conquered by the forces of Babylonian king Nebuchadnezzar and the Jewish people are taken into exile in Babylon.

950 B.C.
850 B.C.
750 B.C.
650 B.C.
550 B.C.

SECULAR HISTORY

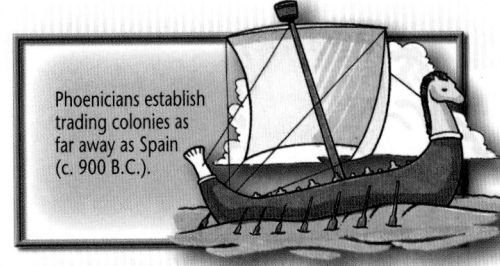

Phoenicians establish trading colonies as far away as Spain (c. 900 B.C.).

Ashurnasirpal II of Assyria has a military campaign every year of his reign (883–859 B.C.).

The royal inscription called the Moabite Stone is made (850 B.C.).

The city of Carthage in northern Africa is founded (c. 825 B.C.).

Athletic contests begin at Olympia (776 B.C.).

Homer's *Iliad* and *Odyssey* descend from oral tradition (c. 750 B.C.).

Greeks start making clay objects using molds (c. 650 B.C.).

The Hanging Gardens of Babylon are built (c. 594 B.C.).

❶ Elijah and Elisha

Elijah and his successor, Elisha, witness boldly against idol worship in Israel. Elijah is vindicated in his contest with the priests of Baal when God consumes his sacrifice with fire on Mount Carmel. Later, Elijah is carried to heaven in a chariot of fire.

❹ Jeremiah

Called "the weeping prophet," Jeremiah warns Judah about their fate at the hands of the Babylonians. After Judah falls, he goes to Egypt with Jewish refugees and continues to prophesy there. He writes the book with his name and also Lamentations.

❺ Daniel

Daniel and his three friends are taken to Babylon as teenagers and keep their faith in God. Daniel predicts future events by interpreting dreams and visions. His friends are protected from harm in a fiery furnace. Daniel is protected by God when he is put in a den of lions.

❽ Esther

A beautiful young Jewish woman wins the heart of Persian king Ahasuerus, becomes his queen, and with her cousin Mordecai saves her people from the plots of the wicked Haman.

❷ Ahab and Jezebel

King Ahab of Israel is attracted to Baal worship by means of his wife, a pagan princess whose name becomes a byword for a wicked woman. She dies a violent death, as Elijah predicted.

❸ Isaiah

Isaiah receives a stirring vision of God in the temple and is called to be a prophet. His ministry spans the time of Israel's fall to the Assyrians. He prophesies several times about the coming Messiah. Isaiah is killed, tradition says, by being sawn in two in the reign of Manasseh of Judah.

❻ Ezra

Persian king Cyrus decrees that the Jews can return to Jerusalem. The scribe and priest Ezra leads them as they rebuild the temple and rededicate themselves to God and His Law.

❼ Nehemiah

As cupbearer to the Persian king Artaxerxes, Nehemiah asks and receives permission to return to Jerusalem as governor with a group of Jews who rebuild the wall of Jerusalem, despite persecution from local opponents.

BIBLICAL HISTORY

Ezekiel sees visions of the future (c. 573 B.C.):
The prophet Ezekiel, in exile in Babylon with his people, sees visions of their future restoration and a magnificent new temple.

Cyrus allows the Jews to rebuild the temple (538–515 B.C.):
Cyrus the Persian's defeat of Babylon brings in a ruler with some religious tolerance. The Jews are given the go-ahead to return and build a new temple in Jerusalem, which they eventually do under Zerubbabel's leadership.

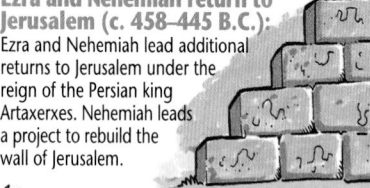
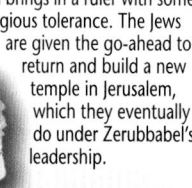
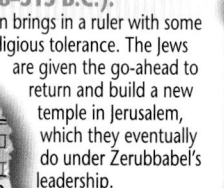

Ezra and Nehemiah return to Jerusalem (c. 458–445 B.C.):
Ezra and Nehemiah lead additional returns to Jerusalem under the reign of the Persian king Artaxerxes. Nehemiah leads a project to rebuild the wall of Jerusalem.

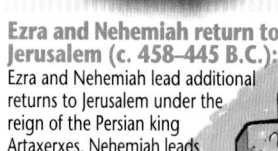

The conquests of Alexander the Great (336–323 B.C.):
Alexander of Macedon's conquered empire covers a huge portion of the ancient world by the time he dies of illness in Babylon at age 32. Greek culture becomes dominant for centuries to come.

Maccabeans and Hasmoneans (166–64 B.C.):
Alexander's successors the Seleucids are defeated by a revolt led by Jewish leader Judas Maccabeus. He and his family restore home rule to the Jews in Judea, followed by their successors the Hasmoneans.

Pompey takes control of Palestine (63 B.C.):
Rule by Rome begins in the Holy Land when the Roman general Pompey captures Jerusalem.

600 B.C.

500 B.C.

400 B.C.

300 B.C.

200 B.C.

100 B.C.

30 B.C.

SECULAR HISTORY

Greeks use saws for cutting (c. 575 B.C.).

Anaximander proposes a mathematical model of the universe (555 B.C.).

Cambyses of Persia builds a naval fleet with Ionians and Phoenicians (530–522 B.C.).

Persians begin a royal mounted messenger service (500 B.C.).

Greek philosophers Socrates (469–399 B.C.), Plato (428–347 B.C.), and Aristotle (384–322 B.C.).

Overshot waterwheel used in the marketplace of Athens (c. 450 B.C.).

Invention of the screw (c. 400 B.C.).

Macedonian armies use catapults for shooting arrows (323 B.C.).

Third Punic War, Rome v. Carthage (149–146 B.C.).

Julius Caesar is assassinated by Brutus and Cassius (44 B.C.)

38 They shall roar together like lions,
    They shall growl like lions' whelps.
39 In their excitement I will prepare
        their feasts;
    I will make them drunk,
    That they may rejoice,
    And sleep a perpetual sleep
    And not awake," says the LORD.
40 "I will bring them down
    Like lambs to the slaughter,
    Like rams with male goats.

41 "Oh, how Sheshach[a] is taken!
    Oh, how the praise of the whole earth
        is seized!
    How Babylon has become desolate
        among the nations!
42 The sea has come up over Babylon;
    She is covered with the multitude of
        its waves.
43 Her cities are a desolation,
    A dry land and a wilderness,
    A land where no one dwells,
    Through which no son of man passes.
44 I will punish Bel in Babylon,
    And I will bring out of his mouth what
        he has swallowed;
    And the nations shall not stream to
        him anymore.
    Yes, the wall of Babylon shall fall.

45 "My people, go out of the midst of her!
    And let everyone deliver himself from
        the fierce anger of the LORD.
46 And lest your heart faint,
    And you fear for the rumor that *will
        be* heard in the land
    (A rumor will come *one* year,
    And after that, in *another* year
    A rumor *will come,*
    And violence in the land,
    Ruler against ruler),
47 Therefore behold, the days are
        coming
    That I will bring judgment on the
        carved images of Babylon;
    Her whole land shall be ashamed,
    And all her slain shall fall in her
        midst.
48 Then the heavens and the earth and
        all that *is* in them
    Shall sing joyously over Babylon;
    For the plunderers shall come to her
        from the north," says the LORD.

49 As Babylon *has caused* the slain of
        Israel to fall,
    So at Babylon the slain of all the
        earth shall fall.
50 You who have escaped the sword,
    Get away! Do not stand still!
    Remember the LORD afar off,
    And let Jerusalem come to your mind.

51 We are ashamed because we have
        heard reproach.
    Shame has covered our faces,
    For strangers have come into the
        sanctuaries of the LORD'S house.

52 "Therefore behold, the days are
        coming," says the LORD,
    "That I will bring judgment on her
        carved images,
    And throughout all her land the
        wounded shall groan.
53 Though Babylon were to mount up to
        heaven,
    And though she were to fortify the
        height of her strength,
    Yet from Me plunderers would come to
        her," says the LORD.

54 The sound of a cry *comes* from
        Babylon,
    And great destruction from the land of
        the Chaldeans,
55 Because the LORD is plundering
        Babylon
    And silencing her loud voice,
    Though her waves roar like great
        waters,
    And the noise of their voice is uttered,
56 Because the plunderer comes against
        her, against Babylon,
    And her mighty men are taken.
    Every one of their bows is broken;
    For the LORD *is* the God of
        recompense,
    He will surely repay.

57 "And I will make drunk
    Her princes and wise men,
    Her governors, her deputies, and her
        mighty men.
    And they shall sleep a perpetual sleep
    And not awake," says the King,
    Whose name *is* the LORD of hosts.

58Thus says the LORD of hosts:

"The broad walls of Babylon shall be
    utterly broken,

51:41 ᵃA code word for Babylon (compare Jeremiah 25:26)

And her high gates shall be burned
with fire;
The people will labor in vain,
And the nations, because of the fire;
And they shall be weary."

Jeremiah's Command to Seraiah

⁵⁹The word which Jeremiah the prophet commanded Seraiah the son of Neriah, the son of Mahseiah, when he went with Zedekiah the king of Judah to Babylon in the fourth year of his reign. And Seraiah *was* the quartermaster. ⁶⁰So Jeremiah wrote in a book all the evil that would come upon Babylon, all these words that are written against Babylon. ⁶¹And Jeremiah said to Seraiah, "When you arrive in Babylon and see it, and read all these words, ⁶²then you shall say, 'O LORD, You have spoken against this place to cut it off, so that none shall remain in it, neither man nor beast, but it shall be desolate forever.' ⁶³Now it shall be, when you have finished reading this book, *that* you shall tie a stone to it and throw it out into the Euphrates. ⁶⁴Then you shall say, 'Thus Babylon shall sink and not rise from the catastrophe that I will bring upon her. And they shall be weary.' "

Thus far *are* the words of Jeremiah.

Priestly Account: Zedekiah and Jeremiah

As with King Jehoiakim, Chronicles gives very little space to King Zedekiah. One detail is added, however. The Chronicler specifies that King Zedekiah did not listen to the prophet Jeremiah (who is never mentioned in the account in Kings). This indicates that by the time Chronicles was written—at least 50 years after Kings, and probably much more—Jeremiah's status was well established. Rejected throughout his life, Jeremiah would at last be recognized as a true prophet of God.

■ 2 Chronicles 36:11, 12

2 Chronicles
Zedekiah Reigns in Judah

36 :11 Zedekiah *was* twenty-one years old when he became king, and he reigned eleven years in Jerusalem. ¹²He did evil in the sight of the LORD his God, *and* did not humble himself before Jere-

miah the prophet, *who spoke* from the mouth of the LORD.

The Book of Ezekiel

The second great prophet of Jerusalem's last days, along with Jeremiah, was Ezekiel. When Nebuchadnezzar captured Jerusalem in 597 B.C., the young priest Ezekiel was one of the Judeans taken into exile in Babylon. Though he would visit Jerusalem in visions (Ezek. 8:3), he appears to have spent the rest of his life and ministry in Babylon.

Being a part of the Jerusalem priestly establishment, Ezekiel must have known of Jeremiah's preaching, and may even have joined the other priests in opposing it. If so, he changed his mind in Babylon. Ezekiel's message to the exiles was much the same as Jeremiah's to those who remained in Jerusalem. To those who felt that this exile would be brief and that soon all would be restored in Jerusalem, Ezekiel prophesied that Jerusalem and even the temple itself would be destroyed. Not until that destruction had taken place (in 586 B.C.) would Ezekiel speak of a future restoration. His oracles of judgment appear in chs. 1—24, followed by his oracles concerning other nations (chs. 25—32). The book concludes with Ezekiel's words of salvation (chs. 33—48).

Ezekiel's priestly heritage shines through his prophecies, especially in his focus on the temple. Judah's sins are sins against true worship and ritual purity, particularly in the temple (see chs. 8—11). Judah's greatest punishment comes when the glory of God leaves the temple (11:23). After that, the temple's destruction is inevitable. Judah's true salvation appears in the form of a new, heavenly temple, to which God's glory would return (chs. 40—48, especially 43:1-5). The priestly focus of Ezekiel's prophecies makes it appropriate to read this prophet in the "Priestly Account" of Israel's history.

Unlike the Book of Jeremiah, Ezekiel's prophecies appear almost entirely in a clearly marked chronological order. Ezekiel received his prophetic call in the 5th year of Jehoiachin's exile (593 B.C.; Ezek. 1:2). The reference in Ezek. 1:1 to the "thirtieth year" may refer to the prophet's age at the time of his call. The account of Ezekiel's first vision of God (1:1—3:21) spans a period of 7 days during the year 593 (3:15, 16).

■ Ezekiel 1:1—3:21

Ezekiel
Ezekiel's Vision of God

1 :1 Now it came to pass in the thirtieth year, in the fourth *month,* on the fifth *day* of the month, as I *was* among the captives by the River Chebar, *that* the heavens were opened and I saw visions[a] of God. 2On the fifth *day* of the month, which *was* in the fifth year of King Jehoiachin's captivity, 3the word of the LORD came expressly to Ezekiel the priest, the son of Buzi, in the land of the Chaldeans[a] by the River Chebar; and the hand of the LORD was upon him there.

4Then I looked, and behold, a whirlwind was coming out of the north, a great cloud with raging fire engulfing itself; and brightness *was* all around it and radiating out of its midst like the color of amber, out of the midst of the fire. 5Also from within it *came* the likeness of four living creatures. And this *was* their appearance: they had the likeness of a man. 6Each one had four faces, and each one had four wings. 7Their legs *were* straight, and the soles of their feet *were* like the soles of calves' feet. They sparkled like the color of burnished bronze. 8The hands of a man *were* under their wings on their four sides; and each of the four had faces and wings. 9Their wings touched one another. *The creatures* did not turn when they went, but each one went straight forward.

10As for the likeness of their faces, *each* had the face of a man; each of the four had the face of a lion on the right side, each of the four had the face of an ox on the left side, and each of the four had the face of an eagle. 11Thus *were* their faces. Their wings stretched upward; two *wings* of each one touched one another, and two covered their bodies. 12And each one went straight forward; they went wherever the spirit wanted to go, and they did not turn when they went.

13As for the likeness of the living creatures, their appearance *was* like burning coals of fire, like the appearance of torches going back and forth among the living creatures. The fire was bright, and out of the fire went lightning. 14And the living creatures ran back and forth, in appearance like a flash of lightning.

15Now as I looked at the living creatures, behold, a wheel *was* on the earth beside each living creature with its four faces. 16The appearance of the wheels and their workings *was* like the color of beryl, and all four had the same likeness. The appearance of their workings *was,* as it were, a wheel in the middle of a wheel. 17When they moved, they went toward any one of four directions; they did not turn aside when they went. 18As for their rims, they were so high they were awesome; and their rims *were* full of eyes, all around the four of them. 19When the living creatures went, the wheels went beside them; and when the living creatures were lifted up from the earth, the wheels were lifted up. 20Wherever the spirit wanted to go, they went, *because* there the spirit went; and the wheels were lifted together with them, for the spirit of the living creatures[a] *was* in the wheels. 21When those went, *these* went; when those stood, *these* stood; and when those were lifted up from the earth, the wheels were lifted up together with them, for the spirit of the living creatures[a] *was* in the wheels.

22The likeness of the firmament above the heads of the living creatures[a] *was* like the color of an awesome crystal, stretched out over their heads. 23And under the firmament their wings *spread out* straight, one toward another. Each one had two which covered one side, and each one had two which covered the other side of the

---

1:1 [a]Following Masoretic Text, Septuagint, and Vulgate; Syriac and Targum read *a vision.*   1:3 [a]Or *Babylonians,* and so elsewhere in this book
1:20 [a]Literally *living creature;* Septuagint and Vulgate read *spirit of life;* Targum reads *creatures.*
1:21 [a]Literally *living creature;* Septuagint and Vulgate read *spirit of life;* Targum reads *creatures.*
1:22 [a]Following Septuagint, Targum, and Vulgate; Masoretic Text reads *living creature.*

RELIGION AND WORSHIP

Ezekiel's vision of God is in effect his call to be a prophet. It seems to have been customary for Judeans in exile to gather for worship near running water, perhaps because ritual washings were involved. The River Chebar (Ezek. 1:1) was probably a canal connected with the Euphrates River in Babylon. Ezekiel's vision caused him to fall down (Ezek. 1:28), much as Isaiah was stunned by the glory of God (Is. 6:5).

A PROPHET IN EXILE (Ezek. 1:1–3)

The River Chebar was located in Babylon, probably a few miles from the city of Nippur. It was there that Ezekiel began his prophetic work as a prophet "among the captives" (Ezek. 1:1)—the Judeans whom the Babylonians had exiled from Judah.

Ezekiel was among a group of Judeans deported by the Babylonians in 597 B.C. (2 Kin. 24:14–16). Upon taking the throne in Judah, King Jehoiachin faced an immediate crisis. His father Jehoiakim had rebelled against the Babylonian king Nebuchadnezzar, but it was Jehoiachin who experienced the consequences of that rebellion. Within 3 months of Jehoiachin's coronation, Nebuchadnezzar had besieged Jerusalem, deposed the new king, and taken him as a prisoner to Babylon (2 Kin. 24:12), along with others, including Ezekiel.

This exile should not be confused with the Babylonian exile of 586 B.C. In 588 B.C., Judah's king Zedekiah revolted against the Babylonians. In response, Nebuchadnezzar destroyed Jerusalem and the temple, taking a large portion of the surviving population into exile to Babylon (2 Kin. 25:1–21).

In 597 B.C., however, Nebuchadnezzar did not destroy Jerusalem. Instead, he "merely" replaced the Judahite king with another king who he thought would not rebel. For good measure, he took the old king, Jehoiachin, and many of Judah's skilled citizens in order to discourage their relatives back home in Judah from further rebellion. By taking this group into exile, Nebuchadnezzar essentially held them hostage.

Ezekiel, therefore, prophesied to a group away from home who most likely had hopes of returning to Jerusalem. If they looked to Ezekiel to fuel this hope, they were disappointed. Rather than hope, Ezekiel saw nothing but God's judgment upon Jerusalem as long as the city stood (Ezek. 15; 16).

---

body. 24When they went, I heard the noise of their wings, like the noise of many waters, like the voice of the Almighty, a tumult like the noise of an army; and when they stood still, they let down their wings. 25A voice came from above the firmament that *was* over their heads; whenever they stood, they let down their wings.

26And above the firmament over their heads *was* the likeness of a throne, in appearance like a sapphire stone; on the likeness of the throne *was* a likeness with the appearance of a man high above it. 27Also from the appearance of His waist and upward I saw, as it were, the color of amber with the appearance of fire all around within it; and from the appearance of His waist and downward I saw, as it were, the appearance of fire with brightness all around. 28Like the appearance of a rainbow in a cloud on a rainy day, so *was* the appearance of the brightness all around it. This *was* the appearance of the likeness of the glory of the LORD.

Ezekiel Sent to Rebellious Israel

So when I saw *it*, I fell on my face, and I heard a voice of One speaking.

2 1And He said to me, "Son of man, stand on your feet, and I will speak to you." 2Then the Spirit entered me when He spoke to me, and set me on my feet; and I heard Him who spoke to me. 3And He said to me: "Son of man, I am sending you to the children of Israel, to a rebellious nation that has rebelled against Me; they and their fathers have transgressed against Me to this very day. 4For *they are* impudent and stubborn children. I am sending you to them, and you shall say to them, 'Thus says the Lord GOD.' 5As for them, whether they hear or whether they refuse—for they *are* a rebellious house—yet they will know that a prophet has been among them.

6"And you, son of man, do not be afraid of them nor be afraid of their words, though briers and thorns *are* with you and you dwell among scorpions; do not be afraid of their words or dismayed by their looks, though they *are* a rebellious house. 7You shall speak My words to them, whether they hear or whether they refuse, for they *are* rebellious. 8But you, son of man, hear what I say to you. Do not be rebellious like that rebellious house; open your mouth and eat what I give you."

9Now when I looked, there was a hand stretched out to me; and behold, a scroll of a book *was* in it. 10Then He spread it before me; and *there was* writing on the inside and on the outside, and written on it *were* lamentations and mourning and woe.

3 1Moreover He said to me, "Son of man, eat what you find; eat this scroll, and go, speak to the house of Israel." 2So I opened my mouth, and He caused me to eat that scroll.

3And He said to me, "Son of man, feed your belly, and fill your stomach with this scroll that I give you." So I ate, and it was in my mouth like honey in sweetness.

4Then He said to me: "Son of man, go to the house of Israel and speak with My words to them. 5For you *are* not sent to a people of unfamiliar speech and of hard language, *but* to the house of Israel, 6not to many people of unfamiliar speech and of hard language, whose words you cannot understand. Surely, had I sent you to them, they would have listened to you. 7But the house of Israel will not listen to you, because they will not listen to Me; for all the house of Israel *are* impudent and hardhearted. 8Behold, I have made your face strong against their faces, and your forehead strong against their foreheads. 9Like adamant stone, harder than flint, I have made your forehead; do not be afraid of them, nor be dismayed at their looks, though they *are* a rebellious house."

10Moreover He said to me: "Son of man, receive into your heart all My words that I speak to you, and hear with your ears. 11And go, get to the captives, to the children of your people, and speak to them and tell them, 'Thus says the Lord GOD,' whether they hear, or whether they refuse."

12Then the Spirit lifted me up, and I heard behind me a great thunderous voice: "Blessed *is* the glory of the LORD from His place!" 13I also *heard* the noise of the wings of the living creatures that touched one another, and the noise of the wheels beside them, and a great thunderous noise. 14So the Spirit lifted me up and took me away, and I went in bitterness, in the heat of my spirit; but the hand of the LORD was strong upon me. 15Then I came to the captives at Tel Abib, who dwelt by the River Chebar; and I sat where they sat, and remained there astonished among them seven days.

Ezekiel Is a Watchman

16Now it came to pass at the end of seven days that the word of the LORD came to me, saying, 17"Son of man, I have made you a watchman for the house of Israel; therefore hear a word from My mouth, and give them warning from Me: 18When I say to the wicked, 'You shall surely die,' and you give him no warning, nor speak to warn the wicked from his wicked way, to save his life, that same wicked *man* shall die in his iniquity; but his blood I will require at your hand. 19Yet, if you warn the wicked, and he does not turn from his wickedness, nor from his wicked way, he shall die in his iniquity; but you have delivered your soul.

20"Again, when a righteous *man* turns from his righteousness and commits iniquity, and I lay a stumbling block before him, he shall die; because you did not give him warning, he shall die in his sin, and his righteousness which he has done shall not be remembered; but his blood I will require at your hand. 21Nevertheless if you warn the righteous *man* that the righteous should not sin, and he does not sin, he shall surely live because he took warning; also you will have delivered your soul."

Prophetic Account: Rebellion Against Babylon

In about 589 B.C. a new king came to power in Egypt, Pharaoh Hophra (or Apries). Hophra appears to have promised his help and convinced Zedekiah to rebel against Nebuchadnezzar. Zedekiah declared independence from Babylon in his 9th year (588 B.C.). Nebuchadnezzar's armies moved swiftly. The siege lasted from the 10th month (perhaps January) of 588 until the summer of 586 B.C. (Zedekiah's 11th year; 2 Kin. 25:2).

■ 2 Kings 24:20—25:3
■ Jeremiah 52:3–6

2 Kings 24:20—25:3

24 :20 For because of the anger of the LORD *this* happened in Jerusalem and Judah, that He finally cast them out from His presence. Then Zedekiah rebelled against the king of Babylon.

25 1Now it came to pass in the ninth year of his reign, in the tenth month, on the tenth *day* of the month, *that*

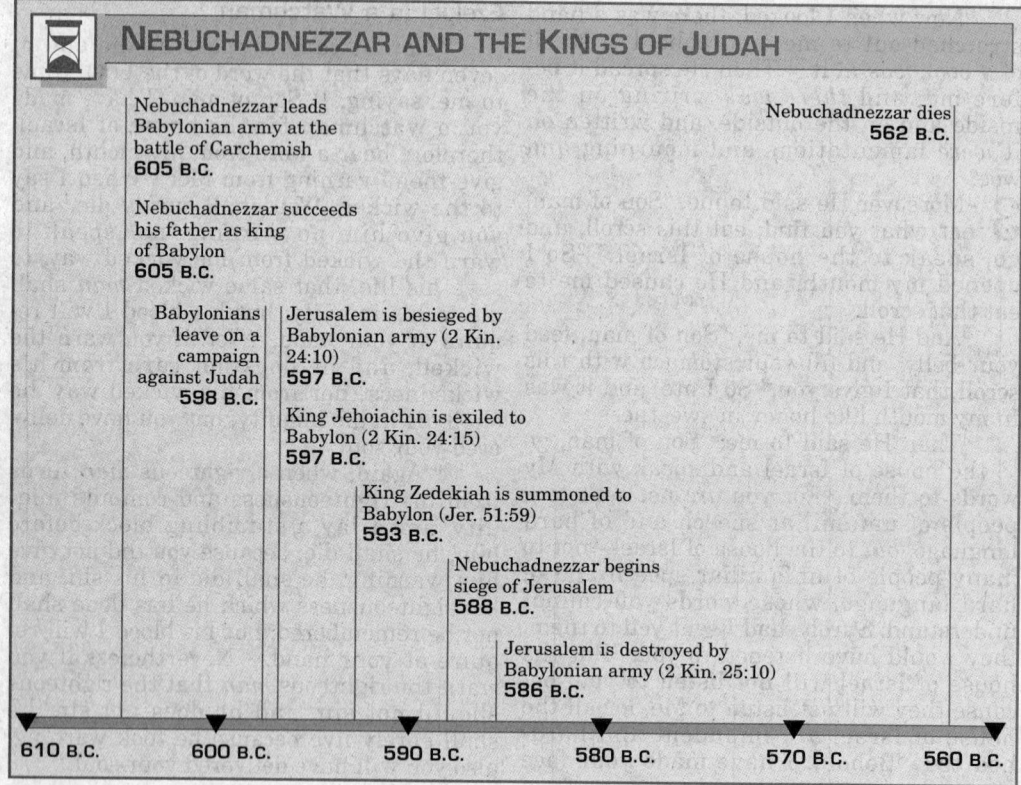

NEBUCHADNEZZAR AND THE KINGS OF JUDAH

Nebuchadnezzar leads
Babylonian army at the
battle of Carchemish
605 B.C.

Nebuchadnezzar succeeds
his father as king
of Babylon
605 B.C.

Nebuchadnezzar dies
562 B.C.

Babylonians
leave on a
campaign
against Judah
598 B.C.

Jerusalem is besieged by
Babylonian army (2 Kin.
24:10)
597 B.C.

King Jehoiachin is exiled to
Babylon (2 Kin. 24:15)
597 B.C.

King Zedekiah is summoned to
Babylon (Jer. 51:59)
593 B.C.

Nebuchadnezzar begins
siege of Jerusalem
588 B.C.

Jerusalem is destroyed by
Babylonian army (2 Kin. 25:10)
586 B.C.

610 B.C.   **600 B.C.**   **590 B.C.**   **580 B.C.**   **570 B.C.**   **560 B.C.**

Nebuchadnezzar king of Babylon and all his army came against Jerusalem and encamped against it; and they built a siege wall against it all around. ²So the city was besieged until the eleventh year of King Zedekiah. ³By the ninth *day* of the *fourth* month the famine had become so severe in the city that there was no food for the people of the land.

Jeremiah 52:3-6
The Fall of Jerusalem Reviewed

52 :3 For because of the anger of the LORD *this* happened in Jerusalem and Judah, till He finally cast them out from His presence. Then Zedekiah rebelled against the king of Babylon.

⁴Now it came to pass in the ninth year of his reign, in the tenth month, on the tenth *day* of the month, *that* Nebuchadnezzar king of Babylon and all his army came against Jerusalem and encamped against it; and *they* built a siege wall against it all around. ⁵So the city was besieged until the eleventh year of King Zedekiah. ⁶By the fourth month, on the ninth day of the month, the famine had become so severe in

the city that there was no food for the people of the land.

The Siege of Jerusalem

It was surely no comfort to Jeremiah to see all his prophecies coming true. He mourned the coming destruction and the ravages of the siege. His prophecies now were addressed to the "inhabitant of the fortress" (Jer. 10:17), the one who was dwelling under the siege. They reflect the horror felt by a person trying to cope with disaster (10:17-25).

Zedekiah may also have seen that Jeremiah had spoken the truth. Though it was far too late, he began to ask Jeremiah's advice and intercession. Jeremiah could give him no comforting answer, though (21:1—22:9). The well-meaning Zedekiah sought to encourage some sort of revival by promoting a return to such covenant obedience as the release of slaves (34:1-22). The Law of Moses called for the release of a Hebrew servant in the 7th year (Ex. 21:2-4; Deut. 15:12-15). Jeremiah approved of this measure, but the reform effort was halfhearted and quickly forgotten (Jer. 34:16), and finally would make no difference in Jerusalem's fate.

- Jeremiah 10:17–25
- Jeremiah 21:1—22:9
- Jeremiah 34:1–22

Jeremiah 10:17–25
The Coming Captivity of Judah

10 :17 Gather up your wares from the land,
O inhabitant of the fortress!

18For thus says the LORD:

"Behold, I will throw out at this time
The inhabitants of the land,
And will distress them,
That they may find it so."

19 Woe is me for my hurt!
My wound is severe.
But I say, "Truly this is an infirmity,
And I must bear it."
20 My tent is plundered,
And all my cords are broken;
My children have gone from me,
And they are no more.
There is no one to pitch my tent anymore,
Or set up my curtains.

21 For the shepherds have become dullhearted,
And have not sought the LORD;
Therefore they shall not prosper,
And all their flocks shall be scattered.
22 Behold, the noise of the report has come,
And a great commotion out of the north country,
To make the cities of Judah desolate,
a den of jackals.

23 O LORD, I know the way of man is not in himself;
It is not in man who walks to direct his own steps.
24 O LORD, correct me, but with justice;
Not in Your anger, lest You bring me to nothing.
25 Pour out Your fury on the Gentiles, who do not know You,

And on the families who do not call on Your name;
For they have eaten up Jacob,
Devoured him and consumed him,
And made his dwelling place desolate.

Jeremiah 21:1—22:9
Jerusalem's Doom Is Sealed

21 :1 The word which came to Jeremiah from the LORD when King Zedekiah sent to him Pashhur the son of Melchiah, and Zephaniah the son of Maaseiah, the priest, saying, 2"Please inquire of the LORD for us, for Nebuchadnezzar[a] king of Babylon makes war against us. Perhaps the LORD will deal with us according to all His wonderful works, that the king may go away from us."

3Then Jeremiah said to them, "Thus you shall say to Zedekiah, 4'Thus says the LORD God of Israel: "Behold, I will turn back the weapons of war that are in your hands, with which you fight against the king of Babylon and the Chaldeans[a] who besiege you outside the walls; and I will assemble them in the midst of this city. 5I Myself will fight against you with an outstretched hand and with a strong arm, even in anger and fury and great wrath. 6I will strike the inhabitants of this city, both man and beast; they shall die of a great pestilence. 7And afterward," says the LORD, "I will deliver Zedekiah king of Judah, his servants and the people, and such as are left in this city from the pestilence and the sword and the famine, into the hand of Nebuchadnezzar king of Babylon, into the hand of their enemies, and into the hand of those who seek their life; and he shall strike them with the edge of the sword. He shall not spare them, or have pity or mercy." '

8"Now you shall say to this people, 'Thus says the LORD: "Behold, I set before you the way of life and the way of death. 9He who remains in this city shall die by the sword, by famine, and by pestilence; but he who goes out and defects to the Chaldeans who besiege you, he shall live, and his life shall be as a prize to him. 10For I have set My face against this city for adversity and not for good," says the LORD. "It shall be given into the hand of the king of Babylon, and he shall burn it with fire." '

Message to the House of David

11"And concerning the house of the king of Judah, say, 'Hear the word of the

---

21:2 aHebrew Nebuchadrezzar, and so elsewhere
21:4 aOr Babylonians

NEBUCHADREZZAR OR NEBUCHADNEZZAR? (Jer. 21:2)

Nebuchadnezzar's name is spelled slightly differently in Hebrew in many references of the books of Jeremiah and Ezekiel. The difference is the subtle change from "r" (Nebuchadrezzar) to "n" (Nebuchadnezzar). See the footnote on Jer. 21:2.

The spelling "Nebuchadrezzar," found in Jeremiah and Ezekiel in the Hebrew Old Testament and in some English translations, is actually closer to the Babylonian spelling, as is proven by Babylonian cuneiform texts. On the other hand, a few verses in Jeremiah also provide the alternate spelling "Nebuchadnezzar" (Jer. 27:6; 28:3; etc.).

The two spellings of Nebuchadnezzar's name may demonstrate a shift in language that was taking place at that time. For hundreds of years the official diplomatic language had been Accadian, a Semitic language centered in Babylon. In the 1st millennium Aramaic, another Semitic language, began to gain in influence. The shift from "r" to "n" in Nebuchadnezzar's name may be evidence of the influence of the Aramaic language. By New Testament times Aramaic was the common spoken language of the region.

LORD, 12O house of David! Thus says the LORD:

"Execute judgment in the morning;
And deliver *him who is* plundered
Out of the hand of the oppressor,
Lest My fury go forth like fire
And burn so that no one can quench
    it,
Because of the evil of your doings.

13 "Behold, I *am* against you,
    O inhabitant of the valley,
    And rock of the plain," says the LORD,
"Who say, 'Who shall come down
    against us?
Or who shall enter our dwellings?'
14 But I will punish you according to the
    fruit of your doings," says the LORD;
"I will kindle a fire in its forest,
And it shall devour all things around
    it." ' "

22 1Thus says the LORD: "Go down to the house of the king of Judah, and there speak this word, 2and say, 'Hear the word of the LORD, O king of Judah, you who sit on the throne of David, you and your servants and your people who enter these gates! 3Thus says the LORD: "Execute judgment and righteousness, and deliver the plundered out of the hand of the oppressor. Do no wrong and do no violence to the stranger, the fatherless, or the widow, nor shed innocent blood in this place. 4For if you indeed do this thing, then shall enter the gates of this house, riding on horses and in chariots, accompanied by servants

and people, kings who sit on the throne of David. 5But if you will not hear these words, I swear by Myself," says the LORD, "that this house shall become a desolation." ' "

6For thus says the LORD to the house of the king of Judah:

"You *are* Gilead to Me,
    The head of Lebanon;
    Yet I surely will make you a
        wilderness,
    Cities *which* are not inhabited.
7   I will prepare destroyers against you,
    Everyone with his weapons;
    They shall cut down your choice
        cedars
    And cast *them* into the fire.

8And many nations will pass by this city; and everyone will say to his neighbor, 'Why has the LORD done so to this great city?' 9Then they will answer, 'Because they have forsaken the covenant of the LORD their God, and worshiped other gods and served them.' "

Jeremiah 34:1–22
Zedekiah Warned by God

34 :1 The word which came to Jeremiah from the LORD, when Nebuchadnezzar king of Babylon and all his army, all the kingdoms of the earth under his dominion, and all the people, fought against Jerusalem and all its cities, saying, 2"Thus says the LORD, the God of Israel: 'Go and speak to Zedekiah king of Judah and tell him, "Thus says the LORD: 'Behold,

LACHISH LETTERS OF DISTRESS (Jer. 34:7)

During Nebuchadnezzar's campaigns against Judah between 598 and 586 B.C., Lachish held a central place in Judahite resistance. Letters, written on broken pieces of pottery, have been found addressed to a military commander of Lachish named "Yaosh." The letters were sent by a strategically placed subordinate serving as a lookout. The lookout's task was to watch for signals from Azekah and Lachish and probably report information to and from Jerusalem.

From the lookout's vantage point, Azekah was probably the halfway point from Lachish. In one letter (Letter IV), he reports that because signals are no longer being received from Azekah he is watching and needing communication from Lachish. Since Azekah was no longer sending out messages, one can only guess that the Babylonians had already conquered that city and that the destruction of Lachish was imminent. The Lachish Letters probably were written shortly before Jerusalem's capture in 586 B.C.

I will give this city into the hand of the king of Babylon, and he shall burn it with fire. ³And you shall not escape from his hand, but shall surely be taken and delivered into his hand; your eyes shall see the eyes of the king of Babylon, he shall speak with you face to face,ᵃ and you shall go to Babylon.' " ⁴Yet hear the word of the LORD, O Zedekiah king of Judah! Thus says the LORD concerning you: 'You shall not die by the sword. ⁵You shall die in peace; as in the ceremonies of your fathers, the former kings who were before you, so they shall burn incense for you and lament for you, *saying,* "Alas, lord!" For I have pronounced the word, says the LORD.' "

⁶Then Jeremiah the prophet spoke all these words to Zedekiah king of Judah in Jerusalem, ⁷when the king of Babylon's army fought against Jerusalem and all the cities of Judah that were left, against Lachish and Azekah; for *only* these fortified cities remained of the cities of Judah.

Treacherous Treatment of Slaves

⁸*This is* the word that came to Jeremiah from the LORD, after King Zedekiah had made a covenant with all the people who *were* at Jerusalem to proclaim liberty to them: ⁹that every man should set free his male and female slave—a Hebrew man or woman—that no one should keep a Jewish brother in bondage. ¹⁰Now when all the princes and all the people, who had entered into the covenant, heard that everyone should set free his male and female slaves, that no one should keep them in bondage

anymore, they obeyed and let *them* go. ¹¹But afterward they changed their minds and made the male and female slaves return, whom they had set free, and brought them into subjection as male and female slaves.

¹²Therefore the word of the LORD came to Jeremiah from the LORD, saying, ¹³"Thus says the LORD, the God of Israel: 'I made a covenant with your fathers in the day that I brought them out of the land of Egypt, out of the house of bondage, saying, ¹⁴"At the end of seven years let every man set free his Hebrew brother, who has been sold to him; and when he has served you six years, you shall let him go free from you." But your fathers did not obey Me nor incline their ear. ¹⁵Then you recently turned and did what was right in My sight—every man proclaiming liberty to his neighbor; and you made a covenant before Me in the house which is called by My name. ¹⁶Then you turned around and profaned My name, and every one of you brought back his male and female slaves, whom you had set at liberty, at their pleasure, and brought them back into subjection, to be your male and female slaves.'

¹⁷"Therefore thus says the LORD: 'You have not obeyed Me in proclaiming liberty, every one to his brother and every one to his neighbor. Behold, I proclaim liberty to you,' says the LORD—'to the sword, to pestilence, and to famine! And I will deliver you to trouble among all the kingdoms of the earth. ¹⁸And I will give the men who have transgressed My covenant, who have not performed the words of the covenant which they made before Me, when they cut the

---

34:3 ᵃLiterally *mouth to mouth*

calf in two and passed between the parts of it— [19]the princes of Judah, the princes of Jerusalem, the eunuchs, the priests, and all the people of the land who passed between the parts of the calf— [20]I will give them into the hand of their enemies and into the hand of those who seek their life. Their dead bodies shall be for meat for the birds of the heaven and the beasts of the earth. [21]And I will give Zedekiah king of Judah and his princes into the hand of their enemies, into the hand of those who seek their life, and into the hand of the king of Babylon's army which has gone back from you. [22]Behold, I will command,' says the LORD, 'and cause them to return to this city. They will fight against it and take it and burn it with fire; and I will make the cities of Judah a desolation without inhabitant.' "

Hophra's Assault

For once, an Egyptian pharaoh kept his promise of aid. While Jerusalem was under siege, Pharaoh Hophra moved north against the Babylonian armies. Hope was reborn in Jerusalem, but Jeremiah declared it to be futile. Egypt could not stand against Babylon (Jer. 46:13–28). Indeed, Jeremiah derisively describes this pharaoh as "but a noise," who "passed by the appointed time" (46:17). Hophra was an indecisive military leader who did not have good relations with his troops.

The Egyptian relief army did force the Babylonians to lift the siege from Jerusalem, but relief lasted only briefly. The Egyptians had to withdraw before the stronger Babylonian armies.

▼   ■ Jeremiah 46:13–28

Jeremiah
Babylonia Will Strike Egypt

46 :13 The word that the LORD spoke to Jeremiah the prophet, how Nebuchadnezzar king of Babylon would come *and* strike the land of Egypt.

[14] "Declare in Egypt, and proclaim in Migdol;
Proclaim in Noph[a] and in Tahpanhes;
Say, 'Stand fast and prepare yourselves,
For the sword devours all around you.'
[15] Why are your valiant *men* swept away?

They did not stand
Because the LORD drove them away.
[16] He made many fall;
Yes, one fell upon another.
And they said, 'Arise!
Let us go back to our own people
And to the land of our nativity
From the oppressing sword.'
[17] They cried there,
'Pharaoh, king of Egypt, *is but* a noise.
He has passed by the appointed time!'

[18] "*As* I live," says the King,
Whose name *is* the LORD of hosts,
"Surely as Tabor *is* among the mountains
And as Carmel by the sea, *so* he shall come.
[19] O you daughter dwelling in Egypt,
Prepare yourself to go into captivity!
For Noph[a] shall be waste and desolate, without inhabitant.

[20] "Egypt *is* a very pretty heifer,
But destruction comes, it comes from the north.
[21] Also her mercenaries are in her midst like fat bulls,
For they also are turned back,
They have fled away together.
They did not stand,
For the day of their calamity had come upon them,
The time of their punishment.
[22] Her noise shall go like a serpent,
For they shall march with an army
And come against her with axes,
Like those who chop wood.

[23] "They shall cut down her forest," says the LORD,

46:14 [a]That is, ancient Memphis   46:19 [a]That is, ancient Memphis

TIME CAPSULE *594 to 593* B.C.

594	*Hanging Gardens of Babylon built*
594	*Aristocrat Solon is appointed archon in Athens*
594	*Solon begins democratic reforms in Greece*
593	*King Zedekiah is summoned to Babylon (Jer. 51:59–64)*
593	*Ezekiel receives his prophetic call*

AMON OF NO (Jer. 46:25)

The prophet Jeremiah warns that Yahweh will use King Nebuchadnezzar of Babylon and his armies to punish "Amon of No" (Jer. 46:25, 26). In Hebrew, "No" referred to the Egyptian designation for Thebes, the main city of Upper Egypt. Thebes (or "No") was a favorite city of the kings of Egypt's 25th Dynasty (780–656 B.C.), who worshiped the god Amon. In the following 26th Dynasty, Pharaoh Psammetichus I (664–610 B.C.) appointed his daughter as the "God's Wife of Amon" in Thebes. In Jeremiah's day, Thebes and Amon represented the power of Egypt, such as it was then.

Amon was the Egyptian god of air, wind, and spirit. The origins of the worship of Amon date back beyond written records. Amon was already among the major deities when his name first appeared in the Pyramid Texts of about 2300 B.C. In the 2nd millennium B.C. Amon was promoted as the central god of Thebes. When the priesthood of Thebes rose to power during Egypt's New Kingdom (after 1550 B.C.), Amon became known as the "king of the gods" and became attached to the god Re in the dual god name "Amon-Re."

Amon was worshiped throughout Egypt as the creator of the world and ruler of Egypt. He kept order not only in Egypt, but in all the physical universe. Yet Jeremiah proclaims Yahweh's superiority over Amon of No (Thebes), the "king of the gods," just as the prophet proclaimed concerning Babylon's god Bel-Marduk (Jer. 50:2; 51:44). This prophecy of Yahweh's justice against Egypt possibly looks toward the confrontation in 587 B.C. between Hophra, also a pharaoh of the 26th Dynasty, and Nebuchadnezzar.

"Though it cannot be searched,
Because they *are* innumerable,
And more numerous than
   grasshoppers.
24 The daughter of Egypt shall be
   ashamed;
She shall be delivered into the hand
Of the people of the north."

25The LORD of hosts, the God of Israel, says: "Behold, I will bring punishment on Amon[a] of No,[b] and Pharaoh and Egypt, with their gods and their kings—Pharaoh and those who trust in him. 26And I will deliver them into the hand of those who seek their lives, into the hand of Nebuchadnezzar king of Babylon and the hand of his servants. Afterward it shall be inhabited as in the days of old," says the LORD.

God Will Preserve Israel

27 "But do not fear, O My servant Jacob,
And do not be dismayed, O Israel!
For behold, I will save you from afar,
And your offspring from the land of
   their captivity;
Jacob shall return, have rest and be at
   ease;
No one shall make *him* afraid.

28 Do not fear, O Jacob My servant," says
   the LORD,
"For I *am* with you;
For I will make a complete end of all
   the nations
To which I have driven you,
But I will not make a complete end of
   you.
I will rightly correct you,
For I will not leave you wholly
   unpunished."

A Lull in the Siege

Hophra's attack succeeded at least temporarily (Jer. 37:1–21). The Babylonians had to pull away from Jerusalem to counter the threat from the south (37:5). Jeremiah warned that the siege would be renewed (37:8), but even he took advantage of the temporary lifting of travel restrictions.

It seems that at this unlikely moment Jeremiah's message changed. On the eve of the greatest calamity in all the history of the kingdom, the prophet began to proclaim salvation. Traveling to his hometown of Anathoth in Zedekiah's 10th year (587 B.C.), Jeremiah officially signed the deed to a plot of land he had inherited (Jer. 32). This he did as a sign that once again the inhabitants of the land would be free landowners (32:13–15). God would keep

---

46:25 [a]A sun god   [b]That is, ancient Thebes

His covenant promises to His people (ch. 33), and His covenant with King David (33:17–22; 23:1–8).

It is possible that all of Jeremiah's messages of hope were delivered at this time, most notably the so-called "Book of Consolation" in Jer. 30; 31. If so, the new message did Jeremiah little good. Upon his return to Jerusalem, he was arrested as a Babylonian sympathizer. Zedekiah continued to consult the imprisoned Jeremiah, but the king feared the leaders in the city, as well as those who had already defected to the Babylonians (Jer. 38). He did not have the courage to make the right choices.

- Jeremiah 37:1–21
- Jeremiah 30:1—33:26
- Jeremiah 23:1–8
- Jeremiah 38:1–28

Jeremiah 37:1–21
Zedekiah's Vain Hope

37 :1 Now King Zedekiah the son of Josiah reigned instead of Coniah the son of Jehoiakim, whom Nebuchadnezzar king of Babylon made king in the land of Judah. ²But neither he nor his servants nor the people of the land gave heed to the words of the LORD which He spoke by the prophet Jeremiah.

³And Zedekiah the king sent Jehucal the son of Shelemiah, and Zephaniah the son of Maaseiah, the priest, to the prophet Jeremiah, saying, "Pray now to the LORD our God for us." ⁴Now Jeremiah was coming and going among the people, for they had not *yet* put him in prison. ⁵Then Pharaoh's army came up from Egypt; and when the Chaldeans who were besieging Jerusalem heard news of them, they departed from Jerusalem.

⁶Then the word of the LORD came to the prophet Jeremiah, saying, ⁷"Thus says the LORD, the God of Israel, 'Thus you shall say to the king of Judah, who sent you to Me to inquire of Me: "Behold, Pharaoh's army which has come up to help you will return to Egypt, to their own land. ⁸And the Chaldeans shall come back and fight against this city, and take it and burn it with fire." ' ⁹Thus says the LORD: 'Do not deceive yourselves, saying, "The Chaldeans will surely depart from us," for they will not depart. ¹⁰For though you had defeated the whole army of the Chaldeans who fight against you, and there remained *only* wounded men among them, they would rise up, every man in his tent, and burn the city with fire.' "

Jeremiah Imprisoned

¹¹And it happened, when the army of the Chaldeans left *the siege* of Jerusalem for fear of Pharaoh's army, ¹²that Jeremiah went out of Jerusalem to go into the land of Benjamin to claim his property there among the people. ¹³And when he was in the Gate of Benjamin, a captain of the guard *was* there whose name *was* Irijah the son of Shelemiah, the son of Hananiah; and he seized Jeremiah the prophet, saying, "You are defecting to the Chaldeans!"

¹⁴Then Jeremiah said, "False! I am not defecting to the Chaldeans." But he did not listen to him.

So Irijah seized Jeremiah and brought him to the princes. ¹⁵Therefore the princes were angry with Jeremiah, and they struck him and put him in prison in the house of Jonathan the scribe. For they had made that the prison.

¹⁶When Jeremiah entered the dungeon and the cells, and Jeremiah had remained there many days, ¹⁷then Zedekiah the king sent and took him *out*. The king asked him secretly in his house, and said, "Is there *any* word from the LORD?"

And Jeremiah said, "There is." Then he said, "You shall be delivered into the hand of the king of Babylon!"

¹⁸Moreover Jeremiah said to King Zedekiah, "What offense have I committed against you, against your servants, or against this people, that you have put me in prison? ¹⁹Where now *are* your prophets who prophesied to you, saying, 'The king of Babylon will not come against you or against this land'? ²⁰Therefore please hear now, O my lord the king. Please, let my petition be accepted before you, and do not make me return to the house of Jonathan the scribe, lest I die there."

²¹Then Zedekiah the king commanded that they should commit Jeremiah to the court of the prison, and that they should give him daily a piece of bread from the bakers' street, until all the bread in the city was gone. Thus Jeremiah remained in the court of the prison.

Jeremiah 30:1—33:26
Restoration of Israel and Judah

30 :1 The word that came to Jeremiah from the LORD, saying, ²"Thus speaks the LORD God of Israel, saying:

THE POLITICS OF THE SIEGE (Jer. 37:1–16)

Siege warfare was—and is—a horrible thing. Israelite cities had little open space within them for food production. Inner city water supplies would often be limited. People from the surrounding countryside would crowd into the city for protection, stretching already thin food, water, and living space to the breaking point.

A city's main defense against a siege, its walls, was also its greatest liability. The enemy could concentrate its forces outside the city's single main gate. While an occasional messenger might escape over the wall, the possibility of goods or people entering or exiting the city was severely limited.

In such a situation, a city could only hope that help would arrive from outside, or that the army outside the city would give up before the people inside starved. The key to survival was not to give up. If morale within the city could be upheld to handle the harsh conditions, the people just might outlast the invading army.

During the siege of Jerusalem by the Babylonian army in 587 B.C., the city leaders asked Jeremiah to support the war effort by praying for the city (Jer. 37:3). Meanwhile, an Egyptian army disrupted the siege, forcing the Babylonian army to withdraw for a time (37:5). Morale among the Jerusalemites doubtlessly soared. Maybe their God would save Jerusalem!

Jeremiah, however, failed to be moved, and responded with more words of judgment: the Babylonians would be back (37:6–10). While the siege was lifted, the prophet attempted to leave the city to take care of personal business outside. Accused of deserting to the enemy, he was imprisoned so as not to adversely affect the effort to win the war (37:11–16). In prison Jeremiah could not disrupt public morale by either desertion or more statements of doom.

'Write in a book for yourself all the words that I have spoken to you. ³For behold, the days are coming,' says the LORD, 'that I will bring back from captivity My people Israel and Judah,' says the LORD. 'And I will cause them to return to the land that I gave to their fathers, and they shall possess it.' "

⁴Now these *are* the words that the LORD spoke concerning Israel and Judah.
⁵"For thus says the LORD:

'We have heard a voice of trembling,
Of fear, and not of peace.
6   Ask now, and see,
Whether a man is ever in labor with
   child?
So why do I see every man *with* his
   hands on his loins
Like a woman in labor,
And all faces turned pale?
7   Alas! For that day *is* great,
So that none *is* like it;
And it *is* the time of Jacob's trouble,
But he shall be saved out of it.

8   'For it shall come to pass in that day,'
Says the LORD of hosts,

'*That* I will break his yoke from your
   neck,
And will burst your bonds;
Foreigners shall no more enslave
   them.
9   But they shall serve the LORD their
   God,
And David their king,
Whom I will raise up for them.

10 'Therefore do not fear, O My servant
   Jacob,' says the LORD,
'Nor be dismayed, O Israel;
For behold, I will save you from afar,
And your seed from the land of their
   captivity.
Jacob shall return, have rest and be
   quiet,
And no one shall make *him* afraid.
11 For I *am* with you,' says the LORD, 'to
   save you;
Though I make a full end of all
   nations where I have scattered
   you,
Yet I will not make a complete end of
   you.
But I will correct you in justice,
And will not let you go altogether
   unpunished.'

12"For thus says the LORD:

'Your affliction *is* incurable,
Your wound *is* severe.
13 *There is* no one to plead your cause,
That you may be bound up;
You have no healing medicines.
14 All your lovers have forgotten you;
They do not seek you;
For I have wounded you with the
     wound of an enemy,
With the chastisement of a cruel one,
For the multitude of your iniquities,
Because your sins have increased.
15 Why do you cry about your affliction?
Your sorrow *is* incurable.
Because of the multitude of your
     iniquities,
Because your sins have increased,
I have done these things to you.

16 'Therefore all those who devour you
     shall be devoured;
And all your adversaries, every one of
     them, shall go into captivity;
Those who plunder you shall become
     plunder,
And all who prey upon you I will
     make a prey.
17 For I will restore health to you
And heal you of your wounds,' says
     the LORD,
'Because they called you an outcast
     saying:
"This *is* Zion;
No one seeks her." '

18"Thus says the LORD:

'Behold, I will bring back the captivity
     of Jacob's tents,
And have mercy on his dwelling
     places;
The city shall be built upon its own
     mound,
And the palace shall remain according
     to its own plan.
19 Then out of them shall proceed
     thanksgiving
And the voice of those who make
     merry;
I will multiply them, and they shall
     not diminish;
I will also glorify them, and they shall
     not be small.
20 Their children also shall be as before,
And their congregation shall be
     established before Me;

And I will punish all who oppress
     them.
21 Their nobles shall be from among
     them,
And their governor shall come from
     their midst;
Then I will cause him to draw near,
And he shall approach Me;
For who *is* this who pledged his heart
     to approach Me?' says the LORD.
22 'You shall be My people,
And I will be your God.' "

23 Behold, the whirlwind of the LORD
Goes forth with fury,
A continuing whirlwind;
It will fall violently on the head of the
     wicked.
24 The fierce anger of the LORD will not
     return until He has done it,
And until He has performed the
     intents of His heart.

In the latter days you will consider it.

The Remnant of Israel Saved

31 1"At the same time," says the LORD,
"I will be the God of all the families
of Israel, and they shall be My people."
2Thus says the LORD:

"The people who survived the sword
Found grace in the wilderness—
Israel, when I went to give him rest."

3 The LORD has appeared of old to me,
     saying:
"Yes, I have loved you with an
     everlasting love;
Therefore with lovingkindness I have
     drawn you.
4 Again I will build you, and you shall
     be rebuilt,
O virgin of Israel!
You shall again be adorned with your
     tambourines,
And shall go forth in the dances of
     those who rejoice.
5 You shall yet plant vines on the
     mountains of Samaria;
The planters shall plant and eat *them*
     as ordinary food.
6 For there shall be a day
When the watchmen will cry on Mount
     Ephraim,
'Arise, and let us go up *to* Zion,
To the LORD our God.' "

THE EXILES RETURN TO SAMARIA (Jer. 31:5, 6)

Originally "Samaria" was the name for the capital of the northern kingdom of Israel. The city had been built by King Omri in the early 9th century B.C., presumably to establish his kingship after a period of civil war and unrest in Israel. Previous Israelite kings had ruled from Tirzah. Later the name "Samaria" would also be associated with the northern kingdom itself.

An earlier name for the region of Israel had been "Ephraim." After the Syro-Ephraimite War (735–732 B.C.), Israel lost some of its outlying territories to Assyria. Under the Assyrian king Tiglath-Pileser III, these areas became Assyrian provinces known as Dor, Megiddo, and Gilead, each being named after the city from which the Assyrian-appointed governor ruled. Israel's borders were reduced to a territory that had belonged to the tribes of Manasseh and Ephraim during the era of the judges. So now what was left of the region of Israel was often called "Ephraim."

After the Assyrian conquest of the city of Samaria in 722 B.C., the Assyrian king Sargon II established another Assyrian province. Following the Assyrian practice of naming a province after its chief city, the name "Samaria" was now used for the region where the city had been.

The prophet Jeremiah mentions "the mountains of Samaria," as well as "Mount Ephraim" (Jer. 31:5, 6). The hill country of Samaria is a harsh, mountainous land full of fissures and valleys. Mountain passes make Samaria's hills accessible. In a message of hope, Jeremiah prophesies that God will return the exiles to the hill country known as Ephraim and Samaria. There they will settle, plant, and travel to Jerusalem (Zion) for worship.

7For thus says the LORD:

"Sing with gladness for Jacob,
And shout among the chief of the
  nations;
Proclaim, give praise, and say,
'O LORD, save Your people,
The remnant of Israel!'
8 Behold, I will bring them from the
  north country,
And gather them from the ends of the
  earth,
Among them the blind and the lame,
The woman with child
And the one who labors with child,
  together;
A great throng shall return there.
9 They shall come with weeping,
And with supplications I will lead them.
I will cause them to walk by the rivers
  of waters,
In a straight way in which they shall
  not stumble;
For I am a Father to Israel,
And Ephraim *is* My firstborn.

10 "Hear the word of the LORD, O nations,
And declare *it* in the isles afar off, and
  say,
'He who scattered Israel will gather
  him,
And keep him as a shepherd *does* his
  flock.'

11 For the LORD has redeemed Jacob,
And ransomed him from the hand of
  one stronger than he.
12 Therefore they shall come and sing in
  the height of Zion,
Streaming to the goodness of the
  LORD—
For wheat and new wine and oil,
For the young of the flock and the
  herd;
Their souls shall be like a well-
  watered garden,
And they shall sorrow no more at all.

13 "Then shall the virgin rejoice in the
  dance,
And the young men and the old,
  together;
For I will turn their mourning to joy,
Will comfort them,
And make them rejoice rather than
  sorrow.
14 I will satiate the soul of the priests
  with abundance,
And My people shall be satisfied with
  My goodness, says the LORD."

Mercy on Ephraim

15Thus says the LORD:

"A voice was heard in Ramah,
Lamentation *and* bitter weeping,

Rachel weeping for her children,
Refusing to be comforted for her
children,
Because they *are* no more."

16Thus says the LORD:

"Refrain your voice from weeping,
And your eyes from tears;
For your work shall be rewarded, says
the LORD,
And they shall come back from the
land of the enemy.
17 There is hope in your future, says the
LORD,
That *your* children shall come back to
their own border.

18 "I have surely heard Ephraim
bemoaning himself:
'You have chastised me, and I was
chastised,
Like an untrained bull;
Restore me, and I will return,
For You *are* the LORD my God.
19 Surely, after my turning, I repented;
And after I was instructed, I struck
myself on the thigh;
I was ashamed, yes, even humiliated,
Because I bore the reproach of my
youth.'
20 *Is* Ephraim My dear son?
Is he a pleasant child?
For though I spoke against him,
I earnestly remember him still;
Therefore My heart yearns for
him;
I will surely have mercy on him, says
the LORD.

21 "Set up signposts,
Make landmarks;
Set your heart toward the highway,
The way in *which* you went.
Turn back, O virgin of Israel,
Turn back to these your cities.
22 How long will you gad about,
O you backsliding daughter?

For the LORD has created a new thing
in the earth—
A woman shall encompass a man."

Future Prosperity of Judah

23Thus says the LORD of hosts, the God
of Israel: "They shall again use this speech
in the land of Judah and in its cities, when
I bring back their captivity: 'The LORD
bless you, O home of justice, *and* mountain
of holiness!' 24And there shall dwell in Judah itself, and in all its cities together,
farmers and those going out with flocks.
25For I have satiated the weary soul, and I
have replenished every sorrowful soul."

26After this I awoke and looked
around, and my sleep was sweet to me.

27"Behold, the days are coming, says
the LORD, that I will sow the house of Israel and the house of Judah with the seed
of man and the seed of beast. 28And it shall
come to pass, *that* as I have watched over
them to pluck up, to break down, to throw
down, to destroy, and to afflict, so I will
watch over them to build and to plant, says
the LORD. 29In those days they shall say no
more:

'The fathers have eaten sour grapes,
And the children's teeth are set on edge.'

30But every one shall die for his own iniquity; every man who eats the sour grapes,
his teeth shall be set on edge.

A New Covenant

31"Behold, the days are coming, says
the LORD, when I will make a new covenant with the house of Israel and with the
house of Judah— 32not according to the
covenant that I made with their fathers in
the day *that* I took them by the hand to
lead them out of the land of Egypt, My
covenant which they broke, though I was a
husband to them,a says the LORD. 33But

31:32 aFollowing Masoretic Text, Targum, and
Vulgate; Septuagint and Syriac read *and I turned away
from them.*

MARRIAGE AND FAMILY

*Ramah was about 5 miles north of Jerusalem, and Rachel's tomb was said to be near
there. As the favorite wife of Jacob and the mother of Benjamin and Joseph, Rachel
represents all of Israel. As their ancestor she is pictured mourning for the generation
that was taken into exile by the Babylonians (Jer. 31:15). The verse is quoted in Matt.
2:18 about the suffering of the infants killed in Bethlehem by Herod.*

this *is* the covenant that I will make with the house of Israel after those days, says the LORD: I will put My law in their minds, and write it on their hearts; and I will be their God, and they shall be My people. ³⁴No more shall every man teach his neighbor, and every man his brother, saying, 'Know the LORD,' for they all shall know Me, from the least of them to the greatest of them, says the LORD. For I will forgive their iniquity, and their sin I will remember no more."

35 Thus says the LORD,
    Who gives the sun for a light by day,
    The ordinances of the moon and the
        stars for a light by night,
    Who disturbs the sea,
    And its waves roar
    (The LORD of hosts *is* His name):

36 "If those ordinances depart
    From before Me, says the LORD,
    Then the seed of Israel shall also
        cease
    From being a nation before Me
        forever."

³⁷Thus says the LORD:

    "If heaven above can be measured,
    And the foundations of the earth
        searched out beneath,
    I will also cast off all the seed of Israel
    For all that they have done, says the
        LORD.

³⁸"Behold, the days are coming, says the LORD, that the city shall be built for the LORD from the Tower of Hananel to the Corner Gate. ³⁹The surveyor's line shall again extend straight forward over the hill Gareb; then it shall turn toward Goath. ⁴⁰And the whole valley of the dead bodies and of the ashes, and all the fields as far as the Brook Kidron, to the corner of the Horse Gate toward the east, *shall be* holy to the LORD. It shall not be plucked up or thrown down anymore forever."

Jeremiah Buys a Field

32 ¹The word that came to Jeremiah from the LORD in the tenth year of Zedekiah king of Judah, which was the eighteenth year of Nebuchadnezzar. ²For then the king of Babylon's army besieged Jerusalem, and Jeremiah the prophet was shut up in the court of the prison, which *was in* the king of Judah's house. ³For Zedekiah king of Judah had shut him up, saying, "Why do you prophesy and say, 'Thus says the LORD: "Behold, I will give this city into the hand of the king of Babylon, and he shall take it; ⁴and Zedekiah king of Judah shall not escape from the hand of the Chaldeans, but shall surely be delivered into the hand of the king of Babylon, and shall speak with him face to face,ᵃ and see him eye to eye; ⁵then he shall lead Zedekiah to Babylon, and there he shall be until I visit him," says the LORD; "though you fight with the Chaldeans, you shall not succeed" '?"

⁶And Jeremiah said, "The word of the LORD came to me, saying, ⁷'Behold, Hanamel the son of Shallum your uncle will come to you, saying, "Buy my field which *is* in Anathoth, for the right of redemption *is* yours to buy *it*." ' ⁸Then Hanamel my uncle's son came to me in the court of the prison according to the word of the LORD, and said to me, 'Please buy my field that *is* in Anathoth, which *is* in the country of Benjamin; for the right of inheritance *is* yours, and the redemption yours; buy *it* for yourself.' Then I knew that this was the word of the LORD. ⁹So I bought the field from Hanamel, the son of my uncle who *was* in Anathoth, and weighed *out to* him the money—seventeen shekels of silver. ¹⁰And I signed the deed and sealed *it,* took witnesses, and weighed the money on the scales. ¹¹So I took the purchase deed, *both* that which was sealed *according* to the law

---

32:4 ᵃLiterally *mouth to mouth*

TRADE AND ECONOMICS

Ancient deeds were prepared in duplicate. One copy was folded or enclosed in the duplicate and then sealed (Jer. 32:10). If a question arose about the deed, the inside copy would show whether someone had tampered with the outside. Seals were applied by pressing a carved stamp into a lump of wet clay. The design of many seals consisted only of a person's name and title.

PROPERTY RIGHTS UNDER SIEGE (Jer. 32:1–15)

In 587 B.C. Jerusalem's fall seemed—and was—at hand. The Babylonian siege against Jerusalem was under way. In response the Judahite king, Zedekiah, had imprisoned Jeremiah (Jer. 32:2). The prophet's portrayal of the siege as God's judgment on Judah's idolatry seriously hindered the people's morale and thus Jerusalem's chances of withstanding the siege (32:3–5).

Prisons were not large bureaucratic institutions with barred cells in ancient Israel. Jeremiah's "crime" was against the king; therefore, his "prison" was a room under guard in the king's palace (32:2). King Zedekiah imprisoned Jeremiah to keep him from speaking in public.

The situation must have seemed quite hopeless to Jeremiah, who was under siege not merely once but twice. While the army of the mightiest empire in the Near East camped outside the city walls, Zedekiah's guard stood outside the prison room. Jeremiah's prophecy of judgment on Judah was playing itself out before everyone's eyes.

Surprisingly, under these circumstances God had Jeremiah purchase property (32:6–8). Free market conditions for the exchange of real estate did not exist in ancient Israel. Land belonged to families. Legal custom insured, as much as possible, that land would stay within family units, rather than fall into the hands of a few. As a nephew of Shallum and cousin of Hanamel (32:7), Jeremiah had the rights of first refusal to land in his hometown of Anathoth. Despite his imprisonment, despite the Babylonian siege, and despite his previous prophecy of annihilation for Jerusalem and Judah, Jeremiah purchased the property.

These actions again were symbolic of Jeremiah's prophetic message. Now that God's judgment was upon Judah, the message shifted to one of hope: judgment would come; yet God still had a future for His people (32:15).

---

and custom, and that which was open; [12]and I gave the purchase deed to Baruch the son of Neriah, son of Mahseiah, in the presence of Hanamel my uncle's *son,* and in the presence of the witnesses who signed the purchase deed, before all the Jews who sat in the court of the prison.

[13]"Then I charged Baruch before them, saying, [14]'Thus says the LORD of hosts, the God of Israel: "Take these deeds, both this purchase deed which is sealed and this deed which is open, and put them in an earthen vessel, that they may last many days." [15]For thus says the LORD of hosts, the God of Israel: "Houses and fields and vineyards shall be possessed again in this land." '

Jeremiah Prays for Understanding

[16]"Now when I had delivered the purchase deed to Baruch the son of Neriah, I prayed to the LORD, saying: [17]'Ah, Lord GOD! Behold, You have made the heavens and the earth by Your great power and outstretched arm. There is nothing too hard for You. [18]*You* show lovingkindness to thousands, and repay the iniquity of the fathers into the bosom of their children after them—the Great, the Mighty God, whose

name *is* the LORD of hosts. [19]*You are* great in counsel and mighty in work, for Your eyes *are* open to all the ways of the sons of men, to give everyone according to his ways and according to the fruit of his doings. [20]You have set signs and wonders in the land of Egypt, to this day, and in Israel and among *other* men; and You have made Yourself a name, as it is this day. [21]You have brought Your people Israel out of the land of Egypt with signs and wonders, with a strong hand and an outstretched arm, and with great terror; [22]You have given them this land, of which You swore to their fathers to give them—"a land flowing with milk and honey."[a] [23]And they came in and took possession of it, but they have not obeyed Your voice or walked in Your law. They have done nothing of all that You commanded them to do; therefore You have caused all this calamity to come upon them.

[24]'Look, the siege mounds! They have come to the city to take it; and the city has been given into the hand of the Chaldeans who fight against it, because of the sword

---

32:22 [a]Exodus 3:8

A God Consuming Human Flesh (Jer. 32:35)

The god Molech was worshiped by sacrificing human children. The ancient world in general was horrified by this practice, and the sacrifice of children to a deity became widely known as a "Molech sacrifice."

Whether the name of this deity was actually "Molech" remains uncertain. The scribes of the Hebrew Bible were so appalled with the worship of Molech that they used the vowels of the Hebrew word *bosheth* (meaning "shame") with this deity's name. The original name apparently meant "king" and could have been understood as a divine title. But it could also have been the actual name of the deity. The prophet Jeremiah mentions Molech together with the god Baal, whose name means "lord" (Jer. 32:35).

While 1 Kin. 11:7 associates the worship of Molech with the Ammonites, it is the Phoenicians and the Judahites who show evidence of practicing child sacrifice. Literary and archaeological sources point to rituals involving the sacrifice of children at the Phoenician colony of Carthage from around 700 to 200 B.C. The central ritual of worship appears to have included the sacrifice of infants and small children, the burning of their bodies, and the burial of the cremated remains.

Jeremiah condemned both the practice of child sacrifice and the city of Jerusalem for allowing it (Jer. 7:30–32; 19:13). The Tophet was a cult site set up in the Valley of Hinnom, near Jerusalem, for human sacrifice. Two Judahite kings, Ahaz (2 Chr. 28:1–3) and Manasseh (2 Chr. 33:1, 6), are reported to have sacrificed children there. We do not know whether what Jeremiah witnessed was the worship of Molech or the incorporation of Molech child sacrifice into the worship of Judah's God Yahweh. But for certain the prophet considered it an abomination (Jer. 32:35).

---

and famine and pestilence. What You have spoken has happened; there You see *it!* ²⁵And You have said to me, O Lord GOD, "Buy the field for money, and take witnesses"!—yet the city has been given into the hand of the Chaldeans.' "

God's Assurance of the People's Return

²⁶Then the word of the LORD came to Jeremiah, saying, ²⁷"Behold, I *am* the LORD, the God of all flesh. Is there anything too hard for Me? ²⁸Therefore thus says the LORD: 'Behold, I will give this city into the hand of the Chaldeans, into the hand of Nebuchadnezzar king of Babylon, and he shall take it. ²⁹And the Chaldeans who fight against this city shall come and set fire to this city and burn it, with the houses on whose roofs they have offered incense to Baal and poured out drink offerings to other gods, to provoke Me to anger; ³⁰because the children of Israel and the children of Judah have done only evil before Me from their youth. For the children of Israel have provoked Me only to anger with the work of their hands,' says the LORD. ³¹'For this city has been to Me *a*

provocation of My anger and My fury from the day that they built it, even to this day; so I will remove it from before My face ³²because of all the evil of the children of Israel and the children of Judah, which they have done to provoke Me to anger— they, their kings, their princes, their priests, their prophets, the men of Judah, and the inhabitants of Jerusalem. ³³And they have turned to Me the back, and not the face; though I taught them, rising up early and teaching *them,* yet they have not listened to receive instruction. ³⁴But they set their abominations in the house which is called by My name, to defile it. ³⁵And they built the high places of Baal which *are* in the Valley of the Son of Hinnom, to cause their sons and their daughters to pass through *the fire* to Molech, which I did not command them, nor did it come into My mind that they should do this abomination, to cause Judah to sin.'

³⁶"Now therefore, thus says the LORD, the God of Israel, concerning this city of which you say, 'It shall be delivered into the hand of the king of Babylon by the sword, by the famine, and by the pestilence: ³⁷Behold, I will gather them out of

all countries where I have driven them in My anger, in My fury, and in great wrath; I will bring them back to this place, and I will cause them to dwell safely. ³⁸They shall be My people, and I will be their God; ³⁹then I will give them one heart and one way, that they may fear Me forever, for the good of them and their children after them. ⁴⁰And I will make an everlasting covenant with them, that I will not turn away from doing them good; but I will put My fear in their hearts so that they will not depart from Me. ⁴¹Yes, I will rejoice over them to do them good, and I will assuredly plant them in this land, with all My heart and with all My soul.'

⁴²For thus says the LORD: 'Just as I have brought all this great calamity on this people, so I will bring on them all the good that I have promised them. ⁴³And fields will be bought in this land of which you say, "It is desolate, without man or beast; it has been given into the hand of the Chaldeans." ⁴⁴Men will buy fields for money, sign deeds and seal them, and take witnesses, in the land of Benjamin, in the places around Jerusalem, in the cities of Judah, in the cities of the mountains, in the cities of the lowland, and in the cities of the South; for I will cause their captives to return,' says the LORD."

Excellence of the Restored Nation

33 ¹Moreover the word of the LORD came to Jeremiah a second time, while he was still shut up in the court of the prison, saying, ²"Thus says the LORD who made it, the LORD who formed it to establish it (the LORD is His name): ³'Call to Me, and I will answer you, and show you great and mighty things, which you do not know.'

⁴"For thus says the LORD, the God of Israel, concerning the houses of this city and the houses of the kings of Judah, which have been pulled down to fortify[a] against the siege mounds and the sword: ⁵They come to fight with the Chaldeans, but only to fill their places[a] with the dead bodies of men whom I will slay in My anger and My fury, all for whose wickedness I have hidden My face from this city. ⁶Behold, I will bring it health and healing; I will heal them and reveal to them the abundance of peace and truth. ⁷And I will cause the captives of Judah and the captives of Israel to return, and will rebuild those places as at the first. ⁸I will cleanse

them from all their iniquity by which they have sinned against Me, and I will pardon all their iniquities by which they have sinned and by which they have transgressed against Me. ⁹Then it shall be to Me a name of joy, a praise, and an honor before all nations of the earth, who shall hear all the good that I do to them; they shall fear and tremble for all the goodness and all the prosperity that I provide for it.'

¹⁰"Thus says the LORD: 'Again there shall be heard in this place—of which you say, "It is desolate, without man and without beast"—in the cities of Judah, in the streets of Jerusalem that are desolate, without man and without inhabitant and without beast, ¹¹the voice of joy and the voice of gladness, the voice of the bridegroom and the voice of the bride, the voice of those who will say:

"Praise the LORD of hosts,
    For the LORD is good,
    For His mercy endures forever"—

and of those who will bring the sacrifice of praise into the house of the LORD. For I will cause the captives of the land to return as at the first,' says the LORD.

¹²"Thus says the LORD of hosts: 'In this place which is desolate, without man and without beast, and in all its cities, there shall again be a dwelling place of shepherds causing their flocks to lie down. ¹³In the cities of the mountains, in the cities of the lowland, in the cities of the South, in the land of Benjamin, in the places around Jerusalem, and in the cities of Judah, the flocks shall again pass under the hands of him who counts them,' says the LORD.

¹⁴'Behold, the days are coming,' says the LORD, 'that I will perform that good thing which I have promised to the house of Israel and to the house of Judah:

15   'In those days and at that time
        I will cause to grow up to David
        A Branch of righteousness;
        He shall execute judgment and
            righteousness in the earth.
16   In those days Judah will be saved,
        And Jerusalem will dwell safely.
        And this is the name by which she will
            be called:

THE LORD OUR RIGHTEOUSNESS.'[a]

33:4 [a]Compare Isaiah 22:10   33:5 [a]Compare
2 Kings 23:14   33:16 [a]Compare 23:5, 6

[17]"For thus says the LORD: 'David shall never lack a man to sit on the throne of the house of Israel; [18]nor shall the priests, the Levites, lack a man to offer burnt offerings before Me, to kindle grain offerings, and to sacrifice continually.' "

The Permanence of God's Covenant

[19]And the word of the LORD came to Jeremiah, saying, [20]"Thus says the LORD: 'If you can break My covenant with the day and My covenant with the night, so that there will not be day and night in their season, [21]then My covenant may also be broken with David My servant, so that he shall not have a son to reign on his throne, and with the Levites, the priests, My ministers. [22]As the host of heaven cannot be numbered, nor the sand of the sea measured, so will I multiply the descendants of David My servant and the Levites who minister to Me.' "

[23]Moreover the word of the LORD came to Jeremiah, saying, [24]"Have you not considered what these people have spoken, saying, 'The two families which the LORD has chosen, He has also cast them off'? Thus they have despised My people, as if they should no more be a nation before them.

[25]"Thus says the LORD: 'If My covenant is not with day and night, and if I have not appointed the ordinances of heaven and earth, [26]then I will cast away the descendants of Jacob and David My servant, so that I will not take any of his descendants to be rulers over the descendants of Abraham, Isaac, and Jacob. For I will cause their captives to return, and will have mercy on them.' "

Jeremiah 23:1–8
The Branch of Righteousness

23 :1 "Woe to the shepherds who destroy and scatter the sheep of My pasture!" says the LORD. [2]Therefore thus says the LORD God of Israel against the shepherds who feed My people: "You have scattered My flock, driven them away, and not attended to them. Behold, I will attend to you for the evil of your doings," says the LORD. [3]"But I will gather the remnant of My flock out of all countries where I have driven them, and bring them back to their folds; and they shall be fruitful and increase. [4]I will set up shepherds over them who will feed them; and they shall fear no more, nor be dismayed, nor shall they be lacking," says the LORD.

5 "Behold, *the* days are coming," says the LORD,
"That I will raise to David a Branch of righteousness;
A King shall reign and prosper,
And execute judgment and righteousness in the earth.
6 In His days Judah will be saved,
And Israel will dwell safely;
Now this *is* His name by which He will be called:

THE LORD OUR RIGHTEOUSNESS.[a]

[7]"Therefore, behold, *the* days are coming," says the LORD, "that they shall no longer say, 'As the LORD lives who brought up the children of Israel from the land of Egypt,' [8]but, 'As the LORD lives who brought up and led the descendants of the house of Israel from the north country and from all the countries where I had driven them.' And they shall dwell in their own land."

Jeremiah 38:1–28
Jeremiah in the Dungeon

38 :1 Now Shephatiah the son of Mattan, Gedaliah the son of Pashhur, Jucal[a] the son of Shelemiah, and Pashhur the son of Malchiah heard the words that Jeremiah had spoken to all the people, saying, [2]"Thus says the LORD: 'He who remains in this city shall die by the sword, by famine, and by pestilence; but he who goes over to the Chaldeans shall live; his life shall be as a prize to him, and he shall live.'[a] [3]Thus says the LORD: 'This city shall surely be given into the hand of the king of Babylon's army, which shall take it.' "

[4]Therefore the princes said to the king, "Please, let this man be put to death, for thus he weakens the hands of the men of war who remain in this city, and the hands of all the people, by speaking such words to them. For this man does not seek the welfare of this people, but their harm."

[5]Then Zedekiah the king said, "Look, he *is* in your hand. For the king can *do* nothing against you." [6]So they took Jeremiah and cast him into the dungeon of Malchiah the king's[a] son, which *was* in the

JEREMIAH'S CALL AND MINISTRY

The prophet Jeremiah is reported to have received the "word of the LORD" in the 13th year of King Josiah, or 627 B.C. (Jer. 1:2). Some think that Jeremiah was a "youth" (Jer. 1:6) at this time. Others suppose that he was "in the womb" (Jer. 1:5) and thus born in 627.

Date	Life of Jeremiah	Kings of Judah
645	Approximate date of Jeremiah's birth if he was a "youth" (Jer. 1:6) in 627 B.C.	
640		Josiah becomes king in Judah
628		Josiah begins early reforms of Judah's pagan religions (2 Chr. 34:3)
627	Jeremiah receives the "word of the LORD" (Jer. 1:2)	
627	Date of Jeremiah's birth if he was called "in the womb" (Jer. 1:5)	
622		Josiah repairs the temple (2 Chr. 34:8)
622		Josiah celebrates the Passover in a climax to his religious reforms (2 Kin. 23:21–23)
612	Jeremiah possibly begins his prophetic ministry (if he was born in 627 B.C.)	
609		Jehoiakim becomes king in Judah
604		Jehoiakim burns Jeremiah's scroll (Jer. 36:9, 22, 23)
597		Zedekiah becomes king in Judah
587		Zedekiah keeps Jeremiah imprisoned (Jer. 37:21)
586	Jeremiah is released by the captain of the Babylonian guard	

court of the prison, and they let Jeremiah down with ropes. And in the dungeon *there was* no water, but mire. So Jeremiah sank in the mire.

7 Now Ebed-Melech the Ethiopian, one of the eunuchs, who was in the king's house, heard that they had put Jeremiah in the dungeon. When the king was sitting at the Gate of Benjamin, 8 Ebed-Melech went out of the king's house and spoke to the king, saying: 9 "My lord the king, these men have done evil in all that they have

AGRICULTURE AND HERDING

In the dry regions of Israel, cisterns for water storage were dug in the ground to a depth of about 15 feet (Jer. 38:6). The opening at the surface was typically small enough to be covered, but below the surface the diameter of the pit increased to 8 or 10 feet. Such a cistern would hold 30 cubic yards or about 6,000 gallons. Rainwater filled the cisterns in the wet season.

done to Jeremiah the prophet, whom they have cast into the dungeon, and he is likely to die from hunger in the place where he is. For *there is* no more bread in the city." [10]Then the king commanded Ebed-Melech the Ethiopian, saying, "Take from here thirty men with you, and lift Jeremiah the prophet out of the dungeon before he dies." [11]So Ebed-Melech took the men with him and went into the house of the king under the treasury, and took from there old clothes and old rags, and let them down by ropes into the dungeon to Jeremiah. [12]Then Ebed-Melech the Ethiopian said to Jeremiah, "Please put these old clothes and rags under your armpits, under the ropes." And Jeremiah did so. [13]So they pulled Jeremiah up with ropes and lifted him out of the dungeon. And Jeremiah remained in the court of the prison.

Zedekiah's Fears and Jeremiah's Advice

[14]Then Zedekiah the king sent and had Jeremiah the prophet brought to him at the third entrance of the house of the LORD. And the king said to Jeremiah, "I will ask you something. Hide nothing from me."

[15]Jeremiah said to Zedekiah, "If I declare *it* to you, will you not surely put me to death? And if I give you advice, you will not listen to me."

[16]So Zedekiah the king swore secretly to Jeremiah, saying, "*As* the LORD lives, who made our very souls, I will not put you to death, nor will I give you into the hand of these men who seek your life."

[17]Then Jeremiah said to Zedekiah, "Thus says the LORD, the God of hosts, the God of Israel: 'If you surely surrender to the king of Babylon's princes, then your soul shall live; this city shall not be burned with fire, and you and your house shall live. [18]But if you do not surrender to the king of Babylon's princes, then this city shall be given into the hand of the Chaldeans; they shall burn it with fire, and you shall not escape from their hand.' "

[19]And Zedekiah the king said to Jeremiah, "I am afraid of the Jews who have defected to the Chaldeans, lest they deliver me into their hand, and they abuse me."

[20]But Jeremiah said, "They shall not deliver *you*. Please, obey the voice of the LORD which I speak to you. So it shall be well with you, and your soul shall live. [21]But if you refuse to surrender, this *is* the ▼

word that the LORD has shown me: [22]'Now behold, all the women who are left in the king of Judah's house *shall be* surrendered to the king of Babylon's princes, and those *women* shall say:

"Your close friends have set upon you
And prevailed against you;
Your feet have sunk in the mire,
And they have turned away again."

[23]'So they shall surrender all your wives and children to the Chaldeans. You shall not escape from their hand, but shall be taken by the hand of the king of Babylon. And you shall cause this city to be burned with fire.' "

[24]Then Zedekiah said to Jeremiah, "Let no one know of these words, and you shall not die. [25]But if the princes hear that I have talked with you, and they come to you and say to you, 'Declare to us now what you have said to the king, and also what the king said to you; do not hide *it* from us, and we will not put you to death,' [26]then you shall say to them, 'I presented my request before the king, that he would not make me return to Jonathan's house to die there.' "

[27]Then all the princes came to Jeremiah and asked him. And he told them according to all these words that the king had commanded. So they stopped speaking with him, for the conversation had not been heard. [28]Now Jeremiah remained in the court of the prison until the day that Jerusalem was taken. And he was *there* when Jerusalem was taken.

Priestly Account: Rebellion Against Babylon

King Zedekiah appears in the Book of Kings as merely a repeat of his brother Jehoiakim and in the Book of Jeremiah as a weak, fearful ruler. The Chronicler has even less patience with this last king of Judah, describing him as one who "stiffened his neck and hardened his heart" (2 Chr. 36:13), words reminiscent of the hated pharaoh of the Exodus (Ex. 8:15). Zedekiah's reign is roundly condemned, especially for the defilement of the house of the Lord (described in Ezek. 8—11), which is the crowning sin to the priestly writer of Chronicles (2 Chr. 36:14).

■ 2 Chronicles 36:13–16

2 Chronicles

36 :13 And he also rebelled against King Nebuchadnezzar, who had made him swear *an oath* by God; but he stiffened his neck and hardened his heart against turning to the LORD God of Israel. 14Moreover all the leaders of the priests and the people transgressed more and more, *according* to all the abominations of the nations, and defiled the house of the LORD which He had consecrated in Jerusalem.

15And the LORD God of their fathers sent *warnings* to them by His messengers, rising up early and sending *them,* because He had compassion on His people and on His dwelling place. 16But they mocked the messengers of God, despised His words, and scoffed at His prophets, until the wrath of the LORD arose against His people, till *there was* no remedy.

Ezekiel's Temple Vision

Ezekiel's visions were very often concerned with the temple (see "The Book of Ezekiel" at Ezek. 1:1). In the 6th year of Jehoiachin's exile (592 B.C.), a year after Ezekiel's prophetic call, the prophet had a vision (Ezek. 8—11). In this vision, he is led through the temple to observe how extensively it had been defiled during Zedekiah's reign. Pagan gods of all kinds were worshiped within the temple precincts. It was more than God would tolerate, and the vision ends with the glory of God departing from the temple (11:22, 23).

■ Ezekiel 8:1—11:25

Ezekiel
Abominations in the Temple

8 :1 And it came to pass in the sixth year, in the sixth *month,* on the fifth *day* of the month, as I sat in my house with the elders of Judah sitting before me, that the hand of the Lord GOD fell upon me there. 2Then I looked, and there was a likeness, like the appearance of fire—from the appearance of His waist and downward, fire; and from His waist and upward, like the appearance of brightness, like the color of amber. 3He stretched out the form of a hand, and took me by a lock of my hair; and the Spirit lifted me up between earth and heaven, and brought me in visions of God to Jerusalem, to the door of the north gate of the inner *court,* where the seat of the image of jealousy *was,* which provokes to jealousy. 4And behold, the glory of the God of Israel *was* there, like the vision that I saw in the plain.

5Then He said to me, "Son of man, lift your eyes now toward the north." So I lifted my eyes toward the north, and there, north of the altar gate, was this image of jealousy in the entrance.

6Furthermore He said to me, "Son of man, do you see what they are doing, the great abominations that the house of Israel commits here, to make Me go far away from My sanctuary? Now turn again, you will see greater abominations." 7So He brought me to the door of the court; and when I looked, there was a hole in the wall. 8Then He said to me, "Son of man, dig into the wall"; and when I dug into the wall, there was a door.

9And He said to me, "Go in, and see the wicked abominations which they are doing there." 10So I went in and saw, and there—every sort of creeping thing, abominable beasts, and all the idols of the house of Israel, portrayed all around on the walls. 11And there stood before them seventy men of the elders of the house of Israel, and in their midst stood Jaazaniah the son of Shaphan. Each man had a censer in his hand, and a thick cloud of incense went up. 12Then He said to me, "Son of man, have you seen what the elders of the house of Israel do in the dark, every man in the room of his idols? For they say, 'The LORD does not see us, the LORD has forsaken the land.'"

13And He said to me, "Turn again, *and* you will see greater abominations that they are doing." 14So He brought me to the door of the north gate of the LORD's house; and to my dismay, women were sitting there weeping for Tammuz.

15Then He said to me, "Have you seen *this,* O son of man? Turn again, you will see greater abominations than these." 16So He brought me into the inner court of the LORD's house; and there, at the door of the temple of the LORD, between the porch and the altar, *were* about twenty-five men with their backs toward the temple of the LORD and their faces toward the east, and they were worshiping the sun toward the east.

17And He said to me, "Have you seen *this,* O son of man? Is it a trivial thing to the house of Judah to commit the abominations which they commit here? For they have filled the land with violence; then

WEEPING FOR TAMMUZ (Ezek. 8:14)

Who was Tammuz that Judean women would weep for him (Ezek. 8:14)? Why was this activity at the temple one of the "great abominations" (Ezek. 8:6, 13–15)?

Tammuz was an imported deity to Judah. The origins of the worship of the god are lost, though the name "Dumuzi" is assumed to have been a ruler of one of the Sumerian city-states before the middle of the 3rd millennium B.C. By the Neo-Sumerian period (c. 2200–1900 B.C.) the Sumerians recognized Dumuzi as a god and usually associated him with the goddess Inanna. In the Accadian cult the god Dumuzi was called Tammuz, and Inanna was identified with Ishtar. This god and goddess are known by both names as Dumuzi/Tammuz and Inanna/Ishtar.

Stories about the goddess Inanna/Ishtar tell of her visit to the underworld to visit a sister, queen of the netherworld. Tricked by her sister into becoming a corpse in the land of the dead, Inanna/Ishtar must find a substitute to take her place or remain among the dead forever. Returning to earth she finds only sympathetic divinities, none of whom she can bring herself to send to her sister. However, when she returns to her own temple, she is greeted by an unconcerned husband, Dumuzi/Tammuz. She has him dragged to the underworld by demons to take her place among the dead.

The poem called the Gilgamesh Epic makes reference to this myth and to an annual weeping that Ishtar establishes to commemorate Tammuz's death. It is this annual weeping for Tammuz which had caught the eye of Ezekiel at the temple in Jerusalem. Women in Judah had taken up the worship of Tammuz and possibly the rituals of Ishtar and Tammuz that involved fertility rites. This would also have been an abomination to God, who through Jeremiah had declared that fertility came only from God (Jer. 5:24). Women weeping in ritual for another deity at the temple dedicated to God clearly was a great abomination.

---

they have returned to provoke Me to anger. Indeed they put the branch to their nose. [18]Therefore I also will act in fury. My eye will not spare nor will I have pity; and though they cry in My ears with a loud voice, I will not hear them."

The Wicked Are Slain

9 [1]Then He called out in my hearing with a loud voice, saying, "Let those who have charge over the city draw near, each *with* a deadly weapon in his hand." [2]And suddenly six men came from the direction of the upper gate, which faces north, each with his battle-ax in his hand. One man among them *was* clothed with linen and had a writer's inkhorn at his side. They went in and stood beside the bronze altar.

[3]Now the glory of the God of Israel had gone up from the cherub, where it had been, to the threshold of the temple.[a] And He called to the man clothed with linen, who *had* the writer's inkhorn at his side; [4]and the LORD said to him, "Go through the midst of the city, through the midst of Je-

rusalem, and put a mark on the foreheads of the men who sigh and cry over all the abominations that are done within it."

[5]To the others He said in my hearing, "Go after him through the city and kill; do not let your eye spare, nor have any pity. [6]Utterly slay old *and* young men, maidens and little children and women; but do not come near anyone on whom *is* the mark; and begin at My sanctuary." So they began with the elders who *were* before the temple. [7]Then He said to them, "Defile the temple, and fill the courts with the slain. Go out!" And they went out and killed in the city.

[8]So it was, that while they were killing them, I was left *alone;* and I fell on my face and cried out, and said, "Ah, Lord GOD! Will You destroy all the remnant of Israel in pouring out Your fury on Jerusalem?"

[9]Then He said to me, "The iniquity of the house of Israel and Judah *is* exceedingly great, and the land is full of bloodshed, and the city full of perversity; for they say, 'The LORD has forsaken the land, and the LORD does not see!' [10]And as for Me also, My eye will neither spare, nor will I have pity, *but* I will recompense their deeds on their own head."

9:3 [a]Literally *house*

GODS ABANDON PEOPLE WHO ABANDON THEIR GODS (Ezek. 10:18)

Ezekiel's vision of the chariot throne carrying Yahweh away from the temple, leaving the city to its destruction (Ezek. 10), fits the theologies of the ancient Near East. Common belief held that when people ignored the laws and rites of their patron gods, the gods abandoned them.

In Sumerian literature are poems (including a long lament over Ur) about the destruction of cities which were given up by their gods. A lament from the period of Sargon of Agade (Accad, c. 2350 B.C.) was written as if from the mouth of a goddess who describes the destruction of her own city and her inability to even find where her temple had been. She regrets that she had fled with the other gods, for she could have stayed and saved her city, but it was now too late.

The god or gods of a city would only put up with a certain amount of disrespect from their people. Marduk, for example, is said to have abandoned Babylon when the people focused on accruing wealth, engaging in immoral behavior, and taking up with the cult of Elam. All the other deities who had lived in Babylon also left the temples for their places in heaven. That left the city open to destruction, as the Assyrians argued to justify their destruction of Babylon in 689 B.C. by their king Sennacherib.

In Ezekiel's vision, the glory of God departs from the threshold of Jerusalem's temple (Ezek. 10:4, 18). His holiness had been rejected so that He would not stay.

11Just then, the man clothed with linen, who *had* the inkhorn at his side, reported back and said, "I have done as You commanded me."

The Glory Departs from the Temple

10 1And I looked, and there in the firmament that was above the head of the cherubim, there appeared something like a sapphire stone, having the appearance of the likeness of a throne. 2Then He spoke to the man clothed with linen, and said, "Go in among the wheels, under the cherub, fill your hands with coals of fire from among the cherubim, and scatter *them* over the city." And he went in as I watched.

3Now the cherubim were standing on the south side of the temple[a] when the man went in, and the cloud filled the inner court. 4Then the glory of the LORD went up from the cherub, *and paused* over the threshold of the temple; and the house was filled with the cloud, and the court was full of the brightness of the LORD's glory. 5And the sound of the wings of the cherubim was heard *even* in the outer court, like the voice of Almighty God when He speaks.

6Then it happened, when He commanded the man clothed in linen, saying, "Take fire from among the wheels, from among the cherubim," that he went in and stood beside the wheels. 7And the cherub stretched out his hand from among the cherubim to the fire that *was* among the cherubim, and took *some of it* and put *it* into the hands of the *man* clothed with linen, who took *it* and went out. 8The cherubim appeared to have the form of a man's hand under their wings.

9And when I looked, there were four wheels by the cherubim, one wheel by one cherub and another wheel by each other cherub; the wheels appeared *to have* the color of a beryl stone. 10As for their appearance, all four looked alike—as it were, a

10:3 aLiterally *house*, also in verses 4 and 18

SCIENCE AND TECHNOLOGY

The sapphire mentioned by Ezekiel (Ezek. 10:1) was probably lapis lazuli, a dark blue, opaque stone found mainly in Afghanistan. It was a most valuable gemstone in ancient times. The modern sapphire is a translucent blue aluminum silicate, chemically the same as ruby. It is extremely hard and could not have been cut or polished by ancient craftsmen. Lapis lazuli is approximately as hard as glass.

THE EAST GATE OF THE TEMPLE (Ezek. 11:1)

The East Gate of Jerusalem's temple was an important social institution. The 25 men, including two "princes," that Ezekiel envisioned there most likely represented the gathering of an official "city council" (Ezek. 11:1).

Right before the exile of 586 B.C., the temple became an important political institution. Entry into the temple's outer courtyard signified full membership in the society. To regulate entry, therefore, the temple had outer gates to keep the impure and the unqualified out. Only the priestly aristocracy were allowed into the inner courtyards. A set of inner gates prohibited nonpriests from violating the temple's sacred space.

The temple gates were not simple doors set on a hinge. Gates were large rooms in which people could gather. It is in one of these rooms that Ezekiel saw the 25 Judeans gather.

The East Gate of the temple, however, bore special significance. It defined a royal and governmental sphere. In Ezekiel's vision of the new temple, the gate is shut except for the Sabbath sacrifices. Then only the prince is allowed into the gate (Ezek. 46:1, 2). The common citizenry, the "people of the land," must worship outside the gate, at—not within—its entrance (46:3). Only the civic leader is allowed into the gate.

It is thus natural that Ezekiel saw two princes, Jaazaniah and Pelatiah, in the East Gate (11:1). The meeting was an important one. The leaders of the city gathered to determine the fate of Jerusalem. The death of Pelatiah at this meeting (11:13), then, signified the depth of divine judgment against these leaders. They had guided Jerusalem on a path that would end in destruction.

---

wheel in the middle of a wheel. [11]When they went, they went toward *any of* their four directions; they did not turn aside when they went, but followed in the direction the head was facing. They did not turn aside when they went. [12]And their whole body, with their back, their hands, their wings, and the wheels that the four had, *were* full of eyes all around. [13]As for the wheels, they were called in my hearing, "Wheel."

[14]Each one had four faces: the first face *was* the face of a cherub, the second face the face of a man, the third the face of a lion, and the fourth the face of an eagle. [15]And the cherubim were lifted up. This *was* the living creature I saw by the River Chebar. [16]When the cherubim went, the wheels went beside them; and when the cherubim lifted their wings to mount up from the earth, the same wheels also did not turn from beside them. [17]When *the cherubim*[a] stood still, *the wheels* stood still, and when *one*[b] was lifted up, *the other*[c] lifted itself up, for the spirit of the living creature *was* in them.

[18]Then the glory of the LORD departed from the threshold of the temple and stood over the cherubim. [19]And the cherubim lifted their wings and mounted up from the earth in my sight. When they went out, the wheels *were* beside them; and they stood at the door of the east gate of the LORD's house, and the glory of the God of Israel *was* above them.

[20]This *is* the living creature I saw under the God of Israel by the River Chebar, and I knew they *were* cherubim. [21]Each one had four faces and each one four wings, and the likeness of the hands of a man *was* under their wings. [22]And the likeness of their faces *was* the same *as* the faces which I had seen by the River Chebar, their appearance and their persons. They each went straight forward.

Judgment on Wicked Counselors

11 [1]Then the Spirit lifted me up and brought me to the East Gate of the LORD's house, which faces eastward; and there at the door of the gate were twenty-five men, among whom I saw Jaazaniah the son of Azzur, and Pelatiah the son of Benaiah, princes of the people. [2]And He said to me: "Son of man, these *are* the men who devise iniquity and give wicked counsel in this city, [3]who say, 'The time is not near to build houses; this *city is* the caldron, and we *are* the meat.' [4]Therefore

---

10:17 [a]Literally *they* [b]Literally *they* [c]Literally *they*

prophesy against them, prophesy, O son of man!"

⁵Then the Spirit of the LORD fell upon me, and said to me, "Speak! 'Thus says the LORD: "Thus you have said, O house of Israel; for I know the things that come into your mind. ⁶You have multiplied your slain in this city, and you have filled its streets with the slain." ⁷Therefore thus says the Lord GOD: "Your slain whom you have laid in its midst, they *are* the meat, and this *city is* the caldron; but I shall bring you out of the midst of it. ⁸You have feared the sword; and I will bring a sword upon you," says the Lord GOD. ⁹"And I will bring you out of its midst, and deliver you into the hands of strangers, and execute judgments on you. ¹⁰You shall fall by the sword. I will judge you at the border of Israel. Then you shall know that I *am* the LORD. ¹¹This *city* shall not be your caldron, nor shall you be the meat in its midst. I will judge you at the border of Israel. ¹²And you shall know that I *am* the LORD; for you have not walked in My statutes nor executed My judgments, but have done according to the customs of the Gentiles which *are* all around you."' "

¹³Now it happened, while I was prophesying, that Pelatiah the son of Benaiah died. Then I fell on my face and cried with a loud voice, and said, "Ah, Lord GOD! Will You make a complete end of the remnant of Israel?"

God Will Restore Israel

¹⁴Again the word of the LORD came to me, saying, ¹⁵"Son of man, your brethren, your relatives, your countrymen, and all the house of Israel in its entirety, *are* those about whom the inhabitants of Jerusalem have said, 'Get far away from the LORD; this land has been given to us as a possession.' ¹⁶Therefore say, 'Thus says the Lord GOD: "Although I have cast them far off among the Gentiles, and although I have scattered them among the countries, yet I shall be a little sanctuary for them in the countries where they have gone."' ¹⁷Therefore say, 'Thus says the Lord GOD: "I will gather you from the peoples, assemble you from the countries where you have been scattered, and I will give you the land of Israel."' ¹⁸And they will go there, and they will take away all its detestable things and all its abominations from there. ¹⁹Then I will give them one heart, and I will put a new spirit within them,ᵃ and take the ▼

stony heart out of their flesh, and give them a heart of flesh, ²⁰that they may walk in My statutes and keep My judgments and do them; and they shall be My people, and I will be their God. ²¹But *as for those* whose hearts follow the desire for their detestable things and their abominations, I will recompense their deeds on their own heads," says the Lord GOD.

²²So the cherubim lifted up their wings, with the wheels beside them, and the glory of the God of Israel *was* high above them. ²³And the glory of the LORD went up from the midst of the city and stood on the mountain, which *is* on the east side of the city.

²⁴Then the Spirit took me up and brought me in a vision by the Spirit of God into Chaldea,ᵃ to those in captivity. And the vision that I had seen went up from me. ²⁵So I spoke to those in captivity of all the things the LORD had shown me.

11:19 ᵃLiterally *you*   11:24 ᵃOr *Babylon*, and so elsewhere in this book

Ezekiel's Oracles Before the Fall of Jerusalem

In the 7th year of Jehoiachin's exile (591 B.C.; Ezek. 20:1), the elders of Israel sat before Ezekiel. The prophet had less than four years of prophetic ministry before Nebuchadnezzar would move against Jerusalem one more time. Ezekiel's message throughout this time was one of judgment, of Jerusalem's certain destruction (20:45—21:17).

The oracles, visions, parables, and allegories given during these years almost all speak of the coming punishment of Jerusalem. The allegory of Ezek. 17, for instance, explicitly condemns Zedekiah's alliance with Egypt that led to Babylon's final assault (17:15–17). Ezekiel condemns the false prophets (ch. 13), the elders of Israel (ch. 14), and the inhabitants of Jerusalem (chs. 15; 16). They all would suffer, not for their ancestors' sins, but for their own (ch. 18; 22:1–22). Judah and Jerusalem had not learned a lesson either from their rebellious past (20:1–44) or from their sister nation Samaria (ch. 23).

- Ezekiel 13:1—18:32
- Ezekiel 20:1—21:17
- Ezekiel 22:1—22
- Ezekiel 23:1—49

Ezekiel 13:1—18:32
Woe to Foolish Prophets

13 :1 And the word of the LORD came to me, saying, [2]"Son of man, prophesy against the prophets of Israel who prophesy, and say to those who prophesy out of their own heart, 'Hear the word of the LORD!' "

[3]Thus says the Lord GOD: "Woe to the foolish prophets, who follow their own spirit and have seen nothing! [4]O Israel, your prophets are like foxes in the deserts. [5]You have not gone up into the gaps to build a wall for the house of Israel to stand in battle on the day of the LORD. [6]They have envisioned futility and false divination, saying, 'Thus says the LORD!' But the LORD has not sent them; yet they hope that the word may be confirmed. [7]Have you not seen a futile vision, and have you not spoken false divination? You say, 'The LORD says,' but I have not spoken."

[8]Therefore thus says the Lord GOD: "Because you have spoken nonsense and envisioned lies, therefore I *am* indeed against you," says the Lord GOD. [9]"My hand will be against the prophets who envision futility and who divine lies; they shall not be in the assembly of My people, nor be written in the record of the house of Israel, nor shall they enter into the land of Israel. Then you shall know that I *am* the Lord GOD.

[10]"Because, indeed, because they have seduced My people, saying, 'Peace!' when *there is* no peace—and one builds a wall, and they plaster it with untempered *mortar*— [11]say to those who plaster *it* with untempered *mortar,* that it will fall. There will be flooding rain, and you, O great hailstones, shall fall; and a stormy wind shall tear *it* down. [12]Surely, when the wall has fallen, will it not be said to you, 'Where *is* the mortar with which you plastered *it?*' "

13:18 [a]Literally *over all the joints of My hands;* Vulgate reads *under every elbow;* Septuagint and Targum read *on all elbows of the hands.*

[13]Therefore thus says the Lord GOD: "I will cause a stormy wind to break forth in My fury; and there shall be a flooding rain in My anger, and great hailstones in fury to consume *it.* [14]So I will break down the wall you have plastered with untempered *mortar,* and bring it down to the ground, so that its foundation will be uncovered; it will fall, and you shall be consumed in the midst of it. Then you shall know that I *am* the LORD.

[15]"Thus will I accomplish My wrath on the wall and on those who have plastered it with untempered *mortar;* and I will say to you, 'The wall *is* no *more,* nor those who plastered it, [16]that is, the prophets of Israel who prophesy concerning Jerusalem, and who see visions of peace for her when *there is* no peace,' " says the Lord GOD.

[17]"Likewise, son of man, set your face against the daughters of your people, who prophesy out of their own heart; prophesy against them, [18]and say, 'Thus says the Lord GOD: "Woe to the *women* who sew *magic* charms on their sleeves[a] and make veils for the heads of people of every height to hunt souls! Will you hunt the souls of My people, and keep yourselves alive? [19]And will you profane Me among My people for handfuls of barley and for pieces of bread, killing people who should not die, and keeping people alive who should not live, by your lying to My people who listen to lies?"

[20]Therefore thus says the Lord GOD: "Behold, I *am* against your *magic* charms by which you hunt souls there like birds. I will tear them from your arms, and let the souls go, the souls you hunt like birds. [21]I will also tear off your veils and deliver My people out of your hand, and they shall no longer be as prey in your hand. Then you shall know that I *am* the LORD. [22]"Because with lies you have made the heart of the righteous sad, whom I have not made sad; and you have strengthened the hands of the wicked, so that he does not turn from his wicked way to save his life. [23]Therefore you shall no longer

---

CULTS AND SUPERNATURAL

A very common form of magic is the "binding spell," whose purpose is to bind or compel the powers to control a person's destiny in a certain way (Ezek. 13:18). Such spells could be cast to fight an enemy, to attract a husband or wife, or to influence the outcome of a race. Items such as amulets, tokens, and figurines were prepared by magicians for their rituals and were given to customers paying for the spell.

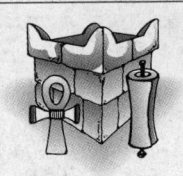

envision futility nor practice divination; for I will deliver My people out of your hand, and you shall know that I *am* the LORD." ' "

Idolatry Will Be Punished

14 ¹Now some of the elders of Israel came to me and sat before me. ²And the word of the LORD came to me, saying, ³"Son of man, these men have set up their idols in their hearts, and put before them that which causes them to stumble into iniquity. Should I let Myself be inquired of at all by them?

⁴"Therefore speak to them, and say to them, 'Thus says the Lord GOD: "Everyone of the house of Israel who sets up his idols in his heart, and puts before him what causes him to stumble into iniquity, and then comes to the prophet, I the LORD will answer him who comes, according to the multitude of his idols, ⁵that I may seize the house of Israel by their heart, because they are all estranged from Me by their idols." '

⁶"Therefore say to the house of Israel, 'Thus says the Lord GOD: "Repent, turn away from your idols, and turn your faces away from all your abominations. ⁷For anyone of the house of Israel, or of the strangers who dwell in Israel, who separates himself from Me and sets up his idols in his heart and puts before him what causes him to stumble into iniquity, then comes to a prophet to inquire of him concerning Me, I the LORD will answer him by Myself. ⁸I will set My face against that man and make him a sign and a proverb, and I will cut him off from the midst of My people. Then you shall know that I *am* the LORD.

⁹"And if the prophet is induced to speak anything, I the LORD have induced that prophet, and I will stretch out My hand against him and destroy him from among My people Israel. ¹⁰And they shall bear their iniquity; the punishment of the prophet shall be the same as the punishment of the one who inquired, ¹¹that the house of Israel may no longer stray from Me, nor be profaned anymore with all their transgressions, but that they may be My people and I may be their God," says the Lord GOD.' "

Judgment on Persistent Unfaithfulness

¹²The word of the LORD came again to me, saying: ¹³"Son of man, when a land sins against Me by persistent unfaithfulness, I will stretch out My hand against it; I will cut off its supply of bread, send famine on it, and cut off man and beast from it. ¹⁴Even *if* these three men, Noah, Daniel, and Job, were in it, they would deliver *only* themselves by their righteousness," says the Lord GOD.

¹⁵"If I cause wild beasts to pass through the land, and they empty it, and make it so desolate that no man may pass through because of the beasts, ¹⁶*even though* these three men *were* in it, *as* I live," says the Lord GOD, "they would deliver neither sons nor daughters; only they would be delivered, and the land would be desolate.

¹⁷"Or *if* I bring a sword on that land, and say, 'Sword, go through the land,' and I cut off man and beast from it, ¹⁸*even though* these three men *were* in it, *as* I live," says the Lord GOD, "they would deliver neither sons nor daughters, but only they themselves would be delivered.

¹⁹"Or *if* I send a pestilence into that land and pour out My fury on it in blood, and cut off from it man and beast, ²⁰*even though* Noah, Daniel, and Job *were* in it, *as* I live," says the Lord GOD, "they would deliver neither son nor daughter; they would deliver *only* themselves by their righteousness."

²¹For thus says the Lord GOD: "How much more it shall be when I send My four severe judgments on Jerusalem—the sword and famine and wild beasts and pestilence—to cut off man and beast from it? ²²Yet behold, there shall be left in it a remnant who will be brought out, *both* sons and daughters; surely they will come out to you, and you will see their ways and their doings. Then you will be comforted concerning the disaster that I have brought

TIME CAPSULE *592 to 589 B.C.*

592 *Ezekiel has vision of the Jerusalem temple*

592 *Elders of Judah sit before Ezekiel (Ezek. 8:1)*

591 *Certain elders inquire of the Lord from Ezekiel (Ezek. 20:1)*

591 *Pharaoh Psammetichus II of Egypt visits Palestine*

591 *Psammetichus marches to Asia*

589 *Ussher's date for the destruction of the temple*

EVEN IF DANIEL WERE HERE! (Ezek. 14:14)

Ezekiel issues a dire warning that even if the great saints—Noah, Daniel, Job—were present, judgment would still come (Ezek. 14:14). Noah was the hero of the Flood (Gen. 6—8); Job, the suffering hero of the Book of Job. Daniel, according to many scholars, is not the Daniel of biblical renown, but another Daniel from the Ugaritic *Legend of Aqhat.* The Hebrew name for "Daniel" is spelled differently in the Hebrew text of Ezek. 14:14 and 28:3 than it is in the Hebrew Book of Daniel.

The *Legend of Aqhat* is a long epic narrative written late in the 2nd millennium B.C. It is one of the texts found at Ugarit, a major Canaanite port city on the Syrian coast of the Mediterranean Sea. The legend is written in the Ugaritic language, which is closely related to the Hebrew language of the Bible.

In the epic, Daniel, the main character, requests an heir from El, the head of the Canaanite pantheon. The request is granted, and Daniel's new son, Aqhat, becomes a great hunter. The goddess Anath desires Aqhat's bow, which had been crafted by the god Kutharu, and when Aqhat refuses to relinquish it, Anath kills him. Aqhat's sister prepares to avenge his death, but the text of the legend is broken at this point, and the story is incomplete.

Whether the Daniel of the *Legend of Aqhat* is the same Daniel named by Ezekiel is not certain. Ezekiel recalls a Daniel who was wise (Ezek. 28:3). There is little evidence that the Ugaritic Daniel is recognized for his great wisdom, although the legend does contain a few wisdom sayings in a list named "Duties of a Son." Since the biblical Daniel was regarded as an expert interpreter of dreams and was renowned for his wisdom (Dan. 5:11, 12), it remains a possibility that Ezekiel had him in mind.

upon Jerusalem, all that I have brought upon it. 23And they will comfort you, when you see their ways and their doings; and you shall know that I have done nothing without cause that I have done in it," says the Lord GOD.

The Outcast Vine

15 1Then the word of the LORD came to me, saying: 2"Son of man, how is the wood of the vine *better* than any other wood, the vine branch which is among the trees of the forest? 3Is wood taken from it to make any object? Or can *men* make a peg from it to hang any vessel on? 4Instead, it is thrown into the fire for fuel; the fire devours both ends of it, and its middle is burned. Is it useful for *any* work? 5Indeed, when it was whole, no object could be made from it. How much less will it be useful for *any* work when the fire has devoured it, and it is burned?

6"Therefore thus says the Lord GOD: 'Like the wood of the vine among the trees of the forest, which I have given to the fire for fuel, so I will give up the inhabitants of Jerusalem; 7and I will set My face against them. They will go out from *one* fire, but *another* fire shall devour them. Then you shall know that I *am* the LORD, when I set

My face against them. 8Thus I will make the land desolate, because they have persisted in unfaithfulness,' says the Lord GOD."

God's Love for Jerusalem

16 1Again the word of the LORD came to me, saying, 2"Son of man, cause Jerusalem to know her abominations, 3and say, 'Thus says the Lord GOD to Jerusalem: "Your birth and your nativity *are* from the land of Canaan; your father *was* an Amorite and your mother a Hittite. 4*As for* your nativity, on the day you were born your navel cord was not cut, nor were you washed in water to cleanse *you;* you were not rubbed with salt nor wrapped in swaddling cloths. 5No eye pitied you, to do any of these things for you, to have compassion on you; but you were thrown out into the open field, when you yourself were loathed on the day you were born.

6"And when I passed by you and saw you struggling in your own blood, I said to you in your blood, 'Live!' Yes, I said to you in your blood, 'Live!' 7I made you thrive like a plant in the field; and you grew, matured, and became very beautiful. *Your* breasts were formed, your hair grew, but you *were* naked and bare.

8"When I passed by you again and looked upon you, indeed your time *was* the time of love; so I spread My wing over you and covered your nakedness. Yes, I swore an oath to you and entered into a covenant with you, and you became Mine," says the Lord GOD.

9"Then I washed you in water; yes, I thoroughly washed off your blood, and I anointed you with oil. 10I clothed you in embroidered cloth and gave you sandals of badger skin; I clothed you with fine linen and covered you with silk. 11I adorned you with ornaments, put bracelets on your wrists, and a chain on your neck. 12And I put a jewel in your nose, earrings in your ears, and a beautiful crown on your head. 13Thus you were adorned with gold and silver, and your clothing *was of* fine linen, silk, and embroidered cloth. You ate *pastry of* fine flour, honey, and oil. You were exceedingly beautiful, and succeeded to royalty. 14Your fame went out among the nations because of your beauty, for it *was* perfect through My splendor which I had bestowed on you," says the Lord GOD.

Jerusalem's Harlotry

15"But you trusted in your own beauty, played the harlot because of your fame, and poured out your harlotry on everyone passing by who *would have* it. 16You took some of your garments and adorned multicolored high places for yourself, and played the harlot on them. *Such* things should not happen, nor be. 17You have also taken your beautiful jewelry from My gold and My silver, which I had given you, and made for yourself male images and played the harlot with them. 18You took your embroidered garments and covered them, and you set My oil and My incense before them. 19Also My food which I gave you—the pastry of fine flour, oil, and honey *which* I fed you— you set it before them as sweet incense; and *so* it was," says the Lord GOD.

20"Moreover you took your sons and your daughters, whom you bore to Me, and these you sacrificed to them to be de-

voured. *Were* your *acts* of harlotry a small matter, 21that you have slain My children and offered them up to them by causing them to pass through *the fire?* 22And in all your abominations and acts of harlotry you did not remember the days of your youth, when you were naked and bare, struggling in your blood.

23"Then it was so, after all your wickedness—'Woe, woe to you!' says the Lord GOD— 24*that* you also built for yourself a shrine, and made a high place for yourself in every street. 25You built your high places at the head of every road, and made your beauty to be abhorred. You offered yourself to everyone who passed by, and multiplied your acts of harlotry. 26You also committed harlotry with the Egyptians, your very fleshly neighbors, and increased your acts of harlotry to provoke Me to anger.

27"Behold, therefore, I stretched out My hand against you, diminished your allotment, and gave you up to the will of those who hate you, the daughters of the Philistines, who were ashamed of your lewd behavior. 28You also played the harlot with the Assyrians, because you were insatiable; indeed you played the harlot with them and still were not satisfied. 29Moreover you multiplied your acts of harlotry as far as the land of the trader, Chaldea; and even then you were not satisfied.

30"How degenerate is your heart!" says the Lord GOD, "seeing you do all these *things,* the deeds of a brazen harlot.

Jerusalem's Adultery

31"You erected your shrine at the head of every road, and built your high place in every street. Yet you were not like a harlot, because you scorned payment. 32*You are* an adulterous wife, *who* takes strangers instead of her husband. 33Men make payment to all harlots, but you made your payments to all your lovers, and hired them to come to you from all around for your harlotry. 34You are the opposite of *other* women in your harlotry, because no

MARRIAGE AND FAMILY

Rubbing a newborn baby with salt was a Palestinian custom (Ezek. 16:4). In caring for a baby during the first days of life, the parents and their society take possession of the child through traditional procedures, such as rubbing. In particular giving the child a name is highly important. In Israel, God took possession of firstborn male children on their 8th day of life, through circumcision (Luke 1:59).

HARLOTRY AFTER OTHER GODS (Ezek. 16:15–30)

The prophet Ezekiel referred to a particular form of religious observance to announce judgment on the Judeans. In many ancient Near Eastern cults of Mesopotamia and Syria-Palestine priestesses engaged in ritual prostitution as an act of religious devotion. Exactly how and why these acts were performed is not clear. Ezekiel accused the Judeans of a form of prostitution in their devotion to gods other than Yahweh. They had "played the harlot" with the representatives of these other gods (Ezek. 16:15–17).

Ezekiel confronted the Judeans about seeking after deities from Canaan, Egypt, and Assyria, while abandoning Yahweh, who had given them all they had. The Canaanite gods, particularly Asherah and Baal, had been worshiped throughout the monarchies of Israel and Judah. Food provided by Yahweh was used in the worship of Baal, the god of storms, who was thought to bring fertility and provide grain in the field (16:19).

Egyptian deities had also been worshiped in Palestine since at least the time of Egyptian hegemony in the 2nd millennium B.C. Images of the divinities Hathor and Bes appeared in the area through the time of the monarchy of Judah. Some Judeans may have worshiped Egyptian deities in Judah's last days, hoping that the gods of their political ally would help them stand against Nebuchadnezzar II (16:26).

At various times in her history, Judah had courted the stronger nations—Assyria (16:28) and Babylonia (Chaldea, 16:29)—both politically and militarily because of a lack of faith in Yahweh as her protector. Such alliances involved acknowledgment of these nations' gods. Some Judeans worshiped the deities of these nations who had conquered them. They believed that the foreign gods had overcome Yahweh and were the current rulers of the universe. Judah indeed had become "a brazen harlot" (16:30).

one solicited you to be a harlot. In that you gave payment but no payment was given you, therefore you are the opposite."

Jerusalem's Lovers Will Abuse Her

35'Now then, O harlot, hear the word of the LORD! 36Thus says the Lord GOD: "Because your filthiness was poured out and your nakedness uncovered in your harlotry with your lovers, and with all your abominable idols, and because of the blood of your children which you gave to them, 37surely, therefore, I will gather all your lovers with whom you took pleasure, all those you loved, *and* all those you hated; I will gather them from all around against you and will uncover your nakedness to them, that they may see all your nakedness. 38And I will judge you as women who break wedlock or shed blood are judged; I will bring blood upon you in fury and jealousy. 39I will also give you into their hand, and they shall throw down your shrines and break down your high places. They shall also strip you of your clothes, take your beautiful jewelry, and leave you naked and bare.

40"They shall also bring up an assembly against you, and they shall stone you with stones and thrust you through with their swords. 41They shall burn your houses with fire, and execute judgments on you in the sight of many women; and I will make you cease playing the harlot, and you shall no longer hire lovers. 42So I will lay to rest My fury toward you, and My jealousy shall depart from you. I will be quiet, and be angry no more. 43Because you did not remember the days of your youth, but agitated Me[a] with all these *things*, surely I will also recompense your deeds on *your own* head," says the Lord GOD. "And you shall not commit lewdness in addition to all your abominations.

More Wicked than Samaria and Sodom

44"Indeed everyone who quotes proverbs will use *this* proverb against you: 'Like mother, like daughter!' 45You *are* your mother's daughter, loathing husband and

16:43 [a]Following Septuagint, Syriac, Targum, and Vulgate; Masoretic Text reads *were agitated with Me.*

children; and you *are* the sister of your sisters, who loathed their husbands and children; your mother *was* a Hittite and your father an Amorite.

⁴⁶"Your elder sister *is* Samaria, who dwells with her daughters to the north of you; and your younger sister, who dwells to the south of you, *is* Sodom and her daughters. ⁴⁷You did not walk in their ways nor act according to their abominations; but, as *if that were* too little, you became more corrupt than they in all your ways.

⁴⁸"*As* I live," says the Lord GOD, "neither your sister Sodom nor her daughters have done as you and your daughters have done. ⁴⁹Look, this was the iniquity of your sister Sodom: She and her daughter had pride, fullness of food, and abundance of idleness; neither did she strengthen the hand of the poor and needy. ⁵⁰And they were haughty and committed abomination before Me; therefore I took them away as I saw *fit*.ᵃ

⁵¹"Samaria did not commit half of your sins; but you have multiplied your abominations more than they, and have justified your sisters by all the abominations which you have done. ⁵²You who judged your sisters, bear your own shame also, because the sins which you committed were more abominable than theirs; they are more righteous than you. Yes, be disgraced also, and bear your own shame, because you justified your sisters.

⁵³"When I bring back their captives, the captives of Sodom and her daughters, and the captives of Samaria and her daughters, then *I will also bring back* the captives of your captivity among them, ⁵⁴that you may bear your own shame and be disgraced by all that you did when you comforted them. ⁵⁵When your sisters, Sodom and her daughters, return to their former state, and Samaria and her daughters return to their former state, then you and your daughters will return to your former state. ⁵⁶For your sister Sodom was not a byword in your mouth in the days of your pride, ⁵⁷before your wickedness was uncovered. It was like the time of the reproach of the daughters of Syriaᵃ and all *those* around her, and of the daughters of the Philistines, who despise you everywhere. ⁵⁸You have paid for your lewdness and your abominations," says the LORD. ⁵⁹For thus says the Lord GOD: "I will deal with you as you have done, who despised the oath by breaking the covenant.

An Everlasting Covenant

⁶⁰"Nevertheless I will remember My covenant with you in the days of your youth, and I will establish an everlasting covenant with you. ⁶¹Then you will remember your ways and be ashamed, when you receive your older and your younger sisters; for I will give them to you for daughters, but not because of My covenant with you. ⁶²And I will establish My covenant with you. Then you shall know that I *am* the LORD, ⁶³that you may remember and be ashamed, and never open your mouth anymore because of your shame, when I provide you an atonement for all you have done," says the Lord GOD.' "

The Eagles and the Vine

17 ¹And the word of the LORD came to me, saying, ²"Son of man, pose a riddle, and speak a parable to the house of Israel, ³and say, 'Thus says the Lord GOD:

"A great eagle with large wings and
       long pinions,
   Full of feathers of various colors,
   Came to Lebanon
   And took from the cedar the highest
       branch.
4   He cropped off its topmost young twig
   And carried it to a land of trade;
   He set it in a city of merchants.
5   Then he took some of the seed of the
       land
   And planted it in a fertile field;
   He placed *it* by abundant waters
   And set it like a willow tree.
6   And it grew and became a spreading
       vine of low stature;
   Its branches turned toward him,
   But its roots were under it.
   So it became a vine,
   Brought forth branches,
   And put forth shoots.

7   "But there was anotherᵃ great eagle
       with large wings and many
       feathers;
   And behold, this vine bent its roots
       toward him,

16:50 ᵃVulgate reads *you saw;* Septuagint reads *he saw;* Targum reads *as was revealed to Me.*
16:57 ᵃFollowing Masoretic Text, Septuagint, Targum, and Vulgate; many Hebrew manuscripts and Syriac read *Edom.*   17:7 ᵃFollowing Septuagint, Syriac, and Vulgate; Masoretic Text and Targum read *one.*

And stretched its branches toward
    him,
From the garden terrace where it had
    been planted,
That he might water it.
8 It was planted in good soil by many
    waters,
To bring forth branches, bear fruit,
And become a majestic vine." '

9"Say, 'Thus says the Lord GOD:

"Will it thrive?
Will he not pull up its roots,
Cut off its fruit,
And leave it to wither?
All of its spring leaves will wither,
And no great power or many people
Will be needed to pluck it up by its
    roots.
10 Behold, *it is* planted,
Will it thrive?
Will it not utterly wither when the
    east wind touches it?
It will wither in the garden terrace
    where it grew." ' "

11Moreover the word of the LORD came
to me, saying, 12"Say now to the rebellious
house: 'Do you not know what these *things
mean?*' Tell *them,* 'Indeed the king of Babylon went to Jerusalem and took its king
and princes, and led them with him to
Babylon. 13And he took the king's offspring,
made a covenant with him, and put him
under oath. He also took away the mighty
of the land, 14that the kingdom might be
brought low and not lift itself up, *but* that
by keeping his covenant it might stand.
15But he rebelled against him by sending
his ambassadors to Egypt, that they might
give him horses and many people. Will he
prosper? Will he who does such *things* escape? Can he break a covenant and still be
delivered?

16'*As* I live,' says the Lord GOD, 'surely
in the place *where* the king *dwells* who
made him king, whose oath he despised
and whose covenant he broke—with him in
the midst of Babylon he shall die. 17Nor
will Pharaoh with *his* mighty army and
great company do anything in the war,
when they heap up a siege mound and

build a wall to cut off many persons.
18Since he despised the oath by breaking
the covenant, and in fact gave his hand
and still did all these *things,* he shall not
escape.' "

19Therefore thus says the Lord GOD:
"*As* I live, surely My oath which he despised, and My covenant which he broke, I
will recompense on his own head. 20I will
spread My net over him, and he shall be
taken in My snare. I will bring him to
Babylon and try him there for the treason
which he committed against Me. 21All his
fugitives[a] with all his troops shall fall by
the sword, and those who remain shall be
scattered to every wind; and you shall
know that I, the LORD, have spoken."

Israel Exalted at Last

22Thus says the Lord GOD: "I will take
also *one* of the highest branches of the high
cedar and set *it* out. I will crop off from the
topmost of its young twigs a tender one,
and will plant *it* on a high and prominent
mountain. 23On the mountain height of Israel I will plant it; and it will bring forth
boughs, and bear fruit, and be a majestic
cedar. Under it will dwell birds of every
sort; in the shadow of its branches they
will dwell. 24And all the trees of the field
shall know that I, the LORD, have brought
down the high tree and exalted the low
tree, dried up the green tree and made the
dry tree flourish; I, the LORD, have spoken
and have done *it.*"

A False Proverb Refuted

18 1The word of the LORD came to me
again, saying, 2"What do you mean
when you use this proverb concerning the
land of Israel, saying:

'The fathers have eaten sour grapes,
And the children's teeth are set on
    edge'?

3"*As* I live," says the Lord GOD, "you
shall no longer use this proverb in Israel.

4 "Behold, all souls are Mine;
The soul of the father
As well as the soul of the son is Mine;
The soul who sins shall die.
5 But if a man is just
And does what is lawful and right;
6 If he has not eaten on the mountains,
Nor lifted up his eyes to the idols of
    the house of Israel,

17:21 [a]Following Masoretic Text and Vulgate; many
Hebrew manuscripts and Syriac read *choice men;*
Targum reads *mighty men;* Septuagint omits *All his
fugitives.*

Nor defiled his neighbor's wife,
Nor approached a woman during her
  impurity;
7 If he has not oppressed anyone,
But has restored to the debtor his
  pledge;
Has robbed no one by violence,
But has given his bread to the hungry
And covered the naked with clothing;
8 If he has not exacted usury
Nor taken any increase,
But has withdrawn his hand from
  iniquity
And executed true judgment between
  man and man;
9 *If* he has walked in My statutes
And kept My judgments faithfully—
He *is* just;
He shall surely live!"
Says the Lord GOD.

10 "If he begets a son *who is* a robber
Or a shedder of blood,
Who does any of these *things*
11 And does none of those *duties,*
But has eaten on the mountains
Or defiled his neighbor's wife;
12 If he has oppressed the poor and
  needy,
Robbed by violence,
Not restored the pledge,
Lifted his eyes to the idols,
Or committed abomination;
13 If he has exacted usury
Or taken increase—
Shall he then live?
He shall not live!
If he has done any of these
  abominations,
He shall surely die;
His blood shall be upon him.

14 "*If,* however, he begets a son
Who sees all the sins which his father
  has done,
And considers but does not do
  likewise;
15 *Who* has not eaten on the mountains,
Nor lifted his eyes to the idols of the
  house of Israel,

Nor defiled his neighbor's wife;
16 Has not oppressed anyone,
Nor withheld a pledge,
Nor robbed by violence,
But has given his bread to the hungry
And covered the naked with clothing;
17 *Who* has withdrawn his hand from the
  poor[a]
And not received usury or increase,
But has executed My judgments
And walked in My statutes—
He shall not die for the iniquity of his
  father;
He shall surely live!

18 "*As for* his father,
Because he cruelly oppressed,
Robbed his brother by violence,
And did what *is* not good among his
  people,
Behold, he shall die for his iniquity.

Turn and Live

19"Yet you say, 'Why should the son not bear the guilt of the father?' Because the son has done what is lawful and right, and has kept all My statutes and observed them, he shall surely live. 20The soul who sins shall die. The son shall not bear the guilt of the father, nor the father bear the guilt of the son. The righteousness of the righteous shall be upon himself, and the wickedness of the wicked shall be upon himself.

21"But if a wicked man turns from all his sins which he has committed, keeps all My statutes, and does what is lawful and right, he shall surely live; he shall not die. 22None of the transgressions which he has committed shall be remembered against him; because of the righteousness which he has done, he shall live. 23Do I have any pleasure at all that the wicked should die?" says the Lord GOD, "and not that he should turn from his ways and live?

18:17 [a]Following Masoretic Text, Targum, and Vulgate; Septuagint reads *iniquity* (compare verse 8).

TRADE AND ECONOMICS

In the ancient world, interest on loans was considered an improper way of making money. The Law of Moses allowed interest to be taken from strangers, but loans to and from Israelites were not permitted to accumulate interest (Ex. 22:25; Lev. 25:35, 36; Deut. 23:20). As Ezekiel summarizes God's law of individual responsibility, he forbids one to gain "increase" by "usury" (Ezek. 18:8).

24"But when a righteous man turns away from his righteousness and commits iniquity, and does according to all the abominations that the wicked *man* does, shall he live? All the righteousness which he has done shall not be remembered; because of the unfaithfulness of which he is guilty and the sin which he has committed, because of them he shall die.

25"Yet you say, 'The way of the Lord is not fair.' Hear now, O house of Israel, is it not My way which is fair, and your ways which are not fair? 26When a righteous *man* turns away from his righteousness, commits iniquity, and dies in it, it is because of the iniquity which he has done that he dies. 27Again, when a wicked *man* turns away from the wickedness which he committed, and does what is lawful and right, he preserves himself alive. 28Because he considers and turns away from all the transgressions which he committed, he shall surely live; he shall not die. 29Yet the house of Israel says, 'The way of the Lord is not fair.' O house of Israel, is it not My ways which are fair, and your ways which are not fair?

30"Therefore I will judge you, O house of Israel, every one according to his ways," says the Lord GOD. "Repent, and turn from all your transgressions, so that iniquity will not be your ruin. 31Cast away from you all the transgressions which you have committed, and get yourselves a new heart and a new spirit. For why should you die, O house of Israel? 32For I have no pleasure in the death of one who dies," says the Lord GOD. "Therefore turn and live!"

Ezekiel 20:1—21:17
The Rebellions of Israel

20 :1 It came to pass in the seventh year, in the fifth *month,* on the tenth *day* of the month, *that* certain of the elders of Israel came to inquire of the LORD, and sat before me. 2Then the word of the LORD came to me, saying, 3"Son of man, speak to the elders of Israel, and say to them, 'Thus says the Lord GOD: "Have you come to inquire of Me? *As* I live," says the Lord GOD, "I will not be inquired of by you." ' 4Will you judge them, son of man, will you judge *them?* Then make known to them the abominations of their fathers.

5"Say to them, 'Thus says the Lord GOD: "On the day when I chose Israel and raised My hand in an oath to the descendants of the house of Jacob, and made Myself known to them in the land of Egypt, I raised My hand in an oath to them, saying, 'I *am* the LORD your God.' 6On that day I raised My hand in an oath to them, to bring them out of the land of Egypt into a land that I had searched out for them, 'flowing with milk and honey,'a the glory of all lands. 7Then I said to them, 'Each of you, throw away the abominations which are before his eyes, and do not defile yourselves with the idols of Egypt. I *am* the LORD your God.' 8But they rebelled against Me and would not obey Me. They did not all cast away the abominations which were before their eyes, nor did they forsake the idols of Egypt. Then I said, 'I will pour out My fury on them and fulfill My anger against them in the midst of the land of Egypt.' 9But I acted for My name's sake, that it should not be profaned before the Gentiles among whom they *were,* in whose sight I had made Myself known to them, to bring them out of the land of Egypt.

10"Therefore I made them go out of the land of Egypt and brought them into the wilderness. 11And I gave them My statutes and showed them My judgments, 'which, *if* a man does, he shall live by them.'a 12Moreover I also gave them My Sabbaths, to be a sign between them and Me, that they might know that I *am* the LORD who sanctifies them. 13Yet the house of Israel rebelled against Me in the wilderness; they did not walk in My statutes; they despised My judgments, 'which, *if* a man does, he shall live by them';a and they greatly defiled My Sabbaths. Then I said I would pour out My fury on them in the wilderness, to consume them. 14But I acted for My name's sake, that it should not be profaned before the Gentiles, in whose sight I had brought them out. 15So I also raised My hand in an oath to them in the wilderness, that I would not bring them into the land which I had given *them,* 'flowing with milk and honey,'a the glory of all lands, 16because they despised My judgments and did not walk in My statutes, but profaned My Sabbaths; for their heart went after their idols. 17Nevertheless My eye spared them from destruction. I did not make an end of them in the wilderness.

20:6 aExodus 3:8   20:11 aLeviticus 18:5
20:13 aLeviticus 18:5   20:15 aExodus 3:8

A CONSULTATION WITH A PROPHET (Ezek. 20:1–3)

Ezekiel pursued his prophetic ministry in public. He continuously went out into the public realm to proclaim a message from God or to engage in symbolic actions that communicated the divine message to the exilic community.

A different situation occurs when the "elders of Israel" approach Ezekiel. These elders, who were the leaders of Ezekiel's exilic community in Babylon, came to the prophet in order to "inquire of the LORD" (Ezek. 20:1).

"Inquiring of a god" recalls the professional prophets that existed throughout the ancient Near East, including Babylon. For a fee individuals or groups could approach a prophet to receive oracular advice in the form of an omen from their deity. Often the prophet, "possessed by the spirit of the god," would enter a trance before presenting the message of the god by offering the appropriate response.

Interestingly, the leaders of Ezekiel's exilic community perceived him this way. Indeed, they "sat before" Ezekiel, as if waiting for a "spirit" to take possession of the prophet (20:1). God, however, rejected this model for Ezekiel. In keeping with God's prohibition (Ezek. 14:1–3), Ezekiel refused to prophesy in answer to the elders' questions. He was not a prophet-for-hire. Rather, the elders received a stinging indictment from God for their behavior (20:4–32), along with God's refusal: "I will not be inquired of by you" (20:3, 31).

18"But I said to their children in the wilderness, 'Do not walk in the statutes of your fathers, nor observe their judgments, nor defile yourselves with their idols. 19I *am* the LORD your God: Walk in My statutes, keep My judgments, and do them; 20hallow My Sabbaths, and they will be a sign between Me and you, that you may know that I *am* the LORD your God.'

21"Notwithstanding, the children rebelled against Me; they did not walk in My statutes, and were not careful to observe My judgments, 'which, *if* a man does, he shall live by them';a but they profaned My Sabbaths. Then I said I would pour out My fury on them and fulfill My anger against them in the wilderness. 22Nevertheless I withdrew My hand and acted for My name's sake, that it should not be profaned in the sight of the Gentiles, in whose sight I had brought them out. 23Also I raised My hand in an oath to those in the wilderness, that I would scatter them among the Gentiles and disperse them throughout the countries, 24because they had not executed My judgments, but had despised My statutes, profaned My Sabbaths, and their eyes were fixed on their fathers' idols.

25"Therefore I also gave them up to statutes *that were* not good, and judgments by which they could not live; 26and I pronounced them unclean because of their ritual gifts, in that they caused all their firstborn to pass through *the fire,* that I might make them desolate and that they might know that I am the LORD." '

27"Therefore, son of man, speak to the house of Israel, and say to them, 'Thus says the Lord GOD: "In this too your fathers have blasphemed Me, by being unfaithful to Me. 28When I brought them into the land *concerning* which I had raised My hand in an oath to give them, and they saw all the high hills and all the thick trees, there they offered their sacrifices and provoked Me with their offerings. There they also sent up their sweet aroma and poured out their drink offerings. 29Then I said to them, 'What *is* this high place to which you go?' So its name is called Bamaha to this day." ' 30Therefore say to the house of Israel, 'Thus says the Lord GOD: "Are you defiling yourselves in the manner of your fathers, and committing harlotry according to their abominations? 31For when you offer your gifts and make your sons pass through the fire, you defile yourselves with all your idols, even to this day. So shall I be inquired of by you, O house of Israel? *As* I live," says the Lord GOD, "I will not be inquired of by you. 32What you have in your mind shall never be, when you say, 'We will be like the Gentiles, like the families in other countries, serving wood and stone.'

20:21 aLeviticus 18:5   20:29 aLiterally *High Place*

God Will Restore Israel

³³"*As* I live," says the Lord GOD, "surely with a mighty hand, with an outstretched arm, and with fury poured out, I will rule over you. ³⁴I will bring you out from the peoples and gather you out of the countries where you are scattered, with a mighty hand, with an outstretched arm, and with fury poured out. ³⁵And I will bring you into the wilderness of the peoples, and there I will plead My case with you face to face. ³⁶Just as I pleaded My case with your fathers in the wilderness of the land of Egypt, so I will plead My case with you," says the Lord GOD.

³⁷"I will make you pass under the rod, and I will bring you into the bond of the covenant; ³⁸I will purge the rebels from among you, and those who transgress against Me; I will bring them out of the country where they dwell, but they shall not enter the land of Israel. Then you will know that I *am* the LORD.

³⁹"As for you, O house of Israel," thus says the Lord GOD: "Go, serve every one of you his idols—and hereafter—if you will not obey Me; but profane My holy name no more with your gifts and your idols. ⁴⁰For on My holy mountain, on the mountain height of Israel," says the Lord GOD, "there all the house of Israel, all of them in the land, shall serve Me; there I will accept them, and there I will require your offerings and the firstfruits of your sacrifices, together with all your holy things. ⁴¹I will accept you as a sweet aroma when I bring you out from the peoples and gather you out of the countries where you have been scattered; and I will be hallowed in you before the Gentiles. ⁴²Then you shall know that I *am* the LORD, when I bring you into the land of Israel, into the country *for* which I raised My hand in an oath to give to your fathers. ⁴³And there you shall remember your ways and all your doings with which you were defiled; and you shall loathe yourselves in your own sight because of all the evils that you have committed. ⁴⁴Then you shall know that I *am* the LORD, when I have dealt with you for My name's sake, not according to your wicked ways nor according to your corrupt doings, O house of Israel," says the Lord GOD.' "

Fire in the Forest

⁴⁵Furthermore the word of the LORD came to me, saying, ⁴⁶"Son of man, set your face toward the south; preach against the south and prophesy against the forest land, the South,^a ⁴⁷and say to the forest of the South, 'Hear the word of the LORD! Thus says the Lord GOD: "Behold, I will kindle a fire in you, and it shall devour every green tree and every dry tree in you; the blazing flame shall not be quenched, and all faces from the south to the north shall be scorched by it. ⁴⁸All flesh shall see that I, the LORD, have kindled it; it shall not be quenched." ' "

⁴⁹Then I said, "Ah, Lord GOD! They say of me, 'Does he not speak parables?' "

Babylon, the Sword of God

21 ¹And the word of the LORD came to me, saying, ²"Son of man, set your face toward Jerusalem, preach against the holy places, and prophesy against the land of Israel; ³and say to the land of Israel, 'Thus says the LORD: "Behold, I *am* against you, and I will draw My sword out of its sheath and cut off both righteous and wicked from you. ⁴Because I will cut off both righteous and wicked from you, therefore My sword shall go out of its sheath against all flesh from south *to* north, ⁵that all flesh may know that I, the LORD, have drawn My sword out of its sheath; it shall not return anymore." ' ⁶Sigh therefore, son of man, with a breaking heart, and sigh with bitterness before their eyes. ⁷And it shall be when they say to you, 'Why are you sighing?' that you shall answer, 'Because of the news; when it comes, every heart will melt, all hands will be feeble, every spirit will faint, and all knees will be weak *as* water. Behold, it is coming and shall be brought to pass,' says the Lord GOD."

⁸Again the word of the LORD came to me, saying, ⁹"Son of man, prophesy and say, 'Thus says the LORD!' Say:

'A sword, a sword is sharpened
And also polished!
¹⁰ Sharpened to make a dreadful
    slaughter,
Polished to flash like lightning!
Should we then make mirth?
It despises the scepter of My son,
As it does all wood.
¹¹ And He has given it to be polished,
That it may be handled;

This sword is sharpened, and it is
     polished
To be given into the hand of the
     slayer.'

12   "Cry and wail, son of man;
     For it will be against My people,
     Against all the princes of Israel.
     Terrors including the sword will be
         against My people;
     Therefore strike *your* thigh.

13   "Because *it is* a testing,
     And what if *the sword* despises even
         the scepter?
     The scepter shall be no *more*,"

says the Lord GOD.

14   "You therefore, son of man, prophesy,
     And strike *your* hands together.
     The third time let the sword do double
         damage.
     It *is* the sword *that* slays,
     The sword that slays the great *men,*
     That enters their private chambers.
15   I have set the point of the sword
         against all their gates,
     That the heart may melt and many
         may stumble.
     Ah! *It is* made bright;
     It is grasped for slaughter:

16   "Swords at the ready!
     Thrust right!
     Set your blade!
     Thrust left—
     Wherever your edge is ordered!

17   "I also will beat My fists together,
     And I will cause My fury to rest;
     I, the LORD, have spoken."

Ezekiel 22:1–22
Sins of Jerusalem

22 :1 Moreover the word of the LORD
came to me, saying, 2"Now, son of
man, will you judge, will you judge the
bloody city? Yes, show her all her abominations! 3Then say, 'Thus says the Lord GOD:
"The city sheds blood in her own midst,
that her time may come; and she makes
idols within herself to defile herself. 4You
have become guilty by the blood which you
have shed, and have defiled yourself with
the idols which you have made. You have
caused your days to draw near, and have
come to *the end of* your years; therefore I

have made you a reproach to the nations,
and a mockery to all countries. 5*Those* near
and *those* far from you will mock you as infamous *and* full of tumult.

6"Look, the princes of Israel: each one
has used his power to shed blood in you.
7In you they have made light of father and
mother; in your midst they have oppressed
the stranger; in you they have mistreated
the fatherless and the widow. 8You have despised My holy things and profaned My
Sabbaths. 9In you are men who slander to
cause bloodshed; in you are those who eat
on the mountains; in your midst they commit lewdness. 10In you men uncover their
fathers' nakedness; in you they violate
women who are set apart during their impurity. 11One commits abomination with
his neighbor's wife; another lewdly defiles
his daughter-in-law; and another in you vi-
olates his sister, his father's daughter. 12In
you they take bribes to shed blood; you
take usury and increase; you have made
profit from your neighbors by extortion,
and have forgotten Me," says the Lord
GOD.

13"Behold, therefore, I beat My fists at
the dishonest profit which you have made,
and at the bloodshed which has been in
your midst. 14Can your heart endure, or
can your hands remain strong, in the days
when I shall deal with you? I, the LORD,
have spoken, and will do *it.* 15I will scatter
you among the nations, disperse you
throughout the countries, and remove your
filthiness completely from you. 16You shall
defile yourself in the sight of the nations;
then you shall know that I *am* the
LORD." ' "

Israel in the Furnace

17The word of the LORD came to me,
saying, 18"Son of man, the house of Israel
has become dross to Me; they *are* all
bronze, tin, iron, and lead, in the midst of a
furnace; they have become dross from silver. 19Therefore thus says the Lord GOD:
'Because you have all become dross, therefore behold, I will gather you into the midst
of Jerusalem. 20*As men* gather silver,
bronze, iron, lead, and tin into the midst of
a furnace, to blow fire on it, to melt *it;* so I
will gather *you* in My anger and in My
fury, and I will leave *you there* and melt
you. 21Yes, I will gather you and blow on
you with the fire of My wrath, and you
shall be melted in its midst. 22As silver is
melted in the midst of a furnace, so shall

you be melted in its midst; then you shall know that I, the LORD, have poured out My fury on you.' "

Ezekiel 23:1–49
Two Harlot Sisters

23 :1 The word of the LORD came again to me, saying:

2 "Son of man, there were two women,
The daughters of one mother.
3 They committed harlotry in Egypt,
They committed harlotry in their youth;
Their breasts were there embraced,
Their virgin bosom was there pressed.
4 Their names: Oholah[a] the elder and Oholibah[b] her sister;
They were Mine,
And they bore sons and daughters.
As for their names,
Samaria *is* Oholah, and Jerusalem *is* Oholibah.

The Older Sister, Samaria

5 "Oholah played the harlot even though she was Mine;
And she lusted for her lovers, the neighboring Assyrians,
6 *Who were* clothed in purple,
Captains and rulers,
All of them desirable young men,
Horsemen riding on horses.
7 Thus she committed her harlotry with them,
All of them choice men of Assyria;
And with all for whom she lusted,
With all their idols, she defiled herself.
8 She has never given up her harlotry *brought* from Egypt,
For in her youth they had lain with her,
Pressed her virgin bosom,
And poured out their immorality upon her.

9 "Therefore I have delivered her
Into the hand of her lovers,
Into the hand of the Assyrians,
For whom she lusted.
10 They uncovered her nakedness,
Took away her sons and daughters,
And slew her with the sword;
She became a byword among women,

For they had executed judgment on her.

The Younger Sister, Jerusalem

11 "Now although her sister Oholibah saw *this,* she became more corrupt in her lust than she, and in her harlotry more corrupt than her sister's harlotry.

12 "She lusted for the neighboring Assyrians,
Captains and rulers,
Clothed most gorgeously,
Horsemen riding on horses,
All of them desirable young men.
13 Then I saw that she was defiled;
Both *took* the same way.
14 But she increased her harlotry;
She looked at men portrayed on the wall,
Images of Chaldeans portrayed in vermilion,
15 Girded with belts around their waists,
Flowing turbans on their heads,
All of them looking like captains,
In the manner of the Babylonians of Chaldea,
The land of their nativity.
16 As soon as her eyes saw them,
She lusted for them
And sent messengers to them in Chaldea.

17 "Then the Babylonians came to her, into the bed of love,
And they defiled her with their immorality;
So she was defiled by them, and alienated herself from them.
18 She revealed her harlotry and uncovered her nakedness.
Then I alienated Myself from her,
As I had alienated Myself from her sister.

19 "Yet she multiplied her harlotry
In calling to remembrance the days of her youth,
When she had played the harlot in the land of Egypt.
20 For she lusted for her paramours,
Whose flesh *is like* the flesh of donkeys,
And whose issue *is like* the issue of horses.
21 Thus you called to remembrance the lewdness of your youth,

---

23:4 [a]Literally *Her Own Tabernacle* [b]Literally *My Tabernacle Is in Her*

When the Egyptians pressed your
   bosom
Because of your youthful breasts.

Judgment on Jerusalem

22"Therefore, Oholibah, thus says the
Lord GOD:

'Behold, I will stir up your lovers
   against you,
From whom you have alienated
   yourself,
And I will bring them against you
   from every side:
23   The Babylonians,
   All the Chaldeans,
   Pekod, Shoa, Koa,
   All the Assyrians with them,
   All of them desirable young men,
   Governors and rulers,
   Captains and men of renown,
   All of them riding on horses.
24   And they shall come against you
   With chariots, wagons, and war-
     horses,
   With a horde of people.
   They shall array against you
   Buckler, shield, and helmet all
     around.

'I will delegate judgment to them,
And they shall judge you according to
   their judgments.
25   I will set My jealousy against you,
   And they shall deal furiously with
     you;
   They shall remove your nose and your
     ears,
   And your remnant shall fall by the
     sword;
   They shall take your sons and your
     daughters,
   And your remnant shall be devoured
     by fire.
26   They shall also strip you of your
     clothes
   And take away your beautiful jewelry.

27   'Thus I will make you cease your
     lewdness and your harlotry

Brought from the land of Egypt,
So that you will not lift your eyes to
   them,
Nor remember Egypt anymore.'

28"For thus says the Lord GOD: 'Surely
I will deliver you into the hand of those you
hate, into the hand *of those* from whom you
alienated yourself. 29They will deal hate-
fully with you, take away all you have
worked for, and leave you naked and bare.
The nakedness of your harlotry shall be
uncovered, both your lewdness and your
harlotry. 30I will do these *things* to you because you have gone as a harlot after the
Gentiles, because you have become defiled
by their idols. 31You have walked in the
way of your sister; therefore I will put her
cup in your hand.'

32"Thus says the Lord GOD:

'You shall drink of your sister's cup,
   The deep and wide one;
You shall be laughed to scorn
   And held in derision;
   It contains much.
33   You will be filled with drunkenness
     and sorrow,
   The cup of horror and desolation,
   The cup of your sister Samaria.
34   You shall drink and drain it,
   You shall break its shards,
   And tear at your own breasts;
   For I have spoken,'
   Says the Lord GOD.

35"Therefore thus says the Lord GOD:

'Because you have forgotten Me and
   cast Me behind your back,
Therefore you shall bear the *penalty*
Of your lewdness and your harlotry.' "

Both Sisters Judged

36The LORD also said to me: "Son of
man, will you judge Oholah and Oholibah?
Then declare to them their abominations.
37For they have committed adultery, and
blood *is* on their hands. They have commit-

POLITICS AND GOVERNMENT

*The cruelty of the Assyrians is proverbial. Their inscriptions boast of how they abused,
mutilated, and killed their prisoners taken in war, whether soldiers or civilians. Their
sculptural reliefs depict scribes taking notes while the condemned hang exposed on
stakes near the city walls. The Babylonians, while not the military nation that Assyria
was, could still be cruel in war (Ezek. 23:25; 2 Kin. 25:6, 7).*

ted adultery with their idols, and even sacrificed their sons whom they bore to Me, passing them through *the fire,* to devour *them.* ³⁸Moreover they have done this to Me: They have defiled My sanctuary on the same day and profaned My Sabbaths. ³⁹For after they had slain their children for their idols, on the same day they came into My sanctuary to profane it; and indeed thus they have done in the midst of My house.

⁴⁰"Furthermore you sent for men to come from afar, to whom a messenger *was* sent; and there they came. And you washed yourself for them, painted your eyes, and adorned yourself with ornaments. ⁴¹You sat on a stately couch, with a table prepared before it, on which you had set My incense and My oil. ⁴²The sound of a carefree multitude *was* with her, and Sabeans *were* brought from the wilderness with men of the common sort, who put bracelets on their wrists and beautiful crowns on their heads. ⁴³Then I said concerning *her who had grown* old in adulteries, 'Will they commit harlotry with her now, and she *with them?*' ⁴⁴Yet they went in to her, as men go in to a woman who plays the harlot; thus they went in to Oholah and Oholibah, the lewd women. ⁴⁵But righteous men will judge them after the manner of adulteresses, and after the manner of women who shed blood, because they *are* adulteresses, and blood *is* on their hands.

⁴⁶"For thus says the Lord GOD: 'Bring up an assembly against them, give them up to trouble and plunder. ⁴⁷The assembly shall stone them with stones and execute them with their swords; they shall slay their sons and their daughters, and burn their houses with fire. ⁴⁸Thus I will cause lewdness to cease from the land, that all women may be taught not to practice your lewdness. ⁴⁹They shall repay you for your lewdness, and you shall pay for your idolatrous sins. Then you shall know that I *am* the Lord GOD.' "

Israel and Ammon Rebel

When Zedekiah made his alliance with Pharaoh Hophra of Egypt and rebelled against Babylon, he was evidently joined by the land of Ammon, on the eastern side of the Jordan (Jer. 27:3). In Ezek. 21:18–23, Ezekiel pictures Nebuchadnezzar, on his way south, stopping to decide which nation to punish first. It would make little difference: neither would escape punishment, and Israel's King Zedekiah, the "profane, wicked prince" (21:25), would be overthrown (21:24–32).

In the 9th year of Jehoiachin's exile (Ezek. 24:1), the siege of Jerusalem began, perhaps in January of 588 B.C. Ezekiel's message—both by word and by deed—was for the exiles to prepare to lose their beloved city and temple (ch. 24).

■ Ezekiel 21:18–32
■ Ezekiel 24:1–27

Ezekiel 21:18–32

21:18 The word of the LORD came to me again, saying: ¹⁹"And son of man, appoint for yourself two ways for the sword of the king of Babylon to go; both of them shall go from the same land. Make a sign; put *it* at the head of the road to the city. ²⁰Appoint a road for the sword to go to Rabbah of the Ammonites, and to Judah, into fortified Jerusalem. ²¹For the king of Babylon stands at the parting of the road, at the fork of the two roads, to use divination: he shakes the arrows, he consults the

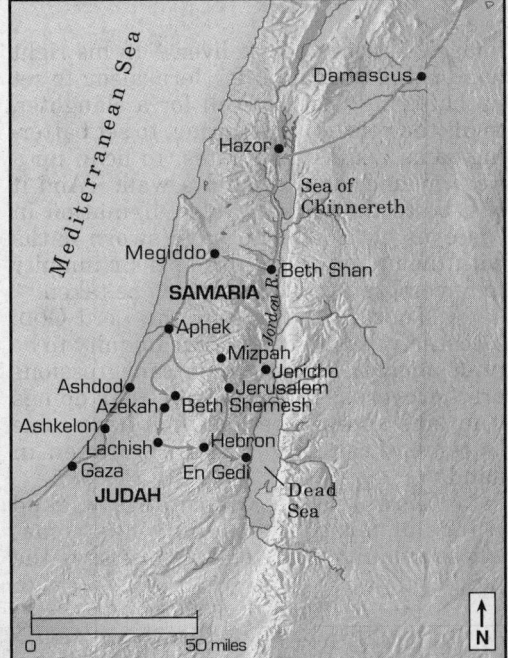

Nebuchadnezzar's Campaigns Against Judah
From 605 to 586 B.C. Nebuchadnezzar conducted several campaigns in Judah. King Jehoiachin was forced to surrender to Nebuchadnezzar in 597 B.C. Jerusalem's destruction came in 586 B.C. as the Babylonians approached from the south.

AMMONITES, A VASSAL PEOPLE (Ezek. 21:19, 20)

The Ammonites were located in central Transjordan along the Jabbok River. Genesis reports that they were descended from Ben-Ammi, the son of an incestuous union between Lot (the nephew of Abraham) and one of Lot's daughters (Gen. 19:36–38).

Although the Ammonites and Israelites were considered to be related, their relationship was often one of conflict. During the judges' period Jephthah successfully defended the Gileadites against an Ammonite attack (Judg. 11:4–6, 32, 33). Saul rescued Jabesh Gilead from a siege by the Ammonite king Nahash (1 Sam. 11:1–3, 11). Conflict again broke out when Hanun succeeded his father Nahash as king of Ammon (2 Sam. 10:1). Israel's king David captured Rabbah, the Ammonite capital, and made the Ammonites a vassal state of Israel (2 Sam. 11:1; 12:26–31).

Documents from the Neo-Assyrian Empire show that the Ammonites were a vassal of Assyria during the period of Assyrian power (c. 742–630 B.C.). The annals of the Assyrian king Tiglath-Pileser III state that about 733 B.C. a certain Shanip of Bit-Ammon paid tribute to him. Two later Assyrian kings, Sennacherib (704–681 B.C.) and Ashurbanipal (668–627 B.C.) also list Ammonite kings who continued the tradition of paying tribute to Assyria.

After the fall of Assyria in 612 B.C. the Ammonites were independent, but not for long. The prophet Ezekiel pictures Babylon's king at a crossroads: one road to Judah's capital Jerusalem; the other to Ammon's Rabbah (Ezek. 21:19, 20). The decision was to proceed to Jerusalem, which fell to the Babylonians in 586 B.C. However, the Ammonites would face a similar fate about 5 years later. The Jewish historian Josephus states that Ammon was defeated by Nebuchadnezzar II of Babylon in 582–581 B.C. (see Ezek. 21:28–32).

images, he looks at the liver. ²²In his right hand is the divination for Jerusalem: to set up battering rams, to call for a slaughter, to lift the voice with shouting, to set battering rams against the gates, to heap up a *siege* mound, and to build a wall. ²³And it will be to them like a false divination in the eyes of those who have sworn oaths with them; but he will bring their iniquity to remembrance, that they may be taken.

²⁴"Therefore thus says the Lord GOD: 'Because you have made your iniquity to be remembered, in that your transgressions are uncovered, so that in all your doings your sins appear—because you have come to remembrance, you shall be taken in hand.

²⁵'Now to you, O profane, wicked prince of Israel, whose day has come, whose iniquity *shall* end, ²⁶thus says the Lord GOD:

"Remove the turban, and take off the crown;
Nothing *shall remain* the same.
Exalt the humble, and humble the exalted.
27 Overthrown, overthrown,
I will make it overthrown!
It shall be no *longer,*
Until He comes whose right it is,
And I will give it *to Him.*"'

A Sword Against the Ammonites

²⁸"And you, son of man, prophesy and say, 'Thus says the Lord GOD concerning the Ammonites and concerning their reproach,' and say:

'A sword, a sword *is* drawn,
Polished for slaughter,
For consuming, for flashing—
29 While they see false visions for you,

CULTS AND SUPERNATURAL

Before going into battle, kings first consulted the gods (Ezek. 21:21). Divination was used to determine the divine will in a certain situation. Arrows were used something like dice, by throwing them and noting how they fell. Priests in Babylon inspected carefully and interpreted the livers of sacrificed animals. The shape and coloring of the liver was interpreted as if it were writing or an enigmatic sign from heaven.

While they divine a lie to you,
To bring you on the necks of the
    wicked, the slain
Whose day has come,
Whose iniquity *shall* end.

30 'Return *it* to its sheath.
I will judge you
In the place where you were created,
In the land of your nativity.
31 I will pour out My indignation on you;
I will blow against you with the fire of
    My wrath,
And deliver you into the hands of
    brutal men *who are* skillful to
    destroy.
32 You shall be fuel for the fire;
Your blood shall be in the midst of the
    land.
You shall not be remembered,
For I the LORD have spoken.' "

Ezekiel 24:1–27
Symbol of the Cooking Pot

24 :1 Again, in the ninth year, in the tenth month, on the tenth *day* of the month, the word of the LORD came to me, saying, 2"Son of man, write down the name of the day, this very day—the king of Babylon started his siege against Jerusalem this very day. 3And utter a parable to the rebellious house, and say to them, 'Thus says the Lord GOD:

"Put on a pot, set *it* on,
And also pour water into it.
4 Gather pieces *of meat* in it,
Every good piece,
The thigh and the shoulder.
Fill *it* with choice cuts;
5 Take the choice of the flock.
Also pile *fuel* bones under it,
Make it boil well,
And let the cuts simmer in it."

6"Therefore thus says the Lord GOD:

"Woe to the bloody city,
To the pot whose scum *is* in it,
And whose scum is not gone from it!
Bring it out piece by piece,
On which no lot has fallen.
7 For her blood is in her midst;
She set it on top of a rock;
She did not pour it on the ground,
To cover it with dust.

8 That it may raise up fury and take
    vengeance,
I have set her blood on top of a rock,
That it may not be covered."

9"Therefore thus says the Lord GOD:

"Woe to the bloody city!
I too will make the pyre great.
10 Heap on the wood,
Kindle the fire;
Cook the meat well,
Mix in the spices,
And let the cuts be burned up.

11 "Then set the pot empty on the coals,
That it may become hot and its bronze
    may burn,
That its filthiness may be melted in it,
That its scum may be consumed.
12 She has grown weary with lies,
And her great scum has not gone from
    her.
Let her scum *be* in the fire!
13 In your filthiness *is* lewdness.
Because I have cleansed you, and you
    were not cleansed,
You will not be cleansed of your
    filthiness anymore,
Till I have caused My fury to rest
    upon you.
14 I, the LORD, have spoken *it;*
It shall come to pass, and I will do *it;*
I will not hold back,
Nor will I spare,
Nor will I relent;
According to your ways
And according to your deeds
They[a] will judge you,"
Says the Lord GOD.' "

The Prophet's Wife Dies

15Also the word of the LORD came to me, saying, 16"Son of man, behold, I take away from you the desire of your eyes with one stroke; yet you shall neither mourn nor weep, nor shall your tears run down. 17Sigh in silence, make no mourning for the dead; bind your turban on your head, and put your sandals on your feet; do not cover *your* lips, and do not eat man's bread *of sorrow*."

18So I spoke to the people in the morning, and at evening my wife died; and the next morning I did as I was commanded.

19And the people said to me, "Will you not tell us what these *things signify* to us, that you behave so?"

20Then I answered them, "The word of the LORD came to me, saying, 21"Speak to

---

24:14 [a]Septuagint, Syriac, Targum, and Vulgate read *I*.

the house of Israel, "Thus says the Lord GOD: 'Behold, I will profane My sanctuary, your arrogant boast, the desire of your eyes, the delight of your soul; and your sons and daughters whom you left behind shall fall by the sword. 22And you shall do as I have done; you shall not cover *your* lips nor eat man's bread *of sorrow.* 23Your turbans shall be on your heads and your sandals on your feet; you shall neither mourn nor weep, but you shall pine away in your iniquities and mourn with one another. 24Thus Ezekiel is a sign to you; according to all that he has done you shall do; and when this comes, you shall know that I *am* the Lord GOD.' "

25"And you, son of man—*will it* not *be* in the day when I take from them their stronghold, their joy and their glory, the desire of their eyes, and that on which they set their minds, their sons and their daughters: 26*that* on that day one who escapes will come to you to let *you* hear *it* with *your* ears? 27On that day your mouth will be opened to him who has escaped; you shall speak and no longer be mute. Thus you will be a sign to them, and they shall know that I *am* the LORD.' "

Ezekiel's Sign Acts

Despite Ezekiel's warnings, news of Zedekiah's rebellion surely sparked hope among the exiles in Babylon that perhaps Jerusalem could indeed gain her independence. Ezekiel vehemently opposed these false hopes. His message to the exiles was the same as Jeremiah's message to those in Jerusalem, but Ezekiel's methods were quite distinct. Where Jeremiah would write soaring, impassioned poetry, Ezekiel communicated in blunt prose or—more distinctively—in pantomime.

In the divine visions Ezekiel received in 593 B.C. (Ezek. 1:1–3; 3:16, 22), he was commanded to enact before the exiles certain sign acts. These symbolic actions (3:22—7:27) dramatically portrayed the horrors of the siege that Jerusalem would undergo from 588 to 586 B.C.

■ Ezekiel 3:22—7:27

Ezekiel

3 :22 Then the hand of the LORD was upon me there, and He said to me, "Arise, go out into the plain, and there I shall talk with you."

23So I arose and went out into the plain, and behold, the glory of the LORD stood there, like the glory which I saw by the River Chebar; and I fell on my face. 24Then the Spirit entered me and set me on my feet, and spoke with me and said to me: "Go, shut yourself inside your house. 25And you, O son of man, surely they will put ropes on you and bind you with them, so that you cannot go out among them. 26I will make your tongue cling to the roof of your mouth, so that you shall be mute and not be one to rebuke them, for they *are* a rebellious house. 27But when I speak with you, I will open your mouth, and you shall say to them, 'Thus says the Lord GOD.' He who hears, let him hear; and he who refuses, let him refuse; for they *are* a rebellious house.

The Siege of Jerusalem Portrayed

4 1"You also, son of man, take a clay tablet and lay it before you, and portray on it a city, Jerusalem. 2Lay siege against it, build a siege wall against it, and heap up a mound against it; set camps against it also, and place battering rams against it all around. 3Moreover take for yourself an iron plate, and set it *as* an iron wall between you and the city. Set your face against it, and it shall be besieged, and you shall lay siege against it. This *will be* a sign to the house of Israel.

4"Lie also on your left side, and lay the iniquity of the house of Israel upon it. *According* to the number of the days that you lie on it, you shall bear their iniquity. 5For I have laid on you the years of their iniquity, according to the number of the days, three hundred and ninety days; so you shall bear the iniquity of the house of Is-

TIME CAPSULE   *589 to 587 B.C.*

589–570	*Hophra, pharaoh of Egypt, resides at Memphis*
588	*King Zedekiah revolts against the Babylonians*
588–586	*Nebuchadnezzar besieges Jerusalem*
587	*Pharaoh Hophra forces the Babylonian armies to lift the siege from Jerusalem (Jer. 37:5)*
587	*Jeremiah attempts to visit Anathoth but is arrested*

HOW TO CONDUCT A SIEGE (Ezek. 4:2, 3)

More than any other prophet, Ezekiel used "street theater" to convey his prophetic message. This prophet graphically portrayed a siege of Jerusalem to indicate God's judgment against the people (Ezek. 4).

The chief defense system of an Israelite city like Jerusalem was its walls. These were huge, thick, massive structures that completely surrounded the city. Already built on elevated land, the city walls made the city like a castle. Usually only one entryway into the city existed—the city gate. Gates, too, were large, complex structures, designed to inhibit a frontal attack on a city.

To counter this, an enemy would build a massive ramp—what Ezekiel calls "a siege wall" (Ezek. 4:2)—at the most vulnerable (that is, the lowest) point of the city wall. Using siege walls, the enemy could gain access to the city through a gradual incline to the height of the wall, rather than attempting to scale the walls like a cliff.

Other strategies that Ezekiel mentions are the siege "mound" and "battering rams" (4:2). The siege mound was a platform of earth, built to put some of the attackers level with the defenders on the wall. Defenders likewise built mounds on the inside of the walls. Battering rams were used to break down the fortifications.

The Judean exiles had just experienced these military techniques when Nebuchadnezzar besieged Jerusalem in 597 B.C. They no doubt heard quite well Ezekiel's message, as he used a scale model or drawings in the dirt to depict the siege machinery that would be brought against the city from 588 to 586 B.C. Ezekiel's street theater was a sign that the captives did not want to see.

---

rael. 6And when you have completed them, lie again on your right side; then you shall bear the iniquity of the house of Judah forty days. I have laid on you a day for each year.

7"Therefore you shall set your face toward the siege of Jerusalem; your arm *shall be* uncovered, and you shall prophesy against it. 8And surely I will restrain you so that you cannot turn from one side to another till you have ended the days of your siege.

9"Also take for yourself wheat, barley, beans, lentils, millet, and spelt; put them into one vessel, and make bread of them for yourself. *During* the number of days that you lie on your side, three hundred and ninety days, you shall eat it. 10And your food which you eat *shall be* by weight, twenty shekels a day; from time to time you shall eat it. 11You shall also drink water by measure, one-sixth of a hin; from time to time you shall drink. 12And you shall eat it *as* barley cakes; and bake it using fuel of human waste in their sight."

13Then the LORD said, "So shall the children of Israel eat their defiled bread among the Gentiles, where I will drive them."

14So I said, "Ah, Lord GOD! Indeed I have never defiled myself from my youth till now; I have never eaten what died of itself or was torn by beasts, nor has abominable flesh ever come into my mouth."

15Then He said to me, "See, I am giving you cow dung instead of human waste, and you shall prepare your bread over it."

16Moreover He said to me, "Son of man, surely I will cut off the supply of bread in Jerusalem; they shall eat bread by weight and with anxiety, and shall drink water by measure and with dread, 17that they may lack bread and water, and be dismayed with one another, and waste away because of their iniquity.

A Sword Against Jerusalem

5 1"And you, son of man, take a sharp sword, take it as a barber's razor, and pass *it* over your head and your beard; then take scales to weigh and divide the hair. 2You shall burn with fire one-third in the midst of the city, when the days of the siege are finished; then you shall take one-third and strike around *it* with the sword, and one-third you shall scatter in the wind: I will draw out a sword after them. 3You shall also take a small number of them and bind them in the edge of your *garment*. 4Then take some of them again and throw

EZEKIEL'S PROPHETIC THEATER (Ezek. 5:1–4)

As ancient Near Eastern prophets proclaimed a message from the gods, they often used more than words to get their message across. Often their very actions and lives illustrated the prophetic oracle. For no prophet was this more true than the prophet Ezekiel.

In one of his acted-out prophecies or sign acts, Ezekiel undergoes a haircut and a shave. The razor in this case, however, was to be a sword (Ezek. 5:1). Ezekiel then was to divide the hair into three parts: one-third to be burned in the midst of the city; a second third to be hit by a sword; another third to be scattered into the wind (5:2). Finally, from the last third, a small amount of hair was to be wrapped in Ezekiel's clothing, and later some of this would be thrown into a fire (5:3, 4).

Such symbolic actions seem bizarre, yet are significant for the prophet's message. First, the cutting of an adult male's hair and beard was a sign of humiliation. Using a sword as the razor, Ezekiel symbolically lived out with his own body the military humiliation that the Jerusalemites would face when the Babylonians conquered their city.

Yet the symbolism was even more precise. The burning of hair in the midst of the city and striking of hair with a sword signified the destruction of people when the Babylonians actually attacked Jerusalem. The scattered hair dramatically portrayed the fleeing of people into the countryside following the attack. The final third showed the destruction of the people after the attack. Only a few hairs, or people, wrapped into Ezekiel's clothing, would survive. Ezekiel's "haircut," thus portrayed an entire drama of death and destruction brought on by the Babylonian attack upon the city.

It is not known where Ezekiel undertook these activities. From his other prophetic behavior, however, we can assume that he performed these actions very much in the public eye, proclaiming Yahweh's message through the most effective media.

---

them into the midst of the fire, and burn them in the fire. From there a fire will go out into all the house of Israel.

5"Thus says the Lord GOD: 'This *is* Jerusalem; I have set her in the midst of the nations and the countries all around her. 6She has rebelled against My judgments by doing wickedness more than the nations, and against My statutes more than the countries that *are* all around her; for they have refused My judgments, and they have not walked in My statutes.' 7Therefore thus says the Lord GOD: 'Because you have multiplied *disobedience* more than the nations that *are* all around you, have not walked in My statutes nor kept My judgments, nor even done[a] according to the judgments of the nations that *are* all around you'— 8therefore thus says the Lord GOD: 'Indeed

I, even I, *am* against you and will execute judgments in your midst in the sight of the nations. 9And I will do among you what I have never done, and the like of which I will never do again, because of all your abominations. 10Therefore fathers shall eat *their* sons in your midst, and sons shall eat their fathers; and I will execute judgments among you, and all of you who remain I will scatter to all the winds.

11"Therefore, *as* I live,' says the Lord GOD, 'surely, because you have defiled My sanctuary with all your detestable things and with all your abominations, therefore I will also diminish *you;* My eye will not

5:7 [a]Following Masoretic Text, Septuagint, Targum, and Vulgate; many Hebrew manuscripts and Syriac read *but have done* (compare 11:12).

ARTS AND LITERATURE

An arrow is a natural symbol for famine and disease, because it comes from afar and does not announce its coming (Ezek. 5:16). In Homer's Iliad, Apollo rains down arrows on the Greek soldiers in order to punish them for insulting a priest. The arrows kill animals and men by means of a plague. Similarly, the Psalms compare disease brought on by God's judgment with arrow wounds (Ps. 38:2).

spare, nor will I have any pity. [12]One-third of you shall die of the pestilence, and be consumed with famine in your midst; and one-third shall fall by the sword all around you; and I will scatter another third to all the winds, and I will draw out a sword after them.

[13]Thus shall My anger be spent, and I will cause My fury to rest upon them, and I will be avenged; and they shall know that I, the LORD, have spoken it in My zeal, when I have spent My fury upon them. [14]Moreover I will make you a waste and a reproach among the nations that are all around you, in the sight of all who pass by.

[15]'So it[a] shall be a reproach, a taunt, a lesson, and an astonishment to the nations that are all around you, when I execute judgments among you in anger and in fury and in furious rebukes. I, the LORD, have spoken. [16]When I send against them the terrible arrows of famine which shall be for destruction, which I will send to destroy you, I will increase the famine upon you and cut off your supply of bread. [17]So I will send against you famine and wild beasts, and they will bereave you. Pestilence and blood shall pass through you, and I will bring the sword against you. I, the LORD, have spoken.' "

Judgment on Idolatrous Israel

6 [1]Now the word of the LORD came to me, saying: [2]"Son of man, set your face toward the mountains of Israel, and prophesy against them, [3]and say, 'O mountains of Israel, hear the word of the Lord GOD! Thus says the Lord GOD to the mountains, to the hills, to the ravines, and to the valleys: "Indeed I, even I, will bring a sword against you, and I will destroy your high places. [4]Then your altars shall be desolate, your incense altars shall be broken, and I will cast down your slain men before your idols. [5]And I will lay the corpses of the children of Israel before their idols, and I will scatter your bones all around your altars. [6]In all your dwelling places the cities shall be laid waste, and the high places shall be desolate, so that your altars may be laid waste and made desolate, your idols may be broken and made to cease, your incense altars may be cut down, and your works may be abolished. [7]The slain shall fall in

your midst, and you shall know that I am the LORD.

[8]"Yet I will leave a remnant, so that you may have some who escape the sword among the nations, when you are scattered through the countries. [9]Then those of you who escape will remember Me among the nations where they are carried captive, because I was crushed by their adulterous heart which has departed from Me, and by their eyes which play the harlot after their idols; they will loathe themselves for the evils which they committed in all their abominations. [10]And they shall know that I am the LORD; I have not said in vain that I would bring this calamity upon them."

[11]'Thus says the Lord GOD: "Pound your fists and stamp your feet, and say, 'Alas, for all the evil abominations of the house of Israel! For they shall fall by the sword, by famine, and by pestilence. [12]He who is far off shall die by the pestilence, he who is near shall fall by the sword, and he who remains and is besieged shall die by the famine. Thus will I spend My fury upon them. [13]Then you shall know that I am the LORD, when their slain are among their idols all around their altars, on every high hill, on all the mountaintops, under every green tree, and under every thick oak, wherever they offered sweet incense to all their idols. [14]So I will stretch out My hand against them and make the land desolate, yes, more desolate than the wilderness toward Diblah, in all their dwelling places. Then they shall know that I am the LORD.' " ' "

Judgment on Israel Is Near

7 [1]Moreover the word of the LORD came to me, saying, [2]"And you, son of man, thus says the Lord GOD to the land of Israel:

'An end! The end has come upon the
    four corners of the land.
3 Now the end has come upon you,
    And I will send My anger against
      you;
  I will judge you according to your
      ways,
  And I will repay you for all your
      abominations.
4 My eye will not spare you,
  Nor will I have pity;
  But I will repay your ways,
  And your abominations will be in your
      midst;

5:15 [a]Septuagint, Syriac, Targum, and Vulgate read you.

Then you shall know that I *am* the
LORD!'

5"Thus says the Lord GOD:

'A disaster, a singular disaster;
Behold, it has come!
6   An end has come,
The end has come;
It has dawned for you;
Behold, it has come!
7   Doom has come to you, you who dwell
in the land;
The time has come,
A day of trouble *is* near,
And not of rejoicing in the mountains.
8   Now upon you I will soon pour out My
fury,
And spend My anger upon you;
I will judge you according to your
ways,
And I will repay you for all your
abominations.

9   'My eye will not spare,
Nor will I have pity;
I will repay you according to your
ways,
And your abominations will be in your
midst.
Then you shall know that I *am* the
LORD who strikes.

10   'Behold, the day!
Behold, it has come!
Doom has gone out;
The rod has blossomed,
Pride has budded.
11   Violence has risen up into a rod of
wickedness;
None of them *shall remain,*
None of their multitude,
None of them;
Nor *shall there be* wailing for them.
12   The time has come,
The day draws near.

'Let not the buyer rejoice,
Nor the seller mourn,
For wrath *is* on their whole multitude.
13   For the seller shall not return to what
has been sold,
Though he may still be alive;
For the vision concerns the whole
multitude,
And it shall not turn back;
No one will strengthen himself
Who lives in iniquity.

14   'They have blown the trumpet and
made everyone ready,
But no one goes to battle;
For My wrath *is* on all their
multitude.
15   The sword *is* outside,
And the pestilence and famine within.
Whoever *is* in the field
Will die by the sword;
And whoever *is* in the city,
Famine and pestilence will devour
him.

16   'Those who survive will escape and be
on the mountains
Like doves of the valleys,
All of them mourning,
Each for his iniquity.
17   Every hand will be feeble,
And every knee will be *as* weak *as*
water.
18   They will also be girded with
sackcloth;
Horror will cover them;
Shame *will be* on every face,
Baldness on all their heads.

19   'They will throw their silver into the
streets,
And their gold will be like refuse;
Their silver and their gold will not be
able to deliver them
In the day of the wrath of the LORD;
They will not satisfy their souls,
Nor fill their stomachs,
Because it became their stumbling
block of iniquity.

20   'As for the beauty of his ornaments,
He set it in majesty;
But they made from it
The images of their abominations—
Their detestable things;
Therefore I have made it
Like refuse to them.
21   I will give it as plunder
Into the hands of strangers,
And to the wicked of the earth as
spoil;
And they shall defile it.
22   I will turn My face from them,
And they will defile My secret place;
For robbers shall enter it and
defile it.

23   'Make a chain,
For the land is filled with crimes of
blood,

And the city is full of violence.
24 Therefore I will bring the worst of the
Gentiles,
And they will possess their houses;
I will cause the pomp of the strong to
cease,
And their holy places shall be defiled.
25 Destruction comes;
They will seek peace, but *there shall
be* none.
26 Disaster will come upon disaster,
And rumor will be upon rumor.
Then they will seek a vision from a
prophet;
But the law will perish from the
priest,
And counsel from the elders.

27 'The king will mourn,
The prince will be clothed with
desolation,
And the hands of the common people
will tremble.
I will do to them according to their
way,
And according to what they deserve I
will judge them;
Then they shall know that I *am* the
LORD!' "

29:3 ªThat is, the Nile   29:5 ªFollowing
Masoretic Text, Septuagint, and Vulgate; some Hebrew
manuscripts and Targum read *buried*.
29:7 ªFollowing Masoretic Text and Vulgate;
Septuagint and Syriac read *hand*.

Pharaoh Hophra's Assault

During a period from the 10th year
(11th month) to the 11th year (3rd month) of
Jehoiachin's exile, Ezekiel received prophetic
messages concerning Egypt (Ezek. 29:1;
30:20; 31:1). This period corresponds to perhaps January through June of 587 B.C. The
siege of Jerusalem had been underway nearly
a year.

The occasion for these prophecies was an
interruption in Nebuchadnezzar's siege of
Jerusalem. Hophra, king of Egypt, came to
Zedekiah's aid, and even temporarily drew the
Babylonian armies away from Jerusalem. In
the city, Jeremiah warned that this lull would
be temporary (Jer. 37:7) and that Egypt would
retreat. In Babylon, Ezekiel had the same message.

In the 6th century B.C. the Egyptians had
already existed beside the Nile for over 3,500

---

years, and for much of that history had been
the supreme ancient Near Eastern power. But
by Ezekiel's time Egypt had not held that position for centuries. Now a weakening Egypt had
to face Babylon's increasing strength (Ezek.
30:20–26). The prophet recalls the fate of the
Assyrian Empire (ch. 31): Egypt could never
match Assyria's greatness, and that nation
had fallen. Like powerful Assyria, Egypt also
would be brought down. After her humiliation
by Nebuchadnezzar, the country would no
longer be among the first rank of world powers
(29:1–16).

■ Ezekiel 29:1–16
■ Ezekiel 30:20—31:18

Ezekiel 29:1–16
Proclamation Against Egypt

29 :1 In the tenth year, in the tenth
month, on the twelfth *day* of the
month, the word of the LORD came to me,
saying, ²"Son of man, set your face against
Pharaoh king of Egypt, and prophesy
against him, and against all Egypt. ³Speak,
and say, 'Thus says the Lord GOD:

"Behold, I *am* against you,
O Pharaoh king of Egypt,
O great monster who lies in the midst
of his rivers,
Who has said, 'My Riverª *is* my own;
I have made *it* for myself.'
4 But I will put hooks in your jaws,
And cause the fish of your rivers to
stick to your scales;
I will bring you up out of the midst of
your rivers,
And all the fish in your rivers will
stick to your scales.
5 I will leave you in the wilderness,
You and all the fish of your rivers;
You shall fall on the open field;
You shall not be picked up or
gathered.ª
I have given you as food
To the beasts of the field
And to the birds of the heavens.

6 "Then all the inhabitants of Egypt
Shall know that I *am* the LORD,
Because they have been a staff of reed
to the house of Israel.
7 When they took hold of you with the
hand,
You broke and tore all their
shoulders;ª

NEBUCHADNEZZAR CAMPAIGNS AGAINST EGYPT (Ezek. 30:21–26)

Egypt and Babylon were adversaries throughout the long reign of Nebuchadnezzar II of Babylon (605–562 B.C.). The spheres of influence for both nations extended to Palestine, and so the tiny kingdom of Judah became a pawn in the rivalry between these two superpowers.

In 605 B.C., while Nebuchadnezzar was yet a crown prince, he defeated Egypt at the great battle of Carchemish in Syria. He thus laid claim to Palestine, and apparently invaded Egypt 4 years later, but was repelled by Egypt's king Necho II (610–595 B.C.).

For practical purposes, Egypt made efforts to defend Judah against the advances of Babylon. The Egyptian king Hophra (589–570 B.C.) attempted to interrupt the Babylonian siege of Jerusalem in 587 B.C., but was forced to withdraw before the stronger army of Nebuchadnezzar. This is probably the situation that the prophet Ezekiel describes: God had "broken the arm of Pharaoh king of Egypt" (Ezek. 30:21). The flexed arm was a common symbol of Egyptian strength; yet God would "strengthen the arms of the king of Babylon" (30:24, 25).

Ezekiel delivered another prophetic message (Ezek. 29:17—30:19) in 571 B.C., just 4 years before another Babylonian invasion to the west. Unfortunately, the Babylonian Chronicle does not discuss this period, and so Nebuchadnezzar's account of this invasion is not known. Apparently Pharaoh Hophra lost control of Egypt in 570 B.C. in a revolt led by the Egyptian general Amasis. In 567 B.C., Nebuchadnezzar attempted to take advantage of Egypt's unstable situation, and Hophra joined with the Babylonians.

Nebuchadnezzar may well have devastated parts of Egypt, and Ezekiel prophesies of Egypt's destruction (30:10–12). However, the Babylonian invasion was repulsed by Amasis, and Pharaoh Hophra died during the battle.

When they leaned on you,
You broke and made all their backs
quiver."

8"Therefore thus says the Lord GOD: "Surely I will bring a sword upon you and cut off from you man and beast. 9And the land of Egypt shall become desolate and waste; then they will know that I *am* the LORD, because he said, 'The River *is* mine, and I have made it.' 10Indeed, therefore, I *am* against you and against your rivers, and I will make the land of Egypt utterly waste and desolate, from Migdol[a] *to* Syene, as far as the border of Ethiopia. 11Neither foot of man shall pass through it nor foot of beast pass through it, and it shall be uninhabited forty years. 12I will make the land of Egypt desolate in the midst of the countries *that are* desolate; and among the cities *that are* laid waste, her cities shall be desolate forty years; and I will scatter the Egyptians among the nations and disperse them throughout the countries."

13"Yet, thus says the Lord GOD: "At the end of forty years I will gather the Egyptians from the peoples among whom they were scattered. 14I will bring back the captives of Egypt and cause them to return to the land of Pathros, to the land of their origin, and there they shall be a lowly kingdom. 15It shall be the lowliest of kingdoms; it shall never again exalt itself above the nations, for I will diminish them so that they will not rule over the nations anymore. 16No longer shall it be the confidence of the house of Israel, but will remind them of *their* iniquity when they turned to follow them. Then they shall know that I *am* the Lord GOD." ' "

Ezekiel 30:20—31:18
Proclamation Against Pharaoh

30 :20 And it came to pass in the eleventh year, in the first *month,* on the seventh *day* of the month, *that* the word of the LORD came to me, saying, 21"Son of man, I have broken the arm of Pharaoh king of Egypt; and see, it has not been bandaged for healing, nor a splint put on to bind it, to make it strong enough to hold a sword. 22Therefore thus says the Lord GOD: 'Surely I *am* against Pharaoh

29:10 [a]Or *tower*

king of Egypt, and will break his arms, both the strong one and the one that was broken; and I will make the sword fall out of his hand. 23I will scatter the Egyptians among the nations, and disperse them throughout the countries. 24I will strengthen the arms of the king of Babylon and put My sword in his hand; but I will break Pharaoh's arms, and he will groan before him with the groanings of a mortally wounded *man.* 25Thus I will strengthen the arms of the king of Babylon, but the arms of Pharaoh shall fall down; they shall know that I *am* the LORD, when I put My sword into the hand of the king of Babylon and he stretches it out against the land of Egypt. 26I will scatter the Egyptians among the nations and disperse them throughout the countries. Then they shall know that I *am* the LORD.' "

Egypt Cut Down Like a Great Tree

31 1Now it came to pass in the eleventh year, in the third *month,* on the first *day* of the month, *that* the word of the LORD came to me, saying, 2"Son of man, say to Pharaoh king of Egypt and to his multitude:

'Whom are you like in your greatness?
3   Indeed Assyria *was* a cedar in
        Lebanon,
    With fine branches that shaded the
        forest,
    And of high stature;
    And its top was among the thick
        boughs.
4   The waters made it grow;
    Underground waters gave it height,
    With their rivers running around the
        place where it was planted,
    And sent out rivulets to all the trees
        of the field.

5   'Therefore its height was exalted above
        all the trees of the field;
    Its boughs were multiplied,
    And its branches became long because
        of the abundance of water,
    As it sent them out.
6   All the birds of the heavens made
        their nests in its boughs;
    Under its branches all the beasts of
        the field brought forth their
        young;

    And in its shadow all great nations
        made their home.

7   'Thus it was beautiful in greatness and
        in the length of its branches,
    Because its roots reached to abundant
        waters.
8   The cedars in the garden of God could
        not hide it;
    The fir trees were not like its boughs,
    And the chestnut[a] trees were not like
        its branches;
    No tree in the garden of God was like
        it in beauty.
9   I made it beautiful with a multitude of
        branches,
    So that all the trees of Eden envied it,
    That *were* in the garden of God.'

10"Therefore thus says the Lord GOD: 'Because you have increased in height, and it set its top among the thick boughs, and its heart was lifted up in its height, 11therefore I will deliver it into the hand of the mighty one of the nations, and he shall surely deal with it; I have driven it out for its wickedness. 12And aliens, the most terrible of the nations, have cut it down and left it; its branches have fallen on the mountains and in all the valleys; its boughs lie broken by all the rivers of the land; and all the peoples of the earth have gone from under its shadow and left it.

13   'On its ruin will remain all the birds of
        the heavens,
    And all the beasts of the field will
        come to its branches—

14"So that no trees by the waters may ever again exalt themselves for their height, nor set their tops among the thick boughs, that no tree which drinks water may ever be high enough to reach up to them.

    'For they have all been delivered to
        death,
    To the depths of the earth,
    Among the children of men who go
        down to the Pit.'

15"Thus says the Lord GOD: 'In the day when it went down to hell, I caused mourning. I covered the deep because of it. I restrained its rivers, and the great waters were held back. I caused Lebanon to mourn for it, and all the trees of the field wilted because of it. 16I made the nations shake at

---

31:8 ªHebrew *armon*

the sound of its fall, when I cast it down to hell together with those who descend into the Pit; and all the trees of Eden, the choice and best of Lebanon, all that drink water, were comforted in the depths of the earth. [17]They also went down to hell with it, with those *slain* by the sword; and *those who were* its *strong* arm dwelt in its shadows among the nations.

[18]'To which of the trees in Eden will you then be likened in glory and greatness? Yet you shall be brought down with the trees of Eden to the depths of the earth; you shall lie in the midst of the uncircumcised, with *those* slain by the sword. This *is* Pharaoh and all his multitude,' says the Lord GOD."

Prophetic Account: The Fall of Jerusalem

As both Jeremiah and Ezekiel predicted, Babylon defeated the Egyptian armies under Pharaoh Hophra and returned to finish off Jerusalem. In Zedekiah's 11th year (586 B.C.), the city fell. The significance of the fall of Jerusalem can hardly be overstated. Israel's identity and the current form of her faith were obliterated at once. For this reason, many Old Testament passages describe the events around that fall. No fewer than four separate narrative accounts (including Chronicles) of the event appear in Scripture. The parallel accounts of 2 Kin. 25:4–26 and Jer. 52:7–30 are supplemented with the longer account found in Jer. 39—44, which may have been written by Jeremiah's scribe Baruch.

Jeremiah's prophecies were fulfilled in these horrible days. By the 4th month (perhaps July) of 586 B.C. the Babylonian army penetrated Jerusalem's walls (Jer. 39:2). When Zedekiah knew that defense was hopeless, he and his army tried to desert the city. The effort was futile; Zedekiah was captured and taken to the Babylonian headquarters at Hamath (Jer. 52:7–11; 39:1–7). One month later (Jer. 52:12), the Babylonian army led by the commander Nebuzaradan trampled the city. The last vestiges of King Solomon's splendor were taken as spoils of war (Jer. 52:12–27; 39:8–10).

- 2 Kings 25:4–7
- Jeremiah 52:7–11
- Jeremiah 39:1–7
- 2 Kings 25:8–21
- Jeremiah 52:12–27
- Jeremiah 39:8–10

2 Kings 25:4–7
The Fall and Captivity of Judah

25 :4 Then the city wall was broken through, and all the men of war *fled* at night by way of the gate between two walls, which was by the king's garden, even though the Chaldeans *were* still encamped all around against the city. And *the king*[a] went by way of the plain.[b] [5]But the army of the Chaldeans pursued the king, and they overtook him in the plains of Jericho. All his army was scattered from him. [6]So they took the king and brought him up to the king of Babylon at Riblah, and they pronounced judgment on him. [7]Then they killed the sons of Zedekiah before his eyes, put out the eyes of Zedekiah, bound him with bronze fetters, and took him to Babylon.

Jeremiah 52:7–11

52 :7 Then the city wall was broken through, and all the men of war fled and went out of the city at night by way of the gate between the two walls, which *was* by the king's garden, even though the Chaldeans *were* near the city all around. And they went by way of the plain.[a]

[8]But the army of the Chaldeans pursued the king, and they overtook Zedekiah in the plains of Jericho. All his army was scattered from him. [9]So they took the king and brought him up to the king of Babylon at Riblah in the land of Hamath, and he pronounced judgment on him. [10]Then the king of Babylon killed the sons of Zedekiah before his eyes. And he killed all the princes of Judah in Riblah. [11]He also put out the eyes of Zedekiah; and the king of Babylon bound him in bronze fetters, took him to Babylon, and put him in prison till the day of his death.

Jeremiah 39:1–7
The Fall of Jerusalem

39 :1 In the ninth year of Zedekiah king of Judah, in the tenth month, Nebuchadnezzar king of Babylon and all his army came against Jerusalem, and besieged it. [2]In the eleventh year of Zedekiah, in the fourth month, on the ninth *day* of the month, the city was penetrated.

25:4 [a]Literally *he*   [b]Or *Arabah*, that is, the Jordan Valley   **Jer. 52:7** [a]Or *the Arabah*, that is, the Jordan Valley

The Last Kings of Judah

Judah (southern kingdom)	**Israel (northern kingdom)**
Jehoiachin, son of Jehoiakim, reigned only 3 months. Nebuchadnezzar of Babylon besieged Jerusalem and carried Jehoiachin into captivity in Babylon (2 Kin. 24:10, 12). Also called Jeconiah and Coniah, Jehoiachin was finally released by the new Babylonian king Evil-Merodach (2 Kin. 25:27).	Fell to the Assyrian Empire in 722 B.C.

Zedekiah, son of Josiah, was an uncle to Jehoiachin. When Nebuchadnezzar exiled Jehoiachin to Babylon, he placed Mattaniah on the throne, giving him the throne name "Zedekiah" (2 Kin. 24:17). Zedekiah was a puppet king ruling over a powerless land of poor farmers and laborers. He was under constant pressure from his advisors to revolt against Babylon. When Jerusalem fell to the Babylonians in 586 B.C., Zedekiah was exiled (2 Kin. 25:7).

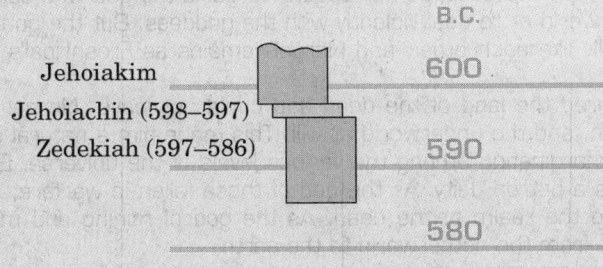

B.C.

Jehoiakim

Jehoiachin (598–597)

Zedekiah (597–586)

600

590

580

---

³Then all the princes of the king of Babylon came in and sat in the Middle Gate: Nergal-Sharezer, Samgar-Nebo, Sarsechim, Rabsaris,ᵃ Nergal-Sarezer, Rabmag,ᵇ with the rest of the princes of the king of Babylon.

⁴So it was, when Zedekiah the king of Judah and all the men of war saw them, that they fled and went out of the city by night, by way of the king's garden, by the gate between the two walls. And he went out by way of the plain.ᵃ ⁵But the Chaldean army pursued them and overtook Zedekiah in the plains of Jericho. And when they had captured him, they brought him up to Nebuchadnezzar king of Babylon, to Riblah

in the land of Hamath, where he pronounced judgment on him. ⁶Then the king of Babylon killed the sons of Zedekiah before his eyes in Riblah; the king of Babylon also killed all the nobles of Judah. ⁷Moreover he put out Zedekiah's eyes, and bound him with bronze fetters to carry him off to Babylon.

2 Kings 25:8–21

25:8 And in the fifth month, on the seventh *day* of the month (which *was* the nineteenth year of King Nebuchadnezzar king of Babylon), Nebuzaradan the captain of the guard, a servant of the king of Babylon, came to Jerusalem. ⁹He burned the house of the LORD and the king's house; all the houses of Jerusalem, that is, all the houses of the great, he burned with fire. ¹⁰And all the army of the Chaldeans who

---

39:3 ᵃA title, probably *Chief Officer;* also verse 13
ᵇA title, probably *Troop Commander;* also verse 13
39:4 ᵃOr *the Arabah,* that is, the Jordan Valley

Politics and Government

The defeat and destruction of a city is a terrible fate. Not only is human life itself destroyed, but with it the visible fruit of human labor and energy. The purpose of salvation is symbolized by a heavenly city, the New Jerusalem (Rev. 21:2), showing how important is the idea of a city. Like the fall of Troy, the destruction of Jerusalem cannot fade from human consciousness (2 Kin. 25:9).

NERGAL AND NERGAL-SHAREZER   (Jer. 39:3, 13)

Among the officials representing Babylon at the siege of Jerusalem was a certain Nergal-Sharezer (Jer. 39:3). His name includes the name of the god Nergal, and means "Nergal, protect the king."

Nergal was the god of the netherworld in 3rd-millennium B.C. Sumer. His official cult center was the city of Cuth. In the 2nd millennium B.C. his worship was incorporated into both Babylonian and Assyrian religions. As each of these states built their empires, they carried the worship of Nergal with them.

The *Myth of Nergal and Ereshkigal* exists in two distinct versions: one from Tell el-Amarna, Egypt, from about 1350 B.C., and another from 7th-century Babylonia. This narrative poem describes how Nergal came to the realm of the dead.

In the myth, Ereshkigal, queen of the dead, is slighted by the gods in heaven and demands that a deity be sent to her realm to assuage her anger. Nergal is the god who comes, prepared either to rule the netherworld or to deal violently with the goddess. But the god and goddess discover that they actually like each other, and Nergal remains as Ereshkigal's husband and as king of the dead.

Unlike other deities who entered the land of the dead and could not leave, Nergal was able to move among heaven, earth, and the underworld at will. This made him a natural deity for any business which required coordination among the various levels of the universe. Especially important were his duties as a patron deity. As the god of those fallen in warfare, Nergal hauled the slain from earth to the realm of the dead. As the god of mining and metalsmiths, he hauled precious metals from the netherworld to the earth.

were with the captain of the guard broke down the walls of Jerusalem all around. ¹¹Then Nebuzaradan the captain of the guard carried away captive the rest of the people *who* remained in the city and the defectors who had deserted to the king of Babylon, with the rest of the multitude. ¹²But the captain of the guard left *some* of the poor of the land as vinedressers and farmers. ¹³The bronze pillars that *were* in the house of the LORD, and the carts and the bronze Sea that *were* in the house of the LORD, the Chaldeans broke in pieces, and carried their bronze to Babylon. ¹⁴They also took away the pots, the shovels, the trimmers, the spoons, and all the bronze utensils with which the priests ministered. ¹⁵The firepans and the basins, the things of solid gold and solid silver, the captain of the guard took away. ¹⁶The two pillars, one Sea, and the carts, which Solomon had made for the house of the LORD, the bronze of all these articles was beyond measure. ¹⁷The height of one pillar *was* eighteen cubits, and the capital on it *was* of bronze. The height of the capital was three cubits, and the network and pomegranates all around the capital were all of bronze. The second pillar was the same, with a network.

¹⁸And the captain of the guard took Seraiah the chief priest, Zephaniah the second priest, and the three doorkeepers. ¹⁹He also took out of the city an officer who had charge of the men of war, five men of the king's close associates who were found in the city, the chief recruiting officer of the army, who mustered the people of the land, and sixty men of the people of the land *who were* found in the city. ²⁰So Nebuzaradan, captain of the guard, took these and brought them to the king of Babylon at Riblah. ²¹Then the king of Babylon struck them and put them to death at Riblah in the land of Hamath. Thus Judah was carried away captive from its own land.

Jeremiah 52:12–27
The Temple and City Plundered and Burned

52:12 Now in the fifth month, on the tenth *day* of the month (which *was* the nineteenth year of King Nebuchadnezzar king of Babylon), Nebuzaradan, the captain of the guard, *who* served the king of Babylon, came to Jerusalem. ¹³He burned the house of the LORD and the king's house; all the houses of Jerusalem, that is, all the houses of the great, he burned with fire. ¹⁴And all the army of the

Chaldeans who *were* with the captain of the guard broke down all the walls of Jerusalem all around. [15]Then Nebuzaradan the captain of the guard carried away captive *some* of the poor people, the rest of the people who remained in the city, the defectors who had deserted to the king of Babylon, and the rest of the craftsmen. [16]But Nebuzaradan the captain of the guard left *some* of the poor of the land as vinedressers and farmers.

[17]The bronze pillars that *were* in the house of the LORD, and the carts and the bronze Sea that *were* in the house of the LORD, the Chaldeans broke in pieces, and carried all their bronze to Babylon. [18]They also took away the pots, the shovels, the trimmers, the bowls, the spoons, and all the bronze utensils with which the priests ministered. [19]The basins, the firepans, the bowls, the pots, the lampstands, the spoons, and the cups, whatever *was* solid gold and whatever *was* solid silver, the captain of the guard took away. [20]The two pillars, one Sea, the twelve bronze bulls which *were* under *it, and* the carts, which King Solomon had made for the house of the LORD—the bronze of all these articles was beyond measure. [21]Now *concerning* the pillars: the height of one pillar *was* eighteen cubits, a measuring line of twelve cubits could measure its circumference, and its thickness *was* four fingers; *it was* hollow. [22]A capital of bronze *was* on it; and the height of one capital *was* five cubits, with a network and pomegranates all around the capital, all of bronze. The second pillar, with pomegranates was the same. [23]There were ninety-six pomegranates on the sides; all the pomegranates, all around on the network, *were* one hundred.

The People Taken Captive to Babylonia

[24]The captain of the guard took Seraiah the chief priest, Zephaniah the second priest, and the three doorkeepers. [25]He also took out of the city an officer who had charge of the men of war, seven men of the king's close associates who were found in the city, the principal scribe of the army who mustered the people of the land, and sixty men of the people of the land who were found in the midst of the city. [26]And Nebuzaradan the captain of the guard took these and brought them to the king of Babylon at Riblah. [27]Then the king of Babylon struck them and put them to

death at Riblah in the land of Hamath. Thus Judah was carried away captive from its own land.

Jeremiah 39:8–10

39 :8 And the Chaldeans burned the king's house and the houses of the people with fire, and broke down the walls of Jerusalem. [9]Then Nebuzaradan the captain of the guard carried away captive to Babylon the remnant of the people who remained in the city and those who defected to him, with the rest of the people who remained. [10]But Nebuzaradan the captain of the guard left in the land of Judah the poor people, who had nothing, and gave them vineyards and fields at the same time.

The Book of Lamentations

The Book of Lamentations consists of five separate poems on the destruction of Jerusalem in 586 B.C. These funeral songs and prayers describe both the horrors of the extended siege (e.g., Lam. 4:4, 5) and the destruction itself. No other book captures so vividly the despair of seeing Zion destroyed, of seeing the holy city and its temple become a mockery to the nations.

Lamentations is traditionally attributed to Jeremiah, which explains its usual placement after the Book of Jeremiah, but the book itself does not name an author. Whether by Jeremiah or an unknown poet, the book is surely an eyewitness account of those wretched days. The five poems were penned, probably not long after Jerusalem's fall in 586, by someone who had seen the slaughter of many of his people, the enslavement of others, and the abject despair of the few survivors.

▼   ■ Lamentations 1:1—5:22

Lamentations
Jerusalem in Affliction

1 :1 How lonely sits the city
    That was full of people!
How like a widow is she,
Who *was* great among the nations!
The princess among the provinces
Has become a slave!

2   She weeps bitterly in the night,
Her tears *are* on her cheeks;
Among all her lovers
She has none to comfort *her.*

LAMENTING FOR THE DEFEATED CITY (Lam. 1:1)

The Book of Lamentations begins with an expression of deep hurt: "How lonely sits the city That was full of people!" (Lam. 1:1). Such laments for defeated cities and destroyed temples were commonplace in the ancient Near East. One of the best known is the *Lament for Ur*, composed sometime after the fall of the 3rd Dynasty of Ur in 2004 B.C.

Ur was a Sumerian kingdom in southern Mesopotamia. The lament was apparently written by the kings of Isin, a nearby city, who attempted to rebuild the city of Ur, and associated themselves with the Ur dynasty. The purpose of the lament was to calm the disquieted spirit of Nanna, the moon god of Ur. It was thus hoped that the moon god would once again rebuild his devastated residence.

The form of the *Lament for Ur* has two parts: the body of the text is a "harp lament," and the ending consists of a "tambourine lament." The first part is sung by Nanna's wife, Ningal, while the second is sung by a singer (or singers) who express the survivors' hope that the city gods will restore the city to greatness.

Scholars believe that the *Lament for Ur* may actually have been performed in the moonlight at the place of the ruined temple of Nanna at Ur. This lament claims that all of the Sumerian gods have abandoned their cities. Later, the lament describes the divine assembly and their fateful decision to evacuate the land. Finally, the tambourine lament makes a plea for Ningal to return to her city. She then makes the same appeal to her husband, Nanna.

There are superficial similarities between the *Lament for Ur* and the Book of Lamentations. Both writings concern a defeated city that has been forsaken by its deity (Lam. 1:15). Both cities have fallen to the enemy (Lam. 2:7). Yet both laments express hope that the deity will restore the city (Lam. 3:22–33).

All her friends have dealt
   treacherously with her;
They have become her enemies.

3 Judah has gone into captivity,
Under affliction and hard servitude;
She dwells among the nations,
She finds no rest;
All her persecutors overtake her in
   dire straits.

4 The roads to Zion mourn
Because no one comes to the set
   feasts.

All her gates are desolate;
Her priests sigh,
Her virgins are afflicted,
And she *is* in bitterness.

5 Her adversaries have become the
   master,
Her enemies prosper;
For the LORD has afflicted her
Because of the multitude of her
   transgressions.
Her children have gone into captivity
   before the enemy.

6 And from the daughter of Zion
All her splendor has departed.
Her princes have become like deer
That find no pasture,
That flee without strength
Before the pursuer.

7 In the days of her affliction and
   roaming,
Jerusalem remembers all her pleasant
   things
That she had in the days of old.
When her people fell into the hand of
   the enemy,
With no one to help her,

TIME CAPSULE 586 B.C.

586	Lachish Letters probably written shortly before Jerusalem's capture
586	Jerusalem falls to the Babylonians
586–538	The exile of Judah to Babylon
586	Hophra accepts Judean refugees in Egypt
586	Gedaliah is appointed governor of Judah

The adversaries saw her
And mocked at her downfall.[a]

8 Jerusalem has sinned gravely,
Therefore she has become vile.[a]
All who honored her despise her
Because they have seen her
nakedness;
Yes, she sighs and turns away.

9 Her uncleanness *is* in her skirts;
She did not consider her destiny;
Therefore her collapse was awesome;
She had no comforter.
"O Lᴏʀᴅ, behold my affliction,
For *the* enemy is exalted!"

10 The adversary has spread his hand
Over all her pleasant things;
For she has seen the nations enter her
sanctuary,
Those whom You commanded
Not to enter Your assembly.

11 All her people sigh,
They seek bread;
They have given their valuables for
food to restore life.
"See, O Lᴏʀᴅ, and consider,
For I am scorned."

12 "*Is it* nothing to you, all you who pass
by?
Behold and see
If there is any sorrow like my sorrow,
Which has been brought on me,
Which the Lᴏʀᴅ has inflicted
In the day of His fierce anger.

13 "From above He has sent fire into my
bones,
And it overpowered them;
He has spread a net for my feet
And turned me back;
He has made me desolate
And faint all the day.

14 "The yoke of my transgressions was
bound;[a]
They were woven together by His
hands,
And thrust upon my neck.

He made my strength fail;
The Lord delivered me into the hands
of *those whom* I am not able to
withstand.

15 "The Lord has trampled underfoot all
my mighty *men* in my midst;
He has called an assembly against me
To crush my young men;
The Lord trampled *as* in a winepress
The virgin daughter of Judah.

16 "For these *things* I weep;
My eye, my eye overflows with water;
Because the comforter, who should
restore my life,
Is far from me.
My children are desolate
Because the enemy prevailed."

17 Zion spreads out her hands,
But no one comforts her;
The Lᴏʀᴅ has commanded concerning
Jacob
That those around him *become* his
adversaries;
Jerusalem has become an unclean
thing among them.

18 "The Lᴏʀᴅ is righteous,
For I rebelled against His
commandment.
Hear now, all peoples,
And behold my sorrow;
My virgins and my young men
Have gone into captivity.

19 "I called for my lovers,
But they deceived me;
My priests and my elders
Breathed their last in the city,
While they sought food
To restore their life.

20 "See, O Lᴏʀᴅ, that I *am* in distress;
My soul is troubled;
My heart is overturned within me,
For I have been very rebellious.
Outside the sword bereaves,
At home *it is* like death.

21 "They have heard that I sigh,
But no one comforts me.
All my enemies have heard of my
trouble;
They are glad that You have done *it*.
Bring on the day You have announced,
That they may become like me.

1:7 [a]Vulgate reads *her Sabbaths.*
1:8 [a]Septuagint and Vulgate read *moved* or
removed.   1:14 [a]Following Masoretic Text and
Targum; Septuagint, Syriac, and Vulgate read *watched
over.*

22 "Let all their wickedness come before
    You,
And do to them as You have done to
    me
For all my transgressions;
For my sighs *are* many,
And my heart *is* faint."

God's Anger with Jerusalem

2 1 How the Lord has covered the
    daughter of Zion
With a cloud in His anger!
He cast down from heaven to the
    earth
The beauty of Israel,
And did not remember His footstool
In the day of His anger.

2 The Lord has swallowed up and has
    not pitied
All the dwelling places of Jacob.
He has thrown down in His wrath
The strongholds of the daughter of
    Judah;
He has brought *them* down to the
    ground;
He has profaned the kingdom and its
    princes.

3 He has cut off in fierce anger
Every horn of Israel;
He has drawn back His right hand
From before the enemy.
He has blazed against Jacob like a
    flaming fire
Devouring all around.

4 Standing like an enemy, He has bent
    His bow;
With His right hand, like an
    adversary,
He has slain all *who were* pleasing to
    His eye;
On the tent of the daughter of Zion,
He has poured out His fury like fire.

5 The Lord was like an enemy.
He has swallowed up Israel,
He has swallowed up all her palaces;
He has destroyed her strongholds,
And has increased mourning and
    lamentation
In the daughter of Judah.

6 He has done violence to His
    tabernacle,
As if it were a garden;
He has destroyed His place of
    assembly;

The LORD has caused
The appointed feasts and Sabbaths to
    be forgotten in Zion.
In His burning indignation He has
    spurned the king and the priest.

7 The Lord has spurned His altar,
He has abandoned His sanctuary;
He has given up the walls of her
    palaces
Into the hand of the enemy.
They have made a noise in the house
    of the LORD
As on the day of a set feast.

8 The LORD has purposed to destroy
The wall of the daughter of Zion.
He has stretched out a line;
He has not withdrawn His hand from
    destroying;
Therefore He has caused the rampart
    and wall to lament;
They languished together.

9 Her gates have sunk into the ground;
He has destroyed and broken her
    bars.
Her king and her princes *are* among
    the nations;
The Law *is* no *more,*
And her prophets find no vision from
    the LORD.

10 The elders of the daughter of Zion
Sit on the ground *and* keep silence;
They throw dust on their heads
And gird themselves with sackcloth.
The virgins of Jerusalem
Bow their heads to the ground.

11 My eyes fail with tears,
My heart is troubled;
My bile is poured on the ground
Because of the destruction of the
    daughter of my people,
Because the children and the infants
Faint in the streets of the city.

12 They say to their mothers,
"Where *is* grain and wine?"
As they swoon like the wounded
In the streets of the city,
As their life is poured out
In their mothers' bosom.

13 How shall I console you?
To what shall I liken you,
O daughter of Jerusalem?

TEMPLE AFIRE (Lam. 2:5–7)

Temples were the focal point of civic life and the target for invaders. The patron deities of the city were believed to dwell in the temples. Festivals were held around temples, and valuables were deposited in them (they were the earliest banks).

For invaders, the capture of the central temple served several purposes, not the least of which was obtaining the wealth stored there. To take the temple was also to show that the gods of the city had chosen the conquerors over the local inhabitants. This meant that the conquerors were now the legitimate rulers of the people, land, and any possessions.

The burning of the central temple was a declaration of unconditional victory. Only if the gods of the city had abandoned that city to its fate would they allow their own home to be destroyed. When Sennacherib destroyed Babylon and the temple of Marduk in 689 B.C., he claimed to have done so on behalf of Marduk, who wished to punish his people for their evil behavior.

The captors were understood to have free rein with the city and its populace. The defeated city had no gods to whom they might appeal for mercy and no hope for a change in their fate. Their gods were believed to have moved to the capital of the victors, where they became patrons of the kings of that city.

The Book of Lamentations says the same thing about Nebuchadnezzar II burning Jerusalem and its temple in 586 B.C. (2 Kin. 25:9). Yahweh Himself had become Judah's enemy (Lam. 2:5) and destroyed His own temple—His "tabernacle" and "place of assembly" (2:6). With Yahweh's permission, Judah's enemy now "made a noise in the house of the LORD" (2:7).

What shall I compare with you, that I
    may comfort you,
O virgin daughter of Zion?
For your ruin *is* spread wide as the
    sea;
Who can heal you?

14 Your prophets have seen for you
    False and deceptive visions;
They have not uncovered your
    iniquity,
To bring back your captives,
But have envisioned for you false
    prophecies and delusions.

15 All who pass by clap *their* hands at
    you;
They hiss and shake their heads
At the daughter of Jerusalem:
"*Is* this the city that is called
'The perfection of beauty,
The joy of the whole earth'?"

16 All your enemies have opened their
    mouth against you;
They hiss and gnash *their* teeth.
They say, "We have swallowed *her* up!
Surely this *is* the day we have waited
    for;
We have found *it*, we have seen *it!*"

17 The LORD has done what He purposed;
He has fulfilled His word
Which He commanded in days of old.
He has thrown down and has not
    pitied,
And He has caused an enemy to
    rejoice over you;
He has exalted the horn of your
    adversaries.

18 Their heart cried out to the Lord,
"O wall of the daughter of Zion,
Let tears run down like a river day
    and night;
Give yourself no relief;
Give your eyes no rest.

19 "Arise, cry out in the night,
At the beginning of the watches;
Pour out your heart like water before
    the face of the Lord.
Lift your hands toward Him
For the life of your young children,
Who faint from hunger at the head of
    every street."

20 "See, O LORD, and consider!
To whom have You done this?
Should the women eat their offspring,

The children they have cuddled?[a]
Should the priest and prophet be slain
In the sanctuary of the Lord?

21 "Young and old lie
On the ground in the streets;
My virgins and my young men
Have fallen by the sword;
You have slain *them* in the day of Your
anger,
You have slaughtered *and* not pitied.

22 "You have invited as to a feast day
The terrors that surround me.
In the day of the LORD's anger
There was no refugee or survivor.
Those whom I have borne and
brought up
My enemies have destroyed."

The Prophet's Anguish and Hope

3 1 I *am* the man *who* has seen
affliction by the rod of His wrath.
2 He has led me and made *me* walk
In darkness and not *in* light.
3 Surely He has turned His hand
against me
Time and time again throughout the
day.

4 He has aged my flesh and my skin,
And broken my bones.
5 He has besieged me
And surrounded *me* with bitterness
and woe.
6 He has set me in dark places
Like the dead of long ago.

7 He has hedged me in so that I cannot
get out;
He has made my chain heavy.
8 Even when I cry and shout,
He shuts out my prayer.
9 He has blocked my ways with hewn
stone;
He has made my paths crooked.

10 He *has been* to me a bear lying in
wait,
Like a lion in ambush.

11 He has turned aside my ways and
torn me in pieces;
He has made me desolate.
12 He has bent His bow
And set me up as a target for the
arrow.

13 He has caused the arrows of His
quiver
To pierce my loins.[a]
14 I have become the ridicule of all my
people—
Their taunting song all the day.
15 He has filled me with bitterness,
He has made me drink wormwood.

16 He has also broken my teeth with
gravel,
And covered me with ashes.
17 You have moved my soul far from
peace;
I have forgotten prosperity.
18 And I said, "My strength and my hope
Have perished from the LORD."

19 Remember my affliction and roaming,
The wormwood and the gall.
20 My soul still remembers
And sinks within me.
21 This I recall to my mind,
Therefore I have hope.

22 *Through* the LORD's mercies we are
not consumed,
Because His compassions fail not.
23 *They are* new every morning;
Great *is* Your faithfulness.
24 "The LORD *is* my portion," says my
soul,
"Therefore I hope in Him!"

25 The LORD *is* good to those who wait for
Him,
To the soul *who* seeks Him.
26 *It is* good that *one* should hope and
wait quietly
For the salvation of the LORD.

2:20 [a]Vulgate reads *a span long.*   3:13 [a]Literally
kidneys

ARTS AND LITERATURE

*Lamentations displays a common technique of Hebrew poetry called acrostic. In an
acrostic poem, each line or group of lines begins with the next letter of the alphabet.
Lam. 3:1–66 has 3 verses for each of the 22 Hebrew letters; the other chapters of
Lamentations have one verse for each letter. The acrostic technique is common in
Arabic and Persian verse, although not in English, which has its own poetic resources.*

27 *It is* good for a man to bear
The yoke in his youth.

28 Let him sit alone and keep silent,
Because *God* has laid *it* on him;
29 Let him put his mouth in the dust—
There may yet be hope.
30 Let him give *his* cheek to the one who
strikes him,
And be full of reproach.

31 For the Lord will not cast off forever.
32 Though He causes grief,
Yet He will show compassion
According to the multitude of His
mercies.
33 For He does not afflict willingly,
Nor grieve the children of men.

34 To crush under one's feet
All the prisoners of the earth,
35 To turn aside the justice *due* a man
Before the face of the Most High,
36 Or subvert a man in his cause—
The Lord does not approve.

37 Who *is* he *who* speaks and it comes to
pass,
When the Lord has not commanded *it?*
38 *Is it* not from the mouth of the Most
High
That woe and well-being proceed?
39 Why should a living man complain,
A man for the punishment of his sins?

40 Let us search out and examine our
ways,
And turn back to the LORD;
41 Let us lift our hearts and hands
To God in heaven.
42 We have transgressed and rebelled;
You have not pardoned.

43 You have covered *Yourself* with anger
And pursued us;
You have slain *and* not pitied.
44 You have covered Yourself with a
cloud,
That prayer should not pass through.
45 You have made us an offscouring and
refuse
In the midst of the peoples.

46 All our enemies
Have opened their mouths against us.

47 Fear and a snare have come upon us,
Desolation and destruction.
48 My eyes overflow with rivers of water
For the destruction of the daughter of
my people.

49 My eyes flow and do not cease,
Without interruption,
50 Till the LORD from heaven
Looks down and sees.
51 My eyes bring suffering to my soul
Because of all the daughters of my
city.

52 My enemies without cause
Hunted me down like a bird.
53 They silenced[a] my life in the pit
And threw stones at me.
54 The waters flowed over my head;
I said, "I am cut off!"

55 I called on Your name, O LORD,
From the lowest pit.
56 You have heard my voice:
"Do not hide Your ear
From my sighing, from my cry for
help."
57 You drew near on the day I called on
You,
And said, "Do not fear!"

58 O Lord, You have pleaded the case for
my soul;
You have redeemed my life.
59 O LORD, You have seen *how* I am
wronged;
Judge my case.
60 You have seen all their vengeance,
All their schemes against me.

61 You have heard their reproach,
O LORD,
All their schemes against me,
62 The lips of my enemies
And their whispering against me all
the day.
63 Look at their sitting down and their
rising up;
I *am* their taunting song.

64 Repay them, O LORD,
According to the work of their hands.
65 Give them a veiled[a] heart;
Your curse *be* upon them!
66 In Your anger,
Pursue and destroy them
From under the heavens of the LORD.

3:53 [a]Septuagint reads *put to death.*   3:65 [a]A
Jewish tradition reads *sorrow of.*

The Degradation of Zion

4 ¹ How the gold has become dim!
How changed the fine gold!
The stones of the sanctuary are
scattered
At the head of every street.

² The precious sons of Zion,
Valuable as fine gold,
How they are regarded as clay pots,
The work of the hands of the potter!

³ Even the jackals present their breasts
To nurse their young;
But the daughter of my people *is*
cruel,
Like ostriches in the wilderness.

⁴ The tongue of the infant clings
To the roof of its mouth for thirst;
The young children ask for bread,
But no one breaks *it* for them.

⁵ Those who ate delicacies
Are desolate in the streets;
Those who were brought up in scarlet
Embrace ash heaps.

⁶ The punishment of the iniquity of the
daughter of my people
Is greater than the punishment of the
sin of Sodom,
Which was overthrown in a moment,
With no hand to help her!

⁷ Her Nazirites[a] were brighter than
snow
And whiter than milk;
They were more ruddy in body than
rubies,
Like sapphire in their appearance.

⁸ *Now* their appearance is blacker than
soot;
They go unrecognized in the streets;
Their skin clings to their bones,
It has become as dry as wood.

⁹ *Those* slain by the sword are better off
Than *those* who die of hunger;
For these pine away,
Stricken *for lack* of the fruits of the
field.

¹⁰ The hands of the compassionate
women
Have cooked their own children;
They became food for them
In the destruction of the daughter of
my people.

¹¹ The LORD has fulfilled His fury,
He has poured out His fierce anger.
He kindled a fire in Zion,
And it has devoured its foundations.

¹² The kings of the earth,
And all inhabitants of the world,
Would not have believed
That the adversary and the enemy
Could enter the gates of Jerusalem—

¹³ Because of the sins of her prophets
And the iniquities of her priests,
Who shed in her midst
The blood of the just.

¹⁴ They wandered blind in the streets;
They have defiled themselves with
blood,
So that no one would touch their
garments.

¹⁵ They cried out to them,
"Go away, unclean!
Go away, go away,
Do not touch us!"
When they fled and wandered,
Those among the nations said,
"They shall no longer dwell *here.*"

¹⁶ The face[a] of the LORD scattered them;
He no longer regards them.
The people do not respect the priests
Nor show favor to the elders.

¹⁷ Still our eyes failed us,
Watching vainly for our help;
In our watching we watched
For a nation *that* could not save *us.*

¹⁸ They tracked our steps
So that we could not walk in our
streets.
Our end was near;
Our days were over,
For our end had come.

¹⁹ Our pursuers were swifter
Than the eagles of the heavens.
They pursued us on the mountains
And lay in wait for us in the
wilderness.

4:7 [a]Or *nobles*   4:16 [a]Targum reads *anger.*

20 The breath of our nostrils, the
     anointed of the LORD,
   Was caught in their pits,
   Of whom we said, "Under his shadow
   We shall live among the nations."

21 Rejoice and be glad, O daughter of
     Edom,
   You who dwell in the land of Uz!
   The cup shall also pass over to you
   And you shall become drunk and
     make yourself naked.

22 *The punishment of* your iniquity is
     accomplished,
   O daughter of Zion;
   He will no longer send you into
     captivity.
   He will punish your iniquity,
   O daughter of Edom;
   He will uncover your sins!

A Prayer for Restoration

5 ¹ Remember, O LORD, what has
        come upon us;
   Look, and behold our reproach!
2 Our inheritance has been turned over
     to aliens,
   And our houses to foreigners.
3 We have become orphans and waifs,
   Our mothers *are* like widows.

4 We pay for the water we drink,
   And our wood comes at a price.
5 *They* pursue at our heels;ᵃ
   We labor *and* have no rest.
6 We have given our hand *to* the
     Egyptians
   And the Assyrians, to be satisfied with
     bread.

7 Our fathers sinned *and are* no more,
   But we bear their iniquities.
8 Servants rule over us;
   There is none to deliver *us* from their
     hand.

9 We get our bread *at the risk* of our
     lives,
   Because of the sword in the
     wilderness.

10 Our skin is hot as an oven,
   Because of the fever of famine.
11 They ravished the women in Zion,
   The maidens in the cities of Judah.
12 Princes were hung up by their hands,
   And elders were not respected.
13 Young men ground at the millstones;
   Boys staggered under *loads of* wood.
14 The elders have ceased *gathering at*
     the gate,
   And the young men from their music.

15 The joy of our heart has ceased;
   Our dance has turned into mourning.
16 The crown has fallen *from* our head.
   Woe to us, for we have sinned!
17 Because of this our heart is faint;
   Because of these *things* our eyes grow
     dim;
18 Because of Mount Zion which is
     desolate,
   With foxes walking about on it.

19 You, O LORD, remain forever;
   Your throne from generation to
     generation.
20 Why do You forget us forever,
   And forsake us for so long a time?
21 Turn us back to You, O LORD, and we
     will be restored;
   Renew our days as of old,
22 Unless You have utterly rejected us,
   And are very angry with us!

Gedaliah the Governor

Nebuchadnezzar had had enough of
kings in Jerusalem. Even his chosen servant
Zedekiah had rebelled. Now there would be no
more royalty. Instead, Nebuchadnezzar appointed a governor, named Gedaliah (2 Kin.
25:22). Archaeological finds indicate that this
Gedaliah had been Zedekiah's chief minister,
but he was not from the line of David. With

5:5 ᵃLiterally *necks*

ARTS AND LITERATURE

*The most prominent feature of Hebrew poetry is repeated thoughts and phrases. There
is little or no rhyme. But there is at least one recognizable meter (or rhythm), usually
used for poems of lament, like the Book of Lamentations. This rhythm is called Qinah
and has five beats divided 3 + 2. The last chapter of Lamentations (5:1–22) follows a
3 + 3 rhythm instead of the Qinah rhythm.*

Jerusalem a heap of rubble, Gedaliah set up his seat of government at Mizpah, while Nebuchadnezzar took still more of the people of Judah into exile to Babylon.

In the confusion of rounding up captives, it seems Jeremiah was arrested by mistake. He was taken to Ramah, a small town a few miles north of Jerusalem, where he was identified and released (Jer. 39:11—40:6). The prophet was offered the chance to leave his land and his people and have full provisions. He chose rather to stay with Gedaliah and the poor survivors.

Gedaliah's father, Ahikam, had once saved Jeremiah's life (Jer. 26:24), and Gedaliah was clearly disposed to follow Jeremiah's advice: he would humbly serve the king of Babylon (Jer. 40:9). Even after all Jeremiah's prophecies had been proven true, though, this advice remained unpopular. Only about 2 months passed (2 Kin. 25:8, 25) between Gedaliah's appointment as governor and his assassination by a certain Ishmael (Jer. 40:7—41:15).

The people, led now by a Judean army commander named Johanan, feared a reprisal by the Babylonians. Despite Jeremiah's prophetic word that they should stay in Judah, they fled to Egypt, taking Jeremiah and Baruch with them (Jer. 41:16—44:30). The last recorded messages of Jeremiah come from Tahpanhes in Egypt. His prophecies concern Pharaoh Hophra's loss of his throne in 570 B.C. to the Egyptian general Amasis (44:30) and Nebuchadnezzar's campaign against Egypt in 567 B.C., during which Hophra was killed (43:8-13).

- 2 Kings 25:22-26
- Jeremiah 39:11—44:30

2 Kings 25:22–26
Gedaliah Made Governor of Judah

25 **:22** Then he made Gedaliah the son of Ahikam, the son of Shaphan, governor over the people who remained in the land of Judah, whom Nebuchadnezzar king of Babylon had left. 23Now when all the captains of the armies, they and *their* men, heard that the king of Babylon had made Gedaliah governor, they came to Gedaliah at Mizpah—Ishmael the son of Nethaniah, Johanan the son of Careah, Seraiah the son of Tanhumeth the Netophathite, and Jaazaniah[a] the son of a Maachathite, they and their men. 24And Gedaliah took an oath before them and their men, and said to them, "Do not be afraid of the servants of the Chaldeans. Dwell in the land and

serve the king of Babylon, and it shall be well with you."

25But it happened in the seventh month that Ishmael the son of Nethaniah, the son of Elishama, of the royal family, came with ten men and struck and killed Gedaliah, the Jews, as well as the Chaldeans who were with him at Mizpah. 26And all the people, small and great, and the captains of the armies, arose and went to Egypt; for they were afraid of the Chaldeans.

Jeremiah 39:11—44:30
Jeremiah Goes Free

39 **:11** Now Nebuchadnezzar king of Babylon gave charge concerning Jeremiah to Nebuzaradan the captain of the guard, saying, 12"Take him and look after him, and do him no harm; but do to him just as he says to you." 13So Nebuzaradan the captain of the guard sent Nebushasban, Rabsaris, Nergal-Sharezer, Rabmag, and all the king of Babylon's chief officers; 14then they sent *someone* to take Jeremiah from the court of the prison, and committed him to Gedaliah the son of Ahikam, the son of Shaphan, that he should take him home. So he dwelt among the people.

15Meanwhile the word of the LORD had come to Jeremiah while he was shut up in the court of the prison, saying, 16"Go and speak to Ebed-Melech the Ethiopian, saying, 'Thus says the LORD of hosts, the God of Israel: "Behold, I will bring My words upon this city for adversity and not for good, and they shall be *performed* in that day before you. 17But I will deliver you in that day," says the LORD, "and you shall not be given into the hand of the men of whom you *are* afraid. 18For I will surely deliver you, and you shall not fall by the sword; but your life shall be as a prize to you, because you have put your trust in Me," says the LORD.' "

Jeremiah with Gedaliah the Governor

40 1The word that came to Jeremiah from the LORD after Nebuzaradan the captain of the guard had let him go from Ramah, when he had taken him bound in chains among all who were carried away captive from Jerusalem and Judah, who were carried away captive to Babylon.

2And the captain of the guard took

25:23 ᵃSpelled *Jezaniah* in Jeremiah 40:8

POLITICAL TURMOIL AFTER JERUSALEM'S FALL (Jer. 40:5)

As Jeremiah had warned, in 586 B.C. the Babylonians utterly destroyed Jerusalem and the temple (2 Kin. 25:8–10). The Judahite leaders who had led the resistance against the Babylonians either died in battle or were exiled. Nevertheless, the Babylonians left some people in the land to produce crops, if for no other reason, to pay tribute to Babylon (2 Kin. 25:12).

The Babylonian king appointed Gedaliah as governor of Judah to oversee the people who remained (Jer. 40:5). He held office only as a representative of the victorious Babylonians; nevertheless, Gedaliah's credentials were impressive. His grandfather was Shaphan, a scribe and high-ranking official during King Josiah's reign (640–609 B.C.) His father Ahikam was also an official of Josiah's court (2 Kin. 22:12), and was instrumental in saving Jeremiah from death (Jer. 26:24). Gedaliah, therefore, came from a family with long ties in the public administration of Judah.

Yet after the conquest, Judah was a tough place to administrate. Jerusalem had been destroyed, so Gedaliah governed from Mizpah (Jer. 40:8), a town north of Jerusalem in the land of the tribe of Benjamin. As might be expected, many of those left in the land resented the havoc and loss caused by the Babylonians. Judah's old society had been destroyed; what remained threatened to fall apart through various factions. It was Gedaliah's job to hold these factions together.

Though initially successful (Jer. 40:12), Gedaliah eventually failed. A member of the royal family named Ishmael assassinated Gedaliah and purged the governor's supporters in an effort to gain the throne of Judah for himself (41:1–3). Yet such was not to be, and Ishmael fled to Ammon as a refugee (41:15). The remaining Judeans, fearing reprisal from the Babylonians, fled to Egypt (41:17). The land, which the Babylonians had left at least marginally inhabited, now was empty.

Jeremiah and said to him: "The LORD your God has pronounced this doom on this place. ³Now the LORD has brought *it,* and has done just as He said. Because you *people* have sinned against the LORD, and not obeyed His voice, therefore this thing has come upon you. ⁴And now look, I free you this day from the chains that *were* on your hand. If it seems good to you to come with me to Babylon, come, and I will look after you. But if it seems wrong for you to come with me to Babylon, remain here. See, all the land *is* before you; wherever it seems good and convenient for you to go, go there."

⁵Now while Jeremiah had not yet gone back, *Nebuzaradan said,* "Go back to Gedaliah the son of Ahikam, the son of Shaphan, whom the king of Babylon has made governor over the cities of Judah, and dwell with him among the people. Or go wherever it seems convenient for you to go." So the captain of the guard gave him rations and a gift and let him go. ⁶Then

Jeremiah went to Gedaliah the son of Ahikam, to Mizpah, and dwelt with him among the people who were left in the land.

⁷And when all the captains of the armies who *were* in the fields, they and their men, heard that the king of Babylon had made Gedaliah the son of Ahikam governor in the land, and had committed to him men, women, children, and the poorest of the land who had not been carried away captive to Babylon, ⁸then they came to Gedaliah at Mizpah—Ishmael the son of Nethaniah, Johanan and Jonathan the sons of Kareah, Seraiah the son of Tanhumeth, the sons of Ephai the Netophathite, and Jezaniah[a] the son of a Maachathite, they and their men. ⁹And Gedaliah the son of Ahikam, the son of Shaphan, took an oath before them and their men, saying, "Do not be afraid to serve the Chaldeans. Dwell in the land and serve the king of Babylon, and it shall be well with you. ¹⁰As for me, I will indeed dwell at Mizpah and serve the Chaldeans who come to us. But you, gather wine and

---

40:8 ªSpelled *Jaazaniah* in 2 Kings 25:23

summer fruit and oil, put *them* in your vessels, and dwell in your cities that you have taken." ¹¹Likewise, when all the Jews who *were* in Moab, among the Ammonites, in Edom, and who *were* in all the countries, heard that the king of Babylon had left a remnant of Judah, and that he had set over them Gedaliah the son of Ahikam, the son of Shaphan, ¹²then all the Jews returned out of all places where they had been driven, and came to the land of Judah, to Gedaliah at Mizpah, and gathered wine and summer fruit in abundance.

¹³Moreover Johanan the son of Kareah and all the captains of the forces that *were* in the fields came to Gedaliah at Mizpah, ¹⁴and said to him, "Do you certainly know that Baalis the king of the Ammonites has sent Ishmael the son of Nethaniah to murder you?" But Gedaliah the son of Ahikam did not believe them.

¹⁵Then Johanan the son of Kareah spoke secretly to Gedaliah in Mizpah, saying, "Let me go, please, and I will kill Ishmael the son of Nethaniah, and no one will know *it*. Why should he murder you, so that all the Jews who are gathered to you would be scattered, and the remnant in Judah perish?"

¹⁶But Gedaliah the son of Ahikam said to Johanan the son of Kareah, "You shall not do this thing, for you speak falsely concerning Ishmael."

Insurrection Against Gedaliah

41 ¹Now it came to pass in the seventh month *that* Ishmael the son of Nethaniah, the son of Elishama, of the royal family and of the officers of the king, came with ten men to Gedaliah the son of Ahikam, at Mizpah. And there they ate bread together in Mizpah. ²Then Ishmael the son of Nethaniah, and the ten men who were with him, arose and struck Gedaliah the son of Ahikam, the son of Shaphan, with the sword, and killed him whom the king of Babylon had made governor over the land. ³Ishmael also struck down all the Jews who were with him, *that is,* with Gedaliah at Mizpah, and the Chaldeans who were found there, the men of war.

⁴And it happened, on the second day after he had killed Gedaliah, when as yet no one knew *it,* ⁵that certain men came from Shechem, from Shiloh, and from Samaria, eighty men with their beards shaved and their clothes torn, having cut themselves, with offerings and incense in their hand, to bring *them* to the house of the LORD. ⁶Now Ishmael the son of Nethaniah went out from Mizpah to meet them, weeping as he went along; and it happened as he met them that he said to them, "Come to Gedaliah the son of Ahikam!" ⁷So it was, when they came into the midst of the city, that Ishmael the son of Nethaniah killed them *and cast them* into the midst of a pit, he and the men who were with him. ⁸But ten men were found among them who said to Ishmael, "Do not kill us, for we have treasures of wheat, barley, oil, and honey in the field." So he desisted and did not kill them among their brethren. ⁹Now the pit into which Ishmael had cast all the dead bodies of the men whom he had slain, because of Gedaliah, *was* the same one Asa the king had made for fear of Baasha king of Israel. Ishmael the son of Nethaniah filled it with *the* slain. ¹⁰Then Ishmael carried away captive all the rest of the people who *were* in Mizpah, the king's daughters and all the people who remained in Mizpah, whom Nebuzaradan the captain of the guard had committed to Gedaliah the son of Ahikam. And Ishmael the son of Nethaniah carried them away captive and departed to go over to the Ammonites.

¹¹But when Johanan the son of Kareah and all the captains of the forces that *were* with him heard of all the evil that Ishmael the son of Nethaniah had done, ¹²they took all the men and went to fight with Ishmael the son of Nethaniah; and they found him by the great pool that *is* in Gibeon. ¹³So it was, when all the people who *were* with Ishmael saw Johanan the son of Kareah, and all the captains of the forces who *were* with him, that they were glad. ¹⁴Then all

DAILY LIFE AND CUSTOMS

When in mourning, people displayed conventional signs of distress, such as tearing their clothes, wearing sackcloth, and putting dust or dirt on themselves (Jer. 41:5). Some mourners cut themselves, although this was forbidden by the Law of Moses (Deut. 14:1). These acts of self-humiliation were powerful expressions of inner turmoil and sorrow. They were not in themselves religious acts (Is. 58:5, 6).

the people whom Ishmael had carried away captive from Mizpah turned around and came back, and went to Johanan the son of Kareah. 15But Ishmael the son of Nethaniah escaped from Johanan with eight men and went to the Ammonites.

16Then Johanan the son of Kareah, and all the captains of the forces that were with him, took from Mizpah all the rest of the people whom he had recovered from Ishmael the son of Nethaniah after he had murdered Gedaliah the son of Ahikam— the mighty men of war and the women and the children and the eunuchs, whom he had brought back from Gibeon. 17And they departed and dwelt in the habitation of Chimham, which is near Bethlehem, as they went on their way to Egypt, 18because of the Chaldeans; for they were afraid of them, because Ishmael the son of Nethaniah had murdered Gedaliah the son of Ahikam, whom the king of Babylon had made governor in the land.

The Flight to Egypt Forbidden

42 1Now all the captains of the forces, Johanan the son of Kareah, Jezaniah the son of Hoshaiah, and all the people, from the least to the greatest, came near 2and said to Jeremiah the prophet, "Please, let our petition be acceptable to you, and pray for us to the LORD your God, for all this remnant (since we are left but a few of many, as you can see), 3that the LORD your God may show us the way in which we should walk and the thing we should do."

4Then Jeremiah the prophet said to them, "I have heard. Indeed, I will pray to the LORD your God according to your words, and it shall be, that whatever the LORD answers you, I will declare it to you. I will keep nothing back from you."

5So they said to Jeremiah, "Let the LORD be a true and faithful witness between us, if we do not do according to everything which the LORD your God sends us by you. 6Whether it is pleasing or displeasing, we will obey the voice of the LORD our God to whom we send you, that it may be well with us when we obey the voice of the LORD our God."

7And it happened after ten days that the word of the LORD came to Jeremiah. 8Then he called Johanan the son of Kareah, all the captains of the forces which were with him, and all the people from the least even to the greatest, 9and said to them, "Thus says the LORD, the God of Israel, to whom you sent me to present your petition before Him: 10'If you will still remain in this land, then I will build you and not pull you down, and I will plant you and not pluck you up. For I relent concerning the disaster that I have brought upon you. 11Do not be afraid of the king of Babylon, of whom you are afraid; do not be afraid of him,' says the LORD, 'for I am with you, to

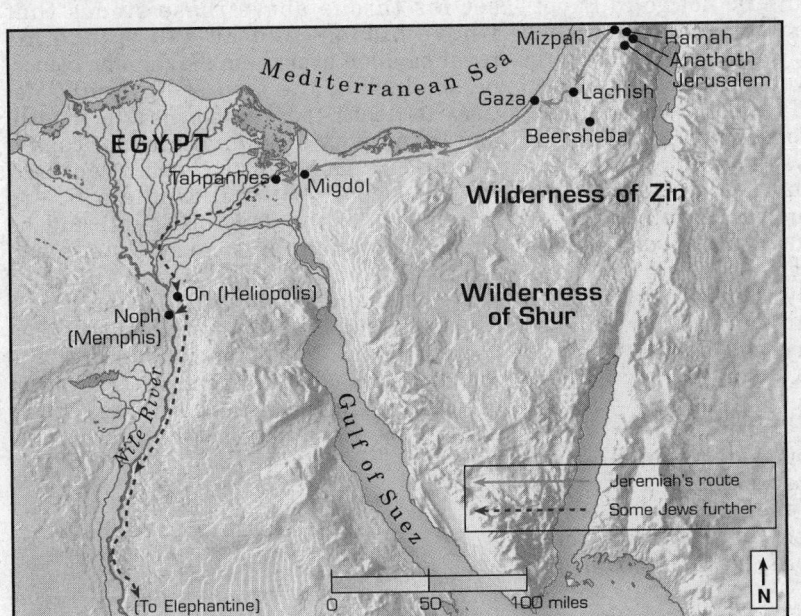

Jeremiah's Journey to Egypt

With the fall of Jerusalem, Jeremiah was taken in chains to Ramah and released. He went on to Mizpah to support the people left in the land. When the governor was killed, Jeremiah prophesied against leaving the land but was taken with the remnant to Tahpanhes in Egypt. His further prophecies to Jews living in Migdol, Noph, and Tahpanhes may have contributed to Jewish settlements being established deeper in Egypt, as far as Yeb (Elephantine).

save you and deliver you from his hand. [12]And I will show you mercy, that he may have mercy on you and cause you to return to your own land.'

[13]"But if you say, 'We will not dwell in this land,' disobeying the voice of the LORD your God, [14]saying, 'No, but we will go to the land of Egypt where we shall see no war, nor hear the sound of the trumpet, nor be hungry for bread, and there we will dwell'— [15]Then hear now the word of the LORD, O remnant of Judah! Thus says the LORD of hosts, the God of Israel: 'If you wholly set your faces to enter Egypt, and go to dwell there, [16]then it shall be *that* the sword which you feared shall overtake you there in the land of Egypt; the famine of which you were afraid shall follow close after you there *in* Egypt; and there you shall die. [17]So shall it be with all the men who set their faces to go to Egypt to dwell there. They shall die by the sword, by famine, and by pestilence. And none of them shall remain or escape from the disaster that I will bring upon them.'

[18]"For thus says the LORD of hosts, the God of Israel: 'As My anger and My fury have been poured out on the inhabitants of Jerusalem, so will My fury be poured out on you when you enter Egypt. And you shall be an oath, an astonishment, a curse, and a reproach; and you shall see this place no more.'

[19]"The LORD has said concerning you, O remnant of Judah, 'Do not go to Egypt!' Know certainly that I have admonished you this day. [20]For you were hypocrites in your hearts when you sent me to the LORD your God, saying, 'Pray for us to the LORD our God, and according to all that the LORD your God says, so declare to us and we will do *it*.' [21]And I have this day declared *it* to you, but you have not obeyed the voice of the LORD your God, or anything which He has sent you by me. [22]Now therefore, know certainly that you shall die by the sword, by famine, and by pestilence in the place where you desire to go to dwell."

Jeremiah Taken to Egypt

43 [1]Now it happened, when Jeremiah had stopped speaking to all the people all the words of the LORD their God, for which the LORD their God had sent him to them, all these words, [2]that Azariah the son of Hoshaiah, Johanan the son of Kareah, and all the proud men spoke, say-ing to Jeremiah, "You speak falsely! The LORD our God has not sent you to say, 'Do not go to Egypt to dwell there.' [3]But Baruch the son of Neriah has set you against us, to deliver us into the hand of the Chaldeans, that they may put us to death or carry us away captive to Babylon." [4]So Johanan the son of Kareah, all the captains of the forces, and all the people would not obey the voice of the LORD, to remain in the land of Judah. [5]But Johanan the son of Kareah and all the captains of the forces took all the remnant of Judah who had returned to dwell in the land of Judah, from all nations where they had been driven— [6]men, women, children, the king's daughters, and every person whom Nebuzaradan the captain of the guard had left with Gedaliah the son of Ahikam, the son of Shaphan, and Jeremiah the prophet and Baruch the son of Neriah. [7]So they went to the land of Egypt, for they did not obey the voice of the LORD. And they went as far as Tahpanhes.

[8]Then the word of the LORD came to Jeremiah in Tahpanhes, saying, [9]"Take large stones in your hand, and hide them in the sight of the men of Judah, in the clay in the brick courtyard which *is* at the entrance to Pharaoh's house in Tahpanhes; [10]and say to them, 'Thus says the LORD of hosts, the God of Israel: "Behold, I will send and bring Nebuchadnezzar the king of Babylon, My servant, and will set his throne above these stones that I have hidden. And he will spread his royal pavilion over them. [11]When he comes, he shall strike the land of Egypt *and deliver* to death *those appointed* for death, and to captivity *those appointed* for captivity, and to the sword *those appointed* for the sword. [12]I[a] will kindle a fire in the houses of the gods of Egypt, and he shall burn them and carry them away captive. And he shall array himself with the land of Egypt, as a shepherd puts on his garment, and he shall go out from there in peace. [13]He shall also break the *sacred* pillars of Beth Shemesh[a] that *are* in the land of Egypt; and the houses of the gods of the Egyptians he shall burn with fire."'"

43:12 [a]Following Masoretic Text and Targum; Septuagint, Syriac, and Vulgate read *He.*
43:13 [a]Literally *House of the Sun,* ancient On; later called Heliopolis

Israelites Will Be Punished in Egypt

44 ¹The word that came to Jeremiah concerning all the Jews who dwell in the land of Egypt, who dwell at Migdol, at Tahpanhes, at Noph,ᵃ and in the country of Pathros, saying, ²"Thus says the LORD of hosts, the God of Israel: 'You have seen all the calamity that I have brought on Jerusalem and on all the cities of Judah; and behold, this day they *are* a desolation, and no one dwells in them, ³because of their wickedness which they have committed to provoke Me to anger, in that they went to burn incense *and* to serve other gods whom they did not know, they nor you nor your fathers. ⁴However I have sent to you all My servants the prophets, rising early and sending *them,* saying, "Oh, do not do this abominable thing that I hate!" ⁵But they did not listen or incline their ear to turn from their wickedness, to burn no incense to other gods. ⁶So My fury and My anger were poured out and kindled in the cities of Judah and in the streets of Jerusalem; and they are wasted *and* desolate, as it is this day.'

⁷"Now therefore, thus says the LORD, the God of hosts, the God of Israel: 'Why do you commit *this* great evil against yourselves, to cut off from you man and woman, child and infant, out of Judah, leaving none to remain, ⁸in that you provoke Me to wrath with the works of your hands, burning incense to other gods in the land of Egypt where you have gone to dwell, that you may cut yourselves off and be a curse and a reproach among all the nations of the earth? ⁹Have you forgotten the wickedness of your fathers, the wickedness of the kings of Judah, the wickedness of their wives, your own wickedness, and the wickedness of your wives, which they committed in the land of Judah and in the streets of Jerusalem? ¹⁰They have not been humbled, to this day, nor have they feared; they have not walked in My law or in My statutes that I set before you and your fathers.'

¹¹"Therefore thus says the LORD of hosts, the God of Israel: 'Behold, I will set My face against you for catastrophe and for cutting off all Judah. ¹²And I will take the remnant of Judah who have set their faces to go into the land of Egypt to dwell there, and they shall all be consumed *and* fall in the land of Egypt. They shall be consumed by the sword *and* by famine. They shall die, from the least to the greatest, by the sword and by famine; and they shall be an oath, an astonishment, a curse and a reproach! ¹³For I will punish those who dwell in the land of Egypt, as I have punished Jerusalem, by the sword, by famine, and by pestilence, ¹⁴so that none of the remnant of Judah who have gone into the land of Egypt to dwell there shall escape or survive, lest they return to the land of Judah, to which they desire to return and dwell. For none shall return except those who escape.' "

¹⁵Then all the men who knew that their wives had burned incense to other gods, with all the women who stood by, a great multitude, and all the people who dwelt in the land of Egypt, in Pathros, answered Jeremiah, saying: ¹⁶"As *for* the word that you have spoken to us in the name of the LORD, we will not listen to you! ¹⁷But we will certainly do whatever has gone out of our own mouth, to burn incense to the queen of heaven and pour out drink offerings to her, as we have done, we and our fathers, our kings and our princes, in the cities of Judah and in the streets of Jerusalem. For *then* we had plenty of food, were well-off, and saw no trouble. ¹⁸But since we stopped burning incense to the queen of heaven and pouring out drink offerings to her, we have lacked everything and have been consumed by the sword and by famine."

¹⁹*The women also said,* "And when we burned incense to the queen of heaven and poured out drink offerings to her, did we make cakes for her, to worship her, and

---

44:1 ᵃThat is, ancient Memphis

CULTS AND SUPERNATURAL

The "queen of heaven" referred to by Jeremiah was a Near Eastern goddess similar to Aphrodite or Venus. Offering cakes to the gods was a common practice, as was pouring out libations (Jer. 44:19). A libation is an offering made by pouring drink onto the ground. Thus, the people offered to a pagan goddess their daily food.

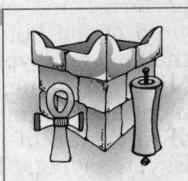

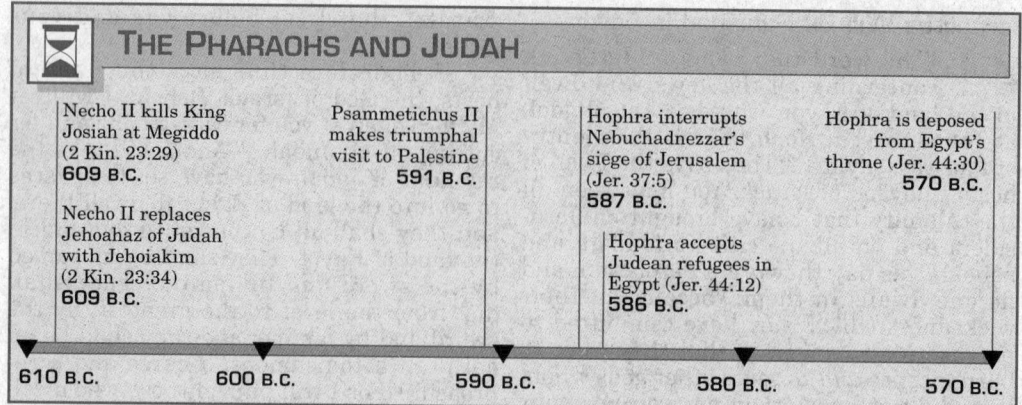

THE PHARAOHS AND JUDAH

Necho II kills King Josiah at Megiddo (2 Kin. 23:29) **609 B.C.**	Psammetichus II makes triumphal visit to Palestine **591 B.C.**	Hophra interrupts Nebuchadnezzar's siege of Jerusalem (Jer. 37:5) **587 B.C.**	Hophra is deposed from Egypt's throne (Jer. 44:30) **570 B.C.**
Necho II replaces Jehoahaz of Judah with Jehoiakim (2 Kin. 23:34) **609 B.C.**		Hophra accepts Judean refugees in Egypt (Jer. 44:12) **586 B.C.**	

610 B.C.   600 B.C.   590 B.C.   580 B.C.   570 B.C.

pour out drink offerings to her without our husbands' *permission?*"

20Then Jeremiah spoke to all the people—the men, the women, and all the people who had given him *that* answer—saying: 21"The incense that you burned in the cities of Judah and in the streets of Jerusalem, you and your fathers, your kings and your princes, and the people of the land, did not the Lord remember them, and did it *not* come into His mind? 22So the Lord could no longer bear *it*, because of the evil of your doings *and* because of the abominations which you committed. Therefore your land is a desolation, an astonishment, a curse, and without an inhabitant, as *it is* this day. 23Because you have burned incense and because you have sinned against the Lord, and have not obeyed the voice of the Lord or walked in His law, in His statutes or in His testimonies, therefore this calamity has happened to you, as *at* this day."

24Moreover Jeremiah said to all the people and to all the women, "Hear the word of the Lord, all Judah who *are* in the land of Egypt! 25Thus says the Lord of hosts, the God of Israel, saying: 'You and your wives have spoken with your mouths and fulfilled with your hands, saying, "We will surely keep our vows that we have made, to burn incense to the queen of heaven and pour out drink offerings to her." You will surely keep your vows and perform your vows!' 26Therefore hear the word of the Lord, all Judah who dwell in the land of Egypt: 'Behold, I have sworn by My great name,' says the Lord, 'that My name shall no more be named in the mouth of any man of Judah in all the land of Egypt, saying, "The Lord God lives." 27Behold, I will watch over them for adversity

and not for good. And all the men of Judah who *are* in the land of Egypt shall be consumed by the sword and by famine, until there is an end to them. 28Yet a small number who escape the sword shall return from the land of Egypt to the land of Judah; and all the remnant of Judah, who have gone to the land of Egypt to dwell there, shall know whose words will stand, Mine or theirs. 29And this *shall be* a sign to you,' says the Lord, 'that I will punish you in this place, that you may know that My words will surely stand against you for adversity.'

30"Thus says the Lord: 'Behold, I will give Pharaoh Hophra king of Egypt into the hand of his enemies and into the hand of those who seek his life, as I gave Zedekiah king of Judah into the hand of Nebuchadnezzar king of Babylon, his enemy who sought his life.' "

Priestly Account: The Fall of Jerusalem

The Chronicler's account of Jerusalem's destruction is brief and, as usual, focuses on the temple. Much is omitted, such as Zedekiah's desperate flight from the doomed city. Chronicles—written long after Kings—adds a reference to the now vindicated prophet Jeremiah (2 Chr. 36:12; see also "Priestly Account: Zedekiah and Jeremiah" at 2 Chr. 36:11). Indeed, the Chronicler was aware not only of the prophet but of some of his specific prophecies: 2 Chr. 36:21 makes a direct reference to the 70 years of captivity that Jeremiah foretold in his letter to the exiles (Jer. 29:10).

■ 2 Chronicles 36:17–21

THE PHARAOH WHO WAS BUT A NOISE (Jer. 44:30)

Hophra, who reigned from 589 to 570 B.C., was the fourth king of the 26th Dynasty of Egypt. Like previous rulers from the capital at Sais, known as the Saite dynasty, he intervened in Palestinian affairs in order to block the advances of Nebuchadnezzar II of Babylon. His attempt to break up Nebuchadnezzar's siege of Jerusalem in 587 B.C. failed, and the city eventually was destroyed (Jer. 37:5–11). Many of Judah's refugees from the Babylonian siege did flee to Egypt, where they were accepted by Hophra and settled.

The Greek historian Diodorus, who from about 60 to 30 B.C. wrote a world history, claims that Hophra was successful in weakening Babylonian rule in Phoenicia and Cyprus at this time. The pharaoh employed Greek mercenaries (Jer. 46:21) from Ionia and Caria (west coast of Turkey) to strengthen his military forces.

The prophet Jeremiah criticizes Hophra as "but a noise," who "passed by the appointed time" (Jer. 46:17). This may describe Hophra's ineffectiveness and indecisiveness as a leader. His attempt to quell a revolt in Cyrene late in his reign was decisively defeated, causing a rebellion in Egypt. In 570 B.C. the Egyptian general Amasis forced Hophra to flee east from Egypt.

In 567 B.C. Hophra returned to side with Nebuchadnezzar in an invasion of Egypt. The effort failed, and Hophra was captured and put to death approximately 20 years after a prophetic statement by Jeremiah (Jer. 44:30). The Greek historian Herodotus claims that Hophra's tomb was still accessible over a century later, during that historian's time (c. 484–425 B.C.).

2 Chronicles
The Fall of Jerusalem

36 :17 Therefore He brought against them the king of the Chaldeans, who killed their young men with the sword in the house of their sanctuary, and had no compassion on young man or virgin, on the aged or the weak; He gave *them* all into his hand. 18And all the articles from the house of God, great and small, the treasures of the house of the LORD, and the treasures of the king and of his leaders, all *these* he took to Babylon. 19Then they burned the house of God, broke down the wall of Jerusalem, burned all its palaces with fire, and destroyed all its precious possessions. 20And those who escaped from the sword he carried away to Babylon, where they became servants to him and his sons until the rule of the kingdom of Persia, 21to fulfill the word of the LORD by the mouth of Jeremiah, until the land had enjoyed her Sabbaths. As long as she lay desolate she kept Sabbath, to fulfill seventy years.

The End of the Siege

When it was clear to all in Jerusalem that there would be no escape from Nebuchadnezzar's siege, King Zedekiah tried to escape. He was captured and brutally blinded (Jer. 39:4–7). Away in Babylon, Ezekiel described the event with uncanny accuracy (Ezek. 12). The end had come for Jerusalem. As Zedekiah's vision was destroyed, Ezekiel's vision was coming true (12:22–28).

■ Ezekiel 12:1–28

Ezekiel
Judah's Captivity Portrayed

12 :1 Now the word of the LORD came to me, saying: 2"Son of man, you dwell in the midst of a rebellious house, which has eyes to see but does not see, and ears to hear but does not hear; for they *are* a rebellious house.

3"Therefore, son of man, prepare your belongings for captivity, and go into captivity by day in their sight. You shall go from your place into captivity to another place in their sight. It may be that they will consider, though they *are* a rebellious house. 4By day you shall bring out your belongings in their sight, as though going into captivity; and at evening you shall go in their sight, like those who go into captivity. 5Dig through the wall in their sight, and carry your belongings out through it. 6In their sight you shall bear *them* on *your* shoulders *and* carry *them* out at twilight;

DIGGING THROUGH A WALL (Ezek. 12:5–7)

God gave Ezekiel a curious command to carry out before his Judean peers. The prophet was to "dig through the wall in their sight," carrying his belongings out through the opening (Ezek. 12:5). Furthermore, he was to undertake this act "at twilight," with his face covered so that he could not see the ground (12:6). This behavior was to be "a sign to the house of Israel."

Ezekiel thus theatrically imitated a clandestine escape from a city under siege. City walls were thick structures, frequently serving as the back wall of private homes. Often the walls were casemate walls: two parallel walls built with 5 to 6 feet of open space between them. Cross walls would regularly link the two. The resulting rooms would be filled with earth or rubble.

City walls protected the inhabitants from enemy attacks, but they also made it difficult to escape the city once a siege was under way. The city gate could be easily guarded, but it provided the only direct access out of the city.

Only two options remained to escape from a city under siege. One could go *over* the wall—though, like a spider on a white wall, the enemy could easily detect you from afar. The other option would be to escape *through* the wall—literally to "dig" your way through it from the back room of your dwelling. Under the cover of darkness—when one could not see the ground—was the best time for such an escape, carrying only one's most valuable personal items.

In this way Ezekiel prophetically acted out someone attempting to escape the siege of Jerusalem before the city fell. He thus was a "sign" of God's judgment to the Judean community in exile.

---

you shall cover your face, so that you cannot see the ground, for I have made you a sign to the house of Israel."

⁷So I did as I was commanded. I brought out my belongings by day, as though going into captivity, and at evening I dug through the wall with my hand. I brought *them* out at twilight, *and* I bore *them* on *my* shoulder in their sight.

⁸And in the morning the word of the LORD came to me, saying, ⁹"Son of man, has not the house of Israel, the rebellious house, said to you, 'What are you doing?' ¹⁰Say to them, 'Thus says the Lord GOD: "This burden *concerns* the prince in Jerusalem and all the house of Israel who are among them." ' ¹¹Say, 'I *am* a sign to you. As I have done, so shall it be done to them; they shall be carried away into captivity.' ¹²And the prince who *is* among them shall bear *his* belongings on *his* shoulder at twilight and go out. They shall dig through the wall to carry *them* out through it. He shall cover his face, so that he cannot see the ground with *his* eyes. ¹³I will also spread My net over him, and he shall be caught in My snare. I will bring him to Babylon, *to* the land of the Chaldeans; yet he shall not see it, though he shall die

there. ¹⁴I will scatter to every wind all who *are* around him to help him, and all his troops; and I will draw out the sword after them.

¹⁵"Then they shall know that I *am* the LORD, when I scatter them among the nations and disperse them throughout the countries. ¹⁶But I will spare a few of their men from the sword, from famine, and from pestilence, that they may declare all their abominations among the Gentiles wherever they go. Then they shall know that I *am* the LORD."

Judgment Not Postponed

¹⁷Moreover the word of the LORD came to me, saying, ¹⁸"Son of man, eat your bread with quaking, and drink your water with trembling and anxiety. ¹⁹And say to the people of the land, 'Thus says the Lord GOD to the inhabitants of Jerusalem *and* to the land of Israel: "They shall eat their bread with anxiety, and drink their water with dread, so that her land may be emptied of all who are in it, because of the violence of all those who dwell in it. ²⁰Then the cities that are inhabited shall be laid waste, and the land shall become desolate; and you shall know that I *am* the LORD." ' "

21And the word of the LORD came to me, saying, 22"Son of man, what *is* this proverb *that* you *people* have about the land of Israel, which says, 'The days are prolonged, and every vision fails'? 23Tell them therefore, 'Thus says the Lord GOD: "I will lay this proverb to rest, and they shall no more use it as a proverb in Israel." But say to them, "The days are at hand, and the fulfillment of every vision. 24For no more shall there be any false vision or flattering divination within the house of Israel. 25For I *am* the LORD. I speak, and the word which I speak will come to pass; it will no more be postponed; for in your days, O rebellious house, I will say the word and perform it," says the Lord GOD.' "

26Again the word of the LORD came to me, saying, 27"Son of man, look, the house of Israel is saying, 'The vision that he sees *is* for many days *from now,* and he prophesies of times far off.' 28Therefore say to them, 'Thus says the Lord GOD: "None of My words will be postponed any more, but the word which I speak will be done," says the Lord GOD.' "

Has God Renounced the Covenant with David?

The superscription to Ps. 89 associates this psalm with Ethan the Ezrahite, an ancient wise man. Ethan is named along with three sons of Mahol as being surpassed in wisdom by Solomon (1 Kin. 4:31). Nevertheless, the content of this psalm almost certainly speaks of the fall of Jerusalem. One passage (89:38–45) describes a successor to King David who was defeated and deposed—possibly Jehoiachin, probably Zedekiah. Perhaps an older psalm was revised sometime after the destruction of 586 B.C. In any case, the question asked by the psalm was surely asked in that crisis: with Jerusalem in ruins and the unbroken line of David apparently ended, where was God's covenant now? The psalm concludes with its question unanswered.

▼ ■ Psalm 89

PSALM 89

Remembering the Covenant with David, and Sorrow for Lost Blessings

A Contemplation[a] *of Ethan the Ezrahite.*

I will sing of the mercies of the LORD
  forever;

89:title ᵃHebrew *Maschil*

With my mouth will I make known
  Your faithfulness to all generations.
2 For I have said, "Mercy shall be built
  up forever;
Your faithfulness You shall establish
  in the very heavens."

3 "I have made a covenant with My
  chosen,
I have sworn to My servant David:
4 'Your seed I will establish forever,
And build up your throne to all
  generations.' "   Selah

5 And the heavens will praise Your
  wonders, O LORD;
Your faithfulness also in the assembly
  of the saints.
6 For who in the heavens can be
  compared to the LORD?
Who among the sons of the mighty can
  be likened to the LORD?
7 God is greatly to be feared in the
  assembly of the saints,
And to be held in reverence by all
  those around Him.
8 O LORD God of hosts,
Who *is* mighty like You, O LORD?
Your faithfulness also surrounds You.
9 You rule the raging of the sea;
When its waves rise, You still them.
10 You have broken Rahab in pieces, as
  one who is slain;
You have scattered Your enemies with
  Your mighty arm.

11 The heavens *are* Yours, the earth also
  is Yours;
The world and all its fullness, You
  have founded them.
12 The north and the south, You have
  created them;
Tabor and Hermon rejoice in Your
  name.
13 You have a mighty arm;
Strong is Your hand, *and* high is Your
  right hand.
14 Righteousness and justice *are* the
  foundation of Your throne;
Mercy and truth go before Your face.
15 Blessed *are* the people who know the
  joyful sound!
They walk, O LORD, in the light of
  Your countenance.
16 In Your name they rejoice all day long,
And in Your righteousness they are
  exalted.

17 For You *are* the glory of their
    strength,
   And in Your favor our horn is exalted.
18 For our shield *belongs* to the LORD,
   And our king to the Holy One of
    Israel.

19 Then You spoke in a vision to Your
    holy one,[a]
   And said: "I have given help to *one
    who is* mighty;
   I have exalted one chosen from the
    people.
20 I have found My servant David;
   With My holy oil I have anointed
    him,
21 With whom My hand shall be
    established;
   Also My arm shall strengthen him.
22 The enemy shall not outwit him,
   Nor the son of wickedness afflict
    him.
23 I will beat down his foes before his
    face,
   And plague those who hate him.

24 "But My faithfulness and My mercy
    shall be with him,
   And in My name his horn shall be
    exalted.
25 Also I will set his hand over the sea,
   And his right hand over the rivers.
26 He shall cry to Me, 'You *are* my
    Father,
   My God, and the rock of my salvation.'
27 Also I will make him *My* firstborn,
   The highest of the kings of the earth.
28 My mercy I will keep for him forever,
   And My covenant shall stand firm
    with him.
29 His seed also I will make *to endure*
    forever,
   And his throne as the days of heaven.

30 "If his sons forsake My law
   And do not walk in My judgments,
31 If they break My statutes
   And do not keep My commandments,

32 Then I will punish their transgression
    with the rod,
   And their iniquity with stripes.
33 Nevertheless My lovingkindness I will
    not utterly take from him,
   Nor allow My faithfulness to fail.
34 My covenant I will not break,
   Nor alter the word that has gone out
    of My lips.
35 Once I have sworn by My holiness;
   I will not lie to David:
36 His seed shall endure forever,
   And his throne as the sun before Me;
37 It shall be established forever like the
    moon,
   Even *like* the faithful witness in the
    sky."   Selah

38 But You have cast off and abhorred,
   You have been furious with Your
    anointed.
39 You have renounced the covenant of
    Your servant;
   You have profaned his crown *by
    casting it* to the ground.
40 You have broken down all his hedges;
   You have brought his strongholds to
    ruin.
41 All who pass by the way plunder him;
   He is a reproach to his neighbors.
42 You have exalted the right hand of his
    adversaries;
   You have made all his enemies rejoice.
43 You have also turned back the edge of
    his sword,
   And have not sustained him in the
    battle.
44 You have made his glory cease,
   And cast his throne down to the
    ground.
45 The days of his youth You have
    shortened;
   You have covered him with shame.
                                       Selah

89:19 [a]Following many Hebrew manuscripts;
Masoretic Text, Septuagint, Targum, and Vulgate read
holy ones.

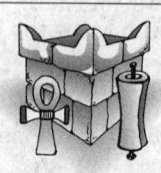

BELIEFS AND IDEAS

The power of kings was visible when they led an army, or when they were surrounded at court by their nobles and subjects. The earthly court is paralleled in the Bible by the heavenly court, where God is attended by an assembly of angels, saints, and "sons of the mighty" (Ps. 89:5–8). None of these lesser divine beings can be compared to God either in greatness or faithfulness (89:6).

46   How long, LORD?
     Will You hide Yourself forever?
     Will Your wrath burn like fire?

47   Remember how short my time is;
     For what futility have You created all
       the children of men?

48   What man can live and not see
       death?
     Can he deliver his life from the power
       of the grave?   Selah

49   Lord, where *are* Your former
      lovingkindnesses,
     Which You swore to David in Your
      truth?

50   Remember, Lord, the reproach of Your
      servants—
     How I bear in my bosom *the reproach*
      of all the many peoples,

51   With which Your enemies have
      reproached, O LORD,
     With which they have reproached the
      footsteps of Your anointed.

52   Blessed *be* the LORD forevermore!
     Amen and Amen.

The News Arrives in Babylon

In the 12th year and 10th month of Jehoiachin's exile (perhaps January, 585 B.C.), news of Jerusalem's end reached the exiles (Ezek. 33:21). Ezekiel (who had evidently been mute for some time) could speak again, and he spoke volumes. The blame for the tragedy should be assigned in general to Judah's abominations (33:25–33). More specifically, blame was due to Judah's faithless rulers. In a lament (ch. 19) over the kings, the "princes of Israel" (19:1), Ezekiel recognized that fire had "come out from a rod" and "devoured her fruit" (19:14). Zedekiah's own unfaithfulness had brought down the whole nation. Furthermore, Judah's prophets, priests, and princes had abused their power for personal gain (ch. 22).

These lamentations and oracles on Jerusalem's fall appear to be reflections on past events rather than predictions of events yet to come. For this reason, their words are appropriate for the days following the tragic events of 586 B.C.

- Ezekiel 33:21–33
- Ezekiel 19:1–14
- Ezekiel 22:23–31

Ezekiel 33:21–33
The Fall of Jerusalem

33 :21 And it came to pass in the twelfth year of our captivity, in the tenth *month,* on the fifth *day* of the month, *that* one who had escaped from Jerusalem came to me and said, "The city has been captured!"

22Now the hand of the LORD had been upon me the evening before the man came who had escaped. And He had opened my mouth; so when he came to me in the morning, my mouth was opened, and I was no longer mute.

The Cause of Judah's Ruin

23Then the word of the LORD came to me, saying: 24"Son of man, they who inhabit those ruins in the land of Israel are saying, 'Abraham was only one, and he inherited the land. But we *are* many; the land has been given to us as a possession.'

25"Therefore say to them, 'Thus says the Lord GOD: "You eat *meat* with blood, you lift up your eyes toward your idols, and shed blood. Should you then possess the land? 26You rely on your sword, you commit abominations, and you defile one another's wives. Should you then possess the land?" '

27"Say thus to them, 'Thus says the Lord GOD: "*As* I live, surely those who *are* in the ruins shall fall by the sword, and the one who *is* in the open field I will give to the beasts to be devoured, and those who *are* in the strongholds and caves shall die of the pestilence. 28For I will make the land most desolate, her arrogant strength shall cease, and the mountains of Israel shall be so desolate that no one will pass through. 29Then they shall know that I *am* the

TIME CAPSULE   585 to 581 B.C.

585–572	Nebuchadnezzar's 13-year siege of Tyre
585	News of Jerusalem's fall reaches the exiles (Ezek. 33:21)
585	The Medes incorporate the kingdom of Ararat into the Median Empire
582–581	Nebuchadnezzar defeats Ammon
581	Babylonian official Nebuzaradan deports captives from Jerusalem (Jer. 52:30)

LORD, when I have made the land most desolate because of all their abominations which they have committed." '

Hearing and Not Doing

30"As for you, son of man, the children of your people are talking about you beside the walls and in the doors of the houses; and they speak to one another, everyone saying to his brother, 'Please come and hear what the word is that comes from the LORD.' 31So they come to you as people do, they sit before you as My people, and they hear your words, but they do not do them; for with their mouth they show much love, but their hearts pursue their own gain. 32Indeed you are to them as a very lovely song of one who has a pleasant voice and can play well on an instrument; for they hear your words, but they do not do them. 33And when this comes to pass—surely it will come—then they will know that a prophet has been among them."

Ezekiel 19:1–14
Israel Degraded

19 :1 "Moreover take up a lamentation for the princes of Israel, 2and say:

'What is your mother? A lioness:
She lay down among the lions;
Among the young lions she nourished
    her cubs.
3 She brought up one of her cubs,
And he became a young lion;
He learned to catch prey,
And he devoured men.
4 The nations also heard of him;
He was trapped in their pit,
And they brought him with chains to
    the land of Egypt.

5 'When she saw that she waited, that
    her hope was lost,
She took another of her cubs and
    made him a young lion.
6 He roved among the lions,
And became a young lion;
He learned to catch prey;
He devoured men.
7 He knew their desolate places,a
And laid waste their cities;
The land with its fullness was
    desolated
By the noise of his roaring.
8 Then the nations set against him from
    the provinces on every side,

And spread their net over him;
He was trapped in their pit.
9 They put him in a cage with chains,
And brought him to the king of
    Babylon;
They brought him in nets,
That his voice should no longer be
    heard on the mountains of Israel.

10 'Your mother was like a vine in your
    bloodline,a
Planted by the waters,
Fruitful and full of branches
Because of many waters.
11 She had strong branches for scepters
    of rulers.
She towered in stature above the thick
    branches,
And was seen in her height amid the
    dense foliage.
12 But she was plucked up in fury,
She was cast down to the ground,
And the east wind dried her fruit.
Her strong branches were broken and
    withered;
The fire consumed them.
13 And now she is planted in the
    wilderness,
In a dry and thirsty land.
14 Fire has come out from a rod of her
    branches
And devoured her fruit,
So that she has no strong branch—a
    scepter for ruling.' "

This is a lamentation, and has become a lamentation.

Ezekiel 22:23–31
Israel's Wicked Leaders

22 :23 And the word of the LORD came to me, saying, 24"Son of man, say to her: 'You are a land that is not cleanseda or rained on in the day of indignation.' 25The conspiracy of her prophetsa in her midst is like a roaring lion tearing the prey; they have devoured people; they have taken treasure and precious things; they have

---

19:7 aSeptuagint reads *He stood in insolence;* Targum reads *He destroyed its palaces;* Vulgate reads *He learned to make widows.*   19:10 aLiterally *blood,* following Masoretic Text, Syriac, and Vulgate; Septuagint reads *like a flower on a pomegranate tree;* Targum reads *in your likeness.*   22:24 aFollowing Masoretic Text, Syriac, and Vulgate; Septuagint reads *showered upon.*   22:25 aFollowing Masoretic Text and Vulgate; Septuagint reads *princes;* Targum reads *scribes.*

Priests Upholding Ritual Purity (Ezek. 22:26)

In ancient Egypt and Mesopotamia it was common for the priests to shave their heads and live in the large temple precincts. As the personal servants or slaves of the god, they were expected to follow regulations for purity which would allow them to enter the presence of the deity and fulfill their roles involving upkeep of the temple, religious sacrifices and festival planning. If a priest became ritually unclean, he would have to leave the divine area until ritually cleansed.

The Jerusalem priests were not required to shave their heads, but were expected to follow similar rules of ritual. Since the priests were the only people who could make the necessary sacrifices before God, they had to be very careful about keeping the ritual correctly and maintaining themselves in the proper stance before God. When the prophet Ezekiel fumed against the Jerusalem priests, it was because they had not kept the precepts which were spelled out in the Levitical laws (Ezek. 22:26).

made many widows in her midst. 26Her priests have violated My law and profaned My holy things; they have not distinguished between the holy and unholy, nor have they made known *the difference* between the unclean and the clean; and they have hidden their eyes from My Sabbaths, so that I am profaned among them. 27Her princes in her midst *are* like wolves tearing the prey, to shed blood, to destroy people, and to get dishonest gain. 28Her prophets plastered them with untempered *mortar,* seeing false visions, and divining lies for them, saying, 'Thus says the Lord GOD,' when the LORD had not spoken. 29The people of the land have used oppressions, committed robbery, and mistreated the poor and needy; and they wrongfully oppress the stranger. 30So I sought for a man among them who would make a wall, and stand in the gap before Me on behalf of the land, that I should not destroy it; but I found no one. 31Therefore I have poured out My indignation on them; I have consumed them with the fire of My wrath; and I have recompensed their deeds on their own heads," says the Lord GOD.

Oracles Against Judah's Neighbors

When Jerusalem fell, the nations around it rejoiced and joined in the plunder. Edom, in particular, appears to have aided Babylon against Judah. Ezekiel pronounced God's judgment on all of these peoples, including Ammon, Moab, and Philistia (Ezek. 25).

The most explicit judgments were reserved for the city of Tyre, on the Phoenician coast, and for Egypt, which had incited Jerusalem's rebellion. The oracles against Tyre (Ezek. 26—28) are actually dated in the 11th year (586 B.C.; 26:1). Nevertheless, Tyre's selfish reaction (26:2) implies that Jerusalem had been destroyed, so these oracles can be read in the context of 585 B.C. when the news of Jerusalem's fall arrived in Babylon (33:21). The oracle includes a description (26:7-14) of Nebuchadnezzar's 13-year siege of Tyre from 585 to 572 B.C.

Ezekiel received the oracle against Egypt (Ezek. 32) in the 12th year and 12th month (perhaps March, 585 B.C.; 32:1). The lament for Pharaoh anticipates the invasion by Nebuchadnezzar's Babylonian army in 567 B.C. (32:11).

■ Ezekiel 25:1—28:26
■ Ezekiel 32:1-32

Ezekiel 25:1—28:26
Proclamation Against Ammon

25 :1 The word of the LORD came to me, saying, 2"Son of man, set your face against the Ammonites, and prophesy against them. 3Say to the Ammonites, 'Hear the word of the Lord GOD! Thus says the Lord GOD: "Because you said, 'Aha!' against My sanctuary when it was profaned, and against the land of Israel when it was desolate, and against the house of Judah when they went into captivity, 4indeed, therefore, I will deliver you as a possession to the men of the East, and they shall set their encampments among you and make their dwellings among you; they shall eat your fruit, and they shall drink your milk. 5And I will make Rabbah a

THE 13-YEAR SIEGE OF TYRE (Ezek. 26:1–8)

According to Ezekiel's prophecy (Ezek. 26:1, 2), the city-state of Tyre was jubilant upon hearing of the destruction of Jerusalem by Nebuchadnezzar II of Babylon in 586 B.C. Tyre was the great Phoenician seaport and commercial center to the north of Samaria and Judah. In her prime, Judah was a commercial link, thus a "gateway" (26:2), between Tyre and Arabia. With Judah out of the way, possibly Tyre imagined even greater opportunities for herself.

Such jubilation, however, would be short lived, as the Babylonian monarch also moved against the Mediterranean coast, including Tyre, soon thereafter. Tyre, along with Sidon, was one of the more prominent Phoenician city-states on the Mediterranean coast. It was actually on an island about 765 yards from land. After Nebuchadnezzar defeated Egypt at the battle of Carchemish (605 B.C.), Tyre became Babylon's chief antagonist in Western Asia.

Josephus, the Jewish historian (A.D. 37–100), quotes presently undiscovered Phoenician sources that Nebuchadnezzar laid siege to Tyre for 13 years (585–572 B.C.). This conflict is mentioned by Ezekiel (Ezek. 29:17, 18), although he makes no reference to the length of the siege. The Babylonian king was unable to capture the city, but he was able to enforce a treaty that Tyre's royal family would now reside in Babylon. Someone from Tyre's royalty was allowed to continue to rule, but only alongside an appointed Babylonian governor. Because of this, Tyre's power was severely weakened, and many of the city's elite classes fled to Carthage.

stable for camels and Ammon a resting place for flocks. Then you shall know that I *am* the LORD."

6"For thus says the Lord GOD: "Because you clapped *your* hands, stamped your feet, and rejoiced in heart with all your disdain for the land of Israel, 7indeed, therefore, I will stretch out My hand against you, and give you as plunder to the nations; I will cut you off from the peoples, and I will cause you to perish from the countries; I will destroy you, and you shall know that I *am* the LORD."

Proclamation Against Moab

8"Thus says the Lord GOD: "Because Moab and Seir say, 'Look! The house of Judah *is* like all the nations,' 9therefore, behold, I will clear the territory of Moab of cities, of the cities on its frontier, the glory of the country, Beth Jeshimoth, Baal Meon, and Kirjathaim. 10To the men of the East I will give it as a possession, together with the Ammonites, that the Ammonites may not be remembered among the nations. 11And I will execute judgments upon Moab, and they shall know that I *am* the LORD."

Proclamation Against Edom

12"Thus says the Lord GOD: "Because of what Edom did against the house of Judah by taking vengeance, and has greatly offended by avenging itself on them," 13therefore thus says the Lord GOD: "I will also stretch out My hand against Edom, cut off man and beast from it, and make it desolate from Teman; Dedan shall fall by the sword. 14I will lay My vengeance on Edom by the hand of My people Israel, that they may do in Edom according to My anger and according to My fury; and they shall know My vengeance," says the Lord GOD.

Proclamation Against Philistia

15"Thus says the Lord GOD: "Because the Philistines dealt vengefully and took vengeance with a spiteful heart, to destroy because of the old hatred," 16therefore thus says the Lord GOD: "I will stretch out My hand against the Philistines, and I will cut off the Cherethites and destroy the remnant of the seacoast. 17I will execute great vengeance on them with furious rebukes; and they shall know that I *am* the LORD, when I lay My vengeance upon them." ' "

Proclamation Against Tyre

26 1And it came to pass in the eleventh year, on the first *day* of the month, *that* the word of the LORD came to me, saying, 2"Son of man, because Tyre has said against Jerusalem, 'Aha! She is broken who *was* the gateway of the peoples; now she is turned over to me; I shall be filled; she is laid waste.'

3"Therefore thus says the Lord GOD: 'Behold, I *am* against you, O Tyre, and will cause many nations to come up against you, as the sea causes its waves to come up. ⁴And they shall destroy the walls of Tyre and break down her towers; I will also scrape her dust from her, and make her like the top of a rock. ⁵It shall be *a place for* spreading nets in the midst of the sea, for I have spoken,' says the Lord GOD; 'it shall become plunder for the nations. ⁶Also her daughter *villages* which *are* in the fields shall be slain by the sword. Then they shall know that I am the LORD.'

⁷For thus says the Lord GOD: 'Behold, I will bring against Tyre from the north Nebuchadnezzarᵃ king of Babylon, king of kings, with horses, with chariots, and with horsemen, and an army with many people. ⁸He will slay with the sword your daughter *villages* in the fields; he will heap up a siege mound against you, build a wall against you, and raise a defense against you. ⁹He will direct his battering rams against your walls, and with his axes he will break down your towers. ¹⁰Because of the abundance of his horses, their dust will cover you; your walls will shake at the noise of the horsemen, the wagons, and the chariots, when he enters your gates, as men enter a city that has been breached. ¹¹With the hooves of his horses he will trample all your streets; he will slay your people by the sword, and your strong pillars will fall to the ground. ¹²They will plunder your riches and pillage your merchandise; they will break down your walls and destroy your pleasant houses; they will lay your stones, your timber, and your soil in the midst of the water. ¹³I will put an end to the sound of your songs, and the sound of your harps shall be heard no more. ¹⁴I will make you like the top of a rock; you shall be *a place for* spreading nets, and you shall never be rebuilt, for I the LORD have spoken,' says the Lord GOD.

¹⁵"Thus says the Lord GOD to Tyre: 'Will the coastlands not shake at the sound

of your fall, when the wounded cry, when slaughter is made in the midst of you? ¹⁶Then all the princes of the sea will come down from their thrones, lay aside their robes, and take off their embroidered garments; they will clothe themselves with trembling; they will sit on the ground, tremble *every* moment, and be astonished at you. ¹⁷And they will take up a lamentation for you, and say to you:

"How you have perished,
O one inhabited by seafaring men,
O renowned city,
Who was strong at sea,
She and her inhabitants,
Who caused their terror *to be* on all
    her inhabitants!
18 Now the coastlands tremble on the
    day of your fall;
Yes, the coastlands by the sea are
    troubled at your departure." '

¹⁹"For thus says the Lord GOD: 'When I make you a desolate city, like cities that are not inhabited, when I bring the deep upon you, and great waters cover you, ²⁰then I will bring you down with those who descend into the Pit, to the people of old, and I will make you dwell in the lowest part of the earth, in places desolate from antiquity, with those who go down to the Pit, so that you may never be inhabited; and I shall establish glory in the land of the living. ²¹I will make you a terror, and you *shall be* no *more;* though you are sought for, you will never be found again,' says the Lord GOD."

Lamentation for Tyre

27 ¹The word of the LORD came again to me, saying, ²"Now, son of man, take up a lamentation for Tyre, ³and say to Tyre, 'You who are situated at the entrance of the sea, merchant of the peoples on many coastlands, thus says the Lord GOD:

"O Tyre, you have said,
'I *am* perfect in beauty.'

GEOGRAPHY AND ENVIRONMENT

Tyre was a Phoenician port about 50 miles south of Berytus (modern Beirut). It had a strong defense because it was built on an offshore island, as is noted by ancient and modern writers. The people of Tyre were expert seafarers, trading and founding colonies around the Mediterranean, including Carthage in North Africa. Tyre (Ezek. 27:2) is mentioned as early as 1800 B.C. in Egyptian texts.

HARAN, A CITY WITH A LONG LIFE (Ezek. 27:23)

Haran was a city in North Syria about 60 miles north of the meeting of the Euphrates and Balikh rivers. The city has a long history, including the report that the patriarch Abraham's family came to this area from Ur of the Chaldeans (Gen. 11:31).

In the late 2nd millennium B.C. Haran became an Assyrian stronghold, having relations with various Assyrian rulers. Adad-nirari I (1307–1274 B.C.) fortified its citadel, while Tiglath-Pileser I (1114–1076 B.C.) restored some of its religious edifices. In 763 B.C., however, the city rebelled against the rule of Ashur-dan III, who then destroyed Haran. The Assyrian king Sennacherib wrote to Judah's king Hezekiah around 701 or 688 B.C., and alluded to the event, boasting that his Assyrian "fathers" had destroyed Haran, among other cities (2 Kin. 19:12).

After the fall of the Neo-Assyrian capital at Nineveh in 612 B.C., Haran became the last center of Assyrian rule until it too fell to the Babylonians in 610 B.C. The city continued to exist, and about 585 B.C. the prophet Ezekiel names Haran as a successful commercial center that traded with Tyre (Ezek. 27:23).

---

4 Your borders *are* in the midst of the
    seas.
  Your builders have perfected your
    beauty.
5 They made all *your* planks of fir trees
    from Senir;
  They took a cedar from Lebanon to
    make you a mast.
6 *Of* oaks from Bashan they made your
    oars;
  The company of Ashurites have inlaid
    your planks
  With ivory from the coasts of Cyprus.[a]
7 Fine embroidered linen from Egypt
    was what you spread for your sail;
  Blue and purple from the coasts of
    Elishah was what covered you.

8 "Inhabitants of Sidon and Arvad were
    your oarsmen;
  Your wise men, O Tyre, were in you;
  They became your pilots.
9 Elders of Gebal and its wise men
  Were in you to caulk your seams;
  All the ships of the sea
  And their oarsmen were in you
  To market your merchandise.

10 "Those from Persia, Lydia,[a] and Libya[b]
  Were in your army as men of war;
  They hung shield and helmet in you;
  They gave splendor to you.
11 Men of Arvad with your army *were* on
    your walls *all* around,
  And the men of Gammad were in your
    towers;

They hung their shields on your walls
  all around;
They made your beauty perfect.

12 "Tarshish *was* your merchant because of your many luxury goods. They gave you silver, iron, tin, and lead for your goods. 13 Javan, Tubal, and Meshech *were* your traders. They bartered human lives and vessels of bronze for your merchandise. 14 Those from the house of Togarmah traded for your wares with horses, steeds, and mules. 15 The men of Dedan *were* your traders; many isles *were* the market of your hand. They brought you ivory tusks and ebony as payment. 16 Syria *was* your merchant because of the abundance of goods you made. They gave you for your wares emeralds, purple, embroidery, fine linen, corals, and rubies. 17 Judah and the land of Israel *were* your traders. They traded for your merchandise wheat of Minnith, millet, honey, oil, and balm. 18 Damascus *was* your merchant because of the abundance of goods you made, because of your many luxury items, with the wine of Helbon and with white wool. 19 Dan and Javan paid for your wares, traversing back and forth. Wrought iron, cassia, and cane were among your merchandise. 20 Dedan *was* your merchant in saddlecloths for riding. 21 Arabia and all the princes of Kedar *were* your regular merchants. They traded

---

27:6 [a]Hebrew *Kittim*, western lands, especially
Cyprus   27:10 [a]Hebrew *Lud* [b]Hebrew *Put*

with you in lambs, rams, and goats. ²²The merchants of Sheba and Raamah *were* your merchants. They traded for your wares the choicest spices, all kinds of precious stones, and gold. ²³Haran, Canneh, Eden, the merchants of Sheba, Assyria, *and* Chilmad *were* your merchants. ²⁴These *were* your merchants in choice items—in purple clothes, in embroidered garments, in chests of multicolored apparel, in sturdy woven cords, which were in your marketplace.

25 "The ships of Tarshish were carriers of
    your merchandise.
  You were filled and very glorious in
    the midst of the seas.
26 Your oarsmen brought you into many
    waters,
  But the east wind broke you in the
    midst of the seas.

27 "Your riches, wares, and merchandise,
  Your mariners and pilots,
  Your caulkers and merchandisers,
  All your men of war who *are* in you,
  And the entire company which *is* in
    your midst,
  Will fall into the midst of the seas on
    the day of your ruin.
28 The common-land will shake at the
    sound of the cry of your pilots.

29 "All who handle the oar,
  The mariners,
  All the pilots of the sea
  Will come down from their ships *and*
    stand on the shore.
30 They will make their voice heard
    because of you;
  They will cry bitterly and cast dust on
    their heads;
  They will roll about in ashes;
31 They will shave themselves
    completely bald because of you,
  Gird themselves with sackcloth,
  And weep for you
  With bitterness of heart *and* bitter
    wailing.
32 In their wailing for you
  They will take up a lamentation,
  And lament for you:
  'What *city is* like Tyre,
  Destroyed in the midst of the sea?

33 'When your wares went out by sea,
  You satisfied many people;
  You enriched the kings of the earth
  With your many luxury goods and
    your merchandise.

34 But you are broken by the seas in the
    depths of the waters;
  Your merchandise and the entire
    company will fall in your midst.
35 All the inhabitants of the isles will be
    astonished at you;
  Their kings will be greatly afraid,
  And *their* countenance will be
    troubled.
36 The merchants among the peoples will
    hiss at you;
  You will become a horror, and *be* no
    more forever.' " ' "

Proclamation Against the King of Tyre

28 ¹The word of the LORD came to me again, saying, ²"Son of man, say to the prince of Tyre, 'Thus says the Lord GOD:

"Because your heart *is* lifted up,
  And you say, 'I *am* a god,
  I sit *in* the seat of gods,
  In the midst of the seas,'
  Yet you *are* a man, and not a god,
  Though you set your heart as the
    heart of a god
3 (Behold, you *are* wiser than Daniel!
  There is no secret that can be hidden
    from you!
4 With your wisdom and your
    understanding
  You have gained riches for yourself,
  And gathered gold and silver into your
    treasuries;
5 By your great wisdom in trade you
    have increased your riches,
  And your heart is lifted up because of
    your riches),"

⁶"Therefore thus says the Lord GOD:

"Because you have set your heart as
    the heart of a god,
7 Behold, therefore, I will bring
    strangers against you,
  The most terrible of the nations;
  And they shall draw their swords
    against the beauty of your wisdom,
  And defile your splendor.
8 They shall throw you down into the
    Pit,
  And you shall die the death of the
    slain
  In the midst of the seas.

9 "Will you still say before him who slays
    you,

MYTH AND THE PRINCE OF TYRE (Ezek. 28:2–10)

Ezekiel's prophecy against the prince of Tyre (Ezek. 28:2–10) brings together elements from the religious and mythological writings of the eastern Mediterranean. The sarcastic description Ezekiel offers of the prince's attitude reflects the cosmopolitan character of the Phoenicians.

Phoenician rulers were seen as subordinate partners with the patron deity of the city. The idea of the ruler himself being a god found some place in Phoenician royal ideology, having been incorporated from Egyptian culture. Thus, the prince of Tyre could boast, "I am a god" (Ezek. 28:2). Ezekiel, however, considered such pretentions to divine status to be merely self-delusion.

A Ugaritic myth presents another example of someone trying to move up the divine hierarchy, though not worthy. The god Athtar attempts to sit on Baal's throne, but Athtar is not equal to the throne, as Baal was, and has to step down. Ezekiel suggests that such is the case with the prince of Tyre: he is not even capable of retaining his royal position, let alone being a god. He is "a man, and not a god" (28:2).

Ezekiel sarcastically mocks the prince about being "wiser than Daniel" (28:3). The Daniel that Ezekiel has in mind is probably the human character in the *Legend of Aqhat*, a narrative from Ugarit. In the legend, Daniel is pious, royal, and wise, but for him life also held bitterness. The Judeans who read Ezekiel's words also may have been reminded of the life of Daniel in exile (Dan. 5:11, 12). Regardless of which Daniel is intended, Tyre's prince was not really wise.

The prince thought much of himself, his heart being "lifted up" (28:5). In Greek mythology, such exaggerated pride or self-confidence is known as hubris, and angers the gods. The myth of Arachne demonstrates the dangers of hubris. Arachne was so good at weaving that she threatened the self-esteem of the goddess Athena. Athena turned her into a spider as punishment. Similarly, Ezekiel warns the prince that God will require his life in payment for his conceit (28:9, 10).

'I *am* a god'?
But you *shall be* a man, and not a god,
In the hand of him who slays you.
10 You shall die the death of the
uncircumcised
By the hand of aliens;
For I have spoken," says the Lord
GOD.' "

Lamentation for the King of Tyre

11Moreover the word of the LORD came to me, saying, 12"Son of man, take up a lamentation for the king of Tyre, and say to him, 'Thus says the Lord GOD:

"You *were* the seal of perfection,
Full of wisdom and perfect in beauty.
13 You were in Eden, the garden of God;
Every precious stone *was* your
covering:
The sardius, topaz, and diamond,
Beryl, onyx, and jasper,
Sapphire, turquoise, and emerald with
gold.

The workmanship of your timbrels
and pipes
Was prepared for you on the day you
were created.

14 "You *were* the anointed cherub who
covers;
I established you;
You were on the holy mountain of
God;
You walked back and forth in the
midst of fiery stones.
15 You *were* perfect in your ways from
the day you were created,
Till iniquity was found in you.

16 "By the abundance of your trading
You became filled with violence
within,
And you sinned;
Therefore I cast you as a profane
thing
Out of the mountain of God;

And I destroyed you, O covering
　　cherub,
From the midst of the fiery stones.

17　"Your heart was lifted up because of
　　　your beauty;
　　You corrupted your wisdom for the
　　　sake of your splendor;
　　I cast you to the ground,
　　I laid you before kings,
　　That they might gaze at you.

18　"You defiled your sanctuaries
　　By the multitude of your iniquities,
　　By the iniquity of your trading;
　　Therefore I brought fire from your
　　　midst;
　　It devoured you,
　　And I turned you to ashes upon the
　　　earth
　　In the sight of all who saw you.
19　All who knew you among the peoples
　　　are astonished at you;
　　You have become a horror,
　　And *shall be* no more forever." ' "

Proclamation Against Sidon

20Then the word of the LORD came to
me, saying, 21"Son of man, set your face toward Sidon, and prophesy against her,
22and say, 'Thus says the Lord GOD:

　　"Behold, I *am* against you, O Sidon;
　　I will be glorified in your midst;
　　And they shall know that I *am* the
　　　LORD,
　　When I execute judgments in her and
　　　am hallowed in her.
23　For I will send pestilence upon her,
　　And blood in her streets;
　　The wounded shall be judged in her
　　　midst
　　By the sword against her on every
　　　side;
　　Then they shall know that I *am* the
　　　LORD.

24"And there shall no longer be a prick-
ing brier or a painful thorn for the house of
Israel from among all *who are* around
them, who despise them. Then they shall
know that I *am* the Lord GOD."

Israel's Future Blessing

25'Thus says the Lord GOD: "When I
have gathered the house of Israel from the
peoples among whom they are scattered,
and am hallowed in them in the sight of

the Gentiles, then they will dwell in their
own land which I gave to My servant Jacob. 26And they will dwell safely there,
build houses, and plant vineyards; yes,
they will dwell securely, when I execute
judgments on all those around them who
despise them. Then they shall know that I
am the LORD their God." ' "

Ezekiel 32:1–32
Lamentation for Pharaoh and Egypt

32 :1 And it came to pass in the twelfth
year, in the twelfth *month,* on the
first *day* of the month, *that* the word of the
LORD came to me, saying, 2"Son of man,
take up a lamentation for Pharaoh king of
Egypt, and say to him:

　　'You are like a young lion among the
　　　nations,
　　And you *are* like a monster in the
　　　seas,
　　Bursting forth in your rivers,
　　Troubling the waters with your feet,
　　And fouling their rivers.'

3"Thus says the Lord GOD:

　　'I will therefore spread My net over
　　　you with a company of many people,
　　And they will draw you up in My net.
4　Then I will leave you on the land;
　　I will cast you out on the open fields,
　　And cause to settle on you all the
　　　birds of the heavens.
　　And with you I will fill the beasts of
　　　the whole earth.
5　I will lay your flesh on the mountains,
　　And fill the valleys with your carcass.

6　'I will also water the land with the
　　　flow of your blood,
　　Even to the mountains;
　　And the riverbeds will be full of you.
7　When *I* put out your light,
　　I will cover the heavens, and make its
　　　stars dark;
　　I will cover the sun with a cloud,
　　And the moon shall not give her light.
8　All the bright lights of the heavens I
　　　will make dark over you,
　　And bring darkness upon your land,'
　　Says the Lord GOD.

9'I will also trouble the hearts of many
peoples, when I bring your destruction
among the nations, into the countries
which you have not known. 10Yes, I will

make many peoples astonished at you, and their kings shall be horribly afraid of you when I brandish My sword before them; and they shall tremble *every* moment, every man for his own life, in the day of your fall.

11"For thus says the Lord GOD: 'The sword of the king of Babylon shall come upon you. 12By the swords of the mighty warriors, all of them the most terrible of the nations, I will cause your multitude to fall.

'They shall plunder the pomp of Egypt,
And all its multitude shall be
destroyed.
13 Also I will destroy all its animals
From beside its great waters;
The foot of man shall muddy them no
more,
Nor shall the hooves of animals
muddy them.
14 Then I will make their waters clear,
And make their rivers run like oil,'
Says the Lord GOD.

15 'When I make the land of Egypt
desolate,
And the country is destitute of all that
once filled it,
When I strike all who dwell in it,
Then they shall know that I *am* the
LORD.

16 'This *is* the lamentation
With which they shall lament her;
The daughters of the nations shall
lament her;
They shall lament for her, for Egypt,
And for all her multitude,'
Says the Lord GOD."

Egypt and Others Consigned to the Pit

17It came to pass also in the twelfth year, on the fifteenth *day* of the month, *that* the word of the LORD came to me, saying:

18 "Son of man, wail over the multitude of
Egypt,

And cast them down to the depths of
the earth,
Her and the daughters of the famous
nations,
With those who go down to the Pit:
19 'Whom do you surpass in beauty?
Go down, be placed with the
uncircumcised.'

20 "They shall fall in the midst of *those*
slain by the sword;
She is delivered to the sword,
Drawing her and all her multitudes.
21 The strong among the mighty
Shall speak to him out of the midst of
hell
With those who help him:
'They have gone down,
They lie with the uncircumcised, slain
by the sword.'

22 "Assyria *is* there, and all her company,
With their graves all around her,
All of them slain, fallen by the sword.
23 Her graves are set in the recesses of
the Pit,
And her company is all around her
grave,
All of them slain, fallen by the sword,
Who caused terror in the land of the
living.

24 "There *is* Elam and all her multitude,
All around her grave,
All of them slain, fallen by the sword,
Who have gone down uncircumcised to
the lower parts of the earth,
Who caused their terror in the land of
the living;
Now they bear their shame with those
who go down to the Pit.
25 They have set her bed in the midst of
the slain,
With all her multitude,
With her graves all around it,
All of them uncircumcised, slain by
the sword;
Though their terror was caused
In the land of the living,

ARTS AND LITERATURE

The crocodile lived in the Nile in Egypt, and was a symbol of the forces of chaos and turmoil. For Ezekiel, this "monster in the seas" represented Egypt's power (Ezek. 32:2). Other symbols of superhuman power were the sun, moon, and stars (32:7). The sun was a principal god in Egypt. Ezekiel's lament over Egypt (32:2–8) shows that God is clearly sovereign over these symbols of the power of Egypt and its pharaoh.

Yet they bear their shame
With those who go down to the Pit;
It was put in the midst of the slain.

26 "There *are* Meshech and Tubal and all
    their multitudes,
With all their graves around it,
All of them uncircumcised, slain by
    the sword,
Though they caused their terror in the
    land of the living.
27 They do not lie with the mighty
Who are fallen of the uncircumcised,
Who have gone down to hell with their
    weapons of war;
They have laid their swords under
    their heads,
But their iniquities will be on their
    bones,
Because of the terror of the mighty in
    the land of the living.
28 Yes, you shall be broken in the midst
    of the uncircumcised,
And lie with *those* slain by the sword.

29 "There *is* Edom,
Her kings and all her princes,
Who despite their might
Are laid beside *those* slain by the
    sword;
They shall lie with the uncircumcised,
And with those who go down to the
    Pit.
30 There *are* the princes of the north,
All of them, and all the Sidonians,
Who have gone down with the slain
In shame at the terror which they
    caused by their might;
They lie uncircumcised with *those*
    slain by the sword,
And bear their shame with those who
    go down to the Pit.

31 "Pharaoh will see them
And be comforted over all his
    multitude,
Pharaoh and all his army,
Slain by the sword,"
Says the Lord GOD.

32 "For I have caused My terror in the
    land of the living;
And he shall be placed in the midst of
    the uncircumcised
With *those* slain by the sword,
Pharaoh and all his multitude,"
Says the Lord GOD.

Despair and Anger

No text more clearly shows how the exiles felt upon hearing of Jerusalem's fall than does Ps. 137, which is in turn achingly beautiful and savagely vindictive. The psalm alternates between love for Jerusalem and hatred for her enemies. The nation of Edom (137:7) was particularly hated for its aid to Babylon.

■ Psalm 137

PSALM 137

Longing for Zion in a Foreign Land

By the rivers of Babylon,
    There we sat down, yea, we wept
    When we remembered Zion.
2 We hung our harps
    Upon the willows in the midst of it.
3 For there those who carried us away
    captive asked of us a song,
And those who plundered us *requested*
    mirth,
Saying, "Sing us *one* of the songs of
    Zion!"

4 How shall we sing the LORD's song
    In a foreign land?
5 If I forget you, O Jerusalem,
    Let my right hand forget *its skill!*
6 If I do not remember you,
    Let my tongue cling to the roof of my
      mouth—
If I do not exalt Jerusalem
    Above my chief joy.

7 Remember, O LORD, against the sons
    of Edom
The day of Jerusalem,
Who said, "Raze *it,* raze *it,*
    To its very foundation!"

8 O daughter of Babylon, who are to be
    destroyed,
Happy the one who repays you as you
    have served us!
9 Happy the one who takes and dashes
    Your little ones against the rock!

The Book of Obadiah

Obadiah's name means "servant of the Lord," but beyond that, nothing certain is known about this prophet. The book's message, though, is clear: judgment upon Edom. The Edomites had acted treacherously against the inhabitants of Jerusalem during their darkest hour. They had laughed at Judah's sorrow, probably looted the hapless people, and helped the Babylonian soldiers find fleeing refugees. Edom, descended from Israel's brother Esau, had betrayed that brotherhood. Now Edom would be punished.

The date of the book is not completely certain; it could be referring to any number of times that Edom opposed Judah. Various verses, however, fit particularly well with the time after the fall of Jerusalem in 586 B.C. Not only does Obadiah refer to the destruction of Jerusalem and a captivity (Obad. 1:11, 12), but he also appears to quote from a prophecy of Jeremiah's (Obad. 1:5; Jer. 49:7-9).

■ Obadiah 1:1-21

Obadiah
The Coming Judgment on Edom

1 :1 The vision of Obadiah.

Thus says the Lord GOD concerning Edom
(We have heard a report from the LORD,
And a messenger has been sent among the nations, *saying,*
"Arise, and let us rise up against her for battle"):

2 "Behold, I will make you small among the nations;
You shall be greatly despised.
3 The pride of your heart has deceived you,
You who dwell in the clefts of the rock,
Whose habitation is high;
You who say in your heart, 'Who will bring me down to the ground?'
4 Though you ascend *as* high as the eagle,
And though you set your nest among the stars,
From there I will bring you down,"
says the LORD.

5 "If thieves had come to you,
If robbers by night—
Oh, how you will be cut off!—
Would they not have stolen till they had enough?
If grape-gatherers had come to you,
Would they not have left *some* gleanings?

6 "Oh, how Esau shall be searched out!
How his hidden treasures shall be sought after!

7 All the men in your confederacy
Shall force you to the border;
The men at peace with you
Shall deceive you *and* prevail against you.
Those who eat your bread shall lay a trap[a] for you.
No one is aware of it.

8 "Will I not in that day," says the LORD,
"Even destroy the wise *men* from Edom,
And understanding from the mountains of Esau?
9 Then your mighty men, O Teman, shall be dismayed,
To the end that everyone from the mountains of Esau
May be cut off by slaughter.

Edom Mistreated His Brother

10 "For violence against your brother Jacob,
Shame shall cover you,
And you shall be cut off forever.
11 In the day that you stood on the other side—
In the day that strangers carried captive his forces,
When foreigners entered his gates
And cast lots for Jerusalem—
Even you *were* as one of them.

12 "But you should not have gazed on the day of your brother
In the day of his captivity;[a]
Nor should you have rejoiced over the children of Judah
In the day of their destruction;
Nor should you have spoken proudly
In the day of distress.
13 You should not have entered the gate of My people
In the day of their calamity.
Indeed, you should not have gazed on their affliction
In the day of their calamity,
Nor laid *hands* on their substance
In the day of their calamity.
14 You should not have stood at the crossroads
To cut off those among them who escaped;
Nor should you have delivered up those among them who remained
In the day of distress.

1:7 [a]Or *wound,* or *plot*   1:12 [a]Literally *on the day he became a foreigner*

15 "For the day of the LORD upon all the
    nations *is* near;
    As you have done, it shall be done to
    you;
    Your reprisal shall return upon your
    own head.
16 For as you drank on My holy
    mountain,
    So shall all the nations drink
    continually;
    Yes, they shall drink, and swallow,
    And they shall be as though they had
    never been.

Israel's Final Triumph

17 "But on Mount Zion there shall be
    deliverance,
    And there shall be holiness;
    The house of Jacob shall possess their
    possessions.
18 The house of Jacob shall be a fire,
    And the house of Joseph a flame;
    But the house of Esau *shall be*
    stubble;
    They shall kindle them and devour
    them,
    And no survivor shall *remain* of the
    house of Esau,"
    For the LORD has spoken.

19 The South^a shall possess the
    mountains of Esau,
    And the Lowland shall possess
    Philistia.
    They shall possess the fields of
    Ephraim
    And the fields of Samaria.
    Benjamin *shall possess* Gilead.
20 And the captives of this host of the
    children of Israel
    Shall possess the land of the
    Canaanites
    As far as Zarephath.
    The captives of Jerusalem who are in
    Sepharad
    Shall possess the cities of the South.^a
21 Then saviors^a shall come to Mount
    Zion
    To judge the mountains of Esau,
    And the kingdom shall be the LORD's.

1:19 ^aHebrew *Negev*   1:20 ^aHebrew *Negev*
1:21 ^aOr *deliverers*

Various Deportations to Babylon

In Jer. 52:28–30 is a historical summary of the various deportations of Judeans from Jerusalem to Babylon. This summary does not occur anywhere else in the Bible. It differs both in dates and numbers of deportees from accounts given by the historian of Kings.

The summary lists three deportations, occurring in the 7th, 18th, and 23rd years of Nebuchadnezzar. The 7th year could refer to the exile of Jehoiachin in 597 B.C., while the 18th year could refer to the exiles deported at Jerusalem's fall in 586. The difference in dates from those reported in 2 Kin. 24:12 and 25:8 could result from different methods of reckoning the 1st year of a king.

The third deportation (52:30) is reported as carried out by Nebuzaradan in 581 B.C. (Nebuchadnezzar's 23rd year). There is no evidence beyond Jeremiah for a deportation in that year. Some scholars suggest that this may have been Babylon's response to the assassination of Gedaliah, the governor appointed by Nebuchadnezzar (Jer. 41:16–18). The amount of time that passed between Jerusalem's fall in 586 and Gedaliah's murder—2 months or 5 years—is not known.

Little is certain about Jeremiah's summary. The vastly greater numbers of deported Judeans given in 2 Kin. 24:14, 16 may be round numbers including women and children. On the other hand, Jer. 52 may refer to smaller deportations that were separate from those of 597 and 586. What the summary does offer is one more reminder of how greatly the inhabitants of Judah suffered in the fall of their nation.

■ Jeremiah 52:28–30

Jeremiah

52 :28 These *are* the people whom Nebuchadnezzar carried away captive: in the seventh year, three thousand and twenty-three Jews; ²⁹in the eighteenth year of Nebuchadnezzar he carried away captive from Jerusalem eight hundred and thirty-two persons; ³⁰in the twenty-third year of Nebuchadnezzar, Nebuzaradan the captain of the guard carried away captive of the Jews seven hundred and forty-five persons. All the persons *were* four thousand six hundred.

EXILE AND RETURN

(586—332 B.C.)

This was a time in which the faith of Israel would become a universal faith, one in which Yahweh would be seen as the saving God of all peoples.

Judah experienced a time of great tragedy when Jerusalem was destroyed and nearly all of Judah's leaders were taken into exile in Babylon. It was a time of despair in Judah's relationship with Yahweh, as well. "How shall we sing the LORD's song in a foreign land?" (Ps. 137:4) was a cry from the heart. What had happened between the exiled people and their God Yahweh?

Chief among the problems facing the Judeans was the question of identity. Prior to the Babylonian exile, they had been an independent, political state, to some extent secured by military power, and with a God-ordained Davidic king on the throne. All this was taken as proof that their God was the true God, the King of the universe. Now, none of these conditions existed. They were a powerless, subject people in a great empire whose rulers thought Yahweh was only one petty god among many.

With their lives now controlled by the Babylonians, the Judeans experienced tremendous temptation to surrender all their previous claims to having an exclusive revelation from God. In addition, they were tempted to surrender those behaviors which had been designed to separate them from the surrounding pagan cultures. Thus, there was a real danger that they would become assimilated into those cultures, preserving some Judean customs, but surrendering the covenants God had made with them.

That this did not happen was largely due to the labors of the prophets Haggai, Zechariah, and Malachi; the priest Ezra; and the governor Nehemiah. Each of these individuals filled a distinctive role, and together they made it possible for the Jews to come to a new understanding of themselves. These five men showed them that their identity was to be a nation of priests, serving God and declaring Him before the world. Their constitution was not to be some political arrangement, but the Law of God. Their covenant with Him was what made them a people. This would be a time in which the faith of Israel would become a universal faith, one in which Yahweh would be seen as the saving God of all peoples.

▶ Archaeology and the Past

Various Babylonian remains elaborate on this period. The Babylonian Chronicle, a collection of documents written on baked clay tablets, describes events leading up to Judah's tragedy. This historical source of the Chaldean kingdom records how Nebuchadnezzar laid siege to Jerusalem in 597 B.C., deposed Jehoiachin of Judah, and appointed a new king in his place. The Babylonian Chronicle pictures Babylon as the new superpower in the Middle East; Judah lived only on sufferance from Babylon. But that relationship did not last, and archaeological surveys reveal that many cities and villages in Judah were destroyed in 586 B.C.

The Babylonian Chronicle recounts nothing after 594 B.C. Another Babylonian record, however, includes receipts for oil and other goods issued to Jehoiachin and his family. These Babylonian cuneiform texts, dating between 595 and 570 B.C., suggest that Judah's royal family, though in exile, lived in relative comfort and freedom at Babylonian expense.

Archaeology also witnesses the Judean return from the Exile. The Cyrus Cylinder, a baked clay document, states that Cyrus was chosen by Marduk, the chief god of Babylon, to be ruler over Babylon and to restore the true worship of the gods. The cylinder clarifies that the return of exiles and freedom of worship were key parts of Cyrus's policy. The language and content of the Cyrus Cylinder is very close to the decree in Ezra 1:2–4.

A document found in Egypt tells of a Persian inquiry into the religious practices of the Jews in Egypt near the end of the 5th century B.C. The letter, known as the Passover Papyrus, is one of the writings sent to the Jewish colony at Elephantine, and is dated in the 5th year of Darius II (419 B.C.), bearing his royal authority. It reminds us that the Persian rulers took an interest in the religious practices of subject peoples and were not above sending commissioners to assure that those practices were observed properly. Such a mission was given to the priest Ezra concerning religious practice in Jerusalem.

Coins and seals further testify to the restoration of Jerusalem. A series of jar handles show seal impressions reading "Judah," "Jerusalem," and "belonging to the king." The language reveals that Hebrew was giving way to Aramaic, which became the common language of the Persian Empire. Before the Persian period, gold and silver were weighed out on scales. Coins, however, made trade and business much simpler. During the second half of the 5th century, coins with Hebrew letters, bearing the name "Judah," appear. The Persian policy of allowing considerable local autonomy to Persian provinces included the right of provinces to strike their own coins.

▶ The Peoples and Groups

During the reign of Babylon's last king, Nabonidus (556–539 B.C.), forces were building that spelled the end of the Babylonian Empire. Cyrus the Great ascended the throne of Persia in 559 B.C. The Persian Empire, founded by Cyrus, became the great superpower of its day. Between 539 B.C., when Cyrus entered Babylon, and 525 B.C., when Cyrus's son Cambyses conquered Egypt, all the Middle East became Persian. At least two Persian emperors tried to capture Greece. Darius I was defeated at Marathon in 490 B.C.; Xerxes I at Salamis in 480.

The Persian Empire, founded by Cyrus, became the great superpower of its day.

The Persian emperors were great builders as well as imperialists. Excavations at Susa have uncovered the palace begun by Darius and finished by Xerxes. The rock carvings on Persian palaces, tombs, and triumphal monuments show us the power and splendor of the Persian kings. Their empire lasted until 331 B.C., finally being defeated by the Macedonian armies of Alexander the Great.

When the exiles returned to Judah, they encountered other peoples already there. Sanballat (Neh. 2:19) is identified as the governor of Samaria in documents from Elephantine. Samaritans were descendants of the mixed marriages between Israelites and peoples whom the Assyrians had imported. When the Jews enjoyed prosperity, the Samaritans were quick to acknowledge their blood relationship. But when the Jews suffered hard times, the Samaritans disowned such kinship, claiming to be descendants of Assyrian immigrants.

Samaritan hostility was coupled with that of the Ammonites in the east and the Arabians in the southeast. Tobiah the Ammonite (Neh. 2:19) may have been the Persian governor of Ammon, just as Nehemiah was governor of Judah. His family was powerful in the Transjordan from the 5th century to at least the 2nd century. Geshem the Arab (Neh. 2:19) was also a governor under Persian rule. The name "Geshem," appearing in inscriptions from Arabia and from a site near the border of Egypt, is associated with peoples of the northwest Arabian peninsula.

▶ The Biblical Literature

Much of this period is related in the Bible by various prophets, as well as by some of the historical books. The prophetical books include Ezekiel, parts of Isaiah, Haggai, Zechariah, Malachi, and Joel. Ezekiel was taken to Babylon in 597 B.C., where he prophesied. He preached hope to the exiles, based on God's own nature and purpose. His book ends with a great vision of a future restoration of the temple. Isaiah's oracles of salvation in Is. 40—55 promise a return from exile and a rebuilding of Jerusalem and the temple. The final chapters (Is. 56—66) presumably speak of the second temple, built during the Persian era.

The second temple is the concern of Haggai and Zechariah, preaching in Jerusalem about 520 B.C. They insisted that the temple had to be rebuilt at all costs. Once done, God would restore the power of the house of David in the person of Zerubbabel, the last known prince of David's line.

Little is known of Joel and Malachi, but it seems they prophesied when a temple was standing, possibly the second temple. Malachi accused the people and priests of indifference, doubt, and immorality. Joel saw a great locust plague as the beginning of the judgment of God, and thus called for national repentance.

Events of the period are narrated in the historical books of Ezra and Nehemiah. The Book of Ezra records the mission of Ezra the priest to inspect religious life in Judah, insisting on ritual purity. The Book of Nehemiah tells of the rebuilding of Jerusalem's walls under the leadership of this Judean governor appointed by the Persians.

The picture of this time is colored by other books. The Book of Esther relates the story of a Jewish heroine who becomes queen of Persia and saves her people at the risk of her own life. Two chapters of the Book of Daniel are set in the reigns of kings of this period: Babylon's Belshazzar, a coregent of Nabonidus (Dan. 5), and Persia's Darius (Dan. 6). Along with these books, we can read various psalms, the wisdom literature of Job and some proverbs, and the genealogical lists of 1 Chronicles.

Exile in Babylon

The Exile lasted about 70 years, witnessing important changes in the faith of the Judeans.

Soon after Nebuchadnezzar, king of Babylon, destroyed Jerusalem, all the ancient Near East fell under the control of the Neo-Babylonian Empire. In the early years of the conquest, the Babylonians were aided by Media, a nation located in the mountainous regions northeast of Babylon. Indeed, Cyaxares, king of the Medes, had been a part of Babylon's overthrow of Nineveh in 612 B.C. (see "The Book of Nahum" at Nah. 1:1). Later on, in 550 B.C., the Medes themselves were conquered by Cyrus the Great and absorbed into Cyrus's Persian Empire. Median troops reinforced the Persian forces that brought about Babylon's downfall. That event of 539 B.C. was still years away.

Nebuchadnezzar became king in 605 B.C., shortly after defeating an Assyrian-Egyptian coalition at Carchemish in Syria. He reigned until 562 B.C., being succeeded by his son Amel-Marduk (the Bible's Evil-Merodach, 2 Kin. 25:27). In 560 B.C., Amel-Marduk was displaced by his brother-in-law Neriglissar (perhaps the Nergal-Sharezer who had been present at the fall of Jerusalem, Jer. 39:3, 13). Neriglissar also reigned only briefly, and his son and successor was deposed by the powerful Babylonian official Nabonidus (556–539 B.C.).

By the end of Nabonidus's reign, the empire was ready to fall apart. Nabonidus was not himself from the city of Babylon, and he did not worship that city's god, Marduk. Instead, he promoted the worship of the moon god Sin, thus angering the official priests of Babylon. Nabonidus moved his capital to an oasis in the Arabian desert and left his son Bel-shar-usur (the Belshazzar of Dan. 5) as his regent in Babylon itself. Seeing Babylon's internal problems, nations on the edges of the empire began to assert their independence from Babylonian influence. The most significant of these was Babylon's former ally, Media.

Under the Medes' last king, Astyages (585–550 B.C.), Media became large enough to be called an empire in its own right. Internal problems developed, however, and in 550 B.C. Astyages was overthrown by a young general named Cyrus, from the Median province of Persia. In 539 B.C., 11 years later, Cyrus the Persian marched almost unopposed into the city of Babylon, thus ending the reign of Nabonidus and conquering the Neo-Babylonian Empire.

The accession of Cyrus also marked the end of the Judean exile in Babylon. That exile had lasted only about 70 years, but those years witnessed important changes in the faith of the Judeans. No longer able to identify the center of their faith in the temple, the exiles focused on Scripture—specifically the Torah, the first five books of the Old Testament. Their worship, meeting in the small gatherings that would later be called synagogues, stressed the reading of the Torah. A new class of religious leader arose, the scribe, whose function was to learn and interpret the Torah. The exiled Judeans became the people of the Book.

Moreover, the exiles had to adapt to their new position as a minority faith. In Babylon, they could not expect the king or the official priesthood to preserve correct worship. They had to define their faith themselves. This they did by emphasizing those laws that distinguished Judeans from other peoples, laws like Sabbath observance, dietary laws, and above all the command: "You shall have no other gods before Me" (Ex. 20:3).

Ezekiel's Message of Hope

Because of the Judeans' new emphasis on the Scriptures, Judah's faith in God survived its shattering grief over the destruction of the temple (see Ps. 137). Indeed Judah's faith did not just survive, it was reborn, in a different form but stronger than ever. That rebirth is already evident in the work of Ezekiel, whose ministry took a new shape after Jerusalem and the temple were destroyed.

Ezekiel begins, in effect, a second ministry, inaugurated by a second vision of the watchman (Ezek. 33:1–20), a vision that had been a part of his original call experience (Ezek. 3:16–21). This second ministry still includes oracles of judgment—against the shepherds of Israel, against Mount Seir (Edom)—but these judgments are followed now by oracles of hope.

Judah was victimized by those closest to her. Kings are often portrayed as shepherds of the people, but many of Judah's kings had enriched themselves at the people's expense (ch. 34). Hope now presented itself in the promise of a true shepherd (34:23, 24). The Edomites were descended from Esau, yet Judah was treacherously attacked by this nation with close kinship ties (ch. 35; see "The Book of Obadiah" at Obad. 1:1). Hope now came through the prophecy of restoration—both physical (36:1–15) and spiritual (36:16–38). Judah's restoration is illustrated by the vision of the valley of dry bones (37:1–14) and by the parable of the two sticks (37:15–28).

■ Ezekiel 33:1–20
■ Ezekiel 34:1—37:28

Ezekiel 33:1–20
The Watchman and His Message

33 :1 Again the word of the LORD came to me, saying, ²"Son of man, speak to the children of your people, and say to them: 'When I bring the sword upon a land, and the people of the land take a man from their territory and make him their watchman, ³when he sees the sword coming upon the land, if he blows the trumpet and warns the people, ⁴then whoever hears the sound of the trumpet and does not take warning, if the sword comes and takes him away, his blood shall be on his *own* head. ⁵He heard the sound of the trumpet, but did not take warning; his blood shall be upon himself. But he who takes warning will save his life. ⁶But if the watchman sees the sword coming and does not blow the trumpet, and the people are not warned, and the sword comes and takes *any* person from among them, he is taken away in his iniquity; but his blood I will require at the watchman's hand.'

⁷"So you, son of man: I have made you a watchman for the house of Israel; therefore you shall hear a word from My mouth and warn them for Me. ⁸When I say to the wicked, 'O wicked *man,* you shall surely die!' and you do not speak to warn the wicked from his way, that wicked *man* shall die in his iniquity; but his blood I will require at your hand. ⁹Nevertheless if you warn the wicked to turn from his way, and he does not turn from his way, he shall die in his iniquity; but you have delivered your soul.

¹⁰"Therefore you, O son of man, say to the house of Israel: 'Thus you say, "If our transgressions and our sins *lie* upon us, and we pine away in them, how can we then live?" ' ¹¹Say to them: '*As* I live,' says the Lord GOD, 'I have no pleasure in the

death of the wicked, but that the wicked turn from his way and live. Turn, turn from your evil ways! For why should you die, O house of Israel?'

The Fairness of God's Judgment

¹²"Therefore you, O son of man, say to the children of your people: 'The righteousness of the righteous man shall not deliver him in the day of his transgression; as for the wickedness of the wicked, he shall not fall because of it in the day that he turns from his wickedness; nor shall the righteous be able to live because of *his righteousness* in the day that he sins.' ¹³When I say to the righteous *that* he shall surely live, but he trusts in his own righteousness and commits iniquity, none of his righteous works shall be remembered; but because of the iniquity that he has committed, he shall die. ¹⁴Again, when I say to the wicked, 'You shall surely die,' if he turns from his sin and does what is lawful and right, ¹⁵*if* the wicked restores the pledge, gives back what he has stolen, and walks in the statutes of life without committing iniquity, he shall surely live; he shall not die. ¹⁶None of his sins which he has committed shall be remembered against him; he has done what is lawful and right; he shall surely live.

¹⁷"Yet the children of your people say, 'The way of the LORD is not fair.' But it is their way which is not fair! ¹⁸When the righteous turns from his righteousness and commits iniquity, he shall die because of it. ¹⁹But when the wicked turns from his wickedness and does what is lawful and right, he shall live because of it. ²⁰Yet you say, 'The way of the LORD is not fair.' O house of Israel, I will judge every one of you according to his own ways."

Ezekiel 34:1—37:28
Irresponsible Shepherds

34 :1 And the word of the LORD came to me, saying, ²"Son of man, prophesy against the shepherds of Israel, prophesy and say to them, 'Thus says the Lord GOD to the shepherds: "Woe to the shepherds of Israel who feed themselves! Should not the shepherds feed the flocks? ³You eat the fat and clothe yourselves with the wool; you slaughter the fatlings, *but* you do not feed the flock. ⁴The weak you have not strengthened, nor have you healed those who were sick, nor bound up the broken, nor brought back what was driven away,

---

TIME CAPSULE *575 to 570 B.C.*

575   *Greeks use saws for cutting*

573   *The prophet Ezekiel receives visions of the new temple*

571   *Ezekiel prophesies 4 years before Babylonian invasion of the west*

570   *Pharaoh Hophra flees Egypt in a revolt led by Egyptian general Amasis*

570– *Pharaoh Amasis allows Greeks to*
526   *settle in Egypt's Delta*

nor sought what was lost; but with force and cruelty you have ruled them. ⁵So they were scattered because *there was* no shepherd; and they became food for all the beasts of the field when they were scattered. ⁶My sheep wandered through all the mountains, and on every high hill; yes, My flock was scattered over the whole face of the earth, and no one was seeking or searching *for them.*"

⁷"Therefore, you shepherds, hear the word of the LORD: ⁸"*As* I live," says the Lord GOD, "surely because My flock became a prey, and My flock became food for every beast of the field, because *there was* no shepherd, nor did My shepherds search for My flock, but the shepherds fed themselves and did not feed My flock"— ⁹therefore, O shepherds, hear the word of the LORD! ¹⁰Thus says the Lord GOD: "Behold, I *am* against the shepherds, and I will require My flock at their hand; I will cause them to cease feeding the sheep, and the shepherds shall feed themselves no more; for I will deliver My flock from their mouths, that they may no longer be food for them."

God, the True Shepherd

¹¹"For thus says the Lord GOD: "Indeed I Myself will search for My sheep and seek them out. ¹²As a shepherd seeks out his flock on the day he is among his scattered sheep, so will I seek out My sheep and deliver them from all the places where they were scattered on a cloudy and dark day. ¹³And I will bring them out from the peoples and gather them from the countries, and will bring them to their own land; I will feed them on the mountains of Israel, in the valleys and in all the inhabited places of the country. ¹⁴I will feed them in good pasture, and their fold shall be on the high mountains of Israel. There they shall lie down in a good fold and feed in rich pasture on the mountains of Israel. ¹⁵I will feed My flock, and I will make them lie down," says the Lord GOD. ¹⁶"I will seek what was lost and bring back what was driven away, bind up the broken and strengthen what was sick; but I will destroy the fat and the strong, and feed them in judgment."

¹⁷"And *as for* you, O My flock, thus says the Lord GOD: "Behold, I shall judge between sheep and sheep, between rams and goats. ¹⁸*Is it* too little for you to have eaten up the good pasture, that you must tread down with your feet the residue of your pasture—and to have drunk of the clear waters, that you must foul the residue with your feet? ¹⁹And *as for* My flock, they eat what you have trampled with your feet, and they drink what you have fouled with your feet."

²⁰"Therefore thus says the Lord GOD to them: "Behold, I Myself will judge between the fat and the lean sheep. ²¹Because you have pushed with side and shoulder, butted all the weak ones with your horns, and scattered them abroad, ²²therefore I will save My flock, and they shall no longer be a prey; and I will judge between sheep and sheep. ²³I will establish one shepherd over them, and he shall feed them—My servant David. He shall feed them and be their shepherd. ²⁴And I, the LORD, will be their God, and My servant David a prince among them; I, the LORD, have spoken.

²⁵"I will make a covenant of peace with them, and cause wild beasts to cease from the land; and they will dwell safely in the wilderness and sleep in the woods. ²⁶I will make them and the places all around My hill a blessing; and I will cause showers to come down in their season; there shall be showers of blessing. ²⁷Then the trees of the field shall yield their fruit, and the earth shall yield her increase. They shall be safe in their land; and they shall know that I *am* the LORD, when I have broken the bands of their yoke and delivered them from the hand of those who enslaved them. ²⁸And they shall no longer be a prey for the nations, nor shall beasts of the land devour them; but they shall dwell safely, and no one shall make *them* afraid. ²⁹I will raise up for them a garden of renown, and they shall no longer be consumed with hunger in the land, nor bear the shame of the Gentiles anymore. ³⁰Thus they shall know that I, the LORD their God, *am* with them, and they, the house of Israel, *are* My people," says the Lord GOD.' "

³¹"You are My flock, the flock of My pasture; you *are* men, *and* I *am* your God," says the Lord GOD.

Judgment on Mount Seir

35 ¹Moreover the word of the LORD came to me, saying, ²"Son of man, set your face against Mount Seir and prophesy against it, ³and say to it, 'Thus says the Lord GOD:

"Behold, O Mount Seir, I *am* against you;

EDOM CARRIES ON ESAU'S HATRED (Ezek. 35:2)

Around January of 585 B.C. the prophet Ezekiel received news of Jerusalem's destruction by the Babylonians, which had occurred in 586 B.C. following a long siege (Ezek. 33:21; see 2 Kin. 25:1–10). The Babylonians, however, were not without allies in their attack on Jerusalem.

The Edomites, a people who dwelt in the desert country southeast of the land of Canaan, seemingly supported the Babylonians in their conquest. The traditions of Judah remember the people of Edom gloating over Jerusalem's destruction (Ps. 137:7; Obad. 1:10–12), as well as acquiring portions of what had once been Judah. Judah's neighbors did not act very "neighborly" in the moment of Judah's distress!

The Edomites are identified with Seir, a geographical name for the mountainous region in which they lived. Seir-Edom was more than Judah's geographical neighbor. The Edomites are also known as decendants of Esau, the older brother of Jacob, the forefather of the Israelites. The Law of Moses warns, "You shall not abhor an Edomite, for he is your brother" (Deut. 23:7). A special kinship link tied Seir to Judah.

It is this tie that the Edomites violated. In response to the hostility of Edom during the Babylonian conquest of Judah and afterwards, God instructed Ezekiel to prophesy against Mount Seir (Ezek. 35:2, 15). Edom had reawakened the "ancient hatred" (Ezek. 35:5) of Esau's grievance against his brother Jacob (Gen. 27:41).

I will stretch out My hand against
   you,
And make you most desolate;
4   I shall lay your cities waste,
And you shall be desolate.
Then you shall know that I *am* the
   LORD.

5"Because you have had an ancient hatred, and have shed *the blood of* the children of Israel by the power of the sword at the time of their calamity, *when* their iniquity *came to an* end, 6therefore, *as* I live," says the Lord GOD, "I will prepare you for blood, and blood shall pursue you; since you have not hated blood, therefore blood shall pursue you. 7Thus I will make Mount Seir most desolate, and cut off from it the one who leaves and the one who returns. 8And I will fill its mountains with the slain; on your hills and in your valleys and in all your ravines those who are slain by the sword shall fall. 9I will make you perpetually desolate, and your cities shall be uninhabited; then you shall know that I *am* the LORD.

10"Because you have said, 'These two nations and these two countries shall be mine, and we will possess them,' although the LORD was there, 11therefore, *as* I live," says the Lord GOD, "I will do according to your anger and according to the envy which you showed in your hatred against them; and I will make Myself known among them when I judge you. 12Then you shall know that I *am* the LORD. I have heard all your blasphemies which you have spoken against the mountains of Israel, saying, 'They are desolate; they are given to us to consume.' 13Thus with your mouth you have boasted against Me and multiplied your words against Me; I have heard *them.*"

14"Thus says the Lord GOD: "The whole earth will rejoice when I make you desolate. 15As you rejoiced because the inheritance of the house of Israel was desolate, so I will do to you; you shall be desolate, O

GEOGRAPHY AND ENVIRONMENT

Mount Seir is another name for Edom (Ezek. 35:2). The Edomites lived in the mountainous territory south and east of the Dead Sea. Through their country ran the King's Highway, the main road from Egypt to Syria and points north and east. Relations between Edom and Judah were usually hostile. Apparently Edom offered no assistance to Judah during the invasions of the Assyrians in 713 and 701 B.C.

Mount Seir, as well as all of Edom—all of it! Then they shall know that I *am* the LORD." '

Blessing on Israel

36 [1]"And you, son of man, prophesy to the mountains of Israel, and say, 'O mountains of Israel, hear the word of the LORD! [2]Thus says the Lord GOD: "Because the enemy has said of you, 'Aha! The ancient heights have become our possession,' " ' [3]therefore prophesy, and say, 'Thus says the Lord GOD: "Because they made *you* desolate and swallowed you up on every side, so that you became the possession of the rest of the nations, and you are taken up by the lips of talkers and slandered by the people"— [4]therefore, O mountains of Israel, hear the word of the Lord GOD! Thus says the Lord GOD to the mountains, the hills, the rivers, the valleys, the desolate wastes, and the cities that have been forsaken, which became plunder and mockery to the rest of the nations all around— [5]therefore thus says the Lord GOD: "Surely I have spoken in My burning jealousy against the rest of the nations and against all Edom, who gave My land to themselves as a possession, with wholehearted joy *and* spiteful minds, in order to plunder its open country." '

[6]"Therefore prophesy concerning the land of Israel, and say to the mountains, the hills, the rivers, and the valleys, 'Thus says the Lord GOD: "Behold, I have spoken in My jealousy and My fury, because you have borne the shame of the nations." [7]Therefore thus says the Lord GOD: "I have raised My hand in an oath that surely the nations that *are* around you shall bear their own shame. [8]But you, O mountains of Israel, you shall shoot forth your branches and yield your fruit to My people Israel, for they are about to come. [9]For indeed I *am* for you, and I will turn to you, and you shall be tilled and sown. [10]I will multiply men upon you, all the house of Israel, all of it; and the cities shall be inhabited and the ruins rebuilt. [11]I will multiply upon you man and beast; and they shall increase and bear young; I will make you inhabited as in former times, and do better *for you* than at your beginnings. Then you shall know that I *am* the LORD. [12]Yes, I will cause men to walk on you, My people Israel; they shall take possession of you, and you shall be their inheritance; no more shall you bereave them *of children*."

[13]Thus says the Lord GOD: "Because they say to you, 'You devour men and bereave your nation *of children,*' [14]therefore you shall devour men no more, nor bereave your nation anymore," says the Lord GOD. [15]Nor will I let you hear the taunts of the nations anymore, nor bear the reproach of the peoples anymore, nor shall you cause your nation to stumble anymore," says the Lord GOD.' "

The Renewal of Israel

[16]Moreover the word of the LORD came to me, saying: [17]"Son of man, when the house of Israel dwelt in their own land, they defiled it by their own ways and deeds; to Me their way was like the uncleanness of a woman in her customary impurity. [18]Therefore I poured out My fury on them for the blood they had shed on the land, and for their idols *with which* they had defiled it. [19]So I scattered them among the nations, and they were dispersed throughout the countries; I judged them according to their ways and their deeds. [20]When they came to the nations, wherever they went, they profaned My holy name— when they said of them, 'These *are* the people of the LORD, *and* yet they have gone out of His land.' [21]But I had concern for My holy name, which the house of Israel had profaned among the nations wherever they went.

[22]"Therefore say to the house of Israel, 'Thus says the Lord GOD: "I do not do *this* for your sake, O house of Israel, but for My holy name's sake, which you have profaned among the nations wherever you went. [23]And I will sanctify My great name, which has been profaned among the nations, which you have profaned in their midst; and the nations shall know that I *am* the LORD," says the Lord GOD, "when I am hallowed in you before their eyes. [24]For I will take you from among the nations, gather you out of all countries, and bring you into your own land. [25]Then I will sprinkle clean water on you, and you shall be clean; I will cleanse you from all your filthiness and from all your idols. [26]I will give you a new heart and put a new spirit within you; I will take the heart of stone out of your flesh and give you a heart of flesh. [27]I will put My Spirit within you and cause you to walk in My statutes, and you will keep My judgments and do *them.* [28]Then you shall dwell in the land that I gave to your fathers; you shall be My people, and I will

THE SACRED AND PROFANE (Ezek. 36:22–26)

While Ezekiel is known chiefly as a prophet, he was also a priest. In fact, priestly concerns, concepts, and terminology fill the Book of Ezekiel. The prophet-priest Ezekiel used terminology related to the temple and its rituals to describe the present situation and future salvation of Israel.

The Jerusalem temple was considered the point where the divine intersected with the earth. As such, the temple, together with its space, utensils, and personnel, was characterized by purity and holiness. To be sanctified or holy was to be set apart from everyday use, devoted solely to the service of God. To use a sanctified object for other reasons or outside the temple was to profane it, thus rendering it impure for use in the temple.

This priestly language makes up the imagery used by Ezekiel (Ezek. 36:22–26). Through the destruction of Jerusalem by the Babylonians in 586 B.C. Israel had come into contact with the nations. Yahweh's name, His status and honor, had been "profaned among the nations" (36:23). Israel's service was no longer confined to Yahweh and Yahweh alone. Contaminated by the nations, Israel had become impure, no longer qualified to enter into the temple area.

Yet Ezekiel saw a different day coming. First, God would again separate Israel from among the nations, returning her to her own land (36:24). Yet Israel's profanity, her impurity had to be removed. In accordance with legislation in the Book of Leviticus, Ezekiel proclaimed that God would cleanse Israel through sprinkling with clean water (36:25). Purified by the ritual cleansing, Israel was sanctified, holy, again set apart for the service of God within the Jerusalem temple.

---

be your God. ²⁹I will deliver you from all your uncleannesses. I will call for the grain and multiply it, and bring no famine upon you. ³⁰And I will multiply the fruit of your trees and the increase of your fields, so that you need never again bear the reproach of famine among the nations. ³¹Then you will remember your evil ways and your deeds that *were* not good; and you will loathe yourselves in your own sight, for your iniquities and your abominations. ³²Not for your sake do I do *this*," says the Lord GOD, "let it be known to you. Be ashamed and confounded for your own ways, O house of Israel!"

³³Thus says the Lord GOD: "On the day that I cleanse you from all your iniquities, I will also enable *you* to dwell in the cities, and the ruins shall be rebuilt. ³⁴The desolate land shall be tilled instead of lying desolate in the sight of all who pass by. ³⁵So they will say, 'This land that was desolate has become like the garden of Eden; and the wasted, desolate, and ruined cities *are now* fortified *and* inhabited.' ³⁶Then the nations which are left all around you shall know that I, the LORD, have rebuilt the ruined places *and* planted what was desolate. I, the LORD, have spoken *it,* and I will do *it.*"

³⁷Thus says the Lord GOD: "I will also let the house of Israel inquire of Me to do this for them: I will increase their men like a flock. ³⁸Like a flock *offered as* holy *sacrifices,* like the flock at Jerusalem on its feast days, so shall the ruined cities be filled with flocks of men. Then they shall know that I *am* the LORD." ' "

The Dry Bones Live

37 ¹The hand of the LORD came upon me and brought me out in the Spirit of the LORD, and set me down in the midst of the valley; and it *was* full of bones. ²Then He caused me to pass by them all around, and behold, *there were* very many in the open valley; and indeed *they were* very dry. ³And He said to me, "Son of man, can these bones live?"

So I answered, "O Lord GOD, You know."

⁴Again He said to me, "Prophesy to these bones, and say to them, 'O dry bones, hear the word of the LORD! ⁵Thus says the Lord GOD to these bones: "Surely I will cause breath to enter into you, and you shall live. ⁶I will put sinews on you and bring flesh upon you, cover you with skin and put breath in you; and you shall live. Then you shall know that I *am* the LORD." ' "

AN OLD BATTLEFIELD (Ezek. 37:1)

One of the most familiar visions received by the prophet Ezekiel took place in a valley "full of bones" (Ezek. 37:1). The vision of the valley of dry bones concerns people who had been dead a long time—the bones were "very dry" (37:2). Yet these dry bones coming to life, animated by the Spirit, provide a powerful image of hope that lies beyond death and destruction.

But why were dry bones in the valley in the first place? Possibly with this imagery Ezekiel envisioned an old battlefield. In the ancient Near East, battles between armies often took place in valleys. The defending army would attempt to set up its line of defense at a pass into a valley. Terrain could restrict the mobility of the attacking army, allowing the defending army to concentrate its forces in a smaller area. If, however, the attacking army broke through the front line, the battle would ensue in the valley, usually with the defending forces retreating.

The valley of dry bones, therefore, symbolized a site of an ancient battle. The enemy force had overwhelmed the defending forces, leaving only bleached bones in their wake. It provided a powerful image of Judah following Jerusalem's destruction by the Babylonians. The reanimation of the bones (37:7–10), therefore, represented the rebirth of Judah and Jerusalem by the Spirit of God. The nation would be restored, given a new body.

---

⁷So I prophesied as I was commanded; and as I prophesied, there was a noise, and suddenly a rattling; and the bones came together, bone to bone. ⁸Indeed, as I looked, the sinews and the flesh came upon them, and the skin covered them over; but *there was* no breath in them.

⁹Also He said to me, "Prophesy to the breath, prophesy, son of man, and say to the breath, 'Thus says the Lord GOD: "Come from the four winds, O breath, and breathe on these slain, that they may live." ' " ¹⁰So I prophesied as He commanded me, and breath came into them, and they lived, and stood upon their feet, an exceedingly great army.

¹¹Then He said to me, "Son of man, these bones are the whole house of Israel. They indeed say, 'Our bones are dry, our hope is lost, and we ourselves are cut off!' ¹²Therefore prophesy and say to them, 'Thus says the Lord GOD: "Behold, O My people, I will open your graves and cause you to come up from your graves, and bring you into the land of Israel. ¹³Then you shall know that I *am* the LORD, when I have opened your graves, O My people, and brought you up from your graves. ¹⁴I will put My Spirit in you, and you shall live, and I will place you in your own land. Then you shall know that I, the LORD, have spoken *it* and performed *it*," says the LORD.' "

One Kingdom, One King

¹⁵Again the word of the LORD came to me, saying, ¹⁶"As for you, son of man, take a stick for yourself and write on it: 'For Judah and for the children of Israel, his companions.' Then take another stick and write on it, 'For Joseph, the stick of Ephraim, and *for* all the house of Israel, his companions.' ¹⁷Then join them one to another for yourself into one stick, and they will become one in your hand.

¹⁸"And when the children of your people speak to you, saying, 'Will you not show us what you *mean* by these?'— ¹⁹say to them, 'Thus says the Lord GOD: "Surely I will take the stick of Joseph, which *is* in the hand of Ephraim, and the tribes of Israel, his companions; and I will join them with it, with the stick of Judah, and make them one stick, and they will be one in My hand." ' ²⁰And the sticks on which you write will be in your hand before their eyes.

²¹"Then say to them, 'Thus says the Lord GOD: "Surely I will take the children of Israel from among the nations, wherever they have gone, and will gather them from every side and bring them into their own land; ²²and I will make them one nation in the land, on the mountains of Israel; and one king shall be king over them all; they shall no longer be two nations, nor shall they ever be divided into two kingdoms again. ²³They shall not defile themselves anymore with their idols, nor with their detestable things, nor with any of their transgressions; but I will deliver them from all their dwelling places in which they have sinned, and will cleanse them. Then

they shall be My people, and I will be their God.

24"David My servant *shall be* king over them, and they shall all have one shepherd; they shall also walk in My judgments and observe My statutes, and do them. 25Then they shall dwell in the land that I have given to Jacob My servant, where your fathers dwelt; and they shall dwell there, they, their children, and their children's children, forever; and My servant David *shall be* their prince forever. 26Moreover I will make a covenant of peace with them, and it shall be an everlasting covenant with them; I will establish them and multiply them, and I will set My sanctuary in their midst forevermore. 27My tabernacle also shall be with them; indeed I will be their God, and they shall be My people. 28The nations also will know that I, the LORD, sanctify Israel, when My sanctuary is in their midst forevermore." ' "

Ezekiel's Apocalyptic Prophecies

Chapters 38 and 39 of Ezekiel are in many ways different from the rest of the book. Their message, the ultimate victory of God over the nations, is perfectly consistent with the preceding chapters, but the manner of describing that victory is distinct. Indeed these chapters are often noted as an early example of what would later be called "apocalyptic" writing, which is best represented in the Bible by Dan. 7—12 and the Book of Revelation.

Apocalyptic literature generally consists of vision reports (the word "apocalypse" comes from a Greek word meaning "revelation"). These visions usually involve a great many symbols, often quite obscure. While the original audience may have had the key to the symbols, such a key is usually left unstated (e.g., who is meant by the "little horn" in Dan. 8:9). The primary purpose of apocalyptic writing appears to be to comfort the persecuted. The message is that while things may be bad now, and indeed may get much worse, in the end God will establish His eternal kingdom and will right all wrongs.

Fitting within this pattern of hidden symbolism is Ezek. 38; 39, which describes the attack and ultimate defeat of the mysterious Gog from the land of Magog. Who is meant by "Gog"? No nation by that name is known. Some have suggested that Ezekiel might have been referring to King Gyges (685–652 B.C.)

of Lydia in Asia Minor. Others suggest it is the name of an otherwise unknown city in Media. Still others, noting that Gog comes from the north (Ezek. 38:6), think the name might refer to the Scythians, a band of barbarous raiders from the area around the Black Sea, north of Babylon.

These very different suggestions refer to groups that Ezekiel himself might have known in his own time. Because nothing in the Bible text itself favors one solution more than any other, though, the question remains open to further interpretation. Every generation since Ezekiel himself has had its own understanding of this passage, seeing the victory over Gog as a prophecy of victory over that generation's own enemies. While this makes the certain identification of Gog still more puzzling, perhaps it is what the prophecy calls for. God's victory over an unidentifiable enemy implies God's victory over any and every enemy.

Not knowing exactly to what the prophecy refers makes it difficult to place the oracle chronologically. It is possible simply to read these chapters in their biblical context, as a part of Ezekiel's second, hopeful ministry. God will no longer use the Gentile nations to punish Israel. Instead, in a future battle God will personally fight for His people and utterly destroy Israel's enemies (38:22). No aggressor can stand against God. Ezekiel's hope includes reunification: God will bring together the once-divided northern and southern kingdoms (39:25).

■ Ezekiel 38:1—39:29

Ezekiel
Gog and Allies Attack Israel

38 :1 Now the word of the LORD came to me, saying, 2"Son of man, set your face against Gog, of the land of Magog, the prince of Rosh,[a] Meshech, and Tubal, and prophesy against him, 3and say, 'Thus says the Lord GOD: "Behold, I *am* against you, O Gog, the prince of Rosh, Meshech, and Tubal. 4I will turn you around, put hooks into your jaws, and lead you out, with all your army, horses, and horsemen, all splendidly clothed, a great company *with* bucklers and shields, all of them handling swords. 5Persia, Ethiopia,[a] and Libya[b] *are* with them, all of them *with* shield and helmet; 6Gomer and all its

---

38:2 [a]Targum, Vulgate, and Aquila read *chief prince of* (also verse 3).   38:5 [a]Hebrew *Cush* [b]Hebrew *Put*

AN EMPIRE FORMS IN PERSIA (Ezek. 38:5)

The land of Persia played a major role in later Old Testament history, especially during the time of Ezra, Nehemiah, and Esther. Like the Medes, the Persians were an Iranian tribal group that entered the region of modern Iran sometime after 1000 B.C. Little is known about the Persians before 559 B.C. when Cyrus the Great ascended the throne of Persia. Nevertheless, the prophet Ezekiel could have known of "Persia" (Ezek. 38:5) some 20 or 30 years before Cyrus. The Assyrian king Ashurbanipal (668–627 B.C.) records in an inscription that a "king of Parsumash" paid him homage around 640 B.C.

The Achaemenid empire of Cyrus (named after one of his supposed ancestors) ruled virtually the entire Near East, Egypt, and the eastern Mediterranean for about 2 centuries (559–331 B.C.). The organization of the Persian administration and its system of royal roads consolidated the state. One could argue that it was the most successful world political power until the advent of Rome.

troops; the house of Togarmah *from* the far north and all its troops—many people *are* with you.

7"Prepare yourself and be ready, you and all your companies that are gathered about you; and be a guard for them. 8After many days you will be visited. In the latter years you will come into the land of those brought back from the sword *and* gathered from many people on the mountains of Israel, which had long been desolate; they were brought out of the nations, and now all of them dwell safely. 9You will ascend, coming like a storm, covering the land like a cloud, you and all your troops and many peoples with you."

10"Thus says the Lord GOD: "On that day it shall come to pass *that* thoughts will arise in your mind, and you will make an evil plan: 11You will say, 'I will go up against a land of unwalled villages; I will go to a peaceful people, who dwell safely, all of them dwelling without walls, and having neither bars nor gates'— 12to take plunder and to take booty, to stretch out your hand against the waste places *that are again* inhabited, and against a people gathered from the nations, who have acquired livestock and goods, who dwell in the midst of the land. 13Sheba, Dedan, the

merchants of Tarshish, and all their young lions will say to you, 'Have you come to take plunder? Have you gathered your army to take booty, to carry away silver and gold, to take away livestock and goods, to take great plunder?' "

14"Therefore, son of man, prophesy and say to Gog, 'Thus says the Lord GOD: "On that day when My people Israel dwell safely, will you not know *it?* 15Then you will come from your place out of the far north, you and many peoples with you, all of them riding on horses, a great company and a mighty army. 16You will come up against My people Israel like a cloud, to cover the land. It will be in the latter days that I will bring you against My land, so that the nations may know Me, when I am hallowed in you, O Gog, before their eyes." 17Thus says the Lord GOD: "Are *you* he of whom I have spoken in former days by My servants the prophets of Israel, who prophesied for years in those days that I would bring you against them?

Judgment on Gog

18"And it will come to pass at the same time, when Gog comes against the land of Israel," says the Lord GOD, "*that* My fury will show in My face. 19For in My jealousy

GEOGRAPHY AND ENVIRONMENT

The places and peoples named in the Old Testament are sometimes difficult or impossible to identify today. Gog and Magog are mentioned only in Ezek. 38; 39 and Rev. 20:8. Since Meshech and Tubal (Ezek. 38:2) were tribes living in what is today Turkey, it is possible that Gog and Magog were peoples in that area. They are reported to come from the north and to be fighters with bow and arrow (Ezek. 39:2, 3).

and in the fire of My wrath I have spoken: 'Surely in that day there shall be a great earthquake in the land of Israel, [20]so that the fish of the sea, the birds of the heavens, the beasts of the field, all creeping things that creep on the earth, and all men who *are* on the face of the earth shall shake at My presence. The mountains shall be thrown down, the steep places shall fall, and every wall shall fall to the ground.' [21]I will call for a sword against Gog throughout all My mountains," says the Lord GOD. "Every man's sword will be against his brother. [22]And I will bring him to judgment with pestilence and bloodshed; I will rain down on him, on his troops, and on the many peoples who *are* with him, flooding rain, great hailstones, fire, and brimstone. [23]Thus I will magnify Myself and sanctify Myself, and I will be known in the eyes of many nations. Then they shall know that I *am* the LORD." '

Gog's Armies Destroyed

39 [1]"And you, son of man, prophesy against Gog, and say, 'Thus says the Lord GOD: "Behold, I *am* against you, O Gog, the prince of Rosh,[a] Meshech, and Tubal; [2]and I will turn you around and lead you on, bringing you up from the far north, and bring you against the mountains of Israel. [3]Then I will knock the bow out of your left hand, and cause the arrows to fall out of your right hand. [4]You shall fall upon the mountains of Israel, you and all your troops and the peoples who *are* with you; I will give you to birds of prey of every sort and *to* the beasts of the field to be devoured. [5]You shall fall on the open field; for I have spoken," says the Lord GOD. [6]"And I will send fire on Magog and on those who live in security in the coastlands. Then they shall know that I *am* the LORD. [7]So I will make My holy name known in the midst of My people Israel, and I will not *let them* profane My holy name anymore. Then the nations shall know that *I am* the LORD, the Holy One in Israel. [8]Surely it is coming, and it shall be done," says the Lord GOD. "This *is* the day of which I have spoken.

[9]"Then those who dwell in the cities of Israel will go out and set on fire and burn the weapons, both the shields and bucklers, the bows and arrows, the javelins and spears; and they will make fires with them for seven years. [10]They will not take wood from the field nor cut down *any* from the forests, because they will make fires with the weapons; and they will plunder those who plundered them, and pillage those who pillaged them," says the Lord GOD.

The Burial of Gog

[11]"It will come to pass in that day *that* I will give Gog a burial place there in Israel, the valley of those who pass by east of the sea; and it will obstruct travelers, because there they will bury Gog and all his multitude. Therefore they will call *it* the Valley of Hamon Gog.[a] [12]For seven months the house of Israel will be burying them, in order to cleanse the land. [13]Indeed all the people of the land will be burying, and they will gain renown for it on the day that I am glorified," says the Lord GOD. [14]"They will set apart men regularly employed, with the help of a search party,[a] to pass through the land and bury those bodies remaining on the ground, in order to cleanse it. At the end of seven months they will make a search. [15]The search party will pass through the land; and *when anyone* sees a man's bone, he shall set up a marker by it, till the buriers have buried it in the Valley of Hamon Gog. [16]*The* name of *the* city *will* also *be* Hamonah. Thus they shall cleanse the land." '

A Triumphant Festival

[17]"And as for you, son of man, thus says the Lord GOD, 'Speak to every sort of bird and to every beast of the field:

TIME CAPSULE   *567 to 560 B.C.*

567   *Hophra joins with Nebuchadnezzar to invade Egypt*

567   *Amasis repels the Babylonians, and Hophra is killed*

562– *Evil-Merodach succeeds Nebuchad-*
560   *nezzar as king of Babylon*

561   *Evil-Merodach releases Jehoiachin from prison (2 Kin. 25:27)*

560– *Neriglissar, king of Babylon, was*
556   *possibly known earlier as Nergal-Sharezer (Jer. 39:3)*

39:1 [a]Targum, Vulgate and Aquila read *chief prince of.*   39:11 [a]Literally *The Multitude of Gog*
39:14 [a]Literally *those who pass through*

"Assemble yourselves and come;
   Gather together from all sides to My
      sacrificial meal
   Which I am sacrificing for you,
   A great sacrificial meal on the
      mountains of Israel,
   That you may eat flesh and drink
      blood.
18 You shall eat the flesh of the mighty,
   Drink the blood of the princes of the
      earth,
   Of rams and lambs,
   Of goats and bulls,
   All of them fatlings of Bashan.
19 You shall eat fat till you are full,
   And drink blood till you are drunk,
   At My sacrificial meal
   Which I am sacrificing for you.
20   You shall be filled at My table
   With horses and riders,
   With mighty men
   And with all the men of war," says the
      Lord GOD.

Israel Restored to the Land

21"I will set My glory among the nations; all the nations shall see My judgment which I have executed, and My hand which I have laid on them. 22So the house of Israel shall know that I *am* the LORD their God from that day forward. 23The Gentiles shall know that the house of Israel went into captivity for their iniquity; because they were unfaithful to Me, therefore I hid My face from them. I gave them into the hand of their enemies, and they all fell by the sword. 24According to their uncleanness and according to their transgressions I have dealt with them, and hidden My face from them." '

25"Therefore thus says the Lord GOD: 'Now I will bring back the captives of Jacob, and have mercy on the whole house of Israel; and I will be jealous for My holy name— 26after they have borne their shame, and all their unfaithfulness in which they were unfaithful to Me, when they dwelt safely in their *own* land and no one made *them* afraid. 27When I have brought them back from the peoples and gathered them out of their enemies' lands, and I am hallowed in them in the sight of many nations, 28then they shall know that I *am* the LORD their God, who sent them into captivity among the nations, but also brought them back to their land, and left none of them captive any longer. 29And I will not hide My face from them

anymore; for I shall have poured out My Spirit on the house of Israel,' says the Lord GOD."

Ezekiel's Second Temple Vision

The 25th year of the Babylonian captivity (Ezek. 40:1) was perhaps April, 573 B.C. Nebuchadnezzar was still king, and the power of Babylon was growing greater each year. But to Ezekiel the turning point had already come, and he saw salvation arriving to replace Israel's shame and punishment. It is appropriate that Ezekiel, who would never forsake his priestly roots, should describe the ultimate salvation with a vision of a new, and better, temple.

Ezekiel's vision of the perfect temple is a companion piece to his earlier temple vision of chs. 8—11 (see "Ezekiel's Temple Vision" at Ezek. 8:1). In that vision, Ezekiel saw abominations and idolatry, and the vision concluded with the glory of God departing from the temple (Ezek. 11:22, 23). This time, Ezekiel sees only perfection. The crowning moment is when "the glory of the LORD came into the temple by way of the gate which faces toward the east . . . and behold, the glory of the LORD filled the temple" (Ezek. 43:4, 5).

Chapters 40—48, like chs. 38; 39, contain a great deal of symbolism. Most of the symbols seem to indicate the absolute perfection of the future temple, but more specific meanings are certainly possible. These chapters too, then, can be described as early "apocalyptic" writing (see "Ezekiel's Apocalyptic Prophecies" at Ezek. 38:1). In fact, the most extensive apocalyptic book in the Bible, the Book of Revelation, also contains an extended vision of a perfect temple in the future, phrased in language very similar to that of Ezekiel (Rev. 21).

These chapters, like chs. 38; 39 before them, are difficult to place chronologically. What temple is referred to here? If it is the actual rebuilt temple mentioned in Ezra 6:14-16, then the prophecy could be associated with that event. But the stunning, perfect temple described in this vision bears little resemblance to the disappointing structure mentioned at that time (see Ezra 3:12).

Perhaps, as is the case with the temple vision of Rev. 21, Ezek. 40—48 is a vision of a future perfection, to come at an unspecified end. Thus it is not intended as a blueprint for an earthly, physical fulfillment. Rather it pictures the purity and spiritual vitality of the ideal place of worship and those who will worship there. In this sense, Ezekiel's vision of the restored temple complements the message of his second, hopeful ministry.

■ Ezekiel 40:1—42:20

Ezekiel
A New City, a New Temple

40 :1 In the twenty-fifth year of our captivity, at the beginning of the year, on the tenth *day* of the month, in the fourteenth year after the city was captured, on the very same day the hand of the LORD was upon me; and He took me there. ²In the visions of God He took me into the land of Israel and set me on a very high mountain; on it toward the south *was* something like the structure of a city. ³He took me there, and behold, *there was* a man whose appearance *was* like the appearance of bronze. He had a line of flax and a measuring rod in his hand, and he stood in the gateway.

⁴And the man said to me, "Son of man, look with your eyes and hear with your ears, and fix your mind on everything I show you; for you *were* brought here so that I might show *them* to you. Declare to the house of Israel everything you see." ⁵Now there was a wall all around the outside of the temple.ᵃ In the man's hand was a measuring rod six cubits *long, each being a* cubit and a handbreadth; and he measured the width of the wall structure, one rod; and the height, one rod.

The Eastern Gateway of the Temple

⁶Then he went to the gateway which faced east; and he went up its stairs and measured the threshold of the gateway, *which was* one rod wide, and the other threshold *was* one rod wide. ⁷Each gate chamber *was* one rod long and one rod wide; between the gate chambers *was a space of* five cubits; and the threshold of the gateway by the vestibule of the inside gate *was* one rod. ⁸He also measured the vestibule of the inside gate, one rod. ⁹Then he measured the vestibule of the gateway, eight cubits; and the gateposts, two cubits. The vestibule of the gate *was* on the inside. ¹⁰In the eastern gateway *were* three gate chambers on one side and three on the other; the three *were* all the same size; also the gateposts were of the same size on this side and that side. ¹¹He measured the width of the en-

trance to the gateway, ten cubits; *and* the length of the gate, thirteen cubits. ¹²*There was* a space in front of the gate chambers, one cubit *on this side* and one cubit on that side; the gate chambers *were* six cubits on this side and six cubits on that side. ¹³Then he measured the gateway from the roof of *one* gate chamber to the roof of the other; the width *was* twenty-five cubits, as door faces door. ¹⁴He measured the gateposts, sixty cubits high, and the court all around the gateway *extended* to the gatepost. ¹⁵*From* the front of the entrance gate to the front of the vestibule of the inner gate *was* fifty cubits. ¹⁶*There were* beveled window *frames* in the gate chambers and in their intervening archways on the inside of the gateway all around, and likewise in the vestibules. *There were* windows all around on the inside. And on each gatepost *were* palm trees.

The Outer Court

¹⁷Then he brought me into the outer court; and *there were* chambers and a pavement made all around the court; thirty chambers faced the pavement. ¹⁸The pavement was by the side of the gateways, corresponding to the length of the gateways; *this was* the lower pavement. ¹⁹Then he measured the width from the front of the lower gateway to the front of the inner court exterior, one hundred cubits toward the east and the north.

The Northern Gateway

²⁰On the outer court was also a gateway facing north, and he measured its length and its width. ²¹Its gate chambers, three on this side and three on that side, its gateposts and its archways, had the same measurements as the first gate; its length *was* fifty cubits and its width twenty-five cubits. ²²Its windows and those of its archways, and also its palm trees, *had* the same measurements as the gateway facing east; it was ascended by seven steps, and its archway *was* in front of it. ²³A gate of the inner court was opposite the northern gateway, just as the eastern *gateway;* and he measured from gateway to gateway, one hundred cubits.

The Southern Gateway

²⁴After that he brought me toward the south, and there a gateway was facing

---

40:5 ᵃLiterally *house,* and so elsewhere in this book

DATES IN THE BOOK OF EZEKIEL

The prophecies in the Book of Ezekiel often provide a date. The dates are counted from the beginning of the exile in 597 B.C., when Nebuchadnezzar captured Jerusalem and carried King Jehoiachin to Babylon (2 Kin. 24:10–16). So each year is a "year in exile," expressed as a certain "year of King Jehoiachin's captivity" (Ezek. 1:2) or "year of our captivity" (Ezek. 33:21; 40:1). One exception is the 30th year of Ezek. 1:1, where "30" is probably Ezekiel's age.

Reference in Ezekiel	Year in Exile	Month	Day	Modern Calendar	Prophecy
1:1	(30th)	4th	5th	July 31, 593 B.C.	Ezekiel's vision of God
1:2	5th	–	5th	July 31, 593 B.C.	Receives the word of the Lord
8:1	6th	6th	5th	Sept. 17, 592 B.C.	Abominations in the temple
20:1	7th	5th	10th	Aug. 9, 591 B.C.	The rebellion of Israel
24:1	9th	10th	10th	Jan. 15, 588 B.C.	The cooking pot
29:1	10th	10th	12th	Jan. 7, 587 B.C.	Proclamation against Egypt
30:20	11th	1st	7th	Apr. 29, 587 B.C.	Proclamation against Pharaoh
31:1	11th	3rd	1st	June 21, 587 B.C.	Assyria an example for Egypt
26:1	11th	–	1st	Feb. 12, 586 B.C.?	Proclamation against Tyre
33:21	12th	10th	5th	Jan. 8, 585 B.C.	News of Jerusalem's capture
32:1	12th	12th	1st	Mar. 3, 585 B.C.	Lamentation for Pharaoh and Egypt
32:17	12th	–	15th	Mar. 17, 585 B.C.	Lamentation for Egypt
40:1	25th	1st	10th	Apr. 28, 573 B.C.	Visions of the new temple
29:17	27th	1st	1st	Apr. 26, 571 B.C.	Egypt is Babylon's wages for Tyre

south; and he measured its gateposts and archways according to these same measurements. ²⁵*There were* windows in it and in its archways all around like those windows; its length *was* fifty cubits and its width twenty-five cubits. ²⁶Seven steps led up to it, and its archway *was* in front of them; and it had palm trees on its gateposts, one on this side and one on that side. ²⁷*There was* also a gateway on the inner court, facing south; and he measured from gateway to gateway toward the south, one hundred cubits.

Gateways of the Inner Court

²⁸Then he brought me to the inner court through the southern gateway; he measured the southern gateway according to these same measurements. ²⁹Also its gate chambers, its gateposts, and its archways *were* according to these same measurements; *there were* windows in it and in its archways all around; *it was* fifty cubits long and twenty-five cubits wide. ³⁰*There were* archways all around, twenty-five cubits long and five cubits wide. ³¹Its archways faced the outer court, palm trees *were* on its gateposts, and going up to it *were* eight steps.

³²And he brought me into the inner court facing east; he measured the gateway according to these same measurements. ³³Also its gate chambers, its gateposts, and its archways *were* according to these same measurements; and *there were* windows in it and in its archways all around; *it was* fifty cubits long and twenty-five cubits wide. ³⁴Its archways faced the outer court, and palm trees *were* on its gateposts on this side and on that side; and going up to it *were* eight steps.

³⁵Then he brought me to the north gateway and measured *it* according to these same measurements— ³⁶also its gate chambers, its gateposts, and its archways. It had windows all around; its length *was* fifty cubits and its width twenty-five cubits. ³⁷Its gateposts faced the outer court, palm trees *were* on its gateposts on this side and on that side, and going up to it *were* eight steps.

Where Sacrifices Were Prepared

³⁸*There was* a chamber and its entrance by the gateposts of the gateway, where they washed the burnt offering. ³⁹In the vestibule of the gateway *were* two tables on this side and two tables on that side, on which to slay the burnt offering, the sin offering, and the trespass offering. ⁴⁰At the outer side of the vestibule, as one goes up to the entrance of the northern

gateway, *were* two tables; and on the other side of the vestibule of the gateway *were* two tables. ⁴¹Four tables *were* on this side and four tables on that side, by the side of the gateway, eight tables on which they slaughtered *the sacrifices.* ⁴²There were also four tables of hewn stone for the burnt offering, one cubit and a half long, one cubit and a half wide, and one cubit high; on these they laid the instruments with which they slaughtered the burnt offering and the sacrifice. ⁴³Inside *were* hooks, a handbreadth wide, fastened all around; and the flesh of the sacrifices *was* on the tables.

Chambers for Singers and Priests

⁴⁴Outside the inner gate *were* the chambers for the singers in the inner court, one facing south at the side of the northern gateway, and the other facing north at the side of the southern gateway. ⁴⁵Then he said to me, "This chamber which faces south *is* for the priests who have charge of the temple. ⁴⁶The chamber which faces north *is* for the priests who have charge of the altar; these *are* the sons of Zadok, from the sons of Levi, who come near the LORD to minister to Him."

Dimensions of the Inner Court and Vestibule

⁴⁷And he measured the court, one hundred cubits long and one hundred cubits wide, foursquare. The altar *was* in front of the temple. ⁴⁸Then he brought me to the vestibule of the temple and measured the doorposts of the vestibule, five cubits on this side and five cubits on that side; and the width of the gateway was three cubits on this side and three cubits on that side. ⁴⁹The length of the vestibule *was* twenty cubits, and the width eleven cubits; and by the steps which led up to it *there were* pillars by the doorposts, one on this side and another on that side.

Dimensions of the Sanctuary

41 ¹Then he brought me into the sanctuaryᵃ and measured the doorposts, six cubits wide on one side and six cubits wide on the other side—the width of the tabernacle. ²The width of the entryway *was* ten cubits, and the side walls of the entrance *were* five cubits on this side and five cubits on the other side; and he measured its length, forty cubits, and its width, twenty cubits.

³Also he went inside and measured the doorposts, two cubits; and the entrance, six cubits *high;* and the width of the entrance, seven cubits. ⁴He measured the length, twenty cubits; and the width, twenty cubits, beyond the sanctuary; and he said to me, "This *is* the Most Holy *Place.*"

The Side Chambers on the Wall

⁵Next, he measured the wall of the temple, six cubits. The width of each side chamber all around the temple *was* four cubits on every side. ⁶The side chambers *were* in three stories, one above the other, thirty chambers in each story; they rested on ledges which *were* for the side chambers all around, that they might be supported, but not fastened to the wall of the temple. ⁷As one went up from story to story, the side chambers became wider all around, because their supporting ledges in the wall of the temple ascended like steps; therefore the width of the structure increased as one went up *from* the lowest *story* to the highest by way of the middle one. ⁸I also saw an elevation all around the temple; it was the foundation of the side chambers, a full rod, *that is,* six cubits *high.* ⁹The thickness of the outer wall of the side chambers *was* five cubits, and so also the remaining terrace by the place of the side chambers of the temple. ¹⁰And between *it and* the *wall* chambers was a width of twenty cubits all around the temple on every side. ¹¹The doors of the side chambers opened on the terrace, one door toward the north and another toward the south; and the width of the terrace *was* five cubits all around.

The Building at the Western End

¹²The building that faced the separating courtyard at its western end *was* seventy cubits wide; the wall of the building *was* five cubits thick all around, and its length ninety cubits.

Dimensions and Design of the Temple Area

¹³So he measured the temple, one hundred cubits long; and the separating courtyard with the building and its walls *was* one hundred cubits long; ¹⁴also the width of the eastern face of the temple, including

---

41:1 ᵃHebrew *heykal,* here the main room of the temple, sometimes called the *holy place* (compare Exodus 26:33)

the separating courtyard, *was* one hundred cubits. ¹⁵He measured the length of the building behind it, facing the separating courtyard, with its galleries on the one side and on the other side, one hundred cubits, as well as the inner temple and the porches of the court, ¹⁶their doorposts and the beveled window frames. And the galleries all around their three stories opposite the threshold were paneled with wood from the ground to the windows—the windows were covered— ¹⁷from the space above the door, even to the inner room,ᵃ as well as outside, and on every wall all around, inside and outside, by measure.

¹⁸And *it was* made with cherubim and palm trees, a palm tree between cherub and cherub. *Each* cherub had two faces, ¹⁹so that the face of a man *was* toward a palm tree on one side, and the face of a young lion toward a palm tree on the other side; thus *it was* made throughout the temple all around. ²⁰From the floor to the space above the door, and on the wall of the sanctuary, cherubim and palm trees *were* carved.

²¹The doorposts of the temple *were* square, *as was* the front of the sanctuary; their appearance was similar. ²²The altar *was* of wood, three cubits high, and its length two cubits. Its corners, its length, and its sides *were* of wood; and he said to me, "This *is* the table that *is* before the LORD."

²³The temple and the sanctuary had two doors. ²⁴The doors had two panels *apiece,* two folding panels: two *panels* for one door and two panels for the other *door.* ²⁵Cherubim and palm trees *were* carved on the doors of the temple just as they *were* carved on the walls. A wooden canopy *was* on the front of the vestibule outside. ²⁶*There were* beveled window *frames* and palm trees on one side and on the other, on the sides of the vestibule—also on the side chambers of the temple and on the canopies.

41:17 ᵃLiterally *house,* here *the Most Holy Place*

The Chambers for the Priests

42 ¹Then he brought me out into the outer court, by the way toward the north; and he brought me into the chamber which *was* opposite the separating courtyard, and which *was* opposite the building toward the north. ²Facing the length, *which was* one hundred cubits (the width was fifty cubits), was the north door. ³Opposite the inner court of twenty *cubits,* and opposite the pavement of the outer court, *was* gallery against gallery in three *stories.* ⁴In front of the chambers, toward the inside, *was* a walk ten cubits wide, at a distance of one cubit; and their doors faced north. ⁵Now the upper chambers *were* shorter, because the galleries took away *space* from them more than from the lower and middle stories of the building. ⁶For they *were* in three *stories* and did not have pillars like the pillars of the courts; therefore *the upper level* was shortened more than the lower and middle levels from the ground up. ⁷And a wall which *was* outside ran parallel to the chambers, at the front of the chambers, toward the outer court; its length *was* fifty cubits. ⁸The length of the chambers toward the outer court *was* fifty cubits, whereas that facing the temple *was* one hundred cubits. ⁹At the lower chambers *was* the entrance on the east side, as one goes into them from the outer court.

¹⁰Also *there were* chambers in the thickness of the wall of the court toward the east, opposite the separating courtyard and opposite the building. ¹¹*There was* a walk in front of them also, and their appearance *was* like the chambers which *were* toward the north; they *were* as long and as wide as the others, and all their exits and entrances *were* according to plan. ¹²And corresponding to the doors of the chambers that *were* facing south, as one enters them, *there was* a door in front of the walk, the way directly in front of the wall toward the east.

¹³Then he said to me, "The north chambers *and* the south chambers, which *are* opposite the separating courtyard, *are*

ARCHITECTURE AND BUILDING

In the religions of the world a perfect square is a common shape for sacred areas. The square represents balance and rational order. This is the shape of the heavenly Jerusalem (Rev. 21:16). The tabernacle and temple in Israel were rectangular, but the most sacred room was square in plan and a cube overall. In Ezekiel's vision the "holy areas" (Ezek. 42:20) are enclosed by walls forming a square.

the holy chambers where the priests who approach the LORD shall eat the most holy offerings. There they shall lay the most holy offerings—the grain offering, the sin offering, and the trespass offering—for the place *is* holy. [14]When the priests enter them, they shall not go out of the holy *chamber* into the outer court; but there they shall leave their garments in which they minister, for they *are* holy. They shall put on other garments; then they may approach *that* which *is* for the people."

Outer Dimensions of the Temple

[15]Now when he had finished measuring the inner temple, he brought me out through the gateway that faces toward the east, and measured it all around. [16]He measured the east side with the measuring rod,[a] five hundred rods by the measuring rod all around. [17]He measured the north side, five hundred rods by the measuring rod all around. [18]He measured the south side, five hundred rods by the measuring rod. [19]He came around to the west side *and* measured five hundred rods by the measuring rod. [20]He measured it on the four sides; it had a wall all around, five hundred *cubits* long and five hundred wide, to separate the holy areas from the common.

> ### The Glory of God Returns
> In perhaps September, 592 B.C., Ezekiel received his first temple vision (Ezek. 8:1). At that time he saw the glory of God depart from the temple (11:22, 23). About 19 years later, perhaps in April, 573 B.C., Ezekiel saw in a second temple vision God's return. As God had left the old temple by the eastern gate, so now He returned by way of the same gate (43:1–5). The East Gate was the outer public entrance to the temple complex.
>
> ▪ Ezekiel 43:1—48:35

Ezekiel
The Temple, the LORD's Dwelling Place

43 :1 Afterward he brought me to the gate, the gate that faces toward the east. [2]And behold, the glory of the God of Israel came from the way of the east. His voice *was* like the sound of many waters; and the earth shone with His glory. [3]*It was* like the appearance of the vision which I saw—like the vision which I saw when I[a] came to destroy the city. The visions *were* like the vision which I saw by the River Chebar; and I fell on my face. [4]And the glory of the LORD came into the temple by way of the gate which faces toward the east. [5]The Spirit lifted me up and brought me into the inner court; and behold, the glory of the LORD filled the temple.

[6]Then I heard *Him* speaking to me from the temple, while a man stood beside me. [7]And He said to me, "Son of man, *this is* the place of My throne and the place of the soles of My feet, where I will dwell in the midst of the children of Israel forever. No more shall the house of Israel defile My holy name, they nor their kings, by their harlotry or with the carcasses of their kings on their high places. [8]When they set their threshold by My threshold, and their doorpost by My doorpost, with a wall between them and Me, they defiled My holy name by the abominations which they committed; therefore I have consumed them in My anger. [9]Now let them put their harlotry and the carcasses of their kings far away from Me, and I will dwell in their midst forever.

[10]"Son of man, describe the temple to the house of Israel, that they may be ashamed of their iniquities; and let them measure the pattern. [11]And if they are ashamed of all that they have done, make known to them the design of the temple and its arrangement, its exits and its entrances, its entire design and all its ordinances, all its forms and all its laws. Write *it* down in their sight, so that they may keep its whole design and all its ordinances, and perform them. [12]This *is* the law of the temple: The whole area surrounding the mountaintop *is* most holy. Behold, this *is* the law of the temple.

Dimensions of the Altar

[13]"These are the measurements of the altar in cubits (the *cubit is* one cubit and a handbreadth): the base one cubit high and one cubit wide, with a rim all around its edge of one span. This *is* the height of the altar: [14]from the base on the ground to the lower ledge, two cubits; the width of the ledge, one cubit; from the smaller ledge to the larger ledge, four cubits; and the width of the ledge, *one* cubit. [15]The altar hearth *is* four cubits high, with four horns extending upward from the hearth. [16]The altar hearth *is* twelve cubits long, twelve

---

42:16 [a]Compare 40:5   43:3 [a]Some Hebrew manuscripts and Vulgate read *He.*

wide, square at its four corners; ¹⁷the ledge, fourteen *cubits* long and fourteen wide on its four sides, with a rim of half a cubit around it; its base, one cubit all around; and its steps face toward the east."

Consecrating the Altar

¹⁸And He said to me, "Son of man, thus says the Lord GOD: 'These *are* the ordinances for the altar on the day when it is made, for sacrificing burnt offerings on it, and for sprinkling blood on it. ¹⁹You shall give a young bull for a sin offering to the priests, the Levites, who are of the seed of Zadok, who approach Me to minister to Me,' says the Lord GOD. ²⁰You shall take some of its blood and put *it* on the four horns of the altar, on the four corners of the ledge, and on the rim around it; thus you shall cleanse it and make atonement for it. ²¹Then you shall also take the bull of the sin offering, and burn it in the appointed place of the temple, outside the sanctuary. ²²On the second day you shall offer a kid of the goats without blemish for a sin offering; and they shall cleanse the altar, as they cleansed *it* with the bull. ²³When you have finished cleansing *it,* you shall offer a young bull without blemish, and a ram from the flock without blemish. ²⁴When you offer them before the LORD, the priests shall throw salt on them, and they will offer them up *as* a burnt offering to the LORD. ²⁵Every day for seven days you shall prepare a goat *for* a sin offering; they shall also prepare a young bull and a ram from the flock, both without blemish. ²⁶Seven days they shall make atonement for the altar and purify it, and so consecrate *it.* ²⁷When these days are over it shall be, on the eighth day and thereafter, that the priests shall offer your burnt offerings and your peace offerings on the altar; and I will accept you,' says the Lord GOD."

The East Gate and the Prince

44 ¹Then He brought me back to the outer gate of the sanctuary which faces toward the east, but it *was* shut. ²And the LORD said to me, "This gate shall be shut; it shall not be opened, and no man shall enter by it, because the LORD God of Israel has entered by it; therefore it shall be shut. ³As *for* the prince, *because* he *is* the prince, he may sit in it to eat bread before the LORD; he shall enter by way of the vestibule of the gateway, and go out the same way."

Those Admitted to the Temple

⁴Also He brought me by way of the north gate to the front of the temple; so I looked, and behold, the glory of the LORD filled the house of the LORD; and I fell on my face. ⁵And the LORD said to me, "Son of man, mark well, see with your eyes and hear with your ears, all that I say to you concerning all the ordinances of the house of the LORD and all its laws. Mark well who may enter the house and all who go out from the sanctuary.

⁶"Now say to the rebellious, to the house of Israel, 'Thus says the Lord GOD: "O house of Israel, let Us have no more of all your abominations. ⁷When you brought in foreigners, uncircumcised in heart and uncircumcised in flesh, to be in My sanctuary to defile it—My house—and when you offered My food, the fat and the blood, then they broke My covenant because of all your abominations. ⁸And you have not kept charge of My holy things, but you have set *others* to keep charge of My sanctuary for you." ⁹Thus says the Lord GOD: "No foreigner, uncircumcised in heart or uncircumcised in flesh, shall enter My sanctuary, including any foreigner who *is* among the children of Israel.

Laws Governing Priests

¹⁰"And the Levites who went far from Me, when Israel went astray, who strayed away from Me after their idols, they shall bear their iniquity. ¹¹Yet they shall be ministers in My sanctuary, *as* gatekeepers of the house and ministers of the house; they shall slay the burnt offering and the sacrifice for the people, and they shall stand before them to minister to them. ¹²Because they ministered to them before their idols

---

TIME CAPSULE   *560 to 556 B.C.*

560   *Anaximander of Miletus is first known Greek prose writer*

559   *Cyrus II ascends throne of Persia and founds the Achaemenid dynasty*

559–   *Achaemenid dynasty marks a pe-*
331   *riod of the Persian Empire's dominance*

559–   *Cyrus the Great of Persia*
530

556–   *Nabonidus, king of Babylon, pro-*
539   *motes the moon god Sin*

and caused the house of Israel to fall into iniquity, therefore I have raised My hand in an oath against them," says the Lord God, "that they shall bear their iniquity. ¹³And they shall not come near Me to minister to Me as priest, nor come near any of My holy things, nor into the Most Holy *Place;* but they shall bear their shame and their abominations which they have committed. ¹⁴Nevertheless I will make them keep charge of the temple, for all its work, and for all that has to be done in it.

¹⁵"But the priests, the Levites, the sons of Zadok, who kept charge of My sanctuary when the children of Israel went astray from Me, they shall come near Me to minister to Me; and they shall stand before Me to offer to Me the fat and the blood," says the Lord God. ¹⁶"They shall enter My sanctuary, and they shall come near My table to minister to Me, and they shall keep My charge. ¹⁷And it shall be, whenever they enter the gates of the inner court, that they shall put on linen garments; no wool shall come upon them while they minister within the gates of the inner court or within the house. ¹⁸They shall have linen turbans on their heads and linen trousers on their bodies; they shall not clothe themselves with *anything that causes* sweat. ¹⁹When they go out to the outer court, to the *outer* court to the people, they shall take off their garments in which they have ministered, leave them in the holy chambers, and put on other garments; and in their holy garments they shall not sanctify the people.

²⁰"They shall neither shave their heads, nor let their hair grow long, but they shall keep their hair well trimmed. ²¹No priest shall drink wine when he enters the inner court. ²²They shall not take as wife a widow or a divorced woman, but take virgins of the descendants of the house of Israel, or widows of priests. ²³"And they shall teach My people *the difference* between the holy and the unholy, and cause them to discern between the unclean and the clean. ²⁴In controversy they shall stand as judges, *and* judge it according to My judgments. They shall keep My laws and My statutes in all My appointed meetings, and they shall hallow My Sabbaths.

²⁵"They shall not defile *themselves* by coming near a dead person. Only for father or mother, for son or daughter, for brother or unmarried sister may they defile themselves. ²⁶After he is cleansed, they shall count seven days for him. ²⁷And on the day that he goes to the sanctuary to minister in the sanctuary, he must offer his sin offering in the inner court," says the Lord God.

²⁸"It shall be, in regard to their inheritance, *that* I *am* their inheritance. You shall give them no possession in Israel, for I *am* their possession. ²⁹They shall eat the grain offering, the sin offering, and the trespass offering; every dedicated thing in Israel shall be theirs. ³⁰The best of all firstfruits of any kind, and every sacrifice of any kind from all your sacrifices, shall be the priest's; also you shall give to the priest the first of your ground meal, to cause a blessing to rest on your house. ³¹The priests shall not eat anything, bird or beast, that died naturally or was torn *by wild beasts.*

The Holy District

45 ¹"Moreover, when you divide the land by lot into inheritance, you shall set apart a district for the Lord, a holy section of the land; its length *shall be* twenty-five thousand *cubits,* and the width ten thousand. It *shall be* holy throughout its territory all around. ²Of this there shall be a square plot for the sanctuary, five hundred by five hundred *rods,* with fifty cubits around it for an open space. ³So this is the district you shall measure: twenty-five thousand *cubits* long and ten thousand wide; in it shall be the sanctuary, the Most Holy *Place.* ⁴It shall be a holy *section* of the land, belonging to the priests, the ministers of the sanctuary, who come near to minister to the Lord; it shall be a place for their houses and a holy place for the sanc-

TRADE AND ECONOMICS

Standard weights from the ancient world show many variations in size. The call for "honest scales" (Ezek. 45:10), however, would be satisfied by maintaining consistency within a certain region and by fair play on the part of sellers. Scales from the Roman world used a pan hanging from one end of a beam. Such scales have been recovered undamaged from the ruins of Pompeii.

tuary. 5*An area* twenty-five thousand *cubits* long and ten thousand wide shall belong to the Levites, the ministers of the temple; they shall have twenty chambers as a possession.[a]

Properties of the City and the Prince

6"You shall appoint as the property of the city *an area* five thousand *cubits* wide and twenty-five thousand long, adjacent to the district of the holy *section;* it shall belong to the whole house of Israel.

7"The prince shall have *a section* on one side and the other of the holy district and the city's property; and bordering on the holy district and the city's property, extending westward on the west side and eastward on the east side, the length *shall be* side by side with one of the *tribal* portions, from the west border to the east border. 8The land shall be his possession in Israel; and My princes shall no more oppress My people, but they shall give *the rest of* the land to the house of Israel, according to their tribes."

Laws Governing the Prince

9Thus says the Lord GOD: "Enough, O princes of Israel! Remove violence and plundering, execute justice and righteousness, and stop dispossessing My people," says the Lord GOD. 10"You shall have honest scales, an honest ephah, and an honest bath. 11The ephah and the bath shall be of the same measure, so that the bath contains one-tenth of a homer, and the ephah one-tenth of a homer; their measure shall be according to the homer. 12The shekel *shall be* twenty gerahs; twenty shekels, twenty-five shekels, *and* fifteen shekels shall be your mina.

13"This *is* the offering which you shall offer: you shall give one-sixth of an ephah from a homer of wheat, and one-sixth of an ephah from a homer of barley. 14The ordinance concerning oil, the bath of oil, *is* one-tenth of a bath from a kor. A kor *is* a homer or ten baths, for ten baths *are* a homer. 15And one lamb shall be given from a flock of two hundred, from the rich pastures of Israel. These shall be for grain offerings, burnt offerings, and peace offerings, to make atonement for them," says the Lord GOD. 16"All the people of the land shall give this offering for the prince in Israel. 17Then it shall be the prince's part *to give* burnt offerings, grain offerings, and drink offerings, at the feasts, the New Moons, the Sabbaths, and at all the appointed seasons of the house of Israel. He shall prepare the sin offering, the grain offering, the burnt offering, and the peace offerings to make atonement for the house of Israel."

Keeping the Feasts

18Thus says the Lord GOD: "In the first *month,* on the first *day* of the month, you shall take a young bull without blemish and cleanse the sanctuary. 19The priest shall take some of the blood of the sin offering and put *it* on the doorposts of the temple, on the four corners of the ledge of the altar, and on the gateposts of the gate of the inner court. 20And so you shall do on the seventh *day* of the month for everyone who has sinned unintentionally or in ignorance. Thus you shall make atonement for the temple.

21"In the first *month,* on the fourteenth day of the month, you shall observe the Passover, a feast of seven days; unleavened bread shall be eaten. 22And on that day the prince shall prepare for himself and for all the people of the land a bull *for* a sin offering. 23On the seven days of the feast he shall prepare a burnt offering to the LORD, seven bulls and seven rams without blemish, daily for seven days, and a kid of the goats daily *for* a sin offering. 24And he shall prepare a grain offering of one ephah for each bull and one ephah for each ram, together with a hin of oil for each ephah.

25"In the seventh *month,* on the fifteenth day of the month, at the feast, he shall do likewise for seven days, according to the sin offering, the burnt offering, the grain offering, and the oil."

The Manner of Worship

46 1Thus says the Lord GOD: "The gateway of the inner court that faces toward the east shall be shut the six working days; but on the Sabbath it shall be opened, and on the day of the New Moon it shall be opened. 2The prince shall enter by way of the vestibule of the gateway from the outside, and stand by the gatepost. The priests shall prepare his burnt offering and his peace offerings. He shall worship at the threshold of the gate. Then he shall go out, but the gate shall not be shut until evening. 3Likewise the people of the land shall worship at the entrance to this

---

45:5 [a]Following Masoretic Text, Targum, and Vulgate; Septuagint reads *a possession, cities of dwelling.*

THE PRINCE IN THE TEMPLE (Ezek. 46:2)

In 586 B.C. the Babylonians destroyed the Jerusalem temple. As part of his prophecy of hope following this destruction, Ezekiel envisioned a new temple in a restored Jerusalem (Ezek. 40—48). The "glory of the LORD," which had departed from the old temple (Ezek. 10:18, 19), returns to this new temple (Ezek. 43:1–5). Ezekiel then described to the people the design for the new temple, including the ordinances and laws related to it (Ezek. 43:10, 11).

A "prince" will rule in this restored Jerusalem. The prince will have certain prerogatives, such as owning special property in Jerusalem around the holy space of the temple (45:6, 7). More significantly, only the prince may enter the east gate (44:1–3), the gate through which God's glory had reentered the temple (43:4).

The prince will be the civil ruler, but also a part of the religious organization. He will lead the people in their proper worship. During the Sabbath sacrifices, the prince offers burnt and peace sacrifices via the east gate, itself a large room, while the people look on from the outside (Ezek. 46:2). Additionally, the sacrificial duty of the prince extends to the monthly New Moon sacrifice (46:6, 7), as well as voluntary burnt and peace offerings (46:12).

Yet the prince must also be along when the people offer their sacrifices. The people are not free to roam in the temple courts; they enter via the north or south gate, escorted by the prince, and leave via the opposite gate (46:9, 10).

In the restored Jerusalem of Ezekiel's vision, then, the prince combines in his own body the civic and the sacred role to maintain the city in purity and righteousness. He orders the life of the people around the temple, which again will be filled with the glory of the Lord.

---

gateway before the LORD on the Sabbaths and the New Moons. ⁴The burnt offering that the prince offers to the LORD on the Sabbath day *shall be* six lambs without blemish, and a ram without blemish; ⁵and the grain offering *shall be one* ephah for a ram, and the grain offering for the lambs, as much as he wants to give, as well as a hin of oil with every ephah. ⁶On the day of the New Moon *it shall be* a young bull without blemish, six lambs, and a ram; they shall be without blemish. ⁷He shall prepare a grain offering of an ephah for a bull, an ephah for a ram, as much as he wants to give for the lambs, and a hin of oil with every ephah. ⁸When the prince enters, he shall go in by way of the vestibule of the gateway, and go out the same way.

⁹"But when the people of the land come before the LORD on the appointed feast days, whoever enters by way of the north gate to worship shall go out by way of the south gate; and whoever enters by way of the south gate shall go out by way of the north gate. He shall not return by way of the gate through which he came, but shall go out through the opposite gate. ¹⁰The prince shall then be in their midst. When they go in, he shall go in; and when they go out, he shall go out. ¹¹At the festivals and the appointed feast days the grain offering shall be an ephah for a bull, an ephah for a ram, as much as he wants to give for the lambs, and a hin of oil with every ephah.

¹²"Now when the prince makes a voluntary burnt offering or voluntary peace offering to the LORD, the gate that faces toward the east shall then be opened for him; and he shall prepare his burnt offering and his peace offerings as he did on the Sabbath day. Then he shall go out, and after he goes out the gate shall be shut.

¹³"You shall daily make a burnt offering to the LORD *of* a lamb of the first year without blemish; you shall prepare it every morning. ¹⁴And you shall prepare a grain offering with it every morning, a sixth of an ephah, and a third of a hin of oil to moisten the fine flour. This grain offering is a perpetual ordinance, to be made regularly to the LORD. ¹⁵Thus they shall prepare the lamb, the grain offering, and the oil, *as* a regular burnt offering every morning."

The Prince and Inheritance Laws

¹⁶'Thus says the Lord GOD: "If the prince gives a gift *of some* of his inheritance to any of his sons, it shall belong to his sons; it is their possession by inheri-

tance. [17]But if he gives a gift of some of his inheritance to one of his servants, it shall be his until the year of liberty, after which it shall return to the prince. But his inheritance shall belong to his sons; it shall become theirs. [18]Moreover the prince shall not take any of the people's inheritance by evicting them from their property; he shall provide an inheritance for his sons from his own property, so that none of My people may be scattered from his property." ' "

How the Offerings Were Prepared

[19]Now he brought me through the entrance, which *was* at the side of the gate, into the holy chambers of the priests which face toward the north; and there a place *was* situated at their extreme western end. [20]And he said to me, "This *is* the place where the priests shall boil the trespass offering and the sin offering, *and* where they shall bake the grain offering, so that they do not bring *them* out into the outer court to sanctify the people." [21]Then he brought me out into the outer court and caused me to pass by the four corners of the court; and in fact, in every corner of the court *there was another* court. [22]In the four corners of the court *were* enclosed courts, forty *cubits* long and thirty wide; all four corners *were* the same size. [23]*There was* a row *of building stones* all around in them, all around the four of them; and cooking hearths were made under the rows of stones all around. [24]And he said to me, "These *are* the kitchens where the ministers of the temple shall boil the sacrifices of the people."

The Healing Waters and Trees

47 [1]Then he brought me back to the door of the temple; and there was water, flowing from under the threshold of the temple toward the east, for the front of the temple faced east; the water was flowing from under the right side of the temple, south of the altar. [2]He brought me out by way of the north gate, and led me around on the outside to the outer gateway that faces east; and there was water, running out on the right side.

[3]And when the man went out to the east with the line in his hand, he measured one thousand cubits, and he brought me through the waters; the water *came up to my* ankles. [4]Again he measured one thousand and brought me through the waters; the water *came up to my* knees. Again he measured one thousand and brought me through; the water *came up to my* waist. [5]Again he measured one thousand, *and it was* a river that I could not cross; for the water was too deep, water in which one must swim, a river that could not be crossed. [6]He said to me, "Son of man, have you seen *this?*" Then he brought me and returned me to the bank of the river.

[7]When I returned, there, along the bank of the river, *were* very many trees on one side and the other. [8]Then he said to me: "This water flows toward the eastern region, goes down into the valley, and enters the sea. *When it* reaches the sea, *its* waters are healed. [9]And it shall be *that* every living thing that moves, wherever the rivers go, will live. There will be a very great multitude of fish, because these waters go there; for they will be healed, and everything will live wherever the river goes. [10]It shall be *that* fishermen will stand by it from En Gedi to En Eglaim; they will be *places* for spreading their nets. Their fish will be of the same kinds as the fish of the Great Sea, exceedingly many. [11]But its swamps and marshes will not be healed; they will be given over to salt. [12]Along the bank of the river, on this side and that, will grow all *kinds of* trees used for food; their leaves will not wither, and their fruit will not fail. They will bear fruit every month, because their water flows from the sanctuary. Their fruit will be for food, and their leaves for medicine."

Borders of the Land

[13]Thus says the Lord GOD: "These *are* the borders by which you shall divide the land as an inheritance among the twelve tribes of Israel. Joseph *shall have two* portions. [14]You shall inherit it equally with one another; for I raised My hand in an oath to give it to your fathers, and this land shall fall to you as your inheritance.

[15]"This *shall be* the border of the land on the north: from the Great Sea, *by* the road to Hethlon, as one goes to Zedad, [16]Hamath, Berothah, Sibraim (which *is* between the border of Damascus and the border of Hamath), to Hazar Hatticon (which *is* on the border of Hauran). [17]Thus the boundary shall be from the Sea to Hazar Enan, the border of Damascus; and as for the north, northward, it is the border of Hamath. *This is* the north side.

[18]"On the east side you shall mark out the border from between Hauran and

Damascus, and between Gilead and the land of Israel, along the Jordan, and along the eastern side of the sea. *This is* the east side.

19"The south side, toward the South,ᵃ *shall be* from Tamar to the waters of Meribah by Kadesh, along the brook to the Great Sea. *This is* the south side, toward the South.

20"The west side *shall be* the Great Sea, from the *southern* boundary until one comes to a point opposite Hamath. This *is* the west side.

21"Thus you shall divide this land among yourselves according to the tribes of Israel. 22It shall be that you will divide it by lot as an inheritance for yourselves, and for the strangers who dwell among you and who bear children among you. They shall be to you as native-born among the children of Israel; they shall have an inheritance with you among the tribes of Israel. 23And it shall be *that* in whatever tribe the stranger dwells, there you shall give *him* his inheritance," says the Lord GOD.

Division of the Land

48 1"Now these *are* the names of the tribes: From the northern border along the road to Hethlon at the entrance of Hamath, to Hazar Enan, the border of Damascus northward, in the direction of Hamath, *there shall be* one *section for* Dan from its east to its west side; 2by the border of Dan, from the east side to the west, one *section for* Asher; 3by the border of Asher, from the east side to the west, one *section for* Naphtali; 4by the border of Naphtali, from the east side to the west, one *section for* Manasseh; 5by the border of Manasseh, from the east side to the west, one *section for* Ephraim; 6by the border of Ephraim, from the east side to the west, one *section for* Reuben; 7by the border of Reuben, from the east side to the west, one *section for* Judah; 8by the border of Judah, from the east side to the west, shall be the district which you shall set apart, twenty-five thousand *cubits* in width, and *in* length the same as one of the *other* portions, from the east side to the west, with the sanctuary in the center.

9"The district that you shall set apart for the LORD *shall be* twenty-five thousand *cubits* in length and ten thousand in width. 10To these—to the priests—the holy district shall belong: on the north twenty-five thousand *cubits in length,* on the west ten thou-sand in width, on the east ten thousand in width, and on the south twenty-five thousand in length. The sanctuary of the LORD shall be in the center. 11*It shall be* for the priests of the sons of Zadok, who are sanctified, who have kept My charge, who did not go astray when the children of Israel went astray, as the Levites went astray. 12And *this* district of land that is set apart shall be to them a thing most holy by the border of the Levites.

13"Opposite the border of the priests, the Levites *shall have an area* twenty-five thousand *cubits* in length and ten thousand in width; its entire length *shall be* twenty-five thousand and its width ten thousand. 14And they shall not sell or exchange any of it; they may not alienate this best *part* of the land, for *it is* holy to the LORD.

15"The five thousand *cubits* in width that remain, along the edge of the twenty-five thousand, shall be for general use by the city, for dwellings and common-land; and the city shall be in the center. 16These *shall be* its measurements: the north side four thousand five hundred *cubits,* the south side four thousand five hundred, the east side four thousand five hundred, and the west side four thousand five hundred. 17The common-land of the city shall be: to the north two hundred and fifty *cubits,* to the south two hundred and fifty, to the east two hundred and fifty, and to the west two hundred and fifty. 18The rest of the length, alongside the district of the holy *section, shall be* ten thousand *cubits* to the east and ten thousand to the west. It shall be adjacent to the district of the holy *section,* and its produce shall be food for the workers of the city. 19The workers of the city, from all the tribes of Israel, shall cultivate it. 20The entire district *shall be* twenty-five thousand *cubits* by twenty-five thousand *cubits,* foursquare. You shall set apart the holy district with the property of the city.

21"The rest *shall belong* to the prince, on one side and on the other of the holy district and of the city's property, next to the twenty-five thousand *cubits* of the *holy* district as far as the eastern border, and westward next to the twenty-five thousand as far as the western border, adjacent to the *tribal* portions; *it shall belong* to the prince. It shall be the holy district, and the sanctuary of the temple *shall be* in the cen-

---

47:19 ᵃHebrew *Negev*

ter. ²²Moreover, apart from the possession of the Levites and the possession of the city *which are* in the midst of what *belongs to* the prince, *the area* between the border of Judah and the border of Benjamin shall belong to the prince.

²³"As for the rest of the tribes, from the east side to the west, Benjamin *shall have* one *section;* ²⁴by the border of Benjamin, from the east side to the west, Simeon *shall have* one *section;* ²⁵by the border of Simeon, from the east side to the west, Issachar *shall have* one *section;* ²⁶by the border of Issachar, from the east side to the west, Zebulun *shall have* one *section;* ²⁷by the border of Zebulun, from the east side to the west, Gad *shall have* one *section;* ²⁸by the border of Gad, on the south side, toward the South,ᵃ the border shall be from Tamar *to* the waters of Meribah *by* Kadesh, along the brook to the Great Sea. ²⁹This *is* the land which you shall divide by lot as an inheritance among the tribes of Israel, and these *are* their portions," says the Lord GOD.

The Gates of the City and Its Name

³⁰"These *are* the exits of the city. On the north side, measuring four thousand five hundred *cubits* ³¹(the gates of the city *shall be* named after the tribes of Israel), the three gates northward: one gate for Reuben, one gate for Judah, and one gate for Levi; ³²on the east side, four thousand five hundred *cubits,* three gates: one gate for Joseph, one gate for Benjamin, and one gate for Dan; ³³on the south side, measuring four thousand five hundred *cubits,* three gates: one gate for Simeon, one gate for Issachar, and one gate for Zebulun; ³⁴on the west side, four thousand five hundred *cubits* with their three gates: one gate for Gad, one gate for Asher, and one gate for Naphtali. ³⁵All the way around *shall be* eighteen thousand *cubits;* and the name of the city from *that* day *shall be:* THE LORD *IS* THERE."ᵃ

48:28 ᵃHebrew *Negev*   48:35 ᵃHebrew *YHWH Shammah*

Nebuchadnezzar's Siege of Tyre

After destroying Jerusalem in 586 B.C., Nebuchadnezzar, king of Babylon, moved north and laid siege to the fortress city of Tyre. This was a formidable task, for not only was Tyre on an island, just off the coast, but it was a great seaport, able to supply itself from the sea. For 13 years, Nebuchadnezzar sought to bring it to heel, but without success. In 572 B.C. he gave up and lifted the siege.

The prophet Ezekiel had had much to say about Tyre in earlier years (Ezek. 27; 28). He had foretold the eventual humbling of Tyre's pride and the desolation of the city. In the 27th year of Jehoiachin's exile (possibly April, 571 B.C.; Ezek. 29:17), after Nebuchadnezzar had lifted the siege, Ezekiel received a new message. He declared that God would allow Nebuchadnezzar to conquer Egypt as a sort of consolation prize for his futile efforts at Tyre (29:17–21). While the prophecies against Egypt in Ezek. 30:1–19 are not dated specifically to this time, they can be understood as a further elaboration of this promise.

■ Ezekiel 29:17–21
■ Ezekiel 30:1–19

Ezekiel 29:17–21
Babylonia Will Plunder Egypt

29 :17 And it came to pass in the twenty-seventh year, in the first *month,* on the first *day* of the month, *that* the word of the LORD came to me, saying, ¹⁸"Son of man, Nebuchadnezzar king of Babylon caused his army to labor strenuously against Tyre; every head *was* made bald, and every shoulder rubbed raw; yet neither he nor his army received wages from Tyre, for the labor which they expended on it. ¹⁹Therefore thus says the Lord GOD: 'Surely I will give the land of Egypt to Nebuchadnezzar king of Babylon; he shall take away her wealth, carry off her spoil, and remove her pillage; and that will be the wages for his army. ²⁰I have given him the land of Egypt *for* his labor, because they worked for Me,' says the Lord GOD.

²¹'In that day I will cause the horn of the house of Israel to spring forth, and I will open your mouth to speak in their midst. Then they shall know that I *am* the LORD.' "

Ezekiel 30:1–19
Egypt and Her Allies Will Fall

30 :1 The word of the LORD came to me again, saying, ²"Son of man, prophesy and say, 'Thus says the Lord GOD:

"Wail, 'Woe to the day!'
3   For the day *is* near,

EGYPT'S CITY OF SUN WORSHIP (Ezek. 30:17)

The prophet Ezekiel pronounced judgment upon several Egyptian cities, one by the name of "Aven" (Ezek. 30:17). In the Hebrew language, "Aven" is probably a different pronunciation for the Hebrew name "On." On was an important Egyptian city in the Delta region. In patriarchal times, Joseph had married the daughter of the priest of On (Gen. 41:45). The city is now identified with Tell Hisn, a site in the northern suburbs of modern Cairo.

Although the city of On was never a major political center, the local priesthood wielded a strong religious influence throughout Egyptian history. On was known primarily for the worship of solar deities and, during Egypt's New Kingdom period (c. 1550–1069 B.C.), played a major role in Egyptian theology of the kingship. Kings were considered to be the image of the sun god on earth.

One of the most controversial monarchs of the New Kingdom, Pharaoh Akhenaten (1352–1336 B.C.), built a temple in honor of the sun disk at On. He introduced the worship of this object to Egypt, describing it as having the attributes of transcendence and even uniqueness. The sun worship so prominent in On is reflected in the later Greek name for the city: Heliopolis, meaning "city of the sun." So also Jeremiah calls the city "Beth Shemesh" (Jer. 43:13), which in Hebrew means "house of the sun."

The prophets Jeremiah and Ezekiel both prophesied of the Babylonian campaign against Egypt in 567 B.C. Jeremiah proclaims that Nebuchadnezzar would "break the sacred pillars of Beth Shemesh" (Jer. 43:10, 13); Ezekiel, that by Nebuchadnezzar's hand "the young men of Aven" would fall (Ezek. 30:10, 17). Both prophets spoke of Egypt's ancient city of On.

Even the day of the LORD *is* near;
It will be a day of clouds, the time of
    the Gentiles.
4 The sword shall come upon Egypt,
And great anguish shall be in
    Ethiopia,
When the slain fall in Egypt,
And they take away her wealth,
And her foundations are broken down.

5"Ethiopia, Libya,[a] Lydia,[b] all the mingled people, Chub, and the men of the lands who are allied, shall fall with them by the sword."
6"Thus says the LORD:

"Those who uphold Egypt shall fall,
And the pride of her power shall come
    down.
From Migdol *to* Syene
Those within her shall fall by the
    sword,"
Says the Lord GOD.

7 "They shall be desolate in the midst of
    the desolate countries,
And her cities shall be in the midst of
    the cities *that are* laid waste.
8 Then they will know that I *am* the
    LORD,
When I have set a fire in Egypt
And all her helpers are destroyed.
9 On that day messengers shall go forth
    from Me in ships
To make the careless Ethiopians
    afraid,
And great anguish shall come upon
    them,
As on the day of Egypt;
For indeed it is coming!"

10"Thus says the Lord GOD:

"I will also make a multitude of Egypt
    to cease

30:5 [a]Hebrew *Put*   [b]Hebrew *Lud*

POLITICS AND GOVERNMENT

The Egyptians employed mercenary soldiers from the countries around them. Ethiopia was to the south, Libya to the west, and Lydia in what is today Turkey. "Chub" (Ezek. 30:5) is possibly another Hebrew term for Libya. The relative strength of Egypt and these countries fluctuated. There were periods when Egypt was ruled by Ethiopians as well as by Libyans.

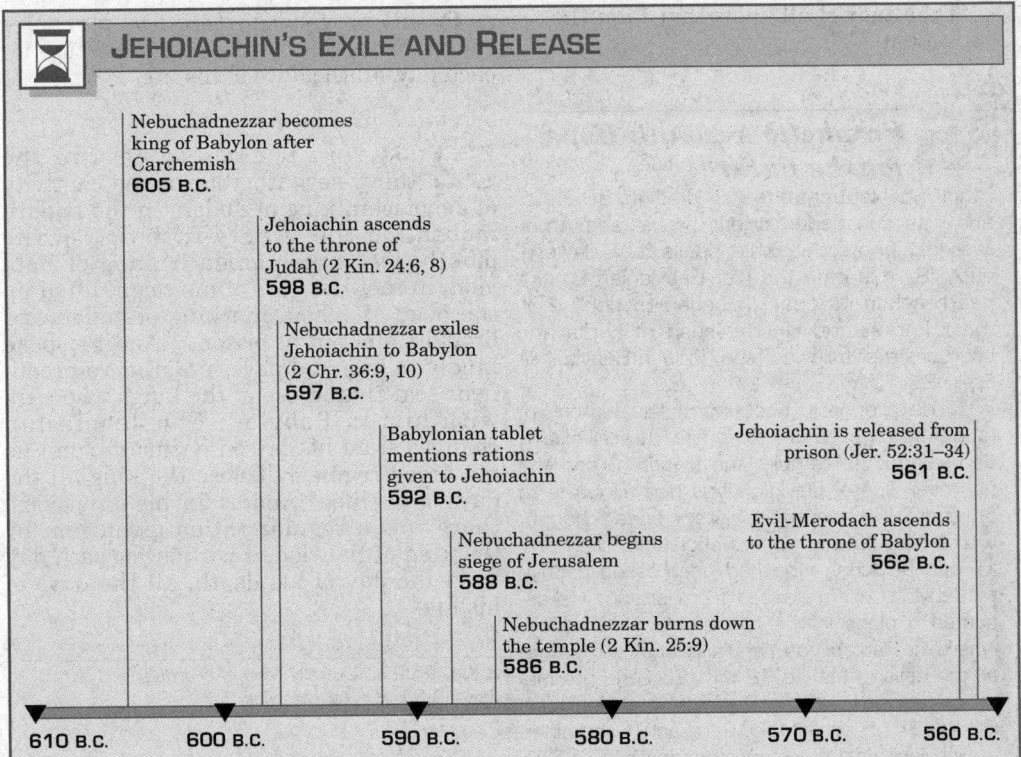

JEHOIACHIN'S EXILE AND RELEASE

Nebuchadnezzar becomes
king of Babylon after
Carchemish
605 B.C.

Jehoiachin ascends
to the throne of
Judah (2 Kin. 24:6, 8)
598 B.C.

Nebuchadnezzar exiles
Jehoiachin to Babylon
(2 Chr. 36:9, 10)
597 B.C.

Babylonian tablet
mentions rations
given to Jehoiachin
592 B.C.

Jehoiachin is released from
prison (Jer. 52:31–34)
561 B.C.

Nebuchadnezzar begins
siege of Jerusalem
588 B.C.

Evil-Merodach ascends
to the throne of Babylon
562 B.C.

Nebuchadnezzar burns down
the temple (2 Kin. 25:9)
586 B.C.

610 B.C.   **600 B.C.**   **590 B.C.**   **580 B.C.**   **570 B.C.**   **560 B.C.**

By the hand of Nebuchadnezzar king
 of Babylon.
11 He and his people with him, the most
 terrible of the nations,
 Shall be brought to destroy the land;
 They shall draw their swords against
 Egypt,
 And fill the land with the slain.
12 I will make the rivers dry,
 And sell the land into the hand of the
 wicked;
 I will make the land waste, and all
 that is in it,
 By the hand of aliens.
 I, the LORD, have spoken."

13"Thus says the Lord GOD:

"I will also destroy the idols,
 And cause the images to cease from
 Noph;ᵃ

There shall no longer be princes from
 the land of Egypt;
 I will put fear in the land of Egypt.
14 I will make Pathros desolate,
 Set fire to Zoan,
 And execute judgments in No.ᵃ
15 I will pour My fury on Sin,ᵃ the
 strength of Egypt;
 I will cut off the multitude of No,
16 And set a fire in Egypt;
 Sin shall have great pain,
 No shall be split open,
 And Noph *shall be in* distress
 daily.
17 The young men of Avenᵃ and Pi
 Beseth shall fall by the sword,
 And these *cities* shall go into captivity.
18 At Tehaphnehesᵃ the day shall also be
 darkened,ᵇ
 When I break the yokes of Egypt
 there.
 And her arrogant strength shall cease
 in her;
 As for her, a cloud shall cover her,
 And her daughters shall go into
 captivity.
19 Thus I will execute judgments on
 Egypt,

30:13 ᵃThat is, ancient Memphis 30:14 ᵃThat
is, ancient Thebes 30:15 ᵃThat is, ancient
Pelusium 30:17 ᵃThat is, ancient On
(Heliopolis) 30:18 ᵃSpelled *Tahpanhes* in Jeremiah
43:7 and elsewhere ᵇFollowing many Hebrew
manuscripts, Bomberg, Septuagint, Syriac, Targum,
and Vulgate; Masoretic Text reads *refrained.*

Then they shall know that I *am* the
LORD." ' "

Prophetic Account: Hope for the Future

King Nebuchadnezzar died in 562 B.C.
and was succeeded briefly by his son Amel-
Marduk, or as the Bible spells it, Evil-Merodach. By this time the Neo-Babylonian Empire
had reached its peak. It began to decline almost immediately in the rush of kings and
usurpers that followed (see "Exile in Babylon" at
Ezek. 33:1).

The prophetic account of the history of
Israel led up to a climactic destruction.
Jerusalem, the temple, the kingdom, and the
unbroken line of Davidic kings had all come to
an end. That prophetic history ends, though,
with a faint note of hope: Jehoiachin, the rightful king of Judah who had been taken captive
to Babylon, was released from prison. He assumed a place in the court of Evil-Merodach,
where he "ate bread regularly before the king
all the days of his life" (2 Kin. 25:29). The historical appendix to the Book of Jeremiah (Jer.
52:31-34) records that Jehoiachin remained
in Babylon "until the day of his death" (52:34).

Jehoiachin's release came in the 37th
year of his captivity (possibly March, 561 B.C.).
As a hope for a restored Israel it was not
much, and the picture of the Davidic king serving in a foreign king's court was hardly flattering to Israel's dignity. Still, the line of David was
not completely cut off, which left some hope of
eventual restoration. After all, David himself
began by serving in another king's court
(1 Sam. 16—20).

■ 2 Kings 25:27-30
■ Jeremiah 52:31-34

2 Kings 25:27-30
Jehoiachin Released from Prison

25 :27 Now it came to pass in the
thirty-seventh year of the captivity
of Jehoiachin king of Judah, in the twelfth
month, on the twenty-seventh *day* of the
month, *that* Evil-Merodach[a] king of Babylon, in the year that he began to reign, released Jehoiachin king of Judah from
prison. 28He spoke kindly to him, and gave
him a more prominent seat than those of
the kings who *were* with him in Babylon.
29So Jehoiachin changed from his prison
garments, and he ate bread regularly before the king all the days of his life. 30And

as for his provisions, *there was* a regular
ration given him by the king, a portion for
each day, all the days of his life.

Jeremiah 52:31-34

52 :31 Now it came to pass in the
thirty-seventh year of the captivity
of Jehoiachin king of Judah, in the twelfth
month, on the twenty-fifth *day* of the
month, *that* Evil-Merodach[a] king of Babylon, in the first *year* of his reign, lifted up
the head of Jehoiachin king of Judah and
brought him out of prison. 32And he spoke
kindly to him and gave him a more prominent seat than those of the kings who *were*
with him in Babylon. 33So Jehoiachin
changed from his prison garments, and he
ate bread regularly before the king all the
days of his life. 34And as for his provisions,
there was a regular ration given him by
the king of Babylon, a portion for each day
until the day of his death, all the days of
his life.

2 Kin. 25:27 [a]Literally *Man of Marduk*
Jer. 52:31 [a]Or *Awil-Marduk*

Isaiah and the Fall of Babylon

The prophet Isaiah, son of Amoz, lived
during the Neo-Assyrian Empire, almost 200
years before the time of the Neo-Babylonian
Empire (626–539 B.C.). Nevertheless, the
Book of Isaiah records some prophecies (Is.
13:1—14:23; 21:1-17) in which Babylon's fall
is described.

Some scholars suggest that these oracles
refer to the Babylon of Isaiah's own day. During
Assyria's rule in the 8th century B.C., Babylon
was a continual thorn in the Assyrian side. The
Babylonian ruler, Merodach-Baladan, twice
managed to declare independence from Assyria (721–710 and 703–702 B.C.). The destruction of Babylon that Isaiah prophesies,
then, would describe the assault of the Assyrian king Sargon in about 710 B.C., which put
down Babylon's first rebellion. While this interpretation is surely possible, it seems odd.
Merodach-Baladan was a guerrilla leader, who
spent much of his time hiding in the swamps.
As such, he bears little resemblance to the
great, world ruler described in Is. 14.

Other scholars understand these oracles
as referring to the later and much greater
Babylon of Nebuchadnezzar and his succes-

EVIL-MERODACH EXTENDS GOODWILL (Jer. 52:31)

Evil-Merodach ruled from 562 to 560 B.C. as the third king of the Chaldean dynasty of Babylon. His Accadian name, Amel-Marduk, means "man of Marduk." Little is known of his short reign, which was quite different from that of his famous father, Nebuchadnezzar II, whom he succeeded. Nebuchadnezzar conducted several campaigns, including the conquering of Jerusalem, while no military engagements of Evil-Merodach are recorded in the known ancient literature.

The only mention of Evil-Merodach in the Bible appears in two virtually identical references to the release of King Jehoiachin of Judah (2 Kin. 25:27; Jer. 52:31). Jehoiachin was taken captive and exiled to Babylon in 597 B.C. by Nebuchadnezzar II. The historian of the books of Kings dates Jehoiachin's release to the 37th year of his captivity, which is usually reckoned as March, 561 B.C. Evil-Merodach did not allow the Judean king to leave, but rather placed him under house arrest, while treating him kindly (2 Kin. 25:28–30).

Greek, Jewish, and Latin sources later than the Bible have more to say about Evil-Merodach. Unfortunately, much of this material is probably more legendary than actual. Some of the stories about Evil-Merodach come from Jewish midrash, which is extensive Jewish commentary on biblical passages. The Babylonian chronicler Berossus does write that Evil-Merodach was assassinated soon after he released Jehoiachin.

sors in the 6th century B.C. This king of Babylon was the one "who made the earth tremble, who shook kingdoms" (Is. 14:16). The Medes (13:17; 21:2) contributed to this later Babylon's downfall. Israel would return from captivity in this Babylon (14:1, 2). All of these details fit the later Babylon far better than the earlier, and so these prophecies can be associated with the Neo-Babylonian Empire.

Although Is. 33—35 do not name Babylon, several strong indicators suggest reading these chapters in light of Babylon's destruction of Jerusalem in 586 B.C. and the aftermath of that event. In Is. 21 Babylon is called a plunderer (21:2, 9), and Is. 33:1 calls down woe on "the plunderer" in very similar language. Also, the judgments of Jer. 49:7–22 and Obadiah condemn Edom for its part in Nebuchadnezzar's destruction of Jerusalem. Reminiscent of these passages is Is. 34, which calls down a curse on Edom in "recompense for the cause of Zion" (34:8). Finally, the promise of Is. 35 that the "ransomed of the LORD" will return to Zion (35:10) makes the most sense when read in light of the Babylonian captivity.

Because these chapters of Isaiah fit the later time period so well, many have suggested that they were not prophesied by the 8th-century Isaiah at all. At the very least, some propose that Isaiah's original words were expanded by 6th-century editors to apply more closely to their own time (see "Isaiah and Cyrus the Persian" at Is. 40:1). Others, though, accept Isaiah as the author and treat these words as a foretelling of the distant future.

- Isaiah 13:1—14:23
- Isaiah 21:1–17
- Isaiah 33:1—35:10

Isaiah 13:1—14:23
Proclamation Against Babylon

13 :1 The burden against Babylon which Isaiah the son of Amoz saw.

2 "Lift up a banner on the high
        mountain,
    Raise your voice to them;
    Wave your hand, that they may enter
        the gates of the nobles.
3 I have commanded My sanctified ones;
    I have also called My mighty ones for
        My anger—
    Those who rejoice in My exaltation."

4 The noise of a multitude in the
        mountains,
    Like that of many people!
    A tumultuous noise of the kingdoms of
        nations gathered together!
    The LORD of hosts musters
    The army for battle.
5 They come from a far country,
    From the end of heaven—
    The LORD and His weapons of
        indignation,
    To destroy the whole land.

6 Wail, for the day of the LORD *is* at
   hand!
   It will come as destruction from the
   Almighty.
7 Therefore all hands will be limp,
   Every man's heart will melt,
8 And they will be afraid.
   Pangs and sorrows will take hold of
   them;
   They will be in pain as a woman in
   childbirth;
   They will be amazed at one another;
   Their faces *will be like* flames.

9 Behold, the day of the LORD comes,
   Cruel, with both wrath and fierce
   anger,
   To lay the land desolate;
   And He will destroy its sinners from
   it.
10 For the stars of heaven and their
   constellations
   Will not give their light;
   The sun will be darkened in its going
   forth,
   And the moon will not cause its light
   to shine.

11 "I will punish the world for *its* evil,
   And the wicked for their iniquity;
   I will halt the arrogance of the proud,
   And will lay low the haughtiness of
   the terrible.
12 I will make a mortal more rare than
   fine gold,
   A man more than the golden wedge of
   Ophir.
13 Therefore I will shake the heavens,
   And the earth will move out of her
   place,
   In the wrath of the LORD of hosts
   And in the day of His fierce anger.
14 It shall be as the hunted gazelle,
   And as a sheep that no man takes up;
   Every man will turn to his own
   people,
   And everyone will flee to his own
   land.
15 Everyone who is found will be thrust
   through,

And everyone who is captured will fall
   by the sword.
16 Their children also will be dashed to
   pieces before their eyes;
   Their houses will be plundered
   And their wives ravished.

17 "Behold, I will stir up the Medes
   against them,
   Who will not regard silver;
   And *as for* gold, they will not delight
   in it.
18 Also *their* bows will dash the young
   men to pieces,
   And they will have no pity on the fruit
   of the womb;
   Their eye will not spare children.
19 And Babylon, the glory of kingdoms,
   The beauty of the Chaldeans' pride,
   Will be as when God overthrew Sodom
   and Gomorrah.
20 It will never be inhabited,
   Nor will it be settled from generation
   to generation;
   Nor will the Arabian pitch tents there,
   Nor will the shepherds make their
   sheepfolds there.
21 But wild beasts of the desert will lie
   there,
   And their houses will be full of owls;
   Ostriches will dwell there,
   And wild goats will caper there.
22 The hyenas will howl in their citadels,
   And jackals in their pleasant palaces.
   Her time *is* near to come,
   And her days will not be prolonged."

Mercy on Jacob

14 [1]For the LORD will have mercy on
   Jacob, and will still choose Israel,
and settle them in their own land. The
strangers will be joined with them, and
they will cling to the house of Jacob. [2]Then
people will take them and bring them to
their place, and the house of Israel will
possess them for servants and maids in the
land of the LORD; they will take them captive whose captives they were, and rule
over their oppressors.

GEOGRAPHY AND ENVIRONMENT

*In the ancient world, the values of life were largely experienced through personal
relations and group activities. So isolated areas, such as deserts, and the animals found
there were viewed with distaste and fear. The ostrich (Is. 13:21) is fitted for desert life.
It eats coarse food and can go for a long time without water. Its head, neck, and legs
have no feathers, helping it remain cool in the desert climate.*

Fall of the King of Babylon

³It shall come to pass in the day the LORD gives you rest from your sorrow, and from your fear and the hard bondage in which you were made to serve, ⁴that you will take up this proverb against the king of Babylon, and say:

"How the oppressor has ceased,
   The goldenª city ceased!
5 The LORD has broken the staff of the wicked,
   The scepter of the rulers;
6 He who struck the people in wrath with a continual stroke,
   He who ruled the nations in anger,
   Is persecuted *and* no one hinders.
7 The whole earth is at rest *and* quiet;
   They break forth into singing.
8 Indeed the cypress trees rejoice over you,
   And the cedars of Lebanon,
   Saying, 'Since you were cut down,
   No woodsman has come up against us.'

9 "Hell from beneath is excited about you,
   To meet *you* at your coming;
   It stirs up the dead for you,
   All the chief ones of the earth;
   It has raised up from their thrones
   All the kings of the nations.
10 They all shall speak and say to you:
   'Have you also become as weak as we?
   Have you become like us?
11 Your pomp is brought down to Sheol,
   And the sound of your stringed instruments;
   The maggot is spread under you,
   And worms cover you.'

The Fall of Lucifer

12 "How you are fallen from heaven,
   O Lucifer,ª son of the morning!
   How you are cut down to the ground,
   You who weakened the nations!

13 For you have said in your heart:
   'I will ascend into heaven,
   I will exalt my throne above the stars of God;
   I will also sit on the mount of the congregation
   On the farthest sides of the north;
14 I will ascend above the heights of the clouds,
   I will be like the Most High.'
15 Yet you shall be brought down to Sheol,
   To the lowest depths of the Pit.

16 "Those who see you will gaze at you,
   And consider you, *saying:*
   '*Is* this the man who made the earth tremble,
   Who shook kingdoms,
17 Who made the world as a wilderness
   And destroyed its cities,
   Who did not open the house of his prisoners?'

18 "All the kings of the nations,
   All of them, sleep in glory,
   Everyone in his own house;
19 But you are cast out of your grave
   Like an abominable branch,
   Like the garment of those who are slain,
   Thrust through with a sword,
   Who go down to the stones of the pit,
   Like a corpse trodden underfoot.
20 You will not be joined with them in burial,
   Because you have destroyed your land
   And slain your people.
   The brood of evildoers shall never be named.
21 Prepare slaughter for his children
   Because of the iniquity of their fathers,
   Lest they rise up and possess the land,
   And fill the face of the world with cities."

14:4 ªOr *insolent*   14:12 ªLiterally *Day Star*

BELIEFS AND IDEAS

The planet Venus was an important subject for ancient mythology. It is bright when it rises, but, when the sun comes up, Venus becomes invisible like any other star. The prophet mocks the king of Babylon, calling him "Lucifer" (Is. 14:12), a translation of the Hebrew word for the Day Star Venus. The king was trying to rival God, like Venus tried to rival the sun, and the prophet rebuked him in these terms.

A FAILED ASSAULT ON HEAVEN (Is. 14:12–15)

The prophet Isaiah uses mythological language in a proverb mocking the king of Babylon (Is. 14:4, 22). His references to the Day Star, the ascent into heaven, the mount of the congregation, and to Sheol (or the Pit) would all have been familiar to his readers from the myths of the ancient Near East.

The name "Lucifer" (Is. 14:12) is a Latin translation of the Hebrew word *helel,* meaning "shining one." Lucifer refers to the Day Star, Venus, and the prophet further identifies him as "son of the morning" (14:12). Similar language appears with the Ugaritic deities Shahar and Shalim. Shahar was the god of dawn or morning; Shalim, the god of dusk or evening. In another Ugaritic text, Shahar (morning) appears together with Athtar, the star deity who is also identified with Venus. So the ancient myths possibly had made Isaiah's readers familiar with the Day Star whose father was the god of morning.

Isaiah's taunt of the Day Star for wanting to ascend into heaven (14:13) may reflect the Ugaritic myth of Athtar, the Venus star deity. Athtar attempts to ascend to the throne of Baal, but is not able and is forced to return to his own, lower position in the pantheon. Athtar was not storming heaven, only sitting on the vacated throne of Baal. He excuses himself from the position upon realizing that he is too small. Nevertheless, a Day Star ascending to heaven was known in Canaanite myth.

In Isaiah's proverb, the Day Star desires to sit on "the mount of the congregation" located "on the farthest sides of the north" (14:13). Similarly, Canaanite myths spoke of the mountain home of Baal on Saphon (the Hebrew word translated "north"), and also of a mount of assembly.

In Isaiah's proverb, the Day Star fails to ascend to heaven and is brought down to Sheol, the netherworld also called the Pit (14:15). Similarly in ancient Near Eastern mythology gods could die and be sent to Mot's netherworld. The reason that Baal's throne was vacant in the Ugaritic myth was that Mot had vanquished Baal and taken him to the realm of the dead.

Babylon Destroyed

22 "For I will rise up against them," says
the LORD of hosts,
"And cut off from Babylon the name
and remnant,
And offspring and posterity," says the
LORD.
23 "I will also make it a possession for the
porcupine,
And marshes of muddy water;
I will sweep it with the broom of
destruction," says the LORD of hosts.

Isaiah 21:1–17
The Fall of Babylon Proclaimed

21 :1 The burden against the Wilderness of the Sea.

As whirlwinds in the South pass
through,
So it comes from the desert, from a
terrible land.
2 A distressing vision is declared to me;
The treacherous dealer deals
treacherously,

And the plunderer plunders.
Go up, O Elam!
Besiege, O Media!
All its sighing I have made to cease.

3 Therefore my loins are filled with
pain;
Pangs have taken hold of me, like the
pangs of a woman in labor.
I was distressed when *I* heard *it;*
I was dismayed when *I* saw *it.*
My heart wavered, fearfulness
frightened me;
The night for which I longed He
turned into fear for me.
5 Prepare the table,
Set a watchman in the tower,
Eat and drink.
Arise, you princes,
Anoint the shield!

6 For thus has the Lord said to me:
"Go, set a watchman,
Let him declare what he sees."
7 And he saw a chariot *with* a pair of
horsemen,

A chariot of donkeys, *and* a chariot of
    camels,
And he listened earnestly with great
    care.
8 Then he cried, "A lion,[a] my Lord!
I stand continually on the watchtower
    in the daytime;
I have sat at my post every night.
9 And look, here comes a chariot of men
    with a pair of horsemen!"
Then he answered and said,
"Babylon is fallen, is fallen!
And all the carved images of her gods
He has broken to the ground."

10 Oh, my threshing and the grain of my
    floor!
That which I have heard from the
    LORD of hosts,
The God of Israel,
I have declared to you.

Proclamation Against Edom

11The burden against Dumah.

He calls to me out of Seir,
"Watchman, what of the night?
Watchman, what of the night?"
12 The watchman said,
"The morning comes, and also the
    night.
If you will inquire, inquire;
Return! Come back!"

Proclamation Against Arabia

13The burden against Arabia.

In the forest in Arabia you will lodge,
O you traveling companies of
    Dedanites.
14 O inhabitants of the land of Tema,
Bring water to him who is thirsty;
With their bread they met him who
    fled.
15 For they fled from the swords, from
    the drawn sword,
From the bent bow, and from the
    distress of war.

16For thus the LORD has said to me:
"Within a year, according to the year of a
hired man, all the glory of Kedar will fail;
17and the remainder of the number of
archers, the mighty men of the people of

Kedar, will be diminished; for the LORD
God of Israel has spoken *it.*"

Isaiah 33:1—35:10
A Prayer in Deep Distress

33 :1 Woe to you who plunder, though
    you *have* not *been* plundered;
And you who deal treacherously,
    though they have not dealt
    treacherously with you!
When you cease plundering,
You will be plundered;
When you make an end of dealing
    treacherously,
They will deal treacherously with you.

2 O LORD, be gracious to us;
We have waited for You.
Be their[a] arm every morning,
Our salvation also in the time of
    trouble.
3 At the noise of the tumult the people
    shall flee;
When You lift Yourself up, the nations
    shall be scattered;
4 And Your plunder shall be gathered
Like the gathering of the caterpillar;
As the running to and fro of locusts,
He shall run upon them.

5 The LORD is exalted, for He dwells on
    high;
He has filled Zion with justice and
    righteousness.
6 Wisdom and knowledge will be the
    stability of your times,
And the strength of salvation;
The fear of the LORD *is* His treasure.

7 Surely their valiant ones shall cry
    outside,

21:8 aDead Sea Scrolls read *Then the observer
cried.*   33:2 aSeptuagint omits *their;* Syriac,
Targum, and Vulgate read *our.*

The ambassadors of peace shall weep
    bitterly.
8   The highways lie waste,
    The traveling man ceases.
    He has broken the covenant,
    He has despised the cities,[a]
    He regards no man.
9   The earth mourns *and* languishes,
    Lebanon is shamed *and* shriveled;
    Sharon is like a wilderness,
    And Bashan and Carmel shake off
        their fruits.

Impending Judgment on Zion

10 "Now I will rise," says the LORD;
    "Now I will be exalted,
    Now I will lift Myself up.
11 You shall conceive chaff,
    You shall bring forth stubble;
    Your breath, *as* fire, shall devour you.
12 And the people shall be *like* the
        burnings of lime;
    Like thorns cut up they shall be
        burned in the fire.
13 Hear, you *who are* afar off, what I
        have done;
    And you *who are* near, acknowledge
        My might."

14 The sinners in Zion are afraid;
    Fearfulness has seized the hypocrites:
    "Who among us shall dwell with the
        devouring fire?
    Who among us shall dwell with
        everlasting burnings?"
15 He who walks righteously and speaks
        uprightly,
    He who despises the gain of
        oppressions,
    Who gestures with his hands, refusing
        bribes,
    Who stops his ears from hearing of
        bloodshed,
    And shuts his eyes from seeing evil:
16 He will dwell on high;
    His place of defense *will be* the
        fortress of rocks;
    Bread will be given him,
    His water *will be* sure.

The Land of the Majestic King

17 Your eyes will see the King in His
        beauty;
    They will see the land that is very far
        off.
18 Your heart will meditate on terror:
    "Where *is* the scribe?
    Where *is* he who weighs?
    Where *is* he who counts the towers?"
19 You will not see a fierce people,
    A people of obscure speech, beyond
        perception,
    Of a stammering tongue *that you*
        cannot understand.

20 Look upon Zion, the city of our
        appointed feasts;
    Your eyes will see Jerusalem, a quiet
        home,
    A tabernacle *that* will not be taken
        down;
    Not one of its stakes will ever be
        removed,
    Nor will any of its cords be broken.
21 But there the majestic LORD *will be*
        for us
    A place of broad rivers *and* streams,
    In which no galley with oars will sail,
    Nor majestic ships pass by
22 (For the LORD *is* our Judge,
    The LORD *is* our Lawgiver,
    The LORD *is* our King;
    He will save us);
23 Your tackle is loosed,
    They could not strengthen their mast,
    They could not spread the sail.

    Then the prey of great plunder is
        divided;
    The lame take the prey.
24 And the inhabitant will not say, "I am
        sick";
    The people who dwell in it *will be*
        forgiven *their* iniquity.

33:8 [a]Following Masoretic Text and Vulgate; Dead Sea
Scrolls read *witnesses;* Septuagint omits *cities;*
Targum reads *They have been removed from their
cities.*

GEOGRAPHY AND ENVIRONMENT

*Lebanon is on the Mediterranean coast north of Israel. Although it is a very small
country, it includes a wide range of climates and is famous even today for the quality and
variety of its fruits and vegetables. Apples, cherries, bananas, and oranges are all grown
in Lebanon. The prophet warned of the destruction of this rich vegetation (Is. 33:9).*

LILITH, A DEADLY DEMON (Is. 34:14)

The prophet Isaiah describes the total desolation which God would visit upon Edom for its hostility to God (Is. 34:2, 5). Among the descriptions of God's wrath is the sole reference in Scripture to a well-known Mesopotamian demon—Lilith.

Later Jewish tradition connected the name "Lilith" with the Hebrew word for "night," giving the traditional English translation "night creature" (Is. 34:14). However as a Mesopotamian name, "Lilith" comes from the Sumerian word *lil*, meaning "wind" (or "spirit").

The earliest records and amulets from Mesopotamia show that people there feared the Lilu, a group of particularly malevolent demons. Lilith herself was believed to attack both babies and mothers in childbirth, eating their flesh and sucking their blood. The only protection from the Lilu was to call upon the king of demons for help.

Jewish inscriptions and amulets describe Lilith in a similar fashion, but with additional features. She was known as a woman with long hair and wings, attacking men who slept alone. Jewish incantation bowls have been found which petition God to defeat and bind Lilith as she seeks her human prey.

For Isaiah, and his listeners, the threat of Lilith finding "a place of rest" (Is. 34:14) amongst humans was nothing but terrifying. Where once the Edomite cities housed wisdom and life and cultured society, there would now be wasteland. Edom would become uninhabitable, the domain of wild animals and wild beasts. The nobility that once led the land would be gone (34:12). No human would dare to dwell in the area (34:10), for Lilith insures its perpetual desolation.

Judgment on the Nations

34 1 Come near, you nations, to hear;
And heed, you people!
Let the earth hear, and all that is in it,
The world and all things that come forth from it.

2 For the indignation of the LORD *is* against all nations,
And *His* fury against all their armies;
He has utterly destroyed them,
He has given them over to the slaughter.

3 Also their slain shall be thrown out;
Their stench shall rise from their corpses,
And the mountains shall be melted with their blood.

4 All the host of heaven shall be dissolved,
And the heavens shall be rolled up like a scroll;
All their host shall fall down
As the leaf falls from the vine,
And as *fruit* falling from a fig tree.

5 "For My sword shall be bathed in heaven;
Indeed it shall come down on Edom,
And on the people of My curse, for judgment.

6 The sword of the LORD is filled with blood,
It is made overflowing with fatness,
With the blood of lambs and goats,
With the fat of the kidneys of rams.
For the LORD has a sacrifice in Bozrah,
And a great slaughter in the land of Edom.

7 The wild oxen shall come down with them,
And the young bulls with the mighty bulls;
Their land shall be soaked with blood,
And their dust saturated with fatness."

8 For *it is* the day of the LORD's vengeance,
The year of recompense for the cause of Zion.

9 Its streams shall be turned into pitch,
And its dust into brimstone;
Its land shall become burning pitch.

10 It shall not be quenched night or day;
Its smoke shall ascend forever.
From generation to generation it shall lie waste;
No one shall pass through it forever and ever.

11 But the pelican and the porcupine
    shall possess it,
   Also the owl and the raven shall dwell
    in it.
   And He shall stretch out over it
   The line of confusion and the stones of
    emptiness.
12 They shall call its nobles to the
    kingdom,
   But none *shall be* there, and all its
    princes shall be nothing.

13 And thorns shall come up in its
    palaces,
   Nettles and brambles in its fortresses;
   It shall be a habitation of jackals,
   A courtyard for ostriches.
14 The wild beasts of the desert shall
    also meet with the jackals,
   And the wild goat shall bleat to its
    companion;
   Also the night creature shall rest
    there,
   And find for herself a place of rest.
15 There the arrow snake shall make her
    nest and lay *eggs*
   And hatch, and gather *them* under her
    shadow;
   There also shall the hawks be
    gathered,
   Every one with her mate.

16 "Search from the book of the LORD, and
    read:
   Not one of these shall fail;
   Not one shall lack her mate.
   For My mouth has commanded it, and
    His Spirit has gathered them.
17 He has cast the lot for them,
   And His hand has divided it among
    them with a measuring line.
   They shall possess it forever;
   From generation to generation they
    shall dwell in it."

The Future Glory of Zion

35 1 The wilderness and the
       wasteland shall be glad for
        them,
      And the desert shall rejoice and
       blossom as the rose;
2 It shall blossom abundantly and
    rejoice,
   Even with joy and singing.
   The glory of Lebanon shall be given to
    it,
   The excellence of Carmel and Sharon.

They shall see the glory of the LORD,
The excellency of our God.

3 Strengthen the weak hands,
   And make firm the feeble knees.
4 Say to those *who are* fearful-hearted,
   "Be strong, do not fear!
   Behold, your God will come *with*
    vengeance,
   With the recompense of God;
   He will come and save you."

5 Then the eyes of the blind shall be
    opened,
   And the ears of the deaf shall be
    unstopped.
6 Then the lame shall leap like a deer,
   And the tongue of the dumb sing.
   For waters shall burst forth in the
    wilderness,
   And streams in the desert.
7 The parched ground shall become a
    pool,
   And the thirsty land springs of water;
   In the habitation of jackals, where
    each lay,
   There shall be grass with reeds and
    rushes.

8 A highway shall be there, and a road,
   And it shall be called the Highway of
    Holiness.
   The unclean shall not pass over it,
   But it *shall be* for others.
   Whoever walks the road, although a
    fool,
   Shall not go astray.
9 No lion shall be there,
   Nor shall *any* ravenous beast go up on
    it;
   It shall not be found there.
   But the redeemed shall walk *there,*
10 And the ransomed of the LORD shall
    return,
   And come to Zion with singing,
   With everlasting joy on their heads.
   They shall obtain joy and gladness,
   And sorrow and sighing shall flee
    away.

Daniel and Belshazzar

Babylon's might declined fastest during the reign of Nabonidus (556–539 B.C.), who left the city of Babylon to live in an oasis in the Arabian desert and worship the moon god Sin (see "Exile in Babylon" at Ezek. 33:1). His son, Bel-shar-usur, was left as regent over the city of Babylon.

The Book of Daniel, which spells Bel-shar-usur as "Belshazzar," refers to Nebuchadnezzar as Belshazzar's father (Dan. 5:2). This could be a metaphorical reference to Nebuchadnezzar as the father (or founder) of the kingdom; Belshazzar was not even related to Nebuchadnezzar. Daniel also calls Belshazzar "king" (5:1), which he never was officially. Still, while his father Nabonidus was absent, he was the closest thing to a king that Babylon had.

Belshazzar served as coregent in Babylon for his father Nabonidus sometime around 545 B.C. Nothing more is heard of Belshazzar after 543 B.C., when Nabonidus returned from Arabian Tema and took sole control of Babylon. Daniel's contempt for this "king," as well as the unflattering comparison made between Belshazzar and the great Nebuchadnezzar (Dan. 5:18–22), suggest that Nabonidus's son was far from deserving his borrowed title.

▼   ■ Daniel 5:1–31

Daniel
Belshazzar's Feast

5 :1 Belshazzar the king made a great feast for a thousand of his lords, and drank wine in the presence of the thousand. ²While he tasted the wine, Belshazzar gave the command to bring the gold and silver vessels which his father Nebuchadnezzar had taken from the temple which *had been* in Jerusalem, that the king and his lords, his wives, and his concubines might drink from them. ³Then they brought the gold vessels that had been taken from the temple of the house of God which *had been* in Jerusalem; and the king and his lords, his wives, and his concubines drank from them. ⁴They drank wine, and praised the gods of gold and silver, bronze and iron, wood and stone.

⁵In the same hour the fingers of a man's hand appeared and wrote opposite the lampstand on the plaster of the wall of the king's palace; and the king saw the part of the hand that wrote. ⁶Then the king's countenance changed, and his thoughts troubled him, so that the joints of his hips were loosened and his knees knocked against each other. ⁷The king cried aloud to bring in the astrologers, the Chaldeans, and the soothsayers. The king

spoke, saying to the wise *men* of Babylon, "Whoever reads this writing, and tells me its interpretation, shall be clothed with purple and *have* a chain of gold around his neck; and he shall be the third ruler in the kingdom." ⁸Now all the king's wise *men* came, but they could not read the writing, or make known to the king its interpretation. ⁹Then King Belshazzar was greatly troubled, his countenance was changed, and his lords were astonished.

¹⁰The queen, because of the words of the king and his lords, came to the banquet hall. The queen spoke, saying, "O king, live forever! Do not let your thoughts trouble you, nor let your countenance change. ¹¹There is a man in your kingdom in whom *is* the Spirit of the Holy God. And in the days of your father, light and understanding and wisdom, like the wisdom of the gods, were found in him; and King Nebuchadnezzar your father—your father the king—made him chief of the magicians, astrologers, Chaldeans, *and* soothsayers. ¹²Inasmuch as an excellent spirit, knowledge, understanding, interpreting dreams, solving riddles, and explaining enigmasª were found in this Daniel, whom the king named Belteshazzar, now let Daniel be called, and he will give the interpretation."

The Writing on the Wall Explained

¹³Then Daniel was brought in before the king. The king spoke, and said to Daniel, "*Are* you that Daniel who is one of the captivesª from Judah, whom my father the king brought from Judah? ¹⁴I have heard of you, that the Spirit of God *is* in you, and *that* light and understanding and excellent wisdom are found in you. ¹⁵Now the wise

---

5:12 ªLiterally *untying knots,* and so in verse 16
5:13 ªLiterally *of the sons of the captivity*

TIME CAPSULE   545 to 539 B.C.

545   Belshazzar is coregent in Babylon with his father Nabonidus

543   Nabonidus returns and assumes sole control of Babylon

540   Nobleman Pisistratus begins benevolent tyranny in Athens

539   Nabonidus fights with the Persian armies at Opis

539   Cyrus conquers Babylon and King Nabonidus

539   Gaubaruwa appointed vice-regent over Mesopotamia by Cyrus

---

BEING KING WHILE FATHER IS GONE (Dan. 5:1)

Belshazzar was the son of Nabonidus, the last monarch of the late Babylonian Empire. Nabonidus ruled from 556 to 539 B.C., and apparently Belshazzar was coregent for at least three of those years while his father was away for a lengthy stay in Arabia. The Book of Daniel describes the coregent Belshazzar as "king" (Dan. 5:1), which was the customary way of referring to an heir-apparent acting in the place of his absent father.

Belshazzar's name has been found on numerous business documents and letters during the first part of the reign of his father. The documents place Belshazzar's rule sometime before 545 B.C. However, we hear nothing more of him after 543 B.C., presumably the year when his father returned and took sole control of the realm.

The Book of Daniel is not the only writing to mention Belshazzar. His name appears also in later Greek, Latin, and rabbinic sources. The rabbis described him as wicked, like an earlier Babylonian king, Nebuchadnezzar. Jewish sources record negative characteristics for both Belshazzar and his father Nabonidus. The Book of Daniel, in prophesying the end of the Babylonian Empire (Dan. 5:22–27), also emphasized Belshazzar's negative traits.

---

men, the astrologers, have been brought in before me, that they should read this writing and make known to me its interpretation, but they could not give the interpretation of the thing. 16And I have heard of you, that you can give interpretations and explain enigmas. Now if you can read the writing and make known to me its interpretation, you shall be clothed with purple and *have* a chain of gold around your neck, and shall be the third ruler in the kingdom."

17Then Daniel answered, and said before the king, "Let your gifts be for yourself, and give your rewards to another; yet I will read the writing to the king, and make known to him the interpretation. 18O king, the Most High God gave Nebuchadnezzar your father a kingdom and majesty, glory and honor. 19And because of the majesty that He gave him, all peoples, nations, and languages trembled and feared before him. Whomever he wished, he executed; whomever he wished, he kept alive; whomever he wished, he set up; and whomever he wished, he put down. 20But when his heart was lifted up, and his spirit was hardened in pride, he was deposed from his kingly throne, and they took his glory from him. 21Then he was driven from the sons of men, his heart was made like the beasts, and his dwelling *was* with the wild donkeys. They fed him with grass like oxen, and his body was wet with the dew of heaven, till he knew that the Most High God rules in the kingdom of men, and appoints over it whomever He chooses.

22"But you his son, Belshazzar, have not humbled your heart, although you knew all this. 23And you have lifted yourself up against the Lord of heaven. They have brought the vessels of His house before you, and you and your lords, your wives and your concubines, have drunk wine from them. And you have praised the gods of silver and gold, bronze and iron, wood and stone, which do not see or hear or know; and the God who *holds* your breath in His hand and owns all your ways, you have not glorified. 24Then the fingersa of the hand were sent from Him, and this writing was written.

25"And this is the inscription that was written:

MENE,a MENE, TEKEL,b UPHARSIN.c

26This *is* the interpretation of *each* word. MENE: God has numbered your kingdom, and finished it; 27TEKEL: You have been weighed in the balances, and found wanting; 28PERES: Your kingdom has been divided, and given to the Medes and Persians."a 29Then Belshazzar gave the command, and they clothed Daniel with purple and *put* a chain of gold around his neck, and made a proclamation concerning him that he should be the third ruler in the kingdom.

5:24 aLiterally *palm*   5:25 aLiterally *a mina* (50 shekels) from the verb "to number"   bLiterally *a shekel* from the verb "to weigh"   cLiterally *and half-shekels* from the verb "to divide"   5:28 aAramaic *Paras,* consonant with *Peres*

Belshazzar's Fall

³⁰That very night Belshazzar, king of the Chaldeans, was slain. ³¹And Darius the Mede received the kingdom, *being* about sixty-two years old.

40:3 ªFollowing Masoretic Text, Targum, and Vulgate; Septuagint omits *in the desert.*   40:6 ªFollowing Masoretic Text and Targum; Dead Sea Scrolls, Septuagint, and Vulgate read *I.*

Isaiah and Cyrus the Persian

The Babylon of King Nabonidus began to totter. In 550 B.C. Cyrus the Persian captured Ecbatana, the capital of the Median Empire and began to look south toward Babylon. To a Babylonian population disgusted with the absentee king Nabonidus and his coregent Belshazzar, the prospect of a Persian conquest was quite attractive. In 539 B.C. Cyrus would march into Babylon as a conqueror, greeted by shouts of joy from the conquered.

The latter chapters of the Book of Isaiah have for centuries been recognized as different from the earlier chapters (see "The Book of Isaiah" at Is. 6:1). The language and style of Is. 40—55 are distinct, but the most remarkable difference is the tone. Whereas Is. 1—39 had spoken almost exclusively of judgment and disaster, the new section begins with God's call: "Comfort, yes, comfort My people!" (40:1). These chapters declare not judgment but salvation, hope, and restoration.

It is not difficult to identify when this salvation is to be: Israel will return from the Babylonian exile. In these chapters, Jerusalem is spoken of as uninhabited and in ruins, and the temple itself as destroyed, but both city and temple will be rebuilt (44:26–28). Israel's return from Babylon is pictured as a second exodus, with God making a way in the wilderness (40:3, 4; 43:19) and causing water to spring up in the desert (43:20; 44:3; 48:21).

God promises to deliver His people from Babylon. Furthermore, through the prophet, God even names the one through whom this great salvation would come about: Cyrus "My shepherd" (44:28; 45:1). These words of comfort seem directed to the Judean exiles in Babylon just before the city of Babylon fell to Cyrus's Persian armies.

There is little argument, then, concerning the time spoken of in Is. 40—55. There is much more disagreement as to when and by whom these chapters were written. Many scholars hold that these oracles came from an unknown prophet who lived in Cyrus's own time, during the Babylonian captivity, and who predicted the approaching end of the Exile. This prophet, often called "Second Isaiah," would have considered himself a disciple of the great Isaiah of Jerusalem. Indeed, some scholars suggest that Second Isaiah may have been the one who preserved the collection of Isaiah's oracles found in Is. 1—39.

Others, though, accept the traditional association of these words with the original Isaiah. The two parts of the book (chs. 1—39 and 40—55) always appear together in the ancient manuscripts, and several key themes appear in both parts. Regardless of who wrote Is. 40—55, these chapters speak of a future event: the glorious return from exile that will be authorized by Cyrus the Persian.

■ Isaiah 40:1—45:25

Isaiah
God's People Are Comforted

40 :1 "Comfort, yes, comfort My people!"
Says your God.

2 "Speak comfort to Jerusalem, and cry out to her,
That her warfare is ended,
That her iniquity is pardoned;
For she has received from the LORD's hand
Double for all her sins."

3 The voice of one crying in the wilderness:
"Prepare the way of the LORD;
Make straight in the desertª
A highway for our God.

4 Every valley shall be exalted
And every mountain and hill brought low;
The crooked places shall be made straight
And the rough places smooth;

5 The glory of the LORD shall be revealed,
And all flesh shall see *it* together;
For the mouth of the LORD has spoken."

6 The voice said, "Cry out!"
And heª said, "What shall I cry?"

"All flesh *is* grass,
And all its loveliness *is* like the flower of the field.

NEEDING COMFORT IN EXILE (Is. 40:1, 2)

The prophet announces God's decree, "Comfort My people!" (Is. 40:1, 2). This message of comfort was very appropriate since, along with the prophecies of Is. 40—55, it addresses the Judean experience of exile to Babylon in the 6th century B.C. Not all of the people of Judah were taken to Babylon (see 2 Kin. 25:8–12). Those who were, the exilic community, were the old Judean aristocracy. Previously they had held positions of power, status, and wealth in Jerusalem. In Babylon, though, life would be very different.

Defeated subjects who were forced from their homeland were allowed to live in ethnic enclaves in Babylon. Initially they probably worked at menial tasks, such as digging ditches to improve the Babylonian irrigation canals. Later on, some Judeans did find prosperity in Babylonian society, largely by assimilating to it. Yet, for people who had been the native aristocracy, the forced move to a Diaspora community was probably like being sent to 20th-century concentration, labor, or refugee camps. Such social change would have stretched to the limit the exilic community's conviction that Yahweh had elected the Judeans from all the people of the earth.

Meanwhile, society in Judah had utterly disintegrated following the fall of Jerusalem in 586 B.C. The deaths caused by the Babylonian invasion, the exile of the aristocracy, and the destruction of the temple gutted Judah of all institutions that had held the society together. Only the tribal area of Benjamin, north of Jerusalem, seemed to escape societal disintegration. In Judah itself, population plummeted 90% following the disaster. Thus the exiles in Babylon could not look to their past for hope; there they found only the consequences of their sin.

What the exiles needed—hope, comfort, tender words, a future—could be found only in the faithfulness of Yahweh, their God. The prophet offers exactly that message in Is. 40, pointing away from the sins of the past, away from the conditions of the present, to a future when the exiles would experience divine faithfulness and be restored to their land.

7 The grass withers, the flower fades,
Because the breath of the LORD blows
    upon it;
Surely the people *are* grass.

8 The grass withers, the flower fades,
But the word of our God stands
    forever."

9 O Zion,
You who bring good tidings,
Get up into the high mountain;
O Jerusalem,
You who bring good tidings,
Lift up your voice with strength,
Lift *it* up, be not afraid;
Say to the cities of Judah, "Behold
    your God!"

10 Behold, the Lord GOD shall come with
    a strong *hand,*
And His arm shall rule for Him;
Behold, His reward *is* with Him,
And His work before Him.

11 He will feed His flock like a shepherd;
He will gather the lambs with His
    arm,

And carry *them* in His bosom,
And gently lead those who are with
    young.

12 Who has measured the waters[a] in the
    hollow of His hand,
Measured heaven with a span
And calculated the dust of the earth in
    a measure?
Weighed the mountains in scales
And the hills in a balance?

13 Who has directed the Spirit of the
    LORD,
Or *as* His counselor has taught
    Him?

14 With whom did He take counsel, and
    who instructed Him,
And taught Him in the path of justice?
Who taught Him knowledge,
And showed Him the way of
    understanding?

40:12 [a]Following Masoretic Text, Septuagint, and Vulgate; Dead Sea Scrolls read *waters of the sea;* Targum reads *waters of the world.*

15 Behold, the nations *are* as a drop in a
    bucket,
    And are counted as the small dust on
      the scales;
    Look, He lifts up the isles as a very
      little thing.
16 And Lebanon *is* not sufficient to burn,
    Nor its beasts sufficient for a burnt
      offering.
17 All nations before Him *are* as nothing,
    And they are counted by Him less
      than nothing and worthless.

18 To whom then will you liken God?
    Or what likeness will you compare to
      Him?
19 The workman molds an image,
    The goldsmith overspreads it with
      gold,
    And the silversmith casts silver
      chains.
20 Whoever *is* too impoverished for *such*
    a contribution
    Chooses a tree *that* will not rot;
    He seeks for himself a skillful
      workman
    To prepare a carved image *that* will
      not totter.

21 Have you not known?
    Have you not heard?
    Has it not been told you from the
      beginning?
    Have you not understood from the
      foundations of the earth?
22 *It is* He who sits above the circle of
    the earth,
    And its inhabitants *are* like
      grasshoppers,
    Who stretches out the heavens like a
      curtain,
    And spreads them out like a tent to
      dwell in.
23 He brings the princes to nothing;
    He makes the judges of the earth
      useless.

24 Scarcely shall they be planted,
    Scarcely shall they be sown,

Scarcely shall their stock take root in
  the earth,
When He will also blow on them,
And they will wither,
And the whirlwind will take them
  away like stubble.

25 "To whom then will you liken Me,
    Or *to whom* shall I be equal?" says the
      Holy One.
26 Lift up your eyes on high,
    And see who has created these *things,*
    Who brings out their host by number;
    He calls them all by name,
    By the greatness of His might
    And the strength of *His* power;
    Not one is missing.

27 Why do you say, O Jacob,
    And speak, O Israel:
    "My way is hidden from the LORD,
    And my just claim is passed over by
      my God"?
28 Have you not known?
    Have you not heard?
    The everlasting God, the LORD,
    The Creator of the ends of the earth,
    Neither faints nor is weary.
    His understanding is unsearchable.
29 He gives power to the weak,
    And to *those who have* no might He
      increases strength.
30 Even the youths shall faint and be
      weary,
    And the young men shall utterly fall,
31 But those who wait on the LORD
    Shall renew *their* strength;
    They shall mount up with wings like
      eagles,
    They shall run and not be weary,
    They shall walk and not faint.

Israel Assured of God's Help

41 ¹ "Keep silence before Me,
          O coastlands,
    And let the people renew *their*
      strength!
    Let them come near, then let them
      speak;

BELIEFS AND IDEAS

*The Bible normally refers to the physical sky with words that portray it as something
stretched out and flattened, like hammered metal, or like a curtain (Is. 40:22). This
imagery emphasizes the immense energy required to create and sustain the framework
of space. The heavens are also remote from human influence and unchanged by time.*

Let us come near together for
judgment.

2   "Who raised up one from the east?
Who in righteousness called him to
His feet?
Who gave the nations before him,
And made *him* rule over kings?
Who gave *them* as the dust *to* his
sword,
As driven stubble to his bow?
3   Who pursued them, *and* passed safely
By the way *that* he had not gone with
his feet?
4   Who has performed and done *it,*
Calling the generations from the
beginning?
'I, the LORD, am the first;
And with the last I *am* He.' "

5   The coastlands saw *it* and feared,
The ends of the earth were afraid;
They drew near and came.
6   Everyone helped his neighbor,
And said to his brother,
"Be of good courage!"
7   So the craftsman encouraged the
goldsmith;
He who smooths *with* the hammer
inspired him who strikes the anvil,
Saying, "It *is* ready for the soldering";
Then he fastened it with pegs,
That it might not totter.

8   "But you, Israel, *are* My servant,
Jacob whom I have chosen,
The descendants of Abraham My
friend.
9   *You* whom I have taken from the ends
of the earth,
And called from its farthest regions,
And said to you,
'You *are* My servant,
I have chosen you and have not cast
you away:
10   Fear not, for I *am* with you;
Be not dismayed, for I *am* your God.
I will strengthen you,
Yes, I will help you,
I will uphold you with My righteous
right hand.'

11   "Behold, all those who were incensed
against you
Shall be ashamed and disgraced;
They shall be as nothing,
And those who strive with you shall
perish.

12   You shall seek them and not find
them—
Those who contended with you.
Those who war against you
Shall be as nothing,
As a nonexistent thing.
13   For I, the LORD your God, will hold
your right hand,
Saying to you, 'Fear not, I will help
you.'

14   "Fear not, you worm Jacob,
You men of Israel!
I will help you," says the LORD
And your Redeemer, the Holy One of
Israel.
15   "Behold, I will make you into a new
threshing sledge with sharp teeth;
You shall thresh the mountains and
beat *them* small,
And make the hills like chaff.
16   You shall winnow them, the wind
shall carry them away,
And the whirlwind shall scatter them;
You shall rejoice in the LORD,
And glory in the Holy One of Israel.

17   "The poor and needy seek water, but
there is none,
Their tongues fail for thirst.
I, the LORD, will hear them;
I, the God of Israel, will not forsake
them.
18   I will open rivers in desolate heights,
And fountains in the midst of the
valleys;
I will make the wilderness a pool of
water,
And the dry land springs of water.
19   I will plant in the wilderness the
cedar and the acacia tree,
The myrtle and the oil tree;
I will set in the desert the cypress tree
and the pine
And the box tree together,
20   That they may see and know,
And consider and understand
together,
That the hand of the LORD has done
this,
And the Holy One of Israel has
created it.

The Futility of Idols

21   "Present your case," says the LORD.
"Bring forth your strong *reasons,*" says
the King of Jacob.

22 "Let them bring forth and show us
     what will happen;
     Let them show the former things,
     what they *were*,
     That we may consider them,
     And know the latter end of them;
     Or declare to us things to come.
23 Show the things that are to come
     hereafter,
     That we may know that you *are* gods;
     Yes, do good or do evil,
     That we may be dismayed and see *it*
     together.
24 Indeed you *are* nothing,
     And your work *is* nothing;
     He who chooses you *is* an
     abomination.

25 "I have raised up one from the north,
     And he shall come;
     From the rising of the sun he shall
     call on My name;
     And he shall come against princes as
     though mortar,
     As the potter treads clay.
26 Who has declared from the beginning,
     that we may know?
     And former times, that we may say,
     '*He is* righteous'?
     Surely *there is* no one who shows,
     Surely *there is* no one who declares,
     Surely *there is* no one who hears your
     words.
27 The first time *I said* to Zion,
     'Look, there they are!'
     And I will give to Jerusalem one who
     brings good tidings.
28 For I looked, and *there was* no man;
     I looked among them, but *there was* no
     counselor,
     Who, when I asked of them, could
     answer a word.
29 Indeed they *are* all worthless;[a]
     Their works *are* nothing;
     Their molded images *are* wind and
     confusion.

The Servant of the LORD

42 1 "Behold! My Servant whom I
     uphold,
     My Elect One *in whom* My soul
     delights!
     I have put My Spirit upon Him;

He will bring forth justice to the
     Gentiles.
2 He will not cry out, nor raise *His*
     voice,
     Nor cause His voice to be heard in the
     street.
3 A bruised reed He will not break,
     And smoking flax He will not quench;
     He will bring forth justice for truth.
4 He will not fail nor be discouraged,
     Till He has established justice in the
     earth;
     And the coastlands shall wait for His
     law."

5 Thus says God the LORD,
     Who created the heavens and
     stretched them out,
     Who spread forth the earth and that
     which comes from it,
     Who gives breath to the people on it,
     And spirit to those who walk on it:
6 "I, the LORD, have called You in
     righteousness,
     And will hold Your hand;
     I will keep You and give You as a
     covenant to the people,
     As a light to the Gentiles,
7 To open blind eyes,
     To bring out prisoners from the
     prison,
     Those who sit in darkness from the
     prison house.
8 I *am* the LORD, that *is* My name;
     And My glory I will not give to
     another,
     Nor My praise to carved images.
9 Behold, the former things have come
     to pass,
     And new things I declare;
     Before they spring forth I tell you of
     them."

Praise to the LORD

10 Sing to the LORD a new song,
     And His praise from the ends of the
     earth,
     You who go down to the sea, and all
     that is in it,
     You coastlands and you inhabitants of
     them!
11 Let the wilderness and its cities lift up
     their voice,
     The villages *that* Kedar inhabits.
     Let the inhabitants of Sela sing,
     Let them shout from the top of the
     mountains.
12 Let them give glory to the LORD,

41:29 [a]Following Masoretic Text and Vulgate; Dead
Sea Scrolls, Syriac, and Targum read *nothing*;
Septuagint omits the first line.

And declare His praise in the
coastlands.
13 The LORD shall go forth like a mighty
man;
He shall stir up *His* zeal like a man of
war.
He shall cry out, yes, shout aloud;
He shall prevail against His enemies.

Promise of the LORD's Help

14 "I have held My peace a long time,
I have been still and restrained
Myself.
Now I will cry like a woman in labor,
I will pant and gasp at once.
15 I will lay waste the mountains and
hills,
And dry up all their vegetation;
I will make the rivers coastlands,
And I will dry up the pools.
16 I will bring the blind by a way they
did not know;
I will lead them in paths they have
not known.
I will make darkness light before
them,
And crooked places straight.
These things I will do for them,
And not forsake them.
17 They shall be turned back,
They shall be greatly ashamed,
Who trust in carved images,
Who say to the molded images,
'You *are* our gods.'

18 "Hear, you deaf;
And look, you blind, that you may see.
19 Who *is* blind but My servant,
Or deaf as My messenger *whom* I
send?
Who *is* blind as *he who is* perfect,
And blind as the LORD's servant?
20 Seeing many things, but you do not
observe;
Opening the ears, but he does not
hear."

Israel's Obstinate Disobedience

21 The LORD is well pleased for His
righteousness' sake;
He will exalt the law and make *it*
honorable.
22 But this *is* a people robbed and
plundered;
All of them are snared in holes,
And they are hidden in prison houses;
They are for prey, and no one delivers;

For plunder, and no one says,
"Restore!"

23 Who among you will give ear to this?
Who will listen and hear for the time
to come?
24 Who gave Jacob for plunder, and
Israel to the robbers?
Was it not the LORD,
He against whom we have sinned?
For they would not walk in His ways,
Nor were they obedient to His law.
25 Therefore He has poured on him the
fury of His anger
And the strength of battle;
It has set him on fire all around,
Yet he did not know;
And it burned him,
Yet he did not take *it* to heart.

The Redeemer of Israel

43 ¹ But now, thus says the LORD,
who created you, O Jacob,
And He who formed you, O Israel:
"Fear not, for I have redeemed you;
I have called *you* by your name;
You *are* Mine.
2 When you pass through the waters, I
will be with you;
And through the rivers, they shall not
overflow you.
When you walk through the fire, you
shall not be burned,
Nor shall the flame scorch you.
3 For I *am* the LORD your God,
The Holy One of Israel, your Savior;
I gave Egypt for your ransom,
Ethiopia and Seba in your place.
4 Since you were precious in My sight,
You have been honored,
And I have loved you;
Therefore I will give men for you,
And people for your life.
5 Fear not, for I *am* with you;
I will bring your descendants from the
east,
And gather you from the west;
6 I will say to the north, 'Give them up!'
And to the south, 'Do not keep them
back!'
Bring My sons from afar,
And My daughters from the ends of
the earth—
7 Everyone who is called by My name,
Whom I have created for My glory;
I have formed him, yes, I have made
him."

CAN GOD REALLY DO THIS "NEW THING"? (Is. 43:19)

If the exiles were to return to Jerusalem, they somehow had to escape the political and military control of the Neo-Babylonian regime. Even in the years just prior to the fall of Babylon in 539 B.C., this would have been a tall order for a small, politically and militarily insignificant community. Yet the prophet claims that this is precisely what will happen: God will do "a new thing" (Is. 43:19).

This "new thing" was a subtle reference to the military defeat of the Babylonians (43:14, 15). The prophet invokes images of the Exodus from Egypt when the Lord defeated Pharaoh and freed the Israelites from slavery (43:16, 17). This time the Lord would lead the exilic community back across the wilderness to their ancestral home in Judah (43:19). What a hopeful announcement this was for the Judeans in Babylon! That God would restore them to the land He had given them was the blunt political reality of the prophet's message.

Yet because the Judeans were still subject to Babylonian power, the announcement was also risky. The message rang of subversion and rebellion, qualities that the Neo-Babylonian regime met with brutal and violent displays of power in their subjected communities. Perhaps this explains why the community did not enthusiastically endorse the prophet's message—why they had not "called upon" the Lord (43:22–24). To do so would have meant really believing that God's power was stronger than the Babylonians, a high stakes political gamble if they were wrong!

8 Bring out the blind people who have
  eyes,
  And the deaf who have ears.
9 Let all the nations be gathered
  together,
  And let the people be assembled.
  Who among them can declare this,
  And show us former things?
  Let them bring out their witnesses,
    that they may be justified;
  Or let them hear and say, "*It is* truth."
10 "You *are* My witnesses," says the LORD,
  "And My servant whom I have chosen,
  That you may know and believe Me,
  And understand that I *am* He.
  Before Me there was no God formed,
  Nor shall there be after Me.
11 I, *even* I, *am* the LORD,
  And besides Me *there is* no savior.
12 I have declared and saved,
  I have proclaimed,
  And *there was* no foreign *god* among
  you;
  Therefore you *are* My witnesses,"
  Says the LORD, "that I *am* God.
13 Indeed before the day *was,* I *am* He;
  And *there is* no one who can deliver
    out of My hand;
  I work, and who will reverse it?"

14 Thus says the LORD, your Redeemer,
  The Holy One of Israel:
  "For your sake I will send to Babylon,

And bring them all down as
  fugitives—
The Chaldeans, who rejoice in their
  ships.
15 I *am* the LORD, your Holy One,
  The Creator of Israel, your King."

16 Thus says the LORD, who makes a way
  in the sea
  And a path through the mighty
  waters,
17 Who brings forth the chariot and
  horse,
  The army and the power
  (They shall lie down together, they
  shall not rise;
  They are extinguished, they are
  quenched like a wick):
18 "Do not remember the former things,
  Nor consider the things of old.
19 Behold, I will do a new thing,
  Now it shall spring forth;
  Shall you not know it?
  I will even make a road in the
  wilderness
  And rivers in the desert.
20 The beast of the field will honor Me,
  The jackals and the ostriches,
  Because I give waters in the
  wilderness
  And rivers in the desert,
  To give drink to My people, My
  chosen.

21 This people I have formed for Myself;
    They shall declare My praise.

Pleading with Unfaithful Israel

22 "But you have not called upon Me,
        O Jacob;
    And you have been weary of Me,
        O Israel.
23 You have not brought Me the sheep
        for your burnt offerings,
    Nor have you honored Me with your
        sacrifices.
    I have not caused you to serve with
        grain offerings,
    Nor wearied you with incense.
24 You have bought Me no sweet cane
        with money,
    Nor have you satisfied Me with the fat
        of your sacrifices;
    But you have burdened Me with your
        sins,
    You have wearied Me with your
        iniquities.

25 "I, *even* I, *am* He who blots out your
        transgressions for My own sake;
    And I will not remember your sins.
26 Put Me in remembrance;
    Let us contend together;
    State your *case,* that you may be
        acquitted.
27 Your first father sinned,
    And your mediators have transgressed
        against Me.
28 Therefore I will profane the princes of
        the sanctuary;
    I will give Jacob to the curse,
    And Israel to reproaches.

God's Blessing on Israel

44 ¹ "Yet hear me now, O Jacob My
        servant,
    And Israel whom I have chosen.
2 Thus says the LORD who made you
    And formed you from the womb, *who*
        will help you:
    'Fear not, O Jacob My servant;
    And you, Jeshurun, whom I have
        chosen.
3 For I will pour water on him who is
        thirsty,
    And floods on the dry ground;
    I will pour My Spirit on your
        descendants,
    And My blessing on your offspring;
4 They will spring up among the grass
    Like willows by the watercourses.'
5 One will say, 'I *am* the LORD's';

Another will call *himself* by the name
    of Jacob;
Another will write *with* his hand, 'The
    LORD's,'
And name *himself* by the name of
    Israel.

There Is No Other God

6 "Thus says the LORD, the King of
        Israel,
    And his Redeemer, the LORD of hosts:
    'I *am* the First and I *am* the Last;
    Besides Me *there is* no God.
7 And who can proclaim as I do?
    Then let him declare it and set it in
        order for Me,
    Since I appointed the ancient people.
    And the things that are coming and
        shall come,
    Let them show these to them.
8 Do not fear, nor be afraid;
    Have I not told you from that time,
        and declared *it?*
    You *are* My witnesses.
    Is there a God besides Me?
    Indeed *there is* no other Rock;
    I know not *one.*' "

Idolatry Is Foolishness

9 Those who make an image, all of them
        are useless,
    And their precious things shall not
        profit;
    They *are* their own witnesses;
    They neither see nor know, that they
        may be ashamed.
10 Who would form a god or mold an
        image
    That profits him nothing?
11 Surely all his companions would be
        ashamed;
    And the workmen, they *are* mere men.
    Let them all be gathered together,
    Let them stand up;
    Yet they shall fear,
    They shall be ashamed together.

12 The blacksmith with the tongs works
        one in the coals,
    Fashions it with hammers,
    And works it with the strength of his
        arms.
    Even so, he is hungry, and his
        strength fails;
    He drinks no water and is faint.

13 The craftsman stretches out *his* rule,
    He marks one out with chalk;

THE TEMPLE SLAVE OF THE LORD (Is. 44:5)

The expression "My servant" (Is. 44:1) is found often throughout Is. 40—55. The designation "the LORD's" in Is. 44:5 possibly gives a clue to the social world from which the image of "My servant" arises. This servant belonged to Yahweh, just as temple slaves in the ancient Near East belonged to the god whose temple they served.

Slavery existed throughout the Neo-Babylonian society. In fact, a large and important group of temple slaves performed much of the work in and around temple properties. Slavery did not necessarily mean low status. Most temple slaves did do menial agricultural work with small compensation. Yet some became important functionaries overseeing the god's economic resources, the resources of the temple and its priests. While temple slaves would never be free, their position could bring a share of power, wealth, and honor.

Neo-Babylonian temple slaves were marked on their foreheads or on the back of their hand with the expression "belonging to . . ." Added to this expression was the name of the Babylonian deity who literally owned them. The prophet's expression "I am the LORD's" (Is. 44:5) draws from this imagery of Neo-Babylonian temple slavery to depict how the Lord "owns" His servant Israel.

We do not know if the Judeans built a temple in Babylon or not. However, when the first group of exiles returned to Jerusalem around 538 or 537 B.C., a class of temple slaves called "the Nethinim" returned with them (Ezra 2:58). When Nehemiah was governor of Judea in 445 B.C., the Nethinim were recognized members of the temple personnel, which also included priests, Levites, gatekeepers, and singers (Neh. 10:28). Anyone familiar with Neo-Babylonian temple slavery as practiced within the Judean exilic community would know the meaning of "I am the LORD's."

He fashions it with a plane,
He marks it out with the compass,
And makes it like the figure of a man,
According to the beauty of a man, that
    it may remain in the house.

14 He cuts down cedars for himself,
And takes the cypress and the oak;
He secures *it* for himself among the
    trees of the forest.
He plants a pine, and the rain
    nourishes *it*.

15 Then it shall be for a man to burn,
For he will take some of it and warm
    himself;
Yes, he kindles *it* and bakes bread;
Indeed he makes a god and worships
    it;
He makes it a carved image, and falls
    down to it.

16 He burns half of it in the fire;
With this half he eats meat;
He roasts a roast, and is satisfied.
He even warms *himself* and says,
"Ah! I am warm,
I have seen the fire."

17 And the rest of it he makes into a
    god,
His carved image.
He falls down before it and worships
    it,
Prays to it and says,
"Deliver me, for you *are* my god!"

18 They do not know nor understand;
For He has shut their eyes, so that
    they cannot see,
And their hearts, so that they cannot
    understand.

19 And no one considers in his heart,

SCIENCE AND TECHNOLOGY

*Blacksmiths (Is. 44:12) work with iron and fire, and in traditional societies are often
regarded with suspicion and fear. They produced weapons and armor as well as plows.
Woodworkers made furniture and other domestic products, including looms and
doorposts. Wood craftsmanship (Is. 44:13) had reached very high standards centuries
before the prophets.*

Nor *is there* knowledge nor
understanding to say,
"I have burned half of it in the fire,
Yes, I have also baked bread on its
coals;
I have roasted meat and eaten *it;*
And shall I make the rest of it an
abomination?
Shall I fall down before a block of
wood?"
20 He feeds on ashes;
A deceived heart has turned him
aside;
And he cannot deliver his soul,
Nor say, "*Is there* not a lie in my right
hand?"

Israel Is Not Forgotten

21 "Remember these, O Jacob,
And Israel, for you *are* My servant;
I have formed you, you *are* My
servant;
O Israel, you will not be forgotten by
Me!
22 I have blotted out, like a thick cloud,
your transgressions,
And like a cloud, your sins.
Return to Me, for I have redeemed
you."

23 Sing, O heavens, for the LORD has
done *it!*
Shout, you lower parts of the earth;
Break forth into singing, you
mountains,
O forest, and every tree in it!
For the LORD has redeemed Jacob,
And glorified Himself in Israel.

Judah Will Be Restored

24 Thus says the LORD, your Redeemer,
And He who formed you from the
womb:
"I *am* the LORD, who makes all *things,*
Who stretches out the heavens all
alone,
Who spreads abroad the earth by
Myself;
25 Who frustrates the signs of the
babblers,
And drives diviners mad;
Who turns wise men backward,
And makes their knowledge
foolishness;
26 Who confirms the word of His servant,
And performs the counsel of His
messengers;

Who says to Jerusalem, 'You shall be
inhabited,'
To the cities of Judah, 'You shall be
built,'
And I will raise up her waste places;
27 Who says to the deep, 'Be dry!
And I will dry up your rivers';
28 Who says of Cyrus, '*He is* My
shepherd,
And he shall perform all My pleasure,
Saying to Jerusalem, "You shall be
built,"
And to the temple, "Your foundation
shall be laid." '

Cyrus, God's Instrument

45 ¹ "Thus says the LORD to His
anointed,
To Cyrus, whose right hand I have
held—
To subdue nations before him
And loose the armor of kings,
To open before him the double doors,
So that the gates will not be shut:
2 'I will go before you
And make the crooked places[a]
straight;
I will break in pieces the gates of
bronze
And cut the bars of iron.
3 I will give you the treasures of
darkness
And hidden riches of secret places,
That you may know that I, the LORD,
Who call *you* by your name,
Am the God of Israel.
4 For Jacob My servant's sake,
And Israel My elect,
I have even called you by your name;
I have named you, though you have
not known Me.
5 I *am* the LORD, and *there is* no other;
There is no God besides Me.
I will gird you, though you have not
known Me,
6 That they may know from the rising
of the sun to its setting
That *there is* none besides Me.
I *am* the LORD, and *there is* no other;
7 I form the light and create darkness,
I make peace and create calamity;
I, the LORD, do all these *things.*'

45:2 ªDead Sea Scrolls and Septuagint read
mountains; Targum reads *I will trample down the walls;*
Vulgate reads *I will humble the great ones of the
earth.*

CYRUS, THE LORD'S ANOINTED (Is. 45:1)

In 559 B.C. Cyrus the Great became the ruler and founder of the Achaemenid dynasty of Persia, which expanded quickly in all directions to become a world empire. Arising from the desert fringes of Mesopotamia, Cyrus ultimately conquered the Neo-Babylonian Empire and absorbed it into his realm in 539 B.C. The defeat of Babylon expanded the Persian Empire to include almost all of the ancient Near East. Only Egypt remained independent.

The ancient mind would ask, "What god has empowered this Persian king, Cyrus?" The Judean prophet answered by identifying Cyrus as a world leader chosen by Yahweh, the God of Israel (Is. 45:1–7). Even more amazingly, the prophet uses language reserved for Israelite and Judean kings to describe God's election of Cyrus. Cyrus is Yahweh's "anointed" (Is. 45:1), the agent by which the Babylonian subjection of the Judean exilic community would be ended.

The social-political force of the prophet's oracle possessed a powder-keg-like quality. Not only did the prophet speak of the military downfall of the ruling junta—the Babylonians, but he also picked a rival monarch as the precise agent of Babylon's demise. This message smacked of political subversion. If heard by the "wrong" people, it could bring a sharp reprisal on himself, and possibly on the whole Judean community by the Babylonian authorities. Ancient Near Eastern regimes were always anxious to beat down a possible uprising before it occurred.

8 "Rain down, you heavens, from above,
   And let the skies pour down
      righteousness;
   Let the earth open, let them bring
      forth salvation,
   And let righteousness spring up
      together.
   I, the LORD, have created it.

9 "Woe to him who strives with his
      Maker!
   Let the potsherd *strive* with the
      potsherds of the earth!
   Shall the clay say to him who forms it,
      'What are you making?'
   Or shall your handiwork *say,* 'He has
      no hands'?
10 Woe to him who says to *his* father,
      'What are you begetting?'
   Or to the woman, 'What have you
      brought forth?' "

11 Thus says the LORD,
   The Holy One of Israel, and his
      Maker:
   "Ask Me of things to come concerning
      My sons;

   And concerning the work of My hands,
      you command Me.
12 I have made the earth,
   And created man on it.
   I—My hands—stretched out the
      heavens,
   And all their host I have commanded.
13 I have raised him up in righteousness,
   And I will direct all his ways;
   He shall build My city
   And let My exiles go free,
   Not for price nor reward,"
   Says the LORD of hosts.

The LORD, the Only Savior

14Thus says the LORD:

"The labor of Egypt and merchandise
      of Cush
   And of the Sabeans, men of stature,
   Shall come over to you, and they shall
      be yours;
   They shall walk behind you,
   They shall come over in chains;
   And they shall bow down to you.
   They will make supplication to you,
   saying, 'Surely God *is* in you,

GEOGRAPHY AND ENVIRONMENT

Cush (Is. 45:14) refers to areas south of Egypt, corresponding roughly to the northern Sudan. The Sabeans came either from this area or from across the Red Sea in southern Arabia. These regions were sources of gold. By means of international trade and control of trade routes through their land, the Sabeans developed into a strong commercial power.

And *there is* no other;'
'*There is* no other God.' "

15 Truly You *are* God, who hide Yourself,
O God of Israel, the Savior!
16 They shall be ashamed
And also disgraced, all of them;
They shall go in confusion together,
Who are makers of idols.
17 *But* Israel shall be saved by the LORD
With an everlasting salvation;
You shall not be ashamed or disgraced
Forever and ever.

18 For thus says the LORD,
Who created the heavens,
Who is God,
Who formed the earth and made it,
Who has established it,
Who did not create it in vain,
Who formed it to be inhabited:
"I *am* the LORD, and *there is* no other.
19 I have not spoken in secret,
In a dark place of the earth;
I did not say to the seed of Jacob,
'Seek Me in vain';
I, the LORD, speak righteousness,
I declare things that are right.

20 "Assemble yourselves and come;
Draw near together,
You *who have* escaped from the
nations.
They have no knowledge,
Who carry the wood of their carved
image,
And pray to a god *that* cannot save.

21 Tell and bring forth *your case;*
Yes, let them take counsel together.
Who has declared this from ancient
time?
Who has told it from that time?
Have not I, the LORD?
And *there is* no other God besides Me,
A just God and a Savior;
There is none besides Me.

22 "Look to Me, and be saved,
All you ends of the earth!
For I *am* God, and *there is* no other.
23 I have sworn by Myself;
The word has gone out of My mouth
in righteousness,
And shall not return,
That to Me every knee shall bow,
Every tongue shall take an oath.
24 He shall say,
'Surely in the LORD I have
righteousness and strength.
To Him *men* shall come,
And all shall be ashamed
Who are incensed against Him.
25 In the LORD all the descendants of
Israel
Shall be justified, and shall glory.' "

Babylon and Her Idols

As Cyrus and his armies were gaining strength, before capturing Babylon in 539 B.C., the prophet proclaimed that Babylon and her gods were doomed. Bel and Nebo, two important Babylonian gods, would themselves be taken into captivity (Is. 46:1, 2). It was common in the ancient Near East to see wars between nations as wars between those nations' respective gods. Thus, Babylon's victory over Assyria would have been considered a victory for Babylon's gods, and the approach of Cyrus as the challenge of Persia's deities.

The prophet radically alters this prevailing view. No section of Scripture declares God's uniqueness so clearly as does Is. 40—55. "I am God, and there is no other; I am God, and there is none like Me" (Is. 46:9; see 45:5, 6, 14, 18). Since there is only one God, Cyrus must not be a representative of Persia's gods. Whether he knows it himself or not, he is sent by the one God, the God of Israel (45:4). Moreover, Babylon's gods will be humiliated, not because they are weaker than another nation's gods but because they are mere idols. Gods that can be carried on cattle (46:1) or on one's shoulders (46:7) are no gods at all.

TIME CAPSULE   538 to 536 B.C.

538 *Cyrus Cylinder announces that Marduk chose Cyrus to conquer the world*

538 *Cyrus issues proclamation of freedom for the Jews (Ezra 1:2–4)*

538 *First group of exiles returns to Jerusalem*

538 *Sheshbazzar returns temple vessels to Jerusalem*

537 *Zerubbabel and Jeshua begin construction of a new temple (Ezra 3:8)*

536 *Work is stopped on the Jerusalem temple*

Babylon's religion involved not only sacrifice to idols but also faith in astrology. The prophet's spirited satire of Babylon's idolatry extended also to her stargazers and soothsayers (47:12, 13). Mostly, though, Babylon adored herself. She claimed to be eternal (47:7), all-powerful (47:8), and all-wise (47:10). Claiming for herself the status of God Himself, she would be desolated suddenly (47:9–11).

■ Isaiah 46:1—48:22

Isaiah
Dead Idols and the Living God

46 :1 Bel bows down, Nebo stoops;
Their idols were on the beasts and on the cattle.
Your carriages *were* heavily loaded,
A burden to the weary *beast.*

2 They stoop, they bow down together;
They could not deliver the burden,
But have themselves gone into captivity.

3 "Listen to Me, O house of Jacob,
And all the remnant of the house of Israel,
Who have been upheld *by Me* from birth,
Who have been carried from the womb:

4 Even to *your* old age, I *am* He,
And *even* to gray hairs I will carry *you!*
I have made, and I will bear;
Even I will carry, and will deliver *you.*

5 "To whom will you liken Me, and make *Me* equal
And compare Me, that we should be alike?

6 They lavish gold out of the bag,
And weigh silver on the scales;
They hire a goldsmith, and he makes it a god;
They prostrate themselves, yes, they worship.

7 They bear it on the shoulder, they carry it
And set it in its place, and it stands;
From its place it shall not move.
Though *one* cries out to it, yet it cannot answer
Nor save him out of his trouble.

8 "Remember this, and show yourselves men;
Recall to mind, O you transgressors.

9 Remember the former things of old,
For I *am* God, and *there is* no other;
I *am* God, and *there is* none like Me,

10 Declaring the end from the beginning,
And from ancient times *things* that are not *yet* done,
Saying, 'My counsel shall stand,
And I will do all My pleasure,'

11 Calling a bird of prey from the east,
The man who executes My counsel, from a far country.
Indeed I have spoken *it;*
I will also bring it to pass.
I have purposed *it;*
I will also do it.

12 "Listen to Me, you stubborn-hearted,
Who *are* far from righteousness:

13 I bring My righteousness near, it shall not be far off;
My salvation shall not linger.
And I will place salvation in Zion,
For Israel My glory.

The Humiliation of Babylon

47 1 "Come down and sit in the dust,
O virgin daughter of Babylon;
Sit on the ground without a throne,
O daughter of the Chaldeans!
For you shall no more be called
Tender and delicate.

2 Take the millstones and grind meal.
Remove your veil,
Take off the skirt,
Uncover the thigh,
Pass through the rivers.

3 Your nakedness shall be uncovered,
Yes, your shame will be seen;
I will take vengeance,
And I will not arbitrate with a man."

4 *As for* our Redeemer, the LORD of hosts *is* His name,
The Holy One of Israel.

5 "Sit in silence, and go into darkness,
O daughter of the Chaldeans;
For you shall no longer be called
The Lady of Kingdoms.

6 I was angry with My people;
I have profaned My inheritance,
And given them into your hand.
You showed them no mercy;
On the elderly you laid your yoke very heavily.

7 And you said, 'I shall be a lady forever,'

No Middle Ground (Is. 47:1)

The prophet uses theological satire relentlessly in attacks upon the Neo-Babylonian society in which the exiled Judeans would find themselves (Is. 41:6, 7; 44:9–20; 46:1, 2). The satire eventually turns directly against the Neo-Babylonians, declaring Babylon's impending doom (Is. 47:1–15).

The image of the "virgin daughter of Babylon" (Is. 47:1) emphasizes the reversal of social and political fortunes that will befall the Babylonians. The Babylonians had showed God's elect, the exilic community, no mercy, even forcing the elderly into forced labor (47:6). The prophet therefore declares that God will remove the privileged Babylonians from their position of wealth, power, and honor. From a situation described as "tender and delicate" (47:1), they would face abject conditions, lacking even the resources to heat their own homes (47:14).

Social, economic, and political issues were at stake behind the prophet's message of deliverance for the exilic community. Cyrus's rise and the exiles' deliverance would mean the end of the Babylonians' luxurious life. Yet the "virgin daughter of Babylon" still controlled the social and political life of the exiled Judean community. Talk of Babylonian demise was risky business.

There was no middle ground. The prophet forced the issue for his people: Should the community stand with the prophet and take the political risk of reprisal by the Neo-Babylonians? Or should the community attempt to maintain the status quo and continue to work with—and under the control of—their Neo-Babylonian overlords? They should listen to what the prophet declared concerning those overlords: no one would save them (47:15).

So that you did not take these *things*
  to heart,
Nor remember the latter end of them.

8 "Therefore hear this now, *you who are*
  given to pleasures,
Who dwell securely,
Who say in your heart, 'I *am,* and
  there is no one else besides me;
I shall not sit *as* a widow,
Nor shall I know the loss of children';
9 But these two *things* shall come to you
In a moment, in one day:
The loss of children, and widowhood.
They shall come upon you in their
  fullness
Because of the multitude of your
  sorceries,
For the great abundance of your
  enchantments.

10 "For you have trusted in your
  wickedness;

You have said, 'No one sees me';
Your wisdom and your knowledge
  have warped you;
And you have said in your heart,
'I *am,* and *there is* no one else besides
  me.'
11 Therefore evil shall come upon you;
You shall not know from where it
  arises.
And trouble shall fall upon you;
You will not be able to put it off.
And desolation shall come upon you
  suddenly,
Which you shall not know.

12 "Stand now with your enchantments
And the multitude of your sorceries,
In which you have labored from your
  youth—
Perhaps you will be able to profit,
Perhaps you will prevail.
13 You are wearied in the multitude of
  your counsels;

Beliefs and Ideas

The belief that the stars control human destiny was widespread in ancient times. Ancient kings maintained astrologers in their courts to give an opinion about whether a certain time was right for a project, or what events to expect (Is. 47:13). In addition to fortune-telling, astrologers had some factual knowledge of astronomy, which they used for establishing a calendar.

Let now the astrologers, the
    stargazers,
And the monthly prognosticators
Stand up and save you
From what shall come upon you.
14 Behold, they shall be as stubble,
The fire shall burn them;
They shall not deliver themselves
From the power of the flame;
It shall not *be* a coal to be warmed by,
Nor a fire to sit before!
15 Thus shall they be to you
With whom you have labored,
Your merchants from your youth;
They shall wander each one to his
    quarter.
No one shall save you.

Israel Refined for God's Glory

48 1 "Hear this, O house of Jacob,
    Who are called by the name of
        Israel,
And have come forth from the
    wellsprings of Judah;
Who swear by the name of the LORD,
And make mention of the God of
    Israel,
But not in truth or in righteousness;
2 For they call themselves after the holy
    city,
And lean on the God of Israel;
The LORD of hosts *is* His name:

3 "I have declared the former things
    from the beginning;
They went forth from My mouth, and
    I caused them to hear it.
Suddenly I did *them,* and they came to
    pass.
4 Because I knew that you *were*
    obstinate,
And your neck *was* an iron sinew,
And your brow bronze,
5 Even from the beginning I have
    declared *it* to you;
Before it came to pass I proclaimed *it*
    to you,
Lest you should say, 'My idol has done
    them,
And my carved image and my molded
    image
Have commanded them.'

6 "You have heard;
See all this.
And will you not declare *it?*
I have made you hear new things from
    this time,

Even hidden things, and you did not
    know them.
7 They are created now and not from
    the beginning;
And before this day you have not
    heard them,
Lest you should say, 'Of course I knew
    them.'
8 Surely you did not hear,
Surely you did not know;
Surely from long ago your ear was not
    opened.
For I knew that you would deal very
    treacherously,
And were called a transgressor from
    the womb.

9 "For My name's sake I will defer My
    anger,
And *for* My praise I will restrain it
    from you,
So that I do not cut you off.
10 Behold, I have refined you, but not as
    silver;
I have tested you in the furnace of
    affliction.
11 For My own sake, for My own sake, I
    will do *it;*
For how should *My name* be
    profaned?
And I will not give My glory to
    another.

God's Ancient Plan to Redeem Israel

12 "Listen to Me, O Jacob,
And Israel, My called:
I *am* He, I *am* the First,
I *am* also the Last.
13 Indeed My hand has laid the
    foundation of the earth,
And My right hand has stretched out
    the heavens;
When I call to them,
They stand up together.

14 "All of you, assemble yourselves, and
    hear!
Who among them has declared these
    things?
The LORD loves him;
He shall do His pleasure on Babylon,
And His arm *shall be against* the
    Chaldeans.
15 I, *even* I, have spoken;
Yes, I have called him,
I have brought him, and his way will
    prosper.

THE NEW EXODUS (Is. 48:20, 21)

With the command "Go forth from Babylon!" (Is. 48:20), the prophet explicitly encouraged the Judean exiles to leave their homes in Babylon and return to their own land. He did not advise them to sneak out, but rather to go publicly and joyously, with "a voice of singing."

The journey would be a new Exodus. The prophet invokes the memory of the Israelites' trip from Egypt to the land of Canaan following the first Exodus (48:21). The people could remember stories of Moses drawing drinking water from a rock (Ex. 17:6). Though now a desert faced the people between Babylon and Judah, they need not worry: as God had provided for Israel's escape from Egyptian tyranny during Moses' time, so would He now provide for these exiles to escape from Babylonian rule.

There was one problem, though. The Babylonians had not yet been removed from power. Still the command "Go!" is given. To leave Babylon would be to take political liberty that the Babylonians were not ready to offer. The prophet challenged the people's faith in God to redeem them, even though their redemption would be rebellion against the Babylonian regime!

---

16 "Come near to Me, hear this:
I have not spoken in secret from the
   beginning;
From the time that it was, I *was*
   there.
And now the Lord GOD and His Spirit
Have[a] sent Me."

17 Thus says the LORD, your Redeemer,
The Holy One of Israel:
"I *am* the LORD your God,
Who teaches you to profit,
Who leads you by the way you should
   go.

18 Oh, that you had heeded My
   commandments!
Then your peace would have been like
   a river,
And your righteousness like the waves
   of the sea.

19 Your descendants also would have
   been like the sand,
And the offspring of your body like the
   grains of sand;
His name would not have been cut off
Nor destroyed from before Me."

20 Go forth from Babylon!
Flee from the Chaldeans!
With a voice of singing,
Declare, proclaim this,
Utter it to the end of the earth;
Say, "The LORD has redeemed
His servant Jacob!"

21 And they did not thirst
When He led them through the
   deserts;
He caused the waters to flow from the
   rock for them;

He also split the rock, and the waters
   gushed out.

22 "*There is* no peace," says the LORD, "for
the wicked."

48:16 [a]The Hebrew verb is singular.

The Servant of the Lord

A "servant of the Lord" is one who voluntarily serves God, as did Abraham (Ps. 105:42). The phrase "My servant" appears frequently in Is. 41—53. Sometimes the phrase describes the entire nation of Israel, God's chosen Jacob (41:8). This meaning is found most often in chs. 41—48. But the nation Israel proved to be an unproductive servant. Assigned to bring "light to the Gentiles, to open blind eyes" (42:6, 7), she herself became blind (42:18—20).

The most important passages concerning "My servant" are the famous Servant Songs (42:1–4; 49:1–6; 50:4–11; 52:13—53:12). Sometimes in these songs, the servant again is identified with the nation of Israel (49:3), but at other times the servant appears to be an individual, working to bring salvation to Israel and the nations (49:4, 5).

It is difficult to know how these poems would have been understood by their first hearers. Perhaps some prophet or king was identified as the servant. Since the time of Christ, however, Christians have identified Jesus Himself as the Servant of the Lord who brought salvation to the Gentiles as well as to the Jews (see Matt. 12:18–21, quoting Is. 42:1–4).

■ Isaiah 49:1—51:23

A LIGHT TO THE GENTILES (Is. 49:3–7)

The tone and subject of the prophet's oracles changed, turning dark. No longer did he speak of Babylon's demise or the exiles' return to Judah, though his oracles seemingly still addressed the same exiled community. Conflict seemed to lurk beneath the prophet's words. His attempt to persuade his people seemingly had produced little, if any, results. He felt as if he had labored "for nothing and in vain" (Is. 49:4).

Instead of narrowing his task, however, God widened the prophet's mission. No longer content to address only the Judean exilic community, God would give the prophet as "a light to the Gentiles" (49:6). In this way, the Judean exilic community's rejection of the prophet's message would lead to the inclusion of all persons, Jews and Gentiles, into the restorative purposes of God. Through His servant, the prophet, God would proclaim "salvation to the ends of the earth" (49:6).

Isaiah
The Servant, the Light to the Gentiles

49

:1 "Listen, O coastlands, to Me,
  And take heed, you peoples
    from afar!
The LORD has called Me from the
  womb;
From the matrix of My mother He has
  made mention of My name.

2 And He has made My mouth like a
    sharp sword;
  In the shadow of His hand He has
    hidden Me,
  And made Me a polished shaft;
  In His quiver He has hidden Me."

3 "And He said to me,
    'You *are* My servant, O Israel,
    In whom I will be glorified.'

4 Then I said, 'I have labored in vain,
    I have spent my strength for nothing
      and in vain;
  Yet surely my just reward *is* with the
    LORD,
  And my work with my God.' "

5 "And now the LORD says,
  Who formed Me from the womb *to be*
    His Servant,
  To bring Jacob back to Him,
  So that Israel is gathered to Him[a]
  (For I shall be glorious in the eyes of
    the LORD,
  And My God shall be My strength),

6 Indeed He says,
    'It is too small a thing that You should
      be My Servant

  To raise up the tribes of Jacob,
  And to restore the preserved ones of
    Israel;
  I will also give You as a light to the
    Gentiles,
  That You should be My salvation to
    the ends of the earth.' "

7 Thus says the LORD,
  The Redeemer of Israel, their Holy
    One,
  To Him whom man despises,
  To Him whom the nation abhors,
  To the Servant of rulers:
  "Kings shall see and arise,
  Princes also shall worship,
  Because of the LORD who is faithful,
  The Holy One of Israel;
  And He has chosen You."

8 Thus says the LORD:

  "In an acceptable time I have heard
    You,
  And in the day of salvation I have
    helped You;
  I will preserve You and give You
  As a covenant to the people,
  To restore the earth,
  To cause them to inherit the desolate
    heritages;

9 That You may say to the prisoners, 'Go
    forth,'
  To those who *are* in darkness, 'Show
    yourselves.'

  "They shall feed along the roads,
  And their pastures *shall be* on all
    desolate heights.

49:5 [a]Qere, Dead Sea Scrolls, and Septuagint read *is gathered to Him;* Kethib reads *is not gathered.*

10 They shall neither hunger nor thirst,
Neither heat nor sun shall strike
    them;
For He who has mercy on them will
    lead them,
Even by the springs of water He will
    guide them.
11 I will make each of My mountains a
    road,
And My highways shall be elevated.
12 Surely these shall come from afar;
Look! Those from the north and the
    west,
And these from the land of Sinim."

13 Sing, O heavens!
Be joyful, O earth!
And break out in singing,
    O mountains!
For the LORD has comforted His
    people,
And will have mercy on His afflicted.

God Will Remember Zion

14 But Zion said, "The LORD has forsaken
    me,
And my Lord has forgotten me."

15 "Can a woman forget her nursing child,
And not have compassion on the son
    of her womb?
Surely they may forget,
Yet I will not forget you.
16 See, I have inscribed you on the palms
    of My hands;
Your walls are continually before Me.
17 Your sons[a] shall make haste;
Your destroyers and those who laid
    you waste
Shall go away from you.
18 Lift up your eyes, look around and
    see;
All these gather together and come to
    you.
As I live," says the LORD,
"You shall surely clothe yourselves
    with them all as an ornament,
And bind them on you as a bride does.

19 "For your waste and desolate places,
And the land of your destruction,
Will even now be too small for the
    inhabitants;
And those who swallowed you up will
    be far away.
20 The children you will have,
After you have lost the others,
Will say again in your ears,

'The place is too small for me;
Give me a place where I may dwell.'
21 Then you will say in your heart,
'Who has begotten these for me,
Since I have lost my children and am
    desolate,
A captive, and wandering to and fro?
And who has brought these up?
There I was, left alone;
But these, where were they?' "

22 Thus says the Lord GOD:

"Behold, I will lift My hand in an oath
    to the nations,
And set up My standard for the
    peoples;
They shall bring your sons in their
    arms,
And your daughters shall be carried
    on their shoulders;
23 Kings shall be your foster fathers,
And their queens your nursing
    mothers;
They shall bow down to you with their
    faces to the earth,
And lick up the dust of your feet.
Then you will know that I am the
    LORD,
For they shall not be ashamed who
    wait for Me."

24 Shall the prey be taken from the
    mighty,
Or the captives of the righteous[a] be
    delivered?

25 But thus says the LORD:

"Even the captives of the mighty shall
    be taken away,
And the prey of the terrible be
    delivered;
For I will contend with him who
    contends with you,
And I will save your children.
26 I will feed those who oppress you with
    their own flesh,
And they shall be drunk with their
    own blood as with sweet wine.
All flesh shall know
That I, the LORD, am your Savior,

49:17 [a]Dead Sea Scrolls, Septuagint, Targum, and
Vulgate read builders.   49:24 [a]Following
Masoretic Text and Targum; Dead Sea Scrolls, Syriac,
and Vulgate read the mighty; Septuagint reads
unjustly.

INTIMIDATION DENIED (Is. 50:4)

A conflict escalated between those who accepted the prophet's message and those who rejected it. On the bright side, the prophet developed a following among those who stood with the prophet (Is. 50:8) and who feared the Lord and obeyed "the voice of His Servant" (50:10). Therefore, the prophet spoke with "the tongue of the learned" (50:4), leading those who would believe.

On the darker side, the prophet also had evoked strong resistance, most likely from within his own community. His faithfulness to proclaim the word of the Lord produced a violent reaction. The prophet received beatings, the pulling of his beard, insults, being spit upon—all tactics to intimidate, humiliate, and discredit him (50:5, 6). The Judean leaders who had accommodated themselves to Babylonian society found his message dangerous and wished to silence him.

Yet the torture did not change the prophet's stance. It seems, instead, to have hardened his resolve: he set his face "like a flint" against his opposition (50:7). The prophet could not be shamed, for torment ultimately awaited those who tormented him (50:11). God, after all, was on his side (50:9).

And your Redeemer, the Mighty One
  of Jacob."

The Servant, Israel's Hope

50 ¹Thus says the LORD:

"Where *is* the certificate of your
  mother's divorce,
Whom I have put away?
Or which of My creditors *is it* to whom
  I have sold you?
For your iniquities you have sold
  yourselves,
And for your transgressions your
  mother has been put away.
² Why, when I came, *was there* no man?
Why, when I called, *was there* none to
  answer?
Is My hand shortened at all that it
  cannot redeem?
Or have I no power to deliver?
Indeed with My rebuke I dry up the
  sea,
I make the rivers a wilderness;
Their fish stink because *there is* no
  water,
And die of thirst.
³ I clothe the heavens with blackness,
And I make sackcloth their covering."

⁴ "The Lord GOD has given Me
The tongue of the learned,
That I should know how to speak
A word in season to *him who is* weary.
He awakens Me morning by morning,
He awakens My ear
To hear as the learned.

⁵ The Lord GOD has opened My ear;
And I was not rebellious,
Nor did I turn away.
⁶ I gave My back to those who struck
  Me,
And My cheeks to those who plucked
  out the beard;
I did not hide My face from shame
  and spitting.

⁷ "For the Lord GOD will help Me;
Therefore I will not be disgraced;
Therefore I have set My face like a
  flint,
And I know that I will not be
  ashamed.
⁸ *He is* near who justifies Me;
Who will contend with Me?
Let us stand together.
Who *is* My adversary?
Let him come near Me.
⁹ Surely the Lord GOD will help Me;
Who *is* he *who* will condemn Me?
Indeed they will all grow old like a
  garment;
The moth will eat them up.

¹⁰ "Who among you fears the LORD?
Who obeys the voice of His Servant?
Who walks in darkness
And has no light?
Let him trust in the name of the LORD
And rely upon his God.
¹¹ Look, all you who kindle a fire,
Who encircle *yourselves* with sparks:
Walk in the light of your fire and in
  the sparks you have kindled—

This you shall have from My hand:
You shall lie down in torment.

The LORD Comforts Zion

51 ¹ "Listen to Me, you who follow
    after righteousness,
You who seek the LORD:
Look to the rock *from which* you were
    hewn,
And to the hole of the pit *from which*
    you were dug.
² Look to Abraham your father,
And to Sarah *who* bore you;
For I called him alone,
And blessed him and increased him."

³ For the LORD will comfort Zion,
He will comfort all her waste places;
He will make her wilderness like
    Eden,
And her desert like the garden of the
    LORD;
Joy and gladness will be found in it,
Thanksgiving and the voice of melody.

⁴ "Listen to Me, My people;
And give ear to Me, O My nation:
For law will proceed from Me,
And I will make My justice rest
As a light of the peoples.
⁵ My righteousness *is* near,
My salvation has gone forth,
And My arms will judge the peoples;
The coastlands will wait upon Me,
And on My arm they will trust.
⁶ Lift up your eyes to the heavens,
And look on the earth beneath.
For the heavens will vanish away like
    smoke,
The earth will grow old like a
    garment,
And those who dwell in it will die in
    like manner;
But My salvation will be forever,
And My righteousness will not be
    abolished.

⁷ "Listen to Me, you who know
    righteousness,

You people in whose heart *is* My law:
Do not fear the reproach of men,
Nor be afraid of their insults.
⁸ For the moth will eat them up like a
    garment,
And the worm will eat them like wool;
But My righteousness will be forever,
And My salvation from generation to
    generation."

⁹ Awake, awake, put on strength,
O arm of the LORD!
Awake as in the ancient days,
In the generations of old.
Are You not *the arm* that cut Rahab
    apart,
And wounded the serpent?

¹⁰ *Are* You not *the One* who dried up the
    sea,
The waters of the great deep;
That made the depths of the sea a
    road
For the redeemed to cross over?
¹¹ So the ransomed of the LORD shall
    return,
And come to Zion with singing,
With everlasting joy on their heads.
They shall obtain joy and gladness;
Sorrow and sighing shall flee away.

¹² "I, *even* I, *am* He who comforts you.
Who *are* you that you should be afraid
Of a man *who* will die,
And of the son of a man *who* will be
    made like grass?
¹³ And you forget the LORD your Maker,
Who stretched out the heavens
And laid the foundations of the earth;
You have feared continually every
    day
Because of the fury of the oppressor,
When *he has* prepared to destroy.
And where *is* the fury of the
    oppressor?
¹⁴ The captive exile hastens, that he may
    be loosed,
That he should not die in the pit,
And that his bread should not fail.

ARTS AND LITERATURE

*The Hebrews were not seafarers, and they found the ocean dangerous and frightening.
In the Bible the sea is usually a symbol for disorder and chaos (Is. 51:10). Rahab (51:9)
was one name given to the chaos monster in pagan mythology. The prophet alludes to
popular literature in describing Israel's escape from Egypt across the Red Sea, which
was a similar conquest over the threatening waters.*

15 But I *am* the LORD your God,
Who divided the sea whose waves
   roared—
The LORD of hosts *is* His name.

16 And I have put My words in your
   mouth;
I have covered you with the shadow of
   My hand,
That I may plant the heavens,
Lay the foundations of the earth,
And say to Zion, 'You *are* My people.' "

God's Fury Removed

17 Awake, awake!
Stand up, O Jerusalem,
You who have drunk at the hand of
   the LORD
The cup of His fury;
You have drunk the dregs of the cup of
   trembling,
And drained *it* out.

18 *There is* no one to guide her
Among all the sons she has brought
   forth;
Nor *is there any* who takes her by the
   hand
Among all the sons she has brought
   up.

19 These two *things* have come to you;
Who will be sorry for you?—
Desolation and destruction, famine
   and sword—
By whom will I comfort you?

20 Your sons have fainted,
They lie at the head of all the streets,
Like an antelope in a net;
They are full of the fury of the LORD,
The rebuke of your God.

21 Therefore please hear this, you
   afflicted,
And drunk but not with wine.

22 Thus says your Lord,
The LORD and your God,
Who pleads the cause of His people:
"See, I have taken out of your hand
The cup of trembling,
The dregs of the cup of My fury;
You shall no longer drink it.

23 But I will put it into the hand of those
   who afflict you,
Who have said to you,[a]
'Lie down, that we may walk over you.'
And you have laid your body like the
   ground,

And as the street, for those who walk
   over."

The Suffering Servant

The Servant of the Lord brings salvation (see "The Servant of the Lord" at Is. 49:1). That salvation comes about in a startling new fashion, though. There will be no wars, plagues, and flight, as when God brought Israel out of Egypt (Is. 52:12). Nor shall this salvation cost Israel (52:3). Instead, salvation shall be brought by the Servant's suffering and death (53:4–6).

To the Judean exiles in Babylon, the message was simply that their suffering was over. God had redeemed His people in a new and marvelous way. Since the passion of Christ, though, Christians have recognized a much more specific fulfillment to the final Servant Song. Christ Himself is the promised Servant. He was the One who bore "our griefs and carried our sorrows" (53:4), and on Him God laid "the iniquity of us all" (53:6). The salvation proclaimed in the New Testament, a salvation that depends not on morality or on earthly power but rather on the Servant's humble self-sacrifice, finds its most powerful expression in Is. 52:13—53:12, written centuries before Christ.

■ Isaiah 52:1—55:13

Isaiah
God Redeems Jerusalem

52 :1 Awake, awake!
Put on your strength, O Zion;
Put on your beautiful garments,
O Jerusalem, the holy city!
For the uncircumcised and the
   unclean
Shall no longer come to you.

2 Shake yourself from the dust, arise;
Sit down, O Jerusalem!
Loose yourself from the bonds of your
   neck,
O captive daughter of Zion!

3 For thus says the LORD:

"You have sold yourselves for nothing,
And you shall be redeemed without
   money."

4 For thus says the Lord GOD:

"My people went down at first
Into Egypt to dwell there;

Then the Assyrian oppressed them
  without cause.
5 Now therefore, what have I here,"
  says the LORD,
  "That My people are taken away for
    nothing?
  Those who rule over them
  Make them wail,"a says the LORD,
  "And My name is blasphemed
    continually every day.
6 Therefore My people shall know My
    name;
  Therefore *they shall know* in that day
  That I *am* He who speaks:
  'Behold, *it is* I.'"

7 How beautiful upon the mountains
  Are the feet of him who brings good
    news,
  Who proclaims peace,
  Who brings glad tidings of good
    things,
  Who proclaims salvation,
  Who says to Zion,
  "Your God reigns!"
8 Your watchmen shall lift up *their*
    voices,
  With their voices they shall sing
    together;
  For they shall see eye to eye
  When the LORD brings back Zion.
9 Break forth into joy, sing together,
  You waste places of Jerusalem!
  For the LORD has comforted His
    people,
  He has redeemed Jerusalem.
10 The LORD has made bare His holy arm
  In the eyes of all the nations;
  And all the ends of the earth shall see
  The salvation of our God.

11 Depart! Depart! Go out from there,
  Touch no unclean *thing;*

Go out from the midst of her,
  Be clean,
  You who bear the vessels of the LORD.
12 For you shall not go out with haste,
  Nor go by flight;
  For the LORD will go before you,
  And the God of Israel *will be* your rear
    guard.

The Sin-Bearing Servant

13 Behold, My Servant shall deal
    prudently;
  He shall be exalted and extolled and
    be very high.
14 Just as many were astonished at you,
  So His visage was marred more than
    any man,
  And His form more than the sons of
    men;
15 So shall He sprinklea many nations.
  Kings shall shut their mouths at Him;
  For what had not been told them they
    shall see,
  And what they had not heard they
    shall consider.

53 ¹ Who has believed our report?
    And to whom has the arm of the
      LORD been revealed?
2 For He shall grow up before Him as a
    tender plant,
  And as a root out of dry ground.
  He has no form or comeliness;
  And when we see Him,
  There is no beauty that we should
    desire Him.
3 He is despised and rejected by men,
  A Man of sorrows and acquainted with
    grief.
  And we hid, as it were, *our* faces from
    Him;
  He was despised, and we did not
    esteem Him.

4 Surely He has borne our griefs
  And carried our sorrows;
  Yet we esteemed Him stricken,
  Smitten by God, and afflicted.
5 But He *was* wounded for our
    transgressions,
  He was bruised for our iniquities;
  The chastisement for our peace *was*
    upon Him,
  And by His stripes we are healed.

52:5 ªDead Sea Scrolls read *Mock;* Septuagint reads
Marvel and wail; Targum reads *Boast themselves;*
Vulgate reads *Treat them unjustly.*   52:15 ªOr
startle

TIME CAPSULE   *530 to 522 B.C.*

530– *Cambyses of Persia builds naval*
522   *fleet with Ionians and Phoenicians*

530   *Capital of Cush is transferred to*
          Meroe

526– *Psammetichus III is last pharaoh of*
525   *Egypt's 26th Dynasty*

525   *Cambyses conquers Sais, capital of*
          Egypt's 26th Dynasty

522   *Cambyses dies while en route to*
          Persia

BEHOLD, MY SERVANT (Is. 52:13)

The words "Behold, My Servant" (Is. 52:13) begin a definitive description of the Servant through whom God would deliver Israel from their sins (Is. 52:13—53:12). From the earliest days of the church, Christians have considered this "Servant" to represent prophetically Jesus Christ, and with good reason. In a very profound sense, the life of Christ reflects and fulfills the life of the Servant.

What is said about the Servant is nothing less than tragic. Like the Servant, Jesus proclaimed good news to the community. Like the Servant, Jesus' good news threatened those who had most accommodated themselves to the foreigners: the prophet's exilic community with the Babylonians; Jesus' Jerusalem priesthood with the Romans. Like the Servant, Jesus did not alter His message, and like the Servant, He paid for it by His life—disgraced, shamed, and held in no account.

Jesus, therefore, relived and fulfilled the theological and social dynamics encountered by the Servant. No one expected that the Messiah would come as a servant: quiet, unassuming, and suffering. This Servant "was wounded for our transgressions"; He was "oppressed" and "afflicted"; yet, by "His stripes we are healed" (53:5, 7). In raising Jesus from the dead, God has allotted Jesus "a portion with the great" (53:12), "exalted and extolled" (52:13). For so many reasons, Christians cannot read Is. 52:13—53:12 without hearing echoes of the life of Christ.

6 All we like sheep have gone astray;
We have turned, every one, to his own way;
And the LORD has laid on Him the iniquity of us all.

7 He was oppressed and He was afflicted,
Yet He opened not His mouth;
He was led as a lamb to the slaughter,
And as a sheep before its shearers is silent,
So He opened not His mouth.

8 He was taken from prison and from judgment,
And who will declare His generation?
For He was cut off from the land of the living;
For the transgressions of My people He was stricken.

9 And they[a] made His grave with the wicked—
But with the rich at His death,
Because He had done no violence,
Nor *was any* deceit in His mouth.

10 Yet it pleased the LORD to bruise Him;
He has put *Him* to grief.

When You make His soul an offering for sin,
He shall see *His* seed, He shall prolong *His* days,
And the pleasure of the LORD shall prosper in His hand.

11 He shall see the labor of His soul,[a]
and be satisfied.
By His knowledge My righteous Servant shall justify many,
For He shall bear their iniquities.

12 Therefore I will divide Him a portion with the great,
And He shall divide the spoil with the strong,
Because He poured out His soul unto death,
And He was numbered with the transgressors,
And He bore the sin of many,
And made intercession for the transgressors.

A Perpetual Covenant of Peace

54 1 "Sing, O barren,
You *who* have not borne!
Break forth into singing, and cry aloud,
You *who* have not labored with child!
For more *are* the children of the desolate
Than the children of the married woman," says the LORD.

53:9 [a]Literally *he* or *He*   53:11 [a]Following Masoretic Text, Targum, and Vulgate; Dead Sea Scrolls and Septuagint read *From the labor of His soul He shall see light.*

The Heritage of Barren "Servants" (Is. 54:17)

The prophet changed his message in a subtle, but important way. No longer did he speak of a single "Servant"; now he spoke of the plural "servants." These servants were the Judean exiles, whose city Jerusalem was in ruins. Yet the prophet offered a message of hope as he turned to address "the heritage of the servants of the LORD" (Is. 54:17).

The situation of these "servants" is similar to that of a barren woman (Is. 54:1). In antiquity a single woman or a woman unable to bear children was in a vulnerable social and economic situation. Such a woman bore social shame from a society which believed infertility indicated a curse from God. Additionally, in a society where children provided "social security," a barren or single woman could be left economically destitute upon the death of her husband. The barren woman provided a powerful image to describe the uncertain situation the people faced when they returned to their desolate city Jerusalem.

But God saw these servants much differently. Though barren, shamed, and a widow, the servants were not destitute. Judah had not been divorced. Her estranged husband would take her back, and she would yet bear children (54:5–10). They were not forsaken; on the contrary, their "husband" owned the wealth of all creation!

The prophet did not deny the servants' current predicament: they were "afflicted" and "not comforted" (54:11). Yet because God was their husband, the future was anything but bleak: God would have mercy on them (54:8). The foundations and walls of their city would be rebuilt and inhabited by their children (54:11–13). This was their "heritage" as God's servants.

---

2 "Enlarge the place of your tent,
And let them stretch out the curtains
of your dwellings;
Do not spare;
Lengthen your cords,
And strengthen your stakes.
3 For you shall expand to the right and
to the left,
And your descendants will inherit the
nations,
And make the desolate cities
inhabited.

4 "Do not fear, for you will not be
ashamed;
Neither be disgraced, for you will not
be put to shame;
For you will forget the shame of your
youth,
And will not remember the reproach
of your widowhood anymore.

5 For your Maker is your husband,
The LORD of hosts is His name;
And your Redeemer is the Holy One of
Israel;
He is called the God of the whole
earth.
6 For the LORD has called you
Like a woman forsaken and grieved in
spirit,
Like a youthful wife when you were
refused,"
Says your God.
7 "For a mere moment I have forsaken
you,
But with great mercies I will gather
you.
8 With a little wrath I hid My face from
you for a moment;
But with everlasting kindness I will
have mercy on you,"
Says the LORD, your Redeemer.

Architecture and Building

The Arabs of the desert, known as the bedouin, live in tents made of dark goat hair. The floor plan of these tents is rectangular with an interior curtain dividing the tent into two parts. A standard tent is made of 6 to 8 lengths of cloth held up by 9 interior poles. The overall size can be up to 6 by 10 yards. Large tents are made twice the size of a standard tent (Is. 54:2).

9 "For this *is* like the waters of Noah to
　　Me;
　For as I have sworn
　That the waters of Noah would no
　　longer cover the earth,
　So have I sworn
　That I would not be angry with you,
　　nor rebuke you.
10 For the mountains shall depart
　And the hills be removed,
　But My kindness shall not depart
　　from you,
　Nor shall My covenant of peace be
　　removed,"
　Says the LORD, who has mercy on
　　you.

11 "O you afflicted one,
　Tossed with tempest, *and* not
　　comforted,
　Behold, I will lay your stones with
　　colorful gems,
　And lay your foundations with
　　sapphires.
12 I will make your pinnacles of rubies,
　Your gates of crystal,
　And all your walls of precious stones.
13 All your children *shall be* taught by
　　the LORD,
　And great *shall be* the peace of your
　　children.
14 In righteousness you shall be
　　established;
　You shall be far from oppression, for
　　you shall not fear;
　And from terror, for it shall not come
　　near you.
15 Indeed they shall surely assemble, *but*
　　not because of Me.
　Whoever assembles against you shall
　　fall for your sake.

16 "Behold, I have created the blacksmith
　Who blows the coals in the fire,
　Who brings forth an instrument for
　　his work;
　And I have created the spoiler to
　　destroy.
17 No weapon formed against you shall
　　prosper,
　And every tongue *which* rises against
　　you in judgment
　You shall condemn.
　This *is* the heritage of the servants of
　　the LORD,
　And their righteousness *is* from Me,"
　Says the LORD.

An Invitation to Abundant Life

55 1 "Ho! Everyone who thirsts,
　　Come to the waters;
　And you who have no money,
　Come, buy and eat.
　Yes, come, buy wine and milk
　Without money and without price.
2 Why do you spend money for *what is*
　　not bread,
　And your wages for *what* does not
　　satisfy?
　Listen carefully to Me, and eat *what is*
　　good,
　And let your soul delight itself in
　　abundance.
3 Incline your ear, and come to Me.
　Hear, and your soul shall live;
　And I will make an everlasting
　　covenant with you—
　The sure mercies of David.
4 Indeed I have given him *as* a witness
　　to the people,
　A leader and commander for the
　　people.
5 Surely you shall call a nation you do
　　not know,
　And nations *who* do not know you
　　shall run to you,
　Because of the LORD your God,
　And the Holy One of Israel;
　For He has glorified you."

6 Seek the LORD while He may be found,
　Call upon Him while He is near.
7 Let the wicked forsake his way,
　And the unrighteous man his
　　thoughts;
　Let him return to the LORD,
　And He will have mercy on him;
　And to our God,
　For He will abundantly pardon.

8 "For My thoughts *are* not your
　　thoughts,
　Nor *are* your ways My ways," says the
　　LORD.
9 "For *as* the heavens are higher than
　　the earth,
　So are My ways higher than your
　　ways,
　And My thoughts than your thoughts.

10 "For as the rain comes down, and the
　　snow from heaven,
　And do not return there,
　But water the earth,
　And make it bring forth and bud,

CYRUS ALLOWS THE JUDEANS TO GO HOME (2 Chr. 36:22, 23)

When Cyrus II ascended the throne of Persia in 559 B.C., he became the founder of the Achaemenid dynasty. In a string of military victories, Cyrus proceeded to conquer the largest territory in known history up to that time, stretching from the Indus River to central Anatolia.

The first major victories allowed Cyrus to successfully unite the Persian tribes and the Medes into a mighty kingdom. After defeating the Median Empire and its last king, Astyages, in 550 B.C., Cyrus declared himself the successor to the Median kings. Just 3 years later, in 547 B.C., a victory over Lydia and their king, Croesus, expanded Cyrus's empire toward Greece. At this point Cyrus turned his attention to his primary enemy, the Neo-Babylonian Empire.

Cyrus's crowning achievement was the conquest of Babylon and their king, Nabonidus, in 539 B.C. Virtually all of the Near East (excluding Egypt) was now under his authority. As with the victory of Media, Cyrus ruled Babylon not as a conquering foreigner, but as a successor to the previous Babylonian kings. This policy meant that the conquered people could maintain their local customs and culture, as well as their deities. Thus Cyrus restored honor and dignity to the Babylonian god Marduk.

Such a tolerant policy of allowing local cultures some autonomy in regard to their traditions had its advantages for Cyrus. This method was in direct contradiction to the harsh policies of deportation employed by the Assyrian and Chaldean kingdoms. Cyrus, though a conquering king, could also appear to be a benevolent king who assisted conquered peoples in preserving their sacred traditions.

Just as Cyrus respected the god Marduk of the Babylonians, so also did he respect the God Yahweh of the Judeans. Cyrus's proclamation (2 Chr. 36:22, 23) allowed the Judeans to return to Judea, to rebuild the Jerusalem temple, and to carry back the sacred objects which were confiscated by Babylon (Ezra 1:7–11). The Judean understanding of this restoration event placed a high view on Cyrus as the one Yahweh had anointed to overcome all nations (Is. 45:1–7).

That it may give seed to the sower
And bread to the eater,
11 So shall My word be that goes forth
    from My mouth;
It shall not return to Me void,
But it shall accomplish what I
    please,
And it shall prosper *in the thing* for
    which I sent it.

12 "For you shall go out with joy,
And be led out with peace;
The mountains and the hills
Shall break forth into singing before
    you,
And all the trees of the field shall clap
    their hands.
13 Instead of the thorn shall come up the
    cypress tree,
And instead of the brier shall come up
    the myrtle tree;
And it shall be to the LORD for a
    name,

For an everlasting sign *that* shall not
    be cut off."

Priestly Account: Hope for the Future

The prediction of Is. 45 that Cyrus the Great would capture Babylon and end the Exile bestows great honor on the Persian leader. He is called God's "anointed" (Is. 45:1; Hebrew *messiah*), but his action was more than just a favor for the Judeans. Archaeological finds from Cyrus's reign (559–530 B.C.) show that it was his standard policy to release all the captive peoples in the lands he conquered. He also allowed religious freedom in his many provinces. These wise policies were continued by his successors, and such tolerance engendered a great deal of loyalty among the Persian Empire's subjects.

Whatever Cyrus's reasons were, in 538 B.C. he proclaimed a release for the peoples held captive by Babylon. The exiled Judeans, recognizing God Himself at work in Cyrus's proclamation of freedom, saw all their hopes fulfilled at once. The prophet Jeremiah's promise that the Exile would end after 70 years (Jer. 29:10) had come true.

It is with Cyrus's proclamation and the promise that it holds for a restored temple that the priestly historian concludes the Book of Chronicles (2 Chr. 36:22, 23). Thus the Chronicler, like the prophetic historian of Kings, ends with a ray of hope. But where 2 Kings ended with a faint hope—the elevation of the captive Jehoiachin to a position in the court of Babylon (2 Kin. 25:27–30)—Chronicles presents a brilliant new future. The exiled Judeans will return to the land of their fathers.

■ 2 Chronicles 36:22, 23

2 Chronicles
The Proclamation of Cyrus

36 :22 Now in the first year of Cyrus king of Persia, that the word of the LORD by the mouth of Jeremiah might be fulfilled, the LORD stirred up the spirit of Cyrus king of Persia, so that he made a proclamation throughout all his kingdom, and also *put it* in writing, saying,

23   Thus says Cyrus king of Persia:
All the kingdoms of the earth the
LORD God of heaven has given me.
And He has commanded me to build
Him a house at Jerusalem which is in
Judah. Who *is* among you of all His
people? May the LORD his God *be* with
him, and let him go up!

Wisdom in the Ancient Near East

> Wisdom teachings dealt with universal matters that apply just as well in every age.

The teaching tradition that is called "wisdom" appears in the Bible in the books of Proverbs, Ecclesiastes, and Job. The wisdom tradition is associated most of all with the figure of Solomon. Ecclesiastes, as well as proverbs ascribed to Solomon, are often read in light of his reputation for wisdom (see "The Book of Proverbs" at Prov. 1:1). The Book of Job and certain other proverbs, though, can be read in light of the larger world of non-Israelite wisdom.

Wisdom teachings appear to have several underlying assumptions. First, the proverbs of the wisdom teachers, or sages, assume that the world is orderly. Everything on earth happens for a just reason. This fairly optimistic premise is followed by an even more hopeful thought: human beings are able to understand that order. The world and its workings are comprehensible; therefore, the goal of the wise is to search out the underlying order of the world. Finally, the source of this knowledge is very human. The way to uncover the fixed principles by which the world operates is, first, through one's own experience and observation, and second, through tradition, which is the experience of those who had come before.

Wisdom, as represented by this general description, is not unique to Israel and the Bible. In fact, the true center of the wisdom tradition in the ancient world seems to have been Egypt. The Egyptian sages were famous throughout the ancient Near East, and enough Egyptian wisdom writings have been discovered to indicate that this fame was deserved. Other wisdom writings have been found in Mesopotamia, especially in Babylon, and the Bible itself testifies to the fame of Edomite sages (Jer. 49:7; Obad. 1:8).

Wisdom teaching, then, was common in many cultures. Following the assumptions of wisdom, many people believed that humans, through their own experience, observation, and tradition, could search out and comprehend the fixed principles behind an orderly world. These assumptions appear essentially unchanged throughout the wisdom literature of the ancient orient. Even more impressive, they remained essentially unchanged by time. Ancient oriental wisdom endured with only minor variations for over 1,000 years, and it was still an important tradition up to and during the time of Christ.

Israel's version of wisdom teaching is somewhat distinct, though. The basic assumptions of wisdom were quite secular. They spoke of worldly matters and had little to say about God. Wisdom was sought through human experience, not through prayer or any direct divine revelation. Israel's sages, not quite comfortable with such a focus, sought to incorporate God more fully. As a result, Israel's central theme was "The fear of the LORD is the beginning of wisdom" (Prov. 9:10). Devotion and obedience to God were seen as prior to and more important than the human quest for wisdom.

Some wisdom teachings are attributed to Solomon, and these can be read in the context of his reign. Most wisdom literature, however, is not so easily associated with a particular person or time. Indeed, wisdom seems rather uninterested in questions of chronological time. The sages sought to expound universal and eternal principles, and were less concerned with specific historical events.

Wisdom teachings largely ignored the fluctuating fortunes of historical kings and kingdoms, which perhaps explains why wisdom did not change greatly over time. Wisdom resisted new ideas and fads, preferring to pass on ancient and deep-rooted traditions. Indeed, many proverb collections are presented as a parent's instruction to a child (Prov. 1:8; 4:1; 31:1). Wisdom teachings dealt with universal matters that apply just as well in every age, such as family relationships, wealth, hard work, and honesty.

Words of the Wise

The Book of Proverbs is a collection of short, pithy instructions. It is, in fact, a collection of collections of proverbs and wisdom teachings. While these collections appear in the Bible, they also show similarities to non-Israelite wisdom. By placing devotion and obedience to God above the human quest for wisdom, the Israelite sages were distinct from other wisdom teachers. But after giving primary position to God, they proceeded to search for wisdom by the same secular methods as other cultures: they stressed personal experience and tradition. As a result, the Book of Proverbs remains one of the most secular of all biblical books.

Two collections in the Book of Proverbs are identified by introductory attributions ascribing these teachings to "the wise" (Prov. 22:17; 24:23). Many of the proverbs found in these collections (Prov. 22:17—24:22 and 24:23–34), as well as the outline by which they are arranged, appear also in a book of Egyptian wisdom, called *The Instruction of Amen-em-hotep*. The relationship is too close to be coincidental. While it is difficult to tell which is oldest, it is clear that both the biblical proverbs and the Egyptian texts are versions of a single wisdom discourse.

■ Proverbs 22:17—24:34

Proverbs
Sayings of the Wise

22 :17 Incline your ear and hear the words of the wise,
And apply your heart to my knowledge;

18 For *it is* a pleasant thing if you keep them within you;
Let them all be fixed upon your lips,

19 So that your trust may be in the LORD;
I have instructed you today, even you.

20 Have I not written to you excellent things
Of counsels and knowledge,

21 That I may make you know the certainty of the words of truth,
That you may answer words of truth
To those who send to you?

22 Do not rob the poor because he *is* poor,
Nor oppress the afflicted at the gate;

23 For the LORD will plead their cause,
And plunder the soul of those who plunder them.

24 Make no friendship with an angry man,
And with a furious man do not go,

25 Lest you learn his ways
And set a snare for your soul.

CULTURE AND SOCIETY

The city gate was the place where trials were conducted, as well as where commercial transactions took place. Warnings about the proper conduct to follow "at the gate" (Prov. 22:22) are directed to those who took part in civic affairs, and to those who held positions of responsibility. The Bible advises those with power to accept God's concern for the poor and weak and make that concern their own (Prov. 29:14).

26 Do not be one of those who shakes
    hands in a pledge,
    One of those who is surety for debts;
27 If you have nothing *with which* to pay,
    Why should he take away your bed
    from under you?

28 Do not remove the ancient landmark
    Which your fathers have set.

29 Do you see a man *who* excels in his
    work?
    He will stand before kings;
    He will not stand before unknown
    men.

23

1 When you sit down to eat with a
    ruler,
    Consider carefully what *is* before you;
2 And put a knife to your throat
    If you *are* a man given to appetite.
3 Do not desire his delicacies,
    For they *are* deceptive food.

4 Do not overwork to be rich;
    Because of your own understanding,
    cease!
5 Will you set your eyes on that which is
    not?
    For *riches* certainly make themselves
    wings;
    They fly away like an eagle *toward*
    heaven.

6 Do not eat the bread of a miser,[a]
    Nor desire his delicacies;
7 For as he thinks in his heart, so *is* he.
    "Eat and drink!" he says to you,
    But his heart is not with you.
8 The morsel you have eaten, you will
    vomit up,
    And waste your pleasant words.

9 Do not speak in the hearing of a fool,
    For he will despise the wisdom of your
    words.

10 Do not remove the ancient landmark,
    Nor enter the fields of the fatherless;
11 For their Redeemer *is* mighty;
    He will plead their cause against you.

12 Apply your heart to instruction,
    And your ears to words of knowledge.

13 Do not withhold correction from a
    child,
    For *if* you beat him with a rod, he will
    not die.
14 You shall beat him with a rod,
    And deliver his soul from hell.[a]

15 My son, if your heart is wise,
    My heart will rejoice—indeed, I
    myself;
16 Yes, my inmost being will rejoice
    When your lips speak right things.

17 Do not let your heart envy sinners,
    But *be zealous* for the fear of the LORD
    all the day;
18 For surely there is a hereafter,
    And your hope will not be cut off.

19 Hear, my son, and be wise;
    And guide your heart in the way.
20 Do not mix with winebibbers,
    Or with gluttonous eaters of meat;
21 For the drunkard and the glutton will
    come to poverty,
    And drowsiness will clothe *a man*
    with rags.

22 Listen to your father who begot you,
    And do not despise your mother when
    she is old.

23 Buy the truth, and do not sell *it*,
    Also wisdom and instruction and
    understanding.

24 The father of the righteous will
    greatly rejoice,
    And he who begets a wise *child* will
    delight in him.
25 Let your father and your mother be
    glad,
    And let her who bore you rejoice.

26 My son, give me your heart,
    And let your eyes observe my ways.
27 For a harlot *is* a deep pit,
    And a seductress *is* a narrow well.
28 She also lies in wait as *for* a victim,
    And increases the unfaithful among
    men.

29 Who has woe?
    Who has sorrow?
    Who has contentions?
    Who has complaints?
    Who has wounds without cause?
    Who has redness of eyes?

23:6 [a]Literally *one who has an evil eye*
23:14 [a]Or *Sheol*

30 Those who linger long at the wine,
Those who go in search of mixed wine.
31 Do not look on the wine when it is red,
When it sparkles in the cup,
When it swirls around smoothly;
32 At the last it bites like a serpent,
And stings like a viper.
33 Your eyes will see strange things,
And your heart will utter perverse
things.
34 Yes, you will be like one who lies down
in the midst of the sea,
Or like one who lies at the top of the
mast, *saying:*
35 "They have struck me, *but* I was not
hurt;
They have beaten me, but I did not
feel *it.*
When shall I awake, that I may seek
another *drink?*"

24

1 Do not be envious of evil men,
Nor desire to be with them;
2 For their heart devises violence,
And their lips talk of troublemaking.

3 Through wisdom a house is built,
And by understanding it is
established;
4 By knowledge the rooms are filled
With all precious and pleasant riches.

5 A wise man *is* strong,
Yes, a man of knowledge increases
strength;
6 For by wise counsel you will wage
your own war,
And in a multitude of counselors *there
is* safety.

7 Wisdom *is* too lofty for a fool;
He does not open his mouth in the
gate.

8 He who plots to do evil
Will be called a schemer.
9 The devising of foolishness *is* sin,
And the scoffer *is* an abomination to
men.

10 *If* you faint in the day of adversity,
Your strength *is* small.

11 Deliver *those who* are drawn toward
death,
And hold back *those* stumbling to the
slaughter.

12 If you say, "Surely we did not know
this,"
Does not He who weighs the hearts
consider *it?*
He who keeps your soul, does He *not*
know *it?*
And will He *not* render to *each* man
according to his deeds?

13 My son, eat honey because *it is* good,
And the honeycomb *which is* sweet to
your taste;
14 So *shall* the knowledge of wisdom *be*
to your soul;
If you have found *it,* there is a
prospect,
And your hope will not be cut off.

15 Do not lie in wait, O wicked *man,*
against the dwelling of the
righteous;
Do not plunder his resting place;
16 For a righteous *man* may fall seven
times
And rise again,
But the wicked shall fall by calamity.

17 Do not rejoice when your enemy falls,
And do not let your heart be glad
when he stumbles;
18 Lest the LORD see *it,* and it displease
Him,
And He turn away His wrath from
him.

19 Do not fret because of evildoers,
Nor be envious of the wicked;
20 For there will be no prospect for the
evil *man;*
The lamp of the wicked will be put
out.

21 My son, fear the LORD and the king;
Do not associate with those given to
change;
22 For their calamity will rise suddenly,
And who knows the ruin those two
can bring?

Further Sayings of the Wise

23 These *things* also *belong* to the wise:

It is not good to show partiality in
judgment.
24 He who says to the wicked, "You *are*
righteous,"
Him the people will curse;
Nations will abhor him.

25 But those who rebuke *the wicked* will
    have delight,
    And a good blessing will come upon
    them.

26 He who gives a right answer kisses
    the lips.

27 Prepare your outside work,
    Make it fit for yourself in the field;
    And afterward build your house.

28 Do not be a witness against your
    neighbor without cause,
    For would you deceive[a] with your lips?

29 Do not say, "I will do to him just as he
    has done to me;
    I will render to the man according to
    his work."

30 I went by the field of the lazy *man,*
    And by the vineyard of the man
    devoid of understanding;

31 And there it was, all overgrown with
    thorns;
    Its surface was covered with nettles;
    Its stone wall was broken down.

32 When I saw *it,* I considered *it* well;
    I looked on *it and* received instruction:

33 A little sleep, a little slumber,
    A little folding of the hands to rest;

34 So shall your poverty come *like* a
    prowler,
    And your need like an armed man.

24:28 ᵃSeptuagint and Vulgate read *Do not
deceive.*

The Wisdom of Agur and Lemuel

The final two chapters of Proverbs are attributed to men named Agur and Lemuel. Neither of these men are mentioned elsewhere.
Appearing in both attributions (Prov. 30:1;
31:1) is the Hebrew word *massa'*, which can
be translated as "burden" or "utterance," as it
is used by the prophets (Is. 17:1; 19:1). The
word might also be the name of a place—
Massa (Gen. 25:14; 1 Chr. 1:30). If so, the
attributions might associate Agur and Lemuel
with a country or city named "Massa." For instance, Prov. 31:1 would begin, "The words of
Lemuel, king of Massa, which his mother
taught him."

Even if these teachers are not from a
place called Massa, they do not appear to be

Israelite. There was no King Lemuel in Israel;
and the name "Agur" is not formed in a typical
Hebrew fashion. Agur's name does appear in
Sabean inscriptions, and in light of that foreign
source, it is interesting that the teachings of
Agur include some of the most religiously ori-
ented of all the proverbs in the book.

■ Proverbs 30:1—31:31

Proverbs
The Wisdom of Agur

30 :1 The words of Agur the son of
Jakeh, *his* utterance. This man declared to Ithiel—to Ithiel and Ucal:

2   Surely I *am* more stupid than *any*
    man,
    And do not have the understanding of
    a man.

3   I neither learned wisdom
    Nor have knowledge of the Holy One.

4   Who has ascended into heaven, or
    descended?
    Who has gathered the wind in His
    fists?
    Who has bound the waters in a
    garment?
    Who has established all the ends of
    the earth?
    What *is* His name, and what *is* His
    Son's name,
    If you know?

5   Every word of God *is* pure;
    He *is* a shield to those who put their
    trust in Him.

6   Do not add to His words,
    Lest He rebuke you, and you be found
    a liar.

7   Two *things* I request of You
    (Deprive me not before I die):

8   Remove falsehood and lies far from
    me;
    Give me neither poverty nor riches—
    Feed me with the food allotted to me;

9   Lest I be full and deny *You,*
    And say, "Who *is* the LORD?"
    Or lest I be poor and steal,
    And profane the name of my God.

10 Do not malign a servant to his
    master,
    Lest he curse you, and you be found
    guilty.

HUMANS IN HEAVEN (Prov. 30:4)

Agur asks in his proverb, "Who has ascended into heaven?" (Prov. 30:1, 4). In the ancient mythology of Mesopotamia and Syria-Palestine, human beings did not enter heaven. The common belief was that the gods had created people for the express purpose of serving on earth. The gods did not have to worry about menial tasks; they had human servants to feed and care for them. The closest humans were allowed to approach heaven was as priests working in the temples.

Myths from Mesopotamia attempt to explain why humans are not in heaven. The story of Adapa is a Mesopotamian myth known from a tablet found at Asshur and at Tell el-Amarna, Egypt, dating from around 1350 B.C. The myth relates how the priest Adapa went to heaven and was offered food that would have made him immortal and allowed him to stay in heaven. He refused the food, for reasons that are not clear, and was cast out of heaven.

The story of Etana is credited as the work of Lu-Nanna, an official in the court of Shulgi, king of Ur (2094–2047 B.C.). It tells how Etana tried to reach heaven by flying up on the back of an eagle, but the gods threw him back to earth. Heaven is for gods; earth is for humans.

In contrast to these Mesopotamian myths is the story of Elijah. This prophet of Yahweh was so important that he was taken, while still alive, into heaven by God (2 Kin. 2:1, 11, 12). Unlike other humans, this one person was worthy of heaven. The story would have been more wondrous in Elijah's time than now, since people then did not think that humans, living or dead, were allowed into the realm of the gods. Agur, in his proverb, is skeptical that heaven is accessible to humans—it is God's realm (Prov. 30:4).

---

11 *There is* a generation *that* curses its
  father,
  And does not bless its mother.
12 *There is* a generation *that is* pure in
  its own eyes,
  Yet is not washed from its filthiness.
13 *There is* a generation—oh, how lofty
  are their eyes!
  And their eyelids are lifted up.
14 *There is* a generation whose teeth *are
  like* swords,
  And whose fangs *are like* knives,
  To devour the poor from off the
  earth,
  And the needy from *among* men.

15 The leech has two daughters—
  Give *and* Give!

  There are three *things that* are never
  satisfied,
  Four never say, "Enough!":
16 The grave,ᵃ
  The barren womb,
  The earth *that* is not satisfied with
  water—
  And the fire never says, "Enough!"

17 The eye *that* mocks *his* father,
  And scorns obedience to *his* mother,

The ravens of the valley will pick it
  out,
  And the young eagles will eat it.

18 There are three *things which* are too
  wonderful for me,
  Yes, four *which* I do not understand:
19 The way of an eagle in the air,
  The way of a serpent on a rock,
  The way of a ship in the midst of the
  sea,
  And the way of a man with a virgin.

20 This *is* the way of an adulterous
  woman:
  She eats and wipes her mouth,
  And says, "I have done no
  wickedness."

21 For three *things* the earth is
  perturbed,
  Yes, for four it cannot bear up:
22 For a servant when he reigns,
  A fool when he is filled with food,
23 A hateful *woman* when she is married,
  And a maidservant who succeeds her
  mistress.

30:16 ᵃOr *Sheol*

24 There are four *things which* are little
　　on the earth,
　　But they *are* exceedingly wise:
25 The ants *are* a people not strong,
　　Yet they prepare their food in the
　　　summer;
26 The rock badgers[a] are a feeble folk,
　　Yet they make their homes in the
　　　crags;
27 The locusts have no king,
　　Yet they all advance in ranks;
28 The spider[a] skillfully grasps with its
　　hands,
　　And it is in kings' palaces.

29 There are three *things which* are
　　majestic in pace,
　　Yes, four *which* are stately in walk:
30 A lion, *which is* mighty among beasts
　　And does not turn away from any;
31 A greyhound,[a]
　　A male goat also,
　　And a king *whose* troops *are* with
　　him.[b]

32 If you have been foolish in exalting
　　yourself,
　　Or if you have devised evil, *put your*
　　hand on *your* mouth.
33 For *as* the churning of milk produces
　　butter,
　　And wringing the nose produces blood,
　　So the forcing of wrath produces
　　strife.

The Words of King Lemuel's Mother

31 ¹The words of King Lemuel, the ut-
　　terance which his mother taught
him:

2 　What, my son?
　　And what, son of my womb?
　　And what, son of my vows?

30:26 ᵃOr *hyraxes*　　30:28 ᵃOr *lizard*
30:31 ᵃExact identity unknown　ᵇA Jewish tradition
reads *a king against whom there is no uprising.*
31:8 ᵃLiterally *sons of passing away*
31:10 ᵃVerses 10 through 31 are an alphabetic
acrostic in Hebrew (compare Psalm 119).　ᵇLiterally *a
wife of valor,* in the sense of all forms of excellence

3 　Do not give your strength to women,
　　Nor your ways to that which destroys
　　　kings.

4 　*It is* not for kings, O Lemuel,
　　It is not for kings to drink wine,
　　Nor for princes intoxicating drink;
5 　Lest they drink and forget the law,
　　And pervert the justice of all the
　　　afflicted.
6 　Give strong drink to him who is
　　perishing,
　　And wine to those who are bitter of
　　heart.
7 　Let him drink and forget his poverty,
　　And remember his misery no more.

8 　Open your mouth for the speechless,
　　In the cause of all *who are* appointed
　　to die.[a]
9 　Open your mouth, judge righteously,
　　And plead the cause of the poor and
　　needy.

The Virtuous Wife

10 Who[a] can find a virtuous[b] wife?
　　For her worth *is* far above rubies.
11 The heart of her husband safely trusts
　　her;
　　So he will have no lack of gain.
12 She does him good and not evil
　　All the days of her life.
13 She seeks wool and flax,
　　And willingly works with her hands.
14 She is like the merchant ships,
　　She brings her food from afar.
15 She also rises while it is yet night,
　　And provides food for her household,
　　And a portion for her maidservants.
16 She considers a field and buys it;
　　From her profits she plants a
　　vineyard.
17 She girds herself with strength,
　　And strengthens her arms.
18 She perceives that her merchandise *is*
　　good,
　　And her lamp does not go out by
　　night.

MARRIAGE AND FAMILY

*The status of women in the ancient world was not the same in every culture. For
example, Roman women were more independent than Greek women. The Book of
Proverbs describes the "virtuous wife" (Prov. 31:10) as a woman who has authority over
her household economy and is free to do many different things. She is industrious
(31:13–15) and resourceful (31:16–19).*

WINE OR INTOXICATING DRINK (Prov. 31:4)

One characteristic of Hebrew poetry is the repetition of similar thoughts in couplets, such as the repeated objects "wine" and "intoxicating drink" in Prov. 31:4. These two items appear in parallel, demonstrating that the author considered them in more or less the same light. In other passages wine and intoxicating drink are similarly mentioned together (Lev. 10:9; 1 Sam. 1:15).

There is evidence, from later times, that the difference between "wine" and "intoxicating drink" was one of concentration rather than of formula. The juice of the grapes was stored in full strength in jars soon after the squeezing process. When it came time to drink the juice, water was mixed with it. The amount of water added determined whether the product was considered "wine" or "intoxicating drink." In New Testament times we know that the most common mixture for "wine" was three or more parts of water for each portion of juice.

"Intoxicating drink" was a mixture of juice and water with a stronger portion of juice. Drinking the juice without diluting it was thought to make one mad. So it was that Hannah protested to the priest Eli that her actions were due to grief, not to drunkenness, because she had not been drinking an "intoxicating drink" or even wine (1 Sam. 1:15, 16). Similarly, kings and princes were warned to abstain from anything that would obscure their reason, causing them to fail in their responsibilities of leadership (Prov. 31:4, 5).

---

19   She stretches out her hands to the
         distaff,
      And her hand holds the spindle.
20   She extends her hand to the poor,
      Yes, she reaches out her hands to the
         needy.
21   She is not afraid of snow for her
         household,
      For all her household *is* clothed with
         scarlet.
22   She makes tapestry for herself;
      Her clothing *is* fine linen and purple.
23   Her husband is known in the gates,
      When he sits among the elders of the
         land.
24   She makes linen garments and sells
         them,
      And supplies sashes for the
         merchants.
25   Strength and honor *are* her clothing;
      She shall rejoice in time to come.
26   She opens her mouth with wisdom,
      And on her tongue *is* the law of
         kindness.
27   She watches over the ways of her
         household,
      And does not eat the bread of idleness.
28   Her children rise up and call her
         blessed;
      Her husband *also,* and he praises her:
29   "Many daughters have done well,
      But you excel them all."
30   Charm *is* deceitful and beauty *is*
         passing,

But a woman *who* fears the LORD, she
   shall be praised.
31   Give her of the fruit of her hands,
      And let her own works praise her in
         the gates.

The Book of Job

The Book of Job is a work of unparalleled magnificence and power. Its depth of thought and feeling, its shining moments of insight, and the transcendent poetry of the central section all give this book a unique place, not only in Scripture but in all of world literature.

This book also stands apart in terms of its historical setting. On the one hand, certain aspects of Job's life sound much like the life of Abraham. His wealth, like Abraham's, was based on numbers of domestic animals. Like Abraham, he offered his own sacrifices to God, without a priestly intermediary. For reasons such as these, many scholars have set the book in Abraham's time during the Middle Bronze Age (2000–1500 B.C.).

Nevertheless, the Book of Job itself offers no historical specificity. Within the Old Testament, where geographical and chronological specificity are common, the introduction of Job has all the vagueness of the traditional opening "Once upon a time, in a far away land." We are told only of "a man in the land of Uz, whose name was Job" (Job 1:1).

The location of the land of Uz is uncertain,

but it was more likely in Edom than in Israel. The name Uz appears several times as an Edomite name (Gen. 36:28; 1 Chr. 1:42). Associating Uz with Edom makes sense. Job's three friends appear as wisdom teachers, and Edom was famous for its wise men (see "Wisdom in the Ancient Near East" at Prov. 22:17). Indeed Job's first friend, Eliphaz the Temanite, also has an Edomite name (see Gen. 36:15, 16). If Job was an Edomite, then he would not come from the time of Abraham, since the Edomites descended from Abraham's grandson Esau.

Besides a geographical setting that is possibly Edomite and at least non-Israelite, all that the Book of Job provides is the intellectual setting of the wisdom tradition. The wisdom setting is by far the most important context. The book both speaks within and speaks against the teaching of the sages, as represented by Job's three friends Eliphaz, Bildad, and Zophar. As these friends try to "comfort" Job, they present the wisdom worldview in speeches that are little more than strings of proverbs. And when Job opposes the friends, he opposes some of wisdom's basic assumptions.

Most significantly, Job rejects wisdom's view that the world is orderly, that all is arranged according to just principles. His tragedy is not just. Righteousness does not always result in good fortune. Bad things do happen to good people. His friends' argument—that Job must have sinned to deserve such suffering—only indicates the poverty of this particular aspect of wisdom teaching. Job also rejects the idea that wisdom is to be sought from tradition. If his three friends represent the teachings of tradition, he wants nothing to do with it (Job 12:2, 3).

Nevertheless, Job does not give up his search for enlightenment and never completely gives up his hope for justice. Nor does he surrender his faith in knowledge by experience. Indeed, it is experience that he seeks: he demands that he be allowed to see God, to present his complaint before Him. Job's wish is granted in God's majestic appearance and speech (Job 38—41). Not all of Job's questions are answered, but it is enough for Job to have experienced God Himself.

The Book of Job belongs in the context of Israel's wisdom tradition, but at what point in the long history of Israel's wisdom? The story of Job was evidently known to the prophet Ezekiel, preaching in exile in Babylon, who used Job as an example of righteousness (Ezek. 14:14, 20). More certain than when Job's story takes place or when the Book of Job was

written is that it came to prominence during and after the Babylonian captivity. It is not hard to imagine why. A people stunned by the destruction of all that they had held dear—their nation, their city, their temple—dealt with the same questions that Job himself confronted.

Since a definite historical setting for the Book of Job is unknown, one can read the book in light of the suffering of the Exile and the questions the exiles faced. The prologue (Job 1; 2) concerns the question of Job's motive for serving God. Satan insinuates that people lead upright lives because of selfishness, not because of love for God. God, however, expresses His complete confidence in His servant Job before the hosts of heaven, citing Job to prove that a person can live a blameless and upright life.

▼   ■ Job 1:1—2:13

Job
Job and His Family in Uz

1:1 There was a man in the land of Uz, whose name *was* Job; and that man was blameless and upright, and one who feared God and shunned evil. ²And seven sons and three daughters were born to him. ³Also, his possessions were seven thousand sheep, three thousand camels, five hundred yoke of oxen, five hundred female donkeys, and a very large household, so that this man was the greatest of all the people of the East.

⁴And his sons would go and feast *in their* houses, each on his *appointed* day, and would send and invite their three sisters to eat and drink with them. ⁵So it was, when the days of feasting had run their course, that Job would send and sanctify them, and he would rise early in the morning and offer burnt offerings *according to* the number of them all. For Job said, "It may be that my sons have sinned and cursedᵃ God in their hearts." Thus Job did regularly.

Satan Attacks Job's Character

⁶Now there was a day when the sons of God came to present themselves before the LORD, and Satanᵃ also came among them. ⁷And the LORD said to Satan, "From where do you come?"

1:5 ᵃLiterally *blessed*, but used here in the evil sense, and so in verse 11 and 2:5, 9
1:6 ᵃLiterally *the Adversary*, and so throughout this book

ENTER THE ADVERSARY—SATAN (Job 1:6–12)

In the scenes of the heavenly assembly (Job 1; 2), only one heavenly being, other than God Himself, is identified. This character is referred to in Hebrew only by his title, which means "the adversary." In English he is called "Satan" (Job 1:6; 2:1). The Adversary is a divine figure, one of the "sons of God," who serves under and reports to Yahweh.

In the human royal courts of the ancient Near East, one officer of the king's court was assigned to seek out and report any behavior contrary to the laws or proclamations of the ruler. The Adversary performed this office for Yahweh in heaven, and so could be considered "the divine prosecuting attorney." It was his responsibility to bring charges and produce proofs. The case being brought against Job is a test, as both God and the Adversary know that Job has been perfect (Job 1:8).

The behavior of the Adversary conforms to the accepted manner of secondary level deities in Canaanite mythology. The Adversary differs in one sense from the deities portrayed in the Ugaritic myths: he accepts orders from his superior and carries them out only within the guidelines established by God, never breaking the rules imposed upon him. The responsibility for Job's ordeal lies with God, who instigated the debate and authorized the activity proposed and carried out by the Adversary (Job 1:12; 2:3).

In the Book of Job the Adversary is a member of the divine court in good standing. The idea for this character could have had its source in almost any human royal court. Later, the idea developed into Satan as the embodiment of all evil, as is found in some New Testament passages (Rom. 16:20). Such a development begins to show in the Chronicler's figure of Satan as a divine being opposing the will of God (1 Chr. 21:1).

So Satan answered the LORD and said, "From going to and fro on the earth, and from walking back and forth on it."

[8]Then the LORD said to Satan, "Have you considered My servant Job, that *there is* none like him on the earth, a blameless and upright man, one who fears God and shuns evil?"

[9]So Satan answered the LORD and said, "Does Job fear God for nothing? [10]Have You not made a hedge around him, around his household, and around all that he has on every side? You have blessed the work of his hands, and his possessions have increased in the land. [11]But now, stretch out Your hand and touch all that he has, and he will surely curse You to Your face!"

[12]And the LORD said to Satan, "Behold, all that he has *is* in your power; only do not lay a hand on his *person*."

So Satan went out from the presence of the LORD.

Job Loses His Property and Children

[13]Now there was a day when his sons and daughters *were* eating and drinking wine in their oldest brother's house; [14]and a messenger came to Job and said, "The oxen were plowing and the donkeys feeding beside them, [15]when the Sabeans[a] raided *them* and took them away—indeed they have killed the servants with the edge of the sword; and I alone have escaped to tell you!"

[16]While he *was* still speaking, another also came and said, "The fire of God fell from heaven and burned up the sheep and

1:15 [a]Literally *Sheba* (compare 6:19)

GEOGRAPHY AND ENVIRONMENT

The raiders who attacked Job may have come from Arabia, south of Israel. Sabeans (Job 1:15) are identified with Saba or Sheba in south Arabia, the home of the queen who visited Solomon (1 Kin. 10:1). The Chaldean raiders (Job 1:17) were not the rulers of the Neo-Babylonian Empire, but rather tribes living in northern Arabia. Such marauders made the wilderness dangerous, even though it might have looked tranquil.

POTSHERDS FROM THE ASHES (Job 2:8)

It may seem curious that Job would scrape himself with a "potsherd" (Job 2:8). Potsherds, though, were one of the most common items in the ancient world.

Clay was used to make everything from cooking pots to large storage jars. Containers were formed by hand, while being rotated to help the forming process. Once crafted, large numbers of pots were collected in ovens, where they were hardened by high-temperature baking.

Large pots, which could reach over 6 feet in height, had pointed bases and were buried in the ground, with the earth becoming the most stable of all settings. Most pots, however, were easily held in one hand. The life expectancy of these pots, especially those used daily, was short, perhaps less than a year. Once a pot was broken, its sherds (or shards) were left where they fell. Archaeologists collect and use these broken pieces to locate and date ancient sites.

That Job used a "potsherd" to scrape his sores tells us that he was sitting in an area of habitation, where pots had been broken. Evidently that potsherd was a broken piece from a cooking pot, since he was sitting among the ashes.

---

the servants, and consumed them; and I alone have escaped to tell you!"

17While he *was* still speaking, another also came and said, "The Chaldeans formed three bands, raided the camels and took them away, yes, and killed the servants with the edge of the sword; and I alone have escaped to tell you!"

18While he *was* still speaking, another also came and said, "Your sons and daughters *were* eating and drinking wine in their oldest brother's house, 19and suddenly a great wind came from across[a] the wilderness and struck the four corners of the house, and it fell on the young people, and they are dead; and I alone have escaped to tell you!"

20Then Job arose, tore his robe, and shaved his head; and he fell to the ground and worshiped. 21And he said:

"Naked I came from my mother's
    womb,
And naked shall I return there.
The LORD gave, and the LORD has
    taken away;
Blessed be the name of the LORD."

22In all this Job did not sin nor charge God with wrong.

Satan Attacks Job's Health

2 1Again there was a day when the sons of God came to present themselves before the LORD, and Satan came also among them to present himself before the LORD. 2And the LORD said to Satan, "From where do you come?"

Satan answered the LORD and said, "From going to and fro on the earth, and from walking back and forth on it."

3Then the LORD said to Satan, "Have you considered My servant Job, that *there is* none like him on the earth, a blameless and upright man, one who fears God and shuns evil? And still he holds fast to his integrity, although you incited Me against him, to destroy him without cause."

4So Satan answered the LORD and said, "Skin for skin! Yes, all that a man has he will give for his life. 5But stretch out Your hand now, and touch his bone and his flesh, and he will surely curse You to Your face!"

6And the LORD said to Satan, "Behold, he *is* in your hand, but spare his life."

7So Satan went out from the presence of the LORD, and struck Job with painful boils from the sole of his foot to the crown of his head. 8And he took for himself a potsherd with which to scrape himself while he sat in the midst of the ashes.

9Then his wife said to him, "Do you still hold fast to your integrity? Curse God and die!"

10But he said to her, "You speak as one of the foolish women speaks. Shall we indeed accept good from God, and shall we not accept adversity?" In all this Job did not sin with his lips.

1:19 [a]Septuagint omits *across.*

Job's Three Friends

[11]Now when Job's three friends heard of all this adversity that had come upon him, each one came from his own place— Eliphaz the Temanite, Bildad the Shuhite, and Zophar the Naamathite. For they had made an appointment together to come and mourn with him, and to comfort him. [12]And when they raised their eyes from afar, and did not recognize him, they lifted their voices and wept; and each one tore his robe and sprinkled dust on his head toward heaven. [13]So they sat down with him on the ground seven days and seven nights, and no one spoke a word to him, for they saw that *his* grief was very great.

Job: May That Day Be Darkness

When Job finally breaks his silence, his words express doubt about the entire wisdom worldview (ch. 3). The wisdom teachers taught first of all that the world was orderly and just. Israel's sages, seeking to incorporate God more fully into the wisdom tradition, emphasized God's role as the wise Creator of this good world (see Prov. 8:22–31). Job's speech, while never actually accusing God, undercuts this comforting picture of benevolent creation.

In the Bible, God begins creation by making light and darkness and naming them day and night (Gen. 1:3–5). Job's speech reverses this picture by calling down curses on day and night (Job 3:3–8) and rejecting the gift of light (3:20, 24). In Genesis, God rested after creating the world, but Job finds no rest on earth (3:26) and wishes for the only rest he can imagine—the rest of death (3:13, 17).

■ Job 3:1–26

Job
Job Deplores His Birth

3:1 After this Job opened his mouth and cursed the day of his *birth*. [2]And Job spoke, and said:

3   "May the day perish on which I was
         born,
     And the night *in which* it was said,
         'A male child is conceived.'
4   May that day be darkness;
     May God above not seek it,
     Nor the light shine upon it.
5   May darkness and the shadow of
         death claim it;

     May a cloud settle on it;
     May the blackness of the day terrify
         it.
6   *As for* that night, may darkness seize
         it;
     May it not rejoice[a] among the days of
         the year,
     May it not come into the number of
         the months.
7   Oh, may that night be barren!
     May no joyful shout come into it!
8   May those curse it who curse the day,
     Those who are ready to arouse
         Leviathan.
9   May the stars of its morning be dark;
     May it look for light, but *have* none,
     And not see the dawning of the day;
10   Because it did not shut up the doors of
         my *mother's* womb,
     Nor hide sorrow from my eyes.

11   "Why did I not die at birth?
     Why did I *not* perish when I came
         from the womb?
12   Why did the knees receive me?
     Or why the breasts, that I should
         nurse?
13   For now I would have lain still and
         been quiet,
     I would have been asleep;
     Then I would have been at rest
14   With kings and counselors of the
         earth,
     Who built ruins for themselves,
15   Or with princes who had gold,
     Who filled their houses *with* silver;
16   Or *why* was I not hidden like a
         stillborn child,
     Like infants who never saw light?
17   There the wicked cease *from*
         troubling,
     And there the weary are at rest.
18   *There* the prisoners rest together;
     They do not hear the voice of the
         oppressor.
19   The small and great are there,
     And the servant *is* free from his
         master.

20   "Why is light given to him who is in
         misery,
     And life to the bitter of soul,
21   Who long for death, but it does not
         come,

3:6 [a]Septuagint, Syriac, Targum, and Vulgate read *be joined.*

And search for it more than hidden
treasures;

22 Who rejoice exceedingly,
And are glad when they can find the
grave?

23 *Why is light given* to a man whose
way is hidden,
And whom God has hedged in?

24 For my sighing comes before I eat,[a]
And my groanings pour out like water.

25 For the thing I greatly feared has
come upon me,
And what I dreaded has happened to
me.

26 I am not at ease, nor am I quiet;
I have no rest, for trouble comes."

Eliphaz: Who Ever Perished Being Innocent?

After Job's first speech (ch. 3), the Book
of Job proceeds with three rounds of
speeches: each friend speaks in turn and is
answered by Job. As the first round (4:1—
14:22) begins, Eliphaz the Temanite defends
the traditional wisdom view of an orderly world
(chs. 4; 5).

In this just and orderly world, the sages
taught, righteousness is rewarded and wickedness is punished. Many proverbs express this
notion. For instance, Prov. 10:27 says, "The
fear of the LORD prolongs days, But the years
of the wicked will be shortened" (see also Prov.
10:3, 24, 28, 30). Eliphaz expresses this view
as an attempt at comfort: Job's own fear of
the Lord should be his hope (Job 4:6).

In the midst of his traditional teachings,
Eliphaz includes a surprising account of an angelic vision (4:12—5:7). This account is curious, first, because wisdom teachers did not
usually rely on direct revelations, and second
because the angel's message that humans
cannot be righteous (4:17) is also uncharacteristic of wisdom. As he closes his speech,
however, Eliphaz returns to the traditional wisdom theme that God will reward righteousness.

■ Job 4:1—5:27

Job
Eliphaz: Job Has Sinned

4 :1 Then Eliphaz the Temanite answered and said:

---

2 "*If* one attempts a word with you, will
you become weary?
But who can withhold himself from
speaking?

3 Surely you have instructed many,
And you have strengthened weak
hands.

4 Your words have upheld him who was
stumbling,
And you have strengthened the feeble
knees;

5 But now it comes upon you, and you
are weary;
It touches you, and you are troubled.

6 *Is* not your reverence your confidence?
And the integrity of your ways your
hope?

7 "Remember now, who *ever* perished
being innocent?
Or where were the upright *ever* cut
off?

8 Even as I have seen,
Those who plow iniquity
And sow trouble reap the same.

9 By the blast of God they perish,
And by the breath of His anger they
are consumed.

10 The roaring of the lion,
The voice of the fierce lion,
And the teeth of the young lions are
broken.

11 The old lion perishes for lack of prey,
And the cubs of the lioness are
scattered.

12 "Now a word was secretly brought to
me,
And my ear received a whisper of it.

13 In disquieting thoughts from the
visions of the night,
When deep sleep falls on men,

14 Fear came upon me, and trembling,
Which made all my bones shake.

15 Then a spirit passed before my face;
The hair on my body stood up.

16 It stood still,
But I could not discern its appearance.
A form *was* before my eyes;
There was silence;
Then I heard a voice *saying:*

17 'Can a mortal be more righteous than
God?
Can a man be more pure than his
Maker?

18 If He puts no trust in His servants,
If He charges His angels with error,

HUMANS ARE NOT PERFECT BEFORE GOD (Job 4:18, 19)

Eliphaz employs a kind of rabbinic logic which argues from an example of greater importance to one of lesser importance. If the point is true of the greater, then it should be true of the lesser. In this case, he argues from angels to humans.

God's angels are His "servants" (Job 4:18). The angels were heavenly beings who carried out the orders of the superior gods. In the Old Testament and in texts from Ugarit, these messengers do exactly as they are commanded; they have no free will. This picture of angels sets up the first stage of Eliphaz's argument.

However powerful they may be, the angels are only servants of God and are not perfect as is God. However innocent of wrongdoing angels may appear to humans, before God even they are not without fault. How, then, can Job, a mere human being who is less than the obedient angels (Job 4:19), claim to be innocent before God? Eliphaz was convinced that no human could claim to be just before God since the angels, who are greater than Job, cannot make such a claim.

19 How much more those who dwell in
    houses of clay,
   Whose foundation is in the dust,
   Who are crushed before a moth?
20 They are broken in pieces from
    morning till evening;
   They perish forever, with no one
    regarding.
21 Does not their own excellence go
    away?
   They die, even without wisdom.'

Eliphaz: Job Is Chastened by God

5 1 "Call out now;
    Is there anyone who will answer
     you?
   And to which of the holy ones will you
    turn?
2 For wrath kills a foolish man,
   And envy slays a simple one.
3 I have seen the foolish taking root,
   But suddenly I cursed his dwelling
    place.
4 His sons are far from safety,
   They are crushed in the gate,
   And *there is* no deliverer.
5 Because the hungry eat up his
    harvest,
   Taking it even from the thorns,[a]
   And a snare snatches their
    substance.[b]
6 For affliction does not come from the
    dust,
   Nor does trouble spring from the
    ground;
7 Yet man is born to trouble,
   As the sparks fly upward.

8 "But as for me, I would seek God,
   And to God I would commit my
    cause—
9 Who does great things, and
    unsearchable,
   Marvelous things without number.
10 He gives rain on the earth,
   And sends waters on the fields.
11 He sets on high those who are lowly,
   And those who mourn are lifted to
    safety.
12 He frustrates the devices of the crafty,
   So that their hands cannot carry out
    their plans.
13 He catches the wise in their own
    craftiness,
   And the counsel of the cunning comes
    quickly upon them.
14 They meet with darkness in the
    daytime,
   And grope at noontime as in the
    night.
15 But He saves the needy from the
    sword,
   From the mouth of the mighty,
   And from their hand.
16 So the poor have hope,
   And injustice shuts her mouth.

17 "Behold, happy *is* the man whom God
    corrects;

5:5 [a]Septuagint reads *They shall not be taken from
evil men;* Vulgate reads *And the armed man shall take
him by violence.*   [b]Septuagint reads *The might shall
draw them off;* Vulgate reads *And the thirsty shall
drink up their riches.*

Therefore do not despise the
chastening of the Almighty.

18 For He bruises, but He binds up;
He wounds, but His hands make
whole.

19 He shall deliver you in six troubles,
Yes, in seven no evil shall touch you.

20 In famine He shall redeem you from
death,
And in war from the power of the
sword.

21 You shall be hidden from the scourge
of the tongue,
And you shall not be afraid of
destruction when it comes.

22 You shall laugh at destruction and
famine,
And you shall not be afraid of the
beasts of the earth.

23 For you shall have a covenant with
the stones of the field,
And the beasts of the field shall be at
peace with you.

24 You shall know that your tent *is* in
peace;
You shall visit your dwelling and find
nothing amiss.

25 You shall also know that your
descendants *shall be* many,
And your offspring like the grass of
the earth.

26 You shall come to the grave at a full
age,
As a sheaf of grain ripens in its
season.

27 Behold, this we have searched out;
It *is* true.
Hear it, and know for yourself."

Job: What Does Your Arguing Prove?

The traditional wisdom expressed by Eliphaz—that in an orderly world the righteous
will prosper—did nothing for Job. Job knows
that he is innocent and yet is suffering. Job is
as disappointed by Eliphaz's heavy-handed comfort as a desert caravan is disappointed by a
dry stream (6:15–20). Job rejects his friend's
words of traditional wisdom as having no bearing on his particular case (6:24–26).

In this second speech (chs. 7; 8), Job still
does not explicitly accuse God. Nevertheless,
his words again reveal his struggle against the
traditional picture of God. In ch. 3 Job questioned the goodness of God's creation. In ch. 7
he questions God's benevolence. The great

hymn of Ps. 8 expresses wonder that God
should love humanity—"What is man that You
are mindful of him?" (Ps. 8:4)—but Job turns
that sentiment on its head and wishes that
God would leave humanity alone. "What is
man, that You should exalt him . . . And test
him every moment?" (Job 7:17, 18).

■ Job 6:1—7:21

Job
Job: My Complaint Is Just

6 :1 Then Job answered and said:

2 "Oh, that my grief were fully weighed,
And my calamity laid with it on the
scales!

3 For then it would be heavier than the
sand of the sea—
Therefore my words have been rash.

4 For the arrows of the Almighty *are*
within me;
My spirit drinks in their poison;
The terrors of God are arrayed against
me.

5 Does the wild donkey bray when it
has grass,
Or does the ox low over its fodder?

6 Can flavorless food be eaten without
salt?
Or is there *any* taste in the white of
an egg?

7 My soul refuses to touch them;
They *are* as loathsome food to me.

8 "Oh, that I might have my request,
That God would grant *me* the thing
that I long for!

9 That it would please God to crush me,
That He would loose His hand and cut
me off!

10 Then I would still have comfort;
Though in anguish I would exult,
He will not spare;
For I have not concealed the words of
the Holy One.

11 "What strength do I have, that I should
hope?
And what *is* my end, that I should
prolong my life?

12 *Is* my strength the strength of stones?
Or is my flesh bronze?

13 *Is* my help not within me?
And is success driven from me?

14 "To him who is afflicted, kindness
should be shown by his friend,

NABONIDUS IN TEMA (Job 6:19)

The city of Tema was at the crossroads of three important trade routes running through northern Arabia. An oasis was nearby, allowing the city to exist in this desert region. Caravans passing through Tema (Job 6:19) would have been familiar with streams that run during the rainy season, but dry up when they are most needed. Such streams were an appropriate illustration for Job to employ in describing his undependable "friends" (Job 6:15-20).

Tema is mentioned in Assyrian sources by the 8th century B.C. Temanite and Sabaean caravans paid tribute to Tiglath-Pileser III (744–727 B.C.). By the end of the 7th century B.C., Tema was in competition with Dedan for control of the incense trade in the region.

The last of the late Babylonian monarchs, Nabonidus (556–539 B.C.), penetrated this area around 553 or 552 B.C. Leaving the capital Babylon to be ruled by his son Belshazzar, Nabonidus camped out at Tema for a decade. It is possible that he saw fit to make Tema his residence for such an extended period in order to control the major trade routes.

Numerous inscriptions, both in Aramaic and in Thamudic (the local Tema script), suggest that Tema continued as a major trading center during the Persian period (559–331 B.C.). Tema in northwest Arabia worked closely with the Sabaeans from Saba (or Sheba) in southwest Arabia to dominate the incense trade. It is natural then that Job should mention Tema and Sheba together (Job 6:19).

Even though he forsakes the fear of
the Almighty.
15 My brothers have dealt deceitfully like
a brook,
Like the streams of the brooks that
pass away,
16 Which are dark because of the ice,
And into which the snow vanishes.
17 When it is warm, they cease to flow;
When it is hot, they vanish from their
place.
18 The paths of their way turn aside,
They go nowhere and perish.
19 The caravans of Tema look,
The travelers of Sheba hope for them.
20 They are disappointed because they
were confident;
They come there and are confused.
21 For now you are nothing,
You see terror and are afraid.
22 Did I ever say, 'Bring *something* to
me'?
Or, 'Offer a bribe for me from your
wealth'?
23 Or, 'Deliver me from the enemy's
hand'?
Or, 'Redeem me from the hand of
oppressors'?
24 "Teach me, and I will hold my tongue;
Cause me to understand wherein I
have erred.
25 How forceful are right words!
But what does your arguing prove?

26 Do you intend to rebuke *my* words,
And the speeches of a desperate one,
which are as wind?
27 Yes, you overwhelm the fatherless,
And you undermine your friend.
28 Now therefore, be pleased to look at
me;
For I would never lie to your face.
29 Yield now, let there be no injustice!
Yes, concede, my righteousness still
stands!
30 Is there injustice on my tongue?
Cannot my taste discern the
unsavory?

Job: My Suffering Is Comfortless

7 ¹ "*Is there* not a time of hard service
for man on earth?
Are not his days also like the days of a
hired man?
2 Like a servant who earnestly desires
the shade,
And like a hired man who eagerly
looks for his wages,
3 So I have been allotted months of
futility,
And wearisome nights have been
appointed to me.
4 When I lie down, I say, 'When shall I
arise,
And the night be ended?'
For I have had my fill of tossing till
dawn.

5   My flesh is caked with worms and
        dust,
     My skin is cracked and breaks out
        afresh.

6   "My days are swifter than a weaver's
        shuttle,
     And are spent without hope.
7   Oh, remember that my life *is* a
        breath!
     My eye will never again see good.
8   The eye of him who sees me will see
        me no *more;*
     While your *eyes* are upon me, I shall
        no longer *be.*
9   *As* the cloud disappears and vanishes
        away,
     So he who goes down to the grave does
        not come up.
10   He shall never return to his house,
     Nor shall his place know him
        anymore.

11   "Therefore I will not restrain my
        mouth;
     I will speak in the anguish of my
        spirit;
     I will complain in the bitterness of my
        soul.
12   *Am* I a sea, or a sea serpent,
     That You set a guard over me?
13   When I say, 'My bed will comfort me,
     My couch will ease my complaint,'
14   Then You scare me with dreams
     And terrify me with visions,
15   So that my soul chooses strangling
     And death rather than my body.[a]
16   I loathe *my life;*
     I would not live forever.
     Let me alone,
     For my days *are but* a breath.

17   "What *is* man, that You should exalt
        him,

That You should set Your heart on
   him,
18   That You should visit him every
        morning,
     And test him every moment?
19   How long?
     Will You not look away from me,
     And let me alone till I swallow my
        saliva?
20   Have I sinned?
     What have I done to You, O watcher of
        men?
     Why have You set me as Your target,
     So that I am a burden to myself?[a]
21   Why then do You not pardon my
        transgression,
     And take away my iniquity?
     For now I will lie down in the dust,
     And You will seek me diligently,
     But I *will* no longer *be.*"

7:15 [a]Literally *my bones*   7:20 [a]Following
Masoretic Text, Targum, and Vulgate; Septuagint and
Jewish tradition read *to You.*

Bildad: Inquire of the Former Age

Job's second friend, Bildad the Shuhite, discards all pretense at offering comfort (ch. 8). Bildad's whole purpose is to defend the traditional wisdom teachings that had been passed from generation to generation. Job's own experience of injustice is unimportant to Bildad, compared with the time-honored teachings of "the former age" and "the things discovered by their fathers" (8:8).

Bildad takes one step beyond the wisdom teaching that the righteous prosper and the wicked suffer. Turning the teaching around, Bildad concludes that Job's children must have been wicked since they died (8:4). Indeed, if Job were really pure, he would not be suffering either (8:6). This reformulation of the teaching might appear logical, but it is unjustified. While biblical wisdom writings, such as appear in Proverbs, do teach that the wicked will suffer, they never permit the reverse reasoning that everyone who suffers is being punished for wickedness.

■ Job 8:1–22

SCIENCE AND TECHNOLOGY

Cloth is woven by passing one thread, the weft, back and forth through fixed threads called the warp. A loom is any device that holds the warp. A shuttle is a spool or frame that carries the weft. It moves back and forth in a repetitive motion, ending its task when the length of cloth is finished. Job compares his passing days to the shuttle shooting to and fro between the warp threads (Job 7:6).

Job
Bildad: Job Should Repent

8 :1 Then Bildad the Shuhite answered and said:

2 "How long will you speak these *things,*
   And the words of your mouth *be like* a
      strong wind?
3 Does God subvert judgment?
   Or does the Almighty pervert justice?
4 If your sons have sinned against Him,
   He has cast them away for their
      transgression.
5 If you would earnestly seek God
   And make your supplication to the
      Almighty,
6 If you *were* pure and upright,
   Surely now He would awake for you,
   And prosper your rightful dwelling
      place.
7 Though your beginning was small,
   Yet your latter end would increase
      abundantly.

8 "For inquire, please, of the former age,
   And consider the things discovered by
      their fathers;
9 For we *were born* yesterday, and know
      nothing,
   Because our days on earth *are* a
      shadow.
10 Will they not teach you and tell you,
   And utter words from their heart?

11 "Can the papyrus grow up without a
      marsh?
   Can the reeds flourish without water?
12 While it *is* yet green *and* not cut
      down,
   It withers before any *other* plant.
13 So *are* the paths of all who forget God;
   And the hope of the hypocrite shall
      perish,
14 Whose confidence shall be cut off,
   And whose trust *is* a spider's web.
15 He leans on his house, but it does not
      stand.
   He holds it fast, but it does not
      endure.
16 He grows green in the sun,
   And his branches spread out in his
      garden.
17 His roots wrap around the rock heap,
   And look for a place in the stones.
18 If he is destroyed from his place,
   Then *it* will deny him, *saying,* 'I have
      not seen you.'

19 "Behold, this is the joy of His way,
   And out of the earth others will grow.
20 Behold, God will not cast away the
      blameless,
   Nor will He uphold the evildoers.
21 He will yet fill your mouth with
      laughing,
   And your lips with rejoicing.
22 Those who hate you will be clothed
      with shame,
   And the dwelling place of the wicked
      will come to nothing."[a]

Job: How Then Can I Answer Him?

In his third speech (chs. 9; 10), Job rejects the whole notion of a just moral order in the world. The righteous do not always prosper, and "the earth is given into the hand of the wicked" (9:24). Job does not see that God makes any distinction between the righteous and the wicked (9:22), and God's power might not always be used for good. The great Creator of the world can also shake the earth and seal off the stars (9:6, 7); the God who fashioned Job can also destroy him (10:8).

Even as Job speaks these despairing words, a part of him refuses to accept this picture of a capricious God. God must be just. Job longs to take his case before God, to plead his innocence in God's presence, but he cannot imagine how a frail human could stand before Almighty God (9:3, 14–16). Believing that God must long for justice, Job envisions a mediator, someone who could stand before God and plead Job's case for him (9:32–35).

▼   ■ Job 9:1—10:22

Job
Job: There Is No Mediator

9 :1 Then Job answered and said:

2 "Truly I know *it is* so,
   But how can a man be righteous
      before God?
3 If one wished to contend with Him,
   He could not answer Him one time out
      of a thousand.
4 *God is* wise in heart and mighty in
      strength.
   Who has hardened *himself* against
      Him and prospered?

8:22 ªLiterally *will not be*

5 He removes the mountains, and they
do not know
When He overturns them in His
anger;

6 He shakes the earth out of its place,
And its pillars tremble;

7 He commands the sun, and it does not
rise;
He seals off the stars;

8 He alone spreads out the heavens,
And treads on the waves of the sea;

9 He made the Bear, Orion, and the
Pleiades,
And the chambers of the south;

10 He does great things past finding out,
Yes, wonders without number.

11 If He goes by me, I do not see *Him;*
If He moves past, I do not perceive
Him;

12 If He takes away, who can hinder
Him?
Who can say to Him, 'What are You
doing?'

13 God will not withdraw His anger,
The allies of the proud[a] lie prostrate
beneath Him.

14 "How then can I answer Him,
And choose my words *to reason* with
Him?

15 For though I were righteous, I could
not answer Him;
I would beg mercy of my Judge.

16 If I called and He answered me,
I would not believe that He was
listening to my voice.

17 For He crushes me with a tempest,
And multiplies my wounds without
cause.

18 He will not allow me to catch my
breath,
But fills me with bitterness.

19 If *it is a matter* of strength, indeed *He
is* strong;
And if of justice, who will appoint my
day *in court?*

20 Though I were righteous, my own
mouth would condemn me;
Though I *were* blameless, it would
prove me perverse.

21 "I am blameless, yet I do not know
myself;
I despise my life.

22 It *is* all one *thing;*
Therefore I say, 'He destroys the
blameless and the wicked.'

23 If the scourge slays suddenly,
He laughs at the plight of the
innocent.

24 The earth is given into the hand of the
wicked.
He covers the faces of its judges.
If it is not *He,* who else could it be?

25 "Now my days are swifter than a
runner;
They flee away, they see no good.

26 They pass by like swift ships,
Like an eagle swooping on its prey.

27 If I say, 'I will forget my complaint,
I will put off my sad face and wear a
smile,'

28 I am afraid of all my sufferings;
I know that You will not hold me
innocent.

29 *If* I am condemned,
Why then do I labor in vain?

30 If I wash myself with snow water,
And cleanse my hands with soap,

31 Yet You will plunge me into the pit,
And my own clothes will abhor me.

32 "For *He is* not a man, as I *am,*
That I may answer Him,
And that we should go to court
together.

33 Nor is there any mediator between us,
Who may lay his hand on us both.

34 Let Him take His rod away from me,
And do not let dread of Him terrify
me.

35 *Then* I would speak and not fear Him,
But it is not so with me.

9:13 [a]Hebrew *rahab*

ARTS AND LITERATURE

*The stars are conventionally grouped into constellations named after mythological figures
(Job 9:9). Orion is the hunter, and can be recognized by three bright stars in a row. The
Pleiades are a faint group of stars. Six can be seen with the naked eye, but according to
tradition there are seven. They are named as an example of distant and mysterious
natural beauty.*

BABYLONIAN JOB AND OTHER INNOCENT SUFFERERS (Job 10:2)

Ancient people believed that gods governed the universe based on some principle of right and wrong. They were confident that pious acts would result in well-being, but aware that wrongdoing would result in misfortune or distress. When misfortune struck, they would consult the gods to discover the cause of their misfortune. If innocent, they would seek divine justice from the gods. So Job, not understanding why he must suffer, calls on God, "Show me why You contend with me" (Job 10:2).

Ancient Near Eastern literary efforts that grapple with the problem of unjust human suffering are not unique to the Scriptures. From Mesopotamia there are at present four known documents that are superficially similar to the Book of Job: *Man and His God; I Will Praise the Lord of Wisdom; The Babylonian Theodicy;* and *Dialogue Between a Master and His Slave.*

In a copy of the Sumerian *Man and His God* from the early 2nd millennium B.C., an individual complains about his plight to his deity. He accuses his god of becoming angry and leaving him unprotected from unscrupulous human enemies, who know that the worshiper's god will not harm them. Finally, the sufferer forgoes his right to protest divine actions and confesses his own guilt. The relationship between himself and his god is repaired.

Despite being unjustly placed in an unfortunate condition, the sufferer in *I Will Praise the Lord of Wisdom* still extols the virtues of his god. He does complain that his god's face is far from him, and concludes that the gods must have a different system of merit that cannot be known by humans. Nonetheless, he encourages humans to continue to perform the proper cultic acts of worship.

The Babylonian Theodicy has often been labeled "The Babylonian Job." The sufferer in this case disputes, like Job, with an educated friend. The sufferer implies that the gods are to be blamed for much of the suffering that occurs. He also maintains that morality is not profitable, as the gods ultimately have no regard for it. The story ends with the sufferer calling upon his god to "pasture his flock."

The *Dialogue Between a Master and His Slave* has only occasional similarities to the Book of Job. Many of the conditions of the master's distress can be compared to that of Job.

Job: I Would Plead with God

10 1 "My soul loathes my life;
I will give free course to my complaint,
I will speak in the bitterness of my soul.

2 I will say to God, 'Do not condemn me;
Show me why You contend with me.

3 *Does it* seem good to You that You should oppress,
That You should despise the work of Your hands,
And smile on the counsel of the wicked?

4 Do You have eyes of flesh?
Or do You see as man sees?

5 *Are* Your days like the days of a mortal man?
Are Your years like the days of a mighty man,

6 That You should seek for my iniquity
And search out my sin,

7 Although You know that I am not wicked,
And *there is* no one who can deliver from Your hand?

8 'Your hands have made me and fashioned me,
An intricate unity;
Yet You would destroy me.

9 Remember, I pray, that You have made me like clay.
And will You turn me into dust again?

10 Did You not pour me out like milk,
And curdle me like cheese,

11 Clothe me with skin and flesh,
And knit me together with bones and sinews?

12 You have granted me life and favor,
And Your care has preserved my spirit.

13 'And these *things* You have hidden in
    Your heart;
    I know that this *was* with You:
14 If I sin, then You mark me,
    And will not acquit me of my iniquity.
15 If I am wicked, woe to me;
    Even *if* I am righteous, I cannot lift up
    my head.
    I am full of disgrace;
    See my misery!
16 If *my head* is exalted,
    You hunt me like a fierce lion,
    And again You show Yourself awesome
    against me.
17 You renew Your witnesses against me,
    And increase Your indignation toward
    me;
    Changes and war are *ever* with me.

18 'Why then have You brought me out of
    the womb?
    Oh, that I had perished and no eye
    had seen me!
19 I would have been as though I had not
    been.
    I would have been carried from the
    womb to the grave.
20 Are not my days few?
    Cease! Leave me alone, that I may
    take a little comfort,
21 Before I go *to the place from which* I
    shall not return,
    To the land of darkness and the
    shadow of death,
22 A land as dark as darkness *itself,*
    As the shadow of death, without any
    order,
    Where even the light *is* like darkness.' "

Zophar: Less Than Your Iniquity Deserves

Believing that the world has a just moral order, Bildad implied that Job's calamities were the result of sin (8:4–6). Now Job's third friend, Zophar the Naamathite, goes the next step and flatly states that Job deserves his suffering. In fact, Job is getting off easy: "Know therefore that God exacts from you less than your iniquity deserves" (11:6).

Much of Zophar's speech (ch. 11) asserts that God is too mysterious for Job, a mere man, to understand (11:7, 8). While this is true, Zophar somewhat spoils the effect by his confidence that he, also a mere man, is able to explain God's ways to Job.

▪ Job 11:1–20

Job
Zophar Urges Job to Repent

11 :1 Then Zophar the Naamathite an-
    swered and said:

2 "Should not the multitude of words be
    answered?
    And should a man full of talk be
    vindicated?
3 Should your empty talk make men
    hold their peace?
    And when you mock, should no one
    rebuke you?
4 For you have said,
    'My doctrine *is* pure,
    And I am clean in your eyes.'
5 But oh, that God would speak,
    And open His lips against you,
6 That He would show you the secrets of
    wisdom!
    For *they would* double *your* prudence.
    Know therefore that God exacts from
    you
    Less than your iniquity *deserves.*

7 "Can you search out the deep things of
    God?
    Can you find out the limits of the
    Almighty?
8 *They are* higher than heaven—what
    can you do?
    Deeper than Sheol—what can you
    know?
9 Their measure *is* longer than the
    earth
    And broader than the sea.

10 "If He passes by, imprisons, and
    gathers *to judgment,*
    Then who can hinder Him?
11 For He knows deceitful men;
    He sees wickedness also.
    Will He not then consider *it?*
12 For an empty-headed man will be
    wise,
    When a wild donkey's colt is born a
    man.

13 "If you would prepare your heart,
    And stretch out your hands toward
    Him;
14 If iniquity *were* in your hand, *and you*
    put it far away,
    And would not let wickedness dwell in
    your tents;
15 Then surely you could lift up your face
    without spot;

Yes, you could be steadfast, and not
fear;

16 Because you would forget *your* misery,
And remember *it* as waters *that have*
passed away,

17 And *your* life would be brighter than
noonday.
Though you were dark, you would be
like the morning.

18 And you would be secure, because
there is hope;
Yes, you would dig *around you, and*
take your rest in safety.

19 You would also lie down, and no one
would make *you* afraid;
Yes, many would court your favor.

20 But the eyes of the wicked will fail,
And they shall not escape,
And their hope—loss of life!"

Job: Your Proverbs of Ashes

As Job's friends grow more bold in their
defense of traditional wisdom and in their accusations against Job, Job himself grows
more frustrated with their trite answers. "Who
does not know such things as these?" he demands (12:3).

Moreover, the friends' answers are
wrong. The wicked *do* prosper (12:5, 6), and
God does not always act benevolently
(12:17–25). The friends' "platitudes are
proverbs of ashes" (13:12) that cannot explain
these facts. Job seeks an explanation from
God Himself, even if getting that answer would
mean Job's death (13:15).

Again, Job's speech (chs. 12—14) concludes with a new hope. Wisdom theology said
almost nothing about a life after death, preferring to focus on this world and this life. With
an inspiration born of sorrow, Job imagines
the possibility that he might find justice after
death (14:14–17).

■ Job 12:1—14:22

Job
Job Answers His Critics

12 :1 Then Job answered and said:

2 "No doubt you *are* the people,
And wisdom will die with you!

3 But I have understanding as well as
you;
I *am* not inferior to you.
Indeed, who does not *know* such
things as these?

4 "I am one mocked by his friends,
Who called on God, and He answered
him,
The just and blameless *who is*
ridiculed.

5 A lamp[a] is despised in the thought of
one who is at ease;
It is made ready for those whose feet
slip.

6 The tents of robbers prosper,
And those who provoke God are
secure—
In what God provides by His hand.

7 "But now ask the beasts, and they will
teach you;
And the birds of the air, and they will
tell you;

8 Or speak to the earth, and it will
teach you;
And the fish of the sea will explain to
you.

9 Who among all these does not know
That the hand of the LORD has done
this,

10 In whose hand *is* the life of every
living thing,
And the breath of all mankind?

11 Does not the ear test words
And the mouth taste its food?

12 Wisdom *is* with aged men,
And with length of days,
understanding.

13 "With Him *are* wisdom and strength,
He has counsel and understanding.

14 If He breaks *a thing* down, it cannot
be rebuilt;
If He imprisons a man, there can be
no release.

15 If He withholds the waters, they dry
up;
If He sends them out, they overwhelm
the earth.

16 With Him *are* strength and prudence.
The deceived and the deceiver *are* His.

17 He leads counselors away plundered,
And makes fools of the judges.

18 He loosens the bonds of kings,
And binds their waist with a belt.

19 He leads princes[a] away plundered,
And overthrows the mighty.

20 He deprives the trusted ones of
speech,

12:5 [a]Or *disaster*   12:19 [a]Literally *priests*, but
not in a technical sense

And takes away the discernment of
the elders.
21 He pours contempt on princes,
And disarms the mighty.
22 He uncovers deep things out of
darkness,
And brings the shadow of death to
light.
23 He makes nations great, and destroys
them;
He enlarges nations, and guides them.
24 He takes away the understanding[a] of
the chiefs of the people of the earth,
And makes them wander in a pathless
wilderness.
25 They grope in the dark without light,
And He makes them stagger like a
drunken *man*.

13
1 "Behold, my eye has seen all
this,
My ear has heard and understood it.
2 What you know, I also know;
I *am* not inferior to you.
3 But I would speak to the Almighty,
And I desire to reason with God.
4 But you forgers of lies,
You *are* all worthless physicians.
5 Oh, that you would be silent,
And it would be your wisdom!
6 Now hear my reasoning,
And heed the pleadings of my lips.
7 Will you speak wickedly for God,
And talk deceitfully for Him?
8 Will you show partiality for Him?
Will you contend for God?
9 Will it be well when He searches you
out?
Or can you mock Him as one mocks a
man?
10 He will surely rebuke you
If you secretly show partiality.
11 Will not His excellence make you
afraid,
And the dread of Him fall upon you?
12 Your platitudes *are* proverbs of ashes,
Your defenses are defenses of clay.

13 "Hold your peace with me, and let me
speak,
Then let come on me what *may!*
14 Why do I take my flesh in my teeth,
And put my life in my hands?

15 Though He slay me, yet will I trust
Him.
Even so, I will defend my own ways
before Him.
16 He also *shall* be my salvation,
For a hypocrite could not come before
Him.
17 Listen carefully to my speech,
And to my declaration with your ears.
18 See now, I have prepared *my* case,
I know that I shall be vindicated.
19 Who *is* he *who* will contend with me?
If now I hold my tongue, I perish.

Job's Despondent Prayer

20 "Only two *things* do not do to me,
Then I will not hide myself from You:
21 Withdraw Your hand far from me,
And let not the dread of You make me
afraid.
22 Then call, and I will answer;
Or let me speak, then You respond to
me.
23 How many *are* my iniquities and sins?
Make me know my transgression and
my sin.
24 Why do You hide Your face,
And regard me as Your enemy?
25 Will You frighten a leaf driven to and
fro?
And will You pursue dry stubble?
26 For You write bitter things against
me,
And make me inherit the iniquities of
my youth.
27 You put my feet in the stocks,
And watch closely all my paths.
You set a limit[a] for the soles of my
feet.

28 "*Man*[a] decays like a rotten thing,
Like a garment that is moth-eaten.

14
1 "Man *who is* born of woman
Is of few days and full of
trouble.
2 He comes forth like a flower and fades
away;
He flees like a shadow and does not
continue.
3 And do You open Your eyes on such a
one,
And bring me[a] to judgment with
Yourself?
4 Who can bring a clean *thing* out of an
unclean?
No one!

12:24 [a]Literally *heart*   13:27 [a]Literally *inscribe a*
print   13:28 [a]Literally *He*   14:3 [a]Septuagint,
Syriac, and Vulgate read *him.*

5   Since his days *are* determined,
    The number of his months *is* with
       You;
    You have appointed his limits, so that
       he cannot pass.
6   Look away from him that he may rest,
    Till like a hired man he finishes his
       day.

7   "For there is hope for a tree,
    If it is cut down, that it will sprout
       again,
    And that its tender shoots will not
       cease.
8   Though its root may grow old in the
       earth,
    And its stump may die in the ground,
9   Yet at the scent of water it will bud
    And bring forth branches like a plant.
10 But man dies and is laid away;
    Indeed he breathes his last
    And where *is* he?
11 *As* water disappears from the sea,
    And a river becomes parched and
       dries up,
12 So man lies down and does not rise.
    Till the heavens *are* no more,
    They will not awake
    Nor be roused from their sleep.

13 "Oh, that You would hide me in the
       grave,
    That You would conceal me until Your
       wrath is past,
    That You would appoint me a set time,
       and remember me!
14 If a man dies, shall he live *again?*
    All the days of my hard service I will
       wait,
    Till my change comes.
15 You shall call, and I will answer You;
    You shall desire the work of Your
       hands.
16 For now You number my steps,
    But do not watch over my sin.
17 My transgression *is* sealed up in a
       bag,
    And You cover[a] my iniquity.

18 "But *as* a mountain falls *and* crumbles
       away,
    And *as* a rock is moved from its place;
19 *As* water wears away stones,
    And as torrents wash away the soil of
       the earth;
    So You destroy the hope of man.
20 You prevail forever against him, and
       he passes on;
    You change his countenance and send
       him away.
21 His sons come to honor, and he does
       not know *it;*
    They are brought low, and he does not
       perceive *it.*
22 But his flesh will be in pain over it,
    And his soul will mourn over it."

Eliphaz: What Wise Men Have Told

The second cycle of speeches (15:1—21:34) repeats many of the issues begun in the first cycle, but the speakers are less polite. The debate has become an angry argument.

Job takes issue with his friends' source of wisdom. The wisdom teachers sought understanding from both personal observation and from tradition. Job, however, finds that his observations do not mesh with traditional understandings, so he rejects tradition (ch. 12). Such independent thinking was shocking to an ancient Near Eastern mind, and Eliphaz devotes much of his second speech (ch. 15) to affirming the value of time-honored wisdom. He asks how Job can claim to know more than "the gray-haired and the aged" (15:10). The rest of Eliphaz's speech comes from ancient and established tradition: "What wise men have told . . . from their fathers" (15:18).

■ Job 15:1–35

Job

Eliphaz Accuses Job of Folly

15 :1 Then Eliphaz the Temanite answered and said:

14:17 [a]Literally *plaster over*

BELIEFS AND IDEAS

Job asserts what seems to be a fatalistic doctrine: the number of days a person will live has already been fixed by God (Job 14:5). His fatalism is pessimistic inasmuch as he compares the days of life to the unending work of the "hired man" (14:6). The tradition of wisdom literature considers such questions in a characteristic way and does not suggest that they can be answered without patience and effort.

BUREAUCRATIC REPORTS IN HEAVEN (Job 15:15)

Eliphaz reflects the belief that humans are not pure, since even God's "saints" in the heavens are not pure (Job 15:15). These saints were members of the heavenly council, an assembly that was prominent in the religious thought of Syria-Palestine and of Edom. In the prologue of Job are scenes of the heavenly council before God (Job 1:6–12; 2:1–6). The members of the council are gods, called the "sons of God" (Job 1:6), who are shown reporting in to the highest deity, Yahweh, their ruler.

Like department chairs, field generals, or vice presidents, deities had days when they were to report their activities to their superior. The action in the heavenly scenes in Job (Job 1:6; 2:1) takes place on the days these reports are due, and the gods show up at God's throne room. Each deity was assigned to care for and control a particular aspect of the universe; the assembly was to make certain all was going well.

The hierarchy of heaven reflected that of a city-state or empire on earth. An earthly king ruled by means of a large bureaucracy, answerable to the head of the hierarchy. Each officer in the human bureaucracy was expected to carry out individual assignments in perfect accord with the desires of the king and to report regularly. The king, in turn, was understood to be responsible to the patron deity of the kingdom and was to render a regular accounting.

The Book of Job, therefore, begins in an ordinary way, describing another day for reports. The gods check in and Yahweh inspects them. It is cosmic bureaucracy at work. The members of the bureaucracy were certainly inferior to Yahweh Himself. They were often found in error (Job 4:18) and did not earn Yahweh's trust (15:15).

---

2 "Should a wise man answer with
  empty knowledge,
  And fill himself with the east wind?
3 Should he reason with unprofitable
  talk,
  Or by speeches with which he can do
  no good?
4 Yes, you cast off fear,
  And restrain prayer before God.
5 For your iniquity teaches your mouth,
  And you choose the tongue of the
  crafty.
6 Your own mouth condemns you, and
  not I;
  Yes, your own lips testify against you.

7 "Are you the first man who was born?
  Or were you made before the hills?
8 Have you heard the counsel of God?
  Do you limit wisdom to yourself?
9 What do you know that we do not
  know?
  What do you understand that is not in
  us?
10 Both the gray-haired and the aged are
  among us,
  Much older than your father.
11 Are the consolations of God too small
  for you,

And the word *spoken* gently[a] with
  you?
12 Why does your heart carry you away,
  And what do your eyes wink at,
13 That you turn your spirit against
  God,
  And let *such* words go out of your
  mouth?

14 "What *is* man, that he could be pure?
  And *he who is* born of a woman, that
  he could be righteous?
15 If *God* puts no trust in His saints,
  And the heavens are not pure in His
  sight,
16 How much less man, *who is*
  abominable and filthy,
  Who drinks iniquity like water!

17 "I will tell you, hear me;
  What I have seen I will declare,
18 What wise men have told,
  Not hiding *anything received* from
  their fathers,
19 To whom alone the land was given,
  And no alien passed among them:
20 The wicked man writhes with pain all
  his days,
  And the number of years is hidden
  from the oppressor.

15:11 [a]Septuagint reads *a secret thing.*

21 Dreadful sounds *are* in his ears;
In prosperity the destroyer comes
upon him.
22 He does not believe that he will return
from darkness,
For a sword is waiting for him.
23 He wanders about for bread, *saying,*
'Where *is it?*'
He knows that a day of darkness is
ready at his hand.
24 Trouble and anguish make him afraid;
They overpower him, like a king ready
for battle.
25 For he stretches out his hand against
God,
And acts defiantly against the
Almighty,
26 Running stubbornly against Him
With his strong, embossed shield.

27 "Though he has covered his face with
his fatness,
And made *his* waist heavy with fat,
28 He dwells in desolate cities,
In houses which no one inhabits,
Which are destined to become ruins.
29 He will not be rich,
Nor will his wealth continue,
Nor will his possessions overspread
the earth.
30 He will not depart from darkness;
The flame will dry out his branches,
And by the breath of His mouth he
will go away.
31 Let him not trust in futile *things,*
deceiving himself,
For futility will be his reward.
32 It will be accomplished before his
time,
And his branch will not be green.
33 He will shake off his unripe grape like
a vine,
And cast off his blossom like an olive
tree.
34 For the company of hypocrites *will be*
barren,
And fire will consume the tents of
bribery.
35 They conceive trouble and bring forth
futility;
Their womb prepares deceit."

Job: My Witness Is in Heaven

Eliphaz's rote recital of traditional wisdom
concerning the fate of the wicked (15:20–35)

leaves Job unmoved. Job calls such trite formulations "words of wind" (16:3). In his reply
(chs. 16; 17), Job again appeals to his own
tragic experience of injustice. In stylized language that is reminiscent of the psalmic
laments, he describes his own pain and shame
(16:7–17; see Ps. 22:7; 38:2).

Despite his suffering, Job does not give
up hope that he might be vindicated before
God. He envisioned a mediator who would take
his case to God (Job 9:33); now he declares
his witness to be "in heaven . . . on high"
(16:19). There must be justice before God,
somehow. Job's hope, depending on an unknown witness, is surely a hope dredged from
the pit of despair, but it is hope nonetheless.
For the first time Job appears not to long for
death (17:13–15).

■ Job 16:1—17:16

Job
Job Reproaches His Pitiless Friends

16 :1 Then Job answered and said:

2 "I have heard many such things;
Miserable comforters *are* you all!
3 Shall words of wind have an end?
Or what provokes you that you
answer?
4 I also could speak as you *do,*
If your soul were in my soul's place.
I could heap up words against you,
And shake my head at you;
5 *But* I would strengthen you with my
mouth,
And the comfort of my lips would
relieve *your grief.*

6 "Though I speak, my grief is not
relieved;
And *if* I remain silent, how am I eased?
7 But now He has worn me out;
You have made desolate all my
company.
8 You have shriveled me up,
And it is a witness *against me;*
My leanness rises up against me
And bears witness to my face.
9 He tears *me* in His wrath, and hates
me;
He gnashes at me with His teeth;
My adversary sharpens His gaze on
me.
10 They gape at me with their mouth,
They strike me reproachfully on the
cheek,
They gather together against me.

11 God has delivered me to the ungodly,
And turned me over to the hands of
the wicked.
12 I was at ease, but He has shattered
me;
He also has taken *me* by my neck, and
shaken me to pieces;
He has set me up for His target,
13 His archers surround me.
He pierces my heartª and does not
pity;
He pours out my gall on the ground.
14 He breaks me with wound upon
wound;
He runs at me like a warrior.ª

15 "I have sewn sackcloth over my skin,
And laid my headª in the dust.
16 My face is flushed from weeping,
And on my eyelids *is* the shadow of
death;
17 Although no violence *is* in my hands,
And my prayer *is* pure.

18 "O earth, do not cover my blood,
And let my cry have no *resting* place!
19 Surely even now my witness *is* in
heaven,
And my evidence *is* on high.
20 My friends scorn me;
My eyes pour out *tears* to God.
21 Oh, that one might plead for a man
with God,
As a man *pleads* for his neighbor!
22 For when a few years are finished,
I shall go the way of no return.

Job Prays for Relief

17 1 "My spirit is broken,
My days are extinguished,
The grave *is ready* for me.
2 *Are* not mockers with me?
And does not my eye dwell on their
provocation?

3 "Now put down a pledge for me with
Yourself.
Who *is he who* will shake hands with
me?
4 For You have hidden their heart from
understanding;
Therefore You will not exalt *them*.

5 He who speaks flattery to *his* friends,
Even the eyes of his children will fail.

6 "But He has made me a byword of the
people,
And I have become one in whose face
men spit.
7 My eye has also grown dim because of
sorrow,
And all my members *are* like shadows.
8 Upright *men* are astonished at this,
And the innocent stirs himself up
against the hypocrite.
9 Yet the righteous will hold to his
way,
And he who has clean hands will be
stronger and stronger.

10 "But please, come back again, all of
you,ª
For I shall not find *one* wise *man*
among you.
11 My days are past,
My purposes are broken off,
Even the thoughts of my heart.
12 They change the night into day;
'The light *is* near,' *they say,* in the face
of darkness.
13 If I wait *for* the grave *as* my house,
If I make my bed in the darkness,
14 If I say to corruption, 'You *are* my
father,'
And to the worm, 'You *are* my mother
and my sister,'
15 Where then *is* my hope?
As for my hope, who can see it?
16 *Will* they go down to the gates of
Sheol?
Shall *we have* rest together in the
dust?"

Bildad: The Light of the Wicked

Bildad's second speech (ch. 18) adds
nothing new to the argument. His theme—that
the wicked will be punished—is the same
theme that Eliphaz presented (ch. 15). Even
the words that Bildad chooses are trite and
repetitive. His assertion "The light of the
wicked indeed goes out" (18:5) is a well-worn
proverbial theme appearing twice in the Book
of Proverbs (Prov. 13:9; 24:20). The friends'
arguments are beginning to sound weary.

■ Job 18:1–21

16:13 ªLiterally *kidneys*   16:14 ªVulgate reads
giant.   16:15 ªLiterally *horn*   17:10 ªFollowing
some Hebrew manuscripts, Septuagint, Syriac, and
Vulgate; Masoretic Text and Targum read *all of
them.*

PARADED BEFORE THE KING OF TERRORS (Job 18:14)

Bildad paints a graphic picture of the terrible fate of the wicked (Job 18:5–21). Death is the end for those who are wicked before God, and Bildad describes the realm of death with many allusions to the Canaanite god Mot and his abode.

In the Ugaritic myths from 1400 to 1200 B.C., Mot is the god of death and the netherworld. He is presented as being ravenous, having an insatiable appetite for the flesh of the living. His land is beneath the earth, where fire, barrenness, darkness, and slime all collect. Where Mot dwells there is no life and no renown. Metals and jewels that are mined are part of his realm, because they are under the ground. Similarly, Pluto, the god of the netherworld in Greek mythology, also ruled over the materials beneath the surface of the earth.

People in ancient Israel believed that everyone who died would go to dwell in the land of the dead. The wicked, it was thought, were condemned to descend to the Pit earlier than the norm. Fear of Mot and his realm of death could be used to frighten the living into behaving. Indeed, one did not want to meet quickly with Mot, the "king of terrors" (Job 18:14) who ruled over the spirits of the dead.

The god Mot is mentioned in the Bible occasionally where Death is described as a person. Yahweh personally addresses "Death" in Hos. 13:14. In Job 28, Job asserts that wisdom belongs only to God, and he quotes the speech of Death. The netherworld (which Job calls "Destruction") and Death say, "We have heard a report," but they do not know of wisdom's whereabouts (Job 28:22). If Mot does not know wisdom, with all the people who ever lived assembled in his realm, and he being a god as well, then wisdom truly is God's and God's alone.

Job

Bildad: The Wicked Are Punished

18 :1 Then Bildad the Shuhite answered and said:

2 "How long *till* you put an end to words?
Gain understanding, and afterward
we will speak.

3 Why are we counted as beasts,
And regarded as stupid in your sight?

4 You who tear yourself in anger,
Shall the earth be forsaken for you?
Or shall the rock be removed from its
place?

5 "The light of the wicked indeed goes
out,
And the flame of his fire does not
shine.

6 The light is dark in his tent,
And his lamp beside him is put out.

7 The steps of his strength are
shortened,
And his own counsel casts him down.

8 For he is cast into a net by his own
feet,
And he walks into a snare.

9 The net takes *him* by the heel,
And a snare lays hold of him.

10 A noose *is* hidden for him on the
ground,
And a trap for him in the road.

11 Terrors frighten him on every side,
And drive him to his feet.

12 His strength is starved,
And destruction *is* ready at his side.

13 It devours patches of his skin;
The firstborn of death devours his
limbs.

14 He is uprooted from the shelter of his
tent,
And they parade him before the king
of terrors.

15 They dwell in his tent *who are* none of
his;
Brimstone is scattered on his
dwelling.

16 His roots are dried out below,
And his branch withers above.

17 The memory of him perishes from the
earth,
And he has no name among the
renowned.[a]

18 He is driven from light into darkness,
And chased out of the world.

18:17 [a]Literally *before the outside*, meaning
distinguished, famous

19 He has neither son nor posterity
   among his people,
   Nor any remaining in his dwellings.
20 Those in the west are astonished at
   his day,
   As those in the east are frightened.
21 Surely such *are* the dwellings of the
   wicked,
   And this *is* the place *of him who* does
   not know God."

Job: My Redeemer Lives

Where Bildad had resorted to the language of proverbial wisdom, Job's response to Bildad (ch. 19) adopts language more like the psalms. To the people of the ancient Near East, the worst fate that could befall someone was to be cut off from one's family and clan. Job describes his condition in terms of this horrible isolation. He is alienated from his family, his servants, and his friends (19:13–22; see Ps. 39:12).

From this isolation, though, Job expresses a most astonishing hope. Elements of all his earlier hopes—for a mediator (9:33), a witness (16:19), even for life after death (14:14–17) are now drawn together. Alienated from his own family, Job declares that *somewhere* there must be a Redeemer who will stand on his side (19:25–27).

■ Job 19:1–29

Job
Job Trusts in His Redeemer

19 :1 Then Job answered and said:

2 "How long will you torment my soul,
   And break me in pieces with words?
3 These ten times you have reproached
   me;
   You are not ashamed *that* you have
   wronged me.ª
4 And if indeed I have erred,
   My error remains with me.

19:3 ªA Jewish tradition reads *make yourselves strange to me.*

5 If indeed you exalt *yourselves* against
  me,
  And plead my disgrace against me,
6 Know then that God has wronged me,
  And has surrounded me with His net.

7 "If I cry out concerning wrong, I am not
  heard.
  If I cry aloud, *there is* no justice.
8 He has fenced up my way, so that I
  cannot pass;
  And He has set darkness in my paths.
9 He has stripped me of my glory,
  And taken the crown *from* my head.
10 He breaks me down on every side,
  And I am gone;
  My hope He has uprooted like a tree.
11 He has also kindled His wrath against
  me,
  And He counts me as *one of* His
  enemies.
12 His troops come together
  And build up their road against me;
  They encamp all around my tent.

13 "He has removed my brothers far from
  me,
  And my acquaintances are completely
  estranged from me.
14 My relatives have failed,
  And my close friends have forgotten
  me.
15 Those who dwell in my house, and my
  maidservants,
  Count me as a stranger;
  I am an alien in their sight.
16 I call my servant, but he gives no
  answer;
  I beg him with my mouth.
17 My breath is offensive to my wife,
  And I am repulsive to the children of
  my own body.
18 Even young children despise me;
  I arise, and they speak against me.
19 All my close friends abhor me,
  And those whom I love have turned
  against me.
20 My bone clings to my skin and to my
  flesh,

ARTS AND LITERATURE

The recording of thoughts or words in writing is a persistent theme in literature. The earliest books so far discovered are in the form of small tablets hinged together like a greeting card. The surfaces of the tablets were coated with wax that was easily written on with a stylus of wood, bone, or metal. The wax was smoothed out and used again. Job, though, wants his words written on stone (Job 19:23, 24).

And I have escaped by the skin of my
teeth.

21 "Have pity on me, have pity on me,
O you my friends,
For the hand of God has struck me!
22 Why do you persecute me as God
does,
And are not satisfied with my flesh?

23 "Oh, that my words were written!
Oh, that they were inscribed in a
book!
24 That they were engraved on a rock
With an iron pen and lead, forever!
25 For I know *that* my Redeemer lives,
And He shall stand at last on the
earth;
26 And after my skin is destroyed, this *I
know,*
That in my flesh I shall see God,
27 Whom I shall see for myself,
And my eyes shall behold, and not
another.
How my heart yearns within me!
28 If you should say, 'How shall we
persecute him?'—
Since the root of the matter is found
in me,
29 Be afraid of the sword for yourselves;
For wrath *brings* the punishment of
the sword,
That you may know *there is* a
judgment."

Zophar: The Portion for a Wicked Man

Job's thoughts may soar upward, ranging
farther at each speech in his search for hope,
but his friends' responses remain solidly earth-
bound. Zophar's second speech (ch. 20) only
repeats the theme presented by Eliphaz and
Bildad—that eventually the wicked will come to
a sticky end (20:12–15).

Like the other friends, Zophar does not
openly accuse Job of being wicked, but the implication is hard to miss. Zophar even twists
Job's own words against him. With transcendent insight, Job had declared that his Redeemer would "stand at last on the earth"
(19:25; literally "on the dust"). Using an almost identical phrase, Zophar says that a
wicked man's strength "will lie down with him in
the dust" (20:11).

■ Job 20:1–29

Job
Zophar's Sermon on the Wicked Man

20 :1 Then Zophar the Naamathite answered and said:

2 "Therefore my anxious thoughts make
me answer,
Because of the turmoil within me.
3 I have heard the rebuke that
reproaches me,
And the spirit of my understanding
causes me to answer.

4 "Do you *not* know this of old,
Since man was placed on earth,
5 That the triumphing of the wicked is
short,
And the joy of the hypocrite is *but* for
a moment?
6 Though his haughtiness mounts up to
the heavens,
And his head reaches to the clouds,
7 *Yet* he will perish forever like his own
refuse;
Those who have seen him will say,
'Where is he?'
8 He will fly away like a dream, and not
be found;
Yes, he will be chased away like a
vision of the night.
9 The eye *that* saw him will *see him* no
more,
Nor will his place behold him
anymore.
10 His children will seek the favor of the
poor,
And his hands will restore his wealth.
11 His bones are full of his youthful
vigor,
But it will lie down with him in the
dust.

12 "Though evil is sweet in his mouth,
And he hides it under his tongue,
13 *Though* he spares it and does not
forsake it,
But still keeps it in his mouth,
14 *Yet* his food in his stomach turns sour;
It becomes cobra venom within him.
15 He swallows down riches
And vomits them up again;
God casts them out of his belly.
16 He will suck the poison of cobras;
The viper's tongue will slay him.
17 He will not see the streams,
The rivers flowing with honey and
cream.

18 He will restore that for which he
      labored,
    And will not swallow *it* down;
    From the proceeds of business
    He will get no enjoyment.
19 For he has oppressed *and* forsaken
      the poor,
    He has violently seized a house which
      he did not build.
20 "Because he knows no quietness in his
      heart,[a]
    He will not save anything he desires.
21 Nothing is left for him to eat;
    Therefore his well-being will not last.
22 In his self-sufficiency he will be in
      distress;
    Every hand of misery will come
      against him.
23 *When* he is about to fill his stomach,
    God will cast on him the fury of His
      wrath,
    And will rain *it* on him while he is
      eating.
24 He will flee from the iron weapon;
    A bronze bow will pierce him through.
25 It is drawn, and comes out of the
      body;
    Yes, the glittering *point comes* out of
      his gall.
    Terrors *come* upon him;
26 Total darkness *is* reserved for his
      treasures.
    An unfanned fire will consume him;
    It shall go ill with him who is left in
      his tent.
27 The heavens will reveal his iniquity,
    And the earth will rise up against
      him.
28 The increase of his house will depart,
    And his goods will flow away in the
      day of His wrath.
29 This *is* the portion from God for a
      wicked man,
    The heritage appointed to him by
      God."

20:20 ªLiterally *belly*   21:13 ªOr *Sheol*

Job: Why Do the Wicked Live?

Throughout the second round of speeches
(chs. 15—21), Job's three friends described in
exhaustive detail the supposed fate of the
wicked. As that round concludes, Job replies
to all three (ch. 21), flatly rejecting traditional
wisdom that the wicked always suffer. Experience does not support that claim. Instead, Job
points out that the wicked often lead long lives,
enjoying the fruits of their evil (21:7–16).

As he speaks, Job mocks the proverb
quoted by Bildad—"The light of the wicked
indeed goes out" (18:5; see Prov. 13:9;
24:20). With obvious scorn, Job queries "How
often is the lamp of the wicked put out?" (Job
21:17). The friends' proverbial wisdom is simply inadequate.

▼   ■ Job 21:1–34

Job
Job's Discourse on the Wicked

21 :1 Then Job answered and said:

2   "Listen carefully to my speech,
      And let this be your consolation.
3   Bear with me that I may speak,
      And after I have spoken, keep
        mocking.

4   "As for me, *is* my complaint against
        man?
      And if *it were,* why should I not be
        impatient?
5   Look at me and be astonished;
      Put *your* hand over *your* mouth.
6   Even when I remember I am terrified,
      And trembling takes hold of my flesh.
7   Why do the wicked live *and* become
        old,
      Yes, become mighty in power?
8   Their descendants are established
        with them in their sight,
      And their offspring before their eyes.
9   Their houses *are* safe from fear,
      Neither *is* the rod of God upon them.
10 Their bull breeds without failure;
      Their cow calves without miscarriage.
11 They send forth their little ones like a
        flock,
      And their children dance.
12 They sing to the tambourine and
        harp,
      And rejoice to the sound of the flute.
13 They spend their days in wealth,
      And in a moment go down to the
        grave.[a]
14 Yet they say to God, 'Depart from us,
      For we do not desire the knowledge of
        Your ways.
15 Who *is* the Almighty, that we should
        serve Him?
      And what profit do we have if we pray
        to Him?'

16 Indeed their prosperity *is* not in their
 hand;
 The counsel of the wicked is far from
 me.

17 "How often is the lamp of the wicked
 put out?
 How often does their destruction come
 upon them,
 The sorrows *God* distributes in His
 anger?
18 They are like straw before the wind,
 And like chaff that a storm carries
 away.
19 *They say,* 'God lays up one's[a] iniquity
 for his children';
 Let Him recompense him, that he may
 know *it.*
20 Let his eyes see his destruction,
 And let him drink of the wrath of the
 Almighty.
21 For what does he care about his
 household after him,
 When the number of his months is cut
 in half?

22 "Can *anyone* teach God knowledge,
 Since He judges those on high?
23 One dies in his full strength,
 Being wholly at ease and secure;
24 His pails[a] are full of milk,
 And the marrow of his bones is moist.
25 Another man dies in the bitterness of
 his soul,
 Never having eaten with pleasure.
26 They lie down alike in the dust,
 And worms cover them.

27 "Look, I know your thoughts,
 And the schemes *with which* you
 would wrong me.
28 For you say,
 'Where *is* the house of the prince?
 And where *is* the tent,[a]
 The dwelling place of the wicked?'
29 Have you not asked those who travel
 the road?
 And do you not know their signs?
30 For the wicked are reserved for the
 day of doom;
 They shall be brought out on the day
 of wrath.
31 Who condemns his way to his face?
 And who repays him *for what* he has
 done?
32 Yet he shall be brought to the grave,
 And a vigil kept over the tomb.

33 The clods of the valley shall be sweet
 to him;
 Everyone shall follow him,
 As countless *have gone* before him.
34 How then can you comfort me with
 empty words,
 Since falsehood remains in your
 answers?"

Eliphaz: Is Not Your Wickedness Great?

The third round of speeches (chs. 22—
31) discards all civility and moves from argument to accusations. In the squabble, the calm
order of speakers is disturbed by interruptions
and words out of order. Zophar is never identified as speaking at all.

In his third speech (ch. 22), Eliphaz takes
the next logical step in the friends' argument:
he accuses Job directly. He imagines Job's
specific sins, and, warming to his theme, describes Job as a heartless villain who had oppressed widows and orphans (22:5–9). The
conclusion is a moving appeal for repentance
(22:21–30), but the effect of this is somewhat
spoiled since Eliphaz calls on Job to repent of
sins that Job has never committed.

■ Job 22:1–30

Job
Eliphaz Accuses Job of Wickedness

22 :1 Then Eliphaz the Temanite answered and said:

2 "Can a man be profitable to God,
 Though he who is wise may be
 profitable to himself?
3 *Is it* any pleasure to the Almighty that
 you are righteous?
 Or *is it* gain *to Him* that you make
 your ways blameless?

4 "Is it because of your fear of Him that
 He corrects you,
 And enters into judgment with you?
5 *Is* not your wickedness great,
 And your iniquity without end?
6 For you have taken pledges from your
 brother for no reason,
 And stripped the naked of their
 clothing.

21:19 [a]Literally *his*   21:24 [a]Septuagint and
Vulgate read *bowels;* Syriac reads *sides;* Targum reads
breasts.   21:28 [a]Vulgate omits *the tent.*

7 You have not given the weary water to
drink,
And you have withheld bread from the
hungry.
8 But the mighty man possessed the
land,
And the honorable man dwelt in it.
9 You have sent widows away empty,
And the strength of the fatherless was
crushed.
10 Therefore snares *are* all around you,
And sudden fear troubles you,
11 Or darkness *so that* you cannot see;
And an abundance of water covers
you.

12 "Is not God in the height of heaven?
And see the highest stars, how lofty
they are!
13 And you say, 'What does God know?
Can He judge through the deep
darkness?
14 Thick clouds cover Him, so that He
cannot see,
And He walks above the circle of
heaven.'
15 Will you keep to the old way
Which wicked men have trod,
16 Who were cut down before their time,
Whose foundations were swept away
by a flood?
17 They said to God, 'Depart from us!
What can the Almighty do to them?'[a]
18 Yet He filled their houses with good
things;
But the counsel of the wicked is far
from me.

19 "The righteous see *it* and are glad,
And the innocent laugh at them:
20 'Surely our adversaries[a] are cut down,
And the fire consumes their remnant.'

21 "Now acquaint yourself with Him, and
be at peace;
Thereby good will come to you.
22 Receive, please, instruction from His
mouth,
And lay up His words in your heart.
23 If you return to the Almighty, you will
be built up;
You will remove iniquity far from your
tents.

24 Then you will lay your gold in the
dust,
And the *gold* of Ophir among the
stones of the brooks.
25 Yes, the Almighty will be your gold[a]
And your precious silver;
26 For then you will have your delight in
the Almighty,
And lift up your face to God.
27 You will make your prayer to Him,
He will hear you,
And you will pay your vows.
28 You will also declare a thing,
And it will be established for you;
So light will shine on your ways.
29 When they cast *you* down, and you
say, 'Exaltation *will come!*'
Then He will save the humble *person.*
30 He will *even* deliver one who is not
innocent;
Yes, he will be delivered by the purity
of your hands."

Job: He Is Not There

Except for a brief assertion that God
knows Job's innocence (23:10–12), Job does
not reply to Eliphaz's accusations. Instead, Job
focuses on the wider issue—the problem of evil
(chs. 23; 24). First, Job says that he seeks
God everywhere, but God is not there (23:8,
9). Next, Job extends God's silence to others
who suffer. The dying and wounded, like Job,
cry aloud to God for help, and like Job, they receive no reply (24:12).

Part of Job's complaint—the absence of
God—will be answered when God shows Himself to Job (chs. 38—41). But Job's other observation—the presence of injustice in the
world—will remain valid, and that injustice
alone is enough to refute the simplistic wisdom
teachings offered by Job's friends.

■ Job 23:1—24:25

Job
Job Proclaims God's Righteous Judgments

23 :1 Then Job answered and said:

2 "Even today my complaint is bitter;
My[a] hand is listless because of my
groaning.
3 Oh, that I knew where I might find
Him,
That I might come to His seat!

22:17 [a]Septuagint and Syriac read *us.*
22:20 [a]Septuagint reads *substance.*   22:25 [a]The
ancient versions suggest *defense;* Hebrew reads *gold*
as in verse 24.   23:2 [a]Following Masoretic Text,
Targum and Vulgate; Septuagint and Syriac read
His.

4   I would present *my* case before Him,
    And fill my mouth with arguments.
5   I would know the words *which* He
        would answer me,
    And understand what He would say to
        me.
6   Would He contend with me in His
        great power?
    No! But He would take *note* of me.
7   There the upright could reason with
        Him,
    And I would be delivered forever from
        my Judge.

8   "Look, I go forward, but He is not
        there,
    And backward, but I cannot perceive
        Him;
9   When He works on the left hand, I
        cannot behold *Him;*
    When He turns to the right hand, I
        cannot see *Him.*
10 But He knows the way that I take;
    When He has tested me, I shall come
        forth as gold.
11 My foot has held fast to His steps;
    I have kept His way and not turned
        aside.
12 I have not departed from the
        commandment of His lips;
    I have treasured the words of His
        mouth
    More than my necessary *food.*

13 "But He *is* unique, and who can make
        Him change?
    And *whatever* His soul desires, *that*
        He does.
14 For He performs *what is* appointed for
        me,
    And many such *things are* with Him.
15 Therefore I am terrified at His
        presence;
    When I consider *this,* I am afraid of
        Him.
16 For God made my heart weak,
    And the Almighty terrifies me;
17 Because I was not cut off from the
        presence of darkness,

And He did *not* hide deep darkness
    from my face.

Job Complains of Violence on the Earth

24 ¹ "*Since* times are not hidden from
        the Almighty,
    Why do those who know Him see not
        His days?

2   "*Some* remove landmarks;
    They seize flocks violently and feed *on*
        them;
3   They drive away the donkey of the
        fatherless;
    They take the widow's ox as a pledge.
4   They push the needy off the road;
    All the poor of the land are forced to
        hide.
5   Indeed, *like* wild donkeys in the
        desert,
    They go out to their work, searching
        for food.
    The wilderness *yields* food for them
        and for *their* children.
6   They gather their fodder in the field
    And glean in the vineyard of the
        wicked.
7   They spend the night naked, without
        clothing,
    And have no covering in the cold.
8   They are wet with the showers of the
        mountains,
    And huddle around the rock for want
        of shelter.

9   "*Some* snatch the fatherless from the
        breast,
    And take a pledge from the poor.
10 They cause *the poor* to go naked,
        without clothing;
    And they take away the sheaves from
        the hungry.
11 They press out oil within their walls,
    And tread winepresses, yet suffer
        thirst.
12 The dying groan in the city,
    And the souls of the wounded cry out;

AGRICULTURE AND HERDING

*In an agricultural and pastoral society it is a serious social crime to steal someone's
sheep, or to confiscate someone's land by moving the boundary markers. Such markers
were erected to indicate the separation of fields and territories. Land in Israel was
supposed to be held by each family in perpetuity as a trust from God. Removing
landmarks violated this trust (Job 24:2).*

Yet God does not charge *them* with
wrong.

13 "There are those who rebel against the
light;
They do not know its ways
Nor abide in its paths.
14 The murderer rises with the light;
He kills the poor and needy;
And in the night he is like a thief.
15 The eye of the adulterer waits for the
twilight,
Saying, 'No eye will see me';
And he disguises *his* face.
16 In the dark they break into houses
Which they marked for themselves in
the daytime;
They do not know the light.
17 For the morning is the same to them
as the shadow of death;
If *someone* recognizes *them,*
They are in the terrors of the shadow
of death.

18 "They *should be* swift on the face of the
waters,
Their portion *should be* cursed in the
earth,
So that no *one would* turn into the
way of their vineyards.
19 As drought and heat consume the
snow waters,
So the grave[a] *consumes those who*
have sinned.
20 The womb *should* forget him,
The worm *should* feed sweetly on him;
He *should* be remembered no more,
And wickedness *should* be broken like
a tree.
21 For he preys on the barren *who* do not
bear,
And does no good for the widow.

22 "But *God* draws the mighty away with
His power;
He rises up, but no *man* is sure of life.
23 He gives them security, and they rely
on it;
Yet His eyes *are* on their ways.
24 They are exalted for a little while,
Then they are gone.
They are brought low;
They are taken out of the way like all
others;
They dry out like the heads of grain.

24:19 [a]Or *Sheol*

25 "Now if *it is* not *so,* who will prove me
a liar,
And make my speech worth nothing?"

Bildad: Man Who Is a Maggot

Of several psalms having echoes in the
Book of Job, the most significant is the great
hymn of Ps. 8. While praising God, Ps. 8 at
the same time exalts humanity as God's particular creation, having a particular relationship
to the Divine. Job has already parodied Ps.
8:4, wishing that God might be a little less particular in his attentions (Job 7:17). Now Bildad
echoes the same psalm, but with a different intention. Using language similar to Ps. 8:3–5,
Bildad demeans humanity as being utterly separated from God (Job 25:5, 6).

Just as Bildad is warming up, though, Job
interrupts. Job has had enough of his friends'
words.

■ Job 25:1–6

Job
Bildad: How Can Man Be Righteous?

25 :1 Then Bildad the Shuhite answered and said:

2 "Dominion and fear *belong* to Him;
He makes peace in His high places.
3 Is there any number to His armies?
Upon whom does His light not rise?
4 How then can man be righteous before
God?
Or how can he be pure *who is* born of
a woman?
5 If even the moon does not shine,
And the stars are not pure in His
sight,
6 How much less man, *who is* a maggot,
And a son of man, *who is* a worm?"

Job: The Fear of the Lord, That Is Wisdom

When Job cuts short Bildad's final
speech, the dialogue falls apart. The ensuing
speeches (chs. 26; 27) are not always clear
as to who is speaking. One passage describes
the fate of the wicked (27:13–23) in phrases
that sound like something Job's friends would
say, not Job. Perhaps this passage is Zophar's
final speech, shouted over Job's words. Or
perhaps here Job is sarcastically mimicking his

friends' teachings. In either case, rational argument is absent.

Because Job has rejected the easy formulations of his friends' wisdom teachings, he might appear to have rejected the wisdom tradition entirely. He does not, though. Instead, Job seeks a deeper wisdom. In a poem of astonishing power and beauty (ch. 28), Job speaks of a profound wisdom, comprehensible only to God (28:23, 24). The greatest wisdom for humans, then, is reverence for that profound God—"the fear of the Lord, that is wisdom" (28:28; see Prov. 9:10).

Job concludes his speech by contrasting the peace and prosperity of his former state to the shame and suffering he experiences now (chs. 29; 30). Then in a solemn fourfold vow he swears to his innocence of wrongdoing (ch. 31). With this vow, "the words of Job are ended" (31:40).

■ Job 26:1—31:40

Job
Job: Man's Frailty and God's Majesty

26
:1 But Job answered and said:

2 "How have you helped *him who is*
      without power?
   How have you saved the arm *that has*
      no strength?
3 How have you counseled *one who has*
      no wisdom?
   And *how* have you declared sound
      advice to many?
4 To whom have you uttered words?
   And whose spirit came from you?

5 "The dead tremble,
   Those under the waters and those
      inhabiting them.
6 Sheol *is* naked before Him,
   And Destruction has no covering.
7 He stretches out the north over empty
      space;
   He hangs the earth on nothing.
8 He binds up the water in His thick
      clouds,
   Yet the clouds are not broken under it.
9 He covers the face of *His* throne,
   And spreads His cloud over it.
10 He drew a circular horizon on the face
      of the waters,
   At the boundary of light and
      darkness.
11 The pillars of heaven tremble,
   And are astonished at His rebuke.

12 He stirs up the sea with His power,
   And by His understanding He breaks
      up the storm.
13 By His Spirit He adorned the heavens;
   His hand pierced the fleeing serpent.
14 Indeed these *are* the mere edges of
      His ways,
   And how small a whisper we hear of
      Him!
   But the thunder of His power who can
      understand?"

Job Maintains His Integrity

27
1 Moreover Job continued his discourse, and said:

2 "As God lives, *who* has taken away my
      justice,
   And the Almighty, *who* has made my
      soul bitter,
3 As long as my breath *is* in me,
   And the breath of God in my nostrils,
4 My lips will not speak wickedness,
   Nor my tongue utter deceit.
5 Far be it from me
   That I should say you are right;
   Till I die I will not put away my
      integrity from me.
6 My righteousness I hold fast, and will
      not let it go;
   My heart shall not reproach *me* as
      long as I live.

7 "May my enemy be like the wicked,
   And he who rises up against me like
      the unrighteous.
8 For what is the hope of the hypocrite,
   Though he may gain *much,*
   If God takes away his life?
9 Will God hear his cry
   When trouble comes upon him?
10 Will he delight himself in the
      Almighty?
   Will he always call on God?

11 "I will teach you about the hand of
      God;
   What *is* with the Almighty I will not
      conceal.
12 Surely all of you have seen *it;*
   Why then do you behave with
      complete nonsense?

13 "This is the portion of a wicked man
      with God,
   And the heritage of oppressors,
      received from the Almighty:

SHEOL FOR ALL THE DEAD WITHOUT DISTINCTION (Job 26:5, 6)

In the world of ancient Judah and Israel people were never expected to enter heaven after death. With the exception of Elijah (2 Kin. 2:11), and possibly of Enoch, who entered heaven alive (Gen. 5:24), humans who died went to a watery domain known as Sheol (Job 26:5, 6).

The understanding of the afterlife in Judah and Israel resembled that current in Mesopotamia and Syria-Palestine. Under the earth, in a dark muddy realm, was Sheol—the netherworld where all the souls of the dead go, whether good or evil. The popular notion in Egypt of an afterlife with a touch of hope for a good eternity did not influence Palestine, despite Egyptian control of Canaan for a millennium. In Palestine, Sheol was understood as a place of darkness, meaninglessness, and hopelessness. Once entering the netherworld, one had to stay there. The prospect of eternity in a most unpleasant place made a long life in this world quite desirable.

The dead retained their individuality in the netherworld, and one could have contact with them. Tubes have been found in the tombs of Palestine from the Bronze Age through the Hellenistic period which allowed food or wine to be dropped into the netherworld. The living sought information from the dead through necromancy, as Saul attempted to consult Samuel's spirit rising from Sheol (1 Sam. 28:11–19). This form of inquiry was forbidden by Israelite law (Deut. 18:10, 11).

The cultures surrounding Judah and Israel had deities who ruled the netherworld. In Mesopotamia the divine couple Nergal and Ereshkigal hanged the corpses of the dead on butchers' hooks like slabs of meat. Egypt's afterlife under the rule of Osiris was more appealing, if you survived the journey to the land of the blessed dead. Syria-Palestine had the god Mot (meaning "death") who was hungry to devour the living. The voraciousness of the netherworld and the mercilessness of its ruler, Mot, is reflected in the "devouring" and "king of terrors" of Job 18:11–14.

14 If his children are multiplied, *it is* for
the sword;
And his offspring shall not be satisfied
with bread.
15 Those who survive him shall be buried
in death,
And their[a] widows shall not weep,
16 Though he heaps up silver like dust,
And piles up clothing like clay—
17 He may pile *it* up, but the just will
wear *it*,
And the innocent will divide the silver.
18 He builds his house like a moth,[a]
Like a booth *which* a watchman
makes.
19 The rich man will lie down,
But not be gathered *up;*[a]
He opens his eyes,
And he *is* no more.

20 Terrors overtake him like a flood;
A tempest steals him away in the
night.
21 The east wind carries him away, and
he is gone;
It sweeps him out of his place.
22 It hurls against him and does not
spare;
He flees desperately from its power.
23 *Men* shall clap their hands at him,
And shall hiss him out of his place.

Job's Discourse on Wisdom

28 ¹ "Surely there is a mine for silver,
And a place *where* gold is
refined.
2 Iron is taken from the earth,
And copper *is* smelted *from* ore.
3 *Man* puts an end to darkness,
And searches every recess
For ore in the darkness and the
shadow of death.
4 He breaks open a shaft away from
people;
In places forgotten by feet

27:15 ᵃLiterally *his*   27:18 ᵃFollowing Masoretic
Text and Vulgate; Septuagint and Syriac read *spider*
(compare 8:14); Targum reads *decay*.
27:19 ᵃFollowing Masoretic Text and Targum;
Septuagint and Syriac read *But shall not add* (that is,
do it again); Vulgate reads *But take away nothing.*

They hang far away from men;
They swing to and fro.

5 *As for* the earth, from it comes bread,
But underneath it is turned up as by fire;

6 Its stones *are* the source of sapphires,
And it contains gold dust.

7 *That* path no bird knows,
Nor has the falcon's eye seen it.

8 The proud lions[a] have not trodden it,
Nor has the fierce lion passed over it.

9 He puts his hand on the flint;
He overturns the mountains at the roots.

10 He cuts out channels in the rocks,
And his eye sees every precious thing.

11 He dams up the streams from trickling;
What is hidden he brings forth to light.

12 "But where can wisdom be found?
And where *is* the place of understanding?

13 Man does not know its value,
Nor is it found in the land of the living.

14 The deep says, '*It is* not in me';
And the sea says, '*It is* not with me.'

15 It cannot be purchased for gold,
Nor can silver be weighed *for* its price.

16 It cannot be valued in the gold of Ophir,
In precious onyx or sapphire.

17 Neither gold nor crystal can equal it,
Nor can it be exchanged for jewelry of fine gold.

18 No mention shall be made of coral or quartz,
For the price of wisdom *is* above rubies.

19 The topaz of Ethiopia cannot equal it,
Nor can it be valued in pure gold.

20 "From where then does wisdom come?
And where *is* the place of understanding?

21 It is hidden from the eyes of all living,
And concealed from the birds of the air.

22 Destruction and Death say,
'We have heard a report about it with our ears.'

23 God understands its way,
And He knows its place.

24 For He looks to the ends of the earth,
And sees under the whole heavens,

25 To establish a weight for the wind,
And apportion the waters by measure.

26 When He made a law for the rain,
And a path for the thunderbolt,

27 Then He saw *wisdom*[a] and declared it;
He prepared it, indeed, He searched it out.

28 And to man He said,
'Behold, the fear of the Lord, that *is* wisdom,
And to depart from evil *is* understanding.' "

Job's Summary Defense

29 ¹Job further continued his discourse, and said:

2 "Oh, that I were as *in* months past,
As *in* the days *when* God watched over me;

3 When His lamp shone upon my head,
And when by His light I walked *through* darkness;

4 Just as I was in the days of my prime,
When the friendly counsel of God *was* over my tent;

5 When the Almighty *was* yet with me,
When my children *were* around me;

6 When my steps were bathed with cream,[a]
And the rock poured out rivers of oil for me!

7 "When I went out to the gate by the city,
When I took my seat in the open square,

28:8 ªLiterally *sons of pride*, figurative of the great lions   28:27 ªLiterally *it*   29:6 ªMasoretic Text reads *wrath*; ancient versions and some Hebrew manuscripts read *cream* (compare 20:17).

SCIENCE AND TECHNOLOGY

From early times people have dug mines in search of metals and precious stones. The first metals to be found and used were gold, silver, iron, and copper—all of which occur in their native state in the earth. Both metals and their ores were the object of searches deep underground (Job 28:1–5). The Greeks lit fires in their mines to create a flow of air for the diggers.

8 The young men saw me and hid,
   And the aged arose *and* stood;
9 The princes refrained from talking,
   And put *their* hand on their mouth;
10 The voice of nobles was hushed,
   And their tongue stuck to the roof of
   their mouth.
11 When the ear heard, then it blessed
   me,
   And when the eye saw, then it
   approved me;
12 Because I delivered the poor who cried
   out,
   The fatherless and *the one who* had no
   helper.
13 The blessing of a perishing *man* came
   upon me,
   And I caused the widow's heart to sing
   for joy.
14 I put on righteousness, and it clothed
   me;
   My justice *was* like a robe and a
   turban.
15 I *was* eyes to the blind,
   And I *was* feet to the lame.
16 I *was* a father to the poor,
   And I searched out the case *that* I did
   not know.
17 I broke the fangs of the wicked,
   And plucked the victim from his teeth.

18 "Then I said, 'I shall die in my nest,
   And multiply *my* days as the sand.
19 My root *is* spread out to the waters,
   And the dew lies all night on my
   branch.
20 My glory *is* fresh within me,
   And my bow is renewed in my hand.'

21 "*Men* listened to me and waited,
   And kept silence for my counsel.
22 After my words they did not speak
   again,
   And my speech settled on them *as*
   dew.

23 They waited for me *as* for the rain,
   And they opened their mouth wide *as*
   for the spring rain.
24 *If* I mocked at them, they did not
   believe *it,*
   And the light of my countenance they
   did not cast down.
25 I chose the way for them, and sat as
   chief;
   So I dwelt as a king in the army,
   As one *who* comforts mourners.

30 1 "But now they mock at me, *men*
        younger than I,
   Whose fathers I disdained to put with
   the dogs of my flock.
2 Indeed, what *profit* is the strength of
   their hands to me?
   Their vigor has perished.
3 *They are* gaunt from want and famine,
   Fleeing late to the wilderness,
   desolate and waste,
4 Who pluck mallow by the bushes,
   And broom tree roots *for* their food.
5 They were driven out from among
   men,
   They shouted at them as *at* a thief.
6 *They had* to live in the clefts of the
   valleys,
   In caves of the earth and the rocks.
7 Among the bushes they brayed,
   Under the nettles they nestled.
8 *They were* sons of fools,
   Yes, sons of vile men;
   They were scourged from the land.

9 "And now I am their taunting song;
   Yes, I am their byword.
10 They abhor me, they keep far from
   me;
   They do not hesitate to spit in my
   face.
11 Because He has loosed my[a] bowstring
   and afflicted me,
   They have cast off restraint before me.
12 At *my* right *hand* the rabble arises;
   They push away my feet,
   And they raise against me their ways
   of destruction.

30:11 [a]Following Masoretic Text, Syriac, and Targum;
Septuagint and Vulgate read *His.*

CULTURE AND SOCIETY

Ostracism, or social rejection, is imposed in traditional or village societies as a way of
punishing offenders and discouraging misbehavior. The rejection is often accompanied by
insulting songs or chants (Job 30:9). This kind of treatment is most effective when a
person's highest social value is honor, rather than wealth or power. Shame and honor
are opposites in these "honor-shame" societies.

13 They break up my path,
They promote my calamity;
They have no helper.

14 They come as broad breakers;
Under the ruinous storm they roll
along.

15 Terrors are turned upon me;
They pursue my honor as the wind,
And my prosperity has passed like a
cloud.

16 "And now my soul is poured out
because of my *plight;*
The days of affliction take hold of me.

17 My bones are pierced in me at night,
And my gnawing pains take no rest.

18 By great force my garment is
disfigured;
It binds me about as the collar of my
coat.

19 He has cast me into the mire,
And I have become like dust and
ashes.

20 "I cry out to You, but You do not
answer me;
I stand up, and You regard me.

21 *But* You have become cruel to me;
With the strength of Your hand You
oppose me.

22 You lift me up to the wind and cause
me to ride *on it;*
You spoil my success.

23 For I know *that* You will bring me *to*
death,
And *to* the house appointed for all
living.

24 "Surely He would not stretch out *His*
hand against a heap of ruins,
If they cry out when He destroys *it.*

25 Have I not wept for him who was in
trouble?
Has *not* my soul grieved for the poor?

26 But when I looked for good, evil came
to me;
And when I waited for light, then
came darkness.

27 My heart is in turmoil and cannot
rest;
Days of affliction confront me.

28 I go about mourning, but not in the
sun;
I stand up in the assembly *and* cry
out for help.

29 I am a brother of jackals,
And a companion of ostriches.

30 My skin grows black and falls from
me;
My bones burn with fever.

31 My harp is *turned* to mourning,
And my flute to the voice of those who
weep.

31

1 "I have made a covenant with my
eyes;
Why then should I look upon a young
woman?

2 For what *is* the allotment of God from
above,
And the inheritance of the Almighty
from on high?

3 *Is* it not destruction for the wicked,
And disaster for the workers of
iniquity?

4 Does He not see my ways,
And count all my steps?

5 "If I have walked with falsehood,
Or if my foot has hastened to deceit,

6 Let me be weighed on honest scales,
That God may know my integrity.

7 If my step has turned from the way,
Or my heart walked after my eyes,
Or if any spot adheres to my hands,

8 *Then* let me sow, and another eat;
Yes, let my harvest be rooted out.

9 "If my heart has been enticed by a
woman,
Or *if* I have lurked at my neighbor's
door,

10 *Then* let my wife grind for another,
And let others bow down over her.

11 For that *would be* wickedness;
Yes, it *would be* iniquity *deserving of*
judgment.

12 For that *would be* a fire *that* consumes
to destruction,
And would root out all my increase.

13 "If I have despised the cause of my
male or female servant
When they complained against me,

14 What then shall I do when God rises
up?
When He punishes, how shall I
answer Him?

15 Did not He who made me in the womb
make them?
Did not the same One fashion us in
the womb?

16 "If I have kept the poor from *their*
desire,

MISTAKING THE SUN AND MOON FOR DEITIES (Job 31:26–28)

As Job takes an oath of innocence (Job 31), he swears that he has never been enticed to worship the sun or moon (31:26, 27). Possibly worshipers threw kisses to these celestial deities, since kissing was part of idol worship (1 Kin. 19:18; Hos. 13:2). Job again swears that he has not gestured such kisses (Job 31:27). Job's oath reflects the popularity of both the sun and the moon as deities in Syria-Palestine.

Yareah, the moon god, is mentioned in the Ugaritic ritual and mythological texts, dating around 1400 to 1200 B.C. In one narrative Yareah is a guest at a drinking feast of the gods, but there is little mention of him otherwise. The moon god Sin of Haran was worshiped throughout Syria-Palestine and Mesopotamia from the 3rd millennium through at least the Hellenistic period (332–37 B.C.). The characteristic crescent moon with dangling tassels, which symbolized this deity, has been found on numerous inscriptions and steles (stone slabs), including those discovered in Judah and Israel.

Much more is known about Shemesh. This deity, who could appear as either feminine (sun goddess) or masculine (sun god), was important in all ancient Near Eastern pantheons. In Ugarit the goddess Shapshu (meaning "sun") was the arbiter of divine judgment as proclaimed by the chief god El. In this she mirrored an image, found from Egypt to Mesopotamia, of the sun as a god of justice.

People of the ancient Near East believed that the sun god rode through the sky by day and the netherworld at night, and thus saw and knew all human activity. Such knowledge made Shemesh useful for locating anyone who was to receive a message from El. In the Ugaritic texts, El sends Shapshu to order Baal and Mot to stop fighting. In Egyptian thought, the sun god (who had several names including Re and Aton) was believed to be the creator of the universe each morning.

Or caused the eyes of the widow to
    fail,
17 Or eaten my morsel by myself,
So that the fatherless could not eat
    of it
18 (But from my youth I reared him as a
    father,
And from my mother's womb I guided
    *the widow*ᵃ);
19 If I have seen anyone perish for lack
    of clothing,
Or any poor *man* without covering;
20 If his heartᵃ has not blessed me,
And *if* he was *not* warmed with the
    fleece of my sheep;
21 If I have raised my hand against the
    fatherless,
When I saw I had help in the gate;
22 *Then* let my arm fall from my
    shoulder,
Let my arm be torn from the socket.
23 For destruction *from* God *is* a terror to
    me,
And because of His magnificence I
    cannot endure.

24 "If I have made gold my hope,
Or said to fine gold, '*You are* my
    confidence';
25 If I have rejoiced because my wealth
    was great,
And because my hand had gained
    much;
26 If I have observed the sunᵃ when it
    shines,
Or the moon moving *in* brightness,
27 So that my heart has been secretly
    enticed,
And my mouth has kissed my hand;
28 This also *would be* an iniquity
    deserving of judgment,
For I would have denied God *who is*
    above.

29 "If I have rejoiced at the destruction of
    him who hated me,
Or lifted myself up when evil found
    him
30 (Indeed I have not allowed my mouth
    to sin
By asking for a curse on his soul);
31 If the men of my tent have not said,
'Who is there that has not been
    satisfied with his meat?'

31:18 ᵃLiterally *her* (compare verse 16)
31:20 ᵃLiterally *loins*   31:26 ᵃLiterally *light*

32 (*But* no sojourner had to lodge in the street,
   For I have opened my doors to the traveler[a]);
33 If I have covered my transgressions as Adam,
   By hiding my iniquity in my bosom,
34 Because I feared the great multitude,
   And dreaded the contempt of families,
   So that I kept silence
   And did not go out of the door—
35 Oh, that I had one to hear me!
   Here is my mark.
   Oh, that the Almighty would answer me,
   That my Prosecutor had written a book!
36 Surely I would carry it on my shoulder,
   And bind it on me *like* a crown;
37 I would declare to Him the number of my steps;
   Like a prince I would approach Him.

38 "If my land cries out against me,
   And its furrows weep together;
39 If I have eaten its fruit[a] without money,
   Or caused its owners to lose their lives;
40 *Then* let thistles grow instead of wheat,
   And weeds instead of barley."

The words of Job are ended.

Elihu: I Am Full of Words

When the argument between Job and his three friends at last collapses into silence, a fifth speaker appears for the first time, a certain Elihu the Buzite. Perhaps Elihu's long monologue (chs. 32—37) is meant to promote some reconciliation between Job and the friends, but it seems unlikely to do so. Elihu makes clear his scorn for all the previous speakers. Job's friends did not speak with wisdom, as expected (32:11, 12), and as for Job, he "speaks without knowledge" (34:35).

Elihu's words, like those of the three friends, often contain passages of great insight, insight that is unfortunately spoiled by its style of delivery. For instance, Elihu speaks with great fervor of God's majesty (36:5—37:24), but that reverent speech is prefaced with Elihu's pompous claim, "Truly my words are not false; One who is perfect in knowledge is with

you" (36:4). Given such a beginning, it is difficult to imagine that Elihu's long-winded reasonings would effect any reconciliation.

   ■ Job 32:1—37:24

Job
Elihu Contradicts Job's Friends

32 :1 So these three men ceased answering Job, because he *was* righteous in his own eyes. [2]Then the wrath of Elihu, the son of Barachel the Buzite, of the family of Ram, was aroused against Job; his wrath was aroused because he justified himself rather than God. [3]Also against his three friends his wrath was aroused, because they had found no answer, and *yet* had condemned Job.

[4]Now because they *were* years older than he, Elihu had waited to speak to Job.[a] [5]When Elihu saw that *there was* no answer in the mouth of these three men, his wrath was aroused.

[6]So Elihu, the son of Barachel the Buzite, answered and said:

"I *am* young in years, and you *are* very old;
   Therefore I was afraid,
   And dared not declare my opinion to you.
7 I said, 'Age[a] should speak,
   And multitude of years should teach wisdom.'
8 But *there is* a spirit in man,
   And the breath of the Almighty gives him understanding.
9 Great men[a] are not *always* wise,
   Nor do the aged *always* understand justice.

10 "Therefore I say, 'Listen to me,
   I also will declare my opinion.'
11 Indeed I waited for your words,
   I listened to your reasonings, while you searched out what to say.
12 I paid close attention to you;
   And surely not one of you convinced Job,
   Or answered his words—
13 Lest you say,
   'We have found wisdom';
   God will vanquish him, not man.

31:32 [a]Following Septuagint, Syriac, Targum, and Vulgate; Masoretic Text reads *road.*
31:39 [a]Literally *its strength*   32:4 [a]Vulgate reads *till Job had spoken.*   32:7 [a]Literally *Days,* that is, years   32:9 [a]Or *Men of many years*

14 Now he has not directed *his* words
　　against me;
　So I will not answer him with your
　　words.

15 "They are dismayed and answer no
　　more;
　Words escape them.
16 And I have waited, because they did
　　not speak,
　Because they stood still *and* answered
　　no more.
17 I also will answer my part,
　I too will declare my opinion.
18 For I am full of words;
　The spirit within me compels me.
19 Indeed my belly *is* like wine *that* has
　　no vent;
　It is ready to burst like new
　　wineskins.
20 I will speak, that I may find relief;
　I must open my lips and answer.
21 Let me not, I pray, show partiality to
　　anyone;
　Nor let me flatter any man.
22 For I do not know how to flatter,
　Else my Maker would soon take me
　　away.

Elihu Contradicts Job

33 1 "But please, Job, hear my
　　　　speech,
　And listen to all my words.
2 Now, I open my mouth;
　My tongue speaks in my mouth.
3 My words *come* from my upright
　　heart;
　My lips utter pure knowledge.
4 The Spirit of God has made me,
　And the breath of the Almighty gives
　　me life.
5 If you can answer me,
　Set *your words* in order before me;
　Take your stand.
6 Truly I *am* as your spokesman[a] before
　　God;
　I also have been formed out of clay.

33:6 ᵃLiterally *as your mouth*

7 Surely no fear of me will terrify you,
　Nor will my hand be heavy on you.

8 "Surely you have spoken in my
　　hearing,
　And I have heard the sound of *your*
　　words, *saying,*
9 'I *am* pure, without transgression;
　I *am* innocent, and *there is* no iniquity
　　in me.
10 Yet He finds occasions against me,
　He counts me as His enemy;
11 He puts my feet in the stocks,
　He watches all my paths.'

12 "Look, *in* this you are not righteous.
　I will answer you,
　For God is greater than man.
13 Why do you contend with Him?
　For He does not give an accounting of
　　any of His words.
14 For God may speak in one way, or in
　　another,
　Yet man does not perceive it.
15 In a dream, in a vision of the night,
　When deep sleep falls upon men,
　While slumbering on their beds,
16 Then He opens the ears of men,
　And seals their instruction.
17 In order to turn man *from his* deed,
　And conceal pride from man,
18 He keeps back his soul from the Pit,
　And his life from perishing by the
　　sword.

19 "*Man* is also chastened with pain on
　　his bed,
　And with strong *pain* in many of his
　　bones,
20 So that his life abhors bread,
　And his soul succulent food.
21 His flesh wastes away from sight,
　And his bones stick out *which once*
　　were not seen.
22 Yes, his soul draws near the Pit,
　And his life to the executioners.

23 "If there is a messenger for him,
　A mediator, one among a thousand,
　To show man His uprightness,

Beliefs and Ideas

Ancient people commonly understood that divine revelation could be received in dreams
(Job 33:14–16). Such dreams were not always self-interpreting, as shown by the
experiences of Joseph (Gen. 40) and Daniel (Dan. 2). In the Iliad, Homer depicts the
gods as appearing to their favorite subjects in dreams. The dreams clarified the
dreamers' thoughts as much as they introduced any new idea.

24 Then He is gracious to him, and says,
'Deliver him from going down to the
Pit;
I have found a ransom';

25 His flesh shall be young like a child's,
He shall return to the days of his
youth.

26 He shall pray to God, and He will
delight in him,
He shall see His face with joy,
For He restores to man His
righteousness.

27 Then he looks at men and says,
'I have sinned, and perverted *what
was* right,
And it did not profit me.'

28 He will redeem his[a] soul from going
down to the Pit,
And his[b] life shall see the light.

29 "Behold, God works all these *things,*
Twice, *in fact,* three *times* with a man,

30 To bring back his soul from the Pit,
That he may be enlightened with the
light of life.

31 "Give ear, Job, listen to me;
Hold your peace, and I will speak.

32 If you have anything to say, answer
me;
Speak, for I desire to justify you.

33 If not, listen to me;
Hold your peace, and I will teach you
wisdom."

Elihu Proclaims God's Justice

34 [1]Elihu further answered and said:

2 "Hear my words, you wise *men;*
Give ear to me, you who have
knowledge.

3 For the ear tests words
As the palate tastes food.

4 Let us choose justice for ourselves;
Let us know among ourselves what *is*
good.

5 "For Job has said, 'I am righteous,
But God has taken away my justice;

6 Should I lie concerning my right?
My wound *is* incurable, *though I am*
without transgression.'

7 What man *is* like Job,
Who drinks scorn like water,

8 Who goes in company with the
workers of iniquity,
And walks with wicked men?

9 For he has said, 'It profits a man
nothing
That he should delight in God.'

10 "Therefore listen to me, you men of
understanding:
Far be it from God *to do* wickedness,
And *from* the Almighty to *commit*
iniquity.

11 For He repays man *according to* his
work,
And makes man to find a reward
according to *his* way.

12 Surely God will never do wickedly,
Nor will the Almighty pervert justice.

13 Who gave Him charge over the earth?
Or who appointed *Him over* the whole
world?

14 If He should set His heart on it,
If He should gather to Himself His
Spirit and His breath,

15 All flesh would perish together,
And man would return to dust.

16 "If *you have* understanding, hear this;
Listen to the sound of my words:

17 Should one who hates justice govern?
Will you condemn *Him who is* most
just?

18 *Is it fitting* to say to a king, 'You are
worthless,'
And to nobles, 'You are wicked'?

19 Yet He is not partial to princes,
Nor does He regard the rich more
than the poor;
For they *are* all the work of His
hands.

20 In a moment they die, in the middle of
the night;
The people are shaken and pass away;
The mighty are taken away without a
hand.

21 "For His eyes *are* on the ways of man,
And He sees all his steps.

22 There is no darkness nor shadow of
death
Where the workers of iniquity may
hide themselves.

23 For He need not further consider a
man,
That he should go before God in
judgment.

24 He breaks in pieces mighty men
without inquiry,
And sets others in their place.

33:28 [a]Or *my* (Kethib) [b]Or *my* (Kethib)

25 Therefore He knows their works;
He overthrows *them* in the night,
And they are crushed.
26 He strikes them as wicked *men*
In the open sight of others,
27 Because they turned back from Him,
And would not consider any of His
ways,
28 So that they caused the cry of the poor
to come to Him;
For He hears the cry of the afflicted.
29 When He gives quietness, who then
can make trouble?
And when He hides *His* face, who
then can see Him,
Whether *it is* against a nation or a
man alone?—
30 That the hypocrite should not reign,
Lest the people be ensnared.

31 "For has *anyone* said to God,
'I have borne *chastening;*
I will offend no more;
32 Teach me *what* I do not see;
If I have done iniquity, I will do no
more'?
33 Should He repay *it* according to your
terms,
Just because you disavow it?
You must choose, and not I;
Therefore speak what you know.

34 "Men of understanding say to me,
Wise men who listen to me:
35 'Job speaks without knowledge,
His words *are* without wisdom.'
36 Oh, that Job were tried to the utmost,
Because *his* answers *are like* those of
wicked men!
37 For he adds rebellion to his sin;
He claps *his hands* among us,
And multiplies his words against
God."

Elihu Condemns Self-Righteousness

35 ¹Moreover Elihu answered and said:

2 "Do you think this is right?
Do you say,
'My righteousness is more than God's'?
3 For you say,
'What advantage will it be to You?
What profit shall I have, more than *if*
I had sinned?'

4 "I will answer you,
And your companions with you.

5 Look to the heavens and see;
And behold the clouds—
They are higher than you.
6 If you sin, what do you accomplish
against Him?
Or, *if* your transgressions are
multiplied, what do you do to Him?
7 If you are righteous, what do you give
Him?
Or what does He receive from your
hand?
8 Your wickedness affects a man such as
you,
And your righteousness a son of man.

9 "Because of the multitude of
oppressions they cry out;
They cry out for help because of the
arm of the mighty.
10 But no one says, 'Where *is* God my
Maker,
Who gives songs in the night,
11 Who teaches us more than the beasts
of the earth,
And makes us wiser than the birds of
heaven?'
12 There they cry out, but He does not
answer,
Because of the pride of evil men.
13 Surely God will not listen to empty
talk,
Nor will the Almighty regard it.
14 Although you say you do not see
Him,
Yet justice *is* before Him, and you
must wait for Him.
15 And now, because He has not
punished in His anger,
Nor taken much notice of folly,
16 Therefore Job opens his mouth in
vain;
He multiplies words without
knowledge."

Elihu Proclaims God's Goodness

36 ¹Elihu also proceeded and said:

2 "Bear with me a little, and I will show
you
That *there are* yet words to speak on
God's behalf.
3 I will fetch my knowledge from afar;
I will ascribe righteousness to my
Maker.
4 For truly my words *are* not false;
One who is perfect in knowledge *is*
with you.

5 "Behold, God *is* mighty, but despises *no one;*
He *is* mighty in strength of understanding.
6 He does not preserve the life of the wicked,
But gives justice to the oppressed.
7 He does not withdraw His eyes from the righteous;
But *they are* on the throne with kings,
For He has seated them forever,
And they are exalted.
8 And if *they are* bound in fetters,
Held in the cords of affliction,
9 Then He tells them their work and their transgressions—
That they have acted defiantly.
10 He also opens their ear to instruction,
And commands that they turn from iniquity.
11 If they obey and serve *Him,*
They shall spend their days in prosperity,
And their years in pleasures.
12 But if they do not obey,
They shall perish by the sword,
And they shall die without knowledge.[a]

13 "But the hypocrites in heart store up wrath;
They do not cry for help when He binds them.
14 They die in youth,
And their life *ends* among the perverted persons.[a]
15 He delivers the poor in their affliction,
And opens their ears in oppression.

16 "Indeed He would have brought you out of dire distress,
Into a broad place where *there is* no restraint;
And what is set on your table *would be* full of richness.
17 But you are filled with the judgment due the wicked;
Judgment and justice take hold *of you.*
18 Because *there is* wrath, *beware* lest He take you away with *one* blow;
For a large ransom would not help you avoid *it.*
19 Will your riches,
Or all the mighty forces,
Keep you from distress?
20 Do not desire the night,
When people are cut off in their place.

21 Take heed, do not turn to iniquity,
For you have chosen this rather than affliction.

22 "Behold, God is exalted by His power;
Who teaches like Him?
23 Who has assigned Him His way,
Or who has said, 'You have done wrong'?

Elihu Proclaims God's Majesty

24 "Remember to magnify His work,
Of which men have sung.
25 Everyone has seen it;
Man looks on *it* from afar.

26 "Behold, God *is* great, and we do not know *Him;*
Nor can the number of His years *be* discovered.
27 For He draws up drops of water,
Which distill as rain from the mist,
28 Which the clouds drop down
And pour abundantly on man.
29 Indeed, can *anyone* understand the spreading of clouds,
The thunder from His canopy?
30 Look, He scatters His light upon it,
And covers the depths of the sea.
31 For by these He judges the peoples;
He gives food in abundance.
32 He covers *His* hands with lightning,
And commands it to strike.
33 His thunder declares it,
The cattle also, concerning the rising *storm.*

37 1 "At this also my heart trembles,
And leaps from its place.
2 Hear attentively the thunder of His voice,
And the rumbling *that* comes from His mouth.
3 He sends it forth under the whole heaven,
His lightning to the ends of the earth.
4 After it a voice roars;
He thunders with His majestic voice,
And He does not restrain them when His voice is heard.
5 God thunders marvelously with His voice;

36:12 [a]Masoretic Text reads *as one without knowledge.*   36:14 [a]Hebrew *qedeshim,* that is, those practicing sodomy and prostitution in religious rituals

He does great things which we cannot comprehend.

6 For He says to the snow, 'Fall *on* the earth';
Likewise to the gentle rain and the heavy rain of His strength.

7 He seals the hand of every man,
That all men may know His work.

8 The beasts go into dens,
And remain in their lairs.

9 From the chamber *of the south* comes the whirlwind,
And cold from the scattering winds *of the north.*

10 By the breath of God ice is given,
And the broad waters are frozen.

11 Also with moisture He saturates the thick clouds;
He scatters His bright clouds.

12 And they swirl about, being turned by His guidance,
That they may do whatever He commands them
On the face of the whole earth.[a]

13 He causes it to come,
Whether for correction,
Or for His land,
Or for mercy.

14 "Listen to this, O Job;
Stand still and consider the wondrous works of God.

15 Do you know when God dispatches them,
And causes the light of His cloud to shine?

16 Do you know how the clouds are balanced,
Those wondrous works of Him who is perfect in knowledge?

17 Why *are* your garments hot,
When He quiets the earth by the south *wind?*

18 With Him, have you spread out the skies,
Strong as a cast metal mirror?

19 "Teach us what we should say to Him,
For we can prepare nothing because of the darkness.

20 Should He be told that I *wish to* speak?
If a man were to speak, surely he would be swallowed up.

21 Even now *men* cannot look at the light *when it is* bright in the skies,
When the wind has passed and cleared them.

22 He comes from the north *as* golden *splendor;*
With God *is* awesome majesty.

23 *As for* the Almighty, we cannot find Him;
He is excellent in power,
In judgment and abundant justice;
He does not oppress.

24 Therefore men fear Him;
He shows no partiality to any *who are* wise of heart."

🧩 Where Were You?

At last God appears, in person, in a whirlwind, and discloses Himself to Job. With a series of rhetorical questions, God presents Himself as the God of creation, magnificent and mysterious (38:1—40:2). God alone created all, and He alone understands His handiwork.

God's message to Job is not entirely new. Eliphaz, Elihu, and Job himself also spoke of God's creative mystery (Job 15:7-9; 28:23-27; 36:26—37:12). Comparable passages appear outside the Book of Job, such as the wisdom teachings of Agur, whose rhetorical question (Prov. 30:4) is strikingly similar to those that God asks Job. Nevertheless, when God Himself speaks this familiar theme, Job is silenced (Job 40:3-5).

■ Job 38:1—40:5

Job

The Lord Reveals His Omnipotence to Job

38 :1 Then the Lord answered Job out of the whirlwind, and said:

2 "Who *is* this who darkens counsel
By words without knowledge?

3 Now prepare yourself like a man;
I will question you, and you shall answer Me.

4 "Where were you when I laid the foundations of the earth?
Tell *Me,* if you have understanding.

5 Who determined its measurements?
Surely you know!
Or who stretched the line upon it?

6 To what were its foundations fastened?
Or who laid its cornerstone,

37:12 [a]Literally *the world of the earth*

WERE YOU THERE AT THE BEGINNING? (Job 38:7)

Public building projects in the ancient Near East were begun with religious rituals, including liturgical singing in praise of the major deities. Kings ritually, if not actually, helped set the foundations of temples and symbolically aided the construction workers in laying walls and fastening gates. In Job 38:4–7, the universe is pictured as a great building project by God. All the inhabitants of heaven sing for joy as the foundations of the earth are laid (Job 38:7).

The heavenly beings who sing and shout are "the morning stars" and "the sons of God" (38:7). In the group of languages called Northwest Semitic, which includes Hebrew, "sons of God" is a standard way to describe the pantheon of deities. The specific mention of the morning stars may reflect Egyptian notions that creation begins anew each morning just as light appears along the horizon. Thus creation begins anew when the morning stars are in the sky. God reminds Job that he was not present, and cannot know what happened at creation when the heavenly choir sang (Job 38:4).

---

7   When the morning stars sang
        together,
    And all the sons of God shouted for
        joy?

8   "Or *who* shut in the sea with doors,
    When it burst forth *and* issued from
        the womb;
9   When I made the clouds its garment,
    And thick darkness its swaddling
        band;
10 When I fixed My limit for it,
    And set bars and doors;
11 When I said,
    'This far you may come, but no farther,
    And here your proud waves must
        stop!'

12 "Have you commanded the morning
        since your days *began,*
    And caused the dawn to know its
        place,
13 That it might take hold of the ends of
        the earth,
    And the wicked be shaken out of it?
14 It takes on form like clay *under* a seal,
    And stands out like a garment.
15 From the wicked their light is
        withheld,
    And the upraised arm is broken.

16 "Have you entered the springs of the
        sea?
    Or have you walked in search of the
        depths?
17 Have the gates of death been revealed
        to you?
    Or have you seen the doors of the
        shadow of death?
18 Have you comprehended the breadth
        of the earth?
    Tell *Me,* if you know all this.

19 "Where *is* the way *to* the dwelling of
        light?
    And darkness, where *is* its place,
20 That you may take it to its territory,
    That you may know the paths *to* its
        home?
21 Do you know *it,* because you were
        born then,
    Or *because* the number of your days *is*
        great?

22 "Have you entered the treasury of
        snow,
    Or have you seen the treasury of hail,
23 Which I have reserved for the time of
        trouble,
    For the day of battle and war?

ARTS AND LITERATURE

While many ancient people believed that the stars were gods and goddesses, Israel believed that God created the constellations. Orion (Job 38:31) is the name of not only one of the constellations, but also of a giant hunter in mythology. The mythological Orion was killed by the goddess Artemis. The Great Bear (38:32) is the constellation Ursa Major. Mazzaroth may mean "constellations" generally.

24 By what way is light diffused,
Or the east wind scattered over the
earth?

25 "Who has divided a channel for the
overflowing *water,*
Or a path for the thunderbolt,
26 To cause it to rain on a land *where
there is* no one,
A wilderness in which *there is* no man;
27 To satisfy the desolate waste,
And cause to spring forth the growth
of tender grass?
28 Has the rain a father?
Or who has begotten the drops of dew?
29 From whose womb comes the ice?
And the frost of heaven, who gives it
birth?
30 The waters harden like stone,
And the surface of the deep is frozen.

31 "Can you bind the cluster of the
Pleiades,
Or loose the belt of Orion?
32 Can you bring out Mazzaroth[a] in its
season?
Or can you guide the Great Bear with
its cubs?
33 Do you know the ordinances of the
heavens?
Can you set their dominion over the
earth?

34 "Can you lift up your voice to the
clouds,
That an abundance of water may
cover you?
35 Can you send out lightnings, that they
may go,
And say to you, 'Here we *are!*'?
36 Who has put wisdom in the mind?[a]
Or who has given understanding to
the heart?
37 Who can number the clouds by
wisdom?
Or who can pour out the bottles of
heaven,
38 When the dust hardens in clumps,
And the clods cling together?

39 "Can you hunt the prey for the lion,
Or satisfy the appetite of the young
lions,
40 When they crouch in *their* dens,
Or lurk in their lairs to lie in wait?

41 Who provides food for the raven,
When its young ones cry to God,
And wander about for lack of food?

39 ¹ "Do you know the time when the
wild mountain goats bear
young?
Or can you mark when the deer gives
birth?
2 Can you number the months *that* they
fulfill?
Or do you know the time when they
bear young?
3 They bow down,
They bring forth their young,
They deliver their offspring.[a]
4 Their young ones are healthy,
They grow strong with grain;
They depart and do not return to
them.

5 "Who set the wild donkey free?
Who loosed the bonds of the onager,
6 Whose home I have made the
wilderness,
And the barren land his dwelling?
7 He scorns the tumult of the city;
He does not heed the shouts of the
driver.
8 The range of the mountains *is* his
pasture,
And he searches after every green
thing.

9 "Will the wild ox be willing to serve
you?
Will he bed by your manger?
10 Can you bind the wild ox in the
furrow with ropes?
Or will he plow the valleys behind
you?
11 Will you trust him because his
strength *is* great?
Or will you leave your labor to him?
12 Will you trust him to bring home your
grain,
And gather it to your threshing floor?

13 "The wings of the ostrich wave proudly,
But are her wings and pinions *like the*
kindly stork's?
14 For she leaves her eggs on the ground,
And warms them in the dust;
15 She forgets that a foot may crush
them,
Or that a wild beast may break them.
16 She treats her young harshly, as
though *they were* not hers;
Her labor is in vain, without concern,

38:32 [a]Literally *Constellations*   38:36 [a]Literally
inward parts   39:3 [a]Literally *pangs,* figurative of
offspring

17 Because God deprived her of wisdom,
And did not endow her with understanding.
18 When she lifts herself on high,
She scorns the horse and its rider.

19 "Have you given the horse strength?
Have you clothed his neck with thunder?[a]
20 Can you frighten him like a locust?
His majestic snorting strikes terror.
21 He paws in the valley, and rejoices in *his* strength;
He gallops into the clash of arms.
22 He mocks at fear, and is not frightened;
Nor does he turn back from the sword.
23 The quiver rattles against him,
The glittering spear and javelin.
24 He devours the distance with fierceness and rage;
Nor does he come to a halt because the trumpet *has* sounded.
25 At *the blast of* the trumpet he says, 'Aha!'
He smells the battle from afar,
The thunder of captains and shouting.

26 "Does the hawk fly by your wisdom,
And spread its wings toward the south?
27 Does the eagle mount up at your command,
And make its nest on high?
28 On the rock it dwells and resides,
On the crag of the rock and the stronghold.
29 From there it spies out the prey;
Its eyes observe from afar.
30 Its young ones suck up blood;
And where the slain *are,* there it *is.*"

40 ¹Moreover the LORD answered Job, and said:

2 "Shall the one who contends with the Almighty correct *Him?*
He who rebukes God, let him answer it."

Job's Response to God

³Then Job answered the LORD and said:

4 "Behold, I am vile;
What shall I answer You?
I lay my hand over my mouth.

5 Once I have spoken, but I will not answer;
Yes, twice, but I will proceed no further."

Behold Behemoth

After Job has bowed before God's presence, God speaks again. Whereas in His first speech (38:1—40:2) God described natural creation, in His second speech (40:6—41:34) He speaks of creatures that transcend the natural. The monsters Behemoth and Leviathan are sometimes associated with the hippopotamus and the crocodile, but in Job 40; 41 they are described in supernatural language, like legendary sea monsters (see 41:19, 20). But even these creatures are subject to God—"Everything under heaven is Mine" (41:11).

■ Job 40:6—41:34

Job
God's Challenge to Job

40 :6 Then the LORD answered Job out of the whirlwind, and said:

7 "Now prepare yourself like a man;
I will question you, and you shall answer Me:

8 "Would you indeed annul My judgment?
Would you condemn Me that you may be justified?
9 Have you an arm like God?
Or can you thunder with a voice like His?
10 Then adorn yourself *with* majesty and splendor,
And array yourself with glory and beauty.
11 Disperse the rage of your wrath;
Look on everyone *who is* proud, and humble him.
12 Look on everyone *who is* proud, *and* bring him low;
Tread down the wicked in their place.
13 Hide them in the dust together,
Bind their faces in hidden *darkness.*
14 Then I will also confess to you
That your own right hand can save you.

39:19 ᵃOr *a mane*

15 "Look now at the behemoth,ᵃ which I
      made *along* with you;
    He eats grass like an ox.
16 See now, his strength *is* in his hips,
    And his power *is* in his stomach
      muscles.
17 He moves his tail like a cedar;
    The sinews of his thighs are tightly
      knit.
18 His bones *are like* beams of bronze,
    His ribs like bars of iron.
19 He *is* the first of the ways of God;
    Only He who made him can bring
      near His sword.
20 Surely the mountains yield food for
      him,
    And all the beasts of the field play
      there.
21 He lies under the lotus trees,
    In a covert of reeds and marsh.
22 The lotus trees cover him *with* their
      shade;
    The willows by the brook surround
      him.
23 Indeed the river may rage,
    Yet he is not disturbed;
    He is confident, though the Jordan
      gushes into his mouth,
24 *Though* he takes it in his eyes,
    Or one pierces *his* nose with a snare.

41

1 "Can you draw out Leviathanᵃ
      with a hook,
    Or *snare* his tongue with a line *which*
      you lower?
2 Can you put a reed through his nose,
    Or pierce his jaw with a hook?
3 Will he make many supplications to
      you?
    Will he speak softly to you?
4 Will he make a covenant with you?
    Will you take him as a servant
      forever?
5 Will you play with him as *with* a
      bird,
    Or will you leash him for your
      maidens?
6 Will *your* companions make a
      banquetᵃ of him?
    Will they apportion him among the
      merchants?

7 Can you fill his skin with harpoons,
    Or his head with fishing spears?
8 Lay your hand on him;
    Remember the battle—
    Never do it again!
9 Indeed, *any* hope of *overcoming* him is
      false;
    Shall *one not* be overwhelmed at the
      sight of him?
10 No one *is so* fierce that he would dare
      stir him up.
    Who then is able to stand against Me?
11 Who has preceded Me, that I should
      pay *him?*
    Everything under heaven is Mine.

12 "I will not concealᵃ his limbs,
    His mighty power, or his graceful
      proportions.
13 Who can remove his outer coat?
    Who can approach *him* with a double
      bridle?
14 Who can open the doors of his face,
    With his terrible teeth all around?
15 *His* rows of scales are *his* pride,
    Shut up tightly *as with* a seal;
16 One is so near another
    That no air can come between them;
17 They are joined one to another,
    They stick together and cannot be
      parted.
18 His sneezings flash forth light,
    And his eyes *are* like the eyelids of the
      morning.
19 Out of his mouth go burning lights;
    Sparks of fire shoot out.
20 Smoke goes out of his nostrils,
    As *from* a boiling pot and burning
      rushes.
21 His breath kindles coals,
    And a flame goes out of his mouth.
22 Strength dwells in his neck,
    And sorrow dances before him.
23 The folds of his flesh are joined
      together;
    They are firm on him and cannot be
      moved.
24 His heart is as hard as stone,
    Even as hard as the lower *millstone.*
25 When he raises himself up, the
      mighty are afraid;
    Because of his crashings they are
      besideᵃ themselves.
26 *Though* the sword reaches him, it
      cannot avail;
    Nor does spear, dart, or javelin.
27 He regards iron as straw,
    And bronze as rotten wood.

40:15 ᵃA large animal, exact identity unknown
41:1 ᵃA large sea creature, exact identity
unknown   41:6 ᵃOr *bargain over him*
41:12 ᵃLiterally *keep silent about*   41:25 ᵃOr
purify themselves

LEVIATHAN, THE SEA SERPENT (Job 41:1)

In Job 41 God continues His speech to Job (see Job 40:1, 6), describing Leviathan, a creature familiar to Job (Job 3:8). This picture of the ultimate sea serpent contrasts the powerlessness of humans against the all-powerful might of God. Although some have supposed that Job 41 speaks of a crocodile or whale, the description of the sea creature is not one that is familiar from nature.

The questions asked of Job stress in minute detail how powerful and how invincible the sea serpent is in the eyes of humans. They cannot even imagine fishing or hunting for this monster. It cannot possibly belong to mere mortals. God Himself, however, created this creature to "play" in the sea (Ps. 104:25, 26). A contrast reveals the unfathomable power of God: While Leviathan terrifies humans, to God it is simply His "little rubber ducky." Leviathan is greater than any other living thing, save One. God alone has no fear of this creature.

There are a number of myths concerning a huge serpent coming from a variety of African cultures. The serpent is presented as an ally of the highest deity. To keep the world from disintegrating, the snake encircles it and grasps its own tail in its mouth, physically holding the universe together. Earthquakes are understood as the serpent moving. Should the serpent die, or cease constricting the land, the world would dissolve back into the sea.

Leviathan appears as Lothan in mythological texts dating around 1400 B.C. In these texts from Ugarit, a Canaanite city-state on the northeast coast of the Mediterranean, the serpent Lothan is associated with the god of the sea, Yam, whom Baal defeats in battle. Possibly a story similar to this Canaanite myth was known in Israel, telling how God defeated Leviathan long ago and placed the serpent in its current status. Imagery from such a story remains in Ps. 74:13, 14, which describes God's victory over Leviathan and the sea serpents.

The original readers of the Book of Job must have recognized in Job 41 the awesome power of God. If at one time in mythological narratives Leviathan was opposed to God, now the sea serpent had become one of God's most impressive servants.

---

28 The arrow cannot make him flee;
    Slingstones become like stubble to
    him.
29 Darts are regarded as straw;
    He laughs at the threat of javelins.
30 His undersides *are* like sharp
    potsherds;
    He spreads pointed *marks* in the mire.
31 He makes the deep boil like a pot;
    He makes the sea like a pot of
    ointment.
32 He leaves a shining wake behind him;
    One would think the deep had white
    hair.
33 On earth there is nothing like him,
    Which is made without fear.
34 He beholds every high *thing;*
    He *is* king over all the children of
    pride."

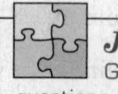

Job: Now My Eye Sees You

God never does answer all of Job's questions, most noticeably the question about why the innocent suffer. Instead, God simply discloses Himself as the source and master of all creation. It is enough. In the presence of God Himself, Job bows and accepts God's mystery (42:1–6).

At last, Job's former glory is reinstated. Perhaps more importantly, though, Job is vindicated. His three friends and their simplistic wisdom are routed, whereas Job's angry questions and profound insights into true wisdom receive God's approval (42:8). In the epilogue of the book (42:7–17) Job's situation is reversed and his blessings restored.

▼   ■ Job 42:1–17

Job

Job's Repentance and Restoration

42 :1 Then Job answered the Lord and said:

2 "I know that You can do everything,
   And that no purpose *of Yours* can be
       withheld from You.
3 *You asked,* 'Who *is* this who hides
       counsel without knowledge?'

Therefore I have uttered what I did
   not understand,
Things too wonderful for me, which I
   did not know.
4 Listen, please, and let me speak;
   You said, 'I will question you, and you
   shall answer Me.'

5 "I have heard of You by the hearing of
   the ear,
   But now my eye sees You.
6 Therefore I abhor *myself,*
   And repent in dust and ashes."

7And so it was, after the LORD had spoken these words to Job, that the LORD said to Eliphaz the Temanite, "My wrath is aroused against you and your two friends, for you have not spoken of Me *what is* right, as My servant Job *has.* 8Now therefore, take for yourselves seven bulls and seven rams, go to My servant Job, and offer up for yourselves a burnt offering; and My servant Job shall pray for you. For I will accept him, lest I deal with you *according to your* folly; because you have not spoken of Me *what is* right, as My servant Job *has.*"

42:10 ªLiterally *Job's captivity,* that is, what was captured from Job

9So Eliphaz the Temanite and Bildad the Shuhite *and* Zophar the Naamathite went and did as the LORD commanded them; for the LORD had accepted Job. 10And the LORD restored Job's lossesª when he prayed for his friends. Indeed the LORD gave Job twice as much as he had before. 11Then all his brothers, all his sisters, and all those who had been his acquaintances before, came to him and ate food with him in his house; and they consoled him and comforted him for all the adversity that the LORD had brought upon him. Each one gave him a piece of silver and each a ring of gold.
12Now the LORD blessed the latter *days* of Job more than his beginning; for he had fourteen thousand sheep, six thousand camels, one thousand yoke of oxen, and one thousand female donkeys. 13He also had seven sons and three daughters. 14And he called the name of the first Jemimah, the name of the second Keziah, and the name of the third Keren-Happuch. 15In all the land were found no women *so* beautiful as the daughters of Job; and their father gave them an inheritance among their brothers.
16After this Job lived one hundred and forty years, and saw his children and grandchildren *for* four generations. 17So Job died, old and full of days.

The Persian Empire

The Persian Empire exceeded the geographic boundaries of any of the earlier empires.

Cyrus the Persian captured the city of Babylon in 539 B.C. The whole of the Neo-Babylonian Empire was his shortly thereafter, including the land of Palestine. He established one of the most successful and enduring of the great ancient empires.

Part of Cyrus's success came from his practice of showing respect for the religious beliefs of his captured peoples. In his first year, according to both Persian records and the biblical account, he proclaimed that all the captive peoples whom the Babylonians had dragged into exile should be allowed to go free (2 Chr. 36:22, 23; Ezra 1:1–4). Cyrus demanded political obedience, particularly regarding the universal requirement of taxes, but unlike the Assyrian and Babylonian rulers, he did not seek to impose his own religion on his subjects.

When Cyrus died in 530 B.C., he was succeeded by his son Cambyses (530–522 B.C.). There are some indications that Cambyses was mentally unstable and perhaps epileptic, but he evidently inherited some of his father's ability as a general. In 525 B.C. Cambyses captured Egypt. The Persian Empire had now exceeded the geographic boundaries of any of the earlier empires.

While Cambyses was returning from the conquest of Egypt, word reached him that he had been deposed by someone claiming to be his brother. For reasons not completely clear, Cambyses committed suicide. One of his officers, named Darius, took his place. Darius put down that rebellion and several others in the next few years, and in the end it was Darius who reigned as the next Persian emperor (522–486 B.C.). Known as Darius the Great, Darius I was as gifted an administrator as Cyrus was a general, and under his rule the extensive organization of the Persian Empire took place. The resulting system of regional governors, satraps, and official inspectors was bulky but effective.

During Darius's reign, a new player appeared in the political life of the ancient Near East: Greece. Darius expanded the Persian Empire through the region of Asia Minor and sought to go the next step, into the Greek peninsula. Greece at this time consisted of many independent city-states, but faced with such a formidable invader, these states joined together. Under Miltiades, a general from the city of Athens, the Greek alliance turned Darius's armies back at the battle of Marathon (490 B.C.).

Darius's son Xerxes I (486–465 B.C.) invaded Greece again in 480 B.C., but after some initial success was also turned back. His successor, Artaxerxes I (465–424 B.C.), ultimately gave up Persian designs on Greek land and signed the Peace of Callias in 449 B.C. The empire was beginning to face internal problems, such as rebellions in Babylon and Egypt. It no longer had the resources to wage new wars of conquest.

Under Persian rule, the Jews faced their own internal disputes. When Cyrus proclaimed that captive peoples could return to their homeland, some of the exiled Jews discovered that they would rather stay where they were. Many had become quite comfortable living in foreign lands, and the prospect of returning home to start over in the ruined city of Jerusalem was daunting.

Several small groups of Jews did return to Jerusalem, though. The first group was led in 538 or 537 B.C. by one Sheshbazzar (Ezra 1:8–11), who became the first Judean governor after the Exile, but otherwise is totally unknown. A second group, led by a direct descendant of King David, named Zerubbabel, was more successful. Under the leadership of Zerubbabel and a priest named Jeshua, this group arrived in Jerusalem and immediately began rebuilding the temple.

In Palestine, though, the returning exiles were confronted by the people who had not been taken to Babylon, who had been on the land all that time, and the confrontation was not friendly. The returned exiles saw those who had stayed in Palestine as mixed-breed Jews who defiled the true worship of God. This was particularly so for the inhabitants of the region of Samaria, the Samaritans, whom the returned exiles regarded with a dislike and suspicion that would still be evident in the New Testament, 500 years later. Both Jews and Samaritans claimed descent from Abraham and worshiped Abraham's God, but they were deeply separated from each other.

So Judaism was divided. First, Jews were divided between those in Palestine (the returned exiles) and those scattered throughout the Persian Empire (the "Diaspora" or "dispersion"). Second, even those in Palestine were split between the returned exiles, who saw themselves as the ethnically and religiously pure remnant of their nation and faith, and the ones who had stayed behind in the land, like the Samaritans.

The Book of Ezra

The story of the Jews' return from exile and the restoration of their ruined temple and city is told in the Book of Ezra and continued in the Book of Nehemiah. The central figure is Ezra, a scribe from a priestly family. But Ezra himself does not appear in the book until ch. 7. The earlier chapters are devoted to the rebuilding of the temple by the returned exiles under the political leader Zerubbabel and the priestly leader Jeshua. To rebuild the temple, they had to overcome opposition from "the people of the land" (Ezra 4:1–5), but in the end they completed the structure.

Tradition holds that the author of the book is Ezra himself. If so, then Ezra may have also been the Chronicler, the author of the priestly history found in 1 and 2 Chronicles, because the Book of Ezra picks up at the precise moment that Chronicles leaves off. Chronicles ends (2 Chr. 36:22, 23), and the Book of Ezra begins (Ezra 1:1–4), with the decree of Cyrus in 538 B.C. that allowed the exiles to return. Other scholars believe that one or more editors compiled the material now known as 1 and 2 Chronicles, Ezra, and Nehemiah.

■ Ezra 1:1—2:70

CYRUS'S RELIGIOUS PROPAGANDA (Ezra 1:2–4)

Cyrus, king of Persia, proclaimed that the God of heaven had given him the empire because of the ruthless deportation practices of the Babylonians. God had called Cyrus to allow peoples displaced by the Babylonians to return to their homes. Judah's God also had commanded him to build the Jerusalem temple (Ezra 1:2).

Apparently Cyrus issued proclamations to specific groups of deported persons. One proclamation, appearing in the Book of Ezra (Ezra 1:2–4), was for the Jews; another for the Babylonians has been found on what is called the Cyrus Cylinder. Both proclamations probably were issued in 538 B.C., at the end of the period in which Cyrus conquered the city of Babylon. While the proclamations announced new freedom for the conquered peoples, they also paid reverence to the captive gods.

In the Cyrus Cylinder, the king announced that the "Lord of the gods" (meaning Babylon's god Marduk) chose him (Cyrus) to conquer the world and set the religious situation in Babylonia right after years of abuse. According to the proclamation, all the sanctuaries were in ruins, and Marduk wished for Cyrus to rebuild them for the Babylonian people. For this reason Marduk allowed Cyrus to conquer Babylon.

Cyrus also claimed it was the will of Marduk to return items that were brought to Babylon during the rule of the Neo-Babylonian Empire. Statues of other gods, along with implements used in their worship, would be returned when conquered peoples returned to their homelands. Temples would be rebuilt and worship restored.

Certainly Cyrus believed that his empire was built with the help of the god who ruled over the entire earth. In writing to various peoples, he called that deity by the name of the highest god of the people to whom he wrote. This might be a classic case of political propaganda, or Cyrus may have assumed that there was one god, who was called different names by different peoples. In either case, Cyrus both appealed to the gods to support his kingship and to the peoples of his new empire to accept him as rightful ruler.

Ezra
End of the Babylonian Captivity

1 :1 Now in the first year of Cyrus king of Persia, that the word of the LORD by the mouth of Jeremiah might be fulfilled, the LORD stirred up the spirit of Cyrus king of Persia, so that he made a proclamation throughout all his kingdom, and also *put it* in writing, saying,

2   Thus says Cyrus king of Persia:
All the kingdoms of the earth the
LORD God of heaven has given me.
And He has commanded me to build
Him a house at Jerusalem which *is* in
Judah. ³Who *is* among you of all His
people? May his God be with him, and
let him go up to Jerusalem which *is* in
Judah, and build the house of the
LORD God of Israel (He *is* God), which
is in Jerusalem. ⁴And whoever is left
in any place where he dwells, let the
men of his place help him with
silver and gold, with goods and
livestock, besides the freewill

offerings for the house of God which *is* in Jerusalem.

⁵Then the heads of the fathers' *houses* of Judah and Benjamin, and the priests and the Levites, with all whose spirits God had moved, arose to go up and build the house of the LORD which *is* in Jerusalem. ⁶And all those who *were* around them encouraged them with articles of silver and gold, with goods and livestock, and with precious things, besides all *that* was willingly offered.

⁷King Cyrus also brought out the articles of the house of the LORD, which Nebuchadnezzar had taken from Jerusalem and put in the temple of his gods; ⁸and Cyrus king of Persia brought them out by the hand of Mithredath the treasurer, and counted them out to Sheshbazzar the prince of Judah. ⁹This *is* the number of them: thirty gold platters, one thousand silver platters, twenty-nine knives, ¹⁰thirty gold basins, four hundred and ten silver basins of a similar *kind, and* one thousand other articles. ¹¹All the articles of gold and

silver *were* five thousand four hundred. All *these* Sheshbazzar took with the captives who were brought from Babylon to Jerusalem.

The Captives Who Returned to Jerusalem

2 [1]Now[a] these *are* the people of the province who came back from the captivity, of those who had been carried away, whom Nebuchadnezzar the king of Babylon had carried away to Babylon, and who returned to Jerusalem and Judah, everyone to his *own* city.

[2]*Those* who came with Zerubbabel *were* Jeshua, Nehemiah, Seraiah, Reelaiah, Mordecai, Bilshan, Mispar,[a] Bigvai, Rehum,[b] *and* Baanah. The number of the men of the people of Israel: [3]the people of Parosh, two thousand one hundred and seventy-two; [4]the people of Shephatiah, three hundred and seventy-two; [5]the people of Arah, seven hundred and seventy-five; [6]the people of Pahath-Moab, of the people of Jeshua *and* Joab, two thousand eight hundred and twelve; [7]the people of Elam, one thousand two hundred and fifty-four; [8]the people of Zattu, nine hundred and forty-five; [9]the people of Zaccai, seven hundred and sixty; [10]the people of Bani,[a] six hundred and forty-two; [11]the people of Bebai, six hundred and twenty-three; [12]the people of Azgad, one thousand two hundred and twenty-two; [13]the people of Adonikam, six hundred and sixty-six; [14]the people of Bigvai, two thousand and fifty-six; [15]the people of Adin, four hundred and fifty-four; [16]the people of Ater of Hezekiah, ninety-eight; [17]the people of Bezai, three hundred and twenty-three; [18]the people of Jorah,[a] one hundred and twelve; [19]the people of

Hashum, two hundred and twenty-three; [20]the people of Gibbar,[a] ninety-five; [21]the people of Bethlehem, one hundred and twenty-three; [22]the men of Netophah, fifty-six; [23]the men of Anathoth, one hundred and twenty-eight; [24]the people of Azmaveth,[a] forty-two; [25]the people of Kirjath Arim,[a] Chephirah, and Beeroth, seven hundred and forty-three; [26]the people of Ramah and Geba, six hundred and twenty-one; [27]the men of Michmas, one hundred and twenty-two; [28]the men of Bethel and Ai, two hundred and twenty-three; [29]the people of Nebo, fifty-two; [30]the people of Magbish, one hundred and fifty-six; [31]the people of the other Elam, one thousand two hundred and fifty-four; [32]the people of Harim, three hundred and twenty; [33]the people of Lod, Hadid, and Ono, seven hundred and twenty-five; [34]the people of Jericho, three hundred and forty-five; [35]the people of Senaah, three thousand six hundred and thirty.

[36]The priests: the sons of Jedaiah, of the house of Jeshua, nine hundred and seventy-three; [37]the sons of Immer, one thousand and fifty-two; [38]the sons of Pashhur, one thousand two hundred and forty-seven; [39]the sons of Harim, one thousand and seventeen.

[40]The Levites: the sons of Jeshua and Kadmiel, of the sons of Hodaviah,[a] seventy-four.

[41]The singers: the sons of Asaph, one hundred and twenty-eight.

[42]The sons of the gatekeepers: the sons of Shallum, the sons of Ater, the sons of Talmon, the sons of Akkub, the sons of Hatita, and the sons of Shobai, one hundred and thirty-nine *in* all.

[43]The Nethinim: the sons of Ziha, the sons of Hasupha, the sons of Tabbaoth, [44]the sons of Keros, the sons of Siaha,[a] the sons of Padon, [45]the sons of Lebanah, the sons of Hagabah, the sons of Akkub, [46]the sons of Hagab, the sons of Shalmai, the sons of Hanan, [47]the sons of Giddel, the sons of Gahar, the sons of Reaiah, [48]the

TIME CAPSULE   *522 to 520 B.C.*

522   *A magi named Gaumata pretends to be Cambyses' younger brother Bardiya*

522–   *Darius I, the Great, kills Gaumata*
486   *and ascends Persia's throne*

521   *Darius suppresses rebellion in Babylonia*

520   *Zechariah and Haggai prophesy to the postexilic community*

520   *Work on the Jerusalem temple is resumed*

2:1 [a]Compare this chapter with Nehemiah 7:6–73.   2:2 [a]Spelled *Mispereth* in Nehemiah 7:7   [b]Spelled *Nehum* in Nehemiah 7:7
2:10 [a]Spelled *Binnui* in Nehemiah 7:15
2:18 [a]Called *Hariph* in Nehemiah 7:24
2:20 [a]Called *Gibeon* in Nehemiah 7:25
2:24 [a]Called *Beth Azmaveth* in Nehemiah 7:28
2:25 [a]Called *Kirjath Jearim* in Nehemiah 7:29
2:40 [a]Spelled *Hodevah* in Nehemiah 7:43
2:44 [a]Spelled *Sia* in Nehemiah 7:47

sons of Rezin, the sons of Nekoda, the sons of Gazzam, [49]the sons of Uzza, the sons of Paseah, the sons of Besai, [50]the sons of Asnah, the sons of Meunim, the sons of Nephusim,[a] [51]the sons of Bakbuk, the sons of Hakupha, the sons of Harhur, [52]the sons of Bazluth,[a] the sons of Mehida, the sons of Harsha, [53]the sons of Barkos, the sons of Sisera, the sons of Tamah, [54]the sons of Neziah, and the sons of Hatipha.

[55]The sons of Solomon's servants: the sons of Sotai, the sons of Sophereth, the sons of Peruda,[a] [56]the sons of Jaala, the sons of Darkon, the sons of Giddel, [57]the sons of Shephatiah, the sons of Hattil, the sons of Pochereth of Zebaim, and the sons of Ami.[a] [58]All the Nethinim and the children of Solomon's servants were three hundred and ninety-two.

[59]And these *were* the ones who came up from Tel Melah, Tel Harsha, Cherub, Addan,[a] and Immer; but they could not identify their father's house or their genealogy,[b] whether they *were* of Israel: [60]the sons of Delaiah, the sons of Tobiah, and the sons of Nekoda, six hundred and fifty-two; [61]and of the sons of the priests: the sons of Habaiah, the sons of Koz,[a] and the sons of Barzillai, who took a wife of the daughters of Barzillai the Gileadite, and was called by their name. [62]These sought their listing *among* those who were registered by genealogy, but they were not found; therefore they *were excluded* from the priesthood as defiled. [63]And the governor[a] said to them that they should not eat of the most holy things till a priest could consult with the Urim and Thummim.

[64]The whole assembly together *was* forty-two thousand three hundred *and* sixty, [65]besides their male and female servants, of whom *there were* seven thousand three hundred and thirty-seven; and they had two hundred men and women singers. [66]Their horses *were* seven hundred and thirty-six, their mules two hundred and forty-five, [67]their camels four hundred and thirty-five, and *their* donkeys six thousand seven hundred and twenty.

[68]*Some* of the heads of the fathers' *houses,* when they came to the house of the LORD which *is* in Jerusalem, offered freely for the house of God, to erect it in its place: [69]According to their ability, they gave to the treasury for the work sixty-one thousand gold drachmas, five thousand minas of silver, and one hundred priestly garments.

[70]So the priests and the Levites, *some* of the people, the singers, the gatekeepers, and the Nethinim, dwelt in their cities, and all Israel in their cities.

Restoring Worship in Jerusalem

The exact dates for the returns led by Sheshbazzar (Ezra 1:11) and by Zerubbabel (Ezra 2:2) are unknown. Some have identified Sheshbazzar with Zerubbabel, but such an identification is not certain. Sheshbazzar could be considered the earlier leader, whose place was later taken by Zerubbabel.

After arriving in Jerusalem, the returnees reestablished their forms of worship, erecting an altar as the first step in restoring the sacrificial system (Ezra 3:3). The 7th month (3:1), corresponding to September-October, was an appropriate time for the people to assemble in Jerusalem, since three holy days were celebrated at that time. Scholars commonly suggest that this 7th month occurred in either 538 or 537 B.C., thus shortly after Cyrus's proclamation. The 2nd year "of their coming" (3:8), when work began on the temple's foundation, would then be either 537 or 536 B.C.

The prophets Haggai and Zechariah encouraged the people to finish their task of rebuilding the temple (Ezra 5:1, 2). The work of both prophets is dated in the 2nd year of Darius I (Hag. 1:1; Zech. 1:1), thus in 520 B.C. Some scholars suppose that the account in Ezra 3:8–13 of laying the temple's foundation actually refers to Zerubbabel's work in 520 B.C. (see Hag. 1:14, 15).

▼   ■ Ezra 3:1—4:5

Ezra
Restoring the Altar

3 **:1** And when the seventh month had come, and the children of Israel *were* in the cities, the people gathered together as one man to Jerusalem. [2]Then Jeshua the son of Jozadak[a] and his brethren the priests, and Zerubbabel the son of Shealtiel and his brethren, arose and built the altar

---

2:50 [a]Spelled *Nephishesim* in Nehemiah 7:52
2:52 [a]Spelled *Bazlith* in Nehemiah 7:54
2:55 [a]Spelled *Perida* in Nehemiah 7:57
2:57 [a]Spelled *Amon* in Nehemiah 7:59
2:59 [a]Spelled *Addon* in Nehemiah 7:61   [b]Literally *seed*   2:61 [a]Or *Hakkoz*   2:63 [a]Hebrew *Tirshatha*   3:2 [a]Spelled *Jehozadak* in 1 Chronicles 6:14

LAYING THE FOUNDATION OF THE SECOND TEMPLE (Ezra 3:8–13)

Judah's temple, the house of Yahweh, had remained desolate since its destruction by the Babylonians in 586 B.C. In the 2nd year after the exiles returned from Babylon, around 537 or 536 B.C., Zerubbabel, a descendant of David, and Jeshua the high priest broke ground to begin the construction of a new temple (Ezra 3:8). The event was met with great ceremony and joy, but also with sadness (3:9–13). The structure was much smaller than the previous temple of King Solomon, which had been built on the same site.

The joy and grief reveal that laying the foundation of the second temple was an event of great importance. The temple had an indispensable theological function to play. It was the very center of God's presence in Judah. It was the point where sacrifices were made in response to Yahweh's gracious choice of Israel as His people.

Yet the temple had important political and economic roles to play in society as well. It was the institution that held all of Judean society together, past as well as present and future. It gave political identity to the people. Access to its courts identified who was properly a citizen and who was excluded.

Economically, rooms in the temple functioned as a treasury—the society's bank. Because of the temple's demands for tithes and offerings, a large portion of the Judean economy passed through temple personnel and storehouses. Without the temple, the Judean people had little chance of pulling together as a coherent society to face the challenges of the future.

The laying of the foundation for this new temple, therefore, represented the rebirth of the kingdom of Judah. Given their past, Judeans could well appreciate that such an event was worthy of both great joy and sadness.

---

of the God of Israel, to offer burnt offerings on it, as *it is* written in the Law of Moses the man of God. ³Though fear *had come* upon them because of the people of those countries, they set the altar on its bases; and they offered burnt offerings on it to the LORD, *both* the morning and evening burnt offerings. ⁴They also kept the Feast of Tabernacles, as *it is* written, and *offered* the daily burnt offerings in the number required by ordinance for each day. ⁵Afterwards *they offered* the regular burnt offering, and *those* for New Moons and for all the appointed feasts of the LORD that were consecrated, and *those* of everyone who willingly offered a freewill offering to the LORD. ⁶From the first day of the seventh month they began to offer burnt offerings to the LORD, although the foundation of the temple of the LORD had not been laid. ⁷They also gave money to the masons and the carpenters, and food, drink, and oil to the people of Sidon and Tyre to bring cedar logs from Lebanon to the sea, to Joppa, according to the permission which they had from Cyrus king of Persia.

Restoration of the Temple Begins

⁸Now in the second month of the second year of their coming to the house of God at Jerusalem, Zerubbabel the son of Shealtiel, Jeshua the son of Jozadak,ᵃ and the rest of their brethren the priests and the Levites, and all those who had come out of the captivity to Jerusalem, began *work* and appointed the Levites from twenty years old and above to oversee the work of the house of the LORD. ⁹Then Jeshua *with* his sons and brothers, Kadmiel *with* his sons, and the sons of Judah,ᵃ arose as one to oversee those working on the house of God: the sons of Henadad *with* their sons and their brethren the Levites.

¹⁰When the builders laid the foundation of the temple of the LORD, the priests stoodᵃ in their apparel with trumpets, and the Levites, the sons of Asaph, with cymbals, to praise the LORD, according to the ordinance of David king of Israel. ¹¹And they sang responsively, praising and giving thanks to the LORD:

"For *He is* good,
  For His mercy *endures* forever toward Israel."ᵃ

3:8 ᵃSpelled *Jehozadak* in 1 Chronicles 6:14
3:9 ᵃOr *Hodaviah* (compare 2:40)
3:10 ᵃFollowing Septuagint, Syriac, and Vulgate; Masoretic Text reads *they stationed the priests.*
3:11 ᵃCompare Psalm 136:1

Then all the people shouted with a great shout, when they praised the LORD, because the foundation of the house of the LORD was laid.

12But many of the priests and Levites and heads of the fathers' *houses,* old men who had seen the first temple, wept with a loud voice when the foundation of this temple was laid before their eyes. Yet many shouted aloud for joy, 13so that the people could not discern the noise of the shout of joy from the noise of the weeping of the people, for the people shouted with a loud shout, and the sound was heard afar off.

Resistance to Rebuilding the Temple

4 1Now when the adversaries of Judah and Benjamin heard that the descendants of the captivity were building the temple of the LORD God of Israel, 2they came to Zerubbabel and the heads of the fathers' *houses,* and said to them, "Let us build with you, for we seek your God as you *do;* and we have sacrificed to Him since the days of Esarhaddon king of Assyria, who brought us here." 3But Zerubbabel and Jeshua and the rest of the heads of the fathers' *houses* of Israel said to them, "You may do nothing with us to build a house for our God; but we alone will build to the LORD God of Israel, as King Cyrus the king of Persia has commanded us." 4Then the people of the land tried to discourage the people of Judah. They troubled them in building, 5and hired counselors against them to frustrate their purpose all the days of Cyrus king of Persia, even until the reign of Darius king of Persia.

Opposition to the Temple
Ezra 4:5 reports that the rebuilding of the temple was frustrated during the last years of Cyrus's reign (539–530 B.C.) until the time of Darius (522–486 B.C.). Strangely, though, the passage that follows (Ezra 4:6–23) describes events that took place during the reigns of the two kings who succeeded

Darius: Ahasuerus (4:6) and Artaxerxes I (4:7, 11, 23). The appearance of Ahasuerus and Artaxerxes at this point in Ezra (4:6, 7) presents a curious chronological problem.

Ahasuerus, also known as Xerxes I (486–465 B.C.), was the son of Darius. Artaxerxes I (465–424 B.C.) was Darius's grandson and Xerxes' son. After describing events during their later reigns (between 486 and 424 B.C.), the narrative returns to the 2nd year of Darius's reign (520 B.C.; Ezra 4:24). Since Xerxes and Artaxerxes reigned after Darius, the events of 4:6–23 are definitely reported out of chronological order. Perhaps this passage was inserted into the middle of Darius's reign to serve as an example of the kind of tactics employed by the "adversaries of Judah and Benjamin" (4:1). See "Opposition to Rebuilding Jerusalem" at Ezra 4:6.

■ Ezra 4:24—5:1

Ezra

4 :24 Thus the work of the house of God which *is* at Jerusalem ceased, and it was discontinued until the second year of the reign of Darius king of Persia.

5 1Then the prophet Haggai and Zechariah the son of Iddo, prophets, prophesied to the Jews who *were* in Judah and Jerusalem, in the name of the God of Israel, *who was* over them.

The Book of Haggai
The "adversaries of Judah and Benjamin," whose help in rebuilding the temple Zerubbabel and Jeshua had rejected (Ezra 4:1–3), were successful in stopping the work on the temple. The foundation had been laid before the work stopped (Ezra 3:10, 11), but nothing further was done from that point. The work stoppage lasted from sometime during Cyrus's reign (c. 536 B.C.) until the 2nd year of Darius I (520 B.C.).

At that time two prophets, Haggai and Zechariah, arose to urge the completion of the temple construction. The ministries of these

---

POLITICS AND GOVERNMENT
Cyrus the Great was the king of Persia who conquered Babylon in 539 B.C. The Babylonians had brought the religious idols of subject peoples to Babylon, and Cyrus allowed these idols to be returned to their original peoples (Ezra 4:3). He was not the only ruler to allow alien religions to exist peacefully in his empire, since this policy made rebellion less likely.

two prophets, who were contemporaries, are dated specifically in 520 B.C. (Ezra 4:24—5:1; Hag. 1:1; Zech. 1:1). The Book of Ezra reports that in that year Haggai and Zechariah prophesied and the Jews "began to build the house of God" (Ezra 5:1, 2). The Book of Haggai consists of the call to complete the temple.

Prophecy in the years after the Exile was different from the great prophecies of such preexilic prophets as Isaiah and Jeremiah. To begin with, the earlier prophets tended to speak about, and to, the kings. But in the restored Judah after the Exile there was no king. Prophets very often spoke to the priests and elders instead. Indeed, many of the prophets themselves seemed to have a priestly perspective. This is certainly true of Haggai, who speaks primarily of the temple and of the particularly priestly concern of ritual defilement (Hag. 2:10–14).

■ Haggai 1:1—2:23

Haggai
The Command to Build God's House

1 :1 In the second year of King Darius, in the sixth month, on the first day of the month, the word of the LORD came by Haggai the prophet to Zerubbabel the son of Shealtiel, governor of Judah, and to Joshua the son of Jehozadak, the high priest, saying, 2"Thus speaks the LORD of hosts, saying: 'This people says, "The time has not come, the time that the LORD's house should be built." ' "

3Then the word of the LORD came by Haggai the prophet, saying, 4"*Is it* time for you yourselves to dwell in your paneled houses, and this temple[a] *to lie* in ruins?" 5Now therefore, thus says the LORD of hosts: "Consider your ways!

6 "You have sown much, and bring in
  little;
  You eat, but do not have enough;
  You drink, but you are not filled with
    drink;
  You clothe yourselves, but no one is
    warm;
  And he who earns wages,
  Earns wages *to put* into a bag with
    holes."

7Thus says the LORD of hosts: "Consider your ways! 8Go up to the mountains

and bring wood and build the temple, that I may take pleasure in it and be glorified," says the LORD. 9"*You* looked for much, but indeed *it came to* little; and when you brought it home, I blew it away. Why?" says the LORD of hosts. "Because of My house that *is in* ruins, while every one of you runs to his own house. 10Therefore the heavens above you withhold the dew, and the earth withholds its fruit. 11For I called for a drought on the land and the mountains, on the grain and the new wine and the oil, on whatever the ground brings forth, on men and livestock, and on all the labor of *your* hands."

The People's Obedience

12Then Zerubbabel the son of Shealtiel, and Joshua the son of Jehozadak, the high priest, with all the remnant of the people, obeyed the voice of the LORD their God, and the words of Haggai the prophet, as the LORD their God had sent him; and the people feared the presence of the LORD. 13Then Haggai, the LORD's messenger, spoke the LORD's message to the people, saying, "I *am* with you, says the LORD." 14So the LORD stirred up the spirit of Zerubbabel the son of Shealtiel, governor of Judah, and the spirit of Joshua the son of Jehozadak, the high priest, and the spirit of all the remnant of the people; and they came and worked on the house of the LORD of hosts, their God, 15on the twenty-fourth day of the sixth month, in the second year of King Darius.

1:4 [a]Literally *house,* and so in verse 8

TIME CAPSULE *518 to 500 B.C.*

518 *Darius I reestablishes order and control in Egypt*

515 *Dedication of the second temple in Jerusalem*

513 *Darius leads expedition into Scythia, expanding the Persian Empire*

509 *Etruscan rule ends and the Roman republic is proclaimed*

500 *Rise of democracy in Athens*

500 *The Babylonians work out a regular 19-year cycle*

500 *Persians begin a royal mounted messenger service*

STARTING OVER IN A DIFFICULT LAND (Hag. 1:6)

The Babylonian destruction of Jerusalem left Judean society in shambles (2 Kin. 25:11, 12). Later, power struggles within the Judean community further emptied the society of necessary leadership and institutions (Jer. 41:1–3). Archaeological surveys suggest that Judah lost 90% of its population during these years. Judean society in the land of Judah had collapsed.

So it remained for approximately 50 years. Then the Persians conquered Babylon in 539 B.C. About 538 B.C. Cyrus the Great decreed that the Jews could return to their land and rebuild the temple and their society. An enthusiastic group of Judean exiles made the journey with high hopes (Ezra 1:11).

Yet the depopulation of the area had taken its toll on the environment. Jerusalem must have been a mess. There is no evidence that anyone attempted to rebuild the city after the destruction of 586 B.C. The returnees to the site of Jerusalem would have been met by wild animals, weeds, dirt, and mounds of debris in the very locations where their ancestors' homes once stood.

The new economy, like the old, depended upon agricultural production. Yet the fields would have suffered from 50 years of neglect. Land would have grown hard and become overgrown with brush. It must have taken intensive manual labor and a lengthy time to get the fields—and thus the economy—to return to productivity again.

Finally, the weather did not cooperate. The prophet Haggai warned of a drought: "the heavens above you withhold the dew, and the earth withholds its fruit" (Hag. 1:10). Difficult circumstances had grown desperate.

Haggai aptly describes the dire straits of the community that had returned to Jerusalem: "You have sown much, and bring in little; You eat, but do not have enough" (Hag. 1:6). The task of starting over in the land had proven to be very difficult.

The Coming Glory of God's House

2 ¹In the seventh *month*, on the twenty-first of the month, the word of the LORD came by Haggai the prophet, saying: ²"Speak now to Zerubbabel the son of Shealtiel, governor of Judah, and to Joshua the son of Jehozadak, the high priest, and to the remnant of the people, saying: ³'Who is left among you who saw this temple[a] in its former glory? And how do you see it now? In comparison with it, *is this* not in your eyes as nothing? ⁴Yet now be strong, Zerubbabel,' says the LORD; 'and be strong, Joshua, son of Jehozadak, the high priest; and be strong, all you people of the land,' says the LORD, 'and work; for I *am* with you,' says the LORD of hosts. ⁵'*According to* the word that I covenanted with you when you came out of Egypt, so My Spirit remains among you; do not fear!'

⁶"For thus says the LORD of hosts: 'Once more (it *is* a little while) I will shake heaven and earth, the sea and dry land;

⁷and I will shake all nations, and they shall come to the Desire of All Nations,[a] and I will fill this temple with glory,' says the LORD of hosts. ⁸'The silver *is* Mine, and the gold *is* Mine,' says the LORD of hosts. ⁹'The glory of this latter temple shall be greater than the former,' says the LORD of hosts. 'And in this place I will give peace,' says the LORD of hosts."

The People Are Defiled

¹⁰On the twenty-fourth *day* of the ninth *month,* in the second year of Darius, the word of the LORD came by Haggai the prophet, saying, ¹¹"Thus says the LORD of hosts: 'Now, ask the priests *concerning the* law, saying, ¹²"If one carries holy meat in the fold of his garment, and with the edge he touches bread or stew, wine or oil, or any food, will it become holy?" ' "

Then the priests answered and said, "No."

¹³And Haggai said, "If *one who is* unclean *because* of a dead body touches any of these, will it be unclean?"

So the priests answered and said, "It shall be unclean."

2:3 [a]Literally *house,* and so in verses 7 and 9
2:7 [a]Or *the desire of all nations*

ZERUBBABEL, GOD'S SIGNET RING (Hag. 2:23)

In the ancient Near East, royalty and other powerful, important people possessed rings bearing a private design and usually including their name and office. After a document had been composed, the person would press his ring into soft clay that sealed the document together. This impression would mark the document as official and legally binding, based upon the authority of the person who owned the ring.

Archaeological digs in Israel have discovered rings, as well as seals and impressions of many Judean officials. Most exciting has been the discovery of the seal of Baruch, with its impressions. Baruch, the scribe and friend of the prophet Jeremiah (Jer. 36:32), even left his fingerprint in the soft clay of one impression!

The prophet Haggai brought to Zerubbabel the message that he had been chosen to become Yahweh's signet ring (Hag. 2:23). The Judeans possibly wondered what real authority and power their local governor had in comparison to the kings and emperors of the major nations. The imagery of the signet ring provided an answer. Zerubbabel's activities would be "pressed" into the soft clay of the early years of the return from exile. The actions of this Davidic governor ultimately bore the authority of Yahweh, the God of Israel.

---

¹⁴Then Haggai answered and said, " 'So is this people, and so is this nation before Me,' says the LORD, 'and so is every work of their hands; and what they offer there is unclean.

Promised Blessing

¹⁵'And now, carefully consider from this day forward: from before stone was laid upon stone in the temple of the LORD— ¹⁶since those *days,* when *one* came to a heap of twenty ephahs, there were *but* ten; when *one* came to the wine vat to draw out fifty baths from the press, there were *but* twenty. ¹⁷I struck you with blight and mildew and hail in all the labors of your hands; yet you did not *turn* to Me,' says the LORD. ¹⁸'Consider now from this day forward, from the twenty-fourth day of the ninth month, from the day that the foundation of the LORD's temple was laid—consider it: ¹⁹Is the seed still in the barn? As yet the vine, the fig tree, the pomegranate, and the olive tree have not yielded *fruit. But* from this day I will bless *you.* ' "

Zerubbabel Chosen as a Signet

²⁰And again the word of the LORD came to Haggai on the twenty-fourth day of the month, saying, ²¹"Speak to Zerubbabel, governor of Judah, saying:

'I will shake heaven and earth.
²² I will overthrow the throne of kingdoms;

I will destroy the strength of the
    Gentile kingdoms.
I will overthrow the chariots
And those who ride in them;
The horses and their riders shall come
    down,
Every one by the sword of his brother.

²³'In that day,' says the LORD of hosts, 'I will take you, Zerubbabel My servant, the son of Shealtiel,' says the LORD, 'and will make you like a signet *ring;* for I have chosen you,' says the LORD of hosts."

The Book of Zechariah

Haggai's companion in prophecy was Zechariah, but Zechariah's work is quite different from Haggai's. He is less exclusively concerned with the temple, for instance, and does not sound quite so priestly. Most obviously, though, he presents his message in a very different fashion. Where Haggai had preached prose sermons, Zechariah describes visionary experiences, often in poetry—or at least in very poetic prose.

Zechariah's visions are every bit as historically specific as Haggai's speeches, though. Both the governor Zerubbabel (Zech. 4:6–10) and the high priest Jeshua (spelled "Joshua" in Zech. 3:1–5) are identified. Zechariah calls these two leaders of the returned exiles the "two anointed ones" (4:14).

Zechariah seems to envision not just a rebuilt temple but a restored nation and a glorious new Jerusalem, with a Davidic king at its head. Zerubbabel, like the Messiah, was from the line of David. The possibilities of this connection would not have been missed by Zechariah's original audience. Jeshua the high priest is also described in messianic language. He is called the "Branch" (Zech. 6:12), a word used by the prophets Isaiah (Is. 4:2) and Jeremiah (Jer. 23:5) to refer to the Messiah.

After chs. 1—8, though, the Book of Zechariah changes dramatically. Chapters 9—14 still include visions, but these visions are much more obscure and no longer come with their own interpretation. The clear references to identifiable historical persons are gone. It becomes much more difficult to date these chapters, but they are different enough from chs. 1—8 that many scholars consider them to be speaking of a later time. See "The Apocalyptic Visions of Zechariah" at Zech. 9:1.

Zechariah's ministry began during the 2nd year of Darius I, approximately in November of 520 B.C. (Zech. 1:1). The foundation of the second temple had been sitting abandoned for possibly 16 years by this time, and Zechariah encourages a disheartened postexilic community. In the month of Shebat (probably February, 519 B.C.), Zechariah received his first vision (Zech. 1:7).

▼ ■ Zechariah 1:1—6:15

Zechariah
A Call to Repentance

1:1 In the eighth month of the second year of Darius, the word of the LORD came to Zechariah the son of Berechiah, the son of Iddo the prophet, saying, 2"The LORD has been very angry with your fathers. 3Therefore say to them, 'Thus says the LORD of hosts: "Return to Me," says the LORD of hosts, "and I will return to you," says the LORD of hosts. 4Do not be like your fathers, to whom the former prophets preached, saying, 'Thus says the LORD of hosts: "Turn now from your evil ways and your evil deeds." ' But they did not hear nor heed Me," says the LORD.

5 "Your fathers, where are they?
    And the prophets, do they live
        forever?
6 Yet surely My words and My statutes,
    Which I commanded My servants the
        prophets,
    Did they not overtake your fathers?

"So they returned and said:

'Just as the LORD of hosts determined
    to do to us,
According to our ways and according
    to our deeds,
So He has dealt with us.' " ' "

Vision of the Horses

7On the twenty-fourth day of the eleventh month, which is the month Shebat, in the second year of Darius, the word of the LORD came to Zechariah the son of Berechiah, the son of Iddo the prophet: 8I saw by night, and behold, a man riding on a red horse, and it stood among the myrtle trees in the hollow; and behind him were horses: red, sorrel, and white. 9Then I said, "My lord, what are these?" So the angel who talked with me said to me, "I will show you what they are."

10And the man who stood among the myrtle trees answered and said, "These are the ones whom the LORD has sent to walk to and fro throughout the earth."

11So they answered the Angel of the LORD, who stood among the myrtle trees, and said, "We have walked to and fro throughout the earth, and behold, all the earth is resting quietly."

The LORD Will Comfort Zion

12Then the Angel of the LORD answered and said, "O LORD of hosts, how long will You not have mercy on Jerusalem and on the cities of Judah, against which You were angry these seventy years?"

13And the LORD answered the angel who talked to me, with good and comforting words. 14So the angel who spoke with me said to me, "Proclaim, saying, 'Thus says the LORD of hosts:

"I am zealous for Jerusalem
    And for Zion with great zeal.
15 I am exceedingly angry with the
        nations at ease;
    For I was a little angry,
    And they helped—but with evil
        intent."

16"Therefore thus says the LORD:

"I am returning to Jerusalem with
    mercy;
My house shall be built in it," says the
    LORD of hosts,
"And a surveyor's line shall be
    stretched out over Jerusalem." '

¹⁷"Again proclaim, saying, 'Thus says the LORD of hosts:

"My cities shall again spread out
    through prosperity;
The LORD will again comfort Zion,
And will again choose Jerusalem."' "

Vision of the Horns

¹⁸Then I raised my eyes and looked, and there *were* four horns. ¹⁹And I said to the angel who talked with me, "What *are* these?"

So he answered me, "These *are* the horns that have scattered Judah, Israel, and Jerusalem."

²⁰Then the LORD showed me four craftsmen. ²¹And I said, "What are these coming to do?"

So he said, "These *are* the horns that scattered Judah, so that no one could lift up his head; but the craftsmen^a are coming to terrify them, to cast out the horns of the nations that lifted up *their* horn against the land of Judah to scatter it."

Vision of the Measuring Line

2 ¹Then I raised my eyes and looked, and behold, a man with a measuring line in his hand. ²So I said, "Where are you going?"

And he said to me, "To measure Jerusalem, to see what *is* its width and what *is* its length."

³And there *was* the angel who talked with me, going out; and another angel was coming out to meet him, ⁴who said to him, "Run, speak to this young man, saying: 'Jerusalem shall be inhabited *as* towns without walls, because of the multitude of men and livestock in it. ⁵For I,' says the LORD, 'will be a wall of fire all around her, and I will be the glory in her midst.' "

Future Joy of Zion and Many Nations

⁶"Up, up! Flee from the land of the north," says the LORD; "for I have spread you abroad like the four winds of heaven," says the LORD. ⁷"Up, Zion! Escape, you who dwell with the daughter of Babylon."

⁸For thus says the LORD of hosts: "He sent Me after glory, to the nations which plunder you; for he who touches you touches the apple of His eye. ⁹For surely I will shake My hand against them, and they shall become spoil for their servants. Then you will know that the LORD of hosts has sent Me.

¹⁰"Sing and rejoice, O daughter of Zion! For behold, I am coming and I will dwell in your midst," says the LORD. ¹¹"Many nations shall be joined to the LORD in that day, and they shall become My people. And I will dwell in your midst. Then you will know that the LORD of hosts has sent Me to you. ¹²And the LORD will take possession of Judah as His inheritance in the Holy Land, and will again choose Jerusalem. ¹³Be silent, all flesh, before the LORD, for He is aroused from His holy habitation!"

Vision of the High Priest

3 ¹Then he showed me Joshua the high priest standing before the Angel of the LORD, and Satan standing at his right hand to oppose him. ²And the LORD said to Satan, "The LORD rebuke you, Satan! The LORD who has chosen Jerusalem rebuke you! *Is* this not a brand plucked from the fire?"

³Now Joshua was clothed with filthy garments, and was standing before the Angel. ⁴Then He answered and spoke to those who stood before Him, saying, "Take away the filthy garments from him." And to him He said, "See, I have removed your iniquity from you, and I will clothe you with rich robes."

⁵And I said, "Let them put a clean turban on his head."

So they put a clean turban on his head, and they put the clothes on him. And the Angel of the LORD stood by.

1:21 ^aLiterally *these*

BELIEFS AND IDEAS

The Hebrew word satan *means "accuser" or "adversary." In time it became the proper name for the chief of the demons. The figure of Satan sometimes appears when God is described as surrounded by His court of angels and other spiritual beings. In heavenly affairs, Satan the Adversary brings charges against humans (Job 1:6–12). In Zechariah's vision (Zech. 3:1, 2), Satan accuses the high priest Joshua.*

CLOTHING, SYMBOLS OF INNER BEING (Zech. 3:1–5)

The Satan who accused the high priest Joshua (or Jeshua; Zech. 3:1) was acting as the Adversary, the heavenly officer in charge of finding those who break the laws of God. God intervened on Joshua's behalf.

Joshua, as high priest, represented the people of Jerusalem before Yahweh. In the ancient Near East high priests interceded for their people with the gods. But no high priest was allowed before any deity when in a state of ritual uncleanness or in improper clerical garments. Anyone who approached a god without the proper garments was punished with death. The official cultic clothing was to be worn properly so that the rituals would be pure and properly performed. A clean garment reflected a clean soul.

The Adversary, Satan, correctly opposed the priest in this case on two grounds. The Jerusalem which Joshua represented before Yahweh had defamed itself, causing the Exile in the first place (2 Kin. 23:26, 27), and for this alone the Adversary had cause to oppose Joshua's appearing before Yahweh. Yet in addition, the priest, while approaching God, wore filthy garments in clear violation of priestly rules.

The Adversary's accusation was accurate, but he did not understand the extent of God's forgiveness. Yahweh had delivered the people of Jerusalem from exile, not so much because they deserved to return, but because God granted them grace. The change in Judah's status is symbolized by God's clothing of Joshua in clean garments (Zech. 3:4, 5). The high priest did not do this for himself, but God, through mercy, reinstated Joshua and Jerusalem—they were "a brand plucked from the fire" (3:2).

The Coming Branch

⁶Then the Angel of the LORD admonished Joshua, saying, ⁷"Thus says the LORD of hosts:

'If you will walk in My ways,
And if you will keep My command,
Then you shall also judge My house,
And likewise have charge of My
    courts;
I will give you places to walk
Among these who stand here.

8 'Hear, O Joshua, the high priest,
You and your companions who sit
    before you,
For they are a wondrous sign;
For behold, I am bringing forth My
    Servant the BRANCH.
9 For behold, the stone
That I have laid before Joshua:
Upon the stone are seven eyes.
Behold, I will engrave its inscription,'
Says the LORD of hosts,
'And I will remove the iniquity of that
    land in one day.
10 In that day,' says the LORD of hosts,
'Everyone will invite his neighbor
Under his vine and under his fig
    tree.' "

Vision of the Lampstand and Olive Trees

4 ¹Now the angel who talked with me came back and wakened me, as a man who is wakened out of his sleep. ²And he said to me, "What do you see?"

So I said, "I am looking, and there is a lampstand of solid gold with a bowl on top of it, and on the stand seven lamps with seven pipes to the seven lamps. ³Two olive trees are by it, one at the right of the bowl and the other at its left." ⁴So I answered and spoke to the angel who talked with me, saying, "What are these, my lord?"

⁵Then the angel who talked with me answered and said to me, "Do you not know what these are?"

And I said, "No, my lord."

⁶So he answered and said to me:

"This is the word of the LORD to
    Zerubbabel:
'Not by might nor by power, but by My
    Spirit,'
Says the LORD of hosts.
7 'Who are you, O great mountain?
Before Zerubbabel you shall become a
    plain!
And he shall bring forth the capstone
With shouts of "Grace, grace to it!" ' "

WICKEDNESS CARRIED TO SHINAR (Zech. 5:11)

In a vision Zechariah describes a woman in a basket who symbolizes Wickedness (Zech. 5:6–8). The basket of Wickedness is carried away to a permanent location "in the land of Shinar" (Zech. 5:10, 11). One could wonder why in this vision Shinar is chosen as the dwelling place for Wickedness.

The name "Shinar" was known from ancient times. In the first list of nations (Gen. 10) Shinar is named as the land in which the legendary Nimrod began his kingdom (Gen. 10:8–10). Nimrod's first cities—Accad, Erech, and Babel—point to a location for the land of Shinar in the southern part of the Tigris-Euphrates valley (now in modern Iraq).

Shinar housed the first known civilization in history. The first cities and temple building were located here, dating as early as the end of the 5th millennium B.C. Moreover, the first writing script has been found at the site of Uruk (Erech), where texts written in Sumerian date to about 3200 B.C. Civilization based on the Sumerian model continued in the Tigris-Euphrates valley until the end of the 1st millennium B.C. Abraham is said to have come from Ur of the Chaldeans (Gen. 11:31), a major Sumerian center in Shinar.

The ancient land of Shinar consisted approximately of the territories later called "Babylonia." Possibly the name "Shinar" was identified in some sense with Babylonia in later times. That would explain why Shinar is listed as a place where the Jews were exiled (Is. 11:11) and as the place to which Nebuchadnezzar, king of Babylon, took vessels from the Jerusalem temple (Dan. 1:2). The translator of the Septuagint (the Greek translation of the Old Testament) even translated the Hebrew word for "Shinar" in Zech. 5:11 with the Greek word for "Babylonia."

Babylon was the place of Judah's captivity. It acquired a reputation as a world power that was hostile to God, and one that would be punished for its hostility (see Jer. 25:12). At the time of Zechariah's prophecy in 520 B.C., the name "Babylon," or its more ancient designation "land of Shinar," would have been considered appropriate for the place where Wickedness would dwell.

---

⁸Moreover the word of the LORD came to me, saying:

9   "The hands of Zerubbabel
    Have laid the foundation of this
        temple;ᵃ
    His hands shall also finish *it*.
    Then you will know
    That the LORD of hosts has sent Me to
        you.
10 For who has despised the day of small
        things?
    For these seven rejoice to see
    The plumb line in the hand of
        Zerubbabel.
    They are the eyes of the LORD,
    Which scan to and fro throughout the
        whole earth."

¹¹Then I answered and said to him, "What *are* these two olive trees—at the right of the lampstand and at its left?" ¹²And I further answered and said to him, "What *are these* two olive branches that *drip* into the receptaclesᵃ of the two gold pipes from which the golden *oil* drains?"

¹³Then he answered me and said, "Do you not know what these *are?*"

And I said, "No, my lord."

¹⁴So he said, "These *are* the two anointed ones, who stand beside the Lord of the whole earth."

Vision of the Flying Scroll

5 ¹Then I turned and raised my eyes, and saw there a flying scroll.

²And he said to me, "What do you see?"

So I answered, "I see a flying scroll. Its length *is* twenty cubits and its width ten cubits."

³Then he said to me, "This *is* the curse that goes out over the face of the whole earth: 'Every thief shall be expelled,' according *to* this side of *the scroll;* and, 'Every perjurer shall be expelled,' according *to* that side of it."

4:9 ᵃLiterally *house of*   4:12 ᵃLiterally *into the hands of*

4 "I will send out *the curse*," says the
     LORD of hosts;
"It shall enter the house of the thief
And the house of the one who swears
     falsely by My name.
It shall remain in the midst of his
     house
And consume it, with its timber and
     stones."

Vision of the Woman in a Basket

5Then the angel who talked with me
came out and said to me, "Lift your eyes
now, and see what this *is* that goes forth."

6So I asked, "What *is* it?" And he said,
"It *is* a basket[a] that is going forth."

He also said, "This *is* their resemblance throughout the earth: 7Here *is* a
lead disc lifted up, and this *is* a woman sitting inside the basket"; 8then he said, "This
is Wickedness!" And he thrust her down
into the basket, and threw the lead cover[a]
over its mouth. 9Then I raised my eyes and
looked, and there *were* two women, coming
with the wind in their wings; for they had
wings like the wings of a stork, and they
lifted up the basket between earth and
heaven.

10So I said to the angel who talked
with me, "Where are they carrying the basket?"

11And he said to me, "To build a house
for it in the land of Shinar;[a] when it is
ready, *the basket* will be set there on its
base."

Vision of the Four Chariots

6 1Then I turned and raised my eyes and
   looked, and behold, four chariots *were*
coming from between two mountains, and
the mountains *were* mountains of bronze.
2With the first chariot *were* red horses,
with the second chariot black horses, 3with
the third chariot white horses, and with
the fourth chariot dappled horses—strong

steeds. 4Then I answered and said to the
angel who talked with me, "What *are*
these, my lord?"

5And the angel answered and said to
me, "These *are* four spirits of heaven, who
go out from *their* station before the Lord of
all the earth. 6The one with the black
horses is going to the north country, the
white are going after them, and the dappled are going toward the south country."
7Then the strong *steeds* went out, eager to
go, that they might walk to and fro
throughout the earth. And He said, "Go,
walk to and fro throughout the earth." So
they walked to and fro throughout the
earth. 8And He called to me, and spoke to
me, saying, "See, those who go toward the
north country have given rest to My Spirit
in the north country."

The Command to Crown Joshua

9Then the word of the LORD came to
me, saying: 10"Receive *the gift* from the captives—from Heldai, Tobijah, and Jedaiah,
who have come from Babylon—and go the
same day and enter the house of Josiah the
son of Zephaniah. 11Take the silver and
gold, make an elaborate crown, and set *it*
on the head of Joshua the son of Jehozadak, the high priest. 12Then speak to
him, saying, 'Thus says the LORD of hosts,
saying:

"Behold, the Man whose name *is* the
     BRANCH!
From His place He shall branch out,
And He shall build the temple of the
     LORD;
13 Yes, He shall build the temple of the
     LORD.
He shall bear the glory,
And shall sit and rule on His throne;
So He shall be a priest on His throne,
And the counsel of peace shall be
     between them both." '

14"Now the elaborate crown shall be for
a memorial in the temple of the LORD for

5:6 [a]Hebrew *ephah*, a measuring container, and so
elsewhere   5:8 [a]Literally *stone*   5:11 [a]That is,
Babylon

ARTS AND LITERATURE

*The colors available to the earliest painters were taken from the earth. Together with
carbon black, they ranged from red to yellow to white. These are possibly the four colors
of Zechariah's chariots (Zech. 6:1–3), although it is not certain what color is meant by
"dappled" (6:3). When no example is given, a color name in a language such as Hebrew
can be impossible to define exactly.*

Helem,[a] Tobijah, Jedaiah, and Hen the son of Zephaniah. ¹⁵Even those from afar shall come and build the temple of the LORD. Then you shall know that the LORD of hosts has sent Me to you. And *this* shall come to pass if you diligently obey the voice of the LORD your God."

Replacing Fasting with Obedience

The occasion for this message was the arrival of a deputation, possibly of Samaritans from Bethel, in the 4th year of Darius (Zech. 7:1, 2). The month of Chislev was probably December, 518 B.C. Since work on the new temple had been underway for about 2 years, they wondered whether to continue the fasts commemorating the burning of the city and temple in 586 B.C. (7:3).

The weeping and fasting in the 5th month recalled the month when the temple had been destroyed (2 Kin. 25:8-10). Such religious actions had been observed for the nearly 70 years since Jerusalem's fall in 586 B.C. (Zech. 7:5). The prophet Zechariah answers that God cares more for righteousness than religious forms.

■ Zechariah 7:1—8:23

Zechariah
Weeping and Fasting

7 :1 Now in the fourth year of King Darius it came to pass *that* the word of the LORD came to Zechariah, on the fourth day of the ninth month, Chislev, ²when *the people*[a] sent Sherezer,[b] with Regem-Melech and his men, *to* the house of God,[c] to pray before the LORD, ³*and* to ask the priests who *were* in the house of the LORD of hosts, and the prophets, saying, "Should I weep in the fifth month and fast as I have done for so many years?"

⁴Then the word of the LORD of hosts came to me, saying, ⁵"Say to all the people of the land, and to the priests: 'When you fasted and mourned in the fifth and seventh *months* during those seventy years, did you really fast for Me—for Me? ⁶When you eat and when you drink, do you not eat and drink *for yourselves*? ⁷Should *you* not *have obeyed* the words which the LORD proclaimed through the former prophets when Jerusalem and the cities around it were inhabited and prosperous, and the South[a] and the Lowland were inhabited?' "

Disobedience Resulted in Captivity

⁸Then the word of the LORD came to Zechariah, saying, ⁹"Thus says the LORD of hosts:

'Execute true justice,
Show mercy and compassion
Everyone to his brother.
10 Do not oppress the widow or the
  fatherless,
The alien or the poor.
Let none of you plan evil in his heart
Against his brother.'

¹¹"But they refused to heed, shrugged their shoulders, and stopped their ears so that they could not hear. ¹²Yes, they made their hearts like flint, refusing to hear the law and the words which the LORD of hosts had sent by His Spirit through the former prophets. Thus great wrath came from the LORD of hosts. ¹³Therefore it happened, *that* just as He proclaimed and they would not hear, so they called out and I would not listen," says the LORD of hosts. ¹⁴"But I scattered them with a whirlwind among all the nations which they had not known. Thus the land became desolate after them, so that no one passed through or returned; for they made the pleasant land desolate."

Jerusalem, Holy City of the Future

8 ¹Again the word of the LORD of hosts came, saying, ²"Thus says the LORD of hosts:

'I am zealous for Zion with great zeal;
With great fervor I am zealous for
  her.'

³"Thus says the LORD:

'I will return to Zion,
And dwell in the midst of Jerusalem.
Jerusalem shall be called the City of
  Truth,
The Mountain of the LORD of hosts,
The Holy Mountain.'

⁴"Thus says the LORD of hosts:

'Old men and old women shall again
  sit

6:14 ᵃFollowing Masoretic Text, Targum, and Vulgate; Syriac reads *for Heldai* (compare verse 10); Septuagint reads *for the patient ones.*
7:2 ᵃLiterally *they* (compare verse 5) ᵇOr *Sar-Ezer*
ᶜHebrew *Bethel*   7:7 ᵃHebrew *Negev*

THE DATES OF HAGGAI AND ZECHARIAH

Haggai and Zechariah provide dates for certain of their prophecies. The dates are counted from the 1st year of Darius I, that is, from April, 521 B.C. Darius actually ascended Persia's throne in September, 522 B.C., but did not secure his position until 521 B.C. The "second year of King Darius" (Hag. 1:1; Zech. 1:1) is reckoned as beginning in April, 520 B.C. The rebuilt temple was dedicated in March, 515 B.C. (Ezra 6:15).

Reference	Month	Day	Year	Modern Calendar
Haggai				
1:1	6th	1st	2nd	August 29, 520 B.C.
1:15	6th	24th		September 21, 520 B.C.
2:1	7th	21st		October 17, 520 B.C.
2:10, 18, 20	9th	24th		December 18, 520 B.C.
Zechariah				
1:1	8th	–	2nd	November, 520 B.C.
1:7	11th	24th		February 15, 519 B.C.
7:1	9th	4th	4th	December 7, 518 B.C.

In the streets of Jerusalem,
Each one with his staff in his hand
Because of great age.
5 The streets of the city
Shall be full of boys and girls
Playing in its streets.'

6"Thus says the LORD of hosts:

'If it is marvelous in the eyes of the
    remnant of this people in these
    days,
Will it also be marvelous in My eyes?'
Says the LORD of hosts.

7"Thus says the LORD of hosts:

'Behold, I will save My people from the
    land of the east
And from the land of the west;
8 I will bring them *back,*
And they shall dwell in the midst of
    Jerusalem.
They shall be My people
And I will be their God,
In truth and righteousness.'

9"Thus says the LORD of hosts:

'Let your hands be strong,
You who have been hearing in these
    days
These words by the mouth of the
    prophets,
Who *spoke* in the day the foundation
    was laid
For the house of the LORD of hosts,
That the temple might be built.

10 For before these days
There were no wages for man nor any
    hire for beast;
There was no peace from the enemy
    for whoever went out or came in;
For I set all men, everyone, against
    his neighbor.

11But now I *will* not *treat* the remnant of
this people as in the former days,' says the
LORD of hosts.

12 'For the seed *shall be* prosperous,
The vine shall give its fruit,
The ground shall give her increase,
And the heavens shall give their
    dew—
I will cause the remnant of this people
To possess all these.
13 And it shall come to pass
That just as you were a curse among
    the nations,
O house of Judah and house of Israel,
So I will save you, and you shall be a
    blessing.
Do not fear,
Let your hands be strong.'

14"For thus says the LORD of hosts:

'Just as I determined to punish you
When your fathers provoked Me to
    wrath,'
Says the LORD of hosts,
'And I would not relent,
15 So again in these days
I am determined to do good

To Jerusalem and to the house of
    Judah.
Do not fear.
16 These *are* the things you shall do:
Speak each man the truth to his
    neighbor;
Give judgment in your gates for truth,
    justice, and peace;
17 Let none of you think evil in your[a]
    heart against your neighbor;
And do not love a false oath.
For all these *are things* that I hate,'
Says the LORD."

18Then the word of the LORD of hosts
came to me, saying, 19"Thus says the LORD
of hosts:

'The fast of the fourth *month,*
The fast of the fifth,
The fast of the seventh,
And the fast of the tenth,
Shall be joy and gladness and cheerful
    feasts
For the house of Judah.
Therefore love truth and peace.'

20"Thus says the LORD of hosts:

'Peoples shall yet come,
Inhabitants of many cities;
21 The inhabitants of one *city* shall go to
    another, saying,
"Let us continue to go and pray before
    the LORD,
And seek the LORD of hosts.
I myself will go also."
22 Yes, many peoples and strong nations
Shall come to seek the LORD of hosts
    in Jerusalem,
And to pray before the LORD.'

23"Thus says the LORD of hosts: 'In
those days ten men from every language of
the nations shall grasp the sleeve of a Jewish man, saying, "Let us go with you, for
we have heard *that* God *is* with you." ' "

Tattenai's Opposition

When Zerubbabel and Jeshua re-
sumed work on the temple in 520 B.C., local
opposition reappeared. Tattenai, one of the
Persian Empire's many local officials, tried to
halt the work through intimidation, taking down
the names of those doing the work (Ezra 5:4,
10). When that failed, he wrote an official let-

ter to King Darius, reporting the Jewish settlers' insubordination. To Tattenai's probable
surprise and dismay, his letter had an opposite
effect from that he intended. Darius discovered that the Jews did indeed have royal permission for their work, and he commanded
Tattenai to help the Jews and to pay their expenses from Tattenai's own regional tax collections (6:8–10).

The portion of the Book of Ezra from Ezra
4:8 through 6:18 is not written in Hebrew, but
rather in the related language of Aramaic.
Since Aramaic evidently served as the trade
language of both the Babylonian and Persian
empires, it is easy to see why the official letters of chs. 5 and 6 (as well as those of chs.
4 and 7) are in that language. Yet the switch
of language may also serve as a reminder that
the Jews, while back in their hereditary land,
were still under foreign control. When the
book describes the Passover celebration, that
most Jewish of observances, the language re-
verts to Hebrew (6:19–22).

The temple was finished and dedicated in
the month of Adar of Darius's 6th year, corresponding to March, 515 B.C. In the following
month of Nisan, the 1st month of the year, the
Jews celebrated the Passover (6:19). Apparently the month name "Nisan" was taken from
the Babylonian language, for this 1st month
had been known by the Canaanite name "Abib"
after the Exodus (Deut. 16:1). Though the
name of the month had changed, the Jews
were again observing Passover at their temple
during their 1st month. The "descendants of
the captivity" (Ezra 6:19) were really the people of the covenant again.

■ Ezra 5:2—6:22

Ezra

Restoration of the Temple Resumed

5 :2 So Zerubbabel the son of Shealtiel
and Jeshua the son of Jozadak[a] rose up
and began to build the house of God which
is in Jerusalem; and the prophets of God
were with them, helping them.

3At the same time Tattenai the governor of *the region* beyond the River[a] and
Shethar-Boznai and their companions
came to them and spoke thus to them:
"Who has commanded you to build this
temple and finish this wall?" 4Then, accordingly, we told them the names of the

---

8:17 [a]Literally *his*
1 Chronicles 6:14

Ezra 5:2 [a]Spelled *Jehozadak* in
5:3 [a]That is, the Euphrates

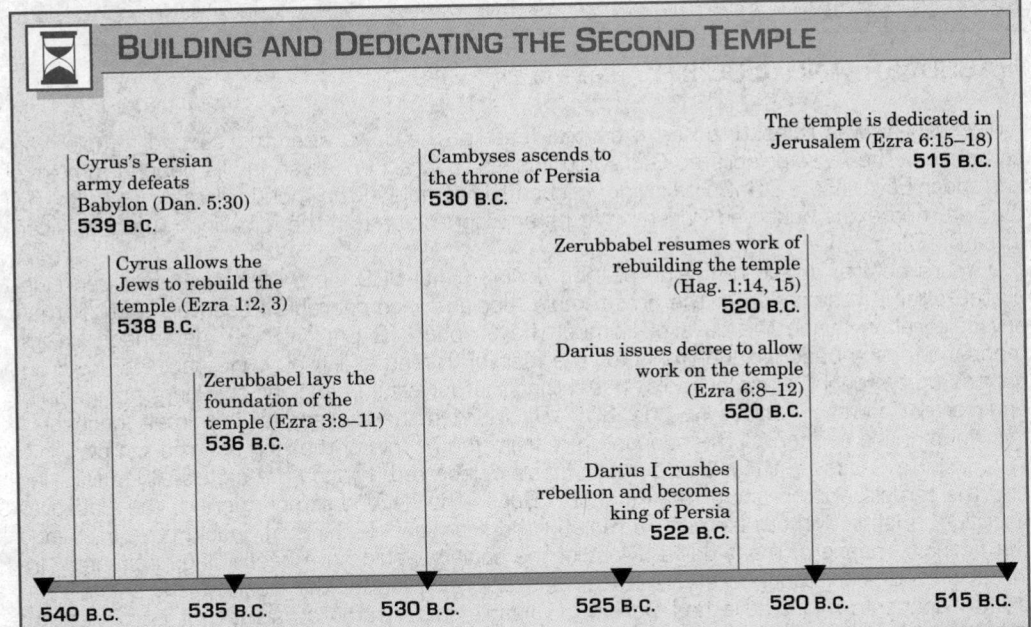

BUILDING AND DEDICATING THE SECOND TEMPLE

The temple is dedicated in
Jerusalem (Ezra 6:15–18)
515 B.C.

Cyrus's Persian
army defeats
Babylon (Dan. 5:30)
539 B.C.

Cambyses ascends to
the throne of Persia
530 B.C.

Zerubbabel resumes work of
rebuilding the temple
(Hag. 1:14, 15)
520 B.C.

Cyrus allows the
Jews to rebuild the
temple (Ezra 1:2, 3)
538 B.C.

Darius issues decree to allow
work on the temple
(Ezra 6:8–12)
520 B.C.

Zerubbabel lays the
foundation of the
temple (Ezra 3:8–11)
536 B.C.

Darius I crushes
rebellion and becomes
king of Persia
522 B.C.

540 B.C.	535 B.C.	530 B.C.	525 B.C.	520 B.C.	515 B.C.

men who were constructing this building. ⁵But the eye of their God was upon the elders of the Jews, so that they could not make them cease till a report could go to Darius. Then a written answer was returned concerning this *matter*. ⁶This is a copy of the letter that Tattenai sent:

The governor of *the region* beyond the River, and Shethar-Boznai, and his companions, the Persians who *were in the region* beyond the River, to Darius the king.

⁷(They sent a letter to him, in which was written thus)

To Darius the king:

All peace.

8 Let it be known to the king that we went into the province of Judea, to the temple of the great God, which is being built with heavy stones, and timber is being laid in the walls; and this work goes on diligently and prospers in their hands.

9 Then we asked those elders, *and* spoke thus to them: "Who commanded you to build this temple and to finish these walls?" ¹⁰We also asked them

their names to inform you, that we might write the names of the men who *were* chief among them.

11 And thus they returned us an answer, saying: "We are the servants of the God of heaven and earth, and we are rebuilding the temple that was built many years ago, which a great king of Israel built and completed. ¹²But because our fathers provoked the God of heaven to wrath, He gave them into the hand of Nebuchadnezzar king of Babylon, the Chaldean, *who* destroyed this temple and carried the people away to Babylon. ¹³However, in the first year of Cyrus king of Babylon, King Cyrus issued a decree to build this house of God. ¹⁴Also, the gold and silver articles of the house of God, which Nebuchadnezzar had taken from the temple that *was* in Jerusalem and carried into the temple of Babylon—those King Cyrus took from the temple of Babylon, and they were given to one named Sheshbazzar, whom he had made governor. ¹⁵And he said to him, 'Take these articles; go, carry them to the temple *site* that *is* in Jerusalem, and let the house of God be rebuilt on its former site.' ¹⁶Then the same Sheshbazzar came *and* laid the foundation of the house

PASSOVER AND SOCIETY (Ezra 6:19, 20)

Passover was reinstituted as a central feast of the Jews after the second temple was completed. The feast celebrated God's faithfulness to Israel in delivering His people from slavery under Egypt (Ex. 12:1–20). Having finished the temple in the month of Adar (Ezra 6:15), the returned exiles observed Passover at its appropriate time in the following month of Nisan (Ezra 6:19).

Years before, during the reign of King Josiah (640–609 B.C.), Passover had been celebrated after a restoration of the first temple. Josiah's incomparable Passover, greater than any celebration "since the days of Samuel the prophet" (2 Chr. 35:18), demanded an immense number of sacrificial animals for the festival to feed all Israel. It was not individual Judahites that brought these animals, but rather the powerful in society; the king, his leaders, and certain powerful Levites (2 Chr. 35:7–9) provided the thousands of animals necessary for the sacrifice and feast. The peasants ate from the bounty of the king and the temple.

Josiah's Passover, then, was a public feast, celebrated through the generosity of the king and the temple aristocracy of the kingdom. But in the second temple period, the Passover sacrifice, a lamb "without blemish, a male of the first year" (Ex. 12:5), would have exceeded the financial means of many Jews. Most of the society would have been village peasants, living at a bare subsistence level. Meat was a luxury reserved for the wealthy; any animals the Jewish peasants might have had were too valuable to consume as a meal! It is interesting, therefore, that the priests and Levites slaughtered lambs for the people (Ezra 6:20), assuming a role not specified for them in the Law of Moses (Ex. 12:3–6).

---

of God which *is* in Jerusalem; but from that time even until now it has been under construction, and it is not finished."

17 Now therefore, if *it seems* good to the king, let a search be made in the king's treasure house, which *is* there in Babylon, whether it is *so* that a decree was issued by King Cyrus to build this house of God at Jerusalem, and let the king send us his pleasure concerning this *matter.*

The Decree of Darius

6 ¹Then King Darius issued a decree, and a search was made in the archives,ᵃ where the treasures were stored in Babylon. ²And at Achmetha,ᵃ in the palace that *is* in the province of Media, a scroll was found, and in it a record *was* written thus:

3 In the first year of King Cyrus, King Cyrus issued a decree *concerning* the house of God at Jerusalem: "Let the house be rebuilt, the place where they offered sacrifices; and let the foundations of it be firmly laid, its height sixty cubits *and* its width sixty cubits, ⁴*with* three rows of heavy

stones and one row of new timber. Let the expenses be paid from the king's treasury. ⁵Also let the gold and silver articles of the house of God, which Nebuchadnezzar took from the temple which *is* in Jerusalem and brought to Babylon, be restored and taken back to the temple which *is* in Jerusalem, *each* to its place; and deposit *them* in the house of God"—

6 Now *therefore,* Tattenai, governor of *the region* beyond the River, and Shethar-Boznai, and your companions the Persians who *are* beyond the River, keep yourselves far from there. ⁷Let the work of this house of God alone; let the governor of the Jews and the elders of the Jews build this house of God on its site.

8 Moreover I issue a decree *as to* what you shall do for the elders of these Jews, for the building of this house of God: Let the cost be paid at the king's expense from taxes *on the region* beyond the River; this is to be given immediately to these men, so that

---

6:1 ᵃLiterally *house of the scrolls*   6:2 ᵃProbably *Ecbatana,* the ancient capital of Media

they are not hindered. ⁹And whatever they need—young bulls, rams, and lambs for the burnt offerings of the God of heaven, wheat, salt, wine, and oil, according to the request of the priests who *are* in Jerusalem—let it be given them day by day without fail, ¹⁰that they may offer sacrifices of sweet aroma to the God of heaven, and pray for the life of the king and his sons.

11 Also I issue a decree that whoever alters this edict, let a timber be pulled from his house and erected, and let him be hanged on it; and let his house be made a refuse heap because of this. ¹²And may the God who causes His name to dwell there destroy any king or people who put their hand to alter it, or to destroy this house of God which is in Jerusalem. I Darius issue a decree; let it be done diligently.

The Temple Completed and Dedicated

¹³Then Tattenai, governor of *the region* beyond the River, Shethar-Boznai, and their companions diligently did according to what King Darius had sent. ¹⁴So the elders of the Jews built, and they prospered through the prophesying of Haggai the prophet and Zechariah the son of Iddo. And they built and finished *it,* according to the commandment of the God of Israel, and according to the command of Cyrus, Darius, and Artaxerxes king of Persia. ¹⁵Now the temple was finished on the third day of the month of Adar, which was in the sixth year of the reign of King Darius. ¹⁶Then the children of Israel, the priests and the Levites and the rest of the descendants of the captivity, celebrated the dedication of this house of God with joy. ¹⁷And they offered sacrifices at the dedication of this house of God, one hundred bulls, two hundred rams, four hundred lambs, and as a sin offering for all Israel twelve male goats, according to the number of the tribes of Israel. ¹⁸They assigned the priests to their divisions and the Levites to their divisions, over the service of God in Jerusalem, as it is written in the Book of Moses.

The Passover Celebrated

¹⁹And the descendants of the captivity kept the Passover on the fourteenth *day* of the first month. ²⁰For the priests and the Levites had purified themselves; all of them *were ritually* clean. And they slaughtered the Passover *lambs* for all the descendants of the captivity, for their brethren the priests, and for themselves. ²¹Then the children of Israel who had returned from the captivity ate together with all who had separated themselves from the filth of the nations of the land in order to seek the Lord God of Israel. ²²And they kept the Feast of Unleavened Bread seven days with joy; for the Lord made them joyful, and turned the heart of the king of Assyria toward them, to strengthen their hands in the work of the house of God, the God of Israel.

Darius the Mede

Of all the chronological puzzles in the Book of Daniel, the most perplexing is the mention of "Darius the Mede." According to the apparent chronology of Daniel, this king *succeeded* Belshazzar, the son of Nabonidus, last of the Babylonian kings (Dan. 5:30, 31). But he apparently ruled *before* Cyrus (Dan. 6:28).

Identifying "Darius the Mede" is difficult since none of the extensive Babylonian or Persian records mention such a Median king in Babylon or anywhere else in the time between Belshazzar and Cyrus. There was a King Darius, but he was a Persian, not a Mede, and he reigned after, not before, Cyrus and Cyrus's son Cambyses (see "The Persian Empire" at Ezra 1:1). So the enigma remains: Who was Darius the Mede?

Some scholars believe that the stories involving Darius the Mede are highly embroidered accounts from which no genuine historical person will ever be identified. Others have suggested that "Darius" actually refers to Cyrus, who did indeed follow Belshazzar in Babylon, and who took that city at the head of both Median and Persian forces. Yet another solution proposes that Darius was not actually king, but was one of Cyrus's officials, named Gaubaruwa, who had been granted certain royal powers. These suggestions locate the story of Dan. 6 sometime around 539 B.C.

A third possibility is that the person intended by "Darius the Mede" was actually the later king of Persia, Darius I (522–486 B.C.). He might have been called a Mede, since his empire and its laws had roots in both Media and Persia. Darius's decree in Dan. 6 is called "the law of the Medes and Persians" (6:12, 15). Moreover, Darius is described as

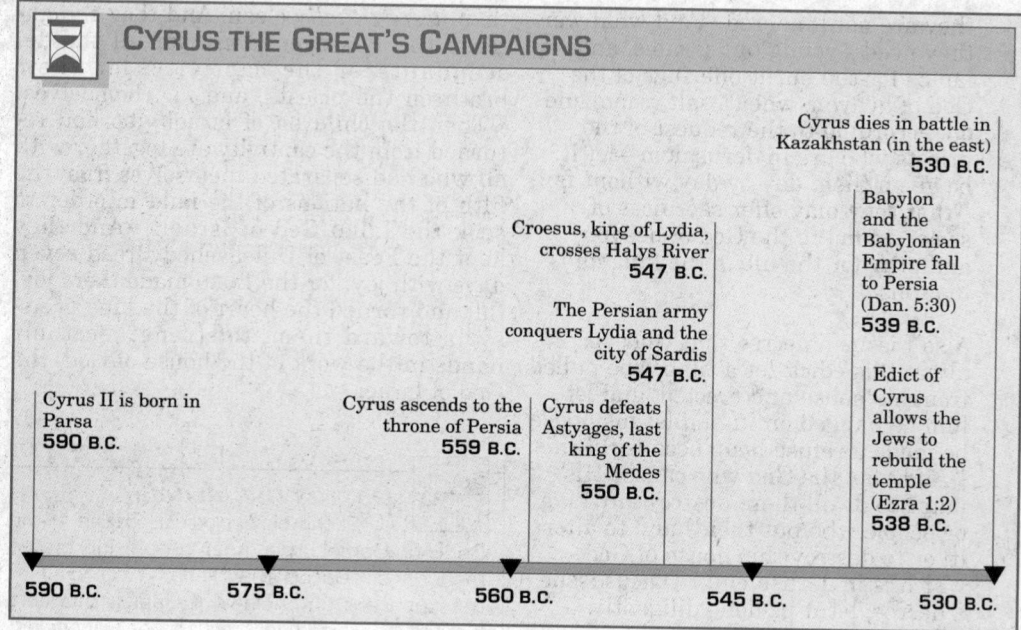

CYRUS THE GREAT'S CAMPAIGNS

Cyrus dies in battle in Kazakhstan (in the east)
530 B.C.

Croesus, king of Lydia, crosses Halys River
547 B.C.

Babylon and the Babylonian Empire fall to Persia (Dan. 5:30)
539 B.C.

The Persian army conquers Lydia and the city of Sardis
547 B.C.

Cyrus II is born in Parsa
590 B.C.

Cyrus ascends to the throne of Persia
559 B.C.

Cyrus defeats Astyages, last king of the Medes
550 B.C.

Edict of Cyrus allows the Jews to rebuild the temple (Ezra 1:2)
538 B.C.

590 B.C.   **575 B.C.**   **560 B.C.**   **545 B.C.**   **530 B.C.**

organizing an official bureaucracy of 120 satraps (Dan. 6:1, 2), which was indeed Darius I's most lasting contribution to the Persian Empire. Reading Dan. 6 in the context of Darius I locates the story around or after 522 B.C.

Darius the Mede may never be identified. Whoever he was, he ruled over the world's greatest empire and issued the world's most solemn decrees ("the law of the Medes and Persians"; Dan. 6:8). But, as Dan. 6 makes clear, neither his worldly power nor his unchangeable laws can stand against the sovereignty of Daniel's God.

■ Daniel 6:1–28

Daniel
The Plot Against Daniel

6 :1 It pleased Darius to set over the kingdom one hundred and twenty satraps, to be over the whole kingdom; [2]and over these, three governors, of whom Daniel *was* one, that the satraps might give account to them, so that the king would suffer no loss. [3]Then this Daniel distinguished himself above the governors and satraps, because an excellent spirit *was* in him; and the king gave thought to setting him over the whole realm. [4]So the governors and satraps sought to find *some* charge against Daniel concerning the kingdom; but they could find no charge or fault, because he *was* faithful; nor was there any error or fault found in him. [5]Then these men said, "We shall not find any charge against this Daniel unless we find *it* against him concerning the law of his God."

[6]So these governors and satraps thronged before the king, and said thus to him: "King Darius, live forever! [7]All the governors of the kingdom, the administrators and satraps, the counselors and advisors, have consulted together to establish a royal statute and to make a firm decree, that whoever petitions any god or man for thirty days, except you, O king, shall be cast into the den of lions. [8]Now, O king, establish the decree and sign the writing, so that it cannot be changed, according to the law of the Medes and Persians, which does not alter." [9]Therefore King Darius signed the written decree.

Daniel in the Lions' Den

[10]Now when Daniel knew that the writing was signed, he went home. And in his upper room, with his windows open toward Jerusalem, he knelt down on his knees three times that day, and prayed and gave thanks before his God, as was his custom since early days.

[11]Then these men assembled and found Daniel praying and making supplication before his God. [12]And they went before the king, and spoke concerning the king's decree: "Have you not signed a decree that

THE MEDES AND PERSIANS (Dan. 6:8)

The kingdom of Media is first mentioned in Assyrian sources describing the 9th-century campaign of Assyria's Shalmaneser III (858–824 B.C.) into the land of the Medes. Media was apparently situated in the area of modern west-central Iran and flourished for the next two centuries, according to the same Assyrian sources.

In the Assyrian texts the Medes are pictured in these centuries as comprised of a group of small autonomous tribes. The Greek historian Herodotus (484–425 B.C.) gives a legendary account of a unification of Median tribes occurring during the 7th century B.C. By the late 7th century the unified Median tribes, led by Cyaxares (c. 625–585 B.C.), were allied with the Chaldeans against Assyria. The unified Medes thus contributed to the downfall of the Assyrian capital of Nineveh in 612 B.C.

The Median kingdom continued under Astyages (c. 585–550 B.C.), successor of Cyaxares, until the middle of the 6th century B.C. In 550 B.C. Cyrus of Persia successfully united the Persian and Median tribes, though it is uncertain whether the Medes were conquered or were peacefully incorporated into Cyrus's empire.

Cyrus was apparently related to the royal houses of both Media and Persia. Thus the union of the two nations may have been accomplished as the result of Cyrus's legal claim to the throne. Media continued to be geographically distinct even under Persian government, and the Medes were second only to the Persians in importance in the Persian Empire. So even after Persia absorbed Media in 550 B.C., the Medes continued to be recognized as a distinct people. This situation is evident in the recurring phrase "the law of the Medes and Persians" (Dan. 6:8, 12, 15).

every man who petitions any god or man within thirty days, except you, O king, shall be cast into the den of lions?"

The king answered and said, "The thing *is* true, according to the law of the Medes and Persians, which does not alter."

13So they answered and said before the king, "That Daniel, who is one of the captivesa from Judah, does not show due regard for you, O king, or for the decree that you have signed, but makes his petition three times a day."

14And the king, when he heard *these* words, was greatly displeased with himself, and set *his* heart on Daniel to deliver him; and he labored till the going down of the sun to deliver him. 15Then these men approached the king, and said to the king, "Know, O king, that *it is* the law of the Medes and Persians that no decree or statute which the king establishes may be changed."

16So the king gave the command, and they brought Daniel and cast *him* into the den of lions. *But* the king spoke, saying to Daniel, "Your God, whom you serve continually, He will deliver you." 17Then a stone

was brought and laid on the mouth of the den, and the king sealed it with his own signet ring and with the signets of his lords, that the purpose concerning Daniel might not be changed.

Daniel Saved from the Lions

18Now the king went to his palace and spent the night fasting; and no musiciansa were brought before him. Also his sleep went from him. 19Then the king arose very early in the morning and went in haste to the den of lions. 20And when he came to the den, he cried out with a lamenting voice to Daniel. The king spoke, saying to Daniel, "Daniel, servant of the living God, has your God, whom you serve continually, been able to deliver you from the lions?"

21Then Daniel said to the king, "O king, live forever! 22My God sent His angel and shut the lions' mouths, so that they have not hurt me, because I was found innocent before Him; and also, O king, I have done no wrong before you."

23Now the king was exceedingly glad for him, and commanded that they should take Daniel up out of the den. So Daniel was taken up out of the den, and no injury whatever was found on him, because he believed in his God.

6:13 aLiterally *of the sons of the captivity*
6:18 aExact meaning unknown

Darius Honors God

24And the king gave the command, and they brought those men who had accused Daniel, and they cast *them* into the den of lions—them, their children, and their wives; and the lions overpowered them, and broke all their bones in pieces before they ever came to the bottom of the den.

25Then King Darius wrote:

To all peoples, nations, and languages that dwell in all the earth:

Peace be multiplied to you.

26   I make a decree that in every
      dominion of my kingdom *men must*
      tremble and fear before the God of
      Daniel.

For He *is* the living God,
And steadfast forever;
His kingdom *is the one* which shall not
   be destroyed,
And His dominion *shall endure* to the
   end.
27   He delivers and rescues,
And He works signs and wonders
In heaven and on earth,
Who has delivered Daniel from the
   power of the lions.

28So this Daniel prospered in the reign of Darius and in the reign of Cyrus the Persian.

Priestly Genealogies

Among the returned exiles in Jerusalem were probably several factions. The most influential of these was the priestly faction. The high priest Jeshua served as a coruler with Zerubbabel, and the next major Jewish leader to appear in Jerusalem would be the priestly scribe Ezra (see "Ezra the Scribe" at Ezra 7:1).

A traditional concern of the Jewish priests was genealogies, the records of who descended from which ancestors. The priests were the ones responsible for maintaining genealogical records, which explains why the genealogies that are preserved tend to be most complete when they describe the priestly families. Perhaps their task to record and preserve the Israelite bloodlines made the priests the ones most concerned about avoiding intermarriage with non-Jews (see Ezra 9; 10).

The priestly history of the kingdom of Israel begins with a series of priestly genealogies (1 Chr. 1—9). These serve as a sort of historical shorthand to bridge the generations from the first man, Adam (1 Chr. 1:1), to the first king, Saul (1 Chr. 9:35–44), after which the historical narrative itself begins in 1 Chr. 10.

That, at least, is the purpose of these genealogies in their current location at the beginning of the Book of 1 Chronicles. But in fact, the genealogies of 1 Chr. 1—9 go much further than just to King Saul. The names in ch. 9 appear to be the names of priests and Levites who lived in Jerusalem after the return from Babylonian exile (see 1 Chr. 9:1, 2). Perhaps the genealogies of 1 Chr. 1—9 were collected originally for the returned exiles and only later were adapted to serve as a brief historical prologue to his history of the kingdom.

These genealogies, as a priestly summary of Israelite history, served two important purposes for the community of returned exiles. First, they demonstrated to that ragtag group of refugees that they were part of a much larger, much more impressive divine plan, which began with Adam and continued through Abraham (1 Chr. 1:28), Israel (Jacob, 2:1), Aaron (6:50), and David (3:1). These lists also stressed that Israel's future hope rested on the priests. Aaron, Moses' priestly brother, receives more space than Moses himself (6:49–53). Moreover, long sections are devoted to the names, duties, and dwellings of the priests and Levites (6:31–81; 9:3–34).

■ 1 Chronicles 1:1—9:34

1 Chronicles
The Family of Adam—Seth to Abraham

1 :1 Adam, Seth, Enosh, 2Cainan,a Mahalalel, Jared, 3Enoch, Methuselah, Lamech, 4Noah,a Shem, Ham, and Japheth.

5The sons of Japheth *were* Gomer, Magog, Madai, Javan, Tubal, Meshech, and Tiras. 6The sons of Gomer *were* Ashkenaz, Diphath,a and Togarmah. 7The sons of Javan *were* Elishah, Tarshishah,a Kittim, and Rodanim.b

8The sons of Ham *were* Cush, Mizraim,

1:2 aHebrew *Qenan*   1:4 aFollowing Masoretic Text and Vulgate; Septuagint adds *the sons of Noah*.   1:6 aSpelled *Riphath* in Genesis 10:3   1:7 aSpelled *Tarshish* in Genesis 10:4   bSpelled *Dodanim* in Genesis 10:4

THESE ARE THE KINGS (1 Chr. 1:43)

One form of genealogical record that was known in ancient Mesopotamia was the "king list." In Assyria, the Assyrian King List preserved a detailed list of Assyrian kings and their general lengths of reign for about 1,000 years. The oldest version of the King List is a 10th-century B.C. manuscript.

The Assyrian King List begins by listing the rulers sequentially, extending from the earliest times of Assyria to Shalmaneser V (726–722 B.C.). Some later narrative sections are short chronicles listing the years of reign, the king's ancestors, and sometimes a prose narration. The King List probably functioned in the later periods as a chronological aid. Yet a broader purpose was to support the belief that kingship in Assyria descended in a continuous line with few interruptions, as if every king officially belonged to the same dynasty.

The King List is divided into a number of sections. The first section is a list of 17 names mentioned without ancestral lists, tribal relationships, or lengths of reign. At the end of the section is the statement, "These are kings who dwelt in tents." The Chronicler uses a very similar statement, "Now these were the kings," in order to introduce his king list for Edom (1:43). The Edomites inhabited the territory of Esau's descendants, so an Edomite King List was an appropriate insertion into the genealogy of Abraham's grandson Esau (1 Chr. 1:28–54).

Put, and Canaan. ⁹The sons of Cush *were* Seba, Havilah, Sabta,ᵃ Raama,ᵇ and Sabtecha. The sons of Raama *were* Sheba and Dedan. ¹⁰Cush begot Nimrod; he began to be a mighty one on the earth. ¹¹Mizraim begot Ludim, Anamim, Lehabim, Naphtuhim, ¹²Pathrusim, Casluhim (from whom came the Philistines and the Caphtorim). ¹³Canaan begot Sidon, his firstborn, and Heth; ¹⁴the Jebusite, the Amorite, and the Girgashite; ¹⁵the Hivite, the Arkite, and the Sinite; ¹⁶the Arvadite, the Zemarite, and the Hamathite.

¹⁷The sons of Shem *were* Elam, Asshur, Arphaxad, Lud, Aram, Uz, Hul, Gether, and Meshech.ᵃ ¹⁸Arphaxad begot Shelah, and Shelah begot Eber. ¹⁹To Eber were born two sons: the name of one *was* Peleg,ᵃ for in his days the earth was divided; and his brother's name *was* Joktan. ²⁰Joktan begot Almodad, Sheleph, Hazarmaveth, Jerah, ²¹Hadoram, Uzal, Diklah, ²²Ebal,ᵃ Abimael, Sheba, ²³Ophir, Havilah, and Jobab. All these *were* the sons of Joktan.

²⁴Shem, Arphaxad, Shelah, ²⁵Eber, Peleg, Reu, ²⁶Serug, Nahor, Terah, ²⁷and Abram, who *is* Abraham. ²⁸The sons of Abraham *were* Isaac and Ishmael.

The Family of Ishmael

²⁹These *are* their genealogies: The firstborn of Ishmael *was* Nebajoth; then Kedar, Adbeel, Mibsam, ³⁰Mishma, Dumah, Massa, Hadad,ᵃ Tema, ³¹Jetur, Naphish, and Kedemah. These *were* the sons of Ishmael.

The Family of Keturah

³²Now the sons born to Keturah, Abraham's concubine, *were* Zimran, Jokshan, Medan, Midian, Ishbak, and Shuah. The sons of Jokshan *were* Sheba and Dedan. ³³The sons of Midian *were* Ephah, Epher, Hanoch, Abida, and Eldaah. All these were the children of Keturah.

The Family of Isaac

³⁴And Abraham begot Isaac. The sons of Isaac *were* Esau and Israel. ³⁵The sons of Esau *were* Eliphaz, Reuel, Jeush, Jaalam, and Korah. ³⁶And the sons of Eliphaz *were* Teman, Omar, Zephi,ᵃ Gatam, *and* Kenaz; and *by* Timna,ᵇ Amalek. ³⁷The sons of Reuel *were* Nahath, Zerah, Shammah, and Mizzah.

The Family of Seir

³⁸The sons of Seir *were* Lotan, Shobal, Zibeon, Anah, Dishon, Ezer, and Dishan.

1:9 ᵃSpelled *Sabtah* in Genesis 10:7   ᵇSpelled *Raamah* in Genesis 10:7   1:17 ᵃSpelled *Mash* in Genesis 10:23   1:19 ᵃLiterally *Division*   1:22 ᵃSpelled *Obal* in Genesis 10:28   1:30 ᵃSpelled *Hadar* in Genesis 25:15   1:36 ᵃSpelled *Zepho* in Genesis 36:11   ᵇCompare Genesis 36:12

[39]And the sons of Lotan *were* Hori and Homam; Lotan's sister *was* Timna. [40]The sons of Shobal *were* Alian,[a] Manahath, Ebal, Shephi,[b] and Onam. The sons of Zibeon *were* Ajah and Anah. [41]The son of Anah *was* Dishon. The sons of Dishon *were* Hamran,[a] Eshban, Ithran, and Cheran. [42]The sons of Ezer *were* Bilhan, Zaavan, *and* Jaakan.[a] The sons of Dishan *were* Uz and Aran.

The Kings of Edom

[43]Now these *were* the kings who reigned in the land of Edom before a king reigned over the children of Israel: Bela the son of Beor, and the name of his city was Dinhabah. [44]And when Bela died, Jobab the son of Zerah of Bozrah reigned in his place. [45]When Jobab died, Husham of the land of the Temanites reigned in his place. [46]And when Husham died, Hadad the son of Bedad, who attacked Midian in the field of Moab, reigned in his place. The name of his city *was* Avith. [47]When Hadad died, Samlah of Masrekah reigned in his place. [48]And when Samlah died, Saul of Rehoboth-by-the-River reigned in his place. [49]When Saul died, Baal-Hanan the son of Achbor reigned in his place. [50]And when Baal-Hanan died, Hadad[a] reigned in his place; and the name of his city was Pai.[b] His wife's name was Mehetabel the daughter of Matred, the daughter of Mezahab. [51]Hadad died also. And the chiefs of Edom were Chief Timnah, Chief Aliah,[a] Chief Jetheth, [52]Chief Aholibamah, Chief Elah, Chief Pinon, [53]Chief Kenaz, Chief Teman, Chief Mibzar, [54]Chief Magdiel, and Chief Iram. These *were* the chiefs of Edom.

The Family of Israel

2 [1]These *were* the sons of Israel: Reuben, Simeon, Levi, Judah, Issachar, Zebulun, [2]Dan, Joseph, Benjamin, Naphtali, Gad, and Asher.

From Judah to David

[3]The sons of Judah *were* Er, Onan, and Shelah. *These* three were born to him by the daughter of Shua, the Canaanitess. Er, the firstborn of Judah, was wicked in the sight of the LORD; so He killed him. [4]And Tamar, his daughter-in-law, bore him Perez and Zerah. All the sons of Judah *were* five.

[5]The sons of Perez *were* Hezron and Hamul. [6]The sons of Zerah *were* Zimri, Ethan, Heman, Calcol, and Dara—five of them in all.

[7]The son of Carmi *was* Achar,[a] the troubler of Israel, who transgressed in the accursed thing.

[8]The son of Ethan *was* Azariah.

[9]Also the sons of Hezron who were born to him *were* Jerahmeel, Ram, and Chelubai.[a] [10]Ram begot Amminadab, and Amminadab begot Nahshon, leader of the children of Judah; [11]Nahshon begot Salma,[a] and Salma begot Boaz; [12]Boaz begot Obed, and Obed begot Jesse; [13]Jesse begot Eliab his firstborn, Abinadab the second, Shimea[a] the third, [14]Nethanel the fourth, Raddai the fifth, [15]Ozem the sixth, *and* David the seventh.

[16]Now their sisters *were* Zeruiah and Abigail. And the sons of Zeruiah *were* Abishai, Joab, and Asahel—three. [17]Abigail bore Amasa; and the father of Amasa *was* Jether the Ishmaelite.[a]

The Family of Hezron

[18]Caleb the son of Hezron had children by Azubah, *his* wife, and by Jerioth. Now these were her sons: Jesher, Shobab, and Ardon. [19]When Azubah died, Caleb took Ephrath[a] as his wife, who bore him Hur. [20]And Hur begot Uri, and Uri begot Bezalel.

TIME CAPSULE   *499 to 490 B.C.*

499   *Aristagora of Miletus leads Ionian rebellion against Persia*

495–400   *The Elephantine Papyri are written in Aramaic*

494   *Persians win naval battle and capture Miletus*

492   *Persian army invades Thrace*

490   *Beginning of the First Persian War*

490   *Darius I is defeated by the Athenians at Marathon*

1:40 [a]Spelled *Alvan* in Genesis 36:23   [b]Spelled *Shepho* in Genesis 36:23   1:41 [a]Spelled *Hemdan* in Genesis 36:26   1:42 [a]Spelled *Akan* in Genesis 36:27   1:50 [a]Spelled *Hadar* in Genesis 36:39 [b]Spelled *Pau* in Genesis 36:39   1:51 [a]Spelled *Alvah* in Genesis 36:40   2:7 [a]Spelled *Achan* in Joshua 7:1 and elsewhere   2:9 [a]Spelled *Caleb* in 2:18, 42   2:11 [a]Spelled *Salmon* in Ruth 4:21 and Luke 3:32   2:13 [a]Spelled *Shammah* in 1 Samuel 16:9 and elsewhere   2:17 [a]Compare 2 Samuel 17:25   2:19 [a]Spelled *Ephrathah* elsewhere

21Now afterward Hezron went in to the daughter of Machir the father of Gilead, whom he married when he *was* sixty years old; and she bore him Segub. 22Segub begot Jair, who had twenty-three cities in the land of Gilead. 23(Geshur and Syria took from them the towns of Jair, with Kenath and its towns—sixty towns.) All these *belonged to* the sons of Machir the father of Gilead. 24After Hezron died in Caleb Ephrathah, Hezron's wife Abijah bore him Ashhur the father of Tekoa.

The Family of Jerahmeel

25The sons of Jerahmeel, the firstborn of Hezron, *were* Ram, the firstborn, and Bunah, Oren, Ozem, *and* Ahijah. 26Jerahmeel had another wife, whose name was Atarah; she was the mother of Onam. 27The sons of Ram, the firstborn of Jerahmeel, were Maaz, Jamin, and Eker. 28The sons of Onam were Shammai and Jada. The sons of Shammai *were* Nadab and Abishur.

29And the name of the wife of Abishur *was* Abihail, and she bore him Ahban and Molid. 30The sons of Nadab *were* Seled and Appaim; Seled died without children. 31The son of Appaim *was* Ishi, the son of Ishi *was* Sheshan, and Sheshan's son *was* Ahlai. 32The sons of Jada, the brother of Shammai, *were* Jether and Jonathan; Jether died without children. 33The sons of Jonathan *were* Peleth and Zaza. These were the sons of Jerahmeel.

34Now Sheshan had no sons, only daughters. And Sheshan had an Egyptian servant whose name *was* Jarha. 35Sheshan gave his daughter to Jarha his servant as wife, and she bore him Attai. 36Attai begot Nathan, and Nathan begot Zabad; 37Zabad begot Ephlal, and Ephlal begot Obed; 38Obed begot Jehu, and Jehu begot Azariah; 39Azariah begot Helez, and Helez begot Eleasah; 40Eleasah begot Sismai, and Sismai begot Shallum; 41Shallum begot Jekamiah, and Jekamiah begot Elishama.

The Family of Caleb

42The descendants of Caleb the brother of Jerahmeel *were* Mesha, his firstborn, who was the father of Ziph, and the sons of Mareshah the father of Hebron. 43The sons of Hebron *were* Korah, Tappuah, Rekem, and Shema. 44Shema begot Raham the father of Jorkoam, and Rekem begot Shammai. 45And the son of Shammai *was* Maon, and Maon *was* the father of Beth Zur.

46Ephah, Caleb's concubine, bore Haran, Moza, and Gazez; and Haran begot Gazez. 47And the sons of Jahdai *were* Regem, Jotham, Geshan, Pelet, Ephah, and Shaaph.

48Maachah, Caleb's concubine, bore Sheber and Tirhanah. 49She also bore Shaaph the father of Madmannah, Sheva the father of Machbenah and the father of Gibea. And the daughter of Caleb *was* Achsah.

50These were the descendants of Caleb: The sons of Hur, the firstborn of Ephrathah, *were* Shobal the father of Kirjath Jearim, 51Salma the father of Bethlehem, *and* Hareph the father of Beth Gader.

52And Shobal the father of Kirjath Jearim had descendants: Haroeh, *and* half of the *families of* Manuhoth.[a] 53The families of Kirjath Jearim *were* the Ithrites, the Puthites, the Shumathites, and the Mishraites. From these came the Zorathites and the Eshtaolites.

54The sons of Salma *were* Bethlehem, the Netophathites, Atroth Beth Joab, half of the Manahethites, and the Zorites. 55And the families of the scribes who dwelt at Jabez *were* the Tirathites, the Shimeathites, *and* the Suchathites. These *were* the Kenites who came from Hammath, the father of the house of Rechab.

The Family of David

3 1Now these were the sons of David who were born to him in Hebron: The firstborn *was* Amnon, by Ahinoam the Jezreelitess; the second, Daniel,[a] by Abigail the Carmelitess; 2the third, Absalom the son of Maacah, the daughter of Talmai, king of Geshur; the fourth, Adonijah the son of Haggith; 3the fifth, Shephatiah, by Abital; the sixth, Ithream, by his wife Eglah.

4*These* six were born to him in Hebron. There he reigned seven years and six months, and in Jerusalem he reigned thirty-three years. 5And these were born to him in Jerusalem: Shimea,[a] Shobab, Nathan, and Solomon—four by Bathshua[b] the daughter of Ammiel.[c] 6Also *there* were Ibhar, Elishama,[a] Eliphelet,[b] 7Nogah,

---

2:52 [a]Same as *the Manahethites,* verse 54
3:1 [a]Called *Chileab* in 2 Samuel 3:3   3:5 [a]Spelled *Shammua* in 14:4 and 2 Samuel 5:14   [b]Spelled *Bathsheba* in 2 Samuel 11:3   [c]Called *Eliam* in 2 Samuel 11:3   3:6 [a]Spelled *Elishua* in 14:5 and 2 Samuel 5:15   [b]Spelled *Elpelet* in 14:5

GENEALOGY AND MESSIANIC HOPES (1 Chr. 3:9)

The books of Chronicles were written after the Jews had rebuilt Jerusalem. The Babylonians had destroyed the city and temple in 586 B.C., carrying many of the Judean people into exile (2 Kin. 25:1–12). When the Judean descendants returned from exile in Babylon about 50 years later, they were concerned about establishing continuity with the life of their people before the Exile. One means of showing continuity was the long genealogical lists of names, as found in 1 Chr. 1—9.

Genealogies recorded the continuity of families through the disaster of exile and beyond. To show an unbroken family line with Judean ancestors before the Exile became a way of establishing continuity and thus claiming a proper role in the postexilic society.

Family lineage became very important in the rebuilding of the Judean society. Certain families had specific roles before the Exile. Without proof of the proper pedigree one could be excluded from these roles in the postexilic community. One such example is the returning Jews who claimed to be priests but could not prove their family's priestly lineage; they were excluded from the priesthood in the postexilic community (Ezra 2:62).

In the preexilic period, the family of David had held a specific and important role in the Judean society—the role of king. Yet following the Exile, after the governorship of Zerubbabel, a descendant of David, native rule of the Judean society went to non-Davidic governors.

The genealogical list of the "sons of David" (1 Chr. 3:1) subtly supports the restoration of a Davidic king in postexilic Jerusalem. The Exile had happened, yet the descendants of David should still be the rightful rulers of Israel. The Davidic genealogy (1 Chr. 3:1–24) reminded the readers that God was not yet done with the line of David in Israel.

Nepheg, Japhia, ⁸Elishama, Eliada,ᵃ and Eliphelet—nine *in all.* ⁹*These were* all the sons of David, besides the sons of the concubines, and Tamar their sister.

The Family of Solomon

¹⁰Solomon's son *was* Rehoboam; Abijahᵃ *was* his son, Asa his son, Jehoshaphat his son, ¹¹Joramᵃ his son, Ahaziah his son, Joashᵇ his son, ¹²Amaziah his son, Azariahᵃ his son, Jotham his son, ¹³Ahaz his son, Hezekiah his son, Manasseh his son, ¹⁴Amon his son, *and* Josiah his son. ¹⁵The sons of Josiah *were* Johanan the firstborn, the second Jehoiakim, the third Zedekiah, and the fourth Shallum.ᵃ ¹⁶The sons of Jehoiakim *were* Jeconiah his son *and* Zedekiahᵃ his son.

The Family of Jeconiah

¹⁷And the sons of Jeconiahᵃ *were* Assir,ᵇ Shealtiel his son, ¹⁸*and* Malchiram, Pedaiah, Shenazzar, Jecamiah, Hoshama, and Nedabiah. ¹⁹The sons of Pedaiah *were* Zerubbabel and Shimei. The sons of Zerubbabel *were* Meshullam, Hananiah, Shelomith their sister, ²⁰and Hashubah, Ohel, Berechiah, Hasadiah, and Jushab-Hesed—five *in all.* ²¹The sons of Hananiah *were* Pelatiah

and Jeshaiah, the sons of Rephaiah, the sons of Arnan, the sons of Obadiah, and the sons of Shechaniah. ²²The son of Shechaniah was Shemaiah. The sons of Shemaiah *were* Hattush, Igal, Bariah, Neariah, and Shaphat—six *in all.* ²³The sons of Neariah *were* Elioenai, Hezekiah, and Azrikam—three *in all.* ²⁴The sons of Elioenai *were* Hodaviah, Eliashib, Pelaiah, Akkub, Johanan, Delaiah, and Anani—seven *in all.*

The Family of Judah

4 ¹The sons of Judah *were* Perez, Hezron, Carmi, Hur, and Shobal. ²And Reaiah the son of Shobal begot Jahath, and Jahath begot Ahumai and Lahad. These *were* the families of the Zorathites. ³These *were* the sons *of the father* of Etam: Jezreel, Ishma, and Idbash; and the name of their sister *was* Hazelelponi; ⁴and Penuel *was* the father of Gedor, and Ezer *was the* father of Hushah.

3:8 ᵃSpelled *Beeliada* in 14:7   3:10 ᵃSpelled *Abijam* in 1 Kings 15:1   3:11 ᵃSpelled *Jehoram* in 2 Kings 1:17 and 8:16   ᵇSpelled *Jehoash* in 2 Kings 12:1   3:12 ᵃCalled *Uzziah* in Isaiah 6:1   3:15 ᵃCalled *Jehoahaz* in 2 Kings 23:31   3:16 ᵃCompare 2 Kings 24:17   3:17 ᵃAlso called *Coniah* in Jeremiah 22:24 and *Jehoiachin* in 2 Kings 24:8   ᵇOr *Jeconiah the captive were*

These *were* the sons of Hur, the first-born of Ephrathah the father of Bethlehem.

5And Ashhur the father of Tekoa had two wives, Helah and Naarah. 6Naarah bore him Ahuzzam, Hepher, Temeni, and Haahashtari. These *were* the sons of Naarah. 7The sons of Helah *were* Zereth, Zohar, and Ethnan; 8and Koz begot Anub, Zobebah, and the families of Aharhel the son of Harum.

9Now Jabez was more honorable than his brothers, and his mother called his name Jabez,[a] saying, "Because I bore *him* in pain." 10And Jabez called on the God of Israel saying, "Oh, that You would bless me indeed, and enlarge my territory, that Your hand would be with me, and that You would keep *me* from evil, that I may not cause pain!" So God granted him what he requested.

11Chelub the brother of Shuhah begot Mehir, who *was* the father of Eshton. 12And Eshton begot Beth-Rapha, Paseah, and Tehinnah the father of Ir-Nahash. These *were* the men of Rechah.

13The sons of Kenaz *were* Othniel and Seraiah. The sons of Othniel *were* Hathath,[a] 14and Meonothai *who* begot Ophrah. Seraiah begot Joab the father of Ge Harashim,[a] for they were craftsmen. 15The sons of Caleb the son of Jephunneh *were* Iru, Elah, and Naam. The son of Elah *was* Kenaz. 16The sons of Jehallelel *were* Ziph, Ziphah, Tiria, and Asarel. 17The sons of Ezrah *were* Jether, Mered, Epher, and Jalon. And *Mered's wife*[a] *bore* Miriam, Shammai, and Ishbah the father of Eshtemoa. 18(His wife Jehudijah[a] bore Jered the father of Gedor, Heber the father of Sochoh, and Jekuthiel the father of Zanoah.) And these were the sons of Bithiah the daughter of Pharaoh, whom Mered took.

19The sons of Hodiah's wife, the sister of Naham, *were* the fathers of Keilah the Garmite and of Eshtemoa the Maachathite. 20And the sons of Shimon *were* Amnon, Rinnah, Ben-Hanan, and Tilon. And the sons of Ishi *were* Zoheth and Ben-Zoheth.

21The sons of Shelah the son of Judah *were* Er the father of Lecah, Laadah the father of Mareshah, and the families of the house of the linen workers of the house of Ashbea; 22also Jokim, the men of Chozeba, and Joash; Saraph, who ruled in Moab, and Jashubi-Lehem. Now the records are ancient. 23These *were* the potters and those who dwell at Netaim[a] and Gederah;[b] there they dwelt with the king for his work.

The Family of Simeon

24The sons of Simeon *were* Nemuel, Jamin, Jarib,[a] Zerah,[b] *and* Shaul, 25Shallum his son, Mibsam his son, and Mishma his son. 26And the sons of Mishma *were* Hamuel his son, Zacchur his son, and Shimei his son. 27Shimei had sixteen sons and six daughters; but his brothers did not have many children, nor did any of their families multiply as much as the children of Judah.

28They dwelt at Beersheba, Moladah, Hazar Shual, 29Bilhah, Ezem, Tolad, 30Bethuel, Hormah, Ziklag, 31Beth Marcaboth, Hazar Susim, Beth Biri, and at Shaaraim. These *were* their cities until the reign of David. 32And their villages *were* Etam, Ain, Rimmon, Tochen, and Ashan— five cities— 33and all the villages that *were* around these cities as far as Baal.[a] These *were* their dwelling places, and they maintained their genealogy: 34Meshobab, Jamlech, and Joshah the son of Amaziah; 35Joel, and Jehu the son of Joshibiah, the son of Seraiah, the son of Asiel; 36Elioenai, Jaakobah, Jeshohaiah, Asaiah, Adiel, Jesimiel, and Benaiah; 37Ziza the son of Shiphi, the son of Allon, the son of Jedaiah, the son of Shimri, the son of Shemaiah— 38these mentioned by name *were* leaders in their families, and their father's house increased greatly.

39So they went to the entrance of Gedor, as far as the east side of the valley, to seek pasture for their flocks. 40And they found rich, good pasture, and the land *was* broad, quiet, and peaceful; for some Hamites formerly lived there.

41These recorded by name came in the days of Hezekiah king of Judah; and they attacked their tents and the Meunites who were found there, and utterly destroyed them, as it is to this day. So they dwelt in their place, because *there was* pasture for their flocks there. 42Now *some* of them, five hundred men of the sons of Simeon, went to Mount Seir, having as their captains

4:9 [a]Literally *He Will Cause Pain*
4:13 [a]Septuagint and Vulgate add *and Meonothai.*
4:14 [a]Literally *Valley of Craftsmen*   4:17 [a]Literally *she*   4:18 [a]Or *His Judean wife*   4:23 [a]Literally *Plants* [b]Literally *Hedges*   4:24 [a]Called *Jachin* in Genesis 46:10 [b]Called *Zohar* in Genesis 46:10
4:33 [a]Or *Baalath Beer* (compare Joshua 19:8)

Pelatiah, Neariah, Rephaiah, and Uzziel, the sons of Ishi. ⁴³And they defeated the rest of the Amalekites who had escaped. They have dwelt there to this day.

The Family of Reuben

5 ¹Now the sons of Reuben the firstborn of Israel—he *was* indeed the firstborn, but because he defiled his father's bed, his birthright was given to the sons of Joseph, the son of Israel, so that the genealogy is not listed according to the birthright; ²yet Judah prevailed over his brothers, and from him *came* a ruler, although the birthright was Joseph's— ³the sons of Reuben the firstborn of Israel were Hanoch, Pallu, Hezron, and Carmi.

⁴The sons of Joel *were* Shemaiah his son, Gog his son, Shimei his son, ⁵Micah his son, Reaiah his son, Baal his son, ⁶and Beerah his son, whom Tiglath-Pileserᵃ king of Assyria carried into captivity. He *was* leader of the Reubenites. ⁷And his brethren by their families, when the genealogy of their generations was registered: the chief, Jeiel, and Zechariah, ⁸and Bela the son of Azaz, the son of Shema, the son of Joel, who dwelt in Aroer, as far as Nebo and Baal Meon. ⁹Eastward they settled as far as the entrance of the wilderness this side of the River Euphrates, because their cattle had multiplied in the land of Gilead. ¹⁰Now in the days of Saul they made war with the Hagrites, who fell by their hand; and they dwelt in their tents throughout the entire *area* east of Gilead.

The Family of Gad

¹¹And the children of Gad dwelt next to them in the land of Bashan as far as Salcah: ¹²Joel *was* the chief, Shapham the next, then Jaanai and Shaphat in Bashan, ¹³and their brethren of their father's house: Michael, Meshullam, Sheba, Jorai, Jachan, Zia, and Eber—seven *in all*. ¹⁴These *were* the children of Abihail the son of Huri, the son of Jaroah, the son of Gilead, the son of Michael, the son of Jeshishai, the son of Jahdo, the son of Buz; ¹⁵Ahi the son of Ab-

diel, the son of Guni, *was* chief of their father's house. ¹⁶And *the Gadites* dwelt in Gilead, in Bashan and in its villages, and in all the common-lands of Sharon within their borders. ¹⁷All these were registered by genealogies in the days of Jotham king of Judah, and in the days of Jeroboam king of Israel.

¹⁸The sons of Reuben, the Gadites, and half the tribe of Manasseh *had* forty-four thousand seven hundred and sixty valiant men, men able to bear shield and sword, to shoot with the bow, and skillful in war, who went to war. ¹⁹They made war with the Hagrites, Jetur, Naphish, and Nodab. ²⁰And they were helped against them, and the Hagrites were delivered into their hand, and all who *were* with them, for they cried out to God in the battle. He heeded their prayer, because they put their trust in Him. ²¹Then they took away their livestock—fifty thousand of their camels, two hundred and fifty thousand of their sheep, and two thousand of their donkeys—also one hundred thousand of their men; ²²for many fell dead, because the war *was* God's. And they dwelt in their place until the captivity.

The Family of Manasseh (East)

²³So the children of the half-tribe of Manasseh dwelt in the land. Their *numbers* increased from Bashan to Baal Hermon, that is, to Senir, or Mount Hermon. ²⁴These *were* the heads of their fathers' houses: Epher, Ishi, Eliel, Azriel, Jeremiah, Hodaviah, and Jahdiel. They were mighty men of valor, famous men, *and* heads of their fathers' houses.

²⁵And they were unfaithful to the God of their fathers, and played the harlot after the gods of the peoples of the land, whom God had destroyed before them. ²⁶So the God of Israel stirred up the spirit of Pul king of Assyria, that is, Tiglath-Pileserᵃ king of Assyria. He carried the Reubenites,

---

5:6 ᵃHebrew *Tilgath-Pilneser*   5:26 ᵃHebrew *Tilgath-Pilneser*

SCIENCE AND TECHNOLOGY

The bow was a deadly weapon of ancient armies (1 Chr. 5:18). Its most advanced form, the composite, recurved bow, was made of specially chosen layers of wood, horn, and sinew. To be strung, the limbs of such a bow had to be bent over backwards. Experienced archers with a large supply of arrows could maintain a devastating rate of fire. The range of a recurved bow was about 150 yards.

THE KING NICKNAMED "PUL" (1 Chr. 5:26)

Tiglath-Pileser III ruled Assyria from 744 to 727 B.C., restoring the empire to military greatness in the mid-8th century B.C. As early as 738 B.C. he began receiving tribute from Samaria, Damascus, and Tyre. That King Menahem of Israel paid tribute to Assyria is confirmed by both biblical (2 Kin. 15:19) and Assyrian sources. In 734 B.C. the Assyrian monarch invaded Palestine and captured Gaza.

Soon thereafter, King Rezin of the Aramean capital Damascus led a rebellion against Assyrian rule, supported by King Pekah of Israel. Damascus was captured by Tiglath-Pileser, and the Aramean kingdom was ended, being incorporated into the Assyrian Empire in 732 B.C. Further, Assyrian sources record that portions of Gilead and Galilee were captured and many of the elite classes were sent into exile.

The Chronicler recorded his genealogies about 3 centuries after Tiglath-Pileser's life. Yet he recalls the Assyrian king who carried so many "into captivity" (1 Chr. 5:5, 26), and who was known as "Pul king of Assyria" (5:26). Until recently it was not understood that the Assyrian king Pul was the same monarch as Tiglath-Pileser. Pul (or Pulu) apparently was a nickname. The king's Assyrian name, Tukulti-apil-esharra, contains the element *apil*, from which Pul probably developed. The nickname has been found in cuneiform records (clay tablets etched with wedge-shaped writing, then baked for permanence).

---

the Gadites, and the half-tribe of Manasseh into captivity. He took them to Halah, Habor, Hara, and the river of Gozan to this day.

The Family of Levi

6 ¹The sons of Levi *were* Gershon, Kohath, and Merari. ²The sons of Kohath *were* Amram, Izhar, Hebron, and Uzziel. ³The children of Amram *were* Aaron, Moses, and Miriam. And the sons of Aaron *were* Nadab, Abihu, Eleazar, and Ithamar. ⁴Eleazar begot Phinehas, *and* Phinehas begot Abishua; ⁵Abishua begot Bukki, and Bukki begot Uzzi; ⁶Uzzi begot Zerahiah, and Zerahiah begot Meraioth; ⁷Meraioth begot Amariah, and Amariah begot Ahitub; ⁸Ahitub begot Zadok, and Zadok begot Ahimaaz; ⁹Ahimaaz begot Azariah, and Azariah begot Johanan; ¹⁰Johanan begot Azariah (it was he who ministered as priest in the temple that Solomon built in Jerusalem); ¹¹Azariah begot Amariah, and Amariah begot Ahitub; ¹²Ahitub begot Zadok, and Zadok begot Shallum; ¹³Shallum begot Hilkiah, and Hilkiah begot Azariah; ¹⁴Azariah begot Seraiah, and Seraiah begot Jehozadak. ¹⁵Jehozadak went *into captivity* when the LORD carried Judah and Jerusalem into captivity by the hand of Nebuchadnezzar.

¹⁶The sons of Levi *were* Gershon,ᵃ Kohath, and Merari. ¹⁷These are the names of the sons of Gershon: Libni and Shimei. ¹⁸The sons of Kohath *were* Amram, Izhar, Hebron, and Uzziel. ¹⁹The sons of Merari *were* Mahli and Mushi. Now these *are* the families of the Levites according to their fathers: ²⁰Of Gershon *were* Libni his son, Jahath his son, Zimmah his son, ²¹Joah his son, Iddo his son, Zerah his son, *and* Jeatherai his son. ²²The sons of Kohath *were* Amminadab his son, Korah his son, Assir his son, ²³Elkanah his son, Ebiasaph his son, Assir his son, ²⁴Tahath his son, Uriel his son, Uzziah his son, and Shaul his son. ²⁵The sons of Elkanah *were* Amasai and Ahimoth. ²⁶*As for* Elkanah,ᵃ the sons of Elkanah *were* Zophaiᵇ his son, Nahathᶜ his son, ²⁷Eliabᵃ his son, Jeroham his son, *and* Elkanah his son. ²⁸The sons of Samuel *were* Joelᵃ the firstborn, and Abijah the second.ᵇ ²⁹The sons of Merari *were* Mahli, Libni his son, Shimei his son, Uzzah his son, ³⁰Shimea his son, Haggiah his son, *and* Asaiah his son.

Musicians in the House of the LORD

³¹Now these are the men whom David appointed over the service of song in the

---

6:16 ᵃHebrew *Gershom* (alternate spelling of *Gershon*, as in verses 1, 17, 20, 43, 62, and 71)   6:26 ᵃCompare verse 35 ᵇSpelled *Zuph* in verse 35 and 1 Samuel 1:1 ᶜCompare verse 34 6:27 ᵃCompare verse 34   6:28 ᵃFollowing Septuagint, Syriac, and Arabic (compare verse 33 and 1 Samuel 8:2) ᵇHebrew *Vasheni*

house of the LORD, after the ark came to rest. [32]They were ministering with music before the dwelling place of the tabernacle of meeting, until Solomon had built the house of the LORD in Jerusalem, and they served in their office according to their order.

[33]And these *are* the ones who ministered with their sons: Of the sons of the Kohathites *were* Heman the singer, the son of Joel, the son of Samuel, [34]the son of Elkanah, the son of Jeroham, the son of Eliel,[a] the son of Toah,[b] [35]the son of Zuph, the son of Elkanah, the son of Mahath, the son of Amasai, [36]the son of Elkanah, the son of Joel, the son of Azariah, the son of Zephaniah, [37]the son of Tahath, the son of Assir, the son of Ebiasaph, the son of Korah, [38]the son of Izhar, the son of Kohath, the son of Levi, the son of Israel. [39]And his brother Asaph, who stood at his right hand, *was* Asaph the son of Berachiah, the son of Shimea, [40]the son of Michael, the son of Baaseiah, the son of Malchijah, [41]the son of Ethni, the son of Zerah, the son of Adaiah, [42]the son of Ethan, the son of Zimmah, the son of Shimei, [43]the son of Jahath, the son of Gershon, the son of Levi.

[44]Their brethren, the sons of Merari, on the left hand, *were* Ethan the son of Kishi, the son of Abdi, the son of Malluch, [45]the son of Hashabiah, the son of Amaziah, the son of Hilkiah, [46]the son of Amzi, the son of Bani, the son of Shamer, [47]the son of Mahli, the son of Mushi, the son of Merari, the son of Levi.

[48]And their brethren, the Levites, *were* appointed to every kind of service of the tabernacle of the house of God.

The Family of Aaron

[49]But Aaron and his sons offered sacrifices on the altar of burnt offering and on the altar of incense, for all the work of the Most Holy *Place*, and to make atonement for Israel, according to all that Moses the servant of God had commanded. [50]Now these *are* the sons of Aaron: Eleazar his son, Phinehas his son, Abishua his son, [51]Bukki his son, Uzzi his son, Zerahiah his son, [52]Meraioth his son, Amariah his son, Ahitub his son, [53]Zadok his son, *and* Ahimaaz his son.

Dwelling Places of the Levites

[54]Now these *are* their dwelling places throughout their settlements in their territory, for they were *given* by lot to the sons of Aaron, of the family of the Kohathites: [55]They gave them Hebron in the land of Judah, with its surrounding common-lands. [56]But the fields of the city and its villages they gave to Caleb the son of Jephunneh. [57]And to the sons of Aaron they gave *one of* the cities of refuge, Hebron; also Libnah with its common-lands, Jattir, Eshtemoa with its common-lands, [58]Hilen[a] with its common-lands, Debir with its common-lands, [59]Ashan[a] with its common-lands, and Beth Shemesh with its common-lands. [60]And from the tribe of Benjamin: Geba with its common-lands, Alemeth[a] with its common-lands, and Anathoth with its common-lands. All their cities among their families *were* thirteen.

[61]To the rest of the family of the tribe of the Kohathites *they gave* by lot ten cities from half the tribe of Manasseh. [62]And to the sons of Gershon, throughout their families, *they gave* thirteen cities from the tribe of Issachar, from the tribe of Asher, from the tribe of Naphtali, and from the tribe of Manasseh in Bashan. [63]To the sons of Merari, throughout their families, *they gave* twelve cities from the tribe of Reuben, from the tribe of Gad, and from the tribe of Zebulun. [64]So the children of Israel gave *these* cities with their common-lands to the Levites. [65]And they gave by lot from the tribe of the children of Judah, from the tribe of the children of Simeon, and from the tribe of the children of Benjamin these cities which are called by *their* names.

[66]Now some of the families of the sons of Kohath *were given* cities as their territory from the tribe of Ephraim. [67]And they gave them *one of* the cities of refuge, Shechem with its common-lands, in the mountains of Ephraim, also Gezer with its common-lands, [68]Jokmeam with its common-lands, Beth Horon with its common-lands, [69]Aijalon with its common-lands, and Gath Rimmon with its common-lands. [70]And from the half-tribe of Manasseh: Aner with its common-lands and Bileam with its common-lands, for the rest of the family of the sons of Kohath.

[71]From the family of the half-tribe of Manasseh the sons of Gershon *were given* Golan in Bashan with its common-lands

---

6:34 [a]Spelled *Elihu* in 1 Samuel 1:1   [b]Spelled *Tohu* in 1 Samuel 1:1   6:58 [a]Spelled *Holon* in Joshua 21:15   6:59 [a]Spelled *Ain* in Joshua 21:16 6:60 [a]Spelled *Almon* in Joshua 21:18

and Ashtaroth with its common-lands. 72And from the tribe of Issachar: Kedesh with its common-lands, Daberath with its common-lands, 73Ramoth with its common-lands, and Anem with its common-lands. 74And from the tribe of Asher: Mashal with its common-lands, Abdon with its common-lands, 75Hukok with its common-lands, and Rehob with its common-lands. 76And from the tribe of Naphtali: Kedesh in Galilee with its common-lands, Hammon with its common-lands, and Kirjathaim with its common-lands.

77From the tribe of Zebulun the rest of the children of Merari *were given* Rimmon[a] with its common-lands and Tabor with its common-lands. 78And on the other side of the Jordan, across from Jericho, on the east side of the Jordan, *they were given* from the tribe of Reuben: Bezer in the wilderness with its common-lands, Jahzah with its common-lands, 79Kedemoth with its common-lands, and Mephaath with its common-lands. 80And from the tribe of Gad: Ramoth in Gilead with its common-lands, Mahanaim with its common-lands, 81Heshbon with its common-lands, and Jazer with its common-lands.

The Family of Issachar

7 1The sons of Issachar *were* Tola, Puah,[a] Jashub, and Shimron—four *in all.* 2The sons of Tola *were* Uzzi, Rephaiah, Jeriel, Jahmai, Jibsam, and Shemuel, heads of their father's house. *The sons of* Tola *were* mighty men of valor in their generations; their number in the days of David *was* twenty-two thousand six hundred. 3The son of Uzzi *was* Izrahiah, and the sons of Izrahiah *were* Michael, Obadiah, Joel, and Ishiah. All five of them *were* chief men. 4And with them, by their generations, according to their fathers' houses, *were* thirty-six thousand troops ready for war; for they had many wives and sons.

5Now their brethren among all the families of Issachar *were* mighty men of valor, listed by their genealogies, eighty-seven thousand in all.

The Family of Benjamin

6*The sons* of Benjamin *were* Bela, Becher, and Jediael—three *in all.* 7The sons of Bela were Ezbon, Uzzi, Uzziel, Jerimoth, and Iri—five *in all.* They *were* heads of *their* fathers' houses, and they were listed by their genealogies, twenty-two thousand and thirty-four mighty men of valor.

8The sons of Becher *were* Zemirah, Joash, Eliezer, Elioenai, Omri, Jerimoth, Abijah, Anathoth, and Alemeth. All these *are* the sons of Becher. 9And they were recorded by genealogy according to their generations, heads of their fathers' houses, twenty thousand two hundred mighty men of valor. 10The son of Jediael *was* Bilhan, and the sons of Bilhan *were* Jeush, Benjamin, Ehud, Chenaanah, Zethan, Tharshish, and Ahishahar.

11All these sons of Jediael *were* heads of their fathers' houses; *there were* seventeen thousand two hundred mighty men of valor fit to go out for war *and* battle. 12Shuppim and Huppim[a] *were* the sons of Ir, *and* Hushim *was* the son of Aher.

The Family of Naphtali

13The sons of Naphtali *were* Jahziel,[a] Guni, Jezer, and Shallum,[b] the sons of Bilhah.

The Family of Manasseh (West)

14The descendants of Manasseh: his Syrian concubine bore him Machir the father of Gilead, the father of Asriel.[a] 15Machir took as his wife *the sister* of Huppim and Shuppim,[a] whose name *was* Maachah. The name of *Gilead's* grandson[b] *was* Zelophehad,[c] but Zelophehad begot only daughters. 16(Maachah the wife of Machir bore a son, and she called his name Peresh. The name of his brother *was* Sheresh, and his sons *were* Ulam and Rakem. 17The son of Ulam *was* Bedan.) These *were* the descendants of Gilead the son of Machir, the son of Manasseh.

18His sister Hammoleketh bore Ishhod, Abiezer, and Mahlah.

19And the sons of Shemida were Ahian, Shechem, Likhi, and Aniam.

The Family of Ephraim

20The sons of Ephraim *were* Shuthelah, Bered his son, Tahath his son, Eladah his son, Tahath his son, 21Zabad his son, Shuthelah his son, and Ezer and Elead. The men of Gath who were born in *that*

6:77 [a]Hebrew *Rimmono,* alternate spelling of *Rimmon;* see 4:32   7:1 [a]Spelled *Puvah* in Genesis 46:13   7:12 [a]Called *Hupham* in Numbers 26:39   7:13 [a]Spelled *Jahzeel* in Genesis 46:24 [b]Spelled *Shillem* in Genesis 46:24   7:14 [a]The son of Gilead (compare Numbers 26:30, 31) 7:15 [a]Compare verse 12   [b]Literally *the second* [c]Compare Numbers 26:30–33

land killed *them* because they came down to take away their cattle. ²²Then Ephraim their father mourned many days, and his brethren came to comfort him.

²³And when he went in to his wife, she conceived and bore a son; and he called his name Beriah,ᵃ because tragedy had come upon his house. ²⁴Now his daughter *was* Sheerah, who built Lower and Upper Beth Horon and Uzzen Sheerah; ²⁵and Rephah *was* his son, *as well* as Resheph, and Telah his son, Tahan his son, ²⁶Laadan his son, Ammihud his son, Elishama his son, ²⁷Nunᵃ his son, and Joshua his son.

²⁸Now their possessions and dwelling places *were* Bethel and its towns: to the east Naaran, to the west Gezer and its towns, and Shechem and its towns, as far as Ayyahᵃ and its towns; ²⁹and by the borders of the children of Manasseh *were* Beth Shean and its towns, Taanach and its towns, Megiddo and its towns, Dor and its towns. In these dwelt the children of Joseph, the son of Israel.

The Family of Asher

³⁰The sons of Asher *were* Imnah, Ishvah, Ishvi, Beriah, and their sister Serah. ³¹The sons of Beriah *were* Heber and Malchiel, who was the father of Birzaith.ᵃ ³²And Heber begot Japhlet, Shomer,ᵃ Hotham,ᵇ and their sister Shua. ³³The sons of Japhlet *were* Pasach, Bimhal, and Ashvath. These *were* the children of Japhlet. ³⁴The sons of Shemer *were* Ahi, Rohgah, Jehubbah, and Aram. ³⁵And the sons of his brother Helem *were* Zophah, Imna, Shelesh, and Amal. ³⁶The sons of Zophah *were* Suah, Harnepher, Shual, Beri, Imrah, ³⁷Bezer, Hod, Shamma, Shilshah, Jithran,ᵃ and Beera. ³⁸The sons of Jether *were* Jephunneh, Pispah, and Ara. ³⁹The sons of Ulla *were* Arah, Haniel, and Rizia.

⁴⁰All these *were* the children of Asher, heads of *their* fathers' houses, choice men, mighty men of valor, chief leaders. And they were recorded by genealogies among the army fit for battle; their number *was* twenty-six thousand.

The Family Tree of King Saul of Benjamin

8 ¹Now Benjamin begot Bela his firstborn, Ashbel the second, Aharahᵃ the third, ²Nohah the fourth, and Rapha the fifth. ³The sons of Bela *were* Addar,ᵃ Gera, Abihud, ⁴Abishua, Naaman, Ahoah, ⁵Gera, Shephuphan, and Huram.

⁶These *are* the sons of Ehud, who were the heads of the fathers' *houses* of the inhabitants of Geba, and who forced them to move to Manahath: ⁷Naaman, Ahijah, and Gera who forced them to move. He begot Uzza and Ahihud.

⁸Also Shaharaim had children in the country of Moab, after he had sent away Hushim and Baara his wives. ⁹By Hodesh his wife he begot Jobab, Zibia, Mesha, Malcam, ¹⁰Jeuz, Sachiah, and Mirmah. These *were* his sons, heads of their fathers' *houses*.

¹¹And by Hushim he begot Abitub and Elpaal. ¹²The sons of Elpaal *were* Eber, Misham, and Shemed, who built Ono and Lod with its towns; ¹³and Beriah and Shema, who *were* heads of their fathers' *houses* of the inhabitants of Aijalon, who drove out the inhabitants of Gath. ¹⁴Ahio, Shashak, Jeremoth, ¹⁵Zebadiah, Arad, Eder, ¹⁶Michael, Ispah, and Joha *were* the sons of Beriah. ¹⁷Zebadiah, Meshullam, Hizki, Heber, ¹⁸Ishmerai, Jizliah, and Jobab *were* the sons of Elpaal. ¹⁹Jakim, Zichri, Zabdi, ²⁰Elienai, Zillethai, Eliel, ²¹Adaiah, Beraiah, and Shimrath *were* the sons of Shimei. ²²Ishpan, Eber, Eliel, ²³Abdon, Zichri, Hanan, ²⁴Hananiah, Elam, Antothijah, ²⁵Iphdeiah, and Penuel *were* the sons of Shashak. ²⁶Shamsherai, Shehariah, Athaliah, ²⁷Jaareshiah, Elijah, and Zichri *were* the sons of Jeroham.

²⁸These *were* heads of the fathers' *houses* by their generations, chief men. These dwelt in Jerusalem.

²⁹Now the father of Gibeon, whose wife's name *was* Maacah, dwelt at Gibeon. ³⁰And his firstborn son *was* Abdon, then Zur, Kish, Baal, Nadab, ³¹Gedor, Ahio, Zecher, ³²and Mikloth, *who* begot Shimeah.ᵃ They also dwelt alongside their relatives in Jerusalem, with their brethren. ³³Nerᵃ begot Kish, Kish begot Saul, and Saul begot Jonathan, Malchishua, Abinadab,ᵇ and Esh-Baal.ᶜ

7:23 ᵃLiterally *In Tragedy*   7:27 ᵃHebrew *Non*
7:28 ᵃMany Hebrew manuscripts, Bomberg, Septuagint, Targum, and Vulgate read *Gazza*.
7:31 ᵃOr *Birzavith* or *Birzoth*   7:32 ᵃSpelled *Shemer* in verse 34   ᵇSpelled *Helem* in verse 35
7:37 ᵃSpelled *Jether* in verse 38   8:1 ᵃSpelled *Ahiram* in Numbers 26:38   8:3 ᵃCalled *Ard* in Numbers 26:40   8:32 ᵃSpelled *Shimeam* in 9:38   8:33 ᵃAlso the son of Gibeon (compare 9:36, 39)   ᵇCalled *Jishui* in 1 Samuel 14:49   ᶜCalled *Ishbosheth* in 2 Samuel 2:8 and elsewhere

[34]The son of Jonathan *was* Merib-Baal,[a] and Merib-Baal begot Micah. [35]The sons of Micah *were* Pithon, Melech, Tarea, and Ahaz. [36]And Ahaz begot Jehoaddah;[a] Jehoaddah begot Alemeth, Azmaveth, and Zimri; and Zimri begot Moza. [37]Moza begot Binea, Raphah[a] his son, Eleasah his son, *and* Azel his son.

[38]Azel had six sons whose names *were* these: Azrikam, Bocheru, Ishmael, Sheariah, Obadiah, and Hanan. All these *were* the sons of Azel. [39]And the sons of Eshek his brother *were* Ulam his firstborn, Jeush the second, and Eliphelet the third.

[40]The sons of Ulam were mighty men of valor—archers. *They* had many sons and grandsons, one hundred and fifty *in all.* These *were* all sons of Benjamin.

9 [1]So all Israel was recorded by genealogies, and indeed, they *were* inscribed in the book of the kings of Israel. But Judah was carried away captive to Babylon because of their unfaithfulness. [2]And the first inhabitants who *dwelt* in their possessions in their cities *were* Israelites, priests, Levites, and the Nethinim.

Dwellers in Jerusalem

[3]Now in Jerusalem the children of Judah dwelt, and some of the children of Benjamin, and of the children of Ephraim and Manasseh: [4]Uthai the son of Ammihud, the son of Omri, the son of Imri, the son of Bani, of the descendants of Perez, the son of Judah. [5]Of the Shilonites: Asaiah the firstborn and his sons. [6]Of the sons of Zerah: Jeuel, and their brethren—six hundred and ninety. [7]Of the sons of Benjamin: Sallu the son of Meshullam, the son of Hodaviah, the son of Hassenuah; [8]Ibneiah the son of Jeroham; Elah the son of Uzzi, the son of Michri; Meshullam the son of Shephatiah, the son of Reuel, the son of Ibnijah; [9]and their brethren, according to their generations—nine hundred and fifty-six. All these men *were* heads of a father's *house* in their fathers' houses.

The Priests at Jerusalem

[10]Of the priests: Jedaiah, Jehoiarib, and Jachin; [11]Azariah the son of Hilkiah, the son of Meshullam, the son of Zadok, the son of Meraioth, the son of Ahitub, the officer over the house of God; [12]Adaiah the son of Jeroham, the son of Pashur, the son of Malchijah; Maasai the son of Adiel, the son of Jahzerah, the son of Meshullam, the son of Meshillemith, the son of Immer; [13]and their brethren, heads of their fathers' *houses*—one thousand seven hundred and sixty. *They were* very able men for the work of the service of the house of God.

The Levites at Jerusalem

[14]Of the Levites: Shemaiah the son of Hasshub, the son of Azrikam, the son of Hashabiah, of the sons of Merari; [15]Bakbakkar, Heresh, Galal, and Mattaniah the son of Micah, the son of Zichri, the son of Asaph; [16]Obadiah the son of Shemaiah, the son of Galal, the son of Jeduthun; and Berechiah the son of Asa, the son of Elkanah, who lived in the villages of the Netophathites.

The Levite Gatekeepers

[17]And the gatekeepers *were* Shallum, Akkub, Talmon, Ahiman, and their brethren. Shallum *was* the chief. [18]Until then *they had been* gatekeepers for the camps of the children of Levi at the King's Gate on the east.

[19]Shallum the son of Kore, the son of Ebiasaph, the son of Korah, and his brethren, from his father's house, the Korahites, *were* in charge of the work of the service, gatekeepers of the tabernacle. Their fathers had been keepers of the entrance to the camp of the LORD. [20]And Phinehas the son of Eleazar had been the officer over them in time past; the LORD *was* with him. [21]Zechariah the son of Meshelemiah *was* keeper of the door of the tabernacle of meeting.

8:34 [a]Called *Mephibosheth* in 2 Samuel 4:4
8:36 [a]Spelled *Jarah* in 9:42　　8:37 [a]Spelled *Rephaiah* in 9:43

TRADE AND ECONOMICS

The temple area contained more than just the building used for worship. Different aspects of social life took place around the temple, not the least of which was the keeping and guarding of public money (1 Chr. 9:26, 27). Pagan temples typically were centers for more than religious activity, and this diversity required large temple staffs. New Testament temples had temple police with powers of arrest.

NOT JUST GUARDING THE GATES (1 Chr. 9:17, 18)

In the genealogies of priestly and Levitical families is a long list of names and assignments of Levitical gatekeepers. We might suppose that there were more important matters to be recorded than the temple's night watchmen and custodians. The books of Chronicles, however, show that the temple gatekeepers played very significant roles in a temple-centered society with crude locks and keys.

In one role the gatekeepers functioned essentially as secret service agents, controlling the inner city security of Jerusalem. For instance, when Joash was established on Judah's throne, Levitical gatekeepers were the security force that ensured a successful transition of power (2 Chr. 23:3–5). After Joash had become king, his safety and the purity of the temple became the responsibility of these same gatekeepers.

The Chronicler also records that some gatekeepers held substantial political power themselves. By guarding doorways a gatekeeper could play the role of the royal "chief of staff," controlling access to the king. A certain Shallum, "the chief," guarded the "King's Gate on the east" (1 Chr. 9:17, 18). Another gatekeeper, a certain Zechariah, is called a "wise counselor" (1 Chr. 26:14), which is a phrase the Chronicler reserves for royal advisors (1 Chr. 27:32, 33).

A significant role for the gatekeepers was their control of temple offerings and the temple payroll. Kore, a gatekeeper of the East Gate, and his kin, gatekeepers all, were "over the freewill offerings to God," a responsibility that included distributing allotments by divisions (2 Chr. 31:14–16). Without bank vaults persons of great integrity were necessary to ensure the proper financial care of the temple and its personnel.

Thus it is evident why Chronicles records the appointment of these officials. Theirs was a "trusted office" (1 Chr. 9:26); they were crucial to the daily operation of Jerusalem and the temple.

22All those chosen as gatekeepers *were* two hundred and twelve. They were recorded by their genealogy, in their villages. David and Samuel the seer had appointed them to their trusted office. 23So they and their children *were* in charge of the gates of the house of the LORD, the house of the tabernacle, by assignment. 24The gatekeepers were assigned to the four directions: the east, west, north, and south. 25And their brethren in their villages *had* to come with them from time to time for seven days. 26For in this trusted office *were* four chief gatekeepers; they were Levites. And they had charge over the chambers and treasuries of the house of God. 27And they lodged *all* around the house of God because they *had* the responsibility, and they *were* in charge of opening *it* every morning.

Other Levite Responsibilities

28Now *some* of them were in charge of the serving vessels, for they brought them in and took them out by count. 29Some of them *were* appointed over the furnishings and over all the implements of the sanctu-

ary, and over the fine flour and the wine and the oil and the incense and the spices. 30And *some* of the sons of the priests made the ointment of the spices.

31Mattithiah of the Levites, the firstborn of Shallum the Korahite, had the trusted office over the things that were baked in the pans. 32And some of their brethren of the sons of the Kohathites *were* in charge of preparing the showbread for every Sabbath.

33These are the singers, heads of the fathers' *houses* of the Levites, *who lodged* in the chambers, *and were* free *from other duties;* for they were employed in *that* work day and night. 34These heads of the fathers' *houses* of the Levites *were* heads throughout their generations. They dwelt at Jerusalem.

The Book of Esther

The reign of the Persian king Darius I (522–486 B.C.) was as successful as it was long. He established a workable system of government, and he built splendid buildings, extensive roads, and even a canal in Egypt between the Nile River and the Red Sea. His only significant failure was his defeat in 490 B.C. in the battle of Marathon, which halted his intended invasion of the Greek peninsula.

Darius was succeeded by his son Xerxes I (486–465 B.C.), who achieved significantly less than his father. Xerxes, called Ahasuerus in the Bible, seemed content to rest on his father's laurels, except that he too tried an invasion of Greece in 480 B.C. He too was driven back.

In the Book of Esther, Ahasuerus is caricatured as a weak and foolish king, with no mind of his own. But the book is not really about Ahasuerus. Like the narratives of Dan. 1—6, the Book of Esther was meant to encourage Jews living in a foreign land. Indeed, during the Persian period, most Jews lived outside of Palestine, surrounded by potential enemies. These Jews of the Diaspora (meaning "dispersion") faced different pressures and different problems than those Jews who had returned to Palestine. Thus the Diaspora Jews began to develop a different religious focus.

The most striking difference between the religion of the Diaspora and the religion of the returned exiles had to do with intermarriage. Where Ezra and Nehemiah would rage at the Palestinian Jews who married outside of the faith (Ezra 9; 10; Neh. 13:23–28), the Book of Esther reports calmly and without apology of Esther's marriage to the Persian Ahasuerus.

Moreover, whereas the Palestinian Jews were vocal and very demonstrative about their beliefs, the Jews of the Diaspora had learned to be prudent with their faith. Esther did not tell her husband that she was a Jew. Even more striking, the story of Esther tells very clearly how God protected His people by providing them an advocate in the king's own court, yet the book recounts God's providence without ever actually mentioning the name of God. The Jews of the Diaspora were willing to die for their faith, but they did not court trouble. Until they had to take a stand, they maintained a sort of underground religion.

Some historical problems pertain to the Book of Esther. In all the royal records and histories from the court of Xerxes, there is no mention of a Queen Vashti, a Queen Esther, a prime minister named Mordecai, or a massacre of Jewish enemies. For this reason, some scholars suggest that the book was not intended as a historical narrative but rather as an instructional work of fiction. Others, though, maintain the book's historicity, noting especially the Feast of Purim, which is still celebrated today. Purim commemorates the events described in the book, and supposedly the Jews would be unlikely to establish such a feast for the plot of a fictional short story.

The narrative begins in the 3rd year of Ahasuerus's reign (Esth. 1:3), which was 483 B.C. The first return of Jews to Jerusalem had already occurred (537 B.C.), but the later returns under Ezra (possibly 458 B.C.) and Nehemiah (445 B.C.) were still in the future. The feast which the king prepared (1:5) should perhaps be identified with the assembly at Shushan that Herodotus, the Greek historian, reports was called by Ahasuerus in 483 B.C. Such magnificence and abundance were undoubtedly calculated to impress the leaders of the empire that the emperor had the power and wealth to rule as he wished.

▼   ■ Esther 1:1–22

Esther
The King Dethrones Queen Vashti

1 :1 Now it came to pass in the days of Ahasuerus[a] (this *was* the Ahasuerus who reigned over one hundred and twenty-seven provinces, from India to Ethiopia), [2]in those days when King Ahasuerus sat on the throne of his kingdom, which *was* in Shushan[a] the citadel, [3]*that* in the third year of his reign he made a feast for all his officials and servants—the powers of Persia and Media, the nobles, and the princes of the provinces *being* before him— [4]when he showed the riches of his glorious kingdom and the splendor of his excellent majesty for many days, one hundred and eighty days *in all.*

[5]And when these days were completed, the king made a feast lasting seven days for all the people who were present in Shushan the citadel, from great to small, in the court of the garden of the king's palace. [6]*There were* white and blue linen *curtains* fastened with cords of fine linen and purple on silver rods and marble pillars; *and the* couches *were* of gold and silver on a *mosaic* pavement of alabaster, turquoise, and white and black marble. [7]And they served drinks in golden vessels, each vessel being different from the other, with royal wine in abundance, according to the generosity of the king. [8]In accordance with the law, the drinking was not compulsory; for so the king had ordered all the

1:1 [a]Generally identified with Xerxes I (486–465 B.C.)   1:2 [a]Or *Susa,* and so throughout this book

THE WEAK AND TEMPERAMENTAL KING (Esth. 1:1)

In the Book of Esther, Ahasuerus (Esth. 1:1) is the king of Persia who chose Esther as his queen. He has been identified with the celebrated Xerxes I (486–465 B.C.), the fourth major king of the Persian Achaemenid dynasty (559–331 B.C.). Shortly after the outset of his reign, Xerxes quelled a rebellion in Babylon, destroying the city and carrying away the statue of Marduk, the city's patron deity.

Xerxes is best known from the writings of Herodotus (484–425 B.C.), the Greek historian who wrote the history of the wars between Greece and Persia. The son of Darius I, the Great (522–486 B.C.), Xerxes continued his father's intervention in Greek affairs, preparing a massive invasion of Greece in 480 B.C. Despite winning the first battle at Thermopylae, the venture proved fatal. The Persian navy was decisively defeated at the Bay of Salamis. Dejected, Xerxes fled Greece before the final defeat of his army at Plataea in 479 B.C.

The Persian name for Ahasuerus means "mighty man," which is ironic in view of this king's description in the Book of Esther and in the writings of Herodotus. Herodotus depicts Xerxes as an incompetent and fickle monarch, not unlike the portrayal of Ahasuerus in Esther. His roller-coaster temperament is witnessed in his reaction to Vashti's rejection (Esth. 1:9–12) and to Esther's plea for her people (Esth. 7:1–10).

---

officers of his household, that they should do according to each man's pleasure.

9Queen Vashti also made a feast for the women *in* the royal palace which *belonged* to King Ahasuerus.

10On the seventh day, when the heart of the king was merry with wine, he commanded Mehuman, Biztha, Harbona, Bigtha, Abagtha, Zethar, and Carcas, seven eunuchs who served in the presence of King Ahasuerus, 11to bring Queen Vashti before the king, *wearing* her royal crown, in order to show her beauty to the people and the officials, for she *was* beautiful to behold. 12But Queen Vashti refused to come at the king's command *brought* by *his* eunuchs; therefore the king was furious, and his anger burned within him.

13Then the king said to the wise men who understood the times (for this *was* the king's manner toward all who knew law and justice, 14those closest to him *being* Carshena, Shethar, Admatha, Tarshish, Meres, Marsena, and Memucan, the seven princes of Persia and Media, who had access to the king's presence, *and* who

ranked highest in the kingdom): 15"What *shall we* do to Queen Vashti, according to law, because she did not obey the command of King Ahasuerus *brought to her* by the eunuchs?"

16And Memucan answered before the king and the princes: "Queen Vashti has not only wronged the king, but also all the princes, and all the people who *are* in all the provinces of King Ahasuerus. 17For the queen's behavior will become known to all women, so that they will despise their husbands in their eyes, when they report, 'King Ahasuerus commanded Queen Vashti to be brought in before him, but she did not come.' 18This very day the *noble* ladies of Persia and Media will say to all the king's officials that they have heard of the behavior of the queen. Thus *there will be* excessive contempt and wrath. 19If it pleases the king, let a royal decree go out from him, and let it be recorded in the laws of the Persians and the Medes, so that it will not be altered, that Vashti shall come no more before King Ahasuerus; and let the king give her royal position to another who is

---

POLITICS AND GOVERNMENT

Ahasuerus displayed the magnificence of his kingdom (Esth. 1:1–4) much like other ancient monarchs, including the pharaohs of Egypt. Kings presented themselves to their people regularly in a formal manner, at designated locations or by parading along a certain route. Sometimes they had ulterior motives. For example, Antony and Cleopatra presented themselves as leaders of a new era, probably trying to challenge the Roman state.

better than she. [20]When the king's decree which he will make is proclaimed throughout all his empire (for it is great), all wives will honor their husbands, both great and small."

[21]And the reply pleased the king and the princes, and the king did according to the word of Memucan. [22]Then he sent letters to all the king's provinces, to each province in its own script, and to every people in their own language, that each man should be master in his own house, and speak in the language of his own people.

Esther Is Made Queen

The process by which a new queen would be chosen involved the bureaucracy of the Persian Empire. Officers were appointed in "all the provinces" (Esth. 2:3), reflecting the administrative structure of governmental provinces, called satrapies, which had been unified under Darius I. Great pains, involving 12 months of preparation (2:12), were taken to ready a woman for one night with the emperor. Not until 4 years had elapsed did Esther enter the royal palace in Ahasuerus's 7th year (2:16). The month of Tebeth corresponds to December-January, 479 B.C.

Mordecai and Esther were cousins, but her response as a daughter to him (2:7) suggests that there may have been a considerable age difference between them. A brief genealogy (2:5, 6) notes that more than a century before, Mordecai's ancestor Kish had been exiled from Jerusalem in 597 B.C. when the Babylonians captured King Jeconiah (Jehoiachin; 2 Kin. 24:10–12).

■ Esther 2:1–23

Esther
Esther Enters the Palace

2 :1 After these things, when the wrath of King Ahasuerus subsided, he remembered Vashti, what she had done, and what had been decreed against her. [2]Then the king's servants who attended him said: "Let beautiful young virgins be sought for the king; [3]and let the king appoint officers in all the provinces of his kingdom, that they may gather all the beautiful young virgins to Shushan the citadel, into the women's quarters, under the custody of Hegai[a] the king's eunuch, custodian of the women. And let beauty preparations be given *them*. [4]Then let the young woman who pleases the king be queen instead of Vashti."

This thing pleased the king, and he did so.

[5]In Shushan the citadel there was a certain Jew whose name *was* Mordecai the son of Jair, the son of Shimei, the son of Kish, a Benjamite. [6]*Kish*[a] had been carried away from Jerusalem with the captives who had been captured with Jeconiah[b] king of Judah, whom Nebuchadnezzar the king of Babylon had carried away. [7]And *Mordecai* had brought up Hadassah, that *is*, Esther, his uncle's daughter, for she had neither father nor mother. The young woman *was* lovely and beautiful. When her father and mother died, Mordecai took her as his own daughter.

[8]So it was, when the king's command and decree were heard, and when many young women were gathered at Shushan the citadel, *under* the custody of Hegai, that Esther also was taken to the king's palace, into the care of Hegai the custodian of the women. [9]Now the young woman pleased him, and she obtained his favor; so he readily gave beauty preparations to her, besides her allowance. Then seven choice maidservants were provided for her from the king's palace, and he moved her and her maidservants to the best *place* in the house of the women.

[10]Esther had not revealed her people or family, for Mordecai had charged her not to reveal *it*. [11]And every day Mordecai paced in front of the court of the women's quarters, to learn of Esther's welfare and what was happening to her.

TIME CAPSULE *486 to 479 B.C.*

486– 465	*Xerxes I of Persia is also known as Ahasuerus*
484– 425	*Greek historian Herodotus*
484	*Herodotus refers to the use of rollers for transporting weights*
480	*Xerxes invades Greece*
480	*Xerxes is defeated by the Athenians at Salamis*
479	*Xerxes' army suffers final defeat at Plataea*

2:3 [a]Hebrew *Hege*   2:6 [a]Literally *Who*   [b]Same as *Jehoiachin*, 2 Kings 24:6 and elsewhere

MORDECAI, ESTHER'S FAMOUS GUARDIAN (Esth. 2:5–7)

One of the main characters in the Book of Esther is Mordecai, who is described as Esther's guardian and adoptive father (Esth. 2:5, 7). The name "Mordecai" is a Gentile name, likely derived from the Babylonian name "Marduk," the head of Babylon's pantheon of gods. Mordecai would have also had a Jewish name, just as Esther's Jewish name was Hadassah (Esth. 2:7).

An official named "Marduka" is mentioned in a Babylonian tablet found in modern central Iraq. The tablet is dated to the reign of Xerxes I (486–465 B.C.), a king identified with the "Ahasuerus" of the Book of Esther (Esth. 1:1). Marduka was a scribe of the governor of Babylon. The same name (written with the consonants *mrdk*) has also been found in Aramaic papyri of the same century, representing an official in northern Mesopotamia.

Some scholars have concluded that either of these Mesopotamian documents could indeed be naming the Mordecai who was Esther's guardian. At least, the existence of officials with the name "Mordecai" in this period supports the picture of Mordecai as a famous person in the Persian Empire (Esth. 9:4).

12Each young woman's turn came to go in to King Ahasuerus after she had completed twelve months' preparation, according to the regulations for the women, for thus were the days of their preparation apportioned: six months with oil of myrrh, and six months with perfumes and preparations for beautifying women. 13Thus *prepared, each* young woman went to the king, and she was given whatever she desired to take with her from the women's quarters to the king's palace. 14In the evening she went, and in the morning she returned to the second house of the women, to the custody of Shaashgaz, the king's eunuch who kept the concubines. She would not go in to the king again unless the king delighted in her and called for her by name.

15Now when the turn came for Esther the daughter of Abihail the uncle of Mordecai, who had taken her as his daughter, to go in to the king, she requested nothing but what Hegai the king's eunuch, the custodian of the women, advised. And Esther obtained favor in the sight of all who saw her. 16So Esther was taken to King Ahasuerus, into his royal palace, in the tenth month, which *is* the month of Tebeth, in the seventh year of his reign. 17The king loved Esther more than all the *other* women, and she obtained grace and favor in his sight more than all the virgins; so he set the royal crown upon her head and made her queen instead of Vashti. 18Then the king made a great feast, the Feast of Esther, for all his officials and servants; and he proclaimed a holiday in the provinces and gave gifts according to the generosity of a king.

Mordecai Discovers a Plot

19When virgins were gathered together a second time, Mordecai sat within the king's gate. 20Now Esther had not revealed her family and her people, just as Mordecai had charged her, for Esther obeyed the command of Mordecai as when she was brought up by him.

21In those days, while Mordecai sat within the king's gate, two of the king's eunuchs, Bigthan and Teresh, doorkeepers, became furious and sought to lay hands on King Ahasuerus. 22So the matter became known to Mordecai, who told Queen Esther, and Esther informed the king in Mordecai's name. 23And when an inquiry was made into the matter, it was confirmed, and both were hanged on a gallows; and it was written in the book of the chronicles in the presence of the king.

Haman's Plot to Destroy the Jews

Haman tried to mask his petty revenge against Mordecai with the slaughter of an entire people. In the 1st month of Ahasuerus's 12th year (March-April, 474 B.C.), the lot was cast to determine the right day for the destruction of the Jews. The lot selected the 12th month, Adar (Esth. 3:7), and the order was sent out to everyone in the administrative chain to execute the tragic operation when that month arrived (3:12, 13). The Feast of Purim, which commemorates the events of this story, takes its name from the Hebrew word *pur,* meaning "lot."

■ Esther 3:1—8:17

Esther
Haman Makes His Request

3 :1 After these things King Ahasuerus promoted Haman, the son of Hammedatha the Agagite, and advanced him and set his seat above all the princes who *were* with him. ²And all the king's servants who *were* within the king's gate bowed and paid homage to Haman, for so the king had commanded concerning him. But Mordecai would not bow or pay homage. ³Then the king's servants who *were* within the king's gate said to Mordecai, "Why do you transgress the king's command?" ⁴Now it happened, when they spoke to him daily and he would not listen to them, that they told *it* to Haman, to see whether Mordecai's words would stand; for *Mordecai* had told them that he *was* a Jew. ⁵When Haman saw that Mordecai did not bow or pay him homage, Haman was filled with wrath. ⁶But he disdained to lay hands on Mordecai alone, for they had told him of the peo-

---

3:7 ᵃSeptuagint adds *to destroy the people of Mordecai in one day;* Vulgate adds *the nation of the Jews should be destroyed.* ᵇFollowing Masoretic Text and Vulgate; Septuagint reads *and the lot fell on the fourteenth of the month.*

---

ple of Mordecai. Instead, Haman sought to destroy all the Jews who *were* throughout the whole kingdom of Ahasuerus—the people of Mordecai.

⁷In the first month, which is the month of Nisan, in the twelfth year of King Ahasuerus, they cast Pur (that *is,* the lot), before Haman to determine the day and the month,ᵃ until *it fell on the* twelfth *month,*ᵇ which *is* the month of Adar.

⁸Then Haman said to King Ahasuerus, "There is a certain people scattered and dispersed among the people in all the provinces of your kingdom; their laws *are* different from all *other* people's, and they do not keep the king's laws. Therefore it *is* not fitting for the king to let them remain. ⁹If it pleases the king, let *a decree* be written that they be destroyed, and I will pay ten thousand talents of silver into the hands of those who do the work, to bring *it* into the king's treasuries."

¹⁰So the king took his signet ring from his hand and gave it to Haman, the son of Hammedatha the Agagite, the enemy of the Jews. ¹¹And the king said to Haman, "The money and the people *are* given to you, to do with them as seems good to you."

¹²Then the king's scribes were called on the thirteenth day of the first month, and *a decree* was written according to all that Haman commanded—to the king's satraps, to the governors who *were* over each province, to the officials of all people, to every province according to its script, and to every people in their language. In

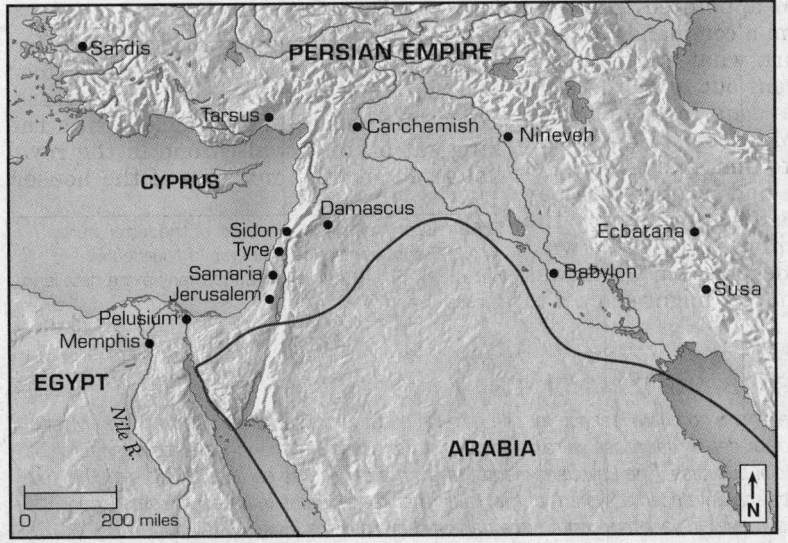

The Persian Empire
The rise of Persia was rapid. In 550 B.C. Cyrus the Persian inherited the kingdom of the Medes. In 547 B.C. he captured the Lydian capital of Sardis. In 539 B.C. he took Babylon without a fight. By 500 B.C. the Persian Empire stretched from India in the east through Asia Minor to Greece in the west, and included Egypt and some of coastal Africa to the south.

the name of King Ahasuerus it was written, and sealed with the king's signet ring. [13]And the letters were sent by couriers into all the king's provinces, to destroy, to kill, and to annihilate all the Jews, both young and old, little children and women, in one day, on the thirteenth *day* of the twelfth *month,* which *is* the month of Adar, and to plunder their possessions.[a] [14]A copy of the document was to be issued as law in every province, being published for all people, that they should be ready for that day. [15]The couriers went out, hastened by the king's command; and the decree was proclaimed in Shushan the citadel. So the king and Haman sat down to drink, but the city of Shushan was perplexed.

Esther Agrees to Help the Jews

4 [1]When Mordecai learned all that had happened, he tore his clothes and put on sackcloth and ashes, and went out into the midst of the city. He cried out with a loud and bitter cry. [2]He went as far as the front of the king's gate, for no one *might* enter the king's gate clothed with sackcloth. [3]And in every province where the king's command and decree arrived, *there was* great mourning among the Jews, with fasting, weeping, and wailing; and many lay in sackcloth and ashes.

[4]So Esther's maids and eunuchs came and told her, and the queen was deeply distressed. Then she sent garments to clothe Mordecai and take his sackcloth away from him, but he would not accept *them.* [5]Then Esther called Hathach, *one* of the king's eunuchs whom he had appointed to attend her, and she gave him a command concerning Mordecai, to learn what and why this *was.* [6]So Hathach went out to Mordecai in the city square that *was* in front of the king's gate. [7]And Mordecai told him all that had happened to him, and the sum of money that Haman had promised to pay into the king's treasuries to destroy the Jews. [8]He also gave him a copy of the written decree for their destruction, which was given at Shushan, that he might show it to Esther and explain it to her, and that he might command her to go in to the king to make supplication to him and plead before him for her people. [9]So Hathach returned and told Esther the words of Mordecai.

[10]Then Esther spoke to Hathach, and gave him a command for Mordecai: [11]"All the king's servants and the people of the king's provinces know that any man or woman who goes into the inner court to the king, who has not been called, *he has* but one law: put *all* to death, except the one to whom the king holds out the golden scepter, that he may live. Yet I myself have not been called to go in to the king these thirty days." [12]So they told Mordecai Esther's words.

[13]And Mordecai told *them* to answer Esther: "Do not think in your heart that you will escape in the king's palace any more than all the other Jews. [14]For if you remain completely silent at this time, relief and deliverance will arise for the Jews from another place, but you and your father's house will perish. Yet who knows whether you have come to the kingdom for *such* a time as this?"

[15]Then Esther told *them* to reply to Mordecai: [16]"Go, gather all the Jews who are present in Shushan, and fast for me; neither eat nor drink for three days, night or day. My maids and I will fast likewise. And so I will go to the king, which *is* against the law; and if I perish, I perish!"

[17]So Mordecai went his way and did according to all that Esther commanded him.[a]

Esther's Banquet

5 [1]Now it happened on the third day that Esther put on *her* royal *robes* and stood in the inner court of the king's palace, across from the king's house, while the king sat on his royal throne in the royal house, facing the entrance of the house.[a]

3:13 [a]Septuagint adds the text of the letter here.
4:17 [a]Septuagint adds a prayer of Mordecai here.   5:1 [a]Septuagint adds many extra details in verses 1 and 2.

TRADE AND ECONOMICS

There was no postal service for the general public until long after biblical times. Most ancient delivery services were a function of the government and were reserved for official business. The Egyptians instituted such a service as early as 2000 B.C. The Persians developed a system of their own that the Romans imitated to some extent. Documents in various scripts were delivered by couriers (Esth. 3:12, 13).

²So it was, when the king saw Queen Esther standing in the court, *that* she found favor in his sight, and the king held out to Esther the golden scepter that *was* in his hand. Then Esther went near and touched the top of the scepter.

³And the king said to her, "What do you wish, Queen Esther? What *is* your request? It shall be given to you—up to half the kingdom!"

⁴So Esther answered, "If it pleases the king, let the king and Haman come today to the banquet that I have prepared for him."

⁵Then the king said, "Bring Haman quickly, that he may do as Esther has said." So the king and Haman went to the banquet that Esther had prepared.

⁶At the banquet of wine the king said to Esther, "What *is* your petition? It shall be granted you. What *is* your request, up to half the kingdom? It shall be done!"

⁷Then Esther answered and said, "My petition and request *is this:* ⁸If I have found favor in the sight of the king, and if it pleases the king to grant my petition and fulfill my request, then let the king and Haman come to the banquet which I will prepare for them, and tomorrow I will do as the king has said."

Haman's Plot Against Mordecai

⁹So Haman went out that day joyful and with a glad heart; but when Haman saw Mordecai in the king's gate, and that he did not stand or tremble before him, he was filled with indignation against Mordecai. ¹⁰Nevertheless Haman restrained himself and went home, and he sent and called for his friends and his wife Zeresh. ¹¹Then Haman told them of his great riches, the multitude of his children, everything in which the king had promoted him, and how he had advanced him above the officials and servants of the king.

¹²Moreover Haman said, "Besides, Queen Esther invited no one but me to come in with the king to the banquet that she prepared; and tomorrow I am again invited by her, along with the king. ¹³Yet all this avails me nothing, so long as I see Mordecai the Jew sitting at the king's gate."

¹⁴Then his wife Zeresh and all his friends said to him, "Let a gallows be made, fifty cubits high, and in the morning suggest to the king that Mordecai be hanged on it; then go merrily with the king to the banquet."

And the thing pleased Haman; so he had the gallows made.

The King Honors Mordecai

6 ¹That night the king could not sleep. So one was commanded to bring the book of the records of the chronicles; and they were read before the king. ²And it was found written that Mordecai had told of Bigthana and Teresh, two of the king's eunuchs, the doorkeepers who had sought to lay hands on King Ahasuerus. ³Then the king said, "What honor or dignity has been bestowed on Mordecai for this?"

And the king's servants who attended him said, "Nothing has been done for him."

⁴So the king said, "Who *is* in the court?" Now Haman had *just* entered the outer court of the king's palace to suggest that the king hang Mordecai on the gallows that he had prepared for him.

⁵The king's servants said to him, "Haman is there, standing in the court."

And the king said, "Let him come in."

⁶So Haman came in, and the king asked him, "What shall be done for the man whom the king delights to honor?"

Now Haman thought in his heart, "Whom would the king delight to honor more than me?" ⁷And Haman answered the king, "*For* the man whom the king delights to honor, ⁸let a royal robe be brought which the king has worn, and a horse on which the king has ridden, which has a royal crest placed on its head. ⁹Then let this robe and horse be delivered to the hand of one of the king's most noble princes, that he may array the man whom the king delights to honor. Then parade him on horseback through the city square, and proclaim before him: 'Thus shall it be done to the man whom the king delights to honor!' "

¹⁰Then the king said to Haman, "Hurry, take the robe and the horse, as you have suggested, and do so for Mordecai the Jew who sits within the king's gate! Leave nothing undone of all that you have spoken."

¹¹So Haman took the robe and the horse, arrayed Mordecai and led him on horseback through the city square, and proclaimed before him, "Thus shall it be done to the man whom the king delights to honor!"

¹²Afterward Mordecai went back to the king's gate. But Haman hurried to his

house, mourning and with his head covered. [13]When Haman told his wife Zeresh and all his friends everything that had happened to him, his wise men and his wife Zeresh said to him, "If Mordecai, before whom you have begun to fall, is of Jewish descent, you will not prevail against him but will surely fall before him."

[14]While they *were* still talking with him, the king's eunuchs came, and hastened to bring Haman to the banquet which Esther had prepared.

Haman Hanged Instead of Mordecai

7 [1]So the king and Haman went to dine with Queen Esther. [2]And on the second day, at the banquet of wine, the king again said to Esther, "What *is* your petition, Queen Esther? It shall be granted you. And what *is* your request, up to half the kingdom? It shall be done!"

[3]Then Queen Esther answered and said, "If I have found favor in your sight, O king, and if it pleases the king, let my life be given me at my petition, and my people at my request. [4]For we have been sold, my people and I, to be destroyed, to be killed, and to be annihilated. Had we been sold as male and female slaves, I would have held my tongue, although the enemy could never compensate for the king's loss."

[5]So King Ahasuerus answered and said to Queen Esther, "Who is he, and where is he, who would dare presume in his heart to do such a thing?"

[6]And Esther said, "The adversary and enemy *is* this wicked Haman!"

So Haman was terrified before the king and queen.

[7]Then the king arose in his wrath from the banquet of wine *and went* into the palace garden; but Haman stood before Queen Esther, pleading for his life, for he saw that evil was determined against him by the king. [8]When the king returned from the palace garden to the place of the banquet of wine, Haman had fallen across the couch where Esther *was*. Then the king said, "Will he also assault the queen while I *am* in the house?"

As the word left the king's mouth, they covered Haman's face. [9]Now Harbonah, one of the eunuchs, said to the king, "Look! The gallows, fifty cubits high, which Haman made for Mordecai, who spoke good on the king's behalf, is standing at the house of Haman."

Then the king said, "Hang him on it!" [10]So they hanged Haman on the gallows that he had prepared for Mordecai. Then the king's wrath subsided.

Esther Saves the Jews

8 [1]On that day King Ahasuerus gave Queen Esther the house of Haman, the enemy of the Jews. And Mordecai came before the king, for Esther had told how he *was related* to her. [2]So the king took off his signet ring, which he had taken from Haman, and gave it to Mordecai; and Esther appointed Mordecai over the house of Haman.

[3]Now Esther spoke again to the king, fell down at his feet, and implored him with tears to counteract the evil of Haman the Agagite, and the scheme which he had devised against the Jews. [4]And the king held out the golden scepter toward Esther. So Esther arose and stood before the king, [5]and said, "If it pleases the king, and if I have found favor in his sight and the thing *seems* right to the king and I am pleasing in his eyes, let it be written to revoke the letters devised by Haman, the son of Hammedatha the Agagite, which he wrote to annihilate the Jews who *are* in all the king's provinces. [6]For how can I endure to see the evil that will come to my people? Or how can I endure to see the destruction of my countrymen?"

[7]Then King Ahasuerus said to Queen Esther and Mordecai the Jew, "Indeed, I have given Esther the house of Haman, and they have hanged him on the gallows because he *tried to* lay his hand on the Jews. [8]You yourselves write *a decree* concerning the Jews, as you please, in the king's name, and seal *it* with the king's signet ring; for whatever is written in the king's name and sealed with the king's signet ring no one can revoke."

[9]So the king's scribes were called at that time, in the third month, which *is* the month of Sivan, on the twenty-third *day;* and it was written, according to all that Mordecai commanded, to the Jews, the satraps, the governors, and the princes of the provinces from India to Ethiopia, one hundred and twenty-seven provinces *in all,* to every province in its own script, to every people in their own language, and to the Jews in their own script and language. [10]And he wrote in the name of King Ahasuerus, sealed *it* with the king's signet ring, and sent letters by couriers on horse-

back, riding on royal horses bred from swift steeds.[a]

[11]By these letters the king permitted the Jews who *were* in every city to gather together and protect their lives—to destroy, kill, and annihilate all the forces of any people or province that would assault them, *both* little children and women, and to plunder their possessions, [12]on one day in all the provinces of King Ahasuerus, on the thirteenth *day* of the twelfth month, which *is* the month of Adar.[a] [13]A copy of the document was to be issued as a decree in every province and published for all people, so that the Jews would be ready on that day to avenge themselves on their enemies. [14]The couriers who rode on royal horses went out, hastened and pressed on by the king's command. And the decree was issued in Shushan the citadel.

[15]So Mordecai went out from the presence of the king in royal apparel of blue and white, with a great crown of gold and a garment of fine linen and purple; and the city of Shushan rejoiced and was glad. [16]The Jews had light and gladness, joy and honor. [17]And in every province and city, wherever the king's command and decree came, the Jews had joy and gladness, a feast and a holiday. Then many of the people of the land became Jews, because fear of the Jews fell upon them.

8:10 [a]Literally *sons of the swift horses*
8:12 [a]Septuagint adds the text of the letter here.

The Countermand to Save the Jews

By Ahasuerus's reign, the Persian Empire had been in existence about 60 years and had assumed the basic form that it was to follow for the next 150. It was thoroughly hierarchical in structure, moving upward from people groups to regions to provinces (satrapies), of which there were 127. Over these the king reigned. While in theory the king was supreme and sovereign, his power was restricted by a system of laws which even he could not annul, and by a bureaucracy that was already becoming calcified.

Because the law giving the enemies of the Jews the right to kill them could not be revoked, another law had to be announced that would nullify the first. This second law gave the Jews the right to retaliate (Esth. 8:11). When the 12th month arrived (Esth. 9:1), God ac-

complished the care of His people through the rise of Mordecai who had faith in God's providential activity (see 9:3, 4; 4:14).

The Book of Esther gives the historical background for the Feast of Purim, one of the Jewish feasts not commanded in the Pentateuch. The one day of feasting at Purim is now observed on two separate days because it was first celebrated in the villages on the 14th day, but in the city of Shushan on the 15th day (9:17–19).

■ Esther 9:1—10:3

Esther
The Jews Destroy Their Tormentors

9 :1 Now in the twelfth month, that *is,* the month of Adar, on the thirteenth day, *the time* came for the king's command and his decree to be executed. On the day that the enemies of the Jews had hoped to overpower them, the opposite occurred, in that the Jews themselves overpowered those who hated them. [2]The Jews gathered together in their cities throughout all the provinces of King Ahasuerus to lay hands on those who sought their harm. And no one could withstand them, because fear of them fell upon all people. [3]And all the officials of the provinces, the satraps, the governors, and all those doing the king's work, helped the Jews, because the fear of Mordecai fell upon them. [4]For Mordecai *was* great in the king's palace, and his fame spread throughout all the provinces; for this man Mordecai became increasingly prominent. [5]Thus the Jews defeated all their enemies with the stroke of the sword, with slaughter and destruction, and did what they pleased with those who hated them.

[6]And in Shushan the citadel the Jews killed and destroyed five hundred men. [7]Also Parshandatha, Dalphon, Aspatha, [8]Poratha, Adalia, Aridatha, [9]Parmashta, Arisai, Aridai, and Vajezatha— [10]the ten sons of Haman the son of Hammedatha, the enemy of the Jews—they killed; but they did not lay a hand on the plunder.

[11]On that day the number of those who were killed in Shushan the citadel was brought to the king. [12]And the king said to Queen Esther, "The Jews have killed and destroyed five hundred men in Shushan the citadel, and the ten sons of Haman. What have they done in the rest of the king's provinces? Now what *is* your

SHUSHAN THE CITADEL AND SHUSHAN (Esth. 9:6–15)

Susa was a great city in the area of modern southwestern Iran, existing as early as the 4th millennium B.C. At one time it was a major city of the Elamites, who inhabited Susa for 3 millenniums. The name "Susa" is spelled "Shushan" in the Bible.

It seems that Susa reached its zenith during the Persian period (559–331 B.C.). Darius I (522–486 B.C.) chose Susa as the main capital of his empire. It is evident that this Persian monarch completely changed the design of the existing city, which he divided into two parts separated by a canal. Susa the citadel, or palace, was the fortified royal city to the west. The writer of the Book of Esther carefully distinguishes between "Shushan the citadel" (Esth. 9:6–12) and the unfortified town to the east, which was simply called "Shushan" (Esth. 9:13–16).

The king's residence was at Susa the citadel, where the women's quarters for the harem were also located (Esth. 2:3). The division of Susa into two halves explains why the writer of the Book of Esther describes the king's command being executed on the 13th day in Susa the citadel (Esth. 9:1, 11, 12) and then on the 14th day in the unfortified Susa (Esth. 9:14, 15).

Almost nothing is known of the lower city, as excavations have been concentrated on the upper citadel which was surrounded by massive fortifications. In Susa the citadel was the immense royal palace, as well as numerous residences presumably designed for the use of the elite classes. The palace was the setting for the Book of Esther, and the writer apparently had a familiarity with the citadel area.

---

petition? It shall be granted to you. Or what *is* your further request? It shall be done."

[13] Then Esther said, "If it pleases the king, let it be granted to the Jews who *are* in Shushan to do again tomorrow according to today's decree, and let Haman's ten sons be hanged on the gallows."

[14] So the king commanded this to be done; the decree was issued in Shushan, and they hanged Haman's ten sons.

[15] And the Jews who *were* in Shushan gathered together again on the fourteenth day of the month of Adar and killed three hundred men at Shushan; but they did not lay a hand on the plunder.

[16] The remainder of the Jews in the king's provinces gathered together and protected their lives, had rest from their enemies, and killed seventy-five thousand of their enemies; but they did not lay a hand on the plunder. [17] *This was* on the thirteenth day of the month of Adar. And on the fourteenth of *the month*[a] they rested and made it a day of feasting and gladness.

The Feast of Purim

[18] But the Jews who *were* at Shushan assembled together on the thirteenth *day,* as well as on the fourteenth; and on the fifteenth of *the month*[a] they rested, and made it a day of feasting and gladness. [19] Therefore the Jews of the villages who dwelt in the unwalled towns celebrated the fourteenth day of the month of Adar *with* gladness and feasting, as a holiday, and for sending presents to one another.

[20] And Mordecai wrote these things and sent letters to all the Jews, near and far, who *were* in all the provinces of King Ahasuerus, [21] to establish among them that they should celebrate yearly the fourteenth and fifteenth days of the month of Adar, [22] as the days on which the Jews had rest from their enemies, as the month which was turned from sorrow to joy for them, and from mourning to a holiday; that they should make them days of feasting and joy, of sending presents to one another and gifts to the poor. [23] So the Jews accepted the custom which they had begun, as Mordecai had written to them, [24] because Haman, the son of Hammedatha the Agagite, the enemy of all the Jews, had plotted against the Jews to annihilate them, and had cast Pur (that *is,* the lot), to consume them and destroy them; [25] but when *Esther*[a] came before the king, he commanded by letter that this[b] wicked plot which *Haman* had devised against the Jews should return on his own head, and that he and his sons should be hanged on the gallows.

9:17 [a]Literally *it*   9:18 [a]Literally *it*
9:25 [a]Literally *she* or *it*   [b]Literally *his*

26So they called these days Purim, after the name Pur. Therefore, because of all the words of this letter, what they had seen concerning this matter, and what had happened to them, 27the Jews established and imposed it upon themselves and their descendants and all who would join them, that without fail they should celebrate these two days every year, according to the written *instructions* and according to the *prescribed* time, 28*that* these days *should be* remembered and kept throughout every generation, every family, every province, and every city, that these days of Purim should not fail *to be observed* among the Jews, and *that* the memory of them should not perish among their descendants.

29Then Queen Esther, the daughter of Abihail, with Mordecai the Jew, wrote with full authority to confirm this second letter about Purim. 30And *Mordecai* sent letters to all the Jews, to the one hundred and twenty-seven provinces of the kingdom of Ahasuerus, *with* words of peace and truth, 31to confirm these days of Purim at their *appointed* time, as Mordecai the Jew and Queen Esther had prescribed for them, and as they had decreed for themselves and their descendants concerning matters of their fasting and lamenting. 32So the decree of Esther confirmed these matters of Purim, and it was written in the book.

Mordecai's Advancement

10 1And King Ahasuerus imposed tribute on the land and *on* the islands of the sea. 2Now all the acts of his power and his might, and the account of the greatness of Mordecai, to which the king advanced him, *are* they not written in the book of the chronicles of the kings of Media and Persia? 3For Mordecai the Jew *was* second to King Ahasuerus, and was great among the Jews and well received by the multitude of his brethren, seeking the good of his people and speaking peace to all his countrymen.[a]

10:3 [a]Literally *seed*. Septuagint and Vulgate add a dream of Mordecai here; Vulgate adds six more chapters.

Opposition to Rebuilding Jerusalem

During the reign of Darius I (522–486 B.C.), the prophets Haggai and Zechariah had encouraged the returned exiles to finish the task of rebuilding the temple (Ezra 5:1, 2). Their neighbors, who were already living in Judah and Jerusalem when the exiles arrived, had opposed the temple project (Ezra 5:3–17). King Darius, however, overruled these objections, and the temple was completed in Darius's 6th year and dedicated in the spring (March, 515 B.C.). Local opposition to the returned exiles did not end there, though. It seems to have resumed under the reign of Darius's son and successor, Xerxes I (Ahasuerus, 486–465 B.C.).

Xerxes' reign was troubled and undistinguished, marked by internal unrest in the conquered lands of Babylon and Egypt and by his failed invasion of Greece in 480 B.C. In 465 B.C. Xerxes was assassinated and succeeded by a younger son, Artaxerxes I (465–424 B.C.). Throughout his long reign, Artaxerxes faced rebellions, notably in Egypt and Cyprus. By the end of his rule, the Persian Empire was considerably less impressive than it had been at its peak, under Darius.

During the reigns of Xerxes and Artaxerxes, the local opponents to the returned exiles waged a letter-writing campaign, complaining about the continued rebuilding of Jerusalem. While this same tactic had been used earlier, during Darius's reign, this time it worked. Artaxerxes consulted the histories and found that Jerusalem had a reputation for being rebellious. Having no desire for more rebellions, he put a stop to the rebuilding. The temple was complete, but the city of Jerusalem was still in ruins.

The Book of Ezra reports this record from the reigns of Ahasuerus and Artaxerxes (4:6–23) before the record from Darius's reign (chs. 5; 6), thus out of sequence. The final editor of the book apparently included it in the earlier context in order to serve as an example of the sort of opposition that had temporarily halted the work on the temple in the days of Darius (see "Opposition to the Temple" at Ezra 4:24).

■ Ezra 4:6–23

Ezra
Later Opposition

4 :6 In the reign of Ahasuerus, in the beginning of his reign, they wrote an accusation against the inhabitants of Judah and Jerusalem.

7In the days of Artaxerxes also, Bishlam, Mithredath, Tabel, and the rest of their companions wrote to Artaxerxes king of Persia; and the letter *was* written in

---

THE GREAT AND NOBLE OSNAPPER (Ezra 4:10)

The king called "Osnapper" and described as "great and noble" was apparently well known to Ezra's readers. He is mentioned in Scripture only in Ezra 4:10, and modern scholars have been unable to determine his identity with certainty.

The letter sent to Artaxerxes I of Persia (465–424 B.C.) claims that Osnapper deported people from Babylonia to Samaria at some undetermined period before Ezra's time (Ezra 4:8–10). The settling of captives in other cities (4:10) fits what is known about Assyrian deportation policies, so Osnapper was possibly an Assyrian king. Such deportations were carried out by the later Assyrian kings, Shalmaneser V (726–722 B.C.) and Sargon II (721–705 B.C.).

Another attempt to identify Osnapper has compared his name to that of Ashurbanipal, the last prominent Assyrian monarch (668–627 B.C.). "Osnapper" may be a Hebrew variation of the more familiar name "Ashurbanipal." This Assyrian king was the destroyer of the Elamites, who are named among the people groups deported to Samaria by Osnapper (Ezra 4:9).

Aramaic script, and translated into the Aramaic language. ⁸Rehum^a the commander and Shimshai the scribe wrote a letter against Jerusalem to King Artaxerxes in this fashion:

9   From^a Rehum the commander, Shimshai the scribe, and the rest of their companions—*representatives* of the Dinaites, the Apharsathchites, the Tarpelites, the people of Persia and Erech and Babylon and Shushan,^b the Dehavites, the Elamites, ¹⁰and the rest of the nations whom the great and noble Osnapper took captive and settled in the cities of Samaria and the remainder beyond the River^a—and so forth.^b

¹¹(This *is* a copy of the letter that they sent him)

To King Artaxerxes from your servants, the men *of the region* beyond the River, and so forth:^a

12   Let it be known to the king that the Jews who came up from you have come to us at Jerusalem, and are building the rebellious and evil city, and are finishing *its* walls and repairing the foundations. ¹³Let it now be known to the king that, if this city is built and the walls completed, they will not pay tax, tribute, or custom, and the king's treasury will be diminished. ¹⁴Now because we receive

support from the palace, it was not proper for us to see the king's dishonor; therefore we have sent and informed the king, ¹⁵that search may be made in the book of the records of your fathers. And you will find in the book of the records and know that this city *is* a rebellious city, harmful to kings and provinces, and that they have incited sedition within the city in former times, for which cause this city was destroyed.

16   We inform the king that if this city is rebuilt and its walls are completed, the result will be that you will have no dominion beyond the River.

¹⁷The king sent an answer:

To Rehum the commander, *to* Shimshai the scribe, *to* the rest of their companions who dwell in Samaria, and *to* the remainder beyond the River:

Peace, and so forth.^a

18   The letter which you sent to us has been clearly read before me. ¹⁹And I gave the command, and a search has

---

4:8 ^aThe original language of Ezra 4:8 through 6:18 is Aramaic.   4:9 ^aLiterally *Then*   ^bOr *Susa*
4:10 ^aThat is, the Euphrates   ^bLiterally *and now*
4:11 ^aLiterally *and now*   4:17 ^aLiterally *and now*

been made, and it was found that this city in former times has revolted against kings, and rebellion and sedition have been fostered in it. ²⁰There have also been mighty kings over Jerusalem, who have ruled over all *the region* beyond the River; and tax, tribute, and custom were paid to them. ²¹Now give the command to make these men cease, that this city may not be built until the command is given by me.

22　Take heed now that you do not fail to do this. Why should damage increase to the hurt of the kings?

²³Now when the copy of King Artaxerxes' letter *was* read before Rehum, Shimshai the scribe, and their companions, they went up in haste to Jerusalem against the Jews, and by force of arms made them cease.

1:1　^aOr *oracle*

The Book of Malachi

Much is uncertain about the prophetic Book of Malachi. Nothing is known of the prophet outside of the words in the book. Indeed, it is not even certain that "Malachi" is a name. In Hebrew, the name "Malachi" (Mal. 1:1) simply means "My messenger" (as it is translated in Mal. 3:1), and it could be understood as an anonymous prophet, designated as God's messenger.

Also uncertain is the book's historical context. When did this prophet live? To whom were these words directed? No one can be completely sure, but some guesses are more probable than others. For instance, Malachi's emphasis on the temple and on correct priestly ritual indicates that he spoke at a time when there was a temple standing, either before the temple was destroyed in 586 B.C. or after the second temple was completed in 515 B.C. The later time is suggested by the reference to Judah's political ruler as "your governor" (Mal. 1:8), since it was during the Persian period that Judah no longer had a king.

Malachi's preaching has a very priestly tone. The sins that he condemns are sins of inappropriate worship: offering blemished sacrifices (1:8, 14), carelessness on the part of priests (2:7, 8), and neglecting the temple tithes (3:8–10). Such an emphasis fits well in the priest-dominated community of returned exiles, though Malachi's criticism of unworthy priests would surely not have been popular among the priests themselves. One period in which Malachi's preaching could have occurred would be the generation after the rebuilding of the temple, when the priests and people had grown complacent.

This at least was the situation that was encountered by Ezra and Nehemiah when they arrived in Jerusalem (around 458 and 445 B.C.). Since both leaders instituted reforms to rectify the very problems that are described in Malachi, perhaps the most likely time for the Book of Malachi is early in the reign of Artaxerxes I (465–424 B.C.), just before the arrival of the reformer Ezra in 458 B.C.

■ Malachi 1:1—4:6

Malachi

1 :1 The burden^a of the word of the LORD to Israel by Malachi.

Israel Beloved of God

2　"I have loved you," says the LORD.
　　"Yet you say, 'In what way have You
　　　　loved us?'
　　Was not Esau Jacob's brother?"
　　Says the LORD.
　　"Yet Jacob I have loved;
3　But Esau I have hated,
　　And laid waste his mountains and his
　　　　heritage
　　For the jackals of the wilderness."

4　Even though Edom has said,
　　"We have been impoverished,
　　But we will return and build the
　　　　desolate places,"

　　Thus says the LORD of hosts:

　　"They may build, but I will throw
　　　　down;
　　They shall be called the Territory of
　　　　Wickedness,
　　And the people against whom the
　　　　LORD will have indignation forever.
5　Your eyes shall see,
　　And you shall say,
　　'The LORD is magnified beyond the
　　　　border of Israel.'

Polluted Offerings

6　"A son honors *his* father,
　　And a servant *his* master.
　　If then I am the Father,

EDOM WILL NOT RETURN (Mal. 1:2–5)

To the south and east of the Dead Sea, between the Dead Sea and the Gulf of Aqaba, lies a hilly, dry land that was called Edom or Seir during Old Testament times. As neighbors, Judah and Edom often encountered each other in the course of their individual histories.

The people of Edom, the Edomites, were related to the Israelites. Edomite origins traced back to Esau, the twin brother of Jacob (Gen. 36:1). As between Esau and Jacob, the sons of Isaac and grandsons of Abraham, rivalry seems to have characterized the relationship between Israel and Edom. This rivalry apparently became especially acute, certainly from the Judean perspective, during the postexilic period.

Though Edomites and the Judeans were related, when the Babylonians utterly destroyed Judah and Jerusalem in 586 B.C., the Edomites either assisted the Babylonians or at least did nothing to aid their relatives. Archaeological results indicate that at this time the Edomites remained unscathed by the Babylonian fury.

The Edomites took Judah's misfortune as an opportunity to settle on Judean land, and, at least from the Judean viewpoint, this encroachment added insult to injury. The Judeans had been either killed or dispersed; the land was empty. The Edomites merely claimed "squatter rights," as they expanded their kingdom to the west. The Jews who returned from exile found much less land available than had once belonged to their ancestors.

In the face of Judah's political misfortunes and the rivalry with Edom which continued to flourish in the postexilic period, the prophet Malachi proclaimed that God loved Judah (Jacob), not Edom (Esau; Mal. 1:2, 3). The Judeans were restored while the Edomites would never again exist as a nation (1:4). Edom was invaded and overthrown by the Nabatean Arabs around the 5th century B.C., and by 312 B.C. Nabateans had gained control of Petra, the former capital of Edom, once known for its strong defenses (Ps. 60:9).

Where *is* My honor?
And if I *am* a Master,
Where *is* My reverence?
Says the LORD of hosts
To you priests who despise My name.
Yet you say, 'In what way have we
  despised Your name?'

7 "You offer defiled food on My altar,
  But say,
  'In what way have we defiled You?'
  By saying,
  'The table of the LORD is contemptible.'
8 And when you offer the blind as a
    sacrifice,
  Is it not evil?
  And when you offer the lame and sick,
  Is it not evil?
  Offer it then to your governor!
  Would he be pleased with you?
  Would he accept you favorably?"
  Says the LORD of hosts.

9 "But now entreat God's favor,
  That He may be gracious to us.
  While this is being *done* by your
    hands,

Will He accept you favorably?"
Says the LORD of hosts.
10 "Who *is there* even among you who
    would shut the doors,
  So that you would not kindle fire *on*
    My altar in vain?
  I have no pleasure in you,"
  Says the LORD of hosts,
  "Nor will I accept an offering from your
    hands.
11 For from the rising of the sun, even to
    its going down,
  My name *shall be* great among the
    Gentiles;
  In every place incense *shall be* offered
    to My name,
  And a pure offering;
  For My name shall be great among
    the nations,"
  Says the LORD of hosts.

12 "But you profane it,
  In that you say,
  'The table of the LORD[a] is defiled;
  And its fruit, its food, *is* contemptible.'

1:12 [a]Following Bomberg; Masoretic Text reads
Lord.

13 You also say,
'Oh, what a weariness!'
And you sneer at it,"
Says the LORD of hosts.
"And you bring the stolen, the lame,
and the sick;
Thus you bring an offering!
Should I accept this from your hand?"
Says the LORD.

14 "But cursed *be* the deceiver
Who has in his flock a male,
And takes a vow,
But sacrifices to the Lord what is
blemished—
For I *am* a great King,"
Says the LORD of hosts,
"And My name *is to be* feared among
the nations.

Corrupt Priests

2 1 "And now, O priests, this
commandment is for you.
2 If you will not hear,
And if you will not take *it* to heart,
To give glory to My name,"
Says the LORD of hosts,
"I will send a curse upon you,
And I will curse your blessings.
Yes, I have cursed them already,
Because you do not take *it* to heart.

3 "Behold, I will rebuke your
descendants
And spread refuse on your faces,
The refuse of your solemn feasts;
And *one* will take you away with it.
4 Then you shall know that I have sent
this commandment to you,
That My covenant with Levi may
continue,"
Says the LORD of hosts.
5 "My covenant was with him, *one* of life
and peace,
And I gave them to him *that he might*
fear *Me;*
So he feared Me
And was reverent before My name.
6 The law of truth[a] was in his mouth,
And injustice was not found on his
lips.
He walked with Me in peace and
equity,
And turned many away from iniquity.

7 "For the lips of a priest should keep
knowledge,
And *people* should seek the law from
his mouth;
For he is the messenger of the LORD of
hosts.
8 But you have departed from the way;
You have caused many to stumble at
the law.
You have corrupted the covenant of
Levi,"
Says the LORD of hosts.
9 "Therefore I also have made you
contemptible and base
Before all the people,
Because you have not kept My ways
But have shown partiality in the
law."

Treachery of Infidelity

10 Have we not all one Father?
Has not one God created us?
Why do we deal treacherously with
one another
By profaning the covenant of the
fathers?
11 Judah has dealt treacherously,
And an abomination has been
committed in Israel and in
Jerusalem,
For Judah has profaned
The LORD's holy *institution* which He
loves:
He has married the daughter of a
foreign god.
12 May the LORD cut off from the tents of
Jacob
The man who does this, being awake
and aware,[a]
Yet who brings an offering to the LORD
of hosts!

TIME CAPSULE	*478 to 465 B.C.*
478– 477	*Athens forms the Delian League alliance on island of Delos*
472	*The Etemenanki destroyed by the Persian king Xerxes I*
469– 399	*Socrates, Greek philosopher*
466	*Athenians defeat Persian forces in Pamphylia*
465– 424	*Artaxerxes I of Persia is known as Longimanus*

2:6 ªOr *true instruction*   2:12 ªTalmud and
Vulgate read *teacher and student.*

13 And this is the second thing you do:
You cover the altar of the LORD with
  tears,
With weeping and crying;
So He does not regard the offering
  anymore,
Nor receive *it* with goodwill from your
  hands.
14 Yet you say, "For what reason?"
Because the LORD has been witness
Between you and the wife of your
  youth,
With whom you have dealt
  treacherously;
Yet she is your companion
And your wife by covenant.
15 But did He not make *them* one,
Having a remnant of the Spirit?
And why one?
He seeks godly offspring.
Therefore take heed to your spirit,
And let none deal treacherously with
  the wife of his youth.

16 "For the LORD God of Israel says
That He hates divorce,
For it covers one's garment with
  violence,"
Says the LORD of hosts.
"Therefore take heed to your spirit,
That you do not deal treacherously."

17 You have wearied the LORD with your
  words;
Yet you say,
"In what way have we wearied *Him*?"
In that you say,
"Everyone who does evil
Is good in the sight of the LORD,
And He delights in them,"
Or, "Where *is* the God of justice?"

The Coming Messenger

3 1 "Behold, I send My messenger,
And he will prepare the way before
  Me.
And the Lord, whom you seek,
Will suddenly come to His temple,
Even the Messenger of the covenant,
In whom you delight.
Behold, He is coming,"
Says the LORD of hosts.

2 "But who can endure the day of His
  coming?
And who can stand when He appears?
For He *is* like a refiner's fire
And like launderers' soap.

3 He will sit as a refiner and a purifier
  of silver;
He will purify the sons of Levi,
And purge them as gold and silver,
That they may offer to the LORD
An offering in righteousness.

4 "Then the offering of Judah and
  Jerusalem
Will be pleasant to the LORD,
As in the days of old,
As in former years.
5 And I will come near you for
  judgment;
I will be a swift witness
Against sorcerers,
Against adulterers,
Against perjurers,
Against those who exploit wage
  earners and widows and orphans,
And against those who turn away an
  alien—
Because they do not fear Me,"
Says the LORD of hosts.

6 "For I *am* the LORD, I do not change;
Therefore you are not consumed,
  O sons of Jacob.
7 Yet from the days of your fathers
You have gone away from My
  ordinances
And have not kept *them*.
Return to Me, and I will return to
  you,"
Says the LORD of hosts.
"But you said,
'In what way shall we return?'

Do Not Rob God

8 "Will a man rob God?
Yet you have robbed Me!
But you say,
'In what way have we robbed You?'
In tithes and offerings.
9 You are cursed with a curse,
For you have robbed Me,
Even this whole nation.
10 Bring all the tithes into the
  storehouse,
That there may be food in My house,
And try Me now in this,"
Says the LORD of hosts,
"If I will not open for you the windows
  of heaven
And pour out for you *such* blessing
That *there will* not *be room* enough *to*
  receive *it*.

Sun God or Sun of Righteousness (Mal. 4:2)

The prophet Malachi borrowed the imagery of sun worship when he mentioned the "wings" of the "Sun of Righteousness" (Mal. 4:2). Another prophet, Ezekiel, saw in his temple vision some two dozen men worshiping the sun (Ezek. 8:16). For Ezekiel, this may have been the worst example of turning away from Yahweh. The prophets knew there was no sun god, but many Judeans still worshiped Shemesh, the Canaanite sun deity.

The sun god was thought to traverse the heavens by day in his chariot drawn by horses. At night the god traveled the length of the underworld. Because this deity was able to see all the living and the dead, the sun god was called upon to witness a person's innocence, and was thus the god of justice.

Worship of the sun in Judah seems to have been a long-standing activity. The horses set up for the god at the temple (2 Kin. 23:11) indicate that worship of the sun was accepted by the priests of Yahweh. Possibly devotees kissed the back of their hands to honor the sun god (Job 31:27). Kissing was a sign of submission, as shown by Assyrian reliefs where dignitaries assume this attitude before the king.

Hymns to the sun god were used in temple worship. Even one of Israel's psalms (Ps. 104:19, 22) appears to be an adapted form of an Egyptian hymn, composed about 1350 B.C. to Egypt's sun god Aten. The psalm was probably taken over from Egyptian or Canaanite sun worship and rewritten to praise Yahweh.

The winged disk was a popular symbol for the sun god in the ancient Near East. Malachi responds that justice or righteousness should not be sought from an Egyptian or Canaanite sun god, but from Yahweh, who "shall arise with healing in His wings" (Mal. 4:2).

11 "And I will rebuke the devourer for
    your sakes,
So that he will not destroy the fruit of
    your ground,
Nor shall the vine fail to bear fruit for
    you in the field,"
Says the LORD of hosts;
12 And all nations will call you blessed,
For you will be a delightful land,"
Says the LORD of hosts.

The People Complain Harshly

13 "Your words have been harsh against
    Me,"
Says the LORD,
"Yet you say,
'What have we spoken against You?'
14 You have said,
'It is useless to serve God;
What profit *is it* that we have kept
    His ordinance,
And that we have walked as mourners
Before the LORD of hosts?
15 So now we call the proud blessed,
For those who do wickedness are
    raised up;
They even tempt God and go free.' "

A Book of Remembrance

16 Then those who feared the LORD spoke
    to one another,
And the LORD listened and heard
    them;
So a book of remembrance was
    written before Him
For those who fear the LORD
And who meditate on His name.

17 "They shall be Mine," says the LORD of
    hosts,
"On the day that I make them My
    jewels.[a]
And I will spare them
As a man spares his own son who
    serves him."
18 Then you shall again discern
Between the righteous and the
    wicked,
Between one who serves God
And one who does not serve Him.

The Great Day of God

4 1 "For behold, the day is coming,
    Burning like an oven,
And all the proud, yes, all who do
    wickedly will be stubble.
And the day which is coming shall
    burn them up,"

3:17 ᵃLiterally *special treasure*

Says the LORD of hosts,
"That will leave them neither root nor
   branch.
2 But to you who fear My name
The Sun of Righteousness shall arise
With healing in His wings;
And you shall go out
And grow fat like stall-fed calves.
3 You shall trample the wicked,
For they shall be ashes under the
   soles of your feet
On the day that I do *this*,"
Says the LORD of hosts.

4 "Remember the Law of Moses, My
   servant,
Which I commanded him in Horeb for
   all Israel,
With the statutes and judgments.
5 Behold, I will send you Elijah the
   prophet
Before the coming of the great and
   dreadful day of the LORD.
6 And he will turn
The hearts of the fathers to the
   children,
And the hearts of the children to their
   fathers,
Lest I come and strike the earth with
   a curse."

Ezra the Scribe

Artaxerxes I may have halted work on the walls of Jerusalem (Ezra 4:21), but it was still Persian policy to permit and encourage captive peoples to worship in their own ways. Following this policy, Artaxerxes allowed yet another group of exiled Jews to return to Jerusalem to establish the worship of Israel's God. Under the leadership of a priestly scribe named Ezra, the group arrived in Jerusalem in the king's 7th year (Ezra 7:8), which for Artaxerxes I was 458 B.C. Some scholars locate this return in 428 B.C. (the 37th year of Artaxerxes I) or in 398 B.C. (the 7th year of Artaxerxes II). See "The Book of Nehemiah" at Neh. 1:1.

In the history of the returned exiles, the figure of Ezra towers above all others. If the return from captivity in Babylon was seen as a new Exodus (and it often was), then Ezra was seen as the new Moses. Like Moses, he led the people through the wilderness with only God for protection (Ezra 8:21–23), settled disputes (Ezra 9; 10), and proclaimed the law (Neh. 8). The picture of Ezra in later Jewish

tradition became even more Mosaic. There is even a legend that the Books of Moses were destroyed when the temple fell, but God miraculously restored them to Ezra.

At the same time, Ezra represents a new type of leader, never before seen in Israel. He was a religious reformer without a king. Although he arrived with the permission and approval of Artaxerxes, he did not use royal authority as a basis for his reforms. Furthermore, although much of Ezra's reform was concentrated on the temple, the temple was not the whole focus of his work, as it seemed to be to earlier priestly leaders such as Jeshua.

Ezra's focus and authority was Scripture, which at that time meant the Books of Moses. In the years before the Exile, Scripture had not been treated as particularly significant. Indeed, when a part of the Law of Moses was found and read during King Josiah's reign, the king and people had evidently never heard such a message before (2 Kin. 22:8–13). Israelite worship had been concentrated on the temple, not the law. During the Exile, though, that changed. Without a temple, the Jews had to find a new center for their faith. They became the people of the Book. In this context, a new kind of religious leader arose. The Hebrew word for these leaders, usually translated "scribes," means in a sense "bookmen," learned men who were able to read and write. Ezra represents this new sort of leader. Although he is from the high priestly line of Aaron (Ezra 7:1–5), his true authority comes from his standing as "a skilled scribe in the Law of Moses" (7:6).

In Ezra 7:27—9:15, the Book of Ezra shifts to a first-person memoir format. Ezra tells his own story. While this may not seem unusual to modern readers, it is a striking new development in biblical history. The thoughts and feelings of the human actor are more clear, but the thoughts of God are less accessible, being presented through that human's consciousness.

The arduous journey from Babylon to Jerusalem took 4 months, from the 1st month to the 5th month of the year (Ezra 7:9; 8:31). Soon upon arriving, Ezra had to address the practice of mixed marriages among the Jewish community in Judah and Jerusalem. This practice had also been a problem for the Israelites at the time of the Exodus from Egypt (Num. 25:1–9). In that original Exodus, the priest Phinehas put a stop to the practice. In this second Exodus, from Babylon, the priest Ezra took charge. An assembly was convened in the

9th month (Ezra 10:9), and a 3-month investigation of the problem undertaken from the 10th month until the 1st month of the following year (10:16, 17). Ezra had to help the Jews arrive at a new understanding of themselves and of the distinctiveness of their faith in God.

▼   ■ Ezra 7:1—10:44

Ezra
The Arrival of Ezra

7 :1 Now after these things, in the reign of Artaxerxes king of Persia, Ezra the son of Seraiah, the son of Azariah, the son of Hilkiah, ²the son of Shallum, the son of Zadok, the son of Ahitub, ³the son of Amariah, the son of Azariah, the son of Meraioth, ⁴the son of Zerahiah, the son of Uzzi, the son of Bukki, ⁵the son of Abishua, the son of Phinehas, the son of Eleazar, the son of Aaron the chief priest— ⁶this Ezra came up from Babylon; and he *was* a skilled scribe in the Law of Moses, which the LORD God of Israel had given. The king granted him all his request, according to the hand of the LORD his God upon him. ⁷*Some* of the children of Israel, the priests, the Levites, the singers, the gatekeepers, and the Nethinim came up to Jerusalem in the seventh year of King Artaxerxes. ⁸And Ezra came to Jerusalem in the fifth month, which *was* in the seventh year of the king. ⁹On the first *day* of the first month he began *his* journey from Babylon, and on the first *day* of the fifth month he came to Jerusalem, according to the good hand of his God upon him. ¹⁰For Ezra had prepared his heart to seek the Law of the LORD, and to do *it,* and to teach statutes and ordinances in Israel.

The Letter of Artaxerxes to Ezra

¹¹This *is* a copy of the letter that King Artaxerxes gave Ezra the priest, the scribe, expert in the words of the commandments of the LORD, and of His statutes to Israel:

12   Artaxerxes,ᵃ king of kings,

To Ezra the priest, a scribe of the Law of the God of heaven:

Perfect *peace,* and so forth.ᵇ

13 I issue a decree that all those of the people of Israel and the priests and Levites in my realm, who volunteer to go up to Jerusalem, may go with you. ¹⁴And whereas you are being sent by the king and his seven counselors to inquire concerning Judah and Jerusalem, with regard to the Law of your God which *is* in your hand; ¹⁵and *whereas you are* to carry the silver and gold which the king and his counselors have freely offered to the God of Israel, whose dwelling *is* in Jerusalem; ¹⁶and *whereas* all the silver and gold that you may find in all the province of Babylon, along with the freewill offering of the people and the priests, *are to be* freely offered for the house of their God in Jerusalem— ¹⁷now therefore, be careful to buy with this money bulls, rams, and lambs, with their grain offerings and their drink offerings, and offer them on the altar of the house of your God in Jerusalem.

18 And whatever seems good to you and your brethren to do with the rest of the silver and the gold, do it according to the will of your God. ¹⁹Also the articles that are given to you for the service of the house of your God, deliver in full before the God of Jerusalem. ²⁰And whatever more may be needed for the house of your God, which you may have occasion to provide, pay *for it* from the king's treasury.

21 And I, *even* I, Artaxerxes the king, issue a decree to all the treasurers who *are in the region* beyond the River, that whatever Ezra the priest, the scribe of the Law of the God of heaven, may require of you, let it be done diligently, ²²up to one hundred talents of silver, one hundred kors of wheat, one hundred baths of wine, one hundred baths of oil, and salt without prescribed limit. ²³Whatever is commanded by the God of heaven, let it diligently be done for the house of the God of heaven. For why should there be wrath against the realm of the king and his sons?

24 Also we inform you that it shall not be lawful to impose tax, tribute, or

---

7:12 ᵃThe original language of Ezra 7:12–26 is Aramaic. ᵇLiterally *and now*

EZRA, NEHEMIAH, AND THE PERSIAN KING (Ezra 7:1)

Three kings of the Achaemenid dynasty of Persia (559–331 B.C.) all bore the name Artaxerxes. Although the Bible does not differentiate between these three, Artaxerxes I, known as Longimanus (465–424 B.C.), is probably the monarch who is mentioned during the period of Ezra and Nehemiah.

Artaxerxes I was the son of Xerxes. Their dynasty experienced serious difficulties during both their reigns. Rebels assassinated the father Xerxes as well as Artaxerxes' brother Darius. As king, Artaxerxes himself faced trouble on different fronts, dealing with an Egyptian rebellion, which was quelled in 455 B.C., and with a rebellion of one of his own satraps in 449 B.C. He was also fearful of a rebellion in Jerusalem. Possibly for this reason Artaxerxes was not interested in continuing the rebuilding of Jerusalem (Ezra 4:7–23).

In Artaxerxes' 7th year (458 B.C.) the Jewish scribe Ezra was sent from Babylon to Jerusalem as an emissary of the Persian king. Evidently Ezra was commissioned to organize the province of Judah along Persian designs (see Ezra 7:25, 26). Artaxerxes established tax-free status for the Jerusalem temple and its personnel (Ezra 7:24).

Later Artaxerxes did allow the walls of Jerusalem to be rebuilt at the request of Nehemiah (Neh. 1:1—2:8). Nehemiah's mission to Jerusalem is dated in Artaxerxes' 20th year (445 B.C.), and the king's decision may show the city's relative political insignificance at that time.

---

custom *on* any of the priests, Levites, singers, gatekeepers, Nethinim, or servants of this house of God. ²⁵And you, Ezra, according to your God-given wisdom, set magistrates and judges who may judge all the people who *are in the region* beyond the River, all such as know the laws of your God; and teach those who do not know *them.* ²⁶Whoever will not observe the law of your God and the law of the king, let judgment be executed speedily on him, whether *it be* death, or banishment, or confiscation of goods, or imprisonment.

²⁷Blessed *be* the LORD God of our fathers, who has put *such a thing* as this in the king's heart, to beautify the house of the LORD which *is* in Jerusalem, ²⁸and has extended mercy to me before the king and his counselors, and before all the king's mighty princes.

So I was encouraged, as the hand of the LORD my God *was* upon me; and I gathered leading men of Israel to go up with me.

Heads of Families Who Returned with Ezra

8 ¹These *are* the heads of their fathers' *houses,* and *this is* the genealogy of those who went up with me from Babylon, in the reign of King Artaxerxes: ²of the sons of Phinehas, Gershom; of the sons of Ithamar, Daniel; of the sons of David, Hattush; ³of the sons of Shecaniah, of the sons of Parosh, Zechariah; and registered with him *were* one hundred and fifty males; ⁴of the sons of Pahath-Moab, Eliehoenai the son of Zerahiah, and with him two hundred males; ⁵of the sons of Shechaniah,^a Ben-Jahaziel, and with him three hundred males; ⁶of the sons of Adin, Ebed the son of Jonathan, and with him fifty males; ⁷of the sons of Elam, Jeshaiah the son of Athaliah,

---

8:5 ^aFollowing Masoretic Text and Vulgate; Septuagint reads *the sons of Zatho,* Shechaniah.

POLITICS AND GOVERNMENT

Kings were considered representatives of the gods of their nations. In Egypt, the pharaoh was honored as if he were divine. The personal, absolute power of kings on their throne was felt on the local level, far from the palace and court, presumably because there was no competing power. The Bible presents God as having direct access to the will of any reigning monarch (Ezra 7:27; Prov. 21:1).

THE LEVITICAL SINGERS (Ezra 7:24)

During the time of Ezra and Nehemiah, various groups were associated with the temple, including priests, Levites, gatekeepers, singers, and Nethinim (Ezra 7:24; Neh. 7:73; 10:28). We should not think that these "singers" of the temple were merely a church choir. The role of Levitical singers went much beyond one of simply making music.

King David appointed Levitical singers to accompany the ark of the covenant as it was brought up to Jerusalem (1 Chr. 15:16–25). They transformed the hard work of a "moving day" into a joyous, holy procession of Yahweh. Levitical singers were also present under King Solomon when the ark of the covenant was placed in the temple and the first temple sacrifices were made (2 Chr. 5:7, 11, 12).

Later Judahite kings employed singers on important occasions. In the Passover celebrations led by kings Hezekiah (2 Chr. 30:21, 22) and Josiah (2 Chr. 35:15, 16), Levitical singers accompanied the sacrifices with songs of praise. Before King Jehoshaphat led his army out to battle a coalition of Ammon, Moab, and Mount Seir (Edom), the Levitical singers sang praises in the temple (2 Chr. 20:18, 19).

The Chronicler reports a function of the Levitical singers that is surprising to us today. When Jehoshaphat led his forces into battle, the singers were advancing before the Judahite army (2 Chr. 20:21, 22). It is common for armies to go into battle by marching to the beat of music. In addition, song or music, particularly the sound of horns or trumpets, was often used in antiquity as a way of communicating battle orders above the din of battle (Judg. 7:16–18; Job 39:24, 25). Thus the Levitical singers had been an important group before the Exile, but still were in Ezra's time, as they were granted tax exemption by the Persian king Artaxerxes (Ezra 7:24).

and with him seventy males; [8]of the sons of Shephatiah, Zebadiah the son of Michael, and with him eighty males; [9]of the sons of Joab, Obadiah the son of Jehiel, and with him two hundred and eighteen males; [10]of the sons of Shelomith,[a] Ben-Josiphiah, and with him one hundred and sixty males; [11]of the sons of Bebai, Zechariah the son of Bebai, and with him twenty-eight males; [12]of the sons of Azgad, Johanan the son of Hakkatan, and with him one hundred and ten males; [13]of the last sons of Adonikam, whose names *are* these—Eliphelet, Jeiel, and Shemaiah—and with them sixty males; [14]also of the sons of Bigvai, Uthai and Zabbud, and with them seventy males.

Servants for the Temple

[15]Now I gathered them by the river that flows to Ahava, and we camped there three days. And I looked among the people and the priests, and found none of the sons of Levi there. [16]Then I sent for Eliezer, Ariel, Shemaiah, Elnathan, Jarib, El-nathan, Nathan, Zechariah, and Meshullam, leaders; also for Joiarib and Elnathan, men of understanding. [17]And I gave them a command for Iddo the chief man at the place Casiphia, and I told them what they should say to Iddo *and* his brethren[a] the Nethinim at the place Casiphia—that they should bring us servants for the house of our God. [18]Then, by the good hand of our God upon us, they brought us a man of understanding, of the sons of Mahli the son of Levi, the son of Israel, namely Sherebiah,

---

8:10 [a]Following Masoretic Text and Vulgate; Septuagint reads *the sons of Banni, Shelomith*.
8:17 [a]Following Vulgate; Masoretic Text reads *to Iddo his brother*; Septuagint reads *to their brethren*.

TIME CAPSULE *464 to 455 B.C.*

464	Athens breaks with Sparta to ally with Argos
462– 461	Pericles leads Athens to replace aristocratic constitution with democracy
460– 404	Conflict between Sparta and Athens
458	Jewish scribe Ezra sent from Babylon to Jerusalem
455– 403	Archives from the house of Murashu

with his sons and brothers, eighteen men; [19]and Hashabiah, and with him Jeshaiah of the sons of Merari, his brothers and their sons, twenty men; [20]also of the Nethinim, whom David and the leaders had appointed for the service of the Levites, two hundred and twenty Nethinim. All of them were designated by name.

Fasting and Prayer for Protection

[21]Then I proclaimed a fast there at the river of Ahava, that we might humble ourselves before our God, to seek from Him the right way for us and our little ones and all our possessions. [22]For I was ashamed to request of the king an escort of soldiers and horsemen to help us against the enemy on the road, because we had spoken to the king, saying, "The hand of our God *is* upon all those for good who seek Him, but His power and His wrath *are* against all those who forsake Him." [23]So we fasted and entreated our God for this, and He answered our prayer.

Gifts for the Temple

[24]And I separated twelve of the leaders of the priests—Sherebiah, Hashabiah, and ten of their brethren with them— [25]and weighed out to them the silver, the gold, and the articles, the offering for the house of our God which the king and his counselors and his princes, and all Israel *who were* present, had offered. [26]I weighed into their hand six hundred and fifty talents of silver, silver articles *weighing* one hundred talents, one hundred talents of gold, [27]twenty gold basins *worth* a thousand drachmas, and two vessels of fine polished bronze, precious as gold. [28]And I said to them, "You *are* holy to the LORD; the articles *are* holy also; and the silver and the gold *are* a freewill offering to the LORD God of your fathers. [29]Watch and keep *them* until you weigh *them* before the leaders of the priests and the Levites and heads of the fathers' *houses* of Israel in Jerusalem, *in* the chambers of the house of the LORD." [30]So the priests and the Levites received the silver and the gold and the articles by weight, to bring *them* to Jerusalem to the house of our God.

The Return to Jerusalem

[31]Then we departed from the river of Ahava on the twelfth *day* of the first month, to go to Jerusalem. And the hand of our God was upon us, and He delivered us from the hand of the enemy and from ambush along the road. [32]So we came to Jerusalem, and stayed there three days.

[33]Now on the fourth day the silver and the gold and the articles were weighed in the house of our God by the hand of Meremoth the son of Uriah the priest, and with him *was* Eleazar the son of Phinehas; with them *were* the Levites, Jozabad the son of Jeshua and Noadiah the son of Binnui, [34]with the number *and* weight of everything. All the weight was written down at that time.

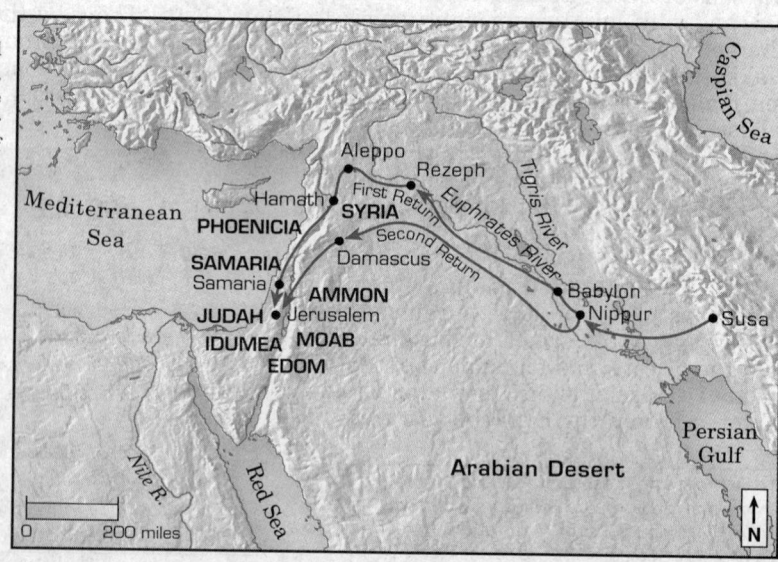

The Return from Exile
Cyrus the Persian captured Babylon in 539 B.C., opening the way for captive Judah to return to her homeland. The Edict of Cyrus in 538 B.C. allowed Jewish exiles not only to return to Judah, but also to rebuild the temple. Two major expeditions are reported among the several returning caravans. The first led by Sheshbazzar occurred soon after the edict, possibly in 537 B.C. The second led by Ezra is placed in either 458, 428, or 398 B.C.

³⁵The children of those who had been carried away captive, who had come from the captivity, offered burnt offerings to the God of Israel: twelve bulls for all Israel, ninety-six rams, seventy-seven lambs, and twelve male goats *as* a sin offering. All *this was* a burnt offering to the LORD.

³⁶And they delivered the king's orders to the king's satraps and the governors *in the region* beyond the River. So they gave support to the people and the house of God.

Intermarriage with Pagans

9 ¹When these things were done, the leaders came to me, saying, "The people of Israel and the priests and the Levites have not separated themselves from the peoples of the lands, with respect to the abominations of the Canaanites, the Hittites, the Perizzites, the Jebusites, the Ammonites, the Moabites, the Egyptians, and the Amorites. ²For they have taken some of their daughters *as wives* for themselves and their sons, so that the holy seed is mixed with the peoples of *those* lands. Indeed, the hand of the leaders and rulers has been foremost in this trespass." ³So when I heard this thing, I tore my garment and my robe, and plucked out some of the hair of my head and beard, and sat down astonished. ⁴Then everyone who trembled at the words of the God of Israel assembled to me, because of the transgression of those who had been carried away captive, and I sat astonished until the evening sacrifice.

⁵At the evening sacrifice I arose from my fasting; and having torn my garment and my robe, I fell on my knees and spread out my hands to the LORD my God. ⁶And I said: "O my God, I am too ashamed and humiliated to lift up my face to You, my God; for our iniquities have risen higher than *our* heads, and our guilt has grown up to the heavens. ⁷Since the days of our fathers to this day we *have been* very guilty, and for our iniquities we, our kings, *and* our priests have been delivered into the hand of the kings of the lands, to the sword, to captivity, to plunder, and to humiliation, as *it is* this day. ⁸And now for a little while grace has been *shown* from the LORD our God, to leave us a remnant to escape, and to give us a peg in His holy place, that our God may enlighten our eyes and give us a measure of revival in our bondage. ⁹For we *were* slaves. Yet our God did not forsake us

in our bondage; but He extended mercy to us in the sight of the kings of Persia, to revive us, to repair the house of our God, to rebuild its ruins, and to give us a wall in Judah and Jerusalem. ¹⁰And now, O our God, what shall we say after this? For we have forsaken Your commandments, ¹¹which You commanded by Your servants the prophets, saying, 'The land which you are entering to possess is an unclean land, with the uncleanness of the peoples of the lands, with their abominations which have filled it from one end to another with their impurity. ¹²Now therefore, do not give your daughters as wives for their sons, nor take their daughters to your sons; and never seek their peace or prosperity, that you may be strong and eat the good of the land, and leave *it* as an inheritance to your children forever.' ¹³And after all that has come upon us for our evil deeds and for our great guilt, since You our God have punished us less than our iniquities *deserve,* and have given us *such* deliverance as this, ¹⁴should we again break Your commandments, and join in marriage with the people *committing* these abominations? Would You not be angry with us until You had consumed *us,* so that *there would be* no remnant or survivor? ¹⁵O LORD God of Israel, You *are* righteous, for we are left as a remnant, as *it is* this day. Here we *are* before You, in our guilt, though no one can stand before You because of this!"

Confession of Improper Marriages

10 ¹Now while Ezra was praying, and while he was confessing, weeping, and bowing down before the house of God, a very large assembly of men, women, and children gathered to him from Israel; for the people wept very bitterly. ²And Shechaniah the son of Jehiel, *one* of the sons of Elam, spoke up and said to Ezra, "We have trespassed against our God, and have taken pagan wives from the peoples of the land; yet now there is hope in Israel in spite of this. ³Now therefore, let us make a covenant with our God to put away all these wives and those who have been born to them, according to the advice of my master and of those who tremble at the commandment of our God; and let it be done according to the law. ⁴Arise, for *this* matter *is* your *responsibility.* We also *are* with you. Be of good courage, and do *it.*"

⁵Then Ezra arose, and made the leaders of the priests, the Levites, and all

Israel swear an oath that they would do according to this word. So they swore an oath. 6Then Ezra rose up from before the house of God, and went into the chamber of Jehohanan the son of Eliashib; and *when* he came there, he ate no bread and drank no water, for he mourned because of the guilt of those from the captivity.

7And they issued a proclamation throughout Judah and Jerusalem to all the descendants of the captivity, that they must gather at Jerusalem, 8and that whoever would not come within three days, according to the instructions of the leaders and elders, all his property would be confiscated, and he himself would be separated from the assembly of those from the captivity.

9So all the men of Judah and Benjamin gathered at Jerusalem within three days. It *was* the ninth month, on the twentieth of the month; and all the people sat in the open square of the house of God, trembling because of *this* matter and because of heavy rain. 10Then Ezra the priest stood up and said to them, "You have transgressed and have taken pagan wives, adding to the guilt of Israel. 11Now therefore, make confession to the LORD God of your fathers, and do His will; separate yourselves from the peoples of the land, and from the pagan wives."

12Then all the assembly answered and said with a loud voice, "Yes! As you have said, so we must do. 13But *there are* many people; *it is* the season for heavy rain, and we are not able to stand outside. Nor *is this* the work of one or two days, for *there are* many of us who have transgressed in this matter. 14Please, let the leaders of our entire assembly stand; and let all those in our cities who have taken pagan wives come at appointed times, together with the elders and judges of their cities, until the fierce wrath of our God is turned away from us in this matter." 15Only Jonathan the son of Asahel and Jahaziah the son of Tikvah opposed this, and Meshullam and Shabbethai the Levite gave them support.

16Then the descendants of the captivity did so. And Ezra the priest, *with* certain heads of the fathers' *households,* were set apart by the fathers' *households,* each of them by name; and they sat down on the first day of the tenth month to examine the matter. 17By the first day of the first month they finished *questioning* all the men who had taken pagan wives.

Pagan Wives Put Away

18And among the sons of the priests who had taken pagan wives *the following* were found of the sons of Jeshua the son of Jozadak,[a] and his brothers: Maaseiah, Eliezer, Jarib, and Gedaliah. 19And they gave their promise that they would put away their wives; and *being* guilty, *they presented* a ram of the flock as their trespass offering.

20Also of the sons of Immer: Hanani and Zebadiah; 21of the sons of Harim: Maaseiah, Elijah, Shemaiah, Jehiel, and Uzziah; 22of the sons of Pashhur: Elioenai, Maaseiah, Ishmael, Nethanel, Jozabad, and Elasah.

23Also of the Levites: Jozabad, Shimei, Kelaiah (the same *is* Kelita), Pethahiah, Judah, and Eliezer.

24Also of the singers: Eliashib; and of the gatekeepers: Shallum, Telem, and Uri.

25And others of Israel: of the sons of Parosh: Ramiah, Jeziah, Malchiah, Mijamin, Eleazar, Malchijah, and Benaiah; 26of the sons of Elam: Mattaniah, Zechariah, Jehiel, Abdi, Jeremoth, and Eliah; 27of the sons of Zattu: Elioenai, Eliashib, Mattaniah, Jeremoth, Zabad, and Aziza; 28of the sons of Bebai: Jehohanan, Hananiah, Zabbai, *and* Athlai; 29of the sons of Bani: Meshullam, Malluch, Adaiah, Jashub, Sheal, *and* Ramoth;[a] 30of the sons of Pahath-Moab: Adna, Chelal, Benaiah, Maaseiah, Mattaniah, Bezalel, Binnui, and Manasseh; 31*of* the sons of Harim: Eliezer, Ishijah, Malchijah, Shemaiah, Shimeon, 32Benjamin, Malluch, *and* Shemariah; 33of the sons of Hashum: Mattenai, Mattattah, Zabad, Eliphelet, Jeremai, Manasseh, *and* Shimei; 34of the sons of Bani: Maadai, Amram, Uel, 35Benaiah, Bedeiah, Cheluh,[a] 36Vaniah, Meremoth, Eliashib, 37Mattaniah, Mattenai, Jaasai,[a] 38Bani, Binnui, Shimei, 39Shelemiah, Nathan, Adaiah, 40Machnadebai, Shashai, Sharai, 41Azarel, Shelemiah, Shemariah, 42Shallum, Amariah, *and* Joseph; 43of the sons of Nebo: Jeiel, Mattithiah, Zabad, Zebina, Jaddai,[a] Joel, *and* Benaiah.

44All these had taken pagan wives, and *some* of them had wives *by whom* they had children.

10:18 [a]Spelled *Jehozadak* in 1 Chronicles 6:14
10:29 [a]Or *Jeremoth*   10:35 [a]Or *Cheluhi,* or *Cheluhu*   10:37 [a]Or *Jaasu*   10:43 [a]Or *Jaddu*

The Book of Nehemiah

Closely associated with the Book of Ezra is the Book of Nehemiah. Where Ezra was the religious leader in Jerusalem, Nehemiah became the secular leader, the official governor of the Persian province of Judah (Neh. 5:14). Nehemiah's great concern was the ruined state of the city, left without walls since Artaxerxes I had earlier halted the repairs (Ezra 4:21). Using his position as a trusted servant in the inner court of Artaxerxes, Nehemiah obtained permission to resume that labor and complete the walls of Jerusalem. He began his work in the 20th year of Artaxerxes' reign (445 B.C.; Neh. 1:1).

The chronology of Ezra and Nehemiah is perplexing. They seem to have been contemporaries in Jerusalem, but neither makes much mention of the other. Although the Book of Nehemiah recounts one incident involving Ezra (Ezra's reading of the Law of Moses to the people; Neh. 8) and twice mentions the two leaders together (Neh. 8:9; 12:26), Ezra and Nehemiah appear to have carried on their reforms separately. Also puzzling is that Ezra put an end to the practice of intermarriage between the returned Jews and the people of the land (Ezra 9; 10), yet Nehemiah had to deal with the same problem (Neh. 13:23–28). The priestly laxity that Nehemiah encountered (13:4–9) is especially strange coming so soon after Ezra's reforms.

For these reasons, many scholars believe that Ezra actually came after Nehemiah, perhaps during the reign of Artaxerxes II (404–359 B.C.). If Ezra arrived in the 7th year of this Artaxerxes' reign (Ezra 7:8), thus in about 398 B.C., Ezra's work would have been the final word in the reform efforts. Using this date, however, makes it impossible for Ezra and Nehemiah to have been contemporaries, despite Neh. 8:9; 12:26. Furthermore, Ezra's proclamation of the Law of Moses (Neh. 8) would have occurred long after Nehemiah's time.

Another proposal speculates that the number now reading "7th year" in Ezra 7:7, 8 was damaged, and originally read "37th year." If Ezra arrived in the 37th year of Artaxerxes I (about 428 B.C.), Ezra's reforms would have occurred after those of Nehemiah, but still during Nehemiah's years in Jerusalem. To change Ezra 7:7, 8 hypothetically, though, is a questionable basis for such a conclusion, and the traditional order of Ezra 7—Neh. 13 seems most likely. Ezra's reforms began in 458 B.C., but like all religious revivals, they did not affect everyone nor did they last forever. When Nehemiah arrived 13 years later, there was still much to be done.

As in the Book of Ezra, parts of the Book of Nehemiah are told in the hero's own words. From these portions, called Nehemiah's memoirs, one not only learns the history, but much about Nehemiah himself: an impatient, often difficult, but incorruptible man who sought no human reward but only to serve his God (Neh. 13:14, 22, 31).

■ Nehemiah 1:1–11

Nehemiah
Nehemiah Prays for His People

1 :1 The words of Nehemiah the son of Hachaliah.

It came to pass in the month of Chislev, *in* the twentieth year, as I was in Shushan[a] the citadel, [2]that Hanani one of my brethren came with men from Judah; and I asked them concerning the Jews who had escaped, who had survived the captivity, and concerning Jerusalem. [3]And they said to me, "The survivors who are left from the captivity in the province *are* there in great distress and reproach. The wall of Jerusalem *is* also broken down, and its gates *are* burned with fire."

[4]So it was, when I heard these words, that I sat down and wept, and mourned *for many* days; I was fasting and praying before the God of heaven.

[5]And I said: "I pray, LORD God of heaven, O great and awesome God, *You* who keep *Your* covenant and mercy with those who love You[a] and observe Your[b] commandments, [6]please let Your ear be attentive and Your eyes open, that You may hear the prayer of Your servant which I pray before You now, day and night, for the children of Israel Your servants, and confess the sins of the children of Israel which we have sinned against You. Both my father's house and I have sinned. [7]We have acted very corruptly against You, and have not kept the commandments, the statutes, nor the ordinances which You commanded Your servant Moses. [8]Remember, I pray, the word that You commanded Your servant Moses, saying, 'If you are unfaithful, I will scatter you among the nations;[a] [9]but *if* you return to Me, and keep My commandments and do them, though some of you

---

1:1 [a]Or *Susa*　　1:5 [a]Literally *Him* [b]Literally *His*　　1:8 [a]Leviticus 26:33

were cast out to the farthest part of the heavens, *yet* I will gather them from there, and bring them to the place which I have chosen as a dwelling for My name.'ᵃ ¹⁰Now these *are* Your servants and Your people, whom You have redeemed by Your great power, and by Your strong hand. ¹¹O Lord, I pray, please let Your ear be attentive to the prayer of Your servant, and to the prayer of Your servants who desire to fear Your name; and let Your servant prosper this day, I pray, and grant him mercy in the sight of this man."

For I was the king's cupbearer.

Nehemiah Sent to Jerusalem

Chislev was the Babylonian name for the 9th month of the Jewish calendar, corresponding to November-December. At that time Nehemiah had received the disquieting news from Jerusalem concerning distress among the returned exiles (Neh. 1:1–3). After more than 3 months had passed, Nehemiah was in the king's presence during Nisan, the 1st month of the Jewish calendar (Neh. 2:1). Both Chislev and Nisan are reckoned in the 20th year of Artaxerxes (445 B.C.).

■ Nehemiah 2:1—6:14

Nehemiah
Nehemiah's Concern for Judah

2 **:1** And it came to pass in the month of Nisan, in the twentieth year of King Artaxerxes, *when* wine *was* before him, that I took the wine and gave it to the king. Now I had never been sad in his presence before. ²Therefore the king said to me, "Why *is* your face sad, since you *are* not sick? This *is* nothing but sorrow of heart."

So I became dreadfully afraid, ³and said to the king, "May the king live forever! Why should my face not be sad, when the city, the place of my fathers' tombs, *lies* waste, and its gates are burned with fire?"

⁴Then the king said to me, "What do you request?"

So I prayed to the God of heaven. ⁵And I said to the king, "If it pleases the king, and if your servant has found favor in your sight, I ask that you send me to Judah, to the city of my fathers' tombs, that I may rebuild it."

⁶Then the king said to me (the queen also sitting beside him), "How long will your journey be? And when will you return?" So it pleased the king to send me; and I set him a time.

⁷Furthermore I said to the king, "If it pleases the king, let letters be given to me for the governors *of the region* beyond the River,ᵃ that they must permit me to pass through till I come to Judah, ⁸and a letter to Asaph the keeper of the king's forest, that he must give me timber to make beams for the gates of the citadel which *pertains* to the temple,ᵃ for the city wall, and for the house that I will occupy." And the king granted *them* to me according to the good hand of my God upon me.

⁹Then I went to the governors *in the region* beyond the River, and gave them the king's letters. Now the king had sent captains of the army and horsemen with me. ¹⁰When Sanballat the Horonite and Tobiah the Ammonite officialᵃ heard *of it,* they were deeply disturbed that a man had come to seek the well-being of the children of Israel.

Nehemiah Views the Wall of Jerusalem

¹¹So I came to Jerusalem and was there three days. ¹²Then I arose in the night, I and a few men with me; I told no one what my God had put in my heart to do at Jerusalem; nor was there any animal with me, except the one on which I rode. ¹³And I went out by night through the Valley Gate to the Serpent Well and the

---

1:9 ᵃDeuteronomy 30:2–5   2:7 ᵃThat is, the Euphrates, and so elsewhere in this book
2:8 ᵃLiterally *house*   2:10 ᵃLiterally *servant,* and so elsewhere in this book

ARTS AND LITERATURE

Ancient itineraries like Nehemiah's (Neh. 2:11–15) are interesting because they can be compared with the features of the land and any buildings that remain on it, in ruins or intact. The Greek writer Pausanias, who lived in the 2nd century A.D., wrote an elaborate account of his travels in Greece. He visited notable buildings and monuments that often can be seen today essentially as he described them.

GESHEM THE ARAB (Neh. 2:19)

Nehemiah names three specific opponents who attempted to thwart his plans for rebuilding the walls of Jerusalem in the mid-5th century B.C. (Neh. 2:19). Sanballat the Horonite is identified as the governor of Samaria in documents from the Jewish colony at Elephantine in southern Egypt. Tobiah, described as an "Ammonite official," was possibly a governor over Ammon. The third opponent, Geshem the Arab, likewise was a governor under Persian rule.

The name "Geshem," which probably means "big man" in Arabic, is often mentioned in Nabatean and northern Arabian inscriptions. Geshem was apparently an important person, since Sanballat threatened to send a letter to the Persian king quoting Geshem. The letter would have contained a false report accusing the Jews of planning to rebel against Persian rule (Neh. 6:5, 6).

Three sources possibly refer to the Geshem who opposed Nehemiah. A 5th-century B.C. Aramaic inscription from Egypt refers to a certain "Qaynu, the son of Gashmu, the king of Kedar." Kedar was one of the main Arab groups in this period. Moreover, both a contemporary account and a king list from Dedan mention Gashmu. If Nehemiah's "Geshem the Arab" was indeed a Kedarite king, his influence would have stretched from northern Arabia to include Judah.

Refuse Gate, and viewed the walls of Jerusalem which were broken down and its gates which were burned with fire. ¹⁴Then I went on to the Fountain Gate and to the King's Pool, but *there was* no room for the animal under me to pass. ¹⁵So I went up in the night by the valley, and viewed the wall; then I turned back and entered by the Valley Gate, and so returned. ¹⁶And the officials did not know where I had gone or what I had done; I had not yet told the Jews, the priests, the nobles, the officials, or the others who did the work.

¹⁷Then I said to them, "You see the distress that we *are* in, how Jerusalem *lies* waste, and its gates are burned with fire. Come and let us build the wall of Jerusalem, that we may no longer be a reproach." ¹⁸And I told them of the hand of my God which had been good upon me, and also of the king's words that he had spoken to me.

So they said, "Let us rise up and build." Then they set their hands to *this* good *work*.

¹⁹But when Sanballat the Horonite, Tobiah the Ammonite official, and Geshem the Arab heard *of it,* they laughed at us and despised us, and said, "What *is* this thing that you are doing? Will you rebel against the king?"

²⁰So I answered them, and said to them, "The God of heaven Himself will prosper us; therefore we His servants will arise and build, but you have no heritage or right or memorial in Jerusalem."

Rebuilding the Wall

3 ¹Then Eliashib the high priest rose up with his brethren the priests and built the Sheep Gate; they consecrated it and hung its doors. They built as far as the Tower of the Hundred,ª *and* consecrated it, then as far as the Tower of Hananel. ²Next to *Eliashib*ª the men of Jericho built. And next to them Zaccur the son of Imri built.

³Also the sons of Hassenaah built the Fish Gate; they laid its beams and hung its doors with its bolts and bars. ⁴And next to them Meremoth the son of Urijah, the son of Koz,ª made repairs. Next to them Meshullam the son of Berechiah, the son of Meshezabel, made repairs. Next to them Zadok the son of Baana made repairs. ⁵Next to them the Tekoites made repairs; but their nobles did not put their shouldersª to the work of their Lord.

⁶Moreover Jehoiada the son of Paseah and Meshullam the son of Besodeiah repaired the Old Gate; they laid its beams and hung its doors, with its bolts and bars. ⁷And next to them Melatiah the Gibeonite, Jadon the Meronothite, the men of Gibeon and Mizpah, repaired the residenceª of the governor *of the region* beyond the River.

3:1 ªHebrew *Hammeah,* also at 12:39
3:2 ªLiterally *On his hand*   3:4 ªOr *Hakkoz*
3:5 ªLiterally *necks*   3:7 ªLiterally *throne*

8Next to him Uzziel the son of Harhaiah, one of the goldsmiths, made repairs. Also next to him Hananiah, one[a] of the perfumers, made repairs; and they fortified Jerusalem as far as the Broad Wall. 9And next to them Rephaiah the son of Hur, leader of half the district of Jerusalem, made repairs. 10Next to them Jedaiah the son of Harumaph made repairs in front of his house. And next to him Hattush the son of Hashabniah made repairs.

11Malchijah the son of Harim and Hashub the son of Pahath-Moab repaired another section, as well as the Tower of the Ovens. 12And next to him was Shallum the son of Hallohesh, leader of half the district of Jerusalem; he and his daughters made repairs.

13Hanun and the inhabitants of Zanoah repaired the Valley Gate. They built it, hung its doors with its bolts and bars, and repaired a thousand cubits of the wall as far as the Refuse Gate.

14Malchijah the son of Rechab, leader of the district of Beth Haccerem, repaired the Refuse Gate; he built it and hung its doors with its bolts and bars.

15Shallun the son of Col-Hozeh, leader of the district of Mizpah, repaired the Fountain Gate; he built it, covered it, hung its doors with its bolts and bars, and repaired the wall of the Pool of Shelah by the King's Garden, as far as the stairs that go down from the City of David. 16After him Nehemiah the son of Azbuk, leader of half the district of Beth Zur, made repairs as far as the place in front of the tombs[a] of David, to the man-made pool, and as far as the House of the Mighty.

17After him the Levites, under Rehum the son of Bani, made repairs. Next to him Hashabiah, leader of half the district of Keilah, made repairs for his district. 18After him their brethren, under Bavai[a] the son of Henadad, leader of the other half of the district of Keilah, made repairs. 19And next to him Ezer the son of Jeshua, the leader of Mizpah, repaired another section in front of the Ascent to the Armory at the buttress. 20After him Baruch the son of Zabbai[a] carefully repaired the other section, from the buttress to the door of the house of Eliashib the high priest. 21After him Meremoth the son of Urijah, the son of Koz,[a] repaired another section, from the door of the house of Eliashib to the end of the house of Eliashib.

22And after him the priests, the men of the plain, made repairs. 23After him Benjamin and Hasshub made repairs opposite their house. After them Azariah the son of Maaseiah, the son of Ananiah, made repairs by his house. 24After him Binnui the son of Henadad repaired another section, from the house of Azariah to the buttress, even as far as the corner. 25Palal the son of Uzai made repairs opposite the buttress, and on the tower which projects from the king's upper house that was by the court of the prison. After him Pedaiah the son of Parosh made repairs.

26Moreover the Nethinim who dwelt in Ophel made repairs as far as the place in front of the Water Gate toward the east, and on the projecting tower. 27After them the Tekoites repaired another section, next to the great projecting tower, and as far as the wall of Ophel.

28Beyond the Horse Gate the priests made repairs, each in front of his own house. 29After them Zadok the son of Immer made repairs in front of his own house. After him Shemaiah the son of Shechaniah, the keeper of the East Gate, made repairs. 30After him Hananiah the son of Shelemiah, and Hanun, the sixth son of Zalaph, repaired another section. After him Meshullam the son of Berechiah made repairs in front of his dwelling. 31After him Malchijah, one of the goldsmiths, made repairs as far as the house of the Nethinim and of the merchants, in front of the Miphkad[a] Gate, and as far as the upper room at the corner. 32And between the upper room at the corner, as far as the Sheep Gate, the goldsmiths and the merchants made repairs.

The Wall Defended Against Enemies

4 1But it so happened, when Sanballat heard that we were rebuilding the wall, that he was furious and very indignant, and mocked the Jews. 2And he spoke before his brethren and the army of Samaria, and said, "What are these feeble Jews doing? Will they fortify themselves? Will they offer sacrifices? Will they com-

---

3:8 [a]Literally the son   3:16 [a]Septuagint, Syriac, and Vulgate read tomb.   3:18 [a]Following Masoretic Text and Vulgate; some Hebrew manuscripts, Septuagint, and Syriac read Binnui (compare verse 24).   3:20 [a]A few Hebrew manuscripts, Syriac, and Vulgate read Zaccai.   3:21 [a]Or Hakkoz   3:31 [a]Literally Inspection or Recruiting

plete it in a day? Will they revive the stones from the heaps of rubbish—*stones that are burned?*"

3Now Tobiah the Ammonite *was* beside him, and he said, "Whatever they build, if even a fox goes up *on it,* he will break down their stone wall."

4Hear, O our God, for we are despised; turn their reproach on their own heads, and give them as plunder to a land of captivity! 5Do not cover their iniquity, and do not let their sin be blotted out from before You; for they have provoked *You* to anger before the builders.

6So we built the wall, and the entire wall was joined together up to half its *height,* for the people had a mind to work.

7Now it happened, when Sanballat, Tobiah, the Arabs, the Ammonites, and the Ashdodites heard that the walls of Jerusalem were being restored and the gaps were beginning to be closed, that they became very angry, 8and all of them conspired together to come *and* attack Jerusalem and create confusion. 9Nevertheless we made our prayer to our God, and because of them we set a watch against them day and night.

10Then Judah said, "The strength of the laborers is failing, and *there is* so much rubbish that we are not able to build the wall."

11And our adversaries said, "They will neither know nor see anything, till we come into their midst and kill them and cause the work to cease."

12So it was, when the Jews who dwelt near them came, that they told us ten

times, "From whatever place you turn, *they will be* upon us."

13Therefore I positioned *men* behind the lower parts of the wall, at the openings; and I set the people according to their families, with their swords, their spears, and their bows. 14And I looked, and arose and said to the nobles, to the leaders, and to the rest of the people, "Do not be afraid of them. Remember the Lord, great and awesome, and fight for your brethren, your sons, your daughters, your wives, and your houses."

15And it happened, when our enemies heard that it was known to us, and *that* God had brought their plot to nothing, that all of us returned to the wall, everyone to his work. 16So it was, from that time on, *that* half of my servants worked at construction, while the other half held the spears, the shields, the bows, and *wore* armor; and the leaders *were* behind all the house of Judah. 17Those who built on the wall, and those who carried burdens, loaded themselves so that with one hand they worked at construction, and with the other held a weapon. 18Every one of the builders had his sword girded at his side as he built. And the one who sounded the trumpet *was* beside me.

19Then I said to the nobles, the rulers, and the rest of the people, "The work *is* great and extensive, and we are separated far from one another on the wall. 20Wherever you hear the sound of the trumpet, rally to us there. Our God will fight for us."

21So we labored in the work, and half of *the men*[a] held the spears from daybreak until the stars appeared. 22At the same time I also said to the people, "Let each man and his servant stay at night in Jerusalem, that they may be our guard by night and a working party by day." 23So neither I, my brethren, my servants, nor the men of the guard who followed me took off our clothes, *except* that everyone took them off for washing.

Nehemiah Deals with Oppression

5 1And there was a great outcry of the people and their wives against their Jewish brethren. 2For there were those who said, "We, our sons, and our daughters *are* many; therefore let us get grain, that we may eat and live."

3There were also *some* who said, "We have mortgaged our lands and vineyards

---

4:21 aLiterally *them*

THE MINISTRIES OF EZRA AND NEHEMIAH

Nehemiah's arrival in Jerusalem in 445 B.C. is supported by contemporary records from Elephantine. But whether Ezra arrived in 458 B.C., well *before* Nehemiah, is questioned. Ezra led several reforms. Yet Nehemiah found many of the immoral behaviors which Ezra supposedly corrected still being practiced. So some scholars suppose Ezra came to Jerusalem *after* Nehemiah, maybe in 428 or 398 B.C.

Date	Event	Reference	Chronology	Comments
538	The Edict of Cyrus allows the first exiles to return to Jerusalem under Sheshbazzar	Ezra 1:1–11	Cyrus conquered Babylon in 539 B.C.	Sheshbazzar may be another name for Zerubbabel (Ezra 2:2; 3:8; Zech. 4:6)
515	The temple is completed and dedicated	Ezra 6:13–18	The 6th year of Darius I is 515 B.C.	
458	Ezra arrives in Jerusalem	Ezra 7:7, 8	The 7th year of Artaxerxes I is 458 B.C.	This dating puts Ezra in Jerusalem before Nehemiah
445	Nehemiah arrives in Jerusalem	Neh. 2:1	The 20th year of Artaxerxes I is 445 B.C.	Records from Elephantine confirm that Nehemiah came during the reign of Artaxerxes I
433	Nehemiah returns to the Persian court for an unknown period of time	Neh. 5:14; 13:6	The 32nd year of Artaxerxes I is 433 B.C.	
428	Another proposal for Ezra's arrival in Jerusalem	Ezra 7:7, 8	The 37th year of Artaxerxes I is 428 B.C.	For this date, Ezra 7:7 has to be changed from 7th to 37th year
398	A third proposal for Ezra's arrival in Jerusalem	Ezra 7:7, 8	The 7th year of Artaxerxes II (not Artaxerxes I) is 398 B.C.	The Bible does not include the numeral I or II to identify the king precisely

and houses, that we might buy grain because of the famine."

⁴There were also those who said, "We have borrowed money for the king's tax *on* our lands and vineyards. ⁵Yet now our flesh *is* as the flesh of our brethren, our children as their children; and indeed we are forcing our sons and our daughters to be slaves, and *some* of our daughters have been brought into slavery. *It is* not in our power *to redeem them,* for other men have our lands and vineyards."

⁶And I became very angry when I heard their outcry and these words. ⁷After serious thought, I rebuked the nobles and rulers, and said to them, "Each of you is exacting usury from his brother." So I called a great assembly against them. ⁸And I said to them, "According to our ability we have redeemed our Jewish brethren who were sold to the nations. Now indeed, will you even sell your brethren? Or should they be sold to us?"

Then they were silenced and found nothing *to* say. ⁹Then I said, "What you are doing *is* not good. Should you not walk in the fear of our God because of the reproach of the nations, our enemies? ¹⁰I also, *with* my brethren and my servants, am lending them money and grain. Please, let us stop this usury! [11]Restore now to them, even this day, their lands, their vineyards, their olive groves, and their houses, also a hundredth of the money and the grain, the new wine and the oil, that you have charged them."

[12]So they said, "We will restore *it,* and will require nothing from them; we will do as you say."

Then I called the priests, and required an oath from them that they would do according to this promise. [13]Then I shook out the fold of my garment[a] and said, "So may God shake out each man from his house, and from his property, who does not perform this promise. Even thus may he be shaken out and emptied."

And all the assembly said, "Amen!" and praised the LORD. Then the people did according to this promise.

The Generosity of Nehemiah

[14]Moreover, from the time that I was appointed to be their governor in the land of Judah, from the twentieth year until the thirty-second year of King Artaxerxes, twelve years, neither I nor my brothers ate the governor's provisions. [15]But the former governors who *were* before me laid burdens on the people, and took from them bread and wine, besides forty shekels of silver. Yes, even their servants bore rule over the people, but I did not do so, because of the fear of God. [16]Indeed, I also continued the work on this wall, and we[a] did not buy any land. All my servants *were* gathered there for the work.

[17]And at my table *were* one hundred and fifty Jews and rulers, besides those who came to us from the nations around us. [18]Now *that* which was prepared daily *was* one ox *and* six choice sheep. Also fowl were prepared for me, and once every ten

days an abundance of all kinds of wine. Yet in spite of this I did not demand the governor's provisions, because the bondage was heavy on this people.

[19]Remember me, my God, for good, *according to* all that I have done for this people.

Conspiracy Against Nehemiah

6 [1]Now it happened when Sanballat, Tobiah, Geshem the Arab, and the rest of our enemies heard that I had rebuilt the wall, and *that* there were no breaks left in it (though at that time I had not hung the doors in the gates), [2]that Sanballat and Geshem sent to me, saying, "Come, let us meet together among the villages in the plain of Ono." But they thought to do me harm.

[3]So I sent messengers to them, saying, "I *am* doing a great work, so that I cannot come down. Why should the work cease while I leave it and go down to you?"

[4]But they sent me this message four times, and I answered them in the same manner.

[5]Then Sanballat sent his servant to me as before, the fifth time, with an open letter in his hand. [6]In it *was* written:

It is reported among the nations, and Geshem[a] says, *that* you and the Jews plan to rebel; therefore, according to these rumors, you are rebuilding the wall, that you may be their king. [7]And you have also appointed prophets to proclaim concerning you at Jerusalem, saying, "*There is* a king in Judah!" Now these matters will be reported to the king. So come, therefore, and let us consult together.

[8]Then I sent to him, saying, "No such things as you say are being done, but you invent them in your own heart."

[9]For they all *were trying to* make us afraid, saying, "Their hands will be weakened in the work, and it will not be done."

Now therefore, O God, strengthen my hands.

5:13 [a]Literally *my lap*   5:16 [a]Following Masoretic Text; Septuagint, Syriac, and Vulgate read *I.*
6:6 [a]Hebrew *Gashmu*

CULTURE AND SOCIETY

The economy of the ancient world had practically no middle class. Like modern corporations, rich men and rulers had many dependents who, socially, were retainers, servants, and slaves. The powerful person was responsible to protect his clients and slaves. It was a mark of shame to a ruler if his dependents were not protected or did not have enough to eat "at his table" (Neh. 5:17).

10Afterward I came to the house of Shemaiah the son of Delaiah, the son of Mehetabel, who *was* a secret informer; and he said, "Let us meet together in the house of God, within the temple, and let us close the doors of the temple, for they are coming to kill you; indeed, at night they will come to kill you."

11And I said, "Should such a man as I flee? And who *is there* such as I who would go into the temple to save his life? I will not go in!" 12Then I perceived that God had not sent him at all, but that he pronounced *this* prophecy against me because Tobiah and Sanballat had hired him. 13For this reason he *was* hired, that I should be afraid and act that way and sin, so *that* they might have *cause* for an evil report, that they might reproach me.

14My God, remember Tobiah and Sanballat, according to these their works, and the prophetess Noadiah and the rest of the prophets who would have made me afraid.

Building the Walls

The rebuilding of the walls was completed in only 52 days (Neh. 6:15). This span of time occurred during the 5th and 6th months, known as Ab and Elul. Faced with difficult circumstances, but with God's help, Nehemiah was able to accomplish his first task just 5 months after requesting permission of the Persian emperor in the 1st month (Nisan) of the Jewish year (Neh. 2:1–5).

▸ ■ Nehemiah 6:15—7:73a

Nehemiah
The Wall Completed

6 :15 So the wall was finished on the twenty-fifth *day* of Elul, in fifty-two days. 16And it happened, when all our enemies heard *of it,* and all the nations around us saw *these things,* that they were very disheartened in their own eyes; for they perceived that this work was done by our God.

17Also in those days the nobles of Judah sent many letters to Tobiah, and *the letters of* Tobiah came to them. 18For many in Judah were pledged to him, because he was the son-in-law of Shechaniah the son of Arah, and his son Jehohanan had married the daughter of Meshullam the son of Berechiah. 19Also they reported his good deeds before me, and reported my words to him. Tobiah sent letters to frighten me.

7 1Then it was, when the wall was built and I had hung the doors, when the gatekeepers, the singers, and the Levites had been appointed, 2that I gave the charge of Jerusalem to my brother Hanani, and Hananiah the leader of the citadel, for he *was* a faithful man and feared God more than many.

3And I said to them, "Do not let the gates of Jerusalem be opened until the sun is hot; and while they stand *guard,* let them shut and bar the doors; and appoint guards from among the inhabitants of Jerusalem, one at his watch station and another in front of his own house."

The Captives Who Returned to Jerusalem

4Now the city *was* large and spacious, but the people in it *were* few, and the houses *were* not rebuilt. 5Then my God put it into my heart to gather the nobles, the rulers, and the people, that they might be registered by genealogy. And I found a register of the genealogy of those who had come up in the first *return,* and found written in it:

6 Thesea *are* the people of the province who came back from the captivity, of those who had been carried away, whom Nebuchadnezzar the king of Babylon had carried away, and who returned to Jerusalem and Judah, everyone to his city.

7 Those who came with Zerubbabel *were* Jeshua, Nehemiah, Azariah, Raamiah, Nahamani, Mordecai, Bilshan, Mispereth,a Bigvai, Nehum, and Baanah.

The number of the men of the people of Israel: 8the sons of Parosh, two thousand one hundred and seventy-two;
9the sons of Shephatiah, three hundred and seventy-two;
10the sons of Arah, six hundred and fifty-two;
11the sons of Pahath-Moab, of the sons of Jeshua and Joab, two thousand eight hundred and eighteen;
12the sons of Elam, one thousand two hundred and fifty-four;

7:6 aCompare verses 6–72 with Ezra 2:1–70
7:7 aSpelled *Mispar* in Ezra 2:2

ARAMAIC WRITINGS AT ELEPHANTINE (Neh. 7:7)

Elephantine is an island in the Nile River in Upper Egypt, near the city of Aswan. The Judeans who settled in Egypt during the Babylonian exile developed thriving Jewish communities there. The Elephantine Jewish colony left an impressive collection of papyri and ostraca (fragmented pottery, often with portions of inscriptions on them). Many of these papyri and ostraca tell us much about the world of these 5th-century B.C. Jews.

In this period, Elephantine was a mercenary garrison of the Achaemenid dynasty of Persia (559–331 B.C.). The Jews of Elephantine wrote in the Aramaic language, the international language of commerce at that time. Included in the Aramaic collection are many literary works which come from the time of Darius I (522–486 B.C.), confirming that this Persian king sent documents throughout the empire (see Dan. 6:25). Over thirty private letters in Aramaic have been uncovered, as well as numerous legal contracts concerning marriage, adoption, property transfer, and release from slavery.

The Elephantine writings also contain lists consisting of Egyptian, Jewish, Aramaic, and Accadian personal names. Many of these names show variant spellings, very similar to the variant spellings found in lists of personal names in the Bible. Among the names listed in Neh. 7 are two examples of differing spellings: Mispereth and Nehum (Neh. 7:7). In the list of people who returned from Babylon with Zerubbabel (Ezra 2), "Mispereth" is spelled "Mispar" and "Nehum" is spelled "Rehum" (Ezra 2:2; see footnote).

13the sons of Zattu, eight hundred and forty-five;
14the sons of Zaccai, seven hundred and sixty;
15the sons of Binnui,a six hundred and forty-eight;
16the sons of Bebai, six hundred and twenty-eight;
17the sons of Azgad, two thousand three hundred and twenty-two;
18the sons of Adonikam, six hundred and sixty-seven;
19the sons of Bigvai, two thousand and sixty-seven;
20the sons of Adin, six hundred and fifty-five;
21the sons of Ater of Hezekiah, ninety-eight;
22the sons of Hashum, three hundred and twenty-eight;
23the sons of Bezai, three hundred and twenty-four;
24the sons of Hariph,a one hundred and twelve;
25the sons of Gibeon,a ninety-five;
26the men of Bethlehem and Netophah, one hundred and eighty-eight;
27the men of Anathoth, one hundred and twenty-eight;
28the men of Beth Azmaveth,a forty-two;
29the men of Kirjath Jearim, Chephirah, and Beeroth, seven hundred and forty-three;
30the men of Ramah and Geba, six hundred and twenty-one;
31the men of Michmas, one hundred and twenty-two;
32the men of Bethel and Ai, one hundred and twenty-three;
33the men of the other Nebo, fifty-two;
34the sons of the other Elam, one thousand two hundred and fifty-four;
35the sons of Harim, three hundred and twenty;
36the sons of Jericho, three hundred and forty-five;
37the sons of Lod, Hadid, and Ono, seven hundred and twenty-one;
38the sons of Senaah, three thousand nine hundred and thirty.

39 The priests: the sons of Jedaiah, of the house of Jeshua, nine hundred and seventy-three;
40the sons of Immer, one thousand and fifty-two;
41the sons of Pashhur, one thousand two hundred and forty-seven;

7:15 aSpelled *Bani* in Ezra 2:10   7:24 aCalled *Jorah* in Ezra 2:18   7:25 aCalled *Gibbar* in Ezra 2:20   7:28 aCalled *Azmaveth* in Ezra 2:24

⁴²the sons of Harim, one thousand and seventeen.

⁴³ The Levites: the sons of Jeshua, of Kadmiel, *and* of the sons of Hodevah,^a seventy-four.

⁴⁴ The singers: the sons of Asaph, one hundred and forty-eight.

⁴⁵ The gatekeepers: the sons of Shallum,
the sons of Ater,
the sons of Talmon,
the sons of Akkub,
the sons of Hatita,
the sons of Shobai, one hundred and thirty-eight.

⁴⁶ The Nethinim: the sons of Ziha,
the sons of Hasupha,
the sons of Tabbaoth,
⁴⁷the sons of Keros,
the sons of Sia,^a
the sons of Padon,
⁴⁸the sons of Lebana,^a
the sons of Hagaba,^b
the sons of Salmai,^c
⁴⁹the sons of Hanan,
the sons of Giddel,
the sons of Gahar,
⁵⁰the sons of Reaiah,
the sons of Rezin,
the sons of Nekoda,
⁵¹the sons of Gazzam,
the sons of Uzza,
the sons of Paseah,
⁵²the sons of Besai,
the sons of Meunim,
the sons of Nephishesim,^a
⁵³the sons of Bakbuk,
the sons of Hakupha,
the sons of Harhur,
⁵⁴the sons of Bazlith,^a
the sons of Mehida,
the sons of Harsha,
⁵⁵the sons of Barkos,
the sons of Sisera,
the sons of Tamah,
⁵⁶the sons of Neziah,
and the sons of Hatipha.

⁵⁷ The sons of Solomon's servants: the sons of Sotai,
the sons of Sophereth,
the sons of Perida,^a
⁵⁸the sons of Jaala,
the sons of Darkon,
the sons of Giddel,
⁵⁹the sons of Shephatiah,
the sons of Hattil,
the sons of Pochereth of Zebaim,
and the sons of Amon.^a
⁶⁰All the Nethinim, and the sons of Solomon's servants, *were* three hundred and ninety-two.

⁶¹ And these *were* the ones who came up from Tel Melah, Tel Harsha, Cherub, Addon,^a and Immer, but they could not identify their father's house nor their lineage, whether they *were* of Israel: ⁶²the sons of Delaiah, the sons of Tobiah, the sons of Nekoda, six hundred and forty-two; ⁶³and of the priests: the sons of Habaiah, the sons of Koz,^a the sons of Barzillai, who took a wife of the daughters of Barzillai the Gileadite, and was called by their name. ⁶⁴These sought their listing *among* those who were registered by genealogy, but it was not found; therefore they were excluded from the priesthood as defiled. ⁶⁵And the governor^a said to them that they should not eat of the most holy things till a priest could consult with the Urim and Thummim.

7:43 ^aSpelled *Hodaviah* in Ezra 2:40
7:47 ^aSpelled *Siaha* in Ezra 2:44
7:48 ^aMasoretic Text reads *Lebanah.* ^bMasoretic Text reads *Hogabah.* ^cOr *Shalmai*, or *Shamlai*
7:52 ^aSpelled *Nephusim* in Ezra 2:50
7:54 ^aSpelled *Bazluth* in Ezra 2:52 7:57 ^aSpelled *Peruda* in Ezra 2:55 7:59 ^aSpelled *Ami* in Ezra 2:57 7:61 ^aSpelled *Addan* in Ezra 2:59
7:63 ^aOr *Hakkoz* 7:65 ^aHebrew *Tirshatha*

TRADE AND ECONOMICS

A daric was a gold coin first issued by the Persian king Darius and named for him. It was one of the very first coinages, appearing in 517 B.C. Darics were widely imitated, and the name was used for amounts of money, not necessarily the literal coin. The name "drachma" (Neh. 7:70) reflects the later spread of coinage to Greece.

66 Altogether the whole assembly *was* forty-two thousand three hundred and sixty, ⁶⁷besides their male and female servants, of whom *there were* seven thousand three hundred and thirty-seven; and they had two hundred and forty-five men and women singers. ⁶⁸Their horses were seven hundred and thirty-six, their mules two hundred and forty-five, ⁶⁹*their* camels four hundred and thirty-five, *and* donkeys six thousand seven hundred and twenty.

70 And some of the heads of the fathers' houses gave to the work. The governorᵃ gave to the treasury one thousand gold drachmas, fifty basins, and five hundred and thirty priestly garments. ⁷¹Some of the heads of the fathers' *houses* gave to the treasury of the work twenty thousand gold drachmas, and two thousand two hundred silver minas. ⁷²And that which the rest of the people gave *was* twenty thousand gold drachmas, two thousand silver minas, and sixty-seven priestly garments.

⁷³So the priests, the Levites, the gatekeepers, the singers, *some* of the people, the Nethinim, and all Israel dwelt in their cities.

7:70 ᵃHebrew *Tirshatha*

Ezra Reads the Law

At Neh. 7:73 the Book of Nehemiah changes. First, the narrative is no longer told in Nehemiah's own words; the governor's memoir is temporarily suspended. Second, the main character in Neh. 7:73—8:18 is not Nehemiah but Ezra the scribe (who is not mentioned at all in Neh. 1—7).

These sudden changes are made much more striking by another curiosity. The apocryphal book of 3 Esdras and the writings of the Jewish historian Josephus both tell the story of Ezra, but in those accounts, the event described in Neh. 8 comes immediately after Ezra 10. In other words, in those ancient texts, Neh. 8 is not a part of the story of Nehemiah at all, but instead a part of the story of Ezra. Many scholars suggest that Neh. 8 was once a part of the Book of Ezra, but was later placed in the middle of the Book of Nehemiah by the editing process that tied these books together.

If Neh. 8 was originally part of the Book of Ezra, then it is uncertain when Ezra read the Law of Moses in the square (Neh. 8:1–3). Nevertheless, it is at least possible to read Neh. 8 following the building of the walls. According to Neh. 8:9, Nehemiah was present at Ezra's reading, and such an event would have been an appropriate way to dedicate the recently completed city walls.

It is also possible to read Neh. 8—10 in the context of the people renewing their covenant with God. The 7th month, Tishri (Neh. 7:73b), corresponding to September-October, was an important time of sacred assemblies. The walls had been completed in the preceding month of Elul (Neh. 6:15), and the timing was now right to gather in Jerusalem for festival celebration and covenant renewal. On the 1st day of the month Ezra read the Law (8:2); for 7 days during the month the people observed the Feast of Tabernacles (8:18); and on the 24th day they made a public confession of sins (9:1–3). Finally, the leaders publicly signed the covenant (10:1–27), and the people, beginning with the priesthood, joined the covenant by taking an oath (10:28, 29).

■ Nehemiah 7:73b—10:39

Nehemiah

7 :73b When the seventh month came, the children of Israel *were* in their cities.

Proclaiming the Mosaic Law

8 ¹Now all the people gathered together as one man in the open square that *was* in front of the Water Gate; and they told Ezra the scribe to bring the Book of the Law of Moses, which the LORD had commanded Israel. ²So Ezra the priest brought the Law before the assembly of men and women and all who *could* hear with understanding on the first day of the seventh month. ³Then he read from it in the open square that *was* in front of the Water Gate from morning until midday, before the men and women and those who could understand; and the ears of all the people *were attentive* to the Book of the Law.

⁴So Ezra the scribe stood on a platform of wood which they had made for the purpose; and beside him, at his right hand, stood Mattithiah, Shema, Anaiah, Urijah, Hilkiah, and Maaseiah; and at his left

hand Pedaiah, Mishael, Malchijah, Hashum, Hashbadana, Zechariah, *and* Meshullam. ⁵And Ezra opened the book in the sight of all the people, for he was *standing* above all the people; and when he opened it, all the people stood up. ⁶And Ezra blessed the LORD, the great God.

Then all the people answered, "Amen, Amen!" while lifting up their hands. And they bowed their heads and worshiped the LORD with *their* faces to the ground.

⁷Also Jeshua, Bani, Sherebiah, Jamin, Akkub, Shabbethai, Hodijah, Maaseiah, Kelita, Azariah, Jozabad, Hanan, Pelaiah, and the Levites, helped the people to understand the Law; and the people *stood* in their place. ⁸So they read distinctly from the book, in the Law of God; and they gave the sense, and helped *them* to understand the reading.

⁹And Nehemiah, who *was* the governor,ᵃ Ezra the priest *and* scribe, and the Levites who taught the people said to all the people, "This day *is* holy to the LORD your God; do not mourn nor weep." For all the people wept, when they heard the words of the Law.

¹⁰Then he said to them, "Go your way, eat the fat, drink the sweet, and send portions to those for whom nothing is prepared; for *this* day *is* holy to our Lord. Do not sorrow, for the joy of the LORD is your strength."

¹¹So the Levites quieted all the people, saying, "Be still, for the day *is* holy; do not be grieved." ¹²And all the people went their way to eat and drink, to send portions and rejoice greatly, because they understood the words that were declared to them.

The Feast of Tabernacles

¹³Now on the second day the heads of the fathers' *houses* of all the people, with the priests and Levites, were gathered to Ezra the scribe, in order to understand the words of the Law. ¹⁴And they found written in the Law, which the LORD had commanded by Moses, that the children of Israel should dwell in booths during the feast of the seventh month, ¹⁵and that they should announce and proclaim in all their cities and in Jerusalem, saying, "Go out to the mountain, and bring olive branches, branches of oil trees, myrtle branches, palm branches, and branches of leafy trees, to make booths, as *it is* written."

¹⁶Then the people went out and brought *them* and made themselves booths,

each one on the roof of his house, or in their courtyards or the courts of the house of God, and in the open square of the Water Gate and in the open square of the Gate of Ephraim. ¹⁷So the whole assembly of those who had returned from the captivity made booths and sat under the booths; for since the days of Joshua the son of Nun until that day the children of Israel had not done so. And there was very great gladness. ¹⁸Also day by day, from the first day until the last day, he read from the Book of the Law of God. And they kept the feast seven days; and on the eighth day *there was* a sacred assembly, according to the *prescribed* manner.

The People Confess Their Sins

9 ¹Now on the twenty-fourth day of this month the children of Israel were assembled with fasting, in sackcloth, and with dust on their heads.ᵃ ²Then those of Israelite lineage separated themselves from all foreigners; and they stood and confessed their sins and the iniquities of their fathers. ³And they stood up in their place and read from the Book of the Law of the LORD their God *for one*-fourth of the day; and *for another* fourth they confessed and worshiped the LORD their God.

⁴Then Jeshua, Bani, Kadmiel, Shebaniah, Bunni, Sherebiah, Bani, *and* Chenani stood on the stairs of the Levites and cried out with a loud voice to the LORD their God. ⁵And the Levites, Jeshua, Kadmiel, Bani, Hashabniah, Sherebiah, Hodijah, Shebaniah, *and* Pethahiah, said:

"Stand up *and* bless the LORD your God
    Forever and ever!

"Blessed be Your glorious name,
    Which is exalted above all blessing
        and praise!
6   You alone *are* the LORD;
    You have made heaven,
    The heaven of heavens, with all their
        host,
    The earth and everything on it,
    The seas and all that is in them,
    And You preserve them all.
    The host of heaven worships You.

7   "You *are* the LORD God,
    Who chose Abram,

8:9 ᵃHebrew *Tirshatha*   9:1 ᵃLiterally *earth on them*

And brought him out of Ur of the
Chaldeans,
And gave him the name Abraham;
8 You found his heart faithful before
You,
And made a covenant with him
To give the land of the Canaanites,
The Hittites, the Amorites,
The Perizzites, the Jebusites,
And the Girgashites—
To give *it* to his descendants.
You have performed Your words,
For You *are* righteous.

9 "You saw the affliction of our fathers in
Egypt,
And heard their cry by the Red Sea.
10 You showed signs and wonders
against Pharaoh,
Against all his servants,
And against all the people of his land.
For You knew that they acted proudly
against them.
So You made a name for Yourself, as *it
is* this day.
11 And You divided the sea before them,
So that they went through the midst
of the sea on the dry land;
And their persecutors You threw into
the deep,
As a stone into the mighty waters.
12 Moreover You led them by day with a
cloudy pillar,
And by night with a pillar of fire,
To give them light on the road
Which they should travel.

13 "You came down also on Mount Sinai,
And spoke with them from heaven,
And gave them just ordinances and
true laws,
Good statutes and commandments.
14 You made known to them Your holy
Sabbath,
And commanded them precepts,
statutes and laws,
By the hand of Moses Your servant.
15 You gave them bread from heaven for
their hunger,
And brought them water out of the
rock for their thirst,

And told them to go in to possess the
land
Which You had sworn to give them.

16 "But they and our fathers acted
proudly,
Hardened their necks,
And did not heed Your
commandments.
17 They refused to obey,
And they were not mindful of Your
wonders
That You did among them.
But they hardened their necks,
And in their rebellion[a]
They appointed a leader
To return to their bondage.
But You *are* God,
Ready to pardon,
Gracious and merciful,
Slow to anger,
Abundant in kindness,
And did not forsake them.

18 "Even when they made a molded calf
for themselves,
And said, 'This *is* your god
That brought you up out of Egypt,'
And worked great provocations,
19 Yet in Your manifold mercies
You did not forsake them in the
wilderness.
The pillar of the cloud did not depart
from them by day,
To lead them on the road;
Nor the pillar of fire by night,
To show them light,
And the way they should go.
20 You also gave Your good Spirit to
instruct them,
And did not withhold Your manna
from their mouth,
And gave them water for their thirst.
21 Forty years You sustained them in the
wilderness;
They lacked nothing;
Their clothes did not wear out[a]
And their feet did not swell.

22 "Moreover You gave them kingdoms
and nations,
And divided them into districts.[a]
So they took possession of the land of
Sihon,
The land of[b] the king of Heshbon,
And the land of Og king of Bashan.
23 You also multiplied their children as
the stars of heaven,

9:17 [a]Following Masoretic Text and Vulgate;
Septuagint reads *in Egypt.*   9:21 [a]Compare
Deuteronomy 29:5   9:22 [a]Literally *corners*
[b]Following Masoretic Text and Vulgate; Septuagint
omits *The land of.*

And brought them into the land
Which You had told their fathers
To go in and possess.
24 So the people went in
And possessed the land;
You subdued before them the
  inhabitants of the land,
The Canaanites,
And gave them into their hands,
With their kings
And the people of the land,
That they might do with them as they
  wished.
25 And they took strong cities and a rich
  land,
And possessed houses full of all goods,
Cisterns *already* dug, vineyards, olive
  groves,
And fruit trees in abundance.
So they ate and were filled and grew
  fat,
And delighted themselves in Your
  great goodness.

26 "Nevertheless they were disobedient
And rebelled against You,
Cast Your law behind their backs
And killed Your prophets, who
  testified against them
To turn them to Yourself;
And they worked great provocations.
27 Therefore You delivered them into the
  hand of their enemies,
Who oppressed them;
And in the time of their trouble,
When they cried to You,
You heard from heaven;
And according to Your abundant
  mercies
You gave them deliverers who saved
  them
From the hand of their enemies.

28 "But after they had rest,
They again did evil before You.
Therefore You left them in the hand of
  their enemies,
So that they had dominion over them;
Yet when they returned and cried out
  to You,
You heard from heaven;
And many times You delivered them
  according to Your mercies,
29 And testified against them,
That You might bring them back to
  Your law.
Yet they acted proudly,
And did not heed Your
  commandments,

But sinned against Your judgments,
'Which if a man does, he shall live by
  them.'ᵃ
And they shrugged their shoulders,
Stiffened their necks,
And would not hear.
30 Yet for many years You had patience
  with them,
And testified against them by Your
  Spirit in Your prophets.
Yet they would not listen;
Therefore You gave them into the
  hand of the peoples of the lands.
31 Nevertheless in Your great mercy
You did not utterly consume them nor
  forsake them;
For You *are* God, gracious and
  merciful.

32 "Now therefore, our God,
The great, the mighty, and awesome
  God,
Who keeps covenant and mercy:
Do not let all the trouble seem small
  before You
That has come upon us,
Our kings and our princes,
Our priests and our prophets,
Our fathers and on all Your people,
From the days of the kings of Assyria
  until this day.
33 However You *are* just in all that has
  befallen us;
For You have dealt faithfully,
But we have done wickedly.
34 Neither our kings nor our princes,
Our priests nor our fathers,
Have kept Your law,
Nor heeded Your commandments and
  Your testimonies,
With which You testified against
  them.
35 For they have not served You in their
  kingdom,
Or in the many good *things* that You
  gave them,
Or in the large and rich land which
  You set before them;
Nor did they turn from their wicked
  works.

36 "Here we *are,* servants today!
And the land that You gave to our
  fathers,
To eat its fruit and its bounty,
Here we *are,* servants in it!

9:29 ᵃLeviticus 18:5

37 And it yields much increase to the
kings
You have set over us,
Because of our sins;
Also they have dominion over our
bodies and our cattle
At their pleasure;
And we *are* in great distress.

38 "And because of all this,
We make a sure *covenant* and write *it;*
Our leaders, our Levites, *and* our
priests seal *it.*"

The People Who Sealed the Covenant

10 ¹Now those who placed *their* seal on
the document were:
Nehemiah the governor, the son of Hac-
aliah, and Zedekiah, ²Seraiah, Azariah,
Jeremiah, ³Pashhur, Amariah, Malchijah,
⁴Hattush, Shebaniah, Malluch, ⁵Harim,
Meremoth, Obadiah, ⁶Daniel, Ginnethon,
Baruch, ⁷Meshullam, Abijah, Mijamin,
⁸Maaziah, Bilgai, *and* Shemaiah. These
were the priests.
⁹The Levites: Jeshua the son of Aza-
niah, Binnui of the sons of Henadad, *and*
Kadmiel.
¹⁰Their brethren: Shebaniah, Hodijah,
Kelita, Pelaiah, Hanan, ¹¹Micha, Rehob,
Hashabiah, ¹²Zaccur, Sherebiah, Sheba-
niah, ¹³Hodijah, Bani, *and* Beninu.
¹⁴The leaders of the people: Parosh,
Pahath-Moab, Elam, Zattu, Bani, ¹⁵Bunni,
Azgad, Bebai, ¹⁶Adonijah, Bigvai, Adin,
¹⁷Ater, Hezekiah, Azzur, ¹⁸Hodijah,
Hashum, Bezai, ¹⁹Hariph, Anathoth,
Nebai, ²⁰Magpiash, Meshullam, Hezir,
²¹Meshezabel, Zadok, Jaddua, ²²Pelatiah,
Hanan, Anaiah, ²³Hoshea, Hananiah, Has-
shub, ²⁴Hallohesh, Pilha, Shobek, ²⁵Re-
hum, Hashabnah, Maaseiah, ²⁶Ahijah,
Hanan, Anan, ²⁷Malluch, Harim, *and*
Baanah.

The Covenant That Was Sealed

²⁸Now the rest of the people—the
priests, the Levites, the gatekeepers, the
singers, the Nethinim, and all those who
had separated themselves from the peoples
of the lands to the Law of God, their wives,
their sons, and their daughters, everyone
who had knowledge and understanding—
²⁹these joined with their brethren, their nobles, and entered into a curse and an oath
to walk in God's Law, which was given by
Moses the servant of God, and to observe
and do all the commandments of the LORD
our Lord, and His ordinances and His
statutes: ³⁰We would not give our daughters as wives to the peoples of the land, nor
take their daughters for our sons; ³¹*if* the
peoples of the land brought wares or any
grain to sell on the Sabbath day, we would
not buy it from them on the Sabbath, or on
a holy day; and we would forego the seventh year's *produce* and the exacting of
every debt.
³²Also we made ordinances for ourselves, to exact from ourselves yearly one-
third of a shekel for the service of the
house of our God: ³³for the showbread, for
the regular grain offering, for the regular
burnt offering of the Sabbaths, the New
Moons, and the set feasts; for the holy
things, for the sin offerings to make atonement for Israel, and all the work of the
house of our God. ³⁴We cast lots among the
priests, the Levites, and the people, for
bringing the wood offering into the house
of our God, according to our fathers'
houses, at the appointed times year by
year, to burn on the altar of the LORD our
God as *it is* written in the Law.
³⁵And *we made ordinances* to bring the
firstfruits of our ground and the firstfruits
of all fruit of all trees, year by year, to the
house of the LORD; ³⁶to bring the firstborn
of our sons and our cattle, as *it is* written
in the Law, and the firstborn of our herds
and our flocks, to the house of our God, to
the priests who minister in the house of
our God; ³⁷to bring the firstfruits of our
dough, our offerings, the fruit from all
kinds of trees, *the* new wine and oil, to the
priests, to the storerooms of the house of
our God; and to bring the tithes of our land
to the Levites, for the Levites should receive the tithes in all our farming commu-

---

CULTURE AND SOCIETY

*A covenant is a written agreement or contract between two or more parties. Covenants
spell out obligations and rights and may also prescribe penalties. In biblical times the
written word had an aura of permanence and authority that is more diluted today when
so much more is recorded. Thus Nehemiah and the leaders speak of the "sure
covenant" which they had written (Neh. 9:38).*

TITHE AND LOYALTY (Neh. 10:37, 38)

An old Canaanite tribute called the "tenth" or "tithe" was payment of a lesser important king to a more powerful one. Tablets from the ancient city of Ugarit, located on the Mediterranean coast, mention such a payment. A king of a smaller village would pay the 10 percent tax, as a representative for his city. His payment was a sign of loyalty to the regional ruler. In return, the more powerful king was obligated to protect those subjects who had paid their tithe.

In the Bible, the payment of tithes became a sign of loyalty to the Israelite God (Mal. 3:8–10). The tithe was taken from the harvest and the herds, both of which were crucial to Israel's physical existence (Deut. 14:22, 23). Bringing God His just due obligated Him to His duties as Savior and Protector (Mal. 3:11). So it was that Nehemiah led the postexilic Jewish community, much in need of God's protection, in the bringing of the tithes to the Levites and to the temple.

nities. **38And the priest, the descendant of Aaron, shall be with the Levites when the Levites receive tithes; and the Levites shall bring up a tenth of the tithes to the house of our God, to the rooms of the storehouse.**

39For the children of Israel and the children of Levi shall bring the offering of the grain, of the new wine and the oil, to the storerooms where the articles of the sanctuary _are, where_ the priests who minister and the gatekeepers and the singers _are;_ and we will not neglect the house of our God.

Wisdom Psalms

The wisdom tradition was one of the most enduring of all ancient Near Eastern traditions, but as time passed it changed slightly, at least in Israel. Some late books of Jewish wisdom place new stress on reverence toward, and obedience to, the Torah. This new Torah-centered teaching, often called "scribal wisdom," was not typical of earlier wisdom writings like the Book of Proverbs. It does appear, however, in the apocryphal book of Ecclesiasticus, written about 180 B.C. and also known as _The Wisdom of Jesus Son of Sirach._

A few hints of scribal wisdom do appear in the "wisdom psalms." These few psalms offer calm and measured advice, drawing simple distinctions between the righteous and the wicked in ways reminiscent of the Book of Proverbs. The entire Book of Psalms is introduced by one of these wisdom psalms (Ps. 1), which describes in stark contrast the lifestyle of the righteous (1:1–3) and of the wicked (1:4, 5). One psalm especially fits the description of scribal wisdom. The longest psalm in the Book ▼

of Psalms (Ps. 119) offers an extended meditation on the beauty and usefulness of the Torah. It even uses the literary device of alphabetic acrostic, which is typical of wisdom writings (for instance, Prov. 31:10–31). Each verse within a particular stanza of the Hebrew Ps. 119 begins with the same letter of the Hebrew alphabet.

Many other psalms, while not as clearly wisdom psalms, contain elements of wisdom thought. For instance, Ps. 49 speaks on a favorite wisdom theme, the vanity of worldly wealth, and Ps. 111 uses the wisdom slogan "the fear of the LORD is the beginning of wisdom" (111:10; see Prov. 1:7). The contrast between the righteous and the wicked appears in parts of Ps. 36, 37, 91, and 112.

Still, most of the psalms that contain wisdom elements are not exclusively wisdom psalms, but can be classed as other psalm types. For example, Ps. 111 is a hymn (see "The Last Word in Praise" at Ps. 104). Even Ps. 91 is a mixed psalm. Its meditative tone and its reflection on the fate of the wicked provide a strong wisdom flavor. Yet Ps. 91 could easily be understood as a song of trust (see "David's Laments" at Ps. 4).

The three psalms (Ps. 1; 91; 119) are without any superscription or any other indication of their date. Nevertheless, the "scribal wisdom" of Ps. 1 and 119 is likely related to the new emphasis on the Scripture that characterized Judaism after the Exile. Just as a new sort of priestly leader developed in the position of the scribe (see "Ezra the Scribe" at Ezra 7:1), so a new Torah-centered type of wisdom developed in the new world that the returned exiles faced.

■ Psalms 1; 91; 119

PSALM 1

The Way of the Righteous and the End of the Ungodly

Blessed *is* the man
Who walks not in the counsel of the
    ungodly,
    Nor stands in the path of sinners,
    Nor sits in the seat of the scornful;
2 But his delight *is* in the law of the
        Lord,
    And in His law he meditates day
        and night.
3 He shall be like a tree
    Planted by the rivers of water,
    That brings forth its fruit in its
        season,
    Whose leaf also shall not wither;
    And whatever he does shall prosper.

4 The ungodly *are* not so,
    But *are* like the chaff which the wind
        drives away.
5 Therefore the ungodly shall not stand
        in the judgment,
    Nor sinners in the congregation of the
        righteous.

6 For the Lord knows the way of the
        righteous,
    But the way of the ungodly shall
        perish.

PSALM 91

Safety of Abiding in the Presence of God

He who dwells in the secret place of the
        Most High
    Shall abide under the shadow of the
        Almighty.
2 I will say of the Lord, "*He is* my
        refuge and my fortress;
    My God, in Him I will trust."

91:3 ᵃThat is, one who catches birds in a trap or
snare

3 Surely He shall deliver you from the
        snare of the fowlerᵃ
    And from the perilous pestilence.
4 He shall cover you with His feathers,
    And under His wings you shall take
        refuge;
    His truth *shall be your* shield and
        buckler.
5 You shall not be afraid of the terror by
        night,
    Nor of the arrow *that* flies by day,
6 *Nor* of the pestilence *that* walks in
        darkness,
    Nor of the destruction *that* lays waste
        at noonday.

7 A thousand may fall at your side,
    And ten thousand at your right hand;
    But it shall not come near you.
8 Only with your eyes shall you look,
    And see the reward of the wicked.

9 Because you have made the Lord, *who
        is* my refuge,
    Even the Most High, your dwelling
        place,
10 No evil shall befall you,
    Nor shall any plague come near your
        dwelling;
11 For He shall give His angels charge
        over you,
    To keep you in all your ways.
12 In *their* hands they shall bear you up,
    Lest you dash your foot against a
        stone.
13 You shall tread upon the lion and the
        cobra,
    The young lion and the serpent you
        shall trample underfoot.

14 "Because he has set his love upon Me,
        therefore I will deliver him;
    I will set him on high, because he has
        known My name.
15 He shall call upon Me, and I will
        answer him;
    I *will be* with him in trouble;
    I will deliver him and honor him.

AGRICULTURE AND HERDING

After grain is harvested, the edible kernels have to be separated from the stem and leaves. This is done by crushing or tearing the plants. The broken grain is thrown into the wind, allowing the waste parts, "the chaff" (Ps. 1:4), to blow away while the heavier kernels fall to the ground. This winnowing of chaff from kernels was a familiar part of village life in Palestine.

¹⁶ With long life I will satisfy him,
And show him My salvation."

PSALM 119

Meditations on the Excellencies of the Word of God

א ALEPH

Blessed *are* the undefiled in the way,
Who walk in the law of the LORD!
2 Blessed *are* those who keep His
testimonies,
Who seek Him with the whole heart!
3 They also do no iniquity;
They walk in His ways.
4 You have commanded *us*
To keep Your precepts diligently.
5 Oh, that my ways were directed
To keep Your statutes!
6 Then I would not be ashamed,
When I look into all Your
commandments.
7 I will praise You with uprightness of
heart,
When I learn Your righteous
judgments.
8 I will keep Your statutes;
Oh, do not forsake me utterly!

ב BETH

9 How can a young man cleanse his
way?
By taking heed according to Your
word.
10 With my whole heart I have sought
You;
Oh, let me not wander from Your
commandments!
11 Your word I have hidden in my heart,
That I might not sin against You.
12 Blessed *are* You, O LORD!
Teach me Your statutes.
13 With my lips I have declared
All the judgments of Your mouth.
14 I have rejoiced in the way of Your
testimonies,
As *much as* in all riches.

15 I will meditate on Your precepts,
And contemplate Your ways.
16 I will delight myself in Your statutes;
I will not forget Your word.

ג GIMEL

17 Deal bountifully with Your servant,
That I may live and keep Your word.
18 Open my eyes, that I may see
Wondrous things from Your law.
19 I *am* a stranger in the earth;
Do not hide Your commandments from
me.
20 My soul breaks with longing
For Your judgments at all times.
21 You rebuke the proud—the cursed,
Who stray from Your commandments.
22 Remove from me reproach and
contempt,
For I have kept Your testimonies.
23 Princes also sit *and* speak against
me,
But Your servant meditates on Your
statutes.
24 Your testimonies also *are* my delight
And my counselors.

ד DALETH

25 My soul clings to the dust;
Revive me according to Your word.
26 I have declared my ways, and You
answered me;
Teach me Your statutes.
27 Make me understand the way of Your
precepts;
So shall I meditate on Your wonderful
works.
28 My soul melts from heaviness;
Strengthen me according to Your
word.
29 Remove from me the way of lying,
And grant me Your law graciously.
30 I have chosen the way of truth;
Your judgments I have laid *before me*.
31 I cling to Your testimonies;
O LORD, do not put me to shame!
32 I will run the course of Your
commandments,
For You shall enlarge my heart.

ARTS AND LITERATURE

The poetic imagery in Ps. 91:5, 6 stands for the calamities that might happen at night or day, whether warfare, sickness, robbery, or death. In the ancient world each of these was thought to be a god. The psalmist thus refers to powers that threaten human life, but also to God's power over all events. God's protection is continuous through night and day.

ה HE

33 Teach me, O LORD, the way of Your
statutes,
And I shall keep it *to* the end.
34 Give me understanding, and I shall
keep Your law;
Indeed, I shall observe it with *my*
whole heart.
35 Make me walk in the path of Your
commandments,
For I delight in it.
36 Incline my heart to Your testimonies,
And not to covetousness.
37 Turn away my eyes from looking at
worthless things,
And revive me in Your way.[a]
38 Establish Your word to Your servant,
Who *is devoted* to fearing You.
39 Turn away my reproach which I
dread,
For Your judgments *are* good.
40 Behold, I long for Your precepts;
Revive me in Your righteousness.

ו WAW

41 Let Your mercies come also to me,
O LORD—
Your salvation according to Your word.
42 So shall I have an answer for him who
reproaches me,
For I trust in Your word.
43 And take not the word of truth utterly
out of my mouth,
For I have hoped in Your ordinances.
44 So shall I keep Your law continually,
Forever and ever.
45 And I will walk at liberty,
For I seek Your precepts.
46 I will speak of Your testimonies also
before kings,
And will not be ashamed.
47 And I will delight myself in Your
commandments,
Which I love.
48 My hands also I will lift up to Your
commandments,

Which I love,
And I will meditate on Your statutes.

ז ZAYIN

49 Remember the word to Your servant,
Upon which You have caused me to
hope.
50 This *is* my comfort in my affliction,
For Your word has given me life.
51 The proud have me in great derision,
Yet I do not turn aside from Your law.
52 I remembered Your judgments of old,
O LORD,
And have comforted myself.
53 Indignation has taken hold of me
Because of the wicked, who forsake
Your law.
54 Your statutes have been my songs
In the house of my pilgrimage.
55 I remember Your name in the night,
O LORD,
And I keep Your law.
56 This has become mine,
Because I kept Your precepts.

ח HETH

57 *You are* my portion, O LORD;
I have said that I would keep Your
words.
58 I entreated Your favor with *my* whole
heart;
Be merciful to me according to Your
word.
59 I thought about my ways,
And turned my feet to Your
testimonies.
60 I made haste, and did not delay
To keep Your commandments.
61 The cords of the wicked have bound
me,
But I have not forgotten Your law.
62 At midnight I will rise to give thanks
to You,
Because of Your righteous judgments.
63 I *am* a companion of all who fear You,
And of those who keep Your precepts.
64 The earth, O LORD, is full of Your
mercy;
Teach me Your statutes.

119:37 ᵃFollowing Masoretic Text, Septuagint, and
Vulgate; Targum reads *Your words.*

ARTS AND LITERATURE

*The acrostic is a common device in biblical poetry. In an acrostic poem, each line or
series of lines begins with a certain letter. Usually the letters follow the order of the
alphabet from beginning to end. The purpose is to aid in memorization (Ps. 119:16), or
to give the composition a sense of completeness. Each of the 22 stanzas in Ps. 119
has lines beginning with the same Hebrew letter.*

ט TETH

65 You have dealt well with Your servant,
O LORD, according to Your word.
66 Teach me good judgment and
knowledge,
For I believe Your commandments.
67 Before I was afflicted I went astray,
But now I keep Your word.
68 You *are* good, and do good;
Teach me Your statutes.
69 The proud have forged a lie against
me,
But I will keep Your precepts with *my*
whole heart.
70 Their heart is as fat as grease,
But I delight in Your law.
71 *It is* good for me that I have been
afflicted,
That I may learn Your statutes.
72 The law of Your mouth *is* better to me
Than thousands of *coins of* gold and
silver.

י YOD

73 Your hands have made me and
fashioned me;
Give me understanding, that I may
learn Your commandments.
74 Those who fear You will be glad when
they see me,
Because I have hoped in Your word.
75 I know, O LORD, that Your judgments
are right,
And *that* in faithfulness You have
afflicted me.
76 Let, I pray, Your merciful kindness be
for my comfort,
According to Your word to Your
servant.
77 Let Your tender mercies come to me,
that I may live;
For Your law *is* my delight.
78 Let the proud be ashamed,
For they treated me wrongfully with
falsehood;
But I will meditate on Your precepts.
79 Let those who fear You turn to me,
Those who know Your testimonies.
80 Let my heart be blameless regarding
Your statutes,
That I may not be ashamed.

כ KAPH

81 My soul faints for Your salvation,
But I hope in Your word.
82 My eyes fail *from searching* Your
word,
Saying, "When will You comfort me?"

83 For I have become like a wineskin in
smoke,
Yet I do not forget Your statutes.
84 How many *are* the days of Your servant?
When will You execute judgment on
those who persecute me?
85 The proud have dug pits for me,
Which *is* not according to Your law.
86 All Your commandments *are* faithful;
They persecute me wrongfully;
Help me!
87 They almost made an end of me on
earth,
But I did not forsake Your precepts.
88 Revive me according to Your
lovingkindness,
So that I may keep the testimony of
Your mouth.

ל LAMED

89 Forever, O LORD,
Your word is settled in heaven.
90 Your faithfulness *endures* to all
generations;
You established the earth, and it
abides.
91 They continue this day according to
Your ordinances,
For all *are* Your servants.
92 Unless Your law *had been* my delight,
I would then have perished in my
affliction.
93 I will never forget Your precepts,
For by them You have given me life.
94 I *am* Yours, save me;
For I have sought Your precepts.
95 The wicked wait for me to destroy me,
But I will consider Your testimonies.
96 I have seen the consummation of all
perfection,
But Your commandment *is* exceedingly
broad.

מ MEM

97 Oh, how I love Your law!
It *is* my meditation all the day.
98 You, through Your commandments,
make me wiser than my enemies;
For they *are* ever with me.
99 I have more understanding than all
my teachers,
For Your testimonies *are* my
meditation.
100 I understand more than the ancients,
Because I keep Your precepts.
101 I have restrained my feet from every
evil way,
That I may keep Your word.

LIGHTS FOR THE NIGHT (Ps. 119:105)

In Old Testament times people used small lamps to furnish artificial light. Ancient lamps were essentially small ceramic bowls that were customized during construction to have a "nose" on one edge. The purpose of this extension was to hold a wick. Wicks of cloth were laid in the nose and extended into the oil in the lamp's bowl.

The light produced was not brilliant but necessary for finding one's way. In Ps. 119:105 the writer compares God's word with a lamp. While the light from that word does not blind the eyes, it does point the way for its hearers.

102 I have not departed from Your
   judgments,
   For You Yourself have taught me.
103 How sweet are Your words to my taste,
   Sweeter than honey to my mouth!
104 Through Your precepts I get
   understanding;
   Therefore I hate every false way.

] NUN
105 Your word *is* a lamp to my feet
   And a light to my path.
106 I have sworn and confirmed
   That I will keep Your righteous
   judgments.
107 I am afflicted very much;
   Revive me, O LORD, according to Your
   word.
108 Accept, I pray, the freewill offerings of
   my mouth, O LORD,
   And teach me Your judgments.
109 My life *is* continually in my hand,
   Yet I do not forget Your law.
110 The wicked have laid a snare for me,
   Yet I have not strayed from Your
   precepts.
111 Your testimonies I have taken as a
   heritage forever,
   For they *are* the rejoicing of my heart.
112 I have inclined my heart to perform
   Your statutes
   Forever, to the very end.

ɔ SAMEK
113 I hate the double-minded,
   But I love Your law.
114 You *are* my hiding place and my shield;
   I hope in Your word.
115 Depart from me, you evildoers,
   For I will keep the commandments of
   my God!
116 Uphold me according to Your word,
   that I may live;
   And do not let me be ashamed of my
   hope.

117 Hold me up, and I shall be safe,
   And I shall observe Your statutes
   continually.
118 You reject all those who stray from
   Your statutes,
   For their deceit *is* falsehood.
119 You put away all the wicked of the
   earth *like* dross;
   Therefore I love Your testimonies.
120 My flesh trembles for fear of You,
   And I am afraid of Your judgments.

ע AYIN
121 I have done justice and righteousness;
   Do not leave me to my oppressors.
122 Be surety for Your servant for good;
   Do not let the proud oppress me.
123 My eyes fail *from seeking* Your
   salvation
   And Your righteous word.
124 Deal with Your servant according to
   Your mercy,
   And teach me Your statutes.
125 I *am* Your servant;
   Give me understanding,
   That I may know Your testimonies.
126 *It is* time for *You* to act, O LORD,
   For they have regarded Your law as
   void.
127 Therefore I love Your commandments
   More than gold, yes, than fine gold!
128 Therefore all *Your* precepts *concerning*
   all *things*
   I consider *to be* right;
   I hate every false way.

פ PE
129 Your testimonies are wonderful;
   Therefore my soul keeps them.
130 The entrance of Your words gives
   light;
   It gives understanding to the simple.
131 I opened my mouth and panted,
   For I longed for Your commandments.

132 Look upon me and be merciful to me,
As Your custom *is* toward those who
love Your name.
133 Direct my steps by Your word,
And let no iniquity have dominion
over me.
134 Redeem me from the oppression of
man,
That I may keep Your precepts.
135 Make Your face shine upon Your
servant,
And teach me Your statutes.
136 Rivers of water run down from my
eyes,
Because *men* do not keep Your law.

צ TSADDE
137 Righteous *are* You, O LORD,
And upright *are* Your judgments.
138 Your testimonies, *which* You have
commanded,
Are righteous and very faithful.
139 My zeal has consumed me,
Because my enemies have forgotten
Your words.
140 Your word *is* very pure;
Therefore Your servant loves it.
141 I *am* small and despised,
Yet I do not forget Your precepts.
142 Your righteousness *is* an everlasting
righteousness,
And Your law *is* truth.
143 Trouble and anguish have overtaken
me,
Yet Your commandments *are* my
delights.
144 The righteousness of Your testimonies
is everlasting;
Give me understanding, and I shall
live.

ק QOPH
145 I cry out with *my* whole heart;
Hear me, O LORD!
I will keep Your statutes.
146 I cry out to You;
Save me, and I will keep Your
testimonies.
147 I rise before the dawning of the
morning,
And cry for help;
I hope in Your word.
148 My eyes are awake through the *night*
watches,
That I may meditate on Your word.
149 Hear my voice according to Your
lovingkindness;

O LORD, revive me according to Your
justice.
150 They draw near who follow after
wickedness;
They are far from Your law.
151 You *are* near, O LORD,
And all Your commandments *are*
truth.
152 Concerning Your testimonies,
I have known of old that You have
founded them forever.

ר RESH
153 Consider my affliction and deliver me,
For I do not forget Your law.
154 Plead my cause and redeem me;
Revive me according to Your word.
155 Salvation *is* far from the wicked,
For they do not seek Your statutes.
156 Great *are* Your tender mercies,
O LORD;
Revive me according to Your
judgments.
157 Many *are* my persecutors and my
enemies,
Yet I do not turn from Your
testimonies.
158 I see the treacherous, and am
disgusted,
Because they do not keep Your word.
159 Consider how I love Your precepts;
Revive me, O LORD, according to Your
lovingkindness.
160 The entirety of Your word *is* truth,
And every one of Your righteous
judgments *endures* forever.

ש SHIN
161 Princes persecute me without a cause,
But my heart stands in awe of Your
word.
162 I rejoice at Your word
As one who finds great treasure.
163 I hate and abhor lying,
But I love Your law.
164 Seven times a day I praise You,
Because of Your righteous judgments.
165 Great peace have those who love Your
law,
And nothing causes them to stumble.
166 LORD, I hope for Your salvation,
And I do Your commandments.
167 My soul keeps Your testimonies,
And I love them exceedingly.
168 I keep Your precepts and Your
testimonies,
For all my ways *are* before You.

ת TAU

169 Let my cry come before You, O LORD;
    Give me understanding according to
    Your word.
170 Let my supplication come before You;
    Deliver me according to Your word.
171 My lips shall utter praise,
    For You teach me Your statutes.
172 My tongue shall speak of Your word,
    For all Your commandments *are*
    righteousness.
173 Let Your hand become my help,
    For I have chosen Your precepts.
174 I long for Your salvation, O LORD,
    And Your law *is* my delight.
175 Let my soul live, and it shall praise
    You;
    And let Your judgments help me.
176 I have gone astray like a lost sheep;
    Seek Your servant,
    For I do not forget Your
    commandments.

The Names of the Returned Exiles

By the end of Nehemiah's labors, when Jerusalem stood whole once more, a new spirit seems to have come over the people. They were proud to be Jews, proud of their holy city, and conscious of having been a part of a great restoration. Perhaps as a part of this new pride, the Jews of Jerusalem had their names preserved and recorded alongside the names of other restoration leaders, from the days of Zerubbabel and Jeshua (Neh. 12:1) to the days of Ezra and Nehemiah (12:26). Now all that was left was to dedicate the new walls of the city (12:27–30).

▼ ■ Nehemiah 11:1—12:30

Nehemiah
The People Dwelling in Jerusalem

11 :1 Now the leaders of the people dwelt at Jerusalem; the rest of the people cast lots to bring one out of ten to dwell in Jerusalem, the holy city, and nine-tenths *were to dwell* in *other* cities. ²And the people blessed all the men who willingly offered themselves to dwell at Jerusalem.

³These *are* the heads of the province who dwelt in Jerusalem. (But in the cities of Judah everyone dwelt in his own possession in their cities—Israelites, priests, Levites, Nethinim, and descendants of Solomon's servants.) ⁴Also in Jerusalem dwelt *some* of the children of Judah and of the children of Benjamin.

The children of Judah: Athaiah the son of Uzziah, the son of Zechariah, the son of Amariah, the son of Shephatiah, the son of Mahalalel, of the children of Perez; ⁵and Maaseiah the son of Baruch, the son of Col-Hozeh, the son of Hazaiah, the son of Adaiah, the son of Joiarib, the son of Zechariah, the son of Shiloni. ⁶All the sons of Perez who dwelt at Jerusalem *were* four hundred and sixty-eight valiant men.

⁷And these are the sons of Benjamin: Sallu the son of Meshullam, the son of Joed, the son of Pedaiah, the son of Kolaiah, the son of Maaseiah, the son of Ithiel, the son of Jeshaiah; ⁸and after him Gabbai *and* Sallai, nine hundred and twenty-eight. ⁹Joel the son of Zichri *was* their overseer, and Judah the son of Senuah[a] *was* second over the city.

¹⁰Of the priests: Jedaiah the son of Joiarib, and Jachin; ¹¹Seraiah the son of Hilkiah, the son of Meshullam, the son of Zadok, the son of Meraioth, the son of Ahitub, *was* the leader of the house of God. ¹²Their brethren who did the work of the house *were* eight hundred and twenty-two; and Adaiah the son of Jeroham, the son of Pelaliah, the son of Amzi, the son of Zechariah, the son of Pashhur, the son of Malchijah, ¹³and his brethren, heads of the fathers' *houses, were* two hundred and forty-two; and Amashai the son of Azarel, the son of Ahzai, the son of Meshillemoth, the son of Immer, ¹⁴and their brethren, mighty men of valor, *were* one hundred and twenty-eight. Their overseer *was* Zabdiel the son of *one of* the great men.[a]

TIME CAPSULE   *447 to 437 B.C.*

**447–
438**   *The Parthenon erected on the Acropolis in Athens*

445   *Athens and Sparta agree to 30-year nonaggression pact*

445   *Nehemiah's mission to Jerusalem*

445   *Nehemiah becomes governor of Judea*

437   *Final walls of Jerusalem completed according to Josephus*

11:9 ᵃOr *Hassenuah*   11:14 ᵃOr *the son of Haggedolim*

ZERUBBABEL THE GOVERNOR (Neh. 12:1)

The name "Zerubbabel" (Neh. 12:1) is a Babylonian name, most likely meaning "seed of Babylon." Zerubbabel was from a Judean family but had grown up in Babylon. In his adult years, however, he had the opportunity to return to his ancestral home in Jerusalem.

Zerubbabel was descended from royalty (1 Chr. 3:17–19). His grandfather had been Jehoiachin (or Jeconiah), the king of Judah whom the Babylonians had taken out of Jerusalem into captivity in 597 B.C. Since Zerubbabel was thus an heir to the throne of David, and the rightful king of Judah, some Judeans hoped that Judah might regain a degree of national power under his leadership. He was compared to a "signet ring" (Hag. 2:23), an instrument belonging to a king, used to impress a seal of his authority.

The political situation of Judah, however, had changed since Zerubbabel's grandfather had ruled. The Persians now were in control. While a Persian king did appoint Zerubbabel to be the governor of the Persian province of Judah, he would not be given the power of a king. The "governor of Judah" (Hag. 1:1) was given charge of the local political situation in Judah and Jerusalem, but would not rule a kingdom.

During Zerubbabel's oversight, the returnees from the Exile completed rebuilding the temple. With Zerubbabel in Jerusalem and the temple completed, hopes were inspired for a rebirth of the Davidic monarchy. Many hoped that Zerubbabel would become more than governor—to rise as Israel's king. But after the temple rebuilding, Zerubbabel no longer appears in any known records. Regardless, a Davidic messianic hope never again departed from Israel.

---

[15]Also of the Levites: Shemaiah the son of Hasshub, the son of Azrikam, the son of Hashabiah, the son of Bunni; [16]Shabbethai and Jozabad, of the heads of the Levites, *had* the oversight of the business outside of the house of God; [17]Mattaniah the son of Micha,[a] the son of Zabdi, the son of Asaph, the leader *who* began the thanksgiving with prayer; Bakbukiah, the second among his brethren; and Abda the son of Shammua, the son of Galal, the son of Jeduthun. [18]All the Levites in the holy city *were* two hundred and eighty-four.

[19]Moreover the gatekeepers, Akkub, Talmon, and their brethren who kept the gates, *were* one hundred and seventy-two.

[20]And the rest of Israel, of the priests *and* Levites, *were* in all the cities of Judah, everyone in his inheritance. [21]But the Nethinim dwelt in Ophel. And Ziha and Gishpa *were* over the Nethinim.

[22]Also the overseer of the Levites at Jerusalem *was* Uzzi the son of Bani, the son of Hashabiah, the son of Mattaniah, the son of Micha, of the sons of Asaph, the singers in charge of the service of the house of God. [23]For *it was* the king's command concerning them that a certain portion should be for the singers, a quota day by day. [24]Pethahiah the son of Meshezabel, of the children of Zerah the son of Judah, *was* the king's deputy[a] in all matters concerning the people.

The People Dwelling Outside Jerusalem

[25]And as for the villages with their fields, *some* of the children of Judah dwelt in Kirjath Arba and its villages, Dibon and its villages, Jekabzeel and its villages; [26]in Jeshua, Moladah, Beth Pelet, [27]Hazar Shual, and Beersheba and its villages; [28]in Ziklag and Meconah and its villages; [29]in En Rimmon, Zorah, Jarmuth, [30]Zanoah, Adullam, and their villages; in Lachish and its fields; in Azekah and its villages. They dwelt from Beersheba to the Valley of Hinnom.

[31]Also the children of Benjamin from Geba *dwelt* in Michmash, Aija, and Bethel, and their villages; [32]in Anathoth, Nob, Ananiah; [33]in Hazor, Ramah, Gittaim; [34]in Hadid, Zeboim, Neballat; [35]in Lod, Ono, *and* the Valley of Craftsmen. [36]Some of the Judean divisions of Levites *were* in Benjamin.

The Priests and Levites

12 [1]Now these *are* the priests and the Levites who came up with Zerubba-

---

11:17 [a]Or *Michah*   11:24 [a]Literally *at the king's hand*

THE PERSIAN KINGS

The Persian Empire profoundly altered the course of Judah's history. For the Jews this was a period of restoration and reconstruction. For the Persians it was a period of imperial expansion. Several Persian kings are mentioned in the Bible.

Date	King	References
559–530 B.C.	Cyrus the Great • conquered Babylon and ordered the temple to be rebuilt, 539 B.C.	Dan. 1:21; Is. 44:28; 2 Chr. 36:22, 23; Ezra 1:1–4
530–522 B.C.	Cambyses II • son of Cyrus • invaded Egypt, 525 B.C.	
522 B.C.	Smerdis • a magi named Gaumata who pretended to be Cambyses' younger brother Bardiya • led a rebellion against Cambyses	
522–486 B.C.	Darius I • defeated by the Athenians at Marathon, 490 B.C.	Ezra 4:5; Hag. 1:1; Zech. 1:1
486–465 B.C.	Xerxes I • also known as Ahasuerus • son of Darius I • defeated by the Athenians at Salamis, 480 B.C.	Ezra 4:6; Esth. 1:1
465–424 B.C.	Artaxerxes I • son of Xerxes I	Ezra 7:7–26; Neh. 2:1–8; 13:6, 7
424 B.C.	Xerxes II • son of Artaxerxes I	
423–404 B.C.	Darius II • son of Artaxerxes I	Neh. 12:22

bel the son of Shealtiel, and Jeshua: Seraiah, Jeremiah, Ezra, ²Amariah, Malluch, Hattush, ³Shechaniah, Rehum, Meremoth, ⁴Iddo, Ginnethoi,ᵃ Abijah, ⁵Mijamin, Maadiah, Bilgah, ⁶Shemaiah, Joiarib, Jedaiah, ⁷Sallu, Amok, Hilkiah, *and* Jedaiah.

These *were* the heads of the priests and their brethren in the days of Jeshua.

⁸Moreover the Levites *were* Jeshua, Binnui, Kadmiel, Sherebiah, Judah, *and* Mattaniah *who led* the thanksgiving *psalms,* he and his brethren. ⁹Also Bakbukiah and Unni, their brethren, *stood* across from them in *their* duties.

¹⁰Jeshua begot Joiakim, Joiakim begot Eliashib, Eliashib begot Joiada, ¹¹Joiada begot Jonathan, and Jonathan begot Jaddua.

¹²Now in the days of Joiakim, the priests, the heads of the fathers' *houses were:* of Seraiah, Meraiah; of Jeremiah, Hananiah; ¹³of Ezra, Meshullam; of Amariah, Jehohanan; ¹⁴of Melichu,ᵃ Jonathan; of Shebaniah,ᵇ Joseph; ¹⁵of Harim,ᵃ Adna; of Meraioth,ᵇ Helkai; ¹⁶of Iddo, Zechariah; of Ginnethon, Meshullam; ¹⁷of Abijah, Zichri; *the son* of Minjamin;ᵃ of Moadiah,ᵇ Piltai; ¹⁸of Bilgah, Shammua;

12:4 ᵃOr *Ginnethon* (compare verse 16)   12:14 ᵃOr *Malluch* (compare verse 2)   ᵇOr *Shechaniah* (compare verse 3)   12:15 ᵃOr *Rehum* (compare verse 3)   ᵇOr *Meremoth* (compare verse 3)   12:17 ᵃOr *Mijamin* (compare verse 5)   ᵇOr *Maadiah* (compare verse 5)

of Shemaiah, Jehonathan; ¹⁹of Joiarib, Mattenai; of Jedaiah, Uzzi; ²⁰of Sallai,ᵃ Kallai; of Amok, Eber; ²¹of Hilkiah, Hashabiah; *and* of Jedaiah, Nethanel.

²²During the reign of Darius the Persian, a record *was also kept* of the Levites and priests *who had been* heads of their fathers' *houses* in the days of Eliashib, Joiada, Johanan, and Jaddua. ²³The sons of Levi, the heads of the fathers' *houses* until the days of Johanan the son of Eliashib, *were* written in the book of the chronicles.

²⁴And the heads of the Levites *were* Hashabiah, Sherebiah, and Jeshua the son of Kadmiel, with their brothers across from them, to praise *and* give thanks, group alternating with group, according to the command of David the man of God. ²⁵Mattaniah, Bakbukiah, Obadiah, Meshullam, Talmon, and Akkub *were* gatekeepers keeping the watch at the storerooms of the gates. ²⁶These *lived* in the days of Joiakim the son of Jeshua, the son of Jozadak,ᵃ and in the days of Nehemiah the governor, and of Ezra the priest, the scribe.

Nehemiah Dedicates the Wall

²⁷Now at the dedication of the wall of Jerusalem they sought out the Levites in all their places, to bring them to Jerusalem to celebrate the dedication with gladness, both with thanksgivings and singing, *with* cymbals and stringed instruments and harps. ²⁸And the sons of the singers gathered together from the countryside around Jerusalem, from the villages of the Netophathites, ²⁹from the house of Gilgal, and from the fields of Geba and Azmaveth; for the singers had built themselves villages all around Jerusalem. ³⁰Then the priests and Levites purified themselves, and purified the people, the gates, and the wall.

🧩 Songs of Ascents

After the workers had finished rebuilding the walls of Jerusalem, the Levitical singers and their instruments were summoned, and the city was formally dedicated in ceremonies that included the singing of psalms. It is impossible to know exactly which psalms were sung, of course. Surely many of the old psalms, from the days of Solomon's temple, were used, but others may have been written specifically for use in the second temple.

One group of psalms (Ps. 120—134), all

linked by the superscription "A Song of Ascents," has a particularly clear connection to temple worship. The title indicates that these songs were sung by worshipers on their way up the hill toward the gates of Jerusalem and the temple. The psalms speak of the joy of worshiping in the Lord's house (Ps. 122; 134), of the need for purity of heart in the true worshiper (Ps. 125; 128; 131), and call for God's blessing in distress (Ps. 120; 129; 130; 132). All the Songs of Ascents appear together, suggesting that at one time they formed an independent collection, a temple songbook, which was later incorporated as a block into the Book of Psalms.

Some of these psalms may be quite old. Several have the superscription "Of David," and one, "Of Solomon" (Ps. 127). Others, though, obviously were composed after the Babylonian exile: one psalmist praises God for His mighty deliverance of "the captivity of Zion" (Ps. 126:1). Such a clear historical reference makes it likely that the Songs of Ascents were put together in this collection for use in the second temple. If so, then some of these psalms may well have been sung at the dedication of the rebuilt Jerusalem, on Mount Zion "which cannot be moved, but abides forever" (Ps. 125:1).

▼

■ Psalms 120—134

PSALM 120

Plea for Relief from Bitter Foes

A Song of Ascents.

In my distress I cried to the LORD,
　　And He heard me.
2　Deliver my soul, O LORD, from lying lips
　　And from a deceitful tongue.

3　What shall be given to you,
　　Or what shall be done to you,
　　You false tongue?
4　Sharp arrows of the warrior,
　　With coals of the broom tree!

5　Woe is me, that I dwell in Meshech,
　　That I dwell among the tents of Kedar!
6　My soul has dwelt too long
　　With one who hates peace.
7　I *am for* peace;
　　But when I speak, they *are* for war.

12:20 ᵃOr *Sallu* (compare verse 7)
12:26 ᵃSpelled *Jehozadak* in 1 Chronicles 6:14

PSALM 121

God the Help of Those Who Seek Him

A Song of Ascents.

I will lift up my eyes to the hills—
   From whence comes my help?
2 My help *comes* from the LORD,
   Who made heaven and earth.

3 He will not allow your foot to be
    moved;
   He who keeps you will not slumber.
4 Behold, He who keeps Israel
   Shall neither slumber nor sleep.

5 The LORD *is* your keeper;
   The LORD *is* your shade at your right
    hand.
6 The sun shall not strike you by day,
   Nor the moon by night.

7 The LORD shall preserve you from all
    evil;
   He shall preserve your soul.
8 The LORD shall preserve your going
    out and your coming in
   From this time forth, and even
    forevermore.

PSALM 122

The Joy of Going to the House of the LORD

A Song of Ascents. Of David.

I was glad when they said to me,
   "Let us go into the house of the LORD."
2 Our feet have been standing
   Within your gates, O Jerusalem!

3 Jerusalem is built
   As a city that is compact together,
4 Where the tribes go up,
   The tribes of the LORD,
   To the Testimony of Israel,
   To give thanks to the name of the
    LORD.

5 For thrones are set there for
    judgment,
   The thrones of the house of David.

6 Pray for the peace of Jerusalem:
   "May they prosper who love you.
7 Peace be within your walls,
   Prosperity within your palaces."
8 For the sake of my brethren and
    companions,
   I will now say, "Peace *be* within you."
9 Because of the house of the LORD our
    God
   I will seek your good.

PSALM 123

Prayer for Relief from Contempt

A Song of Ascents.

U nto You I lift up my eyes,
   O You who dwell in the heavens.
2 Behold, as the eyes of servants *look* to
    the hand of their masters,
   As the eyes of a maid to the hand of
    her mistress,
   So our eyes *look* to the LORD our God,
   Until He has mercy on us.

3 Have mercy on us, O LORD, have
    mercy on us!
   For we are exceedingly filled with
    contempt.
4 Our soul is exceedingly filled
   With the scorn of those who are at
    ease,
   With the contempt of the proud.

PSALM 124

The LORD the Defense of His People

A Song of Ascents. Of David.

"If it had not been the LORD who was on
   our side,"
   Let Israel now say—
2 "If it had not been the LORD who was
    on our side,
   When men rose up against us,

RELIGION AND WORSHIP

The central place of worship was at Jerusalem, and the people were expected to be present there to celebrate the major festivals. Thus they became pilgrims ascending to the temple in the Holy City (Ps. 122:1, 2). The series of psalms called the "Songs of Ascents" (Ps. 120—134) are suitable to accompany such pilgrimages, describing feelings of religious anticipation and delight.

3 Then they would have swallowed us
    alive,
When their wrath was kindled against
    us;
4 Then the waters would have
    overwhelmed us,
The stream would have gone over our
    soul;
5 Then the swollen waters
Would have gone over our soul."

6 Blessed *be* the LORD,
Who has not given us *as* prey to their
    teeth.
7 Our soul has escaped as a bird from
    the snare of the fowlers;[a]
The snare is broken, and we have
    escaped.
8 Our help *is* in the name of the LORD,
Who made heaven and earth.

PSALM 125

The LORD the Strength of His People

A Song of Ascents.

Those who trust in the LORD
    Are like Mount Zion,
    Which cannot be moved, *but* abides
        forever.
2 As the mountains surround
        Jerusalem,
So the LORD surrounds His people
From this time forth and forever.

3 For the scepter of wickedness shall
        not rest
On the land allotted to the righteous,
Lest the righteous reach out their
    hands to iniquity.

4 Do good, O LORD, to *those who are*
    good,
And to *those who are* upright in their
    hearts.

5 As for such as turn aside to their
    crooked ways,

The LORD shall lead them away
With the workers of iniquity.

Peace *be* upon Israel!

PSALM 126

A Joyful Return to Zion

A Song of Ascents.

When the LORD brought back the
    captivity of Zion,
    We were like those who dream.
2 Then our mouth was filled with
        laughter,
And our tongue with singing.
Then they said among the nations,
"The LORD has done great things for
        them."
3 The LORD has done great things for
    us,
And we are glad.

4 Bring back our captivity, O LORD,
As the streams in the South.

5 Those who sow in tears
Shall reap in joy.
6 He who continually goes forth
        weeping,
Bearing seed for sowing,
Shall doubtless come again with
        rejoicing,
Bringing his sheaves *with him*.

PSALM 127

Laboring and Prospering with the LORD

A Song of Ascents. Of Solomon.

Unless the LORD builds the house,
    They labor in vain who build it;
    Unless the LORD guards the city,
    The watchman stays awake in vain.
2 *It is* vain for you to rise up early,
To sit up late,

124:7 [a]That is, persons who catch birds in a trap or
snare

MARRIAGE AND FAMILY

*People in agricultural and nonindustrial economies usually considered it desirable to have
many children. The psalmist described children as a gift or reward from God (Ps.
127:3). The Romans, however, experienced a decline in their birthrate, so severe that
they tried to resist it with different kinds of legislation favoring large families.*

To eat the bread of sorrows;
For so He gives His beloved sleep.

3 Behold, children *are* a heritage from
the LORD,
The fruit of the womb *is* a reward.
4 Like arrows in the hand of a warrior,
So *are* the children of one's youth.
5 Happy *is* the man who has his quiver
full of them;
They shall not be ashamed,
But shall speak with their enemies in
the gate.

PSALM 128

Blessings of Those Who Fear the LORD

A Song of Ascents.

B lessed *is* every one who fears the LORD,
Who walks in His ways.

2 When you eat the labor of your hands,
You *shall be* happy, and *it shall be*
well with you.
3 Your wife *shall be* like a fruitful vine
In the very heart of your house,
Your children like olive plants
All around your table.
4 Behold, thus shall the man be blessed
Who fears the LORD.

5 The LORD bless you out of Zion,
And may you see the good of
Jerusalem
All the days of your life.
6 Yes, may you see your children's
children.

Peace *be* upon Israel!

PSALM 129

Song of Victory over Zion's Enemies

A Song of Ascents.

"M any a time they have afflicted me
from my youth,"
Let Israel now say—
2 "Many a time they have afflicted me
from my youth;
Yet they have not prevailed against
me.
3 The plowers plowed on my back;
They made their furrows long."
4 The LORD *is* righteous;
He has cut in pieces the cords of the
wicked.

5 Let all those who hate Zion
Be put to shame and turned back.
6 Let them be as the grass *on* the
housetops,
Which withers before it grows up,
7 With which the reaper does not fill his
hand,
Nor he who binds sheaves, his arms.
8 Neither let those who pass by them
say,
"The blessing of the LORD *be* upon you;
We bless you in the name of the
LORD!"

PSALM 130

Waiting for the Redemption of the LORD

A Song of Ascents.

O ut of the depths I have cried to You,
O LORD;
2 Lord, hear my voice!
Let Your ears be attentive
To the voice of my supplications.

3 If You, LORD, should mark iniquities,
O Lord, who could stand?
4 But *there is* forgiveness with You,
That You may be feared.

5 I wait for the LORD, my soul waits,
And in His word I do hope.
6 My soul *waits* for the Lord
More than those who watch for the
morning—
Yes, more than those who watch for
the morning.

7 O Israel, hope in the LORD;
For with the LORD *there is* mercy,
And with Him *is* abundant
redemption.
8 And He shall redeem Israel
From all his iniquities.

PSALM 131

Simple Trust in the LORD

A Song of Ascents. Of David.

L ORD, my heart is not haughty,
Nor my eyes lofty.
Neither do I concern myself with great
matters,
Nor with things too profound for me.

2 Surely I have calmed and quieted my
soul,

Like a weaned child with his mother;
Like a weaned child *is* my soul within
    me.

3   O Israel, hope in the LORD
From this time forth and forever.

PSALM 132

The Eternal Dwelling of God in Zion

A Song of Ascents.

LORD, remember David
    And all his afflictions;
2   How he swore to the LORD,
And vowed to the Mighty One of
    Jacob:
3   "Surely I will not go into the chamber
    of my house,
Or go up to the comfort of my bed;
4   I will not give sleep to my eyes
Or slumber to my eyelids,
5   Until I find a place for the LORD,
A dwelling place for the Mighty One of
    Jacob."

6   Behold, we heard of it in Ephrathah;
We found it in the fields of the
    woods.ᵃ
7   Let us go into His tabernacle;
Let us worship at His footstool.
8   Arise, O LORD, to Your resting place,
You and the ark of Your strength.
9   Let Your priests be clothed with
    righteousness,
And let Your saints shout for joy.

10   For Your servant David's sake,
Do not turn away the face of Your
    Anointed.

11   The LORD has sworn *in* truth to
    David;
He will not turn from it:
"I will set upon your throne the fruit of
    your body.
12   If your sons will keep My covenant
And My testimony which I shall teach
    them,
Their sons also shall sit upon your
    throne forevermore."

13   For the LORD has chosen Zion;
He has desired *it* for His dwelling
    place:

14   "This *is* My resting place forever;
Here I will dwell, for I have desired
    it.
15   I will abundantly bless her provision;
I will satisfy her poor with bread.
16   I will also clothe her priests with
    salvation,
And her saints shall shout aloud for
    joy.
17   There I will make the horn of David
    grow;
I will prepare a lamp for My Anointed.
18   His enemies I will clothe with shame,
But upon Himself His crown shall
    flourish."

PSALM 133

Blessed Unity of the People of God

A Song of Ascents. Of David.

Behold, how good and how pleasant *it is*
    For brethren to dwell together in
    unity!

2   *It is* like the precious oil upon the
    head,
Running down on the beard,
The beard of Aaron,
Running down on the edge of his
    garments.
3   *It is* like the dew of Hermon,
Descending upon the mountains of
    Zion;
For there the LORD commanded the
    blessing—
Life forevermore.

PSALM 134

Praising the LORD in His House at Night

A Song of Ascents.

Behold, bless the LORD,
    All *you* servants of the LORD,
Who by night stand in the house of
    the LORD!
2   Lift up your hands *in* the sanctuary,
And bless the LORD.

3   The LORD who made heaven and earth
Bless you from Zion!

132:6 ᵃHebrew *Jaar*

Nehemiah and the Levites

The Book of Nehemiah began as Nehemiah's own memoirs, and Nehemiah himself told the story in the first person. At Neh. 7:73, though, the narrative changed to a third person account, even when speaking of Nehemiah himself (8:9; 12:26). At Neh. 12:31, Nehemiah's own account resumes (except for a brief third-person passage in 12:44–47).

Although Nehemiah represented the secular arm of Jerusalem's revival—with Ezra representing the spiritual aspect—Nehemiah seems to have taken a great deal of interest in the priestly offices of the temple. He even took it upon himself to appoint choirs from the Levitical singers (12:31). Even for the duly appointed Persian governor, Jerusalem's religious life was centered on the priests.

■ Nehemiah 12:31–47

Nehemiah

12 :31 So I brought the leaders of Judah up on the wall, and appointed two large thanksgiving choirs. *One* went to the right hand on the wall toward the Refuse Gate. 32After them went Hoshaiah and half of the leaders of Judah, 33and Azariah, Ezra, Meshullam, 34Judah, Benjamin, Shemaiah, Jeremiah, 35and some of the priests' sons with trumpets—Zechariah the son of Jonathan, the son of Shemaiah, the son of Mattaniah, the son of Michaiah, the son of Zaccur, the son of Asaph, 36and his brethren, Shemaiah, Azarel, Milalai, Gilalai, Maai, Nethanel, Judah, *and* Hanani, with the musical instruments of David the man of God. And Ezra the scribe *went* before them. 37By the Fountain Gate, in front of them, they went up the stairs of the City of David, on the stairway of the wall, beyond the house of David, as far as the Water Gate eastward. 38The other thanksgiving choir went the opposite *way,* and I *was* behind them with half of the people on the wall, going past the Tower of the Ovens as far as the Broad Wall, 39and above the Gate of Ephraim, above the Old Gate, above the Fish Gate, the Tower of Hananel, the Tower of the Hundred, as far as the Sheep Gate; and they stopped by the Gate of the Prison.

40So the two thanksgiving choirs stood in the house of God, likewise I and the half of the rulers with me; 41and the priests, Eliakim, Maaseiah, Minjamin,[a] Michaiah, Elioenai, Zechariah, *and* Hananiah, with trumpets; 42also Maaseiah, Shemaiah, Eleazar, Uzzi, Jehohanan, Malchijah, Elam, and Ezer. The singers sang loudly with Jezrahiah the director.

43Also that day they offered great sacrifices, and rejoiced, for God had made them rejoice with great joy; the women and the children also rejoiced, so that the joy of Jerusalem was heard afar off.

Temple Responsibilities

44And at the same time some were appointed over the rooms of the storehouse for the offerings, the firstfruits, and the tithes, to gather into them from the fields of the cities the portions specified by the Law for the priests and Levites; for Judah rejoiced over the priests and Levites who ministered. 45Both the singers and the gatekeepers kept the charge of their God and the charge of the purification, according to the command of David *and* Solomon his son. 46For in the days of David and Asaph of old *there were* chiefs of the singers, and songs of praise and thanksgiving to God. 47In the days of Zerubbabel and in the days of Nehemiah all Israel gave the portions for the singers and the gatekeepers, a portion for each day. They also consecrated *holy things* for the Levites, and the Levites consecrated *them* for the children of Aaron.

TIME CAPSULE　*434 to 425 B.C.*

434– 404	*Sparta defeats Athens in Peloponnesian War*
433	*Nehemiah returns from Persia to Judah*
428	*Possible date for Ezra's arrival in Jerusalem*
428– 347	*Plato, Greek philosopher*
425– 388	*Aristophanes, Athenian writer of comedy*

12:41　ªOr *Mijamin* (compare verse 5)

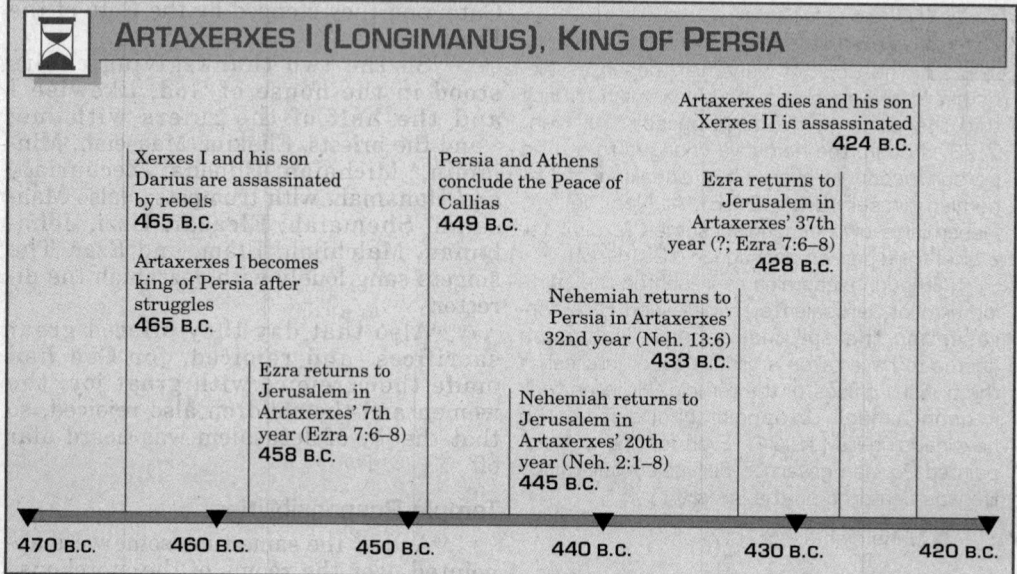

ARTAXERXES I (LONGIMANUS), KING OF PERSIA

Xerxes I and his son
Darius are assassinated
by rebels
465 B.C.

Artaxerxes I becomes
king of Persia after
struggles
465 B.C.

Ezra returns to
Jerusalem in
Artaxerxes' 7th
year (Ezra 7:6–8)
458 B.C.

Persia and Athens
conclude the Peace of
Callias
449 B.C.

Artaxerxes dies and his son
Xerxes II is assassinated
424 B.C.

Ezra returns to
Jerusalem in
Artaxerxes' 37th
year (?; Ezra 7:6–8)
428 B.C.

Nehemiah returns to
Persia in Artaxerxes'
32nd year (Neh. 13:6)
433 B.C.

Nehemiah returns to
Jerusalem in
Artaxerxes' 20th
year (Neh. 2:1–8)
445 B.C.

470 B.C.   **460 B.C.**   **450 B.C.**   **440 B.C.**   **430 B.C.**   **420 B.C.**

The Last Word in Praise

Most of the songs of praise that appear near the end of the Book of Psalms lack superscriptions. Because they are not specified as being psalms of David or of another psalmist, and perhaps because they appear at the end of the biblical book, these hymns are often considered the latest of the psalms. Perhaps they were written during the Persian era, to be sung in the rebuilt temple. Such a hymn as Ps. 136 was certainly intended for use in public worship; one can almost hear the Levitical singer chanting a verse and the congregation responding to each line with the refrain, "For His mercy endures forever."

Many of these late hymns follow the same pattern, beginning and often ending with the refrain "Praise the LORD" (Hebrew *hallelujah;* Ps. 111—113; 117; 135; 146—150). Such a frequent pattern seems to indicate that regular and fairly rigid patterns for public songs of praise had developed in the restored temple. Apparently instrumental accompaniment was common: Ps. 150 calls for various instruments to be used in praising God, just as Levitical instruments were used at the dedication of the walls (Neh. 12:27).

It is significant to find so many hymns near the end of the Book of Psalms. Most of the laments—the songs of complaint and petition to God—appear early in the Psalter, whereas the greatest concentration of hymns of praise is at the end. Reading the Book of Psalms from start to finish, then, is a journey from distress and supplication to thanksgiving and praise.

■ Psalms 104; 107; 111—118; 135; 136; 145—150

PSALM 104

Praise to the Sovereign LORD for His Creation and Providence

Bless the LORD, O my soul!

O LORD my God, You are very great:
You are clothed with honor and
    majesty,
2 Who cover *Yourself* with light as *with*
    a garment,
Who stretch out the heavens like a
    curtain.

3 He lays the beams of His upper
    chambers in the waters,
Who makes the clouds His chariot,
Who walks on the wings of the wind,
4 Who makes His angels spirits,
His ministers a flame of fire.

5 *You who* laid the foundations of the
    earth,
So *that* it should not be moved forever,
6 You covered it with the deep as *with* a
    garment;
The waters stood above the
    mountains.

THE ATEN, THE EGYPTIAN SUN DISK (Ps. 104:10–18)

The *Hymn to the Sun Disk* was composed by the Egyptian king Akhenaten (1352–1336 B.C.). It describes the Aten, which was the Egyptian sun deity, as the creator and sustainer of the universe and of life itself. Akhenaten's hymn exhibits characteristics that some have considered to be monotheistic. These characteristics, however, tend toward what is known as henotheism or monolatry—the worship of one god without denying the existence of others.

There are some detailed but superficial literary similarities between the Egyptian hymn and Ps. 104. For example, the hymn describes the Nile as being in the sky, descending and making waves on the mountains to water the fields. Similarly, Yahweh from His "upper chambers" waters the valleys and hills (Ps. 104:10, 13). The *Hymn to the Sun Disk* mentions beasts that are satisfied with their pasture, along with trees, plants, and birds which fly from their nests. Similarly, Yahweh provides all things necessary to life, caring for animal, plant, and bird life (Ps. 104:11, 12, 14–18).

Clearly, Akhenaten's *Hymn to the Sun Disk* describes the solar deity much the same as Ps. 104 describes Yahweh. Some scholars have supposed, because of common themes in these writings, in many other Egyptian sun hymns, and even in a Mesopotamian hymn to the sun god Shamash, that the psalmist of Ps. 104 used some of these writings as sources. However, more likely there were well-known expressions common to Middle- and Near-Eastern cultures that provided a literary framework within which the psalm was written.

---

7 At Your rebuke they fled;
At the voice of Your thunder they
hastened away.
8 They went up over the mountains;
They went down into the valleys,
To the place which You founded for
them.
9 You have set a boundary that they
may not pass over,
That they may not return to cover the
earth.

10 He sends the springs into the valleys;
They flow among the hills.
11 They give drink to every beast of the
field;
The wild donkeys quench their thirst.
12 By them the birds of the heavens have
their home;
They sing among the branches.
13 He waters the hills from His upper
chambers;
The earth is satisfied with the fruit of
Your works.

14 He causes the grass to grow for the
cattle,
And vegetation for the service of man,
That he may bring forth food from the
earth,

15 And wine *that* makes glad the heart of
man,
Oil to make *his* face shine,
And bread *which* strengthens man's
heart.
16 The trees of the LORD are full *of sap,*
The cedars of Lebanon which He
planted,
17 Where the birds make their nests;
The stork has her home in the fir
trees.
18 The high hills *are* for the wild goats;
The cliffs are a refuge for the rock
badgers.[a]

19 He appointed the moon for seasons;
The sun knows its going down.
20 You make darkness, and it is night,
In which all the beasts of the forest
creep about.
21 The young lions roar after their prey,
And seek their food from God.
22 *When* the sun rises, they gather
together
And lie down in their dens.
23 Man goes out to his work
And to his labor until the evening.

24 O LORD, how manifold are Your
works!
In wisdom You have made them all.
The earth is full of Your possessions—

104:18 ªOr *rock hyrax* (compare Leviticus 11:5)

25 This great and wide sea,
In which *are* innumerable teeming
    things,
Living things both small and great.
26 There the ships sail about;
There is that Leviathan
Which You have made to play there.

27 These all wait for You,
That You may give *them* their food in
    due season.
28 *What* You give them they gather in;
You open Your hand, they are filled
    with good.
29 You hide Your face, they are troubled;
You take away their breath, they die
    and return to their dust.
30 You send forth Your Spirit, they are
    created;
And You renew the face of the earth.

31 May the glory of the Lord endure
    forever;
May the Lord rejoice in His works.
32 He looks on the earth, and it trembles;
He touches the hills, and they smoke.

33 I will sing to the Lord as long as I
    live;
I will sing praise to my God while I
    have my being.
34 May my meditation be sweet to Him;
I will be glad in the Lord.
35 May sinners be consumed from the
    earth,
And the wicked be no more.

Bless the Lord, O my soul!
Praise the Lord!

PSALM 107

Thanksgiving to the Lord for His Great Works of Deliverance

Oh, give thanks to the Lord, for *He is*
    good!
For His mercy *endures* forever.
2 Let the redeemed of the Lord say *so,*
Whom He has redeemed from the
    hand of the enemy,
3 And gathered out of the lands,
From the east and from the west,
From the north and from the south.

4 They wandered in the wilderness in a
    desolate way;
They found no city to dwell in.

5 Hungry and thirsty,
Their soul fainted in them.
6 Then they cried out to the Lord in
    their trouble,
And He delivered them out of their
    distresses.
7 And He led them forth by the right
    way,
That they might go to a city for a
    dwelling place.
8 Oh, that *men* would give thanks to the
    Lord *for* His goodness,
And *for* His wonderful works to the
    children of men!
9 For He satisfies the longing soul,
And fills the hungry soul with
    goodness.

10 Those who sat in darkness and in the
    shadow of death,
Bound in affliction and irons—
11 Because they rebelled against the
    words of God,
And despised the counsel of the Most
    High,
12 Therefore He brought down their
    heart with labor;
They fell down, and *there was* none to
    help.
13 Then they cried out to the Lord in
    their trouble,
And He saved them out of their
    distresses.
14 He brought them out of darkness and
    the shadow of death,
And broke their chains in pieces.
15 Oh, that *men* would give thanks to the
    Lord *for* His goodness,
And *for* His wonderful works to the
    children of men!
16 For He has broken the gates of
    bronze,
And cut the bars of iron in two.

17 Fools, because of their transgression,
And because of their iniquities, were
    afflicted.
18 Their soul abhorred all manner of
    food,
And they drew near to the gates of
    death.
19 Then they cried out to the Lord in
    their trouble,
And He saved them out of their
    distresses.
20 He sent His word and healed them,
And delivered *them* from their
    destructions.

21 Oh, that *men* would give thanks to the
     LORD *for* His goodness,
     And *for* His wonderful works to the
     children of men!
22 Let them sacrifice the sacrifices of
     thanksgiving,
     And declare His works with rejoicing.

23 Those who go down to the sea in
     ships,
     Who do business on great waters,
24 They see the works of the LORD,
     And His wonders in the deep.
25 For He commands and raises the
     stormy wind,
     Which lifts up the waves of the sea.
26 They mount up to the heavens,
     They go down again to the depths;
     Their soul melts because of trouble.
27 They reel to and fro, and stagger like
     a drunken man,
     And are at their wits' end.
28 Then they cry out to the LORD in their
     trouble,
     And He brings them out of their
     distresses.
29 He calms the storm,
     So that its waves are still.
30 Then they are glad because they are
     quiet;
     So He guides them to their desired
     haven.
31 Oh, that *men* would give thanks to the
     LORD *for* His goodness,
     And *for* His wonderful works to the
     children of men!
32 Let them exalt Him also in the
     assembly of the people,
     And praise Him in the company of the
     elders.

33 He turns rivers into a wilderness,
     And the watersprings into dry ground;
34 A fruitful land into barrenness,
     For the wickedness of those who dwell
     in it.
35 He turns a wilderness into pools of
     water,
     And dry land into watersprings.
36 There He makes the hungry dwell,
     That they may establish a city for a
     dwelling place,
37 And sow fields and plant vineyards,
     That they may yield a fruitful harvest.
38 He also blesses them, and they
     multiply greatly;
     And He does not let their cattle
     decrease.

39 When they are diminished and
     brought low
     Through oppression, affliction and
     sorrow,
40 He pours contempt on princes,
     And causes them to wander in the
     wilderness *where there is* no way;
41 Yet He sets the poor on high, far from
     affliction,
     And makes *their* families like a flock.
42 The righteous see *it* and rejoice,
     And all iniquity stops its mouth.

43 Whoever *is* wise will observe these
     things,
     And they will understand the
     lovingkindness of the LORD.

PSALM 111

Praise to God for His Faithfulness and Justice

Praise the LORD!

     I will praise the LORD with *my* whole
     heart,
     In the assembly of the upright and *in*
     the congregation.

2 The works of the LORD *are* great,
     Studied by all who have pleasure in
     them.
3 His work *is* honorable and glorious,
     And His righteousness endures
     forever.
4 He has made His wonderful works to
     be remembered;
     The LORD *is* gracious and full of
     compassion.
5 He has given food to those who fear
     Him;
     He will ever be mindful of His
     covenant.
6 He has declared to His people the
     power of His works,
     In giving them the heritage of the
     nations.

7 The works of His hands *are* verity and
     justice;
     All His precepts *are* sure.
8 They stand fast forever and ever,
     And are done in truth and
     uprightness.
9 He has sent redemption to His people;
     He has commanded His covenant
     forever:
     Holy and awesome *is* His name.

10 The fear of the LORD *is* the beginning
of wisdom;
A good understanding have all those
who do *His commandments.*
His praise endures forever.

PSALM 112

The Blessed State of the Righteous

Praise the LORD!

Blessed *is* the man *who* fears the
LORD,
Who delights greatly in His
commandments.
2 His descendants will be mighty on
earth;
The generation of the upright will be
blessed.
3 Wealth and riches *will be* in his house,
And his righteousness endures
forever.
4 Unto the upright there arises light in
the darkness;
He is gracious, and full of compassion,
and righteous.
5 A good man deals graciously and
lends;
He will guide his affairs with
discretion.
6 Surely he will never be shaken;
The righteous will be in everlasting
remembrance.
7 He will not be afraid of evil tidings;
His heart is steadfast, trusting in the
LORD.
8 His heart *is* established;
He will not be afraid,
Until he sees *his desire* upon his
enemies.
9 He has dispersed abroad,
He has given to the poor;
His righteousness endures forever;
His horn will be exalted with honor.
10 The wicked will see *it* and be grieved;
He will gnash his teeth and melt
away;
The desire of the wicked shall perish.

PSALM 113

The Majesty and Condescension of God

Praise the LORD!

Praise, O servants of the LORD,
Praise the name of the LORD!

2 Blessed be the name of the LORD
From this time forth and forevermore!
3 From the rising of the sun to its going
down
The LORD's name *is* to be praised.

4 The LORD *is* high above all nations,
His glory above the heavens.
5 Who *is* like the LORD our God,
Who dwells on high,
6 Who humbles Himself to behold
The things that are in the heavens
and in the earth?

7 He raises the poor out of the dust,
And lifts the needy out of the ash
heap,
8 That He may seat *him* with princes—
With the princes of His people.
9 He grants the barren woman a home,
Like a joyful mother of children.

Praise the LORD!

PSALM 114

The Power of God in His Deliverance of Israel

When Israel went out of Egypt,
The house of Jacob from a people of
strange language,
2 Judah became His sanctuary,
And Israel His dominion.

3 The sea saw *it* and fled;
Jordan turned back.
4 The mountains skipped like rams,
The little hills like lambs.
5 What ails you, O sea, that you fled?
O Jordan, *that* you turned back?
6 O mountains, *that* you skipped like
rams?
O little hills, like lambs?

7 Tremble, O earth, at the presence of
the Lord,
At the presence of the God of Jacob,
8 Who turned the rock *into* a pool of
water,
The flint into a fountain of waters.

PSALM 115

The Futility of Idols and the Trustworthiness of God

Not unto us, O LORD, not unto us,
But to Your name give glory,

2 Why should the Gentiles say,
"So where *is* their God?"

3 But our God *is* in heaven;
He does whatever He pleases.
4 Their idols *are* silver and gold,
The work of men's hands.
5 They have mouths, but they do not
speak;
Eyes they have, but they do not see;
6 They have ears, but they do not hear;
Noses they have, but they do not smell;
7 They have hands, but they do not
handle;
Feet they have, but they do not walk;
Nor do they mutter through their
throat.
8 Those who make them are like them;
So is everyone who trusts in them.

9 O Israel, trust in the LORD;
He *is* their help and their shield.
10 O house of Aaron, trust in the LORD;
He *is* their help and their shield.
11 You who fear the LORD, trust in the
LORD;
He *is* their help and their shield.

12 The LORD has been mindful of *us;*
He will bless us;
He will bless the house of Israel;
He will bless the house of Aaron.
13 He will bless those who fear the LORD,
Both small and great.

14 May the LORD give you increase more
and more,
You and your children.
15 *May* you *be* blessed by the LORD,
Who made heaven and earth.

16 The heaven, *even* the heavens, *are* the
LORD's;
But the earth He has given to the
children of men.
17 The dead do not praise the LORD,
Nor any who go down into silence.

18 But we will bless the LORD
From this time forth and forevermore.

Praise the LORD!

PSALM 116

Thanksgiving for Deliverance from Death

I love the LORD, because He has heard
My voice *and* my supplications.
2 Because He has inclined His ear to
me,
Therefore I will call *upon Him* as long
as I live.

3 The pains of death surrounded me,
And the pangs of Sheol laid hold of me;
I found trouble and sorrow.
4 Then I called upon the name of the
LORD:
"O LORD, I implore You, deliver my
soul!"

5 Gracious *is* the LORD, and righteous;
Yes, our God *is* merciful.
6 The LORD preserves the simple;
I was brought low, and He saved me.
7 Return to your rest, O my soul,
For the LORD has dealt bountifully
with you.

8 For You have delivered my soul from
death,
My eyes from tears,
And my feet from falling.
9 I will walk before the LORD
In the land of the living.
10 I believed, therefore I spoke,
"I am greatly afflicted."
11 I said in my haste,
"All men *are* liars."

12 What shall I render to the LORD
For all His benefits toward me?
13 I will take up the cup of salvation,
And call upon the name of the LORD.
14 I will pay my vows to the LORD
Now in the presence of all His people.

RELIGION AND WORSHIP

*A religious vow was a voluntary promise made to God, often like a bargain, to be fulfilled
if God answered a certain petition. There was no requirement to make a vow, but if one
was made, the maker was not permitted to break it, unless the vow itself was unlawful.
The payment of a vow was sometimes an expression of thanksgiving (Ps. 116:12, 14).*

15 Precious in the sight of the LORD
   Is the death of His saints.

16 O LORD, truly I *am* Your servant;
   I *am* Your servant, the son of Your
        maidservant;
   You have loosed my bonds.
17 I will offer to You the sacrifice of
        thanksgiving,
   And will call upon the name of the
        LORD.

18 I will pay my vows to the LORD
   Now in the presence of all His people,
19 In the courts of the LORD's house,
   In the midst of you, O Jerusalem.

   Praise the LORD!

PSALM 117

Let All Peoples Praise the LORD

Praise the LORD, all you Gentiles!
   Laud Him, all you peoples!
2 For His merciful kindness is great
        toward us,
   And the truth of the LORD *endures*
        forever.

   Praise the LORD!

PSALM 118

Praise to God for His Everlasting Mercy

Oh, give thanks to the LORD, for *He is*
        good!
   For His mercy *endures* forever.

2 Let Israel now say,
   "His mercy *endures* forever."
3 Let the house of Aaron now say,
   "His mercy *endures* forever."
4 Let those who fear the LORD now say,
   "His mercy *endures* forever."

5 I called on the LORD in distress;
   The LORD answered me *and set me* in
        a broad place.
6 The LORD *is* on my side;
   I will not fear.
   What can man do to me?
7 The LORD is for me among those who
        help me;
   Therefore I shall see *my desire* on
        those who hate me.

8 *It is* better to trust in the LORD
   Than to put confidence in man.
9 *It is* better to trust in the LORD
   Than to put confidence in princes.

10 All nations surrounded me,
   But in the name of the LORD I will
        destroy them.
11 They surrounded me,
   Yes, they surrounded me;
   But in the name of the LORD I will
        destroy them.
12 They surrounded me like bees;
   They were quenched like a fire of
        thorns;
   For in the name of the LORD I will
        destroy them.
13 You pushed me violently, that I might
        fall,
   But the LORD helped me.
14 The LORD *is* my strength and song,
   And He has become my salvation.[a]

15 The voice of rejoicing and salvation
   Is in the tents of the righteous;
   The right hand of the LORD does
        valiantly.
16 The right hand of the LORD is exalted;
   The right hand of the LORD does
        valiantly.
17 I shall not die, but live,
   And declare the works of the LORD.
18 The LORD has chastened me severely,
   But He has not given me over to
        death.

19 Open to me the gates of righteousness;
   I will go through them,
   And I will praise the LORD.
20 This is the gate of the LORD,
   Through which the righteous shall
        enter.

21 I will praise You,
   For You have answered me,
   And have become my salvation.

22 The stone *which* the builders rejected
   Has become the chief cornerstone.
23 This was the LORD's doing;
   It *is* marvelous in our eyes.
24 This *is* the day the LORD has made;
   We will rejoice and be glad in it.

25 Save now, I pray, O LORD;
   O LORD, I pray, send now prosperity.

118:14 [a]Compare Exodus 15:2

AMORITES ON THE MOVE (Ps. 135:11)

The Amorites are well known from Accadian records (c. 2200 B.C.) as the inhabitants of Amurru. The term "Amorite" originally meant "westerner," indicating people living west of Mesopotamia, apparently in a region around the upper Habor (Khabur) and Balikh River valleys in Syria. Here the Amorites employed dry-farming methods and lived in small urban centers.

Amorites eventually migrated east. The Sumerian 3rd Dynasty of Ur (c. 2100 B.C.) records the slow Amorite infiltration of Mesopotamia. After the fall of Ur numerous Amorite dynasties began to appear in Asshur, Babylon, Mari, Uruk, and elsewhere. Both the Babylonians and Assyrians claimed to be of Amorite descent.

Similar Amorite movement occurred along the Mediterranean coast. By 1900 B.C. an Amorite dynasty ruled the city of Ugarit on the Syrian coast. During the Late Bronze Age (1500–1200 B.C.) an Amorite kingdom existed in the Orontes River Valley in Syria, as is recorded in cuneiform texts from Alalakh and from the Amarna archives in Egypt.

The Amorite migration reached farther south into parts of the Transjordan and Palestine. Amorites were among the nations that inhabited Canaan prior to the Israelite conquest (Gen. 15:19–21). "Amorite" became a general term for the peoples of Canaan (Gen. 48:22; Josh. 24:15). The prophet Ezekiel describes the inhabitants of Jerusalem as partly descended from Amorites (Ezek. 16:3).

The migrations of the Amorites thus placed them among the local populations encountered by Israelites during the conquest. Israel's victory over them became fixed in Israelite history as a high point of the invasion. In particular, the defeat of "Sihon king of the Amorites" and his capital at Heshbon was celebrated both in a proverb (Num. 21:26–31) and with psalms (Ps. 135:10, 11; 136:18, 19).

---

26 Blessed *is* he who comes in the name
     of the LORD!
     We have blessed you from the house of
     the LORD.
27 God *is* the LORD,
     And He has given us light;
     Bind the sacrifice with cords to the
     horns of the altar.
28 You *are* my God, and I will praise
     You;
     You are my God, I will exalt You.

29 Oh, give thanks to the LORD, for *He is*
     good!
     For His mercy *endures* forever.

PSALM 135

Praise to God in Creation and Redemption

Praise the LORD!

     Praise the name of the LORD;
     Praise *Him,* O you servants of the
     LORD!
2 You who stand in the house of the
     LORD,
     In the courts of the house of our God,

3 Praise the LORD, for the LORD *is* good;
     Sing praises to His name, for *it is*
     pleasant.
4 For the LORD has chosen Jacob for
     Himself,
     Israel for His special treasure.

5 For I know that the LORD *is* great,
     And our Lord *is* above all gods.
6 Whatever the LORD pleases He does,
     In heaven and in earth,
     In the seas and in all deep places.
7 He causes the vapors to ascend from
     the ends of the earth;
     He makes lightning for the rain;
     He brings the wind out of His
     treasuries.

8 He destroyed the firstborn of Egypt,
     Both of man and beast.
9 He sent signs and wonders into the
     midst of you, O Egypt,
     Upon Pharaoh and all his servants.
10 He defeated many nations
     And slew mighty kings—
11 Sihon king of the Amorites,
     Og king of Bashan,
     And all the kingdoms of Canaan—

12   And gave their land *as* a heritage,
      A heritage to Israel His people.

13   Your name, O LORD, *endures* forever,
      Your fame, O LORD, throughout all
         generations.
14   For the LORD will judge His people,
      And He will have compassion on His
         servants.

15   The idols of the nations *are* silver and
         gold,
      The work of men's hands.
16   They have mouths, but they do not
         speak;
      Eyes they have, but they do not see;
17   They have ears, but they do not hear;
      Nor is there *any* breath in their
         mouths.
18   Those who make them are like them;
      So is everyone who trusts in them.

19   Bless the LORD, O house of Israel!
      Bless the LORD, O house of Aaron!
20   Bless the LORD, O house of Levi!
      You who fear the LORD, bless the
         LORD!
21   Blessed be the LORD out of Zion,
      Who dwells in Jerusalem!

      Praise the LORD!

PSALM 136

Thanksgiving to God for His Enduring Mercy

Oh, give thanks to the LORD, for *He is*
         good!
      For His mercy *endures* forever.
2   Oh, give thanks to the God of gods!
      For His mercy *endures* forever.
3   Oh, give thanks to the Lord of lords!
      For His mercy *endures* forever:

4   To Him who alone does great wonders,
      For His mercy *endures* forever;
5   To Him who by wisdom made the
         heavens,
      For His mercy *endures* forever;
6   To Him who laid out the earth above
         the waters,
      For His mercy *endures* forever;
7   To Him who made great lights,
      For His mercy *endures* forever—
8   The sun to rule by day,
      For His mercy *endures* forever;

9   The moon and stars to rule by night,
      For His mercy *endures* forever.

10   To Him who struck Egypt in their
         firstborn,
      For His mercy *endures* forever;
11   And brought out Israel from among
         them,
      For His mercy *endures* forever;
12   With a strong hand, and with an
         outstretched arm,
      For His mercy *endures* forever;
13   To Him who divided the Red Sea in
         two,
      For His mercy *endures* forever;
14   And made Israel pass through the
         midst of it,
      For His mercy *endures* forever;
15   But overthrew Pharaoh and his army
         in the Red Sea,
      For His mercy *endures* forever;
16   To Him who led His people through
         the wilderness,
      For His mercy *endures* forever;
17   To Him who struck down great kings,
      For His mercy *endures* forever;
18   And slew famous kings,
      For His mercy *endures* forever—
19   Sihon king of the Amorites,
      For His mercy *endures* forever;
20   And Og king of Bashan,
      For His mercy *endures* forever—
21   And gave their land as a heritage,
      For His mercy *endures* forever;
22   A heritage to Israel His servant,
      For His mercy *endures* forever.

23   Who remembered us in our lowly
         state,
      For His mercy *endures* forever;
24   And rescued us from our enemies,
      For His mercy *endures* forever;
25   Who gives food to all flesh,
      For His mercy *endures* forever.

26   Oh, give thanks to the God of heaven!
      For His mercy *endures* forever.

PSALM 145

A Song of God's Majesty and Love

A Praise of David.

I will extol You, my God, O King;
      And I will bless Your name forever
         and ever.
2   Every day I will bless You,

And I will praise Your name forever
and ever.

3 Great *is* the LORD, and greatly to be
praised;
And His greatness *is* unsearchable.

4 One generation shall praise Your
works to another,
And shall declare Your mighty acts.

5 I[a] will meditate on the glorious
splendor of Your majesty,
And on Your wondrous works.[b]

6 *Men* shall speak of the might of Your
awesome acts,
And I will declare Your greatness.

7 They shall utter the memory of Your
great goodness,
And shall sing of Your righteousness.

8 The LORD *is* gracious and full of
compassion,
Slow to anger and great in mercy.

9 The LORD *is* good to all,
And His tender mercies *are* over all
His works.

10 All Your works shall praise You,
O LORD,
And Your saints shall bless You.

11 They shall speak of the glory of Your
kingdom,
And talk of Your power,

12 To make known to the sons of men His
mighty acts,
And the glorious majesty of His
kingdom.

13 Your kingdom *is* an everlasting
kingdom,
And Your dominion *endures*
throughout all generations.[a]

14 The LORD upholds all who fall,
And raises up all *who are* bowed
down.

15 The eyes of all look expectantly to You,
And You give them their food in due
season.

16 You open Your hand
And satisfy the desire of every living
thing.

17 The LORD *is* righteous in all His ways,
Gracious in all His works.

18 The LORD *is* near to all who call upon
Him,
To all who call upon Him in truth.

19 He will fulfill the desire of those who
fear Him;
He also will hear their cry and save
them.

20 The LORD preserves all who love Him,
But all the wicked He will destroy.

21 My mouth shall speak the praise of
the LORD,
And all flesh shall bless His holy
name
Forever and ever.

PSALM 146

The Happiness of Those Whose Help Is the LORD

Praise the LORD!

Praise the LORD, O my soul!

2 While I live I will praise the LORD;
I will sing praises to my God while I
have my being.

3 Do not put your trust in princes,
Nor in a son of man, in whom *there is*
no help.

4 His spirit departs, he returns to his
earth;
In that very day his plans perish.

5 Happy *is he* who *has* the God of Jacob
for his help,
Whose hope *is* in the LORD his God,

6 Who made heaven and earth,
The sea, and all that *is* in them;
Who keeps truth forever,

7 Who executes justice for the
oppressed,
Who gives food to the hungry.
The LORD gives freedom to the
prisoners.

8 The LORD opens *the eyes of* the blind;
The LORD raises those who are bowed
down;
The LORD loves the righteous.

9 The LORD watches over the strangers;
He relieves the fatherless and
widow;
But the way of the wicked He turns
upside down.

145:5 [a]Following Masoretic Text and Targum; Dead
Sea Scrolls, Septuagint, Syriac, and Vulgate read *They.*
[b]Literally *on the words of Your wondrous works*
145:13 [a]Following Masoretic Text and Targum; Dead
Sea Scrolls, Septuagint, Syriac, and Vulgate add *The
LORD is faithful in all His words, And holy in all His
works.*

10 The LORD shall reign forever—
Your God, O Zion, to all generations.

Praise the LORD!

PSALM 147

Praise to God for His Word and Providence

Praise the LORD!
For *it is* good to sing praises to our
God;
For *it is* pleasant, *and* praise is
beautiful.

2 The LORD builds up Jerusalem;
He gathers together the outcasts of
Israel.
3 He heals the brokenhearted
And binds up their wounds.
4 He counts the number of the stars;
He calls them all by name.
5 Great *is* our Lord, and mighty in
power;
His understanding *is* infinite.
6 The LORD lifts up the humble;
He casts the wicked down to the
ground.

7 Sing to the LORD with thanksgiving;
Sing praises on the harp to our God,
8 Who covers the heavens with clouds,
Who prepares rain for the earth,
Who makes grass to grow on the
mountains.
9 He gives to the beast its food,
And to the young ravens that cry.

10 He does not delight in the strength of
the horse;
He takes no pleasure in the legs of a
man.
11 The LORD takes pleasure in those who
fear Him,
In those who hope in His mercy.

12 Praise the LORD, O Jerusalem!
Praise your God, O Zion!

13 For He has strengthened the bars of
your gates;
He has blessed your children within
you.
14 He makes peace *in* your borders,
And fills you with the finest wheat.
15 He sends out His command *to the*
earth;
His word runs very swiftly.
16 He gives snow like wool;
He scatters the frost like ashes;
17 He casts out His hail like morsels;
Who can stand before His cold?
18 He sends out His word and melts
them;
He causes His wind to blow, *and* the
waters flow.
19 He declares His word to Jacob,
His statutes and His judgments to
Israel.
20 He has not dealt thus with any
nation;
And *as for His* judgments, they have
not known them.

Praise the LORD!

PSALM 148

Praise to the LORD from Creation

Praise the LORD!

Praise the LORD from the heavens;
Praise Him in the heights!
2 Praise Him, all His angels;
Praise Him, all His hosts!
3 Praise Him, sun and moon;
Praise Him, all you stars of light!
4 Praise Him, you heavens of heavens,
And you waters above the heavens!

5 Let them praise the name of the LORD,
For He commanded and they were
created.
6 He also established them forever and
ever;
He made a decree which shall not
pass away.

SCIENCE AND TECHNOLOGY

The physical power available to an ancient army was basically the muscle power of men and animals. They did not use explosives or gasoline, kerosene, and oil. Consequently, the "legs of a man" and the "strength of the horse" (Ps. 147:10) refer precisely to military power. Yet God does not delight in physical strength.

PRAISE GOD, ALL HEAVEN AND EARTH (Ps. 148:13)

Hymns from Egypt to Mesopotamia are filled with praises to the deity. On the feast day of any given deity, the hymns named the god as the highest god of the pantheon on that particular day. Whether it was a hymn to Amon of Egypt or to Ishtar of Babylon, the singers praised that deity for creating the world, for ruling over the other gods, for unsurpassed wisdom, and for the blessings which the worshipers had received from the deity. Always, the deity to whom the song was directed was called the greatest of all the gods.

Such a hymn is Ps. 148, possibly composed for a day set aside as holy to Yahweh. After the Exile this psalm could have been sung daily since, at least in Judah's later years, all days were thought holy to Yahweh. In the hymn, the residents of heaven are joined in their praise of Yahweh by inanimate objects, all of creation from heaven to earth (Ps. 148:7–10). Moreover, the song assumes that all peoples everywhere praise God who created them (148:11, 12). Language and motifs that are used elsewhere in the ancient world for other gods are reserved in Ps. 148 exclusively for Yahweh.

The ancient world understood that one never sings hymns of praise alone, but always with the entire universe. This idea of solidarity with the entire created order was carried over into the early church and still remains a central aspect of Orthodox Christian liturgy.

---

7 Praise the LORD from the earth,
    You great sea creatures and all the
        depths;
8 Fire and hail, snow and clouds;
    Stormy wind, fulfilling His word;
9 Mountains and all hills;
    Fruitful trees and all cedars;
10 Beasts and all cattle;
    Creeping things and flying fowl;
11 Kings of the earth and all peoples;
    Princes and all judges of the earth;
12 Both young men and maidens;
    Old men and children.

13 Let them praise the name of the LORD,
    For His name alone is exalted;
    His glory *is* above the earth and
        heaven.
14 And He has exalted the horn of His
        people,
    The praise of all His saints—
    Of the children of Israel,
    A people near to Him.

    Praise the LORD!

PSALM 149

Praise to God for His Salvation and Judgment

Praise the LORD!

    Sing to the LORD a new song,
    And His praise in the assembly of
        saints.

2 Let Israel rejoice in their Maker;
    Let the children of Zion be joyful in
        their King.
3 Let them praise His name with the
        dance;
    Let them sing praises to Him with the
        timbrel and harp.
4 For the LORD takes pleasure in His
        people;
    He will beautify the humble with
        salvation.

5 Let the saints be joyful in glory;
    Let them sing aloud on their beds.
6 *Let* the high praises of God *be* in their
        mouth,
    And a two-edged sword in their hand,
7 To execute vengeance on the nations,
    And punishments on the peoples;
8 To bind their kings with chains,
    And their nobles with fetters of iron;
9 To execute on them the written
        judgment—
    This honor have all His saints.

    Praise the LORD!

PSALM 150

Let All Things Praise the LORD

Praise the LORD!

    Praise God in His sanctuary;
    Praise Him in His mighty firmament!

2 Praise Him for His mighty acts;
  Praise Him according to His excellent
    greatness!

3 Praise Him with the sound of the
    trumpet;
  Praise Him with the lute and harp!
4 Praise Him with the timbrel and
    dance;
  Praise Him with stringed instruments
    and flutes!
5 Praise Him with loud cymbals;
  Praise Him with clashing cymbals!

6 Let everything that has breath praise
    the LORD.

Praise the LORD!

Nehemiah's Religious Reforms

Nehemiah began his term of office in 445 B.C., and his greatest accomplishment was the rebuilding of the city walls. They were completed in only 52 days (Neh. 6:15), but these quickly erected walls may have been just makeshift structures. The Jewish historian Josephus writes that the final walls took over 2 years, being completed in 437 B.C.

Nehemiah remained in Jerusalem until the 32nd year of Artaxerxes (433 B.C.), at which time he returned to Artaxerxes' court (Neh. 13:6). Soon, though, he convinced the Persian king to reappoint him to Judah, and he returned to find matters in an unacceptable state.

Nehemiah, like Ezra, was a purist in religious matters. True worship was only possible by the undefiled, and to Nehemiah that disqualified all of the people who had remained in the land during the Exile. Only the returned exiles, who had kept the faith pure even while in captivity, were acceptable. When Nehemiah found that Tobiah, an Ammonite official (Neh. 2:19), had been given rooms in the temple itself, he was aghast and removed Tobiah with characteristic promptness (Neh. 13:7–9). Nehemiah also restored the official support of the Levitical ministers (13:10–14) and resumed enforcement of Sabbath laws (13:15–22).

The exclusivism of Nehemiah and Ezra is sometimes troubling. Though intended to protect the faith from idolatrous influences, it often seems excessively severe. After all, some of the people so utterly rejected also worshiped the God of Israel. Not everyone felt as

Nehemiah did. The Eliashib who installed Tobiah in his temple apartment was none other than the high priest himself (Neh. 3:1), who evidently regarded his neighbors with more tolerance (see "Isaiah and the Restoration" at Is. 56:1).

■ Nehemiah 13:1–22

Nehemiah
Principles of Separation

13 :1 On that day they read from the Book of Moses in the hearing of the people, and in it was found written that no Ammonite or Moabite should ever come into the assembly of God, 2because they had not met the children of Israel with bread and water, but hired Balaam against them to curse them. However, our God turned the curse into a blessing. 3So it was, when they had heard the Law, that they separated all the mixed multitude from Israel.

Temple, Tithes, and Sabbath

4Now before this, Eliashib the priest, having authority over the storerooms of the house of our God, *was* allied with Tobiah. 5And he had prepared for him a large room, where previously they had stored the grain offerings, the frankincense, the articles, the tithes of grain, the new wine and oil, which were commanded *to be given* to the Levites and singers and gatekeepers, and the offerings for the priests. 6But during all this I was not in Jerusalem, for in the thirty-second year of Artaxerxes king of Babylon I had returned to the king. Then after certain days I obtained leave from the king, 7and I came to Jerusalem and discovered the evil that Eliashib had done for Tobiah, in preparing a room for him in the courts of the house of God. 8And it grieved me bitterly; therefore I threw all the household goods of Tobiah out of the room. 9Then I commanded them to cleanse the rooms; and I brought back into them the articles of the house of God, with the grain offering and the frankincense.

10I also realized that the portions for the Levites had not been given *them;* for each of the Levites and the singers who did the work had gone back to his field. 11So I contended with the rulers, and said, "Why is the house of God forsaken?" And I gathered them together and set them in their place. 12Then all Judah brought the tithe of the grain and the new wine and the oil to

TOBIAH, THE ENEMY OF NEHEMIAH (Neh. 13:7)

Sometime after 433 B.C., Nehemiah returned from Persia to Judah only to find that his personal enemy Tobiah had wormed his way into the temple itself (Neh. 13:7). Tobiah was not a Judean, but an Ammonite. The "evil" that Nehemiah discovered was that the high priest had taken an Ammonite into the temple, something forbidden in the Law of Moses (13:1).

There were several conflicts between Nehemiah and Tobiah. First Tobiah opposed Nehemiah's rebuilding of Jerusalem's walls (Neh. 2:10, 19). Accusations that Nehemiah was rebelling against the Persian king who had appointed him Judah's governor failed to stop the work. Tobiah further ridiculed the walls (Neh. 4:3) and then plotted with others to attack Jerusalem before the walls could be completed (4:11, 15). These attempts likewise failed.

Tobiah was nothing if not persistent. He, with others, attempted to lure Nehemiah away from Jerusalem in order to assassinate him (6:1, 2). Later on, Tobiah sent him threatening letters (6:19).

Attempting to infiltrate the temple was possibly Tobiah's new strategy to undermine Nehemiah's authority. Most likely he wished to rule over Jerusalem himself, even though he was an Ammonite, not a Judean. He most likely desired to absorb Judah into his own realm, since, as an "Ammonite official" (2:19), he possibly held a position in Ammon similar to Sanballat's in Samaria and Nehemiah's in Judah.

Tobiah was from a powerful, wealthy Ammonite family who impacted Jewish history later on. Archaeologists have discovered a palace-fortress just to the east of Judah from a century after Nehemiah's time. The fortress has the name "Tobiah" inscribed at the entrance. Unable to gather control of Jerusalem, Tobiah and his family eventually carved out landholdings and political power in Ammon, just east of the Jordan River.

---

the storehouse. 13And I appointed as treasurers over the storehouse Shelemiah the priest and Zadok the scribe, and of the Levites, Pedaiah; and next to them *was* Hanan the son of Zaccur, the son of Mattaniah; for they were considered faithful, and their task *was* to distribute to their brethren.

14Remember me, O my God, concerning this, and do not wipe out my good deeds that I have done for the house of my God, and for its services!

15In those days I saw *people* in Judah treading wine presses on the Sabbath, and bringing in sheaves, and loading donkeys with wine, grapes, figs, and all *kinds of* burdens, which they brought into Jerusalem on the Sabbath day. And I warned *them* about the day on which they were selling provisions. 16Men of Tyre dwelt there also, who brought in fish and all kinds of goods, and sold *them* on the Sabbath to the children of Judah, and in Jerusalem.

17Then I contended with the nobles of Judah, and said to them, "What evil thing *is* this that you do, by which you profane the Sabbath day? 18Did not your fathers do thus, and did not our God bring all this disaster on us and on this city? Yet you bring added wrath on Israel by profaning the Sabbath."

19So it was, at the gates of Jerusalem, as it began to be dark before the Sabbath, that I commanded the gates to be shut, and charged that they must not be opened till after the Sabbath. Then I posted *some* of my servants at the gates, *so that* no

---

RELIGION AND WORSHIP

The prohibition against work on the Sabbath is a religious obligation, not an arrangement imposed by an employer or government. A man could be executed for "gathering sticks on the Sabbath day" (Num. 15:32–36). Nehemiah did not impose such a strict penalty, but he did try to stop daily work on the 7th day. Working on that day "profanes" it, making it like any other day (Neh. 13:18).

burdens would be brought in on the Sabbath day. 20Now the merchants and sellers of all kinds of wares lodged outside Jerusalem once or twice.

21Then I warned them, and said to them, "Why do you spend the night around the wall? If you do *so* again, I will lay hands on you!" From that time on they came no *more* on the Sabbath. 22And I commanded the Levites that they should cleanse themselves, and that they should go and guard the gates, to sanctify the Sabbath day.

Remember me, O my God, *concerning* this also, and spare me according to the greatness of Your mercy!

The Sabbath After the Exile

When the Jerusalem temple was destroyed in 586 B.C., the Jews in exile had to find and emphasize religious practices that did not require a physical temple. One was Scripture (see "Ezra the Scribe" at Ezra 7:1). Another was the observance of the Sabbath. Although the Sabbath law was one of Israel's most ancient, being the fourth commandment (Ex. 20:8–11), it was not treated as a central truth of the faith until after the temple had been destroyed. To Jews living in foreign lands, the visible distinctive of Sabbath observance became an essential mark of the true believer. It was no less than a public statement of faith.

Even after some exiled Jews returned to Jerusalem and rebuilt the temple, Sabbath observance remained a nonnegotiable element of true worship. When Nehemiah returned to Jerusalem for a second term as governor, one of his first actions was to enforce the Sabbath laws. As always, he was abrupt and severe, even offering threats of physical violence (Neh. 13:21).

For some, the Sabbath day was a reminder and an opportunity to give thanks to God for His great blessings. This, at least, was the perspective of the anonymous psalmist responsible for Ps. 92. Others, though, would simply treat the Sabbath as another law to be followed, and Nehemiah's heavy-handed enforcement of the Sabbath law only added to that legalism. By the time of Christ, legalism had almost obliterated the joy of Sabbath thanksgiving that is so evident in Ps. 92 (see Mark 2:23–28).

■ Psalm 92

PSALM 92

Praise to the LORD for His Love and Faithfulness

A Psalm. A Song for the Sabbath day.

*I*t *is* good to give thanks to the LORD,
And to sing praises to Your name,
   O Most High;
2 To declare Your lovingkindness in the morning,
And Your faithfulness every night,
3 On an instrument of ten strings,
On the lute,
And on the harp,
With harmonious sound.
4 For You, LORD, have made me glad through Your work;
I will triumph in the works of Your hands.

5 O LORD, how great are Your works!
Your thoughts are very deep.
6 A senseless man does not know,
Nor does a fool understand this.
7 When the wicked spring up like grass,
And when all the workers of iniquity flourish,
It is that they may be destroyed forever.

8 But You, LORD, *are* on high forevermore.
9 For behold, Your enemies, O LORD,
For behold, Your enemies shall perish;
All the workers of iniquity shall be scattered.

10 But my horn You have exalted like a wild ox;
I have been anointed with fresh oil.
11 My eye also has seen *my desire* on my enemies;
My ears hear *my desire* on the wicked
Who rise up against me.

12 The righteous shall flourish like a palm tree,
He shall grow like a cedar in Lebanon.
13 Those who are planted in the house of the LORD
Shall flourish in the courts of our God.
14 They shall still bear fruit in old age;
They shall be fresh and flourishing,
15 To declare that the LORD is upright;
He is my rock, and *there is* no unrighteousness in Him.

THE NEHEMIAH MEMOIRS (Neh. 13:31)

Portions of the Book of Nehemiah use the first-person pronouns "I" and "me" in recounting the events of the story. Apparently, the final editor of the book used a firsthand account written by Nehemiah himself to complete the story begun in Chronicles and the Book of Ezra. Called by scholars the "Nehemiah memoirs," the account provides Nehemiah's own perspective of the events and the resistance he faced in attempting to restore Jerusalem to a place of prominence among its neighbors.

The Book of Nehemiah concludes with Nehemiah's short prayer: "Remember me, O my God, for good!" (Neh. 13:31). Nehemiah repeats a similar prayer throughout his memoirs, asking that God remember certain deeds and persons (Neh. 5:19; 6:14; 13:14, 22, 29). As he recounted the events of his life, he was apparently confident that God approved of his actions.

Similar forms of autobiographical inscriptions have been discovered in Egypt from the same historical period as Nehemiah. The statue inscription of Udjahorresnet is from an Egyptian who, like Ezra and Nehemiah, was appointed to an important governmental post by the Persians. The *Long Biographical Inscription of Petosiris* is from a wealthy high priest of the Egyptian god Thoth. Both inscriptions seem to have been written by the individuals, and then posted after their deaths to commemorate their lives before the public and their gods. Both writings ask for people and the gods to "remember" them and their deeds.

Nehemiah may have written his memoirs as part of a similar funerary custom. Following Nehemiah's death, then, his memoirs became an excellent source of Judah's history, dealing with the restoration of the temple and of Jerusalem's walls.

Nehemiah and Foreign Wives

Both Ezra and Nehemiah vehemently (and in Nehemiah's case, violently) opposed the intermarriage of returned exiles and the people of the land. When Ezra heard of such marriages, he tore his clothes and pulled his own hair and beard (Ezra 9:3). Nehemiah, less introspective, pulled the hair of those who had intermarried (Neh. 13:25). To these leaders the problem was serious: any connection with the foreign or unclean could result in an adulterated faith.

Not everyone, not even every religious leader, agreed. The high priest Eliashib himself evidently regarded such marriages with indulgence (Neh. 13:28), and among some of the Jews in exile intermarriage appeared to be unremarkable. The author of the Book of Esther related Esther's marriage to a Persian king without apology or comment (see "The Book of Esther" at Esth. 1:1). The Book of Ruth, which many scholars feel was written sometime during the Persian period, deliberately points out that the great King David himself had a Moabite ancestress (Ruth 1:4; 4:13–22; see Neh. 13:23).

■ Nehemiah 13:23–31

Nehemiah

13 **:23** In those days I also saw Jews *who* had married women of Ashdod, Ammon, *and* Moab. 24And half of their children spoke the language of Ashdod, and could not speak the language of Judah, but spoke according to the language of one or the other people.

25So I contended with them and cursed them, struck some of them and pulled out their hair, and made them swear by God, *saying,* "You shall not give your daughters as wives to their sons, nor take their daughters for your sons or yourselves. 26Did not Solomon king of Israel sin by these things? Yet among many nations there was no king like him, who was beloved of his God; and God made him king over all Israel. Nevertheless pagan women caused even him to sin. 27Should we then hear of your doing all this great evil, transgressing against our God by marrying pagan women?"

28And *one* of the sons of Joiada, the son of Eliashib the high priest, *was* a son-in-law of Sanballat the Horonite; therefore I drove him from me.

29Remember them, O my God, because they have defiled the priesthood and the covenant of the priesthood and the Levites.

³⁰Thus I cleansed them of everything pagan. I also assigned duties to the priests and the Levites, each to his service, ³¹and *to bringing* the wood offering and the firstfruits at appointed times.

Remember me, O my God, for good!

The Book of Joel

Nothing is known about the prophet Joel except for what the Book of Joel itself offers. All information beyond the name of his father Pethuel (Joel 1:1) must be concluded by examining Joel's prophecies.

Joel prophesied in Jerusalem at a time when there was a temple standing (Joel 2:17), but beyond that no one is certain when Joel was active. Some scholars have suggested that Joel was one of the earliest of prophets, prophesying in the 8th century B.C., even before Amos and Hosea. Others place him later, even as late as the Persian period. The book can be read in a context, such as the time of the Persian Empire, when Jerusalem had no king. Joel calls for a national day of fasting and repentance, to be led by the elders and the priests (1:14; 2:15–17). Had Joel prophesied during the monarchy, the king would surely have had a part in such a solemn assembly.

The Persian era suits Joel's prophecies in other ways. Like Malachi, Joel shows a strong priestly orientation. He sees repentance as an official priestly task instead of an individual responsibility (Joel 2:17). He refers once to the Greeks (3:6), a reference that would make the most sense when the Greek city-states were gaining international recognition for their wars against Persia. Finally, Joel shows an amazing awareness of earlier prophecies, quoting extensively from their works. His most interesting quotation (Joel 3:10) reverses an earlier prophecy found in both Isaiah (Is. 2:4) and Micah (Mic. 4:3). Now plowshares would become swords and pruning hooks, spears.

In whatever era Joel spoke, the immediate concern of his prophecy was a plague of locusts. To an agricultural society, the vast swarms of locusts that occasionally appeared in the ancient Near East spelled famine and death. Joel uses one such disaster to call the people back to true faith in God. The locust swarm was a "day of the LORD," and a still more devastating, universal day of the Lord was still to come (Joel 2:30, 31; 3:14–16). Only if the people truly repented could Jerusalem become the holy and eternal city that it was meant to be (3:17, 20, 21).

▼ ■ Joel 1:1—3:21

Joel

1 :1 The word of the LORD that came to Joel the son of Pethuel.

The Land Laid Waste

2   Hear this, you elders,
    And give ear, all you inhabitants of
      the land!
    Has *anything like* this happened in
      your days,
    Or even in the days of your fathers?
3   Tell your children about it,
    Let your children *tell* their children,
    And their children another
      generation.

4   What the chewing locustᵃ left, the
      swarming locust has eaten;
    What the swarming locust left, the
      crawling locust has eaten;
    And what the crawling locust left, the
      consuming locust has eaten.

5   Awake, you drunkards, and weep;
    And wail, all you drinkers of wine,
    Because of the new wine,
    For it has been cut off from your
      mouth.
6   For a nation has come up against My
      land,
    Strong, and without number;
    His teeth *are* the teeth of a lion,
    And he has the fangs of a fierce lion.
7   He has laid waste My vine,
    And ruined My fig tree;
    He has stripped it bare and thrown *it*
      away;
    Its branches are made white.

1:4 ᵃExact identity of these locusts is unknown.

TIME CAPSULE   *424 to 404 B.C.*

424	Xerxes II is assassinated after a few weeks as king
423–404	Darius II defeats his brother in civil war to become king of Persia
410	Temple of Yahweh at Elephantine destroyed by priests of Khnum
407	Darius's son Cyrus becomes commander in chief of the Persian army
404	Amyrtaeus expels Persians from Upper Egypt

The Day of Judgment (Joel 1:15)

Among the Old Testament prophets the phrase "day of the LORD" (or "day of Yahweh") meant disaster and destruction for Judah and Israel. The prophet Joel could only announce, "Alas for the day!" (Joel 1:15). In the ancient Near East, the "day" of a deity meant a time of celebration in which that particular deity was honored as the most powerful god of the pantheon. In the liturgical calendars of Egypt and Mesopotamia there were holy days set aside all through the year for the worship of the various deities.

In the cultures of both Egypt and Mesopotamia, banquets and celebrations marked each god's day. In Egyptian festivals, the image of the god was brought from the temple and carried through the streets. In Mesopotamia, the statues of many gods might be brought in procession to the temple of the god whose day it was to join the celebration. As supreme ruler for that day, the deity was asked to bring justice to the world. Loyal worshipers were expected to be rewarded and the wicked punished.

The people of Judah similarly considered the day of Yahweh to be one of festivals and good times. Prophets like Joel (Joel 1:15) and Amos (Amos 5:18), however, proclaimed a contrasting view. They agreed that Yahweh would indeed bring judgment and true justice on that day. But, since the people had not lived by the rules of God, the judgment that would come would result in their own destruction. The Judeans did not understand that their request for justice was a call for their own condemnation.

---

8 Lament like a virgin girded with
      sackcloth
   For the husband of her youth.
9 The grain offering and the drink
      offering
   Have been cut off from the house of
      the LORD;
   The priests mourn, who minister to
      the LORD.
10 The field is wasted,
   The land mourns;
   For the grain is ruined,
   The new wine is dried up,
   The oil fails.

11 Be ashamed, you farmers,
   Wail, you vinedressers,
   For the wheat and the barley;
   Because the harvest of the field has
      perished.
12 The vine has dried up,
   And the fig tree has withered;
   The pomegranate tree,
   The palm tree also,

And the apple tree—
All the trees of the field are withered;
Surely joy has withered away from the
      sons of men.

Mourning for the Land

13 Gird yourselves and lament, you
      priests;
   Wail, you who minister before the
      altar;
   Come, lie all night in sackcloth,
   You who minister to my God;
   For the grain offering and the drink
      offering
   Are withheld from the house of your
      God.
14 Consecrate a fast,
   Call a sacred assembly;
   Gather the elders
   And all the inhabitants of the land
   Into the house of the LORD your God,
   And cry out to the LORD.

15 Alas for the day!
   For the day of the LORD *is* at hand;

Plants and Animals

The precise meanings of Joel's four kinds of locusts are unclear (Joel 1:4). Locusts are grasshoppers whose form and behavior change when they migrate in large numbers and swarm together. An adult locust has a wingspan of 5 inches and can fly 100 miles in a day. A locust swarm may number billions of locusts and eat several tons of leaves in a day.

It shall come as destruction from the
  Almighty.
16 Is not the food cut off before our eyes,
  Joy and gladness from the house of
    our God?
17 The seed shrivels under the clods,
  Storehouses are in shambles;
  Barns are broken down,
  For the grain has withered.
18 How the animals groan!
  The herds of cattle are restless,
  Because they have no pasture;
  Even the flocks of sheep suffer
    punishment.ᵃ

19 O LORD, to You I cry out;
  For fire has devoured the open
    pastures,
  And a flame has burned all the trees
    of the field.
20 The beasts of the field also cry out to
    You,
  For the water brooks are dried up,
  And fire has devoured the open
    pastures.

The Day of the LORD

2 ¹ Blow the trumpet in Zion,
  And sound an alarm in My holy
    mountain!
  Let all the inhabitants of the land
    tremble;
  For the day of the LORD is coming,
  For it is at hand:
2 A day of darkness and gloominess,
  A day of clouds and thick darkness,
  Like the morning *clouds* spread over
    the mountains.
  A people *come,* great and strong,
  The like of whom has never been;
  Nor will there ever be any *such* after
    them,
  Even for many successive generations.

3 A fire devours before them,
  And behind them a flame burns;
  The land *is* like the Garden of Eden
    before them,
  And behind them a desolate
    wilderness;
  Surely nothing shall escape them.
4 Their appearance is like the
    appearance of horses;
  And like swift steeds, so they run.
5 With a noise like chariots
  Over mountaintops they leap,
  Like the noise of a flaming fire that
    devours the stubble,

Like a strong people set in battle
    array.

6 Before them the people writhe in pain;
  All faces are drained of color.ᵃ
7 They run like mighty men,
  They climb the wall like men of war;
  Every one marches in formation,
  And they do not break ranks.
8 They do not push one another;
  Every one marches in his own
    column.ᵃ
  Though they lunge between the
    weapons,
  They are not cut down.ᵇ
9 They run to and fro in the city,
  They run on the wall;
  They climb into the houses,
  They enter at the windows like a
    thief.

10 The earth quakes before them,
  The heavens tremble;
  The sun and moon grow dark,
  And the stars diminish their
    brightness.
11 The LORD gives voice before His army,
  For His camp is very great;
  For strong *is the One* who executes
    His word.
  For the day of the LORD *is* great and
    very terrible;
  Who can endure it?

A Call to Repentance

12 "Now, therefore," says the LORD,
  "Turn to Me with all your heart,
  With fasting, with weeping, and with
    mourning."
13 So rend your heart, and not your
    garments;
  Return to the LORD your God,
  For He *is* gracious and merciful,
  Slow to anger, and of great kindness;
  And He relents from doing harm.
14 Who knows *if* He will turn and relent,
  And leave a blessing behind Him—
  A grain offering and a drink offering
  For the LORD your God?

15 Blow the trumpet in Zion,
  Consecrate a fast,
  Call a sacred assembly;

1:18 ᵃSeptuagint and Vulgate read *are made
desolate.*   2:6 ᵃSeptuagint, Targum, and Vulgate
read *gather blackness.*   2:8 ᵃLiterally *his own
highway* ᵇThat is, they are not halted by losses

16 Gather the people,
    Sanctify the congregation,
    Assemble the elders,
    Gather the children and nursing
        babes;
    Let the bridegroom go out from his
        chamber,
    And the bride from her dressing room.
17 Let the priests, who minister to the
        LORD,
    Weep between the porch and the altar;
    Let them say, "Spare Your people,
        O LORD,
    And do not give Your heritage to
        reproach,
    That the nations should rule over
        them.
    Why should they say among the
        peoples,
    'Where *is* their God?' "

The Land Refreshed

18 Then the LORD will be zealous for His
        land,
    And pity His people.
19 The LORD will answer and say to His
        people,
    "Behold, I will send you grain and new
        wine and oil,
    And you will be satisfied by them;
    I will no longer make you a reproach
        among the nations.

20 "But I will remove far from you the
        northern *army,*
    And will drive him away into a barren
        and desolate land,
    With his face toward the eastern sea
    And his back toward the western sea;
    His stench will come up,
    And his foul odor will rise,
    Because he has done monstrous
        things."

21 Fear not, O land;
    Be glad and rejoice,
    For the LORD has done marvelous
        things!
22 Do not be afraid, you beasts of the
        field;
    For the open pastures are springing
        up,
    And the tree bears its fruit;
    The fig tree and the vine yield their
        strength.

23 Be glad then, you children of Zion,
    And rejoice in the LORD your God;
    For He has given you the former rain
        faithfully,[a]
    And He will cause the rain to come
        down for you—
    The former rain,
    And the latter rain in the first *month.*
24 The threshing floors shall be full of
        wheat,
    And the vats shall overflow with new
        wine and oil.

25 "So I will restore to you the years that
        the swarming locust has eaten,
    The crawling locust,
    The consuming locust,
    And the chewing locust,[a]
    My great army which I sent among
        you.
26 You shall eat in plenty and be
        satisfied,
    And praise the name of the LORD your
        God,
    Who has dealt wondrously with you;
    And My people shall never be put to
        shame.
27 Then you shall know that I *am* in the
        midst of Israel:
    I *am* the LORD your God
    And there is no other.
    My people shall never be put to
        shame.

God's Spirit Poured Out

28 "And it shall come to pass afterward
    That I will pour out My Spirit on all
        flesh;
    Your sons and your daughters shall
        prophesy,
    Your old men shall dream dreams,
    Your young men shall see visions.
29 And also on *My* menservants and on
        My maidservants
    I will pour out My Spirit in those
        days.

30 "And I will show wonders in the
        heavens and in the earth:
    Blood and fire and pillars of smoke.
31 The sun shall be turned into darkness,
    And the moon into blood,
    Before the coming of the great and
        awesome day of the LORD.
32 And it shall come to pass
    That whoever calls on the name of the
        LORD
    Shall be saved.

2:23 [a]Or *the teacher of righteousness*
2:25 [a]Compare 1:4

TYRE AND SIDON, THE ECONOMIC OPPRESSORS (Joel 3:4–6)

The coastline of Palestine was (and still is) crucially important for the political and economic balance of power in the Near East. The Persians sought to establish a western section of their empire, extending from Egypt, located south of Tyre and Sidon, all the way to Asia Minor and Greece to the north. Tyre and Sidon, as a central point in this western section, were important for providing fleets for trade and for fighting the Greeks.

When the Jews returned to Jerusalem during the Persian period, Tyre and Sidon possessed both wealth and a degree of political importance. In contrast, the small Persian province of Judah was poor and politically important only as the backdoor into Egypt.

City-states along "the coasts of Philistia," as well as Tyre and Sidon (Joel 3:4), seemingly took economic advantage of Judah, their weaker neighbor to the east. For instance, during Nehemiah's governorship of Judah, "men of Tyre" sold fish and other goods in Jerusalem on the Sabbath (Neh. 13:16). While Nehemiah shut down this practice, there is no doubt that Judah operated under a strong trade deficit with coastal city-states like Tyre and Sidon.

Economically, this would have drained Judah of its precious metals and other resources—Yahweh's silver and gold (Joel 3:5). Lacking goods to pay their debts, Judeans would have been forced to trade in the one commodity they possessed—their own sons and daughters. The coastal traders would have sold them to the Greeks, the available market. The Greeks, in turn, would "remove them far from their borders" (Joel 3:6) into Greece or Asia Minor.

Because of such economic exploitation of God's people, the prophet Joel announced God's judgment against "Tyre and Sidon, and all the coasts of Philistia." What they had done to the Judeans would soon happen to them (Joel 3:4, 7, 8).

For in Mount Zion and in Jerusalem
  there shall be deliverance,
As the LORD has said,
Among the remnant whom the LORD
  calls.

God Judges the Nations

3 ¹ "For behold, in those days and at
  that time,
When I bring back the captives of
  Judah and Jerusalem,
² I will also gather all nations,
And bring them down to the Valley of
  Jehoshaphat;
And I will enter into judgment with
  them there
On account of My people, My heritage
  Israel,
Whom they have scattered among the
  nations;
They have also divided up My land.
³ They have cast lots for My people,
Have given a boy *as payment* for a
  harlot,
And sold a girl for wine, that they
  may drink.

⁴ "Indeed, what have you to do with Me,
O Tyre and Sidon, and all the coasts of
  Philistia?

Will you retaliate against Me?
But if you retaliate against Me,
Swiftly and speedily I will return your
  retaliation upon your own head;
⁵ Because you have taken My silver and
  My gold,
And have carried into your temples
  My prized possessions.
⁶ Also the people of Judah and the
  people of Jerusalem
You have sold to the Greeks,
That you may remove them far from
  their borders.

⁷ "Behold, I will raise them
Out of the place to which you have
  sold them,
And will return your retaliation upon
  your own head.
⁸ I will sell your sons and your
  daughters
Into the hand of the people of Judah,
And they will sell them to the
  Sabeans,ᵃ
To a people far off;
For the LORD has spoken."

3:8 ᵃLiterally *Shebaites* (compare Isaiah 60:6 and
Ezekiel 27:22)

9 Proclaim this among the nations:
"Prepare for war!
Wake up the mighty men,
Let all the men of war draw near,
Let them come up.

10 Beat your plowshares into swords
And your pruning hooks into spears;
Let the weak say, 'I *am* strong.' "

11 Assemble and come, all you nations,
And gather together all around.
Cause Your mighty ones to go down
there, O LORD.

12 "Let the nations be wakened, and come
up to the Valley of Jehoshaphat;
For there I will sit to judge all the
surrounding nations.

13 Put in the sickle, for the harvest is
ripe.
Come, go down;
For the winepress is full,
The vats overflow—
For their wickedness *is* great."

14 Multitudes, multitudes in the valley of
decision!
For the day of the LORD *is* near in the
valley of decision.

15 The sun and moon will grow dark,
And the stars will diminish their
brightness.

16 The LORD also will roar from Zion,
And utter His voice from Jerusalem;
The heavens and earth will shake;
But the LORD will be a shelter for His
people,
And the strength of the children of
Israel.

17 "So you shall know that I *am* the LORD
your God,
Dwelling in Zion My holy mountain.
Then Jerusalem shall be holy,
And no aliens shall ever pass through
her again."

God Blesses His People

18 And it will come to pass in that day
That the mountains shall drip with
new wine,
The hills shall flow with milk,
And all the brooks of Judah shall be
flooded with water;
A fountain shall flow from the house
of the LORD
And water the Valley of Acacias.

19 "Egypt shall be a desolation,
And Edom a desolate wilderness,

Because of violence *against* the people
of Judah,
For they have shed innocent blood in
their land.

20 But Judah shall abide forever,
And Jerusalem from generation to
generation.

21 For I will acquit them of the guilt of
bloodshed, whom I had not
acquitted;
For the LORD dwells in Zion."

Isaiah and the Restoration

The chronology of the Book of Isaiah is very complicated. Undoubtedly, different prophecies in the book speak of time periods that are centuries apart. The prophet Isaiah lived in Judah during the reigns of Ahaz (735–715 B.C.) and Hezekiah (715–686 B.C.), and most of the early passages in the book refer to those kings and to the Assyrian Empire, which was expanding at that time. Most of these prophecies are dark and pessimistic, speaking of inevitable judgment and destruction, because Judah had refused to hear God's words.

Strikingly different are the oracles of salvation in Is. 40—55, which promise a return from exile and a rebuilding of Jerusalem and the temple (Is. 44:28). These prophecies explicitly name Cyrus the Persian (44:28; 45:1), identifying the approaching salvation as the restoration of Jerusalem after the Babylonian exile, almost 200 years after the prophet Isaiah himself was active. Scholars differ as to whether the prophecies in these chapters should be understood as foretellings of the distant future by Isaiah himself or rather as the words of an anonymous prophet of the Exile, who saw himself as a spiritual descendant of the great Isaiah (see "Isaiah and Cyrus the Persian" at Is. 40:1).

A third major shift in the Book of Isaiah begins at ch. 56. Where chs. 40—55 spoke of a day when the temple would be restored, chs. 56—66 assume that a temple is standing (56:7; 66:6). Since these final chapters follow immediately after the prophecies of the temple's restoration, it is reasonable to assume that they speak of the second temple, built during the Persian era. As is the case with chs. 40—55, some believe chs. 56—66 are the foretellings of the 8th-century prophet Isaiah, while others consider them the work of a postexilic prophet following in Isaiah's tradition.

If the prophecies of Is. 56—66 do speak of the second temple period, it is remarkable how much their message is in tension with the actual practices of the second temple. All the leaders of the community of returned exiles were meticulous about avoiding foreigners, but the prophet declares that foreigners will be God's servants (Is. 56:3–8). He promises a time when the temple will be "a house of prayer for all nations" (56:7), and when the sacrifices of foreigners will be acceptable on the temple altar. The theme of the faithful Gentiles is resoundingly repeated in chs. 60—62, where the Gentiles will come to God's light (60:3), will build the city walls (60:10), and will see the righteousness of God's people (62:2). If certain members of the restoration community in Jerusalem opposed the exclusivism of Ezra and Nehemiah, as seems likely, they had powerful support in these prophecies.

■ Isaiah 56:1—59:21

Isaiah
Salvation for the Gentiles

56
:1 Thus says the LORD:

"Keep justice, and do righteousness,
For My salvation *is* about to come,
And My righteousness to be revealed.
2   Blessed *is* the man *who* does this,
And the son of man *who* lays hold on
    it;
Who keeps from defiling the Sabbath,
And keeps his hand from doing any
    evil."

3   Do not let the son of the foreigner
Who has joined himself to the LORD
Speak, saying,
"The LORD has utterly separated me
    from His people";
Nor let the eunuch say,
"Here I am, a dry tree."
4   For thus says the LORD:
"To the eunuchs who keep My
    Sabbaths,
And choose what pleases Me,
And hold fast My covenant,
5   Even to them I will give in My house
And within My walls a place and a
    name
Better than that of sons and
    daughters;
I will give them[a] an everlasting
    name
That shall not be cut off.

6   "Also the sons of the foreigner
Who join themselves to the LORD, to
    serve Him,
And to love the name of the LORD, to
    be His servants—
Everyone who keeps from defiling the
    Sabbath,
And holds fast My covenant—
7   Even them I will bring to My holy
    mountain,
And make them joyful in My house of
    prayer.
Their burnt offerings and their
    sacrifices
Will be accepted on My altar;
For My house shall be called a house
    of prayer for all nations."
8   The Lord GOD, who gathers the
    outcasts of Israel, says,
"Yet I will gather to him
Others besides those who are gathered
    to him."

Israel's Irresponsible Leaders
9   All you beasts of the field, come to
    devour,
All you beasts in the forest.
10   His watchmen *are* blind,
They are all ignorant;
They *are* all dumb dogs,
They cannot bark;
Sleeping, lying down, loving to
    slumber.
11   Yes, *they are* greedy dogs
Which never have enough.
And they *are* shepherds
Who cannot understand;
They all look to their own way,
Every one for his own gain,
From his *own* territory.
12   "Come," one says, "I will bring wine,
And we will fill ourselves with
    intoxicating drink;
Tomorrow will be as today,
And much more abundant."

Israel's Futile Idolatry
57
1   The righteous perishes,
    And no man takes *it* to heart;
Merciful men *are* taken away,
While no one considers
That the righteous is taken away from
    evil.
2   He shall enter into peace;
They shall rest in their beds,
Each one walking *in* his uprightness.

56:5 [a]Literally *him*

A EUNUCH AND A FOREIGNER IN GOD'S HOUSE (Is. 56:3)

The prophet addressed the status that two different groups would have in the future Jerusalem: "the son of the foreigner" (Is. 56:3, 6) and the eunuch (56:3). The Book of Deuteronomy excluded both of these groups from taking part in the temple ceremonies (Deut. 23:1–3). They never could be fully a part of God's people.

In God's future Jerusalem, however, a different situation will prevail. In the future temple, ethnic origin or physical defects will no longer determine one's status. Rather, what matters will be obedience to God's covenant, particularly keeping the Sabbath (Is. 56:2, 4, 6).

The future, therefore, would bring about a reversal of the present status of these excluded people. Eunuchs were restricted by the Law of Moses because self-mutilation was often performed in honor of a heathen god (1 Kin. 18:28). In addition, a person with a defect was deemed unfit for service to God. Faithful eunuchs, however, will have a place within the future temple that will more than compensate for their lack of descendants (Is. 56:5).

The faithful "sons of the foreigner" can also become God's servants (56:6). They will have more than just access to the temple. God will grant them full participation as part of His own people by accepting their sacrifices. The temple will indeed become "a house of prayer for all nations" (56:7).

---

3 "But come here,
    You sons of the sorceress,
    You offspring of the adulterer and the
       harlot!
4 Whom do you ridicule?
    Against whom do you make a wide
       mouth
    And stick out the tongue?
    Are you not children of transgression,
    Offspring of falsehood,
5 Inflaming yourselves with gods under
       every green tree,
    Slaying the children in the valleys,
    Under the clefts of the rocks?
6 Among the smooth *stones* of the
       stream
    Is your portion;
    They, they, *are* your lot!
    Even to them you have poured a drink
       offering,
    You have offered a grain offering.
    Should I receive comfort in these?

7 "On a lofty and high mountain
    You have set your bed;

8 Even there you went up
    To offer sacrifice.
    Also behind the doors and their posts
    You have set up your remembrance;
    For you have uncovered yourself *to*
       those other than Me,
    And have gone up to them;
    You have enlarged your bed
    And made *a covenant* with them;
    You have loved their bed,
    Where you saw *their* nudity.ᵃ
9 You went to the king with ointment,
    And increased your perfumes;
    You sent your messengers far off,
    And *even* descended to Sheol.
10 You are wearied in the length of your
       way;
    Yet you did not say, 'There is no hope.'
    You have found the life of your hand;
    Therefore you were not grieved.

11 "And of whom have you been afraid, or
       feared,
    That you have lied
    And not remembered Me,
    Nor taken *it* to your heart?

57:8 ᵃLiterally *hand*, a euphemism

CULTS AND SUPERNATURAL

Archaeological evidence reveals that child sacrifice was practiced in the ancient Mediterranean area (Is. 57:5). The bodies were buried in clay urns, and inscriptions written on the urns have been found stating to which god the child was sacrificed. The largest burial area so far discovered is in ancient Carthage, the city in north Africa that the Romans destroyed in 146 B.C.

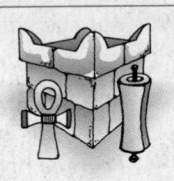

Is it not because I have held My peace
   from of old
That you do not fear Me?
12 I will declare your righteousness
And your works,
For they will not profit you.
13 When you cry out,
Let your collection *of idols* deliver you.
But the wind will carry them all away,
A breath will take *them.*
But he who puts his trust in Me shall
   possess the land,
And shall inherit My holy mountain."

Healing for the Backslider

14 And one shall say,
"Heap it up! Heap it up!
Prepare the way,
Take the stumbling block out of the
   way of My people."

15 For thus says the High and Lofty One
Who inhabits eternity, whose name *is*
   Holy:
"I dwell in the high and holy *place,*
With him *who* has a contrite and
   humble spirit,
To revive the spirit of the humble,
And to revive the heart of the contrite
   ones.
16 For I will not contend forever,
Nor will I always be angry;
For the spirit would fail before Me,
And the souls *which* I have made.
17 For the iniquity of his covetousness
I was angry and struck him;
I hid and was angry,
And he went on backsliding in the
   way of his heart.
18 I have seen his ways, and will heal
   him;
I will also lead him,
And restore comforts to him
And to his mourners.

19 "I create the fruit of the lips:
Peace, peace to *him who is* far off and
   to *him who is* near,"
Says the LORD,
"And I will heal him."
20 But the wicked *are* like the troubled
   sea,
When it cannot rest,
Whose waters cast up mire and dirt.

21 "*There is* no peace,"
Says my God, "for the wicked."

Fasting that Pleases God

58 1 "Cry aloud, spare not;
Lift up your voice like a
   trumpet;
Tell My people their transgression,
And the house of Jacob their sins.
2 Yet they seek Me daily,
And delight to know My ways,
As a nation that did righteousness,
And did not forsake the ordinance of
   their God.
They ask of Me the ordinances of
   justice;
They take delight in approaching God.
3 'Why have we fasted,' *they say,* 'and
   You have not seen?
Why have we afflicted our souls, and
   You take no notice?'

"In fact, in the day of your fast you find
   pleasure,
And exploit all your laborers.
4 Indeed you fast for strife and debate,
And to strike with the fist of
   wickedness.
You will not fast as *you do* this day,
To make your voice heard on high.
5 Is it a fast that I have chosen,
A day for a man to afflict his soul?
Is it to bow down his head like a
   bulrush,
And to spread out sackcloth and
   ashes?
Would you call this a fast,
And an acceptable day to the LORD?

6 "*Is* this not the fast that I have chosen:
To loose the bonds of wickedness,
To undo the heavy burdens,
To let the oppressed go free,
And that you break every yoke?

TIME CAPSULE   *404 to 386 B.C.*

404–359	*Artaxerxes II becomes king of Persia, defeating his younger brother Cyrus*
401	*Chariots with sickles on the wheels used at Cunaxa*
400	*Invention of the screw*
398	*Possible date for Ezra's arrival in Jerusalem*
390	*Rome is sacked by the Gauls*
386	*Artaxerxes claims all Greek cities in the Peace of Antalkidas*

TOUGH TIMES IN JERUSALEM (Is. 58:10)

In Is. 58:1-14 the prophet most likely describes the situation in Jerusalem soon after the exiles returned home. Life was hard upon their return. Not only did the community have to reclaim the land for farming and reconstruct the city, they had to rebuild all their economic institutions from the ground up.

The prophet criticized the Judean leaders for the way religious devotion had become a substitute for ethical behavior. These people exhibited an active piety in beseeching God's blessing on their new endeavor to pick up the pieces in Jerusalem. One cannot fault their religious sincerity. They were daily in prayer (Is. 58:2) and pursued an active program of fasting (58:3). They obeyed the proper guidelines—the "ordinances of justice" (58:2)—for their religious behavior.

Yet God was not impressed. No matter how properly "religious" their behavior was, it did not address the real need of the community: the need to share the scarce resources that were available to the returnees. The leaders possessed what little wealth had awaited the exiles when they returned to Jerusalem.

The situation in Jerusalem after the Exile showed a huge gap between the "haves" and the "have-nots." Jerusalem had its share of the hungry, the homeless, and those who lacked adequate clothing (58:7). These people were a part of the exilic community; they were from the Judean leaders' "own flesh" (58:7). Nevertheless, the "haves" did not see the necessity of relating their religious devotion to their social and economic practice.

God thought that they should. The prophetic oracle promised the full restoration of Jerusalem (58:12), but only if the "haves" would extend themselves to those hungry and afflicted (58:10).

---

7 *Is it* not to share your bread with the hungry,
And that you bring to your house the poor who are cast out;
When you see the naked, that you cover him,
And not hide yourself from your own flesh?

8 Then your light shall break forth like the morning,
Your healing shall spring forth speedily,
And your righteousness shall go before you;
The glory of the LORD shall be your rear guard.

9 Then you shall call, and the LORD will answer;
You shall cry, and He will say, 'Here I am.'

"If you take away the yoke from your midst,
The pointing of the finger, and speaking wickedness,

10 *If* you extend your soul to the hungry
And satisfy the afflicted soul,
Then your light shall dawn in the darkness,

And your darkness shall *be* as the noonday.

11 The LORD will guide you continually,
And satisfy your soul in drought,
And strengthen your bones;
You shall be like a watered garden,
And like a spring of water, whose waters do not fail.

12 Those from among you
Shall build the old waste places;
You shall raise up the foundations of many generations;
And you shall be called the Repairer of the Breach,
The Restorer of Streets to Dwell In.

13 "If you turn away your foot from the Sabbath,
From doing your pleasure on My holy day,
And call the Sabbath a delight,
The holy *day* of the LORD honorable,
And shall honor Him, not doing your own ways,
Nor finding your own pleasure,
Nor speaking *your own* words,

14 Then you shall delight yourself in the LORD;

A Mound of Ruins (Is. 58:12)

Since rainfall occurs only during the winter months in Canaan, cities there needed to be built near perennial springs. For defensive purposes cities also needed to be built on higher ground. Thus in ancient times cities were built on the hills closest to a perennial water source.

Because Canaan was on the major path of Egyptians going toward Asia and of Asians going toward Egypt, the cities and towns of Canaan were regularly destroyed by invaders. In addition, Canaan regularly suffered from the effects of earthquakes and other natural disasters. Once destroyed, ancient cities were most often just rebuilt on top of the ruins of the old cities. The old city was already in the most defensible location closest to the water, so the city inhabitants just rebuilt on the same spot.

During the rebuilding process, some stones could be easily reused and were. Others were just allowed to become part of the foundation. Mud bricks, a common building material, were often displaced and, thus, became unusable. After a time, the original small hills grew into large mounds, many of which can still be seen today. Some of these hills, called "tells," are made up of 20 and more cities that were built, destroyed, and rebuilt.

The prophet described this process by noting that some powers that were then strong would become a "ruinous heap" (Is. 17:1) and some of them would never again be rebuilt (Is. 25:2). Yet there was a message of hope for Judah: certain Judeans would return to Judah's ruined cities and rebuild "the old waste places" with new foundations (Is. 58:12).

And I will cause you to ride on the
    high hills of the earth,
And feed you with the heritage of
    Jacob your father.
The mouth of the LORD has spoken."

Separated from God

59 ¹ Behold, the LORD's hand is not
    shortened,
That it cannot save;
Nor His ear heavy,
That it cannot hear.

2 But your iniquities have separated
    you from your God;
And your sins have hidden *His* face
    from you,
So that He will not hear.

3 For your hands are defiled with blood,
And your fingers with iniquity;
Your lips have spoken lies,
Your tongue has muttered perversity.

4 No one calls for justice,
Nor does *any* plead for truth.
They trust in empty words and speak
    lies;
They conceive evil and bring forth
    iniquity.

5 They hatch vipers' eggs and weave the
    spider's web;
He who eats of their eggs dies,
And *from* that which is crushed a
    viper breaks out.

6 Their webs will not become garments,
Nor will they cover themselves with
    their works;
Their works *are* works of iniquity,
And the act of violence *is* in their
    hands.

7 Their feet run to evil,
And they make haste to shed innocent
    blood;
Their thoughts *are* thoughts of
    iniquity;
Wasting and destruction *are* in their
    paths.

8 The way of peace they have not
    known,
And *there is* no justice in their ways;
They have made themselves crooked
    paths;
Whoever takes that way shall not
    know peace.

Sin Confessed

9 Therefore justice is far from us,
Nor does righteousness overtake us;
We look for light, but there is
    darkness!
For brightness, *but* we walk in
    blackness!

10 We grope for the wall like the blind,
And we grope as if *we had* no eyes;
We stumble at noonday as at twilight;
We are as dead *men* in desolate places.

11 We all growl like bears,
And moan sadly like doves;
We look for justice, but *there is* none;
For salvation, *but* it is far from us.
12 For our transgressions are multiplied
before You,
And our sins testify against us;
For our transgressions *are* with us,
And *as for* our iniquities, we know
them:
13 In transgressing and lying against the
LORD,
And departing from our God,
Speaking oppression and revolt,
Conceiving and uttering from the
heart words of falsehood.
14 Justice is turned back,
And righteousness stands afar off;
For truth is fallen in the street,
And equity cannot enter.
15 So truth fails,
And he *who* departs from evil makes
himself a prey.

The Redeemer of Zion

Then the LORD saw *it,* and it
displeased Him
That *there was* no justice.
16 He saw that *there was* no man,
And wondered that *there was* no
intercessor;
Therefore His own arm brought
salvation for Him;
And His own righteousness, it
sustained Him.
17 For He put on righteousness as a
breastplate,
And a helmet of salvation on His head;
He put on the garments of vengeance
for clothing,
And was clad with zeal as a cloak.
18 According to *their* deeds, accordingly
He will repay,
Fury to His adversaries,
Recompense to His enemies;
The coastlands He will fully repay.
19 So shall they fear
The name of the LORD from the west,
And His glory from the rising of the
sun;
When the enemy comes in like a flood,
The Spirit of the LORD will lift up a
standard against him.

20 "The Redeemer will come to Zion,
And to those who turn from
transgression in Jacob,"
Says the LORD.

21 "As for Me," says the LORD, "this *is*
My covenant with them: My Spirit who *is*
upon you, and My words which I have put
in your mouth, shall not depart from your
mouth, nor from the mouth of your descendants, nor from the mouth of your descendants' descendants," says the LORD, "from
this time and forevermore."

God's Glory upon God's City

The oracles of the first section of the
Book of Isaiah (chs. 1—39) speak predominantly of sin and judgment. By contrast, the
prophecies of Is. 40—55 proclaim only salvation and joy (see "Isaiah and Cyrus the Persian"
at Is. 40:1). The final section of the Book of
Isaiah (chs. 56—66) contains both words of
judgment (such as Is. 59) and words of salvation (such as Is. 60—62). The oracles of hope
in Is. 60—62 are of surpassing power, though,
and easily overpower the prophet's condemnations.

The hopeful tone begins at Is. 60:1 with
the announcement: "Arise, shine; For your
light has come!" The darkness of Jerusalem's
broken walls and temple would be replaced
with light and brightness as God's glory rose
upon the city. Israel would be nurtured rather
than oppressed by the mighty nations (Is.
60:10–12).

God's plan for Jerusalem included an un-
fading glory that is actually God's presence.
God would glorify Mount Zion and His people
with His glory (60:19). This theme emerges
from the three poems of chs. 60—62. While
ch. 60 emphasizes the brilliance of God's city,
ch. 61 announces glory in the form of justice
to the poor (61:8), and ch. 62 reveals God's
purpose for Jerusalem: the city would demonstrate His righteousness to all the earth
(62:1, 2, 7, 11, 12).

■ Isaiah 60:1—66:24

Isaiah
The Gentiles Bless Zion

60 :1 Arise, shine;
For your light has come!
And the glory of the LORD is risen
upon you.
2 For behold, the darkness shall cover
the earth,
And deep darkness the people;
But the LORD will arise over you,
And His glory will be seen upon you.

JERUSALEM, THE FUTURE WORLD CENTER (Is. 60:14)

In Is. 60 is a vision of a new Jerusalem which would become the world imperial center. All the nations would converge upon Jerusalem, bringing their wealth as tribute to the city's king, the Lord God (Is. 60:4–7).

Very similar imagery is found in pictures in the ceremonial hall in Persepolis, the capital of the Persian Empire. On the stairway that leads up to the throne of the Persian king, who was considered the "King of Kings," stand carvings of other kings in various ethnic dress. Each king bears a valuable, unique gift from his own country to offer to the Great King.

The Great King is not directly represented in the pictures—he is there in concept. Yet in the center, accompanying the king, is an image of the Persian god, Ahura Mazda. Ahura Mazda was represented by a winged sun, indicating his rule of light over "all the earth" to fight back the forces of darkness. The Great King, therefore, was considered to be Ahura Mazda's representative.

The prophet uses very similar imagery to articulate God's promise to Jerusalem. The city's gates will be "open continually," allowing kings to approach "in procession," bringing "the wealth of the Gentiles" (60:11). Jerusalem, not Persepolis, will be the imperial center of the world.

Furthermore, the prophet depicts God in solar imagery similar to that found at Persepolis. Yet this imagery represents, not Ahura Mazda, the Persian god, but Yahweh, the God of Israel at the center of the city. Yahweh, not Ahura Mazda, will rule in Jerusalem. Yahweh, not Ahura Mazda, will be "an everlasting light" (60:19).

These prophecies offered great hope for the returnees, a hope reechoed for all people in the Book of Revelation (Rev. 21:23). Though a "deep darkness" may cover the earth, Yahweh will arise over Jerusalem as a sunrise, and His glory will attract peoples from afar (Is. 60:1–3).

---

3   The Gentiles shall come to your light,
     And kings to the brightness of your
         rising.

4   "Lift up your eyes all around, and see:
     They all gather together, they come to
         you;
     Your sons shall come from afar,
     And your daughters shall be nursed at
         your side.

5   Then you shall see and become
         radiant,
     And your heart shall swell with joy;
     Because the abundance of the sea
         shall be turned to you,
     The wealth of the Gentiles shall come
         to you.

6   The multitude of camels shall cover
         your *land,*

     The dromedaries of Midian and
         Ephah;
     All those from Sheba shall come;
     They shall bring gold and incense,
     And they shall proclaim the praises of
         the LORD.

7   All the flocks of Kedar shall be
         gathered together to you,
     The rams of Nebaioth shall minister
         to you;
     They shall ascend with acceptance on
         My altar,
     And I will glorify the house of My
         glory.

8   "Who *are* these *who* fly like a cloud,
     And like doves to their roosts?

9   Surely the coastlands shall wait for
         Me;

ARTS AND LITERATURE

The Greek poet Hesiod lists the four ages of man as gold, silver, bronze, and iron. A similar list of materials in decreasing order of value is found in Dan. 2:32, and with some variation in Is. 60:17. The metals are listed in order of their prestige and rarity. In the New Testament, Paul uses a similar figure in 1 Cor. 3:12.

And the ships of Tarshish *will come* first,
To bring your sons from afar,
Their silver and their gold with them,
To the name of the LORD your God,
And to the Holy One of Israel,
Because He has glorified you.

10 "The sons of foreigners shall build up your walls,
And their kings shall minister to you;
For in My wrath I struck you,
But in My favor I have had mercy on you.

11 Therefore your gates shall be open continually;
They shall not be shut day or night,
That *men* may bring to you the wealth of the Gentiles,
And their kings in procession.

12 For the nation and kingdom which will not serve you shall perish,
And *those* nations shall be utterly ruined.

13 "The glory of Lebanon shall come to you,
The cypress, the pine, and the box tree together,
To beautify the place of My sanctuary;
And I will make the place of My feet glorious.

14 Also the sons of those who afflicted you
Shall come bowing to you,
And all those who despised you shall fall prostrate at the soles of your feet;
And they shall call you The City of the LORD,
Zion of the Holy One of Israel.

15 "Whereas you have been forsaken and hated,
So that no one went through *you,*
I will make you an eternal excellence,
A joy of many generations.

16 You shall drink the milk of the Gentiles,
And milk the breast of kings;
You shall know that I, the LORD, *am* your Savior
And your Redeemer, the Mighty One of Jacob.

17 "Instead of bronze I will bring gold,
Instead of iron I will bring silver,
Instead of wood, bronze,

And instead of stones, iron.
I will also make your officers peace,
And your magistrates righteousness.

18 Violence shall no longer be heard in your land,
Neither wasting nor destruction within your borders;
But you shall call your walls Salvation,
And your gates Praise.

God the Glory of His People

19 "The sun shall no longer be your light by day,
Nor for brightness shall the moon give light to you;
But the LORD will be to you an everlasting light,
And your God your glory.

20 Your sun shall no longer go down,
Nor shall your moon withdraw itself;
For the LORD will be your everlasting light,
And the days of your mourning shall be ended.

21 Also your people *shall* all *be* righteous;
They shall inherit the land forever,
The branch of My planting,
The work of My hands,
That I may be glorified.

22 A little one shall become a thousand,
And a small one a strong nation.
I, the LORD, will hasten it in its time."

The Good News of Salvation

61 1 "The Spirit of the Lord GOD *is* upon Me,
Because the LORD has anointed Me
To preach good tidings to the poor;
He has sent Me to heal the brokenhearted,
To proclaim liberty to the captives,
And the opening of the prison to *those who are* bound;

2 To proclaim the acceptable year of the LORD,
And the day of vengeance of our God;
To comfort all who mourn,

3 To console those who mourn in Zion,
To give them beauty for ashes,
The oil of joy for mourning,
The garment of praise for the spirit of heaviness;
That they may be called trees of righteousness,
The planting of the LORD, that He may be glorified."

4 And they shall rebuild the old ruins,
They shall raise up the former
  desolations,
And they shall repair the ruined
  cities,
The desolations of many generations.

5 Strangers shall stand and feed your
  flocks,
And the sons of the foreigner
Shall be your plowmen and your
  vinedressers.

6 But you shall be named the priests of
  the LORD,
They shall call you the servants of our
  God.
You shall eat the riches of the
  Gentiles,
And in their glory you shall boast.

7 Instead of your shame *you shall have*
  double *honor,*
And *instead of* confusion they shall
  rejoice in their portion.
Therefore in their land they shall
  possess double;
Everlasting joy shall be theirs.

8 "For I, the LORD, love justice;
I hate robbery for burnt offering;
I will direct their work in truth,
And will make with them an
  everlasting covenant.

9 Their descendants shall be known
  among the Gentiles,
And their offspring among the people.
All who see them shall acknowledge
  them,
That they *are* the posterity *whom* the
  LORD has blessed."

10 I will greatly rejoice in the LORD,
My soul shall be joyful in my God;
For He has clothed me with the
  garments of salvation,
He has covered me with the robe of
  righteousness,
As a bridegroom decks *himself* with
  ornaments,
And as a bride adorns *herself* with her
  jewels.

11 For as the earth brings forth its bud,
As the garden causes the things that
  are sown in it to spring forth,
So the Lord GOD will cause
  righteousness and praise to spring
  forth before all the nations.

Assurance of Zion's Salvation

62 ¹ For Zion's sake I will not hold
      My peace,
And for Jerusalem's sake I will not
  rest,
Until her righteousness goes forth as
  brightness,
And her salvation as a lamp *that*
  burns.

2 The Gentiles shall see your
  righteousness,
And all kings your glory.
You shall be called by a new name,
Which the mouth of the LORD will
  name.

3 You shall also be a crown of glory
In the hand of the LORD,
And a royal diadem
In the hand of your God.

4 You shall no longer be termed
  Forsaken,
Nor shall your land any more be
  termed Desolate;
But you shall be called Hephzibah,[a]
  and your land Beulah;[b]
For the LORD delights in you,
And your land shall be married.

5 For *as* a young man marries a virgin,
So shall your sons marry you;
And *as* the bridegroom rejoices over
  the bride,
So shall your God rejoice over you.

6 I have set watchmen on your walls,
  O Jerusalem;
They shall never hold their peace day
  or night.
You who make mention of the LORD,
  do not keep silent,

7 And give Him no rest till He
  establishes
And till He makes Jerusalem a praise
  in the earth.

62:4 [a]Literally *My Delight Is in Her*   [b]Literally
Married

TIME CAPSULE   *384 to 356 B.C.*

384– 322	*Aristotle, Greek philosopher*
360	*The Great Revolt of the Satraps (against Persia)*
359– 336	*Philip II becomes king of Macedon*
359– 338	*Artaxerxes III is poisoned by Bagoas*
356	*Alexander the Great is born to Philip II of Macedon*

NO LONGER FORSAKEN (Is. 62:4, 12)

The prophet had encouraging news for the people of Jerusalem. The difficulties of the present time in Jerusalem would not compare with the glories to come in the new, restored Jerusalem of the future.

The years Jerusalem spent under foreign rulers had taken their toll. Things must have been hard, for we learn that Jerusalem was nicknamed "Forsaken" and its surrounding land, "Desolate" (Is. 62:4). High rates of Persian taxation contributed to Jerusalem's economic troubles.

In the Persian Empire taxation was done, not by the exchange of money, but in agricultural produce. Though the Judeans had worked hard to grow their produce, much of the crop went to support the Persian king, his court, and his armies. In other words, Judean grain became food for Judah's enemies, and foreigners drank her wine (Is. 62:8). Economic resources were taken out of the community, rather than used within it to spur the local economy.

God promised to change this situation. In the future Jerusalem, those who gather their crops will also eat of them; those who produce wine will also drink of it (62:9). Then Jerusalem's name will no longer be "Forsaken," but rather "A City Not Forsaken" (62:12).

---

8   The LORD has sworn by His right
     hand
     And by the arm of His strength:
     "Surely I will no longer give your
       grain
     As food for your enemies;
     And the sons of the foreigner shall not
       drink your new wine,
     For which you have labored.
9   But those who have gathered it shall
       eat it,
     And praise the LORD;
     Those who have brought it together
       shall drink it in My holy courts."

10   Go through,
     Go through the gates!
     Prepare the way for the people;
     Build up,
     Build up the highway!
     Take out the stones,
     Lift up a banner for the peoples!

11   Indeed the LORD has proclaimed
     To the end of the world:
     "Say to the daughter of Zion,
     'Surely your salvation is coming;
     Behold, His reward *is* with Him,
     And His work before Him.' "
12   And they shall call them The Holy
       People,
     The Redeemed of the LORD;
     And you shall be called Sought Out,
     A City Not Forsaken.

The LORD in Judgment and Salvation

63   1   Who *is* this who comes from
       Edom,
     With dyed garments from Bozrah,
     This *One who is* glorious in His
       apparel,
     Traveling in the greatness of His
       strength?—

     "I who speak in righteousness, mighty
       to save."

2   Why *is* Your apparel red,
     And Your garments like one who
       treads in the winepress?

3   "I have trodden the winepress alone,
     And from the peoples no one *was* with
       Me.
     For I have trodden them in My anger,
     And trampled them in My fury;
     Their blood is sprinkled upon My
       garments,
     And I have stained all My robes.
4   For the day of vengeance *is* in My
       heart,
     And the year of My redeemed has
       come.
5   I looked, but *there was* no one to help,
     And I wondered
     That *there was* no one to uphold;
     Therefore My own arm brought
       salvation for Me;
     And My own fury, it sustained Me.

6 I have trodden down the peoples in
    My anger,
  Made them drunk in My fury,
  And brought down their strength to
    the earth."

God's Mercy Remembered

7 I will mention the lovingkindnesses of
    the LORD
  And the praises of the LORD,
  According to all that the LORD has
    bestowed on us,
  And the great goodness toward the
    house of Israel,
  Which He has bestowed on them
    according to His mercies,
  According to the multitude of His
    lovingkindnesses.
8 For He said, "Surely they *are* My
    people,
  Children *who* will not lie."
  So He became their Savior.
9 In all their affliction He was afflicted,
  And the Angel of His Presence saved
    them;
  In His love and in His pity He
    redeemed them;
  And He bore them and carried them
  All the days of old.
10 But they rebelled and grieved His
    Holy Spirit;
  So He turned Himself against them as
    an enemy,
  And He fought against them.

11 Then he remembered the days of old,
  Moses *and* his people, *saying:*
  "Where *is* He who brought them up out
    of the sea
  With the shepherd of His flock?
  Where *is* He who put His Holy Spirit
    within them,
12 Who led *them* by the right hand of
    Moses,
  With His glorious arm,
  Dividing the water before them
  To make for Himself an everlasting
    name,
13 Who led them through the deep,
  As a horse in the wilderness,
  That they might not stumble?"

14 As a beast goes down into the valley,
  And the Spirit of the LORD causes him
    to rest,
  So You lead Your people,
  To make Yourself a glorious name.

A Prayer of Penitence

15 Look down from heaven,
  And see from Your habitation, holy
    and glorious.
  Where *are* Your zeal and Your
    strength,
  The yearning of Your heart and Your
    mercies toward me?
  Are they restrained?
16 Doubtless You *are* our Father,
  Though Abraham was ignorant of us,
  And Israel does not acknowledge us.
  You, O LORD, *are* our Father;
  Our Redeemer from Everlasting *is*
    Your name.
17 O LORD, why have You made us stray
    from Your ways,
  And hardened our heart from Your
    fear?
  Return for Your servants' sake,
  The tribes of Your inheritance.
18 Your holy people have possessed *it* but
    a little while;
  Our adversaries have trodden down
    Your sanctuary.
19 We have become *like* those of old, over
    whom You never ruled,
  Those who were never called by Your
    name.

64 1 Oh, that You would rend the
      heavens!
  That You would come down!
  That the mountains might shake at
    Your presence—
2 As fire burns brushwood,
  As fire causes water to boil—
  To make Your name known to Your
    adversaries,
  That the nations may tremble at Your
    presence!
3 When You did awesome things *for
    which* we did not look,
  You came down,
  The mountains shook at Your
    presence.
4 For since the beginning of the world
  Men have not heard nor perceived by
    the ear,
  Nor has the eye seen any God besides
    You,
  Who acts for the one who waits for
    Him.
5 You meet him who rejoices and does
    righteousness,
  Who remembers You in Your ways.
  You are indeed angry, for we have
    sinned—

A PETITION TO OUR FATHER IN HEAVEN (Is. 64:8–12)

The exiles faced a sorry state of affairs in Jerusalem immediately following their return from Babylon. The city of Jerusalem and its temple were still in ruins (Is. 64:10, 11). The Babylonians had laid siege to the city for 18 months, eventually destroying it in 586 B.C. (2 Kin. 25:1, 2). What was left were ashes, arrowheads, and fallen buildings. In fact, the whole region, the "holy cities" (Is. 64:10), was laid waste. Apparently, both Jerusalem and Judah were mostly uninhabited during the time between 586 and 538 B.C.

The prophet, as a representative of the whole community, turned to God for aid. He called upon the Lord as "Father," invoking the special relationship between Israel and her God (64:8). The term "Father" should not be understood according to our modern conceptions of fatherhood. "Father" was not so much a term of endearment, as it was a word of authority and ownership. Under Israelite law a man's children were legally his property, over which he exercised much power.

The community was helpless before God as "Father" like clay in the hands of a potter (64:8). The prophet interceded for the people for forgiveness so that God's faithfulness might be revealed again in a restored Jerusalem.

In these ways we continue;
And we need to be saved.

6 But we are all like an unclean *thing,*
And all our righteousnesses *are* like
    filthy rags;
We all fade as a leaf,
And our iniquities, like the wind,
Have taken us away.
7 And *there is* no one who calls on Your
    name,
Who stirs himself up to take hold of
    You;
For You have hidden Your face from
    us,
And have consumed us because of our
    iniquities.

8 But now, O LORD,
You *are* our Father;
We *are* the clay, and You our potter;
And all we *are* the work of Your hand.
9 Do not be furious, O LORD,
Nor remember iniquity forever;
Indeed, please look—we all *are* Your
    people!
10 Your holy cities are a wilderness,
Zion is a wilderness,
Jerusalem a desolation.
11 Our holy and beautiful temple,
Where our fathers praised You,
Is burned up with fire;
And all our pleasant things are laid
    waste.
12 Will You restrain Yourself because of
    these *things,* O LORD?

Will You hold Your peace, and afflict
    us very severely?

The Righteousness of God's Judgment

65 1 "I was sought by *those who* did
        not ask *for Me;*
I was found by *those who* did not seek
    Me.
I said, 'Here I am, here I am,'
To a nation *that* was not called by My
    name.
2 I have stretched out My hands all day
    long to a rebellious people,
Who walk in a way *that is* not good,
According to their own thoughts;
3 A people who provoke Me to anger
    continually to My face;
Who sacrifice in gardens,
And burn incense on altars of brick;
4 Who sit among the graves,
And spend the night in the tombs;
Who eat swine's flesh,
And the broth of abominable things is
    in their vessels;
5 Who say, 'Keep to yourself,
Do not come near me,
For I am holier than you!'
These *are* smoke in My nostrils,
A fire that burns all the day.

6 "Behold, *it is* written before Me:
I will not keep silence, but will
    repay—
Even repay into their bosom—
7 Your iniquities and the iniquities of
    your fathers together,"

FEEDING THE GODS OF FORTUNE (Is. 65:11)

It was a common practice throughout the ancient world to set out fine feasts for the gods. In the large temple complexes of Mesopotamia and Egypt the statues of the deities were served with regular meals daily by the priests. Other offerings of food were brought by devotees as gifts, along with their petitions for help from the gods.

The prophet accused a group of Judeans of ignoring God and turning their attention to other deities. Rather than the old Canaanite gods and goddesses, however, the Judeans worshiped Gad and Meni. Apparently, these gods were honored with the practice of serving meals, since the prophet charges the worshipers with providing "a table" and "drink offering" for the deities (Is. 65:11).

Gad, whose name means literally "fortune," was a god of luck or fortune. This deity is mentioned in a number of inscriptions which have been recovered from Jordan to Spain, covering a period from 300 to 180 B.C. Meni, whose name means literally "destiny," appears to be a god of fortune. Although Meni was a male deity, he was possibly related to the Arabian goddess Manât. The Koran identifies Manât as one of the deities worshiped by the pre-Islamic Arabs. Perhaps given the struggles of rebuilding Jerusalem, the returned exiles thought that "Fortune" and "Destiny" might assist them in their building project.

Deities of fortune, like the Greek god Tyche, could bring either good or bad fortunes. Worshipers assumed that these deities could wreak havoc on a person's life should they take a dislike to an individual. The meal and drink were intended to gain the favor of these gods so that they would direct the worshipers' destinies toward a good life. The prophet condemns the Judeans for assuming that these gods could affect life, and thus rejecting God as the sole power in the world.

Says the LORD,
"Who have burned incense on the
  mountains
And blasphemed Me on the hills;
Therefore I will measure their former
  work into their bosom."

⁸Thus says the LORD:

"As the new wine is found in the
  cluster,
And *one* says, 'Do not destroy it,
For a blessing *is* in it,'
So will I do for My servants' sake,
That I may not destroy them all.
9   I will bring forth descendants from
      Jacob,
And from Judah an heir of My
  mountains;
My elect shall inherit it,
And My servants shall dwell there.

10   Sharon shall be a fold of flocks,
And the Valley of Achor a place for
  herds to lie down,
For My people who have sought Me.

11   "But you *are* those who forsake the
      LORD,
Who forget My holy mountain,
Who prepare a table for Gad,ᵃ
And who furnish a drink offering for
  Meni.ᵇ
12   Therefore I will number you for the
      sword,
And you shall all bow down to the
  slaughter;
Because, when I called, you did not
  answer;
When I spoke, you did not hear,

65:11 ᵃLiterally *Troop* or *Fortune*, a pagan deity
ᵇLiterally *Number* or *Destiny*, a pagan deity

FOOD AND DRINK

The products of the vineyard were extremely important in ancient times. Wine was put up in large clay jars and shipped all over the Mediterranean. The cultivation of grapes was a well-developed skill. Ancient writers described how to plant, prune, and tend grapevines. This occupation required time and patience, flourishing only in times of peace (Is. 65:21).

But did evil before My eyes,
And chose *that* in which I do not
delight."

13Therefore thus says the Lord GOD:

"Behold, My servants shall eat,
But you shall be hungry;
Behold, My servants shall drink,
But you shall be thirsty;
Behold, My servants shall rejoice,
But you shall be ashamed;
14 Behold, My servants shall sing for joy
of heart,
But you shall cry for sorrow of heart,
And wail for grief of spirit.
15 You shall leave your name as a curse
to My chosen;
For the Lord GOD will slay you,
And call His servants by another
name;
16 So that he who blesses himself in the
earth
Shall bless himself in the God of
truth;
And he who swears in the earth
Shall swear by the God of truth;
Because the former troubles are
forgotten,
And because they are hidden from My
eyes.

The Glorious New Creation

17 "For behold, I create new heavens and
a new earth;
And the former shall not be
remembered or come to mind.
18 But be glad and rejoice forever in
what I create;
For behold, I create Jerusalem *as* a
rejoicing,
And her people a joy.
19 I will rejoice in Jerusalem,
And joy in My people;
The voice of weeping shall no longer
be heard in her,
Nor the voice of crying.

20 "No more shall an infant from there
live but a few days,
Nor an old man who has not fulfilled
his days;
For the child shall die one hundred
years old,
But the sinner *being* one hundred
years old shall be accursed.
21 They shall build houses and inhabit
them;

They shall plant vineyards and eat
their fruit.
22 They shall not build and another
inhabit;
They shall not plant and another eat;
For as the days of a tree, *so shall be*
the days of My people,
And My elect shall long enjoy the
work of their hands.
23 They shall not labor in vain,
Nor bring forth children for trouble;
For they *shall be* the descendants of
the blessed of the LORD,
And their offspring with them.

24 "It shall come to pass
That before they call, I will answer;
And while they are still speaking, I
will hear.
25 The wolf and the lamb shall feed
together,
The lion shall eat straw like the ox,
And dust *shall be* the serpent's food.
They shall not hurt nor destroy in all
My holy mountain,"
Says the LORD.

True Worship and False

66 1Thus says the LORD:

"Heaven *is* My throne,
And earth *is* My footstool.
Where *is* the house that you will build
Me?
And where *is* the place of My rest?
2 For all those *things* My hand has
made,
And all those *things* exist,"
Says the LORD.
"But on this *one* will I look:

TIME CAPSULE *351 to 336 B.C.*

351–350	Persia suffers defeat by Egypt
343	Persian army regains domination of Egypt
338–336	Arses, son of Artaxerxes III, is poisoned by Bagoas
338	The Macedonians defeat Athens and Thebes
338	Philip II founds the Corinthian League to liberate Greek cities
336	Assassination of Alexander's father

On *him who is* poor and of a contrite
spirit,
And who trembles at My word.

3 "He who kills a bull *is as if* he slays a
man;
He who sacrifices a lamb, *as if* he
breaks a dog's neck;
He who offers a grain offering, *as if he
offers* swine's blood;
He who burns incense, *as if* he blesses
an idol.
Just as they have chosen their own
ways,
And their soul delights in their
abominations,
4 So will I choose their delusions,
And bring their fears on them;
Because, when I called, no one
answered,
When I spoke they did not hear;
But they did evil before My eyes,
And chose *that* in which I do not
delight."

The LORD Vindicates Zion

5 Hear the word of the LORD,
You who tremble at His word:
"Your brethren who hated you,
Who cast you out for My name's sake,
said,
'Let the LORD be glorified,
That we may see your joy.'
But they shall be ashamed."

6 The sound of noise from the city!
A voice from the temple!
The voice of the LORD,
Who fully repays His enemies!

7 "Before she was in labor, she gave
birth;
Before her pain came,
She delivered a male child.
8 Who has heard such a thing?
Who has seen such things?
Shall the earth be made to give birth
in one day?
Or shall a nation be born at once?
For as soon as Zion was in labor,
She gave birth to her children.
9 Shall I bring to the time of birth, and
not cause delivery?" says the LORD.
"Shall I who cause delivery shut up *the
womb?*" says your God.
10 "Rejoice with Jerusalem,
And be glad with her, all you who love
her;

Rejoice for joy with her, all you who
mourn for her;
11 That you may feed and be satisfied
With the consolation of her bosom,
That you may drink deeply and be
delighted
With the abundance of her glory."

12For thus says the LORD:

"Behold, I will extend peace to her like
a river,
And the glory of the Gentiles like a
flowing stream.
Then you shall feed;
On *her* sides shall you be carried,
And be dandled on *her* knees.
13 As one whom his mother comforts,
So I will comfort you;
And you shall be comforted in
Jerusalem."

The Reign and Indignation of God

14 When you see *this,* your heart shall
rejoice,
And your bones shall flourish like
grass;
The hand of the LORD shall be known
to His servants,
And *His* indignation to His enemies.
15 For behold, the LORD will come with
fire
And with His chariots, like a
whirlwind,
To render His anger with fury,
And His rebuke with flames of fire.
16 For by fire and by His sword
The LORD will judge all flesh;
And the slain of the LORD shall be
many.

17 "Those who sanctify themselves and
purify themselves,
To go to the gardens
After an *idol* in the midst,
Eating swine's flesh and the
abomination and the mouse,
Shall be consumed together," says the
LORD.

18"For I *know* their works and their
thoughts. It shall be that I will gather all
nations and tongues; and they shall come
and see My glory. 19I will set a sign among
them; and those among them who escape I
will send to the nations: *to* Tarshish and

Pul[a] and Lud, who draw the bow, and Tubal and Javan, *to* the coastlands afar off who have not heard My fame nor seen My glory. And they shall declare My glory among the Gentiles. [20]Then they shall bring all your brethren for an offering to the LORD out of all nations, on horses and in chariots and in litters, on mules and on camels, to My holy mountain Jerusalem," says the LORD, "as the children of Israel bring an offering in a clean vessel into the house of the LORD. [21]And I will also take some of them for priests *and* Levites," says the LORD.

22 "For as the new heavens and the new earth
      Which I will make shall remain before Me," says the LORD,
    "So shall your descendants and your name remain.
23 And it shall come to pass
      That from one New Moon to another,
    And from one Sabbath to another,
    All flesh shall come to worship before Me," says the LORD.

24 "And they shall go forth and look
    Upon the corpses of the men
    Who have transgressed against Me.
    For their worm does not die,
    And their fire is not quenched.
    They shall be an abhorrence to all flesh."

66:19 [a]Following Masoretic Text and Targum; Septuagint reads *Put* (compare Jeremiah 46:9).
Zech. 9:1 [a]Or *oracle*

The Apocalyptic Visions of Zechariah

The prophet Zechariah prophesied during the reign of Darius I (522–486 B.C.). Along with his fellow prophet Haggai, he inspired the newly returned exiles in Jerusalem to finish rebuilding the temple (Zech. 1:1; Ezra 5:1; see "The Book of Zechariah" at Zech. 1:1). The oracles of Zech. 1—8 are filled with symbolic vision reports, but they are still very specific. Such restoration leaders as Zerubbabel and Jeshua (or Joshua) the high priest are mentioned by name (Zech. 3:1; 4:6–10).

At ch. 9, though, the Book of Zechariah changes. Symbolic visions are no longer interpreted by a helpful angelic guide, as were the visions in the first half of the book. Indeed, the prophecies of Zech. 9—14 are among the most difficult to place in historical context. Some scholars place them in Darius's reign, along with the first half of the book, while others date them much later in the Persian period, or even after the Persian Empire had been replaced by the Greek Empire of Alexander the Great (see "The Greek Empire" at Dan. 7:1).

Reading Zech. 9—14 in the Greek era is suggested by the mention of Greece (Zech. 9:13), and by the list of conquered cities (9:1–8), which supposedly follow the path of Alexander the Great's conquest of Palestine in 332 B.C. The destruction of Tyre (9:2–4) is particularly telling, since Alexander was the only conqueror of the ancient world who succeeded in capturing that island fortress. Still, a list of cities and one mention of Greece does not mean that these chapters were written after Alexander. Greece had been an important international player at least since the Greek alliance defeated Darius I at Marathon in 490 B.C.

The prophecies of Zech. 9—14 do not appear to be speaking of the same historical context as Zech. 1—8. What time they do speak of, however, is uncertain. It was a time when the Persian province of Judah was under bad leadership (10:2, 3), faced economic oppression and distress (11:5), and had turned to idolatry (13:1, 2). Such conditions could have existed either before the arrival of Nehemiah as governor in 445 B.C. or sometime after his tenure had ended.

■ Zechariah 9:1—10:12

Zechariah
Israel Defended Against Enemies

9 :1 The burden[a] of the word of the LORD
    Against the land of Hadrach,
    And Damascus its resting place
    (For the eyes of men
    And all the tribes of Israel
    Are on the LORD);
2 Also *against* Hamath, *which* borders on it,
    And *against* Tyre and Sidon, though they are very wise.

3 For Tyre built herself a tower,
    Heaped up silver like the dust,
    And gold like the mire of the streets.
4 Behold, the LORD will cast her out;
    He will destroy her power in the sea,
    And she will be devoured by fire.

ALEXANDER'S SIEGE OF TYRE (Zech. 9:3, 4)

Tyre's fortunes changed through a dramatic event at the end of the Persian period (559–331 B.C.). The city had furnished troops, ships, and a seemingly impregnable port for Persian naval encounters in the Mediterranean during two centuries. The prophet Zechariah describes Tyre's demise with a prophecy often related to this time period. God would destroy Tyre's "power in the sea" (Zech. 9:3, 4).

Alexander the Great was the first to completely subdue Tyre. His Greco-Macedonian armies laid siege to the island in 332 B.C., successfully storming the city after 7 months. The campaign required the building of a massive causeway, 300 yards wide and about half a mile long, extending from the mainland to the island, using the remains of destroyed buildings. Reputedly, over 30,000 citizens of Tyre were sold into slavery, and 2,000 of that city-state's leaders were crucified. Tyre never again reached the economic and political prominence it had enjoyed in previous centuries.

5   Ashkelon shall see *it* and fear;
    Gaza also shall be very sorrowful;
    And Ekron, for He dried up her
        expectation.
    The king shall perish from Gaza,
    And Ashkelon shall not be inhabited.

6   "A mixed race shall settle in Ashdod,
    And I will cut off the pride of the
        Philistines.

7   I will take away the blood from his
        mouth,
    And the abominations from between
        his teeth.
    But he who remains, even he *shall be*
        for our God,
    And shall be like a leader in Judah,
    And Ekron like a Jebusite.

8   I will camp around My house
    Because of the army,
    Because of him who passes by and
        him who returns.
    No more shall an oppressor pass
        through them,
    For now I have seen with My eyes.

The Coming King

9   "Rejoice greatly, O daughter of Zion!
    Shout, O daughter of Jerusalem!
    Behold, your King is coming to you;
    He *is* just and having salvation,

    Lowly and riding on a donkey,
    A colt, the foal of a donkey.

10 I will cut off the chariot from Ephraim
    And the horse from Jerusalem;
    The battle bow shall be cut off.
    He shall speak peace to the nations;
    His dominion *shall be* 'from sea to sea,
    And from the River to the ends of the
        earth.'[a]

God Will Save His People

11 "As for you also,
    Because of the blood of your covenant,
    I will set your prisoners free from the
        waterless pit.

12 Return to the stronghold,
    You prisoners of hope.
    Even today I declare
    That I will restore double to you.

13 For I have bent Judah, My *bow*,
    Fitted the bow with Ephraim,
    And raised up your sons, O Zion,
    Against your sons, O Greece,
    And made you like the sword of a
        mighty man."

14 Then the LORD will be seen over them,
    And His arrow will go forth like
        lightning.

9:10 [a]Psalm 72:8

AGRICULTURE AND HERDING

The relative prestige of a riding animal is determined by several factors, including size, rarity, and cost. Although horses are not always as useful as mules or donkeys (Zech. 9:9, 10), they have maintained a high rank in many cultures. The nomads of northern Arabia kept horses even when their camels had to carry water for the horses to drink.

WHATEVER HAPPENED TO THE PHILISTINES? (Zech. 9:6)

During the 9th century B.C. the Philistines were in decline. They paid tribute to Judah while Jehoshaphat was king (872–848 B.C.; 2 Chr. 17:10, 11), although they tried to become independent under Jehoshaphat's son Jehoram (848–841 B.C.; 2 Chr. 21:16, 17). Toward the end of the century, when the Assyrians began to raid Palestine, Philistia faced another master. The Assyrian king Adad-nirari III (810–783 B.C.) claims in his inscriptions to have placed Philistine cities under heavy tribute in his 5th year (c. 805 B.C.).

Philistia did not fall under complete Assyrian domination until the invasion of Tiglath-Pileser III in 734 B.C. During that campaign Philistine towns were subdued and became vassals of Assyria. The Assyrians allowed the Philistine city-states a degree of self-government as long as they paid tribute. That arrangement crumbled, however, when the city of Ashdod rebelled against Assyrian rule in 713 B.C. The rebellion was subsequently crushed by the Assyrian king Sargon II during campaigns in 713 and 712, and the region was incorporated into the empire as an Assyrian province.

By the end of the 8th century B.C., the Philistine cities became established as a buffer zone between Assyria and hostile Egypt to the south. Eventually Egypt was able to dominate Philistia after the fall of Assyria in 612 B.C. The Egyptian pharaoh Psammetichus I (664–610 B.C.) besieged Ashdod for 29 years, eventually conquering the city.

During the Persian period (559–331 B.C.) the Philistines lost their distinct identity and were mixed with other Palestinian cultural peoples. The prophet Zechariah warned of the decline of the Philistines, and particularly of a "mixed race" that would inhabit Ashdod (Zech. 9:6).

The Lord GOD will blow the trumpet,
And go with whirlwinds from the
　　south.
15 The LORD of hosts will defend them;
They shall devour and subdue with
　　slingstones.
They shall drink *and* roar as if with
　　wine;
They shall be filled *with blood* like
　　basins,
Like the corners of the altar.
16 The LORD their God will save them in
　　that day,
As the flock of His people.
For they *shall be like* the jewels of a
　　crown,
Lifted like a banner over His land—
17 For how great is its[a] goodness
And how great its[b] beauty!
Grain shall make the young men
　　thrive,
And new wine the young women.

Restoration of Judah and Israel

10 1 Ask the LORD for rain
　　In the time of the latter rain.[a]

The LORD will make flashing clouds;
He will give them showers of rain,
Grass in the field for everyone.

2 For the idols[a] speak delusion;
The diviners envision lies,
And tell false dreams;
They comfort in vain.
Therefore *the people* wend their way
　　like sheep;
They are in trouble because *there is* no
　　shepherd.

3 "My anger is kindled against the
　　shepherds,
And I will punish the goatherds.
For the LORD of hosts will visit His
　　flock,
The house of Judah,
And will make them as His royal
　　horse in the battle.
4 From him comes the cornerstone,
From him the tent peg,
From him the battle bow,
From him every ruler[a] together.
5 They shall be like mighty men,
Who tread down *their enemies*
In the mire of the streets in the battle.
They shall fight because the LORD is
　　with them,

9:17 [a]Or *His* [b]Or *His* 　10:1 [a]That is, spring
rain 　10:2 [a]Hebrew *teraphim* 　10:4 [a]Or
despot

And the riders on horses shall be put
to shame.

6 "I will strengthen the house of Judah,
And I will save the house of Joseph.
I will bring them back,
Because I have mercy on them.
They shall be as though I had not cast
them aside;
For I *am* the LORD their God,
And I will hear them.
7 *Those of* Ephraim shall be like a
mighty man,
And their heart shall rejoice as if with
wine.
Yes, their children shall see *it* and be
glad;
Their heart shall rejoice in the LORD.
8 I will whistle for them and gather
them,
For I will redeem them;
And they shall increase as they once
increased.

9 "I will sow them among the peoples,
And they shall remember Me in far
countries;
They shall live, together with their
children,
And they shall return.
10 I will also bring them back from the
land of Egypt,
And gather them from Assyria.
I will bring them into the land of
Gilead and Lebanon,
Until no *more room* is found for them.
11 He shall pass through the sea with
affliction,
And strike the waves of the sea:
All the depths of the River[a] shall dry
up.
Then the pride of Assyria shall be
brought down,
And the scepter of Egypt shall depart.

12 "So I will strengthen them in the LORD,
And they shall walk up and down in
His name,"
Says the LORD.

The Vision of the Shepherds

A good illustration of the difficulty in dating
the prophecies of Zechariah is the vision of the
shepherds (Zech. 11:4–17). In this vision God
dismisses three shepherds in one month

(11:8). The term "shepherd" is a frequent
term for a ruler, but which three rulers are
these? Several guesses have been offered: the
flurry of short-lived kings in the northern kingdom of Israel just before Assyria destroyed it in
722 B.C.; or some otherwise unknown high
priests or governors during the Persian era; or
high priests in Jerusalem during the late Greek
period (about 100 B.C.). The guesses range
over more than half a millennium, and none is
any more certain than any other.

If Zech. 9—14 speaks of the time during
the Persian period, after the reforms of Ezra
and Nehemiah, then the shepherds may have
been governors of that era. In the tiny Persian
province of Judah of the later Persian Empire,
governors were frequent and usually oppressive (12:5, 6). Zechariah's vision of God's coming eternal kingdom (ch. 14) would have been
as living waters (14:8) to the oppressed people of Jerusalem.

▼ ■ Zechariah 11:1—13:9

Zechariah
Desolation of Israel

11 :1 Open your doors, O Lebanon,
That fire may devour your
cedars.
2 Wail, O cypress, for the cedar has
fallen,
Because the mighty *trees* are ruined.
Wail, O oaks of Bashan,
For the thick forest has come down.
3 *There is* the sound of wailing
shepherds!
For their glory is in ruins.
There is the sound of roaring lions!

10:11 [a]That is, the Nile

TIME CAPSULE   *336 to 332 B.C.*

336–331	Darius III is the last Persian king
334	Alexander wins battle at Granicus River against Persia
333	Darius suffers severe defeat at battle of Issos
332–37	Hellenistic period
332	Alexander's armies lay siege to the island of Tyre

For the pride[a] of the Jordan is in
ruins.

Prophecy of the Shepherds

[4]Thus says the LORD my God, "Feed
the flock for slaughter, [5]whose owners
slaughter them and feel no guilt; those who
sell them say, 'Blessed be the LORD, for I
am rich'; and their shepherds do not pity
them. [6]For I will no longer pity the inhabitants of the land," says the LORD. "But indeed I will give everyone into his neighbor's hand and into the hand of his king.
They shall attack the land, and I will not
deliver *them* from their hand."

[7]So I fed the flock for slaughter, in particular the poor of the flock.[a] I took for myself two staffs: the one I called Beauty,[b]
and the other I called Bonds;[c] and I fed the
flock. [8]I dismissed the three shepherds in
one month. My soul loathed them, and
their soul also abhorred me. [9]Then I said,
"I will not feed you. Let what is dying die,
and what is perishing perish. Let those
that are left eat each other's flesh." [10]And I
took my staff, Beauty, and cut it in two,
that I might break the covenant which I
had made with all the peoples. [11]So it was
broken on that day. Thus the poor[a] of the
flock, who were watching me, knew that it
was the word of the LORD. [12]Then I said to
them, "If it is agreeable to you, give *me* my
wages; and if not, refrain." So they weighed
out for my wages thirty *pieces* of silver.

[13]And the LORD said to me, "Throw it
to the potter"—that princely price they set
on me. So I took the thirty *pieces* of silver
and threw them into the house of the LORD
for the potter. [14]Then I cut in two my
other staff, Bonds, that I might break the
brotherhood between Judah and Israel.

[15]And the LORD said to me, "Next, take
for yourself the implements of a foolish
shepherd. [16]For indeed I will raise up a
shepherd in the land *who* will not care for
those who are cut off, nor seek the young,
nor heal those that are broken, nor feed
those that still stand. But he will eat the
flesh of the fat and tear their hooves in
pieces.

[17] "Woe to the worthless shepherd,
Who leaves the flock!
A sword *shall be* against his arm
And against his right eye;
His arm shall completely wither,
And his right eye shall be totally
blinded."

The Coming Deliverance of Judah

12 [1]The burden[a] of the word of the
LORD against Israel. Thus says the
LORD, who stretches out the heavens, lays
the foundation of the earth, and forms the
spirit of man within him: [2]"Behold, I will
make Jerusalem a cup of drunkenness to
all the surrounding peoples, when they lay
siege against Judah and Jerusalem. [3]And
it shall happen in that day that I will make
Jerusalem a very heavy stone for all peoples; all who would heave it away will
surely be cut in pieces, though all nations
of the earth are gathered against it. [4]In
that day," says the LORD, "I will strike
every horse with confusion, and its rider
with madness; I will open My eyes on the
house of Judah, and will strike every horse
of the peoples with blindness. [5]And the
governors of Judah shall say in their heart,
'The inhabitants of Jerusalem *are* my
strength in the LORD of hosts, their God.'
[6]In that day I will make the governors of
Judah like a firepan in the woodpile, and
like a fiery torch in the sheaves; they shall
devour all the surrounding peoples on the
right hand and on the left, but Jerusalem
shall be inhabited again in her own place—
Jerusalem.

[7]"The LORD will save the tents of Judah first, so that the glory of the house of
David and the glory of the inhabitants of
Jerusalem shall not become greater than
that of Judah. [8]In that day the LORD will
defend the inhabitants of Jerusalem; the
one who is feeble among them in that day
shall be like David, and the house of David
shall be like God, like the Angel of the
LORD before them. [9]It shall be in that day
that I will seek to destroy all the nations
that come against Jerusalem.

Mourning for the Pierced One

[10]"And I will pour on the house of David and on the inhabitants of Jerusalem
the Spirit of grace and supplication; then
they will look on Me whom they pierced.
Yes, they will mourn for Him as one
mourns for *his* only *son*, and grieve for Him
as one grieves for a firstborn. [11]In that day

11:3 [a]Or *floodplain, thicket*   11:7 [a]Following
Masoretic Text, Targum, and Vulgate; Septuagint reads
for the Canaanites.   [b]Or *Grace,* and so in verse 10
[c]Or *Unity,* and so in verse 14   11:11 [a]Following
Masoretic Text, Targum, and Vulgate; Septuagint reads
the Canaanites.   12:1 [a]Or *oracle*

CUTTING OFF THE NAMES (Zech. 13:2)

The prophet Zechariah proclaims a time when the worship of other gods in Judah will be ended, the names of the gods will be removed, and they will be forgotten by the people of the land. Yahweh specifically says, "I will cut off the names of the idols from the land" (Zech. 13:2). Zechariah's prophecy (Zech. 13:1–6) reflects a hope for the future of Judah when its religion shall be purified of both idolatry and false prophecy. Such a reform has a historical precedent in Egypt's Amarna period.

The Amarna period of Egypt (c. 1360–1333 B.C.) essentially coincided with the reign of Pharaoh Amenhotep IV (1352–1336 B.C.). This time saw a vast change in the theology of Egypt. The new king reduced the official pantheon to the sun-disk god Aten and himself as Aten's loyal regent. The reform of the official Egyptian cult included building an entire new capital at Amarna, where the god-king would live and Aten alone would be worshiped.

As Zechariah announced the cutting off of idols' names, so also did Amenhotep. The king ordered the names of other gods to be removed from the monuments of Egypt. The names were literally cut out with chisels, even from inscriptions of personal names that included the god's name. The pharaoh even changed his own name from Amenhotep, which included the divine name Amen (or Amon), to Akhenaten, which contained his patron deity's name Aten.

When Akhenaten died, the worshipers of the other gods in the Egyptian pantheon had their revenge. They took their chisels and chipped out the name of Aten from Akhenaten's monumental buildings. The capital at Amarna was abandoned and, for much of the rest of ancient Egyptian history, the rule of Akhenaten and his sun-disk god were effectively forgotten.

---

there shall be a great mourning in Jerusalem, like the mourning at Hadad Rimmon in the plain of Megiddo.[a] 12And the land shall mourn, every family by itself: the family of the house of David by itself, and their wives by themselves; the family of the house of Nathan by itself, and their wives by themselves; 13the family of the house of Levi by itself, and their wives by themselves; the family of Shimei by itself, and their wives by themselves; 14all the families that remain, every family by itself, and their wives by themselves.

Idolatry Cut Off

13 1"In that day a fountain shall be opened for the house of David and for the inhabitants of Jerusalem, for sin and for uncleanness.

2"It shall be in that day," says the LORD of hosts, "*that* I will cut off the names of the idols from the land, and they shall no longer be remembered. I will also cause the prophets and the unclean spirit to depart from the land. 3It shall come to pass *that* if anyone still prophesies, then his father and mother who begot him will say to him, 'You shall not live, because you have spoken lies in the name of the LORD.' And his father and mother who begot him shall thrust him through when he prophesies.

4"And it shall be in that day *that* every prophet will be ashamed of his vision when he prophesies; they will not wear a robe of coarse hair to deceive. 5But he will say, 'I *am* no prophet, I *am* a farmer; for a man taught me to keep cattle from my youth.' 6And *one* will say to him, 'What are these wounds between your arms?'[a] Then he will answer, '*Those* with which I was wounded in the house of my friends.'

The Shepherd Savior

7 "Awake, O sword, against My
       Shepherd,
   Against the Man who is My
       Companion,"
   Says the LORD of hosts.
   "Strike the Shepherd,
   And the sheep will be scattered;
   Then I will turn My hand against the
       little ones.
8 And it shall come to pass in all the
       land,"
   Says the LORD,
   "*That* two-thirds in it shall be cut off
       and die,
   But *one*-third shall be left in it:
9 I will bring the *one*-third through the
       fire,

12:11 ^aHebrew *Megiddon*   13:6 ^aOr *hands*

Will refine them as silver is refined,
And test them as gold is tested.
They will call on My name,
And I will answer them.
I will say, 'This *is* My people';
And each one will say, 'The LORD *is*
  my God.' "

The Last Battle Won

The prophecies of Zech. 9—14 are often called apocalyptic writing, a literary style that included many symbolic visions. Apocalyptic literature offered consolation to oppressed and persecuted people, and very often included a comforting vision of God's eternal kingdom, which will replace all the oppressive kingdoms of this present world (see "Ezekiel's Apocalyptic Prophecies" at Ezek. 38:1). The vision of Zech. 14, with its picture of a final battle (14:3) and an eternal spring of living waters (14:8) has much in common with both Ezek. 38 and 39 and with Rev. 20—22, two other apocalyptic visions. To struggling Jewish settlers oppressed by wicked and self-serving governors (Zech. 12:5, 6), Zechariah offered a future hope.

Like the prophecies of Is. 56—66, those of Zech. 9—14 speak of the restored Jerusalem, but without the priestly emphasis of such Persian era prophets as Haggai and Malachi. Where the priestly prophets stressed the role of God's holy temple, Zechariah offered a radical vision of a time when no temple will be necessary. Instead, everything in Jerusalem, from the harnesses of the horses to the pots and pans of the kitchen, will be holy to God (14:20, 21). Also like Is. 56—66, Zechariah rejects the exclusivism of such leaders as Ezra and Nehemiah. All nations and families of the earth will be able to worship God and keep the Jewish celebration of the Feast of Tabernacles (14:16—19).

▼   ■ Zechariah 14:1–21

Zechariah
The Day of the LORD

14 :1 Behold, the day of the LORD is
         coming,
And your spoil will be divided in your
  midst.
2   For I will gather all the nations to
    battle against Jerusalem;

The city shall be taken,
The houses rifled,
And the women ravished.
Half of the city shall go into captivity,
But the remnant of the people shall
  not be cut off from the city.

3   Then the LORD will go forth
    And fight against those nations,
    As He fights in the day of battle.
4   And in that day His feet will stand on
      the Mount of Olives,
    Which faces Jerusalem on the east.
    And the Mount of Olives shall be split
      in two,
    From east to west,
    Making a very large valley;
    Half of the mountain shall move
      toward the north
    And half of it toward the south.

5   Then you shall flee *through* My
      mountain valley,
    For the mountain valley shall reach to
      Azal.
    Yes, you shall flee
    As you fled from the earthquake
    In the days of Uzziah king of Judah.

    Thus the LORD my God will come,
    And all the saints with You.[a]

6   It shall come to pass in that day
    That there will be no light;
    The lights will diminish.
7   It shall be one day
    Which is known to the LORD—
    Neither day nor night.
    But at evening time it shall happen
    That it will be light.

8   And in that day it shall be
    That living waters shall flow from
      Jerusalem,
    Half of them toward the eastern sea
    And half of them toward the western
      sea;
    In both summer and winter it shall
      occur.
9   And the LORD shall be King over all
      the earth.
    In that day it shall be—
    "The LORD *is* one,"[a]
    And His name one.

10All the land shall be turned into a
plain from Geba to Rimmon south of Jerusalem. *Jerusalem*[a] shall be raised up and

14:5 [a]Or *you;* Septuagint, Targum, and Vulgate read
Him.   14:9 [a]Compare Deuteronomy 6:4
14:10 [a]Literally *She*

inhabited in her place from Benjamin's Gate to the place of the First Gate and the Corner Gate, and *from* the Tower of Hananel to the king's winepresses.

11 *The people* shall dwell in it;
    And no longer shall there be utter destruction,
    But Jerusalem shall be safely inhabited.

¹²And this shall be the plague with which the LORD will strike all the people who fought against Jerusalem:

Their flesh shall dissolve while they stand on their feet,
Their eyes shall dissolve in their sockets,
And their tongues shall dissolve in their mouths.

13 It shall come to pass in that day
    That a great panic from the LORD will be among them.
    Everyone will seize the hand of his neighbor,
    And raise his hand against his neighbor's hand;

14 Judah also will fight at Jerusalem.
    And the wealth of all the surrounding nations
    Shall be gathered together:
    Gold, silver, and apparel in great abundance.

15 Such also shall be the plague
    On the horse *and* the mule,

On the camel and the donkey,
And on all the cattle that will be in those camps.
So *shall* this plague *be*.

The Nations Worship the King

¹⁶And it shall come to pass *that* everyone who is left of all the nations which came against Jerusalem shall go up from year to year to worship the King, the LORD of hosts, and to keep the Feast of Tabernacles. ¹⁷And it shall be *that* whichever of the families of the earth do not come up to Jerusalem to worship the King, the LORD of hosts, on them there will be no rain. ¹⁸If the family of Egypt will not come up and enter in, they *shall have* no rain; they shall receive the plague with which the LORD strikes the nations who do not come up to keep the Feast of Tabernacles. ¹⁹This shall be the punishment of Egypt and the punishment of all the nations that do not come up to keep the Feast of Tabernacles.

²⁰In that day "HOLINESS TO THE LORD" shall be *engraved* on the bells of the horses. The pots in the LORD's house shall be like the bowls before the altar. ²¹Yes, every pot in Jerusalem and Judah shall be holiness to the LORD of hosts.[a] Everyone who sacrifices shall come and take them and cook in them. In that day there shall no longer be a Canaanite in the house of the LORD of hosts.

14:21 [a]Or *on every pot . . . shall be* (engraved) *"HOLINESS TO THE LORD OF HOSTS"*

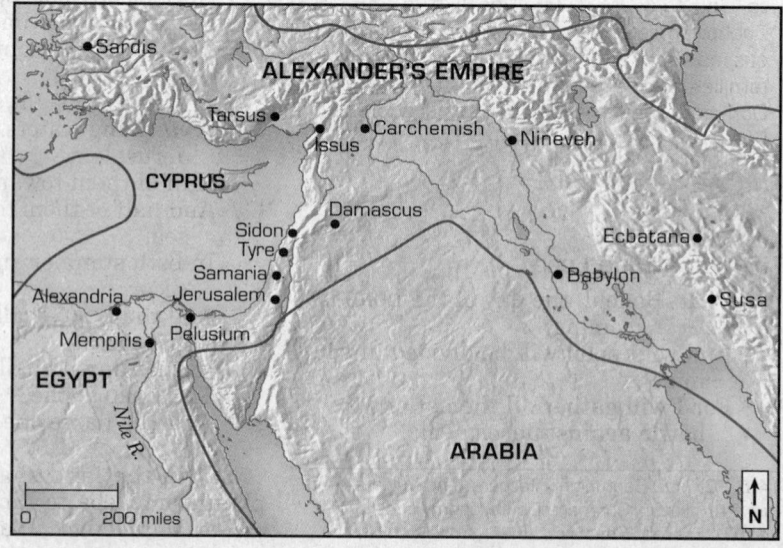

Alexander's Greek Empire
In 334 B.C. a 22-year-old Alexander began a military quest to destroy the Persian Empire. Moving from west to east, he was victorious in battle at Issus in 333 B.C. against the Persian Darius III. Moving south, Alexander defeated the Phoenicians at Tyre in 332 B.C., swept through Palestine, and conquered Egypt in 331 B.C. Darius III was defeated again near Nineveh. Alexander's campaigns secured vast territory for the Greek Empire before he died in 323 B.C.

Sardis
ALEXANDER'S EMPIRE
Tarsus
Carchemish
Issus
Nineveh
CYPRUS
Damascus
Sidon
Ecbatana
Tyre
Samaria
Babylon
Alexandria
Jerusalem
Susa
Memphis
Pelusium
EGYPT
Nile R.
ARABIA
0   200 miles
N

BETWEEN THE TWO TESTAMENTS

(332—37 B.C.)

During this time, that is little known to the Bible but fully attested in the Apocrypha, the faith of the Jewish people was tested both by oppression and freedom.

The Old Testament provides scant information on events following the end of the Persian period (c. 331 B.C.). One prophecy of Zechariah (Zech. 9) possibly refers to the conquests of Alexander the Great in 332 B.C. At least one interpretation of Daniel's later visions (particularly Dan. 8—11) refers to events after Alexander's Greek kingdom was divided, resulting eventually in the Ptolemies and the Seleucids of the 2nd century B.C. Yet, for the most part, the Old Testament is silent on the approximately 300 years before the birth of Jesus Christ (c. 5 B.C.). This epoch is known appropriately as "the Intertestamental Period" since it is the time between the testaments—between the last writings of the Old Testament and the first writings of the New.

For Judea, the epoch is characterized not only as "between the testaments," but also as between Persian rule and Greek rule, between Greek rule and Judean independence, between independence and Roman rule, with Herod the Great on the throne. It was a time when the faith of the Jewish people was tested, both by oppression and freedom. It is a time little known to the Bible, but fully attested in the Apocrypha.

▶ Archaeology and the Past

Archaeology hints of extensive building and rebuilding during this period. All over Palestine, cities were rebuilt by the Greek Ptolemies from Egypt, or by the Greek Seleucids from Syria. Samaria was settled by colonists from Macedonia, and coastal cities in Palestine became Greek. East of the Jordan River, there were many Greek colonies (called the Decapolis in the Gospels). Specific archaeological data is scanty because so much of the building material was reused by later peoples.

The Jewish colony in Egypt continued to thrive. Papyrus documents list Jewish names in Alexandria and all the way up the Nile to present-day Aswan. The Nash Papyrus, a small fragment from this period containing the Ten Commandments in Hebrew, shows that at least some Jews in Egypt could still read Hebrew.

In Palestine itself, one important monument is the painted tombs of Marisa, in southern Judah. These tombs were carved out of the rock and painted elaborately, with the spaces between the paintings being filled with inscriptions and graffiti. The city of Marisa had been the capital of Edomite territory in southern Judah, a region eventually influenced by Greek culture. Names recovered from the tombs are Greek, Phoenician, and Idumean (all of southern Palestine eventually became known as Idumea).

Coins in Palestine show the succession of rulers. Many coins are from the Seleucid rulers of Syria, but coins dated after the Maccabean revolt of 166 B.C. indicate a free Judea. The Judean coins show the Hasmonean rulers becoming more and more secular. ("Hasmonean" derives from the family to which the Maccabees belonged. It was the name applied to the dynasty of Maccabean high priests and kings who ruled Judea between 142 B.C. and 63 B.C.)

One of the most famous archaeological remains from the period is the early occupation at Qumran, south of Jericho on the shores of the Dead Sea. Qumran was apparently settled by a sect of strict Jews who did not approve of the Hasmoneans being both kings and high priests. Josephus, the Jewish historian of the 1st century A.D., tells us that the founders of Qumran were the Essenes, a kind of monastic community. Their settlement was later abandoned and then resettled. It was near Qumran that the famous Dead Sea Scrolls were found in 1947.

▶ The Peoples and Groups

At the beginning of the period the most influential people were the Greeks and their successors. Alexander the Great founded colonies for his soldiers all over his empire. His generals who succeeded him ruled in Syria (the Seleucids) and in Egypt (the Ptolemies), and continued the ancient struggle between Asia and Africa for control of Palestine. While they fought each other over Palestine, both agreed on the importance of establishing Greek culture in the land. The increasing Greek influence would lead ultimately to revolt on the part of the Jews and to defeat of the ruling Seleucids. The incredible struggle of the Jewish people against Greek culture culminated in a Jewish political kingdom independent of Gentile control.

Other peoples figure importantly in this time of Jewish history. The Edomites, who had long been an enemy of Israel, lost their territory in Transjordan and the Sinai to the rising power of the Nabatean Arabs. Many Edomites moved to southern Judah, where they became known as Idumeans. The Idumeans were conquered by the Jews and forced to convert to Judaism, but, ironically, an Idumean would come to rule the Jewish state. Not only was Herod the Great an Idumean, but his brother-in-law was descended from the priests of Koze, an ancient Edomite god.

By 312 B.C. the Nabateans established themselves at Petra, the former capital of Edom, and in this great center they carved homes and temples out of the sandstone. By controlling the desert highways south of the Dead Sea, they became great traders, dominating much of the spice trade in the Middle East.

The Samaritans inhabited the area immediately north of Jerusalem and Judea. Tension between Samaritans and Jews goes back at least to the reconstruction of the Jerusalem temple (538 B.C.). Yet a definite break between these groups occurred around either 388 or 332 B.C. when the Samaritans built a rival temple on Mount Gerizim, claiming Shechem rather than Jerusalem as the location of the true house of God. Both the temple and the city were destroyed by the Jewish ruler John Hyrcanus around 129 B.C.

At the close of the period the most powerful people were the Romans. The first record of Romans in Palestine is the treaty entered into by Judas Maccabeus and the Senate of Rome. Judea and Rome became allies just as Rome was beginning to consolidate its power and expand its territory. The alliance was helpful to the Jews for a few decades, then the Romans moved into Palestine and took control in 63 B.C. Pompey, Julius Caesar, Mark Antony (and Cleopatra), Augustus, and Crassus are Romans associated with Jewish history. Herod the Great was a friend of Caesar, Antony, and Augustus, changing sides with the changes of power in Rome.

▶ The Biblical Literature

The books associated with this period are found primarily in the Apocrypha. The books of Maccabees exalt Jewish martyrs and encourage the Jews to be strong in their faith. The history of the Jewish revolt that began in 166 B.C. is told in 1 and 2 Maccabees. Stories about the Jews' struggle with Greek culture are found in 3 and 4 Maccabees. The Wisdom of Jesus Son of Sirach (also called Ecclesiasticus) covers ethics in public life, standing in the tradition of Proverbs and Ecclesiastes. The writer wrote in Jerusalem around 180 B.C.

These apocryphal books provide the background for a period almost unknown to the Old Testament, except for the last chapters of the Book of Daniel. The apocalyptic visions of Dan. 7; 8 reveal the kingdoms that came after Babylon, extending at least as far as the Greek Empire established by Alexander and possibly to the Roman Empire. Daniel's vision of 70 weeks (Dan. 9) points toward either Greek or Roman times of the 2nd or 1st century B.C. The Greek kingdoms that controlled Palestine during the 2nd century B.C., particularly the reign of Antiochus IV (175–164 B.C.), come into view in Dan. 10—12.

> *The visions of Daniel reveal that the trials of God's people would get worse before they got better.*

These visions of Daniel reveal that the trials of God's people would get worse before they got better. Other empires would succeed Babylon, and the later ones would persecute the Jews for their religion, threatening not only their lives, but the continued worship of God. But there is a further message: the pagan kings would not be able to ignore or defy God. Exalt themselves as they might, they would be brought low before the God of Israel. The final outcome would be determined not by earthly armies, but by heavenly ones.

The Greek Empire

> Alexander's conquests, in their swiftness and effectiveness, are the stuff of military legend.

The Persian Empire continued for another century after the death of Artaxerxes I (424 B.C.). Various kings of varying ability ruled Persia, but no great advances were made by the empire, and no new territories were added. Indeed, some of the empire's conquered territories were lost. Egypt, at the far southwestern end of the empire, rebelled several times, and in 404 B.C. finally won independence from its Persian overlords.

Besides rebellions within its own dominion, Persia's most significant threat continued to be the growing power of the independent city-states of Greece. Both Darius I (522–486 B.C.) and Xerxes I (486–465 B.C.) attempted to invade Greece but were turned back. Later Persian kings gave up plans for conquest, being content simply to keep the Greeks from encroaching on Persian territory. This goal was made easier by wars between the fiercely independent Greek city-states, such as the Peloponnesian War between Athens and Sparta (434–404 B.C.). While the Greeks fought each other, the Persian kings Artaxerxes I (465–424 B.C.), Xerxes II (424 B.C.), and Darius II (423–404 B.C.) were able to concentrate their military forces in Asia Minor, making that area a buffer between Greece and the rest of the Persian Empire.

Despite continuous conflict between the Greek city-states, this century was the golden age in Greece. The city of Athens, which had led the Greek alliance against Darius I and Xerxes I, became the center of Greek politics, literature, and philosophy. In Athenian politics, this was the age of Pericles. In literature, this century saw such Greek dramatists as Aeschylus,

Sophocles, and Euripides. Athenian philosophers of this time included Socrates, Plato, and near the end of the century, Aristotle.

Despite great diversity, Greek art and thought shared a few significant presuppositions. Most important of these was a new emphasis on the beauty and value of the human being. Before this time, most cultures saw people as weak creatures, helpless before the more powerful forces of nature and of the gods. In 5th-century Greece, this view changed. Humans came to be perceived as having intrinsic value as well as the strength to overcome (or at least endure) the worst that fate or the gods could offer. The Stoic philosopher Protagoras summarized this humanism with his dictum, "Man is the measure of all things." This philosophical position was to prove much more enduring and influential in world history than any of the military or political achievements of Athens.

No human glory lasts forever, and the glory of Persia and of the Greek city-states began to fail simultaneously. In Persia, the collapse came from within. After Artaxerxes II (404–359 B.C.), Persia was ruled by a series of violent, ambitious men, most of whom gained the throne by assassinating their predecessor and all possible rivals. One of these, Artaxerxes III (359–338 B.C.) seemed to be restoring Persian might—he even recaptured Egypt in 343 B.C.—but that return to glory was illusory. Artaxerxes III was poisoned and replaced by his son Arses (338–336 B.C.).

The threat to Greece came from without, from the land of Macedon to the north. The king of Macedon, Philip II (359–336 B.C.), marched his armies south and by 338 B.C. had captured the whole Greek peninsula. Although not a Greek himself, Philip had his son tutored in Greek thought by none other than the great Greek thinker Aristotle. When Philip was murdered in 336 B.C., his son was ready to expand both the kingdom of Macedon and the culture of Greece into Persian territory. Philip's son was named Alexander (336–323 B.C.).

Alexander the Great's conquests, in their swiftness and effectiveness, are the stuff of military legend. In 334 B.C. Alexander crossed the Hellespont into Asia Minor and overcame all opposition. He met the main Persian force, under Darius III (336–331 B.C.) in 333 B.C. and routed it, sending Darius himself fleeing. Before pressing on into Mesopotamia, the center of Persian power, Alexander marched south and conquered Palestine and Egypt in 332 B.C. Moving north again, he took Mesopotamia in 331 B.C. and everything else he could find to conquer by 327 B.C. The new Greek Empire stretched from Macedon to Egypt, from Greece to India. Alexander himself died of a fever in Babylon in 323 B.C. at the age of 33.

Upon Alexander's death, his generals began fighting over his newly acquired empire. The next few decades were marked by a series of shifting alliances, intrigues, and wars. No one general was strong enough to take control of the whole empire. At first the empire was divided into four parts, but by 280 B.C. three separate dynasties were established: the Antigonids in Macedonia, the Ptolemies in Egypt, and the Seleucids in Persia and Syria.

The land of Palestine, which included Judah and Jerusalem, was at first a part of the Ptolemaic kingdom, centered in Egypt. In about 200 B.C., however, Palestine was captured by the Seleucid king Antiochus III (223–187 B.C.). Now Judah was part of the Seleucid kingdom, based in Syria. The Jews, who had been largely left alone under Ptolemaic rule, now faced danger. The Seleucid king Antiochus IV Epiphanes (175–164 B.C.) sought to establish Greek religion and culture in his realm and to wipe out all rival beliefs. He outlawed the Jewish faith, burned all copies he could find of the Jewish Scripture, and in 167 B.C. sacrificed pigs to Zeus on the altar of the Jerusalem temple. Faithful Jews rebelled and in 164 B.C. were able to cleanse and rededicate the temple, a rededication still celebrated today in the Feast of Dedication, or Hanukkah.

For 300 years after the death of Alexander, the ancient world was controlled by the descendants of his Greek generals. Greek became the official language of trade, and Greek culture found its way into every land. As early as 215 B.C., though, a rival to Greek power began to appear to the west—Rome. In 30 B.C. the last of the Hellenistic (Greek) kingdoms, the Ptolemaic dynasty in Egypt, was absorbed into the new Roman Empire.

The Apocalyptic Visions of Daniel

The young Jewish exile Daniel interpreted a dream for the king of Babylon, Nebuchadnezzar (Dan. 2). That interpretation was a foretelling of future kingdoms and empires, starting with the Babylonians and moving through the Persian and Greek empires. Since Daniel's dream interpretation was part of a narrative from the time of Nebuchadnezzar (Dan. 2), it could be read in that context (see "Daniel's Time in Babylon" at Dan. 2:1).

Several of Daniel's own visions appear to parallel Nebuchadnezzar's dream narrated in Dan. 2. Like that dream, the visions of Dan. 7; 8 describe the kingdoms that will follow the kingdom of Babylon and extend at least as far as the Greek Empire established by Alexander. Unlike that dream, these visions are not part of a narrative. They are dated as received in Belshazzar's 1st and 3rd years (Dan. 7:1; 8:1), but it is not known when he began to rule. Some think that Belshazzar's father Nabonidus left him as regent over the city of Babylon when Nabonidus departed for Tema in 553 B.C., though that is not certain. The dates report only that Daniel received these visions sometime before 545 B.C. The content of the visions, however, extends far beyond the time of Daniel and Belshazzar, and so can be read in light of the Greek Empire.

Daniel's visions are the best examples of apocalyptic literature in all the Old Testament. Apocalyptic literature was a particularly Jewish form of writing, fairly common in the centuries after the destruction of Jerusalem in 586 B.C. Apocalyptic texts usually presented symbolic visions, with every detail appearing to have a specific hidden meaning, though not always explaining it. The primary purpose of apocalyptic writing was to comfort those who were persecuted for their faith. Such comfort was found in knowing that all the kingdoms of earth, however powerful they might appear, would one day be crushed and replaced by God's eternal kingdom, in which the faithful would be vindicated (Dan. 2:44, 45; 7:27; 8:25).

Apocalyptic visions thus refer to two or even three separate time frames. First, there is the time of the visionary, which in Dan. 7; 8 is the reign of Nabonidus and Belshazzar. Second, there is the time of persecution to which the comfort is offered. That time, for Dan. 7; 8, may be the time of Daniel, or it may be a much later persecution, the time of the future events described in the visions. Finally, there is the final time—an ultimate day of the Lord, when all will be set right, a time sometime after the persecutions.

The visions of Dan. 7; 8 speak of a series of kingdoms, beginning with the Babylonian Empire. Exactly which kingdoms is not completely clear, however. The four beasts (Dan. 7:3–7), for instance, might refer to (1) Babylon (the lion), (2) Media (the bear), (3) Persia (the leopard), and (4) Greece (the dreadful beast). Alternately, the last three kingdoms could be Persia, Greece, and Rome. Thus the last beast, in which Daniel is most interested, could be either the Greek Empire or the Roman Empire.

The "little horn" of Dan. 7:8, then, would be a proud king of this last kingdom, who would greatly persecute God's people. Should that kingdom be Greece, the little horn might refer to Antiochus IV, the Seleucid ruler who defiled the Jerusalem temple in 167 B.C. References to Greece in Daniel give this interpretation some support: the vision of Dan. 8 specifically identifies the final kingdom as Greece (Dan. 8:21), and Dan. 10; 11 include some clear references to the time of Antiochus (see "Daniel and the Greeks" at Dan. 10:1). Other scholars, interpreting the fourth kingdom as Rome, have identified the little horn as Nero Caesar, or as some other figure who persecuted Christians.

The indeterminate nature of the vision has resulted in other interpretations throughout history. During the English Civil War of the 17th century, for instance, the Puritan rebels against the throne identified the little horn as the English king. At the same time, the royalist Sir Thomas More identified the little horn as Oliver Cromwell, the Puritan leader. By nature, apocalyptic literature always appears to apply to one's own time. To interpret an apocalyptic vision it is important to seek the original reference of the vision—the Greek or Roman persecutions, for instance. Having done this, it is still appropriate to seek one's own situation in the vision's symbols and to find one's own comfort in its promises.

■ Daniel 7:1–28

Daniel
Vision of the Four Beasts

7 :1 In the first year of Belshazzar king of Babylon, Daniel had a dream and visions of his head *while* on his bed. Then he wrote down the dream, telling the main facts.[a]

7:1 [a]Literally *the head* (or *chief*) *of the words*

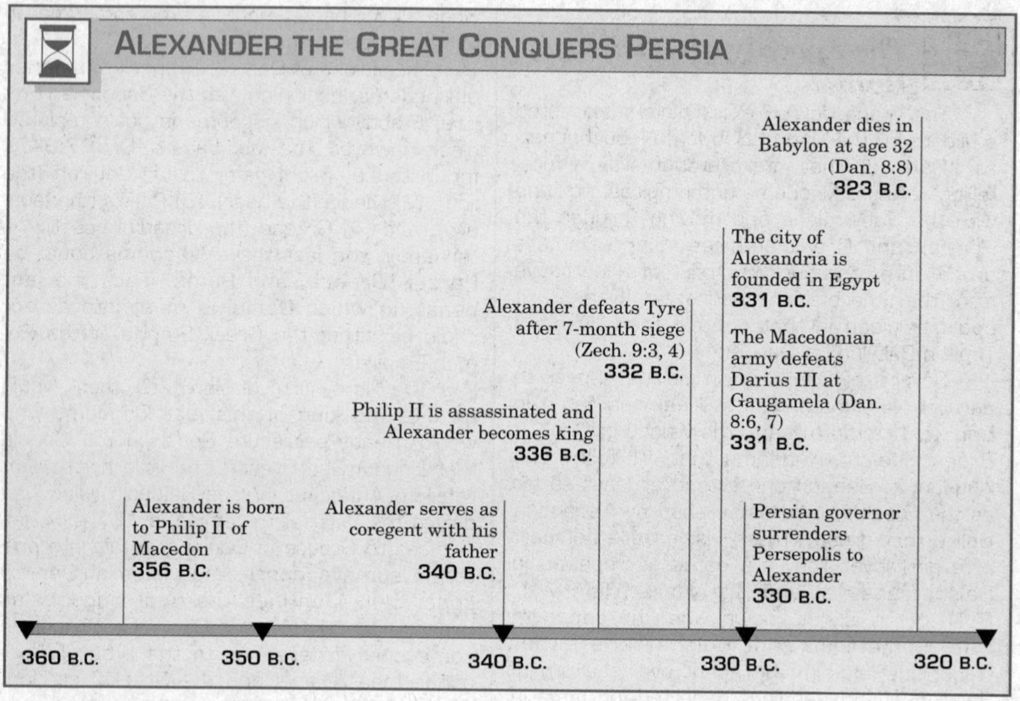

⧗ ALEXANDER THE GREAT CONQUERS PERSIA

Alexander dies in
Babylon at age 32
(Dan. 8:8)
323 B.C.

The city of
Alexandria is
founded in Egypt
331 B.C.

Alexander defeats Tyre
after 7-month siege
(Zech. 9:3, 4)
332 B.C.

The Macedonian
army defeats
Darius III at
Gaugamela (Dan.
8:6, 7)
331 B.C.

Philip II is assassinated and
Alexander becomes king
336 B.C.

Alexander is born
to Philip II of
Macedon
356 B.C.

Alexander serves as
coregent with his
father
340 B.C.

Persian governor
surrenders
Persepolis to
Alexander
330 B.C.

360 B.C.   **350 B.C.**   **340 B.C.**   **330 B.C.**   **320 B.C.**

²Daniel spoke, saying, "I saw in my vision by night, and behold, the four winds of heaven were stirring up the Great Sea. ³And four great beasts came up from the sea, each different from the other. ⁴The first *was* like a lion, and had eagle's wings. I watched till its wings were plucked off; and it was lifted up from the earth and made to stand on two feet like a man, and a man's heart was given to it.

⁵"And suddenly another beast, a second, like a bear. It was raised up on one side, and *had* three ribs in its mouth between its teeth. And they said thus to it: 'Arise, devour much flesh!'

⁶"After this I looked, and there was another, like a leopard, which had on its back four wings of a bird. The beast also had four heads, and dominion was given to it.

⁷"After this I saw in the night visions, and behold, a fourth beast, dreadful and terrible, exceedingly strong. It had huge iron teeth; it was devouring, breaking in pieces, and trampling the residue with its feet. It *was* different from all the beasts that *were* before it, and it had ten horns. ⁸I was considering the horns, and there was another horn, a little one, coming up among them, before whom three of the first horns were plucked out by the roots. And there, in this horn, *were* eyes like the eyes of a man, and a mouth speaking pompous words.

Vision of the Ancient of Days

9   "I watched till thrones were put in
          place,
      And the Ancient of Days was seated;
      His garment *was* white as snow,
      And the hair of His head *was* like
          pure wool.
      His throne *was* a fiery flame,
      Its wheels a burning fire;

PLANTS AND ANIMALS

The Syrian bear is a type of European brown bear, closely related to the grizzly bear but not so large. Brown bears can grow to over 500 pounds, making them about the same size as a lion. Their diet is mostly vegetable, although they can eat meat (Dan. 7:5). They are not aggressive toward humans, but are ferocious if their cubs are threatened.

10 A fiery stream issued
And came forth from before Him.
A thousand thousands ministered to
Him;
Ten thousand times ten thousand
stood before Him.
The court[a] was seated,
And the books were opened.

11"I watched then because of the sound of the pompous words which the horn was speaking; I watched till the beast was slain, and its body destroyed and given to the burning flame. 12As for the rest of the beasts, they had their dominion taken away, yet their lives were prolonged for a season and a time.

13 "I was watching in the night visions,
And behold, *One* like the Son of Man,
Coming with the clouds of heaven!
He came to the Ancient of Days,
And they brought Him near before
Him.
14 Then to Him was given dominion and
glory and a kingdom,
That all peoples, nations, and
languages should serve Him.
His dominion *is* an everlasting
dominion,
Which shall not pass away,
And His kingdom *the one*
Which shall not be destroyed.

Daniel's Visions Interpreted

15"I, Daniel, was grieved in my spirit within *my* body, and the visions of my head troubled me. 16I came near to one of those who stood by, and asked him the truth of all this. So he told me and made known to me the interpretation of these things: 17"Those great beasts, which are four, *are* four kings[a] *which* arise out of the earth. 18But the saints of the Most High shall receive the kingdom, and possess the kingdom forever, even forever and ever.'

19"Then I wished to know the truth about the fourth beast, which was different from all the others, exceedingly dreadful, *with* its teeth of iron and its nails of bronze, *which* devoured, broke in pieces, and trampled the residue with its feet; 20and the ten horns that *were* on its head, and the other *horn* which came up, before

which three fell, namely, that horn which had eyes and a mouth which spoke pompous words, whose appearance *was* greater than his fellows. 21"I was watching; and the same horn was making war against the saints, and prevailing against them, 22until the Ancient of Days came, and a judgment was made *in favor* of the saints of the Most High, and the time came for the saints to possess the kingdom.

23"Thus he said:

'The fourth beast shall be
A fourth kingdom on earth,
Which shall be different from all *other*
kingdoms,
And shall devour the whole earth,
Trample it and break it in pieces.
24 The ten horns *are* ten kings
Who shall arise from this kingdom.
And another shall rise after them;
He shall be different from the first
ones,
And shall subdue three kings.
25 He shall speak *pompous* words
against the Most High,
Shall persecute[a] the saints of the Most
High,
And shall intend to change times and
law.
Then *the saints* shall be given into his
hand
For a time and times and half a time.

26 'But the court shall be seated,
And they shall take away his
dominion,
To consume and destroy *it* forever.
27 Then the kingdom and dominion,
And the greatness of the kingdoms
under the whole heaven,

TIME CAPSULE   *331 to 327 B.C.*

331 *Darius retreats to Ecbatana, as Alexander takes Babylon and Susa*

330 *The Persian governor surrenders Persepolis to Alexander*

330 *Darius is assassinated by Bessos, satrap of Bactria*

330 *Lycurgus rebuilds Dionysus theater in Athens*

327 *Alexander conquers all of Persia before age 30*

Shall be given to the people, the
    saints of the Most High.
His kingdom *is* an everlasting
    kingdom,
And all dominions shall serve and
    obey Him.'

[28] "This *is* the end of the account.[a] As
for me, Daniel, my thoughts greatly troubled me, and my countenance changed; but
I kept the matter in my heart."

Daniel and Alexander

Though the vision of Dan. 7 could refer ultimately to either the Greek Empire or the
Roman Empire, the vision of Dan. 8 clearly
speaks of Greece. The ram, with which the
dream begins, is the Medo-Persian Empire
(8:3, 4, 20). This ram is conquered by a goat
from the west, which can hardly refer to anything except the Macedonian and Greek
armies under Alexander that swept the old
Persian Empire away (8:21).

The "horns" of Dan. 8 reflect the Greek
Empire. At first the goat has one "notable
horn," representing Alexander himself (8:5,
21). After this horn is broken off, four horns
replace it, representing the four generals who
replaced Alexander (8:8, 22). The little horn
which grew "toward the south" (8:9), and blasphemed and defiled the temple (8:11, 12),
sounds very much like the Seleucid king Antiochus IV Epiphanes (see "The Greek Empire" at
Dan. 7:1).

■ Daniel 8:1–27

Daniel
Vision of a Ram and a Goat

8 :1 In the third year of the reign of King
Belshazzar a vision appeared *to* me—to
me, Daniel—after the one that appeared to
me the first time. [2] I saw in the vision, and
it so happened while I was looking, that I
was in Shushan, the citadel, which *is* in
the province of Elam; and I saw in the vision that I was by the River Ulai. [3] Then I
lifted my eyes and saw, and there, standing
beside the river, was a ram which had two
horns, and the two horns *were* high; but
one *was* higher than the other, and the
higher *one* came up last. [4] I saw the ram
pushing westward, northward, and southward, so that no animal could withstand
him; nor *was there any* that could deliver

from his hand, but he did according to his
will and became great.

[5] And as I was considering, suddenly a
male goat came from the west, across the
surface of the whole earth, without touching the ground; and the goat *had* a notable
horn between his eyes. [6] Then he came to
the ram that had two horns, which I had
seen standing beside the river, and ran at
him with furious power. [7] And I saw him
confronting the ram; he was moved with
rage against him, attacked the ram, and
broke his two horns. There was no power
in the ram to withstand him, but he cast
him down to the ground and trampled him;
and there was no one that could deliver the
ram from his hand.

[8] Therefore the male goat grew very
great; but when he became strong, the
large horn was broken, and in place of it
four notable ones came up toward the four
winds of heaven. [9] And out of one of them
came a little horn which grew exceedingly
great toward the south, toward the east,
and toward the Glorious *Land.* [10] And it
grew up to the host of heaven; and it cast
down *some* of the host and *some* of the
stars to the ground, and trampled them.
[11] He even exalted *himself* as high as the
Prince of the host; and by him the daily
sacrifices were taken away, and the place of
His sanctuary was cast down. [12] Because of
transgression, an army was given over *to
the horn* to oppose the daily *sacrifices;* and
he cast truth down to the ground. He did
all this and prospered.

[13] Then I heard a holy one speaking;
and *another* holy one said to that certain
one who was speaking, "How long *will* the
vision *be, concerning* the daily *sacrifices*
and the transgression of desolation, the
giving of both the sanctuary and the host
to be trampled underfoot?"

[14] And he said to me, "For two thousand three hundred days;[a] then the sanctuary shall be cleansed."

Gabriel Interprets the Vision

[15] Then it happened, when I, Daniel,
had seen the vision and was seeking the
meaning, that suddenly there stood before
me one having the appearance of a man.
[16] And I heard a man's voice between *the
banks* of the Ulai, who called, and said,
"Gabriel, make this *man* understand the

7:28 [a]Literally *the word*   8:14 [a]Literally *evening-
mornings*

THE PERSIAN PROVINCE OF ELAM (Dan. 8:2)

By the time of Daniel (6th century B.C.), the territory of Elam was already a very ancient land. Located in modern southwest Iran in the province of Khuzistan, Elam shows evidence of beginning urbanization as early as the late 4th millennium B.C., with Susa (Shushan in the Bible) as its major center. The Elamites flourished there until the 7th century B.C. when they were overrun by the Medes and Persians.

Susa was the religious center of Elam during the Neo-Elamite kingdom of the 8th century B.C. The Assyrians waged various campaigns against the Neo-Elamite kings, and in 646 B.C. the Assyrian king Ashurbanipal destroyed the city.

The Persians eventually took the part of Elam called Anshan. After the Assyrian Empire was destroyed (609 B.C.), the Medes annexed most of Elam. When the Persians, in turn, began to control Media, all of Elam became a Persian administrative district. After the 6th century B.C., Elam was never again an independent nation.

The fortunes of Susa turned for the better under the Persian Empire. During the reign of King Darius I (522–486 B.C.), Susa was restored to its position of influence and power in the region. It was evidently the winter capital of the Achaemenid kings of Persia. The rebuilt city consisted of two parts separated by a canal: a lower city and a fortified royal city.

Daniel's vision placed him in the Persian "province of Elam" (Dan. 8:2). In the vision was the city of Susa (or Shushan) and the fortified royal city, referred to as "the citadel" (8:2). The River Ulai, by which Daniel stood, flowed north of Susa. Some scholars believe that Ulai was an artificial irrigation canal and not a natural river. Possibly Ulai was the canal separating the two parts of Susa.

---

vision." [17]So he came near where I stood, and when he came I was afraid and fell on my face; but he said to me, "Understand, son of man, that the vision *refers* to the time of the end."

[18]Now, as he was speaking with me, I was in a deep sleep with my face to the ground; but he touched me, and stood me upright. [19]And he said, "Look, I am making known to you what shall happen in the latter time of the indignation; for at the appointed time the end *shall be.* [20]The ram which you saw, having the two horns—*they are* the kings of Media and Persia. [21]And the male goat *is* the kingdom[a] of Greece. The large horn that *is* between its eyes *is* the first king. [22]As for the broken *horn* and the four that stood up in its place, four kingdoms shall arise out of that nation, but not with its power.

23   "And in the latter time of their kingdom,
    When the transgressors have reached their fullness,
    A king shall arise,

    Having fierce features,
    Who understands sinister schemes.
24 His power shall be mighty, but not by his own power;
    He shall destroy fearfully,
    And shall prosper and thrive;
    He shall destroy the mighty, and *also* the holy people.

25 "Through his cunning
    He shall cause deceit to prosper under his rule;[a]
    And he shall exalt *himself* in his heart.
    He shall destroy many in *their* prosperity.
    He shall even rise against the Prince of princes;
    But he shall be broken without *human* means.[b]

26 "And the vision of the evenings and mornings
    Which was told is true;
    Therefore seal up the vision,
    For *it refers* to many days *in the future.*"

8:21 [a]Literally *king,* representing his kingdom (compare 7:17, 23)   8:25 [a]Literally *hand*
[b]Literally *hand*

[27]And I, Daniel, fainted and was sick for days; afterward I arose and went about

the king's business. I was astonished by the vision, but no one understood it.

Daniel
Daniel's Prayer for the People

9 :1 In the first year of Darius the son of Ahasuerus, of the lineage of the Medes, who was made king over the realm of the Chaldeans— ²in the first year of his reign I, Daniel, understood by the books the number of the years *specified* by the word of the LORD through Jeremiah the prophet, that He would accomplish seventy years in the desolations of Jerusalem.

³Then I set my face toward the Lord God to make request by prayer and supplications, with fasting, sackcloth, and ashes. ⁴And I prayed to the LORD my God, and made confession, and said, "O Lord, great and awesome God, who keeps His covenant and mercy with those who love Him, and with those who keep His commandments, ⁵we have sinned and committed iniquity, we have done wickedly and rebelled, even by departing from Your precepts and Your judgments. ⁶Neither have we heeded Your servants the prophets, who spoke in Your name to our kings and our princes, to our fathers and all the people of the land. ⁷O Lord, righteousness *belongs* to You, but to us shame of face, as *it is* this day—to the men of Judah, to the inhabitants of Jerusalem and all Israel, those near and those far off in all the countries to which You have driven them, because of the unfaithfulness which they have committed against You.

⁸"O Lord, to us *belongs* shame of face, to our kings, our princes, and our fathers, because we have sinned against You. ⁹To the Lord our God *belong* mercy and forgiveness, though we have rebelled against Him. ¹⁰We have not obeyed the voice of the LORD our God, to walk in His laws, which He set before us by His servants the prophets. ¹¹Yes, all Israel has transgressed Your law, and has departed so as not to obey Your voice; therefore the curse and the oath written in the Law of Moses the servant of God have been poured out on us, because we have sinned against Him. ¹²And He has confirmed His words, which He spoke against us and against our judges who judged us, by bringing upon us a great disaster; for under the whole heaven such has never been done as what has been done to Jerusalem. ¹³"As *it is* written in the Law of Moses, all this disaster has come upon us; yet we have not made our prayer before the LORD

The Seventy Weeks

Biblical texts concerning the future are not usually specific about dates. One exception to this rule is Jeremiah's prophecy that the exiles in Babylon would return to Jerusalem, but not until 70 years had passed (Jer. 25:11, 12; 29:10). Even here, Jeremiah emphasizes not a specific date, but rather that the exiles should not expect the return to occur in their own lifetime. We cannot be certain of either the exact beginning point or the exact end point of Jeremiah's 70-year period.

Jeremiah had prophesied that the Exile in Babylon would last 70 years. The fall of Babylon caused the exiled Daniel to recall Jeremiah's 70 years (Dan. 9:2) and pray for restoration. The vision that Daniel receives (Dan. 9:24–27) does not explain the 70 years, but does offer a second interpretation. Full restoration would come not in 70 years but in 70 weeks (Dan. 9:24). If the 70 weeks represent 70 periods of 7 years each (thus 70 × 7 = 490 years), the vision would be pointing to some time in the 2nd or 1st century B.C.

Despite the apparent specificity of the prophecy, the exact years represented by the vision's 70 weeks cannot be calculated. To begin with, it is not certain where to begin counting—70 weeks starting when? Perhaps it is from 538 B.C., the year of Cyrus's decree allowing the exiles to return and rebuild Jerusalem (Dan. 9:25). Or it may be from 520 B.C., the date of the actual rebuilding of the temple. Or perhaps it is from the date of the vision itself. But that date itself is unclear, because the vision is dated from the 1st year of "Darius the son of Ahasuerus, of the lineage of the Medes" (Dan. 9:1, 2). The first Darius to be king was not a Mede, but a Persian, and Ahasuerus (Xerxes) was his son, not his father (see "Darius the Mede" at Dan. 6:1).

In the end, the exact dates are less important than the theological message of the chapter. Full restoration of the punished people of God cannot and will not be immediate. Just as the sins of the Jews were long-standing sins, stubbornly clung to by unfaithful Israel, so the restoration will take longer than just one generation to be completed. As in chs. 7 and 8, Dan. 9 points toward the final years of the 1st millennium B.C., to some great salvation in either Greek or Roman times.

■ Daniel 9:1–27

ALEXANDER THE GREAT (Dan. 8:21)

Alexander the Great, born to Philip II of Macedon and Olympias of Epirus in 356 B.C., is depicted in Daniel's vision (Dan. 8:5, 21) and prophecy (Dan. 11:3). After the assassination of his father in 336 B.C., Alexander inherited the rising kingdom of Macedon, the Greek-speaking state north of modern Greece. He was able to sustain his father's recent conquests in Greece and then manipulate the Greek city-states to join him in the conquest of the great Persian Empire.

Before the age of thirty (327 B.C.) Alexander had conquered all of Persia, from Lycia to the Indus River. He then returned to Babylon and prepared to make the city his new capital. Some have suggested that Alexander attempted to create a universal state that broke down the cultural barriers between Greece and Persia. He may also have contemplated the conquest of the western Mediterranean world, but if so, that ambition was cut off by his premature death in 323 B.C.

Following the decease of Alexander, the empire broke up and was divided among four of his generals, symbolized by the four horns (Dan. 8:8, 22) and the four winds (Dan. 11:4). One of these generals, Ptolemy I, founded the Ptolemaic dynasty of Egypt, which he ruled himself from 305 to 282 B.C. The Ptolemies initially controlled Palestine until being defeated by the Seleucids in 200 B.C.

Alexander's conquests had far-reaching effects on the Near East. Greek language and culture were introduced to this area, considerably reshaping Near Eastern civilization. This mixture of Greek and Near Eastern civilizations became known as Hellenism.

Hellenism greatly influenced Israel's culture, especially through the Septuagint, a Greek translation of the Hebrew Old Testament. The Septuagint became the Scripture of the early Christians. New Testament writers frequently quoted the Septuagint (as does Paul in Rom. 15:12) as a source of inspired teaching (see Rom. 15:4). Other Jewish writers, such as Philo and Josephus, interpreted the Septuagint allegorically and quoted it often.

our God, that we might turn from our iniquities and understand Your truth. [14]Therefore the LORD has kept the disaster in mind, and brought it upon us; for the LORD our God *is* righteous in all the works which He does, though we have not obeyed His voice. [15]And now, O Lord our God, who brought Your people out of the land of Egypt with a mighty hand, and made Yourself a name, as *it is* this day—we have sinned, we have done wickedly!

[16]"O Lord, according to all Your righteousness, I pray, let Your anger and Your fury be turned away from Your city Jerusalem, Your holy mountain; because for our sins, and for the iniquities of our fathers, Jerusalem and Your people *are* a reproach to all *those* around us. [17]Now therefore, our God, hear the prayer of Your servant, and his supplications, and for the Lord's sake cause Your face to shine on Your sanctuary, which is desolate. [18]O my God, incline Your ear and hear; open Your eyes and see our desolations, and the city which is called by Your name; for we do not present our supplications before You because of our righteous deeds, but because of Your great mercies. [19]O Lord, hear! O Lord, forgive! O Lord, listen and act! Do not delay for Your own sake, my God, for Your city and Your people are called by Your name."

The Seventy-Weeks Prophecy

[20]Now while I *was* speaking, praying, and confessing my sin and the sin of my people Israel, and presenting my supplication before the LORD my God for the holy mountain of my God, [21]yes, while I *was* speaking in prayer, the man Gabriel, whom I had seen in the vision at the beginning, being caused to fly swiftly, reached me about the time of the evening offering. [22]And he informed *me,* and talked with me, and said, "O Daniel, I have now come forth to give you skill to understand. [23]At the beginning of your supplications the command went out, and I have come to tell *you,* for you *are* greatly beloved; therefore consider the matter, and understand the vision:

THE 70 YEARS OF JEREMIAH

Jeremiah prophesied that Israel would be captive in Babylon for 70 years (Jer. 25:11, 12; 29:10). His prophecy was recalled in the writings of the Chronicler (2 Chr. 36:20, 21) and of the prophets (Dan. 9:2; and probably Zech. 1:12).

Various important events have been interpreted as marking either the beginning point or end point of the 70-year period. The actual spans of years between any of the possible beginning points (612, 605, 586 B.C.) and the possible end points (538, 520, 515 B.C.) do not provide any interval of exactly 70 years. The number 70 is probably a round figure, which represents the length of one lifetime (Ps. 90:10). In other words, any of the exact spans (of 74, 67, 66, or 71 years) could correspond to the significant number 70.

Beginning Year and Event	Span	Ending Year and Event
612 B.C. Babylon conquers Nineveh (Nah. 1:1, 14)	74 years	538 B.C. Cyrus allows Jews to rebuild temple (Ezra 1:1–4)
605 B.C. Battle of Carchemish; Nebuchadnezzar becomes king (Jer. 46:2)	67 years	538 B.C. Cyrus allows Jews to rebuild temple (Ezra 1:1–4)
586 B.C. Fall of Jerusalem (Jer. 52:12)	66 years	520 B.C. Jews resume rebuilding the temple (Hag. 1:14, 15)
586 B.C. Fall of Jerusalem (Jer. 52:12)	71 years	515 B.C. Jews celebrate the dedication of the temple (Ezra 6:15–18)

24 "Seventy weeks[a] are determined
For your people and for your holy city,
To finish the transgression,
To make an end of[b] sins,
To make reconciliation for iniquity,
To bring in everlasting righteousness,
To seal up vision and prophecy,
And to anoint the Most Holy.

25 "Know therefore and understand,
That from the going forth of the command
To restore and build Jerusalem
Until Messiah the Prince,
There shall be seven weeks and sixty-two weeks;
The street[a] shall be built again, and the wall,[b]
Even in troublesome times.

26 "And after the sixty-two weeks
Messiah shall be cut off, but not for Himself;
And the people of the prince who is to come

Shall destroy the city and the sanctuary.
The end of it *shall be* with a flood,
And till the end of the war desolations are determined.

27 Then he shall confirm a covenant with many for one week;
But in the middle of the week
He shall bring an end to sacrifice and offering.
And on the wing of abominations shall be one who makes desolate,
Even until the consummation, which is determined,
Is poured out on the desolate."

9:24 [a]Literally *sevens,* and so throughout the chapter [b]Following Qere, Septuagint, Syriac, and Vulgate; Kethib and Theodotion read *To seal up.*   9:25 [a]Or *open square* [b]Or *moat*

Daniel and the Greeks

The final vision of the Book of Daniel (Dan. 10—12) is the clearest in terms of its historical context. Although it certainly may be reinterpreted to apply to other and later times, it also certainly speaks of events in the 2nd century B.C., when the Greek kingdoms controlled Palestine.

The vision begins with a description of the heavenly messenger who brought the vision to Daniel (Dan. 10:4–9). This messenger is clad in radiant gold and his eyes are fiery. Daniel is frightened, but the messenger gives him courage to face the vision (10:10, 18). The apocalyptic visions of the New Testament writer John, described in the Book of Revelation, begin in almost exactly the same way (Rev. 1:12–20).

As the vision itself is revealed (Dan. 11:2—12:3), its relation to the historical events of the Greek Empire becomes apparent. As the last kings of Persia are ruling, a great king shall arise in Greece who will "rule with great dominion" (11:2, 3). This king must be Alexander (336–323 B.C.). After the great king dies, though, his kingdom will be divided among those who are not his heirs (11:4), the Greek generals who divided Alexander's empire. After this, the vision is only interested in two of those kingdoms, the ones most closely concerned with the land of Judah and Jerusalem. These are the kings of the South (the Ptolemies, based in Egypt) and the kings of the North (the Seleucids, based in Syria).

The vision describes the relations between the Ptolemies and the Seleucids in amazing detail. For instance, the attempted marriage alliance between the two kingdoms (11:6) probably refers to an event of 250 B.C. The Ptolemies and Seleucids were briefly united in the troubled marriage of Berenice, daughter of Ptolemy II (285–246 B.C.), to the Seleucid king Antiochus II (261–246 B.C.).

Various Seleucid kings are alluded to in Dan. 11. Antiochus III (223–187 B.C.) was the king who finally captured Judah and Jerusalem from the Ptolemies (11:11–19). His immediate successor, Seleucus IV (187–175 B.C.), had a mostly peaceful reign, though in the end he was murdered (11:20). The hated Antiochus IV (175–164 B.C.) attempted to stamp out all religions except those of Greece and showed a particular hatred for the religion of the Jews (11:21–45). The vision first describes his military campaigns against Egypt (11:25–28), then his persecutions of the Jews (11:30–39). Antiochus IV outlawed Jewish religion, forced Jews to eat pork or die, burned the Jewish Scriptures, and in the worst act of all, set up an altar to the Greek god Zeus in the Jerusalem temple (the "abomination of desolation," 11:31).

The rest of the vision is somewhat less specific. The distant future seems to be the focus of ch. 12, which offers the general prediction that all such evil worldly kingdoms will fall at the last day before the eternal victory of Israel's God (12:1–3). Although it is easy to be diverted by the specifics of the historical visions, this is the heart of all apocalyptic writing: the promise that God will one day right all wrongs and His faithful will dwell with Him "like the stars forever and ever" (12:3).

Historical specificity such as appears in Dan. 11 is rare in biblical prophecy. It is especially remarkable since Daniel's exile is placed more than 400 years before the events so minutely described in the vision (Dan. 1:1–7). Because of this, many scholars suggest that the visions of Dan. 7—12 were actually written in Palestine during the persecutions of Antiochus IV (167 B.C.), and attributed after the fact to the famous exile Daniel. Such late attributions are fairly common in other apocalyptic writings of Greek and Roman times and would have been a familiar literary device to the original readers.

Other scholars emphasize that accurate foretelling of the future is possible for God, even down to minute details, and accept Daniel's authorship. Whether these visions were written during the Babylonian exile (597–538 B.C.) or during the reign of Antiochus IV (175–164 B.C.), the message is the same: the faithful ones who are persecuted, particularly those persecuted by Antiochus, can take heart. God will overcome His enemies at last.

■ Daniel 10:1—12:13

Daniel
Vision of the Glorious Man

10 :1 In the third year of Cyrus king of Persia a message was revealed to Daniel, whose name was called Belteshazzar. The message *was* true, but the appointed time *was* long;[a] and he understood the message, and had understanding of the vision. [2]In those days I, Daniel, was mourning three full weeks. [3]I ate no pleasant food, no meat or wine came into my mouth, nor did I anoint myself at all, till three whole weeks were fulfilled.

[4]Now on the twenty-fourth day of the first month, as I was by the side of the

---

10:1 [a]Or *and of great conflict*

great river, that *is,* the Tigris,[a] [5]I lifted my eyes and looked, and behold, a certain man clothed in linen, whose waist *was* girded with gold of Uphaz! [6]His body *was* like beryl, his face like the appearance of lightning, his eyes like torches of fire, his arms and feet like burnished bronze in color, and the sound of his words like the voice of a multitude.

[7]And I, Daniel, alone saw the vision, for the men who were with me did not see the vision; but a great terror fell upon them, so that they fled to hide themselves. [8]Therefore I was left alone when I saw this great vision, and no strength remained in me; for my vigor was turned to frailty in me, and I retained no strength. [9]Yet I heard the sound of his words; and while I heard the sound of his words I was in a deep sleep on my face, with my face to the ground.

Prophecies Concerning Persia and Greece

[10]Suddenly, a hand touched me, which made me tremble on my knees and *on* the palms of my hands. [11]And he said to me, "O Daniel, man greatly beloved, understand the words that I speak to you, and stand upright, for I have now been sent to you." While he was speaking this word to me, I stood trembling.

[12]Then he said to me, "Do not fear, Daniel, for from the first day that you set your heart to understand, and to humble yourself before your God, your words were heard; and I have come because of your words. [13]But the prince of the kingdom of Persia withstood me twenty-one days; and behold, Michael, one of the chief princes, came to help me, for I had been left alone there with the kings of Persia. [14]Now I have come to make you understand what will happen to your people in the latter days, for the vision *refers to many* days yet *to come.*"

[15]When he had spoken such words to me, I turned my face toward the ground and became speechless. [16]And suddenly, one having the likeness of the sons[a] of men touched my lips; then I opened my mouth and spoke, saying to him who stood before me, "My lord, because of the vision my sorrows have overwhelmed me, and I have retained no strength. [17]For how can this servant of my lord talk with you, my lord? As for me, no strength remains in me now, nor is any breath left in me."

[18]Then again, *the one* having the likeness of a man touched me and strengthened me. [19]And he said, "O man greatly beloved, fear not! Peace *be* to you; be strong, yes, be strong!"

So when he spoke to me I was strengthened, and said, "Let my lord speak, for you have strengthened me."

[20]Then he said, "Do you know why I have come to you? And now I must return to fight with the prince of Persia; and when I have gone forth, indeed the prince of Greece will come. [21]But I will tell you what is noted in the Scripture of Truth. (No one upholds me against these, except Michael your prince.

11 [1]"Also in the first year of Darius the Mede, I, *even* I, stood up to confirm and strengthen him.) [2]And now I will tell you the truth: Behold, three more kings will arise in Persia, and the fourth shall be far richer than *them* all; by his strength, through his riches, he shall stir up all against the realm of Greece. [3]Then a mighty king shall arise, who shall rule with great dominion, and do according to his will. [4]And when he has arisen, his kingdom shall be broken up and divided toward the four winds of heaven, but not among his posterity nor according to his dominion with which he ruled; for his kingdom shall be uprooted, even for others besides these.

Warring Kings of North and South

[5]"Also the king of the South shall become strong, as well as *one* of his princes; and he shall gain power over him and have

---

10:4 [a]Hebrew *Hiddekel*   10:16 [a]Theodotion and Vulgate read *the son;* Septuagint reads *a hand.*

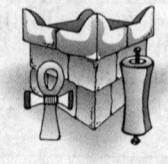

BELIEFS AND IDEAS

Ancient people believed that the destinies of nations were determined by a council of heavenly beings. Each nation was assigned to a certain heavenly power or prince (Dan. 10:13). In the Bible this relation of heaven and earth expresses God's interest in human affairs and also His power over them. God can act in the nations by dispatching an appropriate messenger (Dan. 10:11).

WHO WAS DARIUS THE MEDE? (Dan. 11:1)

A date for the 1st year of "Darius the Mede" (Dan. 11:1) is uncertain because the identity of this Darius is uncertain. The Book of Daniel reports that "Darius the Mede" took over the Chaldean-Babylonian kingdom following the death of Babylon's king Belshazzar (Dan. 5:30, 31). Both Greek and Babylonian sources, however, give credit to Cyrus the Great of Persia for conquering Babylon in 539 B.C. Who, then, was Darius the Mede?

There is no mention of anyone by the name of Darius the Mede outside of the Bible. Nor is there any mention of this Darius in the Bible outside of the Book of Daniel. The other "Darius" in Scripture is Darius I (522–486 B.C.), the king of Persia named in the books of Ezra (Ezra 4:5, 24) and Nehemiah (Neh. 12:22), who ruled years after the fall of Babylon. Thus, ancient sources do not answer the question, Who was Darius the Mede?

Some scholars identify Darius the Mede with a governor of Gutium named Gaubaruwa. Gaubaruwa could be considered "a Mede" since Gutium was a Babylonian term for Media in this period. A royal inscription known as the Nabonidus Chronicle relates how Gaubaruwa captured Babylon on behalf of Cyrus. Gaubaruwa was then appointed by Cyrus to be vice-regent over the whole of Mesopotamia, a rule cut short by Gaubaruwa's death less than a year later. The Book of Daniel might refer to this appointment in noting that Darius "was made king" (Dan. 9:1).

It is plausible that Gaubaruwa was Darius the Mede. Several kings bore the name "Darius," and it could have been used by Gaubaruwa as a throne name. If this Darius really was an older man of 62 years when assuming rule of Babylon (Dan. 5:31), his quick death would be understandable. Nevertheless, scholars have not yet been able to explain the relationship of Darius with the little-known Gaubaruwa.

---

dominion. His dominion *shall be* a great dominion. 6And at the end of *some* years they shall join forces, for the daughter of the king of the South shall go to the king of the North to make an agreement; but she shall not retain the power of her authority,[a] and neither he nor his authority[b] shall stand; but she shall be given up, with those who brought her, and with him who begot her, and with him who strengthened her in *those* times. 7But from a branch of her roots *one* shall arise in his place, who shall

---

11:6 [a]Literally *arm*   [b]Literally *arm*

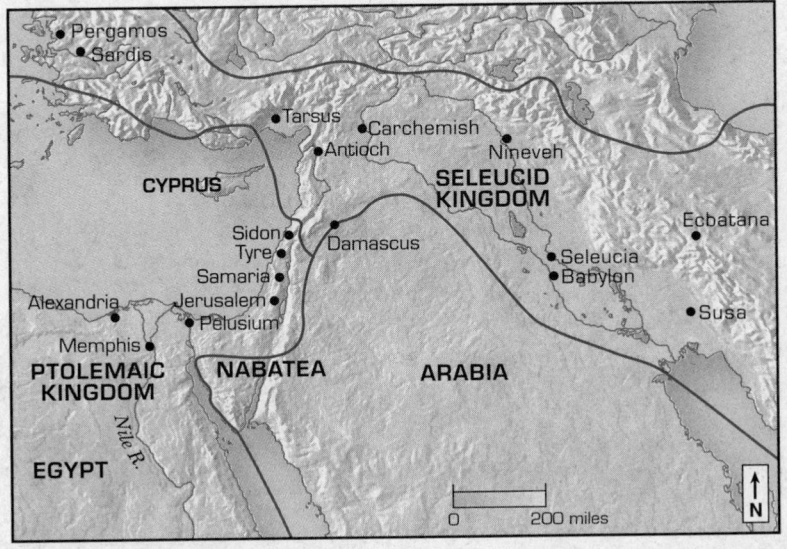

Ptolemaic Control of Palestine

Alexander's death resulted in the breakup of his empire into smaller kingdoms ruled by his generals. Two of those generals, Ptolemy and Seleucus, became established in the regions around Palestine. By 275 B.C. the Ptolemies were controlling Egypt, Palestine, Cyrene, Phoenicia, Cyprus, and the coast of Asia Minor. The Seleucids controlled Mesopotamia, Syria, and most of Asia Minor and Iran.

come with an army, enter the fortress of the king of the North, and deal with them and prevail. 8And he shall also carry their gods captive to Egypt, with their princes[a] *and* their precious articles of silver and gold; and he shall continue *more* years than the king of the North.

9"Also *the king of the North* shall come to the kingdom of the king of the South, but shall return to his own land. 10However his sons shall stir up strife, and assemble a multitude of great forces; and *one* shall certainly come and overwhelm and pass through; then he shall return to his fortress and stir up strife.

11"And the king of the South shall be moved with rage, and go out and fight with him, with the king of the North, who shall muster a great multitude; but the multitude shall be given into the hand of his *enemy.* 12When he has taken away the multitude, his heart will be lifted up; and he will cast down tens of thousands, but he will not prevail. 13For the king of the North will return and muster a multitude greater than the former, and shall certainly come at the end of some years with a great army and much equipment.

14"Now in those times many shall rise up against the king of the South. Also, violent men[a] of your people shall exalt themselves in fulfillment of the vision, but they shall fall. 15So the king of the North shall come and build a siege mound, and take a fortified city; and the forces[a] of the South

shall not withstand *him.* Even his choice troops *shall have* no strength to resist. 16But he who comes against him shall do according to his own will, and no one shall stand against him. He shall stand in the Glorious Land with destruction in his power.[a]

17"He shall also set his face to enter with the strength of his whole kingdom, and upright ones[a] with him; thus shall he do. And he shall give him the daughter of women to destroy it; but she shall not stand *with him,* or be for him. 18After this he shall turn his face to the coastlands, and shall take many. But a ruler shall bring the reproach against them to an end; and with the reproach removed, he shall turn back on him. 19Then he shall turn his face toward the fortress of his own land; but he shall stumble and fall, and not be found.

20"There shall arise in his place one who imposes taxes *on* the glorious kingdom; but within a few days he shall be destroyed, but not in anger or in battle. 21And in his place shall arise a vile person, to whom they will not give the honor of royalty; but he shall come in peaceably, and seize the kingdom by intrigue. 22With the force[a] of a flood they shall be swept away

---

11:8 [a]Or *molded images*   11:14 [a]Or *robbers,* literally *sons of breakage*   11:15 [a]Literally *arms*   11:16 [a]Literally *hand*   11:17 [a]Or *bring equitable terms*   11:22 [a]Literally *arms*

Seleucid Control of Palestine

Antiochus III, king of Syria, expanded the boundaries of the Seleucid Kingdom in numerous battles with the Ptolemies. In 221 B.C. he captured part of Palestine, only to lose most of it in 217 B.C. Returning in 201 B.C., he finally defeated the Ptolemies in 198 B.C. with the aid and support of the Jews. Palestine enjoyed freedom until 175 B.C., when Antiochus IV oppressed the Jews, causing the Maccabean revolt in 167 B.C.

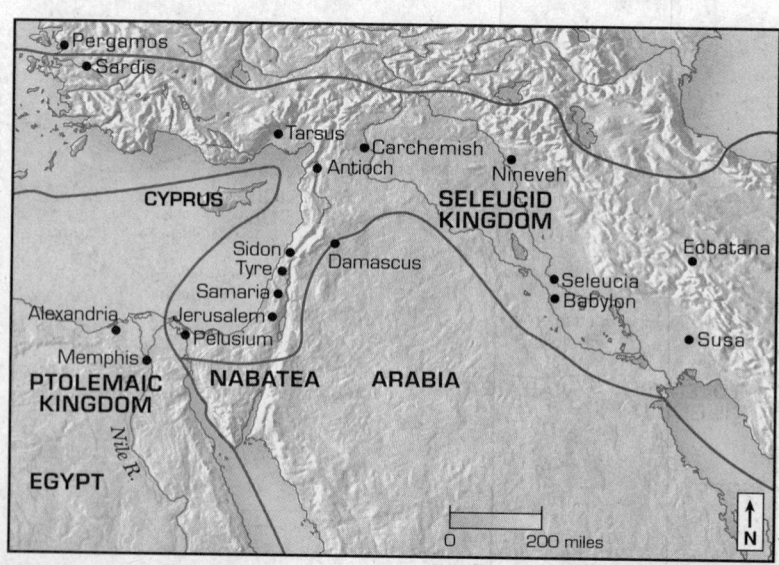

ANTIOCHUS IV—EPIPHANES OR EPIMANES? (Dan. 11:21–31)

Thirteen kings of the Greek Seleucid dynasty from Syria bore the name of Antiochus. Antiochus III (223–187 B.C.), the great conqueror, was eventually defeated by the Romans at Magnesia in 190 B.C. and forced to send his son as a hostage to Rome. That son, Antiochus IV (175–164 B.C.), would return from Rome to become one of the cruelest rulers of the Seleucid dynasty. He is likely the "king of the North" alluded to in Daniel's prophecy (11:21–45).

Ancient historians describe the character of Antiochus as volatile and unstable. The Greek historian Polybius (who published about 145 B.C.) gave him the nickname Epimanes, meaning "mad." Like his father, Antiochus sought to create a united Seleucid empire from a variety of diverse elements, not only politically, but culturally and religiously. Those who refused to be fully assimilated, such as the Jews, were considered a threat and forced into a policy of Hellenization.

In 169 B.C. Antiochus attacked the city of Jerusalem and looted the temple (2 Macc. 5:11–21). Two years later he again attacked that Jewish city on a Sabbath, killing the male children and enslaving other inhabitants. The city walls were demolished and a military garrison was established. After prohibiting any Jewish religious rituals and forbidding the reading of the Scriptures, Antiochus performed a pagan sacrifice to Zeus in the temple, erecting an altar to Zeus over the altar of burnt offering. This desecration is alluded to as the "abomination of desolation" (Dan. 11:31).

Soon thereafter came violent resistance from the Jews. By 164 B.C. Judas Maccabeus had freed Jerusalem from Seleucid hands. Antiochus died in October of that year, during a campaign against Persia. The nickname Epimanes ("mad") was possibly more relevant than his surname Epiphanes (meaning "the manifest god"). The Seleucid ruler had insanely persecuted the Jews, but his persecutions did not last. In December, 164 B.C., exactly 3 years after he defiled the temple and just 2 months after his death, Judas dedicated a new altar of burnt offering.

from before him and be broken, and also the prince of the covenant. ²³And after the league *is made* with him he shall act deceitfully, for he shall come up and become strong with a small *number of* people. ²⁴He shall enter peaceably, even into the richest places of the province; and he shall do *what his fathers have not done, nor his forefathers*: he shall disperse among them the plunder, spoil, and riches; and he shall devise his plans against the strongholds, but *only* for a time.

²⁵"He shall stir up his power and his courage against the king of the South with a great army. And the king of the South shall be stirred up to battle with a very great and mighty army; but he shall not stand, for they shall devise plans against him. ²⁶Yes, those who eat of the portion of his delicacies shall destroy him; his army shall be swept away, and many shall fall down slain. ²⁷Both these kings' hearts *shall be* bent on evil, and they shall speak lies at the same table; but it shall not prosper, for the end *will* still *be* at the appointed time. ²⁸While returning to his land with great riches, his heart shall be *moved* against the holy covenant; so he shall do *damage* and return to his own land.

The Northern King's Blasphemies

²⁹"At the appointed time he shall return and go toward the south; but it shall not be like the former or the latter. ³⁰For ships from Cyprusᵃ shall come against him; therefore he shall be grieved, and return in rage against the holy covenant, and do *damage*.

"So he shall return and show regard for those who forsake the holy covenant.

11:30 ᵃHebrew *Kittim*, western lands, especially Cyprus

³¹And forces[a] shall be mustered by him, and they shall defile the sanctuary fortress; then they shall take away the daily *sacrifices,* and place *there* the abomination of desolation. ³²Those who do wickedly against the covenant he shall corrupt with flattery; but the people who know their God shall be strong, and carry out *great exploits.* ³³And those of the people who understand shall instruct many; yet *for many* days they shall fall by sword and flame, by captivity and plundering. ³⁴Now when they fall, they shall be aided with a little help; but many shall join with them by intrigue. ³⁵And *some* of those of understanding shall fall, to refine them, purify *them,* and make *them* white, *until* the time of the end; because *it is* still for the appointed time.

³⁶"Then the king shall do according to his own will: he shall exalt and magnify himself above every god, shall speak blasphemies against the God of gods, and shall prosper till the wrath has been accomplished; for what has been determined shall be done. ³⁷He shall regard neither the God[a] of his fathers nor the desire of women, nor regard any god; for he shall exalt himself above *them* all. ³⁸But in their place he shall honor a god of fortresses; and a god which his fathers did not know he shall honor with gold and silver, with precious stones and pleasant things. ³⁹Thus he shall act against the strongest fortresses with a foreign god, which he shall acknowledge, *and* advance *its* glory; and he shall cause them to rule over many, and divide the land for gain.

The Northern King's Conquests

⁴⁰"At the time of the end the king of the South shall attack him; and the king of the North shall come against him like a whirlwind, with chariots, horsemen, and with many ships; and he shall enter the countries, overwhelm *them,* and pass through. ⁴¹He shall also enter the Glorious Land, and many *countries* shall be overthrown; but these shall escape from his hand: Edom, Moab, and the prominent people of Ammon. ⁴²He shall stretch out his hand against the countries, and the land of Egypt shall not escape. ⁴³He shall have power over the treasures of gold and silver, and over all the precious things of Egypt; also the Libyans and Ethiopians *shall fol-*

11:31 [a]Literally *arms*   11:37 [a]Or *gods*

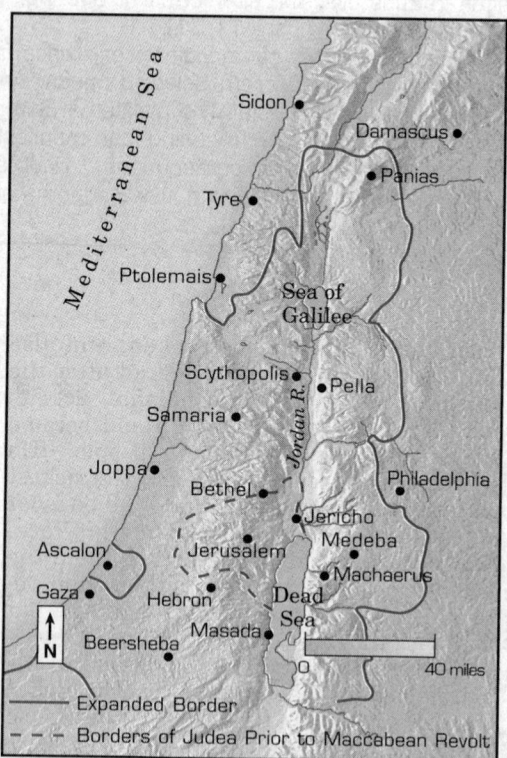

Expansion of Palestine Under the Maccabees
At the time of the Maccabean revolt, the Jewish leaders controlled a very small portion of their former land. Between 166 and 76 B.C., however, several men led the Jews to expand their area of control: Jonathan, brother and successor to Judas Maccabeus; John Hyrcanus; Aristobulus; and Alexander Jannaeus.

TIME CAPSULE   *327 to 323 B.C.*

327   *Alexander marries the Iranian princess Roxane*

327   *Alexander's army begins campaign against India*

323   *Macedonian armies use catapults for shooting arrows*

323   *Alexander dies prematurely of fever*

323   *Alexander's empire divided among four of his generals*

323   *Ptolemy I hijacks Alexander's body and takes it to Egypt*

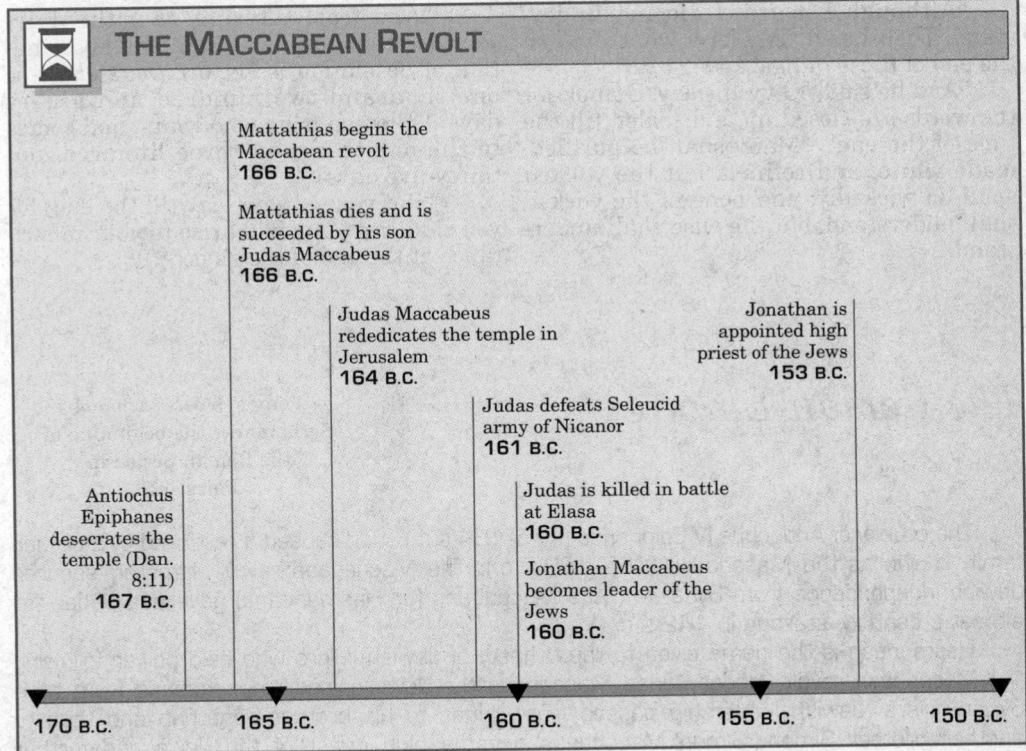

THE MACCABEAN REVOLT

Mattathias begins the
Maccabean revolt
166 B.C.

Mattathias dies and is
succeeded by his son
Judas Maccabeus
166 B.C.

Judas Maccabeus
rededicates the temple in
Jerusalem
164 B.C.

Jonathan is
appointed high
priest of the Jews
153 B.C.

Judas defeats Seleucid
army of Nicanor
161 B.C.

Antiochus
Epiphanes
desecrates the
temple (Dan.
8:11)
167 B.C.

Judas is killed in battle
at Elasa
160 B.C.

Jonathan Maccabeus
becomes leader of the
Jews
160 B.C.

170 B.C.   **165 B.C.**   **160 B.C.**   **155 B.C.**   **150 B.C.**

low at his heels. ⁴⁴But news from the east and the north shall trouble him; therefore he shall go out with great fury to destroy and annihilate many. ⁴⁵And he shall plant the tents of his palace between the seas and the glorious holy mountain; yet he shall come to his end, and no one will help him.

Prophecy of the End Time

12 ¹"At that time Michael shall stand up,
The great prince who stands _watch_
over the sons of your people;
And there shall be a time of
trouble,
Such as never was since there was a
nation,
Even to that time.
And at that time your people shall be
delivered,
Every one who is found written in the
book.
² And many of those who sleep in the
dust of the earth shall awake,
Some to everlasting life,

Some to shame _and_ everlasting
contempt.
³ Those who are wise shall shine
Like the brightness of the firmament,
And those who turn many to
righteousness
Like the stars forever and ever.

⁴"But you, Daniel, shut up the words, and seal the book until the time of the end; many shall run to and fro, and knowledge shall increase."

⁵Then I, Daniel, looked; and there stood two others, one on this riverbank and the other on that riverbank. ⁶And _one_ said to the man clothed in linen, who _was_ above the waters of the river, "How long shall the fulfillment of these wonders _be?_"

⁷Then I heard the man clothed in linen, who _was_ above the waters of the river, when he held up his right hand and his left hand to heaven, and swore by Him who lives forever, that _it shall be_ for a time, times, and half _a time;_ and when the power of the holy people has been completely shattered, all these _things_ shall be finished.

[8]Although I heard, I did not understand. Then I said, "My lord, what *shall be* the end of these *things?*"

[9]And he said, "Go *your way*, Daniel, for the words *are* closed up and sealed till the time of the end. [10]Many shall be purified, made white, and refined, but the wicked shall do wickedly; and none of the wicked shall understand, but the wise shall understand.

[11]"And from the time *that* the daily *sacrifice* is taken away, and the abomination of desolation is set up, *there shall be* one thousand two hundred and ninety days. [12]Blessed *is* he who waits, and comes to the one thousand three hundred and thirty-five days.

[13]"But you, go *your way* till the end; for you shall rest, and will arise to your inheritance at the end of the days."

The Roman Empire

Pompey's occupation of Syria marks the beginning of the Roman period in Palestine.

The cruelty of Antiochus IV Epiphanes (175–164 B.C.) soon caused a revolt led by a Jewish family known as the Maccabees (166–160 B.C.). The Maccabean revolt ultimately secured Jewish independence from Syria, and the Maccabees (or Hasmoneans) governed Judea for almost a century, starting in 142 B.C.

Hasmonean is the name given to the dynasty of Jewish rulers who held power following the Maccabean revolt. Under Judas Maccabeus the Jews gained independence from their Syrian rulers. Jewish leadership passed from Judas to his brother Jonathan and then to another brother Simon. Simon Maccabeus became high priest of the Jews and further established the family in power. When Simon's son, John Hyrcanus I (135–104 B.C.), succeeded his father, this signaled the beginning of the Hasmonean dynasty. Their rule continued under Aristobulus (104–103 B.C.), Alexander Jannaeus (103–76 B.C.), Salome Alexandra (76–67 B.C.), and Aristobulus II (67–63 B.C.).

The Hasmonean rulers were recognized by Rome, but their period of rule was troubled by constant war with their neighbors, political infighting, murder, terrorism, and conflict between the Pharisees and the Sadducees. Although Judea was nominally still a province of Syria, in practical terms the country was independent and remained so until 63 B.C., when Rome invaded. The Romans sent the famous general Pompey the Great to end Hasmonean rule and to establish Roman authority in Jerusalem.

According to tradition, Rome was founded in 753 B.C. by Romulus, who became its first king. The little kingdom grew in size and importance, absorbing its immediate neighbors through the reign of seven kings, until the tyranny of Tarquinius Superbus drove the people to revolt and to take the government into their own hands. A republic was established, and Roman citizens had a voice in governmental affairs.

During the period of the republic, Rome extended her borders throughout all of Italy and much of the known world. The Roman occupation of Syria under Pompey in 63 B.C. marks the beginning of the Roman period in Palestine, and for the next century Roman soldiers were stationed in Jerusalem. Under the watchful eye of Rome, Herod the Great (37–4 B.C.) became governor of Galilee (47 B.C.) and later ruler of Judea (37 B.C.). As king, Herod controlled not only the political life in Judea, but also the important office of high priest, although the religious affairs of the nation were led by the Pharisees and Sadducees.

By defeating Antony and Cleopatra in 31 B.C., Octavian became the head of the Roman Empire. He ruled under the title of Augustus, bringing a period of peace and prosperity to the empire until his death in A.D. 14. It was during the reign of Augustus, and just before the death of Herod the Great, that Jesus Christ was born (about 5 B.C.). With this event the chronology of the Old Testament era formally comes to an end.

TIME CAPSULE *319 to 223 B.C.*

319   Ptolemy I unsuccessfully attempts to control Palestine

312–250   The early Seleucid kings found many cities with the name "Antioch"

312   Nabateans gain control of Petra, the former capital of Edom

305–282   Ptolemy I founds the Ptolemaic dynasty of Egypt

305–281   Seleucus I founds the dating system known as the Seleucid Era

305–240   Callimachus, Greek poet

301   Seleucus conquers Syria; Ptolemy controls Palestine

285–246   Ptolemy II corules with his sister Arsinoe II

281–261   Antiochus I establishes Seleucid ruler cult

280   Dynasty of the Antigonids established in Macedonia

280   Dynasty of the Ptolemies established in Egypt

280   Dynasty of the Seleucids established in Persia and Syria

274–271   First Syrian War (Antiochus I vs. Ptolemy II)

264–241   First Punic War (Rome vs. Carthage)

261–246   Antiochus II marries his half sister Laodice

260–253   Second Syrian War (Antiochus II vs. Ptolemy II)

250   Ptolemies and Seleucids are united in the marriage of Berenice and Antiochus II (Dan. 11:6)

246–241   Third Syrian War (Seleucus II vs. Ptolemy III)

246–225   Seleucus II invades Egypt but is repulsed (Dan. 11:9)

246–222   Ptolemy III retaliates against Seleucids for his sister's death (Dan. 11:7, 8)

238–224   The Parthian Empire

225–223   Seleucus III and his brother Antiochus III are defeated by Egypt (Dan. 11:10)

223–187   Antiochus III rules the Greek Seleucid dynasty of Syria

TIME CAPSULE *221 to 166 B.C.*

221–217   Fourth Syrian War (Antiochus III vs. Ptolemy IV)

222–204   Ptolemy IV loses control of Upper Egypt to Nubian kings

218–201   Second Punic War (Rome vs. Carthage)

218   Romans take control of the island of Malta

217   Ptolemy IV defeats Antiochus III at battle of Raphia (Dan. 11:11, 12)

215   Rome begins to rival Greek power in the West

204–180   Ptolemy V marries Cleopatra I (Dan. 11:17)

202–200   Fifth Syrian War (Antiochus III vs. Ptolemy V)

200   Ptolemies lose control of Palestine to the Seleucids (Dan. 11:13–15)

192–189   War between Rome and the Seleucids

190   The Romans defeat Antiochus III at Magnesia (Dan. 11:18, 19)

188   Treaty of Apamea between Antiochus III and Rome

187–175   Seleucus IV raises monies to pay the Romans (Dan. 11:20)

180   Jesus, son of Sirach, writes Ecclesiasticus

175–164   Antiochus IV is one of the cruelest rulers of the Seleucid dynasty

175   Antiochus deposes Onias III as high priest and appoints Jason

172   Menelaus supplants Jason as high priest

170   Antiochus invades Egypt (Dan. 11:25–28)

169   Antiochus attacks Jerusalem and loots the temple (2 Macc. 5:11–21)

168   Romans force Antiochus to leave Egypt (Dan. 11:29, 30)

168–30   Ptolemies fall under Roman control

167   Antiochus offers sacrifices to Zeus on the altar of the temple (Dan. 11:31)

166–160   The Maccabees lead revolt against Seleucids

TIME CAPSULE *164 to 76 B.C.*

164 Judas Maccabeus frees Jerusalem from the Seleucids

164 Antiochus IV dies during campaign against Persia

164 Judas Maccabeus dedicates new altar of burnt offering

162 Demetrius I seizes control in Syria

160 Judas Maccabeus dies and Jonathan assumes command

152 Jonathan becomes high priest

149–146 Third Punic War (Rome vs. Carthage)

146 Romans destroy Greek Corinth

145 Greek historian Polybius publishes

143 Jonathan Maccabeus is murdered

142 Simon Maccabeus is recognized as high priest

142 Hasmonean dynasty governs an independent Judea

135–104 John Hyrcanus I inscribes his own name on coins

129 John Hyrcanus destroys the Samaritan temple on Mount Gerizim

104–103 Aristobulus I conquers Galilee

103–76 Alexander Jannaeus is supported by Sadducees

90–85 Pharisees rebel against Jannaeus

76–67 Salome Alexandra, widow of Jannaeus, rules as queen

76 Alexandra makes peace with the Pharisees

76 Alexandra appoints her son Hyrcanus II as high priest

TIME CAPSULE *67 to 37 B.C.*

67–63 Aristobulus II seizes throne with support of Sadducees

65 Hyrcanus II besieges Jerusalem

64 Roman general Pompey ends Seleucid rule in Syria

63 Pompey takes control of Palestine

63 Gaius Octavius (Augustus Caesar) is born

63 Pompey captures Jerusalem, and Rome takes control of Palestine

63–40 Hyrcanus II serves as high priest in Judea

60–30 Diodorus Siculus writes a world history

48 Julius Caesar defeats Pompey to become Roman ruler

47 City of Tarsus adopts name "Iuliopolis" in honor of Julius Caesar

47 Herod the Great becomes governor of Galilee

44 Romans rebuild Corinth

44 Julius Caesar is assassinated by Brutus and Cassius

44 Julius Caesar's will makes Gaius Octavius his adopted son

42 The Triumvirate gains victory over Caesar's murderers

42 Tarsus made a free city by Antony

40 Roman Senate appoints Herod the Great to rule Judea

37–4 Herod the Great rules as king of Judea

37 The Romans conquer Jerusalem for Herod the Great

THE COMING OF THE MESSIAH

(37 B.C.—A.D. 30)

**The Herods are overshadowed by the great events
that occurred during their time: the ministry,
crucifixion, and resurrection of the Messiah.**

The epoch that witnessed the Messiah's coming actually began with the rise to power of King Herod the Great. The lives of Herod and his sons were closely connected with the earthly life of the Messiah, Jesus of Nazareth. According to the Gospel of Matthew, Herod the Great ordered the deaths of all male children in Bethlehem who were under the age of two (Matt. 2), an order that forced Joseph to flee, taking his wife and young Child to Egypt.

After Herod's death, his sons continued to impact the life of the Messiah. One of Herod's sons was partly responsible for the Messiah becoming known as "Jesus of Nazareth." When Joseph returned from Egypt with Mary and Jesus, he chose to avoid Judea. Herod's son, Archelaus, ruled over Judea and was worse than his father, so Joseph (with Jesus) settled in Nazareth of Galilee. Herod Antipas, another son of Herod the Great, ordered the death of John the Baptist and held a mock "hearing" of Jesus after His arrest. Despite having positions of power, the Herodian family was overshadowed by the great events that occurred during their time: the ministry, crucifixion, and resurrection of the Messiah, bringing victory over sin, death, and the devil.

▶ Archaeology and the Past

Archaeological discoveries in the Holy Land from the Roman period (37 B.C.–A.D. 325) fall into two categories: those which shed light on the Roman world, and those which shed light on the life of Jesus. Sometimes the same archaeological find fits into both categories.

The Roman period, archaeologically, is the world of Herod the Great. Among his many building accomplishments is the great seaport Caesarea Maritima. Excavations have uncovered the theater, the harbor, vast warehouses, temples, and one important inscription. A stone bearing the name of Pontius Pilate, the governor, reminds us that Caesarea was also the headquarters of Roman forces occupying the land. Military installations were placed all over Judea, since it was a border province. Roman Jericho, built on a site different from both Old Testament Jericho and the modern city, was also the work of Herod. The ruins of a magnificent palace and baths have been uncovered in Jericho's excavations.

In Jerusalem are more remains of Herod's building programs. The Wailing Wall is actually part of the great retaining wall Herod built around the Temple Mount to make a surface large enough for the temple rebuilding project. On the western side of the Old City, at a site called the Tower of David, are the remains of one of the towers Herod built to defend the city. It is probably the tower called Phasael, as described by Josephus. Either in one of these towers, or in his great palace nearby, Herod and his soldiers mocked Jesus.

The ministry of Jesus is illumined by archaeology. In Galilee, the famous "Jesus boat" was discovered in a lake during a drought. One can picture Jesus, Peter, and the others setting out across the lake in such a boat, since it is much like the ones used by fishermen of the 1st century. In Capernaum, the center of Jesus' Galilean ministry, are at least two possible links to Jesus. The synagogue that visitors see is dated to the 4th century, but more recent excavations have shown the foundations of a 1st-century building underneath it. Since synagogues were always built on the same site, the 1st-century synagogue may have been where Jesus preached. Nearby are the ruins of an octagonal church. Archaeologists believe that this ancient church is on the site of Peter's house, and that the foundations discovered underneath the church are literally the remains of the building where Jesus stayed while in Capernaum.

Around Jerusalem are many reminders of Jesus' ministry. Just over the Mount of Olives is the village of Bethany, where we find a 1st-century tomb belonging to a wealthy family. This is the traditional tomb of Lazarus, having a vestibule chamber and a small inner chamber. Somewhere on the Mount of Olives is the Garden of Gethsemane. Whether it was located at the Church of All Nations or nearby at the "Tomb of Mary" is debated. But beyond debate is the reality that Jesus prayed in this vicinity.

Excavations at the southern end of the Temple Mount have uncovered the steps that led up to the temple. Several steps remain in an unrestored condition, and represent the way 1st-century persons, including Jesus, usually entered the temple. The steps are also identified as the "rabbis' teaching steps," meaning that Jesus likely sat on them, teaching His disciples and the crowds.

On the north end of the Old City are twin pools which possibly represent the Pool of Bethesda, where Jesus healed a lame man. The porches mentioned in John's Gospel (John 5:2) stood along the sides of the pools and on the causeway between them. Back on the south end of the city are the remains of the Essene Gate, a 1st-century gate that led into Jerusalem. Nearby the gate are the remains of the house of Caiaphas, who was high priest at the time of Jesus' trial. A dank, cold basement cell reminds us that Jesus may have been imprisoned there for at least a few hours. A paved courtyard above reminds us of Peter's denial by the high priest's house.

The steps are the "rabbis' teaching steps"; Jesus likely sat on them, teaching His disciples and the crowds.

One of the most powerful archaeological remains is the discovery of a man who had been crucified. Johanan, the name inscribed in the stone box that held his bones, had nail marks in his wrists, and one nail driven through the heel bones. The wood of the cross had been cut apart and buried with him. Johanan's bones illustrate crucifixion, a common method of execution for the Romans, and possibly suggest the way Jesus Himself was executed.

Archaeologists almost universally agree that the site of Jesus' tomb is located inside the Church of the Holy Sepulchre. At two points in the church, one can actually see what is left of the hill of Calvary. The traditional site of Jesus' burial is found very near other 1st-century tombs.

▶ The Peoples and Groups

Peoples outside Judea and Galilee were also prominent in this period. The Nabateans were an Arabic people, with their capital at Petra to the south. The daughter of the Nabatean king Aretas IV married Herod Antipas. When Antipas threw her over for his own sister-in-law Herodias, war broke out between Herod Antipas and the Nabateans. This was the same Herod who beheaded John the Baptist and held a hearing for Jesus at the request of Pilate.

Southeast of the Sea of Galilee were the cities of the Decapolis. Founded by Greeks and Macedonians, the Decapolis was united not by political organization, but by Hellenistic culture and institutions. Gerasa has been excavated, and one can see the city walls, temples, the marketplace, and paved streets with colonnades. The only remains of 1st-century Philadelphia are the ruins of a Roman theater, near the downtown heart of a bustling, modern city.

The Gospels mention such groups as the Samaritans, Pharisees, Sadducees, and Zealots. The Samaritans and Jews suffered a long history of hatred for each other, going back to the fall of Israel in 722 B.C. But out of this background of hatred, Jesus identified a Samaritan as one who was truly a neighbor to a Jewish person in need. The Sadducees were the priestly aristocracy in Jerusalem, the leaders of the people. They walked a fine line between Jewish nationalism and keeping the peace with their Roman overlords. The Pharisees were a group of laymen dedicated to the keeping of the Law (Torah). They had a saying: if all Israel would keep Torah perfectly for just one day, the Messiah would come. Some Pharisees opposed Jesus; others befriended Him—warning Him of trouble, speaking for Him at His trial, providing a place for His burial. The Zealots were the revolutionary underground. Jesus' disciple Simon "the Zealot" probably belonged to one of the 1st-century groups who actively opposed Roman rule.

▶ The Biblical Literature

The biblical books relating the time of the Messiah are the Gospels—Matthew, Mark, Luke, and John. Although they tell us almost everything we know about the life and teachings of Jesus, they are not true biographies. Rather, they are theological documents telling who Jesus is and why He is important. They say little about Jesus' family background and youth, and nothing about His physical appearance. They concentrate almost totally on Jesus' ministry, but even here they do not give enough information to reconstruct the history of those years with absolute certainty. Rather, they focus on Jesus' person and His teachings, and give considerable attention to His death and resurrection and the surrounding events.

Matthew, Mark, and Luke are called the Synoptic Gospels. The name "Synoptic" means that they view the life of Jesus from a common perspective. After introducing Jesus in different ways depending on their purpose, they relate the ministry of John the Baptist, the baptism and temptation of Jesus, His ministry in Galilee, His journey to Judea and ministry there, His final week in Jerusalem, His death, and His resurrection.

The Gospel of John differs from the Synoptics in a number of ways. It tells us more about Jesus' early ministry in Judea. John also records long thematic discourses by Jesus instead of the usual shorter sayings of the Synoptics. More than the Synoptics, John includes theological reflection on the meaning of Jesus' life and death. The four Gospels together give us a more complete picture of Jesus than any one of them would by itself.

Introductions to Jesus Christ

Jesus Christ marked a new beginning in God's dealings with His people.

Each of the four Gospels uniquely introduces the story of Jesus Christ as marking a new beginning in God's dealings with His people. The Gospel of Mark uses a brief superscription (Mark 1:1) and prophetic announcement (1:2, 3) to make it clear that Jesus Christ is the Son of God, a truth previously declared by the prophets. Matthew begins his Gospel with a genealogy (Matt. 1:1–17), showing his Jewish readers that Jesus is truly the Messiah by tracing His ancestors back to David. That Jesus' ancestry goes back also to Abraham evidences Jesus' fulfillment of God's promises to Israel.

Two Gospel writers, John and Luke, alert their readers concerning their purpose for writing a Gospel. Luke provides a brief preface (Luke 1:1–4) in which he sets out his intention. In a prologue, John begins with a clear statement about Jesus' preexistence and divinity. He wanted his readers to know and believe that "Jesus is the Christ, the Son of God" (John 20:30, 31).

The Prehistory of Jesus

The prologue of John's Gospel locates the beginning of the story of Jesus in timeless eternity, before the dawn of creation (see Phil. 2:5–11; Col. 1:15–20). John at once identifies "the Word" as God *the Son* and distinguishes Him from God *the Father.* Although there was a time when Jesus of Nazareth did not exist, there never was a time when the Word did not exist.

Yet John announces a time when "the Word became flesh" (John 1:14). The Word became incarnate in this Jesus. This event, the Incarnation, marks the time when the Revealer of God became a specific human being. After the Incarnation, John's Gospel never again refers to Jesus as "the Word." Since the Incarnation, God may be known in the person and work of Jesus.

■ John 1:1–18

John
The Eternal Word

1 **:1** In the beginning was the Word, and the Word was with God, and the Word was God. ²He was in the beginning with God. ³All things were made through Him, and without Him nothing was made that was made. ⁴In Him was life, and the life was the light of men. ⁵And the light shines in the darkness, and the darkness did not comprehendª it.

John's Witness: The True Light

⁶There was a man sent from God, whose name *was*ª John. ⁷This man came for a witness, to bear witness of the Light, that all through him might believe. ⁸He was not that Light, but *was sent* to bear witness of that Light. ⁹That was the true Light which gives light to every man coming into the world.ª

¹⁰He was in the world, and the world was made through Him, and the world did not know Him. ¹¹He came to His own,ª and His ownᵇ did not receive Him. ¹²But as many as received Him, to them He gave the right to become children of God,

---

1:5 ªOr *overcome*   1:6 ªWords in italic type have been added for clarity. They are not found in the original Greek.   1:9 ªOr *That was the true Light which, coming into the world, gives light to every man.*   1:11 ªThat is, His own things or domain ᵇThat is, His own people

---

THE WORD BECOMES FLESH (John 1:14)

John's Gospel describes Jesus' preexistence by identifying Him as the divine "Word" (John 1:1), or, as expressed in the Greek language, the *Logos*. Many Greek philosophers spoke of the *Logos* as universal Reason. People familiar with Greek thought could have understood John to be proclaiming Jesus as the organizing principle or "Reason" behind the universe.

Some Jewish people adapted the Greek idea of *Logos* to fit the traditional Jewish idea of the Word. But more thought of the Word in traditionally Jewish categories. They identified God's creative Word with divine Wisdom, which they also identified with God's Law (the Torah). They brought various ideas together: that God created all things through the Law or Wisdom (John 1:3), that the Word was life and light (1:4), and that Wisdom had been with God from the beginning (1:2).

In the prologue of his Gospel, John declares something that neither the Greek philosophers nor the Jewish teachers conceived: the Word became flesh and dwelt among His people. To the Greeks *Logos* was invisible reason, not part of the material world. To the Jewish teachers Wisdom was a divine attribute of Yahweh. But to John the Word was the divine Christ who became a human being. The Word's glory was "full of grace and truth," revealing to us the full character of God (John 1:14, 17, 18).

---

to those who believe in His name: ¹³who were born, not of blood, nor of the will of the flesh, nor of the will of man, but of God.

The Word Becomes Flesh

¹⁴And the Word became flesh and dwelt among us, and we beheld His glory, the glory as of the only begotten of the Father, full of grace and truth.

¹⁵John bore witness of Him and cried out, saying, "This was He of whom I said, 'He who comes after me is preferred before me, for He was before me.' "

¹⁶Andᵃ of His fullness we have all received, and grace for grace. ¹⁷For the law was given through Moses, *but* grace and truth came through Jesus Christ. ¹⁸No one has seen God at any time. The only begotten Son,ᵃ who is in the bosom of the Father, He has declared *Him*.

1:16 ᵃNU-Text reads *For.*   1:18 ᵃNU-Text reads *only begotten God.*   **Luke** 1:1 ᵃOr *are most surely believed*

Introduction and Dedication

The author of the third Gospel introduces his historical work, identifying his sources and purpose. Luke's Gospel is dedicated to a distinguished patron, Theophilus, whose name in Greek means "lover of God." Theophilus already had been instructed in Christian teachings, but Luke wished to provide him with "certainty" (Luke 1:4). Luke is alone among the Gospel writers in beginning his account with a preface that explains in some detail his procedure and desire to write an "orderly account" (1:3).

■ Luke 1:1–4

Luke
Dedication to Theophilus

1 **:1** Inasmuch as many have taken in hand to set in order a narrative of those things which have been fulfilledᵃ among us, ²just as those who from the beginning were eyewitnesses and ministers of the word delivered them to us, ³it

---

ARTS AND LITERATURE

Ancient books were often dedicated to a noble or prominent person. The title "most excellent" indicates that Theophilus was a person of high standing (Luke 1:3). He probably helped Luke with time, space, and materials for his work. The formal style of Luke's dedication announces that the book is the serious work of a responsible person.

seemed good to me also, having had perfect understanding of all things from the very first, to write to you an orderly account, most excellent Theophilus, [4]that you may know the certainty of those things in which you were instructed.

Early Lives of John the Baptist and Jesus

Even before birth, these babies were named and set apart for unique missions.

Elizabeth and Mary, the mothers of John and Jesus, were either blood relatives or close kinswomen (Luke 1:36). The angel Gabriel appeared to both families—to Elizabeth's husband and to Mary herself—and announced their future sons John and Jesus. Even before birth, these babies were named (Luke 1:13, 31) and set apart for unique missions (1:16, 17, 32, 33).

Practically nothing is known of John's boyhood, except that he "grew and became strong in spirit" (Luke 1:80). Only slightly more is known of Jesus' upbringing. Early in His life Jesus was taken to Nazareth, a town of Galilee, and there raised by His mother, Mary, and her husband, Joseph, a carpenter by trade. Hence the Child was known as "Jesus of Nazareth" (Mark 1:24).

Jesus was His mother's firstborn child; he had four brothers (James, Joses, Judas, and Simon) and an unspecified number of sisters (Mark 6:3). The only incident preserved from His first 30 years (after His infancy) was His trip to Jerusalem with Joseph and Mary when He was 12 years old (Luke 2:41–50). Occurring in the year that, as a Jewish boy, He attained the age of religious responsibility, the trip was at a crucial juncture of His development.

The Birth of John the Baptist

Luke gives an extraordinary glimpse of ordinary, pious Jews at the time. We should not imagine that everyone was as spiritually bankrupt as the Jewish leaders who later opposed Jesus. The lives of the barren, old Elizabeth and the young, virgin Mary intersect at the point of God's unexpected favor to His humble servants. Elizabeth was from the tribe of Levi (Luke 1:5) and was also related to Mary (1:36). Because Elizabeth was barren and elderly, the birth of John the Baptist is presented by Luke as a special work of God.

Luke implies that John was born 6 months before Jesus (Luke 1:26) and that the two were relatives (1:36). No other Gospel mentions their kinship, and John's Gospel raises a question: If Jesus and John the Baptist were related, why did John not recognize Jesus at the time of His baptism (John 1:31)? Some think that the Baptist knew Jesus, but did not recognize Him as the Messiah. Geography allows for another possibility: Luke indicates that John was raised in the wilderness of Judea (Luke 1:80), whereas Jesus was raised in Nazareth of Galilee (2:39). During their early years they were separated by quite a distance by ancient standards, possibly dis-

tant enough to be unfamiliar with each other as adults.

■ Luke 1:5–80

Luke
John's Birth Announced to Zacharias

1:5 There was in the days of Herod, the king of Judea, a certain priest named Zacharias, of the division of Abijah. His wife *was* of the daughters of Aaron, and her name *was* Elizabeth. [6]And they were both righteous before God, walking in all the commandments and ordinances of the Lord blameless. [7]But they had no child, because Elizabeth was barren, and they were both well advanced in years.

[8]So it was, that while he was serving as priest before God in the order of his division, [9]according to the custom of the priesthood, his lot fell to burn incense when he went into the temple of the Lord. [10]And the whole multitude of the people was praying outside at the hour of incense. [11]Then an angel of the Lord appeared to him, standing on the right side of the altar of incense. [12]And when Zacharias saw *him,* he was troubled, and fear fell upon him.

[13]But the angel said to him, "Do not be afraid, Zacharias, for your prayer is heard;

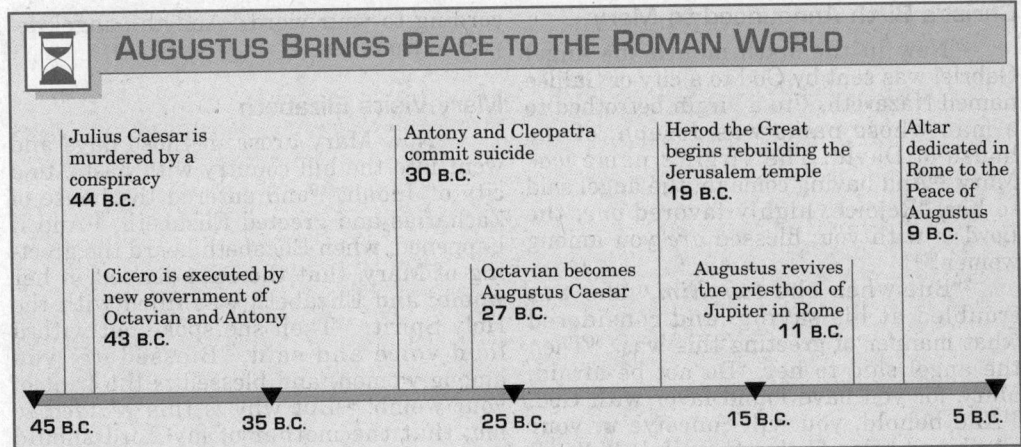

AUGUSTUS BRINGS PEACE TO THE ROMAN WORLD

Julius Caesar is murdered by a conspiracy **44 B.C.**	Antony and Cleopatra commit suicide **30 B.C.**	Herod the Great begins rebuilding the Jerusalem temple **19 B.C.**	Altar dedicated in Rome to the Peace of Augustus **9 B.C.**
Cicero is executed by new government of Octavian and Antony **43 B.C.**	Octavian becomes Augustus Caesar **27 B.C.**	Augustus revives the priesthood of Jupiter in Rome **11 B.C.**	

45 B.C.   **35 B.C.**   **25 B.C.**   **15 B.C.**   **5 B.C.**

and your wife Elizabeth will bear you a son, and you shall call his name John. [14]And you will have joy and gladness, and many will rejoice at his birth. [15]For he will be great in the sight of the Lord, and shall drink neither wine nor strong drink. He will also be filled with the Holy Spirit, even from his mother's womb. [16]And he will turn many of the children of Israel to the Lord their God. [17]He will also go before Him in the spirit and power of Elijah, *'to turn the hearts of the fathers to the children,'*[a] and the disobedient to the wisdom of the just, to make ready a people prepared for the Lord."

[18]And Zacharias said to the angel, "How shall I know this? For I am an old man, and my wife is well advanced in years."

[19]And the angel answered and said to him, "I am Gabriel, who stands in the presence of God, and was sent to speak to you and bring you these glad tidings. [20]But behold, you will be mute and not able to speak until the day these things take place, because you did not believe my words which will be fulfilled in their own time."

[21]And the people waited for Zacharias, and marveled that he lingered so long in the temple. [22]But when he came out, he could not speak to them; and they perceived that he had seen a vision in the temple, for he beckoned to them and remained speechless.

[23]So it was, as soon as the days of his service were completed, that he departed to his own house. [24]Now after those days his wife Elizabeth conceived; and she hid herself five months, saying, [25]"Thus the Lord has dealt with me, in the days when He looked on *me,* to take away my reproach among people."

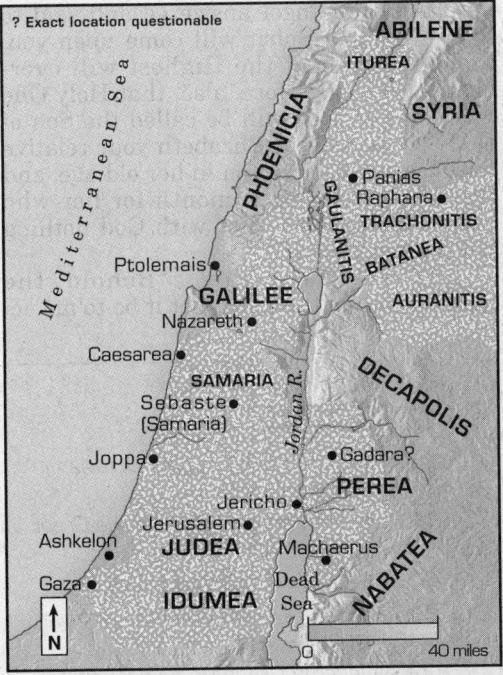

Herod's Kingdom at Jesus' Birth

Born in Idumea, Herod the Great was a Jew by religion, but was also immersed in Greek culture and politically loyal to Rome. The Roman emperor Augustus Caesar appointed Herod over a kingdom including the regions of Idumea, Judea, Perea, Samaria, Gaulanitis, Iturea, Trachonitis, Batanea, and Auranitis.

1:17 [a]Malachi 4:5, 6. Words in oblique type in the New Testament are quoted from the Old Testament.

Christ's Birth Announced to Mary

26Now in the sixth month the angel Gabriel was sent by God to a city of Galilee named Nazareth, 27to a virgin betrothed to a man whose name was Joseph, of the house of David. The virgin's name *was* Mary. 28And having come in, the angel said to her, "Rejoice, highly favored *one,* the Lord *is* with you; blessed *are* you among women!"a

29But when she saw *him,*a she was troubled at his saying, and considered what manner of greeting this was. 30Then the angel said to her, "Do not be afraid, Mary, for you have found favor with God. 31And behold, you will conceive in your womb and bring forth a Son, and shall call His name JESUS. 32He will be great, and will be called the Son of the Highest; and the Lord God will give Him the throne of His father David. 33And He will reign over the house of Jacob forever, and of His kingdom there will be no end."

34Then Mary said to the angel, "How can this be, since I do not know a man?"

35And the angel answered and said to her, "*The* Holy Spirit will come upon you, and the power of the Highest will overshadow you; therefore, also, that Holy One who is to be born will be called the Son of God. 36Now indeed, Elizabeth your relative has also conceived a son in her old age; and this is now the sixth month for her who was called barren. 37For with God nothing will be impossible."

38Then Mary said, "Behold the maidservant of the Lord! Let it be to me according to your word." And the angel departed from her.

Mary Visits Elizabeth

39Now Mary arose in those days and went into the hill country with haste, to a city of Judah, 40and entered the house of Zacharias and greeted Elizabeth. 41And it happened, when Elizabeth heard the greeting of Mary, that the babe leaped in her womb; and Elizabeth was filled with the Holy Spirit. 42Then she spoke out with a loud voice and said, "Blessed *are* you among women, and blessed *is* the fruit of your womb! 43But why *is* this *granted* to me, that the mother of my Lord should come to me? 44For indeed, as soon as the voice of your greeting sounded in my ears, the babe leaped in my womb for joy. 45Blessed *is* she who believed, for there will be a fulfillment of those things which were told her from the Lord."

The Song of Mary

46And Mary said:

"My soul magnifies the Lord,
47   And my spirit has rejoiced in God my Savior.
48   For He has regarded the lowly state of His maidservant;
   For behold, henceforth all generations will call me blessed.

1:28 aNU-Text omits *blessed are you among women.*
1:29 aNU-Text omits *when she saw him.*

49 For He who is mighty has done great
    things for me,
    And holy *is* His name.
50 And His mercy *is* on those who fear
    Him
    From generation to generation.
51 He has shown strength with His
    arm;
    He has scattered *the* proud in the
    imagination of their hearts.
52 He has put down the mighty from
    their thrones,
    And exalted *the* lowly.
53 He has filled *the* hungry with good
    things,
    And *the* rich He has sent away
    empty.
54 He has helped His servant Israel,
    In remembrance of *His* mercy,
55 As He spoke to our fathers,
    To Abraham and to his seed forever."

56And Mary remained with her about three months, and returned to her house.

Birth of John the Baptist

57Now Elizabeth's full time came for her to be delivered, and she brought forth a son. 58When her neighbors and relatives heard how the Lord had shown great mercy to her, they rejoiced with her.

Circumcision of John the Baptist

59So it was, on the eighth day, that they came to circumcise the child; and they would have called him by the name of his father, Zacharias. 60His mother answered and said, "No; he shall be called John."

61But they said to her, "There is no one among your relatives who is called by this name." 62So they made signs to his father—what he would have him called.

63And he asked for a writing tablet, and wrote, saying, "His name is John." So they all marveled. 64Immediately his mouth was opened and his tongue *loosed,* and he spoke, praising God. 65Then fear came on all who dwelt around them; and all these sayings were discussed throughout all the hill country of Judea. 66And all those who heard *them* kept *them* in their hearts, saying, "What kind of child will this be?" And the hand of the Lord was with him.

Zacharias's Prophecy

67Now his father Zacharias was filled with the Holy Spirit, and prophesied, saying:

68 "Blessed *is* the Lord God of Israel,
    For He has visited and redeemed His
    people,
69 And has raised up a horn of salvation
    for us
    In the house of His servant David,
70 As He spoke by the mouth of His holy
    prophets,
    Who *have been* since the world began,
71 That we should be saved from our
    enemies
    And from the hand of all who hate us,
72 To perform the mercy *promised* to our
    fathers
    And to remember His holy covenant,
73 The oath which He swore to our father
    Abraham:
74 To grant us that we,
    Being delivered from the hand of our
    enemies,
    Might serve Him without fear,
75 In holiness and righteousness before
    Him all the days of our life.

76 "And you, child, will be called the
    prophet of the Highest;
    For you will go before the face of the
    Lord to prepare His ways,
77 To give knowledge of salvation to His
    people
    By the remission of their sins,
78 Through the tender mercy of our God,
    With which the Dayspring from on
    high has visited[a] us;
79 To give light to those who sit in
    darkness and the shadow of death,
    To guide our feet into the way of
    peace."

80So the child grew and became strong in spirit, and was in the deserts till the day of his manifestation to Israel.

The Genealogy of Jesus

The first Gospel begins, like 1 Chronicles, with a genealogy. This account of the ancestors of Jesus Christ sets His story within the sacred history of the people of Israel. As Abraham's descendant, Jesus is identified as a Jew. As David's descendant, He is located more narrowly in Israel's royal family.

1:78 [a]NU-Text reads *shall visit.*

Matthew's account follows Chronicles, but omits some generations, apparently grouping the descendants into sets of fourteen (Matt. 1:17). The mention of four non-Jewish women—Tamar (1:3), Rahab, Ruth (1:5), Uriah's wife (1:6)—anticipates the Gospel's conclusion, which calls for the evangelization of all nations.

Numerous attempts have been made to account for disagreements between Matthew's and Luke's genealogies (see "The Genealogy of Jesus" at Luke 3:23). Some have proposed that Matthew provides Joseph's genealogy and Luke, Mary's. But Luke describes Mary as related to Elizabeth from the tribe of Levi (Luke 1:5, 36) while placing Jesus in the tribe of Judah (3:33), making it improbable that Luke's genealogy is actually Mary's. Probably the discrepancies between the genealogies arise from the different sources used by the two evangelists.

▼   ■ Matthew 1:1–17

Matthew
From Abraham to Christ

1 :1 The book of the genealogy of Jesus Christ, the Son of David, the Son of Abraham:

²Abraham begot Isaac, Isaac begot Jacob, and Jacob begot Judah and his brothers. ³Judah begot Perez and Zerah by Tamar, Perez begot Hezron, and Hezron begot Ram. ⁴Ram begot Amminadab, Amminadab begot Nahshon, and Nahshon begot Salmon. ⁵Salmon begot Boaz by Rahab, Boaz begot Obed by Ruth, Obed begot Jesse, ⁶and Jesse begot David the king.

David the king begot Solomon by her *who had been the wife* of Uriah. ⁷Solomon begot Rehoboam, Rehoboam begot Abijah, and Abijah begot Asa.ᵃ ⁸Asa begot Jehoshaphat, Jehoshaphat begot Joram, and Joram begot Uzziah. ⁹Uzziah begot Jotham, Jotham begot Ahaz, and Ahaz begot Hezekiah. ¹⁰Hezekiah begot Manasseh, Manasseh begot Amon,ᵃ and Amon begot Josiah. ¹¹Josiah begot Jeconiah and his

brothers about the time they were carried away to Babylon.

¹²And after they were brought to Babylon, Jeconiah begot Shealtiel, and Shealtiel begot Zerubbabel. ¹³Zerubbabel begot Abiud, Abiud begot Eliakim, and Eliakim begot Azor. ¹⁴Azor begot Zadok, Zadok begot Achim, and Achim begot Eliud. ¹⁵Eliud begot Eleazar, Eleazar begot Matthan, and Matthan begot Jacob. ¹⁶And Jacob begot Joseph the husband of Mary, of whom was born Jesus who is called Christ.

¹⁷So all the generations from Abraham to David *are* fourteen generations, from David until the captivity in Babylon *are* fourteen generations, and from the captivity in Babylon until the Christ *are* fourteen generations.

1:7 ᵃNU-Text reads *Asaph.*   1:10 ᵃNU-Text reads *Amos.*

The Birth of Jesus

No one knows precisely when Jesus was born. Even His year of birth is only an educated guess based on the information available. The intention of the medieval creators of our calendar was to set the date of Jesus' birth at A.D. 1. They simply miscalculated. The Jewish historian Josephus places the death of Herod the Great in 4 B.C., and both Matthew (Matt. 2:1) and Luke (Luke 1:5) presume that Herod was king at the time of Jesus' birth. But it is not clear how much before Herod's death Jesus was born.

We know that Herod became king of the Jews in 37 B.C. Outside of Matthew (Matt. 2:16), no historical record mentions Herod's slaughter of the infants in Bethlehem. Josephus does write that Herod ordered the murders of members of his own family to protect his throne. So it is not surprising that a few peasant children in Bethlehem went unnoticed among Herod's many atrocities, leaving us no help with dating. Since Herod's calculations led him to target children under two years old, Jesus' birth likely occurred one or two years before Herod's death—in either 6 or 5 B.C.

CULTURE AND SOCIETY

An honorable genealogy was necessary for a person to have a place in society. The genealogy given by Matthew is divided into three groups of fourteen (Matt. 1:17), a system recalling the numbers 3 and 7, which ancient people thought were significant or perfect. David and the Babylonian captivity are the high and low points of the period covered.

A date of about 5 B.C. would fit with Luke's note that Augustus, who reigned from 27 B.C. to A.D. 14, was the Roman emperor when Jesus was born (Luke 2:1). Luke's mention of Quirinius (2:2), however, creates a problem. After Herod died, Rome divided his territory among his surviving sons. Archelaus ruled in Judea (see Matt. 2:22) until he was deposed by the Romans in A.D. 6. Only then was Quirinius appointed governor, after serving for more than a decade as commander of the Roman troops in the area. Perhaps Luke simply identified him by his later office.

Some have tried to specify Jesus' birth date by appeal to astronomical phenomena that might explain the star of Bethlehem (Matt. 2:2, 7, 9, 10). Halley's comet appeared in 12 or 11 B.C. and another comet in 5 B.C. But in antiquity comets were thought to forecast evil, not blessed, events. In 7 B.C. a rare (once every 794 years) conjunction of the planets Jupiter, Venus, and Saturn occurred in the constellation Pisces. Whether Matthew's star was any of these is pure speculation. For ancient people the star confirmed again that Jesus was the Messiah who fulfilled Balaam's star prophecy (Num. 24:17).

- Matthew 1:18–25
- Luke 2:1–20

Matthew 1:18–25
The Virgin Birth

1 :18 Now the birth of Jesus Christ was as follows: After His mother Mary was betrothed to Joseph, before they came together, she was found with child of the Holy Spirit. 19Then Joseph her husband, being a just *man,* and not wanting to make her a public example, was minded to put her away secretly. 20But while he thought about these things, behold, an angel of the Lord appeared to him in a dream, saying, "Joseph, son of David, do not be afraid to take to you Mary your wife, for that which is conceived in her is of the Holy Spirit. 21And she will bring forth a Son, and you shall call His name JESUS, for He will save His people from their sins."

22So all this was done that it might be fulfilled which was spoken by the Lord through the prophet, saying: 23*"Behold, the virgin shall be with child, and bear a Son, and they shall call His name Immanuel,"*[a] which is translated, "God with us."

24Then Joseph, being aroused from sleep, did as the angel of the Lord commanded him and took to him his wife, 25and did not know her till she had brought forth her firstborn Son.[a] And he called His name JESUS.

Luke 2:1–20
Christ Born of Mary

2 :1 And it came to pass in those days *that* a decree went out from Caesar Augustus that all the world should be registered. 2This census first took place while Quirinius was governing Syria. 3So all went to be registered, everyone to his own city.

4Joseph also went up from Galilee, out of the city of Nazareth, into Judea, to the city of David, which is called Bethlehem, because he was of the house and lineage of David, 5to be registered with Mary, his betrothed wife,[a] who was with child. 6So it was, that while they were there, the days were completed for her to be delivered. 7And she brought forth her firstborn Son, and wrapped Him in swaddling cloths, and laid Him in a manger, because there was no room for them in the inn.

Glory in the Highest

8Now there were in the same country shepherds living out in the fields, keeping watch over their flock by night. 9And

1:23 [a]Isaiah 7:14   1:25 [a]NU-Text reads *a Son.*   **Luke 2:5** [a]NU-Text omits *wife.*

BETRAYAL AND BETROTHAL (Matt. 1:18)

The betrothal of Mary and Joseph (Matt. 1:18) involved much more than engagement does today. Even though a young Jewish man was considered an adult around age 13, he would work for a few years to save up for his marriage, around the age of 18 or 20. After the making of a legal contract between the two families, the young man and the woman (who was normally between the ages of 12 and 16) were "betrothed."

That Mary became pregnant after their betrothal, but before their wedding, prompted Joseph "to put her away" (Matt. 1:19). A betrothed couple could not sleep together before the wedding. In fact, Galilean parents normally kept the man and woman from spending time together privately until the wedding (normally a year after betrothal). Thus, Joseph would not have known Mary very well, and should not be blamed for mistrusting her and deciding to end the betrothal.

The commitment of a betrothal was so legally binding that a divorce was required to break it off (1:19). Joseph had little choice. If a man's betrothed wife became pregnant, people would assume that she had regarded him as an inadequate man and this would publicly humiliate him. Worse yet, should he not divorce her most people would assume that he was the one who had gotten her pregnant, and he would bear great shame in a culture that was obsessed with shame and honor.

Jewish law required a man to divorce a wife who had been unfaithful. Joseph could have divorced Mary publicly in a court. The court would not only establish his innocence, but also profit him financially: he would get to keep all of Mary's dowry (the money her father gave her for her marriage). By planning to divorce her privately (writing out a certificate of divorce for her in front of two witnesses), Joseph elected to forfeit profit rather than shame her any further.

---

behold,[a] an angel of the Lord stood before them, and the glory of the Lord shone around them, and they were greatly afraid. [10]Then the angel said to them, "Do not be afraid, for behold, I bring you good tidings of great joy which will be to all people. [11]For there is born to you this day in the city of David a Savior, who is Christ the Lord. [12]And this *will be* the sign to you: You will find a Babe wrapped in swaddling cloths, lying in a manger."

[13]And suddenly there was with the angel a multitude of the heavenly host praising God and saying:

[14] "Glory to God in the highest,
      And on earth peace, goodwill toward
         men!"[a]

[15]So it was, when the angels had gone away from them into heaven, that the shepherds said to one another, "Let us now go to Bethlehem and see this thing that has come to pass, which the Lord has made known to us." [16]And they came with haste and found Mary and Joseph, and the Babe lying in a manger. [17]Now when they had seen *Him,* they made widely[a] known the saying which was told them concerning this Child. [18]And all those who heard *it* marveled at those things which were told them by the shepherds. [19]But Mary kept all these things and pondered *them* in her

2:9 [a]NU-Text omits *behold.*   2:14 [a]NU-Text reads *toward men of goodwill.*   2:17 [a]NU-Text omits *widely.*

TRADE AND ECONOMICS

The gifts given to Jesus by the foreign rulers were luxury items (Matt. 2:11), like the symbolic gifts exchanged by rulers today, and like the wealth brought by Gentiles to Israel's king (Ps. 72:10; Is. 60:6). Frankincense and myrrh are resins or gums taken from plants that grow in Arabia or the Horn of Africa. They were used for incense and perfume.

AUGUSTUS, THE FIRST ROMAN EMPEROR (Luke 2:1)

Luke refers to "Caesar Augustus" as the Roman emperor who ruled the Mediterranean world during the birth and youth of Jesus (Luke 2:1). The Roman Senate gave the title "Augustus" to this ruler in 27 B.C. He was born Gaius Octavius in 63 B.C., the great-nephew of the famous Julius Caesar.

In his will Julius Caesar made Octavius his adopted son. The untimely death of the dictator in 44 B.C. by assassination was the beginning of Octavius's path to the emperorship. He changed his name to Gaius Julius Caesar Octavian.

Octavian, as he was now called, sided with Mark Antony against the assassins of his adopted father. He initiated a coalition of three dictators—himself, Antony, and Marcus Lepidus—known as "the Triumvirate." The three not only gained victory over Caesar's murderers by 42 B.C., but also carried out the bloodiest purge in Rome's history. From 36 to 33 B.C. there was a break in relations between Octavian and Antony, culminating in Octavian's dominion over the empire by 31 B.C.

After 27 B.C. Octavian became known as "Augustus," the name bestowed on him by the Senate. He was the first Roman emperor, reigning solely as ruler of the Roman realm for more than 40 years (27 B.C.–A.D. 14). In essence, Augustus was the second founder of Rome, reorganizing it as an empire, and presiding over the Silver Age of Latin literature, dominated by names like Virgil, Livy, and Ovid.

Augustus did not change foreign policy in Palestine much from that of his predecessors. He continued the employment of client kingdoms in the remote parts of the Roman Empire and in 30 B.C. confirmed Herod the Great as ruler of Judea.

---

heart. 20Then the shepherds returned, glorifying and praising God for all the things that they had heard and seen, as it was told them.

Jesus Presented in the Temple

Luke indicates that "eight days were completed" for the circumcision of Jesus (Luke 2:21). Since the Jews considered the day of birth as the first day, this would be 7 days by our way of counting. The mother of a newborn son was deemed ceremonially unclean for 7 days (Lev. 12:2), after which the parents had to take the child to the temple for circumcision. She was then considered unclean for an additional 33 days, after which she would go to the temple to offer a sacrifice for her purification (Luke 2:22).

▼ ■ Luke 2:21–38

Luke
Circumcision of Jesus

2 **:21** And when eight days were completed for the circumcision of the

Child,a His name was called JESUS, the name given by the angel before He was conceived in the womb.

Jesus Presented to God

22Now when the days of her purification according to the law of Moses were completed, they brought Him to Jerusalem to present *Him* to the Lord 23(as it is written in the law of the Lord, *"Every male who opens the womb shall be called holy to the LORD"*),a 24and to offer a sacrifice according to what is said in the law of the Lord, *"A pair of turtledoves or two young pigeons."*a

Simeon Sees God's Salvation

25And behold, there was a man in Jerusalem whose name was Simeon, and this man was just and devout, waiting for the Consolation of Israel, and the Holy Spirit was upon him. 26And it had been revealed to him by the Holy Spirit that he would not see death before he had seen the Lord's Christ. 27So he came by the Spirit into the temple. And when the parents brought in the Child Jesus, to do for Him according to the custom of the law, 28he took Him up in his arms and blessed God and said:

2:21 aNU-Text reads *for His circumcision.*
2:23 aExodus 13:2, 12, 15   2:24 aLeviticus 12:8

29 "Lord, now You are letting Your servant
      depart in peace,
      According to Your word;
30 For my eyes have seen Your salvation
31 Which You have prepared before the
      face of all peoples,
32 A light to *bring* revelation to the
      Gentiles,
   And the glory of Your people Israel."

33And Joseph and His mother[a] marveled at those things which were spoken of Him. 34Then Simeon blessed them, and said to Mary His mother, "Behold, this *Child* is destined for the fall and rising of many in Israel, and for a sign which will be spoken against 35(yes, a sword will pierce through your own soul also), that the thoughts of many hearts may be revealed."

Anna Bears Witness to the Redeemer

36Now there was one, Anna, a prophetess, the daughter of Phanuel, of the tribe of Asher. She was of a great age, and had lived with a husband seven years from her virginity; 37and this woman *was* a widow of about eighty-four years,[a] who did not depart from the temple, but served *God* with fastings and prayers night and day. 38And coming in that instant she gave thanks to the Lord,[a] and spoke of Him to all those who looked for redemption in Jerusalem.

Jesus Escapes to Egypt

The visit of the wise men occurred some months after the birth of Jesus. Joseph and Mary were no longer in the stable, but living in a house (see Matt. 2:11) in Bethlehem, a village about 5 miles south of Jerusalem. The family fled from there to Egypt to escape the plot of Herod, who apparently feared the new King would replace him.

Herod died in 4 B.C., and Matt. 2:16, 19 suggests that Jesus may have been one to two years old at that time (see "The Birth of Jesus" at Matt. 1:18). Herod's death meant that Joseph could take his young Child and wife Mary back to Israel (Matt. 2:19–21).

■ Matthew 2:1–21

Matthew
Wise Men from the East

2 :1 Now after Jesus was born in Bethlehem of Judea in the days of Herod the king, behold, wise men from the East came to Jerusalem, 2saying, "Where is He who has been born King of the Jews? For we have seen His star in the East and have come to worship Him."

3When Herod the king heard *this,* he was troubled, and all Jerusalem with him. 4And when he had gathered all the chief priests and scribes of the people together, he inquired of them where the Christ was to be born.

5So they said to him, "In Bethlehem of Judea, for thus it is written by the prophet:

6 '*But you, Bethlehem, in the land of
      Judah,
   Are not the least among the rulers of
      Judah;
   For out of you shall come a Ruler
   Who will shepherd My people
      Israel.'*"[a]

7Then Herod, when he had secretly called the wise men, determined from them what time the star appeared. 8And he sent them to Bethlehem and said, "Go and search carefully for the young Child, and when you have found *Him,* bring back word to me, that I may come and worship Him also."

9When they heard the king, they departed; and behold, the star which they had seen in the East went before them, till it came and stood over where the young Child was. 10When they saw the star, they

---

2:33 [a]NU-Text reads *And His father and mother.*
2:37 [a]NU-Text reads *a widow until she was eighty-four.*   2:38 [a]NU-Text reads *to God.*
Matt. 2:6 [a]Micah 5:2

TIME CAPSULE   *17 to 12 B.C.*

17	*Augustus appoints the children of M. V. Agrippa as his heirs*
15	*M. V. Agrippa presents sacrifices at the temple in Jerusalem*
15	*Veterans of two legions colonize Berytus (Beirut)*
15	*Quirinius becomes praetor of Rome*
15	*Herod invites M. V. Agrippa to visit Judea*
12	*Augustus becomes "high priest" of Rome, the "Pontifex Maximus"*
12	*Quirinius elected consul of Rome*

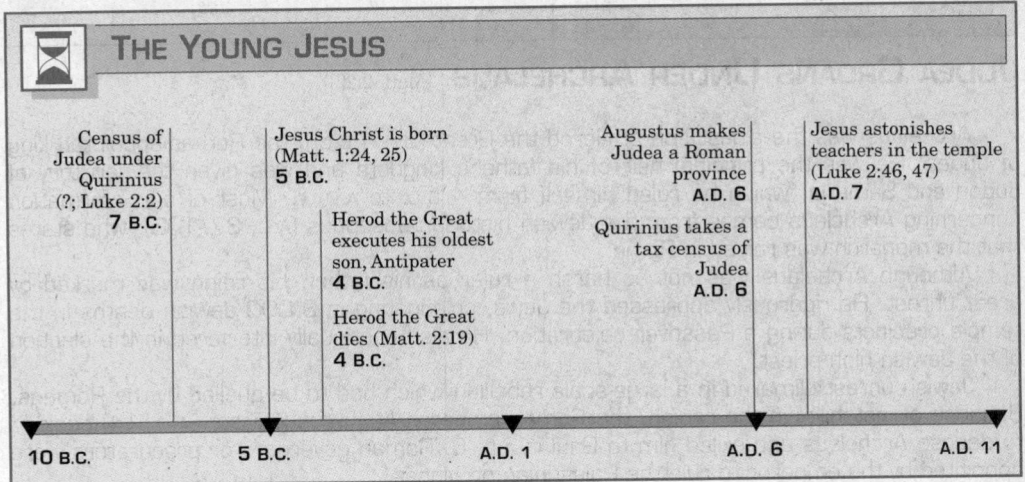

THE YOUNG JESUS

Census of Judea under Quirinius (?; Luke 2:2) **7 B.C.**	Jesus Christ is born (Matt. 1:24, 25) **5 B.C.**	Augustus makes Judea a Roman province **A.D. 6**	Jesus astonishes teachers in the temple (Luke 2:46, 47) **A.D. 7**
	Herod the Great executes his oldest son, Antipater **4 B.C.**	Quirinius takes a tax census of Judea **A.D. 6**	
	Herod the Great dies (Matt. 2:19) **4 B.C.**		

| 10 B.C. | 5 B.C. | A.D. 1 | A.D. 6 | A.D. 11 |

rejoiced with exceedingly great joy. ¹¹And when they had come into the house, they saw the young Child with Mary His mother, and fell down and worshiped Him. And when they had opened their treasures, they presented gifts to Him: gold, frankincense, and myrrh.

2:15 ªHosea 11:1   2:18 ªJeremiah 31:15

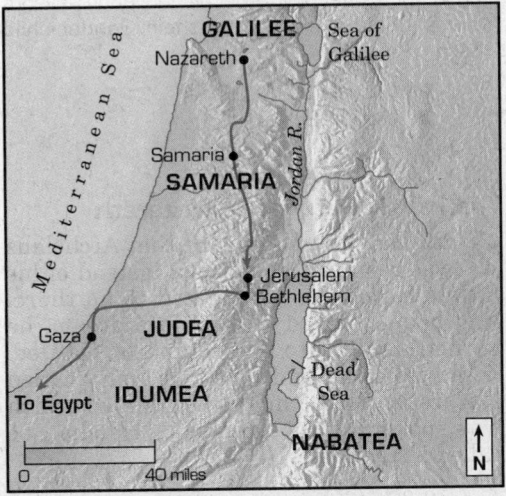

The Journeys of Jesus' Birth

The decree of Caesar Augustus required Mary and Joseph to leave the Galilean city of Nazareth and register for the census in the Judean city of Bethlehem. After Jesus was born and circumcised, His parents took Him to the temple in Jerusalem (Luke 2:1–40).

Joseph fled from Bethlehem, taking his family to Egypt to escape from Herod the Great. Returning from Egypt after Herod's death, Jesus' family settled in Nazareth (Matt. 2:13–23).

¹²Then, being divinely warned in a dream that they should not return to Herod, they departed for their own country another way.

The Flight into Egypt

¹³Now when they had departed, behold, an angel of the Lord appeared to Joseph in a dream, saying, "Arise, take the young Child and His mother, flee to Egypt, and stay there until I bring you word; for Herod will seek the young Child to destroy Him."

¹⁴When he arose, he took the young Child and His mother by night and departed for Egypt, ¹⁵and was there until the death of Herod, that it might be fulfilled which was spoken by the Lord through the prophet, saying, *"Out of Egypt I called My Son."*ª

Massacre of the Innocents

¹⁶Then Herod, when he saw that he was deceived by the wise men, was exceedingly angry; and he sent forth and put to death all the male children who were in Bethlehem and in all its districts, from two years old and under, according to the time which he had determined from the wise men. ¹⁷Then was fulfilled what was spoken by Jeremiah the prophet, saying:

18 *"A voice was heard in Ramah,*
    Lamentation, weeping, and great
       mourning,
    Rachel weeping for her children,
    Refusing to be comforted,
    *Because they are no more."*ª

JUDEA GROANS UNDER ARCHELAUS (Matt. 2:22)

Archelaus was the eldest son of Herod the Great (37–4 B.C.), the Roman-appointed king of Judea. He was the principal heir of his father's kingdom and was given the territory of Judea and Samaria, which he ruled himself from 4 B.C. to A.D. 6. Most of our information concerning Archelaus comes from the Jewish historian Josephus (A.D. 37–100), who states that the monarch was raised in Rome.

Although Archelaus was not as harsh a ruler as his father, his reign was marked by great unrest. He rigorously oppressed the Jews, culminating in 3,000 Jewish deaths in the temple precincts during a Passover celebration. He also continually interfered in the election of the Jewish high priest.

Jewish unrest climaxed in a large-scale rebellion which had to be quelled by the Romans. Because of instability in the region, the Roman emperor Augustus (27 B.C.–A.D. 14) decided to depose Archelaus and exiled him to Gaul in A.D. 6. Roman governors or procurators were appointed by the emperor to rule the Palestinian provinces.

Joseph's fear of returning to Judea with the young Jesus (Matt. 2:22) is understandable in light of the conditions during the short time Archelaus was in office. Tension and unrest in Judea probably made Galilee seem a much safer region in which to raise a child.

19Now when Herod was dead, behold, an angel of the Lord appeared in a dream to Joseph in Egypt, 20saying, "Arise, take the young Child and His mother, and go to the land of Israel, for those who sought the young Child's life are dead." 21Then he arose, took the young Child and His mother, and came into the land of Israel.

Jesus' Childhood in Nazareth of Galilee

Matthew's Gospel does not specify Joseph's hometown, but indicates that he decided not to return to Bethlehem of Judea to avoid living in the territory of Archelaus. The choice to settle instead in Nazareth of Galilee fulfilled a messianic prophecy (Matt. 2:23), for which no corresponding verse is found in the Old Testament.

Luke's Gospel, however, presumes that Joseph and Mary were residents of Nazareth (Luke 1:26; 2:4, 39). Jesus' birth in Bethlehem occurred because of a census that required His parents to return to their ancestral home (2:1–4). Not mentioning the family's flight to Egypt, Luke reports only that from Bethlehem they traveled to Jerusalem (2:21–38) before returning home to Nazareth where Jesus was raised.

Obviously, the details of Jesus' childhood were buried in obscurity. Such things did not matter when He was thought to be only the son of simple peasants. After His death and

resurrection, these differing accounts of His childhood did agree on two central points: He was born in Bethlehem in fulfillment of popular messianic expectations, but He was better known as "Jesus of Nazareth" (Matt. 26:71; Mark 1:24; 16:6; Luke 18:37). The so-called "Infancy Gospels" among the New Testament apocrypha offer wild speculation about events surrounding the youth of their wonder-child hero.

- Matthew 2:22, 23
- Luke 2:39, 40

Matthew 2:22, 23
The Family Returns to Nazareth

2 :22 But when he heard that Archelaus was reigning over Judea instead of his father Herod, he was afraid to go there. And being warned by God in a dream, he turned aside into the region of Galilee. 23And he came and dwelt in a city called Nazareth, that it might be fulfilled which was spoken by the prophets, "He shall be called a Nazarene."

Luke 2:39, 40

2 :39 So when they had performed all things according to the law of the Lord, they returned to Galilee, to their *own* city, Nazareth. 40And the Child grew and became strong in spirit,[a] filled with wisdom; and the grace of God was upon Him.

Luke 2:40 [a]NU-Text omits *in spirit.*

Jesus Visits the Temple

The date of Jesus' visit to the temple depends on the year of His birth (see "The Birth of Jesus" at Matt. 1:18). If He were born in 5 B.C., this temple event could have occurred about A.D. 7. However, the date also depends on how exact we understand the age 12 (Luke 2:42).

The circumstances described in this event do not present Jesus as a child-prodigy. A Jewish boy was considered a man, accountable to the Law's demands, following his bar mitzvah at age 13. (Bar mitzvah, meaning "son of the commandment," is a religious rite of passage comparable to catechism and confirmation in some Christian traditions.) It was customary for Jewish parents to take their son to the temple one or two years before he turned 13. Thus Jesus' visit to the temple at this age, as well as His questions of and by the teachers of the Law are consistent with normal Jewish practice. He took His relationship with God seriously. What was exceptional was His level of understanding (Luke 2:47).

■ Luke 2:41–52

Luke
The Boy Jesus Amazes the Scholars

2 **:41** His parents went to Jerusalem every year at the Feast of the Passover.

2:43 ᵃNU-Text reads *And His parents.*

⁴²And when He was twelve years old, they went up to Jerusalem according to the custom of the feast. ⁴³When they had finished the days, as they returned, the Boy Jesus lingered behind in Jerusalem. And Joseph and His motherᵃ did not know *it;* ⁴⁴but supposing Him to have been in the company, they went a day's journey, and sought Him among *their* relatives and acquaintances. ⁴⁵So when they did not find Him, they returned to Jerusalem, seeking Him. ⁴⁶Now so it was *that* after three days they found Him in the temple, sitting in the midst of the teachers, both listening to them and asking them questions. ⁴⁷And all who heard Him were astonished at His understanding and answers. ⁴⁸So when they saw Him, they were amazed; and His mother said to Him, "Son, why have You done this to us? Look, Your father and I have sought You anxiously."

⁴⁹And He said to them, "Why did you seek Me? Did you not know that I must be about My Father's business?" ⁵⁰But they did not understand the statement which He spoke to them.

Jesus Advances in Wisdom and Favor

⁵¹Then He went down with them and came to Nazareth, and was subject to them, but His mother kept all these things in her heart. ⁵²And Jesus increased in wisdom and stature, and in favor with God and men.

Beginning of Jesus' Ministry

John the Baptist prepared the way, announcing Jesus as the Coming One.

John the Baptist prepared the way for Jesus' ministry. The silence of John's early years was broken by his thundering call to repentance sometime around A.D. 26 or 27, shortly before Jesus began His ministry. Matthew's Gospel pictures John preaching in the wilderness of Judea (Matt. 3:1), calling people to repentance and baptism (3:3–10), announcing Jesus as the Coming One (3:11, 12), and baptizing Him (3:13–17).

According to the Synoptic Gospels, the main phase of Jesus' ministry began in Galilee after John's imprisonment by Herod Antipas. Possibly John's arrest was a signal for Jesus to proclaim His message in Galilee: "The time is fulfilled, and the kingdom of God is at hand" (Mark 1:14, 15). In the Gospel of John, however, there is indication that Jesus ministered for a short time in Judea, while John the Baptist was still preaching (John 3:22—4:3). Some of John's disciples even became concerned because Jesus "baptized more disciples than John" (John 3:36; 4:1). John reassured his followers: Jesus' ministry was given to Him by God; John himself was only a forerunner (3:27, 28).

John the Baptist

The description of John the Baptist in Matthew and Mark (Matt. 3:4; Mark 1:6) resembles that of Elijah in 2 Kin. 1:8. There were popular expectations of an Elijah-like figure who would prepare for the coming of the Messiah, and both Gospels explicitly report that Jesus identified John as the fulfillment (Matt. 11:14; 17:10–13; Mark 9:11–13). But according to the Fourth Gospel, John himself denied this identification (John 1:21, 25). Possibly the Baptist did not realize the true significance of his role. He could only describe himself as a herald preparing the way for the Lord's coming (John 1:23).

Luke dates the beginning of John's ministry as the 15th year of the Roman emperor Tiberius (Luke 3:1). Tiberius had a 2-year co-regency with Augustus, his adoptive father, before Augustus died. Depending on whether Luke refers to the beginning of the coregency or of Tiberius's independent rule, the 15th year would be A.D. 26 or 28. Pontius Pilate was the Roman procurator (or governor) of Judea from A.D. 26 to 36. Caiaphas was the Jewish high priest from A.D. 18 to 36.

■ Matthew 3:1–12
■ Mark 1:1–8
■ Luke 3:1–18
■ John 1:19–28

Matthew 3:1–12
John the Baptist Prepares the Way

3 :1 In those days John the Baptist came preaching in the wilderness of Judea, ²and saying, "Repent, for the kingdom of heaven is at hand!" ³For this is he who was spoken of by the prophet Isaiah, saying:

> "The voice of one crying in the
>   wilderness:
> 'Prepare the way of the LORD;
>   Make His paths straight.' "ᵃ

⁴Now John himself was clothed in camel's hair, with a leather belt around his waist; and his food was locusts and wild honey. ⁵Then Jerusalem, all Judea, and all the region around the Jordan went out to him ⁶and were baptized by him in the Jordan, confessing their sins.

⁷But when he saw many of the Pharisees and Sadducees coming to his baptism, he said to them, "Brood of vipers! Who warned you to flee from the wrath to come? ⁸Therefore bear fruits worthy of repentance, ⁹and do not think to say to yourselves, 'We have Abraham as *our* father.' For I say to you that God is able to raise up children to Abraham from these stones. ¹⁰And even now the ax is laid to the root of the trees. Therefore every tree which does not bear good fruit is cut down and thrown into the fire. ¹¹I indeed baptize you with water unto repentance, but He who is coming after me is mightier than I, whose sandals I am not worthy to carry. He will baptize you with the Holy Spirit and fire.ᵃ ¹²His winnowing fan *is* in His hand, and He will thoroughly clean out His threshing floor, and gather His wheat into the barn; but He will burn up the chaff with unquenchable fire."

Mark 1:1–8
Preparation for Jesus' Ministry

1 :1 The beginning of the gospel of Jesus Christ, the Son of God. ²As it is written in the Prophets:ᵃ

> "Behold, I send My messenger before
>   Your face,
> Who will prepare Your way before
>   You."ᵇ

³ "The voice of one crying in the
>   wilderness:
> 'Prepare the way of the LORD;
>   Make His paths straight.' "ᵃ

⁴John came baptizing in the wilderness and preaching a baptism of repentance for the remission of sins. ⁵Then all

---

3:3 ᵃIsaiah 40:3   3:11 ᵃM-Text omits *and fire.*
Mark 1:2 ᵃNU-Text reads *Isaiah the prophet.*
ᵇMalachi 3:1   1:3 ᵃIsaiah 40:3

CULTURE AND SOCIETY

John the Baptist's rough appearance probably reminded his hearers of Elijah (2 Kin. 1:7, 8). The camel hair of John's garb was more rustic than linen or wool. His visible isolation and independence correspond to his spiritual and ethical independence. Thus he was preaching his message in the wilderness, not in the town (Matt. 3:1, 4; 11:7–9).

JOHN'S BAPTISM OF REPENTANCE (Mark 1:4)

Some people who claimed to be especially holy lived in the wilderness. Also, Jewish people anticipated a new exodus through the wilderness (Is. 40:3), so many who claimed to be prophets or messiahs gathered followings in wilderness areas. Only there were they usually safe from interference by the established Jewish and Roman authorities. Thus John the Baptist began his ministry "in the wilderness" (Mark 1:4).

Like other ancient peoples, Jewish people had many symbolic rituals involving water. They washed themselves before festivals and after contact with anything they considered impure. A washing ritual was also performed when a person was initiated into a wilderness sect like the Essenes (who wrote the Dead Sea Scrolls). But John's baptism was different from these ritual washings; it was a once-for-all baptism, like the kind Gentiles experienced when they converted to Judaism.

In John's day, Jewish people had special ways to practice baptism. Normally a person would strip naked, step down into the baptismal pool, and dunk himself or herself completely under water. But John's baptisms were different. The persons baptized did not perform the rite on themselves, and so presumably did not strip naked. Jewish people generally detested nakedness, and *public* nude baptisms would have been scandalous.

John had a message for those who came for baptism: water alone could not change them; they needed genuine repentance. This was also true for baptisms of Gentiles into Judaism and baptisms of Jews becoming Essenes; both required a pure heart as well as water. Yet while Jewish people often spoke of "repentance" as a regular act each time one sinned, John preached a special repentance, a turning from sin to God. John thus expected from his own people the kind of repentance they expected of Gentiles who converted to Judaism (Matt. 3:8, 9).

---

the land of Judea, and those from Jerusalem, went out to him and were all baptized by him in the Jordan River, confessing their sins.

6Now John was clothed with camel's hair and with a leather belt around his waist, and he ate locusts and wild honey. 7And he preached, saying, "There comes One after me who is mightier than I, whose sandal strap I am not worthy to stoop down and loose. 8I indeed baptized you with water, but He will baptize you with the Holy Spirit."

Luke 3:1–18
Ministry of the Baptist

3 :1 Now in the fifteenth year of the reign of Tiberius Caesar, Pontius Pilate being governor of Judea, Herod being tetrarch of Galilee, his brother Philip tetrarch of Iturea and the region of Trachonitis, and Lysanias tetrarch of Abilene, 2while Annas and Caiaphas were high priests,ᵃ the word of God came to John the son of Zacharias in the wilderness. 3And he went into all the region around the Jordan, preaching a baptism of repentance for the remission of sins, 4as it is written in the book of the words of Isaiah the prophet, saying:

"The voice of one crying in the
   wilderness:
  '*Prepare the way of the LORD;*
  Make His paths straight.

TIME CAPSULE   12 to 10 B.C.

12   Death of Augustus's friend and son-in-law (M. V. Agrippa)

12   An altar is dedicated to Roma and Augustus in Lyon, France

11   Augustus revives the priesthood of Jupiter in Rome

10   Dedication of Caesarea, Herod's seaport

10   Herod Antipas gives a display of gladiators at Caesarea

10   Birth of Herod Agrippa I (Acts 12:1)

3:2 ᵃNU-Text and M-Text read *in the high priesthood of Annas and Caiaphas.*

5   Every valley shall be filled
    And every mountain and hill brought
       low;
    The crooked places shall be made
       straight
    And the rough ways smooth;
6   And all flesh shall see the salvation of
       God.' "ᵃ

John Preaches to the People

⁷Then he said to the multitudes that came out to be baptized by him, "Brood of vipers! Who warned you to flee from the wrath to come? ⁸Therefore bear fruits worthy of repentance, and do not begin to say to yourselves, 'We have Abraham as *our* father.' For I say to you that God is able to raise up children to Abraham from these stones. ⁹And even now the ax is laid to the root of the trees. Therefore every tree which does not bear good fruit is cut down and thrown into the fire."

¹⁰So the people asked him, saying, "What shall we do then?"

¹¹He answered and said to them, "He who has two tunics, let him give to him who has none; and he who has food, let him do likewise."

¹²Then tax collectors also came to be baptized, and said to him, "Teacher, what shall we do?"

¹³And he said to them, "Collect no more than what is appointed for you."

¹⁴Likewise the soldiers asked him, saying, "And what shall we do?"

So he said to them, "Do not intimidate anyone or accuse falsely, and be content with your wages."

¹⁵Now as the people were in expectation, and all reasoned in their hearts about John, whether he was the Christ *or* not, ¹⁶John answered, saying to all, "I indeed baptize you with water; but One mightier than I is coming, whose sandal strap I am not worthy to loose. He will baptize you with the Holy Spirit and fire. ¹⁷His winnowing fan *is* in His hand, and He will thoroughly clean out His threshing floor, and gather the wheat into His barn; but the chaff He will burn with unquenchable fire."

¹⁸And with many other exhortations he preached to the people.

John 1:19–28
A Voice in the Wilderness

1 :19 Now this is the testimony of John, when the Jews sent priests and Levites from Jerusalem to ask him, "Who are you?"

²⁰He confessed, and did not deny, but confessed, "I am not the Christ."

²¹And they asked him, "What then? Are you Elijah?"

He said, "I am not."

"Are you the Prophet?"

And he answered, "No."

²²Then they said to him, "Who are you, that we may give an answer to those who sent us? What do you say about yourself?"

²³He said: "I *am*

'The voice of one crying in the
    wilderness:
"Make straight the way of the LORD," 'ᵃ

as the prophet Isaiah said."

²⁴Now those who were sent were from the Pharisees. ²⁵And they asked him, saying, "Why then do you baptize if you are not the Christ, nor Elijah, nor the Prophet?"

²⁶John answered them, saying, "I baptize with water, but there stands One among you whom you do not know. ²⁷It is He who, coming after me, is preferred before me, whose sandal strap I am not worthy to loose."

²⁸These things were done in Bethabaraᵃ beyond the Jordan, where John was baptizing.

3:6 ᵃIsaiah 40:3–5   **John** 1:23 ᵃIsaiah 40:3
1:28 ᵃNU-Text and M-Text read *Bethany.*

 ## The Baptism of Jesus

In the Synoptic Gospels Jesus' baptism marks His inauguration as the servant Messiah and the dawning of the new age of the Spirit. The Spirit is the agent of a new beginning. The open heaven, the descending dove, and the confirming heavenly voice highlight the ultimate revelatory significance of the baptism. Jesus was anointed by the Spirit of God as the Messiah and the Servant of the Lord described centuries earlier by the prophet Isaiah (Is. 11:2; 42:1; 61:1).

Mark's account of Jesus' baptism was open to several possible false interpretations. Readers of his Gospel might conclude (1) that Jesus was a repentant sinner (see Mark 1:4, 9), or (2) that He was inferior to John who baptized Him (1:9), or (3) that He became the Son of God at His baptism (1:10, 11). The other evangelists denied such speculations early in their Gospels. The birth narratives in Matthew and Luke emphasize that Jesus was conceived of the Holy Spirit (Matt. 1:20), and even as a baby was the Christ (Luke 2:11). He was neither sinful nor inferior prior to His baptism. John's prologue makes it clear that Jesus did not become the Son of God through baptism, but had been such from eternity (John 1:1–18).

Each evangelist further reformulates the baptism story to preclude any confusion Mark's account might allow. Matthew introduces a dialogue between John and Jesus in which Jesus explained His true motive for receiving baptism ("to fulfill all righteousness," Matt. 3:15) and John acknowledged his inferiority to Jesus (3:14). Luke reports the imprisonment of John (Luke 3:19, 20) before describing Jesus' baptism. In his baptism narrative Luke nowhere refers to John and describes the Spirit as coming upon Jesus in response to His own prayer (3:21).

The Fourth Gospel stresses John's inferiority to Jesus (John 1:6–8, 19–37) and never mentions Jesus' baptism by John nor John's preaching of repentance. John served only as a witness to Jesus: (1) that Jesus received the abiding Spirit; (2) that He is the One who baptizes with the Spirit; and (3) that He is the Son of God (John 1:32–34).

- Matthew 3:13–17
- Mark 1:9–11
- Luke 3:21, 22
- John 1:29–34

Matthew 3:13–17
John Baptizes Jesus

3 **:13** Then Jesus came from Galilee to John at the Jordan to be baptized by him. ¹⁴And John *tried to* prevent Him, saying, "I need to be baptized by You, and are You coming to me?"

¹⁵But Jesus answered and said to him, "Permit *it to be so* now, for thus it is fitting for us to fulfill all righteousness." Then he allowed Him.

¹⁶When He had been baptized, Jesus came up immediately from the water; and behold, the heavens were opened to Him, and He[a] saw the Spirit of God descending like a dove and alighting upon Him. ¹⁷And suddenly a voice *came* from heaven, saying, "This is My beloved Son, in whom I am well pleased."

Matt. 3:16 [a]Or *he* **Mark** 1:10 [a]NU-Text reads *out of.*

Mark 1:9–11

1 **:9** It came to pass in those days *that* Jesus came from Nazareth of Galilee, and was baptized by John in the Jordan. ¹⁰And immediately, coming up from[a] the water, He saw the heavens parting and the Spirit descending upon Him like a dove. ¹¹Then a voice came from heaven, "You are My beloved Son, in whom I am well pleased."

Luke 3:21, 22

3 **:21** When all the people were baptized, it came to pass that Jesus also was baptized; and while He prayed, the heaven was opened. ²²And the Holy Spirit descended in bodily form like a dove upon Him, and a voice came from heaven which said, "You are My beloved Son; in You I am well pleased."

John 1:29–34
The Lamb of God

1 **:29** The next day John saw Jesus coming toward him, and said, "Behold! The Lamb of God who takes away the sin of the world! ³⁰This is He of whom I said, 'After me comes a Man who is preferred before me, for He was before me.' ³¹I did not know Him; but that He should be revealed to Israel, therefore I came baptizing with water."

³²And John bore witness, saying, "I saw the Spirit descending from heaven like a dove, and He remained upon Him. ³³I did not know Him, but He who sent me to baptize with water said to me, 'Upon whom you see the Spirit descending, and remaining on Him, this is He who baptizes with the Holy Spirit.' ³⁴And I have seen and testified that this is the Son of God."

The Genealogy of Jesus

The genealogy in Luke's Gospel moves in reverse of the order found in Matthew's genealogy (see "The Genealogy of Jesus" at Matt. 1:1). Luke continues beyond Abraham, all the way back to Adam, thus setting the story of Jesus within the history of God's dealings with all humanity.

Luke introduces the genealogy with the comment that Jesus "began His ministry" (Luke 3:23). By referring to the beginning of Jesus' ministry before relating the temptation, Luke makes Jesus' victory over Satan's temptations the first event of His ministry. Matthew and Mark begin Jesus' ministry after the temptation (see "Early Ministry in Galilee" at Matt. 4:12).

According to the Synoptics, Jesus did not begin His ministry until John completed his. Matthew's and Mark's Gospels place Jesus' ministry in Galilee after the arrest of John the Baptist (Matt. 4:12; Mark 1:14). In Luke's presentation, John's arrest is recorded before Jesus' baptism, as well as before His ministry (Luke 3:19, 20, 23). Only in the Fourth Gospel do Jesus and John seem to minister simultaneously before John fades from the scene.

Luke puts Jesus' age at "about thirty years" at the time He began to minister (Luke 3:23). If Jesus were born in 5 B.C., He would have been 30 during part of A.D. 26 and A.D. 27. It is possible chronologically that Jesus and John could have ministered at the same time around A.D. 26 (see "John the Baptist" at Matt. 3:1). However, we should not attempt precise dates since the Gospels offer different conceptions as to what marked the beginning of Jesus' ministry.

■ Luke 3:23–38

Luke
From Jesus to Adam

3 **:23** Now Jesus Himself began *His ministry at* about thirty years of age, being (as was supposed) *the* son of Joseph, *the son* of Heli, [24]*the son* of Matthat,[a] *the son of* Levi, *the son* of Melchi, *the son* of Janna, *the son* of Joseph, [25]*the son* of Mattathiah, *the son* of Amos, *the son* of Nahum, *the son* of Esli, *the son* of Naggai, [26]*the son* of Maath, *the son* of Mattathiah, *the son* of Semei, *the son* of Joseph, *the son* of Judah, [27]*the son* of Joannas, *the son* of Rhesa, *the son* of Zerubbabel, *the son* of Shealtiel, *the son* of Neri, [28]*the son* of Melchi, *the son* of

Addi, *the son* of Cosam, *the son* of Elmodam, *the son* of Er, [29]*the son* of Jose, *the son* of Eliezer, *the son* of Jorim, *the son* of Matthat, *the son* of Levi, [30]*the son* of Simeon, *the son* of Judah, *the son* of Joseph, *the son* of Jonan, *the son* of Eliakim, [31]*the son* of Melea, *the son* of Menan, *the son* of Mattathah, *the son* of Nathan, *the son* of David, [32]*the son* of Jesse, *the son* of Obed, *the son* of Boaz, *the son* of Salmon, *the son* of Nahshon, [33]*the son* of Amminadab, *the son* of Ram, *the son* of Hezron, *the son* of Perez, *the son* of Judah, [34]*the son* of Jacob, *the son* of Isaac, *the son* of Abraham, *the son* of Terah, *the son* of Nahor, [35]*the son* of Serug, *the son* of Reu, *the son* of Peleg, *the son* of Eber, *the son* of Shelah, [36]*the son* of Cainan, *the son* of Arphaxad, *the son* of Shem, *the son* of Noah, *the son* of Lamech, [37]*the son* of Methuselah, *the son* of Enoch, *the son* of Jared, *the son* of Mahalalel, *the son* of Cainan, [38]*the son* of Enosh, *the son* of Seth, *the son* of Adam, *the son* of God.

3:24 [a]This and several other names in the genealogy are spelled somewhat differently in the NU-Text. Since the New King James Version uses the Old Testament spelling for persons mentioned in the New Testament, these variations, which come from the Greek, have not been footnoted.

The Temptation of Jesus

In all three Synoptics Jesus' temptation is not that of any ordinary individual, but of the Messiah, the Spirit-anointed Servant and Son of God (Ps. 2:7; Is. 42:1), as the heavenly voice affirmed at His baptism (Matt. 3:17). The Spirit led Jesus to face the question of what kind of Messiah He would be.

During the Intertestamental Period many Jews had come to believe that somehow Satan had wrested from God control of this earth. Thus, when Jesus emerged victorious from His test by Satan, He could announce the good news of the nearness of the kingdom of God (Mark 1:15; Matt. 4:17), the messianic age (Luke 4:14–22), or the age of the Spirit (John 4:23, 24; 7:37–39).

The order of the three temptations is different in Matthew and Luke. Matthew's order moves toward a more logical climax: "turn stones to bread" (Matt. 4:3); "throw Yourself from the temple" (4:6); "give You all things" (4:9). Luke's order, making the temple the last temptation, moves Jesus once again toward

TIME CAPSULE   9 to 7 B.C.

9–7   *Sentius Saturninus, governor of Syria, conducts census*

9   *Aretas IV becomes ruler of Nabatea (southwest of Judea)*

9   *Dedication in Rome of the altar to the Peace of Augustus*

8   *Augustus conducts census*

8   *Death of the Roman poet Horace*

7   *Herod the Great executes his sons Alexander and Aristobulus*

LUKE AND THE CAREER OF QUIRINIUS

Luke's Gospel lists a census that was conducted at the time of Jesus' birth, "while Quirinius was governing Syria" (Luke 2:1, 2). Further, Luke indicates that John the Baptist began preaching in the 15th year of Tiberius Caesar (3:1) and that Jesus was about 30 years old when He began to minister (3:23). Scholars are uncertain how to coordinate Luke's chronological information with the varied career of P. Sulpicius Quirinius.

Year	Event
31 B.C.	Augustus Caesar becomes emperor of Rome (31 B.C.–A.D. 14)
15 B.C.	Quirinius becomes praetor of Rome
14 B.C.	Quirinius, as governor of Crete and Cyrene, defeats desert tribe
12 B.C.	Quirinius elected consul of Rome
5 B.C.	Quirinius, as governor of Pamphylia and Galatia, subdues tribes in south Galatia
5 B.C.	Jesus is born 1 or 2 years before Herod's death (Matt. 2:1, 16), and about 30 years before Tiberius's 15th year
4 B.C.	Herod the Great dies in March; Archelaus is made ruler of Judea at Passover in April
A.D. 2	Quirinius becomes chief advisor to Augustus's grandson Gaius
A.D. 6	Archelaus is deposed, and Judea becomes a Roman province, subject to taxes by census
A.D. 6	Quirinius, as governor of Syria, conducts census in Syria and surrounding territories
A.D. 14	Tiberius Caesar becomes emperor of Rome (A.D. 14–37)
A.D. 21	Public funeral for Quirinius
A.D. 26	15th year of Tiberius, counting from his coregency with Augustus

The census taken by Quirinius in A.D. 6 is too late for Jesus' birth. Some think that Quirinius was governor of Syria twice, taking a census both times. Others think it would be highly unusual for Quirinius to conduct a census before his appointment in A.D. 6. While some historians regard Luke's information as flawed, others accept his statements as proof that Quirinius's career was unusual.

His destiny in Jerusalem: "turn stone to bread" (Luke 4:3); "give You all things" (4:6, 7); "throw Yourself from the temple" (4:9). See "Jesus' Final Journey" at Matt. 8:18.

■ Matthew 4:1–11
■ Mark 1:12, 13
■ Luke 4:1–13

Matthew 4:1–11
Satan Tempts Jesus

4 :1 Then Jesus was led up by the Spirit into the wilderness to be tempted by the devil. 2And when He had fasted forty days and forty nights, afterward He was hungry. 3Now when the tempter came to Him, he said, "If You are the Son of God, command that these stones become bread."

4But He answered and said, "It is written, *'Man shall not live by bread alone, but by every word that proceeds from the mouth of God.'*[a]

5Then the devil took Him up into the holy city, set Him on the pinnacle of the temple, 6and said to Him, "If You are the Son of God, throw Yourself down. For it is written:

'He shall give His angels charge over you,'

and,

'In their hands they shall bear you up, Lest you dash your foot against a stone.'[a]

7Jesus said to him, "It is written again, *'You shall not tempt the LORD your God.'*[a]

4:4 aDeuteronomy 8:3   4:6 aPsalm 91:11, 12
4:7 aDeuteronomy 6:16

[8]Again, the devil took Him up on an exceedingly high mountain, and showed Him all the kingdoms of the world and their glory. [9]And he said to Him, "All these things I will give You if You will fall down and worship me."

[10]Then Jesus said to him, "Away with you,[a] Satan! For it is written, *'You shall worship the LORD your God, and Him only you shall serve.'*"[b]

[11]Then the devil left Him, and behold, angels came and ministered to Him.

Mark 1:12, 13

1 :12 Immediately the Spirit drove Him into the wilderness. [13]And He was there in the wilderness forty days, tempted by Satan, and was with the wild beasts; and the angels ministered to Him.

Luke 4:1–13

4 :1 Then Jesus, being filled with the Holy Spirit, returned from the Jordan and was led by the Spirit into[a] the wilderness, [2]being tempted for forty days by the devil. And in those days He ate nothing, and afterward, when they had ended, He was hungry.

[3]And the devil said to Him, "If You are the Son of God, command this stone to become bread."

[4]But Jesus answered him, saying,[a] "It is written, *'Man shall not live by bread alone, but by every word of God.'*"[b]

[5]Then the devil, taking Him up on a high mountain, showed Him[a] all the kingdoms of the world in a moment of time. [6]And the devil said to Him, "All this authority I will give You, and their glory; for

this has been delivered to me, and I give it to whomever I wish. [7]Therefore, if You will worship before me, all will be Yours."

[8]And Jesus answered and said to him, "Get behind Me, Satan![a] For[b] it is written, *'You shall worship the LORD your God, and Him only you shall serve.'*"[c]

[9]Then he brought Him to Jerusalem, set Him on the pinnacle of the temple, and said to Him, "If You are the Son of God, throw Yourself down from here. [10]For it is written:

'He shall give His angels charge over
   you,
    To keep you,'

[11]and,

'In their hands they shall bear you up,
Lest you dash your foot against a
   stone.'"[a]

[12]And Jesus answered and said to him, "It has been said, *'You shall not tempt the LORD your God.'*"[a]

[13]Now when the devil had ended every temptation, he departed from Him until an opportune time.

Matt. 4:10 [a]M-Text reads *Get behind Me.*
[b]Deuteronomy 6:13   **Luke** 4:1 [a]NU-Text reads *in.*
4:4 [a]Deuteronomy 8:3   [b]NU-Text omits *but by every word of God.*   4:5 [a]NU-Text reads *And taking Him up, he showed Him.*   4:8 [a]NU-Text omits *Get behind Me, Satan.*   [b]NU-Text and M-Text omit *For.*
[c]Deuteronomy 6:13   4:11 [a]Psalm 91:11, 12
4:12 [a]Deuteronomy 6:16

The Galilean Ministry

John's Gospel includes trips between Galilee and Judea not mentioned by the Synoptic Gospels.

Jesus' ministry is traditionally divided into segments: a Galilean ministry, a journey toward Jerusalem, a Judean ministry, and the Passion Week in Jerusalem. Whereas Matthew, Mark, and Luke narrate only one visit to Jerusalem as the climax of Jesus' ministry, John recounts that Jesus regularly followed the practice of Palestinian Jews by observing the pilgrimage feasts. The three feasts of Passover (Unleavened Bread), Pentecost (Weeks), and Tabernacles involved pilgrimages to Jerusalem (Deut. 16:16; see John 5:1; 7:2–10). As a consequence of this attention to feasts, John's Gospel includes several trips back and forth between Galilee and Judea that are not mentioned by the Synoptic Gospels. What emerges from a comparison of the four Gospels is a complementary view of Jesus' public ministry: Matthew, Mark, and Luke emphasize His activities in His native Galilee; John gives most of his attention to Jesus' work in Jerusalem and surrounding Judea.

Beginning of the Public Ministry

The Fourth Gospel emphasizes that John the Baptist was the one who came "to bear witness of the Light" (John 1:6, 7, 34). In keeping with this emphasis, the Gospel writer John begins his account of Jesus' ministry by reporting that the first persons to follow Jesus were responding to the Baptist's testimony. Previously Andrew had been a disciple of the Baptist (1:35–37, 40).

The place where the Baptist had been baptizing disciples is reported in John 1:28 as Bethabara of Judea in some Greek manuscripts and as Bethany of Perea in others. Neither place can be located with certainty. Many of Jesus' earliest followers, however, were from areas farther north surrounding the Sea of Galilee, such as Bethsaida (1:44). This group of followers increased as they told family members and friends about Jesus (1:41, 45), and as Jesus Himself summoned people, "Follow Me" (1:43). Jesus shortly left the region of the Baptist's ministry at the Jordan River and went to Galilee (1:43).

■ John 1:35–51

John
The First Disciples

1 :35 Again, the next day, John stood with two of his disciples. 36And looking at Jesus as He walked, he said, "Behold the Lamb of God!"

37The two disciples heard him speak, and they followed Jesus. 38Then Jesus

---

1:42 ªNU-Text reads *John.*

TIME CAPSULE *7 to 4 B.C.*

7 *Census of Judea under Quirinius (?; Luke 2:2)*

5 *Birth of Jesus Christ (Matt. 1:24, 25)*

4 *Wise men from the East visit Jesus (Matt. 2:1–12)*

4 *Herod the Great executes his oldest son, Antipater*

4 *Herod the Great slaughters children under two years (Matt. 2:13–15)*

4 *Death of Herod the Great (Matt. 2:19)*

---

turned, and seeing them following, said to them, "What do you seek?"

They said to Him, "Rabbi" (which is to say, when translated, Teacher), "where are You staying?"

39He said to them, "Come and see." They came and saw where He was staying, and remained with Him that day (now it was about the tenth hour).

40One of the two who heard John *speak,* and followed Him, was Andrew, Simon Peter's brother. 41He first found his own brother Simon, and said to him, "We have found the Messiah" (which is translated, the Christ). 42And he brought him to Jesus.

Now when Jesus looked at him, He said, "You are Simon the son of Jonah.ª You shall be called Cephas" (which is translated, A Stone).

Philip and Nathanael

43The following day Jesus wanted to go to Galilee, and He found Philip and said to him, "Follow Me." 44Now Philip was from

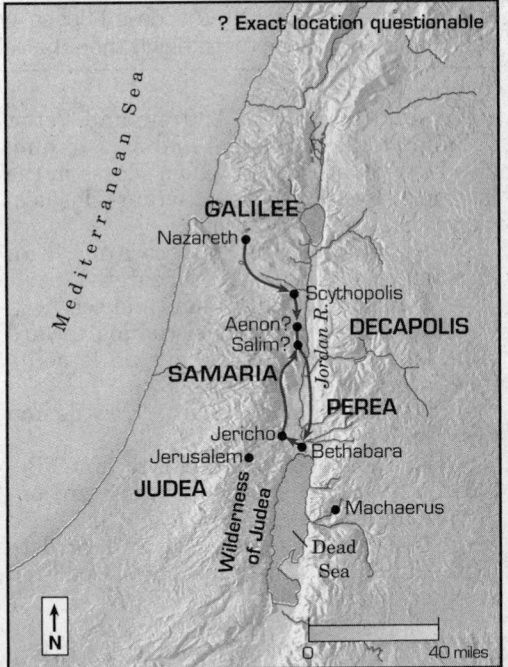

Jesus' Baptism and Temptation
Jesus came from Nazareth in Galilee to be baptized by John the Baptist. While John had been baptizing near Aenon and Salim (John 3:23), the exact location of Jesus' baptism is uncertain. Immediately after His baptism, Jesus was led by the Holy Spirit into the wilderness of Judea below Jericho.

WATERPOTS FOR PURIFICATION (John 2:6)

On several occasions, such as before festivals (John 11:55) and after contracting ritual impurity, Jewish people would ceremonially purify themselves. One purification ritual involved a tank of water known as a *mikveh,* and for a *mikveh* to be valid, it had to contain at least 40 seahs of water (about 120 gallons, each seah equaling approximately 3 gallons). The amount of water at the Cana wedding Jesus attended would have been more than enough to fill a *mikveh* tank; each of the 6 stone vessels held 20 or more gallons (John 2:1, 6).

The 6 waterpots were available at the wedding because of the "manner of purification" (John 2:6), and the large amount of water would suggest a *mikveh.* Very religious Jews, however, insisted on using only "living water" for a *mikveh*—that is, rainwater or fresh water from a stream, rather than water drawn from a well. Some Jews even settled for dirty, stagnant rainwater to avoid violating custom by using drawn water. Only more lenient Jews would use the drawn water in the Cana waterpots for a *mikveh.*

Possibly the waterpots at Cana were used specifically for ritual washing of the hands, rather than for the *mikveh.* The tradition of some Jews called for pouring water over the hands before eating (Mark 7:3). Since John's Gospel does not specify what type of purification ritual was connected with the waterpots, we cannot know whether Jesus' Cana host was any more or less observant of proper Jewish custom than his contemporaries.

Jewish tradition greatly praised weddings, but did not approve using for wedding wine any vessels set aside for ritual purposes. Holy vessels set aside for sacred purposes were not to be used for profane purposes. Jesus, however, knew that the host would be the laughingstock of his community for years to come if he ran out of wine at his wedding. (Wedding celebrations normally lasted 7 days.) Jesus' wedding gift—filling the waterpots with wine—valued His friend's honor more highly than the religious tradition of His contemporaries.

Bethsaida, the city of Andrew and Peter. [45]Philip found Nathanael and said to him, "We have found Him of whom Moses in the law, and also the prophets, wrote—Jesus of Nazareth, the son of Joseph."

[46]And Nathanael said to him, "Can anything good come out of Nazareth?"

Philip said to him, "Come and see."

[47]Jesus saw Nathanael coming toward Him, and said of him, "Behold, an Israelite indeed, in whom is no deceit!"

[48]Nathanael said to Him, "How do You know me?"

Jesus answered and said to him, "Before Philip called you, when you were under the fig tree, I saw you."

[49]Nathanael answered and said to Him, "Rabbi, You are the Son of God! You are the King of Israel!"

[50]Jesus answered and said to him, "Because I said to you, 'I saw you under the fig tree,' do you believe? You will see greater things than these." [51]And He said to him, "Most assuredly, I say to you, hereafter[a] you shall see heaven open, and the angels of God ascending and descending upon the Son of Man."

1:51 [a]NU-Text omits *hereafter.*

The First of Seven Signs

In Cana of Galilee Jesus performed the first of several signs. John's account of Jesus' public ministry (John 1:19—12:50) is often called "the Book of Signs," because John had a special interest in the role that signs

RELIGION AND WORSHIP

Baptism is a ritual of bathing that was practiced by the Jews before New Testament times. Forms of baptism were used in other religions as well. It is a natural symbol of cleansing or purification. Baptism announces the beginning of a new life, marking the transition from paganism to Judaism, or for the church, from unbelief to Christ (John 2:11; 3:22).

played in revealing Jesus' relationship with the Father (see John 20:30, 31). Traditionally, seven miracles have been isolated as being particular "signs" for John: transformation of water into wine (2:1–11), healing of a nobleman's son (4:46–54), cure of a paralytic (5:1–15), the feeding of the 5,000 (6:1–15), walking on the sea (6:16–21), healing a blind man (ch. 9), and raising Lazarus (ch. 11).

Two of these signs are specifically numbered (2:11; 4:54), causing some scholars to think that John had access to a "signs source." Supposedly, this signs source was a collection of stories about wonders performed by Jesus. When writing his Gospel, John would have drawn from this source, which was known in his community. If such a source existed, we cannot determine its specific content. Interspersed among the seven miracles are statements that Jesus performed many other signs (see 2:23; 3:2; 6:2).

■ John 2:1–12

John
Water Turned to Wine

2 :1 On the third day there was a wedding in Cana of Galilee, and the mother of Jesus was there. ²Now both Jesus and His disciples were invited to the wedding. ³And when they ran out of wine, the mother of Jesus said to Him, "They have no wine."

⁴Jesus said to her, "Woman, what does your concern have to do with Me? My hour has not yet come."

⁵His mother said to the servants, "Whatever He says to you, do *it*."

⁶Now there were set there six waterpots of stone, according to the manner of purification of the Jews, containing twenty or thirty gallons apiece. ⁷Jesus said to them, "Fill the waterpots with water." And they filled them up to the brim. ⁸And He said to them, "Draw *some* out now, and take *it* to the master of the feast." And they took *it*. ⁹When the master of the feast had tasted the water that was made wine, and did not know where it came from (but the servants who had drawn the water knew), the master of the feast called the bridegroom. ¹⁰And he said to him, "Every man at the beginning sets out the good wine, and when the *guests* have well drunk, then the inferior. You have kept the good wine until now!"

¹¹This beginning of signs Jesus did in Cana of Galilee, and manifested His glory; and His disciples believed in Him.

¹²After this He went down to Capernaum, He, His mother, His brothers, and His disciples; and they did not stay there many days.

Jesus' First Visit to Jerusalem

Matthew, Mark, and Luke mention only one visit of Jesus to Jerusalem during His ministry (see "The Galilean Ministry" at John 1:35). Thus Jesus' "cleansing of the temple" raises a chronological question regarding when this incident in Jerusalem may have occurred. All four evangelists report Jesus' prophetic demonstration, which provoked direct challenges to His authority from the religious leadership in Jerusalem (Matt. 21:23–27; Mark 11:27–33; Luke 20:1–8; John 2:18–22).

Comparing John with the Synoptics leads us to ask whether the temple cleansing occurred once or twice, and whether it happened at the beginning or end of Jesus' ministry. John reports the incident early in his Gospel account. The other evangelists, though, associate it with the events of Jesus' Passion (see "Monday: Cleansing the Temple" at Matt. 21:12). Some suggest that Jesus "cleansed" the temple both at the outset and at the conclusion of His ministry. Others believe that John and the Synoptics report a single event at different points in their Gospels for theological or literary reasons. Supposedly John located the cleansing early to emphasize that Jesus encountered opposition from priests even at the beginning of His ministry.

The Jewish leaders misunderstood Jesus' saying regarding the temple (John 2:19). Jesus' body was the temple that would be destroyed in His crucifixion, but raised up in His resurrection (2:21, 22). He was not speaking of the building that Herod had begun to reconstruct 46 years previously. The task of rebuilding the temple began in Herod's 18th year (c. 20–19 B.C.) and continued beyond his lifetime. A passage of 46 years would date this Jerusalem visit of Jesus in about A.D. 27, at the spring Passover celebration.

■ John 2:13–25

John
Jesus Cleanses the Temple

2 :13 Now the Passover of the Jews was at hand, and Jesus went up to

Jerusalem. ¹⁴And He found in the temple those who sold oxen and sheep and doves, and the money changers doing business. ¹⁵When He had made a whip of cords, He drove them all out of the temple, with the sheep and the oxen, and poured out the changers' money and overturned the tables. ¹⁶And He said to those who sold doves, "Take these things away! Do not make My Father's house a house of merchandise!" ¹⁷Then His disciples remembered that it was written, *"Zeal for Your house has eaten*ᵃ *Me up."*ᵇ

¹⁸So the Jews answered and said to Him, "What sign do You show to us, since You do these things?"

¹⁹Jesus answered and said to them, "Destroy this temple, and in three days I will raise it up."

²⁰Then the Jews said, "It has taken forty-six years to build this temple, and will You raise it up in three days?" ²¹But He was speaking of the temple of His body. ²²Therefore, when He had risen from the dead, His disciples remembered that He had said this to them;ᵃ and they believed the Scripture and the word which Jesus had said.

The Discerner of Hearts

²³Now when He was in Jerusalem at the Passover, during the feast, many believed in His name when they saw the signs which He did. ²⁴But Jesus did not commit Himself to them, because He knew all *men,* ²⁵and had no need that anyone should testify of man, for He knew what was in man.

Nicodemus, the Pharisee

John's mention of the Passover (John 2:13, 23) gives the impression that Nicodemus came to Jesus during this feast, immediately following the temple cleansing. This Pharisee, who was a member of Judea's ruling class (3:1), asserted that Jesus' signs revealed Him to be "a teacher come from God" (3:2; see 2:18, 23). Such a statement from one who himself was a prominent "teacher of Israel" (3:10) emphasizes John's view that the conflict between Jesus and the Jewish religious leaders would focus on authority, or more particularly the origin of authority.

John is clear about the origin of Jesus' own authority and that of His followers: it comes "from above." As the "Son of Man" who "came down from heaven" (3:13), Jesus could reveal "heavenly things" (3:12). Likewise, His followers knew about these heavenly things, for they had been "born again" or "from above" (3:3, 5–7). After Jesus had left Jerusalem, John the Baptist emphasized this same point during a controversy with Jewish leaders (3:22–36).

■ John 3:1–36

John
The New Birth

3 :1 There was a man of the Pharisees named Nicodemus, a ruler of the Jews. ²This man came to Jesus by night and said to Him, "Rabbi, we know that You are a teacher come from God; for no one can do these signs that You do unless God is with him."

³Jesus answered and said to him, "Most assuredly, I say to you, unless one is born again, he cannot see the kingdom of God."

⁴Nicodemus said to Him, "How can a man be born when he is old? Can he enter a second time into his mother's womb and be born?"

⁵Jesus answered, "Most assuredly, I say to you, unless one is born of water and the Spirit, he cannot enter the kingdom of God. ⁶That which is born of the flesh is flesh, and that which is born of the Spirit is spirit. ⁷Do not marvel that I said to you, 'You must be born again.' ⁸The wind blows where it wishes, and you hear the sound of

---

TIME CAPSULE *4 to 2 B.C.*

4	*The Jews petition Rome not to leave the Herods in power*
4	*Herod's kingdom is divided for three of his sons*
4– A.D. 6	*Archelaus rules as ethnarch of Judea and Samaria (Matt. 2:22)*
4– A.D. 39	*Herod Antipas rules as tetrarch of Galilee and Perea*
4– A.D. 34	*Philip rules as tetrarch of Gaulanitis*
2	*Augustus is named the "father of his country"*

2:17 ᵃNU-Text and M-Text read *will eat.* ᵇPsalm 69:9   2:22 ᵃNU-Text and M-Text omit *to them.*

BORN OF WATER AND THE SPIRIT (John 3:5)

When Jesus spoke of being "born again" (John 3:3), He literally meant "from above," that is, "from God." Nicodemus failed to understand, so Jesus explained the concept in more familiar terms: "born of water and the Spirit" (3:5).

Not certain, however, is what the expression "born of water and the Spirit" meant to Jesus and Nicodemus. One possibility is that "born of water" was compared to Jewish baptism. A Gentile who converted to Judaism came to be viewed as a new person, cleansed from his or her former life. Converted Gentiles immersed themselves in water to symbolize the cleansing of their former impurity as Gentiles. If this is what Jesus wanted Nicodemus to grasp, He was treating him like a spiritual Gentile: though a teacher of Israel, Nicodemus himself needed to convert to the true faith promised to Israel—a new life given by the Holy Spirit to those believing in Jesus.

Yet Jesus may have intended not a *physical* water for conversion, but a sort of *spiritual* water. The Gospel of John applies the symbolism of water to the Spirit (John 7:37–39), possibly reflecting God's promise to purify His people someday from spiritual uncleanness and put His Spirit within them (Ezek. 36:25–27). If Jesus intended water as such a symbol, then "born of water and the Spirit" would refer not to two different experiences, but to a single one. In other words, Jesus meant not a physical Jewish proselyte baptism, but a *spiritual* proselyte baptism, a conversion by the Spirit of God.

In the exchange with Nicodemus, Jesus saw the Pharisee's real need and came immediately to the heart of the matter. A transformation of the heart by the Holy Spirit would enable him to see fullness of life in the kingdom of God.

---

it, but cannot tell where it comes from and where it goes. So is everyone who is born of the Spirit."

⁹Nicodemus answered and said to Him, "How can these things be?"

¹⁰Jesus answered and said to him, "Are you the teacher of Israel, and do not know these things? ¹¹Most assuredly, I say to you, We speak what We know and testify what We have seen, and you do not receive Our witness. ¹²If I have told you earthly things and you do not believe, how will you believe if I tell you heavenly things? ¹³No one has ascended to heaven but He who came down from heaven, *that is,* the Son of Man who is in heaven.[a] ¹⁴And as Moses lifted up the serpent in the wilderness, even so must the Son of Man be lifted up, ¹⁵that whoever believes in Him should not perish but[a] have eternal life. ¹⁶For God so loved the world that He gave His only begotten Son, that whoever believes in Him should not perish but have everlasting life. ¹⁷For God did not send His Son into the world to condemn the world, but that the world through Him might be saved.

¹⁸"He who believes in Him is not con-demned; but he who does not believe is condemned already, because he has not believed in the name of the only begotten Son of God. ¹⁹And this is the condemnation, that the light has come into the world, and men loved darkness rather than light, because their deeds were evil. ²⁰For everyone practicing evil hates the light and does not come to the light, lest his deeds should be exposed. ²¹But he who does the truth comes to the light, that his deeds may be clearly seen, that they have been done in God."

John the Baptist Exalts Christ

²²After these things Jesus and His disciples came into the land of Judea, and there He remained with them and baptized. ²³Now John also was baptizing in Aenon near Salim, because there was much water there. And they came and were baptized. ²⁴For John had not yet been thrown into prison.

²⁵Then there arose a dispute between *some* of John's disciples and the Jews about purification. ²⁶And they came to John and said to him, "Rabbi, He who was with you beyond the Jordan, to whom you have testified—behold, He is baptizing, and all are coming to Him!"

3:13 ᵃNU-Text omits *who is in heaven.*
3:15 ᵃNU-Text omits *not perish but.*

27John answered and said, "A man can receive nothing unless it has been given to him from heaven. 28You yourselves bear me witness, that I said, 'I am not the Christ,' but, 'I have been sent before Him.' 29He who has the bride is the bridegroom; but the friend of the bridegroom, who stands and hears him, rejoices greatly because of the bridegroom's voice. Therefore this joy of mine is fulfilled. 30He must increase, but I *must* decrease. 31He who comes from above is above all; he who is of the earth is earthly and speaks of the earth. He who comes from heaven is above all. 32And what He has seen and heard, that He testifies; and no one receives His testimony. 33He who has received His testimony has certified that God is true. 34For He whom God has sent speaks the words of God, for God does not give the Spirit by measure. 35The Father loves the Son, and has given all things into His hand. 36He who believes in the Son has everlasting life; and he who does not believe the Son shall not see life, but the wrath of God abides on him."

Through Samaria to Galilee

John's remark that Jesus "needed to go through Samaria" to return to Galilee (John 4:4) may reflect a spiritual necessity of His ministry. Most Jews en route to Galilee traveled through the region of Perea east of the Jordan River rather than take the more direct route through Samaria. There were deep-seated prejudices between the Jews and the Samaritans, going back to at least the period of the restoration of Judah following the Babylonian exile. Jesus, however, had a mission to Samaritans as well as to Jews.

Figuring prominently in John 4 are two aspects of Jewish and Samaritan religious differences: the place of worship and the promised Messiah. The Samaritans had opposed the reconstruction of the Jerusalem temple in 538 B.C. (Ezra 4:1–5). Furthermore, they had constructed their own temple to the God of Abraham on Mount Gerizim in either 388 or 332 B.C. Wishing to divert attention from her personal life, the Samaritan woman posed a theological question about the place where one ought to worship (John 4:19, 20).

The second aspect—the coming Messiah—develops from the sacred Scriptures used by Jews and Samaritans. The Jews already recognized two divisions of Scripture—

the Law and the Prophets (Matt. 5:17). Believing that Israel's prophets had supported the rival Jerusalem temple, the Samaritans rejected the division called "the Prophets" and accepted only the Law of Moses or Torah (the books of Genesis through Deuteronomy) as Scripture. Thus, Samaritan expectations about the Messiah centered in the promise of a "Prophet like Moses" (Deut. 18:15–19) who would be a teacher (John 4:25), rather than a political figure like the messianic Son of David expected by many Jews. As was previously the case with Nicodemus (John 3:4, 9), both the Samaritan woman (4:11, 12, 15) and Jesus' own disciples (4:31–33) were so fixed on the literal, physical meaning of His words that they failed to understand the spiritual significance.

■ John 4:1–45

John
A Samaritan Woman Meets Her Messiah

4:1 Therefore, when the Lord knew that the Pharisees had heard that Jesus made and baptized more disciples than John 2(though Jesus Himself did not baptize, but His disciples), 3He left Judea and departed again to Galilee. 4But He needed to go through Samaria.

5So He came to a city of Samaria which is called Sychar, near the plot of ground that Jacob gave to his son Joseph. 6Now Jacob's well was there. Jesus therefore, being wearied from *His* journey, sat thus by the well. It was about the sixth hour.

7A woman of Samaria came to draw water. Jesus said to her, "Give Me a drink." 8For His disciples had gone away into the city to buy food.

9Then the woman of Samaria said to Him, "How is it that You, being a Jew, ask a drink from me, a Samaritan woman?" For Jews have no dealings with Samaritans.

10Jesus answered and said to her, "If you knew the gift of God, and who it is who says to you, 'Give Me a drink,' you would have asked Him, and He would have given you living water."

11The woman said to Him, "Sir, You have nothing to draw with, and the well is deep. Where then do You get that living water? 12Are You greater than our father Jacob, who gave us the well, and drank from it himself, as well as his sons and his livestock?"

13Jesus answered and said to her,

MARVELING OVER JESUS WITH A WOMAN (John 4:27)

Jesus' encounter with a woman at Jacob's well could look very ambiguous (John 4:6–8). In fact, 1st-century cultural norms gave Jesus' disciples reason to be troubled. Jesus had crossed ethnic, moral, and gender barriers that most of His contemporaries felt should not be crossed.

A history of ethnic conflict had left little chance of positive interaction between Jewish people and the Samaritans (4:9). They ridiculed each other's holy places, and once the Samaritans had even defiled the Jerusalem temple. The Judeans for their part had completely destroyed the Samaritan temple on Mount Gerizim nearly two centuries before. By Jewish standards, Samaritan drinking vessels were technically unclean, so Jesus' request for water probably led the woman to think that He was not very religious (4:7).

Jesus also crossed a moral barrier. This woman came alone to draw water from the well (4:7), maybe because she was not welcome among the other women of the village. Her personal life was probably considered loose by Samaritan standards, since she had been married five times and was not married to the man with whom she was living. Talking with this woman at a well was an ambiguous situation. Even the Samaritan woman, telling Jesus that she was unmarried, may have misread His motives, though He quickly set the matter straight (4:17, 18).

Finally, Jesus crossed a gender barrier in force among His fellow Jews. Many sages, such as Jesus son of Sirach, warned against being seen speaking with women, offering two reasons. First, one could easily fall prey to temptation; second, one could get a bad reputation because of what people might think, even if the woman turned out to be one's sister.

That the disciples were astonished to find Jesus talking with this woman fits their culture. That they said nothing shows their respect for and trust in Jesus (4:27).

"Whoever drinks of this water will thirst again, [14]but whoever drinks of the water that I shall give him will never thirst. But the water that I shall give him will become in him a fountain of water springing up into everlasting life."

[15]The woman said to Him, "Sir, give me this water, that I may not thirst, nor come here to draw."

[16]Jesus said to her, "Go, call your husband, and come here."

[17]The woman answered and said, "I have no husband."

Jesus said to her, "You have well said, 'I have no husband,' [18]for you have had five husbands, and the one whom you now have is not your husband; in that you spoke truly."

[19]The woman said to Him, "Sir, I perceive that You are a prophet. [20]Our fathers worshiped on this mountain, and you *Jews* say that in Jerusalem is the place where one ought to worship."

[21]Jesus said to her, "Woman, believe Me, the hour is coming when you will neither on this mountain, nor in Jerusalem, worship the Father. [22]You worship what you do not know; we know what we worship, for salvation is of the Jews. [23]But the hour is coming, and now is, when the true worshipers will worship the Father in spirit and truth; for the Father is seeking such to worship Him. [24]God *is* Spirit, and those who worship Him must worship in spirit and truth."

[25]The woman said to Him, "I know that Messiah is coming" (who is called Christ). "When He comes, He will tell us all things."

[26]Jesus said to her, "I who speak to you am *He*."

The Whitened Harvest

[27]And at this *point* His disciples came, and they marveled that He talked with a woman; yet no one said, "What do You seek?" or, "Why are You talking with her?"

[28]The woman then left her waterpot, went her way into the city, and said to the men, [29]"Come, see a Man who told me all things that I ever did. Could this be the Christ?" [30]Then they went out of the city and came to Him.

³¹In the meantime His disciples urged Him, saying, "Rabbi, eat."

³²But He said to them, "I have food to eat of which you do not know."

³³Therefore the disciples said to one another, "Has anyone brought Him *anything* to eat?"

³⁴Jesus said to them, "My food is to do the will of Him who sent Me, and to finish His work. ³⁵Do you not say, 'There are still four months and *then* comes the harvest'? Behold, I say to you, lift up your eyes and look at the fields, for they are already white for harvest! ³⁶And he who reaps receives wages, and gathers fruit for eternal life, that both he who sows and he who reaps may rejoice together. ³⁷For in this the saying is true: 'One sows and another reaps.' ³⁸I sent you to reap that for which you have not labored; others have labored, and you have entered into their labors."

The Savior of the World

³⁹And many of the Samaritans of that city believed in Him because of the word of the woman who testified, "He told me all that I *ever* did." ⁴⁰So when the Samaritans had come to Him, they urged Him to stay with them; and He stayed there two days. ⁴¹And many more believed because of His own word.

⁴²Then they said to the woman, "Now we believe, not because of what you said, for we ourselves have heard *Him* and we know that this is indeed the Christ,ᵃ the Savior of the world."

Welcome at Galilee

⁴³Now after the two days He departed from there and went to Galilee. ⁴⁴For Jesus Himself testified that a prophet has no honor in his own country. ⁴⁵So when He came to Galilee, the Galileans received Him, having seen all the things He did in Jerusalem at the feast; for they also had gone to the feast.

Early Ministry in Galilee

Matthew and Mark begin their accounts of Jesus' Galilean ministry by summarizing the content of His preaching in a virtual slogan: "Repent, for the kingdom of heaven is at hand" (Matt. 4:17; see Mark 1:15). Simon Peter, Andrew, James, and John immediately accepted Jesus' call. Matthew is particularly interested in the events of Jesus' life that fulfill Old Testament prophecies (Matt. 1:22, 23;

2:5, 6). Both the inception of the ministry in Galilee and its positive reception are for Matthew yet further fulfillments of prophecy (Matt. 4:13–16).

Luke, however, begins his account with Jesus' rejection in the synagogue of His hometown of Nazareth (Luke 4:14–30). This choice may seem a strange illustration that Jesus "taught in their synagogues, being glorified by all" (4:15). Nevertheless, Jesus' reading of Is. 61:1, 2 provides a more extensive summary of His ministry. Although Jesus was met by opposition from the beginning, Luke insists that "Joseph's son" ministered "in the power of the Spirit" (Luke 4:14, 18, 22).

■ Matthew 4:12–22
■ Mark 1:14–20
■ Luke 4:14–30

Matthew 4:12–22
Jesus Begins His Galilean Ministry

4:12 Now when Jesus heard that John had been put in prison, He departed to Galilee. ¹³And leaving Nazareth, He came and dwelt in Capernaum, which is by the sea, in the regions of Zebulun and Naphtali, ¹⁴that it might be fulfilled which was spoken by Isaiah the prophet, saying:

¹⁵ "The land of Zebulun and the land of
        Naphtali,
      By the way of the sea, beyond the
        Jordan,
      Galilee of the Gentiles:
¹⁶ The people who sat in darkness have
        seen a great light,
      And upon those who sat in the region
        and shadow of death
      Light has dawned."ᵃ

4:42 ᵃNU-Text omits *the Christ.*
Matt. 4:16 ᵃIsaiah 9:1, 2

TIME CAPSULE *A.D. 2 to 6*

2 *Death of Lucius, son of M. V. Agrippa and heir of Augustus*

4 *Death of Gaius, grandchild and designated successor of Augustus*

4 *The* Lex Aelia Sentia *provides for registration of Roman citizens*

5 *Ovid composes* Metamorphoses

6 *Caesarea becomes the provincial capital*

¹⁷From that time Jesus began to preach and to say, "Repent, for the kingdom of heaven is at hand."

Four Fishermen Called as Disciples

¹⁸And Jesus, walking by the Sea of Galilee, saw two brothers, Simon called Peter, and Andrew his brother, casting a net into the sea; for they were fishermen. ¹⁹Then He said to them, "Follow Me, and I will make you fishers of men." ²⁰They immediately left *their* nets and followed Him.

²¹Going on from there, He saw two other brothers, James *the son* of Zebedee, and John his brother, in the boat with Zebedee their father, mending their nets. He called them, ²²and immediately they left the boat and their father, and followed Him.

Mark 1:14–20
Calling Disciples in Galilee

1 :14 Now after John was put in prison, Jesus came to Galilee, preaching the gospel of the kingdomᵃ of God, ¹⁵and saying, "The time is fulfilled, and the kingdom of God is at hand. Repent, and believe in the gospel."

¹⁶And as He walked by the Sea of Galilee, He saw Simon and Andrew his brother casting a net into the sea; for they were fishermen. ¹⁷Then Jesus said to them, "Follow Me, and I will make you become fishers of men." ¹⁸They immediately left their nets and followed Him.

¹⁹When He had gone a little farther from there, He saw James the *son* of Zebedee, and John his brother, who also *were* in the boat mending their nets. ²⁰And immediately He called them, and they left their father Zebedee in the boat with the hired servants, and went after Him.

Luke 4:14–30
Jesus Rejected at Nazareth

4 :14 Then Jesus returned in the power of the Spirit to Galilee, and news of Him went out through all the surrounding region. ¹⁵And He taught in their synagogues, being glorified by all.

¹⁶So He came to Nazareth, where He had been brought up. And as His custom was, He went into the synagogue on the Sabbath day, and stood up to read. ¹⁷And He was handed the book of the prophet Isaiah. And when He had opened the book, He found the place where it was written:

18   "The Spirit of the LORD is upon Me,
       Because He has anointed Me
       To preach the gospel to the poor;
       He has sent Me to heal the
          brokenhearted,ᵃ
       To proclaim liberty to the captives
       And recovery of sight to the blind,
       To set at liberty those who are
          oppressed;
19   To proclaim the acceptable year of the
          LORD."ᵃ

²⁰Then He closed the book, and gave *it* back to the attendant and sat down. And the eyes of all who were in the synagogue were fixed on Him. ²¹And He began to say to them, "Today this Scripture is fulfilled in your hearing." ²²So all bore witness to Him, and marveled at the gracious words which proceeded out of His mouth. And they said, "Is this not Joseph's son?"

²³He said to them, "You will surely say this proverb to Me, 'Physician, heal yourself! Whatever we have heard done in Capernaum,ᵃ do also here in Your country.'" ²⁴Then He said, "Assuredly, I say to you, no prophet is accepted in his own country. ²⁵But I tell you truly, many widows were in Israel in the days of Elijah, when the heaven was shut up three years and six months, and there was a great famine

---

1:14 ᵃNU-Text omits *of the kingdom.*
Luke 4:18 ᵃNU-Text omits *to heal the brokenhearted.*
4:19 ᵃIsaiah 61:1, 2   4:23 ᵃHere and elsewhere the NU-Text spelling is *Capharnaum.*

GEOGRAPHY AND ENVIRONMENT

The Sea of Galilee is about 13 miles by 8 miles in size. This freshwater lake, once known by the names Chinnereth, Gennesar, and Tiberias, supports a great number of fish (Matt. 4:18). The steep hills surrounding the small lake can channel the winds and cause sudden dangerous storms upon the water's surface (Mark 4:37).

throughout all the land; ²⁶but to none of them was Elijah sent except to Zarephath,ᵃ *in the region* of Sidon, to a woman *who was* a widow. ²⁷And many lepers were in Israel in the time of Elisha the prophet, and none of them was cleansed except Naaman the Syrian."

²⁸So all those in the synagogue, when they heard these things, were filled with wrath, ²⁹and rose up and thrust Him out of the city; and they led Him to the brow of the hill on which their city was built, that they might throw Him down over the cliff. ³⁰Then passing through the midst of them, He went His way.

Teaching with Authority

Mark and Luke both associate Jesus' teaching with His authority over evil spirits (Mark 1:22, 27; Luke 4:32, 36). Mark, though, goes so far as to identify such actions by Jesus as being themselves a "new doctrine" (Mark 1:27). More space in Mark's Gospel is devoted to Jesus' miraculous works and less space to His "sayings" than any of the other Gospels. Mark is particularly interested in associating Jesus the miracle worker with Jesus the teacher. For Mark, what Jesus does is as much a part of His teaching as what He says.

■ Mark 1:21–28
■ Luke 4:31–37

Mark 1:21–28
Jesus Casts Out an Unclean Spirit

1 :21 Then they went into Capernaum, and immediately on the Sabbath He entered the synagogue and taught. ²²And they were astonished at His teaching, for He taught them as one having authority, and not as the scribes.

²³Now there was a man in their synagogue with an unclean spirit. And he cried out, ²⁴saying, "Let *us* alone! What have we to do with You, Jesus of Nazareth? Did You come to destroy us? I know who You are—the Holy One of God!"

²⁵But Jesus rebuked him, saying, "Be quiet, and come out of him!" ²⁶And when the unclean spirit had convulsed him and cried out with a loud voice, he came out of him. ²⁷Then they were all amazed, so that they questioned among themselves, saying, "What is this? What new doctrine *is* this? For with authorityᵃ He commands even the unclean spirits, and they obey Him." ²⁸And immediately His fame spread throughout all the region around Galilee.

Luke 4:31–37
Ministry in Capernaum

4 :31 Then He went down to Capernaum, a city of Galilee, and was teaching them on the Sabbaths. ³²And they were astonished at His teaching, for His word was with authority. ³³Now in the synagogue there was a man who had a spirit of an unclean demon. And he cried out with a loud voice, ³⁴saying, "Let *us* alone! What have we to do with You, Jesus of Nazareth? Did You come to destroy us? I know who You are—the Holy One of God!"

³⁵But Jesus rebuked him, saying, "Be quiet, and come out of him!" And when the demon had thrown him in *their* midst, it came out of him and did not hurt him. ³⁶Then they were all amazed and spoke among themselves, saying, "What a word this *is!* For with authority and power He commands the unclean spirits, and they come out." ³⁷And the report about Him went out into every place in the surrounding region.

4:26 ᵃGreek *Sarepta*   **Mark** 1:27 ᵃNU-Text reads *What is this? A new doctrine with authority.*

Healing the Sick

The brief accounts of the healings of Peter's mother-in-law and of others in the village highlight particular interests of the evangelists. Matthew once again links the details of Jesus' life with Israel's prophetic tradition (Matt. 8:17 cites Is. 53:4).

Mark uses this episode to introduce his theme of the "messianic secret" (Mark 1:43,

HEALTH AND MEDICINE

Several proverbs concerning doctors, such as "Physician, heal yourself!" (Luke 4:23), are known in the ancient world. Herodotus (died about 425 B.C.) describes a public area where the sick could meet and exchange what they knew about their problems and what treatments were effective. Minor surgery was fairly common. At its best the medical treatment of antiquity was marked by compassion and common sense.

SIMON PETER'S HOUSE AT CAPERNAUM (Mark 1:29)

Capernaum was a city on the northwest bank of the Sea of Galilee. After leaving Nazareth, Jesus moved to this city, where He began His early ministry in Galilee (Matt. 4:13). One place Jesus visited in Capernaum was the house of Simon Peter, which is sometimes identified by the disciple's name (Matt. 8:14; Mark 1:29; Luke 4:38), but other times as simply "the house" (Matt. 17:24, 25; Mark 9:33).

Archaeologists have recently discovered in Capernaum what they consider to be Simon Peter's house. The plan of the house had three courts arranged around a series of living rooms. It appears to have been built in the Hellenistic period (332–37 B.C.)—possibly two centuries before Peter's occupation. Later in the apostolic period, portions of the house were transformed into a house church.

44; 3:11, 12). For Mark, only Jesus' death on the cross can reveal what it really means for Jesus to be the Messiah and "Son of God" (Mark 15:39). So in Mark's presentation, Jesus is careful to keep His identity secret so as to avoid the popular misconceptions about what the work of the Messiah would be. For that reason, Jesus "did not allow the demons to speak, because they knew Him" (Mark 1:34).

- Matthew 8:14–17
- Mark 1:29–34
- Luke 4:38–41

Matthew 8:14–17
Peter's Mother-in-Law Healed

8 **:14** Now when Jesus had come into Peter's house, He saw his wife's mother lying sick with a fever. [15]So He touched her hand, and the fever left her. And she arose and served them.[a]

[16]When evening had come, they brought to Him many who were demon-possessed. And He cast out the spirits with a word, and healed all who were sick, [17]that it might be fulfilled which was spoken by Isaiah the prophet, saying:

"*He Himself took our infirmities*
And bore our sicknesses."[a]

8:15 [a]NU-Text and M-Text read *Him.*
8:17 [a]Isaiah 53:4

Mark 1:29–34
In Simon Peter's House

1 **:29** Now as soon as they had come out of the synagogue, they entered the house of Simon and Andrew, with James and John. [30]But Simon's wife's mother lay sick with a fever, and they told Him about her at once. [31]So He came and took her by the hand and lifted her up, and immediately the fever left her. And she served them.

[32]At evening, when the sun had set, they brought to Him all who were sick and those who were demon-possessed. [33]And the whole city was gathered together at the door. [34]Then He healed many who were sick with various diseases, and cast out many demons; and He did not allow the demons to speak, because they knew Him.

Luke 4:38–41
Many Healed After Sabbath Sunset

4 **:38** Now He arose from the synagogue and entered Simon's house. But Simon's wife's mother was sick with a high fever, and they made request of Him concerning her. [39]So He stood over her and rebuked the fever, and it left her. And immediately she arose and served them.

[40]When the sun was setting, all those who had any that were sick with various

---

RELIGION AND WORSHIP
The word "synagogue" (Luke 4:38) comes from a Greek word meaning "meeting place" or "congregation." By the time of Jesus, the Jews had established synagogues everywhere they lived. The oldest synagogue excavated so far in Judea dates from about A.D. 100. It was located near the city gates, a traditional place for public business.

diseases brought them to Him; and He laid His hands on every one of them and healed them. ⁴¹And demons also came out of many, crying out and saying, "You are the Christ,ᵃ the Son of God!"

And He, rebuking *them,* did not allow them to speak, for they knew that He was the Christ.

Departing Capernaum

Matthew and Mark emphasized the radical obedience exhibited by Jesus' first disciples in accepting His call (Matt. 4:18–22; Mark 1:16–20). Luke, however, provides further insight into an experience with Jesus that led Simon Peter, James, and John to leave their businesses to follow Jesus. They witnessed a catch of fish so large that it astounded even these professional fishermen.

Having heard Jesus' teaching (Luke 5:3), Peter said to Him, "at Your word I will let down the net" (5:5), even though they had met with no success in their fishing endeavors that night. Jesus then used their extraordinary success as a kind of parable, telling the fishermen, "From now on you will catch men" (5:10). During these earliest stages of Jesus' Galilean ministry (Luke 4:38–41, 44), including here at the lakeshore, His followers received personal knowledge of His teaching and miracles. In response, they were willing to accept His call to discipleship.

- Matthew 4:23–25
- Mark 1:35–39
- Luke 4:42—5:11

Matthew 4:23–25
Jesus Heals a Great Multitude

4 :23 And Jesus went about all Galilee, teaching in their synagogues, preaching the gospel of the kingdom, and healing all kinds of sickness and all kinds of disease among the people. ²⁴Then His fame went throughout all Syria; and they brought to Him all sick people who were afflicted with various diseases and torments, and those who were demon-possessed, epileptics, and paralytics; and He healed them. ²⁵Great multitudes followed Him—from Galilee, and *from* Decapolis, Jerusalem, Judea, and beyond the Jordan.

Mark 1:35–39
Preaching in Galilee

1 :35 Now in the morning, having risen a long while before daylight, He went out

and departed to a solitary place; and there He prayed. ³⁶And Simon and those *who were* with Him searched for Him. ³⁷When they found Him, they said to Him, "Everyone is looking for You."

³⁸But He said to them, "Let us go into the next towns, that I may preach there also, because for this purpose I have come forth."

³⁹And He was preaching in their synagogues throughout all Galilee, and casting out demons.

Luke 4:42—5:11

4 :42 Now when it was day, He departed and went into a deserted place. And the crowd sought Him and came to Him, and tried to keep Him from leaving them; ⁴³but He said to them, "I must preach the kingdom of God to the other cities also, because for this purpose I have been sent." ⁴⁴And He was preaching in the synagogues of Galilee.ᵃ

Four Fishermen Called as Disciples

5 ¹So it was, as the multitude pressed about Him to hear the word of God, that He stood by the Lake of Gennesaret, ²and saw two boats standing by the lake; but the fishermen had gone from them and were washing *their* nets. ³Then He got into one of the boats, which was Simon's, and asked him to put out a little from the land. And He sat down and taught the multitudes from the boat.

⁴When He had stopped speaking, He said to Simon, "Launch out into the deep and let down your nets for a catch."

⁵But Simon answered and said to Him, "Master, we have toiled all night and caught nothing; nevertheless at Your word I will let down the net." ⁶And when they had done this, they caught a great number of fish, and their net was breaking. ⁷So they signaled to *their* partners in the other boat to come and help them. And they came and filled both the boats, so that they began to sink. ⁸When Simon Peter saw *it,* he fell down at Jesus' knees, saying, "Depart from me, for I am a sinful man, O Lord!"

⁹For he and all who were with him were astonished at the catch of fish which they had taken; ¹⁰and so also *were* James and John, the sons of Zebedee, who were

---

Luke 4:41   ᵃNU-Text omits *the Christ.*
4:44   ᵃNU-Text reads *Judea.*

partners with Simon. And Jesus said to Simon, "Do not be afraid. From now on you will catch men." [11]So when they had brought their boats to land, they forsook all and followed Him.

Cleansing the Leper

The cleansing and healing of a leper, an outcast from society, is a second instance of Mark's "messianic secret" theme (see "Healing the Sick" at Matt. 8:14). Mark highlights two dynamics of Jesus' secret identity. First, those who did not completely understand Jesus' messiahship, supposing Him to be only a miracle worker or healer, could in fact hinder His ability to accomplish His ministry. Because of their reactions, Jesus "could no longer openly enter the city" (Mark 1:45). Second, Mark shows that those whose lives had genuinely been changed by the gospel were not able to contain their excitement and enthusiasm about what God had done for them (see Mark 5:18–20).

Luke's narrative does not mention the leper spreading the news of his cleansing. Perhaps Luke wished to downplay any appearance of the leper disobeying Jesus' instructions. It is enough for Luke to note simply that a report concerning Jesus did spread as a result of this healing (Luke 5:15).

- ■ Matthew 8:1–4
- ■ Mark 1:40–45
- ■ Luke 5:12–16

Matthew 8:1–4
The Compassion of Jesus

8 :1 When He had come down from the mountain, great multitudes followed Him. [2]And behold, a leper came and worshiped Him, saying, "Lord, if You are willing, You can make me clean."

[3]Then Jesus put out *His* hand and touched him, saying, "I am willing; be cleansed." Immediately his leprosy was cleansed.

[4]And Jesus said to him, "See that you tell no one; but go your way, show yourself to the priest, and offer the gift that Moses commanded, as a testimony to them."

Mark 1:40–45
A Miracle of Healing

1 :40 Now a leper came to Him, imploring Him, kneeling down to Him and saying to Him, "If You are willing, You can make me clean."

[41]Then Jesus, moved with compassion, stretched out *His* hand and touched him, and said to him, "I am willing; be cleansed." [42]As soon as He had spoken, immediately the leprosy left him, and he was cleansed. [43]And He strictly warned him and sent him away at once, [44]and said to him, "See that you say nothing to anyone; but go your way, show yourself to the priest, and offer for your cleansing those things which Moses commanded, as a testimony to them."

[45]However, he went out and began to proclaim *it* freely, and to spread the matter, so that Jesus could no longer openly enter the city, but was outside in deserted places; and they came to Him from every direction.

Luke 5:12–16
Jesus Cleanses a Leper

5 :12 And it happened when He was in a certain city, that behold, a man who was full of leprosy saw Jesus; and he fell on *his* face and implored Him, saying, "Lord, if You are willing, You can make me clean."

[13]Then He put out *His* hand and touched him, saying, "I am willing; be cleansed." Immediately the leprosy left him. [14]And He charged him to tell no one, "But go and show yourself to the priest, and make an offering for your cleansing, as a testimony to them, just as Moses commanded."

[15]However, the report went around concerning Him all the more; and great multitudes came together to hear, and to be healed by Him of their infirmities. [16]So He Himself *often* withdrew into the wilderness and prayed.

CULTS AND SUPERNATURAL

By the time of Augustus (27 B.C.–A.D. 14), one of the most popular religious cults was the worship of Asclepius. Much like the multitudes sought out Jesus (Luke 5:15), people would go to temples hoping that Asclepius would heal their sicknesses. They stayed overnight at the temple, and the god was supposed to visit them in a dream in the night, bringing them healing.

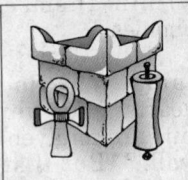

Events in Capernaum

Each of the Synoptic Gospels recounts a cluster of exchanges in Capernaum between Jesus and certain Jewish religious teachers. The encounters emphasize the importance of forgiveness in Jesus' ministry, a focus which is established in the opening report of the healing of a paralytic. Jesus used His ability to perform miraculous healings as proof "that the Son of Man has power on earth to forgive sins" (Mark 2:10).

Eating a meal in a tax collector's house was the occasion to show that God's forgiveness was now readily available to all. Jesus could now fellowship with "sinners" without being tainted by the ritual impurity that concerned the scribes and Pharisees (Luke 5:30). Although Jesus came to call sinners to repentance (Mark 2:17), His ministry was a time to celebrate this forgiveness rather than to fast or mourn (Matt. 9:14, 15).

Traditional religion believed that God alone forgave sins (Luke 5:21). So Jesus' new offer of forgiveness marked a radical change in God's dealings with humanity. Jesus did not reject all Jewish practice. The time would come when His own disciples would resume the spiritual discipline of fasting (Luke 5:35). But to try to force Jesus' ministry into the traditional religious patterns would have resulted in both His own failure and the unnecessary destruction of what God had done in the past. This point is illustrated by a parable of garments and wineskins (Luke 5:36–39).

■ Matthew 9:1–17
■ Mark 2:1–22
■ Luke 5:17–39

Matthew 9:1–17
Authority to Forgive Sins

9 :1 So He got into a boat, crossed over, and came to His own city. ²Then behold, they brought to Him a paralytic lying on a bed. When Jesus saw their faith, He said to the paralytic, "Son, be of good cheer; your sins are forgiven you."

³And at once some of the scribes said within themselves, "This Man blasphemes!"

⁴But Jesus, knowing their thoughts, said, "Why do you think evil in your hearts? ⁵For which is easier, to say, 'Your sins are forgiven you,' or to say, 'Arise and walk'? ⁶But that you may know that the Son of Man has power on earth to forgive

sins"—then He said to the paralytic, "Arise, take up your bed, and go to your house." ⁷And he arose and departed to his house.

⁸Now when the multitudes saw it, they marveledᵃ and glorified God, who had given such power to men.

Matthew the Tax Collector

⁹As Jesus passed on from there, He saw a man named Matthew sitting at the tax office. And He said to him, "Follow Me." So he arose and followed Him.

¹⁰Now it happened, as Jesus sat at the table in the house, that behold, many tax collectors and sinners came and sat down with Him and His disciples. ¹¹And when the Pharisees saw it, they said to His disciples, "Why does your Teacher eat with tax collectors and sinners?"

¹²When Jesus heard that, He said to them, "Those who are well have no need of a physician, but those who are sick. ¹³But go and learn what this means: 'I desire mercy and not sacrifice.'ᵃ For I did not come to call the righteous, but sinners, to repentance."ᵇ

9:8 ᵃNU-Text reads were afraid.   9:13 ᵃHosea 6:6   ᵇNU-Text omits to repentance.

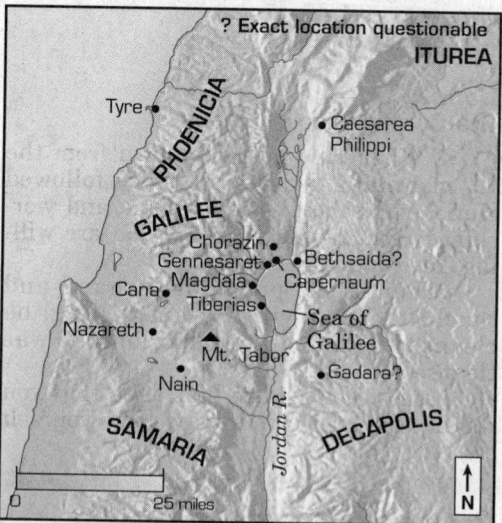

? Exact location questionable

ITUREA

Tyre
PHOENICIA
Caesarea Philippi

GALILEE
Chorazin
Gennesaret · Bethsaida?
Cana · Magdala
Capernaum
Tiberias
Nazareth · Sea of Galilee
Mt. Tabor
Gadara?
Nain
Jordan R.
SAMARIA
DECAPOLIS

0   25 miles   ↑ N

Jesus' Galilean Ministry

Jesus began His public ministry at Cana, turning water into wine. When His hometown of Nazareth rejected Him, He established a base of ministry in the prosperous fishing town of Capernaum (Mark 2:1). Healing miracles occurred at Nain, Gennesaret, and Bethsaida.

Jesus Is Questioned About Fasting

14Then the disciples of John came to Him, saying, "Why do we and the Pharisees fast often,[a] but Your disciples do not fast?"

15And Jesus said to them, "Can the friends of the bridegroom mourn as long as the bridegroom is with them? But the days will come when the bridegroom will be taken away from them, and then they will fast. 16No one puts a piece of unshrunk cloth on an old garment; for the patch pulls away from the garment, and the tear is made worse. 17Nor do they put new wine into old wineskins, or else the wineskins break, the wine is spilled, and the wineskins are ruined. But they put new wine into new wineskins, and both are preserved."

Mark 2:1–22
Your Sins Are Forgiven

2 :1 And again He entered Capernaum after *some* days, and it was heard that He was in the house. 2Immediately[a] many gathered together, so that there was no longer room to receive *them,* not even near the door. And He preached the word to them. 3Then they came to Him, bringing a paralytic who was carried by four *men.* 4And when they could not come near Him because of the crowd, they uncovered the roof where He was. So when they had broken through, they let down the bed on which the paralytic was lying.

5When Jesus saw their faith, He said to the paralytic, "Son, your sins are forgiven you."

6And some of the scribes were sitting there and reasoning in their hearts, 7"Why does this *Man* speak blasphemies like this? Who can forgive sins but God alone?"

8But immediately, when Jesus perceived in His spirit that they reasoned thus within themselves, He said to them, "Why do you reason about these things in your hearts? 9Which is easier, to say to the paralytic, '*Your* sins are forgiven you,' or to say, 'Arise, take up your bed and walk'? 10But that you may know that the Son of Man has power on earth to forgive sins"—He said to the paralytic, 11"I say to you, arise, take up your bed, and go to your house." 12Immediately he arose, took up the bed, and went out in the presence of them all, so that all were amazed and glorified God, saying, "We never saw *anything* like this!"

Levi's Call

13Then He went out again by the sea; and all the multitude came to Him, and He taught them. 14As He passed by, He saw Levi the *son* of Alphaeus sitting at the tax office. And He said to him, "Follow Me." So he arose and followed Him.

15Now it happened, as He was dining in *Levi's* house, that many tax collectors and sinners also sat together with Jesus and His disciples; for there were many, and they followed Him. 16And when the scribes and[a] Pharisees saw Him eating with the tax collectors and sinners, they said to His disciples, "How *is it* that He eats and drinks with tax collectors and sinners?"

17When Jesus heard *it,* He said to them, "Those who are well have no need of a physician, but those who are sick. I did not come to call *the* righteous, but sinners, to repentance."[a]

Fasting and the Bridegroom

18The disciples of John and of the Pharisees were fasting. Then they came and said to Him, "Why do the disciples of John and of the Pharisees fast, but Your disciples do not fast?"

19And Jesus said to them, "Can the friends of the bridegroom fast while the bridegroom is with them? As long as they have the bridegroom with them they cannot fast. 20But the days will come when the bridegroom will be taken away from them, and then they will fast in those days. 21No

---

9:14 [a]NU-Text brackets *often* as disputed.
Mark 2:2 [a]NU-Text omits *Immediately.*
2:16 [a]NU-Text reads *of the.*   2:17 [a]NU-Text omits *to repentance.*

one sews a piece of unshrunk cloth on an old garment; or else the new piece pulls away from the old, and the tear is made worse. ²²And no one puts new wine into old wineskins; or else the new wine bursts the wineskins, the wine is spilled, and the wineskins are ruined. But new wine must be put into new wineskins."

Luke 5:17–39
Jesus Forgives and Heals a Paralytic

5 **:17** Now it happened on a certain day, as He was teaching, that there were Pharisees and teachers of the law sitting by, who had come out of every town of Galilee, Judea, and Jerusalem. And the power of the Lord was *present* to heal them.ᵃ ¹⁸Then behold, men brought on a bed a man who was paralyzed, whom they sought to bring in and lay before Him. ¹⁹And when they could not find how they might bring him in, because of the crowd, they went up on the housetop and let him down with *his* bed through the tiling into the midst before Jesus.

²⁰When He saw their faith, He said to him, "Man, your sins are forgiven you."

²¹And the scribes and the Pharisees began to reason, saying, "Who is this who speaks blasphemies? Who can forgive sins but God alone?"

²²But when Jesus perceived their thoughts, He answered and said to them, "Why are you reasoning in your hearts? ²³Which is easier, to say, 'Your sins are forgiven you,' or to say, 'Rise up and walk'? ²⁴But that you may know that the Son of Man has power on earth to forgive sins"— He said to the man who was paralyzed, "I say to you, arise, take up your bed, and go to your house."

²⁵Immediately he rose up before them, took up what he had been lying on, and departed to his own house, glorifying God. ²⁶And they were all amazed, and they glorified God and were filled with fear, saying, "We have seen strange things today!"

Levi Follows Jesus

²⁷After these things He went out and saw a tax collector named Levi, sitting at the tax office. And He said to him, "Follow Me." ²⁸So he left all, rose up, and followed Him.

²⁹Then Levi gave Him a great feast in his own house. And there were a great number of tax collectors and others who sat down with them. ³⁰And their scribes and the Phariseesᵃ complained against His disciples, saying, "Why do You eat and drink with tax collectors and sinners?"

³¹Jesus answered and said to them, "Those who are well have no need of a physician, but those who are sick. ³²I have not come to call *the* righteous, but sinners, to repentance."

New Garments and Wine

³³Then they said to Him, "Why doᵃ the disciples of John fast often and make prayers, and likewise those of the Pharisees, but Yours eat and drink?"

³⁴And He said to them, "Can you make the friends of the bridegroom fast while the bridegroom is with them? ³⁵But the days will come when the bridegroom will be taken away from them; then they will fast in those days."

³⁶Then He spoke a parable to them: "No one puts a piece from a new garment on an old one;ᵃ otherwise the new makes a tear, and also the piece that was *taken* out of the new does not match the old. ³⁷And no one puts new wine into old wineskins; or else the new wine will burst the wineskins and be spilled, and the wineskins will be ruined. ³⁸But new wine must be put into new wineskins, and both are preserved.ᵃ ³⁹And no one, having drunk old *wine,* im-

---

5:17 ᵃNU-Text reads *present with Him to heal.*
5:30 ᵃNU-Text reads *But the Pharisees and their scribes.*   5:33 ᵃNU-Text omits *Why do,* making the verse a statement.   5:36 ᵃNU-Text reads *No one tears a piece from a new garment and puts it on an old one.*   5:38 ᵃNU-Text omits *and both are preserved.*

Food and Drink

Cups and jars were made of pottery and metal. Another more portable kind of vessel was made of leather, typically from a single goatskin. New wine put into such a bottle would ferment. A new bottle would be strong and could stretch without breaking under the pressure of the gases produced by fermentation, but an old one might burst (Luke 5:37, 38).

mediately^a desires new; for he says, 'The old is better.' "^b

Lord of the Sabbath

Two events—the disciples plucking grain and Jesus healing a man's hand on the Sabbath—have often been understood as expressing Jesus' authority over the Law of Moses. This concern is certainly expressed in the assertion: "the Son of Man is Lord even of the Sabbath" (Matt. 12:8). But the evangelists have a more primary concern. In both events Jesus emphasized that keeping the spirit and intent of the law was more important than strictly adhering to the letter of its ritual requirements.

This point is emphasized by Jesus' question to those in the synagogue: "Is it lawful on the Sabbath to do good or to do evil, to save a life or to kill?" (Mark 3:4). Both Matthew and Mark address this issue in the story about the grain. Mark recounts Jesus' interpretation that the law was given for humanity's benefit; humanity was not created for the sake of the law (Mark 2:27). Matthew reports Jesus' reference to Hos. 6:6, stressing God's desire for humans to put mercy, concern for people, before sacrifice as legalistic ritual observance (Matt. 12:7).

- Matthew 12:1–14
- Mark 2:23—3:6
- Luke 6:1–11

Matthew 12:1–14
Jesus Is Lord of the Sabbath

12 **:1** At that time Jesus went through the grainfields on the Sabbath. And His disciples were hungry, and began to pluck heads of grain and to eat. ²And when the Pharisees saw *it,* they said to Him, "Look, Your disciples are doing what is not lawful to do on the Sabbath!"

³But He said to them, "Have you not read what David did when he was hungry, he and those who were with him: ⁴how he entered the house of God and ate the showbread which was not lawful for him to eat, nor for those who were with him, but only for the priests? ⁵Or have you not read in the law that on the Sabbath the priests in the temple profane the Sabbath, and are blameless? ⁶Yet I say to you that in this

place there is *One* greater than the temple. ⁷But if you had known what *this* means, '*I desire mercy and not sacrifice,*'^a you would not have condemned the guiltless. ⁸For the Son of Man is Lord even^a of the Sabbath."

Healing on the Sabbath

⁹Now when He had departed from there, He went into their synagogue. ¹⁰And behold, there was a man who had a withered hand. And they asked Him, saying, "Is it lawful to heal on the Sabbath?"—that they might accuse Him.

¹¹Then He said to them, "What man is there among you who has one sheep, and if it falls into a pit on the Sabbath, will not lay hold of it and lift *it* out? ¹²Of how much more value then is a man than a sheep? Therefore it is lawful to do good on the Sabbath." ¹³Then He said to the man, "Stretch out your hand." And he stretched *it* out, and it was restored as whole as the other. ¹⁴Then the Pharisees went out and plotted against Him, how they might destroy Him.

Mark 2:23—3:6
Sabbath Keeping

2 **:23** Now it happened that He went through the grainfields on the Sabbath; and as they went His disciples began to pluck the heads of grain. ²⁴And the Pharisees said to Him, "Look, why do they do what is not lawful on the Sabbath?"

²⁵But He said to them, "Have you never read what David did when he was in need and hungry, he and those with him: ²⁶how he went into the house of God *in the days* of Abiathar the high priest, and ate the showbread, which is not lawful to eat

---

5:39 ^aNU-Text omits *immediately.*   ^bNU-Text reads *good.*   **Matt.** 12:7 ^aHosea 6:6
12:8 ^aNU-Text and M-Text omit *even.*

TIME CAPSULE   A.D. 6

6–15   *Annas is high priest in Jerusalem (Luke 3:2)*

6–9   *Coponius is prefect or governor of Judea*

6   *Augustus deposes Archelaus and exiles him to Gaul*

6   *Augustus makes Judea a Roman province*

6   *Quirinius conducts a tax census of Syria and Judea*

6–7   *Judas the Galilean leads resistance against Romans (Acts 5:37)*

except for the priests, and also gave some to those who were with him?"

27And He said to them, "The Sabbath was made for man, and not man for the Sabbath. 28Therefore the Son of Man is also Lord of the Sabbath."

3 1And He entered the synagogue again, and a man was there who had a withered hand. 2So they watched Him closely, whether He would heal him on the Sabbath, so that they might accuse Him. 3And He said to the man who had the withered hand, "Step forward." 4Then He said to them, "Is it lawful on the Sabbath to do good or to do evil, to save life or to kill?" But they kept silent. 5And when He had looked around at them with anger, being grieved by the hardness of their hearts, He said to the man, "Stretch out your hand." And he stretched it out, and his hand was restored as whole as the other.a 6Then the Pharisees went out and immediately plotted with the Herodians against Him, how they might destroy Him.

Luke 6:1–11
Sabbath Conflicts

6 :1 Now it happened on the second Sabbath after the firsta that He went through the grainfields. And His disciples plucked the heads of grain and ate *them,* rubbing *them* in *their* hands. 2And some of the Pharisees said to them, "Why are you doing what is not lawful to do on the Sabbath?"

3But Jesus answering them said, "Have you not even read this, what David did when he was hungry, he and those who were with him: 4how he went into the house of God, took and ate the showbread, and also gave some to those with him, which is not lawful for any but the priests to eat?" 5And He said to them, "The Son of Man is also Lord of the Sabbath."

6Now it happened on another Sabbath, also, that He entered the synagogue and taught. And a man was there whose right hand was withered. 7So the scribes and Pharisees watched Him closely, whether He would heal on the Sabbath, that they might find an accusation against Him. 8But He knew their thoughts, and said to the man who had the withered hand, "Arise and stand here." And he arose and stood. 9Then Jesus said to them, "I will ask you one thing: Is it lawful on the Sabbath to do good or to do evil, to save life or to destroy?"a 10And when He had looked around

at them all, He said to the man,a "Stretch out your hand." And he did so, and his hand was restored as whole as the other.b 11But they were filled with rage, and discussed with one another what they might do to Jesus.

Jesus' Followers

Mark presents the continuing growth of Jesus' ministry by contrasting two groups of His followers: a "great multitude" (Mark 3:7) and the "twelve" (3:14). These groups differ not only in their size, but also in their relationship to Jesus. The exuberance of the multitude remained a potential hazard to Jesus' ministry (3:9), so Jesus continued to silence the unclean spirits that exclaimed His identity (3:11, 12; see "Healing the Sick" at Matt. 8:14). In contrast to the hindering multitude, Jesus selected twelve men who would "be with Him" and extend His preaching and healing ministry (Mark 3:14, 15).

Luke likewise mentions both the multitude and the twelve, although in the opposite order. He may have placed the multitude last as a transition to his "Sermon on the Plain." The sermon is so-named because it was preached in a "level place" (Luke 6:17). The multitude, along with "a crowd of His disciples," thus became the extended audience for that sermon (6:17, 20).

Matthew mentions only the multitude in this account, having already listed the twelve apostles earlier (Matt. 10:2–4). In keeping with his interest in prophetic fulfillment, Matthew compares Jesus' efforts to limit the spread of His fame to the unassuming attitude of the Servant in the prophecies of Isaiah (Matt. 12:18–21; Is. 42:1–4). Jesus came in humility and gentleness as the prophesied Servant.

■ Matthew 12:15–21
■ Mark 3:7–19
■ Luke 6:12–19

Matthew 12:15–21
Behold, My Servant

12 :15 But when Jesus knew *it,* He withdrew from there. And great multitudesa followed Him, and He healed

3:5 aNU-Text omits *as whole as the other.*
Luke 6:1 aNU-Text reads *on a Sabbath.*
6:9 aM-Text reads *to kill.*   6:10 aNU-Text and M-Text read *to him.*   bNU-Text omits *as whole as the other.*   **Matt.12:15** aNU-Text brackets *multitudes* as disputed.

them all. ¹⁶Yet He warned them not to make Him known, ¹⁷that it might be fulfilled which was spoken by Isaiah the prophet, saying:

18   "Behold! My Servant whom I have
        chosen,
      My Beloved in whom My soul is well
        pleased!
      I will put My Spirit upon Him,
      And He will declare justice to the
        Gentiles.
19   He will not quarrel nor cry out,
      Nor will anyone hear His voice in the
        streets.
20   A bruised reed He will not break,
      And smoking flax He will not quench,
      Till He sends forth justice to victory;
21   And in His name Gentiles will trust."^a

Mark 3:7–19
A Great Multitude Follows Jesus

3 :7 But Jesus withdrew with His disciples to the sea. And a great multitude from Galilee followed Him, and from Judea ⁸and Jerusalem and Idumea and beyond the Jordan; and those from Tyre and Sidon, a great multitude, when they heard how many things He was doing, came to Him. ⁹So He told His disciples that a small boat should be kept ready for Him because of the multitude, lest they should crush Him. ¹⁰For He healed many, so that as many as had afflictions pressed about Him to touch Him. ¹¹And the unclean spirits, whenever they saw Him, fell down before Him and cried out, saying, "You are the Son of God." ¹²But He sternly warned them that they should not make Him known.

The Twelve Chosen

¹³And He went up on the mountain and called to *Him* those He Himself wanted. And they came to Him. ¹⁴Then He appointed twelve,^a that they might be with Him and that He might send them out to preach, ¹⁵and to have power to heal sicknesses and^a to cast out demons: ¹⁶Simon,^a to whom He gave the name Peter; ¹⁷James the *son* of Zebedee and John the brother of James, to whom He gave the name Boanerges, that is, "Sons of Thunder"; ¹⁸Andrew, Philip, Bartholomew, Matthew,

Thomas, James the *son* of Alphaeus, Thaddaeus, Simon the Cananite; ¹⁹and Judas Iscariot, who also betrayed Him. And they went into a house.

Luke 6:12–19
The Twelve Apostles

6 :12 Now it came to pass in those days that He went out to the mountain to pray, and continued all night in prayer to God. ¹³And when it was day, He called His disciples to *Himself;* and from them He chose twelve whom He also named apostles: ¹⁴Simon, whom He also named Peter, and Andrew his brother; James and John; Philip and Bartholomew; ¹⁵Matthew and Thomas; James the *son* of Alphaeus, and Simon called the Zealot; ¹⁶Judas *the son* of James, and Judas Iscariot who also became a traitor.

Jesus Heals a Great Multitude

¹⁷And He came down with them and stood on a level place with a crowd of His disciples and a great multitude of people from all Judea and Jerusalem, and from the seacoast of Tyre and Sidon, who came to hear Him and be healed of their diseases, ¹⁸as well as those who were tormented with unclean spirits. And they were healed. ¹⁹And the whole multitude sought to touch Him, for power went out from Him and healed *them* all.

Sermon on the Mount or Plain

The presentations of Jesus' teachings in Matthew's "Sermon on the Mount" (Matt. 5—7) and Luke's "Sermon on the Plain" (Luke 6:20–49) illustrate the so-called "Synoptic problem." There are tremendous similarities between their presentations, but also differences. The name "Synoptic" means that the Gospels view the life of Jesus from a common perspective. Yet the three Synoptic Gospels vary in what material they include and in how they arrange specific events, and such differences are apparent between Matthew's and Luke's sermons.

Some believe these differences resulted because Jesus repeated His teachings on various occasions and each evangelist provided only a summary of Jesus' teaching in each episode. Thus, Luke's "Sermon" is about a third the length of Matthew's. Others think these differences show that both Matthew and

ZEALOTS AGAINST THE ROMANS (Luke 6:15)

The Jewish historian Josephus (A.D. 37–100) provides the main source of information concerning a group known as the Zealots. The term "Zealots" refers to those who had a "zeal" for the Law (the Torah). Yet such zeal went beyond the Law. This mix of malcontents in Judea led the land against Rome during the Jewish War (A.D. 66–70). Their ranks appear to have included priests, bandit refugees, and others, and their goal was political independence from Rome.

Josephus reports about a number of Jerusalemites, under the leadership of the priest Eleazar, who in A.D. 66 stopped the sacrifices being made in the city on behalf of Caesar. This was considered by Rome a declaration of political independence, and it precipitated a civil war in the area. Eleazar's forces were joined by other revolutionaries and were successful in holding off a Roman legion in A.D. 68. It is to this coalition that Josephus first referred by the term "Zealots."

Eleazar ultimately used the temple as his fortress against the advances of the Roman general Vespasian. When Vespasian became emperor in A.D. 69, his son Titus assumed command of the war against the Jews. A great number of the Zealots were killed during Titus's siege of Jerusalem in A.D. 70. The term "Zealot" eventually came to refer not only to the coalition of forces under Eleazar, but to all revolutionary groups who struggled against the Romans in the 1st century A.D.

One of Jesus' disciples, Simon, was "called the Zealot" (Luke 6:15). Certainly, Simon was not involved with the Zealot movement during the Jewish Wars, which occurred almost 40 years after Jesus' death. Probably "the Zealot" was applied to Simon in a general way because he was a malcontent who wanted the end of Roman rule in Palestine.

Luke used an earlier collection of Jesus' teachings that did not reveal the original setting in which the teachings were given. Thus, Matthew gathers a number of sayings from this collection or source for his "Sermon on the Mount," whereas Luke independently uses the source in forming his "Sermon on the Plain" and later treatment of prayer (see "Unassuming Godliness" at Matt. 6:1). The source is usually called the "Q" source, apparently from the German word *Quelle*, meaning "source."

Matthew had a theological interest in presenting Jesus as a "new Moses" who calls into being the church as a "new Israel." Comparisons with Moses develop this theme. Matthew presents five major sermons by Jesus (Matt. 5—7; 10; 13:1–52; 18; 24; 25), possibly alluding to the traditional "Five Books of Moses." The first of Matthew's sermons is set "on a mountain" (Matt. 5:1) and discusses fulfilling the law (5:17–48), recalling Moses receiving the law on Mount Sinai.

■ Matthew 5:1–48
■ Luke 6:20–36

Matthew 5:1–48
The Beatitudes

5 :1 And seeing the multitudes, He went up on a mountain, and when He was seated His disciples came to Him. ²Then He opened His mouth and taught them, saying:

3 "Blessed *are* the poor in spirit,
   For theirs is the kingdom of heaven.
4 Blessed *are* those who mourn,
   For they shall be comforted.
5 Blessed *are* the meek,
   For they shall inherit the earth.
6 Blessed *are* those who hunger and
      thirst for righteousness,
   For they shall be filled.
7 Blessed *are* the merciful,
   For they shall obtain mercy.
8 Blessed *are* the pure in heart,
   For they shall see God.
9 Blessed *are* the peacemakers,
   For they shall be called sons of God.
10 Blessed *are* those who are persecuted
      for righteousness' sake,
   For theirs is the kingdom of heaven.

THE TINY HEBREW *YOD* (Matt. 5:18)

Jewish people learned the Bible from early childhood, and Gentile observers sometimes praised them as a "nation of philosophers" because of their devotion to learning. Jewish teachers emphasized the absolute importance of the law in many ways. One way was to point out the necessity of keeping even the least commandment of the law. Yet another way was to emphasize the details of the law.

Such details might concern which commandments were more or less important. For instance, the teachers often regarded the law about the bird's nest (Deut. 22:6, 7) as the least commandment, and honoring one's parents (Ex. 20:12; Deut. 5:16) as the greatest. Both commandments included the promises "it may be well with you" and "your days may be long" (which Jewish teachers sometimes interpreted as "have eternal life"). Thus God would give people the same reward for keeping the least commandment as for the greatest.

This equal reward was to Jewish teachers a graphic way of saying, "Do not neglect even the smallest commandment" (Matt. 5:19). While they acknowledged that everyone, including themselves, had sinned, they warned that a person could not pick and choose among commandments, deciding that one was small enough to be ignored. To purposely reject any commandment was tantamount to rejecting God's right to rule one's life.

Jewish stories also emphasized the importance of keeping the details of the law. When Sarai's name was changed to Sarah, the letter *yod* (the smallest Hebrew letter) was removed from her name. According to some Jewish teachers, the *yod* cried out from generation to generation, lamenting, "God, You have taken me from the Bible. When will You restore me to the Bible?" Finally, when Moses' servant received the name "Joshua," the *yod* was restored.

In another story Solomon tried to uproot a *yod* from the Bible, whereupon God promised that a thousand Solomons would come and go, but God would not let a single *yod* be taken from the Bible. "So you see," said the teachers, "not even the smallest letter can pass from God's Word." Jesus probably alluded to a popular story line: not a single "jot," meaning a *yod*, would pass from the Bible (Matt. 5:18). Thus disciples should pay attention to all that the Bible teaches.

11Blessed are you when they revile and persecute you, and say all kinds of evil against you falsely for My sake. 12Rejoice and be exceedingly glad, for great *is* your reward in heaven, for so they persecuted the prophets who were before you.

Believers Are Salt and Light

13"You are the salt of the earth; but if the salt loses its flavor, how shall it be seasoned? It is then good for nothing but to be thrown out and trampled underfoot by men.

14"You are the light of the world. A city that is set on a hill cannot be hidden. 15Nor do they light a lamp and put it under a basket, but on a lampstand, and it gives light to all *who are* in the house. 16Let your light so shine before men, that they may see your good works and glorify your Father in heaven.

Christ Fulfills the Law

17"Do not think that I came to destroy the Law or the Prophets. I did not come to destroy but to fulfill. 18For assuredly, I say to you, till heaven and earth pass away, one jot or one tittle will by no means pass from the law till all is fulfilled. 19Whoever therefore breaks one of the least of these

---

FOOD AND DRINK

The salt used in ancient times was not refined, and there was always some proportion of chemicals present in addition to sodium chloride. If the fraction useful for flavoring food was leached away by dampness, what remained was without value. It was sometimes strewn on paths like gravel, since it was "then good for nothing" (Matt. 5:13).

commandments, and teaches men so, shall be called least in the kingdom of heaven; but whoever does and teaches *them,* he shall be called great in the kingdom of heaven. ²⁰For I say to you, that unless your righteousness exceeds *the righteousness* of the scribes and Pharisees, you will by no means enter the kingdom of heaven.

Murder Begins in the Heart

²¹"You have heard that it was said to those of old, *'You shall not murder,*ᵃ and whoever murders will be in danger of the judgment.' ²²But I say to you that whoever is angry with his brother without a causeᵃ shall be in danger of the judgment. And whoever says to his brother, 'Raca!' shall be in danger of the council. But whoever says, 'You fool!' shall be in danger of hell fire. ²³Therefore if you bring your gift to the altar, and there remember that your brother has something against you, ²⁴leave your gift there before the altar, and go your way. First be reconciled to your brother, and then come and offer your gift. ²⁵Agree with your adversary quickly, while you are on the way with him, lest your adversary deliver you to the judge, the judge hand you over to the officer, and you be thrown into prison. ²⁶Assuredly, I say to you, you will by no means get out of there till you have paid the last penny.

Adultery in the Heart

²⁷"You have heard that it was said to those of old,ᵃ *'You shall not commit adultery.'*ᵇ ²⁸But I say to you that whoever looks at a woman to lust for her has already committed adultery with her in his heart. ²⁹If your right eye causes you to sin, pluck it out and cast *it* from you; for it is more profitable for you that one of your members perish, than for your whole body to be cast into hell. ³⁰And if your right hand causes you to sin, cut it off and cast *it* from you; for it is more profitable for you that one of your members perish, than for your whole body to be cast into hell.

Marriage Is Sacred and Binding

³¹"Furthermore it has been said, 'Whoever divorces his wife, let him give her a certificate of divorce.' ³²But I say to you that whoever divorces his wife for any reason except sexual immoralityᵃ causes her to commit adultery; and whoever marries a woman who is divorced commits adultery.

Jesus Forbids Oaths

³³"Again you have heard that it was said to those of old, 'You shall not swear falsely, but shall perform your oaths to the Lord.' ³⁴But I say to you, do not swear at all: neither by heaven, for it is God's throne; ³⁵nor by the earth, for it is His footstool; nor by Jerusalem, for it is the city of the great King. ³⁶Nor shall you swear by your head, because you cannot make one hair white or black. ³⁷But let your 'Yes' be 'Yes,' and your 'No,' 'No.' For whatever is more than these is from the evil one.

Go the Second Mile

³⁸"You have heard that it was said, *'An eye for an eye and a tooth for a tooth.'*ᵃ ³⁹But I tell you not to resist an evil person. But whoever slaps you on your right cheek, turn the other to him also. ⁴⁰If anyone wants to sue you and take away your tunic, let him have *your* cloak also. ⁴¹And whoever compels you to go one mile, go with him two. ⁴²Give to him who asks you, and from him who wants to borrow from you do not turn away.

Love Your Enemies

⁴³"You have heard that it was said, *'You shall love your neighbor*ᵃ and hate your enemy.' ⁴⁴But I say to you, love your enemies, bless those who curse you, do good to those who hate you, and pray for those who spitefully use you and persecute

---

5:21 ᵃExodus 20:13; Deuteronomy 5:17
5:22 ᵃNU-Text omits *without a cause.*
5:27 ᵃNU-Text and M-Text omit *to those of old.*
ᵇExodus 20:14; Deuteronomy 5:18   5:32 ᵃOr
fornication   5:38 ᵃExodus 21:24; Leviticus 24:20;
Deuteronomy 19:21   5:43 ᵃCompare Leviticus
19:18

you,a 45that you may be sons of your Father in heaven; for He makes His sun rise on the evil and on the good, and sends rain on the just and on the unjust. 46For if you love those who love you, what reward have you? Do not even the tax collectors do the same? 47And if you greet your brethrena only, what do you do more *than others?* Do not even the tax collectorsb do so? 48Therefore you shall be perfect, just as your Father in heaven is perfect."

Luke 6:20–36
The Beatitudes

6 **:20** Then He lifted up His eyes toward His disciples, and said:

"Blessed *are you* poor,
    For yours is the kingdom of God.
21 Blessed *are you* who hunger now,
    For you shall be filled.
  Blessed *are you* who weep now,
    For you shall laugh.
22 Blessed are you when men hate you,
    And when they exclude you,
    And revile *you,* and cast out your
      name as evil,
    For the Son of Man's sake.
23 Rejoice in that day and leap for joy!
    For indeed your reward *is* great in
      heaven.
    For in like manner their fathers did
      to the prophets.

Jesus Pronounces Woes

24 "But woe to you who are rich,
    For you have received your
      consolation.
25 Woe to you who are full,
    For you shall hunger.
  Woe to you who laugh now,
    For you shall mourn and weep.
26 Woe to youa when allb men speak well
      of you,
    For so did their fathers to the false
      prophets.

Love Your Enemies

27"But I say to you who hear: Love your enemies, do good to those who hate

you, 28bless those who curse you, and pray for those who spitefully use you. 29To him who strikes you on the *one* cheek, offer the other also. And from him who takes away your cloak, do not withhold *your* tunic either. 30Give to everyone who asks of you. And from him who takes away your goods do not ask *them* back. 31And just as you want men to do to you, you also do to them likewise.

32"But if you love those who love you, what credit is that to you? For even sinners love those who love them. 33And if you do good to those who do good to you, what credit is that to you? For even sinners do the same. 34And if you lend *to those* from whom you hope to receive back, what credit is that to you? For even sinners lend to sinners to receive as much back. 35But love your enemies, do good, and lend, hoping for nothing in return; and your reward will be great, and you will be sons of the Most High. For He is kind to the unthankful and evil. 36Therefore be merciful, just as your Father also is merciful."

Unassuming Godliness

Common religious practices included giving (Matt. 6:2–4), praying (6:5–15), and fasting (6:16–18). The Jewish religious leaders considered keeping the law and these three practices as the most important proofs of piety. Jesus did not condemn these pious deeds or rebuke the expectation of reward, but He did warn that these practices should not be done to receive human recognition.

Jesus offered the Lord's Prayer as a pattern for His disciples. Luke associates the teachings about prayer (Luke 11:1–13) with Jesus' journey to Jerusalem (Luke 9—18), and does not include them with the Sermon on the Plain (Luke 6). See "Jesus' Final Journey" at Matt. 8:18.

Both Matthew and Luke contrasted trusting in material wealth for security with seeking the kingdom of God (Matt. 6:19–34; Luke 12:22–34). True treasures are to be found "in heaven," not "on earth" (Matt. 6:19, 20). Again Luke associates these teachings not with the Sermon, but with the journey to Jerusalem (Luke 12).

■ Matthew 6:1–34
■ Luke 11:1–4
■ Luke 12:22–34

5:44 aNU-Text omits three clauses from this verse, leaving, *"But I say to you, love your enemies and pray for those who persecute you."* 5:47 aM-Text reads *friends.* bNU-Text reads *Gentiles.*
Luke 6:26 aNU-Text and M-Text omit *to you.* bM-Text omits *all.*

PRAYING TO OUR FATHER (Matt. 6:7, 9)

Jesus cautioned His disciples not to pray "as the heathen do," using "vain repetitions" and "many words" (Matt. 6:7). When Greeks and Romans prayed, they often called deities by as many different names and titles as possible. Also, their prayers frequently reminded the deity of any favors he or she owed the worshiper because of sacrifices the worshiper had offered.

Jewish people, however, were not supposed to barter with God or try to impress Him with titles. They were to approach God with confidence that He was their Father, as the Old Testament taught them (see Ex. 4:22; Is. 63:16). Most children in the ancient world saw their father as a strong provider and protector (with whom they did not need to bargain). Jewish prayers therefore regularly invoked God as "Our Father in heaven," and trusted Him to provide (Matt. 6:8, 9; 7:7–11).

Teaching His disciples to pray (Matt. 6:9, 10), Jesus adapted a fairly common Jewish prayer called the *Kaddish* that came to be prayed regularly in the synagogues: "Exalted and hallowed be His great name . . . and may He cause His kingdom to rule . . ." This was a prayer for the future kingdom. The Jewish people longed for the ultimate coming of God's reign when He would rule the earth unchallenged and restore justice and mercy in all the world. At that time God's name would be "hallowed," shown to be holy (Ezek. 39:7, 27); people would no longer "profane" it by swearing oaths by it lightly or living in such a way as to dishonor it.

"Hallowing God's name" was a central principle of Jewish ethics: Live even among the Gentiles in such a manner that people will honor God. The reverse of such honorable behavior, "profaning God's name," was considered so odious that some teachers insisted those plotting to do evil should disguise themselves as Gentiles first! Those who would utter this prayer in sincerity—who yearn for God's name to be shown holy in the age to come—must live in the present in such a way as to honor that name now.

Matthew 6:1–34
Do Good to Please God

6 :1 "Take heed that you do not do your charitable deeds before men, to be seen by them. Otherwise you have no reward from your Father in heaven. ²Therefore, when you do a charitable deed, do not sound a trumpet before you as the hypocrites do in the synagogues and in the streets, that they may have glory from men. Assuredly, I say to you, they have their reward. ³But when you do a charitable deed, do not let your left hand know what your right hand is doing, ⁴that your charitable deed may be in secret; and your Father who sees in secret will Himself reward you openly.ᵃ

The Model Prayer

⁵"And when you pray, you shall not be like the hypocrites. For they love to pray standing in the synagogues and on the corners of the streets, that they may be seen by men. Assuredly, I say to you, they have their reward. ⁶But you, when you pray, go into your room, and when you have shut your door, pray to your Father who *is* in the secret *place;* and your Father who sees in secret will reward you openly.ᵃ ⁷And when you pray, do not use vain repetitions as the heathen *do.* For they think that they will be heard for their many words.

⁸"Therefore do not be like them. For your Father knows the things you have need of before you ask Him. ⁹In this manner, therefore, pray:

Our Father in heaven,
Hallowed be Your name.
10   Your kingdom come.
Your will be done
On earth as *it is* in heaven.
11   Give us this day our daily bread.
12   And forgive us our debts,
As we forgive our debtors.
13   And do not lead us into temptation,
But deliver us from the evil one.

6:4 ᵃNU-Text omits *openly.*   6:6 ᵃNU-Text omits *openly.*

For Yours is the kingdom and the
    power and the glory forever. Amen.[a]

[14]"For if you forgive men their trespasses, your heavenly Father will also forgive you. [15]But if you do not forgive men
their trespasses, neither will your Father
forgive your trespasses.

Fasting to Be Seen Only by God

[16]"Moreover, when you fast, do not be
like the hypocrites, with a sad countenance. For they disfigure their faces that
they may appear to men to be fasting. Assuredly, I say to you, they have their reward. [17]But you, when you fast, anoint
your head and wash your face, [18]so that
you do not appear to men to be fasting, but
to your Father who *is* in the secret *place;*
and your Father who sees in secret will reward you openly.[a]

Lay Up Treasures in Heaven

[19]"Do not lay up for yourselves treasures on earth, where moth and rust destroy and where thieves break in and steal;
[20]but lay up for yourselves treasures in
heaven, where neither moth nor rust destroys and where thieves do not break in
and steal. [21]For where your treasure is,
there your heart will be also.

The Lamp of the Body

[22]"The lamp of the body is the eye. If
therefore your eye is good, your whole body
will be full of light. [23]But if your eye is bad,
your whole body will be full of darkness. If
therefore the light that is in you is darkness, how great *is* that darkness!

You Cannot Serve God and Riches

[24]"No one can serve two masters; for either he will hate the one and love the
other, or else he will be loyal to the one and
despise the other. You cannot serve God
and mammon.

Do Not Worry

[25]"Therefore I say to you, do not worry
about your life, what you will eat or what
you will drink; nor about your body, what

you will put on. Is not life more than food
and the body more than clothing? [26]Look at
the birds of the air, for they neither sow
nor reap nor gather into barns; yet your
heavenly Father feeds them. Are you not of
more value than they? [27]Which of you by
worrying can add one cubit to his stature?
[28]"So why do you worry about clothing?
Consider the lilies of the field, how they
grow: they neither toil nor spin; [29]and yet I
say to you that even Solomon in all his
glory was not arrayed like one of these.
[30]Now if God so clothes the grass of the
field, which today is, and tomorrow is
thrown into the oven, *will He* not much
more *clothe* you, O you of little faith?
[31]"Therefore do not worry, saying,
'What shall we eat?' or 'What shall we
drink?' or 'What shall we wear?' [32]For after
all these things the Gentiles seek. For your
heavenly Father knows that you need all
these things. [33]But seek first the kingdom
of God and His righteousness, and all these
things shall be added to you. [34]Therefore
do not worry about tomorrow, for tomorrow
will worry about its own things. Sufficient
for the day *is* its own trouble."

Luke 11:1–4
The Model Prayer

11 :1 Now it came to pass, as He was
praying in a certain place, when He
ceased, *that* one of His disciples said to
Him, "Lord, teach us to pray, as John also
taught his disciples."

[2]So He said to them, "When you pray,
say:

Our Father in heaven,[a]
Hallowed be Your name.
Your kingdom come.[b]
Your will be done
On earth as *it is* in heaven.
3   Give us day by day our daily bread.
4   And forgive us our sins,
For we also forgive everyone who is
    indebted to us.
And do not lead us into temptation,
But deliver us from the evil one."[a]

Luke 12:22–34
True Security

12 :22 Then He said to His disciples,
"Therefore I say to you, do not worry
about your life, what you will eat; nor
about the body, what you will put on. [23]Life
is more than food, and the body *is more*
than clothing. [24]Consider the ravens, for

6:13 [a]NU-Text omits *For Yours* through *Amen.*
6:18 [a]NU-Text and M-Text omit *openly.*
Luke 11:2 [a]NU-Text omits *Our* and *in heaven.*
[b]NU-Text omits the rest of this verse.
11:4 [a]NU-Text omits *But deliver us from the evil
one.*

they neither sow nor reap, which have neither storehouse nor barn; and God feeds them. Of how much more value are you than the birds? 25And which of you by worrying can add one cubit to his stature? 26If you then are not able to do *the* least, why are you anxious for the rest? 27Consider the lilies, how they grow: they neither toil nor spin; and yet I say to you, even Solomon in all his glory was not arrayed like one of these. 28If then God so clothes the grass, which today is in the field and tomorrow is thrown into the oven, how much more *will He clothe* you, O *you* of little faith?

29"And do not seek what you should eat or what you should drink, nor have an anxious mind. 30For all these things the nations of the world seek after, and your Father knows that you need these things. 31But seek the kingdom of God, and all these thingsa shall be added to you.

32"Do not fear, little flock, for it is your Father's good pleasure to give you the kingdom. 33Sell what you have and give alms; provide yourselves money bags which do not grow old, a treasure in the heavens that does not fail, where no thief approaches nor moth destroys. 34For where your treasure is, there your heart will be also."

Doing the Will of God

Both Matthew and Luke end their sermons with Jesus' emphasis on doing God's will. At the end of Matthew's Sermon on the Mount, Jesus challenged His listeners to enter the "narrow gate" (Matt. 7:13, 14). Both evangelists close with an illustration emphasizing the supreme importance of obedience. The obedient person is likened to one who builds his house on a rock that stands the storms (Matt. 7:24–27; Luke 6:46–49).

- Matthew 7:1–29
- Luke 6:37–49
- Luke 11:5–13

Matthew 7:1–29
Do Not Judge

7 :1 "Judge not, that you be not judged. 2For with what judgment you judge, you will be judged; and with the measure you use, it will be measured back to you. 3And why do you look at the speck in your brother's eye, but do not consider the plank in your own eye? 4Or how can you say to

your brother, 'Let me remove the speck from your eye'; and look, a plank *is* in your own eye? 5Hypocrite! First remove the plank from your own eye, and then you will see clearly to remove the speck from your brother's eye.

6"Do not give what is holy to the dogs; nor cast your pearls before swine, lest they trample them under their feet, and turn and tear you in pieces.

Keep Asking, Seeking, Knocking

7"Ask, and it will be given to you; seek, and you will find; knock, and it will be opened to you. 8For everyone who asks receives, and he who seeks finds, and to him who knocks it will be opened. 9Or what man is there among you who, if his son asks for bread, will give him a stone? 10Or if he asks for a fish, will he give him a serpent? 11If you then, being evil, know how to give good gifts to your children, how much more will your Father who is in heaven give good things to those who ask Him! 12Therefore, whatever you want men to do to you, do also to them, for this is the Law and the Prophets.

The Narrow Way

13"Enter by the narrow gate; for wide *is* the gate and broad *is* the way that leads to destruction, and there are many who go in by it. 14Becausea narrow *is* the gate and difficult *is* the way which leads to life, and there are few who find it.

You Will Know Them by Their Fruits

15"Beware of false prophets, who come to you in sheep's clothing, but inwardly they are ravenous wolves. 16You will know them by their fruits. Do men gather grapes from thornbushes or figs from thistles? 17Even so, every good tree bears good fruit, but a bad tree bears bad fruit. 18A good tree cannot bear bad fruit, nor *can* a bad tree bear good fruit. 19Every tree that does not bear good fruit is cut down and thrown into the fire. 20Therefore by their fruits you will know them.

I Never Knew You

21"Not everyone who says to Me, 'Lord, Lord,' shall enter the kingdom of heaven, but he who does the will of My Father in

---

12:31 aNU-Text reads *His kingdom, and these things.*   **Matt.** 7:14 aNU-Text and M-Text read *How . . . !*

heaven. [22]Many will say to Me in that day, 'Lord, Lord, have we not prophesied in Your name, cast out demons in Your name, and done many wonders in Your name?' [23]And then I will declare to them, 'I never knew you; depart from Me, you who practice lawlessness!'

Build on the Rock

[24]"Therefore whoever hears these sayings of Mine, and does them, I will liken him to a wise man who built his house on the rock: [25]and the rain descended, the floods came, and the winds blew and beat on that house; and it did not fall, for it was founded on the rock.

[26]"But everyone who hears these sayings of Mine, and does not do them, will be like a foolish man who built his house on the sand: [27]and the rain descended, the floods came, and the winds blew and beat on that house; and it fell. And great was its fall."

[28]And so it was, when Jesus had ended these sayings, that the people were astonished at His teaching, [29]for He taught them as one having authority, and not as the scribes.

Luke 6:37–49
Do Not Judge

6 :37 "Judge not, and you shall not be judged. Condemn not, and you shall not be condemned. Forgive, and you will be forgiven. [38]Give, and it will be given to you: good measure, pressed down, shaken together, and running over will be put into your bosom. For with the same measure that you use, it will be measured back to you."

[39]And He spoke a parable to them: "Can the blind lead the blind? Will they not both fall into the ditch? [40]A disciple is not above his teacher, but everyone who is perfectly trained will be like his teacher. [41]And

6:45 [a]NU-Text omits *treasure of his heart.*
6:48 [a]NU-Text reads *for it was well built.*
6:49 [a]NU-Text reads *collapsed.*

why do you look at the speck in your brother's eye, but do not perceive the plank in your own eye? [42]Or how can you say to your brother, 'Brother, let me remove the speck that *is* in your eye,' when you yourself do not see the plank that *is* in your own eye? Hypocrite! First remove the plank from your own eye, and then you will see clearly to remove the speck that is in your brother's eye.

A Tree Is Known by Its Fruit

[43]"For a good tree does not bear bad fruit, nor does a bad tree bear good fruit. [44]For every tree is known by its own fruit. For *men* do not gather figs from thorns, nor do they gather grapes from a bramble bush. [45]A good man out of the good treasure of his heart brings forth good; and an evil man out of the evil treasure of his heart[a] brings forth evil. For out of the abundance of the heart his mouth speaks.

Build on the Rock

[46]"But why do you call Me 'Lord, Lord,' and not do the things which I say? [47]Whoever comes to Me, and hears My sayings and does them, I will show you whom he is like: [48]He is like a man building a house, who dug deep and laid the foundation on the rock. And when the flood arose, the stream beat vehemently against that house, and could not shake it, for it was founded on the rock.[a] [49]But he who heard and did nothing is like a man who built a house on the earth without a foundation, against which the stream beat vehemently; and immediately it fell.[a] And the ruin of that house was great."

Luke 11:5–13
A Friend Comes at Midnight

11 :5 And He said to them, "Which of you shall have a friend, and go to him at midnight and say to him, 'Friend, lend me three loaves; [6]for a friend of mine has come to me on his journey, and I have

---

CULTURE AND SOCIETY

In traditional societies the protocols of hospitality are formal at every level of society, not just in the courts of state or diplomacy. A householder has the duty to receive guests and help them on their way (Luke 11:8). He also has the responsibility of protecting the society from interlopers or people who are not what they seem.

nothing to set before him'; 7and he will answer from within and say, 'Do not trouble me; the door is now shut, and my children are with me in bed; I cannot rise and give to you'? 8I say to you, though he will not rise and give to him because he is his friend, yet because of his persistence he will rise and give him as many as he needs.

Keep Asking, Seeking, Knocking

9"So I say to you, ask, and it will be given to you; seek, and you will find; knock, and it will be opened to you. 10For everyone who asks receives, and he who seeks finds, and to him who knocks it will be opened. 11If a son asks for bread[a] from any father among you, will he give him a stone? Or if *he asks* for a fish, will he give him a serpent instead of a fish? 12Or if he asks for an egg, will he offer him a scorpion? 13If you then, being evil, know how to give good gifts to your children, how much more will *your* heavenly Father give the Holy Spirit to those who ask Him!"

In Capernaum and Nain

Since the 2nd century A.D. Christian theologians have discussed the relationship of John's "second sign" (John 4:54; see "The First of Seven Signs" at John 2:1) to the healing stories in Matt. 8:5–13 and Luke 7:1–10. The similarities in the stories have suggested to some that the same healing is described in all three accounts. In addition, the Greek word which Matthew uses for "servant" (Matt. 8:6) can designate either a "servant" (Luke 7:7) or a "son" (John 4:46 uses the usual Greek word for "son"). All agree that at least Matthew and Luke are recounting a single incident.

Matthew contrasts the faith of the Gentile centurion with that of many of Jesus' fellow Jews (Matt. 8:10–12). Possibly Jesus and the centurion speak directly with each other in Matthew's account to highlight this contrast. Luke's account indicates that the centurion sent Jewish intermediaries (Luke 7:3–5). Luke also describes the boy as "ready to die" (7:2), and follows his healing with the report of Jesus raising the dead son of a widow residing in Nain (7:11–17). Thus Luke prepares for Jesus' response to John the Baptist: "the dead are raised" (7:22).

■ Matthew 8:5–13
■ Luke 7:1–17
■ John 4:46–54

Matthew 8:5–13
Jesus Heals a Centurion's Servant

8 :5 Now when Jesus had entered Capernaum, a centurion came to Him, pleading with Him, 6saying, "Lord, my servant is lying at home paralyzed, dreadfully tormented."

7And Jesus said to him, "I will come and heal him."

8The centurion answered and said, "Lord, I am not worthy that You should come under my roof. But only speak a word, and my servant will be healed. 9For I also am a man under authority, having soldiers under me. And I say to this *one*, 'Go,' and he goes; and to another, 'Come,' and he comes; and to my servant, 'Do this,' and he does *it*."

10When Jesus heard *it*, He marveled, and said to those who followed, "Assuredly, I say to you, I have not found such great faith, not even in Israel! 11And I say to you that many will come from east and west, and sit down with Abraham, Isaac, and Jacob in the kingdom of heaven. 12But the sons of the kingdom will be cast out into outer darkness. There will be weeping and gnashing of teeth." 13Then Jesus said to the centurion, "Go your way; and as you have believed, *so* let it be done for you." And his servant was healed that same hour.

Luke 7:1–17
Such Great Faith

7 :1 Now when He concluded all His sayings in the hearing of the people, He entered Capernaum. 2And a certain centurion's servant, who was dear to him, was

---

11:11 [a]NU-Text omits the words from *bread* through *for* in the next sentence.

TIME CAPSULE A.D. 13 to 15

13	Tiberius begins coregency with Augustus
14–31	Sejanus, prefect of Rome, increases size of Praetorian guard
14	Augustus dies and Tiberius becomes emperor (Luke 3:1)
14	The Senate makes Augustus one of the gods of Rome
15–26	Valerius Gratus is prefect or governor of Judea

sick and ready to die. ³So when he heard about Jesus, he sent elders of the Jews to Him, pleading with Him to come and heal his servant. ⁴And when they came to Jesus, they begged Him earnestly, saying that the one for whom He should do this was deserving, ⁵"for he loves our nation, and has built us a synagogue."

⁶Then Jesus went with them. And when He was already not far from the house, the centurion sent friends to Him, saying to Him, "Lord, do not trouble Yourself, for I am not worthy that You should enter under my roof. ⁷Therefore I did not even think myself worthy to come to You. But say the word, and my servant will be healed. ⁸For I also am a man placed under authority, having soldiers under me. And I say to one, 'Go,' and he goes; and to another, 'Come,' and he comes; and to my servant, 'Do this,' and he does it."

⁹When Jesus heard these things, He marveled at him, and turned around and said to the crowd that followed Him, "I say to you, I have not found such great faith, not even in Israel!" ¹⁰And those who were sent, returning to the house, found the servant well who had been sick.ᵃ

Jesus Raises the Son of the Widow of Nain

¹¹Now it happened, the day after, that He went into a city called Nain; and many of His disciples went with Him, and a large crowd. ¹²And when He came near the gate of the city, behold, a dead man was being carried out, the only son of his mother; and she was a widow. And a large crowd from the city was with her. ¹³When the Lord saw her, He had compassion on her and said to her, "Do not weep." ¹⁴Then He came and touched the open coffin, and those who carried him stood still. And He said, "Young man, I say to you, arise." ¹⁵So he who was dead sat up and began to speak. And He presented him to his mother.

¹⁶Then fear came upon all, and they glorified God, saying, "A great prophet has risen up among us"; and, "God has visited His people." ¹⁷And this report about Him went throughout all Judea and all the surrounding region.

John 4:46–54
A Nobleman's Son Healed

4 :46 So Jesus came again to Cana of Galilee where He had made the water wine. And there was a certain nobleman whose son was sick at Capernaum. ⁴⁷When he heard that Jesus had come out of Judea into Galilee, he went to Him and implored Him to come down and heal his son, for he was at the point of death. ⁴⁸Then Jesus said to him, "Unless you people see signs and wonders, you will by no means believe."

⁴⁹The nobleman said to Him, "Sir, come down before my child dies!"

⁵⁰Jesus said to him, "Go your way; your son lives." So the man believed the word that Jesus spoke to him, and he went his way. ⁵¹And as he was now going down, his servants met him and told him, saying, "Your son lives!"

⁵²Then he inquired of them the hour when he got better. And they said to him, "Yesterday at the seventh hour the fever left him." ⁵³So the father knew that it was at the same hour in which Jesus said to him, "Your son lives." And he himself believed, and his whole household.

⁵⁴This again is the second sign Jesus did when He had come out of Judea into Galilee.

Jesus Allays John's Doubts

Matthew's and Luke's accounts of the delegation from John the Baptist to Jesus agree almost word for word. Only brief sections in the middle of this story differ (see Matt. 11:12–14 and Luke 7:29, 30).

Three basic issues were at stake as John the Baptist sent his followers to ask Jesus if He was truly the "Coming One," the promised

---

7:10　ᵃNU-Text omits who had been sick.

POLITICS AND GOVERNMENT

A centurion was a soldier in the Roman legions who had command of a unit of approximately 80 men (thus not 100 men, as one might conclude from the name "centurion"). Centurions were generally practical career men. It was a responsible position (Luke 7:6–8), and centurions sometimes accumulated a certain amount of wealth during their careers.

Messiah (Matt. 11:2, 3; Luke 7:19). First, was the Baptist to maintain his belief that Jesus was indeed the Coming One? It may have been that the Baptist was expecting more emphasis upon judgment in Jesus' ministry (see Matt. 3:7–12). Jesus responded by directing John's attention to other signs of His Galilean ministry fulfilling prophetic expectation (Matt. 11:4–6).

The second issue concerned Jesus' identification of the Baptist as the prophet who would prepare for the coming Messiah (Luke 7:24–28). The Jewish expectation for the future was for Elijah to return, as promised in the Old Testament (Mal. 4:5). In Matthew's account Jesus identified the Baptist as fulfilling the promise (Matt. 11:14).

Finally, Jesus criticized those in "this generation" who rejected both His own ministry and that of the Baptist (Matt. 11:16–19). Luke's account points out that the Pharisees and lawyers, by rejecting the Baptist, had rejected the very will and purpose of God (Luke 7:29, 30).

■ Matthew 11:2–19
■ Luke 7:18–35

Matthew 11:2–19
Jesus Explains John's Ministry

11 :2 And when John had heard in prison about the works of Christ, he sent two of[a] his disciples ³and said to Him, "Are You the Coming One, or do we look for another?"

⁴Jesus answered and said to them, "Go and tell John the things which you hear and see: ⁵*The* blind see and *the* lame walk; *the* lepers are cleansed and *the* deaf hear; *the* dead are raised up and *the* poor have the gospel preached to them. ⁶And blessed is he who is not offended because of Me."

⁷As they departed, Jesus began to say to the multitudes concerning John: "What did you go out into the wilderness to see? A reed shaken by the wind? ⁸But what did you go out to see? A man clothed in soft garments? Indeed, those who wear soft *clothing* are in kings' houses. ⁹But what did you go out to see? A prophet? Yes, I say to you, and more than a prophet. ¹⁰For this is *he* of whom it is written:

'Behold, I send My messenger before
    Your face,
Who will prepare Your way before
    You.'[a]

¹¹"Assuredly, I say to you, among those born of women there has not risen one greater than John the Baptist; but he who is least in the kingdom of heaven is greater than he. ¹²And from the days of John the Baptist until now the kingdom of heaven suffers violence, and the violent take it by force. ¹³For all the prophets and the law prophesied until John. ¹⁴And if you are willing to receive *it,* he is Elijah who is to come. ¹⁵He who has ears to hear, let him hear!

¹⁶"But to what shall I liken this generation? It is like children sitting in the marketplaces and calling to their companions, ¹⁷and saying:

'We played the flute for you,
    And you did not dance;
We mourned to you,
    And you did not lament.'

¹⁸For John came neither eating nor drinking, and they say, 'He has a demon.' ¹⁹The Son of Man came eating and drinking, and they say, 'Look, a glutton and a winebibber, a friend of tax collectors and sinners!' But wisdom is justified by her children."[a]

Luke 7:18–35
John the Baptist Sends Messengers to Jesus

7 :18 Then the disciples of John reported to him concerning all these things. ¹⁹And John, calling two of his disciples to *him,* sent *them* to Jesus,[a] saying, "Are You the Coming One, or do we look for another?"

²⁰When the men had come to Him, they said, "John the Baptist has sent us to You, saying, 'Are You the Coming One, or do we look for another?' " ²¹And that very hour He cured many of infirmities, afflictions, and evil spirits; and to many blind He gave sight.

²²Jesus answered and said to them, "Go and tell John the things you have seen and heard: that *the* blind see, *the* lame walk, *the* lepers are cleansed, *the* deaf hear, *the* dead are raised, *the* poor have the gospel preached to them. ²³And blessed is *he* who is not offended because of Me."

²⁴When the messengers of John had departed, He began to speak to the multi-

---

11:2 ᵃNU-Text reads *by* for *two of.*
11:10 ᵃMalachi 3:1   11:19 ᵃNU-Text reads *works.*   **Luke** 7:19 ᵃNU-Text reads *the Lord.*

MATTHEW AND OLD TESTAMENT FULFILLMENT (Matt. 11:10)

Matthew quotes the words of Malachi, which in the Old Testament read "Behold, I send My messenger, And he will prepare the way before Me" (Mal. 3:1). The Old Testament words seemed to speak of an agent Yahweh would send to prepare for a coming day of judgment. This messenger was identified as the prophet Elijah (Mal. 4:5), who became a major figure in Jewish hope for the future age. Matthew, though, reinterpreted Mal. 3:1 to refer to John the Baptist: "this is he of whom it is written" (Matt. 11:9–11).

By preparing the way for Jesus, John the Baptist fulfilled the role prophesied of Elijah. In his Gospel, Matthew emphasizes the fulfillment of Old Testament prophecy, so he makes it clear to his readers that Jesus identified John as Elijah (Matt. 17:11–13) and that John was the one spoken of by the prophets (Matt. 3:3).

Matthew also announced fulfillment of Hosea's prophecy, "Out of Egypt I called My Son" (Matt. 2:15). The first line of this verse in the Old Testament (Hos. 11:1) shows that the prophet was actually referring to God calling Israel out of Egypt in the Exodus. But Matthew reinterpreted the words as a picture of God's providing salvation by bringing the child Jesus back from Egypt.

Some critics have accused Matthew of quoting the Old Testament out of context. They fail, however, to recognize Matthew's method of applying the Old Testament. The problem is not that Matthew does not know the Hosea passage, but that he applies it in a different way than most modern readers would expect.

When Matthew cites from the prophet Hosea, he is making a broader point about Jesus' place in Israel's history. Jesus was the heir of Israel's history (Matt. 1:1–17), who went into exile in Egypt as Judah did in Babylon, and who spent 40 days being tested in the wilderness (4:1, 2) as Israel spent 40 years in the wilderness. Ancient Jewish readers, conversant in the Bible and more accustomed to various methods of applying Scripture, would have caught Matthew's point more readily than do modern readers.

---

tudes concerning John: "What did you go out into the wilderness to see? A reed shaken by the wind? 25But what did you go out to see? A man clothed in soft garments? Indeed those who are gorgeously appareled and live in luxury are in kings' courts. 26But what did you go out to see? A prophet? Yes, I say to you, and more than a prophet. 27This is *he* of whom it is written:

'Behold, I send My messenger before
    Your face,
Who will prepare Your way before
    You.'a

28For I say to you, among those born of women there is not a greater prophet than John the Baptist;a but he who is least in the kingdom of God is greater than he."

29And when all the people heard *Him,* even the tax collectors justified God, having been baptized with the baptism of John. 30But the Pharisees and lawyers rejected the will of God for themselves, not having been baptized by him.

31And the Lord said,a "To what then shall I liken the men of this generation, and what are they like? 32They are like children sitting in the marketplace and calling to one another, saying:

'We played the flute for you,
    And you did not dance;
We mourned to you,
    And you did not weep.'

33For John the Baptist came neither eating bread nor drinking wine, and you say, 'He has a demon.' 34The Son of Man has come eating and drinking, and you say, 'Look, a glutton and a winebibber, a friend of tax collectors and sinners!' 35But wisdom is justified by all her children."

7:27 aMalachi 3:1   7:28 aNU-Text reads *there is none greater than John.*   7:31 aNU-Text and M-Text omit *And the Lord said.*

Anointing in Galilee

Luke's report of a woman anointing Jesus focuses on the question of Jesus' identity. Since the woman who anointed Jesus "was a sinner" (Luke 7:37), Simon the Pharisee began to question within himself whether Jesus was genuinely a prophet (7:39). By His response, Jesus validated His prophetic credentials. Not only was He aware of her sinful past (7:47), but He also knew Simon's thoughts as well. By forgiving the woman's sins (7:48), Jesus made clear to those assembled that He was more than just a prophet (7:49). The woman possibly already believed that Jesus brought forgiveness, and thus offered duties which went well beyond the usual customs of hospitality and respect (7:44–47).

The other Gospels relate similar stories about a woman who anointed Jesus (see Matt. 26:6–13; Mark 14:3–9; John 12:1–8). Their accounts, however, are located specifically in Bethany and focus on the preparation for Jesus' burial. See "Plot, Anointing, Betrayal" at Matt. 26:1.

▼ ■ Luke 7:36–50

Luke
A Sinful Woman Forgiven

7:36 Then one of the Pharisees asked Him to eat with him. And He went to the Pharisee's house, and sat down to eat. 37And behold, a woman in the city who was a sinner, when she knew that *Jesus* sat at the table in the Pharisee's house, brought an alabaster flask of fragrant oil, 38and stood at His feet behind *Him* weeping; and she began to wash His feet with her tears, and wiped *them* with the hair of her head; and she kissed His feet and anointed *them* with the fragrant oil. 39Now when the Pharisee who had invited Him saw *this,* he spoke to himself, saying, "This Man, if He were a prophet, would know who and what manner of woman *this is* who is touching Him, for she is a sinner."

40And Jesus answered and said to him, "Simon, I have something to say to you."

So he said, "Teacher, say it."

41"There was a certain creditor who had two debtors. One owed five hundred denarii, and the other fifty. 42And when they had nothing with which to repay, he freely forgave them both. Tell Me, therefore, which of them will love him more?"

43Simon answered and said, "I suppose the *one* whom he forgave more."

And He said to him, "You have rightly judged." 44Then He turned to the woman and said to Simon, "Do you see this woman? I entered your house; you gave Me no water for My feet, but she has washed My feet with her tears and wiped *them* with the hair of her head. 45You gave Me no kiss, but this woman has not ceased to kiss My feet since the time I came in. 46You did not anoint My head with oil, but this woman has anointed My feet with fragrant oil. 47Therefore I say to you, her sins, *which are* many, are forgiven, for she loved much. But to whom little is forgiven, *the same* loves little."

48Then He said to her, "Your sins are forgiven."

49And those who sat at the table with Him began to say to themselves, "Who is this who even forgives sins?"

50Then He said to the woman, "Your faith has saved you. Go in peace."

Jesus and Beelzebub

Each of the Synoptic Gospels reports Jesus' opponents claiming that His power came from Beelzebub and that His supernatural deeds resulted from demonic influence. Mark indicates that at least some of Jesus' own people, His family and relatives, had this concern, thinking He was "out of His mind" (Mark 3:21, 31–35). Matthew and Luke, though, separate Jesus' family from this allegation. In Matthew's account, the family did not arrive for their visit until after Jesus had countered the charge by the Pharisees (Matt. 12:24, 46–50). Luke reports the family's visit at an earlier stage of Jesus' ministry (Luke 8:19–21), thus not connecting it with the Beelzebub accusation. Only Luke tells of a woman who showed the proper response to Jesus' healings and exorcisms: rather than associate Him with demons, she offered a blessing for His mother (Luke 11:27, 28).

■ Matthew 12:22–50
■ Mark 3:20–35
■ Luke 11:14–36
▼ ■ Luke 8:19–21

Matthew 12:22–50
A House Divided Cannot Stand

12:22 Then one was brought to Him who was demon-possessed, blind and mute; and He healed him, so that the blind and[a] mute man both spoke and saw.

12:22 [a]NU-Text omits *blind and.*

OFFSPRING OF VIPERS (Matt. 12:34)

Jesus' contemporaries considered the Pharisees to be model religious people. Yet in some of Jesus' encounters with Pharisees (Matt. 3:7; 12:24), He called them a "brood of vipers" (Matt. 12:34), that is, "offspring of snakes." Calling someone a snake was an insult, but calling someone the "child of a snake" was even worse.

Even though the Greek historian Herodotus (484–425 B.C.) lived 5 centuries before Jesus, an idea that Herodotus had about Arabian vipers was still associated with vipers in general by many people of Jesus' day. Although most reptiles lay eggs, people believed that viper eggs hatched inside their mother's stomach. The baby vipers would then eat their way through their mother's stomach to be born, killing their mother in the process. According to some ancient writers (including Herodotus), mother vipers ate the father vipers while the mothers were pregnant, so the baby vipers avenged their father by killing the mother.

Murdering one's mother or father was the crime ancient people thought most horrible. Even if one killed one parent to avenge the murder of the other, Greeks thought the child who committed this avenging murder would be hounded by avenging spirits called the "Furies." Jewish people also considered the murder of parents or other blood relatives to be an inconceivably wicked crime.

By calling the religious Pharisees "children of vipers," Jesus may have compared them with parent murderers, thus implying that they were the most vile and evil people possible. Since He openly associated the title with murder and bloodshed (Matt. 23:33–35), the Pharisees were no doubt offended.

23And all the multitudes were amazed and said, "Could this be the Son of David?"

24Now when the Pharisees heard *it* they said, "This *fellow* does not cast out demons except by Beelzebub,[a] the ruler of the demons."

25But Jesus knew their thoughts, and said to them: "Every kingdom divided against itself is brought to desolation, and every city or house divided against itself will not stand. 26If Satan casts out Satan, he is divided against himself. How then will his kingdom stand? 27And if I cast out demons by Beelzebub, by whom do your sons cast *them* out? Therefore they shall be your judges. 28But if I cast out demons by the Spirit of God, surely the kingdom of God has come upon you. 29Or how can one enter a strong man's house and plunder his goods, unless he first binds the strong man? And then he will plunder his house. 30He who is not with Me is against Me, and he who does not gather with Me scatters abroad.

The Unpardonable Sin

31"Therefore I say to you, every sin and blasphemy will be forgiven men, but the blasphemy *against* the Spirit will not be forgiven men. 32Anyone who speaks a word against the Son of Man, it will be forgiven him; but whoever speaks against the Holy Spirit, it will not be forgiven him, either in this age or in the *age* to come.

A Tree Known by Its Fruit

33"Either make the tree good and its fruit good, or else make the tree bad and its fruit bad; for a tree is known by *its* fruit. 34Brood of vipers! How can you, being evil, speak good things? For out of the abundance of the heart the mouth speaks. 35A good man out of the good treasure of his heart[a] brings forth good things, and an evil man out of the evil treasure brings forth evil things. 36But I say to you that for every idle word men may speak, they will give account of it in the day of judgment. 37For by your words you will be justified, and by your words you will be condemned."

The Scribes and Pharisees Ask for a Sign

38Then some of the scribes and Pharisees answered, saying, "Teacher, we want to see a sign from You."

39But He answered and said to them, "An evil and adulterous generation seeks after a sign, and no sign will be given to it

---

12:24 aNU-Text and M-Text read *Beelzebul.*
12:35 aNU-Text and M-Text omit *of his heart.*

except the sign of the prophet Jonah. ⁴⁰For as Jonah was three days and three nights in the belly of the great fish, so will the Son of Man be three days and three nights in the heart of the earth. ⁴¹The men of Nineveh will rise up in the judgment with this generation and condemn it, because they repented at the preaching of Jonah; and indeed a greater than Jonah *is* here. ⁴²The queen of the South will rise up in the judgment with this generation and condemn it, for she came from the ends of the earth to hear the wisdom of Solomon; and indeed a greater than Solomon *is* here.

An Unclean Spirit Returns

⁴³"When an unclean spirit goes out of a man, he goes through dry places, seeking rest, and finds none. ⁴⁴Then he says, 'I will return to my house from which I came.' And when he comes, he finds *it* empty, swept, and put in order. ⁴⁵Then he goes and takes with him seven other spirits more wicked than himself, and they enter and dwell there; and the last *state* of that man is worse than the first. So shall it also be with this wicked generation."

Jesus' Mother and Brothers Send for Him

⁴⁶While He was still talking to the multitudes, behold, His mother and brothers stood outside, seeking to speak with Him. ⁴⁷Then one said to Him, "Look, Your mother and Your brothers are standing outside, seeking to speak with You."

⁴⁸But He answered and said to the one who told Him, "Who is My mother and who are My brothers?" ⁴⁹And He stretched out His hand toward His disciples and said, "Here are My mother and My brothers! ⁵⁰For whoever does the will of My Father in heaven is My brother and sister and mother."

TIME **C**APSULE *A.D. 15 to 18*

15 *Annas is deposed from the high priesthood*

17 *Gnaeus Piso is made legate of Syria*

17 *Syria and Judea petition Rome to lower their taxes*

18–36 *Caiaphas is high priest in Jerusalem (Matt. 26:3, 57)*

18 *Ovid, the Roman poet, dies in exile*

Mark 3:20–35
Sin Against the Holy Spirit

3 :20 Then the multitude came together again, so that they could not so much as eat bread. ²¹But when His own people heard *about this,* they went out to lay hold of Him, for they said, "He is out of His mind."

²²And the scribes who came down from Jerusalem said, "He has Beelzebub," and, "By the ruler of the demons He casts out demons."

²³So He called them to *Himself* and said to them in parables: "How can Satan cast out Satan? ²⁴If a kingdom is divided against itself, that kingdom cannot stand. ²⁵And if a house is divided against itself, that house cannot stand. ²⁶And if Satan has risen up against himself, and is divided, he cannot stand, but has an end. ²⁷No one can enter a strong man's house and plunder his goods, unless he first binds the strong man. And then he will plunder his house.

²⁸"Assuredly, I say to you, all sins will be forgiven the sons of men, and whatever blasphemies they may utter; ²⁹but he who blasphemes against the Holy Spirit never has forgiveness, but is subject to eternal condemnation"— ³⁰because they said, "He has an unclean spirit."

Jesus' Mother and Brothers Seek Him

³¹Then His brothers and His mother came, and standing outside they sent to Him, calling Him. ³²And a multitude was sitting around Him; and they said to Him, "Look, Your mother and Your brothersᵃ are outside seeking You."

³³But He answered them, saying, "Who is My mother, or My brothers?" ³⁴And He looked around in a circle at those who sat about Him, and said, "Here are My mother and My brothers! ³⁵For whoever does the will of God is My brother and My sister and mother."

Luke 11:14–36
With the Finger of God

11 :14 And He was casting out a demon, and it was mute. So it was, when the demon had gone out, that the mute spoke; and the multitudes marveled. ¹⁵But some

3:32 ᵃNU-Text and M-Text add *and Your sisters.*

of them said, "He casts out demons by Beelzebub,ᵃ the ruler of the demons."

¹⁶Others, testing *Him,* sought from Him a sign from heaven. ¹⁷But He, knowing their thoughts, said to them: "Every kingdom divided against itself is brought to desolation, and a house *divided* against a house falls. ¹⁸If Satan also is divided against himself, how will his kingdom stand? Because you say I cast out demons by Beelzebub. ¹⁹And if I cast out demons by Beelzebub, by whom do your sons cast *them* out? Therefore they will be your judges. ²⁰But if I cast out demons with the finger of God, surely the kingdom of God has come upon you. ²¹When a strong man, fully armed, guards his own palace, his goods are in peace. ²²But when a stronger than he comes upon him and overcomes him, he takes from him all his armor in which he trusted, and divides his spoils. ²³He who is not with Me is against Me, and he who does not gather with Me scatters.

An Unclean Spirit Returns

²⁴"When an unclean spirit goes out of a man, he goes through dry places, seeking rest; and finding none, he says, 'I will return to my house from which I came.' ²⁵And when he comes, he finds *it* swept and put in order. ²⁶Then he goes and takes with *him* seven other spirits more wicked than himself, and they enter and dwell there; and the last *state* of that man is worse than the first."

Keeping the Word

²⁷And it happened, as He spoke these things, that a certain woman from the crowd raised her voice and said to Him, "Blessed *is* the womb that bore You, and *the* breasts which nursed You!"

²⁸But He said, "More than that, blessed *are* those who hear the word of God and keep it!"

Seeking a Sign

²⁹And while the crowds were thickly gathered together, He began to say, "This is an evil generation. It seeks a sign, and no sign will be given to it except the sign of Jonah the prophet.ᵃ ³⁰For as Jonah became a sign to the Ninevites, so also the Son of Man will be to this generation. ³¹The queen of the South will rise up in the judgment

with the men of this generation and condemn them, for she came from the ends of the earth to hear the wisdom of Solomon; and indeed a greater than Solomon *is* here. ³²The men of Nineveh will rise up in the judgment with this generation and condemn it, for they repented at the preaching of Jonah; and indeed a greater than Jonah *is* here.

The Lamp of the Body

³³"No one, when he has lit a lamp, puts *it* in a secret place or under a basket, but on a lampstand, that those who come in may see the light. ³⁴The lamp of the body is the eye. Therefore, when your eye is good, your whole body also is full of light. But when *your eye* is bad, your body also *is* full of darkness. ³⁵Therefore take heed that the light which is in you is not darkness. ³⁶If then your whole body *is* full of light, having no part dark, *the* whole *body* will be full of light, as when the bright shining of a lamp gives you light."

Luke 8:19–21

Jesus' Mother and Brothers Come to Him

8 **:19** Then His mother and brothers came to Him, and could not approach Him because of the crowd. ²⁰And it was told Him *by some,* who said, "Your mother and Your brothers are standing outside, desiring to see You."

²¹But He answered and said to them, "My mother and My brothers are these who hear the word of God and do it."

Parables by the Sea

Each of the Synoptic Gospels relates Jesus' parable of the sower with His purpose for teaching in parables. Jesus used parables not only to reveal spiritual truth, but also to conceal it from those who were "outside" (Mark 4:11). The somewhat atypical parable of the sower works well to illustrate this purpose. It is really an allegory where each type of soil symbolizes a type of response to the gospel. Since the symbolism was not immediately obvious, Jesus had to explain it to His disciples if they were to understand it properly (Matt. 13:18–23; Mark 4:13–20; Luke 8:11–15).

The same is true of the parable of the tares which Jesus also explained as an allegory (Matt. 13:24–30, 36–43). Contrasting these two parables with others Jesus told shows that most of His parables were very

---

11:15 ᵃNU-Text and M-Text read *Beelzebul.*
11:29 ᵃNU-Text omits *the prophet.*

short stories that clearly illustrated a single spiritual truth. Most of the parables are to be interpreted as either simple metaphors or similes rather than as allegories.

- Matthew 13:1–52
- Mark 4:1–34
- Luke 8:1–18
- Luke 13:18–21

Matthew 13:1–52
The Parable of the Sower

13 :1 On the same day Jesus went out of the house and sat by the sea. ²And great multitudes were gathered together to Him, so that He got into a boat and sat; and the whole multitude stood on the shore.

³Then He spoke many things to them in parables, saying: "Behold, a sower went out to sow. ⁴And as he sowed, some *seed* fell by the wayside; and the birds came and devoured them. ⁵Some fell on stony places, where they did not have much earth; and they immediately sprang up because they had no depth of earth. ⁶But when the sun was up they were scorched, and because they had no root they withered away. ⁷And some fell among thorns, and the thorns sprang up and choked them. ⁸But others fell on good ground and yielded a crop: some a hundredfold, some sixty, some thirty. ⁹He who has ears to hear, let him hear!"

The Purpose of Parables

¹⁰And the disciples came and said to Him, "Why do You speak to them in parables?"

¹¹He answered and said to them, "Because it has been given to you to know the mysteries of the kingdom of heaven, but to them it has not been given. ¹²For whoever has, to him more will be given, and he will have abundance; but whoever does not have, even what he has will be taken away from him. ¹³Therefore I speak to them in parables, because seeing they do not see, and hearing they do not hear, nor do they understand. ¹⁴And in them the prophecy of Isaiah is fulfilled, which says:

'Hearing you will hear and shall not
   understand,
And seeing you will see and not
   perceive;
15   For the hearts of this people have
      grown dull.
Their ears are hard of hearing,
And their eyes they have closed,
Lest they should see with their eyes
   and hear with their ears,
Lest they should understand with
   their hearts and turn,
So that I should ª heal them.'ᵇ

¹⁶But blessed *are* your eyes for they see, and your ears for they hear; ¹⁷for assuredly, I say to you that many prophets and righteous *men* desired to see what you see, and did not see *it,* and to hear what you hear, and did not hear *it.*

The Parable of the Sower Explained

¹⁸"Therefore hear the parable of the sower: ¹⁹When anyone hears the word of the kingdom, and does not understand *it,* then the wicked *one* comes and snatches away what was sown in his heart. This is he who received seed by the wayside. ²⁰But he who received the seed on stony places, this is he who hears the word and immediately receives it with joy; ²¹yet he has no root in himself, but endures only for a while. For when tribulation or persecution arises because of the word, immediately he stumbles. ²²Now he who received seed among the thorns is he who hears the word, and the cares of this world and the deceitfulness of riches choke the word, and he becomes unfruitful. ²³But he who received seed on the good ground is he who hears the word and understands *it,* who indeed bears fruit and produces: some a hundredfold, some sixty, some thirty."

13:15 ªNU-Text and M-Text read *would.*
ᵇIsaiah 6:9, 10

AGRICULTURE AND HERDING

Jesus' parables taught spiritual truths through practical illustrations, such as sowing of seed. Plowing in ancient Israel was not deep, and it could be done either before or after the sower scattered the seed. Rainfall was irregular and often inadequate. The success of a growing season in a particular plot could not be predicted, and for that reason a good harvest was all the more appreciated (Matt. 13:8).

The Parable of the Wheat and the Tares

24Another parable He put forth to them, saying: "The kingdom of heaven is like a man who sowed good seed in his field; 25but while men slept, his enemy came and sowed tares among the wheat and went his way. 26But when the grain had sprouted and produced a crop, then the tares also appeared. 27So the servants of the owner came and said to him, 'Sir, did you not sow good seed in your field? How then does it have tares?' 28He said to them, 'An enemy has done this.' The servants said to him, 'Do you want us then to go and gather them up?' 29But he said, 'No, lest while you gather up the tares you also uproot the wheat with them. 30Let both grow together until the harvest, and at the time of harvest I will say to the reapers, "First gather together the tares and bind them in bundles to burn them, but gather the wheat into my barn." ' "

The Parable of the Mustard Seed

31Another parable He put forth to them, saying: "The kingdom of heaven is like a mustard seed, which a man took and sowed in his field, 32which indeed is the least of all the seeds; but when it is grown it is greater than the herbs and becomes a tree, so that the birds of the air come and nest in its branches."

The Parable of the Leaven

33Another parable He spoke to them: "The kingdom of heaven is like leaven, which a woman took and hid in three measures[a] of meal till it was all leavened."

Prophecy and the Parables

34All these things Jesus spoke to the multitude in parables; and without a parable He did not speak to them, 35that it might be fulfilled which was spoken by the prophet, saying:

13:33 [a]Greek *sata*, approximately two pecks in all
13:35 [a]Psalm 78:2

"I will open My mouth in parables;
I will utter things kept secret from the
foundation of the world."[a]

The Parable of the Tares Explained

36Then Jesus sent the multitude away and went into the house. And His disciples came to Him, saying, "Explain to us the parable of the tares of the field."

37He answered and said to them: "He who sows the good seed is the Son of Man. 38The field is the world, the good seeds are the sons of the kingdom, but the tares are the sons of the wicked *one*. 39The enemy who sowed them is the devil, the harvest is the end of the age, and the reapers are the angels. 40Therefore as the tares are gathered and burned in the fire, so it will be at the end of this age. 41The Son of Man will send out His angels, and they will gather out of His kingdom all things that offend, and those who practice lawlessness, 42and will cast them into the furnace of fire. There will be wailing and gnashing of teeth. 43Then the righteous will shine forth as the sun in the kingdom of their Father. He who has ears to hear, let him hear!

The Parable of the Hidden Treasure

44"Again, the kingdom of heaven is like treasure hidden in a field, which a man found and hid; and for joy over it he goes and sells all that he has and buys that field.

The Parable of the Pearl of Great Price

45"Again, the kingdom of heaven is like a merchant seeking beautiful pearls, 46who, when he had found one pearl of great price, went and sold all that he had and bought it.

The Parable of the Dragnet

47"Again, the kingdom of heaven is like a dragnet that was cast into the sea and gathered some of every kind, 48which, when it was full, they drew to shore; and they sat down and gathered the good into

---

GEOGRAPHY AND ENVIRONMENT

The Sea of Galilee is a freshwater lake, small but deep, with good fishing (Matt. 13:47). Fishermen threw their dragnets by hand from small boats, and dragged the nets along the bottom of the lake. The edge of the net was pulled down by weights to snare the fish. Fish were a very important part of the Roman diet, and the Mediterranean Sea provided them.

vessels, but threw the bad away. [49]So it will be at the end of the age. The angels will come forth, separate the wicked from among the just, [50]and cast them into the furnace of fire. There will be wailing and gnashing of teeth."

[51]Jesus said to them,[a] "Have you understood all these things?"

They said to Him, "Yes, Lord."[b]

[52]Then He said to them, "Therefore every scribe instructed concerning[a] the kingdom of heaven is like a householder who brings out of his treasure *things* new and old."

Mark 4:1–34
The Parable of the Sower

4:1 And again He began to teach by the sea. And a great multitude was gathered to Him, so that He got into a boat and sat *in it* on the sea; and the whole multitude was on the land facing the sea. [2]Then He taught them many things by parables, and said to them in His teaching:

[3]"Listen! Behold, a sower went out to sow. [4]And it happened, as he sowed, *that* some *seed* fell by the wayside; and the birds of the air[a] came and devoured it. [5]Some fell on stony ground, where it did not have much earth; and immediately it sprang up because it had no depth of earth. [6]But when the sun was up it was scorched, and because it had no root it withered away. [7]And some *seed* fell among thorns; and the thorns grew up and choked it, and it yielded no crop. [8]But other *seed* fell on good ground and yielded a crop that sprang up, increased and produced: some thirtyfold, some sixty, and some a hundred."

[9]And He said to them,[a] "He who has ears to hear, let him hear!"

The Purpose of Parables

[10]But when He was alone, those around Him with the twelve asked Him about the parable. [11]And He said to them, "To you it has been given to know the mystery of the kingdom of God; but to those who are outside, all things come in parables, [12]so that

'Seeing they may see and not perceive,
And hearing they may hear and not understand;
Lest they should turn,
And their sins be forgiven them.'"[a]

The Parable of the Sower Explained

[13]And He said to them, "Do you not understand this parable? How then will you understand all the parables? [14]The sower sows the word. [15]And these are the ones by the wayside where the word is sown. When they hear, Satan comes immediately and takes away the word that was sown in their hearts. [16]These likewise are the ones sown on stony ground who, when they hear the word, immediately receive it with gladness; [17]and they have no root in themselves, and so endure only for a time. Afterward, when tribulation or persecution arises for the word's sake, immediately they stumble. [18]Now these are the ones sown among thorns; *they are* the ones who hear the word, [19]and the cares of this world, the deceitfulness of riches, and the desires for other things entering in choke the word, and it becomes unfruitful. [20]But these are the ones sown on good ground, those who hear the word, accept *it,* and bear fruit: some thirtyfold, some sixty, and some a hundred."

Light Under a Basket

[21]Also He said to them, "Is a lamp brought to be put under a basket or under a bed? Is it not to be set on a lampstand? [22]For there is nothing hidden which will not be revealed, nor has anything been kept secret but that it should come to light. [23]If anyone has ears to hear, let him hear." [24]Then He said to them, "Take heed what you hear. With the same measure you use, it will be measured to you; and to you

TIME CAPSULE A.D. 18 to 26

18 Antipas builds city of Tiberias by the Sea of Galilee

19 Tiberius expels the Jews from Rome

26–36 Pontius Pilate is prefect of Judea (Mark 15:1)

26 The 15th year of Tiberius (counting from his coregency)

26 Tiberius begins period of retirement on island of Capri

13:51 [a]NU-Text omits *Jesus said to them.* [b]NU-Text omits *Lord.*   13:52 [a]Or *for*
Mark 4:4 [a]NU-Text and M-Text omit *of the air.*
4:9 [a]NU-Text and M-Text omit *to them.*
4:12 [a]Isaiah 6:9, 10

How to Understand a Parable (Mark 4:2)

Ministers today often use sermon illustrations to help their hearers understand a sermon's point. In the same way, ancient Jewish teachers often told stories to illustrate whatever moral principle they were trying to communicate. Sometimes these parables had one central point. In other cases, such as Jesus' parable of the sower and the four soils (Mark 4:2–8), parables included several points of comparison.

Sometimes sages would tell a parable or a riddle which hearers would understand only if they had the key to interpretation. Usually only disciples of that teacher who spent enough time with him to learn his teachings would understand his point. This might happen with Jewish teachers who felt that some subjects in particular were best discussed only in private or in very small gatherings.

With some parables, then, the details had symbolic significance. This teaching device was a way of encouraging students to consider deeply the teacher's words and to weed out the uncommitted. The stories conveyed truth to attentive hearers who were eager to understand. At the same time the figurative language sometimes veiled truth from persons who did not want to believe it. While the multitude heard Jesus' parable (Mark 4:1, 2), only His disciples sought its meaning in private (Mark 4:10; Luke 8:9).

Because Jewish parables were usually stories, we understand Jesus' parables best when we consider them as stories. For the disciples, Jesus interpreted the details of the parable of the sower (Mark 4:13–20). For the most part, however, rather than reading meaning into every detail, we should try to catch the lesson or lessons of the story as a whole.

who hear, more will be given. ²⁵For whoever has, to him more will be given; but whoever does not have, even what he has will be taken away from him."

The Parable of the Growing Seed

²⁶And He said, "The kingdom of God is as if a man should scatter seed on the ground, ²⁷and should sleep by night and rise by day, and the seed should sprout and grow, he himself does not know how. ²⁸For the earth yields crops by itself: first the blade, then the head, after that the full grain in the head. ²⁹But when the grain ripens, immediately he puts in the sickle, because the harvest has come."

The Parable of the Mustard Seed

³⁰Then He said, "To what shall we liken the kingdom of God? Or with what parable shall we picture it? ³¹*It is* like a mustard seed which, when it is sown on the ground, is smaller than all the seeds on earth; ³²but when it is sown, it grows up and becomes greater than all herbs, and shoots out large branches, so that the birds of the air may nest under its shade."

Jesus' Use of Parables

³³And with many such parables He spoke the word to them as they were able to hear *it*. ³⁴But without a parable He did not speak to them. And when they were alone, He explained all things to His disciples.

Luke 8:1–18
Many Women Minister to Jesus

8 :1 Now it came to pass, afterward, that He went through every city and village, preaching and bringing the glad tidings of the kingdom of God. And the twelve *were* with Him, ²and certain women who had been healed of evil spirits and infirmities—Mary called Magdalene, out of whom had come seven demons, ³and Joanna the wife of Chuza, Herod's steward, and Susanna, and many others who provided for Him^a from their substance.

The Parable of the Sower

⁴And when a great multitude had gathered, and they had come to Him from every city, He spoke by a parable: ⁵"A sower went out to sow his seed. And as he sowed, some fell by the wayside; and it was trampled down, and the birds of the air devoured it. ⁶Some fell on rock; and as soon

8:3 ^aNU-Text and M-Text read *them*.

as it sprang up, it withered away because it lacked moisture. [7]And some fell among thorns, and the thorns sprang up with it and choked it. [8]But others fell on good ground, sprang up, and yielded a crop a hundredfold." When He had said these things He cried, "He who has ears to hear, let him hear!"

The Purpose of Parables

[9]Then His disciples asked Him, saying, "What does this parable mean?"

[10]And He said, "To you it has been given to know the mysteries of the kingdom of God, but to the rest *it is given* in parables, that

> 'Seeing they may not see,
> And hearing they may not
>   understand.'[a]

The Parable of the Sower Explained

[11]"Now the parable is this: The seed is the word of God. [12]Those by the wayside are the ones who hear; then the devil comes and takes away the word out of their hearts, lest they should believe and be saved. [13]But the ones on the rock *are those* who, when they hear, receive the word with joy; and these have no root, who believe for a while and in time of temptation fall away. [14]Now the ones *that* fell among thorns are those who, when they have heard, go out and are choked with cares, riches, and pleasures of life, and bring no fruit to maturity. [15]But the ones *that* fell on the good ground are those who, having heard the word with a noble and good heart, keep *it* and bear fruit with patience.

The Parable of the Revealed Light

[16]"No one, when he has lit a lamp, covers it with a vessel or puts *it* under a bed, but sets *it* on a lampstand, that those who enter may see the light. [17]For nothing is secret that will not be revealed, nor *anything* hidden that will not be known and come to light. [18]Therefore take heed how you hear. For whoever has, to him *more* will be given; and whoever does not have, even what he seems to have will be taken from him."

Luke 13:18–21
The Parable of the Mustard Seed

13 :18 Then He said, "What is the kingdom of God like? And to what shall I compare it? [19]It is like a mustard seed, which a man took and put in his garden; and it grew and became a large[a] tree, and the birds of the air nested in its branches."

The Parable of the Leaven

[20]And again He said, "To what shall I liken the kingdom of God? [21]It is like leaven, which a woman took and hid in three measures[a] of meal till it was all leavened."

8:10 [a]Isaiah 6:9   13:19 [a]NU-Text omits *large.*   13:21 [a]Greek *sata,* approximately two pecks in all

---

Crossing to the East Shore

Jesus' brief visit to the region of the Decapolis, east of the Sea of Galilee, was marked by two episodes: the calming of a storm and the healing of demon possession. Both episodes focus on the fear and awe of those who witnessed the happenings (Luke 8:25, 34–37), and on Jesus' ability to bring peace. Jesus demonstrated His authority over both the natural and supernatural realms by calming the storm on the lake (Mark 4:39) and by ending the violence caused by the unclean spirits named "Legion" (Mark 5:2–5, 9, 15).

Matthew's account of the exorcism provides considerably less detail than do the accounts of Mark and Luke. Such matters as the man's living conditions among the tombs (Mark 5:2–5; Luke 8:27, 29) and the name "Legion" (Mark 5:9; Luke 8:30) are not mentioned. More significantly, Matthew states that there were "two demon-possessed men" (Matt. 8:28). Similarly Matthew reports the healing of

---

SCIENCE AND TECHNOLOGY

Clay lamps from as early as 3000 B.C. have been found in Mesopotamia. The typical clay lamp has a reservoir for the oil and a channel or groove to hold the wick (Luke 8:16). Different kinds of oil were used for fuel, notably olive oil and other vegetable oils, but other fuels included fish or animal fat, and possibly petroleum.

two blind men (Matt. 20:29–34), whereas Mark and Luke mention only one (Mark 10:46–52; Luke 18:35–43). Some have suggested that Matthew mentions two men in both cases to confirm the validity of their testimony in accordance with Deut. 19:15 (see Matt. 18:16).

- ■ Matthew 8:23–34
- ■ Mark 4:35—5:20
- ■ Luke 8:22–39

Matthew 8:23–34
Lord of the Tempest

8 **:23** Now when He got into a boat, His disciples followed Him. [24]And suddenly a great tempest arose on the sea, so that the boat was covered with the waves. But He was asleep. [25]Then His disciples came to *Him* and awoke Him, saying, "Lord, save us! We are perishing!"

[26]But He said to them, "Why are you fearful, O you of little faith?" Then He arose and rebuked the winds and the sea, and there was a great calm. [27]So the men marveled, saying, "Who can this be, that even the winds and the sea obey Him?"

Two Demon-Possessed Men Healed

[28]When He had come to the other side, to the country of the Gergesenes,[a] there met Him two demon-possessed *men,* coming out of the tombs, exceedingly fierce, so that no one could pass that way. [29]And suddenly they cried out, saying, "What have we to do with You, Jesus, You Son of God? Have You come here to torment us before the time?"

[30]Now a good way off from them there was a herd of many swine feeding. [31]So the demons begged Him, saying, "If You cast us out, permit us to go away[a] into the herd of swine."

[32]And He said to them, "Go." So when they had come out, they went into the herd of swine. And suddenly the whole herd of swine ran violently down the steep place into the sea, and perished in the water. [33]Then those who kept *them* fled; and they went away into the city and told everything, including what *had happened* to the demon-possessed *men.* [34]And behold,

the whole city came out to meet Jesus. And when they saw Him, they begged *Him* to depart from their region.

Mark 4:35—5:20
Wind and Wave Obey Jesus

4 **:35** On the same day, when evening had come, He said to them, "Let us cross over to the other side." [36]Now when they had left the multitude, they took Him along in the boat as He was. And other little boats were also with Him. [37]And a great windstorm arose, and the waves beat into the boat, so that it was already filling. [38]But He was in the stern, asleep on a pillow. And they awoke Him and said to Him, "Teacher, do You not care that we are perishing?"

[39]Then He arose and rebuked the wind, and said to the sea, "Peace, be still!" And the wind ceased and there was a great calm. [40]But He said to them, "Why are you so fearful? How *is it* that you have no faith?"[a] [41]And they feared exceedingly, and said to one another, "Who can this be, that even the wind and the sea obey Him!"

Casting Out Demons

5 [1]Then they came to the other side of the sea, to the country of the Gadarenes.[a] [2]And when He had come out of the boat, immediately there met Him out of the tombs a man with an unclean spirit, [3]who had *his* dwelling among the tombs; and no one could bind him,[a] not even with chains, [4]because he had often been bound with shackles and chains. And the chains had been pulled apart by him, and the shackles broken in pieces; neither could anyone tame him. [5]And always, night and day, he was in the mountains and in the tombs, crying out and cutting himself with stones.

[6]When he saw Jesus from afar, he ran and worshiped Him. [7]And he cried out with a loud voice and said, "What have I to do with You, Jesus, Son of the Most High God? I implore You by God that You do not torment me."

[8]For He said to him, "Come out of the man, unclean spirit!" [9]Then He asked him, "What *is* your name?"

And he answered, saying, "My name *is* Legion; for we are many." [10]Also he begged Him earnestly that He would not send them out of the country.

8:28 [a]NU-Text reads *Gadarenes.*　　8:31 [a]NU-Text reads *send us.*　　**Mark** 4:40 [a]NU-Text reads *Have you still no faith?*　　5:1 [a]NU-Text reads *Gerasenes.*　　5:3 [a]NU-Text adds *anymore.*

CITIES OF THE DECAPOLIS (Mark 5:20)

After crossing the Sea of Galilee, also known as Lake Tiberias (John 6:1), Jesus and His disciples encountered a demon-possessed man in the "country of the Gadarenes" (Mark 5:1). Gadara was one of several cities which were known as "the Decapolis." The Greek word *dekapolis* means "ten cities," and in Jesus' time it referred to a group of Hellenistic cities on the east side of the Jordan River in the vicinity of Lake Tiberias.

The cities of the Decapolis were founded by Greeks and Macedonians soon after Alexander's conquest of Palestine in the late 4th century B.C. Although commonly assumed to be a league of independent entities, the cities were actually associated because of their Hellenistic character. Various Greek cultural attributes, such as religion, architecture, sculpture, painting, and town planning, contributed to their unity. This Hellenistic culture made the Decapolis distinct from nearby towns of Jewish, Nabatean, and other cultures.

The Decapolis was also a distinct administrative region set up by the Romans and appended to the province of Syria. Just as the Romans assigned Pontius Pilate to serve as governor over the province of Judea, so was a provincial governor, according to a Greek inscription, assigned to the Decapolis region.

The demon-possessed man who was cured by Jesus spread the news of the healing to other cities of the Decapolis (Mark 5:20). People in these Gentile cities often feared miracle workers as some sort of magicians, so word of mouth might possibly calm their misunderstandings. No rejection of Jesus is reported when He Himself traveled through the Decapolis region (Mark. 7:31).

---

¹¹Now a large herd of swine was feeding there near the mountains. ¹²So all the demons begged Him, saying, "Send us to the swine, that we may enter them." ¹³And at once Jesusᵃ gave them permission. Then the unclean spirits went out and entered the swine (there were about two thousand); and the herd ran violently down the steep place into the sea, and drowned in the sea.

¹⁴So those who fed the swine fled, and they told *it* in the city and in the country. And they went out to see what it was that had happened. ¹⁵Then they came to Jesus, and saw the one *who had been* demon-possessed and had the legion, sitting and clothed and in his right mind. And they were afraid. ¹⁶And those who saw it told them how it happened to him *who had been* demon-possessed, and about the swine. ¹⁷Then they began to plead with Him to depart from their region.

¹⁸And when He got into the boat, he who had been demon-possessed begged Him that he might be with Him. ¹⁹However, Jesus did not permit him, but said to him, "Go home to your friends, and tell them what great things the Lord has done for you, and how He has had compassion on you." ²⁰And he departed and began to proclaim in Decapolis all that Jesus had done for him; and all marveled.

Luke 8:22–39
Who Can This Be?

8 :22 Now it happened, on a certain day, that He got into a boat with His disciples. And He said to them, "Let us cross over to the other side of the lake." And they launched out. ²³But as they sailed He fell asleep. And a windstorm came down on the lake, and they were filling *with water,* and were in jeopardy. ²⁴And they came to Him and awoke Him, saying, "Master, Master, we are perishing!"

Then He arose and rebuked the wind and the raging of the water. And they ceased, and there was a calm. ²⁵But He said to them, "Where is your faith?"

And they were afraid, and marveled, saying to one another, "Who can this be? For He commands even the winds and water, and they obey Him!"

Jesus Controls Demons

²⁶Then they sailed to the country of the Gadarenes,ᵃ which is opposite Galilee. ²⁷And when He stepped out on the land, there met Him a certain man from the city who had demons for a long time. And he

---

5:13 ᵃNU-Text reads *And He gave.*
Luke 8:26 ᵃNU-Text reads *Gerasenes.*

wore no clothes,ᵃ nor did he live in a house but in the tombs. ²⁸When he saw Jesus, he cried out, fell down before Him, and with a loud voice said, "What have I to do with You, Jesus, Son of the Most High God? I beg You, do not torment me!" ²⁹For He had commanded the unclean spirit to come out of the man. For it had often seized him, and he was kept under guard, bound with chains and shackles; and he broke the bonds and was driven by the demon into the wilderness.

³⁰Jesus asked him, saying, "What is your name?"

And he said, "Legion," because many demons had entered him. ³¹And they begged Him that He would not command them to go out into the abyss.

³²Now a herd of many swine was feeding there on the mountain. So they begged Him that He would permit them to enter them. And He permitted them. ³³Then the demons went out of the man and entered the swine, and the herd ran violently down the steep place into the lake and drowned.

³⁴When those who fed *them* saw what had happened, they fled and told *it* in the city and in the country. ³⁵Then they went out to see what had happened, and came to Jesus, and found the man from whom the demons had departed, sitting at the feet of Jesus, clothed and in his right mind. And they were afraid. ³⁶They also who had seen *it* told them by what means he who had been demon-possessed was healed. ³⁷Then the whole multitude of the surrounding region of the Gadarenesᵃ asked Him to depart from them, for they were seized with great fear. And He got into the boat and returned.

³⁸Now the man from whom the demons had departed begged Him that he might be with Him. But Jesus sent him away, saying, ³⁹"Return to your own house, and tell what great things God has done for you." And he went his way and proclaimed throughout the whole city what great things Jesus had done for him.

8:27 ᵃNU-Text reads *who had demons and for a long time wore no clothes.*   8:37 ᵃNU-Text reads *Gerasenes.*

Returning to the West Shore

As with the reports of the exorcism of Legion (see "Crossing to the East Shore" at Matt.

8:23), Matthew recounts the healings of Jairus's daughter and of the woman with a hemorrhage in considerably less detail than do Mark and Luke. Matthew's emphasis is on the role of faith in the healings rather than on the manner in which they were accomplished. While Mark relates Jesus' foreign language phrase, *Talitha, cumi* (Mark 5:41), Matthew omits such detail, possibly because it resembles incantations of the Hellenistic magic texts. Instead, he reports the additional healings of two blind men and a mute demon-possessed man, again explicitly emphasizing the blind men's faith (Matt. 9:28, 29).

Keeping a secret of the new life given Jairus's previously deceased daughter would have been impossible (Matt. 9:26). So some have thought that when Jesus charged her parents "to tell no one what had happened" (Luke 8:56) He was referring specifically to what had transpired in the girl's room. Perhaps Jesus wanted to leave open the possibility in the minds of some that the girl had actually only been sleeping (Matt. 9:24; Mark 5:39; Luke 8:52), lest His fame for raising the dead should become a hindrance to His continuing ministry (see "Healing the Sick" at Matt. 8:14).

■ Matthew 9:18–34
■ Mark 5:21–43
■ Luke 8:40–56

Matthew 9:18–34
A Girl Restored to Life and a Woman Healed

9:18 While He spoke these things to them, behold, a ruler came and worshiped Him, saying, "My daughter has just died, but come and lay Your hand on her and she will live." ¹⁹So Jesus arose and followed him, and so *did* His disciples.

²⁰And suddenly, a woman who had a flow of blood for twelve years came from behind and touched the hem of His garment. ²¹For she said to herself, "If only I may touch His garment, I shall be made well." ²²But Jesus turned around, and when He saw her He said, "Be of good cheer, daughter; your faith has made you well." And the woman was made well from that hour.

²³When Jesus came into the ruler's house, and saw the flute players and the noisy crowd wailing, ²⁴He said to them, "Make room, for the girl is not dead, but sleeping." And they ridiculed Him. ²⁵But when the crowd was put outside, He went

in and took her by the hand, and the girl arose. ²⁶And the report of this went out into all that land.

Two Blind Men Healed

²⁷When Jesus departed from there, two blind men followed Him, crying out and saying, "Son of David, have mercy on us!" ²⁸And when He had come into the house, the blind men came to Him. And Jesus said to them, "Do you believe that I am able to do this?"

They said to Him, "Yes, Lord."

²⁹Then He touched their eyes, saying, "According to your faith let it be to you." ³⁰And their eyes were opened. And Jesus sternly warned them, saying, "See *that* no one knows *it*." ³¹But when they had departed, they spread the news about Him in all that country.

A Mute Man Speaks

³²As they went out, behold, they brought to Him a man, mute and demon-possessed. ³³And when the demon was cast out, the mute spoke. And the multitudes marveled, saying, "It was never seen like this in Israel!"

³⁴But the Pharisees said, "He casts out demons by the ruler of the demons."

Mark 5:21–43
Faith Born in Desperation

5 :21 Now when Jesus had crossed over again by boat to the other side, a great multitude gathered to Him; and He was by the sea. ²²And behold, one of the rulers of the synagogue came, Jairus by name. And when he saw Him, he fell at His feet ²³and begged Him earnestly, saying, "My little daughter lies at the point of death. Come and lay Your hands on her, that she may be healed, and she will live." ²⁴So *Jesus* went with him, and a great multitude followed Him and thronged Him.

²⁵Now a certain woman had a flow of blood for twelve years, ²⁶and had suffered many things from many physicians. She had spent all that she had and was no bet-

ter, but rather grew worse. ²⁷When she heard about Jesus, she came behind *Him* in the crowd and touched His garment. ²⁸For she said, "If only I may touch His clothes, I shall be made well."

²⁹Immediately the fountain of her blood was dried up, and she felt in *her* body that she was healed of the affliction. ³⁰And Jesus, immediately knowing in Himself that power had gone out of Him, turned around in the crowd and said, "Who touched My clothes?"

³¹But His disciples said to Him, "You see the multitude thronging You, and You say, 'Who touched Me?' "

³²And He looked around to see her who had done this thing. ³³But the woman, fearing and trembling, knowing what had happened to her, came and fell down before Him and told Him the whole truth. ³⁴And He said to her, "Daughter, your faith has made you well. Go in peace, and be healed of your affliction."

³⁵While He was still speaking, *some* came from the ruler of the synagogue's *house* who said, "Your daughter is dead. Why trouble the Teacher any further?"

³⁶As soon as Jesus heard the word that was spoken, He said to the ruler of the synagogue, "Do not be afraid; only believe." ³⁷And He permitted no one to follow Him except Peter, James, and John the brother of James. ³⁸Then He came to the house of the ruler of the synagogue, and saw a tumult and those who wept and wailed loudly. ³⁹When He came in, He said to them, "Why make this commotion and weep? The child is not dead, but sleeping."

⁴⁰And they ridiculed Him. But when He had put them all outside, He took the father and the mother of the child, and those *who were* with Him, and entered where the child was lying. ⁴¹Then He took the child by the hand, and said to her, "Talitha, cumi," which is translated, "Little girl, I say to you, arise." ⁴²Immediately the girl arose and walked, for she was twelve years *of age.* And they were overcome with great amazement. ⁴³But He commanded

---

ARTS AND LITERATURE

Aramaic is a Semitic language, closely related to Arabic and Hebrew. It was widely used in Syria by 1000 B.C. In the 6th century B.C. the Persians made it the language of diplomacy and official business, and from that time it was common all over the Near East. Aramaic is found in the Dead Sea Scrolls and was the language spoken by Jesus, as represented by the Aramaic phrase, "Talitha, cumi" (Mark 5:41).

SCANDALOUS FAITH (Luke 8:43, 44)

The rationale behind some of Israel's laws is not always clear to us. So it is with legislation governing the uncleanness of bloody discharges from the body. According to the Law of Moses (Lev. 15:25–28), a flow of blood rendered a woman ceremonially unclean, and communicated uncleanness to anyone she touched. The woman Jesus encountered (Luke 8:43, 44) had experienced a continual flow of blood (not simply a monthly discharge) that most likely forced her to remain single. If the problem started after her marriage, it probably led her husband to divorce her. In her case, ceremonial uncleanness made her an outcast of her society.

Since she had had the problem for 12 years, much of her life had been consumed by this illness. Because many people died in their forties, her problem probably began some time after puberty; she may have felt like half her adult life was already lost. Furthermore, in a culture where women remained economically dependent on men, this woman's disease had exhausted "her livelihood" (8:43). She was desperate—so desperate that she would allow *nothing* to deter her from Jesus.

Anyone this woman touched would be rendered unclean, so it was scandalous for her to press her way to Jesus through the crowd. Even touching Jesus' garment would make Him unclean. If she was going to touch Him, she must do so without announcing her intentions (see Lev. 15:26, 27).

Once the woman was healed, Jesus was unashamed to be identified publicly with her hardship (Luke 8:46). His greater concern was that she, as well as those looking on, should realize that her "faith" (8:48) was the source of the healing. Jesus' power, unlike that of some other proclaimed wonder-workers of His day, was not simply "magic."

them strictly that no one should know it, and said that *something* should be given her to eat.

Luke 8:40–56
Healing a Hemorrhage and Restoring Life

8 **:40** So it was, when Jesus returned, that the multitude welcomed Him, for they were all waiting for Him. [41]And behold, there came a man named Jairus, and he was a ruler of the synagogue. And he fell down at Jesus' feet and begged Him to come to his house, [42]for he had an only daughter about twelve years of age, and she was dying.

But as He went, the multitudes thronged Him. [43]Now a woman, having a flow of blood for twelve years, who had spent all her livelihood on physicians and could not be healed by any, [44]came from behind and touched the border of His garment. And immediately her flow of blood stopped.

[45]And Jesus said, "Who touched Me?"

When all denied it, Peter and those with him[a] said, "Master, the multitudes throng and press You, and You say, 'Who touched Me?' "[b] [46]But Jesus said, "Somebody touched Me, for I perceived power going out from Me." [47]Now when the woman saw that she was not hidden, she came trembling; and falling down before Him, she declared to Him in the presence of all the people the reason she had touched Him and how she was healed immediately.

[48]And He said to her, "Daughter, be of

8:45 [a]NU-Text omits *and those with him.* [b]NU-Text omits *and You say, 'Who touched Me?'*

TIME CAPSULE *A.D. 26 to 27*

26 *John the Baptist begins to preach (Matt. 3:1)*

26 *Annas is named along with Caiaphas as co-high priests (Luke 3:2)*

27 *John baptizes Jesus (Matt. 3:13)*

27 *Jesus changes water into wine (John 2:7–9)*

27 *Rebuilding of the temple still in progress after 46 years (John 2:20)*

good cheer;[a] your faith has made you well. Go in peace."

⁴⁹While He was still speaking, someone came from the ruler of the synagogue's *house,* saying to him, "Your daughter is dead. Do not trouble the Teacher."[a]

⁵⁰But when Jesus heard *it,* He answered him, saying, "Do not be afraid; only believe, and she will be made well." ⁵¹When He came into the house, He permitted no one to go in[a] except Peter, James, and John,[b] and the father and mother of the girl. ⁵²Now all wept and mourned for her; but He said, "Do not weep; she is not dead, but sleeping." ⁵³And they ridiculed Him, knowing that she was dead.

⁵⁴But He put them all outside,[a] took her by the hand and called, saying, "Little girl, arise." ⁵⁵Then her spirit returned, and she arose immediately. And He commanded that she be given *something* to eat. ⁵⁶And her parents were astonished, but He charged them to tell no one what had happened.

Rejection at Nazareth

Even at the midpoint of His Galilean ministry, Jesus continued to be met with resistance and unbelief in His hometown of Nazareth (see Luke 4:16–30). Mark once again closely connects Jesus' miracles and His teachings: the people wondered "what wisdom" Jesus possessed to be able to perform "such mighty works" (Mark 6:2; see "Teaching with Authority" at Mark 1:21).

Matthew characteristically maintains more of a distinction between teaching and miracles, speaking of them individually: "this wisdom and these mighty works" (Matt. 13:54). Being attracted to Jesus' miraculous works is not sufficient to make one a true disciple of His. Faith, for Matthew, is crucial, and the limited miracles performed in Nazareth are directly attributed to the people's "unbelief" (Matt. 13:58; see "Returning to the West Shore" at Matt. 9:18).

- Matthew 13:53–58
- Mark 6:1–6

Matthew 13:53–58
Jesus Rejected

13 :53 Now it came to pass, when Jesus had finished these parables, that He departed from there. ⁵⁴When He had come to His own country, He taught them in their synagogue, so that they were aston-

ished and said, "Where did this *Man* get this wisdom and *these* mighty works? ⁵⁵Is this not the carpenter's son? Is not His mother called Mary? And His brothers James, Joses,[a] Simon, and Judas? ⁵⁶And His sisters, are they not all with us? Where then did this *Man* get all these things?" ⁵⁷So they were offended at Him.

But Jesus said to them, "A prophet is not without honor except in his own country and in his own house." ⁵⁸Now He did not do many mighty works there because of their unbelief.

Mark 6:1–6
Without Honor in His Own Country

6 :1 Then He went out from there and came to His own country, and His disciples followed Him. ²And when the Sabbath had come, He began to teach in the synagogue. And many hearing *Him* were astonished, saying, "Where *did* this Man *get* these things? And what wisdom *is* this which is given to Him, that such mighty works are performed by His hands! ³Is this not the carpenter, the Son of Mary, and brother of James, Joses, Judas, and Simon? And are not His sisters here with us?" So they were offended at Him.

⁴But Jesus said to them, "A prophet is not without honor except in his own country, among his own relatives, and in his own house." ⁵Now He could do no mighty work there, except that He laid His hands on a few sick people and healed *them.* ⁶And He marveled because of their unbelief. Then He went about the villages in a circuit, teaching.

8:48 [a]NU-Text omits *be of good cheer.* 8:49 [a]NU-Text adds *anymore.*   8:51 [a]NU-Text adds *with Him.* [b]NU-Text and M-Text read *Peter, John, and James.*   8:54 [a]NU-Text omits *put them all outside.* **Matt.** 13:55 [a]NU-Text reads *Joseph.*

Jesus' Second Visit to Jerusalem

According to John's Gospel, Jesus returned to Jerusalem to attend a pilgrimage feast (see "The Galilean Ministry" at John 1:35). During this visit, He healed a lame man at the Pool of Bethesda. When, at Jesus' instruction, the man carried his bed away from the pool, he came into violation of the Sabbath prohibition against work (John 5:8–10). Jesus defended His healing works by associating them with those of His "Father," but the opposition from the Jewish religious authorities only continued to mount. Not only had Jesus broken the Sabbath, but now He had also "said that God was His Father, making Himself equal with God" (5:17, 18). John records Jesus' extended defense of His special relationship with the Father and of the witnesses that testified to that relationship.

It is impossible to identify the "feast of the Jews" (5:1), which forms the setting for this healing account. It could have been Pentecost. John explicitly identified Passover as the occasion for Jesus' previous pilgrimage (John 2:13, 23), and Pentecost is the next feast after the combined festival of Passover and Unleavened Bread. Furthermore, the Feast of Pentecost was traditionally associated with the giving of the law to Moses at Mount Sinai. Thus Jesus' allusions to the writings of Moses (5:39, 45–47) were possibly prompted by the occasion of Pentecost.

Jesus' first Jerusalem pilgrimage might be dated to the spring Passover celebration of A.D. 27 (see "Jesus' First Visit to Jerusalem" at John 2:13). This second pilgrimage could represent the Pentecost occurring only several weeks later, or be understood as Pentecost of the following year, early summer of A.D. 28. On the other hand, it could have been Passover of spring, A.D. 28, or the Feast of Tabernacles in fall, A.D. 28.

▼   ■ John 5:1–47

John
A Man Healed at the Pool of Bethesda

5 :1 After this there was a feast of the Jews, and Jesus went up to Jerusalem. [2]Now there is in Jerusalem by the Sheep *Gate* a pool, which is called in Hebrew, Bethesda,[a] having five porches. [3]In these lay a great multitude of sick people, blind, lame, paralyzed, waiting for the moving of the water. [4]For an angel went down at a certain time into the pool and stirred up the water; then whoever stepped in first, after the stirring of the water, was made well of whatever disease he had.[a] [5]Now a certain man was there who had an infirmity thirty-eight years. [6]When Jesus saw him lying there, and knew that he already

had been *in that condition* a long time, He said to him, "Do you want to be made well?"

[7]The sick man answered Him, "Sir, I have no man to put me into the pool when the water is stirred up; but while I am coming, another steps down before me."

[8]Jesus said to him, "Rise, take up your bed and walk." [9]And immediately the man was made well, took up his bed, and walked.

And that day was the Sabbath. [10]The Jews therefore said to him who was cured, "It is the Sabbath; it is not lawful for you to carry your bed."

[11]He answered them, "He who made me well said to me, 'Take up your bed and walk.'"

[12]Then they asked him, "Who is the Man who said to you, 'Take up your bed and walk'?" [13]But the one who was healed did not know who it was, for Jesus had withdrawn, a multitude being in *that* place. [14]Afterward Jesus found him in the temple, and said to him, "See, you have been made well. Sin no more, lest a worse thing come upon you."

[15]The man departed and told the Jews that it was Jesus who had made him well.

Honor the Father and the Son

[16]For this reason the Jews persecuted Jesus, and sought to kill Him,[a] because He had done these things on the Sabbath. [17]But Jesus answered them, "My Father has been working until now, and I have been working."

[18]Therefore the Jews sought all the more to kill Him, because He not only broke the Sabbath, but also said that God was His Father, making Himself equal with God. [19]Then Jesus answered and said to them, "Most assuredly, I say to you, the Son can do nothing of Himself, but what He sees the Father do; for whatever He does, the Son also does in like manner. [20]For the Father loves the Son, and shows Him all things that He Himself does; and He will show Him greater works than these, that you may marvel. [21]For as the Father raises the dead and gives life to *them,* even so the Son gives life to whom He will. [22]For the Father judges no one, but has committed all judgment to the Son, [23]that all should honor the Son just as they honor the Father. He who does not honor the Son does not honor the Father who sent Him.

5:2 [a]NU-Text reads *Bethzatha.*   5:4 [a]NU-Text omits *waiting for the moving of the water* at the end of verse 3, and all of verse 4.   5:16 [a]NU-Text omits *and sought to kill Him.*

THE POOL OF BETHESDA (John 5:2)

John's Gospel mentions a pool that was known in Hebrew as "Bethesda" or, as listed in some manuscripts, "Bethzatha" (John 5:2). The exact site of the pool has not been determined, although one of the Dead Sea Scrolls indicates that people who visited Jerusalem in Jesus' day knew where it was.

The "five porches" of Bethesda (5:2) have led to comparisons with the porticoes, or porches, of the ancient twin pools archaeologists found under St. Anne's monastery in Jerusalem. Porches ran along all four sides of the pools, plus one through the center, dividing them. In the vicinity of the pools archaeologists discovered a votive offering that looks just like what pagans offered to gods at healing sanctuaries. If Bethesda is the same site as these twin pools, it continued to be used for healing long after Jesus' day.

Regardless of whether the twin pools represent the actual site of the Pool of Bethesda, the lame man's hope in the pool resembles the practices of surrounding cultures. Many people in antiquity went to healing sanctuaries, which often included a pool, to seek healing from gods like Asclepius or Apollo. Likewise, the lame man was probably hoping for an angel to heal him. The statement about the angel stirring the waters (John 5:3b, 4) is missing in many early Greek manuscripts of John's Gospel, but may reflect an early tradition or local customs related to the pool.

The man was no doubt weak and hopeless after 38 years of confinement and affliction (John 5:5). Jesus, unlike the water of the pool, offered him real healing.

Life and Judgment Are Through the Son

24"Most assuredly, I say to you, he who hears My word and believes in Him who sent Me has everlasting life, and shall not come into judgment, but has passed from death into life. 25Most assuredly, I say to you, the hour is coming, and now is, when the dead will hear the voice of the Son of God; and those who hear will live. 26For as the Father has life in Himself, so He has granted the Son to have life in Himself, 27and has given Him authority to execute judgment also, because He is the Son of Man. 28Do not marvel at this; for the hour is coming in which all who are in the graves will hear His voice 29and come forth—those who have done good, to the resurrection of life, and those who have done evil, to the resurrection of condemnation. 30I can of Myself do nothing. As I hear, I judge; and My judgment is righteous, because I do not seek My own will but the will of the Father who sent Me.

The Fourfold Witness

31"If I bear witness of Myself, My witness is not true. 32There is another who bears witness of Me, and I know that the witness which He witnesses of Me is true. 33You have sent to John, and he has borne witness to the truth. 34Yet I do not receive testimony from man, but I say these things that you may be saved. 35He was the burning and shining lamp, and you were willing for a time to rejoice in his light. 36But I have a greater witness than John's; for the works which the Father has given Me to finish—the very works that I do—bear witness of Me, that the Father has sent Me. 37And the Father Himself, who sent Me, has testified of Me. You have neither heard His voice at any time, nor seen His form. 38But you do not have His word abiding in you, because whom He sent, Him you do

TIME CAPSULE   A.D. 27 to 29

27   Jesus attends the spring Passover in Jerusalem (John 2:13)

28   The 15th year of Tiberius (based on his sole reign)

28   Jesus attends a feast (Passover?) in Jerusalem (John 5:1)

29   Herod Antipas orders the death of John the Baptist (Mark 6:27)

29   Pontius Pilate strikes coins in Jerusalem and Caesarea

not believe. ³⁹You search the Scriptures, for in them you think you have eternal life; and these are they which testify of Me. ⁴⁰But you are not willing to come to Me that you may have life.

⁴¹"I do not receive honor from men. ⁴²But I know you, that you do not have the love of God in you. ⁴³I have come in My Father's name, and you do not receive Me; if another comes in his own name, him you will receive. ⁴⁴How can you believe, who receive honor from one another, and do not seek the honor that *comes* from the only God? ⁴⁵Do not think that I shall accuse you to the Father; there is *one* who accuses you—Moses, in whom you trust. ⁴⁶For if you believed Moses, you would believe Me; for he wrote about Me. ⁴⁷But if you do not believe his writings, how will you believe My words?"

9:35 ᵃNU-Text omits *among the people.*
9:36 ᵃNU-Text and M-Text read *harassed.*
10:3 ᵃNU-Text omits *Lebbaeus, whose surname was.*   10:4 ᵃNU-Text reads *Cananaean.*
10:8 ᵃNU-Text reads *raise the dead, cleanse the lepers;* M-Text omits *raise the dead.*

Mission of the Twelve

Mark and Luke treat the mission of the twelve disciples during Jesus' Galilean ministry in summary fashion. Matthew, on the other hand, was especially interested in the mission of the church (see Matt. 28:18–20) and so devotes considerable attention to Jesus' instructions to His disciples regarding their mission.

Jesus' instruction on mission is the second of Matthew's five major teaching sections (see "Sermon on the Mount or Plain" at Matt. 5:1). Matthew presents the disciples' mission as an extension of Jesus' own continuing ministry. Jesus' compassion for people and His prayer that God would "send out laborers" (9:35–38) introduces the episode. During the disciples' mission Jesus actively continued His own ministry (11:1). Whereas Mark and Luke listed the names of the twelve apostles much earlier in their accounts of Jesus' ministry (Mark 3:13–19; Luke 6:13–16), Matthew reserves the listing until this occasion (Matt. 10:2–4).

■ Matthew 9:35—11:1
■ Mark 6:7–13
■ Luke 9:1–6

Matthew 9:35—11:1
The Compassion of Jesus

9 **:35** Then Jesus went about all the cities and villages, teaching in their synagogues, preaching the gospel of the kingdom, and healing every sickness and every disease among the people.ᵃ ³⁶But when He saw the multitudes, He was moved with compassion for them, because they were wearyᵃ and scattered, like sheep having no shepherd. ³⁷Then He said to His disciples, "The harvest truly *is* plentiful, but the laborers *are* few. ³⁸Therefore pray the Lord of the harvest to send out laborers into His harvest."

The Twelve Apostles

10 ¹And when He had called His twelve disciples to *Him,* He gave them power *over* unclean spirits, to cast them out, and to heal all kinds of sickness and all kinds of disease. ²Now the names of the twelve apostles are these: first, Simon, who is called Peter, and Andrew his brother; James the *son* of Zebedee, and John his brother; ³Philip and Bartholomew; Thomas and Matthew the tax collector; James the *son* of Alphaeus, and Lebbaeus, whose surname wasᵃ Thaddaeus; ⁴Simon the Cananite,ᵃ and Judas Iscariot, who also betrayed Him.

Sending Out the Twelve

⁵These twelve Jesus sent out and commanded them, saying: "Do not go into the way of the Gentiles, and do not enter a city of the Samaritans. ⁶But go rather to the lost sheep of the house of Israel. ⁷And as you go, preach, saying, 'The kingdom of heaven is at hand.' ⁸Heal the sick, cleanse the lepers, raise the dead,ᵃ cast out demons. Freely you have received, freely give. ⁹Provide neither gold nor silver nor copper in your money belts, ¹⁰nor bag for *your* journey, nor two tunics, nor sandals, nor staffs; for a worker is worthy of his food.

¹¹"Now whatever city or town you enter, inquire who in it is worthy, and stay there till you go out. ¹²And when you go into a household, greet it. ¹³If the household is worthy, let your peace come upon it. But if it is not worthy, let your peace return to you. ¹⁴And whoever will not receive you nor hear your words, when you depart from that house or city, shake off the dust from your feet. ¹⁵Assuredly, I say to you, it

will be more tolerable for the land of Sodom and Gomorrah in the day of judgment than for that city!

Persecutions Are Coming

16"Behold, I send you out as sheep in the midst of wolves. Therefore be wise as serpents and harmless as doves. 17But beware of men, for they will deliver you up to councils and scourge you in their synagogues. 18You will be brought before governors and kings for My sake, as a testimony to them and to the Gentiles. 19But when they deliver you up, do not worry about how or what you should speak. For it will be given to you in that hour what you should speak; 20for it is not you who speak, but the Spirit of your Father who speaks in you.

21"Now brother will deliver up brother to death, and a father *his* child; and children will rise up against parents and cause them to be put to death. 22And you will be hated by all for My name's sake. But he who endures to the end will be saved. 23When they persecute you in this city, flee to another. For assuredly, I say to you, you will not have gone through the cities of Israel before the Son of Man comes.

24"A disciple is not above *his* teacher, nor a servant above his master. 25It is enough for a disciple that he be like his teacher, and a servant like his master. If they have called the master of the house Beelzebub,ᵃ how much more *will they call* those of his household! 26Therefore do not fear them. For there is nothing covered that will not be revealed, and hidden that will not be known.

Jesus Teaches the Fear of God

27"Whatever I tell you in the dark, speak in the light; and what you hear in the ear, preach on the housetops. 28And do not fear those who kill the body but cannot kill the soul. But rather fear Him who is able to destroy both soul and body in hell. 29Are not two sparrows sold for a copper coin? And not one of them falls to the ground apart from your Father's will. 30But the very hairs of your head are all numbered. 31Do not fear therefore; you are of more value than many sparrows.

Confess Christ Before Men

32"Therefore whoever confesses Me before men, him I will also confess before My Father who is in heaven. 33But whoever denies Me before men, him I will also deny before My Father who is in heaven.

Christ Brings Division

34"Do not think that I came to bring peace on earth. I did not come to bring peace but a sword. 35For I have come to *set a man against his father, a daughter against her mother, and a daughter-in-law against her mother-in-law*; 36and *'a man's enemies will be those of his own household.'*ᵃ 37He who loves father or mother more than Me is not worthy of Me. And he who loves son or daughter more than Me is not worthy of Me. 38And he who does not take his cross and follow after Me is not worthy of Me. 39He who finds his life will lose it, and he who loses his life for My sake will find it.

A Cup of Cold Water

40"He who receives you receives Me, and he who receives Me receives Him who sent Me. 41He who receives a prophet in the name of a prophet shall receive a prophet's reward. And he who receives a righteous man in the name of a righteous man shall receive a righteous man's reward. 42And whoever gives one of these little ones only a cup of cold *water* in the name of a disciple, assuredly, I say to you, he shall by no means lose his reward."

11 ¹Now it came to pass, when Jesus finished commanding His twelve disciples, that He departed from there to teach and to preach in their cities.

10:25 ᵃNU-Text and M-Text read *Beelzebul.*
10:36 ᵃMicah 7:6

GEOGRAPHY AND ENVIRONMENT

The Samaritans (Matt. 10:5) lived in the area immediately to the north of Jerusalem and Judea. They called themselves Israelites, claiming that their ancestors survived the fall of Israel to Assyria in 722 B.C. But Judeans thought Samaritans were descended from colonists brought to Samaria by the Assyrians. Samaritan worshipers followed the five books of Moses, and established a temple of their own on Mount Gerizim.

Mark 6:7–13
Sending Out the Twelve

6 :7 And He called the twelve to *Himself,* and began to send them out two *by* two, and gave them power over unclean spirits. 8He commanded them to take nothing for the journey except a staff—no bag, no bread, no copper in *their* money belts— 9but to wear sandals, and not to put on two tunics.

10Also He said to them, "In whatever place you enter a house, stay there till you depart from that place. 11And whoevera will not receive you nor hear you, when you depart from there, shake off the dust under your feet as a testimony against them.b Assuredly, I say to you, it will be more tolerable for Sodom and Gomorrah in the day of judgment than for that city!"

12So they went out and preached that *people* should repent. 13And they cast out many demons, and anointed with oil many who were sick, and healed *them.*

Luke 9:1–6
Mission of the Twelve

9 :1 Then He called His twelve disciples together and gave them power and authority over all demons, and to cure diseases. 2He sent them to preach the kingdom of God and to heal the sick. 3And He said to them, "Take nothing for the journey, neither staffs nor bag nor bread nor money; and do not have two tunics apiece.

4"Whatever house you enter, stay there, and from there depart. 5And whoever will not receive you, when you go out of that city, shake off the very dust from your feet as a testimony against them."

6So they departed and went through the towns, preaching the gospel and healing everywhere.

6:11 aNU-Text reads *whatever place.* bNU-Text omits the rest of this verse.

Death of John the Baptist

The Jewish historian Josephus wrote in his *Antiquities of the Jews* that John the Baptist was imprisoned and executed by Herod Antipas. Antipas, who ruled as tetrarch of Galilee and Perea (4 B.C.–A.D. 39), apparently perceived the Baptist to be a threat to lead an insurrection.

The Gospel of Mark provides the most extensive and detailed account of the circumstances surrounding the death of the Baptist. But even all Mark's detail did not prevent later writers from embellishing the story with legendary elements. The New Testament does not mention either the name of "Herodias' daughter" (Mark 6:22) or her "seven veils." The traditional name "Salome" probably comes from Josephus, who wrote that Herod Philip was married to a daughter of Herodias by that name.

Both Matthew and Mark recount the Baptist's imprisonment and execution by Herod as a kind of literary flashback. There was a superstitious belief that Jesus was actually the resurrected John the Baptist, and even Herod himself was inclined toward this superstition (Matt. 14:1, 2; Mark 6:14).

Luke's treatment differs considerably. John's imprisonment is reported before beginning the account of Jesus' public ministry (Luke 3:19, 20). Maybe Luke wished to avoid the insinuation that Jesus and the Baptist were engaged in rival ministries. Only Luke connects the superstition that Jesus was a resurrected prophet with the reason Herod was curious about Jesus and desired "to see Him" (Luke 9:9). Herod's curiosity prepares the way literarily for Jesus' "trial" before Herod, which only Luke reports (Luke 23:6–12).

- Matthew 14:1–12
- Mark 6:14–29
- Luke 3:19, 20
- Luke 9:7–9

Matthew 14:1–12
John the Baptist Beheaded

14 :1 At that time Herod the tetrarch heard the report about Jesus 2and said to his servants, "This is John the Baptist; he is risen from the dead, and therefore these powers are at work in him." 3For Herod had laid hold of John and bound him, and put *him* in prison for the sake of Herodias, his brother Philip's wife. 4Because John had said to him, "It is not lawful for you to have her." 5And although he wanted to put him to death, he feared the multitude, because they counted him as a prophet.

6But when Herod's birthday was celebrated, the daughter of Herodias danced before them and pleased Herod. 7Therefore he promised with an oath to give her whatever she might ask.

8So she, having been prompted by her

HEROD AND JUDEA UNDER ROME'S AUGUSTUS

In early 30 B.C. Herod the Great met with Octavian and bargained to keep his life and throne. From that time on, Herod remained a client of Rome. After his death, Herod's sons squandered the favor with Rome that Herod had enjoyed.

Year	Event
31 B.C.	Octavian, great-nephew of Julius Caesar, defeats his rivals in the battle of Actium
27 B.C.	Octavian becomes "Caesar Augustus"
19 B.C.	In Jerusalem, Herod the Great begins construction of the temple
18 B.C.	Herod the Great visits Rome
12 B.C.	Augustus is named "high priest" of Rome and worshiped in the provinces
10 B.C.	Herod names a city "Caesarea" in honor of Augustus Caesar
4 B.C.	Herod the Great dies and his kingdom is divided into three parts for his sons Archelaus, Antipas, and Philip
2 B.C.	Augustus is named "father of his country"
A.D. 6	Archelaus is deposed and Judea becomes a Roman province
A.D. 14	Augustus dies and the Senate makes him one of the gods of Rome
A.D. 28	Herod Antipas beheads John the Baptist (Matt. 14:1–11)
A.D. 39	Antipas is deposed by the emperor Caligula

mother, said, "Give me John the Baptist's head here on a platter."

⁹And the king was sorry; nevertheless, because of the oaths and because of those who sat with him, he commanded *it* to be given to *her.* ¹⁰So he sent and had John beheaded in prison. ¹¹And his head was brought on a platter and given to the girl, and she brought *it* to her mother. ¹²Then his disciples came and took away the body and buried it, and went and told Jesus.

Mark 6:14–29
Herodias Requests John's Death

6 :14 Now King Herod heard *of Him,* for His name had become well known. And he said, "John the Baptist is risen from the dead, and therefore these powers are at work in him."

¹⁵Others said, "It is Elijah."

And others said, "It is the Prophet, or[a] like one of the prophets."

¹⁶But when Herod heard, he said, "This is John, whom I beheaded; he has been raised from the dead!" ¹⁷For Herod himself had sent and laid hold of John, and bound him in prison for the sake of Herodias, his brother Philip's wife; for he had married her. ¹⁸Because John had said to

Herod, "It is not lawful for you to have your brother's wife."

¹⁹Therefore Herodias held it against him and wanted to kill him, but she could not; ²⁰for Herod feared John, knowing that he *was* a just and holy man, and he protected him. And when he heard him, he did many things, and heard him gladly.

²¹Then an opportune day came when Herod on his birthday gave a feast for his nobles, the high officers, and the chief *men* of Galilee. ²²And when Herodias' daughter herself came in and danced, and pleased Herod and those who sat with him, the king said to the girl, "Ask me whatever you want, and I will give *it* to you." ²³He also swore to her, "Whatever you ask me, I will give you, up to half my kingdom."

²⁴So she went out and said to her mother, "What shall I ask?"

And she said, "The head of John the Baptist!"

²⁵Immediately she came in with haste to the king and asked, saying, "I want you to give me at once the head of John the Baptist on a platter."

²⁶And the king was exceedingly sorry;

6:15 ᵃNU-Text and M-Text omit *or.*

IMMORALITY AND HEROD'S POLITICS (Mark 6:17)

Herod Antipas was the tetrarch of Galilee and Perea (4 B.C.–A.D. 39). Reports of Jesus' works made Herod's guilty conscience remember his crime against John the Baptist (Mark 6:14). John had boldly denounced Herod's immorality in marrying his brother's wife (6:18). The law prohibited adultery and incest; sleeping with one's brother's wife was considered incestuous as well as adulterous (Lev. 18:16). But given his political problems in 1st-century Galilee, Antipas may have viewed John's moral criticisms as a political threat that could stir unrest.

While Antipas was planning to marry his brother's wife, his first wife realized that he was also planning to divorce her. She fled home to her father, Aretas IV, ruler of the Nabatean Arabs, reporting Antipas's intentions, and Aretas was enraged that Antipas would treat his daughter so lightly. This created friction between the two kingdoms, and some Nabateans living in Antipas's territory of Perea made his father-in-law's enmity even more delicate. Aretas invaded Antipas's kingdom in A.D. 36 (sometime after Herod had executed John), and would have destroyed it had not the Romans intervened. Many Galileans felt this defeat was God's judgment on Antipas for executing the Baptist.

This political embarrassment was not the last problem Antipas's liaison with Herodias caused him. When in A.D. 37 her brother Agrippa I was appointed "king" of Gaulanitis, Herodias persuaded her husband Herod Antipas to request the same title. So enraged was the emperor at Antipas for making such a request, however, that he banished him to Gaul in A.D. 39, and Herodias went off into exile with him. The Gospel of Mark ironically refers to Antipas as "King Herod" (Mark 6:14), even though he was technically only a "tetrarch" (Matt. 14:1). Possibly under Herodias's influence Antipas thought himself a king.

---

yet, because of the oaths and because of those who sat with him, he did not want to refuse her. ²⁷Immediately the king sent an executioner and commanded his head to be brought. And he went and beheaded him in prison, ²⁸brought his head on a platter, and gave it to the girl; and the girl gave it to her mother. ²⁹When his disciples heard *of it,* they came and took away his corpse and laid it in a tomb.

Luke 3:19, 20

3 :19 But Herod the tetrarch, being rebuked by him concerning Herodias, his brother Philip's wife,ᵃ and for all the evils which Herod had done, ²⁰also added this, above all, that he shut John up in prison.

Luke 9:7–9
Herod Seeks to See Jesus

9 :7 Now Herod the tetrarch heard of all that was done by Him; and he was perplexed, because it was said by some that John had risen from the dead, ⁸and by some that Elijah had appeared, and by others that one of the old prophets had risen

again. ⁹Herod said, "John I have beheaded, but who is this of whom I hear such things?" So he sought to see Him.

Feeding the 5,000

The feeding of 5,000 people is the only event from Jesus' ministry preceding His last week in Jerusalem that is reported in all four New Testament Gospels. All the accounts agree upon the basic matters: the number fed totaled 5,000; the available food was "five loaves and two fish"; the quantity of leftovers was "twelve baskets full." Only Matthew explicitly notes that the number 5,000 did not include "women and children" (Matt. 14:21).

The miraculous supply of bread in "a deserted place" (Matt. 14:15) calls to mind Moses' provision of manna during the Exodus (Ex. 16). According to John's Gospel, the miracle convinced some that Jesus was in fact the long-expected "Prophet" like Moses (John 6:14; see Deut. 18:15).

John's Gospel places this miracle just before a Passover (John 6:4), the second of three Passovers mentioned in the Fourth Gospel. The first (John 2:13, 23) was possibly in A.D. 27 (see "Jesus' First Visit to Jerusalem"

3:19 ᵃNU-Text reads *his brother's wife.*

at John 2:13). Thus, this feeding story should be dated to the spring of either A.D. 28 or 29. If the undesignated "feast of the Jews" in John 5:1 is Pentecost or Tabernacles, the 5,000 feeding could have occurred in A.D. 28. If the "feast" of John 5:1 is Passover, then the 5,000 were fed in A.D. 29 (see "Jesus' Second Visit to Jerusalem" at John 5:1). The third Passover mentioned by John was the occasion of Jesus' death (John 13:1), usually dated to A.D. 30.

- Matthew 14:13–21
- Mark 6:30–44
- Luke 9:10–17
- John 6:1–15

Matthew 14:13–21

14 **:13** When Jesus heard *it,* He departed from there by boat to a deserted place by Himself. But when the multitudes heard it, they followed Him on foot from the cities. ¹⁴And when Jesus went out He saw a great multitude; and He was moved with compassion for them, and healed their sick. ¹⁵When it was evening, His disciples came to Him, saying, "This is a deserted place, and the hour is already late. Send the multitudes away, that they may go into the villages and buy themselves food."

¹⁶But Jesus said to them, "They do not need to go away. You give them something to eat."

¹⁷And they said to Him, "We have here only five loaves and two fish."

¹⁸He said, "Bring them here to Me." ¹⁹Then He commanded the multitudes to sit down on the grass. And He took the five loaves and the two fish, and looking up to heaven, He blessed and broke and gave the loaves to the disciples; and the disciples gave to the multitudes. ²⁰So they all ate and were filled, and they took up twelve baskets full of the fragments that remained. ²¹Now those who had eaten were about five thousand men, besides women and children.

Mark 6:30–44

6 **:30** Then the apostles gathered to Jesus and told Him all things, both what they had done and what they had taught. ³¹And He said to them, "Come aside by yourselves to a deserted place and rest a while." For there were many coming and going, and they did not even have time to eat. ³²So they departed to a deserted place in the boat by themselves.

³³But the multitudes[a] saw them departing, and many knew Him and ran there on foot from all the cities. They arrived before them and came together to Him. ³⁴And Jesus, when He came out, saw a great multitude and was moved with compassion for them, because they were like sheep not having a shepherd. So He began to teach them many things. ³⁵When the day was now far spent, His disciples came to Him and said, "This is a deserted place, and already the hour *is* late. ³⁶Send them away, that they may go into the surrounding country and villages and buy themselves bread;[a] for they have nothing to eat."

³⁷But He answered and said to them, "You give them something to eat."

And they said to Him, "Shall we go and buy two hundred denarii worth of bread and give them *something* to eat?"

³⁸But He said to them, "How many loaves do you have? Go and see."

And when they found out they said, "Five, and two fish."

³⁹Then He commanded them to make them all sit down in groups on the green grass. ⁴⁰So they sat down in ranks, in hundreds and in fifties. ⁴¹And when He had taken the five loaves and the two fish, He looked up to heaven, blessed and broke the loaves, and gave *them* to His disciples to set before them; and the two fish He divided among *them* all. ⁴²So they all ate and

---

6:33 ᵃNU-Text and M-Text read *they.*
6:36 ᵃNU-Text reads *something to eat* and omits the rest of this verse.

BELIEFS AND IDEAS

The ancients considered remote or deserted places distasteful and threatening. The positive values of community, civilization, and safety from animals or outlaws were found in towns and cities, not in the wilderness. People had to have a certain level of motivation before they would follow Jesus or John the Baptist to the desert (Matt. 14:13).

were filled. ⁴³And they took up twelve baskets full of fragments and of the fish. ⁴⁴Now those who had eaten the loaves were aboutᵃ five thousand men.

Luke 9:10–17

9 **:10** And the apostles, when they had returned, told Him all that they had done. Then He took them and went aside privately into a deserted place belonging to the city called Bethsaida. ¹¹But when the multitudes knew *it,* they followed Him; and He received them and spoke to them about the kingdom of God, and healed those who had need of healing. ¹²When the day began to wear away, the twelve came and said to Him, "Send the multitude away, that they may go into the surrounding towns and country, and lodge and get provisions; for we are in a deserted place here."

¹³But He said to them, "You give them something to eat."

And they said, "We have no more than five loaves and two fish, unless we go and buy food for all these people." ¹⁴For there were about five thousand men.

Then He said to His disciples, "Make them sit down in groups of fifty." ¹⁵And they did so, and made them all sit down.

¹⁶Then He took the five loaves and the two fish, and looking up to heaven, He blessed and broke *them,* and gave *them* to the disciples to set before the multitude. ¹⁷So they all ate and were filled, and twelve baskets of the leftover fragments were taken up by them.

John 6:1–15

6 **:1** After these things Jesus went over the Sea of Galilee, which is *the Sea* of Tiberias. ²Then a great multitude followed Him, because they saw His signs which He performed on those who were diseased. ³And Jesus went up on the mountain, and there He sat with His disciples.

⁴Now the Passover, a feast of the Jews, was near. ⁵Then Jesus lifted up *His* eyes, and seeing a great multitude coming toward Him, He said to Philip, "Where shall we buy bread, that these may eat?" ⁶But this He said to test him, for He Himself knew what He would do.

⁷Philip answered Him, "Two hundred denarii worth of bread is not sufficient for them, that every one of them may have a little."

⁸One of His disciples, Andrew, Simon Peter's brother, said to Him, ⁹"There is a lad here who has five barley loaves and two small fish, but what are they among so many?"

¹⁰Then Jesus said, "Make the people sit down." Now there was much grass in the place. So the men sat down, in number about five thousand. ¹¹And Jesus took the loaves, and when He had given thanks He distributed *them* to the disciples, and the disciplesᵃ to those sitting down; and likewise of the fish, as much as they wanted. ¹²So when they were filled, He said to His disciples, "Gather up the fragments that remain, so that nothing is lost." ¹³Therefore they gathered *them* up, and filled twelve baskets with the fragments of the five barley loaves which were left over by those who had eaten. ¹⁴Then those men, when they had seen the sign that Jesus did, said, "This is truly the Prophet who is to come into the world."

¹⁵Therefore when Jesus perceived that they were about to come and take Him by force to make Him king, He departed again to the mountain by Himself alone.

Walking on the Water

Each evangelist closely ties Jesus' walking on water with the preceding story of feeding the 5,000. For Mark, the inability of the disciples to understand that earlier miracle affected their understanding of who Jesus truly was in this instance as well (Mark 6:52; see John 6:26, 27). Some think that Jesus' walking on water is parallel to Old Testament theophanies or visionary appearances in which God strides across the waters as a symbol of control over evil and chaos (see Ps. 77:19; 107:23–29; Job 9:8).

While in Mark, the disciples lacked understanding, Matthew stresses that the miracle of walking on water confirmed their belief that Jesus was "the Son of God" (Matt. 14:33). Only Matthew reports Peter's walking on the sea, and his subsequent sinking illustrates the weakness of faith that is diminished by doubt (14:31). Faith must remain focused upon Jesus and not have its attention divided by harsh circumstances (Matt. 14:28–30).

■ Matthew 14:22–33
■ Mark 6:45–52
■ John 6:16–21

Mark 6:44 ᵃNU-Text and M-Text omit *about.*
John 6:11 ᵃNU-Text omits *to the disciples, and the disciples.*

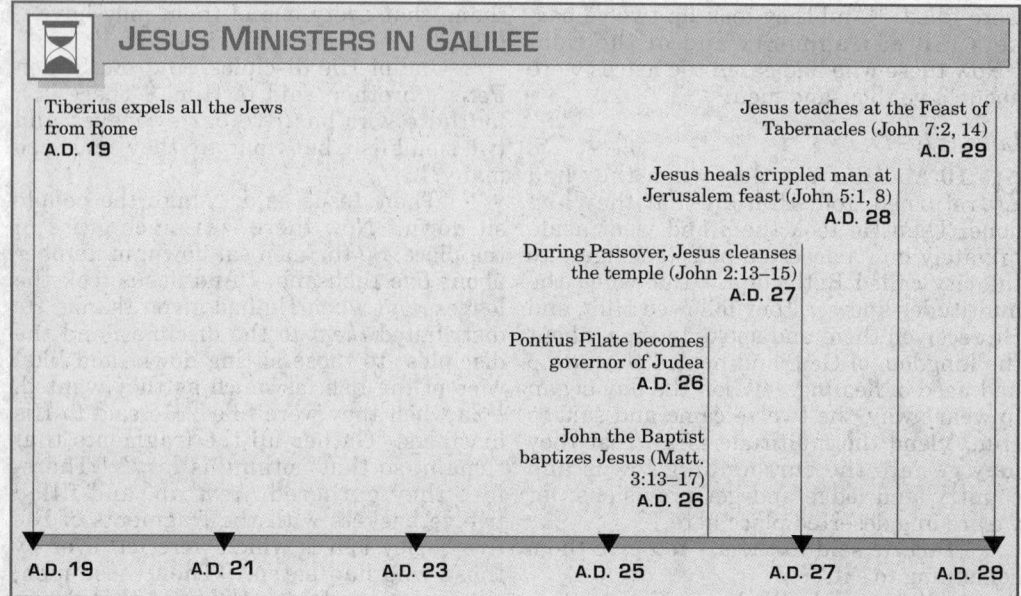

JESUS MINISTERS IN GALILEE

Tiberius expels all the Jews
from Rome
A.D. 19

Jesus teaches at the Feast of
Tabernacles (John 7:2, 14)
A.D. 29

Jesus heals crippled man at
Jerusalem feast (John 5:1, 8)
A.D. 28

During Passover, Jesus cleanses
the temple (John 2:13–15)
A.D. 27

Pontius Pilate becomes
governor of Judea
A.D. 26

John the Baptist
baptizes Jesus (Matt.
3:13–17)
A.D. 26

A.D. 19   **A.D. 21**   **A.D. 23**   **A.D. 25**   **A.D. 27**   **A.D. 29**

Matthew 14:22–33
It Is I

14 **:22** Immediately Jesus made His disciples get into the boat and go before Him to the other side, while He sent the multitudes away. ²³And when He had sent the multitudes away, He went up on the mountain by Himself to pray. Now when evening came, He was alone there. ²⁴But the boat was now in the middle of the sea,ᵃ tossed by the waves, for the wind was contrary.

²⁵Now in the fourth watch of the night Jesus went to them, walking on the sea. ²⁶And when the disciples saw Him walking on the sea, they were troubled, saying, "It is a ghost!" And they cried out for fear.

²⁷But immediately Jesus spoke to them, saying, "Be of good cheer! It is I; do not be afraid."

²⁸And Peter answered Him and said, "Lord, if it is You, command me to come to You on the water."

²⁹So He said, "Come." And when Peter had come down out of the boat, he walked on the water to go to Jesus. ³⁰But when he saw that the wind *was* boisterous,ᵃ he was afraid; and beginning to sink he cried out, saying, "Lord, save me!"

³¹And immediately Jesus stretched out *His* hand and caught him, and said to him, "O you of little faith, why did you doubt?" ³²And when they got into the boat, the wind ceased.

³³Then those who were in the boat came andᵃ worshiped Him, saying, "Truly You are the Son of God."

Mark 6:45–52
The Disciples Are Amazed

6 **:45** Immediately He made His disciples get into the boat and go before Him to the other side, to Bethsaida, while He sent the multitude away. ⁴⁶And when He had sent them away, He departed to the mountain to pray. ⁴⁷Now when evening came, the boat was in the middle of the sea; and He *was* alone on the land. ⁴⁸Then He saw them straining at rowing, for the wind was against them. Now about the fourth watch of the night He came to them, walking on the sea, and would have passed them by. ⁴⁹And when they saw Him walking on the sea, they supposed it was a ghost, and cried out; ⁵⁰for they all saw Him and were troubled. But immediately He talked with them and said to them, "Be of good cheer! It is I; do not be afraid." ⁵¹Then He went up into the boat to them, and the wind ceased. And they were greatly amazed in themselves beyond measure, and marveled. ⁵²For they had not understood about the loaves, because their heart was hardened.

14:24 ᵃNU-Text reads *many furlongs away from the land.*   14:30 ᵃNU-Text brackets *that* and *boisterous* as disputed.   14:33 ᵃNU-Text omits *came and.*

John 6:16–21

6 :16 Now when evening came, His disciples went down to the sea, [17]got into the boat, and went over the sea toward Capernaum. And it was already dark, and Jesus had not come to them. [18]Then the sea arose because a great wind was blowing. [19]So when they had rowed about three or four miles,[a] they saw Jesus walking on the sea and drawing near the boat; and they were afraid. [20]But He said to them, "It is I; do not be afraid." [21]Then they willingly received Him into the boat, and immediately the boat was at the land where they were going.

John 6:19 ªLiterally *twenty-five or thirty stadia*
Matt. 14:34 ªNU-Text reads *came to land at.*
John 6:22 ªNU-Text omits *that* and *which His disciples had entered.*

Popularity at Gennesaret and Capernaum

Much of Jesus' early ministry occurred on the northwest shore of the Sea of Galilee. Matthew and Mark each provide brief comments about the success of Jesus' ministry in Gennesaret, where the crowds flocked for healing, bringing the sick with them, and hoping for a brief encounter with Jesus.

John provides a longer treatment about a controversy that arose in the nearby city of Capernaum (about 3 miles east of Gennesaret along the shore of the Sea of Galilee). Jesus' popularity was still increasing because of the miracles which He performed, yet the people misunderstood the true meaning of His works. Although they had eaten the multiplied loaves, they had not understood the miracle as a "sign" that would give spiritual insight (John 6:26, 27; see "The First of Seven Signs" at John 2:1). The people longed only for Jesus to improve the circumstances of their physical lives (see John 6:15). Rather, Jesus was "the bread of life" that would forever provide the spiritual nourishment they needed (John 6:48–51).

Some suggest that with this episode (especially John 6:53–58) the Gospel of John explains the Lord's Supper. When John recounts the Last Supper (John 13), he does not report the institution of the sacrament, as do the Synoptic Gospels (Matt. 26:26–29; Mark 14:22–25; Luke 22:15–20).

■ Matthew 14:34–36
■ Mark 6:53–56
■ John 6:22–71

Matthew 14:34–36
Many Touch Him and Are Made Well

14 :34 When they had crossed over, they came to the land of[a] Gennesaret. [35]And when the men of that place recognized Him, they sent out into all that surrounding region, brought to Him all who were sick, [36]and begged Him that they might only touch the hem of His garment. And as many as touched *it* were made perfectly well.

Mark 6:53–56

6 :53 When they had crossed over, they came to the land of Gennesaret and anchored there. [54]And when they came out of the boat, immediately the people recognized Him, [55]ran through that whole surrounding region, and began to carry about on beds those who were sick to wherever they heard He was. [56]Wherever He entered, into villages, cities, or the country, they laid the sick in the marketplaces, and begged Him that they might just touch the hem of His garment. And as many as touched Him were made well.

John 6:22–71
The Bread from Heaven

6 :22 On the following day, when the people who were standing on the other side of the sea saw that there was no other boat there, except that one which His disciples had entered,[a] and that Jesus had not entered the boat with His disciples, but His disciples had gone away alone— [23]however, other boats came from Tiberias, near the place where they ate bread after the Lord had given thanks— [24]when the people therefore saw that Jesus was not there, nor His disciples, they also got into boats and came to Capernaum, seeking Jesus. [25]And when they found Him on the other side of the sea, they said to Him, "Rabbi, when did You come here?"

[26]Jesus answered them and said, "Most assuredly, I say to you, you seek Me, not because you saw the signs, but because you ate of the loaves and were filled. [27]Do not labor for the food which perishes, but for the food which endures to everlasting life, which the Son of Man will give you, because God the Father has set His seal on Him."

[28]Then they said to Him, "What shall we do, that we may work the works of God?"

[29]Jesus answered and said to them,

"This is the work of God, that you believe in Him whom He sent."

³⁰Therefore they said to Him, "What sign will You perform then, that we may see it and believe You? What work will You do? ³¹Our fathers ate the manna in the desert; as it is written, *'He gave them bread from heaven to eat.'*ᵃ

³²Then Jesus said to them, "Most assuredly, I say to you, Moses did not give you the bread from heaven, but My Father gives you the true bread from heaven. ³³For the bread of God is He who comes down from heaven and gives life to the world."

³⁴Then they said to Him, "Lord, give us this bread always."

³⁵And Jesus said to them, "I am the bread of life. He who comes to Me shall never hunger, and he who believes in Me shall never thirst. ³⁶But I said to you that you have seen Me and yet do not believe. ³⁷All that the Father gives Me will come to Me, and the one who comes to Me I will by no means cast out. ³⁸For I have come down from heaven, not to do My own will, but the will of Him who sent Me. ³⁹This is the will of the Father who sent Me, that of all He has given Me I should lose nothing, but should raise it up at the last day. ⁴⁰And this is the will of Him who sent Me, that everyone who sees the Son and believes in Him may have everlasting life; and I will raise him up at the last day."

Rejected by His Own

⁴¹The Jews then complained about Him, because He said, "I am the bread which came down from heaven." ⁴²And they said, "Is not this Jesus, the son of Joseph, whose father and mother we know? How is it then that He says, 'I have come down from heaven'?"

⁴³Jesus therefore answered and said to them, "Do not murmur among yourselves. ⁴⁴No one can come to Me unless the Father who sent Me draws him; and I will raise him up at the last day. ⁴⁵It is written in the prophets, *'And they shall all be taught by God.'*ᵃ Therefore everyone who has heard and learnedᵇ from the Father comes to Me. ⁴⁶Not that anyone has seen the Father, except He who is from God; He has seen the Father. ⁴⁷Most assuredly, I say to you, he who believes in Meᵃ has everlasting life. ⁴⁸I am the bread of life. ⁴⁹Your fathers ate the manna in the wilderness, and are dead. ⁵⁰This is the bread which comes down from heaven, that one may eat of it and not die. ⁵¹I am the living bread which came down from heaven. If anyone eats of this bread, he will live forever; and the bread that I shall give is My flesh, which I shall give for the life of the world."

⁵²The Jews therefore quarreled among themselves, saying, "How can this Man give us *His* flesh to eat?"

⁵³Then Jesus said to them, "Most assuredly, I say to you, unless you eat the flesh of the Son of Man and drink His blood, you have no life in you. ⁵⁴Whoever eats My flesh and drinks My blood has eternal life, and I will raise him up at the last day. ⁵⁵For My flesh is food indeed,ᵃ and My blood is drink indeed. ⁵⁶He who eats My flesh and drinks My blood abides in Me, and I in him. ⁵⁷As the living Father sent Me, and I live because of the Father, so he who feeds on Me will live because of Me. ⁵⁸This is the bread which came down from heaven—not as your fathers ate the manna, and are dead. He who eats this bread will live forever."

⁵⁹These things He said in the synagogue as He taught in Capernaum.

Many Disciples Turn Away

⁶⁰Therefore many of His disciples, when they heard *this,* said, "This is a hard saying; who can understand it?"

⁶¹When Jesus knew in Himself that His disciples complained about this, He said to them, "Does this offend you? ⁶²*What* then if you should see the Son of Man ascend where He was before? ⁶³It is the Spirit who gives life; the flesh profits nothing. The words that I speak to you are spirit, and *they* are life. ⁶⁴But there are some of you who do not believe." For Jesus knew from the beginning who they were who did not believe, and who would betray Him. ⁶⁵And He said, "Therefore I have said to you that no one can come to Me unless it has been granted to him by My Father."

⁶⁶From that *time* many of His disciples went back and walked with Him no more. ⁶⁷Then Jesus said to the twelve, "Do you also want to go away?"

⁶⁸But Simon Peter answered Him, "Lord, to whom shall we go? You have the words of eternal life. ⁶⁹Also we have come

---

6:31 ᵃExodus 16:4; Nehemiah 9:15; Psalm 78:24   6:45 ᵃIsaiah 54:13   ᵇM-Text reads *hears and has learned.*   6:47 ᵃNU-Text omits *in Me.* 6:55 ᵃNU-Text reads *true food* and *true drink.*

to believe and know that You are the Christ, the Son of the living God."[a]

70Jesus answered them, "Did I not choose you, the twelve, and one of you is a devil?" 71He spoke of Judas Iscariot, *the son* of Simon, for it was he who would betray Him, being one of the twelve.

Controversy over Traditions

The "tradition of the elders" [Matt. 15:2] contained hundreds of rules, which Jewish teachers had developed over the centuries to ensure that the people properly kept God's law. Jesus called these teachers "hypocrites" because they emphasized the many commandments of their human tradition, being concerned only with outward conduct while they ignored the inner dynamic and moral demands of the law. This is the only episode in which Mark reports Jesus referring to His Pharisaic opponents as "hypocrites" [Mark 7:6]. Matthew, by contrast, recounts several such instances [especially in Matt. 23].

The details of this particular controversy show that "hypocrisy" for Jesus was not "saying one thing and doing another." The Pharisees did observe the ritual washings which Jesus' disciples had occasionally neglected [Mark 7:2, 3]. In the Jewish literature of this period written in Greek, a "hypocrite" was a godless person who substituted human standards and desires for God's commandments. Thus, when people scrupulously observed traditions that had the effect of countering God's command [Matt. 15:3–6; Mark 7:9–13], they became "hypocrites" not because their actions were inconsistent but because they consistently ignored God's will. Ritual purity cannot cleanse a person defiled by his or her own evil actions [Matt. 15:17–20; Mark 7:15, 18–23].

■ Matthew 15:1–20
■ Mark 7:1–23

Matthew 15:1–20
Defilement Comes from Within

15 :1 Then the scribes and Pharisees who were from Jerusalem came to Jesus, saying, 2"Why do Your disciples transgress the tradition of the elders? For they do not wash their hands when they eat bread."

3He answered and said to them, "Why do you also transgress the commandment of God because of your tradition? 4For God commanded, saying, *'Honor your father and your mother'*;[a] and, *'He who curses father or mother, let him be put to death.'*[b] 5But you say, 'Whoever says to his father or mother, "Whatever profit you might have received from me *is* a gift *to God*"— 6then he need not honor his father or mother.'[a] Thus you have made the commandment[b] of God of no effect by your tradition. 7Hypocrites! Well did Isaiah prophesy about you, saying:

8 *'These people draw near to Me with their mouth,*
   And[a] *honor Me with their lips,*
   But their heart is far from Me.
9 *And in vain they worship Me,*
   Teaching as doctrines the commandments of men.'"[a]

10When He had called the multitude to *Himself*, He said to them, "Hear and understand: 11Not what goes into the mouth defiles a man; but what comes out of the mouth, this defiles a man."

12Then His disciples came and said to Him, "Do You know that the Pharisees were offended when they heard this saying?"

13But He answered and said, "Every plant which My heavenly Father has not planted will be uprooted. 14Let them alone. They are blind leaders of the blind. And if the blind leads the blind, both will fall into a ditch."

15Then Peter answered and said to Him, "Explain this parable to us."

16So Jesus said, "Are you also still without understanding? 17Do you not yet understand that whatever enters the mouth goes into the stomach and is eliminated? 18But those things which proceed out of the mouth come from the heart, and they defile a man. 19For out of the heart proceed evil thoughts, murders, adulteries, fornications, thefts, false witness, blasphemies. 20These are *the things* which defile a man, but to eat with unwashed hands does not defile a man."

6:69 [a]NU-Text reads *You are the Holy One of God.*   **Matt.** 15:4 [a]Exodus 20:12; Deuteronomy 5:16   [b]Exodus 21:17   15:6 [a]NU-Text omits *or mother.*   [b]NU-Text reads *word.*   15:8 [a]NU-Text omits *draw near to Me with their mouth, And.*   15:9 [a]Isaiah 29:13

Mark 7:1–23
True Purity

7:1 Then the Pharisees and some of the scribes came together to Him, having come from Jerusalem. 2Now when[a] they saw some of His disciples eat bread with defiled, that is, with unwashed hands, they found fault. 3For the Pharisees and all the Jews do not eat unless they wash *their* hands in a special way, holding the tradition of the elders. 4*When they come* from the marketplace, they do not eat unless they wash. And there are many other things which they have received and hold, *like* the washing of cups, pitchers, copper vessels, and couches.

5Then the Pharisees and scribes asked Him, "Why do Your disciples not walk according to the tradition of the elders, but eat bread with unwashed hands?"

6He answered and said to them, "Well did Isaiah prophesy of you hypocrites, as it is written:

'This people honors Me with their lips,
But their heart is far from Me.
7   And in vain they worship Me,
Teaching as doctrines the
    commandments of men.'[a]

8For laying aside the commandment of God, you hold the tradition of men[a]—the washing of pitchers and cups, and many other such things you do."

9He said to them, "*All too* well you reject the commandment of God, that you may keep your tradition. 10For Moses said, *'Honor your father and your mother'*;[a] and, *'He who curses father or mother, let him be put to death.'*[b] 11But you say, 'If a man says to his father or mother, "Whatever profit you might have received from me *is* Corban"—' (that is, a gift *to God*), 12then you no longer let him do anything for his father or his mother, 13making the word of God of no effect through your tradition which you have handed down. And many such things you do."

14When He had called all the multi-tude to *Himself,* He said to them, "Hear Me, everyone, and understand: 15There is nothing that enters a man from outside which can defile him; but the things which come out of him, those are the things that defile a man. 16If anyone has ears to hear, let him hear!"[a]

17When He had entered a house away from the crowd, His disciples asked Him concerning the parable. 18So He said to them, "Are you thus without understanding also? Do you not perceive that whatever enters a man from outside cannot defile him, 19because it does not enter his heart but his stomach, and is eliminated, *thus* purifying all foods?"[a] 20And He said, "What comes out of a man, that defiles a man. 21For from within, out of the heart of men, proceed evil thoughts, adulteries, fornications, murders, 22thefts, covetousness, wickedness, deceit, lewdness, an evil eye, blasphemy, pride, foolishness. 23All these evil things come from within and defile a man."

7:2 [a]NU-Text omits *when* and *they found fault.*
7:7 [a]Isaiah 29:13   7:8 [a]NU-Text omits the rest of this verse.   7:10 [a]Exodus 20:12; Deuteronomy 5:16   [b]Exodus 21:17   7:16 [a]NU-Text omits this verse.   7:19 [a]NU-Text ends quotation with *eliminated,* setting off the final clause as Mark's comment that Jesus has declared all foods clean.

Ministry in Gentile Regions

The "region of Tyre and Sidon" (Matt. 15:21; Mark 7:24) and the Decapolis (Mark 7:31), which bordered the southeastern shore of the Sea of Galilee, were predominantly Gentile territories. Jesus may have come here in order to teach His disciples privately, but His ministry soon extended to non-Jews.

Matthew's and Mark's accounts of Jesus' ministry in these areas reveal the special interests of each writer. As he did earlier in his Gospel (see "Returning to the West Shore" at Matt. 9:18), Matthew omits any details which

---

RELIGION AND WORSHIP

The Jews maintained a clear distinction between themselves and the cultures around them. Their regulations about food and drink were a constant reminder that they belonged to the God who had delivered them from Egypt. Their traditions expanded; the "tradition of the elders" (Mark 7:3) contained hundreds of rules which Jewish teachers had developed over the centuries.

have possible magical connotations, such as the healing of the deaf man (see Mark 7:33, 34). Rather he emphasizes the role of faith, evident in the exorcism of the Canaanite woman's daughter (Matt. 15:28).

Mark continues to develop his theme of the "messianic secret" (Mark 7:24, 36; see "Healing the Sick" at Matt. 8:14). But the more earnestly Jesus commanded the people to remain silent about what He had done, "the more widely they proclaimed it" (7:36).

- Matthew 15:21–31
- Mark 7:24–37

Matthew 15:21–31
A Gentile Shows Her Faith

15 **:21** Then Jesus went out from there and departed to the region of Tyre and Sidon. 22And behold, a woman of Canaan came from that region and cried out to Him, saying, "Have mercy on me, O Lord, Son of David! My daughter is severely demon-possessed."

23But He answered her not a word.

And His disciples came and urged Him, saying, "Send her away, for she cries out after us."

24But He answered and said, "I was not sent except to the lost sheep of the house of Israel."

25Then she came and worshiped Him, saying, "Lord, help me!"

26But He answered and said, "It is not good to take the children's bread and throw it to the little dogs."

27And she said, "Yes, Lord, yet even the little dogs eat the crumbs which fall from their masters' table."

28Then Jesus answered and said to her, "O woman, great is your faith! Let it be to you as you desire." And her daughter was healed from that very hour.

Jesus Heals Great Multitudes

29Jesus departed from there, skirted the Sea of Galilee, and went up on the mountain and sat down there. 30Then great multitudes came to Him, having with them the lame, blind, mute, maimed, and many others; and they laid them down at Jesus' feet, and He healed them. 31So the multitude marveled when they saw the mute speaking, the maimed made whole, the lame walking, and the blind seeing; and they glorified the God of Israel.

Mark 7:24–37
Gentiles Believe

7 **:24** From there He arose and went to the region of Tyre and Sidon.[a] And He entered a house and wanted no one to know it, but He could not be hidden. 25For a woman whose young daughter had an unclean spirit heard about Him, and she came and fell at His feet. 26The woman was a Greek, a Syro-Phoenician by birth, and she kept asking Him to cast the demon out of her daughter. 27But Jesus said to her, "Let the children be filled first, for it is not good to take the children's bread and throw it to the little dogs."

28And she answered and said to Him, "Yes, Lord, yet even the little dogs under the table eat from the children's crumbs."

29Then He said to her, "For this saying go your way; the demon has gone out of your daughter."

30And when she had come to her house, she found the demon gone out, and her daughter lying on the bed.

Jesus Heals a Deaf-Mute

31Again, departing from the region of Tyre and Sidon, He came through the midst of the region of Decapolis to the Sea of Galilee. 32Then they brought to Him one who was deaf and had an impediment in his speech, and they begged Him to put His hand on him. 33And He took him aside from the multitude, and put His fingers in his ears, and He spat and touched his tongue. 34Then, looking up to heaven, He sighed, and said to him, "Ephphatha," that is, "Be opened."

35Immediately his ears were opened, and the impediment of his tongue was loosed, and he spoke plainly. 36Then He commanded them that they should tell no one; but the more He commanded them, the more widely they proclaimed it. 37And they were astonished beyond measure, saying, "He has done all things well. He makes both the deaf to hear and the mute to speak."

Feeding the 4,000

The feeding of 4,000 people is a miracle similar to the feeding of the 5,000 (see "Feeding the 5,000" at Matt. 14:13). Indeed, the similarities between the two feeding miracles has led some to suggest that the story of feeding 4,000 is simply a variation of the ear-

7:24 [a]NU-Text omits and Sidon.

WHO GETS THE CHILDREN'S BREAD? (Mark 7:27)

While Jesus was in the Gentile territory of Phoenicia, He was approached by a woman who was "a Greek, a Syro-Phoenician by birth" (Mark 7:26). She was a member of the Greek-speaking ruling class of Phoenicia. Citizens of Phoenician cities like Tyre and Sidon had long been influenced by Greek culture. This particular woman belonged to a class of people who often took for themselves the grain raised by poor Jews living in these regions.

That this powerful woman must come to a Jewish prophet and beg help for her daughter suggests a reversal of roles (Mark 7:25). Jesus challenged the woman's faith. Just as her class may have been taking the bread of poor Jews in neighboring areas, the "bread" of miracles from Israel's God belonged to Israel first of all. Israel had priority before Gentiles during Jesus' earthly ministry just as one's children had priority over dogs (7:27).

Jesus put the woman off with the expression "little dogs," but He did not insult her as harshly as it may sound to our ears today. Jewish people viewed dogs negatively, as scavengers, the way we today might view rats. As a well-to-do Greek, however, the woman was more likely to think of dogs as household pets. By willingly acknowledging her secondary place, yet also refusing to settle for anything less than a miracle, she demonstrated her humility and faith, and thus won her request.

---

lier account. It seems implausible that Jesus' disciples would respond in precisely the same way on this later occasion—questioning how to feed so many people (Matt. 15:33)—if they had witnessed the earlier miracle (see Matt. 14:15–17).

Still, others suggest that this miracle in Gentile territory is the complement to the previous miraculous feeding of Jews. The numbers of loaves, baskets, and people in the two stories differ. Furthermore, the disciples simply could not comprehend the true power of God in Jesus' miracles. Mark commented specifically that they did not properly understand the first feeding miracle (Mark 6:52). Both he and Matthew report that Jesus later chastised His disciples for failing to remember His ability to provide bread, demonstrated by these two miracles (Matt. 16:9, 10; Mark 8:17–21).

■ Matthew 15:32–39
■ Mark 8:1–10

Matthew 15:32–39

15 :32 Now Jesus called His disciples to *Himself* and said, "I have compassion on the multitude, because they have now continued with Me three days and have nothing to eat. And I do not want to send them away hungry, lest they faint on the way."

33Then His disciples said to Him, "Where could we get enough bread in the wilderness to fill such a great multitude?"

34Jesus said to them, "How many loaves do you have?"

And they said, "Seven, and a few little fish."

35So He commanded the multitude to sit down on the ground. 36And He took the seven loaves and the fish and gave thanks, broke *them* and gave *them* to His disciples; and the disciples *gave* to the multitude. 37So they all ate and were filled, and they took up seven large baskets full of the fragments that were left. 38Now those who ate were four thousand men, besides women and children. 39And He sent away the multitude, got into the boat, and came to the region of Magdala.ᵃ

Mark 8:1–10

8 :1 In those days, the multitude being very great and having nothing to eat, Jesus called His disciples *to Him* and said to them, 2"I have compassion on the multitude, because they have now continued with Me three days and have nothing to eat. 3And if I send them away hungry to their own houses, they will faint on the way; for some of them have come from afar."

4Then His disciples answered Him, "How can one satisfy these people with bread here in the wilderness?"

5He asked them, "How many loaves do you have?"

15:39 ᵃNU-Text reads *Magadan*.

And they said, "Seven."

⁶So He commanded the multitude to sit down on the ground. And He took the seven loaves and gave thanks, broke *them* and gave *them* to His disciples to set before *them;* and they set *them* before the multitude. ⁷They also had a few small fish; and having blessed them, He said to set them also before *them.* ⁸So they ate and were filled, and they took up seven large baskets of leftover fragments. ⁹Now those who had eaten were about four thousand. And He sent them away, ¹⁰immediately got into the boat with His disciples, and came to the region of Dalmanutha.

16:3 ªNU-Text omits *Hypocrites.*   16:4 ªNU-Text omits *the prophet.*   16:8 ªNU-Text reads *you have no bread.*

Teaching About the Pharisees

The Gospel of Mark, in one of its characteristic features, consistently describes Jesus' disciples as having trouble understanding their Teacher. That tendency toward misunderstanding is evident in two accounts from Mark and Matthew concerning the Pharisees. Following a dispute with the Pharisees regarding Jesus' miracles (Mark 8:11, 12), Jesus warned His disciples to "beware of the leaven of the Pharisees" (8:15). His disciples believed He was chastising them for a lack of provisions (8:16). A lack of food was certainly no problem for Jesus, and reminding them of the two miraculous feedings, Jesus asked, "How is it you do not understand?" (8:21).

Mark seems to use the story of a blind man in Bethsaida to illustrate the disciple's own plight. Just as the man only gradually regained his sight through Jesus' ministry (Mark 8:23–25), so also the disciples only gradually, and with much repeated effort, came to see who Jesus was (see "The Christ and His Disciples" at Matt. 16:13).

By contrast Matthew shows the disciples being able to understand what Jesus was teaching them, albeit with a little prompting (Matt. 16:8–12). The Pharisees and Sadducees were more interested in testing Jesus (16:1) than in considering the significance of His ministry, and this spiritual insensitivity receives more attention in Matthew's Gospel.

■ Matthew 16:1–12
■ Mark 8:11–26

Matthew 16:1–12
The Pharisees and Sadducees Seek a Sign

16 :1 Then the Pharisees and Sadducees came, and testing Him asked that He would show them a sign from heaven. ²He answered and said to them, "When it is evening you say, '*It will be* fair weather, for the sky is red'; ³and in the morning, '*It will be* foul weather today, for the sky is red and threatening.' Hypocrites!ª You know how to discern the face of the sky, but you cannot *discern* the signs of the times. ⁴A wicked and adulterous generation seeks after a sign, and no sign shall be given to it except the sign of the prophetª Jonah." And He left them and departed.

The Leaven of the Pharisees and Sadducees

⁵Now when His disciples had come to the other side, they had forgotten to take bread. ⁶Then Jesus said to them, "Take heed and beware of the leaven of the Pharisees and the Sadducees."

⁷And they reasoned among themselves, saying, "*It is* because we have taken no bread."

⁸But Jesus, being aware of *it,* said to them, "O you of little faith, why do you reason among yourselves because you have brought no bread?ª ⁹Do you not yet understand, or remember the five loaves of the five thousand and how many baskets you took up? ¹⁰Nor the seven loaves of the four thousand and how many large baskets you took up? ¹¹How is it you do not understand that I did not speak to you concerning bread?—*but* to beware of the leaven of the Pharisees and Sadducees." ¹²Then they understood that He did not tell *them* to beware of the leaven of bread, but of the doctrine of the Pharisees and Sadducees.

Mark 8:11–26
The Pharisees Seek a Sign

8 :11 Then the Pharisees came out and began to dispute with Him, seeking from Him a sign from heaven, testing Him. ¹²But He sighed deeply in His spirit, and said, "Why does this generation seek a sign? Assuredly, I say to you, no sign shall be given to this generation."

Beware of the Leaven of the Pharisees and Herod

¹³And He left them, and getting into the boat again, departed to the other side.

14Now the disciples[a] had forgotten to take bread, and they did not have more than one loaf with them in the boat. 15Then He charged them, saying, "Take heed, beware of the leaven of the Pharisees and the leaven of Herod."

16And they reasoned among themselves, saying, "It is because we have no bread."

17But Jesus, being aware of it, said to them, "Why do you reason because you have no bread? Do you not yet perceive nor understand? Is your heart still[a] hardened? 18Having eyes, do you not see? And having ears, do you not hear? And do you not remember? 19When I broke the five loaves for the five thousand, how many baskets full of fragments did you take up?"

They said to Him, "Twelve."

20"Also, when I broke the seven for the four thousand, how many large baskets full of fragments did you take up?"

And they said, "Seven."

21So He said to them, "How is it you do not understand?"

A Blind Man Healed at Bethsaida

22Then He came to Bethsaida; and they brought a blind man to Him, and begged Him to touch him. 23So He took the blind man by the hand and led him out of the town. And when He had spit on his eyes and put His hands on him, He asked him if he saw anything.

24And he looked up and said, "I see men like trees, walking."

25Then He put His hands on his eyes again and made him look up. And he was restored and saw everyone clearly. 26Then He sent him away to his house, saying, "Neither go into the town, nor tell anyone in the town."[a]

The Christ and His Disciples

Peter's confession at Caesarea Philippi, identifying Jesus as "the Christ of God" (Luke 9:20), marked an important milestone in Jesus' ministry. Nevertheless, the disciples still needed to learn much about the nature of Jesus' messiahship, as was demonstrated when Peter rejected Jesus' first prediction of His eventual death and resurrection in Jerusalem (Matt. 16:21–23). They were still focused not on "the things of God, but the things of men" (Mark 8:33).

Jesus' disciples still held the popular conception that the Messiah would bring political and economic success to God's people. Their misconception was exposed by the call for a true disciple to "deny himself, and take up his cross" (Matt. 16:24; Mark 8:34). Thus, Jesus emphasized placing spiritual life ahead of physical life (Mark 8:36). The Son of Man Himself was willing to lose His life to bring spiritual benefit to all.

- Matthew 16:13–28
- Mark 8:27—9:1
- Luke 9:18–27

Matthew 16:13–28
Peter's Confession of Faith

16 :13 When Jesus came into the region of Caesarea Philippi, He asked His disciples, saying, "Who do men say that I, the Son of Man, am?"

14So they said, "Some say John the Baptist, some Elijah, and others Jeremiah or one of the prophets."

15He said to them, "But who do you say that I am?"

16Simon Peter answered and said, "You are the Christ, the Son of the living God."

17Jesus answered and said to him, "Blessed are you, Simon Bar-Jonah, for flesh and blood has not revealed this to you, but My Father who is in heaven. 18And I also say to you that you are Peter, and on this rock I will build My church, and the gates of Hades shall not prevail against it. 19And I will give you the keys of the kingdom of heaven, and whatever you bind on earth will be bound in heaven, and whatever you loose on earth will be loosed[a] in heaven."

20Then He commanded His disciples that they should tell no one that He was Jesus the Christ.

The Way of the Cross

21From that time Jesus began to show to His disciples that He must go to Jerusalem, and suffer many things from the elders and chief priests and scribes, and be killed, and be raised the third day.

22Then Peter took Him aside and began to rebuke Him, saying, "Far be it from You, Lord; this shall not happen to You!"

8:14 [a]NU-Text and M-Text read they.
8:17 [a]NU-Text omits still.   8:26 [a]NU-Text reads "Do not even go into the town."   **Matt. 16:19** [a]Or will have been bound . . . will have been loosed

THE CITY OF SEVERAL NAMES (Matt. 16:13)

In the city of Caesarea Philippi, about 25 miles north of the Sea of Galilee, Jesus asked His disciples, "Who do you say that I am?" They first answered with several names—John the Baptist, Elijah, Jeremiah—before one disciple acknowledged Jesus as Israel's promised Savior (Matt. 16:13–16). Interestingly, Jesus' question would be answered in a city that went through a series of name changes, each time to honor some god or man other than the Son of God.

The name this city had before the Hellenistic period (beginning c. 332 B.C.) is unknown. According to the Greek historian Polybius, by the time of the Seleucid king Antiochus III (c. 223–187 B.C.) the site was called "Panion," after the Greek god Pan.

The northern district of Galilee was given to Herod the Great in 20 B.C. Herod subsequently built a great temple there in honor of the emperor Augustus Caesar. According to the Jewish historian Josephus, this district was bequeathed to Herod's son Philip when he succeeded his father in 4 B.C. Philip enlarged the city and renamed it "Caesarea" in honor of Caesar. "Philippi" was added to the name to distinguish it from Caesarea Maritima, the great Mediterranean coastal city.

Five decades later Agrippa II enlarged the city even more and renamed it "Neronias," after the Roman emperor Nero. This name seems to have been used only rarely, and the name reverted back to Paneas (i.e., Panion) during the Byzantine period (after A.D. 330).

The compound name Caesarea Philippi was thus the name of the town when Jesus visited there (Matt. 16:13). In a city whose various names remembered Pan, Caesar, Nero, and Philip the tetrarch, a disciple answered his Teacher, "You are the Christ, the Son of the living God" (Matt. 16:16).

---

²³But He turned and said to Peter, "Get behind Me, Satan! You are an offense to Me, for you are not mindful of the things of God, but the things of men."

²⁴Then Jesus said to His disciples, "If anyone desires to come after Me, let him deny himself, and take up his cross, and follow Me. ²⁵For whoever desires to save his life will lose it, but whoever loses his life for My sake will find it. ²⁶For what profit is it to a man if he gains the whole world, and loses his own soul? Or what will a man give in exchange for his soul? ²⁷For the Son of Man will come in the glory of His Father with His angels, and then He will reward each according to his works. ²⁸Assuredly, I say to you, there are some standing here who shall not taste death till they see the Son of Man coming in His kingdom."

Mark 8:27—9:1
Christ and the Cross

8 :27 Now Jesus and His disciples went out to the towns of Caesarea Philippi; and on the road, He asked His disciples, saying to them, "Who do men say that I am?"

²⁸So they answered, "John the Baptist; but some *say,* Elijah; and others, one of the prophets."

²⁹He said to them, "But who do you say that I am?"

Peter answered and said to Him, "You are the Christ."

³⁰Then He strictly warned them that they should tell no one about Him.

³¹And He began to teach them that the Son of Man must suffer many things, and be rejected by the elders and chief priests and scribes, and be killed, and after three

---

RELIGION AND WORSHIP

"Christ" is a transliteration of the Greek word christos *meaning "anointed" (Matt. 16:16). "Messiah" comes from the Hebrew word* mashiach *also meaning "anointed." Anointing is a ritual of applying oil to something. Ancient people were anointed to mark them as having a public appointment from God as a political or religious leader. The Jews anticipated a messianic King who would bring deliverance and salvation for His people.*

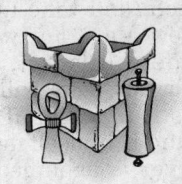

days rise again. ³²He spoke this word openly. Then Peter took Him aside and began to rebuke Him. ³³But when He had turned around and looked at His disciples, He rebuked Peter, saying, "Get behind Me, Satan! For you are not mindful of the things of God, but the things of men."

³⁴When He had called the people to *Himself,* with His disciples also, He said to them, "Whoever desires to come after Me, let him deny himself, and take up his cross, and follow Me. ³⁵For whoever desires to save his life will lose it, but whoever loses his life for My sake and the gospel's will save it. ³⁶For what will it profit a man if he gains the whole world, and loses his own soul? ³⁷Or what will a man give in exchange for his soul? ³⁸For whoever is ashamed of Me and My words in this adulterous and sinful generation, of him the Son of Man also will be ashamed when He comes in the glory of His Father with the holy angels."

9 ¹And He said to them, "Assuredly, I say to you that there are some standing here who will not taste death till they see the kingdom of God present with power."

Luke 9:18–27
Peter's Confession of Christ

9 :18 And it happened, as He was alone praying, *that* His disciples joined Him, and He asked them, saying, "Who do the crowds say that I am?"

¹⁹So they answered and said, "John the Baptist, but some *say* Elijah; and others *say* that one of the old prophets has risen again."

²⁰He said to them, "But who do you say that I am?"

Peter answered and said, "The Christ of God."

²¹And He strictly warned and commanded them to tell this to no one, ²²saying, "The Son of Man must suffer many things, and be rejected by the elders and chief priests and scribes, and be killed, and be raised the third day."

²³Then He said to *them* all, "If anyone desires to come after Me, let him deny himself, and take up his cross daily,ᵃ and follow Me. ²⁴For whoever desires to save his life will lose it, but whoever loses his life for My sake will save it. ²⁵For what profit is it to a man if he gains the whole world, and is himself destroyed or lost? ²⁶For whoever is ashamed of Me and My words, of him the Son of Man will be ashamed when

He comes in His *own* glory, and *in His* Father's, and of the holy angels. ²⁷But I tell you truly, there are some standing here who shall not taste death till they see the kingdom of God."

The Transfiguration

Jesus' transfiguration was a visionary revelation (Matt. 17:9) of the divine glory that the Son (Mark 9:7) possessed from His incarnation (see John 1:14). A brief scene in Luke's Gospel clarifies what was at stake, not only in the vision, but in Jesus' ministry: Jesus discussed His "decease" with Moses and Elijah (Luke 9:31). The Greek word translated "decease" (*exodos*) refers in literary Greek to the process of "death." It recalls the "Exodus" from Egypt as an earlier process of divine redemption. Thus, Jesus' impending death and resurrection, also an "Exodus," would further extend God's redemption to humanity.

- Matthew 17:1–13
- Mark 9:2–13
- Luke 9:28–36

Matthew 17:1–13
Jesus Transfigured on the Mount

17 :1 Now after six days Jesus took Peter, James, and John his brother, led them up on a high mountain by themselves; ²and He was transfigured before them. His face shone like the sun, and His clothes became as white as the light. ³And behold, Moses and Elijah appeared to them, talking with Him. ⁴Then Peter answered and said to Jesus, "Lord, it is good for us to be here; if You wish, let usᵃ make here three tabernacles: one for You, one for Moses, and one for Elijah."

⁵While he was still speaking, behold, a bright cloud overshadowed them; and suddenly a voice came out of the cloud, saying, "This is My beloved Son, in whom I am well pleased. Hear Him!" ⁶And when the disciples heard *it,* they fell on their faces and were greatly afraid. ⁷But Jesus came and touched them and said, "Arise, and do not be afraid." ⁸When they had lifted up their eyes, they saw no one but Jesus only.

⁹Now as they came down from the mountain, Jesus commanded them, saying, "Tell the vision to no one until the Son of Man is risen from the dead."

Luke 9:23 ᵃM-Text omits *daily.*
Matt. 17:4 ᵃNU-Text reads *I will.*

¹⁰And His disciples asked Him, saying, "Why then do the scribes say that Elijah must come first?"

¹¹Jesus answered and said to them, "Indeed, Elijah is coming first[a] and will restore all things. ¹²But I say to you that Elijah has come already, and they did not know him but did to him whatever they wished. Likewise the Son of Man is also about to suffer at their hands." ¹³Then the disciples understood that He spoke to them of John the Baptist.

Mark 9:2–13

9:2 Now after six days Jesus took Peter, James, and John, and led them up on a high mountain apart by themselves; and He was transfigured before them. ³His clothes became shining, exceedingly white, like snow, such as no launderer on earth can whiten them. ⁴And Elijah appeared to them with Moses, and they were talking with Jesus. ⁵Then Peter answered and said to Jesus, "Rabbi, it is good for us to be here; and let us make three tabernacles: one for You, one for Moses, and one for Elijah"— ⁶because he did not know what to say, for they were greatly afraid.

⁷And a cloud came and overshadowed them; and a voice came out of the cloud, saying, "This is My beloved Son. Hear Him!" ⁸Suddenly, when they had looked around, they saw no one anymore, but only Jesus with themselves.

⁹Now as they came down from the mountain, He commanded them that they should tell no one the things they had seen, till the Son of Man had risen from the dead. ¹⁰So they kept this word to themselves, questioning what the rising from the dead meant.

¹¹And they asked Him, saying, "Why do the scribes say that Elijah must come first?"

¹²Then He answered and told them, "Indeed, Elijah is coming first and restores all things. And how is it written concerning the Son of Man, that He must suffer many things and be treated with contempt? ¹³But I say to you that Elijah has also come, and they did to him whatever they wished, as it is written of him."

Luke 9:28–36

9:28 Now it came to pass, about eight days after these sayings, that He took Peter, John, and James and went up on the mountain to pray. ²⁹As He prayed, the appearance of His face was altered, and His robe *became* white *and* glistening. ³⁰And behold, two men talked with Him, who were Moses and Elijah, ³¹who appeared in glory and spoke of His decease which He was about to accomplish at Jerusalem. ³²But Peter and those with him were heavy with sleep; and when they were fully awake, they saw His glory and the two men who stood with Him. ³³Then it happened, as they were parting from Him, *that* Peter said to Jesus, "Master, it is good for us to be here; and let us make three tabernacles: one for You, one for Moses, and one for Elijah"—not knowing what he said.

³⁴While he was saying this, a cloud came and overshadowed them; and they were fearful as they entered the cloud. ³⁵And a voice came out of the cloud, saying, "This is My beloved Son.[a] Hear Him!" ³⁶When the voice had ceased, Jesus was found alone. But they kept quiet, and told no one in those days any of the things they had seen.

Faithless Generation

The disciples continued in their struggle to develop a faithful response to what God was doing in Jesus. Their inability to perform an exorcism led Jesus to despair about the "faithless generation" and the limited time remaining for Him to reach them (Mark 9:19). Continuing his characteristic emphasis on faith, Matthew explained that the disciples' failure to do Jesus' work was rooted in their own "unbelief" (Matt. 17:19, 20). They still had not grasped the spiritual aspect of Jesus'

17:11 [a]NU-Text omits *first*.   Luke 9:35 [a]NU-Text reads *This is My Son, the Chosen One.*

DAILY LIFE AND CUSTOMS

A kind of soap was used in Mesopotamia in very early times, although it was not refined or made into bars. But soap was hardly known in Egypt or Palestine, and launderers used other means to "whiten" clothing (Mark 9:3). Ashes or natural substances like sodium carbonate and fuller's earth (a kind of superfine clay) were used to remove grease and dirt. Also, wet clothes were pounded on stones.

messianic mission, so they could only respond to the predictions of His impending death and resurrection with misunderstanding (Mark 9:31, 32; Luke 9:44, 45) and sorrow (Matt. 17:22, 23).

■ Matthew 17:14–23
■ Mark 9:14–32
■ Luke 9:37–45

Matthew 17:14–23
The Need for Faith

17 :14 And when they had come to the multitude, a man came to Him, kneeling down to Him and saying, 15"Lord, have mercy on my son, for he is an epileptic[a] and suffers severely; for he often falls into the fire and often into the water. 16So I brought him to Your disciples, but they could not cure him."

17Then Jesus answered and said, "O faithless and perverse generation, how long shall I be with you? How long shall I bear with you? Bring him here to Me." 18And Jesus rebuked the demon, and it came out of him; and the child was cured from that very hour.

19Then the disciples came to Jesus privately and said, "Why could we not cast it out?"

20So Jesus said to them, "Because of your unbelief;[a] for assuredly, I say to you, if you have faith as a mustard seed, you will say to this mountain, 'Move from here to there,' and it will move; and nothing will be impossible for you. 21However, this kind does not go out except by prayer and fasting."[a]

22Now while they were staying[a] in Galilee, Jesus said to them, "The Son of Man is about to be betrayed into the hands of men, 23and they will kill Him, and the third day He will be raised up." And they were exceedingly sorrowful.

Mark 9:14–32
O Faithless Generation

9 :14 And when He came to the disciples, He saw a great multitude around them, and scribes disputing with them. 15Immediately, when they saw Him, all the people were greatly amazed, and running to *Him,* greeted Him. 16And He asked the scribes, "What are you discussing with them?"

17Then one of the crowd answered and said, "Teacher, I brought You my son, who has a mute spirit. 18And wherever it seizes him, it throws him down; he foams at the mouth, gnashes his teeth, and becomes rigid. So I spoke to Your disciples, that they should cast it out, but they could not."

19He answered him and said, "O faithless generation, how long shall I be with you? How long shall I bear with you? Bring him to Me." 20Then they brought him to Him. And when he saw Him, immediately the spirit convulsed him, and he fell on the ground and wallowed, foaming at the mouth.

21So He asked his father, "How long has this been happening to him?"

And he said, "From childhood. 22And often he has thrown him both into the fire and into the water to destroy him. But if You can do anything, have compassion on us and help us."

23Jesus said to him, "If you can believe,[a] all things *are* possible to him who believes."

24Immediately the father of the child cried out and said with tears, "Lord, I believe; help my unbelief!"

25When Jesus saw that the people came running together, He rebuked the unclean spirit, saying to it, "Deaf and dumb spirit, I command you, come out of him and enter him no more!" 26Then *the spirit* cried out, convulsed him greatly, and came out of him. And he became as one dead, so that many said, "He is dead." 27But Jesus took

17:15 aLiterally *moonstruck*   17:20 aNU-Text reads *little faith.*   17:21 aNU-Text omits this verse.   17:22 aNU-Text reads *gathering together.*   **Mark 9:23** aNU-Text reads " 'If You can!' All things . . . . "

GEOGRAPHY AND ENVIRONMENT

A possible location for the Mount of Transfiguration (Luke 9:28) is Mount Hermon, in modern Lebanon. This is part of a long mountain range. In the highest reaches there is beautiful snow in the descending valleys, providing a source of water for the fields below. Snow is rare in Jerusalem and most of the surrounding country.

him by the hand and lifted him up, and he arose.

28And when He had come into the house, His disciples asked Him privately, "Why could we not cast it out?"

29So He said to them, "This kind can come out by nothing but prayer and fasting."a

30Then they departed from there and passed through Galilee, and He did not want anyone to know it. 31For He taught His disciples and said to them, "The Son of Man is being betrayed into the hands of men, and they will kill Him. And after He is killed, He will rise the third day." 32But they did not understand this saying, and were afraid to ask Him.

Luke 9:37–45
A Boy Is Healed

9 :37 Now it happened on the next day, when they had come down from the mountain, that a great multitude met Him. 38Suddenly a man from the multitude cried out, saying, "Teacher, I implore You, look on my son, for he is my only child. 39And behold, a spirit seizes him, and he suddenly cries out; it convulses him so that he foams at the mouth; and it departs from him with great difficulty, bruising him. 40So I implored Your disciples to cast it out, but they could not."

41Then Jesus answered and said, "O faithless and perverse generation, how long shall I be with you and bear with you? Bring your son here." 42And as he was still coming, the demon threw him down and convulsed him. Then Jesus rebuked the unclean spirit, healed the child, and gave him back to his father.

Jesus Again Predicts His Death

43And they were all amazed at the majesty of God.

But while everyone marveled at all the things which Jesus did, He said to His disciples, 44"Let these words sink down into your ears, for the Son of Man is about to be betrayed into the hands of men." 45But they did not understand this saying, and it was hidden from them so that they did not

perceive it; and they were afraid to ask Him about this saying.

Being Christ's Disciple

During a visit to Capernaum, Jesus began teaching His disciples about the differences between the kingdom of God that He proclaimed and the political kingdom which most people expected the Messiah to establish. Matthew's unique story about the temple tax (Matt. 17:24–27) points out that membership in God's kingdom is not about domination, such as receiving tribute from "customs or taxes," but about becoming children of God. Each of the Synoptic Gospels emphasizes that one's status in God's kingdom depends upon receiving others and being received oneself as a child (Matt. 18:1–5; Mark 9:33–38; Luke 9:46–48).

Jesus made two points regarding membership in the kingdom. First, membership in God's kingdom is open to a broad range of people. All are to be considered God's children unless their actions in opposition to God's work demand that they be excluded (Mark 9:40; Luke 9:49, 50). Jesus' second point identified such opposing acts. Any action that caused one of these "little ones" to fall was in danger of judgment (Mark 9:42; see Matt. 18:6–9) and of being removed from the community of faith (Matt. 18:7).

■ Matthew 17:24—18:9
■ Mark 9:33–50
■ Luke 9:46–50

Matthew 17:24—18:9
Peter and His Master Pay Their Taxes

17 :24 When they had come to Capernaum,a those who received the temple tax came to Peter and said, "Does your Teacher not pay the temple tax?"

25He said, "Yes."

And when he had come into the house, Jesus anticipated him, saying, "What do you think, Simon? From whom do the kings of the earth take customs or taxes, from their sons or from strangers?"

26Peter said to Him, "From strangers."

Jesus said to him. "Then the sons are free. 27Nevertheless, lest we offend them, go to the sea, cast in a hook, and take the fish that comes up first. And when you have opened its mouth, you will find a piece of money;a take that and give it to them for Me and you."

Who Is the Greatest?

18 ¹At that time the disciples came to Jesus saying, "Who then is greatest in the kingdom of heaven?"

²Then Jesus called a little child to Him, set him in the midst of them, ³and said, "Assuredly, I say to you, unless you are converted and become as little children, you will by no means enter the kingdom of heaven. ⁴Therefore whoever humbles himself as this little child is the greatest in the kingdom of heaven. ⁵Whoever receives one little child like this in My name receives Me.

Allow No Occasion for Sin

⁶"Whoever causes one of these little ones who believe in Me to sin, it would be better for him if a millstone were hung around his neck, and he were drowned in the depth of the sea. ⁷Woe to the world because of offenses! For offenses must come, but woe to that man by whom the offense comes!

⁸"If your hand or foot causes you to sin, cut it off and cast *it* from you. It is better for you to enter into life lame or maimed, rather than having two hands or two feet, to be cast into the everlasting fire. ⁹And if your eye causes you to sin, pluck it out and cast *it* from you. It is better for you to enter into life with one eye, rather than having two eyes, to be cast into hell fire."

Mark 9:33–50
The Way of Discipleship

9 :33 Then He came to Capernaum. And when He was in the house He asked them, "What was it you disputed among yourselves on the road?" ³⁴But they kept silent, for on the road they had disputed among themselves who *would be the* greatest. ³⁵And He sat down, called the twelve, and said to them, "If anyone desires to be first, he shall be last of all and servant of all." ³⁶Then He took a little child and set him in the midst of them. And when He had taken him in His arms, He said to them, ³⁷"Whoever receives one of these little children in My name receives Me; and whoever receives Me, receives not Me but Him who sent Me."

³⁸Now John answered Him, saying, "Teacher, we saw someone who does not follow us casting out demons in Your name, and we forbade him because he does not follow us."

³⁹But Jesus said, "Do not forbid him, for no one who works a miracle in My name can soon afterward speak evil of Me. ⁴⁰For he who is not against us is on our[a] side. ⁴¹For whoever gives you a cup of water to drink in My name, because you belong to Christ, assuredly, I say to you, he will by no means lose his reward.

Jesus Warns of Offenses

⁴²"But whoever causes one of these little ones who believe in Me to stumble, it would be better for him if a millstone were hung around his neck, and he were thrown into the sea. ⁴³If your hand causes you to sin, cut it off. It is better for you to enter into life maimed, rather than having two hands, to go to hell, into the fire that shall never be quenched— ⁴⁴where

> 'Their worm does not die
> And the fire is not quenched.'[a]

⁴⁵And if your foot causes you to sin, cut it off. It is better for you to enter life lame, rather than having two feet, to be cast into hell, into the fire that shall never be quenched— ⁴⁶where

> 'Their worm does not die
> And the fire is not quenched.'[a]

9:40 [a]M-Text reads *against you is on your side.* 9:44 [a]NU-Text omits this verse.   9:46 [a]NU-Text omits the last clause of verse 45 and all of verse 46.

GEOGRAPHY AND ENVIRONMENT

Capernaum was a village on the north shore of the Sea of Galilee. According to the Gospels (Matt. 4:13), the city became a kind of headquarters for Jesus and His disciples. Often the Gospel accounts mention a house in Capernaum, sometimes describing it simply as "the house" (Mark 9:33). It probably belonged to Simon Peter, and has been the object of excavation in recent decades.

⁴⁷And if your eye causes you to sin, pluck it out. It is better for you to enter the kingdom of God with one eye, rather than having two eyes, to be cast into hell fire— ⁴⁸where

'Their worm does not die
And the fire is not quenched.'^a

Tasteless Salt Is Worthless

⁴⁹"For everyone will be seasoned with fire,^a and every sacrifice will be seasoned with salt. ⁵⁰Salt *is* good, but if the salt loses its flavor, how will you season it? Have salt in yourselves, and have peace with one another."

Luke 9:46–50
True Greatness

9:46 Then a dispute arose among them as to which of them would be greatest. ⁴⁷And Jesus, perceiving the thought of their heart, took a little child and set him by Him, ⁴⁸and said to them, "Whoever receives this little child in My name receives Me; and whoever receives Me receives Him who sent Me. For he who is least among you all will be great."

Jesus Forbids Sectarianism

⁴⁹Now John answered and said, "Master, we saw someone casting out demons in Your name, and we forbade him because he does not follow with us."

⁵⁰But Jesus said to him, "Do not forbid *him,* for he who is not against us^a is on our^b side."

Mark 9:48 ^aIsaiah 66:24   9:49 ^aNU-Text omits the rest of this verse.   **Luke** 9:50 ^aNU-Text reads *you.*   ^bNU-Text reads *your.*

From Galilee to Jerusalem

The Teacher was moving steadfastly toward the climax of His earthly ministry.

The second traditional segment of Jesus' ministry is His journey from His native Galilee toward Jerusalem during the final year of His life. The Synoptic Gospels relate only one visit to Jerusalem by Jesus during His ministry (Matt. 19:1), a visit that ended with His crucifixion. The Gospel of John, however, reports a series of visits corresponding to the traditional Jewish pilgrimage feasts (see "The Galilean Ministry" at John 1:35).

Only Luke gives extended attention to Jesus' specific journey from Galilee to Judea. Much of the information about Jesus' ministry that is unique to the Gospel of Luke is found in a large section (Luke 9:51—18:14) in which Luke emphasizes Jesus' ultimate destination (see Luke 9:53; 13:22, 33). Teachings on the meaning of discipleship are given by a Teacher who was moving steadfastly toward the climax of His earthly ministry. See "Jesus' Final Journey" at Matt. 8:18.

Attending the Feast of Tabernacles

One of Jesus' several visits to Jerusalem recorded in the Gospel of John was to attend the Feast of Tabernacles. Jesus made that trip to Jerusalem secretly, but began to openly teach in the temple about midway through the feast (John 7:2, 10–14). If the unidentified feast of John 5:1 refers to either Passover or Tabernacles of A.D. 28, this Feast of Tabernacles would have occurred during the fall of A.D. 29 (see "Jesus' Second Visit to Jerusalem" at John 5:1).

At the time of this celebration of the Feast of Tabernacles opposition to Jesus' ministry continued to mount (John 7:1, 2). Yet John's Gospel shows that Jesus remained firmly in control of the events: His "time" was not governed by the world's schedule, but by the Father (7:6, 8). Jesus refused to be manipulated by His family into revealing Himself before this divinely ordained time (7:3–8), and His opponents failed in their attempt to seize Him "because His hour had not yet come" (7:30).

Jesus used the traditional practices of the Jewish religious festival to set the stage for His message. The Feast of Tabernacles had come to be closely associated with prayers for the fall rains that were necessary to assure a bountiful springtime harvest. On the final day of the festival, the priest would present a special offering of water, along with the daily drink offering of wine, in thanksgiving and prayer to the God who supplies the life-giving rains. It may have been at the very moment of that ritual that Jesus announced, "If anyone thirsts, let him come to Me and drink" (7:37).

Worshipers at the Feast of Tabernacles may have also made associations between the feast and the ancient Israelites' wanderings in the wilderness. In such a case, Jesus could have suggested a connection with the rock that miraculously provided the Israelites with water in the wilderness (Ex. 17:1–6). His promise of "rivers of living water" (John 7:38) is identified by John as referring to the Holy Spirit (7:39).

▼ ■ John 7:1–52

John
Jesus' Brothers Disbelieve

7 **:1** After these things Jesus walked in Galilee; for He did not want to walk in Judea, because the Jews[a] sought to kill Him. ²Now the Jews' Feast of Tabernacles was at hand. ³His brothers therefore said to Him, "Depart from here and go into Judea, that Your disciples also may see the works that You are doing. ⁴For no one does anything in secret while he himself seeks to be known openly. If You do these things, show Yourself to the world." ⁵For even His brothers did not believe in Him.

⁶Then Jesus said to them, "My time has not yet come, but your time is always ready. ⁷The world cannot hate you, but it hates Me because I testify of it that its works are evil. ⁸You go up to this feast. I am not yet[a] going up to this feast, for My time has not yet fully come." ⁹When He had said these things to them, He remained in Galilee.

The Heavenly Scholar

¹⁰But when His brothers had gone up, then He also went up to the feast, not openly, but as it were in secret. ¹¹Then the Jews sought Him at the feast, and said, "Where is He?" ¹²And there was much complaining among the people concerning Him.

Some said, "He is good"; others said, "No, on the contrary, He deceives the people." ¹³However, no one spoke openly of Him for fear of the Jews.

¹⁴Now about the middle of the feast Jesus went up into the temple and taught. ¹⁵And the Jews marveled, saying, "How does this Man know letters, having never studied?"

¹⁶Jesus[a] answered them and said, "My doctrine is not Mine, but His who sent Me. ¹⁷If anyone wills to do His will, he shall know concerning the doctrine, whether it is from God or *whether* I speak on My own *authority.* ¹⁸He who speaks from himself seeks his own glory; but He who seeks the glory of the One who sent Him is true, and no unrighteousness is in Him. ¹⁹Did not Moses give you the law, yet none of you keeps the law? Why do you seek to kill Me?"

²⁰The people answered and said, "You have a demon. Who is seeking to kill You?"

²¹Jesus answered and said to them, "I did one work, and you all marvel. ²²Moses therefore gave you circumcision (not that it is from Moses, but from the fathers), and you circumcise a man on the Sabbath. ²³If a man receives circumcision on the Sabbath, so that the law of Moses should not be broken, are you angry with Me because I made a man completely well on the Sabbath? ²⁴Do not judge according to appearance, but judge with righteous judgment."

Could This Be the Christ?

²⁵Now some of them from Jerusalem said, "Is this not He whom they seek to kill? ²⁶But look! He speaks boldly, and they say nothing to Him. Do the rulers know indeed that this is truly[a] the Christ? ²⁷However, we know where this Man is from; but when the Christ comes, no one knows where He is from."

7:1 ᵃThat is, the ruling authorities   7:8 ᵃNU-Text omits *yet.*   7:16 ᵃNU-Text and M-Text read *So Jesus.*   7:26 ᵃNU-Text omits *truly.*

ARTS AND LITERATURE

The literacy rate of any ancient society is hard to estimate. Inscriptions on public buildings, casual graffiti scratched on the walls of Pompeii, and the wide range of things written on papyrus show that writing was not confined to a caste of priests. When the people in Jerusalem were amazed at how Jesus the Galilean could "know letters" (John 7:15), they were surprised that He could teach, not that He could read.

THE SPIRIT AND RIVERS OF LIVING WATER (John 7:38)

The Feast of Tabernacles was celebrated at the end of the grape harvest in September and October. With all harvests completed, the 7 days of this feast were a time for great joy. About halfway through the celebration, Jesus began teaching at the temple (John 7:2, 14), and on the last day He appealed to "the Scripture" (7:37, 38).

What Scripture Jesus had in mind is a mystery since the Old Testament does not speak of "rivers of living water" flowing from a person's heart. There were passages, however, from which Jewish people seem to have read during the Feast of Tabernacles, such as Zechariah 14 and Ezekiel 47. These texts talked about rivers of living water flowing from Jerusalem or from the temple, and in Jesus' day, Jewish people often spoke of Jerusalem and the temple as the "navel of the earth." So it seems that Jesus appealed to the prophecy of water flowing from the temple in the end time.

Most 1st-century Jews would have known of this prophecy. Visitors to the festival watched priests march in solemn procession from the Pool of Siloam into the temple, where they poured out sacred water at the base of the altar. This ritual pointed to the coming rivers of water that the prophets had promised. Those who witnessed the festival event returned home to tell others, and souvenir jars depicting the ritual have been found in other parts of the ancient world.

The Gospel writer John explains Jesus' promise of "rivers of living water" as referring to the Spirit (John 7:39). His interpretation borrows from the Old Testament prophets who sometimes portrayed the "pouring out" of the Spirit as water (Is. 44:3; Ezek. 36:25–27). In the "rivers of living water" John saw the Holy Spirit which Jesus would send after He had been glorified (John 20:22).

28Then Jesus cried out, as He taught in the temple, saying, "You both know Me, and you know where I am from; and I have not come of Myself, but He who sent Me is true, whom you do not know. 29But[a] I know Him, for I am from Him, and He sent Me."

30Therefore they sought to take Him; but no one laid a hand on Him, because His hour had not yet come. 31And many of the people believed in Him, and said, "When the Christ comes, will He do more signs than these which this *Man* has done?"

Jesus and the Religious Leaders

32The Pharisees heard the crowd murmuring these things concerning Him, and the Pharisees and the chief priests sent officers to take Him. 33Then Jesus said to them,[a] "I shall be with you a little while longer, and *then* I go to Him who sent Me. 34You will seek Me and not find *Me,* and where I am you cannot come."

35Then the Jews said among themselves, "Where does He intend to go that we shall not find Him? Does He intend to go to the Dispersion among the Greeks and teach the Greeks? 36What is this thing that He said, 'You will seek Me and not find Me, and where I am you cannot come'?"

The Promise of the Holy Spirit

37On the last day, that great *day* of the feast, Jesus stood and cried out, saying, "If anyone thirsts, let him come to Me and drink. 38He who believes in Me, as the

---

7:29 ªNU-Text and M-Text omit *But.*
7:33 ªNU-Text and M-Text omit *to them.*

CULTURE AND SOCIETY

Educational practice during Jesus' time was influenced by Greek education (John 7:35), whose centerpiece was the poems of Homer. Hebrew education was less formal, but the parents were charged with teaching their children the history, customs, and laws that in effect make up the Pentateuch, the first five books of the Bible. The Romans had a set of traditional laws that all children were supposed to memorize.

Scripture has said, out of his heart will flow rivers of living water." ³⁹But this He spoke concerning the Spirit, whom those believingª in Him would receive; for the Holyᵇ Spirit was not yet *given,* because Jesus was not yet glorified.

Who Is He?

⁴⁰Therefore manyª from the crowd, when they heard this saying, said, "Truly this is the Prophet." ⁴¹Others said, "This is the Christ."

But some said, "Will the Christ come out of Galilee? ⁴²Has not the Scripture said that the Christ comes from the seed of David and from the town of Bethlehem, where David was?" ⁴³So there was a division among the people because of Him. ⁴⁴Now some of them wanted to take Him, but no one laid hands on Him.

Rejected by the Authorities

⁴⁵Then the officers came to the chief priests and Pharisees, who said to them, "Why have you not brought Him?"

⁴⁶The officers answered, "No man ever spoke like this Man!"

⁴⁷Then the Pharisees answered them, "Are you also deceived? ⁴⁸Have any of the rulers or the Pharisees believed in Him? ⁴⁹But this crowd that does not know the law is accursed."

⁵⁰Nicodemus (he who came to Jesus by night,ª being one of them) said to them, ⁵¹"Does our law judge a man before it hears him and knows what he is doing?"

⁵²They answered and said to him, "Are you also from Galilee? Search and look, for no prophet has arisenª out of Galilee."

TIME CAPSULE A.D. 29

29 In spring, Jesus attends the Passover in Jerusalem (John 6:4)

29 Jesus walks on the water (John 6:19)

29 Peter confesses that Jesus is the Christ (Luke 9:20)

29 Jesus attends the fall Feast of Tabernacles (John 7:2, 14)

29 Jesus attends the winter Feast of Dedication (John 10:22)

Forgiving an Adulteress

In this memorable story about a woman caught in adultery, Jesus doodled in the dirt while the crowd, whom He had confronted with their own sins, slowly departed without stoning her. Scholars are divided, however, over whether the story was originally part of the Gospel of John. It is found in the vast majority of Greek manuscripts of the Fourth Gospel, but is not found in any of the earliest manuscripts. In some Greek manuscripts it appears in three other places in the Gospel of John (after John 7:36; 7:44; 21:25) or even in the Gospel of Luke (after Luke 21:38). Moreover, the Greek in John 7:53—8:11 is of a markedly different style and character than that found in the remainder of the Fourth Gospel. Though it is uncertain whether the story was an original part of John's Gospel, it is still possible that it preserves an actual event from Jesus' ministry.

■ John 7:53—8:11

John

7 :53 And everyone went to his *own* house.ª

An Adulteress Faces the Light of the World

8 ¹But Jesus went to the Mount of Olives.

²Now earlyª in the morning He came again into the temple, and all the people came to Him; and He sat down and taught them. ³Then the scribes and Pharisees brought to Him a woman caught in adultery. And when they had set her in the midst, ⁴they said to Him, "Teacher, this woman was caughtª in adultery, in the very act. ⁵Now Moses, in the law, commandedª us that such should be stoned.ᵇ But what do You say?"ᶜ ⁶This they said, testing Him, that they might have *something* of which to accuse Him. But Jesus stooped down and

---

7:39 ªNU-Text reads *who believed.*   ᵇNU-Text omits *Holy.*   7:40 ªNU-Text reads *some.*
7:50 ªNU-Text reads *before.*   7:52 ªNU-Text reads *is to rise.*   7:53 ªThe words *And everyone* through *sin no more* (8:11) are bracketed by NU-Text as not original. They are present in over 900 manuscripts.   8:2 ªM-Text reads *very early.*
8:4 ªM-Text reads *we found this woman.*
8:5 ªM-Text reads *in our law Moses commanded.* ᵇNU-Text and M-Text read *to stone such.*   ᶜM-Text adds *about her.*

wrote on the ground with *His* finger, as though He did not hear.ᵃ

⁷So when they continued asking Him, He raised Himself upᵃ and said to them, "He who is without sin among you, let him throw a stone at her first." ⁸And again He stooped down and wrote on the ground. ⁹Then those who heard *it,* being convicted by *their* conscience,ᵃ went out one by one, beginning with the oldest *even* to the last. And Jesus was left alone, and the woman standing in the midst. ¹⁰When Jesus had raised Himself up and saw no one but the woman, He said to her,ᵃ "Woman, where are those accusers of yours?ᵇ Has no one condemned you?"

¹¹She said, "No one, Lord."

And Jesus said to her, "Neither do I condemn you; go andᵃ sin no more."

Discussions with the Pharisees

Another debate with the Pharisees continues Jesus' teaching on the occasion of the Feast of Tabernacles (see "Attending the Feast of Tabernacles" at John 7:1). Given associations between the feast and the Israelites' wilderness wanderings, Jesus' statement, "I am the light of the world" (John 8:12) possibly recalled the presence of God as a pillar of fire leading the Israelites in the wilderness (Ex. 13:21).

The recurring theme of Jesus' discussions was His relationship with God the Father. His use of the phrase "I AM" as a type of personal address (John 8:58) indicates His unique relationship with the Father. Among Jesus' Jewish contemporaries this phrase was understood as an expression of God's personal name (see Ex. 3:14), so for Jesus to claim it for Himself was to claim unity with God.

■ John 8:12–59

John
Jesus Defends His Self-Witness

8:12 Then Jesus spoke to them again, saying, "I am the light of the world. He who follows Me shall not walk in darkness, but have the light of life."

¹³The Pharisees therefore said to Him, "You bear witness of Yourself; Your witness is not true."

¹⁴Jesus answered and said to them, "Even if I bear witness of Myself, My witness is true, for I know where I came from and where I am going; but you do not know where I come from and where I am going. ¹⁵You judge according to the flesh; I judge no one. ¹⁶And yet if I do judge, My judgment is true; for I am not alone, but I *am* with the Father who sent Me. ¹⁷It is also written in your law that the testimony of two men is true. ¹⁸I am One who bears witness of Myself, and the Father who sent Me bears witness of Me."

¹⁹Then they said to Him, "Where is Your Father?"

Jesus answered, "You know neither Me nor My Father. If you had known Me, you would have known My Father also."

²⁰These words Jesus spoke in the treasury, as He taught in the temple; and no one laid hands on Him, for His hour had not yet come.

Jesus Predicts His Departure

²¹Then Jesus said to them again, "I am going away, and you will seek Me, and will die in your sin. Where I go you cannot come."

²²So the Jews said, "Will He kill Himself, because He says, 'Where I go you cannot come'?"

²³And He said to them, "You are from beneath; I am from above. You are of this world; I am not of this world. ²⁴Therefore I said to you that you will die in your sins; for if you do not believe that I am *He,* you will die in your sins."

²⁵Then they said to Him, "Who are You?"

And Jesus said to them, "Just what I have been saying to you from the beginning. ²⁶I have many things to say and to judge concerning you, but He who sent Me is true; and I speak to the world those things which I heard from Him."

²⁷They did not understand that He spoke to them of the Father.

²⁸Then Jesus said to them, "When you lift up the Son of Man, then you will know that I am *He,* and *that* I do nothing of Myself; but as My Father taught Me, I speak these things. ²⁹And He who sent Me is with Me. The Father has not left Me alone, for I

8:6 ᵃNU-Text and M-Text omit *as though He did not hear.*   8:7 ᵃM-Text reads *He looked up.*
8:9 ᵃNU-Text and M-Text omit *being convicted by their conscience.*   8:10 ᵃNU-Text omits *and saw no one but the woman;* M-Text reads *He saw her and said.* ᵇNU-Text and M-Text omit *of yours.*
8:11 ᵃNU-Text and M-Text add *from now on.*

always do those things that please Him."
³⁰As He spoke these words, many believed
in Him.

The Truth Shall Make You Free

³¹Then Jesus said to those Jews who
believed Him, "If you abide in My word,
you are My disciples indeed. ³²And you
shall know the truth, and the truth shall
make you free."

³³They answered Him, "We are Abraham's descendants, and have never been in
bondage to anyone. How *can* You say, 'You
will be made free'?"

³⁴Jesus answered them, "Most assuredly, I say to you, whoever commits sin
is a slave of sin. ³⁵And a slave does not
abide in the house forever, *but* a son abides
forever. ³⁶Therefore if the Son makes you
free, you shall be free indeed.

Abraham's Seed and Satan's

³⁷"I know that you are Abraham's descendants, but you seek to kill Me, because
My word has no place in you. ³⁸I speak
what I have seen with My Father, and you
do what you have seen with[a] your father."

³⁹They answered and said to Him,
"Abraham is our father."

Jesus said to them, "If you were Abraham's children, you would do the works of
Abraham. ⁴⁰But now you seek to kill Me, a
Man who has told you the truth which I
heard from God. Abraham did not do this.
⁴¹You do the deeds of your father."

Then they said to Him, "We were not
born of fornication; we have one Father—
God."

⁴²Jesus said to them, "If God were your
Father, you would love Me, for I proceeded
forth and came from God; nor have I come
of Myself, but He sent Me. ⁴³Why do you
not understand My speech? Because you
are not able to listen to My word. ⁴⁴You are
of *your* father the devil, and the desires of
your father you want to do. He was a murderer from the beginning, and does not
stand in the truth, because there is no
truth in him. When he speaks a lie, he
speaks from his own *resources,* for he is a
liar and the father of it. ⁴⁵But because I tell
the truth, you do not believe Me. ⁴⁶Which
of you convicts Me of sin? And if I tell the
truth, why do you not believe Me? ⁴⁷He
who is of God hears God's words; therefore
you do not hear, because you are not of
God."

Before Abraham Was, I AM

⁴⁸Then the Jews answered and said to
Him, "Do we not say rightly that You are a
Samaritan and have a demon?"

⁴⁹Jesus answered, "I do not have a demon; but I honor My Father, and you dishonor Me. ⁵⁰And I do not seek My *own*
glory; there is One who seeks and judges.
⁵¹Most assuredly, I say to you, if anyone
keeps My word he shall never see death."

⁵²Then the Jews said to Him, "Now we
know that You have a demon! Abraham is
dead, and the prophets; and You say, 'If
anyone keeps My word he shall never taste
death.' ⁵³Are You greater than our father
Abraham, who is dead? And the prophets
are dead. Who do You make Yourself out to
be?"

⁵⁴Jesus answered, "If I honor Myself,
My honor is nothing. It is My Father who
honors Me, of whom you say that He is
your[a] God. ⁵⁵Yet you have not known Him,
but I know Him. And if I say, 'I do not
know Him,' I shall be a liar like you; but I
do know Him and keep His word. ⁵⁶Your
father Abraham rejoiced to see My day, and
he saw *it* and was glad."

⁵⁷Then the Jews said to Him, "You are
not yet fifty years old, and have You seen
Abraham?"

⁵⁸Jesus said to them, "Most assuredly,
I say to you, before Abraham was, I AM."

⁵⁹Then they took up stones to throw at
Him; but Jesus hid Himself and went out
of the temple,[a] going through the midst of
them, and so passed by.

8:38 ªNU-Text reads *heard from.*   8:54 ªNU-Text
and M-Text read *our.*   8:59 ªNU-Text omits the
rest of this verse.

 ### *Healing the Man Born Blind*

Jesus proclaimed, "I am the light of the
world" (John 8:12; 9:5) and demonstrated
what He meant by healing a man with congeni-
tal blindness. Jesus' presence in the world as
"light" served first as a source of revelation,
revealing "the works of God" (John 9:3) in
overcoming affliction. But this "light" was also
a source of judgment (see John 3:19–21).
The healing provoked a crisis because it was
performed on the Sabbath (9:16; see "Lord
of the Sabbath" at Matt. 12:1). By self-
righteously condemning Jesus as a "sinner" for
this breach of Sabbath observance traditions,

Jesus' Pharisaic opponents brought themselves under judgment (John 9:39–41).

Conversely, the man who was healed received not only physical sight but also increasing spiritual insight. As he reflected upon what had happened to him, he gradually proceeded from referring to his benefactor as "a Man called Jesus" (9:11) to saying that "He is a prophet" (9:17), and ultimately to confessing belief that He is "the Son of God" (9:35–38).

▼ ■ John 9:1–41

John
Jesus, the Light of the World

9 :1 Now as *Jesus* passed by, He saw a man who was blind from birth. 2And His disciples asked Him, saying, "Rabbi, who sinned, this man or his parents, that he was born blind?"

3Jesus answered, "Neither this man nor his parents sinned, but that the works of God should be revealed in him. 4Ia must work the works of Him who sent Me while it is day; *the* night is coming when no one can work. 5As long as I am in the world, I am the light of the world."

6When He had said these things, He spat on the ground and made clay with the saliva; and He anointed the eyes of the blind man with the clay. 7And He said to him, "Go, wash in the pool of Siloam" (which is translated, Sent). So he went and washed, and came back seeing.

8Therefore the neighbors and those who previously had seen that he was blinda said, "Is not this he who sat and begged?"

9Some said, "This is he." Others *said,* "He is like him."a

He said, "I am *he.*"

10Therefore they said to him, "How were your eyes opened?"

11He answered and said, "A Man called Jesus made clay and anointed my eyes and said to me, 'Go to the pool ofa Siloam and wash.' So I went and washed, and I received sight."

12Then they said to him, "Where is He?"

He said, "I do not know."

The Pharisees Excommunicate the Healed Man

13They brought him who formerly was blind to the Pharisees. 14Now it was a Sab-

bath when Jesus made the clay and opened his eyes. 15Then the Pharisees also asked him again how he had received his sight. He said to them, "He put clay on my eyes, and I washed, and I see."

16Therefore some of the Pharisees said, "This Man is not from God, because He does not keep the Sabbath."

Others said, "How can a man who is a sinner do such signs?" And there was a division among them.

17They said to the blind man again, "What do you say about Him because He opened your eyes?"

He said, "He is a prophet."

18But the Jews did not believe concerning him, that he had been blind and received his sight, until they called the parents of him who had received his sight. 19And they asked them, saying, "Is this your son, who you say was born blind? How then does he now see?"

20His parents answered them and said, "We know that this is our son, and that he was born blind; 21but by what means he now sees we do not know, or who opened his eyes we do not know. He is of age; ask him. He will speak for himself." 22His parents said these *things* because they feared the Jews, for the Jews had agreed already that if anyone confessed *that* He *was* Christ, he would be put out of the synagogue. 23Therefore his parents said, "He is of age; ask him."

24So they again called the man who was blind, and said to him, "Give God the glory! We know that this Man is a sinner."

25He answered and said, "Whether He is a sinner *or not* I do not know. One thing I know: that though I was blind, now I see."

26Then they said to him again, "What did He do to you? How did He open your eyes?"

27He answered them, "I told you already, and you did not listen. Why do you want to hear *it* again? Do you also want to become His disciples?"

28Then they reviled him and said, "You are His disciple, but we are Moses' disciples. 29We know that God spoke to Moses; *as for* this *fellow,* we do not know where He is from."

30The man answered and said to them, "Why, this is a marvelous thing, that you do not know where He is from; yet He has opened my eyes! 31Now we know that God does not hear sinners; but if anyone is a

---

9:4 aNU-Text reads *We.*   9:8 aNU-Text reads *a beggar.*   9:9 aNU-Text reads *"No, but he is like him."*   9:11 aNU-Text omits *the pool of.*

PUT OUT OF THE SYNAGOGUE (John 9:22)

In Jesus' day various groups competed for power in Jerusalem. The Sadducees held the most formal power, since they were backed by the Romans. The Pharisees, however, were more popular with the people, and often held prominent roles in the Jerusalem synagogues. Ironically, the Pharisees used their control of the synagogues to wield authority over the very people whom they were supposed to be serving.

When Jesus miraculously helped a blind man receive his sight, the people brought the healed man to the Pharisees (John 9:8–13). Because the healing occurred on a Sabbath, the Pharisees were much concerned about Jesus violating their interpretation of Sabbath laws. In their view, a Sabbath-breaker could not have healed anyone by God's power (9:16).

The blind man's parents, being questioned concerning their son's healing, dared not counter the Pharisees' view (9:20–22). John's Gospel makes it clear that the parents feared being "put out of the synagogue" (9:22). This could mean excommunication, that is exclusion from the synagogue community. Severely erring members of synagogues were sometimes disciplined by beatings, or by temporary or long-term exclusion from their synagogues.

By the time John wrote his Gospel, more than 60 years after Jesus' death, Jewish Christians were being threatened with excommunication from their synagogues because of their belief in Jesus as the Messiah. John warns of this conflict (John 16:2). By retelling the time that Jesus healed the blind man and defended him against those who persecuted him for his faith, John encouraged his own readers in their situation: Jesus would be with them as well.

worshiper of God and does His will, He hears him. ³²Since the world began it has been unheard of that anyone opened the eyes of one who was born blind. ³³If this Man were not from God, He could do nothing."

³⁴They answered and said to him, "You were completely born in sins, and are you teaching us?" And they cast him out.

³⁵Jesus heard that they had cast him out; and when He had found him, He said to him, "Do you believe in the Son of God?"ᵃ

³⁶He answered and said, "Who is He, Lord, that I may believe in Him?"

³⁷And Jesus said to him, "You have both seen Him and it is He who is talking with you."

³⁸Then he said, "Lord, I believe!" And he worshiped Him.

³⁹And Jesus said, "For judgment I have come into this world, that those who do not see may see, and that those who see may be made blind."

⁴⁰Then *some* of the Pharisees who were with Him heard these words, and said to Him, "Are we blind also?"

⁴¹Jesus said to them, "If you were blind, you would have no sin; but now you say, 'We see.' Therefore your sin remains."

9:35 ᵃNU-Text reads *Son of Man.*

Jesus, the Good Shepherd

It is uncertain how closely Jesus' parable of the good shepherd (John 10:1–6) should be tied to the healing of the blind man (see "Healing the Man Born Blind" at John 9:1). Some scholars believe this exchange with Jewish leaders occurred sometime later, during the 2-month period separating Jesus' visits to Jerusalem for the Feast of Tabernacles (John 7:2) and for the Feast of Dedication (now known as Hanukkah; John 10:22). Others, though, since there is no introductory statement in John 10:1, consider this parable to be the continuation of Jesus' response to "some of the Pharisees" following the blind man's healing (see John 9:40, 41). Some of those who heard Jesus' teaching on this parable did refer back to the healing of the blind man (10:21).

Whether or not Jesus' parable continued His response to the controversy over the blind man's healing, the illustration of the shepherd's relationship to his sheep can be read as an allegory of that event. Just as the sheep know the voice of the shepherd and follow only him and not strangers (10:4, 5), so the healed blind man refused to heed those who advised him to renounce Jesus (see John 9:24–33). Those who had sought to bar others from fellowship with God's people (9:22) can be likened to "a thief and a robber" within the sheepfold (10:1).

■ John 10:1–21

John
The Shepherd's Flock

10 :1 "Most assuredly, I say to you, he who does not enter the sheepfold by the door, but climbs up some other way, the same is a thief and a robber. ²But he who enters by the door is the shepherd of the sheep. ³To him the doorkeeper opens, and the sheep hear his voice; and he calls his own sheep by name and leads them out. ⁴And when he brings out his own sheep, he goes before them; and the sheep follow him, for they know his voice. ⁵Yet they will by no means follow a stranger, but will flee from him, for they do not know the voice of strangers." ⁶Jesus used this illustration, but they did not understand the things which He spoke to them.

⁷Then Jesus said to them again, "Most assuredly, I say to you, I am the door of the sheep. ⁸All who *ever* came before Meᵃ are thieves and robbers, but the sheep did not hear them. ⁹I am the door. If anyone enters by Me, he will be saved, and will go in and out and find pasture. ¹⁰The thief does not come except to steal, and to kill, and to destroy. I have come that they may have life, and that they may have *it* more abundantly.

¹¹"I am the good shepherd. The good shepherd gives His life for the sheep. ¹²But a hireling, *he who is* not the shepherd, one who does not own the sheep, sees the wolf coming and leaves the sheep and flees; and the wolf catches the sheep and scatters them. ¹³The hireling flees because he is a hireling and does not care about the sheep. ¹⁴I am the good shepherd; and I know My *sheep,* and am known by My own. ¹⁵As the Father knows Me, even so I know the Father; and I lay down My life for the sheep. ¹⁶And other sheep I have which are not of this fold; them also I must bring, and they will hear My voice; and there will be one flock *and* one shepherd.

¹⁷"Therefore My Father loves Me, because I lay down My life that I may take it again. ¹⁸No one takes it from Me, but I lay it down of Myself. I have power to lay it down, and I have power to take it again. This command I have received from My Father."

¹⁹Therefore there was a division again among the Jews because of these sayings. ²⁰And many of them said, "He has a demon and is mad. Why do you listen to Him?"

²¹Others said, "These are not the words of one who has a demon. Can a demon open the eyes of the blind?"

10:8 ᵃM-Text omits *before Me.*

Jesus' Final Journey

Luke's "travel narrative" is a unique account of Jesus' journey from Galilee to Jerusalem.

The Galilean portion of His ministry now completed, Jesus began a journey to Jerusalem to meet His destiny, a destiny of which He was well aware and which He faced willingly (Mark 8:31; 9:30, 31). In the Synoptic Gospels, this journey is Jesus' only visit to Jerusalem, while in John it is simply the last of several journeys. Though the Gospels differ concerning the number of journeys, they necessarily agree that Jesus made a final such journey shortly before His death. About this final journey the Gospels differ only in the amount of information they provide concerning its various events.

By far the greatest amount of information on Jesus' teachings and deeds while on this journey is in the Gospel of Luke. Luke's unique account of the journey from Galilee to Jerusalem (Luke 9:51—18:14) is called his "travel narrative." There are only a few places in the narrative where the other Gospels offer parallels to Luke's version of events, and these occur mostly toward the end of the journey when Jesus is in Judea but has not yet arrived at Jerusalem.

Matthew and Luke report some of Jesus' same teachings, but do so in different settings. While in Luke's Gospel these teachings were spoken on the road to Jerusalem (Luke 9:57), Matthew places most of them earlier in Jesus' ministry (Matt. 8:18, 19). Many scholars believe that most of Luke's information for the travel narrative came from two written sources, one which was apparently available only to him (called the "L" source for "Luke"), and one which was also employed by Matthew (called the "Q" source).

Through Samaria Toward Jerusalem

Luke begins his account of the journey to Jerusalem with Jesus traveling to Judea through Samaria, the region directly between Galilee and Judea (Luke 9:52). Mark and Matthew do not mention this direct route through Samaria, but rather a route around Samaria through Perea, called "the region of Judea beyond the Jordan" (Matt. 19:1; Mark 10:1).

Luke's report of Jesus' rejection by a Samaritan village (Luke 9:53) reflects the hostility between Jews and Samaritans. Jesus knew that He would face opposition in Samaria and wished to encounter it head-on, demonstrating His courage and His determination to fulfill His destiny in spite of all opposition. The Samaritan encounter also allowed Him to teach His disciples how to handle such opposition, a lesson they surely needed. They would have called down fire from heaven to punish this village for rejecting their Master. But Jesus rebukes the disciples: lashing out in anger is not the way to handle opposition (Luke 9:55).

Since following Jesus would involve rejection and suffering, His followers could not be halfhearted. Both Luke and Matthew record Jesus' teachings that disciples must be completely committed (Matt. 8:20–22; Luke 9:58–62). They could not allow excuses, such as the death of a loved one or the need to say farewell to family members, to delay them from following.

■ Matthew 8:18–22
■ Luke 9:51–62

Matthew 8:18–22
The Cost of Discipleship

8 **:18** And when Jesus saw great multitudes about Him, He gave a command to depart to the other side. 19Then a certain scribe came and said to Him, "Teacher, I will follow You wherever You go." 20And Jesus said to him, "Foxes have holes and birds of the air *have* nests, but the Son of Man has nowhere to lay *His* head." 21Then another of His disciples said to Him, "Lord, let me first go and bury my father." 22But Jesus said to him, "Follow Me, and let the dead bury their own dead."

Luke 9:51–62
A Samaritan Village Rejects the Savior

9 **:51** Now it came to pass, when the time had come for Him to be received up, that He steadfastly set His face to go to Jerusalem, 52and sent messengers before His face. And as they went, they entered a village of the Samaritans, to prepare for Him. 53But they did not receive Him, because His face was *set* for the journey to Jerusalem. 54And when His disciples James and John saw *this,* they said, "Lord, do You want us to command fire to come down from heaven and consume them, just as Elijah did?"[a]

55But He turned and rebuked them,[a] and said, "You do not know what manner of spirit you are of. 56For the Son of Man did not come to destroy men's lives but to save *them.*"[a] And they went to another village.

I Will Follow You

57Now it happened as they journeyed on the road, *that* someone said to Him, "Lord, I will follow You wherever You go." 58And Jesus said to him, "Foxes have holes and birds of the air *have* nests, but the Son of Man has nowhere to lay *His* head." 59Then He said to another, "Follow Me."

But he said, "Lord, let me first go and bury my father." 60Jesus said to him, "Let the dead bury their own dead, but you go and preach the kingdom of God." 61And another also said, "Lord, I will follow You, but let me first go *and* bid them farewell who are at my house." 62But Jesus said to him, "No one, having put his hand to the plow, and looking back, is fit for the kingdom of God."

9:54 [a]NU-Text omits *just as Elijah did.*
9:55 [a]NU-Text omits the rest of this verse.
9:56 [a]NU-Text omits the first sentence of this verse.

Mission of the 70 Disciples

Jesus sent out a large group of disciples to prepare the way for Him (Luke 10:1). Just as harvest workers must labor with great haste to bring in their crops before it is too late, so too did Jesus instruct these disciples to hurry and not to concern themselves with insignificant matters such as what they would eat or where they would stay (10:7, 8). They would face great opposition along the way, and Jesus instructed them on how to handle being rejected by a town. Such unreceptive Galilean cities as Chorazin, Bethsaida, and Capernaum were more guilty than the Gentile cities of Phoenicia, who would have repented if they had witnessed Jesus' work (10:13–15).

Only Luke suggests that Jesus ever sent out such a large group of disciples. All three Synoptic Gospels agree that Jesus sent out the twelve disciples to preach and to heal (Luke 9:1–6). Luke, however, mentions this second mission with a much larger group of 70 disciples. The other evangelists do not give the impression that Jesus had such a large and devoted group of followers, while Luke presents the "workers" as more plentiful and the "harvest" as more abundant.

Most of the material in Luke's story of the mission of 70 disciples is also found in Matthew. The different sayings of Jesus in Luke 10:1–24 are sprinkled throughout Matt. 9—11 (Matt. 9:37; 10:7-16, 40; 11:20-27). Possibly both evangelists found these sayings in a common source, each choosing to fit them into his account in a different way.

- Matthew 11:20–30
- Luke 10:1–24

Matthew 11:20–30
Woe to the Impenitent Cities

11 **:20** Then He began to rebuke the cities in which most of His mighty

works had been done, because they did not repent: [21]"Woe to you, Chorazin! Woe to you, Bethsaida! For if the mighty works which were done in you had been done in Tyre and Sidon, they would have repented long ago in sackcloth and ashes. [22]But I say to you, it will be more tolerable for Tyre and Sidon in the day of judgment than for you. [23]And you, Capernaum, who are exalted to heaven, will be[a] brought down to Hades; for if the mighty works which were done in you had been done in Sodom, it would have remained until this day. [24]But I say to you that it shall be more tolerable for the land of Sodom in the day of judgment than for you."

Jesus Gives True Rest

[25]At that time Jesus answered and said, "I thank You, Father, Lord of heaven and earth, that You have hidden these things from *the* wise and prudent and have revealed them to babes. [26]Even so, Father, for so it seemed good in Your sight. [27]All things have been delivered to Me by My Father, and no one knows the Son except the Father. Nor does anyone know the Father except the Son, and *the one* to whom the Son wills to reveal *Him.* [28]Come to Me, all *you* who labor and are heavy laden, and I will give you rest. [29]Take My yoke upon you and learn from Me, for I am gentle and lowly in heart, and you will find rest for your souls. [30]For My yoke *is* easy and My burden is light."

Luke 10:1–24
The Seventy Sent Out

10 **:1** After these things the Lord appointed seventy others also,[a] and sent them two by two before His face into every city and place where He Himself was about to go. [2]Then He said to them, "The harvest truly *is* great, but the laborers *are* few; therefore pray the Lord of the harvest to send out laborers into His harvest. [3]Go your way; behold, I send you out as lambs among wolves. [4]Carry neither money bag, knapsack, nor sandals; and greet no one

---

11:23 [a]NU-Text reads *will you be exalted to heaven? No, you will be.*   **Luke** 10:1 [a]NU-Text reads *seventy-two others.*

GEOGRAPHY AND ENVIRONMENT

Chorazin and Bethsaida, located close to the north shore of Lake Galilee, are named along with Capernaum in Jesus' announcement of judgment against the cities of Galilee (Matt. 11:21, 23). Chorazin was a town of medium size and, according to Jewish literature, a center for producing wheat. "Bethsaida of Galilee" was the home of some of Jesus' disciples, particularly Philip, Andrew, and Peter (John 1:44; 12:21).

WAITING TO BURY THEIR DEAD (Matt. 8:21)

One of Jesus' disciples requested, "Let me first go and bury my father" (Matt. 8:21). This request may sound reasonable to modern readers who suppose that the disciple's father had just died and the burial would not take long. That was not the case, however, in 1st-century Jewish culture.

Immediately after a person died, family members and professional mourners would gather to weep and wail. As soon as the body was ready, they would carry it on a stretcher to the family tomb, while other people in town who heard or saw the procession would quickly join it to share the family's sorrow. Members of the immediate family would continue heavy grieving for one week, while friends and neighbors would bring food or other items to relieve the family of its other obligations.

For 1st-century Jews, honoring parents was one of life's highest obligations, and burying one's parents was considered a most important way to honor them. No son whose father had just died would be talking with Jesus in public before the father's body had been laid in a tomb. The son would be preparing the body for immediate transport to the tomb.

So what was this disciple asking of Jesus? Possibly the father was not yet dead. Even today in the Middle East, the expression "Wait until I bury my father" expresses a desire to wait until the father has died before embarking too far from home. The disciple may have wanted to wait until his aged father died before following Jesus.

Yet it is also possible that the disciple's father had been dead for some time. Jewish people in the 1st century let the flesh rot off of a corpse's bones for a year, then returned to the tomb and gathered the bones into a box which they deposited into a slot in the tomb wall. If the disciple was referring to such a reburial, known as *secondary* burial, then he was asking for as much as a year's delay in following Jesus.

Some teachers claimed special honor, but no other teacher claimed that following him was as important as burying one's parents. Only God Himself warranted that role. Those who did not recognize Jesus' true identity may have viewed Him as arrogant or anti-family to demand, "Let the dead bury their own dead" (8:22).

along the road. ⁵But whatever house you enter, first say, 'Peace to this house.' ⁶And if a son of peace is there, your peace will rest on it; if not, it will return to you. ⁷And remain in the same house, eating and drinking such things as they give, for the laborer is worthy of his wages. Do not go from house to house. ⁸Whatever city you enter, and they receive you, eat such things as are set before you. ⁹And heal the sick there, and say to them, 'The kingdom of God has come near to you.' ¹⁰But whatever city you enter, and they do not receive you, go out into its streets and say, ¹¹'The very dust of your city which clings to usᵃ we wipe off against you. Nevertheless know this, that the kingdom of God has come near you.' ¹²Butᵃ I say to you that it will be more tolerable in that Day for Sodom than for that city.

Woe to the Impenitent Cities

¹³"Woe to you, Chorazin! Woe to you, Bethsaida! For if the mighty works which

were done in you had been done in Tyre and Sidon, they would have repented long ago, sitting in sackcloth and ashes. ¹⁴But it will be more tolerable for Tyre and Sidon at the judgment than for you. ¹⁵And you, Capernaum, who are exalted to heaven, will be brought down to Hades.ᵃ ¹⁶He who hears you hears Me, he who rejects you rejects Me, and he who rejects Me rejects Him who sent Me."

The Seventy Return with Joy

¹⁷Then the seventyᵃ returned with joy, saying, "Lord, even the demons are subject to us in Your name."

¹⁸And He said to them, "I saw Satan fall like lightning from heaven. ¹⁹Behold, I give you the authority to trample on ser-

10:11 ᵃNU-Text reads *our feet.*   10:12 ᵃNU-Text and M-Text omit *But.*   10:15 ᵃNU-Text reads *will you be exalted to heaven? You will be thrust down to Hades!*   10:17 ᵃNU-Text reads *seventy-two.*

pents and scorpions, and over all the power of the enemy, and nothing shall by any means hurt you. [20]Nevertheless do not rejoice in this, that the spirits are subject to you, but rather[a] rejoice because your names are written in heaven."

Jesus Rejoices in the Spirit

[21]In that hour Jesus rejoiced in the Spirit and said, "I thank You, Father, Lord of heaven and earth, that You have hidden these things from *the* wise and prudent and revealed them to babes. Even so, Father, for so it seemed good in Your sight. [22]All[a] things have been delivered to Me by My Father, and no one knows who the Son

is except the Father, and who the Father is except the Son, and *the one* to whom the Son wills to reveal *Him*."

[23]Then He turned to *His* disciples and said privately, "Blessed *are* the eyes which see the things you see; [24]for I tell you that many prophets and kings have desired to see what you see, and have not seen *it,* and to hear what you hear, and have not heard *it.*"

10:20 [a]NU-Text and M-Text omit *rather.*
10:22 [a]M-Text reads *And turning to the disciples He said, "All* . . . .

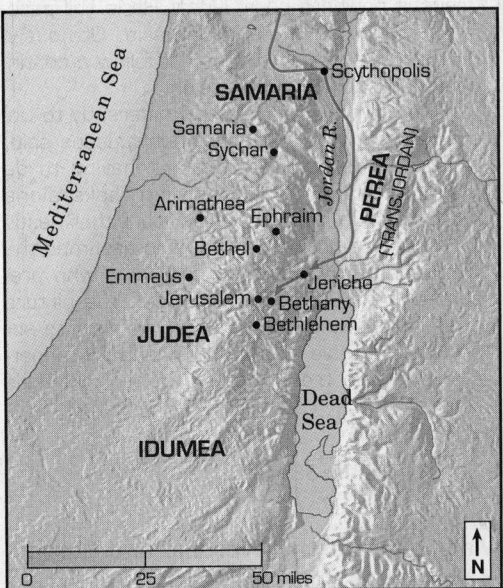

Last Journey to Jerusalem
On His last trip to Jerusalem, Jesus apparently took the longer route from Scythopolis, crossing to the east bank of the Jordan River to travel south. Recrossing the Jordan River near Jericho, He ascended the mountain to Bethany and finally arrived at Jerusalem. This route bypassed Samaria altogether.

Compassion and Mercy from a Samaritan

A lawyer tested Jesus with a question about how to inherit eternal life. Both Mark and Matthew include a similar story, in which a scribe (Mark 12:28) and a Pharisee (Matt. 22:34–36) question Jesus concerning which is the greatest commandment. Only in Luke's Gospel does the lawyer ask a second question. Having been told that to inherit eternal life he must love his neighbor as himself, he asks Jesus, "And who is my neighbor?" (Luke 10:29). In answer, Jesus delivered one of the best known of His parables: the parable of the good Samaritan.

On the surface, this parable offers the simple teaching that a "neighbor" is anyone with whom one comes into contact, especially those in need. The specific identities of the characters involved, however, moves the parable beyond a simple moral lesson. The man who is beaten and robbed was traveling "from Jerusalem to Jericho" (Luke 10:30), which marks him almost certainly as a Jew. The priest and Levite passed by without helping the man, perhaps because they did not wish to defile themselves by contact with blood or with (presumably) a dead body. The Samaritan, a mortal enemy of all Jews, took pity on the man and offered him an extraordinary degree of assistance.

If Jesus' sole intention had been to say that one's neighbor includes everyone, there would have been no need to identify the actors as a "Levite," a "priest," and a "Samaritan." Jesus was also critiquing the heartlessness of

---

GEOGRAPHY AND ENVIRONMENT

Tyre and Sidon (Luke 10:13, 14) are ancient seaports along the Mediterranean coast, between Israel and Berytus. Today Berytus is Beirut. Tyre was defeated by Alexander the Great in 332 B.C. after a 7-month siege and a hard struggle, including the building of a causeway from the mainland to the island. Just north of Tyre is Sidon, which had the reputation of being the oldest Phoenician port.

those Jews who allowed the Law to thwart their humanity. With this parable Luke continues a favorite theme: the inclusion of all nations in the people of God. Even a Samaritan can aspire to eternal life!

▼ ■ Luke 10:25–37

Luke
The Parable of the Good Samaritan

10 **:25** And behold, a certain lawyer stood up and tested Him, saying, "Teacher, what shall I do to inherit eternal life?"

26He said to him, "What is written in the law? What is your reading *of it?*"

27So he answered and said, "*'You shall love the* LORD *your God with all your heart, with all your soul, with all your strength, and with all your mind,'*a and *'your neighbor as yourself.'*"b

28And He said to him, "You have answered rightly; do this and you will live."

29But he, wanting to justify himself, said to Jesus, "And who is my neighbor?"

30Then Jesus answered and said: "A certain *man* went down from Jerusalem to Jericho, and fell among thieves, who stripped him of his clothing, wounded *him,* and departed, leaving *him* half dead. 31Now by chance a certain priest came down that road. And when he saw him, he passed by on the other side. 32Likewise a Levite, when he arrived at the place, came and looked, and passed by on the other side. 33But a certain Samaritan, as he journeyed, came where he was. And when he saw him, he had compassion. 34So he went to *him* and bandaged his wounds, pouring on oil and wine; and he set him on his own animal, brought him to an inn, and took care of him. 35On the next day, when he departed,a he took out two denarii, gave *them* to the innkeeper, and said to him, 'Take care of him; and whatever more you spend, when I come again, I will repay you.' 36So which of these three do you think was neighbor to him who fell among the thieves?"

37And he said, "He who showed mercy on him."

Then Jesus said to him, "Go and do likewise."

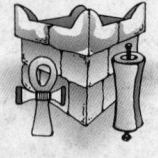

Visiting in Bethany
On the journey toward Jerusalem, Jesus was welcomed into the home of two sisters, Mary and Martha. Luke does not indicate a location, but John's Gospel informs us that Mary and Martha were from Bethany, where they lived with their brother Lazarus (John 11:1). Since Bethany is in Judea just outside of Jerusalem, Jesus' journey would have been almost complete, having already passed through all of Samaria and northern Judea. Yet Luke makes comments later that the journey continued for quite some time (Luke 13:22; 17:11), and even at these later points Jesus is nowhere near Judea; He is still passing through Galilee and Samaria. Obviously, Luke's travel narrative does not follow a continuous geographical progression.

The two women reacted differently to Jesus' arrival. Mary listened to what Jesus said, while Martha complained about having to do the customarily female serving tasks alone (Luke 10:40). It is highly significant that Jesus took the side not of Martha, who assumed the traditional female role, but of Mary, who presumed to act like a male disciple. The picture of Jesus allowing and encouraging Mary to act as would a male disciple continues the generally favorable treatment of women in Luke's Gospel (Luke 1:24–63; 2:36–38; 8:1–3; 24:1–10).

▼ ■ Luke 10:38–42

Luke
Mary and Martha Worship and Serve

10 **:38** Now it happened as they went that He entered a certain village; and a certain woman named Martha welcomed Him into her house. 39And she had a

10:27 aDeuteronomy 6:5   bLeviticus 19:18
10:35 aNU-Text omits *when he departed.*

RELIGION AND WORSHIP
The Pharisees were not the only ones concerned about ritual matters (Luke 11:39). The approved religion of Rome focused on performing rituals exactly as they were prescribed. If an error was made in the ritual, the Romans displayed their piety by starting over from the beginning, and continuing this way until everything was correct. Otherwise they felt that their religious service was ineffective.

sister called Mary, who also sat at Jesus'[a] feet and heard His word. 40But Martha was distracted with much serving, and she approached Him and said, "Lord, do You not care that my sister has left me to serve alone? Therefore tell her to help me."

41And Jesus[a] answered and said to her, "Martha, Martha, you are worried and troubled about many things. 42But one thing is needed, and Mary has chosen that good part, which will not be taken away from her."

10:39 [a]NU-Text reads *the Lord's*.
10:41 [a]NU-Text reads *the Lord*.   11:44 [a]NU-Text omits *scribes and Pharisees, hypocrites*.
11:53 [a]NU-Text reads *And when He left there*.

Hypocrisy of the Lawyers and Pharisees

Jesus' invitation to dine with a Pharisee results in a wide-ranging series of curses directed against His opponents, the scribes (lawyers) and Pharisees (Luke 11:37–52). Jesus condemned the Pharisees for being excessively concerned with trivial matters, such as ritual purity and tithing, while failing to pursue important matters such as social justice and ethical behavior. The lawyers also are denounced for sharing in the perpetuation of injustice, but they are singled out for criticism for their fathers' part in killing the prophets (Luke 11:47).

On this occasion Jesus' opponents began laying a trap in order to accuse Him of some crime (Luke 11:53, 54). By noting this, Luke anticipates Jesus' arrest, trials, and crucifixion, which all the evangelists do in different ways.

Luke presents these sayings of Jesus as a single speech, given while a guest in the house of a Pharisee. While for Luke this event occurred during the journey from Galilee to Jerusalem, Matthew shows Jesus giving these sayings on several occasions, in a different order, and at times both before and after the journey, but not during it.

Unlike the scribes and Pharisees, who receive nothing but condemnation, the disciples are both warned and reassured. Jesus reassured them of God's love and concern for them, but counseled them on the price of unbelief and the rewards of faith (Luke 12:1–12).

▼   ■ Luke 11:37—12:12

Luke
Woe to the Pharisees and Lawyers

11 :37 And as He spoke, a certain Pharisee asked Him to dine with him. So He went in and sat down to eat. 38When the Pharisee saw *it*, he marveled that He had not first washed before dinner.

39Then the Lord said to him, "Now you Pharisees make the outside of the cup and dish clean, but your inward part is full of greed and wickedness. 40Foolish ones! Did not He who made the outside make the inside also? 41But rather give alms of such things as you have; then indeed all things are clean to you.

42"But woe to you Pharisees! For you tithe mint and rue and all manner of herbs, and pass by justice and the love of God. These you ought to have done, without leaving the others undone. 43Woe to you Pharisees! For you love the best seats in the synagogues and greetings in the marketplaces. 44Woe to you, scribes and Pharisees, hypocrites![a] For you are like graves which are not seen, and the men who walk over *them* are not aware *of them*."

45Then one of the lawyers answered and said to Him, "Teacher, by saying these things You reproach us also."

46And He said, "Woe to you also, lawyers! For you load men with burdens hard to bear, and you yourselves do not touch the burdens with one of your fingers. 47Woe to you! For you build the tombs of the prophets, and your fathers killed them. 48In fact, you bear witness that you approve the deeds of your fathers; for they indeed killed them, and you build their tombs. 49Therefore the wisdom of God also said, 'I will send them prophets and apostles, and *some* of them they will kill and persecute,' 50that the blood of all the prophets which was shed from the foundation of the world may be required of this generation, 51from the blood of Abel to the blood of Zechariah who perished between the altar and the temple. Yes, I say to you, it shall be required of this generation.

52"Woe to you lawyers! For you have taken away the key of knowledge. You did not enter in yourselves, and those who were entering in you hindered."

53And as He said these things to them,[a] the scribes and the Pharisees began to assail *Him* vehemently, and to cross-examine Him about many things, 54lying in wait for Him, and seeking to catch Him in something He might say, that they might accuse Him.[a]

Beware of Hypocrisy

12 ¹In the meantime, when an innumerable multitude of people had gathered together, so that they trampled one another, He began to say to His disciples first *of all,* "Beware of the leaven of the Pharisees, which is hypocrisy. ²For there is nothing covered that will not be revealed, nor hidden that will not be known. ³Therefore whatever you have spoken in the dark will be heard in the light, and what you have spoken in the ear in inner rooms will be proclaimed on the housetops.

Jesus Teaches the Fear of God

⁴"And I say to you, My friends, do not be afraid of those who kill the body, and after that have no more that they can do. ⁵But I will show you whom you should fear: Fear Him who, after He has killed, has power to cast into hell; yes, I say to you, fear Him!

⁶"Are not five sparrows sold for two copper coins?[a] And not one of them is forgotten before God. ⁷But the very hairs of your head are all numbered. Do not fear therefore; you are of more value than many sparrows.

Confess Christ Before Men

⁸"Also I say to you, whoever confesses Me before men, him the Son of Man also will confess before the angels of God. ⁹But he who denies Me before men will be denied before the angels of God.

¹⁰"And anyone who speaks a word against the Son of Man, it will be forgiven him; but to him who blasphemes against the Holy Spirit, it will not be forgiven.

¹¹"Now when they bring you to the synagogues and magistrates and authorities, do not worry about how or what you should answer, or what you should say. ¹²For the Holy Spirit will teach you in that very hour what you ought to say."

Earthly or Heavenly Treasures

Some parts of Jesus' teaching about this lifetime which Luke places with the journey to Jerusalem are covered by Matthew in his Sermon on the Mount. Luke's lessons on seeking treasures in heaven rather than security on earth (Luke 12:22–34) are paralleled in Matthew's Sermon (see "Unassuming Godliness" at Matt. 6:1). Others, including the parable of the rich fool, appear only in Luke (Luke 12:13–21). The message of all these teachings is the same: people should not concern themselves excessively with their material needs, but should concentrate on their spiritual development and worry about answering for themselves at the final judgment. They should not worry as much about this life as about the next.

■ Luke 12:13–21

Luke
The Parable of the Rich Fool

12 **:13** Then one from the crowd said to Him, "Teacher, tell my brother to divide the inheritance with me."

¹⁴But He said to him, "Man, who made Me a judge or an arbitrator over you?" ¹⁵And He said to them, "Take heed and beware of covetousness,[a] for one's life does not consist in the abundance of the things he possesses."

¹⁶Then He spoke a parable to them, saying: "The ground of a certain rich man yielded plentifully. ¹⁷And he thought within himself, saying, 'What shall I do, since I have no room to store my crops?' ¹⁸So he said, 'I will do this: I will pull down my barns and build greater, and there I will store all my crops and my goods. ¹⁹And I will say to my soul, "Soul, you have many

---

11:54 ᵃNU-Text omits *and seeking* and *that they might accuse Him.*   12:6 ᵃGreek *assarion,* a coin of very small value   12:15 ᵃNU-Text reads *all covetousness.*

SCIENCE AND TECHNOLOGY

An ancient key was a piece of wood or metal that could be passed through a hole in a door and used to move a latch or crossbar inside. Protection was provided by making the shape of the key complex. The Egyptians put wooden pins in the crossbar that kept it from moving until the right key was used to push the pins just the right amount. The illustration of "keys" signified access to spiritual teaching (Luke 11:52; Matt. 16:19).

goods laid up for many years; take your ease; eat, drink, *and* be merry." ' ²⁰But God said to him, 'Fool! This night your soul will be required of you; then whose will those things be which you have provided?'

²¹"So *is* he who lays up treasure for himself, and is not rich toward God."

Be Watchful for the Son of Man

Using parables of servants, stewards, and masters, Jesus commented about being watchful and prepared. His teachings apply equally well both to one's own death and to the end of the world. In both cases, people cannot simply assume that they have all the time in the world to prepare themselves. Death as well as the Second Coming of Christ may occur at any time, and believers should always be ready for both. While some of Jesus' comments (Luke 12:42–48) may be taken in either of these two ways, others (12:49–59) are more clearly directed toward the Second Coming and the end of the world.

Although Jesus had come to bring "peace" (see Luke 2:14, 19:38), ironically the effect of His coming was just the opposite. He inspired passionate responses on two sides: devotion and acceptance by some and utter rejection by others. Because each side's response to Jesus meant so much to them, His coming caused division among people, even schisms among families (Luke 12:52, 53). Unfortunately, many were not able to see how near their judgment was, in spite of all the signs Jesus had given (12:54–59).

▪ Luke 12:35–59

Luke
The Faithful Servant and the Evil Servant

12 :35 "Let your waist be girded and *your* lamps burning; ³⁶and you yourselves be like men who wait for their mas-

ter, when he will return from the wedding, that when he comes and knocks they may open to him immediately. ³⁷Blessed *are* those servants whom the master, when he comes, will find watching. Assuredly, I say to you that he will gird himself and have them sit down *to eat,* and will come and serve them. ³⁸And if he should come in the second watch, or come in the third watch, and find *them* so, blessed are those servants. ³⁹But know this, that if the master of the house had known what hour the thief would come, he would have watched andª not allowed his house to be broken into. ⁴⁰Therefore you also be ready, for the Son of Man is coming at an hour you do not expect."

⁴¹Then Peter said to Him, "Lord, do You speak this parable *only* to us, or to all *people?*"

⁴²And the Lord said, "Who then is that faithful and wise steward, whom *his* master will make ruler over his household, to give *them their* portion of food in due season? ⁴³Blessed *is* that servant whom his master will find so doing when he comes. ⁴⁴Truly, I say to you that he will make him ruler over all that he has. ⁴⁵But if that servant says in his heart, 'My master is delaying his coming,' and begins to beat the male and female servants, and to eat and drink and be drunk, ⁴⁶the master of that servant will come on a day when he is not looking for *him,* and at an hour when he is not aware, and will cut him in two and appoint *him* his portion with the unbelievers. ⁴⁷And that servant who knew his master's will, and did not prepare *himself* or do according to his will, shall be beaten with many *stripes.* ⁴⁸But he who did not know, yet committed things deserving of stripes, shall be beaten with few. For everyone to whom much is given, from him much will be required; and to whom much has been committed, of him they will ask the more.

Christ Brings Division

⁴⁹"I came to send fire on the earth, and how I wish it were already kindled! ⁵⁰But I

12:39 ªNU-Text reads *he would not have allowed.*

A POOL AND TOWER IN SILOAM (Luke 13:4)

The Gihon spring was a major water source for the city of Jerusalem from the time of David and Solomon (10th century B.C.; 1 Kin. 1:33, 45). Water was channeled from the western side of the Kidron Valley outside of Jerusalem and collected into reservoirs or pools.

In the 8th century B.C. King Hezekiah constructed a tunnel to bring water from the Gihon spring for storage in a reservoir within the city. The project was done in anticipation of a siege of Jerusalem by the Assyrians (2 Kin. 20:20); thus, the water supply of the city would be secure during the siege, which finally occurred in 701 B.C. Water from the southern end of Hezekiah's tunnel is still used today by Jerusalem's inhabitants.

Most scholars think that Hezekiah's tunnel emptied into what is known today as the Pool of Siloam. It was possibly called the "upper pool" in Hezekiah's time (2 Kin. 18:17; Is. 7:3). The Jewish historian Josephus (A.D. 37–100) described Siloam as a fountain, and located it near the tunnel that Hezekiah constructed. In Jesus' time, Siloam was a well-known area, containing both a pool, where Jesus sent a blind man to wash (John 9:7, 11), as well as a tower. Although there is no material evidence for a "tower in Siloam" (Luke 13:4), presumably it was near the pool of the same name.

have a baptism to be baptized with, and how distressed I am till it is accomplished! ⁵¹Do *you* suppose that I came to give peace on earth? I tell you, not at all, but rather division. ⁵²For from now on five in one house will be divided: three against two, and two against three. ⁵³Father will be divided against son and son against father, mother against daughter and daughter against mother, mother-in-law against her daughter-in-law and daughter-in-law against her mother-in-law."

Discern the Time

⁵⁴Then He also said to the multitudes, "Whenever *you see* a cloud rising out of the west, immediately you say, 'A shower is coming'; and so it is. ⁵⁵And when you see the south wind blow, you say, 'There will be hot weather'; and there is. ⁵⁶Hypocrites! You can discern the face of the sky and of the earth, but how *is it* you do not discern this time?

Make Peace with Your Adversary

⁵⁷"Yes, and why, even of yourselves, do you not judge what is right? ⁵⁸When you go with your adversary to the magistrate, make every effort along the way to settle with him, lest he drag you to the judge, the judge deliver you to the officer, and the officer throw you into prison. ⁵⁹I tell you, you shall not depart from there till you have paid the very last mite."

Necessity of Repentance

Receiving the news about a group of Galileans killed by the Roman governor Pontius Pilate, Jesus taught the crowds once more that death may come at any moment, and stressed the consequent need for repentance. The Galileans were deliberately murdered; they did not die because they were especially guilty, any more than did the Judeans who were accidentally killed when a tower fell on them. Death often comes unexpectedly, and not just to the guilty (Luke 13:4).

Those who are alive, unlike the dead, still have the chance to repent, but their time is short. Just as a planter will not wait forever for his fig tree to bear fruit, neither will God wait forever for evildoers to repent (13:6–9).

■ Luke 13:1–9

Luke
Repent or Perish

13 :1 There were present at that season some who told Him about the Galileans whose blood Pilate had mingled with their sacrifices. ²And Jesus answered and said to them, "Do you suppose that these Galileans were worse sinners than all *other* Galileans, because they suffered such things? ³I tell you, no; but unless you repent you will all likewise perish. ⁴Or those eighteen on whom the tower in Siloam fell and killed them, do you think that they were worse sinners than all *other* men who dwelt in Jerusalem? ⁵I tell you, no; but unless you repent you will all likewise perish."

The Parable of the Barren Fig Tree

⁶He also spoke this parable: "A certain *man* had a fig tree planted in his vineyard, and he came seeking fruit on it and found none. ⁷Then he said to the keeper of his vineyard, 'Look, for three years I have come seeking fruit on this fig tree and find none. Cut it down; why does it use up the ground?' ⁸But he answered and said to him, 'Sir, let it alone this year also, until I dig around it and fertilize *it*. ⁹And if it bears fruit, *well*. But if not, after that[a] you can cut it down.' "

Restoring a Deformed Body

Somewhere in Jewish territory, possibly still in Galilee, Jesus stopped at a synagogue. His act of healing a woman on the Sabbath brought criticism from the "ruler of the synagogue" (Luke 13:14). Jesus had clashed several times previously with the Pharisees and scribes on precisely this issue (Matt. 12:9–14; Mark 3:1–6; Luke 6:6–11).

On this occasion Jesus pointed out the inconsistency and lack of compassion of His Jewish opponents (Luke 13:15, 16). Leading one's animals to water on the Sabbath was a common and accepted practice, even though technically it counted as "working" on the supposed day of rest. If this was accepted, why should not Jesus be allowed to heal on the Sabbath? Is not a human being at least as valuable as a farm animal?

▼ ■ Luke 13:10–17

Luke
A Spirit of Infirmity

13 :10 Now He was teaching in one of the synagogues on the Sabbath. ¹¹And behold, there was a woman who had a spirit of infirmity eighteen years, and was bent over and could in no way raise *herself* up. ¹²But when Jesus saw her, He called *her* to *Him* and said to her, "Woman, you are loosed from your infirmity." ¹³And He laid *His* hands on her, and immediately she was made straight, and glorified God.

¹⁴But the ruler of the synagogue answered with indignation, because Jesus had healed on the Sabbath; and he said to the crowd, "There are six days on which men ought to work; therefore come and be healed on them, and not on the Sabbath day."

¹⁵The Lord then answered him and said, "Hypocrite![a] Does not each one of you on the Sabbath loose his ox or donkey from the stall, and lead *it* away to water it? ¹⁶So ought not this woman, being a daughter of Abraham, whom Satan has bound—think of it—for eighteen years, be loosed from this bond on the Sabbath?" ¹⁷And when He said these things, all His adversaries were put to shame; and all the multitude rejoiced for all the glorious things that were done by Him.

Entry into the Kingdom

When questioned concerning the number of people who will be saved, Jesus hinted that it will be only a few (Luke 13:23, 24). Stressing that the way to salvation is more difficult than the way to damnation, He urged people to enter by the "narrow gate." Moreover, He warned that those who try entering by this gate only after it is too late would not succeed (13:25). Contrary to popular Jewish belief, Jesus insisted that not every Israelite would be saved, and neither is salvation restricted to Israel: those who are saved will come from all directions (13:29).

Luke reminds his readers that Jesus' ultimate destination is Jerusalem (13:22). Surprisingly, some Pharisees warned Jesus of Herod's desire to kill Him, advising Him to "depart from here" (13:31). The death threat implies that Jesus was still in Galilee, because Herod Antipas was tetrarch of Galilee and Perea from 4 B.C. until A.D. 39. Jesus' response (13:32, 33) emphasized again that He was still on the way to Jerusalem, even if He had not yet left Galilee or had returned there momentarily. It was His destiny to die in Jerusalem, and nothing could stop Him short of that city.

▼ ■ Luke 13:22–35

Luke
The Narrow Way

13 :22 And He went through the cities and villages, teaching, and journeying toward Jerusalem. ²³Then one said to

---

13:9 ªNU-Text reads *And if it bears fruit after that, well. But if not, you can cut it down.*
13:15 ªNU-Text and M-Text read *Hypocrites.*

Him, "Lord, are there few who are saved?"

And He said to them, [24]"Strive to enter through the narrow gate, for many, I say to you, will seek to enter and will not be able. [25]When once the Master of the house has risen up and shut the door, and you begin to stand outside and knock at the door, saying, 'Lord, Lord, open for us,' and He will answer and say to you, 'I do not know you, where you are from,' [26]then you will begin to say, 'We ate and drank in Your presence, and You taught in our streets.' [27]But He will say, 'I tell you I do not know you, where you are from. Depart from Me, all you workers of iniquity.' [28]There will be weeping and gnashing of teeth, when you see Abraham and Isaac and Jacob and all the prophets in the kingdom of God, and yourselves thrust out. [29]They will come from the east and the west, from the north and the south, and sit down in the kingdom of God. [30]And indeed there are last who will be first, and there are first who will be last."

[31]On that very day[a] some Pharisees came, saying to Him, "Get out and depart from here, for Herod wants to kill You."

[32]And He said to them, "Go, tell that fox, 'Behold, I cast out demons and perform cures today and tomorrow, and the third *day* I shall be perfected.' [33]Nevertheless I must journey today, tomorrow, and the *day* following; for it cannot be that a prophet should perish outside of Jerusalem.

Jesus Laments over Jerusalem

[34]"O Jerusalem, Jerusalem, the one who kills the prophets and stones those who are sent to her! How often I wanted to gather your children together, as a hen *gathers* her brood under *her* wings, but you were not willing! [35]See! Your house is left to you desolate; and assuredly,[a] I say to you, you shall not see Me until *the time* comes when you say, 'Blessed is He who comes in the name of the LORD!'"[b]

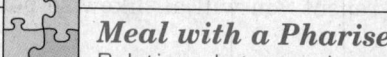

Meal with a Pharisee

Relations between Jesus and the Pharisees were not always hostile. On several occasions Pharisees invited Him to eat with them (Luke 7:36; 11:37; 14:1). Controversy erupted, however, over Jesus healing on the Sabbath (Luke 14:2–6; see 6:6–11; 13:10–17). There were exceptions to the rule about work on the Sabbath, and Jesus argued that His extraordinary work of healing should certainly be an exception (Luke 14:5).

The selfish behavior of the guests, vying for the best places at the dinner, led Jesus to comment on the "reversal of fortunes." Those who seek prestige and honor for themselves will not find it, while those who humble themselves will be honored above all the rest (14:7–14).

The parable of the great supper (14:15–24) illustrates the "reversal of fortunes" theme: the rich and powerful are debased, while the poor and unfortunate are exalted. The irony of the parable is that those who are invited do not even accept the invitation, let alone seek the "best places." Their families and businesses are more important to them, so the host invites instead people who would otherwise be considered undesirable: the poor, the maimed, the lame, the blind (14:21). The analogy is probably to the scribes and Pharisees, who, though reputed for their wisdom and piety, rejected Jesus, while those of poor reputation, both Jews of lesser social standing and Gentiles, followed Him immediately.

■ Luke 14:1–24

Luke
A Man with Dropsy Healed on the Sabbath

14 :1 Now it happened, as He went into the house of one of the rulers of the Pharisees to eat bread on the Sabbath,

---

13:31 [a]NU-Text reads *In that very hour.*
13:35 [a]NU-Text and M-Text omit *assuredly.* [b]Psalm 118:26

GEOGRAPHY AND ENVIRONMENT

Jerusalem is in the hill country of Judea and is not a natural crossroads or the center of an agricultural region. The city was a political and religious center (Luke 13:33), and its commercial importance derived from this function. The population in Jesus' time was 25,000 or 30,000, but grew to five times that number during pilgrimage festivals (Luke 2:42).

that they watched Him closely. ²And behold, there was a certain man before Him who had dropsy. ³And Jesus, answering, spoke to the lawyers and Pharisees, saying, "Is it lawful to heal on the Sabbath?"ᵃ ⁴But they kept silent. And He took *him* and healed him, and let him go. ⁵Then He answered them, saying, "Which of you, having a donkeyᵃ or an ox that has fallen into a pit, will not immediately pull him out on the Sabbath day?" ⁶And they could not answer Him regarding these things.

Take the Lowly Place

⁷So He told a parable to those who were invited, when He noted how they chose the best places, saying to them: ⁸"When you are invited by anyone to a wedding feast, do not sit down in the best place, lest one more honorable than you be invited by him; ⁹and he who invited you and him come and say to you, 'Give place to this man,' and then you begin with shame to take the lowest place. ¹⁰But when you are invited, go and sit down in the lowest place, so that when he who invited you comes he may say to you, 'Friend, go up higher.' Then you will have glory in the presence of those who sit at the table with you. ¹¹For whoever exalts himself will be humbled, and he who humbles himself will be exalted."

¹²Then He also said to him who invited Him, "When you give a dinner or a supper, do not ask your friends, your brothers, your relatives, nor rich neighbors, lest they also invite you back, and you be repaid. ¹³But when you give a feast, invite *the* poor, *the* maimed, *the* lame, *the* blind. ¹⁴And you will be blessed, because they cannot repay you; for you shall be repaid at the resurrection of the just."

The Parable of the Great Supper

¹⁵Now when one of those who sat at the table with Him heard these things, he said to Him, "Blessed *is* he who shall eat breadᵃ in the kingdom of God!"

¹⁶Then He said to him, "A certain man gave a great supper and invited many, ¹⁷and sent his servant at supper time to say to those who were invited, 'Come, for all things are now ready.' ¹⁸But they all with one *accord* began to make excuses. The first said to him, 'I have bought a piece

of ground, and I must go and see it. I ask you to have me excused.' ¹⁹And another said, 'I have bought five yoke of oxen, and I am going to test them. I ask you to have me excused.' ²⁰Still another said, 'I have married a wife, and therefore I cannot come.' ²¹So that servant came and reported these things to his master. Then the master of the house, being angry, said to his servant, 'Go out quickly into the streets and lanes of the city, and bring in here *the* poor and *the* maimed and *the* lame and *the* blind.' ²²And the servant said, 'Master, it is done as you commanded, and still there is room.' ²³Then the master said to the servant, 'Go out into the highways and hedges, and compel *them* to come in, that my house may be filled. ²⁴For I say to you that none of those men who were invited shall taste my supper.' "

Calling for Commitment

Total commitment is necessary for discipleship, and devotion to one's family is not a legitimate excuse for failing to heed Jesus' call. The idea of following Jesus was so radical and so new that a decision to become His disciple could very well lead to a split within families (see Luke 12:51–53). Because of this, Jesus' disciples must be prepared for the family hatred that might result from their unpopular decisions, and be willing to go so far as to lose their families altogether (Luke 14:26).

With the demands of discipleship being so rigorous, Jesus advised people to consider well whether they had what it takes to follow Him (14:28, 31). Just as salt can lose its flavor, so too can disciples lose their zeal when faced with poverty and persecution (14:34, 35).

▶ ■ Luke 14:25–35

Luke
Leaving All to Follow Christ

14 **:25** Now great multitudes went with Him. And He turned and said to them, ²⁶"If anyone comes to Me and does not hate his father and mother, wife and children, brothers and sisters, yes, and his own life also, he cannot be My disciple. ²⁷And whoever does not bear his cross and come after Me cannot be My disciple. ²⁸For which of you, intending to build a tower, does not sit down first and count the cost, whether he has *enough* to finish *it*— ²⁹lest, after he has laid the foundation, and is not

---

14:3 ᵃNU-Text adds *or not.*   14:5 ᵃNU-Text and M-Text read *son.*   14:15 ᵃM-Text reads *dinner.*

able to finish, all who see *it* begin to mock him, ³⁰saying, 'This man began to build and was not able to finish.' ³¹Or what king, going to make war against another king, does not sit down first and consider whether he is able with ten thousand to meet him who comes against him with twenty thousand? ³²Or else, while the other is still a great way off, he sends a delegation and asks conditions of peace. ³³So likewise, whoever of you does not forsake all that he has cannot be My disciple.

Tasteless Salt Is Worthless

³⁴"Salt *is* good; but if the salt has lost its flavor, how shall it be seasoned? ³⁵It is neither fit for the land nor for the dunghill, *but* men throw it out. He who has ears to hear, let him hear!"

🧩 *Parables of the Lost*

In three parables Jesus spoke about things that are lost and then found: a sheep, a coin, and a son. Matthew reports only the lost sheep parable, using it to emphasize the Father's desire that none of the "little ones" be lost (Matt. 18:10, 14). Luke suggests that the teachings all occurred on one occasion when the scribes and Pharisees complained about Jesus' association with tax collectors and sinners.

Judging from the manner in which Jesus answered His opponents, they must have thought He cared more for sinners than for the righteous. They seemed resentful of the disproportionate amount of attention Jesus was giving to the lowest people in Jewish society. Jesus answered that God will always take the initiative in seeking out what is lost, and there is always great rejoicing when that which was lost is found (Luke 15:7).

With the parable of the prodigal son (Luke 15:11–32), Jesus made two points clear. First, He was not neglecting the righteous to look for sinners. The father deals very fairly with the elder son, who still receives his inheritance (15:31). Second, Jesus associated with tax collectors and sinners precisely because

they were in need of repentance and because they exhibited a willingness to repent. The younger son is grieved by his sins, and it is his sincere repentance that leads to his acceptance by his father (15:21, 24).

In many ways, the parable of the prodigal son is more about the extraordinary love of the father than it is about either of the two sons. Similarly, God's love and mercy are greater than the scribes and Pharisees could understand.

■ Matthew 18:10–14
■ Luke 15:1–32

Matthew 18:10–14
The Parable of the Lost Sheep

18 :10 "Take heed that you do not despise one of these little ones, for I say to you that in heaven their angels always see the face of My Father who is in heaven. ¹¹For the Son of Man has come to save that which was lost.ᵃ

¹²"What do you think? If a man has a hundred sheep, and one of them goes astray, does he not leave the ninety-nine and go to the mountains to seek the one that is straying? ¹³And if he should find it, assuredly, I say to you, he rejoices more over that *sheep* than over the ninety-nine that did not go astray. ¹⁴Even so it is not the will of your Father who is in heaven that one of these little ones should perish."

Luke 15:1–32
The Parable of the Lost Sheep

15 :1 Then all the tax collectors and the sinners drew near to Him to hear Him. ²And the Pharisees and scribes complained, saying, "This Man receives sinners and eats with them." ³So He spoke this parable to them, saying:

⁴"What man of you, having a hundred sheep, if he loses one of them, does not leave the ninety-nine in the wilderness, and go after the one which is lost until he finds it? ⁵And when he has found *it*, he lays

18:11 ᵃNU-Text omits this verse.

POLITICS AND GOVERNMENT

Roman citizens traditionally did not have to pay taxes. The tax collectors appointed by Rome collected tax from the colonies and allies of the Roman Empire. Collectors often exploited the people, and were classed with robbers, thieves, and sinners (Luke 15:1). In Syria, ill will toward taxation erupted in resistance and unrest over a census, which was the first step for imposing property and personal taxes.

BIBLICAL HISTORY

Herod the Great's reign (37–4 B.C.):
Not really a Jew, but an Idumean, Herod serves as Rome's puppet king in Judea. He begins a new temple in 19 B.C. He attempts to deceive the Magi at the time of Jesus' birth, and orders the "massacre of the innocents."

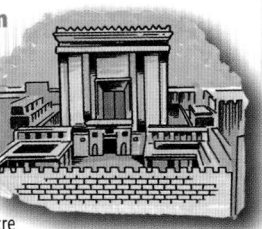

Jesus is born (c. 5 B.C.):
Mary gives birth to the Son of God in a humble stable in Bethlehem.

Jesus astonishes teachers in the temple (c. A.D. 7):
At age twelve, the missing Jesus is found by Mary and Joseph as He amazes the teachers in the temple in Jerusalem with His wisdom and insights.

Tiberius becomes emperor of Rome (A.D. 14):
Tiberius Caesar, adopted son and successor to Augustus, rules the Roman Empire during the time of the ministry of Christ. He sends Pontius Pilate to be procurator, Rome's appointed ruler, in Judea.

John the Baptist baptizes Jesus (c. A.D. 26):
Christ's cousin John is baptizing people in the River Jordan for repentance and re-mission of sins. Jesus is without sin, but He submits to John's baptism "to fulfill all righteousness," and His public ministry begins.

Crucifixion and resurrection of Jesus (A.D. 30):
The crowd's cries of "Hosanna!" on Palm Sunday turn to "Crucify!" less than a week later. The Son of God is led to His death on a cross at Calvary—then He rises again on the third day.

35 B.C.

20 B.C.

10 B.C.

10 A.D.

20 A.D.

30 A.D.

SECULAR HISTORY

Defeated by Octavian (Augustus), the Roman leader Mark Antony and Egyptian queen Cleopatra commit suicide (30 B.C.).

Veterans of two Roman legions colonize Berytus (Beirut) (15 B.C.).

Augustus revives the priesthood of Jupiter in Rome (11 B.C.).

Herod Antipas puts on a gladiator display at Caesarea (10 B.C.).

Herod the Great executes his sons Alexander and Aristobulus (7 B.C.).

Caesar Augustus dies and the Senate of Rome declares him a god (A.D. 14).

Syria and Judea petition Rome to lower their taxes (A.D. 17).

The emperor Tiberius begins his retirement on the Isle of Capri (A.D. 26).

(EPOCHS 8 AND 9,

❶ Zechariah, Elizabeth, and John the Baptist

The priest Zechariah and his wife Elizabeth have had no children, but John is born to them and grows to become the prophet who prepares the way for the Savior. Herod Antipas has John beheaded.

❷ Joseph and Mary

Young Mary of Nazareth becomes pregnant by the Holy Spirit. Confused and dismayed, Joseph wants to end their wedding plans. But an angel reassures him, and he becomes Mary's husband. They take the baby Jesus to Egypt to escape from Herod. Mary survives her husband by several years, and lives to see the church begin.

❸ Jesus

The Son of God becomes a man, lives a perfect life, and gives it up on a cross as the ultimate sacrifice for sinners. He is buried, rises again, appears to many, and ascends to heaven where He sits at His Father's right hand until it is time for Him to return.

❹ Martha, Mary, and Lazarus

Two sisters and their brother in Bethany are Jesus' very good friends. Martha loves to serve Him and Mary loves to listen to Him teach. Lazarus dies, and Jesus demonstrates His power by restoring him to life.

37 B.C. TO A.D. 100)

❺ Mary Magdalene

Jesus casts seven demons out of this Mary, and she becomes His grateful and devoted follower. She is among the first to bear witness to His resurrection.

❻ John

This son of Zebedee becomes a disciple, and forms an especially close friendship with Jesus. Authorship of the fourth gospel is attributed to him, along with several other New Testament books.

❼ Peter

A brusque and impulsive fisherman is one of Jesus' most loyal and trusted disciples. But he denies even knowing Jesus on the night He is betrayed. Peter repents of his denial and the risen Christ forgives him. He becomes an important leader in the early church.

❽ Paul

Originally named Saul, this zealous Pharisee dearly wants to destroy the new church, but God has other plans. Saul travels to Damascus to arrest Christians, but he is converted to faith when Christ reveals Himself to him on the way. Paul travels throughout the Roman Empire preaching to Jews and Gentiles and founding churches in many cities.

EPOCH 9
A.D. 30 TO 100

BIBLICAL HISTORY

Pentecost (A.D. 30):
After Christ ascends to heaven, His followers are filled with the Holy Spirit as they assemble together in Jerusalem. Beginning at Jerusalem and spreading from there, they are empowered to share the gospel.

Saul is converted (A.D. 34):
Saul, a zealous Pharisee bent on persecuting the young church, is converted to faith in Christ when the risen Savior appears to him on the road to Damascus.

Paul's first missionary journey (A.D. 46):
Saul, renamed Paul, goes on his first journey to preach the gospel with Barnabas. They travel through Cyprus and several towns in Asia Minor.

Paul preaches on Mars Hill in Athens (A.D. 50):
On his second missionary journey, Paul tells Athenians that their "unknown god" is none other than the one true God who sent His Son Jesus and raised Him from the dead.

Paul is sent to Rome (A.D. 57–59):
Paul is arrested in Jerusalem and takes his fourth journey, this time as a prisoner. After surviving shipwreck, he gets his wish to visit Rome. He shares his faith there in chains and eventually is executed under the persecutions of the emperor Nero (c. A.D. 67).

The Romans destroy Jerusalem (A.D. 69–70):
Judea rebels against Rome, and Rome sends armies under the command of Titus who set up a siege of Jerusalem. After a valiant defense, the city is taken and the temple is destroyed.

John is exiled on Patmos (c. A.D. 95):
John sees visions of Christ's future glorious triumph and writes the Book of Revelation while exiled on the island of Patmos off the western coast of Asia Minor.

SECULAR HISTORY

Pontius Pilate is recalled to Rome for misconduct (A.D. 36).

The emperor Caligula orders his statue to be placed in the temple, and Herod Agrippa persuades him not to (A.D. 40).

Caligula is assassinated (A.D. 41).

Famine, as predicted by the prophet Agabus (A.D. 44–48).

The emperor Nero compels senators to fight in the stadium (A.D. 57).

Nero orders his own mother to be put to death (A.D. 59).

Rome burns and Nero blames the Christians (A.D. 64).

Masada, the last Jewish stronghold, falls to the Romans and its defenders commit suicide (A.D. 74).

The volcano Vesuvius erupts, burying Pompeii and Herculaneum (A.D. 79).

The Council of Jamnia meets and begins to settle the canon of the Hebrew Scriptures (A.D. 90).

Timeline
30 A.D. · 50 A.D. · 70 A.D. · 85 A.D. · 100 A.D.

ROBE, RING, SANDALS, AND CALF (Luke 15:22, 23)

In the parable of the prodigal son (Luke 15:11–32), Jesus stressed the value of a lost sinner. The way ancient stories normally went, Jesus' hearers would expect the wayward son to get his just deserts: he had grievously insulted his father, so he should spend the remainder of his life feeding unclean pigs. Instead, Jesus portrayed the son returning home to a father who graciously receives him. Although running was considered undignified for older Jewish men, the father throws his dignity to the wind to embrace his beloved son (15:20).

The son seeks not to regain his status in his father's house, but only to be a "hired servant" (15:19). Yet the father, not answering directly, responds in a manner much more dramatic. He calls for the fatted calf—enough food to feed the whole village, normally reserved for the most special of occasions. He also calls for the best robe in the house, most probably his own, and for a ring, in all likelihood the family signet ring, symbolizing reinstatement to sonship. Lastly he furnishes sandals, worn by the sons of well-to-do households but rarely by hired servants.

The father's answer through these actions represents God's mercy to repentant sinners: "No! I will not receive you as a servant. I will receive you only as a son." The elder brother, protesting that he had been "serving" in the fields, saw himself as a faithful servant who had not received any reward (15:29), yet he needed to learn a lesson: It is always "right" (15:32) to rejoice over a life that is restored.

---

it on his shoulders, rejoicing. 6And when he comes home, he calls together *his* friends and neighbors, saying to them, 'Rejoice with me, for I have found my sheep which was lost!' 7I say to you that likewise there will be more joy in heaven over one sinner who repents than over ninety-nine just persons who need no repentance.

The Parable of the Lost Coin

8"Or what woman, having ten silver coins,ᵃ if she loses one coin, does not light a lamp, sweep the house, and search carefully until she finds *it?* 9And when she has found *it,* she calls *her* friends and neighbors together, saying, 'Rejoice with me, for I have found the piece which I lost!' 10Likewise, I say to you, there is joy in the presence of the angels of God over one sinner who repents."

The Parable of the Lost Son

11Then He said: "A certain man had two sons. 12And the younger of them said to *his* father, 'Father, give me the portion of goods that falls *to me.*' So he divided to them *his* livelihood. 13And not many days after, the younger son gathered all together, journeyed to a far country, and there wasted his possessions with prodigal living. 14But when he had spent all, there arose a severe famine in that land, and he began to be in want. 15Then he went and joined himself to a citizen of that country, and he sent him into his fields to feed swine. 16And he would gladly have filled his stomach with the pods that the swine ate, and no one gave him *anything.*

17"But when he came to himself, he said, 'How many of my father's hired servants have bread enough and to spare, and I perish with hunger! 18I will arise and go to my father, and will say to him, "Father, I have sinned against heaven and before you, 19and I am no longer worthy to be called your son. Make me like one of your hired servants." '

20"And he arose and came to his father. But when he was still a great way off, his father saw him and had compassion, and ran and fell on his neck and kissed him. 21And the son said to him, 'Father, I have sinned against heaven and in your sight, and am no longer worthy to be called your son.'

22"But the father said to his servants, 'Bringᵃ out the best robe and put *it* on him, and put a ring on his hand and sandals on *his* feet. 23And bring the fatted calf here and kill *it,* and let us eat and be merry; 24for this my son was dead and is alive

---

15:8 ᵃGreek *drachma,* a valuable coin often worn in a ten-piece garland by married women
15:22 ᵃNU-Text reads *Quickly bring.*

again; he was lost and is found.' And they began to be merry.

25"Now his older son was in the field. And as he came and drew near to the house, he heard music and dancing. 26So he called one of the servants and asked what these things meant. 27And he said to him, 'Your brother has come, and because he has received him safe and sound, your father has killed the fatted calf.'

28"But he was angry and would not go in. Therefore his father came out and pleaded with him. 29So he answered and said to *his* father, 'Lo, these many years I have been serving you; I never transgressed your commandment at any time; and yet you never gave me a young goat, that I might make merry with my friends. 30But as soon as this son of yours came, who has devoured your livelihood with harlots, you killed the fatted calf for him.'

31"And he said to him, 'Son, you are always with me, and all that I have is yours. 32It was right that we should make merry and be glad, for your brother was dead and is alive again, and was lost and is found.' "

Parables on Wealth

In two separate parables Luke treats the dangers of wealth, although in different ways. In between these parables is a series of wisdom sayings from Jesus.

The parable of the unjust steward (16:1–8) is one of the most puzzling in the Gospels. A dishonest manager, informed that he will be fired, provides for his future economic security by making friends of his master's debtors. The lesson is not that Christians should be dishonest and self-serving. Indeed, it is not the manager's apparent commission of fraud that is praiseworthy, but rather his prudence and resourcefulness. He used the means available to him to maximum benefit.

The wisdom sayings (16:9–18) include a warning to "money-loving" Pharisees. The wealthy may appear to others to be upright and may think to themselves that they have God's approval, but God's standards of judgment are different from those of humans (16:14, 15).

The parable of the rich man and Lazarus (16:19–31) illustrates again Luke's theme of the reversal of fortunes (see "Meal with a Pharisee" at Luke 14:1). Lazarus, who is not described as virtuous but only as poor, is comforted after death with Abraham. The rich man, whose only sin is that he is rich (and perhaps that he did not feed a hungry Lazarus), is faced with eternal torment in Hades. Abraham advises that those who do not heed "Moses and the prophets" will not be convinced to repent even by a resurrection (16:31). This saying obviously foreshadows the rejection that will continue to greet the Christian message even after the resurrection of Jesus.

■ Luke 16:1–31

Luke
The Parable of the Unjust Steward

16 :1 He also said to His disciples: "There was a certain rich man who had a steward, and an accusation was brought to him that this man was wasting his goods. 2So he called him and said to him, 'What is this I hear about you? Give an account of your stewardship, for you can no longer be steward.'

3"Then the steward said within himself, 'What shall I do? For my master is taking the stewardship away from me. I cannot dig; I am ashamed to beg. 4I have resolved what to do, that when I am put out of the stewardship, they may receive me into their houses.'

5"So he called every one of his master's debtors to *him,* and said to the first, 'How much do you owe my master?' 6And he said, 'A hundred measuresª of oil.' So he said to him, 'Take your bill, and sit down quickly and write fifty.' 7Then he said to another, 'And how much do you owe?' So he said, 'A hundred measuresª of wheat.' And he said to him, 'Take your bill, and write eighty.' 8So the master commended the unjust steward because he had dealt shrewdly. For the sons of this world are more shrewd in their generation than the sons of light.

9"And I say to you, make friends for yourselves by unrighteous mammon, that when you fail,ª they may receive you into an everlasting home. 10He who *is* faithful in *what is* least is faithful also in much; and he who is unjust in *what is* least is unjust also in much. 11Therefore if you have not been faithful in the unrighteous mammon, who will commit to your trust the

---

16:6 ªGreek *batos,* eight or nine gallons each (Old Testament *bath*)   16:7 ªGreek *koros,* ten or twelve bushels each (Old Testament *kor*)   16:9 ªNU-Text reads *it fails.*

true *riches?* 12And if you have not been faithful in what is another man's, who will give you what is your own? 13"No servant can serve two masters; for either he will hate the one and love the other, or else he will be loyal to the one and despise the other. You cannot serve God and mammon."

The Law, the Prophets, and the Kingdom

14Now the Pharisees, who were lovers of money, also heard all these things, and they derided Him. 15And He said to them, "You are those who justify yourselves before men, but God knows your hearts. For what is highly esteemed among men is an abomination in the sight of God. 16"The law and the prophets *were* until John. Since that time the kingdom of God has been preached, and everyone is pressing into it. 17And it is easier for heaven and earth to pass away than for one tittle of the law to fail.

18"Whoever divorces his wife and marries another commits adultery; and whoever marries her who is divorced from *her* husband commits adultery.

The Rich Man and Lazarus

19"There was a certain rich man who was clothed in purple and fine linen and fared sumptuously every day. 20But there was a certain beggar named Lazarus, full of sores, who was laid at his gate, 21desiring to be fed with the crumbs which fell[a] from the rich man's table. Moreover the dogs came and licked his sores. 22So it was that the beggar died, and was carried by the angels to Abraham's bosom. The rich man also died and was buried. 23And being in torments in Hades, he lifted up his eyes and saw Abraham afar off, and Lazarus in his bosom. 24"Then he cried and said, 'Father Abraham, have mercy on me, and send Lazarus that he may dip the tip of his finger in water and cool my tongue; for I am tormented in this flame.' 25But Abraham said, 'Son, remember that in your lifetime you received your good things, and likewise Lazarus evil things; but now he is comforted and you are tormented. 26And besides all this, between us and you there is a great gulf fixed, so that those who want

to pass from here to you cannot, nor can those from there pass to us.' 27"Then he said, 'I beg you therefore, father, that you would send him to my father's house, 28for I have five brothers, that he may testify to them, lest they also come to this place of torment.' 29Abraham said to him, 'They have Moses and the prophets; let them hear them.' 30And he said, 'No, father Abraham; but if one goes to them from the dead, they will repent.' 31But he said to him, 'If they do not hear Moses and the prophets, neither will they be persuaded though one rise from the dead.'"

Guidelines for Disciples

Jesus offered guidelines to the disciples on how to handle sin. First, disciples must avoid leading others into temptation (Matt. 18:6, 7; Luke 17:1, 2). The punishment for this offense would be severe. Second, if other disciples sin, they must be taken aside and corrected (Matt. 18:15–20; Luke 17:3). Third, if disciples repent, they must *always* be forgiven (Matt. 18:21, 22; Luke 17:3, 4).

Matthew's Gospel illustrates these guidelines with the parable of the unforgiving servant (Matt. 18:23–35), emphasizing two themes. First, God will always forgive sins, no matter how serious, as long as there is sincere repentance. The amount of the debt that is forgiven by the king is an incredibly huge sum (18:24). The second theme is also found in the Lord's Prayer (Matt. 6:9–15): the only thing that can cause God not to forgive our sins is our refusal to forgive the sins of others.

■ Matthew 18:15–35
■ Luke 17:1–10

Matthew 18:15–35
Dealing with a Sinning Brother

18 :15 "Moreover if your brother sins against you, go and tell him his fault between you and him alone. If he hears you, you have gained your brother. 16But if he will not hear, take with you one or two more, that *'by the mouth of two or three witnesses every word may be established.'*[a] 17And if he refuses to hear them, tell *it* to the church. But if he refuses even to hear the church, let him be to you like a heathen and a tax collector.

18"Assuredly, I say to you, whatever

16:21 [a]NU-Text reads *with what fell.*
Matt. 18:16 [a]Deuteronomy 19:15

you bind on earth will be bound in heaven, and whatever you loose on earth will be loosed in heaven.

19"Again I say[a] to you that if two of you agree on earth concerning anything that they ask, it will be done for them by My Father in heaven. 20For where two or three are gathered together in My name, I am there in the midst of them."

The Parable of the Unforgiving Servant

21Then Peter came to Him and said, "Lord, how often shall my brother sin against me, and I forgive him? Up to seven times?"

22Jesus said to him, "I do not say to you, up to seven times, but up to seventy times seven. 23Therefore the kingdom of heaven is like a certain king who wanted to settle accounts with his servants. 24And when he had begun to settle accounts, one was brought to him who owed him ten thousand talents. 25But as he was not able to pay, his master commanded that he be sold, with his wife and children and all that he had, and that payment be made. 26The servant therefore fell down before him, saying, 'Master, have patience with me, and I will pay you all.' 27Then the master of that servant was moved with compassion, released him, and forgave him the debt.

28"But that servant went out and found one of his fellow servants who owed him a hundred denarii; and he laid hands on him and took him by the throat, saying, 'Pay me what you owe!' 29So his fellow servant fell down at his feet[a] and begged him, saying, 'Have patience with me, and I will pay you all.'[b] 30And he would not, but went and threw him into prison till he should pay the debt. 31So when his fellow servants saw what had been done, they were very grieved, and came and told their master all that had been done. 32Then his master, after he had called him, said to him, 'You wicked servant! I forgave you all that debt because you begged me. 33Should you not also have had compassion on your fellow servant, just as I had pity on you?' 34And his master was angry, and delivered him to the torturers until he should pay all that was due to him.

35"So My heavenly Father also will do to you if each of you, from his heart, does not forgive his brother his trespasses."[a]

Luke 17:1–10
Jesus Warns of Offenses

17 :1 Then He said to the disciples, "It is impossible that no offenses should come, but woe *to him* through whom they do come! 2It would be better for him if a millstone were hung around his neck, and he were thrown into the sea, than that he should offend one of these little ones. 3Take heed to yourselves. If your brother sins against you,[a] rebuke him; and if he repents, forgive him. 4And if he sins against you seven times in a day, and seven times in a day returns to you,[a] saying, 'I repent,' you shall forgive him."

Faith and Duty

5And the apostles said to the Lord, "Increase our faith."

6So the Lord said, "If you have faith as a mustard seed, you can say to this mulberry tree, 'Be pulled up by the roots and be planted in the sea,' and it would obey you. 7And which of you, having a servant plowing or tending sheep, will say to him when he has come in from the field, 'Come at once and sit down to eat'? 8But will he not rather say to him, 'Prepare something for my supper, and gird yourself and serve me till I have eaten and drunk, and afterward you will eat and drink'? 9Does he thank that servant because he did the things that were commanded him? I think not.[a] 10So likewise you, when you have done all those things which you are commanded, say, 'We are unprofitable servants. We have done what was our duty to do.' "

18:19 [a]NU-Text and M-Text read *Again, assuredly, I say.*   18:29 [a]NU-Text omits *at his feet.*   [b]NU-Text and M-Text omit *all.*   18:35 [a]NU-Text omits *his trespasses.*   **Luke** 17:3 [a]NU-Text omits *against you.*   17:4 [a]M-Text omits *to you.*
17:9 [a]NU-Text ends verse with *commanded;* M-Text omits *him.*

Passing Through Samaria and Galilee

The miracle which Jesus performed while journeying through Samaria and Galilee is strongly reminiscent of an earlier healing of leprosy which took place near the beginning of His Galilean ministry (see "Cleansing the Leper" at Matt. 8:1). The point of difference between the two healings is not simply that Jesus healed ten lepers instead of one, but that only one of the lepers returned to praise God. Furthermore, the grateful leper was a Samaritan (Luke 17:16), while presumably the other nine lepers were Jews. Just as in the parable of the good Samaritan (Luke 10:29–37), the behavior of a hated Samaritan proved to be better than that of the Jews themselves.

Luke's Gospel continues its theme of inclusiveness. Faith arises from unexpected sources: women, tax collectors, and Samaritans. The leper who was shunned by Jewish society was the only one who expressed his thanks.

■ Luke 17:11–19

Luke
Ten Lepers Cleansed

17 **:11** Now it happened as He went to Jerusalem that He passed through the midst of Samaria and Galilee. ¹²Then as He entered a certain village, there met Him ten men who were lepers, who stood

afar off. ¹³And they lifted up *their* voices and said, "Jesus, Master, have mercy on us!"

¹⁴So when He saw *them,* He said to them, "Go, show yourselves to the priests." And so it was that as they went, they were cleansed.

¹⁵And one of them, when he saw that he was healed, returned, and with a loud voice glorified God, ¹⁶and fell down on *his* face at His feet, giving Him thanks. And he was a Samaritan.

¹⁷So Jesus answered and said, "Were there not ten cleansed? But where *are* the nine? ¹⁸Were there not any found who returned to give glory to God except this foreigner?" ¹⁹And He said to him, "Arise, go your way. Your faith has made you well."

The Coming of the Kingdom

In response to a question posed to Him by some Pharisees about the kingdom of God, Jesus suggested that those who ask when the kingdom will come are misunderstanding it. Although He had previously hinted that one could "see" the kingdom of God (Luke 9:27), Jesus also taught His followers that the kingdom of God is not a place and does not come at a particular time. Indeed, the kingdom had "come near" (Luke 10:9) to them and had "come upon" them (Luke 11:20). When Jesus said to the Pharisees, "The kingdom of God is *within* you" (17:21), He possibly meant that it was in their midst in the person of Himself or that it was within their reach, if only they would repent and believe.

Jesus did distinguish, apparently, between the kingdom of God and the "days of the Son of Man" (17:22). These "days" will occur at a definite time and be accompanied by certain events (17:22–37). Not everything is known about the timing of the end, and Jesus cautioned against trying to decipher its coming from any supposed "signs." But He did provide a dire warning: the end of the age will be characterized by a great judgment, resulting in destruction for some and salvation for others.

■ Luke 17:20–37

Jewish Pilgrimage to Jerusalem

Galilean Jews traveled to Jerusalem for three major Jewish festivals. The route from Capernaum to Ginae on through Samaria and Bethel was the most direct pilgrimage route. It was also cooler in hot weather to travel along the mountain ridges. An alternate route went south from Scythopolis along the west bank of the Jordan River to Jericho.

Luke
The Day of the Son of Man

17 **:20** Now when He was asked by the Pharisees when the kingdom of God would come, He answered them and said, "The kingdom of God does not come with observation; [21]nor will they say, 'See here!' or 'See there!'[a] For indeed, the kingdom of God is within you."

[22]Then He said to the disciples, "The days will come when you will desire to see one of the days of the Son of Man, and you will not see *it.* [23]And they will say to you, 'Look here!' or 'Look there!'[a] Do not go after *them* or follow *them.* [24]For as the lightning that flashes out of one *part* under heaven shines to the other *part* under heaven, so also the Son of Man will be in His day. [25]But first He must suffer many things and be rejected by this generation. [26]And as it was in the days of Noah, so it will be also in the days of the Son of Man: [27]They ate, they drank, they married wives, they were given in marriage, until the day that Noah entered the ark, and the flood came and destroyed them all. [28]Likewise as it was also in the days of Lot: They ate, they drank, they bought, they sold, they planted, they built; [29]but on the day that Lot went out of Sodom it rained fire and brimstone from heaven and destroyed *them* all. [30]Even so will it be in the day when the Son of Man is revealed.

[31]"In that day, he who is on the housetop, and his goods *are* in the house, let him not come down to take them away. And likewise the one who is in the field, let him not turn back. [32]Remember Lot's wife. [33]Whoever seeks to save his life will lose it, and whoever loses his life will preserve it. [34]I tell you, in that night there will be two *men* in one bed: the one will be taken and the other will be left. [35]Two *women* will be grinding together: the one will be taken and the other left. [36]Two *men* will be in the field: the one will be taken and the other left."[a]

[37]And they answered and said to Him, "Where, Lord?"

So He said to them, "Wherever the body is, there the eagles will be gathered together."

Parables on Prayer

Luke's unique travel narrative comes to an end with two parables about prayer. The parable of the unjust judge (Luke 18:1–8) concerns the efficacy of prayer and the reward for persistence. If a judge who lacks respect for people (Luke 18:2) will finally listen to the plea of a determined widow, *how much more* then will a loving and gracious God listen to the prayers of the faithful? Similar teachings encouraging prayer are the parable of the persistent friend (Luke 11:5–8) and one from Matthew's Sermon on the Mount, in which Jesus compares God's good gifts to the simple requests that most people grant their children (Matt. 7:11).

The parable of the Pharisee and the tax collector (Luke 18:9–14) concerns the necessity of humility and true repentance in prayer. Certainly, fasts and tithes are pleasing to God, but the Pharisee's self-righteousness and self-congratulatory attitude are not. Pride in good works prevents the Pharisee from being "justified," while the tax collector—whose profession was notorious for immoral and even criminal behavior—humbly acknowledges his sin in true repentance and is redeemed in God's eyes.

■ Luke 18:1–14

Luke
The Parable of the Persistent Widow

18 **:1** Then He spoke a parable to them, that men always ought to pray and not lose heart, [2]saying: "There was in a certain city a judge who did not fear God nor regard man. [3]Now there was a widow in that city; and she came to him, saying, 'Get justice for me from my adversary.' [4]And he would not for a while; but afterward he said within himself, 'Though I do not fear God nor regard man, [5]yet because this widow troubles me I will avenge her, lest by her continual coming she weary me.'"

17:21 [a]NU-Text reverses *here* and *there.*
17:23 [a]NU-Text reverses *here* and *there.*
17:36 [a]NU-Text and M-Text omit verse 36.

POLITICS AND GOVERNMENT

The Roman consul Marius (died 88 B.C.) gave each Roman legion a silver eagle as its symbolic standard. In 20 B.C. Augustus, working by diplomacy rather than by open fighting, was able to retrieve Roman military standards that had been captured by the Parthians, Rome's enemies beyond Syria to the east. In A.D. 70 the Romans destroyed the Jerusalem temple and offered sacrifices to their silver eagle standards (Luke 17:37).

⁶Then the Lord said, "Hear what the unjust judge said. ⁷And shall God not avenge His own elect who cry out day and night to Him, though He bears long with them? ⁸I tell you that He will avenge them speedily. Nevertheless, when the Son of Man comes, will He really find faith on the earth?"

The Parable of the Pharisee and the Tax Collector

⁹Also He spoke this parable to some who trusted in themselves that they were righteous, and despised others: ¹⁰"Two men went up to the temple to pray, one a Pharisee and the other a tax collector. ¹¹The Pharisee stood and prayed thus with himself, 'God, I thank You that I am not like other men—extortioners, unjust, adulterers, or even as this tax collector. ¹²I fast twice a week; I give tithes of all that I possess.' ¹³And the tax collector, standing afar off, would not so much as raise *his* eyes to heaven, but beat his breast, saying, 'God, be merciful to me a sinner!' ¹⁴I tell you, this man went down to his house justified *rather* than the other; for everyone who exalts himself will be humbled, and he who humbles himself will be exalted."

Final Ministry in Judea

> Judea was a dangerous place for Jesus, yet He continued to preach until arriving in Jerusalem.

Luke presents the teachings of his long travel narrative (Luke 9:51—18:14) as taking place while Jesus was on the way from Galilee to Jerusalem. In contrast, Matthew and Mark indicate very briefly that Jesus departed from Galilee and arrived in Judea (Matt. 19:1; Mark 10:1). No direct announcement of Jesus' entry into Judea appears in Luke's Gospel, but Jesus' location "near Jericho" (Luke 18:35), which is in Judea, is a clear sign that Luke's much longer account of Jesus' journey is nearing its conclusion.

The narration of Jesus' ministry in John's Gospel indicates several trips between Galilee and Judea, while Jesus attended the feasts in Jerusalem (see "The Galilean Ministry" at John 1:35). Thus much more of John's story takes place in Judea than does that of the Synoptics. Some events of John's account occur in Judea shortly before the last week of Jesus' life, and these can be considered in connection with His final ministry there. Judea was a very dangerous place for Jesus, yet in spite of this danger He continued to preach and heal right up until the time of His arrival in Jerusalem.

Marriage, Divorce, and Children

Judaism, based on the Law of Moses, allowed males to obtain a divorce easily. Jesus overturned this "easy" divorce law, an interpretation of Deut. 24:1–4, and pointed to a more important scriptural principle in the story of creation. In marriage a man and a woman become "one flesh" and cannot then be separated (Gen. 2:24). Jesus further argued that the divorce law was only granted by God because of the Jews' hardness of heart (Matt. 19:8).

The essence of Jesus' teaching on divorce appears in all three Gospels, though Luke presents it in a very brief form while Jesus was on the way to Jerusalem (Luke 16:18). While Mark and Luke indicate a total prohibition on divorce, Matthew allows an exception for "sexual immorality" (Matt. 19:9; see Matt. 5:32). While Matthew and Luke follow Jewish mar-

riage customs which allowed only men to divorce their wives, Mark includes also the Roman custom allowing women to divorce their husbands. Only Matthew's Gospel shows the disciples questioning the wisdom of marriage altogether (Matt. 19:10).

The Synoptics relate an episode in which the disciples try to prevent some children (or infants) from being brought to Jesus. Perhaps they thought Jesus had more important things to do. But Jesus indignantly corrected them: the kingdom of God "belongs" to such as children (Matt. 19:14). This may be so because children believe things easily and are not skeptical and doubting like many adults, or because children (like women, Samaritans, the sick, and tax collectors) had little or no status in Jewish society in comparison to their place in the kingdom of God.

- Matthew 19:1–15
- Mark 10:1–16
- Luke 18:15–17

No Divorce—Except for Immorality (Matt. 19:3–9)

Two leading schools of Pharisees debated over what constituted appropriate grounds for divorce. The school of Hillel said that divorce was unfortunate, but that a man could divorce his wife for simply burning his toast. By contrast, the school of Shammai declared that a man could divorce his wife only if she had been sexually unfaithful in some manner, either by adultery or some other form of promiscuity.

Jesus entered the debate over grounds for divorce when the Pharisees questioned Him whether a man could divorce his wife "for just any reason" (Matt. 19:3). While the Shammaites objected to divorces based on weak grounds, they never went so far as Jesus. He replied by allowing divorce in only one situation: when the wife had committed "sexual immorality" (19:9). To divorce and remarry for any other reason was, to Jesus, adultery.

Scholars debate what exactly Jesus had in mind by "sexual immorality." Many think that He was referring to incest or other specific forms of immorality. Normally, though, when the term "sexual immorality" appears without explanation it refers to sexual misconduct of any sort. It would be natural in Jesus' culture for Him to comment on marital unfaithfulness in general while speaking of divorce. When ancient divorces went to court, a charge of immorality could determine who got the wife's dowry.

In Mark's and Luke's Gospels, Jesus' prohibition of divorce offers no exceptions—not even that of sexual immorality (Mark 10:11, 12; Luke 16:18). Some scholars understand these sayings to be rhetorical overstatements, a common Jewish teaching technique. Jesus used the technique when commenting on the seriousness of sin (Matt. 5:29) and on loving riches more than God (Matt. 19:24). This would not weaken Jesus' opposition to divorce, but would recognize that He considered the innocent party in a divorce, and allowed exceptions for those divorced or betrayed against their will (Matt. 5:32; see 1 Cor. 7:15).

Matthew 19:1–15
Marriage and Divorce

19 :1 Now it came to pass, when Jesus had finished these sayings, *that* He departed from Galilee and came to the region of Judea beyond the Jordan. ²And great multitudes followed Him, and He healed them there.

³The Pharisees also came to Him, testing Him, and saying to Him, "Is it lawful for a man to divorce his wife for *just* any reason?"

⁴And He answered and said to them, "Have you not read that He who made*ᵃ* *them* at the beginning 'made them male and female,'*ᵇ* ⁵and said, 'For this reason a man shall leave his father and mother and be joined to his wife, and the two shall become one flesh'?*ᵃ* ⁶So then, they are no longer two but one flesh. Therefore what God has joined together, let not man separate."

⁷They said to Him, "Why then did Moses command to give a certificate of divorce, and to put her away?"

⁸He said to them, "Moses, because of the hardness of your hearts, permitted you to divorce your wives, but from the beginning it was not so. ⁹And I say to you, whoever divorces his wife, except for sexual immorality,*ᵃ* and marries another, commits adultery; and whoever marries her who is divorced commits adultery."

¹⁰His disciples said to Him, "If such is the case of the man with *his* wife, it is better not to marry."

Jesus Teaches on Celibacy

¹¹But He said to them, "All cannot accept this saying, but only *those* to whom it has been given: ¹²For there are eunuchs who were born thus from *their* mother's womb, and there are eunuchs who were made eunuchs by men, and there are eunuchs who have made themselves eunuchs for the kingdom of heaven's sake. He who is able to accept *it*, let him accept *it*."

19:4 ᵃNU-Text reads *created.*   ᵇGenesis 1:27; 5:2
19:5 ᵃGenesis 2:24   19:9 ᵃOr *fornication*

Jesus Opposes Divorce (Mark 10:11, 12)

Many people in the ancient world believed that divorce was unfortunate; a few Jewish teachers, such as those in the school of Shammai, even believed that it was usually contrary to Scripture. But divorce was quite common, and no one went as far as Jesus in condemning it. To Him, anyone who divorced husband or wife and married another was committing adultery (Mark 10:11, 12).

Jesus confronted ancient concepts of marriage by declaring remarriage after a divorce to be adultery. Many scholars understand Him to imply that a man who divorces without legitimate grounds remains married, in God's sight, to his original wife. Thus he commits adultery against her if he remarries. Other scholars point out that Jesus, like many ancient teachers, often offered general statements of principle which did not cover every circumstance or articulate every exception. Thus it makes sense that Jesus would have allowed divorce in the case of a spouse's unfaithfulness (Matt. 5:32; 19:9) or abandonment (1 Cor. 7:15).

Many scholars also think that Jesus was protecting the innocent party in a divorce. Both schools of Pharisees limited the right of divorce to the husband alone. Jewish men had the right to divorce their wives, but the reverse was not true: women did not divorce; they "were divorced" (Matt. 5:32; Luke 16:18). Jesus possibly was defending women against being divorced frivolously.

A few women in Jesus' time could divorce their husbands. Among the Romans either the husband or the wife could initiate a divorce. So Mark, who writes his Gospel to Gentile readers, mentions the circumstance of a woman divorcing her husband (Mark 10:12). An upper-class Jewish woman, such as Herodias (Mark 6:17), being influenced by Greek custom, might also initiate a divorce. To all Jesus stressed that the psychological and physical bonds formed by marriage must not be broken—by husband or wife.

Jesus Blesses Little Children

13Then little children were brought to Him that He might put *His* hands on them and pray, but the disciples rebuked them. 14But Jesus said, "Let the little children come to Me, and do not forbid them; for of such is the kingdom of heaven." 15And He laid *His* hands on them and departed from there.

Mark 10:1–16
God's Plan for Marriage

10 :1 Then He arose from there and came to the region of Judea by the other side of the Jordan. And multitudes gathered to Him again, and as He was accustomed, He taught them again.

2The Pharisees came and asked Him, "Is it lawful for a man to divorce *his* wife?" testing Him.

3And He answered and said to them, "What did Moses command you?"

4They said, "Moses permitted *a man* to write a certificate of divorce, and to dismiss her."

5And Jesus answered and said to them, "Because of the hardness of your heart he wrote you this precept. 6But from the beginning of the creation, God *'made them male and female.'*[a] 7*'For this reason a man shall leave his father and mother and be joined to his wife,* 8*and the two shall become one flesh';*[a] so then they are no longer two, but one flesh. 9Therefore what God has joined together, let not man separate."

10In the house His disciples also asked Him again about the same *matter.* 11So He said to them, "Whoever divorces his wife and marries another commits adultery against her. 12And if a woman divorces her husband and marries another, she commits adultery."

Receive the Kingdom as a Child

13Then they brought little children to Him, that He might touch them; but the disciples rebuked those who brought *them.* 14But when Jesus saw *it,* He was greatly displeased and said to them, "Let the little children come to Me, and do not forbid

10:6 aGenesis 1:27; 5:2   10:8 aGenesis 2:24

them; for of such is the kingdom of God. ¹⁵Assuredly, I say to you, whoever does not receive the kingdom of God as a little child will by no means enter it." ¹⁶And He took them up in His arms, laid *His* hands on them, and blessed them.

Luke 18:15–17
Jesus Blesses Little Children

18 :15 Then they also brought infants to Him that He might touch them; but when the disciples saw *it,* they rebuked them. ¹⁶But Jesus called them to *Him* and said, "Let the little children come to Me, and do not forbid them; for of such is the kingdom of God. ¹⁷Assuredly, I say to you, whoever does not receive the kingdom of God as a little child will by no means enter it."

Riches and Discipleship

A rich young man asked Jesus what he must do to inherit eternal life. Following the commandments was a requirement the young man expected, but he became shocked and went away grieving when told to sell all of his possessions. Jesus perceived that the rich young man's problem was not that he owned many possessions, but that he *cared more* about them than he did about doing God's will.

The disciples too were shocked to hear Jesus comment about how hard it is for the rich to enter the kingdom of heaven. Traditional Jewish wisdom held that great riches were a sign of God's favor and blessing, while sickness and poverty were a sign of God's curse. Peter reminded Jesus that the disciples had given up everything to follow Him, and Jesus assured Peter that there would be rewards for all who faithfully followed Him (Matt. 19:27–29). Nevertheless, such rewards would be based on God's graciousness, not on human merit (see "The Laborers in the Vineyard" at Matt. 20:1).

■ Matthew 19:16–30
■ Mark 10:17–31
■ Luke 18:18–30

Matthew 19:16–30
Jesus Counsels a Rich Ruler

19 :16 Now behold, one came and said to Him, "Goodᵃ Teacher, what good thing shall I do that I may have eternal life?"

¹⁷So He said to him, "Why do you call Me good?ᵃ No one *is* good but One, *that is,* God.ᵇ But if you want to enter into life, keep the commandments."

¹⁸He said to Him, "Which ones?"

Jesus said, "*'You shall not murder,' 'You shall not commit adultery,' 'You shall not steal,' 'You shall not bear false witness,'* ¹⁹*'Honor your father and your mother,'*ᵃ and, *'You shall love your neighbor as yourself.'*"ᵇ

²⁰The young man said to Him, "All these things I have kept from my youth.ᵃ What do I still lack?"

²¹Jesus said to him, "If you want to be perfect, go, sell what you have and give to the poor, and you will have treasure in heaven; and come, follow Me."

²²But when the young man heard that saying, he went away sorrowful, for he had great possessions.

With God All Things Are Possible

²³Then Jesus said to His disciples, "Assuredly, I say to you that it is hard for a rich man to enter the kingdom of heaven. ²⁴And again I say to you, it is easier for a camel to go through the eye of a needle than for a rich man to enter the kingdom of God."

²⁵When His disciples heard *it,* they were greatly astonished, saying, "Who then can be saved?"

²⁶But Jesus looked at *them* and said to them, "With men this is impossible, but with God all things are possible."

²⁷Then Peter answered and said to

19:16 ᵃNU-Text omits *Good.*   19:17 ᵃNU-Text reads *Why do you ask Me about what is good?* ᵇNU-Text reads *There is One who is good.* 19:19 ᵃExodus 20:12–16; Deuteronomy 5:16–20 ᵇLeviticus 19:18   19:20 ᵃNU-Text omits *from my youth.*

ARTS AND LITERATURE

Jesus' saying about a camel is a kind of proverb, a colorful illustration of impossibility. A rich man who loves his riches more than God can no more enter God's kingdom than a camel can pass through the "eye of a needle" (Matt. 19:24). Many people at that time would have been puzzled to hear that the rich were at a disadvantage in anything, since money opened so many doors.

Him, "See, we have left all and followed You. Therefore what shall we have?"

28So Jesus said to them, "Assuredly I say to you, that in the regeneration, when the Son of Man sits on the throne of His glory, you who have followed Me will also sit on twelve thrones, judging the twelve tribes of Israel. 29And everyone who has left houses or brothers or sisters or father or mother or wifea or children or lands, for My name's sake, shall receive a hundred-fold, and inherit eternal life. 30But many who are first will be last, and the last first."

Mark 10:17–31
Earthly Riches

10:17 Now as He was going out on the road, one came running, knelt before Him, and asked Him, "Good Teacher, what shall I do that I may inherit eternal life?"

18So Jesus said to him, "Why do you call Me good? No one *is* good but One, *that is,* God. 19You know the commandments: *'Do not commit adultery,' 'Do not murder,' 'Do not steal,' 'Do not bear false witness,' 'Do not defraud,' 'Honor your father and your mother.'"a*

20And he answered and said to Him, "Teacher, all these things I have kept from my youth."

21Then Jesus, looking at him, loved him, and said to him, "One thing you lack: Go your way, sell whatever you have and give to the poor, and you will have treasure in heaven; and come, take up the cross, and follow Me."

22But he was sad at this word, and went away sorrowful, for he had great possessions.

Heavenly Rewards

23Then Jesus looked around and said to His disciples, "How hard it is for those who have riches to enter the kingdom of God!" 24And the disciples were astonished at His words. But Jesus answered again and said to them, "Children, how hard it is for those who trust in richesa to enter the kingdom of God! 25It is easier for a camel to go through the eye of a needle than for a rich man to enter the kingdom of God."

26And they were greatly astonished, saying among themselves, "Who then can be saved?"

27But Jesus looked at them and said, "With men *it is* impossible, but not with God; for with God all things are possible."

28Then Peter began to say to Him, "See, we have left all and followed You."

29So Jesus answered and said, "Assuredly, I say to you, there is no one who has left house or brothers or sisters or father or mother or wifea or children or lands, for My sake and the gospel's, 30who shall not receive a hundredfold now in this time—houses and brothers and sisters and mothers and children and lands, with persecutions—and in the age to come, eternal life. 31But many who are first will be last, and the last first."

Luke 18:18–30
Jesus Counsels the Rich Young Ruler

18:18 Now a certain ruler asked Him, saying, "Good Teacher, what shall I do to inherit eternal life?"

19So Jesus said to him, "Why do you call Me good? No one *is* good but One, *that is,* God. 20You know the commandments: *'Do not commit adultery,' 'Do not murder,' 'Do not steal,' 'Do not bear false witness,' 'Honor your father and your mother.'"a*

21And he said, "All these things I have kept from my youth."

22So when Jesus heard these things, He said to him, "You still lack one thing. Sell all that you have and distribute to the poor, and you will have treasure in heaven; and come, follow Me."

23But when he heard this, he became very sorrowful, for he was very rich.

The Danger of Riches

24And when Jesus saw that he became very sorrowful, He said, "How hard it is for those who have riches to enter the kingdom of God! 25For it is easier for a camel to go through the eye of a needle than for a rich man to enter the kingdom of God."

26And those who heard it said, "Who then can be saved?"

27But He said, "The things which are impossible with men are possible with God."

28Then Peter said, "See, we have left alla and followed You."

29So He said to them, "Assuredly, I say to you, there is no one who has left house or parents or brothers or wife or children,

---

19:29 aNU-Text omits *or wife.*
Mark 10:19 aExodus 20:12–16; Deuteronomy 5:16–20   10:24 aNU-Text omits *for those who trust in riches.*   10:29 aNU-Text omits *or wife.*
Luke 18:20 aExodus 20:12–16; Deuteronomy 5:16–20   18:28 aNU-Text reads *our own.*

for the sake of the kingdom of God, ³⁰who shall not receive many times more in this present time, and in the age to come eternal life."

The Laborers in the Vineyard

Only Matthew's Gospel relates the parable of the laborers in the vineyard. The point of the parable is that the owner of the vineyard was not unfair to the workers hired early in the morning, since he paid them exactly what he had promised. If he is more generous to the workers who come later, he is within his rights to do so. Likewise, God's rewards are not earned by the time we serve or the energy we expend. They are His gracious gifts to all who follow Him faithfully. Matthew's parable explains the proverb "first will be last" (Matt. 19:30; 20:16).

■ Matthew 20:1–16

Matthew
The Parable of the Laborers

20 :1 "For the kingdom of heaven is like a landowner who went out early in the morning to hire laborers for his vineyard. ²Now when he had agreed with the laborers for a denarius a day, he sent them into his vineyard. ³And he went out about the third hour and saw others standing idle in the marketplace, ⁴and said to them, 'You also go into the vineyard, and whatever is right I will give you.' So they went. ⁵Again he went out about the sixth and the ninth hour, and did likewise. ⁶And about the eleventh hour he went out and found others standing idle,^a and said to them, 'Why have you been standing here idle all day?' ⁷They said to him, 'Because no one hired us.' He said to them, 'You also go into the vineyard, and whatever is right you will receive.'^a

⁸"So when evening had come, the owner of the vineyard said to his steward, 'Call the laborers and give them *their* wages, beginning with the last to the first.' ⁹And when those came who *were hired* about the eleventh hour, they each received a denarius. ¹⁰But when the first came, they supposed that they would receive more; and they likewise received each a denarius. ¹¹And when they had received *it,* they complained against the landowner, ¹²saying, 'These last *men* have worked *only* one hour, ▼

and you made them equal to us who have borne the burden and the heat of the day.' ¹³But he answered one of them and said, 'Friend, I am doing you no wrong. Did you not agree with me for a denarius? ¹⁴Take *what is* yours and go your way. I wish to give to this last man *the same* as to you. ¹⁵Is it not lawful for me to do what I wish with my own things? Or is your eye evil because I am good?' ¹⁶So the last will be first, and the first last. For many are called, but few chosen."^a

---

20:6 ^aNU-Text omits *idle.*   20:7 ^aNU-Text omits the last clause of this verse.   20:16 ^aNU-Text omits the last sentence of this verse.

At the Feast of Dedication

John reports that Jesus was in Jerusalem during the Feast of Dedication (Hanukkah). This feast was celebrated in winter (John 10:22), and the particular feast visited by Jesus was probably in December of A.D. 29 (see "Attending the Feast of Tabernacles" at John 7:1). It is not clear whether Jesus had remained in Jerusalem during the 2 months since the Feast of Tabernacles or had recently returned to the city.

Jesus disputed with His opponents over two issues concerning His identity. First, they challenged Him to state "plainly" whether He was "the Christ" (that is, the Messiah; John 10:24). The nationalist character of the Feast of Dedication would have encouraged questions about Israel's Messiah. The festival commemorated the rededication of the temple in 165 B.C. by Judas Maccabeus, who had led Judea's war of independence against the Seleucid ruler Antiochus Epiphanes.

Jesus' opponents raised a second issue, charging that Jesus had committed "blasphemy" by making Himself God (10:33). He had performed messianic "works" and claimed that these works bore witness to Him (10:25). Jewish leaders would not have considered that claim in itself blasphemous, for they did not believe that the Messiah would be a divine figure. Rather, it was Jesus' claim of a unique relationship with God that sparked their charge: He actually said, "I and My Father are one" (10:30). The continued opposition Jesus met in Jerusalem (10:39) was quite a contrast to the acceptance He found in Perea, on the east side of the Jordan River (10:41, 42).

■ John 10:22–42

THE TEMPLES OF YAHWEH

The "Solomon's porch" (John 10:23) through which Jesus walked was a colonnade on the east side of Herod's temple. In order to gain favor with the Jews, Herod the Great began rebuilding the Jerusalem temple in his 18th year (20–19 B.C.). The main structure was completed in 18 months, but the project was still under way in Jesus' time (John 2:20). Herod's building was one of a series of structures constructed over the years for the worship of Yahweh.

Building	Date	Size	Location	Reference
Tabernacle under Moses	Completed in 1445 B.C. or 1274 B.C.	15 x 45 feet	A movable sanctuary	Ex. 40:17
First temple under Solomon	Completed in 959 B.C. Destroyed by the Babylonians in 586 B.C.	30 x 90 feet	Jerusalem	1 Kin. 6:37, 38
Second temple under Zerubbabel and Joshua	Completed and dedicated in 515 B.C.	30 x 90 feet	Jerusalem	Ezra 6:15, 16
Third temple under Herod the Great	Begun in 20–19 B.C. Still under way after A.D. 26. Destroyed by the Romans in A.D. 70	30 x 90 feet inside, surrounded by 35 acres of pavement, courtyards, and buildings	Jerusalem	John 2:20; Mark 13:1, 2

John
The Shepherd Knows His Sheep

10 **:22** Now it was the Feast of Dedication in Jerusalem, and it was winter. 23And Jesus walked in the temple, in Solomon's porch. 24Then the Jews surrounded Him and said to Him, "How long do You keep us in doubt? If You are the Christ, tell us plainly."

25Jesus answered them, "I told you, and you do not believe. The works that I do in My Father's name, they bear witness of Me. 26But you do not believe, because you are not of My sheep, as I said to you.ᵃ 27My sheep hear My voice, and I know them, and they follow Me. 28And I give them eternal life, and they shall never perish; neither shall anyone snatch them out of My hand. 29My Father, who has given *them* to Me, is greater than all; and no one is able to snatch *them* out of My Father's hand. 30I and *My* Father are one."

10:26 ᵃNU-Text omits *as I said to you.*

TRADE AND ECONOMICS

The denarius was a common unit of currency in the Roman Empire for over 4 centuries (Matt. 20:9). First minted in 211 B.C., this silver coin weighed about an eighth of an ounce, a weight between that of a penny and a nickel. Julius Caesar paid soldiers 225 denarii per year, and Augustus paid the same but supplemented it with awards and gifts.

Renewed Efforts to Stone Jesus

[31]Then the Jews took up stones again to stone Him. [32]Jesus answered them, "Many good works I have shown you from My Father. For which of those works do you stone Me?"

[33]The Jews answered Him, saying, "For a good work we do not stone You, but for blasphemy, and because You, being a Man, make Yourself God."

[34]Jesus answered them, "Is it not written in your law, 'I said, "You are gods" '?[a] [35]If He called them gods, to whom the word of God came (and the Scripture cannot be broken), [36]do you say of Him whom the Father sanctified and sent into the world, 'You are blaspheming,' because I said, 'I am the Son of God'? [37]If I do not do the works of My Father, do not believe Me; [38]but if I do, though you do not believe Me, believe the works, that you may know and believe[a] that the Father is in Me, and I in Him." [39]Therefore they sought again to seize Him, but He escaped out of their hand.

The Believers Beyond Jordan

[40]And He went away again beyond the Jordan to the place where John was baptizing at first, and there He stayed. [41]Then many came to Him and said, "John performed no sign, but all the things that John spoke about this Man were true." [42]And many believed in Him there.

The Raising of Lazarus

The story of Jesus raising Lazarus from the dead is the turning point in John's Gospel. Not only is this miracle the last of the "signs" emphasized by John (John 11:47; see "The First of Seven Signs" at John 2:1), it is also the climax of Jesus' public ministry. Repeatedly John mentions how this miracle revealed Jesus and led people to believe (11:4, 15, 25–27, 40, 42, 45).

Raising Lazarus from the dead dramatically concluded Jesus' public ministry among the Jews (11:54). While some came to believe in Him because of this great miracle, His opponents, alarmed at Jesus' growing popularity, resolved "to put Him to death" (11:53). A threat of execution had already hung over Jesus (11:8, 16), but now the religious authorities decided that His popularity threatened to provoke intervention by the Roman military. The priest Caiaphas advised that Jesus must die so that the Romans would not take away the privileges of the Jewish nation (11:48). But John interprets the priest's political calculation as an indirect prophecy that Jesus would die for the salvation of the Jews and of people everywhere who would believe in Him (11:51, 52).

■ John 11:1–57

John
The Death of Lazarus

11 :1 Now a certain *man* was sick, Lazarus of Bethany, the town of Mary and her sister Martha. [2]It was *that* Mary who anointed the Lord with fragrant oil and wiped His feet with her hair, whose brother Lazarus was sick. [3]Therefore the sisters sent to Him, saying, "Lord, behold, he whom You love is sick."

[4]When Jesus heard *that,* He said, "This sickness is not unto death, but for the glory of God, that the Son of God may be glorified through it."

[5]Now Jesus loved Martha and her sister and Lazarus. [6]So, when He heard that he was sick, He stayed two more days in the place where He was. [7]Then after this He said to *the* disciples, "Let us go to Judea again."

[8]*The* disciples said to Him, "Rabbi, lately the Jews sought to stone You, and are You going there again?"

[9]Jesus answered, "Are there not twelve hours in the day? If anyone walks in the day, he does not stumble, because he sees the light of this world. [10]But if one walks in the night, he stumbles, because the light is not in him." [11]These things He said, and after that He said to them, "Our friend Lazarus sleeps, but I go that I may wake him up."

[12]Then His disciples said, "Lord, if he sleeps he will get well." [13]However, Jesus spoke of his death, but they thought that He was speaking about taking rest in sleep.

[14]Then Jesus said to them plainly, "Lazarus is dead. [15]And I am glad for your sakes that I was not there, that you may believe. Nevertheless let us go to him."

[16]Then Thomas, who is called the Twin, said to his fellow disciples, "Let us also go, that we may die with Him."

10:34 [a]Psalm 82:6   10:38 [a]NU-Text reads *understand.*

I Am the Resurrection and the Life

[17]So when Jesus came, He found that he had already been in the tomb four days. [18]Now Bethany was near Jerusalem, about two miles[a] away. [19]And many of the Jews had joined the women around Martha and Mary, to comfort them concerning their brother.

[20]Now Martha, as soon as she heard that Jesus was coming, went and met Him, but Mary was sitting in the house. [21]Now Martha said to Jesus, "Lord, if You had been here, my brother would not have died. [22]But even now I know that whatever You ask of God, God will give You."

[23]Jesus said to her, "Your brother will rise again."

[24]Martha said to Him, "I know that he will rise again in the resurrection at the last day."

[25]Jesus said to her, "I am the resurrection and the life. He who believes in Me, though he may die, he shall live. [26]And whoever lives and believes in Me shall never die. Do you believe this?"

[27]She said to Him, "Yes, Lord, I believe that You are the Christ, the Son of God, who is to come into the world."

Jesus and Death, the Last Enemy

[28]And when she had said these things, she went her way and secretly called Mary her sister, saying, "The Teacher has come

and is calling for you." [29]As soon as she heard *that,* she arose quickly and came to Him. [30]Now Jesus had not yet come into the town, but was[a] in the place where Martha met Him. [31]Then the Jews who were with her in the house, and comforting her, when they saw that Mary rose up quickly and went out, followed her, saying, "She is going to the tomb to weep there."[a]

[32]Then, when Mary came where Jesus was, and saw Him, she fell down at His feet, saying to Him, "Lord, if You had been here, my brother would not have died."

[33]Therefore, when Jesus saw her weeping, and the Jews who came with her weeping, He groaned in the spirit and was troubled. [34]And He said, "Where have you laid him?"

They said to Him, "Lord, come and see."

[35]Jesus wept. [36]Then the Jews said, "See how He loved him!"

[37]And some of them said, "Could not this Man, who opened the eyes of the blind, also have kept this man from dying?"

Lazarus Raised from the Dead

[38]Then Jesus, again groaning in Himself, came to the tomb. It was a cave, and a stone lay against it. [39]Jesus said, "Take away the stone."

Martha, the sister of him who was dead, said to Him, "Lord, by this time there is a stench, for he has been *dead* four days."

[40]Jesus said to her, "Did I not say to you that if you would believe you would see

---

11:18 [a]Literally *fifteen stadia*   11:30 [a]NU-Text adds *still.*   11:31 [a]NU-Text reads *supposing that she was going to the tomb to weep there.*

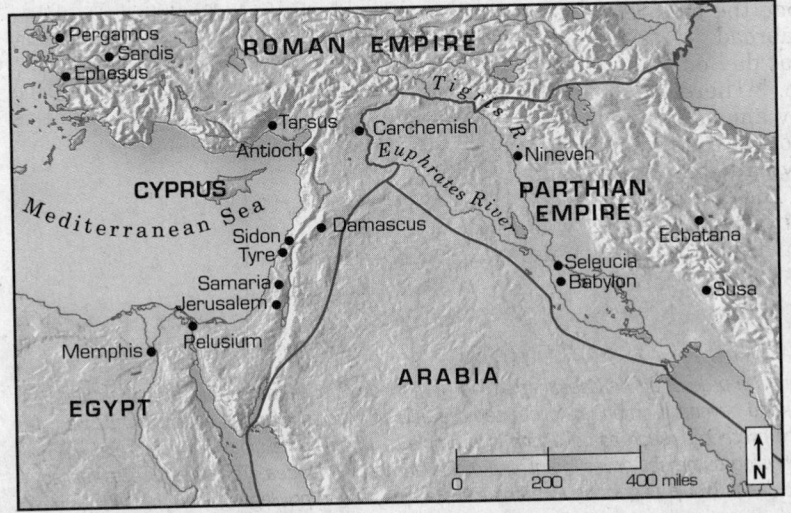

Roman Control of Palestine

Following a successful military campaign against the Seleucids in 64 B.C., Pompey turned the Roman armies southward and took control of Jerusalem in 63 B.C. Initially the Roman army had been invited by some of the Jews to protect them from the Nabateans. Once the Romans became established in Palestine, they never left, despite repeated Jewish revolts against Roman control. In Jesus' time, Jewish leaders feared the strength of Rome (John 11:48).

the glory of God?" 41Then they took away the stone *from the place* where the dead man was lying.ª And Jesus lifted up *His* eyes and said, "Father, I thank You that You have heard Me. 42And I know that You always hear Me, but because of the people who are standing by I said *this,* that they may believe that You sent Me." 43Now when He had said these things, He cried with a loud voice, "Lazarus, come forth!" 44And he who had died came out bound hand and foot with graveclothes, and his face was wrapped with a cloth. Jesus said to them, "Loose him, and let him go."

The Plot to Kill Jesus

45Then many of the Jews who had come to Mary, and had seen the things Jesus did, believed in Him. 46But some of them went away to the Pharisees and told them the things Jesus did. 47Then the chief priests and the Pharisees gathered a council and said, "What shall we do? For this Man works many signs. 48If we let Him alone like this, everyone will believe in Him, and the Romans will come and take away both our place and nation."

49And one of them, Caiaphas, being high priest that year, said to them, "You know nothing at all, 50nor do you consider that it is expedient for usª that one man should die for the people, and not that the whole nation should perish." 51Now this he did not say on his own *authority;* but being high priest that year he prophesied that Jesus would die for the nation, 52and not for that nation only, but also that He would gather together in one the children of God who were scattered abroad.

53Then, from that day on, they plotted to put Him to death. 54Therefore Jesus no longer walked openly among the Jews, but went from there into the country near the wilderness, to a city called Ephraim, and there remained with His disciples.

55And the Passover of the Jews was near, and many went from the country up ▼

to Jerusalem before the Passover, to purify themselves. 56Then they sought Jesus, and spoke among themselves as they stood in the temple, "What do you think—that He will not come to the feast?" 57Now both the chief priests and the Pharisees had given a command, that if anyone knew where He was, he should report *it,* that they might seize Him.

11:41 ªNU-Text omits *from the place where the dead man was lying.*   11:50 ªNU-Text reads *you.*

Greatness and Discipleship

Shortly before His Triumphal Entry into Jerusalem, Jesus predicted His passion for a third and final time. Since Jesus' humiliating death on a cross was such a stumbling block for so many people, each of the Synoptic writers repeat continually the message that Jesus knew beforehand He would die and faced death willingly, and that the crucifixion was part of God's plan for the forgiveness of sins for all people. The idea of a suffering Messiah was strange to most Jews of the time, as shown in part by the befuddled reaction of the disciples to the passion prediction (Luke 18:34).

According to Mark's Gospel, James and John reacted to the passion prediction by seeking honor from Jesus when He is in His glory (Mark 10:37). Their selfish request shows that they were still thinking in terms of an earthly kingdom for Jesus and were preoccupied with greatness, fame, and glory. They had not yet taken to heart Jesus' repeated message that Christian discipleship is really about service to others. Matthew's Gospel lessens the negative image of James and John by depicting their mother, not the disciples themselves, as the one making the request (Matt. 20:20).

- Matthew 20:17–28
- Mark 10:32–45
- Luke 18:31–34

POLITICS AND GOVERNMENT

From the time of Julius Caesar (died 44 B.C.) through the time of Augustus (died A.D. 14) and beyond, Roman law protected the Jewish religion. Various aspects of Jewish life were protected, such as collecting the temple tax, holding religious services, and exercising some self-government and police authority in Judea. The chief priests feared that Jesus would cause the Romans to take away these privileges (John 11:48).

Matthew 20:17–28
Jesus a Third Time Predicts His Death and Resurrection

20 :17 Now Jesus, going up to Jerusalem, took the twelve disciples aside on the road and said to them, 18"Behold, we are going up to Jerusalem, and the Son of Man will be betrayed to the chief priests and to the scribes; and they will condemn Him to death, 19and deliver Him to the Gentiles to mock and to scourge and to crucify. And the third day He will rise again."

Greatness Is Serving

20Then the mother of Zebedee's sons came to Him with her sons, kneeling down and asking something from Him.

21And He said to her, "What do you wish?"

She said to Him, "Grant that these two sons of mine may sit, one on Your right hand and the other on the left, in Your kingdom."

22But Jesus answered and said, "You do not know what you ask. Are you able to drink the cup that I am about to drink, and be baptized with the baptism that I am baptized with?"a

They said to Him, "We are able."

23So He said to them, "You will indeed drink My cup, and be baptized with the baptism that I am baptized with;a but to sit on My right hand and on My left is not Mine to give, but it is for those for whom it is prepared by My Father."

24And when the ten heard it, they were greatly displeased with the two brothers. 25But Jesus called them to Himself and said, "You know that the rulers of the Gentiles lord it over them, and those who are great exercise authority over them. 26Yet it shall not be so among you; but whoever desires to become great among you, let him be your servant. 27And whoever desires to be first among you, let him be your slave— 28just as the Son of Man did not come to be served, but to serve, and to give His life a ransom for many."

Mark 10:32–45
Service: Christ's Way to Greatness

10 :32 Now they were on the road, going up to Jerusalem, and Jesus was

going before them; and they were amazed. And as they followed they were afraid. Then He took the twelve aside again and began to tell them the things that would happen to Him: 33"Behold, we are going up to Jerusalem, and the Son of Man will be betrayed to the chief priests and to the scribes; and they will condemn Him to death and deliver Him to the Gentiles; 34and they will mock Him, and scourge Him, and spit on Him, and kill Him. And the third day He will rise again."

35Then James and John, the sons of Zebedee, came to Him, saying, "Teacher, we want You to do for us whatever we ask."

36And He said to them, "What do you want Me to do for you?"

37They said to Him, "Grant us that we may sit, one on Your right hand and the other on Your left, in Your glory."

38But Jesus said to them, "You do not know what you ask. Are you able to drink the cup that I drink, and be baptized with the baptism that I am baptized with?"

39They said to Him, "We are able."

So Jesus said to them, "You will indeed drink the cup that I drink, and with the baptism I am baptized with you will be baptized; 40but to sit on My right hand and on My left is not Mine to give, but it is for those for whom it is prepared."

41And when the ten heard it, they began to be greatly displeased with James and John. 42But Jesus called them to Himself and said to them, "You know that those who are considered rulers over the Gentiles lord it over them, and their great ones exercise authority over them. 43Yet it shall not be so among you; but whoever desires to become great among you shall be your servant. 44And whoever of you desires to be first shall be slave of all. 45For even the Son of Man did not come to be served, but to serve, and to give His life a ransom for many."

Luke 18:31–34
The Third Prediction

18 :31 Then He took the twelve aside and said to them, "Behold, we are going up to Jerusalem, and all things that are written by the prophets concerning the Son of Man will be accomplished. 32For He will be delivered to the Gentiles and will be mocked and insulted and spit upon. 33They will scourge Him and kill Him. And the third day He will rise again."

34But they understood none of these

20:22 aNU-Text omits and be baptized with the baptism that I am baptized with.   20:23 aNU-Text omits and be baptized with the baptism that I am baptized with.

things; this saying was hidden from them, and they did not know the things which were spoken.

Passing Through Jericho Toward Jerusalem

All three Synoptic Gospels recount how Jesus healed a blind beggar while passing through the city of Jericho on His way to Jerusalem. Matthew's Gospel mentions the healing of two blind men (Matt. 20:30, 34), of which one may have been Bartimaeus (Mark 10:46). This episode is another in a long line of stories which illustrate (in varying degrees in the different Gospels) the remarkable faith of the people that Jesus healed. Bartimaeus proclaimed his faith in Jesus as the Messiah by calling Him "Son of David" (Mark 10:47; 12:35). The blind man was fully confident in Jesus' power to heal him.

Two episodes unique to Luke's Gospel continue Jesus' progress toward Jerusalem. In the city of Jericho Jesus sought out a tax collector, a story illustrating Luke's favorite theme of Jesus' concern for the "lost" and the outcast (Luke 19:1–10). Contrary to the assumptions of the crowd, Jesus proclaimed Zacchaeus to be a faithful son of Abraham (19:9). Even a tax collector such as Zacchaeus could be saved.

In another unique account (19:11–27), Luke explains that Jesus told the parable of the pounds to correct the mistaken impression that the kingdom of God would appear immediately. Jesus was now "near Jerusalem" (19:11), and some Jews expected a political revolution to take place in the city.

- Matthew 20:29–34
- Mark 10:46–52
- Luke 18:35—19:27

Matthew 20:29–34
Two Blind Men Receive Their Sight

20 **:29** Now as they went out of Jericho, a great multitude followed Him. ³⁰And behold, two blind men sitting by the road, when they heard that Jesus was passing by, cried out, saying, "Have mercy on us, O Lord, Son of David!"

³¹Then the multitude warned them that they should be quiet; but they cried out all the more, saying, "Have mercy on us, O Lord, Son of David!"

³²So Jesus stood still and called them,

and said, "What do you want Me to do for you?"

³³They said to Him, "Lord, that our eyes may be opened." ³⁴So Jesus had compassion and touched their eyes. And immediately their eyes received sight, and they followed Him.

Mark 10:46–52
Jesus Heals Blind Bartimaeus

10 **:46** Now they came to Jericho. As He went out of Jericho with His disciples and a great multitude, blind Bartimaeus, the son of Timaeus, sat by the road begging. ⁴⁷And when he heard that it was Jesus of Nazareth, he began to cry out and say, "Jesus, Son of David, have mercy on me!"

⁴⁸Then many warned him to be quiet; but he cried out all the more, "Son of David, have mercy on me!"

⁴⁹So Jesus stood still and commanded him to be called.

Then they called the blind man, saying to him, "Be of good cheer. Rise, He is calling you."

⁵⁰And throwing aside his garment, he rose and came to Jesus.

⁵¹So Jesus answered and said to him, "What do you want Me to do for you?"

The blind man said to Him, "Rabboni, that I may receive my sight."

⁵²Then Jesus said to him, "Go your way; your faith has made you well." And immediately he received his sight and followed Jesus on the road.

Luke 18:35—19:27
A Blind Man Receives His Sight

18 **:35** Then it happened, as He was coming near Jericho, that a certain blind man sat by the road begging. ³⁶And hearing a multitude passing by, he asked what it meant. ³⁷So they told him that Jesus of Nazareth was passing by. ³⁸And he cried out, saying, "Jesus, Son of David, have mercy on me!"

³⁹Then those who went before warned him that he should be quiet; but he cried out all the more, "Son of David, have mercy on me!"

⁴⁰So Jesus stood still and commanded him to be brought to Him. And when he had come near, He asked him, ⁴¹saying, "What do you want Me to do for you?"

He said, "Lord, that I may receive my sight."

⁴²Then Jesus said to him, "Receive

your sight; your faith has made you well." [43]And immediately he received his sight, and followed Him, glorifying God. And all the people, when they saw *it,* gave praise to God.

Jesus Comes to Zacchaeus's House

19 [1]Then *Jesus* entered and passed through Jericho. [2]Now behold, *there was* a man named Zacchaeus who was a chief tax collector, and he was rich. [3]And he sought to see who Jesus was, but could not because of the crowd, for he was of short stature. [4]So he ran ahead and climbed up into a sycamore tree to see Him, for He was going to pass that *way.* [5]And when Jesus came to the place, He looked up and saw him,[a] and said to him, "Zacchaeus, make haste and come down, for today I must stay at your house." [6]So he made haste and came down, and received Him joyfully. [7]But when they saw *it,* they all complained, saying, "He has gone to be a guest with a man who is a sinner."

[8]Then Zacchaeus stood and said to the Lord, "Look, Lord, I give half of my goods to the poor; and if I have taken anything from anyone by false accusation, I restore fourfold."

[9]And Jesus said to him, "Today salvation has come to this house, because he also is a son of Abraham; [10]for the Son of Man has come to seek and to save that which was lost."

The Parable of the Minas

[11]Now as they heard these things, He spoke another parable, because He was near Jerusalem and because they thought the kingdom of God would appear immediately. [12]Therefore He said: "A certain nobleman went into a far country to receive for himself a kingdom and to return. [13]So he called ten of his servants, delivered to them ten minas,[a] and said to them, 'Do business till I come.' [14]But his citizens hated him, and sent a delegation after him, saying, 'We will not have this *man* to reign over us.'

[15]"And so it was that when he returned, having received the kingdom, he then commanded these servants, to whom he had given the money, to be called to him, that he might know how much every man had gained by trading. [16]Then came the first, saying, 'Master, your mina has earned ten minas.' [17]And he said to him, 'Well *done,* good servant; because you were faithful in a very little, have authority over ten cities.' [18]And the second came, saying, 'Master, your mina has earned five minas.' [19]Likewise he said to him, 'You also be over five cities.'

[20]"Then another came, saying, 'Master, here is your mina, which I have kept put away in a handkerchief. [21]For I feared you, because you are an austere man. You collect what you did not deposit, and reap what you did not sow.' [22]And he said to him, 'Out of your own mouth I will judge you, *you* wicked servant. You knew that I was an austere man, collecting what I did not deposit and reaping what I did not sow. [23]Why then did you not put my money in the bank, that at my coming I might have collected it with interest?'

[24]"And he said to those who stood by, 'Take the mina from him, and give *it* to him who has ten minas.' [25](But they said to him, 'Master, he has ten minas.') [26]'For I say to you, that to everyone who has will be given; and from him who does not have, even what he has will be taken away from him. [27]But bring here those enemies of mine, who did not want me to reign over them, and slay *them* before me.' "

Returning to Bethany Before the Passover

All four Gospels relate stories of a woman who anoints Jesus. There are significant differences among these accounts, with only Matthew and Mark being in close agreement (see "Plot, Anointing, Betrayal" at Matt. 26:1). Some scholars suppose that the different accounts arose from only a single anointing incident. Others have concluded that there were three separate anointings—one reported by Luke, another by John, and a third by Matthew and Mark. Yet others see just two separate incidents—one related by Luke, and the other by Matthew, Mark, and John.

The anointing account in John's Gospel is closer to Matthew's and Mark's than to Luke's. Only Luke places the incident in the house of a Pharisee who questions why Jesus is anointed by "a sinner" (see "Anointing in Galilee" at Luke 7:36–50). John concurs with Matthew and Mark that the anointing occurred in Bethany

---

19:5 [a]NU-Text omits *and saw him.*   19:13 [a]The *mina* (Greek *mna,* Hebrew *minah*) was worth about three months' salary.

and figuratively prepared Jesus for His later burial (John 12:7).

On other details John differs from Matthew and Mark. The exact location in Bethany where the anointing took place is the house of Lazarus, Mary, and Martha in John's Gospel, but the house of Simon the leper in Mark's and Matthew's Gospels. Also different is John's timing of the event. He places it "six days before the Passover" (John 12:1), thus before the Triumphal Entry (see "Sunday: The Triumphal Entry" at Matt. 21:1). In contrast, Matthew and Mark place it only two days before Passover (Mark 14:1, 3) and thus after Jesus' entry into Jerusalem.

■ John 12:1–11

John
The Anointing at Bethany

12 :1 Then, six days before the Passover, Jesus came to Bethany, where Lazarus was who had been dead,ᵃ whom He had raised from the dead. ²There they made Him a supper; and Martha served, but Lazarus was one of those who sat at the table with Him. ³Then Mary took a pound of very costly oil of spikenard, anointed the feet of Jesus, and wiped His feet with her hair. And the house was filled with the fragrance of the oil.

⁴But one of His disciples, Judas Iscariot, Simon's *son,* who would betray Him, said, ⁵"Why was this fragrant oil not sold for three hundred denariiᵃ and given to the poor?" ⁶This he said, not that he cared for the poor, but because he was a thief, and had the money box; and he used to take what was put in it.

⁷But Jesus said, "Let her alone; she has keptᵃ this for the day of My burial. ⁸For the poor you have with you always, but Me you do not have always."

The Plot to Kill Lazarus

⁹Now a great many of the Jews knew that He was there; and they came, not for Jesus' sake only, but that they might also see Lazarus, whom He had raised from the dead. ¹⁰But the chief priests plotted to put Lazarus to death also, ¹¹because on account of him many of the Jews went away and believed in Jesus.

12:1 ᵃNU-Text omits *who had been dead.*
12:5 ᵃAbout one year's wages for a worker
12:7 ᵃNU-Text reads *that she may keep.*

Jesus' Final Week in Jerusalem

During the final week of His life, often called "Passion Week," Jesus fulfilled His mission.

All four Gospels stress the importance of Jesus' final week in Jerusalem. The account of this week occupies fully the last half of the Fourth Gospel (John 12—21) and roughly the last one-third of both Matthew (Matt. 21—28) and Mark (Mark 11—16). Early in his own Gospel, Luke announces that Jesus "set His face to go to Jerusalem" (Luke 9:51).

As Jesus determined to move steadfastly toward Jerusalem, He thus moved toward His own death. The final week of His life is often called "Passion Week," an appropriate name since the word "passion" is derived from the Latin word for "suffering." Each of the Gospels reveals that Jerusalem was the place where Jesus fulfilled His mission by being handed over to the rulers, dying for the sins of the world, and being raised from the dead on the 3rd day.

Sunday: The Triumphal Entry

Jesus' entry into Jerusalem was hailed by the populace as a decisive event. His foreknowledge of where to find a colt on which He was to ride (Matt. 21:2) indicates that this event played a predetermined role in His mission. Large crowds welcomed Him along the approach down the Mount of Olives to the Kidron Valley and up the hill to the Temple Mount. They chanted a refrain from the Psalms, "Hosanna! 'Blessed is He who comes in the name of the LORD!'" (Mark 11:9; Ps. 118:25, 26).

The Gospel writers capture the full significance of Jesus' climactic arrival in Jerusalem. Both Matthew (Matt. 21:5) and John (John 12:15) interpret the Triumphal Entry according to the prophecy of Zech. 9:9—Jesus is the messianic King coming to His bride, Zion (Jerusalem). He was greeted by the hailing of the multitudes, and the response, John reports, like the raising of Lazarus before, aroused fears of a popular uprising in the minds of the religious leaders who opposed Jesus (John 12:19).

In spite of such acclamation, Jesus wept over the city. Only Luke's Gospel presents Jesus as aware that He would be rejected by the people, and that destruction lay ahead for them (Luke 19:41–44). Such destruction tragically occurred during the Roman occupation of A.D. 70.

■ Matthew 21:1–11
■ Mark 11:1–11
■ Luke 19:28–44
■ John 12:12–19

Matthew 21:1–11
Hosanna to the Son of David

21 :1 Now when they drew near Jerusalem, and came to Bethphage,[a] at the Mount of Olives, then Jesus sent two disciples, 2saying to them, "Go into the village opposite you, and immediately you will find a donkey tied, and a colt with her. Loose *them* and bring *them* to Me. 3And if anyone says anything to you, you shall say, 'The Lord has need of them,' and immediately he will send them."

4All[a] this was done that it might be fulfilled which was spoken by the prophet, saying:

5   *"Tell the daughter of Zion,*
    'Behold, your King is coming to you,
    Lowly, and sitting on a donkey,
    A colt, the foal of a donkey.' "[a]

6So the disciples went and did as Jesus commanded them. 7They brought the don-

key and the colt, laid their clothes on them, and set *Him*[a] on them. 8And a very great multitude spread their clothes on the road; others cut down branches from the trees and spread *them* on the road. 9Then the multitudes who went before and those who followed cried out, saying:

"Hosanna to the Son of David!
'Blessed is He who comes in the name
of the LORD!'[a]
Hosanna in the highest!"

10And when He had come into Jerusalem, all the city was moved, saying, "Who is this?"
11So the multitudes said, "This is Jesus, the prophet from Nazareth of Galilee."

Mark 11:1–11
The Kingdom of Our Father David

11 :1 Now when they drew near Jerusalem, to Bethphage[a] and Bethany, at the Mount of Olives, He sent two of His disciples; 2and He said to them, "Go into the village opposite you; and as soon as you have entered it you will find a colt tied, on which no one has sat. Loose it and bring *it*. 3And if anyone says to you, 'Why are you doing this?' say, 'The Lord has need of it,' and immediately he will send it here."

4So they went their way, and found the[a] colt tied by the door outside on the street, and they loosed it. 5But some of those who stood there said to them, "What are you doing, loosing the colt?"
6And they spoke to them just as Jesus had commanded. So they let them go. 7Then they brought the colt to Jesus and threw their clothes on it, and He sat on it. 8And many spread their clothes on the road, and others cut down leafy branches from the trees and spread *them* on the road. 9Then those who went before and those who followed cried out, saying:

21:1 [a]M-Text reads *Bethsphage.*   21:4 [a]NU-Text omits *All.*   21:5 [a]Zechariah 9:9   21:7 [a]NU-Text reads *and He sat.*   21:9 [a]Psalm 118:26   **Mark** 11:1 [a]M-Text reads *Bethsphage.*   11:4 [a]NU-Text and M-Text read *a.*

ARCHITECTURE AND BUILDING

For his spectacular reconstruction of the temple Herod the Great prepared a platform more than 33 acres in size, five times the area of the Acropolis in Athens. The result was a temple precinct that included courts, porches, a fortress, and other buildings in addition to the sanctuary. Each year at Passover more than 100,000 pilgrims visited Herod's Temple Mount for the feast. Thus Jesus observed a crowded and busy scene (Mark 11:11).

"Hosanna!
'Blessed is He who comes in the name
    of the LORD!'[a]
10 Blessed is the kingdom of our father
    David
    That comes in the name of the Lord![a]
    Hosanna in the highest!"

[11]And Jesus went into Jerusalem and into
the temple. So when He had looked around
at all things, as the hour was already late,
He went out to Bethany with the twelve.

Luke 19:28–44
The Stones Would Cry Out

19 :28 When He had said this, He went
on ahead, going up to Jerusalem.
[29]And it came to pass, when He drew near
to Bethphage[a] and Bethany, at the mountain called Olivet, that He sent two of His
disciples, [30]saying, "Go into the village opposite you, where as you enter you will find
a colt tied, on which no one has ever sat.
Loose it and bring it here. [31]And if anyone
asks you, 'Why are you loosing it?' thus you
shall say to him, 'Because the Lord has
need of it.' "

[32]So those who were sent went their
way and found it just as He had said to
them. [33]But as they were loosing the colt,
the owners of it said to them, "Why are you
loosing the colt?"

[34]And they said, "The Lord has need of
him." [35]Then they brought him to Jesus.
And they threw their own clothes on the
colt, and they set Jesus on him. [36]And as
He went, many spread their clothes on the
road.

[37]Then, as He was now drawing near
the descent of the Mount of Olives, the
whole multitude of the disciples began to
rejoice and praise God with a loud voice for
all the mighty works they had seen, [38]say-
ing:

" 'Blessed is the King who comes in the
    name of the LORD!'[a]
    Peace in heaven and glory in the
    highest!"

[39]And some of the Pharisees called to
Him from the crowd, "Teacher, rebuke Your
disciples."

[40]But He answered and said to them,
"I tell you that if these should keep silent,
the stones would immediately cry out."

Jesus Weeps over Jerusalem

[41]Now as He drew near, He saw the
city and wept over it, [42]saying, "If you had
known, even you, especially in this your
day, the things that make for your peace!
But now they are hidden from your eyes.
[43]For days will come upon you when your
enemies will build an embankment around
you, surround you and close you in on
every side, [44]and level you, and your children within you, to the ground; and they
will not leave in you one stone upon another, because you did not know the time of
your visitation."

John 12:12–19
Your King Is Coming

12 :12 The next day a great multitude
that had come to the feast, when
they heard that Jesus was coming to
Jerusalem, [13]took branches of palm trees
and went out to meet Him, and cried
out:

"Hosanna!
'Blessed is He who comes in the name
    of the LORD!'[a]
The King of Israel!"

[14]Then Jesus, when He had found a
young donkey, sat on it; as it is written:

15 "Fear not, daughter of Zion;
    Behold, your King is coming,
    Sitting on a donkey's colt."[a]

[16]His disciples did not understand
these things at first; but when Jesus was
glorified, then they remembered that these
things were written about Him and that
they had done these things to Him.

[17]Therefore the people, who were with
Him when He called Lazarus out of his
tomb and raised him from the dead, bore
witness. [18]For this reason the people also
met Him, because they heard that He had
done this sign. [19]The Pharisees therefore
said among themselves, "You see that you
are accomplishing nothing. Look, the world
has gone after Him!"

11:9 [a]Psalm 118:26   11:10 [a]NU-Text omits in
the name of the Lord.   **Luke 19:29** [a]M-Text
reads Bethsphage.   19:38 [a]Psalm 118:26
John 12:13 [a]Psalm 118:26   12:15 [a]Zechariah
9:9

Monday: Cleansing the Temple

Due to overcrowding in the city, perhaps, Jesus and the disciples stayed with friends in Bethany, a small village over the crest of the Mount of Olives, two miles to the east of Jerusalem (Mark 11:11). In Mark's account, they reentered the city on "the next day" (11:12), thus on Monday, and on this day Jesus cursed the fig tree (11:14) and cleansed the temple (11:15). Matthew's account, however, presents a different sequence: Jesus cleansed the temple while it was still the 1st day (Sunday), and only then retreated to Bethany (Matt. 21:17).

The Law of Moses commanded worship and sacrifice to be celebrated at a central sanctuary, a place that "God chooses" (Deut. 12:5–7). This place came to be identified with Jerusalem, and naturally Israel's most solemn festival, Passover, was held in that city. Passover was a pilgrim festival, drawing 100,000 or more pilgrims to Jerusalem each spring. Like other observant Jews, Jesus and His followers arrived early in order to purchase a lamb for slaughter, to procure a place to celebrate the feast, and to undergo the necessary rites of purification.

The commercial ventures of the temple were overseen by the Sadducees and were very lucrative. Jesus justified His attack on the animal dealers and currency exchangers by quoting the prophet Isaiah, "My house shall be called a house of prayer for all nations" (Is. 56:7). Matthew, who writes his Gospel for a primarily Jewish audience, omits the phrase "for all nations," being irrelevant for his audience. Mark possibly includes the phrase to show that Jesus is also Savior of the Gentiles. The commercialization of the temple took place in the Court of the Gentiles, depriving Gentiles of their only place to worship. Jesus responded to such profiteering with anger and decisive action.

The Synoptic Gospels place the temple cleansing during Jesus' final week in Jerusalem. The Gospel of John, however, places it at the outset of Jesus' ministry (John 2:13–22). One way of reconciling this difference is to assume that there were two temple cleansings, one early in Jesus' ministry (John's Gospel) and one late (the Synoptics). John's early placement of the episode is probably theologically motivated, maybe to show the opposition to Jesus at the beginning of His ministry (see "Jesus' First Visit to Jerusalem" at John 2:13).

- Matthew 21:12–17
- Mark 11:12–19
- Luke 19:45–48

Matthew 21:12–17
Out of the Mouth of Babes

21 **:12** Then Jesus went into the temple of God[a] and drove out all those who bought and sold in the temple, and overturned the tables of the money changers and the seats of those who sold doves. [13]And He said to them, "It is written, *'My house shall be called a house of prayer,'*[a] but you have made it a *'den of thieves.'"*[b]

[14]Then *the* blind and *the* lame came to Him in the temple, and He healed them. [15]But when the chief priests and scribes saw the wonderful things that He did, and the children crying out in the temple and saying, "Hosanna to the Son of David!" they were indignant [16]and said to Him, "Do You hear what these are saying?"

And Jesus said to them, "Yes. Have you never read,

*'Out of the mouth of babes and
　nursing infants
　You have perfected praise'?"* [a]

[17]Then He left them and went out of the city to Bethany, and He lodged there.

21:12 [a]NU-Text omits *of God.*　　21:13 [a]Isaiah 56:7　[b]Jeremiah 7:11　　21:16 [a]Psalm 8:2

RELIGION AND WORSHIP

The temple area had been rebuilt by Herod so as to include not only the main building but other buildings, gates, and porches. Animals and birds to be used for sacrifice were sold there, and the foreign currency of visitors was exchanged for the coins required for offerings and taxes (Matt. 21:12). The temple was the most important social center for Jews, and crowds gathered there every day.

Money Changers in the Temple Court (Matt. 21:12)

The temple in Jerusalem had always been divided into courts. Even in Solomon's temple there was a court to which some were forbidden. All the people had access to the outer court called the "great court" (1 Kin. 7:12). The inner court, however, was reserved only for priests, and was thus called the "court of the priests" (2 Chr. 4:9).

Herod's temple, though still under construction in Jesus' time (Matt. 21:12), was enormously impressive, consisting of four courts. The large outer Court of the Gentiles was an open-air quadrangle measuring some 500 yards long by 325 yards wide, enclosed by rows of tall columns. This was the only part of the temple open to Gentiles (non-Jews).

Each of the remaining three courts of the temple was restricted to certain people. All three courts—the Court of Women, the Court of Israel, the Court of Priests—were located in the temple proper, a sublime edifice measuring some 150 yards by 100 yards. This complex stood in the middle of the Court of the Gentiles, but only Jews were allowed to enter its first court—the Court of Women. Only Jewish men were admitted to the Court of Israel.

When Jesus observed the tables of the money changers who "sold in the temple" (Matt. 21:12), He was standing in the Court of the Gentiles. Only in this area were the merchants allowed to sell sheep and doves for sacrifice at Passover, and to exchange foreign currency for the required temple offering. This outer court was the site of Jesus' dramatic temple cleansing.

Mark 11:12–19
The Fig Tree Withered

11 **:12** Now the next day, when they had come out from Bethany, He was hungry. ¹³And seeing from afar a fig tree having leaves, He went to see if perhaps He would find something on it. When He came to it, He found nothing but leaves, for it was not the season for figs. ¹⁴In response Jesus said to it, "Let no one eat fruit from you ever again."

And His disciples heard *it*.

Jesus Cleanses the Temple

¹⁵So they came to Jerusalem. Then Jesus went into the temple and began to drive out those who bought and sold in the temple, and overturned the tables of the money changers and the seats of those who sold doves. ¹⁶And He would not allow anyone to carry wares through the temple. ¹⁷Then He taught, saying to them, "Is it not written, *'My house shall be called a house of prayer for all nations'*?ᵃ But you have made it a *'den of thieves.'"*ᵇ

¹⁸And the scribes and chief priests heard it and sought how they might destroy Him; for they feared Him, because all the people were astonished at His teaching. ¹⁹When evening had come, He went out of the city.

Luke 19:45–48
The House of Prayer

19 **:45** Then He went into the temple and began to drive out those who bought and sold in it,ᵃ ⁴⁶saying to them, "It is written, *'My house is*ᵃ *a house of prayer,'*ᵇ but you have made it a *'den of thieves.'"*ᶜ

⁴⁷And He was teaching daily in the temple. But the chief priests, the scribes, and the leaders of the people sought to destroy Him, ⁴⁸and were unable to do anything; for all the people were very attentive to hear Him.

11:17 ᵃIsaiah 56:7   ᵇJeremiah 7:11
Luke 19:45 ᵃNU-Text reads *those who were selling.*   19:46 ᵃNU-Text reads *shall be.*   ᵇIsaiah 56:7   ᶜJeremiah 7:11

Tuesday: Faith and Forgiveness

As He did after the 1st day (Mark 11:11), Jesus withdrew from the city at the close of the 2nd day also (11:19). Mark's account now indicates the beginning of the 3rd day, "in the morning" (11:20), thus Tuesday. On this day Mark describes the withering of the fig tree (11:21), which Jesus had cursed the previous day. Like Mark, Matthew notes the beginning of a new day "in the morning" (Matt. 21:18). For Matthew, though, this is only the 2nd day

HOUSE OF PRAYER, DEN OF THIEVES (Mark 11:15–17)

The ground plan of courts in Herod's temple restricted the access of some people. Jewish women were kept out of the Court of Israel, which was on a higher level than the Court of Women. Gentiles were kept farther out, forbidden also from the Court of Women. Jewish people were extremely concerned that Gentiles not move from the Court of the Gentiles to the rest of the temple. Posted signs warned that any Gentile proceeding further would do so at the cost of his or her life. One of the accusations hurled against the apostle Paul was that he "brought Greeks into the temple" (Acts 21:28).

Those who came to the temple for Passover needed to buy lambs and other animals. They also needed money changers because the local currencies of the places they came from were different from the standard used in the temple. Merchants performed these services in the Court of the Gentiles, but in doing so were distracting the Gentiles who came to worship God. In reaction, Jesus quoted the prophet Isaiah (Is. 56:7) to emphasize God's plan for His temple: "My house shall be called a house of prayer for all nations" (Mark 11:17).

Jesus also quoted the prophet Jeremiah's words about treating the temple court like a "den of thieves" (Jer. 7:11; Mark 11:17). Just as thieves feel safe when bringing their loot to their den, Jeremiah's contemporaries believed that, regardless of how they lived, God would not destroy His own temple (Jer. 7:4). The prophet warned them, however, that because of their disobedience they should not seek refuge in God's house—He would destroy their temple (Jer. 7:14).

Jesus had a similar message of judgment for His generation. They should not trust in the temple to protect them while they neither understood nor obeyed God's message. As Jeremiah had smashed a pot to symbolize the city's destruction (Jer. 19:10–12), Jesus similarly announced the temple's impending doom (Mark 13:2).

(Monday), and the fig tree is cursed and withers on this same day (21:19–22).

Both Matthew and Mark relate the cleansing of the temple to the cursing of the fig tree. The activity in the temple, like the fig tree, had the appearance of life but could be as fruitless as was the greed of the money changers. Mark links the two events by recording the cursing of the tree before the temple episode and the withering of the tree after (Mark 11:14, 21). The fig tree was often a symbol of judgment upon Israel in the Old Testament (Jer. 8:13), and Mark uses this symbolism to represent judgment upon the religious observances in the temple.

- Matthew 21:18–22
- Mark 11:20–26

Matthew 21:18–22
The Fig Tree Withered

21:18 Now in the morning, as He returned to the city, He was hungry. 19And seeing a fig tree by the road, He came to it and found nothing on it but leaves, and said to it, "Let no fruit grow on you ever again." Immediately the fig tree withered away.

The Lesson of the Withered Fig Tree

20And when the disciples saw *it,* they marveled, saying, "How did the fig tree wither away so soon?"

21So Jesus answered and said to them, "Assuredly, I say to you, if you have faith and do not doubt, you will not only do what was done to the fig tree, but also if you say to this mountain, 'Be removed and be cast into the sea,' it will be done. 22And whatever things you ask in prayer, believing, you will receive."

Mark 11:20–26
The Lesson of the Withered Fig Tree

11:20 Now in the morning, as they passed by, they saw the fig tree dried up from the roots. 21And Peter, remembering, said to Him, "Rabbi, look! The fig tree which You cursed has withered away."

22So Jesus answered and said to them, "Have faith in God. 23For assuredly, I say to you, whoever says to this mountain, 'Be removed and be cast into the sea,' and does not doubt in his heart, but believes that those things he says will be done, he will have whatever he says. 24Therefore I say to you, whatever things you ask when you pray, believe that you receive *them,* and you will have *them.*

Forgiveness and Prayer

25"And whenever you stand praying, if you have anything against anyone, forgive him, that your Father in heaven may also forgive you your trespasses. 26But if you do not forgive, neither will your Father in heaven forgive your trespasses."a

Questioning Jesus' Authority

Opposition to Jesus came not from the Jewish people in general, but primarily from their religious leaders and rulers, especially from the high Jewish council, the Sanhedrin. The center of this opposition was located in Jerusalem, and particularly in the temple. So it was in the temple precincts that various opposing factions engaged Jesus in a series of verbal altercations.

The Gospel writers record a number of these controversies as occurring during Jesus' final week in Jerusalem. The challenges to Jesus appear as a series of rapid-fire encounters during a single day (see Matt. 22:23), but they may have taken place over a longer period of time.

Jesus' questioners were those who considered themselves religious: the Pharisees, Herodians, Sadducees, and scribes. Only Matthew's Gospel relates the parable of the two sons (Matt. 21:28–32), which condemns the self-righteous attitude of the Jewish leaders. While the first son (21:29) in the parable represents those who responded to the preaching of John the Baptist, the second son (21:30) represents those who claimed to be religious but rejected Jesus (21:31).

■ Matthew 21:23–32
■ Mark 11:27–33
■ Luke 20:1–8

Matthew 21:23–32
By What Authority?

21 :23 Now when He came into the temple, the chief priests and the elders of the people confronted Him as He was teaching, and said, "By what authority are You doing these things? And who gave You this authority?"

24But Jesus answered and said to them, "I also will ask you one thing, which

if you tell Me, I likewise will tell you by what authority I do these things: 25The baptism of John—where was it from? From heaven or from men?"

And they reasoned among themselves, saying, "If we say, 'From heaven,' He will say to us, 'Why then did you not believe him?' 26But if we say, 'From men,' we fear the multitude, for all count John as a prophet." 27So they answered Jesus and said, "We do not know."

And He said to them, "Neither will I tell you by what authority I do these things.

The Parable of the Two Sons

28"But what do you think? A man had two sons, and he came to the first and said, 'Son, go, work today in my vineyard.' 29He answered and said, 'I will not,' but afterward he regretted it and went. 30Then he came to the second and said likewise. And he answered and said, 'I *go,* sir,' but he did not go. 31Which of the two did the will of *his* father?"

They said to Him, "The first."

Jesus said to them, "Assuredly, I say to you that tax collectors and harlots enter the kingdom of God before you. 32For John came to you in the way of righteousness, and you did not believe him; but tax collectors and harlots believed him; and when you saw *it,* you did not afterward relent and believe him."

Mark 11:27–33
Jesus Is Challenged

11 :27 Then they came again to Jerusalem. And as He was walking in the temple, the chief priests, the scribes, and the elders came to Him. 28And they said to Him, "By what authority are You doing these things? And who gave You this authority to do these things?"

29But Jesus answered and said to them, "I also will ask you one question; then answer Me, and I will tell you by what authority I do these things: 30The baptism of John—was it from heaven or from men? Answer Me."

31And they reasoned among themselves, saying, "If we say, 'From heaven,' He will say, 'Why then did you not believe him?' 32But if we say, 'From men' "—they feared the people, for all counted John to have been a prophet indeed. 33So they an-

---

11:26 aNU-Text omits this verse.

swered and said to Jesus, "We do not know."

And Jesus answered and said to them, "Neither will I tell you by what authority I do these things."

Luke 20:1–8
Jesus Silences His Opponents

20 :1 Now it happened on one of those days, as He taught the people in the temple and preached the gospel, *that* the chief priests and the scribes, together with the elders, confronted *Him* ²and spoke to Him, saying, "Tell us, by what authority are You doing these things? Or who is he who gave You this authority?"

³But He answered and said to them, "I also will ask you one thing, and answer Me: ⁴The baptism of John—was it from heaven or from men?"

⁵And they reasoned among themselves, saying, "If we say, 'From heaven,' He will say, 'Why then^a did you not believe him?' ⁶But if we say, 'From men,' all the people will stone us, for they are persuaded that John was a prophet." ⁷So they answered that they did not know where *it was* from.

⁸And Jesus said to them, "Neither will I tell you by what authority I do these things."

20:5 ªNU-Text and M-Text omit *then*.
Matt. 21:42 ªPsalm 118:22, 23

Matthew 21:33—22:14
The Parable of the Wicked Vinedressers

21 :33 "Hear another parable: There was a certain landowner who planted a vineyard and set a hedge around it, dug a winepress in it and built a tower. And he leased it to vinedressers and went into a far country. ³⁴Now when vintage-time drew near, he sent his servants to the vinedressers, that they might receive its fruit. ³⁵And the vinedressers took his servants, beat one, killed one, and stoned another. ³⁶Again he sent other servants, more than the first, and they did likewise to them. ³⁷Then last of all he sent his son to them, saying, 'They will respect my son.' ³⁸But when the vinedressers saw the son, they said among themselves, 'This is the heir. Come, let us kill him and seize his inheritance.' ³⁹So they took him and cast *him* out of the vineyard and killed *him*.

⁴⁰"Therefore, when the owner of the vineyard comes, what will he do to those vinedressers?"

⁴¹They said to Him, "He will destroy those wicked men miserably, and lease *his* vineyard to other vinedressers who will render to him the fruits in their seasons."

⁴²Jesus said to them, "Have you never read in the Scriptures:

'The stone which the builders rejected
Has become the chief cornerstone.
This was the LORD's doing,
And it is marvelous in our eyes'?^a

⁴³"Therefore I say to you, the kingdom of God will be taken from you and given to a nation bearing the fruits of it. ⁴⁴And whoever falls on this stone will be broken; but on whomever it falls, it will grind him to powder."

⁴⁵Now when the chief priests and Pharisees heard His parables, they perceived that He was speaking of them. ⁴⁶But when they sought to lay hands on Him, they feared the multitudes, because they took Him for a prophet.

AGRICULTURE AND HERDING

Grapes were an important crop that yielded fruit, fruit juice, wine, and raisins. Vineyards required skill and care to manage successfully (Matt. 21:33), and wine was shipped in jars marked with the place of origin to indicate its quality. In all, the cultivation of grapes was considered to be a sign of peace and civilization.

LANDOWNERS OF GALILEE (Mark 12:9)

Jesus' parables are geographically set in Galilee, the northern part of Judean territory in New Testament times. A parable about owners of vineyards (Mark 12:1–9) was quite appropriate for Jesus' audience in the rural economic conditions of Galilee.

The name "Galilee" likely means "the circle" or "district," and appears in the expression "Galilee (district) of the Gentiles" (Matt. 4:15). The Jewish historian Josephus gives a detailed description of the area and its administrative structure. Except for a few notable larger cities, such as Chorazin, Sepphoris, Bethsaida, and Capernaum, Galilee was a rural area.

Josephus describes Galilee as an agriculturally fertile area which grew grapes, figs, olives, and wheat. Galilee was also well situated to take advantage of already existing trade routes. The Via Maris, a major highway, forked on its way north at Megiddo, with one branch going by the Sea of Galilee to Hazor. Caravans of traders would use this route when traveling from Damascus towards the Mediterranean coast.

During the Hellenistic period (after 332 B.C.), Galilee flourished with landowners of large estates, employing sharecroppers and unskilled laborers. The Zenon papyri (3rd century B.C.) describe a certain Zenon, who toured and inspected a number of estates in the region. This source, along with a handful of others, presents Galilee as an area of concentrated agricultural production, increasingly concerned with water supply and tenant housing. While some of Jesus' parables show evidence of small family estates, others reflect the existence of absentee landlords who lived away from their land (Mark 12:1).

Social structure in Galilee likely depended on whether an individual owned land. While many Galileans were small landowners, there were a number of elites in the region. Certainly among the upper class were the "chief men of Galilee" (Mark 6:21), who attended Herod's birthday feast.

The Parable of the Wedding Feast

22 ¹And Jesus answered and spoke to them again by parables and said: ²"The kingdom of heaven is like a certain king who arranged a marriage for his son, ³and sent out his servants to call those who were invited to the wedding; and they were not willing to come. ⁴Again, he sent out other servants, saying, 'Tell those who are invited, "See, I have prepared my dinner; my oxen and fatted cattle *are* killed, and all things *are* ready. Come to the wedding." ' ⁵But they made light of it and went their ways, one to his own farm, another to his business. ⁶And the rest seized his servants, treated *them* spitefully, and killed *them*. ⁷But when the king heard *about it,* he was furious. And he sent out his armies, destroyed those murderers, and burned up their city. ⁸Then he said to his servants, 'The wedding is ready, but those who were invited were not worthy. ⁹Therefore go into the highways, and as many as you find, invite to the wedding.' ¹⁰So those servants went out into the highways and gathered together all whom they found, both bad and good. And the wedding *hall* was filled with guests.

¹¹"But when the king came in to see the guests, he saw a man there who did not have on a wedding garment. ¹²So he said to him, 'Friend, how did you come in here without a wedding garment?' And he was speechless. ¹³Then the king said to the servants, 'Bind him hand and foot, take him

CULTURE AND SOCIETY

A wedding party was a substantial, almost public affair. Guests wore their best clothes as participants in an important ritual of the social order. A person who attended without being properly dressed proclaimed indifference, not so much to the one holding the party, but to the people of the village and their common interests. Jesus' hearers would sense the dishonor of a guest lacking the appropriate wedding garment (Matt. 22:11).

DIVISION OF HEROD'S KINGDOM

The territories under Herod the Great's rule included Judea, Galilee, and Gaulanitis, as well as surrounding regions. Upon Herod's death, his kingdom was divided among three sons. Archelaus received Judea, the primary portion of the kingdom. Antipas and Philip received lesser positions as tetrarchs over small territories. The Herodian dynasty gradually lost power, with Herod's grandson Agrippa I and great-grandson Agrippa II the last descendants to rule.

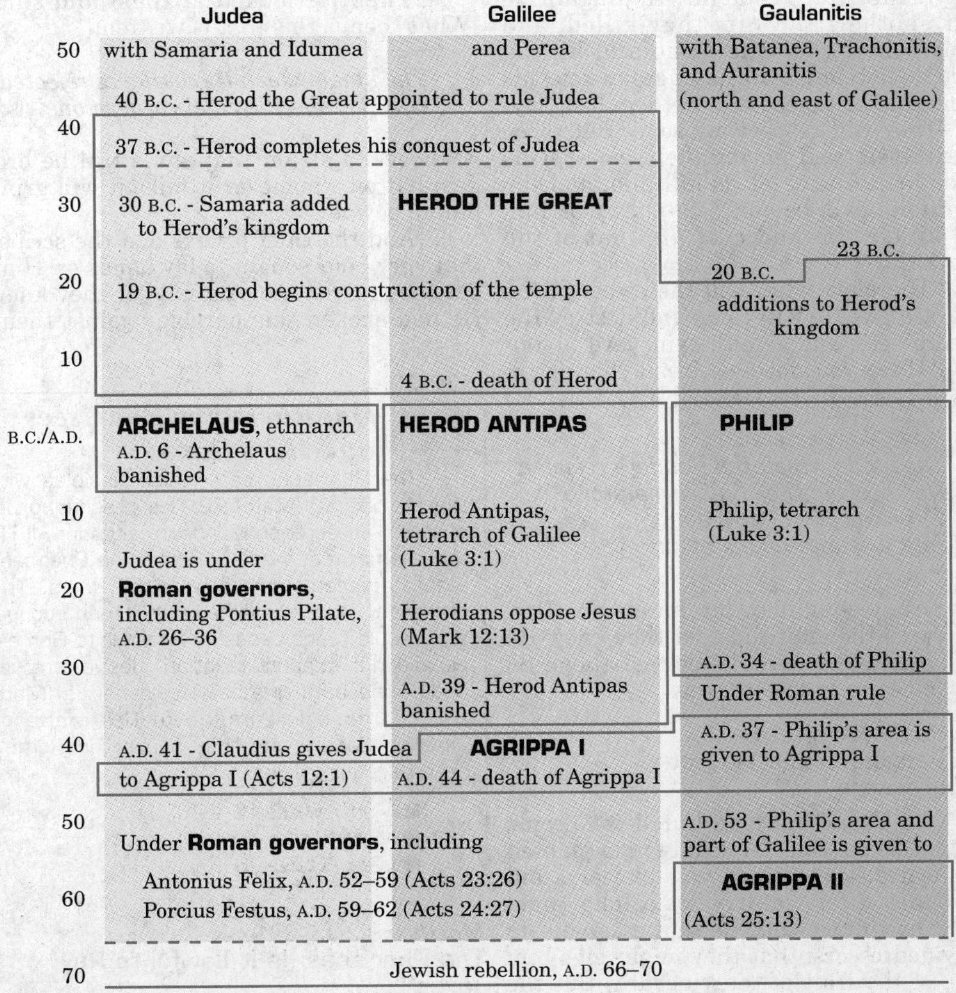

	Judea	Galilee	Gaulanitis
50	with Samaria and Idumea	and Perea	with Batanea, Trachonitis, and Auranitis (north and east of Galilee)
	40 B.C. - Herod the Great appointed to rule Judea		
40	37 B.C. - Herod completes his conquest of Judea		
30	30 B.C. - Samaria added to Herod's kingdom	**HEROD THE GREAT**	
20	19 B.C. - Herod begins construction of the temple		23 B.C. / 20 B.C. additions to Herod's kingdom
10		4 B.C. - death of Herod	
B.C./A.D.	**ARCHELAUS**, ethnarch A.D. 6 - Archelaus banished	**HEROD ANTIPAS**	**PHILIP**
10	Judea is under	Herod Antipas, tetrarch of Galilee (Luke 3:1)	Philip, tetrarch (Luke 3:1)
20	**Roman governors**, including Pontius Pilate, A.D. 26–36	Herodians oppose Jesus (Mark 12:13)	
30		A.D. 39 - Herod Antipas banished	A.D. 34 - death of Philip Under Roman rule
40	A.D. 41 - Claudius gives Judea to Agrippa I (Acts 12:1)	**AGRIPPA I** A.D. 44 - death of Agrippa I	A.D. 37 - Philip's area is given to Agrippa I
50	Under **Roman governors**, including		A.D. 53 - Philip's area and part of Galilee is given to
60	Antonius Felix, A.D. 52–59 (Acts 23:26) Porcius Festus, A.D. 59–62 (Acts 24:27)		**AGRIPPA II** (Acts 25:13)
70	Jewish rebellion, A.D. 66–70		

After the fall of Jerusalem in A.D. 70, Palestine became an imperial colony, with Caesarea Maritima as the capital.

away, and[a] cast *him* into outer darkness; there will be weeping and gnashing of teeth.'

¹⁴"For many are called, but few *are* chosen."

22:13 ᵃNU-Text omits *take him away, and.*

Mark 12:1–12

The Parable of the Wicked Vinedressers

12 :1 Then He began to speak to them in parables: "A man planted a vineyard and set a hedge around *it,* dug *a place* for the wine vat and built a tower. And he leased it to vinedressers and went into a far country. ²Now at vintage-time he sent a servant to the vinedressers, that he might receive some of the fruit of the vineyard from the vinedressers. ³And they took *him* and beat him and sent *him* away empty-handed. ⁴Again he sent them another servant, and at him they threw stones,ᵃ wounded *him* in the head, and sent *him* away shamefully treated. ⁵And again he sent another, and him they killed; and many others, beating some and killing some. ⁶Therefore still having one son, his beloved, he also sent him to them last, saying, 'They will respect my son.' ⁷But those vinedressers said among themselves, 'This is the heir. Come, let us kill him, and the inheritance will be ours.' ⁸So they took him and killed *him* and cast *him* out of the vineyard.

⁹"Therefore what will the owner of the vineyard do? He will come and destroy the vinedressers, and give the vineyard to others. ¹⁰Have you not even read this Scripture:

'The stone which the builders rejected
Has become the chief cornerstone.
11   This was the LORD's doing,
And it is marvelous in our eyes'? "ᵃ

¹²And they sought to lay hands on Him, but feared the multitude, for they knew He had spoken the parable against them. So they left Him and went away.

Luke 20:9–19
The Parable of the Wicked Vinedressers

20 :9 Then He began to tell the people this parable: "A certain man planted a vineyard, leased it to vinedressers, and went into a far country for a long time. ¹⁰Now at vintage-time he sent a servant to the vinedressers, that they might give him some of the fruit of the vineyard. But the vinedressers beat him and sent *him* away empty-handed. ¹¹Again he sent another servant; and they beat him also, treated *him* shamefully, and sent *him* away empty-handed. ¹²And again he sent a third; and they wounded him also and cast *him* out.

¹³"Then the owner of the vineyard said, 'What shall I do? I will send my beloved son. Probably they will respect *him* when they see him.' ¹⁴But when the vinedressers saw him, they reasoned among themselves,

saying, 'This is the heir. Come, let us kill him, that the inheritance may be ours.' ¹⁵So they cast him out of the vineyard and killed *him*. Therefore what will the owner of the vineyard do to them? ¹⁶He will come and destroy those vinedressers and give the vineyard to others."

And when they heard *it* they said, "Certainly not!"

¹⁷Then He looked at them and said, "What then is this that is written:

'The stone which the builders rejected
Has become the chief cornerstone'?ᵃ

¹⁸Whoever falls on that stone will be broken; but on whomever it falls, it will grind him to powder."

¹⁹And the chief priests and the scribes that very hour sought to lay hands on Him, but they feared the peopleᵃ—for they knew He had spoken this parable against them.

Questioned by Pharisees and Herodians

The Pharisees sent "their disciples with the Herodians" (Matt. 22:16), presenting Jesus with an apparently "no-win" situation. If He told them to pay taxes to Rome, the Pharisees would discredit Jesus with the Jews. The Herodians, who supported the Roman occupation, would brand Jesus as a traitor to Rome if He did not support taxation. Jesus' answer challenged both groups. The denarius (Matt. 22:18) bore the image of the emperor Tiberius Caesar and thus supported Rome's right to require taxes.

■ Matthew 22:15–22
■ Mark 12:13–17
■ Luke 20:20–26

Matthew 22:15–22
The Pharisees: Is It Lawful to Pay Taxes?

22 :15 Then the Pharisees went and plotted how they might entangle Him in *His* talk. ¹⁶And they sent to Him their disciples with the Herodians, saying, "Teacher, we know that You are true, and teach the way of God in truth; nor do You

---

12:4 ᵃNU-Text omits *and at him they threw stones.*   12:11 ᵃPsalm 118:22, 23
Luke 20:17 ᵃPsalm 118:22   20:19 ᵃM-Text reads *but they were afraid.*

care about anyone, for You do not regard the person of men. [17]Tell us, therefore, what do You think? Is it lawful to pay taxes to Caesar, or not?"

[18]But Jesus perceived their wickedness, and said, "Why do you test Me, *you* hypocrites? [19]Show Me the tax money."

So they brought Him a denarius.

[20]And He said to them, "Whose image and inscription *is* this?"

[21]They said to Him, "Caesar's."

And He said to them, "Render therefore to Caesar the things that are Caesar's, and to God the things that are God's." [22]When they had heard *these words,* they marveled, and left Him and went their way.

Mark 12:13–17
To Caesar What Is Caesar's

12 :13 Then they sent to Him some of the Pharisees and the Herodians, to catch Him in *His* words. [14]When they had come, they said to Him, "Teacher, we know that You are true, and care about no one; for You do not regard the person of men, but teach the way of God in truth. Is it lawful to pay taxes to Caesar, or not? [15]Shall we pay or shall we not pay?"

But He, knowing their hypocrisy, said to them, "Why do you test Me? Bring Me a denarius that I may see *it.*" [16]So they brought *it.*

And He said to them, "Whose image and inscription *is* this?" They said to Him, "Caesar's."

[17]And Jesus answered and said to them, "Render to Caesar the things that are Caesar's, and to God the things that are God's."

And they marveled at Him.

Luke 20:20–26
Paying Tribute

20 :20 So they watched *Him,* and sent spies who pretended to be righteous, that they might seize on His words, in order to deliver Him to the power and the authority of the governor.

[21]Then they asked Him, saying, "Teacher, we know that You say and teach rightly, and You do not show personal favoritism, but teach the way of God in truth: [22]Is it lawful for us to pay taxes to Caesar or not?"

[23]But He perceived their craftiness, and said to them, "Why do you test Me?[a] [24]Show Me a denarius. Whose image and inscription does it have?"

They answered and said, "Caesar's."

[25]And He said to them, "Render therefore to Caesar the things that are Caesar's, and to God the things that are God's."

[26]But they could not catch Him in His words in the presence of the people. And they marveled at His answer and kept silent.

Questioned by Sadducees

The Sadducees were the priestly sect among the Jews that had charge of the temple sacrificial system. They were more aristocratic than the other sects, and being theologically more liberal, they did not believe in an afterlife or the resurrection. The story of the seven brothers may have been one of their stock illustrations to ridicule the idea of a resurrection. While the doctrine of the Sadducees was opposed to the Pharisees, they were like the Pharisees in trying to discredit Jesus.

- Matthew 22:23–33
- Mark 12:18–27
- Luke 20:27–40

Matthew 22:23–33
The Sadducees: What About the Resurrection?

22 :23 The same day the Sadducees, who say there is no resurrection, came to Him and asked Him, [24]saying: "Teacher, Moses said that if a man dies, having no children, his brother shall marry his wife and raise up offspring for his brother. [25]Now there were with us seven

20:23 [a]NU-Text omits *Why do you test Me?*

TRADE AND ECONOMICS

The coins in circulation in Palestine included both Roman and local issues. The typical Roman coin had on one side a portrait of the emperor or another important person (Matt. 22:20). On the other side was a symbolic design, like a temple. The lettering around the imperial portraits had recently begun to include the letters "DIV," signifying "divine." Julius Caesar was the first living person to appear on official Roman coins.

brothers. The first died after he had married, and having no offspring, left his wife to his brother. ²⁶Likewise the second also, and the third, even to the seventh. ²⁷Last of all the woman died also. ²⁸Therefore, in the resurrection, whose wife of the seven will she be? For they all had her."

²⁹Jesus answered and said to them, "You are mistaken, not knowing the Scriptures nor the power of God. ³⁰For in the resurrection they neither marry nor are given in marriage, but are like angels of God^a in heaven. ³¹But concerning the resurrection of the dead, have you not read what was spoken to you by God, saying, ³²*'I am the God of Abraham, the God of Isaac, and the God of Jacob'?*^a God is not the God of the dead, but of the living." ³³And when the multitudes heard *this,* they were astonished at His teaching.

Mark 12:18–27
Life in Heaven Is Different

12 **:18** Then *some* Sadducees, who say there is no resurrection, came to Him; and they asked Him, saying: ¹⁹"Teacher, Moses wrote to us that if a man's brother dies, and leaves *his* wife behind, and leaves no children, his brother should take his wife and raise up offspring for his brother. ²⁰Now there were seven brothers. The first took a wife; and dying, he left no offspring. ²¹And the second took her, and he died; nor did he leave any offspring. And the third likewise. ²²So the seven had her and left no offspring. Last of all the woman died also. ²³Therefore, in the resurrection, when they rise, whose wife will she be? For all seven had her as wife."

²⁴Jesus answered and said to them, "Are you not therefore mistaken, because you do not know the Scriptures nor the power of God? ²⁵For when they rise from the dead, they neither marry nor are given in marriage, but are like angels in heaven. ²⁶But concerning the dead, that they rise, have you not read in the book of Moses, in the *burning* bush *passage,* how God spoke to him, saying, *'I am the God of Abraham, the God of Isaac, and the God of Jacob'?*^a ²⁷He is not the God of the dead, but the God of the living. You are therefore greatly mistaken."

Luke 20:27–40
Marriage in the Resurrection?

20 **:27** Then some of the Sadducees, who deny that there is a resurrec-

tion, came to *Him* and asked Him, ²⁸saying: "Teacher, Moses wrote to us *that* if a man's brother dies, having a wife, and he dies without children, his brother should take his wife and raise up offspring for his brother. ²⁹Now there were seven brothers. And the first took a wife, and died without children. ³⁰And the second^a took her as wife, and he died childless. ³¹Then the third took her, and in like manner the seven also; and they left no children,^a and died. ³²Last of all the woman died also. ³³Therefore, in the resurrection, whose wife does she become? For all seven had her as wife."

³⁴Jesus answered and said to them, "The sons of this age marry and are given in marriage. ³⁵But those who are counted worthy to attain that age, and the resurrection from the dead, neither marry nor are given in marriage; ³⁶nor can they die anymore, for they are equal to the angels and are sons of God, being sons of the resurrection. ³⁷But even Moses showed in the *burning* bush *passage* that the dead are raised, when he called the Lord *'the God of Abraham, the God of Isaac, and the God of Jacob.'*^a ³⁸For He is not the God of the dead but of the living, for all live to Him."

³⁹Then some of the scribes answered and said, "Teacher, You have spoken well." ⁴⁰But after that they dared not question Him anymore.

22:30 ^aNU-Text omits *of God.*   22:32 ^aExodus 3:6, 15   **Mark** 12:26 ^aExodus 3:6, 15
Luke 20:30 ^aNU-Text ends verse 30 here.
20:31 ^aNU-Text and M-Text read *the seven also left no children.*   20:37 ^aExodus 3:6, 15

Questioned by a Scribe
While some Jewish leaders tried to trap Jesus into making discrediting statements, one sincere scribe asked about God's true purpose (Matt. 22:36). In Matthew's Gospel, Jesus returned a question to the Pharisees, challenging the false understanding of who Christ would be. He would not be only a human "Son of David" (22:42), an earthly king. David himself had called the Messiah his "Lord" (Ps. 110:1). How then could the Pharisees call Him anything less?

- Matthew 22:34–46
- Mark 12:28–37
- Luke 20:41–44

Matthew 22:34–46
The Scribe: Which Is the First Commandment of All?

22 **:34** But when the Pharisees heard that He had silenced the Sadducees, they gathered together. ³⁵Then one of them, a lawyer, asked *Him a question,* testing Him, and saying, ³⁶"Teacher, which *is* the great commandment in the law?"

³⁷Jesus said to him, " *'You shall love the LORD your God with all your heart, with all your soul, and with all your mind.'*ᵃ ³⁸This is *the* first and great commandment. ³⁹And *the* second is like it: *'You shall love your neighbor as yourself.'*ᵃ ⁴⁰On these two commandments hang all the Law and the Prophets."

Jesus: How Can David Call His Descendant Lord?

⁴¹While the Pharisees were gathered together, Jesus asked them, ⁴²saying, "What do you think about the Christ? Whose Son is He?"

They said to Him, *"The Son* of David."

⁴³He said to them, "How then does David in the Spirit call Him *'Lord,'* saying:

⁴⁴　*'The LORD said to my Lord,*
　　"Sit at My right hand,
　　　Till I make Your enemies Your
　　　　*footstool" '?*ᵃ

⁴⁵If David then calls Him *'Lord,'* how is He his Son?" ⁴⁶And no one was able to answer Him a word, nor from that day on did anyone dare question Him anymore.

Mark 12:28–37
The Greatest Commandment

12 **:28** Then one of the scribes came, and having heard them reasoning together, perceivingᵃ that He had answered

them well, asked Him, "Which is the first commandment of all?"

²⁹Jesus answered him, "The first of all the commandments *is: 'Hear, O Israel, the* LORD *our God, the* LORD *is one.* ³⁰*And you shall love the* LORD *your God with all your heart, with all your soul, with all your mind, and with all your strength.'*ᵃ This *is* the first commandment.ᵇ ³¹And the second, like *it, is* this: *'You shall love your neighbor as yourself.'*ᵃ There is no other commandment greater than these."

³²So the scribe said to Him, "Well *said,* Teacher. You have spoken the truth, for there is one God, and there is no other but He. ³³And to love Him with all the heart, with all the understanding, with all the soul,ᵃ and with all the strength, and to love one's neighbor as oneself, is more than all the whole burnt offerings and sacrifices."

³⁴Now when Jesus saw that he answered wisely, He said to him, "You are not far from the kingdom of God."

But after that no one dared question Him.

Greater than David

³⁵Then Jesus answered and said, while He taught in the temple, "How *is it* that the scribes say that the Christ is the Son of David? ³⁶For David himself said by the Holy Spirit:

　'The LORD said to my Lord,
　"Sit at My right hand,
　　Till I make Your enemies Your
　　　*footstool." '*ᵃ

³⁷Therefore David himself calls Him *'Lord';* how is He *then* his Son?"

And the common people heard Him gladly.

Luke 20:41–44
David's Son and Lord

20 **:41** And He said to them, "How can they say that the Christ is the Son of David? ⁴²Now David himself said in the Book of Psalms:

22:37 ᵃDeuteronomy 6:5　　22:39 ᵃLeviticus 19:18　　22:44 ᵃPsalm 110:1
Mark 12:28 ᵃNU-Text reads *seeing.*
12:30 ᵃDeuteronomy 6:4, 5　　ᵇNU-Text omits this sentence.　　12:31 ᵃLeviticus 19:18
12:33 ᵃNU-Text omits *with all the soul.*
12:36 ᵃPsalm 110:1

POLITICS AND GOVERNMENT
The traditional Law of Israel was part of the education of all Jews (Matt. 22:40). The Romans also had a traditional law called the Twelve Tables, that their children memorized. This law had civil, criminal, and religious provisions. Unlike the Law of Moses, the text of Twelve Tables has been preserved only in fragments.

'The LORD said to my Lord,
" Sit at My right hand,
43   Till I make Your enemies Your
      footstool." 'ᵃ

⁴⁴Therefore David calls Him *'Lord'*; how is
He then his Son?"

Beware of the Scribes

Only Matthew's Gospel provides Jesus' long condemnation of the scribes and Pharisees (Matt. 23:1–36), denouncing their hypocrisy and disobedience, and pronouncing seven judgments of woe on them. They are characterized as selfish religious officials who "devour widows' houses" (Matt. 23:14; Mark 12:40). Apparently the scribes mismanaged the property of widows which had been entrusted to them in the wills of the widows' dead husbands.

Mark and Luke contrast these scribes, who took advantage of others, with the widow who had little (Mark 12:42; Luke 21:2). She put in all that she had; her love was not calculating.

- Matthew 23:1–39
- Mark 12:38–44
- Luke 20:45—21:4

Matthew 23:1–39
Woe to the Scribes and Pharisees

23 **:1** Then Jesus spoke to the multitudes and to His disciples, ²saying: "The scribes and the Pharisees sit in Moses' seat. ³Therefore whatever they tell you to observe,ᵃ *that* observe and do, but do not do according to their works; for they say, and do not do. ⁴For they bind heavy burdens, hard to bear, and lay *them* on men's shoulders; but they *themselves* will not move them with one of their fingers. ⁵But all their works they do to be seen by men. They make their phylacteries broad and enlarge the borders of their garments. ⁶They love the best places at feasts, the best seats in the synagogues, ⁷greetings in

the marketplaces, and to be called by men, 'Rabbi, Rabbi.' ⁸But you, do not be called 'Rabbi'; for One is your Teacher, the Christ,ᵃ and you are all brethren. ⁹Do not call anyone on earth your father; for One is your Father, He who is in heaven. ¹⁰And do not be called teachers; for One is your Teacher, the Christ. ¹¹But he who is greatest among you shall be your servant. ¹²And whoever exalts himself will be humbled, and he who humbles himself will be exalted.

¹³"But woe to you, scribes and Pharisees, hypocrites! For you shut up the kingdom of heaven against men; for you neither go in *yourselves,* nor do you allow those who are entering to go in. ¹⁴Woe to you, scribes and Pharisees, hypocrites! For you devour widows' houses, and for a pretense make long prayers. Therefore you will receive greater condemnation.ᵃ

¹⁵"Woe to you, scribes and Pharisees, hypocrites! For you travel land and sea to win one proselyte, and when he is won, you make him twice as much a son of hell as yourselves.

¹⁶"Woe to you, blind guides, who say, 'Whoever swears by the temple, it is nothing; but whoever swears by the gold of the temple, he is obliged *to perform it.*' ¹⁷Fools and blind! For which is greater, the gold or the temple that sanctifiesᵃ the gold? ¹⁸And, 'Whoever swears by the altar, it is nothing; but whoever swears by the gift that is on it, he is obliged *to perform it.*' ¹⁹Fools and blind! For which is greater, the gift or the altar that sanctifies the gift? ²⁰Therefore he who swears by the altar, swears by it and by all things on it. ²¹He who swears by the temple, swears by it and by Him who dwellsᵃ in it. ²²And he who swears by heaven, swears by the throne of God and by Him who sits on it.

20:43 ᵃPsalm 110:1   **Matt.** 23:3 ᵃNU-Text omits *to observe.*   23:8 ᵃNU-Text omits *the Christ.*
23:14 ᵃNU-Text omits this verse.
23:17 ᵃNU-Text reads *sanctified.*   23:21 ᵃM-Text reads *dwelt.*

RELIGION AND WORSHIP

Jesus' statement that the Pharisees went over land and sea to make converts does not mean that they sent out missionaries (Matt. 23:15). Rather, it expressed the arrogant assumption of some Pharisees that they should make others just like themselves. Judaism itself attracted people because of its moral standards and its pure monotheism, but Pharisaic teachings did not necessarily make a convert a better person.

Weightier Matters of the Law (Matt. 23:23)

The scribes and Pharisees were among the most respected religious people of Jesus' day. Jesus, however, criticized them as teachers who were preoccupied with petty rules and ignored the truly important religious principles. Although some other outsiders (as well as certain later Jewish teachers) also criticized the scribes and Pharisees, most people thought highly of them and would have been shocked by Jesus' criticisms.

In Old Testament times the Israelites mainly lived on livestock and crops, and, following the Law of Moses, gathered a tithe (one tenth) of their produce into storehouses or granaries (Mal. 3:10). The law commanded the Israelites to use the tithes to support the priests and Levites, who spiritually served God and the people (Num. 18:21–24). At the end of every third year, a part of the tithe was used for the poor, as well as for the Levites (Deut. 14:28, 29; 26:12).

In Jesus' day the Pharisees were particularly scrupulous about tithing. According to Matthew, they tithed mint, anise, and cummin—all common garden herbs (Matt. 23:23). Luke mentions another herb, rue (Luke 11:42). In Aramaic, Jesus' native language in Galilee, the word "rue" sounds very similar to the word "anise," which possibly explains why Matthew names one and Luke the other. Because the law emphasized tithing foods, some Pharisees debated whether one need tithe such vegetables as these, especially cummin. Jesus called these very conservative Pharisees "hypocrites" (Matt. 23:23), because they were concerned only with outward matters, while neglecting inward purity.

23"Woe to you, scribes and Pharisees, hypocrites! For you pay tithe of mint and anise and cummin, and have neglected the weightier *matters* of the law: justice and mercy and faith. These you ought to have done, without leaving the others undone. 24Blind guides, who strain out a gnat and swallow a camel!

25"Woe to you, scribes and Pharisees, hypocrites! For you cleanse the outside of the cup and dish, but inside they are full of extortion and self-indulgence.[a] 26Blind Pharisee, first cleanse the inside of the cup and dish, that the outside of them may be clean also.

27"Woe to you, scribes and Pharisees, hypocrites! For you are like whitewashed tombs which indeed appear beautiful outwardly, but inside are full of dead *men's* bones and all uncleanness. 28Even so you also outwardly appear righteous to men, but inside you are full of hypocrisy and lawlessness.

29"Woe to you, scribes and Pharisees, hypocrites! Because you build the tombs of the prophets and adorn the monuments of the righteous, 30and say, 'If we had lived in the days of our fathers, we would not have been partakers with them in the blood of the prophets.'

31"Therefore you are witnesses against yourselves that you are sons of those who murdered the prophets. 32Fill up, then, the measure of your fathers' *guilt.* 33Serpents, brood of vipers! How can you escape the condemnation of hell? 34Therefore, indeed, I send you prophets, wise men, and scribes: *some* of them you will kill and crucify, and *some* of them you will scourge in your synagogues and persecute from city to city, 35that on you may come all the righteous blood shed on the earth, from the blood of righteous Abel to the blood of Zechariah, son of Berechiah, whom you murdered between the temple and the altar. 36Assuredly, I say to you, all these things will come upon this generation.

Jesus Laments over Jerusalem

37"O Jerusalem, Jerusalem, the one who kills the prophets and stones those who are sent to her! How often I wanted to gather your children together, as a hen gathers her chicks under *her* wings, but you were not willing! 38See! Your house is left to you desolate; 39for I say to you, you shall see Me no more till you say, 'Blessed is He who comes in the name of the Lord!'"[a]

23:25 [a]M-Text reads *unrighteousness.*
23:39 [a]Psalm 118:26

Mark 12:38–44
All That She Had

12 :38 Then He said to them in His teaching, "Beware of the scribes, who desire to go around in long robes, *love* greetings in the marketplaces, ³⁹the best seats in the synagogues, and the best places at feasts, ⁴⁰who devour widows' houses, and for a pretense make long prayers. These will receive greater condemnation."

⁴¹Now Jesus sat opposite the treasury and saw how the people put money into the treasury. And many *who were* rich put in much. ⁴²Then one poor widow came and threw in two mites,ᵃ which make a quadrans. ⁴³So He called His disciples to *Himself* and said to them, "Assuredly, I say to you that this poor widow has put in more than all those who have given to the treasury; ⁴⁴for they all put in out of their abundance, but she out of her poverty put in all that she had, her whole livelihood."

Luke 20:45—21:4
The Widow's Two Mites

20 :45 Then, in the hearing of all the people, He said to His disciples, ⁴⁶"Beware of the scribes, who desire to go around in long robes, love greetings in the marketplaces, the best seats in the synagogues, and the best places at feasts, ⁴⁷who devour widows' houses, and for a pretense make long prayers. These will receive greater condemnation."

21 ¹And He looked up and saw the rich putting their gifts into the treasury, ²and He saw also a certain poor widow putting in two mites. ³So He said, "Truly I say to you that this poor widow has put in more than all; ⁴for all these out of their abundance have put in offerings for God,ᵃ but she out of her poverty put in all the livelihood that she had."

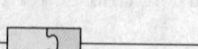

Discourse While on the Mount of Olives

The Kidron Valley falls away beneath the Mount of Olives, leaving a spectacular panorama of Jerusalem and the Temple Mount to the west. The vista from the Mount of Olives provides the setting for a final discourse of Jesus on future events.

The discourse warns of approaching tribulation. The first focus is the near future and the destruction of Jerusalem by the Roman army. All three Synoptics warn of this impending catastrophe, but Luke provides an explicit allusion to the sack of Jerusalem under Titus in A.D. 70. Some scholars think that Luke's writing of Jerusalem being "surrounded by armies" (Luke 20:21) and "trampled by Gentiles" (21:24) indicates that the fall of Jerusalem in that year had already taken place, thus Luke recorded Jesus' words in light of the actual calamity that befell the city. Other scholars suppose that Luke 21:20 is an actual prediction of the Romans crushing the Jewish revolt.

The second focus of the Mount of Olives discourse is the distant future. "Eschatology" is the technical term in Judaism that refers to events attending the end of time. The destruction of Jerusalem was seen by Jesus and the Gospel writers as a symbol or anticipation of the catastrophes of the end time, before which the Son of Man will return in glory. Jesus' instruction to the disciples on what to say when they are hailed before the authorities is included by Mark and Luke in this eschatological discourse (Mark 13:9–13; Luke 12:12–19). Matthew's Gospel reports these words earlier as part of Jesus' mission instructions to the twelve disciples (Matt. 10:17–22). See "Mission of the Twelve" at Matt. 9:35.

■ Matthew 24:1–35
■ Mark 13:1–31
■ Luke 21:5–33

Matthew 24:1–35
Conditions Before Christ's Return

24 :1 Then Jesus went out and departed from the temple, and His disciples came up to show Him the buildings of the temple. ²And Jesus said to them, "Do you not see all these things? Assuredly, I say to you, not *one* stone shall be left here upon another, that shall not be thrown down."

³Now as He sat on the Mount of Olives, the disciples came to Him privately, saying, "Tell us, when will these things be? And what *will be* the sign of Your coming, and of the end of the age?"

⁴And Jesus answered and said to them: "Take heed that no one deceives you. ⁵For many will come in My name, saying, 'I am the Christ,' and will deceive many. ⁶And you will hear of wars and rumors of wars. See that you are not troubled; for allᵃ

12:42 ᵃGreek *lepta*, very small copper coins worth a fraction of a penny   **Luke 21:4** ᵃNU-Text omits *for God*.   **Matt. 24:6** ᵃNU-Text omits *all*.

HEROD, THE GREAT BUILDER (Matt. 24:1)

More architectural remains in Israel date from the reign of Herod the Great (37–4 B.C.) than from any other historical personality. He initiated numerous diverse projects, including temples, gymnasiums, harbors, and other buildings.

Herod was born in the late 70s B.C. to a noble family in Idumea. His Idumean ancestors had been forcibly converted to Judaism by the late 2nd century B.C. Antipater, Herod's father, had been a close confidant of Hyrcanus II, one of the Jewish Hasmonean kings. The Romans conquered Judea in 63 B.C., and Herod, who became governor of Galilee in 47 B.C., knew that to be successful he would need to cooperate with Rome. After numerous struggles, Herod was able with Roman help to claim the throne of Judea in 37 B.C., and to rule there for 33 years.

In Jerusalem alone Herod had a number of important building projects. The Antonia Fortress, a combined palace and fortress which dominated the Temple Mount, was named after Mark Antony. The central palace was the largest of Herod's palaces. His building activity produced a theater and amphitheater, numerous fortifications, and the most famous of all his projects—the Temple Mount. Unfortunately, because of the Roman destruction of the city in A.D. 70, nearly all of the material remains of Herod's period have disappeared.

In his 18th year (20–19 B.C.), Herod began rebuilding the Jerusalem temple and enlarging the sacred precincts surrounding it. The new temple probably followed the original plan of the second temple, but on a more elaborate scale. Modern excavations have exposed large parts of the western and southern Temple Mount walls, as well as a monumental stairway, gates, a plaza, and evidence of adjoining roads. The "buildings of the temple" (Matt. 24:1) were certainly impressive in Jesus' day, even though secondary construction around the temple was still in progress.

---

these things must come to pass, but the end is not yet. ⁷For nation will rise against nation, and kingdom against kingdom. And there will be famines, pestilences,ᵃ and earthquakes in various places. ⁸All these *are* the beginning of sorrows.

⁹"Then they will deliver you up to tribulation and kill you, and you will be hated by all nations for My name's sake. ¹⁰And then many will be offended, will betray one another, and will hate one another. ¹¹Then many false prophets will rise up and deceive many. ¹²And because lawlessness will abound, the love of many will grow cold. ¹³But he who endures to the end shall be saved. ¹⁴And this gospel of the kingdom will be preached in all the world as a witness to all the nations, and then the end will come.

The Abomination of Desolation

¹⁵"Therefore when you see the *'abomination of desolation,'*ᵃ spoken of by Daniel the prophet, standing in the holy place"

(whoever reads, let him understand), ¹⁶"then let those who are in Judea flee to the mountains. ¹⁷Let him who is on the housetop not go down to take anything out of his house. ¹⁸And let him who is in the field not go back to get his clothes. ¹⁹But woe to those who are pregnant and to those who are nursing babies in those days! ²⁰And pray that your flight may not be in winter or on the Sabbath. ²¹For then there will be great tribulation, such as has not been since the beginning of the world until this time, no, nor ever shall be. ²²And unless those days were shortened, no flesh would be saved; but for the elect's sake those days will be shortened.

²³"Then if anyone says to you, 'Look, here *is* the Christ!' or 'There!' do not believe it. ²⁴For false christs and false prophets will rise and show great signs and wonders to deceive, if possible, even the elect. ²⁵See, I have told you beforehand.

²⁶"Therefore if they say to you, 'Look, He is in the desert!' do not go out; *or* 'Look, *He is* in the inner rooms!' do not believe *it*. ²⁷For as the lightning comes from the east and flashes to the west, so also will the

---

24:7 ᵃNU-Text omits *pestilences*.   24:15 ᵃDaniel 11:31; 12:11

coming of the Son of Man be. ²⁸For wherever the carcass is, there the eagles will be gathered together.

The Coming of the Son of Man

²⁹"Immediately after the tribulation of those days the sun will be darkened, and the moon will not give its light; the stars will fall from heaven, and the powers of the heavens will be shaken. ³⁰Then the sign of the Son of Man will appear in heaven, and then all the tribes of the earth will mourn, and they will see the Son of Man coming on the clouds of heaven with power and great glory. ³¹And He will send His angels with a great sound of a trumpet, and they will gather together His elect from the four winds, from one end of heaven to the other.

The Parable of the Fig Tree

³²"Now learn this parable from the fig tree: When its branch has already become tender and puts forth leaves, you know that summer *is* near. ³³So you also, when you see all these things, know that itᵃ is near—at the doors! ³⁴Assuredly, I say to you, this generation will by no means pass away till all these things take place. ³⁵Heaven and earth will pass away, but My words will by no means pass away."

Mark 13:1–31
Jesus Predicts Destruction

13 :1 Then as He went out of the temple, one of His disciples said to Him, "Teacher, see what manner of stones and what buildings *are here!*"

²And Jesus answered and said to him, "Do you see these great buildings? Not *one* stone shall be left upon another, that shall not be thrown down."

The Signs of the Times and the End of the Age

³Now as He sat on the Mount of Olives opposite the temple, Peter, James, John, and Andrew asked Him privately, ⁴"Tell us, when will these things be? And what *will*

be the sign when all these things will be fulfilled?"

⁵And Jesus, answering them, began to say: "Take heed that no one deceives you. ⁶For many will come in My name, saying, 'I am *He,'* and will deceive many. ⁷But when you hear of wars and rumors of wars, do not be troubled; for *such things* must happen, but the end *is* not yet. ⁸For nation will rise against nation, and kingdom against kingdom. And there will be earthquakes in various places, and there will be famines and troubles.ᵃ These *are* the beginnings of sorrows.

⁹"But watch out for yourselves, for they will deliver you up to councils, and you will be beaten in the synagogues. You will be broughtᵃ before rulers and kings for My sake, for a testimony to them. ¹⁰And the gospel must first be preached to all the nations. ¹¹But when they arrest *you* and deliver you up, do not worry beforehand, or premeditateᵃ what you will speak. But whatever is given you in that hour, speak that; for it is not you who speak, but the Holy Spirit. ¹²Now brother will betray brother to death, and a father *his* child; and children will rise up against parents and cause them to be put to death. ¹³And you will be hated by all for My name's sake. But he who endures to the end shall be saved.

The Great Tribulation

¹⁴"So when you see the *'abomination of desolation,'*ᵃ spoken of by Daniel the prophet,ᵇ standing where it ought not" (let the reader understand), "then let those who are in Judea flee to the mountains. ¹⁵Let him who is on the housetop not go down into the house, nor enter to take anything out of his house. ¹⁶And let him who is in the field not go back to get his clothes.

24:33 ᵃOr *He*   **Mark 13:8** ᵃNU-Text omits *and troubles.*   13:9 ᵃNU-Text and M-Text read *will stand.*   13:11 ᵃNU-Text omits *or premeditate.* 13:14 ᵃDaniel 11:31; 12:11   ᵇNU-Text omits *spoken of by Daniel the prophet.*

PLANTS AND ANIMALS

The fig tree has been cultivated around the Mediterranean for thousands of years. This large tree gives fruit from early to late summer. Like grapes, figs can be eaten fresh or dried. In the winter, the leaves fall off, but new shoots appear in spring and so announce that summer is near (Matt. 24:32). Jesus' parable of the fig tree encouraged people to watch for the coming of God's future kingdom (Luke 21:31).

THE ABOMINATION OF DESOLATION (Mark 13:14)

Matthew and Mark refer to the "abomination of desolation," assuming that their readers will know what it is (Matt. 24:15; Mark 13:14). Modern scholars differ among themselves as to whether this "abomination" will be repeated in the future, but most agree that at least part of it has already occurred. The prophecies of Daniel speak of an abomination which would lead to desolation (Dan. 9:27; 11:31; 12:11). Later writings, such as 1 Maccabees and the Psalms of Solomon, use Daniel's terms to describe the repeated attacks on Jerusalem's temple.

One Jewish historian who lived in the 1st century A.D., Josephus, describes the war of A.D. 66–70 similarly as a desolating sacrilege. Josephus believed that when Jewish patriots slaughtered the priests in the Jerusalem temple, they defiled the temple, hence inviting destruction (see Matt. 23:38—24:2). Early Christian writers tell us that before the Romans closed in on Jerusalem, the Jewish patriots began to seize control of the city, forcing the Christians to flee.

In A.D. 70, just 3½ years after the desecrating slaughter in the temple, the Romans finally took Jerusalem. They slaughtered or enslaved most of the Jerusalemites, but according to Josephus self-proclaimed prophets promised those who were taking refuge in the temple that God would protect the sacred building. But God did not, and after the Romans burned the temple they placed on it their standards, bearing the insignia of the emperor who was worshiped as a god.

Most Jewish people, including the Essenes who wrote the Dead Sea Scrolls, considered the Roman standards to be idolatrous. Some preferred to die rather than allow the standards into Jerusalem. Tragically, the Romans now offered sacrifices to their standards on the site of the temple. Judean Jews revolted again in A.D. 132, and were again brutally suppressed by the Romans around 135. After that, the Romans built a pagan temple on the site once reserved for the worship of Israel's God. These acts were truly "abominations."

17But woe to those who are pregnant and to those who are nursing babies in those days! 18And pray that your flight may not be in winter. 19For *in* those days there will be tribulation, such as has not been since the beginning of the creation which God created until this time, nor ever shall be. 20And unless the Lord had shortened those days, no flesh would be saved; but for the elect's sake, whom He chose, He shortened the days. 21"Then if anyone says to you, 'Look, here *is* the Christ!' or, 'Look, *He is* there!' do not believe it. 22For false christs and false prophets will rise and show signs and wonders to deceive, if possible, even the elect. 23But take heed; see, I have told you all things beforehand.

The Coming of the Son of Man

24"But in those days, after that tribulation, the sun will be darkened, and the moon will not give its light; 25the stars of heaven will fall, and the powers in the heavens will be shaken. 26Then they will see the Son of Man coming in the clouds with great power and glory. 27And then He will send His angels, and gather together His elect from the four winds, from the farthest part of earth to the farthest part of heaven.

The Parable of the Fig Tree

28"Now learn this parable from the fig tree: When its branch has already become tender, and puts forth leaves, you know that summer is near. 29So you also, when you see these things happening, know that ita is near—at the doors! 30Assuredly, I say to you, this generation will by no means pass away till all these things take place. 31Heaven and earth will pass away, but My words will by no means pass away."

Luke 21:5–33
The Destruction of the Temple

21 :5 Then, as some spoke of the temple, how it was adorned with beautiful stones and donations, He said, 6"These things which you see—the days will come

13:29 aOr *He*

in which not *one* stone shall be left upon another that shall not be thrown down."

Signs and Persecutions

⁷So they asked Him, saying, "Teacher, but when will these things be? And what sign *will there be* when these things are about to take place?"

⁸And He said: "Take heed that you not be deceived. For many will come in My name, saying, 'I am *He*,' and, 'The time has drawn near.' Therefore[a] do not go after them. ⁹But when you hear of wars and commotions, do not be terrified; for these things must come to pass first, but the end *will not come* immediately."

¹⁰Then He said to them, "Nation will rise against nation, and kingdom against kingdom. ¹¹And there will be great earthquakes in various places, and famines and pestilences; and there will be fearful sights and great signs from heaven. ¹²But before all these things, they will lay their hands on you and persecute *you,* delivering *you* up to the synagogues and prisons. You will be brought before kings and rulers for My name's sake. ¹³But it will turn out for you as an occasion for testimony. ¹⁴Therefore settle *it* in your hearts not to meditate beforehand on what you will answer; ¹⁵for I will give you a mouth and wisdom which all your adversaries will not be able to contradict or resist. ¹⁶You will be betrayed even by parents and brothers, relatives and friends; and they will put *some* of you to death. ¹⁷And you will be hated by all for My name's sake. ¹⁸But not a hair of your head shall be lost. ¹⁹By your patience possess your souls.

The Destruction of Jerusalem

²⁰"But when you see Jerusalem surrounded by armies, then know that its desolation is near. ²¹Then let those who are in Judea flee to the mountains, let those who are in the midst of her depart, and let not those who are in the country enter her. ²²For these are the days of vengeance, that all things which are written may be ful-

filled. ²³But woe to those who are pregnant and to those who are nursing babies in those days! For there will be great distress in the land and wrath upon this people. ²⁴And they will fall by the edge of the sword, and be led away captive into all nations. And Jerusalem will be trampled by Gentiles until the times of the Gentiles are fulfilled.

The Coming of the Son of Man

²⁵"And there will be signs in the sun, in the moon, and in the stars; and on the earth distress of nations, with perplexity, the sea and the waves roaring; ²⁶men's hearts failing them from fear and the expectation of those things which are coming on the earth, for the powers of the heavens will be shaken. ²⁷Then they will see the Son of Man coming in a cloud with power and great glory. ²⁸Now when these things begin to happen, look up and lift up your heads, because your redemption draws near."

The Parable of the Fig Tree

²⁹Then He spoke to them a parable: "Look at the fig tree, and all the trees. ³⁰When they are already budding, you see and know for yourselves that summer is now near. ³¹So you also, when you see these things happening, know that the kingdom of God is near. ³²Assuredly, I say to you, this generation will by no means pass away till all things take place. ³³Heaven and earth will pass away, but My words will by no means pass away."

21:8 ªNU-Text omits *Therefore.*

Parables from the Mount of Olives

Portions of Jesus' teaching appear in different contexts in the different Gospels. Matthew supplements the eschatological discourse on the Mount of Olives by the addition of five parables, none of which appear in

POLITICS AND GOVERNMENT

At the death of Augustus in A.D. 14, the Roman army numbered about 260,000 men. About half were Roman citizens, 22 legions of 5,000 to 6,000 men each. Legions were subdivided into cohorts and centuries, with a centurion over each century. The noncitizen troops were "auxiliaries" drawn from tribes, allies, and provincials, and organized in regiments. These Roman armies "surrounded" Jerusalem in A.D. 70 (Luke 21:20).

Mark's Gospel. The last of these parables, the judgment of the nations (Matt. 25:31–46), is found only in Matthew's Gospel. The other four parables are reported by Luke as well as by Matthew: the flood (Matt. 24:37–44); the faithful and evil servants (24:45–51); the ten virgins (25:1–13); the talents (25:14–30). Luke's Gospel, however, places these parables in different contexts, all prior to Jesus' final week in Jerusalem.

Various explanations have been offered to account for these differences in the placement of Jesus' sayings and parables. In some instances it is reasonable to assume that Jesus taught the same things more than once, and that the different Gospels preserve the teachings at various points in His ministry. The differing arrangements of sayings, however, suggest yet another explanation. The early church often remembered a saying but not its context. Shorn of a context, a saying or parable depended on the discretion and purpose of each Gospel writer for its placement in the Gospel. The church father Papias (who died in A.D. 135) recognized this early in the 2nd century, writing, "Mark wrote accurately all that [Peter] taught about Jesus, though not always in the order of the things said and done by Jesus."

■ Matthew 24:36—25:46
■ Mark 13:32–37
■ Luke 21:34–38

Matthew 24:36—25:46
Be Ready!

24 :36 "But of that day and hour no one knows, not even the angels of heaven,ᵃ but My Father only. 37But as the days of Noah *were,* so also will the coming of the Son of Man be. 38For as in the days before the flood, they were eating and drinking, marrying and giving in marriage, until the day that Noah entered the ark, 39and did not know until the flood came and took them all away, so also will the coming of the Son of Man be. 40Then two *men* will be in the field: one will be taken and the other left. 41Two *women will be* grinding at the mill: one will be taken and the other left. 42Watch therefore, for you do not know what hourᵃ your Lord is coming. 43But know this, that if the master of the

house had known what hour the thief would come, he would have watched and not allowed his house to be broken into. 44Therefore you also be ready, for the Son of Man is coming at an hour you do not expect.

The Faithful Servant and the Evil Servant

45"Who then is a faithful and wise servant, whom his master made ruler over his household, to give them food in due season? 46Blessed *is* that servant whom his master, when he comes, will find so doing. 47Assuredly, I say to you that he will make him ruler over all his goods. 48But if that evil servant says in his heart, 'My master is delaying his coming,'ᵃ 49and begins to beat *his* fellow servants, and to eat and drink with the drunkards, 50the master of that servant will come on a day when he is not looking for *him* and at an hour that he is not aware of, 51and will cut him in two and appoint *him* his portion with the hypocrites. There shall be weeping and gnashing of teeth.

The Parable of the Wise and Foolish Virgins

25 1"Then the kingdom of heaven shall be likened to ten virgins who took their lamps and went out to meet the bridegroom. 2Now five of them were wise, and five *were* foolish. 3Those who *were* foolish took their lamps and took no oil with them, 4but the wise took oil in their vessels with their lamps. 5But while the bridegroom was delayed, they all slumbered and slept.

6"And at midnight a cry was *heard:* 'Behold, the bridegroom is coming;ᵃ go out to meet him!' 7Then all those virgins arose and trimmed their lamps. 8And the foolish said to the wise, 'Give us *some* of your oil, for our lamps are going out.' 9But the wise answered, saying, 'No, lest there should not be enough for us and you; but go rather to those who sell, and buy for yourselves.' 10And while they went to buy, the bridegroom came, and those who were ready went in with him to the wedding; and the door was shut.

11"Afterward the other virgins came also, saying, 'Lord, Lord, open to us!' 12But he answered and said, 'Assuredly, I say to you, I do not know you.'

13"Watch therefore, for you know

24:36 ᵃNU-Text adds *nor the Son.*
24:42 ᵃNU-Text reads *day.*   24:48 ᵃNU-Text omits *his coming.*   25:6 ᵃNU-Text omits *is coming.*

neither the day nor the hour[a] in which the Son of Man is coming.

The Parable of the Talents

14"For *the kingdom of heaven is* like a man traveling to a far country, *who* called his own servants and delivered his goods to them. 15And to one he gave five talents, to another two, and to another one, to each according to his own ability; and immediately he went on a journey. 16Then he who had received the five talents went and traded with them, and made another five talents. 17And likewise he who *had received* two gained two more also. 18But he who had received one went and dug in the ground, and hid his lord's money. 19After a long time the lord of those servants came and settled accounts with them.

20"So he who had received five talents came and brought five other talents, saying, 'Lord, you delivered to me five talents; look, I have gained five more talents besides them.' 21His lord said to him, 'Well *done,* good and faithful servant; you were faithful over a few things, I will make you ruler over many things. Enter into the joy of your lord.' 22He also who had received two talents came and said, 'Lord, you delivered to me two talents; look, I have gained two more talents besides them.' 23His lord said to him, 'Well *done,* good and faithful servant; you have been faithful over a few things, I will make you ruler over many things. Enter into the joy of your lord.'

24"Then he who had received the one talent came and said, 'Lord, I knew you to be a hard man, reaping where you have not sown, and gathering where you have not scattered seed. 25And I was afraid, and went and hid your talent in the ground. Look, *there* you have *what is* yours.'

26"But his lord answered and said to him, 'You wicked and lazy servant, you knew that I reap where I have not sown, and gather where I have not scattered seed. 27So you ought to have deposited my money with the bankers, and at my coming I would have received back my own with interest. 28So take the talent from him, and give *it* to him who has ten talents.

29"For to everyone who has, more will be given, and he will have abundance; but from him who does not have, even what he has will be taken away. 30And cast the unprofitable servant into the outer darkness. There will be weeping and gnashing of teeth.'

The Son of Man Will Judge the Nations

31"When the Son of Man comes in His glory, and all the holy[a] angels with Him, then He will sit on the throne of His glory. 32All the nations will be gathered before Him, and He will separate them one from another, as a shepherd divides *his* sheep from the goats. 33And He will set the sheep on His right hand, but the goats on the left. 34Then the King will say to those on His right hand, 'Come, you blessed of My Father, inherit the kingdom prepared for you from the foundation of the world: 35for I was hungry and you gave Me food; I was thirsty and you gave Me drink; I was a stranger and you took Me in; 36I *was* naked and you clothed Me; I was sick and you visited Me; I was in prison and you came to Me.'

37"Then the righteous will answer Him, saying, 'Lord, when did we see You hungry and feed *You,* or thirsty and give *You* drink? 38When did we see You a stranger and take *You* in, or naked and clothe *You?* 39Or when did we see You sick, or in prison, and come to You?' 40And the King will answer and say to them, 'Assuredly, I say to you, inasmuch as you did *it* to one of the least of these My brethren, you did *it* to Me.'

41"Then He will also say to those on the left hand, 'Depart from Me, you cursed, into the everlasting fire prepared for the devil and his angels: 42for I was hungry and you gave Me no food; I was thirsty and you gave Me no drink; 43I was a stranger and you did not take Me in, naked and you did not clothe Me, sick and in prison and you did not visit Me.'

44"Then they also will answer Him,[a] saying, 'Lord, when did we see You hungry or thirsty or a stranger or naked or sick or in prison, and did not minister to You?' 45Then He will answer them, saying, 'Assuredly, I say to you, inasmuch as you did not do *it* to one of the least of these, you did not do *it* to Me.' 46And these will go away into everlasting punishment, but the righteous into eternal life."

Mark 13:32–37
No One Knows the Day or Hour

13 :32 "But of that day and hour no one knows, not even the angels in

---

25:13 [a]NU-Text omits the rest of this verse.
25:31 [a]NU-Text omits *holy.*   25:44 [a]NU-Text and M-Text omit *Him.*

heaven, nor the Son, but only the Father. ³³Take heed, watch and pray; for you do not know when the time is. ³⁴*It is* like a man going to a far country, who left his house and gave authority to his servants, and to each his work, and commanded the doorkeeper to watch. ³⁵Watch therefore, for you do not know when the master of the house is coming—in the evening, at midnight, at the crowing of the rooster, or in the morning— ³⁶lest, coming suddenly, he find you sleeping. ³⁷And what I say to you, I say to all: Watch!"

Luke 21:34–38
The Importance of Watching

21 :34 "But take heed to yourselves, lest your hearts be weighed down with carousing, drunkenness, and cares of this life, and that Day come on you unexpectedly. ³⁵For it will come as a snare on all those who dwell on the face of the whole earth. ³⁶Watch therefore, and pray always that you may be counted worthyª to escape all these things that will come to pass, and to stand before the Son of Man."

³⁷And in the daytime He was teaching in the temple, but at night He went out and stayed on the mountain called Olivet. ³⁸Then early in the morning all the people came to Him in the temple to hear Him.

21:36 ªNU-Text reads *may have strength.*

Discourse on His Own Death

Between the Triumphal Entry and the Last Supper, the Synoptics record the great controversies in the temple, the parables, and the eschatological discourse on the Mount of Olives. The Gospel of John passes over in silence all of these. The only echo of them in John is a simple but trenchant quotation from the prophet Isaiah about the blindness of the people and their hardness of heart (John 12:39–41).

The Triumphal Entry and the Last Supper are connected in the Fourth Gospel instead by a brief soliloquy of Jesus on His impending death. His powerful illustration of the dying and germinating of a seed symbolizes the meaning of His death: the grain of wheat must die before it can reproduce itself (John 12:24). Similarly, the Son of Man must be "lifted up" on a cross to draw "all peoples" to Himself (John 12:32–34).

▼ ■ John 12:20–50

John
The Fruitful Grain of Wheat

12 :20 Now there were certain Greeks among those who came up to worship at the feast. ²¹Then they came to Philip, who was from Bethsaida of Galilee, and asked him, saying, "Sir, we wish to see Jesus."

²²Philip came and told Andrew, and in turn Andrew and Philip told Jesus.

²³But Jesus answered them, saying, "The hour has come that the Son of Man should be glorified. ²⁴Most assuredly, I say to you, unless a grain of wheat falls into the ground and dies, it remains alone; but if it dies, it produces much grain. ²⁵He who loves his life will lose it, and he who hates his life in this world will keep it for eternal life. ²⁶If anyone serves Me, let him follow Me; and where I am, there My servant will be also. If anyone serves Me, him *My* Father will honor.

Jesus Predicts His Death on the Cross

²⁷"Now My soul is troubled, and what shall I say? 'Father, save Me from this hour'? But for this purpose I came to this hour. ²⁸Father, glorify Your name."

Then a voice came from heaven, *saying,* "I have both glorified *it* and will glorify *it* again."

²⁹Therefore the people who stood by and heard *it* said that it had thundered. Others said, "An angel has spoken to Him."

³⁰Jesus answered and said, "This voice did not come because of Me, but for your sake. ³¹Now is the judgment of this world; now the ruler of this world will be cast out. ³²And I, if I am lifted up from the earth, will draw all *peoples* to Myself." ³³This He said, signifying by what death He would die.

³⁴The people answered Him, "We have heard from the law that the Christ remains forever; and how *can* You say, 'The Son of Man must be lifted up'? Who is this Son of Man?"

³⁵Then Jesus said to them, "A little while longer the light is with you. Walk while you have the light, lest darkness overtake you; he who walks in darkness does not know where he is going. ³⁶While you have the light, believe in the light, that you may become sons of light." These things Jesus spoke, and departed, and was hidden from them.

Who Has Believed Our Report?

37But although He had done so many signs before them, they did not believe in Him, 38that the word of Isaiah the prophet might be fulfilled, which he spoke:

"Lord, who has believed our report?
And to whom has the arm of the LORD
*been revealed?"*a

39Therefore they could not believe, because Isaiah said again:

40 *"He has blinded their eyes and*
hardened their hearts,
Lest they should see with their eyes,
Lest they should understand with
their hearts and turn,
*So that I should heal them."*a

41These things Isaiah said whena he saw His glory and spoke of Him.

Walk in the Light

42Nevertheless even among the rulers many believed in Him, but because of the Pharisees they did not confess *Him*, lest they should be put out of the synagogue; 43for they loved the praise of men more than the praise of God.

44Then Jesus cried out and said, "He who believes in Me, believes not in Me but in Him who sent Me. 45And he who sees Me sees Him who sent Me. 46I have come *as a* light into the world, that whoever believes in Me should not abide in darkness. 47And if anyone hears My words and does not believe,a I do not judge him; for I did not come to judge the world but to save the world. 48He who rejects Me, and does not receive My words, has that which judges him—the word that I have spoken will judge him in the last day. 49For I have not spoken on My own *authority;* but the Father who sent Me gave Me a command, what I should say and what I should

speak. 50And I know that His command is everlasting life. Therefore, whatever I speak, just as the Father has told Me, so I speak."

Plot, Anointing, Betrayal

Judas Iscariot, one of the twelve disciples, entered into conspiracy with the chief priests to betray Jesus into their hands. The chief priests stood at the pinnacle of the Sanhedrin, the Jewish ruling council, and Judas's pact with them indicates that the plot against Jesus was hatched by the Jewish leaders rather than by the people as a whole.

The motive for Judas's betrayal is obscure. As treasurer of the twelve disciples, he must have enjoyed rank among them, but evidently either his person or office inclined him to opportunism and even greed (John 12:4–6). Luke (Luke 22:3) and John (John 13:2, 27) ascribe his betrayal of Jesus as the work of Satan. Only Matthew records the betrayal price of thirty silver pieces, recalling perhaps Zech. 11:12 and assuring his readers that this monstrous deed was foreseen by God.

Between the plotting of the Jewish leaders and Judas's betrayal, Matthew and Mark include a story of Jesus' anointing by an unnamed woman of Bethany. A similar though not identical story appears in John's Gospel (John 12:1–8), where the woman is identified as Mary, the sister of Lazarus, from Bethany (12:3). A third anointing of Jesus by a contrite woman who washed His feet with her tears and wiped them with her hair in the house of Simon the Pharisee appears early in Luke's Gospel (Luke 7:36–50).

The exact relation of these stories to each other is uncertain, given the differences between them (see "Returning to Bethany Before the Passover" at John 12:1). Luke's story is the most remote from the others. John's story is possibly a different version of Matthew's and Mark's anointing at Bethany, and may even preserve the anointing's more historical placement before the Triumphal Entry. Mark frequently sandwiches two different stories together to achieve a single theological purpose,

12:38 aIsaiah 53:1   12:40 aIsaiah 6:10
12:41 aNU-Text reads *because.*   12:47 aNU-Text reads *keep them.*

DAILY LIFE AND CUSTOMS

Alabaster is a soft, translucent stone that can be easily carved and polished. It was often used as a substitute for glass. Alabaster perfume bottles were sealed, disposable containers that were opened by breaking and then discarded when empty (Matt. 26:7). The value of spices, ointments, and perfumes was much higher relative to other goods than it is today.

and in the placement of the anointing could have been followed by Matthew.

Mark indicates the timing of the chief priests' plotting: the Passover and Feast of Unleavened Bread were only two days away (Mark 14:1; see Matt. 26:2). Because Mark and John disagree on whether the Last Supper was a Passover meal (see "Thursday: Preparation for the Last Supper" at Matt. 26:17), it is impossible to know certainly that the Passover was on Friday, and whether "two days before Passover" was thus a Wednesday.

- Matthew 26:1–16
- Mark 14:1–11
- Luke 22:1–6

Matthew 26:1–16
The Plot to Kill Jesus

26 :1 Now it came to pass, when Jesus had finished all these sayings, *that* He said to His disciples, 2"You know that after two days is the Passover, and the Son of Man will be delivered up to be crucified."

3Then the chief priests, the scribes,a and the elders of the people assembled at the palace of the high priest, who was called Caiaphas, 4and plotted to take Jesus by trickery and kill *Him.* 5But they said, "Not during the feast, lest there be an uproar among the people."

The Anointing at Bethany

6And when Jesus was in Bethany at the house of Simon the leper, 7a woman came to Him having an alabaster flask of very costly fragrant oil, and she poured *it* on His head as He sat *at the table.* 8But when His disciples saw *it,* they were indignant, saying, "Why this waste? 9For this fragrant oil might have been sold for much and given to *the* poor."

10But when Jesus was aware of *it,* He said to them, "Why do you trouble the woman? For she has done a good work for Me. 11For you have the poor with you always, but Me you do not have always. 12For in pouring this fragrant oil on My body, she did *it* for My burial. 13Assuredly, I say to you, wherever this gospel is preached in the whole world, what this woman has done will also be told as a memorial to her."

Judas Agrees to Betray Jesus

14Then one of the twelve, called Judas Iscariot, went to the chief priests 15and said, "What are you willing to give me if I deliver Him to you?" And they counted out to him thirty pieces of silver. 16So from that time he sought opportunity to betray Him.

Mark 14:1–11
A Woman Anoints Jesus

14 :1 After two days it was the Passover and *the Feast* of Unleavened Bread. And the chief priests and the scribes sought how they might take Him by trickery and put *Him* to death. 2But they said, "Not during the feast, lest there be an uproar of the people."

3And being in Bethany at the house of Simon the leper, as He sat at the table, a woman came having an alabaster flask of very costly oil of spikenard. Then she broke the flask and poured *it* on His head. 4But there were some who were indignant among themselves, and said, "Why was this fragrant oil wasted? 5For it might have been sold for more than three hundred denarii and given to the poor." And they criticized her sharply.

6But Jesus said, "Let her alone. Why do you trouble her? She has done a good work for Me. 7For you have the poor with you always, and whenever you wish you may do them good; but Me you do not have always. 8She has done what she could. She has come beforehand to anoint My body for burial. 9Assuredly, I say to you, wherever this gospel is preached in the whole world, what this woman has done will also be told as a memorial to her."

10Then Judas Iscariot, one of the twelve, went to the chief priests to betray Him to them. 11And when they heard *it,* they were glad, and promised to give him money. So he sought how he might conveniently betray Him.

Luke 22:1–6
The Betrayal by Judas

22 :1 Now the Feast of Unleavened Bread drew near, which is called Passover. 2And the chief priests and the scribes sought how they might kill Him, for they feared the people.

3Then Satan entered Judas, surnamed Iscariot, who was numbered among the twelve. 4So he went his way and conferred with the chief priests and captains, how he might betray Him to them. 5And they were glad, and agreed to give him money. 6So he promised and sought opportunity to betray Him to them in the absence of the multitude.

26:3 aNU-Text omits *the scribes.*

Thursday: Preparation for the Last Supper

The four Gospels record that Jesus shared a farewell meal with His disciples on the eve of His crucifixion. All of the Gospels agree that Jesus was placed in the tomb on late Friday, immediately before the Sabbath began at sundown. Friday was known as the Preparation Day—the day before the Sabbath (Mark 15:42; Luke 23:54; John 19:31). So the last supper of Jesus with His disciples was eaten on Thursday, the previous night.

The Synoptics present the Last Supper as being the Passover meal. Passover began at sunset with the meal ushering in the new day, the 15th of Nisan. The celebration was the focal point of a week-long festival in Jerusalem commemorating the Exodus from Egypt. Each of the Synoptics relates that Jesus knew where He and His disciples would "eat the Passover," and sent them to prepare (Mark 14:12–16).

In John's Gospel, the Last Supper was not the Passover meal. John does not report Jesus sending the disciples ahead into Jerusalem to prepare the Passover room, nor does he record Jesus' familiar words of institution during the course of the meal (Mark 14:22–25). Rather he suggests that Jesus was crucified on the day *before* Passover began—"the Preparation Day of the Passover" (John 19:14, 16). In John's sequence, the Last Supper was celebrated on Passover eve, and Jesus was tried the next day while the Jewish authorities themselves were preparing to eat the Passover meal (18:28).

Various suggestions attempt to account for the discrepancy between John and the Synoptics. One possibility is that John's account follows a different calendar. More probably, however, John makes Jesus' death coincide with the sacrifice of the Passover lamb in the temple. This powerfully signifies that Jesus is "the Lamb of God" (John 1:29) who is killed at the same time the lambs are being prepared for the evening Passover meal (19:14).

All four Gospels set the Last Supper in the context of Judas's betrayal of Jesus. In each account, Jesus announces that the betrayer is present among them at the meal. Matthew (Matt. 26:25) and John (John 13:26) specifically identify the betrayer to be Judas. In ancient Judaism, table fellowship was the supreme act of intimacy and trust. Judas's betrayal at a meal—and in the Synop-

tics, a Passover meal—thus heightens its treachery.

- Matthew 26:17–29
- Mark 14:12–25
- Luke 22:7–30
- John 13:18–30

Matthew 26:17–29
Passover with the Disciples

26 **:17** Now on the first *day of the Feast* of Unleavened Bread the disciples came to Jesus, saying to Him, "Where do You want us to prepare for You to eat the Passover?"

18 And He said, "Go into the city to a certain man, and say to him, 'The Teacher says, "My time is at hand; I will keep the Passover at your house with My disciples."'"

19 So the disciples did as Jesus had directed them; and they prepared the Passover.

20 When evening had come, He sat down with the twelve. 21 Now as they were eating, He said, "Assuredly, I say to you, one of you will betray Me."

22 And they were exceedingly sorrowful, and each of them began to say to Him, "Lord, is it I?"

23 He answered and said, "He who dipped *his* hand with Me in the dish will betray Me. 24 The Son of Man indeed goes just as it is written of Him, but woe to that man by whom the Son of Man is betrayed! It would have been good for that man if he had not been born."

25 Then Judas, who was betraying Him, answered and said, "Rabbi, is it I?"

He said to him, "You have said it."

Institution of the Lord's Supper

26 And as they were eating, Jesus took bread, blessed[a] and broke *it,* and gave *it* to the disciples and said, "Take, eat; this is My body."

27 Then He took the cup, and gave thanks, and gave *it* to them, saying, "Drink from it, all of you. 28 For this is My blood of the new[a] covenant, which is shed for many for the remission of sins. 29 But I say to you, I will not drink of this fruit of the vine from now on until that day when I drink it new with you in My Father's kingdom."

26:26 [a]M-Text reads *gave thanks for.*
26:28 [a]NU-Text omits *new.*

HIS BODY, HIS BLOOD, AND PASSOVER (Mark 14:22, 24)

The Synoptic Gospels present Jesus sharing the Passover meal as His last supper with the disciples. He reinterpreted the common elements of the celebration in the light of a new covenant. The unleavened bread became His body (Mark 14:22) and the wine became His blood (14:26).

Customarily, the head of a Jewish household would explain each of the elements of the Passover meal. When explaining the bread, he would announce, "This is the bread of affliction which our ancestors ate when they came from the land of Egypt." He was not suggesting that it was the literal bread eaten by their ancestors, which was by then over 1,000 years old, but that it represented the bread their ancestors ate. This was one way Jewish people could identify with their ancestors whom God had first redeemed from captivity.

The head of the household normally blessed the bread and wine at other meals as well, but at Passover, when four cups of red wine were drunk, he would lift the cup a handbreadth above the table and recite a special blessing. Jewish men normally sat in chairs for meals, but they reclined on couches in typical Greek fashion when eating at banquets like the Passover. With their feet pointed away from the center of the room (see Luke 7:38) and their heads more toward the center (see John 13:23), they generally reclined on one elbow, using the other arm to reach the food on the table beside them.

Jesus' remark about the "blood of the new covenant" (14:24) looked back to when God redeemed Israel from Egypt (Ex. 24:8). By His blood being "shed for many," Jesus possibly alluded to the suffering Servant pouring out His life (Is. 53:12). He saw Himself as redeeming His people by His own death.

Jewish people customarily finished their meal by singing more psalms from the Hallel (Ps. 113—118). Likewise, Jesus' disciples sang "a hymn" (Mark 14:26) before departing for Gethsemane, where they would in the end desert Jesus.

Mark 14:12–25
Jesus Celebrates the Passover

14 :12 Now on the first day of Unleavened Bread, when they killed the Passover *lamb,* His disciples said to Him, "Where do You want us to go and prepare, that You may eat the Passover?"

13And He sent out two of His disciples and said to them, "Go into the city, and a man will meet you carrying a pitcher of water; follow him. 14Wherever he goes in, say to the master of the house, 'The Teacher says, "Where is the guest room in which I may eat the Passover with My disciples?" ' 15Then he will show you a large upper room, furnished *and* prepared; there make ready for us."

16So His disciples went out, and came into the city, and found it just as He had said to them; and they prepared the Passover.

17In the evening He came with the twelve. 18Now as they sat and ate, Jesus said, "Assuredly, I say to you, one of you who eats with Me will betray Me."

19And they began to be sorrowful, and to say to Him one by one, "*Is* it I?" And another *said,* "*Is* it I?"[a]

20He answered and said to them, "*It is* one of the twelve, who dips with Me in the dish. 21The Son of Man indeed goes just as it is written of Him, but woe to that man by whom the Son of Man is betrayed! It would have been good for that man if he had never been born."

Jesus Institutes the Lord's Supper

22And as they were eating, Jesus took bread, blessed and broke *it,* and gave *it* to them and said, "Take, eat;[a] this is My body."

23Then He took the cup, and when He had given thanks He gave *it* to them, and they all drank from it. 24And He said to them, "This is My blood of the new[a] covenant, which is shed for many. 25Assuredly, I say to you, I will no longer drink of the fruit of the vine until that day when I drink it new in the kingdom of God."

14:19 [a]NU-Text omits this sentence.
14:22 [a]NU-Text omits *eat.*   14:24 [a]NU-Text omits *new.*

Luke 22:7–30
The Last Supper

22 :7 Then came the Day of Unleavened Bread, when the Passover must be killed. 8And He sent Peter and John, saying, "Go and prepare the Passover for us, that we may eat."

9So they said to Him, "Where do You want us to prepare?"

10And He said to them, "Behold, when you have entered the city, a man will meet you carrying a pitcher of water; follow him into the house which he enters. 11Then you shall say to the master of the house, 'The Teacher says to you, "Where is the guest room where I may eat the Passover with My disciples?"' 12Then he will show you a large, furnished upper room; there make ready."

13So they went and found it just as He had said to them, and they prepared the Passover.

The Cup and Bread

14When the hour had come, He sat down, and the twelve[a] apostles with Him. 15Then He said to them, "With *fervent* desire I have desired to eat this Passover with you before I suffer; 16for I say to you, I will no longer eat of it until it is fulfilled in the kingdom of God."

17Then He took the cup, and gave thanks, and said, "Take this and divide *it* among yourselves; 18for I say to you,[a] I will not drink of the fruit of the vine until the kingdom of God comes."

19And He took bread, gave thanks and broke *it,* and gave *it* to them, saying, "This is My body which is given for you; do this in remembrance of Me."

20Likewise He also *took* the cup after supper, saying, "This cup *is* the new covenant in My blood, which is shed for you. 21But behold, the hand of My betrayer *is* with Me on the table. 22And truly the Son of Man goes as it has been determined, but woe to that man by whom He is betrayed!"

23Then they began to question among themselves, which of them it was who would do this thing.

The Disciples Argue About Greatness

24Now there was also a dispute among them, as to which of them should be considered the greatest. 25And He said to them, "The kings of the Gentiles exercise lordship over them, and those who exercise authority over them are called 'benefactors.' 26But not so *among* you; on the contrary, he who is greatest among you, let him be as the younger, and he who governs as he who serves. 27For who *is* greater, he who sits at the table, or he who serves? *Is* it not he who sits at the table? Yet I am among you as the One who serves.

28"But you are those who have continued with Me in My trials. 29And I bestow upon you a kingdom, just as My Father bestowed *one* upon Me, 30that you may eat and drink at My table in My kingdom, and sit on thrones judging the twelve tribes of Israel."

John 13:18–30
Jesus Identifies His Betrayer

13 :18 "I do not speak concerning all of you. I know whom I have chosen; but that the Scripture may be fulfilled, *'He who eats bread with Me*[a] *has lifted up his heel against Me.'*[b] 19Now I tell you before it comes, that when it does come to pass, you may believe that I am *He.* 20Most assuredly, I say to you, he who receives whomever I send receives Me; and he who receives Me receives Him who sent Me."

21When Jesus had said these things, He was troubled in spirit, and testified and said, "Most assuredly, I say to you, one of you will betray Me." 22Then the disciples looked at one another, perplexed about whom He spoke.

23Now there was leaning on Jesus' bosom one of His disciples, whom Jesus loved. 24Simon Peter therefore motioned to him to ask who it was of whom He spoke. 25Then, leaning back[a] on Jesus' breast, he said to Him, "Lord, who is it?"

26Jesus answered, "It is he to whom I shall give a piece of bread when I have dipped *it.*" And having dipped the bread, He gave *it* to Judas Iscariot, *the son* of Simon. 27Now after the piece of bread, Satan entered him. Then Jesus said to him, "What you do, do quickly." 28But no one at the table knew for what reason He said this to him. 29For some thought, because Judas had the money box, that Jesus had said to him, "Buy *those things* we need for

---

22:14 [a]NU-Text omits *twelve.*   22:18 [a]NU-Text adds *from now on.*   **John** 13:18 [a]NU-Text reads *My bread.* [b]Psalm 41:9   13:25 [a]NU-Text and M-Text add *thus.*

the feast," or that he should give something to the poor.

30Having received the piece of bread, he then went out immediately. And it was night.

Jesus Washes the Disciples' Feet

The four Gospels differ regarding the purpose of the solemn meal that Jesus shared with His disciples during Passion Week. For the Synoptics, the Last Supper was the inauguration of a new covenant in the body and blood of Jesus. John's Gospel alludes to the Last Supper, but does so for the purpose of introducing the new commandment of love.

John omits the words of institution found in the Synoptics (see Mark 14:22–25), but instead recounts the footwashing of the disciples. The Passover meal included a handwashing ritual called *rehaz*, and Jesus may have altered the ritual into a footwashing. It is not certain whether the ritual occurred during or after the meal, since some Greek manuscripts read "during supper" in John 13:2, instead of "supper being ended."

There was no precedent for a footwashing at the Passover ritual. Indeed, even a Jewish slave could not be required to wash his master's feet; such an act was only required of a non-Jewish slave! This abject deed demonstrates the sacrificial humility and love of Jesus, which is subsequently interpreted by the new commandment (John 13:31–35). The washing of the disciples' feet is a demonstration of the love that Jesus' disciples are to have for one another.

■ John 13:1–17
■ John 13:31–35

John 13:1–17
Jesus, Lord and Servant

13 :1 Now before the Feast of the Passover, when Jesus knew that His hour had come that He should depart from this world to the Father, having loved His own who were in the world, He loved them to the end.

2And supper being ended,ᵃ the devil having already put it into the heart of Judas Iscariot, Simon's *son,* to betray Him, 3Jesus, knowing that the Father had given all things into His hands, and that He had come from God and was going to God, 4rose from supper and laid aside His garments, took a towel and girded Himself. 5After that, He poured water into a basin and began to wash the disciples' feet, and to wipe *them* with the towel with which He was girded. 6Then He came to Simon Peter. And *Peter* said to Him, "Lord, are You washing my feet?"

7Jesus answered and said to him, "What I am doing you do not understand now, but you will know after this."

8Peter said to Him, "You shall never wash my feet!"

Jesus answered him, "If I do not wash you, you have no part with Me."

9Simon Peter said to Him, "Lord, not my feet only, but also *my* hands and *my* head!"

10Jesus said to him, "He who is bathed needs only to wash *his* feet, but is completely clean; and you are clean, but not all of you." 11For He knew who would betray Him; therefore He said, "You are not all clean."

12So when He had washed their feet, taken His garments, and sat down again, He said to them, "Do you know what I have done to you? 13You call Me Teacher and Lord, and you say well, for *so* I am. 14If I then, *your* Lord and Teacher, have washed your feet, you also ought to wash one another's feet. 15For I have given you an example, that you should do as I have done to you. 16Most assuredly, I say to you, a servant is not greater than his master; nor is he who is sent greater than he who sent him. 17If you know these things, blessed are you if you do them."

John 13:31–35
The New Commandment

13 :31 So, when he had gone out, Jesus said, "Now the Son of Man is glorified, and God is glorified in Him. 32If God is glorified in Him, God will also glorify Him in Himself, and glorify Him immediately. 33Little children, I shall be with you a little while longer. You will seek Me; and as I said to the Jews, 'Where I am going, you cannot come,' so now I say to you. 34A new commandment I give to you, that you love one another; as I have loved you, that you also love one another. 35By this all will know that you are My disciples, if you have love for one another."

13:2 ᵃNU-Text reads *And during supper.*

Warnings About Denial

Following the Last Supper, each of the Gospels records a conversation between Jesus and Peter. Jesus predicts Peter's defection along with the disciples, but Peter vigorously protests his willingness and even ability to follow Jesus to death if necessary. Then follows the famous pronouncement that Peter will deny Jesus three times before the cock crows.

Luke's Gospel regards the defection of Peter, as it regarded the defection of Judas (Luke 22:3), as a Satanic temptation that could be resisted only by divine assistance and intervention (Luke 22:31, 32). The saying of Jesus about procuring a money bag, knapsack, and a sword appears in no other Gospel (Luke 22:35–38). Though this picturesque saying was intended to prepare the disciples for future tribulations, they took it literally. When two swords were actually presented, Jesus ended the conversation with "Enough" (of such nonsense).

■ Matthew 26:30–35
■ Mark 14:26–31
■ Luke 22:31–38
■ John 13:36–38

Matthew 26:30–35

26 **:30** And when they had sung a hymn, they went out to the Mount of Olives.

Jesus Predicts Peter's Denial

[31]Then Jesus said to them, "All of you will be made to stumble because of Me this night, for it is written:

'I will strike the Shepherd,
And the sheep of the flock will be
    scattered.'[a]

[32]But after I have been raised, I will go before you to Galilee."

[33]Peter answered and said to Him, "Even if all are made to stumble because of You, I will never be made to stumble."

[34]Jesus said to him, "Assuredly, I say to you that this night, before the rooster crows, you will deny Me three times."

[35]Peter said to Him, "Even if I have to die with You, I will not deny You!" And so said all the disciples.

Mark 14:26–31

14 **:26** And when they had sung a hymn, they went out to the Mount of Olives.

The Sheep Will Be Scattered

[27]Then Jesus said to them, "All of you will be made to stumble because of Me this night,[a] for it is written:

'I will strike the Shepherd,
And the sheep will be scattered.'[b]

[28]"But after I have been raised, I will go before you to Galilee."

[29]Peter said to Him, "Even if all are made to stumble, yet I *will* not *be*."

[30]Jesus said to him, "Assuredly, I say to you that today, *even* this night, before the rooster crows twice, you will deny Me three times."

[31]But he spoke more vehemently, "If I have to die with You, I will not deny You!"

And they all said likewise.

Luke 22:31–38
Satan Tempts Simon Peter

22 **:31** And the Lord said,[a] "Simon, Simon! Indeed, Satan has asked for you, that he may sift *you* as wheat. [32]But I have prayed for you, that your faith should not fail; and when you have returned to *Me*, strengthen your brethren."

[33]But he said to Him, "Lord, I am ready to go with You, both to prison and to death."

[34]Then He said, "I tell you, Peter, the rooster shall not crow this day before you will deny three times that you know Me."

26:31 [a]Zechariah 13:7   **Mark** 14:27 [a]NU-Text omits *because of Me this night.*   [b]Zechariah 13:7
Luke 22:31 [a]NU-Text omits *And the Lord said.*

Supplies for the Road

³⁵And He said to them, "When I sent you without money bag, knapsack, and sandals, did you lack anything?"

So they said, "Nothing."

³⁶Then He said to them, "But now, he who has a money bag, let him take *it,* and likewise a knapsack; and he who has no sword, let him sell his garment and buy one. ³⁷For I say to you that this which is written must still be accomplished in Me: *'And He was numbered with the transgressors.'*[a] For the things concerning Me have an end."

³⁸So they said, "Lord, look, here *are* two swords."

And He said to them, "It is enough."

John 13:36–38
You Cannot Follow Now

13 :36 Simon Peter said to Him, "Lord, where are You going?"

Jesus answered him, "Where I am going you cannot follow Me now, but you shall follow Me afterward."

³⁷Peter said to Him, "Lord, why can I not follow You now? I will lay down my life for Your sake."

³⁸Jesus answered him, "Will you lay down your life for My sake? Most assuredly, I say to you, the rooster shall not crow till you have denied Me three times."

22:37 [a]Isaiah 53:12   **John** 14:2 [a]Literally *dwellings* [b]NU-Text adds a word which would cause the text to read either *if it were not so, would I have told you that I go to prepare a place for you?* or *if it were not so I would have told you; for I go to prepare a place for you.*   14:14 [a]NU-Text adds *Me.* 14:15 [a]NU-Text reads *you will keep.*

Farewell Discourses with Disciples

The Fourth Gospel presents a more distinctive portrait of Jesus than do the other three Gospels. One of John's most important characteristics is his extensive discourse material, especially the series of discourses delivered by Jesus to the disciples in an upper room following the Last Supper. These farewell discourses, which are entirely absent in the Synoptic Gospels, comprise four chapters in John (chs. 14—17). Jesus prepares His disciples for His death and departure to the Father. Among His final instructions to them are commandments to abide in His life and love, fore-warnings of hatred and persecutions, and a final prayer (ch. 17) for the unity of His followers.

■ John 14:1–24

John
The Way, the Truth, and the Life

14 :1 "Let not your heart be troubled; you believe in God, believe also in Me. ²In My Father's house are many mansions;[a] if *it were* not *so,* I would have told you. I go to prepare a place for you.[b] ³And if I go and prepare a place for you, I will come again and receive you to Myself; that where I am, *there* you may be also. ⁴And where I go you know, and the way you know."

⁵Thomas said to Him, "Lord, we do not know where You are going, and how can we know the way?"

⁶Jesus said to him, "I am the way, the truth, and the life. No one comes to the Father except through Me.

The Father Revealed

⁷"If you had known Me, you would have known My Father also; and from now on you know Him and have seen Him."

⁸Philip said to Him, "Lord, show us the Father, and it is sufficient for us."

⁹Jesus said to him, "Have I been with you so long, and yet you have not known Me, Philip? He who has seen Me has seen the Father; so how can you say, 'Show us the Father'? ¹⁰Do you not believe that I am in the Father, and the Father in Me? The words that I speak to you I do not speak on My own *authority;* but the Father who dwells in Me does the works. ¹¹Believe Me that I *am* in the Father and the Father in Me, or else believe Me for the sake of the works themselves.

The Answered Prayer

¹²"Most assuredly, I say to you, he who believes in Me, the works that I do he will do also; and greater *works* than these he will do, because I go to My Father. ¹³And whatever you ask in My name, that I will do, that the Father may be glorified in the Son. ¹⁴If you ask[a] anything in My name, I will do *it.*

Jesus Promises Another Helper

¹⁵"If you love Me, keep[a] My commandments. ¹⁶And I will pray the Father, and He will give you another Helper, that He

may abide with you forever— ¹⁷the Spirit of truth, whom the world cannot receive, because it neither sees Him nor knows Him; but you know Him, for He dwells with you and will be in you. ¹⁸I will not leave you orphans; I will come to you.

Indwelling of the Father and the Son

¹⁹"A little while longer and the world will see Me no more, but you will see Me. Because I live, you will live also. ²⁰At that day you will know that I *am* in My Father, and you in Me, and I in you. ²¹He who has My commandments and keeps them, it is he who loves Me. And he who loves Me will be loved by My Father, and I will love him and manifest Myself to him."

²²Judas (not Iscariot) said to Him, "Lord, how is it that You will manifest Yourself to us, and not to the world?"

²³Jesus answered and said to him, "If anyone loves Me, he will keep My word; and My Father will love him, and We will come to him and make Our home with him. ²⁴He who does not love Me does not keep My words; and the word which you hear is not Mine but the Father's who sent Me."

Help from the Holy Spirit

The most unique aspect of the farewell discourses is Jesus' teaching about the Holy Spirit, whom He calls "the Helper" (John 15:26), the advocate of believers. The Holy Spirit testifies of Jesus and guides disciples "into all truth" (16:13–15). Continuing the work of Jesus, the Spirit teaches and brings to remembrance the words and teachings of Jesus (14:26). Many scholars believe that such statements about the Spirit help explain the uniqueness of the Gospel of John. John's presentation of Jesus, in other words, is determined less by the exact words and deeds of Jesus than by the *meaning* of the Incarnation as revealed by later inspiration from the Holy Spirit.

▼

■ John 14:25—16:33

John
The Gift of His Peace

14 **:25** "These things I have spoken to you while being present with you. ²⁶But the Helper, the Holy Spirit, whom the Father will send in My name, He will teach you all things, and bring to your remembrance all things that I said to you. ²⁷Peace I leave with you, My peace I give to you; not as the world gives do I give to you. Let not your heart be troubled, neither let it be afraid. ²⁸You have heard Me say to you, 'I am going away and coming *back* to you.' If you loved Me, you would rejoice because I said,ᵃ 'I am going to the Father,' for My Father is greater than I.

²⁹"And now I have told you before it comes, that when it does come to pass, you may believe. ³⁰I will no longer talk much with you, for the ruler of this world is coming, and he has nothing in Me. ³¹But that the world may know that I love the Father, and as the Father gave Me commandment, so I do. Arise, let us go from here.

The True Vine

15 ¹⁴"I am the true vine, and My Father is the vinedresser. ²Every branch in Me that does not bear fruit He takes away;ᵃ and every *branch* that bears fruit He prunes, that it may bear more fruit. ³You are already clean because of the word which I have spoken to you. ⁴Abide in Me, and I in you. As the branch cannot bear fruit of itself, unless it abides in the vine, neither can you, unless you abide in Me.

⁵"I am the vine, you *are* the branches. He who abides in Me, and I in him, bears much fruit; for without Me you can do nothing. ⁶If anyone does not abide in Me, he is cast out as a branch and is withered; and they gather them and throw *them* into the fire, and they are burned. ⁷If you abide in Me, and My words abide in you, you willᵃ ask what you desire, and it shall be done for you. ⁸By this My Father is glori-

14:28 ᵃNU-Text omits *I said.*   15:2 ᵃOr *lifts up*   15:7 ᵃNU-Text omits *you will.*

ARCHITECTURE AND BUILDING

In 9 B.C. Augustus dedicated the Altar of Peace in Rome, a marble altar in an enclosure 38 by 35 feet. The altar was decorated with carved garlands and other sculptures illustrating the peace and prosperity that Augustus announced as his gift to the world. Jesus announced yet a greater peace from the indwelling Holy Spirit (John 14:27).

FRIENDSHIP WITH THE MASTER (John 15:15)

In the Roman world, a "friend" was often a political ally who owed one a favor, or a more powerful patron on whom one could depend. But the traditional Greek concept of friendship remained influential even during the apostle Paul's day. Paul had urged the financially well-off Christians of Corinth to treat Christians in Jerusalem as friends by sharing all things in common. Friends treated one another as "equals" (2 Cor. 8:13, 14).

Jesus said to His disciples: "I have called you friends" (John 15:15). While He was not implying that as His friends they were His equals, He was offering to share with them what belonged to Him. John's Gospel describes this assurance specifically as the promise of the Spirit sharing Jesus' *words* with the disciples, so they would know Jesus' heart (see 16:13–15).

The intimacy pictured between Jesus and the disciples fits the ancient ideal of friendship, which stressed both loyalty and the sharing of secrets. Among the Greeks, the highest expression of a friend's loyalty was to die for a friend, and Jesus summoned His disciples to lay down their lives for Him and for one another, as He was about to do for them (15:12–14). But servants often proved no less loyal than friends, so Jesus spoke of an intimacy greater than that between the average master and servant. Greek literature often stressed how friends share secrets with one another in confidence, and Jesus had shared with the disciples all the words He had heard from His Father (15:15).

Some Jewish writers in Jesus' day stressed that being God's friend, as exemplified by Abraham and Moses, was even greater than being God's servant. Jesus thus bestowed on His disciples such an honor of intimacy with Himself.

---

fied, that you bear much fruit; so you will be My disciples.

Love and Joy Perfected

9"As the Father loved Me, I also have loved you; abide in My love. 10If you keep My commandments, you will abide in My love, just as I have kept My Father's commandments and abide in His love.

11"These things I have spoken to you, that My joy may remain in you, and *that* your joy may be full. 12This is My commandment, that you love one another as I have loved you. 13Greater love has no one than this, than to lay down one's life for his friends. 14You are My friends if you do whatever I command you. 15No longer do I call you servants, for a servant does not know what his master is doing; but I have called you friends, for all things that I heard from My Father I have made known to you. 16You did not choose Me, but I chose you and appointed you that you should go and bear fruit, and *that* your fruit should remain, that whatever you ask the Father in My name He may give you. 17These things I command you, that you love one another.

The World's Hatred

18"If the world hates you, you know that it hated Me before *it hated* you. 19If you were of the world, the world would love its own. Yet because you are not of the world, but I chose you out of the world, therefore the world hates you. 20Remember the word that I said to you, 'A servant is not greater than his master.' If they persecuted Me, they will also persecute you. If they kept My word, they will keep yours also. 21But all these things they will do to you for My name's sake, because they do not know Him who sent Me. 22If I had not come and spoken to them, they would have no sin, but now they have no excuse for their sin. 23He who hates Me hates My Father also. 24If I had not done among them the works which no one else did, they would have no sin; but now they have seen and also hated both Me and My Father. 25But *this happened* that the word might be fulfilled which is written in their law, *'They hated Me without a cause.'*[a]

The Coming Rejection

26"But when the Helper comes, whom I shall send to you from the Father, the Spirit of truth who proceeds from the

15:25 [a]Psalm 69:4

Father, He will testify of Me. ²⁷And you also will bear witness, because you have been with Me from the beginning.

16 ¹"These things I have spoken to you, that you should not be made to stumble. ²They will put you out of the synagogues; yes, the time is coming that whoever kills you will think that he offers God service. ³And these things they will do to you[a] because they have not known the Father nor Me. ⁴But these things I have told you, that when the[a] time comes, you may remember that I told you of them.

"And these things I did not say to you at the beginning, because I was with you.

The Work of the Holy Spirit

⁵"But now I go away to Him who sent Me, and none of you asks Me, 'Where are You going?' ⁶But because I have said these things to you, sorrow has filled your heart. ⁷Nevertheless I tell you the truth. It is to your advantage that I go away; for if I do not go away, the Helper will not come to you; but if I depart, I will send Him to you. ⁸And when He has come, He will convict the world of sin, and of righteousness, and of judgment: ⁹of sin, because they do not believe in Me; ¹⁰of righteousness, because I go to My Father and you see Me no more; ¹¹of judgment, because the ruler of this world is judged.

¹²"I still have many things to say to you, but you cannot bear *them* now. ¹³However, when He, the Spirit of truth, has come, He will guide you into all truth; for He will not speak on His own *authority,* but whatever He hears He will speak; and He will tell you things to come. ¹⁴He will glorify Me, for He will take of what is Mine and declare *it* to you. ¹⁵All things that the Father has are Mine. Therefore I said that He will take of Mine and declare *it* to you.[a]

Sorrow Will Turn to Joy

¹⁶"A little while, and you will not see Me; and again a little while, and you will see Me, because I go to the Father."

¹⁷Then *some* of His disciples said among themselves, "What is this that He says to us, 'A little while, and you will not see Me; and again a little while, and you will see Me'; and, 'because I go to the Father'?" ¹⁸They said therefore, "What is this that He says, 'A little while'? We do not know what He is saying."

¹⁹Now Jesus knew that they desired to ask Him, and He said to them, "Are you inquiring among yourselves about what I said, 'A little while, and you will not see Me; and again a little while, and you will see Me'? ²⁰Most assuredly, I say to you that you will weep and lament, but the world will rejoice; and you will be sorrowful, but your sorrow will be turned into joy. ²¹A woman, when she is in labor, has sorrow because her hour has come; but as soon as she has given birth to the child, she no longer remembers the anguish, for joy that a human being has been born into the world. ²²Therefore you now have sorrow; but I will see you again and your heart will rejoice, and your joy no one will take from you.

²³"And in that day you will ask Me nothing. Most assuredly, I say to you, whatever you ask the Father in My name He will give you. ²⁴Until now you have asked nothing in My name. Ask, and you will receive, that your joy may be full.

Jesus Christ Has Overcome the World

²⁵"These things I have spoken to you in figurative language; but the time is coming when I will no longer speak to you in figurative language, but I will tell you plainly about the Father. ²⁶In that day you will ask in My name, and I do not say to you that I shall pray the Father for you; ²⁷for the Father Himself loves you, because you have loved Me, and have believed that I came forth from God. ²⁸I came forth from

---

16:3 ªNU-Text and M-Text omit *to you.*
16:4 ªNU-Text reads *their.*   16:15 ªNU-Text and M-Text read *He takes of Mine and will declare it to you.*

HEALTH AND MEDICINE

In ancient times babies were born at home, not in hospitals. Assisting the process of birth were midwives, local women with experience, rather than doctors. Since practically no scientific medical knowledge existed, a high mortality rate was common for infants and children. Yet in the people's everyday experience of these natural events, the joy of birth was greater than the anguish of the birth process (John 16:21).

the Father and have come into the world. Again, I leave the world and go to the Father."

29His disciples said to Him, "See, now You are speaking plainly, and using no figure of speech! 30Now we are sure that You know all things, and have no need that anyone should question You. By this we believe that You came forth from God."

31Jesus answered them, "Do you now believe? 32Indeed the hour is coming, yes, has now come, that you will be scattered, each to his own, and will leave Me alone. And yet I am not alone, because the Father is with Me. 33These things I have spoken to you, that in Me you may have peace. In the world you willa have tribulation; but be of good cheer, I have overcome the world."

Jesus' High Priestly Prayer

The longest recorded prayer of Jesus (John 17:1–26) is called the High Priestly Prayer. On the eve of the crucifixion Jesus interceded for His people, praying this prayer for all who would believe in Him throughout time (John 17:20).

■ John 17:1–26

John
Jesus Prays for Himself

17 :1 Jesus spoke these words, lifted up His eyes to heaven, and said: "Father, the hour has come. Glorify Your Son, that Your Son also may glorify You, 2as You have given Him authority over all flesh, that He shoulda give eternal life to as many as You have given Him. 3And this is eternal life, that they may know You, the only true God, and Jesus Christ whom You have sent. 4I have glorified You on the earth. I have finished the work which You have given Me to do. 5And now, O Father, glorify Me together with Yourself, with the glory which I had with You before the world was.

Jesus Prays for His Disciples

6"I have manifested Your name to the men whom You have given Me out of the world. They were Yours, You gave them to Me, and they have kept Your word. 7Now they have known that all things which You have given Me are from You. 8For I have given to them the words which You have given Me; and they have received *them,* and have known surely that I came forth from You; and they have believed that You sent Me.

9"I pray for them. I do not pray for the world but for those whom You have given Me, for they are Yours. 10And all Mine are Yours, and Yours are Mine, and I am glorified in them. 11Now I am no longer in the world, but these are in the world, and I come to You. Holy Father, keep through Your name those whom You have given Me,a that they may be one as We *are.* 12While I was with them in the world,a I kept them in Your name. Those whom You gave Me I have kept;b and none of them is lost except the son of perdition, that the Scripture might be fulfilled. 13But now I come to You, and these things I speak in the world, that they may have My joy fulfilled in themselves. 14I have given them Your word; and the world has hated them because they are not of the world, just as I am not of the world. 15I do not pray that You should take them out of the world, but that You should keep them from the evil one. 16They are not of the world, just as I am not of the world. 17Sanctify them by Your truth. Your word is truth. 18As You sent Me into the world, I also have sent them into the world. 19And for their sakes I sanctify Myself, that they also may be sanctified by the truth.

Jesus Prays for All Believers

20"I do not pray for these alone, but also for those who willa believe in Me through their word; 21that they all may be one, as You, Father, *are* in Me, and I in You; that they also may be one in Us, that the world may believe that You sent Me. 22And the glory which You gave Me I have given them, that they may be one just as We are one: 23I in them, and You in Me; that they may be made perfect in one, and that the world may know that You have sent Me, and have loved them as You have loved Me.

24"Father, I desire that they also whom

You gave Me may be with Me where I am, that they may behold My glory which You have given Me; for You loved Me before the foundation of the world. ²⁵O righteous Father! The world has not known You, but I have known You; and these have known that You sent Me. ²⁶And I have declared to them Your name, and will declare *it,* that the love with which You loved Me may be in them, and I in them."

Jesus' Prayer and Arrest in Gethsemane

After the Last Supper, Jesus retired to an olive grove in the Kidron Valley. Matthew and Mark call the place "Gethsemane," a Hebrew word meaning "olive press" (Matt. 26:36; Mark 14:32), whereas John simply designates it a garden (John 18:1). There, according to the Synoptic Gospels, Jesus prayed in great anguish and sorrow to be spared the ordeal of crucifixion. But the Father remained silent and the disciples succumbed to sleep.

The Gospel of John omits the account of Jesus' prayerful agony and records only His arrest in Gethsemane. The presence of a "detachment of troops" in the garden (John 18:3) indicates that Roman as well as Jewish authorities were responsible for the arrest. John underscores Jesus' royal authority by recording a hesitancy and trepidation on the part of the soldiers at the moment of encounter (18:4–9).

According to the Synoptic Gospels, the arrest occurred on the heels of Jesus' prayer. Matthew reminds his readers that Jesus was not powerless to prevent His seizure, but allows it in fulfillment of God's will (Matt. 26:52–54; see John 18:11). Mark includes a singular and curious note about a young man fleeing naked in the wake of Jesus' arrest (Mark 14:51, 52). As some have supposed, the Gospel writer is possibly making a disguised reference to himself.

- Matthew 26:36–56
- Mark 14:32–52
- Luke 22:39–53
- John 18:1–11

Matthew 26:36–56
The Prayer in the Garden

26 **:36** Then Jesus came with them to a place called Gethsemane, and said to the disciples, "Sit here while I go and pray over there." ³⁷And He took with Him Peter and the two sons of Zebedee, and He began to be sorrowful and deeply distressed. ³⁸Then He said to them, "My soul is exceedingly sorrowful, even to death. Stay here and watch with Me."

³⁹He went a little farther and fell on His face, and prayed, saying, "O My Father, if it is possible, let this cup pass from Me; nevertheless, not as I will, but as You *will.*"

⁴⁰Then He came to the disciples and found them sleeping, and said to Peter, "What! Could you not watch with Me one hour? ⁴¹Watch and pray, lest you enter into temptation. The spirit indeed *is* willing, but the flesh *is* weak."

⁴²Again, a second time, He went away and prayed, saying, "O My Father, if this cup cannot pass away from Me unlessᵃ I drink it, Your will be done." ⁴³And He came and found them asleep again, for their eyes were heavy.

⁴⁴So He left them, went away again, and prayed the third time, saying the same words. ⁴⁵Then He came to His disciples and said to them, "Are *you* still sleeping and resting? Behold, the hour is at hand, and the Son of Man is being betrayed into the hands of sinners. ⁴⁶Rise, let us be going. See, My betrayer is at hand."

Betrayal and Arrest in Gethsemane

⁴⁷And while He was still speaking, behold, Judas, one of the twelve, with a great multitude with swords and clubs, came from the chief priests and elders of the people.

⁴⁸Now His betrayer had given them a sign, saying, "Whomever I kiss, He is the One; seize Him." ⁴⁹Immediately he went up to Jesus and said, "Greetings, Rabbi!" and kissed Him.

⁵⁰But Jesus said to him, "Friend, why have you come?"

Then they came and laid hands on Jesus and took Him. ⁵¹And suddenly, one of those *who were* with Jesus stretched out *his* hand and drew his sword, struck the servant of the high priest, and cut off his ear.

⁵²But Jesus said to him, "Put your sword in its place, for all who take the sword will perishᵃ by the sword. ⁵³Or do

---

26:42 ᵃNU-Text reads *if this may not pass away unless.*   26:52 ᵃM-Text reads *die.*

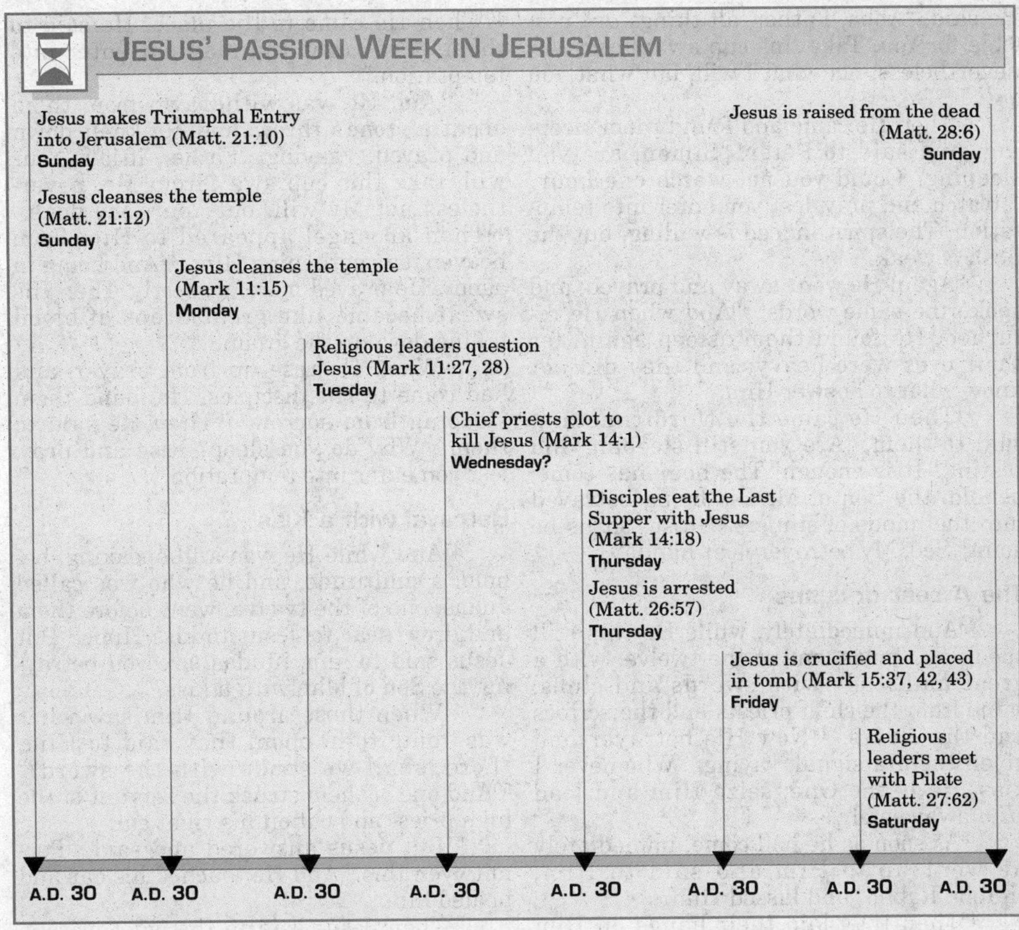

JESUS' PASSION WEEK IN JERUSALEM

Jesus makes Triumphal Entry
into Jerusalem (Matt. 21:10)
Sunday

Jesus cleanses the temple
(Matt. 21:12)
Sunday

Jesus cleanses the temple
(Mark 11:15)
Monday

Religious leaders question
Jesus (Mark 11:27, 28)
Tuesday

Chief priests plot to
kill Jesus (Mark 14:1)
Wednesday?

Disciples eat the Last
Supper with Jesus
(Mark 14:18)
Thursday

Jesus is arrested
(Matt. 26:57)
Thursday

Jesus is raised from the dead
(Matt. 28:6)
Sunday

Jesus is crucified and placed
in tomb (Mark 15:37, 42, 43)
Friday

Religious
leaders meet
with Pilate
(Matt. 27:62)
Saturday

A.D. 30   A.D. 30   A.D. 30   A.D. 30   A.D. 30   A.D. 30   A.D. 30   A.D. 30

you think that I cannot now pray to My Father, and He will provide Me with more than twelve legions of angels? ⁵⁴How then could the Scriptures be fulfilled, that it must happen thus?"

⁵⁵In that hour Jesus said to the multitudes, "Have you come out, as against a robber, with swords and clubs to take Me? I sat daily with you, teaching in the temple, and you did not seize Me. ⁵⁶But all this was done that the Scriptures of the prophets might be fulfilled."

Then all the disciples forsook Him and fled.

Mark 14:32–52
Your Will Be Done

14 **:32** Then they came to a place which was named Gethsemane; and He said to His disciples, "Sit here while I pray." ³³And He took Peter, James, and John with Him, and He began to be troubled and deeply distressed. ³⁴Then He said to them, "My soul is exceedingly sorrowful, *even* to death. Stay here and watch."

³⁵He went a little farther, and fell on the ground, and prayed that if it were possible, the hour might pass from Him. ³⁶And

ARTS AND LITERATURE

A cup is a common symbol for a person's destiny in life, prepared by God and given from heaven through the unfolding of temporal events. A bitter cup would symbolize trials and hardship, such as Jesus' cup symbolizing His suffering and death (Mark 14:36). In the Iliad Homer describes the divine sovereignty in terms of two jars, one of good and one of suffering.

He said, "Abba, Father, all things *are* possible for You. Take this cup away from Me; nevertheless, not what I will, but what You *will*."

37Then He came and found them sleeping, and said to Peter, "Simon, are you sleeping? Could you not watch one hour? 38Watch and pray, lest you enter into temptation. The spirit indeed *is* willing, but the flesh *is* weak."

39Again He went away and prayed, and spoke the same words. 40And when He returned, He found them asleep again, for their eyes were heavy; and they did not know what to answer Him.

41Then He came the third time and said to them, "Are you still sleeping and resting? It is enough! The hour has come; behold, the Son of Man is being betrayed into the hands of sinners. 42Rise, let us be going. See, My betrayer is at hand."

The Arrest of Jesus

43And immediately, while He was still speaking, Judas, one of the twelve, with a great multitude with swords and clubs, came from the chief priests and the scribes and the elders. 44Now His betrayer had given them a signal, saying, "Whomever I kiss, He is the One; seize Him and lead *Him* away safely."

45As soon as he had come, immediately he went up to Him and said to Him, "Rabbi, Rabbi!" and kissed Him.

46Then they laid their hands on Him and took Him. 47And one of those who stood by drew his sword and struck the servant of the high priest, and cut off his ear.

48Then Jesus answered and said to them, "Have you come out, as against a robber, with swords and clubs to take Me? 49I was daily with you in the temple teaching, and you did not seize Me. But the Scriptures must be fulfilled."

50Then they all forsook Him and fled.

A Young Man Flees Naked

51Now a certain young man followed Him, having a linen cloth thrown around *his* naked *body*. And the young men laid hold of him, 52and he left the linen cloth and fled from them naked.

Luke 22:39–53
Jesus' Gethsemane Prayer

22 :39 Coming out, He went to the Mount of Olives, as He was accustomed, and His disciples also followed Him.

40When He came to the place, He said to them, "Pray that you may not enter into temptation."

41And He was withdrawn from them about a stone's throw, and He knelt down and prayed, 42saying, "Father, if it is Your will, take this cup away from Me; nevertheless not My will, but Yours, be done." 43Then an angel appeared to Him from heaven, strengthening Him. 44And being in agony, He prayed more earnestly. Then His sweat became like great drops of blood falling down to the ground.a

45When He rose up from prayer, and had come to His disciples, He found them sleeping from sorrow. 46Then He said to them, "Why do you sleep? Rise and pray, lest you enter into temptation."

Betrayal with a Kiss

47And while He was still speaking, behold, a multitude; and he who was called Judas, one of the twelve, went before them and drew near to Jesus to kiss Him. 48But Jesus said to him, "Judas, are you betraying the Son of Man with a kiss?"

49When those around Him saw what was going to happen, they said to Him, "Lord, shall we strike with the sword?" 50And one of them struck the servant of the high priest and cut off his right ear.

51But Jesus answered and said, "Permit even this." And He touched his ear and healed him.

52Then Jesus said to the chief priests, captains of the temple, and the elders who had come to Him, "Have you come out, as against a robber, with swords and clubs? 53When I was with you daily in the temple, you did not try to seize Me. But this is your hour, and the power of darkness."

John 18:1–11
I Am He

18 :1 When Jesus had spoken these words, He went out with His disciples over the Brook Kidron, where there was a garden, which He and His disciples entered. 2And Judas, who betrayed Him, also knew the place; for Jesus often met there with His disciples. 3Then Judas, having received a detachment *of troops,* and officers from the chief priests and Pharisees, came there with lanterns, torches, and weapons. 4Jesus therefore, knowing all

22:44 aNU-Text brackets verses 43 and 44 as not in the original text.

things that would come upon Him, went forward and said to them, "Whom are you seeking?"

⁵They answered Him, "Jesus of Nazareth."

Jesus said to them, "I am *He.*" And Judas, who betrayed Him, also stood with them. ⁶Now when He said to them, "I am *He,*" they drew back and fell to the ground. ⁷Then He asked them again, "Whom are you seeking?"

And they said, "Jesus of Nazareth."

⁸Jesus answered, "I have told you that I am *He.* Therefore, if you seek Me, let these go their way," ⁹that the saying might be fulfilled which He spoke, "Of those whom You gave Me I have lost none."

¹⁰Then Simon Peter, having a sword, drew it and struck the high priest's servant, and cut off his right ear. The servant's name was Malchus.

¹¹So Jesus said to Peter, "Put your sword into the sheath. Shall I not drink the cup which My Father has given Me?"

26:59 ªNU-Text omits *the elders.*
26:60 ªNU-Text puts a comma after *but found none,* does not capitalize *Even,* and omits *they found none.*
ᵇNU-Text omits *false witnesses.*

Jesus' Trial Before the Sanhedrin

Following His arrest, Jesus underwent two trials: one before the Sanhedrin and a second before the Roman governor, Pontius Pilate. The Sanhedrin, the high Jewish council, was given complete freedom by the Roman government over religious affairs and limited freedom in political affairs. It consisted of seventy elders and scribes (who could be either Sadducees or Pharisees), plus a presider known as the high priest, who was elected annually to renewable terms in office.

Jesus was hauled before the Sanhedrin on false charges of plotting to overthrow the temple (Matt. 26:61; Mark 14:58). The Synoptic Gospels record a hearing before Caiaphas, who was high priest from A.D. 18 to 36, whereas John records a preliminary hearing before Annas, the father-in-law of Caiaphas (John 18:13). Jesus remained silent until pressed by the high priest to answer whether He was the Son of God or not. According to Mark, Jesus affirmed the question (Mark 14:62). Yet even the ambiguous responses recorded by Matthew and Luke (Matt. 26:64; Luke 22:70) are not a denial of the question,

since they were understood as blasphemy deserving of death.

All four Gospels interweave Peter's courtyard experience with the Sanhedrin trial, contrasting the faithful confession of Jesus with the denial by Peter. Jesus' hearing in "the high priest's house" (Luke 22:54) permitted Him a view of Peter standing in the courtyard (22:55, 61). The Fourth Gospel appears to base its knowledge of the trial, in part at least, on "the other disciple" (John 18:16), which may refer to the apostle John. Otherwise all the disciples had fled (Mark 14:50), and their absence may account for the greater divergences in the Gospel reports of the trial.

- Matthew 26:57–75
- Mark 14:53–72
- Luke 22:54–71
- John 18:12–27

Matthew 26:57–75
Trial Before Caiaphas

26 :57 And those who had laid hold of Jesus led *Him* away to Caiaphas the high priest, where the scribes and the elders were assembled. ⁵⁸But Peter followed Him at a distance to the high priest's courtyard. And he went in and sat with the servants to see the end.

⁵⁹Now the chief priests, the elders,ª and all the council sought false testimony against Jesus to put Him to death, ⁶⁰but found none. Even though many false witnesses came forward, they found none.ª But at last two false witnessesᵇ came forward ⁶¹and said, "This *fellow* said, 'I am able to destroy the temple of God and to build it in three days.'"

⁶²And the high priest arose and said to Him, "Do You answer nothing? What *is it* these men testify against You?" ⁶³But Jesus kept silent. And the high priest answered and said to Him, "I put You under oath by the living God: Tell us if You are the Christ, the Son of God!"

⁶⁴Jesus said to him, "*It is as* you said. Nevertheless, I say to you, hereafter you will see the Son of Man sitting at the right hand of the Power, and coming on the clouds of heaven."

⁶⁵Then the high priest tore his clothes, saying, "He has spoken blasphemy! What further need do we have of witnesses? Look, now you have heard His blasphemy! ⁶⁶What do you think?"

They answered and said, "He is deserving of death."

ANNAS AND CAIAPHAS THE HIGH PRIESTS (Matt. 26:57)

Caiaphas was the Jewish high priest at the time of Jesus' crucifixion, exercising an active role in His trial proceedings (Matt. 26:3, 57, 62). However, another high priest, Annas, seems to have been influential at the same time as Caiaphas. Since the office of high priest was usually occupied by only one person, the situation of these two high priests is somewhat perplexing.

The Jewish historian Josephus makes clear the relationship between Annas and Caiaphas. He writes that Annas was appointed high priest by the Romans in A.D. 6 and deposed in A.D. 15. Caiaphas was high priest at a later time, being appointed in A.D. 18 and not deposed until A.D. 36. Caiaphas's approximately 18-year tenure as high priest was a relatively long time compared to most Roman appointees. At any rate, he had a very close relationship with the Roman authorities, which likely explains his long tenure in office.

Luke's writings, both his Gospel and Acts, place Annas's influence as high priest much later than A.D. 15, the date when Josephus states Annas was deposed. Luke names Annas and Caiaphas together as co-high priests in about A.D. 26 (the 15th year of Tiberius; Luke 3:2). Furthermore, Acts 4:6 lists Annas as high priest and Caiaphas as belonging to the family of the high priest, not long after Jesus' death, about A.D. 30 or 31.

Apparently, Annas's influence continued long beyond A.D. 15, the date when he last served officially as high priest. According to Josephus, five of Annas's sons were also appointed high priest at various times. Moreover, John's Gospel informs us that Annas was a relative (father-in-law) of Caiaphas (John 18:13). Possibly Annas retained a position of leadership within the high priestly family, while his son-in-law, Caiaphas, served as the appointed high priest.

67Then they spat in His face and beat Him; and others struck *Him* with the palms of their hands, 68saying, "Prophesy to us, Christ! Who is the one who struck You?"

I Do Not Know the Man!

69Now Peter sat outside in the courtyard. And a servant girl came to him, saying, "You also were with Jesus of Galilee."

70But he denied it before *them* all, saying, "I do not know what you are saying."

71And when he had gone out to the gateway, another *girl* saw him and said to those *who were* there, "This *fellow* also was with Jesus of Nazareth."

72But again he denied with an oath, "I do not know the Man!"

73And a little later those who stood by came up and said to Peter, "Surely you also are *one* of them, for your speech betrays you."

74Then he began to curse and swear, *saying,* "I do not know the Man!"

Immediately a rooster crowed. 75And Peter remembered the word of Jesus who had said to him, "Before the rooster crows, you will deny Me three times." So he went out and wept bitterly.

Mark 14:53–72
Trial Before the Sanhedrin

14 :53 And they led Jesus away to the high priest; and with him were assembled all the chief priests, the elders, and the scribes. 54But Peter followed Him at a distance, right into the courtyard of the high priest. And he sat with the servants and warmed himself at the fire.

55Now the chief priests and all the council sought testimony against Jesus to put Him to death, but found none. 56For many bore false witness against Him, but their testimonies did not agree.

57Then some rose up and bore false witness against Him, saying, 58"We heard Him say, 'I will destroy this temple made with hands, and within three days I will build another made without hands.' " 59But not even then did their testimony agree.

60And the high priest stood up in the midst and asked Jesus, saying, "Do You answer nothing? What *is it* these men testify against You?" 61But He kept silent and answered nothing.

Again the high priest asked Him, saying to Him, "Are You the Christ, the Son of the Blessed?"

62Jesus said, "I am. And you will see the Son of Man sitting at the right hand of the Power, and coming with the clouds of heaven."

63Then the high priest tore his clothes and said, "What further need do we have of witnesses? 64You have heard the blasphemy! What do you think?"

And they all condemned Him to be deserving of death.

65Then some began to spit on Him, and to blindfold Him, and to beat Him, and to say to Him, "Prophesy!" And the officers struck Him with the palms of their hands.a

Peter in the Courtyard

66Now as Peter was below in the courtyard, one of the servant girls of the high priest came. 67And when she saw Peter warming himself, she looked at him and said, "You also were with Jesus of Nazareth."

68But he denied it, saying, "I neither know nor understand what you are saying." And he went out on the porch, and a rooster crowed.

69And the servant girl saw him again, and began to say to those who stood by, "This is one of them." 70But he denied it again.

And a little later those who stood by said to Peter again, "Surely you are *one* of them; for you are a Galilean, and your speech shows *it*."a

71Then he began to curse and swear, "I do not know this Man of whom you speak!"

72A second time *the* rooster crowed. Then Peter called to mind the word that Jesus had said to him, "Before the rooster crows twice, you will deny Me three times." And when he thought about it, he wept.

Luke 22:54–71
Peter Weeps Bitterly

22 :**54** Having arrested Him, they led Him and brought Him into the high priest's house. But Peter followed at a distance. 55Now when they had kindled a fire in the midst of the courtyard and sat down together, Peter sat among them. 56And a certain servant girl, seeing him as he sat by the fire, looked intently at him and said, "This man was also with Him."

57But he denied Him,a saying, "Woman, I do not know Him."

58And after a little while another saw him and said, "You also are of them."

But Peter said, "Man, I am not!"

59Then after about an hour had passed, another confidently affirmed, saying, "Surely this *fellow* also was with Him, for he is a Galilean."

60But Peter said, "Man, I do not know what you are saying!"

Immediately, while he was still speaking, the roostera crowed. 61And the Lord turned and looked at Peter. Then Peter remembered the word of the Lord, how He had said to him, "Before the rooster crows,a you will deny Me three times." 62So Peter went out and wept bitterly.

Jesus Mocked and Beaten

63Now the men who held Jesus mocked Him and beat Him. 64And having blindfolded Him, they struck Him on the face and asked Him,a saying, "Prophesy! Who is the one who struck You?" 65And many other things they blasphemously spoke against Him.

Jesus Faces the Sanhedrin

66As soon as it was day, the elders of the people, both chief priests and scribes, came together and led Him into their council, saying, 67"If You are the Christ, tell us."

But He said to them, "If I tell you, you will by no means believe. 68And if I also ask *you,* you will by no means answer Me or let *Me* go.a 69Hereafter the Son of Man will sit on the right hand of the power of God."

70Then they all said, "Are You then the Son of God?"

So He said to them, "You *rightly* say that I am."

71And they said, "What further testimony do we need? For we have heard it ourselves from His own mouth."

John 18:12–27
Trial Before Annas

18 :**12** Then the detachment *of troops* and the captain and the officers of the Jews arrested Jesus and bound Him.

14:65 aNU-Text reads *received Him with slaps.*
14:70 aNU-Text omits *and your speech shows it.*
Luke 22:57 aNU-Text reads *denied it.*
22:60 aNU-Text and M-Text read *a rooster.*
22:61 aNU-Text adds *today.*   22:64 aNU-Text reads *And having blindfolded Him, they asked Him.*
22:68 aNU-Text omits *also* and *Me or let Me go.*

¹³And they led Him away to Annas first, for he was the father-in-law of Caiaphas who was high priest that year. ¹⁴Now it was Caiaphas who advised the Jews that it was expedient that one man should die for the people.

Peter Denies Jesus

¹⁵And Simon Peter followed Jesus, and so *did* another[a] disciple. Now that disciple was known to the high priest, and went with Jesus into the courtyard of the high priest. ¹⁶But Peter stood at the door outside. Then the other disciple, who was known to the high priest, went out and spoke to her who kept the door, and brought Peter in. ¹⁷Then the servant girl who kept the door said to Peter, "You are not also *one* of this Man's disciples, are you?"

He said, "I am not."

¹⁸Now the servants and officers who had made a fire of coals stood there, for it was cold, and they warmed themselves. And Peter stood with them and warmed himself.

Jesus Questioned by the High Priest

¹⁹The high priest then asked Jesus about His disciples and His doctrine. ²⁰Jesus answered him, "I spoke openly to the world. I always taught in synagogues and in the temple, where the Jews always meet,[a] and in secret I have said nothing. ²¹Why do you ask Me? Ask those who have heard Me what I said to them. Indeed they know what I said."

²²And when He had said these things, one of the officers who stood by struck Jesus with the palm of his hand, saying, "Do You answer the high priest like that?"

²³Jesus answered him, "If I have spoken evil, bear witness of the evil; but if well, why do you strike Me?"

²⁴Then Annas sent Him bound to Caiaphas the high priest.

Peter Denies Twice More

²⁵Now Simon Peter stood and warmed himself. Therefore they said to him, "You are not also *one* of His disciples, are you?"

He denied *it* and said, "I am not!"

²⁶One of the servants of the high priest, a relative *of him* whose ear Peter

cut off, said, "Did I not see you in the garden with Him?" ²⁷Peter then denied again; and immediately a rooster crowed.

Friday: Before Pilate the Governor

On the morning of the next day, Friday, Jesus faced the second of two trials: a hearing before Pontius Pilate. Pilate was procurator or governor of Judea from A.D. 26 to 36. As might be expected, the charges before Pilate changed from Jewish legal allegations to political allegations, especially that Jesus claimed to be "King of the Jews" (Mark 15:2).

The Synoptic Gospels report that Jesus remained silent during the interrogation, responding only briefly and vaguely to Pilate's questions (Matt. 27:14). John's Gospel, however, relates how Pilate engaged Jesus in reluctant conversation, with Jesus explaining that His kingdom is not of this world (John 18:36).

The hearing before Pilate is augmented by three incidents. Judas's remorse at betraying Jesus resulted in an attempt to return the ransom money, and in Judas's suicide by hanging (see Acts 1:18). Only Matthew includes this story (Matt. 27:3–10), likely to show his Jewish readers a fulfillment of Old Testament prophecy. The Old Testament quotation in Matt. 27:9, 10 is largely from Zech. 11:12, 13, but Matthew may have ascribed it to the better-known prophet Jeremiah because he refers to the buying of a field (Jer. 32:6–9).

A second incident is the warning about Jesus' innocence that Pilate received from his wife (Matt. 27:19). Although Matthew's source for this information is unknown, it effectively heightens Pilate's guilt in the sentencing of Jesus.

Only Luke's Gospel reports the third incident: an additional hearing of Jesus before Herod Antipas (Luke 23:6–12). That Pilate would refer Jesus to Antipas is understandable, since Roman rulers were customarily in Jerusalem during Jewish festivals, and since Jesus came from Galilee, over which Antipas had jurisdiction. Luke may have included this incident because it supported the prophecy of Ps. 2:1, 2, wherein kings and rulers plotted against God's anointed (see Acts 4:25–28).

Pilate deserves no sympathy for his dilemma in sentencing Jesus. As governor, he was authorized with plenary power by Rome, so his weakness and vacillation should not be mistaken for virtue. Josephus recounts Pilate's effective and indeed ruthless use of that power on a number of occasions. By choosing the path of least resistance in Jesus' case, Pilate was responsible for a monstrous evil: the release of a convicted assassin and the condemning of the righteous Son of God to torture and death.

■ Matthew 27:1–26
■ Mark 15:1–15
■ Luke 23:1–25
■ John 18:28–40

Matthew 27:1–26
Jesus Handed Over to Pontius Pilate

27 :1 When morning came, all the chief priests and elders of the people plotted against Jesus to put Him to death. ²And when they had bound Him, they led Him away and delivered Him to Pontius[a] Pilate the governor.

Judas Hangs Himself

³Then Judas, His betrayer, seeing that He had been condemned, was remorseful and brought back the thirty pieces of silver to the chief priests and elders, ⁴saying, "I have sinned by betraying innocent blood."

And they said, "What *is that* to us? You see *to it!*"

⁵Then he threw down the pieces of silver in the temple and departed, and went and hanged himself.

⁶But the chief priests took the silver pieces and said, "It is not lawful to put them into the treasury, because they are the price of blood." ⁷And they consulted together and bought with them the potter's field, to bury strangers in. ⁸Therefore that field has been called the Field of Blood to this day.

⁹Then was fulfilled what was spoken by Jeremiah the prophet, saying, *"And they took the thirty pieces of silver, the value of Him who was priced,* whom they of the children of Israel priced, ¹⁰*and gave them for the potter's field, as the LORD directed me."*[a]

Jesus Faces Pilate

¹¹Now Jesus stood before the governor. And the governor asked Him, saying, "Are You the King of the Jews?"

Jesus said to him, "*It is as* you say."

¹²And while He was being accused by the chief priests and elders, He answered nothing. ¹³Then Pilate said to Him, "Do You not hear how many things they testify against You?" ¹⁴But He answered him not one word, so that the governor marveled greatly.

Barabbas or Jesus?

¹⁵Now at the feast the governor was accustomed to releasing to the multitude one prisoner whom they wished. ¹⁶And at that time they had a notorious prisoner called Barabbas.[a] ¹⁷Therefore, when they had gathered together, Pilate said to them, "Whom do you want me to release to you? Barabbas, or Jesus who is called Christ?" ¹⁸For he knew that they had handed Him over because of envy.

¹⁹While he was sitting on the judgment seat, his wife sent to him, saying, "Have nothing to do with that just Man, for I have suffered many things today in a dream because of Him."

²⁰But the chief priests and elders persuaded the multitudes that they should ask for Barabbas and destroy Jesus. ²¹The governor answered and said to them, "Which of the two do you want me to release to you?"

They said, "Barabbas!"

²²Pilate said to them, "What then shall I do with Jesus who is called Christ?"

They all said to him, "Let Him be crucified!"

²³Then the governor said, "Why, what evil has He done?"

But they cried out all the more, saying, "Let Him be crucified!"

²⁴When Pilate saw that he could not prevail at all, but rather *that* a tumult was rising, he took water and washed *his* hands before the multitude, saying, "I am innocent of the blood of this just[a] Person. You see *to it.*"

²⁵And all the people answered and said, "His blood *be* on us and on our children."

²⁶Then he released Barabbas to them; and when he had scourged Jesus, he delivered *Him* to be crucified.

Mark 15:1–15
Trial Before Pilate

15 :1 Immediately, in the morning, the chief priests held a consultation with the elders and scribes and the whole

---

27:2 [a]NU-Text omits *Pontius*.   27:10 [a]Jeremiah 32:6–9   27:16 [a]NU-Text reads *Jesus Barabbas*.
27:24 [a]NU-Text omits *just*.

GOVERNOR PILATE'S UNHAPPY CONSTITUENTS (Mark 15:7)

In A.D. 26, Pontius Pilate replaced Valerius Gratus as governor of Judea. Pilate is mentioned not only in the Gospel accounts, but also by the Jewish writers Josephus (A.D. 37–100) and Philo (20 B.C.–A.D. 50), and by the Roman historian Tacitus (A.D. 56–117?). In addition, the name "Pilate" appears on coins, and in an inscription found at Caesarea Maritima.

As a governor, Pilate was responsible for the administration of the province of Judea, including judicial matters. Josephus states that Pilate had the power to "execute." He was also responsible for collecting taxes and tribute, disbursing funds to the provinces, and sending revenues to Rome. Even so, the office of governor of Judea was not the most prestigious in the Roman Empire.

A number of incidents occurred during Pilate's rule (A.D. 26–36) that resulted in skirmishes between the governor and the Jews. Pilate got off to a bad start when he introduced into Jerusalem images in honor of the reigning emperor, Tiberius. These articles, religiously offensive to the Jews, aroused such a protest that Pilate transported the items to Caesarea.

In another incident, Pilate constructed an aqueduct with the use of Jewish funds, giving rise to rebellion that was put down with bloodshed. Josephus, however, reports that the Jews were upset not over the money involved, but over what was done with the water. Scholars have concluded that the unrest was due to the lack of concern by Pilate for the water's ritual purity as it came into Jerusalem.

Tensions sometimes erupted into riots. Mark's Gospel reports "the rebellion" (Mark 15:7) that apparently was well known in Jesus' time, though now unknown. The Gospel of Luke describes an encounter with "Galileans whose blood Pilate had mingled with their sacrifices" (Luke 13:1). Josephus and Philo also report events which may be connected to these Gospel references. Jesus' opponents made the most of these tensions between a Roman governor and his Jewish constituency, accusing Jesus of rebelling "against Caesar" (John 19:12).

council; and they bound Jesus, led *Him* away, and delivered *Him* to Pilate. ²Then Pilate asked Him, "Are You the King of the Jews?"

He answered and said to him, *"It is as you say."*

³And the chief priests accused Him of many things, but He answered nothing. ⁴Then Pilate asked Him again, saying, "Do You answer nothing? See how many things they testify against You!"^a ⁵But Jesus still answered nothing, so that Pilate marveled.

Taking the Place of Barabbas

⁶Now at the feast he was accustomed to releasing one prisoner to them, whomever they requested. ⁷And there was one named Barabbas, *who was* chained with his fellow rebels; they had committed murder in the rebellion. ⁸Then the multitude, crying aloud,^a began to ask *him to do* just as he had always done for them. ⁹But Pilate answered them, saying, "Do you want me to release to you the King of the Jews?" ¹⁰For he knew that the chief priests had handed Him over because of envy.

¹¹But the chief priests stirred up the crowd, so that he should rather release Barabbas to them. ¹²Pilate answered and

15:4 ^aNU-Text reads *of which they accuse You.*
15:8 ^aNU-Text reads *going up.*

POLITICS AND GOVERNMENT

Pontius Pilate was the governor of Judea from A.D. 26 to 36 (Mark 15:1). He was appointed as "prefect," his exact title, by the emperor, to whom he reported directly. The prefect or governor (later called procurator) had the power to impose the death penalty, as well as having a certain military authority. The official residence of the governor was Caesarea.

said to them again, "What then do you want me to do *with Him* whom you call the King of the Jews?"

¹³So they cried out again, "Crucify Him!"

¹⁴Then Pilate said to them, "Why, what evil has He done?"

But they cried out all the more, "Crucify Him!"

¹⁵So Pilate, wanting to gratify the crowd, released Barabbas to them; and he delivered Jesus, after he had scourged *Him,* to be crucified.

Luke 23:1–25
Jesus Brought Before Pontius Pilate

23 :1 Then the whole multitude of them arose and led Him to Pilate. ²And they began to accuse Him, saying, "We found this *fellow* perverting theᵃ nation, and forbidding to pay taxes to Caesar, saying that He Himself is Christ, a King."

³Then Pilate asked Him, saying, "Are You the King of the Jews?"

He answered him and said, *"It is as you say."*

⁴So Pilate said to the chief priests and the crowd, "I find no fault in this Man."

⁵But they were the more fierce, saying, "He stirs up the people, teaching throughout all Judea, beginning from Galilee to this place."

Jesus Faces Herod

⁶When Pilate heard of Galilee,ᵃ he asked if the Man were a Galilean. ⁷And as soon as he knew that He belonged to Herod's jurisdiction, he sent Him to Herod, who was also in Jerusalem at that time. ⁸Now when Herod saw Jesus, he was exceedingly glad; for he had desired for a long *time* to see Him, because he had heard many things about Him, and he hoped to see some miracle done by Him. ⁹Then he questioned Him with many words, but He answered him nothing. ¹⁰And the chief priests and scribes stood and vehemently accused Him. ¹¹Then Herod, with his men of war, treated Him with contempt and mocked *Him,* arrayed Him in a gorgeous robe, and sent Him back to Pilate. ¹²That very day Pilate and Herod became friends with each other, for previously they had been at enmity with each other.

Jesus Sentenced to Crucifixion

¹³Then Pilate, when he had called together the chief priests, the rulers, and the people, ¹⁴said to them, "You have brought this Man to me, as one who misleads the people. And indeed, having examined *Him* in your presence, I have found no fault in this Man concerning those things of which you accuse Him; ¹⁵no, neither did Herod, for I sent you back to him;ᵃ and indeed nothing deserving of death has been done by Him. ¹⁶I will therefore chastise Him and release *Him*" ¹⁷(for it was necessary for him to release one to them at the feast).ᵃ

¹⁸And they all cried out at once, saying, "Away with this *Man,* and release to us Barabbas"— ¹⁹who had been thrown into prison for a certain rebellion made in the city, and for murder.

²⁰Pilate, therefore, wishing to release Jesus, again called out to them. ²¹But they shouted, saying, "Crucify *Him,* crucify Him!"

²²Then he said to them the third time, "Why, what evil has He done? I have found no reason for death in Him. I will therefore chastise Him and let *Him* go."

²³But they were insistent, demanding with loud voices that He be crucified. And the voices of these men and of the chief priestsᵃ prevailed. ²⁴So Pilate gave sentence that it should be as they requested. ²⁵And he released to themᵃ the one they requested, who for rebellion and murder had been thrown into prison; but he delivered Jesus to their will.

John 18:28–40
In Pilate's Court

18 :28 Then they led Jesus from Caiaphas to the Praetorium, and it was early morning. But they themselves did not go into the Praetorium, lest they should be defiled, but that they might eat the Passover. ²⁹Pilate then went out to them and said, "What accusation do you bring against this Man?"

³⁰They answered and said to him, "If He were not an evildoer, we would not have delivered Him up to you."

³¹Then Pilate said to them, "You take Him and judge Him according to your law."

Therefore the Jews said to him, "It is not lawful for us to put anyone to death," ³²that the saying of Jesus might be fulfilled

---

23:2 ᵃNU-Text reads *our.*   23:6 ᵃNU-Text omits *of Galilee.*   23:15 ᵃNU-Text reads *for he sent Him back to us.*   23:17 ᵃNU-Text omits verse 17.
23:23 ᵃNU-Text omits *and of the chief priests.*
23:25 ᵃNU-Text and M-Text omit *to them.*

A KINGDOM OF TRUTH (John 18:36)

The concept of "kingdom" in Jesus' time was rooted in the Old Testament: "kingdom" most often referred to the reign or royal authority of a king. Jewish people prayed daily for the coming of God's reign. When they prayed for His kingdom, they did not doubt that God reigned over His creation in the present. Yet they longed for the day when God would rule unchallenged and all peoples would acknowledge Him. Most Jews associated this kingdom with the coming of a Jewish king who would lead his people to victory over their enemies.

The Romans, however, guarded the title "king." Anyone who, without the emperor's permission, claimed to be even a client king was committing the offense of high treason. Jewish leaders, like the high priest Caiaphas and the Jerusalem aristocracy who helped keep peace for the Romans, therefore wanted to stop any would-be kings who might stir up trouble with Rome (John 11:47–50).

The governor, by contrast, understood Jesus' kingdom in very different terms. As a Roman, he knew reports of Cynic philosophers who wandered around claiming to be kings while possessing nothing. Such philosophers lacked respect for rulers, yet were without political ambition for themselves. As thinkers, they spoke about truth and about reigning, but to a Roman pragmatist they were at worst insane but harmless. Pilate, therefore, did not see Jesus as a threat, as did the Jewish religious leaders. Although Pilate asked Jesus, "Are You a king then?" (John 18:37), he actually misapprehended the nature of the mission Jesus claimed to fulfill (18:36).

---

which He spoke, signifying by what death He would die.

33Then Pilate entered the Praetorium again, called Jesus, and said to Him, "Are You the King of the Jews?"

34Jesus answered him, "Are you speaking for yourself about this, or did others tell you this concerning Me?"

35Pilate answered, "Am I a Jew? Your own nation and the chief priests have delivered You to me. What have You done?"

36Jesus answered, "My kingdom is not of this world. If My kingdom were of this world, My servants would fight, so that I should not be delivered to the Jews; but now My kingdom is not from here."

37Pilate therefore said to Him, "Are You a king then?"

Jesus answered, "You say *rightly* that I am a king. For this cause I was born, and for this cause I have come into the world, that I should bear witness to the truth. Everyone who is of the truth hears My voice."

38Pilate said to Him, "What is truth?" And when he had said this, he went out again to the Jews, and said to them, "I find no fault in Him at all.

Release Barabbas!

39"But you have a custom that I should release someone to you at the Passover. Do you therefore want me to release to you the King of the Jews?"

40Then they all cried again, saying, "Not this Man, but Barabbas!" Now Barabbas was a robber.

Sentenced to Crucifixion

Jesus was delivered by Pilate to be scourged before execution. Commonly practiced before crucifixion, the scourge consisted of a leather whip with bone, rock, or metal in the ends that ripped the flesh from a prisoner's back. Scourging severely weakened a prisoner, thereby hastening death on the cross, or sometimes was fatal itself. In addition to the scourge, Jesus was subjected to the soldiers' mockery about Him being "King of the Jews."

The scourging and mocking took place in the Praetorium. This area, which John identifies as "the Pavement" (John 19:13), functioned as the Roman governor's headquarters. It was often also the governor's residence, and Mark describes it as a "hall" (Mark 15:16). Some think that the Praetorium was located at Herod the Great's palace in the western part of Jerusalem. One archaeologist identified the Praetorium with the square in front of the palace, which Herod built in 23 B.C.

The accounts of Matthew and Mark re-

MOCKING THE SO-CALLED KING (John 19:2)

Often playing games to pass time, soldiers were known to beat and ridicule those they were about to execute. So they mocked Jesus, kneeling before Him to imitate the eastern Mediterranean custom of bowing before kings. Their salutation "Hail!" was the standard way Romans saluted their emperor. Many Romans and especially Greeks disliked the Jews, hence as the soldiers mocked a condemned Jewish man as "King of the Jews" (John 19:3), they may have been mocking the land of Judea as a whole.

Part of the soldiers' charade involved placing upon Jesus the regalia of a king: crown, robe, and scepter. The reed parodies a scepter (Matt. 27:29). The soldiers may have had a bamboo cane available, since they frequently used such for military floggings. Roman soldiers wore scarlet robes, so the robe they draped on Jesus was possibly a faded scarlet (Matt. 27:28), if it was one of theirs. Possibly they imitated the purple robe (John 19:2) of the Greek rulers who reigned in the eastern Mediterranean before the Roman conquest.

The soldiers mocked Jesus with words they thought were false, yet some of those words turned out, in the end, to be true. The Jewish people expected a king who would deliver them from the Romans, and the crowds hailed Jesus during His Triumphal Entry into Jerusalem. The Romans, who executed anyone they considered to be a threat to Judea's political stability, crucified Jesus on the charge of claiming to be "King of the Jews." They failed to realize that Jesus' kingship was real, just not of this world.

port Jesus being crucified following the flagellation, but John's Gospel relates a continuation of the hearing (John 19:8–11). The effect of this long hearing before the governor reinforces Jesus' innocence. Pilate appealed for Jesus' release, but ceased such efforts when faced with a new political threat. The governor would not risk accusations of disloyalty to Caesar (John 19:12, 15). In the end, the blame for Jesus' death falls on the religious leaders and the crowd, as well as Pilate.

- ■ Matthew 27:27–31
- ■ Mark 15:16–20
- ■ John 19:1–16

Matthew 27:27–31
The Soldiers Mock Jesus

27 :27 Then the soldiers of the governor took Jesus into the Praetorium and gathered the whole garrison around Him. 28And they stripped Him and put a scarlet robe on Him. 29When they had twisted a crown of thorns, they put *it* on His head, and a reed in His right hand. And they bowed the knee before Him and mocked Him, saying, "Hail, King of the Jews!" 30Then they spat on Him, and took the reed and struck Him on the head. 31And when they had mocked Him, they

19:3 ªNU-Text reads *And they came up to Him and said.*

took the robe off Him, put His *own* clothes on Him, and led Him away to be crucified.

Mark 15:16–20
Hail, King of the Jews

15 :16 Then the soldiers led Him away into the hall called Praetorium, and they called together the whole garrison. 17And they clothed Him with purple; and they twisted a crown of thorns, put it on His *head,* 18and began to salute Him, "Hail, King of the Jews!" 19Then they struck Him on the head with a reed and spat on Him; and bowing the knee, they worshiped Him. 20And when they had mocked Him, they took the purple off Him, put His own clothes on Him, and led Him out to crucify Him.

John 19:1–16
Pilate's Decision

19 :1 So then Pilate took Jesus and scourged *Him.* 2And the soldiers twisted a crown of thorns and put *it* on His head, and they put on Him a purple robe. 3Then they said,ª "Hail, King of the Jews!" And they struck Him with their hands.

4Pilate then went out again, and said to them, "Behold, I am bringing Him out to you, that you may know that I find no fault in Him."

⁵Then Jesus came out, wearing the crown of thorns and the purple robe. And *Pilate* said to them, "Behold the Man!"

⁶Therefore, when the chief priests and officers saw Him, they cried out, saying, "Crucify *Him, crucify Him!*"

Pilate said to them, "You take Him and crucify *Him,* for I find no fault in Him."

⁷The Jews answered him, "We have a law, and according to ourᵃ law He ought to die, because He made Himself the Son of God."

⁸Therefore, when Pilate heard that saying, he was the more afraid, ⁹and went again into the Praetorium, and said to Jesus, "Where are You from?" But Jesus gave him no answer.

¹⁰Then Pilate said to Him, "Are You not speaking to me? Do You not know that I have power to crucify You, and power to release You?"

¹¹Jesus answered, "You could have no power at all against Me unless it had been given you from above. Therefore the one who delivered Me to you has the greater sin."

¹²From then on Pilate sought to release Him, but the Jews cried out, saying, "If you let this Man go, you are not Caesar's friend. Whoever makes himself a king speaks against Caesar."

¹³When Pilate therefore heard that saying, he brought Jesus out and sat down in the judgment seat in a place that is called *The* Pavement, but in Hebrew, Gabbatha. ¹⁴Now it was the Preparation Day of the Passover, and about the sixth hour. And he said to the Jews, "Behold your King!"

¹⁵But they cried out, "Away with *Him,* away with *Him!* Crucify Him!"

Pilate said to them, "Shall I crucify your King?"

The chief priests answered, "We have no king but Caesar!"

¹⁶Then he delivered Him to them to be crucified. Then they took Jesus and led *Him* away.ᵃ

Crucifixion at Golgotha

The crucifixion of Jesus is related in all the Gospels with reserve and brevity and without sentimentality. The dominant theme lies on the mockery rather than on the physical suffering of Jesus.

The details of the crucifixion, however, vary in the Gospel accounts more than usual, doubtlessly due to the different theological emphases of the Gospel writers. Only Luke, from his interest in outsiders and the outcast, reports Jesus' compassion on the women of Jerusalem (Luke 23:27–32) and on the repentant thief on the cross (23:39–43). Only Matthew reports the opening of the tombs at the death of Jesus and the entry of the saints into the Holy City. This unusual story (Matt. 27:51–53) may reflect Matthew's purpose of showing that the Old Covenant leads to and is fulfilled by Jesus Christ.

Significant variations are found in the Fourth Gospel. Only John records the argument between Pilate and the chief priests about the sign on the cross reading "The King of the Jews" (John 19:19–22). Only John mentions that Jesus' tunic was not divided (19:24; see Ps. 22:18). Only John tells how Jesus entrusted His mother to the beloved disciple at the cross (19:25–27), an episode that heightens the authority of that disciple in John's Gospel.

Another account unique to John provides a final reminder that Jesus is the true Passover lamb (19:31–37). The soldiers forego the breaking of Jesus' legs, fulfilling the words of Ps. 34:20: "Not one of His bones shall be broken" (John 19:36). The piercing of Jesus' side, at which blood and water flow forth (symbolizing Holy Communion and baptism), further emphasizes that the Christian sacraments originate from and supersede the Jewish Passover celebration.

■ Matthew 27:32–56
■ Mark 15:21–41
■ Luke 23:26–49
■ John 19:17–37

Matthew 27:32–56
Crucified with Two Robbers

27 **:32** Now as they came out, they found a man of Cyrene, Simon by name. Him they compelled to bear His cross. ³³And when they had come to a place called Golgotha, that is to say, Place of a Skull, ³⁴they gave Him sourᵃ wine mingled with gall to drink. But when He had tasted *it,* He would not drink.

³⁵Then they crucified Him, and divided His garments, casting lots,ᵃ that it might

---

19:7 ᵃNU-Text reads *the law.*   19:16 ᵃNU-Text omits *and led Him away.*   **Matt.** 27:34 ᵃNU-Text omits *sour.*   27:35 ᵃNU-Text and M-Text omit the rest of this verse.

be fulfilled which was spoken by the prophet:

> "They divided My garments among them,
> And for My clothing they cast lots."[b]

36Sitting down, they kept watch over Him there. 37And they put up over His head the accusation written against Him:

THIS IS JESUS THE KING
OF THE JEWS.

38Then two robbers were crucified with Him, one on the right and another on the left.

39And those who passed by blasphemed Him, wagging their heads 40and saying, "You who destroy the temple and build it in three days, save Yourself! If You are the Son of God, come down from the cross."

41Likewise the chief priests also, mocking with the scribes and elders,[a] said, 42"He saved others; Himself He cannot save. If He is the King of Israel,[a] let Him now come down from the cross, and we will believe Him.[b] 43He trusted in God; let Him deliver Him now if He will have Him; for He said, 'I am the Son of God.' "

44Even the robbers who were crucified with Him reviled Him with the same thing.

The Opening of the Graves

45Now from the sixth hour until the ninth hour there was darkness over all the land. 46And about the ninth hour Jesus cried out with a loud voice, saying, "Eli, Eli, lama sabachthani?" that is, *"My God, My God, why have You forsaken Me?"*[a]

47Some of those who stood there, when they heard *that*, said, "This Man is calling

for Elijah!" 48Immediately one of them ran and took a sponge, filled *it* with sour wine and put *it* on a reed, and offered it to Him to drink.

49The rest said, "Let Him alone; let us see if Elijah will come to save Him."

50And Jesus cried out again with a loud voice, and yielded up His spirit.

51Then, behold, the veil of the temple was torn in two from top to bottom; and the earth quaked, and the rocks were split, 52and the graves were opened; and many bodies of the saints who had fallen asleep were raised; 53and coming out of the graves after His resurrection, they went into the holy city and appeared to many.

54So when the centurion and those with him, who were guarding Jesus, saw the earthquake and the things that had happened, they feared greatly, saying, "Truly this was the Son of God!"

55And many women who followed Jesus from Galilee, ministering to Him, were there looking on from afar, 56among whom were Mary Magdalene, Mary the mother of James and Joses,[a] and the mother of Zebedee's sons.

Mark 15:21–41
The King on a Cross

15:21 Then they compelled a certain man, Simon a Cyrenian, the father of Alexander and Rufus, as he was coming out of the country and passing by, to bear His cross. 22And they brought Him to the place Golgotha, which is translated, Place of a Skull. 23Then they gave Him wine mingled with myrrh to drink, but He did not take it. 24And when they crucified Him, they divided His garments, casting lots for them to determine what every man should take.

25Now it was the third hour, and they crucified Him. 26And the inscription of His accusation was written above:

THE KING OF THE JEWS.

27With Him they also crucified two robbers, one on His right and the other on His left.

27:35 [b]Psalm 22:18   27:41 [a]M-Text reads *with the scribes, the Pharisees, and the elders.*
27:42 [a]NU-Text reads *He is the King of Israel!*
[b]NU-Text and M-Text read *we will believe in Him.*
27:46 [a]Psalm 22:1   27:56 [a]NU-Text reads *Joseph.*

RELIGION AND WORSHIP

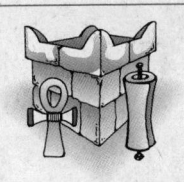

Jesus was crucified during the Passover feast. The exact day of Passover is determined by the lunar calendar, and always falls during the full moon. In a solar eclipse, the moon passes in front of the sun, which cannot occur when the moon is full. This means that the darkness during the crucifixion was not the effect of an eclipse (Matt. 27:45).

²⁸So the Scripture was fulfilled^a which says, *"And He was numbered with the transgressors."*^b

²⁹And those who passed by blasphemed Him, wagging their heads and saying, "Aha! *You* who destroy the temple and build *it* in three days, ³⁰save Yourself, and come down from the cross!"

³¹Likewise the chief priests also, mocking among themselves with the scribes, said, "He saved others; Himself He cannot save. ³²Let the Christ, the King of Israel, descend now from the cross, that we may see and believe."^a

Even those who were crucified with Him reviled Him.

Jesus Dies on the Cross

³³Now when the sixth hour had come, there was darkness over the whole land until the ninth hour. ³⁴And at the ninth hour Jesus cried out with a loud voice, saying, "Eloi, Eloi, lama sabachthani?" which is translated, *"My God, My God, why have You forsaken Me?"*^a

³⁵Some of those who stood by, when they heard *that,* said, "Look, He is calling for Elijah!" ³⁶Then someone ran and filled a sponge full of sour wine, put *it* on a reed, and offered *it* to Him to drink, saying, "Let Him alone; let us see if Elijah will come to take Him down."

³⁷And Jesus cried out with a loud voice, and breathed His last.

³⁸Then the veil of the temple was torn in two from top to bottom. ³⁹So when the centurion, who stood opposite Him, saw that He cried out like this and breathed His last,^a he said, "Truly this Man was the Son of God!"

⁴⁰There were also women looking on from afar, among whom were Mary Magdalene, Mary the mother of James the Less and of Joses, and Salome, ⁴¹who also followed Him and ministered to Him when He was in Galilee, and many other women who came up with Him to Jerusalem.

Luke 23:26–49
Compassion for Women and a Criminal

23 **:26** Now as they led Him away, they laid hold of a certain man, Simon a Cyrenian, who was coming from the country, and on him they laid the cross that he might bear *it* after Jesus.

²⁷And a great multitude of the people followed Him, and women who also mourned and lamented Him. ²⁸But Jesus, turning to them, said, "Daughters of Jerusalem, do not weep for Me, but weep for yourselves and for your children. ²⁹For indeed the days are coming in which they will say, 'Blessed *are* the barren, wombs that never bore, and breasts which never nursed!' ³⁰Then they will begin *'to say to the mountains, "Fall on us!" and to the hills, "Cover us!"* '^a ³¹For if they do these things in the green wood, what will be done in the dry?"

³²There were also two others, criminals, led with Him to be put to death. ³³And when they had come to the place called Calvary, there they crucified Him, and the criminals, one on the right hand and the other on the left. ³⁴Then Jesus said, "Father, forgive them, for they do not know what they do."^a

And they divided His garments and cast lots. ³⁵And the people stood looking on. But even the rulers with them sneered, saying, "He saved others; let Him save Himself if He is the Christ, the chosen of God."

³⁶The soldiers also mocked Him, coming and offering Him sour wine, ³⁷and saying, "If You are the King of the Jews, save Yourself."

³⁸And an inscription also was written over Him in letters of Greek, Latin, and Hebrew:^a

---

15:28 ^aIsaiah 53:12 ^bNU-Text omits this verse.
15:32 ^aM-Text reads *believe Him.*   15:34 ^aPsalm 22:1   15:39 ^aNU-Text reads *that He thus breathed His last.*   Luke 23:30 ^aHosea 10:8   23:34 ^aNU-Text brackets the first sentence as a later addition.   23:38 ^aNU-Text omits *written* and *in letters of Greek, Latin, and Hebrew.*

ARTS AND LITERATURE

The Hebrew Bible represents some of the earliest writings to be translated into another language. The Hebrew was translated into Greek between the 3rd and 1st centuries B.C. This translation is known as the Septuagint, abbreviated LXX, because tradition said it was made by 70 scholars working independently. By Jesus' time people were familiar with the same content appearing in Greek, Latin, and Hebrew (Luke 23:38).

THIS IS THE KING OF THE JEWS.

[39]Then one of the criminals who were hanged blasphemed Him, saying, "If You are the Christ,[a] save Yourself and us."

[40]But the other, answering, rebuked him, saying, "Do you not even fear God, seeing you are under the same condemnation? [41]And we indeed justly, for we receive the due reward of our deeds; but this Man has done nothing wrong." [42]Then he said to Jesus, "Lord,[a] remember me when You come into Your kingdom."

[43]And Jesus said to him, "Assuredly, I say to you, today you will be with Me in Paradise."

I Commit My Spirit

[44]Now it was[a] about the sixth hour, and there was darkness over all the earth until the ninth hour. [45]Then the sun was darkened,[a] and the veil of the temple was torn in two. [46]And when Jesus had cried out with a loud voice, He said, "Father, *'into Your hands I commit My spirit.'*"[a] Having said this, He breathed His last.

[47]So when the centurion saw what had happened, he glorified God, saying, "Certainly this was a righteous Man!"

[48]And the whole crowd who came together to that sight, seeing what had been done, beat their breasts and returned. [49]But all His acquaintances, and the women who followed Him from Galilee, stood at a distance, watching these things.

John 19:17–37
Jesus Is Crucified

19 :17 And He, bearing His cross, went out to a place called *the Place* of a Skull, which is called in Hebrew, Golgotha, [18]where they crucified Him, and two others with Him, one on either side, and Jesus in the center. [19]Now Pilate wrote a title and put *it* on the cross. And the writing was:

JESUS OF NAZARETH, THE KING
OF THE JEWS.

[20]Then many of the Jews read this title, for the place where Jesus was crucified was near the city; and it was written in Hebrew, Greek, *and* Latin.

[21]Therefore the chief priests of the Jews said to Pilate, "Do not write, 'The King of the Jews,' but, 'He said, "I am the King of the Jews." ' "

[22]Pilate answered, "What I have written, I have written."

[23]Then the soldiers, when they had crucified Jesus, took His garments and made four parts, to each soldier a part, and also the tunic. Now the tunic was without seam, woven from the top in one piece. [24]They said therefore among themselves, "Let us not tear it, but cast lots for it, whose it shall be," that the Scripture might be fulfilled which says:

*"They divided My garments among
    them,
And for My clothing they cast lots."*[a]

Therefore the soldiers did these things.

Behold Your Mother

[25]Now there stood by the cross of Jesus His mother, and His mother's sister, Mary the *wife* of Clopas, and Mary Magdalene. [26]When Jesus therefore saw His mother, and the disciple whom He loved standing by, He said to His mother, "Woman, behold your son!" [27]Then He said to the disciple, "Behold your mother!" And from that hour that disciple took her to his own *home.*

It Is Finished

[28]After this, Jesus, knowing[a] that all things were now accomplished, that the Scripture might be fulfilled, said, "I thirst!" [29]Now a vessel full of sour wine was sitting there; and they filled a sponge with sour wine, put *it* on hyssop, and put *it* to His

---

23:39 [a]NU-Text reads *Are You not the Christ?*
23:42 [a]NU-Text reads *And he said, "Jesus, remember me.*   23:44 [a]NU-Text adds *already.*
23:45 [a]NU-Text reads *obscured.*   23:46 [a]Psalm 31:5   **John** 19:24 [a]Psalm 22:18
19:28 [a]M-Text reads *seeing.*

HEALTH AND MEDICINE

A crucified person could not breathe freely. When exhaustion set in, death came by suffocation, which could take several days. But the legs were needed to raise the body for breathing, and death came much more quickly when the victim's legs were broken. Since Jewish law forbade leaving a body exposed overnight, the Jews requested the breaking of the legs (John 19:31–33).

mouth. ³⁰So when Jesus had received the sour wine, He said, "It is finished!" And bowing His head, He gave up His spirit.

Jesus' Side Is Pierced

³¹Therefore, because it was the Preparation *Day,* that the bodies should not remain on the cross on the Sabbath (for that Sabbath was a high day), the Jews asked Pilate that their legs might be broken, and *that* they might be taken away. ³²Then the soldiers came and broke the legs of the first and of the other who was crucified with Him. ³³But when they came to Jesus and saw that He was already dead, they did not break His legs. ³⁴But one of the soldiers pierced His side with a spear, and immediately blood and water came out. ³⁵And he who has seen has testified, and his testimony is true; and he knows that he is telling the truth, so that you may believe. ³⁶For these things were done that the Scripture should be fulfilled, *"Not one of His bones shall be broken."*ª ³⁷And again another Scripture says, *"They shall look on Him whom they pierced."*ª

The Burial of Jesus

After the crucifixion, Joseph of Arimathea asked Pilate for the body of Jesus. Joseph is presented as a righteous seeker of the kingdom of God (Mark 15:43) and a secret follower of Jesus (John 19:38). Though he was a member of the Sanhedrin, the council that delivered Jesus to the Roman authorities, he did not consent to the council's actions (Luke 23:50, 51). Upon receiving permission from Pilate, Joseph took Jesus' body down from the cross and placed it in a rock tomb near the site of the crucifixion before the onset of the Sabbath. A group of women (Luke 23:55), including Mary Magdalene (Matt. 27:61), observed the burial.

Nicodemus, a Pharisee, came to Joseph of Arimathea to assist in the burial of Jesus (John 19:39). Earlier he had come to Jesus "by night" (John 3:1, 2), possibly because he wished their meeting to be secret. When the Pharisees pushed for Jesus' arrest, Nicodemus argued a legitimate point of law that Jesus deserved a hearing (7:50–52). The plea fell on deaf ears. Appearing only in John's Gospel, Nicodemus is an example of one whose regard for Jesus as a teacher from God was based primarily on Jesus' miraculous signs. He seems to have been sincere in his approach to Jesus, but lacked understanding of the salvation He offered.

Friday was the "Day of Preparation" for the Sabbath (Matt. 27:62). The conference of the priests and Pharisees with Pilate occurred on Saturday, the Sabbath day itself. Only Matthew's Gospel records this incident, revealing the insincere piety of the Jewish leaders: they were so concerned about Jesus' claim to rise "after three days" (27:63) that they were willing to violate the Jewish Sabbath.

■ Matthew 27:57–66
■ Mark 15:42–47
■ Luke 23:50–56
■ John 19:38–42

Matthew 27:57–66
Jesus' Body Buried

27 **:57** Now when evening had come, there came a rich man from Arimathea, named Joseph, who himself had also become a disciple of Jesus. ⁵⁸This man went to Pilate and asked for the body of Jesus. Then Pilate commanded the body to be given to him. ⁵⁹When Joseph had taken the body, he wrapped it in a clean linen cloth, ⁶⁰and laid it in his new tomb which he had hewn out of the rock; and he rolled a large stone against the door of the tomb, and departed. ⁶¹And Mary Magdalene was there, and the other Mary, sitting opposite the tomb.

Pilate Sets a Guard

⁶²On the next day, which followed the Day of Preparation, the chief priests and Pharisees gathered together to Pilate,

---

19:36 ªExodus 12:46; Numbers 9:12; Psalm 34:20   19:37 ªZechariah 12:10

CULTURE AND SOCIETY

In the ancient world people considered it extremely important how and where the dead were buried. In Palestine, tombs were rooms or groups of rooms cut into the hillsides. The individual chambers and the tomb as a whole needed to be shut securely because of animals and vandals. Joseph's "new tomb" (Matt. 27:60) was possibly a family burial crypt, which generally held more than one body.

63saying, "Sir, we remember, while He was still alive, how that deceiver said, 'After three days I will rise.' 64Therefore command that the tomb be made secure until the third day, lest His disciples come by night[a] and steal Him *away,* and say to the people, 'He has risen from the dead.' So the last deception will be worse than the first." 65Pilate said to them, "You have a guard; go your way, make *it* as secure as you know how." 66So they went and made the tomb secure, sealing the stone and setting the guard.

Mark 15:42–47
Jesus' Burial

15 :42 Now when evening had come, because it was the Preparation Day, that is, the day before the Sabbath, 43Joseph of Arimathea, a prominent council member, who was himself waiting for the kingdom of God, coming and taking courage, went in to Pilate and asked for the body of Jesus. 44Pilate marveled that He was already dead; and summoning the centurion, he asked him if He had been dead for some time. 45So when he found out from the centurion, he granted the body to Joseph. 46Then he bought fine linen, took Him down, and wrapped Him in the linen. And he laid Him in a tomb which had been hewn out of the rock, and rolled a stone against the door of the tomb. 47And Mary Magdalene and Mary *the mother* of Joses observed where He was laid.

Luke 23:50–56
Jesus Buried in Joseph's Tomb

23 :50 Now behold, *there was* a man named Joseph, a council member, a good and just man. 51He had not consented to their decision and deed. *He was* from Arimathea, a city of the Jews, who himself was also waiting[a] for the kingdom of God. 52This man went to Pilate and asked for the body of Jesus. 53Then he took it down,

wrapped it in linen, and laid it in a tomb *that was* hewn out of the rock, where no one had ever lain before. 54That day was the Preparation, and the Sabbath drew near. 55And the women who had come with Him from Galilee followed after, and they observed the tomb and how His body was laid. 56Then they returned and prepared spices and fragrant oils. And they rested on the Sabbath according to the commandment.

John 19:38–42
Buried in a Garden Tomb

19 :38 After this, Joseph of Arimathea, being a disciple of Jesus, but secretly, for fear of the Jews, asked Pilate that he might take away the body of Jesus; and Pilate gave *him* permission. So he came and took the body of Jesus. 39And Nicodemus, who at first came to Jesus by night, also came, bringing a mixture of myrrh and aloes, about a hundred pounds. 40Then they took the body of Jesus, and bound it in strips of linen with the spices, as the custom of the Jews is to bury. 41Now in the place where He was crucified there was a garden, and in the garden a new tomb in which no one had yet been laid. 42So there they laid Jesus, because of the Jews' Preparation *Day,* for the tomb was nearby.

Sunday: Morning at the Tomb

The Gospels agree that Jesus was raised bodily from the dead on Sunday, the first day of the week. They also agree that Mary Magdalene was the first witness of the empty tomb, and most probably of the resurrected Lord. This is an important piece of historical evidence, since the testimony of a woman was of no legal value in ancient Jewish society. Had some early church writers invented a story of the resurrection, they would not have emphasized Mary's witness in the narrative.

Like the crucifixion accounts, the resur-

27:64 [a]NU-Text omits *by night.*
Luke 23:51 [a]NU-Text reads *who was waiting.*

BELIEFS AND IDEAS
Burial within city limits was objectionable for reasons of health if nothing else [John 19:41, 42]. The oldest Roman law, the Twelve Tables, prohibited burial within the traditional limits of the city of Rome. This particular law was observed until the 4th century A.D., though a special exception was made for the ashes of the emperor Trajan in A.D. 117.

rection accounts diverge in a number of particulars. Only Matthew reports an earthquake and the rolling away of the stone from the tomb (Matt. 28:2). Since Matthew also reported an earthquake at the crucifixion (27:51), the second earthquake may show the equal significance of the resurrection. Matthew and Mark speak of one angel at the tomb (Matt. 28:5; Mark 16:5), whereas Luke and John speak of two (Luke 24:4; John 20:12). Matthew and Mark report only the women visiting the empty tomb, while Luke and John tell of a visit by Peter (Luke 24:12), with John relating a footrace between Peter and the beloved disciple to the tomb (John 20:3–8).

- Matthew 28:1–8
- Mark 16:1–8
- Luke 24:1–12
- John 20:1–13

Matthew 28:1–8
The Risen Lord

28 :1 Now after the Sabbath, as the first *day* of the week began to dawn, Mary Magdalene and the other Mary came to see the tomb. ²And behold, there was a great earthquake; for an angel of the Lord descended from heaven, and came and rolled back the stone from the door,ᵃ and sat on it. ³His countenance was like lightning, and his clothing as white as snow. ⁴And the guards shook for fear of him, and became like dead *men*.

⁵But the angel answered and said to the women, "Do not be afraid, for I know that you seek Jesus who was crucified. ⁶He is not here; for He is risen, as He said. Come, see the place where the Lord lay. ⁷And go quickly and tell His disciples that He is risen from the dead, and indeed He is going before you into Galilee; there you will see Him. Behold, I have told you."

⁸So they went out quickly from the tomb with fear and great joy, and ran to bring His disciples word.

Mark 16:1–8
The Empty Tomb

16 :1 Now when the Sabbath was past, Mary Magdalene, Mary *the mother* of James, and Salome bought spices, that they might come and anoint Him. ²Very early in the morning, on the first *day* of the week, they came to the tomb when the sun

had risen. ³And they said among themselves, "Who will roll away the stone from the door of the tomb for us?" ⁴But when they looked up, they saw that the stone had been rolled away—for it was very large. ⁵And entering the tomb, they saw a young man clothed in a long white robe sitting on the right side; and they were alarmed.

⁶But he said to them, "Do not be alarmed. You seek Jesus of Nazareth, who was crucified. He is risen! He is not here. See the place where they laid Him. ⁷But go, tell His disciples—and Peter—that He is going before you into Galilee; there you will see Him, as He said to you."

⁸So they went out quicklyᵃ and fled from the tomb, for they trembled and were amazed. And they said nothing to anyone, for they were afraid.

28:2 ᵃNU-Text omits *from the door.*
Mark 16:8 ᵃNU-Text and M-Text omit *quickly.*

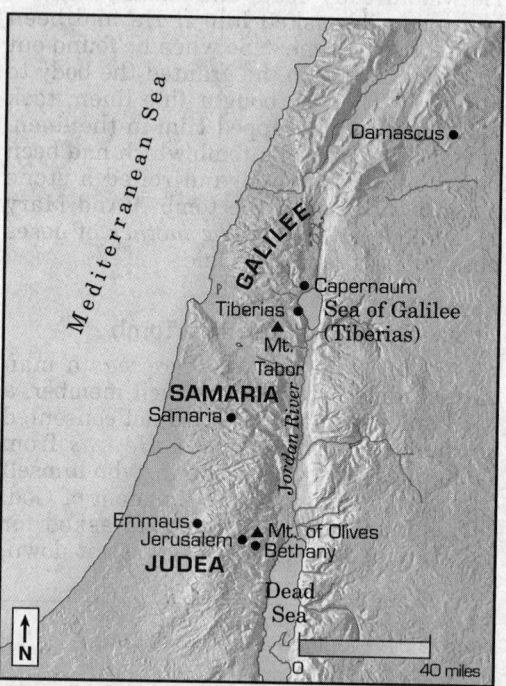

Appearances of the Risen Christ
The event of Jesus' resurrection is evident in various Gospel accounts which record His post-resurrection appearances. Several appearances occurred in and around Jerusalem, but Jesus was seen also beyond Jerusalem—on the way to the village of Emmaus and in Galilee by the Sea of Galilee. Not the least is Paul's vision of the resurrected Christ on the road to Damascus.

Luke 24:1–12
He Is Risen

24 :1 Now on the first *day* of the week, very early in the morning, they, and certain *other women* with them,[a] came to the tomb bringing the spices which they had prepared. 2But they found the stone rolled away from the tomb. 3Then they went in and did not find the body of the Lord Jesus. 4And it happened, as they were greatly[a] perplexed about this, that behold, two men stood by them in shining garments. 5Then, as they were afraid and bowed *their* faces to the earth, they said to them, "Why do you seek the living among the dead? 6He is not here, but is risen! Remember how He spoke to you when He was still in Galilee, 7saying, 'The Son of Man must be delivered into the hands of sinful men, and be crucified, and the third day rise again.' "

8And they remembered His words. 9Then they returned from the tomb and told all these things to the eleven and to all the rest. 10It was Mary Magdalene, Joanna, Mary *the mother* of James, and the other *women* with them, who told these things to the apostles. 11And their words seemed to them like idle tales, and they did not believe them. 12But Peter arose and ran to the tomb; and stooping down, he saw the linen cloths lying[a] by themselves; and he departed, marveling to himself at what had happened.

John 20:1–13
Risen from the Tomb

20 :1 Now the first *day* of the week Mary Magdalene went to the tomb early, while it was still dark, and saw *that* the stone had been taken away from the tomb. 2Then she ran and came to Simon Peter, and to the other disciple, whom Jesus loved, and said to them, "They have taken away the Lord out of the tomb, and we do not know where they have laid Him."

3Peter therefore went out, and the other disciple, and were going to the tomb. 4So they both ran together, and the other disciple outran Peter and came to the tomb first. 5And he, stooping down and looking in, saw the linen cloths lying *there;* yet he did not go in. 6Then Simon Peter came, following him, and went into the tomb; and he saw the linen cloths lying *there,* 7and the handkerchief that had been around His head, not lying with the linen cloths, but folded together in a place by itself. 8Then the other disciple, who came to the tomb first, went in also; and he saw and believed. 9For as yet they did not know the Scripture, that He must rise again from the dead. 10Then the disciples went away again to their own homes.

Mary Magdalene Sees the Risen Lord

11But Mary stood outside by the tomb weeping, and as she wept she stooped down *and looked* into the tomb. 12And she saw two angels in white sitting, one at the head and the other at the feet, where the body of Jesus had lain. 13Then they said to her, "Woman, why are you weeping?"

She said to them, "Because they have taken away my Lord, and I do not know where they have laid Him."

24:1 aNU-Text omits *and certain other women with them.* 24:4 aNU-Text omits *greatly.* 24:12 aNU-Text omits *lying.*

TIME CAPSULE A.D. 30 to 31

30 *Jesus is crucified (John 19:17, 18)*

30 *Jesus ascends to heaven (Luke 24:51)*

31 *Sejanus is executed for plotting against Caligula*

31 *Annas is named along with Caiaphas as co-high priests (Acts 4:6)*

Early Resurrection Appearances

The women met the resurrected Lord outside the tomb, near Jerusalem, and again were instructed to tell the disciples to go to Galilee (Matt. 28:7, 10). Jesus' appearance to one woman, Mary Magdalene, is specifically noted by John and Mark. Overcome by grief, and with tear-dimmed eyes, Mary did not immediately recognize the Lord.

Matthew is the only evangelist to report the Jewish religious leaders' cover-up of the resurrection (Matt. 28:11–15). Since Matthew's Gospel is intended for Jewish readers, this story helps explain the disappointing response of Jews to the gospel.

■ Matthew 28:9–15
■ Mark 16:9–11
■ John 20:14–18

Matthew 28:9–15
The Women Worship the Risen Lord

28 :9 And as they went to tell His disciples,[a] behold, Jesus met them, saying, "Rejoice!" So they came and held Him by the feet and worshiped Him. [10]Then Jesus said to them, "Do not be afraid. Go *and* tell My brethren to go to Galilee, and there they will see Me."

The Soldiers Are Bribed

[11]Now while they were going, behold, some of the guard came into the city and reported to the chief priests all the things that had happened. [12]When they had assembled with the elders and consulted together, they gave a large sum of money to the soldiers, [13]saying, "Tell them, 'His disciples came at night and stole Him *away* while we slept.' [14]And if this comes to the governor's ears, we will appease him and make you secure." [15]So they took the money and did as they were instructed; and this saying is commonly reported among the Jews until this day.

Mark 16:9–11
Mary Magdalene and the Risen Lord

16 :9 Now when *He* rose early on the first *day* of the week, He appeared first to Mary Magdalene, out of whom He had cast seven demons. [10]She went and told those who had been with Him, as they mourned and wept. [11]And when they heard that He was alive and had been seen by her, they did not believe.

John 20:14–18

20 :14 Now when she had said this, she turned around and saw Jesus standing *there,* and did not know that it was Jesus. [15]Jesus said to her, "Woman, why are you weeping? Whom are you seeking?"

She, supposing Him to be the gardener, said to Him, "Sir, if You have carried Him away, tell me where You have laid Him, and I will take Him away."

[16]Jesus said to her, "Mary!"

She turned and said to Him,[a] "Rabboni!" (which is to say, Teacher).

[17]Jesus said to her, "Do not cling to Me, for I have not yet ascended to My Father; but go to My brethren and say to them, 'I am ascending to My Father and your Father, and *to* My God and your God.' "

[18]Mary Magdalene came and told the disciples that she had seen the Lord,[a] and *that* He had spoken these things to her.

Appearances in Judea: Emmaus and Jerusalem

Jesus next appeared to two disciples who were walking from Jerusalem to Emmaus, an encounter Luke describes in considerable detail (Luke 24:13–35), but which Mark alludes to only briefly (Mark 16:12, 13). These two disciples thought Jesus would set up a political kingdom; therefore, His death was to them a tragedy (Luke 24:21).

Another appearance of the resurrected Jesus was to the disciples gathered in Jerusalem. Jesus demonstrated that He was not a ghost by revealing His scars (Luke 24:39, 40; John 20:20). Commanding the disciples to remain in Jerusalem and await "power from on high" (Luke 24:49) signified the coming of the Holy Spirit. This power arrived, according to Luke's sequel in the Book of Acts (Acts 2:1–13), at the Day of Pentecost, 40 days after the Ascension. For Luke, Pentecost begins the dispensation of the Holy Spirit, just as the baptism of Jesus began the dispensation of the Incarnation.

The Gospel of John, by contrast, suggests that the Holy Spirit was bestowed while the resurrected Jesus was still with the disciples. The effects of the Spirit are not described by John, however. Some understand Jesus' injunction "Receive the Holy Spirit" (John 20:22) to anticipate the coming of the Spirit at Pentecost. Others see it as a fulfillment of the promise of the Holy Spirit emphasized prominently in John 15; 16.

- Mark 16:12, 13
- Luke 24:13–49
- John 20:19–31

Mark 16:12, 13
Jesus Appears to Two Disciples

16 :12 After that, He appeared in another form to two of them as they walked and went into the country. [13]And they went and told *it* to the rest, *but* they did not believe them either.

28:9 [a]NU-Text omits the first clause of this verse.
John 20:16 [a]NU-Text adds *in Hebrew.*
20:18 [a]NU-Text reads *disciples, "I have seen the Lord," . . .*

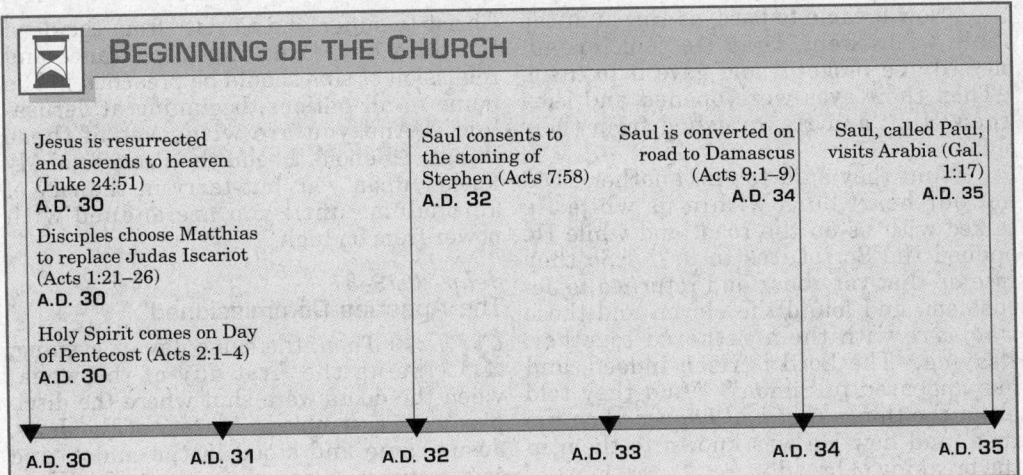

BEGINNING OF THE CHURCH

Jesus is resurrected and ascends to heaven (Luke 24:51)
A.D. 30

Disciples choose Matthias to replace Judas Iscariot (Acts 1:21–26)
A.D. 30

Holy Spirit comes on Day of Pentecost (Acts 2:1–4)
A.D. 30

Saul consents to the stoning of Stephen (Acts 7:58)
A.D. 32

Saul is converted on road to Damascus (Acts 9:1–9)
A.D. 34

Saul, called Paul, visits Arabia (Gal. 1:17)
A.D. 35

| A.D. 30 | A.D. 31 | A.D. 32 | A.D. 33 | A.D. 34 | A.D. 35 |

Luke 24:13–49
The Road to Emmaus

24 **:13** Now behold, two of them were traveling that same day to a village called Emmaus, which was seven miles[a] from Jerusalem. ¹⁴And they talked together of all these things which had happened. ¹⁵So it was, while they conversed and reasoned, that Jesus Himself drew near and went with them. ¹⁶But their eyes were restrained, so that they did not know Him.

¹⁷And He said to them, "What kind of conversation *is* this that you have with one another as you walk and are sad?"[a]

¹⁸Then the one whose name was Cleopas answered and said to Him, "Are You the only stranger in Jerusalem, and have You not known the things which happened there in these days?"

¹⁹And He said to them, "What things?"

So they said to Him, "The things concerning Jesus of Nazareth, who was a Prophet mighty in deed and word before God and all the people, ²⁰and how the chief priests and our rulers delivered Him to be condemned to death, and crucified Him. ²¹But we were hoping that it was He who was going to redeem Israel. Indeed, besides all this, today is the third day since these things happened. ²²Yes, and certain women of our company, who arrived at the tomb early, astonished us. ²³When they did not find His body, they came saying that they had also seen a vision of angels who said He was alive. ²⁴And certain of those *who were* with us went to the tomb and found *it* just as the women had said; but Him they did not see."

²⁵Then He said to them, "O foolish ones, and slow of heart to believe in all that the prophets have spoken! ²⁶Ought not the Christ to have suffered these things and to enter into His glory?" ²⁷And beginning at Moses and all the Prophets, He expounded to them in all the Scriptures the things concerning Himself.

The Disciples' Eyes Opened

²⁸Then they drew near to the village where they were going, and He indicated that He would have gone farther. ²⁹But they constrained Him, saying, "Abide with us, for it is toward evening, and the day is far spent." And He went in to stay with them.

24:13 ªLiterally *sixty stadia*   24:17 ªNU-Text reads *as you walk? And they stood still, looking sad.*

BELIEFS AND IDEAS

The Law of Moses prohibited omen interpretation, magic, and divination (Deut. 18:10, 11). Yet at the same time God was able to communicate by means of dreams (Matt. 2:12), visions (Luke 24:23), or movements of the stars (Matt. 2:9). An obvious factor in this distinction is that no one can compel God to reveal the future. Efforts to do so were not only futile, but condemned as evil.

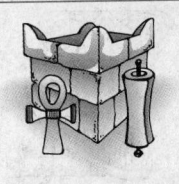

³⁰Now it came to pass, as He sat at the table with them, that He took bread, blessed and broke *it,* and gave it to them. ³¹Then their eyes were opened and they knew Him; and He vanished from their sight.

³²And they said to one another, "Did not our heart burn within us while He talked with us on the road, and while He opened the Scriptures to us?" ³³So they rose up that very hour and returned to Jerusalem, and found the eleven and those *who were* with them gathered together, ³⁴saying, "The Lord is risen indeed, and has appeared to Simon!" ³⁵And they told about the things *that had happened* on the road, and how He was known to them in the breaking of bread.

Jesus Appears to His Disciples

³⁶Now as they said these things, Jesus Himself stood in the midst of them, and said to them, "Peace to you." ³⁷But they were terrified and frightened, and supposed they had seen a spirit. ³⁸And He said to them, "Why are you troubled? And why do doubts arise in your hearts? ³⁹Behold My hands and My feet, that it is I Myself. Handle Me and see, for a spirit does not have flesh and bones as you see I have."

⁴⁰When He had said this, He showed them His hands and His feet.ᵃ ⁴¹But while they still did not believe for joy, and marveled, He said to them, "Have you any food here?" ⁴²So they gave Him a piece of a broiled fish and some honeycomb.ᵃ ⁴³And He took *it* and ate in their presence.

The Scriptures Opened

⁴⁴Then He said to them, "These *are* the words which I spoke to you while I was still with you, that all things must be fulfilled which were written in the Law of Moses and *the* Prophets and *the* Psalms concerning Me." ⁴⁵And He opened their understanding, that they might comprehend the Scriptures.

⁴⁶Then He said to them, "Thus it is written, and thus it was necessary for the Christ to suffer and to riseᵃ from the dead the third day, ⁴⁷and that repentance and remission of sins should be preached in His name to all nations, beginning at Jerusalem. ⁴⁸And you are witnesses of these things. ⁴⁹Behold, I send the Promise of My Father upon you; but tarry in the city of Jerusalemᵃ until you are endued with power from on high."

John 20:19–31
The Apostles Commissioned

20:19 Then, the same day at evening, being the first *day* of the week, when the doors were shut where the disciples were assembled,ᵃ for fear of the Jews, Jesus came and stood in the midst, and said to them, "Peace *be* with you." ²⁰When He had said this, He showed them *His* hands and His side. Then the disciples were glad when they saw the Lord.

²¹So Jesus said to them again, "Peace to you! As the Father has sent Me, I also send you." ²²And when He had said this, He breathed on *them,* and said to them, "Receive the Holy Spirit. ²³If you forgive the sins of any, they are forgiven them; if you retain the *sins* of any, they are retained."

Seeing and Believing

²⁴Now Thomas, called the Twin, one of the twelve, was not with them when Jesus came. ²⁵The other disciples therefore said to him, "We have seen the Lord."

So he said to them, "Unless I see in His hands the print of the nails, and put my finger into the print of the nails, and put my hand into His side, I will not believe."

²⁶And after eight days His disciples

24:40 ᵃSome printed New Testaments omit this verse. It is found in nearly all Greek manuscripts.
24:42 ᵃNU-Text omits *and some honeycomb.*
24:46 ᵃNU-Text reads *written, that the Christ should suffer and rise.*   24:49 ᵃNU-Text omits *of Jerusalem.*   **John 20:19** ᵃNU-Text omits *assembled.*

Science and Technology

Thomas was invited to touch Jesus' side where He was pierced (John 20:27). The Roman javelin was 5 to 7 feet long, with a long metal point hardened only at the end. It would bend and stick into a shield, making both useless. If the spear hit the ground it would still bend and could not be thrown back at the Romans. The soldier's thrust with his spear into Jesus was to make sure that He was dead (John 19:34).

BREATHING NEW LIFE (John 20:22)

Many Jewish people thought long and hard about Adam's fall into sin, and expected the end time to resemble the primeval paradise, before that fall. In the Creation story, God first creates Adam in paradise, personally breathing into him "the breath of life" (Gen. 2:7). Through the Old Testament prophets, God also promised someday to send the breath of His Spirit again to bring new life to His people (Ezek. 37:4–14). Some Jewish interpreters seem to have connected Genesis 2:7 with Ezekiel 37, anticipating God's breathing of new life through the Spirit.

By "breathing" on His disciples (John 20:22), Jesus probably symbolized this promise of new life associated with the coming of God's Spirit. Later Jewish writings connected the Spirit's coming with empowerment to prophesy for God, and similarly John's Gospel connects the Spirit with empowerment of the disciples to witness about Jesus (John 20:23; see 15:26, 27).

The disciples should have understood these connections, because Jewish tradition of their day emphasized two aspects of the Spirit's work in the Old Testament: purification and prophetic empowerment. Some Jewish groups, especially the Essenes, associated the Spirit with purification of one's heart. Most Jewish people (including the Essenes), however, associated the Spirit with the empowerment the biblical prophets possessed to hear from God and to speak for Him. Jesus provided for His disciples both the purifying gift of new life and empowerment for their mission.

---

were again inside, and Thomas with them. Jesus came, the doors being shut, and stood in the midst, and said, "Peace to you!" 27Then He said to Thomas, "Reach your finger here, and look at My hands; and reach your hand *here,* and put *it* into My side. Do not be unbelieving, but believing."

28And Thomas answered and said to Him, "My Lord and my God!"

29Jesus said to him, "Thomas,[a] because you have seen Me, you have believed. Blessed *are* those who have not seen and *yet* have believed."

That You May Believe

30And truly Jesus did many other signs in the presence of His disciples, which are not written in this book; 31but these are written that you may believe that Jesus is the Christ, the Son of God, and that believing you may have life in His name.

20:29 [a]NU-Text and M-Text omit *Thomas.*

Later Appearances in Galilee

Matthew, Mark, and John each record appearances of Jesus to the disciples in Galilee. Each account is quite different, suggesting that

Jesus made several post-resurrection appearances to His followers. According to Matthew's Gospel, the disciples were visited by Jesus as they gathered on a mountain (Matt. 28:16), as He had earlier predicted (28:10). As they worshiped Jesus, He delivered the Great Commission to go and make disciples of all nations (28:19).

In John's Gospel, Jesus appears to the disciples by the Sea of Tiberias (John 21:1). The Sea of Galilee had been renamed for the Roman emperor Tiberius Caesar. During a meal with the disciples on the shore, Jesus told Peter to "feed" His sheep (21:17), a metaphorical way of describing the Great Commission.

Resembling Matthew's Great Commission, Mark's Gospel presents Jesus instructing the disciples to go and preach the gospel (Mark 16:15, 16). Several signs are predicted for believers, including speaking in tongues, handling deadly serpents, and drinking poison without being harmed (16:17, 18). These miraculous signs (see Matt. 10:1; Luke 10:19) are regarded as signs of faith in the ending of Mark.

The Galilean appearance of Jesus in Mark's Gospel is recorded in what is known as Mark's "secondary ending" (Mark 16:9–20). These last twelve verses of Mark are absent from the earliest Greek manuscripts. They are a secondary ending combining elements from the resurrection appearances of the other three Gospels. Scholars suppose that Mark's Gospel originally ended at 16:8, with the abrupt ending there indicating either the loss of the original ending of the manuscript or perhaps Mark's death before he finished the Gospel.

- Matthew 28:16–20
- Mark 16:14–18
- John 21:1–25

Matthew 28:16–20
The Great Commission

28 :16 Then the eleven disciples went away into Galilee, to the mountain which Jesus had appointed for them. ¹⁷When they saw Him, they worshiped Him; but some doubted.

¹⁸And Jesus came and spoke to them, saying, "All authority has been given to Me in heaven and on earth. ¹⁹Go therefore^a and make disciples of all the nations, baptizing them in the name of the Father and of the Son and of the Holy Spirit, ²⁰teaching them to observe all things that I have commanded you; and lo, I am with you always, *even* to the end of the age." Amen.^a

Mark 16:14–18
Jesus Commissions the Disciples

16 :14 Later He appeared to the eleven as they sat at the table; and He rebuked their unbelief and hardness of heart, because they did not believe those who had seen Him after He had risen. ¹⁵And He said to them, "Go into all the world and preach the gospel to every creature. ¹⁶He who believes and is baptized will be saved; but he who does not believe will be condemned. ¹⁷And these signs will follow those who believe: In My name they will cast out demons; they will speak with new tongues; ¹⁸they^a will take up serpents; and if they drink anything deadly, it will by no means hurt them; they will lay hands on the sick, and they will recover."

John 21:1–25
Breakfast by the Sea

21 :1 After these things Jesus showed Himself again to the disciples at the Sea of Tiberias, and in this way He showed *Himself:* ²Simon Peter, Thomas called the Twin, Nathanael of Cana in Galilee, the *sons* of Zebedee, and two others of His disciples were together. ³Simon Peter said to them, "I am going fishing."

They said to him, "We are going with you also." They went out and immediately^a got into the boat, and that night they caught nothing. ⁴But when the morning had now come, Jesus stood on the shore; yet the disciples did not know that it was Jesus. ⁵Then Jesus said to them, "Children, have you any food?"

They answered Him, "No."

⁶And He said to them, "Cast the net on the right side of the boat, and you will find *some.*" So they cast, and now they were not able to draw it in because of the multitude of fish.

⁷Therefore that disciple whom Jesus loved said to Peter, "It is the Lord!" Now when Simon Peter heard that it was the Lord, he put on *his* outer garment (for he had removed it), and plunged into the sea. ⁸But the other disciples came in the little boat (for they were not far from land, but about two hundred cubits), dragging the net with fish. ⁹Then, as soon as they had come to land, they saw a fire of coals there, and fish laid on it, and bread. ¹⁰Jesus said to them, "Bring some of the fish which you have just caught."

¹¹Simon Peter went up and dragged the net to land, full of large fish, one hundred and fifty-three; and although there were so many, the net was not broken. ¹²Jesus said to them, "Come *and* eat breakfast." Yet none of the disciples dared ask Him, "Who are You?"—knowing that it was the Lord. ¹³Jesus then came and took the bread and gave it to them, and likewise the fish.

¹⁴This *is* now the third time Jesus showed Himself to His disciples after He was raised from the dead.

Jesus Restores Peter

¹⁵So when they had eaten breakfast, Jesus said to Simon Peter, "Simon, *son of* Jonah,^a do you love Me more than these?"

He said to Him, "Yes, Lord; You know that I love You."

He said to him, "Feed My lambs."

¹⁶He said to him again a second time, "Simon, *son of* Jonah,^a do you love Me?"

He said to Him, "Yes, Lord; You know that I love You."

28:19 ^aM-Text omits *therefore.*   28:20 ^aNU-Text omits *Amen.*   **Mark** 16:18 ^aNU-Text reads *and in their hands they will.*   **John** 21:3 ^aNU-Text omits *immediately.*   21:15 ^aNU-Text reads *John.* 21:16 ^aNU-Text reads *John.*

He said to him, "Tend My sheep."

[17]He said to him the third time, "Simon, *son* of Jonah,[a] do you love Me?" Peter was grieved because He said to him the third time, "Do you love Me?"

And he said to Him, "Lord, You know all things; You know that I love You."

Jesus said to him, "Feed My sheep. [18]Most assuredly, I say to you, when you were younger, you girded yourself and walked where you wished; but when you are old, you will stretch out your hands, and another will gird you and carry *you* where you do not wish." [19]This He spoke, signifying by what death he would glorify God. And when He had spoken this, He said to him, "Follow Me."

The Beloved Disciple and His Book

[20]Then Peter, turning around, saw the disciple whom Jesus loved following, who also had leaned on His breast at the supper, and said, "Lord, who is the one who betrays You?" [21]Peter, seeing him, said to Jesus, "But Lord, what *about* this man?"

[22]Jesus said to him, "If I will that he remain till I come, what *is that* to you? You follow Me."

[23]Then this saying went out among the brethren that this disciple would not die. Yet Jesus did not say to him that he would not die, but, "If I will that he remain till I come, what *is that* to you?"

[24]This is the disciple who testifies of these things, and wrote these things; and we know that his testimony is true.

[25]And there are also many other things that Jesus did, which if they were written one by one, I suppose that even the world itself could not contain the books that would be written. Amen.

Jesus Ascends from the Mount of Olives

Mark and Luke conclude their Gospels with the ascension of Jesus. The disciples watched as Jesus was taken into heaven from the Mount of Olives at Bethany to the east of Jerusalem (Luke 24:50). Mark's Gospel shows the disciples fulfilling their commission as they went forth "everywhere" and preached (Mark 16:20). Luke's emphasis, however, is that the disciples would not begin their missionary activity until after they received the Holy Spirit at Pentecost (see Acts 1:12–14). Thus his Gospel closes with the disciples returning to Jerusalem and devoting themselves to worship in the temple (Luke 24:52, 53).

■ Mark 16:19, 20
■ Luke 24:50–53

Mark 16:19, 20
Ascending to God's Right Hand

16 :19 So then, after the Lord had spoken to them, He was received up into heaven, and sat down at the right hand of God. [20]And they went out and preached everywhere, the Lord working with *them* and confirming the word through the accompanying signs. Amen.[a]

Luke 24:50–53
The Ascension

24 :50 And He led them out as far as Bethany, and He lifted up His hands and blessed them. [51]Now it came to pass, while He blessed them, that He was parted from them and carried up into heaven. [52]And they worshiped Him, and returned to Jerusalem with great joy, [53]and were continually in the temple praising and[a] blessing God. Amen.[b]

21:17 [a]NU-Text reads *John*.
Mark 16:20 [a]Verses 9–20 are bracketed in NU-Text as not original. They are lacking in Codex Sinaiticus and Codex Vaticanus, although nearly all other manuscripts of Mark contain them.
Luke 24:53 [a]NU-Text omits *praising and*.   [b]NU-Text omits *Amen*.

THE CHURCH AGE

(A.D. 30—100)

As the gospel spread beyond Judea to Samaria and the Gentile world, many converted to the belief that "Jesus Christ is the Son of God" (Acts 8:37).

The beginning of the church is a fascinating story of the Holy Spirit at work, leading the followers of Jesus into new ways and new worlds. The period from roughly A.D. 30 to 100 saw the glory of the first Pentecost, the struggle of the church to organize for mission, the conversion of Saul (Paul), the mission to the Gentiles, and the spread of the faith to Rome, Alexandria, and Antioch (the three greatest cities of the Roman Empire). Dozens of other cities and villages in Asia Minor, Greece, and Egypt would hear the Good News concerning the Man of Nazareth: "This Jesus God has raised up" (Acts 2:32).

As the gospel spread beyond Judea to Samaria and the Gentile world, many converted to the belief that "Jesus Christ is the Son of God" (Acts 8:37). The new believers met with opposition. Gentiles called these disciples of Christ by the name "Christians" (Acts 26:28; 1 Pet. 4:16), but did so with an element of scorn. Another scornful label for the early Christian movement was "the Way" (Acts 19:9). The term was appropriate, though, for Christ had made a "new and living way" for people to enter into the presence of God (Heb. 10:20).

▶ Archaeology and the Past

Archaeological finds from this period are a rich treasure, even when narrowly restricted to those directly connected with the church. The most significant of the riches are those associated with Jerusalem and the journeys of Paul.

In Jerusalem are two inscriptions that possibly reflect this period. The Theodotus Inscription, discovered on the hill known as the Ophel, describes a synagogue built specifically for visitors and immigrants from abroad. This Ophel synagogue has been identified with the Synagogue of the Freedmen, some of whose members opposed Stephen (Acts 6:9). A second inscription once stood in the temple, marking the boundaries beyond which Gentiles were not permitted to go, on pain of death. A crowd accused Paul of bringing a Gentile into the temple, in direct violation of this ban (Acts 21:28).

The destruction of Jerusalem by the Romans in A.D. 70 left ruins, some of which have remained. The most famous of these is a restored room from the lowest floors of the home of a member of one of the high priestly families, the house of Kathros. The Christians left Jerusalem at the outbreak of the Jewish revolt in A.D. 66 and went to Pella (modern Jordan), escaping the destruction of the city. They returned after the war and built a church under the leadership of Simeon, a cousin of Jesus. Many archaeologists believe that a small part of that church can still be seen today, behind what is called "David's Tomb."

Archaeological treasures abound in the cities of Paul's journeys. In Antioch of Pisidia, for example, is the *Monumentum Ancyranum,* on which is carved the deeds of Augustus Caesar and the hope for universal peace. Christianity was able to spread quickly in a Roman world because of the Roman peace. The excavated city square in Antioch featured a temple of the Anatolian god Men, showing that Christianity existed also in a cosmopolitan world, steeped in ancient cultures and religions, all under the aegis of Rome.

The ancient city of Ephesus has remains that reflect Paul's long ministry there. The temple and the statues of the Greek goddess Artemis, who became identified with the Roman goddess Diana, help explain why the Ephesians might riot when the worship of Artemis was threatened by Christianity. In Asia, Artemis assumed characteristics of the mother goddess, and her temple was one of the Seven Wonders of the ancient world, still magnificent in ruins. Also among the excavations in Ephesus were a collection of papyri with magical formulas written on them. The ancient world was much taken with magic, used both as a blessing and a curse, and the papyri recall the magic books that were burned during Paul's time (Acts 19:19).

Christianity existed in a cosmopolitan world, steeped in ancient cultures and religions.

The accounts of Paul's travels mention his experiences in the agora, or marketplace, of two cities. Philippi was a trading city, and Lydia, one of Paul's converts, likely operated her business (she bought and sold expensive purple cloth) near what is now the ruins of the agora (Acts 16:14, 19). The ruins of another agora still exists in Athens, where Paul first encountered the Athenian philosophers (Acts 17:17).

Archaeological finds are rich in Corinth, in the city that existed in Paul's day. Corinthian ruins include the marketplace and a stone bench identified as the bema, the judgment seat where Paul was brought before the proconsul Gallio. Also from Corinth is an inscription mentioning Gallio. Everywhere he went, Paul was in touch with Roman authorities, either because he was in trouble with them, or because they were protecting him, or both. Inscriptions from Corinth identify the meat market, and also name "Lucian the butcher." Butchers and meat markets recall Paul's writing to the Corinthian church over the issue of eating meat from the market that had been sacrificed to idols (1 Cor. 10:25).

The ruins of Rome, Paul's final destination, are overwhelming, and remind us of the persecution that the church endured. The Colosseum was the site of athletic events, chariot races, and gladiatorial combats. It is quite likely that Christians lost their lives there, thrown to the lions or other forms of torture. The magnificent arch of Titus is a monument to the Roman victory over the Jews and the destruction of Jerusalem. On it are carved Roman soldiers carrying the menorah (the golden lampstand) and table from the temple. The catacombs, or underground cemeteries, of Rome remind us that Christians were an illegal organization, and they often met in secret in the cemeteries.

▶ The Peoples and Groups

All of the New Testament story unfolds under the reign of emperors of the Roman Empire, which reached the height of its power from about A.D. 100 to 175. Of the various emperors who ruled during the New Testament period, Claudius was responsible for expelling the Jews from Rome (Acts 18:2), and Nero was the emperor to whom Paul appealed his case (Acts 25:11). The destruction of Jerusalem was accomplished in the year A.D. 70 by the Roman general Titus, who later became emperor himself.

Christianity developed amongst a rich mixture of religious cults represented in the Roman world. The most striking feature of Roman religion was its ability to merge the best features of several religions. As the empire expanded, it imported and assimilated many religious ideas and pagan gods from Greece and the Orient. Roman gods were fused and identified with the gods of the Greeks. Buildings, temples, and monuments to these gods were erected. Astrological beliefs and magical practices flourished.

An "imperial ruler cult" developed in the 1st century B.C. when the Roman Senate voted to deify Julius Caesar and to dedicate a temple to his honor. Among all the emperors, only Julius Caesar, Augustus, and Claudius were deified. This phenomenon apparently had more political than religious meaning.

▶ The Biblical Literature

The beginnings of the Christian church are related in the Book of Acts, the letters of Paul, and the general letters that make up the rest of the New Testament. Acts might more accurately be called the "Acts of the Holy Spirit," for Luke shows the role of the Spirit in guiding and strengthening the church. The Spirit's activity is prominent in the founding of the church through the work of Stephen, Philip, Peter, and especially Paul.

Paul's letters are the oldest Christian documents we have, and make up the bulk of the New Testament. Galatians was possibly the earliest letter. Shortly thereafter are 1 and 2 Thessalonians, written on Paul's second missionary journey, and 1 and 2 Corinthians and Romans, written on the third journey. The letters of Ephesians, Philippians, Colossians, and Philemon all give indication of being written in prison. The letters of 1 and 2 Timothy and Titus are called the Pastoral Epistles, addressing not churches, but pastors. Paul's letters tell us a great deal about the problems the churches faced as a result of their faith; opposition came from outside (pagan and public hostility) and from inside (heresies and persons struggling for position and power).

The General Epistles and the Book of Revelation tell us most of what we know about the early church beyond Paul. Hebrews was written to Jewish Christians. It emphasizes the humanity of Jesus, His perfect sacrifice, and His bringing forgiveness to all. The letter of James reminds Christians that real faith leads to faithful living, affecting the little acts of daily life.

The key to 1 Peter is hope in Christ, even in times of persecution. It was written for the church in Asia Minor, and may originally have been a treatise on the meaning of baptism for daily life. The letters of Jude and 2 Peter were written to counter false teachers. The early church expected Jesus to return at any minute, and 2 Peter calls on the church to live faithfully in anticipation of that return. Jude reminds its readers that God's grace is not an excuse for immoral living.

Of the three letters associated with John, 1 John is a sermon, calling for a return to the fundamental of the faith: Jesus came in the flesh for our salvation. Of the two letters written by "the Elder," 2 John emphasizes the commandment to love, while 3 John is a warning against a false teacher (already appearing in the church!).

The Book of Revelation calls the church to be faithful and stand firm. In the great cosmic struggle between good and evil, a struggle in which Christ will prevail, faithful Christians will share in His final triumph.

The Gospel to the Jews

> In its early years, Christianity was regarded by Rome as a sect of Judaism, and was ignored.

Under Roman rule the Jews were given a special status with certain legal rights. They were permitted to practice their own religion and to build their synagogues. They also were exempt from military service and were not required to appear in court on the Sabbath. Relationships between the Jews and the Romans were mostly positive. The birth and development of Christianity took place among the Jews and within the borders of the Roman Empire. In its early years, Christianity was regarded by Rome as a sect of Judaism, and was thus ignored.

The Gospels ended with an emphasis on the ascension of the risen Christ (Mark 16:19, 20; Luke 24:50–53). The Book of Acts opens with special attention to this important event in Christian history (Acts 1:1–11). The eleven apostles, and many other Jewish believers, were joyous after witnessing the Ascension. Yet they were at a loss to know what to do next, other than selecting a successor to Judas. All this mingling of hope and uncertainty vanished at Pentecost.

Henceforth, with courage and power, they gave witness to their conviction that Jesus was alive. Their claim was confirmed by undeniable miracles performed in His name (Acts 4:14). The witness of these Christians brought consternation to persons responsible for Jesus' death. Those who killed Him thought they had disposed of Him. Now His authority and power were stirring Jerusalem more than ever. There was intense opposition led by Saul of Tarsus and the rulers in Jerusalem. Yet the gospel spread rapidly to Judea, Samaria, and the entire Mediterranean world.

The Book of Acts

The Book of Acts is the second of a two-volume set, the first volume being the Gospel of Luke. Both books are addressed to Theophilus and written by one of Paul's associates named Luke "the beloved physician" (Col. 4:14). The author of Acts was a companion of Paul in many of his journeys, as implied by his use of the pronoun "we" to indicate he was traveling with Paul (see Acts 16:10). He was also with Paul during his imprisonment in Rome (2 Tim. 4:11).

Luke shows the link between what he reported in his Gospel and what he now reports in this book: the events of Jesus' ministry are the foundation for the results obtained by the message of His Spirit-inspired witnesses. Since the risen Christ was not seen in public, the burden of proof for the resurrection event lay with those who had firsthand experience of His postresurrection appearances (see 1 Cor. 15:4–8). The Gospels, Acts, and Paul's letters are at great pains to convince the reader that Jesus' appearances were not fantasy or the result of wishful thinking, but rather "hard evidence" which calls for faith.

The date of Luke's writing is not easily determined. The author possibly concluded his account 2 years after Paul's imprisonment in Rome, about A.D. 62 (Acts 28:30). Luke writes to Theophilus (meaning "lover of God"), who was probably a prominent Gentile believer. Theophilus had been "instructed" concerning matters related in Luke's Gospel (see Luke 1:3, 4), and so may have assisted Luke in his research.

■ Acts 1:1–8

Acts
Prologue

1 **:1 The former account I made, O Theophilus, of all that Jesus began both to do and teach, ²until the day in which He was taken up, after He through the Holy Spirit had given commandments to the apostles whom He had chosen, ³to whom He also presented Himself alive after His suffering by many infallible proofs, being seen by them during forty days and speaking of the things pertaining to the kingdom of God.**

The Holy Spirit Promised

⁴And being assembled together with *them,* **He commanded them not to depart from Jerusalem, but to wait for the**

Promise of the Father, "which," *He said,* "you have heard from Me; [5]for John truly baptized with water, but you shall be baptized with the Holy Spirit not many days from now." [6]Therefore, when they had come together, they asked Him, saying, "Lord, will You at this time restore the kingdom to Israel?" [7]And He said to them, "It is not for you to know times or seasons which the Father has put in His own authority. [8]But you shall receive power when the Holy Spirit has come upon you; and you shall be witnesses to Me[a] in Jerusalem, and in all Judea and Samaria, and to the end of the earth."

The Ascension

As does the Gospel of John, Luke emphasizes Jesus' departure to the Father. This was the last the disciples were to see of their Master—something they had long dreaded (John 14:5). Luke reports a period of approximately 40 days (Acts 1:3) after Jesus' resurrection during which He appeared alive to His disciples. The climax of these appearances came on the Mount of Olives (or Olivet), a ridge east of Jerusalem that is slightly higher than the parallel ridge on which Jerusalem itself lies. Here, only "a Sabbath day's journey" (Acts 1:12; about ⅔ mile) from the city, Jesus ascended into heaven. Now the disciples were alone until He returned in the Person of "another Helper" (John 14:16) at Pentecost.

■ Acts 1:9–26

Acts
Jesus Ascends to Heaven

1:9 Now when He had spoken these things, while they watched, He was taken up, and a cloud received Him out of their sight. [10]And while they looked steadfastly toward heaven as He went up, behold, two men stood by them in white apparel, [11]who also said, "Men of Galilee, why do you stand gazing up into heaven? This *same* Jesus, who was taken up from you into heaven, will so come in like manner as you saw Him go into heaven."

The Upper Room Prayer Meeting

[12]Then they returned to Jerusalem from the mount called Olivet, which is near Jerusalem, a Sabbath day's journey. [13]And when they had entered, they went up into the upper room where they were staying: Peter, James, John, and Andrew; Philip

and Thomas; Bartholomew and Matthew; James *the son* of Alphaeus and Simon the Zealot; and Judas *the son* of James. [14]These all continued with one accord in prayer and supplication,[a] with the women and Mary the mother of Jesus, and with His brothers.

Matthias Chosen

[15]And in those days Peter stood up in the midst of the disciples[a] (altogether the number of names was about a hundred and twenty), and said, [16]"Men *and* brethren, this Scripture had to be fulfilled, which the Holy Spirit spoke before by the mouth of David concerning Judas, who became a guide to those who arrested Jesus; [17]for he was numbered with us and obtained a part in this ministry."

[18](Now this man purchased a field with the wages of iniquity; and falling headlong, he burst open in the middle and all his entrails gushed out. [19]And it became known to all those dwelling in Jerusalem; so that field is called in their own language, Akel Dama, that is, Field of Blood.)

[20]"For it is written in the Book of Psalms:

'Let his dwelling place be desolate,
    And let no one live in it'; [a]

and,

'Let [b] another take his office.' [c]

[21]"Therefore, of these men who have accompanied us all the time that the Lord Jesus went in and out among us, [22]begin-

---

1:8 [a]NU-Text reads *My witnesses.*   1:14 [a]NU-Text omits *and supplication.*   1:15 [a]NU-Text reads *brethren.*   1:20 [a]Psalm 69:25   [b]Psalm 109:8 [c]Greek *episkopen,* position of overseer

---

TIME CAPSULE   A.D. 30 to 31

30	*Jesus ascends to heaven (Acts 1:9)*
30	*The disciples choose Matthias to replace Judas Iscariot (Acts 1:26)*
30	*The Day of Pentecost (Acts 2:1)*
30	*Peter addresses the Sanhedrin (Acts 4:5)*
31	*Annas is named along with Caiaphas as co-high priests (Acts 4:6)*

THE NUMBER "12" (Acts 1:26)

Soon after the apostle Judas Iscariot had betrayed Jesus, Judas met with a rather ignoble end (Acts 1:18). The disciples felt it essential to fill the vacancy left by Judas, thus maintaining the number of 12 apostles. So a certain Matthias "was numbered with the eleven apostles" (Acts 1:26). His appointment restored Jesus' apostles to their original number of 12.

It does not take a mathematical wizard to see that the number 12 played an important role. Why? Why replace Judas anyway? The group of Jesus' followers gathered in the upper room had nominated both Matthias and a certain Joseph Barsabas (Acts 1:23). Why not add both Matthias and Joseph? What is the significance of the number 12?

Various numbers in ancient times had symbolic significance. The number "7" was particularly favored, but so also was the number "12." This number reaches far back in the Book of Genesis to the 12 sons of Jacob, named Israel. These 12 sons became the 12 tribes of Israel, the totality of the people of Israel, the kingdom of the Jews. Any Jew of the day would recognize the political significance of the number 12.

Perhaps the number 12 also represented the 12 tribes of the new "Israel." Israel would now live on in the church! Matthias's appointment as a "witness" of Jesus' resurrection (1:22) again brought the apostles' number to completion. They were now prepared for the future, whatever lay ahead.

During the Last Supper, Jesus had granted a kingdom to the disciples, telling them that they would "sit on thrones judging the twelve tribes of Israel" (Luke 22:29, 30). They had not forgotten. Before Jesus ascended into heaven, the apostles asked Him when He would "restore the kingdom to Israel" (Acts 1:6). By bringing their number back to 12, they prepared themselves for God to fulfill His promises to Israel. With the Day of Pentecost approaching, they did not have long to wait.

---

ning from the baptism of John to that day when He was taken up from us, one of these must become a witness with us of His resurrection."

23And they proposed two: Joseph called Barsabas, who was surnamed Justus, and Matthias. 24And they prayed and said, "You, O Lord, who know the hearts of all, show which of these two You have chosen 25to take part in this ministry and apostleship from which Judas by transgression fell, that he might go to his own place." 26And they cast their lots, and the lot fell on Matthias. And he was numbered with the eleven apostles.

2:1 ªNU-Text reads *together.*

🧩 *The Day of Pentecost*

The Day of Pentecost came 50 days after the offering of the firstfruits (Lev. 23:10, 15, 16) at the Passover observances. It was a celebration of the wheat harvest, with pilgrims gathering from various nations of the Roman world. The crowd included Jews living outside of Palestine, as well as proselytes (Gentiles who had accepted the Jewish faith). Luke lists their homelands beginning in the East (Acts 2:9), then in Asia Minor (2:9, 10), and on to other Mediterranean areas—North Africa, Rome, and Crete (2:11).

Less than 2 months had passed since Jesus had been executed. In a sermon to the crowd on this occasion, Peter solemnly charged the Jewish leaders with crucifying the "Man attested by God," their Messiah. Yet while they were responsible, Jesus' death was no accident: He was "delivered by the determined purpose and foreknowledge of God" (Acts 2:22, 23).

■ Acts 2:1–47

Acts
Coming of the Holy Spirit

2 :1 When the Day of Pentecost had fully come, they were all with one accordª in one place. 2And suddenly there came a sound from heaven, as of a rushing mighty wind, and it filled the whole house where they were sitting. 3Then there appeared to them divided tongues, as of fire, and *one*

THE SPIRIT OF PROPHECY (Acts 2:17)

Old Testament passages associate the Spirit with creation, with new life, and with empowerment for various divine missions, most often for the mission of a prophet. By Jesus' day, Jewish interpreters most frequently emphasized prophetic empowerment: the Spirit empowered God's servants to hear Him and to speak His message the way He desired.

Many Jewish people believed that God had withdrawn the Spirit after the death of the prophets Haggai, Zechariah, and Malachi. The general assumption was that prophecy continued occasionally on a lower level, but the full restoration of the Spirit was yet to come. Prophets like Isaiah and Ezekiel had promised the final restoration of the Spirit (Is. 44:3; Ezek. 39:29). Nevertheless, the Spirit was not expected until the end time, in the period in which the Messiah would come, and most Jewish people did not believe that the Messiah had come yet.

Peter, recognizing that the Messiah had come in Jesus and that the Spirit who empowered the prophets was now fully active among God's people, chose an Old Testament text about the outpouring of the Spirit of prophecy (Joel 2:28–32). To make it clear that Joel's prophecy refers to the end time, Peter added explanatory words to his quote of Joel: "in the last days" (Acts 2:17).

Further, Peter was teaching that the end time had already begun because the Messiah had already come and taken His heavenly throne (2:34–36). Thus *some* "signs in the earth" (2:19) had been fulfilled by Jesus (2:22). This in turn meant that the time of salvation of which Joel spoke had also arrived. Thus Peter viewed the Spirit of prophecy as an end-time gift. God's servants should consider themselves to be empowered by the same Spirit who empowered Isaiah, Jeremiah, Huldah, Samuel, Deborah, and others.

So thoroughly did Peter wish to emphasize this point that he took a liberty used sometimes by Jewish interpreters in his day. He added some more explanatory words to the text he was quoting: "And they shall prophesy" (2:18).

---

sat upon each of them. ⁴And they were all filled with the Holy Spirit and began to speak with other tongues, as the Spirit gave them utterance.

The Crowd's Response

⁵And there were dwelling in Jerusalem Jews, devout men, from every nation under heaven. ⁶And when this sound occurred, the multitude came together, and were confused, because everyone heard them speak in his own language. ⁷Then they were all amazed and marveled, saying to one another, "Look, are not all these who speak Galileans? ⁸And how *is it that* we hear, each in our own language in which we were born? ⁹Parthians and Medes and Elamites, those dwelling in Mesopotamia, Judea and Cappadocia, Pontus and Asia, ¹⁰Phrygia and Pamphylia, Egypt and the parts of Libya adjoining Cyrene, visitors from Rome, both Jews and proselytes, ¹¹Cretans and Arabs—we hear them speaking in our own tongues the wonderful works of God." ¹²So they were all amazed and perplexed, saying to one another, "Whatever could this mean?"

¹³Others mocking said, "They are full of new wine."

Peter's Sermon

¹⁴But Peter, standing up with the eleven, raised his voice and said to them, "Men of Judea and all who dwell in Jerusa-

---

GEOGRAPHY AND ENVIRONMENT

Many nations of the Roman world were represented among the gathering of pilgrims in Jerusalem for the Day of Pentecost. The list of peoples (Acts 2:8–11) includes the Parthians to the east of Jerusalem and Rome to the west. North it includes Asia Minor (modern Turkey), and south the coast of Africa (Libya). The largest community of Jews outside Judea was in Egypt.

lem, let this be known to you, and heed my words. ¹⁵For these are not drunk, as you suppose, since it is *only* the third hour of the day. ¹⁶But this is what was spoken by the prophet Joel:

17   'And it shall come to pass in the last
         days, says God,
      That I will pour out of My Spirit on all
         flesh;
      Your sons and your daughters shall
         prophesy,
      Your young men shall see visions,
      Your old men shall dream dreams.
18   And on My menservants and on My
         maidservants
      I will pour out My Spirit in those
         days;
      And they shall prophesy.
19   I will show wonders in heaven above
      And signs in the earth beneath:
      Blood and fire and vapor of smoke.
20   The sun shall be turned into
         darkness,
      And the moon into blood,
      Before the coming of the great and
         awesome day of the LORD.
21   And it shall come to pass
      That whoever calls on the name of the
         LORD
      Shall be saved.'ᵃ

2:21 ᵃJoel 2:28–32   2:23 ᵃNU-Text omits *have taken.*   2:28 ᵃPsalm 16:8–11   2:30 ᵃNU-Text omits *according to the flesh, He would raise up the Christ* and completes the verse with *He would seat one on his throne.*

²²"Men of Israel, hear these words: Jesus of Nazareth, a Man attested by God to you by miracles, wonders, and signs which God did through Him in your midst, as you yourselves also know— ²³Him, being delivered by the determined purpose and foreknowledge of God, you have takenᵃ by lawless hands, have crucified, and put to death; ²⁴whom God raised up, having loosed the pains of death, because it was not possible that He should be held by it. ²⁵For David says concerning Him:

      'I foresaw the LORD always before my
         face,
      For He is at my right hand, that I
         may not be shaken.
26   Therefore my heart rejoiced, and my
         tongue was glad;
      Moreover my flesh also will rest in
         hope.
27   For You will not leave my soul in
         Hades,
      Nor will You allow Your Holy One to
         see corruption.
28   You have made known to me the ways
         of life;
      You will make me full of joy in Your
         presence.'ᵃ

²⁹"Men *and* brethren, let *me* speak freely to you of the patriarch David, that he is both dead and buried, and his tomb is with us to this day. ³⁰Therefore, being a prophet, and knowing that God had sworn with an oath to him that of the fruit of his body, according to the flesh, He would raise up the Christ to sit on his throne,ᵃ ³¹he,

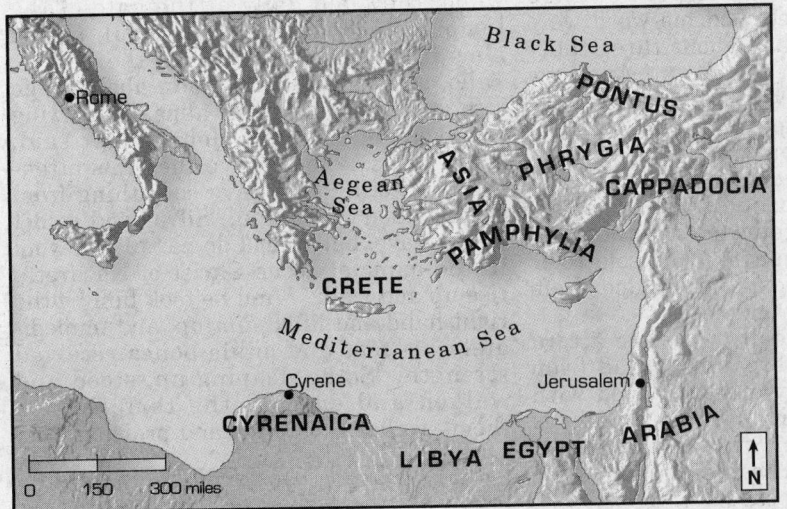

The Nations of Pentecost
In the 1st century A.D., Jewish communities were located primarily in the eastern part of the Roman Empire, where Greek was the common language, but also existed as far west as Italy and as far east as Babylonia. In addition to people from the nations shown here, those present on the Day of Pentecost (Acts 2:9–11) included visitors from Mesopotamia and even farther east, from Parthia, Media, and Elam (present-day Iran).

foreseeing this, spoke concerning the resurrection of the Christ, that His soul was not left in Hades, nor did His flesh see corruption. ³²This Jesus God has raised up, of which we are all witnesses. ³³Therefore being exalted to the right hand of God, and having received from the Father the promise of the Holy Spirit, He poured out this which you now see and hear.

³⁴"For David did not ascend into the heavens, but he says himself:

'The LORD said to my Lord,
  "Sit at My right hand,
35 Till I make Your enemies Your
      footstool." ' ª

³⁶"Therefore let all the house of Israel know assuredly that God has made this Jesus, whom you crucified, both Lord and Christ."

³⁷Now when they heard *this,* they were cut to the heart, and said to Peter and the rest of the apostles, "Men *and* brethren, what shall we do?"

³⁸Then Peter said to them, "Repent, and let every one of you be baptized in the name of Jesus Christ for the remission of sins; and you shall receive the gift of the Holy Spirit. ³⁹For the promise is to you and to your children, and to all who are afar off, as many as the Lord our God will call."

A Vital Church Grows

⁴⁰And with many other words he testified and exhorted them, saying, "Be saved from this perverse generation." ⁴¹Then those who gladlyª received his word were baptized; and that day about three thousand souls were added *to them.* ⁴²And they continued steadfastly in the apostles' doctrine and fellowship, in the breaking of bread, and in prayers. ⁴³Then fear came upon every soul, and many wonders and signs were done through the apostles. ⁴⁴Now all who believed were together, and had all things in common, ⁴⁵and sold their possessions and goods, and divided them among all, as anyone had need.

⁴⁶So continuing daily with one accord in the temple, and breaking bread from house to house, they ate their food with gladness and simplicity of heart, ⁴⁷praising God and having favor with all the people. And the Lord added to the churchª daily those who were being saved.

The Early Christians in Jerusalem

The healing of the lame man (Acts 3:1—4:31) and the miraculous deliverance of Peter and John from prison (5:12–42) are examples of the witness of the early Christians in Jerusalem. This witness brought them into conflict with the Jewish authorities, for the "notable miracle" performed by the disciples (4:16) was done publicly and therefore placed the religious leaders in an embarrassing position. The people had accepted the explanation given by the disciples—God had healed the lame man.

While the early Christians lacked temporal resources, they were not short on spiritual power. Some people supposed that these followers of Jesus were just another sect of Judaism, or were trying to start a new mystery religion around Jesus of Nazareth. But miracles were convincing others that the disciples were truly serving God, so the temple officials moved to suppress the people's interest in the new religion. One Pharisee, the highly respected Gamaliel, suggested that this movement might fail, as had that led in A.D. 6 or 7 by the insurrectionist Judas the Galilean (Acts 5:37–39).

■ Acts 3:1—5:42

Acts

A Lame Man Healed

3 :1 Now Peter and John went up together to the temple at the hour of prayer, the ninth *hour.* ²And a certain man lame from his mother's womb was carried, whom they laid daily at the gate of the temple which is called Beautiful, to ask alms from those who entered the temple; ³who, seeing Peter and John about to go into the temple, asked for alms. ⁴And fixing his eyes on him, with John, Peter said, "Look at us." ⁵So he gave them his attention, expecting to receive something from them. ⁶Then Peter said, "Silver and gold I do not have, but what I do have I give you: In the name of Jesus Christ of Nazareth, rise up and walk." ⁷And he took him by the right hand and lifted *him* up, and immediately his feet and ankle bones received strength. ⁸So he, leaping up, stood and walked and entered the temple with them—walking, leaping, and praising God.

2:35 ªPsalm 110:1   2:41 ªNU-Text omits
gladly.   2:47 ªNU-Text omits *to the church.*

BEGGING AT THE GATE OF THE TEMPLE (Acts 3:2)

The Jerusalem temple was a unique type of religious building. Unlike churches and synagogues, the temple was not meant to seat large numbers of people for prayer and worship. It was understood quite literally as the "house of Yahweh."

As the dwelling place of God, the temple was a holy place. The closer a person moved to the Most Holy Place in the middle of the temple itself, the more restricted was the access. Barriers served to keep out those who might profane the sacred space. The temple stood as an isolated building in the midst of a series of courtyards enclosed by walls. Gates regulated access to the courtyards.

The temple was built for God to inhabit, not for humans. The only humans meant to live regularly in the temple precincts were priests, whose job was to "serve" the Lord, overseeing the sacrifices and maintaining the temple property. Others were merely guests, visitors who might linger in the outer courts and/or offer sacrifices for the priests to place on the altar. Sacrifices were no doubt often offered in hopes of receiving some favor from God in return.

The architecture and social dynamics of the temple explain the presence of a lame beggar at the gate (Acts 3:2). Whereas the man's lameness itself would not necessarily have hindered him, lameness was frowned upon within the temple courtyards. Lame priests were prohibited from offering sacrifices in the temple (Lev. 21:18), and lame animals could not serve as sacrifices (Deut. 15:21). Thus the lame beggar remained outside the temple walls.

For his purpose, however, a temple gate was the perfect place to be. There he was assured of a constant traffic flow of those most able to give to him. Furthermore, those visiting the courtyard to seek the beneficence of God perhaps would recognize as well God's desire for them to exercise beneficence toward others. If the secret to success in business is location, location, location, the lame man was in the prime spot for his "work." Yet when Peter and John came by (Acts 3:6), he got more than he ever bargained for!

---

⁹And all the people saw him walking and praising God. ¹⁰Then they knew that it was he who sat begging alms at the Beautiful Gate of the temple; and they were filled with wonder and amazement at what had happened to him.

Preaching in Solomon's Portico

¹¹Now as the lame man who was healed held on to Peter and John, all the people ran together to them in the porch which is called Solomon's, greatly amazed. ¹²So when Peter saw it, he responded to the people: "Men of Israel, why do you marvel at this? Or why look so intently at us, as though by our own power or godliness we had made this man walk? ¹³The God of Abraham, Isaac, and Jacob, the God of our fathers, glorified His Servant Jesus, whom you delivered up and denied in the presence of Pilate, when he was determined to let Him go. ¹⁴But you denied the Holy One and the Just, and asked for a murderer to be granted to you, ¹⁵and killed the Prince of life, whom God raised from the dead, of which we are witnesses. ¹⁶And His name,

through faith in His name, has made this man strong, whom you see and know. Yes, the faith which *comes* through Him has given him this perfect soundness in the presence of you all.

¹⁷"Yet now, brethren, I know that you did *it* in ignorance, as *did* also your rulers. ¹⁸But those things which God foretold by the mouth of all His prophets, that the Christ would suffer, He has thus fulfilled. ¹⁹Repent therefore and be converted, that your sins may be blotted out, so that times

TIME CAPSULE A.D. 32 to 34

32	A temple to Bel is dedicated in Palmyra
32	Philip the evangelist preaches to an Ethiopian official
34	Philip the tetrarch dies (Luke 3:1)
34	Saul is converted (Acts 9:3)
34–37	Saul spends 3 years in Arabia and Damascus (Gal. 1:17)

of refreshing may come from the presence of the Lord, [20]and that He may send Jesus Christ, who was preached to you before,[a] [21]whom heaven must receive until the times of restoration of all things, which God has spoken by the mouth of all His holy prophets since the world began. [22]For Moses truly said to the fathers, *'The LORD your God will raise up for you a Prophet like me from your brethren. Him you shall hear in all things, whatever He says to you. [23]And it shall be that every soul who will not hear that Prophet shall be utterly destroyed from among the people.'*[a] [24]Yes, and all the prophets, from Samuel and those who follow, as many as have spoken, have also foretold[a] these days. [25]You are sons of the prophets, and of the covenant which God made with our fathers, saying to Abraham, *'And in your seed all the families of the earth shall be blessed.'*[a] [26]To you first, God, having raised up His Servant Jesus, sent Him to bless you, in turning away every one *of you* from your iniquities."

Peter and John Arrested

4 [1]Now as they spoke to the people, the priests, the captain of the temple, and the Sadducees came upon them, [2]being greatly disturbed that they taught the people and preached in Jesus the resurrection from the dead. [3]And they laid hands on them, and put *them* in custody until the next day, for it was already evening. [4]However, many of those who heard the word believed; and the number of the men came to be about five thousand.

Addressing the Sanhedrin

[5]And it came to pass, on the next day, that their rulers, elders, and scribes, [6]as well as Annas the high priest, Caiaphas, John, and Alexander, and as many as were of the family of the high priest, were gathered together at Jerusalem. [7]And when they had set them in the midst, they asked, "By what power or by what name have you done this?"

[8]Then Peter, filled with the Holy Spirit, said to them, "Rulers of the people and elders of Israel: [9]If we this day are judged for a good deed *done* to a helpless man, by what means he has been made well, [10]let it be known to you all, and to all the people of Israel, that by the name of Jesus Christ of Nazareth, whom you crucified, whom God raised from the dead, by

Him this man stands here before you whole. [11]This is the *'stone which was rejected by you builders, which has become the chief cornerstone.'*[a] [12]Nor is there salvation in any other, for there is no other name under heaven given among men by which we must be saved."

The Name of Jesus Forbidden

[13]Now when they saw the boldness of Peter and John, and perceived that they were uneducated and untrained men, they marveled. And they realized that they had been with Jesus. [14]And seeing the man who had been healed standing with them, they could say nothing against it. [15]But when they had commanded them to go aside out of the council, they conferred among themselves, [16]saying, "What shall we do to these men? For, indeed, that a notable miracle has been done through them *is* evident to all who dwell in Jerusalem, and we cannot deny *it*. [17]But so that it spreads no further among the people, let us severely threaten them, that from now on they speak to no man in this name."

[18]So they called them and commanded them not to speak at all nor teach in the name of Jesus. [19]But Peter and John answered and said to them, "Whether it is right in the sight of God to listen to you more than to God, you judge. [20]For we cannot but speak the things which we have seen and heard." [21]So when they had further threatened them, they let them go, finding no way of punishing them, because of the people, since they all glorified God for what had been done. [22]For the man was over forty years old on whom this miracle of healing had been performed.

Prayer for Boldness

[23]And being let go, they went to their own *companions* and reported all that the chief priests and elders had said to them. [24]So when they heard that, they raised their voice to God with one accord and said: "Lord, You *are* God, who made heaven and earth and the sea, and all that is in them, [25]who by the mouth of Your servant David[a] have said:

3:20 [a]NU-Text and M-Text read *Christ Jesus, who was ordained for you before.*   3:23 [a]Deuteronomy 18:15, 18, 19   3:24 [a]NU-Text and M-Text read *proclaimed.*   3:25 [a]Genesis 22:18; 26:4; 28:14   4:11 [a]Psalm 118:22   4:25 [a]NU-Text reads *who through the Holy Spirit, by the mouth of our father, Your servant David.*

'Why did the nations rage,
And the people plot vain things?
26 *The kings of the earth took their*
stand,
And the rulers were gathered together
Against the LORD and against His
Christ.'[a]

27"For truly against Your holy Servant Jesus, whom You anointed, both Herod and Pontius Pilate, with the Gentiles and the people of Israel, were gathered together 28to do whatever Your hand and Your purpose determined before to be done. 29Now, Lord, look on their threats, and grant to Your servants that with all boldness they may speak Your word, 30by stretching out Your hand to heal, and that signs and wonders may be done through the name of Your holy Servant Jesus."

31And when they had prayed, the place where they were assembled together was shaken; and they were all filled with the Holy Spirit, and they spoke the word of God with boldness.

Sharing in All Things

32Now the multitude of those who believed were of one heart and one soul; neither did anyone say that any of the things he possessed was his own, but they had all things in common. 33And with great power the apostles gave witness to the resurrection of the Lord Jesus. And great grace was upon them all. 34Nor was there anyone among them who lacked; for all who were possessors of lands or houses sold them, and brought the proceeds of the things that were sold, 35and laid *them* at the apostles' feet; and they distributed to each as anyone had need.

36And Joses,[a] who was also named Barnabas by the apostles (which is translated Son of Encouragement), a Levite of the country of Cyprus, 37having land, sold *it,* and brought the money and laid *it* at the apostles' feet.

Lying to the Holy Spirit

5 1But a certain man named Ananias, with Sapphira his wife, sold a possession. 2And he kept back *part* of the proceeds, his wife also being aware *of it,* and brought a certain part and laid *it* at the apostles' feet. 3But Peter said, "Ananias,

why has Satan filled your heart to lie to the Holy Spirit and keep back *part* of the price of the land for yourself? 4While it remained, was it not your own? And after it was sold, was it not in your own control? Why have you conceived this thing in your heart? You have not lied to men but to God."

5Then Ananias, hearing these words, fell down and breathed his last. So great fear came upon all those who heard these things. 6And the young men arose and wrapped him up, carried *him* out, and buried *him.*

7Now it was about three hours later when his wife came in, not knowing what had happened. 8And Peter answered her, "Tell me whether you sold the land for so much?"

She said, "Yes, for so much."

9Then Peter said to her, "How is it that you have agreed together to test the Spirit of the Lord? Look, the feet of those who have buried your husband *are* at the door, and they will carry you out." 10Then immediately she fell down at his feet and breathed her last. And the young men came in and found her dead, and carrying *her* out, buried *her* by her husband. 11So great fear came upon all the church and upon all who heard these things.

Continuing Power in the Church

12And through the hands of the apostles many signs and wonders were done among the people. And they were all with one accord in Solomon's Porch. 13Yet none of the rest dared join them, but the people esteemed them highly. 14And believers were increasingly added to the Lord, multitudes of both men and women, 15so that they brought the sick out into the streets and laid *them* on beds and couches, that at least the shadow of Peter passing by might fall on some of them. 16Also a multitude gathered from the surrounding cities to Jerusalem, bringing sick people and those who were tormented by unclean spirits, and they were all healed.

Imprisoned Apostles Freed

17Then the high priest rose up, and all those who *were* with him (which is the sect of the Sadducees), and they were filled with indignation, 18and laid their hands on the apostles and put them in the common prison. 19But at night an angel of the Lord opened the prison doors and brought them

---

4:26 [a]Psalm 2:1, 2　　4:36 [a]NU-Text reads Joseph.

FOOD FOR THE HELLENIST WIDOWS (Acts 6:1)

Tensions developed in the Jerusalem church over alleged discrimination on the basis of language and culture. Scholars differ in their descriptions of the two opposing groups: the "Hebrews" and the "Hellenists." The Hebrews are often described as Aramaic-speaking Jews native to Palestine. The Hellenists were possibly Greek-speaking Jews from outside of Palestine. Most Jews in Jerusalem, however, would have spoken Greek as at least one language, so more likely the Hellenists were Diaspora (foreign) Jews, or their children, who had settled in Jerusalem. Some of these foreign Jews probably had come from places such as Cyrene, Alexandria, Cilicia, or Asia (Acts 6:9).

Widows were a disadvantaged segment of ancient society, invariably poor and easily oppressed. Jewish people traditionally cared for the widows and other poor through the charity collections of local synagogues. The Hellenist synagogues, however, probably had more widows to care for than other synagogues, hence were stretched to the limit in their capacity to help. Since it was considered pious to spend one's last days in Jerusalem, many foreign Jewish men moved to Jerusalem when they retired, eventually leaving an inordinate number of foreign Jewish widows needing support.

This broader societal problem spilled over into the church: how would they care for the foreign Jewish widows among them? And how could they be sure to keep this minority group within the church from feeling second-class? Most people in antiquity simply told offended minorities to be quiet, but the apostles had a different solution: they selected members of the Hellenist minority to run the food distribution program. All seven of those selected have Greek names (6:5), suggesting that all or most were foreign Jews. These seven Hellenists were commissioned for the office of charity distributor, a highly respected position in Jerusalem (6:6).

out, and said, 20"Go, stand in the temple and speak to the people all the words of this life."

21And when they heard *that,* they entered the temple early in the morning and taught. But the high priest and those with him came and called the council together, with all the elders of the children of Israel, and sent to the prison to have them brought.

Apostles on Trial Again

22But when the officers came and did not find them in the prison, they returned and reported, 23saying, "Indeed we found the prison shut securely, and the guards standing outside[a] before the doors; but when we opened them, we found no one inside!" 24Now when the high priest,[a] the captain of the temple, and the chief priests heard these things, they wondered what the outcome would be. 25So one came and told them, saying,[a] "Look, the men whom you put in prison are standing in the temple and teaching the people!"

26Then the captain went with the officers and brought them without violence, for they feared the people, lest they should be stoned. 27And when they had brought them, they set *them* before the council. And the high priest asked them, 28saying, "Did we not strictly command you not to teach in this name? And look, you have filled Jerusalem with your doctrine, and intend to bring this Man's blood on us!"

5:23 [a]NU-Text and M-Text omit *outside.*
5:24 [a]NU-Text omits *the high priest.*
5:25 [a]NU-Text and M-Text omit *saying.*

BELIEFS AND IDEAS

Peter and the apostles boldly proclaimed the principle that even supreme human authorities, like the high priest and the council, must yield to the law of God (Acts 5:27–29). A similar principle provides the theme of the Greek tragedy Antigone. There Antigone says that no human being can overrule the unwritten, unchangeable laws of heaven.

²⁹But Peter and the *other* apostles answered and said: "We ought to obey God rather than men. ³⁰The God of our fathers raised up Jesus whom you murdered by hanging on a tree. ³¹Him God has exalted to His right hand *to be* Prince and Savior, to give repentance to Israel and forgiveness of sins. ³²And we are His witnesses to these things, and *so* also *is* the Holy Spirit whom God has given to those who obey Him."

Gamaliel's Advice

³³When they heard *this,* they were furious and plotted to kill them. ³⁴Then one in the council stood up, a Pharisee named Gamaliel, a teacher of the law held in respect by all the people, and commanded them to put the apostles outside for a little while. ³⁵And he said to them: "Men of Israel, take heed to yourselves what you intend to do regarding these men. ³⁶For some time ago Theudas rose up, claiming to be somebody. A number of men, about four hundred, joined him. He was slain, and all who obeyed him were scattered and came to nothing. ³⁷After this man, Judas of Galilee rose up in the days of the census, and drew away many people after him. He also perished, and all who obeyed him were dispersed. ³⁸And now I say to you, keep away from these men and let them alone; for if this plan or this work is of men, it will come to nothing; ³⁹but if it is of God, you cannot overthrow it—lest you even be found to fight against God."

⁴⁰And they agreed with him, and when they had called for the apostles and beaten *them,* they commanded that they should not speak in the name of Jesus, and let them go. ⁴¹So they departed from the presence of the council, rejoicing that they were counted worthy to suffer shame for His^a name. ⁴²And daily in the temple, and in every house, they did not cease teaching and preaching Jesus *as* the Christ.

5:41 ^aNU-Text reads *the name;* M-Text reads *the name of Jesus.*   6:1 ^aThat is, Greek-speaking Jews

---

Stephen, the First Martyr

The church grew so rapidly that the disciples had to appoint men to distribute goods. With the choice of seven deacons from among the Greek-speaking Jews (Acts 6:1–7), the gospel began to reach beyond Palestinian Judaism. One of the deacons, Stephen, directly challenged the central role of the temple

and the law, bringing him into conflict with the Synagogue of the Freedmen (6:9–14).

The synagogue was a local assembly of Jews who met for prayer and scripture exposition. In cities throughout the Roman world, synagogues became the focal point of Jewish life. The Synagogue of the Freedmen included Greek-speaking (Hellenist) Jews whose ancestors had been slaves of the Romans, later set free. Thus Stephen, a Hellenist himself, was accused of blasphemy by those of his own cultural group.

Stephen was ultimately brought before the Sanhedrin ("the council," 6:12), which consisted of religious leaders from the various Jewish sects in Jerusalem. There he spoke on a theme that was not well received by his audience: Israel's rejection of God's leaders had now climaxed in the Jewish authorities' rejection of Jesus. Further, he used the history of Israel to show that God does not dwell in the temple (7:44–50). Stephen's execution sometime around A.D. 32 marked the beginning of "a great persecution" against the early Christians (7:57—8:3). A young Pharisee named Saul, who served as custodian for Stephen's executioners (7:58), would lead that persecution.

▪ Acts 6:1—8:3

Acts
Seven Chosen to Serve

6 :1 Now in those days, when *the number of* the disciples was multiplying, there arose a complaint against the Hebrews by the Hellenists,^a because their widows were neglected in the daily distribution. ²Then the twelve summoned the multitude of the disciples and said, "It is not desirable that we should leave the word of God and serve tables. ³Therefore, brethren, seek out from among you seven men of *good* reputation, full of the Holy Spirit and wisdom, whom we may appoint over this business; ⁴but we will give ourselves continually to prayer and to the ministry of the word."

⁵And the saying pleased the whole multitude. And they chose Stephen, a man full of faith and the Holy Spirit, and Philip, Prochorus, Nicanor, Timon, Parmenas, and Nicolas, a proselyte from Antioch, ⁶whom they set before the apostles; and when they had prayed, they laid hands on them.

⁷Then the word of God spread, and the number of the disciples multiplied greatly in Jerusalem, and a great many of the priests were obedient to the faith.

JEWS OF CYRENE VISIT JERUSALEM (Acts 6:9)

Cyrene was a major city in North Africa founded by the Greeks in the 7th century B.C. It became a flourishing city, blessed with a fertile surrounding countryside. Specific individuals from Cyrene appear in Scripture. One Cyrenian named Simon was forced by the Romans to carry the cross of Jesus (Luke 23:26). Another, Lucius, was a principal teacher of the Christians at the church in Antioch (Acts 13:1).

Like Crete, Cyrene had a large Jewish population that was settled there by the Ptolemaic kings of Egypt, beginning with Ptolemy I in the 4th century B.C. This population was apparently still substantial during the New Testament period, and traveled from Cyrene to Jerusalem. Cyrenians are named among the Jews who were in Jerusalem for the Day of Pentecost (Acts 2:1, 5, 10). They are also among the Jews who attended the Synagogue of the Freedmen in Jerusalem (Acts 6:9).

What exactly the Synagogue of the Freedmen was is not certain. The name "Freedmen" indicates the worshipers were either Jews that had been freed from slavery, or were Jews descended from slaves. The groups named in Acts 6:9 (Cyrenians, Alexandrians, Cilicians, Asians) could have attended one synagogue, or each group could have had their own synagogue in Jerusalem.

Cities with large Jewish populations often had several synagogues, and certainly Jerusalem did. A Synagogue of the Alexandrians in Jerusalem is known to have belonged to a Rabbi Zadok around A.D. 100. An inscription found just south of Jerusalem reports that someone named Theodotus built a synagogue complete with a guesthouse for those "coming from abroad." We do not know that Jews of Cyrene actually stayed in this guesthouse, but Cyrenians were among those who came "from abroad" to visit Jerusalem, and may have been populous enough to have their own synagogue.

Stephen Accused of Blasphemy

8And Stephen, full of faith[a] and power, did great wonders and signs among the people. 9Then there arose some from what is called the Synagogue of the Freedmen (Cyrenians, Alexandrians, and those from Cilicia and Asia), disputing with Stephen. 10And they were not able to resist the wisdom and the Spirit by which he spoke. 11Then they secretly induced men to say, "We have heard him speak blasphemous words against Moses and God." 12And they stirred up the people, the elders, and the scribes; and they came upon *him,* seized him, and brought *him* to the council. 13They also set up false witnesses who said, "This man does not cease to speak blasphemous[a] words against this holy place and the law; 14for we have heard him say that this Jesus of Nazareth will destroy this place and change the customs which Moses delivered to us." 15And all who sat in the council, looking steadfastly at him, saw his face as the face of an angel.

Stephen's Address: The Call of Abraham

7 1Then the high priest said, "Are these things so?"

2And he said, "Brethren and fathers, listen: The God of glory appeared to our father Abraham when he was in Mesopotamia, before he dwelt in Haran, 3and said to him, 'Get out of your country and from your relatives, and come to a land that I will show you.'[a] 4Then he came out of the land of the Chaldeans and dwelt in

TIME CAPSULE A.D. 35 to 36

35 The Roman army crosses the Euphrates River

35 Saul preaches Christ in Damascus (Acts 9:20)

35 Peter restores Dorcas to life

35 Peter meets the centurion Cornelius (Acts 10:25)

36 Agrippa I meets Emperor Tiberius on the island of Capri

6:8 [a]NU-Text reads *grace.*   6:13 [a]NU-Text omits *blasphemous.*   7:3 [a]Genesis 12:1

Haran. And from there, when his father was dead, He moved him to this land in which you now dwell. [5]And *God* gave him no inheritance in it, not even *enough* to set his foot on. But even when *Abraham* had no child, He promised to give it to him for a possession, and to his descendants after him. [6]But God spoke in this way: that his descendants would dwell in a foreign land, and that they would bring them into bondage and oppress *them* four hundred years. [7]*'And the nation to whom they will be in bondage I will judge,'* [a] said God, *'and after that they shall come out and serve Me in this place.'* [b] [8]Then He gave him the covenant of circumcision; and so *Abraham* begot Isaac and circumcised him on the eighth day; and Isaac *begot* Jacob, and Jacob *begot* the twelve patriarchs.

The Patriarchs in Egypt

[9]"And the patriarchs, becoming envious, sold Joseph into Egypt. But God was with him [10]and delivered him out of all his troubles, and gave him favor and wisdom in the presence of Pharaoh, king of Egypt; and he made him governor over Egypt and all his house. [11]Now a famine and great trouble came over all the land of Egypt and Canaan, and our fathers found no sustenance. [12]But when Jacob heard that there was grain in Egypt, he sent out our fathers first. [13]And the second *time* Joseph was made known to his brothers, and Joseph's family became known to the Pharaoh. [14]Then Joseph sent and called his father Jacob and all his relatives to *him,* seventy-five[a] people. [15]So Jacob went down to Egypt; and he died, he and our fathers. [16]And they were carried back to Shechem and laid in the tomb that Abraham bought for a sum of money from the sons of Hamor, *the father* of Shechem.

God Delivers Israel by Moses

[17]"But when the time of the promise drew near which God had sworn to Abraham, the people grew and multiplied in Egypt [18]till another king arose who did not know Joseph. [19]This man dealt treacherously with our people, and oppressed our forefathers, making them expose their babies, so that they might not live. [20]At this time Moses was born, and was well pleasing to God; and he was brought up in his father's house for three months. [21]But when he was set out, Pharaoh's daughter took him away and brought him up as her own son. [22]And Moses was learned in all the wisdom of the Egyptians, and was mighty in words and deeds.

[23]"Now when he was forty years old, it came into his heart to visit his brethren, the children of Israel. [24]And seeing one of *them* suffer wrong, he defended and avenged him who was oppressed, and struck down the Egyptian. [25]For he supposed that his brethren would have understood that God would deliver them by his hand, but they did not understand. [26]And the next day he appeared to two of them as they were fighting, and *tried to* reconcile them, saying, 'Men, you are brethren; why do you wrong one another?' [27]But he who did his neighbor wrong pushed him away, saying, *'Who made you a ruler and a judge over us? [28]Do you want to kill me as you did the Egyptian yesterday?'* [a] [29]Then, at this saying, Moses fled and became a dweller in the land of Midian, where he had two sons.

[30]"And when forty years had passed, an Angel of the Lord[a] appeared to him in a flame of fire in a bush, in the wilderness of Mount Sinai. [31]When Moses saw *it,* he marveled at the sight; and as he drew near to observe, the voice of the Lord came to him, [32]*saying, 'I am the God of your fathers—the God of Abraham, the God of Isaac, and the God of Jacob.'* [a] And Moses trembled and dared not look. [33]*Then the* LORD *said to him, "Take your sandals off your feet, for the place where you stand is holy ground. [34]I have surely seen the oppression of My people who are in Egypt; I have heard their groaning and have come down to deliver them. And now come, I will send you to Egypt." '* [a]

[35]"This Moses whom they rejected, saying, *'Who made you a ruler and a judge?'* [a] is the one God sent *to be* a ruler and a deliverer by the hand of the Angel who appeared to him in the bush. [36]He brought them out, after he had shown wonders and signs in the land of Egypt, and in the Red Sea, and in the wilderness forty years.

7:7 [a]Genesis 15:14   [b]Exodus 3:12   7:14 [a]Or *seventy* (compare Exodus 1:5)   7:28 [a]Exodus 2:14   7:30 [a]NU-Text omits *of the Lord.* 7:32 [a]Exodus 3:6, 15   7:34 [a]Exodus 3:5, 7, 8, 10   7:35 [a]Exodus 2:14

Israel Rebels Against God

37"This is that Moses who said to the children of Israel,[a] 'The LORD your God will raise up for you a Prophet like me from your brethren. Him you shall hear.'[b]

38"This is he who was in the congregation in the wilderness with the Angel who spoke to him on Mount Sinai, and with our fathers, the one who received the living oracles to give to us, 39whom our fathers would not obey, but rejected. And in their hearts they turned back to Egypt, 40saying to Aaron, 'Make us gods to go before us; as for this Moses who brought us out of the land of Egypt, we do not know what has become of him.'[a] 41And they made a calf in those days, offered sacrifices to the idol, and rejoiced in the works of their own hands. 42Then God turned and gave them up to worship the host of heaven, as it is written in the book of the Prophets:

> 'Did you offer Me slaughtered animals
>   and sacrifices during forty years in
>   the wilderness,
>   O house of Israel?
> 43 You also took up the tabernacle of
>   Moloch,
>   And the star of your god Remphan,
>   Images which you made to worship;
>   And I will carry you away beyond
>   Babylon.'[a]

God's True Tabernacle

44"Our fathers had the tabernacle of witness in the wilderness, as He appointed, instructing Moses to make it according to the pattern that he had seen, 45which our fathers, having received it in turn, also brought with Joshua into the land possessed by the Gentiles, whom God drove out before the face of our fathers until the days of David, 46who found favor before God and asked to find a dwelling for the God of Jacob. 47But Solomon built Him a house.

48"However, the Most High does not dwell in temples made with hands, as the prophet says:

> 49 'Heaven is My throne,
>   And earth is My footstool.
>   What house will you build for Me?
>   says the LORD,
>   Or what is the place of My rest?

> 50 Has My hand not made all these
>   things?'[a]

Israel Resists the Holy Spirit

51"You stiff-necked and uncircumcised in heart and ears! You always resist the Holy Spirit; as your fathers did, so do you. 52Which of the prophets did your fathers not persecute? And they killed those who foretold the coming of the Just One, of whom you now have become the betrayers and murderers, 53who have received the law by the direction of angels and have not kept it."

Stephen the Martyr

54When they heard these things they were cut to the heart, and they gnashed at him with their teeth. 55But he, being full of the Holy Spirit, gazed into heaven and saw the glory of God, and Jesus standing at the right hand of God, 56and said, "Look! I see the heavens opened and the Son of Man standing at the right hand of God!"

57Then they cried out with a loud voice, stopped their ears, and ran at him with one accord; 58and they cast him out of the city and stoned him. And the witnesses laid down their clothes at the feet of a young man named Saul. 59And they stoned Stephen as he was calling on God and saying, "Lord Jesus, receive my spirit." 60Then he knelt down and cried out with a loud voice, "Lord, do not charge them with this sin." And when he had said this, he fell asleep.

Saul Persecutes the Church

8 ¹Now Saul was consenting to his death. At that time a great persecution arose against the church which was at Jerusalem; and they were all scattered throughout the regions of Judea and Samaria, except the apostles. 2And devout men carried Stephen to his burial, and made great lamentation over him.

3As for Saul, he made havoc of the church, entering every house, and dragging off men and women, committing them to prison.

7:37 [a]Deuteronomy 18:15   [b]NU-Text and M-Text omit Him you shall hear.   7:40 [a]Exodus 32:1, 23   7:43 [a]Amos 5:25–27   7:50 [a]Isaiah 66:1, 2

The Gospel to the Gentiles

Soon the gospel was taken to the Samaritans and to the "God-fearers."

Following Jesus' ascension in rapid succession was Pentecost and the birth of the church, as distinct from a mere Jewish sect. Thousands of Jews became believers. This new church met in the temple courts and the Jewish synagogues, as well as in private homes of believers (Acts 5:42). Yet the Good News would not be contained in Jerusalem; soon it was taken to the Samaritans and to the "God-fearers" in Caesarea and Antioch (10:2; 11:19, 20).

God Himself made it clear that Gentiles should be included in His church. Philip was sent and directed by an angel (8:26) and by the Spirit (8:29) to the desert region near Gaza where he made the first Gentile convert, a court official who served Candace, the queen of the Ethiopians. An angel also directed the Roman officer Cornelius to send for Peter (10:3, 5). By a vision (10:9–16) and by the Spirit (10:19) Peter was instructed to go.

As Peter preached on Jesus' resurrection, the Holy Spirit fell upon the Gentiles. This miracle of divine grace was God's gift to the Gentile believers and His answer to those who questioned sharing the gospel with non-Jews. Eventually, the Jerusalem church acknowledged acceptance of Gentiles (11:18), and Antioch became a center of the Gentile church (11:26). Nevertheless, the first non-Jews to be evangelized by the early church were the Samaritans.

Philip and the Samaritan Pentecost

Philip "preached Christ" to the Samaritans (Acts 8:5) in fulfillment of his Master's mandate (Acts 1:8). Their reception of Philip's message about the kingdom of God and about Jesus Christ was a significant step in the spread of the gospel. Samaritans, who were considered heretics by orthodox Jews, had received Christ. Perhaps the Samaritans accepted the gospel more readily than Jews because they did not have to unlearn previous misconceptions about the coming Messiah.

Though the Samaritans were baptized with water in the name of Jesus, they still needed to receive the baptism with the Holy Spirit, as had the disciples on the Day of Pentecost. So the Jerusalem church sent Peter and John in order that these new believers might hear the message about the Holy Spirit (8:15). As the apostles continued to preach in many villages of Samaria, Samaritans became an accepted part of the church (8:25).

▼ ■ Acts 8:4–40

Acts
Christ Is Preached in Samaria

8 **:4** Therefore those who were scattered went everywhere preaching the word. 5Then Philip went down to thea city of Sa-

maria and preached Christ to them. 6And the multitudes with one accord heeded the things spoken by Philip, hearing and seeing the miracles which he did. 7For unclean spirits, crying with a loud voice, came out of many who were possessed; and many who were paralyzed and lame were healed. 8And there was great joy in that city.

The Sorcerer's Profession of Faith

9But there was a certain man called Simon, who previously practiced sorcery in the city and astonished the people of Samaria, claiming that he was someone great, 10to whom they all gave heed, from the least to the greatest, saying, "This man is the great power of God." 11And they heeded him because he had astonished them with his sorceries for a long time. 12But when they believed Philip as he preached the things concerning the kingdom of God and the name of Jesus Christ, both men and women were baptized. 13Then Simon himself also believed; and when he was baptized he continued with Philip, and was amazed, seeing the miracles and signs which were done.

The Sorcerer's Sin

14Now when the apostles who were at Jerusalem heard that Samaria had received the word of God, they sent Peter and John to them, 15who, when they had come

SIMON MAGUS, THE GREAT POWER (Acts 8:9–11)

In the city of Samaria was one Samaritan who considered himself "someone great" (Acts 8:9). The wonder-worker Simon is even reported to have been called "the great power of God" by the people of Samaria (8:10). Simon is well known outside of Scripture. According to early Christian sources, he was from Gitta, a Samaritan village. Later Christian sources describe him as a *Magus,* or magician, and suggest that he used his abilities for propagandistic purposes.

Later writers disagreed with Simon's title "great power of God." Justin Martyr, in the 2nd century A.D., claimed that Simon used demonic forces to imitate Christianity, reporting that he performed wonders by demons in Rome during the reign of Claudius (A.D. 41–54). Justin claims that Simon had a large following.

Simon's teachings were labeled heretical. Irenaeus, in the late 2nd century A.D., stated that Simon was the source of all heresies, even identifying himself with the Christian Trinity. He was usually associated by the early church with some of the Gnostic heresies. Hippolytus wrote in the early 3rd century A.D. of Simon's claim that he would be raised on the third day after his death. The resurrection claims were not fulfilled, since, as Hippolytus explains, Simon was "not the Christ."

Other Christian literature portrayed Simon as a fake and an antichrist, and even as a disciple of John the Baptist! In sum, Simon was a Samaritan who practiced elements of syncretism—mixing Christian and non-Christian elements. In Acts, Luke reports Peter's rebuke of Simon (Acts 8:20–23). The magician was later condemned by the church, which likely embellished tales about him, seeing him as a model of the anti-Christ.

down, prayed for them that they might receive the Holy Spirit. ¹⁶For as yet He had fallen upon none of them. They had only been baptized in the name of the Lord Jesus. ¹⁷Then they laid hands on them, and they received the Holy Spirit.

¹⁸And when Simon saw that through the laying on of the apostles' hands the Holy Spirit was given, he offered them money, ¹⁹saying, "Give me this power also, that anyone on whom I lay hands may receive the Holy Spirit."

²⁰But Peter said to him, "Your money perish with you, because you thought that the gift of God could be purchased with money! ²¹You have neither part nor portion in this matter, for your heart is not right in the sight of God. ²²Repent therefore of this your wickedness, and pray God if perhaps the thought of your heart may be forgiven you. ²³For I see that you are poisoned by bitterness and bound by iniquity."

²⁴Then Simon answered and said, "Pray to the Lord for me, that none of the things which you have spoken may come upon me."

²⁵So when they had testified and preached the word of the Lord, they returned to Jerusalem, preaching the gospel in many villages of the Samaritans.

Christ Is Preached to an Ethiopian

²⁶Now an angel of the Lord spoke to Philip, saying, "Arise and go toward the south along the road which goes down from Jerusalem to Gaza." This is desert. ²⁷So he arose and went. And behold, a man of Ethiopia, a eunuch of great authority under Candace the queen of the Ethiopians, who had charge of all her treasury, and had come to Jerusalem to worship, ²⁸was re-

CULTURE AND SOCIETY

The word "eunuch" referred literally to castrated males. In Judea, eunuchs were viewed as impaired persons (Deut. 23:1), and Jewish people opposed their appointment to important positions. In other nations, though, eunuchs were considered safe to hire as attendants or custodians of women, and many were servants to royalty (Acts 8:27). The historian Josephus reports that a eunuch served as cupbearer for Herod the Great.

CANDACE'S EUNUCH BELIEVES (Acts 8:27)

Luke gives us much information about the person that Philip evangelized and eventually baptized. The man was from Ethiopia, was a eunuch, served a queen as her treasurer, and had gone to worship in Jerusalem (Acts 8:27). This new convert's background makes his conversion to Christianity significant.

Ethiopia was an area south of Egypt. Because Ethiopia and Egypt were so close geographically, they are often mentioned together in Scripture (see Ps. 68:31; Ezek. 30:4; Nah. 3:9). But Ethiopia is not close to Jerusalem, so Candace's eunuch had traveled from a distant location. Being from Ethiopia may have given him some prominence. The Greek historian Herodotus (484?–425? B.C.) described Ethiopians as taller and more handsome than any people.

The eunuch served "under Candace." Candace is not a personal name, but a title, like pharaoh. As the pharaoh was king of Egypt, so the candace was queen of Meroe, a kingdom on the Nile River south of Egypt. From Acts 8:27 it appears that "Candace" could be used as a name for Meroe's queens just as "Pharaoh" was used as a name for Egypt's kings. The eunuch worked for someone of high authority.

His position added to his status since as the queen's treasurer he exercised "great authority." It was common in Eastern countries for eunuchs to hold positions of high authority in a queen's court. This eunuch was an important person.

Nevertheless, he was a eunuch, and eunuchs were excluded from religious service in Israel (Deut. 23:1). The law prohibited them from serving as priests, who were required to have a whole body, free from blemishes (Lev. 21:17–20). The eunuch could worship in Jerusalem and read the sacred Scriptures (Acts 8:28), but could not be a full member of the Jewish religion.

This eunuch represents a significant conversion to Christianity. With him, the Christian faith reached out to a distant land, to someone in the service of a queen, to someone who himself had high position. More importantly, it reached out to one who previously was an "outsider" to Israel's religion.

---

turning. And sitting in his chariot, he was reading Isaiah the prophet. 29Then the Spirit said to Philip, "Go near and overtake this chariot."

30So Philip ran to him, and heard him reading the prophet Isaiah, and said, "Do you understand what you are reading?"

31And he said, "How can I, unless someone guides me?" And he asked Philip to come up and sit with him. 32The place in the Scripture which he read was this:

"He was led as a sheep to the
    slaughter;
And as a lamb before its shearer is
    silent,
So He opened not His mouth.
33   In His humiliation His justice was
    taken away,

*And who will declare His generation?
For His life is taken from the earth."*[a]

34So the eunuch answered Philip and said, "I ask you, of whom does the prophet say this, of himself or of some other man?" 35Then Philip opened his mouth, and beginning at this Scripture, preached Jesus to him. 36Now as they went down the road, they came to some water. And the eunuch said, "See, *here is* water. What hinders me from being baptized?"

37Then Philip said, "If you believe with all your heart, you may."

And he answered and said, "I believe that Jesus Christ is the Son of God."[a]

38So he commanded the chariot to stand still. And both Philip and the eunuch went down into the water, and he baptized him. 39Now when they came up out of the water, the Spirit of the Lord caught Philip away, so that the eunuch saw him no more; and he went on his way rejoicing. 40But

---

8:33 [a]Isaiah 53:7, 8   8:37 [a]NU-Text and M-Text omit this verse. It is found in Western texts, including the Latin tradition.

Philip was found at Azotus. And passing through, he preached in all the cities till he came to Caesarea.

Spreading Beyond Judea and Samaria

Christians continued to disperse from Jerusalem and the surrounding regions, eventually reaching Damascus in Syria. Because of extradition permits authorized by Rome, letters from the high priest gave Saul jurisdiction over Jews in Damascus. On the way there, however, Saul met the risen Jesus (Acts 9:5). Through this dramatic encounter, Saul, the zealous Pharisee who led and intensified the persecution against the disciples, became God's "chosen vessel" (9:15) to bear Christ's name before the Gentiles.

The new Christian Saul confounded the Jews by his training, experience, and boldness. But the persecutor became the persecuted, and Saul was forced to flee Damascus. He finally arrived in Jerusalem in A.D. 37. Despite his 3-year absence visiting Arabia and reports of his ministry in Damascus, the disciples in Jerusalem could not believe Saul had become a Christian (9:26). Some miracles seem incredible.

The period following Saul's conversion was one of relative calm for the church. Peter began to evangelize outside of Jerusalem, healing the sick and raising the dead in the power of Jesus, as Jesus Himself had done. These miracles led to a widespread acceptance of the gospel (9:35, 42).

▼   ■ Acts 9:1–43

Acts
The Damascus Road: Saul Converted

9 :1 Then Saul, still breathing threats and murder against the disciples of the Lord, went to the high priest ²and asked letters from him to the synagogues of Damascus, so that if he found any who were of the Way, whether men or women, he might bring them bound to Jerusalem.

³As he journeyed he came near Damascus, and suddenly a light shone around him from heaven. ⁴Then he fell to the ground, and heard a voice saying to him, "Saul, Saul, why are you persecuting Me?"

⁵And he said, "Who are You, Lord?"

Then the Lord said, "I am Jesus, whom you are persecuting.ᵃ It *is* hard for you to kick against the goads."

⁶So he, trembling and astonished, said, "Lord, what do You want me to do?"

Then the Lord *said* to him, "Arise and go into the city, and you will be told what you must do."

⁷And the men who journeyed with him stood speechless, hearing a voice but seeing no one. ⁸Then Saul arose from the ground, and when his eyes were opened he saw no one. But they led him by the hand and brought *him* into Damascus. ⁹And he was three days without sight, and neither ate nor drank.

Ananias Baptizes Saul

¹⁰Now there was a certain disciple at Damascus named Ananias; and to him the Lord said in a vision, "Ananias."

And he said, "Here I am, Lord."

¹¹So the Lord *said* to him, "Arise and go to the street called Straight, and inquire at the house of Judas for *one* called Saul of Tarsus, for behold, he is praying. ¹²And in a vision he has seen a man named Ananias coming in and putting *his* hand on him, so that he might receive his sight."

¹³Then Ananias answered, "Lord, I have heard from many about this man, how much harm he has done to Your saints in Jerusalem. ¹⁴And here he has authority from the chief priests to bind all who call on Your name."

¹⁵But the Lord said to him, "Go, for he is a chosen vessel of Mine to bear My name before Gentiles, kings, and the children of Israel. ¹⁶For I will show him how many things he must suffer for My name's sake."

¹⁷And Ananias went his way and en-

9:5 ᵃNU-Text and M-Text omit the last sentence of verse 5 and begin verse 6 with *But arise and go.*

TIME CAPSULE   A.D. 36 to 37

36	*Pontius Pilate recalled to Rome for misconduct*
36	*Caiaphas is deposed from the high priesthood*
37–41	*Caligula is emperor of Rome*
37–44	*Herod Agrippa I*
37–100	*Life of Jewish historian Josephus*
37	*In Rome a temple is dedicated to "the Divine Augustus"*

tered the house; and laying his hands on him he said, "Brother Saul, the Lord Jesus,[a] who appeared to you on the road as you came, has sent me that you may receive your sight and be filled with the Holy Spirit." 18Immediately there fell from his eyes *something* like scales, and he received his sight at once; and he arose and was baptized.

19So when he had received food, he was strengthened. Then Saul spent some days with the disciples at Damascus.

Saul Preaches Christ

20Immediately he preached the Christ[a] in the synagogues, that He is the Son of God.

21Then all who heard were amazed, and said, "Is this not he who destroyed those who called on this name in Jerusalem, and has come here for that purpose, so that he might bring them bound to the chief priests?"

22But Saul increased all the more in strength, and confounded the Jews who dwelt in Damascus, proving that this *Jesus* is the Christ.

Saul Escapes Death

23Now after many days were past, the Jews plotted to kill him. 24But their plot became known to Saul. And they watched the gates day and night, to kill him. 25Then the disciples took him by night and let *him* down through the wall in a large basket.

Saul at Jerusalem

26And when Saul had come to Jerusalem, he tried to join the disciples; but they were all afraid of him, and did not believe that he was a disciple. 27But Barnabas took him and brought *him* to the apostles. And he declared to them how he had seen the Lord on the road, and that He had spoken to him, and how he had preached boldly at

Damascus in the name of Jesus. 28So he was with them at Jerusalem, coming in and going out. 29And he spoke boldly in the name of the Lord Jesus and disputed against the Hellenists, but they attempted to kill him. 30When the brethren found out, they brought him down to Caesarea and sent him out to Tarsus.

The Church Prospers

31Then the churches[a] throughout all Judea, Galilee, and Samaria had peace and were edified. And walking in the fear of the Lord and in the comfort of the Holy Spirit, they were multiplied.

Aeneas Healed

32Now it came to pass, as Peter went through all *parts of the country,* that he also came down to the saints who dwelt in Lydda. 33There he found a certain man named Aeneas, who had been bedridden eight years and was paralyzed. 34And Peter said to him, "Aeneas, Jesus the Christ heals you. Arise and make your bed." Then he arose immediately. 35So all who dwelt at Lydda and Sharon saw him and turned to the Lord.

Dorcas Restored to Life

36At Joppa there was a certain disciple named Tabitha, which is translated Dorcas. This woman was full of good works and charitable deeds which she did. 37But it happened in those days that she became sick and died. When they had washed her, they laid *her* in an upper room. 38And since Lydda was near Joppa, and the disciples had heard that Peter was there, they sent two men to him, imploring *him* not to delay in coming to them. 39Then Peter arose and went with them. When he had come, they brought *him* to the upper room. And all the widows stood by him weeping, showing the tunics and garments which Dorcas had made while she was with them. 40But Peter put them all out, and knelt down and prayed. And turning to the body he said, "Tabitha, arise." And she opened her eyes,

---

9:17 [a]M-Text omits *Jesus.*   9:20 [a]NU-Text reads *Jesus.*   9:31 [a]NU-Text reads *church . . . was edified.*

SCIENCE AND TECHNOLOGY

Tanning (Acts 9:43) is the process of treating animal skin to make it into leather.
Organic and inorganic chemicals are used to prevent decomposition and to make the
leather flexible, strong, and attractive. Hard leather was used for shields and containers;
soft leather was used for clothing and shoes. Parchment was a smooth, thin leather
that was prepared for writing.

and when she saw Peter she sat up. ⁴¹Then he gave her *his* hand and lifted her up; and when he had called the saints and widows, he presented her alive. ⁴²And it became known throughout all Joppa, and many believed on the Lord. ⁴³So it was that he stayed many days in Joppa with Simon, a tanner.

Peter's Missionary Work

The Book of Acts records two missionary journeys made by Peter. On his first trip he confirmed the evangelistic work of Philip in Samaria (Acts 8:14). Peter subsequently made a trip along the Mediterranean coast from Joppa to Caesarea, where a Roman garrison was commanded by the officer Cornelius. Peter's ministry to the Gentile household of Cornelius was accepted by the Jerusalem church only when Peter convinced them that the Gentiles had become believers in the same sense as Jesus' followers, who were filled with the Holy Spirit on the Day of Pentecost (11:1–18).

The church continued to grow as a result of persecution, for the scattered Christians shared their faith in their new home cities (11:19). Meanwhile, in Jerusalem, opposition to the church continued to mount: Herod Agrippa I, whom the emperor Caligula had given the title "king," had James executed and arrested Peter. Agrippa died in A.D. 44 of abdominal pains, according to Josephus (12:23).

The first church to include Gentile Christians was the church at Antioch. More innovative than the Jerusalem church, Antioch became the center of missionary outreach to Gentiles, yet still maintained close ties with Jerusalem. Josephus and other historians record the famine that occurred in A.D. 46 or 47, during the reign of Claudius Caesar (A.D. 41–54). Christians at Antioch sent to Judea by way of Barnabas and Saul their collection for famine relief (11:27–30).

■ Acts 10:1—12:25

Acts
Cornelius Sends a Delegation

10 :1 There was a certain man in Caesarea called Cornelius, a centurion of what was called the Italian Regiment, ²a devout *man* and one who feared God with all his household, who gave alms generously to the people, and prayed to God always. ³About the ninth hour of the day he saw clearly in a vision an angel of God coming in and saying to him, "Cornelius!"

⁴And when he observed him, he was afraid, and said, "What is it, lord?"

So he said to him, "Your prayers and your alms have come up for a memorial before God. ⁵Now send men to Joppa, and send for Simon whose surname is Peter. ⁶He is lodging with Simon, a tanner, whose house is by the sea.ᵃ He will tell you what you must do." ⁷And when the angel who spoke to him had departed, Cornelius called two of his household servants and a devout soldier from among those who waited on him continually. ⁸So when he had explained all *these* things to them, he sent them to Joppa.

Peter's Vision

⁹The next day, as they went on their journey and drew near the city, Peter went up on the housetop to pray, about the sixth hour. ¹⁰Then he became very hungry and wanted to eat; but while they made ready, he fell into a trance ¹¹and saw heaven opened and an object like a great sheet bound at the four corners, descending to him and let down to the earth. ¹²In it were all kinds of four-footed animals of the earth, wild beasts, creeping things, and birds of the air. ¹³And a voice came to him, "Rise, Peter; kill and eat."

¹⁴But Peter said, "Not so, Lord! For I have never eaten anything common or unclean."

¹⁵And a voice *spoke* to him again the second time, "What God has cleansed you

---

10:6 ᵃNU-Text and M-Text omit the last sentence of this verse.

TIME CAPSULE A.D. 37 to 38

37 Herod Agrippa I becomes king of Philip's part of Syria

37 Josephus, the Jewish historian, is born in Jerusalem

37 Saul escapes from Damascus in a basket (Acts 9:25)

37 Saul visits Jerusalem, then goes to Syria (Gal. 1:21)

37 Roman emperor Nero is born

38 Agrippa I returns to Palestine with the favor of Caligula

WHO WAS THE GOD-FEARING CORNELIUS? (Acts 10:1, 2)

Caesarea Maritima, the coastal city and home of Cornelius, served as the capital for the province of Judea. As such, the city contained the residence for the Roman governor of Judea, as well as a regular Roman garrison (Acts 10:1). A legion of the Roman army was comprised of ten cohorts; five cohorts of about 600 soldiers each were stationed at Caesarea, while another cohort remained garrisoned on the Temple Mount in Jerusalem.

Centurions, like Cornelius, commanded units, called centuries, that generally averaged 80 men. In contrast to high-class Romans who aspired to higher offices, centurions usually began as regular soldiers and worked their way up through the ranks. Army service for males usually began around age 17, and roughly half of the enlisters who survived the required 20 years of service were highly rewarded.

The devout Cornelius (10:2) was a member of the "God-fearers," a class of religious people named in many ancient Jewish sources. God-fearers, while not full converts to Judaism, did respect Israel's God and His teachings. Inscriptions reveal that many soldiers were interested in foreign religions like Judaism.

Just who was part of Cornelius's household is uncertain, since Roman regulations prohibited soldiers from marrying. Officials usually looked the other way while soldiers stationed in various places held illegal concubines, but centurions, who were moved more frequently, probably developed less relationships even with concubines. Unless Cornelius was retired or (as often happened) was breaking official rules, his household may have consisted primarily of servants (10:7).

Roman custom expected members of a household (whether wives and children or servants) to follow the religion of the head of the household. It was thus natural for Cornelius to have spread his faith to "all his household" (10:2).

---

must not call common." [16]This was done three times. And the object was taken up into heaven again.

Summoned to Caesarea

[17]Now while Peter wondered within himself what this vision which he had seen meant, behold, the men who had been sent from Cornelius had made inquiry for Simon's house, and stood before the gate. [18]And they called and asked whether Simon, whose surname was Peter, was lodging there.

[19]While Peter thought about the vision, the Spirit said to him, "Behold, three men are seeking you. [20]Arise therefore, go down and go with them, doubting nothing; for I have sent them."

[21]Then Peter went down to the men who had been sent to him from Cornelius,[a] and said, "Yes, I am he whom you seek. For what reason have you come?"

[22]And they said, "Cornelius *the* centurion, a just man, one who fears God and has a good reputation among all the nation of the Jews, was divinely instructed by a holy angel to summon you to his house, and to hear words from you." [23]Then he invited them in and lodged *them*.

On the next day Peter went away with them, and some brethren from Joppa accompanied him.

Peter Meets Cornelius

[24]And the following day they entered Caesarea. Now Cornelius was waiting for

---

10:21 [a]NU-Text and M-Text omit *who had been sent to him from Cornelius.*

GEOGRAPHY AND ENVIRONMENT

Caesarea was the capital of the Roman province of Judea (Acts 10:24), and was called Caesarea Maritima to distinguish it from another Caesarea. Herod the Great refurbished the harbor at great expense, even building huge piers that are now underwater. Before these piers were discovered, the ancient descriptions of them seemed to be obvious exaggerations.

them, and had called together his relatives and close friends. 25As Peter was coming in, Cornelius met him and fell down at his feet and worshiped *him.* 26But Peter lifted him up, saying, "Stand up; I myself am also a man." 27And as he talked with him, he went in and found many who had come together. 28Then he said to them, "You know how unlawful it is for a Jewish man to keep company with or go to one of another nation. But God has shown me that I should not call any man common or unclean. 29Therefore I came without objection as soon as I was sent for. I ask, then, for what reason have you sent for me?"

30So Cornelius said, "Four days ago I was fasting until this hour; and at the ninth houra I prayed in my house, and behold, a man stood before me in bright clothing, 31and said, 'Cornelius, your prayer has been heard, and your alms are remembered in the sight of God. 32Send therefore to Joppa and call Simon here, whose surname is Peter. He is lodging in the house of Simon, a tanner, by the sea.a When he comes, he will speak to you.' 33So I sent to you immediately, and you have done well to come. Now therefore, we are all present before God, to hear all the things commanded you by God."

Preaching to Cornelius's Household

34Then Peter opened *his* mouth and said: "In truth I perceive that God shows no partiality. 35But in every nation whoever fears Him and works righteousness is accepted by Him. 36The word which *God* sent to the children of Israel, preaching peace through Jesus Christ—He is Lord of all— 37that word you know, which was proclaimed throughout all Judea, and began from Galilee after the baptism which John preached: 38how God anointed Jesus of Nazareth with the Holy Spirit and with power, who went about doing good and healing all who were oppressed by the devil, for God was with Him. 39And we are witnesses of all things which He did both in the land of the Jews and in Jerusalem, whom theya killed by hanging on a tree. 40Him God raised up on the third day, and showed Him openly, 41not to all the people, but to witnesses chosen before by God, *even* to us who ate and drank with Him after He arose from the dead. 42And He commanded us to preach to the people, and to testify that it is He who was ordained by God *to be* Judge of the living and the dead. 43To Him

all the prophets witness that, through His name, whoever believes in Him will receive remission of sins."

The Holy Spirit Falls on the Gentiles

44While Peter was still speaking these words, the Holy Spirit fell upon all those who heard the word. 45And those of the circumcision who believed were astonished, as many as came with Peter, because the gift of the Holy Spirit had been poured out on the Gentiles also. 46For they heard them speak with tongues and magnify God.

Then Peter answered, 47"Can anyone forbid water, that these should not be baptized who have received the Holy Spirit just as we *have?*" 48And he commanded them to be baptized in the name of the Lord. Then they asked him to stay a few days.

Peter Defends God's Grace

11 1Now the apostles and brethren who were in Judea heard that the Gentiles had also received the word of God. 2And when Peter came up to Jerusalem, those of the circumcision contended with him, 3saying, "You went in to uncircumcised men and ate with them!"

4But Peter explained *it* to them in order from the beginning, saying: 5"I was in the city of Joppa praying; and in a trance I saw a vision, an object descending like a great sheet, let down from heaven by four corners; and it came to me. 6When I observed it intently and considered, I saw

10:30 aNU-Text reads *Four days ago to this hour, at the ninth hour.* 10:32 aNU-Text omits the last sentence of this verse. 10:39 aNU-Text and M-Text add *also.*

TIME CAPSULE A.D. 38 to 41

38	*The Jews in Alexandria, Egypt, suffer severe persecution*
38	*Riots in Alexandria between Jews and Gentiles*
39	*Herod Antipas is deposed and sent into exile*
40	*Caligula orders his statue to be placed in the temple*
40	*Herod Agrippa I persuades Caligula not to set up the statue*
41	*Caligula is assassinated*

THOSE "CHRISTIANS" IN ANTIOCH (Acts 11:26)

When Barnabas came to Antioch, he found a group of people who were already disciples of Jesus Christ as Lord (Acts 11:22–24). Soon Saul joined Barnabas, teaching many disciples in the city. It is here in Antioch that these disciples were identified with the term "Christian," a term appearing only here and twice elsewhere in Scripture (Acts 26:28; 1 Pet. 4:16).

The word "Christian" is commonly assumed to be of Latin derivation, being found in the 2nd-century A.D. writings of such Latin authors as Tacitus, Suetonius, and Pliny the Younger. Pliny, the Roman governor of Bithynia and Pontus, writes around A.D. 111 to the emperor Trajan that those who admitted to being "Christians" were thus persecuted.

But the Romans were probably not the first to refer to certain people as "Christians." In the 1st century, followers of a certain leader were identified by attaching the ending "-ians" to the leader's name. Thus the followers of Herod were called "Herodians" (Mark 3:6). In the same way, those who followed Christ and were devoted to Him were eventually called "Christians."

There is no evidence that the followers of Jesus used the term to describe themselves. In fact, the other two occurrences of the term "Christian" in Scripture seem to imply an element of scorn. In Acts 26:28 Agrippa does not really intend to become a "Christian" himself, and in 1 Pet. 4:16 Peter possibly speaks of those who were suffering precisely because they claimed to be "Christians."

The term "Christian" probably originated with the Gentile population in Antioch, rather than with the followers of Christ themselves. The Gentiles, being unfamiliar with Jewish religion, could have thought "Christ" was a name, rather than recognizing it as a title for the Messiah. Thus, by about A.D. 46, the Antiochan Gentiles had distinguished the "Christians" from both Jews and pagans.

---

four-footed animals of the earth, wild beasts, creeping things, and birds of the air. 7And I heard a voice saying to me, 'Rise, Peter; kill and eat.' 8But I said, 'Not so, Lord! For nothing common or unclean has at any time entered my mouth.' 9But the voice answered me again from heaven, 'What God has cleansed you must not call common.' 10Now this was done three times, and all were drawn up again into heaven. 11At that very moment, three men stood before the house where I was, having been sent to me from Caesarea. 12Then the Spirit told me to go with them, doubting nothing. Moreover these six brethren accompanied me, and we entered the man's house. 13And he told us how he had seen an angel standing in his house, who said to him, 'Send men to Joppa, and call for Simon whose surname is Peter, 14who will tell you words by which you and all your household will be saved.' 15And as I began to speak, the Holy Spirit fell upon them, as upon us at the beginning. 16Then I remembered the word of the Lord, how He said, 'John indeed baptized with water, but you

shall be baptized with the Holy Spirit.' 17If therefore God gave them the same gift as *He gave* us when we believed on the Lord Jesus Christ, who was I that I could withstand God?"

18When they heard these things they became silent; and they glorified God, saying, "Then God has also granted to the Gentiles repentance to life."

Barnabas and Saul at Antioch

19Now those who were scattered after the persecution that arose over Stephen traveled as far as Phoenicia, Cyprus, and Antioch, preaching the word to no one but the Jews only. 20But some of them were men from Cyprus and Cyrene, who, when they had come to Antioch, spoke to the Hellenists, preaching the Lord Jesus. 21And the hand of the Lord was with them, and a great number believed and turned to the Lord.

22Then news of these things came to the ears of the church in Jerusalem, and they sent out Barnabas to go as far as Antioch. 23When he came and had seen the grace of God, he was glad, and encouraged them all that with purpose of heart they should continue with the Lord. 24For he was a good man, full of the Holy Spirit and of faith. And a great many people were added to the Lord.

25Then Barnabas departed for Tarsus to seek Saul. 26And when he had found him, he brought him to Antioch. So it was that for a whole year they assembled with the church and taught a great many people. And the disciples were first called Christians in Antioch.

Relief to Judea

27And in these days prophets came from Jerusalem to Antioch. 28Then one of them, named Agabus, stood up and showed by the Spirit that there was going to be a great famine throughout all the world, which also happened in the days of Claudius Caesar. 29Then the disciples, each according to his ability, determined to send relief to the brethren dwelling in Judea. 30This they also did, and sent it to the elders by the hands of Barnabas and Saul.

Herod's Violence to the Church

12 1Now about that time Herod the king stretched out *his* hand to harass some from the church. 2Then he killed James the brother of John with the sword. 3And because he saw that it pleased the Jews, he proceeded further to seize Peter also. Now it was *during* the Days of Unleavened Bread. 4So when he had arrested him, he put *him* in prison, and delivered *him* to four squads of soldiers to keep him, intending to bring him before the people after Passover.

Peter Freed from Prison

5Peter was therefore kept in prison, but constant[a] prayer was offered to God for him by the church. 6And when Herod was about to bring him out, that night Peter was sleeping, bound with two chains between two soldiers; and the guards before the door were keeping the prison. 7Now behold, an angel of the Lord stood by *him,* and a light shone in the prison; and he struck Peter on the side and raised him up, saying, "Arise quickly!" And his chains fell off *his* hands. 8Then the angel said to him, "Gird yourself and tie on your sandals"; and so he did. And he said to him, "Put on your garment and follow me." 9So he went out and followed him, and did not know

that what was done by the angel was real, but thought he was seeing a vision. 10When they were past the first and the second guard posts, they came to the iron gate that leads to the city, which opened to them of its own accord; and they went out and went down one street, and immediately the angel departed from him.

11And when Peter had come to himself, he said, "Now I know for certain that the Lord has sent His angel, and has delivered me from the hand of Herod and *from* all the expectation of the Jewish people."

12So, when he had considered *this,* he came to the house of Mary, the mother of John whose surname was Mark, where many were gathered together praying. 13And as Peter knocked at the door of the gate, a girl named Rhoda came to answer. 14When she recognized Peter's voice, because of *her* gladness she did not open the gate, but ran in and announced that Peter stood before the gate. 15But they said to her, "You are beside yourself!" Yet she kept insisting that it was so. So they said, "It is his angel."

16Now Peter continued knocking; and when they opened *the door* and saw him, they were astonished. 17But motioning to them with his hand to keep silent, he declared to them how the Lord had brought him out of the prison. And he said, "Go, tell these things to James and to the brethren." And he departed and went to another place.

18Then, as soon as it was day, there was no small stir among the soldiers about what had become of Peter. 19But when Herod had searched for him and not found him, he examined the guards and commanded that *they* should be put to death.

And he went down from Judea to Caesarea, and stayed *there.*

Herod's Violent Death

20Now Herod had been very angry with the people of Tyre and Sidon; but they came to him with one accord, and having made Blastus the king's personal aide their friend, they asked for peace, because their country was supplied with food by the king's *country.*

21So on a set day Herod, arrayed in royal apparel, sat on his throne and gave an oration to them. 22And the people kept shouting, "The voice of a god and not of a

12:5 ªNU-Text reads *constantly* (or *earnestly*).

WORSHIP THE EMPEROR (Acts 12:20–23)

Reverence for rulers or emperors did not begin in Rome. In fact, the Romans were rather late in accepting such a practice. While they revered the spirits of their dead ancestors—and especially the spirit of the head of their family—they regarded their political leaders as merely men.

The worship of living rulers was practiced in many nations, including Egypt, Persia, and Greece. Alexander the Great established his own cult of worshipers in Alexandria in Egypt.

Augustus Caesar (27 B.C.–A.D. 14) was the first Roman emperor to combine the ideas of ruler worship and ancestor worship in creating an imperial cult. He made it a sign of his subjects' loyalty to him and the Roman state. He did, however, exempt the Jews from this cult.

Caligula (A.D. 37–41), who was known for being somewhat unbalanced, proclaimed himself a god and loved to dress up as Jupiter. In A.D. 40 he even ordered that a statue of himself as Jupiter be erected in the temple in Jerusalem. Faced with a likely revolt by the Jewish populace, the Roman governor Petronius managed to get the order canceled.

It is surprising that Herod Agrippa I (A.D. 41–44), just a few years after the incident with Caligula, would allow himself to be worshiped as a god (Acts 12:20–23). According to Acts, his failure to discourage the shouts of the people, "The voice of a god and not of a man!" (v. 22), and give glory to God, resulted in a violent death. The Jewish historian Josephus recorded that Agrippa died 5 days after an attack of abdominal pains.

man!" 23Then immediately an angel of the Lord struck him, because he did not give glory to God. And he was eaten by worms and died.

24But the word of God grew and multiplied.

25And Barnabas and Saul returned from^a Jerusalem when they had fulfilled *their* ministry, and they also took with them John whose surname was Mark.

12:25 ^aNU-Text and M-Text read *to*.

The Gospel to the Gentile World

> This new initiative into the Gentile world was begun by the church at Antioch.

The entire Book of Acts is an expansion and fulfillment of the promise "you shall be witnesses . . . in Jerusalem, . . . Judea and Samaria, and to the end of the earth" (Acts 1:8). The gospel had already spread beyond Judea to the Samaritans (8:5), to an Ethiopian (8:27), to God-fearing Gentiles in the household of Cornelius (10:44, 45), and to Hellenists at Antioch (11:20). In the remainder of the account of Acts, Luke describes how the gospel was carried into the Gentile world. This new initiative was begun by the church at Antioch sending out Barnabas and Saul (13:2, 3).

The change of thrust towards pagan non-Jews rather than to skeptical Jews is made clear by Paul's announcement in Antioch of Pisidia: "we turn to the Gentiles" (13:46). Paul (Saul's Roman name) now focused his strategy on Gentile evangelism. His sermons, as recorded in Acts, indicate the way the Good News was presented to Gentiles (13:16–41) and to a sophisticated audience (17:22–31), emphasizing the activity of the Holy Spirit and the power of Jesus' resurrection.

The great increase of Gentile converts caused alarm among many of the Jewish Christians in Judea. They feared that too many Gentiles would hurt the character of the church. Militant Jewish nationalists were already beginning a movement to require Gentile converts to become circumcised and follow the Jewish law. The stage was set for a Jerusalem conference of church leaders (Acts 15); the problem was how to reconcile the new communities of believers with the customs of Jewish law.

Paul's First Missionary Journey

Paul's first missionary journey took him to Cyprus, and then to Asia Minor where he visited Pisidian Antioch, Iconium, Lystra, and Derbe. This journey, setting out around A.D. 46, marked the first time a church had purposefully sent out missionaries. It was natural for Paul and Barnabas to evangelize first in Cyprus since it was Barnabas's home (see Acts 4:36).

The missionary strategy was to reach out first to the Jewish population. Since the synagogues were the centers of Jewish community life in the cities that Paul visited, they were the most appropriate places to begin preaching Christ. Only when rejected by the Jews did Paul and Barnabas turn to the Gentiles with the gospel (Acts 13:46).

■ Acts 13:1—14:28

Acts
Barnabas and Saul Appointed

13 :1 Now in the church that was at Antioch there were certain prophets and teachers: Barnabas, Simeon who was called Niger, Lucius of Cyrene, Manaen who had been brought up with Herod the tetrarch, and Saul. ²As they ministered to the Lord and fasted, the Holy Spirit said, "Now separate to Me Barnabas and Saul for the work to which I have called them." ³Then, having fasted and prayed, and laid hands on them, they sent *them* away.

Preaching in Cyprus

⁴So, being sent out by the Holy Spirit, they went down to Seleucia, and from there they sailed to Cyprus. ⁵And when they arrived in Salamis, they preached the word of God in the synagogues of the Jews. They also had John as *their* assistant.

⁶Now when they had gone through the island[a] to Paphos, they found a certain sorcerer, a false prophet, a Jew whose name *was* Bar-Jesus, ⁷who was with the proconsul, Sergius Paulus, an intelligent man. This man called for Barnabas and Saul and sought to hear the word of God. ⁸But Elymas the sorcerer (for so his name is translated) withstood them, seeking to turn the proconsul away from the faith. ⁹Then Saul, who also *is called* Paul, filled with the Holy Spirit, looked intently at him ¹⁰and said, "O full of all deceit and all fraud, *you* son of the devil, *you* enemy of all righteousness, will you not cease perverting the straight ways of the Lord? ¹¹And now, indeed, the hand of the Lord *is* upon you, and you shall be blind, not seeing the sun for a time."

And immediately a dark mist fell on him, and he went around seeking someone to lead him by the hand. ¹²Then the proconsul believed, when he saw what had been done, being astonished at the teaching of the Lord.

At Antioch in Pisidia

¹³Now when Paul and his party set sail from Paphos, they came to Perga in Pam-

13:6 ªNU-Text reads *the whole island.*

Paul Goes to Galatia
Paul and Barnabas were sent out from the church at Antioch to the cities of Galatia in Asia Minor. This first missionary journey (Acts 13; 14) took them to Cyprus, and then to Pisidian Antioch, Iconium, Lystra, and Derbe. The Jewish synagogues in these cities provided Paul a platform for preaching the gospel. At times, however, he encountered opposition even from the synagogues.

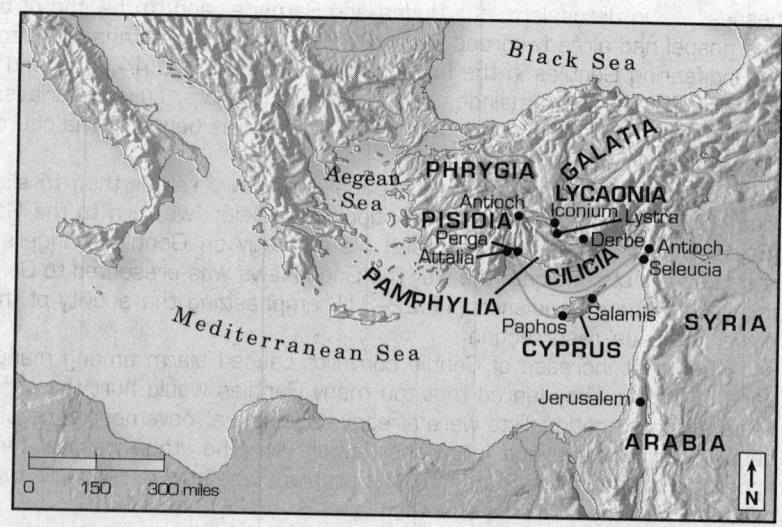

MULTICULTURAL PROPHETS AT ANTIOCH (Acts 13:1)

Five leaders are named as prophets and teachers in the church at Antioch of Syria: Barnabas, Simeon, Lucius, Manaen, and Saul (Acts 13:1). Most 1st-century Jewish people believed that prophecy was rare in their own time, so the leadership of "prophets" in the Antioch church would have struck them forcefully.

Simeon and Manaen (which in Hebrew is "Menahem") are common Jewish names. Simeon's surname "Niger" was a frequent Roman name, making it possible that he, like Saul (Paul), was a Roman citizen. On the other hand, "Niger" seems to be a nickname rather than his birth name, and its Latin meaning ("black") could suggest that Simeon was descended from North African converts to Judaism.

Manaen had been "brought up" (13:1) with Herod Antipas, the tetrarch of Galilee. This phrase sometimes described those who shared the same wet nurse, meaning that Manaen possibly had been a high-status servant in the royal household. When slaves grew up with a master's son, the two often became close, and the son often freed the slave after inheriting him. Even when not freed, slaves of royal families wielded considerable power and status in society, sometimes more power than local aristocrats.

In Greek society, friendships from youth often led to political alliances and favors in adulthood. But Herod Antipas, Manaen's patron, had lost his position when the emperor banished him to Gaul in A.D. 39. Manaen's influence undoubtedly had dwindled by A.D. 46 when Paul and Barnabas were sent out by the Antioch church.

Lucius was a common Greek name, but that does not determine his ethnic background. Many Jews had Greek names, especially outside Palestine. Cyrene, his place of origin, had a very large Jewish population, so Lucius was possibly a Hellenistic Jew.

The other named Antioch prophets were Barnabas, a Levite who originated from Cyprus (Acts 4:36), and Saul, the Pharisee from Cilicia (Acts 22:3; 23:6). The combined cultural backgrounds of these five individuals brought to the church a diversified staff of prophetic leaders.

---

phylia; and John, departing from them, returned to Jerusalem. ¹⁴But when they departed from Perga, they came to Antioch in Pisidia, and went into the synagogue on the Sabbath day and sat down. ¹⁵And after the reading of the Law and the Prophets, the rulers of the synagogue sent to them, saying, "Men *and* brethren, if you have any word of exhortation for the people, say on."

¹⁶Then Paul stood up, and motioning with *his* hand said, "Men of Israel, and you who fear God, listen: ¹⁷The God of this people Israel[a] chose our fathers, and exalted the people when they dwelt as strangers in the land of Egypt, and with an uplifted arm He brought them out of it. ¹⁸Now for a time of about forty years He put up with their ways in the wilderness. ¹⁹And when He had destroyed seven nations in the land of Canaan, He distributed their land to them by allotment.

²⁰"After that He gave *them* judges for about four hundred and fifty years, until Samuel the prophet. ²¹And afterward they asked for a king; so God gave them Saul the son of Kish, a man of the tribe of Benjamin, for forty years. ²²And when He had removed him, He raised up for them David as king, to whom also He gave testimony and said, 'I have found David[a] the *son* of Jesse, *a man after My own heart,* who will do all My will.'[b] ²³From this man's seed, according to *the* promise, God raised up for Israel a Savior—Jesus—[a] ²⁴after John had first preached, before His coming, the baptism of repentance to all the people of Israel. ²⁵And as John was finishing his course, he said, 'Who do you think I am? I am not *He.* But behold, there comes One after me, the sandals of whose feet I am not worthy to loose.'

²⁶"Men *and* brethren, sons of the family of Abraham, and those among you who

13:17 ᵃM-Text omits *Israel.*   13:22 ᵃPsalm 89:20 ᵇ1 Samuel 13:14   13:23 ᵃM-Text reads *for Israel salvation.*

fear God, to you the word of this salvation has been sent. ²⁷For those who dwell in Jerusalem, and their rulers, because they did not know Him, nor even the voices of the Prophets which are read every Sabbath, have fulfilled *them* in condemning *Him*. ²⁸And though they found no cause for death *in Him*, they asked Pilate that He should be put to death. ²⁹Now when they had fulfilled all that was written concerning Him, they took *Him* down from the tree and laid *Him* in a tomb. ³⁰But God raised Him from the dead. ³¹He was seen for many days by those who came up with Him from Galilee to Jerusalem, who are His witnesses to the people. ³²And we declare to you glad tidings—that promise which was made to the fathers. ³³God has fulfilled this for us their children, in that He has raised up Jesus. As it is also written in the second Psalm:

'You are My Son,
Today I have begotten You.'ᵃ

³⁴And that He raised Him from the dead, no more to return to corruption, He has spoken thus:

'I will give you the sure mercies of David.'ᵃ

³⁵Therefore He also says in another *Psalm*:

'You will not allow Your Holy One to see corruption.'ᵃ

³⁶"For David, after he had served his own generation by the will of God, fell asleep, was buried with his fathers, and saw corruption; ³⁷but He whom God raised up saw no corruption. ³⁸Therefore let it be known to you, brethren, that through this Man is preached to you the forgiveness of sins; ³⁹and by Him everyone who believes is justified from all things from which you could not be justified by the law of Moses. ⁴⁰Beware therefore, lest what has been spoken in the prophets come upon you:

⁴¹   'Behold, you despisers,
     Marvel and perish!
     For I work a work in your days,
     A work which you will by no means believe,
     Though one were to declare it to you.'"ᵃ

Blessing and Conflict at Antioch

⁴²So when the Jews went out of the synagogue,ᵃ the Gentiles begged that these words might be preached to them the next Sabbath. ⁴³Now when the congregation had broken up, many of the Jews and devout proselytes followed Paul and Barnabas, who, speaking to them, persuaded them to continue in the grace of God.

⁴⁴On the next Sabbath almost the whole city came together to hear the word of God. ⁴⁵But when the Jews saw the multitudes, they were filled with envy; and contradicting and blaspheming, they opposed the things spoken by Paul. ⁴⁶Then Paul and Barnabas grew bold and said, "It was necessary that the word of God should be spoken to you first; but since you reject it, and judge yourselves unworthy of everlasting life, behold, we turn to the Gentiles. ⁴⁷For so the Lord has commanded us:

'I have set you as a light to the Gentiles,
That you should be for salvation to the ends of the earth.'"ᵃ

⁴⁸Now when the Gentiles heard this, they were glad and glorified the word of the Lord. And as many as had been appointed to eternal life believed. ⁴⁹And the word of the Lord was being

---

13:33 ᵃPsalm 2:7   13:34 ᵃIsaiah 55:3
13:35 ᵃPsalm 16:10   13:41 ᵃHabakkuk 1:5
13:42 ᵃOr *And when they went out of the synagogue of the Jews*; NU-Text reads *And when they went out of the synagogue, they begged.*   13:47 ᵃIsaiah 49:6

TIME CAPSULE *A.D. 41 to 44*

41   The Roman army declares Claudius emperor

41   Agrippa I reads from Deuteronomy at the Feast of Tabernacles

43   The emperor Claudius travels to Britain

44–48 Famine, as predicted by Agabus (Acts 11:28)

44   Herod Agrippa I dies suddenly in Caesarea (Acts 12:23)

44   Judea again becomes a Roman province

PROMINENT WOMEN OF ANTIOCH IN PISIDIA (Acts 13:50)

Many cities with the name "Antioch" were founded by the early Seleucid kings from about 312 to 250 B.C. Two of the most important were Antioch in Pisidia and Antioch in Syria, both mentioned in the New Testament.

Antioch in Pisidia passed into Roman hands in 25 B.C. during the reign of Augustus Caesar (27 B.C.–A.D. 14). Augustus transformed the city into a Roman colony and transplanted large numbers of Roman citizens to live there. In fact, inscriptions from Antioch show a preponderance of Roman personal names as well as a substantial minority of Jewish inhabitants. Antioch was a prominent city. A large number of its citizenry entered into the Roman Senate, and numerous building projects were completed there.

The apostle Paul visited Antioch in Pisidia at least once during his missionary journeys. The city was a natural target for Paul since many prominent Roman citizens lived there. On his first journey, about A.D. 46, his visit began in the Jewish synagogue (Acts 13:13, 14), but his preaching reached both Jew and Gentile (13:42, 48).

When some members of the Jewish community reacted against Paul, they enlisted the support of "devout and prominent women" in opposition to him (13:50). These women probably belonged to some of the Roman families brought by Augustus to colonize the city. The Jewish faith had found some converts among aristocratic women who had influence through their wealthy and politically powerful husbands. Such public clout forced Paul and Barnabas to leave town (13:50, 51).

spread throughout all the region. ⁵⁰But the Jews stirred up the devout and prominent women and the chief men of the city, raised up persecution against Paul and Barnabas, and expelled them from their region. ⁵¹But they shook off the dust from their feet against them, and came to Iconium. ⁵²And the disciples were filled with joy and with the Holy Spirit.

At Iconium

14 ¹Now it happened in Iconium that they went together to the synagogue of the Jews, and so spoke that a great multitude both of the Jews and of the Greeks believed. ²But the unbelieving Jews stirred up the Gentiles and poisoned their minds against the brethren. ³Therefore they stayed there a long time, speaking boldly in the Lord, who was bearing witness to the word of His grace, granting signs and wonders to be done by their hands.

⁴But the multitude of the city was divided: part sided with the Jews, and part with the apostles. ⁵And when a violent attempt was made by both the Gentiles and Jews, with their rulers, to abuse and stone them, ⁶they became aware of it and fled to Lystra and Derbe, cities of Lycaonia, and to the surrounding region. ⁷And they were preaching the gospel there.

Idolatry at Lystra

⁸And in Lystra a certain man without strength in his feet was sitting, a cripple from his mother's womb, who had never walked. ⁹*This* man heard Paul speaking. Paul, observing him intently and seeing that he had faith to be healed, ¹⁰said with a loud voice, "Stand up straight on your feet!" And he leaped and walked. ¹¹Now when the people saw what Paul had done, they raised their voices, saying in the Lycaonian *language,* "The gods have come down to us in the likeness of men!" ¹²And Barnabas they called Zeus, and Paul, Hermes, because he was the chief speaker. ¹³Then the priest of Zeus, whose temple was in front of their city, brought oxen and garlands to the gates, intending to sacrifice with the multitudes.

¹⁴But when the apostles Barnabas and Paul heard this, they tore their clothes and ran in among the multitude, crying out ¹⁵and saying, "Men, why are you doing these things? We also are men with the same nature as you, and preach to you that you should turn from these useless things to the living God, who made the heaven, the earth, the sea, and all things that are in them, ¹⁶who in bygone generations allowed all nations to walk in their own ways. ¹⁷Nevertheless He did not leave

Himself without witness, in that He did good, gave us rain from heaven and fruitful seasons, filling our hearts with food and gladness." ¹⁸And with these sayings they could scarcely restrain the multitudes from sacrificing to them.

Stoning, Escape to Derbe

¹⁹Then Jews from Antioch and Iconium came there; and having persuaded the multitudes, they stoned Paul *and* dragged *him* out of the city, supposing him to be dead. ²⁰However, when the disciples gathered around him, he rose up and went into the city. And the next day he departed with Barnabas to Derbe.

Strengthening the Converts

²¹And when they had preached the gospel to that city and made many disciples, they returned to Lystra, Iconium, and Antioch, ²²strengthening the souls of the disciples, exhorting *them* to continue in the faith, and *saying,* "We must through many tribulations enter the kingdom of God." ²³So when they had appointed elders in every church, and prayed with fasting, they commended them to the Lord in whom they had believed. ²⁴And after they had passed through Pisidia, they came to Pamphylia. ²⁵Now when they had preached the word in Perga, they went down to Attalia. ²⁶From there they sailed to Antioch, where they had been commended to the grace of God for the work which they had completed.

²⁷Now when they had come and gathered the church together, they reported all that God had done with them, and that He had opened the door of faith to the Gentiles. ²⁸So they stayed there a long time with the disciples.

Conference in Jerusalem

The many Gentiles won to Christ precipitated the Jerusalem Council, where it was decided that circumcision would not be required of Gentile Christians. Attempts to place this conference chronologically are compli-

cated by apparent differences between Luke's description of the event and Paul's account in Gal. 2:1–10. The most notable difference in the accounts is the issue of circumcision itself. In Luke's account, circumcision is the central concern. In Paul's account, circumcision was at best incidental to the conference. If the issue had been decisively settled there, he could have simply appealed to the "apostolic decree" (Acts 15:23–29) when he was disputing with the Judaizers in Galatia.

Several suggestions have been offered for relating Luke's and Paul's accounts. A first proposal holds that, despite the differences, the similarities between Acts 15 and Gal. 2 suggest that these accounts are two reports of the same event. A second proposal, though, identifies the events described in Gal. 2 with Paul's second visit to Jerusalem, correlating that visit with the famine-relief trip mentioned in Acts 11:27–30. (Paul's first visit to Jerusalem is mentioned in Gal. 1:18.) In both of these views, the Jerusalem Council is usually dated around A.D. 49.

A third proposal arises because during Paul's final visit to Jerusalem, James appeared to inform him for the first time about the ruling of the conference (see Acts 21:17–25). So, it is supposed, Paul was not at the meeting during which the decision regarding circumcision of Gentiles was reached. In this view, the events described by Paul in Gal. 2 are usually associated with the visit to Jerusalem mentioned in Acts 18:22, and dated about A.D. 52.

The conference settled the matter. The Gentiles were not required to keep the law or to be circumcised. They were directed to abstain from practices that were offensive to the Jews and made it particularly hard for them to have table fellowship with Gentiles (Acts 15:29).

■ Acts 15:1–35

Acts

Conflict over Circumcision

15 :1 And certain *men* came down from Judea and taught the brethren, "Unless you are circumcised according to

GEOGRAPHY AND ENVIRONMENT

Today Antioch (Acts 14:26) is not very well known, but in New Testament times it was one of the largest cities in the Roman world, comparable to Rome or Alexandria in population. Antioch of Syria (to distinguish it from Antioch in Pisidia) is 310 miles north of Jerusalem and about 12 miles inland from the Mediterranean coast, on the banks of the Orontes River.

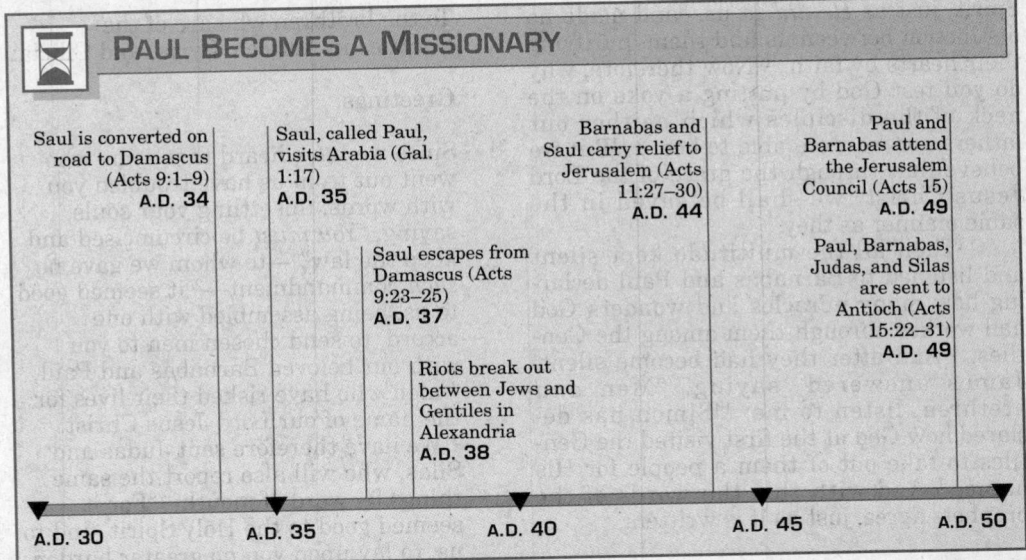

PAUL BECOMES A MISSIONARY

Saul is converted on road to Damascus (Acts 9:1–9) **A.D. 34**	Saul, called Paul, visits Arabia (Gal. 1:17) **A.D. 35**	Barnabas and Saul carry relief to Jerusalem (Acts 11:27–30) **A.D. 44**	Paul and Barnabas attend the Jerusalem Council (Acts 15) **A.D. 49**
	Saul escapes from Damascus (Acts 9:23–25) **A.D. 37**		Paul, Barnabas, Judas, and Silas are sent to Antioch (Acts 15:22–31) **A.D. 49**
	Riots break out between Jews and Gentiles in Alexandria **A.D. 38**		

A.D. 30   A.D. 35   A.D. 40   A.D. 45   A.D. 50

the custom of Moses, you cannot be saved." ²Therefore, when Paul and Barnabas had no small dissension and dispute with them, they determined that Paul and Barnabas and certain others of them should go up to Jerusalem, to the apostles and elders, about this question.

³So, being sent on their way by the church, they passed through Phoenicia and Samaria, describing the conversion of the Gentiles; and they caused great joy to all the brethren. ⁴And when they had come to Jerusalem, they were received by the church and the apostles and the elders; and they reported all things that God had done with them. ⁵But some of the sect of the Pharisees who believed rose up, saying, "It is necessary to circumcise them, and to command *them* to keep the law of Moses."

The Jerusalem Council

⁶Now the apostles and elders came together to consider this matter. ⁷And when there had been much dispute, Peter rose up and said to them: "Men and brethren, you know that a good while ago God chose among us, that by my mouth the Gentiles should hear the word of the gospel and believe. ⁸So God, who knows the heart, acknowledged them by giving them the Holy

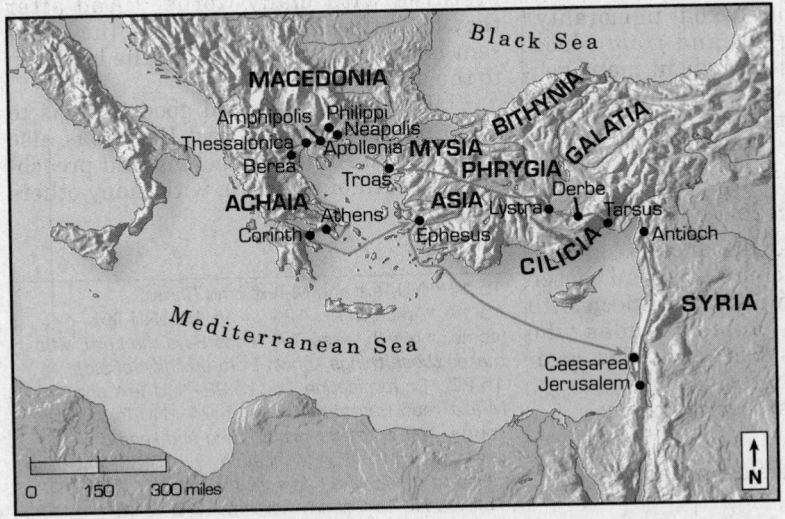

Paul Goes to Greece
Paul's second missionary journey (Acts 15:39—18:22) took him, along with Silas, back to Asia Minor, then over to Europe to the cities of Philippi, Thessalonica, Berea, Athens, and Corinth. Young Timothy joined them in Lystra, accompanying them through Macedonia and Achaia (present-day Greece). The gospel spread further as Paul came into contact with Roman authorities and Greek philosophers.

Spirit, just as *He did* to us, 9and made no distinction between us and them, purifying their hearts by faith. 10Now therefore, why do you test God by putting a yoke on the neck of the disciples which neither our fathers nor we were able to bear? 11But we believe that through the grace of the Lord Jesus Christ[a] we shall be saved in the same manner as they."

12Then all the multitude kept silent and listened to Barnabas and Paul declaring how many miracles and wonders God had worked through them among the Gentiles. 13And after they had become silent, James answered, saying, "Men *and* brethren, listen to me: 14Simon has declared how God at the first visited the Gentiles to take out of them a people for His name. 15And with this the words of the prophets agree, just as it is written:

16   'After this I will return
      And will rebuild the tabernacle of
         David, which has fallen down;
      I will rebuild its ruins,
      And I will set it up;
17   So that the rest of mankind may seek
         the LORD,
      Even all the Gentiles who are called
         by My name,
      Says the LORD who does all these
         things.'[a]

18"Known to God from eternity are all His works.[a] 19Therefore I judge that we should not trouble those from among the Gentiles who are turning to God, 20but that we write to them to abstain from things polluted by idols, *from* sexual immorality,[a] *from* things strangled, and *from* blood. 21For Moses has had throughout many generations those who preach him in every city, being read in the synagogues every Sabbath."

The Jerusalem Decree

22Then it pleased the apostles and elders, with the whole church, to send chosen men of their own company to Antioch with Paul and Barnabas, *namely,* Judas who was also named Barsabas,[a] and Silas, leading men among the brethren. 23They wrote this, *letter* by them:

The apostles, the elders, and the brethren,

To the brethren who are of the Gentiles in Antioch, Syria, and Cilicia:

Greetings.

24 Since we have heard that some who went out from us have troubled you with words, unsettling your souls, saying, "*You must* be circumcised and keep the law"[a]—to whom we gave no *such* commandment—25it seemed good to us, being assembled with one accord, to send chosen men to you with our beloved Barnabas and Paul, 26men who have risked their lives for the name of our Lord Jesus Christ. 27We have therefore sent Judas and Silas, who will also report the same things by word of mouth. 28For it seemed good to the Holy Spirit, and to us, to lay upon you no greater burden than these necessary things: 29that you abstain from things offered to idols, from blood, from things strangled, and from sexual immorality.[a] If you keep yourselves from these, you will do well.

Farewell.

Continuing Ministry in Syria

30So when they were sent off, they came to Antioch; and when they had gathered the multitude together, they delivered the letter. 31When they had read it, they rejoiced over its encouragement. 32Now Judas and Silas, themselves being prophets also, exhorted and strengthened the brethren with many words. 33And after they had stayed *there* for a time, they were sent back with greetings from the brethren to the apostles.[a]

34However, it seemed good to Silas to remain there.[a] 35Paul and Barnabas also remained in Antioch, teaching and preaching the word of the Lord, with many others also.

15:11 [a]NU-Text and M-Text omit *Christ.*
15:17 [a]Amos 9:11, 12   15:18 [a]NU-Text
(combining with verse 17) reads *Says the Lord, who makes these things known from eternity (of old).*
15:20 [a]Or *fornication*   15:22 [a]NU-Text and M-Text read *Barsabbas.*   15:24 [a]NU-Text omits *saying, "You must be circumcised and keep the law."*   15:29 [a]Or *fornication*   15:33 [a]NU-Text reads *to those who had sent them.*
15:34 [a]NU-Text and M-Text omit this verse.

The Letter to the Galatians

The most crucial factor in dating the letter to the Galatians is the relationship between the journey of Paul to Jerusalem mentioned in Gal. 2:1 and the Jerusalem Council mentioned in Acts 15 (see "Conference in Jerusalem" at Acts 15:1). If the decision of the council in Acts 15 had been common knowledge when the letter was written, Paul would surely have used the council's decision in defense of Gentile freedom and especially in his rebuke of Peter (Gal. 2:11–13). It is therefore possible that Galatians is Paul's earliest letter, and was written by A.D. 49 just prior to the Jerusalem Council of Acts 15. Those who associate Paul's account in Gal. 2:1–10 with the Jerusalem visit mentioned in Acts 18:22 date this letter to about A.D. 53, and thus after the Thessalonian letters.

The destination of this letter to Galatia was a group of churches that Paul himself had founded (Gal. 1:2, 8, 9; 4:19). His close relationship with them is reflected in 4:11–14. Until the 18th century most readers understood "Galatia" to be the territory in the heart of Asia Minor whose boundaries included Bithynia and Pontus on the north, Phrygia on the southwest, and Cappadocia on the east. However, the Book of Acts offers no record of Paul evangelizing in this "North Galatian" area, apart from brief hints (Acts 16:6; 18:23).

The "South Galatian" theory understands Galatia to refer to the Roman province of Paul's day, which included Pisidia, Lycaonia, and parts of Phrygia and Cappadocia. Also included were the cities of Antioch, Lystra, Derbe, and Iconium which Paul visited on both his first (Acts 13; 14) and second (Acts 16) missionary journeys.

■ Galatians 1:1–24

Galatians
Greeting

1 :1 Paul, an apostle (not from men nor through man, but through Jesus Christ and God the Father who raised Him from the dead), ²and all the brethren who are with me,

To the churches of Galatia:

³Grace to you and peace from God the Father and our Lord Jesus Christ, ⁴who gave Himself for our sins, that He might deliver us from this present evil age, according to the will of our God and Father, ⁵to whom *be* glory forever and ever. Amen.

Only One Gospel

⁶I marvel that you are turning away so soon from Him who called you in the grace of Christ, to a different gospel, ⁷which is not another; but there are some who trouble you and want to pervert the gospel of Christ. ⁸But even if we, or an angel from heaven, preach any other gospel to you than what we have preached to you, let him be accursed. ⁹As we have said before, so now I say again, if anyone preaches any other gospel to you than what you have received, let him be accursed.

¹⁰For do I now persuade men, or God? Or do I seek to please men? For if I still pleased men, I would not be a bondservant of Christ.

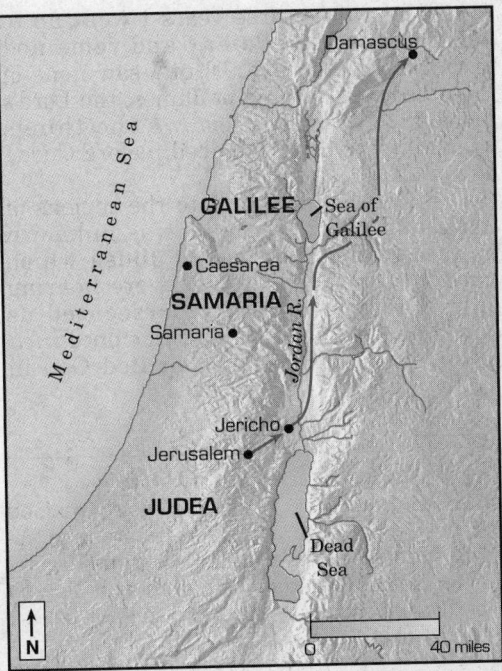

Paul on the Road to Damascus

Following Stephen's death, Paul became actively involved in the Jewish persecution of Christians (Gal. 1:13). Armed with letters from the high priest, Paul set out from Jerusalem to Damascus intending to bring back any followers of Christ as prisoners. But while approaching Damascus, he was confronted by the resurrected Jesus in a blinding encounter.

Call to Apostleship

[11]But I make known to you, brethren, that the gospel which was preached by me is not according to man. [12]For I neither received it from man, nor was I taught *it*, but *it came* through the revelation of Jesus Christ.

[13]For you have heard of my former conduct in Judaism, how I persecuted the church of God beyond measure and *tried to destroy it*. [14]And I advanced in Judaism beyond many of my contemporaries in my own nation, being more exceedingly zealous for the traditions of my fathers.

[15]But when it pleased God, who separated me from my mother's womb and called *me* through His grace, [16]to reveal His Son in me, that I might preach Him among the Gentiles, I did not immediately confer with flesh and blood, [17]nor did I go up to Jerusalem to those *who were* apostles before me; but I went to Arabia, and returned again to Damascus.

Contacts at Jerusalem

[18]Then after three years I went up to Jerusalem to see Peter,[a] and remained with him fifteen days. [19]But I saw none of the other apostles except James, the Lord's brother. [20](Now *concerning* the things which I write to you, indeed, before God, I do not lie.)

[21]Afterward I went into the regions of Syria and Cilicia. [22]And I was unknown by face to the churches of Judea which *were* in Christ. [23]But they were hearing only, "He who formerly persecuted us now preaches the faith which he once *tried to destroy*." [24]And they glorified God in me.

Known to scholars as "the Judaizers," this heretical group maintained that all Christians, whether of Jewish or of Gentile ancestry, must observe the Mosaic law. Precisely when the Judaizers raised the issue of circumcision is not known, but Paul offered two types of response to their teaching. First, he appealed to the precedent of how the Jewish leadership of the church had received Gentile converts in the past, including his earlier confrontation with Peter over this very issue in Antioch (2:1–21). Second, he developed a theological argument about the purpose of the law and the responsibilities of Christian life (3:1–6:18).

■ Galatians 2:1—6:18

Galatians
Defending the Gospel

2 :1 Then after fourteen years I went up again to Jerusalem with Barnabas, and also took Titus with *me*. [2]And I went up by revelation, and communicated to them that gospel which I preach among the Gentiles, but privately to those who were of reputation, lest by any means I might run, or had run, in vain. [3]Yet not even Titus who *was* with me, being a Greek, was compelled to be circumcised. [4]And *this occurred* because of false brethren secretly brought in (who came in by stealth to spy out our liberty which we have in Christ Jesus, that they might bring us into bondage), [5]to whom we did not yield submission even for an hour, that the truth of the gospel might continue with you.

[6]But from those who seemed to be something—whatever they were, it makes no difference to me; God shows personal favoritism to no man—for those who seemed *to be something* added nothing to me. [7]But

1:18 [a]NU-Text reads *Cephas*.

🧩 **Paul Corrects Peter**
Paul took Titus, an uncircumcised Gentile convert, to Jerusalem in order to establish that Gentiles did not have to be circumcised to be Christians. This second visit to Jerusalem occurred, according to Paul, after a period of 14 years (Gal. 2:1). If Paul means 14 years after his conversion (Gal. 1:15), the date would be about A.D. 37–38; however, if he means 14 years after his first Jerusalem visit (Gal. 1:18), the date would be about A.D. 51–52.

Within a very short time after Paul's presentation of the gospel to them, the Galatians were influenced by an outside group (Gal. 1:6).

TIME CAPSULE A.D. 46

46–120	Life of Plutarch, Greek philosopher
46–48	Sergius Paulus rules as proconsul
46	Barnabas and Saul (Paul) appointed
46	Beginning of Paul's first missionary journey (Acts 13:4)
46	Paul visits Antioch in Pisidia
46	Josephus's date for the revolt by Theudas (Acts 5:36)

CHRISTIANS OF ANTIOCH IN SYRIA (Gal. 2:11)

The city of Antioch in Syria was founded by the first Seleucid king, Seleucus I (c. 300 B.C.). Situated on the Orontes River, it was the largest of all cities that bore the name "Antioch." Ancient estimates of its size vary from 200,000 to 600,000 inhabitants. According to the Jewish historian Josephus (A.D. 37–100), the city also had a substantial Jewish population (*Antiquities of the Jews*, 12.119).

The Roman general Pompey took Antioch in 64 B.C. and declared it a free city. It then became the capital of the Roman province of Syria and the third largest city in the empire. The extant buildings, temples, aqueduct, masonry works, hippodrome, and gridlike street plan of Antioch attest to its great importance.

This great city became a center for Christianity. Many believers fled there after the stoning of Stephen and preached to Antioch's Jewish population (Acts 11:19). But in Antioch were also Gentiles who had converted to Judaism. Some of them, such as Nicolas, called "a proselyte from Antioch" (Acts 6:5), also accepted Christianity. Soon the church in Antioch faced the task of unifying its Jewish and Gentile members.

The Antioch Christian community prospered. For a year Barnabas and Paul taught these believers, who were the first to be called "Christians" (Acts 11:25, 26). That this church had ample resources can be seen by their sending relief to the Jerusalem church (Acts 11:27–30).

Questions arose, however, concerning Jewish-Gentile relations. Eventually the Antioch congregation sent a delegation (including Paul and Barnabas) to Jerusalem to debate the issue of the circumcision of the Gentiles (Acts 14:26—15:2). That issue found some degree of resolution, but other tensions would surface. So the church of Antioch in Syria became the scene for another debate, this time over whether Jewish Christians should eat together with Gentile Christians (Gal. 2:11–13).

---

on the contrary, when they saw that the gospel for the uncircumcised had been committed to me, as *the gospel* for the circumcised *was* to Peter [8](for He who worked effectively in Peter for the apostleship to the circumcised also worked effectively in me toward the Gentiles), [9]and when James, Cephas, and John, who seemed to be pillars, perceived the grace that had been given to me, they gave me and Barnabas the right hand of fellowship, that we *should go* to the Gentiles and they to the circumcised. [10]*They desired* only that we should remember the poor, the very thing which I also was eager to do.

No Return to the Law

[11]Now when Peter[a] had come to Antioch, I withstood him to his face, because he was to be blamed; [12]for before certain men came from James, he would eat with the Gentiles; but when they came, he withdrew and separated himself, fearing those who were of the circumcision. [13]And the rest of the Jews also played the hypocrite with him, so that even Barnabas was carried away with their hypocrisy.

[14]But when I saw that they were not straightforward about the truth of the gospel, I said to Peter before *them* all, "If you, being a Jew, live in the manner of Gentiles and not as the Jews, why do you[a] compel Gentiles to live as Jews?[b] [15]We *who are* Jews by nature, and not sinners of the Gentiles, [16]knowing that a man is not justified by the works of the law but by faith in Jesus Christ, even we have believed in Christ Jesus, that we might be justified by faith in Christ and not by the works of the law; for by the works of the law no flesh shall be justified.

[17]"But if, while we seek to be justified by Christ, we ourselves also are found sinners, *is* Christ therefore a minister of sin? Certainly not! [18]For if I build again those things which I destroyed, I make myself a transgressor. [19]For I through the law died to the law that I might live to God. [20]I have

2:11 [a]NU-Text reads *Cephas*.   2:14 [a]NU-Text reads *how can you.*   [b]Some interpreters stop the quotation here.

been crucified with Christ; it is no longer I who live, but Christ lives in me; and the *life* which I now live in the flesh I live by faith in the Son of God, who loved me and gave Himself for me. 21I do not set aside the grace of God; for if righteousness *comes* through the law, then Christ died in vain."

Justification by Faith

3 1O foolish Galatians! Who has bewitched you that you should not obey the truth,a before whose eyes Jesus Christ was clearly portrayed among youb as crucified? 2This only I want to learn from you: Did you receive the Spirit by the works of the law, or by the hearing of faith? 3Are you so foolish? Having begun in the Spirit, are you now being made perfect by the flesh? 4Have you suffered so many things in vain—if indeed *it was* in vain?

5Therefore He who supplies the Spirit to you and works miracles among you, *does He do it* by the works of the law, or by the hearing of faith?— 6just as Abraham *"believed God, and it was accounted to him for righteousness."* a 7Therefore know that *only* those who are of faith are sons of Abraham. 8And the Scripture, foreseeing that God would justify the Gentiles by faith, preached the gospel to Abraham beforehand, *saying, "In you all the nations shall be blessed."* a 9So then those who *are* of faith are blessed with believing Abraham.

The Law Brings a Curse

10For as many as are of the works of the law are under the curse; for it is written, *"Cursed is everyone who does not continue in all things which are written in the book of the law, to do them."* a 11But that no one is justified by the law in the sight of God *is* evident, for *"the just shall live by faith."* a 12Yet the law is not of faith, but *"the man who does them shall live by them."* a

13Christ has redeemed us from the curse of the law, having become a curse for us (for it is written, *"Cursed is everyone who hangs on a tree"* a), 14that the blessing of Abraham might come upon the Gentiles in Christ Jesus, that we might receive the promise of the Spirit through faith.

The Changeless Promise

15Brethren, I speak in the manner of men: Though *it is* only a man's covenant, yet *if it is* confirmed, no one annuls or adds to it. 16Now to Abraham and his Seed were the promises made. He does not say, "And to seeds," as of many, but as of one, *"And to your Seed,"* a who is Christ. 17And this I say, *that* the law, which was four hundred and thirty years later, cannot annul the covenant that was confirmed before by God in Christ,a that it should make the promise of no effect. 18For if the inheritance *is* of the law, *it is* no longer of promise; but God gave *it* to Abraham by promise.

Purpose of the Law

19What purpose then *does* the law *serve?* It was added because of transgressions, till the Seed should come to whom the promise was made; *and it was* appointed through angels by the hand of a mediator. 20Now a mediator does not *mediate* for one *only,* but God is one.

21*Is* the law then against the promises of God? Certainly not! For if there had been a law given which could have given life, truly righteousness would have been by the law. 22But the Scripture has confined all under sin, that the promise by faith in Jesus Christ might be given to those who believe. 23But before faith came, we were kept under guard by the law, kept for the faith which would afterward be revealed. 24Therefore the law was our tutor *to bring us* to Christ, that we might be justified by faith. 25But after faith has come, we are no longer under a tutor.

TIME CAPSULE   A.D. 48 to 49

48   *Paul and Barnabas return to Antioch in Syria*

49   *Paul and Barnabas attend the Jerusalem Council (Acts 15)*

49   *Claudius expels Jews from Rome (Acts 18:2)*

49   *Seneca becomes Nero's tutor*

49   *Paul's letter to the Galatians (if to "South Galatia")*

3:1 aNU-Text omits *that you should not obey the truth.* bNU-Text omits *among you.*   3:6 aGenesis 15:6   3:8 aGenesis 12:3; 18:18; 22:18; 26:4; 28:14   3:10 aDeuteronomy 27:26
3:11 aHabakkuk 2:4   3:12 aLeviticus 18:5
3:13 aDeuteronomy 21:23   3:16 aGenesis 12:7; 13:15; 24:7   3:17 aNU-Text omits *in Christ.*

Sons and Heirs

²⁶For you are all sons of God through faith in Christ Jesus. ²⁷For as many of you as were baptized into Christ have put on Christ. ²⁸There is neither Jew nor Greek, there is neither slave nor free, there is neither male nor female; for you are all one in Christ Jesus. ²⁹And if you *are* Christ's, then you are Abraham's seed, and heirs according to the promise.

4 ¹Now I say *that* the heir, as long as he is a child, does not differ at all from a slave, though he is master of all, ²but is under guardians and stewards until the time appointed by the father. ³Even so we, when we were children, were in bondage under the elements of the world. ⁴But when the fullness of the time had come, God sent forth His Son, born^a of a woman, born under the law, ⁵to redeem those who were under the law, that we might receive the adoption as sons.

⁶And because you are sons, God has sent forth the Spirit of His Son into your hearts, crying out, "Abba, Father!" ⁷Therefore you are no longer a slave but a son, and if a son, then an heir of ^a God through Christ.

Fears for the Church

⁸But then, indeed, when you did not know God, you served those which by nature are not gods. ⁹But now after you have known God, or rather are known by God, how *is it that* you turn again to the weak and beggarly elements, to which you desire again to be in bondage? ¹⁰You observe days and months and seasons and years. ¹¹I am afraid for you, lest I have labored for you in vain.

¹²Brethren, I urge you to become like me, for I *became* like you. You have not injured me at all. ¹³You know that because of physical infirmity I preached the gospel to

you at the first. ¹⁴And my trial which was in my flesh you did not despise or reject, but you received me as an angel of God, *even* as Christ Jesus. ¹⁵What^a then was the blessing you *enjoyed?* For I bear you witness that, if possible, you would have plucked out your own eyes and given them to me. ¹⁶Have I therefore become your enemy because I tell you the truth?

¹⁷They zealously court you, *but* for no good; yes, they want to exclude you, that you may be zealous for them. ¹⁸But it is good to be zealous in a good thing always, and not only when I am present with you. ¹⁹My little children, for whom I labor in birth again until Christ is formed in you, ²⁰I would like to be present with you now and to change my tone; for I have doubts about you.

Two Covenants

²¹Tell me, you who desire to be under the law, do you not hear the law? ²²For it is written that Abraham had two sons: the one by a bondwoman, the other by a freewoman. ²³But he *who was* of the bondwoman was born according to the flesh, and he of the freewoman through promise, ²⁴which things are symbolic. For these are the^a two covenants: the one from Mount Sinai which gives birth to bondage, which is Hagar— ²⁵for this Hagar is Mount Sinai in Arabia, and corresponds to Jerusalem which now is, and is in bondage with her children— ²⁶but the Jerusalem above is free, which is the mother of us all. ²⁷For it is written:

> "Rejoice, O barren,
> You who do not bear!
> Break forth and shout,
> You who are not in labor!
> For the desolate has many more
> children
> Than she who has a husband." ^a

²⁸Now we, brethren, as Isaac *was*, are children of promise. ²⁹But, as he who was born according to the flesh then persecuted

---

4:4 ^aOr *made*   4:7 ^aNU-Text reads *through God* and omits *through Christ.*   4:15 ^aNU-Text reads *Where.*   4:24 ^aNU-Text and M-Text omit *the.* 4:27 ^aIsaiah 54:1

ARTS AND LITERATURE

Allegory was a method of interpretation that had been used by the Greeks in reading Homer. In allegory, the characters, actions, and other parts of a story are understood to be symbols standing for other things. In metaphor, there is a comparison, but in allegory, the symbols are like a code used to make assertions about things for which they stand. Paul's allegory interprets the Old Testament (Gal. 4:24).

ABBA, FATHER (Gal. 4:6)

Following some Old Testament models, Jewish prayers often addressed God as "Father," "our Father," or "our Father in heaven." They normally avoided, however, the more familiar title "Abba" (although one early sage is said to have compared God with an "abba").

Children called their fathers "Abba," a title of endearment, intimacy, and respect. Adults continued the practice, though apparently less frequently, again emphasizing the intimacy of the father-child relationship. Jesus' use of this title in prayer (Mark 14:36) demonstrated His distinctive intimacy with the heavenly Father, an intimacy which provided the model for those who followed Him by the Spirit (Rom. 8:15).

Jesus' native language was Aramaic (a Semitic language related to Hebrew), and *abba* is an Aramaic word. The Gospels, however, were written in Greek rather than in Aramaic, "Abba" being one of the few original Aramaic words preserved in a Gospel. What is most surprising is that Paul's Greek-speaking readers in Galatia already knew what "Abba" meant (Gal. 4:6). Especially the Roman readers (Rom. 8:15) could not have learned from Paul since he had not visited Rome before writing his letter there. Possibly the early Christians picked up Jesus' use of "Abba" to represent the intimacy with God which Jesus had provided for them as well.

To understand what "father" meant in Jesus' world may be helpful to many Christians today who grow up in broken homes or other family structures that are quite different from ancient Mediterranean families. Children generally viewed their fathers as strong and dependable, as affectionate, and as providers (Matt. 7:9-11). For the early Christians to call God "Abba" was for them to recognize a special intimacy with the heavenly Father on whom they depended.

---

him *who was born* according to the Spirit, even so *it is* now. [30]Nevertheless what does the Scripture say? *"Cast out the bondwoman and her son, for the son of the bondwoman shall not be heir with the son of the freewoman."* [a] [31]So then, brethren, we are not children of the bondwoman but of the free.

Christian Liberty

5 [1]Stand fast therefore in the liberty by which Christ has made us free,[a] and do not be entangled again with a yoke of bondage. [2]Indeed I, Paul, say to you that if you become circumcised, Christ will profit you nothing. [3]And I testify again to every man who becomes circumcised that he is a debtor to keep the whole law. [4]You have become estranged from Christ, you who *attempt to* be justified by law; you have fallen from grace. [5]For we through the Spirit eagerly wait for the hope of righteousness by faith. [6]For in Christ Jesus neither circumcision nor uncircumcision avails anything, but faith working through love.

Love Fulfills the Law

[7]You ran well. Who hindered you from obeying the truth? [8]This persuasion does not *come* from Him who calls you. [9]A little leaven leavens the whole lump. [10]I have confidence in you, in the Lord, that you will have no other mind; but he who troubles you shall bear his judgment, whoever he is.

[11]And I, brethren, if I still preach circumcision, why do I still suffer persecu-

---

4:30 [a]Genesis 21:10   5:1 [a]NU-Text reads *For freedom Christ has made us free; stand fast therefore.*

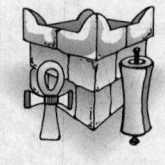

RELIGION AND WORSHIP

Circumcision, the operation to remove a fold of skin from the male parts, is usually performed on infants. All Jews practiced it as a sign of the covenant that God made with them through Abraham. If a person converted to Judaism, circumcision was a definitive step to take. When Christians said it was not necessary, they were clearly separating themselves from Judaism (Gal. 5:3-6; 6:13).

tion? Then the offense of the cross has ceased. ¹²I could wish that those who trouble you would even cut themselves off!

¹³For you, brethren, have been called to liberty; only do not *use* liberty as an opportunity for the flesh, but through love serve one another. ¹⁴For all the law is fulfilled in one word, *even* in this: *"You shall love your neighbor as yourself."* ᵃ ¹⁵But if you bite and devour one another, beware lest you be consumed by one another!

Walking in the Spirit

¹⁶I say then: Walk in the Spirit, and you shall not fulfill the lust of the flesh. ¹⁷For the flesh lusts against the Spirit, and the Spirit against the flesh; and these are contrary to one another, so that you do not do the things that you wish. ¹⁸But if you are led by the Spirit, you are not under the law.

¹⁹Now the works of the flesh are evident, which are: adultery,ᵃ fornication, uncleanness, lewdness, ²⁰idolatry, sorcery, hatred, contentions, jealousies, outbursts of wrath, selfish ambitions, dissensions, heresies, ²¹envy, murders,ᵃ drunkenness, revelries, and the like; of which I tell you beforehand, just as I also told *you* in time past, that those who practice such things will not inherit the kingdom of God.

²²But the fruit of the Spirit is love, joy, peace, longsuffering, kindness, goodness, faithfulness, ²³gentleness, self-control. Against such there is no law. ²⁴And those *who are* Christ's have crucified the flesh with its passions and desires. ²⁵If we live in the Spirit, let us also walk in the Spirit. ²⁶Let us not become conceited, provoking one another, envying one another.

Bear and Share the Burdens

6 ¹Brethren, if a man is overtaken in any trespass, you who *are* spiritual restore such a one in a spirit of gentleness, considering yourself lest you also be tempted. ²Bear one another's burdens, and so fulfill the law of Christ. ³For if anyone thinks himself to be something, when he is nothing, he deceives himself. ⁴But let each one examine his own work, and then he will have rejoicing in himself alone, and not in another. ⁵For each one shall bear his own load.

Be Generous and Do Good

⁶Let him who is taught the word share in all good things with him who teaches.

⁷Do not be deceived, God is not mocked; for whatever a man sows, that he will also reap. ⁸For he who sows to his flesh will of the flesh reap corruption, but he who sows to the Spirit will of the Spirit reap everlasting life. ⁹And let us not grow weary while doing good, for in due season we shall reap if we do not lose heart. ¹⁰Therefore, as we have opportunity, let us do good to all, especially to those who are of the household of faith.

Glory Only in the Cross

¹¹See with what large letters I have written to you with my own hand! ¹²As many as desire to make a good showing in the flesh, these *would* compel you to be circumcised, only that they may not suffer persecution for the cross of Christ. ¹³For not even those who are circumcised keep the law, but they desire to have you circumcised that they may boast in your flesh. ¹⁴But God forbid that I should boast except in the cross of our Lord Jesus Christ, by whomᵃ the world has been crucified to me, and I to the world. ¹⁵For in Christ Jesus neither circumcision nor uncircumcision avails anything, but a new creation.

Blessing and a Plea

¹⁶And as many as walk according to this rule, peace and mercy *be* upon them, and upon the Israel of God.

¹⁷From now on let no one trouble me, for I bear in my body the marks of the Lord Jesus.

¹⁸Brethren, the grace of our Lord Jesus Christ *be* with your spirit. Amen.

5:14 ᵃLeviticus 19:18   5:19 ᵃNU-Text omits *adultery.*   5:21 ᵃNU-Text omits *murders.*
6:14 ᵃOr *by which* [the cross]

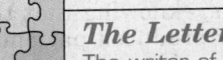

The Letter of James

The writer of this letter identifies himself only as "James, a bondservant of God and of the Lord Jesus Christ" [1:1]. The name "James" has usually been identified with the James who led the church in Jerusalem [Acts 15:13]. Paul referred to this James as "the Lord's brother" [see Mark 6:3] and included him among the "apostles" [Gal. 1:19]. He also characterized him as one of the "pillars" of the church [Gal. 2:9]. When Peter left Palestine [Acts 12:17], James seems to have become the leader of the Jerusalem church.

Since the early centuries, however, there has been disagreement about whether James, the Lord's brother, actually wrote this letter. There are no allusions to a personal relationship with Jesus, and indeed Jesus is only mentioned twice (James 1:1; 2:1). Both the quality of the letter's Greek and the structure of its arguments have suggested to some that the author was a Hellenistic Jew rather than a Jew from Palestine. If so, then the letter is pseudonymous, and the actual author associated the work with James the Just (as he was later known) by using his name. It is also possible the letter was written by a Hellenistic Jew actually named "James," who is otherwise unknown to us.

No evidence determines exactly when the letter was written. Scholars who believe the letter to be an authentic work of James the Just necessarily date it before his martyrdom in A.D. 62. Since the letter does not hint at any controversy over the issue of circumcision, some would date it around A.D. 45, before the Jerusalem Council (see "Conference in Jerusalem" at Acts 15:1). Others, however, would place it late in James's life after the controversy had diminished. Those who view the letter as pseudonymous usually date it in the last quarter of the 1st century (c. 75–100).

■ James 1:1—5:20

James
Greeting to the Twelve Tribes

1 :1 James, a bondservant of God and of the Lord Jesus Christ,

To the twelve tribes which are scattered abroad:

Greetings.

Profiting from Trials

2My brethren, count it all joy when you fall into various trials, 3knowing that the testing of your faith produces patience. 4But let patience have *its* perfect work, that you may be perfect and complete, lacking nothing. 5If any of you lacks wisdom, let him ask of God, who gives to all liberally and without reproach, and it will be given to him. 6But let him ask in faith, with no doubting, for he who doubts is like a wave of the sea driven and tossed by the wind. 7For let not that man suppose that he will receive anything from the Lord; 8*he is* a double-minded man, unstable in all his ways.

The Perspective of Rich and Poor

9Let the lowly brother glory in his exaltation, 10but the rich in his humiliation, because as a flower of the field he will pass away. 11For no sooner has the sun risen with a burning heat than it withers the grass; its flower falls, and its beautiful appearance perishes. So the rich man also will fade away in his pursuits.

Loving God Under Trials

12Blessed *is* the man who endures temptation; for when he has been approved, he will receive the crown of life which the Lord has promised to those who love Him. 13Let no one say when he is tempted, "I am tempted by God"; for God cannot be tempted by evil, nor does He Himself tempt anyone. 14But each one is tempted when he is drawn away by his own desires and enticed. 15Then, when desire has conceived, it gives birth to sin; and sin, when it is full-grown, brings forth death.

16Do not be deceived, my beloved brethren. 17Every good gift and every perfect gift is from above, and comes down from the Father of lights, with whom there is no variation or shadow of turning. 18Of His own will He brought us forth by the word of truth, that we might be a kind of firstfruits of His creatures.

Qualities Needed in Trials

19So then,a my beloved brethren, let every man be swift to hear, slow to speak, slow to wrath; 20for the wrath of man does not produce the righteousness of God.

Doers—Not Hearers Only

21Therefore lay aside all filthiness and overflow of wickedness, and receive with meekness the implanted word, which is able to save your souls.

22But be doers of the word, and not hearers only, deceiving yourselves. 23For if anyone is a hearer of the word and not a doer, he is like a man observing his natural face in a mirror; 24for he observes himself, goes away, and immediately forgets what kind of man he was. 25But he who looks into the perfect law of liberty and continues *in it,* and is not a forgetful hearer but a doer of the work, this one will be blessed in what he does.

1:19 aNU-Text reads *Know this* or *This you know.*

VARIOUS TRIALS OF THE POOR (James 1:2)

The letter of James seems especially to address the trials of the poor (James 1:2), suggesting a right response to poverty and suffering. In Judea at this time, wealthy Sadducean priests were seizing the tithes that rightfully belonged to the poorer priests. In Galilee, rich landlords were repressing the poor peasants who worked on their estates. Similar situations existed throughout much of the Roman Empire, which was therefore primed for violence. In Rome, shortages of grain often led to riots.

Conditions like these partially contributed to a revolt against Rome in Judea in the year A.D. 66—a revolt which led to widespread destruction and enslavement. Meanwhile a wave of violence was unleashed in Rome itself, and before Jerusalem fell in A.D. 70 Rome had discarded four emperors. Wealth, poverty, repression, and violence were the standard fare of the day.

The letter of James was written to encourage Christians who were suffering. The opening prologue summarizes the appropriate responses to their trials, responses which the rest of the letter discusses: wisdom (1:5), faith (1:6–8), and endurance (1:9–11). The letter also describes tensions between the rich and the poor: The wealthy are arrogant against the poor (2:1–4), and even repress them (2:6, 7) and withhold their wages (5:4). Yet the poor are advised not to retaliate with violence in deed (4:1, 2) or, perhaps more tempting, in words (4:11; 5:9).

26If anyone among you[a] thinks he is religious, and does not bridle his tongue but deceives his own heart, this one's religion *is* useless. 27Pure and undefiled religion before God and the Father is this: to visit orphans and widows in their trouble, *and* to keep oneself unspotted from the world.

Beware of Personal Favoritism

2 1My brethren, do not hold the faith of our Lord Jesus Christ, *the Lord* of glory, with partiality. 2For if there should come into your assembly a man with gold rings, in fine apparel, and there should also come in a poor man in filthy clothes, 3and you pay attention to the one wearing the fine clothes and say to him, "You sit here in a good place," and say to the poor man, "You stand there," or, "Sit here at my footstool," 4have you not shown partiality among yourselves, and become judges with evil thoughts?

5Listen, my beloved brethren: Has God not chosen the poor of this world *to be* rich in faith and heirs of the kingdom which He promised to those who love Him? 6But you have dishonored the poor man. Do not the rich oppress you and drag you into the courts? 7Do they not blaspheme that noble name by which you are called?

8If you really fulfill *the* royal law according to the Scripture, *"You shall love your neighbor as yourself,"*[a] you do well; 9but if you show partiality, you commit sin, and are convicted by the law as transgressors. 10For whoever shall keep the whole law, and yet stumble in one *point,* he is guilty of all. 11For He who said, *"Do not commit adultery,"*[a] also said, *"Do not murder."*[b] Now if you do not commit adultery, but you do murder, you have become a transgressor of the law. 12So speak and so do as those who will be judged by the law of liberty. 13For judgment is without mercy

---

1:26 [a]NU-Text omits *among you.*   2:8 [a]Leviticus
19:18   2:11 [a]Exodus 20:14; Deuteronomy 5:18
[b]Exodus 20:13; Deuteronomy 5:17

DAILY LIFE AND CUSTOMS

Ancient societies did not change their fashion of clothing every year. Certain garments and styles could persist for generations. At the same time, there was room for people to exercise vanity and to advertise their rank in society (James 2:2). Rings and other items of jewelry clearly had such functions.

to the one who has shown no mercy. Mercy triumphs over judgment.

Faith Without Works Is Dead

14What *does it* profit, my brethren, if someone says he has faith but does not have works? Can faith save him? 15If a brother or sister is naked and destitute of daily food, 16and one of you says to them, "Depart in peace, be warmed and filled," but you do not give them the things which are needed for the body, what *does it* profit? 17Thus also faith by itself, if it does not have works, is dead.

18But someone will say, "You have faith, and I have works." Show me your faith without your[a] works, and I will show you my faith by my[b] works. 19You believe that there is one God. You do well. Even the demons believe—and tremble! 20But do you want to know, O foolish man, that faith without works is dead?[a] 21Was not Abraham our father justified by works when he offered Isaac his son on the altar? 22Do you see that faith was working together with his works, and by works faith was made perfect? 23And the Scripture was fulfilled which says, *"Abraham believed God, and it was accounted to him for righteousness."*[a] And he was called the friend of God. 24You see then that a man is justified by works, and not by faith only.

25Likewise, was not Rahab the harlot also justified by works when she received the messengers and sent *them* out another way?

26For as the body without the spirit is dead, so faith without works is dead also.

The Untamable Tongue

3 1My brethren, let not many of you become teachers, knowing that we shall receive a stricter judgment. 2For we all stumble in many things. If anyone does not stumble in word, he *is* a perfect man, able also to bridle the whole body. 3Indeed,[a] we put bits in horses' mouths that they may obey us, and we turn their whole body. 4Look also at ships: although they are so large and are driven by fierce winds, they are turned by a very small rudder wherever the pilot desires. 5Even so the tongue is a little member and boasts great things.

See how great a forest a little fire kindles! 6And the tongue *is* a fire, a world of iniquity. The tongue is so set among our members that it defiles the whole body, and sets on fire the course of nature; and it is set on fire by hell. 7For every kind of beast and bird, of reptile and creature of the sea, is tamed and has been tamed by mankind. 8But no man can tame the tongue. *It is* an unruly evil, full of deadly poison. 9With it we bless our God and Father, and with it we curse men, who have been made in the similitude of God. 10Out of the same mouth proceed blessing and cursing. My brethren, these things ought not to be so. 11Does a spring send forth fresh *water* and bitter from the same opening? 12Can a fig tree, my brethren, bear olives, or a grapevine bear figs? Thus no spring yields both salt water and fresh.[a]

Heavenly Versus Demonic Wisdom

13Who *is* wise and understanding among you? Let him show by good conduct *that* his works *are done* in the meekness of wisdom. 14But if you have bitter envy and self-seeking in your hearts, do not boast and lie against the truth. 15This wisdom does not descend from above, but *is* earthly, sensual, demonic. 16For where envy and self-seeking *exist,* confusion and every evil thing *are* there. 17But the wisdom that is from above is first pure, then peaceable, gentle, willing to yield, full of mercy and good fruits, without partiality and without hypocrisy. 18Now the fruit of righteousness is sown in peace by those who make peace.

Pride Promotes Strife

4 1Where do wars and fights *come* from among you? Do *they* not *come* from your *desires for* pleasure that war in your members? 2You lust and do not have. You murder and covet and cannot obtain. You fight and war. Yet[a] you do not have because you do not ask. 3You ask and do not receive, because you ask amiss, that you may spend *it* on your pleasures. 4Adulterers and[a] adulteresses! Do you not know that friendship with the world is enmity with God? Whoever therefore wants to be a friend of the world makes himself an enemy of God. 5Or do you think that the Scripture says in vain, "The Spirit who dwells in us yearns jealously"?

2:18 [a]NU-Text omits *your.* [b]NU-Text omits *my.*
2:20 [a]NU-Text reads *useless.* 2:23 [a]Genesis 15:6 3:3 [a]NU-Text reads *Now if.*
3:12 [a]NU-Text reads *Neither can a salty spring produce fresh water.* 4:2 [a]NU-Text and M-Text omit *Yet.* 4:4 [a]NU-Text omits *Adulterers and.*

[6]But He gives more grace. Therefore He says:

"*God resists the proud,
But gives grace to the humble.*"[a]

Humility Cures Worldliness

[7]Therefore submit to God. Resist the devil and he will flee from you. [8]Draw near to God and He will draw near to you. Cleanse *your* hands, *you* sinners; and purify *your* hearts, *you* double-minded. [9]Lament and mourn and weep! Let your laughter be turned to mourning and *your* joy to gloom. [10]Humble yourselves in the sight of the Lord, and He will lift you up.

Do Not Judge a Brother

[11]Do not speak evil of one another, brethren. He who speaks evil of a brother and judges his brother, speaks evil of the law and judges the law. But if you judge the law, you are not a doer of the law but a judge. [12]There is one Lawgiver,[a] who is able to save and to destroy. Who[b] are you to judge another?[c]

Do Not Boast About Tomorrow

[13]Come now, you who say, "Today or tomorrow we will[a] go to such and such a city, spend a year there, buy and sell, and make a profit"; [14]whereas you do not know what *will happen* tomorrow. For what *is* your life? It is even a vapor that appears for a little time and then vanishes away. [15]Instead you *ought* to say, "If the Lord wills, we shall live and do this or that." [16]But now you boast in your arrogance. All such boasting is evil.

[17]Therefore, to him who knows to do good and does not do *it,* to him it is sin.

Rich Oppressors Will Be Judged

5 [1]Come now, *you* rich, weep and howl for your miseries that are coming upon *you!* [2]Your riches are corrupted, and your garments are moth-eaten. [3]Your gold and silver are corroded, and their corrosion will be a witness against you and will eat your flesh like fire. You have heaped up treasure in the last days. [4]Indeed the wages of the laborers who mowed your fields, which you kept back by fraud, cry out; and the cries of the reapers have reached the ears of the Lord of Sabaoth.[a] [5]You have lived on the earth in pleasure and luxury; you have fattened your hearts as[a] in a day of slaughter. [6]You have condemned, you have murdered the just; he does not resist you.

Be Patient and Persevering

[7]Therefore be patient, brethren, until the coming of the Lord. See *how* the farmer waits for the precious fruit of the earth, waiting patiently for it until it receives the early and latter rain. [8]You also be patient. Establish your hearts, for the coming of the Lord is at hand.

[9]Do not grumble against one another, brethren, lest you be condemned.[a] Behold, the Judge is standing at the door! [10]My brethren, take the prophets, who spoke in the name of the Lord, as an example of suffering and patience. [11]Indeed we count them blessed who endure. You have heard of the perseverance of Job and seen the end *intended by* the Lord—that the Lord is very compassionate and merciful.

[12]But above all, my brethren, do not swear, either by heaven or by earth or with any other oath. But let your "Yes" be "Yes," and *your* "No," "No," lest you fall into judgment.[a]

Meeting Specific Needs

[13]Is anyone among you suffering? Let him pray. Is anyone cheerful? Let him sing psalms. [14]Is anyone among you sick? Let him call for the elders of the church, and let them pray over him, anointing him with oil in the name of the Lord. [15]And the prayer of faith will save the sick, and the Lord will raise him up. And if he has committed sins, he will be forgiven. [16]Confess *your* trespasses[a] to one another, and pray for one another, that you may be healed. The effective, fervent prayer of a righteous man avails much. [17]Elijah was a man with a nature like ours, and he prayed earnestly that it would not rain; and it did not rain on the land for three years and six months. [18]And he prayed again, and the heaven gave rain, and the earth produced its fruit.

Bring Back the Erring One

[19]Brethren, if anyone among you wanders from the truth, and someone turns

---

4:6 [a]Proverbs 3:34　　4:12 [a]NU-Text adds *and Judge.* [b]NU-Text and M-Text read *But who.* [c]NU-Text reads *a neighbor.* 4:13 [a]M-Text reads *let us.* 5:4 [a]Literally, in Hebrew, *Hosts* 5:5 [a]NU-Text omits *as.* 5:9 [a]NU-Text and M-Text read *judged.* 5:12 [a]M-Text reads *hypocrisy.* 5:16 [a]NU-Text reads *Therefore confess your sins.*

him back, ²⁰let him know that he who turns a sinner from the error of his way will save a soulᵃ from death and cover a multitude of sins.

Paul's Second Missionary Journey

Paul's second missionary journey took him back to Asia Minor, then over to Europe to the cities of Philippi (Acts 16:11–40), Thessalonica (17:1–9), Berea (17:10–15), Athens (17:16–34), and Corinth (18:1–17). Most scholars agree that this trip ended about A.D. 52 when Paul returned to Antioch (18:22), but the beginning of the trip is variously dated between 46 and 50.

A disagreement between Paul and Barnabas over whether John Mark should accompany them on the new mission resulted in two missions instead of only one (15:37–40). Barnabas and Mark went one direction, while Paul ministered with Silas throughout this journey (15:40), with Timothy joining them at Lystra (16:1–3). The gospel spread further as Paul came into contact with Roman authorities and Greek philosophers.

▼ ■ Acts 15:36—18:11

Acts
Division over John Mark

15 :36 Then after some days Paul said to Barnabas, "Let us now go back and visit our brethren in every city where we have preached the word of the Lord, *and see* how they are doing." ³⁷Now Barnabas was determined to take with them John called Mark. ³⁸But Paul insisted that they should not take with them the one who had departed from them in Pamphylia, and had not gone with them to the work. ³⁹Then the contention became so sharp that they parted from one another. And so Barnabas took Mark and sailed to Cyprus; ⁴⁰but Paul chose Silas and departed, being commended by the brethren to the grace of God. ⁴¹And he went through Syria and Cilicia, strengthening the churches.

Timothy Joins Paul and Silas

16 ¹Then he came to Derbe and Lystra. And behold, a certain disciple was there, named Timothy, *the* son of a certain Jewish woman who believed, but his father *was* Greek. ²He was well spoken of by the

brethren who were at Lystra and Iconium. ³Paul wanted to have him go on with him. And he took *him* and circumcised him because of the Jews who were in that region, for they all knew that his father was Greek. ⁴And as they went through the cities, they delivered to them the decrees to keep, which were determined by the apostles and elders at Jerusalem. ⁵So the churches were strengthened in the faith, and increased in number daily.

The Macedonian Call

⁶Now when they had gone through Phrygia and the region of Galatia, they were forbidden by the Holy Spirit to preach the word in Asia. ⁷After they had come to Mysia, they tried to go into Bithynia, but the Spiritᵃ did not permit them. ⁸So passing by Mysia, they came down to Troas. ⁹And a vision appeared to Paul in the night. A man of Macedonia stood and pleaded with him, saying, "Come over to Macedonia and help us." ¹⁰Now after he had seen the vision, immediately we sought to go to Macedonia, concluding that the Lord had called us to preach the gospel to them.

Lydia Baptized at Philippi

¹¹Therefore, sailing from Troas, we ran a straight course to Samothrace, and the next *day* came to Neapolis, ¹²and from there to Philippi, which is the foremost city of that part of Macedonia, a colony. And we were staying in that city for some days. ¹³And on the Sabbath day we went out of the city to the riverside, where prayer was customarily made; and we sat down and spoke to the women who met *there.* ¹⁴Now a certain woman named Lydia heard *us.* She was a seller of purple from the city of Thyatira, who worshiped God. The Lord opened her heart to heed the things spoken by Paul. ¹⁵And when she and her household were baptized, she begged *us,* saying, "If you have judged me to be faithful to the Lord, come to my house and stay." So she persuaded us.

Paul and Silas Imprisoned

¹⁶Now it happened, as we went to prayer, that a certain slave girl possessed with a spirit of divination met us, who brought her masters much profit by

5:20 ᵃNU-Text reads *his soul.*
Acts 16:7 ᵃNU-Text adds *of Jesus.*

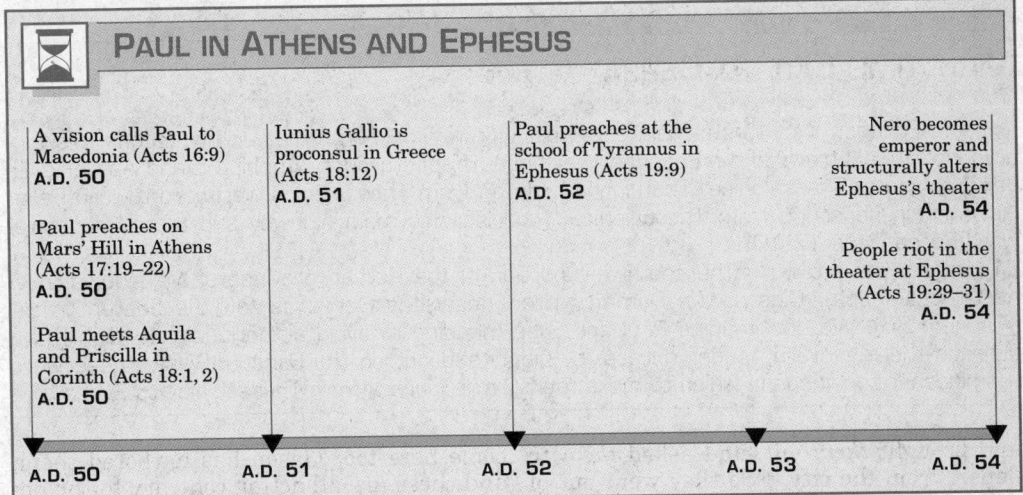

PAUL IN ATHENS AND EPHESUS

A vision calls Paul to Macedonia (Acts 16:9) **A.D. 50**	Iunius Gallio is proconsul in Greece (Acts 18:12) **A.D. 51**	Paul preaches at the school of Tyrannus in Ephesus (Acts 19:9) **A.D. 52**	Nero becomes emperor and structurally alters Ephesus's theater **A.D. 54**
Paul preaches on Mars' Hill in Athens (Acts 17:19–22) **A.D. 50**			People riot in the theater at Ephesus (Acts 19:29–31) **A.D. 54**
Paul meets Aquila and Priscilla in Corinth (Acts 18:1, 2) **A.D. 50**			

A.D. 50　　　**A.D. 51**　　　**A.D. 52**　　　**A.D. 53**　　　**A.D. 54**

fortune-telling. ¹⁷This girl followed Paul and us, and cried out, saying, "These men are the servants of the Most High God, who proclaim to us the way of salvation." ¹⁸And this she did for many days.

But Paul, greatly annoyed, turned and said to the spirit, "I command you in the name of Jesus Christ to come out of her." And he came out that very hour. ¹⁹But when her masters saw that their hope of profit was gone, they seized Paul and Silas and dragged *them* into the marketplace to the authorities.

²⁰And they brought them to the magistrates, and said, "These men, being Jews, exceedingly trouble our city; ²¹and they teach customs which are not lawful for us, being Romans, to receive or observe." ²²Then the multitude rose up together against them; and the magistrates tore off their clothes and commanded *them* to be beaten with rods. ²³And when they had laid many stripes on them, they threw *them* into prison, commanding the jailer to keep them securely. ²⁴Having received such a charge, he put them into the inner prison and fastened their feet in the stocks.

The Philippian Jailer Saved

²⁵But at midnight Paul and Silas were praying and singing hymns to God, and the prisoners were listening to them. ²⁶Suddenly there was a great earthquake, so that the foundations of the prison were shaken; and immediately all the doors were opened and everyone's chains were loosed. ²⁷And the keeper of the prison, awaking from sleep and seeing the prison

doors open, supposing the prisoners had fled, drew his sword and was about to kill himself. ²⁸But Paul called with a loud voice, saying, "Do yourself no harm, for we are all here."

²⁹Then he called for a light, ran in, and fell down trembling before Paul and Silas. ³⁰And he brought them out and said, "Sirs, what must I do to be saved?"

³¹So they said, "Believe on the Lord Jesus Christ, and you will be saved, you and your household." ³²Then they spoke the word of the Lord to him and to all who were in his house. ³³And he took them the same hour of the night and washed *their* stripes. And immediately he and all his family were baptized. ³⁴Now when he had brought them into his house, he set food before them; and he rejoiced, having believed in God with all his household.

Paul Refuses to Depart Secretly

³⁵And when it was day, the magistrates sent the officers, saying, "Let those men go."

³⁶So the keeper of the prison reported these words to Paul, saying, "The magistrates have sent to let you go. Now therefore depart, and go in peace."

³⁷But Paul said to them, "They have beaten us openly, uncondemned Romans, *and* have thrown *us* into prison. And now do they put us out secretly? No indeed! Let them come themselves and get us out."

³⁸And the officers told these words to the magistrates, and they were afraid when they heard that they were Romans. ³⁹Then they came and pleaded with them

NIGHTTIME EXIT TO BEREA (Acts 17:10)

The Egnatian Way was a main east-west highway in Paul's time. On his second mission-ary journey Paul traveled the Egnatian Way from Philippi through Amphipolis and Apollonia, fi-nally arriving at Thessalonica. The highway ran on from Thessalonica westward toward Pella. However, in departing from Thessalonica, Paul left this main highway and turned south to-ward Berea (Acts 17:10).

Berea was a town in the southwest portion of the Roman province of Macedonia (now northern Greece). Cicero, the Roman writer, describes Berea as "off the beaten track" (*Pisonem* 36). We can imagine Paul and Silas, needing to avoid authorities that might have pursued them, traveling under duress, by night, and not on the Egnatian Way. These were not pleasant conditions in which to make the 50-mile journey from Thessalonica to Berea.

and brought *them* out, and asked *them* to depart from the city. ⁴⁰So they went out of the prison and entered *the house of* Lydia; and when they had seen the brethren, they encouraged them and departed.

Preaching Christ at Thessalonica

17 ¹Now when they had passed through Amphipolis and Apollonia, they came to Thessalonica, where there was a synagogue of the Jews. ²Then Paul, as his custom was, went in to them, and for three Sabbaths reasoned with them from the Scriptures, ³explaining and dem-onstrating that the Christ had to suffer and rise again from the dead, and *saying*, "This Jesus whom I preach to you is the Christ." ⁴And some of them were per-suaded; and a great multitude of the de-vout Greeks, and not a few of the leading women, joined Paul and Silas.

Assault on Jason's House

⁵But the Jews who were not per-suaded, becoming envious,ᵃ took some of the evil men from the marketplace, and gathering a mob, set all the city in an up-roar and attacked the house of Jason, and sought to bring them out to the people. ⁶But when they did not find them, they dragged Jason and some brethren to the rulers of the city, crying out, "These who have turned the world upside down have

come here too. ⁷Jason has harbored them, and these are all acting contrary to the de-crees of Caesar, saying there is another king—Jesus." ⁸And they troubled the crowd and the rulers of the city when they heard these things. ⁹So when they had taken security from Jason and the rest, they let them go.

Ministering at Berea

¹⁰Then the brethren immediately sent Paul and Silas away by night to Berea. When they arrived, they went into the syn-agogue of the Jews. ¹¹These were more fair-minded than those in Thessalonica, in that they received the word with all readiness, and searched the Scriptures daily *to find out* whether these things were so. ¹²There-fore many of them believed, and also not a few of the Greeks, prominent women as well as men. ¹³But when the Jews from Thessalonica learned that the word of God was preached by Paul at Berea, they came there also and stirred up the crowds. ¹⁴Then immediately the brethren sent Paul away, to go to the sea; but both Silas and Timothy remained there. ¹⁵So those who conducted Paul brought him to Athens; and receiving a command for Silas and Timothy

17:5 ᵃNU-Text omits *who were not persuaded*; M-Text omits *becoming envious*.

GEOGRAPHY AND ENVIRONMENT

Paul spoke at the Areopagus, whose name was associated with Ares, the Greek god of war (Acts 17:22). In Greek, the name "Areopagus" means "hill of Ares" or "Mars' Hill." It is the name of a hill below the Acropolis in Athens, and also of the traditional law court of Athens, which once met on or near the hill. A little farther from the Acropolis and below the Areopagus was the agora, the city marketplace.

STOICS, EPICUREANS, AND A BABBLER (Acts 17:18)

In Athens, Paul encountered the Epicurean and Stoic philosophers (Acts 17:18). Epicureans, who held little influence outside the academic elite of their day, dismissed popular Greek notions about the gods. If deities existed, Epicureans argued, one could know them only in terms of physical phenomena like stars or planets. In Epicurean philosophy the supreme goal was pleasure, defined especially as the absence of pain.

By contrast, the more popular Stoics opposed pleasure, criticized Epicureans, and usually professed belief in the gods. Nevertheless, Stoics had interpretations of the gods that were quite different from those held by the common people. Sometimes Stoics focused on the supreme deity, whom they saw as ruling and permeating the universe.

Paul could not appeal simultaneously to both of these groups as he addressed them at the Areopagus. Most of what he says fits both Christian and Stoic teaching (Acts 17:22–29). Only after he had won his audience's ear did he present distinctive Christian theology (17:30, 31).

In 399 B.C. the council of the Areopagus had accused Socrates of introducing new gods, so with the charge against Paul of proclaiming "foreign gods" (17:18) the Athenians were treating him as they had their most famous thinker. Such a charge had once been a capital offense in Athens; they had stoned to death a priestess for the same crime.

Paul's philosophic critics called him a "babbler" (17:18). In Greek, the term originally referred to birds pecking up grain, but by Paul's time it meant worthless persons—perhaps somewhat like the traditional American insult "birdbrain." Yet this "babbler's" sermon was not a failure, and resulted in new believers including the influential Dionysius (17:33, 34). A tradition from Eusebius reports that Dionysius the Areopagite became the first Christian bishop of Athens.

---

to come to him with all speed, they departed.

The Philosophers at Athens

16Now while Paul waited for them at Athens, his spirit was provoked within him when he saw that the city was given over to idols. 17Therefore he reasoned in the synagogue with the Jews and with the *Gentile* worshipers, and in the marketplace daily with those who happened to be there. 18Then[a] certain Epicurean and Stoic philosophers encountered him. And some said, "What does this babbler want to say?"

Others said, "He seems to be a proclaimer of foreign gods," because he preached to them Jesus and the resurrection.

19And they took him and brought him to the Areopagus, saying, "May we know what this new doctrine *is* of which you speak? 20For you are bringing some strange things to our ears. Therefore we want to know what these things mean." 21For all the Athenians and the foreigners who were there spent their time in nothing else but either to tell or to hear some new thing.

Addressing the Areopagus

22Then Paul stood in the midst of the Areopagus and said, "Men of Athens, I perceive that in all things you are very religious; 23for as I was passing through and considering the objects of your worship, I even found an altar with this inscription:

TO THE UNKNOWN GOD.

Therefore, the One whom you worship without knowing, Him I proclaim to you: 24God, who made the world and everything in it, since He is Lord of heaven and earth, does not dwell in temples made with hands. 25Nor is He worshiped with men's hands, as though He needed anything, since He gives to all life, breath, and all things. 26And He has made from one blood[a] every nation of men to dwell on all the face of the earth, and has determined their preappointed times and the boundaries of their dwellings, 27so that they should seek the Lord, in the hope that they might grope

---

17:18 ᵃNU-Text and M-Text add *also*.
17:26 ᵃNU-Text omits *blood*.

PAUL BEFORE THE AREOPAGUS (Acts 17:19)

In A.D. 50 Paul visited Athens and began preaching in the agora, the marketplace which in ancient Greece served as the center of public life (Acts 17:17). Paul was summoned by the Athenians to the Areopagus, where he preached his sermon about the "unknown God" (Acts 17:19–23). The purpose of his visit to the Areopagus and its council is not certain, but he may have been on trial to defend his beliefs. We know of one individual from the Areopagus council, Dionysius, who became convinced of the truthfulness of Paul's message (Acts 17:34).

The Areopagus was a prominent hill in Athens (nearly 400 feet high) that was associated with the Greek god of war, Ares. Although ancient references to the council of the Areopagus are few, it is evident that it was an aristocratic body that advised the king. It then assumed royal functions after the Athenians deposed their monarchy (sometime before 800 B.C.). With the rise of democracy in 500 B.C. the council lost some of its power and became largely an esteemed group with religious functions.

By the 1st century A.D. the council of the Areopagus had regained much of its former authority. The assembly to which Paul preached was again the chief governing body in Athens, a position it would keep until the advent of Christian domination in the 4th century A.D.

---

for Him and find Him, though He is not far from each one of us; 28for in Him we live and move and have our being, as also some of your own poets have said, 'For we are also His offspring.' 29Therefore, since we are the offspring of God, we ought not to think that the Divine Nature is like gold or silver or stone, something shaped by art and man's devising. 30Truly, these times of ignorance God overlooked, but now commands all men everywhere to repent, 31because He has appointed a day on which He will judge the world in righteousness by the Man whom He has ordained. He has given assurance of this to all by raising Him from the dead."

32And when they heard of the resurrection of the dead, some mocked, while others said, "We will hear you again on this *matter.*" 33So Paul departed from among them. 34However, some men joined him and believed, among them Dionysius the Areopagite, a woman named Damaris, and others with them.

Ministering at Corinth

18 1After these things Paul departed from Athens and went to Corinth. 2And he found a certain Jew named Aquila, born in Pontus, who had recently come from Italy with his wife Priscilla (because Claudius had commanded all the Jews to depart from Rome); and he came to them. 3So, because he was of the same trade, he stayed with them and worked; for by occu-

pation they were tentmakers. 4And he reasoned in the synagogue every Sabbath, and persuaded both Jews and Greeks.

5When Silas and Timothy had come from Macedonia, Paul was compelled by the Spirit, and testified to the Jews *that* Jesus *is* the Christ. 6But when they opposed him and blasphemed, he shook *his* garments and said to them, "Your blood *be* upon your *own* heads; I *am* clean. From now on I will go to the Gentiles." 7And he departed from there and entered the house of a certain *man* named Justus,a *one* who worshiped God, whose house was next door to the synagogue. 8Then Crispus, the ruler of the synagogue, believed on the Lord with all his household. And many of the Corinthians, hearing, believed and were baptized.

9Now the Lord spoke to Paul in the night by a vision, "Do not be afraid, but speak, and do not keep silent; 10for I am with you, and no one will attack you to hurt you; for I have many people in this city." 11And he continued *there* a year and six months, teaching the word of God among them.

18:7 aNU-Text reads *Titius Justus.*

The First Letter to the Thessalonians

Paul, Silas, and Timothy came to Thessalonica on Paul's second missionary journey

(Acts 17:1–9). Paul's stay at Thessalonica was brief, at most only a few months. From there he went to Berea (17:10), on to Athens (17:15), and then to Corinth (18:1). From Athens Paul sent Timothy to encourage the Thessalonians, and when Timothy returned to him at Corinth, the apostle was overjoyed at the news of the strong faith of the Thessalonians. From Corinth he wrote the first Thessalonian letter in late A.D. 50 or early 51. First Thessalonians is one of the earliest of Paul's letters, and thus also one of the first books in the New Testament to be written.

Thessalonica, now called Salonika, was an ancient Greek city, the capital of the Roman province of Macedonia. Paul began his ministry there in the Jewish synagogue; however, the church that resulted included not only Jews, but also a number of devout Greeks and many leading women. Many Jews of Thessalonica did not become believers, and the synagogue rulers eventually rejected Paul and drove him from the town (Acts 17:10).

Paul had not had time in Thessalonica to instruct his converts as thoroughly as he would have liked. Thus, in this letter he wanted to express his joy at their steadfastness, encourage them in the midst of suffering, and correct misconceptions about the Lord's return.

▼   ■ 1 Thessalonians 1:1—2:20

1 Thessalonians
Greeting

1 :1 Paul, Silvanus, and Timothy,

To the church of the Thessalonians in God the Father and the Lord Jesus Christ:

Grace to you and peace from God our Father and the Lord Jesus Christ.[a]

Their Good Example

2 We give thanks to God always for you all, making mention of you in our prayers,

---

1:1 [a]NU-Text omits *from God our Father and the Lord Jesus Christ.*   2:2 [a]NU-Text and M-Text omit *even.*

3 remembering without ceasing your work of faith, labor of love, and patience of hope in our Lord Jesus Christ in the sight of our God and Father, 4 knowing, beloved brethren, your election by God. 5 For our gospel did not come to you in word only, but also in power, and in the Holy Spirit and in much assurance, as you know what kind of men we were among you for your sake.

6 And you became followers of us and of the Lord, having received the word in much affliction, with joy of the Holy Spirit, 7 so that you became examples to all in Macedonia and Achaia who believe. 8 For from you the word of the Lord has sounded forth, not only in Macedonia and Achaia, but also in every place. Your faith toward God has gone out, so that we do not need to say anything. 9 For they themselves declare concerning us what manner of entry we had to you, and how you turned to God from idols to serve the living and true God, 10 and to wait for His Son from heaven, whom He raised from the dead, *even* Jesus who delivers us from the wrath to come.

Paul's Conduct

2 1 For you yourselves know, brethren, that our coming to you was not in vain. 2 But even[a] after we had suffered before and were spitefully treated at Philippi, as you know, we were bold in our God to speak to you the gospel of God in much conflict. 3 For our exhortation *did* not *come* from error or uncleanness, nor *was it* in deceit.

4 But as we have been approved by God to be entrusted with the gospel, even so we speak, not as pleasing men, but God who tests our hearts. 5 For neither at any time did we use flattering words, as you know, nor a cloak for covetousness—God *is* witness. 6 Nor did we seek glory from men, either from you or from others, when we might have made demands as apostles of Christ. 7 But we were gentle among you, just as a nursing *mother* cherishes her own children. 8 So, affectionately longing for

GEOGRAPHY AND ENVIRONMENT
Thessalonica (1 Thess. 1:1) was located about 200 miles north of Athens, on the main road leading from Rome to Byzantium (that is, Istanbul). As the capital of the province of Macedonia, the city had been Pompey's headquarters during the civil war that he lost to Julius Caesar. It was a prosperous trading city, as well as the home of Paul's coworkers, Aristarchus and Secundus (Acts 20:4).

you, we were well pleased to impart to you not only the gospel of God, but also our own lives, because you had become dear to us. ⁹For you remember, brethren, our labor and toil; for laboring night and day, that we might not be a burden to any of you, we preached to you the gospel of God.

¹⁰You *are* witnesses, and God *also,* how devoutly and justly and blamelessly we behaved ourselves among you who believe; ¹¹as you know how we exhorted, and comforted, and charged[a] every one of you, as a father *does* his own children, ¹²that you would walk worthy of God who calls you into His own kingdom and glory.

Their Conversion

¹³For this reason we also thank God without ceasing, because when you received the word of God which you heard from us, you welcomed *it* not *as* the word of men, but as it is in truth, the word of God, which also effectively works in you who believe. ¹⁴For you, brethren, became imitators of the churches of God which are in Judea in Christ Jesus. For you also suffered the same things from your own countrymen, just as they *did* from the Judeans, ¹⁵who killed both the Lord Jesus and their own prophets, and have persecuted us; and they do not please God and are contrary to all men, ¹⁶forbidding us to speak to the Gentiles that they may be saved, so as always to fill up *the measure of* their sins; but wrath has come upon them to the uttermost.

Longing to See Them

¹⁷But we, brethren, having been taken away from you for a short time in presence, not in heart, endeavored more eagerly to see your face with great desire. ¹⁸Therefore we wanted to come to you—even I, Paul, time and again—but Satan hindered us. ¹⁹For what *is* our hope, or joy, or crown of rejoicing? *Is it* not even you in the presence of our Lord Jesus Christ at His coming? ²⁰For you are our glory and joy.

Good News from Thessalonica

From Thessalonica the missionaries had gone to Berea (Acts 17:10–15). Silas and Timothy stayed there, while Paul went on to Athens. Anxious because of the severe persecution the Christians faced at Thessalonica, he

asked Timothy to return to that city and encourage them (1 Thess. 3:2). Paul went on to Corinth, where Timothy later joined him with news of the faith and courage of the Thessalonians (Acts 18:1, 5).

How the missionary loved his converts! After such deep anxiety over them, their standing "fast in the Lord" (1 Thess. 3:8) gave him a new lease on life. Yet the faith of the Thessalonians still lacked full instruction because Paul's stay with them had been cut short, so now he wrote, providing the needed instruction (4:1—5:24).

▼   ■ 1 Thessalonians 3:1—5:28

1 Thessalonians
Concern for Their Faith

3 :1 Therefore, when we could no longer endure it, we thought it good to be left in Athens alone, ²and sent Timothy, our brother and minister of God, and our fellow laborer in the gospel of Christ, to establish you and encourage you concerning your faith, ³that no one should be shaken by these afflictions; for you yourselves know that we are appointed to this. ⁴For, in fact, we told you before when we were with you that we would suffer tribulation, just as it happened, and you know. ⁵For this reason, when I could no longer endure it, I sent to know your faith, lest by some means the tempter had tempted you, and our labor might be in vain.

Encouraged by Timothy

⁶But now that Timothy has come to us from you, and brought us good news of your faith and love, and that you always have good remembrance of us, greatly desiring to see us, as we also *to see* you—⁷therefore, brethren, in all our affliction and distress we were comforted concerning you by your faith. ⁸For now we live, if you stand fast in the Lord.

⁹For what thanks can we render to God for you, for all the joy with which we rejoice for your sake before our God, ¹⁰night and day praying exceedingly that we may see your face and perfect what is lacking in your faith?

Prayer for the Church

¹¹Now may our God and Father Himself, and our Lord Jesus Christ, direct our way to you. ¹²And may the Lord make you

2:11 ªNU-Text and M-Text read *implored.*

ALONE IN THE CITY OF PHILOSOPHERS (1 Thess. 3:1)

In A.D. 50 Paul sent Timothy to minister in Thessalonica while he remained alone in Athens (1 Thess. 3:1–3). Paul was confronted by what was considered the city with the greatest academic tradition of the region. Here Paul met various philosophers (Acts 17:18). Here he met Athenians who spent much time discussing and debating "some new thing" (Acts 17:21). The city's intellectual life had a long history prior to Paul's visit.

The Greek city-state of Athens was composed of the city of Athens proper, along with the entire peninsula of Attica, more than 1,000 square miles. By the 7th century B.C. the Attic peninsula was unified under the control of Athens, and the Athenian monarchy had been replaced with a ruling class aristocracy.

All philosophy did not originate in the region; however, Athens did become the center of Greek philosophy in the 4th century B.C. Socrates (469–399 B.C.), Plato (428–347 B.C.), and Aristotle (384–322 B.C.) all made their greatest contributions while residing in Athens. During the Hellenistic period (beginning around 332 B.C.) Athens continued to house some of the most important philosophical schools in the Mediterranean world, including representatives of the Stoics, Cynics, Skeptics, and Epicureans.

Athens finally became subject to Rome in the early part of the 1st century B.C. Although Athenians lost their international political autonomy, the Romans were content to allow them local political rule. Roman senators sent their sons to study in Athens, which continued its preeminence in the field of philosophy and culture on into the 1st century A.D. In Paul's time, discussions of philosophical matters flourished in the agora (or marketplace), and there certain Athenian philosophers discovered Paul and his "new doctrine" (Acts 17:17–19).

increase and abound in love to one another and to all, just as we *do* to you, [13]so that He may establish your hearts blameless in holiness before our God and Father at the coming of our Lord Jesus Christ with all His saints.

Plea for Purity

4 [1]Finally then, brethren, we urge and exhort in the Lord Jesus that you should abound more and more, just as you received from us how you ought to walk and to please God; [2]for you know what commandments we gave you through the Lord Jesus.

[3]For this is the will of God, your sanctification: that you should abstain from sexual immorality; [4]that each of you should know how to possess his own vessel in sanctification and honor, [5]not in passion of lust, like the Gentiles who do not know God; [6]that no one should take advantage of and defraud his brother in this matter, because the Lord *is* the avenger of all such, as we also forewarned you and testified. [7]For God did not call us to uncleanness, but in holiness. [8]Therefore he who rejects *this* does not reject man, but God, who has also given[a] us His Holy Spirit.

A Brotherly and Orderly Life

[9]But concerning brotherly love you have no need that I should write to you, for you yourselves are taught by God to love one another; [10]and indeed you do so toward all the brethren who are in all Macedonia. But we urge you, brethren, that you increase more and more; [11]that you also aspire to lead a quiet life, to mind your own

---

TIME CAPSULE A.D. 50

50 Claudius adopts Nero

50 Beginning of Paul's second missionary journey (Acts 15:36)

50 Plutarch, author of the Lives, is born

50 A vision calls Paul to Macedonia

50 Paul preaches on Mars' Hill in Athens (Acts 17)

50–51 Paul writes 1 Thessalonians from Corinth

4:8 [a]NU-Text reads *who also gives.*

PICTURES OF THE END TIME (1 Thess. 4:16)

The "voice of an archangel" and the "trumpet of God" (1 Thess. 4:16) emphasize the divine authority behind Paul's description of Jesus' return. The images and pictures Paul uses for the end time overlap with those of other Jews of his time, though he omits most elements found in contemporary Jewish descriptions. What Paul does describe especially matches Jesus' picture of the end time (trumpet, clouds, angels, times and seasons, sudden destruction).

Jewish readers familiar with the Old Testament recognized the importance of trumpets for gathering the assembly, sometimes to battle. Gentile readers probably knew the Roman use of trumpets to gather troops or to send signals in battle. Most relevant, Jewish tradition, as emphasized in a daily synagogue prayer, portrayed the gathering of Israel in the end time as accompanied by the sounding of a trumpet.

The highest archangel, according to Jewish tradition, was Michael (Dan. 10:13), who was also the special patron for Israel. Each nation had a guardian angel, but Michael was especially powerful, as the guardian of God's chosen people. Jewish traditions sometimes gave Michael special prominence in the final battle, though, for Paul, Jesus fulfilled this function Himself (1 Thess. 4:16).

The "shout," conjoined with the trumpet, may picture the battle cry offered by a commander. The Old Testament sometimes portrays God as a divine warrior, occasionally mentioning His battle cry (Is. 42:13).

Jesus' teaching about the end time (Matt. 24) is probably the background for Paul's own teaching, which he claimed was by "the word of the Lord" (1 Thess. 4:15). As Jesus described the coming Son of Man, He applied to Himself a variety of end-time descriptions that the Old Testament and Judaism normally reserved only for God (Matt. 24:30, 31). Similarly, Paul applies these same descriptions to the coming Christ.

---

business, and to work with your own hands, as we commanded you, 12that you may walk properly toward those who are outside, and *that* you may lack nothing.

The Comfort of Christ's Coming

13But I do not want you to be ignorant, brethren, concerning those who have fallen asleep, lest you sorrow as others who have no hope. 14For if we believe that Jesus died and rose again, even so God will bring with Him those who sleep in Jesus.a

15For this we say to you by the word of the Lord, that we who are alive *and* remain until the coming of the Lord will by no means precede those who are asleep. 16For the Lord Himself will descend from heaven with a shout, with the voice of an archangel, and with the trumpet of God. And the dead in Christ will rise first. 17Then we who are alive *and* remain shall be caught up together with them in the clouds to meet the Lord in the air. And thus we shall always be with the Lord. 18Therefore comfort one another with these words.

The Day of the Lord

5 1But concerning the times and the seasons, brethren, you have no need that I should write to you. 2For you yourselves know perfectly that the day of the Lord so comes as a thief in the night. 3For when they say, "Peace and safety!" then sudden destruction comes upon them, as labor pains upon a pregnant woman. And they shall not escape. 4But you, brethren, are not in darkness, so that this Day should overtake you as a thief. 5You are all sons of light and sons of the day. We are not of the night nor of darkness. 6Therefore let us not sleep, as others *do,* but let us watch and be sober. 7For those who sleep, sleep at night, and those who get drunk are drunk at night. 8But let us who are of the day be sober, putting on the breastplate of faith and love, and *as* a helmet the hope of salvation. 9For God did not appoint us to wrath, but to obtain salvation through our Lord Jesus Christ, 10who died for us, that whether we wake or sleep, we should live together with Him.

4:14 aOr *those who through Jesus sleep*

¹¹Therefore comfort each other and edify one another, just as you also are doing.

Various Exhortations

¹²And we urge you, brethren, to recognize those who labor among you, and are over you in the Lord and admonish you, ¹³and to esteem them very highly in love for their work's sake. Be at peace among yourselves.

¹⁴Now we exhort you, brethren, warn those who are unruly, comfort the fainthearted, uphold the weak, be patient with all. ¹⁵See that no one renders evil for evil to anyone, but always pursue what is good both for yourselves and for all.

¹⁶Rejoice always, ¹⁷pray without ceasing, ¹⁸in everything give thanks; for this is the will of God in Christ Jesus for you.

¹⁹Do not quench the Spirit. ²⁰Do not despise prophecies. ²¹Test all things; hold fast what is good. ²²Abstain from every form of evil.

Blessing and Admonition

²³Now may the God of peace Himself sanctify you completely; and may your whole spirit, soul, and body be preserved blameless at the coming of our Lord Jesus Christ. ²⁴He who calls you *is* faithful, who also will do *it*.

²⁵Brethren, pray for us.

²⁶Greet all the brethren with a holy kiss.

²⁷I charge you by the Lord that this epistle be read to all the holyᵃ brethren.

²⁸The grace of our Lord Jesus Christ *be* with you. Amen.

5:27 ᵃNU-Text omits *holy.*

The Second Letter to the Thessalonians

It appears that several issues Paul addressed in 1 Thessalonians were still very much alive when the second Thessalonian letter was written: the suffering of Christians, idleness, and the Lord's return. Thus, Paul

could have written this letter from Corinth a few months after writing 1 Thessalonians, probably late in A.D. 51.

While both letters are very concerned with the Second Coming of Christ, some scholars question whether Paul is the author of both. In 1 Thessalonians, Paul was so certain of the nearness of Christ's return that he anticipated both himself and some of the Thessalonians being alive to see it (1 Thess. 4:15). A somewhat different view is expressed in 2 Thessalonians. Several specific events, some involving "the man of sin," must transpire before the Lord's coming (2 Thess. 2:1–12). Those who are convinced that Paul's theology about the end of time could not have changed to this degree in only a few months conclude that 2 Thessalonians is a pseudonymous letter. Some later writer, writing sometime after Paul's death (A.D. 80–100), but using his name (2 Thess. 3:17), addressed mounting concerns about the delay in Christ's return.

■ 2 Thessalonians 1:1—3:18

2 Thessalonians
Greeting

1 :1 Paul, Silvanus, and Timothy,

To the church of the Thessalonians in God our Father and the Lord Jesus Christ:

²Grace to you and peace from God our Father and the Lord Jesus Christ.

God's Final Judgment and Glory

³We are bound to thank God always for you, brethren, as it is fitting, because your faith grows exceedingly, and the love of every one of you all abounds toward each other, ⁴so that we ourselves boast of you among the churches of God for your patience and faith in all your persecutions and tribulations that you endure, ⁵*which is* manifest evidence of the righteous judgment of God, that you may be counted worthy of the kingdom of God, for which you also suffer; ⁶since *it is* a righteous thing with God to repay with tribulation those

---

DAILY LIFE AND CUSTOMS

Kisses were a common greeting for family, friends, and respected acquaintances. The "holy kiss" (1 Thess. 5:26) was not a romantic kiss on the lips or face. For example, in one form known today, as the parties shook hands they leaned forward repeatedly, bowing and repeating stylized formulas of greeting near the other person's ear.

who trouble you, [7]and to *give* you who are troubled rest with us when the Lord Jesus is revealed from heaven with His mighty angels, [8]in flaming fire taking vengeance on those who do not know God, and on those who do not obey the gospel of our Lord Jesus Christ. [9]These shall be punished with everlasting destruction from the presence of the Lord and from the glory of His power, [10]when He comes, in that Day, to be glorified in His saints and to be admired among all those who believe,[a] because our testimony among you was believed.

[11]Therefore we also pray always for you that our God would count you worthy of *this* calling, and fulfill all the good pleasure of *His* goodness and the work of faith with power, [12]that the name of our Lord Jesus Christ may be glorified in you, and you in Him, according to the grace of our God and the Lord Jesus Christ.

The Great Apostasy

2 [1]Now, brethren, concerning the coming of our Lord Jesus Christ and our gathering together to Him, we ask you, [2]not to be soon shaken in mind or troubled, either by spirit or by word or by letter, as if from us, as though the day of Christ[a] had come. [3]Let no one deceive you by any means; for *that Day will not come* unless the falling away comes first, and the man of sin[a] is revealed, the son of perdition, [4]who opposes and exalts himself above all that is called God or that is worshiped, so that he sits as God[a] in the temple of God, showing himself that he is God.

[5]Do you not remember that when I was still with you I told you these things? [6]And now you know what is restraining, that he may be revealed in his own time. [7]For the mystery of lawlessness is already at work; only He[a] who now restrains *will do so* until He[b] is taken out of the way. [8]And then the lawless one will be revealed, whom the Lord will consume with the breath of His mouth and destroy with the brightness of His coming. [9]The coming of the *lawless one*

is according to the working of Satan, with all power, signs, and lying wonders, [10]and with all unrighteous deception among those who perish, because they did not receive the love of the truth, that they might be saved. [11]And for this reason God will send them strong delusion, that they should believe the lie, [12]that they all may be condemned who did not believe the truth but had pleasure in unrighteousness.

Stand Fast

[13]But we are bound to give thanks to God always for you, brethren beloved by the Lord, because God from the beginning chose you for salvation through sanctification by the Spirit and belief in the truth, [14]to which He called you by our gospel, for the obtaining of the glory of our Lord Jesus Christ. [15]Therefore, brethren, stand fast and hold the traditions which you were taught, whether by word or our epistle.

[16]Now may our Lord Jesus Christ Himself, and our God and Father, who has loved us and given *us* everlasting consolation and good hope by grace, [17]comfort your hearts and establish you in every good word and work.

Pray for Us

3 [1]Finally, brethren, pray for us, that the word of the Lord may run *swiftly* and be glorified, just as *it is* with you, [2]and that we may be delivered from unreasonable and wicked men; for not all have faith. [3]But the Lord is faithful, who will establish you and guard *you* from the evil one. [4]And we have confidence in the Lord concerning you, both that you do and will do the things we command you.

[5]Now may the Lord direct your hearts into the love of God and into the patience of Christ.

1:10 [a]NU-Text and M-Text read *have believed.*
2:2 [a]NU-Text reads *the Lord.*   2:3 [a]NU-Text reads *lawlessness.*   2:4 [a]NU-Text omits *as God.*
2:7 [a]Or he [b]Or he

TRADE AND ECONOMICS

Some of the philosophers of the ancient world considered themselves above everyday work. The Cynics styled themselves as wandering beggars, proud of their otherworldliness and not ashamed to beg. Their refusal to work (2 Thess. 3:6–8) did not result from simple laziness, but rather from their rejection of community standards and tradition.

GALLIO RULES THE PROVINCE OF ACHAIA (Acts 18:12)

L. Iunius Gallio Annaeanus was the brother of the celebrated Latin writer and Stoic philosopher Seneca. Gallio held a number of important administrative posts within the Roman Empire, including that of proconsul of Achaia (southern Greece). Apparently, Paul visited Corinth, the capital of Achaia, during Gallio's term of office as proconsul (Acts 18:12).

Gallio is often mentioned in the writings of Seneca, as well as in those of Pliny the Elder. Moreover, a number of fragments from an inscription at Delphi dated to A.D. 52 mention Iunius Gallio. The text of the inscription, which has been interpreted as a letter from Emperor Claudius to Delphi, appears to concern the resettlement of Delphi.

Because of the mention of Gallio in the Delphi inscription and in Acts, scholars have supposed that Paul's first stay in Corinth must have occurred around A.D. 51–52, the date usually set for Gallio's term of office. The account of Paul before Gallio shows conflict between Paul and the Jews, as well as the hesitancy of Roman officials to become involved with religious quarrels.

Paul's Jewish opponents attempted to use legal means to silence his preaching. Their appeal to the Jewish Law of Moses failed, however, as Gallio, the Roman proconsul, refused to accept the Jewish charges, telling them to settle the matter themselves. His response is in accord with Roman legal tradition followed in Rome's conquered provinces.

What Gallio thought of the Jews or of the Christians is not known. He did not allow Paul to defend himself, as Paul was able to do in other instances (Acts 24:10). Furthermore, he "took no notice" of the beating of Sosthenes, the synagogue ruler (Acts 18:17). Possibly Gallio was influenced by his brother Seneca, who criticized some Jewish customs, stating that the "vanquished" (meaning the Jews) had given laws to "their victors" (the Romans).

Warning Against Idleness

⁶But we command you, brethren, in the name of our Lord Jesus Christ, that you withdraw from every brother who walks disorderly and not according to the tradition which heᵃ received from us. ⁷For you yourselves know how you ought to follow us, for we were not disorderly among you; ⁸nor did we eat anyone's bread free of charge, but worked with labor and toil night and day, that we might not be a burden to any of you, ⁹not because we do not have authority, but to make ourselves an example of how you should follow us. ¹⁰For even when we were with you, we commanded you this: If anyone will not work, neither shall he eat. ¹¹For we hear that there are some who walk among you in a disorderly manner, not working at all, but are busybodies. ¹²Now those who are such we command and exhort through our Lord Jesus Christ that they work in quietness and eat their own bread.

¹³But as for you, brethren, do not grow weary in doing good. ¹⁴And if anyone does not obey our word in this epistle, note that person and do not keep company with him, that he may be ashamed. ¹⁵Yet do not count him as an enemy, but admonish him as a brother.

Benediction

¹⁶Now may the Lord of peace Himself give you peace always in every way. The Lord be with you all.

¹⁷The salutation of Paul with my own hand, which is a sign in every epistle; so I write.

¹⁸The grace of our Lord Jesus Christ be with you all. Amen.

Paul Before Gallio

The emperor Claudius Caesar (A.D. 41–54), while favorable toward the Jews early in his reign, later forbade their assembly. Suetonius, a Roman historian, indicates that Claudius "expelled from Rome the Jews, who were constantly rioting under the leadership of Chrestus." Two Jewish refugees affected by this expulsion (which is dated in A.D. 49 by Orosius, a church historian) were Aquila and Priscilla. Luke records that when Paul stayed with them in Corinth, they "had recently come

3:6 ᵃNU-Text and M-Text read they.

from Italy" because of Claudius's edict (Acts 18:2, 3).

During a period of 18 months Paul established a flourishing Christian congregation (18:11). In A.D. 51 he was brought before Gallio, the Roman proconsul of Achaia (southern Greece). The archaeological remains of Gallio's judgment hall have now been discovered. Perhaps more important, however, is an inscription found at Delphi that mentions Gallio and fixes his brief proconsulship over Achaia (about one year) in A.D. 51–52. The likelihood, then, that Paul founded the church in Corinth in A.D. 51 is one of the most certain points for establishing the chronology of Paul's ministry.

After leaving Corinth, Paul accompanied Priscilla and Aquila to Ephesus. He left them there and sailed to Caesarea. He next greeted the church at Jerusalem before returning to his home base in Antioch.

▼   ■ Acts 18:12–22

Acts

18:12 When Gallio was proconsul of Achaia, the Jews with one accord rose up against Paul and brought him to the judgment seat, 13saying, "This *fellow* persuades men to worship God contrary to the law."

14And when Paul was about to open *his* mouth, Gallio said to the Jews, "If it were a matter of wrongdoing or wicked crimes, O Jews, there would be reason why I should bear with you. 15But if it is a question of words and names and your own law, look *to it* yourselves; for I do not want to be a judge of such *matters*." 16And he drove them from the judgment seat. 17Then all the Greeksa took Sosthenes, the ruler of the synagogue, and beat *him* before the judgment seat. But Gallio took no notice of these things.

Paul Returns to Antioch

18So Paul still remained a good while. Then he took leave of the brethren and sailed for Syria, and Priscilla and Aquila ▼

were with him. He had *his* hair cut off at Cenchrea, for he had taken a vow. 19And he came to Ephesus, and left them there; but he himself entered the synagogue and reasoned with the Jews. 20When they asked *him* to stay a longer time with them, he did not consent, 21but took leave of them, saying, "I must by all means keep this coming feast in Jerusalem;a but I will return again to you, God willing." And he sailed from Ephesus.

22And when he had landed at Caesarea, and gone up and greeted the church, he went down to Antioch.

18:17 aNU-Text reads *they all.*
18:21 aNU-Text omits *I must* through *Jerusalem.*

Paul's Third Missionary Journey

On Paul's third missionary journey he visited the places in Galatia and Phrygia (Acts 18:23) which he had evangelized on his first journey. He also revisited Macedonia and Greece (20:1–3), evangelized on his second. But the focus of the third journey was Ephesus in western Asia Minor (19:1—20:1). Here the gospel dramatically overturned paganism and its magic (see "Commotion in Ephesus" at Acts 19:23). This journey concluded with Paul's fateful trip to Jerusalem (21:1–14).

Paul taught daily in Ephesus as he had done in Corinth. Ephesus was the political and religious center of the province of Asia, so visitors, as well as residents, heard and shared the gospel. After teaching for 3 months in the Jewish synagogue, Paul retreated to the school of Tyrannus (19:8, 9). Luke indicates a long ministry for Paul over a 2-year period (19:10), while his total stay in Ephesus lasted approximately 3 years (20:31), usually dated from A.D. 52 to 55. One result of this Asian ministry was the planting of the church at Colosse by Epaphras (see Col. 4:12).

■ Acts 18:23—19:22

POLITICS AND GOVERNMENT

A judgment seat was a platform something like the outdoor stages used today for concerts or speakers. The courts conducted their business from such a platform. The judgment seat in Corinth has been excavated, and it is possible today to stand where Paul stood in A.D. 51, and face the deserted platform where Gallio sat to preside over the court (Acts 18:12).

Acts

18

:23 After he had spent some time *there,* he departed and went over the region of Galatia and Phrygia in order, strengthening all the disciples.

Ministry of Apollos

24Now a certain Jew named Apollos, born at Alexandria, an eloquent man *and* mighty in the Scriptures, came to Ephesus. 25This man had been instructed in the way of the Lord; and being fervent in spirit, he spoke and taught accurately the things of the Lord, though he knew only the baptism of John. 26So he began to speak boldly in the synagogue. When Aquila and Priscilla heard him, they took him aside and explained to him the way of God more accurately. 27And when he desired to cross to Achaia, the brethren wrote, exhorting the disciples to receive him; and when he arrived, he greatly helped those who had believed through grace; 28for he vigorously refuted the Jews publicly, showing from the Scriptures that Jesus is the Christ.

Paul at Ephesus

19

1And it happened, while Apollos was at Corinth, that Paul, having passed through the upper regions, came to Ephesus. And finding some disciples 2he said to them, "Did you receive the Holy Spirit when you believed?"

So they said to him, "We have not so much as heard whether there is a Holy Spirit."

19:13 aNU-Text reads *I.*

3And he said to them, "Into what then were you baptized?"

So they said, "Into John's baptism."

4Then Paul said, "John indeed baptized with a baptism of repentance, saying to the people that they should believe on Him who would come after him, that is, on Christ Jesus."

5When they heard *this,* they were baptized in the name of the Lord Jesus. 6And when Paul had laid hands on them, the Holy Spirit came upon them, and they spoke with tongues and prophesied. 7Now the men were about twelve in all.

8And he went into the synagogue and spoke boldly for three months, reasoning and persuading concerning the things of the kingdom of God. 9But when some were hardened and did not believe, but spoke evil of the Way before the multitude, he departed from them and withdrew the disciples, reasoning daily in the school of Tyrannus. 10And this continued for two years, so that all who dwelt in Asia heard the word of the Lord Jesus, both Jews and Greeks.

Miracles Glorify Christ

11Now God worked unusual miracles by the hands of Paul, 12so that even handkerchiefs or aprons were brought from his body to the sick, and the diseases left them and the evil spirits went out of them. 13Then some of the itinerant Jewish exorcists took it upon themselves to call the name of the Lord Jesus over those who had evil spirits, saying, "Wea exorcise you by the Jesus whom Paul preaches." 14Also

Asia and Greece Revisited

On the third missionary journey (Acts 18:23—21:16), Paul visited the places in Galatia and Phrygia which he had evangelized on his first journey. He also revisited Macedonia and Greece, evangelized on his second journey. But the focus of the third journey was Ephesus in western Asia Minor, where he settled for more than two years. Here the gospel dramatically overturned paganism and its magic.

EARLY JEWISH MISSIONARIES   (Acts 19:13, 14)

Missionary work among the Jews in the Greco-Roman world took place in the everyday lives of the people. Jewish "missionaries" were active in the marketplace, competing for devotion to their God amidst various other persons who were advocating devotion to their own god. Such competition often occurred in displays of power over spiritual forces. The missionary whose god proved his or her power by signs of superiority over other gods could make a strong case for a person to change religious devotion.

These "missionaries," both Jewish and non-Jewish, therefore were often wanderers, migrants who traveled from city to city to show the power of their deity. Their missionary work was also their livelihood. In response to their activity, the missionaries hoped to receive adequate compensation to keep their operations afloat. A century later, the Christian critic Celsus described such Jewish and non-Jewish missionary activity in a not-so-complimentary way: "There are many who, although of no name, are moved without scruples and on the slightest occasion, whether within or without the cultic places, gesturing like inspired persons, they beg and roam in cities and camps" (Origen, *Contra Celsum* 7.8–10).

Competitive missionary activity is the setting behind the "itinerant Jewish exorcists" and the "seven sons of Sceva" (Acts 19:13, 14). Impressed by the works of Paul, these missionaries sought to prove their God's superiority over other gods in order to convert people to the synagogue, and they even appealed to "the name of the Lord Jesus" (19:13). Yet the evil spirit knew the difference between the Jewish missionaries and the Christian Paul, turning on the missionaries (19:15, 16).

This public display strengthened the credibility of the Christian missionaries in Ephesus. The name of Jesus was "magnified," leading many to convert from pagan magical arts (19:17–19). The Jewish missionaries had inadvertently turned into missionaries for Christ and His church!

---

there were seven sons of Sceva, a Jewish chief priest, who did so.

15And the evil spirit answered and said, "Jesus I know, and Paul I know; but who are you?"

16Then the man in whom the evil spirit was leaped on them, overpowereda them, and prevailed against them,b so that they fled out of that house naked and wounded. 17This became known both to all Jews and Greeks dwelling in Ephesus; and fear fell on them all, and the name of the Lord Jesus was magnified. 18And many who had believed came confessing and telling their deeds. 19Also, many of those who had practiced magic brought their books together and burned *them* in the sight of all. And they counted up the value of them, and *it* totaled fifty thousand *pieces* of silver. 20So the word of the Lord grew mightily and prevailed.

21When these things were accomplished, Paul purposed in the Spirit, when he had passed through Macedonia and Achaia, to go to Jerusalem, saying, "After I have been there, I must also see Rome." 22So he sent into Macedonia two of those who ministered to him, Timothy and Erastus, but he himself stayed in Asia for a time.

TIME CAPSULE   A.D. 51 to 52

51   Silas and Timothy arrive in Corinth from Macedonia (Acts 18:5)

51   Paul writes 2 Thessalonians from Corinth

51   Paul appears before Gallio (Acts 18:12)

52–59   Antonius Felix is procurator or governor of Judea (Acts 23:26)

52   Ananias is summoned to Rome to explain local unrest

52   Paul, Priscilla, and Aquila sail from Corinth (Acts 18:18)

19:16 aM-Text reads *and they overpowered.*
bNU-Text reads *both of them.*

The First Letter to the Corinthians

The apostle Paul is almost universally recognized as the author of 1 Corinthians. In the letter, probably written about A.D. 55 during the third missionary journey, he remarked, "I will tarry in Ephesus until Pentecost" (1 Cor. 16:8). Since he was planning his departure, he probably wrote 1 Corinthians during the last of his 3 years in Ephesus (Acts 20:31).

The Corinth which Paul knew had been founded as a Roman colony during the century before Christ. It was strategically located in the Roman province of Achaia on a narrow strip of land between the Aegean Sea and the Adriatic, with two adjoining ports. Corinth's location made it a center of the trade routes passing from east to west. Prosperity brought luxury and immorality. The expression "To live like a Corinthian" to one Athenian writer meant living in gross immorality.

The church which Paul had established in Corinth during his second missionary journey (Acts 18:1–17) was very diverse, including men and women, rich and poor. The report from Chloe's household informed Paul of divisions in the church; they were developing conflicting loyalties to different human teachers (1 Cor. 1:10–13). He wanted them to understand that salvation is not based on human wisdom or personalities, but on Christ crucified and the work of God in building His church.

■ 1 Corinthians 1:1—4:21

1 Corinthians
Greeting

1 :1 Paul, called *to be* an apostle of Jesus Christ through the will of God, and Sosthenes *our* brother,

2To the church of God which is at Corinth, to those who are sanctified in Christ Jesus, called *to be* saints, with all who in every place call on the name of Jesus Christ our Lord, both theirs and ours:

3Grace to you and peace from God our Father and the Lord Jesus Christ.

Spiritual Gifts at Corinth

4I thank my God always concerning you for the grace of God which was given to you by Christ Jesus, 5that you were enriched in everything by Him in all utterance and all knowledge, 6even as the testimony of Christ was confirmed in you, 7so that you come short in no gift, eagerly waiting for the revelation of our Lord Jesus Christ, 8who will also confirm you to the end, *that you may be* blameless in the day of our Lord Jesus Christ. 9God *is* faithful, by whom you were called into the fellowship of His Son, Jesus Christ our Lord.

Sectarianism Is Sin

10Now I plead with you, brethren, by the name of our Lord Jesus Christ, that you all speak the same thing, and *that* there be no divisions among you, but *that* you be perfectly joined together in the same mind and in the same judgment. 11For it has been declared to me concerning you, my brethren, by those of Chloe's *household,* that there are contentions among you. 12Now I say this, that each of you says, "I am of Paul," or "I am of Apollos," or "I am of Cephas," or "I am of Christ." 13Is Christ divided? Was Paul crucified for you? Or were you baptized in the name of Paul? 14I thank God that I baptized none of you except Crispus and Gaius, 15lest anyone should say that I had baptized in my own name. 16Yes, I also baptized the household of Stephanas. Besides, I do not know whether I baptized any other. 17For Christ did not send me to baptize, but to preach the gospel, not with wisdom of words, lest the cross of Christ should be made of no effect.

Christ the Power and Wisdom of God

18For the message of the cross is foolishness to those who are perishing, but to

GEOGRAPHY AND ENVIRONMENT

Corinth was located near the isthmus of land joining the mainland of Greece to the peninsula called the Peloponnesus (1 Cor. 1:2). It was the site of the Isthmian Games, an important competition similar to the Olympic Games. Not only men but women competed in these games, with the prize being a sprig of celery. The Isthmian Games were held in A.D. 49 and 51.

us who are being saved it is the power of God. ¹⁹For it is written:

> *"I will destroy the wisdom of the wise,*
> *And bring to nothing the*
> *understanding of the prudent."* ᵃ

²⁰Where *is* the wise? Where *is* the scribe? Where *is* the disputer of this age? Has not God made foolish the wisdom of this world? ²¹For since, in the wisdom of God, the world through wisdom did not know God, it pleased God through the foolishness of the message preached to save those who believe. ²²For Jews request a sign, and Greeks seek after wisdom; ²³but we preach Christ crucified, to the Jews a stumbling block and to the Greeksᵃ foolishness, ²⁴but to those who are called, both Jews and Greeks, Christ the power of God and the wisdom of God. ²⁵Because the foolishness of God is wiser than men, and the weakness of God is stronger than men.

Glory Only in the Lord

²⁶For you see your calling, brethren, that not many wise according to the flesh, not many mighty, not many noble, *are called.* ²⁷But God has chosen the foolish things of the world to put to shame the wise, and God has chosen the weak things of the world to put to shame the things which are mighty; ²⁸and the base things of the world and the things which are despised God has chosen, and the things which are not, to bring to nothing the things that are, ²⁹that no flesh should glory in His presence. ³⁰But of Him you are in Christ Jesus, who became for us wisdom from God—and righteousness and sanctification and redemption— ³¹that, as it is written, *"He who glories, let him glory in the LORD."* ᵃ

Christ Crucified

2 ¹And I, brethren, when I came to you, did not come with excellence of speech or of wisdom declaring to you the testimonyᵃ of God. ²For I determined not to know anything among you except Jesus Christ and Him crucified. ³I was with you in weakness, in fear, and in much trembling. ⁴And my speech and my preaching *were* not with persuasive words of humanᵃ wisdom, but in demonstration of the Spirit and of power, ⁵that your faith should not be in the wisdom of men but in the power of God.

Spiritual Wisdom

⁶However, we speak wisdom among those who are mature, yet not the wisdom of this age, nor of the rulers of this age, who are coming to nothing. ⁷But we speak the wisdom of God in a mystery, the hidden *wisdom* which God ordained before the ages for our glory, ⁸which none of the rulers of this age knew; for had they known, they would not have crucified the Lord of glory. ⁹But as it is written:

> *"Eye has not seen, nor ear heard,*
> *Nor have entered into the heart of*
> *man*
> *The things which God has prepared*
> *for those who love Him."* ᵃ

¹⁰But God has revealed *them* to us through His Spirit. For the Spirit searches all things, yes, the deep things of God. ¹¹For what man knows the things of a man except the spirit of the man which is in him? Even so no one knows the things of God except the Spirit of God. ¹²Now we have received, not the spirit of the world, but the Spirit who is from God, that we might know the things that have been freely given to us by God. ¹³These things we also speak, not in words which man's wisdom teaches but which the Holyᵃ Spirit teaches, comparing spiritual things with spiritual. ¹⁴But the natural man does not receive the things of

---

1:19 ᵃIsaiah 29:14   1:23 ᵃNU-Text reads *Gentiles.*   1:31 ᵃJeremiah 9:24   2:1 ᵃNU-Text reads *mystery.*   2:4 ᵃNU-Text omits *human.*   2:9 ᵃIsaiah 64:4   2:13 ᵃNU-Text omits *Holy.*

ARTS AND LITERATURE

The highest skill taught in ancient education was public address and debate. People were familiar with the distinction between what someone said and how they said it, and from the time of Socrates they were reminded to be suspicious of speakers with exceptional skills in rhetoric (1 Cor. 2:4). Someone clever but unprincipled might use such skill to deceive and mislead.

OF PAUL OR APOLLOS? PATRONAGE AT CORINTH (1 Cor. 3:1–9)

Modern western societies teach their citizens that all persons should have equal access to the goods and services provided by the society. Despite all evidence to the contrary, it is supposedly not "*who* you know" but "*what* you know" that obtains for a person what is desired in life. We are taught that "equal rights" means "equal opportunity," and equal rights are equally possessed by all.

The Greco-Roman world, however, did not operate under such an illusion, but according to a different principle: it was who you knew that really mattered. Access to the society's goods and services arose from knowing the right person in the right place. Such a social system is called "patronage," a system built on the presupposition of social inequality. The more powerful person in the relationship (the patron) had access to goods and services that the person of lower status (the client) needed or wanted.

In return for a favor, a client granted the patron loyalty and honor that increased the patron's status and influence. Possibly the Christians at Corinth reflected the patronage system when they expressed their loyalty to particular Christian leaders. Perhaps the Gentile Christians claimed to be "of Paul" (1 Cor. 3:4), considering themselves his disciples. The intellectuals of the Corinthian church may have supported the Alexandrian leader Apollos, who had ministered in Corinth (Acts 19:1). Rather, Paul preferred for himself and Apollos to be viewed only as ministers who served the church according to the gifts and abilities they had received from God (3:5).

---

the Spirit of God, for they are foolishness to him; nor can he know *them,* because they are spiritually discerned. ¹⁵But he who is spiritual judges all things, yet he himself is *rightly* judged by no one. ¹⁶For *"who has known the mind of the LORD that he may instruct Him?"* ᵃ But we have the mind of Christ.

Sectarianism Is Carnal

3 ¹And I, brethren, could not speak to you as to spiritual *people* but as to carnal, as to babes in Christ. ²I fed you with milk and not with solid food; for until now you were not able *to receive it,* and even now you are still not able; ³for you are still carnal. For where *there are* envy, strife, and divisions among you, are you not carnal and behaving like *mere* men? ⁴For when one says, "I am of Paul," and another, "I *am* of Apollos," are you not carnal?

Watering, Working, Warning

⁵Who then is Paul, and who *is* Apollos, but ministers through whom you believed, as the Lord gave to each one? ⁶I planted, Apollos watered, but God gave the increase. ⁷So then neither he who plants is anything, nor he who waters, but God who gives the increase. ⁸Now he who plants and he who waters are one, and each one will receive his own reward according to his own labor.

⁹For we are God's fellow workers; you are God's field, *you are* God's building. ¹⁰According to the grace of God which was given to me, as a wise master builder I have laid the foundation, and another builds on it. But let each one take heed how he builds on it. ¹¹For no other foundation can anyone lay than that which is laid, which is Jesus Christ. ¹²Now if anyone builds on this foundation *with* gold, silver, precious stones, wood, hay, straw, ¹³each one's work will become clear; for the Day will declare it, because it will be revealed by fire; and the fire will test each one's work, of what sort it is. ¹⁴If anyone's work which he has built on *it* endures, he will receive a reward. ¹⁵If anyone's work is burned, he will suffer loss; but he himself will be saved, yet so as through fire.

¹⁶Do you not know that you are the temple of God and *that* the Spirit of God dwells in you? ¹⁷If anyone defiles the temple of God, God will destroy him. For the temple of God is holy, which *temple* you are.

Avoid Worldly Wisdom

¹⁸Let no one deceive himself. If anyone among you seems to be wise in this age, let him become a fool that he may become

---

2:16 ᵃIsaiah 40:13

PATRONS, CLIENTS, AND PUFFED-UP CHRISTIANS (1 Cor. 4:6)

In a patronage system, social power and status was not so much based on wealth, but on friendships. The greater the number and status of those friends who owed you honor, the more your influence increased in the society. Even a client's own status depended on the status and influence of the patron being honored. Having friends in high places helped "broker" situations into results that were desired.

Of course, this led to great social competition between clients of different patrons and between the patrons themselves. Who a person "belonged to" could determine how much access that person had to what the Greco-Roman world offered. This seems to be the background for the divisions in the church at Corinth. Rather than one church, the body of Christ, the Corinthians seemed to think of themselves as clients of specific Christian leaders, perhaps of those by whose ministry they had come to believe in Jesus Christ. Perhaps they even saw these leaders as special "brokers" to God.

Apparently, inner-church patronage systems led to competition, even jealousy and quarreling within the church. By allowing their conduct to mirror the surrounding social world, these puffed-up Corinthian Christians were in danger of fragmenting their fragile unity (1 Cor. 4:6). Paul saw these divisions as a sign of the spiritual immaturity of these believers. In his view, the patronage system belonged to the world, "this present evil age" (Gal. 1:4). Ultimately, for Paul, not patronage, but cooperation mattered in the church, for it was neither the planter nor the waterer, but God who provided "the increase" (1 Cor. 3:8).

wise. ¹⁹For the wisdom of this world is foolishness with God. For it is written, *"He catches the wise in their own craftiness"*;ᵃ ²⁰and again, *"The LORD knows the thoughts of the wise, that they are futile."*ᵃ ²¹Therefore let no one boast in men. For all things are yours: ²²whether Paul or Apollos or Cephas, or the world or life or death, or things present or things to come—all are yours. ²³And you *are* Christ's, and Christ *is* God's.

Stewards of the Mysteries of God

4 ¹Let a man so consider us, as servants of Christ and stewards of the mysteries of God. ²Moreover it is required in stewards that one be found faithful. ³But with me it is a very small thing that I should be judged by you or by a human court.ᵃ In fact, I do not even judge myself. ⁴For I know of nothing against myself, yet I am not justified by this; but He who judges me is the Lord. ⁵Therefore judge nothing before the time, until the Lord comes, who will both bring to light the hidden things of darkness and reveal the counsels of the hearts. Then each one's praise will come from God.

Fools for Christ's Sake

⁶Now these things, brethren, I have figuratively transferred to myself and Apollos for your sakes, that you may learn in us not to think beyond what is written, that none of you may be puffed up on behalf of one against the other. ⁷For who makes you differ *from another?* And what do you have that you did not receive? Now if you did indeed receive *it,* why do you boast as if you had not received *it?*

⁸You are already full! You are already rich! You have reigned as kings without us—and indeed I could wish you did reign, that we also might reign with you! ⁹For I think that God has displayed us, the apostles, last, as men condemned to death; for we have been made a spectacle to the world, both to angels and to men. ¹⁰We *are* fools for Christ's sake, but you *are* wise in Christ! We *are* weak, but you *are* strong! You *are* distinguished, but we *are* dishonored! ¹¹To the present hour we both hunger and thirst, and we are poorly clothed, and beaten, and homeless. ¹²And we labor, working with our own hands. Being reviled, we bless; being persecuted, we endure; ¹³being defamed, we entreat. We have been made as the filth of the world, the offscouring of all things until now.

3:19 ᵃJob 5:13   3:20 ᵃPsalm 94:11
4:3 ᵃLiterally *day*

Paul's Paternal Care

¹⁴I do not write these things to shame you, but as my beloved children I warn *you.* ¹⁵For though you might have ten thousand instructors in Christ, yet *you do* not *have* many fathers; for in Christ Jesus I have begotten you through the gospel. ¹⁶Therefore I urge you, imitate me. ¹⁷For this reason I have sent Timothy to you, who is my beloved and faithful son in the Lord, who will remind you of my ways in Christ, as I teach everywhere in every church.

¹⁸Now some are puffed up, as though I were not coming to you. ¹⁹But I will come to you shortly, if the Lord wills, and I will know, not the word of those who are puffed up, but the power. ²⁰For the kingdom of God *is* not in word but in power. ²¹What do you want? Shall I come to you with a rod, or in love and a spirit of gentleness?

5:1 ᵃNU-Text omits *named.*
5:5 ᵃNU-Text omits *Jesus.*
5:7 ᵃNU-Text omits *for us.*

Paul's Authority and Epistle

Paul addressed three specific areas in which the Corinthians had rejected his authority: They had condoned incest by one of their members (1 Cor. 5:1–13), compromised their Christian witness by suing one another in the secular courts (6:1–11), and allowed some of their members to visit prostitutes (6:12–20). In an earlier letter (5:9), he had already written to the Corinthians dealing with some of these matters.

This "earlier letter" would necessarily have predated what is now known to us as 1 Corinthians. Some scholars believe it may be preserved in what is now known as 2 Corinthians (supposing that 2 Corinthians itself is made up of parts of several letters; see "The Second Letter to the Corinthians" at 2 Cor. 1:1). Others, though, point out that sexual immorality—the topic of the earlier letter (1 Cor. 5:9)—is addressed only in 2 Cor. 12:21. They conclude that this "earlier letter" was simply not preserved, perhaps being lost by the early church.

▼   ■ 1 Corinthians 5:1—6:20

1 Corinthians
Immorality Defiles the Church

5 :1 It is actually reported *that there is* sexual immorality among you, and such sexual immorality as is not even namedᵃ among the Gentiles—that a man has his father's wife! ²And you are puffed up, and have not rather mourned, that he who has done this deed might be taken away from among you. ³For I indeed, as absent in body but present in spirit, have already judged (as though I were present) him who has so done this deed. ⁴In the name of our Lord Jesus Christ, when you are gathered together, along with my spirit, with the power of our Lord Jesus Christ, ⁵deliver such a one to Satan for the destruction of the flesh, that his spirit may be saved in the day of the Lord Jesus.ᵃ

⁶Your glorying *is* not good. Do you not know that a little leaven leavens the whole lump? ⁷Therefore purge out the old leaven, that you may be a new lump, since you truly are unleavened. For indeed Christ, our Passover, was sacrificed for us.ᵃ ⁸Therefore let us keep the feast, not with old leaven, nor with the leaven of malice and wickedness, but with the unleavened *bread* of sincerity and truth.

Immorality Must Be Judged

⁹I wrote to you in my epistle not to keep company with sexually immoral people. ¹⁰Yet *I* certainly *did* not *mean* with the sexually immoral people of this world, or with the covetous, or extortioners, or idolaters, since then you would need to go out of the world. ¹¹But now I have written to you not to keep company with anyone named a brother, who is sexually immoral, or covetous, or an idolater, or a reviler, or a

TIME CAPSULE *A.D. 52 to 54*

52	*Paul returns to Antioch in Syria*
52	*Paul preaches in the school of Tyrannus in Ephesus (Acts 19:9)*
53	*Herod Agrippa II receives parts of Syria*
53	*Paul's letter to the Galatians (if to "North Galatia")*
54	*Nero becomes emperor*
54	*The riot at Ephesus (Acts 19:23)*

drunkard, or an extortioner—not even to eat with such a person.

[12]For what *have* I *to do* with judging those also who are outside? Do you not judge those who are inside? [13]But those who are outside God judges. Therefore *"put away from yourselves the evil person."* [a]

Do Not Sue the Brethren

6 [1]Dare any of you, having a matter against another, go to law before the unrighteous, and not before the saints? [2]Do you not know that the saints will judge the world? And if the world will be judged by you, are you unworthy to judge the smallest matters? [3]Do you not know that we shall judge angels? How much more, things that pertain to this life? [4]If then you have judgments concerning things pertaining to this life, do you appoint those who are least esteemed by the church to judge? [5]I say this to your shame. Is it so, that there is not a wise man among you, not even one, who will be able to judge between his brethren? [6]But brother goes to law against brother, and that before unbelievers!

[7]Now therefore, it is already an utter failure for you that you go to law against one another. Why do you not rather accept wrong? Why do you not rather *let yourselves* be cheated? [8]No, you yourselves do wrong and cheat, and *you do* these things *to your* brethren! [9]Do you not know that the unrighteous will not inherit the kingdom of God? Do not be deceived. Neither fornicators, nor idolaters, nor adulterers, nor homosexuals,[a] nor sodomites, [10]nor thieves, nor covetous, nor drunkards, nor revilers, nor extortioners will inherit the kingdom of God. [11]And such were some of you. But you were washed, but you were sanctified, but you were justified in the name of the Lord Jesus and by the Spirit of our God.

Glorify God in Body and Spirit

[12]All things are lawful for me, but all things are not helpful. All things are lawful for me, but I will not be brought under the power of any. [13]Foods for the stomach and the stomach for foods, but God will destroy both it and them. Now the body *is* not for sexual immorality but for the Lord, and the Lord for the body. [14]And God both raised up the Lord and will also raise us up by His power.

[15]Do you not know that your bodies are members of Christ? Shall I then take the members of Christ and make *them* members of a harlot? Certainly not! [16]Or do you not know that he who is joined to a harlot is one body *with her?* For *"the two,"* He says, *"shall become one flesh."* [a] [17]But he who is joined to the Lord is one spirit *with Him.*

[18]Flee sexual immorality. Every sin that a man does is outside the body, but he who commits sexual immorality sins against his own body. [19]Or do you not know that your body is the temple of the Holy Spirit *who is* in you, whom you have from God, and you are not your own? [20]For you were bought at a price; therefore glorify God in your body[a] and in your spirit, which are God's.

5:13 [a]Deuteronomy 17:7; 19:19; 22:21, 24; 24:7   6:9 [a]That is, catamites   6:16 [a]Genesis 2:24   6:20 [a]NU-Text ends the verse at *body.*

Questions from the Corinthians

Paul's writing of 1 Corinthians was apparently prompted by the visit with him in Ephesus of a delegation from the Corinthian church. This delegation from "Chloe's household" (1 Cor. 1:11) may also have included Stephanas (the head of another important household), Fortunatus, and Achaicus (16:15–17). They seem to have brought not only an oral report (5:1), but perhaps also a formal letter.

Paul answered each of the questions raised in their letter to him, usually indicating his transition from topic to topic by the phrase "now concerning" (see 7:1, 25; 8:1; 12:1; 16:1, 12). His instructions to them covered Christian marriage and sexual practice (7:1–40). They might eat food that had been offered to idols, but they should do nothing that gave even the appearance of idol worship (8:1—11:1). Church worship should be conducted decently and with consideration for others (11:2–34). Spiritual gifts should be used for building up others (12:1–31) in true Christian love (13:1–13). Prophecy is better than tongues because it edifies (14:1–40). Because Christ has risen (15:1–11), we too will rise (15:12–34) with a new spiritual body (15:35–58).

■ 1 Corinthians 7:1—15:58

1 Corinthians
Principles of Marriage

7 :1 Now concerning the things of which you wrote to me:

It is good for a man not to touch a woman. ²Nevertheless, because of sexual immorality, let each man have his own wife, and let each woman have her own husband. ³Let the husband render to his wife the affection due her, and likewise also the wife to her husband. ⁴The wife does not have authority over her own body, but the husband *does*. And likewise the husband does not have authority over his own body, but the wife *does*. ⁵Do not deprive one another except with consent for a time, that you may give yourselves to fasting and prayer; and come together again so that Satan does not tempt you because of your lack of self-control. ⁶But I say this as a concession, not as a commandment. ⁷For I wish that all men were even as I myself. But each one has his own gift from God, one in this manner and another in that.

⁸But I say to the unmarried and to the widows: It is good for them if they remain even as I am; ⁹but if they cannot exercise self-control, let them marry. For it is better to marry than to burn *with passion.*

Keep Your Marriage Vows

¹⁰Now to the married I command, *yet* not I but the Lord: A wife is not to depart from *her* husband. ¹¹But even if she does depart, let her remain unmarried or be reconciled to *her* husband. And a husband is not to divorce *his* wife.

¹²But to the rest I, not the Lord, say: If any brother has a wife who does not believe, and she is willing to live with him, let him not divorce her. ¹³And a woman who has a husband who does not believe, if he is willing to live with her, let her not divorce him. ¹⁴For the unbelieving husband is sanctified by the wife, and the unbelieving wife is sanctified by the husband; otherwise your children would be unclean, but now they are holy. ¹⁵But if the unbeliever departs, let him depart; a brother or a sister is not under bondage in such *cases.* But God has called us to peace. ¹⁶For how do you know, O wife, whether you will save *your* husband? Or how do you know, O husband, whether you will save *your* wife?

Live as You Are Called

¹⁷But as God has distributed to each one, as the Lord has called each one, so let him walk. And so I ordain in all the churches. ¹⁸Was anyone called while circumcised? Let him not become uncircumcised. Was anyone called while uncircumcised? Let him not be circumcised. ¹⁹Circumcision is nothing and uncircumcision is nothing, but keeping the commandments of God *is what matters.* ²⁰Let each one remain in the same calling in which he was called. ²¹Were you called *while* a slave? Do not be concerned about it; but if you can be made free, rather use *it.* ²²For he who is called in the Lord *while* a slave is the Lord's freedman. Likewise he who is called *while* free is Christ's slave. ²³You were bought at a price; do not become slaves of men. ²⁴Brethren, let each one remain with God in that *state* in which he was called.

To the Unmarried and Widows

²⁵Now concerning virgins: I have no commandment from the Lord; yet I give judgment as one whom the Lord in His mercy *has made* trustworthy. ²⁶I suppose therefore that this is good because of the present distress—that *it is* good for a man to remain as he is: ²⁷Are you bound to a wife? Do not seek to be loosed. Are you loosed from a wife? Do not seek a wife. ²⁸But even if you do marry, you have not sinned; and if a virgin marries, she has not sinned. Nevertheless such will have trouble in the flesh, but I would spare you.

²⁹But this I say, brethren, the time *is* short, so that from now on even those who have wives should be as though they had none, ³⁰those who weep as though they did not weep, those who rejoice as though they did not rejoice, those who buy as though they did not possess, ³¹and those who use

MARRIAGE AND FAMILY

Jewish people regarded marriage as the natural duty of men and women. In line with Jewish tradition, Paul suggested that a person should marry in order to avoid sexual immorality (1 Cor. 7:9). The apostle also understood marriage and celibacy to be gifts of God (7:7). When he advocated remaining single (7:8), he was conscious of people's usual expectation that adult men, and especially religious leaders, would marry.

DIVORCE AND REMARRIAGE AT CORINTH (1 Cor. 7:15)

Jewish law permitted only the husband to initiate a divorce. Only under extreme circumstances could the wife request a court to compel a husband to divorce her. By contrast, Roman law viewed marriage as a matter of mutual consent, and so dissolved a marriage if either party requested it. Under Roman divorce, the children went to the father. Rapid remarriage was customary and society encouraged it (especially for young women), so the church congregation in Corinth probably included some new converts who had been remarried one or more times before their conversion.

Paul addressed the Christians who wanted to divorce spiritually incompatible spouses. Offering his own judgment, he contended that spiritual incompatibility did not provide adequate grounds for a divorce (1 Cor. 7:12–14). In addition, by giving the command of "the Lord" (1 Cor. 7:10, 11), he seemed to cite Jesus' general prohibition of divorce (Mark 10:11, 12).

Ancient interpreters commonly qualified general principles, modifying or interpreting them to account for specific situations. In this manner Paul interprets Jesus' general principle as needing to be qualified for those who are divorced against their will. In cases in which an unbelieving mate deserted the marriage, Paul declared, the believer was "not under bondage" (7:15).

In using the phrase "not under bondage," Paul was echoing the exact language of ancient divorce contracts, which spoke of marriage as "binding" a woman to her husband and divorce as "loosing" or "freeing" a woman for remarriage. Such divorce terminology appears in Jewish texts, such as the Mishnah, and in actual 1st-century Jewish divorce contracts that have been recovered. Ancient readers would have understood "not under bondage" as Paul's permission for an abandoned person to remarry.

---

this world as not misusing *it*. For the form of this world is passing away.

³²But I want you to be without care. He who is unmarried cares for the things of the Lord—how he may please the Lord. ³³But he who is married cares about the things of the world—how he may please *his* wife. ³⁴There is[a] a difference between a wife and a virgin. The unmarried woman cares about the things of the Lord, that she may be holy both in body and in spirit. But she who is married cares about the things of the world—how she may please *her* husband. ³⁵And this I say for your own profit, not that I may put a leash on you, but for what is proper, and that you may serve the Lord without distraction.

³⁶But if any man thinks he is behaving improperly toward his virgin, if she is past the flower of youth, and thus it must be, let him do what he wishes. He does not sin; let them marry. ³⁷Nevertheless he who stands steadfast in his heart, having no necessity, but has power over his own will, and has so determined in his heart that he will keep his virgin,[a] does well. ³⁸So then he who gives her[a] in marriage does well, but he who does not give *her* in marriage does better.

³⁹A wife is bound by law as long as her husband lives; but if her husband dies, she is at liberty to be married to whom she wishes, only in the Lord. ⁴⁰But she is happier if she remains as she is, according to my judgment—and I think I also have the Spirit of God.

Be Sensitive to Conscience

8 ¹Now concerning things offered to idols: We know that we all have knowledge. Knowledge puffs up, but love edifies. ²And if anyone thinks that he knows anything, he knows nothing yet as he ought to know. ³But if anyone loves God, this one is known by Him.

⁴Therefore concerning the eating of things offered to idols, we know that an idol *is* nothing in the world, and that *there is* no other God but one. ⁵For even if there are so-called gods, whether in heaven or on earth (as there are many gods and many lords), ⁶yet for us *there is* one God, the Father, of whom *are* all things, and we for Him; and one Lord Jesus Christ, through

---

7:34 [a]M-Text adds *also*.   7:37 [a]Or *virgin daughter*   7:38 [a]NU-Text reads *his own virgin.*

whom *are* all things, and through whom we *live*.

7However, *there is* not in everyone that knowledge; for some, with consciousness of the idol, until now eat *it* as a thing offered to an idol; and their conscience, being weak, is defiled. 8But food does not commend us to God; for neither if we eat are we the better, nor if we do not eat are we the worse.

9But beware lest somehow this liberty of yours become a stumbling block to those who are weak. 10For if anyone sees you who have knowledge eating in an idol's temple, will not the conscience of him who is weak be emboldened to eat those things offered to idols? 11And because of your knowledge shall the weak brother perish, for whom Christ died? 12But when you thus sin against the brethren, and wound their weak conscience, you sin against Christ. 13Therefore, if food makes my brother stumble, I will never again eat meat, lest I make my brother stumble.

A Pattern of Self-Denial

9 1Am I not an apostle? Am I not free? Have I not seen Jesus Christ our Lord? Are you not my work in the Lord? 2If I am not an apostle to others, yet doubtless I am to you. For you are the seal of my apostleship in the Lord.

3My defense to those who examine me is this: 4Do we have no right to eat and drink? 5Do we have no right to take along a believing wife, as *do* also the other apostles, the brothers of the Lord, and Cephas? 6Or *is it* only Barnabas and I *who* have no right to refrain from working? 7Who ever goes to war at his own expense? Who plants a vineyard and does not eat of its fruit? Or who tends a flock and does not drink of the milk of the flock?

8Do I say these things as a *mere* man? Or does not the law say the same also? 9For it is written in the law of Moses, *"You shall not muzzle an ox while it treads out the grain."* a Is it oxen God is concerned about? 10Or does He say *it* altogether for our sakes? For our sakes, no doubt, *this* is written, that he who plows should plow in hope, and he who threshes in hope should

be partaker of his hope. 11If we have sown spiritual things for you, *is it* a great thing if we reap your material things? 12If others are partakers of *this* right over you, *are we* not even more?

Nevertheless we have not used this right, but endure all things lest we hinder the gospel of Christ. 13Do you not know that those who minister the holy things eat *of the things* of the temple, and those who serve at the altar partake of *the offerings of* the altar? 14Even so the Lord has commanded that those who preach the gospel should live from the gospel.

15But I have used none of these things, nor have I written these things that it should be done so to me; for it *would be* better for me to die than that anyone should make my boasting void. 16For if I preach the gospel, I have nothing to boast of, for necessity is laid upon me; yes, woe is me if I do not preach the gospel! 17For if I do this willingly, I have a reward; but if against my will, I have been entrusted with a stewardship. 18What is my reward then? That when I preach the gospel, I may present the gospel of Christ a without charge, that I may not abuse my authority in the gospel.

Serving All Men

19For though I am free from all *men,* I have made myself a servant to all, that I might win the more; 20and to the Jews I became as a Jew, that I might win Jews; to those *who are* under the law, as under the law, a that I might win those *who are* under the law; 21to those *who are* without law, as without law (not being without law toward God, a but under law toward Christ b), that I might win those *who are* without law; 22to the weak I became as a weak, that I might win the weak. I have become all things to all *men,* that I might by all means save some. 23Now this I do for the gospel's sake, that I may be partaker of it with *you.*

Striving for a Crown

24Do you not know that those who run in a race all run, but one receives the prize? Run in such a way that you may obtain *it.* 25And everyone who competes *for the prize* is temperate in all things. Now they *do it* to obtain a perishable crown, but we *for* an imperishable *crown.* 26Therefore I run thus: not with uncertainty. Thus I fight: not as *one who* beats the air. 27But I discipline my body and bring *it* into

---

9:9 aDeuteronomy 25:4   9:18 aNU-Text omits *of Christ.*   9:20 aNU-Text adds *though not being myself under the law.*   9:21 aNU-Text reads *God's law.*   bNU-Text reads *Christ's law.*   9:22 aNU-Text omits *as.*

RUNNING IN THE OLYMPICS (1 Cor. 9:24–27)

Foot racing was the most important event at the famous Olympic Games of Greece. The Olympic Games were held every 4 years in Olympia, a plain located about 125 miles west of Athens, and 75 miles west of Corinth. It was the main shrine of the Greek god Zeus.

Paul's Corinthian readers would have been well familiar with runners in the Games (1 Cor. 9:24). The athletic contests at Olympia were founded in 776 B.C. and held continuously for more than a thousand years. They did not cease until A.D. 393 when the Roman emperor Theodosius abolished them because they were pagan.

The Corinthians were also familiar with the crown that was the winning prize (1 Cor. 9:25). Statues show the athletes completely naked, but probably they had some covering. The prize for the winner was a crown made of laurel leaves, or an imitation crown made of golden leaves. With this crown went great fame, if not a stipend of money from the city.

Athletic events were very popular, and thus a good illustration for preaching. Paul wanted his readers to understand that the need to train and the desire to win applies to spiritual life as it does to athletic contests. Like a runner Paul disciplined his own body (1 Cor. 9:27). His prize would be imperishable (1 Cor. 9:25), and thus of much greater value than the athlete's prize of leaves.

---

subjection, lest, when I have preached to others, I myself should become disqualified.

Old Testament Examples

10 ¹Moreover, brethren, I do not want you to be unaware that all our fathers were under the cloud, all passed through the sea, ²all were baptized into Moses in the cloud and in the sea, ³all ate the same spiritual food, ⁴and all drank the same spiritual drink. For they drank of that spiritual Rock that followed them, and that Rock was Christ. ⁵But with most of them God was not well pleased, for *their bodies* were scattered in the wilderness.

⁶Now these things became our examples, to the intent that we should not lust after evil things as they also lusted. ⁷And do not become idolaters as *were* some of them. As it is written, *"The people sat down to eat and drink, and rose up to play."*ᵃ ⁸Nor let us commit sexual immorality, as some of them did, and in one day twenty-three thousand fell; ⁹nor let us tempt Christ, as some of them also tempted, and were destroyed by serpents; ¹⁰nor complain, as some of them also com-

plained, and were destroyed by the destroyer. ¹¹Now allᵃ these things happened to them as examples, and they were written for our admonition, upon whom the ends of the ages have come.

¹²Therefore let him who thinks he stands take heed lest he fall. ¹³No temptation has overtaken you except such as is common to man; but God *is* faithful, who will not allow you to be tempted beyond what you are able, but with the temptation will also make the way of escape, that you may be able to bear *it*.

Flee from Idolatry

¹⁴Therefore, my beloved, flee from idolatry. ¹⁵I speak as to wise men; judge for yourselves what I say. ¹⁶The cup of blessing which we bless, is it not the communion of the blood of Christ? The bread which we break, is it not the communion of the body of Christ? ¹⁷For we, *though* many, are one bread *and* one body; for we all partake of that one bread.

10:7 ᵃExodus 32:6   10:11 ᵃNU-Text omits *all*.

CULTS AND SUPERNATURAL

Meat was eaten frequently in connection with religious sacrifices. Birds were sacrificed often; oxen on special occasions. Leftover meat was kept by the priests and worshipers. What they did not use themselves would be sold in the marketplace, with or without information that it had been sacrificed. Paul warned against eating this meat in a pagan temple, but allowed it to be eaten in a household (1 Cor. 8:10; 10:25).

[18]Observe Israel after the flesh: Are not those who eat of the sacrifices partakers of the altar? [19]What am I saying then? That an idol is anything, or what is offered to idols is anything? [20]Rather, that the things which the Gentiles sacrifice they sacrifice to demons and not to God, and I do not want you to have fellowship with demons. [21]You cannot drink the cup of the Lord and the cup of demons; you cannot partake of the Lord's table and of the table of demons. [22]Or do we provoke the Lord to jealousy? Are we stronger than He?

All to the Glory of God

[23]All things are lawful for me,[a] but not all things are helpful; all things are lawful for me,[b] but not all things edify. [24]Let no one seek his own, but each one the other's *well-being.*

[25]Eat whatever is sold in the meat market, asking no questions for conscience' sake; [26]for *"the earth is the LORD's, and all its fullness."* [a]

[27]If any of those who do not believe invites you *to dinner,* and you desire to go, eat whatever is set before you, asking no question for conscience' sake. [28]But if anyone says to you, "This was offered to idols," do not eat it for the sake of the one who told you, and for conscience' sake;[a] for *"the earth is the LORD's, and all its fullness."* [b] [29]"Conscience," I say, not your own, but that of the other. For why is my liberty judged by another *man's* conscience? [30]But if I partake with thanks, why am I evil spoken of for *the food* over which I give thanks?

[31]Therefore, whether you eat or drink, or whatever you do, do all to the glory of God. [32]Give no offense, either to the Jews or to the Greeks or to the church of God, [33]just as I also please all *men* in all *things,* not seeking my own profit, but the *profit* of many, that they may be saved.

11 [1]Imitate me, just as I also *imitate* Christ.

Head Coverings

[2]Now I praise you, brethren, that you remember me in all things and keep the traditions just as I delivered *them* to you. [3]But I want you to know that the head of every man is Christ, the head of woman *is* man, and the head of Christ *is* God. [4]Every man praying or prophesying, having *his* head covered, dishonors his head. [5]But every woman who prays or prophesies with *her* head uncovered dishonors her head, for that is one and the same as if her head were shaved. [6]For if a woman is not covered, let her also be shorn. But if it is shameful for a woman to be shorn or shaved, let her be covered. [7]For a man indeed ought not to cover *his* head, since he is the image and glory of God; but woman is the glory of man. [8]For man is not from woman, but woman from man. [9]Nor was man created for the woman, but woman for the man. [10]For this reason the woman ought to have *a symbol of* authority on *her* head, because of the angels. [11]Nevertheless, neither *is* man independent of woman, nor woman independent of man, in the Lord. [12]For as woman *came* from man, even so man also *comes* through woman; but all things are from God.

[13]Judge among yourselves. Is it proper for a woman to pray to God with her head uncovered? [14]Does not even nature itself teach you that if a man has long hair, it is a dishonor to him? [15]But if a woman has long hair, it is a glory to her; for *her* hair is given to her[a] for a covering. [16]But if anyone seems to be contentious, we have no such custom, nor *do* the churches of God.

Conduct at the Lord's Supper

[17]Now in giving these instructions I do not praise *you,* since you come together not for the better but for the worse. [18]For first of all, when you come together as a church, I hear that there are divisions among you, and in part I believe it. [19]For there must also be factions among you, that those who are approved may be recognized among you. [20]Therefore when you come together in one place, it is not to eat the Lord's Supper. [21]For in eating, each one takes his own supper ahead of *others;* and one is hungry and another is drunk. [22]What! Do you not have houses to eat and drink in? Or do you despise the church of God and shame those who have nothing? What shall I say to you? Shall I praise you in this? I do not praise *you.*

Institution of the Lord's Supper

[23]For I received from the Lord that which I also delivered to you: that the Lord Jesus on the *same* night in which He was

---

10:23 [a]NU-Text omits *for me.* [b]NU-Text omits *for me.* 10:26 [a]Psalm 24:1 10:28 [a]NU-Text omits the rest of this verse. [b]Psalm 24:1 11:15 [a]M-Text omits *to her.*

COVERING A WOMAN'S HEAD   (1 Cor. 11:5, 6)

Proper conduct in worship is expressed in different ways in different times and places. Paul was concerned that the conduct of women at the church in Corinth was not following the then current customs for public worship (1 Cor. 11:5, 6). Accepted social custom called for Jewish and Christian women to cover their hair.

Customs varied somewhat. Lower-class women in much of the Mediterranean world covered their heads, especially in the eastern Mediterranean. Far to the east, conservative women veiled even their faces; in most other places, they simply wore a shawl that covered their hair. Many ancient texts inform us why married women needed to cover their heads: hair was the crown of the woman's beauty, and for a wife to expose this to the public gaze was to act promiscuous. Thus uncovered hair could symbolize seductiveness.

Not all women in Corinth were this conservative, however. Upper-class women were especially prone to showing off their hairstyles, requiring them to keep their heads uncovered. Because the Corinthian churches met in well-to-do members' homes, affluent and poorer women came into contact with one another, producing a clash of different views concerning covering their heads. To one group, uncovered heads represented progressive freedom; to the other, ostentation and seduction.

Paul thus faced a serious conflict in the church that had to be addressed gently. Arraying a variety of arguments—some traditionally Jewish, some more in keeping with Greco-Roman moralists' tastes—he acknowledged the Corinthian women's freedom but called on them to use it responsibly for the sake of others who might stumble. Those who might still be contentious about this issue should bow to custom: other Christian churches did not allow women to worship with uncovered heads; neither should the Corinthians (11:16).

---

betrayed took bread; ²⁴and when He had given thanks, He broke *it* and said, "Take, eat;^a this is My body which is broken^b for you; do this in remembrance of Me." ²⁵In the same manner *He* also *took* the cup after supper, saying, "This cup is the new covenant in My blood. This do, as often as you drink *it,* in remembrance of Me."

²⁶For as often as you eat this bread and drink this cup, you proclaim the Lord's death till He comes.

Examine Yourself

²⁷Therefore whoever eats this bread or drinks *this* cup of the Lord in an unworthy manner will be guilty of the body and blood^a of the Lord. ²⁸But let a man examine himself, and so let him eat of the bread and drink of the cup. ²⁹For he who eats and drinks in an unworthy manner^a eats and drinks judgment to himself, not discerning the Lord's^b body. ³⁰For this reason many *are* weak and sick among you, and many sleep. ³¹For if we would judge ourselves, we would not be judged. ³²But when we are judged, we are chastened by the Lord, that we may not be condemned with the world.

³³Therefore, my brethren, when you come together to eat, wait for one another. ³⁴But if anyone is hungry, let him eat at home, lest you come together for judgment. And the rest I will set in order when I come.

Spiritual Gifts: Unity in Diversity

12 ¹Now concerning spiritual *gifts,* brethren, I do not want you to be ignorant: ²You know that^a you were Gentiles, carried away to these dumb idols, however you were led. ³Therefore I make known to you that no one speaking by the Spirit of God calls Jesus accursed, and no one can say that Jesus is Lord except by the Holy Spirit.

⁴There are diversities of gifts, but the same Spirit. ⁵There are differences of ministries, but the same Lord. ⁶And there are diversities of activities, but it is the same God who works all in all. ⁷But the manifes-

---

11:24 ^aNU-Text omits *Take, eat.* ^bNU-Text omits *broken.* 11:27 ^aNU-Text and M-Text read *the blood.* 11:29 ^aNU-Text omits *in an unworthy manner.* ^bNU-Text omits *Lord's.* 12:2 ^aNU-Text and M-Text add *when.*

tation of the Spirit is given to each one for the profit *of all:* [8]for to one is given the word of wisdom through the Spirit, to another the word of knowledge through the same Spirit, [9]to another faith by the same Spirit, to another gifts of healings by the same[a] Spirit, [10]to another the working of miracles, to another prophecy, to another discerning of spirits, to another *different* kinds of tongues, to another the interpretation of tongues. [11]But one and the same Spirit works all these things, distributing to each one individually as He wills.

Unity and Diversity in One Body

[12]For as the body is one and has many members, but all the members of that one body, being many, are one body, so also *is* Christ. [13]For by one Spirit we were all baptized into one body—whether Jews or Greeks, whether slaves or free—and have all been made to drink into[a] one Spirit. [14]For in fact the body is not one member but many.

[15]If the foot should say, "Because I am not a hand, I am not of the body," is it therefore not of the body? [16]And if the ear should say, "Because I am not an eye, I am not of the body," is it therefore not of the body? [17]If the whole body *were* an eye, where *would be* the hearing? If the whole *were* hearing, where *would be* the smelling? [18]But now God has set the members, each one of them, in the body just as He pleased. [19]And if they *were* all one member, where *would* the body *be?*

[20]But now indeed *there are* many members, yet one body. [21]And the eye cannot say to the hand, "I have no need of you"; nor again the head to the feet, "I have no need of you." [22]No, much rather, those members of the body which seem to be weaker are necessary. [23]And those *members* of the body which we think to be less honorable, on these we bestow greater honor; and our unpresentable *parts* have greater modesty, [24]but our presentable *parts* have no need. But God composed the body, having given greater honor to that *part* which lacks it, [25]that there should be no schism in the body, but *that* the mem-

bers should have the same care for one another. [26]And if one member suffers, all the members suffer with *it;* or if one member is honored, all the members rejoice with *it.*

[27]Now you are the body of Christ, and members individually. [28]And God has appointed these in the church: first apostles, second prophets, third teachers, after that miracles, then gifts of healings, helps, administrations, varieties of tongues. [29]*Are* all apostles? *Are* all prophets? *Are* all teachers? *Are* all workers of miracles? [30]Do all have gifts of healings? Do all speak with tongues? Do all interpret? [31]But earnestly desire the best[a] gifts. And yet I show you a more excellent way.

The Greatest Gift

13 [1]Though I speak with the tongues of men and of angels, but have not love, I have become sounding brass or a clanging cymbal. [2]And though I have *the gift of* prophecy, and understand all mysteries and all knowledge, and though I have all faith, so that I could remove mountains, but have not love, I am nothing. [3]And though I bestow all my goods to feed *the poor,* and though I give my body to be burned,[a] but have not love, it profits me nothing.

[4]Love suffers long *and* is kind; love does not envy; love does not parade itself, is not puffed up; [5]does not behave rudely, does not seek its own, is not provoked, thinks no evil; [6]does not rejoice in iniquity, but rejoices in the truth; [7]bears all things, believes all things, hopes all things, endures all things.

[8]Love never fails. But whether *there are* prophecies, they will fail; whether *there are* tongues, they will cease; whether *there is* knowledge, it will vanish away. [9]For we know in part and we prophesy in part. [10]But when that which is perfect has come, then that which is in part will be done away.

[11]When I was a child, I spoke as a child, I understood as a child, I thought as a child; but when I became a man, I put away childish things. [12]For now we see in a mirror, dimly, but then face to face. Now I know in part, but then I shall know just as I also am known.

[13]And now abide faith, hope, love, these three; but the greatest of these *is* love.

12:9 [a]NU-Text reads *one.*   12:13 [a]NU-Text omits *into.*   12:31 [a]NU-Text reads *greater.*
13:3 [a]NU-Text reads *so I may boast.*

IN A MIRROR OR FACE TO FACE (1 Cor. 13:12)

Ancient people often made mirrors from bronze, and the bronze of Corinth was especially famous as the best bronze of the ancient Mediterranean world. Some Corinthian bronze had even been imported to Jerusalem for use in the temple. Nevertheless, the best of ancient mirrors provided only an imperfect reflection, leading some philosophers to use the analogy of an imperfect mirror to depict mortals' imperfect attempts to understand the deity.

Paul apparently uses the same analogy. The present, partial state of our knowledge of God compares to seeing "in a mirror, dimly" (1 Cor. 13:12). This contrasts with the full knowledge of God available when Christ returns, which will be like seeing "face to face."

Jewish traditions likewise contrasted Moses' face-to-face revelation of God with the partial revelation seen by most other prophets (Num. 12:8; Deut. 34:10). In the present, God's people receive spiritual gifts that partly reveal God, but in the future, such gifts will be unnecessary because believers will know God face to face, as Moses did.

Paul anticipated this future age when he would know God directly (1 Cor. 13:12; see Jer. 31:31–34), and his expectation influenced his ideas about spiritual gifts. The gifts which the Corinthians valued so highly were only for this life, and in the future age there would be no more need for the gifts of prophecies, tongues, or knowledge (13:8–10). The reflection of the dim mirror would become a face-to-face view.

Prophecy and Tongues

14 ¹Pursue love, and desire spiritual *gifts,* but especially that you may prophesy. ²For he who speaks in a tongue does not speak to men but to God, for no one understands *him;* however, in the spirit he speaks mysteries. ³But he who prophesies speaks edification and exhortation and comfort to men. ⁴He who speaks in a tongue edifies himself, but he who prophesies edifies the church. ⁵I wish you all spoke with tongues, but even more that you prophesied; for[a] he who prophesies *is* greater than he who speaks with tongues, unless indeed he interprets, that the church may receive edification.

Tongues Must Be Interpreted

⁶But now, brethren, if I come to you speaking with tongues, what shall I profit you unless I speak to you either by revelation, by knowledge, by prophesying, or by teaching? ⁷Even things without life, whether flute or harp, when they make a sound, unless they make a distinction in the sounds, how will it be known what is piped or played? ⁸For if the trumpet makes an uncertain sound, who will prepare for battle? ⁹So likewise you, unless you utter by the tongue words easy to understand, how will it be known what is spoken? For you will be speaking into the air. ¹⁰There are, it may be, so many kinds of languages in the world, and none of them *is* without significance. ¹¹Therefore, if I do not know the meaning of the language, I shall be a foreigner to him who speaks, and he who speaks *will be* a foreigner to me. ¹²Even so you, since you are zealous for spiritual *gifts, let it be* for the edification of the church *that* you seek to excel.

¹³Therefore let him who speaks in a tongue pray that he may interpret. ¹⁴For if I pray in a tongue, my spirit prays, but my understanding is unfruitful. ¹⁵What is *the conclusion* then? I will pray with the spirit, and I will also pray with the understanding. I will sing with the spirit, and I will also sing with the understanding. ¹⁶Otherwise, if you bless with the spirit, how will he who occupies the place of the uninformed say "Amen" at your giving of thanks, since he does not understand what you say? ¹⁷For you indeed give thanks well, but the other is not edified.

¹⁸I thank my God I speak with tongues more than you all; ¹⁹yet in the church I would rather speak five words with my understanding, that I may teach others also, than ten thousand words in a tongue.

Tongues a Sign to Unbelievers

²⁰Brethren, do not be children in understanding; however, in malice be babes, but in understanding be mature.

14:5 [a]NU-Text reads *and.*

ASK AT HOME, NOT AT CHURCH (1 Cor. 14:34, 35)

Although specific conditions varied from one part of the ancient Mediterranean to another, the Roman world valued the quietness and subordination of wives. Some writers even longed for earlier days when Roman matrons had been even more quiet and submissive. Paul appears to be respecting the culture of his time when he says, "Let your women keep silent in the churches" (1 Cor. 14:34).

The specific sort of quietness Paul intends is debated. It is doubtful that he calls for *absolute* silence of women in church, because he permitted prayer and prophecy under appropriate conditions (1 Cor. 11:4, 5). Suggestions as to what Paul was prohibiting women from doing include teaching Scripture or judging prophecy (14:29). But the only clue in his letter points to the asking of questions (14:35). Possibly Paul exhorted the women to ask their questions privately rather than publicly.

In ancient lecture settings, including Jewish teachers who expounded Torah, the Law, hearers learned more by asking questions than by simply listening. Yet, as Plutarch wrote in *On Lectures,* it was considered rude for the unlearned to ask questions because their questioning slowed everyone else down. Women were on the whole far less educated than men (although exceptions existed) and prone to ask less educated questions. An additional problem for a place like Corinth may have been the cultural impropriety of women asking questions in what was normally a male-dominated lecture setting.

What is striking in view of 1st-century culture is not Paul's limitation of the Corinthian women but his concern for their learning. Only rarely did ancient writers exhort husbands to take an interest in their wives' education (Greek men were on average more than a decade older than their wives). When writers did suggest instructing wives, they sometimes added words like, "For if left to themselves, women produce only base passion and folly." Paul's concern that husbands take an interest in their wives' learning was among the more progressive voices of his day.

21In the law it is written:

"*With men of other tongues and other lips
I will speak to this people;
And yet, for all that, they will not hear Me,*" a

says the Lord.

22Therefore tongues are for a sign, not to those who believe but to unbelievers; but prophesying is not for unbelievers but for those who believe. 23Therefore if the whole church comes together in one place, and all speak with tongues, and there come in *those who are* uninformed or unbelievers, will they not say that you are out of your mind? 24But if all prophesy, and an unbeliever or an uninformed person comes in, he is convinced by all, he is convicted by all. 25And thusa the secrets of his heart are revealed; and so, falling down on *his* face,

he will worship God and report that God is truly among you.

Order in Church Meetings

26How is it then, brethren? Whenever you come together, each of you has a psalm, has a teaching, has a tongue, has a revelation, has an interpretation. Let all things be done for edification. 27If anyone speaks in a tongue, *let there be* two or at the most three, *each* in turn, and let one interpret. 28But if there is no interpreter, let him keep silent in church, and let him speak to himself and to God. 29Let two or three prophets speak, and let the others judge. 30But if *anything* is revealed to another who sits by, let the first keep silent. 31For you can all prophesy one by one, that all may learn and all may be encouraged. 32And the spirits of the prophets are subject to the prophets. 33For God is not *the author* of confusion but of peace, as in all the churches of the saints.

34Let youra women keep silent in the churches, for they are not permitted to

---

14:21 aIsaiah 28:11, 12   14:25 aNU-Text omits
And thus.   14:34 aNU-Text omits *your.*

speak; but *they are* to be submissive, as the law also says. ³⁵And if they want to learn something, let them ask their own husbands at home; for it is shameful for women to speak in church.

³⁶Or did the word of God come *originally* from you? Or *was it* you only that it reached? ³⁷If anyone thinks himself to be a prophet or spiritual, let him acknowledge that the things which I write to you are the commandments of the Lord. ³⁸But if anyone is ignorant, let him be ignorant. ᵃ

³⁹Therefore, brethren, desire earnestly to prophesy, and do not forbid to speak with tongues. ⁴⁰Let all things be done decently and in order.

The Risen Christ, Faith's Reality

15 ¹Moreover, brethren, I declare to you the gospel which I preached to you, which also you received and in which you stand, ²by which also you are saved, if you hold fast that word which I preached to you—unless you believed in vain.

³For I delivered to you first of all that which I also received: that Christ died for our sins according to the Scriptures, ⁴and that He was buried, and that He rose again the third day according to the Scriptures, ⁵and that He was seen by Cephas, then by the twelve. ⁶After that He was seen by over five hundred brethren at once, of whom the greater part remain to the present, but some have fallen asleep. ⁷After that He was seen by James, then by all the apostles. ⁸Then last of all He was seen by me also, as by one born out of due time.

⁹For I am the least of the apostles, who am not worthy to be called an apostle, because I persecuted the church of God. ¹⁰But by the grace of God I am what I am, and His grace toward me was not in vain; but I labored more abundantly than they all, yet not I, but the grace of God *which was* with me. ¹¹Therefore, whether *it was* I or they, so we preach and so you believed.

The Risen Christ, Our Hope

¹²Now if Christ is preached that He has been raised from the dead, how do some among you say that there is no resurrection of the dead? ¹³But if there is no resurrection of the dead, then Christ is not risen. ¹⁴And if Christ is not risen, then our preaching *is* empty and your faith *is* also empty. ¹⁵Yes, and we are found false witnesses of God, because we have testified of God that He raised up Christ, whom He did not raise up—if in fact the dead do not rise. ¹⁶For if *the* dead do not rise, then Christ is not risen. ¹⁷And if Christ is not risen, your faith *is* futile; you are still in your sins! ¹⁸Then also those who have fallen asleep in Christ have perished. ¹⁹If in this life only we have hope in Christ, we are of all men the most pitiable.

The Last Enemy Destroyed

²⁰But now Christ is risen from the dead, *and* has become the firstfruits of those who have fallen asleep. ²¹For since by man *came* death, by Man also *came* the resurrection of the dead. ²²For as in Adam all die, even so in Christ all shall be made alive. ²³But each one in his own order: Christ the firstfruits, afterward those *who are* Christ's at His coming. ²⁴Then *comes* the end, when He delivers the kingdom to God the Father, when He puts an end to all rule and all authority and power. ²⁵For He must reign till He has put all enemies under His feet. ²⁶The last enemy *that* will be destroyed *is* death. ²⁷For *"He has put all things under His feet."* ᵃ But when He says "all things are put under *Him,"* *it is* evident that He who put all things under Him is excepted. ²⁸Now when all things are made subject to Him, then the Son Himself will also be subject to Him who put all things under Him, that God may be all in all.

Effects of Denying the Resurrection

²⁹Otherwise, what will they do who are baptized for the dead, if the dead do not rise at all? Why then are they baptized for

---

14:38 ᵃNU-Text reads *if anyone does not recognize this, he is not recognized.*   15:27 ᵃPsalm 8:6

CULTURE AND SOCIETY

Public contests to entertain people with the spectacle of death were extremely popular in the Roman world. Throughout the empire Romans built stadiums where professional gladiators, prisoners, and slaves fought wild animals and each other to the death for sport. Paul's figure of speech "fought with beasts" (1 Cor. 15:32) probably describes his human enemies as wild animals, not claiming that he actually fought in the arena.

the dead? [30]And why do we stand in jeopardy every hour? [31]I affirm, by the boasting in you which I have in Christ Jesus our Lord, I die daily. [32]If, in the manner of men, I have fought with beasts at Ephesus, what advantage *is it* to me? If *the* dead do not rise, *"Let us eat and drink, for tomorrow we die!"* [a]

[33]Do not be deceived: "Evil company corrupts good habits." [34]Awake to righteousness, and do not sin; for some do not have the knowledge of God. I speak *this* to your shame.

A Glorious Body

[35]But someone will say, "How are the dead raised up? And with what body do they come?" [36]Foolish one, what you sow is not made alive unless it dies. [37]And what you sow, you do not sow that body that shall be, but mere grain—perhaps wheat or some other *grain.* [38]But God gives it a body as He pleases, and to each seed its own body.

[39]All flesh *is* not the same flesh, but *there is* one *kind of* flesh[a] of men, another flesh of animals, another of fish, *and* another of birds.

[40]*There are* also celestial bodies and terrestrial bodies; but the glory of the celestial *is* one, and the *glory* of the terrestrial *is* another. [41]*There is* one glory of the sun, another glory of the moon, and another glory of the stars; for *one* star differs from *another* star in glory.

[42]So also *is* the resurrection of the dead. *The body* is sown in corruption, it is raised in incorruption. [43]It is sown in dishonor, it is raised in glory. It is sown in weakness, it is raised in power. [44]It is sown a natural body, it is raised a spiritual body. There is a natural body, and there is a spiritual body. [45]And so it is written, *"The first man Adam became a living being."* [a] The last Adam *became* a life-giving spirit.

[46]However, the spiritual is not first, but the natural, and afterward the spiritual. [47]The first man *was* of the earth, *made* of dust; the second Man *is* the Lord[a] from heaven. [48]As *was* the *man* of dust, so also *are* those *who are* made of dust; and as *is* the heavenly *Man,* so also *are* those *who are* heavenly. [49]And as we have borne the image of the *man* of dust, we shall also bear[a] the image of the heavenly *Man.*

Our Final Victory

[50]Now this I say, brethren, that flesh and blood cannot inherit the kingdom of God; nor does corruption inherit incorruption. [51]Behold, I tell you a mystery: We shall not all sleep, but we shall all be changed— [52]in a moment, in the twinkling of an eye, at the last trumpet. For the trumpet will sound, and the dead will be raised incorruptible, and we shall be changed. [53]For this corruptible must put on incorruption, and this mortal *must* put on immortality. [54]So when this corruptible has put on incorruption, and this mortal has put on immortality, then shall be brought to pass the saying that is written: *"Death is swallowed up in victory."* [a]

[55]   *"O Death, where is your sting?* [a]
      O Hades, where is your victory?" [b]

[56]The sting of death *is* sin, and the strength of sin *is* the law. [57]But thanks *be* to God, who gives us the victory through our Lord Jesus Christ.

[58]Therefore, my beloved brethren, be steadfast, immovable, always abounding in the work of the Lord, knowing that your labor is not in vain in the Lord.

🧩 ***Paul's Future Plans***

As is typical of his letters, Paul concluded with final instructions and greetings. He also related future plans for himself and his missionary companions, which included receiving the Corinthians' gift for Jerusalem (1 Cor. 16:1–3). Paul had organized a collection from the Gentile churches to help the poor believers in Jerusalem. The collection was widespread, being contributed by churches from at least Galatia, Macedonia, and Achaia (see Rom. 15:26, 27; 2 Cor. 9:1, 2).

Future plans also included a visit of Paul to Corinth. He would continue his ministry in Ephesus until the Day of Pentecost (16:8), in late spring of A.D. 55. His original plans had been to travel at that time from Ephesus straight to Corinth, and he was apparently criticized for deciding to pass through Macedonia first (16:5, 6; 2 Cor. 1:15–17). From Ephesus Paul did send Timothy to Macedonia along with Erastus, the commissioner of public works for

---

15:32 [a]Isaiah 22:13   15:39 [a]NU-Text and M-Text omit *of flesh.*   15:45 [a]Genesis 2:7
15:47 [a]NU-Text omits *the Lord.*   15:49 [a]M-Text reads *let us also bear.*   15:54 [a]Isaiah 25:8
15:55 [a]Hosea 13:14   [b]NU-Text reads *O Death, where is your victory? O Death, where is your sting?*

EVIDENCE FOR DATING NEW TESTAMENT EVENTS

A number of events recorded in the New Testament can be dated with reasonable certainty. The evidence that allows us to determine specific dates comes from a variety of sources.

Event	Date	Evidence Source	New Testament Connection	Reference
Reign of Augustus Caesar	27 B.C.– A.D. 14	Roman history	Reigned during NT times	Luke 2:1
Death of Herod the Great	4 B.C.	An eclipse of the moon mentioned by Josephus	Jesus was born before Herod died	Matt. 2:19
15th year of Tiberius Caesar	A.D. 26 or 28	Possible definitions of when his rule began	Date is cited by Luke	Luke 3:1
Passover during Passion Week	A.D. 30 or 33	Astronomical calculation of the phases of the moon	Last Supper and crucifixion of Jesus	Luke 22:15; John 19:14
Death of Herod Agrippa I	A.D. 44	Josephus	Event is described in Acts	Acts 12:20–23
Famine	A.D. 44–48	Ancient writers	Famine relief sent from Antioch to Jerusalem	Acts 11:28–30
Edict of Claudius	A.D. 49	Orosius, writing in A.D. 416–417	Aquila and Priscilla left Rome for Corinth	Acts 18:1, 2; 1 Cor. 16:19
Term of office for Gallio	A.D. 51–52	Ancient inscription discovered at Delphi, Greece	Paul appeared before Gallio	Acts 18:12

Corinth (Acts 19:22; Rom. 16:23). That trip probably included Timothy's visit to the Corinthian church (1 Cor. 4:17; 16:10).

■ 1 Corinthians 16:1–24

1 Corinthians
Collection for the Saints

16 :1 Now concerning the collection for the saints, as I have given orders to the churches of Galatia, so you must do also: ²On the first *day* of the week let each one of you lay something aside, storing up as he may prosper, that there be no collections when I come. ³And when I come, whomever you approve by *your* letters I will send to bear your gift to Jerusalem. ⁴But if it is fitting that I go also, they will go with me.

Personal Plans

⁵Now I will come to you when I pass through Macedonia (for I am passing through Macedonia). ⁶And it may be that I will remain, or even spend the winter with you, that you may send me on my journey, wherever I go. ⁷For I do not wish to see you now on the way; but I hope to stay a while with you, if the Lord permits.

⁸But I will tarry in Ephesus until Pentecost. ⁹For a great and effective door has opened to me, and *there are* many adversaries.

¹⁰And if Timothy comes, see that he may be with you without fear; for he does the work of the Lord, as I also *do*. ¹¹Therefore let no one despise him. But send him on his journey in peace, that he may come

to me; for I am waiting for him with the brethren.

12Now concerning *our* brother Apollos, I strongly urged him to come to you with the brethren, but he was quite unwilling to come at this time; however, he will come when he has a convenient time.

Final Exhortations

13Watch, stand fast in the faith, be brave, be strong. 14Let all *that* you *do* be done with love.

15I urge you, brethren—you know the household of Stephanas, that it is the first-fruits of Achaia, and *that* they have devoted themselves to the ministry of the saints— 16that you also submit to such, and to everyone who works and labors with *us*.

17I am glad about the coming of Stephanas, Fortunatus, and Achaicus, for what was lacking on your part they supplied. 18For they refreshed my spirit and yours. Therefore acknowledge such men.

Greetings and a Solemn Farewell

19The churches of Asia greet you. Aquila and Priscilla greet you heartily in the Lord, with the church that is in their house. 20All the brethren greet you.

Greet one another with a holy kiss.

21The salutation with my own hand— Paul's.

22If anyone does not love the Lord Jesus Christ, let him be accursed.[a] O Lord, come![b]

23The grace of our Lord Jesus Christ *be* with you. 24My love *be* with you all in Christ Jesus. Amen.

16:22 [a]Greek *anathema* [b]Aramaic *Maranatha*
Acts 19:24 [a]Greek *Artemis* 19:27 [a]NU-Text reads *she be deposed from her magnificence.*

Commotion in Ephesus

Paul's work in Ephesus during his third missionary journey (c. A.D. 54) began to turn the allegiance of some from paganism to Christ. When the success of the gospel threatened the trade of silversmiths in Ephesus, money motivated an attack against Paul. A civil disturbance was instigated by Demetrius, a silversmith who manufactured devotional shrines for the worship of Diana (the Greek goddess Artemis).

"Diana of the Ephesians" (Acts 19:34)

was the mother goddess of Asia. Her temple in Ephesus was one of the Seven Wonders of the ancient world, and people came from all parts of the Roman world to worship her. A legend told of an "image which fell down from Zeus" that was kept in Diana's temple (19:35). The "image" may have been a meteorite similar to others that were venerated at various places in the ancient world, most notably the "image of the Great Mother" brought to Rome from Pessinus.

■ Acts 19:23—20:1

Acts
The Riot at Ephesus

19 :23 And about that time there arose a great commotion about the Way. 24For a certain man named Demetrius, a silversmith, who made silver shrines of Diana,[a] brought no small profit to the craftsmen. 25He called them together with the workers of similar occupation, and said: "Men, you know that we have our prosperity by this trade. 26Moreover you see and hear that not only at Ephesus, but throughout almost all Asia, this Paul has persuaded and turned away many people, saying that they are not gods which are made with hands. 27So not only is this trade of ours in danger of falling into disrepute, but also the temple of the great goddess Diana may be despised and her magnificence destroyed,[a] whom all Asia and the world worship."

28Now when they heard *this,* they were full of wrath and cried out, saying, "Great *is* Diana of the Ephesians!" 29So the whole city was filled with confusion, and rushed into the theater with one accord, having seized Gaius and Aristarchus, Macedonians, Paul's travel companions. 30And when Paul wanted to go in to the people, the disciples would not allow him. 31Then some of the officials of Asia, who were his friends, sent to him pleading that he would not venture into the theater. 32Some therefore cried one thing and some another, for the assembly was confused, and most of them did not know why they had come together. 33And they drew Alexander out of the multitude, the Jews putting him forward. And Alexander motioned with his hand, and wanted to make his defense to the people. 34But when they found out that he was a Jew, all with one voice cried out for about two hours, "Great *is* Diana of the Ephesians!"

PAUL VERSUS THE GODDESS DIANA (Acts 19:24–28)

The Ephesian silversmith Demetrius incited a riot against Paul for preaching in Ephesus that gods "made with hands" are not really gods (Acts 19:26). Ephesus had as many as a quarter million inhabitants, making it the largest city in the province of Asia. Its size was reason enough for Paul to found a church in Ephesus, but another significant factor was religion: Ephesus was the cult center for the worship of Artemis or Diana.

Artemis was a very popular Greek goddess. In Greek religion she was the virgin goddess of the hunt and the moon, and the daughter of the Greek god Zeus. In Roman religion she was identified as the goddess Diana.

Part of what made Artemis important to Ephesus was her temple. It was the largest temple in Asia Minor (modern Turkey). The top of the platform it was built on (that would be the floor of the temple) was 168 feet, 9 inches wide by 365 feet, 9 inches long. The columns were 6 feet in diameter and almost 58 feet tall. By comparison, the floor of the Parthenon at Athens was only about two-thirds the size of the temple at Ephesus, and the Parthenon's columns were only a little more than 34 feet high.

The temple of Artemis was one of the Seven Wonders of the ancient world. Its size and magnificence made it an attraction for tourists and pilgrims. For Ephesus, it was a place for worship, but also a treasury and a storehouse.

Paul took on a sizeable opponent in Diana or Artemis. She had become the guardian deity of Ephesus. She influenced the politics, culture, and economy of the city. The people of Ephesus were prepared to defend Artemis against any who would threaten her, and Paul's gospel threatened to destroy the profit of the craftsmen who made silver shrines of the goddess.

35And when the city clerk had quieted the crowd, he said: "Men of Ephesus, what man is there who does not know that the city of the Ephesians is temple guardian of the great goddess Diana, and of the *image* which fell down from Zeus? 36Therefore, since these things cannot be denied, you ought to be quiet and do nothing rashly. 37For you have brought these men here who are neither robbers of temples nor blasphemers of youra goddess. 38Therefore, if Demetrius and his fellow craftsmen have a case against anyone, the courts are open and there are proconsuls. Let them bring charges against one another. 39But if you have any other inquiry to make, it shall be determined in the lawful assembly. 40For we are in danger of being called in question for today's uproar, there being no reason which we may give to account for this disorderly gathering." 41And when he had said these things, he dismissed the assembly.

20 1After the uproar had ceased, Paul called the disciples to *himself,* embraced *them,* and departed to go to Macedonia.

19:37 aNU-Text reads *our.*

The Second Letter to the Corinthians

The letter of 2 Corinthians was written perhaps 6 months to a year after Paul wrote 1 Corinthians, possibly in A.D. 55 at the end of his long ministry in Ephesus (Acts 20:31). The Corinthian church required Paul's continual care. Shortly after his founding mission in

ARCHITECTURE AND BUILDING

The Greek goddess Artemis was Diana to the Romans (Acts 19:34). Her temple at Ephesus was one of the largest Greek temples, with columns 58 feet high standing on a platform 169 by 366 feet. Surviving copies of the statue of Diana of Ephesus are decorated with what appear to be numerous breasts, but which also could represent grapes, olives, or eggs.

Corinth, he sent a letter instructing the church "not to keep company with sexually immoral people" (1 Cor. 5:9). Later, a delegation from Corinth came to Ephesus asking for Paul's guidance; they returned, possibly carrying the letter of 1 Corinthians with them (1 Cor. 16:17–19). Timothy visited Corinth (1 Cor. 4:17; 16:10, 11) and probably returned to Paul in Ephesus with news of opposition to Paul and continued division in the church.

Such unchristian practices in Corinth required correction. Paul made a "sorrowful" visit (2 Cor. 1:23—2:1), which did not resolve these problems. He then sent a "severe" letter delivered to the Corinthians by Titus (2 Cor. 2:3–5). When finally Paul was reconciled to the church, he wrote to them both to celebrate their restored relationship and to have them prepare for yet another visit (2 Cor. 1:13–16).

Scholars disagree over whether 2 Corinthians is a single letter, or was compiled from several shorter letters. Some think there were four letters: Paul's "earlier" letter (1 Cor. 5:9); 1 Corinthians; the "severe" letter (2 Cor. 2:3); and 2 Corinthians. In this case, 1 Corinthians would have been the second letter Paul wrote to the Corinthian church; and 2 Corinthians, at least the fourth. Thus, one option is to accept that 2 Corinthians was originally written as it now appears in the New Testament, and suppose that the "earlier" letter against sexual immorality and the "severe" letter have been lost.

An alternative is to suppose that the "earlier" letter, warning against sexual immorality, is part of 2 Corinthians (see "Paul's Authority and Epistle" at 1 Cor. 5:1). Similarly, the four final chapters (2 Cor. 10—13) are considered to be the so-called "severe" letter, the letter written "out of much affliction and anguish" (2 Cor. 2:4). Those favoring this option point to a marked contrast: the positive relationship between Paul and the Corinthians evidenced in the early chapters of 2 Corinthians versus Paul's harsh attacks on some in Corinth in 2 Cor. 10—13.

▼ ■ 2 Corinthians 1:1—2:11

2 Corinthians
Greeting

1 **:1** Paul, an apostle of Jesus Christ by the will of God, and Timothy *our* brother,

To the church of God which is at Corinth, with all the saints who are in all Achaia:

2Grace to you and peace from God our Father and the Lord Jesus Christ.

Comfort in Suffering

3Blessed *be* the God and Father of our Lord Jesus Christ, the Father of mercies and God of all comfort, 4who comforts us in all our tribulation, that we may be able to comfort those who are in any trouble, with the comfort with which we ourselves are comforted by God. 5For as the sufferings of Christ abound in us, so our consolation also abounds through Christ. 6Now if we are afflicted, *it is* for your consolation and salvation, which is effective for enduring the same sufferings which we also suffer. Or if we are comforted, *it is* for your consolation and salvation. 7And our hope for you *is* steadfast, because we know that as you are partakers of the sufferings, so also *you will partake* of the consolation.

Delivered from Suffering

8For we do not want you to be ignorant, brethren, of our trouble which came to us in Asia: that we were burdened beyond measure, above strength, so that we despaired even of life. 9Yes, we had the sentence of death in ourselves, that we should not trust in ourselves but in God who raises the dead, 10who delivered us from so great a death, and doesa deliver us; in whom we trust that He will still deliver *us,* 11you also helping together in prayer for us, that thanks may be given by many persons on oura behalf for the gift *granted* to us through many.

Paul's Sincerity

12For our boasting is this: the testimony of our conscience that we conducted ourselves in the world in simplicity and godly sincerity, not with fleshly wisdom but by the grace of God, and more abundantly toward you. 13For we are not writing any other things to you than what you read or understand. Now I trust you will understand, even to the end 14(as also you have understood us in part), that we are your boast as you also *are* ours, in the day of the Lord Jesus.

Sparing the Church

15And in this confidence I intended to come to you before, that you might have a

1:10 aNU-Text reads *shall.*   1:11 aM-Text reads *your behalf.*

second benefit— ¹⁶to pass by way of you to Macedonia, to come again from Macedonia to you, and be helped by you on my way to Judea. ¹⁷Therefore, when I was planning this, did I do it lightly? Or the things I plan, do I plan according to the flesh, that with me there should be Yes, Yes, and No, No? ¹⁸But *as* God *is* faithful, our word to you was not Yes and No. ¹⁹For the Son of God, Jesus Christ, who was preached among you by us—by me, Silvanus, and Timothy—was not Yes and No, but in Him was Yes. ²⁰For all the promises of God in Him *are* Yes, and in Him Amen, to the glory of God through us. ²¹Now He who establishes us with you in Christ and has anointed us *is* God, ²²who also has sealed us and given us the Spirit in our hearts as a guarantee.

²³Moreover I call God as witness against my soul, that to spare you I came no more to Corinth. ²⁴Not that we have dominion over your faith, but are fellow workers for your joy; for by faith you stand.

2 ¹But I determined this within myself, that I would not come again to you in sorrow. ²For if I make you sorrowful, then who is he who makes me glad but the one who is made sorrowful by me?

Forgive the Offender

³And I wrote this very thing to you, lest, when I came, I should have sorrow over those from whom I ought to have joy, having confidence in you all that my joy is *the joy* of you all. ⁴For out of much affliction and anguish of heart I wrote to you, with many tears, not that you should be grieved, but that you might know the love which I have so abundantly for you.

⁵But if anyone has caused grief, he has not grieved me, but all of you to some extent—not to be too severe. ⁶This punishment which *was inflicted* by the majority *is* sufficient for such a man, ⁷so that, on the contrary, you *ought* rather to forgive and comfort *him,* lest perhaps such a one be swallowed up with too much sorrow. ⁸Therefore I urge you to reaffirm *your* love

to him. ⁹For to this end I also wrote, that I might put you to the test, whether you are obedient in all things. ¹⁰Now whom you forgive anything, I also *forgive.* For if indeed I have forgiven anything, I have forgiven that one[a] for your sakes in the presence of Christ, ¹¹lest Satan should take advantage of us; for we are not ignorant of his devices.

Paul Seeks a Report from Titus

Instead of leaving Ephesus and visiting Corinth on the way to Macedonia, Paul went to Troas (see 2 Cor. 1:8, 16). Having previously sent Titus to Corinth with the letter commanding punishment of the offender (2:3–8), Paul was anxious to meet Titus in Troas to receive word from Corinth. Not finding him there, Paul left Troas for Macedonia, possibly to meet Titus as he returned.

It seems strange that in ch. 7 Paul returns to discussing his and Titus's travels without any renewed introduction (7:5–16). That sudden change of topic to Paul's travel plans and his sending of Titus to Corinth might suggest that the portion of 2 Corinthians in 2:14—7:4 is part of another letter, and was inserted (after 2:13) by a later editor who compiled 2 Corinthians as it now appears in the New Testament. This brief letter (2:14—7:4), describing Paul's view of an apostle's ministry, would have been written between his writing of 1 Corinthians and his "sorrowful visit" to Corinth (see "The Second Letter to the Corinthians" at 2 Cor. 1:1).

■ 2 Corinthians 2:12—7:16

2 Corinthians
Triumph in Christ

2 :12 Furthermore, when I came to Troas to *preach* Christ's gospel, and a door was opened to me by the Lord, ¹³I had no rest in my spirit, because I did not find Ti-

---

2:10 ᵃNU-Text reads *For indeed, what I have forgiven, if I have forgiven anything, I did it.*

POLITICS AND GOVERNMENT

The triumph was a tradition of the Roman state. A general who had won an important victory in war was entitled to ride in a splendid chariot with his troops marching fully armed, leading prisoners and booty captured in the fighting. During the celebration, which could last several days, important prisoners were executed. Paul pictured the spread of the gospel as a parade of victory (2 Cor. 2:14).

LETTERS OF COMMENDATION (2 Cor. 3:1–3)

Western culture has a long history of personal references. Without phones or faxes, the typical recommendations in the Greco-Roman world took the form of letters. The writer of the letter often requested, on the basis of his or her previous relationship with the recipient, that the recipient welcome, provide hospitality for, and cooperate with the person being commended.

Usually the commended person also delivered the letter. The writer, who was well known to and respected by the letter's recipient, would thus presuppose a face-to-face encounter between the one he was commending and the recipient. Someone who lacked a letter of commendation could appear to be a vagrant out to take advantage of the hospitality of others.

The letters could be quite short. After an initial greeting, the sender would identify the commended person, providing a brief background introduction. A specific request and the purpose of the recommendation was followed by a statement of appreciation. In closing, the sender would often provide a "blessing," a wish for the well-being of the recipient.

Early Christians wrote these letters to form a support network among the widely dispersed churches. One group of "brethren" wrote a letter of commendation for the Alexandrian Jewish Christian named Apollos, "exhorting the disciples to receive him" (Acts 18:27). The apostle Paul recommended Epaphroditus to the Philippian church, including a commendation within his broader letter (Phil. 2:25–30).

Paul saw no need to provide "letters of commendation" on his behalf to the church at Corinth (2 Cor. 3:1). Recommendations served to introduce strangers who lacked credibility. Paul, on the other hand, had started the Corinthian church—he was, in a sense, their Christian father (see 1 Cor. 4:15).

Nor did Paul need commendation from the Corinthian believers themselves. Their own lives authenticated his mission, proving his apostolic authority better than any letter could. They were a commendation "written not with ink but by the Spirit of the living God" (2 Cor. 3:3). What better commendation could one get!

---

tus my brother; but taking my leave of them, I departed for Macedonia.

14Now thanks *be* to God who always leads us in triumph in Christ, and through us diffuses the fragrance of His knowledge in every place. 15For we are to God the fragrance of Christ among those who are being saved and among those who are perishing. 16To the one *we are* the aroma of death *leading* to death, and to the other the aroma of life *leading* to life. And who *is* sufficient for these things? 17For we are not, as so many,a peddling the word of God; but as of sincerity, but as from God, we speak in the sight of God in Christ.

Christ's Epistle

3 1Do we begin again to commend ourselves? Or do we need, as some *others,* epistles of commendation to you or *letters* of commendation from you? 2You are our epistle written in our hearts, known and read by all men; 3clearly *you are* an epistle of Christ, ministered by us, written not with ink but by the Spirit of the living God, not on tablets of stone but on tablets of flesh, *that is,* of the heart.

The Spirit, Not the Letter

4And we have such trust through Christ toward God. 5Not that we are sufficient of ourselves to think of anything as *being* from ourselves, but our sufficiency *is* from God, 6who also made us sufficient as ministers of the new covenant, not of the letter but of the Spirit;a for the letter kills, but the Spirit gives life.

Glory of the New Covenant

7But if the ministry of death, written *and* engraved on stones, was glorious, so that the children of Israel could not look steadily at the face of Moses because of the glory of his countenance, which *glory* was passing away, 8how will the ministry of the Spirit not be more glorious? 9For if the

---

2:17 aM-Text reads *the rest.*   3:6 aOr *spirit*

ministry of condemnation *had* glory, the ministry of righteousness exceeds much more in glory. [10]For even what was made glorious had no glory in this respect, because of the glory that excels. [11]For if what is passing away *was* glorious, what remains *is* much more glorious.

[12]Therefore, since we have such hope, we use great boldness of speech— [13]unlike Moses, *who* put a veil over his face so that the children of Israel could not look steadily at the end of what was passing away. [14]But their minds were blinded. For until this day the same veil remains unlifted in the reading of the Old Testament, because the *veil* is taken away in Christ. [15]But even to this day, when Moses is read, a veil lies on their heart. [16]Nevertheless when one turns to the Lord, the veil is taken away. [17]Now the Lord is the Spirit; and where the Spirit of the Lord *is,* there *is* liberty. [18]But we all, with unveiled face, beholding as in a mirror the glory of the Lord, are being transformed into the same image from glory to glory, just as by the Spirit of the Lord.

The Light of Christ's Gospel

4 [1]Therefore, since we have this ministry, as we have received mercy, we do not lose heart. [2]But we have renounced the hidden things of shame, not walking in craftiness nor handling the word of God deceitfully, but by manifestation of the truth commending ourselves to every man's conscience in the sight of God. [3]But even if our gospel is veiled, it is veiled to those who are perishing, [4]whose minds the god of this age has blinded, who do not believe, lest the light of the gospel of the glory of Christ, who is the image of God, should shine on them. [5]For we do not preach ourselves, but Christ Jesus the Lord, and ourselves your bondservants for Jesus' sake. [6]For it is the God who commanded light to shine out of darkness, who has shone in our hearts to *give* the light of the knowledge of the glory of God in the face of Jesus Christ.

Cast Down but Unconquered

[7]But we have this treasure in earthen vessels, that the excellence of the power may be of God and not of us. [8]*We are* hard-pressed on every side, yet not crushed; *we are* perplexed, but not in despair; [9]persecuted, but not forsaken; struck down, but not destroyed— [10]always carrying about in the body the dying of the Lord Jesus, that the life of Jesus also may be manifested in our body. [11]For we who live are always delivered to death for Jesus' sake, that the life of Jesus also may be manifested in our mortal flesh. [12]So then death is working in us, but life in you.

[13]And since we have the same spirit of faith, according to what is written, *"I believed and therefore I spoke,"* [a] we also believe and therefore speak, [14]knowing that He who raised up the Lord Jesus will also raise us up with Jesus, and will present *us* with you. [15]For all things *are* for your sakes, that grace, having spread through the many, may cause thanksgiving to abound to the glory of God.

Seeing the Invisible

[16]Therefore we do not lose heart. Even though our outward man is perishing, yet the inward *man* is being renewed day by day. [17]For our light affliction, which is but for a moment, is working for us a far more exceeding *and* eternal weight of glory, [18]while we do not look at the things which are seen, but at the things which are not seen. For the things which are seen *are* temporary, but the things which are not seen *are* eternal.

Assurance of the Resurrection

5 [1]For we know that if our earthly house, *this* tent, is destroyed, we have a building from God, a house not made with hands, eternal in the heavens. [2]For in this we groan, earnestly desiring to be clothed with our habitation which is from heaven,

4:13 [a]Psalm 116:10

³if indeed, having been clothed, we shall not be found naked. ⁴For we who are in *this* tent groan, being burdened, not because we want to be unclothed, but further clothed, that mortality may be swallowed up by life. ⁵Now He who has prepared us for this very thing *is* God, who also has given us the Spirit as a guarantee.

⁶So *we are* always confident, knowing that while we are at home in the body we are absent from the Lord. ⁷For we walk by faith, not by sight. ⁸We are confident, yes, well pleased rather to be absent from the body and to be present with the Lord.

The Judgment Seat of Christ

⁹Therefore we make it our aim, whether present or absent, to be well pleasing to Him. ¹⁰For we must all appear before the judgment seat of Christ, that each one may receive the things *done* in the body, according to what he has done, whether good or bad. ¹¹Knowing, therefore, the terror of the Lord, we persuade men; but we are well known to God, and I also trust are well known in your consciences.

Be Reconciled to God

¹²For we do not commend ourselves again to you, but give you opportunity to boast on our behalf, that you may have *an answer* for those who boast in appearance and not in heart. ¹³For if we are beside ourselves, *it is* for God; or if we are of sound mind, *it is* for you. ¹⁴For the love of Christ compels us, because we judge thus: that if One died for all, then all died; ¹⁵and He died for all, that those who live should live no longer for themselves, but for Him who died for them and rose again.

¹⁶Therefore, from now on, we regard no one according to the flesh. Even though we have known Christ according to the flesh, yet now we know *Him thus* no longer. ¹⁷Therefore, if anyone *is* in Christ, *he is* a new creation; old things have passed away; behold, all things have become new. ¹⁸Now

6:2 ᵃIsaiah 49:8

all things *are* of God, who has reconciled us to Himself through Jesus Christ, and has given us the ministry of reconciliation, ¹⁹that is, that God was in Christ reconciling the world to Himself, not imputing their trespasses to them, and has committed to us the word of reconciliation.

²⁰Now then, we are ambassadors for Christ, as though God were pleading through us: we implore *you* on Christ's behalf, be reconciled to God. ²¹For He made Him who knew no sin *to be* sin for us, that we might become the righteousness of God in Him.

Marks of the Ministry

6 ¹We then, *as* workers together *with Him* also plead with *you* not to receive the grace of God in vain. ²For He says:

> "In an acceptable time I have heard you,
> And in the day of salvation I have helped you." ᵃ

Behold, now *is* the accepted time; behold, now *is* the day of salvation.

³We give no offense in anything, that our ministry may not be blamed. ⁴But in all *things* we commend ourselves as ministers of God: in much patience, in tribulations, in needs, in distresses, ⁵in stripes, in imprisonments, in tumults, in labors, in sleeplessness, in fastings; ⁶by purity, by knowledge, by longsuffering, by kindness, by the Holy Spirit, by sincere love, ⁷by the word of truth, by the power of God, by the armor of righteousness on the right hand and on the left, ⁸by honor and dishonor, by evil report and good report; as deceivers, and *yet* true; ⁹as unknown, and *yet* well known; as dying, and behold we live; as chastened, and *yet* not killed; ¹⁰as sorrowful, yet always rejoicing; as poor, yet making many rich; as having nothing, and *yet* possessing all things.

Be Holy

¹¹O Corinthians! We have spoken openly to you, our heart is wide open. ¹²You

---

SCIENCE AND TECHNOLOGY

A yoke was usually a wooden beam shaped to fit over the necks of two animals, harnessing them to a plow or similar tool. Oxen were the most common animals used for working the land, and a yoke linking a pair of oxen together allowed them to work efficiently. An ox and a donkey put in a yoke would be "unequally yoked" (2 Cor. 6:14; see Deut. 22:10). They could not pull the load evenly and might want to go different directions.

are not restricted by us, but you are restricted by your *own* affections. ¹³Now in return for the same (I speak as to children), you also be open.

¹⁴Do not be unequally yoked together with unbelievers. For what fellowship has righteousness with lawlessness? And what communion has light with darkness? ¹⁵And what accord has Christ with Belial? Or what part has a believer with an unbeliever? ¹⁶And what agreement has the temple of God with idols? For you[a] are the temple of the living God. As God has said:

> *"I will dwell in them*
> *And walk among them.*
> *I will be their God,*
> *And they shall be My people."*[b]

¹⁷Therefore

> *"Come out from among them*
> *And be separate, says the Lord.*
> *Do not touch what is unclean,*
> *And I will receive you."*[a]
> ¹⁸ *"I will be a Father to you,*
> *And you shall be My sons and*
> *daughters,*
> *Says the LORD Almighty."*[a]

7 ¹Therefore, having these promises, beloved, let us cleanse ourselves from all filthiness of the flesh and spirit, perfecting holiness in the fear of God.

The Corinthians' Repentance

²Open *your hearts* to us. We have wronged no one, we have corrupted no one, we have cheated no one. ³I do not say *this* to condemn; for I have said before that you are in our hearts, to die together and to live together. ⁴Great *is* my boldness of speech toward you, great *is* my boasting on your behalf. I am filled with comfort. I am exceedingly joyful in all our tribulation.

⁵For indeed, when we came to Macedonia, our bodies had no rest, but we were troubled on every side. Outside *were* conflicts, inside *were* fears. ⁶Nevertheless God, who comforts the downcast, comforted us by the coming of Titus, ⁷and not only by his coming, but also by the consolation with which he was comforted in you, when he told us of your earnest desire, your mourning, your zeal for me, so that I rejoiced even more.

⁸For even if I made you sorry with my letter, I do not regret it; though I did regret it. For I perceive that the same epistle made you sorry, though only for a while. ⁹Now I rejoice, not that you were made sorry, but that your sorrow led to repentance. For you were made sorry in a godly manner, that you might suffer loss from us in nothing. ¹⁰For godly sorrow produces repentance *leading* to salvation, not to be regretted; but the sorrow of the world produces death. ¹¹For observe this very thing, that you sorrowed in a godly manner: What diligence it produced in you, *what* clearing *of yourselves, what* indignation, *what* fear, *what* vehement desire, *what* zeal, *what* vindication! In all *things* you proved yourselves to be clear in this matter. ¹²Therefore, although I wrote to you, *I did* not *do it* for the sake of him who had done the wrong, nor for the sake of him who suffered wrong, but that our care for you in the sight of God might appear to you.

The Joy of Titus

¹³Therefore we have been comforted in your comfort. And we rejoiced exceedingly more for the joy of Titus, because his spirit has been refreshed by you all. ¹⁴For if in anything I have boasted to him about you, I am not ashamed. But as we spoke all things to you in truth, even so our boasting to Titus was found true. ¹⁵And his affections are greater for you as he remembers the obedience of you all, how with fear and trembling you received him. ¹⁶Therefore I rejoice that I have confidence in you in everything.

TIME CAPSULE *A.D. 54 to 55*

54–55 *Paul imprisoned in Ephesus (?)*

55 *Paul writes 1 Corinthians from Ephesus*

55 *Paul writes 2 Corinthians from Ephesus*

55 *Pallas loses his position as financial secretary*

55 *Paul leaves Ephesus after Day of Pentecost (1 Cor. 16:8)*

55–56 *Paul travels through Macedonia to Greece (Acts 20:1)*

6:16 [a]NU-Text reads *we.*   [b]Leviticus 26:12; Jeremiah 32:38; Ezekiel 37:27   6:17 [a]Isaiah 52:11; Ezekiel 20:34, 41   6:18 [a]2 Samuel 7:14

The Offering for Jerusalem's Christians

On his third missionary journey Paul raised an offering to relieve the poverty of the Christians in Jerusalem and to demonstrate the unity of the Jewish and Gentile churches (see 1 Cor. 16:1–4; Rom. 15:25–28). Corinth was in Achaia, just south of Macedonia from which Paul was writing. The Christians in Corinth, a great commercial center, were better off financially than those in Macedonia and Jerusalem, yet Paul encouraged the Corinthians to participate in this offering by praising the generosity of the Macedonians (2 Cor. 8:1–4).

The apparent repetition of instructions regarding the offering (compare 8:1–6 with 9:1–5) suggests that 2 Cor. 9 may be part of a brief letter that Paul wrote to the Corinthians just in advance of his third and final visit with them. If so, a previous letter, written after the tensions between Paul and the Corinthians had been relieved, could have consisted of 2 Cor. 1:3—2:13 and 7:5—8:24. See "The Second Letter to the Corinthians" at 2 Cor. 1:1.

■ 2 Corinthians 8:1—9:15

2 Corinthians
Excel in Giving

8:1 Moreover, brethren, we make known to you the grace of God bestowed on the churches of Macedonia: 2that in a great trial of affliction the abundance of their joy and their deep poverty abounded in the riches of their liberality. 3For I bear witness that according to *their* ability, yes, and beyond *their* ability, *they were* freely willing, 4imploring us with much urgency that we would receive[a] the gift and the fellowship of the ministering to the saints. 5And not *only* as we had hoped, but they first gave themselves to the Lord, and *then* to us

---

8:4 [a]NU-Text and M-Text omit *that we would receive,* thus changing text to *urgency for the favor and fellowship* . . . .   8:15 [a]Exodus 16:18
8:16 [a]NU-Text reads *has put.*

by the will of God. 6So we urged Titus, that as he had begun, so he would also complete this grace in you as well. 7But as you abound in everything—in faith, in speech, in knowledge, in all diligence, and in your love for us—*see* that you abound in this grace also.

Christ Our Pattern

8I speak not by commandment, but I am testing the sincerity of your love by the diligence of others. 9For you know the grace of our Lord Jesus Christ, that though He was rich, yet for your sakes He became poor, that you through His poverty might become rich.

10And in this I give advice: It is to your advantage not only to be doing what you began and were desiring to do a year ago; 11but now you also must complete the doing *of it;* that as *there was* a readiness to desire *it,* so *there* also *may be* a completion out of what *you* have. 12For if there is first a willing mind, *it is* accepted according to what one has, *and* not according to what he does not have.

13For *I do* not *mean* that others should be eased and you burdened; 14but by an equality, *that* now at this time your abundance *may supply* their lack, that their abundance also may supply your lack—that there may be equality. 15As it is written, *"He who gathered much had nothing left over, and he who gathered little had no lack."*[a]

Collection for the Judean Saints

16But thanks *be* to God who puts[a] the same earnest care for you into the heart of Titus. 17For he not only accepted the exhortation, but being more diligent, he went to you of his own accord. 18And we have sent with him the brother whose praise *is* in the gospel throughout all the churches, 19and not only *that,* but who was also chosen by the churches to travel with us with this gift, which is administered by us to the glory of the Lord Himself and *to show* your ready mind, 20avoiding this: that anyone

---

GEOGRAPHY AND ENVIRONMENT
The Macedonian churches had produced an example of generosity. Among the provinces, Macedonia was worse off economically than Achaia, in which Corinth was located. Since Corinth was a great commercial center, the Christians there were much better off financially than those in either Macedonia or Jerusalem. In spite of their poverty, the Macedonians gave far beyond what one would expect (2 Cor. 8:1–4).

PAUL'S COLLECTION FOR JERUSALEM (2 Cor. 8:16–24)

Paul's letters addressed the specific issues that arose within the congregations he had planted. One issue, however, that Paul consistently addressed was of his own making: a financial offering for the church in Jerusalem.

This collection for the Jerusalem church seems to have originated at the so-called "Jerusalem Council" (Acts 15; Gal. 2:1–10). While the apostles and elders of the council agreed that Paul could pursue his mission to the Gentiles, they asked that he "remember the poor" (Gal. 2:10), indirectly referring to an offering for the Jerusalem church. The collection, therefore, stood at the very foundation of Paul's missionary work.

The offering remained a cornerstone in Paul's ministry. He mentioned the collection in writing to churches at Corinth (1 Cor. 16:1–4) and at Rome (Rom. 15:25–27). He praised churches in Macedonia and Achaia for their generosity in giving (Rom. 15:26; 2 Cor. 8:1–4).

Why would Jerusalem ask for such an offering, and why would Paul keep the offering central to his mission among the Gentiles, the non-Jews? Possibly because he saw his ministry as fulfilling the promises of the Jewish Scriptures, the Old Testament. In the resurrection of Jesus Christ, as Paul believed, the end time had already begun, and through Jesus, God had begun to fulfill the end time promises found in the Scriptures. Among these eschatological promises, especially those in the Book of Isaiah, Jerusalem bore special prominence. Isaiah looks toward a new age centered in Jerusalem, where God unites both Jew and Gentile in worship to Him (Is. 66:18–21).

No wonder the collection was central to Paul's mission; it *was* Paul's mission. The offering brought the wealth of the Gentiles to Jerusalem, signaling the fulfillment of God's plan for Israel through Jesus. Paul finally returned to Jerusalem with the offering and delivered it to the church there around A.D. 57 (Acts 21:15–17; 24:17).

should blame us in this lavish gift which is administered by us— [21]providing honorable things, not only in the sight of the Lord, but also in the sight of men.

[22]And we have sent with them our brother whom we have often proved diligent in many things, but now much more diligent, because of the great confidence which *we have* in you. [23]If *anyone inquires* about Titus, *he is* my partner and fellow worker concerning you. Or if our brethren *are inquired about, they are* messengers of the churches, the glory of Christ. [24]Therefore show to them, and[a] before the churches, the proof of your love and of our boasting on your behalf.

Administering the Gift

9 [1]Now concerning the ministering to the saints, it is superfluous for me to write to you; [2]for I know your willingness, about which I boast of you to the Macedonians, that Achaia was ready a year ago; and your zeal has stirred up the majority. [3]Yet I have sent the brethren, lest our boasting of you should be in vain in this respect, that, as I said, you may be ready; [4]lest if *some* Macedonians come with me and find you unprepared, we (not to mention you!) should be ashamed of this confident boasting.[a] [5]Therefore I thought it necessary to exhort the brethren to go to you ahead of time, and prepare your generous gift beforehand, which *you had* previously promised, that it may be ready as *a matter of* generosity and not as a grudging obligation.

TIME CAPSULE A.D. 56 to 57

56 Roman historian Tacitus is born

56 Paul sends the letter to the Romans from Corinth

57 Nero compels senators to fight in the stadium

57 Paul encourages the Ephesian elders in Miletus

57 Paul sails from Miletus to Tyre

8:24 [a]NU-Text and M-Text omit *and.*
9:4 [a]NU-Text reads *this confidence.*

The Cheerful Giver

⁶But this *I say:* He who sows sparingly will also reap sparingly, and he who sows bountifully will also reap bountifully. ⁷*So let* each one *give* as he purposes in his heart, not grudgingly or of necessity; for God loves a cheerful giver. ⁸And God *is* able to make all grace abound toward you, that you, always having all sufficiency in all *things,* may have an abundance for every good work. ⁹As it is written:

> "He has dispersed abroad,
> He has given to the poor;
> His righteousness endures forever."ᵃ

¹⁰Now mayᵃ He who supplies seed to the sower, and bread for food, supply and multiply the seed you have *sown* and increase the fruits of your righteousness, ¹¹while *you are* enriched in everything for all liberality, which causes thanksgiving through us to God. ¹²For the administration of this service not only supplies the needs of the saints, but also is abounding through many thanksgivings to God, ¹³while, through the proof of this ministry, they glorify God for the obedience of your confession to the gospel of Christ, and for *your* liberal sharing with them and all *men,* ¹⁴and by their prayer for you, who long for you because of the exceeding grace of God in you. ¹⁵Thanks *be* to God for His indescribable gift!

9:9 ᵃPsalm 112:9   9:10 ᵃNU-Text reads *Now He who supplies . . . will supply . . . .*
10:7 ᵃNU-Text reads *even as we are.*
10:8 ᵃNU-Text omits *us.*

Paul's Third Visit to Corinth

In the final chapters of 2 Corinthians Paul defends himself against false teachers who had come to Corinth and claimed authority greater than his. They mistook the "gentleness of Christ" (2 Cor. 10:1) in Paul's life for weakness, claiming that he was braver in his letters than he would be in a face-to-face encounter (10:10). In response Paul argues that the authority they claim is based on comparing themselves with each other and not on having the commendation of God (10:18).

Paul wrote this defense of his apostolic authority in advance of his third visit to Corinth (12:14; 13:1), and thus after his "sorrowful"

visit (see 1:23—2:1). Paul's uncharacteristic personal boasts (12:1) and his harsh condemnations of his opponents are in stark contrast to his warm regard for the Corinthians in other parts of 2 Corinthians (see 7:8—11, 16). Possibly these chapters were written soon after the "sorrowful" visit while emotions were still high on both sides, whereas the earlier chapters were written later once Paul and the Corinthians had been reconciled (see "The Offering for Jerusalem's Christians" at 2 Cor. 8:1).

Still, 2 Corinthians could have been written by Paul as it now appears in the New Testament. The apostle could have made reconciliation with some of the Corinthians while yet dealing with other opponents in the church.

▼   ■ 2 Corinthians 10:1—13:14

2 Corinthians
The Spiritual War

10 :1 Now I, Paul, myself am pleading with you by the meekness and gentleness of Christ—who in presence *am* lowly among you, but being absent am bold toward you. ²But I beg *you* that when I am present I may not be bold with that confidence by which I intend to be bold against some, who think of us as if we walked according to the flesh. ³For though we walk in the flesh, we do not war according to the flesh. ⁴For the weapons of our warfare *are* not carnal but mighty in God for pulling down strongholds, ⁵casting down arguments and every high thing that exalts itself against the knowledge of God, bringing every thought into captivity to the obedience of Christ, ⁶and being ready to punish all disobedience when your obedience is fulfilled.

Reality of Paul's Authority

⁷Do you look at things according to the outward appearance? If anyone is convinced in himself that he is Christ's, let him again consider this in himself, that just as he *is* Christ's, even so we *are* Christ's.ᵃ ⁸For even if I should boast somewhat more about our authority, which the Lord gave usᵃ for edification and not for your destruction, I shall not be ashamed— ⁹lest I seem to terrify you by letters. ¹⁰"For *his* letters," they say, "*are* weighty and powerful, but *his* bodily presence *is* weak, and *his* speech contemptible." ¹¹Let such a person consider this, that what we are in word by letters when we are absent, such

we will also *be* in deed when we are present.

Limits of Paul's Authority

¹²For we dare not class ourselves or compare ourselves with those who commend themselves. But they, measuring themselves by themselves, and comparing themselves among themselves, are not wise. ¹³We, however, will not boast beyond measure, but within the limits of the sphere which God appointed us—a sphere which especially includes you. ¹⁴For we are not overextending ourselves (as though *our authority* did not extend to you), for it was to you that we came with the gospel of Christ; ¹⁵not boasting of things beyond measure, *that is,* in other men's labors, but having hope, *that* as your faith is increased, we shall be greatly enlarged by you in our sphere, ¹⁶to preach the gospel in the *regions* beyond you, *and* not to boast in another man's sphere of accomplishment. ¹⁷But *"he who glories, let him glory in the LORD."* ᵃ ¹⁸For not he who commends himself is approved, but whom the Lord commends.

Concern for Their Faithfulness

11 ¹Oh, that you would bear with me in a little folly—and indeed you do bear with me. ²For I am jealous for you with godly jealousy. For I have betrothed you to one husband, that I may present *you as* a chaste virgin to Christ. ³But I fear, lest somehow, as the serpent deceived Eve by his craftiness, so your minds may be corrupted from the simplicityᵃ that is in Christ. ⁴For if he who comes preaches another Jesus whom we have not preached, or *if* you receive a different spirit which you have not received, or a different gospel which you have not accepted—you may well put up with it!

Paul and False Apostles

⁵For I consider that I am not at all inferior to the most eminent apostles. ⁶Even though *I am* untrained in speech, yet *I am* not in knowledge. But we have been thoroughly manifestedᵃ among you in all things.

⁷Did I commit sin in humbling myself that you might be exalted, because I preached the gospel of God to you free of charge? ⁸I robbed other churches, taking wages *from them* to minister to you. ⁹And when I was present with you, and in need, I was a burden to no one, for what I lacked the brethren who came from Macedonia supplied. And in everything I kept myself from being burdensome to you, and so I will keep *myself.* ¹⁰As the truth of Christ is in me, no one shall stop me from this boasting in the regions of Achaia. ¹¹Why? Because I do not love you? God knows!

¹²But what I do, I will also continue to do, that I may cut off the opportunity from those who desire an opportunity to be regarded just as we are in the things of which they boast. ¹³For such *are* false apostles, deceitful workers, transforming themselves into apostles of Christ. ¹⁴And no wonder! For Satan himself transforms himself into an angel of light. ¹⁵Therefore *it is* no great thing if his ministers also transform themselves into ministers of righteousness, whose end will be according to their works.

Reluctant Boasting

¹⁶I say again, let no one think me a fool. If otherwise, at least receive me as a fool, that I also may boast a little. ¹⁷What I speak, I speak not according to the Lord, but as it were, foolishly, in this confidence of boasting. ¹⁸Seeing that many boast according to the flesh, I also will boast. ¹⁹For you put up with fools gladly, since you *yourselves* are wise! ²⁰For you put up with it if one brings you into bondage, if one devours *you,* if one takes *from you,* if one exalts himself, if one strikes you on the face. ²¹To *our* shame I say that we were too

---

10:17 ᵃJeremiah 9:24   11:3 ᵃNU-Text adds *and purity.*   11:6 ᵃNU-Text omits *been.*

CULTURE AND SOCIETY

In the culture of the 1st century, exchanging gifts was an important way of establishing and continuing particular social relations. A person's refusal of a gift could be interpreted as a refusal to accept the giver as an equal, or as a declaration that no social relation was desired. In other words, Paul's refusal was open to serious misinterpretation (2 Cor. 11:7).

weak for that! But in whatever anyone is bold—I speak foolishly—I am bold also.

Suffering for Christ

22Are they Hebrews? So *am* I. Are they Israelites? So *am* I. Are they the seed of Abraham? So *am* I. 23Are they ministers of Christ?—I speak as a fool—I *am* more: in labors more abundant, in stripes above measure, in prisons more frequently, in deaths often. 24From the Jews five times I received forty *stripes* minus one. 25Three times I was beaten with rods; once I was stoned; three times I was shipwrecked; a night and a day I have been in the deep; 26*in* journeys often, *in* perils of waters, *in* perils of robbers, *in* perils of *my own* countrymen, *in* perils of the Gentiles, *in* perils in the city, *in* perils in the wilderness, *in* perils in the sea, *in* perils among false brethren; 27in weariness and toil, in sleeplessness often, in hunger and thirst, in fastings often, in cold and nakedness— 28besides the other things, what comes upon me daily: my deep concern for all the churches. 29Who is weak, and I am not weak? Who is made to stumble, and I do not burn *with indignation?*

30If I must boast, I will boast in the things which concern my infirmity. 31The God and Father of our Lord Jesus Christ, who is blessed forever, knows that I am not lying. 32In Damascus the governor, under Aretas the king, was guarding the city of the Damascenes with a garrison, desiring to arrest me; 33but I was let down in a basket through a window in the wall, and escaped from his hands.

The Vision of Paradise

12 1It is doubtless[a] not profitable for me to boast. I will come to visions and revelations of the Lord: 2I know a man in Christ who fourteen years ago—whether in the body I do not know, or whether out of the body I do not know, God knows—

such a one was caught up to the third heaven. 3And I know such a man—whether in the body or out of the body I do not know, God knows— 4how he was caught up into Paradise and heard inexpressible words, which it is not lawful for a man to utter. 5Of such a one I will boast; yet of myself I will not boast, except in my infirmities. 6For though I might desire to boast, I will not be a fool; for I will speak the truth. But I refrain, lest anyone should think of me above what he sees me *to be* or hears from me.

The Thorn in the Flesh

7And lest I should be exalted above measure by the abundance of the revelations, a thorn in the flesh was given to me, a messenger of Satan to buffet me, lest I be exalted above measure. 8Concerning this thing I pleaded with the Lord three times that it might depart from me. 9And He said to me, "My grace is sufficient for you, for My strength is made perfect in weakness." Therefore most gladly I will rather boast in my infirmities, that the power of Christ may rest upon me. 10Therefore I take pleasure in infirmities, in reproaches, in needs, in persecutions, in distresses, for Christ's sake. For when I am weak, then I am strong.

Signs of an Apostle

11I have become a fool in boasting;[a] you have compelled me. For I ought to have been commended by you; for in nothing was I behind the most eminent apostles, though I am nothing. 12Truly the signs of an apostle were accomplished among you with all perseverance, in signs and wonders and mighty deeds. 13For what is it in which you were inferior to other churches, except that I myself was not burdensome to you? Forgive me this wrong!

Love for the Church

14Now *for* the third time I am ready to come to you. And I will not be burdensome to you; for I do not seek yours, but you. For

---

12:1 [a]NU-Text reads *necessary, though not profitable, to boast.*   12:11 [a]NU-Text omits *in boasting.*

HOW IMMORAL WAS CORINTH? (2 Cor. 12:21)

Corinth was a large Greek city on the northeast coast of the Peloponnesus, the peninsula that forms the south part of Greece. Paul wrote at least two letters (1 and 2 Corinthians) to the Christians there. He was aware of the undesirable behavior of some in the church, behavior which he names as "uncleanness, fornication, and lewdness" (2 Cor. 12:21). Such behavior might be expected in a city that had been characterized as sexually immoral.

Actually, history had witnessed two Corinths. The "Greek Corinth" was well known from classical antiquity as a major power in the Greek world. The Romans destroyed that city in 146 B.C., and not until about a century later did they rebuild "Roman Corinth" in 44 B.C. Within a half century, Corinth had regained its economic preeminence in the Aegean world, as well as its leadership of the Isthmian Games. The new Roman Corinth, like the old Greek city, was a prosperous commercial center.

This prosperity resulted in jealousy of a rival Greek city. Athens could look back on its past as a glorious age. But it could not match the commercial and financial success of Corinth. Jealousy may explain why it was often Athenians who made slanderous remarks concerning Corinth's character, identifying Greek Corinth with fornication. Aristophanes was an Athenian writer of comedy, producing plays between 425 and 388 B.C. He used the phrase "to Corinthianize" or "to live like a Corinthian" as an expression of immoral conduct. Plato (427–347 B.C.), the great philosopher of Athens, used the phrase "a Corinthian girl" to refer to a prostitute.

Roman Corinth also was associated with immoral behavior. The novelist Apuleius, writing a humorous work called *Metamorphoses* in the 2nd century A.D., tells of sexual misconduct in Corinth. But Apuleius was partly educated in Athens, and it was possibly there that he heard of Corinth's reputation.

Such characterizations could reflect that Corinth really was more immoral than other Greek cities. On the other hand, the immoral reputation of Corinth could have been enhanced by Athenian authors who were antagonistic towards the city. In reality then, Corinth, though immoral, was possibly no more corrupt than any other contemporary Greek trading city.

---

the children ought not to lay up for the parents, but the parents for the children. ¹⁵And I will very gladly spend and be spent for your souls; though the more abundantly I love you, the less I am loved.

¹⁶But be that *as it may,* I did not burden you. Nevertheless, being crafty, I caught you by cunning! ¹⁷Did I take advantage of you by any of those whom I sent to you? ¹⁸I urged Titus, and sent our brother with *him.* Did Titus take advantage of you? Did we not *walk* in the same spirit? Did *we* not *walk* in the same steps?

¹⁹Again, do you think[a] that we excuse ourselves to you? We speak before God in Christ. But *we do* all things, beloved, for your edification. ²⁰For I fear lest, when I come, I shall not find you such as I wish, and *that* I shall be found by you such as you do not wish; lest *there be* contentions, jealousies, outbursts of wrath, selfish ambitions, backbitings, whisperings, conceits,

tumults; ²¹lest, when I come again, my God will humble me among you, and I shall mourn for many who have sinned before and have not repented of the uncleanness, fornication, and lewdness which they have practiced.

Coming with Authority

13 ¹This *will be* the third *time* I am coming to you. *"By the mouth of two or three witnesses every word shall be established."*[a] ²I have told you before, and foretell as if I were present the second time, and now being absent I write[a] to those who have sinned before, and to all the rest, that if I come again I will not spare— ³since you seek a proof of Christ speaking in me, who is not weak toward

---

12:19 [a]NU-Text reads *You have been thinking for a long time* . . . .   13:1 [a]Deuteronomy 19:15
13:2 [a]NU-Text omits *I write.*

you, but mighty in you. [4]For though He was crucified in weakness, yet He lives by the power of God. For we also are weak in Him, but we shall live with Him by the power of God toward you.

[5]Examine yourselves *as to* whether you are in the faith. Test yourselves. Do you not know yourselves, that Jesus Christ is in you?—unless indeed you are disqualified. [6]But I trust that you will know that we are not disqualified.

Paul Prefers Gentleness

[7]Now I[a] pray to God that you do no evil, not that we should appear approved, but that you should do what is honorable, though we may seem disqualified. [8]For we can do nothing against the truth, but for the truth. [9]For we are glad when we are weak and you are strong. And this also we pray, that you may be made complete. [10]Therefore I write these things being absent, lest being present I should use sharpness, according to the authority which the Lord has given me for edification and not for destruction.

Greetings and Benediction

[11]Finally, brethren, farewell. Become complete. Be of good comfort, be of one mind, live in peace; and the God of love and peace will be with you.

[12]Greet one another with a holy kiss. [13]All the saints greet you.

[14]The grace of the Lord Jesus Christ, and the love of God, and the communion of the Holy Spirit *be* with you all. Amen.

13:7 [a]NU-Text reads *we.*

Paul's Trip Through Macedonia

After leaving Ephesus, Paul sailed across to Macedonia, possibly in the winter of A.D. 55–56, and later went to Greece. Most of the 3-month stay in Greece (Acts 20:3) was probably spent in Corinth with Gaius, the city's treasurer. From Gaius's large house, Paul wrote the letter to the Romans (Rom. 16:23). This was Paul's third and final visit to Corinth, after which he returned to Macedonia and sailed from Philippi to Troas en route to Jerusalem.

■ Acts 20:2, 3a

Acts
Journey to Greece

20 :2 Now when he had gone over that region and encouraged them with many words, he came to Greece [3]and stayed three months.

The Letter to the Romans

From the earliest time, no one has questioned that the author of this epistle was Paul. Paul probably wrote Romans from Corinth. Gaius, who was Paul's host at the time of writing (Rom. 16:23), had been one of the prominent converts of his ministry in Corinth (1 Cor. 1:14). Phoebe, who delivered the epistle, was a member of the church in Cenchrea, a harbor town near Corinth (16:1, 2).

The letter is to be dated toward the latter part of Paul's missionary work when he was engaged in the collection of a fund for the church in Jerusalem. When Paul wrote to the Corinthians while traveling from Ephesus to Corinth, the collection was still incomplete (2 Cor. 8:1–7). At the time he wrote to the Romans, this collection seems to have been completed (15:26–28). Therefore, it is likely that Paul wrote the epistle to the Romans from Corinth when he stayed there for 3 months in A.D. 56 at the end of his third missionary journey, before he traveled to Jerusalem (15:25; Acts 20:2, 3).

■ Romans 1:1—15:13

Romans
Greeting

1 :1 Paul, a bondservant of Jesus Christ, called *to be* an apostle, separated to the gospel of God [2]which He promised before through His prophets in the Holy Scriptures, [3]concerning His Son Jesus Christ our Lord, who was born of the seed of David according to the flesh, [4]*and* declared *to be* the Son of God with power according to the Spirit of holiness, by the resurrection from the dead. [5]Through Him we have received grace and apostleship for obedience to the faith among all nations for His name, [6]among whom you also are the called of Jesus Christ;

[7]To all who are in Rome, beloved of God, called *to be* saints:

Grace to you and peace from God our Father and the Lord Jesus Christ.

VILE PASSIONS AND UNNATURAL LUSTS (Rom. 1:27)

Greek culture rarely frowned upon, and indeed frequently promoted, male homosexual intercourse. Many well-to-do males lusted after boys and had sex with them. Because most males did not marry much before age 30, younger men had three primary opportunities for sex: with slaves, with prostitutes (respectable high-class ones or other people's slaves), or with each other. Close male bonds in many parts of Greek society made sex with other males a frequent option.

By the 1st century, many upper-class Roman males had adopted Greek values toward homosexual behavior, exhibiting such conduct at fashionable parties. At the same time, Roman society as a whole was far less disposed to such practices than Greek society had been (especially that of Athens). Some Roman philosophers, like Seneca, spoke against homosexual practice. Some philosophers regarded sex with members of a person's own gender as "against nature."

Jewish society opposed homosexual behavior even more. Literature from early Jewish sources gives indication of Jewish adulterers, Jewish fornicators, and Jewish males committing sexual sins, but homosexual behavior is treated in Jewish writings as a distinctively *Gentile* sin. Jewish writers also viewed homosexual behavior as "against nature," and as a sin which warranted God's judgment.

As Paul discussed how God judges Jews and Gentiles, he made a point that Jewish Christian readers who looked down on Gentiles would quickly grasp. First he addressed sins that his readers would agree are sinful as a prelude to mentioning other sins that they themselves possibly did not condemn. If they agreed that homosexual practices were "vile passions" (Rom. 1:26, 27), how could they approve of other "such things" (Rom. 1:29–32)? Thus he prepared his readers for the realization that "*all* have sinned" (Rom. 3:23).

Desire to Visit Rome

⁸First, I thank my God through Jesus Christ for you all, that your faith is spoken of throughout the whole world. ⁹For God is my witness, whom I serve with my spirit in the gospel of His Son, that without ceasing I make mention of you always in my prayers, ¹⁰making request if, by some means, now at last I may find a way in the will of God to come to you. ¹¹For I long to see you, that I may impart to you some spiritual gift, so that you may be established— ¹²that is, that I may be encouraged together with you by the mutual faith both of you and me.

¹³Now I do not want you to be unaware, brethren, that I often planned to come to you (but was hindered until now), that I might have some fruit among you also, just as among the other Gentiles. ¹⁴I am a debtor both to Greeks and to barbarians, both to wise and to unwise. ¹⁵So, as much as is in me, *I am* ready to preach the gospel to you who are in Rome also.

The Just Live by Faith

¹⁶For I am not ashamed of the gospel of Christ,^a for it is the power of God to salva-

tion for everyone who believes, for the Jew first and also for the Greek. ¹⁷For in it the righteousness of God is revealed from faith to faith; as it is written, *"The just shall live by faith."* ^a

God's Wrath on Unrighteousness

¹⁸For the wrath of God is revealed from heaven against all ungodliness and unrighteousness of men, who suppress the truth in unrighteousness, ¹⁹because what may be known of God is manifest in them, for God has shown *it* to them. ²⁰For since the creation of the world His invisible *attributes* are clearly seen, being understood by the things that are made, *even* His eternal power and Godhead, so that they are without excuse, ²¹because, although they knew God, they did not glorify *Him* as God, nor were thankful, but became futile in their thoughts, and their foolish hearts were darkened. ²²Professing to be wise, they became fools, ²³and changed the glory of the incorruptible God into an image

1:16 ^aNU-Text omits *of Christ*.   1:17 ^aHabakkuk 2:4

made like corruptible man—and birds and four-footed animals and creeping things.

24Therefore God also gave them up to uncleanness, in the lusts of their hearts, to dishonor their bodies among themselves, 25who exchanged the truth of God for the lie, and worshiped and served the creature rather than the Creator, who is blessed forever. Amen.

26For this reason God gave them up to vile passions. For even their women exchanged the natural use for what is against nature. 27Likewise also the men, leaving the natural use of the woman, burned in their lust for one another, men with men committing what is shameful, and receiving in themselves the penalty of their error which was due.

28And even as they did not like to retain God in *their* knowledge, God gave them over to a debased mind, to do those things which are not fitting; 29being filled with all unrighteousness, sexual immorality,a wickedness, covetousness, maliciousness; full of envy, murder, strife, deceit, evil-mindedness; *they are* whisperers, 30backbiters, haters of God, violent, proud, boasters, inventors of evil things, disobedient to parents, 31undiscerning, untrustworthy, unloving, unforgiving,a unmerciful; 32who, knowing the righteous judgment of God, that those who practice such things are deserving of death, not only do the same but also approve of those who practice them.

God's Righteous Judgment

2 1Therefore you are inexcusable, O man, whoever you are who judge, for in whatever you judge another you condemn yourself; for you who judge practice the same things. 2But we know that the judgment of God is according to truth against those who practice such things. 3And do you think this, O man, you who judge those practicing such things, and doing the same, that you will escape the judgment of God? 4Or do you despise the riches of His goodness, forbearance, and longsuffering, not knowing that the goodness of God leads you to repentance? 5But in accordance with your hardness and your impenitent heart you are treasuring up for yourself wrath in the day of wrath and revelation of the righteous judgment of God, 6who *"will render to each one according to his deeds"*:a 7eternal life to those who by patient continuance in doing good seek for glory, honor, and immortality; 8but to those who are self-seeking and do not obey the truth, but obey unrighteousness—indignation and wrath, 9tribulation and anguish, on every soul of man who does evil, of the Jew first and also of the Greek; 10but glory, honor, and peace to everyone who works what is good, to the Jew first and also to the Greek. 11For there is no partiality with God.

12For as many as have sinned without law will also perish without law, and as many as have sinned in the law will be judged by the law 13(for not the hearers of the law *are* just in the sight of God, but the doers of the law will be justified; 14for when Gentiles, who do not have the law, by nature do the things in the law, these, although not having the law, are a law to themselves, 15who show the work of the law written in their hearts, their conscience also bearing witness, and between themselves *their* thoughts accusing or else excusing *them*) 16in the day when God will judge the secrets of men by Jesus Christ, according to my gospel.

The Jews Guilty as the Gentiles

17Indeeda you are called a Jew, and rest on the law, and make your boast in God, 18and know *His* will, and approve the things that are excellent, being instructed out of the law, 19and are confident that you yourself are a guide to the blind, a light to those who are in darkness, 20an instructor

---

1:29 aNU-Text omits *sexual immorality.*
1:31 aNU-Text omits *unforgiving.*   2:6 aPsalm
62:12; Proverbs 24:12   2:17 aNU-Text reads
But if.

ARCHITECTURE AND BUILDING

Temples were public buildings used not only for religion but also as treasuries. Thus the Parthenon in Athens safeguarded the gold and silver of the Athenians, although in one emergency it was coined and used to finance a war. To call people temple robbers (Rom. 2:22) was to describe them as openly disregarding universal standards of religion and morality.

of the foolish, a teacher of babes, having the form of knowledge and truth in the law. ²¹You, therefore, who teach another, do you not teach yourself? You who preach that a man should not steal, do you steal? ²²You who say, "Do not commit adultery," do you commit adultery? You who abhor idols, do you rob temples? ²³You who make your boast in the law, do you dishonor God through breaking the law? ²⁴For *"the name of God is blasphemed among the Gentiles because of you,"* ᵃ as it is written.

Circumcision of No Avail

²⁵For circumcision is indeed profitable if you keep the law; but if you are a breaker of the law, your circumcision has become uncircumcision. ²⁶Therefore, if an uncircumcised man keeps the righteous requirements of the law, will not his uncircumcision be counted as circumcision? ²⁷And will not the physically uncircumcised, if he fulfills the law, judge you who, *even* with *your* written *code* and circumcision, *are* a transgressor of the law? ²⁸For he is not a Jew who *is one* outwardly, nor *is* circumcision that which *is* outward in the flesh; ²⁹but *he is* a Jew who *is one* inwardly; and circumcision *is that* of the heart, in the Spirit, not in the letter; whose praise *is* not from men but from God.

God's Judgment Defended

3 ¹What advantage then has the Jew, or what *is* the profit of circumcision? ²Much in every way! Chiefly because to them were committed the oracles of God. ³For what if some did not believe? Will their unbelief make the faithfulness of God without effect? ⁴Certainly not! Indeed, let God be true but every man a liar. As it is written:

"That You may be justified in Your words,
And may overcome when You are judged." ᵃ

⁵But if our unrighteousness demonstrates the righteousness of God, what shall we say? *Is* God unjust who inflicts wrath? (I speak as a man.) ⁶Certainly not! For then how will God judge the world?

⁷For if the truth of God has increased through my lie to His glory, why am I also still judged as a sinner? ⁸And *why* not *say,* "Let us do evil that good may come"?—as we are slanderously reported and as some affirm that we say. Their condemnation is just.

All Have Sinned

⁹What then? Are we better *than they?* Not at all. For we have previously charged both Jews and Greeks that they are all under sin.

¹⁰As it is written:

"There is none righteous, no, not one;
11   There is none who understands;
There is none who seeks after God.
12   They have all turned aside;
They have together become unprofitable;
There is none who does good, no, not one." ᵃ
13   "Their throat is an open tomb;
With their tongues they have practiced deceit"; ᵃ
"The poison of asps is under their lips"; ᵇ
14   "Whose mouth is full of cursing and bitterness." ᵃ
15   "Their feet are swift to shed blood;
16   Destruction and misery are in their ways;
17   And the way of peace they have not known." ᵃ
18   "There is no fear of God before their eyes." ᵃ

¹⁹Now we know that whatever the law says, it says to those who are under the law, that every mouth may be stopped, and all the world may become guilty before

---

TIME CAPSULE *A.D. 57*

57 *Agabus warns Paul not to go to Jerusalem (Acts 21:10)*

57 *Paul, Luke, and disciples from Caesarea proceed to Jerusalem*

57 *Paul visits the temple and is arrested there (Acts 21:30)*

57 *Paul appears before Felix (Acts 24)*

57–59 *Paul imprisoned in Caesarea*

2:24 ᵃIsaiah 52:5; Ezekiel 36:22   3:4 ᵃPsalm 51:4   3:12 ᵃPsalms 14:1–3; 53:1–3; Ecclesiastes 7:20   3:13 ᵃPsalm 5:9 ᵇPsalm 140:3   3:14 ᵃPsalm 10:7   3:17 ᵃIsaiah 59:7, 8   3:18 ᵃPsalm 36:1

God. 20Therefore by the deeds of the law no flesh will be justified in His sight, for by the law *is* the knowledge of sin.

God's Righteousness Through Faith

21But now the righteousness of God apart from the law is revealed, being witnessed by the Law and the Prophets, 22even the righteousness of God, through faith in Jesus Christ, to all and on alla who believe. For there is no difference; 23for all have sinned and fall short of the glory of God, 24being justified freely by His grace through the redemption that is in Christ Jesus, 25whom God set forth *as* a propitiation by His blood, through faith, to demonstrate His righteousness, because in His forbearance God had passed over the sins that were previously committed, 26to demonstrate at the present time His righteousness, that He might be just and the justifier of the one who has faith in Jesus.

Boasting Excluded

27Where *is* boasting then? It is excluded. By what law? Of works? No, but by the law of faith. 28Therefore we conclude that a man is justified by faith apart from the deeds of the law. 29Or *is* He the God of the Jews only? *Is He* not also the God of the Gentiles? Yes, of the Gentiles also, 30since *there is* one God who will justify the circumcised by faith and the uncircumcised through faith. 31Do we then make void the law through faith? Certainly not! On the contrary, we establish the law.

Abraham Justified by Faith

4 1What then shall we say that Abraham our father has found according to the flesh?a 2For if Abraham was justified by works, he has *something* to boast about, but not before God. 3For what does the Scripture say? *"Abraham believed God, and it was accounted to him for righteousness."*a 4Now to him who works, the wages are not counted as grace but as debt.

David Celebrates the Same Truth

5But to him who does not work but believes on Him who justifies the ungodly, his faith is accounted for righteousness, 6just

as David also describes the blessedness of the man to whom God imputes righteousness apart from works:

7   *"Blessed are those whose lawless deeds*
        are forgiven,
     And whose sins are covered;
8   *Blessed is the man to whom the* LORD
        *shall not impute sin."*a

Abraham Justified Before Circumcision

9*Does* this blessedness then *come* upon the circumcised *only,* or upon the uncircumcised also? For we say that faith was accounted to Abraham for righteousness. 10How then was it accounted? While he was circumcised, or uncircumcised? Not while circumcised, but while uncircumcised. 11And he received the sign of circumcision, a seal of the righteousness of the faith which *he had while still* uncircumcised, that he might be the father of all those who believe, though they are uncircumcised, that righteousness might be imputed to them also, 12and the father of circumcision to those who not only *are* of the circumcision, but who also walk in the steps of the faith which our father Abraham *had while still* uncircumcised.

The Promise Granted Through Faith

13For the promise that he would be the heir of the world *was* not to Abraham or to his seed through the law, but through the righteousness of faith. 14For if those who are of the law *are* heirs, faith is made void and the promise made of no effect, 15because the law brings about wrath; for where there is no law *there is* no transgression.

16Therefore *it is* of faith that *it might be* according to grace, so that the promise might be sure to all the seed, not only to those who are of the law, but also to those who are of the faith of Abraham, who is the father of us all 17(as it is written, *"I have made you a father of many nations"*a) in the presence of Him whom he believed—God, who gives life to the dead and calls those things which do not exist as though they did; 18who, contrary to hope, in hope believed, so that he became the father of many nations, according to what was spoken, *"So shall your descendants be."*a 19And not being weak in faith, he did not consider his own body, already dead (since he was about a hundred years old), and the deadness of Sarah's womb. 20He did not

3:22 aNU-Text omits *and on all.*   4:1 aOr *Abraham our (fore)father according to the flesh has found?*   4:3 aGenesis 15:6   4:8 aPsalm 32:1, 2   4:17 aGenesis 17:5   4:18 aGenesis 15:5

waver at the promise of God through unbelief, but was strengthened in faith, giving glory to God, [21]and being fully convinced that what He had promised He was also able to perform. [22]And therefore *"it was accounted to him for righteousness."*[a]

[23]Now it was not written for his sake alone that it was imputed to him, [24]but also for us. It shall be imputed to us who believe in Him who raised up Jesus our Lord from the dead, [25]who was delivered up because of our offenses, and was raised because of our justification.

Faith Triumphs in Trouble

5 [1]Therefore, having been justified by faith, we have[a] peace with God through our Lord Jesus Christ, [2]through whom also we have access by faith into this grace in which we stand, and rejoice in hope of the glory of God. [3]And not only *that,* but we also glory in tribulations, knowing that tribulation produces perseverance; [4]and perseverance, character; and character, hope. [5]Now hope does not disappoint, because the love of God has been poured out in our hearts by the Holy Spirit who was given to us.

Christ in Our Place

[6]For when we were still without strength, in due time Christ died for the ungodly. [7]For scarcely for a righteous man will one die; yet perhaps for a good man someone would even dare to die. [8]But God demonstrates His own love toward us, in that while we were still sinners, Christ died for us. [9]Much more then, having now been justified by His blood, we shall be saved from wrath through Him. [10]For if when we were enemies we were reconciled to God through the death of His Son, much more, having been reconciled, we shall be saved by His life. [11]And not only *that,* but we also rejoice in God through our Lord Jesus Christ, through whom we have now received the reconciliation.

Death in Adam, Life in Christ

[12]Therefore, just as through one man sin entered the world, and death through sin, and thus death spread to all men, because all sinned— [13](For until the law sin was in the world, but sin is not imputed when there is no law. [14]Nevertheless death reigned from Adam to Moses, even over those who had not sinned according to the likeness of the transgression of Adam, who

is a type of Him who was to come. [15]But the free gift *is* not like the offense. For if by the one man's offense many died, much more the grace of God and the gift by the grace of the one Man, Jesus Christ, abounded to many. [16]And the gift *is* not like *that which came* through the one who sinned. For the judgment *which came* from one *offense resulted* in condemnation, but the free gift *which came* from many offenses *resulted* in justification. [17]For if by the one man's offense death reigned through the one, much more those who receive abundance of grace and of the gift of righteousness will reign in life through the One, Jesus Christ.)

[18]Therefore, as through one man's offense *judgment* came to all men, resulting in condemnation, even so through one Man's righteous act *the free gift came* to all men, resulting in justification of life. [19]For as by one man's disobedience many were made sinners, so also by one Man's obedience many will be made righteous.

[20]Moreover the law entered that the offense might abound. But where sin abounded, grace abounded much more, [21]so that as sin reigned in death, even so grace might reign through righteousness to eternal life through Jesus Christ our Lord.

Dead to Sin, Alive to God

6 [1]What shall we say then? Shall we continue in sin that grace may abound? [2]Certainly not! How shall we who died to sin live any longer in it? [3]Or do you not know that as many of us as were baptized into Christ Jesus were baptized into His death? [4]Therefore we were buried with Him through baptism into death, that just as Christ was raised from the dead by the glory of the Father, even so we also should walk in newness of life.

[5]For if we have been united together in the likeness of His death, certainly we also shall be *in the likeness* of *His* resurrection, [6]knowing this, that our old man was crucified with *Him,* that the body of sin might be done away with, that we should no longer be slaves of sin. [7]For he who has died has been freed from sin. [8]Now if we died with Christ, we believe that we shall also live with Him, [9]knowing that Christ, having been raised from the dead, dies no more. Death no longer has dominion over

---

4:22 [a]Genesis 15:6   5:1 [a]Another ancient reading is, *let us have peace.*

Him. [10]For *the death* that He died, He died to sin once for all; but *the life* that He lives, He lives to God. [11]Likewise you also, reckon yourselves to be dead indeed to sin, but alive to God in Christ Jesus our Lord.

[12]Therefore do not let sin reign in your mortal body, that you should obey it in its lusts. [13]And do not present your members *as* instruments of unrighteousness to sin, but present yourselves to God as being alive from the dead, and your members *as* instruments of righteousness to God. [14]For sin shall not have dominion over you, for you are not under law but under grace.

From Slaves of Sin to Slaves of God

[15]What then? Shall we sin because we are not under law but under grace? Certainly not! [16]Do you not know that to whom you present yourselves slaves to obey, you are that one's slaves whom you obey, whether of sin *leading* to death, or of obedience *leading* to righteousness? [17]But God be thanked that *though* you were slaves of sin, yet you obeyed from the heart that form of doctrine to which you were delivered. [18]And having been set free from sin, you became slaves of righteousness. [19]I speak in human *terms* because of the weakness of your flesh. For just as you presented your members *as* slaves of uncleanness, and of lawlessness *leading* to *more* lawlessness, so now present your members *as* slaves *of* righteousness for holiness.

[20]For when you were slaves of sin, you were free in regard to righteousness. [21]What fruit did you have then in the things of which you are now ashamed? For the end of those things *is* death. [22]But now having been set free from sin, and having become slaves of God, you have your fruit to holiness, and the end, everlasting life. [23]For the wages of sin *is* death, but the gift of God *is* eternal life in Christ Jesus our Lord.

Freed from the Law

7 [1]Or do you not know, brethren (for I speak to those who know the law), that the law has dominion over a man as long as he lives? [2]For the woman who has a husband is bound by the law to *her* husband as long as he lives. But if the husband dies, she is released from the law of *her* husband. [3]So then if, while *her* husband lives, she marries another man, she will be called an adulteress; but if her husband dies, she is free from that law, so that she is no adulteress, though she has married another man. [4]Therefore, my brethren, you also have become dead to the law through the body of Christ, that you may be married to another—to Him who was raised from the dead, that we should bear fruit to God. [5]For when we were in the flesh, the sinful passions which were aroused by the law were at work in our members to bear fruit to death. [6]But now we have been delivered from the law, having died to what we were held by, so that we should serve in the newness of the Spirit and not *in* the oldness of the letter.

Sin's Advantage in the Law

[7]What shall we say then? *Is* the law sin? Certainly not! On the contrary, I would not have known sin except through the law. For I would not have known covetousness unless the law had said, *"You shall not covet."*[a] [8]But sin, taking opportunity by the commandment, produced in me all *manner of* evil desire. For apart from the law sin *was* dead. [9]I was alive once without the law, but when the commandment came, sin revived and I died. [10]And the commandment, which *was* to *bring* life, I found to *bring* death. [11]For sin, taking occasion by the commandment, deceived me, and by it killed *me.* [12]Therefore the law *is* holy, and the commandment holy and just and good.

Law Cannot Save from Sin

[13]Has then what is good become death to me? Certainly not! But sin, that it might appear sin, was producing death in me through what is good, so that sin through the commandment might become exceedingly sinful. [14]For we know that the law is spiritual, but I am carnal, sold under sin. [15]For what I am doing, I do not understand. For what I will to do, that I do not practice; but what I hate, that I do. [16]If, then, I do what I will not to do, I agree with the law that *it is* good. [17]But now, *it is* no longer I who do it, but sin that dwells in me. [18]For I know that in me (that is, in my flesh) nothing good dwells; for to will is present with me, but *how* to perform what is good I do not find. [19]For the good that I will *to do,* I do not do; but the evil I will not *to do,* that I practice. [20]Now if I do what I will not *to do,* it is no longer I who do it, but sin that dwells in me.

7:7 [a]Exodus 20:17; Deuteronomy 5:21

WARRING WITH THE EVIL IMPULSE WITHIN (Rom. 7:21–23)

When Paul wrote about living life under the law of God (Rom. 7), perhaps he was describing, from his new Christian perspective, his own genuine experience under the law. The Church Fathers were divided (as are modern readers) on whether Paul wrote of his present experience or of his preconversion experience. Whichever, he agonized over the battle to do God's will, saying, "Evil is present with me" (Rom. 7:21).

Jewish people commonly believed that a child was born with a *yetzer hara,* an evil impulse. When a Jewish boy entered adulthood, he would accept responsibility for the commandments (a custom which later evolved into bar mitzvah, the religious rite of passage). According to Jewish belief, once a boy accepted the commandments, he found in God's law strength to overcome his evil impulse. After this, two impulses—good and evil—would battle within him, in a struggle similar to Paul's description.

Philosophers also discussed a struggle, one between human reason and human passion. In the philosophers' view, a person overcame passions by depending on reason. Jewish teachers felt that one overcame the evil impulse by learning Torah, the Law. For Paul, however, the battle appeared futile, because mere knowledge without transformation of character could not bring victory. Any solution to the struggle depending on human effort, whether on a person's reason or on knowledge of Torah, was inadequate.

Victory was possible, Paul realized, through God's Spirit (8:2–4). Interestingly, one strand of Jewish tradition emphasized that in the end time, when the Messiah came, God would publicly slay the evil impulse. For Paul, the Messiah's work of delivering from sin was an accomplished act of history (Rom. 6:5, 11), and the gift of the Spirit was the foretaste of future glory (8:23).

---

²¹I find then a law, that evil is present with me, the one who wills to do good. ²²For I delight in the law of God according to the inward man. ²³But I see another law in my members, warring against the law of my mind, and bringing me into captivity to the law of sin which is in my members. ²⁴O wretched man that I am! Who will deliver me from this body of death? ²⁵I thank God—through Jesus Christ our Lord!

So then, with the mind I myself serve the law of God, but with the flesh the law of sin.

Free from Indwelling Sin

8 ¹*There is* therefore now no condemnation to those who are in Christ Jesus,ᵃ who do not walk according to the flesh, but according to the Spirit. ²For the law of the Spirit of life in Christ Jesus has made me free from the law of sin and death. ³For what the law could not do in that it was weak through the flesh, God *did* by sending His own Son in the likeness of sinful flesh, on account of sin: He condemned sin in the flesh, ⁴that the righteous requirement of the law might be fulfilled in us who do not walk according to the flesh but according to the Spirit. ⁵For those who live according to the flesh set their minds on the things of the flesh, but those *who live* according to the Spirit, the things of the Spirit. ⁶For to be carnally minded *is* death, but to be spiritually minded *is* life and peace. ⁷Because the carnal mind *is* enmity against God; for it is not subject to the law of God, nor indeed can be. ⁸So then, those who are in the flesh cannot please God.

⁹But you are not in the flesh but in the Spirit, if indeed the Spirit of God dwells in you. Now if anyone does not have the Spirit of Christ, he is not His. ¹⁰And if Christ *is* in you, the body *is* dead because of sin, but the Spirit *is* life because of righteousness. ¹¹But if the Spirit of Him who raised Jesus from the dead dwells in you, He who raised Christ from the dead will also give life to your mortal bodies through His Spirit who dwells in you.

Sonship Through the Spirit

¹²Therefore, brethren, we are debtors—not to the flesh, to live according to the flesh. ¹³For if you live according to the

---

8:1 ᵃNU-Text omits the rest of this verse.

flesh you will die; but if by the Spirit you put to death the deeds of the body, you will live. [14]For as many as are led by the Spirit of God, these are sons of God. [15]For you did not receive the spirit of bondage again to fear, but you received the Spirit of adoption by whom we cry out, "Abba, Father." [16]The Spirit Himself bears witness with our spirit that we are children of God, [17]and if children, then heirs—heirs of God and joint heirs with Christ, if indeed we suffer with *Him,* that we may also be glorified together.

From Suffering to Glory

[18]For I consider that the sufferings of this present time are not worthy *to be compared* with the glory which shall be revealed in us. [19]For the earnest expectation of the creation eagerly waits for the revealing of the sons of God. [20]For the creation was subjected to futility, not willingly, but because of Him who subjected *it* in hope; [21]because the creation itself also will be delivered from the bondage of corruption into the glorious liberty of the children of God. [22]For we know that the whole creation groans and labors with birth pangs together until now. [23]Not only *that,* but we also who have the firstfruits of the Spirit, even we ourselves groan within ourselves, eagerly waiting for the adoption, the redemption of our body. [24]For we were saved in this hope, but hope that is seen is not hope; for why does one still hope for what he sees? [25]But if we hope for what we do not see, we eagerly wait for *it* with perseverance.

[26]Likewise the Spirit also helps in our weaknesses. For we do not know what we should pray for as we ought, but the Spirit Himself makes intercession for us[a] with groanings which cannot be uttered. [27]Now He who searches the hearts knows what the mind of the Spirit *is,* because He makes intercession for the saints according to *the will of* God.

[28]And we know that all things work together for good to those who love God, to those who are the called according to *His* purpose. [29]For whom He foreknew, He also predestined *to be* conformed to the image of His Son, that He might be the firstborn among many brethren. [30]Moreover whom He predestined, these He also called; whom He called, these He also justified; and whom He justified, these He also glorified.

God's Everlasting Love

[31]What then shall we say to these things? If God *is* for us, who *can be* against us? [32]He who did not spare His own Son, but delivered Him up for us all, how shall He not with Him also freely give us all things? [33]Who shall bring a charge against God's elect? *It is* God who justifies. [34]Who *is* he who condemns? *It is* Christ who died, and furthermore is also risen, who is even at the right hand of God, who also makes intercession for us. [35]Who shall separate us from the love of Christ? *Shall* tribulation, or distress, or persecution, or famine, or nakedness, or peril, or sword? [36]As it is written:

*"For Your sake we are killed all day
    long;
We are accounted as sheep for the
    slaughter."* [a]

[37]Yet in all these things we are more than conquerors through Him who loved us. [38]For I am persuaded that neither death nor life, nor angels nor principalities nor powers, nor things present nor things to come, [39]nor height nor depth, nor any other created thing, shall be able to separate us from the love of God which is in Christ Jesus our Lord.

Israel's Rejection of Christ

9 [1]I tell the truth in Christ, I am not lying, my conscience also bearing me witness in the Holy Spirit, [2]that I have great sorrow and continual grief in my heart. [3]For I could wish that I myself were accursed from Christ for my brethren, my countrymen[a] according to the flesh, [4]who are Israelites, to whom *pertain* the adoption, the glory, the covenants, the giving of the law, the service *of God,* and the promises; [5]of whom *are* the fathers and from whom, according to the flesh, Christ *came,* who is over all, *the* eternally blessed God. Amen.

Israel's Rejection and God's Purpose

[6]But it is not that the word of God has taken no effect. For they *are* not all Israel who *are* of Israel, [7]nor *are they* all children because they are the seed of Abraham; but, *"In Isaac your seed shall be called."* [a] [8]That

---

8:26 [a]NU-Text omits *for us.*   8:36 [a]Psalm
44:22   9:3 [a]Or *relatives*   9:7 [a]Genesis
21:12

is, those who *are* the children of the flesh, these *are* not the children of God; but the children of the promise are counted as the seed. ⁹For this *is* the word of promise: *"At this time I will come and Sarah shall have a son."* ᵃ

¹⁰And not only *this,* but when Rebecca also had conceived by one man, *even* by our father Isaac ¹¹(for *the children* not yet being born, nor having done any good or evil, that the purpose of God according to election might stand, not of works but of Him who calls), ¹²it was said to her, *"The older shall serve the younger."* ᵃ ¹³As it is written, *"Jacob I have loved, but Esau I have hated."* ᵃ

Israel's Rejection and God's Justice

¹⁴What shall we say then? *Is there* unrighteousness with God? Certainly not! ¹⁵For He says to Moses, *"I will have mercy on whomever I will have mercy, and I will have compassion on whomever I will have compassion."* ᵃ ¹⁶So then *it is* not of him who wills, nor of him who runs, but of God who shows mercy. ¹⁷For the Scripture says to the Pharaoh, *"For this very purpose I have raised you up, that I may show My power in you, and that My name may be declared in all the earth."* ᵃ ¹⁸Therefore He has mercy on whom He wills, and whom He wills He hardens.

¹⁹You will say to me then, "Why does He still find fault? For who has resisted His will?" ²⁰But indeed, O man, who are you to reply against God? Will the thing formed say to him who formed *it,* "Why have you made me like this?" ²¹Does not the potter have power over the clay, from the same lump to make one vessel for honor and another for dishonor?

²²*What* if God, wanting to show *His* wrath and to make His power known, endured with much longsuffering the vessels of wrath prepared for destruction, ²³and that He might make known the riches of His glory on the vessels of mercy, which He had prepared beforehand for glory, ²⁴*even*

us whom He called, not of the Jews only, but also of the Gentiles? ²⁵As He says also in Hosea:

*"I will call them My people, who were not My people,
And her beloved, who was not beloved."* ᵃ
26 *"And it shall come to pass in the place where it was said to them,
'You are not My people,'
There they shall be called sons of the living God."* ᵃ

²⁷Isaiah also cries out concerning Israel:ᵃ

*"Though the number of the children of Israel be as the sand of the sea,
The remnant will be saved.
28 For He will finish the work and cut it short in righteousness,
Because the LORD will make a short work upon the earth."* ᵃ

²⁹And as Isaiah said before:

*"Unless the LORD of Sabaoth*ᵃ *had left us a seed,
We would have become like Sodom,
And we would have been made like Gomorrah."* ᵇ

Present Condition of Israel

³⁰What shall we say then? That Gentiles, who did not pursue righteousness, have attained to righteousness, even the righteousness of faith; ³¹but Israel, pursuing the law of righteousness, has not attained to the law of righteousness.ᵃ ³²Why?

9:9 ᵃGenesis 18:10, 14　　9:12 ᵃGenesis 25:23　　9:13 ᵃMalachi 1:2, 3　　9:15 ᵃExodus 33:19　　9:17 ᵃExodus 9:16　　9:25 ᵃHosea 2:23　　9:26 ᵃHosea 1:10　　9:27 ᵃIsaiah 10:22, 23　　9:28 ᵃNU-Text reads *For the LORD will finish the work and cut it short upon the earth.* 9:29 ᵃLiterally, in Hebrew, *Hosts* ᵇIsaiah 1:9 9:31 ᵃNU-Text omits *of righteousness.*

SCIENCE AND TECHNOLOGY

Pottery is one of the oldest and most widely known technologies. The raw material is clay, which is abundant and has no economic value until it is formed into a vessel and dried or fired. The same store of clay is easily transformed into whatever shape the potter intends, or that the client may have specified (Rom. 9:21). Some pottery is so cheap it is thrown away after one use.

Because *they did* not *seek it* by faith, but as it were, by the works of the law.[a] For they stumbled at that stumbling stone. 33As it is written:

> "Behold, I lay in Zion a stumbling
>   stone and rock of offense,
> And whoever believes on Him will not
>   be put to shame."[a]

Israel Needs the Gospel

10 1Brethren, my heart's desire and prayer to God for Israel[a] is that they may be saved. 2For I bear them witness that they have a zeal for God, but not according to knowledge. 3For they being ignorant of God's righteousness, and seeking to establish their own righteousness, have not submitted to the righteousness of God. 4For Christ *is* the end of the law for righteousness to everyone who believes.

5For Moses writes about the righteousness which is of the law, *"The man who does those things shall live by them."*[a] 6But the righteousness of faith speaks in this way, *"Do not say in your heart, 'Who will ascend into heaven?'"*[a] (that is, to bring Christ down *from above*) 7or, *"'Who will descend into the abyss?'"*[a] (that is, to bring Christ up from the dead). 8But what does it say? *"The word is near you, in your mouth and in your heart"*[a] (that is, the word of faith which we preach): 9that if you confess with your mouth the Lord Jesus and believe in your heart that God has raised Him from the dead, you will be saved. 10For with the heart one believes unto righteousness, and with the mouth confession is made unto salvation. 11For the Scripture says, *"Whoever believes on Him will not be put to shame."*[a] 12For there is no distinction between Jew and Greek, for the same Lord over all is rich to all who call upon Him. 13For *"whoever calls on the name of the LORD shall be saved."*[a]

Israel Rejects the Gospel

14How then shall they call on Him in whom they have not believed? And how shall they believe in Him of whom they have not heard? And how shall they hear without a preacher? 15And how shall they preach unless they are sent? As it is written:

> "How beautiful are the feet of those
>   who preach the gospel of peace,[a]
> Who bring glad tidings of good
>   things!"[b]

16But they have not all obeyed the gospel. For Isaiah says, *"LORD, who has believed our report?"*[a] 17So then faith *comes* by hearing, and hearing by the word of God.

18But I say, have they not heard? Yes indeed:

> "Their sound has gone out to all the
>   earth,
> And their words to the ends of the
>   world."[a]

19But I say, did Israel not know? First Moses says:

> "I will provoke you to jealousy by those
>   who are not a nation,
> I will move you to anger by a foolish
>   nation."[a]

20But Isaiah is very bold and says:

> "I was found by those who did not seek
>   Me;
> I was made manifest to those who did
>   not ask for Me."[a]

21But to Israel he says:

> "All day long I have stretched out My
>   hands
> To a disobedient and contrary
>   people."[a]

Israel's Rejection Not Total

11 1I say then, has God cast away His people? Certainly not! For I also am an Israelite, of the seed of Abraham, *of* the tribe of Benjamin. 2God has not cast away His people whom He foreknew. Or do you not know what the Scripture says of Elijah, how he pleads with God against Israel, saying, 3*"LORD, they have killed Your*

9:32 ªNU-Text reads *by works.*   9:33 ªIsaiah
8:14; 28:16   10:1 ªNU-Text reads *them.*
10:5 ªLeviticus 18:5   10:6 ªDeuteronomy
30:12   10:7 ªDeuteronomy 30:13
10:8 ªDeuteronomy 30:14   10:11 ªIsaiah
28:16   10:13 ªJoel 2:32   10:15 ªNU-Text
omits *preach the gospel of peace, Who.*   ᵇIsaiah
52:7; Nahum 1:15   10:16 ªIsaiah 53:1
10:18 ªPsalm 19:4   10:19 ªDeuteronomy
32:21   10:20 ªIsaiah 65:1   10:21 ªIsaiah
65:2

prophets and torn down Your altars, and I alone am left, and they seek my life"? [a] [4] But what does the divine response say to him? *"I have reserved for Myself seven thousand men who have not bowed the knee to Baal."* [a] [5] Even so then, at this present time there is a remnant according to the election of grace. [6] And if by grace, then *it is* no longer of works; otherwise grace is no longer grace. [a] But if *it is* of works, it is no longer grace; otherwise work is no longer work.

[7] What then? Israel has not obtained what it seeks; but the elect have obtained it, and the rest were blinded. [8] Just as it is written:

"God has given them a spirit of stupor,
Eyes that they should not see
And ears that they should not hear,
To this very day." [a]

[9] And David says:

"Let their table become a snare and a
*   trap,*
A stumbling block and a recompense
*   to them.*
[10] *Let their eyes be darkened, so that*
*   they do not see,*
And bow down their back always." [a]

Israel's Rejection Not Final

[11] I say then, have they stumbled that they should fall? Certainly not! But through their fall, to provoke them to jealousy, salvation *has come* to the Gentiles. [12] Now if their fall *is* riches for the world, and their failure riches for the Gentiles, how much more their fullness!

[13] For I speak to you Gentiles; inasmuch as I am an apostle to the Gentiles, I magnify my ministry, [14] if by any means I may provoke to jealousy *those who are* my flesh and save some of them. [15] For if their being cast away *is* the reconciling of the world, what *will* their acceptance *be* but life from the dead?

[16] For if the firstfruit *is* holy, the lump *is* also *holy;* and if the root *is* holy, so *are* the branches. [17] And if some of the branches were broken off, and you, being a wild olive tree, were grafted in among them, and with them became a partaker of the root and fatness of the olive tree, [18] do not boast against the branches. But if you do boast, *remember that* you do not support the root, but the root supports you.

[19] You will say then, "Branches were broken off that I might be grafted in." [20] Well *said.* Because of unbelief they were broken off, and you stand by faith. Do not be haughty, but fear. [21] For if God did not spare the natural branches, He may not spare you either. [22] Therefore consider the goodness and severity of God: on those who fell, severity; but toward you, goodness, [a] if you continue in *His* goodness. Otherwise you also will be cut off. [23] And they also, if they do not continue in unbelief, will be grafted in, for God is able to graft them in again. [24] For if you were cut out of the olive tree which is wild by nature, and were grafted contrary to nature into a cultivated olive tree, how much more will these, who *are* natural *branches,* be grafted into their own olive tree?

[25] For I do not desire, brethren, that you should be ignorant of this mystery, lest you should be wise in your own opinion, that blindness in part has happened to Israel until the fullness of the Gentiles has come in. [26] And so all Israel will be saved, [a] as it is written:

"The Deliverer will come out of Zion,
And He will turn away ungodliness
*   from Jacob;*
[27] *For this is My covenant with them,*
When I take away their sins." [a]

[28] Concerning the gospel *they are* enemies for your sake, but concerning the election *they are* beloved for the sake of the fathers. [29] For the gifts and the calling of God *are* irrevocable. [30] For as you were once disobedient to God, yet have now obtained mercy through their disobedience, [31] even so these also have now been disobedient, that through the mercy shown you they also may obtain mercy. [32] For God has committed them all to disobedience, that He might have mercy on all.

[33] Oh, the depth of the riches both of the wisdom and knowledge of God! How unsearchable *are* His judgments and His ways past finding out!

11:3 [a]1 Kings 19:10, 14   11:4 [a]1 Kings
19:18   11:6 [a]NU-Text omits the rest of this
verse.   11:8 [a]Deuteronomy 29:4; Isaiah
29:10   11:10 [a]Psalm 69:22, 23
11:22 [a]NU-Text adds *of God.*   11:26 [a]Or
delivered   11:27 [a]Isaiah 59:20, 21

34 *"For who has known the mind of the*
    LORD?
    Or who has become His counselor?" a
35 *"Or who has first given to Him*
    And it shall be repaid to him?" a

36For of Him and through Him and to
Him *are* all things, to whom *be* glory forever. Amen.

Living Sacrifices to God

12 1I beseech you therefore, brethren,
by the mercies of God, that you present your bodies a living sacrifice, holy,
acceptable to God, *which is* your reasonable service. 2And do not be conformed to
this world, but be transformed by the renewing of your mind, that you may prove
what *is* that good and acceptable and perfect will of God.

Serve God with Spiritual Gifts

3For I say, through the grace given to
me, to everyone who is among you, not to
think *of himself* more highly than he ought
to think, but to think soberly, as God has
dealt to each one a measure of faith. 4For
as we have many members in one body, but
all the members do not have the same
function, 5so we, *being* many, are one body
in Christ, and individually members of one
another. 6Having then gifts differing according to the grace that is given to us, *let
us use them*: if prophecy, *let us prophesy* in
proportion to our faith; 7or ministry, *let us
use it* in *our* ministering; he who teaches,
in teaching; 8he who exhorts, in exhortation; he who gives, with liberality; he who
leads, with diligence; he who shows mercy,
with cheerfulness.

Behave Like a Christian

9*Let* love *be* without hypocrisy. Abhor
what is evil. Cling to what is good. 10*Be*
kindly affectionate to one another with

11:34 aIsaiah 40:13; Jeremiah 23:18
11:35 aJob 41:11   12:19 aDeuteronomy
32:35   12:20 aProverbs 25:21, 22

brotherly love, in honor giving preference
to one another; 11not lagging in diligence,
fervent in spirit, serving the Lord; 12rejoic-
ing in hope, patient in tribulation, continuing steadfastly in prayer; 13distributing to
the needs of the saints, given to hospitality.

14Bless those who persecute you; bless
and do not curse. 15Rejoice with those who
rejoice, and weep with those who weep.
16Be of the same mind toward one another.
Do not set your mind on high things, but
associate with the humble. Do not be wise
in your own opinion.

17Repay no one evil for evil. Have regard for good things in the sight of all men.
18If it is possible, as much as depends on
you, live peaceably with all men. 19Beloved,
do not avenge yourselves, but *rather* give
place to wrath; for it is written, *"Vengeance
is Mine, I will repay,"* a says the Lord.
20Therefore

"If your enemy is hungry, feed him;
If he is thirsty, give him a drink;
For in so doing you will heap coals of
    fire on his head." a

21Do not be overcome by evil, but overcome
evil with good.

Submit to Government

13 1Let every soul be subject to the governing authorities. For there is no
authority except from God, and the authorities that exist are appointed by God.
2Therefore whoever resists the authority
resists the ordinance of God, and those who
resist will bring judgment on themselves.
3For rulers are not a terror to good works,
but to evil. Do you want to be unafraid of
the authority? Do what is good, and you
will have praise from the same. 4For he is
God's minister to you for good. But if you
do evil, be afraid; for he does not bear the
sword in vain; for he is God's minister, an
avenger to *execute* wrath on him who practices evil. 5Therefore *you* must be subject,
not only because of wrath but also for conscience' sake. 6For because of this you also
pay taxes, for they are God's ministers

POLITICS AND GOVERNMENT

The governing authorities in Palestine were the emperor of Rome and those approved or
appointed by him (Rom. 13:1). Augustus was the first emperor of Rome, and he ruled in
peace for more than 40 years. Most of the regions familiar to Paul were ruled by a
Roman provincial governor, or by the family of the Herods. In Jerusalem, the Jewish
governing authorities had a temple police and could collect some taxes.

THE ROMAN EMPIRE RULES PALESTINE

The people of Rome developed the last civilization of the ancient world in the West, and had a significant impact upon Palestine during the New Testament era. During the apostle Paul's ministry, the Romans were the "governing authorities" (Rom. 13:1) to whom he urged Christians to submit.

Date	Event
A.D. 37	Nero is born. Caligula succeeds Tiberius as emperor.
A.D. 40	Caligula orders a statue of himself to be placed in the temple at Jerusalem. Herod Agrippa I persuades him to cancel the order.
A.D. 41	Caligula is assassinated. The new emperor appoints Herod Agrippa I to rule Judea.
A.D. 44	Herod Agrippa I dies (Acts 12). Judea becomes a province again.
A.D. 52–59	Antonius Felix is governor of Judea (Acts 23:24).
A.D. 54	Claudius dies, probably poisoned by his wife, and Nero becomes emperor.
A.D. 59–62	Porcius Festus is governor of Judea (Acts 24:27—25:1).
A.D. 64	The Great Fire burns in the city of Rome (July 19–28). Nero blames it on the Christians and persecutes them.
A.D. 66	The Jews in Palestine rebel against Rome.
A.D. 68	Nero commits suicide.
A.D. 70	Jerusalem is conquered by Titus. Jews are forbidden to live there.

attending continually to this very thing. ⁷Render therefore to all their due: taxes to whom taxes *are due,* customs to whom customs, fear to whom fear, honor to whom honor.

Love Your Neighbor

⁸Owe no one anything except to love one another, for he who loves another has fulfilled the law. ⁹For the commandments, *"You shall not commit adultery," "You shall not murder," "You shall not steal," "You shall not bear false witness,"* ᵃ *"You shall not covet,"* ᵇ and if *there is* any other commandment, are *all* summed up in this saying, namely, *"You shall love your neighbor as yourself."* ᶜ ¹⁰Love does no harm to a neighbor; therefore love *is* the fulfillment of the law.

Put on Christ

¹¹And *do* this, knowing the time, that now *it is* high time to awake out of sleep; for now our salvation *is* nearer than when we *first* believed. ¹²The night is far spent, the day is at hand. Therefore let us cast off the works of darkness, and let us put on the armor of light. ¹³Let us walk properly, as in the day, not in revelry and drunkenness, not in lewdness and lust, not in strife and envy. ¹⁴But put on the Lord Jesus Christ, and make no provision for the flesh, to *fulfill its* lusts.

The Law of Liberty

14 ¹Receive one who is weak in the faith, *but* not to disputes over doubtful things. ²For one believes he may eat all things, but he who is weak eats *only* vegetables. ³Let not him who eats despise him who does not eat, and let not him who does not eat judge him who eats; for God has received him. ⁴Who are you to judge another's servant? To his own master he

---

13:9 ᵃNU-Text omits *"You shall not bear false witness."* ᵇExodus 20:13–15, 17; Deuteronomy 5:17–19, 21 ᶜLeviticus 19:18

CULTURE AND SOCIETY

The Romans obtained many of their slaves through warfare. In addition, some criminals and pirates engaged in the business of capturing people and selling them as slaves. Slaves could be bought in markets without their origin being known, while children of slaves were slaves from birth. Paul did not discuss the abolition of slavery, but did speak to masters and slaves on how to live within that culture's institutions (Rom. 14:4).

stands or falls. Indeed, he will be made to stand, for God is able to make him stand.

5One person esteems *one* day above another; another esteems every day *alike.* Let each be fully convinced in his own mind. 6He who observes the day, observes *it* to the Lord;a and he who does not observe the day, to the Lord he does not observe *it.* He who eats, eats to the Lord, for he gives God thanks; and he who does not eat, to the Lord he does not eat, and gives God thanks. 7For none of us lives to himself, and no one dies to himself. 8For if we live, we live to the Lord; and if we die, we die to the Lord. Therefore, whether we live or die, we are the Lord's. 9For to this end Christ died and rosea and lived again, that He might be Lord of both the dead and the living. 10But why do you judge your brother? Or why do you show contempt for your brother? For we shall all stand before the judgment seat of Christ.a 11For it is written:

> "As I live, says the LORD,
> Every knee shall bow to Me,
> And every tongue shall confess to
> 　God."a

12So then each of us shall give account of himself to God. 13Therefore let us not judge one another anymore, but rather resolve this, not to put a stumbling block or a cause to fall in *our* brother's way.

The Law of Love

14I know and am convinced by the Lord Jesus that *there is* nothing unclean of itself; but to him who considers anything to be unclean, to him *it is* unclean. 15Yet if your brother is grieved because of *your* food, you are no longer walking in love. Do not destroy with your food the one for whom Christ died. 16Therefore do not let your good be spoken of as evil; 17for the kingdom of God is not eating and drinking, but righteousness and peace and joy in the Holy Spirit. 18For he who serves Christ in these thingsa *is* acceptable to God and approved by men.

19Therefore let us pursue the things *which make* for peace and the things by which one may edify another. 20Do not destroy the work of God for the sake of food. All things indeed *are* pure, but *it is* evil for the man who eats with offense. 21*It is* good neither to eat meat nor drink wine nor *do anything* by which your brother stumbles or is offended or is made weak.a 22Do you have faith?a Have *it* to yourself before God. Happy *is* he who does not condemn himself in what he approves. 23But he who doubts is condemned if he eats, because *he does* not *eat* from faith; for whatever *is* not from faith is sin.a

Bearing Others' Burdens

15 1We then who are strong ought to bear with the scruples of the weak, and not to please ourselves. 2Let each of us please *his* neighbor for *his* good, leading to edification. 3For even Christ did not please Himself; but as it is written, *"The reproaches of those who reproached You fell on Me."* a 4For whatever things were written before were written for our learning, that we through the patience and comfort of the Scriptures might have hope. 5Now may the God of patience and comfort grant you to be like-minded toward one another, according to Christ Jesus, 6that you may with one mind *and* one mouth glorify the God and Father of our Lord Jesus Christ.

Glorify God Together

7Therefore receive one another, just as Christ also received us,a to the glory of God. 8Now I say that Jesus Christ has become a servant to the circumcision for the truth of God, to confirm the promises *made* to the fathers, 9and that the Gentiles might glorify God for *His* mercy, as it is written:

> "For this reason I will confess to You
> 　among the Gentiles,
> 　And sing to Your name."a

10And again he says:

> "Rejoice, O Gentiles, with His people!" a

11And again:

> "Praise the LORD, all you Gentiles!
> Laud Him, all you peoples!" a

14:6 aNU-Text omits the rest of this sentence.
14:9 aNU-Text omits *and rose.*　14:10 aNU-Text reads *of God.*　14:11 aIsaiah 45:23
14:18 aNU-Text reads *this.*　14:21 aNU-Text omits *or is offended or is made weak.*
14:22 aNU-Text reads *The faith which you have—* have.　14:23 aM-Text puts Romans 16:25–27 here.　15:3 aPsalm 69:9　15:7 aNU-Text and M-Text read *you.*　15:9 a2 Samuel 22:50; Psalm 18:49　15:10 aDeuteronomy 32:43
15:11 aPsalm 117:1

¹²And again, Isaiah says:

> "There shall be a root of Jesse;
> And He who shall rise to reign over
>   the Gentiles,
> In Him the Gentiles shall hope."ᵃ

¹³Now may the God of hope fill you with all joy and peace in believing, that you may abound in hope by the power of the Holy Spirit.

Paul's Ministry to the Gentiles

Having ministered in the eastern Mediterranean area for many years, Paul planned to take the gospel farther west to Spain and to visit the Romans on his way (Rom. 15:24). Even though Paul had never been to Rome, many Roman Christians who had labored with Paul elsewhere knew him. Among them were Priscilla and Aquila (Acts 18:2, 3), as well as Rufus and his mother (Rom. 16:13). Paul hoped that Rome could serve as the home base for his missions in the West, as Antioch had in the East, and may have written this letter in order to solicit support from the Roman church for his mission.

That Paul sent so many greetings (16:3–15) and apparently knew so many people in a city he had yet to visit strikes some scholars as odd. He also seems to have written a conclusion to the letter already in Rom. 15:30–33. Since many of the people who receive personal greetings in ch. 16 are associated with Ephesus elsewhere in the New Testament, some scholars suggest that Paul had two copies of the letter made. One copy, ending at 15:33, was sent to the church at Rome. Paul then added a personal postscript to the other copy and had it delivered to the church at Ephesus.

■ Romans 15:14—16:27

Romans
From Jerusalem to Illyricum

15 :14 Now I myself am confident concerning you, my brethren, that you also are full of goodness, filled with all knowledge, able also to admonish one another.ᵃ ¹⁵Nevertheless, brethren, I have written more boldly to you on *some* points, as reminding you, because of the grace given to me by God, ¹⁶that I might be a minister of Jesus Christ to the Gentiles,

ministering the gospel of God, that the offering of the Gentiles might be acceptable, sanctified by the Holy Spirit. ¹⁷Therefore I have reason to glory in Christ Jesus in the things *which pertain* to God. ¹⁸For I will not dare to speak of any of those things which Christ has not accomplished through me, in word and deed, to make the Gentiles obedient— ¹⁹in mighty signs and wonders, by the power of the Spirit of God, so that from Jerusalem and round about to Illyricum I have fully preached the gospel of Christ. ²⁰And so I have made it my aim to preach the gospel, not where Christ was named, lest I should build on another man's foundation, ²¹but as it is written:

> "To whom He was not announced, they
>   shall see;
> And those who have not heard shall
>   understand."ᵃ

Plan to Visit Rome

²²For this reason I also have been much hindered from coming to you. ²³But now no longer having a place in these parts, and having a great desire these many years to come to you, ²⁴whenever I journey to Spain, I shall come to you.ᵃ For I hope to see you on my journey, and to be helped on my way there by you, if first I may enjoy your *company* for a while. ²⁵But now I am going to Jerusalem to minister to the saints. ²⁶For it pleased those from Macedonia and Achaia to make a certain contribution for the poor among the saints who are in Jerusalem. ²⁷It pleased them indeed, and they are their debtors. For if the Gentiles have been partakers of their spiritual things, their duty is also to minister to them in material things. ²⁸Therefore, when I have performed this and have sealed to them this fruit, I shall go by way of you to Spain. ²⁹But I know that when I come to you, I shall come in the fullness of the blessing of the gospelᵃ of Christ.

³⁰Now I beg you, brethren, through the Lord Jesus Christ, and through the love of the Spirit, that you strive together with me in prayers to God for me, ³¹that I may be delivered from those in Judea who do not believe, and that my service for Jerusalem

---

15:12 ᵃIsaiah 11:10   15:14 ᵃM-Text reads *others.*   15:21 ᵃIsaiah 52:15
15:24 ᵃNU-Text omits *I shall come to you* (and joins *Spain* with the next sentence).   15:29 ᵃNU-Text omits *of the gospel.*

SERVANT OF THE CHURCH AT CENCHREA (Rom. 16:1, 2)

Located on the prosperous isthmus of Corinth, Cenchrea was a port city, 7 miles east of Corinth. Much of Corinth's wealth came from this town, which by Paul's time hosted many foreign religions and was more religiously tolerant than some other less cosmopolitan locations. Phoebe, a woman of the church at Cenchrea, delivered Paul's letter to the Roman Christians (Rom. 16:1).

Paul calls Phoebe a "servant of the church" (16:1). By "servant" Paul could have meant a "minister" of the gospel, as he described himself, Apollos (1 Cor. 3:5), and Timothy (1 Thess. 3:2), or the more particular office of "deacon." The word "deacon" might describe Phoebe as the owner of the home in which the church met. Paul also calls her a "helper" (Rom. 16:2), which in Greek generally referred to "patrons" who hosted religious associations, like churches, in their homes. Women patrons, although in the minority, did exist in ancient times.

The phrase "servant of the church" may well correspond to the Jewish title *chazzan*, the person in charge of the synagogue building. (Like churches, synagogues without adequate resources to build special structures typically began in homes.) Jewish synagogues highly respected the office of *chazzan*, which was usually filled by men.

Though women's roles had improved in much of Greco-Roman society, 1st-century cultural prejudices still restricted opportunities for the average woman. Paul, though, did not hesitate to support women's roles to his Roman readers. He commends various ministries of many women, including Phoebe, Priscilla (16:3), Mary (16:6), and Junia, whom he calls an apostle (16:7).

may be acceptable to the saints, ³²that I may come to you with joy by the will of God, and may be refreshed together with you. ³³Now the God of peace *be* with you all. Amen.

Sister Phoebe Commended

16 ¹I commend to you Phoebe our sister, who is a servant of the church in Cenchrea, ²that you may receive her in the Lord in a manner worthy of the saints, and assist her in whatever business she has need of you; for indeed she has been a helper of many and of myself also.

Greeting Roman Saints

³Greet Priscilla and Aquila, my fellow workers in Christ Jesus, ⁴who risked their own necks for my life, to whom not only I give thanks, but also all the churches of the Gentiles. ⁵Likewise *greet* the church that is in their house.

Greet my beloved Epaenetus, who is the firstfruits of Achaiaᵃ to Christ. ⁶Greet Mary, who labored much for us. ⁷Greet Andronicus and Junia, my countrymen and my fellow prisoners, who are of note among the apostles, who also were in Christ before me.

⁸Greet Amplias, my beloved in the Lord. ⁹Greet Urbanus, our fellow worker in Christ, and Stachys, my beloved. ¹⁰Greet Apelles, approved in Christ. Greet those who are of the *household* of Aristobulus. ¹¹Greet Herodion, my countryman.ᵃ Greet those who are of the *household* of Narcissus who are in the Lord.

¹²Greet Tryphena and Tryphosa, who have labored in the Lord. Greet the beloved

16:5 ᵃNU-Text reads *Asia*.   16:11 ᵃOr *relative*

Persis, who labored much in the Lord. [13]Greet Rufus, chosen in the Lord, and his mother and mine. [14]Greet Asyncritus, Phlegon, Hermas, Patrobas, Hermes, and the brethren who are with them. [15]Greet Philologus and Julia, Nereus and his sister, and Olympas, and all the saints who are with them.

[16]Greet one another with a holy kiss. The[a] churches of Christ greet you.

Avoid Divisive Persons

[17]Now I urge you, brethren, note those who cause divisions and offenses, contrary to the doctrine which you learned, and avoid them. [18]For those who are such do not serve our Lord Jesus[a] Christ, but their own belly, and by smooth words and flattering speech deceive the hearts of the simple. [19]For your obedience has become known to all. Therefore I am glad on your behalf; but I want you to be wise in what is good, and simple concerning evil. [20]And the God of peace will crush Satan under your feet shortly.

The grace of our Lord Jesus Christ *be* with you. Amen.

Greetings from Paul's Friends

[21]Timothy, my fellow worker, and Lucius, Jason, and Sosipater, my countrymen, greet you.

[22]I, Tertius, who wrote *this* epistle, greet you in the Lord.

[23]Gaius, my host and *the host* of the whole church, greets you. Erastus, the treasurer of the city, greets you, and Quartus, a brother. [24]The grace of our Lord Jesus Christ *be* with you all. Amen.[a]

Benediction

[25]Now to Him who is able to establish you according to my gospel and the preaching of Jesus Christ, according to the revelation of the mystery kept secret since the world began [26]but now made manifest, and by the prophetic Scriptures made known to all nations, according to the commandment of the everlasting God, for obedience to the faith— [27]to God, alone wise, *be* glory through Jesus Christ forever. Amen.[a]

En Route to Jerusalem

The account of Paul's travels to Jerusalem at the end of his third missionary journey (Acts 20:3b—21:16) is one of three segments in the Book of Acts known as the "we" passages (also 16:10-18; 27:1—28:16). These accounts appear to relate first-hand reports of events at which the author of Acts was personally present.

Scholars differ over the significance the "we" passages have concerning the authorship of Acts as a whole. Since Paul was known to have had an associate named Luke (Philem. 1:24; Col. 4:14; 2 Tim. 4:11), these firsthand accounts might support the traditional view that Luke wrote Acts. Other scholars suggest that the "we" passages may represent a source used by the author of Acts. In this case, the author of the source for the "we" passages need not have been the author of the entire book.

At Tyre Paul heard the first Spirit-inspired prediction of trouble facing him at Jerusalem (Acts 21:4). But Paul was undeterred. His destination was Jerusalem, hoping to be there by the Day of Pentecost in A.D. 57. After that, he planned to visit Rome (see 19:21).

■ Acts 20:3b—21:16

Acts

20 :3b And when the Jews plotted against him as he was about to sail to Syria, he decided to return through Macedonia. [4]And Sopater of Berea accompanied him to Asia—also Aristarchus and Secundus of the Thessalonians, and Gaius of Derbe, and Timothy, and Tychicus and Trophimus of Asia. [5]These men, going ahead, waited for us at Troas. [6]But we sailed away from Philippi after the Days of Unleavened Bread, and in five days joined them at Troas, where we stayed seven days.

Ministering at Troas

[7]Now on the first *day* of the week, when the disciples came together to break bread, Paul, ready to depart the next day, spoke to them and continued his message until midnight. [8]There were many lamps in the upper room where they[a] were gathered together. [9]And in a window sat a certain young man named Eutychus, who was sinking into a deep sleep. He was overcome by sleep; and as Paul continued speaking, he fell down from the third story and was

16:16 [a]NU-Text reads *All the churches.*
16:18 [a]NU-Text and M-Text omit *Jesus.*
16:24 [a]NU-Text omits this verse. 16:27 [a]M-Text puts Romans 16:25–27 after Romans 14:23.
Acts 20:8 [a]NU-Text and M-Text read *we.*

taken up dead. ¹⁰But Paul went down, fell on him, and embracing *him* said, "Do not trouble yourselves, for his life is in him." ¹¹Now when he had come up, had broken bread and eaten, and talked a long while, even till daybreak, he departed. ¹²And they brought the young man in alive, and they were not a little comforted.

From Troas to Miletus

¹³Then we went ahead to the ship and sailed to Assos, there intending to take Paul on board; for so he had given orders, intending himself to go on foot. ¹⁴And when he met us at Assos, we took him on board and came to Mitylene. ¹⁵We sailed from there, and the next *day* came opposite Chios. The following *day* we arrived at Samos and stayed at Trogyllium. The next *day* we came to Miletus. ¹⁶For Paul had decided to sail past Ephesus, so that he would not have to spend time in Asia; for he was hurrying to be at Jerusalem, if possible, on the Day of Pentecost.

The Ephesian Elders Exhorted

¹⁷From Miletus he sent to Ephesus and called for the elders of the church. ¹⁸And when they had come to him, he said to them: "You know, from the first day that I came to Asia, in what manner I always lived among you, ¹⁹serving the Lord with all humility, with many tears and trials which happened to me by the plotting of the Jews; ²⁰how I kept back nothing that was helpful, but proclaimed it to you, and taught you publicly and from house to house, ²¹testifying to Jews, and also to Greeks, repentance toward God and faith toward our Lord Jesus Christ. ²²And see, now I go bound in the spirit to Jerusalem, not knowing the things that will happen to me there, ²³except that the Holy Spirit testifies in every city, saying that chains and tribulations await me. ²⁴But none of these things move me; nor do I count my life dear to myself,^a so that I may finish my race with joy, and the ministry which I received from the Lord Jesus, to testify to the gospel of the grace of God. ²⁵"And indeed, now I know that you all, among whom I have gone preaching the kingdom of God, will see my face no

more. ²⁶Therefore I testify to you this day that I *am* innocent of the blood of all *men.* ²⁷For I have not shunned to declare to you the whole counsel of God. ²⁸Therefore take heed to yourselves and to all the flock, among which the Holy Spirit has made you overseers, to shepherd the church of God^a which He purchased with His own blood. ²⁹For I know this, that after my departure savage wolves will come in among you, not sparing the flock. ³⁰Also from among yourselves men will rise up, speaking perverse things, to draw away the disciples after themselves. ³¹Therefore watch, and remember that for three years I did not cease to warn everyone night and day with tears.

³²"So now, brethren, I commend you to God and to the word of His grace, which is able to build you up and give you an inheritance among all those who are sanctified. ³³I have coveted no one's silver or gold or apparel. ³⁴Yes,^a you yourselves know that these hands have provided for my necessities, and for those who were with me. ³⁵I have shown you in every way, by laboring like this, that you must support the weak. And remember the words of the Lord Jesus, that He said, 'It is more blessed to give than to receive.' "

³⁶And when he had said these things, he knelt down and prayed with them all. ³⁷Then they all wept freely, and fell on Paul's neck and kissed him, ³⁸sorrowing most of all for the words which he spoke, that they would see his face no more. And they accompanied him to the ship.

Warnings on the Journey to Jerusalem

21 ¹Now it came to pass, that when we had departed from them and set sail, running a straight course we came to Cos, the following *day* to Rhodes, and from there to Patara. ²And finding a ship sailing over to Phoenicia, we went aboard and set sail. ³When we had sighted Cyprus, we passed it on the left, sailed to Syria, and landed at Tyre; for there the ship was to unload her cargo. ⁴And finding disciples,^a we stayed there seven days. They told Paul through the Spirit not to go up to Jerusalem. ⁵When we had come to the end of those days, we departed and went on our way; and they all accompanied us, with wives and children, till *we were* out of the city. And we knelt down on the shore and prayed. ⁶When we had taken our leave of one another, we boarded the ship, and they returned home.

20:24 ^aNU-Text reads *But I do not count my life of any value or dear to myself.* 20:28 ^aM-Text reads *of the Lord and God.* 20:34 ^aNU-Text and M-Text omit *Yes.* 21:4 ^aNU-Text reads *the disciples.*

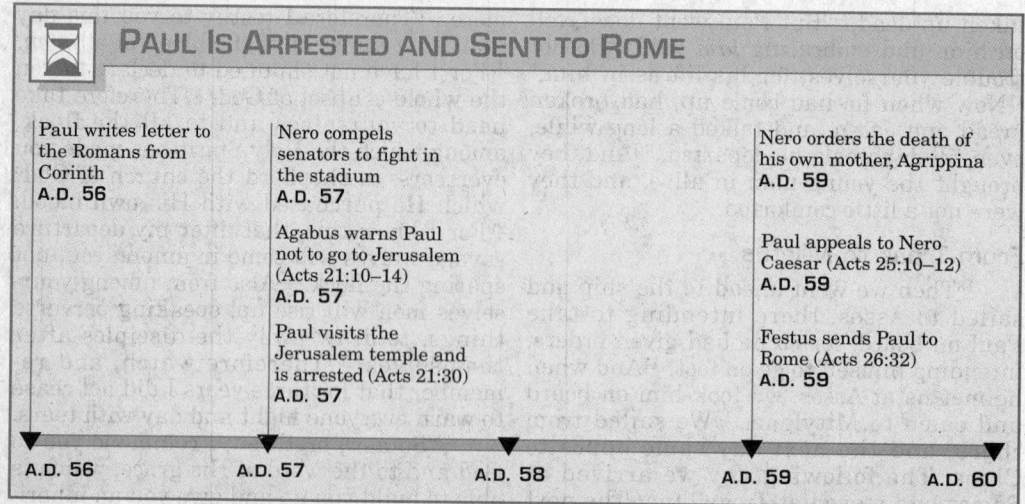

PAUL IS ARRESTED AND SENT TO ROME

Paul writes letter to the Romans from Corinth **A.D. 56**	Nero compels senators to fight in the stadium **A.D. 57**	Nero orders the death of his own mother, Agrippina **A.D. 59**
	Agabus warns Paul not to go to Jerusalem (Acts 21:10–14) **A.D. 57**	Paul appeals to Nero Caesar (Acts 25:10–12) **A.D. 59**
	Paul visits the Jerusalem temple and is arrested (Acts 21:30) **A.D. 57**	Festus sends Paul to Rome (Acts 26:32) **A.D. 59**

A.D. 56   **A.D. 57**   **A.D. 58**   **A.D. 59**   **A.D. 60**

⁷And when we had finished *our* voyage from Tyre, we came to Ptolemais, greeted the brethren, and stayed with them one day. ⁸On the next *day* we who were Paul's companionsª departed and came to Caesarea, and entered the house of Philip the evangelist, who was *one* of the seven, and stayed with him. ⁹Now this man had four virgin daughters who prophesied. ¹⁰And as we stayed many days, a certain prophet named Agabus came down from Judea. ¹¹When he had come to us, he took Paul's belt, bound his *own* hands and feet, and said, "Thus says the Holy Spirit, 'So shall the Jews at Jerusalem bind the man who owns this belt, and deliver *him* into the hands of the Gentiles.' "

¹²Now when we heard these things, both we and those from that place pleaded with him not to go up to Jerusalem. ¹³Then Paul answered, "What do you mean by weeping and breaking my heart? For I am ready not only to be bound, but also to die at Jerusalem for the name of the Lord Jesus." ¹⁴So when he would not be persuaded, we ceased, saying, "The will of the Lord be done."

Paul Urged to Make Peace

¹⁵And after those days we packed and went up to Jerusalem. ¹⁶Also some of the disciples from Caesarea went with us and brought with them a certain Mnason of Cyprus, an early disciple, with whom we were to lodge.

21:8 ªNU-Text omits *who were Paul's companions.*

The Gospel from Jerusalem to Rome

 God used Paul's imprisonment to bring him to Rome, the heart of the world.

Acts presents Rome as the guardian of law and order, a situation which often worked to the advantage of Paul and the gospel. Christians were expected to observe Roman law and not to get involved in disorderly, suspicious, or treasonous activity. The Romans, for their part, recognized Christianity as a legal and valid religion with the right to exist.

Paul's Roman citizenship granted him certain privileges as well as protection from Jewish fanaticism. His defense before the Roman governors Felix and Festus, as well as his specific appeal to plead his case before Caesar (Acts 25:10–12) are examples of Roman civil and legal law protecting Christianity.

The final chapters of Acts portray Paul as a witness for Jesus Christ on trial for the gospel. He defends himself before a Jerusalem crowd (Acts 22:1–21), before Felix (24:10–21), and before King Agrippa (26:1–32). He was not found guilty of any crime by the

Romans, but they kept him in prison to satisfy the Jews. In the view of the author of Acts, God used Paul's imprisonment to bring him to Rome, the heart of the world, and to make him a witness there.

Paul's appearance in Rome was ironic, because he came as a prisoner and not as a missionary (Acts 28:19, 20). In a Roman house he was held in confinement awaiting a trial that apparently never took place.

Paul Arrested in the Temple

After arriving in Jerusalem, Paul went to James, the brother of Jesus, and to the elders telling them about his work among the Gentiles. The leaders of the church rejoiced over the conversion of Gentiles, but they were worried about Jewish hostility. Rumors were circulating that Paul had taught Jews living outside of Palestine not to keep the Jewish law. To avoid a dispute, Paul was urged to join with four men who had taken a Nazirite vow. By accompanying them to the temple and paying the expenses of the sacrificial offerings, Paul would demonstrate that as a Jew he was keeping the law, despite his witnessing to Gentiles.

Paul was also accused of profaning the temple by bringing a Gentile into its inner courts. Gentiles were allowed in the outer court, called appropriately the Court of the Gentiles, but they were forbidden to come into the Court of Women or the Court of Israel. Signs warned that Gentiles entering these courts would be put to death.

Though Paul had not brought Gentiles into the temple, accusations of such led to an attack against him. The mob stopped beating Paul only because the Roman soldiers intervened to save his life.

■ Acts 21:17—23:22

Acts

21 **:17** And when we had come to Jerusalem, the brethren received us gladly. [18]On the following *day* Paul went in

21:22 ªNU-Text reads *What then is to be done? They will certainly.*   21:25 ªNU-Text omits *that they should observe no such thing, except.*

with us to James, and all the elders were present. [19]When he had greeted them, he told in detail those things which God had done among the Gentiles through his ministry. [20]And when they heard *it,* they glorified the Lord. And they said to him, "You see, brother, how many myriads of Jews there are who have believed, and they are all zealous for the law; [21]but they have been informed about you that you teach all the Jews who are among the Gentiles to forsake Moses, saying that they ought not to circumcise *their* children nor to walk according to the customs. [22]What then? The assembly must certainly meet, for they willª hear that you have come. [23]Therefore do what we tell you: We have four men who have taken a vow. [24]Take them and be purified with them, and pay their expenses so that they may shave *their* heads, and that all may know that those things of which they were informed concerning you are nothing, but *that* you yourself also walk orderly and keep the law. [25]But concerning the Gentiles who believe, we have written *and* decided that they should observe no such thing, exceptª that they should keep themselves from *things* offered to idols, from blood, from things strangled, and from sexual immorality."

Arrested in the Temple

[26]Then Paul took the men, and the next day, having been purified with them, entered the temple to announce the expiration of the days of purification, at which time an offering should be made for each one of them.

[27]Now when the seven days were almost ended, the Jews from Asia, seeing him in the temple, stirred up the whole

---

CULTURE AND SOCIETY

Tensions in Judea grew worse and worse during the decades leading up to the war between Judea and Rome. The historian Josephus describes a new kind of assassin called sicarii, *who would approach a target in daytime in a crowded place, stab the victim with daggers, and then disappear into the crowd (Acts 21:38). The Latin word* sica *means "dagger" and* sicarii *means "dagger men."*

RABBI GAMALIEL, PAUL'S TEACHER (Acts 22:3)

Gamaliel was a leading Pharisee and a member of the Jewish Sanhedrin in the New Testament period. As a rabbi, he was well known for his ability to interpret the Torah, having the respect of "all the people" (Acts 5:34). According to one tradition, he was the disciple of the famous rabbi Hillel, whose rabbinical school he represented. Yet another tradition knew Gamaliel to be Hillel's grandson.

Later Jewish sources applauded Gamaliel for upholding the purity of the Law (Torah) and for maintaining its dietary regulations. In other matters, though, he is reported to have held liberal views concerning divorce, keeping the Sabbath, and accepting the Targums (Jewish commentary upon the Torah). This more liberal side of Gamaliel is consistent with his counseling of the Sanhedrin, as Luke relates in Acts. When the Sanhedrin would have killed Peter and some of the apostles, Gamaliel rose to urge a wait-and-see attitude (Acts 5:33–35). The council should let God take care of misguided radicals like the apostles, Gamaliel advised (5:38, 39).

Paul claimed to have been a disciple of Gamaliel, "brought up" or instructed at the rabbi's feet (Acts 22:3). In one sense, though, Paul the disciple did not follow in his teacher's steps. While Gamaliel had urged restraint in dealing with Jesus' followers, Paul persecuted them zealously until his conversion.

---

crowd and laid hands on him, ²⁸crying out, "Men of Israel, help! This is the man who teaches all *men* everywhere against the people, the law, and this place; and furthermore he also brought Greeks into the temple and has defiled this holy place." ²⁹(For they had previouslyᵃ seen Trophimus the Ephesian with him in the city, whom they supposed that Paul had brought into the temple.)

³⁰And all the city was disturbed; and the people ran together, seized Paul, and dragged him out of the temple; and immediately the doors were shut. ³¹Now as they were seeking to kill him, news came to the commander of the garrison that all Jerusalem was in an uproar. ³²He immediately took soldiers and centurions, and ran down to them. And when they saw the commander and the soldiers, they stopped beating Paul. ³³Then the commander came near and took him, and commanded *him* to be bound with two chains; and he asked who he was and what he had done. ³⁴And some among the multitude cried one thing and some another.

So when he could not ascertain the truth because of the tumult, he commanded him to be taken into the barracks. ³⁵When he reached the stairs, he had to be carried by the soldiers because of the violence of the mob. ³⁶For the multitude of the people followed after, crying out, "Away with him!"

Addressing the Jerusalem Mob

³⁷Then as Paul was about to be led into the barracks, he said to the commander, "May I speak to you?"

He replied, "Can you speak Greek? ³⁸Are you not the Egyptian who some time ago stirred up a rebellion and led the four thousand assassins out into the wilderness?"

³⁹But Paul said, "I am a Jew from Tarsus, in Cilicia, a citizen of no mean city; and I implore you, permit me to speak to the people."

⁴⁰So when he had given him permission, Paul stood on the stairs and motioned with his hand to the people. And when there was a great silence, he spoke to *them* in the Hebrew language, saying,

22 ¹"Brethren and fathers, hear my defense before you now." ²And when they heard that he spoke to them in the Hebrew language, they kept all the more silent.

Then he said: ³"I am indeed a Jew, born in Tarsus of Cilicia, but brought up in this city at the feet of Gamaliel, taught according to the strictness of our fathers' law, and was zealous toward God as you all are today. ⁴I persecuted this Way to the death, binding and delivering into prisons both men and women, ⁵as also the high priest

---

21:29 ᵃM-Text omits *previously*.

bears me witness, and all the council of the elders, from whom I also received letters to the brethren, and went to Damascus to bring in chains even those who were there to Jerusalem to be punished.

6"Now it happened, as I journeyed and came near Damascus at about noon, suddenly a great light from heaven shone around me. 7And I fell to the ground and heard a voice saying to me, 'Saul, Saul, why are you persecuting Me?' 8So I answered, 'Who are You, Lord?' And He said to me, 'I am Jesus of Nazareth, whom you are persecuting.'

9"And those who were with me indeed saw the light and were afraid,a but they did not hear the voice of Him who spoke to me. 10So I said, 'What shall I do, Lord?' And the Lord said to me, 'Arise and go into Damascus, and there you will be told all things which are appointed for you to do.' 11And since I could not see for the glory of that light, being led by the hand of those who were with me, I came into Damascus.

12"Then a certain Ananias, a devout man according to the law, having a good testimony with all the Jews who dwelt there, 13came to me; and he stood and said to me, 'Brother Saul, receive your sight.' And at that same hour I looked up at him. 14Then he said, 'The God of our fathers has chosen you that you should know His will, and see the Just One, and hear the voice of His mouth. 15For you will be His witness to all men of what you have seen and heard. 16And now why are you waiting? Arise and be baptized, and wash away your sins, calling on the name of the Lord.'

17"Now it happened, when I returned to Jerusalem and was praying in the temple, that I was in a trance 18and saw Him saying to me, 'Make haste and get out of Jerusalem quickly, for they will not receive your testimony concerning Me.' 19So I said, 'Lord, they know that in every synagogue I imprisoned and beat those who believe on You. 20And when the blood of Your martyr Stephen was shed, I also was standing by consenting to his death,a and guarding the clothes of those who were killing him.' 21Then He said to me, 'Depart, for I will send you far from here to the Gentiles.' "

Paul's Roman Citizenship

22And they listened to him until this word, and *then* they raised their voices and said, "Away with such a *fellow* from the earth, for he is not fit to live!" 23Then, as they cried out and tore off *their* clothes and threw dust into the air, 24the commander ordered him to be brought into the barracks, and said that he should be examined under scourging, so that he might know why they shouted so against him. 25And as they bound him with thongs, Paul said to the centurion who stood by, "Is it lawful for you to scourge a man who is a Roman, and uncondemned?"

26When the centurion heard *that,* he went and told the commander, saying, "Take care what you do, for this man is a Roman."

27Then the commander came and said to him, "Tell me, are you a Roman?"

He said, "Yes."

28The commander answered, "With a large sum I obtained this citizenship."

And Paul said, "But I was born *a citizen.*"

29Then immediately those who were about to examine him withdrew from him; and the commander was also afraid after he found out that he was a Roman, and because he had bound him.

The Sanhedrin Divided

30The next day, because he wanted to know for certain why he was accused by the Jews, he released him from *his* bonds, and commanded the chief priests and all their council to appear, and brought Paul down and set him before them.

23 1Then Paul, looking earnestly at the council, said, "Men *and* brethren, I have lived in all good conscience before God until this day." 2And the high priest Ananias commanded those who stood by him to strike him on the mouth. 3Then Paul said to him, "God will strike you, *you* whitewashed wall! For you sit to judge me according to the law, and do you command me to be struck contrary to the law?"

4And those who stood by said, "Do you revile God's high priest?"

5Then Paul said, "I did not know, brethren, that he was the high priest; for it is written, 'You shall not speak evil of a ruler of your people.' "a

6But when Paul perceived that one part were Sadducees and the other

---

22:9　aNU-Text omits *and were afraid.*
22:20　aNU-Text omits *to his death.*
23:5　aExodus 22:28

Pharisees, he cried out in the council, "Men *and* brethren, I am a Pharisee, the son of a Pharisee; concerning the hope and resurrection of the dead I am being judged!"

⁷And when he had said this, a dissension arose between the Pharisees and the Sadducees; and the assembly was divided. ⁸For Sadducees say that there is no resurrection—and no angel or spirit; but the Pharisees confess both. ⁹Then there arose a loud outcry. And the scribes of the Pharisees' party arose and protested, saying, "We find no evil in this man; but if a spirit or an angel has spoken to him, let us not fight against God."ᵃ

¹⁰Now when there arose a great dissension, the commander, fearing lest Paul might be pulled to pieces by them, commanded the soldiers to go down and take him by force from among them, and bring *him* into the barracks.

The Plot Against Paul

¹¹But the following night the Lord stood by him and said, "Be of good cheer, Paul; for as you have testified for Me in Jerusalem, so you must also bear witness at Rome."

¹²And when it was day, some of the Jews banded together and bound themselves under an oath, saying that they would neither eat nor drink till they had killed Paul. ¹³Now there were more than forty who had formed this conspiracy. ¹⁴They came to the chief priests and elders, and said, "We have bound ourselves under a great oath that we will eat nothing until we have killed Paul. ¹⁵Now you, therefore, together with the council, suggest to the commander that he be brought down to you tomorrow,ᵃ as though you were going to make further inquiries concerning him; but we are ready to kill him before he comes near."

¹⁶So when Paul's sister's son heard of their ambush, he went and entered the barracks and told Paul. ¹⁷Then Paul called one of the centurions to *him* and said, "Take this young man to the commander, for he has something to tell him." ¹⁸So he took him and brought *him* to the commander and said, "Paul the prisoner called me to *him* and asked *me* to bring this young man to you. He has something to say to you."

¹⁹Then the commander took him by the hand, went aside, and asked privately, "What is it that you have to tell me?"

²⁰And he said, "The Jews have agreed to ask that you bring Paul down to the council tomorrow, as though they were going to inquire more fully about him. ²¹But do not yield to them, for more than forty of them lie in wait for him, men who have bound themselves by an oath that they will neither eat nor drink till they have killed him; and now they are ready, waiting for the promise from you."

²²So the commander let the young man depart, and commanded *him*, "Tell no one that you have revealed these things to me."

Paul Escorted to Caesarea

Citizens of Rome had special privileges including freedom from punishment until they had been tried and convicted. Because Paul had appealed for protection and a legal hearing under his rights as a Roman citizen, he was conducted by a military contingent to the governor's residence in the port city of Caesarea. Paul received an initial hearing before the Roman governor Antonius Felix within a week of arriving (Acts 24:1), but Felix declined to issue a ruling in the case. Even 2 years later (24:27), probably in July of A.D. 59, Paul's case still awaited adjudication. Felix was succeeded as governor by Porcius Festus at that time.

■ Acts 23:23—24:27

Acts
Sent to Felix

23 :23 And he called for two centurions, saying, "Prepare two hundred soldiers, seventy horsemen, and two hundred spearmen to go to Caesarea at the third hour of the night; ²⁴and provide mounts to set Paul on, and bring *him* safely to Felix the governor." ²⁵He wrote a letter in the following manner:

26   Claudius Lysias,

To the most excellent governor Felix:

Greetings.

27   This man was seized by the Jews and was about to be killed by them.

23:9 ᵃNU-Text omits last clause and reads *what if a spirit or an angel has spoken to him?*
23:15 ᵃNU-Text omits *tomorrow.*

BEFORE THE GOVERNOR AT CAESAREA (Acts 23:23, 24)

The seaport of Caesarea on the Mediterranean coast was first founded as a trading station by the Sidonian king Strato in the 4th century B.C. It was subsequently occupied by the Ptolemies and Hasmoneans, among others, and eventually made into a fortified port city with an expanded harbor. But it is Herod the Great (37–4 B.C.) who is known as the builder of the city.

Caesarea was in a ruined state when Herod began building operations in 22 B.C. His dream was to have an international port built in a Roman provincial style that would challenge Egypt's Alexandria as the leading trading center in the eastern Mediterranean. The city was completed in about a dozen years according to the Jewish historian Josephus (our primary source of information about Herod's Caesarea). It was an engineering wonder, with many unique features. The builders used a siltation system and made use of hydraulic concrete (poured into the sea as liquid but hardened underwater). The harbor complex was the most elaborate of its day.

After Herod's time, the Roman procurators made Caesarea the official seat of rule. During Jesus' time Pontius Pilate governed Judea from Caesarea, and archaeologists have discovered a fragment of an inscription bearing Pilate's name at the theater there. Antonius Felix was the procurator (or governor) ruling at Caesarea between A.D. 52 and 59, which explains why Paul the prisoner was taken there to stand before him (Acts 23:23, 24).

Coming with the troops I rescued him, having learned that he was a Roman. 28And when I wanted to know the reason they accused him, I brought him before their council. 29I found out that he was accused concerning questions of their law, but had nothing charged against him deserving of death or chains. 30And when it was told me that the Jews lay in wait for the man,ᵃ I sent him immediately to you, and also commanded his accusers to state before you the charges against him.

Farewell.

31Then the soldiers, as they were commanded, took Paul and brought *him* by night to Antipatris. 32The next day they left the horsemen to go on with him, and returned to the barracks. 33When they came to Caesarea and had delivered the letter to the governor, they also presented Paul to him. 34And when the governor had read *it,* he asked what province he was from. And when he understood that *he was* from Cilicia, 35he said, "I will hear you when your accusers also have come." And he commanded him to be kept in Herod's Praetorium.

Accused of Sedition

24 1Now after five days Ananias the high priest came down with the elders and a certain orator *named* Tertullus. These gave evidence to the governor against Paul.

2And when he was called upon, Tertullus began his accusation, saying: "Seeing that through you we enjoy great peace, and prosperity is being brought to this nation by your foresight, 3we accept *it* always and in all places, most noble Felix, with all thankfulness. 4Nevertheless, not to be tedious to you any further, I beg you to hear, by your courtesy, a few words from us. 5For we have found this man a plague, a creator of dissension among all the Jews throughout the world, and a ringleader of the sect of the Nazarenes. 6He even tried to profane the temple, and we seized him,ᵃ and wanted to judge him according to our law. 7But the commander Lysias came by and with great violence took *him* out of our hands, 8commanding his accusers to come to you. By examining him yourself you may ascertain all these things of which we accuse him." 9And the Jews also assented,ᵃ maintaining that these things were so.

23:30 ᵃNU-Text reads *there would be a plot against the man.*   24:6 ᵃNU-Text ends the sentence here and omits the rest of verse 6, all of verse 7, and the first clause of verse 8.   24:9 ᵃNU-Text and M-Text read *joined the attack.*

WHEN DID FESTUS TAKE OFFICE? (Acts 24:27)

Luke comments in Acts on a transfer of power that occurred while Paul was held in prison. The Roman procurator (or governor) of Judea, Antonius Felix, was replaced by Porcius Festus (Acts 24:27). The new procurator faced a situation left by Felix: Paul had been detained in prison while Felix dealt with other matters (Acts 24:24–26). Now Festus would need to hear Paul's case and decide whether to grant him passage to Rome for trial. The Jewish historian Josephus had a high regard for Festus, whom he contrasted with Felix, Festus's predecessor.

Just when Festus succeeded Felix as procurator is not exactly known. Both Josephus and Luke claim that he followed Felix. Josephus further says that Festus died 4 years before the Jewish war against Rome, which began in A.D. 66, thus making it A.D. 62 when Festus was succeeded by the next procurator, Albinus. But when Festus first took office and judged Paul's case is not as easy to determine.

One later source, Jerome's Latin version of Eusebius, claims that Festus took office in the emperor Nero's 2nd year, that is, A.D. 56. Complicating this date, though, is Josephus's statement that the previous procurator, Felix, received support from his brother Pallas when Felix left office and returned to Rome. Pallas lost his own position as financial secretary in A.D. 55, making it questionable whether he could have helped his brother after that time. Festus, then, would have taken office by A.D. 55.

The information regarding when Felix left office and Festus took over simply prevents any definite date from being established. Pallas is described as extremely wealthy by two Roman historians, Tacitus and Dio Cassius, so even after he was no longer financial secretary his wealth would have allowed him to help his brother Felix. It is also known that Felix was in office in A.D. 53 and ruled for "many years" (Acts 24:10), and Josephus writes considerably of Felix's time in office. While a specific year remains unsettled, most scholars suggest that Festus succeeded Felix around A.D. 59, ruling until his death in A.D. 62.

The Defense Before Felix

[10]Then Paul, after the governor had nodded to him to speak, answered: "Inasmuch as I know that you have been for many years a judge of this nation, I do the more cheerfully answer for myself, [11]because you may ascertain that it is no more than twelve days since I went up to Jerusalem to worship. [12]And they neither found me in the temple disputing with anyone nor inciting the crowd, either in the synagogues or in the city. [13]Nor can they prove the things of which they now accuse me. [14]But this I confess to you, that according to the Way which they call a sect, so I worship the God of my fathers, believing all things which are written in the Law and in the Prophets. [15]I have hope in God, which they themselves also accept, that there will be a resurrection of *the* dead,[a] both of *the* just and *the* unjust. [16]This *being* so, I myself always strive to have a conscience without offense toward God and men.

[17]"Now after many years I came to bring alms and offerings to my nation, [18]in the midst of which some Jews from Asia found me purified in the temple, neither with a mob nor with tumult. [19]They ought to have been here before you to object if they had anything against me. [20]Or else let those who are *here* themselves say if they found any wrongdoing[a] in me while I stood before the council, [21]unless *it is* for this one statement which I cried out, standing among them, 'Concerning the resurrection of the dead I am being judged by you this day.'"

Felix Procrastinates

[22]But when Felix heard these things, having more accurate knowledge of *the* Way, he adjourned the proceedings and said, "When Lysias the commander comes down, I will make a decision on your case." [23]So he commanded the centurion to keep Paul and to let *him* have liberty, and told

24:15 [a]NU-Text omits *of the dead.*
24:20 [a]NU-Text and M-Text read *say what wrongdoing they found.*

him not to forbid any of his friends to provide for or visit him.

²⁴And after some days, when Felix came with his wife Drusilla, who was Jewish, he sent for Paul and heard him concerning the faith in Christ. ²⁵Now as he reasoned about righteousness, self-control, and the judgment to come, Felix was afraid and answered, "Go away for now; when I have a convenient time I will call for you." ²⁶Meanwhile he also hoped that money would be given him by Paul, that he might release him.ᵃ Therefore he sent for him more often and conversed with him.

²⁷But after two years Porcius Festus succeeded Felix; and Felix, wanting to do the Jews a favor, left Paul bound.

24:26 ᵃNU-Text omits *that he might release him.*
Phil. 1:1 ᵃLiterally *overseers*

The Letter to the Philippians

Paul's immediate purpose for writing a letter to the Philippians was to thank them for a gift they had sent him (Phil. 4:14–18). Their messenger, Epaphroditus, had recovered from a serious illness and could carry this letter as he returned to Philippi (2:25–30). Paul's authorship of the letter to the Philippians has never been seriously questioned. There has been frequent and vigorous debate, however, over the date as well as the place of writing.

One view is that Paul wrote Philippians from Rome between A.D. 61 and 63. Paul was in prison (Phil. 1:12–14), and references to the "palace guard" (1:13) and "Caesar's household" (4:22) might suggest imprisonment in Rome. If so, this letter would have been written sometime after Paul was first placed under Roman guard (Acts 28:16).

Other scholars believe that Philippians was written earlier, either around A.D. 54 or 55 during Paul's ministry in Ephesus (Acts 19), or about A.D. 57–59 during his imprisonment at Caesarea (Acts 24—26). The terms "Caesar's household" and "palace guard," important evidence for a Roman imprisonment, could instead refer to Roman authorities in provincial cities like Ephesus or Caesarea. The location of Ephesus is favored because of hints that frequent travels were made between the prison and Philippi (Phil. 1:26; 2:19, 23–26; 4:18), suggesting that Paul was nearer to Philippi than imprisonment in Rome would allow.

That Paul wrote this letter from either Ephesus or Caesarea can be questioned. The Book of Acts does not mention Paul's ever being in prison in Ephesus, although Paul did write from Ephesus about some threat that he faced in Asia, the Roman province of which Ephesus was the chief city (2 Cor. 1:8–11). The Book of Acts does refer to a Caesarean imprisonment, but Caesarea was much farther from Philippi than was either Ephesus or Rome.

Wherever Paul was imprisoned, the Philippians supported him (Phil. 1:7). In one of his most personal letters, Paul is concerned, yet confident, that God will bring the Philippians' faith to maturity (2:15).

■ Philippians 1:1—4:23

Philippians
Greeting

1 :1 Paul and Timothy, bondservants of Jesus Christ,

To all the saints in Christ Jesus who are in Philippi, with the bishopsᵃ and deacons:

²Grace to you and peace from God our Father and the Lord Jesus Christ.

Thankfulness and Prayer

³I thank my God upon every remembrance of you, ⁴always in every prayer of mine making request for you all with joy, ⁵for your fellowship in the gospel from the first day until now, ⁶being confident of this very thing, that He who has begun a good

---

TIME CAPSULE   A.D. *58 to 59*

58   Domitius Corbulo is procurator or governor of Syria

59–62   Porcius Festus is procurator or governor of Judea (Acts 24:27)

59   Nero orders the death of his mother, Agrippina

59   Paul appeals to Caesar (Acts 25:11)

59   Festus decides to send Paul to Rome

59   Paul appears before Agrippa II and Bernice

59   Paul shipwrecked on the island of Malta

work in you will complete *it* until the day of Jesus Christ; ⁷just as it is right for me to think this of you all, because I have you in my heart, inasmuch as both in my chains and in the defense and confirmation of the gospel, you all are partakers with me of grace. ⁸For God is my witness, how greatly I long for you all with the affection of Jesus Christ.

⁹And this I pray, that your love may abound still more and more in knowledge and all discernment, ¹⁰that you may approve the things that are excellent, that you may be sincere and without offense till the day of Christ, ¹¹being filled with the fruits of righteousness which *are* by Jesus Christ, to the glory and praise of God.

Christ Is Preached

¹²But I want you to know, brethren, that the things *which happened* to me have actually turned out for the furtherance of the gospel, ¹³so that it has become evident to the whole palace guard, and to all the rest, that my chains are in Christ; ¹⁴and most of the brethren in the Lord, having become confident by my chains, are much more bold to speak the word without fear.

¹⁵Some indeed preach Christ even from envy and strife, and some also from goodwill: ¹⁶The former[a] preach Christ from selfish ambition, not sincerely, supposing to add affliction to my chains; ¹⁷but the latter out of love, knowing that I am appointed for the defense of the gospel. ¹⁸What then? Only *that* in every way, whether in pretense or in truth, Christ is preached; and in this I rejoice, yes, and will rejoice.

To Live Is Christ

¹⁹For I know that this will turn out for my deliverance through your prayer and the supply of the Spirit of Jesus Christ, ²⁰according to my earnest expectation and hope that in nothing I shall be ashamed, but with all boldness, as always, so now also Christ will be magnified in my body, whether by life or by death. ²¹For to me, to live *is* Christ, and to die *is* gain. ²²But if *I* live on in the flesh, this *will mean* fruit from *my* labor; yet what I shall choose I cannot tell. ²³For[a] I am hard-pressed between the two, having a desire to depart and be with Christ, *which is* far better. ²⁴Nevertheless to remain in the flesh *is* more needful for you. ²⁵And being confident of this, I know that I shall remain and continue with you all for your progress and joy

of faith, ²⁶that your rejoicing for me may be more abundant in Jesus Christ by my coming to you again.

Striving and Suffering for Christ

²⁷Only let your conduct be worthy of the gospel of Christ, so that whether I come and see you or am absent, I may hear of your affairs, that you stand fast in one spirit, with one mind striving together for the faith of the gospel, ²⁸and not in any way terrified by your adversaries, which is to them a proof of perdition, but to you of salvation,[a] and that from God. ²⁹For to you it has been granted on behalf of Christ, not only to believe in Him, but also to suffer for His sake, ³⁰having the same conflict which you saw in me and now hear *is* in me.

Unity Through Humility

2 ¹Therefore if *there is* any consolation in Christ, if any comfort of love, if any fellowship of the Spirit, if any affection and mercy, ²fulfill my joy by being like-minded, having the same love, *being* of one accord, of one mind. ³*Let* nothing *be done* through selfish ambition or conceit, but in lowliness of mind let each esteem others better than himself. ⁴Let each of you look out not only for his own interests, but also for the interests of others.

The Humbled and Exalted Christ

⁵Let this mind be in you which was also in Christ Jesus, ⁶who, being in the form of God, did not consider it robbery to be equal with God, ⁷but made Himself of no reputation, taking the form of a bond-servant, *and* coming in the likeness of men. ⁸And being found in appearance as a man, He humbled Himself and became obedient to *the point of* death, even the death of the cross. ⁹Therefore God also has highly exalted Him and given Him the name which is above every name, ¹⁰that at the name of Jesus every knee should bow, of those in heaven, and of those on earth, and of those under the earth, ¹¹and *that* every tongue should confess that Jesus Christ *is* Lord, to the glory of God the Father.

Light Bearers

¹²Therefore, my beloved, as you have always obeyed, not as in my presence only,

---

1:16 [a]NU-Text reverses the contents of verses 16 and 17.   1:23 [a]NU-Text and M-Text read *But.*
1:28 [a]NU-Text reads *of your salvation.*

but now much more in my absence, work out your own salvation with fear and trembling; [13]for it is God who works in you both to will and to do for *His* good pleasure.

[14]Do all things without complaining and disputing, [15]that you may become blameless and harmless, children of God without fault in the midst of a crooked and perverse generation, among whom you shine as lights in the world, [16]holding fast the word of life, so that I may rejoice in the day of Christ that I have not run in vain or labored in vain.

[17]Yes, and if I am being poured out *as a drink offering* on the sacrifice and service of your faith, I am glad and rejoice with you all. [18]For the same reason you also be glad and rejoice with me.

Timothy Commended

[19]But I trust in the Lord Jesus to send Timothy to you shortly, that I also may be encouraged when I know your state. [20]For I have no one like-minded, who will sincerely care for your state. [21]For all seek their own, not the things which are of Christ Jesus. [22]But you know his proven character, that as a son with *his* father he served with me in the gospel. [23]Therefore I hope to send him at once, as soon as I see how it goes with me. [24]But I trust in the Lord that I myself shall also come shortly.

Epaphroditus Praised

[25]Yet I considered it necessary to send to you Epaphroditus, my brother, fellow worker, and fellow soldier, but your messenger and the one who ministered to my need; [26]since he was longing for you all, and was distressed because you had heard that he was sick. [27]For indeed he was sick almost unto death; but God had mercy on him, and not only on him but on me also, lest I should have sorrow upon sorrow. [28]Therefore I sent him the more eagerly, that when you see him again you may re-

joice, and I may be less sorrowful. [29]Receive him therefore in the Lord with all gladness, and hold such men in esteem; [30]because for the work of Christ he came close to death, not regarding his life, to supply what was lacking in your service toward me.

All for Christ

3 [1]Finally, my brethren, rejoice in the Lord. For me to write the same things to you *is* not tedious, but for you *it is* safe.

[2]Beware of dogs, beware of evil workers, beware of the mutilation! [3]For we are the circumcision, who worship God in the Spirit,[a] rejoice in Christ Jesus, and have no confidence in the flesh, [4]though I also might have confidence in the flesh. If anyone else thinks he may have confidence in the flesh, I more so: [5]circumcised the eighth day, of the stock of Israel, *of* the tribe of Benjamin, a Hebrew of the Hebrews; concerning the law, a Pharisee; [6]concerning zeal, persecuting the church; concerning the righteousness which is in the law, blameless.

[7]But what things were gain to me, these I have counted loss for Christ. [8]Yet indeed I also count all things loss for the excellence of the knowledge of Christ Jesus my Lord, for whom I have suffered the loss of all things, and count them as rubbish, that I may gain Christ [9]and be found in Him, not having my own righteousness, which *is* from the law, but that which *is* through faith in Christ, the righteousness which is from God by faith; [10]that I may know Him and the power of His resurrection, and the fellowship of His sufferings, being conformed to His death, [11]if, by any means, I may attain to the resurrection from the dead.

Pressing Toward the Goal

[12]Not that I have already attained, or am already perfected; but I press on, that I may lay hold of that for which Christ Jesus has also laid hold of me. [13]Brethren, I do not count myself to have apprehended; but

3:3 [a]NU-Text and M-Text read *who worship in the Spirit of God.*

RELIGION AND WORSHIP

Every morning and evening an animal sacrifice accompanied by a drink offering was presented at the temple. For this the priests took somewhat more than a quart of wine and poured it out on the ground at the base of the altar. Paul likens his own life to the animal sacrifice and libation that were familiar practices in the ancient world (Phil. 2:17).

PAUL'S PEDIGREE AS A PHARISEE (Phil. 3:4–6)

Much has been written about the Pharisees in the time of Jesus, yet remarkably little was written by them. Firsthand writings exist from only two persons who identified themselves with the Pharisees: Josephus, the 1st-century Jewish historian and apologist, and Paul of Tarsus, also known as the apostle Paul. Neither Josephus nor Paul resembles the Pharisees written about elsewhere!

Paul recognized that his time as a Pharisee established for him a pedigree within Judaism that was quite impressive. His own summary of his pre-Christian life (Phil. 3:4–6), therefore, gives us insight into the convictions of at least some Pharisees. For one thing, to be a Pharisee meant for Paul that he interpreted the Law, the Jewish Torah in a certain way (3:5). Josephus also writes that Pharisees had their own interpretation of the Law.

Another conviction that Paul links to his pedigree as a Pharisee is zeal. "Zeal" characterizes those within Judaism who used violence against other Jews for violating the Torah. These Pharisees lived by their particular interpretations, and they were zealous to preserve the traditions of the fathers (Gal. 1:14) and Israel's integrity. The Pharisee Saul demonstrated his own zeal for Judaism by "persecuting the church" (Phil. 3:6).

Another example of such zeal appeared during the Maccabean war (166–160 B.C.), 200 years before Paul's time. The war broke out when the priest Mattathias "burned with zeal" and killed a fellow Jew who was sacrificing to Greek gods in violation of the Torah (1 Macc. 2:23–26). Mattathias cried out, "Let every one who is zealous for the law and supports the covenant come out with me!" (1 Macc. 2:27).

Reflecting on his time as a Pharisee, Paul counted himself amongst the most intense followers of the Law, zealous to the point of using violence to protect Israel from Torah desecration. No wonder he persecuted the church. In the view of the Pharisees, the first Christians, as a Jewish group that was lax in the observance of the Law, represented the defilement of Israel! Saul the Pharisee had lived out his commitment to Israel through the Law; Paul the apostle would live it out through Jesus Christ (Phil. 3:7–9).

---

one thing *I do,* forgetting those things which are behind and reaching forward to those things which are ahead, [14]I press toward the goal for the prize of the upward call of God in Christ Jesus.

[15]Therefore let us, as many as are mature, have this mind; and if in anything you think otherwise, God will reveal even this to you. [16]Nevertheless, to *the degree* that we have already attained, let us walk by the same rule,[a] let us be of the same mind.

Our Citizenship in Heaven

[17]Brethren, join in following my example, and note those who so walk, as you have us for a pattern. [18]For many walk, of whom I have told you often, and now tell you even weeping, *that they are* the enemies of the cross of Christ: [19]whose end *is* destruction, whose god *is their* belly, and *whose* glory *is* in their shame—who set their mind on earthly things. [20]For our citizenship is in heaven, from which we also eagerly wait for the Savior, the Lord Jesus Christ, [21]who will transform our lowly body that it may be conformed to His glorious body, according to the working by which He is able even to subdue all things to Himself.

4 [1]Therefore, my beloved and longed-for brethren, my joy and crown, so stand fast in the Lord, beloved.

Be United, Joyful, and in Prayer

[2]I implore Euodia and I implore Syntyche to be of the same mind in the Lord. [3]And[a] I urge you also, true companion, help these women who labored with me in the gospel, with Clement also, and the rest of my fellow workers, whose names *are* in the Book of Life.

[4]Rejoice in the Lord always. Again I will say, rejoice!

3:16 [a]NU-Text omits *rule* and the rest of the verse.   4:3 [a]NU-Text and M-Text read *Yes.*

WOMEN LEADERS IN THE PHILIPPIAN CHURCH (Phil. 4:2, 3)

Paul's letters provide insight into the social makeup of the small early Christian communities in the Greco-Roman world. In his letter to the Philippian church, the first two persons he mentions by name are women: Euodia and Syntyche (Phil. 4:2). When Paul describes them as "these women who labored with me in the gospel" and includes them in the category of "fellow workers" (4:3), he indicates that they joined with him as equal partners in his missionary and teaching activity.

The exact nature of their leadership roles in the church at Philippi is not certain. The authority of both women in the church was sufficient, however, for Paul to encourage them to seek harmony with one another (4:2). He even called on someone addressed as "true companion" to "help these women" (4:3). Perhaps he was concerned that competition between them for the Philippian's loyalty and affection might fracture the young Philippian church. Perhaps the church met in the houses of these two women; competition between them, then, would have been a temptation.

Paul was concerned that Euodia and Syntyche "be of the same mind in the Lord" (4:2). His concern could not have run too deep, though. Along with Clement, he believed that both Euodia's and Syntyche's names were "in the Book of Life" (4:3). Nevertheless, both women needed to seek the mind of Christ, not their own.

Women played important leadership roles in Paul's churches, two examples being Phoebe in the church at Cenchrea (Rom. 16:1) and Priscilla in Ephesus (1 Cor. 16:19). Particularly in Macedonia, where women often assumed prominent roles in religious cults, it would be natural to find female leaders in a church. Paul supported women's roles in the Christian communities and instructed believers: "there is neither male nor female; for you are all one in Christ Jesus" (Gal. 3:28).

---

[5]Let your gentleness be known to all men. The Lord *is* at hand.

[6]Be anxious for nothing, but in everything by prayer and supplication, with thanksgiving, let your requests be made known to God; [7]and the peace of God, which surpasses all understanding, will guard your hearts and minds through Christ Jesus.

Meditate on These Things

[8]Finally, brethren, whatever things are true, whatever things *are* noble, whatever things *are* just, whatever things *are* pure, whatever things *are* lovely, whatever things *are* of good report, if *there is* any virtue and if *there is* anything praiseworthy—meditate on these things. [9]The things which you learned and received and heard and saw in me, these do, and the God of peace will be with you.

Philippian Generosity

[10]But I rejoiced in the Lord greatly that now at last your care for me has flourished again; though you surely did care, but you lacked opportunity. [11]Not that I speak in regard to need, for I have learned in whatever state I am, to be content: [12]I know how to be abased, and I know how to abound. Everywhere and in all things I have learned both to be full and to be hungry, both to abound and to suffer need. [13]I can do all things through Christ[a] who strengthens me.

[14]Nevertheless you have done well that you shared in my distress. [15]Now you Philippians know also that in the beginning of the gospel, when I departed from Macedonia, no church shared with me concerning giving and receiving but you only. [16]For even in Thessalonica you sent *aid* once and again for my necessities. [17]Not that I seek the gift, but I seek the fruit that abounds to your account. [18]Indeed I have all and abound. I am full, having received from Epaphroditus the things *sent* from you, a sweet-smelling aroma, an acceptable sacrifice, well pleasing to God. [19]And my God shall supply all your need according to His riches in glory by Christ Jesus. [20]Now to our God and Father *be* glory forever and ever. Amen.

4:13 [a]NU-Text reads *Him who.*

Greeting and Blessing

²¹Greet every saint in Christ Jesus. The brethren who are with me greet you. ²²All the saints greet you, but especially those who are of Caesar's household.

²³The grace of our Lord Jesus Christ be with you all.ᵃ Amen.

Paul Appeals to Caesar

Felix was succeeded as governor by Porcius Festus in the summer of A.D. 59 or 60. Like his predecessor Felix, Festus wanted to please the Jewish leadership, so he asked Paul to stand trial in Jerusalem. Paul, though, refused and used his prerogative as a Roman citizen to appeal, over the jurisdiction of the governor, to the emperor.

After Paul's appeal, Festus decided to present the problem to King Agrippa II. He and Bernice were children of Herod Agrippa I, who died at Caesarea (Acts 12:23). The king apparently welcomed the opportunity to hear Paul. Paul was equally pleased to bear witness before such a distinguished audience and a relatively friendly king. Both Festus and Agrippa II concurred that Paul's appeal to Caesar had removed the case from their legal jurisdiction (25:12; 26:32).

▼   ■ Acts 25:1—26:32

Acts
Paul Before Festus

25 :1 Now when Festus had come to the province, after three days he went up from Caesarea to Jerusalem. ²Then the high priestᵃ and the chief men of the Jews informed him against Paul; and they petitioned him, ³asking a favor against him, that he would summon him to Jerusalem—while *they* lay in ambush along the road to kill him. ⁴But Festus answered that Paul should be kept at Caesarea, and that he himself was going *there* shortly. ⁵"Therefore," he said, "let those who have authority among you go down with *me* and accuse this man, to see if there is any fault in him."

⁶And when he had remained among them more than ten days, he went down to Caesarea. And the next day, sitting on the judgment seat, he commanded Paul to be brought. ⁷When he had come, the Jews who had come down from Jerusalem stood about and laid many serious complaints against Paul, which they could not prove, ⁸while he answered for himself, "Neither against the law of the Jews, nor against the temple, nor against Caesar have I offended in anything at all."

⁹But Festus, wanting to do the Jews a favor, answered Paul and said, "Are you willing to go up to Jerusalem and there be judged before me concerning these things?"

¹⁰So Paul said, "I stand at Caesar's judgment seat, where I ought to be judged. To the Jews I have done no wrong, as you very well know. ¹¹For if I am an offender, or have committed anything deserving of death, I do not object to dying; but if there is nothing in these things of which these men accuse me, no one can deliver me to them. I appeal to Caesar."

¹²Then Festus, when he had conferred with the council, answered, "You have appealed to Caesar? To Caesar you shall go!"

Paul Before Agrippa

¹³And after some days King Agrippa and Bernice came to Caesarea to greet Festus. ¹⁴When they had been there many days, Festus laid Paul's case before the king, saying: "There is a certain man left a prisoner by Felix, ¹⁵about whom the chief priests and the elders of the Jews informed *me*, when I was in Jerusalem, asking for a judgment against him. ¹⁶To them I answered, 'It is not the custom of the Romans to deliver any man to destructionᵃ before the accused meets the accusers face to face, and has opportunity to answer for himself concerning the charge against him.' ¹⁷Therefore when they had come together,

---

4:23 ᵃNU-Text reads *your spirit.*
Acts 25:2 ᵃNU-Text reads *chief priests.*
25:16 ᵃNU-Text omits *to destruction,* although it is implied.

POLITICS AND GOVERNMENT

In A.D. 54 the Roman Senate conferred the powers of emperor on Nero, who was the Caesar at the time Paul stood trial (Acts 25:10). Nero's mother Agrippina seems to have poisoned her husband Claudius so that her son could become emperor in his place. Nero was proud, cruel, and in the end a victim of delusions. He executed members of his own family. His enemies forced him to commit suicide in A.D. 68.

AGRIPPA, PAUL'S JUDGE (Acts 25:23)

Marcus Julius Agrippa was the Roman name of Agrippa II, the last of the Herodian dynasty of five Roman-appointed kings in Palestine. He and his father, Agrippa I, were descended from the Jewish-born Herod the Great, ruler of Judea at the time of Christ's birth (Matt. 2:1).

The writings of the Jewish historian Josephus (A.D. 37–100) provide the most information about Agrippa. Since he was too young to receive the throne of Judea in A.D. 44 when his father died, the Romans appointed a governor. Agrippa himself was given other territories to rule, notably in Galilee.

At the beginning of the Jewish revolt in A.D. 66 Agrippa came to Jerusalem to quell the disorder. Unsuccessful in this venture, he became an ardent Roman sympathizer. Josephus (The Wars of the Jews 2:345) attributes a speech to Agrippa in which he warned that the Romans were much too strong for the Jews to resist, and thus they should side with them. After the revolt in A.D. 70 the Romans gave Agrippa additional territory in reward for his loyalty.

In A.D. 59 the apostle Paul stood trial before Agrippa, who was considered an expert on Jewish affairs, and was interested in Paul's case (Acts 25:13—26:32). The king was accompanied at the trial by his sister Bernice (25:13, 23). Rumors about Agrippa, who apparently never married, having an incestuous relationship with Bernice were denied by Josephus while supported by the Roman writer Juvenal. Paul's judge was a Jewish king, a Roman sympathizer, and a man of questionable moral reputation. As Paul defended his Christian faith, he appealed to Agrippa's Jewish background, challenging even him to become a believing Jew (26:2, 3, 26, 27).

---

without any delay, the next day I sat on the judgment seat and commanded the man to be brought in. 18When the accusers stood up, they brought no accusation against him of such things as I supposed, 19but had some questions against him about their own religion and about a certain Jesus, who had died, whom Paul affirmed to be alive. 20And because I was uncertain of such questions, I asked whether he was willing to go to Jerusalem and there be judged concerning these matters. 21But when Paul appealed to be reserved for the decision of Augustus, I commanded him to be kept till I could send him to Caesar."

22Then Agrippa said to Festus, "I also would like to hear the man myself."

"Tomorrow," he said, "you shall hear him."

23So the next day, when Agrippa and Bernice had come with great pomp, and had entered the auditorium with the commanders and the prominent men of the city, at Festus' command Paul was brought in. 24And Festus said: "King Agrippa and all the men who are here present with us, you see this man about whom the whole assembly of the Jews petitioned me, both at Jerusalem and here, crying out that he

was not fit to live any longer. 25But when I found that he had committed nothing deserving of death, and that he himself had appealed to Augustus, I decided to send him. 26I have nothing certain to write to my lord concerning him. Therefore I have brought him out before you, and especially before you, King Agrippa, so that after the examination has taken place I may have something to write. 27For it seems to me unreasonable to send a prisoner and not to specify the charges against him."

Paul's Early Life

26 1Then Agrippa said to Paul, "You are permitted to speak for yourself."

So Paul stretched out his hand and answered for himself: 2"I think myself happy, King Agrippa, because today I shall answer for myself before you concerning all the things of which I am accused by the Jews, 3especially because you are expert in all customs and questions which have to do with the Jews. Therefore I beg you to hear me patiently.

4"My manner of life from my youth, which was spent from the beginning among my own nation at Jerusalem, all the Jews know. 5They knew me from the first, if they were willing to testify, that according to the strictest sect of our religion I lived a Pharisee. 6And now I stand and am judged for the hope of the promise made by God to our fathers. 7To this *promise* our twelve tribes, earnestly serving *God* night and day, hope to attain. For this hope's sake, King Agrippa, I am accused by the Jews. 8Why should it be thought incredible by you that God raises the dead?

9"Indeed, I myself thought I must do many things contrary to the name of Jesus of Nazareth. 10This I also did in Jerusalem, and many of the saints I shut up in prison, having received authority from the chief priests; and when they were put to death, I cast my vote against *them*. 11And I punished them often in every synagogue and compelled *them* to blaspheme; and being exceedingly enraged against them, I persecuted *them* even to foreign cities.

Paul Recounts His Conversion

12"While thus occupied, as I journeyed to Damascus with authority and commission from the chief priests, 13at midday, O king, along the road I saw a light from heaven, brighter than the sun, shining around me and those who journeyed with me. 14And when we all had fallen to the ground, I heard a voice speaking to me and saying in the Hebrew language, 'Saul, Saul, why are you persecuting Me? *It is* hard for you to kick against the goads.' 15So I said, 'Who are You, Lord?' And He said, 'I am Jesus, whom you are persecuting. 16But rise and stand on your feet; for I have appeared to you for this purpose, to make you a minister and a witness both of the things which you have seen and of the things which I will yet reveal to you. 17I will deliver you from the *Jewish* people, as well as *from* the Gentiles, to whom I nowa send you, 18to open their eyes, *in order* to turn *them* from darkness to light, and *from* the power of Satan to God, that they may receive forgiveness of sins and an inheritance among those who are sanctified by faith in Me.'

Paul's Post-Conversion Life

19"Therefore, King Agrippa, I was not disobedient to the heavenly vision, 20but declared first to those in Damascus and in Jerusalem, and throughout all the region of Judea, and *then* to the Gentiles, that they should repent, turn to God, and do works befitting repentance. 21For these

reasons the Jews seized me in the temple and tried to kill *me*. 22Therefore, having obtained help from God, to this day I stand, witnessing both to small and great, saying no other things than those which the prophets and Moses said would come— 23that the Christ would suffer, that He would be the first to rise from the dead, and would proclaim light to the *Jewish* people and to the Gentiles."

Agrippa Parries Paul's Challenge

24Now as he thus made his defense, Festus said with a loud voice, "Paul, you are beside yourself! Much learning is driving you mad!"

25But he said, "I am not mad, most noble Festus, but speak the words of truth and reason. 26For the king, before whom I also speak freely, knows these things; for I am convinced that none of these things escapes his attention, since this thing was not done in a corner. 27King Agrippa, do you believe the prophets? I know that you do believe."

28Then Agrippa said to Paul, "You almost persuade me to become a Christian."

29And Paul said, "I would to God that not only you, but also all who hear me today, might become both almost and altogether such as I am, except for these chains."

30When he had said these things, the king stood up, as well as the governor and Bernice and those who sat with them; 31and when they had gone aside, they talked among themselves, saying, "This man is doing nothing deserving of death or chains."

32Then Agrippa said to Festus, "This man might have been set free if he had not appealed to Caesar."

26:17 aNU-Text and M-Text omit *now*.

The Voyage to Rome

All the participants in the trial at Caesarea, even Agrippa, agreed that Paul was innocent. Christianity was not a crime before a Roman court, and Paul should rightfully have been set free (Acts 26:32). Instead, after having spent approximately 2 years in Roman custody in Caesarea, Paul was sent by ship to Rome (c. A.D. 59 or 60).

The voyage to Rome did not turn out to be a pleasure cruise. Contrary winds had delayed the grain ship until fall weather made sailing dangerous (Acts 27:7, 8). It was already late September or early October, the time when the fast on the Day of Atonement was observed (27:9). This late season, plus Paul's God-given foresight, led to his bold prediction: "this voyage will end with disaster" (27:9, 10). After departing the island of Crete late in the fall, his party was shipwrecked on Malta during a storm.

    Paul spent the 3 winter months ministering on the island of Malta. According to Pliny the Elder, the seas could open up for safe sailing as early as February, though weather conditions could delay a voyage until sometime in March. So it was possibly in the spring of A.D. 60 that Paul's journey finally reached Italy. Appii Forum, 43 miles from Rome, and Three Inns, 33 miles from Rome (Acts 28:15), were well-known stopping places on the main highway from southern Italy to Rome.

    ■ Acts 27:1—28:15

Acts
The Voyage Begins

27 :1 And when it was decided that we should sail to Italy, they delivered Paul and some other prisoners to *one* named Julius, a centurion of the Augustan Regiment. ²So, entering a ship of Adramyttium, we put to sea, meaning to sail along the coasts of Asia. Aristarchus, a Macedonian of Thessalonica, was with us. ³And the next *day* we landed at Sidon. And Julius treated Paul kindly and gave *him* liberty to go to his friends and receive care. ⁴When we had put to sea from there, we sailed under *the shelter of* Cyprus, because the winds were contrary. ⁵And when we had sailed over the sea which is off Cilicia and Pamphylia, we came to Myra, *a city* of Lycia. ⁶There the centurion found an Alexandrian ship sailing to Italy, and he put us on board.

27:14 ªNU-Text reads *Euraquilon.*
27:16 ªNU-Text reads *Cauda.*   27:17 ªM-Text reads *Syrtes.*

⁷When we had sailed slowly many days, and arrived with difficulty off Cnidus, the wind not permitting us to proceed, we sailed under *the shelter of* Crete off Salmone. ⁸Passing it with difficulty, we came to a place called Fair Havens, near the city *of* Lasea.

Paul's Warning Ignored

⁹Now when much time had been spent, and sailing was now dangerous because the Fast was already over, Paul advised them, ¹⁰saying, "Men, I perceive that this voyage will end with disaster and much loss, not only of the cargo and ship, but also our lives." ¹¹Nevertheless the centurion was more persuaded by the helmsman and the owner of the ship than by the things spoken by Paul. ¹²And because the harbor was not suitable to winter in, the majority advised to set sail from there also, if by any means they could reach Phoenix, a harbor of Crete opening toward the southwest and northwest, *and* winter there.

In the Tempest

¹³When the south wind blew softly, supposing that they had obtained *their* desire, putting out to sea, they sailed close by Crete. ¹⁴But not long after, a tempestuous head wind arose, called Euroclydon.ª ¹⁵So when the ship was caught, and could not head into the wind, we let *her* drive. ¹⁶And running under *the shelter of* an island called Clauda,ª we secured the skiff with difficulty. ¹⁷When they had taken it on board, they used cables to undergird the ship; and fearing lest they should run aground on the Syrtisª *Sands,* they struck sail and so were driven. ¹⁸And because we were exceedingly tempest-tossed, the next *day* they lightened the ship. ¹⁹On the third *day* we threw the ship's tackle overboard with our own hands. ²⁰Now when neither sun nor stars appeared for many days, and no small tempest beat on *us,* all hope that we would be saved was finally given up.

²¹But after long abstinence from food,

Trade and Economics

Merchant ships in the 1st century were made of wood and powered by sail. They were mostly from 50 to 120 feet long, and thus could carry 200 to 300 tons of cargo. Passengers also traveled on cargo ships (Acts 27:6). The weather was dangerous after mid-September, and except for emergencies, the sea was closed to shipping between November 12 and March 10.

then Paul stood in the midst of them and said, "Men, you should have listened to me, and not have sailed from Crete and incurred this disaster and loss. 22And now I urge you to take heart, for there will be no loss of life among you, but only of the ship. 23For there stood by me this night an angel of the God to whom I belong and whom I serve, 24saying, 'Do not be afraid, Paul; you must be brought before Caesar; and indeed God has granted you all those who sail with you.' 25Therefore take heart, men, for I believe God that it will be just as it was told me. 26However, we must run aground on a certain island."

27Now when the fourteenth night had come, as we were driven up and down in the Adriatic *Sea*, about midnight the sailors sensed that they were drawing near some land. 28And they took soundings and found *it* to be twenty fathoms; and when they had gone a little farther, they took soundings again and found *it* to be fifteen fathoms. 29Then, fearing lest we should run aground on the rocks, they dropped four anchors from the stern, and prayed for day to come. 30And as the sailors were seeking to escape from the ship, when they had let down the skiff into the sea, under pretense of putting out anchors from the prow, 31Paul said to the centurion and the soldiers, "Unless these men stay in the ship, you cannot be saved." 32Then the soldiers cut away the ropes of the skiff and let it fall off.

33And as day was about to dawn, Paul implored *them* all to take food, saying, "Today is the fourteenth day you have waited and continued without food, and eaten nothing. 34Therefore I urge you to take nourishment, for this is for your survival, since not a hair will fall from the head of any of you." 35And when he had said these things, he took bread and gave thanks to God in the presence of them all; and when he had broken *it* he began to eat. 36Then they were all encouraged, and also took food themselves. 37And in all we were two hundred and seventy-six persons on the ship. 38So when they had eaten enough, they lightened the ship and threw out the wheat into the sea.

Shipwrecked on Malta

39When it was day, they did not recognize the land; but they observed a bay with a beach, onto which they planned to run the ship if possible. 40And they let go the anchors and left *them* in the sea, meanwhile loosing the rudder ropes; and they hoisted the mainsail to the wind and made for shore. 41But striking a place where two seas met, they ran the ship aground; and the prow stuck fast and remained immovable, but the stern was being broken up by the violence of the waves.

42And the soldiers' plan was to kill the prisoners, lest any of them should swim away and escape. 43But the centurion, wanting to save Paul, kept them from *their* purpose, and commanded that those who could swim should jump *overboard* first and get to land, 44and the rest, some on boards and some on *parts* of the ship. And so it was that they all escaped safely to land.

Paul's Ministry on Malta

28 1Now when they had escaped, they then found out that the island was called Malta. 2And the natives showed us unusual kindness; for they kindled a fire and made us all welcome, because of the rain that was falling and because of the cold. 3But when Paul had gathered a bundle of sticks and laid *them* on the fire, a viper came out because of the heat, and fastened on his hand. 4So when the natives saw the creature hanging from his hand, they said to one another, "No doubt this man is a murderer, whom, though he has escaped the sea, yet justice does not allow to live." 5But he shook off the creature into the fire and suffered no harm. 6However, they were expecting that he would swell up or suddenly fall down dead. But after they had looked for a long time and saw no harm come to him, they changed their minds and said that he was a god.

7In that region there was an estate of

TIME CAPSULE *A.D. 60 to 61*

60 *The Romans defeat the Druids and stop their human sacrifices*

60 *Boudicca (Boadicea) leads a revolt against the Romans in Britain*

60 *Paul and Luke arrive at Rome (Acts 28:16)*

60 *Earthquake strikes Anatolia near Colosse and Laodicea*

61 *Nero puts Gentiles over Caesarea, capital of Judea*

THE NATIVES OF MALTA (Acts 28:1, 2)

Late in the autumn of A.D. 59 a ship carrying the apostle Paul to Rome was shipwrecked on a small island. About 60 miles south of Sicily lies the island of Malta, and on the northern part of Malta is the site traditionally called "St. Paul's Bay." Some scholars believe that St. Paul's Bay fits the description of Acts 27:39 which mentions "a bay with a beach," meaning a bay with a beach suitable to run aground a ship.

Before 700 B.C. Malta was a Phoenician trading colony. Diodorus Siculus, who between 60 to 30 B.C. wrote a world history, described Malta as the place where traders stopped off for trade with Spain. The island was also located on the shipping route from Rome to Egypt.

Phoenician culture and language existed on Malta long after the Romans took control of the island in 218 B.C. The Maltese people spoke Punic, a Phoenician language of ancient Carthage. Luke refers to them as "natives" (Acts 28:2, 4), but he does not mean they were primitive or uncivilized. The Greek word *barbaros,* which is translated "native," was used by Greeks for foreigners, meaning those who were not Greek. Luke calls the Maltese people *barbaros* only because they were of Phoenician descent and did not speak Greek.

The Maltese natives were a religious people. One of their beliefs was that someone guilty of murder, or some such crime, who escaped a tragic death (such as Paul did at sea) would soon face some other form of death. So they concluded that a Phoenician deity had caused Paul's viper attack. Luke expresses their idea in Greek thought: the goddess Justice will not allow a "guilty" Paul to live (Acts 28:4).

When Paul survived, the natives' pagan beliefs led them to mistake Paul himself for a god (28:6). But the writer Luke credits the safety of Paul and those with him to another deity: God is the true protector who had a mission for Paul to fulfill (Acts 27:21–26).

---

the leading citizen of the island, whose name was Publius, who received us and entertained us courteously for three days. 8And it happened that the father of Publius lay sick of a fever and dysentery. Paul went in to him and prayed, and he laid his hands on him and healed him. 9So when this was done, the rest of those on the island who had diseases also came and were healed. 10They also honored us in many ways; and when we departed, they provided such things as were necessary.

Arrival at Rome

11After three months we sailed in an Alexandrian ship whose figurehead was the Twin Brothers, which had wintered at the island. 12And landing at Syracuse, we

On to Rome
In Jerusalem following his third missionary journey, Paul struggled with Jews who accused him of profaning the temple (Acts 21:26–34). He was placed in Roman custody in Caesarea for two years, but, after appealing to the emperor, was sent by ship to Rome. During this fourth journey (Acts 27:1–28:16), Paul's party departed from the island of Crete only to be shipwrecked on Malta by a great storm. Three months later he finally arrived at the imperial city.

stayed three days. ¹³From there we circled round and reached Rhegium. And after one day the south wind blew; and the next day we came to Puteoli, ¹⁴where we found brethren, and were invited to stay with them seven days. And so we went toward Rome. ¹⁵And from there, when the brethren heard about us, they came to meet us as far as Appii Forum and Three Inns. When Paul saw them, he thanked God and took courage.

Imprisonment in Rome

According to the Book of Acts, Paul spent 2 years under house arrest in Rome (Acts 28:16, 30). Acts is silent, however, regarding what happened to him at the end of that time, in late A.D. 62 or early 63. Some scholars argue that Luke intended the prophecy of Paul's martyrdom (Acts 20:24, 38) to inform the reader about his fate. Paul's execution under Nero sometime between the summers of A.D. 62 and 64 would also fit with two developments in Roman history of this period. First, Nero reinstated laws against treason in early 62, and Paul's execution may have been ordered based on such a charge (though Paul claims innocence of such; see Acts 25:8). Second, Nero married Poppaea in the spring of A.D. 62. Her strong support of the Jews may have negatively influenced the disposition of Paul's case.

Other scholars have suggested that Paul, after 2 years of imprisonment, was released about A.D. 63. He then carried on further missionary work in Macedonia (see 1 Tim. 1:3) and, according to some early Christian traditions, possibly also in Spain (see Rom. 15:28). Details of the end of Paul's life are unknown. Apparently he was subsequently rearrested and imprisoned, and Tertullian describes Paul's execution by beheading. Eusebius, the church historian, dates Paul's death in A.D. 67.

■ Acts 28:16–31

Acts

28 **:16** Now when we came to Rome, the centurion delivered the prisoners to the captain of the guard; but Paul was permitted to dwell by himself with the soldier who guarded him.

Paul's Ministry at Rome

¹⁷And it came to pass after three days that Paul called the leaders of the Jews together. So when they had come together, he said to them: "Men *and* brethren, though I have done nothing against our people or the customs of our fathers, yet I was delivered as a prisoner from Jerusalem into the hands of the Romans, ¹⁸who, when they had examined me, wanted to let *me* go, because there was no cause for putting me to death. ¹⁹But when the Jewsᵃ spoke against *it,* I was compelled to appeal to Caesar, not that I had anything of which to accuse my nation. ²⁰For this reason therefore I have called for you, to see *you* and speak with *you,* because for the hope of Israel I am bound with this chain."

²¹Then they said to him, "We neither received letters from Judea concerning you, nor have any of the brethren who came reported or spoken any evil of you. ²²But we desire to hear from you what you think; for concerning this sect, we know that it is spoken against everywhere."

²³So when they had appointed him a day, many came to him at *his* lodging, to whom he explained and solemnly testified of the kingdom of God, persuading them concerning Jesus from both the Law of Moses and the Prophets, from morning till evening. ²⁴And some were persuaded by the things which were spoken, and some disbelieved. ²⁵So when they did not agree among themselves, they departed after Paul had said one word: "The Holy Spirit spoke rightly through Isaiah the prophet to ourᵃ fathers, ²⁶saying,

> 'Go to this people and say:
> "Hearing you will hear, and shall not
>   understand;
> And seeing you will see, and not
>   perceive;
27   For the hearts of this people have
>   grown dull.
> Their ears are hard of hearing,
> And their eyes they have closed,
> Lest they should see with their eyes
>   and hear with their ears,
> Lest they should understand with
>   their hearts and turn,
> So that I should heal them." 'ᵃ

²⁸"Therefore let it be known to you that the salvation of God has been sent to the Gentiles, and they will hear it!" ²⁹And when he had said these words, the Jews

28:19 ᵃThat is, the ruling authorities
28:25 ᵃNU-Text reads *your.*   28:27 ᵃIsaiah 6:9,
10

departed and had a great dispute among themselves.[a]

30Then Paul dwelt two whole years in his own rented house, and received all who came to him, 31preaching the kingdom of God and teaching the things which concern the Lord Jesus Christ with all confidence, no one forbidding him.

28:29 [a]NU-Text omits this verse.
Philem. 1:2 [a]NU-Text reads *to our sister Apphia.*
1:6 [a]NU-Text and M-Text read *us.*   1:7 [a]NU-Text
reads *had.*   [b]M-Text reads *thanksgiving.*
1:12 [a]NU-Text reads *back to you in person, that is,
my own heart.*

The Letter to Philemon

Philemon probably lived in the Lycus Valley where Colosse and Laodicea were located (see Col. 4:15). He was a close friend of Paul, indebted to him spiritually, and a helper in his ministry (Philem. 1:1, 19). Onesimus, Philemon's slave, had run away and been converted by Paul. Paul offers two reasons for writing this letter to Philemon: (1) an appeal for him to receive Onesimus as a brother in Christ (1:10–17), and (2) a request for him to prepare a guest room for Paul's coming visit (1:22).

The letters to Philemon and to the Colossians were possibly written by Paul at the same time, about A.D. 62, during his imprisonment at Rome (Acts 28:16–31). Paul described himself both as a prisoner (Philem. 1:1, 9, 23) and as being aged (1:9). Many of the people mentioned in Philemon are also mentioned in Colossians: Archippus (Col. 4:17), Onesimus (Col. 4:9), Epaphras (Col. 1:7; 4:12), Mark, Aristarchus (Col. 4:10), Demas, and Luke (Col. 4:14). Onesimus and Tychicus (Col. 4:7–9) were the bearers of these letters.

An earlier imprisonment, either in Ephesus around A.D. 54 or 55 or in Caesarea, has also been suggested as the time of Paul's writing (see "The Letter to the Philippians" at Phil. 1:1). Ephesus is closer to Colosse than is Rome, thus the close proximity of Ephesus would make more likely both the capture of the runaway slave Onesimus, as well as Paul's own hopes to visit Philemon in the near future (Philem. 1:22). Nevertheless, the chance that Paul wrote from his Caesarean imprisonment (see "Paul Escorted to Caesarea" at Acts 23:23) has been considered, although Caesarea is even farther from Colosse than Rome.

■ Philemon 1:1–25

Philemon

Greeting

1 :1 Paul, a prisoner of Christ Jesus, and Timothy *our* brother,

To Philemon our beloved *friend* and fellow laborer, 2to the beloved[a] Apphia, Archippus our fellow soldier, and to the church in your house:

3Grace to you and peace from God our Father and the Lord Jesus Christ.

Philemon's Love and Faith

4I thank my God, making mention of you always in my prayers, 5hearing of your love and faith which you have toward the Lord Jesus and toward all the saints, 6that the sharing of your faith may become effective by the acknowledgment of every good thing which is in you[a] in Christ Jesus. 7For we have[a] great joy[b] and consolation in your love, because the hearts of the saints have been refreshed by you, brother.

The Plea for Onesimus

8Therefore, though I might be very bold in Christ to command you what is fitting, 9yet for love's sake I rather appeal *to you*—being such a one as Paul, the aged, and now also a prisoner of Jesus Christ— 10I appeal to you for my son Onesimus, whom I have begotten *while* in my chains, 11who once was unprofitable to you, but now is profitable to you and to me.

12I am sending him back.[a] You therefore receive him, that is, my own heart, 13whom I wished to keep with me, that on your behalf he might minister to me in my chains for the gospel. 14But without your consent I wanted to do nothing, that your good deed might not be by compulsion, as it were, but voluntary.

15For perhaps he departed for a while for this *purpose,* that you might receive him forever, 16no longer as a slave but more than a slave—a beloved brother, especially to me but how much more to you, both in the flesh and in the Lord.

Philemon's Obedience Encouraged

17If then you count me as a partner, receive him as *you would* me. 18But if he has wronged you or owes anything, put that on my account. 19I, Paul, am writing with my own hand. I will repay—not to mention to

MORE THAN A SLAVE (Philem. 1:16)

Roman law in some respects treated slaves as persons but also viewed them economically as property. While slaves could hold property and buy their freedom, they also could be beaten and interrogated under torture. In the rare case where a head of a household was murdered by one of his slaves, all of his slaves would be executed. Thus, the term "beloved brother" (Philem. 1:16), as Paul calls Onesimus, indicated something more than a slave.

Onesimus was probably a household slave, the only type of slave addressed in Paul's letters, which were written to urban congregations. Household slaves had greater opportunities for social advancement than did free peasants, and, in prominent households, often became powerful. Indeed, some noble women even married slaves of Caesar, thereby becoming slaves, to increase their social status! By saving money on the side, household slaves often purchased their freedom, and, with help from their former slaveholders, sometimes attained social prominence and wealth.

Slaveholders would send their trusted slaves, especially the more educated ones, on errands, often with money. Occasionally a slave chose to escape rather than return home, dangerous as such a venture was. Such may be the situation faced by Onesimus.

Roman law required Paul to return Onesimus to his master Philemon, or else face severe punishment. Paul does not advise Philemon to receive back Onesimus as a slave; he invites Philemon to embrace him as a brother. The letter to Philemon took the form of a "letter of recommendation," in which a person of equal or higher status asked a favor for a person of lower status.

Escaped slaves, once recaptured, normally received severe punishment. One option for the slave was to seek out an advocate who would beseech the slaveowner on the slave's behalf. In one situation, a close parallel to Paul's letter, a Roman writer requested clemency for an escaped slave. Paul, however, asks not merely for clemency, but for Onesimus's freedom.

---

you that you owe me even your own self besides. ²⁰Yes, brother, let me have joy from you in the Lord; refresh my heart in the Lord.

²¹Having confidence in your obedience, I write to you, knowing that you will do even more than I say. ²²But, meanwhile, also prepare a guest room for me, for I trust that through your prayers I shall be granted to you.

Farewell

²³Epaphras, my fellow prisoner in Christ Jesus, greets you, ²⁴as do Mark, Aristarchus, Demas, Luke, my fellow laborers.

²⁵The grace of our Lord Jesus Christ be with your spirit. Amen.

The Letter to the Colossians

The Book of Colossians is closely related to the books of Ephesians and Philemon. Colossians was probably written before Ephesians, with which it shares main ideas and a general outline. Ephesians seems to expand some of the key ideas of Colossians.

Paul wrote this epistle from prison, as he did Philippians and Philemon. Some scholars believe this was during a first imprisonment in Rome (see "Imprisonment in Rome" at Acts 28:16). Colossians could then have been written about A.D. 62, not long before Paul's release. Yet others would place the writing of this letter during an Ephesian imprisonment around A.D. 54 or 55 (see "The Letter to the

POLITICS AND GOVERNMENT

In the Roman Empire, slaves were not permitted to marry, and any children they did have belonged to their owners. Slaves were at the service of their owners, male or female, who were free to punish or kill any slave who "wronged" them (Philem. 1:18). Even though there were few slave revolts, the fear that slaves would revolt or harm their owners was always present.

Philippians" at Phil. 1:1, and "The Letter to Philemon" at Philem. 1:1).

The significant difference of the Greek vocabulary and style in Colossians from that of other Pauline letters raises a question whether Paul actually wrote Colossians. Some scholars argue that the theology of the letter and the understanding and organization of the church are more developed than in letters Paul himself wrote. This may indicate that Colossians was written by one of Paul's associates in the decade following his death (perhaps between A.D. 70–75).

Colosse was located on the south bank of the Lycus River near Laodicea and Hierapolis in western Asia Minor, about 100 miles east of Ephesus on the important trade route between Ephesus and the Euphrates Valley. Paul had never visited Colosse, but the gospel had been preached there, as well as in Laodicea and Hierapolis, while he was in Ephesus.

This letter deals primarily with doctrinal heresy that possibly mixed Judaism with some early form of Gnosticism. Jesus was superhuman, but not truly God. He was greater than human beings, but not great enough to be the Savior. Those who believe in Christ must go through angels to get to the deeper levels of spirituality. Paul built a positive case for the Christian truth in order to show the Colossians the futility of ideas such as these.

■ Colossians 1:1—4:18

Colossians
Greeting

1 :1 Paul, an apostle of Jesus Christ by the will of God, and Timothy our brother,

2To the saints and faithful brethren in Christ *who are* in Colosse:

Grace to you and peace from God our Father and the Lord Jesus Christ.ᵃ

1:2 ᵃNU-Text omits *and the Lord Jesus Christ.*
1:6 ᵃNU-Text and M-Text add *and growing.*
1:14 ᵃNU-Text and M-Text omit *through His blood.*

Their Faith in Christ

3We give thanks to the God and Father of our Lord Jesus Christ, praying always for you, 4since we heard of your faith in Christ Jesus and of your love for all the saints; 5because of the hope which is laid up for you in heaven, of which you heard before in the word of the truth of the gospel, 6which has come to you, as *it has* also in all the world, and is bringing forth fruit,ᵃ as *it is* also among you since the day you heard and knew the grace of God in truth; 7as you also learned from Epaphras, our dear fellow servant, who is a faithful minister of Christ on your behalf, 8who also declared to us your love in the Spirit.

Preeminence of Christ

9For this reason we also, since the day we heard it, do not cease to pray for you, and to ask that you may be filled with the knowledge of His will in all wisdom and spiritual understanding; 10that you may walk worthy of the Lord, fully pleasing *Him,* being fruitful in every good work and increasing in the knowledge of God; 11strengthened with all might, according to His glorious power, for all patience and longsuffering with joy; 12giving thanks to the Father who has qualified us to be partakers of the inheritance of the saints in the light. 13He has delivered us from the power of darkness and conveyed *us* into the kingdom of the Son of His love, 14in whom we have redemption through His blood,ᵃ the forgiveness of sins.

15He is the image of the invisible God, the firstborn over all creation. 16For by Him all things were created that are in heaven and that are on earth, visible and invisible, whether thrones or dominions or principalities or powers. All things were created through Him and for Him. 17And He is before all things, and in Him all things consist. 18And He is the head of the body, the church, who is the beginning, the firstborn from the dead, that in all things He may have the preeminence.

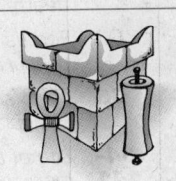

RELIGION AND WORSHIP

Among the most popular religions of the ancient world were the so-called mystery religions. Details of the initiations, rituals, and doctrines of these religions were kept secret from outsiders. Standard elements were purification, fasting, sacrifice, and ceremonial banquets. Early Christianity showed similarities to the mystery religions, including the idea of "mystery" (Col. 1:25–27).

Reconciled in Christ

[19]For it pleased *the Father that* in Him all the fullness should dwell, [20]and by Him to reconcile all things to Himself, by Him, whether things on earth or things in heaven, having made peace through the blood of His cross.

[21]And you, who once were alienated and enemies in your mind by wicked works, yet now He has reconciled [22]in the body of His flesh through death, to present you holy, and blameless, and above reproach in His sight— [23]if indeed you continue in the faith, grounded and steadfast, and are not moved away from the hope of the gospel which you heard, which was preached to every creature under heaven, of which I, Paul, became a minister.

Sacrificial Service for Christ

[24]I now rejoice in my sufferings for you, and fill up in my flesh what is lacking in the afflictions of Christ, for the sake of His body, which is the church, [25]of which I became a minister according to the stewardship from God which was given to me for you, to fulfill the word of God, [26]the mystery which has been hidden from ages and from generations, but now has been revealed to His saints. [27]To them God willed to make known what are the riches of the glory of this mystery among the Gentiles: which[a] is Christ in you, the hope of glory. [28]Him we preach, warning every man and teaching every man in all wisdom, that we may present every man perfect in Christ Jesus. [29]To this *end* I also labor, striving according to His working which works in me mightily.

Not Philosophy but Christ

2 [1]For I want you to know what a great conflict I have for you and those in Laodicea, and *for* as many as have not seen my face in the flesh, [2]that their hearts may be encouraged, being knit together in love, and *attaining* to all riches of the full assurance of understanding, to the knowledge of the mystery of God, both of the Father and[a] of Christ, [3]in whom are hidden all the treasures of wisdom and knowledge.

[4]Now this I say lest anyone should deceive you with persuasive words. [5]For though I am absent in the flesh, yet I am with you in spirit, rejoicing to see your *good* order and the steadfastness of your faith in Christ.

[6]As you therefore have received Christ Jesus the Lord, so walk in Him, [7]rooted and built up in Him and established in the faith, as you have been taught, abounding in it[a] with thanksgiving.

[8]Beware lest anyone cheat you through philosophy and empty deceit, according to the tradition of men, according to the basic principles of the world, and not according to Christ. [9]For in Him dwells all the fullness of the Godhead bodily; [10]and you are complete in Him, who is the head of all principality and power.

Not Legalism but Christ

[11]In Him you were also circumcised with the circumcision made without hands, by putting off the body of the sins[a] of the flesh, by the circumcision of Christ, [12]buried with Him in baptism, in which you also were raised with *Him* through faith in the working of God, who raised Him from the dead. [13]And you, being dead in your trespasses and the uncircumcision of your flesh, He has made alive together with Him, having forgiven you all trespasses, [14]having wiped out the handwriting of requirements that was against us, which was contrary to us. And He has taken it out of the way, having nailed it to the cross. [15]Having disarmed principalities and powers, He made a public spectacle of them, triumphing over them in it.

[16]So let no one judge you in food or in drink, or regarding a festival or a new moon or sabbaths, [17]which are a shadow of

---

TIME CAPSULE *A.D. 62 to 64*

62 *Paul writes to Philemon from Rome*

62 *Paul writes to the Colossians and Ephesians from Rome (?)*

62 *The apostle James is stoned to death*

62 *Festus is succeeded by Albinus as procurator*

63 *Nero sends a military expedition to Ethiopia*

64– 141 *Life of the Greek writer Philo of Byblos*

1:27 [a]M-Text reads *who.* 2:2 [a]NU-Text omits *both of the Father and.* 2:7 [a]NU-Text omits *in it.* 2:11 [a]NU-Text omits *of the sins.*

things to come, but the substance is of Christ. [18]Let no one cheat you of your reward, taking delight in *false* humility and worship of angels, intruding into those things which he has not[a] seen, vainly puffed up by his fleshly mind, [19]and not holding fast to the Head, from whom all the body, nourished and knit together by joints and ligaments, grows with the increase *that is* from God.

[20]Therefore,[a] if you died with Christ from the basic principles of the world, why, as *though* living in the world, do you subject yourselves to regulations— [21]"Do not touch, do not taste, do not handle," [22]which all concern things which perish with the using—according to the commandments and doctrines of men? [23]These things indeed have an appearance of wisdom in self-imposed religion, *false* humility, and neglect of the body, *but are* of no value against the indulgence of the flesh.

Not Carnality but Christ

3 [1]If then you were raised with Christ, seek those things which are above, where Christ is, sitting at the right hand of God. [2]Set your mind on things above, not on things on the earth. [3]For you died, and your life is hidden with Christ in God. [4]When Christ *who is* our life appears, then you also will appear with Him in glory.

[5]Therefore put to death your members which are on the earth: fornication, uncleanness, passion, evil desire, and covetousness, which is idolatry. [6]Because of these things the wrath of God is coming upon the sons of disobedience, [7]in which you yourselves once walked when you lived in them.

[8]But now you yourselves are to put off all these: anger, wrath, malice, blasphemy, filthy language out of your mouth. [9]Do not lie to one another, since you have put off the old man with his deeds, [10]and have put on the new *man* who is renewed in knowledge according to the image of Him who created him, [11]where there is neither Greek nor Jew, circumcised nor uncircumcised, barbarian, Scythian, slave *nor* free, but Christ *is* all and in all.

Character of the New Man

[12]Therefore, as *the* elect of God, holy and beloved, put on tender mercies, kindness, humility, meekness, longsuffering; [13]bearing with one another, and forgiving one another, if anyone has a complaint against another; even as Christ forgave you, so you also *must do*. [14]But above all these things put on love, which is the bond of perfection. [15]And let the peace of God rule in your hearts, to which also you were called in one body; and be thankful. [16]Let the word of Christ dwell in you richly in all wisdom, teaching and admonishing one another in psalms and hymns and spiritual songs, singing with grace in your hearts to the Lord. [17]And *whatever* you do in word or deed, *do* all in the name of the Lord Jesus, giving thanks to God the Father through Him.

The Christian Home

[18]Wives, submit to your own husbands, as is fitting in the Lord.

[19]Husbands, love your wives and do not be bitter toward them.

[20]Children, obey your parents in all things, for this is well pleasing to the Lord.

[21]Fathers, do not provoke your children, lest they become discouraged.

[22]Bondservants, obey in all things your masters according to the flesh, not with eyeservice, as men-pleasers, but in sincerity of heart, fearing God. [23]And whatever you do, do it heartily, as to the Lord and not to men, [24]knowing that from the Lord you will receive the reward of the inheritance; for[a] you serve the Lord Christ. [25]But he who does wrong will be repaid for what he has done, and there is no partiality.

4 [1]Masters, give your bondservants what is just and fair, knowing that you also have a Master in heaven.

Christian Graces

[2]Continue earnestly in prayer, being vigilant in it with thanksgiving; [3]meanwhile praying also for us, that God would open to us a door for the word, to speak the mystery of Christ, for which I am also in chains, [4]that I may make it manifest, as I ought to speak.

[5]Walk in wisdom toward those *who are* outside, redeeming the time. [6]*Let* your speech always *be* with grace, seasoned with salt, that you may know how you ought to answer each one.

2:18 [a]NU-Text omits *not*.   2:20 [a]NU-Text and M-Text omit *Therefore*.   3:24 [a]NU-Text omits *for*.

FAMILY VALUES IN THE HOUSEHOLD (Col. 3:18, 19)

Romans in the 1st century felt that religions from the East, such as Judaism, Christianity, and the worship of Isis, undermined traditional Roman family values. Because religious groups were sometimes expelled from Rome, members of persecuted minority religions often adopted traditional "household codes" to prove that they would uphold traditional Roman values. Philosophers from the time of Aristotle onward detailed these "household codes," which showed the male head of the household how to rule his wife, children, and slaves.

The structure of these traditional codes was adopted in Christian letters, including wives, husbands (and fathers), children, slaves, and slaveholders (Col. 3:18—4:1). The Christian adaptation balanced commands for those who were socially inferior (wives, children, bondservants) with responsibilities for the socially superior (husbands, fathers, masters).

The Christian codes, such as one in Eph. 5, differ considerably from traditional household codes. They address wives, children, and slaves themselves, and not just the male head of the household. They do not tell the husband how to "rule" his wife, but how to love her (Eph. 5:25). Although traditional Greek and Roman values demanded the wife's quiet obedience, the Christian code defines "submission" primarily in terms of respect (Eph. 5:33). The wife's submission was based on the broader Christian virtue of servanthood, which applied to all Christians—husbands as well as wives (Eph. 5:21).

Final Greetings

7Tychicus, a beloved brother, faithful minister, and fellow servant in the Lord, will tell you all the news about me. 8I am sending him to you for this very purpose, that he[a] may know your circumstances and comfort your hearts, 9with Onesimus, a faithful and beloved brother, who is *one* of you. They will make known to you all things which *are happening* here.

10Aristarchus my fellow prisoner greets you, with Mark the cousin of Barnabas (about whom you received instructions: if he comes to you, welcome him), 11and Jesus who is called Justus. These *are* my only fellow workers for the kingdom of God who are of the circumcision; they have proved to be a comfort to me.

12Epaphras, who is *one* of you, a bondservant of Christ, greets you, always laboring fervently for you in prayers, that you may stand perfect and complete[a] in all the will of God. 13For I bear him witness that he has a great zeal[a] for you, and those who are in Laodicea, and those in Hierapolis. 14Luke the beloved physician and Demas greet you. 15Greet the brethren who are in Laodicea, and Nymphas and the church that *is* in his[a] house.

Closing Exhortations and Blessing

16Now when this epistle is read among you, see that it is read also in the church of the Laodiceans, and that you likewise read the epistle from Laodicea. 17And say to Archippus, "Take heed to the ministry which you have received in the Lord, that you may fulfill it."

18This salutation by my own hand—Paul. Remember my chains. Grace *be* with you. Amen.

4:8 [a]NU-Text reads *you may know our circumstances and he may.* 4:12 [a]NU-Text reads *fully assured.* 4:13 [a]NU-Text reads *concern.*
4:15 [a]NU-Text reads *Nympha . . . her house.*

HEALTH AND MEDICINE

The range of medical tools that have been recovered by archaeologists, especially from the ruins of Pompeii and Herculaneum, show that physicians, such as Luke (Col. 4:14), performed many kinds of physical procedures. The equipment for childbirth and delivery is quite modern in its appearance, although made of bronze rather than steel.

CITIES IN THE LYCUS VALLEY (Col. 4:12, 13)

Near the end of Paul's letter to the Colossians is a comment concerning a Christian named Epaphras. Apparently, Epaphras had worked fervently for the cause of Christians in Colosse, as well as for those in Laodicea and Hierapolis (Col. 4:12, 13). These three cities— Colosse, Laodicea, Hierapolis—were the largest cities in the Lycus Valley of Anatolian Phrygia.

All three cities were situated near the Lycus River: Colosse being about 11 miles south-east of Laodicea and 15 miles southeast of Hierapolis. Their locations positioned them on a major trade route from the Orient to the Aegean coast, and all were prosperous in the textile industry. Colosse, in particular, was known primarily for its purple wool.

The city of Colosse had been a major center for at least 5 centuries before Paul's time. However, it was eventually overshadowed in influence by Laodicea. The Colosse addressed in Paul's letter, now part of the Roman province of Asia Minor, was a smaller, less important city, while Laodicea had become the most prominent city in the Lycus Valley. At the letter's close, the Colossians are urged to forward the writing to the church in Laodicea, and also to read what was sent to Laodicea (Col. 4:16).

In the early A.D. 60s an earthquake rocked this area of Anatolia. Laodicea, though de-stroyed by the natural disaster, was able to rebuild. The threat of such earthquakes, however, may have caused the local population of Colosse to relocate to the nearby town of Chonaz.

The Letter to the Ephesians

Although the first verse in most manu-scripts of this letter reads "To the saints who are in Ephesus," other early copies lack the words "in Ephesus." The letter also does not follow Paul's usual practice of including per-sonal greetings to many friends in the city to which he wrote. One 2nd-century writer even cites this letter by the title "To the Laodiceans." It may be that Paul sent copies of this letter to a number of churches in the region, either supplying the name of each city in the opening greeting or leaving the destination out if the copy was to circulate to several churches.

Ephesians is closely related to Colossians. No other two letters are so similar as these, either in outline and outlook, or in general theme. Half of the verses in Ephesians contain expressions identical to those in Colossians. It is as though Paul wrote Colossians first to meet some special needs of the church there, and then felt that a letter to be circulated among all the churches in Asia Minor ought to elaborate on some of the Colossian themes. The similarities could suggest that both letters were written at about the same time, being composed during Paul's Caesarean or Roman imprisonments (see "The Letter to the Colos-sians" at Col. 1:1).

As is the case with Colossians, there are doubts whether Paul actually wrote the letter to the Ephesians. Like Colossians, the lan-guage and theological development in Ephe-sians is more elaborate than that found in Paul's earlier letters. The tremendous similari-ties between these two letters leads some to conclude that Ephesians was actually based on Colossians. Some have even suggested that Ephesians may have been written as a kind of introduction to Paul's theology by an associate who was collecting Paul's letters in the years after his death.

Ephesus was a chief city of the west coast of Asia Minor, situated at the mouth of the Cayster River. Paul visited the city on the re-turn part of his second missionary journey, staying only briefly (Acts 18:19–21). He re-turned on his third journey to spend more than two years strengthening the church (Acts 19). The letter to the Ephesians was also intended to strengthen them, making them more con-scious of their oneness in Christ.

■ Ephesians 1:1—6:24

Ephesians
Greeting

1 :1 Paul, an apostle of Jesus Christ by the will of God,

To the saints who are in Ephesus, and faithful in Christ Jesus:

2 Grace to you and peace from God our Father and the Lord Jesus Christ.

WRITERS OF THE EARLY CHURCH

The "Apostolic Fathers" were a group of writers of the early Christian church who are thought to have been affiliated with the apostles or with their disciples. One of the fathers, Ignatius, was familiar with Paul's letters, especially the letter to the Ephesians, and himself wrote to the church "in Ephesus" (Eph. 1:1).

Writer/Writings	Date	Description
Clement	died A.D. 96	Bishop of Rome. His first letter mentions the deaths of Peter and Paul.
Ignatius	A.D. 35–107	Bishop of Antioch, executed at Rome. He wrote seven letters to the churches.
Papias	A.D. 60–130	A friend of Polycarp. He discusses how Matthew and Mark wrote their Gospels.
Polycarp	A.D. 69–155	An important church leader executed because he would not renounce Christ. He had probably met the apostle John.
Didache	1st century	The Didache ("Teaching") describes the "two ways" of life and death, and tells about worship and order in the church.
Barnabas	1st century	The Letter of Barnabas (not the apostle Barnabas) is about Judaism and Christianity.
Diognetus	2nd century	An anonymous letter of Christian instruction written to Diognetus, who is otherwise unknown.
Hermas	2nd century	Hermas wrote *The Shepherd*, a book of instruction that was highly regarded in the early church.

Redemption in Christ

³Blessed *be* the God and Father of our Lord Jesus Christ, who has blessed us with every spiritual blessing in the heavenly *places* in Christ, ⁴just as He chose us in Him before the foundation of the world, that we should be holy and without blame before Him in love, ⁵having predestined us to adoption as sons by Jesus Christ to Himself, according to the good pleasure of His will, ⁶to the praise of the glory of His grace, by which He made us accepted in the Beloved.

⁷In Him we have redemption through His blood, the forgiveness of sins, according to the riches of His grace ⁸which He made to abound toward us in all wisdom and prudence, ⁹having made known to us the mystery of His will, according to His good pleasure which He purposed in Himself, ¹⁰that in the dispensation of the fullness of the times He might gather together in one all things in Christ, both ͣ which are in heaven and which are on earth—in Him. ¹¹In Him also we have obtained an inheri-

tance, being predestined according to the purpose of Him who works all things according to the counsel of His will, ¹²that we who first trusted in Christ should be to the praise of His glory.

¹³In Him you also *trusted,* after you heard the word of truth, the gospel of your salvation; in whom also, having believed, you were sealed with the Holy Spirit of promise, ¹⁴whoͣ is the guarantee of our inheritance until the redemption of the purchased possession, to the praise of His glory.

Prayer for Spiritual Wisdom

¹⁵Therefore I also, after I heard of your faith in the Lord Jesus and your love for all the saints, ¹⁶do not cease to give thanks for you, making mention of you in my prayers: ¹⁷that the God of our Lord Jesus Christ, the Father of glory, may give to you the spirit of wisdom and revelation in the

1:10 ͣNU-Text and M-Text omit *both.*
1:14 ͣNU-Text reads *which.*

knowledge of Him, [18]the eyes of your understanding[a] being enlightened; that you may know what is the hope of His calling, what are the riches of the glory of His inheritance in the saints, [19]and what *is* the exceeding greatness of His power toward us who believe, according to the working of His mighty power [20]which He worked in Christ when He raised Him from the dead and seated *Him* at His right hand in the heavenly *places,* [21]far above all principality and power and might and dominion, and every name that is named, not only in this age but also in that which is to come.

[22]And He put all *things* under His feet, and gave Him *to be* head over all *things* to the church, [23]which is His body, the fullness of Him who fills all in all.

By Grace Through Faith

2 [1]And you *He made alive,* who were dead in trespasses and sins, [2]in which you once walked according to the course of this world, according to the prince of the power of the air, the spirit who now works in the sons of disobedience, [3]among whom also we all once conducted ourselves in the lusts of our flesh, fulfilling the desires of the flesh and of the mind, and were by nature children of wrath, just as the others.

[4]But God, who is rich in mercy, because of His great love with which He loved us, [5]even when we were dead in trespasses, made us alive together with Christ (by grace you have been saved), [6]and raised *us* up together, and made *us* sit together in the heavenly *places* in Christ Jesus, [7]that in the ages to come He might show the exceeding riches of His grace in *His* kindness toward us in Christ Jesus. [8]For by grace you have been saved through faith, and that not of yourselves; *it is* the gift of God, [9]not of works, lest anyone should boast. [10]For we are His workmanship, created in Christ Jesus for good works, which God prepared beforehand that we should walk in them.

1:18 [a]NU-Text and M-Text read *hearts.*

Brought Near by His Blood

[11]Therefore remember that you, once Gentiles in the flesh—who are called Uncircumcision by what is called the Circumcision made in the flesh by hands— [12]that at that time you were without Christ, being aliens from the commonwealth of Israel and strangers from the covenants of promise, having no hope and without God in the world. [13]But now in Christ Jesus you who once were far off have been brought near by the blood of Christ.

Christ Our Peace

[14]For He Himself is our peace, who has made both one, and has broken down the middle wall of separation, [15]having abolished in His flesh the enmity, *that is,* the law of commandments *contained* in ordinances, so as to create in Himself one new man *from* the two, *thus* making peace, [16]and that He might reconcile them both to God in one body through the cross, thereby putting to death the enmity. [17]And He came and preached peace to you who were afar off and to those who were near. [18]For through Him we both have access by one Spirit to the Father.

Christ Our Cornerstone

[19]Now, therefore, you are no longer strangers and foreigners, but fellow citizens with the saints and members of the household of God, [20]having been built on the foundation of the apostles and prophets, Jesus Christ Himself being the chief corner*stone,* [21]in whom the whole building, being fitted together, grows into a holy temple in the Lord, [22]in whom you also are being built together for a dwelling place of God in the Spirit.

The Mystery Revealed

3 [1]For this reason I, Paul, the prisoner of Christ Jesus for you Gentiles— [2]if indeed you have heard of the dispensation of the grace of God which was given to me for

ARCHITECTURE AND BUILDING

The temple built by Herod the Great was standing throughout the New Testament period up to the fall of Jerusalem in A.D. 70. In the temple area there was a wall about four and a half feet high that only Jews could go beyond (Eph. 2:14). There were warning notices carved in the wall, one of which was discovered almost intact in 1871.

you, ³how that by revelation He made known to me the mystery (as I have briefly written already, ⁴by which, when you read, you may understand my knowledge in the mystery of Christ), ⁵which in other ages was not made known to the sons of men, as it has now been revealed by the Spirit to His holy apostles and prophets: ⁶that the Gentiles should be fellow heirs, of the same body, and partakers of His promise in Christ through the gospel, ⁷of which I became a minister according to the gift of the grace of God given to me by the effective working of His power.

Purpose of the Mystery

⁸To me, who am less than the least of all the saints, this grace was given, that I should preach among the Gentiles the unsearchable riches of Christ, ⁹and to make all see what *is* the fellowshipᵃ of the mystery, which from the beginning of the ages has been hidden in God who created all things through Jesus Christ;ᵇ ¹⁰to the intent that now the manifold wisdom of God might be made known by the church to the principalities and powers in the heavenly *places,* ¹¹according to the eternal purpose which He accomplished in Christ Jesus our Lord, ¹²in whom we have boldness and access with confidence through faith in Him. ¹³Therefore I ask that you do not lose heart at my tribulations for you, which is your glory.

Appreciation of the Mystery

¹⁴For this reason I bow my knees to the Father of our Lord Jesus Christ,ᵃ ¹⁵from whom the whole family in heaven and earth is named, ¹⁶that He would grant you, according to the riches of His glory, to be strengthened with might through His Spirit in the inner man, ¹⁷that Christ may dwell in your hearts through faith; that you, being rooted and grounded in love, ¹⁸may be able to comprehend with all the saints what *is* the width and length and depth and height— ¹⁹to know the love of Christ which passes knowledge; that you may be filled with all the fullness of God.

²⁰Now to Him who is able to do exceedingly abundantly above all that we ask or think, according to the power that works in us, ²¹to Him *be* glory in the church by Christ Jesus to all generations, forever and ever. Amen.

Walk in Unity

4 ¹I, therefore, the prisoner of the Lord, beseech you to walk worthy of the calling with which you were called, ²with all lowliness and gentleness, with longsuffering, bearing with one another in love, ³endeavoring to keep the unity of the Spirit in the bond of peace. ⁴*There is* one body and one Spirit, just as you were called in one hope of your calling; ⁵one Lord, one faith, one baptism; ⁶one God and Father of all, who *is* above all, and through all, and in youᵃ all.

Spiritual Gifts

⁷But to each one of us grace was given according to the measure of Christ's gift. ⁸Therefore He says:

"When He ascended on high,
He led captivity captive,
*And gave gifts to men."*ᵃ

⁹(Now this, *"He ascended"*—what does it mean but that He also firstᵃ descended into the lower parts of the earth? ¹⁰He who descended is also the One who ascended far above all the heavens, that He might fill all things.)

¹¹And He Himself gave some *to be* apostles, some prophets, some evangelists, and some pastors and teachers, ¹²for the equipping of the saints for the work of ministry, for the edifying of the body of Christ, ¹³till we all come to the unity of the faith and of the knowledge of the Son of God, to a perfect man, to the measure of the stature of the fullness of Christ; ¹⁴that we should no longer be children, tossed to and fro and carried about with every wind of doctrine, by the trickery of men, in the cunning craftiness of deceitful plotting, ¹⁵but, speaking the truth in love, may grow up in all things into Him who is the head— Christ— ¹⁶from whom the whole body, joined and knit together by what every joint supplies, according to the effective working by which every part does its share, causes growth of the body for the edifying of itself in love.

3:9 ᵃNU-Text and M-Text read *stewardship* (dispensation). ᵇNU-Text omits *through Jesus Christ.*   3:14 ᵃNU-Text omits *of our Lord Jesus Christ.*   4:6 ᵃNU-Text omits *you;* M-Text reads *us.*
4:8 ᵃPsalm 68:18   4:9 ᵃNU-Text omits *first.*

The New Man

17This I say, therefore, and testify in the Lord, that you should no longer walk as the rest of a the Gentiles walk, in the futility of their mind, 18having their understanding darkened, being alienated from the life of God, because of the ignorance that is in them, because of the blindness of their heart; 19who, being past feeling, have given themselves over to lewdness, to work all uncleanness with greediness.

20But you have not so learned Christ, 21if indeed you have heard Him and have been taught by Him, as the truth is in Jesus: 22that you put off, concerning your former conduct, the old man which grows corrupt according to the deceitful lusts, 23and be renewed in the spirit of your mind, 24and that you put on the new man which was created according to God, in true righteousness and holiness.

Do Not Grieve the Spirit

25Therefore, putting away lying, *"Let each one of you speak truth with his neighbor,"* a for we are members of one another. 26*"Be angry, and do not sin":*a do not let the sun go down on your wrath, 27nor give place to the devil. 28Let him who stole steal no longer, but rather let him labor, working with *his* hands what is good, that he may have something to give him who has need. 29Let no corrupt word proceed out of your mouth, but what is good for necessary edification, that it may impart grace to the hearers. 30And do not grieve the Holy Spirit of God, by whom you were sealed for the day of redemption. 31Let all bitterness, wrath, anger, clamor, and evil speaking be put away from you, with all malice. 32And be kind to one another, tenderhearted, forgiving one another, even as God in Christ forgave you.

Walk in Love

5 1Therefore be imitators of God as dear children. 2And walk in love, as Christ also has loved us and given Himself for us, an offering and a sacrifice to God for a sweet-smelling aroma.

3But fornication and all uncleanness or covetousness, let it not even be named among you, as is fitting for saints; 4neither filthiness, nor foolish talking, nor coarse jesting, which are not fitting, but rather giving of thanks. 5For this you know,a that no fornicator, unclean person, nor covetous man, who is an idolater, has any inheritance in the kingdom of Christ and God. 6Let no one deceive you with empty words, for because of these things the wrath of God comes upon the sons of disobedience. 7Therefore do not be partakers with them.

Walk in Light

8For you were once darkness, but now *you are* light in the Lord. Walk as children of light 9(for the fruit of the Spirita *is* in all goodness, righteousness, and truth), 10finding out what is acceptable to the Lord. 11And have no fellowship with the unfruitful works of darkness, but rather expose *them.* 12For it is shameful even to speak of those things which are done by them in secret. 13But all things that are exposed are made manifest by the light, for whatever makes manifest is light. 14Therefore He says:

"Awake, you who sleep,
Arise from the dead,
And Christ will give you light."

Walk in Wisdom

15See then that you walk circumspectly, not as fools but as wise, 16redeeming the time, because the days are evil. 17Therefore do not be unwise, but understand what the will of the Lord *is.* 18And do not be drunk with wine, in which is dissipation; but be filled with the Spirit, 19speaking to one another in psalms and hymns and spiritual songs, singing and making melody in your heart to the Lord, 20giving thanks always for all things to God the Father in the name of our Lord Jesus Christ, 21submitting to one another in the fear of God.a

Marriage—Christ and the Church

22Wives, submit to your own husbands, as to the Lord. 23For the husband is head of the wife, as also Christ is head of the church; and He is the Savior of the body. 24Therefore, just as the church is subject to Christ, so *let* the wives *be* to their own husbands in everything. 25Husbands, love your wives, just as

---

4:17 aNU-Text omits the rest of.
4:25 aZechariah 8:16   4:26 aPsalm 4:4
5:5 aNU-Text reads For know this.   5:9 aNU-Text reads light.   5:21 aNU-Text reads Christ.

WIVES SUBMITTING TO HUSBANDS (Eph. 5:22)

The nature of marriage in Asia Minor was very different from marriage today. In the Greek culture that was dominant in and around Ephesus, husbands were on average 12 or more years older than their wives, were usually more educated, and held much higher social status, than their wives. In one traditional Greek formulation, men used prostitutes for pleasure and wives only to bear them legitimate children.

In most of the Greco-Roman world, marital practices placed women at a disadvantage. Marriage contracts forbade a woman to leave the marital home without her husband's permission. In parts of the eastern Mediterranean a wife not wearing a shawl over her hair in public could be divorced for unfaithfulness, and a woman not divorced or widowed was under the legal control of her father or husband.

Paul's command "Wives, submit to your own husbands" (Eph. 5:22) is at least partly related to concern for Christian witness within the surrounding culture, and is quite mild in comparison to the rest of his culture. What is significant is that Paul modified the culture's values, calling on all believers to submit (5:21), and allowing the husband-wife relationship to be affected by the God-human relationship. Wives were to submit "as to the Lord" (Eph. 5:22), and husbands were to love their wives "as Christ also loved the church" (5:25). While Romans and Greeks supposed that husbands would love their wives, Paul listed such as a command.

Christ also loved the church and gave Himself for her, 26that He might sanctify and cleanse her with the washing of water by the word, 27that He might present her to Himself a glorious church, not having spot or wrinkle or any such thing, but that she should be holy and without blemish. 28So husbands ought to love their own wives as their own bodies; he who loves his wife loves himself. 29For no one ever hated his own flesh, but nourishes and cherishes it, just as the Lord *does* the church. 30For we are members of His body,[a] of His flesh and of His bones. 31*"For this reason a man shall leave his father and mother and be joined to his wife, and the two shall become one flesh."* [a] 32This is a great mystery, but I speak concerning Christ and the church. 33Nevertheless let each one of you in particular so love his own wife as himself, and let the wife *see* that she respects *her* husband.

Children and Parents

6 1Children, obey your parents in the Lord, for this is right. 2*"Honor your father and mother,"* which is the first commandment with promise: 3*"that it may be well with you and you may live long on the earth."* [a]

4And you, fathers, do not provoke your children to wrath, but bring them up in the training and admonition of the Lord.

Bondservants and Masters

5Bondservants, be obedient to those who are your masters according to the flesh, with fear and trembling, in sincerity of heart, as to Christ; 6not with eyeservice, as men-pleasers, but as bondservants of Christ, doing the will of God from the heart, 7with goodwill doing service, as to the Lord, and not to men, 8knowing that whatever good anyone does, he will receive the same from the Lord, whether *he is* a slave or free.

9And you, masters, do the same things to them, giving up threatening, knowing that your own Master also[a] is in heaven, and there is no partiality with Him.

The Whole Armor of God

10Finally, my brethren, be strong in the Lord and in the power of His might. 11Put on the whole armor of God, that you may be able to stand against the wiles of the devil. 12For we do not wrestle against flesh and blood, but against principalities, against powers, against the rulers of the darkness of this age,[a] against spiritual *hosts* of wickedness in the heavenly *places.*

5:30 [a]NU-Text omits the rest of this verse.
5:31 [a]Genesis 2:24   6:3 [a]Deuteronomy
5:16   6:9 [a]NU-Text reads *He who is both their Master and yours.*   6:12 [a]NU-Text reads *rulers of this darkness.*

BONDSERVANTS, BE OBEDIENT! (Eph. 6:5–9)

Paul had no reason to address the issue of slavery per se in his letters to churches. He touched on the behavior of different groups within the churches, discussing how slaves should respond to their situation, but he did not write concerning whether or not slavery itself should be abolished. His advice to slaves was to "be obedient," serving as if doing the will of God (Eph. 6:5, 6).

Advocating revolt was not a practical solution. Individual slaves often escaped and some small groups revolted, but all three earlier, full-scale slave wars which occurred in the Roman world, seeking to liberate more slaves, had ended in violent defeat. In view of the persecution Christians faced as a small sect sometimes viewed as socially subversive, it was far more important to urge all Christians to work for the time being within the social system that already existed.

Some philosophers (especially the Stoics) affirmed the theoretical equality of masters and servants. What these philosophers meant by equality was probably that slaves were personally equal in humanity, rather than that all slaves should be freed. Nevertheless, some did question whether slavery should exist, and long before Paul's time Aristotle (384–322 B.C.) had complained of philosophers who suggested that slavery was against nature, by which they meant that it was immoral.

Paul explains his position somewhat more fully than did the philosophers. After calling on slaves to serve their masters, he calls on masters to "serve" their slaves—"do the same things to them" (Eph. 6:9). Such advice was hardly conventional in the traditional household codes, which instructed masters how to *rule* their slaves. Instead, Paul advises Christian masters to serve Christ by acting differently than pagan masters. Their "Master in heaven" (6:9) would judge both them and their slaves on the same basis. We can imagine that, had the question been put to him, Paul would have regarded slavery itself as contrary to God's will.

¹³Therefore take up the whole armor of God, that you may be able to withstand in the evil day, and having done all, to stand. ¹⁴Stand therefore, having girded your waist with truth, having put on the breastplate of righteousness, ¹⁵and having shod your feet with the preparation of the gospel of peace; ¹⁶above all, taking the shield of faith with which you will be able to quench all the fiery darts of the wicked one. ¹⁷And take the helmet of salvation, and the sword of the Spirit, which is the word of God; ¹⁸praying always with all prayer and supplication in the Spirit, being watchful to this end with all perseverance and supplication for all the saints— ¹⁹and for me, that utterance may be given to me, that I may open my mouth boldly to make known the mystery of the gospel, ²⁰for which I am an ambassador in chains; that in it I may speak boldly, as I ought to speak.

A Gracious Greeting

²¹But that you also may know my affairs *and* how I am doing, Tychicus, a beloved brother and faithful minister in the Lord, will make all things known to you; ²²whom I have sent to you for this very purpose, that you may know our affairs, and *that* he may comfort your hearts.

²³Peace to the brethren, and love with faith, from God the Father and the Lord

SCIENCE AND TECHNOLOGY

The Roman shield as depicted on the Trajan column of A.D. 113 was a curved rectangle, like part of the side of a cylinder. It covered from the shoulders to the middle of the thighs and was decorated with stylized lightning bolts. Julius Caesar described how a group of soldiers could interlock their shields like roof tiles and march together protected that way (Eph. 6:16).

Jesus Christ. ²⁴Grace *be* with all those who love our Lord Jesus Christ in sincerity. Amen.

The First Letter to Timothy

The letters of 1 and 2 Timothy and Titus constitute a subgroup among the letters of Paul. They are addressed not to churches, but to pastors, Paul's younger colleagues in ministry. Therefore, since the 18th century, these three letters, sharing similar characteristics and contents, have been called the Pastoral Epistles. They presume a time after the close of the Book of Acts and near the end of Paul's life.

The first verse of each letter identifies Paul as the author. Some scholars, however, dispute this claim, since the differences in language and style between these letters and Paul's other letters seem very great. These three short books contain more than 300 words found in no other book that names Paul as its author. Moreover, if Paul was martyred around A.D. 64 at the end of his Roman imprisonment (see "Imprisonment in Rome" at Acts 28:16), he would not have had opportunity to write these letters. In that case, an editor or compiler could have produced these letters in the last quarter of the 1st century or first quarter of the 2nd century.

Yet Paul's authorship of the Pastoral Epistles is accepted by those who argue that Paul was released from his Roman imprisonment in late A.D. 62 or early A.D. 63. The only specific historical reference (1 Tim. 1:3) hints at a period of further travel and ministry, during which Paul had stationed Timothy at Ephesus. The letter known as 1 Timothy could then have been written about A.D. 65, in order to provide pastoral care and guidance to a young church leader.

Timothy, a native of Lystra in Asia Minor, was the son of a Jewish mother and Gentile father (Acts 16:1, 2). He was a convert of the apostle Paul, who had evangelized Lystra on his first missionary journey. Timothy joined Paul and Silas on the second missionary journey and traveled with them to Greece. Paul sent him to visit the Thessalonian and Corinthian churches (see 1 Cor. 4:17; 1 Thess. 3:2). In the letter, Timothy is warned against false teaching and given guidance on how to handle it.

▼   ■ 1 Timothy 1:1—6:21

1 Timothy
Greeting

1 :1 Paul, an apostle of Jesus Christ, by the commandment of God our Savior and the Lord Jesus Christ, our hope,

²To Timothy, a true son in the faith:

Grace, mercy, *and* peace from God our Father and Jesus Christ our Lord.

No Other Doctrine

³As I urged you when I went into Macedonia—remain in Ephesus that you may charge some that they teach no other doctrine, ⁴nor give heed to fables and endless genealogies, which cause disputes rather than godly edification which is in faith. ⁵Now the purpose of the commandment is love from a pure heart, *from* a good conscience, and *from* sincere faith, ⁶from which some, having strayed, have turned aside to idle talk, ⁷desiring to be teachers of the law, understanding neither what they say nor the things which they affirm.

⁸But we know that the law *is* good if one uses it lawfully, ⁹knowing this: that the law is not made for a righteous person, but for *the* lawless and insubordinate, for *the* ungodly and for sinners, for *the* unholy and profane, for murderers of fathers and murderers of mothers, for manslayers, ¹⁰for fornicators, for sodomites, for kidnappers, for liars, for perjurers, and if there is any other thing that is contrary to sound doctrine, ¹¹according to the glorious gospel of the blessed God which was committed to my trust.

Glory to God for His Grace

¹²And I thank Christ Jesus our Lord who has enabled me, because He counted me faithful, putting *me* into the ministry, ¹³although I was formerly a blasphemer, a persecutor, and an insolent man; but I obtained mercy because I did *it* ignorantly in unbelief. ¹⁴And the grace of our Lord was exceedingly abundant, with faith and love which are in Christ Jesus. ¹⁵This *is* a faithful saying and worthy of all acceptance, that Christ Jesus came into the world to save sinners, of whom I am chief. ¹⁶However, for this reason I obtained mercy, that in me first Jesus Christ might show all longsuffering, as a pattern to those who are going to believe on Him for everlasting life. ¹⁷Now to the King eternal, immortal, invis-

LEARN QUIETLY BUT DO NOT TEACH (1 Tim. 2:11, 12)

Although exceptions existed in antiquity, women were generally far less educated than men. Jewish women were far less likely to be trained in the law. Although they heard it taught in the synagogue, they were not accepted as students for study under Jewish teachers. There is evidence of only one woman fully trained as a rabbi in early Judaism, and most male rabbis refused to heed her. In such a context, the admonition for women to "learn in silence" (1 Tim. 2:11) might prove more striking for its emphasis on learning than for an emphasis on doing so quietly, which was considered the appropriate way for all novices to learn.

Understanding the situation addressed in the letter of 1 Timothy helps explain the instruction not to "permit a woman to teach" (2:12). Men rarely respected and still less often promoted women's leadership. Minority sects like Christianity were sometimes accused of subverting the traditional Roman social order, which supported male dominance. If female authority was allowed in the church, opposition may have increased against the small Christian community.

More significant was the local situation in the church. False teachers had apparently found support in homes headed by widows (1 Tim. 1:6, 7; 5:13–15). False teaching was apparently still a problem for "gullible women" when the letter of 2 Timothy was written (2 Tim. 3:6, 7). So the instructions for a woman to "learn" but not to "teach" may be aimed at keeping the women, who in this congregation had proved particularly susceptible to false teaching, from spreading it.

---

ible, to God who alone is wise,[a] *be* honor and glory forever and ever. Amen.

Fight the Good Fight

[18]This charge I commit to you, son Timothy, according to the prophecies previously made concerning you, that by them you may wage the good warfare, [19]having faith and a good conscience, which some having rejected, concerning the faith have suffered shipwreck, [20]of whom are Hymenaeus and Alexander, whom I delivered to Satan that they may learn not to blaspheme.

Pray for All Men

2 [1]Therefore I exhort first of all that supplications, prayers, intercessions, *and* giving of thanks be made for all men, [2]for kings and all who are in authority, that we

may lead a quiet and peaceable life in all godliness and reverence. [3]For this *is* good and acceptable in the sight of God our Savior, [4]who desires all men to be saved and to come to the knowledge of the truth. [5]For *there is* one God and one Mediator between God and men, *the* Man Christ Jesus, [6]who gave Himself a ransom for all, to be testified in due time, [7]for which I was appointed a preacher and an apostle—I am speaking the truth in Christ[a] *and* not lying—a teacher of the Gentiles in faith and truth.

Men and Women in the Church

[8]I desire therefore that the men pray everywhere, lifting up holy hands, without wrath and doubting; [9]in like manner also, that the women adorn themselves in modest apparel, with propriety and moderation, not with braided hair or gold or pearls or costly clothing, [10]but, which is proper for women professing godliness, with good

---

1:17 [a]NU-Text reads *to the only God.*
2:7 [a]NU-Text omits *in Christ.*

RELIGION AND WORSHIP

The Jewish people had the duty to offer sacrifices to God in the temple regularly on behalf of the Roman emperor (1 Tim. 2:2). In A.D. 66, Eleazar, the son of the high priest Ananias, ended this traditional observance. According to the contemporary historian Josephus, Eleazar's affront to the Romans was the beginning of the war that ended in A.D. 70 with the destruction of Jerusalem and the temple.

HUSBAND OF ONE WIFE (1 Tim. 3:2, 12)

One of the qualifications for being a bishop or deacon in the early church was to be the "husband of one wife" (1 Tim. 3:2, 12). Just what this qualification means concerning the marital history of a man desiring to become a church leader is debated.

One interpretation understands the meaning to be the "husband of only one wife in a lifetime." A widower would thus be prohibited from remarrying and serving as a bishop. Yet few people in the ancient world thought it praiseworthy for widowers to remain single.

Another interpretation is the "husband of one living wife." A widower could thus remarry and be a bishop, but a divorced man could not. No one in the ancient world, however, regarded a validly divorced husband as still married to his previous wife.

Yet a third interpretation is the "husband of one wife at a time." In this case, only a man involved in polygamy would be prohibited from service as a bishop. But polygamy was not practiced either in Ephesus (1 Tim. 1:3) or in Crete (Titus 1:5), where the letters of 1 Timothy and Titus were written.

More likely, "husband of one wife" carries a similar meaning to "wife of one husband" (1 Tim. 5:9), and addresses the more pervasive issue of being faithful in a marriage. Greek men apparently used the phrase "wife of one husband" to mean "a wife so faithful and loving that I never needed to divorce her." So a "husband of one wife" could refer to "a committed and faithful husband."

Husbands faithful to their current wives were needed to lead the church in Ephesus. False teachers were forbidding marriage (1 Tim. 4:3) and apparently manipulating some of the widows (2 Tim. 3:6, 7). Since the false teachers were taking advantage of unstable families, stable heads of households were desired to occupy positions of prominence and leadership in the church.

---

works. ¹¹Let a woman learn in silence with all submission. ¹²And I do not permit a woman to teach or to have authority over a man, but to be in silence. ¹³For Adam was formed first, then Eve. ¹⁴And Adam was not deceived, but the woman being deceived, fell into transgression. ¹⁵Nevertheless she will be saved in childbearing if they continue in faith, love, and holiness, with self-control.

Qualifications of Overseers

3 ¹This is a faithful saying: If a man desires the position of a bishop,ᵃ he desires a good work. ²A bishop then must be blameless, the husband of one wife, temperate, sober-minded, of good behavior, hospitable, able to teach; ³not given to wine, not violent, not greedy for money,ᵃ but gentle, not quarrelsome, not covetous; ⁴one who rules his own house well, having his children in submission with all reverence ⁵(for if a man does not know how to rule his own house, how will he take care of the church of God?); ⁶not a novice, lest being puffed up with pride he fall into the same condemnation as the devil. ⁷Moreover he must have a good testimony among those who are outside, lest he fall into reproach and the snare of the devil.

Qualifications of Deacons

⁸Likewise deacons must be reverent, not double-tongued, not given to much wine, not greedy for money, ⁹holding the mystery of the faith with a pure conscience. ¹⁰But let these also first be tested; then let them serve as deacons, being found blameless. ¹¹Likewise, their wives must be reverent, not slanderers, temperate, faithful in all things. ¹²Let deacons be the husbands of one wife, ruling their children and their own houses well. ¹³For those who have served well as deacons obtain for themselves a good standing and great boldness in the faith which is in Christ Jesus.

The Great Mystery

¹⁴These things I write to you, though I hope to come to you shortly; ¹⁵but if I am delayed, I write so that you may know how you ought to conduct yourself in the house

3:1 ᵃLiterally overseer   3:3 ᵃNU-Text omits not greedy for money.

of God, which is the church of the living God, the pillar and ground of the truth. [16]And without controversy great is the mystery of godliness:

> God[a] was manifested in the flesh,
> Justified in the Spirit,
> Seen by angels,
> Preached among the Gentiles,
> Believed on in the world,
> Received up in glory.

The Great Apostasy

4 [1]Now the Spirit expressly says that in latter times some will depart from the faith, giving heed to deceiving spirits and doctrines of demons, [2]speaking lies in hypocrisy, having their own conscience seared with a hot iron, [3]forbidding to marry, *and commanding* to abstain from foods which God created to be received with thanksgiving by those who believe and know the truth. [4]For every creature of God *is* good, and nothing is to be refused if it is received with thanksgiving; [5]for it is sanctified by the word of God and prayer.

A Good Servant of Jesus Christ

[6]If you instruct the brethren in these things, you will be a good minister of Jesus Christ, nourished in the words of faith and of the good doctrine which you have carefully followed. [7]But reject profane and old wives' fables, and exercise yourself toward godliness. [8]For bodily exercise profits a little, but godliness is profitable for all things, having promise of the life that now is and of that which is to come. [9]This *is* a faithful saying and worthy of all acceptance. [10]For to this *end* we both labor and suffer reproach,[a] because we trust in the living God, who is *the* Savior of all men, especially of those who believe. [11]These things command and teach.

Take Heed to Your Ministry

[12]Let no one despise your youth, but be an example to the believers in word, in conduct, in love, in spirit,[a] in faith, in purity. [13]Till I come, give attention to reading, to exhortation, to doctrine. [14]Do not neglect the gift that is in you, which was given to you by prophecy with the laying on of the hands of the eldership. [15]Meditate on these things; give yourself entirely to them, that your progress may be evident to all. [16]Take heed to yourself and to the doctrine. Continue in them, for in doing this you will save both yourself and those who hear you.

Treatment of Church Members

5 [1]Do not rebuke an older man, but exhort *him* as a father, younger men as brothers, [2]older women as mothers, younger women as sisters, with all purity.

Honor True Widows

[3]Honor widows who are really widows. [4]But if any widow has children or grandchildren, let them first learn to show piety at home and to repay their parents; for this is good and[a] acceptable before God. [5]Now she who is really a widow, and left alone, trusts in God and continues in supplications and prayers night and day. [6]But she who lives in pleasure is dead while she lives. [7]And these things command, that they may be blameless. [8]But if anyone does not provide for his own, and especially for those of his household, he has denied the faith and is worse than an unbeliever.

[9]Do not let a widow under sixty years old be taken into the number, *and not unless* she has been the wife of one man, [10]well reported for good works: if she has brought up children, if she has lodged strangers, if she has washed the saints' feet, if she has relieved the afflicted, if she has diligently followed every good work.

[11]But refuse *the* younger widows; for when they have begun to grow wanton against Christ, they desire to marry, [12]having condemnation because they have cast off their first faith. [13]And besides they learn *to be* idle, wandering about from house to house, and not only idle but also

---

TIME CAPSULE *A.D. 64*

64   *Nero begins construction of his "Golden Palace"*

64   *Fire rages in Rome for 9 days*

64   *Nero blames Christians for the Great Fire*

64   *Peter and Paul executed under Nero (?)*

64–65   *Paul travels to Macedonia (?; if released)*

3:16 [a]NU-Text reads *Who.*   4:10 [a]NU-Text reads *we labor and strive.*   4:12 [a]NU-Text omits *in spirit.*   5:4 [a]NU-Text and M-Text omit *good and.*

WIDOWS IN THE HOUSEHOLD (1 Tim. 5:8)

The fundamental social institution of the Greco-Roman world was the household. The ancient household included far more people than the modern nuclear family of a husband, wife, and two and one-third children. Everyone involved in the "family business" under the rule of a male administrator, called the "father," was part of the household. Thus the Greco-Roman household consisted of relatives plus various dependents: the father's wife, his slaves, children, as well as clients—those who gave the father honor and influence in exchange for material favors.

Households, particularly the fathers, ranked themselves socially in terms of honor, prestige, and influence. The more honor a father received, the more prestige and influence he gathered. Wealth, therefore, was not important to accumulate in order to gain more wealth. Wealth was important so that a father might parade his honor. Wealth enabled a father to lavish gifts on his dependents, thereby making more people honor their father as their benefactor.

One household member who especially needed protection was the widow. In New Testament times, widows had virtually no means of supporting themselves. The early church felt responsible to care for Christian widows, but problems arose in ministering to their needs. As new structures and guidelines had to be developed, the church eventually distinguished between widows who really needed support and those who should be commended to the care of their household (1 Tim. 5:3–5, 8). A Christian father who did not provide for a widow of his household was deemed "worse than an unbeliever" (5:8). Even in non-Christian households of the Greco-Roman world, the head of the household supported poor widows.

gossips and busybodies, saying things which they ought not. ¹⁴Therefore I desire that *the* younger *widows* marry, bear children, manage the house, give no opportunity to the adversary to speak reproachfully. ¹⁵For some have already turned aside after Satan. ¹⁶If any believing man or[a] woman has widows, let them relieve them, and do not let the church be burdened, that it may relieve those who are really widows.

Honor the Elders

¹⁷Let the elders who rule well be counted worthy of double honor, especially those who labor in the word and doctrine. ¹⁸For the Scripture says, *"You shall not muzzle an ox while it treads out the grain,"*[a] and, *"The laborer is worthy of his wages."*[b] ¹⁹Do not receive an accusation against an elder except from two or three witnesses. ²⁰Those who are sinning rebuke in the presence of all, that the rest also may fear.

²¹I charge *you* before God and the Lord Jesus Christ and the elect angels that you observe these things without prejudice, doing nothing with partiality. ²²Do not lay hands on anyone hastily, nor share in other people's sins; keep yourself pure.

²³No longer drink only water, but use a little wine for your stomach's sake and your frequent infirmities.

²⁴Some men's sins are clearly evident, preceding *them* to judgment, but those of some *men* follow later. ²⁵Likewise, the good works *of some* are clearly evident, and those that are otherwise cannot be hidden.

Honor Masters

6 ¹Let as many bondservants as are under the yoke count their own masters worthy of all honor, so that the name of God and *His* doctrine may not be blasphemed. ²And those who have believing masters, let them not despise *them* because they are brethren, but rather serve *them* because those who are benefited are believers and beloved. Teach and exhort these things.

Error and Greed

³If anyone teaches otherwise and does not consent to wholesome words, *even* the words of our Lord Jesus Christ, and to the doctrine which accords with godliness, ⁴he is proud, knowing nothing, but is obsessed with disputes and arguments over words,

5:16 ªNU-Text omits *man* or.
5:18 ªDeuteronomy 25:4   ᵇLuke 10:7

from which come envy, strife, reviling, evil suspicions, [5]useless wranglings[a] of men of corrupt minds and destitute of the truth, who suppose that godliness is a *means of* gain. From such withdraw yourself.[b]

[6]Now godliness with contentment is great gain. [7]For we brought nothing into *this* world, *and it is* certain[a] we can carry nothing out. [8]And having food and clothing, with these we shall be content. [9]But those who desire to be rich fall into temptation and a snare, and *into* many foolish and harmful lusts which drown men in destruction and perdition. [10]For the love of money is a root of all *kinds of* evil, for which some have strayed from the faith in their greediness, and pierced themselves through with many sorrows.

The Good Confession

[11]But you, O man of God, flee these things and pursue righteousness, godliness, faith, love, patience, gentleness. [12]Fight the good fight of faith, lay hold on eternal life, to which you were also called and have confessed the good confession in the presence of many witnesses. [13]I urge you in the sight of God who gives life to all things, and *before* Christ Jesus who witnessed the good confession before Pontius Pilate, [14]that you keep *this* commandment without spot, blameless until our Lord Jesus Christ's appearing, [15]which He will manifest in His own time, *He who is* the blessed and only Potentate, the King of kings and Lord of lords, [16]who alone has immortality, dwelling in unapproachable light, whom no man has seen or can see, to whom *be* honor and everlasting power. Amen.

Instructions to the Rich

[17]Command those who are rich in this present age not to be haughty, nor to trust in uncertain riches but in the living God,

who gives us richly all things to enjoy. [18]*Let them* do good, that they be rich in good works, ready to give, willing to share, [19]storing up for themselves a good foundation for the time to come, that they may lay hold on eternal life.

Guard the Faith

[20]O Timothy! Guard what was committed to your trust, avoiding the profane *and* idle babblings and contradictions of what is falsely called knowledge— [21]by professing it some have strayed concerning the faith.

Grace *be* with you. Amen.

The Letter to Titus

Considerable doubts have been raised about whether Paul actually wrote this letter to Titus (see "The First Letter to Timothy" at 1 Tim. 1:1). Those who accept Paul's authorship believe the letter to Titus was probably written shortly after 1 Timothy, but before the apostle's rearrest and imprisonment in A.D. 66. Paul had left Titus in Crete to oversee the work on that island (Titus 1:5).

Little is known about Titus (he is never mentioned in Acts). He was an uncircumcised Greek who was apparently converted to Christianity under Paul's ministry (Gal. 2:1). He played an important role in Paul's relationship with the Corinthian church (2 Cor. 7:6, 7; 8:16; 12:18).

The letter was written to encourage Titus in his task of organizing, instructing, and appointing leaders for the churches of Crete (Titus 1:5). It was also intended to help him stop the false teachers who threatened church authority, unity, and morality (1:10–16; 3:9–11).

■ Titus 1:1—3:15

6:5 [a]NU-Text and M-Text read *constant friction.*
[b]NU-Text omits this sentence.   6:7 [a]NU-Text omits *and it is certain.*

Titus
Greeting

1 :1 Paul, a bondservant of God and an apostle of Jesus Christ, according to the faith of God's elect and the acknowledgment of the truth which accords with godliness, [2]in hope of eternal life which God,

---

CULTS AND SUPERNATURAL

The Gnostics proclaimed a kind of "knowledge" which could help certain spiritual people to escape from the deception and futility of a world dominated by an evil god. Gnostic ideas were already circulating in the 1st century, but it is not known how close their followers were to Christianity or Judaism. Certainly, the early church faced human speculations that were "falsely called knowledge" (1 Tim. 6:20).

AN ANCIENT PROPHET FROM CRETE (Titus 1:12)

Crete is a large southern Aegean island with a very ancient past going back as early as 6000 B.C. The earliest civilization in European history was found at Crete, dating as early as the 3rd millennium B.C. The small states that were built around palaces and flourishing sea-trading routes have been named the Minoan civilization, reminiscent of King Minos of Greek legend. The Minoan period experienced its high point from about 2000 B.C. (when the first palace was built) until around 1400 B.C.

When the Minoan civilization ended, Cretan culture declined, until dominated mostly by traders and soldiers. Decline is possibly reflected in the description of Cretans as "liars, evil beasts, lazy gluttons" (Titus 1:12; also quoted in Acts 17:28), which comes from Epimenides, a Cretan poet of about 600 B.C. Cretans were described in a similar manner (as liars and gluttons) in the writings of various authors, such as Greek poet Callimachus (c. 305–240 B.C.), Roman historian Livy (59 B.C.–A.D. 17), and Greek philosopher Plutarch (c. A.D. 46–120).

In New Testament times there was a substantial Jewish population on this Roman-controlled island. Some of these Cretan Jews apparently took on similar characteristics to those named by Epimenides, and the quote from Epimenides illustrates the charge that these members of the Jewish community were insubordinate. Titus was appointed to Crete partly to stop the Judaizing tendencies of this group called "those of the circumcision" (Titus 1:10).

who cannot lie, promised before time began, ³but has in due time manifested His word through preaching, which was committed to me according to the commandment of God our Savior;

⁴To Titus, a true son in *our* common faith:

Grace, mercy, *and* peace from God the Father and the Lord Jesus Christᵃ our Savior.

Qualified Elders

⁵For this reason I left you in Crete, that you should set in order the things that are lacking, and appoint elders in every city as I commanded you— ⁶if a man is blameless, the husband of one wife, having faithful children not accused of dissipation or insubordination. ⁷For a bishopᵃ must be blameless, as a steward of God, not self-willed, not quick-tempered, not given to wine, not violent, not greedy for money, ⁸but hospitable, a lover of what is good, sober-minded, just, holy, self-controlled, ⁹holding fast the faithful word as he has been taught, that he may be able, by sound doctrine, both to exhort and convict those who contradict.

The Elders' Task

¹⁰For there are many insubordinate, both idle talkers and deceivers, especially

those of the circumcision, ¹¹whose mouths must be stopped, who subvert whole households, teaching things which they ought not, for the sake of dishonest gain. ¹²One of them, a prophet of their own, said, "Cretans *are* always liars, evil beasts, lazy gluttons." ¹³This testimony is true. Therefore rebuke them sharply, that they may be sound in the faith, ¹⁴not giving heed to Jewish fables and commandments of men who turn from the truth. ¹⁵To the pure all things are pure, but to those who are defiled and unbelieving nothing is pure; but even their mind and conscience are defiled. ¹⁶They profess to know God, but in works they deny Him, being abominable, disobedient, and disqualified for every good work.

Qualities of a Sound Church

2 ¹But as for you, speak the things which are proper for sound doctrine: ²that the older men be sober, reverent, temperate, sound in faith, in love, in patience; ³the older women likewise, that they be reverent in behavior, not slanderers, not given to much wine, teachers of good things— ⁴that they admonish the young women to love their husbands, to love their children, ⁵to be discreet, chaste, homemakers, good,

---

1:4 ᵃNU-Text reads *and Christ Jesus.*
1:7 ᵃLiterally *overseer*

obedient to their own husbands, that the word of God may not be blasphemed.

[6]Likewise, exhort the young men to be sober-minded, [7]in all things showing yourself *to be* a pattern of good works; in doctrine *showing* integrity, reverence, incorruptibility,[a] [8]sound speech that cannot be condemned, that one who is an opponent may be ashamed, having nothing evil to say of you.[a]

[9]*Exhort* bondservants to be obedient to their own masters, to be well pleasing in all *things,* not answering back, [10]not pilfering, but showing all good fidelity, that they may adorn the doctrine of God our Savior in all things.

Trained by Saving Grace

[11]For the grace of God that brings salvation has appeared to all men, [12]teaching us that, denying ungodliness and worldly lusts, we should live soberly, righteously, and godly in the present age, [13]looking for the blessed hope and glorious appearing of our great God and Savior Jesus Christ, [14]who gave Himself for us, that He might redeem us from every lawless deed and purify for Himself *His* own special people, zealous for good works.

[15]Speak these things, exhort, and rebuke with all authority. Let no one despise you.

Graces of the Heirs of Grace

3 [1]Remind them to be subject to rulers and authorities, to obey, to be ready for every good work, [2]to speak evil of no one, to be peaceable, gentle, showing all humility to all men. [3]For we ourselves were also once foolish, disobedient, deceived, serving various lusts and pleasures, living in malice and envy, hateful and hating one another. [4]But when the kindness and the love of God our Savior toward man appeared, [5]not by works of righteousness which we have done, but according to His mercy He saved us, through the washing of regeneration and renewing of the Holy Spirit, [6]whom He poured out on us abundantly through Jesus Christ our Savior, [7]that having been justified by His grace we should become heirs according to the hope of eternal life.

[8]This is a faithful saying, and these things I want you to affirm constantly, that those who have believed in God should be careful to maintain good works. These things are good and profitable to men.

Avoid Dissension

[9]But avoid foolish disputes, genealogies, contentions, and strivings about the law; for they are unprofitable and useless. [10]Reject a divisive man after the first and second admonition, [11]knowing that such a person is warped and sinning, being self-condemned.

Final Messages

[12]When I send Artemas to you, or Tychicus, be diligent to come to me at Nicopolis, for I have decided to spend the winter there. [13]Send Zenas the lawyer and Apollos on their journey with haste, that they may lack nothing. [14]And let our *people* also learn to maintain good works, to *meet* urgent needs, that they may not be unfruitful.

Farewell

[15]All who *are* with me greet you. Greet those who love us in the faith.

Grace *be* with you all. Amen.

The Second Letter to Timothy

As with the other Pastoral Epistles, the letter of 2 Timothy is often not considered to be an original letter of Paul's (see "The First Letter to Timothy" at 1 Tim. 1:1). Those who do accept Paul's authorship believe that 2 Timothy was probably written in A.D. 67, after Paul had been rearrested. Companions who were recently with him had departed (2 Tim. 4:10), leaving him alone—"Only Luke is with me" (4:11). Presumably, Timothy was still in Ephesus (4:19), where Paul had left Priscilla and Aquila at the end of his second journey (Acts 18:18, 19), and where he had stationed Timothy to oversee the work in Asia Minor (see 1 Tim. 1:3).

The letter of 2 Timothy describes Paul as a prisoner in Rome at the time of writing (2 Tim. 1:16, 17). The apostle had already endured a "first defense" (4:16) and had been delivered (4:17). Presumably that was a preliminary hearing; he now faced formal trial. Paul expected a negative verdict and the death sentence. He had reached the end of his course in this life; death was imminent (4:6). The primary object of this letter was to strengthen Timothy so that he would endure in the face of opposition from false teachers. He is encouraged to carry on the gospel ministry and to train others who will take up that ministry after he is gone.

■ 2 Timothy 1:1—4:22

2 Timothy
Greeting

1 :1 Paul, an apostle of Jesus Christ[a] by the will of God, according to the promise of life which is in Christ Jesus,

²To Timothy, a beloved son:

Grace, mercy, *and* peace from God the Father and Christ Jesus our Lord.

Timothy's Faith and Heritage

³I thank God, whom I serve with a pure conscience, as *my* forefathers *did,* as without ceasing I remember you in my prayers night and day, ⁴greatly desiring to see you, being mindful of your tears, that I may be filled with joy, ⁵when I call to remembrance the genuine faith that is in you, which dwelt first in your grandmother Lois and your mother Eunice, and I am persuaded is in you also. ⁶Therefore I remind you to stir up the gift of God which is in you through the laying on of my hands. ⁷For God has not given us a spirit of fear, but of power and of love and of a sound mind.

Not Ashamed of the Gospel

⁸Therefore do not be ashamed of the testimony of our Lord, nor of me His prisoner, but share with me in the sufferings for the gospel according to the power of God, ⁹who has saved us and called *us* with a holy calling, not according to our works, but according to His own purpose and grace which was given to us in Christ Jesus before time began, ¹⁰but has now been revealed by the appearing of our Savior Jesus Christ, *who* has abolished death and brought life and immortality to light through the gospel, ¹¹to which I was appointed a preacher, an apostle, and a teacher of the Gentiles.[a] ¹²For this reason I also suffer these things; nevertheless I am not ashamed, for I know whom I have believed and am persuaded that He is able to keep what I have committed to Him until that Day.

Be Loyal to the Faith

¹³Hold fast the pattern of sound words which you have heard from me, in faith and love which are in Christ Jesus. ¹⁴That good thing which was committed to you, keep by the Holy Spirit who dwells in us.

¹⁵This you know, that all those in Asia have turned away from me, among whom are Phygellus and Hermogenes. ¹⁶The Lord grant mercy to the household of Onesiphorus, for he often refreshed me, and was not ashamed of my chain; ¹⁷but when he arrived in Rome, he sought me out very zealously and found *me.* ¹⁸The Lord grant to him that he may find mercy from the Lord in that Day—and you know very well how many ways he ministered *to me*[a] at Ephesus.

Be Strong in Grace

2 ¹You therefore, my son, be strong in the grace that is in Christ Jesus. ²And the things that you have heard from me among many witnesses, commit these to faithful men who will be able to teach others also. ³You therefore must endure[a] hardship as a good soldier of Jesus Christ. ⁴No one engaged in warfare entangles himself with the affairs of *this* life, that he may please him who enlisted him as a soldier. ⁵And also if anyone competes in athletics, he is not crowned unless he competes according to the rules. ⁶The hardworking farmer must be first to partake of the crops. ⁷Consider what I say, and may[a] the Lord give you understanding in all things.

⁸Remember that Jesus Christ, of the seed of David, was raised from the dead according to my gospel, ⁹for which I suffer trouble as an evildoer, *even* to the point of chains; but the word of God is not chained. ¹⁰Therefore I endure all things for the sake of the elect, that they also may obtain the salvation which is in Christ Jesus with eternal glory.

¹¹*This is* a faithful saying:

For if we died with *Him,*
    We shall also live with *Him.*
¹² If we endure,
    We shall also reign with *Him.*

1:1 [a]NU-Text and M-Text read *Christ Jesus.*
1:11 [a]NU-Text omits *of the Gentiles.*   1:18 [a]*To me* is from the Vulgate and a few Greek manuscripts.
2:3 [a]NU-Text reads *You must share.*
2:7 [a]NU-Text reads *the Lord will give you.*

THE WHO'S WHO OF BANQUETING (2 Tim. 2:20, 21)

The Greco-Roman society developed intricate social customs and rituals in order to rank people as honorable or shameful, socially superior or inferior. One of these rituals was the banquet. As a formal dinner party, the banquet helped mark people in their proper "rank" within the society.

As the host, the head of the household, called the "father," occupied the social pinnacle at the banquet. People would not usually attend the banquet given by someone of lesser social standing than themselves. Various arrangements of the banquet ranked the participants socially, such as the seating or reclining assignments. The closer an attendee was to the host, the more status or honor that one possessed at the banquet.

In a spacious "great house" (2 Tim. 2:20) of an extremely wealthy household, a banquet could involve many, many people, all indebted to the father or head of household. Not only access to the host, but also food and serving dishes would mark "who's who" at the banquet. Those possessing sufficient honor or status would eat from platters of precious metals; the common freemen would eat from earthenware with wooden utensils.

The banquet and its social code possibly provide the background for the imagery of vessels in the letter of 2 Timothy (2 Tim. 2:20, 21). Within the "great house" of God the Father, moral purity is the distinguishing mark of a vessel "for honor"; implied, though not stated, is that impurity marks a vessel "for dishonor." Thus in the visible church are people of various kinds—some for good, others regrettably unworthy.

If we deny *Him,*
> He also will deny us.
13 If we are faithless,
> He remains faithful;
> He cannot deny Himself.

Approved and Disapproved Workers

14Remind *them* of these things, charging *them* before the Lord not to strive about words to no profit, to the ruin of the hearers. 15Be diligent to present yourself approved to God, a worker who does not need to be ashamed, rightly dividing the word of truth. 16But shun profane *and* idle babblings, for they will increase to more ungodliness. 17And their message will spread like cancer. Hymenaeus and Philetus are of this sort, 18who have strayed concerning the truth, saying that the resurrection is already past; and they overthrow the faith of some. 19Nevertheless the solid foundation of God stands, having this seal: "The Lord knows those who are His," and, "Let everyone who names the name of Christa depart from iniquity."

20But in a great house there are not only vessels of gold and silver, but also of wood and clay, some for honor and some for dishonor. 21Therefore if anyone cleanses himself from the latter, he will be a vessel for honor, sanctified and useful for the Master, prepared for every good work. 22Flee also youthful lusts; but pursue righteousness, faith, love, peace with those who call on the Lord out of a pure heart. 23But avoid foolish and ignorant disputes, knowing that they generate strife. 24And a servant of the Lord must not quarrel but be gentle to all, able to teach, patient, 25in humility correcting those who are in opposition, if God perhaps will grant them repentance, so that they may know the truth, 26and *that* they may come to their senses *and escape* the snare of the devil, having been taken captive by him to *do* his will.

Perilous Times and Perilous Men

3 1But know this, that in the last days perilous times will come: 2For men will be lovers of themselves, lovers of money, boasters, proud, blasphemers, disobedient to parents, unthankful, unholy, 3unloving, unforgiving, slanderers, without self-control, brutal, despisers of good, 4traitors, headstrong, haughty, lovers of pleasure rather than lovers of God, 5having a form of godliness but denying its power. And from such people turn away! 6For of this sort are those who creep into households and make captives of gullible women loaded down with sins, led away by various lusts, 7always learning and never able to

---

2:19 aNU-Text and M-Text read *the Lord.*

come to the knowledge of the truth. ⁸Now as Jannes and Jambres resisted Moses, so do these also resist the truth: men of corrupt minds, disapproved concerning the faith; ⁹but they will progress no further, for their folly will be manifest to all, as theirs also was.

The Man of God and the Word of God

¹⁰But you have carefully followed my doctrine, manner of life, purpose, faith, longsuffering, love, perseverance, ¹¹persecutions, afflictions, which happened to me at Antioch, at Iconium, at Lystra—what persecutions I endured. And out of *them* all the Lord delivered me. ¹²Yes, and all who desire to live godly in Christ Jesus will suffer persecution. ¹³But evil men and impostors will grow worse and worse, deceiving and being deceived. ¹⁴But you must continue in the things which you have learned and been assured of, knowing from whom you have learned *them,* ¹⁵and that from childhood you have known the Holy Scriptures, which are able to make you wise for salvation through faith which is in Christ Jesus. ¹⁶All Scripture *is* given by inspiration of God, and *is* profitable for doctrine, for reproof, for correction, for instruction in righteousness, ¹⁷that the man of God may be complete, thoroughly equipped for every good work.

Preach the Word

4 ¹I charge *you* therefore before God and the Lord Jesus Christ, who will judge the living and the dead atª His appearing and His kingdom: ²Preach the word! Be ready in season *and* out of season. Convince, rebuke, exhort, with all longsuffering and teaching. ³For the time will come when they will not endure sound doctrine, but according to their own desires, *because* they have itching ears, they will heap up for themselves teachers; ⁴and they will turn *their* ears away from the truth, and be turned aside to fables. ⁵But you be watchful in all things, endure afflictions, do the work of an evangelist, fulfill your ministry.

Paul's Valedictory

⁶For I am already being poured out as a drink offering, and the time of my departure is at hand. ⁷I have fought the good fight, I have finished the race, I have kept the faith. ⁸Finally, there is laid up for me the crown of righteousness, which the Lord, the righteous Judge, will give to me on that Day, and not to me only but also to all who have loved His appearing.

The Abandoned Apostle

⁹Be diligent to come to me quickly; ¹⁰for Demas has forsaken me, having loved this present world, and has departed for Thessalonica—Crescens for Galatia, Titus for Dalmatia. ¹¹Only Luke is with me. Get Mark and bring him with you, for he is useful to me for ministry. ¹²And Tychicus I have sent to Ephesus. ¹³Bring the cloak that I left with Carpus at Troas when you come—and the books, especially the parchments.

¹⁴Alexander the coppersmith did me much harm. May the Lord repay him according to his works. ¹⁵You also must beware of him, for he has greatly resisted our words.

¹⁶At my first defense no one stood with me, but all forsook me. May it not be charged against them.

The Lord Is Faithful

¹⁷But the Lord stood with me and strengthened me, so that the message might be preached fully through me, and *that* all the Gentiles might hear. Also I was delivered out of the mouth of the lion. ¹⁸And the Lord will deliver me from every evil work and preserve *me* for His heavenly kingdom. To Him *be* glory forever and ever. Amen!

4:1 ªNU-Text omits *therefore* and reads *and by* for *at.*

CULTURE AND SOCIETY

The awards given in Greek athletic competition were wreaths, or crowns woven from leaves, or else gold imitations of such crowns. The honor of these awards overshadowed whatever money accompanied them. Aspects of athletic competition, such as the "race" and "crown" (2 Tim. 4:7, 8), were appropriate figures to describe the finish of life as a faithful Christian.

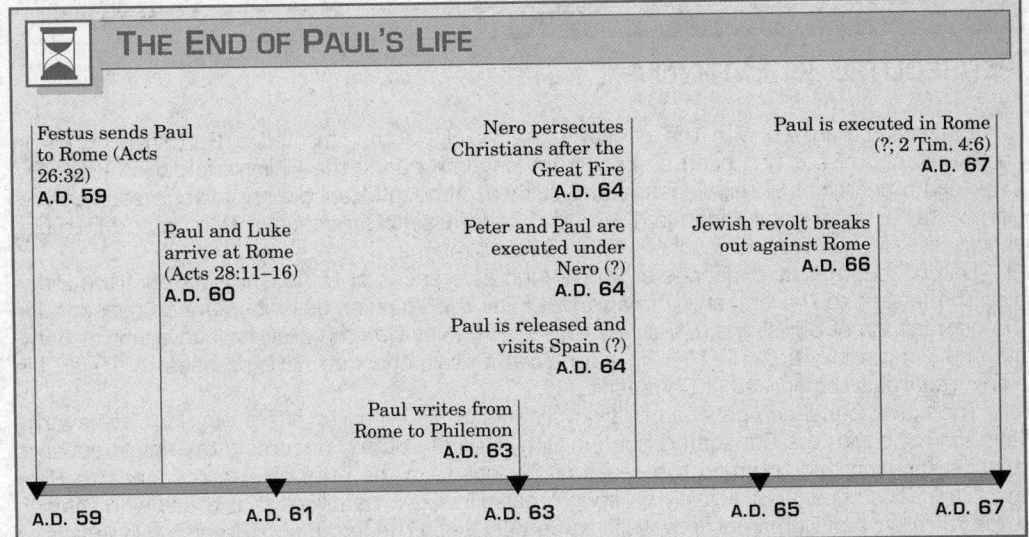

THE END OF PAUL'S LIFE

Festus sends Paul
to Rome (Acts
26:32)
A.D. 59

Paul and Luke
arrive at Rome
(Acts 28:11–16)
A.D. 60

Nero persecutes
Christians after the
Great Fire
A.D. 64

Peter and Paul are
executed under
Nero (?)
A.D. 64

Paul is released and
visits Spain (?)
A.D. 64

Paul writes from
Rome to Philemon
A.D. 63

Paul is executed in Rome
(?; 2 Tim. 4:6)
A.D. 67

Jewish revolt breaks
out against Rome
A.D. 66

A.D. 59   **A.D. 61**   **A.D. 63**   **A.D. 65**   **A.D. 67**

Come Before Winter

¹⁹Greet Prisca and Aquila, and the household of Onesiphorus. ²⁰Erastus stayed in Corinth, but Trophimus I have left in Miletus sick.

²¹Do your utmost to come before winter.

Eubulus greets you, as well as Pudens, Linus, Claudia, and all the brethren.

Farewell

²²The Lord Jesus Christ^a be with your spirit. Grace be with you. Amen.

4:22 ^aNU-Text omits *Jesus Christ*.

The First Letter of Peter

If Simon Peter was the author of the letter of 1 Peter, he probably wrote it around A.D. 63 or 64, shortly before the beginning of Nero's persecution of Christians at Rome. The name "Babylon" (1 Pet. 5:13), then, is likely a figurative description of Rome. According to early church tradition, Peter was martyred during the reign of Nero in about A.D. 64. Peter's scribe, Sylvanus (5:12) may have been responsible for much of the letter's style and vocabulary.

Some scholars reject Peter's authorship: the good style and extensive literary vocabulary of the author could not have come from a Galilean fisherman. Moreover, the letter shows the influence of Paul's theology and vocabulary, such as the expression "in Christ."

If Peter was not the author, the letter could have been written sometime after A.D. 70. The symbolic reference to Rome as "Babylon," found in several early Christian writings (see Rev. 17:5), probably resulted from Rome's destruction of Jerusalem in A.D. 70, a tragic event that repeated the conquest by Babylon in 586 B.C. The link between being "a Christian" and criminal offenses (4:14–16) might suggest a date around A.D. 90–95, well after Peter's death. The earliest evidence for an official governmental persecution being enforced on more than a local basis is found during the reign of the emperor Domitian (A.D. 81–96).

The Christians who received this letter lived in Pontus, Galatia, Cappadocia, Asia, and Bithynia (1 Pet. 1:1), regions located in Asia Minor. Many of them seem to have been Gentiles (2:10) who were facing persecution from non-Christians around them and perhaps also from government officials. This letter was written primarily to bring them a message of hope and encouragement.

■ 1 Peter 1:1—5:14

1 Peter
Greeting to the Elect Pilgrims

1 :1 Peter, an apostle of Jesus Christ,

To the pilgrims of the Dispersion in Pontus, Galatia, Cappadocia, Asia, and Bithynia, ²elect according to the foreknowledge of God the Father, in sanctification of

PERSECUTED IN BITHYNIA (1 Pet. 1:1)

Bithynia, combined with the nearby territory of Pontus, formed a Roman province in northwest Anatolia. It had been an important kingdom during the Hellenistic period (332–37 B.C.), and a center of Greek language and culture. Although Paul did not evangelize in the region (Acts 16:7), the salutation in 1 Pet. 1:1, addressing Christians in Pontus and Bithynia, shows that Christianity had reached there by other means.

One of the earliest evidences of the Roman awareness of Christianity comes from Bithynia. The letters to the emperor Trajan from Pliny the Younger describe various reasons for the persecution of Christians (*Epistulae* 10.95–96). Pliny was the provincial governor of Bithynia and Pontus in A.D. 111–113. In his official correspondence he expresses to Trajan his alarm regarding the spread of Christianity.

The correspondence between this governor and his emperor offers one look at how the Romans dealt with the Christian religion in Bithynia and Pontus. According to Pliny, it appears that persecution had trimmed the ranks of Christians in the area. Trajan responds to Pliny that Christians should not actively be sought out. However, he allows that those who refused to perform certain Roman orders were to be punished. The letter of 1 Peter to Christians in Bithynia, Pontus, and other regions, offers encouragement during similar persecutions (1 Pet. 1:6, 7).

---

the Spirit, for obedience and sprinkling of the blood of Jesus Christ:

Grace to you and peace be multiplied.

A Heavenly Inheritance

3Blessed *be* the God and Father of our Lord Jesus Christ, who according to His abundant mercy has begotten us again to a living hope through the resurrection of Jesus Christ from the dead, 4to an inheritance incorruptible and undefiled and that does not fade away, reserved in heaven for you, 5who are kept by the power of God through faith for salvation ready to be revealed in the last time.

6In this you greatly rejoice, though now for a little while, if need be, you have been grieved by various trials, 7that the genuineness of your faith, *being* much more precious than gold that perishes, though it is tested by fire, may be found to praise, honor, and glory at the revelation of Jesus Christ, 8whom having not seen[a] you love. Though now you do not see *Him,* yet

---

1:8 [a]M-Text reads *known.*

Regions of the Dispersion
The letter of 1 Peter is addressed to "the pilgrims of the Dispersion in Pontus, Galatia, Cappadocia, Asia, and Bithynia" (1 Pet. 1:1). The author wrote from Rome, as indicated by the code name "Babylon" (1 Pet. 5:13), and encouraged these pilgrims in various areas of Asia Minor to be strong in the faith as they encountered persecutions.

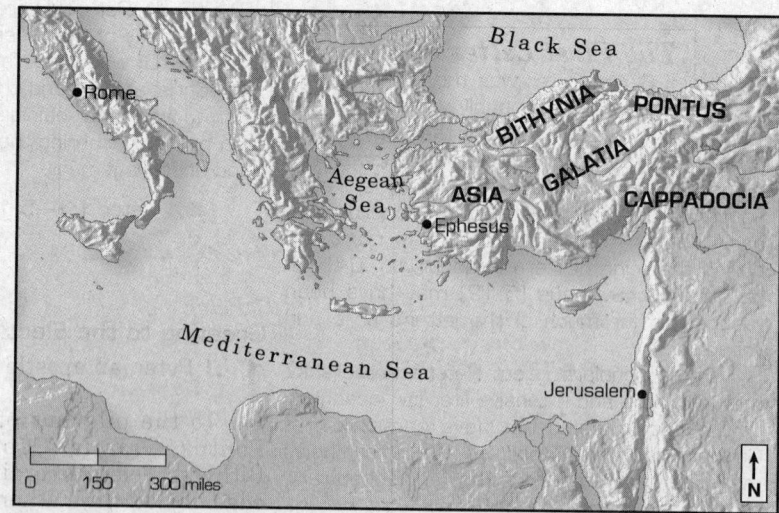

believing, you rejoice with joy inexpressible and full of glory, [9]receiving the end of your faith—the salvation of *your* souls.

[10]Of this salvation the prophets have inquired and searched carefully, who prophesied of the grace *that would come* to you, [11]searching what, or what manner of time, the Spirit of Christ who was in them was indicating when He testified beforehand the sufferings of Christ and the glories that would follow. [12]To them it was revealed that, not to themselves, but to us[a] they were ministering the things which now have been reported to you through those who have preached the gospel to you by the Holy Spirit sent from heaven—things which angels desire to look into.

Living Before God Our Father

[13]Therefore gird up the loins of your mind, be sober, and rest *your* hope fully upon the grace that is to be brought to you at the revelation of Jesus Christ; [14]as obedient children, not conforming yourselves to the former lusts, *as* in your ignorance; [15]but as He who called you *is* holy, you also be holy in all *your* conduct, [16]because it is written, *"Be holy, for I am holy."*[a]

[17]And if you call on the Father, who without partiality judges according to each one's work, conduct yourselves throughout the time of your stay *here* in fear; [18]knowing that you were not redeemed with corruptible things, *like* silver or gold, from your aimless conduct *received* by tradition from your fathers, [19]but with the precious blood of Christ, as of a lamb without blemish and without spot. [20]He indeed was foreordained before the foundation of the world, but was manifest in these last times for you [21]who through Him believe in God, who raised Him from the dead and gave Him glory, so that your faith and hope are in God.

The Enduring Word

[22]Since you have purified your souls in obeying the truth through the Spirit[a] in sincere love of the brethren, love one another fervently with a pure heart, [23]having been born again, not of corruptible seed but incorruptible, through the word of God which lives and abides forever,[a] [24]because

"All flesh is as grass,
  And all the glory of man[a] as the flower
    of the grass.
The grass withers,
  And its flower falls away,
25 *But the word of the LORD endures*
    forever."[a]

Now this is the word which by the gospel was preached to you.

2 [1]Therefore, laying aside all malice, all deceit, hypocrisy, envy, and all evil speaking, [2]as newborn babes, desire the pure milk of the word, that you may grow thereby,[a] [3]if indeed you have tasted that the Lord *is* gracious.

The Chosen Stone and His Chosen People

[4]Coming to Him *as to* a living stone, rejected indeed by men, but chosen by God *and* precious, [5]you also, as living stones, are being built up a spiritual house, a holy priesthood, to offer up spiritual sacrifices acceptable to God through Jesus Christ. [6]Therefore it is also contained in the Scripture,

"Behold, I lay in Zion
  A chief cornerstone, elect, precious,
  And he who believes on Him will by
    no means be put to shame."[a]

[7]Therefore, to you who believe, *He is* precious; but to those who are disobedient,[a]

1:12 [a]NU-Text and M-Text read *you*.
1:16 [a]Leviticus 11:44, 45; 19:2; 20:7
1:22 [a]NU-Text omits *through the Spirit*.
1:23 [a]NU-Text omits *forever*.   1:24 [a]NU-Text reads *all its glory*.   1:25 [a]Isaiah 40:6–8
2:2 [a]NU-Text adds *up to salvation*.   2:6 [a]Isaiah 28:16   2:7 [a]NU-Text reads *to those who disbelieve*.

ARTS AND LITERATURE

Poets commonly compare human life that is fragile and short to the brief life of plants that bloom and die in a single season. By contrast, the king was compared to a tree that bore fruit year after year. Such comparisons of human life to plants are used many times in Scripture with different nuances (1 Pet. 1:24).

THE PERSECUTION OF THE CHURCH

The letter of 1 Peter was written primarily to bring a message of hope and encouragement to Christians under persecution. Many of them were being persecuted by non-Christians around them, and perhaps also by government officials. Christians faced animosity particularly from several Roman emperors.

Date	Emperor
A.D. **64**	Nero (54–68)
	Nero blamed the Christians for the Great Fire in Rome and punished them cruelly.
A.D. **95**	Domitian (81–96)
	Domitian accused some high-ranking people of atheism. There is some evidence of persecution in the provinces especially.
A.D. **111**	Trajan (98–117)
	Pliny the Younger corresponded with the emperor Trajan. The decision was that Christians should be punished if known, but should not be hunted down.
A.D. **125**	Hadrian (117–138)
	Hadrian continued Trajan's policy; Christians were entitled to due process and should not be hunted down.
A.D. **155**	Antoninus Pius (138–161)
	Polycarp was martyred in Syria for refusal to serve pagan gods. Another possible date for this event is 167–168, during the reign of Marcus Aurelius (161–180).
A.D. **202**	Septimius Severus (193–211)
	Severus made it against the law for anyone to be converted to Judaism or to Christianity.

"The stone which the builders rejected
Has become the chief cornerstone,"[b]

8and

"A stone of stumbling
And a rock of offense."[a]

They stumble, being disobedient to the word, to which they also were appointed.

9But you *are* a chosen generation, a royal priesthood, a holy nation, His own special people, that you may proclaim the praises of Him who called you out of darkness into His marvelous light; 10who once *were* not a people but *are* now the people of God, who had not obtained mercy but now have obtained mercy.

Living Before the World

11Beloved, I beg *you* as sojourners and pilgrims, abstain from fleshly lusts which war against the soul, 12having your conduct honorable among the Gentiles, that when they speak against you as evildoers, they may, by *your* good works which they observe, glorify God in the day of visitation.

Submission to Government

13Therefore submit yourselves to every ordinance of man for the Lord's sake, whether to the king as supreme, 14or to governors, as to those who are sent by him for the punishment of evildoers and *for the* praise of those who do good. 15For this is the will of God, that by doing good you may put to silence the ignorance of foolish men— 16as free, yet not using liberty as a cloak for vice, but as bondservants of God. 17Honor all *people.* Love the brotherhood. Fear God. Honor the king.

Submission to Masters

18Servants, *be* submissive to *your* masters with all fear, not only to the good and gentle, but also to the harsh. 19For this *is* commendable, if because of conscience toward God one endures grief, suffering wrongfully. 20For what credit *is it* if, when you are beaten for your faults, you take it patiently? But when you do good and suffer, if you take it patiently, this *is* com-

2:7 bPsalm 118:22   2:8 aIsaiah 8:14

mendable before God. ²¹For to this you were called, because Christ also suffered for us,ª leaving usᵇ an example, that you should follow His steps:

²² *"Who committed no sin,*
　　Nor was deceit found in His mouth";ª

²³who, when He was reviled, did not revile in return; when He suffered, He did not threaten, but committed *Himself* to Him who judges righteously; ²⁴who Himself bore our sins in His own body on the tree, that we, having died to sins, might live for righteousness—by whose stripes you were healed. ²⁵For you were like sheep going astray, but have now returned to the Shepherd and Overseerª of your souls.

Submission to Husbands

3 ¹Wives, likewise, *be* submissive to your own husbands, that even if some do not obey the word, they, without a word, may be won by the conduct of their wives, ²when they observe your chaste conduct *accompanied* by fear. ³Do not let your adornment be *merely* outward—arranging the hair, wearing gold, or putting on *fine* apparel— ⁴rather *let it be* the hidden person of the heart, with the incorruptible *beauty* of a gentle and quiet spirit, which is very precious in the sight of God. ⁵For in this manner, in former times, the holy women who trusted in God also adorned themselves, being submissive to their own husbands, ⁶as Sarah obeyed Abraham, calling him lord, whose daughters you are if you do good and are not afraid with any terror.

A Word to Husbands

⁷Husbands, likewise, dwell with *them* with understanding, giving honor to the wife, as to the weaker vessel, and as *being*

heirs together of the grace of life, that your prayers may not be hindered.

Called to Blessing

⁸Finally, all *of you be* of one mind, having compassion for one another; love as brothers, *be* tenderhearted, *be* courteous;ª ⁹not returning evil for evil or reviling for reviling, but on the contrary blessing, knowing that you were called to this, that you may inherit a blessing. ¹⁰For

　　"He who would love life
　　　And see good days,
　　Let him refrain his tongue from evil,
　　　And his lips from speaking deceit.
11　　*Let him turn away from evil and do*
　　　good;
　　Let him seek peace and pursue it.
12　　*For the eyes of the Lᴏʀᴅ are on the*
　　　righteous,
　　And His ears are open to their
　　　prayers;
　　But the face of the Lᴏʀᴅ is against
　　　*those who do evil."*ª

Suffering for Right and Wrong

¹³And who *is* he who will harm you if you become followers of what is good? ¹⁴But even if you should suffer for righteousness' sake, *you are* blessed. *"And do not be afraid of their threats, nor be troubled."*ª ¹⁵But sanctify the Lord Godª in your hearts, and always *be* ready to *give* a defense to everyone who asks you a reason for the hope that is in you, with meekness and fear; ¹⁶having a good conscience, that when they defame you as evildoers, those who revile your good conduct in Christ may be ashamed. ¹⁷For *it is* better, if it is the will of God, to suffer for doing good than for doing evil.

Christ's Suffering and Ours

¹⁸For Christ also suffered once for sins, the just for the unjust, that He might bring usª to God, being put to death in the flesh but made alive by the Spirit, ¹⁹by whom also He went and preached to the spirits in

CULTURE AND SOCIETY

The women of the Roman Empire are known for the care they expended on their hairstyles (1 Pet. 3:3). This outward emphasis is apparent in the numerous surviving portrait sculptures which show the exact way the hair was piled up, coiled, and fastened. Roman writers sometimes criticized these excesses when they attacked luxury and recommended the simplicity of the past.

WIVES, HUSBANDS, AND RELIGION (1 Pet. 3:1)

In the Roman world, wives were expected to follow their husband's religion. Many women, however, were drawn to other religious groups, like Judaism and Christianity, often provoking their husbands' anger. This marital conflict over religion often caused religious groups to face hostility, and the groups frequently responded by upholding Greek and Roman traditional family values, insofar as they could accommodate them.

The letter of 1 Peter advocates submission to all the authority figures of that day, including kings, governors, slave masters, and husbands (1 Pet. 2:13, 14, 18; 3:1). Similarly, ancient writers who delineated proper societal roles usually included sections on how the male head of the household should rule both wife and slaves.

An emphasis on the adornment of the heart rather than on outward appearance (3:3) was common in ancient speeches and writings. Greek and Roman ideals for wifely behavior included submission, meekness, and quietness. Greek and Roman moralists exhorted wives to a meekness that included avoiding all ostentation, dressing simply rather than drawing attention to oneself. These moralists typically pointed out that women could "adorn" themselves with meekness rather than costly garments.

Moralists often drew on examples from the past, because people generally thought that past matrons had been more obedient than were those of their own day. Jewish readers, as well as Gentiles who had begun learning the Old Testament, would recognize Sarah as an ultimate example of proper behavior. Sarah's address of Abraham as "lord" (3:6) probably reflects the standard Hebrew title of respect for husbands (although her use of this title is most frequent in the apocryphal Testament of Abraham written in Greek).

The letter of 1 Peter exhorts wives whose husbands may have already been distrustful of Christian teaching, suspecting it would subvert their wives' obedience. The model for how to best win over these husbands to Christianity involves adopting the societal norms of a wife's submissiveness and loyalty to her husband.

---

prison, [20]who formerly were disobedient, when once the Divine longsuffering waited[a] in the days of Noah, while the ark was being prepared, in which a few, that is, eight souls, were saved through water. [21]There is also an antitype which now saves us—baptism (not the removal of the filth of the flesh, but the answer of a good conscience toward God), through the resurrection of Jesus Christ, [22]who has gone into heaven and is at the right hand of God, angels and authorities and powers having been made subject to Him.

4 [1]Therefore, since Christ suffered for us[a] in the flesh, arm yourselves also with the same mind, for he who has suffered in the flesh has ceased from sin, [2]that he no longer should live the rest of his time in the flesh for the lusts of men, but for the will of God. [3]For we have spent enough of our past lifetime[a] in doing the will of the Gentiles—when we walked in lewdness, lusts, drunkenness, revelries, drinking parties, and abominable idolatries. [4]In regard to these, they think it strange that you do not run with them in the same flood of dissipation, speaking evil of you. [5]They will give an account to Him who is ready to judge the living and the dead. [6]For this reason the gospel was preached also to those who are dead, that they might be judged according to men in the flesh, but live according to God in the spirit.

Serving for God's Glory

[7]But the end of all things is at hand; therefore be serious and watchful in your prayers. [8]And above all things have fervent love for one another, for "love will cover a multitude of sins." [a] [9]Be hospitable to one another without grumbling. [10]As each one has received a gift, minister it to one another, as good stewards of the manifold

---

3:20 [a]NU-Text and M-Text read when the longsuffering of God waited patiently. 4:1 [a]NU-Text omits for us. 4:3 [a]NU-Text reads time. 4:8 [a]Proverbs 10:12

grace of God. [11]If anyone speaks, *let him speak* as the oracles of God. If anyone ministers, *let him do it* as with the ability which God supplies, that in all things God may be glorified through Jesus Christ, to whom belong the glory and the dominion forever and ever. Amen.

Suffering for God's Glory

[12]Beloved, do not think it strange concerning the fiery trial which is to try you, as though some strange thing happened to you; [13]but rejoice to the extent that you partake of Christ's sufferings, that when His glory is revealed, you may also be glad with exceeding joy. [14]If you are reproached for the name of Christ, blessed *are you,* for the Spirit of glory and of God rests upon you.[a] On their part He is blasphemed, but on your part He is glorified. [15]But let none of you suffer as a murderer, a thief, an evildoer, or as a busybody in other people's matters. [16]Yet if *anyone suffers* as a Christian, let him not be ashamed, but let him glorify God in this matter.[a] [17]For the time *has come* for judgment to begin at the house of God; and if *it begins* with us first, what will *be* the end of those who do not obey the gospel of God? [18]Now

---

4:14 [a]NU-Text omits the rest of this verse.
4:16 [a]NU-Text reads *name.*   4:18 [a]Proverbs
11:31   5:2 [a]NU-Text adds *according to God.*
5:5 [a]Proverbs 3:34   5:8 [a]NU-Text and M-Text omit *because.*   5:10 [a]NU-Text reads *But the God of all grace . . . will perfect, establish, strengthen, and settle you.*   [b]NU-Text and M-Text read *you.*

TIME CAPSULE   A.D. 65 to 67

65 *Nero orders his tutor Seneca to commit suicide*

66 *Roman procurator Florus takes treasure from the Jerusalem temple*

66 *Outbreak of the Jewish revolt against Rome*

67 *Nero orders his general Domitius Corbulo to kill himself*

67 *Roman forces kill 11,000 Samaritans*

67 *Paul is arrested and executed in Rome (?)*

"If the righteous one is scarcely saved,
Where will the ungodly and the sinner
appear?" [a]

[19]Therefore let those who suffer according to the will of God commit their souls *to Him* in doing good, as to a faithful Creator.

Shepherd the Flock

5 [1]The elders who are among you I exhort, I who am a fellow elder and a witness of the sufferings of Christ, and also a partaker of the glory that will be revealed: [2]Shepherd the flock of God which is among you, serving as overseers, not by compulsion but willingly,[a] not for dishonest gain but eagerly; [3]nor as being lords over those entrusted to you, but being examples to the flock; [4]and when the Chief Shepherd appears, you will receive the crown of glory that does not fade away.

Submit to God, Resist the Devil

[5]Likewise you younger people, submit yourselves to *your* elders. Yes, all of *you* be submissive to one another, and be clothed with humility, for

"God resists the proud,
But gives grace to the humble." [a]

[6]Therefore humble yourselves under the mighty hand of God, that He may exalt you in due time, [7]casting all your care upon Him, for He cares for you.

[8]Be sober, be vigilant; because[a] your adversary the devil walks about like a roaring lion, seeking whom he may devour. [9]Resist him, steadfast in the faith, knowing that the same sufferings are experienced by your brotherhood in the world. [10]But may[a] the God of all grace, who called us[b] to His eternal glory by Christ Jesus, after you have suffered a while, perfect, establish, strengthen, and settle *you.* [11]To Him *be* the glory and the dominion forever and ever. Amen.

Farewell and Peace

[12]By Silvanus, our faithful brother as I consider him, I have written to you briefly, exhorting and testifying that this is the true grace of God in which you stand.

[13]She who is in Babylon, elect together with *you,* greets you; and *so does* Mark my son. [14]Greet one another with a kiss of love.

Peace to you all who are in Christ Jesus. Amen.

The Letter of Jude

The Jude (or Judas) named as the author of this letter (1:1) is most probably the half brother of Jesus (see Matt. 13:55). He is identified as the "brother of James" (Jude 1:1), another half brother of Jesus. Some scholars have doubted whether Jude actually wrote this letter, raising questions similar to those raised about James's authorship of the letter bearing his name (see "The Letter of James" at James 1:1). As with the letter of James, however, others accept the book as an authentic letter by Jude himself.

Exactly when Jude wrote the letter depends to some extent on its relationship with the letter of 2 Peter. The marked similarity of wording between Jude 1:4–19 and 2 Peter 2:1—3:3 indicates direct literary dependence. Yet it cannot be proven whether the 2 Peter passage was borrowed from Jude, or Jude borrowed from 2 Peter, or both letters used ideas from a common source that no longer exists. The apparent literary relationship between the two letters might mean that Jude was written at roughly the same time as 2 Peter (see "The Second Letter of Peter" at 2 Pet. 1:1).

Jude wrote this letter to a group of Christians who were being led astray by false teachers. He urges them to fight for the truth (Jude 1:3).

■ Jude 1:1–25

Jude
Greeting to the Called

1 :1 Jude, a bondservant of Jesus Christ, and brother of James,

To those who are called, sanctified[a] by God the Father, and preserved in Jesus Christ:

²Mercy, peace, and love be multiplied to you.

Contend for the Faith

³Beloved, while I was very diligent to write to you concerning our common salvation, I found it necessary to write to you exhorting you to contend earnestly for the faith which was once for all delivered to the saints. ⁴For certain men have crept in unnoticed, who long ago were marked out for this condemnation, ungodly men, who turn the grace of our God into lewdness and deny the only Lord God[a] and our Lord Jesus Christ.

Old and New Apostates

⁵But I want to remind you, though you once knew this, that the Lord, having saved the people out of the land of Egypt, afterward destroyed those who did not believe. ⁶And the angels who did not keep their proper domain, but left their own abode, He has reserved in everlasting chains under darkness for the judgment of the great day; ⁷as Sodom and Gomorrah, and the cities around them in a similar manner to these, having given themselves over to sexual immorality and gone after strange flesh, are set forth as an example, suffering the vengeance of eternal fire.

⁸Likewise also these dreamers defile the flesh, reject authority, and speak evil of dignitaries. ⁹Yet Michael the archangel, in contending with the devil, when he disputed about the body of Moses, dared not bring against him a reviling accusation, but said, "The Lord rebuke you!" ¹⁰But these speak evil of whatever they do not know; and whatever they know naturally, like brute beasts, in these things they corrupt themselves. ¹¹Woe to them! For they have gone in the way of Cain, have run greedily in the error of Balaam for profit, and perished in the rebellion of Korah.

Apostates Depraved and Doomed

¹²These are spots in your love feasts, while they feast with you without fear, serving *only* themselves. *They are* clouds without water, carried about[a] by the winds; late autumn trees without fruit, twice dead, pulled up by the roots; ¹³raging waves of the sea, foaming up their own shame; wandering stars for whom is reserved the blackness of darkness forever.

¹⁴Now Enoch, the seventh from Adam, prophesied about these men also, saying, "Behold, the Lord comes with ten thousands of His saints, ¹⁵to execute judgment on all, to convict all who are ungodly among them of all their ungodly deeds which they have committed in an ungodly way, and of all the harsh things which ungodly sinners have spoken against Him."

1:1 ªNU-Text reads *beloved.*   1:4 ªNU-Text omits *God.*   1:12 ªNU-Text and M-Text read *along.*

Apostates Predicted

16These are grumblers, complainers, walking according to their own lusts; and they mouth great swelling *words,* flattering people to gain advantage. 17But you, beloved, remember the words which were spoken before by the apostles of our Lord Jesus Christ: 18how they told you that there would be mockers in the last time who would walk according to their own ungodly lusts. 19These are sensual persons, who cause divisions, not having the Spirit.

Maintain Your Life with God

20But you, beloved, building yourselves up on your most holy faith, praying in the Holy Spirit, 21keep yourselves in the love of God, looking for the mercy of our Lord Jesus Christ unto eternal life.

22And on some have compassion, making a distinction;a 23but others save with fear, pulling *them* out of the fire,a hating even the garment defiled by the flesh.

Glory to God

24   Now to Him who is able to keep youa
      from stumbling,
   And to present *you* faultless
   Before the presence of His glory with
      exceeding joy,
25   To God our Savior,a
   Who alone is wise,b
   Be glory and majesty,
   Dominion and power,c
   Both now and forever.
   Amen.

1:22 aNU-Text reads *who are doubting* (or *making distinctions*).   1:23 aNU-Text adds *and on some have mercy with fear* and omits *with fear* in first clause.   1:24 aM-Text reads *them.*
1:25 aNU-Text reads *To the only God our Savior.* bNU-Text omits *Who . . . is wise* and adds *Through Jesus Christ our Lord.*   cNU-Text adds *Before all time.*

The Second Letter of Peter

Two New Testament letters bear the name of Simon Peter (1 Pet. 1:1; 2 Pet. 1:1). The two have little in common with each other, and the differences in style, vocabulary, and theology between 1 and 2 Peter have led some scholars to doubt whether Peter was the author of 2 Peter. Other scholars recognize these differences, but still accept Peter's authorship of the second letter. Differences in style and vocabulary are explained as the re-

sult of Peter using a different secretary to write the second letter, and by treating differing subject matter.

The author of the letter refers to "our beloved brother Paul" and to "all his epistles" (2 Pet. 3:15, 16). Some suppose that if Peter wrote the letter he would never have implied that Paul's writings were equal to "the rest of the Scriptures" (3:16). Moreover, it seems unlikely that Paul's letters would have been gathered into a formal collection prior to Peter's and Paul's martyrdoms under Nero. Nevertheless, others point out that the apostles wrote and taught with a consciousness of having divine authority, as Paul did in his earliest letters (1 Cor. 2:13; Gal. 1:1).

Those who accept Peter's authorship believe he probably wrote in the early 60s, not long before his death. Since the letter of 2 Peter apparently acknowledges the existence of 1 Peter (2 Pet. 3:1), it would necessarily have been written after 1 Peter. If an unknown author wrote the letter, its composition might date to the late 1st century or early 2nd century.

The similarities between 2 Peter and Jude do not necessarily determine when 2 Peter may have been written. While 2 Pet. 2:1—3:3 appears to quote word for word from Jude 1:4–19 (see "The Letter of Jude" at Jude 1:1), it is possible that 2 Peter depended on Jude, or that Peter and Jude used a common source, or even that Jude copied Peter.

The letter is written out of pastoral concern to counter false teachings and their influence on the lives of early Christians. Certain teachers, for their own personal gain, were promising that people could be Christians and still live immoral lives. The writer of this letter is concerned that there be a check against this false teaching and immoral living even after he is gone (1:12–15).

■ 2 Peter 1:1—3:18

2 Peter
Greeting the Faithful

1 :1 Simon Peter, a bondservant and apostle of Jesus Christ,

To those who have obtained like precious faith with us by the righteousness of our God and Savior Jesus Christ:

2Grace and peace be multiplied to you in the knowledge of God and of Jesus our Lord, 3as His divine power has given to us all things that *pertain* to life and godliness, through the knowledge of Him who called us by glory and virtue, [4]by which have been given to us exceedingly great and precious promises, that through these you may be partakers of the divine nature, having escaped the corruption *that is* in the world through lust.

Fruitful Growth in the Faith

[5]But also for this very reason, giving all diligence, add to your faith virtue, to virtue knowledge, [6]to knowledge self-control, to self-control perseverance, to perseverance godliness, [7]to godliness brotherly kindness, and to brotherly kindness love. [8]For if these things are yours and abound, *you will be* neither barren nor unfruitful in the knowledge of our Lord Jesus Christ. [9]For he who lacks these things is shortsighted, even to blindness, and has forgotten that he was cleansed from his old sins. [10]Therefore, brethren, be even more diligent to make your call and election sure, for if you do these things you will never stumble; [11]for so an entrance will be supplied to you abundantly into the everlasting kingdom of our Lord and Savior Jesus Christ.

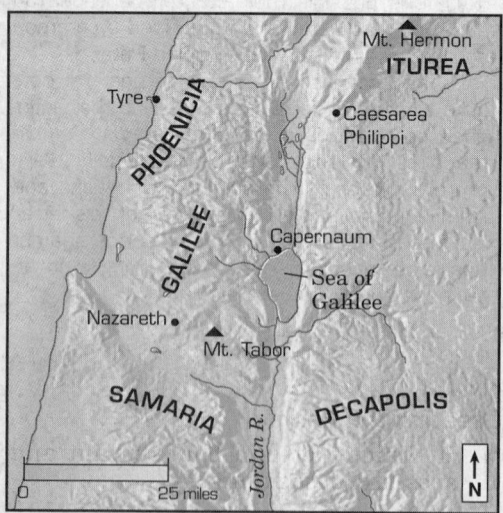

Sites of the Transfiguration
None of the gospel accounts exactly locate the high mountain on which the transfiguration of Jesus took place (2 Pet. 1:16–18). Matthew and Mark link the event closely to Peter's prior confession of faith made in Caesarea Philippi, thus suggesting Mt. Hermon to the north as a plausible site. The account in Luke ties the event closely to Jesus' departure from Galilee en route to Jerusalem, making Mt. Tabor a credible possibility as well.

Peter's Approaching Death

[12]For this reason I will not be negligent to remind you always of these things, though you know and are established in the present truth. [13]Yes, I think it is right, as long as I am in this tent, to stir you up by reminding *you,* [14]knowing that shortly I *must* put off my tent, just as our Lord Jesus Christ showed me. [15]Moreover I will be careful to ensure that you always have a reminder of these things after my decease.

The Trustworthy Prophetic Word

[16]For we did not follow cunningly devised fables when we made known to you the power and coming of our Lord Jesus Christ, but were eyewitnesses of His majesty. [17]For He received from God the Father honor and glory when such a voice came to Him from the Excellent Glory: "This is My beloved Son, in whom I am well pleased." [18]And we heard this voice which came from heaven when we were with Him on the holy mountain.

[19]And so we have the prophetic word confirmed,[a] which you do well to heed as a light that shines in a dark place, until the day dawns and the morning star rises in your hearts; [20]knowing this first, that no prophecy of Scripture is of any private interpretation,[a] [21]for prophecy never came by the will of man, but holy men of God[a] spoke *as they were* moved by the Holy Spirit.

Destructive Doctrines

2 [1]But there were also false prophets among the people, even as there will be false teachers among you, who will secretly bring in destructive heresies, even denying the Lord who bought them, *and* bring on themselves swift destruction. [2]And many will follow their destructive ways, because of whom the way of truth will be blasphemed. [3]By covetousness they will exploit you with deceptive words; for a long time their judgment has not been idle, and their destruction does[a] not slumber.

Doom of False Teachers

[4]For if God did not spare the angels who sinned, but cast *them* down to hell and delivered *them* into chains of darkness, to

---

1:19 [a]Or *We also have the more sure prophetic word.*   1:20 [a]Or *origin*   1:21 [a]NU-Text reads *but men spoke from God.*   2:3 [a]M-Text reads *will not.*

QUOTATIONS OF GREEK LITERATURE

The New Testament quotes often from the Septuagint, the Greek translation of the Old Testament, and once from the Jewish apocryphal book of 1 Enoch (see Jude 1:14, 15). New Testament writers also referred to Greek literature, quoting the works of Greek authors dating as far back as 600 B.C.

Quotation: "Cretans are always liars, evil beasts, lazy gluttons" (Titus 1:12)
From: *De oraculis* by Epimenides (about 600 B.C.)

Epimenides was a wandering religious teacher. The quotation in Titus also resembles a line from Hesiod's *Theogony*, a better-known poem.

Quotation: "a sow, having washed, to her wallowing in the mire" (2 Pet. 2:22)
From: A fragment of Heraclitus (about 500 B.C.)

Heraclitus was an early philosopher. There is a proverb known from other sources that seems to be closer than Heraclitus's fragment to what Peter is saying.

Quotation: "It is hard for you to kick against the goads" (Acts 26:14)
From: *Bacchae*, 794, by Euripides (485–406 B.C.)

The line is a familiar proverb, and the phrase in Acts 26 may not be quoted directly from Euripides.

Quotation: "Evil company corrupts good habits" (1 Cor. 15:33)
From: *Thais* by Menander (343–293 B.C.)

Menander, a writer of dramatic comedy, was from Athens. The quotation was a common proverb by Paul's time.

Quotation: "For we are also His offspring" (Acts 17:28)
From: *Phenomena*, 5, by Aratus (314–240 B.C.)

The *Phenomena* was a famous poem, dealing mainly with astronomy.

be reserved for judgment; [5]and did not spare the ancient world, but saved Noah, *one of* eight *people,* a preacher of righteousness, bringing in the flood on the world of the ungodly; [6]and turning the cities of Sodom and Gomorrah into ashes, condemned *them* to destruction, making *them* an example to those who afterward would live ungodly; [7]and delivered righteous Lot, *who was* oppressed by the filthy conduct of the wicked [8](for that righteous man, dwelling among them, tormented *his* righteous soul from day to day by seeing and hearing *their* lawless deeds)— [9]*then* the Lord knows how to deliver the godly out of temptations and to reserve the unjust under punishment for the day of judgment, [10]and especially those who walk according to the flesh in the lust of uncleanness and despise authority. *They are* presumptuous, self-willed. They are not afraid to speak evil of dignitaries, [11]whereas angels, who are greater in power and might, do not bring a reviling accusation against them before the Lord.

Depravity of False Teachers

[12]But these, like natural brute beasts made to be caught and destroyed, speak evil of the things they do not understand, and will utterly perish in their own corruption, [13]*and* will receive the wages of unrighteousness, *as* those who count it pleasure to carouse in the daytime. *They are* spots and blemishes, carousing in their own deceptions while they feast with you, [14]having eyes full of adultery and that cannot cease from sin, enticing unstable souls.

BELIEFS AND IDEAS

The official and unofficial religions practiced in the Roman world included many fables or stories about various gods. It was known that these stories were not historical accounts, and the expression "cunningly devised fables" (2 Pet. 1:16), like the English word "myth," was used as an insult meaning "false." People who heard the gospel knew the difference between myth and history.

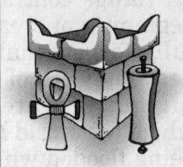

They have a heart trained in covetous practices, *and are* accursed children. [15]They have forsaken the right way and gone astray, following the way of Balaam the *son* of Beor, who loved the wages of unrighteousness; [16]but he was rebuked for his iniquity: a dumb donkey speaking with a man's voice restrained the madness of the prophet.

[17]These are wells without water, clouds[a] carried by a tempest, for whom is reserved the blackness of darkness forever.[b]

Deceptions of False Teachers

[18]For when they speak great swelling *words* of emptiness, they allure through the lusts of the flesh, through lewdness, the ones who have actually escaped[a] from those who live in error. [19]While they promise them liberty, they themselves are slaves of corruption; for by whom a person is overcome, by him also he is brought into bondage. [20]For if, after they have escaped the pollutions of the world through the knowledge of the Lord and Savior Jesus Christ, they are again entangled in them and overcome, the latter end is worse for them than the beginning. [21]For it would have been better for them not to have known the way of righteousness, than having known *it,* to turn from the holy commandment delivered to them. [22]But it has happened to them according to the true proverb: *"A dog returns to his own vomit,"*[a] and, "a sow, having washed, to her wallowing in the mire."

God's Promise Is Not Slack

3 [1]Beloved, I now write to you this second epistle (in *both of* which I stir up your pure minds by way of reminder), [2]that you may be mindful of the words which were spoken before by the holy prophets, and of the commandment of us,[a] the apostles of the Lord and Savior, [3]knowing this first: that scoffers will come in the last days, walking according to their own lusts, [4]and saying, "Where is the promise of His coming? For since the fathers fell asleep, all things continue as *they were* from the beginning of creation." [5]For this they willfully forget: that by the word of God the heavens were of old, and the earth standing out of water and in the water, [6]by which the world *that* then existed perished, being flooded with water. [7]But the heavens and the earth *which* are now preserved by the same word, are reserved for fire until the day of judgment and perdition of ungodly men.

[8]But, beloved, do not forget this one thing, that with the Lord one day *is* as a thousand years, and a thousand years as one day. [9]The Lord is not slack concerning *His* promise, as some count slackness, but is longsuffering toward us,[a] not willing that any should perish but that all should come to repentance.

The Day of the Lord

[10]But the day of the Lord will come as a thief in the night, in which the heavens will pass away with a great noise, and the elements will melt with fervent heat; both the earth and the works that are in it will be burned up.[a] [11]Therefore, since all these things will be dissolved, what manner *of persons* ought you to be in holy conduct and godliness, [12]looking for and hastening the coming of the day of God, because of which the heavens will be dissolved, being on fire, and the elements will melt with fervent heat? [13]Nevertheless we, according to His promise, look for new heavens and a new earth in which righteousness dwells.

2:17 [a]NU-Text reads *and mists.* [b]NU-Text omits *forever.* 2:18 [a]NU-Text reads *are barely escaping.* 2:22 [a]Proverbs 26:11 3:2 [a]NU-Text and M-Text read *commandment of the apostles of your Lord and Savior* or *commandment of your apostles of the Lord and Savior.* 3:9 [a]NU-Text reads *you.* 3:10 [a]NU-Text reads *laid bare* (literally *found*).

TIME CAPSULE A.D. *68 to 71*

68	Nero, age 30, is forced to commit suicide
69	Troops in Caesarea hail Vespasian as emperor
69	An impostor pretends to be Nero in Greece
70	Titus defeats Jerusalem and burns down the temple
70	Prayer becomes a substitute for sacrifices in the temple
70–75	Followers of Paul write Colossians and Ephesians (?)
71	Titus celebrates a triumph for his victory over Judea

Be Steadfast

¹⁴Therefore, beloved, looking forward to these things, be diligent to be found by Him in peace, without spot and blameless; ¹⁵and consider *that* the longsuffering of our Lord *is* salvation—as also our beloved brother Paul, according to the wisdom given to him, has written to you, ¹⁶as also in all his epistles, speaking in them of these things, in which are some things hard to understand, which untaught and unstable *people* twist to their own destruction, as *they do* also the rest of the Scriptures.

¹⁷You therefore, beloved, since you know *this* beforehand, beware lest you also fall from your own steadfastness, being led away with the error of the wicked; ¹⁸but grow in the grace and knowledge of our Lord and Savior Jesus Christ.

To Him *be* the glory both now and forever. Amen.

1:3 ᵃNU-Text omits *by Himself.* ᵇNU-Text omits *our.*   1:5 ᵃPsalm 2:7   ᵇ2 Samuel 7:14
1:6 ᵃDeuteronomy 32:43 (Septuagint, Dead Sea Scrolls); Psalm 97:7   1:7 ᵃPsalm 104:4

The Letter to the Hebrews

Unlike the letters recognized as written by Paul, the letter to the Hebrews is not signed by its author, nor are the addressees named. It is not a circular letter to be read in several churches. The many exhortations remind us of a sermon. Hebrews deals with Christ's priesthood and sacrifice much more thoroughly than any other New Testament book.

Even the early church fathers were uncertain who wrote this letter. The mention of Timothy (Heb. 13:23) has led some to think that Paul or one of his associates wrote the letter. Apollos has been suggested because the style and content of Hebrews reflect a Jew versed in Greek learning and literary style (see Acts 18:24-28). Other suggestions include Barnabas, Luke, Silas, Aquila, or Priscilla as possible authors. But after considering all the evidence, many scholars agree that the authorship of this letter remains unknown.

Hebrews was certainly written during the last half of the 1st century. It is quoted at length in a letter written about A.D. 95 to the church at Corinth by Clement, a leader in the church at Rome. If not written during the lifetime of Paul, Hebrews was most likely written during the lifetime of Paul's younger associate, Timothy (13:23).

Almost all of Hebrews is exposition of Old Testament passages. The author uses Jewish methods of interpretation common in the synagogues of his day. He differs from Jewish interpreters, however, in that he sees Christ as the fulfillment of the Old Testament. The letter is a masterful description of the salvation obtained by Christ's priesthood and sacrifice interwoven with exhortation for Christians to persevere in the benefits of this salvation.

▼ ■ Hebrews 1:1—13:25

Hebrews
God's Supreme Revelation

1:1 God, who at various times and in various ways spoke in time past to the fathers by the prophets, ²has in these last days spoken to us by *His* Son, whom He has appointed heir of all things, through whom also He made the worlds; ³who being the brightness of *His* glory and the express image of His person, and upholding all things by the word of His power, when He had by Himselfᵃ purged ourᵇ sins, sat down at the right hand of the Majesty on high, ⁴having become so much better than the angels, as He has by inheritance obtained a more excellent name than they.

The Son Exalted Above Angels

⁵For to which of the angels did He ever say:

"You are My Son,
Today I have begotten You"?ᵃ

And again:

"I will be to Him a Father,
And He shall be to Me a Son"?ᵇ

⁶But when He again brings the firstborn into the world, He says:

"Let all the angels of God worship Him."ᵃ

⁷And of the angels He says:

"Who makes His angels spirits
And His ministers a flame of fire."ᵃ

⁸But to the Son He *says:*

"Your throne, O God, is forever and ever;

A scepter of righteousness is the
     scepter of Your kingdom.
9   You have loved righteousness and
          hated lawlessness;
     Therefore God, Your God, has
          anointed You
     With the oil of gladness more than
          Your companions." a

10And:

"You, LORD, in the beginning laid the
     foundation of the earth,
And the heavens are the work of Your
     hands.
11   They will perish, but You remain;
     And they will all grow old like a
          garment;
12   Like a cloak You will fold them up,
     And they will be changed.
     But You are the same,
     And Your years will not fail." a

13But to which of the angels has He
ever said:

"Sit at My right hand,
     Till I make Your enemies Your
          footstool"?a

14Are they not all ministering spirits sent
forth to minister for those who will inherit
salvation?

Do Not Neglect Salvation

2 1Therefore we must give the more
     earnest heed to the things we have
heard, lest we drift away. 2For if the word
spoken through angels proved steadfast,
and every transgression and disobedience
received a just reward, 3how shall we escape if we neglect so great a salvation,
which at the first began to be spoken by
the Lord, and was confirmed to us by those
who heard Him, 4God also bearing witness
both with signs and wonders, with various
miracles, and gifts of the Holy Spirit, according to His own will?

The Son Made Lower than Angels

5For He has not put the world to come,
of which we speak, in subjection to angels.
6But one testified in a certain place, saying:

"What is man that You are mindful of
     him,
Or the son of man that You take care
     of him?
7   You have made him a little lower than
          the angels;
     You have crowned him with glory and
          honor,a
     And set him over the works of Your
          hands.
8   You have put all things in subjection
          under his feet." a

For in that He put all in subjection under
him, He left nothing that is not put under
him. But now we do not yet see all things
put under him. 9But we see Jesus, who was
made a little lower than the angels, for the
suffering of death crowned with glory and
honor, that He, by the grace of God, might
taste death for everyone.

Bringing Many Sons to Glory

10For it was fitting for Him, for whom
are all things and by whom are all things,
in bringing many sons to glory, to make the
captain of their salvation perfect through
sufferings. 11For both He who sanctifies
and those who are being sanctified are all
of one, for which reason He is not ashamed
to call them brethren, 12saying:

"I will declare Your name to My
     brethren;
In the midst of the assembly I will
     sing praise to You." a

1:9 aPsalm 45:6, 7   1:12 aPsalm
102:25–27   1:13 aPsalm 110:1
2:7 aNU-Text and M-Text omit the rest of verse 7.
2:8 aPsalm 8:4–6   2:12 aPsalm 22:22

RELIGION AND WORSHIP

*Angels apparently played some role when Moses received the law on Mount Sinai (Gal.
3:19). The Old Testament already described the presence of a heavenly army of angels
at Sinai (Ps. 68:17 and probably Deut. 33:2, if "saints" refers to angels). Jewish
tradition outside the Bible further developed the idea of "the word spoken through
angels" (Heb. 2:2).*

13And again:

> "I will put My trust in Him."a

And again:

> "Here am I and the children whom God has given Me."b

14Inasmuch then as the children have partaken of flesh and blood, He Himself likewise shared in the same, that through death He might destroy him who had the power of death, that is, the devil, 15and release those who through fear of death were all their lifetime subject to bondage. 16For indeed He does not give aid to angels, but He does give aid to the seed of Abraham. 17Therefore, in all things He had to be made like *His* brethren, that He might be a merciful and faithful High Priest in things *pertaining* to God, to make propitiation for the sins of the people. 18For in that He Himself has suffered, being tempted, He is able to aid those who are tempted.

The Son Was Faithful

3 1Therefore, holy brethren, partakers of the heavenly calling, consider the Apostle and High Priest of our confession, Christ Jesus, 2who was faithful to Him who appointed Him, as Moses also *was faithful* in all His house. 3For this One has been counted worthy of more glory than Moses, inasmuch as He who built the house has more honor than the house. 4For every house is built by someone, but He who built all things *is* God. 5And Moses indeed *was* faithful in all His house as a servant, for a testimony of those things which would be spoken *afterward,* 6but Christ as a Son over His own house, whose house we are if we hold fast the confidence and the rejoicing of the hope firm to the end.a

Be Faithful

7Therefore, as the Holy Spirit says:

> "Today, if you will hear His voice,
> 8 Do not harden your hearts as in the rebellion,
> In the day of trial in the wilderness,
> 9 Where your fathers tested Me, tried Me,
> And saw My works forty years.

> 10 Therefore I was angry with that generation,
> And said, 'They always go astray in their heart,
> And they have not known My ways.'
> 11 So I swore in My wrath,
> 'They shall not enter My rest.' "a

12Beware, brethren, lest there be in any of you an evil heart of unbelief in departing from the living God; 13but exhort one another daily, while it is called *"Today,"* lest any of you be hardened through the deceitfulness of sin. 14For we have become partakers of Christ if we hold the beginning of our confidence steadfast to the end, 15while it is said:

> "Today, if you will hear His voice,
> Do not harden your hearts as in the rebellion."a

Failure of the Wilderness Wanderers

16For who, having heard, rebelled? Indeed, *was it* not all who came out of Egypt, *led* by Moses? 17Now with whom was He angry forty years? *Was it* not with those who sinned, whose corpses fell in the wilderness? 18And to whom did He swear that they would not enter His rest, but to those who did not obey? 19So we see that they could not enter in because of unbelief.

The Promise of Rest

4 1Therefore, since a promise remains of entering His rest, let us fear lest any of you seem to have come short of it. 2For indeed the gospel was preached to us as well as to them; but the word which they heard

---

2:13 a2 Samuel 22:3; Isaiah 8:17   bIsaiah 8:18
3:6 aNU-Text omits *firm to the end.*   3:11 aPsalm 95:7–11   3:15 aPsalm 95:7, 8

TIME CAPSULE   A.D. 74 to 80

74	Masada falls to the Romans and its defenders commit suicide
75	Vessels from the Jerusalem temple are displayed at Rome
75	Josephus publishes The Jewish War
75	Trajan (later emperor) is in Syria as a soldier
79	The volcano Vesuvius erupts, burying Pompeii and Herculaneum
80– 100	Unknown author writes letter of 2 Thessalonians (?)

did not profit them,[a] not being mixed with faith in those who heard *it*. [3]For we who have believed do enter that rest, as He has said:

"So I swore in My wrath,
  'They shall not enter My rest,' "[a]

although the works were finished from the foundation of the world. [4]For He has spoken in a certain place of the seventh *day* in this way: *"And God rested on the seventh day from all His works";*[a] [5]and again in this place: *"They shall not enter My rest."*[a]

[6]Since therefore it remains that some *must* enter it, and those to whom it was first preached did not enter because of disobedience, [7]again He designates a certain day, saying in David, *"Today,"* after such a long time, as it has been said:

"Today, if you will hear His voice,
  Do not harden your hearts."[a]

[8]For if Joshua had given them rest, then He would not afterward have spoken of another day. [9]There remains therefore a rest for the people of God. [10]For he who has entered His rest has himself also ceased from his works as God *did* from His.

The Word Discovers Our Condition

[11]Let us therefore be diligent to enter that rest, lest anyone fall according to the same example of disobedience. [12]For the word of God *is* living and powerful, and sharper than any two-edged sword, piercing even to the division of soul and spirit, and of joints and marrow, and is a discerner of the thoughts and intents of the heart. [13]And there is no creature hidden from His sight, but all things *are* naked and open to the eyes of Him to whom we *must give* account.

Our Compassionate High Priest

[14]Seeing then that we have a great High Priest who has passed through the heavens, Jesus the Son of God, let us hold fast *our* confession. [15]For we do not have a High Priest who cannot sympathize with our weaknesses, but was in all *points* tempted as *we are*, yet without sin. [16]Let us therefore come boldly to the throne of grace, that we may obtain mercy and find grace to help in time of need.

Qualifications for High Priesthood

5 [1]For every high priest taken from among men is appointed for men in things *pertaining* to God, that he may offer both gifts and sacrifices for sins. [2]He can have compassion on those who are ignorant and going astray, since he himself is also subject to weakness. [3]Because of this he is required as for the people, so also for himself, to offer *sacrifices* for sins. [4]And no man takes this honor to himself, but he who is called by God, just as Aaron *was*.

A Priest Forever

[5]So also Christ did not glorify Himself to become High Priest, *but it* was He who said to Him:

"You are My Son,
  Today I have begotten You."[a]

[6]As *He* also *says* in another *place:*

"You are a priest forever
  According to the order of
    Melchizedek";[a]

[7]who, in the days of His flesh, when He had offered up prayers and supplications, with vehement cries and tears to Him who was able to save Him from death, and was heard because of His godly fear, [8]though He was a Son, *yet* He learned obedience by the things which He suffered. [9]And having been perfected, He became the author of eternal salvation to all who obey Him, [10]called by God as High Priest *"according to the order of Melchizedek,"* [11]of whom we have much to say, and hard to explain, since you have become dull of hearing.

Spiritual Immaturity

[12]For though by this time you ought to be teachers, you need *someone* to teach you again the first principles of the oracles of God; and you have come to need milk and not solid food. [13]For everyone who partakes *only* of milk *is* unskilled in the word of righteousness, for he is a babe. [14]But solid food belongs to those who are of full age, *that is,* those who by reason of use have

---

4:2 [a]NU-Text and M-Text read *profit them, since they were not united by faith with those who heeded it.*
4:3 [a]Psalm 95:11   4:4 [a]Genesis 2:2
4:5 [a]Psalm 95:11   4:7 [a]Psalm 95:7, 8
5:5 [a]Psalm 2:7   5:6 [a]Psalm 110:4

MELCHIZEDEK IN JEWISH TRADITION (Heb. 5:8–10)

The author of Hebrews uses the figure of Melchizedek to clarify the nature of the priesthood of Christ. Melchizedek, whose name means "king of righteousness" (Heb. 7:2), appears briefly in Genesis as the king of Salem (Gen. 14:18–20). Despite being mentioned only in Genesis and one psalm (Ps. 110:4), the mystery of Melchizedek's figure inspired much interpretive activity in Judaism during the second temple period.

Such intrigue was not lost on serious interpreters of the Old Testament in antiquity. Melchizedek emerges as the central figure in a fragmentary document found at Qumran. This document, entitled "11QMelchizedek," consists largely of interpretive comments on Old Testament passages, and presents Melchizedek as an important figure in God's judgment upon the earth in the end times.

Another fragmentary text, called "Melchizedek," was found at Nag Hammadi in Egypt. It seemingly contains much older traditions from a group of Jews who found the origins of their theology in the person of Seth, the son of Adam born after Cain killed Abel (Gen. 4:25). In this tradition Melchizedek, "priest of God Most High," receives special revelations concerning Jesus from heavenly messengers. In a second group of revelations Melchizedek himself becomes Jesus, and is both crucified and raised as savior! Such ideas make Jesus the new appearance of Melchizedek.

The author of Hebrews reads the Melchizedek tradition in a restrained manner compared to the speculations current at that time. Ultimately, he is not so much interested in Melchizedek, as in Christ, who was the High Priest "according to the order of Melchizedek" (Heb. 5:8–10). Christ's heavenly priesthood surpasses any earthly priesthood, even the priesthood of the king of Salem (Heb. 7:15–17).

---

their senses exercised to discern both good and evil.

The Peril of Not Progressing

6 ¹Therefore, leaving the discussion of the elementary *principles* of Christ, let us go on to perfection, not laying again the foundation of repentance from dead works and of faith toward God, ²of the doctrine of baptisms, of laying on of hands, of resurrection of the dead, and of eternal judgment. ³And this we willᵃ do if God permits.

⁴For *it is* impossible for those who were once enlightened, and have tasted the heavenly gift, and have become partakers of the Holy Spirit, ⁵and have tasted the good word of God and the powers of the age to come, ⁶if they fall away,ᵃ to renew them again to repentance, since they crucify again for themselves the Son of God, and put *Him* to an open shame.

⁷For the earth which drinks in the rain that often comes upon it, and bears herbs useful for those by whom it is cultivated, receives blessing from God; ⁸but if it bears thorns and briers, *it is* rejected and near to being cursed, whose end *is* to be burned.

A Better Estimate

⁹But, beloved, we are confident of better things concerning you, yes, things that accompany salvation, though we speak in this manner. ¹⁰For God *is* not unjust to forget your work and labor of ᵃ love which you have shown toward His name, *in that* you have ministered to the saints, and do minister. ¹¹And we desire that each one of you show the same diligence to the full assurance of hope until the end, ¹²that you do not become sluggish, but imitate those who through faith and patience inherit the promises.

God's Infallible Purpose in Christ

¹³For when God made a promise to Abraham, because He could swear by no one greater, He swore by Himself, ¹⁴saying, *"Surely blessing I will bless you, and multiplying I will multiply you."* ᵃ ¹⁵And so, after he had patiently endured, he obtained the promise. ¹⁶For men indeed swear by the greater, and an oath for confirmation *is* for them an end of all dispute. ¹⁷Thus God,

---

6:3 ᵃM-Text reads *let us do.*   6:6 ᵃOr *and have fallen away*   6:10 ᵃNU-Text omits *labor of.*
6:14 ᵃGenesis 22:17

determining to show more abundantly to the heirs of promise the immutability of His counsel, confirmed *it* by an oath, [18]that by two immutable things, in which it *is* impossible for God to lie, we might[a] have strong consolation, who have fled for refuge to lay hold of the hope set before *us.*

[19]This *hope* we have as an anchor of the soul, both sure and steadfast, and which enters the *Presence* behind the veil, [20]where the forerunner has entered for us, *even* Jesus, having become High Priest forever according to the order of Melchizedek.

The King of Righteousness

7 [1]For this Melchizedek, king of Salem, priest of the Most High God, who met Abraham returning from the slaughter of the kings and blessed him, [2]to whom also Abraham gave a tenth part of all, first being translated "king of righteousness," and then also king of Salem, meaning "king of peace," [3]without father, without mother, without genealogy, having neither beginning of days nor end of life, but made like the Son of God, remains a priest continually.

[4]Now consider how great this man *was,* to whom even the patriarch Abraham gave a tenth of the spoils. [5]And indeed those who are of the sons of Levi, who receive the priesthood, have a commandment to receive tithes from the people according to the law, that is, from their brethren, though they have come from the loins of Abraham; [6]but he whose genealogy is not derived from them received tithes from Abraham and blessed him who had the

promises. [7]Now beyond all contradiction the lesser is blessed by the better. [8]Here mortal men receive tithes, but there he *receives them,* of whom it is witnessed that he lives. [9]Even Levi, who receives tithes, paid tithes through Abraham, so to speak, [10]for he was still in the loins of his father when Melchizedek met him.

Need for a New Priesthood

[11]Therefore, if perfection were through the Levitical priesthood (for under it the people received the law), what further need *was there* that another priest should rise according to the order of Melchizedek, and not be called according to the order of Aaron? [12]For the priesthood being changed, of necessity there is also a change of the law. [13]For He of whom these things are spoken belongs to another tribe, from which no man has officiated at the altar.

[14]For *it is* evident that our Lord arose from Judah, of which tribe Moses spoke nothing concerning priesthood.[a] [15]And it is yet far more evident if, in the likeness of Melchizedek, there arises another priest [16]who has come, not according to the law of a fleshly commandment, but according to the power of an endless life. [17]For He testifies:[a]

> "You are a priest forever
> According to the order of
>   Melchizedek."[b]

[18]For on the one hand there is an annulling of the former commandment because of its weakness and unprofitableness, [19]for the law made nothing perfect; on the other hand, *there is the* bringing in of a better hope, through which we draw near to God.

Greatness of the New Priest

[20]And inasmuch as *He was* not *made priest* without an oath [21](for they have become priests without an oath, but He with an oath by Him who said to Him:

> "The LORD has sworn
> And will not relent,
> 'You are a priest forever[a]
> According to the order of
>   Melchizedek' ")[b],

6:18 [a]M-Text omits *might.*   7:14 [a]NU-Text reads *priests.*   7:17 [a]NU-Text reads *it is testified.* [b]Psalm 110:4   7:21 [a]NU-Text ends the quotation here. [b]Psalm 110:4

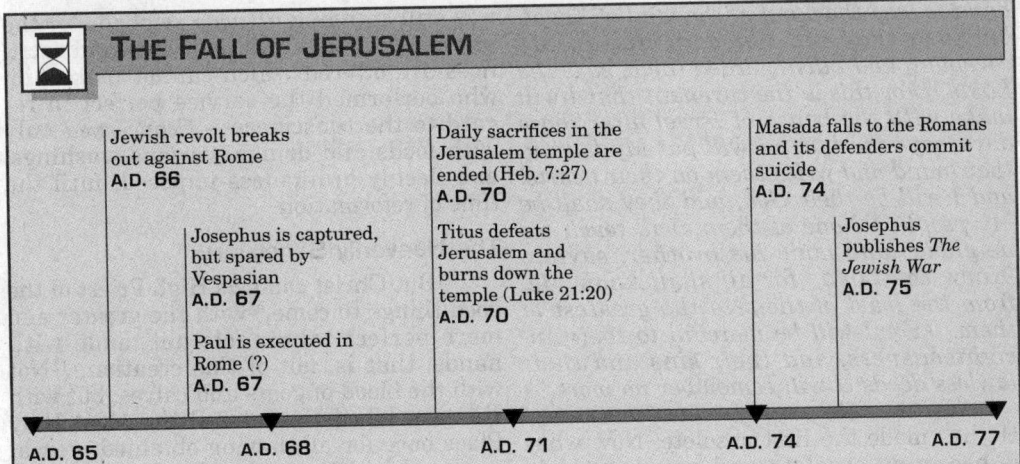

THE FALL OF JERUSALEM

Jewish revolt breaks out against Rome **A.D. 66**	Daily sacrifices in the Jerusalem temple are ended (Heb. 7:27) **A.D. 70**	Masada falls to the Romans and its defenders commit suicide **A.D. 74**
Josephus is captured, but spared by Vespasian **A.D. 67**	Titus defeats Jerusalem and burns down the temple (Luke 21:20) **A.D. 70**	Josephus publishes *The Jewish War* **A.D. 75**
Paul is executed in Rome (?) **A.D. 67**		

A.D. 65   **A.D. 68**   **A.D. 71**   **A.D. 74**   **A.D. 77**

22by so much more Jesus has become a surety of a better covenant.

23Also there were many priests, because they were prevented by death from continuing. 24But He, because He continues forever, has an unchangeable priesthood. 25Therefore He is also able to save to the uttermost those who come to God through Him, since He always lives to make intercession for them.

26For such a High Priest was fitting for us, *who is* holy, harmless, undefiled, separate from sinners, and has become higher than the heavens; 27who does not need daily, as those high priests, to offer up sacrifices, first for His own sins and then for the people's, for this He did once for all when He offered up Himself. 28For the law appoints as high priests men who have weakness, but the word of the oath, which came after the law, *appoints* the Son who has been perfected forever.

The New Priestly Service

8 1Now *this is* the main point of the things we are saying: We have such a High Priest, who is seated at the right hand of the throne of the Majesty in the heavens, 2a Minister of the sanctuary and of the true tabernacle which the Lord erected, and not man.

3For every high priest is appointed to offer both gifts and sacrifices. Therefore *it is* necessary that this One also have something to offer. 4For if He were on earth, He would not be a priest, since there are priests who offer the gifts according to the law; 5who serve the copy and shadow of the heavenly things, as Moses was divinely instructed when he was about to make the tabernacle. For He said, *"See that you make all things according to the pattern shown you on the mountain."* a 6But now He has obtained a more excellent ministry, inasmuch as He is also Mediator of a better covenant, which was established on better promises.

A New Covenant

7For if that first *covenant* had been faultless, then no place would have been sought for a second. 8Because finding fault with them, He says: *"Behold, the days are coming, says the LORD, when I will make a new covenant with the house of Israel and with the house of Judah— 9not according to the covenant that I made with their fathers in the day when I took them by the*

8:5 ªExodus 25:40

RELIGION AND WORSHIP

Jewish priests offered sacrifices at only one location—the temple in Jerusalem (Heb. 7:27; 10:11). Every morning and every night a lamb was sacrificed, as required by the Law of Moses (Ex. 29:38–42). The body was divided without breaking the bones and then burned on the altar. On Sabbaths and holidays other sacrifices were scheduled, and individuals and families could bring sacrifices of their own.

hand to lead them out of the land of Egypt; because they did not continue in My covenant, and I disregarded them, says the LORD. [10]For this is the covenant that I will make with the house of Israel after those days, says the LORD: I will put My laws in their mind and write them on their hearts; and I will be their God, and they shall be My people. [11]None of them shall teach his neighbor, and none his brother, saying, 'Know the LORD,' for all shall know Me, from the least of them to the greatest of them. [12]For I will be merciful to their unrighteousness, and their sins and their lawless deeds[a] I will remember no more."[b]

[13]In that He says, "A new covenant," He has made the first obsolete. Now what is becoming obsolete and growing old is ready to vanish away.

The Earthly Sanctuary

9 [1]Then indeed, even the first *covenant* had ordinances of divine service and the earthly sanctuary. [2]For a tabernacle was prepared: the first *part,* in which *was* the lampstand, the table, and the showbread, which is called the sanctuary; [3]and behind the second veil, the part of the tabernacle which is called the Holiest of All, [4]which had the golden censer and the ark of the covenant overlaid on all sides with gold, in which *were* the golden pot that had the manna, Aaron's rod that budded, and the tablets of the covenant; [5]and above it were the cherubim of glory overshadowing the mercy seat. Of these things we cannot now speak in detail.

Limitations of the Earthly Service

[6]Now when these things had been thus prepared, the priests always went into the first part of the tabernacle, performing *the services.* [7]But into the second part the high priest *went* alone once a year, not without blood, which he offered for himself and *for* the people's sins *committed* in ignorance; [8]the Holy Spirit indicating this, that the way into the Holiest of All was not yet made manifest while the first tabernacle

was still standing. [9]It *was* symbolic for the present time in which both gifts and sacrifices are offered which cannot make him who performed the service perfect in regard to the conscience— [10]*concerned* only with foods and drinks, various washings, and fleshly ordinances imposed until the time of reformation.

The Heavenly Sanctuary

[11]But Christ came *as* High Priest of the good things to come,[a] with the greater and more perfect tabernacle not made with hands, that is, not of this creation. [12]Not with the blood of goats and calves, but with His own blood He entered the Most Holy Place once for all, having obtained eternal redemption. [13]For if the blood of bulls and goats and the ashes of a heifer, sprinkling the unclean, sanctifies for the purifying of the flesh, [14]how much more shall the blood of Christ, who through the eternal Spirit offered Himself without spot to God, cleanse your conscience from dead works to serve the living God? [15]And for this reason He is the Mediator of the new covenant, by means of death, for the redemption of the transgressions under the first covenant, that those who are called may receive the promise of the eternal inheritance.

The Mediator's Death Necessary

[16]For where there *is* a testament, there must also of necessity be the death of the testator. [17]For a testament *is* in force after men are dead, since it has no power at all while the testator lives. [18]Therefore not even the first *covenant* was dedicated without blood. [19]For when Moses had spoken every precept to all the people according to the law, he took the blood of calves and goats, with water, scarlet wool, and hyssop, and sprinkled both the book itself and all the people, [20]saying, *"This is the blood of the covenant which God has commanded*

8:12 [a]NU-Text omits *and their lawless deeds.*
[b]Jeremiah 31:31–34   9:11 [a]NU-Text reads *that have come.*

you." a 21Then likewise he sprinkled with blood both the tabernacle and all the vessels of the ministry. 22And according to the law almost all things are purified with blood, and without shedding of blood there is no remission.

Greatness of Christ's Sacrifice

23Therefore *it was* necessary that the copies of the things in the heavens should be purified with these, but the heavenly things themselves with better sacrifices than these. 24For Christ has not entered the holy places made with hands, *which are* copies of the true, but into heaven itself, now to appear in the presence of God for us; 25not that He should offer Himself often, as the high priest enters the Most Holy Place every year with blood of another— 26He then would have had to suffer often since the foundation of the world; but now, once at the end of the ages, He has appeared to put away sin by the sacrifice of Himself. 27And as it is appointed for men to die once, but after this the judgment, 28so Christ was offered once to bear the sins of many. To those who eagerly wait for Him He will appear a second time, apart from sin, for salvation.

Animal Sacrifices Insufficient

10 1For the law, having a shadow of the good things to come, *and* not the very image of the things, can never with these same sacrifices, which they offer continually year by year, make those who approach perfect. 2For then would they not have ceased to be offered? For the worshipers, once purified, would have had no more consciousness of sins. 3But in those *sacrifices there is* a reminder of sins every year. 4For *it is* not possible that the blood of bulls and goats could take away sins.

Christ's Death Fulfills God's Will

5Therefore, when He came into the world, He said:

"Sacrifice and offering You did not desire,
　But a body You have prepared for Me.
6　In burnt offerings and sacrifices for sin

You had no pleasure.
7　Then I said, 'Behold, I have come—
　In the volume of the book it is written of Me—
　To do Your will, O God.' " a

8Previously saying, *"Sacrifice and offering, burnt offerings, and offerings for sin You did not desire, nor had pleasure in them"* (which are offered according to the law), 9then He said, *"Behold, I have come to do Your will, O God."* a He takes away the first that He may establish the second. 10By that will we have been sanctified through the offering of the body of Jesus Christ once *for all.*

Christ's Death Perfects the Sanctified

11And every priest stands ministering daily and offering repeatedly the same sacrifices, which can never take away sins. 12But this Man, after He had offered one sacrifice for sins forever, sat down at the right hand of God, 13from that time waiting till His enemies are made His footstool. 14For by one offering He has perfected forever those who are being sanctified.

15But the Holy Spirit also witnesses to us; for after He had said before,

16*"This is the covenant that I will make with them after those days, says the* LORD: *I will put My laws into their hearts, and in their minds I will write them,"* a 17*then He adds, "Their sins and their lawless deeds I will remember no more."* a 18Now where there is remission of these, *there is* no longer an offering for sin.

Hold Fast Your Confession

19Therefore, brethren, having boldness to enter the Holiest by the blood of Jesus, 20by a new and living way which He consecrated for us, through the veil, that is, His flesh, 21and *having* a High Priest over the house of God, 22let us draw near with a true heart in full assurance of faith, having our hearts sprinkled from an evil conscience and our bodies washed with pure water. 23Let us hold fast the confession of *our* hope without wavering, for He who promised *is* faithful. 24And let us consider one another in order to stir up love and good works, 25not forsaking the assembling of ourselves together, as *is* the manner of some, but exhorting *one another,* and so much the more as you see the Day approaching.

9:20 aExodus 24:8　　10:7 aPsalm 40:6–8
10:9 aNU-Text and M-Text omit *O God.*
10:16 aJeremiah 31:33　　10:17 aJeremiah 31:34

HOLDING FAST THE CONFESSION (Heb. 10:23–25)

The writer of Hebrews addresses Christians faced with persecution from a Roman society that threatened the church's morale. To prevent the church from disintegrating from within, the writer encourages these Christians: "hold fast the confession of our hope" (Heb. 10:23–25). A series of letters between the Roman governor Pliny and the emperor Trajan offers the Roman perspective on the process whereby Christians were examined in times of persecution.

Pliny writes the emperor for advice on how to treat Christians. It seems that local merchants were upset because Christians refused to participate in the civic religious rites, thus cutting down the meat sales at festivals. Pliny states, "I have never been present at an examination of Christians. Consequently, I do not know the nature or the extent of the punishments usually meted out to them, nor the grounds for starting an investigation and how far it should be pressed" (*Epistulae* 96).

Trajan's reply provides some insight into the nature of a Christian's examination. The emperor made the practice of Christianity illegal, responding that when Christians "are brought before you and the charge against them is proved, they must be punished, but in the case of anyone who denies that he is a Christian, and makes it clear that he is not by offering prayers to our gods, he is to be pardoned" (*Epistulae* 10.97).

Apparently, a person accused of being a Christian was brought into court before the governor. Asked if he or she was a Christian, the accused could offer a quick public prayer to the Roman gods, quite possibly to the emperor himself. Refusal to do so meant execution. For Christians to "hold fast the confession," publicly confessing Jesus Christ as Lord, was tantamount to signing their own death warrant.

The Just Live by Faith

26For if we sin willfully after we have received the knowledge of the truth, there no longer remains a sacrifice for sins, 27but a certain fearful expectation of judgment, and fiery indignation which will devour the adversaries. 28Anyone who has rejected Moses' law dies without mercy on the testimony of two or three witnesses. 29Of how much worse punishment, do you suppose, will he be thought worthy who has trampled the Son of God underfoot, counted the blood of the covenant by which he was sanctified a common thing, and insulted the Spirit of grace? 30For we know Him who said, *"Vengeance is Mine, I will repay,"*a says the Lord.b And again, *"The* LORD *will judge His people."*c 31It is a fearful thing to fall into the hands of the living God.

32But recall the former days in which, after you were illuminated, you endured a great struggle with sufferings: 33partly while you were made a spectacle both by reproaches and tribulations, and partly while you became companions of those who were so treated; 34for you had compassion on mea in my chains, and joyfully accepted the plundering of your goods, knowing that you have a better and an enduring possession for yourselves in heaven.b 35Therefore do not cast away your confidence, which has great reward. 36For you have need of endurance, so that after you have done the will of God, you may receive the promise:

37   *"For yet a little while,*
    *And He*a *who is coming will come and*
        will not tarry.
38   *Now the*a *just shall live by faith;*
    But if anyone draws back,
    *My soul has no pleasure in him."*b

39But we are not of those who draw back to perdition, but of those who believe to the saving of the soul.

By Faith We Understand

11 1Now faith is the substance of things hoped for, the evidence of things not

---

10:30 aDeuteronomy 32:35   bNU-Text omits *says the Lord.*   cDeuteronomy 32:36   10:34 aNU-Text reads *the prisoners* instead of *me in my chains.*   bNU-Text omits *in heaven.*   10:37 aOr *that which*   10:38 aNU-Text reads *My just one.*   bHabakkuk 2:3, 4

seen. ²For by it the elders obtained a *good* testimony.

³By faith we understand that the worlds were framed by the word of God, so that the things which are seen were not made of things which are visible.

Faith at the Dawn of History

⁴By faith Abel offered to God a more excellent sacrifice than Cain, through which he obtained witness that he was righteous, God testifying of his gifts; and through it he being dead still speaks.

⁵By faith Enoch was taken away so that he did not see death, *"and was not found, because God had taken him"*,ᵃ for before he was taken he had this testimony, that he pleased God. ⁶But without faith *it is* impossible to please *Him,* for he who comes to God must believe that He is, and *that* He is a rewarder of those who diligently seek Him.

⁷By faith Noah, being divinely warned of things not yet seen, moved with godly fear, prepared an ark for the saving of his household, by which he condemned the world and became heir of the righteousness which is according to faith.

Faithful Abraham

⁸By faith Abraham obeyed when he was called to go out to the place which he would receive as an inheritance. And he went out, not knowing where he was going. ⁹By faith he dwelt in the land of promise as *in* a foreign country, dwelling in tents with Isaac and Jacob, the heirs with him of the same promise; ¹⁰for he waited for the city which has foundations, whose builder and maker *is* God.

¹¹By faith Sarah herself also received strength to conceive seed, and she bore a childᵃ when she was past the age, because she judged Him faithful who had promised.

11:5 ᵃGenesis 5:24   11:11 ᵃNU-Text omits *she bore a child.*   11:13 ᵃNU-Text and M-Text omit *were assured of them.*   11:18 ᵃGenesis 21:12

¹²Therefore from one man, and him as good as dead, were born *as many* as the stars of the sky in multitude—innumerable as the sand which is by the seashore.

The Heavenly Hope

¹³These all died in faith, not having received the promises, but having seen them afar off were assured of them,ᵃ embraced *them* and confessed that they were strangers and pilgrims on the earth. ¹⁴For those who say such things declare plainly that they seek a homeland. ¹⁵And truly if they had called to mind that *country* from which they had come out, they would have had opportunity to return. ¹⁶But now they desire a better, that is, a heavenly *country*. Therefore God is not ashamed to be called their God, for He has prepared a city for them.

The Faith of the Patriarchs

¹⁷By faith Abraham, when he was tested, offered up Isaac, and he who had received the promises offered up his only begotten *son,* ¹⁸of whom it was said, *"In Isaac your seed shall be called,"* ᵃ ¹⁹concluding that God *was* able to raise *him* up, even from the dead, from which he also received him in a figurative sense.

²⁰By faith Isaac blessed Jacob and Esau concerning things to come.

²¹By faith Jacob, when he was dying, blessed each of the sons of Joseph, and worshiped, *leaning* on the top of his staff.

²²By faith Joseph, when he was dying, made mention of the departure of the children of Israel, and gave instructions concerning his bones.

The Faith of Moses

²³By faith Moses, when he was born, was hidden three months by his parents, because they saw *he was* a beautiful child; and they were not afraid of the king's command.

²⁴By faith Moses, when he became of age, refused to be called the son of Pharaoh's daughter, ²⁵choosing rather to suffer

---

Beliefs and Ideas

The Hebrews thought it very important how and where a person was buried. Abraham's negotiations for a burial plot are carefully recorded (Gen. 23:3–9). Joseph's dying words include instructions about his burial (Gen. 50:25), as the New Testament itself notices (Heb. 11:22). It was a calamity for a person's body to be left in the open or in some other way disgraced.

THE TORTURED "OTHERS" (Heb. 11:35–38)

The author of Hebrews provides a long list of characters whose faithfulness to God was exemplary for the author's audience (Heb. 11:4–35). Yet also listed vaguely are unnamed "others" who were tortured, refusing to deny their faith (11:35, 36).

The Greek word translated "tortured" (11:35) refers to a means of execution in which a prisoner was stretched out on a rack or a wheel and beaten to death. Such was the case with a certain Eleazar, a Jewish martyr of the Maccabean period. This priest refused to violate Jewish law by eating pork, and, "welcoming death with honor rather than life with pollution, went up to the rack on his own accord, spitting out the flesh" (2 Macc. 6:19).

The types of persecutions that some faithful had endured are frightening: scourging, chains, imprisonment, stoning, being sawn in two, wandering in deserts, mountains, and caves (Heb. 11:36–38). An early Christian story called the *Acts of Thekla* details such a situation. Through the miraculous intervention of God, Thekla, a female convert under Paul's teaching, survived two civil proceedings that threatened to take her life. In the end, though, there was no place for her as an unwed Christian woman in the city. She thus "dwelt in a cave seventy-two years, living upon herbs and water. And she enlightened many by the word of God."

These various tortures may also represent possible situations that the recipients of the letter to the Hebrews themselves had to face. The author of Hebrews himself was put into chains (Heb. 10:34), and the community to which he wrote had already endured persecution "with sufferings" (10:32), even having their goods confiscated (10:34). If they remained faithful, they would be spiritual heirs of the tortured "others."

---

affliction with the people of God than to enjoy the passing pleasures of sin, 26esteeming the reproach of Christ greater riches than the treasures in[a] Egypt; for he looked to the reward.

27By faith he forsook Egypt, not fearing the wrath of the king; for he endured as seeing Him who is invisible. 28By faith he kept the Passover and the sprinkling of blood, lest he who destroyed the firstborn should touch them.

29By faith they passed through the Red Sea as by dry *land, whereas* the Egyptians, attempting *to do* so, were drowned.

By Faith They Overcame

30By faith the walls of Jericho fell down after they were encircled for seven days. 31By faith the harlot Rahab did not perish with those who did not believe, when she had received the spies with peace.

32And what more shall I say? For the time would fail me to tell of Gideon and Barak and Samson and Jephthah, also *of* David and Samuel and the prophets: 33who through faith subdued kingdoms, worked righteousness, obtained promises, stopped the mouths of lions, 34quenched the violence of fire, escaped the edge of the sword,

out of weakness were made strong, became valiant in battle, turned to flight the armies of the aliens. 35Women received their dead raised to life again.

Others were tortured, not accepting deliverance, that they might obtain a better resurrection. 36Still others had trial of mockings and scourgings, yes, and of chains and imprisonment. 37They were stoned, they were sawn in two, were tempted,[a] were slain with the sword. They wandered about in sheepskins and goatskins, being destitute, afflicted, tormented— 38of whom the world was not worthy. They wandered in deserts and mountains, *in* dens and caves of the earth.

39And all these, having obtained a good testimony through faith, did not receive the promise, 40God having provided something better for us, that they should not be made perfect apart from us.

The Race of Faith

12 1Therefore we also, since we are surrounded by so great a cloud of witnesses, let us lay aside every weight, and the sin which so easily ensnares *us,* and let

---

11:26 [a]NU-Text and M-Text read *of.*
11:37 [a]NU-Text omits *were tempted.*

us run with endurance the race that is set before us, [2]looking unto Jesus, the author and finisher of *our* faith, who for the joy that was set before Him endured the cross, despising the shame, and has sat down at the right hand of the throne of God.

The Discipline of God

[3]For consider Him who endured such hostility from sinners against Himself, lest you become weary and discouraged in your souls. [4]You have not yet resisted to bloodshed, striving against sin. [5]And you have forgotten the exhortation which speaks to you as to sons:

> "*My son, do not despise the chastening of the LORD,*
> *Nor be discouraged when you are rebuked by Him;*
> [6] *For whom the LORD loves He chastens,*
> *And scourges every son whom He receives.*"[a]

[7]If[a] you endure chastening, God deals with you as with sons; for what son is there whom a father does not chasten? [8]But if you are without chastening, of which all have become partakers, then you are illegitimate and not sons. [9]Furthermore, we have had human fathers who corrected *us,* and we paid *them* respect. Shall we not much more readily be in subjection to the Father of spirits and live? [10]For they indeed for a few days chastened *us* as seemed *best* to them, but He for *our* profit, that *we* may be partakers of His holiness. [11]Now no chastening seems to be joyful for the present, but painful; nevertheless, afterward it yields the peaceable fruit of righteousness to those who have been trained by it.

Renew Your Spiritual Vitality

[12]Therefore strengthen the hands which hang down, and the feeble knees, [13]and make straight paths for your feet, so that what is lame may not be dislocated, but rather be healed.

[14]Pursue peace with all *people,* and holiness, without which no one will see the Lord: [15]looking carefully lest anyone fall short of the grace of God; lest any root of bitterness springing up cause trouble, and by this many become defiled; [16]lest there *be* any fornicator or profane person like Esau, who for one morsel of food sold his birthright. [17]For you know that afterward, when he wanted to inherit the blessing, he was rejected, for he found no place for repentance, though he sought it diligently with tears.

The Glorious Company

[18]For you have not come to the mountain that[a] may be touched and that burned with fire, and to blackness and darkness[b] and tempest, [19]and the sound of a trumpet and the voice of words, so that those who heard *it* begged that the word should not be spoken to them anymore. [20](For they could not endure what was commanded: "*And if so much as a beast touches the mountain, it shall be stoned*[a] *or shot with an arrow.*"[b] [21]And so terrifying was the sight *that* Moses said, "*I am exceedingly afraid and trembling.*"[a])

[22]But you have come to Mount Zion and to the city of the living God, the heavenly Jerusalem, to an innumerable company of angels, [23]to the general assembly and church of the firstborn *who are* registered in heaven, to God the Judge of all, to the spirits of just men made perfect, [24]to Jesus the Mediator of the new covenant, and to the blood of sprinkling that speaks better things than *that of* Abel.

Hear the Heavenly Voice

[25]See that you do not refuse Him who speaks. For if they did not escape who refused Him who spoke on earth, much more *shall we not escape* if we turn away from Him who *speaks* from heaven, [26]whose voice then shook the earth; but now He has promised, saying, "*Yet once more I shake*[a] *not only the earth, but also heaven.*"[b] [27]Now this, "*Yet once more,*" indicates the removal of those things that are being shaken, as of things that are made, that the things which cannot be shaken may remain.

[28]Therefore, since we are receiving a kingdom which cannot be shaken, let us have grace, by which we may[a] serve God acceptably with reverence and godly fear. [29]For our God *is* a consuming fire.

12:6 [a]Proverbs 3:11, 12　　12:7 [a]NU-Text and M-Text read *It is for discipline that you endure; God . . . .*　　12:18 [a]NU-Text reads *to that which.* [b]NU-Text reads *gloom.*　　12:20 [a]NU-Text and M-Text omit the rest of this verse. [b]Exodus 19:12, 13　　12:21 [a]Deuteronomy 9:19　　12:26 [a]NU-Text reads *will shake.* [b]Haggai 2:6　　12:28 [a]M-Text omits *may.*

Concluding Moral Directions

13 ¹Let brotherly love continue. ²Do not forget to entertain strangers, for by so *doing* some have unwittingly entertained angels. ³Remember the prisoners as if chained with them—those who are mistreated—since you yourselves are in the body also.

⁴Marriage *is* honorable among all, and the bed undefiled; but fornicators and adulterers God will judge.

⁵*Let your* conduct *be* without covetousness; *be* content with such things as you have. For He Himself has said, *"I will never leave you nor forsake you."* ᵃ ⁶So we may boldly say:

> *"The LORD is my helper;*
> *I will not fear.*
> *What can man do to me?"* ᵃ

Concluding Religious Directions

⁷Remember those who rule over you, who have spoken the word of God to you, whose faith follow, considering the outcome of *their* conduct. ⁸Jesus Christ *is* the same yesterday, today, and forever. ⁹Do not be carried aboutᵃ with various and strange doctrines. For *it is* good that the heart be established by grace, not with foods which have not profited those who have been occupied with them.

¹⁰We have an altar from which those who serve the tabernacle have no right to eat. ¹¹For the bodies of those animals, whose blood is brought into the sanctuary by the high priest for sin, are burned outside the camp. ¹²Therefore Jesus also, that He might sanctify the people with His own blood, suffered outside the gate. ¹³Therefore let us go forth to Him, outside the camp, bearing His reproach. ¹⁴For here we have no continuing city, but we seek the one to come. ¹⁵Therefore by Him let us continually offer the sacrifice of praise to God, that is, the fruit of *our* lips, giving thanks to His name. ¹⁶But do not forget to do good and to share, for with such sacrifices God is well pleased.

¹⁷Obey those who rule over you, and be submissive, for they watch out for your souls, as those who must give account. Let them do so with joy and not with grief, for that would be unprofitable for you.

Prayer Requested

¹⁸Pray for us; for we are confident that we have a good conscience, in all things desiring to live honorably. ¹⁹But I especially urge *you* to do this, that I may be restored to you the sooner.

Benediction, Final Exhortation, Farewell

²⁰Now may the God of peace who brought up our Lord Jesus from the dead, that great Shepherd of the sheep, through the blood of the everlasting covenant, ²¹make you complete in every good work to do His will, working in youᵃ what is well pleasing in His sight, through Jesus Christ, to whom *be* glory forever and ever. Amen.

²²And I appeal to you, brethren, bear with the word of exhortation, for I have written to you in few words. ²³Know that *our* brother Timothy has been set free, with whom I shall see you if he comes shortly.

²⁴Greet all those who rule over you, and all the saints. Those from Italy greet you.

²⁵Grace *be* with you all. Amen.

13:5 ᵃDeuteronomy 31:6, 8; Joshua 1:5
13:6 ᵃPsalm 118:6   13:9 ᵃNU-Text and M-Text read *away.*   13:21 ᵃNU-Text and M-Text read *us.*

The First Letter of John

The writer of 1 John does not mention his own name or his position in the church, as does the author of 2 and 3 John who identifies himself as "the Elder" (2 John 1:1; 3 John 1:1). Early church tradition held that 1 John, like the Gospel of John, was written by the apostle John, son of Zebedee. Ire-

---

POLITICS AND GOVERNMENT

Imprisonment involved physical suffering, but in addition it exposed the prisoner to extreme shame. The legal system incorporated disgrace and the destruction of personal dignity (Mark 14:65) into the punishments that were imposed. As a result, prisoners were usually deserted by all but the truest friends (2 Tim. 4:10, 11). Yet Christians were advised to sympathize with those who so suffered (Heb. 13:3).

naeus, a 2nd-century church father, quoted John's disciple, Polycarp, to confirm John's authorship of this letter.

There have been debates about the authorship of the Johannine letters going back to the 2nd century. One view is that John the apostle wrote all the New Testament books that bear his name. Another view is that the Gospel and 1 John were written by the same author (who may or may not have been John the apostle), while 2 and 3 John were written by another "Elder" of the churches around Ephesus. Such was the view already of Jerome and possibly also Origen. Finally, some believe all three letters (1, 2, and 3 John) to be by the same author, but not the author who wrote the Gospel.

Many scholars suppose that the Johannine letters were written in the general sequence indicated by their arrangement in the New Testament. Thus, after the Gospel of John, 1 John was the first letter written and was followed later by the roughly contemporaneous letters 2 and 3 John. Those who accept authorship by John, the son of Zebedee, for the Gospel, letters, and Revelation (see "The Revelation to John" at Rev. 1:1) place the letters before his exile to Patmos, where he wrote the Book of the Revelation. John lived until about A.D. 100, and the letter of 1 John is often dated between A.D. 85 and 95.

This letter was probably sent to a group of Christians living in Asia Minor who were troubled by false teachers. Although these teachers had left the church, they were trying to persuade Christians to follow their false teaching. John writes to show that no true knowledge of God is possible without commitment to the divine-human Son of God (1 John 5:13). Fellowship with God will be evidenced by faith in Christ, obedience to His commands, and love for others.

■ 1 John 1:1—5:21

1 John
What Was Heard, Seen, and Touched

1 :1 That which was from the beginning, which we have heard, which we have seen with our eyes, which we have looked upon, and our hands have handled, concerning the Word of life— ²the life was manifested, and we have seen, and bear witness, and declare to you that eternal life

which was with the Father and was manifested to us— ³that which we have seen and heard we declare to you, that you also may have fellowship with us; and truly our fellowship *is* with the Father and with His Son Jesus Christ. ⁴And these things we write to you that your[a] joy may be full.

Fellowship with Him and One Another

⁵This is the message which we have heard from Him and declare to you, that God is light and in Him is no darkness at all. ⁶If we say that we have fellowship with Him, and walk in darkness, we lie and do not practice the truth. ⁷But if we walk in the light as He is in the light, we have fellowship with one another, and the blood of Jesus Christ His Son cleanses us from all sin.

⁸If we say that we have no sin, we deceive ourselves, and the truth is not in us. ⁹If we confess our sins, He is faithful and just to forgive us *our* sins and to cleanse us from all unrighteousness. ¹⁰If we say that we have not sinned, we make Him a liar, and His word is not in us.

2 ¹My little children, these things I write to you, so that you may not sin. And if anyone sins, we have an Advocate with the Father, Jesus Christ the righteous. ²And He Himself is the propitiation for our sins, and not for ours only but also for the whole world.

The Test of Knowing Him

³Now by this we know that we know Him, if we keep His commandments. ⁴He who says, "I know Him," and does not keep His commandments, is a liar, and the truth is not in him. ⁵But whoever keeps His word, truly the love of God is perfected in him. By this we know that we are in Him. ⁶He who says he abides in Him ought himself also to walk just as He walked.

⁷Brethren,[a] I write no new commandment to you, but an old commandment which you have had from the beginning. The old commandment is the word which you heard from the beginning.[b] ⁸Again, a new commandment I write to you, which thing is true in Him and in you, because the darkness is passing away, and the true light is already shining.

⁹He who says he is in the light, and hates his brother, is in darkness until now. ¹⁰He who loves his brother abides in the light, and there is no cause for stumbling in him. ¹¹But he who hates his brother is in

---

1:4 [a]NU-Text and M-Text read *our.*   2:7 [a]NU-Text reads *Beloved.*   [b]NU-Text omits *from the beginning.*

darkness and walks in darkness, and does not know where he is going, because the darkness has blinded his eyes.

Their Spiritual State

12 I write to you, little children,
    Because your sins are forgiven you
        for His name's sake.
13 I write to you, fathers,
    Because you have known Him *who
        is* from the beginning.
    I write to you, young men,
    Because you have overcome the
        wicked one.
    I write to you, little children,
    Because you have known the
        Father.
14 I have written to you, fathers,
    Because you have known Him *who
        is* from the beginning.
    I have written to you, young men,
    Because you are strong, and the
        word of God abides in you,
    And you have overcome the wicked
        one.

Do Not Love the World

15Do not love the world or the things in the world. If anyone loves the world, the love of the Father is not in him. 16For all that *is* in the world—the lust of the flesh, the lust of the eyes, and the pride of life—is not of the Father but is of the world. 17And the world is passing away, and the lust of it; but he who does the will of God abides forever.

Deceptions of the Last Hour

18Little children, it is the last hour; and as you have heard that the[a] Antichrist is coming, even now many antichrists have come, by which we know that it is the last hour. 19They went out from us, but they were not of us; for if they had been of us, they would have continued with us; but *they went out* that they might be made manifest, that none of them were of us.

20But you have an anointing from the Holy One, and you know all things.[a] 21I have not written to you because you do not know the truth, but because you know it, and that no lie is of the truth.

22Who is a liar but he who denies that Jesus is the Christ? He is antichrist who denies the Father and the Son. 23Whoever denies the Son does not have the Father either; he who acknowledges the Son has the Father also.

Let Truth Abide in You

24Therefore let that abide in you which you heard from the beginning. If what you heard from the beginning abides in you, you also will abide in the Son and in the Father. 25And this is the promise that He has promised us—eternal life.

26These things I have written to you concerning those who *try to* deceive you. 27But the anointing which you have received from Him abides in you, and you do not need that anyone teach you; but as the same anointing teaches you concerning all things, and is true, and is not a lie, and just as it has taught you, you will[a] abide in Him.

The Children of God

28And now, little children, abide in Him, that when[a] He appears, we may have confidence and not be ashamed before Him at His coming. 29If you know that He is righteous, you know that everyone who practices righteousness is born of Him.

3 1Behold what manner of love the Father has bestowed on us, that we should be called children of God![a] Therefore the world does not know us,[b] because it did not know Him. 2Beloved, now we are children of God; and it has not yet been revealed what we shall be, but we know that when He is revealed, we shall be like Him, for we shall see Him as He is. 3And everyone who has this hope in Him purifies himself, just as He is pure.

2:18 [a]NU-Text omits *the*.   2:20 [a]NU-Text reads *you all know*.   2:27 [a]NU-Text reads *you abide*.
2:28 [a]NU-Text reads *if*.   3:1 [a]NU-Text adds *And we are*.   [b]M-Text reads *you*.

Sin and the Child of God

⁴Whoever commits sin also commits lawlessness, and sin is lawlessness. ⁵And you know that He was manifested to take away our sins, and in Him there is no sin. ⁶Whoever abides in Him does not sin. Whoever sins has neither seen Him nor known Him.

⁷Little children, let no one deceive you. He who practices righteousness is righteous, just as He is righteous. ⁸He who sins is of the devil, for the devil has sinned from the beginning. For this purpose the Son of God was manifested, that He might destroy the works of the devil. ⁹Whoever has been born of God does not sin, for His seed remains in him; and he cannot sin, because he has been born of God.

The Imperative of Love

¹⁰In this the children of God and the children of the devil are manifest: Whoever does not practice righteousness is not of God, nor *is* he who does not love his brother. ¹¹For this is the message that you heard from the beginning, that we should love one another, ¹²not as Cain *who* was of the wicked one and murdered his brother. And why did he murder him? Because his works were evil and his brother's righteous.

¹³Do not marvel, my brethren, if the world hates you. ¹⁴We know that we have passed from death to life, because we love the brethren. He who does not love *his* brother[a] abides in death. ¹⁵Whoever hates his brother is a murderer, and you know that no murderer has eternal life abiding in him.

The Outworking of Love

¹⁶By this we know love, because He laid down His life for us. And we also ought to lay down *our* lives for the brethren. ¹⁷But whoever has this world's goods, and sees his brother in need, and shuts up his heart from him, how does the love of God abide in him?

¹⁸My little children, let us not love in word or in tongue, but in deed and in truth. ¹⁹And by this we know[a] that we are of the truth, and shall assure our hearts before Him. ²⁰For if our heart condemns us, God is greater than our heart, and knows all things. ²¹Beloved, if our heart does not condemn us, we have confidence toward God. ²²And whatever we ask we receive from Him, because we keep His commandments and do those things that are pleasing in His sight. ²³And this is His commandment: that we should believe on the name of His Son Jesus Christ and love one another, as He gave us[a] commandment.

The Spirit of Truth and the Spirit of Error

²⁴Now he who keeps His commandments abides in Him, and He in him. And by this we know that He abides in us, by the Spirit whom He has given us.

4 ¹Beloved, do not believe every spirit, but test the spirits, whether they are of God; because many false prophets have gone out into the world. ²By this you know the Spirit of God: Every spirit that confesses that Jesus Christ has come in the flesh is of God, ³and every spirit that does not confess that[a] Jesus Christ has come in the flesh is not of God. And this is the *spirit* of the Antichrist, which you have heard was coming, and is now already in the world.

⁴You are of God, little children, and have overcome them, because He who is in you is greater than he who is in the world. ⁵They are of the world. Therefore they speak *as* of the world, and the world hears them. ⁶We are of God. He who knows God hears us; he who is not of God does not hear us. By this we know the spirit of truth and the spirit of error.

3:14 aNU-Text omits *his brother*.   3:19 aNU-Text reads *we shall know*.   3:23 aM-Text omits *us*. 4:3 aNU-Text omits *that* and *Christ has come in the flesh*.

Beliefs and Ideas

From the earliest days the Christian church was plagued by proponents of false teaching. The New Testament does not describe any systems of false doctrine, but false teachers arose from within the congregations and appeared as visitors (Acts 20:29). John's advice was that the truth has one origin, God. Though having many disguises, the false teachers were consistent in their denial of Christ (1 John 4:2, 3).

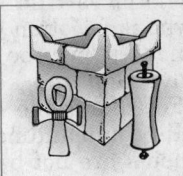

Knowing God Through Love

[7]Beloved, let us love one another, for love is of God; and everyone who loves is born of God and knows God. [8]He who does not love does not know God, for God is love. [9]In this the love of God was manifested toward us, that God has sent His only begotten Son into the world, that we might live through Him. [10]In this is love, not that we loved God, but that He loved us and sent His Son *to be* the propitiation for our sins. [11]Beloved, if God so loved us, we also ought to love one another.

Seeing God Through Love

[12]No one has seen God at any time. If we love one another, God abides in us, and His love has been perfected in us. [13]By this we know that we abide in Him, and He in us, because He has given us of His Spirit. [14]And we have seen and testify that the Father has sent the Son *as* Savior of the world. [15]Whoever confesses that Jesus is the Son of God, God abides in him, and he in God. [16]And we have known and believed the love that God has for us. God is love, and he who abides in love abides in God, and God in him.

The Consummation of Love

[17]Love has been perfected among us in this: that we may have boldness in the day of judgment; because as He is, so are we in this world. [18]There is no fear in love; but perfect love casts out fear, because fear involves torment. But he who fears has not been made perfect in love. [19]We love Him[a] because He first loved us.

Obedience by Faith

[20]If someone says, "I love God," and hates his brother, he is a liar; for he who does not love his brother whom he has seen, how can[a] he love God whom he has not seen? [21]And this commandment we have from Him: that he who loves God *must* love his brother also.

5 [1]Whoever believes that Jesus is the Christ is born of God, and everyone who loves Him who begot also loves him who is begotten of Him. [2]By this we know that we love the children of God, when we love God and keep His commandments. [3]For this is the love of God, that we keep His commandments. And His commandments are not burdensome. [4]For whatever is born of God overcomes the world. And

this is the victory that has overcome the world—our[a] faith. [5]Who is he who overcomes the world, but he who believes that Jesus is the Son of God?

The Certainty of God's Witness

[6]This is He who came by water and blood—Jesus Christ; not only by water, but by water and blood. And it is the Spirit who bears witness, because the Spirit is truth. [7]For there are three that bear witness in heaven: the Father, the Word, and the Holy Spirit; and these three are one. [8]And there are three that bear witness on earth:[a] the Spirit, the water, and the blood; and these three agree as one.

[9]If we receive the witness of men, the witness of God is greater; for this is the witness of God which[a] He has testified of His Son. [10]He who believes in the Son of God has the witness in himself; he who does not believe God has made Him a liar, because he has not believed the testimony that God has given of His Son. [11]And this is the testimony: that God has given us eternal life, and this life is in His Son. [12]He who has the Son has life; he who does not have the Son of God does not have life. [13]These things I have written to you who believe in the name of the Son of God, that you may know that you have eternal life,[a] and that you may *continue to* believe in the name of the Son of God.

Confidence and Compassion in Prayer

[14]Now this is the confidence that we have in Him, that if we ask anything according to His will, He hears us. [15]And if we know that He hears us, whatever we ask, we know that we have the petitions that we have asked of Him.

[16]If anyone sees his brother sinning a sin *which does* not *lead* to death, he will ask, and He will give him life for those who commit sin not *leading* to death. There is sin *leading* to death. I do not say that he should pray about that. [17]All unrighteousness is sin, and there is sin not *leading* to death.

4:19 [a]NU-Text omits *Him*.   4:20 [a]NU-Text reads *he cannot*.   5:4 [a]M-Text reads *your*.
5:8 [a]NU-Text and M-Text omit the words from *in heaven* (verse 7) through *on earth* (verse 8). Only four or five very late manuscripts contain these words in Greek.   5:9 [a]NU-Text reads *God, that*.
5:13 [a]NU-Text omits the rest of this verse.

Knowing the True—Rejecting the False

[18]We know that whoever is born of God does not sin; but he who has been born of God keeps himself,[a] and the wicked one does not touch him.

[19]We know that we are of God, and the whole world lies *under the sway of* the wicked one.

[20]And we know that the Son of God has come and has given us an understanding, that we may know Him who is true; and we are in Him who is true, in His Son Jesus Christ. This is the true God and eternal life.

[21]Little children, keep yourselves from idols. Amen.

5:18 [a]NU-Text reads *him.*   **2 John** 1:3 [a]NU-Text and M-Text read *us.*   1:8 [a]NU-Text reads *you.* [b]NU-Text reads *you.*   1:9 [a]NU-Text reads *goes ahead.*

The Second Letter of John

According to early church tradition, the letter of 2 John was written by the apostle John, the same person who wrote 1 John. Yet the author does not refer to himself as an apostle, but rather as "the Elder" (2 John 1:1). "Elder" was a term of respect used by both Jews and Christians for venerated religious teachers, and could have been used of John later in his life (see 1 Pet. 5:1). Some scholars suppose that the elder John who wrote this letter may have been a disciple of the apostle John (see "The First Letter of John" at 1 John 1:1).

The letter of 2 John was probably written in the final decade of the 1st century. It has the form and size of a normal personal letter of the 1st century. The address—"To the elect lady and her children" (2 John 1:1)—may well have been a figurative way of referring to a local church and its members, probably in Asia Minor.

The false teachers threatening this church held the same error as those confronted in 1 John. This letter is an earnest plea to continue to love one another and so obey Christ's commandment. The other side of the admonition is to reject the subtle deceivers who deny that Jesus Christ truly became a human being.

■ 2 John 1:1–13

2 John
Greeting the Elect Lady

1 :1 The Elder,

To the elect lady and her children, whom I love in truth, and not only I, but also all those who have known the truth, [2]because of the truth which abides in us and will be with us forever:

[3]Grace, mercy, *and* peace will be with you[a] from God the Father and from the Lord Jesus Christ, the Son of the Father, in truth and love.

Walk in Christ's Commandments

[4]I rejoiced greatly that I have found *some* of your children walking in truth, as we received commandment from the Father. [5]And now I plead with you, lady, not as though I wrote a new commandment to you, but that which we have had from the beginning: that we love one another. [6]This is love, that we walk according to His commandments. This is the commandment, that as you have heard from the beginning, you should walk in it.

Beware of Antichrist Deceivers

[7]For many deceivers have gone out into the world who do not confess Jesus Christ *as* coming in the flesh. This is a deceiver and an antichrist. [8]Look to yourselves, that we[a] do not lose those things we worked for, but *that* we[b] may receive a full reward.

[9]Whoever transgresses[a] and does not abide in the doctrine of Christ does not have God. He who abides in the doctrine of Christ has both the Father and the Son. [10]If anyone comes to you and does not bring this doctrine, do not receive him into

---

TRADE AND ECONOMICS

The paper (2 John 1:12) of the 1st century was made of papyrus, a tall reed found abundantly in Egypt, which still grows further south along the Nile. Making this paper was an important industry, and the Egyptians exported it all over the Mediterranean world. Tens of thousands of original papyrus documents have survived, including numerous personal letters (though none of the New Testament).

your house nor greet him; ¹¹for he who greets him shares in his evil deeds.

John's Farewell Greeting

¹²Having many things to write to you, I did not wish *to do so* with paper and ink; but I hope to come to you and speak face to face, that our joy may be full.

¹³The children of your elect sister greet you. Amen.

The Third Letter of John

The letter of 3 John was probably written by the author of 1 and 2 John sometime in the last decade of the first century (see "The First Letter of John" at 1 John 1:1). The subjects discussed are less doctrinal and more administrative than in 1 and 2 John, applying Christian principles to church life. The letter addresses an individual named Gaius, who probably attended a church in a city of Asia Minor, and reflects a time when Christian evangelists traveled from town to town preaching the gospel. These missionaries depended on the hospitality of local Christians.

It is apparent that Diotrephes had gained control of the church, and in his arrogance had rejected the leadership of "the Elder" and his representatives. Gaius is commended for continuing to walk in Christian truth, showing generosity to local church members, and aiding traveling evangelists. Diotrephes is condemned for his prideful rejection of the apostle, domination of the local church, and refusal to give hospitality. Finally, Demetrius, a fellow Christian and perhaps the bearer of this letter, is recommended to the confidence of the church.

■ 3 John 1:1–14

3 John
Greeting to Gaius

1:1 The Elder,

To the beloved Gaius, whom I love in truth:

²Beloved, I pray that you may prosper in all things and be in health, just as your soul prospers. ³For I rejoiced greatly when brethren came and testified of the truth *that is* in you, just as you walk in the truth. ⁴I have no greater joy than to hear that my children walk in truth.ᵃ

Gaius Commended for Generosity

⁵Beloved, you do faithfully whatever you do for the brethren andᵃ for strangers, ⁶who have borne witness of your love before the church. *If* you send them forward on their journey in a manner worthy of God, you will do well, ⁷because they went forth for His name's sake, taking nothing from the Gentiles. ⁸We therefore ought to receiveᵃ such, that we may become fellow workers for the truth.

Diotrephes and Demetrius

⁹I wrote to the church, but Diotrephes, who loves to have the preeminence among them, does not receive us. ¹⁰Therefore, if I come, I will call to mind his deeds which he does, prating against us with malicious words. And not content with that, he himself does not receive the brethren, and forbids those who wish to, putting *them* out of the church.

¹¹Beloved, do not imitate what is evil, but what is good. He who does good is of God, butᵃ he who does evil has not seen God.

¹²Demetrius has a *good* testimony from all, and from the truth itself. And we also bear witness, and you know that our testimony is true.

Farewell Greeting

¹³I had many things to write, but I do not wish to write to you with pen and ink; ¹⁴but I hope to see you shortly, and we shall speak face to face.

Peace to you. Our friends greet you. Greet the friends by name.

---

3 John 1:4 ᵃNU-Text reads *the truth*.
1:5 ᵃNU-Text adds *especially*.   1:8 ᵃNU-Text reads *support*.   1:11 ᵃNU-Text and M-Text omit *but*.

CULTURE AND SOCIETY

It was customary for some teachers to travel about, being supported by their students in the towns they visited. Christian teachers as well as pagan philosophers did this. The system was open to abuse, because travelers could easily conceal their background. The New Testament advises the aiding of traveling evangelists (3 John 1:6–8), while warning of people who use religion for private ends (2 John 1:10).

Apocalyptic Writings and the End Time

> Biblical prophecy was not given in order that we might create a timetable for future events.

Several of the later prophets, especially Ezekiel, Daniel, and Zechariah, share certain literary characteristics which are also found in the Olivet Discourse (Mark 13) and the Book of Revelation. Some of these characteristics are the use of fantastic imagery, vivid colors, and numbers with symbolic significance. In the view of some interpreters, these writings also seem to give more attention to explaining the upheavals which will attend the end of time than to contemporary events. Because they explain these otherwise mysterious events, the writings are often called "apocalyptic" from the Greek word *apokalyptō,* meaning "to disclose, uncover."

There is also a body of nonbiblical Jewish literature which falls into the category known as apocalyptic. These writings share several common themes: (1) a pessimism over the present; (2) a belief that God will miraculously intervene at the end of time to save His own; (3) the belief that God has secretly disclosed to a chosen few the secrets of the end time; (4) the conviction that these secrets are hidden from the common people in special visions which include secret numbers, strange images, and key phrases. The biblical writings classified as apocalyptic share in the literary features of this noncanonical apocalyptic literature.

Throughout history apocalyptic literature has been most popular when current conditions have turned chaotic. At such times there has been a tendency to find remarkable similarities between one's own situation and the biblical prophecies. This tendency should be resisted. Biblical prophecy was not given in order that we might create a timetable for future events. Rather its authors intended to stimulate obedience to and confidence in God, who remained firmly in control of both contemporary events and the future.

The Revelation to John

The tradition that John the apostle wrote Revelation was widely held during the 2nd century. While the author often names himself as "John," the term "apostle" is never added, although he appears to be a man of stature in the churches (Rev. 1:1, 4, 9). He never claims to have been an eyewitness of Jesus.

There are significant differences between the Greek style of the Revelation and that of the Gospel and letters of John. In the 3rd century these variations of the original language prompted scholars to question the apostle John's authorship of the Revelation. A debate still continues over whether the John who wrote this book is to be identified with John the apostle, John the Elder (see "The First Letter of John" at 1 John 1:1), or an otherwise unknown John.

Dating the composition of Revelation is complicated, but Nero (A.D. 54–68) and Domitian (A.D. 81–96) are the Roman emperors whose reigns correspond most closely with the persecutions reflected in the book. The intensity of these persecutions fits better in Domitian's reign than in Nero's.

Four broad schools of interpretation have ▼ been applied to the visions and symbolism of Rev. 4—22. (1) "Preterists" view these chapters as referring only to the period of the Roman Empire during John's lifetime and immediately after. (2) "Historicists" view them as describing events that would occur throughout the church age from the ascension of Jesus to His Second Coming. (3) "Futurists" maintain that chs. 4—22 deal chiefly with events of the end times that surround Christ's Second Coming. (4) "Idealists" maintain that these chapters do not prophesy actual events, but paint a symbolic picture of the cosmic conflict between the kingdom of God and the forces of evil.

Elements from all of these views are helpful in understanding the Revelation. This book certainly had relevance to the situation that surrounded its first readers. Yet its primary focus seems to be on events associated with the return of Christ. Also the conflict between God and Satan is often reflected by different symbolic pictures throughout the book. The differing interpretations come closer to each other when we remember that the events of the end time are often an intensification of what Christians have faced throughout the church age.

■ Revelation 1:1—3:22

Revelation
Introduction and Benediction

1 :1 The Revelation of Jesus Christ, which God gave Him to show His servants—things which must shortly take place. And He sent and signified *it* by His angel to His servant John, ²who bore witness to the word of God, and to the testimony of Jesus Christ, to all things that he saw. ³Blessed *is* he who reads and those who hear the words of this prophecy, and keep those things which are written in it; for the time *is* near.

Greeting the Seven Churches

⁴John, to the seven churches which are in Asia:

Grace to you and peace from Him who is and who was and who is to come, and from the seven Spirits who are before His throne, ⁵and from Jesus Christ, the faithful witness, the firstborn from the dead, and the ruler over the kings of the earth.

To Him who loved us and washedᵃ us from our sins in His own blood, ⁶and has made us kingsᵃ and priests to His God and Father, to Him *be* glory and dominion forever and ever. Amen.

⁷Behold, He is coming with clouds, and every eye will see Him, even they who pierced Him. And all the tribes of the earth will mourn because of Him. Even so, Amen.

⁸"I am the Alpha and the Omega, *the* Beginning and *the* End,"ᵃ says the Lord,ᵇ "who is and who was and who is to come, the Almighty."

Vision of the Son of Man

⁹I, John, bothᵃ your brother and companion in the tribulation and kingdom and patience of Jesus Christ, was on the island that is called Patmos for the word of God and for the testimony of Jesus Christ. ¹⁰I was in the Spirit on the Lord's Day, and I heard behind me a loud voice, as of a trumpet, ¹¹saying, "I am the Alpha and the Omega, the First and the Last,"ᵃ and, "What you see, write in a book and send *it* to the seven churches which are in Asia:ᵇ to Ephesus, to Smyrna, to Pergamos, to Thyatira, to Sardis, to Philadelphia, and to Laodicea."

¹²Then I turned to see the voice that spoke with me. And having turned I saw seven golden lampstands, ¹³and in the midst of the seven lampstands *One* like the Son of Man, clothed with a garment down to the feet and girded about the chest with a golden band. ¹⁴His head and hair *were* white like wool, as white as snow, and His eyes like a flame of fire; ¹⁵His feet *were* like fine brass, as if refined in a furnace, and His voice as the sound of many waters; ¹⁶He had in His right hand seven stars, out of His mouth went a sharp two-edged

---

1:5 ᵃNU-Text reads *loves us and freed;* M-Text reads *loves us and washed.*   1:6 ᵃNU-Text and M-Text read *a kingdom.*   1:8 ᵃNU-Text and M-Text omit *the Beginning and the End.*   ᵇNU-Text and M-Text add *God.*   1:9 ᵃNU-Text and M-Text omit *both.*
1:11 ᵃNU-Text and M-Text omit *I am* through third *and.*   ᵇNU-Text and M-Text omit *which are in Asia.*

The Seven Churches of Revelation

The churches of seven cities (Rev. 1:11) were recipients of an apocalyptic letter from God, which John was called to write while exiled on the island of Patmos. By commendation, rebuke, and warning, the people of God were exhorted to remain faithful in adversity. These churches held significant roles in the Christian experience of Asia Minor as a result of their location within a transportation network linking different parts of the region.

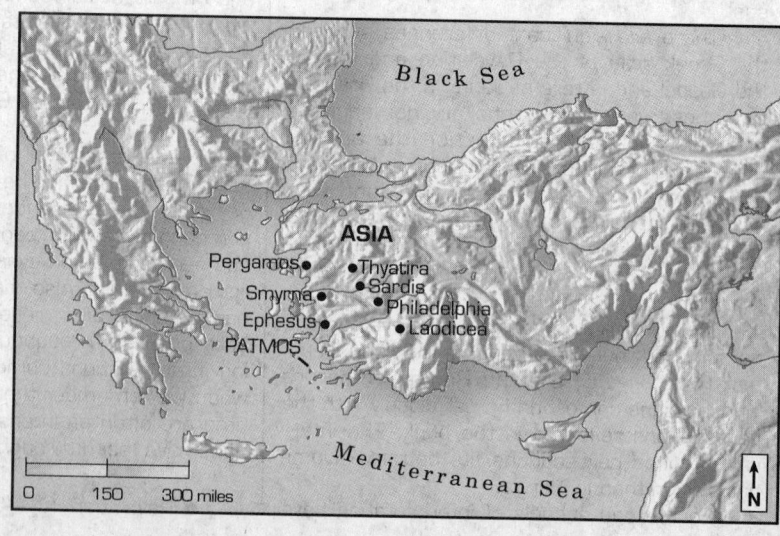

Map showing the Black Sea, ASIA, Pergamos, Thyatira, Smyrna, Sardis, Ephesus, Philadelphia, Laodicea, PATMOS, and the Mediterranean Sea. Scale: 0, 150, 300 miles. N

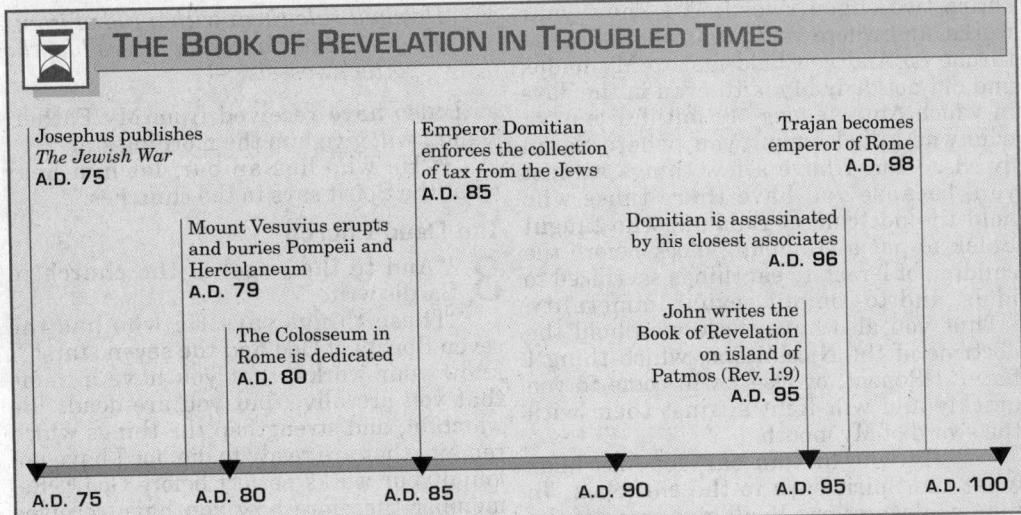

THE BOOK OF REVELATION IN TROUBLED TIMES

Josephus publishes
The Jewish War
A.D. 75

Mount Vesuvius erupts
and buries Pompeii and
Herculaneum
A.D. 79

The Colosseum in
Rome is dedicated
A.D. 80

Emperor Domitian
enforces the collection
of tax from the Jews
A.D. 85

Domitian is assassinated
by his closest associates
A.D. 96

John writes the
Book of Revelation
on island of
Patmos (Rev. 1:9)
A.D. 95

Trajan becomes
emperor of Rome
A.D. 98

A.D. 75　**A.D. 80**　**A.D. 85**　**A.D. 90**　**A.D. 95**　**A.D. 100**

sword, and His countenance *was* like the sun shining in its strength. [17]And when I saw Him, I fell at His feet as dead. But He laid His right hand on me, saying to me,[a] "Do not be afraid; I am the First and the Last. [18]I *am* He who lives, and was dead, and behold, I am alive forevermore. Amen. And I have the keys of Hades and of Death. [19]Write[a] the things which you have seen, and the things which are, and the things which will take place after this. [20]The mystery of the seven stars which you saw in My right hand, and the seven golden lampstands: The seven stars are the angels of the seven churches, and the seven lampstands which you saw[a] are the seven churches.

The Loveless Church

2 [1]"To the angel of the church of Ephesus write,

'These things says He who holds the seven stars in His right hand, who walks in the midst of the seven golden lampstands: [2]"I know your works, your labor, your patience, and that you cannot bear those who are evil. And you have tested those who say they are apostles and are not, and have found them liars; [3]and you have persevered and have patience, and have labored for My name's sake and have not become weary. [4]Nevertheless I have *this* against you, that you have left your first love. [5]Remember therefore from where you have fallen; repent and do the first works, or else I will come to you quickly and remove your lampstand from its place—unless you repent. [6]But this you have, that you hate the deeds of the Nicolaitans, which I also hate.

[7]"He who has an ear, let him hear what the Spirit says to the churches. To him who overcomes I will give to eat from the tree of life, which is in the midst of the Paradise of God." '

The Persecuted Church

[8]"And to the angel of the church in Smyrna write,

'These things says the First and the Last, who was dead, and came to life: [9]"I know your works, tribulation, and poverty (but you are rich); and I *know* the blasphemy of those who say they are Jews and are not, but *are* a synagogue of Satan. [10]Do not fear any of those things which you are about to suffer. Indeed, the devil is about to throw *some* of you into prison, that you may be tested, and you will have tribulation ten days. Be faithful until death, and I will give you the crown of life.

[11]"He who has an ear, let him hear what the Spirit says to the churches. He who overcomes shall not be hurt by the second death." '

The Compromising Church

[12]"And to the angel of the church in Pergamos write,

'These things says He who has the

1:17 [a]NU-Text and M-Text omit *to me.*
1:19 [a]NU-Text and M-Text read *Therefore, write.*
1:20 [a]NU-Text and M-Text omit *which you saw.*

sharp two-edged sword: [13]"I know your works, and where you dwell, where Satan's throne *is*. And you hold fast to My name, and did not deny My faith even in the days in which Antipas *was* My faithful martyr, who was killed among you, where Satan dwells. [14]But I have a few things against you, because you have there those who hold the doctrine of Balaam, who taught Balak to put a stumbling block before the children of Israel, to eat things sacrificed to idols, and to commit sexual immorality. [15]Thus you also have those who hold the doctrine of the Nicolaitans, which thing I hate.[a] [16]Repent, or else I will come to you quickly and will fight against them with the sword of My mouth.

[17]"He who has an ear, let him hear what the Spirit says to the churches. To him who overcomes I will give some of the hidden manna to eat. And I will give him a white stone, and on the stone a new name written which no one knows except him who receives *it*." '

The Corrupt Church

[18]"And to the angel of the church in Thyatira write,

'These things says the Son of God, who has eyes like a flame of fire, and His feet like fine brass: [19]"I know your works, love, service, faith,[a] and your patience; and *as* for your works, the last *are* more than the first. [20]Nevertheless I have a few things against you, because you allow[a] that woman[b] Jezebel, who calls herself a prophetess, to teach and seduce[c] My servants to commit sexual immorality and eat things sacrificed to idols. [21]And I gave her time to repent of her sexual immorality, and she did not repent.[a] [22]Indeed I will cast her into a sickbed, and those who commit adultery with her into great tribulation, unless they repent of their[a] deeds. [23]I will kill her children with death, and all the churches shall know that I am He who searches the minds and hearts. And I will give to each one of you according to your works.

[24]"Now to you I say, and[a] to the rest in Thyatira, as many as do not have this doctrine, who have not known the depths of Satan, as they say, I will[b] put on you no other burden. [25]But hold fast what you have till I come. [26]And he who overcomes, and keeps My works until the end, to him I will give power over the nations—

[27] 'He shall rule them with a rod of iron;
        They shall be dashed to pieces like the
        potter's vessels'[a]—

as I also have received from My Father; [28]and I will give him the morning star.

[29]"He who has an ear, let him hear what the Spirit says to the churches." '

The Dead Church

3 [1]"And to the angel of the church in Sardis write,

'These things says He who has the seven Spirits of God and the seven stars: "I know your works, that you have a name that you are alive, but you are dead. [2]Be watchful, and strengthen the things which remain, that are ready to die, for I have not found your works perfect before God.[a] [3]Remember therefore how you have received and heard; hold fast and repent. Therefore if you will not watch, I will come upon you as a thief, and you will not know what hour I will come upon you. [4]You[a] have a few names even in Sardis who have not defiled their garments; and they shall walk with Me in white, for they are worthy. [5]He who overcomes shall be clothed in white garments, and I will not blot out his name from the Book of Life; but I will confess his name before My Father and before His angels.

[6]"He who has an ear, let him hear what the Spirit says to the churches." '

The Faithful Church

[7]"And to the angel of the church in Philadelphia write,

'These things says He who is holy, He who is true, *"He who has the key of David, He who opens and no one shuts, and shuts and no one opens"*.[a] [8]"I know your works. See, I have set before you an open door, and no one can shut it;[a] for you have a lit-

---

2:15 [a]NU-Text and M-Text read *likewise* for *which thing I hate.* 2:19 [a]NU-Text and M-Text read *faith, service.* 2:20 [a]NU-Text and M-Text read *I have against you that you tolerate.* [b]M-Text reads *your wife Jezebel.* [c]NU-Text and M-Text read *and teaches and seduces.* 2:21 [a]NU-Text and M-Text read *time to repent, and she does not want to repent of her sexual immorality.* 2:22 [a]NU-Text and M-Text read *her.* 2:24 [a]NU-Text and M-Text omit *and.* [b]NU-Text and M-Text omit *will.* 2:27 [a]Psalm 2:9 3:2 [a]NU-Text and M-Text read *My God.* 3:4 [a]NU-Text and M-Text read *Nevertheless you have a few names in Sardis.* 3:7 [a]Isaiah 22:22 3:8 [a]NU-Text and M-Text read *which no one can shut.*

tle strength, have kept My word, and have not denied My name. [9]Indeed I will make *those* of the synagogue of Satan, who say they are Jews and are not, but lie—indeed I will make them come and worship before your feet, and to know that I have loved you. [10]Because you have kept My command to persevere, I also will keep you from the hour of trial which shall come upon the whole world, to test those who dwell on the earth. [11]Behold,[a] I am coming quickly! Hold fast what you have, that no one may take your crown. [12]He who overcomes, I will make him a pillar in the temple of My God, and he shall go out no more. I will write on him the name of My God and the name of the city of My God, the New Jerusalem, which comes down out of heaven from My God. And *I will write on him* My new name.

[13]"He who has an ear, let him hear what the Spirit says to the churches." '

The Lukewarm Church

[14]"And to the angel of the church of the Laodiceans[a] write,

'These things says the Amen, the Faithful and True Witness, the Beginning of the creation of God: [15]"I know your works, that you are neither cold nor hot. I could wish you were cold or hot. [16]So then, because you are lukewarm, and neither cold nor hot,[a] I will vomit you out of My mouth. [17]Because you say, 'I am rich, have become wealthy, and have need of nothing'—and do not know that you are wretched, miserable, poor, blind, and naked— [18]I counsel you to buy from Me gold refined in the fire, that you may be rich; and white garments, that you may be clothed, *that* the shame of your nakedness may not be revealed; and anoint your eyes with eye salve, that you may see. [19]As

---

3:11 [a]NU-Text and M-Text omit *Behold.*
3:14 [a]NU-Text and M-Text read *in Laodicea.*
3:16 [a]NU-Text and M-Text read *hot nor cold.*
4:3 [a]M-Text omits *And He who sat there was* (which makes the description in verse 3 modify the throne rather than God).

---

many as I love, I rebuke and chasten. Therefore be zealous and repent. [20]Behold, I stand at the door and knock. If anyone hears My voice and opens the door, I will come in to him and dine with him, and he with Me. [21]To him who overcomes I will grant to sit with Me on My throne, as I also overcame and sat down with My Father on His throne.

[22]"He who has an ear, let him hear what the Spirit says to the churches." ' "

A Revelation of Heaven

The open "door" (Rev. 4:1) gave opportunity for John to see things transpiring in heaven. The vision of God's throne in chs. 4; 5, revealing the adoration of God the Creator by all the inhabitants of heaven, lays the foundation for the rest of Revelation. The God whom John saw is beyond description, but His throne fills the entire scene giving us an awareness of His power.

The "scroll" (Rev. 5:1) contained God's plan for His creation as revealed in the remaining chapters of Revelation: judgment on the wicked, deliverance for the righteous, and establishment of His kingdom. In ch. 5 Christ is the Lamb who by His death and resurrection has brought about the salvation of humanity. Thus He alone is worthy to open the scroll of destiny and to share equal praise with God the Father. Because God is both the Creator and Redeemer, the future is secure in His hands.

■ Revelation 4:1—5:14

Revelation
The Throne Room of Heaven

4:1 After these things I looked, and behold, a door *standing* open in heaven. And the first voice which I heard *was* like a trumpet speaking with me, saying, "Come up here, and I will show you things which must take place after this."

[2]Immediately I was in the Spirit; and behold, a throne set in heaven, and *One* sat on the throne. [3]And He who sat there was[a] like a jasper and a sardius stone in

---

SCIENCE AND TECHNOLOGY

Sardius, also called carnelian, is a translucent, reddish variety of chalcedony (Rev. 4:3). Chemically it is a type of quartz. "Jasper" translates a Hebrew word that came over into Greek from the Old Testament (Ex. 28:20). It is not known what stone is meant, though some have said it is diamond. The ancients could not polish diamonds or other hard stones.

appearance; and *there was* a rainbow around the throne, in appearance like an emerald. 4Around the throne *were* twenty-four thrones, and on the thrones I saw twenty-four elders sitting, clothed in white robes; and they had crowns[a] of gold on their heads. 5And from the throne proceeded lightnings, thunderings, and voices.[a] Seven lamps of fire *were* burning before the throne, which are the[b] seven Spirits of God.

6Before the throne *there was*[a] a sea of glass, like crystal. And in the midst of the throne, and around the throne, *were* four living creatures full of eyes in front and in back. 7The first living creature *was* like a lion, the second living creature like a calf, the third living creature had a face like a man, and the fourth living creature *was* like a flying eagle. 8*The* four living creatures, each having six wings, were full of eyes around and within. And they do not rest day or night, saying:

"Holy, holy, holy,[a]
Lord God Almighty,
Who was and is and is to come!"

9Whenever the living creatures give glory and honor and thanks to Him who sits on the throne, who lives forever and ever, 10the twenty-four elders fall down before Him who sits on the throne and worship Him who lives forever and ever, and cast their crowns before the throne, saying:

11 "You are worthy, O Lord,[a]
To receive glory and honor and power;
For You created all things,
And by Your will they exist[b] and were created."

The Lamb Takes the Scroll

5 1And I saw in the right *hand* of Him who sat on the throne a scroll written inside and on the back, sealed with seven seals. 2Then I saw a strong angel proclaiming with a loud voice, "Who is worthy to open the scroll and to loose its seals?" 3And no one in heaven or on the earth or under the earth was able to open the scroll, or to look at it.

4So I wept much, because no one was found worthy to open and read[a] the scroll, or to look at it. 5But one of the elders said to me, "Do not weep. Behold, the Lion of the tribe of Judah, the Root of David, has prevailed to open the scroll and to loose[a] its seven seals."

6And I looked, and behold,[a] in the midst of the throne and of the four living creatures, and in the midst of the elders, stood a Lamb as though it had been slain, having seven horns and seven eyes, which are the seven Spirits of God sent out into all the earth. 7Then He came and took the scroll out of the right hand of Him who sat on the throne.

Worthy Is the Lamb

8Now when He had taken the scroll, the four living creatures and the twenty-four elders fell down before the Lamb, each having a harp, and golden bowls full of incense, which are the prayers of the saints. 9And they sang a new song, saying:

"You are worthy to take the scroll,
And to open its seals;
For You were slain,
And have redeemed us to God by Your blood
Out of every tribe and tongue and people and nation,
10   And have made us[a] kings[b] and priests to our God;
And we[c] shall reign on the earth."

4:4 [a]NU-Text and M-Text read *robes, with crowns.*   4:5 [a]NU-Text and M-Text read *voices, and thunderings.*   [b]M-Text omits *the.* 4:6 [a]NU-Text and M-Text add *something like.* 4:8 [a]M-Text has *holy* nine times.   4:11 [a]NU-Text and M-Text read *our Lord and God.*   [b]NU-Text and M-Text read *existed.*   5:4 [a]NU-Text and M-Text omit *and read.*   5:5 [a]NU-Text and M-Text omit *to loose.*   5:6 [a]NU-Text and M-Text read *I saw in the midst . . . a Lamb standing.*   5:10 [a]NU-Text and M-Text read *them.*   [b]NU-Text reads *a kingdom.* [c]NU-Text and M-Text read *they.*

Trade and Economics

Until after New Testament times, papyrus documents were normally rolled rather than folded. Like a school diploma, they were tied with strings or ribbons. For contracts and wills, the knots could be sealed with wax to keep any unauthorized person from secretly changing the contents. In most cases, papyrus scrolls were not "written inside and on the back" (Rev. 5:1).

The Heavenly Scroll (Rev. 5:1–5)

The "throne" is an important theological image in the Book of Revelation. The throne is the seat of God, from whence He rules both heaven and earth. God rules, not merely over souls, but over all aspects of His creation. In this royal setting appears the image of the heavenly scroll containing God's plan for His creation. Seven seals prevent any created being from opening the scroll (Rev. 5:1–5).

In the ancient Near East, sealed scrolls were the means by which royal authority was exercised over a king's domain. A royal official would inscribe the king's will onto a scroll. The king would seal the scroll with a ring pressed into a wax seal. The scroll would remain bound until it was unsealed and read by the properly designated royal official. Then the king's will could be carried out in the kingdom.

In the ancient Near East this administrative method was transferred to the divine realm. The high god was imaged as possessing heavenly books, sealed shut. It was believed that the future of the world was inscribed on these books, and, at the proper time, the designated heavenly figure would unseal a book, releasing the events recorded in it to take place upon the earth.

The vision of John utilizes the scroll metaphor to depict the unfolding of the will of God on earth. Yet without any properly authorized person to open the scroll, God's will remained merely inscribed in the scroll, and not actualized on earth. Unchecked by the divine will, injustice could continue to reign upon the earth. Thus John wept, for no one was found worthy to unseal the scroll (Rev. 5:4).

Yet One was found who is worthy—the "Lion of the tribe of Judah" appearing as a Lamb standing "as though it had been slain" (5:5, 6). The Lion-Lamb, the one who conquers through death, was worthy to open the seals. Through Him the will of God could unfold upon the earth. As the seals are opened, God's judgment springs forth that ultimately leads to the new, purified, just creation. "Worthy is the Lamb who was slain!" (5:12).

---

[11]Then I looked, and I heard the voice of many angels around the throne, the living creatures, and the elders; and the number of them was ten thousand times ten thousand, and thousands of thousands, [12]saying with a loud voice:

"Worthy is the Lamb who was slain
To receive power and riches and wisdom,
And strength and honor and glory and blessing!"

[13]And every creature which is in heaven and on the earth and under the earth and such as are in the sea, and all that are in them, I heard saying:

"Blessing and honor and glory and power
Be to Him who sits on the throne,
And to the Lamb, forever and ever!"[a]

[14]Then the four living creatures said, "Amen!" And the twenty-four[a] elders fell down and worshiped Him who lives forever and ever.[b]

The Sevenfold Plagues

Three series of sevenfold plagues (seven seals, seven trumpets, seven bowls) form the center of John's vision. Some believe the seven seals (Rev. 6:1—8:5) represent the suffering of the world throughout church history, leading up to the end time. The seven trumpets (8:6—9:21; 11:15–19) and the seven bowls (15:1—16:21) would represent the intensified sufferings that immediately precede the return of Christ. Others think the seals, trumpets, and bowls all describe with increasing intensity the suffering immediately before Christ returns. For still others, the seals, trumpets, and bowls do not form a chronological sequence, but rather symbolize the intensity of evil and chaos experienced by John and his readers. In any case, the sufferings described differ more in degree than in kind from

---

5:13 [a]M-Text adds *Amen.*   5:14 [a]NU-Text and M-Text omit *twenty-four.*   [b]NU-Text and M-Text omit *Him who lives forever and ever.*

those some Christians have always experienced.

The plagues are interrupted by two interludes. Following trumpets one through six is an interlude (10:1—11:14) before the seventh trumpet sounds (11:15-19). The angel assures Christians that there will be no further delay; the time of the seventh trumpet is the time of the end (10:5-7). Another interlude (12:1—14:20) separates the seven trumpets and the seven bowls. The purpose of this series of visions (14:1-20) is to give Christians courage, and to assure them of their ultimate triumph. This will be especially needed as they face intense persecution (ch. 13).

■ Revelation 6:1—16:21

Revelation
First Seal: The Conqueror

6 :1 Now I saw when the Lamb opened one of the seals;[a] and I heard one of the four living creatures saying with a voice like thunder, "Come and see." [2]And I looked, and behold, a white horse. He who sat on it had a bow; and a crown was given to him, and he went out conquering and to conquer.

Second Seal: Conflict on Earth

[3]When He opened the second seal, I heard the second living creature saying, "Come and see."[a] [4]Another horse, fiery red, went out. And it was granted to the one who sat on it to take peace from the earth, and that *people* should kill one another; and there was given to him a great sword.

Third Seal: Scarcity on Earth

[5]When He opened the third seal, I heard the third living creature say, "Come and see." So I looked, and behold, a black horse, and he who sat on it had a pair of scales in his hand. [6]And I heard a voice in the midst of the four living creatures saying, "A quart[a] of wheat for a denarius,[b] and three quarts of barley for a denarius; and do not harm the oil and the wine."

Fourth Seal: Widespread Death on Earth

[7]When He opened the fourth seal, I heard the voice of the fourth living creature saying, "Come and see." [8]So I looked, and behold, a pale horse. And the name of him who sat on it was Death, and Hades followed with him. And power was given to them over a fourth of the earth, to kill with

sword, with hunger, with death, and by the beasts of the earth.

Fifth Seal: The Cry of the Martyrs

[9]When He opened the fifth seal, I saw under the altar the souls of those who had been slain for the word of God and for the testimony which they held. [10]And they cried with a loud voice, saying, "How long, O Lord, holy and true, until You judge and avenge our blood on those who dwell on the earth?" [11]Then a white robe was given to each of them; and it was said to them that they should rest a little while longer, until both *the number of* their fellow servants and their brethren, who would be killed as they *were,* was completed.

Sixth Seal: Cosmic Disturbances

[12]I looked when He opened the sixth seal, and behold,[a] there was a great earthquake; and the sun became black as sackcloth of hair, and the moon[b] became like blood. [13]And the stars of heaven fell to the earth, as a fig tree drops its late figs when it is shaken by a mighty wind. [14]Then the sky receded as a scroll when it is rolled up, and every mountain and island was moved out of its place. [15]And the kings of the earth, the great men, the rich men, the commanders,[a] the mighty men, every slave and every free man, hid themselves in the caves and in the rocks of the mountains, [16]and said to the mountains and rocks,

---

6:1 [a]NU-Text and M-Text read *seven seals.*
6:3 [a]NU-Text and M-Text omit *and see.*
6:6 [a]Greek *choinix;* that is, approximately one quart
[b]This was approximately one day's wage for a worker.   6:12 [a]NU-Text and M-Text omit *behold.*
[b]NU-Text and M-Text read *the whole moon.*
6:15 [a]NU-Text and M-Text read *the commanders, the rich men.*

TIME CAPSULE *A.D. 96 to 107*

96 *Domitian is assassinated by his closest associates*

98 *Trajan becomes emperor*

100 *The Alexandrians have a synagogue in Jerusalem*

107 *Ignatius, early Christian writer, is executed in Rome*

107 *Trajan sponsors 123 days of games with 10,000 gladiators*

SEALED JUDGMENTS (Rev. 6:5, 6)

People in the 1st-century Mediterranean world tied shut legal documents with strings, which then were fixed in place by having hot wax seals (often seven) stamped over them. These seals authenticated the contents of a document. To open the document a person had to break the seals; thus unbroken seals affirmed that no one had tampered with the document. In John's vision, the opening of the first four seals revealed God's judgment on the world (Rev. 6:1–8).

Opening the third seal resulted in severe famine (6:5, 6). The "pair of scales" (6:5) probably implies rationing of wheat and barley, which constituted the basic staples of a common person's diet. The low supply of wheat had driven its price ten times its average: a quart of wheat was only a day's worth of food, yet it cost a denarius, a day's wage (6:6). Thus heads of families would have to buy the cheaper barley instead, so their families could eat as well. Still, even the three quarts of barley (that also cost a denarius) would barely feed the whole family. Families were often large, and in conditions such as these some children in peasant families would die.

People regularly used oil and wine. They used oil for washing and anointing, as well as for lighting lamps. They mixed wine with (on average) two parts water to drink with many meals. Still, oil and wine were not necessities for life like the wheat and barley, and their availability may have underscored the reality of God's judgment on some crops but not others. The food shortages were not caused by mere drought conditions; God Himself was responsible.

"Fall on us and hide us from the face of Him who sits on the throne and from the wrath of the Lamb! [17]For the great day of His wrath has come, and who is able to stand?"

The Sealed of Israel

7 [1]After these things I saw four angels standing at the four corners of the earth, holding the four winds of the earth, that the wind should not blow on the earth, on the sea, or on any tree. [2]Then I saw another angel ascending from the east, having the seal of the living God. And he cried with a loud voice to the four angels to whom it was granted to harm the earth and the sea, [3]saying, "Do not harm the earth, the sea, or the trees till we have sealed the servants of our God on their foreheads." [4]And I heard the number of those who were sealed. One hundred *and* forty-four thousand of all the tribes of the children of Israel *were* sealed:

[5]   of the tribe of Judah twelve thousand *were* sealed;[a]
     of the tribe of Reuben twelve thousand *were* sealed;

of the tribe of Gad twelve thousand *were* sealed;
[6] of the tribe of Asher twelve thousand *were* sealed;
of the tribe of Naphtali twelve thousand *were* sealed;
of the tribe of Manasseh twelve thousand *were* sealed;
[7] of the tribe of Simeon twelve thousand *were* sealed;
of the tribe of Levi twelve thousand *were* sealed;
of the tribe of Issachar twelve thousand *were* sealed;
[8] of the tribe of Zebulun twelve thousand *were* sealed;
of the tribe of Joseph twelve thousand *were* sealed;
of the tribe of Benjamin twelve thousand *were* sealed.

A Multitude from the Great Tribulation

[9]After these things I looked, and behold, a great multitude which no one could number, of all nations, tribes, peoples, and tongues, standing before the throne and before the Lamb, clothed with white robes, with palm branches in their hands, [10]and crying out with a loud voice, saying, "Salvation *belongs* to our God who sits on the throne, and to the Lamb!" [11]All the angels stood around the throne and the elders and

---

7:5 [a]In NU-Text and M-Text *were sealed* is stated only in verses 5a and 8c; the words are understood in the remainder of the passage.

the four living creatures, and fell on their faces before the throne and worshiped God, [12]saying:

> "Amen! Blessing and glory and
>   wisdom,
> Thanksgiving and honor and power
>   and might,
> *Be* to our God forever and ever.
>   Amen."

[13]Then one of the elders answered, saying to me, "Who are these arrayed in white robes, and where did they come from?"

[14]And I said to him, "Sir,[a] you know."

So he said to me, "These are the ones who come out of the great tribulation, and washed their robes and made them white in the blood of the Lamb. [15]Therefore they are before the throne of God, and serve Him day and night in His temple. And He who sits on the throne will dwell among them. [16]They shall neither hunger anymore nor thirst anymore; the sun shall not strike them, nor any heat; [17]for the Lamb who is in the midst of the throne will shepherd them and lead them to living fountains of waters.[a] And God will wipe away every tear from their eyes."

Seventh Seal: Prelude to the Seven Trumpets

8 [1]When He opened the seventh seal, there was silence in heaven for about half an hour. [2]And I saw the seven angels who stand before God, and to them were given seven trumpets. [3]Then another angel, having a golden censer, came and stood at the altar. He was given much incense, that he should offer *it* with the prayers of all the saints upon the golden altar which was before the throne. [4]And the smoke of the incense, with the prayers of the saints, ascended before God from the angel's hand. [5]Then the angel took the censer, filled it with fire from the altar, and threw *it* to the earth. And there were noises, thunderings, lightnings, and an earthquake.

[6]So the seven angels who had the seven trumpets prepared themselves to sound.

First Trumpet: Vegetation Struck

[7]The first angel sounded: And hail and fire followed, mingled with blood, and they were thrown to the earth.[a] And a third of the trees were burned up, and all green grass was burned up.

Second Trumpet: The Seas Struck

[8]Then the second angel sounded: And *something* like a great mountain burning with fire was thrown into the sea, and a third of the sea became blood. [9]And a third of the living creatures in the sea died, and a third of the ships were destroyed.

Third Trumpet: The Waters Struck

[10]Then the third angel sounded: And a great star fell from heaven, burning like a torch, and it fell on a third of the rivers and on the springs of water. [11]The name of the star is Wormwood. A third of the waters became wormwood, and many men died from the water, because it was made bitter.

Fourth Trumpet: The Heavens Struck

[12]Then the fourth angel sounded: And a third of the sun was struck, a third of the moon, and a third of the stars, so that a third of them were darkened. A third of the day did not shine, and likewise the night.

[13]And I looked, and I heard an angel[a] flying through the midst of heaven, saying with a loud voice, "Woe, woe, woe to the inhabitants of the earth, because of the remaining blasts of the trumpet of the three angels who are about to sound!"

Fifth Trumpet: The Locusts from the Bottomless Pit

9 [1]Then the fifth angel sounded: And I saw a star fallen from heaven to the earth. To him was given the key to the bottomless pit. [2]And he opened the bottomless pit, and smoke arose out of the pit like the smoke of a great furnace. So the sun and the air were darkened because of the smoke of the pit. [3]Then out of the smoke locusts came upon the earth. And to them was given power, as the scorpions of the earth have power. [4]They were commanded not to harm the grass of the earth, or any green thing, or any tree, but only those men who do not have the seal of God on their foreheads. [5]And they were not given *authority* to kill them, but to torment them *for* five months. Their torment *was* like the torment of a scorpion when it strikes a man. [6]In those days men will seek death

---

7:14 [a]NU-Text and M-Text read *My lord.*
7:17 [a]NU-Text and M-Text read *to fountains of the waters of life.*   8:7 [a]NU-Text and M-Text add *and a third of the earth was burned up.*   8:13 [a]NU-Text and M-Text read *eagle.*

THE FATE OF JERUSALEM

Jerusalem, as the capital of Palestine, faced attack from various armies, contending for control of the territory surrounding the sacred city. Eventually the Roman Empire reduced Jerusalem to a city-state under Roman domination.

Date	Event
332 B.C.	Palestine is conquered by Alexander the Great.
167 B.C.	Antiochus IV dedicates the Jerusalem temple to Zeus, the Greek god of Olympus. The Maccabean revolt begins.
164 B.C.	The Maccabees rededicate the temple to God.
142 B.C.	Simon Maccabeus is made high priest. Palestine is independent until 63.
63 B.C.	The Roman general Pompey takes advantage of a struggle between the Jewish rulers of Palestine and captures Jerusalem for Rome.
40 B.C.	The Romans return Herod the Great to Judea as a king under Roman authority.
A.D. 6	The Romans grow tired of unrest in Palestine and make Judea, Samaria, and Idumea (Edom) into the Roman province of Judea.
A.D. 39	The emperor Gaius Caligula tries to erect a statue of himself in the temple.
A.D. 66	The Jews rebel against Roman authority.
A.D. 70	The Romans defeat Jerusalem, destroy the temple, and begin to gather the temple tax as a Roman government tax.
A.D. 115–118	Fierce Jewish rebellion occurs in the provinces outside Palestine, but is put down by the Romans.
A.D. 132	Bar Kochba leads a Jewish revolt in Palestine. "Kochba" means "star" (Num. 24:17).
A.D. 135	The Bar Kochba rebellion is defeated. Jerusalem is renamed "Aelia Capitolina" as a Roman colony and Jews are forbidden to live there.

and will not find it; they will desire to die, and death will flee from them.

7The shape of the locusts was like horses prepared for battle. On their heads were crowns of something like gold, and their faces *were* like the faces of men. 8They had hair like women's hair, and their teeth were like lions' *teeth*. 9And they had breastplates like breastplates of iron, and the sound of their wings *was* like the sound of chariots with many horses running into battle. 10They had tails like scorpions, and there were stings in their tails. Their power *was* to hurt men five months. 11And they had as king over them the angel of the bottomless pit, whose name in Hebrew *is* Abaddon, but in Greek he has the name Apollyon.

12One woe is past. Behold, still two more woes are coming after these things.

Sixth Trumpet: The Angels from the Euphrates

13Then the sixth angel sounded: And I heard a voice from the four horns of the golden altar which is before God, 14saying to the sixth angel who had the trumpet, "Release the four angels who are bound at the great river Euphrates." 15So the four angels, who had been prepared for the hour and day and month and year, were released to kill a third of mankind. 16Now the number of the army of the horsemen *was* two hundred million; I heard the number of them. 17And thus I saw the horses in the vision: those who sat on them had breastplates of fiery red, hyacinth blue, and sulfur yellow; and the heads of the horses *were* like the heads of lions; and out of their mouths came fire, smoke, and brimstone. 18By these three *plagues* a third of mankind was killed—by the fire and the smoke and the brimstone which came out of their mouths. 19For their power[a] is in their mouth and in their tails; for their

9:19 [a]NU-Text and M-Text read *the power of the horses.*

tails *are* like serpents, having heads; and with them they do harm.

20But the rest of mankind, who were not killed by these plagues, did not repent of the works of their hands, that they should not worship demons, and idols of gold, silver, brass, stone, and wood, which can neither see nor hear nor walk. 21And they did not repent of their murders or their sorceries[a] or their sexual immorality or their thefts.

The Mighty Angel with the Little Book

10 1I saw still another mighty angel coming down from heaven, clothed with a cloud. And a rainbow *was* on his head, his face *was* like the sun, and his feet like pillars of fire. 2He had a little book open in his hand. And he set his right foot on the sea and *his* left *foot* on the land, 3and cried with a loud voice, as *when* a lion roars. When he cried out, seven thunders uttered their voices. 4Now when the seven thunders uttered their voices,[a] I was about to write; but I heard a voice from heaven saying to me,[b] "Seal up the things which the seven thunders uttered, and do not write them."

5The angel whom I saw standing on the sea and on the land raised up his hand[a] to heaven 6and swore by Him who lives forever and ever, who created heaven and the things that are in it, the earth and the things that are in it, and the sea and the things that are in it, that there should be delay no longer, 7but in the days of the sounding of the seventh angel, when he is about to sound, the mystery of God would be finished, as He declared to His servants the prophets.

John Eats the Little Book

8Then the voice which I heard from heaven spoke to me again and said, "Go, take the little book which is open in the hand of the angel who stands on the sea and on the earth."

9So I went to the angel and said to him, "Give me the little book."

And he said to me, "Take and eat it; and it will make your stomach bitter, but it will be as sweet as honey in your mouth."

10Then I took the little book out of the angel's hand and ate it, and it was as sweet as honey in my mouth. But when I had eaten it, my stomach became bitter. 11And he[a] said to me, "You must prophesy again about many peoples, nations, tongues, and kings."

The Two Witnesses

11 1Then I was given a reed like a measuring rod. And the angel stood,[a] saying, "Rise and measure the temple of God, the altar, and those who worship there. 2But leave out the court which is outside the temple, and do not measure it, for it has been given to the Gentiles. And they will tread the holy city underfoot *for* forty-two months. 3And I will give *power* to my two witnesses, and they will prophesy one thousand two hundred and sixty days, clothed in sackcloth."

4These are the two olive trees and the two lampstands standing before the God[a] of the earth. 5And if anyone wants to harm them, fire proceeds from their mouth and devours their enemies. And if anyone wants to harm them, he must be killed in this manner. 6These have power to shut heaven, so that no rain falls in the days of their prophecy; and they have power over waters to turn them to blood, and to strike the earth with all plagues, as often as they desire.

The Witnesses Killed

7When they finish their testimony, the beast that ascends out of the bottomless pit will make war against them, overcome them, and kill them. 8And their dead bodies *will lie* in the street of the great city

---

TIME CAPSULE A.D. 111 to 116

111– 113	Pliny is procurator or governor in Bithynia
111	Trajan and Pliny correspond about Christians
115	Trajan is in Antioch during an earthquake
115– 117	Armed revolt by Jews in North Africa, Egypt, and elsewhere
115	Mesopotamia becomes a Roman province
116	Trajan reaches the Persian Gulf, but does not go to India

---

9:21 [a]NU-Text and M-Text read *drugs.*
10:4 [a]NU-Text and M-Text read *sounded.* [b]NU-Text and M-Text omit *to me.* 10:5 [a]NU-Text and M-Text read *right hand.* 10:11 [a]NU-Text and M-Text read *they.* 11:1 [a]NU-Text and M-Text omit *And the angel stood.* 11:4 [a]NU-Text and M-Text read *Lord.*

which spiritually is called Sodom and Egypt, where also our[a] Lord was crucified. [9]Then *those* from the peoples, tribes, tongues, and nations will see their dead bodies three-and-a-half days, and not allow[a] their dead bodies to be put into graves. [10]And those who dwell on the earth will rejoice over them, make merry, and send gifts to one another, because these two prophets tormented those who dwell on the earth.

The Witnesses Resurrected

[11]Now after the three-and-a-half days the breath of life from God entered them, and they stood on their feet, and great fear fell on those who saw them. [12]And they[a] heard a loud voice from heaven saying to them, "Come up here." And they ascended to heaven in a cloud, and their enemies saw them. [13]In the same hour there was a great earthquake, and a tenth of the city fell. In the earthquake seven thousand people were killed, and the rest were afraid and gave glory to the God of heaven.

[14]The second woe is past. Behold, the third woe is coming quickly.

Seventh Trumpet: The Kingdom Proclaimed

[15]Then the seventh angel sounded: And there were loud voices in heaven, saying, "The kingdoms[a] of this world have become *the kingdoms* of our Lord and of His Christ, and He shall reign forever and ever!" [16]And the twenty-four elders who sat before God on their thrones fell on their faces and worshiped God, [17]saying:

> "We give You thanks, O Lord God
> Almighty,

> The One who is and who was and who
> is to come,[a]
> Because You have taken Your great
> power and reigned.
> The nations were angry, and Your
> wrath has come,
> And the time of the dead, that they
> should be judged,
> And that You should reward Your
> servants the prophets and the
> saints,
> And those who fear Your name, small
> and great,
> And should destroy those who destroy
> the earth."

18

[19]Then the temple of God was opened in heaven, and the ark of His covenant[a] was seen in His temple. And there were lightnings, noises, thunderings, an earthquake, and great hail.

The Woman, the Child, and the Dragon

12 [1]Now a great sign appeared in heaven: a woman clothed with the sun, with the moon under her feet, and on her head a garland of twelve stars. [2]Then being with child, she cried out in labor and in pain to give birth.

[3]And another sign appeared in heaven: behold, a great, fiery red dragon having seven heads and ten horns, and seven diadems on his heads. [4]His tail drew a third of the stars of heaven and threw them to the earth. And the dragon stood before the woman who was ready to give birth, to devour her Child as soon as it was born. [5]She bore a male Child who was to rule all nations with a rod of iron. And her Child was caught up to God and His throne. [6]Then the woman fled into the wilderness, where she has a place prepared by God, that they should feed her there one thousand two hundred and sixty days.

Satan Thrown Out of Heaven

[7]And war broke out in heaven: Michael and his angels fought with the dragon; and

---

AGRICULTURE AND HERDING

The olive tree is a small tree characterized by a long life. Its hardwood, which shows a rich grain when finished, was used for ornamental carpentry. Its fruit was pressed for oil, and the oil used for cooking or as a fuel for lamps (Rev. 11:4). The Mediterranean cultural area can almost be defined as the area where olives are grown.

SYMBOLIC PICTURES OF HEAVENLY CONFLICT (Rev. 12:1)

The Book of Revelation frequently uses visons, symbols, and images that the first readers would have understood. The vision of the woman clothed with the sun, moon, and stars (Rev. 12) portrays the salvation struggle between good and evil.

Throughout the Greco-Roman world people told stories of divine deliverers destined to defeat evil dragons. The dragon tried to slay the newborn deliverer, but the deliverer miraculously survived, grew up, and returned to slay the dragon. In one version of the story, the emperor seems to have claimed to be the dragon-slayer. In Revelation, the wicked emperor is himself a pawn of the dragon, and the true ruler, the Child Jesus, is the One who will triumph over all the world's kingdoms (Rev. 12:5).

The writer of Revelation has interwoven echoes from the Old Testament. The woman with sun, moon, and twelve stars can be interpreted as Israel (see Gen. 37:9), as in some later Jewish traditions about twelve stars. The Old Testament portrays the faithful remnant of Israel as God's virgin bride, in contrast to a portrayal of unfaithful Israel as a prostitute. The Old Testament and the Dead Sea Scrolls portray the righteous remnant of Israel laboring and giving birth to a child, symbolizing the future restoration of God's people (Is. 66:7–10; Mic. 5:3).

In Revelation, the woman's first Child (Rev. 12:2–5) is often interpreted as Jesus and her other "offspring" as Christian believers (12:17). As John wrote to 1st-century churches in Asia (Rev. 1:4, 11), his imagery of a woman birthing her Child and of conflict with the dragon would have been familiar to his readers.

the dragon and his angels fought, ⁸but they did not prevail, nor was a place found for them[a] in heaven any longer. ⁹So the great dragon was cast out, that serpent of old, called the Devil and Satan, who deceives the whole world; he was cast to the earth, and his angels were cast out with him.

¹⁰Then I heard a loud voice saying in heaven, "Now salvation, and strength, and the kingdom of our God, and the power of His Christ have come, for the accuser of our brethren, who accused them before our God day and night, has been cast down. ¹¹And they overcame him by the blood of the Lamb and by the word of their testimony, and they did not love their lives to the death. ¹²Therefore rejoice, O heavens, and you who dwell in them! Woe to the inhabitants of the earth and the sea! For the devil has come down to you, having great wrath, because he knows that he has a short time."

The Woman Persecuted

¹³Now when the dragon saw that he had been cast to the earth, he persecuted the woman who gave birth to the male *Child*. ¹⁴But the woman was given two wings of a great eagle, that she might fly into the wilderness to her place, where she is nourished for a time and times and half a time, from the presence of the serpent. ¹⁵So the serpent spewed water out of his mouth like a flood after the woman, that he might cause her to be carried away by the flood. ¹⁶But the earth helped the woman, and the earth opened its mouth and swallowed up the flood which the dragon had spewed out of his mouth. ¹⁷And the dragon was enraged with the woman, and he went to make war with the rest of her offspring, who keep the command-

---

12:8 ᵃM-Text reads *him*.

BELIEFS AND IDEAS

Some teachers said it was necessary to know the names of angels in order to gain access to the heavens (see Col. 2:18). By contrast, the names of only two angels appear in the Bible: Michael (Dan. 10:13; Rev. 12:7) and Gabriel (Dan. 8:16; Luke 1:19). A third angel, Raphael, appears in the apocryphal book Tobit. According to Tobit, Raphael is one of seven angels that stand before God (Tob. 12:15).

IS NERO'S NUMBER 666? (Rev. 13:18)

How did ancients "calculate the number" of a person (Rev. 13:18)? There is a well-known system for both Hebrew and Greek in which the letters of the alphabet are used for numbers. The first letter of the alphabet is the number "one," the second letter is "two," and so forth. In this system the letters of a name are changed to numbers, and the numbers are then added to arrive at a total.

No one knows the identity of the man or beast whose number is 666 (Rev. 13:18); however, one candidate is Nero. When the Hebrew consonants of "Nero Caesar" are calculated, the total is 666. These consonants, NRWN QSR, have been discovered written just this way in a manuscript, dated about A.D. 55–56, found 15 miles southeast of Jerusalem.

Like the beast, Nero was also a persecutor of the church. He was born in A.D. 37 and became emperor in A.D. 54, when he was only 17 years old. After a few years in office he began to use his powers to put to death anyone he wanted out of the way.

In A.D. 64 a terrible fire burned down about half of the city of Rome. Nero was rumored to have started this fire himself, but afterward he said the Christians were to blame for it. Reports say that Nero used Christians as lamps, burning them to death in his garden.

Nero killed his closest advisors and members of his own family. Eventually, other politicians rose against him; he was deserted, had to flee Rome, and committed suicide in A.D. 68, not quite 30 years old. After he died, there were persistent rumors that he would return from the grave (see Rev. 13:3, 12, 14 where the first beast lived again). All this does not prove that Nero is the man of Rev. 13:18; however, it is possible that the number 666 was associated with his name by the time Revelation was written.

---

ments of God and have the testimony of Jesus Christ.[a]

The Beast from the Sea

13 [1]Then I[a] stood on the sand of the sea. And I saw a beast rising up out of the sea, having seven heads and ten horns,[b] and on his horns ten crowns, and on his heads a blasphemous name. [2]Now the beast which I saw was like a leopard, his feet were like *the feet of* a bear, and his mouth like the mouth of a lion. The dragon gave him his power, his throne, and great authority. [3]And *I saw* one of his heads as if it had been mortally wounded, and his deadly wound was healed. And all the world marveled and followed the beast. [4]So they worshiped the dragon who gave authority to the beast; and they worshiped the beast, saying, "Who *is* like the beast? Who is able to make war with him?"

[5]And he was given a mouth speaking great things and blasphemies, and he was given authority to continue[a] for forty-two months. [6]Then he opened his mouth in blasphemy against God, to blaspheme His name, His tabernacle, and those who dwell in heaven. [7]It was granted to him to make war with the saints and to overcome them. And authority was given him over every tribe,[a] tongue, and nation. [8]All who dwell on the earth will worship him, whose names have not been written in the Book of Life of the Lamb slain from the foundation of the world.

[9]If anyone has an ear, let him hear. [10]He who leads into captivity shall go into captivity; he who kills with the sword must be killed with the sword. Here is the patience and the faith of the saints.

The Beast from the Earth

[11]Then I saw another beast coming up out of the earth, and he had two horns like a lamb and spoke like a dragon. [12]And he exercises all the authority of the first beast in his presence, and causes the earth and those who dwell in it to worship the first beast, whose deadly wound was healed. [13]He performs great signs, so that he even makes fire come down from heaven on the earth in the sight of men. [14]And he

---

12:17 [a]NU-Text and M-Text omit *Christ*.
13:1 [a]NU-Text reads *he*.   [b]NU-Text and M-Text read *ten horns and seven heads*.   13:5 [a]M-Text reads *make war*.   13:7 [a]NU-Text and M-Text add *and people*.

deceives those[a] who dwell on the earth by those signs which he was granted to do in the sight of the beast, telling those who dwell on the earth to make an image to the beast who was wounded by the sword and lived. [15]He was granted *power* to give breath to the image of the beast, that the image of the beast should both speak and cause as many as would not worship the image of the beast to be killed. [16]He causes all, both small and great, rich and poor, free and slave, to receive a mark on their right hand or on their foreheads, [17]and that no one may buy or sell except one who has the mark or[a] the name of the beast, or the number of his name.

[18]Here is wisdom. Let him who has understanding calculate the number of the beast, for it is the number of a man: His number *is* 666.

The Lamb and the 144,000

14 [1]Then I looked, and behold, a[a] Lamb standing on Mount Zion, and with Him one hundred *and* forty-four thousand, having[b] His Father's name written on their foreheads. [2]And I heard a voice from heaven, like the voice of many waters, and like the voice of loud thunder. And I heard the sound of harpists playing their harps. [3]They sang as it were a new song before the throne, before the four living creatures, and the elders; and no one could learn that song except the hundred *and* forty-four thousand who were redeemed from the earth. [4]These are the ones who were not defiled with women, for they are virgins. These are the ones who follow the Lamb wherever He goes. These were redeemed[a] from *among* men, *being* firstfruits to God and to the Lamb. [5]And in their mouth was

found no deceit,[a] for they are without fault before the throne of God.[b]

The Proclamations of Three Angels

[6]Then I saw another angel flying in the midst of heaven, having the everlasting gospel to preach to those who dwell on the earth—to every nation, tribe, tongue, and people— [7]saying with a loud voice, "Fear God and give glory to Him, for the hour of His judgment has come; and worship Him who made heaven and earth, the sea and springs of water."

[8]And another angel followed, saying, "Babylon[a] is fallen, is fallen, that great city, because she has made all nations drink of the wine of the wrath of her fornication."

[9]Then a third angel followed them, saying with a loud voice, "If anyone worships the beast and his image, and receives *his* mark on his forehead or on his hand, [10]he himself shall also drink of the wine of the wrath of God, which is poured out full strength into the cup of His indignation. He shall be tormented with fire and brimstone in the presence of the holy angels and in the presence of the Lamb. [11]And the smoke of their torment ascends forever and ever; and they have no rest day or night, who worship the beast and his image, and whoever receives the mark of his name."

[12]Here is the patience of the saints; here *are* those[a] who keep the commandments of God and the faith of Jesus.

[13]Then I heard a voice from heaven saying to me,[a] "Write: 'Blessed *are* the dead who die in the Lord from now on.'"

"Yes," says the Spirit, "that they may rest from their labors, and their works follow them."

Reaping the Earth's Harvest

[14]Then I looked, and behold, a white cloud, and on the cloud sat *One* like the Son of Man, having on His head a golden crown, and in His hand a sharp sickle.

TIME CAPSULE *A.D. 117 to 130*

117 *Hadrian becomes emperor*

122 *Hadrian's Wall becomes the Roman border in Britain*

129 *Hadrian is in Antioch, Syria*

130 *A triumphal arch is dedicated to Hadrian in Arabia*

130 *Hadrian plans a temple to Jupiter at Jerusalem*

130 *Hadrian is in Egypt*

13:14 [a]M-Text reads *my own people.*
13:17 [a]NU-Text and M-Text omit *or.*
14:1 [a]NU-Text and M-Text read *the.* [b]NU-Text and M-Text add *His name and.*   14:4 [a]M-Text adds *by Jesus.*   14:5 [a]NU-Text and M-Text read *falsehood.* [b]NU-Text and M-Text omit *before the throne of God.*   14:8 [a]NU-Text reads *Babylon the great is fallen, is fallen, which has made;* M-Text reads *Babylon the great is fallen. She has made.*
14:12 [a]NU-Text and M-Text omit *here are those.*
14:13 [a]NU-Text and M-Text omit *to me.*

15And another angel came out of the temple, crying with a loud voice to Him who sat on the cloud, "Thrust in Your sickle and reap, for the time has come for You[a] to reap, for the harvest of the earth is ripe." 16So He who sat on the cloud thrust in His sickle on the earth, and the earth was reaped.

Reaping the Grapes of Wrath

17Then another angel came out of the temple which is in heaven, he also having a sharp sickle.

18And another angel came out from the altar, who had power over fire, and he cried with a loud cry to him who had the sharp sickle, saying, "Thrust in your sharp sickle and gather the clusters of the vine of the earth, for her grapes are fully ripe." 19So the angel thrust his sickle into the earth and gathered the vine of the earth, and threw it into the great winepress of the wrath of God. 20And the winepress was trampled outside the city, and blood came out of the winepress, up to the horses' bridles, for one thousand six hundred furlongs.

Prelude to the Bowl Judgments

15 1Then I saw another sign in heaven, great and marvelous: seven angels having the seven last plagues, for in them the wrath of God is complete.

2And I saw something like a sea of glass mingled with fire, and those who have the victory over the beast, over his image and over his mark[a] and over the number of his name, standing on the sea of glass, having harps of God. 3They sing the song of Moses, the servant of God, and the song of the Lamb, saying:

"Great and marvelous are Your works,
  Lord God Almighty!
Just and true are Your ways,
  O King of the saints![a]
4   Who shall not fear You, O Lord, and
  glorify Your name?

For You alone are holy.
For all nations shall come and
  worship before You,
For Your judgments have been
  manifested."

5After these things I looked, and behold,[a] the temple of the tabernacle of the testimony in heaven was opened. 6And out of the temple came the seven angels having the seven plagues, clothed in pure bright linen, and having their chests girded with golden bands. 7Then one of the four living creatures gave to the seven angels seven golden bowls full of the wrath of God who lives forever and ever. 8The temple was filled with smoke from the glory of God and from His power, and no one was able to enter the temple till the seven plagues of the seven angels were completed.

16 1Then I heard a loud voice from the temple saying to the seven angels, "Go and pour out the bowls[a] of the wrath of God on the earth."

First Bowl: Loathsome Sores

2So the first went and poured out his bowl upon the earth, and a foul and loathsome sore came upon the men who had the mark of the beast and those who worshiped his image.

Second Bowl: The Sea Turns to Blood

3Then the second angel poured out his bowl on the sea, and it became blood as of a dead man; and every living creature in the sea died.

Third Bowl: The Waters Turn to Blood

4Then the third angel poured out his bowl on the rivers and springs of water, and they became blood. 5And I heard the angel of the waters saying:

"You are righteous, O Lord,[a]
The One who is and who was and who
  is to be,[b]
Because You have judged these things.
6   For they have shed the blood of saints
  and prophets,
And You have given them blood to
  drink.
For[a] it is their just due."

7And I heard another from[a] the altar saying, "Even so, Lord God Almighty, true and righteous are Your judgments."

14:15 [a]NU-Text and M-Text omit for You.
15:2 [a]NU-Text and M-Text omit over his mark.
15:3 [a]NU-Text and M-Text read nations.
15:5 [a]NU-Text and M-Text omit behold.
16:1 [a]NU-Text and M-Text read seven bowls.
16:5 [a]NU-Text and M-Text omit O Lord. [b]NU-Text and M-Text read who was, the Holy One.
16:6 [a]NU-Text and M-Text omit For.
16:7 [a]NU-Text and M-Text omit another from.

Fourth Bowl: Men Are Scorched

[8]Then the fourth angel poured out his bowl on the sun, and power was given to him to scorch men with fire. [9]And men were scorched with great heat, and they blasphemed the name of God who has power over these plagues; and they did not repent and give Him glory.

Fifth Bowl: Darkness and Pain

[10]Then the fifth angel poured out his bowl on the throne of the beast, and his kingdom became full of darkness; and they gnawed their tongues because of the pain. [11]They blasphemed the God of heaven because of their pains and their sores, and did not repent of their deeds.

Sixth Bowl: Euphrates Dried Up

[12]Then the sixth angel poured out his bowl on the great river Euphrates, and its water was dried up, so that the way of the kings from the east might be prepared. [13]And I saw three unclean spirits like frogs *coming* out of the mouth of the dragon, out of the mouth of the beast, and out of the mouth of the false prophet. [14]For they are spirits of demons, performing signs, *which* go out to the kings of the earth and[a] of the whole world, to gather them to the battle of that great day of God Almighty.

[15]"Behold, I am coming as a thief. Blessed *is* he who watches, and keeps his garments, lest he walk naked and they see his shame."

[16]And they gathered them together to the place called in Hebrew, Armageddon.[a]

Seventh Bowl: The Earth Utterly Shaken

[17]Then the seventh angel poured out his bowl into the air, and a loud voice came out of the temple of heaven, from the throne, saying, "It is done!" [18]And there were noises and thunderings and lightnings; and there was a great earthquake, such a mighty and great earthquake as had not occurred since men were on the earth. [19]Now the great city was divided into three parts, and the cities of the nations fell. And great Babylon was remembered before God, to give her the cup of the wine of the fierceness of His wrath. [20]Then every island fled away, and the mountains were not found. [21]And great hail from heaven fell upon men, *each hailstone* about the weight of a talent. Men blasphemed God because of the plague of the hail, since that plague was exceedingly great.

The Sinful City and the Antichrist

The great harlot, identified with Babylon (Rev. 17:5), is a powerful and wealthy center of human civilization that leads the kings and all the earth in rebellion against God. As ancient Babylon led people away from God and into idolatry and wickedness, so the harlot sets the nations against Him. Rome in the 1st century may have been one manifestation of the harlot; the "seven mountains" (17:9) could recall the original city of Rome that was built on seven hills.

Other societies and governments in human history have also seemed to be in open rebellion against God. This great harlot is empowered by the beast, the Antichrist. The church, by contrast, is likened to a wife united with her Husband, Christ, at His return (19:7, 8). John's vision continues as the beast and his armies prepare for a battle that cannot be won. Christ has already secured the victory. The beast and his prophet are captured, and his armies are destroyed by the sword from Christ's mouth (19:15).

■ Revelation 17:1—19:21

Revelation
The Scarlet Woman and the Scarlet Beast

17 :1 Then one of the seven angels who had the seven bowls came and talked with me, saying to me,[a] "Come, I will show you the judgment of the great harlot who sits on many waters, [2]with whom the kings of the earth committed fornication, and the inhabitants of the earth were made drunk with the wine of her fornication."

[3]So he carried me away in the Spirit into the wilderness. And I saw a woman sitting on a scarlet beast *which was* full of names of blasphemy, having seven heads and ten horns. [4]The woman was arrayed in purple and scarlet, and adorned with gold and precious stones and pearls, having in her hand a golden cup full of abominations

---

16:14 [a]NU-Text and M-Text omit *of the earth and.*   16:16 [a]M-Text reads *Megiddo.*
17:1 [a]NU-Text and M-Text omit *to me.*

SEVEN KINGS AND SEVEN MOUNTAINS (Rev. 17:9–11)

John is shown a vision of a woman on a scarlet beast, a beast described as "having seven heads" (Rev. 17:3). The first interpretation, which identifies the seven heads as seven mountains (17:9), is obvious enough: ancients called Rome the "city on seven hills." Rome annually celebrated a festival recalling its origin on "seven mountains," and this was the city that was currently reigning over the nations (17:18). Without question, in John's day the epitome of the world system was Rome.

The second interpretation, identifying the seven heads with seven kings (17:10, 11), is more complicated. The sixth king is announced as reigning at that time ("one is," 17:10). If the Book of Revelation was written during the reign of the emperor Domitian, it would be possible to count back from Domitian and determine which ruler might qualify to be the one that was to return and "continue a short time" (17:10). One such calculation points to Nero.

Once Vespasian's dynasty (which included his sons Titus and Domitian) had been established, few people would have considered the three brief usurpers who followed Nero (Galba, Otho, Vitellius) as true kings. Some calculations skip these three emperors, thus allowing the six kings to include both Nero and Domitian. Many people anticipated Nero's return even well into Domitian's reign. Indeed, shortly before the Book of Revelation was written, a Nero impostor even tricked the Parthian armies into following him into the Roman Empire (though he was quickly proved an impostor).

Many scholars do not identify the seven kings precisely with seven specific Roman emperors. More importantly, John's interpretation of seven kings does not imply that in writing Revelation he supposed that Nero would literally return from the dead. Rather, he probably uses the popular image of a new "Nero" to communicate a message: "If you thought Nero was bad, wait till you see the final evil ruler." Besides claiming to be a god, Nero was the first emperor to actively martyr Christians. He is a fitting model for other evil rulers of history, especially the final one often known as the Antichrist (1 John 2:18).

---

and the filthiness of her fornication.[a] ⁵And on her forehead a name *was* written:

MYSTERY,
BABYLON THE GREAT,
THE MOTHER OF HARLOTS
AND OF THE ABOMINATIONS
OF THE EARTH.

⁶I saw the woman, drunk with the blood of the saints and with the blood of the martyrs of Jesus. And when I saw her, I marveled with great amazement.

The Meaning of the Woman and the Beast

⁷But the angel said to me, "Why did you marvel? I will tell you the mystery of the woman and of the beast that carries her, which has the seven heads and the ten horns. ⁸The beast that you saw was, and is not, and will ascend out of the bottomless pit and go to perdition. And those who dwell on the earth will marvel, whose names are not written in the Book of Life from the foundation of the world, when they see the beast that was, and is not, and yet is.[a]

⁹"Here *is* the mind which has wisdom: The seven heads are seven mountains on

---

GEOGRAPHY AND ENVIRONMENT

The city of Rome was famous for being built on seven hills (Rev. 17:9). At the time of Cicero, these hills were known as the Palatine, Capitoline, Caelian, Aventine, Esquiline, Viminal, and Quirinal. In 378 B.C. all of the hills except the Esquiline were enclosed by the Wall of Servius. The Palatine was the location of the Roman emperor's residence, from which he did official business.

which the woman sits. ¹⁰There are also seven kings. Five have fallen, one is, *and* the other has not yet come. And when he comes, he must continue a short time. ¹¹The beast that was, and is not, is himself also the eighth, and is of the seven, and is going to perdition.

¹²"The ten horns which you saw are ten kings who have received no kingdom as yet, but they receive authority for one hour as kings with the beast. ¹³These are of one mind, and they will give their power and authority to the beast. ¹⁴These will make war with the Lamb, and the Lamb will overcome them, for He is Lord of lords and King of kings; and those *who are* with Him *are* called, chosen, and faithful."

¹⁵Then he said to me, "The waters which you saw, where the harlot sits, are peoples, multitudes, nations, and tongues. ¹⁶And the ten horns which you saw onᵃ the beast, these will hate the harlot, make her desolate and naked, eat her flesh and burn her with fire. ¹⁷For God has put it into their hearts to fulfill His purpose, to be of one mind, and to give their kingdom to the beast, until the words of God are fulfilled. ¹⁸And the woman whom you saw is that great city which reigns over the kings of the earth."

The Fall of Babylon the Great

18 ¹After these things I saw another angel coming down from heaven, having great authority, and the earth was illuminated with his glory. ²And he cried mightilyᵃ with a loud voice, saying, "Babylon the great is fallen, is fallen, and has become a dwelling place of demons, a prison for every foul spirit, and a cage for every unclean and hated bird! ³For all the nations have drunk of the wine of the wrath of her fornication, the kings of the earth have committed fornication with her, and the merchants of the earth have become rich through the abundance of her luxury."

⁴And I heard another voice from heaven saying, "Come out of her, my people, lest you share in her sins, and lest you receive of her plagues. ⁵For her sins have reachedᵃ to heaven, and God has remembered her iniquities. ⁶Render to her just as she rendered to you,ᵃ and repay her double according to her works; in the cup which she has mixed, mix double for her. ⁷In the measure that she glorified herself and lived luxuriously, in the same measure give her torment and sorrow; for she says in her heart, 'I sit *as* queen, and am no widow, and will not see sorrow.' ⁸Therefore her plagues will come in one day—death and mourning and famine. And she will be utterly burned with fire, for strong *is* the Lord God who judgesᵃ her.

The World Mourns Babylon's Fall

⁹"The kings of the earth who committed fornication and lived luxuriously with her will weep and lament for her, when they see the smoke of her burning, ¹⁰standing at a distance for fear of her torment, saying, 'Alas, alas, that great city Babylon, that mighty city! For in one hour your judgment has come.'

¹¹"And the merchants of the earth will weep and mourn over her, for no one buys their merchandise anymore: ¹²merchandise of gold and silver, precious stones and pearls, fine linen and purple, silk and scarlet, every kind of citron wood, every kind of object of ivory, every kind of object of most precious wood, bronze, iron, and marble; ¹³and cinnamon and incense, fragrant oil and frankincense, wine and oil, fine flour and wheat, cattle and sheep, horses and chariots, and bodies and souls of men. ¹⁴The fruit that your soul longed for has gone from you, and all the things which are rich and splendid have gone from you,ᵃ and you shall find them no more at all. ¹⁵The merchants of these things, who became rich by her, will stand at a distance for fear of her torment, weeping and wailing, ¹⁶and saying, 'Alas, alas, that great city that was clothed in fine linen, purple, and scarlet, and adorned with gold and precious stones and pearls! ¹⁷For in one hour such great riches came to nothing.' Every shipmaster, all who travel by ship, sailors, and as many as trade on the sea, stood at a distance ¹⁸and cried out when they saw the smoke of her burning, saying, 'What *is* like this great city?'

¹⁹"They threw dust on their heads and cried out, weeping and wailing, and saying, 'Alas, alas, that great city, in which all who had ships on the sea became rich by her

---

17:16 ᵃNU-Text and M-Text read *saw, and the beast.*
18:2 ᵃNU-Text and M-Text omit *mightily.*
18:5 ᵃNU-Text and M-Text read *have been heaped up.*
18:6 ᵃNU-Text and M-Text omit *to you.*
18:8 ᵃNU-Text and M-Text read *has judged.*
18:14 ᵃNU-Text and M-Text read *been lost to you.*

A TRAGIC LOSS OF BUSINESS! (Rev. 18:12)

John received a series of visions revealing the fall of the evil kingdom. The woes of the coming judgments are echoed in various dirges, one given by merchants (Rev. 18:11–18). These merchants mourn because their financial profit from the wicked city has come to an end: "no one buys their merchandise anymore" (18:11).

The items described in Rev. 18:12 represent many of the luxurious products that were imported by Rome and other cities in John's day. One product, purple dye, recalls the city of Thyatira, in Asia Minor, which was known as an industrial center and manufacturer of the dye. The few inscriptions found there show a thriving civic and social life for about 5 centuries until the 3rd century A.D. Not only was Thyatira known for its purple dye, it was a major center of wool trade.

Josephus describes a Jewish colony in Thyatira. Thus, it is not surprising that Paul could encounter a Jewish "seller of purple" who hailed from Thyatira (Acts 16:11). Lydia was a wealthy woman who engaged in the trade of the purple dye, and owned her own home, emphasizing her financial independence. In fact, she hosted a gathering of Jesus' followers at her home (Acts 16:40), typical of many Jewish women at that time who were benefactors of synagogues.

Merchants, such as Lydia, became rich by trading luxuries, like purple dye, that could be afforded only by a few. The wicked city in John's vision represented a great trading center, and the loss of business from such a place would indeed provoke the merchants' demonstration of grief and mourning (Rev. 18:19).

---

wealth! For in one hour she is made desolate.'

20"Rejoice over her, O heaven, and *you* holy apostles[a] and prophets, for God has avenged you on her!"

Finality of Babylon's Fall

21Then a mighty angel took up a stone like a great millstone and threw *it* into the sea, saying, "Thus with violence the great city Babylon shall be thrown down, and shall not be found anymore. 22The sound of harpists, musicians, flutists, and trumpeters shall not be heard in you anymore. No craftsman of any craft shall be found in you anymore, and the sound of a millstone shall not be heard in you anymore. 23The

light of a lamp shall not shine in you anymore, and the voice of bridegroom and bride shall not be heard in you anymore. For your merchants were the great men of the earth, for by your sorcery all the nations were deceived. 24And in her was found the blood of prophets and saints, and of all who were slain on the earth."

Heaven Exults over Babylon

19 1After these things I heard[a] a loud voice of a great multitude in heaven, saying, "Alleluia! Salvation and glory and honor and power *belong* to the Lord[b] our God! 2For true and righteous *are* His judgments, because He has judged the great harlot who corrupted the earth with her fornication; and He has avenged on her the blood of His servants *shed* by her." 3Again they said, "Alleluia! Her smoke rises up forever and ever!" 4And the twenty-four elders and the four living creatures fell down

18:20 [a]NU-Text and M-Text read *saints and apostles.*   19:1 [a]NU-Text and M-Text add *something like.*   [b]NU-Text and M-Text omit *the Lord.*

SCIENCE AND TECHNOLOGY

Linen is a cloth made from fibers of the flax plant. The Egyptians could make linen cloth so fine (Rev. 19:8) it was practically transparent, as well as coarse and thick like canvas. The techniques for preparing and weaving linen were known from the earliest recorded times in Egypt, as evidenced by wall paintings in tombs.

and worshiped God who sat on the throne, saying, "Amen! Alleluia!" [5]Then a voice came from the throne, saying, "Praise our God, all you His servants and those who fear Him, both[a] small and great!"

[6]And I heard, as it were, the voice of a great multitude, as the sound of many waters and as the sound of mighty thunderings, saying, "Alleluia! For the[a] Lord God Omnipotent reigns! [7]Let us be glad and rejoice and give Him glory, for the marriage of the Lamb has come, and His wife has made herself ready." [8]And to her it was granted to be arrayed in fine linen, clean and bright, for the fine linen is the righteous acts of the saints.

[9]Then he said to me, "Write: 'Blessed *are* those who are called to the marriage supper of the Lamb!' " And he said to me, "These are the true sayings of God." [10]And I fell at his feet to worship him. But he said to me, "See *that you do* not *do that!* I am your fellow servant, and of your brethren who have the testimony of Jesus. Worship God! For the testimony of Jesus is the spirit of prophecy."

Christ on a White Horse

[11]Now I saw heaven opened, and behold, a white horse. And He who sat on him *was* called Faithful and True, and in righteousness He judges and makes war. [12]His eyes *were* like a flame of fire, and on His head *were* many crowns. He had[a] a name written that no one knew except Himself. [13]He *was* clothed with a robe dipped in blood, and His name is called The Word of God. [14]And the armies in heaven, clothed in fine linen, white and clean,[a] followed Him on white horses. [15]Now out of His mouth goes a sharp[a] sword, that with it He should strike the nations. And He Himself will rule them with a rod of iron. He Himself treads the winepress of the fierceness and wrath of Almighty God. [16]And He has on *His* robe and on His thigh a name written:

KING OF KINGS
AND LORD OF LORDS.

The Beast and His Armies Defeated

[17]Then I saw an angel standing in the sun; and he cried with a loud voice, saying to all the birds that fly in the midst of heaven, "Come and gather together for the supper of the great God,[a] [18]that you may

eat the flesh of kings, the flesh of captains, the flesh of mighty men, the flesh of horses and of those who sit on them, and the flesh of all *people,* free[a] and slave, both small and great."

[19]And I saw the beast, the kings of the earth, and their armies, gathered together to make war against Him who sat on the horse and against His army. [20]Then the beast was captured, and with him the false prophet who worked signs in his presence, by which he deceived those who received the mark of the beast and those who worshiped his image. These two were cast alive into the lake of fire burning with brimstone. [21]And the rest were killed with the sword which proceeded from the mouth of Him who sat on the horse. And all the birds were filled with their flesh.

19:5 [a]NU-Text and M-Text omit *both.*
19:6 [a]NU-Text and M-Text read *our.*
19:12 [a]M-Text adds *names written, and.*
19:14 [a]NU-Text and M-Text read *pure white linen.*
19:15 [a]M-Text adds *two-edged.*   19:17 [a]NU-Text and M-Text read *the great supper of God.*
19:18 [a]NU-Text and M-Text read *both free.*

The Millennium

The term "millennium," coming from the Latin *mille,* "one thousand," is used to identify the 1,000-year rule of Christ with His saints (Rev. 20:4–7). This is the only place in the New Testament where such a period is described. Christians are divided over how to interpret the 1,000-year reign and the events surrounding it.

Some believe that the binding of Satan represents Christ's victory on the cross. The 1,000 years is, then, symbolic of the church age during which the saints will rule spiritually with Christ. Satan's rebellion at the end of the 1,000 years is his final desperate attempt to challenge God before the return of Christ to judge the world. This view is called amillennialism because it does not believe in a millennial period separate from the church age.

Others believe that the victories of Christ (19:1–21) and the binding of Satan (20:1–3) represent the gradual triumph of the gospel throughout the church age. The millennium is, then, symbolic of an indeterminate time of earthly harmony after the progress of the gospel has resulted in the kingdom of God on earth. Only after this time will Christ return to finally defeat Satan (20:7–10) and judge the world (20:11–15). This view is known as postmillennialism because it teaches that Christ will not return until after the millennium.

Other Christians believe that 19:1–21 depicts Christ's Second Coming which will culminate in the binding of Satan (20:1–3), after which the saints will be raised and rule with Christ on earth for a period symbolized by 1,000 years (20:4–6). At the end of this period Satan will be released for one last rebellion and will be destroyed (20:7–10). Then the unrighteous will be raised and all will be judged (20:11–15). This position is called premillennialism since it teaches the return of Christ before the millennium.

▼ ■ Revelation 20:1–15

Revelation
Satan Bound 1,000 Years

20 :1 Then I saw an angel coming down from heaven, having the key to the bottomless pit and a great chain in his hand. ²He laid hold of the dragon, that serpent of old, who is *the* Devil and Satan, and bound him for a thousand years; ³and he cast him into the bottomless pit, and shut him up, and set a seal on him, so that he should deceive the nations no more till the thousand years were finished. But after these things he must be released for a little while.

The Saints Reign with Christ 1,000 Years

⁴And I saw thrones, and they sat on them, and judgment was committed to them. Then *I saw* the souls of those who

---

20:4 ªM-Text reads *the*.   20:10 ªNU-Text and M-Text add *also*.   20:12 ªNU-Text and M-Text read *the throne*.   20:14 ªNU-Text and M-Text add *the lake of fire*.

TIME CAPSULE   A.D. 132 to 139

132   The Jews in Palestine revolt under Bar Kochba

135   The Romans defeat and kill Bar Kochba

135   The Jews are sold into slavery and expelled from Jerusalem

135   Jerusalem is destroyed

139   The Romans rename Judea "Syria Palestina"

---

had been beheaded for their witness to Jesus and for the word of God, who had not worshiped the beast or his image, and had not received *his* mark on their foreheads or on their hands. And they lived and reigned with Christ for aª thousand years. ⁵But the rest of the dead did not live again until the thousand years were finished. This *is* the first resurrection. ⁶Blessed and holy *is* he who has part in the first resurrection. Over such the second death has no power, but they shall be priests of God and of Christ, and shall reign with Him a thousand years.

Satanic Rebellion Crushed

⁷Now when the thousand years have expired, Satan will be released from his prison ⁸and will go out to deceive the nations which are in the four corners of the earth, Gog and Magog, to gather them together to battle, whose number *is* as the sand of the sea. ⁹They went up on the breadth of the earth and surrounded the camp of the saints and the beloved city. And fire came down from God out of heaven and devoured them. ¹⁰The devil, who deceived them, was cast into the lake of fire and brimstone whereª the beast and the false prophet *are*. And they will be tormented day and night forever and ever.

The Great White Throne Judgment

¹¹Then I saw a great white throne and Him who sat on it, from whose face the earth and the heaven fled away. And there was found no place for them. ¹²And I saw the dead, small and great, standing before God,ª and books were opened. And another book was opened, which is *the* Book of Life. And the dead were judged according to their works, by the things which were written in the books. ¹³The sea gave up the dead who were in it, and Death and Hades delivered up the dead who were in them. And they were judged, each one according to his works. ¹⁴Then Death and Hades were cast into the lake of fire. This is the second death.ª ¹⁵And anyone not found written in the Book of Life was cast into the lake of fire.

A New Heaven and a New Earth

The dominant theme of Rev. 6—20 is tribulation and death. A new mood is set in chs. 21; 22 that moves from time into eternity and provides a description of the eternal blessedness of God's people in the renewed creation. John's first vision depicts this blessedness in general (21:1–8). When God dwells with humanity, He Himself will tenderly remove every "sorrow" and "pain" just as He promised (21:4, 5; see 7:17).

The second vision describes the New Jerusalem (21:9–21) and life in it (21:22—22:5). The description of this city as made of shining "precious stones" and translucent "gold" suggests a glory and beauty that surpass human experience and imagination—realities for which there are no human words (21:18–21). God's splendor will be fully revealed. It will be the source of joy and light. Life in the New Jerusalem will surpass the blessings of the Garden of Eden.

In all this John's message is that God's victory has already been won. The Lamb is "King of kings and Lord of lords."

■ Revelation 21:1—22:21

Revelation
All Things Made New

21 :1 Now I saw a new heaven and a new earth, for the first heaven and the first earth had passed away. Also there was no more sea. ²Then I, John,ᵃ saw the holy city, New Jerusalem, coming down out of heaven from God, prepared as a bride adorned for her husband. ³And I heard a loud voice from heaven saying, "Behold, the tabernacle of God *is* with men, and He will dwell with them, and they shall be His people. God Himself will be with them *and be* their God. ⁴And God will wipe away every tear from their eyes; there shall be no more death, nor sorrow, nor crying. There shall be no more pain, for the former things have passed away."

⁵Then He who sat on the throne said, "Behold, I make all things new." And He said to me,ᵃ "Write, for these words are true and faithful."

⁶And He said to me, "It is done!ᵃ I am the Alpha and the Omega, the Beginning and the End. I will give of the fountain of the water of life freely to him who thirsts. ⁷He who overcomes shall inherit all things,ᵃ and I will be his God and he shall be My son. ⁸But the cowardly, unbelieving,ᵃ abominable, murderers, sexually immoral, sorcerers, idolaters, and all liars shall have their part in the lake which burns with fire and brimstone, which is the second death."

The New Jerusalem

⁹Then one of the seven angels who had the seven bowls filled with the seven last plagues came to meᵃ and talked with me, saying, "Come, I will show you the bride, the Lamb's wife."ᵇ ¹⁰And he carried me away in the Spirit to a great and high mountain, and showed me the great city, the holyᵃ Jerusalem, descending out of heaven from God, ¹¹having the glory of God. Her light *was* like a most precious stone, like a jasper stone, clear as crystal. ¹²Also she had a great and high wall with twelve gates, and twelve angels at the gates, and names written on them, which are *the names* of the twelve tribes of the children of Israel: ¹³three gates on the east, three gates on the north, three gates on the south, and three gates on the west.

¹⁴Now the wall of the city had twelve foundations, and on them were the namesᵃ of the twelve apostles of the Lamb. ¹⁵And he who talked with me had a gold reed to measure the city, its gates, and its wall. ¹⁶The city is laid out as a square; its length is as great as its breadth. And he measured the city with the reed: twelve thousand furlongs. Its length, breadth, and height are equal. ¹⁷Then he measured its wall: one hundred *and* forty-four cubits, *according* to the measure of a man, that is, of an angel. ¹⁸The construction of its wall was *of* jasper; and the city *was* pure gold, like clear glass. ¹⁹The foundations of the wall of the city *were* adorned with all kinds of precious stones: the first foundation *was* jasper, the second sapphire, the third chalcedony, the fourth emerald, ²⁰the fifth sardonyx, the sixth sardius, the seventh chrysolite, the eighth beryl, the ninth topaz, the tenth chrysoprase, the eleventh jacinth, and the twelfth amethyst. ²¹The twelve gates *were* twelve pearls: each individual gate was of one pearl. And the street of the city *was* pure gold, like transparent glass.

21:2 ᵃNU-Text and M-Text omit *John.*
21:5 ᵃNU-Text and M-Text omit *to me.*
21:6 ᵃM-Text omits *It is done.*   21:7 ᵃM-Text reads *overcomes, I shall give him these things.*
21:8 ᵃM-Text adds *and sinners.*   21:9 ᵃNU-Text and M-Text omit *to me.*   ᵇM-Text reads *I will show you the woman, the Lamb's bride.*   21:10 ᵃNU-Text and M-Text omit *the great* and read *the holy city, Jerusalem.*   21:14 ᵃNU-Text and M-Text read *twelve names.*

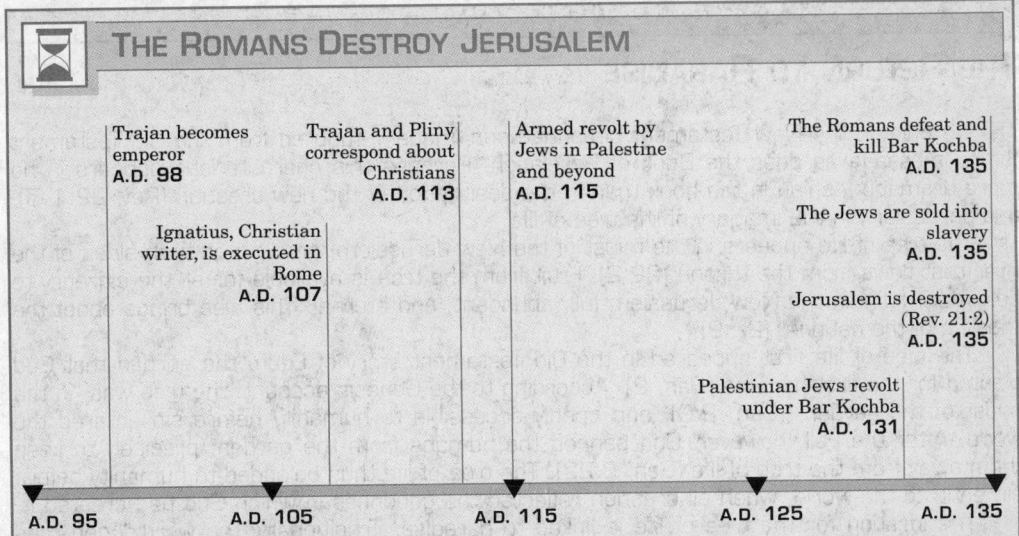

The Glory of the New Jerusalem

²²But I saw no temple in it, for the Lord God Almighty and the Lamb are its temple. ²³The city had no need of the sun or of the moon to shine in it,ᵃ for the gloryᵇ of God illuminated it. The Lamb *is* its light. ²⁴And the nations of those who are savedᵃ shall walk in its light, and the kings of the earth bring their glory and honor into it.ᵇ ²⁵Its gates shall not be shut at all by day (there shall be no night there). ²⁶And they shall bring the glory and the honor of the nations into it.ᵃ ²⁷But there shall by no means enter it anything that defiles, or causesᵃ an abomination or a lie, but only those who are written in the Lamb's Book of Life.

The River of Life

22 ¹And he showed me a pureᵃ river of water of life, clear as crystal, proceeding from the throne of God and of the Lamb. ²In the middle of its street, and on either side of the river, *was* the tree of life, which bore twelve fruits, each *tree* yielding its fruit every month. The leaves of the tree *were* for the healing of the nations. ³And there shall be no more curse, but the throne of God and of the Lamb shall be in it, and His servants shall serve Him. ⁴They shall see His face, and His name *shall be* on their foreheads. ⁵There shall be no night there: They need no lamp nor light of the sun, for the Lord God gives them light. And they shall reign forever and ever.

The Time Is Near

⁶Then he said to me, "These words *are* faithful and true." And the Lord God of the holyᵃ prophets sent His angel to show His servants the things which must shortly take place.

⁷"Behold, I am coming quickly! Blessed *is* he who keeps the words of the prophecy of this book."

⁸Now I, John, saw and heardᵃ these things. And when I heard and saw, I fell down to worship before the feet of the angel who showed me these things.

⁹Then he said to me, "See *that you do not do that.* Forᵃ I am your fellow servant, and of your brethren the prophets, and of those who keep the words of this book. Worship God." ¹⁰And he said to me, "Do not seal the words of the prophecy of this book, for the time is at hand. ¹¹He who is unjust, let him be unjust still; he who is filthy, let him be filthy still; he who is righteous, let him be righteousᵃ still; he who is holy, let him be holy still."

21:23 ᵃNU-Text and M-Text omit *in it.* ᵇM-Text reads *the very glory.* 21:24 ᵃNU-Text and M-Text omit *of those who are saved.* ᵇM-Text reads *the glory and honor of the nations to Him.* 21:26 ᵃM-Text adds *that they may enter in.* 21:27 ᵃNU-Text and M-Text read *anything profane, nor one who causes.* 22:1 ᵃNU-Text and M-Text omit *pure.* 22:6 ᵃNU-Text and M-Text read *spirits of the prophets.* 22:8 ᵃNU-Text and M-Text read *am the one who heard and saw.* 22:9 ᵃNU-Text and M-Text omit *For.* 22:11 ᵃNU-Text and M-Text read *do right.*

The Return to Paradise (Rev. 22:1-5)

No book in the New Testament depends upon imagery supplied from the Old Testament for its message as does the Book of Revelation. Perhaps this characteristic appears in no more dramatic fashion in the book than in the description of the new creation (Rev. 22:1–5), and particularly in the imagery of the tree of life.

The tree of life appears in the midst of the New Jerusalem, growing on both sides of the river that flows from the throne (22:2). Fruit from the tree is available for all the citizenry to eat, making life in the New Jerusalem full, abundant, and eternal. This tree brings about the "healing of the nations" (22:2).

The tree of life first appeared in the Old Testament story of Eden, the garden that God planted for the first humans (Gen. 2). According to the Genesis account, the tree was "in the midst of the garden" (Gen. 2:9), and openly accessible to humanity before sin entered the world. After the Fall, however, God banned the humans from the garden, precisely to keep them away from the tree of life (Gen. 3:22). The tree of life thus belonged to humanity before sin entered the world, when all creation reflected the goodness in which God had created it.

The location for the tree of life is linked to paradise. Traditionally, the word "Eden" has been viewed as meaning "delight" or "luxury." This view is reflected in the Septuagint, where the Greek translation for "garden of Eden" is "paradise of Delight." Again in the *First Book of Enoch* the tree of life appears in paradise. Enoch journeys to God's mountain paradise where the tree of life is kept. The tree's fruit will be given to the righteous when the tree is planted in the New Jerusalem (1 Enoch 24:2—25:7).

John's vision repeats these allusions. Fruit from the tree of life, located in the "Paradise of God," is promised to "him who overcomes" (Rev. 2:7). The inexpressible abundance of the tree is symbolized in its yield being available "every month" (22:7).

Jesus Testifies to the Churches

[12]"And behold, I am coming quickly, and My reward *is* with Me, to give to every one according to his work. [13]I am the Alpha and the Omega, *the* Beginning and *the* End, the First and the Last."[a]

[14]Blessed *are* those who do His commandments,[a] that they may have the right to the tree of life, and may enter through the gates into the city. [15]But[a] outside *are* dogs and sorcerers and sexually immoral and murderers and idolaters, and whoever loves and practices a lie.

[16]"I, Jesus, have sent My angel to testify to you these things in the churches. I am the Root and the Offspring of David, the Bright and Morning Star."

[17]And the Spirit and the bride say, "Come!" And let him who hears say, "Come!" And let him who thirsts come. Whoever desires, let him take the water of life freely.

A Warning

[18]For[a] I testify to everyone who hears the words of the prophecy of this book: If anyone adds to these things, God will add[b] to him the plagues that are written in this book; [19]and if anyone takes away from the words of the book of this prophecy, God shall take away[a] his part from the Book[b] of Life, from the holy city, and *from* the things which are written in this book.

I Am Coming Quickly

[20]He who testifies to these things says, "Surely I am coming quickly."

Amen. Even so, come, Lord Jesus!

[21]The grace of our Lord Jesus Christ *be* with you all.[a] Amen.

22:13 [a]NU-Text and M-Text read *the First and the Last, the Beginning and the End.* 22:14 [a]NU-Text reads *wash their robes.* 22:15 [a]NU-Text and M-Text omit *But.* 22:18 [a]NU-Text and M-Text omit *For.* [b]M-Text reads *may God add.* 22:19 [a]M-Text reads *may God take away.* [b]NU-Text and M-Text read *tree of life.* 22:21 [a]NU-Text reads *with all;* M-Text reads *with all the saints.*

INDEX OF SCRIPTURE PASSAGES

The Old Testament

Passage	Pages
Genesis 1:1—4:26	4–9
Genesis 5:1—6:22	10–12
Genesis 7:1—11:32	13–21
Genesis 12:1—15:21	25–29
Genesis 16:1—20:18	30–35
Genesis 21:1—24:67	35–42
Genesis 25:1—36:43	42–61
Genesis 37:1—46:34	61–75
Genesis 47:1—50:26	75–80
Exodus 1:1—2:15	83–85
Exodus 2:16—6:30	85–90
Exodus 7:1—12:36	91–98
Exodus 12:37—18:27	99–108
Exodus 19:1—40:38	108–135
Leviticus 1:1—15:33	135–152
Leviticus 16:1—22:33	153–161
Leviticus 23:1—24:23	161–165
Leviticus 25:1—27:34	165–170
Numbers 1:1—8:26	171–182
Numbers 9:1—12:16	182–187
Numbers 13:1–33	187–189
Numbers 14:1—20:13	189–198
Numbers 20:14—36:13	198–220
Deuteronomy 1:1–4	221
Deuteronomy 1:5—4:43	221–226
Deuteronomy 4:44—28:68	227–256
Deuteronomy 29:1—33:29	256–264
Deuteronomy 34:1–12	264–265
Joshua 1:1—5:15	267–272
Joshua 6:1—14:5	272–284
Joshua 14:6—24:33	284–297
Judges 1:1—3:6	301–305
Judges 3:7—21:25	305–336
Ruth 1:1—4:12	336–340
Ruth 4:13–22	340–341
1 Samuel 1:1—6:21	341–349
1 Samuel 7:1–17	349–350
1 Samuel 8:1–22	351–352
1 Samuel 9:1—12:25	352–358
1 Samuel 13:1—16:23	358–364
1 Samuel 17:1—19:17	365–370
1 Samuel 19:18—21:15	371–374
1 Samuel 22:1–23	376–377

Passage	Pages
1 Samuel 23:1–29	378–379
1 Samuel 24:1–22	380–381
1 Samuel 25:1–44	382–384
1 Samuel 26:1—30:31	385–391
1 Samuel 31:1–13	391
2 Samuel 1:1–27	391–392
2 Samuel 2:1—4:12	395–399
2 Samuel 5:1—7:29	399–403
2 Samuel 8:1—12:15a	438–443
2 Samuel 12:15b—14:33	444–449
2 Samuel 15:1–37	449–451
2 Samuel 16:1–14	451–452
2 Samuel 16:15—20:26	453–460
2 Samuel 21:1–22	461–462
2 Samuel 22:1—23:39	462–465
2 Samuel 24:1–25	469–471
1 Kings 1:1—2:35	472–475
1 Kings 2:36–46	475–476
1 Kings 3:1—4:34	529–532
1 Kings 5:1–18	556–557
1 Kings 6:1–38	557–559
1 Kings 7:1—9:14	559–564
1 Kings 9:15—10:29	565–567
1 Kings 11:1–8	578–579
1 Kings 11:9–43	587–588
1 Kings 12:1–24	604–605
1 Kings 12:25—14:20	606–609
1 Kings 14:21—15:24	609–611
1 Kings 15:25—16:20	611–614
1 Kings 16:21–34	622–623
1 Kings 17:1—19:21	624–629
1 Kings 20:1—22:40	629–634
1 Kings 22:41–50	634–635
1 Kings 22:51–53	641
2 Kings 1:1–18	641–642
2 Kings 2:1—8:15	643–653
2 Kings 8:16–29	653
2 Kings 9:1—10:36	654–659
2 Kings 11:1—12:21	660–663
2 Kings 13:1–25	663–665
2 Kings 14:1–22	666–668
2 Kings 14:23–29	674
2 Kings 15:1–7	702–703
2 Kings 15:8–31	713–714
2 Kings 15:32—16:4	715
2 Kings 16:5–9	716
2 Kings 16:10–20	724–725
2 Kings 17:1–4	735
2 Kings 17:5–41	740–742
2 Kings 18:1–12	743

Passage	Pages
2 Kings 18:13–16	767–768
2 Kings 18:17—19:7	768–769
2 Kings 19:8–37	771–773
2 Kings 20:1–11	764
2 Kings 20:12–19	766–767
2 Kings 20:20, 21	775
2 Kings 21:1–18	789–791
2 Kings 21:19–26	791–792
2 Kings 22:1–20	793
2 Kings 23:1–25	798–800
2 Kings 23:26, 27	808
2 Kings 23:28–34	825
2 Kings 23:35–37	831
2 Kings 24:1–4	856
2 Kings 24:5–9	863
2 Kings 24:10–17	865–866
2 Kings 24:18, 19	877
2 Kings 24:20—25:3	899–900
2 Kings 25:4–7	948
2 Kings 25:8–21	949–950
2 Kings 25:22–26	960
2 Kings 25:27–30	1012
1 Chronicles 1:1—9:34	1124–1136
1 Chronicles 9:35–44	403
1 Chronicles 10:1—11:47	404–406
1 Chronicles 12:1—15:29	406–410
1 Chronicles 16:1–43	418–420
1 Chronicles 17:1–27	437–438
1 Chronicles 18:1–13	466
1 Chronicles 18:14—20:8	467–469
1 Chronicles 21:1–30	476–478
1 Chronicles 22:1–19	504–505
1 Chronicles 23:1—26:19	505–509
1 Chronicles 26:20—29:30	517–521
2 Chronicles 1:1—2:18	588–591
2 Chronicles 3:1—4:22	591–593
2 Chronicles 5:1—7:22	593–597
2 Chronicles 8:1—9:31	597–600
2 Chronicles 10:1—11:23	615–616
2 Chronicles 12:1—13:22	616–618
2 Chronicles 14:1—16:14	618–622
2 Chronicles 17:1—19:11	636–639
2 Chronicles 20:1–37	639–641
2 Chronicles 21:1—22:9	659–660
2 Chronicles 22:10—23:21	668–670
2 Chronicles 24:1—25:28	670–673
2 Chronicles 26:1–23	711–713
2 Chronicles 27:1—28:27	733–734
2 Chronicles 29:1—31:21	782–786
2 Chronicles 32:1–23	787–788
2 Chronicles 32:24–31	786–787

Passage	Pages	Passage	Pages	Passage	Pages
2 Chronicles 32:32, 33	788–789	Psalm 5	478–479	Psalm 62	425
2 Chronicles 33:1—35:19	801–805	Psalm 6	479	Psalm 63	380
2 Chronicles 35:20—36:4	826–827	Psalm 7	452–453	Psalm 64	494
2 Chronicles 36:5–10	866–867	Psalm 8	411	Psalm 65	414
2 Chronicles 36:11, 12	896	Psalm 9	479–480	Psalm 66	806–807
2 Chronicles 36:13–16	918	Psalm 10	480–481	Psalm 67	807
2 Chronicles 36:17–21	967	Psalm 11	481	Psalm 68	414–416
2 Chronicles 36:22, 23	1049	Psalm 12	481	Psalm 69	494–495
		Psalm 13	481–482	Psalm 70	495
Ezra 1:1—2:70	1103–1105	Psalm 14	482	Psalm 71	496
Ezra 3:1—4:5	1105–1107	Psalm 15	509	Psalm 72	523–524
Ezra 4:6–23	1147–1149	Psalm 16	482–483	Psalm 73	426–427
Ezra 4:24—5:1	1107	Psalm 17	483–484	Psalm 74	427–428
Ezra 5:2—6:22	1118–1121	Psalm 18	393–395	Psalm 75	428
Ezra 7:1—10:44	1155–1160	Psalm 19	411–412	Psalm 76	428–429
		Psalm 20	522–523	Psalm 77	429
Nehemiah 1:1–11	1161–1162	Psalm 21	523	Psalm 78	429–432
Nehemiah 2:1—6:14	1162–1168	Psalm 22	484–485	Psalm 79	432
Nehemiah 6:15—7:73a	1168–1171	Psalm 23	364–365	Psalm 80	432–434
Nehemiah 7:73b—10:39	1171–1176	Psalm 24	509–510	Psalm 81	434
Nehemiah 11:1—12:30	1183–1186	Psalm 25	485	Psalm 82	434
Nehemiah 12:31–47	1191	Psalm 26	485–486	Psalm 83	434–435
Nehemiah 13:1–22	1204–1206	Psalm 27	486–487	Psalm 84	515–516
Nehemiah 13:23–31	1207–1208	Psalm 28	487	Psalm 85	516
		Psalm 29	412–413	Psalm 86	497
Esther 1:1–22	1137–1139	Psalm 30	505	Psalm 87	516–517
Esther 2:1–23	1139–1140	Psalm 31	487–488	Psalm 88	436–437
Esther 3:1—8:17	1141–1145	Psalm 32	413	Psalm 89	969–971
Esther 9:1—10:3	1145–1147	Psalm 33	805–806	Psalm 90	265–266
		Psalm 34	375–376	Psalm 91	1177–1178
Job 1:1—2:13	1057–1060	Psalm 35	488–489	Psalm 92	1206
Job 3:1–26	1060–1061	Psalm 36	489–490	Psalm 93	524
Job 4:1—5:27	1061–1063	Psalm 37	502–503	Psalm 94	524–525
Job 6:1—7:21	1063–1065	Psalm 38	490	Psalm 95	525
Job 8:1–22	1066	Psalm 39	424–425	Psalm 96	420–421
Job 9:1—10:22	1066–1069	Psalm 40	490–491	Psalm 97	525–526
Job 11:1–20	1069–1070	Psalm 41	491–492	Psalm 98	526
Job 12:1—14:22	1070–1072	Psalm 42	510	Psalm 99	526–527
Job 15:1–35	1072–1074	Psalm 43	510–511	Psalm 100	807
Job 16:1—17:16	1074–1075	Psalm 44	511–512	Psalm 101	527
Job 18:1–21	1076–1077	Psalm 45	512–513	Psalm 102	497–498
Job 19:1–29	1077–1078	Psalm 46	513	Psalm 103	416–417
Job 20:1–29	1078–1079	Psalm 47	514	Psalm 104	1192–1194
Job 21:1–34	1079–1080	Psalm 48	514	Psalm 105	421–422
Job 22:1–30	1080–1081	Psalm 49	515	Psalm 106	422–424
Job 23:1—24:25	1081–1083	Psalm 50	425–426	Psalm 107	1194–1195
Job 25:1–6	1083	Psalm 51	443	Psalm 108	417–418
Job 26:1—31:40	1084–1090	Psalm 52	378	Psalm 109	498–499
Job 32:1—37:24	1090–1095	Psalm 53	492	Psalm 110	527–528
Job 38:1—40:5	1095–1098	Psalm 54	384–385	Psalm 111	1195–1196
Job 40:6—41:34	1098–1100	Psalm 55	492–493	Psalm 112	1196
Job 42:1–17	1100–1101	Psalm 56	375	Psalm 113	1196
		Psalm 57	381	Psalm 114	1196
Psalm 1	1177	Psalm 58	493	Psalm 115	1196–1197
Psalm 2	552	Psalm 59	370–371	Psalm 116	1197–1198
Psalm 3	451	Psalm 60	467	Psalm 117	1198
Psalm 4	478	Psalm 61	493–494	Psalm 118	1198–1199

Passage	Pages	Passage	Pages	Passage	Pages
Psalm 119	1178–1183	Isaiah 24:1—27:13	778–782	Jeremiah 52:1, 2	877
Psalm 120	1186	Isaiah 28:1—29:24	735–740	Jeremiah 52:3–6	900
Psalm 121	1187	Isaiah 30:1—32:20	759–763	Jeremiah 52:7–11	948
Psalm 122	1187	Isaiah 33:1—35:10	1017–1020	Jeremiah 52:12–27	950–951
Psalm 123	1187	Isaiah 36:1	767	Jeremiah 52:28–30	983
Psalm 124	1187–1188	Isaiah 36:2—37:7	769–771	Jeremiah 52:31–34	1012
Psalm 125	1188	Isaiah 37:8–38	773–775		
Psalm 126	1188	Isaiah 38:1–22	764–766	Lamentations 1:1—5:22	951–959
Psalm 127	1188–1189	Isaiah 39:1–8	767		
Psalm 128	1189	Isaiah 40:1—45:25	1023–1034	Ezekiel 1:1—3:21	897–899
Psalm 129	1189	Isaiah 46:1—48:22	1035–1038	Ezekiel 3:22—7:27	940–945
Psalm 130	1189	Isaiah 49:1—51:23	1039–1043	Ezekiel 8:1—11:25	918–922
Psalm 131	1189–1190	Isaiah 52:1—55:13	1043–1048	Ezekiel 12:1–28	967–969
Psalm 132	1190	Isaiah 56:1—59:21	1214–1219	Ezekiel 13:1—18:32	923–931
Psalm 133	1190	Isaiah 60:1—66:24	1219–1229	Ezekiel 19:1–14	972
Psalm 134	1190			Ezekiel 20:1—21:17	931–934
Psalm 135	1199–1200	Jeremiah 1:1—6:30	809–820	Ezekiel 21:18–32	937–939
Psalm 136	1200	Jeremiah 7:1—8:3	832–834	Ezekiel 22:1–22	934
Psalm 137	981	Jeremiah 8:4—10:16	851–855	Ezekiel 22:23–31	972–973
Psalm 138	418	Jeremiah 10:17–25	901	Ezekiel 23:1–49	935–937
Psalm 139	499–500	Jeremiah 11:1—12:17	835–837	Ezekiel 24:1–27	939–940
Psalm 140	500–501	Jeremiah 13:1–14	839–840	Ezekiel 25:1—28:26	973–979
Psalm 141	501	Jeremiah 13:15–27	864–865	Ezekiel 29:1–16	945–946
Psalm 142	381–382	Jeremiah 14:1—15:9	846–847	Ezekiel 29:17–21	1009
Psalm 143	501–502	Jeremiah 15:10–21	845	Ezekiel 30:1–19	1009–1011
Psalm 144	528	Jeremiah 16:1—17:27	848–851	Ezekiel 30:20—31:18	946–948
Psalm 145	1200–1201	Jeremiah 18:1–17	840–841	Ezekiel 32:1–32	979–981
Psalm 146	1201–1202	Jeremiah 18:18—20:18	860–863	Ezekiel 33:1–20	988
Psalm 147	1202	Jeremiah 21:1—22:9	901–902	Ezekiel 33:21–33	971–972
Psalm 148	1202–1203	Jeremiah 22:10–17	825–826	Ezekiel 34:1—37:28	988–994
Psalm 149	1203	Jeremiah 22:18–30	863–864	Ezekiel 38:1—39:29	994–997
Psalm 150	1203–1204	Jeremiah 23:1–8	915	Ezekiel 40:1—42:20	998–1002
		Jeremiah 23:9–40	858–860	Ezekiel 43:1—48:35	1002–1009
Proverbs 1:1—9:18	532–540	Jeremiah 24:1–10	867		
Proverbs 10:1—15:33	540–548	Jeremiah 25:1–14	842–843	Daniel 1:1—21	868–870
Proverbs 16:1—22:16	548–556	Jeremiah 25:15–38	883–884	Daniel 2:1—4:37	870–876
Proverbs 22:17—24:34	1050–1053	Jeremiah 26:1–6	831–832	Daniel 5:1–31	1021–1023
Proverbs 25:1—29:27	748–754	Jeremiah 26:7–24	834–835	Daniel 6:1–28	1122–1124
Proverbs 30:1—31:31	1053–1056	Jeremiah 27:1–11	877–878	Daniel 7:1–28	1241–1244
		Jeremiah 27:12—28:17	884–886	Daniel 8:1–27	1244–1245
Ecclesiastes 1:1—12:14	567–578	Jeremiah 29:1–32	886–887	Daniel 9:1–27	1246–1248
		Jeremiah 30:1—33:26	906–915	Daniel 10:1—12:13	1249–1256
Song of Solomon 1:1—8:14	579–586	Jeremiah 34:1–22	902–904		
		Jeremiah 35:1–19	856–857	Hosea 1:1—3:5	689–691
Isaiah 1:1—5:30	705–711	Jeremiah 36:1–10	841–842	Hosea 4:1—5:7	692–693
Isaiah 6:1–13	703–704	Jeremiah 36:11–32	843–844	Hosea 5:8—6:11	693–694
Isaiah 7:1—10:4	716–722	Jeremiah 37:1–21	906	Hosea 7:1—14:9	695–702
Isaiah 10:5—12:6	744–748	Jeremiah 38:1–28	915–917		
Isaiah 13:1—14:23	1013–1016	Jeremiah 39:1–7	948–949	Joel 1:1—3:21	1208–1213
Isaiah 14:24–32	724	Jeremiah 39:8–10	951		
Isaiah 15:1—16:14	757–759	Jeremiah 39:11—44:30	960–966	Amos 1:1—6:7	678–684
Isaiah 17:1–14	722–723	Jeremiah 45:1–5	844–845	Amos 6:8—7:9	685
Isaiah 18:1—20:6	754–757	Jeremiah 46:1–12	838–839	Amos 7:10—9:15	686–689
Isaiah 21:1–17	1016–1017	Jeremiah 46:13–28	904–905		
Isaiah 22:1–14	775–777	Jeremiah 47:1–7	837–838	Obadiah 1:1–21	982–983
Isaiah 22:15–25	759	Jeremiah 48:1—49:39	878–883		
Isaiah 23:1–18	777–778	Jeremiah 50:1—51:64	888–896	Jonah 1:1—4:11	675–677

Passage	Pages	Passage	Pages	Passage	Pages
Micah 1:1—2:13	725–727	Matthew 16:13–28	1346–1347	Mark 7:24–37	1343
Micah 3:1—7:20	727–732	Matthew 17:1–13	1348–1349	Mark 8:1–10	1344–1345
		Matthew 17:14–23	1350	Mark 8:11–26	1345–1346
Nahum 1:1—3:19	820–824	Matthew 17:24—18:9	1351–1352	Mark 8:27—9:1	1347–1348
		Matthew 18:10–14	1374	Mark 9:2–13	1349
Habakkuk 1:1—3:19	827–831	Matthew 18:15–35	1377–1378	Mark 9:14–32	1350–1351
		Matthew 19:1–15	1382–1383	Mark 9:33–50	1352–1353
Zephaniah 1:1—3:20	794–798	Matthew 19:16–30	1384–1385	Mark 10:1–16	1383–1384
		Matthew 20:1–16	1386	Mark 10:17–31	1385
Haggai 1:1—2:23	1108–1110	Matthew 20:17–28	1391	Mark 10:32–45	1391
		Matthew 20:29–34	1392	Mark 10:46–52	1392
Zechariah 1:1—6:15	1111–1116	Matthew 21:1–11	1395	Mark 11:1–11	1395–1396
Zechariah 7:1—8:23	1116–1118	Matthew 21:12–17	1397	Mark 11:12–19	1398
Zechariah 9:1—10:12	1229–1232	Matthew 21:18–22	1399	Mark 11:20–26	1399–1400
Zechariah 11:1—13:9	1232–1234	Matthew 21:23–32	1400	Mark 11:27–33	1400
Zechariah 14:1–21	1235–1236	Matthew 21:33—22:14	1401–1403	Mark 12:1–12	1403–1404
		Matthew 22:15–22	1404–1405	Mark 12:13–17	1405
Malachi 1:1—4:6	1149–1154	Matthew 22:23–33	1405–1406	Mark 12:18–27	1406
		Matthew 22:34–46	1407	Mark 12:28–37	1407
		Matthew 23:1–39	1408–1409	Mark 12:38–44	1410
The New Testament		Matthew 24:1–35	1410–1412	Mark 13:1–31	1412–1413
		Matthew 24:36—25:46	1415–1416	Mark 13:32–37	1416–1417
Matthew 1:1–17	1268	Matthew 26:1–16	1419	Mark 14:1–11	1419
Matthew 1:18–25	1269	Matthew 26:17–29	1420	Mark 14:12–25	1421
Matthew 2:1–21	1272–1274	Matthew 26:30–35	1424	Mark 14:26–31	1424
Matthew 2:22, 23	1274	Matthew 26:36–56	1430–1431	Mark 14:32–52	1431–1432
Matthew 3:1–12	1276	Matthew 26:57–75	1433–1434	Mark 14:53–72	1434–1435
Matthew 3:13–17	1279	Matthew 27:1–26	1437	Mark 15:1–15	1437–1439
Matthew 4:1–11	1281–1282	Matthew 27:27–31	1441	Mark 15:16–20	1441
Matthew 4:12–22	1290–1291	Matthew 27:32–56	1442–1443	Mark 15:21–41	1443–1444
Matthew 4:23–25	1294	Matthew 27:57–66	1446–1447	Mark 15:42–47	1447
Matthew 5:1–48	1302–1305	Matthew 28:1–8	1448	Mark 16:1–8	1448
Matthew 6:1–34	1306–1307	Matthew 28:9–15	1450	Mark 16:9–11	1450
Matthew 7:1–29	1308–1309	Matthew 28:16–20	1454	Mark 16:12, 13	1450
Matthew 8:1–4	1295			Mark 16:14–18	1454
Matthew 8:5–13	1310	Mark 1:1–8	1276–1277	Mark 16:19, 20	1455
Matthew 8:14–17	1293	Mark 1:9–11	1279		
Matthew 8:18–22	1362	Mark 1:12, 13	1282	Luke 1:1–4	1263–1264
Matthew 8:23–34	1323	Mark 1:14–20	1291	Luke 1:5–80	1264–1267
Matthew 9:1–17	1296–1297	Mark 1:21–28	1292	Luke 2:1–20	1269–1271
Matthew 9:18–34	1325–1326	Mark 1:29–34	1293	Luke 2:21–38	1271–1272
Matthew 9:35—11:1	1331–1332	Mark 1:35–39	1294	Luke 2:39, 40	1274
Matthew 11:2–19	1312	Mark 1:40–45	1295	Luke 2:41–52	1275
Matthew 11:20–30	1363	Mark 2:1–22	1297–1298	Luke 3:1–18	1277–1278
Matthew 12:1–14	1299	Mark 2:23—3:6	1299–1300	Luke 3:19, 20	1335
Matthew 12:15–21	1300–1301	Mark 3:7–19	1301	Luke 3:21, 22	1279
Matthew 12:22–50	1314–1316	Mark 3:20–35	1316	Luke 3:23–38	1280
Matthew 13:1–52	1318–1320	Mark 4:1–34	1320–1321	Luke 4:1–13	1282
Matthew 13:53–58	1328	Mark 4:35—5:20	1323–1324	Luke 4:14–30	1291–1292
Matthew 14:1–12	1333–1334	Mark 5:21–43	1326	Luke 4:31–37	1292
Matthew 14:13–21	1336	Mark 6:1–6	1328	Luke 4:38–41	1293–1294
Matthew 14:22–33	1338	Mark 6:7–13	1333	Luke 4:42—5:11	1294–1295
Matthew 14:34–36	1339	Mark 6:14–29	1334–1335	Luke 5:12–16	1295
Matthew 15:1–20	1341	Mark 6:30–44	1336–1337	Luke 5:17–39	1298
Matthew 15:21–31	1343	Mark 6:45–52	1338	Luke 6:1–11	1300
Matthew 15:32–39	1344	Mark 6:53–56	1339	Luke 6:12–19	1301
Matthew 16:1–12	1345	Mark 7:1–23	1342	Luke 6:20–36	1305

Passage	Pages	Passage	Pages	Passage	Pages
Luke 6:37–49	1309	Luke 23:1–25	1439	Acts 15:1–35	1488–1490
Luke 7:1–17	1310–1311	Luke 23:26–49	1444–1445	Acts 15:36—18:11	1502–1506
Luke 7:18–35	1312–1313	Luke 23:50–56	1447	Acts 18:12–22	1513–1514
Luke 7:36–50	1314	Luke 24:1–12	1449	Acts 18:23—19:22	1515–1516
Luke 8:1–18	1321–1322	Luke 24:13–49	1451–1452	Acts 19:23—20:1	1535–1536
Luke 8:19–21	1317	Luke 24:50–53	1455	Acts 20:2, 3a	1549
Luke 8:22–39	1324–1325			Acts 20:3b—21:16	1566–1568
Luke 8:40–56	1327–1328	John 1:1–18	1262–1263	Acts 21:17—23:22	1569–1572
Luke 9:1–6	1333	John 1:19–28	1278	Acts 23:23—24:27	1572–1575
Luke 9:7–9	1335	John 1:29–34	1279	Acts 25:1—26:32	1580–1582
Luke 9:10–17	1337	John 1:35–51	1283–1284	Acts 27:1—28:15	1583–1586
Luke 9:18–27	1348	John 2:1–12	1285	Acts 28:16–31	1586–1587
Luke 9:28–36	1349	John 2:13–25	1285–1286		
Luke 9:37–45	1351	John 3:1–36	1286–1288	Romans 1:1—15:13	1549–1564
Luke 9:46–50	1353	John 4:1–45	1288–1290	Romans 15:14—16:27	1564–1566
Luke 9:51–62	1362	John 4:46–54	1311		
Luke 10:1–24	1363–1365	John 5:1–47	1329–1331	1 Corinthians 1:1—4:21	1517–1521
Luke 10:25–37	1366	John 6:1–15	1337	1 Corinthians 5:1—6:20	1521–1522
Luke 10:38–42	1366–1367	John 6:16–21	1339	1 Corinthians 7:1—15:58	1523–1533
Luke 11:1–4	1307	John 6:22–71	1339–1341	1 Corinthians 16:1–24	1534–1535
Luke 11:5–13	1309–1310	John 7:1–52	1354–1356		
Luke 11:14–36	1316–1317	John 7:53—8:11	1356–1357	2 Corinthians 1:1—2:11	1537–1538
Luke 11:37—12:12	1367–1368	John 8:12–59	1357–1358	2 Corinthians 2:12—7:16	1538–1542
Luke 12:13–21	1368–1369	John 9:1–41	1359–1360	2 Corinthians 8:1—9:15	1543–1545
Luke 12:22–34	1307–1308	John 10:1–21	1361	2 Corinthians 10:1—13:14	1545–1549
Luke 12:35–59	1369–1370	John 10:22–42	1387–1388		
Luke 13:1–9	1370–1371	John 11:1–57	1388–1390	Galatians 1:1–24	1491–1492
Luke 13:10–17	1371	John 12:1–11	1394	Galatians 2:1—6:18	1492–1497
Luke 13:18–21	1322	John 12:12–19	1396		
Luke 13:22–35	1371–1372	John 12:20–50	1417–1418	Ephesians 1:1—6:24	1593–1600
Luke 14:1–24	1372–1373	John 13:1–17	1423		
Luke 14:25–35	1373–1374	John 13:18–30	1422–1423	Philippians 1:1—4:23	1575–1580
Luke 15:1–32	1374–1376	John 13:31–35	1423		
Luke 16:1–31	1376–1377	John 13:36–38	1425	Colossians 1:1—4:18	1589–1592
Luke 17:1–10	1378	John 14:1–24	1425–1426		
Luke 17:11–19	1379	John 14:25—16:33	1426–1429	1 Thessalonians 1:1—2:20	1507–1508
Luke 17:20–37	1379–1380	John 17:1–26	1429–1430	1 Thessalonians 3:1—5:28	1508–1511
Luke 18:1–14	1380–1381	John 18:1–11	1432–1433		
Luke 18:15–17	1384	John 18:12–27	1435–1436	2 Thessalonians 1:1—3:18	1511–1513
Luke 18:18–30	1385–1386	John 18:28–40	1439–1440		
Luke 18:31–34	1391	John 19:1–16	1441–1442	1 Timothy 1:1—6:21	1600–1605
Luke 18:35—19:27	1392–1393	John 19:17–37	1445–1446		
Luke 19:28–44	1396	John 19:38–42	1447	2 Timothy 1:1—4:22	1608–1611
Luke 19:45–48	1398	John 20:1–13	1449		
Luke 20:1–8	1401	John 20:14–18	1450	Titus 1:1—3:15	1605–1607
Luke 20:9–19	1404	John 20:19–31	1452–1453		
Luke 20:20–26	1405	John 21:1–25	1454–1455	Philemon 1:1–25	1587–1588
Luke 20:27–40	1406				
Luke 20:41–44	1407–1408	Acts 1:1–8	1459–1460	Hebrews 1:1—13:25	1623–1636
Luke 20:45—21:4	1410	Acts 1:9–26	1460–1461		
Luke 21:5–33	1413–1414	Acts 2:1–47	1461–1464	James 1:1—5:20	1498–1502
Luke 21:34–38	1417	Acts 3:1—5:42	1464–1468		
Luke 22:1–6	1419	Acts 6:1—8:3	1469–1472	1 Peter 1:1—5:14	1611–1617
Luke 22:7–30	1422	Acts 8:4–40	1473–1475		
Luke 22:31–38	1424–1425	Acts 9:1–43	1476–1478	2 Peter 1:1—3:18	1619–1623
Luke 22:39–53	1432	Acts 10:1—12:25	1478–1483		
Luke 22:54–71	1435	Acts 13:1—14:28	1484–1488	1 John 1:1—5:21	1637–1641

Passage	Pages	Passage	Pages	Passage	Pages
2 John 1:1–13	1641–1642	Revelation 1:1—3:22	1644–1647	Revelation 17:1—19:21	1660–1664
3 John 1:1–14	1642	Revelation 4:1—5:14	1647–1649	Revelation 20:1–15	1665
Jude 1:1–25	1618–1619	Revelation 6:1—16:21	1650–1660	Revelation 21:1—22:21	1666–1668

CULTURAL AND HISTORICAL TOPICS

The background notes in *The So That's Why! Bible* offer cultural and historical information on several topics, which are grouped under eight categories:

Art and Literature
Daily Life and Customs
Gods and Goddesses
Peoples and Nations

Personalities
Places and Geography
Politics and Government
Religion and Worship

The topics listed below are followed by the titles and page numbers of background notes where information is found on that topic. For example, to locate information on the deity Dagon see the category "Gods and Goddesses" which references the background note titled *Dagon Breaks Before God* on page 347.

Art and Literature

Topic	Page
Accadian	
The First World Empire	17
Acts of Thekla	
The Tortured "Others"	1634
Adapa myth	
Adapa Misses Out on Immortality	258
Humans in Heaven	1054
Amarna documents	
Adapa Misses Out on Immortality	258
Shechem in the Amarna Letters	317
Humans in Heaven	1054
Apuleius	
How Immoral Was Corinth?	1548
Aristophanes	
How Immoral Was Corinth?	1548
Assyrian annals	
Sennacherib Fails to Open the Cage	765
A Bird in a Cage	789
The City of Failed Revolts	838
Assyrian Doomsday Book	
Counting Heads	471
Assyrian King List	
These Are the Kings	1125
Assyrian law codes	
Middle Assyrian Laws	251
autobiography	
The Nehemiah Memoirs	1207
Babylonian Chronicle	
Jehoiachin's Exile in Babylon	865
Nebuchadnezzar, King of Babylon	873
Babylonian Theodicy	
Babylonian Job and Other Innocent Sufferers	1068
Black Obelisk	
Jehu Encounters Shalmaneser and Hazael	655
cherubim	
Cherubim, the Divine Guardians	433
Curse of Agade	
The First World Empire	17
Cyrus Cylinder	
Cyrus's Religious Propaganda	1103
De Dea Syria	
Technical Prophecy Seeks Divine Knowledge	157
Mocking Canaanite Religious Ritual	626
Diodorus Siculus	
The Natives of Malta	1585
Djoser's Tradition	
Egypt's Seven Lean Years	68
dragons	
Symbolic Pictures of Heavenly Conflict	1656
Edict of Horemhab	
Appointing Just Judges	241
Elephantine writings	
Aramaic Writings at Elephantine	1169
Emar texts	
Swearing to the Gods	212
Enmerkar	
Enmerkar and the Heavy Mouth	87
Enoch	
The Return to Paradise	1668
Enuma Anu Enlil	
Oracles in Heaven	854
Enuma Elish	
Creation by Conquest in Babylon	5
When the Heavens Go to War	271
Marduk Ascends the Divine Ranks	889
A Festival for Bel Marduk	894
Epic of Erra	
When God Is Angry	416
Epimenides	
An Ancient Prophet from Crete	1606

Topic	Page	Topic	Page
Etana		**Lamentations**	
Humans in Heaven	1054	*Lamenting for the Defeated City*	952
flood		**Legend of Aqhat**	
King of the Universe	413	*Even If Daniel Were Here!*	925
folklore		*Myth and the Prince of Tyre*	978
The Birth of Sargon	84	**Legend of Keret**	
Gilgamesh Epic		*A Quick Cure for Snakebite*	200
When the Bird Does Not Return	15	**Logos**	
God's Bow or a Goddess's Necklace	16	*The Word Becomes Flesh*	1263
The Sleep of Death	482	**Ludlul bel Nemeqi**	
Death Is Our Lot; Enjoy Life	574	*Manasseh's Repentance and Forgiveness*	848
What the Dead Know	575	**magical texts**	
Weeping for Tammuz	919	*Dueling Deities: Magic and Magicians in Egypt*	91
great flood accounts		**Mari tablets**	
The Sumerian King List	10	*The Habiru—Refugees or Outlaws?*	27
The Flood Through Other Eyes	12	*The Mari Tablet Towns*	48
When the Gods Tire of Noisy Humans	13	*Benjamin—Sons of the South*	59
When the Bird Does Not Return	15	*Dagon Breaks Before God*	347
God's Bow or a Goddess's Necklace	16	*A Prophet Prophesies Against the Prophets*	728
Hammurabi		*The Ox That Gored*	111
The Code of Hammurabi	113	**Matthew**	
Hammurabi's "Eye for an Eye"	164	*Matthew and Old Testament Fulfillment*	1313
Herodotus		**Melchizedek**	
The Weak and Temperamental King	1138	*Melchizedek in Jewish Tradition*	1627
Offspring of Vipers	1315	**Menander**	
Hittite text		*Founding Solomon's Temple*	558
Abram's Ceremony and a Hittite Ritual	28	**Moabite Stone**	
household codes		*Ahab the Religious Compromiser*	623
Family Values in the Household	1592	*The Moabite Stone and King Mesha*	666
Hymn to the Sun Disk		*Omri's Name Lives On*	731
The Aten, the Egyptian Sun Disk	1193	**Myth of Nergal**	
hymns		*Nergal and Nergal-Sharezer*	950
There Are gods and Then There Is God	420	**Nag Hammadi**	
I Will Praise the Lord of Wisdom		*Melchizedek in Jewish Tradition*	1627
Babylonian Job and Other Innocent Sufferers	1068	**Nehemiah**	
Israel Stele		*The Nehemiah Memoirs*	1207
Merenptah, the Subduer of Gezer	286	**Nineveh**	
The Israel Stele of Merenptah	335	*The Siege of Lachish*	788
ivory		**Nippur**	
The Ivory House	634	*The Slandered Bride from Nippur*	247
Josephus		**numerology**	
Founding Solomon's Temple	558	*Is Nero's Number 666?*	1657
Before the Governor at Caesarea	1573	**Nuzi texts**	
When Did Festus Take Office?	1574	*The Habiru—Refugees or Outlaws?*	27
Paul's Pedigree as a Pharisee	1578	*A Slave of a Wife Becomes a Mother!*	36
Agrippa, Paul's Judge	1581	*The Ox That Gored*	111
Justin Martyr		*The Household Gods of Nuzi*	330
Simon Magus, the Great Power	1474	**omen texts**	
Karnak		*When God Listened to a Man*	279
The City of Failed Revolts	838	**Origen**	
Kuntillet 'Ajrud		*Early Jewish Missionaries*	1516
Asherah, Queen Mother of the Gods	621	**parables**	
Lachish		*How to Understand a Parable*	1321
Signal-Fires in Beth Haccerem	819	**Pliny the Younger**	
Lachish Letters of Distress	903	*Persecuted in Bithynia*	1612
Lament for Ur		*Holding Fast the Confession*	1632
Lamenting for the Defeated City	952		

Topic	Page
Prism of Esarhaddon	
The King of Assyria Deports Manasseh	802
psalms	
David the Sweet Psalmist	464
Punic	
The Natives of Malta	1585
pyramids	
The Great Pyramid at Giza	25
Qumran	
Melchizedek in Jewish Tradition	1627
Saqqara Papyrus	
Ekron Drinks God's Wine Cup of Fury	884
Seneca	
Vile Passions and Unnatural Lusts	1550
Siloam inscription	
Hezekiah's Tunnel	776
song	
The Levitical Singers	1157
Song of Moses	
God Among the Warrior Deities	103
Sumer	
Sumerian Cities of Refuge	292
Gods Abandon People Who Abandon Their Gods	920
Babylonian Job and Other Innocent Sufferers	1068
Sumerian King List	
The Sumerian King List	10
Sumerian texts	
Sumerian Abominations	750
Tale of Sinuhe	
Sinuhe Visits a Fertile Palestine	194
Tale of Two Brothers	
The Tale of Two Brothers	66
temples	
Paul Versus the Goddess Diana	1536
tree of life	
The Return to Paradise	1668
Ugarit	
Annihilation of the Golden Calf	233
Taxes in Ugarit	239
Anath, Goddess of War	306
Baal, God of Storms	312
Angel: Messenger and Presence of God	376
Storm God Imagery	412
When Gods Go Bad	435
A Human Sacrifice for a Hopeless War	646
A Covenant with Death	737
God Punishes Gods and Kings	779
Mourning at the Banquet Hall	850
Even If Daniel Were Here!	925
Myth and the Prince of Tyre	978
Mistaking the Sun and Moon for Deities	1089
Leviathan, the Sea Serpent	1100
Utnapishtim	
When the Bird Does Not Return	15
yod	
The Tiny Hebrew Yod	1303

Topic	Page
ziggurats	
Babel and Its Tower	20

Daily Life and Customs

Topic	Page
Abba	
Abba, Father	1496
adoption	
My Servant Is My Heir!	39
The Household Gods of Nuzi	330
banquets	
The Who's Who of Banqueting	1609
bronze	
In a Mirror or Face to Face	1530
burial	
Buried in the Cave of Machpelah	43
calendar	
Months of the Yearly Calendar	372
camels	
Bedouins and Their Camels	389
caves	
Buried in the Cave of Machpelah	43
chariots	
Chariots and Chariot Cities	598
Christians	
Those "Christians" in Antioch	1481
cisterns	
The Pools of Heshbon	585
Broken Cisterns	811
city gates	
Gates and Fortified Cities	468
city walls	
Towers of Safety	315
Digging Through a Wall	968
close relative	
Naomi's Close Relative	338
commerce	
Taking Off the Sandals	250
concubine	
The Sort of Wife	397
death	
Waiting to Bury Their Dead	1364
deeds	
Business Documents at Ebla	38
divorce	
Divorce and Remarriage at Corinth	1524
dogs	
You Dirty Dead Dog!	440
drinking	
Mourning at the Banquet Hall	850
Epicureans	
Stoics, Epicureans, and a Babbler	1505

Topic	Page	Topic	Page
eunuchs		**letters**	
Candace's Eunuch Believes	1475	*Letters of Commendation*	1539
exile		**magic**	
Tough Times in Jerusalem	1217	*Dueling Deities: Magic and Magicians in Egypt*	91
famine		*A Quick Cure for Snakebite*	200
Sealed Judgments	1651	**manners**	
fathers		*Sumerian Abominations*	750
Widows in the Household	1604	**marriage**	
food		*A Slave of a Wife Becomes a Mother!*	36
Eating the Good Foods of Egypt	185	*Levirate Marriage and Sandal Ceremony*	340
footwashing		*The Sort of Wife*	397
They Washed Their Feet	331	*A Prophet Without a Family*	849
friendship		*Betrayal and Betrothal*	1270
Friendship with the Master	1427	*No Divorce—Except for Immorality*	1382
garbage		*Jesus Opposes Divorce*	1383
Broken Pieces in the Garbage Dump	861	*Divorce and Remarriage at Corinth*	1524
gatekeepers		*Wives Submitting to Husbands*	1598
Not Just Guarding the Gates	1136	*Husband of One Wife*	1602
gates		*Wives, Husbands, and Religion*	1616
Solomon and His Architecture	565	**marriage and divorce**	
genealogy		*The Slandered Bride from Nippur*	247
Genealogy and Messianic Hopes	1128	**metalworking**	
Gihon spring		*From Copper to Bronze to Iron*	359
Hezekiah's Tunnel	776	*Jonah Sails for Tarshish*	676
gold		*Destroying Their Idols*	696
Egypt and Its Gold	98	**Millo**	
head covering		*What Was the Millo?*	405
Covering a Woman's Head	1528	**millstones**	
Hellenism		*The Old-Time Bread Machine*	318
Alexander the Great	1247	**missionaries**	
Alone in the City of Philosophers	1509	*Early Jewish Missionaries*	1516
Hellenists		**mourning**	
Food for the Hellenist Widows	1469	*Ashes of Sorrow*	446
homosexuality		*Mourning at the Banquet Hall*	850
Vile Passions and Unnatural Lusts	1550	**numerology**	
honor		*The Number "12"*	1461
Widows in the Household	1604	**Olympic Games**	
The Who's Who of Banqueting	1609	*Running in the Olympics*	1526
household codes		**Passover**	
Family Values in the Household	1592	*His Body, His Blood, and Passover*	1421
household gods		**patronage**	
The Household Gods of Nuzi	330	*Of Paul or Apollos? Patronage at Corinth*	1519
iron		**perfume**	
From Copper to Bronze to Iron	359	*Is Beauty Judged by the Nose?*	351
lamps		**Pharisees**	
Lights for the Night	1181	*Paul's Pedigree as a Pharisee*	1578
language		**potsherds**	
Israel's Southern Drawl	323	*Potsherds from the Ashes*	1059
laws		**poverty**	
The Ox That Gored	111	*Various Trials of the Poor*	1499
The Code of Hammurabi	113	**prodigal son**	
Hammurabi's "Eye for an Eye"	164	*Robe, Ring, Sandals, and Calf*	1375
lectures		**purple**	
Ask at Home, Not at Church	1531	*A Tragic Loss of Business!*	1663
		sandals	
		Taking Off the Sandals	250

Topic	Page	Topic	Page
seals		**Ahura Mazda**	
A Faithful Friend and Scribe	844	Satan, Initiating Evil for Israel	477
Zerubbabel, God's Signet Ring	1110	Jerusalem, the Future World Center	1220
servants		**Amon-Re**	
Servant of the Church at Cenchrea	1565	The Creator God Is Not Sun or Moon	4
shaving		Amon of No	905
Priests Upholding Ritual Purity	973	**Anath**	
Shibboleth		Anath, Goddess of War	306
Israel's Southern Drawl	323	**Angra Mainyu**	
slavery		Satan, Initiating Evil for Israel	477
The Temple Slave of the Lord	1031	**Anubis**	
More Than a Slave	1588	The Tale of Two Brothers	66
Bondservants, Be Obedient!	1599	**Artemis**	
sling		Paul Versus the Goddess Diana	1536
From the Pocket of a Sling	383	**Asherah**	
snakes		Organizing a Pantheon of Many Gods	304
Offspring of Vipers	1315	The Person of Lady Wisdom	539
Stoics		Asherah, Queen Mother of the Gods	621
Stoics, Epicureans, and a Babbler	1505	**Ashtoreth**	
Bondservants, Be Obedient!	1599	Worshiping Your Neighbors' Gods	319
stone tools		**Asshur**	
Circumcised with Flint Knives	270	Okay, the Assyrians Really Serve Asshur	770
sword		**Assyrian gods**	
Is the Armor Too Big, or the Crown?	367	The Curses of Disobedience	255
Jonathan Transfers Claim to the Throne	368	Gods of the Assyrian Exiles in Israel	742
temples		**Aten**	
Temple Afire	955	Jerusalem's Apostasies and Other Gods	795
Not Just Guarding the Gates	1136	Cutting Off the Names	1234
teraphim		**Athena**	
The Household Gods of Nuzi	330	Myth and the Prince of Tyre	978
throne		**Aton**	
King of the Universe	413	The Creator God Is Not Sun or Moon	4
towers		**Baal**	
Towers of Safety	315	Anath, Goddess of War	306
trumpets		Baal, God of Storms	312
Pictures of the End Time	1510	Worshiping Your Neighbors' Gods	319
		Storm God Imagery	412
widows		Mocking Canaanite Religious Ritual	626
Food for the Hellenist Widows	1469	Baal Worship in Samaria	658
Widows in the Household	1604	Baal Worship in Jerusalem	669
wine		Jerusalem's Apostasies and Other Gods	795
Wine or Intoxicating Drink	1056	**Baal of Peor**	
women		Chasing the Gods of Moab	206
Ask at Home, Not at Church	1531	**Baal-Zebub**	
Servant of the Church at Cenchrea	1565	The Lord of the Flies	642
Learn Quietly but Do Not Teach	1601	**Bel Marduk**	
Wives, Husbands, and Religion	1616	Marduk Ascends the Divine Ranks	889
writing		A Festival for Bel Marduk	894
The First Major City	18	**Canaanite gods**	
		The Temple Pantheon of Jerusalem	803
		Harlotry After Other Gods	927
Gods and Goddesses		**Chemosh**	
		Gods' Lands, Gods' Peoples	321
Topic	Page	**Dagon**	
Adonis		Dagon Breaks Before God	347
Is This a Ritual for a Dying God?	723		

Topic	Page
Day Star	
A Failed Assault on Heaven	1016
death	
Death Comes Through Your Windows	853
Diana	
Paul Versus the Goddess Diana	1536
Dumuzi	
Weeping for Tammuz	919
Egypt	
Harlotry After Other Gods	927
El	
Calves, Cows, and Bulls Representing the Divine	124
Organizing a Pantheon of Many Gods	304
God Punishes Gods and Kings	779
Erra	
When God Is Angry	416
Gad	
Feeding the Gods of Fortune	1226
Hadad	
Baal, God of Storms	312
heavenly bureaucracy	
Bureaucratic Reports in Heaven	1073
Inanna	
Weeping for Tammuz	919
Ishtar	
The Birth of Sargon	84
God Among the Warrior Deities	103
Weeping for Tammuz	919
Leviathan	
Leviathan, the Sea Serpent	1100
Lilith	
Lilith, a Deadly Demon	1019
Lucifer	
A Failed Assault on Heaven	1016
Marduk	
Creation by Conquest in Babylon	5
God Is in the Midst of His City	513
Adopting Their Idols	673
Should We Correct a Cult Gone Astray?	792
Marduk Ascends the Divine Ranks	889
Gods Abandon People Who Abandon Their Gods	920
Cyrus's Religious Propaganda	1103
Meni	
Feeding the Gods of Fortune	1226
Milcom	
Cleaning Out Solomon's High Places	800
Molech	
A God Consuming Human Flesh	913
moon god	
Mistaking the Sun and Moon for Deities	1089
Mot	
A Covenant with Death	737
Death Comes Through Your Windows	853
Paraded Before the King of Terrors	1076
Nanna	
Lamenting for the Defeated City	952

Topic	Page
Nergal	
Nergal and Nergal-Sharezer	950
Ningirsu	
Ritual for an Audience with God	342
Ninhursag	
God's Bow or a Goddess's Necklace	16
Ninurta	
Sumerian Cities of Refuge	292
Celestial Idols	683
patron deities	
Each with Their Own God	729
Ptah	
The Creator God Is Not Sun or Moon	4
queen of heaven	
Family Worship of the Queen of Heaven	833
Re	
The Creator God Is Not Sun or Moon	4
Satan	
Satan, Initiating Evil for Israel	477
Enter the Adversary—Satan	1058
Clothing, Symbols of Inner Being	1113
Saturn	
Celestial Idols	683
Shamash	
The Creator God Is Not Sun or Moon	4
Sin	
The Brothers and the Moon God	296
sons of God	
Were You There at the Beginning?	1096
sun god	
Mistaking the Sun and Moon for Deities	1089
Sun God or Sun of Righteousness	1153
The Aten, the Egyptian Sun Disk	1193
Tammuz	
Weeping for Tammuz	919
Tefnut	
The Creator God Is Not Sun or Moon	4
Tiamat	
Creation by Conquest in Babylon	5
Tyche	
Feeding the Gods of Fortune	1226
Ugarit	
Organizing a Pantheon of Many Gods	304
wisdom	
The Person of Lady Wisdom	539
Yahweh	
Arad in the Inscriptions	302
Testing the Presence of God	348
Storm God Imagery	412
King of the Universe	413
When God Is Angry	416
When Gods Go Bad	435
God Is in the Midst of His City	513
Kings as Vice-Regents	522
Davidic Kings in the Cosmic Order	527
Asherah, Queen Mother of the Gods	621

Topic	Page
Baal Worship in Samaria	658
Baal Worship in Jerusalem	669
God Is the God of All Peoples	688
Isaiah Encounters the Seraphim	704
No King-Priests in Judah	712
Each with Their Own God	729
Assyrians Worship Yahweh	741
God Punishes Gods and Kings	779
Jerusalem's Apostasies and Other Gods	795
Gods Abandon People Who Abandon Their Gods	920
The Sacred and Profane	992
Bureaucratic Reports in Heaven	1073

Peoples and Nations

Topic	Page
Ammonites	
Gods' Lands, Gods' Peoples	321
Ammonites, a Vassal People	938
Amorites	
Amorites on the Move	1199
Aram-Damascus	
King, Dog, and Son of a Nobody	652
Vassal to Sovereign to Vassal	717
Arameans	
Laban of Aram-naharaim	54
Chaldeans Become Babylonians	828
Assyria	
The Assyrians Make a Comeback	700
Assyrians Worship Yahweh	741
A Chaldean Thorn Pricks Mighty Assyria	766
Okay, the Assyrians Really Serve Asshur	770
Ararat—Assyria's Enemy to the North	774
Avoiding Ungodly Alliances	812
Assyria's Capital Is Destroyed	821
The City of Failed Revolts	838
Ammonites, a Vassal People	938
Babylon	
Creation by Conquest in Babylon	5
Protecting the Weak in the Jubilee Year	166
Chaldeans Become Babylonians	828
Cyrus, the Lord's Anointed	1033
Wickedness Carried to Shinar	1114
bedouins	
Bedouins and Their Camels	389
Bene-yamina	
Benjamin—Sons of the South	59
Chaldeans	
Chaldeans Become Babylonians	828
Cushites	
Ethiopians Ruling in Egypt	757
Edom	
Edom Will Not Return	1150
Edomites	
The Horites of Mount Seir	60
Edom—Judah's Unwanted Neighbor	746
Edom Carries On Esau's Hatred	990
Egypt	
The Creator God Is Not Sun or Moon	4
Joseph Goes to Egypt	65
Dueling Deities: Magic and Magicians in Egypt	91
Egypt and Its Gold	98
Eating the Good Foods of Egypt	185
Pharaoh, King of Egypt	231
Shishak Campaigns Against Solomon's Son	614
Worshiping Moles and Bats	707
Avoiding Ungodly Alliances	812
Habiru	
The Habiru—Refugees or Outlaws?	27
Shechem in the Amarna Letters	317
Hebrews	
The Habiru—Refugees or Outlaws?	27
Hittites	
Kings of the Neo-Hittites	589
Horites	
The Horites of Mount Seir	60
Hurrians	
The Horites of Mount Seir	60
Hyksos	
Joseph Goes to Egypt	65
Ishmael	
An Arabian Tribal Confederacy	436
Jebusites	
Jebus, City of the Jebusites	289
Up the Jebusite Water Shaft	400
Jews	
Origins of the Passover Meal	97
Medes	
Ararat—Assyria's Enemy to the North	774
The Medes and Persians	1123
Minoans	
An Ancient Prophet from Crete	1606
Moab	
The Moabite Stone and King Mesha	666
Neo-Babylonians	
No Middle Ground	1036
Nimrod	
The First Major City	18
Palestine	
Shishak Campaigns Against Solomon's Son	614
Persia	
An Empire Forms in Persia	995
The Medes and Persians	1123
Philistines	
The Sea Peoples Settle in Philistia	283
Royal Cities of the Philistine Lords	386
Pelesets, Philistines, and Palestine	409
Whatever Happened to the Philistines?	1231
Phoenicians	
The Natives of Malta	1585
Rechabites	
The Obedient Rechabites	857
Sabeans	
Solomon and the Queen of Sheba	599

Topic	Page
Samaria	
Marveling over Jesus with a Woman	1289
Sea Peoples	
The Sea Peoples Settle in Philistia	283
Pelesets, Philistines, and Palestine	409
From a Capital to a Vassal City	679
Ugarit	
Taxes in Ugarit	239

Personalities

Topic	Page
Abraham	
The Great Pyramid at Giza	25
The Habiru—Refugees or Outlaws?	27
Abram's Ceremony and a Hittite Ritual	28
Passing Between the Halves	29
Business Documents at Ebla	38
My Servant Is My Heir!	39
Buried in the Cave of Machpelah	43
The Brothers and the Moon God	296
Haran, a City with a Long Life	976
Absalom	
Absalom's Monument	456
Achan	
Accursed and Under the Ban	274
Agrippa I	
Immorality and Herod's Politics	1335
Agrippa II	
Agrippa, Paul's Judge	1581
Ahab	
Ahab the Religious Compromiser	623
The Uptown Girl	628
The Ivory House	634
Heaven Plans an Assassination	638
Ahaz	
Edom—Judah's Unwanted Neighbor	746
Ahaziah	
The Lord of the Flies	642
Akhenaten	
Egypt's City of Sun Worship	1010
The Aten, the Egyptian Sun Disk	1193
Cutting Off the Names	1234
Alexander	
Alexander's Siege of Tyre	1230
Alexander the Great	1247
Worship the Emperor	1483
Amos	
From a Capital to a Vassal City	679
Celestial Idols	683
The Decline of Hamath the Great	684
God Is the God of All Peoples	688
Annas	
Annas and Caiaphas the High Priests	1434
Antiochus IV	
Antiochus IV—Epiphanes or Epimanes?	1253

Topic	Page
Archelaus	
Judea Groans Under Archelaus	1274
Aretas IV	
Immorality and Herod's Politics	1335
Artaxerxes	
Ezra, Nehemiah, and the Persian King	1156
Athaliah	
Baal Worship in Jerusalem	669
Augustus	
Augustus, the First Roman Emperor	1271
Judea Groans Under Archelaus	1274
Worship the Emperor	1483
Balaam	
Balaam: Prophet for Hire	202
Baruch	
A Faithful Friend and Scribe	844
Belshazzar	
Being King While Father Is Gone	1022
Ben-Hadad	
The Declining Kingdom of Ben-Hadad	664
Benjamin	
Benjamin—Sons of the South	59
Bernice	
Agrippa, Paul's Judge	1581
Boaz	
Naomi's Close Relative	338
Caiaphas	
Annas and Caiaphas the High Priests	1434
Caleb	
Long Gone but Never Forgotten—the Nephilim	188
Caligula	
Worship the Emperor	1483
candace	
Candace's Eunuch Believes	1475
Cornelius	
Who Was the God-Fearing Cornelius?	1479
Cyrus II	
Adopting Their Idols	673
Cyrus, the Lord's Anointed	1033
Cyrus Allows the Judeans to Go Home	1048
Cyrus's Religious Propaganda	1103
Starting Over in a Difficult Land	1109
The Medes and Persians	1123
Daniel	
Even If Daniel Were Here!	925
Myth and the Prince of Tyre	978
Darius the Mede	
Who Was Darius the Mede?	1251
David	
Is the Armor Too Big, or the Crown?	367
Jonathan Transfers Claim to the Throne	368
What Was the Millo?	405
Idrimi Returns to His Kingdom	458
Cherethites and Pelethites	460
David the Sweet Psalmist	464
Counting Heads	471
Genealogy and Messianic Hopes	1128

Topic	Page
Diodorus Siculus	
The Pharaoh Who Was But a Noise	967
Dionysius	
Stoics, Epicureans, and a Babbler	1505
Eleazar	
The Tortured "Others"	1634
Eliezer	
My Servant Is My Heir!	39
Elijah	
Mocking Canaanite Religious Ritual	626
The Lord of the Flies	642
Elisha	
Life from a Spring	644
Esarhaddon	
The King of Assyria Deports Manasseh	802
Evil-Merodach	
Evil-Merodach Extends Goodwill	1013
Ezekiel	
A Prophet in Exile	898
Digging Through a Wall	968
The Sacred and Profane	992
An Old Battlefield	993
Felix	
When Did Festus Take Office?	1574
Festus	
When Did Festus Take Office?	1574
Gallio	
Gallio Rules the Province of Achaia	1514
Gamaliel	
Rabbi Gamaliel, Paul's Teacher	1570
Gaubaruwa	
Who Was Darius the Mede?	1251
Gedaliah	
Political Turmoil After Jerusalem's Fall	961
Geshem	
Geshem the Arab	1163
Gideon	
Baal, God of Storms	312
Goliath	
How Big Is a Giant?	366
Gudea	
Ritual for an Audience with God	342
Hadadezer	
Hadadezer Falls to King David	439
Hammurabi	
Babel and Its Tower	20
The Mari Tablet Towns	48
Hammurabi's "Eye for an Eye"	164
Hanno	
From a Capital to a Vassal City	679
Hazael	
King, Dog, and Son of a Nobody	652
Herod Agrippa I	
Worship the Emperor	1483

Topic	Page
Herod Antipas	
Immorality and Herod's Politics	1335
Multicultural Prophets at Antioch	1485
Herod the Great	
Herod, the Great Builder	1411
Before the Governor at Caesarea	1573
Herodias	
Immorality and Herod's Politics	1335
Hezekiah	
Hezekiah's Tunnel	776
Hezekiah Brings Revival to Judah	785
A Pool and Tower in Siloam	1370
Hiram	
Hiram, King of Tyre	590
Hophra	
Nebuchadnezzar Campaigns Against Egypt	946
The Pharaoh Who Was But a Noise	967
Idrimi	
Idrimi Returns to His Kingdom	458
Isaac	
Blessed Are the Blessed	76
Isaiah	
Smoldering Ends of Burnt-Out Logs	718
Is This a Ritual for a Dying God?	723
Jacob	
Family Leadership and Household Gods	53
Blessed Are the Blessed	76
Jehoiachin	
Jehoiachin's Exile in Babylon	865
A Prophet in Exile	898
Evil-Merodach Extends Goodwill	1013
Jehoiada	
Priests Wielding Political Power	671
Jehoiakim	
Jehoiakim Resists Babylon's Control	842
Jehu	
Jehu Encounters Shalmaneser and Hazael	655
Jephthah	
Gods' Lands, Gods' Peoples	321
Jeremiah	
Avoiding Ungodly Alliances	812
Jeremiah in the Days of King Josiah	814
A Faithful Friend and Scribe	844
A Prophet Without a Family	849
True or False Prophet?	859
Property Rights Under Siege	912
The Pharaoh Who Was But a Noise	967
Jeroboam I	
Holy Cows	607
Jezebel	
Ahab the Religious Compromiser	623
The Uptown Girl	628
John the Baptist	
John's Baptism of Repentance	1277
Jonathan	
Jonathan Transfers Claim to the Throne	368

Topic	Page
Joseph	
Joseph Goes to Egypt	65
The Tale of Two Brothers	66
Egypt's Seven Lean Years	68
Betrayal and Betrothal	1270
Josephus	
Zealots Against the Romans	1302
The Abomination of Desolation	1413
Annas and Caiaphas the High Priests	1434
Joshua	
Long Gone but Never Forgotten—the Nephilim	188
When the Heavens Go to War	271
When God Listened to a Man	279
Clothing, Symbols of Inner Being	1113
Josiah	
Should We Correct a Cult Gone Astray?	792
Cleaning Out Solomon's High Places	800
The Temple Pantheon of Jerusalem	803
Jeremiah in the Days of King Josiah	814
Laban	
Family Leadership and Household Gods	53
Laban of Aram-naharaim	54
Lydia	
A Tragic Loss of Business!	1663
Maachah	
Asherah, Queen Mother of the Gods	621
Manaen	
Multicultural Prophets at Antioch	1485
Manasseh	
The Long, Dark Years of Manasseh	791
Manasseh's Repentance and Forgiveness	848
Marduka	
Mordecai, Esther's Famous Guardian	1140
Mary	
Betrayal and Betrothal	1270
Mattathias	
Paul's Pedigree as a Pharisee	1578
Melchizedek	
Melchizedek in Jewish Tradition	1627
Mephibosheth	
You Dirty Dead Dog!	440
Merenptah	
Merenptah, the Subduer of Gezer	286
The Israel Stele of Merenptah	335
Merodach-Baladan	
A Chaldean Thorn Pricks Mighty Assyria	766
Mesha	
A Human Sacrifice for a Hopeless War	646
The Moabite Stone and King Mesha	666
Micah	
Omri's Name Lives On	731
Micaiah	
Heaven Plans an Assassination	638
Mordecai	
Mordecai, Esther's Famous Guardian	1140
Moses	
The Birth of Sargon	84
Enmerkar and the Heavy Mouth	87

Topic	Page
Dueling Deities: Magic and Magicians in Egypt	91
In a Mirror or Face to Face	1530
Nabonidus	
Should We Correct a Cult Gone Astray?	792
Nabonidus in Tema	1064
Nabopolassar	
A New King Rises and a Capital Dies	796
Nadab and Abihu	
Right or Wrong Ritual: Life or Death	145
Nahor	
The Brothers and the Moon God	296
Naomi	
Naomi's Close Relative	338
Levirate Marriage and Sandal Ceremony	340
Nebuchadnezzar I	
Adopting Their Idols	673
Nebuchadnezzar II	
The City of Failed Revolts	838
Who's Controlling Carchemish?	839
Jehoiakim Resists Babylon's Control	842
Nebuchadnezzar, King of Babylon	873
A Prophet in Exile	898
Nebuchadrezzar or Nebuchadnezzar?	902
Nebuchadnezzar Campaigns Against Egypt	946
Temple Afire	955
The 13-Year Siege of Tyre	974
Necho	
Who's Controlling Carchemish?	839
Pharaoh Necho Battles the Babylonians	863
Nehemiah	
Tobiah, the Enemy of Nehemiah	1205
Nero	
Is Nero's Number 666?	1657
Seven Kings and Seven Mountains	1661
Nicodemus	
Born of Water and the Spirit	1287
Nimrod	
The First World Empire	17
Omri	
Omri's Name Lives On	731
Omri Builds a Capital at Samaria	745
Osnapper	
The Great and Noble Osnapper	1148
Osorkon IV	
King So or Dynasty So	736
Paul	
Paul's Pedigree as a Pharisee	1578
Philemon	
More Than a Slave	1588
Phoebe	
Servant of the Church at Cenchrea	1565
Pilate	
Governor Pilate's Unhappy Constituents	1438
Pompey	
Christians of Antioch in Syria	1493
queen of Sheba	
Solomon and the Queen of Sheba	599

Topic	Page
Rabshakeh	
The Assyrians Serve God, So They Say	769
Okay, the Assyrians Really Serve Asshur	770
A Bird in a Cage	789
Rachel	
Family Leadership and Household Gods	53
Where Was Rachel's Tomb?	354
Ramesses III	
The Sea Peoples Settle in Philistia	283
Pelesets, Philistines, and Palestine	409
From a Capital to a Vassal City	679
Rezin	
Vassal to Sovereign to Vassal	717
Smoldering Ends of Burnt-Out Logs	718
Samson	
Samson the Nazirite	328
Sarah	
A Slave of a Wife Becomes a Mother!	36
Sargon	
The First World Empire	17
The Birth of Sargon	84
Sargon II	
The Tartan Comes to Ashdod	756
Sargon II Devours Israel	890
The Exiles Return to Samaria	909
Saul	
Saul the King?	356
Is the Armor Too Big, or the Crown?	367
Seneca	
Gallio Rules the Province of Achaia	1514
Sennacherib	
Sennacherib Fails to Open the Cage	765
A Chaldean Thorn Pricks Mighty Assyria	766
The Siege of Lachish	788
A Bird in a Cage	789
Should We Correct a Cult Gone Astray?	792
Assyria's Capital Is Destroyed	821
Servant, the	
Behold, My Servant	1045
Shalman	
Remember the Brutal Shalman	698
Shalmaneser	
Remember the Brutal Shalman	698
Shalmaneser III	
Jehu Encounters Shalmaneser and Hazael	655
Shishak	
Arad in the Inscriptions	302
Shishak Campaigns Against Solomon's Son	614
Simon Magus	
Simon Magus, the Great Power	1474
Simon the Zealot	
Zealots Against the Romans	1302
So	
King So or Dynasty So	736
Socrates	
Stoics, Epicureans, and a Babbler	1505

Topic	Page
Solomon	
Solomon Marries Pharaoh's Daughter	530
Solomon Worships the Gods of His Wives	578
Hiram, King of Tyre	590
Chariots and Chariot Cities	598
Syro-Phoenician woman	
Who Gets the Children's Bread?	1344
Tamar	
Ashes of Sorrow	446
Tefnakht I	
King So or Dynasty So	736
Terah	
The Brothers and the Moon God	296
Tiglath-Pileser III	
The King Nicknamed "Pul"	1131
Tirhakah	
Tirhakah, King of Ethiopia and Egypt	771
Tobiah	
Tobiah, the Enemy of Nehemiah	1205
Trajan	
Persecuted in Bithynia	1612
Holding Fast the Confession	1632
Uzziah	
No King-Priests in Judah	712
Xerxes I	
The Weak and Temperamental King	1138
Zedekiah	
Property Rights Under Siege	912
Zephaniah	
Jerusalem's Apostasies and Other Gods	795
Zerubbabel	
Zerubbabel, God's Signet Ring	1110
Zerubbabel the Governor	1184
Zoroaster	
Satan, Initiating Evil for Israel	477

Places and Geography

Topic	Page
Accad	
The First World Empire	17
Alalakh	
Idrimi Returns to His Kingdom	458
Amarna	
Cutting Off the Names	1234
Antioch in Pisidia	
Prominent Women of Antioch in Pisidia	1487
Antioch in Syria	
Christians of Antioch in Syria	1493
Arad	
Arad in the Inscriptions	302
Aram-Damascus	
The Declining Kingdom of Ben-Hadad	664
Ararat	
Ararat—Assyria's Enemy to the North	774

Topic	Page	Topic	Page
Areopagus		**Edom**	
Paul Before the Areopagus	1506	The Horites of Mount Seir	60
Ashdod		Seir Is Edom	640
The Tartan Comes to Ashdod	756	**Egnatian Way**	
Athens		Nighttime Exit to Berea	1504
Alone in the City of Philosophers	1509	**Egypt**	
How Immoral Was Corinth?	1548	The River of Egypt	218
Azekah		**Ekron**	
Lachish Letters of Distress	903	Ekron Drinks God's Wine Cup of Fury	884
Babylon		**Elam**	
Babel and Its Tower	20	The Persian Province of Elam	1245
Berea		**En Gedi**	
Nighttime Exit to Berea	1504	En Gedi, an Oasis in a Mountain	580
Beth Arbel		**En es-Sultan**	
Remember the Brutal Shalman	698	Life from a Spring	644
Beth Haccerem		**Ephesus**	
Signal-Fires in Beth Haccerem	819	Paul Versus the Goddess Diana	1536
Bethesda		**Ephraim**	
The Pool of Bethesda	1330	The Exiles Return to Samaria	909
Bithynia		**Erech**	
Persecuted in Bithynia	1612	The First Major City	18
Caesarea		**Ethiopia**	
Before the Governor at Caesarea	1573	Ethiopians Ruling in Egypt	757
Caesarea Maritima		Candace's Eunuch Believes	1475
Who Was the God-Fearing Cornelius?	1479	**Galilee**	
Caesarea Philippi		Landowners of Galilee	1402
The City of Several Names	1347	**Gath**	
Canaan		Gittites Fight with David	450
Long Gone but Never Forgotten—the Nephilim	188	**Gaza**	
Capernaum		From a Capital to a Vassal City	679
Simon Peter's House at Capernaum	1293	**Gehenna**	
Carchemish		Tophet Burns with Much Wood	761
Who's Controlling Carchemish?	839	**Gezer**	
Jehoiakim Resists Babylon's Control	842	Merenptah, the Subduer of Gezer	286
Pharaoh Necho Battles the Babylonians	863	**Gihon spring**	
Nebuchadnezzar, King of Babylon	873	Up the Jebusite Water Shaft	400
Carthage		A Pool and Tower in Siloam	1370
A Place for Burning Babies to the Gods	834	**Gilgal**	
A God Consuming Human Flesh	913	Gilgal, Place of Covenant	277
Colosse		Saul the King?	356
Cities in the Lycus Valley	1593	**Giza**	
Corinth		The Great Pyramid at Giza	25
How Immoral Was Corinth?	1548	**Hamath**	
Crete		The Decline of Hamath the Great	684
An Ancient Prophet from Crete	1606	**Haran**	
Cyrene		Haran, a City with a Long Life	976
Jews of Cyrene Visit Jerusalem	1470	**Hazor**	
Decapolis		Solomon and His Architecture	565
Cities of the Decapolis	1324	**Hermopolis**	
East Gate		Family Worship of the Queen of Heaven	833
The East Gate of the Temple	921	**Heshbon**	
Ebla		The Pools of Heshbon	585
Business Documents at Ebla	38	**Jebus**	
Eden		Jebus, City of the Jebusites	289
Where Was Eden?	6		

Topic	Page	Topic	Page
Jericho		**Rabbah**	
Accursed and Under the Ban	274	*Rabbah, Capital of the Ammonites*	445
Life from a Spring	644	**Rameses**	
Jerusalem		*Eating the Good Foods of Egypt*	185
Jebus, City of the Jebusites	289	**Red Sea**	
Shechem in the Amarna Letters	317	*Where Was the Red Sea?*	95
The Politics of the Siege	907	**Rome**	
Jerusalem, the Future World Center	1220	*Seven Kings and Seven Mountains*	1661
Jerusalem temple		**Samaria**	
Money Changers in the Temple Court	1398	*The Ivory House*	634
House of Prayer, Den of Thieves	1399	*The Assyrians Make a Comeback*	700
Herod, the Great Builder	1411	*Omri Builds a Capital at Samaria*	745
Lachish		*The Exiles Return to Samaria*	909
The Siege of Lachish	788	**Seir**	
A Bird in a Cage	789	*The Horites of Mount Seir*	60
Signal-Fires in Beth Haccerem	819	*Seir Is Edom*	640
Lachish Letters of Distress	903	*Edom Carries On Esau's Hatred*	990
Laodicea		**Shechem**	
Cities in the Lycus Valley	1593	*Shechem in the Amarna Letters*	317
Lycus River		**Shinar**	
Cities in the Lycus Valley	1593	*Wickedness Carried to Shinar*	1114
Machpelah		**Sidon**	
Buried in the Cave of Machpelah	43	*The Uptown Girl*	628
Malta		*Tyre and Sidon, the Economic Oppressors*	1212
The Natives of Malta	1585	**Siloam**	
Mari		*A Pool and Tower in Siloam*	1370
The Mari Tablet Towns	48	**Sumer**	
Megiddo		*The Sumerian King List*	10
Megiddo in Solomon's Districts	531	*The First Major City*	18
Solomon and His Architecture	565	**Susa**	
Memphis		*Shushan the Citadel and Shushan*	1146
Tirhakah, King of Ethiopia and Egypt	771	*The Persian Province of Elam*	1245
Mesopotamia		**Tarshish**	
Laban of Aram-naharaim	54	*Jonah Sails for Tarshish*	676
Nile		**tells**	
The River of Egypt	218	*A Mound of Ruins*	1218
Nineveh		**Tema**	
A New King Rises and a Capital Dies	796	*Nabonidus in Tema*	1064
Assyria's Capital Is Destroyed	821	**Thyatira**	
No		*A Tragic Loss of Business!*	1663
Amon of No	905	**Tophet**	
On		*Tophet Burns with Much Wood*	761
Egypt's City of Sun Worship	1010	*A Place for Burning Babies to the Gods*	834
Palestine		**Tyre**	
Sinuhe Visits a Fertile Palestine	194	*The 13-Year Siege of Tyre*	974
Panion		*Myth and the Prince of Tyre*	978
The City of Several Names	1347	*Tyre and Sidon, the Economic Oppressors*	1212
Persepolis		*Alexander's Siege of Tyre*	1230
Jerusalem, the Future World Center	1220	**Uruk**	
Philippi		*The First Major City*	18
Women Leaders in the Philippian Church	1579	*Wickedness Carried to Shinar*	1114
Philistine Pentapolis		**Valley of Hinnom**	
Ekron Drinks God's Wine Cup of Fury	884	*Broken Pieces in the Garbage Dump*	861
Pontus		**way of Horus**	
Persecuted in Bithynia	1612	*The Road Through Philistia*	101

Topic	Page
Ziklag	
Royal Cities of the Philistine Lords	386

Politics and Government

Topic	Page
Benjamin	
Where Was Rachel's Tomb?	354
Carchemish	
Nebuchadnezzar Campaigns Against Egypt	946
census taking	
Counting Heads	471
centurions	
Who Was the God-Fearing Cornelius?	1479
cities	
Theology of Palace and Temple Districts	560
covenants	
Passing Between the Halves	29
Cyrus II	
Cyrus Allows the Judeans to Go Home	1048
East Gate	
The East Gate of the Temple	921
Egypt	
Kings as Vice-Regents	522
Ethiopians Ruling in Egypt	757
Tirhakah, King of Ethiopia and Egypt	771
exile	
Needing Comfort in Exile	1024
Can God Really Do This "New Thing"?	1029
The New Exodus	1038
Starting Over in a Difficult Land	1109
Jubilee year	
Protecting the Weak in the Jubilee Year	166
judges	
Appointing Just Judges	241
kingdom	
A Kingdom of Truth	1440
Mocking the So-Called King	1441
kings	
Davidic Kings in the Cosmic Order	527
laws	
Middle Assyrian Laws	251
marriage	
Solomon Marries Pharaoh's Daughter	530
Solomon Worships the Gods of His Wives	578
mercenaries	
Gittites Fight with David	450
Cherethites and Pelethites	460
murder	
Finding a Dead Body	246
persecution	
Seven Kings and Seven Mountains	1661
Pharaoh	
Pharaoh, King of Egypt	231

Topic	Page
priests	
Priests Wielding Political Power	671
prophets	
Heaven Plans an Assassination	638
refuge	
Sumerian Cities of Refuge	292
scrolls	
The Heavenly Scroll	1649
seals	
Sealed Judgments	1651
siege warfare	
The Politics of the Siege	907
Property Rights Under Siege	912
How to Conduct a Siege	941
Digging Through a Wall	968
Solomon	
Megiddo in Solomon's Districts	531
Syro-Ephraimite War	
Smoldering Ends of Burnt-Out Logs	718
Edom—Judah's Unwanted Neighbor	746
taxes	
Taxes in Ugarit	239
No Longer Forsaken	1223
temples	
Theology of Palace and Temple Districts	560
tithe	
Tithe and Loyalty	1176
torture	
The Tortured "Others"	1634
vassals	
The Long, Dark Years of Manasseh	791
Zealots	
Zealots Against the Romans	1302

Religion and Worship

Topic	Page
altars	
Forbidden Religious Objects	127
ancestor worship	
Worshiping Ancestors as Gods	423
angels	
Angel: Messenger and Presence of God	376
Humans Are Not Perfect Before God	1062
Pictures of the End Time	1510
ark of the covenant	
A Throne for God	131
Testing the Presence of God	348
Asherim	
Forbidden Religious Objects	127
baptism	
John's Baptism of Repentance	1277
Born of Water and the Spirit	1287
blessing	
Blessed Are the Blessed	76

Topic	Page
cities	
God Is in the Midst of His City	513
clothing	
Clothing, Symbols of Inner Being	1113
collection	
Paul's Collection for Jerusalem	1544
covenants	
Abram's Ceremony and a Hittite Ritual	28
Passing Between the Halves	29
death	
The Sleep of Death	482
Death Is Our Lot; Enjoy Life	574
What the Dead Know	575
Paraded Before the King of Terrors	1076
Sheol for All the Dead Without Distinction	1085
divination	
Technical Prophecy Seeks Divine Knowledge	157
Omens, Spells, and Other Abominations	243
Testing the Presence of God	348
divine curses	
The Curses of Disobedience	255
divine wars	
When the Heavens Go to War	271
Accursed and Under the Ban	274
Egypt	
Were You There at the Beginning?	1096
emperor worship	
Worship the Emperor	1483
Father	
A Petition to Our Father in Heaven	1225
Feast of Tabernacles	
The Spirit and Rivers of Living Water	1355
festivals	
The Day of Judgment	1209
forgiveness	
Manasseh's Repentance and Forgiveness	848
fungus	
Rituals Against Fungus	150
healing	
The Pool of Bethesda	1330
high places	
The Evil High Places	353
Cleaning Out Solomon's High Places	800
human sacrifice	
A Human Sacrifice for a Hopeless War	646
Tophet Burns with Much Wood	761
Cleaning Out Solomon's High Places	800
A Place for Burning Babies to the Gods	834
A God Consuming Human Flesh	913
hymns	
Praise God, All Heaven and Earth	1203
idols	
Calves, Cows, and Bulls Representing the Divine	124
How Is an Idol a God?	228
Annihilation of the Golden Calf	233
Holy Cows	607
Mocking Canaanite Religious Ritual	626

Topic	Page
Adopting Their Idols	673
Destroying Their Idols	696
Worshiping Moles and Bats	707
The Temple Pantheon of Jerusalem	803
Jerusalem temple	
House of Prayer, Den of Thieves	1399
The Abomination of Desolation	1413
kings	
No King-Priests in Judah	712
local deities	
Worshiping Your Neighbors' Gods	319
Gods' Lands, Gods' Peoples	321
Messiah	
The Spirit of Prophecy	1462
mountains	
Where the Gods Live: Sacred Mountains	109
Nazirite vow	
Samson the Nazirite	328
necromancy	
What the Dead Know	575
New Moon festival	
Months of the Yearly Calendar	372
omens	
Should We Correct a Cult Gone Astray?	792
Passover	
Origins of the Passover Meal	97
Passover and Society	1120
His Body, His Blood, and Passover	1421
pillars	
Forbidden Religious Objects	127
prayer	
Ritual for an Audience with God	342
Praying to Our Father	1306
Abba, Father	1496
prophecy	
Balaam: Prophet for Hire	202
Prophets Between God and Humanity	508
A Consultation with a Prophet	932
Ezekiel's Prophetic Theater	942
The Sacred and Profane	992
The Spirit of Prophecy	1462
prophets	
Samson the Nazirite	328
A Prophet Prophesies Against the Prophets	728
True or False Prophet?	859
Intimidation Denied	1041
Multicultural Prophets at Antioch	1485
purification	
Waterpots for Purification	1284
Scandalous Faith	1327
rabbis	
Learn Quietly but Do Not Teach	1601
ritual	
Right or Wrong Ritual: Life or Death	145
Rituals Against Fungus	150
Annihilation of the Golden Calf	233
Finding a Dead Body	246
Is This a Ritual for a Dying God?	723

Topic	Page	Topic	Page
Family Worship of the Queen of Heaven	833	A Eunuch and a Foreigner in God's House	1215
A Festival for Bel Marduk	894	Begging at the Gate of the Temple	1465
ritual prostitution		**tithe**	
Harlotry After Other Gods	927	Weightier Matters of the Law	1409
ritual purity		**Torah**	
Priests Upholding Ritual Purity	973	The Tiny Hebrew Yod	1303
sacrifice		**Urim and Thummim**	
Chasing the Gods of Moab	206	Technical Prophecy Seeks Divine Knowledge	157
scapegoat		Omens, Spells, and Other Abominations	243
Animals That Carry Away Sin	154	A Guide for Divine Wisdom	387
seraphim		**vows**	
Isaiah Encounters the Seraphim	704	Swearing to the Gods	212
singers		**washing**	
The Levitical Singers	1157	Waterpots for Purification	1284
snakes		**weather**	
Isaiah Encounters the Seraphim	704	Oracles in Heaven	854
Spirit of God		**women**	
Breathing New Life	1453	Family Worship of the Queen of Heaven	833
symbolic actions		Ask at Home, Not at Church	1531
Ezekiel's Prophetic Theater	942	Women Leaders in the Philippian Church	1579
synagogue		**ziggurats**	
Put Out of the Synagogue	1360	Babel and Its Tower	20
temples		Where the Gods Live: Sacred Mountains	109
The Prince in the Temple	1006	**zodiac**	
Laying the Foundation of the Second Temple	1106	Oracles in Heaven	854

GLOSSARY

When we read about the life and times of ancient biblical peoples, we encounter many names, places, and things that are unfamiliar to us today. The Glossary describes and explains many of the subjects mentioned in the notes of *The So That's Why! Bible.*

ACCAD A city in Mesopotamia that Sargon the Great (c. 2350 B.C.) made the capital of his empire; also spelled Agade. Sargon's dynasty controlled Mesopotamia for 2 centuries, until Accad fell, to be succeeded by Ur.

ACCADIAN The language of Accad, a Semitic language that continued in use and influence long after the fall of Accad in about 2100 B.C. It used the Sumerian writing system.

ACHAEMENID The dynasty ruling the Persian Empire founded by Cyrus the Great when he conquered Babylon, 559 B.C. Darius, Xerxes, and Ahasuerus belong to this dynasty. It was finally overthrown by Alexander the Great in 330 B.C.

ACHAIA The Roman province corresponding to modern Greece, south of Macedonia.

ADAD Along with Shamash, an Assyrian deity in charge of omens. *See* SHAMASH.

ADAD-NIRARI I Ruler of Assyria 1308–1274 B.C.

ADAD-NIRARI III Ruler of Assyria 810–783 B.C.

ADAPA Character in an Accadian myth who must remain outside heaven.

ADAR The 12th month of the Babylonian calendar. Adar begins in March of the modern calendar.

ADONIS Originally a Phoenician god of vegetation and fertility worshiped at Byblos (near modern Beirut, Lebanon) and introduced to the Greeks probably via Cyprus. Adonis spends part of the year with Aphrodite and another part in Hades.

ADRAMMELECH The name of a son of Sennacherib; also, a deity worshiped by Syrians in Samaria after the Assyrian conquest of 722 B.C.

AEGEAN The Aegean Sea is 150 miles wide, lying between Greece and Asia Minor (modern Turkey); Macedonia and Thrace are to its north and Crete to the south. There are many islands in the Aegean.

AGADE *See* ACCAD.

AGORA The Greek word for *marketplace.*

AGRIPPA I, II *See* HEROD AGRIPPA I, II.

AHASUERUS Or Xerxes I, the son of Darius I the Great and the ruler of Persia 486–465 B.C. Xerxes's navy was defeated by Athens at the battle of Salamis, 479 B.C.

AHURA MAZDA The Persian God, proclaimed by Zoroaster, and represented by a solar disk with wings. As the force of light he fights against darkness. The king of Persia was his representative.

AKHENATEN *See* AMENHOTEP IV.

ALALAKH A city located on the Orontes river 20 miles east of Antioch, in northern Syria. Alalakh was conquered by the Hittites about 1370 B.C., and abandoned after the invasion of the Sea Peoples in 1194 B.C.

ALTAR A platform or table for religious offerings, typically animal sacrifices.

AMALEKITES Nomadic people who lived south of Israel and toward Egypt; descendants of Esau. They were traditional enemies of Israel.

AMARNA A city on the Nile, 200 miles south of Cairo; founded by Amenhotep IV (1352–1336 B.C.). In 1887 several hundred clay tablets were discovered there, consisting of correspondence between Egypt and other countries.

AMASIS *See* HOPHRA.

AMENEMHET I Ruler of Egypt 1963–1934 B.C., first pharaoh of the twelfth dynasty; this dynasty promoted irrigation and mining, and was in power for more than two hundred years.

AMENHOTEP III   Ruler of Egypt 1390–1352 B.C. Amenhotep's reign was peaceful and prosperous. His diplomatic correspondence is extensively recorded in the Amarna letters.

AMENHOTEP IV   Also called Akhenaten; ruler of Egypt 1352–1336 B.C. His wife was Nefertiti. Akhenaten instituted exclusive worship of the sun god Aten, but his reforms did not survive him. He built a new capital at Amarna.

AMMONITES   A people reportedly descended from Lot. The Ammonites lived east of the Jordan and were traditional enemies of Israel.

AMON   The god of the Egyptian city of Thebes, and the primary god of the Egyptians. Akhenaten tried to replace Amon with Aten, the sun god, but his reforms were reversed by his son Tutankhamun.

AMORITES   Ancient inhabitants of northern Mesopotamia and the area to the west as far as Syria and Palestine. They were at Ugarit by 1900 B.C. and at Byblos by 1800 B.C. Hammurabi of Babylon (1792–1750 B.C.) was an Amorite; many texts relating to the Amorites were discovered at Mari.

AN   The chief deity of Uruk and head of the Sumerian pantheon.

ANAMMELECH   A deity who, like Adrammelech, was worshiped in Samaria after the Assyrian conquest of 722 B.C. *See* ADRAMMELECH.

ANATH   A goddess of war worshiped in Palestine, also regarded as the sister or spouse of the storm god Baal.

ANATOLIA   Asia Minor; the large peninsula separating the eastern Mediterranean from the Black Sea; this is today eastern Turkey.

ANNALS   History written year by year; a continuous account of current events.

ANTIOCH   An important city of the ancient world, located in northern Syria near the Mediterranean coast. Antioch was comparable in size to Rome and Alexandria. Pisidian Antioch is another city, much smaller, 300 miles to the west in Anatolia.

ANTIOCHUS IV EPIPHANES   Ruler of Syria 175–164 B.C., one of the Seleucid kings. He desecrated the Jerusalem temple and made Judaism unlawful, precipitating the Maccabean revolt. *See* JUDAS MACCABEUS.

APOCALYPTIC   Writings about what has been revealed concerning the end of the age, with its associated upheavals and changes, and the divine interventions.

APOCRYPHA   Several books often included in Bibles along with the 27 books of the Old Testament; also called Deuterocanonicals.

APSU   One of the two original gods in the Babylonian creation story; Apsu and Tiamat were gods of fresh and salt water.

AQUEDUCT   A pipe or channel for water supply, especially those built by the Romans going cross-country on arches.

ARABIA   The world's largest peninsula, between Africa, Mesopotamia, and Persia. The southwest boundary is the Red Sea, and beyond it lie Egypt and Sudan.

ARACHNE   A young woman in Greek mythology who challenges the goddess Athena to a contest of weaving. The goddess drives Arachne to suicide, and then transforms her into a spider that must weave forever.

ARAD   An archaeological site in Judah, about halfway between Masada and Beersheba. There are remains of an ancient city dating from 3000–2700 B.C., and additional remains of a fortified city and a temple dating from 1200 B.C.

ARAM   The Hebrew word *aram,* often translated Syria, refers to the ancient nation north and east of Israel, in the same area as the modern country of Syria. The capital was Damascus.

ARAMAIC   A Semitic language similar to Hebrew. Aramaic was the common international commercial speech of the ancient Near East throughout the Persian period (559–331 B.C.). It was still the primary language of Palestine in the time of Jesus.

ARARAT   A country made famous by Noah's ark (Gen. 8:4), which came to rest in its mountains. Ararat included parts of modern Iran, Iraq, and southern Russia.

ARCHANGEL   A higher order of heavenly being; the Bible names Gabriel and

Michael as archangels, and Raphael is named in the Book of Tobit, in the Apocrypha.

AREOPAGUS The traditional law court of Athens, which originally met on a small hill below the Acropolis. The name means "hill of Ares," Ares being Mars, the god of war.

ARK OF THE COVENANT A wood and gold chest specially built to hold the two tablets of the law given to Moses. It was kept in the inner part of the tabernacle and was also carried into battle.

ARPAD A province and capital city near Hamath in northern Syria. Arpad was conquered by the Assyrians in 740 B.C. and again in 720 B.C.

ARTAXERXES I Also called Artaxerxes Longimanus; ruler of Persia 465–424 B.C.

ARTEMIS *See* DIANA.

ARYANS Related groups of nomadic peoples that moved into northwestern India in 1500 B.C. They spread across Mesopotamia, including Media and Persia. Ultimately they migrated to Europe, and are also called Indo-Europeans. *See* MEDIA; PERSIA.

ASHDOD One of the five main cities of the Philistines, remembered for its part in capturing the ark of the covenant (1 Sam. 5:1–7).

ASHERAH Goddess of ancient Palestine; at Ugarit the wife of El and mother of Baal. The name *asherah* is also used for the sacred poles or trees that marked the sites where the goddess was worshiped.

ASHIMA A god worshiped by Syrians living in Samaria. The name may refer to Asherah, the Canaanite goddess. *See* ASHERAH.

ASHKELON One of the five main cities of the Philistines.

ASHTORETH A fertility goddess worshiped in ancient Palestine. She was called Ishtar in Babylon and Astarte in Ugarit. The plural form of Ashtoreth is Ashtaroth.

ASHUR-DAN III Ruler of Assyria who destroyed the city of Haran in 763 B.C.

ASHUR-UBALLIT Ruler of Assyria 1363–1328 B.C. During his reign Nineveh

was incorporated into the Assyrian Empire. *See* NINEVEH.

ASHURNASIRPAL II Ruler of Assyria 883–859 B.C.; father of Shalmaneser III. He conducted successful military campaigns in the west, exacting tribute from the Phoenicians. His capital was at Calah. *See* CALAH.

ASHURBANIPAL The last powerful king of Assyria, c. 668–627 B.C. He conquered Memphis and Thebes. The large library that he established at Nineveh was discovered in 1853.

ASIA MINOR Anatolia. *See* ANATOLIA.

ASSHUR The first capital of Assyria, located 56 miles south of ancient Nineveh. *Asshur* is also the name of the main god of Assyria, and as such appears in many Assyrian names.

ASSYRIA Ancient empire in Mesopotamia, north of Babylonia. The main cities were Asshur, Calah, and Nineveh. Notable kings were Shalmaneser I, Tiglath-Pileser I, and Ashurbanipal. The empire ended with the fall of Nineveh in 612 B.C.

ASSYRIAN KING LIST An ancient list of the kings of Assyria with the lengths of their reigns, covering about 1,000 years.

ASSYRIAN REVIVAL The period of Assyrian power under the reigns of Tiglath-Pileser III, Shalmaneser V, Sargon II, and Sennacherib, spanning 744 to 681 B.C.

ASTARTE *See* ASHTORETH.

ASTROLOGY The study of the sun, moon, stars, and planets in order to discern their supposed influence on human affairs.

ASTYAGES Ruler of the Median Empire 585–550 B.C.; grandfather of Cyrus the Great.

ATEN The ancient Egyptian name for the solar disk, which Amenhotep IV (1352–1336 B.C.) attempted to establish as the supreme god in Egypt. His reforms were reversed by his son Tutankhamun.

ATHENA The Greek goddess, said to have sprung fully armed from the head of Zeus. Athena commonly appears as a warrior but is also known for her skill in crafts, or intelligence. She is associated with the city of Athens, and the Parthenon was her main temple.

ATHTAR A Ugaritic god who tried unsuccessfully to usurp the throne of Baal.

ATON *See* ATEN.

ATRAHASIS Hero from a myth that is similar to the Gilgamesh Epic.

AVEN An important ancient city of Egypt in the northern Nile delta.

AZEKAH A fortified city 17 miles southwest of Jerusalem and 12 miles northeast of Lachish.

BAAL The main god of the Canaanites, a storm and fertility god; prominent in Ugaritic myths. "Baal" means "lord" or "owner." Baal was given particular names, associated with different locations or types of worship.

BABEL Hebrew for "Babylon." The tower of Babel was possibly a ziggurat.

BABYLON Literally "gate of god," an ancient city on the Euphrates River, about 50 miles south of modern Baghdad. It reached its greatest height under Nebuchadnezzar II, and was conquered by the forces of Alexander the Great in 330 B.C.

BABYLONIA Ancient empire in Mesopotamia, south of Assyria; the capital was Babylon. Notable kings were Hammurabi, Nebuchadnezzar I, and Nebuchadnezzar II. Babylon was often under the power of Assyria; in 559 B.C. it was conquered by Persia.

BABYLONIAN CHRONICLES Records kept by the ancient Babylonians that give a brief report of yearly events, preserved on clay tablets of different shapes and sizes.

BASALT A very fine-grained black rock, often used by the Egyptians for architecture and sculpture.

BDELLIUM A tree from east of Persia, whose gum becomes clear and waxy, so that it looks like pearl.

BEDOUIN Arab nomadic tribes that have a distinctive culture.

BEL MARDUK *See* MARDUK.

BELSHAZZAR Son of Nabonidus, the last king of Babylon. Belshazzar ruled as coregent alongside Nabonidus (ruled 556–539 B.C.) for 3 years or more.

BEN-HADAD The name of two and possibly three kings of Syria. The name is similar to a title, and it is not always clear which Ben-Hadad is meant. *See* HAZAEL.

BENJAMIN The youngest son of Jacob, and the tribe descending from him. The name means "son of the right hand" or "son of the south." Also, a tribe mentioned in the Mari tablets (c. 1800 B.C.).

BETH SHEMESH The name of three cities in ancient Israel: one in upper Galilee in the area of Naphtali (Josh. 19:38); one in lower Galilee in Issachar (19:22); and a third, the most important, in Judah (Josh. 15:10).

BITHYNIA Roman province, organized by Pompey in 63 B.C.; it occupied the northwest coast of Asia Minor (modern Turkey), north of Galatia and Asia.

BLESSING The communication of good intentions, normally from a superior to an inferior. Blessing was regarded as a purposeful and effective act, not merely a social form.

BONDSERVANT Another word for "slave."

BRONZE AGE The archaeological period during which bronze was the most important metal in use. Bronze is a hard, strong alloy of copper and tin. It was displaced by iron, especially for weapons, after about 1200 B.C.

BYBLOS One of the world's oldest cities, near Beirut, Lebanon. It was already inhabited in 5000 B.C., and in the 2nd millennium B.C. was a Phoenician seaport.

BYZANTINE The time and culture associated with Byzantium (Constantinople, modern Istanbul), from about A.D. 400 to 1450.

CALAH The capital of Assyria, also called Nimrud, on the east bank of the Tigris River south of Nineveh. The city was rebuilt by Shalmaneser I (1273–1244 B.C.), then abandoned until being restored by Ashurnasirpal II (883–859 B.C.).

CALAMUS Or "sweet flag," a plant with two rows of flat, swordlike leaves 3 to 6 feet long. It produces a perfume and a kind of medicine.

CANAAN The area east of the Mediterranean occupied by Israel after leaving Egypt under Moses.

CARCHEMISH A Hittite city on the northern Euphrates, 100 miles east of the Mediterranean Sea. At Carchemish in 605 B.C., Nebuchadnezzar II defeated the Egyptians and forced them out of Palestine.

CARTHAGE A Phoenician colony and seaport on the north African coast, founded about 800 B.C. The Romans fought several wars with Carthage and destroyed it in 146 B.C. In 29 B.C. it was rebuilt by Augustus.

CASSIA A tree with a fragrance resembling cinnamon. The buds are a substitute for cloves, and the small leaves have medicinal value.

CHALDEANS A people from southern Mesopotamia, adjacent to the Persian Gulf. The term Chaldean is sometimes a synonym for Babylonian.

CHEBAR A river or large canal near Babylon (Ezek. 1:1). *See* EUPHRATES; BABYLON.

CHEMOSH The national god of Moab. Evidently Chemosh was worshiped with human sacrifice (2 Kin. 3:26, 27).

CHERUBIM Superior spiritual beings close to God; the Hebrew word *cherubim* is the plural of *cherub*. Translated "living creatures" in Ezekiel and Revelation.

CHRONICLER The conventional name for the author of 1 and 2 Chronicles, understood to have a particular point of view.

CISTERN A large container for storing water, usually dug or built underground. In ancient Palestine there were both public and private cisterns.

CONCUBINE An additional wife or mistress whose legal status is lower than that of a normal wife.

CONSUL The highest office in the Roman republic; there were always two consuls, newly elected each year. The consulship continued in the Roman Empire, but no longer as the highest office.

CORINTH Prosperous port city in Greece, on the isthmus (3.7 miles wide) separating the mainland from the Peloponnesus.

COVENANT A solemn agreement or promise between two or more parties. A covenant was established with a docu-ment or ceremony that expressed and underlined the terms of agreement. For example, the sacrifice of animals could illustrate the consequences of breaking a covenant.

CUBIT A linear measure of about 18 inches, corresponding to the distance from elbow to fingertips.

CULT Religious service or acts of worship; a particular religion.

CUNEIFORM An ancient method of writing, using marks pressed into clay with a triangular pen or stylus. If the clay was baked or burned afterward, it became a permanent record.

CUSH *See* ETHIOPIA.

CUTH A Sumerian and Babylonian city located about 20 miles northeast of Babylon.

CYAXERES Ruler of Media 625–585 B.C.; he extended Median power throughout Assyria and as far west as Anatolia (Asia Minor).

CYNICISM A popular Greek philosophy, whose teachers and disciples advertised their independence by refusing to work and by flaunting social standards.

CYRUS CYLINDER A clay cylinder with a cuneiform inscription in which Cyrus the Great tells how he conquered and administered Babylon. The cylinder is 10 inches long and was discovered in about 1880.

CYRUS II Cyrus the Great, who reigned 559–530 B.C. He founded the Persian Achaemenid empire, which came to an end when it was conquered by Alexander the Great in 331 B.C.

DAGON Or "Dagan", a god of agriculture or fertility, the chief god of the Philistines, but also known in Ugarit, Mari, and Sumer.

DAMASCUS Ancient and modern capital of Syria. The name sometimes refers to Syria as a whole.

DARIUS I Ruler of the Medo-Persian Empire 522–486 B.C. "Darius" was the name or throne name of at least three Persian rulers, Darius I being the most prominent.

DAY STAR The morning star (Venus) referred to in Is. 14:5; the Hebrew is literally "shining one." This was translated "Lucifer" in Latin, meaning literally "light carrier."

DEACON An official worker in the early church, distinguished from teachers and preachers.

DEBIR Another name for Kirjath Sepher, an ancient city near Hebron. It was captured by Joshua's army, recaptured by the Canaanites, and finally taken again by Caleb (Josh. 15:13–17).

DELTA REGION The Nile delta is the semicircular, fertile region formed by branches of the Nile flowing into the Mediterranean Sea. It is about 165 miles east to west.

DENARIUS The main unit of Roman currency in New Testament times. It was a silver coin weighing about 4 grams, and was one day's wage for common workers.

DIANA A Roman goddess of the moon, women, and the wilderness; the same as the Greek goddess Artemis. Her main shrine was at Aricia, near Rome.

DIASPORA A term referring to Jews outside Israel, taken from a Greek word meaning "scattered."

DIODORUS A Greek historian from Sicily, Diodorus Siculus wrote over a period of 30 years a history of the world in 40 books, of which 15 have survived.

DIVINERS Persons considered to have supernatural powers of understanding or predicting events.

DOMITIAN Emperor of Rome A.D. 81 to 96. There is some evidence that Christians were persecuted during his reign.

DOR A stronghold on the northern Palestinian coast occupied by Israel in the time of David. It was for a time the capital of an Assyrian province.

DYNASTY A succession of rulers from a particular family. Thus, the "12th dynasty" of Egypt would refer to the twelfth of the series of families and their descendants who ruled Egypt.

EBLA Ancient city in northern Syria, 50 miles east of Ugarit and the Mediterranean and about 35 miles southwest of Aleppo; an important trading center. The city archives have yielded many thousands of clay tablets, mostly economic records. The language is Semitic.

ECSTATIC A person who experiences a trance, vision, or reverie.

EDOM The country southeast of the Dead Sea and south of Moab, often at war with Israel, sometimes called "Seir." The original inhabitants were the Horites.

EGYPTIAN EXECRATION TEXTS Curses written on broken pieces of pottery dating from about 1800 B.C. These texts name cities and kings of the time, including Jerusalem, and as such are important historical evidence.

EKRON The most northern of the five leading cities of Philistia. It was not captured by the Jews until after the death of Joshua.

EL The chief god in the Canaanite pantheon or council of gods. El is also a general word for deity, especially the supreme deity, and is used of God in the Bible.

ELAMITES A people from what is today Iran. Their origins appear to go back to Elam, son of Shem (Gen. 10:22), although some maintain they were Caucasian and not Semitic. After the Assyrians conquered Samaria, they sent Elamites there.

ELEPHANTINE A Jewish colony that was settled in southern Egypt 550 B.C. or before, and was supposed to defend the southern border of Egypt. Many papyrus documents from this colony have been discovered and published.

ELLIL The warrior god who is angered by the survival of the few humans in the Babylonian flood story.

EMMER A variety of wheat.

ENLIL Sumerian god of the city of Nippur, the most important religious center of Sumer. *See* SUMER.

ENMERKAR A Sumerian king and character in a 3rd-millennium epic.

ENUMA ELISH A Babylonian poem relating the story of the creation of the physical world. The poem was composed about the time of Nebuchadnezzar I (1133–1116 B.C.) to honor Marduk as king of the gods.

EPHRAIMITES   The Hebrew tribe descended from Ephraim, the second son born to Joseph in Egypt.

EPICUREANS   Followers of the philosophy of Epicurus (341–270 B.C.), who held that the highest goal was rational happiness, or tranquillity, in this life.

ERECH   *See* URUK.

ERESHKIGAL   A female deity in ancient Babylonian myth, the queen of the dead and the wife of Nergal, king of the dead.

ESARHADDON   Ruler of Assyria 680–669 B.C., maintaining its dominance over Babylon. He was also active in building.

ESHNUNNA   One of the cities in Mesopotamia overpowered by Amorites about 2000 B.C.

ESSENES   A Jewish religious group of New Testament times that pursued asceticism, separation, and purity. The Dead Sea Scrolls are a collection of literature hidden by Essenes before A.D. 70.

ETANA   Character in a Sumerian myth who tries but fails to enter heaven.

ETHIOPIA   Conventional translation of the Hebrew word *Cush,* referring to the remote region of southern Egypt and beyond; it is not the same as modern Ethiopia.

EUNUCH   A male person who has been neutered. Ancient kings and the Roman emperors often employed eunuchs at court.

EUPHRATES   An important river that flows from Armenia to the southwest, then turns southeast, and finally empties into the Persian Gulf. The Euphrates passes close to the Tigris River. Mesopotamia is the area bounded by these two rivers.

EUSEBIUS   Bishop of Caesarea and the first important church historian; died A.D. 339.

EVIL-MERODACH   Ruler of Babylon 562–560 B.C., the third king of the Babylonian Chaldean dynasty and the son of Nebuchadnezzar II. *See* MARDUK.

EXILES   Usual designation of the Jewish captives taken to Babylon following the Babylonian conquest of Judah. Such de-

portations occurred in 597 and 586 B.C. In 538 B.C. Cyrus the Great permitted the exiles to return to Jerusalem.

EXODUS   The name of the second book of the Old Testament, from the Greek for "going out." Also, the miraculous departure of Israel from Egypt.

FRANKINCENSE   The resin of trees from north India and Arabia producing a hard, fragrant yellow gum.

GAD   Like Meni, a god of fortune or luck worshiped in Judah after the Babylonian exile. *See* MENI.

GALATIA   A region in middle Anatolia (modern Turkey). The name refers specifically to the Roman province Galatia, or else to an undefined area north of it, where Galatian people lived.

GALBANUM   A gum extracted from an herb that grows in Palestine. The hardened gum gives a strong but pleasant scent when burned.

GALLIO   Brother of the Roman writer Seneca. Gallio was proconsul in Greece and heard Paul's case, A.D. 51 (Acts 18:12).

GAMES   The ancient Greeks held organized athletic contests at four main locations; these were the Isthmian, Nemean, Olympian, and Pythian games. There was also a contest at Athens (the Panathenaia), as well as other lesser ones.

GATEKEEPERS   Officials at the Jerusalem temple who controlled offerings and pay for the priests, and were a security force to guarantee a smooth transition of power when a ruler died.

GATH   One of the five main cities of the Philistines; its inhabitants were called "Gittites."

GAZA   The most important of the five main cities of the Philistines, on the Mediterranean coast 50 miles from Jerusalem. Gaza was the capital of Canaan for several centuries (1550–1150 B.C.).

GEDALIAH   Appointed governor of Judah by Nebuchadnezzar II and assassinated after 2 months in office.

GENTILE   Any person who is not a Jew.

GESHEM THE ARAB   One of the three opponents of Nehemiah's program to rebuild the walls of Jerusalem.

GIHON SPRING   The main source of water for Jerusalem in Old Testament times. In 701 B.C. Hezekiah built the Siloam tunnel to bring its waters into the city.

GILEADITES   Israelites who lived on the east side of the Jordan River. There was also an Israelite tribe called Gilead.

GILGAL   The first camp established by Joshua after crossing the Jordan. Gilgal became a town close to the northern border of Judah.

GILGAMESH EPIC   A Sumerian poem 3,000 lines long describing the legendary deeds of Gilgamesh, king of Uruk. This popular epic dates from as early as 2000 B.C. and contains a flood story.

GUDEA   Ruler of the Sumerians about 2000 B.C. He was guided by a dream to build a temple to the god Ningirsu at Lagash, north of Ur.

GULF OF AQABA   The northeastern extension of the Red Sea, between the Sinai Peninsula and Arabia. Ezion Geber is at the north end of the gulf.

HABIRU   Or "Hapiru"; bandits, migrants, or refugees noticed all over the Middle East from about 2000 to 1000 B.C. It has been suggested that the Hebrews were Habiru.

HADAD   Another name for Baal.

HALLEL   A Hebrew word meaning "praise," referring to Psalms 113—118.

HAMATH   A Syrian city on the Orontes River about 125 miles north of Damascus. Hamath became the capital of a small Hittite kingdom, but was finally subjugated by Assyria.

HAMMURABI   Ammorite king of Babylon (1792–1750 B.C.), who made Babylon a great city. His law code inscribed on a column of hard stone (diorite) was discovered in 1901 and is now in the Louvre.

HARAN   A city in northwestern Mesopotamia, 60 miles east of Carchemish; located on important trade routes; home of Laban (Gen. 27:43).

HASMONEAN   A name given to the Jewish dynasty founded by Judas Maccabeus in 167 B.C. See JUDAS MACCABEUS.

HAZAEL   Ruled Aram (also called Syria) about 842–800 B.C. Hazael made northern Israel a vassal of Aram. Southern Israel (Judah) also paid tribute to Aram during Hazael's reign.

HAZOR   An ancient city about 9 miles north of the Sea of Galilee. Hazor was destroyed by the Hebrews in the 13th century B.C. (Josh. 11:10, 11) and was rebuilt during Solomon's reign.

HELLENISTIC   Influenced by the international Greek culture that developed outside Greece itself following the conquests of Alexander the Great.

HELLENISTS   In the New Testament, those Jews who spoke Greek rather than Aramaic or Hebrew.

HENOTHEISM   Worshiping one god as supreme, but without denying the existence of others.

HEROD AGRIPPA I   That is, Iulius Agrippa I, grandson of Herod the Great. In A.D. 37 he succeeded as tetrarch to the areas ruled by Philip, and in 39 to those of Herod Antipas. He died suddenly in Caesarea in 44 (Acts 12).

HEROD AGRIPPA II   That is, Iulius Agrippa II, son of Iulius Agrippa I. He ruled part of Lebanon, and then Galilee and Judea, A.D. 50–66. He helped the Romans during the revolt of A.D. 66–70 and received additional territory. His sister was Bernice (Acts 25:13).

HEROD ANTIPAS   Son of Herod the Great; became tetrarch of Galilee in 4 B.C. (see Luke 3:1; 9:7–9; 23:6–12). Herod Antipas was deposed and exiled by the emperor Gaius Caligula in A.D. 39.

HEROD THE GREAT   Ruler of Judea, 37 to 4 B.C.; famous for his building programs and for his outrage at Jesus' birth (Matt. 2).

HERODOTUS   The first Greek historian (484–425 B.C.), often called "the father of history." He traveled throughout the Near East and wrote a history of the world.

HIGH PLACES   Places where the gods of early Palestine were worshiped, usually having altars and sacred poles.

HILLEL   The founder of one of two schools (or "houses") of Pharisaic tradition; active at the end of the 1st century B.C. The tradition of Hillel was less strict than that of Shammai.

HIRAM   King of Tyre during the reigns of David and Solomon. Hiram sent materials and artisans to help build David's house and Solomon's temple and palace.

HITTITES   An Indo-European people who controlled Anatolia (today eastern Turkey) by 1800 B.C. Their capital was at Hattusa (Boghazköy). Later their power extended south into Syria.

HOPHRA   Ruler of Egypt 589–570 B.C. He resisted Babylonian power in Palestine. In 570 B.C. his general Amasis overthrew him, and he died in battle in 567 B.C.

HORITES   The original inhabitants of Edom.

HORUS   Egyptian god of the sky, light, and goodness. Horus was the son of Isis, the goddess of nature, and of Osiris, the god of the underworld.

HOUSEHOLD GODS   Called "teraphim," after the Hebrew word; small idols belonging to a particular household.

HURRIANS   A people from northeastern Mesopotamia who lived in many parts of the Near East, becoming powerful and influential in the late 2nd millennium B.C. Thousands of cuneiform texts illustrating Hurrian family laws were found at Nuzi, a city in what is now northern Iraq. *See* NUZI.

HYKSOS   A people of mixed Semitic and Asiatic origin who ruled Egypt for more than a century (1648–1540 B.C.).

INANNA   The Sumerian goddess of love, whose yearly reunion with the god Dumuzi was thought to bring renewed fertility to the earth.

INDUS RIVER   A river 1,700 miles long, originating in western Tibet from a meeting of glacial streams. It flows northwest and then turns south through Pakistan, and at last empties into the Arabian Sea.

IRENAEUS   Bishop of Lyons (France); Christian writer and theologian; lived about A.D. 130–202.

ISHTAR   The Mesopotamian goddess of love and war, worshiped throughout the Old Testament period.

ISIN   A city between the Tigris and the Euphrates, 70 miles southeast of Babylon. It was a Sumerian power for over 225 years, until defeated by Hammurabi in about 1781 B.C.

ISIS   The most popular Egyptian goddess, worshiped also at Rome. Isis was the goddess of life, the wife of Osiris, and the mother of Horus.

IVAH   A city in Syria.

JABBOK RIVER   A river 60 miles long that empties into the Jordan from the east. The Ammonites lived along this river.

JEBUSITES   The original inhabitants of Jerusalem.

JERICHO   An ancient city 5 miles west of the Jordan and 7 miles north of the Dead Sea; 840 feet below sea level. Jericho is called "the city of palm trees" in Deut. 34:3.

JEROBOAM   First king of northern Israel c. 930–909 B.C., formed by the division of Israel into ten northern tribes (Israel) and two southern (Judah). Jeroboam promoted idolatry and corrupted the priesthood. *See* REHOBOAM.

JEROBOAM II   King of northern Israel, 793–753 B.C.

JEROME   Christian monk, scholar, and writer who died about A.D. 420. Jerome knew Hebrew as well as Greek. His standard translation of the Bible into Latin is called the Vulgate.

JERUSALEM   The biblical city, 33 miles east of the Mediterranean and 2,500 feet above sea level. Jerusalem is first mentioned by name in Egyptian texts of the 19th century B.C.

JESUS CHRIST   These words come from the Greek rendering of two Hebrew words, the first being a personal name (Joshua) meaning "God saves," and the second a word meaning "anointed one" or "Messiah."

JEZREEL VALLEY   The east-west valley separating Samaria and Galilee, providing a way from the Mediterranean coast to the Jordan River. During biblical times many battles were fought in this valley.

JOSEPHUS Jewish historian who lived c. A.D. 37–100. Captured during the Jewish revolt against Rome, Josephus gained the favor of the Roman general Vespasian and was spared. He wrote an official history of the war, including the fall of Jerusalem, which he witnessed.

JUDAHITES People of Judah.

JUDAS MACCABEUS Leader of the Jewish revolt against Antiochus IV Epiphanes, beginning in 169 B.C. In 164 B.C. Judas rededicated the Jerusalem temple. He founded the Hasmonean dynasty, which remained in power until 63 B.C.

JUSTIN MARTYR A Christian writer who was martyred at Rome about A.D. 165. His writings are a defense of Christianity against paganism.

JUVENAL Roman writer of Latin satire; died about A.D. 130.

KARNAK A city on the Nile near ancient Thebes, 300 miles south of Memphis. Karnak is famous for its remains of temples, which occupied a square mile, built by Thutmose III, Ramesses II, and others.

KENITES The name "Kenite" is derived from a Hebrew word denoting smiths or metalworkers. The Kenites were a people found in southern Palestine from earliest times.

KETHIB Literally meaning "written," used to indicate a designated word or phrase as it stands in the traditional Hebrew Bible. *See* QERE.

KINGU A subsidiary god in Babylonian myth.

KIR HARASETH A Moabite city, also called "Kir of Moab," located just east of the Dead Sea.

LACHISH An ancient city in Judah, 30 miles southwest of Jerusalem and west of Hebron. Lachish was destroyed by Joshua in the 13th century B.C., by Sennacherib in 701 B.C. (2 Kin. 18:13–15), and by the Babylonians in 587 B.C. Lachish is a very important archaeological site, especially for pottery and ostraca (pieces of pottery used for writing on).

LACHISH LETTERS Letters found at Lachish, near Jerusalem, dating from the time of Nebuchadnezzar's conquest of Jerusalem, 586 B.C. The letters are written on fragments of pottery (ostraca) and document the coming fall of Lachish.

LAMENT FOR UR A Sumerian poem written in response to the fall of Ur in 2004 B.C.

LAURIUM A location southeast of Athens where the ancient Greeks had mines for silver.

LEGEND OF AQHAT A Ugaritic legend from the 2nd millennium B.C. A certain Daniel is the main character. Daniel's son Aqhat is killed by the goddess Anath; Aqhat's sister determines to take revenge, and then the story breaks off.

LEVIRATE MARRIAGE A law in Israel (Deut. 25:5) providing that when a man died leaving a wife but not a son, the man's brother or nearest male relative must marry the widow and bear a son in the dead relative's name. This would keep the man's inheritance within his family. *Levir* is the Latin word for "brother-in-law."

LEVITES The descendants of Levi, the third son of the patriarch Jacob. The Levites were appointed to be priests and to care for the temple.

LIBYA In ancient times, the northern part of Africa west of Egypt.

LILITH A Mesopotamian demon believed to attack babies and mothers in childbirth. The name is derived from a Sumerian word meaning "wind."

LOGOS The Greek word usually translated "word" or "idea," used philosophically with related meanings.

LOTHAN A mythical sea monster identified in Ugaritic texts with the sea god Yam, who is defeated in battle by Baal.

LYCUS RIVER A river in Anatolia (Asia Minor) that joins the Maeander river near Colosse.

LYDIA A district in western Anatolia Asia Minor whose main city was Sardis.

MACCABEES The early rulers of the Hasmonean dynasty that began in 167 B.C. with Judas Maccabeus. *See* JUDAS MACCABEUS.

MAGIC The attempt to govern events and human experience through supernatural means, commonly associated with the occult.

MAGUS A magician or astrologer (from a Greek word).

MARDUK The chief god of Babylon, who appears as the chief deity in the Babylonian epic, the Enuma Elish. Also spelled Merodach.

MARI An ancient city on the Euphrates River, halfway between Babylon and the Mediterranean Sea; occupied as early as 3000 B.C. Thousands of clay tablets were discovered at Mari, mostly administrative archives, dating from the decades just before the conquest of Mari by Hammurabi in about 1760 B.C.

MASORETIC TEXT The text of the Bible as preserved by Jewish scholars from ancient times to the middle ages.

MEDIA An Indo-European nation occupying what is now northwestern Iran. The Medes became part of the Persian Empire through the efforts of Cyrus the Great, who defeated them in battle in 550 B.C.

MEGIDDO An ancient city near Mt. Carmel. Megiddo is in the Jezreel Valley, that connects the coast with the interior; it is also on the main road from Egypt to Damascus. As a result, Megiddo has been the site of important battles in both ancient and modern times.

MENI Like Gad, a god of fortune or luck worshiped in Judah after the Babylonian exile. Possibly related to the goddess Mani worshiped by the Arabs before the coming of Islam.

MERENPTAH (or Merneptah) Ruler of Egypt after the death of Ramesses II. His armies fought in Palestine, and he mentioned Israel on a famous stone monument (a stele) commemorating his victories.

MERODACH Alternate spelling of Marduk. *See* MARDUK.

MERODACH-BALADAN II Ruler of Babylonia 721–710 B.C. and 703–702 B.C.

An outstanding king who resisted the Assyrians. He was defeated in 710, and again in 702 after a brief return to power.

MESOPOTAMIA The region between and next to the Tigris and Euphrates rivers, two rivers that flow from Armenia southeast to the Persian Gulf. Assyria, Babylonia, and Sumer were in Mesopotamia.

MIDDLE ASSYRIAN EMPIRE The period of Assyrian history beginning with the reign of Shalmaneser I (1273–1244 B.C.). He enlarged Assyria's borders and successfully resisted invasions by the Babylonians and other powers in the region. *See* SHALMANESER I.

MILLSTONES Large stones used in pairs to grind grain into flour. An upper stone is rubbed back and forth or rotated against a lower stone, milling the grain in between.

MITANNI A Hurrian state in northern Mesopotamia, including more than a single city. Mitanni was the leading power in the region from about 1500 to 1350 B.C., fostering wide travel, trade, and diplomacy. *See* HITTITES.

MIZPAH A place not certainly identified but probably about 10 miles north of Jerusalem.

MOAB Moab was located on the plateau southeast of the Dead Sea. The Moabites descended from Lot and were traditional enemies of Israel.

MOABITE STONE An inscribed basalt slab 28 by 44 inches in size, now in the Louvre, Paris. It was made about 850 B.C. to record a Moabite victory over Israel.

MOLECH (or Milcom) A god probably first worshiped by the Phoenicians. The name as given in the Old Testament combines the Hebrew words *melech* and *bosheth,* meaning "king" and "shame." Molech was worshiped by sacrificing children in fire. *See* PHOENICIA.

MONOLATRY Worshiping one god only.

MOT The god of death in Ugaritic mythology, a monster who swallows the living. Mot is in conflict with Baal and is defeated by him.

MYRRH A small plant found in Palestine whose gum gives off a pleasant perfume.

NABATEA   An Arab kingdom whose capital was at Petra, south of the Dead Sea, and whose influence extended far into the surrounding territory. The Nabateans flourished during the period between the Old and New Testaments. *See* EDOM; NEGEV.

NABONIDUS   Last king of Babylonia (556–539 B.C.). During part of his reign he was in Tema, Arabia, while his son Belshazzar ruled for him in Babylon.

NABOPOLASSAR   Ruler of Babylonia and Assyria 626–605 B.C.; father of Nebuchadnezzar II.

NAG HAMMADI   A location in Egypt where a collection of Gnostic books written on papyrus was discovered in 1947.

NANNA   The Sumerian moon god in the 2nd millennium B.C. *See* LAMENT FOR UR.

NARD   Also called spikenard; an East Indian plant producing a pleasant fragrance.

NEBUCHADNEZZAR I   Ruler of Babylonia 1133–1116 B.C. He conquered the Elamites and returned a statue of Marduk to Babylonia, proclaiming Marduk to be the creator and ruler of all things. *See* ELAMITES; ENUMA ELISH.

NEBUCHADNEZZAR II   Ruler of Babylonia 605–562 B.C.; built the hanging gardens of Babylon. He defeated Pharaoh Necho at Carchemish in 605 B.C., and destroyed Jerusalem in 589 B.C.

NECHO II   Ruler of Egypt 610–595 B.C. He occupied parts of Palestine but was pushed back by Nebuchadnezzar II after the battle of Carchemish, 605 B.C.

NECROMANCY   The practice of magic through supposed contact with the dead.

NEGEV   The desert region of southern Judah. The Hebrew word is sometimes translated simply "the South."

NEHUSHTAN   The name given to the bronze serpent set up by Moses in the desert (2 Kin. 18:4).

NEO-ASSYRIAN EMPIRE   The period of Assyrian rule dating from Ashur-dan II (934–912 B.C.) to the fall of Nineveh in 612 B.C. The period includes Shalmaneser III, who set up the Black Obelisk that mentions King Jehu of Israel submitting to Assyria.

NERGAL SHAREZER   A Babylonian official present at the siege of Jerusalem in 588–586 B.C.

NERO   Born A.D. 37; became emperor of Rome in A.D. 54. After he murdered his own mother in 59, Nero became uncontrolled and cruel, if not insane. He was forced to commit suicide in 68.

NETHINIM   A class of temple servants that returned from the Babylonian exile. The Nethinim were one of five groups associated with the temple, along with priests, Levites, gatekeepers, and singers.

NIMRUD   *See* CALAH.

NINEVEH   One of the world's oldest cities, on the Tigris River 300 miles northwest of Babylon and 600 miles northwest of the Persian Gulf. Nineveh became the capital of the Assyrian Empire under Sennacherib (704–681 B.C.); it fell to the Babylonians in 612 B.C.

NINHURSAG   A goddess appearing in the Babylonian flood story.

NINURTA   A deity of the Assyrian pantheon.

NO   The Hebrew name for the city of Thebes in Egypt. *See* THEBES.

NUZI   A city of the 2nd millennium B.C., 9 miles from modern Kirkut in Iraq. Many texts concerning family law and dating from approximately 1400 B.C. have been recovered at Nuzi.

OBELISK   A kind of monument consisting of a freestanding tapered stone column with flat sides.

OMRI   Ruled northern Israel sometime between 885 and 874 B.C. He was made king by the army but did not have the support of the nation. Samaria was his capital. *See* JEROBOAM.

OSIRIS   A principal god of ancient Egypt, the brother and husband of Isis, and the father of Horus.

OSTRACA   A Greek word referring to broken pieces of pottery, used in ancient times as something to write on. Many historically valuable ostraca have been unearthed in Egypt and southern Judah.

PADAN ARAM Abraham's home in northern Mesopotamia; also known as Aram-naharaim.

PALESTINE The general area occupied by Israel in the Bible, on the east coast of the Mediterranean Sea. The name is derived from the Hebrew word for "Philistia."

PALMYRA A city in Syria 120 miles northeast of Damascus, once wealthy and powerful, but now a ruin in an oasis.

PANTHEON An array of gods, usually with different powers, worshiped by a group or race of people. The word comes from Greek and means "of all gods."

PAPYRUS A tall reed native to the Nile, and also the paper that the ancient Egyptians manufactured from it. Papyrus was sold in rolls made by gluing together single sheets.

PARABLE A brief moral story or comparison like those used by Jesus.

PASSOVER The festival celebrating Israel's escape from Egypt under Moses, which was also the occasion of the original Passover.

PATRONAGE A social system in which the rich and powerful support dependents called clients, who give them their allegiance. It was typical of the Roman world.

PEKAH Ruled northern Israel 740–732 B.C. Pekah and the king of Syria, Rezin, made war against the southern kingdom for refusing to help them in a fight against Assyria. The Assyrians killed Rezin, and Pekah was assassinated.

PERSEPOLIS Persia's ancient capital. The Persian monarch decorated the ceremonial hall with sculptures and pictures depicting his claim to world sovereignty.

PERSIA A plateau east of Mesopotamia, surrounded by mountain ranges. The Persian Empire was expanded by Cyrus the Great beginning in 550 B.C. At one time it included Anatolia, Palestine, Mesopotamia, and east to the Indus River, an extent of 2,700 miles.

PHARAOH The title used for the rulers of ancient Egypt.

PHARISEES A section or party of the Jews prominent during New Testament times, known for their dedication to religion, especially matters concerning ritual purity.

PHILISTINES The people living on the Mediterranean coast west of Israel. There were five main cities in the Philistine federation: Ashdod, Ashkelon, Ekron, Gaza, and Gath.

PHILO Jewish philosopher and scholar from Alexandria (20 B.C.–A.D. 50). Philo wrote biblical commentaries and philosophy, and is remembered for his allegorical exegesis of the Old Testament.

PHOENICIA The Mediterranean country north of Israel, including the ports of Tyre, Sidon, and Berytus (modern Beirut). The Phoenicians engaged in shipping all over the Mediterranean; they had an important colony at Carthage, north Africa.

PISIDIAN ANTIOCH *See* ANTIOCH.

PLINY Roman writer and provincial governor; died about A.D. 112. He described the eruption of Vesuvius as an eyewitness, and his correspondence mentions the persecution of Christians.

POLEMIC A kind of writing or speech whose purpose is to argue against opposing views.

POSTEXILIC Events after the exile of the Jews to Babylon, that is, after 538 B.C., when refugees began to return from Babylon to Jerusalem.

POTSHERD A broken piece of pottery. *See* OSTRACA.

PREEXILIC Events before the exile of the Jews to Babylon, that is, before the fall of Jerusalem in 586 B.C.

PREEXISTENCE The existence of Jesus Christ before He was incarnated and born to Mary.

PRISM An inscribed tablet or stone in the shape of a cylinder with flat sides.

PROCONSUL A kind of Roman provincial governor.

PROCURATOR A civil servant of the Roman emperor. There were many different levels of procurator.

PROSELYTE A convert.

PSAMMETICHUS I Ruler of Egypt 664–610 B.C., an ally of Assyria; son of

Necho I and father of Necho II. Psammetichus I captured Memphis and Thebes, reuniting Egypt. His capital was at Sais, and he began what is called the Saite dynasty.

PSEUDONYMOUS   Published or circulated under another name than that of the actual author.

PTOLEMAIC DYNASTY   Ptolemy I (ruled 305–282 B.C.) was one of four generals who inherited Alexander the Great's empire when he died. Ptolemy received Egypt, and his family formed the Ptolemaic dynasty, which controlled Egypt until defeated by the Seleucids in 200 B.C. *See* SELEUCID.

PUL   Another name for Assyria's King Tiglath-Pileser III.

QERE   Meaning "to be read," a marginal notation in the Hebrew Bible indicating a traditional alternative reading for a word or phrase in the text. *See* KETHIB.

QUEEN HATSHEPSUT   Ruler of Egypt 1479–1457 B.C., although her nephew Thutmose III (1479–1425) was nominally pharaoh during her rule.

QUEEN OF HEAVEN   A fertility goddess mentioned in Jeremiah (Jer. 7:18; 44:17) and possibly to be identified with Astarte.

QUMRAN   A community near the Dead Sea where the Dead Sea Scrolls were found. *See* ESSENES.

RABBI   The conventional Hebrew title for a teacher.

RABSHAKEH   A high-ranking officer in the ancient Assyrian army, similar to a modern chief of staff.

RAMESSES II   Ruler of Egypt 1279–1213 B.C. He was active in war and as a builder. He concluded a peace treaty with the Hittites.

RAMESSES III   Ruler of Egypt 1184–1153 B.C., in the 20th Dynasty. He was the last of Egypt's great kings and a brilliant soldier, who repelled several powerful invaders. He was also a great builder.

RAS SHAMRA   The modern location of ancient Ugarit, in Syria. *See* UGARIT.

RE   (or Ra) The sun god of ancient Egypt, having a human body and the head of a hawk.

RECHABITES   A religious community founded by Jonadab (often spelled Jehonadab). Apparently the object of this group was to maintain the purity of the Hebrew religion.

RED SEA   The conventional translation of a Hebrew name, more correctly translated "Reed Sea" or "Marsh Sea." This sea formed the boundary between Egypt and the desert to the east, while the Red Sea itself extends far to the south.

REHOBOAM   Ruler of Judah c. 930–913 B.C., after his father Solomon. Rehoboam alienated the northern tribes of Israel, splitting the kingdom into north and south. Judah and Benjamin became the southern kingdom, and the other ten tribes were the northern kingdom, with Jeroboam as their king.

RELIGION   Beliefs about the divine, and practices depending on these beliefs.

REZIN   Ruler of Damascus c. 740 B.C., and died resisting the Assyrian invasion under Tiglath-Pileser III, 732 B.C.

RITUAL   Religious actions or ceremonies performed in a way prescribed by tradition or law.

ROME   The city on the Tiber River in Italy; traditionally founded by Romulus and Remus, 753 B.C.; capital of the Roman Empire, which was founded 27 B.C. by Augustus Caesar.

SABA   The country of the Sabeans in southwestern Arabia; also called Sheba. The Sabeans had contact with Africa across the Red Sea and with Tema in northern Arabia.

SACRIFICE   A religious offering, often an animal. Animal sacrifice was a normal part of ancient religion, practiced everywhere, and subject to many different interpretations.

SADDUCEES   An aristocratic, conservative party of the Jews prominent during New Testament times. As a distinct party they did not survive the destruction of Jerusalem in A.D. 70.

SAFFRON   A plant grown from a bulb, with a pleasant aroma and an extract used as a food coloring.

SAMARIA   The capital city of the northern kingdom of Israel during the period of divided monarchy after Solomon (1 Kin. 12). Samaria can also refer to the northern kingdom as a whole. *See* JEROBOAM; REHOBOAM.

SAMARITAN   A person from Samaria, the country north of Judea.

SAMARITAN PENTATEUCH   The text of the first five books of the Hebrew Bible as preserved from ancient times by the Samaritans.

SANBALLAT   One of the opponents of Nehemiah's rebuilding of the walls of Jerusalem in the 5th century B.C. Documents from the Jewish colony at Elephantine in southern Egypt record that Sanballat was governor of Samaria.

SARGON OF ACCAD   King of Sumer, c. 2350 B.C. Because of Sargon's conquests, Sumer is generally regarded as the first world empire.

SARGON II   King of Assyria 721–705 B.C.; he deported people from Samaria to Assyria. He also defeated an Egyptian army at the border of Egypt.

SCYTHIA   The region northeast of the Roman Empire, including what is today Poland, Hungary, and the Ukraine.

SCYTHIANS   Nomads who emigrated to the Near East from the Caucasus in the 8th century B.C. For some reason they became a stock example of uncivilized barbarians.

SEA PEOPLES   Groups of people who invaded the Middle East, destroying many cities, in the 12th century B.C.

SEIR   Another name for Edom. *See* EDOM.

SELEUCID   Refers to the kingdom north of Palestine, founded and called Syria in 312 B.C. by Seleucus, one of Alexander the Great's surviving generals.

SEMINOMADS   More or less settled tribes, not living in villages or towns.

SEMIPRECIOUS STONES   Ornamental stones of many kinds used in jewelry, crafts, and architecture, but not including the "precious" stones (diamond, emerald, ruby, sapphire), which are much more rare.

SEMITIC   The Semitic languages are a family of related languages that includes Arabic, Aramaic, Hebrew, and Ugaritic. The Semitic peoples are the original speakers of these languages, nominally descended from Shem.

SENNACHERIB   Ruler of Assyria 704–681 B.C.; son of Sargon II. His capital was Nineveh. He threatened Jerusalem in 691 B.C. but was suddenly turned back; he destroyed Babylon in 689 B.C. He was assassinated by his sons.

SEPHARVAIM   A place whose inhabitants the Assyrians brought to Samaria after 722 B.C.; the exact location is unknown.

SEPTUAGINT   The Greek version of the Old Testament, translated in Alexandria between 250 and 150 B.C. The name "Septuagint" and the abbreviation LXX come from the tradition that there were seventy translators.

SERAPHIM   Superior guardian angels in the presence of God.

SESOSTRIS I   Ruler of Egypt 1943–1898 B.C., including 10 years as coruler with his father Amenemhet I.

SHAHAR   Ugaritic deity, the god of dawn.

SHALIM   Ugaritic deity, the god of dusk or evening.

SHALMAN   An abbreviation of the name Shalmaneser used by several Assyrian kings.

SHALMANESER I   Ruler of Assyria 1273–1244 B.C. He was the greatest warrior of the Middle Assyrian period. He conquered the Hittites, Hurrians, and Arameans, and defeated the Egyptians at Carchemish.

SHALMANESER III   Ruler of Assyria 858–824 B.C. He tried repeatedly to conquer the regions west of Assyria, including Damascus.

SHALMANESER V   Ruler of Assyria 726–722 B.C. He continued the western conquests and the collection of tribute begun by Shalmaneser I through IV.

SHAMASH   The Mesopotamian sun god, also associated with justice. In the ancient Middle East worship of the sun was widespread.

SHAMMAI   The founder of a school of thought within the Pharisees, active at the end of the 1st century B.C. The other school is that of Hillel. *See* HILLEL.

SHAMSHI-ADAD I   Ruler of the city-state of Asshur 1813–1781 B.C. He extended Assyrian power as far as the Mediterranean Sea, making Assyria in effect an empire. After he died, Assyria was overrun by Hammurabi of Babylon.

SHAPSHU   A Ugaritic sun goddess.

SHECHEM   An ancient fortified city 30 miles north of Jerusalem in the hill country of Palestine. Shechem was prosperous during the 2nd millennium B.C.

SHEMESH   The sun god prominent in ancient Near-Eastern pantheons, whether as feminine or masculine (goddess or god).

SHEOL   The Hebrew word for the realm of the dead, thought of as dark and gloomy. The word is used in poetic descriptions.

SHILOH   A town in central Palestine, where Joshua put the tabernacle along with the ark of the covenant after his conquest of Canaan. Shiloh was then the center of worship until the ark was brought to Jerusalem by King David.

SHINAR   The biblical name for the region of southern Mesopotamia, also called Babylon.

SHISHAK   Ruler of Egypt c. 945–924 B.C., and founder of Egypt's 22nd Dynasty. In the 5th year of Rehoboam, Shishak raided Judah (1 Kin. 14:25–28).

SHULAMITE   Or "Shunammite," a person from Shunem, a town in Issachar, north of the Jezreel Valley.

SHUSHAN   Also spelled "Susa," a town and a fortified citadel in southwestern Iran. The city was at the height of its power under the Persians in the 6th century B.C.

SIDON   The oldest Phoenician seaport, about 22 miles south of modern Beirut. Sidon is closely associated with the nearby city of Tyre.

SIEGE WALL   A wall built by an army to prevent movement of the enemy. Another kind of siege wall was a ramp leading from ground level to the top of a city wall to give the attackers a way up.

SIHOR   (or Shihor) The Nile River or one of its eastern branches.

SIN   A moon god worshiped in Syria, Palestine, and Mesopotamia from the 3rd millennium B.C. through at least the Hellenistic period (332–37 B.C.).

SINAI PENINSULA   The triangle-shaped desert between Israel and Egypt. The north boundary is the Mediterranean Sea, and the south is the two northern extensions of the Red Sea, one ending at Suez and one at Ezion Geber. *See* GULF OF AQABA.

SKEPTICS   Followers of the philosophy that nothing can be known for certain.

SO   Identified as the king of Egypt in 2 Kin. 17:4; possibly Osorkon IV (730–715 B.C.); or an Egyptian general; or a geographical name.

SODOM   One of the "cities of the plain" (Gen. 13:12). Any possible remains of the city are now thought to be submerged in the Dead Sea.

STELE   A column or pillar of stone with inscriptions.

STOICS   Followers of the philosophical school founded by Zeno, who came to Athens 313 B.C. Stoicism emphasized ethics, responsibility, and rational behavior.

STRABO   Greek historian, probably a Roman citizen; lived about 64 B.C. to A.D. 21 and wrote about geography and politics.

SUCCOTH-BENOTH   A deity worshiped by Babylonians resettled in Samaria after the Assyrian conquest of Samaria in 722 B.C. This god was a consort of Marduk. *See* MARDUK.

SUMER   Ancient nation in southern Mesopotamia, dating from about 3000 to 2000 B.C.; sometimes referred to as Shinar. A considerable amount of Sumerian literature survives; the language continued to be used for long after the political end of Sumer.

SUZERAIN   A person or state exercising rule over other less powerful persons or states, called vassals.

SYNAGOGUE   A Greek term meaning "congregation," normally referring to the regular meetings and meeting places of the Jews.

SYRIA   An important Roman province, whose boundaries fluctuated but typically included what is today Israel, Jordan,

Lebanon, and Syria. In the Old Testament Syria is a translation of the Hebrew word *aram*. *See* ARAM.

SYRIAC   Syriac is a Semitic language and a branch of Aramaic. The Syriac versions are early translations of the Bible, both Old and New Testaments, made between about the 2nd and 6th centuries A.D.

SYRO-PHOENICIAN   From the area including Syria and Phoenicia, or the eastern Mediterranean coast and interior.

TABERNACLE   A tent or shelter. In the Bible the term refers to the movable structure housing the ark, and to the temporary shelters used for the Feast of Tabernacles.

TALMUD   The written record of Jewish traditions concerning the Bible, law, ethics, and many other subjects, essentially completed by A.D. 500.

TAMARISK   A small tree common in the Middle East.

TAMMUZ   A deity in Sumerian myth, the husband and brother of Ishtar. His yearly return from the underworld was said to restore the earth's fertility.

TARGUM   Ancient Aramaic translations of the Hebrew Bible.

TARTAN   Commander or commander in chief in the Assyrian army (2 Kin. 18:17; Is. 20:1).

TELL   A mound (*tell* in Arabic) covering the remains of an ancient city. Successive populations built their buildings on the ruins of what went before them, resulting in a hill with the earliest buildings at the lowest levels. Such tells are often the sites of modern towns.

TEMA   An oasis in northern Arabia; the name derives from the Hebrew word meaning "south country."

TETRARCH   A name used by the Romans for a local king ruling with their help.

THEBES   A city 400 miles south of Cairo; second largest city of ancient Egypt. Flourished during the 16th to 11th centuries B.C. In Hebrew called *No Amon* (Nah. 3:8).

THEODICY   An argument that defends God's justice, especially one that explains why there is evil in nature and society.

THEOPHANY   An appearance of God, for example, at the burning bush or on Mount Sinai.

THUTMOSE I   Ruler of Egypt 1504–1492 B.C. He expanded Egypt to the south, and in the East his armies reached the Euphrates. He was the first ruler to be buried in what became the Valley of the Kings.

THUTMOSE III   Ruler of Egypt 1479–1425 B.C. He succeeded Hatshepsut to the throne, and then in a series of campaigns conquered Palestine and Syria as far as Carchemish and the Euphrates. His rule made Egypt powerful and prosperous.

TIAMAT   Ruler of the chaotic waters who is defeated by Marduk, in the Gilgamesh Epic.

TIGLATH-PILESER I   Ruler of Assyria 1114–1076 B.C. He wanted to establish a world empire, but his reign was followed by several centuries of national weakness.

TIGLATH-PILESER III   Ruler of Assyria 744–727 B.C., a successful commander whose conquests reached as far as Egypt.

TIGRIS   A river flowing from the region of Lake Van in Armenia southeast to the Persian Gulf. Mesopotamia is the area between the Tigris and the Euphrates.

TIRHAKAH   Pharaoh of Egypt 690–664 B.C.; he was from Ethiopia (that is, Cush, or southern Egypt and Sudan).

TIRZAH   The capital of northern Israel in the early 9th century B.C.

TISHBITE   From Tishbe, a place evidently in Gilead, east of the Jordan.

TITHE   Literally, a "tenth," a conventional assessment of taxes.

TOBIAH   One of the three opponents of Nehemiah's rebuilding the walls of Jerusalem.

TOPHET   Or "Topheth", a place in the Valley of the Son of Hinnom (2 Kin. 23:10) where the god Molech was worshiped by sacrificing children in fire. This valley is on the south side of Jerusalem and is called Gehenna in the New Testament.

TORAH The Law, that is, the five books of Moses: Genesis, Exodus, Leviticus, Numbers, and Deuteronomy.

TRANSJORDAN The territory across the Jordan River, that is, on the east bank.

TRIBUTE A tax that those who are defeated are forced to pay to the victor.

TUKULTI-NINURTA I Ruler of Assyria c. 1243–1207 B.C.; conquered Babylon.

TUTANKHAMUN Ruler of Egypt 1336–1327 B.C. His tomb, practically intact and containing fabulous wealth, was discovered by Lord Carnarvon and Howard Carter in 1922.

TYCHE The Greek word for fortune, or fate, often personified as a goddess.

TYRE A Phoenician port on a small island off the Mediterranean coast north of Israel. Tyre repelled all foreign invaders until 332 B.C., when Alexander the Great built a causeway to the island and conquered it.

UGARIT An ancient seaport in north Syria, occupied from 6000 B.C. to 1180 B.C.; today called Ras Shamra. Ugarit traded widely with other ancient nations. Excavation there has yielded the oldest example of the alphabet written down in order, and other important cuneiform documents.

ULAI A river near the fortified city of Shushan (Susa) in Persia. The Ulai may have been an artificial canal.

UNLEAVENED Made without yeast, or leaven, like crackers and tortillas.

UR An important Sumerian city on the Euphrates River, 150 miles southeast of Babylon; the original home of Abraham. Excavations at Ur uncovered rich royal tombs containing remains of servants buried with their king.

URARTU A small nation north of ancient Assyria that had threatened Assyria with conquest but was ultimately conquered during the reign of Tiglath-Pileser III.

URUK Biblical "Erech" (Gen. 10:10; Ezra 4:9). Ancient city 40 miles southeast of Ur, occupied from before 3500 B.C. The earliest known ziggurat is here, as also the earliest written documents, clay tablets with Sumerian inscriptions.

USSHER, JAMES Archbishop of Armagh (Ireland), who prepared a chronology of the Bible. He died in A.D. 1656.

UTNAPISHTIM The survivor of the flood in the Gilgamesh Epic.

VALLEY OF HINNOM A valley below Jerusalem where children were sacrificed by fire to Baal, Chemosh, or Molech. The valley is called Gehenna in the New Testament.

VASSAL A person or state ruled by another, more powerful person or state, in an arrangement established by convention or treaty.

VICE-REGENT A person who rules for and in the place of another.

VULGATE The standard Latin translation of the Bible prepared by Jerome, who died about A.D. 420.

WILDERNESS A term used in the Bible for the uninhabited areas of the Middle East, typically desert or near-desert.

YAHWEH The probable pronunciation of the personal name of God, recorded in Hebrew as four consonants without vowels (YHWH). Translations usually write "LORD" instead of Yahweh.

YAREAH A moon god of Ugarit.

ZERUBBABEL Appointed by the Persian king to be governor of the Jews returning to Judah from Babylon. Zerubbabel began the rebuilding of the Jerusalem temple around 537 or 536 B.C.

ZIGGURAT A pyramidlike tower, built in step formation with stairways to the top. More than two dozen ziggurats are known to have existed in ancient Mesopotamia. The gods were thought to dwell at the tops of these buildings.

ZODIAC The constellations of stars through which the sun, moon, and planets seem to pass during the year as seen from the earth. Twelve prominent constellations on this path yield the twelve signs of the zodiac.

ZOROASTRIANISM The religion of Persia, founded by Zoroaster in the 6th century or possibly the 10th century B.C. This prophet, also called Zarathustra, taught that there were two gods, one good and one evil, fighting for universal control. In the end the good god, Ahura Mazda, would prevail.